W0231599

New Rock Record

2nd Edition

A SIDE

Terry Hounsome

A COLLECTORS' DIRECTORY OF ROCK ALBUMS AND MUSICIANS

BLANDFORD PRESS
POOLE · DORSET

First published in the U.K. in 1981 by Blandford Press
Link House, West Street, Poole, Dorset BH15 1LL.

Reprinted (January) 1982
Reprinted (October) 1982
Second Edition 1983
Reprinted 1983
Reprinted 1984

This book is based upon the original limited edition 'Rockmaster' 1978 and its revised , expanded edition 'Rock Record' 1979 Both of which were published and produced by Terry Hounsome.

British Library Cataloguing in Publication Data

New rock record.—2nd ed.
1. Rock music—Discography
I. Hounsome, Terry
016.7899'12454 ML156.4.R6

ISBN 0 7137 1305 4

Printed in Great Britain by
Butler & Tanner, Frome and London

Contents

Introduction

This second edition of NEW ROCK RECORD has taken 7 years to produce in its present form. It lists groups and artistes together with their LP records and the musicians who have played with them. It includes an index to all the groups and musicians.

This edition now contains some 6,000 entries; 40,000 LP records and 35,000 different musicians. It takes in all forms of"Rock" music from its roots to the present day; as well as mainstream Rock it also contains much information on Pop, Soul, Reggae, Jazzrock, Blues, Country and Folk.

Imports (to Britain) and reissues (with different catalogue numbers) are listed together with some EPs, but singles and bootlegs are beyond the scope of this edition. Catalogue numbers are listed from many countries but only if this number is different from the British release. It is not intended to list every countries release of a particular record. The current availibility of any record is not listed as albums are continually being reissued from many countries. The dates stated in the entries are generally the date on the album or cover. Material has been added to early 1983.

The aim of NEW ROCK RECORD is to provide a useful and as accurate as possible guide to rock music albums and the people who have made them. As a discography its main purpose is to aid identification: It does not set out to review the records or musicians, for this reason, apart from a few factual notes, no text has been included.

The size of each entry is governed by the amount of information available not the relative importance of each group or artiste. Each entry carries a code symbol consisting of its initial letter and running order number. Check in the index for the symbol of any particular group or artistes precise location.

In many entries musicians have been linked by symbols to the albums or dates on which they played; musicians are listed even if they have played only on one track of a particular LP. Many musicians play more than one instrument and where space permits these have been listed but not the make or specific type of instrument, this abbreviation should be taken as a general indication. Instruments are listed in groups, e.g. Guitar covers all types of guitar. String sections and orchestras are described as such and not by individual musicians.

Wherever possible the appearance of a musician on an album has been indicated by coding the album alphabetically or numerically and placing the code after the musicians name and instrument.Where musicians have been known to belong to a group at a particular date, the date has been stated and coded. In some cases where both albums and dates are listed, a mixture of alphabetical and numerical symbols have been used.

The entries run in alphabetical order , though some entries are not in totally strict order. Also, some entries were allocated numbers but have been subsequently withdrawn as unsuitable for inclusion in this edition. Some entries have been continued over to the next page, these have been indicated at the top and bottom of the relevant pages.

The editor is aware that some entries are incomplete and that there are some omissions. Anyone-musicians or collectors- who is able to supply further information or any other suggestions is invited to contact him by letter or telephone at the address given below. Correspondents requiring a reply are requested to enclose a stamped addressed envelope or an international reply coupon.

Terry Hounsome,
13, Stanton Road,
Regents Park,
Southampton,
Hampshire,
England.
SOI 4HF
Tele. 0703 771639.

How to use this book

CODE SYMBOL — LINK SYMBOL — RECORD TITLE — ENTRY NAME — DATE OF ISSUE — RECORD COMPANY — COUNTRY OF ORIGIN — CATALOGUE NUMBER

```
                                                   ACE
A7
 PHIL  HARRIS   G     (AB          (A) FIVE A SIDE                      1974  ANCHOR   UK    ANCL2001
 ALAN KING      G     (ABC         (B) TIME FOR ANOTHER                 1975  ANCHOR   UK    ANCL2013
 PAUL CARRACK   V     (ABC         (C) NO STRINGS                       1977  ANCHOR   UK    ANCL2020
 TERRY COMER    B     (ABC
 FRAN BYRNE           (ABC
 JOHN WOODHEAD  G     (C     CHRIS HUGHES     HRNS (A   BUD BEADLE    HRNS  (A    TIM RENWICK  G    (
 MICK EVE       HRNS  (A     JIM PRICE        HRNS (C   STEVE MADAIO  TPT   (C    TREVOR LAWRENCE TROM(C
 BOBBY KEYS     HRNS  (C     RUSTY YOUNG      STEEL(B
```

MUSICIANS NAMES — INSTRUMENTS PLAYED

Acknowledgements

I would like to thank the following people, [friends, musicians and readers] from all over the world for the help, sympathy, encouragement, inspiration, the many letters and the odd record or tape.

Clive Ablett,
Ross John Angel,
Bjerkem Brynjar,
Louis Behlals,
Paul Barber,
B.N.Broomfield,
M Brusselman,
Paul Cole,
Cob Records,
Gerald Chute,
Chris Curry,
Pete Drewson,
George Davenport,
Geoff Eldridge,
D.A. Eames
Neal Farnsworth,
Peter Fippl,
M. Fitzgerald,
D.Goodyear,
Paul Gilbert,
Josh Greer,
Ron Hockings,
John Huggins,
Peter Hiley,
Michael Harris,
John Harrelson,
Arlo Hegler,
Tom Jasivkowiez,
Bernard Koob,
Dieter Kiefer,
Alan Lord,
Logo Records,
Allan Levine,
G lewis,
Bernd Matheja,
Paul Mann,
Alasdair Macdonald,
Barry Margolis
Andy Neal
Jack Nadelle,
Terry Osborn,
Ted Pinch,
Pye
David Powell,
Jeff Parr,
G.R.Ritchie,
Red Lightnin',
Wilhelm Reber,
Dave Smith,
Shades,
R Slaymaker,
R Sturgen,
Wolfgang Siebert,
Gary Stokes,
John Tobler
Uwe Tessnow,
Crofton Thorpe,
Mark Volman,
C Wood,
Francis M Ward,
Jeff Wells,
Kirmo Wilen,
Clifton Yorks,
Brett 'Buddy' Ascott,
Armadillo Records,
Jeff Brown,
Michael Bates,
Phil Broughton,
Walter Becker,
Tim Chambre,
Geoff Cox,
Cruisin' Records,
Paul Cross,
Fred Dellar,
Tim Deal,
K.Disney,
E.MI. Records,
John Eagle,
Scott Friedberg,
John Farrah,
Kurt Glaso,
G.I Records,
Natalie Gomillian,
Bill Gurney,
Phil Harwood
Derek Henderson,
Stephen Hammonds,
Jurgen Heeger,
Christian Hanell,
Wolfgang Jensen,
Neil Jeffries,
Detlef Krug,
Phil King,
Bernard leonard,
Neil Littman,
Chris Lorimer,
Andy Lynch,
Hugh Maclain,
J Matlathronas,
Ed Mechem,
Rob Morrish,
Zbignew Nowara,
Lars Nilsson,
Norbert Obermanns,
Bob Pearce,
John Philpin,
Maurizio Petitti,
Les Raphael,
Peter Redman,
Peter Ried,
Tony Reynolds,
Eiji Sashida,
Carol Shipp
Jim Seymour,
Rainer Steinike,
John B Sacksteder,
Henning Sander,
Gerhard Taufer,
Dick Tomli,
Tumbleweed Connection,
Virgin Records,
Ludwig Webel ,
Paul Williams,
Muddy Waters,
Deena Weinstein,
Steve York,
Roy Arblaster,
Ash & Gloria,
Marc Barthemy,
Hugh Byron,
Adrian Booth,
Olaf Benzinger,
John Clare
Roger Chapman,
Chilli Charles,
Andrew Craven,
Decca Records,
Andy Dobbs,
Pete Drewery,
Everly Brothers,
John W. Edwards
George Forrester,
Klaus Freestad,
Kurt Galle,
Dave Greenhaulgh,
Stephen Green,
Andrew Gibbons,
Guy Hamilton,
Steve Hammond,
E.P.Hopper,
Phill Hall,
Jim Hill,
Ian Jones,
Derek King,
Nigel Keatley,
Ferninand Kother,
Spencer Liegh,
Jeff Lambert,
Ian Lumsden,
Bob Lyons,
Steve Morgan,
Andy Maunder,
Rod Mortimer,
Gordon Mackay,
Richard Norris,
Knut Olsson,
Oasis,
Frank Plouright,
Deb Pal,
Anthony Parr,
Andy Read,
Paul Renk,
Jermy Robinson,
Peter Richmond,
Richard Sadler,
Paul Soper,
George Sepetjian,
Harvey Shields,
Willie Sugg,
Malc Tipping,
David Thompson,
Julian Thomas,
United Artist,
Vinyl Solution,
Paul Williams,
Arthur Wood,
Stephen Weeks,
Stephen Young,
Pete York,
Erroll Antzis,
R.G.Allen,
David Bragg,
Vytenis Babrauskas,
Beano's
Steve Blamire
Henry's Records
Randy California,
Bill Cullen,
Max Cripps,
Alan Dawson,
C.D.Davies,
Klaus Damrau,
Ezy Ryder Records
T Evans,
Donald Fagen,
Steven Feigenbaum,
John Grave,
David Ginsburg,
John Guest,
Wolfgang Giese,
Bruno Haas,
Stuart Heather,
David Hayhoe,
Richard Hughes,
Bernie Hein,
Robert Jackson,
Freddie King,
William.F.Krober,
Howard Kaylan,
Line Records (Germany)
Bri Lockyear,
Graham liddell,
Barry Lazell,
Gary Moberley,
Bert Muirhead,
Bob Metcalfe,
Torben Nielsen,
Chris Newby,
Ingrid Olsson,
Olaf Owre,
Polydor,
Chris Pouncy
Charlie Pritchard,
Norman Read,
Replay's,
L Rogoff,
Wilf Roach,
Summit Records,
Harry Shapiro,
Roger Seaman,
John Stewart,
Martin Storkman,
Mike Tesise,
David Teeitlel,
Mark Tyrell,
Jan Van Neck,
Ian Walker,
W.E.A. ,
Mel Wright,
George Walker,
Paul Yaersley,
J Young.

And all the others i have forgotten or missed.

And a special thanks to my family, Chris, my wife, for the typing, indexing, sorting and a LOT of patience. My children : Claire, Steven and Jonathan for the coffee they have made and the help they have given.

Abbreviations

ACC	ACCORDIAN
A'HARP	AUTOHARP
B	BASS
BAN	BANJO
BAZ	BAZOUKI
BOD	BODHRAN
BOMBA	BOMBARDE
CLAR	CLARINET
COMP	COMPILATION ALBUM
CONC	CONCERTINA
D	DRUMS
DBL	DOUBLE ALBUM SET
DOB	DOBRO GUITAR
DULC	DULCIMER
EURO	EUROPEAN
FDL	FIDDLE
FLT	FLUTE
FR	FRANCE
G	GUITAR
GERM	GERMANY
HCA	HARMONICA
HRNS	HORNS(TRUMPETS,TROMBONES, TUBA ETC)
IT	ITALY
JAP	JAPAN
K	KEYBOARDS(ALL TYPES)
MAND	MANDOLIN
MEL	MELODEON
NOR	NORWAY
ORG	ORGAN
PERC	PERCUSSION
PNO	PIANO
R I	RE ISSUE
SAX	SAXOPHONE
SIT	SITAR
STEEL	STEEL GUITAR /PEDAL STEEL GUITAR
STR	STRINGS(VIOLIN, CELLO, BASS VIOLA)
SYN	SYNTHESIZER
SWED	SWEDEN
TPT	TRUMPET
TROM	TROMBONE
UK	GREAT BRITAIN
US	UNITED STATES OF AMERICA
V	VOCALS/ BACKING VOCALS
VLA	VIOLA
VLN	VIOLIN
WIND	SAXOPHONE,FLUTE, CLARINET ETC

THIS BOOK IS DEDICATED TO:

Freddie King – Roger Chapman
Randy California – Steely Dan
Muddy Waters – Kraan
Fabulous Thunderbirds – Z Z Top

Musicians & Record Collectors
Everywhere

Chris, Claire, Steven & Jon

And
All my friends & family

DIRECTORY

Directory

A1 — A B SKHY — A1

JIM MARCOTTE B (AB — (A) A B SKHY — 1969 MGM SE4628
DENNIS GEYER G/V (AB — (B) RAMBLING ON — 1970 MGM SE4676
TERRY ANDERSEN D/V (A
HOWARD WALES K (A — RICK JAEGER D (B — CURLEY COOKE G (B — JIM LIBAN HCA(A
OTIS HALE FLT (A — RUSSELL DASHIELL G (A — LAROON HOLT TPT (A — MARVIN BROWN TPT(A
BUD BRISBOIS TPT (A — PHILLIP PRUDEN SAX (A — JIM HORN SAX (A — DONALD WALDROP TROM(A
DAVE ROBERTS TROM (A — SAM McCUE G V (A — BEN SIDRAN K (B — ELVIN BISHOP G (B
WALLY ROSE PNO (B

A2 — AC.DC — A2

ANGUS YOUNG G (ABCDEFGH — (A) HIGH VOLTAGE — 1976 ATLANTIC UK K50257 US SD36142
MALCOLM YOUNG G (ABCDEFGH — (B) DIRTY DEEDS DONE CHEAP — 1976 ATLANTIC UK K50323 US 16033
PHIL RUDD D (ABCDEFGH — (C) LET THERE BE ROCK — 1977 ATLANTIC UK K50366 US SD36151
BRIAN JOHNSON V (GH — (D) POWERAGE — 1978 ATLANTIC UK K50483 US SD19180
BON SCOTT V (ABCDEF — (E) IF YOU WANT BLOOD — 1978 ATLANTIC UK K50532 US 19212
CLIFF WILLIAMS B (DEFGH — (F) HIGHWAY TO HELL — 1979 ATLANTIC UK K50628 US 19244
MARK EVANS (ABC — (G) BACK IN BLACK — 1980 ATLANTIC UK K50735 US 16018
ROBERT JOHN LANGE PROD (GH — (H) FOR THOSE ABOUT TO ROCK — 1981 ATLANTIC UK K50851 US 11111

A2A — AALON — A2A

AALON BUTLER — (A) CREAM CITY — 19 ARISTA US 4127

A2B — ADC BAND — A2B

(A) RENAISSANCE — 1980 COTILLION US 5221
(B) BROTHER LUCK — 1981 ATLANTIC UK K50795 US 16041

A2C — AK BAND — A2C

(A) MANHOLE KIDS — 1981 RCA LP 5024

A2D — THE A's — A2D

RICHARD BUSH V (AB — (A) THE A's — 1981 ARISTA US 4238
RICK DiFONZO G (AB — (B) A WOMANS GOT THE POWER — 1981 ARISTA US 9554
TERRY BORTMAN B (AB
MIKE SNYDER D (AB — ROCCO NOTTE K (AB

A2E — A TO Z — A2E

CHRIS SLACK G (— (A) WITCH OF BERKELEY — 1980 POLYDOR UK 2383 587
CHRIS HOWARD B (
JOHN THORNE D (— MARV ? G (— JULA HARRINGTON V (

A3 — AARDVARK — A3

FRANK CLARK D (AB — (A) PRE LP LINE UP
DAVE SKILLIN V (AB — (B) AARDVARK — 1970 NOVA GER 12024 UK SDN .17
STAN ALDOUS B (AB
PADDY COULTER K (A — STEVE MILLINER K (B

A3A — ABACUS — A3A

CHRIS WILLIAMS V (— (A) ABACUS — 1971
CHARLY SCHADE G (— (B) EVERYTHING YOU NEED — 1972 ZEBRA GER 2949 002
CHRIS BARUTZKY K SYN(— (C) JUST A DAYS JOURNEY AWAY — 1972 POLYDOR 2371 270
KLAUS KOHHASE B (— (D) MIDWAY — 1974 ZEBRA GER 2949 013
ALLAN WARREN D (

A4 — ABBA — A4

ANNA ULVAEUS V (123A>Z — (A) RING RING — 1973 POLAR SWED 242 RCA AUST 102323
BENNY ANDERSSON K V (4 A>Z — (B) WATERLOO — 1974 EPIC UK 80179 ATLANTIC US 18101
ANNIFRID LYNGSTAD-FREDRIKSSON V(A>Z — (B) WATERLOO — 1974 POLAR SWED 252 RCA AUST 14003
BJORN ULVAEUS G V (4 A>Z — (B) WATERLOO — 1974 VOGUE FR 28047 POLYDOR GER 2374111
(B) WATERLOO — 19 EPIC UK 32009
ANDERS DAHL STR (E — (C) ABBA — 1975 EPIC UK 80835 ATLANTIC US 18146
MALANDO GASSAMA PERC (BEGJ — (C) ABBA — 1975 POLAR SWED 262 RCA AUST 14013
AKE GUNKVIST PERC (KZ — (C) ABBA — 1975 VOGUE FR 28039
JANNE SCHAFFER G (BCDEGJK — (D) GREATEST HITS — 1976 EPIC UK 69218 ATLANTIC US 18189
ANDREW EIJAS HRNS (JZ — (D) GREATEST HITS — 1976 POLAR SWED 266 RCA AUST 14020
PER LINDVALL D (K — (D) GREATEST HITS — 1976 VOGUE FR 28047 ATLANTIC CAN 19114
KAJTEK WOJCIECHOWSKI SAX(JK — (E) ARRIVAL — 1976 EPIC UK 86018 ATLANTIC US 18207
JANNE KLING WIND (J — (E) ARRIVAL — 1976 VOGUE FR 20238 RCA AUST 14034
PAUL HARRIS PNO (J — (E) ARRIVAL — 1976 POLAR SWED 272
LASSE WELLANDER G (CEGJK — (F) GOLDEN DOUBLE — 1977 VOGUE FR 685
LARS CARLSSON HRNS (EGJK — (G) THE ALBUM — 1977 EPIC UK 86052 ATLANTIC US 19164
ULF ANDERSSON SAX (C — (G) THE ALBUM — 1977 POLAR SWED 282 RCA AUST 14060
PER SAHLBERG B (B — (H) LES PLUS GRANDS SUCCES — 197 RCA FR 13036
CHRISTER EKLUND SAX (B — (J) VOULEZ VOUS — 1979 EPIC UK 86086 ATLANTIC US 16000
RUTGER GUNNARSON B (BCEGJK — (J) VOULEZ VOUS — 1979 POLAR SWED 292 RCA AUST 14135
MIKE WATSON B (CJK — (K) SUPER TROUPER — 1980 EPIC UK 10022 ATLANTIC US 16023
ANDERS GLENMARK G (E — (K) SUPER TROUPER — 1980 POLAR SWED 322
OLA BRUNKERT D (BCEGJK — (L) GREATEST HITS VOL 2 — 1980 EPIC UK 10017 ATLANTIC US 16009
FINN SJOBERG G (B — (L) GREATEST HITS VOL 2 — 1980 POLAR SWED 312
ROGER PALM D (CEF — (M) VISITORS — 1981 EPIC UK 10032 ATLANTIC US 19332
BRUNO GLENMARK TPT (C — (M) VISITORS — 1981 POLAR SWED 342
JOE GALDO D (J — (Z) LIVE LINE-UP NOV 1979
ARNOLD PASEIRO B (J — ( ) CIRACIAS POR LAS MUSICA — 1981 EPIC UK 86123
ISH LEDESMA G (J — SOLO ALBUMS
GEORGE TERRY G (J — (1) AGNETHA(ANNA) — 1968 CUPOL SWED 1002
HALLDOR PALSSON SAX (J — (2) AGNETHA 2(ANNA) — 1969 CUPOL SWED 1003
JOHAN STENGARD SAX (J — (3) AGNETHA — 1974 EMBASSY UK 31094
NILS LANDGREN TROM (J — (4) LYCKA(BENNY & BJORN) — 1970 POLAR SWED 113
ROLF ALEX D (J — ( ) SORN JAG AR — 1970
JAN RISBERG OBOE (J — ( ) 11 WOMEN IN A HOUSE — 1972
MATS RONANDER G (Z — ( ) BASTA (AGNETHA) — 1973
( ) TEN YEARS WITH (AGNETHA) — 1979

A4A

JOHN ABERCROMBIE

A4A

JOHN ABERCROMBIE G (ALL — (A) FRIENDS — 1971 OBLIVION US 003
DAVE HOLLAND D (CDI — (A) FRIENDS — 1975 CAROLINE UK 1511
JACK DEJOHNETTE D (BCDGI — (B) TIMELESS — 1975 ECM 1047
RALPH TOWNER (H — (C) GATEWAY — 1975 ECM 1061
JAN HAMMER K (B — (D) CLOUD DANCE — 1976 ECM 1062
JEFF WILLLIAMS G (A — (E) PILGRIM & THE STARS — 1976 ECM 1063
CLINT HOUSTON B (A — (F) UNTITLED — 197 ECM 1074
MARC COHEN SAX (A — (G) PICTURES — 1977 ECM 1079
RICHIE BEIRACH PNO (KL — (H) SARGASSA SEA — 1976 ECM 1080
GEORGE MRAZ B (KL — (I) GATEWAY 2 — 1978 ECM 1105
PETER DONALDSON D (JK — (J) CHARACTERS — 1978 ECM 1117
COLIN WALCOTT TABLA(D — (K) ARCADE — 1979 ECM 1133
(L) M — 1980 ECM 1191
(M) STRAIGHT FLIGHT — 1982 JAM 5001

A5

MICK ABRAHAMS

A5

MICK ABRAHAMS G V (ALL — (A) MICK ABRAHAMS — 1971 CHRYSALIS UK 9147 US A&M 4312
BOB SARGEANT G V K(AB — (B) AT LAST — 1972 CHRYSALIS US 1005
RITCHIE DHARMA D (AB — (C) LEARNING TO PLAY GUITAR WITH.. — 1975 SRT SRTM 73313
WALT MONAGHAN B (AB — (1) AUG> SEPT 1978
JACK LANCASTER WIND (B
TOM DOWNING FDL G(1 — DAVE BRISTOW PNO (1 — PETE CLEMMINS (B

A5A

ABSOLUTELY ELSEWHERE

A5A

PAUL FISHMAN K (A — (A) IN SEARCH OF ANCIENT GODS — 1976 WB UK K56192
BILL BRUFORD D (A
PHILIP SAATCHI G (A — JON ASTROP B (A

A5B

NATHAN ABSHIRE & THE PINEGROVE BOYS

A5B

NATHAN ABSHIRE ACC (— (A) THE LEGENDARY JAY MILLER SESSION VOL 13 1978 FLYRIGHT LP 535

A5C

MIKE ABSALOM

A5C

MIKE ABSALOM (ALL — (A) SAVE THE LAST GHERKIN FOR ME — 1969 SAYDISC SDL162
(B) MIKE ABSALOM — 1971 VERTIGO 6360 053
(C) HECTOR AND OTHER PECCADILLOS — 1973 PHILIPS

A6

ABYSSINIANS

A6

BERNARD COLLINS (— (A) FORWARD TO ZION — 19 KLIK KLP9023
DONALD MANNING (— (B) ARISE — 1978 FRONT LINE FL1019
UNFORD MANNING
JAH JERRY G (AB — FRANKLYN WAUL K (AB — EARL SMITH G (AB — CARLTON MANNING G (A
ROBBIE SHAKESPEARE B (AB — PABLO BLACK K (AB — SLY DUNBAR D (AB — MICHAEL COOPER K (AB
DEVON RICHARDSON D (AB — RAS JAWBONE D (AB — LLOYD PARKS B (AB — BONGO HERMAN PERC (AB
WINSTON BOWEN G (AB — GLEN DE COSTA SAX (A — CEDRIC BROOKS SAX (AB — BOBBY ELLIS TPT (AB
HERMAN MARQUIS SAX (AB — GEORGE FULLWOOD B (AB — SANTA D (AB — TONY CHIN G (AB
TOMMY McCOOK WIND (AB — VIVIAN HALL TPT (AB

A6A

ACCOLADE

A6A

GORDON GILTRAP G (1 — (A) ACCOLADE — 1970 COLUMBIA UK SCX 6405
DON PARTRIDGE G (1 — (B) ACCOLADE 2 — 1971 REGAL ZONOPHONE UK SLRZ 1024
BRIAN CRESSWELL (1 — (1) 1969
MALCOLM POOLE B (1 — IAN HOLT (1

A6B

ACADEMY

A6B

POLLY PERKINS V (A — (A) POP LORE ACCORDING TO .. — 1969 MORGAN BLUE TOWN UK 5001
DAMON J HARDY V (A
RICHARD COBBY G (A — DICK WALTER FLT (A

A6C

ACCELERATES

A6C

CHRIS MARTIN V (A — (A) THE ACCELERATES(EP) — 1979 SPIV RECORDS UK
TONY DOYLE B V (A
MARTIN SMITH G (A — BRIAN DAMAGE D (A — KATHY FREEMAN G (A

A6D

ACCEPT

A6D

UDO DIRKSCHNEIDER V (A — (A) ACCEPT — 1979 BRAIN UK 0060 188
PETER BALTES B V (A — (B) I'M A REBEL — 1980 LOGO UK 1025 PASSPORT US 9849
WOLF HOFFMAN G (A
JORG FISCHER G (A — STEFAN KAUFMAN D (A — FRANK FRIEDRICH D (A

A6E

ACCIDENTS

A6E

(A) KISS ME ON THE APOCALYPSE — 19 HOOK LINE & SINKER

A7

ACE

A7

PHIL HARRIS G (AB — (A) FIVE A SIDE — 1974 ANCHOR UK ANCL 2001
ALAN BAM KING G (ABC — (B) TIME FOR ANOTHER — 1975 ANCHOR UK ANCL 2013
PAUL CARRACK V (ABC — (C) NO STRINGS — 1977 ANCHOR UK ANCL 2020
TERRY COMER B (ABC — (C) NO STRINGS — 1977 CARRERE FR 68037
FRAN BYRNE D (ABC
JOHN WOODHEAD G (C — CHRIS HUGHES HRNS (A — BUD BEADLE HRNS (A — TIM RENWICK G (
MICK EVE HRNS (A — JIM PRICE HRNS (C — STEVE MADAIO TPT (C — TREVOR LAWRENCE TROM(C
BOBBY KEYS HRNS (C — RUSTY YOUNG STEEL(B — STEVE WITHERINGTON D (

A7A

JOHNNY ACE

A7A

JOHNNY ACE (A — (A) JOHNNY ACE MEMORIAL ALBUM — 1971 DUKE ? RI 1981 ACE UK CH40

A7B

ACE SPECTRUM

A7B

(A) JUST LIKE THE MOVIES — 19 ATLANTIC US 18185

A8

ACES

A8

LOUIS MYERS V G HCA(ABC — (A) CHICAGO BEAT — 1976 BLACK & BLUE 33508
DAVE MYERS B (ABC — (B) ACES & GUESTS — 1977 MCM FR 900293
FRED BELOW D (C — (C) KINGS OF CHICAGO BLUES — 19 VOGUE FR 30174
SAM LAWHORN G (C
EDDIE TAYLOR G (C

A8A

ACHE

A8A

STEEN TOFT ANDERSEN B HCA(B — (A) DE HOMINE URBANO — 1970 PHILIPS? 841906
GLENN FISCHER D PERC(A — (B) BLÅ SOM ALTID — 1977 KHF DK ROLP 6570
JOHNNIE GELLETT V K G (B
PETER MELLIN K G (A — FINN OLAFSSON G K (AB — TORSTEN OLAFSSON B V (A — GERT SMEDEGARD D (B
PER WIUM K (B

A9 DAVID ACKLES A9

DAVID ACKLES V (ALL (A) DAVID ACKLES 1968 ELEKTRA US EKS 74022 UK 71 K42020
MICHAEL FONFARA ORG (A (B) SUBWAY TO THE COUNTRY 1970 ELEKTRA US EKS 74060 UK 71 K42092
DOUG HASTINGS G (A (C) AMERICAN GOTHIC 1972 ELEKTRA US EKS 75032 UK K42112
JOHN KELIEHOR PERC (A (D) FIVE & DIME 1973 CBS US 32466
DAWN WEIS PICC (D
GEORGINA MOHAMMED FLT (D LOREN PICKFORD WIND (D EARL DUMLER WIND (D JAMES KANTER CLAR (D
EUGENE CIPRIANO SAX (D TODD MILLAR HRNS (D ROBERT HENDERSON HRNS (D RUSSELL KIDD TPT (D
ZIGMANT KANSTUL TPT (D JOHN DALEY TROM (D EDMOND WELTER TUBA (D COLIN BAILEY PERC (D
LOU ANNE NEILL HARP (D BRUCE LANGHORNE G (D JAMIE GRAHAM G (D RED RHODES STEEL (D
DEAN TORRANCE V (D DOUGLAS GRAHAM V (D DANNY WEIS G (A JERRY PENROD B (A

A9A BARBARA ACKLIN A9A

BARBARA ACKLIN V (AB (A) LOVE MAKES A WOMAN 19 BRUNSWICK US 754137
(B) SEVEN DAYS OF NIGHT 19 BRUNSWICK US 754148

A9B ACQUA FRAGILE A9B

PIERO CANAVERA D G V(AB (A) ACQUA FRAGILE 1973 NUMERO UNO IT 55656
GINO CAMPANINI G V (AB (B) MASS MEDIA STARS 1974 DISCHI IT 6150 IMPORT 1005
FRANZ DOND B (AB
BERNARDO LANZETTI V G (AB MAURIZIO MORI K V (AB CLAUDIO FABI PNO (B

A9C ACTION A9C

ALAN BAM KING G (A (A) THE ULTIMATE ACTION 1980 EDSEL UK ED 101
REG KING V (A
PETE WATSON G (A MIKE EVANS B (A ROGER POWELL D (A GEORGE MARTIN PROD(A

A9D ACROBAT A9D

BILLY JONES G (A (A) ACROBAT 1972 TMI US 1004

A10 ADAM & THE ANTS A10

ADAM ANT V (ALL (1) NOVEMBER 1977
JOHNNY BIVOUAC G (1 (A) DIRK WEARS WHITE SOX 1979 DO IT RIDE 3
ANDY WATSON B (1 (B) KINGS OF THE WILD FRONTIER 1980 CBS UK 84549 US 37033
DAVE BARB D (1 (C) STAND AND DELIVER 1981
MATTHEW ASHMAN G K (A (D) PRINCE CHARMING 1981
ANDREW WARREN B (A
KEVIN MOONEY B (BCD MARCO PIRRONI G (BCD TERRY LEE MIALL D(BCD CHRIS 'MERRICK'HUGHES D(BCD

A11 ARTHUR ADAMS A11

ARTHUR ADAMS G V (ABC (A) ITS PRIVATE TONIGHT 1972 BLUE THUMB BT 543
PHIL UPCHURCH G (A (B) HOME BREW 197 FANTASY US 9479
WILTON FELDER B (A (C) MIDNIGHT SERENADE 19 FANTASY 9523
JOE SAMPLE K (A (D) I LOVE LOVE LOVE MY LADY 1979 A&M US 4752
SHIRLEY MATTHEWS V (A
GENE ESTES VIBES(A ERNIE WATTS HRS (A PAUL HUMPHREY D (A MIKE ALTSCHUL HRS (A
JACK KELSO HRS (A PAUL HUBINON HRS (A BILL GREEN HRS (A CHUCK FINDLEY HRS (A
BOBBYE HALL PERC(A GEORGE BOHANON HRS (A JAMES JAMESON B (B DENNIS COFFEY G (B
EARL PALMER D (B VANETTA FIELDS V (A CLYDIE KING V (A

A11A DOUGLAS ADAMS A11A

DOUGLAS ADAMS V (A (A) THE HITCHIKERS GUIDE TO THE GALAXY 1979 ORIGINAL UK ORA42
BERNIE LEADON (A
TIM SOUSTER (A PADDY KINGSLAND (A

A11B JAY BOY ADAMS A11B

JAY BOY ADAMS (AB (A) JAY BOY ADAMS 1978 ATLANTIC US 18221
(B) FORK 1980 ATLANTIC US 19195

A12 JOHNNY ADAMS A12

JOHNNY ADAMS (ABC (A) HEART & SOUL 19 SSS INT US SSS5
(A) HEART & SOUL 19 CHARLY UK CR 30154
(B) AFTER ALL THE GOOD IS GONE 19 ARIOLA US SW 50036
(C) STAND BY ME 19 CHELSEA US S 25
(D) RECONSIDER ME 1976 CHARLY EP CEP 102

A12A DANNY ADLER A12A

DANNY ADLER G K V(A (A) THE DANNY ADLER STORY 1979 DO IT RIDE 2
NICK PLYTAS K (A
JULIAN SCOTT B (A JUSTIN HILDRITH D (A NICK MONNAS D (A

A12B ADVENTURERS A12B

(A) CANT STOP TWISTING 19 COLUMBIA 1747

A13 ADVERTISING A13

TOT TAYLOR G K (A (A) JINGLES 1978 EMI UK EMC 3253
PAUL BULTITUDE D (A
DENNIS SMITH B (A SIMON BOSWELL G (A

A14 ADVERTS A14

GAYE ADVERT B (A1B (1) MARCH 1978 GIG
T V SMITH V (A1B (A) CROSSING THE RED SEA 1978 BRIGHT UK BRL 201
TOM NEWMAN SYN (B (A) CROSSING THE RED SEA 1981 BUTT RI ALSO002
LAURIE DRIVER D (A (B) CAST OF THOUSANDS 1979 RCA UK PL25246
HOWARD PICKUP G (A1B
JOHN TOWE D (1 TIM GROSS K (C ROD LATTER D (B RICHARD STRANGE SYN (B

A15 AERIAL A15

LAURIE CURRIE D V (A (A) IN THE MIDDLE OF THE NIGHT 1978 CAPITOL GER 8590 UK/US 11828
MALCOLM BUCHANAN K (A
BRIAN MIESSNER B V G (A GARY O'CONNOR G B V (

A16 AEROSMITH A16

STEVE TYLER HCA PERC K B V(ABCDEF (A) AEROSMITH 1973 CBS UK 65486 US 32005
BRAD WHITFORD G (BCD EF (B) GET YOUR WINGS 1974 CBS UK 80015 US 32847
JOEY KRAMER D V (BCDEF (C) TOYS IN THE ATTIC 1975 CBS UK 80773 US 33479
SCOTT CUSHNIE PNO (C (D) ROCKS 1976 CBS UK 81379 US 34165
JOE PERRY V B G PERC (ABCDEF (E) DRAW THE LINE 1977 CBS UK 82147 US 34865
TOM HAMILTON B G (BCDEF (F) LIVE BOOTLEG 1978 CBS UK 88325 US 35564
JAY MESSINA PERC (C (G) NIGHT IN THE RUTS 1979 CBS UK 83680 US 36050
PAUL PRESTOPINO BANJ (D (H) GREATEST HITS 1980 CBS UK 84704 US 36865

A17 **AFFINITY** A17

LINDA HOYLE V (A — (A) AFFINITY — 1970 VERTIGO UK 6360004
MIKE JOPP G (A — (A) AFFINITY — 1970 PARAMOUNT US PAS5027
MO FOSTER B (A
GRANT SERPELL D (A — LYNTON NAIFF K (A

A18 **AFTER TEA** A18

(A) AFTER TEA — 19 ACE OF CLUBS UK SCLR 1251

A19 **AFTER THE FIRE** A19

PETER BANKS K (BCD — (A) SIGNS OF CHANGE — 1978 RAPID UK RR 001
IVOR TWIDELL D (B — (B) LASER LOVE — 1979 CBS UK 83795
ANDY PIERCY V G B (BCD — (C) 80F — 1980 EPIC UK 84545
TIM HAYWELL B (— (D) BATTERIES NOT INCLUDED — 1982 CBS UK 85566
NICK BATTLE B (
JOHN RUSSELL G (BCD — PETE KING D (CD

A19A **AGITATION FREE** A19A

LUTZ ULBRICH G K (ABC — (A) MALESCH — 1972 VERTIGO UK 6360 607
ULI POP BONGO (A — (A) MALESCH — 1978 ATMOSPHERE IRI 5001
JORG SCHWENKE G (AC — (B) 2ND ALBUM — 1973 VERTIGO UK 6360 615
ERHARD GROSSKOPF (C — (B) 2ND ALBUM — 1979 ATMOSPHERE IRI 5002
MICHEL GUNTER B (ABC — (C) LAST — 1976 BARCLAY FR 80615
MICHAEL HOENIG K SYN (ABC
BURGHARD RAUSCH K D V (ABC — GUSTAV LUTHJENS G (— PETER MICHAEL HAMEL K (A — STEFAN DIEZ G (B
DIETMAR BURMEISTER D (C

A19C **AGAIN AGAIN** A19C

(A) THE WAY WE WERE(EP) — 1979 DO IT UK DUN IT 7

A19D **AGGREGATION** A19D

(A) MIND ODYSSEY — 19 LHI US 12008

A20 **AGNES STRANGE** A20

JOHN WESTWOOD G (A — (A) STRANGE FLAVOUR — 1975 BIRDSNEST UK BRL 9000
ALAN GREEN B (A
DAVE RODWELL D (A

A20A **AGORA** A20A

ROBERTO BACCHIOCCHI K V (A — (A) AGORA — 1975 ATLANTIC EURO 50171
RENATO GASPARINI G (A
OVIDIO URBANI SAX V(A — PAOLO COLA FRANCESCO B V (A — MAURA MENCARONI D V (A

A21 **DON AGRATI** A21

DON AGRATI V K B D (A — (A) HOME GROWN — 1973 ELEKTRA UK K42141 US EKS 75057
JAMES GANDUGLIA PERC (A
GIL ROGERS G (A — RIC RICCIO FLT (A — KARLA PAYNE B (A — SKIP SHORTLEDGE HRS
PHIL AYLING HRS (A — BOB CASSENS B (A — MIKE FRANCIS HRS (A — FRED LAWRENCE HRS (A
LIZA REY HARP (A — DAVE KAUFMAN HRS (A — JIM STOUDER CLAR (A

A21A **AIM** A21A

MICHAEL OVERLY V FLT(A — (A) AIM FOR THE HIGHEST — 1973 BLUE THUMB US BTS 64
WARREN PEMBERTON D (A
DAVID M SHERR OBOE (A — ALAN ESTES CONGA(A — LOREN NEWKIRK K (A — PATRICK O'CONNOR (A

A22 **CHARLIE AINLEY** A22

CHARLIE AINLEY V G (AB — (A) TOO MUCH IS NOT ENOUGH — 1978 NEMPEROR US35080
HENRY SPINETTI D (A — (B) BANG YOUR DOOR — 1978 NEMPEROR US 35648 EMI UK 3285
ROB HENDRY G (1 — (1) LIVE DATE NOV 1979
CHARLIE HARRISON B (A
RICHARD WORTHY G (AB — JOHN PORTER G B (A — PRESTON HEYMAN PERC (A — TOM WILDY HCA (A
MEL COLLINS HRS (A — KOKOMO V (A — JO PARTRIDGE G MAND(A — MICK WEAVER K (A
PETE WINGFIELD K (A — MIKE STOREY K (A — DAVID HENTSCHEL SYN (A — STUART ELLIOTT D PERC(B
CHAS HODGES B (B — HOWIE CASEY HRS (B — TONY ASHTON ORG (B — MARTIN FRITH HRNS(B
ROBIN BIBI G (1 — SAM HARLEY B (1 — RON TELEMACQUE D (1

A22A **AIR** A22A

TOM COPPOLA K (A — (A) AIR — 1971 EMBRYO US SD733
JOHN SIEGLER B (A
GOOGIE K V (A — MARK ROSENHAGEN D (A

A22B **AIR RAID** A22B

RICK BROWN D (A — (A)AIR RAID — 1981 20th CENTURY
ARTHUR OFFEN V K (A
RICK HINKLE G (A — TOMMY WALKER B (A

A22C **AIR SUPPLY** A22C

RUSSELL HITCHCOCK V (AB — (A) LOST IN LOVE — 1980 ARISTA US 4268 UK SPART 1138
GRAHAM RUSSELL G V (AB — (B) THE ONE THAT YOU LOVE — 1981 ARISTA US 9551 UK SPART 1169
TOMMY EMMANUEL G (A
RALPH COOPER D (AB — FRANK ESTER SMITH K (AB — DAVID MOYSE G V (AB — REX GOH B V (B
CRISTON BARKER B V (A — DAVID GREEN K (B — SAM McNALLY K (A

A22D **AIRBORNE** A22D

LARRY STEWART V G K(A — (A) AIRBORNE — 1979 CBS US 36076
BEAU HILL V G K(A
JOHN PEARCE B V (A — MIKE BAIRD D (A — DAVID ZYCHEK G V (A

A23 **JANE AIRE & BELVEDERES** A23

JANE AIRE V (A — (A) JANE AIRE & THE BELVEDERES — 1979 VIRGIN UK V2134
CHRIS PYNE TROM (A — (B) JANE AIRE — 19 STIFF UK SEEZ 11
PIETRO NARDINI G K (A
GALEN STUDEBAKER D (— EMILY RUTH VLN — FRANCOIS DE CHANCY GK — CHRIS BUTLER B
ROBERT LU EDMUNDS G (A — GAVIN POVEY K (A — GLYN HAVARD B (A — JOHN MOSS D (A
CHRIS JENKINS G (A — MARTIN DROVER TPT (A — MIKE DAVIS TPT (A — MALCOLM GRIFFITHS TROM (A
GEOFF DALEY SAX (A — RAY WARLEIGH SAX (A — JOAN ASHLEY V (A — KIRSTY MACCOLL V (A
RACHEL SWEET V (A — DAVID ARNOLD PERC (A

A24 **AIRTO** A24

AIRTO MOREIRA PERC V D(ALL — (A) SEEDS ON THE GROUND — 19 POLYDOR 2310 040 BUDDAH 5085
FLORA PURIM V PERC(BJH — (B) FINGERS — 1973 CTI CTI18 6028
HUGO FATTORUSO K V (B — (C) VIRGIN LAND — 1974 CTI CTI23 SALVATION 701
RINGO THIELMANN B V (B — (D) IN CONCERT — 1974 CTI CTI21
SIVUCA G (J — (E) FREE — 19 CTI 6020
HERMETO K FLT(J — (G) IDENTITY — 1976 ARISTA UK ARTY119 PATHE FR 4068
(CONTINUED)

A24 AIRTO (CONTINUED) A24

DEODATO (D — (H) PROMISES OF THE SUN — 1976 ARISTA US AL4116 PATHE FR 98770
STANLEY CLARKE B (F — (I) I'M FINE — 19 WEA K59420
JOE FARRELL (F — (J) THE ESSENTIAL AIRTO — 19 BUDDAH 25668 87003/2
CHICK COREA K (F — (K) NATURAL FEELINGS — 197 SKYE US 21
DAVID AMARO G (BG
JORGE FATTORUSO D V (B — RON CARTER B (J — KEITH JARRETT K (F

A25 (GINGER BAKERS) AIRFORCE A25

GINGER BAKER D (ABCD — (A) AIRFORCE — 1970 POLYDOR UK 2662 001 US ATCO 703
STEVE WINWOOD K V G(A — (B) AIRFORCE 2 — 1970 POLYDOR UK 2383 029 US ATCO 33343
RICK GRECH B (AB — (C) FREE KINGS — 19 KARUSSELL GERM 2499 018
CHRIS WOOD SAX (A — (D) POP GIANTS VOL 10 — 19 BRUNSWICK 2011 521
HAROLD McNAIR SAX (AB
PHIL SEAMAN D (A — DENNY LAINE G V (AB — GRAHAM BOND K SAX(AB — BUD BEADLE WIND (A
DIANE STEWART V (B — REMI KABAKA PERC (A — KEN CRADDOCK K (B — ALIKI ASHMAN V(B
STEVE GREGORY HRNS (B — COLIN GIBSON B (B — NEEMOI ACQUAYE PERC (B — CATHERINE JAMES B(B
ROCKY DIDZORNU PERC (B

A25A AIRPLAY A25A

DAVID FOSTER K V (A — (A) AIRPLAY — 1980 RCA US 1 3099
JAY GRAYDON G V (A
TOMMY FUNDERBURK V (A — JEFF PORCARO D (A — MIKE BAIRD D (A

A26 AIRWAVES A26

RAY MARTINEZ G V K(AB — (A) NEW DAY — 1978 MERCURY UK 9109 613 A&M US 4689
DAVE CHARLES D (AB — (B) NEXT STOP — 1979 MERCURY UK 9109 625 A&M US 4763
JOHN DAVID V K G(AB
PAUL COBBOLD CELLO(AB — TED BUNTIN (B — PAT MORAN PROD (A

A26A AIZZ A26A

(A) THE WITCH OF BERKELY — 1980 POLYDOR UK 2383 587

A26B AKA & THE CHARLATANS A26B

(A) HEROES ARE LOSERS — 1978 VANITY (EP) VEIN 1

A26C AKIDO A26C

NEEMOI SPEEDY ACQUAYE PERC(A — (A) AKIDO — 1972 MERCURY US SRM1 644

A27 JAN AKKERMAN A27

JAN AKKERMAN G (ALL — (A) PROFILE — 1972 HARVEST UK SHSP4026 US SIRE 7407
KAZ LUX V (D — (B) GUITAR FOR SALE — 1973 BOVEMA EURO 51105
JOACHIM KUHN B (E — (C) TABERNAKEL — 1974 ATLANTIC UK K 40522 US ATCO 7032
BRUNO CASTELUCCI D (EG — (D) ELI — 1977 ATLANTIC UK K 50320 US ATCO 18210
RAY LUCAS D (C — (E) JAN AKKERMAN — 1978 ATLANTIC UK K 50420 US ATCO 19159
CARMINE APPICE D (C — (F) ARANJUEZ — 1978 CBS UK 81843
GEORGE FLYNN K (C — (G) LIVE — 1979 ATLANTIC UK K 50560
BERT RUITER B (A — (H) TALENT FOR SALE — 19 M F P NL 5036
PIERRE VAN DER LINDEN D(ADE — (J) 3 — 1979 ATLANTIC UK K50664
HENRY RONDE STEEL(J — (K) TRANSPARENTAL — 1980 ARIOLA NL 203 043
DANIEL WAITZMAN FLT (C — (L) BEST OF — 1980 ATLANTIC NL 50740
FRANS SMIT D (A — (M) ALL IN THE FAMILY — 1981 ARIOLA 655 137
FERRY MAAT PNO (A — (N) MEDITATION — 19 POLYDOR EURO 2441 089
JIM CHAMPAGNOLA SAX (M — ( ) A PHENOMENON — 1979 EMI EURO 26189
AF TOMBOEL PERC (M
EDDIE CONRAD PERC (M — JAAP VAN EYCK B (A — JASPER VAN'T HOF K (DG — TOM BARLAGE SAX K (G
WILLEM ENNES K (G — RICK VAN DER LINDEN K (D — WARWICK READING B (D — RICHARD DE BOIS D (D
MARGARET ESHUIS V (D — MAGGIE McNEAL V (D — PATRICIA PAAY V (D — CEES VAN DER LAARSE B(EG
NEPPIE NOYA PERC (DEGJ — TIM BOGERT B (C — PETER SCHON K (J — DUANE HITCHINS K (J
BUNNY BRUNEL B (J — DAVID KELFIELD D (J — YVETTE CASON V (J — WILLY DEE V (J
JODY PYPER V (J — KIMM HEKKER V (J — MARGO THUNDER V (J — RON BIJTELELAAR B(B
SINEY WACHTEL D (B — COCKY AKKERMAN D (B — GENE SANTION B (J — JON FADDIS TPT(J
ALAN RUBIN HRNS (J — TOM MALONE TROM (J — DAVID TAYLOR TROM (J — JIM ODGREN SAX (J
TONY SCOTT WLAR V(N — CEES SCHNOMA K (N — WIM ESSED B (N — BRUNO CASTELUCCI D (JN
JON CLARK HRNS (J — HOWARD JHOA SAX (J — PETE GORDON HRNS (J — MIKE BRECKER SAX (J

A27A ALABAMA A27A

RANDY OWEN G V (AB — (A) MY HOME'S IN ALABAMA — 1980 RCA 1 3644
TEDDY GENTRY B V (AB — (B) FEELS SO RIGHT — 1981 RCA 5025
MARK HERNDON D V (AB
JEFF COOK G K V (AB

A28 ALABAMA STATE TROUPERS A28

DON NIX G V (A — (A) ALABAMA STATE TROUPERS — 1972 ELEKTRA US EKS75022
FURRY LEWIS V G (A
CLAYTON IVEY PNO (A — TIPPY ARMSTRONG G (A — FRED PROOTY D (A — BOB WRAY B (A
KEN WOODLEY K (A — CAROLYN WATKINS V (A — JEANNIE GREENE V (A — BRENDA PATTERSON V(A
WAYNE PERKINS G (A — MARIANNE WATKINS V (A — MARLINE GREENE V (A — MARY ANDERSON V (A
TARP TARRANT D (A

A28A ALAMO A28A

KEN WOODLEY K V (A — (A) ALAMO — 1971 ATLANTIC US 8279
LARRY RASPBERRY G (A
RICHARD ROSEBROUGH G (A — LARRY DAVIS B (A

A28B ALBATROSS A28B

PETER BARRON B (B — (A) ALBATROSS — 19? ?
KIM BRYANT D (B — (B) A BREATH OF FRESH AIR — 19? REPRISE US 4002
LINDSAY BJERRE G V (B — (C) GOING EASY — 19 HARVEST US SMAS 671

A28C ALBERT A28C

OTIS SMITH V (AB — (A) ALBERT — 1970 PERCEPTION US
PAUL DICKLER G (B — (B) THE ALBERT — 1971 PERCEPTION US 9
MICHAEL GIBSON TROM (AB
BARRY LAZAROWITZ D (AB — HOWARD WYETH K (AB — RICHARD MEISTERMAN TPT (B — FRANK VICARI SAX (B
JAY SILVA TPT (B — PETER PETRUCCELLI B(B — JON HUSTON HRNS (AB — MIKE MATTIO TPT (A
JAY THOMAS TPT (A — JOE BRAZIL SAX (A — STEVE McCORD G B (A — BILLY ELMIGER B (A

A29 ALBERTO Y LOS TRIOS PARANOIAS A29

CHRIS LEE V G (ABCD — (A) ALBERTO Y LOS TRIOS PARANOIAS — 1976 TRANSATLANTIC TRA 316
BOB HARDING V G B (ABCD — (B) ITALIANS FROM OUTER SPACE — 1977 TRANSATLANTIC TRA 349
BRUCE MITCHELL PERC (ABCD — (C) SNUFF ROCK (EP) — 1977 STIFF LAST 2

(CONTINUED)

A29 (CONTINUED)

ALBERTO Y LOS TRIOS PARANOIAS

A29

TONY BOWERS G B (ABCD (D) SKITE 1978 LOGO 1009
SIMON WHITE STEEL (ABCD (E) WORST OF THE BERTS 1980 LOGO 4008
JIMMY HIBBERT V B (ABCD
LES PRYOR V (ABCD CHAS JANKEL K (D ROGER RUSKIN SPEAR SAX(D ALBIE DONNELLY HRS(A
GRAHAM ROBERTSON HRS (A DAVE TOMLINSON CLAR SYN (A ANTHONY MOORE ORG (A PETER TENNER PROD(A

A30

THE ALBION BAND

A30

ASHLEY HUTCHINGS B V (ALL THE ALBION COUNTRY BAND
MARTIN CARTHY V G (EFMO (A) JAN 1972 (B) JAN OCT 1972 (C) OCT 1972 (D) DEC 1972 (E) 1973
SUE HARRIS V OBOE DULC(EF (F) BATTLE OF THE FIELD 1976 ISLAND UK HELP 25
JOHN KIRKPATRICK V CONC(AEFO ETCHINGHAM STEAM BAND
MARTIN NICHOLLS SACKBUTS(F (G) JAN 1974 JULY 1974 (H) SUMMER 1974 (J) APRIL 1975
SIMON NICOL V G K DULC (ABCDEFKLMN ALBION DANCE BAND
ROGER SWALLOW D (EF (K) FORMED 1975
DAVE MATTACKS D (BCEFJKLM (L) THE PROSPECT BEFORE US 1977 HARVEST UK SHSP4059
JOHN IVESON SACKBUTS(F ALBION BAND
COLIN SHEEN SACKBUTS (F (M) RISE UP LIKE THE SUN 1978 HARVEST UK SHSP4092 FR 06612
PAUL BEER SACKBUTS(F (N) ALBION RIVER HYMN MARCH 1979
STEVE ASHLEY V G HCA (B (O) LARK RISE TO CANDLEFORD 1980 CHARISMA UK CD 54020
ROYSTON WOOD V CONC (AB
SUE DRAHEIM FDL BANJO(ABC ANDY FAIRWEATHER LOW V(M RICHARD THOMPSON G V(ACDM LINDA THOMPSON V (CDM
BILL CADDICK V PERC(O SHIRLEY COLLINS V (DGHJKL JOHN WATCHAM (D TERRY POTTER HCA(GJ
PETER KNIGHT FDL (J JOHN RODD V CONC(KL WILL DUKE CONC MEL(K MADDY PRIOR V (N
JOHN SOTHCOTT VIELLE(KLN PHIL PICKETT WIND K (LMN MICHAEL GREGORY D (KLMO PETE BULLOCK K WIND(MNO
JOHN TAMS V MEL(LMO RIC SANDERS VLN (M GRAEME TAYLOR G K (LMO DAVE BRISTOW K (M
KATE McGARRIGLE V (M JULIE COVINGTON V (M PAT DONALDSON V (M HOWARD EVANS HRNS(O
DOUG MORTER G (O BRIAN PROTHEROE K V O STEVE SAUNDERS TROM (O MARTIN SIMPSON BAN(O
IAN HOLDER ACC (GHJ VIC GAMMON (HJ EDDIE UPTON V HCA(JKL

A30A

ALCO

A30A

TIM CAESAR V (A (A) THREADS OF LIFE 1972 ALCO ALC 530
JULIAN CAESAR D V K(A
PAUL FIDLIN B G V (A BEN BROOKE G B V (A MARTIN KENNARD V (A RICHARD WILLIAMS V (A
JONATHAN PALMER V (A STEPHEN HARBACH V (A NORMAN FRASER V (A RAY DAVISON V (A
ITCHEN ORCHESTRA (A

A30B

ALDA RESERVE

A30B

BRAD ELLIS K V (A (A) LOVE GOES ON 1979 SIRE GERM 201 042 UK SRK 6079
MARK SUALL G V (A
MATTHEW PATUTO D V (A TONY SHANAHAN B V (A

A31

ALESSI BROTHERS

A31

BOBBY ALESSI V G (ABC (A) ALESSI 1977 A&M UK AMLH64608 US 4608
BILLY ALESSI K V (ABC (B) ALL FOR A REASON 1978 A&M UK AMLH68446 US 4657
JAMES DIVISEK D (C (C) DRIFTIN' 1978 A&M UK AMLH64713 US 4713
DENNIS BELFIELD B (C (D) WORDS & MUSIC 1979 A&M UK AMLH64776 US 4776
JIM SEALS SAX (C
LOUIE SHELTON G (C BRIAN WHITCOMB K (C STEVE PORCARO SYN (C ALAN ESTES PERC (C
VINCE CHARLES PERC (C ED GREENE D (C DAVID HUNGATE B (C LEE RITENOUR G (C
MELVIN WATSON G (C GREG PHILLINGANES K (C ABE LABORIEL B (C RICHIE HAVENS V (C
MICHAEL BAIRD D (C DASH CROFTS V (C GREG MATHIESON K (C DON MENZA SAX (C
MIKE MELVION G (A DENNID BUDIMIR G (A RAY PARKER G (A JIM HUGHART (A
SCOTTY EDWARDS B (A JEFF PORCARO D (A HAL BLAINE D (A JOHN GUERIN D (A
TOM SCOTT WIND (A VIC FELDMAN VIBES(A EMIL RICHARDS VIBES(A BONAS HOWE PERC(A
FRANK RIVIOLI D (A STEVE GADD D (B ANDY NEWMARK D (B WILL LEE B (B
RICHARD TEE K (B JOHN TROPEA G (B CHARLIE BROWN SAX (B DAVID SPINOZZA G (B
MICHAEL CHIMES (B BOB RILEY (B RAPHAEL GOLDFIELD B (B JIMMY RIPPETOE G (B
DAWN KAROL (B DAVID SANBORN HRNS (B RANDY BRECKER HRNS (B MICHAEL BRECKER HRN(B
ALAN RUBIN HRNS (B GEORGE YOUNG HRNS (B RONNIE CUBER HRNS (B WAYNE ANDREA HRN(B
JOE DEANGELES HRNS (B

A31A

ARTHUR ALEXANDER

A31A

ARTHUR ALEXANDER V (ALL (A) ALEXANDER THE GREAT 19 LONDON RED 1364
(B) ARTHUR ALEXANDER 19 LONDON RED 1401
(C) YOU BETTER MOVE ON 1962 LONDON UK HAD 2457
(C) YOU BETTER MOVE ON 1962 DOT US 25434
(D) ARTHUR ALEXANDER 197 WB US 2567

A32

WILLY ALEXANDER & THE BOOM BOOM BAND

A32

WILLY ALEXANDER V K (AB (A) WILLY ALEXANDER & BOOM BOOM BAND 1978 MCA UK MCF 2835 US 2323
BILLY LOOSIGIAN G (AB (B) MEAN WHILE BACK IN THE STATES 1979 MCA UK MCF 2876 US 3052
SEVERIN GROSSMAN B (AB
DAVID McLEAN D PERC(AB

A32A

ALEXANDER RABBIT

A32A

C HOLMER (A (A) THE HUNCHBACK OF NOTRE DAME 1970 MERCURY US 61291
B BRADBURY (A
L DEMSKI (A S SCHEIER (A C J BRODOWICZ (A

A32B

ALEXIS

A32B

RANDY REEDER D (A (A) ALEXIS 1977 MCA US 2260
LARRY BRADEN B V (A
DAVE PETERS SAX K(A ROBBIE FALLBERO G (A EDDIE ULIBARRI K V (A DICK WALKER K V(A

A33

ALFALPHA

A33

NICK LAIRD CLOWES V HCA G (A (A) ALFALPHA 1977 EMI UK EMC 3213
ANDY HARLEY V G (A
SAM HARLEY B G (A STEVE CHAPMAN D (A ADRIAN REA D (A RAY COOPER PERC(A
JIM CUOMO SAX K(A B J COLE STEEL(A JOHN MEALING PNO (A DEL NEWMAN K (A
FRED SHUSTER G (A ISAAC GUILLORY G (A

A33A

ALICE

A33A

DOUDON WEISS D (AB (A) ALICE 1970 METRONOME FR MLP15391
ALAN SUZAN V B (AB (A) ALICE 19 BYG FR 529016
PAUL SEMANA G (B (B) ARRETEZ LA MONDE 1973 POLYDOR FR 2393 043
LUC BERTIN K (B
IAN GELFS G V (B BRUNO BESSE G (A SYLVAIN DUPLANT B V (A

A33B
ALIAS
A33B

JOJO BILLINGSLEY V (A — (A) CONTRABAND — 1979 MERCURY US SRM1 3800
DORMAN COGBURN G (A
JIMMY DAUGHERTY V (A — BARRY HARWOOD G (A — ARTIMUS PYLE D (A — RICKY POWELL B (A
BILLY POWELL K (A — LEON WILKESON B (A

A33C
ALIBI
A33C

(A) FRIENDS — 1980 MAGNET UK 5034 POLYDOR US 6292

A33D
ALIEN
A33D

(A) SONS OF THE UNIVERSE — 1980 ELEKTRA US 221

A33E
ALIOTTA HAYNES
A33E

MITCH ALIOTTA G B V(ABCD — (A) ALIOTTA HAYNES MUSIC — 1970 AMPEX US 10108
SKIP HAYNES B G V(ABCD — (B) ALIOTTA HAYNES JEREMIAH — 1970 AMPEX US 10119
TED ALIOTTA B V (A — (C) LAKE SHORE DRIVE — 19 BIG FOOT US 714
JOHN JEREMIAH K V (BCD — (D) SLIPPIN AWAY — 1977 LITTLE FOOT US 711
RON ZETA D (B
BOB PARISIO D V (D

A33F
ALIVE & KICKIN'
A33F

(A) ALIVE & KICKIN' — 197 ROULETTE US 47052

A34
ALKATRAZ
A34

WILL YOUATT G (A — (A) DOING A MOONLIGHT — 1976 UA/ROCKFIELD UAS 30001
JAMES DAVIES G (A
JEFF SINGER B (A — STUART HALLIDAY G (A — JIMMY JEWEL SAX (A — CLIVE JOHN K (A
RAY MARTINEZ G (A

A34A
ALKATRAZZ
A34A

CRAIG STEVENS V (A — (A) YOUNGBLOOD — 1981 RCA UK 5023
BOB JENNER G (A
GARY BEVEN B (A — NICK PARSONS D (A

A34B
BARRY ALLEN
A34B

BARRY ALLEN (— (A) BARRY ALLEN — 19 UNI US 73104

A35
DAEVID ALLEN
A35

DAEVID ALLEN V G (ALL — (A) OBSOLETE(DASHIELL HEDAYAT) — 1971 SHANDAR FR 10009 CBS UK 83512
DASHIELL HEDAYAT (A — (B) BANANA MOON — 1975 CAROLINE UK C1512
ROBERT WYATT G D V(B — (B) BANANA MOON — 1971 BYG FR 529 345
ARCHIE LEGGET B (B — (B) BANANA MOON — 197 CHARLY CR 30165
GARY WRIGHT VLN (B — (C) GOOD MORNING — 1976 VIRGIN UK V2054
GERRY FIELDS VLN (B — (D) NOW IS THE HAPPIEST TIME..........1977 AFFINITY AFF3
BARRY ST JOHN V (B — (E) N'EXISTE PAS — 1979 CHARLY UK CRL5015
PIP PYLE D (AB
CHRISTIAN TRITSCH G (AB — NICK EVANS TROM (B — GILLIE'SHAKTI YONI'SMYTH V(ABC — DIDIER MALHERBE FLT (A
MAGGIE BELL V (B — WILLIAM BURROUGHS V (A — SAM WYATT V (A — PEPE MILAN G (CDE
ANN CAMPS V (C — TONY PASCUAL K G (C — TONY ARES B (C — JUAN BIBLIONI G (D
TONI TREE FERNANDEZ G (C — SAM GOPAL PERC (D — VICTOR PERAINO K (D — VERA VIOLIN VLN(D
XAVER RIBA VLN (D — CHRIS CUTLER D (E — ANGEL ADUANA BANJO (E — RONALD WALTHEN (E
BRIAN DAMAGE D (E — GEORGE BISHOP SAX (E

A35A
LUTHER ALLISON
A35A

LUTHER ALLISON G V (AB — (A) LOVE ME MAMA(BLUES NEBULAE) — 1969 DELMARK us DS625
WITH — (B) NIGHT LIFE — 1976 GORDY US US G 974V1
RICHARD TEE K (B — (C) LUTHERS BLUES — 1973 GORDY US 967
ROBIN KENYATTA SAX (B — (D) BA NEWS IS COMING — 1973 GORDY US 964 VOGUE 523023
GERRY BROWN D (B
K J KNIGHT D (C — STEVE KHAN G (B — JOHN LEE B (B — JEFFREY ALDRICH B (B
MICHAEL CARVIN D (B — LARRY BYRNE K (B — DR JOHN K (B — RAY ANDERSON TROM(B
JIM SOLBERG G (B — RALPH McDONALD PERC (B — RANDY BRECKER TPT (B — MICHAEL BRECKER SAX(B
LEW DEL GATTO SAX (B — RICHARD DRAKE SAX (B — BRUCE JOHNSTONE SAX (B — TASHA THOMAS V (B
MAERETHA STEWART V (B — HILDA HARRIS V (B — GAIL KANTOR V (B — DAVID NEWMAN SAX(B
ANDREW SMITH D (CD — BOB BABBITT B (C — GARY DEAM D (C — PAUL WHITE K (CD
TOM CURRY K (C — RAY GOODMAN G (CD — GENE BLOCK G (C
GARFILED ANYOVE HCA (D

A35B
MICHAEL ALLEN
A35B

MICHAEL ALLEN (ALL — (A) ACT ONE — 19? LONDON US 544
(B) LOVE OF MIKE — 19? LONDON US
(C) SOMETHING SPECIAL — 19 MGM US 4762

A35C
PETER ALLEN
A35C

PETER ALLEN K V (ALL — (A) CONTINENTAL AMERICA — 1975 A&M UK AMLS 63643
FRED THALER D (C — (B) TAUGHT BY EXPERTS — 1976 A&M UK AMLH 64584
DAVE PARLATO B (C — (C) IT IS TIME FOR PETER ALLEN — 1977 A&M UK AMLH 63706
RUBIN RIVERA CELLO(C — (D) I COULD HAVE BEEN A SAILOR — 1979 A&M UK AMLH 64739
MIKE WARREN G (C — (E) BI-COASTAL — 1980 A&M UK AMLH 64825
JOHN GUTH G (C
TIM MAY G (C — MARSHALL ROSENBERG PERC (C — DAVID FOSTER K (C — ED GREENE D (E
MIKE PORCARO B (E — DAVID WILLIAMS G (E — PAULINHO DACOSTA PERC (E — EUGENE MEROS SAX(E
RICHARD PAGE V (E — STEVE GEORGE V (E — TOM KEANE K (E — STEVE LUKATHER G (E
GARY HERBIG SAX (E — RALPH HUMPHRIES D (E — DAVE McDANIEL B (E — LON PRICE SAX (E
CARLOS VEGA D (E — RICHIE ZITO G (E — LARRY WILLIAMS K (E — JAY GRAYDON G (E
ERICH BULLING STR (E — JOSE ROSSY PERC (E — JERRY HEY HRNS (E

A35D
TERRY ALLEN
A35D

TERRY ALLEN K V (ALL — (A) JUAREZ — 1975 LANDFALL 1394
LLOYD MAINES G V (BC — (B) LUBBOCK — 1978 FATE 33997
KENNY MAINES B V (BC — (C) SMOKIN' THE DUMMY — 1980 FATE 38121
DONNIE MAINES D V (C
RICHARD BOWDEN FDL V(BC — JESSE TAYLOR G V (C — JOE ELY HCA (BC — PONT BOONE ACC (BC
ALAN SHINN PERC (BC — MIKE MEYERS PERC (C — MONTE WILLIAMS K SYN (C — TOMMIE ANDERSON HRNS(BC
MARK ANTHONY HRNS (BC — JACK DELAHUNTY CLAR (C — DON CALDWELL SAX (C — JO HARVEY ALLEN V (BC
GREG DOUGLAS G (A — PETER KAUKONEN G (A — DIANE HARRIS V (A — JIMMY HOWELL PROD(A
CURTIS McBRIDE D (B — LUIS MARTINEZ G (B — JESSE TAYLOR G (B — RUSS STANDEFER HRN (B
SYLVESTER RICE V (B — GIVEN HEWITT V (B — SUZANNE PAULK V (B — FREDDY PRIDE V (B
MIKE AUSTIN V (B — VINCENT THOMAS V (B — JIMMY SAMPSON V (B — STRINGS & BAND (B

A36 DUANE ALLMAN A36

DUANE ALLMAN G (ALL (A) ANTHOLOGY 1972 CAPRICORN UK K 67502 US 0108
(A) ANTHOLOGY 1974 CAPRICORN UK 2659 035
(B) ANTHOLOGY VOL 2 1974 CAPRICORN UK 2659037 US 0139
(C) BEST OF DUANE ALLMAN 1979 CAPRICORN UK 2429 187

A37 GREGG ALLMAN A37

GREGG ALLMAN K V (ALL (A) LAID BACK 1973 CAPRICORN UK 2429 103 K47508
CHER V (D (A) LAID BACK 1973 CAPRICORN US CP 0116
NEIL LARSEN K (CD (B) GREGG ALLMAN TOUR (DBL) 1974 CAPRICORN UK 2659 038 US 0141
MAC REBENNACK K (C (C) PLAYIN' UP A STORM 1977 CAPRICORN UK 2473 131 US 0181
DAVID LUELL SAX (C (D) TWO THE HARD WAY 1977 W B UK K 56436 US 3120
BILL STEWART D (ABCD
JOHN HUG G (CD RICKY HIRSCH G (CD FRED BECKMAIER B (C WILLIE WEEKS B (CD
RED CALLENDER B (C STEVE MADAIO HRNS (C MILT HOLLAND PERC (C PAT RIZZO HRNS(C
CLYDIE KING V (CD SHIRLEY MATTHEWS V (CD VANETTA FIELDS V (CD JIM HORN HRNS(D
RON EADES SAX (D HARRISON CALLOWAY HRS (D PAT HENDERSON V (D DOUG HAYWOOD V (D
DENNIS GOODE TROM (D HARVEY THOMPSON SAX (D TIM SCHMIT V (D SID SHARP STRINGS(D
BOBBYE HALL PERC (D SCOTT BOYER G (ABD FRED TACKETT G (D MICKEY RAPHAEL HCA (D
RANDALL BRAMBLETT SAX (D BEN CAULEY TPT (D RUSSELL MORRIS V (D STEVE BECKMAIER G (C
BILL PAYNE K (C VICTOR FELDMAN PERC (C TOMMY TALTON G (AB JOHNNY LEE JOHNSON D(B
KENNY TIBBETTS B (B CHUCK LEAVELL PNO (AB DAVID BROWN SAX (B ED FREEMAN STR(A
HAROLD WILLIAMS SAX (B TODD LOGAN TPT (B PETER EKLUND TPT (B ANNIE SUTTON V (B
ERIN DICKINS V (B LYNN RUBIN V (B JOHNNY SANDLIN PROD (AB RUSS TITELMAN PROD(C
LENNY WARONKER PROD (C BUZZ FEITEN G (A CHARLIE HAYWARD B (A DAVID NEWMAN SAX (A
JAIMOE JAI JOHANSON PERC(A PAUL HORNSBY K (A JIMMY NAILS G (A BUTCH TRUCKS PERC (A
MAERETHA STEWART V (A HELENE MILES V (A HILDA HARRIS V (A ALBERT ROBINSON V (A
CARL HALL V (A JUNE McGRUDER V (A LYNDA NOVEMBER V (A EILEEN GILBERT V (A
EMILY HOUSTON V (A

A38 ALLMAN BROTHERS BAND A38

GREGG ALLMAN K V (ALL (A) THE ALLMAN BROTHERS BAND 1969 ATCO US SD33308
DUANE ALLMAN G (ABCDI (A) THE ALLMAN BROTHERS BAND 1969 CAPRICORN UK 228 033
BERRY OAKLEY B (ABCDE (A) THE ALLMAN BROTHERS BAND 1969 CAPRICORN US 0196
RICHARD BETTS G V (ABCDEFGHJKL (B) IDLEWILD SOUTH 1970 ATCO US SD 33342
JAI JOHANSON PERC (ABCDEFHJL (B) IDLEWILD SOUTH 1970 CAPRICORN UK 2400 032
BUTCH TRUCKS PERC (ABCDEFHJKL (B) IDLEWILD SOUTH 1970 CAPRICORN US 0197
THOM DOUCETTE HCA (B (C) LIVE AT FILLMORE EAST (DBL) 1971 CAPRICORN UK K 60011
CHUCK LEAVELL SYN PNO V (EFH (C) LIVE AT FILLMORE EAST (DBL) 1971 CAPRICORN UK 2659 039
LAMAR WILLIAMS B (EFH (C) LIVE AT FILLMORE EAST (DBL) 1971 CAPRICORN US 2/802 0131
LES DUDEK G (E (C) LIVE AT FILLMORE EAST (DBL) 1971 POLYDOR 2639 102
TOMMY TALTON G (G (D) EAT A PEACH (DBL) 1972 CAPRICORN UK K 67501
JOHNNY SANDLIN G PERC(F (D) EAT A PEACH (DBL) 1972 CAPRICORN UK 2659 034
BILL STEWART PERC (F (D) EAT A PEACH (DBL) 1972 CAPRICORN US 2C4 0102
DAN TOLER G (JKL (D) EAT A PEACH (DBL) 1972 POLYDOR 2639 101
DAVID GOLDFLIES B (JKL (E) BROTHERS & SISTERS 1973 CAPRICORN US CP 0111
DAVID TOLER D (KL (E) BROTHERS & SISTERS 1971 CAPRICORN UK 2429 102
CHARLIE DANIELS FDL (KL (E) BROTHERS & SISTERS 1974 CAPRICORN UK K 47507
CHIP YOUNG V (L (F) WIN LOOSE OR DRAW 1975 CAPRICORN UK 2476 116
MARK MORRIS PERC (KL (F) WIN LOOSE OR DRAW 1975 CAPRICORN US CP 0156
JOHNNY COBB V PNO (L (G) THE ROAD GOES ON FOREVER (DBL) 1975 CAPRICORN UK 2637 101
TOM COBB V (L (G) THE ROAD GOES ON FOREVER (DBL) 1975 CAPRICORN US 2CP 0164
THOMAS CAINE V (L (H) WIPE THE WINDOWS,....... (DBL) 1976 CAPRICORN UK 2637 103
MIKE LAWLER K (KL (H) WIPE THE WINDOWS,....... (DBL) 1976 CAPRICORN US CP 0177
JIMMY HALL SAX V (KL (J) ENLIGHTENED ROGUES 1979 CAPRICORN UK POLD5016
JIM ESSERY HCA (JK (K) REACH FOR THE SKY 1980 ARISTA US 9535 UK SPART 1146
SHERRY CAINE V (L (K) REACH FOR THE SKY 1980 ARISTA NL 202 843
BONNIE BRAMLETT V (J (L) BROTHERS OF THE ROAD 1981 ARISTA UK SPART 1176
MIMI HART V (J
JOE LALA PERC (J (AB) BEGINNINGS (DBL) 1973 ATCO US SD 2 805
GREG GUIDRY V (L (AB) BEGINNINGS (DBL) 1974 CAPRICORN UK 2569 040
JOY LANNON V (L (AB) BEGINNINGS (DBL) 1974 CAPRICORN UK K 60046
DONNA McELROY V (L (AB) BEGINNINGS (DBL) 1974 CAPRICORN US 2CX 0123
KEITH ENGLAND V (L ( ) THE ALLMAN BROTHERS (DBL) 19 ATLANTIC K 60070
JEFF SILVERMAN V (L ( ) ALL MENS BROTHERS (DBL) 19 ATCO US 40424
RANDALL HART V (L ( ) THE BEST OF 1980 CAPRICORN UK 2429 198
PETER KINGSBERRY V (L ( ) DUANE & GREGG 1973 POLYDOR UK 2310 235
JOE PIZZULO V (L ( ) DUANE & GREGG 197 SPRINGBOARD US 4046
JOHN RYAN PROD (L ( ) DUANE & GREGG 1972 POLYDOR GER 2310 235
( ) DUANE & GREGG 19 BOLD 33301

A39 ALLMAN JOYS A39

GREGG ALLMAN K V (A (A) ALLMANJOYS 1973 DIAL US DL6005
DUANE ALLMAN G V (A (A) ALLMANJOYS 197 MERCURY UK 6398 005
RALPH BALINGER D (A
RONNIE WILKIN PNO (A TOMMY AMATO D (A BOBBY DENNIS G (A JACK JACKSON G (A

A39A ALMA ATA A39A

PHIL DRESHER V (A (A) DREAMS 19 CAIN GERM CL 4793
LESLIE FORSTER B (A
DAGMAR HORN G V (A JOE SCHAFER G V (A TOMMY VIEWEG D (A RANDY KWIZOROWSKI K V(A
LUDWIG GOTZ TROM (A JORG SEEMAN TPT (A MARTI URIGSHARDT SAX (A

A40 JOHNNY ALMOND A40

JOHNNY ALMOND SAX K(ALL (A) MUSIC MACHINE PATENT PENDING 1969 DERAM UK SML 1043 US 18030
WITH (B) MUSIC MACHINE HOLLYWOOD BLUES 1970 DERAM UK SML 1057 US 18037
JEFF CONDON HRNS (A
JIMMY CRAWFORD G (A ROGER SUTTON B (A JOHNNY WIGGINS K (A STEVE HAMMOND G (A
ALAN WHITE D (A CHARLES KYNARD ORG (B JOE PASS G (B RAY NEOPOLITAN B (B
EARL PALMER B (B JOE HARRIS HRS (B HADLEY CALIMAN HRS (B CURTIS AMY SAX(B
PAUL WILLIAMS (A ZOOT MONEY (A

A41 ALPHA BAND A41

STEVE SOLES V G (ABC | (A) ALPHA BAND | 1977 ARISTA UK ARTY 143 US AB 4102
T BONE BURNETT V G (ABC | (B) SPARK IN THE DARK | 1977 ARISTA UK US AB 4145
DAVID JACKSON B (A | (B) SPARK IN THE DARK | 1977 PATHE FR 06860066
MATT BETTON D (AB | (C) STATUE MAKERS OF HOLLYWOOD | 1978 ARISTA UK SPART1039US AB 4279
DAVID MINER B (BC | (C) STATUE MAKERS OF HOLLYWOOD | 1978 PATHE FR 06860885
CINDY BULLENS V (BC
EVERETT BRYSON PERC (C | LEE PASTORA (C | K O THOMAS K (AB | DAVID MANSFIELD G (ABC
ROSCOE WEST V (A | ROSANNA TAPLIN V (A | JOE CORRERO D (B | BILLY MAXWELL (BC
RINGO STARR D (B | MIKE UTLEY K (B | OSAU KITAJIMA KOTO (B | GEOFFREY HALES D (B

A41A ALPHA RALPHA A41A

MICHAEL MARESKA G (A | (A) ALPHA RALPHA | 19 WEA K 56330
CHARLIE CHARRIROW B (A
EMMANUEL LACORDAIRE PERC(A | CLAUDE ALVAREZ PERC G(A | JEAN GARDET K (A

A41B ALPHATAURAS A41B

PIETRO PELLEGRINI K (A | (A) ALPHATAURAS | 1973 MAGMA ITALY 18001
GUIDO WASSERMAN G (A
GIORGIO SANTANDEREA D (A | ALFONSO OLIVE B (A | MICHELE BAVARO V (A

A42 ALQUIN A42

FERDINAND BAKKER G K V(ABCDEF | (A) MARKS | 1972 POLYDOR 2646 101 UK 2480 152
THUNDERTHIGHS V (| (A) MARKS | 1972 POLYDOR 2419 060
RONALD OTTENHOFF HRS (ABCDEF | (B) MOUNTAIN QUEEN | 1973 POLYDOR UK 2480 179
DICK FRANSSEN K (ABCDEF | (C) NOBODY CAN WAIT FOREVER | 19 POLYDOR 2925 045 UK 2480 262
MICHAEL VAN DIJK V (CDEF | (C) NOBODY CAN WAIT FOREVER | 1975 RCA US APLI 1061
HEIN MARS B (ABC | (D) CRASH | 19 POLYDOR 2646 101
PAUL WESTSTRATE D (ABC | (E) BEST KEPT SECRET | 1976 POLYDOR 2925 045
JOB TARENSKEEN WIND (ABCDEF | (F) ON TOUR | 1976 POLYDOR 2441 067
JAN VISSEN B (F

A42A SHIRLEY ALSTON A42A

SHIRLEY ALSTON V (ALL | (A) WITH ALITTLE HELP | 1975 LONDON SHA 8491
FLAMINGO'S V (A | (B) LADY ROSE | 1977 STRAWBERRY US STW 6004
THE DRIFTERS V (A | (C) SINGS SHIRELLES GREATEST HITS | 1977 STRAWBERRY US STW 6006
BELMONTS V (A
HERMANS HERMITS V (A | THE 5 SATINS V (A | DANNY & THE JUNIORS V (A
SHEP & THE LIMLITES V (A

A42B ALTERED IMAGES A42B

CLARE GROGAN V (A | (A) HAPPY BIRTHDAY | 1981 EPIC UK 84893

A43 ALTERNATIVE T V A43

MICKY SMITH B (1 | (A) THE IMAGE HAS CRACKED | 1978 DEPTFORD FUN CITY DPL 01
ALEX FERGUSSON G (123D | (B) WHAT YOU SEE IS WHAT YOU ARE | 1978 DEPTFORD FUN CITY DLP 02
MARK PERRY V G (ABCD12345 | (C) VIBING UP THE SENILE MAN | 1979 DEPTFORD FUN CITY DLP 03
JOHN TOWE D (12 | (D) LIVE AT THE RAT CLUB 77 | 1979 CRYSTAL CLP 001
DAVE GEORGE D (C5 | (E) ACTION TIME VISION (COMP) | 1979 DEPTFORD FUN CITY LPS005
MARK LINEHAM G (| (F) STRANGE KICKS | 1981 IRS UK 70023
TYRONE THOMAS B (A234D | (1) APRIL 1977 | (2)MAY JULY 1977 | (3) AUG OCT 1977
CHRIS BENNETT D (AD34 | (4) OCT 1977 1978 | (5) 1979 | (B) WITH HERE & NOW
DENNIS BURNS B (ABC45

A43A ALTERNATIVES A43A

(A) ALTERNATIVES | 197 WB US 31873

A44 ALTHEA & DONNA A44

ALTHEA V (A | (A) UPTOWN TOP RANKING | 1978 FRONT LINE FL 1012
DONNA V (A

A45 AMAZING RHYTHM ACES A45

BARRY BYRD BURTON V G (ABCD | (A) STACKED DECK | 1975 ABC UK ABCL5152 US ABCD 913
BILLY EARHEART K (ABCDEF | (B) TOO STUFFED TOO JUMP | 1976 ABC UK ABCL5160 US ABCD 940
JIM KERSHAW G (A | (B) TOO STUFFED TO JUMP | 1976 CARRERE FR 68024
BUTCH McDADE V D (ABCDEF | (C) TOUCAN DO IT TOO | 1976 ABC UK ABCL5219 US AB 1005
JAMES HOOKER K V (ABCDEF | (C) TOUCAN DO IT TOO | 1976 CARRERE FR 1005
JEFF DAVIS B (ABCDEF | (D) BURNING THE BALLROOM DOWN | 1978 ABC UK ABCL5244 US AA 1063
RUSSELL SMITH V G (ABCDEF | (D) BURNING THE BALLROOM DOWN | 1978 CARRERE FR 68057
DUNCAN CAMERON G V (EF | (E) AMAZING RHYTHM ACES | 1979 ABC UK ABCL5267 CBS US 36083
JIMMY JOHNSON G (E | (F) HOW THE HELL DO YOU SPELL RHYTHUM | 1980 WB UK K 56859 US 3476
ROGER HAWKINS D (E
HARRISON CALLOWAY TPT (E | RONNIE EADES SAX (E | HARVEY THOMPSON SAX (E
CHARLES ROSE TROM (E | LLOYD BARRY TPT (E | BEN CAULEY TPT (E
JOAN BAEZ V (E | LIZA GILKYSON V (E

A47 AMBERGRIS A47

LARRY HARLOW K PERC(A | (A) AMBERGRIS | 1970 PARAMOUNT PAS 5014
JERRY WEISS B K (A
CHARLIE CAMILLARI TPT (A | HARRY MAX B VLN TPT(A | GIL FIELDS D (A
GLEN JOHN MILLER TROM (A | JIMMY MAELEN V PERC (A | LEWIS KAHN TROM VLA(A
BILLY SHAY G HCA (A

A47A AMBROSE SLADE A47A

JIM LEE B VLN (A | (A) AMBROSE SLADE | 1969 FONTANA SRF67598
DON POWELL D (| (A) BEGINNINGS | 1969 FONTANA STL 5492
NODDY HOLDER G V (A
DAVE HILL G (A

A48 AMBROSIA A48

CHRISTOPHER NORTH K V (ABCDE | (A) AMBROSIA | 1975 20th CENTURY BT 434
DAVID PACK G K V (ABCDE | (A) AMBROSIA | 1975 DISCODIS FR 199
JOE PUERTA B G V (ABCDE | (B) SOMEWHERE I'VE NEVER TRAVELLED | 1976 20th CENTURY BTH 510
BURLEIGH DRUMMOND D PERC V(ABCDE | (B) SOMEWHERE I'VE NEVER TRAVELLED | 1976 DISCODIS FR 224
IAN UNDERWOOD SAX (AB | (C) LIFE BEYOND L A | 1978 W B US 3135 UK K 56525
RUTH UNDERWOOD MARIMBA(AB | (D) ONE EIGHTY | 1980 W B US 3368 UK K 56811
JIM HORN SAX (E | (E) ROAD ISLAND | 1982 W B US 3638 UK K 56968
DAVID LEWIS K (DE
ROYCE JONES V (DE | ERNIE WATTS SAX (D | JOE SAMPLE PNO (C
CLIFF WOOLLEY HCA (C | DANIEL KOBIALKA VLN (CD | MARTY KRYSTALL SAX (C
JAMES WEST V (C | JAMES GUTHRIE SAX (E

AME SON

A48A

	Year	Label		No.
(A) AME SON	19	BYG	FR	529 325
(A) CATALYSE	19	METRONOME	GER MLP	15 373

MARK BLANC	D	(
BERNARD LAVIALLE	G	(
PATRICK FONTAINE	B	(
FRANCOIS GARRELL	FLT	(

AMEN CORNER

A49

	Year	Label		No.
(A) ROUND AMEN CORNER	1968	DERAM	UK	DML 1021
(B) NATIONAL WELSH COAST LIVE	1979	IMMEDIATE	UK	IMSP 023
(C) FAREWELL MAGNIFICENT SEVEN	1969	IMMEDIATE	UK	IMSP 028
(D) WORLD OF AMEN CORNER	1969	DECCA	UK	SPA 33
(E) AMEN CORNER & SMALL FACES	1975	NEW WORLD		NW 6001
(F) RETURN OF THE MAGNIFICENT SEVEN	1976	IMMEDIATE	UK	IML 1004
(G) GREATEST HITS	1978	IMMEDIATE	UK	IML 2004

ANDY FAIRWEATHER LOW	V G	(ALL
NEIL JONES	G	(
BLUE WEAVER	K	(
ALAN JONES	SAX	(
MIKE SMITH	SAX	(
CLIVE TAYLOR	B	(
DENNIS BRYON	D	(

AMERICA

A50

	Year	Label		US
(A) AMERICA	1971	WB UK K 46093	US	2576
(B) HORSE WITH NO NAME	19	WB UK K 46157		
(C) HOMECOMING	1972	WB UK K 46180	US	2655
(D) HAT TRICK	1973	WB UK K 56016	US	2728
(E) HOLIDAY	1974	WB UK K 56046	US	2808
(F) HEARTS	1975	WB UK K 56115	US	2852
(G) HISTORY (GREATEST HITS)	1975	WB UK K 56169	US	3110
(H) HIDEAWAY	1976	WB UK K 56236	US	2932
(I) HARBOR	1976	WB UK K 56351	US	3017
(J) LIVE	1977	WB UK K 56434	US	3136
(K) SILENT LETTER	1979	CAPITOL	UK US	11950
(L) ALIBI	1980	CAPITOL	UK US	12098
(M) VIEW FROM THE GROUND	1982	CAPITOL		12209

GERRY BECKLEY	G V	(ALL
DEWEY BUNNELL	D G V	(ALL
DAN PEEK	G V	(ABCDEFGHIJ
DAVE ATTWOOD	D	(AG
RAY COOPER	PERC	(AG
JOE OSBORN	B	(CG
DAVID DICKEY	B	(FGHIJK
GEORGE MARTIN	PNO	(H
JIMMY CALIRE	K SAX	(IJK
CLYDIE KING	V	(FG
JESSICA SMITH	V	(FG
HAL BLAINE	D	(CG
DAVID LINDLEY	STEEL	(A
RUSS BALLARD	V	(M
GARY MALLABER	D	(C
WILLIE LEACOX	D	(HIJGKM
LARRY CARLTON	SITAR	(J
DEAN PARKS	G	(M
CARL WILSON	V	(M
TIM SCHMIDT	V	(M
ALVIN TAYLOR	D	(M
SARA TAYLOR	V	(M
HADLEY HECKENSMITH	G	(M
JAI WINDING	K SYN	(M
HENRY DILTZ	BAN	(CG
VANETTA FIELDS	V	(FG
CHESTER McCRACKEN	PERC	(G
STEVE LUKATHER	G	(M
CHRISTOPHER CROSS	V	(M
BRAD PALMER	B	(M
RICK NEIGHER	G	(M
CHUCK KIRKPATRICK	V	(M
BILL MUMY	G	(M
TOM WALSH	PERC	(IJKM
MIKE WOODS	G	(K
KIM HAWORTH	D	(G
MARK ISHAM	SYN	(M
TOM KELLY	V	(M
CHRIS SOTE	K SYN	(M
MIKE PORCARO	B	(M
BOBBY COLLOMBY	PROD	(M
JEFF PORCARO	D	(M

AMERICAN BLUES LEGENDS

A50A

	Year	Label	
(A) AMERICAN BLUES LEGENDS	1972	POLYDOR	2460 186
(A) AMERICAN BLUES LEGENDS	1974	BIG BEAR USBM150202 UK	BEAR 1
( ) AMERICAN BLUES LEGENDS	1975	BIG BEAR	BEAR 8

JOHNNY BARNES	CLAR	(A
EDDIE TAYLOR	G	(A
BIG JOHN WRENCHER	V HCA	(A
DR ROSS	V G HCA	(A
COUSIN JOE PLEASANT	V PNO	(A
BOB BRUNNING	B	(A
GRAHAM GALLERY	B	(A
G P JACKSON	V G	(A
PETE YORK	D	(A
GEORGE CHISHOLM	TROM	(A
BOB HALL	PNO	(A
ROGER HILL	G	(A
COLIN SMITH	TPT	(A

AMERICAN BREED

A51

	Year	Label	No.
(A) AMERICAN BREED	1967	DOT DOLP0255 ATLANTIC	38002
(B) BEND ME SHAPE ME	1968	DOT SLPD 502 ATLANTIC	38003
(C) PUMPKIN,POWDER,SCARLET & GREEN	1968	ATLANTIC	38006
(D) LONELY SIDE OF THE CITY	1968	ATLANTIC	38008

GARY LOIZZO	V G	(ABC
CHUCK COLBERT	B	(ABC
AL CINER	G	(ABC
LEE GRAZIANO	D	(ABC
SKEET BRUSHOR		(C
RALPH CRAIG		(C
ART HOYLE		(C
BOB KEENE		(C
BOBBY LEWIS		(C
JOEL VANCE		(C
CLARK WEBER		(C
LEN DRUSS		(C
JOHN HOWELL		(C

AMERICAN DREAM

A51A

	Year	Label		No.
(A) AMERICAN DREAM	197	AMPEX	US	81001

NICK JACKSON	G K V	(A
DON LEE VAN WINKLE	G V	(A
NICKY INDELICATO	G V	(A
DON FERRIS	B V	(A
MICKY BROOKS	D	(A

AMERICAN EAGLE

A51B

	Year	Label		No.
(A) AMERICAN EAGLE	1970	DECCA	US	75258

GREG BECK	G V	(A
GENE HUBBARD	K V B	(A
ROBERT LOWERY	V	(A
FRED ZEUFELDT	D V	(A

AMERICAN ECHOES

A51C

	Year	Label	No.
(A) LAST TRAIN TO CLARKESVILLE	19	BLUEPORT	BLU 7

AMERICAN FLYER

A52

	Year	Label		No.
(A) AMERICAN FLYER	1976	UA	US	UALA 650
(A) AMERICAN FLYER	1976	UA	UK	UAS29991
(B) SPIRIT OF A WOMAN	1977	UAS	UK	UAS30078
(B) SPIRIT OF A WOMAN	1977	UA	US	UALA 720

STEVE KATZ		(AB
ERIC KAZ		(AB
DOUG YULE		(AB
CRAIG FULLER		(AB
J D SOUTHER		(B
LINDA RONSTADT	V	(B
BEN MINK		(B
BOBBY KEYS	HRS	(B
ALVIN TAYLOR	D	(B
SCOTT EDWARDS	B	(A
JOE SAMPLE	K	(A
BYRON BERLINE	FDL	(A
HARRY BLUESTONE	STRINGS	(A
SYLVIA TYSON	V	(B
WHITEY GLAN	D	(B
JERRY SCHEFF		(B
FRED BECKMAIER	B	(A
GARY COLEMAN	PERC	(A
LELAND SKLAR	B	(A
EARL DUMLER	HRN	(A
TRACY NELSON	V	(B
PRAKASH JOHN	B	(B
JOHN KAPEC		(B
LARRY CARLTON	G	(A
RUSTY YOUNG	STEEL	(A
ERNIE WATTS	SAX	(A
VINCE DEROSA	HRNS	(A

AMERICAN GYPSY (1)

A53

	Year	Label	No.
(A) AMERICAN GYPSY	1975	CHESS/CADET	CH 60034
( ) AMERICAN GYPSY	1975	BTM	BTM 1001
( ) AMERICAN GYPSY	1975	CHESS	BTM 5003
( ) ANGEL EYES	19	PHILIPS	6410 066

JOE SKEEFE	B V K	(A
STEVE CLISBY	K HCA V	(A
MICHAEL HAMANE	G V	(
DALE HARREL Jr	G V	(A
RICHARD JAMES	PERC D	(A
LORENZO MILLS	PERC V	(A

A53A AMERICAN GYPSY (2) A53A

Member	Instr.	Albums
JOE LALA	PERC	(B
WILLIE WEEKS	B	(B
BILL LORDAN	D	(A
JAMES WALSH	V K D	(ABD
ENRICO ROSENBAUM	PERC V G	(ABD
JAY EPSTEIN	D	(A
JAMES JOHNSON	V G	(ABD
DONI LARSON	B	(A

	Title	Release
(A)	GYPSY	1971 CBS UK 66270 METROMEDIA US 1031
(B)	IN THE GARDEN	1972 METROMEDIA US 1044
(C)	UNLOCK THE DEAD GATES	1973 RCA US APLI0093
(D)	ANTITHESIS	1972 RCA US LSP 4775

A54 AMERICAN NOISE A54

Member	Instr.	Albums
TOMMY RICH	D	(A
CRAIG BLAZER	G	(A
GEORGE SIPL	K	(A
JERRY MORAN	K	(A
BRUCE BLAZER	G	(A

	Title	Release
(A)	AMERICAN NOISE	1980 PLANET NL 52236 US P8

A54A AMERICAN STANDARD BAND A54A

	Title	Release
(A)	AMERICAN STANDARD BAND	1979 ISLAND ILPS9450

A55 AMERICAN TEARS A55

Member	Instr.	Albums
MARK MANGOLD	K V	(ABC
GLENN KITHCART	D	(C
KIRK POWERS	B V	(C
CRAIG EVAN BROOKS	G V	(C
GARY SONNY	B	(A
TOMMY GUNN	D	(AB
GREG BAZE	B	(B

	Title	Release
(A)	BRANDED BAD	1974 CBS US KC 33038
(B)	TEARGAS	1975 CBS US PC 33847
(C)	POWERHOUSE	1977 CBS US PC 34676

A56 AMERICAN TRAIN A56

Member	Instr.	Albums
TOM HOWE	G	(
CHRIS SCHINDLER	B	
MIKE SKINNER	D	
JOHN SULLIVAN	V	

A56A AMM II A56A

Member	Instr.	Albums
KEITH ROWE	G	(A
EDDIE PROVOST	D	(A
LOU GARE	SAX	(A

	Title	Release
(A)	IT HAS BEEN AN ORDINARY DAY	1980 JAPO 60031

A57 AMON DUUL A57

Member	Instr.	Albums
RAINER BAUER	G V	(ABCDEF
ULLRICH LEOPOLD	B	(ABCDEF
PETER LEOPOLD	D	(ABDE
HELGE FILANDA	V PERC	(ABCDEF
WOLFGANG KRISCHKE	K PERC	(ABDEF
ELLA BAUER	V PERC	(ABCDEF
ANGELIKA FILANDA	V PERC	(ABDEf
USCHI OBERMEIER	PERC	(ABDE
KLAUS ESSER	G	(C

	Title	Release
(A)	AMON DUUL	1969 PROPHESY 1003
(B)	COLLAPSING	1969 METRONOME SMLP 012
(C)	PARA DIESWARTS DUUL	1969 OHR GER 56068
(D)	DISTASTER	1971 BASF GER 29 290 79/4
(E)	THIS IS AMON DUUL	1973 BRAIN GER 200 146
(F)	MINNELIED	1975 BRAIN GER 0040 149

A57A AMON DUUL II A57A

Member	Instr.	Albums
CHRIS KARRER	SAX G V	(ABCDEFGHJKLP
JOHN WEINZIERL	G	(ABCDEFGHJLO
FALK ROGNER	B	(ABCDEFGHJK
RENATE KNAUP	V	(ABCDEFGHJK
CHRISTIAN 'STRAT'THIELE	VLN V	(AB
DIETER SERFAS	D	(A
PETER LEOPOLD	D	(ABCDEFGHJKOP
DAVE ANDERSON	B	(AB
RAINER BAUER	G V	(B
ULLRICH LEOPOLD	B	(B
THOMAS KEYSERLING	FLT	(B
LOTHAR MEID	B V	(CDEGHJ
KARL HEINZ HAUSMANN	K	(CD
JIMMY JACKSON	K	(CE
AL GROMER	SITAR	(CE
ROLF ZACHER	V	(CE
OLAF KUBLER	PROD SAX	(ABCDEFH
PAUL HEYDA	VLN	(E
PANDIT SHANKAR	TABLA	(E
LIZ VAN NEIENHOFF	TABLA	(E
ROBBY HEIBL	B G VLN V	(FK
LEE HARPER	TPT	(HK
BOBBY JONES	SAX	(HK
HERMANN JALOWITZKI	PERC	(H
PETER KRAMPER	SYN	(EF
HELMUT SONNLEIFNER	VLN	(K
ERIK EBERT		(P
DANNY FICHELSCHER	D PERC	(DEG
KEITH FORSEY	PERC	(F
LUDWIG POPP	HRN	(H
RUDY NAGORA	SAX	(H
WILD WILLY	ACC V	(H
NANDO TISCHER	G V	(K
KLAUS EBERT	B	(LO
JOY ALASKA	V	(D
CHRIS BALDER	STR	(H
BOB CHATWIN	TPT	(H
THOR BALDURSSON	K	(HK
HEINZ BECKER	PERC	(K
JURGEN KORULETSCH	V	(K
STEFAN ZAUNER	K	(LOP
DESMOND BONNER	V	(F

	Title	Release
(A)	PHALLUS DEI	1969 LIBERTY LBS 83279
(A)	PHALLUS DEI	1972 SUNSET RI 50257
(B)	YETI	1970 LIBERTY LSP 101/2 83359/60
(C)	DANCE OFTHE LEMMINGS (DBL)	1971 UA US 9954 UK 60003/4
(C)	TANZ DER LEMMINGE (DBL)	1971 LIBERTY GER 83473 /74
(D)	CARNIVAL IN BABYLON	1972 UA US 5586 UK UAG 29327
(E)	WOLF CITY	1972 UA US LA 017 UK UAG 29406
(F)	VIVA LA TRANCE	1973 UA US LA 198 UK UAS 29504
(G)	LIVE IN LONDON	1974 UA USP 102 UK UAS 29466
(H)	HI JACK	1974 NOVA GER 6/22056
(H)	HI JACK	1974 ATCO US 36108 UK ATLANTIC K50136
(J)	LEMMINGMANIA	1975 UA UAS 29723
(K)	MADE IN GERMANY	1975 NOVA 628350
(K)	MADE IN GERMANY	1975 ATCO US 36119 UK ATLANTIC K50182
(L)	PYRAGONY	1976 NOVA 622890
(M)	CLASSIC GERMAN ROCK SCENE	197 SONOPRESSE FR 29770/71
(O)	ALMOST LIVE	1977 NOVA GER 623305
(P)	ONLY HUMAN	1978 STRAUD GER 623561
(P)	ONLY HUMAN	1978 VINYL UK LV 1004

A57B ANARCHIC SYSTEM A57B

	Title	Release
(A)	CHERIE SHA LA LA	19 DISCODIS FR 85064/65
(B)	GENERATION	19 DISCODIS FR 7 00005
(C)	SPECIAL CLUBS	19 DISCO DIS FR 70008/9

A58 ANCIENT GREASE A58

Member	Instr.	Albums
JOHN WEATHERS	D	(A
GARY PICKFORD HOPKINS	V	(A
PHIL RYAN	K	(A

	Title	Release
(A)	WOMEN & CHILDREN FIRST	1970 MERCURY UK 6338 033 US 61305

A59 ERIC ANDERSEN A59

Member	Instr.	Albums
ERIC ANDERSEN	HCA V G	(ALL
WITH		
DEBBIE GREENE	G PNO	(ABCDEJ
DEBORAH ANDERSEN	V	(K
JOHN GUERIN	D	(K
RUSS KUNKEL	D	(K
SCOTT EDWARDS	B	(K
DEAN PARKS	G	(K
TOM HENSLEY	PNO	(K
HOWARD EMERSON	G	(K
GARY COLEMAN	PERC	(K
TOM SCOTT	SAX	(KL
TOM SELLERS	K	(K
EMANUEL MOSS	VLN	(K
CHRIS BOND	G	(K

	Title	Release
(A)	TODAY IS THE HIGHWAY	1965 FONTANA UK TFL6061
(A)	TODAY IS THE HIGHWAY	1965 VANGUARD VSD 79157
(B)	'BOUT CHANGES & THINGS	1966 VANGUARD VSD 79206
(C)	'BOUT CHANGES & THINGS TAKE 2	1968 FONTANA UK STFL 6068
(C)	'BOUT CHANGES & THINGS TAKE 2	1967 VANGUARD VSD 79236
(D)	MORE HITS FROM TIN CAN ALLEY	1968 VANGUARD SVRL19003
(D)	MORE HITS FROM TIN CAN ALLEY	1968 VANGUARD VSD 79271
(E)	A COUNTRY DREAM	1969 VANGUARD VSD 6540
(F)	AVALANCHE	1970 W B US WS 1748
(G)	ERIC ANDERSEN	1970 W B US WS 1806
(H)	THE BEST OF ERIC ANDERSEN (DBL)	1971 VANGUARD VSD 7/8
(J)	BLUE RIVER	1973 CBS UK 65145
(J)	BLUE RIVER	1973 CBS US 31062
(K)	BE TRUE TO YOU	1975 ARISTA UK ARTY 114
(K)	BE TRUE TO YOU	1975 ARISTA US 4033

(CONTINUED)

A59 (CONTINUED) **ERIC ANDERSEN** A59

RICHARD BENNETT	G	(K	(L) SWEET SUPRISE	1976	ARISTA	US	4075
ERNIE WATTS	SAX	(K	(M) THE BEST SONGS	1977	ARISTA	US	4128
ANDY ROBINSON	V	(K	(M) THE BEST SONGS	1977	PATHE	FR	4148
ALAN LINDGREN	K	(K	(N) STAGE	19	CBS	US	65571
DENNIS ST JOHN	D	(K					

EMORY GORDY	B	(K	JENNIFER WARREN	V	(K	MAXINE WILLARD	V	(K	GINGER BLAKE	V	(K
JULIA TILLMAN	V	(K	DOUG HAYWOOD	V	(K	JACKSON BROWNE	V	(K	HERB PEDERSEN	V	(K
MIKE CONDELLO	V	(K	JONI MITCHELL	V	(KJ	RAY BUCKWICH	V	(K	ORWIN MIDDLETON	V	(K
MARIA MULDAUR	V	(K	PAUL HARRIS	K	(CDG	HARVEY BROOKS	B	(BC	HERBIE LOVELL	D	(CDE
MARK SPORER	B	(KJ	JESSE EHRLICH	CELLO	(K	ANDY JOHNSON	G VIBES	(EFJ	GARRY CARRIGAN	PERC	(J
NORBERT PUTNAM	B	(DJ	WELDON MYRICK	STEEL	(EJ	TEMPLE RISES	V	(J	KENNY BUTTREY	D	(DJ
GLEN SPREEN	K	(J	EDDIE HINTON	G	(J	DAVID BRIGGS	K	(DJ	FARRELL MORRIS	VIBES	(J
HUGH McCRACKEN	G	(D	GRADY MARTIN	G	(J	JIM McKEVITT	D	(J	BOB RAFKIN	G	(D
DAVID BROMBERG	G	(J	DON THOMAS	G	(D	KEVIN KELLY	ACC	(J	RICHARD SCHLOSSER	D	(J
AL COOPER	G	(D	LAVERNA MOORE	V	(J	MILLE KIRKHAM	V	(J	AMOS GARRETT	G	(D
SONJA MONTGOMERY	V	(G	JORDANAIRES	V	(J	BOB BUSHELL	B	(D	FLORENCE WARNER	V	(J
JOE MACK	B	(D	STEVE ANANDER	B	(DF	PAUL GRIFFIN	PNO	(D	AL ROGERS	D	(D
BOBBY GREGG	D	(D	DOC BUTLER	HRN	(E	GREGG DEVINS	PERC	(D	BILL PURSELL	PNO	(E
JACK JENNINGS	PERC	(D	LEE CRABTREE	PNO	(F	CHARLIE McCOY	HCA	(E	CHUCK RAUNEY	B	(F
BRUCE LANGHORN	G B	(F	JAYDEE MANNESS	G	(F	ERIC GALE	G	(F	CHRIS PARKER	D	(L
RICHARD BELL	K	(L	TONY BROWN	B	(L	ARLEN ROTH	G	(L	DAVID MANSFIELD	VLN STEEL	(L
ANTONIO RAMOS	PERC	(L	TOM SELLERS	K	(L	SISTER JOON	G	(L	TIM SCHMIT	V	(L
BEN KEITH	STEEL	(L	JOHN BATDORF	V	(L	BRENT MYDLAND	V	(L	TOM P SALISBURY	K	(O
RANDY CIARLANTE	D	(O	BRAD STAHL	B V	(O	ROBERT LUSTGARTTEN	G	(O			

A59A **AL ANDERSON** A59A

AL ANDERSON	K G V	(A	(A) AL ANDERSON	1972	VANGUARD	US	79324	VSQ 40018
TOM STALEY	D	(A						
TERRY ADAMS	PNO	(A	DON ADAMS TROM (A	AL LEPAK	B	(A		

A59B **CASEY ANDERSON** A59B

CASEY ANDERSON	G V	(ALL	(A) GOIN' PLACES	196	ELEKTRA	US	7192
CARL LYNCH	G	(E	(B) BAG I'M IN	196	ATCO	US	33149
BOBBY BUSHNELL	B	(E	(C) MORE PRETTY GIRLS THAN ONE	196	ATCO	US	33166
PANAMA FRANCIS	D	(E	(D) LIVE AT THE ICEHOUSE	1964	ATCO	US	33172
			(E) BLUES IS A WOMAN GONE	1965	ATCO	US	33176

A59B **DON ANDERSON** A59B

DON ANDERSON	V PNO	(AB	(A) FEELIN' ALRIGHT			1972	INTERCORD	26007/5
KEITH FORSEY	D	(A	(B) EAGLE FLIES			1973	INTERCORD	26012/5
LOTHAR MEID	B	(A						
ANDY MANX	G	(A	VILKO ZANKI	G B	(AB	PAUL VINCENT	G	(A
JOY FLEMING	V	(A	MAX GREGER JR	K	(A	RAINER PIETSCH	HCA K V	(A
RALF MOWY	WIND	(A	THOR BALDERURSSON	K V	(B	GERHARD SPIRKA	B	(B
ERNST VOSTER	G V	(B	ROLF BAUM	D	(B	FREDERIC RABOLD	HRNS	(B

A60 **IAN A ANDERSON** A60

IAN A ANDERSON	V G	(ALL	(A) STEREO DEATH BREAKDOWN	1969	LIBERTY		LBS83242
AL JONES	G	(B	(B) BOOK OF CHANGES	1970	FONTANA		STL 5542
DAVE JEFF	HCA	(B	(C) ROYAL YORK CRESENT	1970	VILLAGE THING	UK	VTS 3
PICK WITHERS	D	(D	(D) A VULTURE IS NOT A BIRD YOU CAN...	1971	VILLAGE THING	UK	VTS 9
KIPPS BROWN	ORG	(D	(E) SINGER SLEEPS ON	197	VILLAGE THING	UK	VTS 18
JOHN TURNER	B	(BD	(1) COUNTRY BLUES BAND 1968				
KEITH WARMINGTON	HCA	(D	(2) COUNTRY BLUES BAND 1968				
PAUL ROWAN	HCA	(1					

BOB ROWE	B	(12AB	CHRIS TURNER		(2A	PETE MORAN	V	(E
PETE SIDDONS	BOUZ	(E	MIKE COOPER	G	(E	LES CALVERT	K B	(E
IAN FOSTER	D	(E	BILL BOAZMAN	G V	(E	MAGGIE HOLLAND	G	(E
BOB HALL	PNO	(B	KEITH CHRISTMAS	D	(B	RON NEEDS	MAND	(A
PETE HOSSELL	JUG	(A	MEL RIGHT	D	(B	BRIAN CLAXTON		(A

A60A **JON ANDERSON** A60A

JON ANDERSON	ALL	(AB	(A) OLIAS OF SUNHILLOW	1976	ATLANTIC	UK	K50261	US	SD18180
BRIAN GAYLOR	SYN	(A	(B) SONG OF SEVEN	1980	ATLANTIC	UK	K50756	US	16021
DAVE LAWSON		(C	(C) ANIMATION	1982	ATLANTIC			US	19355
KEN FREEMAN	STR	(A							

IAN BARINSON	G B V	(B	JOHN GIBLIN	B	(BC	RONNIE LEAHY	K	(BC
MORRIS PERT	D	(BC	DICK MORRISSEY	SAX	(BC	CHRISTOPHER RAINBOW	V	(BC
JOHNNY DANKWORTH	SAX	(B	SIMON PHILIPS	D	(BC	JACK BRUCE	B	(BC
CLEM CLEMPSON	G	(BC	MEL	B	(B	DAVE SANCIOUS		(C
STEFANO CERRI		(C	BROTHER JAMES		(C	BILLY KRISTIAN		(C
BRETT MORGAN		(C	BLUE WEAVER	K	(C	IAN WALLACE	D	(C
TONY STANTON		(C	CHRIS PYNE		(C	HENRY LOWTHER	HRNS	(C
DELMAY STRING QUARTET		(C						

A61 **MILLER ANDERSON** A61

MILLER ANDERSON	G V	(A	(A) BRIGHT CITY	1971	DERAM	UK	SDL 3	US	18062	
WITH										

MICK WEAVER	K	(A	PETER DINES	K	(A	GARY THAIN	B	(A
ERIC DILLON	D	(A	NEIL HUBBARD	G	(A	LYN DOBSON	FLT	(A
HAROLD BECKETT	HRNS	(A	MADELINE BELL	V	(A	LIZA STRIKE	V	(A
TRACY MILLER	V	(A						

A62 **HARVEY ANDREWS** A62

HARVEY ANDREWS	V G	(ALL	(A) PLACES & FACES	1970	DECCA		SDN 9
WITH			(B) WRITER OF SONGS	1972	CUBE		HIFLY 10
TED TAYLOR	K	(B	(B) WRITER OF SONGS	1981	BEESWING	UK RI	LBEE 002
MIKE MORAN	PNO	(C	(C) FRIENDS OF MINE	1977	ELECTRICAL		GNAT 2
GRAHAM COOPER	G	(CD	(C) FRIENDS OF MINE	1973	FLY		HIFLY 15
TERRY COX	D	(C	(D) FANTASIES FROM A CORNER SEAT	1975	TRANSATLANTIC		TRA 298
ROY BABBINGTON	B	(BC	(E) SOMEDAY	1976	TRANSATLANTIC		TRA 329
CHRIS KARAN	D	(C	(F) BRAND NEW DAY	1980	POLYDOR		2383 595
GEOFF BODENHAM	G V	(F					

PHIL KENZIE	SAX	(C	DAVE COXHILL	SAX	(C	JIMMY HELMS	TPT	(C

(CONTINUED)

A62 HARVEY ANDREWS (CONTINUED)

Member	Instrument	Albums
MIKE BAILEY	TPT	(C
BOB JONES	G	(E
JIM TOOMEY	D	(E
RON CARTHY	TPT	(E
DAVE MATTACKS	D	(BC
MIKE PAGE	SAX	(C
LINDA THOMPSON	V	(D
RALPH McTELL	G	(B
IAN THOMPSON	B	(B
BERNIE HOLLAND	G	(E
PETE WILLSHER	STEEL	(E
MO FOSTER	B	(E
GRAHAM PRESKETT	MAN VLN	(C
DAVE CARTWRIGHT	G HCA	(C
PAT DONALDSON	B	(D
BOB FALLOON	G	(B
DAVE PEGG	B	(B
RICK WAKEMAN	K	(B
MARK WARNER	G	(E
PETE WINGFIELD	K	(DE
CHRIS MERCER	SAX	(E
PAUL KEOGH	G	(BC
FRANCIS MONKMAN	K	(C
RICHARD THOMPSON	G	(D
STAN GORMAN	D	(B
COZY POWELL	D	(B
LES THATCHER	G	(B

A62A MARK ANDREWS & THE GENTS

Member	Instrument	Albums
MARK ANDREWS	K V	(A
MARTIN SAWTELL	B V	(A
LARRY TOLFREE	D	(A
BRIAN KEMP	K V	(A
BARRY LINES	G V	(A

Album	Year	Label		
(A) BIG BOY	1979	A&M US 4812	UK	AMLH68513

A63 ANDROMEDA

Member	Instrument	Albums
JOHN CANN	G V	(A
MICK HAWKSWORTH	B V	(A
IAN McCLANE	D V	(A

Album	Year	Label		
(A) ANDROMEDA	1969	RCA		SF 8031

A63A ANDWELLA'S DREAM

Member	Instrument	Albums
DAVE LEWIS	G K V	(ABC
NIGEL SMITH	B	(ABC
GORDON BARTON	D	(ABC
DAVE McDOUGALL	K	(BC
DAVE STRUTHERS	B V	(C
JACK McCULLOCH	D	(B
BOB DOWNES	FLT PERC	(A
PHIL GILLIN	PROD	C
DORIS TROY	V	(C
LIZA STRIKE	V	(C

Album	Year	Label		
(A) LOVE & POETRY	1969	CBS		63673
(B) WORLD'S END	1970	REFLECTION	UK	REF 1010
(B) WORLD'S END	1970	DUNHILL	US	50095
(C) PEOPLE'S PEOPLE	1971	REFLECTION	UK	REFL 10
(C) PEOPLE'S PEOPLE	1971	DUNHILL	US	50105

A64 ANGE

Member	Instrument	Albums
DANIEL HAAS	B G	(BCDE
FRANCIS DECAMPS	K V	(BCDEFGH
JEAN MICHEL BREZOVAR	G V	(BCDE
JEAN PIERRE GUICHARD	D	(H
GERALD JELSCH	D	(BCD
GUENOLE BIGER	G D	(E
CHRISTIAN DECAMPS	K V	(BCDEFGH
ERIC BIBONNE	V	(D
HENRY LOUSTAU	VLN	(D
MICHEL LEFLOCH	V	(D
CLAUDE LEMET	G B FLT	(H
GERALD RENARD	B	(H

Album	Year	Label		
(A) IN CONCERT	1971	RCA		PL 37153
(B) CARICATURES	1972	PHILIPS 6325 181		6332 066
(C) LA CIMETIERE DES ARLEQUINS	1974	PHILIPS 6325 037		9101 022
(D) AU DELA DU DELIRE	1975	PHILIPS		9101 004
(E) EMILE JACOTEY	1975	PHILIPS		9101 012
(F) PAR LE FILS DU MANDARIN	1976	PHILIPS		9101 090
(G) ANGE TOME (DBL)	1977	PHILIPS		6641 715
(H) GUET APENS	1978	PHILIPS		9101 184

A65 ANGEL

Member	Instrument	Albums
BARRY BRANT	D V	(ABCDEF
'PUNKY' EDWIN MEADOWS	G	(ABCDEF
FRANK DIMINO	V	(ABCDEF
FELIX ROBINSON	B	(DEF
GREGG GIUFFRIA	K	(ABCDEF
MICKEY JONES	B	(ABC

Album	Year	Label		
(A) ANGEL	1976	CASABLANCA UK CBC 4007	US	7021
(B) HELLUVA BAND	1976	CASABLANCA UK CBC 4010	US	7028
(C) ON EARTH AS IT IS IN HEAVEN	1977	CASABLANCA UK CAL 2002	US	7043
(C) ON EARTH AS IT IS IN HEAVEN	1977	CASABLANCA	FR	CBLA71007
(D) WHITE HOT	1978	CASABLANCA UK CSL 2023	US	7085
(E) SINFUL	1979	CASABLANCA	US	7127
(F) LIVE WITHOUT A NET	1980	CASABLANCA UK 2703	US	7203

A65A ANGEL CITY

Member	Instrument	Albums
DOC NEESON	V	(C
JOHN BREWSTER	G V	(C
RICK BREWSTER	G K	(C
GRAHAM BIDSTRUP	D	(
CHRIS BAILEY	B V	(C
MURRAY BURNS	K	(A
BRENT ECLLES	D	(C

Album	Year	Label		
(A) FACE TO FACE	1978	EPIC US 36344	UK	84253
(B) DARKROOM	1980	EPIC US 36543	UK	84502
(C) NIGHT ATTACK	1981	EPIC	UK	85480

A65A ANGELIC UPSTARTS

Member	Instrument	Albums
MENSI	V	(
STEVE	B	(
MOND	G	(
STICKS	D	(

Album	Year	Label		
(A) WE GOTTA GET OUT OF THIS PLACE	1980	WB	UK	K56806
(B) LIVE	1981	EMI	UK	ZEM 102
(C) 2,000,000 VOICES	1981	ZONOPHONE	UK	ZONC104

A65C ANGELO

Member	Instrument	Albums
ANGELO	V K	(A
LEE RITENOUR	G	(A
DAVID AMARO	G	(A
LAUDIR DE OLIVEIRA	PERC	(A
LEE LOUGHNAME	TPT	(A
PETER CETERA	V	(A
BILL DICKENSON	B	(A
DAVID SERAPHINE	D	(A
MIKE BARONE	TROM	(A
CARL WILSON	V	(A
JIM GORDON	D	(A
TOM SCOTT	WIND	(A
DONALD BYRD	HRN	(A

Album	Year	Label		
(A) ANGELO	1977	FANTASY		F9507

A65D ANGELWITCH

Member	Instrument	Albums
KEVIN HEYBOURNE	G	(
KEVIN RIDDLES	B	
DAVE HOGG	D	(

Album	Year	Label		
(A) ANGELWITCH	1980	BRONZE	UK	BRON 532

A66 ANGLETRAX

Member	Instrument	Albums
JERRY MINGE	K	(A
MARTIN HEATH	B	(A
RENE RENNO	G	
LIN JAMMET	G	(A
WENDY HERMAN	V	(A
DAN WHO	D	(A

Album	Year	Label		
(A) ANGLETRAX	1979	ARIOLA		AHAL8009

A67 ANIMALS

Member	Instrument	Albums
ALAN PRICE	K	(ABCDEI
JOHN STEEL	D	(ABCDEI
HILTON VALENTINE	G	(ABCDEFGI
CHAS CHANDLER	B	(ABCDEFGI
ERIC BURDON	V	(ABCDEFGHIM
DAVE ROWEBERRY	K	(G
JOHN WEIDER	B G	(LMN
VIC BRIGGS	G B	(LM
DANNY McCULLOCH	B G V	(LM
BARRY JENKINS	D	(GLMN
ANDY SOMERS(SUMMERS)	G	(N
ZOOT MONEY	K	(N
GEORGE BRUNO	K V	(L

(CONTINUED)

Album	Year	Label		
(A) IN THE BEGINNING (EP)	1965	DECCA DFE8643		WAND 690
(B) THE ANIMALS	1964	COLUMBIA	UK	33SX1669
(B) THE ANIMALS	1969	STARLINE	UK	SRS 5006
(C) THE ANIMALS	1964	M G M	US	SE 4264
(C) GET YOURSELF A COLLEGE GIRL	1965	M G M	US	SE 4273
(D) ANIMALS ON TOUR	1965	M G M	US	SE 4281
(E) ANIMAL TRACKS	1965	COLUMBIA	UK	33SX1708
(E) ANIMAL TRACKS	1965	M G M	US	SE 4305
(F) BRITISH GO GO	1965	M G M	US	SE 4306
(G) ANIMALISM	1966	DECCA	UK	LK 4797
(G) ANIMALISM	1966	M G M	US	SE 4414
(H) AMINALIZATION	1966	M G M	US	SE 4384
(I) MOST OF THE ANIMALS	1966	COLUMBIA	UK	SX 6035
(I) MOST OF THE ANIMALS	1973	M F P	UK	MFP 5218

A67 (CONTINUED)

ANIMALS A67

	Title		Year	Label	Country	Number
(J)	WIND OF CHANGE		1967	M G M	US	CS 8052
(J)	WIND OF CHANGE		1971	M G M	UK	2354 001
(J)	WIND OF CHANGE		1967	M G M	US	SE 4484
(K)	ERIC IS HERE		1967	M G M	US	SE 4433
(L)	EVERYONE OF US		1968	M G M	US	SE 4553
(M)	TWAIN SHALL MEET		1968	M G M		CS 8074
(M)	TWAIN SHALL MEET		1968	M G M	US	SE 4537
(N)	LOVE IS	(DBL)	1969	VERVE		6651 09/10
(N)	LOVE IS		1969	M G M		CS 8104
(N)	LOVE IS		1968	M G M	US	SE 4591
(N)	LOVE IS		1971	M G M	UK	2619 002
(N)	LOVE IS		1972	M G M	US	690
(JM)	WIND OF CHANGE/TWAIN SHALL MEET		19	M G M		2642 004
( )	ANIMALS ANTHOLOGY 64 65		19	RAK	EURO	184 97238/9
( )	BEST OF THE ANIMALS		1966	M G M	US	SE 4324
( )	BEST OF THE ANIMALS		1967	M G M	US	4454
( )	BEST OF THE ANIMALS	(DBL)	1973	ABCKO		AB 4226
( )	BEST OF THE ANIMALS		19	SPRINGBOARD	US	4025
( )	BEST OF THE ANIMALS		19	PATHE	FR	C062 91190
( )	BEST OF VOL2		1967	M G M	US	SE 4454
( )	GREATEST HITS		1969	M G M	US	SE 4602
( )	IN THE BEGINNING		1973	WAND		V6 5083
( )	ERIC BURDON & THE ANIMALS		1975	POLYDOR		2356 142
( )	NEWCASTLE 63		1976	D J M		DJSL 069
( )	NEWCASTLE 63		1977	CHARLY	UK	CR 30016
( )	LIVE IN NEWCASTLE		1976	D J M		DJB26069
( )	WITH SONNY BOY WILLIAMSON 63		1977	CHARLY	UK	CR 30018
( )	WILD ANIMALS		1966	DECCA	IMP	XLB 646028
( )	HITS OF THE ANIMALS		1969	COLUMBIA	IMP	SGHX 10048
( )	HOUSE OF THE RISING SUN		1970	EMI	IMP	048 50731
( )	STAR PORTRAIT		1971	M G M	IMP	665 102
( )	POP HISTORY		1971	M G M	IMP	2625 011
( )	MADMAN		1971	M G M	IMP	2674 044
( )	EARLY ANIMALS WITH ERIC BURDON		1973	PICKWICK	IMP	SPS 3330
( )	BEFORE WE WERE SO RUDELY INTERUPTED		77	BARN		2314 104
( )	BEFORE WE WERE SO RUDELY INTERUPTED		77	JET	US	JTLA790H
( )	NIGHTTIME IS THE RIGHT TIME		19	SPRINGBOARD	US	4065
( )	LET IT ROCK		1980	INTERCORD	NL	128611
( )	ERIC BURDON & THE ANIMALS		19	CHARLY		30197

(EP's)

Title	Year	Label	Country	Number
ANIMALS IS HERE	1964	COLUMBIA	UK	SEG 8374
ANIMALS(BOOM BOOM)	1965	COLUMBIA	UK	SEG 8400
ANIMALS No2(I'M IN LOVE AGAIN)	1965	COLUMBIA	UK	SEG 8439
ARE BACK	1966	COLUMBIA	UK	SEG 8452
ANIMAL TRACKS	1966	COLUMBIA	UK	SEG 8499

A67A ANNEXUS QUAM A67A

UWE BICK D V (A
JURGENS JONUSCHIES B V (A
WERNER HOSTERMANN K V (A
HANS KAMPER G V (AB
MARTIN HABENICHT B (B

	Title	Year	Label	Country	Number
(A)	ANNEXUS QUAM(OSMOSE)	1970	OHR	GER	56007
(B)	BEZIEHUNGEN	1972	OHR	GER	556028

HARALD KLEMM G FLT V(AB OVE VOLQUARTZ SAX (AB

A67C ANY TROUBLE A67C

CLIVE GREGSON G V (A
NICK SIMPSON (
MEL HARLEY D (A
PHIL BARNES

	Title	Year	Label
(A)	WHERE ARE ALL THE NICE GIRLS	1980	STIFF UK SEEZ 25 US USE 6
(B)	WHEELS IN MOTION	1981	STIFF UK SEEZ 37

CHRIS PARKS G V (A

A67D AORTA A67D

BILLY JONES
JIM DONLINGER
JIM NYEHOLT
BILLY HERMAN

	Title	Year	Label	Country	Number
(A)	AORTA	1969	CBS		CS 9785
(B)	AORTA 2	1970	HAPPY TIGER	US	1010

A67E APHRODOITES CHILD A67E

VANGELIS PAPATHANASSIOU K B (ALL
DEMIS ROUSSOS V B G (ALL
LUCAS SIDERAS D V (ALL
WITH

SILVER KOULOURIS G PERC AC
VANNIS TSAROUCHIS V (C
IRENE PAPAS V (C
JOHN FROST V (C
ARRIS HALKITIS B SAX V PERC (C
MICHEL RIPOCHE TROM SAX (C

	Title	Year	Label	Country	Number
(A)	END OF THE WORLD	1969	MERCURY	UK	SMCL20140
(AF)	END OF THE WORLD RAIN & TEARS	19	VERTIGO		6333 008
(B)	ITS FIVE O'CLOCK	19	VERTIGO		6333 009
(C)	666,APOCALYPSE OF JOHN	1972	VERTIGO		6673 001
(C)	666,APOCALYPSE OF JOHN	1972	VERTIGO		6641 581
(C)	666,APOCALYPSE OF JOHN	197	VERTIGO	US	500
(D)	APHRODITES CHILD	1978	MERCURY		6886 650
(D)	APHRODITES CHILD	19	MERCURY	US	VEL 2 500
(D)	APHRODITES CHILD	1975	MERCURY		138 351
(E)	BEST OF	1975	MERCURY		6333 002
(E)	BEST OF	19	VERTIGO		6583 025
(F)	RAIN & TEARS	1975	VERTIGO/PHILIPS		6483 035
(H)	GREATEST HITS	1981	FONTANA		6420 006

A67F ANIMATED EGG A67F

	Title	Year	Label	Country	Number
(A)	ANIMATED EGG	196	ALSHIRE	US	5104

A67G ANNO DOMINI A67G

DAVE MERCER G B V (A
'TIGER' TAYLOR G V (A
KERRY SCOTT V PER (A

	Title	Year	Label	Number
(A)	ON THE NEW DAY	1971	DERAM	SLM 1085

JOHN JONES G (A

A67H ANTHEM A67H

BARTHOLOMEW G V (A
BOBBY HOWE D V (A
GREGG HOLLISTER B V (A

	Title	Year	Label	Country	Number
(A)	ANTHEM	1970	BUDDAH	US	5071

A67J ANTI PASTI A67J

	Title	Year	Label	Country	Number
(A)	THE LAST CALL	1981	RONDELET	UK	ABOUT 5

A67K

ANYONES DAUGHTER

A67K

HARALD BARETH B V (A — (A) ADONIS — 1979 BRAIN 0060 186
UWE KARPA G (A
KONO KONOPIK D (A — MATTHIAS ULMER K (A

A67L

APPALOOSA

A67L

AL KOOPER K (A — (A) APPALOOSA — 1971 CBS US 9819
JOHN CROMPTON V (A
ROBIN BATTEAU VLN (A — GENO ROSOU STR (A — DAVID REISER B (A

A67M

APPLEJACKS

A67M

AL JACKSON V (A — (A) APPLEJACKS — 1964 DECCA UK LK 4635
MARTIN BAGGOTT G (A
PHIL CASH G (A — MEGAN DAVIES B (A — DON GOULD K (A
GERRY FREEMAN D (A

A67N

CARMINE APPICE

A67N

CARMINE APPICE D V (A — (A) CARMINE APPICE — 1981 WEA UK K99196
DANNY JOHNSON G (A
JAY DAVIS B (A — DUANE HITCHINGS K (A

A67P

APACHE

A67P

JOE MESSINA V (A — (A) APACHE — 1981 ATCO UK K50826
GARY T AMOS D (A
TOM CLIFFORD B (A — DENNIS SHEAHAN G (A — PETER ARENDT G K (A

A68

APPLETREE THEATRE

A68

TERENCE BOYLAN (— (A) PLAYBACK — 19 POLYDOR UK 2353 051 US VERVE3042
JOHN BOYLAN (A
LARRY CORYELL G (A — CHUCK RAINEY B (A — CHUCK ISRAELS (A
HERB LOVELLE (A — ERIC GALE G (A

A68A

APPLE PIE MOTHERHOOD

A68A

JEFF LABES K (AB — (A) APPLE PIE MOTHERHOOD BAND — 1968 ATLANTIC US SD 8189
TED DEMOS G V (AB — (B) APPLE PIE — 1969 ATLANTIC US SD 8233
JOE CASTAGNO G (A
JACK BRUNO G V (AB — DICK BARNABY B (AB — BRUCE PAINE V (B
ADAM MEYERS HCA V (A — MICHAEL SORAFINE G V (A

A68B

APPLE & APPLEBERRY

A68B

(A) APPLE & APPLEBERRY — 1974 ABC US 802

A69

APRIL WINE

A69

RICK MORRISON SAX (A — (A) ON RECORD — 1972 AQUARIUS US 503
BRIAN GREENWAY G V (HJKL — (A) APRIL WINE — 1972 BIG TREE US 2012
JERRY MERCER D V (BCDEFGHJK — (B) ELECTRIC JEWELS — 1973 AQUARIUS US AQR 504
STEVE LANG B V (EFGHJKL — (C) LIVE — 1974 AQUARIUS US AQR 505
JIM CLENCH B V (ABCD — (D) STAND BACK — 1975 BIG TREE US89506 AQUARIUS506
MYLES GOODWYN V G K (ALL — (E) WHOLE WORLDS GONE CRAZY — 1976 LONDON UK SHU 8503
GARY MOFFET G V (BCDEFGHJK — (E) WHOLE WORLDS GONE CRAZY — 1976 LONDON US PS 675
DAVID HENMAN G (AB — (F) FOREVER FOR NOW — 1976 AQUARIUS AQR 511
RITCHIE HENMAN D (AB — (G) LIVE AT THE EL MOCAMBO — 1977 LONDON UK SHU 8510
KEITH JOLLIMORE FLT (A — (G) LIVE AT THE EL MOCAMBO — 1977 LONDON US PS 699
RICHARD NEWELL HCA (B — (H) FIRST GLANCE — 1978 CAPITOL 11852
PIERRE SENECAL K (B — (J) HARDER ...FASTER — 19 CAPITOL US 12013
AL NICHOLS V (B — (K) GREATEST HITS — 1979 AQUARIUS US AQR 525
PAM MARSH V (BF — (L) NATURE OF THE BEAST — 1981 CAPITOL 12125
MARY LOU GAUTHIER V (A — (EP) UNRELEASED LIVE — 1979 CAPITOL 12CL18
DWAYNE FORD K (E
FRANK LUDWIG K (E — FRANK MARINI G (E — SERGE LUCAS K (E
BILLY SZAWLOWSKI V (E — BARRY KEAN PERC (F — JUDY RICHARDS V (F
GAIL MEZO V (F — TONY GRANT V (F — BRIAN GREENWAY G V (HJ

A70

AQUARIAN DREAM

A70

(A) FANTASY — 1978 ELEKTRA K 52109
(B) NORMAN CONNORS PRESENTS A' DREAM — 19 BUDDAH US 5672
(C) AQUARIAN DREAM — 1980 BUDDAH UK 08
(D) CHANCE TO DANCE — 1980 ELEKTRA US 205

A71

AQUILA

A71

RALPH DENYER V G (A — (A) AQUILA — 1970 RCA SF 8126
PHIL CHILDS B K (A
GEORGE LEE WIND (A — MARTIN WOODWARD K (A — JAMES SMITH D (A

A71A

AQSAK MABOUL

A71A

MARC HOLLANDER K WIND(A — (A) UN PEU DE L'AME DES BANDITS — 1979 ATEM BELG 002
CATHERINE JAUNIAUX V (A
FRED FRITH G VLN B(A — MICHEL BERCKMANS WIND (A — FRANK WUYTS D (A
CHRIS CUTLER D (A — DENIS VAN HECKE STR G (A

A71B

AQUATONES

A71B

(A) THE AQUATONES SING — 19 FARGO 5001

A72

ARBRE

A72

PAUL CAFFREY V G (AB — (A) TIME & AGAIN — 1976 DJM DJF20480
TONY DAVISON B (AB — (B) ARBRE — 1978 DJM DJF20527
ROGER ASKEW G PNO (AB
BILL BISSET D (AB — PHIL CAFFREY V G (AB — PETER CAFFREY G V (AB

A72A

DAN ARBRAS

A72A

DAN ARBRAS G V (ALL — (A) DOUAR NEVEZ — 1977 HEXAGONE FR 883 009
PATRIG MOLARD WIND (ABC — (B) ALLEZ DIRE A LA VILLE — 1978 HEXAGONE FR 883 021
BENOIT WIDEMANN K SYN AABC — (C) THE EARTH LAMENT — 1979 HEXAGONE FR 883 034
DAVE PEGG B (A
MICHEL SANTANGELI D (ABC — MARC CHANTEREAU PERC (A — EMMANUELLE PARRENIN VIELLE (A
GUY DELACROIX B (B — FRANCIS MOZE B (BC — PATRICK AUDOIN K (BC
DONINIQUE WIDIEZ (B

A72B

ARC (US)

A72B

BOBBY SAVENE B V (A — (A) ARC — 1978 LIFESONG US 35413
WAYNE GEORGE K V (A
EDDIE KOSOWSKI G V (A — STEVE SZCZESNIAK D V (A

A73 ARC A73

MICK GALLAGHER K G V (A
JOHN TURNBULL G (A
TOM DUFFY B V (A
DAVID MONTGOMERY D (A

(A) ARC AT THIS 1971 DECCA SKLR5077

A73A ARCADIUM A73A

GRAHAM BEST B V (A
ALAN ELLWOOD K V (A
JOHN PARKER D (A
ROBERT ELLWOOD (A
MIGUEL SEGIDES (A

(A) ARCADIUM(BREATHE AWHILE) 1969 MIDDLE EARTH MDLS 302

A74 NEIL ARDLEY A74

NEIL ARDLEY K SYN (ALL
TONY REEVES B (A
JON HISEMAN D (AD
JACK BRUCE B (BC
JEFF CLYNE B (CD
BOB BERTLES WIND (E
PAUL BUCKMASTER CELLO(E
IAN CARR HRNS (EABCDEF
GEOFF CASTLE K (EF
TONY COE WIND (EF
DAVE McCRAE K (E
ROGER SELLERS D (E
KEN SHAW G (E
BRIAN SMITH WIND (E
ROGER SUTTON B (E
BARBARA THOMPSON WIND (EF
TREVOR TOMKINS PERC (EF
STAN SULZMANN WIND (E
JOHN TAYLOR K (E
JOHN MARTYN G (F
BILLY KRISTIAN B (F
RICHARD BURGESS D (F
PEPI LEMER V (F
NORMA WINSTONE V (F
MICK PALMER HRNS (A
TONY DUDLEY HRNS (A
BOB LEAPER HRNS(A
MIKE PHILLIPSON HRNS (A
JOHN MUMFORD HRNS (A
PAUL RUTTERFORD HRNS (A
PETER HARVEY HRNS(A
DICK HART HRNS (AD
LES CARTER WIND (A
TREVOR WATTS WIND (A
DAVE GELLY WIND K(ABD
TOM HARRIS WIND (A
SEBASTIAN FREUDENBERG WIND(A
MIKE BARRETT K (A
DEREK WATKINS HRNS(BD
HARRY BECKETT HRNS (BD
HENRY LOWTHER HRNS (BD
MIKE GIBBS HRNS (BC
DEREK WADSWORTH HRNS(BD
TONY RUSSELL HRNS (B
GEORGE SMITH HRNS (B
JIM PHILLIPS WIND (B
JOHN MARSHALL D (C
DICK HECKSTAL SMITH WIND(BD
FRANK RICOTTI PERC (BCD
DON RENDELL HRNS (CD
KARL JENKINS WIND K (CD
NIGEL CARTER HRNS (D
JOHN CLEMENSON WIND (D
RAY PREMRU HRNS (D
BUNNY GOULD WIND(D
STAN TRACEY K (D
ALAN BRANSCOMBE K (D
CHRIS LAURENCE B (D
NORMA WINSTON V (D
IVOR CUTLER V (D

(A) WESTERN UNION 1965 DECCA UK SKL 4690
(B) DEJEUNER SUR L'HERBE 1969 VERVE UK SVLP 9236
(C) GREEK VARIATIONS(1 SIDE) 1970 COLUMBIA UK SCX 6414
(D) SYMPHONY OF AMARANTHS 1972 REGAL ZONOPHONE SLRZ 1028
(E) KALEIDOSCOPE OF RAINBOWS 1976 GULL UK GULP 1018
(F) HARMONY OF SPHERES 1979 DECCA UK TXSR 133

A74A AREA A74A

DEMETRIO STATOS V K (AB
ARES TAVOLAZZI B (A
PATRIZIO FARISELLI K (AB
GIAMPAOLO TOFANI G (AB
PATRICK ERARD OJIVAS B (B

(A) CRAC 19 BARCLAY IT 940 512
(B) ARBEIT MACHT FREI 1973 CRAMPS 5101

A74B ARDO DOMBEC A74B

HELMUT HECHMAN WIND (A
WOLFGANG SPILLNER D V (A
HARALD GLEN G V (A
MICHAEL UFER B (A

(A) ARDO DOMBEC 1971 BASF/PILZ GER 2021095/2

A75 AREA CODE 615 A75

WELDON MYRICK STEEL G (AB
BOBBY THOMPSON BAN K (AB
BUDDY SPICHER FDL (AB
CHARLIE McCOY HCA (AB
MAC GAYDEN G (AB
WAYNE MOSS B G (AB
KENNY BUTTREY D (AB
DAVID BRIGGS PNO (B
NORBERT PUTNAM B (AB
KEN LAUBER PNO (A

(A) AREA CODE 615 1969 POLYDOR UK 583572
(A) AREA CODE 615 1969 POLYDOR US 24 4002
(B) A TRIP IN THE COUNTRY 1970 POLYDOR 2425 023
(B) A TRIP IN THE COUNTRY 1970 POLYDOR US 24 4025
(AB)AREA CODE/A TRIP (DBL) 1974 POLYDOR 2683 040

A76 JOSE 'CHEPITO' AREAS A76

JOSE CHEPITO AREAS PERC (A

(A) JOSE CHEPITO AREAS 1974 CBS US 33062 UK 80296

A77 ARGENT A77

ROD ARGENT K V (ABCDEFGH
ROBERT HENRIT D (ABCDEFGH
JIM RODFORD B (ABCDEFGH
RUSS BALLARD G V (ABCDEF
JOHN VERITY V (GH
JOHN GRIMALDI G (GH
PHIL COLLINS PERC (H
DEREK GRIFFITHS G (D

(A) ARGENT 1970 CBS UK 63781
(A) ARGENT 1970 EPIC US 26525
(B) RING OF HANDS 1971 EPIC UK 64190
(B) RING OF HAND 1971 EPIC US 30128
(C) ALL TOGETHER NOW 1972 CBS UK 64962
(C) ALL TOGETHER NOW 1972 EPIC US 31556
(D) IN DEEP 1973 EPIC UK 65475
(D) IN DEEP 1973 EPIC US 32195
(E) NEXUS 1974 EPIC UK 65924
(E) NEXUS 1974 EPIC US 32573
(F) ENCORE (DBL) 1974 EPIC UK 88063
(F) ENCORE (DBL) 1974 EPIC US 33079
(G) CIRCUS 1975 EPIC UK 80691
(G) CIRCUS 1975 EPIC US 33422
(H) COUNTERPOINT 1975 RCA UK RS 1020
(H) COUNTERPOINT 1975 U A US LA 560G
( ) BEST OF ARGENT 1976 EPIC UK 81321
( ) HOLD YOUR HEAD UP 1978 EMBASSY UK 31640
( ) ANTHOLOGY 197 EPIC US 33955
( ) SILVER PLATED 197 EPIC US 26285

A78 ROD ARGENT A78

ROD ARGENT K V (A
WITH
PHIL COLLINS PERC (A
CLIVE CHAMAN B (A
MORRIS PERT PERC (A
GARY MOORE G (A
ALPHONSO JOHNSON B (A
JACK LANCASTER WIND (A

(A) MOVING HOME 1978 MCA MCF 2854

A79 ARIEL A79

MICHAEL RUDD V G (AB
WILLIAM PUTT B (AB
HARVEY JAMES G (B
JOHN LEE D (B
NIGEL MACARA D V (A
JOHN MILLS K (A
TIM GAZE G V (A

(A) STRANGE FANTASTIC DREAM 1973 HARVEST SHSP4028
(B) ROCK N ROLL SCARS 1974 HARVEST SHSP4039

A80 ARIZONA A80

PETER KUCH (B
DOUG HOLZWARTH (B
MARY DOBBINS (B
WILLIE KNOWLES (B
PAT MURPHY (B
KEN ASHBY (B

(A) ARIZONA 1976 RCA SF 8465
(A) ARIZONA 1976 RCA US LPL1 5123
(B) LOWDOWN 1977 RCA PL 25103

A81

ARMAGEDDON

A81

KEITH RELF V HCA (A | (A) ARMAGEDDON | 1975 A&M US SP4513 UK AMLH 64513
LOUIS CENNAMO B (A
BOBBY CALDWELL D V (A | MARTIN PUGH G (A

A82

JOAN ARMATRADING

A82

JOAN ARMATRADING V G (ALL | (A) WHATEVERS FOR US | 1974 CUBE 2338 023 UK HIFLY 12
RAY COOPER PERC(AJ | (A) WHATEVERS FOR US | 1972 A&M US 4382
HENRY SPINETTI D (ADE | (B) BACK TO THE NIGHT | 1975 A&M US 4525 UK AMLH 68305
ROBBIE SHAKESPEARE B (J | (B) BACK TO THE NIGHT | 1982 A&M UK RI AMID 112
DAVEY JOHNSTONE G (A | (C) JOAN ARMATRADING | 1976 A&M US 4588 UK AMLH64588
KENNEY JONES D (CD | (D) SHOW SOME EMOTION | 1977 A&M US 4663 UK AMLH 68433
TONY CARR D (BC | (E) TO THE LIMIT | 1978 A&M AMLH 64732
CHRIS KARAN PERC(B | (F) STEPPING OUT | 1979 A&M AMLH 64789
LON PRICE WIND(F | (G) ME MYSELF I | 1980 A&M AMLH 64809
RON MATTHEWSON B (B | (H) HOW CRUEL ½ LP | 1980 A&M US 3302 NL 63302
DAVE MARKEE B (CDE | (J) WALK UNDER LADDERS | 1981 A&M UK AMLH 64876
DAVE BROOKS SAX (B | (1) 1975 TOUR (2) 1975 TOUR (3) 1977 IN CONCERT TV SHOW
COLIN PINCOTT G (B
JEAN ROUSSEL K (B | JOHN HALSEY D (B | ANDY SOMERS G (B | PETE GAGE K G (B
BERNIE HOLLAND G (B | SHAMSI SARUMI PERC (B | PHIL CHEN B (B | TONY NEWMAN D (B
GASPAR LAWAL PERC(B | JERRY DONAHUE G (CD23 | DAVE MATTACKS D (C2 | JIMMY JEWELL SAX (C
B J COLE STEEL(C | PAT DONALDSON B (2 | GERRY CONWAY D (AB | BRYAN GAROFALO B (D3
DAVID KEMPER D (D3 | JOHN BUNDRICK K (D | GEORGIE FAME K (D | PETE CLARKE V (D
JOE SCOTT V (D | MEL COLLINS SAX (DJ | TIM HINKLEY K (D | GRAHAM LYLE G (C
PETE WOOD K (C | BRYN HAWORTH G MAND(2C | ALBERT LEE G (2 | QUITMAN DENNIS SAX (E3
RED YOUNG K (3EF | PHILIP PALMER G (E | THE MOVIES (1 | DICK SIMS K (E
MARCUS MILLER B (G | STEVE YORK B HCA (B | WILL LEE B (G | ANTON FIG D (G
CHRIS SPEDDING G (G | HIRAM BULLOCK G (G | RICKY HIRSCH G (FG | DANNY FEDERICI K (G
PAUL SCHAEFFER PNO (G | CLIFFORD CARTER PNO (G | PHILLIP ST JOHN PNO (G | CLARENCE CLEMONS SAX (G
GEORGE KERR V (G | SAMMY TURNER K (F | RITCHIE HAYWARD D (F | BILL BODINE B (F
LARRY STEELE B (A | PAM NESTER V (A | JERRY MAROTTA D V (J | TONY LEVIN B (J
HUGH BURNS G (J | THOMAS DOLBY SYN (J | GARY SANFORD G (J | NICK PLYTAS K (J
DICK CUTHELL HRNS(J | RICO RODRIGUEZ HRNS (J | ANDY PARTRIDGE G (J | JULIAN DIGGLE PERC (J
SLY DUNBAR D (J

A82A

FRANKIE ARMSTRONG

A82A

FRANKIE ARMSTRONG V (AB | (A) LOVELY ON THE WATER | 1972 TOPIC UK 12TS 216
JEFF LOWE DULC/WIND (A | (B) SONGS & BALLADS | 1975 TOPIC UK 12TS 273
JACK WARSHAW G BAN(A | (C) AND THE MUSIC PLAYS | 1981 BRIAR US 4211
ANDREW BROWN FDL (B
GRAHAM GOFFEE G (B | SUSIE ROTHFIELD DULC V(B | HEATHER WOOD V (B | BRIAN PEARSON V (B

A82B

KEVIN ARMSTRONG

A82B

KEVIN ARMSTRONG (A | (A) HOW THE WEST WAS WON | 1981 NEW OPIUM UK OVAL302

A82C

THE ARNOLD

A82C

ROB JONES V (A | (A) WHEN | 1980 ACE (EP) ACE 20
ROB HILL G (A
JAIME CORTINAS B (A | GARY FOSTER D (A | ANDY BRISCOE SYN (A | PHIL MARTIN G (A

A83

BILLY BOY ARNOLD

A83

BILLY BOY ARNOLD V HCA(ALL | (A) KING OF CHICAGO BLUES VOL 3 | 1975 VOGUE 30285
WITH | (B) BLOW THE BACK OFF IT | 1975 RED LIGHTNIN RL 0012
JOHNNY WALKER PNO (C | (C) SINNERS PRAYER | 1976 RED LIGHTNIN RL 0014
CHRIS MOSS D (C | (D) MORE BLUES ON THE SOUTH SIDE | 197 BELLAPHON 40108 PRESTIGE 7389
ODELL CAMPBELL B (BC | (E) CHECKIN' IT OUT | 1979 RED LIGHTNIN RL 0024
LOUIS MYERS G (C | (F) CRYING & PLEADING | 1980 CHARLY CRB 1016
SAMMY LAWHORN G (C | (G) I WISH YOU WOULD (EP) | 1980 CHARLY UK CTD 117
PETER SHERTSER PROD (E
BO DIDDLEY G (B | OTIS SPAN PNO (B | JEROME GREEN PERC (B | FRED BELOW D (D
REYNOLDS HOWARD D (B | JAMES BRADFORD B (B | CLIFTON JAMES D (B | HENRY GRAY PNO (B
JODY WILLIAMS G (B | SUNNYLAND SLIM PNO (B | MILTON RECTOR B (B | EARL PHILLIPS D (B
QUINN WILSON B (B | SYLVESTER THOMPSON G (B | MACK THOMPSON G (B | MIGHTY JOE YOUNG G (E
LAFAYETTE LEAKE PNO (D | JEROME ARNOLD B (D | JUNIOR BLACKMAN D (D | TONY McPHEE G (E
WILGER CAMPBELL D (E | ALAN FISH B (E

A84

P P ARNOLD

A84

P P ARNOLD V (ALL | (A) FIRST LADY | 1967 IMMEDIATE IMSP 011
LEE JACKSON B (| (B) KAFUNTA | 1968 IMMEDIATE IMSP017
KEITH EMERSON K (| (C) GREATEST HITS | 1977 IMMEDIATE IML2006
DAVY O'LIST G (
BRIAN DAVISON D (

A85

ARRIVAL

A85

DYAN BIRCH V (ABC | (A) ARRIVAL | 1970 LONDON US 576
FRANK COLLINS V (ABC | (A) ARRIVAL | 1970 DECCA SKL5055
PADDY McHUGH V (ABC | (B) HEARTBREAK KID | 1973 CBS 70125
TONY O'MALLEY V K (ABC | (C) ARRIVAL | 1972 CBS 64733
CARROLL CARTER V (ABC
RALPH PEREIRA G (C | LEE SUTHERLAND B (C | GLEN LEFLEUR D (C | DON HUME B (A
LLOYD COURTENAY D (A | RON CARTHY TPT (D | ED RAY-SMITH TROM (B | ROY CARTER OBOE (D
PETE ZORN HRNS (D | PHIL CHEN B (D | GEORGE LEE SAX (C

A85A

ARROGANCE

A85A

DON NIXON B V PERC(AB | (A) RUMOURS | 1976 VANGUARD US VSD 79369
ROBERT KIRKLAND G V PERC(AB | (B) SUDDENLY | 1980 WB US 3429
SCOTT DAVISON D PERC (AB
MARTY STOOT K (AB | DON BROOKS HCA (A | LARRY PACKER FDL (A | ERIC WEISSBERG BANJ(A
SANFORD ALLEN (A | STRING SECTION (A

A85B

ARROWS

A85B

DAVIE ALLAN G V (A | (A) APACHE'65 | 1965 TOWER US 5002
STEVE PUGH B (A | (B) BLUES THEME | 1967 TOWER US 5078
LARRY BROWN D (A | (C) CYCLE DELIC SOUNDS | 1968 TOWER US 5094
PAUL JOHNSON G (A | (D) WILD IN THE STREETS | 196 TOWER US 5139

A86 — ARS NOVA

Member	Instruments
JOHN PIERSON	TROM V(AB
WYATT DAY	G K V (AB
WARREN BERNHARDT	K (B
MAURY BAKER	PERC K (A
GIOVANNI PAPALIA	G (A
ART KOENIG	B (B
SAM BROWN	G (B
JOE HUNT	D (B
JIMMY OWENS	TPT (B
JONATHAN RASKIN	B G V(A
BILL FOLWELL	TPT B(A

Album	Year	Label	Country	Catalogue
(A) ARS NOVA	1968	ELEKTRA	US	EKS74020
(B) SUNSHINE & SHADOWS	1969	ATLANTIC		SD 8221
(B) SUNSHINE & SHADOWS	1969	ATLANTIC		588 196

A87 — ART

Member	Instruments
LUTHER GROSVENOR	G (A
MIKE KELLIE	D (A
MIKE HARRISON	V K (A
GREG RIDLEY	B (A

Album	Year	Label	Country	Catalogue
(A) SUPERNATURAL FAIRYTALES	1967	ISLAND		ILP 967

A87A — ART & LANGUAGE

Member	Instruments
MAYO THOMPSON	(A
JESSE CHAMBERLAIN	(

Album	Year	Label	Country	Catalogue
(A) CORRECTED SLOGANS	197	MUSIC LANGUAGE	US	1848

A88 — ART BEARS

Member	Instruments
FRED FRITH	G VLN K(ABC
CHRIS CUTLER	D PERC(ABC
DAGMAR KRAUSE	V (ABC
GEORGE BORN	V (A
LINDSAY COOPER	WIND (A
TIM HODGKINSON	K WIND(A

Album	Year	Label	Country	Catalogue
(A) HOPES & FEARS	1978	RE		2188
(A) HOPES & FEARS	1978	RANDOM RADAR		RRR 004
(B) WINTER SONGS	1979	RE		RE0618
(C) THE WORLD AS IT IS TODAY	1981	RE		6622

A89 — ART ENSEMBLE OF CHICAGO

Member	Instruments
ROSCOE MITCHELL	SAX (ALL
LESTER BOWIE	TPT (ALL
MALACHI FAVORS	B (ALL
JOESEPH JARMAN	WIND (ALL
DON MOYE	D (ALL
FONTELLA BASS	V (BJP

Album	Year	Label	Country	Catalogue
(A) PHASE ONE	19	AMERICA		AM 6116
(A) PHASE ONE	19	PRESTIGE	US	10064
(B) WITH FONTELLA BASS	19	AMERICA		AM 6117
(B) WITH FONTELLA BASS	19	PRESTIGE		PR 10049
(C) SPIRITUAL	1974	POLYDOR		2383 098
(C) SPIRITUAL	1974	FREEDOM		28 428
(D) FANFARE FOR WARRIORS	1974	ATLANTIC	US	SD 1651
(D) FANFARE FOR WARRIORS	1977	ATLANTIC	UK	K 50304
(E) TUTAMKHAMUN	1975	FREEDOM		28 473
(F) PEOPLE IN SORROW	19	PATHE		2C062 10523
(F) PEOPLE IN SORROW	19	NESSA	US	N3
(G JACKS ONLY YOUR HOUSE	1978	AFFINITY		AFF 9
(I) CHI CONGA	19	PAULA	US	LPS 4001
(J) LES STANCES A SOPHIE	19	NESSA	US	N4
(K) THE PARIS SESSION (1969)	1975	FREEDOM	US	AL 1903
(K) THE PARIS SESSION (DBL)	197	FREEDOM		41106 /7
(L) CERTAIN BLACKS	19	INNERCITY	US	IC 1004
(M) NICE GUYS	1979	ECM		ECM 1126
(N) REESE & THE SMOOTH ONES	197	FREEDOM		AFF 22
(O) LIVE PART ONE	197			
(P) LIVE PART TWO	197	BYG	FR	2401
(Q) FULL FORCE	1980	ECM		1167

A89A — ART OBJECTS

Album	Year	Label	Country	Catalogue
(A) BAGPIPE MUSIC	1981	HEARTBEAT		HB5

A89B — ART ZOYD

Member	Instruments
ROCCO FERNANDEZ	G V (ABC
THIERRY ZABOITZEFF	B V (ABC
JEAN PIERRE SOAREZ	TPT (ABC
FRANK CARDON	VLN (B
ALAIN ECKERT	G PERC(AC
MICHEL BERCKMANS	WIND (B
GILLES RENARD	SAX (C
GERERD HOURBETTE	VLN SAX(ABC
DANIEL DENIS	PERC (BC
MICHEL THOMAS	SAX (B
PATRICIA DALLIO	PNO (C

Album	Year	Label	Country	Catalogue
(A) SYMPHONIE POUR LE JOUR...	1976	ART ZOYD		001
(B) MUSIQUE POUR L'ODYSSEE	1979	ATEM GER 7002	UK RE	RR3
(C) GENERATION SANS FUTUR	1980	ATEM	GER	7007

A90 — ARTFUL DODGER

Member	Instruments
STEVE BRIGADA	B PERC(ABCD
STEVE COOPER	B (ABCD
GARY COX	G V (ABC
GARY HERREWIG	G V (ABCD
BILL PALISELLI	V (ABCD
PETE BONTA	K G (D

Album	Year	Label	Country	Catalogue
(A) ARTFUL DODGER	1975	CBS	US	PC 33811
(B) HONOUR AMONG THIEVES	1976	CBS	US	PC 34273
(C) BABES ON BROADWAY	1977	CBS	US	PC 34846
(D) RAVE ON	1980	ARIOLA US 1503	NL	202 804

A91 — ARTI & MESTIERI

Member	Instruments
FURIO CHIRICO	D PERC(A
BEPPE CROVELLA	K SYN (A
MARCO GALLESI	B (A
ARTURO VITALE	WIND (A
GIGI VENEGONI	G SYN (A

Album	Year	Label	Country	Catalogue
(A) TILT	1974	CRAMPS	IT	CRSLP5501
(B) GIRO DI VALZEPER	19	BARCLAY		940 518

A91A — ARTISTICS

Album	Year	Label	Country	Catalogue
(A) I'M GONNA MISS YOU	19	BRUNSWICK		754123
(B) ARTICULATE	19	BRUNSWICK		754139
(C) WHAT HAPPENED	19	BRUNSWICK		754153
(D) GET MY HANDS ON SOME LOVIN'	19	OKEH		14119

A92 — ARTWOODS

Member	Instruments
ART WOOD	V (A
JON LORD	K (A
KEEF HARTLEY	D (A
DEREK GRIFFITHS	G (A
MALCOLM POOLE	B (A

Album	Year	Label	Country	Catalogue
(A) ART GALLERY	1964	DECCA		LK 4830
(A) ARTWOODS	1973	SPARK		SRLM2006
(B) ART GALLERY	1974	ECLIPSE		ECS 2025
(C) JAZZ IN JEANS (EP)	1966	DECCA		DFE 8654

A92A — ARZACHEL

Member	Instruments
STEVE HILLAGE	G V (A
MONT CAMPBELL	B (A
CLIVE BROOKS	D (A
DAVE STEWART	K (A

Album	Year	Label	Country	Catalogue
(A) ARZACHEL	1969	EGG EURO ROULETTE	US	42036

A93 — ASCEND

Member	Instruments
AMIN MOHAMMED	SITAR B (A
CHRIS BISCOE	SAX (A
NICK JONES	G (A
GRAHAME SMITH	VLN (A
EDDY SAYER	D (A
PETER LEMER	K (A

Album	Year	Label	Country	Catalogue
(A) CREATURES OF LIGhT & DARKNESS	1978			

A94 ASGARD A94

JAMES SMITH V (A
TED BARTLETT V (A
RODNEY HARRISON G V (A
IAN SNOW D (A
PETER ORGIL VLN (A
DAVE COOK B (A

(A) IN THE REALM OF — 1972 THRESHOLD THS 6

A95 DOUG ASHDOWN A95

DOUG ASHDOWN G V (A
MARK PONCH G (A
TIM PARTRIDGE B (A
STU BASEORE STEEL (A
LAURIE LONDON D (A
KIM RYRIE SYN (A
DECLAN AFFLEY WIND (A
NORMA STONEMAN V (A
PEE WEE CLARK STEEL (A
RUSSELL DUNLOP D (A
DAVID BRIGGS PNO (A
ROY RITCHIE K (A
JOHN JACKSON G (A
DAVID COOPER V (A
JOE ALLAN B (A
TONY BUCHANAN WIND (A
WAYNE FINDLAY K (A
TROY SEALS G (A
IAN BLOXSOM PERC (A

(A) A WINTER IN AMERICA — 1977 DECCA TXSR 125

A96 ASHFORD & SIMPSON A96

NICKOLAS ASHFORD V PROD(ALL
VALERIE SIMPSON V K PROD(ALL
ELLIOTT RANDALL G (C
RICHARD TEE K (CK
FRANCISCO CENTENO B (CFBDJK
RALPH McDONALD PERC (ABCFJ
RICK MAROTTA D (C
STEVE JORDAN D (F
JOHN DAVID HRNS (F
STEVE GADD D (C
JOHN SUSSEWELL D (F
LEROY PENDARVIS HRNS (ABJ
RAY SIMPSON V (CBDF
RAY CHEW K (FDJK
ERIC GALE G (CFDJK
ROBERT KREINER BABBIT B (AB
ANDREW SMITH D (AB
DAVID TOFANI SAX (K
CHARLES COLLINS D (AB
DAVID CAREY PERC (ABD
ROB MOUNSEY SYN HRNS(JK
JOSHIE ARMSTEAD V (ABC
DON GROLNICK K (C
PAUL RISER STRINGS(FABDJ
HUGH McCRACKEN G (C
PHILLIP WOO SYN (D
YOGI HORTON D (K
STEVE KHAN G (D
FRANK OWENS K (B
CHRIS PARKER D (DJK
JOHN SUSSWELL D (D
JEFF MIRANOV G (C
GEORGE YOUNG HRNS (CJ
ULLANDA McCULLOUGH V (FDJK
JERRY FRIEDMANN G (AB
EDDIE DANIELS FLT (J
CORNELL DUPREE G (B
JOHN TROPEA G (A
KEITH LOVING ILLEDGE G (B
ROBERT SOBINO K (B
CRUSHER BENNETT PERC (K

(A) GIMME SOMETHING REAL — 1974 WB UK K 46283 US BS 2739
(B) I WANNA BE SELFISH — 1974 WB UK K 56050 US BS 2789
(C) COME AS YOU ARE — 1976 WB UK K 56159 US BS 2858
(D) SEND IT — 1977 WB UK K US BS 3088
(E) SO SO SATISFIED — 1977 WB US BS 2992
(F) IS IT STILL GOOD TO YOU — 1978 WB UK K 56547 US BS 3219
(G) KEEP IT COMING — 197 TAMLA US T 7351
(H) STAY FREE — 1979 WB UK K 56703 US 3357
(J) A MUSICAL AFFAIR — 1980 WB UK K 56840 US 3458
(K) SECRET OPERA — 1982 EMI UK 12207

A97 ASHKAN A97

STEVE BAILEY V (A
RON BENDING B V (A
TERRY SIMS PERC (A
BOB WESTON G V (A

(A) IN FROM THE COLD — 1970 NOVA UK SRNR 1 US SIRE 97017

A98 STEVE ASHLEY A98

STEVE ASHLEY HCA V G (AB
RICHARD BYERS G (B
ROYSTON MITCHELL K (B
MADDY PRIOR SPOONS(B
DAVE MATTACKS D (B
BARRY DRANSFIELD (A
SIMON NICOL G (A
RAINER SCHUELEIN (A
SUE DRAHEIM (A
ROYSTON WOOD (A
DARRYL RUNSWICK B (A
DENNIS LOPEZ PERC (B
LYLE HARPER B (B
ASHLEY HUTCHINGS B (A
B J COLE STEEL (A
DANNY THOMPSON B (A
REDD McREADY (A
THOM FRIEDLEIN (A
RICHARD TAYLOR (A
DAVE PEGG B (B
SIMON PHILLIPS D (B
LEA NICHOLSON (B
CLAIRE DAWSON (A
BRIAN DIPROVE (A
CHRISTOPHER TAYLOR (A
CHRIS KARAN PERC (A

(A) STROLL ON — 1974 GULL US 6-401 UK GULP1003
(B) SPEEDY RETURN — 1975 GULL UK GULP1012

A98A ASHMAN REYNOLDS A98A

ALIKI ASHMAN V (A
HARRY REYNOLDS B G V (A
BOB WESTON G (A
KEITH BOYCE D (A
LIZA STRIKE V (A
MICKEY KEEN G (A
TONY CLARKE PERC (A
LADBROKE HORNS HRNS (A
ROD EDWARDS K V G (A
MADELINE BELL V (A

(A) STOP OFF — 1972 POLYDOR US 5507 UK 2383 114

A99 ASH RA (TEMPLE) A99

MANUEL GOETTSCHING G SYN (ALL
UDI ARNDT G (H
LUTZ ULBRICH G (I
KLAUS SCHULZE K (ADF
HARMUT ENKE B G (ABCD
WOLFGANG MULLER B (B
HARALD GROSSKOPF D SYN (EI
MATHIAS WEHLER SAX (B
ROSI MULLER V PERC(ED
ULI POP PERC (B
DIETER DIERKS B PERC(CE
MIKKY DOWE V FLT(C
STEVE SCHROYDER K (C
DIETMAR BURMEISTER D (C
HARALD GROSSKOPF D (E
TOMMIE ENGEL D (C
ROLF ULRICH KAISER PROD (D

(A) ASH RA TEMPLE — 1971 OHR OMM 556013
(B) SCHWINGUNGEN — 1972 OHR OMM 556020
(C) SEVEN UP — 1973 KOMISCHE KM 58001
(D) JOIN IN — 1973 OHR OMM 556032
(E) STARRING ROSI — 1973 KOMISCHE KM 58007
(F) INVENTIONS FOR ELECTRIC GUITAR — 19 KOMISCHE KM 58015
(F) INVENTIONS FOR ELECTRIC GUITAR — 19 BARCLAY 840066
(G) NEW AGE OF EARTH — 1977 VIRGIN V 2080
(G) NEW AGE OF EARTH — 1977 ISADORA ISA 9003
(H) BLACKOUTS — 1977 VIRGIN V 2091
(H) BLACKOUTS — 1977 POLYDOR 2373 740
(I) CORRELATIONS — 1979 VIRGIN NL V 2117
(J) BELLE ALLIANCE — 1980 VIRGIN NL 202 284

A99A MARK ASHTON A99A

MARK ASHTON G V (AB
STEVE GOULD G (B
MICK FEAT B (B
PETER VAN HOOKE D (B
TONY BRAUNAGEL D (B
CHRIS FLETCHER PERC (B
PHIL WAINMAN D (B
TERRY WILSON B (B
MIGUEL BARRADOS D (B
WINSTON DELANDRO G (B
BOB WESTON G (B
DEREK AUSTIN K (B
PETE WILLSHER STEEL(B

(A)MARK ASHTON — 1978 20TH CENTURY US 520
(B) SOLO — 1979 ARISTA ARL 5023

A99B ASIA A99B

JOHN WETTON B V K (A
STEVE HOWE G V (A
GEOFFREY DOWNES K (A
CARL PALMER D (A

(A) ASIA — 1982 GEFFEN UK 85577 GHS 2008

A100 ASHTON & LORD A100

TONY ASHTON K V (A
JON LORD (A

(A) FIRST OF THE BIG BANDS — 1974 PURPLE UK 3507 US WB 2778
(A) FIRST OF THE BIG BANDS — 1974 PATHE FR 2C064 95592

A101 ASHTON GARDNER & DYKE A101

TONY ASHTON K V (ABCD (A) ASHTON GARDNER & DYKE 1969 POLYDOR 583 081
KIM GARDNER B (ABCD (B) WHAT A BLOODY LONG DAY ITS BEEN 1972 CAPITOL EAST 862
ROY DYKE D (ABCD (C) THE WORST OF 1971 CAPITOL EST 563
JOHN MUMFORD TPT (B (D) THE LAST REBEL (SOUNDTRACK) 1971 CAPITOL
DAVE CASWELL TPT (B
LYLE JENKINS WIND (B MICK LIBER G (BC JIM PRICE TPT (C
STAN WEBB G (C GEORGE OHARA SMITH G (C PAUL PILNIK G (C
ROSETTA HIGHTOWER V (C CHRIS BARBER TROM (C P P ARNOLD V (C
MADELINE POULET(BELL?) V (C B J COLE STEEL (C CEDRIC CLAYTON G (C
ROMULUS WOODWORTH G (C MOXY HCA (C PHIL & BOOGIE BAND (C

A101A RICHARD ASHWORTH & WHITE DUB A101A

RICHARD ASHWORTH (AB (A) M 3 REVISITED (EP) 19 OVERDRIVE ORDER 1
(B) SURREY SKYLINE (EP) 19 OVERDRIVE ORDER 2

A102 ASLEEP AT THE WHEEL A102

RAY BENSON G V (ABCDEFGHI (A) COMIN' RIGHT AT YA 1973 UA US LA 038 UK UAS29454
LEROY PRESTON G D V(ABCDEFGHI (B) COMIN' RIGHT AT YA 1978 SUNSET UK SNS50415
CHRIS O'CONNELL V G (ABCDEFGHI (B) ASLEEP AT THE WHEEL 1974 EPIC US 33097
FLOYD DOMINO PNO (ABCDEFGHI (C) TEXAS GOLD 1975 CAPITOL UK EST11441
TONY GARNIER B (DFG (D) WHEELIN 'N' DEALIN 1976 CAPITOL EST11546
DANNY LEVIN MAN FDL(CDFG((E) TEXAS COUNTRY (ONE SIDE) 1976 UA US UALA 574
ED VIZARD SAX (C (F) THE WHEEL 1977 CAPITOL EST11620
SCOTT HENNIGE D (CD (G) COLLISION COURSE 1978 CAPITOL EST11726
LINK DAVIS FDL SAX(DFG (H) SERVED LIVE 1979 CAPITOL ST 11945
JOHNNY GIMBLE FDL (ABCD (I) FATHERS & SONS (DBL)1WHEEL 1 WILLS197 EPIC US 33782
LUCKY OCEANS D STEEL(ABCDEFGHI (J) FRAMED 1980 MCA US 5131
BILLY JOOR TPT (C
BILLY BRIGGS SAX (C DAVID POE SAX (C TOMMY ALLSUP B (C BOBBY WOMMACK TPT(C
MIKE O'DOWD WIND (C HURSHAL W WIGGINGTON V (C BILL MABRY FDL (DFG DENNIS SOLEE SAX(D
JOEL SONNIER ACC (D LINDA HARGROVE G (D BUCKY MEADOWS G (D TINY MOORE MAND(D
ELDON SHAMLIN G (D JACO WIND (F ED FREEMAN PNO (GENE DOBKIN B (A
BUDDY SPICHER FDL (A RICHARD CASONA FDL (A ANDREW STEIN FDL (AG LEON RAUSCH V (F
PAT RYAN WIND (FG CHRIS YORK D (FG DOLORES HALL V (G BENNY DIGGS V (G
PHILLIP BALLOU V (G BOB WILLS FDL HRN (I ARNETT COBB SAX (D

A103 VERA & GARY ASPEY A103

VERA ASPEY V G (AB (A) FROM THE NORTH 1975 TOPIC 12TS 255
GARY ASPEY V G (AB (B) A TASTE OF HOTPOT 1976 TOPIC 12TS 299
BERNARD WRIGLEY V CONC(A
WILF DARLINGTON V MAND(A

A104 VERA ASPEY A104

VERA ASPEY V G (A (A) THE BLACKBIRD 1977 TOPIC 12TS 356
DAVE GOTLIFFE PNO (A
JOHN LUCE G (A

A104A ASSASSIN OF SILENCE A104A

JIM CURNUTTE V SYN G B(A (A) BENEATH ALL THE MADNESS 1979 NEUROLOGICAL 5001
JANE CHAFIN K V (A
ELLIOT THORNE D V (A ROBIN JAMESON B (A WILLIE MAC B (A
MARK SEGAL D (A PHIL CULP B (A KEVIN LAMB PNO FLT(A

A105 ASSAGAI A105

LOUIS MOHOLO D (AB (A) ASSAGAI 1971 VERTIGO 6360 030
DUDU PUKWANA SAX (AB (B) ZIMBABWE 1972 PHILIPS 6308 079
MONGEZI FEZA TPT (AB ( ) ASSAGAI 1975 CONTOUR 2879 394
BIZO MNGQIKANA SAX (AB ( ) AFROROCK 1971 SOUNDS SUPERB UK SPR 90054
FRED COKER G (A
CHARLES ONONOGBO B (A TERRI QUAYE CONGA (B FRED FREDERICKS SAX (B
MARTHA MDENGE V (B TONY DUHIG (B JON FIELD (B
GLYN HAVARD (B SMILEY DE JONNES PERC (B

A105A ASSOCIATES A105A

BILLY McKENZIE V (A (A) AFFECTIONATE PUNCH 1980 FICTION UK FIX 1 2383 585
ALAN RANKINE G B K (A
NIGEL GLOCKLER D (A ROBERT SMITH V (A JOHN MURPHY D (
MICHAEL DEMPSEY B (

A105B ASSEMBLED MULTITUDE A105B

(A) ASSEMBLED MULTITUDE 197 ATLANTIC US 8262

A106 ASSOCIATION A106

RUSS GIGUERE G V (ABCDEFGH (A) AND THEN...ALONG CAME ASSOCIATION 1966 VALIENT US VLS 25002
JIM YESTER SAX V G K (ABCDEFGHIJ(A) AND THEN ..ALONG CAME ASSOCIATION 1966 LONDON UK HAT 8305
TED BLUECHEL D V (ABCDEFGHIJ(A) AND THEN...ALONG CAME ASSOCIATION 1966 W B US 1702
BRIAN COLE CLAR B V (ABCDEFGHIJ(B) RENAISSANCE 1967 VALIENT US VLS 25004
TERRY KIRKMAN D V WIND (ABCDEFGHIJ(B) RENAISSANCE 1967 LONDON UK HAT 8313
GARY ALEXANDER G V (ABEGHIJ (B) RENAISSANCE 1967 W B US WS 1704
LARRY RAMOS SAX HCA G V (CDEFGHIJ (C) INSIGHT OUT 1967 LONDON UK MHAT 8342
RICHARD THOMPSON G V (IJ (C) INSIGHT OUT 1967 WB US WS 1696
(D) BIRTHDAY 1968 WB US WS 1733
(E) GREATEST HITS 1969 WB US WS 1767
(F) GOODBYE COLUMBUS (SOUNDTRACK) 1969 WB US WS 1786
(G) ASSOCIATION 1969 WB US WS 1800
(H) LIVE (DBL) 1970 WB US 2WS 1868
(I) STOP YOUR MOTOR 1971 WB US WS 1927
(J) WATERBEDS IN TRINIDAD 1972 CBS UK S 65009
(J) WATERBEDS IN TRINIDAD 1972 CBS US KC 31348
(K) THE ASSOCIATION 1981 WB UK K26012

A106A ASTRONAUTS A106A

BOB DEMMON G TPT K(AB (A) SURFIN' WITH THE ASTRONAUTS 1963 RCA US 2760
RICH FIFIELD G V (A (B) TRAVELIN' MAN 1967 RCA US 3733
DENNIS LINDSEY G (A
JIM GALLAGHER D (A STORMY PATTERSON B V (A

A107 ASWAD A107

Personnel	Instr.		Record	Year	Label		Number
BRINSLEY FORDE	PERC G V	(AB	(A) ASWAD	1976	ISLAND	UK	ILPS9399
DON GRIFFITHS	PERC G V	(ABC	(B) HULET	1980	ISLAND UK 9611 GROVE		GMLP 6
BUNNY McKENZIE	HCA	(A	(C) SHOWCASE	1981	GROVE		ASWAD 1
COURTNEY HEMMINGS	PERC V K	(AC					

GEORGE OBAN	PERC B	(ABC	ANGUS GAYE	D K	(AB	CANDY McKENZIE	V	(A
TREVOR BOW	PERC	(A	DELROY WASHINGTON	V	(A	ADETOKUMBA ILLORIN	G	(A
TONY GADD	K V	(B	KARL PITTERSON		(C	BONGO LEVI	V	(C
VIN GORDON	TPT	(C	MIKE ROSE	TPT	(C			

A108 ATACAMA A108

Record	Year	Label		Number
(A) ATACAMA	1971	CHARISMA	UK	CAS 1039
(B) SUN BURNS UP ABOVE	1972	CHARISMA	UK	CAS 1060

A108A ATHLETICO SPIZZ 80 A108A

Record	Year	Label		Number
(A) DO A RUNNER	1980	A&M	UK	AMLE 68514

A109 PETE ATKIN A109

Personnel	Instr.		Record	Year	Label		Number
PETE ATKIN	G V PNO	(ALL	(A) BEWARE OF THE BEAUTIFUL STRANGER	1970	FONTANA	UK	6309 011
STEVE COOK	B	(A	(A) BEWARE OF THE BEAUTIFUL STRANGER	1974	RCA		SF 8387
BRIAN ODGERS	B	(A	(B) DRIVING THROUGH MYTHICAL AMERICA	1971	PHILIPS		6308 070
TONY MARSH	D	(A	(B) DRIVING THROUGH MYTHICAL AMERICA	1974	RCA		SF 8386
HENRY MACKENZIE	CLAR	(A	(C) A KING AT NIGHTFALL	1973	RCA		SF 8336
RUSSELL DAVIES	HRNS	(A	(D) THE ROAD OF SILK	1974	RCA		LPLI 5014
ALBERT HALL	HRNS	(A	(E) SECRET DRINKER	1974	RCA		LPLI 5062
FRANK RICOTTI	PERC	(D	(F) LIVE LIBEL	1975	RCA		RS 1013
CHRIS SPEDDING	G	(BC	( ) MASTER OF REVELS (BEST OF)	1977	RCA		PL 25041
HERBIE FLOWERS	B	(BC	(G) RIDERS TO THE WORLDS END (CASS)	19	RCA		PK 11677
KENNY CLARE	D	(B					
DENNIS CLIFT	TPT		(NOTE (A) RECORDS HAVE ONE DIFFERENT TRACK)				
LEON CALVERT	HRNS	(B					

DAI DAVIS	TROM	(B	JIM WORTLEY	TROM	(B	RICHARD IHNATON WIEZ	WIND	(B
ALAN PARKER	G	(B	BARRY MORGAN	D	(BC	DAVE BELL	B	(B
TONY COE	WIND	(D	CLIVE BAKER	TPT	(BC	DARRYL RUNSWICK	B	(DEF
ALAN WAKEMAN	WIND	(BC	DON FAY	SAX	(B	BARRY DE SOUZA	D	(E
MIKE MORAN	K	(CD	RAY COOPER	PERC	(C	TERRY COX	D	(D
RALPH IZEN	TPT	(C	NAT PECK	TROM	(C	BILL GELDARD	TROM	(C
DICK HART	TUBA	(C	BOB SYDOR	WIND	(C	MIKE PAGE	WIND	(C
RONNIE ROSS	SAX	(E	HOWARD BALL	STRINGS	(C	CLIVE JAMES	LYRICS	(
NEIL CAMPBELL	G	(F	DICK LEVENS	B	(F	JEFF SEOPARDIE	D	(F
GAYE BROWN	V	(F	DIANE LANGTON	V	(F	ANNABEL LEVENTON	V	(F

A110 CHET ATKINS A110

Title	Label	Year	Number
CHET ATKINS AT HOME	RCA	1958	LPM 1544
SESSION WITH	RCA	1959	LPM 1090
STRINGING ALONG WITH	RCA	1959	LPM 1236
IN THREE DIMENSIONS	RCA	1959	LPM 1197
FINGER STYLE GUITAR	RCA	1959	LPM 1383
HI FI FOCUS	RCA	1959	LPM 1577
IN HOLLYWOOD	RCA	195	LPM 1993
HUM & STRUM ALONG	RCA	1959	LPM 2025
MISTER GUITAR	RCA	1960	LPM 2103
TEENSVILLE	RCA	1960	LPM 2161
TEENSVILLE	RCA UK	1960	RD 27168
THE OTHER CHET ATKINS	RCA	1960	LPM 2175
WORKSHOP	RCA	1961	RD 27214
WORKSHOP	RCA	1961	LPM 2232
MOST POPULAR GUITAR	RCA	1961	LPM 2346
& HIS GUITAR	CAMDEN	1961	CDN 160
BACK HOME HYMNS	RCA	1962	LSA 2007
DOWN HOME	CAMDEN	1962	CDN 165
DOWN HOME	RCA	1962	LSP 2450
DOWN HOME	CAMDEN	1962	SND 5016
CARRIBBEAN GUITAR	RCA	1962	LSP 2549
CHRISTMAS WITH CHET	RCA	1962	LSP 2423
THE POPS GOES COUNTRY	RCA	196	LSC 2070
CHET PICKS ON THE POPS	RCA	196	LSC 3104
RELAXIN' WITH CHET	RCA	1969	INTS 1004
RELAXING WITH CHET	RCA	1969	CAM 2292
TRAVELLIN' GUITAR	RCA	19	INTS 1141
TRAVELLIN'	RCA	19	LSP 2678
THE EARLY YEARS	CAMDEN	19	CAS 659
OUR MAN IN NASHVILLE	RCA	1963	LSP 2616
OUR MAN IN NASHVILLE	RCA	19	SE 7529
GUITAR COUNTRY	RCA	1964	LSP 2783
PROGRESSIVE PICKIN'	RCA	1964	LSP 2908
BEST OF	RCA	1964	LSP 2887
BEST OF	RCA	196	RD 7664
& HIS OTHER GUITAR	RCA	19	
PICKS ON THE POPS	RCA	19	LSC 3104
IN CONCERT	CAMDEN	19	CPL2 1014
PICKIN' MY WAY	RCA	19	LSA 3051
PICKIN' MY WAY	RCA	1970	LSP 4585
MY FAVOURITE GUITARS	RCA	1965	LSP 3316
MY FAVOURITE GUITARS	RCA	1965	RD 7710
MORE OF THAT GUITAR COUNTRY	RCA	1965	LSP 3429
TEENSCENE	RCA	19	ACLI 7005
TEENSCENE	RCA	19	SF 7602
AMERICAN SALUTE	RCA	19	LSC 3277
GUITAR COUNTRY	RCA	1965	
PICKS ON THE BEATLES	RCA	1966	LSP 3531
PICKS ON THE BEATLES	RCA	1966	SF LSP 7813
BEST OF VOL 2	RCA	1965	LSP 3558
BEST OF VOL 2	CAMDEN	19	CAS 10261
PICKS ON THE BEATLES(REISSUE)	RCA	1977	ANLA 2002
BEST OF CHET ATKINS	RCA	1966	
MUSIC FROM NASHVILLE	CAMDEN	1966	CAM 981
THE GUITAR GENIUS	CAMDEN	1963	CDS 1067
THE GUITAR GENIUS	CAMDEN	1963	CAS 753
FROM NASHVILLE WITH LOVE	RCA	1966	
GUITAR WORLD	RCA	1967	LSP 3728
PICKS THE BEST	RCA	1967	LSP 3818
PICKS THE BEST	RCA	1967	ANLI 0981
MR ATKINS GUITAR PICKER	CAMDEN	196	CDS 1090
MR ATKINS GUITAR PICKER	CAMDEN	196	CASX2464E
CLASS GUITAR	RCA	1967	LSP 3885
CHET	CAMDEN	1967	CDS 1014
CHET	CAMDEN	196	2182
SOLO FLIGHTS	RCA	1968	LSP 3922
SOLO FLIGHTS	RCA	1968	RD 7934
COUNTRY PICKIN'	RCA	19	X9006
REMINISCING (HANK SNOW)	RCA	1964	RD 7691
REMINISCING (HANK SNOW)	RCA	1964	LSP 2952
SOLID GOLD 68	RCA	1968	LSP 4061
HOMETOWN GUITAR	RCA	1968	LSP 4017
LOVERS GUITAR	RCA	1969	LSP 4035
SOLID GOLD 69	RCA	1969	LSP 4244
C B ATKINS & C E SNOW	RCA	1969	LSP 4254
THIS IS CHET ATKINS	RCA	19	VPS 4254
BY SPECIAL REQUEST	RCA	1970	LSP 5254
SOLID GOLD 70	RCA	1970	LSP 4244
SOLID GOLD 70	RCA	1970	SF 0092
ME & JERRY	RCA	19	LSA 3033
ME & JERRY	RCA	1971	LSP 4396
GUITAR PICKER	CAMDEN	1971	2464
YESTERGROOVIN'	RCA	1970	LSP 4331
YESTERGROOVIN'	RCA	1970	SF 8130
ME & CHET	RCA	19	LSA 3091
ME & CHET	RCA	1972	ANLI 2167
FOR THE GOOD TIMES	RCA	1971	LSP 4464
NOW & THEN	RCA	1972	6079
NASHVILLE GOLD	RCA	1972	CAS 2551
FINGER PICKIN' GOOD	RCA	19	CAS 2600
PICKS THE HITS	RCA	1973	LSA 3121
STRUM ALONG GUITAR METHOD	RCA	1973	PRP 36932
PICKS THE HITS	RCA	19	LSP 4754
PICKS ON JERRY REED	RCA	1974	APLI 0545
SUPERPICKERS	RCA	1974	APLI 0329
ALONE	RCA	19	APLI 0159
GOES TO THE MOVIES	RCA	19	APLI 0845
THE NIGHT ATLANTA BURNED	RCA	1975	APLI 1233
FAMOUS COUNTRY MUSIC MAKERS	RCA	1975	DPS 2063
LOVE LETTERS	CAMDEN	19	ACLI 7042
CHET & BOOTS	CAMDEN	19	CAS 2523
THE BEST OF CHET & FRIENDS	RCA	1976	APLI 1985
CHESTER & LESTER	RCA	1976	APLI 1167
CHESTER & LESTER	RCA	1977	LPS 3290
ME & MY GUITAR	RCA	1977	PL 12405
CHET FLOYD & DANNY	RCA	1977	APLI 2311
GUITAR MONSTERS (LES PAUL)	RCA	1978	PL 1286
GUITAR MONSTERS (LES PAUL)	RCA	1978	APLI 2786
LEGENDARY PERFORMER	RCA	1978	PL 12503
FIRST NASHVILLE GUIT QUARTET	RCA	1979	AHLI 3302

A111 ATLANTA RHYTHM SECTION A111

Musician	Instr	Albums
PAUL GODDARD	B G	(ALL
BARRY BAILEY	G B	(ALL
J R COBB	G B V	(ALL
RONNIE HAMMOND	V	(ALL
DEAN DAUGHTRY	K	(ALL
ROBERT NIX	D V	(ABCDEFGHI
MYLON LEFEVRE	V	(C
MIKE HUEY	CONGA	(C
PAUL DAVIS	V	(G
ROY YEAGER	D	(IJK
BUDDY BUIE	V	(K
STEVE McRAY	K V	(K
BILLY LEE RILEY	HCA	(B
HUGH BABY JARRET	V	(C
JO JO BILLINGSLEY	V	(G
ARTIMUS PYLE	PERC	(G
MARK DENNY	SYN	(K
STRAY STRATON		(J
STEVE HAMMOND	V	(J
RODNEY JUSTO	V	(A
RICK MAXWELL	STEEL	(J

Album	Year	Label	Catalogue
(A) ATLANTA RHYTHM SECTION	1972	MCA	UK MAPS 5594
(A) ATLANTA RHYTHM SECTION	1972	DECCA	US 5265
(B) BACK UP AGAINST THE WALL	1974	MCA	UK MCF 2670 6465
(B) BACK UP AGAINST THE WALL	1974	DECCA	US 5390
(C) THIRD ANNUAL PIPE DREAM	1975	POLYDOR	UK 2391 136 US 6027
(D) DOG DAYS	1976	POLYDOR	UK 2391 179 US 6041
(E) RED TAPE	1976	POLYDOR	UK 2391 223 US 6060
(F) ROCK'N'ROLL ALTERNATIVE	1977	POLYDOR	UK 2391 255 US 6080
(G) CHAMPAGNE JAM	1978	POLYDOR	UK 2391 319 US 6134
(H) ARE YOU READY (DBL)	1980	POLYDOR	UK 2672 050 US 6236
(I) UNDERDOG	1979	POLYDOR	UK 2391 398 US 6200
(J) BOYS FROM DORAVILLE(DIFF US/UK)	1980	POLYDOR	UK 2391 467 US 6285
(AB) ATLANTA RHYTHM SECTION(DBL)	19	MCA	US 4114
(K) QUINELLA	1981	CBS	UK 85320

A112 ATLANTIC BRIDGE A112

Musician	Instr	Albums
MIKE TRAVIS	D	(A
MIKE McNAUGHT	K	(A
JIM PHILLIPS	SAX	(A
DARYL RUNSWICK	B	(A

Album	Year	Label	Catalogue
(A) ATLANTIC BRIDGE	1970	DAWN	DNLS 3014
(B) I CANT LIE TO YOU (EP)	1971	DAWN	DNX 2507

A112A ATLANTICS A112A

Musician	Instr	Albums
RAY BOY FERNANDES	D PERC	(A
FRED PINEAU	G	(A
B WILKINSON	B V K	(A
TOM HAUCK	G V	(A
BOBBY MARRON	V	(A

Album	Year	Label	Catalogue
(A) BIG CITY ROCK	1979	ABC	US AA 1134

A113 ATLANTIS A113

Musician	Instr	Albums
GASPAR LAWAL	PERC	(B
INGA RUMPF	V PERC	(ALL
JEAN JACQUES KRAVETZ	K	(ABCD
RINGO FUNK	D	(BCDFGH
CURT CRESS	D	(A
KARL HEINZ SCHOTT	B	(ALL
DIETER BORNSCHLEGEL	G	(B
RAINER MARZ	G V	(GH
REEBOP BAAH	PERC	(A
JEAN ROUSSEL	K	(a
INGO BISCHOFF	K	(G
LINDA FIELD	V	(C
ADRIAN ASKEW	K G V	(CDEGH
GERALD HARTWIG	B	(G
JACKIE DIEZ	V	(A
ALEX CONTI	G V	(CDF
FRANK DIEZ		(Agh
JASPER VAN'T' HOF	PNO	(C

Album	Year	Label	Catalogue
(A) ATLANTIS	1973	VERTIGO	UK 6360 609 US VEL1016
(B) ITS GETTING BETTER	1974	VERTIGO	UK 6360 614 US VEL1018
(C) ATLANTIS	1974	POLYDOR	UK 2391 176 US PD 6513
(D) OH BABY	1974	VERTIGO	UK 6360 621
(D) OH BABY	1974	VENUS	US 1009
(E) ALLEY CAT	19	VERTIGO	UK 6360 127
(F) LIVE (DBL)	1974	VERTIGO	6623 900
(F) LIVE (DBL)	19	VENUS	US 1010
(G) TOP OF THE BILL	1976	VENUS	F1002
(H) GET ON BOARD	1975	VENUS	1011

A113A ATLAS A113A

Musician	Instr	Albums
DARREL WILKES	G V	(A
PAUL GREENWOOD	K B	(A
N H K PLEASANT	D PERC	(A

Album	Year	Label	Catalogue
(A) AGAINST ALL THE ODDS	1978	ATLAS	WIL 001

A114 ATOLL A114

Musician	Instr	Albums
MICHEL TAILLET	K	(AB
RICHARD AUBERT	VLN	(A
CHRISTIAN BEYA	G	(AB
ANDRE BALZER	PERC	(AB
ALAIN GOZZO	D	(AB
JEAN LUC THILLOT	B	(AB

Album	Year	Label	Catalogue
(A) L'ARAIGNEE MAL	1975	EURODISC	FR 913 002
(B) TERTIO	1978	ARIOLA	ARL 5008
(B) TERTIOS	1978	EURODISC	FR 913 132

A115 ATOMIC ROOSTER A115

Musician	Instr	Albums
VINCENT CRANE	K	(ALL
CARL PALMER	D	(A
NICK GRAHAM	B	(A
RICK PARNELL	D	(DEF
STEVE BOLTON	G	(D
JOHN MANDELLA	G	(EF
PRESTON HEYMAN	D	(H
CHRIS FARLOWE	V	(DEF
JOHN CANN	G	(BC
PAUL HAMMOND	D	(BC
DORIS TROY	V	(D
BILL SMITH	B	(D
LIZA STRIKE	V	(D
PETER FRENCH	V	(C

Album	Year	Label	Catalogue
(A) ATOMIC ROOSTER	1970	B &C	UK CAS 1010
(B) DEATH WALKS BEHIND YOU	1970	B & C	UK CAS 2026
(B) DEATH WALKS BEHIND YOU	1971	ELEKTRA	US EKS 74094
(C) IN HEARING OF	1971	PEGASUS	UK PEG 1
(C) IN HEARING OF	1971	ELEKTRA	US 74109
(D) MADE IN ENGLAND	1972	DAWN	UK DNLS 3038
(D) MADE IN ENGLAND	1972	ELEKTRA	US 75039
(E) ATOMIC ROOSTER IV	1973	ELEKTRA	US EKS 75074
(F) NICE & GREASY	1973	DAWN	UK DNLS3049 GER BRAIN 1033
(G) ASSORTMENT	1974	B & C	UK CS 9
(H) HOME TO ROOST	1977	MOONCREST	UK CDR 2
(I) THIS IS ATOMIC ROOSTER	1977	BRAIN	GER 200 151
(J) ATOMIC ROOSTER	1980	EMI	UK EMC 3341

A115A ATTILA A115A

Musician	Instr	Albums
BILLY JOEL	K V	(A
JON SMALL	D	(A

Album	Year	Label	Catalogue
(A) ATTILA	1970	EPIC	30030 26282

A116 ATTITUDES A116

Musician	Instr	Albums
DANNY KOOTCH	G	(AB
JIM KELTNER	D	(AB
PAUL STALLWORTH	B V	(AB
DAVID FOSTER	K	(AB

WITH

Musician	Instr	Albums
VENETTE GLOUD	V	(A
COSMO DE AGUERO	CONGA	(A
WADDY WACHTEL	G	(B
MARVIN BRAXTON	HCA	(B
JAY GRAYDON	G	(B
RINGO STARR	D	(B
CARMEN TWILLIE	V	(A
CHUCK HIGGINS	V	(AB
JESSE ED DAVIS	G	(A
TOWER OF POWER	HRNS	(B
JAY LEWIS	G	(B
EMIL RICHARDS	PERC	(B
BOOKER T JONES	K	(B
KATHRYN COLLIER	V	(A
PAT MURPHY	CONGA	(AB
VINCE CHARLES	PERC	(Ab
DONNY GERRARD	V	(B
GEORGE BELL	FLT	(B
JORGE CALDERON	V	(B
YVONNE RANKIN	V	(B

Album	Year	Label	Catalogue
(A) ATTITUDES	1975	DARK HORSE	AMLH22008
(B) GOOD NEWS	1977	DARK HORSE	K 56385
(B) GOOD NEWS	1977	DARK HORSE	US 3021

A116A ATTRACTIONS A116A

Album	Year	Label	Catalogue
(A) MAD ABOUT THE WRONG BOY	1980	F BEAT	UK 8UK WEA NL 58158

A116B AU PAIRS A116B

Musician	Instr	Albums
LESLEY	G V	(A
PAUL	G V	(A
JANE	B	(A
PETE	D	(A

Album	Year	Label	Catalogue
(A) PLAYING WITH A DIFFERENCE SEX	1981	HUMAN	UK HUMAN 1

A117 AUBREY SMALL A117

- PETER PINCKNEY G V (A
- ROD TAYLOR K V (A
- ALAN CHRISTMAS G (A
- DAVID YEARLEY B (A
- GRAHAM HUNT D G V(A

- (A) AUBREY SMALL 1971 POLYDOR UK 2383 048

A118 AUDIENCE A118

- TONY CONNOR D (ABCDE
- GUS DUDGEON PROD PERC (CD
- TREVOR WILLIAMS B K V (ABCDE
- KEITH GEMMELL WIND (ABCDE
- JIM PRICE HRNS (D
- BOBBY KEYS SAX (D
- NICK JUDD K (D
- HOWARD WERTH G V (ABCDE
- CHRIS BROUGH PROD (A

- (A) AUDIENCE 1969 POLYDOR 583 065
- (B) FRIENDS FRIENDS FRIENDS 1970 CHARISMA CAS 1012
- (C) HOUSE ON THE HILL 1971 CHARISMA CAS 1032
- (C) HOUSE ON THE HILL 1971 ELEKTRA US EKS 74100
- (D) LUNCH 1972 CHARISMA UK CAS 1054
- (D) LUNCH 1972 ELEKTRA US EKS 75026
- (E) YOU CANT BEAT THEM 1973 CHARISMA UK CS 7

A119 MICK AUDSLEY A119

- MICK AUDSLEY

- (A) DARK & DEVIL WATERS 1973 SONET SNTF 641
- (B) STORYBOARD 1974 SONET SNTF 659

A120 BRIAN AUGER A120

- BRIAN AUGER K V (ALL
- ROY SWINFIELD FLT (B
- JIMMY PAGE G (M
- I BEERS WIND (B
- JULIE DRISCOLL(TIPPETTS) V(ACORS
- RICK LAIRD B (
- PHIL KINORRA D (
- GLEN HUGHES SAX (
- MICK WALLER D (MS
- ROD STEWART V (
- DAVE AMBROSE B (ABCDR
- CLIVE THACKER D (ABCDRS
- COLIN ALLEN D (D
- JACK MILLS G (HJKLNX
- JOHN McLAUGHLIN G (
- DAVID DOYLE D (X
- STEVE FERRONE D (JKL
- ROGER SUTTON B (DS
- JIM MULLEN G (EFG
- GODFREY MACLEAN D (H
- MIRZA AL SHARIF PERC (J
- DAVE CRIGGER D (O
- CLEM CATTINI D (S
- ALEX LIGERTWOOD V (GKLNX
- LENNOX LAINGTON (HJNX
- DAVID McDANIELS B (O
- GEORGE DOERING G (O
- MAXINE WILLARD V (O
- LENNY WHITE D (N
- A McGAVIN WIND (B
- J BUCK FLT (B
- RICK BROWN B (MS
- LONG JOHN BALDRY V (
- CLIVE CHAMAN B (NX
- ALAN SKIDMORE SAX (M
- BARRY REEVES D (D
- JESSICA SMITH V (O
- GREG BOWEN TPT (B
- DEREK HEALEY TPT (B
- CLIFF HARDIE TROM (B
- P POUCHER TROM (B
- SONNY BOY WILLIAMSON (RICE MILLER) HCA (M
- VIC BRIGGS G (S
- BARRY DEAN G (EFGHJKL
- STRING SECTION (B
- DEREK WATKINS TPT (B
- S REYNOLDS TPT (B
- ALF REECE TROM (B
- B ALTRAM TROM (B
- JOE HARRIOT SAX (M
- GARY BOYLE G (ADR
- ROBBIE McINTOSH D (EFG
- ALBERT HALL TPT (B
- LENNIE CALVERT TPT(D
- D CAMPBELL TPT (B
- J SIMCOCK TROM (B
- T RANDALL WIND (B

- (A) OPEN 1967 ATCO US 33256 MARMALADE 607 002
- (A) OPEN 19 POLYDOR RI 2438 304
- (B) DEFINITELY WHAT 1968 ATCO US 33273 MARMALADE 607 003
- (B) DEFINITELY WHAT 19 POLYDOR RI GER 184 182
- (C) STREETNOISE (DBL) 1968 ATCO US 2701 MARMALADE 608005/6
- (C) STREETNOISE (DBL) 1968 KARUSSELL RI GER 2674 014
- (D) BEFOUR 1970 RCA US 4372 UK SF 8101
- (E) OBLIVION EXPRESS 1971 RCA US 4462 UK SF 8170
- (F) A BETTER LAND 1971 RCA US 4540 UK POLYDOR 2383 062
- (G) SECOND WIND 1972 RCA US 4703 UK POLYDOR 2383 104
- (H) CLOSER TO IT 1973 RCA US 0140 UK CBS 65625
- (J) STRAIGHT AHEAD 1974 RCA US 0454 UK CBS 80058
- (K) LIVE OBLIVION VOL 1 1974 RCA US 2481 US 0645
- (L) LIVE OBLIVION VOL 2 (DBL) 1974 RCAUS 1230
- (X) REINFORCEMENTS 1974 RCA US 1210
- (M) DONT SEND ME NO FLOWERS 1969 MARMALADE 608 004
- (M) JAM SESSION 1975 CHARLY UK 30011
- (N) HAPPINESS HEARTACHES 1977 WB US BS2981 UK 56326
- (O) ENCORE 1978 WB US BSK3153 UK K56458
- (P) BEST OF BRIAN AUGER & TRINITY 1970 POLYDOR 2334 004
- (Q) BRIAN AUGER & THE TRINITY 19 POLYDOR 2384 062
- (R) GENESIS(TRINITY) 1975 POLYDOR US 6505 UK 2383 277
- (S) LONDON 1964 67 1977 CHARLY UK CR300019
- (T) THIS IS 1975 METRONOME GER 200149
- ( ) STAR PORTRAIT(DBL COMP) 19 POLYDOR 2625 008
- ( ) BRIAN AUGER 19 SPRINGBOARD US SPB 4044
- ( ) THE BEST OF BRIAN AUGER 19 RCA US 2249
- ( ) JULIE DRISCOLL & BRIAN AUGER 1968 MFP 1265
- ( ) ATTENTION 19 FONTANA 9294 901
- ( ) POP HISTORY VOL 26 1972 POLYDOR 26680
- ( ) IN & OUT 1969 KARUSSELL 2345 004

A121 MIKE AULDRIDGE A121

- MIKE AULDRIDGE DOBRO V G(ALL
- DAVID BROMBERG G (AB
- VASSAR CLEMENTS FDL (AB
- CHARLIE WALLER G (A
- BUCK GRAVES DOB (A
- BILL EMERSON BANJO(A
- JOHN DUFFY G MAND(AB
- ED FERRIS B (A
- JOHN STARLING G (B
- LOWELL GEORGE G (B
- PAUL CRAFT G (B
- DOYLE LAWSON MAND G (AB
- STEVE BURGH B (A
- RICK SCAGGS G (B
- TOM GUIDERA G (B
- TOM GREY B (AB
- BILL YATES B (A
- BOB LAWRENCE D (B
- FAYSSOUX STARLING V (B
- BEN ELDRIDGE BAN G(AB
- JEFF NEWMAN (E
- GERRY MULE G (B
- LINDA RONSTADT V (B

- (A) DOBRO 1972 SONET UK SNTF657 US TAKOMA 1033
- (B) BLUES & BLUEGRASS 1977 SONET UK SNTF673 US TAKOMA 1041
- (C) MIKE AULDRIDGE 1976 FLYING FISH US FF029+FLY 0003
- (D) OLD DOG 19 FLYING FISH US FF054+FLY 0004
- (E) SLIDIN' SMOKE 1979 FLYING FISH US FF080

A121A AUM A121A

- LARRY MARTIN D V (AB
- WAYNE CEBALLOS HCA V G K(AB
- KEN NEWELL B V (AB

- (A) BLUESVIBES 1969 SIRE LONDON US 97007
- (B) RESURRECTION 1969 FILLMORE/CBS US 30002

A121B AURA A121B

- AL LATHAN V PERC(A
- BILL WALDNER G (A
- FRED ENTESARI SAX (A
- ANDY FOERTSCH TROM (A
- SAM ALESSI K (A
- DENNIS HORAN D (A
- CHUCK GREENBERG WIND (A
- JERRY SMITH B V (A
- TERRY QUAYE PERC (A
- GEORGE BARR TPT V (A

- (A) AURA 1971 MERCURY US SRM1 620
- (B) AURA II? 1972 GUINNESS US

A122 AURACLE A122

- BILL STAEBELL B (AB
- RON WAGNER D (AB
- RICHARD C BRAUN TPT (AB
- STEPHEN KUJALA WIND (AB
- STACEY O'BRIEN V (B
- JEFF TKAZYAK HRNS (B
- TIM MAY G (B
- STEVEN REHBEIN PERC (AB
- GLORIA O'BRIEN V (B
- STEVE JOHNSON HRNS (B
- AFREEA TREES V (B
- JOHN SERRY JNR K (A
- DONNA DELORY V (B
- ROBERT PAYNE HRNS (B
- GLORIA GOLDSMITH V (B
- BIFF HANNON PNO (B
- LEE RITENOUR G (B
- STACY CLINGER V (B

- (A) GLIDER 1978 CHRYSALIS US/UK CHR 1172
- (B) CITY SLICKER 1979 CHRYSALIS US/UK CHR 1210

A123 PATTI AUSTIN A123

Title	Year/Label	Catalogue
(A) END OF A RAINBOW	1976 CTI	CTI 5001
(B) HAVANA CANDY	1977 CTI	CTI 5006
(C) LIVE AT THE BOTTOM LINE	1979 CTI	7086
(D) BODY LANGUAGE	1980 CTI UK 2406 013 · US	36503
(E) EVERY HOME SHOULD HAVE ONE	1980 QWEST UK	K56931

PATTI AUSTIN	V	(ALL									
WITH											
DAVE GRUSIN	PNO	(B									
ERIC GALE	G	(ABE									
STEVE KHAN	G	(AB									
HUGH McCRACKEN	G	(B									
WILL LEE	B	(BCD	STEVE JORDAN	D	(B	RALPH McDONALD	PERC	(BE	ERNIE WATTS	SAX	(E
CHRIS PARKER	D	(E	MICHAEL BRECKER	SAX	(ABCD	RICHARD TEE	K	(ABE	FRANCISCO CENTENO	B	(B
ANTHONY JACKSON	B	(BE	BOB JAMES	K	(E	EDDIE WATKINS	B	(E	ROD TEMPERTON	SYN	(E
DAVE VALENTIN	PERC	(B	FRANK GRAVIS	B	(B	ALAN RUBIN	TPT	(B	MARVIN STAMM	TPT	(B
WAYNE ANDRE	TROM	(B	GERRY NIEWOOD	SAX	(B	LOU MARINI	SAX	(B	RONNIE CUBER	SAX	(B
LANI GROVES	V	(B	GWEN GUTHRIE	V	(B	YOLANDA McCULLOUGH	V	(B	KEN WILLIAMS	V	(B
JEFF BERLIN	B	(A	STEVE GADD	D	(A	RANDY BRECKER	HRNS	(AD	STRINGS		(B
GLORIA AGOSTINI	HARP	(A	RANDY McCORMACK	K	(D	JEREMY WALL	K	(D	DUNCAN CAMERON	G	(D
DAVID HOOD	B	(D	ROGER HAWKINS	D	(D	MICKEY BUCKINS	PERC	(D	JOHN TROPEA	G	(D
JERRY DODGION	SAX	(D	JIM PUGH	TROM	(D	AVA ALDRIDGE	V	(D	MARIE TOMLINSON CLARKE	V	(D
CINDI RICHARDSON	V	(D	JAMES INGRAM	V	(E	LOUIS JOHNSON	B	(E	JOHN ROBINSON	D	(E
GREG PHILLINGANES	K SYN	(E	DAVID FOSTER	SYN	(E	MICHAEL BODDICKER	SYN	(E	PAULINHO DA COSTA	PERC	(E
STEVE LUKATHER	G	(E	LEON PENDARVIS	K	(C	CRUSHER BENNETT	PERC	(C	BABI FLOYD	V	(C
DAVID SPINOZZA	G	(C	PAT REBILLOT	K	(C	FRANK FLOYD	V	(C	WILLIAM McCULLOUGH	V	(C
CHARLES COLLINS	D	(C									

A124 SIL AUSTIN A124

SIL AUSTIN SAX (

Title	Year	Label	Catalogue
( ) HONEY SAX	19	POLYDOR 583 758	US SSS SSST 4
( ) SLOW ROCK ROCK	19	WING	US MGW 12168
( ) EVERYTHINGS SHAKIN'	19	MERCURY	US MG 20320
( ) GO SIL GO	19	MERCURY	US 3348
( ) SILVER SCREEN	19	SSS	US SSS 14
( ) PLAYS PRETTY	19	MERCURY	US 60096
( ) SOFT SOUL	19	SSS	US SSS 8

A125 TOM AUSTIN A125

(A) EMPTY NIGHTS 1977 FIRST AMERICAN US 7707

TOM AUSTIN	K V	(A						
CHRIS LEIGHTON	D	(A						
DAVE RAYNOR	G V	(A	TERRY LAUBER	STEEL	(A	DON McKINNEY	V	(A
JOE CHEMAY	B	(A	DALE BOBBIT	B	(A	RICH OLSON	G	(A
MARDI SHERIDAN	G	(A	ROGER PEASE	CONGA	(A	KELLEY HARLAND	V	(A
JIM BREDOUW	V	(A						

A126 AUTOMATIC FINE TUNING A126

(A) AUTOMATIC FINE TUNING 1976 CHARISMA CAS 1122

PAT McDONNELL	G	(A
ROBERT CROSS	G	(A
DAVID BALL	D	(A
TREVOR DARKS	B	(A

A127 AUTOMATIC MAN A127

(A) AUTOMATIC MAN 1976 ISLAND UK ILPS9397

(B) VISITORS 1977 ISLAND UK ILPS9429 ANTILLES US 7062

MICHAEL SHRIEVE	D	(A						
PAT THRALL	G V	(AB						
BAYETE	K V	(AB						
DON HARVEY	B	(AB	JEROME RIMSON	B	(B	GLENN SYMMONDS	D	(B
TODD COCHRAN	K V	(AB						

A129 AUTOSALVAGE A129

(A) AUTOSALVAGE 1968 RCA US LSP3940

THOMAS DANAHER	V G	(A
DARIUS DAVENPORT	V G K B	(A
RICK TURNER	DULC BANJO G	(A
SKIP BOONE	B PNO	(A

A130 AUTUMN PEOPLE A130

(A) AUTUMN PEOPLE 1976 SOUNDTECH US 3020

LARRY CLARK	G V	(A
DANNY POFF	K V	(A
CLIFF SPIEGEL	B V	(A
STEVE BARRAZA	D V	(A

A130A AVALANCHE A130A

Title	Year	Label	Catalogue
(A) AVALANCHE	1976	BOOTLEG	AUSTRALIA 059
(A) AVALANCHE	1977	ABC	US 1000

ADRIAN CAMPBELL	V	(A
TONY NAYLOR	G V	(A
CLIVE HARRISON	B V	(A
GEOFF COX	D	(A

A130B JOHNNY AVERAGE BAND A130B

(A) SOME PEOPLE 1981 WB US 3514

JOHNNY AVERAGE (A

A131 AVERAGE WHITE BAND A131

Title	Release
(A) SHOW YOUR HAND	1973 MCA UK MUPS 486 74 MCF2514
(A) SHOW YOUR HAND	1973 MCA US 345
(B) AVERAGE WHITE BAND	1974 ATLANTIC UK K50058 US 7308
(B) AVERAGE WHITE BAND	197 ATLANTIC US RI 19116
(B) AVERAGE WHITE BAND	1980 RCA INT UK 5049
(C) CUT THE CAKE	1975 ATLANTIC UK K50146 US18140
(D) PUT IT WHERE YOU WANT IT	1975 MCA UK MCF 270 US 475
(E) SOUL SEARCHIN'	1976 ATLANTIC UK K50272 US 18179
(E) SOUL SEARCHIN'	1980 RCA INT UK 5058
(F) PERSON TO PERSON	1976 ATLANTIC UK K60127 US 1002
(G) BENNY & US	1977 ATLANTIC UK K50384 US 19105
(H) WARMER COMMUNICATIONS	1978 RCA UK XL 13053
(H) WARMER COMMUNICATIONS	1978 ATLANTIC US SD 19162
(J) FEEL NO FRET	1979 RCA UK 3063 RI 81 INT5140
(K) VOL7	1980 ATLANTIC RI US 19266
(L) THE BEST OF	1979 RCA UK 3101 RI INTS 5139
(M) SHINE	1980 ARISTA US 9523
(M) SHINE	1980 RCA UK 3123
(N) CUPIDS IN FASHION	1982 RCA RCALP6052

(NB) (D) IS A SLIGHTLY DIFFERENT REISSUE OF (A)

ALAN GORRIE	V G B	(ALL									
ROBBIE McINTOSH	D	(ABCD									
ROGER BALL	K SAX	(ALL									
ONNIE McINTYRE	V G	(ALL									
HAMISH STUART	G B V	(ALL									
MALCOLM DUNCAN	SAX	(ALL									
STEVE FERRONE	D	(CEFGHJKLMN									
CORNELL DUPREE	G	(H									
RANDY BRECKER	HRNS	(BEHJN									
MICHAEL BRECKER	HRNS	(BEHJ									
MARVIN STAMM	TPT	(BE									
AIRTO MOREIRA	PERC	(J									
LEW DELGATTO	SAX	(HJ									
MEL DAVIS	TPT	(B									
BEN E KING	V	(G									
KEN BISCEL	K	(B									
ROBIM CLARK	V	(H									
ZECA DA CUICA		(J									
DAVID FOSTER	PROD K	(KM									
DEBRA GRAY	V	(G									
RALPH McDONALD	PERC	(B									
LUIS DOS SANTOS		(J	RAY BARRETTO	CONGA	(CH	GLENN FERRIS	TROM	(B	LUTHER VANDROSS	V	(J
TOM MALONE	TROM	(H	RONNIE CUBER	SAX	(E	BARRY ROGERS	TROM	(EH	JIM MULLEN	G	(E
CARLOS MARTIN	PERC	(E	DAVE BRIGATI	V	(E	EDDIE BRIGATI	V	(E	RUBENS BASSINI	PERC	(H
NICHOLAS MARRERO	PERC	(G	PAIL LANI	PERC	(M	BRENDA RUSSELL	V	(M	LENNY CASTRO	PERC	(M
PAULINHO DACOSTA	PERC	(M	GARY GRANT	TPT	(KM	LEW McCREARY	TROM	(M	ERNIE WATTS	SAX	(KM
DAN HARTMAN	K V PROD	(N	RICHIE STOOTS	G	(N	JERRY HEY	HRNS	(KM	LARRY HALL	TPT	(M
BILL REICHENBACH	TROM	(KM	KIM HUTCHCROFT	SAX	(M	ARIF MARDIN	PROD	(K	JEFF BOVA	SYN	(N
SAMMY FIGUERA	PERC	(N	JOE MELOTTI	V	(N						

A131A

AVIARY

A131A

BRAD LOVE K V (A — (A) AVIARY — 1979 EPIC US 35716 UK EPC 83572
PAUL MADDEN K (A
KEN STEINMONTS B V (A TOBY BOWEN G (A RICHARD BRYANS D V (A

A131B

AVIATOR

A131B

MICK ROGERS G V (AB — (A) AVIATOR — 1979 HARVEST UK SHSP4096 US EMI17012
CLIVE BUNKER D (AB — (B) TURBULENCE — 1980 HARVEST UK SHSP4107
JOHN G PERRY B V (AB
JACK LANCASTER WIND (A

A131C

AXE

A131C

MICHAEL TURPIN B V (AB — (A) AXE — 1979 MCA US 3171
TEDDY MUELLER D (AB — (B) LIVING ON THE EDGE — 1980 MCA US 3224 UK 3033
BOBBY BARTH G V (AB
EDGAR RILEY JR. K V (AB MICHAEL OSBORNE G V (AB

A131D

DAVID AXELROD

A131D

DAVID AXELROD V (ALL — (A) SONGS OF INNOCENCE — 1968 CAPITOL UK ST2982 US 11362
WITH — (B) ROCK MESSIAH — 1972 RCA US 4636
NDUGU LEON CHANCLER D (D — (C) THE AUCTION — 1974 MCA UK MCF2664 US DECCA 75355
MAILTO CORREA PERC (D — (D) SERIOUSLY DEEP — 1975 POLYDOR UK 2391 193 US 6050
JIM HUGHART B (DF — (E) HEAVY AXE — 1975 FANTASY US 9456
GARY COLEMAN VIBES (AD — (F) STRANGE LADIES — 1978 MCA US 2283
BILLY FENDER G (DF — (G) MARCHIN' — 1980 MCA US 3199
JOHN MORELL G (D
STRINGS (A EUGENE SNOOKYYOUNG TPT (D JIMMY CLEVELAND TROM (DF DICK HYDE TROM (D
JEROME RICHARDSON SAX (D ERNIE WATTS WIND (DF JAY MIGLIORI WIND (D GENE CIPRIANO WIND(D
JOE SAMPLE K (D BENJAMIN BARRETT (A ARNOLD BELNICK (A AL CASEY G (C
VINCENT DE ROSA HRNS (A ALVIN DINKIN (C ALLEN DI RIENZO (A GENE ESTES PERC (A
FREDDIE HILL TPT (A BILL HINSHAW (A HARRY HYAMS (A TONY TERRAN (A
PETE WYANT (A CAROLE KAYE B (A RICHARD LEITH TROM (A ARTHUR MANEBE HRNS (A
LEW McCREARY HRNS (A OLLIE MITCHELL TPT (A EARL PALMER D (A HOWARD ROBERTS G (A
NATHAN ROSS (A MYRON SANDLER (A HAROLD SCHNEIER (A HENRY SIGISMONTI WIND(A
MARSHALL SOSSON (A DON RANDI K (E BOBBY BRYANT TPT (E

A131E

AXISPOINT

A131E

EDDIE HARDIN K V (AB — (A) AXIS POINT — 1979 RCA PL 30039
CHARLIE WITNEY G (AB — (B) BOAST OF THE TOWN — 1980 RCA PL 25277
CHARLIE McCRACKEN B V (AB
ROB TOWNSEND D (AB JOHN GUSTAFSON B (A LOUIE AUSTIN V (A LES BINKS D (A
COLIN JENNINGS PERC (A

A131F

AXIS(ITALY)

A131F

DEMIS VISVIKIS K V (ALL — (A) ELA ELA /OSANNA — 1971 RIVIERA IT 521 192
GEORGE CHATZIATHANASSIOU D V(AB — (B) AXIS — 1971 RIVIERA IT 95010
ALECOS CARACANDAS G V (AB — (C) AXIS — 1973 RIVIERA IT 95014
ALEXANDROS FANTIS B (C
CHRIS STASSINOPOULOS D (C GEORGE HADJIATHNASSIOU D (C

A131G

AXIS(US)

A131G

VINNY APPICE D V (A — (A) ITS A CIRCUS WORLD — 1978 RCA US AFLI 2950
DANNY JOHNSON G (A
KEN AARONSON B (A JAY DAVIS B V (A

A132

HOYT AXTON

A132

HOYT AXTON G V (ALL — (A) GREENBACK DOLLAR — 1964 STATESIDE UK SL10082 US HORIZON 1601
MIKE BOTTS D (LN — (B) THUNDER & LIGHTNIN' — 1964 STATESIDE UK SL10096 US HORIZON 1613
DAVID JACKSON PNO B(JLN — (C) EXPLODES — 196 JOY JOYS119 US VEEJAY 1098
FRANCISCO ARELLANO TPT (N — (D) SINGS BETTY SMITH — 196 EXODUS US 301
SAMMY CREASON D (JN — (E) JOY TO THE WORLD — 196 CAPITOL US EST 788
MIKE UTLEY K (JN — (F) SATURDAYS CHILD — 196 VEEJAY US 1127
JAMES BURTON G (JLNQ — (G) COUNTRY ANTHEM — 19 CAPITOL US SMA9830
RED RHODES STEEL(JN — (H) LESS THAN A SONG — 1973 A&M UK AMLH 64376 US A&M 4376
RALPH MOONEY STEEL(JN — (J) LIFE MACHINE — 1974 A&M UK AMLH 63604 US A&M 3604
JEFF BAXTER G (LNOQ — (K) MY GRIFFIN IS GONE — 1974 CBS US 33103
HANK DEVITO STEEL(N — (L) SOUTHBOUND — 1975 A&M UK AMLH 64510 US A&M 4510
BOB WILSON K (N — (M) FEARLESS — 1976 A&M UK AMLH 64571 US A&M 4571
WILLIAM GRIFFIN V(N — (N) ROADSONGS — 1977 A&M UK AMLH 64669 US A&M 4669
RONEE BLAKLEY V (JN — (O) SNOW BLIND FRIEND — 1977 MCA UK MCF 2803 US MCA 2263
BOB LIND G (J — (P) FREE SAILIN' — 1978 MCA UK MCF 2831 US MCA 2319
ROGER JOHNSON AUTOHARP(LN — (Q) RUSTY OLD HALO — 1979 YOUNGBLOOD UK 800 US JEREMIAH 5000
MAX BENNETT B (LN — (Q) RUSTY OLD HALO — 1980 MFP UK 50520
JIM KELTNER D (JN — (R) WHERE DID THE MONEY GO — 1980 US JEREMIAH 5001
LOREN NEWKIRK PNO (JN — (R) EVERYBODY'S GOIN ON ROAD — 1980 YOUNGBLOOD UK 4BP120
MARK VOLMAN V (JN — (S) LIVE (DBL) — 1981 US JEREMIAH 5002
HOWARD KAYLAN V (JN
LARRY CARLTON G (N BEN BENAY G (N MIKE OMARTIAN K (N JOE SAMPLE K (N
GARY COLEMAN PERC (N MARC EDELSTEIN V (N CLAUDIA LENNEAR V (N DONNA WEISS V (N
ROBERT ROGERS V (N RONALD WHITE V (N KATHY SMITH V (N LARRY MUHOBERAC PNO (N
NICOLETTE LARSON V (N LINDA RONSTADT V (JN JERRY SCHEFF B (LN DICK HYDE TROM(N
GAIL DAVIES TAMB (LN LEE SKLAR B (JN TEDA BRACCI V (N RON CORNELIUS G (N
MAC GAYDEN G (N KARL HIMMEL D (N TIM DRUMMOND B (N TOM SCOTT WIND(N
TERRY REID G (J DR ERIC HORD G (J DOUG DILLARD BANJ (JL MILT HOLLAND PERC(J
LEE MONTGOMERY V (JL CLYDIE KING V (J MERRY CLAYTON V (J SHIRLEY MATTHEWS V (J
SKITCHY WASHBURN V (J DENNY BROOKS V (J MIMI FARINA V (O KATHY WARD V (O
DONNA ROBERTS K (O JACK SKINNER B (O ALAN THORNHILL G (O PETE GRANT AUTOHARP (O
GARY WATTMAN D (O PIERRE LA PORTE HCA (O JIM MESSINA G (O BYRON BERLINE FDL MAN(O
JOE LAMANO B (L GEORGE CLINTON PNO (L MARTY HOWARD G (L DICK ROSMINI G (LN
VICTOR FELDMAN PERC (L PAUL LEWINSON K (L JOHNNY ROTELLA WIND (L JOHN GUERIN D (L
JOHN HARTFORD FDL (L FRANK REKARD G (L JUDY ELLIOTT V (L ERNIE CARLSON TROM(N
EMORY GORDY B (JNQ GUSTAVO RAMOS TPT (N RENEE ARMAND V (JLN JEFF PORCARO D (N
ED KOLLIS HCA (N DANA BRADY V (JN WARREN MOORE V (N MARK DAWSON G V (JLNO
GARTH HUDSON K (Q STEPHEN STILLS G V (Q JOHN McUEN (Q PAUL BUTTERFIELD HCA (Q
Dr JOHN K (Q MARLENE PRINS V (Q DAVID WOODFORD (Q DICK STEWART (Q
GLEN HARDIN K (Q BOB FRAZIER (Q BAMBI ROBERTS V (Q DONNA WASHBURN V (N

A133 KEVIN AYERS A133

KEVIN AYERS PROD V G (ALL — (A) JOY OF A TOY — 1970 HARVEST UK SHVL 763
WITH — (B) SHOOTING AT THE MOON — 1971 HARVEST UK SHSP 4005
TONY CARR D (CH — (AB)JOY OF A TOY/SHOOTING AT THE MOON — 1975 HARVEST DBL UK SHDW 407
JOHN VAN DERRICK VLN (C — (AB)JOY OF A TOY/SHOOTING AT THE MOON — 19 PATHE DBL FR C18452277/8
ROBERT WYATT D V (ABCDF — (C) WHATEVERSHEBRINGSWESING — 1972 HARVEST UK SHVL 800
ROB TAIT D (A — (D) BANANAMOUR — 1973 HARVEST UK SHVL 807
DIDIER MALHERBE WIND (C — (CD)WHATEVERSHEBRINGSWESING/BANANAMOUR — PATHE DBL FR C15052507/8
MIKE RATLEDGE K (ABDE — (E) CONFESSIONS OF DR DREAM — 1974 ISLAND UK ILPS 9263
HUGH HOPPER B (A — (F) JUNE 1st 1974 — 1974 ISLAND UK ILPS 9291
DAVID BEDFORD K (ABCDH — (G) SWEET DECEIVER — 1975 ISLAND UK ILPS 9322
LOL COXHILL SAX (BEH — (H) ODD DITTIES — 1976 HARVEST UK SHSM 2005
MIKE OLDFIELD G B V (BCEHF — (J) YES WE HAVE NO MANANAS — 1976 HARVEST UK SHSP 4057
WILLIAM MURRAY D (C — (J) YES WE HAVE NO MANANAS — 1976 ABC US ABC 1021
RICHARD SINCLAIR B (BH — (K) RAINBOW TAKEAWAY — 1978 HARVEST UK SHSP 4085
DAVE DUFORT D (CH — (L) THATS WHAT YOU GET BABE — 1980 HARVEST UK SHSP 4016
GERRY FIELD VLN (C — (L) THATS WHAT YOU GET BABE — 1980 HARVEST NL 062 63637
HOWIE CASEY G (D
ROY SMITH-FIELD PICC (H — ARCHIE LEGGET B (DFH — DAVE CASWELL TPT (D — MICK FINCHER D (HB
KEITH BATCHELOR FLT (H — LYLE JENKINS SAX (D — RICHARD COUGHLAN D (H — ROB TOWNSEND D (JK
TRISTAM FRY PERC (D — DAVE SINCLAIR K (H — BILLY LIVSEY K (JK — OLLIE HALSALL B G(EFGJK
B J COLE STEEL(J — RICK WILLS B (J — MARK WARNER G (E — TONY NEWMAN D (J
EDDIE SPARROW PERC (DHF — SAMMY MITCHELL G (E — ROGER POPE D (J — RON PRICE PNO(DH
RUPERT HINE K (E — RAY COOPER PERC (E — LIZA STRIKE V (DH — JOHN PERRY B (E
SEAN MILLIGAN V (E — BARRY ST JOHN V (DH — MIKE GILES D (E — LADYBIRDS V (H
DORIS TROY V (DEH — ROSETTA HIGHTOWER V (E — JOHN ALTMAN CLAR (G — GEORGE ZOOT MONEY K (J
CHARLIE McCRACKEN B G (JK — DUNCAN BROWN TPT (H — JACOB MAGNUSSON V K (G — CAL BATCHELOR G (E
CHARLIE ROSE HRNS (G — BRIDGET ST JOHN V (BH — RONNIE EADES HRNS (G — HENRY CRALLAN PNO (E
HARRISON CALLOWAY HRNS (G — JOANNE WILLIAMS V (E — STEVE NYE ORG (E — STEVE HILLAGE G (D
HARRY SMITH (H — MIKE MORAN PNO (E — FRED SMITH D (G — ELTON JOHN PNO (G
NICO V (EF — BIAS BOSHELL PNO (G — CHILI CHARLES D (G — MICK FEAT B (J
ANDY ROBERTS G (J — NICK ROWLEY K (J — FUZZY SAMUELS B (G — TREVOR JONES B (E
JOHN GUSTAFSON B (E — HARVEY THOMPSON HRNS (G — GRAHAM PRESKETT VLN (K — BARRY DE SOUZA D (K
ROGER SAUNDERS G (J — ANTHONY MOORE (K — DAEVID ALLEN (B — HULLOO CHOIR V (E
BRIAN ENO V SYN (F — JOHN CALE VIOLA (F — RABBIT BUNDRICK K (F — PETER JENNER PROD (ABH
ANDREW KING PROD (CDH — MALCOLM JONES PROD (H

A134 ROY AYERS A134

ROY AYERS — ( ) VIRGO VIBES — 19 ATLANTIC US SD 1488
WAYNE HENDERSON (* — ( ) DADDY BUG & FRIEND — 19 ATCO US SD 1692
( ) UBIQUITY — 1975 POLYDOR US PD 6046
( ) TEARS TO A SMILE — 19 POLYDOR US
( ) MYSTIC VOYAGE — 1975 POLYDOR US PD 6057
( ) RED BLACK & GREEN — 197 POLYDOR US PD 1-6078
( ) VIBRATIONS — 1976 POLYDOR UK 2391 256
( ) EVERYBODY LOVES THE SUNSHINE — 1976 POLYDOR US PD 16070
( ) LIFELINE — 1977 POLYDOR US 2391 292
( ) YOU SEND ME — 1978 POLYDOR UK 2391 365
( ) LETS DO IT — 1978 POLYDOR UK 2490 145
(*) STEP INTO OUR LIFE — 1978 POLYDOR US PD 16179
(*) STEP INTO OUR LIFE — 1978 POLYDOR UK 2391 380
(*) STEP INTO OUR LIFE — 1978 POLYDOR UK POLS 1004
( ) FEVER — 1979 POLYDOR UK 2391 396
( ) THE BEST OF (LOVE FANTASY) — 1979 POLYDOR UK 2391 429
( ) AFRICA CENTRE OF THE WORLD — 1981 POLYDOR UK 2391 157

A134A AYERS ROCK A134A

CHRIS BROWN G V (AB — (A) BIG RED ROCK — 1975 A&M US 4523 UK AMLH64523
COL COUGHNAN WIND V(AB — (B) BEYOND — 1976 A&M US 4565
JAMES DOYLE G (AB
DUNCAN McGUIRE B (AB — MARK KENNEDY D (AB

A135 AZTEC TWO STEP A135

NEAL SHULMAN V G (ALL — (A) AZTEC TWO STEP — 1972 ELEKTRA UK K42118 US EKS 75031
DAVID VAUGHT B (A — (B) SECOND STEP — 1975 RCA UK RS1034 US AFLI 1161
SPANKY McFARLANE V (A — (C) TWOS COMPANY — 197 RCA US AFLI 1497
PETER KLIEMES BANJO(A — (D) ADJOINING SUITES — 197 RCA US AFLI 2453
BOBBY TORRES CONGA(A
REX FOWLER G V (ALL — JOHN SEITER D (A — JERRY YESTER BANJO V PNO(A — RANDY BENSON V (A
DOUG DILLARD BANJO(A — JOHN SEBASTIAN HCA (A — DENNIS WITCHER V (A — JOHN TROPEA G (B
KEN ASCHER K (B — DON PAYNE B (B — ALLEN SCHWARZBERG D (B — EMILE LATIMER PERC (B
DON ELLIOTT VIBES(B — FRANK SIMS V (B — GEORGE SIMS V (B — DAVID KONDZIELA V (B

A136 AZTECA A136

BOB FERREIRA WIND (B — (A) AZTECA — 197 CBS 65011
PAT O'HARA TROM (B — (B) PYRAMID OF THE SUN — 1973 CBS US KC 32451
TOM HARREL HRNS (B
MEL MARTIN WIND (B — WENDY HAAS V (B — ERROL KNOWLES V (B — PETE ESCOVEDO PER V(B
PAUL JACKSON B (B — BILL COURTIAL G (B — GEORGE MURIBUS K (B — FLIP NUNEZ ORG (B
GEORGE DI QUATRO K (B — COKE ESCOVEDO PERC (B — VICTOR PANTOJA CONGA(B — JOHN BRINCK D (B
LENNY WHITE D (B — RICO REYES V (B — TOM RUTLEY B (B — TONY JUNCALE B (B
MIKE NOCK K (B — NEAL SCHON G (B

A137 AZTECS A137

BILLY THORPE G V (B — (A) LIVE AT SUNBURY (DBL) — 19 HAVOC NZ HST4003/4
PAUL WHEELER B (B — (B) THE HOAX IS OVER — 1970 INFINITY AUS 934 092
KEVIN MURPHY PERC (B
WARREN MORGAN K (B — LOBBY LOYDE G (A

B1 B BUMBLE & THE STINGERS B1

WILLIAM 'B' BUMBLE G (A — (A) PIANO STYLINGS OF B BUMBLE (EP) — 19 STATESIDE UK SE 1001
RON BRADY D (A
FRED RICHARD PNO (A

B2

B B BLUNDER

(A) WORKERS PLAYTIME — 1971 U A UK UAG 29156

BRIAN GODDING V PNO G K (A
KEVIN WESTLAKE D G (A
BRIAN BELSHAW B V (A
BRIAN AUGER K (A
CHRIS KIMSEY PNO (A
JULIE DRISCOLL V (A
MARK CHARIG TPT (A
NICK EVANS TROM (A
BARRY JENKINS D (A
MICK TAYLOR G (A
GRAHAM SMITH PERC (A

B2A

B52s

(A) B52'S — 1979 ISLAND UK ILPS9580 US WB 3255
(B) WILD PLANET — 1980 ISLAND UK ILPS9622 US WB 3471
(C) PARTY MIX — 1981 ISLAND UK IPM 1001

KEITH STRICKLAND D (ABC
CINDY WILSON V G (ABC
RICKY WILSON G (ABC
FRED SCHNEIDER K V (ABC
KATE PIERSON V G K (ABC
CHRIS BLACKWELL PROD(AB

B2B

B MOVIES

(A) TAKE THREE (EP) — 1980 DEAD GOOD UK DEAD9

B3

B T EXPRESS

(A) DO IT TILL YOURE SATISFIED — 1975 PYE UK NSPL28207
(A) DO IT TILL YOURE SATISFIED — 1975 ROADSHOW US SDS 5117
(B) NON STOP — 1976 EMI UK INA 1501
(B) NON STOP — 1976 ROADSHOW US RS 41001
(C) ENERGY TO BURN — 1977 EMI UK INA 1502
(C) ENERGY TO BURN — 1977 CBS US PC 34178
(D) FUNCTION AT THE JUNCTION — 19 CBS US 34702
(D) FUNCTION AT THE JUNCTION — 1977 EMI UK INS 3009
(E) SHOUT — 19 CBS US JC 35078
(E) SHOUT — 1978 EMI UK INS 3016
(F) 1980 — 1980 EXCALIBRE UK 5002 US 36333
(G) GREATEST HITS — 1980 CBS US 36923
(H) OLD GOLD , FUTURE GOLD — 1980 EXCALIBRE UK 5001

JAMAL RASOOL B V (E
LESLIE MING D (E
RICHARD THOMPSON G V (E
KASHIF SALEEM K V (E
DENNIS ROWE PERC V(E
CARLOS WARD WIND K V (E

B3A

B Z N

(A) MAKING A NAME — 19 NEGRAM NN2
( ) GREATEST HITS — 1980 MERCURY NL 9198 681
( ) IN THE BEGINNING — 1980 POLYDOR NL 2426 024
( ) GREEN VALLEYS — 1980 MERCURY NL 6423 371
( ) BEST OF — 1980 M F P NL 58018

B4

REBOP KWAKU BAAH

(A) REBOP — 1972 ISLAND US SW 9304
(B) ANTHONY REBOP KWAKU BAAH — 1973 PHILIPS SWED 6316 008
(C) TRANCE — 1977 ISLAND UK ILPS 9491

REBOP KWAKU BAAH PERC (ABC
STEVE WINWOOD K G V(A
CHRIS WOOD FLT (A
ROSCO GEE B (A
DELISLE HARPER B (A
JEAN ROUSSEL K (A
PETER VANDERPUIJE WIND (A
GEORGE LEE WIND (A
THE VOICE OF AFRICA V (A
GUNNAR BERGSTEN SAX (B
BENGT DAHLEN B (B
RUNE CARLSSON D (B
ABDELLA EL HILALLI PERC (C
SIDI JILLALA (C
CONRAD ISADORE D (A
GORDON HUNTE G (A
CHRIS MERCER WIND (A
KENNY WHEELER TPT (A
MAFFY FALAY TPT (B
BOBO STENSON K (B
LUKAS LINDHOLM B (B
ABDELLCADA ZEF ZEF V (C
BEN MOHAMED ZAIN FLT (C
GANOUS ENSEMBLE V (C
JUNIOR KERR G (A
RABBIT K (A
ROGER CAWKWELL WIND (A
EDDIE QUANSAH TPT (A
ULF ANDERSSON SAX (B
JANNE SCHAFFER G (B
ERIK DAHLBACK D (B
MOHAMED BEN HAMOU SAIDI (C

B5

BABE RUTH

(A) FIRST BASE — 1972 HARVEST UK SHSP4022 US11151
(B) AMAR CABALLERO — 1973 HARVEST UK SHVL812 US 11275
(C) BABE RUTH — 1975 HARVEST UK SHSP4038 US 11367
(D) STEALIN HOME — 1975 CAPITOL US/UK 11451
(E) KIDS STUFF — 1976 CAPITOL UK 23739 US 11515
(F) BEST OF — 1977 HARVEST UK SHSM2019

(1) 1971 (2) 1973 (3) 1975 (4) 1975 (5) 1976 (6) 1976

DAVE PUNSHON K (A1
ALAN SHACKLOCK G (123ABC
DAVE HEWITT B (A12345BC
JENNY HAAN V (ABC1234
ED SPEVOCK D (23456CDE
BERNIE MARSDEN G (456E
ELLIE HOPE V (56E
GASPAR LAWAL PERC (AB
RAY KNOTT B (6
CHRIS HOLMES K (2
JEFF ALLEN D (A
STEVE GREGORY SAX (D
RAY PREMRU TROM (B
RON CARTHY TPT (B
ANGELITO PEREZ V PERC(B
FRANK RICOTTI VIBES (E
HARRY MIER OBOE (A
DICK POWELL D (AB1
RAY HARRIS HRNS (B
DAVE WHITE FLT (B
JACK ELLORY FLT (B
BUD BEADLE SAX (B
NEIL MURRAY B (E
TONY CARR PERC (E
BRENT CARTER SAX (A
DUNCAN LAMONT FLT (B
KEITH CHRISTIE TROM (B
BRIAN WARREN FLT (B
NICK MOBBS PERC (B
DON AIREY K SYN(E
CHRIS KARAN PERC (E

B6

BABY

(A) BABY — 1976 MERCURY US 1 1062 LONESTARR 6264
(B) WHERE DID ALL THE MONEY GO — 1977 CHELSEA CHL 517

JOHNNY LEE SCHELL V K G (AB
TOM SCOTT WIND (B
STEVE CRANE B V (AB
WOODIE PUTMAN D (B
JOHN MARK CAMP G V (B

B7

BABY GRAND

(A) BABY GRAND — 1978 ARISTA UK SPART1061 US AB4148
(B) ANCIENT MEDICINE — 1979 ARISTA US 4200

DAVID KAGAN V (AB
ERIC BAZILIAN G V (AB
ROB HYMAN K V (AB
RALPH SCHUCKETT K (A
MICHAEL BRECKER HRNS (A
JOHN SIEGLER B (A
DAVID DARTH PRATER D (A
RICK CHERTHOFF PERC (A
RICK MAROTTA D (A

B7A

BABY RAY

(A) WHERE THE SOUL IS — 19 IMPERIAL US 12335

BABY RAY (A

B7B

BABYFACE

(A) BABYFACE — 1977 ASI US 213

EDGAR RILEY K V (A
BOB MILES D (A
MICHAEL TURPIN B V (A
BOBBY BARTH G V (A

B8

BABYS

(A) BABYS — 1976 CHRYSALIS 1129
(B) BROKEN HEART — 1977 CHRYSALIS 1150
(C) HEAD FIRST — 1979 CHRYSALIS 1195
(D) UNION JACKS — 1980 CHRYSALIS 1267
(E) ON THE EDGE — 1980 CHRYSALIS 1305
(F) ANTHOLOGY — 1981 CHRYSALIS 1351

JOHN WAITE B V (ABCDE
MIKE CORBY K G (ABC
WALT STOCKER G (ABCDE
TONY BROCK D V (ABCDE
MARTI McCALL V (C
JONATHAN CAIN G K V (DE
DIANA LEE V (C

(CONTINUED)

B8 BABYS (CONTINUED) B8

ROBB LAWRENCE MAND (C
MIKE JAPP V (C
JOHN SINCLAIR SYN (C
JACK CONRAD B (C
PAT HENDERSON V (BC
BOBBYE HALL PERC (C
RICKY PHILLIPS B (CDE
ANNE MARIE LECLERC V (DE
KEVIN KELLY PNO (C
MYRNA MATTHEWS V (BC
LISA ROBERTS V (BC

B8A BACHDENKEL B8A

PETER KIMBERLEY B K V (AB
COLIN SWINBURNE G V (AB
BRIAN SMITH D (AB
KAREL BEER K G (AB
IRVIN MOWREY V (A
ANDY SCOTT K (A

(A) STALINGRAD 1977 INITIAL IRL 002
(B) LEMMINGS 1978 INITIAL IRL 001

B9 RANDY BACHMAN B9

RANDY BACHMAN G V B (AB
WITH
BURTON CUMMINGS K (A
JEFF PORCARO D (A
IAN GARDINER D (A
PATTY BROOKS V (A
TOM SCOTT SAX (A
PETSYE POWELL V (A
BECKY LOPEZ (A

(A) SURVIVOR 1978 POLYDOR UK 2490 146
(A) SURVIVOR 1978 POLYDOR US PD1 6141
(B) AXE 19 RCA US LSP 4349

B10 BACHMAN TURNER OVERDRIVE B10

RANDY BACHMAN G V (ALL
TIM BACHMAN V (AB
BLAIR THORNTON G V B (CDEFGHJ
ROBBIE BACHMAN PERC D V (ABCDGJ
FRED TURNER B V (ALL
JIM CLENCH D (JH
FRANK TROWBRIDGE G (C
BARRY KEANE PERC (A

(A) BACHMAN TURNER OVERDRIVE 1973 MERCURY UK 6499 509 US SRM1 673
(B) BACHMAN TURNER OVERDRIVE 2 1974 MERCURY UK 6338 482 US SRM1 693
(C) NOT FRAGILE 1974 MERCURY UK 9100 007 US SRM11004
(D) FOUR WHEEL DRIVE 1975 MERCURY UK 9100 012 US SRM11027
(D) FOUR WHEEL DRIVE 1975 MERCURY GERM 6338 566
(E) AS BRAVE BELT 1975 WB UK K 54036 US MS 2210
(F) HEAD ON 1976 MERCURY UK 9100 020 US SRM11067
( ) THE BEST OF 1976 MERCURY UK 9100 026 US SRM11101
(G) FREEWAYS 1977 MERCURY UK 9100 035 US SRM13700
(H) STREET ACTION 1978 MERCURY UK 9100 051 US SRM13713
(J) ROCK'N'ROLL NIGHTS 1979 MERCURY US SRM13748
(K) GREATEST 1980 MERCURY NL 9279 123

B11 BACK DOOR B11

COLIN HODGKINSON B (ALL
FELIX PAPPALARDI K (C
ADRIAN TILBROOK D (
RON ASPERY K FLT SAX (ALL
TONY HICKS D (ABC
BERNIE HOLLAND G (C
PETER THORUP V (C
DAVE McRAE K (C

(A) BACK DOOR 1972 BLAKEY BLP 5989
(A) BACK DOOR 1973 WB K 46231
(A) BACK DOOR 1973 WB US BS 2753
(B) EIGHTH STREET NITES 1973 WB K 46265
(C) ANOTHER FINE MESS 1975 WB K 56098
(D) ACTIVATE 1976 WB K 56243

B11A BACKSTAGE B11A

(A) BACKSTAGE 1979 SONET UK SNTF 852

B12 BACK STREET CRAWLER B12

PAUL KOSSOFF G (AB
TERRY WILSON-SLESSER V (AB
MIKE MONTGOMERY K (AB
TONY BRAUNAGEL D V((AB
TERRY WILSON B V (AB
GEORGE LARNYOH WIND (A
GEOFF WHITEHORN G (B
EDDIE QUANSAH HRNS (A
PETE VANDER PUIJE SAX (A
JOHN RABBIT BUNDRICK V (B

(A) THE BAND PLAYS ON 1975 ATLANTIC K 50173
(A) THE BAND PLAYS ON 1975 ATCO 36125
(B) SECOND STREET 1976 ATLANTIC K 50267

B12A BACKHAUSEN B12A

PETER BACKHAUSEN V K G D (A
KARL GILLAUT G (A
STEFFI STEPHAN B (A
KARL SCHOTT B (A
WILLY TJON AJONG K (A
BERTRAM ENGEL D (A
GEOFF PEACEY K (A
SIDDARTHA GAUTAMA D (A
GEORG FUNKE B (A

(A) PLANET SHOW 1979 SKY SKY 037

B13 BACONFAT B13

GEORGE SMITH V HCA (B
BUDDY REED G V (AB
DICK INNES Jr D (AB
GREGG SCHAEFER G HCA (AB
J D NICHOLSON V PNO (AB
JERRY SMITH B (AB
ROD GINGERMAN PIAZZA V HCA (AB

(A) GREASE ONE FOR ME 1970 BLUE HORIZON 7 63858
(B) TOUGH DUDE 1971 BLUE HORIZON 2431 001

B13A BAD BOY B13A

STEVE GRIMM G V (ABC
JOE LAVIE K G V (AB
JOHN MARCELLI B (ABC
LARS HANSON D (AB
EARL SLICK G (B
SCOTT STEPHAN G V (C
HECTOR'JACKIE'RAMES D V (C
BARRY GOLDBERG K (B
STEVE HUNTER G (A
CLAUDE PEPPER D (B

(A)THE BAND THAT MADE MILWALKEE FAMOUS 1977 UA US LA 781
(B) BACK TO BACK 1978 UA US LA 869
(C) PRIVATE PARTY 1980 STREETWISE US 4321

B14 BAD COMPANY B14

PAUL RODGERS PNO V G (ALL
SIMON KIRKE D (ALL
BOZ BURRELL B (ALL
MICK RALPHS G K (ALL
MEL COLLINS SAX (AD
SUE & SUNNY V (A

(A) BAD COMPANY 1974 ISLAND UK ILPS 9279
(A) BAD COMPANY 1974 SWANSONG US 8410 RI 77 8510
(B) STRAIGHT SHOOTER 1975 ISLAND UK ILPS 9304
(B) STRAIGHT SHOOTER 1975 SWANSONG US 8413 RI 8502
(C) RUN WITH THE PACK 1976 ISLAND UK ILPS 9346
(C) RUN WITH THE PACK 1976 SWANSONG US 8415 RI 77 8503
(D) BURNING SKY 1977 ISLAND UK ILPS 9441
(D) BURNING SKY 1977 SWANSONG US 8500
(E) DESOLATION ANGELS 1979 SWANSONG UK SSK59408
(E) DESOLATION ANGELS 1979 SWANSONG US 8506
(F) ROUGH DIAMONDS 1982 SWANSONG US SSK 59419

B15 BAD MANNERS B15

BUSTER BLOODVESSEL V (

(A) SKA'N'B 1980 MAGNET UK 5033
(B) LOONIE TUNES 1980 MAGNET UK 5038
(C) GOSH IT'S.. 1980 MAGNET UK 5043

B16 BADFINGER

Musician	Inst	Albums
PETE HAM	V G	(ABCDEF
TOM EVANS	V B	(ABCDEFGH
JOEY MOLLAND	G V	(ABCDEFGH
PETER CLARK		(G
DAVID MALLONY	V	(G
DUANE HITCHINGS	SYN	(G
ANDY NEWMARK	D	(G
STEVE FORMAN	PERC	(G
KEN HARCK	D	(G
MIKE GIBBINS	D	(ABCDEF
TONY KAYE	K	(GH
JOE TANSIN	G	(G
RICHARD BRYANS	D	(H
NICKY HOPKINS	K	(G
GLENN SHERBA	G	(H

Album	Year	Label	UK	US
(A) MAGIC CHRISTIAN MUSIC	1970	APPLE	UK SAPCOR12	US 3364
(B) NO DICE	1970	APPLE	UK SAPCOR 16	US 3367
(C) STRAIGHT UP	1972	APPLE	UK SAPCOR 19	US 3387
(D) BADFINGER	1974	WB	UK K56023	US 2762
(E) ASS	1974	APPLE	UK SAPCOR 27	US 3411
(F) WISH YOU WERE HERE	1975	WB		US 2827
(G) AIRWAVES	1979	ELEKTRA	UK K52129	US 6E 129
(H) SAY NO MORE	1981	RADIO RECORD		16030

B17 BADGER

Musician	Inst	Albums
TONY KAYE	K	(AB
ROY DYKE	D	(AB
DAVID FOSTER	B V	(A
BRIAN PARRISH	G V	(A
BRY HAWORTH	G	(B
JOHN LANGO	TROM	(B
BOBBY MONTGOMERY	V	(B
JESSIE SMITH	V	(B
MERCEDES DAVIS	V	(B
JACKIE LOMAX	G V	(B
PAUL PILNICK	G	(B
KIM GARDNER	B	(B
TERESIPA HENRY	V	(B
JEFF BECK	G	(B
ALLEN TOUSSAINT	K PERC	(B
JOAN HARMON	V	(B
BARRY BAILEY	G	(B
LESTER CALISTE	TPT	(B
CARL BLOUIN	WIND	(B
ALVIN THOMAS	SAX	(B

Album	Year	Label	UK	US
(A) ONE LIVE BADGER	1973	ATLANTIC	UK K40473	US 7022
(B) WHITE LADY	1974	EPIC	UK 80009	US 32831

B17A JOAN BAEZ

Musician	Inst	Albums
JOAN BAEZ	G V	(ALL
WITH		
HAL RUGG	G	(LM
JERRY REED	G	(LM
JERRY KENNEDY	G	(LM
HAROLD BRADLEY	G	(LM
PETE WADE	G	(LMR
TOMMY JACKSON	FDL	(LM
BUDDY SPICHER	FDL	(LM
JUNIOR HUSKY	B	(LM
NORBERT PUTNAM	B	(LMQR
HARGUS PIG ROBBINS	K	(LM
KENNY BUTTREY	D	(LMQR
FRED CARTER	MAND	(LM
BILL PURCELL	K	(LM
GRADY MARTIN	G	(LMQ
JIM GORDON	D	(
LARRY CARLTON	G	(X
DEAN PARKS	G	(1X
JOE SAMPLE	K	(X
DAVID PAICH	K	(X
LARRY KNECHTEL	K	(X
REINHOLD PRESS	B	(1X
RED RHODES	STEEL	(X
JIM HORN	SAX	(X
MALCOLM CECIL	SYN	(X1
HAMPTON HAWES	K	(X
TOM SCOTT	WIND	(UX
MAX BENNETT	B	(X
JOHN GUERIN	D	(X
RICK LOTEMPIO	G	(X
OLLIE MITCHELL	TPT	(X
DONALD DUNN	B	(1
JONI MITCHELL	V	(UX
BUCK MONARI	TPT	(X
BILL WOOD	V	(9
TED ALEVIZOS	V	(9
PETE DRAKE	STEEL	(LM
JOHNNY GIMBLE		(L
DAVID BRIGGS		(LR
STEPHEN STILLS		(L
MILT HOLLAND	PERC	(U
JIM HUGHART	B	(U
LALO LINDGRON	HARP	(U
EDGARLUSTGARTEN	CELLO	(U
SALLY STEVENS	V	(U
TOMMY TEDESCO	G	(U
JACKIE WARD	V	(U
ANDRA WILLIS	V	(U
BRUCE LANGHORN	G	(F
RALPH RINZLER	MAND	(F
RUSS SAVAKUS	B	(F
RICHARD FESTINGER	G	(Q
FARRELL MORRIS	PERC	(R
JOHN BUCK WILKINS	G	(R
RICHARD ROMOFF	B	(F
STUART BASORE	STEEL	(R
WELDON MYRICK	STEEL	(R
DAVID HARRIS	V	(Q
CHARLIE McCOY	HCA	(R
GLEN SPREEN	K	(R

Album	Year	Label	Catalogue	Catalogue
(A) JOAN BAEZ	1960	VANGUARD	VSD79073	VSD 2077
(A) JOAN BAEZ	1960	FONTANA		STFL 6002
(B) JOAN BAEZ 2	1961	VANGUARD	VSD 79094	VSD 2097
(B) JOAN BAEZ 2	1961	FONTANA		STFL 6025
(C) IN CONCERT	1962	VANGUARD	VSD79112	VSD 2122
(C) IN CONCERT	1962	FONTANA		STFL 6033
(D) IN CONCERT 2	1963	VANGUARD	VSD79113	VSD 2133
(D) IN CONCERT 2	1963	FONTANA		STFL 6035
(E) JOAN BAEZ 5	1964	VANGUARD		VSD79160
(E) JOAN BAEZ 5	1964	FONTANA		STFL 6043
(F) FAREWELL ANGELINA	1965	VANGUARD	VSD79200	VSD 23006
(F) FAREWELL ANGELINA	1965	FONTANA		STFL 6058
(G) NOEL	1966	VANGUARD	VSD79230	VSD 23018
(G) NOEL	1966	FONTANA		STFL 6078
(H) PORTRAIT	1966	VANGUARD		SVRL19025
(J) JOAN	1967	VANGUARD	VSD79240	VSD 23011
(J) JOAN	1967	FONTANA		STFL 6082
(K) BAPTISM	1968	VANGUARD	SVRL19000	VSD 79275
(L) ANY DAY NOW	1968	VANGUARD	VSD79306/7	55/66
(M) DAVIDS ALBUM	1969	VANGUARD	VSD79308	SVRL19050
(N) ONE DAY AT A TIME	1970	VANGUARD	VSD79310	VSD 23010
(O) FIRST TEN YEARS	1970	VANGUARD		VSD 6560
(P) BLESSED ARE	1971	VANGUARD		VSD6570/1
(Q) CARRY IT ON	1972	VANGUARD	VSD79313	519042
(R) COME FROM THE SHADOWS	1972	A&M	US 4339	UK AMLH64339
(S) THE BALLAD BOOK	1972	VANGUARD		VSD 41/42
(T) WHERE ARE YOU NOW MY SON	1973	A&M	US 4390	UK AMLH64390
(U) GRACIAS A LA VIDA (HERES TO LIFE)	1974	A&M		AMLH63614
(V) CONTEMPORARY BALLAD BOOK	1974	VANGUARD		VSD 49/50
(W) PROFILES	1974	IRL		IC054 95128
(X) DIAMONDS & RUST	1975	A&M	AMLH64527	
(Y) LIVE IN JAPAN	1975	VANGUARD		GP 315
(Z) LOVE SONG ALBUM	1976	VANGUARD		VSD 79/80
( ) FROM EVERY STAGE	1976	A&M	US 3704	UK AMLH64704
(1) GULF WINDS	1976	A&M	US 4603	UK AMLH64603
( ) BLOWING AWAY	1977	PORTRAIT	US 34697	UK 82011
( ) GOLDEN HOUR	1972	PYE	GH 843	
( ) HITS THE GREATEST & OTHERS	1973	VANGUARD		VSD 79332
( ) GREATEST HITS	19	IRL		IC062 93622
( ) BEST OF	1977	A&M	AMLH64665	
( ) INTRODUCTION TO/FAREWELL ANGELINA	1976	ARL	IC18892665/6	
(9) THE BEST OF	1968	SAGA	EROS	8075
( ) GOLDEN HOUR VOL 2	19	PYE	GH 863	
( ) HOUSE OF THE RISING SUN	1978	MUSIDISC		1367
( ) SUPER DISC OF JOAN BAEZ	19	A&M	GXM 9002	
( ) HONEST LULABY	1979	PORTRAIT		PRT 83474
( ) COUNTRY MUSIC	1979	VANGUARD		VSD 105
( ) SPOTLIGHT ON	1980	PORTRAIT		1008
( ) LIVE IN CONCERT	1980	PORTRAIT	UK	84790
( ) MAGIC OF JOAN BAEZ	1981	K TEL	UK	NE 1114

B17B HENRY BADOWSKI

Musician	Inst	Albums
HENRY BADOWSKI	V SAX B K	(A
JAMES STEPHENSON	G B	(A
ALEXSANDER KOLKOWSKI	VLN	(A
WALLY BRILL	PROD	(A

Album	Year	Label	UK
(A) LIFE IS GRAND	1981	A&M	UK AMLH 68527

B17C BAG

Musician	Inst	Albums
JIMMY CURTISS		(A

Album	Year	Label	US
(A) REAL	1969	DECCA	US 75057

B17D EDDIE BAIRD

Musician	Inst	Albums
EDDIE BAIRD	G K V	(A

Album	Year	Label	UK
(A) HARD GRAFT	1976	DJM	UK 467

B18 DUCK BAKER

Musician	Inst	Albums
DUCK BAKER	G V	(ALL
WITH		
STEFAN GROSSMAN	G	(C
MIKE PIGGOTT	VLN	(C

Album	Year	Label	US	UK
(A) THERES SOMETHING FOR EVERYONE	1977	KICKING MULE	US 124	UK SNKF116
(B) WHEN YOU WORE A TULIP	19	KICKING MULE	US 135	UK SNKF123
(C) KING OF BONGO BONG	1977	KICKING MULE	US 144	UK SNKF137
(D) FINGER STYLE JAZZ GUITAR	1979	KICKING MULE		UK SNKF154

B19 GINGER BAKER B19

GINGER BAKER D (ALL — (A)STRATAVARIOUS — 1972 POLYDOR UK 2383 133 US ATCO 7015
CHRIS SPEDDING G (E — (B) FELI RANSOME KUTI & THE AFRICA BAND 72 REGAL ZONOPHONE UK SLRZ 1023
RICK GRECH B V (E — (C) AT HIS BEST — 1973 POLYDOR UK 2659 023 US 3504
HENRY THOMAS B (1 — (D) POP HISTORY — 19 POLYDOR 2668 002
MIKE DAVIS G (1 — (E) ELEVEN SIDES OF BAKER — 1977 MOUNTAIN UK 5005 US SIRE 7532
JOHN MIZAROLLI G (1 — (E) ELEVEN SIDES OF BAKER — 1977 PHONOGRAM 6370 419
FELI RANSOME KUTI (B — (1) 1980 LIVE BAND
DELISLE HARPER B (E
LOUISE ARTHURWORREY V (E — KOFI OSAPANIN PERC (E — OLU GEORGE PERC (E
STAN SULZMANN SAX (E — JEFF DALY SAX (E — DEREK WADSWORTH TROM (E
SNIPS V (E — KUMA HARADA B (E — HERBIE FLOWERS B (E
EUNICE A GREEN V (E — MIKE DEACON K (E — KOJO OSAPANIN PERC (E
IAN HAMER TPT (E — ALAN SKIDMORE SAX (E — EDDIE MORDUE SAX (E
WALLY SMITH TROM (E

B20 BAKER GURVITZ ARMY B20

GINGER BAKER D PERC(ABC — (A) BAKER GURVITZ ARMY — 1974 VERTIGO UK 9103 201
ADRIAN GURVITZ G V (ABC — (A) BAKER GURVITZ ARMY — 1974 JANUS US 7015
PAUL GURVITZ B V (ABC — (B) ELYSIAN ENCOUNTER — 1975 MOUNTAIN UK TOPS 101
SNIPS V (BC — (B) ELYSIAN ENCOUNTER — 1975 ATCO US 36123
PETER LEMER K (B — (C) HEARTS ON FIRE — 1976 MOUNTAIN UK TOPS 111
JOHN NORMAN MITCHELL VIBES K(A — (C) HEARTS ON FIRE — 1976 PHONOGRAM EURO 9103 206
MADELINE BELL V (A — (C) HEARTS ON FIRE — 1976 ATCO US 36137
ROSETTA HIGHTOWER V (A
BARRY ST JOHN V (A — LIZA STRIKE V (A

B20A LAVERN BAKER B20A

LAVERN BAKER V (ALL — (A) LET ME BELONG TO YOU — 1974 BRUNSWICK US 754160
(B) SINGS BESSIE SMITH — 1976 ATLANTIC GER ATL51241
(C) HER GREATEST RECORDINGS — 19 ATLANTIC US

B21 MICKEY BAKER B21

MICKEY BAKER G (ALL — (A) TAKE A LOOK INSIDE — 1975 BIG BEAR BEAR 5
WILLY MABON K HCA (A — (B) THE BLUES IN ME — 1975 BLACK & BLUE 33507
FRITZ OZMEC D (C — (C) UP ON THE HILL — 1975 ROOTS US SL 517
DAN ARMSTRONG B (A — (D) BLUES & JAZZ GUITAR OF M BAKER — 197 KICKING MULE UK SNKF127 US 142
PETE MORGAN B (A — (E) JAZZ ROCK GUITAR — 1978 KICKING MULE UK SNKF145 US 140
PETE YORK B (A
KIERAN O'CONNOR PERC (A — KEN ELLIOTT K (A — DYAN BIRCH V (A
PADDY McHUGH V (A — FRANK COLLINS V (A — MARTIN WICHTL SAX (C
FRANK MANTOOTH PNO (C — KARL KRBAVAC B HCA (C

B22 BAKERLOO B22

DAVE CLEMPSON G HCA K (A — (A) BAKERLOO — 1969 HARVEST UK SHVL 762
TERRY POOLE B (A
KEITH BAKER D (A — JERRY SALISBURY TPT (A

B22A BALANCE B22A

PEPPY CASTRO V (AB — (A) BALANCE — 1981 PORTRAIT
BOB KULICK G (AB — (B) IN FOR THE COUNT — 1982 PORTRAIT UK 85787
DOUG KATSAROS K V (AB
JOHN SIEGLER B (A — ANDY NEWMARK D (A — CHUCK BURGI D (B
DENNIS FELDMAN B (B

B23 LONG JOHN BALDRY B23

LONG JOHN BALDRY V HCA(ALL — (A) LONG JOHNS BLUES — 1964 U A ULP1081 ASCOT US 13022
WITH — (A) LONG JOHNS BLUES — 1971 UA US UAS5545
RAY JACKSON MAND (E — (B) LOOKING AT LONG JOHN — 1966 U A SULP1146 SUNSET 50109
KATHI McDONALD V (K — (C) LET THE HEARTACHE BEGIN — 1968 PYE UK NSPL 18208
ALAN MURPHY G (KJ — (D) LET THERE BE LONG JOHN — 1968 PYE UK NSPL 18228
IAN ARMITT K (AEFJ — (E) IT AINT EASY — 1971 WB US 1921 UK K 46008
RONNIE WOOD G (E — (F) EVERYTHING STOPS FOR TEA — 1972 WB K 46160
SAM MITCHELL STEEL(EF — (G) HEARTACHES (GOLDEN HOUR) — 1974 PYE GH 572
MAGGIE BELL V (E — (H) GOOD TO BE ALIVE — 1976 CASABLANCA US 7012
MICKEY WALLER PERC (F — (J) WELCOME TO THE CLUB — 1977 CASABLANCA US 7035
ALAN SKIDMORE SAX (E — (K) BALDRY'S OUT — 1979 EMI US 17015 UK AML3002
JIMMY HOROWITZ K (FHJK — (L) BLUES(HOOCHIE COOCHIE MEN) — 19 UA US 5543
JEFF BRADFORD G HCA(A — (M) LONG JOHN BALDRY — 1980 EMI US 17038 NL 86263
CLIFF BARTON B (A — ( ) WAIT FOR ME — 1969 JANUS US 7002
RICK BROWN B (F
BILL LAW D (A — ELTON JOHN PNO (EF — CALEB QUAYE G (E — DAVE GLOVER B (E
IAN DUCK V HCA(E — ROGER POPE D (E — DAVEY JOHNSTONE G (F — NIGEL OLSSON D (F
KLAUS VOORMANN B (F — RAY COOPER PERC (F — STEFAN DELFT VLA (F — JAMES LITHERLAND G (F
ROBERT WESTON G (F — BILL SMITH B (F — JOHN DENTITH D (F — LIZA STRIKE V (FHJ
DORIS TROY V (F — BARRY ST JOHN V (F — TERRY STANNARD D (F — JOHN PORTER B (F
ROD STEWART BANJ (F — MADELINE BELL V (FJ — DAVID BALL G (H — DENNIS BALL B (H
TONY NEWMAN D (H — JON FIELD FDL (H — ANDY BOWN G (HJ — JOHN MEALING ORG (H
LESLEY DUNCAN V (HJ — SUE GLOVER V (H — NEIL SHEPHERD V (H — JESSE ED DAVIS G (J
JOHN JARVIS PNO (J — PETER GAVIN D (J — KLAUS VOORMANN B (J — GEORGE CHISHOLM TROM (J
NEIL LANCASTER V (J — MICK CLARKE G (K — ROY YOUNG K V (K — SAM MITCHELL G (HJ
TERRY COX D (H — MIKE FRENCH FDL (H — PETE STANLEY BANJ (H — CHRIS HUGHES SAX (H
BOB COHEN G (H — MIKE DRISCOL D (H — KAY GARNER V (HJ — FRED TACKETT G (J
JIM KELTNER D (J — TOM BROWN SAX (J — DAVID SNELL HARP (J — TONY BURROWS V (J
CHAS MILLS V (J — JAMES LEE FISH B (K — JEFF SEITZ D (K — CAROL BECKER V (K
TRACY BALIN V (K — MICHAEL ICEBERG SYN (K — RAY WARLEIGH SAX (K — TIM SADLER V (K
KIM KELLY V (K — STEPHEN BRUCE V (K — ORCHESTRA (F

B23A MARTY BALIN B23A

MARTY BALIN G V (A — (A) BALIN — 1981 EMI US 17054
JOHN JARVIS K (A
JOHNNY DECARO G V (A — MARK CUMMINGS K V (A — BILLY LEE LEWIS D V (A
RICHARD BASSIL B V (A — NEIL LARSEN K (A — MICHAEL BODDICKER K (A
JOHN HUG G (A — KEN WATSON PERC (A — BOBBYE HALL PERC (A
STEVE FORMAN PERC (A — BILL CHAMPLIN V (A — RICK NOWELS V (A
DAVID E LANDAU V (A

B23B MARCIA BALL

MARCIA BALL V (A

(A) CIRSUIT QUEEN	1978	CAPITOL	US	ST	11752
(B) FREDA & THE FIREDOGS LIVE	1980	BIG WHEEL	US	NR	10876

B24 HANK BALLARD

HANK BALLARD V (ALL
WITH
LAWSON SMITH
NORMAN THRASHER
BILLY DAVIS
HENRY BOOTH
CHARLES SUTTON
ARTHUR PORTER
SONNY WOODS

(A) HANK BALLARD & THE MIDNIGHTERS	19	STARDAY	US		K5003X
( ) HANK BALLARD & THE MIDNIGHTERS	19	POWERPAK	US	PO	276
( ) HANK BALLARD BIGGEST HITS	19				
( ) THOSE LAZY LAZY DAYS	19				
( ) GLAD SONGS SAD SONGS	19				
( ) JUMPIN' HANK BALLARD	19	LONDON HA 8101	US	KING	793
( ) GREATEST JUKE BOX HITS	19	KING	US		541
( ) HANGING WITH HANK	19	STANG	US	ST	1031
( ) SPOTLIGHT ON HANK BALLARD	19	STARDAY GUSTO	US	SK	740
( ) CANT KEEP A GOOD MAN DOWN	19	KING	US		1052
( ) FINGER POPPIN TIME	19	KING	US		700

B24A LARRY BALLARD

LARRY BALLARD V (ALL

(A) YOUNG BLOOD & SWEET COUNTRY MUSIC	1974	ELEKTRA	US		7E1024
(B) HONKY TONK HEAVEN	1976	CAPITOL	US	ST	11520
(C) WAITING IN THE WINGS	1977	CAPITOL	US	ST	11662

B25 RUSS BALLARD

RUSS BALLARD V D K B G HCA (ALL
NICK NEWELL SAX (AB
CHRIS MERCER SAX (AB
STEVE GREGORY SAX (A
MICK EVE SAX (A
RABBIT BUNDRICK K (B
DENNIS BELFIELD B (A
STEVE FREDIANI HRNS (C
BOBBYE HALL PERC (C
DAVE HENSON V (C
MIKE PORCARO B (C
TOM KELLY V (C
CHRIS KARAN PERC (B
TERRY STARR TPT (B
SUNNY LESLIE V (B
DAVE WINTOUR B (DE
RICHARD BLANSHARD V (DE

(A) RUSS BALLARD	1974	EPIC US 33252	UK EPC 80341
(B) WINNING	1976	EPIC US 34093	UK EPC 69210
(C) AT THE THIRD STROKE	1978	EPIC US 35035	UK EPC 82629
(D) RUSS BALLARD & THE BARNET DOGS	1980	EPIC US 36186	UK EPC 83867
(E) INTO THE FIRE	1981	EPIC US 36993	

MIKE BAIRD D (C
TOM SCOTT SAX (C
DAVID FOSTER K (C
LEE SKLAR B (C
KEITH OLSEN PERC (C
DAVE MATTACKS D (B
GEOFF SKATES (B
PIP WILLIAMS (B
JOANNE WILLIAMS V (B
BILL ROBERTS G V (DE
LESLIE MORGAN D (D
CRAIG DOERGE K (C
DAVID HUNGATE B (C
FRED TACKETT G (C
JEFF PORCARO D (C
DAVID PAICH K (C
DAVE MARKEE B (B
PETE ZORN B (B
MADELINE BELL V (B
LIZA STRIKE V (B
ROB HENRIT D (DE

B25A BALLIN' JACK

GLENN THOMAS G (A
LUTHER RABB B V (A
JIM COILE WIND (A
RONNIE HAMMON D (A
TIM McFARLAND PNO (A
JIM WALTERS TPT (A

(A) BALLIN' JACK	1970	CBS US 30344	UK	64210
(B) BUZZARD LUCK	1972	CBS US 31468		
(C) SPECIAL PRIDE	1973	MERCURY	US	1 672
(D) LIVE AND IN COLOR	1974	MERCURY	US	1 700

B26 BALLS

TREVOR BURTON B (ABCD
DENNY LAINE G V (ABCD
ALAN WHITE D (B
MIKE KELLIE D (CD
RICHARD TANDY K (A

(A) 1969 (B) 1969 (C) 1970 SUMMER (D) 1970 LATE

JACKIE LOMAX G V (C
DAVE MORGAN B (A
STEVE GIBBONS V G (D
KEITH SMART D (A

B26A BALTIK

JANNE SCHAFFER G (A
BJORN JASON LINDH FLT (A
JOHN GUSTAFSON B (A

(A) BALTIK 1973 CBS SWED 65581

B26B BAMA

(A) GHETTO'S OF MY MIND 1974 CHESS 50032

B27 BAMBOO

DAVE RAY HCA V G (A
WILL DONIGHT V B PNO (A
DANIEL LEE HALL V K G (A
PETER HODGSON B (A

(A) BAMBOO 1969 ELEKTRA US EKS 74048

SANFORD KONIKOFF D (A
BRENDAN HARKIN PERC (A
RED RHODES STEEL (A
KEN JENKINS B (A

B27A BAMBOO ZOO

(A) LOOK, LISTEN, CONSUME 1981 PHONEY UK PHOG8101

B27B BANCHEE

PETER ALONGI G V (B
JOSE MIGUEL DE JESUS G V (B
FERNANDO ROMAN PERC V (B
MICHAEL MARINE B V (B

(A) BANCHEE	1969	ATLANTIC	US
(B) THINKIN'	1971	POLYDOR US 24 4066	UK 242507?

VICTOR DIGILIE D (B

B28 BANCO

PIER LUIGI CALDERONI D (D
FRANCESCO DI GIACOMO V (D
RENATO D'ANGELO B G (D
GIANNA NOCENZI K CLAR (D
VITTORIO NOCENZI K (D

( ) BANCO DEL MUTUO SOCCORSO	1972	ORIZZONTE	ITAL	ORL	8041
( ) DARWIN	1972	ORIZZONTE	ITAL	ORL	8094
( ) LO SONO NATO LIBERO	1973	ORIZZONTE	ITAL	ORL	8202
(D) BANCO	1975	MANTICORE	UK	K	53507
(D) BANCO	1975	MANTICORE	US	MA6	505
( ) GAROGANO ROSSO	1976	ORIZZONTE	ITAL	ORL	8334
( ) AS IN A LAST SUPPER	1976	MANTICORE			28004
( ) DI TEARO	19	DISCHI	ITAL	SMRL	6226
( ) CANTO DI PRIMAVERA	19	DISCHI	ITAL	SMRL	6247
( ) CAPOLINEA	19	DISCHI	ITAL	SMRL	6260

B29 THE BAND

ROBBIE ROBERTSON G V K (ALL
RICK DANKO B V VLN (ALL
RICHARD MANUEL D K V (ALL
LEVON HELM V D G (ALL
GARTH HUDSON K SAX (ALL
WITH
TOM MALONE HRNS (HJ
JIM GORDON HRNS (HJ
(CONTINUED)

(A) MUSIC FROM THE BIG PINK	1968	CAPITOL		ST 2955
(B) THE BAND	1969	CAPITOL		EST 132
(AB)MILESTONES	1973	EMI	IMP	5C18450195/6
(C) STAGE FRIGHT	1970	CAPITOL		EASW 425
(D) CAHOOTS	1971	CAPITOL		EAST 651
(E) ROCK OF AGES	1972	CAPITOL		EASSP 11
(E) ROCK OF AGES	1972	CAPITOL		SABB11045
(F) MOONDOG MATINEE	1973	CAPITOL		ESW 11214

B29 THE BAND (CONTINUED) B29

Member	Instr.	Albums	Album	Year	Label		Catalogue
JOHN SIMON	K HRNS	(BEHJ	(G) NORTHERN LIGHTS SOUTHERN CROSS	1975	CAPITOL		EST 11440
LARRY PACKER	VLN	(HJ	(H) ISLANDS	1977	CAPITOL		EST 11602
VAN MORRISON	V	(DJ	(J) THE LAST WALTZ TRIPLE	1978	WB	UK	K 66076
ALLEN TOUSSAINT	K	(D	(J) THE LAST WALTZ TRIPLE	1978	WB	US	3WS 3146
SNOOKY YOUNG	HRNS	(E	( ) THE BEST OF THE BAND	1976	CAPITOL		EAST23927
HOWARD JOHNSON	HRNS	(EJ	( ) THE BEST OF THE BAND	1976	CAPITOL	US	ST 11553
DOC POMUS		(E	( ) THE BEST OF THE BAND	1976	CAPITOL	UK	ST 3927
JOE FARRELL	HRNS	(E	( ) MASTERS OF ROCK	1975	EMI INT		IC 054 81735
EARL McINTYRE	TROM	(E	( ) IN CONCERT	1973	EMI IMP		5C 054 81466
J D PARRAN	WIND	(E	( ) ANTHOLOGY	1978	CAPITOL		ESTSP 19
BOBBY CHARLES	V	(EJ	( ) ANTHOLOGY	1978	CAPITOL	US	SKBO11856
BOB DYLAN	V G	(EJ					
Dr JOHN	K PERC	(EJ					
RICH COOPER	HRNS	(J					
RONNIE HAWKINS	V	(J					
NEIL DIAMOND	V G	(J					
MUDDY WATERS	G V	(J					
ERIC CLAPTON	G V	(J					
EMMYLOU HARRIS	V G	(J					

BILLY MUNDI (F — BEN KEITH (F
JERRY HEY HRNS (J — CHARLIE KEAGLE HRNS (J
NEIL YOUNG V G (J — JONI MITCHELL V G (J
DENNIS ST JOHN D (J — PAUL BUTTERFIELD HCA V (J
BOB MARGOLIN G (J — PINETOP PERKINS K (J
RINGO STARR D (J — RON WOOD G (J
STAPLES SINGERS V (J — BYRON BERLINE FDL (G

B30 BAND OF JOY B30

ROBERT PLANT V (
JOHN BONHAM D (
PAUL LOCKEY G V (
MICHAEL CHETWOOD K (

(A) BAND OF JOY — 1978 POLYDOR US 6133 UK 2310 588

KEVIN HAMMOND G V (— JOHN PASTERNAK B V (
FRANCESCO NIZZA D (

B30A BAND OF THIEVES B30A

(A) BAND OF THIEVES — 1979 OVAL US 1727

B31 BANDIT B31

JAMES LITHERLAND G (A
GRAHAM BROAD D K (A
DANNY McINTOSH G V (AB*
JIM DIAMOND V (A
CLIFF WILLIAMS B V (A
TONY LESTER B V (B
TWO DIFFERENT COVERS GIVING DIFFERENT GUITARIST

(A) BANDIT — 1977 ARISTA US 4113 UK ARTY 148
*(B) PARTNERS IN CRIME — 1978 ARIOLA US 50042 UK ARL 5010
(C) HIT & RUN — 1980 ARIOLA US 50067

THEODORE THUNDER D V (B — GERRY TREW V (B
MICK GRABHAM G V (B*

B31A BANDIT (US) B31A

JOEY NEWMAN G V (A
KEVIN BARNHILL B V G (A
TIMOTHY EATON V (A

(A) BANDIT — 1975 ABC US 918

DAVID DELLA ROSSA GV (A — DANNY GORMAN D (A

B31B BANDERA B31B

(A) HYPE INTO SELLING YOUR HEAD — 1980 JSP UK 1018

B32 BANDOGGS B32

TONY ROSE (
NIC JONES (
PETE COE (

(A) BANDOGGS — 1978 TRANSATLANTIC LTRA 504

CHRIS COE

B32A BANG B32A

TONY D'IORIO D (A
FRANK FERRARA B V (ABC
FRANK GLICKEN G V (ABC
DURIS MAXWELL D (B
BRUCE GARY D (BC
SHIRLEY MATTHEWS V (B

(A) BANG — 1972 CAPITOL US 11015
(B) MOTHER/BOW TO THE KING — 1972 CAPITOL US 11110
(C) BANG MUSIC — 1973 CAPITOL US 11190

JEFFREY CHEEN PERC (B — CLYDIE KING V (B
VANETTA FIELDS V (B

B33 BANGOR FLYING CIRCUS B33

MICHAEL TEGZA D PERC (A
DAVID WOLINSKI PERC K V B (A
ALAN DE CARLO PERC G V (A

(A) BANGOR FLYING CIRCUS — 1969 STATESIDE UK SSL5022 US DUNHILL 50069

B33A DARRELL BANKS B33A

DARRELL BANKS (A

(A) DARRELL BANKS IS HERE — 19 ATCO US SD 33216 VOLT US 6002

B34 PETER BANKS B34

PETER BANKS G (ABC
JAN AKKERMAN G (AB
STEVE HACKETT G (B
RAY BENNETT B (B
JOHN WETTON B (B

(A) PETER BANKS & JAN AKKERMAN — 19 SOVEREIGN SVNA 7250
(B) PETER BANKS — 1973 SOVEREIGN SVNA 7256
(B) TWO SIDES OF PETER BANKS — 1973 CAPITOL SMAS11217

PHIL COLLINS D (B — MIKE HOUGH D (B

B34A ROSE BANKS B34A

ROSE BANKS V (A

(A) ROSE — 1976 MOTOWN US 6/845 UK STML 12024

B34B TONY BANKS B34B

TONY BANKS K G B (A
KIM BEACON V (A
CHESTER THOMPSON D (A

(A) A CURIOUS FEELING — 1979 CHARISMA US 2207 UK CAS 1148

B35 BANZAI B35

EVERT VERHEES G V K B (A
PETER TORFS K V (A
JOHN McO G V (A

(A) HORANATA — 19 DELTA DG 10 001

LUDWIG KERMAT VIBES PERC (A — ERRY FOX D PERC (A

B36 BAR KAYS B36

Member	Albums	Album	Year	Label		Catalogue
JIMMY KING	(*	( ) SOUL FINGER	19	ATCO		228 030
RONNIE CALDWELL	(*	( ) SOUL FINGER	19	ATCO		SD 33287
PHALIN JONES	(*	( ) SOUL FINGER	19	ATLANTIC		K 40184
CARL CUNNINGHAM	(*	( ) GOTTA GROOVE	1969	STAX STATS1009		RI 80 4130
FRANK THOMPSON	(	( ) GOTTA GROOVE	1969	VOLT		6004
JAMES ALEXANDER	(	( ) BLACK ROCK	19	POLYDOR		2362 003
BEN CAULEY	(	( ) DO YOU SEE	19	POLYDOR		2325 087
LLOYD SMITH	(	( ) COLD BLOODED	1976	STAX		STX 1033
CHARLES ALLEN	(	( ) TOO HOT TO STOP	1976	MERCURY		SRM 11099
MICHAEL BEARD	(	( ) FLYING HIGH ON YOUR LOVE	1978	MERCURY	UK	9100 048
WINSTON STEWART	(	( ) FLYING HIGH ON YOUR LOVE	1978	MERCURY		SRM 1181
HARVEY HENDERSON	(	( ) MONEY TALKS	1979	STAX		STX 3023
	(	( ) MONEY TALKS	1979	STAX		4106
		( ) DO YOU SEE WHAT I SEE	19	VOLT	US	8001

(CONTINUED)

B36 (CONTINUED)

BAR KAYS B36

Title	Year	Label	Country	Number
( ) IN JOY	1980	MERCURY		3781
( ) LIGHT OF LIFE	1980	MERCURY		3732
( ) AS ONE	1981	MERCURY	UK	6337 108
( ) BLACK LIGHT	19	VOLT	US	6011

(*) THE FOUR MEMBERS WHO DIED WITH OTIS REDDING(*)

B36A BARBARELLA B36A

Member	Instr	Records
GERNER BRESSEN	V FLY	(A
HENNING POLD	V B	(A
TERJE BARNHOLDT	D	(A
KAARE BARKOU	K V	(A
KENNETH CARTER	G V	(A

Title	Year	Label	Country	Number
(A) FIRST LOVE	1975	ARTIST	DENMARK	515
(B) BARBARELLA?	1976	ARTIST	DENMARK	?

B36B BARBARIANS B36B

Member	Instr	Records
JERRY CAUSI	B	(A
JEFF MORRIS	G	(A
BRUCE BENSON	G	(A
VICTOR MOULTON	D V	(A

Title	Year	Label	Country	Number
(A) THE BARBARIANS	1979	RHINO	US RI	008

B36C BILL BARCLAY B36C

Member	Instr	Records
BILL BARCLAY	V	(ALL

Title	Year	Label	Country	Number
(A) ALMOST ALIVE	1974	GM		GHL 1016
(B) THERE WAS THIS BLOKE	1975	RUBBER		RUB 010
(C) VIVA DUNBAR	1976	PYE		PKL 5555
(D) HALF ALIVE	1979	SAFARI		BOOB 1

B37 BARCLAY JAMES HARVEST B37

Member	Instr	Records
JOHN LEES	G V	(ALL
STEWART WOLSTENHOLME	K	(A>L
MEL PRITCHARD	D	(ALL
LES HOLROYD	B	(ALL
ALAN PARSONS	J HARP	(B
KEVIN McALEA	K	(M
BARRY THOMAS	V	(D
BILL NEWTON	V	(D
NORMAN BROWN	V	(D
NAT WHITWORTH	V	(D
GEORGE WALL	V	(D
DAVE BROWNING	TPT	(D
LENNIE MOAKES	TPT	(D
DON BANKS	TPT	(D
BROM HARVEY	TPT	(D
FRANK DIXON	TROM	(D
MUFF KING	TROM	(D
FRANK BRIERLEY	TROM	(D
AUSTIN GLEAVE	TROM	(D
KEVIN McALEA	K	(M
ALAN FAWKES	SAX	(M
SYMPH ORCH		(ABCD

Title	Year	Label	Country	Number
(A) BARCLAY JAMES HARVEST	1970	HARVEST		SHVL 770
(B) ONCE AGAIN	1971	HARVEST		SHVL 788
(C) OTHER SHORT STORIES	1971	HARVEST		SHVL 794
(D) BABY JAMES HARVEST	1972	HARVEST		SHSP 4023
( ) EARLY MORNING ONWARDS	1972	STARLINE	UK	SRS 5126
(E) EVERYONE IS EVERYBODY ELSE	1974	POLYDOR		2383 286
(F) LIVE	1974	POLYDOR		2683 052
(G) TIME HONOURED GHOSTS	1975	POLYDOR		2383 361
(G) TIME HONOURED GHOSTS	1975	POLYDOR	US	6517
(H) OCTOBERON	1976	POLYDOR		2442 144
(H) OCTOBERON	1976	MCA	US	2234
( ) BEST OF VOL 1	1977	HARVEST	UK	SHSM 2013
(I) GONE TO EARTH	1978	POLYDOR		2442 148
(I) GONE TO EARTH	1978	MCA	US	2302
(J) LIVE TAPES	1978	POLYDOR		PODV 2001
(K) NUMBER 12	1978	POLYDOR		2442 153
(K) NUMBER 12	1978	POLYDOR		POLD 5006
( ) BEST OF VOL 2	1979	HARVEST		SHSM 2023
(L) MOCKINGBIRD (THE EARLY YEARS	1980	HARVEST	EURO	05607236
(M) EYES OF THE UNIVERSE	1980	POLYDOR		POLD 5029
( ) BEST OF VOL 3	1981	HARVEST	UK	SHSM 2033
(N) TURN OF THE TIDE	1981	POLYDOR	UK	POLD 5040
(O) CONCERT FOR THE PEOPLE	1982	POLYDOR	UK	POLD 5052

B38 NICKEY BARCLAY B38

Member	Instr	Records
NICKEY BARCLAY		(
WITH		
WADDY WACHTEL	G	(A
JEFF RICH	B	(A
BUGS PEMBERTON	D	(A

Title	Year	Label	Country	Number
(A) DIAMOND IN A JUNKYARD	1976	ARIOLA		AAS 1503
(A) DIAMOND IN A JUNKYARD	1976	ARIOLA	US	ST 5006

B39 PETER BARDENS B39

Member	Instr	Records
PETER BARDENS	K V	(ALL
WITH		
ANDY GEE	G	(ABC
BRUCE THOMAS	B	(AC
ALAN MARSHALL	V PERC	(AC
STEVE ELLIS	V	(AC
REG ISADOR	D	(ABC
ROCKY	PERC	(AC
DAVID WOOLEY	V	(AC
JOHN OWEN	B	(BC
VIC LINTON	G	(C
MAXINE OFFLA	V	(BC
GUS ISADORE	G V	(D
PETE SHADE	VIBES	(D
LINDA LEWIS	V	(ABC
VICTOR BROX	VLN V	(B
JUDY POWELL	V	(BC
PETER VAN HOOKE	D	(D
MEL COLLINS	SAX	(D
PETER GREEN	G	(C
LIZA STRIKE	V	(BC
ANITA POLLINGER	V	(BC
STAN SCRIVENER	B	(D
CHRIS KARAN	PERC	(D

Title	Year	Label	Country	Number
(A) THE ANSWER	1970	TRANSATLANTIC	UK	TRA 222
(A) THE ANSWER	1970	VERVE	US	3088
(A) THE ANSWER	1970	METRONOME	IMP	MPL 15 389
(B) PETER BARDENS	1971	TRANSATLANTIC	UK	TRA 243
(B) WRITE MY NAME IN DUST	1971	VERVE MGM	US	3091
(C) VINTAGE 69	1976	TRANSATLANTIC	UK	TRASAM36
(D) HEART TO HEART	1979	ARISTA		SPART1108

B40 BARDOT B40

Member	Instr	Records
RAY McRINER	V G	(A
CHRIS BRADFORD	V	(A
LAURIE ANDREW	V	(A
GEOFF WESTBY	K	(A
BOB YOUNG	HCA	(A
PIP	G	(A
MIKE GILES	D	(A
FRANK RICOTTI	D	(A
DAVE MARKEE	B	(A

Title	Year	Label	Country	Number
(A) ROCKIN IN RHYTHM	1978	RCA		PL 25121

B41 BAREFOOT JERRY B41

Member	Instr	Records
WAYNE MOSS	G V K B PERC	(ALL
MAC GAYDEN	G V K	(A
JOHN HARRIS	K	(ABC
KEN BUTTREY	D	(A
RUSS HICKS	STEEL G V HRS	(BCDEF
KENNY MALONE	D	(BC
BUDDY SPICHER	FDL	(BC
DAN FLICKENGER	K	(B
TOM KNOX	K	(B
BUDDY BLACKMON	BANJ DOBRO	(F
DAVE DORAN	B V G	(C
FRED NEWELL	V B BANJO	(CD
BARRY CHANCE	K B G	(EF
COSTO DAVIS	STRING	(E
CHARLIE McCOY	HCA V FLT PNO	(DEF
JIM COLVARD	G B	(DE
BOBBY THOMPSON	B V G	(BCD
BUDDY SKIPPER	HRNS V PERC	(CD
JIM ISBELL		(D
MIKE McBRIDE	B G PERC	(F
SI EDWARDS	PERC	(CDEF
JOHN MOSS	HRNS	(EF
TERRY DEARMORE	B G	(DE
STEVE DAVIS	K	(E
WARREN HARTMAN	K	(DE
BILLY SWAN	V	(D

Title	Year	Label	Country	Number
(A) SOUTHERN DELIGHT	1971	CAPITOL		EST 786
(B) BAREFOOT JERRY	1972	WB	US	BS 2641
(B) BAREFOOT JERRY	1972	WB	UK	K 46268
(C) WATCHIN' TV	1974	MONUMENT KZ32926		MC 6631
(C) WATCHIN' TV	1979	CRIMINAL	UK RI	TAKE 2
(D) YOU CANT GET OFF WITH YOUR SHOES ON	75	MONUMENT		MNT 80695
(D) YOU CANT GET OFF WITH YOUR SHOES ON	75	MONUMENT		MC 6631
(D) YOU CANT GET OFF WITH YOUR SHOES ON	75	MONUMENT		KZ 33381
(E) KEYS TO THE COUNTRY	1976	CBS		34252
(E) KEYS TO THE COUNTRY	1976	MONUMENT	US	MG 7605
(F) BAREFOOTIN'	1977	MONUMENT		MG 7610
(F) BAREFOOTIN'	1977	MONUMENT		MNT 82413
(AB)GROCERY DBLE	1976	MONUMENT		KZ 33381
(AB)GROCERY DBL	1976	MONUMENT		33909
(AB)GROCERY DBL	1976	MONUMENT		MP 8603

B41A PATRICK BARNES

(A) GUITAR — 1980 STIFF SEEZ 22

PATRICK BARNES G (A

B41B JESSE BARISH

(A) JESSE BARISH — 1979 RCA US 1 2555
(B) MERCURY SHOES — 1980 RCA US 1 3420

JESSE BARISH G V FLT(ALL
JAY DAVID D V (B
AUSTIN DELONO K V G (B
DOUG KILLMER B V (B
JOHN HUG G (B
STEVE FORMAN PERC (B
JAMES RALSTON G V (B
MARTY BALIN V (AB
TOMMY VIG PERC (B
JOHNNY FONTAYNE DECARO G V (B
GREG PHILLINGANES SYN (B
ALTO REED SAX (B

B41C MAX D BARNES

(A) ROUGH AROUND THE EDGES — 1980 OVATION US 1749

MAX D BARNES (A

B42 BAROOGA BANDIT

(A) COME SOFTLY — 1979 CAPITOL EST 11924

BRUCE MECHAN G V (A
DAN O'CONNELL B V (A
MAT DE RAAD K V (A
CHARLIE MARTIN PERC V(A
MICHAEL STOKES PERC (A
FRANZ DE RAAD D V (A
TOM NEME G (A
DREW ABBOTT G (A
ALTO REED WIND (A

B42A BAROQUES

(A) THE BAROQUES — 1967 CHESS US 1516

DEAN NIMMER D (A
RICK BIENIEWSKI B (A
JAY BERKENHAGEN G K V (A
JACQUES HUTCHINSON G V (A

B42B WALTER BARR

(A) FIRST VISIT — 1978 MUSE US 5172
(B) EAST WINDS — 1979 MUSE US 5210

WALT BARR G (ABC
ROY BEAVERMAN K (ABC
DOUG HODGES B (A
JACK TURCHIN D (A
BRIAN ROSE D (C
JULIE LONG V (B
BILL KUHNE B (B
BRYAN TILFORD B (C
JACK LECOMPTE PERC (B
MARK LEON D (B
SANFORD PERC (C

B43 BARRABAS

(A) POWER — 1973 RCA US SPLI 2000
(B) BARRABAS — 1975 ATLANTIC K 50152
(B) BARRABAS — 1975 ATLANTIC US 913 092
(B) BARRABAS — 1975 ATCO US 36110
(C) RELEASE — 1975 ATLANTIC 913 207
(D) HEART OF THE CITY — 1975 ATLANTIC ATC 9590
(D) HEART OF THE CITY — 1975 ATCO US 36 118
(D) HEART OF THE CITY — 1975 ATLANTIC 913 039
(E) HI JACK — 19 ATLANTIC 87912
(F) WATCH OUT — 19 ATCO US 36 136
(F) WATCH OUT — 1976 ATLANTIC UK K50285

JOAN A VIDAL K (ABCDE
JOSE LUIS TEJADA V HCA (ABCDE
ENRIQUE MORALES G V (ABCDE
ERNESTO DUARTE WIND PERC V(ABCDE
MIGUEL MORALES G B V (ABCDE
DANIEL LOUIS D (DE
JOSE MARIA MOLL D (AB
MAXINE WATERS V (B
PATTI WATERS V (B
JULIA WATERS V (B
HERNANOS MORALES V (B

B43A BARRELHOUSE

(A) BARRELHOUSE — 1974 MUNICH BM 150205
(B) WHO'S MISSING — 1975 MUNICH BM 150213
(C) HARD TO COVER — 1977 MUNICH BM 150214
(D) BEWARE — 1979 ARIOLA NL 200 895
(E) GOT TO GET TOGETHER — 1981 ARIOLA NL 203 461

JOHNNY LA PORTE G (ABCDE
TINEKE SCHOEMAKER V (ABCDE
BARRELHOUSE BAILEY PNO (A
BOB DROS D (ABCDE
JAY WALKER B (A
HAN VAN DAM PNO (BC
JAN WILLEM SLIGTING B (BC
JEFF REYNOLDS TPT (E
GUS LA PORTE G (CDE
ROB VAN DONSELAAR K (E
HANS DULFER SAX (DE

B43B BARRELHOUSE BUCK

(A) BARRELHOUSE BUCK — 19 FOLKWAYS 3554

B43C ELIZABETH BARRACLOUGH

(A) ELIZABETH BARRACLOUGH — 1978 BEARSVILLE UK K55520 US 6978
(B) HI — 1979 BEARSVILLE US 6992

ELIZABETH BARRACLOUGH G V (ALL
DAVE LEWIS D (A
KENNY BUTTREY D (A
CHARLIE McCOY HCA (A
IAN HAMPTON B (A
BOB BOUCHER B (A
PAUL BUTTERFIELD HCA (AB
WILLIE MITCHELL PNO (B
ERMA SHAW V (B
MALCOLM MORTIMORE D (A
RUSS HICKS G (A
TODD RUNDGREN G (A
LEROY HODGES B (B
JACK HOLDER SYN (B
ELIZABETH SMITH V (B
MIKE LEECH B (A
MICK HODGKINSON K B G(A
AARON NESBIT K (B
GENE CHRISMAN D (B
ANDREW LOVE SAX (B
ROMELL GREENLEE V (B

B43D BARRACUDAS

(A) DROP OUT WITH — 1981 REGAL ZONOPHONE UK ZONO103

JEREMY GLUCK V (A
ROBIN WILLS G (A
NICK TURNER D (A
DAVID BUCKLEY B (A

B43E BARRATT BAND

(A) PLAYING IN THE CITY — 1981 CHAPEL LANE UK 8005

NORMAN BARRATT G V (A
TIM HATWELL B V (A
RUSSELL CALDWELL D (A
DAVE MORRIS K V (A
WALTER BOLLARD K (A

B44 SYD BARRETT

(A) MADCAP LAUGHS — 1970 HARVEST SHVL 765
(A) MADCAP LAUGHS — 1970 HARVEST US SABB11314
(B) BARRETT — 1970 HARVEST SHSP 4007
(AB) MADCAP/BARRETT (DBL) — 1974 HARVEST SHDW 404
(AB) MADCAP/BARRETT (DBL) — 197 PATHE FR C18450350/1

SYD BARRETT G V (AB
JERRY SHIRLEY D (B
DAVID GILMOUR PROD B G (AB
RICHARD WRIGHT PROD K (B
ROGER WATERS PROD B(A
MALCOLM JONES PROD (A
MIKE RATLEDGE K (A
WILLIE WILSON D (AB
ROBERT WYATT D (A
VIC SEYWELL HRN (A
HUGH HOPPER B (A

B44A RONNIE BARRON

(A) REVEREND ETHER — 1971 DECCA US DL 75303

RONNIE BARRON (A

B44B BARRINO BROTHERS

(A) I SHALL NOT BE MOVED — 19 INVICTUS US 7308

B45 BARRON KNIGHTS B45

Musician	Instr	Albums
DUKE D'MOND	V	(ALL
BARRON ANTHONY	V	(ALL
PEANUTS LANGFORD	G V	(ALL
BUTCH BAKER	G V	(ALL
DAVE BALLINGER	D	(ALL

Album	Year	Label	Country	No.
( ) CALL UP THE GROUPS	1964	COLUMBIA	UK	33SX 1648
( ) BARRON KNIGHTS	1966	COLUMBIA	UK	SX 6007
( ) SCRIBED	1967	COLUMBIA	UK	SCX 6176
( ) KNIGHTS OF LAUGHTER	1975	PENNYFARTHING		PAGS 533
( ) ONE MANS MEAT	1973	PENNYFARTHING		PELS 536
( ) LIVE IN TROUBLE	1977	EPIC		EPC 82451
( ) NIGHT GALLERY	1978	EPIC		EPC 83221
( ) KNIGHTS OF LAUGHTER	1979	PICKWICK		SHM 981
( ) TEACH THE WORLD TO LAUGH	1979	CBS		83891
( ) JESTA GIGGLE	1980	epic	UK	84550

B45A NEIL BASHAN B45A

Musician	Instr	Albums
NEIL BASHAN		(AB
PETE VAN HOOKE	D	(AB
ROY BABINGTON	B	(B
PAUL WESTWOOD	B	(B
VICKY BROWN	V	(B
GARY OSBORNE	V	(B
RAY RUSSELL	G	(B
HELEN CHAPELL	V	(B
LYNTON NAIFF	K	(B
LIZA STRIKE	V	(B

Album	Year	Label	Country	No.
(A) YOU GOT THE POWER	1978	ARIOLA		ARL 5005
(B) HIGH ON A EASY FEELING	1979	ARIOLA		ARL 5026

B45B JON BARTEL B45B

Musician	Instr	Albums
JON BARTEL	K	(AB
LOU STELLUTE	HRNS	(B
LARRY O'BRIAN	STR	(B
ABE BLASINGAME	PERC	(B

Album	Year	Label	Country	No.
(A) JON BARTEL	1968	PERCEPTION	US	
(B) THE JON BARTEL THING	1969	CAPITOL	US	274

B45C MICHAEL BARTON & THE GROOVERS B45C

Musician	Instr	Albums
MICHAEL BARTON	V K PERC	(A
MICKEY FINN	PERC	(A
ROB LUCAS	K G	(A
RICHARD JOHNS	SAX	(A
ROYSTON LUCAS	B V	(A
ROY BACKHOUSE	K	(A
MONKEY	K V	(A
VALERIE BURROWES	V	(A

Album	Year	Label	Country	No.
(A) ST GEORGE IS CROSS RUPERT	1981	CERBENIS BITE	UK	

B45D GARY BARTZ B45D

Musician	Instr	Albums
GARY BARTZ		(A

Album	Year	Label	Country	No.
(A) BARTZ	1980	ARISTA	US	4263

B45E ROBBIE BASHO B45E

Musician	Instr	Albums
ROBBIE BASHO	G V	(ALL
KREHE RITTER	HRNS	(C
MOREEN LIBET	VLA	(C
VICTOR CHANCELLOR	G	(C

Album	Year	Label	Country	No.
(A) THE FALCONERS ARM 1	1967	TAKOMA	US	1017
(B) THE FALCONERS ARM 2	1968	TAKOMA	US	1018
(C) VENUS IN CANCER	1969	BLUE THUMB	US	10
(D) SONG OF THE STALLION	1972	TAKOMA	US	1031
(E) VISIONS OF THE COUNTRY	1979	WINDHAM HILL	US	1005
(F) ART OF ACOUSTIC STEEL GUITAR	1980	WINDHAN HILL	US	1010

B45F BASEMENT FIVE B45F

Musician	Instr	Albums
DENNIS MORRIS		(A
RICHARD DUDANSKI		(A
J R		(A
LEO		(A

(A) 1965/80 — 1980 ISLAND UK ILPS9641 ANTILLES US7082

B46 MICHAEL BASS B46

Musician	Instr	Albums
MICHAEL BASS	PERC K V TROM	(A
WITH		
DAVE NEWHOUSE	WIND K V	(A
GLENN WISER	B G V	(A

Album	Year	Label	Country	No.
(A) PARCHESI PIE	1978	RANDOM RADAR		RRR 3 14

B47 BASTARD B47

Musician	Instr	Albums
CARLOS BASTARDOS	V B	(AB
KEITH KOSSOFF	G	(AB
THEO TREMOLO	G	(AB
TOTO PETTICOATO	D	(AB
ULI MEIBER	G	(B
KARL ROTHERT	B	(B

Album	Year	Label	Country	No.
(A) BACK TO NATURE	1977	NOVA		6 23288
(B) TEARING NIGHTS	1978	NOVA		6 23619
(C) LIVE & ALIVE	1980	LAVA		TCH 80535

B47A BATDORF & RODNEY B47A

Musician	Instr	Albums
MARK RODNEY	G V K	(ALL
JOHN BATDORF	G V K	(ALL
RUSS KUNKEL	D	(C
SCOTT EDWARDS	B	(C
RICK CARLOS	B	(C
TOM HENSLEY	K	(C
JULIA TILLMAN	V	(C
TOM SELLERS	K	(C
JOHN MAUCERI	D	(B
JOHN BARBATA	D	(A
DAVID HOOD	B	(A
DEAN PARKS	G	(C
GINGER BLAKE	V	(C
MARTY GWINN	V	(C
STRINGS		(C
JIM HASKELL	K	(B
BARRY BECKETT	K	(A
GARY COLEMAN	PERC	(C
MAXINE WILLARD	V	(C
JOE SIDORE	V	(C
RICK CARLOS	B	(B
CHRIS ETHRIDGE	B	(A
ROGER HAWKINS	D	(A

Album	Year	Label	Country	No.
(A) OFF THE SHELF	1971	WEA	US	SD 8298
(B) BATDORF & RODNEY	1972	ASYLUM		5056
(C) LIFE IS YOU	1975	ARISTA US 4041	UK	ARTY 112

B47B MIKE BATT B47B

Musician	Instr	Albums
MIKE BATT		(
FRANK RICOTTI	PERC	(C
FRANK McDONALD	B	(C
CLEM CATTINI	D	(B
CHRIS SPEDDING	G	(B
RAY COOPER	PERC	(B
ROGER CHAPMAN	V	(B
B J COLE	STEEL	(BC
JIM CREGAN	G	(BC
HAROLD FISHER	D	(B
ROY MORGAN	PERC	(B
RORY GALLAGHER	G	(B
COLIN BLUNSTONE	V	(B
TERRY COX	D	(B
RAY RUSSELL	G	(C
MEL COLLINS	SAX	(BC
NIGEL JENKINS	G	(C
FRANK McDONALD	B	(B
MARTIN KERSHAW	G	(B
RAY COOPER	PERC	(B
TONY McPHEE	G	(B
RICK KEMP	B	(B
EDDIE COWARD	CONG	(C
TREVOR MORAIS	D	(CB
AMSTERDAM CHAMBER ORCH		(C
TONY CARR	PERC	(B
RICKY HITCHCOCK	G	(B
LES THATCHER	G	(B
CHRIS KARAN	PERC	(B

Album	Year	Label	Country	No.
( ) SCHIZOPHONIA	1977	EPIC		EPC 82001
(B) TAROT SUITE	1979	EPIC		EPC 86099
(C) WAVES	1980	EPIC		EPC 84617
(D) 6 DAYS IN BERLIN	1981	EPIC		85149

B47C DAVID BATTEAU B47C

Musician	Instr	Albums
DAVID BATTEAU	V G	(A
WITH		
WILLIE WEEKS	B	(A
MILT HOLLAND	PERC	(A
DAVID SPINOZZA	G	(A
MICHAEL BAILEY	TPT	(A
DENIECE WILLIAMS	V	(A
JOAN SLIWIN	V	(A
KENNY ALTMAN	B	(A
DAVID PAICH	K	(A
ROBERT AHWAI	G	(A
MARTIN DROVER	TPT	(A
JULIA TILLMAN	V	(A
JEFF PORCARO	D	(A
ROY DAVIES	K	(A
STEVE GREGORY	FLT	(A
CHRIS MERCER	SAX	(A
MAXINE WILLARD	V	(A

Album	Year	Label	Country	No.
(A) HAPPY IN HOLLYWOOD	1976	A&M		AMLH64576

B47D STIV BATORS B47D

STIV BATORS V (A — (A) DISCONNECTED — 1980 BOMP BLP 4015
FRANK SECICH B V (A
GEORGIE HAMSON G V (A — DAVID QUINTON D (A — GREG SHAW PROD (A
THOM WILSON PROD (A

B47E BATTEAUX B47E

DAVID BATTEAU G V (A — (A) BATTEAUX — 1974 CBS US 32063
ROBIN BATTEAU VLN G V(A
PETER FREIBERGER B (A — ANDY NEWMARK D (A — MILT HOLLAND PERC (A
ROBIN LANE V (A — SALLY STEVENS V (A — DOUG McCLARAN K (A
JOHN GUERIN D (A — TOM SCOTT WIND (A — JACKIE WARD V (A
SHELBY FLINT V (A

B48 BATTI MAMZELLE B48

PETER DUPREY B V (A — (A) I SEE THE LIGHT — 1974 CUBE HI FLY 17 2326 037
WINSTON DELANDRO G K (A
RICHARD BAILEY D V (A — MIGUEL BARRADAS PERC (A — RALPH RICHARDSON PERC (A
RUSSELL VALDEZ PERC (A — FRANK INCE CONGA (A — JIMMY CHAMBERS CONGAS(A

B48A BATTERED ORNAMENTS B48A

NISAR AHMED KHAN FLT V (A — (A) MANTLE PIECE — 1969 HARVEST UK SHVL 758
CHRIS SPEDING G K V (A
ROGER POTTER B V (A — PETE BAILEY PERC V (A — ROB TAIT D V (A

B49 SKIP BATTIN B49

SKIP BATTIN B V (AB — (A) SKIP — 1973 SIGNPOST UK SG4255 US 8408
CLARENCE WHITE G (A — (B) NAVIGATOR — 1981 APPALOOSA IT 014
BILLY MUNDI D (A
JOHN GUERIN D (A — ROGER McGUINN G V (A — SPANKY McFARLANE V (A
SNEAKY PETE KLEINOW STEEL (B — DAVID HINES G (B — GREGG HARRIS G (B
GAIL KANTOR V (B — JACK BRUNO D (B — BRIAN ELLIOT PNO (B
NADRA THOMAS V (B — BRYAN POLAND PERC (B

B50 LUCIO BATTISTI B50

LUCIO BATTISTI V (ALL — (A) IL MIO CANTO LIBERO — 1973 COLUMBIA SCX 6540
RAY PARKER G (D — (B) IL NOSTRO CARO ANGELO — 1975 VOGUE LDM 30254
DENNIS BUDIMIR G (D — (C) ANIMA LATINA — 1975 VOGUE LDM 30282
DANNY FERGUSON G (D — (D) IMAGES — 1978 RCA PL 31889
MIKE MELVOIN K (D
SCOTTY EDWARDS B (D — JIM HUGHART B (D — ED GREENE D (D
HAL BLAINE D (D — MICHAEL BODDICKER K (D

B51 BATTLEFIELD BAND B51

ALAN REID G V K SYN (ALL — (A) BATTLEFIELD BAND — 1976 ARFOLK FR 349
BRIAN McNEILL VLN V (ALL — (B) THE BATTLEFIELD — 1977 TOPIC UK 12TS313
RICKY SCAGGS WIND (AC — (C) BATTLEFIELD BAND 2 — 1977 ARFOLK FR 358
JAMIE McMEMEMY G MAN V(BD — (D) AT THE FRONT — 1978 TOPIC UK 12TS381
JOHN GAHAGAN CONC (B — (E) STAND EASY — 1979 TOPIC UK 12TS404
JENNY CLARK G V (E — (F) PREVIEW (EP) — 1980 TEMPLE UK ETP 10
DUNCAN McGILLIVRAY WIND G V(EFG — (G) HOME IS WHERE THE VAN IS — 1980 TEMPLE UK TP 005
ALEC DUDGEON D (E — (G) HOME IS WHERE THE VAN IS — 1981 FLYING FISH US 250
PAT KILBRIDE G V (D
SYLVIA BARNES G V (F — GED FOLEY G MAND V WIND(G

B51A BAUHAUS B51A

KEVIN HASKINS D (ABC — (A) IN THE FLAT FIELD — 1980 4AD UK CAD 13
DAVID JAY B (ABC — (B) MASK — 1981 BEGGARS BANQUET UK BEGA 29
PETER MURPHY V (ABC — (C) THE SKY'S GONE OUT — 1982 BEGGARS BANQUET UK BEGA 45
DANIEL ASH G (ABc — (C+) PRESS THE EJECT(FREE WITH C) — 1982 BEGGARS BANQUET UK BEGA 38

B52 PETER BAUMANN B52

PETER BAUMANN K (AB — (A) ROMANCE 76 — 1977 VIRGIN UK 2069
W THIERFELD D (B — (B) TRANS HARMONIC NIGHTS — 1979 VIRGIN 2124
B JOBSKI HRNS (B — (C) REPEAT REPEAT — 1981 VIRGIN 2214
CARSTEN BOHN K D (C
MIKE DAWE D (C — RITCHIE FLIEGLER G (C — JOHN TROPEA G (A
LINDSAY KAY BRYNAN V (C

B52A BAUTISTA B52A

ROLAND BAUTISTA G V (A — (A) BAUTISTA — 1977 ABC US 1003
CHIP STEEN PERC (A
BOBBY LYLE K SYN (A — STEVE GUTIERREZ D (A — VICTOR FELDMAN VIBES(A
DONALD BECK B (A

B52B BAXTER B52B

STEVE BELGRADE G V (A — (A) BAXTER — 1973 PARAMOUNT US 6050
DOUG ARIOLI G V (A
LAWRENCE DI NATALE D (A — STEVEN KIRSHENBAUM K SYN (A — EDWIN PERRY B V (A

B53 CAROL BAYER SAGER B53

CAROL BAYER SAGER V (ALL — (A) CAROL BAYER SAGER — 1977 ELEKTRA US 7E1100 UK K52059
LEE SKLAR B (ABC — (B) TOO — 1978 ELEKTRA US 6E 151 UK K52093
JOHNNY VASTANO G V (A — (C) SOMETIMES LATE AT NIGHT — 1981 EPIC UK 85110
ARTIE BUTLER K (A

PETER ALLEN	V K	(A	LANCE QUINN	G	(A	ALAN ESTES	PERC	(A	BRENDA RUSSELL	V	(A
GENE PAGE	STR	(A	EMORY GORDY	B	(A	PAUL BUCKMASTER	SYN	(A	WILL LEE	B	(A
JERRY FRIEDMAN	G	(A	MADELINE KOHN	V	(A	HUGH McCRACKEN	G	(A	ANDY NEWMARK	D	(A
NINO TEMPO	SAX	(B	ED GREENE	D	(B	DAVID FOSTER	K STR	(BC	STEVE FORMAN	PERC	(B
BILL CHAMPLIN	V	(B	REINNE PRESS	B	(BC	ALICE COOPER	V	(B	IRA NEWBORN	G	(B
JEFF PORCARO	D	(C	BURT BACHARACH	PNO	(C	GEORGE YOUNG	SAX	(C	STEVE GEORGE	V	(C
MICHAEL JACKSON	V	(C	FRANN GOLDE	V	(C	JERRY HEY	HRNS	(C	FRED TACKETT	G	(C
DENNIS ST JOHN	D	(C	RICHARD BENNETT	G	(C	THOM HENSLEY	PNO	(C	KING ERRISSON	PERC	(C
WARREN LUENING	HRNS	(C	RAY GRAYDEN	G	(BC	MELISSA MANCHESTER	K V	(ABC	LEE RITENOUR	G	(ABC
NICKY HOPKINS	K	(A	RUSS KUNKEL	D	(AB	BOB CRANSHAW	B	(A	ALAN SCHWARTZBERG	D	(A
ABIGAIL HANESS	V	(A	TONY ORLANDO	V	(A	MARVIN HAMLISCH	G STR	(ABC	JIM KELTNER	D	(AC
BRUCE ROBERTS	V PNO	(ABC	AL GORGONI	G	(A	ROY MARKOWITZ	D	(A	THOM COTELLA	G	(AB
GARNETT BROWN	TROM	(A	BETTE MIDLER	V	(A	DON COSTA	STR	(B	DAVID HUNGATE	B	(B

(CONTINUED)

B53 (CONTINUED) **CAROL BAYER SAGER** B53

STEVE LUKATHER	G	(BC	MICHAEL McDONALD	V	(B	JIM GORDON	D	(B	STEVE PORCARO	SYN	(B
CRAIG DOERGE	K	(B	DAVID CAMPBELL	STR	(B	MICHAEL LANG	K	(C	ED WALSH	SYN	(C
RICHARD PAGE	V	(C	PAUL JACKSON	G	(C	PAULINHO DACOSTA	PERC	(C	JOANN HARRIS	V	(C
TIM MAY	G	(C	IAN UNDERWOOD	SYN	(C	NEIL DIAMOND	G	(C	DOUG RHONE	G	(C
ALAN LINDGREN	SYN	(C	VINCE CHARLES	PERC	(C	VENNETTE GLOUD	V	(C	JENNIFER SLOAN	V	(B
CARMEN TWILLIE	V	(B	RICHIE ZITO	G	(B	DAVID LASLEY	V	(B	LUTHER VANDROSS	V	(B
RICHARD DAVID	B	(B	JIM HUGHART	B	(B	SKIP REDWINE	K	(B	MICHAEL RUBINI	G	(B

B53A **BAZAAR** B53A

(A) ORIENTAL WIND 1981 SONET UK SNTF 864

B54 **BE BOP DELUXE** B54

BILL NELSON	G V	(ALL	(A) AXE VICTIM	1974 HARVEST US SM 11689 UK SHVL 813
ROBERT BRYAN	B	(AH	(B) FUTURAMA	1975 HARVEXT US ST 11432 UK SHSP4045
NICHOLAS DEW	D	(AH	(C) SUNBURST FINISH	1976 HARVEST US ST 11478 UK SHSP4053
IAN PARKIN	G	(AH	(D) MODERN MUSIC	1976 HARVEST US ST 11575 UK SHSP4058
RICHARD BROWN	K	(	(E) HOT VALVES (EP)	1976 HARVEST UK HAR 5117
MILTON REAME JAMES	K	(	(F) LIVE IN THE AIR AGE (DBL)	1977 HARVEST US 11666 UK SHVL 816
PAUL JEFFREYS	B	(	(G) DRASTIC PLASTIC	1978 HARVEST FR 06598 UK SHSP4091
SIMON FOX	D	(BCDEFGH	(H) THE BEST OF & THE REST (DBL)	1978 HARVEST UK SHDW 410
CHARLIE TUMAHAI	B	(BCDEFGH		
ANDREW CLARK	K	(CDEFGH	NICK CLARK G (JENNY HAAN V (A	

B56 **BEACH BOYS** B56

BRIAN WILSON		(	MIKE LOVE		(	AL JARDINE	G	(	DENNIS WILSON		(
BRUCE JOHNSTON		(	BLONDI CHAPMAN		(	CARL WILSON		(	RICK FATAAR	D	(
JAMES GUERCIO		(	DAVID MATTS		(	GLEN CAMPBELL		(			
WITH											
TONI TENNILLE	V	(	MARILYN WILSON	V	(	STEVE DOUGLAS	SAX	(	JACK NIMITZ	SAX	(
MIKE ALTSCHUL	SAX	(	DENNIS DREITH	SAX	(	JOHN J KELSO	SAX	(	JAY MIGLIORI	SAX	(
PLAS JOHNSON	SAX	(	JULES JACOBS	CLAR	(	CAROL LEE MILLER	A'HARP	(	GENE ESTES	PERC	(
JULIUS WECHTER	PERC	(	HAL BLAINE	D	(	DENNIS DRAGON	D	(	RON ALTBACH	PNO	(
ED CARTER	G	(	BILLY HINSCHE	G	(	BEN BENAY	G	(	JERRY COLE	G	(
TOMMY TEDESCO	G	(	LYLE RITZ	B	(	TIM DRUMMOND	B	(	RAY POLMAN	B	(
JAMES HUGHART	B	(	BOBBY SHEW	TPT	(	GARY GRIFFIN	K	(	MIKE KOWALSKI	D	(
CHRIS MIDDAUGH	STEEL	(	MICHAEL ANDREAS	HRNS	(	CHARLES LLOYD	HRNS	(	LANCE BUTLER	HRNS	(
JOHN FOSS	HRNS	(	VICTOR FELDMAN	PERC	(	STEVE FORMAN	PERC	(	MIKE MAROS	K	(
BOB ESTY	SYN	(	WAH WAH WATSON	G	(	JOE CHEANAY	B	(	ED CARTER	G B	(
CARLOS FIGUEORA	D	(	JIM GUERICO	B	(	STERLING SMITH	K	(	PHIL SHENDALE		(
JOEL PERSKIN	SAX	(	GARY MALLABER	D	(	RITCHIE ZITO	G	(	MIKE BAIRD	D	(
JIMMY LYONS	G	(									

SURFIN SAFARI	1962	CAPITOL	T1808
SURFIN SAFARI	1962	CAPITOL	SY 4572
SURFIN SAFARI	1981	GREENLIGHT UK	2014
SURFIN U S A	1963	CAPITOL	ST 1890
SURFER GIRL	1963	CAPITOL	ST 1981
SURFER GIRL	19	PICKWICK	SPC3351
GREAT CONCERT	19	PICKWICK	SPC 3309
LITTLE DEUCE COUPE	1963	CAPITOL	ST 1998
LITTLE DEUCE COUPE	1981	GREENLIGHT UK	2025
SHUT DOWN VOL 2	1964	CAPITOL	ST 2027
ALL SUMMER LONG	1964	CAPITOL	ST 2110
ALL SUMMER LONG	1973	MFP	50065
CHRISTMAS ALBUM	1964	CAPITOL	ST 2164
CHRISTMAS ALBUM	1977	CAPITOL	CAP1014
BEACH BOYS CONCERT	1964	CAPITOL	ST 2198
BEACH BOYS TODAY	1965	CAPITOL	ST 2269
SUMMER DAYS SUMMER NIGHTS	1965	CAPITOL	ST 2354
SUMMER DAYS SUMMER NIGHTS	1978	CAPITOL	CAPS 1023
BEACH BOYS PARTY	1965	CAPITOL	ST 2398
BEACH BOYS PARTY	1965	CAPITOL	MAS 2398
PET SOUNDS	1966	CAPITOL	ST 2458
PET SOUNDS	1966	CAPITOL	MS 2197
PET SOUNDS	19	BROTHER US	2083
PET SOUNDS	1981	GREENLIGHT UK	2002
BEST OF THE BEACH BOYS	1966	CAPITOL	ST 2545
BEST OF THE BEACH BOYS	1966	CAPITOL	ST20856
SMILEY SMILE	1967	CAPITOL	ST 9001
SMILEY SMILE (GERM)	1967	CAPITOL	SMK 74330
SMILEY SMILE	19	BROTHER	9001
BEST OF VOL 2	1967	CAPITOL	ST 2706
BEST OF VOL 2	1967	CAPITOL	ST20956
WILD HONEY	1968	CAPITOL	ST 2859
FRIENDS	1968	CAPITOL	ST 2895
FRIENDS (GERM)	1968	CAPITOL	SMK 74456
CALIFORNIA GIRLS (FRENCH)	19	CAPITOL	T 20740
BEST OF VOL 3	1968	CAPITOL	ST 2945
BEST OF VOL 3	1968	CAPITOL	ST21142
BEACH BOYS	1970	M F P	MFP 1382
20/20	1969	CAPITOL	EST 133
CLOSE UP	1969	CAPITOL	EST 253
LONDON 69	1969	CAPITOL	ST 11584
SUNFLOWER	1970	REPRISE	6382
SUNFLOWER	1970	STATESIDE	SSLA 8251
SUNFLOWER	1980	CARIBOU UK	RI 31773
BUG IN	1970	STARLINE	SRS 5014
GREATEST HITS	1970	CAPITOL	ST21628
SURFS UP	1971	REPRISE	6453
SURFS UP	1971	STATESIDE	SSL10313
SURFS UP	1980	EMBASSY	UK 31774
BEACH BOYS	1971	STARLINE	SRS 5074
LIVE IN LONDON	1972	CAPITOL	ST21715
LIVE IN LONDON	1977	M F P	50345
SO TOUGH	1972	REPRISE	K 44184
SO TOUGH	1972	REPRISE	2083
SO TOUGH	19	BROTHER	2090
HOLLAND	1973	REPRISE	K 54008
HOLLAND	1973	BROTHER	2118
SUNFLOWER/SURFS UP (DBL)	1973	EMI	5C184502156
IN CONCERT	1973	REPRISE	84001
ENDLESS SUMMER	1974	CAPITOL	EAST11307
ENDLESS SUMMER	1981	MFP	50528
FRIENDS /SMILEY SMILE DBL	1974	REPRISE	2MS 2167
VERY BEST OF 63-69	1974	ELECTROLA	IC15281482
STARS OF THE SIXTIES	1974	BOVEMA	5C05081596
DO YOU WANNA DANCE	1975	EMI	140502545
DO YOU WANNA DANCE	1971	MFP	5235
WILD HONEY/20 20 (DBL)	1975	REPRISE US	2MS 2166
WILD HONEY/FRIENDS	1975	CAPITOL	ESTSP 14
OLDIES	1975	EMI	048 0776
GOOD VIBRATIONS BEST OF	19	REPRISE	K 2280
GOOD VIBRATIONS	1975	REPRISE	K 52223
GOOD VIBRATIONS	1975	REPRISE	6484
GOOD VIBRATIONS(BEST OF)	1975	BROTHER	2223
GOOD VIBRATIONS	197	M F P	50234
GOOD VIBRATIONS	197	PICKWICK	SPC3769
SPIRIT OF AMERICA DBL	1975	CAPITOL	SVBB11384
SPIRIT OF AMERICA DBL	1975	CAPITOL	VMP1007
15 BIG ONES	1976	REPRISE	2251
15 BIG ONES	1976	REPRISE	K 54079
STACK O TRACKS	1976	CAPITOL	DKAD2893
STACK O TRACKS	1977	CAPITOL	EST24009
20 GOLDEN GREATS	1977	CAPITOL	EMTV1
LOVE YOU	1977	REPRISE	K 54087
LOVE YOU	1977	REPRISE	MSK 2258
M I U	1978	REPRISE	MSK 2268
M I U	1978	REPRISE	K 54102
40 GREAT HITS (DBL)	19	CAPITOL	CAPITOL 1/2
30 GREATEST HITS'TRIPLE)	19	CAPITOL	2813
BEACH BOYS	19	PICKWICK US	SPC3221
FUN FUN FUN (DBL)	19	CAPITOL	SF702/703
FUN FUN FUN (DBL)	19	CAPITOL US	STB 701
GIRLS	19	CAPITOL GER	05480 627
L A LIGHT ALBUM	1979	CARIBOU UK	86081
GIRLS ON THE BEACH	19	CAPITOL	CAPS 1037
ALL SUMMER LONG CALIFORNIS	19	CAPITOL US	500
1962/65 (DBL)	1980	CAPITOL	82292
1966/69 (DBL)	1980	CAPITOL	82294
KEEP THE SUMMER ALIVE	1980	CARIBOU UK	86109
KEEP THE SUMMER ALIVE	1980	CARIBOU US	36283
(EPs)			
SURFIN USA	196	CAPITOL	20540
FUN FUN FUN	196	CAPITOL	20603
4 BY THE BEACH BOYS	196	CAPITOL	1/ 5267
SAIL ON SAILOR	1977	REPRISE	k14481

B57 BEACON STREET UNION B57

PAUL TARTACHNY G V (AB
WAYNE ULAKY B V (AB
JOHN WRIGHT V PERC(AB
RICHARD WEISBURG D (AB
ROBERT RHODES K WIND (AB

(A) EYES OF THE BEACON STREET UNION 1968 MGM UK 8069 US SE 4517
(B) CLOWN DIED IN MARVIN GARDENS 1968 MGM US SE 4568

B57A RICHARD T BEAR B57A

RICHARD T BEAR K (A
ALLAN SCHWARZBERG D PERC(A
LES DUDEK G (A
ELLIOTT RANDALL G (A
STEVE GELFAND B (A
GEORGE GOMEZ G (A
JOHN BARRANCO V (A
DIVA GRAY V (A
TRACY RICHARDSON V (A
CHRISTINE FAITH V (A
RANDY BRECKER HRNS (A
RON CUBER HRNS (A
MIKE FINNIGAN K (A
PAUL SCHAEFFER K (A
BOB GURLAND TPT (A
SHARON LEE WILLIAMS V (A
BILLY SQUIER G (A
DAVE WOODS TPT (A
MICHAEL BRECKER HRNS (A
TONY PRICE HRNS (A
NEIL JASON B (A
GORDON GRODY V (A
ANNIE SUTTON V (A
ZULEMA CUSSEAUX V (A
KATHY INGRAHAM V (A
JACK ZAZA ACC (A
GEORGE YOUNG HRNS (A
TOM MALONE HRNS (A

(A) RED HOT & BLUE 1979 RCA PL 12927
(B) BEAR 1980 RCA 13313

B57B BEADGAME B57B

(A) WELCOME 19 AVCO US 33009

B57C BEANS B57C

(A) BEANS 1972 AVALANCHE US 9200

B57D BEAR B57D

ARTIE TRAUM G V (A
ERIC KAZ K V (A
DARIUS DAVENPORT D (A

(A) BEAR 1968 VERVE US 3059

B57E BEAR MOUNTAIN B57E

FRANK FORD D (A
BILL KEISLER B (A
CAM EMPENS K V (A
BILL RICHARDSON G V (A

(A) ONE MORE DAY 19 PREDATOR US 1001

B57F BEARFOOT B57F

DWAYNE FORD FLT K G V (ABC
TERRY DANKE B V (AB
JIM ATKINSON G V (ABC
HUGH BROCKIE G BAN(ABC
GARY HOLT B (C
KENNY MALONE D (C
BRUCE PENNYCOOK HRNS (C
WHITEY GLAN D (C
DANNY McBRIDE G (C
PRAKASH JOHN B (C
DAVE McMURDOW HRNS (C
LARRY LONDON PERC (C
BRIAN HILTEN D (A
CHRIS VICKERY B (C
MALCOLM TOMLINSON PERC (C

(A) BEARFOOT 1973 EPIC US 32146
(B) FRIENDS 1973 EPIC CAN 32653
(C) PASSING TIME 1975 EPIC CAN 33530

B58 BEARS B58

GEORGE GIL G (
RON WEST B
CALLY D
KRIS KERSHAW SAX

(A) BEARS 1981 OK UK 3001

B58A THE BEAST B58A

DAVID RAINES V (AB
ROBERT YEAZEL G V (AB
GERRY FIKE K (AB
LARRY FERRIS D (AB
DOMINICK TODERO TPT (A
MICHAEL KERNS WIND (AB
ROBERT BRYANT B (B
KEN PASSARELLI B HCA(A

(A) PRELUDE FOR TODAY 1969 COTILLION US 9012
(B) BEAST 1970 EVOLUTION US 2017

B58B BEAT B58B

DAVE WAKELING G (ABC
ANDY COX G (AB
RANKIN ROGER V (AB
SAXA SAX (AB
EVERETT MARTIN D (A
DAVID STEELE B (A
BOB SARGEANT PROD (A
DAVID WRIGHT K (A
BUCK CHARLERY V (

(A) I JUST CANT STOP IT 1980 BEAT UK 001 SIRE US 6091
(B) WHA'APPEN ?? 1981 GO FEET UK BEET 3

B58C BEATPUMP B58C

FIVE MONTH PLAN 1980 SLOWLORRIES UK SLOW 1

B59 THE BEATLES B59

JOHN LENNON G V K (ALL
PAUL McCARTNEY B G K V(ALL
GEORGE HARRISON G V (ALL
RINGO STARR D V (ALL
WITH
PETE BEST D
STUART SUTCLIFFE G
KLAUS VOORMANN B
ERIC CLAPTON G
GEORGE MARTIN K
BILLY PRESTON K
TONY SHERIDAN G V
ANDY WHITE D
MICK JAGGER V
KEITH RICHARD V
YOKO ONO V
MARIANNE FAITHFUL V
PATTI BOYD V
GARY LEEDS V
JANE ASHER V
KEITH MOON V
GRAHAM NASH V
SOUNDS INC
LES CONDON HRN
IAN HAMER HRN
EDDIE THORNTON HRN
ALAN BRANSCOMBE SAX
PETER COE SAX
BLACK DYKE MILLS BAND
RONNIE SCOTT SAX
BILL JACKMAN SAX
BILL POVEY SAX
HARRY KLEIN SAX
DAVID JONES TPT
NEIL ASPINAL V
GEOFF EMERICK V
FRANK CLARKE B
ANIL BHAGWAT V
PHIL JONES TPT
NICKY HOPKINS K
JESSIE ROBINS V
BRIAN JONES SAX

EPs

BEATLES HITS	1963	PARLOPHONE	GEP 8880
TWIST & SHOUT	1963	PARLOPHONE	GEP 8882
BEATLES NO 1	1963	PARLOPHONE	GEP 8883
ALL MY LOVIN'	1964	PARLOPHONE	GEP 8891
LONG TALL SALLY	1964	PARLOPHONE	GEP 8913
HARD DAYS NIGHT	1964	PARLOPHONE	GEP 8920
HARD DAYS NIGHT 2	1964	PARLOPHONE	GEP 8924
BEATLES FOR SALE	1965	PARLOPHONE	GEP 8931
BEATLES FOR SALE 2	1965	PARLOPHONE	GEP 8938
MILLION SELLERS	1965	PARLOPHONE	GEP 8946
YESTERDAY	1965	PARLOPHONE	GEP 8948
NOWHERE MAN	1966	PARLOPHONE	GEP 8952
MAGICAL MYSTERY TOUR	1967	PARLOPHONE	SMMT 1
MY BONNIE	19	POLYDOR	H 21 610

(CONTINUED)

LPs

Title		Year	Label	Country	Number
THE BEATLES & TONY SHERIDAN		1962	CONTOUR		CN 2007
THE EARLY YEARS		1962	CONTOUR		2870111
THE BEATLES FIRST		19	POLYDOR		24001
IN THE BEGINNING		19	POLYDOR		2664 107
THIS IS WHERE IT STARTED		19			
PLEASE PLEASE ME	MONO	1963	PARLOPHONE	UK	PMC 1202
"	MONO	1963	PARLOPHONE	UK	PCS 3042
"		1963	EMI	EURO	04219
"		1966	ODEON	JAP	7548
"		1969	APPLE	JAP	AP8675
"		1976	APPLE	JAP	80550
WITH THE BEATLES	MONO	1963	PARLOPHONE	UK	PMC 1206
"	STEREO	1963	PARLOPHONE	UK	PCS 3045
"		196	EMI	EURO	04181
"		1966	ODEON	JAP	7549
"		1969	APPLE	JAP	AP 8678
"		1976	APPLE	JAP	80551
INTRODUCING THE BEATLES		1964	VEE JAY	US	SR1062
NUMBER 2		1964	ODEON	JAP	7058
"		1967	ODEON	JAP	8027
"		1970	APPLE	JAP	8027
"		1976	APPLE	JAP	70101
THE BEATLES		1964	MGM	US	4215
"		1964	ODEON	JAP	7041
"		1967	ODEON	JAP	8026
"		1970	APPLE	JAP	8026
"		1976	APPLE	JAP	70100
MEET THE BEATLES		1964	CAPITOL	US	2047
"		1970	APPLE	JAP	AP 80011
"		1975	APPLE	JAP	80562
NUMBER 5		1964	ODEON	JAP	7103
"		1967	ODEON	JAP	8028
"		1970	APPLE	JAP	8028
"		1976	APPLE	JAP	70102
BEATLES SECOND		1964	CAPITOL	US	2080
"		1970	APPLE	JAP	AP80012
"		1976	APPLE	JAP	80563
SOMETHING NEW		1964	CAPITOL	US	2108
"		19	EMI	EURO	04600
"		1970	APPLE	JAP	80033
"		1976	APPLE	JAP	80564
AINT SHE SWEET		1964		US	
BEATLES STORY		1964	CAPITOL	US	2222
"		1966	ODEON	JAP	7553
"		1969	APPLE	JAP	8676/7
"		1976	APPLE	JAP	77007/8
HARD DAYS NIGHT	MONO	1964	PARLOPHONE	UK	PMC 1230
"	STEREO	1964	PARLOPHONE	UK	PCS 3058
"		1964	EMI	EURO	04145
"		1964	ODEON	JAP	7123
"		1967	ODEON	JAP	8147
"		1970	APPLE	JAP	AP8147
"		1976	APPLE	JAP	80552
"		1964	U A	US	3366 64
BEATLES FOR SALE	MONO	1964	PARLOPHONE	UK	PMC 1240
"	STEREO	1964	PARLOPHONE	UK	PCS 3062
"		1964	EMI	EURO	04200
"		1965	ODEON	JAP	7179
"		1968	ODEON	JAP	8442
"		1976	APPLE	JAP	80553
BEATLES 65		1965	CAPITOL	US	2228
"		1965	EMI	EURO	04201
EARLY BEATLES		1965	CAPITOL	US	2309
"		1970	APPLE	JAP	80034
"		1976	APPLE	JAP	80565
BEATLES VI		1965	CAPITOL	US	2358
"		1970	APPLE	JAP	80035
"		1976	APPLE	JAP	80566
HELP		1965	PARLOPHONE	UK	PMC 1255
"	STEREO	1965	PARLOPHONE	UK	PCS 3071
"		1965	EMI	EURO	04257
"		1965	ODEON	JAP	7387
"		1967	ODEON	JAP	8151
"		1970	APPLE	JAP	8151
"		1970	APPLE	JAP	80060
"		1965	CAPITOL	US	2386
"		1976	APPLE	JAP	80567
RUBBER SOUL	MONO	1966	PARLOPHONE	UK	PMC 1267
"	STEREO	1966	PARLOPHOONE	UK	PCS 3075
"		1966	CAPITOL	US	2442
"		1966	EMI	EURO	04115
"		1966	ODEON	JAP	7450
"		1967	ODEON	JAP	8156
"		1970	APPLE	JAP	8156
"		1976	APPLE	JAP	80555
YESTERDAY & TODAY		1966	CAPITOL	US	2553
"		1970	APPLE	JAP	80061
"					

Title		Year	Label	Country	Number
REVOLVER		1966	PARLOPHONE	UK	PCS 7009
"		1966	CAPITOL	US	2576
"		1966	EMI	EURO	04097
"		1966	ODEON	JAP	7600
"		1968	ODEON	JAP	8443
"		1969	APPLE	JAP	8443
"		1976	APPLE	JAP	80556
COLLECTION OF OLDIES		1967	PARLOPHONE	UK	PCS 7016
"		1967	ODEON	JAP	8016
"		1970	APPLE	JAP	8016
"		1976	APPLE	JAP	80557
SGT PEPPER		1967	PARLOPHONE	UK	PCS 7027
"		1967	CAPITOL	US	2653
"		1967	EMI	EURO	04177
"		1967	ODEON	JAP	8163
"		1969	APPLE	JAP	8163
"		1976	APPLE	JAP	80668
MAGICAL MYSTERY TOUR		1968	CAPITOL	US	2835
"		1976	EMI	UK	PCTC 255
"		1969	APPLE	JAP	9728
"		1976	APPLE	JAP	80569
THE BEATLES WHITE (DBL)		1968	PARLOPHONE	UK	PCS7067/8
"		1968	APPLE	US	101
"		1969	APPLE	JAP	8570/1
"		1976	APPLE	JAP	77001/2
YELLOW SUBMARINE		1969	APPLE	UK	PCS 7070
"		1969	APPLE	IMP	74585
"		1969	EMI	EURO	04002
"		1969	APPLE	JAP	8610
"		1976	APPLE	JAP	80559
"		1969	CAPITOL	US	153
ABBEY ROAD		1969	APPLE	UK	PCS 7088
"		1969	CAPITOL	US	SO 383
"		1969	EMI	EURO	04243
"		1969	APPLE	JAP	8815
"		1976	APPLE	JAP	80560
BEATLES AGAIN		19	EMI	EURO	04348
"		19	APPLE	JAP	8940
LET IT BE		1970	APPLE	UK	PCS 7096
"		1970	APPLE	US	34001
"	BOX SET	1970	APPLE		PXS1
"		1970	EMI	EURO	04433
"		1970	APPLE	JAP	9009
"		1971	APPLE	JAP	AP 80189
"		1976	APPLE	JAP	80561
HEY JUDE		1970	CAPITOL	US	SW 385
"		1970	APPLE		CPCS 106
"		1970	APPLE	JAP	8940
"		1976	APPLE	JAP	80570
1962 66	DBL	1973	PARLOPHONE	UK	PCSP 717
"	DBL	1973	CAPITOL	US	SEBX11842
"	DBL	1973	CAPITOL	US	3403
"	DBL	1973	EMI	EURO	05307
"	DBL	1973	APPLE	JAP	AP 9032
"	DBL	1976	APPLE	JAP	77003/4
1967 70	DBL	1973	PARLOPHONE	UK	PCSP 718
"	DBL	1973	CAPITOL	US	SEBX11843
"	DBL	1973	CAPITOL	US	3404
"	DBL	1973	EMI	EURO	05309/0
"	DBL	1973	APPLE	JAP	AP 9033
"	DBL	1976	APPLE	JAP	77005/6
THE EARLY YEARS		1973	EMI	IMP	2870 111
"		1975	APPLE		2309
PORTRAIT OF		1975	POLYDOR		
RARITIES		19	PARLOPHONE	UK	PMC 1001
LIVE AT THE STAR CLUB HAMBURG		1977	BELLAPHON	GERM	BLS 5560
"		1977	ATLANTIC	US	SD2 7001
"		1977	RCA		7375
LIVE AT THE HOLLYWOOD BOWL		1977	EMI	UK	EMTV 4
"		1977	EMI	EURO	06377
"		1977	CAPITOL	US	SMAS11638
ROCK'N'ROLL		1976	PARLOPHONE	UK	PCSP 719
"		1976	CAPITOL	US	SKBO11537
"		1976	EMI	EURO	06137/8
"		1976	ODEON	JAP	77009
LOVE SONGS		1977	PARLOPHONE	UK	PCS 7211
"		1977	CAPITOL	US	SKBL11711
"		1977	PATHE	FR	C15406550/1
BEATLES BEAT		19	PATHE	FR	C07204363
BEATLES GREATEST		19	PATHE	FR	C06204207
BEATLES TAPES		1977	POLYDOR		2683 068
LIVE AT THE STAR CLUB		1977	LINGASONG		LNL1
LIVE AT THE STAR CLUB		1977	BELLAPHON		15233
BEATLES BALLADS		1980	PARLOPHONE		PCS 7214
HEAR THE BEATLES TELL ALL		1981	CHARLY		CRV 202

B59A BEATLES REVIVAL BAND B59A

Member	Instrument	Records		Title	Year	Label	Country	Number
RICHARD KERSEY	G V	(A		(A) LIVE	1977	TELDEC	GER	623179
ROBBY MATTHES	B V	(A		(B) TAKING MY TIME	1980	INTERCORD	NL	148504
KLAUS LARISEL	G V	(A						
CHRISTIAN ENGEL	D V	(A						

B60 BEAU B60

Member	Instr	LPs
C J T MIDGLEY(BEAU)	G V	(AB
JIM MILNE		(B
STEVE CLAYTON		(B

LP	Year	Label	Country	No.
(A) BEAU	1969	DANDELION	UK	63751
(B) CREATION	1971	DANDELION	UK	DAN 8006

B61 BEAU BRUMMELS B61

Member	Instr	LPs
SAL VALENTINO	V	(ABCDEFGHJ
RON ELLIOTT	G v	(ABCDEFGHJ
RON MEAGHER	G B V	(ABDEFJ
DECLAN MULLIGAN	BG V	(AJ
JON PETERSON	D	(AJBD
WITH		
VAN DYKE PARKS	K	(E
JERRY REED	G	(H
NORBERT PUTNAM	B	(H
DAVID BRIGGS	K	(H
KENNY BUTTREY	D	(H
DAN LEVITT	G BAN	(J
MARK JORDAN	PNO	(J
VICTOR FELDMAN	PERC	(J

LP	Year	Label	Country	No.
(A) INTRODUCING	1965	AUTUMN		SLP 103
(B) BEAU BRUMMELS	19	AUTUMN		SLP 104
(C) BEAU BRUMMELS	1966	PYE		NPL 28062
(D) BEAU BRUMMELS 66	1966	W B		WS 1644
(E) TRIANGLE	1967	W B		WS 1692
(F) BEST OF	1967	VAULT		LPS 114
(G) VOL 44	196	VAULT		LPS 121
(H) BRADLEYS BARN	1968	W B		WS 1760
(J) THE BEAU BRUMMELS	1975	W B		WS 2842
(K) GREATEST HITS	19	JAS		JAS 5000
( ) BEAU BRUMMELS SING	19	POST	US	6000
( ) BEST OF 1964/68	1981	RHINO	US	101

B61A BEAUREGARD B61A

LP	Year	Label	Country	No.
(A) BEAUREGARD	19	SOUND PROD		

B61B D BEAVER B61B

Member	Instr	LPs
D BEAVER	K V	(A
PAUL ALLAN TAYLOR	G V	(A
JIMMY JAMISON	V	(A
CARL MARSH	WIND	(A
JIMMY TARBUTTON	G	(A
LEO LEBLANC	STEEL	(A
TOMMY CATHEY	B	(A
J A SPELL	FDL	(A
DAVID MAYO	V PNO	(A
RUDY GARNER	CLAR	(A
JOEL WILLIAMS	G D	(A
STEVE SPEAR	B	(A
RENI CROOK	V	(A
JACKIE COOK	V	(A

LP	Year	Label	Country	No.
(A) COMBINATIONS	1973	TMI		BTLI 0118

B62 BEAVER BROTHERS B62

Member	Instr	LPs
GEOFF GILL	V K G B D	(A
CLIFF WADE	K V	(A
CAPRIOL SINGERS	V	(A

LP	Year	Label	Country	No.
(A) VENTRILOQUISMS	197	AURA		AUL 701

B63 BEAVER & KRAUSE B63

Member	Instr	LPs
PAUL BEAVER	K SYN	(ALL
BERNARD KRAUSE	K SYN	(ALL
WITH		
MIKE BLOOMFIELD	G	(C
RAY BROWN	B	(C
RIK ELSWIT	G	(C
LEE CHARLTON	D	(C
ROD ELLICOTT	B	(C
LAMONT JOHNSON	K	(C
GEORGE MARCH	D	(C
HOWARD ROBERTS	G	(ABC
CLYDIE KING	V	(C
MILT HOLLAND	PERC	(AB
RON LEE HICKLIN	V	(CD
EDNA WRIGHT	V	(CD
ADRIENNE ANDERSON	V	(D
MIKE LANG	K	(C
RONNIE MONTROSE	G	(C
BUD SHANK	SAX	(AAB
PAUL LAGOS	D	(A
EVENGELINE CARMICHAEL	V	(CD
BILL KING	V	(CD
ELIZABETH WILSON	V	(D
GAIL LANGTON	HARP	(C
GERRY MULLIGAN	SAX	(C
PATRICE HOLLOWAY	V	(C
DAVE GRUISIN	K	(A
VANETTA FIELDS	V	(CD
LEWIS MOCFORD	C	(CD
CRIS WILLIAMSON	V	(D

LP	Year	Label	Country	No.
(A) RAGNAROK ELECTRONIC FUNK	1969	LIMELIGHT	US	86069
(B) IN A WILD SANCTUARY	1970	W B		WS 1850
(C) GANDHARVA	1971	W B	US	WS 1909
(C) GANDHARVA	1971	W B	UK	K 46130
(D) ALL GOOD MEN	1972	W B	UK	K 46184
(D) ALL GOOD MEN	1972	W B	US	BS 2624
(E) GUIDE TO ELECTRONIC MUSIC	1975	NONSUCH	UK	K 73018

B63A BEAVERTEETH B63A

LP	Year	Label	Country	No.
(A) BEAVER TEETH	1977	RCA		1 2076
(B) DAM IT	1978	RCA		1 2574

B64 JEFF BECK B64

Member	Instr	LPs
JEFF BECK	G B	(ALL
WITH		
JET HARRIS	B	(1
VIV PRINCE	D	(1
RAY COOK	D	(2
RON WOOD	G	(AB2
ROD STEWART	V	(AB2
NICKY HOPKINS	K	(AB
TONY NEWMAN	D	(B
MAX MIDDLETON	K	(CDEF
COZY POWELL	D	(CDX
BOB TENCH	G V	(CDX
PHIL CHEN	B	(E
WILBUR BASCOMB	B	(F
FERNANDO SAUNDERS	B V G	(G
JOHN PAUL JONES	ORG	(A
SIMON PHILLIPS	D	(H
TONY HYMAS	K	(H
MO FOSTER	B	(H
STEVE KINDLER	VLN K	(G
TONY SMITH	D V	(G
JAN HAMMER	K	(FGH
MICK WALLER	D	(A
RICHARD BAILEY	D	(EF
AYNSLEY DUNBAR	D	(A
NARADA MICHAEL WALDEN	D	(F
KEITH MOON	D	(A
CLIVE CHAMAN	B	(CDMX

(1) PRE FIRST LP LINE UP (2) PRE FIRST LP LINE UP

LP	Year	Label	Country	No.
(A) TRUTH	1968	COLUMBIA	UK	SCX 6293
(A) TRUTH	1968	EPIC	US	PE 26413
(B) BECK OLA	1969	COLUMBIA	UK	SCX 6351
(B) BECK OLA	1973	PATHE	FE	2C062 90496
(B) BECK OLA	1975	EPIC	US	BN 26478
(AB)TRUTH/ BECK OLA	19	EPIC	US	BC 33779
(C) ROUGH & READY	1971	EPIC UK 64619	US	30973
(D) THE JEFF BECK GROUP	1972	EPIC UK 64899	US	31331
(CD) ROUGH & READY/JEFF BECK GROUP DB	19	EPIC	US	PE 30973
(E) BLOW BY BLOW	1975	EPIC UK 69117	US	33409
(F) WIRED	1976	EPIC UK 86012	US	33849
(G) LIVE	1977	EPIC UK 86025	US	34433
(H) THERE & BACK	1980	EPIC UK 83288		
( ) MASTER OF ROCK	1974	EMI 054 92207 FR	PATHE	06295122
(B) THE MOST OF JEFF BECK	1971	M F P	UK	MFP 5219
( ) BEST OF JEFF BECK	19	CBS	HOLL	92207
(X) GOT THE FEELING & OTHERS (EP)	1972	PLAYBACK		1026
(X) GOT THE FEELING	1972	CBS	US	31546
( ) JEFF BECK GOLDEN DISC	1974	CBS SONY	JAP	ECPN 23

B64A BECK BOGERT & APPICE B64A

Member	Instr	LPs
JEFF BECK	G	(AB
CARMINE APPICE	D	(AB
TIM BOGERT	B	(AB
DANNY HUTTON	V	(A
DUANE HITCHINGS	K	(A
JIM GREENSPOON	PNO	(A

LP	Year	Label	Country	No.
(A) BECK BOGERT & APPICE	1973	EPIC	UK	EPC 65455
(A) BECK BOGERT & APPICE	1973	EPIC	US	KE 32140
(B) LIVE IN JAPAN	1975	EPIC	JAP	EPCO 58
(C) LIVE IN JAPAN (DBL)	1973	CBS/SONY	JAP	ECPJ11/12
(D) ALIVE	1974	EPIC		22001

B65 JOE BECK B65

Musician	Instrument	Albums
JOE BECK	G V	(ALL
STEVE KHAN	G	(C
DON GROLNICK	K	(C
WILL LEE	B	(C
CHRIS PARKER	D	(C
DAVID SANBORN	SAX	(C
SABICAS	G	(D

Album	Year	Label	Country	Number
(A) NATURE BOY	1969	VERVE	US	FTS 3081
(B) WATCH THE TIME	1977	POLYDOR		2391 257
(B) WATCH THE TIME	1977	POLYDOR	US	PD 6092
(C) BECK	1977	KUDU		KU 21
(C) BECK	1975	KUDU	US	KU 2151
(D) ROCK ENCOUNTER	19	POLYDOR		2925 024

B66 BECKETT B66

Musician	Instrument	Albums
ROBERT BARTON	G V	(A
KENNY MOUNTAIN	G V	(A
TERRY WILSON-SLESSER	V	(A
IAN MURRAY	B	(A
KEITH FISHER	D	(A
TIM HINKLEY	K	(A
FRANKIE GIBBONS	B	(

Album	Year	Label	Country	Number
(A) BECKETT	1974	RAFT	UK	RA 48502

B67 HARRY BECKETT B67

Musician	Instrument	Albums
HARRY BECKETT	HRND	(ALL
JOHN SURMAN	SAX	(A
MIKE OSBORNE	SAX	(ABC
ALAN SKIDMORE	SAX	(AC
FRANK RICOTTI	VIBES PERC	(ABC
JOHN TAYLOR	K	(ABC
CHRIS LAURENCE	B	(ABC
JOHN WEBB	D	(ABCE
DARYL RUNSWICK	B	(DE
ROBIN JONES	PERC	(E
ROY BABBINGTON	B	(F
RAY RUSSELL	G	(DEF
NIGEL MORRIS	D	(D
PETE LEMER	K	(F
BRIAN MILLER	K	(DE
MARTIN DAVID	PERC	(DF
ALAN JACKSON	D	(F

Album	Year	Label	Country	Number
(A) FLARE UP	1971	PHILIPS		6308 026
(B) WARM SMILES	1972	RCA		SF 8225
(C) THEME FOR FEGA	1973	RCA		SF 8264
(D) JOY UNLIMITED	1975	CADILLAC		SGC 1004
(E) MEMORIES OF BACARES	1976	OGUN		OG 800
(F) GOT IT MADE	1978	OGUN		OG 020

B68 BECKIES B68

Musician	Instrument	Albums
MICHAEL BROWN	K	(A
MAYO JAMES McALLISTER		(A
GARY HODGDEN		(A
SCOTT TRUSTY		(A

Album	Year	Label	Country	Number
(A) THE BECKIES	1976	SIRE	US	SASD 7159

B68A BECKMEIER BROTHERS B68A

Musician	Instrument	Albums
FRED BECKMEIER	V B	(A
STEVE BECKMEIER	G	(A
DAVID KALISH	G	(A
DAVID SHAW	D	(A
R A MARTIN	K HRNS	(A
GARY FERGUSON	D	(A
NEIL LARSEN	K	(A
RICHIE HAYWARD	D	(A
STEVE BERLIN	SAX	(A

Album	Year	Label	Country	Number
(A) BECKMEIER BROTHERS	1979	CASABLANCA	US	7147

B69 DAVID BEDFORD B69

Musician	Instrument	Albums
DAVID BEDFORD	K	(ALL
WITH		
MICHAEL OLDFIELD	G B	(ABCDEF
CHRIS CUTLER	PERC	(B
DIANE COULSON	V	(D
LUCY BLACKBURN	V	(D
KEVIN AYERS	V	(A
DARYL RUNSWICK	B	(B
MIKE RATLEDGE	SYN	(F
GILBERT BIBERIAN	G	(A
JOHN PEEL	REC	(A
ANDY SUMMERS	G	(E
LAYNE HALSTEAD	OBOE	(E
SOPHIE DICKSON	V	(E
MEGAN POWELL	V	(E
JUDY PLANT	V	(E
OMEGA PLAYERS	G	(A
SEBASTIAN BELL	FLT	(A
ANNE MURRAY	REC	(E
NICOLETTE ALVEY	K V	(E
ELLY LEMOS		(E
DAISY GOODWIN	V	(E
QUEEN'S COLLEGE CHOIR	V	(ADE
ROBERT POWELL	V	(D
ROSALIND KANDLER	REC	(E
VICKY COOPER	V	(E
SERENA MACREADY-SELLARS		(E
MAI DICKSON	V	(E

Album	Year	Label	Country	Number
(A) NURSES SONG WITH ELEPHANTS	1972	DANDELION		2310 165
(B) STARS END	1974	VIRGIN		V 2020
(C) ORCHESTRAL TUBULAR BELLS	1975	VIRGIN		V 2026
(D) RIME OF THE ANCIENT MARINER	1975	VIRGIN		V 2038
(E) ODYSSEY	1976	VIRGIN		V 2070
(E) ODYSSEY	1976	POLYDOR		2933 735
(F) INSTRUCTIONS FOR ANGELS	1977	VIRGIN		V 2090
(F) INSTRUCTIONS FOR ANGELS	1977	POLYDOR		2437 738

B70 BEDLAM B70

Musician	Instrument	Albums
COZY POWELL	D	(A
FRANCESCO AIELLO	V	(A
DENNIS BALL	B	(A
DABE BALL	G	(A
FELIX PAPPALARDI	K	(A
MAX MIDDLETON	K	(A

Album	Year	Label	Country	Number
(A) BEDLAM	1973	CHRYSALIS		CHR 1048

B71 BEE GEES B71

Musician	Instrument	Albums
MAURICE GIBB	V	(ALL
ROBIN GIBB	V	(ALL
COLIN PETERSEN	D	(ABCDEG
DENNIS BYRON	D	(TWZabY
BARRY GIBB	V G	(ALL
VINCE MELOUNEY	G	(ABCD
ALAN KENDALL	G B	(TWYZab
BLUE WEAVER	K	(TWZabY
GARY BROWN	SAX	(a
HAROLD COWART	B	(ac
JOE LALA	PERC	(aWY
HERBIE MANN	FLT	(a
GEORGE TERRY	G	(ac
DANIEL BEN ZEBULON	PERC	(a
BILL PURSE	HRNS	(a
STAN WEBB	HRNS	(a
NEIL BONSANTI	HRNS	(a
PETER GRAVES	HRNS	(a
WHIT SIDENER	HRNS	(a
KENNY FAULK	HRNS	(a
JAMES PANKOW	HRNS	(a
WALTER PARAZAIDER	HRNS	(a
LEE LOUGHNANE	HRNS	(a
JIM WESTLEY	K	(
BRIAN GLASCOCK	D	(
GEOFF BRIDGEFORD	D	(
JIM KELTNER	D	(O
SNEAKY PETE	STEEL	(O
RICK GRECH	B	(O
MANHATTAN HORNS		(
BONAROO HRNS		(WYac
ARIF MARIN	PROD	(T
RAY BARETTO	D	(T
STEPHEN STILLS	PERC	(W

Album	Year	Label	UK	US
(A) BEE GEES FIRST	1967	POLYDOR	UK 583 012	US ATCO 33223
(B) HORIZONTAL	1968	POLYDOR	UK 583 020	US ATCO 33233
(C) RARE PRECIOUS & BEAUTIFUL	1968	POLYDOR	UK 236 221	US ATCO 33264
(D) IDEA	1968	POLYDOR	UK 583 036	US ATCO 33253
(E) RARE PRECIOUS & BEAUTIFUL VOL 2	1968	POLYDOR	UK 236 513	US ATCO 33321
(F) RARE PRECIOUS & BEATIFUL VOL 3	1969	POLYDOR	UK 236 556	
(G) ODESSA	1969	POLYDOR	UK 582049/50	US ATCO 2702
(G) ODESSA	1969	POLYDOR		US RSO 3007
(H) THE BEST OF	1969	POLYDOR	UK 583 063	
(I) CUCUMBER CASTLE	1970	POLYDOR	UK 2383 010	US 33327
(J) SOUND OF LOVE	1970	POLYDOR	UK 2447 005	
(K) TWO YEARS ON	1970	POLYDOR	UK 2310 069	US 33353
(L) MARLEY PURT DRIVE	1970	POLYDOR	UK 2447 012	
(M) TRAFALGAR	1971	POLYDOR	UK 2383 052	US ATCO 7003
(N) TO WHOM IT MAY CONCERN	1972	POLYDOR	UK 2383 139	US ATCO 7012
(O) LIFE IN A TIN CAN	1973	RSO	UK 2394 102	
(P) THE BEST OF VOL 2	1973	RSO	UK 2394 106	US SO 875
(Q) GOTTA GET A MESSAGE TO YOU	1973	CONTOUR	2870 404	
(R) MrNATURAL	1974	RSO	UK 2394 132	
(T) MAIN COURSE	1975	RSO	UK 2394 150	US 3024
(U) PORTRAIT	1975	POLYDOR	UK 2482 092	
(V) S W A L K (SOUNDTRACK)	197	POLYDOR	UK 2383 043	
(W) CHILDREN OF THE WORLD	1976	RSO		US 1 3003
(X) GOLD	197	RSO		US 1 3006
(Y) HERE AT LAST.....LIVE	1977	RSO	UK 2658 120	US 1 3901
(Z) SATURDAY NIGHT FEVER(SOUNDTRACK)	1977	RSO	UK 2658 123	US 2 4001
(a) SPIRITS HAVING FLOWN	1979	RSO	UK RSBG 1	US 1 3041
(b) BEE GEES GREATEST	1979	RSO	UK RSDX001	US 4200
(c) LIVING EYES	1981	RSO	UK RSBG 002	
EARLY DAYS VOL 1	1978	PICKWICK		SHM 971
EARLY DAYS VOL 2	1978	PICKWICK		SHM 973
EARLY DAYS VOL 3	1978	PICKWICK		SHM 982
BONANZA	1978	PICKWICK		PDA 048

(CONTINUED)

B71 (CONTINUED) BEE GEES B71

ALBHY GALUTEN	SYN B PROD	(WYac						
KARL RICHARDSON	PROD	(WYac	JOEY MURCIA	G	(Y	JEFF PORCARO	D	(c
GEORGE BITZER	PROD SYN	(c	CHUCK KIRKPATRICK	G	(c	DON FELDER	G	(c
BOB GLAUB	B	(c	JOE GALDO	D	(c	JOE FARRELL	SAX	(T
DONNY BROOKS	HCA	(c	GARY BROWN	SAX	(Wa	GEORGE PERRY	B	(W
GEOFF WESTLEY	K	(Y	RICHARD TEE	K	(c	RALPH McDONALD	PERC	(c
STEVE GADD	D	(c	RUSS KUNKEL	D	(c	DAVID WOLINSKI	K	(c

B72 CAPTAIN BEEFHEART B72

CAPTAIN BEEFHEART			(A) SAFE AS MILK	1967	BUDDAH	US	BDS 5001
(DON VAN VLIET)	G V HCA	(ALL	(A) SAFE AS MILK	1970	BUDDAH	US	BDS 5063
			(A) SAFE AS MILK	1968	PYE INT	UK	NPL 28110
RY COODER	G	(A	(B) DROP OUT BOOGIE	1967	BUDDAH		2349 002
			(C) STRICTLY PERSONAL	1968	LIBERTY LBR1006		83172
ANTENNAE JIM SEMENS)			(C) STRICTLY PERSONAL	19	UA UAS29540	SUNSET	50208
(JEFF COTTON)	G	(ACDEH	(C) STRICTLY PERSONAL	1968	BLUE THUMB	US	BTS 1
			(C) STRICTLY PERSONAL(ROCKFILE)	19	LIBERTY		LBR 1006
			(D) TROUT MASK REPLICA(DBL)	1969	STRAIGHT	US	STS 1053
ZOOT HORN ROLLO			(D) TROUT MASK REPLICA(DBL)	1969	REPRISE		K 64026
(BILL HARKLEROAD)	G	(DEFGJ	(D) TROUT MASK REPLICA(DBL)	1969	REPRISE	US	RS 2027
			(E) LICK MY DECALS OFF	1970	STRAIGHT	US	STS 1063
ROCKETTE MORTON			(E) LICK MY DECALS OFF	1970	REPRISE		K 44244
(MARK BOSTON)	B G	(DEFGJ	(E) LICK MY DECALS OFF	1970	REPRISE	US	RS 6240
			(E) LICK MY DECALS OFF	19	ELECTROLA		IC 062 92092
ED MARIMBA(ART TRIPP)	K D	(FGJ	(F) SPOTLIGHT KID	1971	REPRISE	UK	K 44162
			(F) SPOTLIGHT KID	1971	REPRISE	US	RS 2050
OREJON (ROY ESTRADA)	B	(G	(G) CLEAR SPOT	1972	REPRISE		UK K54007
			(G) CLEAR SPOT	1972	REPRISE	US	MS 2115
SNOUFFER(ALEX ST CLAIRE)	G	(ACHJ	(H) MIRROR MAN	1971	BUDDAH		2365 022
			(H) MIRROR MAN	1974	BUDDAH		BDLP 4004
DRUMBO (JOHN FRENCH)	D	(ACDEFHLM	(H) MIRROR MAN	19	BUDDAH	US	BDS 5077
			(J) UNCONDITIONALLY GUARANTEED	1974	VIRGIN	UK	V 2015
			(J) UNCONDITIONALLY GUARANTEED	1974	MERCURY	US	SRM1 709
WINGED EEL FINGERLING			(K) BLUEJEANS & MOONBEAMS	1974	VIRGIN	UK	V 2123
(ELLIOT INGBER)	G	(1FK	(K) SHINEY BEAST BAT CHAIN PULLER	1978	W B	US	BSK 3256
JEFF MORRIS TEPPER	G	(LM	(L) CAPT BEEFHEART FILE	1977	PYE	UK	FILD 008
ERIC DREW FELDMAN	B K	(LM	(M) DOC AT THE RADAR STATION	1980	VIRGIN	UK	V 2172
ROBERT WILLIAMS	D	(LM	( ) PLASTIC FACTORY	19	BUDDAH	GER	2318 014
MARC MARCELLINO	K	(CH	(1) LIVE TOUR BAND				
BRUCE FOWLER	TROM	(LM	( ) BONGO FURY	1975	DISCREET		2334
MASCARA SNAKE	CLAR	(DE					

JERRY HANDLEY	B	(ACDEH	HERB BETMEN		(A	RUSS TITELMAN	G	(A
ANDY DIMARTINO	G	(J	DEL SIMMONS	WIND	(J	RHYS CLARK	D	(F
JIMMY CARL BLACK	D	(1	GREG DAVIDSON	G	(1	DOUG MOON	G	(DE
TED CACTUS		(F	MILT HOLLAND	PERC	(G	DEAN SMITH	G	(K
TY GRIMES	PERC	(K	BOB WEST	B	(K	MICHAEL SMOTHERMAN	K V	(K
MARK GIBBONS	K	(K	GENE PELLO	D	(K	JIMMY CARAVAN	K	(K
GARY LEWIS	G	(LM						

B73 BEES MAKE HONEY B73

BARRY RICHARDSON	B SAX	(ABCDE	(A) MUSIC EVERY NIGHT	1972	EMI		EMC 3013
RUAN O'LOCHLAINN	G K SAX	(AB	(B) 1971/72 (C) 1973 (D) 1974 (E) 1974				
MICK MOLLOY	G	(ABCD	( ) BEES MAKE HONEY (SYVIE) (EP)	1977	CHARLY		CEP 117
DEKE O'BRIEN	G	(ABCD					
BOB CEEMANBERG	D	(AB					

FRAN BYRNE	D	(ABCD	CLIFF BILLETT	TPT	(A	GERRY HOGAN	STEEL	(A
MALCOLM MORLEY	G	(C	ROD DEMICK	B	(DE	ED DEAN	G	(E
KEVIN McALEA	PNO	(E	WILLIE FINLAYSON	G	(E	JEDD KELLY	D	(A

B74 BEGGARS OPERA B74

MARTIN GRIFFITHS	V PERC	(ABC	(A) ACT ONE	1970	VERTIGO		6360 018
ALAN PARK	K	(ABCDE	(A) ACT ONE	197	VERVE	US	5080
RAYMOND WILSON	D	(ABC	(B) WATERS OF CHANGE	1971	VERTIGO	UK	6360 054
RICKY GARDINER	G V	(ABCDEF	(C) PATHFINDER	1972	VERTIGO	UK	6360 073
MARSHALL ERSKINE	B FLT	(AB	(D) GET YOUR DOG OFF ME	1973	VERTIGO	UK	6360 090
GORDON SELLAR	B G V	(BCDEF	(E) SAGITTARY	19	JUPITER	GER	88907
VIRGINIA SCOTT	V	(BEF	(F) BEGGARS CANT BE CHOOSERS	19	JUPITER	GER	27702
LINNIE PATERSON	V	(D	(G) LIFELINE	197	VERTIGO	GER	6350 060
COLIN FAIRLIE	D	(DE					
PETE SCOTT	V	(F	CLEM CATTINI	D	(F		

B74A ADRIAN BELEW B74A

ADRIAN BELEW	G D V	(A	(A) LONE RAUNO	1982	ISLAND	UK	ILPS 9675
CHRISTY BLEY	K V	(A					
WILLIAM JANSSEN	SAX V	(A	AUDIE BELEW K (A		J CLIFTON MAYHUGH	B V	(A

B75 GRAHAM BELL B75

GRAHAM BELL	V G	(A	(A) GRAHAM BELL		1972	CHARISMA	UK	CAS 1061
MEL COLLINS	SAX	(A						
RON CORNELIUS	G	(A	TIM DRUMMOND	B	(A	IAN WALLACE	D	(A
TIM HINKLEY	K	(A	BOB WILSON	K	(A	GASPAR LAWAL	PERC	(A
DEREK QUINN	PERC	(A						

B75A JIMMY BELL B75A

JIMMY BELL	PNO	(A	(A) STRANGER IN YOUR TOWN	197	JSP	UK	1007

B76 MADELINE BELL B76

MADELINE BELL	V	(ALL	BELLS A POPPIN'	1967	PHILIPS	SBL 7818
			DOIN' THINGS	1969	PHILIPS	SBL 7865
			MADELINE BELL	1971	PHILIPS	6308 053
			16 STAR TRACKS BY MADELINE BELL	1971	PHILIPS	6308 066
			COMIN' ATCHA	1974	RCA	SF 8393
			THIS IS ONE GIRL	1976	PYE	NSPL18483

B77 MAGGIE BELL B77

Album	Year	Label	Country	Catalogue
(A) QUEEN OF THE NIGHT	1973	POLYDOR		2383 239
(A) QUEEN OF THE NIGHT	1973	ATLANTIC	US	7293
(B) SUICIDE SAL	1975	POLYDOR		2383 313
(B) SUICIDE SAL	1975	SWANSONG	US	SS 8412
(D) GREAT ROCK SENSATION	19	POLYDOR	IMP	2499 107

- MAGGIE BELL V (ABC
- WITH
- REGGIE YOUNG G (A
- CORNELL DUPREE G (A
- JOHN HUGHEY STEEL (A
- MICKEY KEENE G (B
- HUGH McCRACKEN G (A
- LEON PENDARVIS K (A
- BILL SALTER B (A
- SWEET INSPIRATION V (A
- PETE WINGFIELD K (B
- TERRY G (B
- RAY GLYNN G (B
- BILLY LAWRIE V (B
- RICHARD TEE K (A
- BARRY GOLDBERG K (A
- STEVE GADD D (A
- PAUL FRANCIS D (B
- ROY DAVIES K (B
- HUGH BURNS G (B
- JIMMY JEWELL SAX (B
- MARK LONDON V (B
- ARTHUR JENKINS K (A
- CHUCK RAINEY B (A
- RALPH McDONALD PERC (A
- DELISLE HARPER B (B
- BRIAN BREEZE G V (B
- JIMMY PAGE G (B
- CUDDLEY JUDD BAGPIPES (B

B78 WILLIAM BELL B78

Album	Year	Label	US	Country	Catalogue
PHASES OF REALITY	19	STAX	US 3005		2362 027
BOUND TO HAPPEN	1974	STAX			2363 002
COMIN BACK FOR MORE	1977	MERCURY			9100 038
COMIN BACK FOR MORE	19	MERCURY		US	SRM1 1146
ITS TIME YOU TOOK ANOTHER LISTEN	19	MERCURY		US	SRM1 1193
(X) RELATING	19	STAX	US 5502		STX 1010
BOUND TO HAPPEN	19	STAX	US 2014		STX 1050
WOW WILLIAM BELL	19	STAX	US 2037		

- WILLIAM BELL V (ALL
- SWEET INSPIRATION V
- BOOKER T JONES
- AL JACKSON PERC (X
- CARSON WHITSETT K (X
- HORACE SHIPP JR G (X
- DUCK DUNN B (X
- JAMES McDUFF K (X
- HAROLD BEANE G (X
- BOBBY MANUEL G (X

B79 BELL & ARC B79

Album	Year	Label	Country	Catalogue
(A) BELL & ARC	1971	CHARISMA	UK	CAS 1053
(A) BELL & ARC	1971	CBS	US	31142

- MICK GALLAGHER K (A
- GRAHAM BELL V G (A
- TOM DUFFY B (A
- JOHN WOODS PERC (A
- STEVE GREGORY SAX (A
- JEFF CONDON CORNET(A
- ALAN WHITE PERC D(A
- BUD BEADLE SAX (A
- KEN CRADDOCK G (A
- JOHN TURNBULL G (A
- ROB TAIT D (A

B79A BELL &JAMES B79A

Album	Year	Label	Country	Catalogue
(A) BELL & JAMES	1978	A&M US 4728	UK	AMLH64728

- LEROY BELL G D PERC(A
- THOM BELL PROD (A
- CASEY JAMES G B K SYN (A
- YVETTE BENTON V (A
- CARLA BENSON V (A
- M F S B ORCHESTRA (A
- HARRIET THARPE V (A

B80 BELLAMY BROTHERS B80

Album	Year	Label	Country	Catalogue
(A) LET YOUR LOVE FLOW	1976	W B US 2941	UK	K56242
(B) PLAIN & FANCY	1977	W B US 3034	UK	K56357
(C) BEAUTIFUL FRIENDS	1978	W B US 3176	UK	K56485
(D) TWO & ONLY	1979	W B 337		
(E) YOU CAN GET CRAZY	1980	W B	UK	K56777
(F) SONS OF THE SUN	1980	W B	UK	K56872

- DAVID BELLAMY V G(ALL
- HOWARD BELLAMY V G(ALL
- RICHARD BENNETT G (ABC
- DOUG RHONE G (AC
- DENNIS ST JOHN D (A
- ALAN LINDGREN K (ABC
- KING ERRISON PERC (AB
- EMORY GORDY B (AC
- ALAN ESTES PERC (E
- CARL CHAMBERS G (E
- JESSE CHAMBERS B (EF
- BOBBIE HALL PERC (F
- RANDY FERRELL G (F
- MIKE HUEY D (B
- BOBBY BRUCE FDL (E
- JON LAFRANDE K (EF
- CARLOS VEGA D (E
- REINIE PRESS B (C
- MICHAEL LLOYD PROD (F
- JOHN SELK B (B
- DANNY JONES STEEL(EF
- RODNEY PRICE D (EF
- RICKY SKAGGS FDL MAND(F
- RICK SCHLOSSER D (C

B80A BELMONTS B80A

Album	Year	Label	Country	Catalogue
(A) CARNIVAL OF HITS	196	SABRINA	US	5001
(B) SUMMER LOVE	196	DOT	US	25949
(C) CIGARS ACAPPELLA CANDY	1972	BUDDAH	US	5123

- FRED MILANE V (ABC
- ANGELO D'ALEO V (ABC
- FRANK LYNDON V (C
- CARLO MASTRANGELO V (A

B80B PAT BENATAR B80B

Album	Year	Label	Catalogue
(A) IN THE HEAT OF THE NIGHT	1979	CHRYSALIS	CHR1236
(B) CRIME OF PASSION	1980	CHRYSALIS	CHR1245
(C) PRECIOUS TIME	1981	CHRYSALIS	CHR1346
(D) GET NERVOUS	1982	CHRYSALIS	CHR1396

- PAT BENATAR V (ALL
- SCOTT ST CLAIR SHEETS G(ABC
- ROGER CAPPS B V (ABCD
- NEIL GERALDO G K V (ABCD
- MYRON GROMBACHER D (ABCD
- GLEN HAMILTON D (B
- CHARLIE GIORDANO K (D

B81 DAVID BENDETH B81

Album	Year	Label	Catalogue
(A) ADRENALIN	1979	SIDEWALK	SWK 2004
(B) JUST DESERT	1981	ENSIGN	ENVY 502

- DAVID BENDETH PROD G V (AB
- JOHN CLEVELAND HUGHES K (AB
- MARCUS MILLER B (A
- LENNY WHITE D (A
- MEMO ACEVEDO PERC (AB
- FRED BOYER V (AB
- CHUCK BURGI D (B
- MIKE MALONE TPT (B
- DAVID DUNLOP TPT (A
- RANDY BRAMWELL B (AB
- ROBERT BOYER V (AB
- BILLY COBHAM D (AB
- SELWYN PITT V (B
- DON ENGLARD SAX (B
- DAVID SPAN D (A
- JOHN JOHNSON SAX (A
- LOU POMANTI K SYN(B
- MICHAEL STUART SAX (B
- TERRY LUKISKI TROM (B

B81A BRIAN BENNETT B81A

Album	Year	Label	Country	Catalogue
(A) CHANGE OF DIRECTION	1968	COLUMBIA	UK	SCX 6144
(B) THE ILLUSTRATED LONDON PRIDE	1969	STUDIO 2	UK	TWO 268
(C) ROCK DREAMS	1977	DJM	UK	20499
(D) VOYAGE	1978	DJM	UK	20532

- BRIAN BENNETT D (ALL
- ALAN PARKER G (C
- ALAN HAWKSHAW K (C
- LES HURDLE B (C
- TONY RIVERS V (C
- JOHN PERRY V (C
- PETE WILLSHER STEEL (C
- JOE FAGIN V (C
- GRAHAM TODD PNO (C
- STUART CALVER V (C
- JOE BROWN V (C
- TERRY BRITON G (C
- CLIFF RICHARD V (C
- JIM LAWLESS CONGA(C
- ALAN TARNEY B (C

B82 CLIFF BENNETT B82

Musician	Inst	LPs
CLIFF BENNETT	V	(ALL
ROY YOUNG	K V	(B
MICK BURT	D	(B
CHAS HODGES	G	(
MOSS GROVES	SAX	(B
SID PHILLIPS	SAX	(B
JOHN GRAY	B	(E
MAREK KLUCZYNSKI	FLT	(E
DEREK WIER	PERC	(E
ROBERT SMITH	G	(E
BOBBY THOMPSON	B	(B
DAVE WENDELLS	B	(B

LP	Year	Label	Country	Cat. No.
(A)CLIFF BENNETT & THE REBEL ROUSERS	1964	PARLOPHONE	UK	PMC 1242
(B) DRIVING YOU WILD	1966	REGAL ZONOPHONE		REG 1035
(B) DRIVING YOU WILD	1966	M F P	UK	MFP 1121
(C) GOT TO GET YOU INTO MY LIFE	1968	PARLOPHONE	UK	PCS 7017
(D) BRANCHES OUT	1968	PARLOPHONE	UK	PCS 7054
(E) REBELLION	1971	CBS	US	64487
(F) CLIFF BENNETT & THE REBEL ROUSERS	1978	EMI	UK	NUT 14

B83 DUSTER BENNETT B83

Musician	Inst	LPs
DUSTER BENNETT	V G HCA PERC	(ALL
WITH		
PETER GREEN	G	(A
JOHN McVIE	B	(A
HAM RICHMOND	K	(A
STELLA SUTTON	V	(AB
MICK FLEETWOOD	D	(A
TOP TOPHAM	G	(BC
TONY MILLS	B	(BC
NICKY HOPKINS	K	(D
JOHN SIOMOS	D	(D
RICK WILLS	B	(D
HUGH BURNS	G	(D
MORRIS PERT	PERC	(D
PETER FRAMPTON	G	(D
TERRY STANNARD	D	(D
LIZA STRIKE	V	(D
ROB ROBERTSON	B	(D
PHIL WAINMAN	D	(D
PETE WINGFIELD	K	(D
PIP WILLIAMS	G	(D
BARRY ST JOHN	V	(D
LINDA KENDRICK	V	(D
ANN SIMMONDS	V	(D
BOZ BURRELL	B	(D
IAN WALLACE	D	(D
BILLY GRAHAM	HRNS	(D
HOWIE CASEY	HRNS	(D
DICK PARRY	HRNS	(D
REG BROOKS	HRNS	(D
CECIL MOSS	HRNS	(D
JOHNNY HUCKRIDGE	HRNS	(D
MIKE DAVIS	HRNS	(D
JOHN DONNELLY	HRNS	(D
PETER BLUE	B	(B

LP	Year	Label	Country	Cat. No.
(A) SMILING LIKE IM HAPPY	1968	BLUE HORIZON		7 63208
(B) BRIGHT LIGHTS	1969	BLUE HORIZON		7 63221
(C) 12 DBs	1970	BLUE HORIZON		7 63868
(D) FINGERTIPS	1974	TOADSTOOL	AUSTRALIA	L 35436
(E) BENNETT	19	BLUE HORIZON	US	4812
(F) JUSTA	19	BLUE HORIZON	US	4804

B83A BENNINGHOFF'S BAD ROCK BLUES BAND B83A

LP	Year	Label	Country	Cat. No.
(A) CHURCH BACH	1972	SSS	US	17

B84 MARC BENNO B84

Musician	Inst	LPs
MARC BENNO	G V K	(ALL
WITH		
CLARENCE WHITE	G	(B
JESSE ED DAVIS	G	(BC
BOBBY WOMACK	G	(B
JERRY McGEE	G	(AB
CARL RADLE	B	(BCD
JERRY SCHEFF	B	(BA
CHUCK COMANICO	B	(B
GARY ILLINGSWORTH	K	(B
JIM KELTNER	D	(BCD
NICK DE CARO	ACC	(B
RITA COOLIDGE	V	(BA
CLYDIE KING	V	(B
VENETTA FIELDS	V	(B
MIKE UTLEY	K	(C
BOBBY KEYS	SAX	(C
BOOKER T JONES	HRNS G	(C
RAY BROWN	B	(C
BONNIE BRAMLETT	V	(C
ALBERT LEE	G	(D
ERIC CLAPTON	G V	(D
DICK SIMS	K	(D
DICK MORRISSEY	SAX	(D
BOOKER T JONES	K	(A
RY COODER	G	(A
JIM HORN	WIND	(A
JIMMY KARSTEIN	D	(A
SANDY KONIKOFF	TROM	(A
PRISCILLA COOLIDGE	V	(A

LP	Year	Label	Country	Cat. No.
(A) MARC BENNO	1970	A&M	US	SP 4273
(B) MINNOWS	1971	A&M	UK	AMLS64303
(B) MINNOWS	1971	A&M	US	SP 4303
(C) AMBUSH	1972	A&M	UK	AMLS64634
(C) AMBUSH	1972	A&M	US	SP 4364
(D) LOST IN AUSTIN	1979	A&M US 4769	UK	AMLH64767

B84A BENOIT B84A

Musician	Inst	LPs
DAVE BENOIT	K SYN	(AB
DAVE WILLIAMS	B	(A
GARY FERGUSON	D	(AB
WADE SHORT	B	(B
DAVID SHERR	WIND	(A
JOHN WHELLOCK	G	(B
LAURIN RINDER	PERC	(A
MARCELINE VALDEZ	PERC	(B
RON KINK	TPT	(A

LP	Year	Label	Country	Cat. No.
(A) HEAVIER THAN YESTERDAY	1977	AVI	US	6025
(B) CAN YOU IMAGINE	1980	AVI	US	6074

B85 GEORGE BENSON B85

Musician	Inst	LPs
GEORGE BENSON	G V	(ALL
WITH		
RON CUBER	SAX	(ATXI
JIMMY LOVELACE	D	(A
LONNIE SMITH	K	(A
PHIL UPCHURCH	G	(LPTX
JORGE DALTO	K	(LPX
HARVEY MASON	D	(LPX
RALPH McDONALD	PERC	(LPX
LEE RITENOUR	G	(WX
GEORGE DUKE	K	(W
HERBIE HANCOCK	K	(WFX
JOE FARRELL	HRNS	(JYX
RONNIE FOSTER	K	(LPTX
STANLEY BANKS	B	(LPX
JACK McDUFF	K	(RV
DON GROLNICK	K	(TJ
CLIFF CARTER	K	(T
WILBUR BASCOMB	B	(T
WAYNE DOCKERY	B	(TK
MARVIN CHAPELL	D	(TK
RAY ARMANDO	PERC	(TK
JOHNNY GRIGGS	PERC	(TK
SUE EVANS	PERC	(TX
FRED WESLEY	TROM	(T
STEVE LUKATHER	G	(X
JAY BERLINER	G	(XF
RON CARTER	B	(XF
BILLY COBHAM	D	(XF
AIRTO MOREIRA	PERC	(XF
PHIL KRAUS	PERC	(X
STEVE GADD	D	(KTX
ROBERT POWELL	B	(X
CHARLES CONVINTON	K	(X
LEO MORRIS	B	(X
JOHNNY PACHECO	PERC	(X
BURT COLLINS	TPT	(X
JOE SHEPLEY	TPT	(X
MARVIN STAMM	WIND	(X
WAYNE ANDRE	HRNS	(X
ALAN RAPH	HRNS	(X
BUDDY LUCAS	SAX	(X
WILL LEE	B	(KTXJ
EARL KLUGH	G	(XF
DON ASHWORTH	K	(X
GEROME RICHARDSON	K	(X
BOB JAMES	K	(X
ERNIE HAYES	K	(X
GERRY JEMMOTT	B	(X
JEFF PORCARO	D	(X
JAY GRAYDON	G SYN	(X
DAVID PAICH	SYN	(XW
CHUCK FINDLEY	TPT	(X
GARY HERBIG	WIND	(X
VANETTE GLOUD	V	(X
CARMEN TWILLEY	V	(X
BILL CHAMPLIN	V	(X
BILL REICHENBACH	TROM	(X
MIKE BAIRD	PERC	(X
DAVID FOSTER	K SYN	(XW
JAI WINDING	PNO	(X
ARETHA FRANKLIN	V	(X
LOUIS JORDAN	B	(X
BUZZY FEITEN	G	(X
PAULINHO DA COSTA	PERC	(XW
EDDIE DANIELS	SAX	(X

(CONTINUED)

LP	Year	Label	Country	Cat. No.
(A) ITS UPTOWN	1966	CBS	US	CS 9325
(B) GEORGE BENSON COOKBOOK	19	CBS	US	CS 9413
(C) BENSON DURNER (DBL)	19	CBS	US	CH 33569
(D) WILLOW WEEP FOR ME	19	CBS		63533
(E) BEYOND THE BLUE HORIZON	19	CTI	US	CTI 6009
(F) WHITE RABBIT	1972	CTI US 6015	UK	CTI 6
(G) BODY TALK	1974	CTI US 6033	UK	CTI 20
(H) BAD BENSON	1974	CTI	US	CTI 6045
(I) GOOD KING BAD	1976	CTI	UK	CTI 6062
(J) BENSON & FARRELL	1977	CTI	US	CTI 6069
(K) IN CONCERT	1977	CTI	US	CTI 6072
(L) BREEZIN'	1976	W B US 3111	UK	K 56199
(M) SHAPE OF THINGS TO COME	1976	A&M	US	SP 3014
(N) TELL IT LIKE IT IS	197	A&M	US	SP 3020
(O) THE OTHER SIDE OF ABBEY ROAD	1976	A&M	US	SP 3028
(P) IN FLIGHT	1977	W B US 2983	UK	K 56327
(Q) SUMMERTIME	1977	EMBASSY	UK	EMB 31566
(R) BENSON & McDUFF	1977	PRESTIGE	UK	PR 2407
(S) WEEKEND IN L.A. (LIVE) (DBL)	1978	W B	UK	K 66074
(T) SPACE ALBUM	1978	CTI		7085
(U) STORMY WEATHER	19	EMBASSY	UK	EMB 31689
(V) LIVING INSIDE YOUR LOVE	1979	WB	UK	K 66085
(W) GIVE ME THE NIGHT	1980	WB US 3453	UK	K 56823
(X) THE GEORGE BENSON COLLECTION	1981	WB	UK	K 66107
(Y) THE BEST OF	19	CTI		66035

B85 GEORGE BENSON (CONTINUED) B85

MARCY LEVY	V	(X	MARK STEVENS	V	(X	ABRAHAM LABORIEL	B	(XW	JOHN ROBINSON	D	(XW
RICHARD TEE	K	(XW	MICHAEL BODDICKER	SYN	(XW	PATTI AUSTIN	V	(XW	DIVA GRAY	V	(XW
JOCELYN ALLEN	V	(XW	TOM BAHLER	V	(XW	JIM GILSTRAP	V	(XW	JERRY HEY	TPT	(WX
KIM HUTCHCROFT	WIND	(WX	LARRY WILLIAMS	WIND	(WX	ERIC GALE	G	(TXJ	BOBBY LYLE	K	(X
GARY KING	B	(JX	ANDY NEWMARK	D	(KTXJ	DAVID FRIEDMAN	PERC	(X	FRANK VICARI	SAX	(X
GREG PHILLINGANES	PNO	(XW	MICHAEL OMARTIAN	K	(X	HERBERT LAWS	FLT	(KTX	JEROME RICHARDSON	FLT	(X
PHIL BODNER	WIND	(X	PATTI AUSTIN	V	(X	CHAKA KHAN	V	(X	ARTHUR JENKINS	PNO	(X
HAMISH STUART	G	(X	STEVE FERRONE	D	(X	RALPH CRUZ	PERC	(X	EDDIE DANIELS	FLT	(XJ
GEORGE MARGE	FLT	(X	KEN BISCHEL	SYN	(X	RANDY BRECKER	TPT	(TX	GEORGE YOUNG	SAX	(X
MICHAEL BRECKER	SAX	(X	BARRY ROGERS	TROM	(X	MICHAEL MASSER	PNO	(X	QUINCY JONES	PROD	(WX
CARLOS VEGA	D	(W	CLAIRE FISCHER	K	(W	ARIF MARDIN	PROD	(X	SUE EVANS	PERC	(X
NEIL STUBENHAUS	B	(X	TOMMY LIPUMA	PROD	(X	GEORGE RICCI	CELLO	(X	MAX POLLIKOFF	VLN	(X
RONNIE CUBER	SAX	(X	CREED TAYLOR	PROD	(X	EMANUEL VARDI	VLA	(X	RAOWL POLIKIAN	VLN	(X
NICKY MARRERO	PERC	(J	DAVID TOFANI	FLT	(J	SONNY BRAVO	PNO	(J	STEVE KHAN	G	(J
JOSE MADERA	PERC	(J	MICHAEL COLLAZA	PERC	(J						

B85A OSCAR BENTON BLUES BAND B85A

OSCAR BENTON	G V	(ALL	(A) FEEL SO GOOD	1969	DECCA	no 418
H J B HAWKINS	B	(A	(B) BENTON 71	1971	DECCA	SLK 16724
BARRELHOUSE BAILEY	PNO	(ABC	(C) DRAGGIN' AROUND	197	IMPERIAL	054 24550
LONESOME TANNY LANT	D	(AB				
JAY WALKER	B D	(BC				

GUS LAPORTE	G B	(BC	JOHNNY LAPORTE	G	(C	RUUEL BRINK	SAX	(C

B85B > BUSTER BENTON B85B

BUSTER BENTON	G V	(ABC	(A) BLUES BUSTER	19	RED LIGHTNIN' UK	RL 0026
RON SCOTT	SAX	(AB	(B) SPIDER IN MY STEW	1978	RONN US 7536 JAP P VINE	3502
CAREY BELL	HCA	(AB	(C) IS THE FELLING	1980	RONN US 7535	
LAFAYETTE LEAKE	PNO	(AB	(AB) HAVE 8 TRACKS THE SAME)			
JIMMY JOHNSON	G	(AB	(EP) SWEET 94	1980	CHARLY	CTD 119
NOLAN STRUCK	B	(AB				
RAY ALLISON	D	(AB				
BILLY DAVENPORT	D	(B				

MIGHTY JOE YOUNG	G	(B	WILLIE DIXON	B	(B	JAMES GREEN	B	(B

B85C BERLIN BLONDES B85C

(A) BERLIN BLONDES	1980	EMI	UK	3346

B86 BYRON BERLINE B86

BYRON BERLINE	FDL	(ALL	(A) & SUNDANCE	1977	MCA US	2217
			(B) LIVE AT McCABES	1978	TAKAMO US 1061 RI 80	7061

B87 CHUCK BERRY B87

			( ) ROCK ROCK	19	CHESS	US	1515
CHUCK BERRY	G V	(ALL	( ) AFTER SCHOOL SESSIONS	1958	CHESS	US	LP 1426
WITH			( ) ONE DOZEN BERRY'S	1958	CHESS	US	LP 1432
			( ) ONE DOZEN BERRY'S	1958	LONDON	UK	2132
BO DIDDLEY	G	(	( ) CHUCK BERRY IS ON TOP	19	CHESS	US	LP 1435
JOHNNY JOHNSON	PNO	(	( ) ROCKIN' AT THE HOPS	19	CHESS	US	LP 1448
WILLIE DIXON	B	(	( ) NEW JUKE BOX HITS	19	CHESS	US	LP 1456
JASPER THOMAS	D	(	( ) NEW JUKE BOX HITS	1960	PYE INT	UK	NPL 28019
JEROME GREEN	PERC	(	( ) CHUCK BERRY	1960	PYE INT	UK	NPL 28024
OTIS SPANN	PNO	(	( ) CHUCK BERRY	19	CHESS	US	60032
EDDIE HARDY	D	(	( ) CHUCK BERRY	1967	MARBLE ARCH	UK	MAL 611
L C DAVIS	SAX	(	( ) ON STAGE	1960	CHESS	US	LP 1480
JIMMIE ROGERS	G	(	( ) ON STAGE	1960	PYE INT	UK	NPL 28027
FRED BELOW	D	(	( ) MORE CHUCK BERRY	1960	CHESS	US	LP 1465
LAFAYETTE LEAKE	PNO	(	( ) MORE CHUCK BERRY	1960	PYE INT	UK	NPL 28028
G SMITH	B	(	( ) TWIST	1960	CHESS	US	LP 1466
MATT MURPHY	G	(	( ) LATEST & GREATEST	196	PYE INT	UK	NPL 28031
ODIE PAYNE	D	(	( ) YOU NEVER CAN TELL	1964	PYE INT	UK	NPL 28039
PAUL WILLIAMS	PNO	(	( ) YOU NEVER CAN TELL	1967	MARBLE ARCH	UK	MAL 702
THE FIVE DIMENSIONS(GB)		(	( ) GREATEST HITS	1964	CHESS	US	LP 321
MARTHA BERRY	V	(	( ) GREATEST HITS	1964	CHESS	US	LP 1485
WAYNE GABRIEL	G	(	( ) GREATEST HITS	1967	MARBLE ARCH	UK	MAL 660
ADAM IPPOLITO	PNO	(	( ) 2 GREAT GUITARS	1964	PYE INT	UK	NPL 28047
GARY VAN SCYOC	B	(	( ) CHUCK BERRY IN LONDON	1965	CHESS	UK	4005
STAN BRONSTEIN	SAX	(	( ) CHUCK BERRY IN LONDON	1965	CHESS	US	LP 1495
RICK FRANK	D	(	( ) FRESH BERRYS	1965	CHESS	UK	4506
BILLY PEEK	G	(	( ) FRESH BERRYS	1965	CHESS	US	LP 1498
RON NEED	D	(	( ) ST LOUIS TO LIVERPOOL	196	CHESS	US	LP 1488
GREY EDRICK	B	(	( )BACK HOME	196	CHESS	US	LP 1550
ELLIOTT RANDALL	G	(	( ) GOLDEN HITS	1967	MERCURY		61103
WILBUR BASCOMB	B	(	( ) FROM ST LOUIS TO FRISCO	19	MERCURY		6463 015
ERNIE HAYES	PNO	(	( ) AT THE FILLMORE	1967	MERCURY		6463 016
INGRID BERRY	V	(	( ) AT THE FILLMORE	19	MERCURY		SMCL20110
EQUADORS	V	(	( ) MEDLEY	1967	MERCURY		6851 002
STEVE MILLER BAND		(	( ) IN MEMPHIS	1967	MERCURY		6430 022
KENNY BUTTREY	D	(	( ) IN MEMPHIS	19	MERCURY		SMCL20110
JIM MARSALA	B	(	( ) CONCERTO IN B GOODE	1969	MERCURY		61233
BOB WRAY	B	(	( )HOME AGAIN	1971	CHESS		6310 113
PETER JOHN HOGAN	HCA	(	( )ST LOUIS TO FRISCO TO MEMPHIS DBL	1972	PHILIPS		6619 008
CHUCK BERNARD		(	( )ST LOUIS TI FRISCO TO MEMPHIS DBL	1972	MERCURY	US	2 6501
DEREK GRIFFITHS	G	(	( ) THE LONDON SESSIONS	1972	CHESS	UK	6310 122
IAN McLAGEN	K	(	( ) THE LONDON SESSIONS	1972	CHESS	US	50001
KENNY JONES	D	(	( ) THE LONDON SESSIONS	19	CHESS	US	60020
ONNIE McINTYRE	G	(	( ) SAN FRANCISCO DUES	1972	CHESS	UK	6310 115
DAVE KAFINETTI	K	(	( ) SAN FRANCISCO DUES	1972	CHESS		50008
NIC POTTER	B	(	( ) BACK HOME	1972	CHESS		50024
ROBBIE McINTOSH	D	(	( ) GOLDEN DECADE	1972	CHESS	US	1514
			( ) GOLDEN DECADE	1972	CHESS		6641 018
			( ) GOLDEN DECADE VOL 2	1973	CHESS		6641 058
			( ) GOLDEN DECADE VOL 2	1973	CHESS	US	60023
			( ) BIO	1973	CHESS		50043
			( ) BIO	1973	CHESS		6499 650

(CONTINUED)

B87 (CONTINUED)

CHUCK BERRY

B87

	Title		Year	Label	Country	Number
( )	BACK IN THE USA		1973	PHILIPS		6336 216
( )	ALLTIME GREATEST R'N'R PARTY HITS		1974	CHESS		6310 130
( )	ALLTIME GREATEST R'N'R PARTY HITS		1974	CHESS	US	ACB 00208
( )	GOLDEN DECADE VOL 3		1974	CHESS		6641 177
( )	GOLDEN DECADE VOL 3		1974	CHESS		50039
( )	GOLDEN DECADE VOL 3		1974	CHESS	US	60028
( )	I'M A ROCKER		1975	CONTOUR CAN 2019	UK	6870 638
( )	CHUCK BERRY 75		1975	CHESS	UK	9109 101
( )	CHUCK BERRY 75		1975	CHESS US 60032		50047
( )	MOTORVATIN'		1976	CHESS	UK	9286 690
( )	MOTORVATIN'		1976	CHESS	NL	9283 020
( )	GREATEST HITS		1977	ARCHIVE	US	321
( )	SWEET LITTLE SIXTEEN R'N' R HITS		1976	PHILIPS	UK	SON 006
( )	ROCKIT		1979	ATLANTIC	UK	K 50648
( )	ROCKIT		1979	ATCO	US	SD38118
( )	CHUCK BERRY		19	IMPACT	FR	6499671
( )	LOUISIANA		19	CHESS	US	26 130
( )	THE SECOND COMING		19	W B	US	0598
( )	WILD BERRY'S		19	PICKWICK	US	SPC 3392
( )	AMERICA'S HOTEST WAX		19	REELIN'	US	001
( )	FLASHBACK	DBL	19	PICKWICK	US	PTP 2061
( )	THE BEST OF		19	STARDAY	US	
( )	CHUCK BERRY VOL I		19	IMPACT	FR	6886 403
( )	CHUCK BERRY VOL 2		19	IMPACT	FR	6886 407
( )	CHUCK BERRY		19	IMPACT	FR	6995 402
( )	CHUCK BERRY & FRIENDS		19	ARISTOCRAT	US	BR 100
( )	20 GOLDEN GREATS		1979	HAMMER	UK	HMR 9003
( )	SPOTLIGHT		1980	CHESS	UK	1003
( )	MODS & ROCKERS		1980	MERCURY	UK	6336 635
()	GREATEST HITS		1981	WHITE DOVE	UK	957
( )	ROCKIN' WITH		1981	MERCURY	UK	9279140
(EP)	CHUCK & BO		196	PYE INT	UK	NEP 44009
(EP)	CHUCK BERRY		196	PYE INT	UK	NEP 44011
(EP)	CHUCK & BO 2		196	PYE INT	UK	NEP 44012
(EP)	THIS IS CHUCK BERRY		196	PYE INT	UK	NEP 44013
(EP)	CHUCK & BO 3		196	PYE INT	UK	NEP 44017
(EP)	BEST OF		1964	PYE INT	UK	NEP 44018
(EP)	HITS		1964	PYE INT	UK	NEP 44028
(EP)	BLUE MOOD		1965	PYE INT	UK	NEP 44033
(EP)	PROMISED LAND		1964	CHESS	UK	CRE 6002
(EP)	COME ON		1965	CHESS	UK	CRE 6005
(EP)	R& B WITH CHUCK BERRY		196	LONDON	UK	EPU 1053
(EP)	REELIN & ROCKIN		196	LONDON	UK	EPM 1188
(EP)	I GOT A BOOKING		19	CHESS	UK	CRE 6012
(EP)	YOU CAME A LONG WAY FROM ST LOUIS		19	CHESS	UK	CRS 6016

B88

DAVE BERRY

B88

Member	Instr.	
DAVE BERRY	V	(ALL

	Title	Year	Label	Country	Number
(A)	DAVE BERRY	1964	DECCA	UK	LK 4653
(B)	A DOZEN BERRY'S	1966	ACE OF CLUBS	UK	SCL 1218
(C)	SPECIAL SOUND OF DAVE BERRY	1968	DECCA	UK	LK 4823
(D)	DAVE BERRY 68	1968	DECCA	UK	LK 4932
(E)	REMEMBERING	1976	DECCA	UK	REM 3

B89

MIKE BERRY

B89

Member	Instr.	
MIKE BERRY	V	(ALL
MEL JONES	D	(B
GERRY CONWAY	D	(B
KEN LUNDGREN	B	(B
BILLY KUY	G	(B
GEOFF WHITEHORN	G	(B
TERRY BRITTON	G	(B
KEN FREEMAN	SYN	(B
CHAS HODGES	K	(B
CLEM CATTINI	D	(B
ANDY PARKER	G	(B
GRAHAM TODD	K	(B

	Title	Year	Label	Country	Number
(A)	DRIFT AWAY	1972	YORK	UK	FYK 409
(B)	ROCKS IN MY HEAD	1976	POLYDOR	UK	2383 392
(B)	ROCKS IN MY HEAD	1976	SIRE	US	7524
(C)	I'M A ROCKER	1980	EPIC	US	36071

B89A

PETE BEST

B89A

Member	Instr.	
PETE BEST	D V	(A
GEORGE HARRISON	G V	(A
PAUL McCARTNEY	B V G	(A
JOHN LENNON	G V	(A
STUART SUTCLIFFE	B	(A

(A) THE PETE BEST STORY — 1966 SAVAGE 71/2 BEST FAN CLUB 100

B89B

BETHLEHAM ASYLUM

B89B

Member	Instr.	
DANNY FINLAY	G V	(AB
CHARLES DECHANT	WIND V	(AB
CHRISTIAN GANDH	K FLT	(AB
JIMMY NEIMAN	B V	(AB
BUDDY HELM	D	(AB

	Title	Year	Label	Country	Number
(A)	COMMIT THYSELF	1970	AMPEX	US	10106
(B)	BETHLEHEM ASYLUM	1971	AMPEX	US	10124

B90

BETHNAL

B90

Member	Instr.	
GEORGE CSAPO	V K VLN	(AB
EVERTON WILLIAMS	B V	(AB
PETE DOWLING	D	(AB
NICK MICHAELS	G	(AB

	Title	Year	Label	Country	Number
(A)	DANGEROUS TIMES	1978	VERTIGO	UK	9102 020
(B)	CRASH LANDING	1978	VERTIGO	UK	9102 029

B91

DICKIE BETTS

B91

Member	Instr.	
RICHARD(DICKIE)BETTS	G V	(ALL
WITH		
DAVE TOLER	D	(1C
DAN TOLER	G V	(BC
KEN TIBBETTS	B	(B
TOM BROOME	K V	(B
DONNIE SHARBONO	D	(1BC
JERRY THOMPSON	PERC	(
DAVID GOLDFLIES	B	(1C
MICHAEL WORKMAN	K V	(1
DON JOHNSON	V	(B
TOPPER PRICE	HCA	(BC
MICKEY THOMAS	V	(B
VASSAR CLEMENTS	FDL	(A
BUCK	V	(A
BONNIE BRAMLETT	V	(C
CHUCK LEAVELL	PNO	(A
JOHN HUGHEY	STEEL	(A
TOMMY TALTON	G	(A
WALTER POINDEXTER	BAN V	(A
OSCAR UNDERWOOD	MAND	(A
JEFF HANNA	G	(A
DOTTIE	V	(A
CLYDIE KING	V	(C
DAVID WALSHAW	D PERC	(A
JOHNNY SANDLIN	B PERC	(A
STRAY STRATON	B V	(A
FRANK POINDEXTER	DOBRO V	(A
LEON POINDEXTER	G V	(A
REESE WYNANS	HCA	(AC
REBA	V	(A
SHIRLEY MATTHEWS	V (	(C

	Title	Year	Label	Country	Number
(A)	HIGHWAY CALL	1975	CAPRICORN	UK	2429 117
(A)	HIGHWAY CALL	1975	CAPRICORN	US	0123
(B)	DICKIE BETTS & GREAT SOUTHERN	1977	ARISTA	UK	SPARTY 1005
(B)	DICKIE BETTS & GREAT SOUTHERN	1977	ARISTA	US	4123
(C)	ATLANTA BURNING DOWN	1978	ARISTA	UK	SPARTY 1046
(C)	ATLANTA BURNING DOWN	1978	ARISTA	US	4168
(1)	1978 UK TOURING BAND				

B91A BETWEEN B91A

ROBERTO DETREE G (ABCD
JIMMY J GALWAY FLT (A
ROBERT ELISCU WIND (ABCD
COTCH BLACK PERC D(ABC
ULRICH STRANZ (A
PETER MICHAEL HAMEL K (ABCD
GARY TODD B (C
AL GROMER SIT (D
CHARLES CAMPBELL CONGA (CD
FRANZ LEHRNDORFER K (D

(A) EINSTIEG 19 VERTIGO GER 1001
(B) AND THE WATERS OPENED 19 VERTIGO GER 6360 612
(C) DHARANA 19 VERTIGO GER 6360 619
(D) HESSE BETWEEN MUSIC 19 ELECTROLA GER 062 29546

ANATOL ARKUS SYN (C
JERZY ZIEMBROWSKI B (D
PETER MULLER (D
APARNA CHAKRAVARTI TAMB (C
GERT WESTPHAL V (D
TOM VANDERGELD VIBES (D
HOLGER BRANDT D (D
DURU OMSON D (B
BOBBY JONES WIND (D

B91B ALEX BEVAN B91B

ALEX BEVAN G V (A
ROLLY BROWN G (A
JIM NICE B (A

(A) NO TRUTH TO SELL 1971 BIG TREE US 2006

TOM BAKER PNO (A

B91C BHAGAVAN DAS B91C

BHAGAVAN DAS V PERC(A

(A) AH (DBL) 1972 BHAGAVAN DAS US 1080

B91D HANSI BIEBL BAND B91D

HANSI BIEBL G V (A
MICHAEL KASZUBOWSKI B (A
PETER KRAUSE D (A

(A) FIRST 1979 AMIGA GDR 855716

BERND KLEINOW HARP (A

B92 BIG BALLS & THE GREAT WHITE IDIOT B92

ATLI GRUND G V (A
ALFRED GRUND B V (A
PETER GRUND D V (A

(A) BIG BALLS & THE GREAT WHITE IDIOT 1977 NOVA 6 23280

WOLFGANG LORENZ G V (A
BARON ADOLF KAISER V (A

B93 BIG BOPPER B93

BIG BOPPER(J P RICHARDSON V
DIED 1959 IN PLANE CRASH WITH
BUDDY HOLLY

(A) CHANTILLY LACE 1958 MERCURY 20432
(A) CHANTILLY LACE 1974 CONTOUR 6870 531
(A) CHANTILLY LACE 19 PICKWICK US 3565

B93A BIG BROTHER B93A

CHRIS SHAKESPEARE V
NICK GUYLER G
ARNIE COTRELL G V
SIMON TILLEY D
CHRIS BROWN G

(A) ROLLS ON & ROCKS OFF(4 TRACKS) CASSETTE ONLY COMP

RONNIE TAYLOR SAX
BOB PETTIT SAX
JOSS JONES B (
MARTIN WHITE TROM

B94 BIG BROTHER & THE HOLDING COMPANY B94

JANIS JOPLIN V (AB
SAM ANDREWS G B V (ABCD
JAMES GURLEY B (ABCD
DAVID GETZ D PNO (ABCD
PETE ALBIN B G (ABCD
NICK GRAVENITES V (CD
DAVID SCHALLOCK G V (CD
MIKE FINNIGAN K V (CD
KATHY McDONALD V (CD
IRA KAMIN K (C
TOWER OF POWER HRNS (C

(A) BIG BROTHER & THE HOLDING COMPANY 1968 LONDON UK SHT 8377
(A) BIG BROTHER & THE HOLDING COMPANY 1967 FONTANA TL 5457
(A) BIG BROTHER & THE HOLDING COMPANY 1967 MAINSTREAM US 6099
(A) BIG BROTHER & THE HOLDING COMPANY 1967 CBS 9700 US KC 30631
(B) CHEAP THRILLS 1968 CBS UK 63392
(B) CHEAP THRILLS 1968 CBS US PC 9700
(C) BE A BROTHER 1971 CBS UK 64118
(C) BE A BROTHER 1971 CBS US KC 30222
(D) HOW HARD IT IS 1971 CBS US KC 30738

JOHN SIMON PNO (B

B94A BIG DADDY B94A

FRANKIE BRUNSON V (A

(A) BIG DADDY'S BLUES 196 GEE US 704
(B) TWIST PARTY 196 REGENT US 6106

B94B BIG FOOT B94B

ART MUNSON G V (A
VIRGIL BECKHAM B V (A
SPENCER EARNSHAW D (A

(A) BIG FOOT 1968 WINRE US 1004

GERARD BELISLE HRNS V (A
DAVID GARLAND K HRNS V(A

B94C BIG HORN B94C

JOE SHIKANY G V (A
MICHAEL IPSEN B V (A
STEVE ADAMEK D V (A

(A) BIG HORN 1978 CBS US 35618

BOB MARCY WIND V(A
PETER DAVIS K V (A

B95 BIG JOHNS ROCK'N'ROLL CIRCUS B95

BIG JOHN GOODISON V (ALL
PIP WILLIAMS G (A
COLIN FLETCHER K V (A
MIKE GREGORY D (A
PHIL WAINMAN D V (A

(A) ACT 1 1974 DJM DJLPS 438
(B) ACT 2 1975 DJM DJLPS 463
(C) ON THE ROAD 1977 DJM DJF 30511

B95A BIG JOE B95A

BIG JOE V (A
SLY DUNBAR D (A
JOHNNY CLARKE PNO (A
CARLTON DAVIS D (A
EARL SMITH G (A
ANSEL COLLINS ORG (A

(A) KEEP ROCKING & SWINGING 197 ? LAP 001
(B) AFRICAN PRINCESS 1978 TROJAN UK TRLS 152

ROBBIE SHAKESPEARE B (A
BOOFA G (A
BERNARD HARVEY ORG (A
LLOYD SPARKS B (A
TONY CHIN G (A
AUSSIE HEBERT PNO (A

B95B BIG MACEO B95B

MACEO MERRYWEATHER V PNO(A
TAMPA RED G (B
ALFRED ELKINS B (B
CLIFFORD JONES D (B
BIG CRAWFORD B (B

(A) VOLUME ONE 1976 RCA 17204
(B) BIG MACEO 19 RCA FR 730 577

LITTLE T(TYRELL DIXON) D (B
EDDIE BOYD PNO (B
CHARLIE SANDERS D (B

B95C BIG MOUTH B95C

(A) BIG MOUTH 19 SPINDIZZY US 31024

B96 BIG SLEEP B96

JOHN WEATHERS D (A
PHIL RYAN K (A
GARY PICKFORD HOPKINS V G

(A) BLUEBELL WOOD 1971 PEGASUS UK PEG 4

RAY TAFF WILLIAMS G (A
RITCHIE FRANCIS B PNO V (A

B97 BIG STAR B97

ALEX CHILTON V (ABC
CHRIS BELL G V (A
ANDY HUMMELL B (AB
JODY STEPHENS D (ABC
TOMMY CATHY B (C
STEVE CROPPER G (C
CARL MARSH SYN (C
LEE BAKER G (C
TOMMY McCLURE B (C

(A) RADIO CITY 1971 ARDENT US ADS 2803
(B) BIG STAR 1972 ARDENT US ADS 1501
(AB) RADIO CITY/BIG STAR 1978 STAX SXSP 302
(C) THIRD ALBUM 1978 AURA AUL 703
(C) THIRD ALBUM 1978 PVC US 7903

RICHARD ROSEBROUGH D (BC
JIM DICKINSON K G PROD(C
TAPT TARRENT D (C
WILLIAM MURPHY B (C
DANNY JONES (B

B98

BIG THREE (UK)

BRIAN GRIFFITHS G (AB
JOHN GUSTAFSON B (AB
JOHN HUTCHINSON D (A
PETER ROBINSON PNO (B
LES THATCHER BANJO (B
HENRY LOWTHER HRN (B
MICK GRABHAM G (B
JOHN SMITH TUBA (B
NIGEL OLSSON D (B

(A) LIVE AT THE CAVERN (EP) 1963 DECCA UK DFE 8552
(B) RESURECTION 1973 POLYDOR UK 2383 199

B99

BIG THREE (US)

CASS ELLIOTT V (
TIM ROSE V (
DENNY DOHERTY V (

(A) BIG THREE 196 ROULETTE US 42000
( ) BIG THREE 19 FM US 307
( ) LIVE AT RECORDING STUDIO 19 FM US 311

B101

BIG YOUTH

BIG YOUTH PERC V(ALL
TONY CHIN G (E
KEITH STERLING PNO (E
EARL SMITH G (E
SANTA D (E
GEORGE FULLWOOD B (E
EARL LINDO K (E
VINCENT GORDON TROM (E
HERMAN MARQUIS SAX (E
BOBBY ELLIS TPT (E
S MORRIS PERC (E
JUDY MOWATT V (E
STICKY PERC (E
SKINFLESH & BONES BAND (D
RITA MARLEY V (E

(A) SCREAMING TARGET 1973 TROJAN TRLS 61
(B) NATTY CULTURAL DREAD 1976 TROJAN TRLS 123
(C) HIT THE ROAD JACK 1976 TROJAN TRLS 137
(D) DREADLOCKS DREAD 1976 KLIK KLP 9001
(D) DREADLOCKS DREAD 1978 FRONT LINE FL 1014
(E) ISAIAH FIRST PROPHET OF OLD 1978 FRONT LINE FL 1011
(F) REGGAE GI DEM DUB 1979
(G) REGGAE PHENOMENON 1977 BIG YOUTH BYD 1
(H) EVERYDAY SKANK(BEST OF) 19 TROJAN TRLS 189

B101A

TRAVIS BIGGS

TRAVIS BIGGS (A

(A) SOLAR FUNK 1980 MCA US 3154

B102

BIJOU

VINCENT PALMER G V (ABCDE
PHILIPPE DAUGA B V (ABCDE
DYNAMITE YAN D (ABCDE
JEAN WILLIAM THOURY PROD (ABDE
RON MAEL PROD (C
RUSSELL MAEL PROD (C

(A) DANSE AVEC MOI 1977 PHILIPS 9101 138
(B) OK CAROLE 1978 PHILIPS 9101 178
(C) PAS DORMIR 1979 PHILIPS 9101 272
(D) EN PUBLIC 1980 PHILIPS 6313 059
(E) FAMOUS DIMPLES 1981 PHILIPS 6313 139

B103

BILLION DOLLAR BABIES

MICHAEL BRUCE G V (A
NEAL SMITH D (A
DENNIS DUNAWAY B (A
BOB DOLIN K (A
MIKE MARCONI G V (A

(A) BATTLE AXE 1977 POLYDOR UK 2391 273
(A) BATTLE AXE 1977 POLYDOR US 1 6100

B104

TREVOR BILLMUSS

TREVOR BILLMUSS (A

(A) FAMILY APOLOGY 1970 CHARISMA CAS 1017

B104A

BINTANGS

JIM CUOMO WIND (C
LEO PERC (C
GUS PLEINES V HCA (CDE
JAPIE CASTRICUM G PNO (C
JACK VAN SCHIE G (CDE
FRANK KRAAIJEVELD B V (C
HARRY SCHIERBEEK D PERC(C
ALBERT SCHIERBEEK PERC G (C
WILLEM PERC(C

(A) BLUES ON THE CEILING 1969 DECCA NL 6440 676
(B) RIDIN' ON THE 1970 DECCA
(C) GENUINE BULL 1975 RCA NL YHPL10982
(D) NIGHT FIGHTER 1979 ARIOLA NL 200 525
(E) MICKEY FINN 1980 ARIOLA NL 202 119

B104B

BILLY & THE BEATERS

BILLY VERA G V (A
JEFF BAXTER G (A
BRYAN CUMMINGS SAX (A
GEORGE MARINELLI G (A
RON VIOLA SAX (A
JIM EHINGER PNO (A
JERRY PETERSON SAX (A
BEAU SEGAL D (A
CHUCK FIORE B (A
LON PRICE SAX (A

(A) BILLY & THE BEATERS 1981 ALFA

B105

TONY BIRD

TONY BIRD V G (AB
WITH
EMMANUEL RENTZOS K (A
WINSTON DELANDRO G (A
LUCKY RANKU G (A
JOHN KIRKPATRICK CONC/ACC (A
KWA ZULU SINGERS V (A
STEPHEN AMAZING B (A
JOEL REIFF B (B
FRANK CENTENO B (B
BARRY LAZAROWITZ PERC (B
JOHN LISSAUER V K PERC (B
DAVID SAMUELS PERC (B
JOHN CROWDER V (B
RON GETMAN V (B
THEMBA NTINGA V (B
RICHARD BAILEY D (A
JAMES MENE D (A
GRAHAM SMITH HCA (A
T L BEDEAU SAX (A
JEREMY TAYLOR G (A
JOHN SIEGLER B (B
CHRISTOPHER PARKER D (B
CRUSHER BENNETT PERC (B
DOMINIC CORTESE ACC (B
MAERETHA STEWART V (B
LINDA TSHABALALA V (B
GORDON GRODY V (B
FANA DAVID KEKANA V (B
ERNEST BAIDO B (A
ERNEST MOTHLE B (A
SETH SIDANDA V (B
GEORGE LEE SAX (A
ARLEN ROTH G BAN(B
STU WOODS B (B
RICHARD CROOKS D (B
FALUMI PRINCE PERC (B
MORRIS GOLDBERG WIND (B
DEBORAH MACDUFFIE V (B
SELAELO DAN MAREDI V (B
THEMBI MISHALI V (B

(A) TONY BIRD 1976 CBS US 34324 UK 81183
(B) BIRD OF PARADISE 1978 CBS US 34988 UK 82498

B106

BIRDS

RON WOOD G
ALISTAIR McKENZIE V
KIM GARDNER B
TONY MUNROE G
PETE McDANIELS D

(A) HARD UP HEROES (1TRACK) 1974 DECCA DPA 3009/ 10

B107

BIRTH CONTROL

BERND NOSKE D PERC V (ABCFGHI
DIRK STEFFENS G V (D
BRUNO FRENZEL G V (ABCDEFGHI
PETER FEOLLER B V (DFG
HORST STACHELHAUS B (HI
MANFRED VON BOHR D (HI
ZEUS B HELD V SAX K (DFGHI
REINHOLD SOBOTTA K (A
WOLFGANG NEUSER K (C
BERND KOSCHMIDDER B (ABC
JOCKEN VAN GRUMBKOW CELLO (F
FRIEDEMANN LEINER FLT (F
CHRIS NOPPENEY VLA (F
BERND NOSKE D V (K
BRUNO FRENZEL G V (K
JURGEN GOLDSCHMIDT B (K
WOLFGANG HOM K (K

(A) BIRTH CONTROLL 1969 METRONOME MLP15 336
(A) BIRTH CONTROL 1971 CHARISMA CAS1036 PROPHESY US1002
(B) OPERATION 1971 OHR GER 556 015
( ) GOLD ROCK 1973 METRONOME 0040 019
(C) HOODOO MAN 1974 CBS 65316
(D) RE BIRTH 1974 CBS 65963
(E) LIVE 1974 CBS 88088
(F) PLASTIC PEOPLE 1975 CBS 80921
(G) BACKDOOR POSSIBILITIES 1976 BRAIN 0060 019
(H) INCREASE 1977 BRAIN 0060 019 0040 122
(I) TITANIC 1978 BRAIN 0060 149
(J) LIVE 79 1979 BRAIN 0060 240
(K) DEAL DONE AT NIGHT 1980 ARIOLA 203 423

B108 BIRTHA B108

SHELE PINIZZOTTO G V (AB — (A) BIRTHA 1972 PROBE SPBA 6267
LIVER FAVELA V PERC D (AB — (A) BIRTHA 1972 ABC DUNHILL DSK 50127
SHERRY HAGLER K (AB — (B) CANT STOP THE MADNESS 1973 PROBE SPBA 6272
ROSEMARY BUTLER B V (AB

B108A BIRTHDAY PARTY B108A

NICK CAVE V (A — (A) PRAYERS ON FIRE 1981 4AD UK CAD 104
ROWLAND HOWARD G (A
MICK HARVEY G K (A — TRACY PEW WIND (A — PHIL CALVERT D (A

B108B BISCUIT DAVIS B108B

TOM BAILEN G V (A — (A) PLAYING ON THE MOON 1973 FLYING DUTCHMAN US 12014
TODD ZIMMERMAN B (A
BOB THIELE G K V (A — DERRICK HOITSMAN G VLN V(A — ROBERT ANTHOINE D (A

B109 ELVIN BISHOP B109

ELVIN BISHOP G V (ALL — (A) ELVIN BISHOP 1969 FILLMORE 30001
WITH — (B) FEEL IT 1970 CBS 30239
STEVEN MILLER PNO (ABEC — (B) FEEL IT 1970 EPIC 64180
JOHN CHAMBERS D (ABC — (C) ROCK MY SOUL 19 EPIC 31563
APPLEJACK HCA (A — (C) APPLEJACK 19 EPIC 65295
ALBERT GIANQUINTO PNO (A — (D) BEST OF (CRABSHAW RISING) 1972 EPIC 33693
ART STAVRO B (A — (E) LET IT FLOW 1974 CAPRICORN UK 2429116
JO BAKER V PERC(BEFC — (E) LET IT FLOW 1974 CAPRICORN US CP 0134
KIP MAERCKLEIN B (BC — (F) JUKE JOINT JUMP 1975 CAPRICORN UK 2429 127
PERRY WALSH V HCA (BC — (F) JUKE JOINT JUMP 1975 CAPRICORN US CP 0151
MIKE CARABELLO PERC (B — (G) STRUTTIN' MY STUFF 1976 CAPRICORN UK 2429 136
CHEPITO AREAS PERC (B — (G) STRUTTIN' MY STUFF 1976 CAPRICORN US CP 0165
POINTER SISTERS V (B — (H) HOMETOWN BOY MAKES GOOD 1976 CAPRICORN UK 2429 147
PHIL AABERG K (EFGHJ — (H) HOMETOWN BOY MAKES GOOD 1976 CAPRICORN US CP 0176
DON BALDWIN D V (EFGHIJ — (I) RAISIN' HELL 1977 CAPRICORN UK 2637 104
JOHN VERNAZZA G (EFGHIJ — (I) RAISIN' HELL 1977 CAPRICORN US 2CP 0185
MICK THOMAS V (EFGHIJ — (J) THE BEST OF 1979 CAPRICORN UK 2429 189
TOY CALDWELL STEEL (E
JOHN SANDLIN G PERC(EF — DICKIE BETTS G (EF — SLY STONE K (E — CHARLIE DANIELS V FDLG(E
ROSS MASON B (F — RICK KELLOGG HCA (F — STEPHEN STILLS G V (F — ROSS HAYASHIDA V (FH
BILL SLAIS K (GHIJ — MIKE KECK K (G — TERRY HANCK SAX (G — RENI SLAIS V (H
DEBBIE CATHEY V (EI — MELVIN SEALS K (IJ — CHUCK BROOKE HRNS (IJ — BOB CLAIRE HRNS (IJ
DAVE GROVER HRNS (IJ — BILL LAMB HRNS (IJ — MIC GILLETTE HRNS (HI — STEVE KUPKA HRNS (HI
GREG ADAMS HRNS (HI — PAUL HORNSBY K (E — BILL MEEKER D (EC — JEROME JOSEPH CONGA(E
DAVID WALSHAW PERC (E — RANDALL BRAMBLETT SAX (E — DAVID BROWN SAX (E — HAROLD WILLIAMS SAX(E
VASSAR CLEMENTS STRINGS(E — GIDEON DANIELS V (E — ANNIE SAMPSON V (E — TOWER OF POWER HRNS(H
JUNE POINTER V (F — MICHAEL BROOKS B(EFGHJI — RON STALLINGS V SAX(C — MILT HOLLAND PERC(C
MEL ELLISON SAX (C — DENNIS MARCELINO SAX (C — DELANEY BRAMLETT G PROD V(C — JIM GORDON CLAR(C
BOBBY BLACK FDL (C — CLYDIE KING V (C — VANETTA FIELDS V (C — GLORIA JONES V (C
SHIRLEY MATTHEWS V (C

B110 STEPHEN BISHOP B110

STEPHEN BISHOP TROM V G(ALL — (A) CARELESS 1976 ABC US 954 UK ABCL 5201
ANDREW GOLD G (A — (B) BISH 1978 ABC US 1082 UK ABCL 5252
MAC CRIDLIN B (A — (C) RED CAB TO MANHATTAN 1980 WB US 3473 UK K 56853
TOMMY VIG PERC (B
MICHAEL STATON V STEEL(AB — VICTOR FELDMAN PERC (A — STEVE PORCARO SYN (B — STEVE PAIETTA ACC (A
LARRY BROWN D (A — LEE RITENOUR G (A — CRAIG DOERGE K (A — REINIE PRESS B (A
JIM GORDON D (A — CHAKA KHAN V (AB — ALAN LINDGREN SYN (A — LARRY KNECHTEL K (A
ERIC CLAPTON G (AC — RAY PIZZI SAX (A — MAX BENNETT B (A — JOHN GUERIN D (A
ART GARFUNKEL V (ABC — TOMMY TEDESCO MAND (A — JEFFREY STATON G V B (ABC — LEAH KUNKEL V (AB
ED SHAUGHNESSY D (B — RAY BROWN B (B — RICK SCHLOSSER D (B — DAVID FOSTER K (B
GREG PHILLINGANES K (B — MIKE McDONALD V (B — LEE SKLAR B (B — ABE LABORIEL B (B
DAVID HUNGATE B (B — JOHN JARVIS K (AB — TOM SCOTT SAX (B — RAY POUNDS D (B
NATHAN WATTS B (B — MICHAEL SEMBELLO G (B — RAY PARKER G (B — PAULINHO DA COSTA PERC(B
KEITH HOLLAR B (B — BILL PAYNE K (B — STEVE CROPPER G (B — NATALIE COLE V (B
HAL ATKINSON D (B — DAVID SHIELDS B (B — BOBBY CHADWICK K (B — ANDY NEWMARK D (C
WILLIE WEEKS B (C — DON GROLNICK K (C — DAVID SPINOZZA G (C — SID McGINNIS G (C
CHRIS STAINTON PNO (C — CLIVE ANSTEE STR (C — JOHN GIBLIN B (C — PHIL COLLINS D (C
CHRIS PARKER D (C — NEIL JASON B (C — HUGH McCRACKEN G (C — JEFF MIRONOV G (C
PHOEBE SNOW V (C — NEIL LARSEN K (C — STEVE GADD D (C — DENNIS BELFIELD D (C
GARY BROOKER PNO (C — JOHN TROPEA G (C — DEAN PARKS G (C — BUZZY FEITEN G (C
MIKE MAINIERI SYN (C — LENNY CASTRO PERC (C — DAVID LASLEY V (C — ARNOLD McCULLER V (C
JAY GRAYDON G (A — BARLOW JARVIS K (A — RUSS KUNKEL D (C

B110A BIZARROS B110A

NICK NICKOLLS V (— (A) LADY DUBONETTE (EP) 1976 GORILLA
GERRY PARKINS G (— (B) BIZARROS 1979 MERCURY US
TERRY WALKER G (— (C) RUBBER CITY REBELS 19 CLONE UK CL001

B111 BILL BLACK COMBO B111

BILL BLACK B (
BOB TUCKER G V (* — BILL BLACK COMBO 19 ZODIAC US 5006
RONNIE SCAIFE G (* — SAXY JAZZ 1960 HI US 32002
ROBERT GLADNEY SAX V (* — SOLID & RAUNCHY 1962 HI US 32003 LONDON UK 2310
PHIL MUNSEY B (* — THAT WONDERFUL FEELING 1961 HI US 32004
BILL COMPTON D (* — MOVIN' 1962 HI US 32004 LONDON UK 2433
GIL MICHAEL STEEL FDL (* — RECORD HOP 196 HI US 32006
LARRY ROGERS HCA (* — LETS TWIST 196 HI US 32006 LONDON UK 2427
DANNY HOGAN V (* — UNTOUCHABLE SOUND 1963 HI US 32009 LONDON UK 8080
BUTCH CARTER V (* — GREATEST HITS 1963 HI US 32012 LONDON UK 8113
PLAYS THE BLUES 196 HI US 32015
PLAYS CHUCK BERRY 1964 HI US 32017 LONDON UK 8187
GOES BIG BAND 1964 HI US 32020
MORE SOULID & RAUNCHY 1965 HI US 32023
ALL TIMERS 1966 HI US 32032
BLACK LACE 1967 HI US 32033
KING OF THE ROAD 1967 HI US 32036
THE MEMPHIS SCENE 1967 MEGA US 1008
THE BEAT GOES ON 1968 HI US 32041 LONDON UK 8367
TURN ON YOUR LOVE LIGHT 1969 HI US 32044 LONDON UK 8373
(CONTINUED) — SOULIN' THE BLUES 1969 HI US 32047 LONDON UK 8389

RAINDROPS KEEP FALLING	1970 CBS	59957
JUKE BOX FAVOURITES	19 MEGA	US 1014 NASHVILLE UK 2003
MORE MAGIC	19 HI	US 32061
ROCK'N'ROLL FOREVER	1973 MEGA	US 5008 NASHVILLE uk 2005
BILL BLACK IS BACK	1974 MEGA	US 600 NASHVILLE UK 2007
GREATEST HITS VOL 2	19 HI	US 32078
SOLID & COUNTRY	1975 HI	US 32088
WORLDS GREATEST HONKY TONK BAND	1975 HI	US 32093
(*) ITS HONKY TONK TIME	1977 HI	US 32104 LONDON UK 140
BLACK WITH SUGAR	19 CBS	UK 63672
MR BEAT	19 HI	US 52604
MEMPHIS TENNESSEE	1977 HI	US 5006
AWARD WINNERS	1977 HI	US 8004

B111A

PABLO BLACK

B111A

PAUL DIXON (

( ) MR MUSIC ORIGINALLY — 1978 STUDIO ONE

B111B

BLACK ACE

B111B

(A) BLACK ACE — 19 ARHOOLIE US 1003

B112

BLACK CAT BONES

B112

(A) BARBED WIRE SANDWICH — 1970 NOVA SDN 15

SIMON KIRKE	D	(
PAUL KOSSOFF	G	(
STU BROOKS	B	(A
TERRY SIMMS		(
ROD PRICE	G V	(A
ROBIN SYLVESTER	PNO	(A
DEREK BROOKS	G	(A
PAUL TILLER		(
STEVE MILLINER	PNO	(A
BOB WESTON	G	(
BRIAN SHORT	V	(A
PHIL LENOIR	D	(A

B113

BLACK HEAT

B113

( ) BLACK HEAT	19	ATLANTIC	US	7237
( ) NO TIME TO BURN	1973	JAM		JAL 104
( ) NO TIME TO BURN	1974	ATLANTIC	US	SD 7294
( ) KEEP ON RUNNING	1975	ATLANTIC	US	18128

B113A

BLACK IVORY

B113A

( ) DONT TURN AROUND	1972	TODAY		1005
( ) FEEL IT	1976	BUDDAH	US	5644
( ) BLACK IVORY	1977	BUDDAH	US	5658
( ) HEAVY HEAVY	1980	BUDDAH	US	5722

B113B

BLACK MERDA

B113B

ANTHONY HAWKINS	G	(A
CHARLES HAWKINS	G	(A
TYRONE HITE	D	(A

(A) BLACK MERDA	197	CHESS 1511		569517
(B) LONG BURN THE FIRE	197	JANUS	US	3042

B114

BLACK OAK ARKANSAS

B114

JIM DANDY MANGRUM	V	(ALL
RICKY REYNOLDS	G	(ABCDEFGHIJN
JIMMY HENDERSON	G	(HIJKLMO
STAN KNIGHT	G	(ABCDEFGHIJKLN
PAT DAUGHERTY	B	(ABCDEFGHIJKLN
RUBY STARR	V	(FKLN
TOMMY ALDRIDGE	D	(CDEFGHIJKLN
A K A DORK JACKSON		
HARVEY JETT	G	(ACEN
GREG REDING	G V K	(
JACK HOLDER	SAX G K	(MO
JOEL WILLIAMS	D	(MO
WAYNE EVANS	D	(ABGN
ANDY TANAS	V B	(MO

( ) THE KNOWBODY ELSE	1969	STAX	US	
(A) BLACK OAK ARKANSAS	1971	ATLANTIC UK 2400180 US ATCO 33354		
(B) BLACK OAK ARKANSAS	19	ATLANTIC	UK	K 40215
(B) KEEP THE FAITH	1972	ATCO	US	SD 33381
(C) IF AN ANGEL CAME TO SEE YOU	1972	ATCO	US	SD 7008
(D) RAUNCH & ROLL	1973	ATLANTIC UK K40451 US ATCO 7019		
(E) HIGH ON A HOG	1974	ATLANTIC	UK	K 40538
(E) HIGH ON A HOG	1974	ATCO	US	SD 7035
(F) STREET PARTY	1974	ATLANTIC	UK	K 50057
(F) STREET PARTY	1974	ATCO	US	36101
(G) HOT & NASTY	1974	ATLANTIC	UK	K 20083
(H) AINT LIFE GRAND	1975	ATLANTIC	UK	K 50150
(I) X RATED	1975	MCA	UK	MCF 2734
(I) X RATED	1975	MCA	US	2155
( ) EARLY TIMES	1975	STAX	US	5504
(J) LIVE MUTHA	1976	ATLANTIC	UK	K50220
(J) LIVE MUTHA	1976	ATCO	US	36128
(K) BALLS OF FIRE	1976	MCA UK 2762	US MCA	2199
(L) 10 YEAR OVERNIGHT SUCCESS	1976	MCA	US	2224
(M) RACE WITH THE DEVIL	1977	CAPRICORN	UK	2429 156
(M) RACE WITH THE DEVIL	1977	CAPRICORN	US	CP 0191
(N) BEST OF	1977	ATCO	US	SD 36150
(O) I'D RATHER BE SAILING	1978	CAPRICORN	US	CP 0207

B114A

BLACK PEARL

B114A

B B FIELDINGS		(A
GEOFF MORRIS		(A
JERRY CAUSI		(A
MOULTY	D	(A

(A) BLACK PEARL	1969	ATLANTIC	US	8220
(B) LIVE	19	PROPHESY	US	1001

B114B

BLACK ROSE

B114B

(A) BLACK ROSE — 1980 CASABLANCA NBLP 7234

LES DUDEK	G V	(A
CHER	V	(A
MAX GRONENTHAL	V	(A
MICHAEL FINNIGAN	K V	(A
TREY THOMPSON	B	(A
DAVID PAICH	V	(A
JOHN TOWNSEND	V	(A
WARREN HAM	V	(A
STEVE PORCARO	K	(A
JAMES NEWTON HOWARD	K	(A
GARY FERGUSON	D	(A
RON RITCHOTTE	G V	(A
MICHAEL BODDICKER	K	(A
PHIL BROWN	G	(A

B115

BLACK SABBATH

B115

TONY IOMMI	G	(ALL
GEEZER BUTLER	B	(ALL
BILL WARD	D V	(ABCDEFGHJ
OZZIE OSBOURNE	V HCA	(ABCDEFGHJ
GERALD WOODRUFFE	K	(G
RONNIE JAMES DIO	V	(JKI
RICK WAKEMAN	K	(E
VINNIE APPICE	D	(K
ROGER BAIN	PROD	(AB

(A) BLACK SABBATH	1970	VERTIGO	UK	V06
(A) "	1974	WWA		WWA 006
(A) "	1977	NEMS	UK	NEL 6002
(A) "	197	WB	US	1871
(A) "	197	WEA		913 193
(A) "	1980	NEMS	UK	6017
(B) PARANOID	1970	VERTIGO	UK	6360 011
(B) "	1975	WB	US	WS4 1887
(B) "	1977	NEMS	UK	NEL 6003
(B) "	19	WB	US	K 3104
(B) "	1980	ARIOLA	NL	203 148
(B) "	19	WEA		913 194

(CONTINUED)

B115 (CONTINUED)

BLACK SABBATH B115

(C) MASTER OF REALITY	1971	VERTIGO	UK	6360 050
(C) "	1974	WWA		WWA 008
(C) "	1977	NEMS	UK	NEL 6004
(C) "	1971	WB	US	BS 2562
(C) "	197	WEA		913 195
(D) BLACK SABBATH 4	1972	VERTIGO	UK	6360 071
(D) "	1974	WWA		WWA 009
(D) "	1977	NEMS	UK	NEL 6005
(D) "	197	WB	US	BS 2602
(D) "	197	WEA		913 196
(E) SABBATH BLOODY SABBATH	1973	VERTIGO	UK	6360 115
(E) "	1974	WWA		WWA 005
(E) 2	197	WB	US	BS 2695
(F) SABOTAGE	1975	VERTIGO	UK	9119 001
(F) "	197	WB	US	BS 2822
(F) "	1980	NEMS	UK	6018
(G) TECHNICAL ECSTACY	1976	VERTIGO	UK	9102 750
(G) "	1976	WB	US	BS 2969
(H) NEVER SAY DIE	1978	VERTIGO	UK	9102 751
(H) "	197	WB	US	K 3186
(I) HEAVEN & HELL	1980	VERTIGO	UK	9102 752
(I) "	1980	VERTIGO	NL	6302 017
(I) "	1980	WB	US	3372
(J) LIVE AT LAST	1980	NEMS CASSETTE	UK	BSC 001
(J) "	1980	ARIOLA	NL	203 049
(K) MOB RULES	1981	VERTIGO	UK	6302 119

COMPILATION ALBUMS

( ) ATTENTION (	1975	VERTIGO		6438 057
( ) ATTENTION (	19	WWA		WWA 101
( ) BLACK SABBATH VOL 2(COMP)	1975	VERTIGO	UK	9199 133
( ) WE SOLD OUR SOULS FOR ROCK'N'ROLL	1976	VERTIGO	UK	6641 335
( ) WE SOLD OUR SOULS FOR ROCK'N'ROLL	1977	NEMS	UK	NALD 101
( ) WE SOLD OUR SOUL FOR ROCK'N'ROLL	19	WB	US	BS 2923
( ) GREATEST HITS	1977	NEMS	UK	NELS 6009
( ) GREATEST HITS	1977	WEA		913 192

B115A BLACK SHEEP B115A

LOUIS GRAMMATICE V (AB
BRUCE TURGEN B (AB
LARRY CROZIER K (AB
DONALD MANCUSE G (AB
RON ROCCO D (A
MIKE BENAFEDE D (B

(A) BLACK SHEEP	1975	CAPITOL	US	11369
(B) ENCOURAGING WORDS	1975	CAPITOL	US	11447

B116 BLACK SLATE B116

DESMOND MAHONEY D (A
KEITH DRUMMOND V (A
CHRIS HANSON G (A
ELROY BAILEY B (A
NICKY RIDGUARD TROM (A
RAY CARNESS SAX (A
CLEDWYN ROGERS G (A
RUDY HOLMES SAX (A
ANTHONY BRIGHTLY K (A
HERSCHEL HOLDER TPT (A

(A) AMIGO	1980	TCD TLDLP 1	ENSIGN	ENVY15
(B) SIRENS IN THE CITY	1981	ENSIGN		ENVY505

B116A BLACK SUN B116A

JACK SIDNEY PERC (A
RONNIE COBEN D (A
STEVE McLOGAN B (A
ARFAN DERSON G (A
WALLY HAMILTON K (A
STEVE LASKER SYN (A
SAM BUCCO G (A
PHIL WALTER K V (A
JEFF SHAPER K (A
LENNY GARCIA V (A
JOHN SPRINGFIELD G V (A
BRUCE McGUINNS K (A
RICHARD ELSON SYN (A
MICHAEL LEONARDO HRNS (A

(A) BLACK SUN	1978	ROCKLAND		2424 181

B117 BLACK UHURU B117

MICHAEL ROSE V (CFFG
PUMA JONES V (CFG
DICKIE SIMPSON V (CFG
SLY DUNBAR D (CDFG
ROBBIE SHAKESPEARE B G (CFG
RUDOLF DENNIS (
DON CARLOS (
DOUGIE BRYAN G (FG
KEITH STERLING ORG (CF
BARRY REYNOLDS G (FG
WINSTON WRIGHT ORG (C
STICKY THOMPSON PERC (FG
SKY JUICE PERC (G
RADCLIFFE BRYAN G (CF
MIKEY CHUNG G (FG
ANSELL COLLINS K (G
RANCHIE McLEAN ORG (FG
ROBERT LYN PNO (FG

(A) LOVE CRISIS	1978	THIRD WORLD		TWS 925
(B) SHOWCASE	197	D ROY		
(C) BLACK UHURU	1979	VIRGIN	UK	1004
(C) BLACK UHURU	1980	BUTT	UK	ONLY2
(D) SINSEMILLA	1980	ISLAND	UK	ILPS 9593
(E) BLACKSOUND OF FREEDOM	1981	GREENSLEEVES	UK	GREL 23
(F) RED	1981	ISLAND	UK	ILPS 9625
(F) RED	1981	ISLAND	GER	203 775
(G) CHILL OUT	1982	ISLAND	GER	204 698

B118 BLACK VELVET B118

PETE MORRIS
CLINTON CREASEY
LYNTON STEEL
BRIAN CLARK

(A) THIS IS BLACK VELVET	1971	BEACON		BENS 16
(B) PEOPLE OF THE WORLD	1972	PYE		NSPL18392
(C) CAN YOU FEEL IT	1973	SEVEN SUN		SUN LP1
(D) LOVE CITY	19	OKEH	US	14130

B119 BLACK WIDOW B119

JIM GANNON V G VIBES (AB
ZOOT TAYLOR K (ABC
KIP TREVOR V G (ABC
CLIVE JONES WIND (ABC
BOB BOND B (A
ROMEO CHALLENGER D (BC
JOHN CULLEY G V (C
GEOFF GRIFFITHS B V (BC
CLIVE BOX D (A

(A) SACRIFICE	1970	CBS US 6786	UK	63948
(B) BLACK WIDOW	1970	CBS		64133
(C) THREE	1971	CBS		64562

B120 BLACKBEARD B120

DENNIS 'BLACKBEARD'BOVELL B G K(AB
NICK BAILEY SYN (B
TONY ROBINSON K (B
ANGUS GAYE D (B
JOHN KPIAYE G (B
JAH BUNNY D (B
PATRICK TENYUE K V (
JULIO FINN HCA (B

(A) STRICTLY DUB WIZE	1978	TEMPUS		TEM 001
(A) STRICTLY DUB WISE	197	LIBERTY (ROCKFILE)		LBR 1013
(B) I WAH DUB	1980	MORE CUT		RDC 2002

B121 BLACKBLOOD B121

BLACKBLOOD

Album	Year	Label	Country	Number
( ) BLACKBLOOD	1976	BRADLEY	UK	BLAK 9001
( ) BLACKBLOOD	19	MAINSTREAM	US	416
( ) BLOOD BROTHER BLOOD SISTER	19	CHRYSALIS	US	1144

B122 BLACKBYRDS B122

Member	Instrument	Albums
KEVIN TONEY	K	(E
KEITH KILLGO	D	(E
JOE HALL	B	(E
ORVILLE SAUNDERS	G	(E
STEPHEN JOHNSON	SAX	(E

Album	Year	Label	Country	Number
(A) BLACKBYRDS FIRST	1975	FANTASY		FT 9444
(B) FLYING START	197	FANTASY		FT 522
(B) FLYING START	197	FANTASY	US	FT 9472
(C) CITY LIFE	197	FANTASY	US	FT 9490
(D) UNFINISHED BUSINESS	197	FANTASY	US	FT 9518
(E) ACTION	1978	FANTASY	UK	FT 534
(E) ACTION	1978	FANTASY	US	FT 9535
(F) BETTER DAYS	1980	FANTASY	UK	9602

B123 BLACKFOOT B123

Member	Instrument	Albums
GREG WALKER	B	(ABCDEF
RICK MEDLOCKE	G V	(ABCDEF
JACKSON SPIRES	D V	(ABCDEF
PAT McCAFFREY	K	(CDE
CHARLIE HARGRETT	G	(ABCDEF
CYNTHIA DOUGLAS	V	(C
ROGER HAWKINS		(
BARRY BECKETT		(
BARBARA WYRICK		(
PAMELA VINCENT	V	(CDE
PETER RUTH	HCA	(D
MELODY McCULLY	V	(D
SUZI STORM	V	(
SHORTY MEDLOCKE	HCA BAN	(DE
HENRY WEEK	PERC	(CDE
DAVID CAVENDER	HRNS	(E
LAURA STRUZICK	V	(
DONNA DAVIS	V	(CDE
DR DAVE CAVENDER	TPT	(E
CUB CODA	HCA	(C

Album	Year	Label	Country	Number
(A) NO RESERVATIONS	1975	ISLAND	UK	ILPS 9326
(B) FLYIN' HIGH	1976	EPIC	US	PE 34378
(C) STRIKES	1979	ATCO US 38112	UK	K50603
(D) TOMCATTIN'	1980	ATCO US 32101	UK	K 50702
(E) MARAUDER	1981	ATCO US 32107	UK	K 50799
(F) HIGHWAY SONG'LIVE'	1982	ATCO	UK	K 50910

B123A J D BLACKFOOT B123A

Member	Instrument	Albums
J D BLACKFOOT		(ALL
STERLING SMITH	B G	(A
JEFF WHITLOCK	G	(A
CRAIG FULLER	G	(A
PHIL STOKES	B	(A
BUDD FOWLER	B K V	(A
DAN WALDRON	D	(A
BILLY CARROLL	D V	(A
GEORGE MOBLEY	G	(A

Album	Year	Label	Country	Number
(A) THE ULTIMATE PROPHECY	1970	MERCURY	US	61288
(B) SONG OF CRAZY HORSE	1974	FANTASY	US	9468
(C) SOUTHBOUND & GONE	1975	FANTASY	US	9487

B124 BLACKFOOT SUE B124

Member	Instrument	Albums
TOM FARMER		(A
DAVE FARMERS		(A
EDDIE GALGA		(A
ALAN JONES		(A

Album	Year	Label	Country	Number
(A) NOTHING TO HIDE	1973	JAM		JAL 104
(B) GUN RUNNING	1975	DJM		DJLPS 455
(C) STRANGERS	1974		US	1007

B124A BLACKJACK B124A

Member	Instrument	Albums
MICHAEL BOLOTIN	V	(AB
BRUCE KULICK	G	(AB
SANDY GENNARO	D	(AB
JIMMY HASLIP	B	(AB
TONY BATTAGLIA	V	(A
JAN MULLANEY	K	(A
CHUCK KIRKPATRICK	V	(A

Album	Details
(A) BLACKJACK	1979 POLYDOR US PD16215 UK 2391 411
(B) WORLDS APART	1980 POLYDOR US PD16279

B124B BLACKSTONE(CAN) B124B

Member	Instrument	Albums
JOHN FINLAY	V	(A
MICHAEL FONFARA	K	(A
PETER HODGSON	B	(A
ZEKE SHEPPARD	HCA V	(A
LARRY LEISHMAN	G V HCA	(A
RICHARD STEINBERG	D	(A
DANNY WEIS	G	(A

Album	Year	Label	Country	Number
(A) ON THE LINE	1972	GRT	CAN	9230 1025

B124C BLACKSTONE(US) B124C

Member	Instrument	Albums
TOM FLYNN	V	(A
KEVIN COLLINS	K	(A
TOM BUTLER	B	(A
DAVE DESROCHERS	G	(A
MAX WEINBERG	D	(A

Album	Year	Label	Country	Number
BLACKSTONE	1971	EPIC	US	30470

B125 BLACKWATER JUNCTION B125

Album	Year	Label	Country	Number
( ) BLACKWATER JUNCTION	1973	MCA		MUPS 469
( ) BLACKWATER JUNCTION	1974	MCA		MCF 2663
( ) BLACKWATER JUNCTION	196	DJM		DJF 20465

B125A TIM BLAKE B125A

Member	Instrument	Albums
TIM BLAKE	SYN	(AB

Album	Year	Label	Country	Number
(A) CRYSTAL MACHINE	1977	EGG		900 545
(B) BLAKES NEW JERUSALEM	1978	EGG 90288 BARCLAY		7005

B125B BLACKWELL B125B

Member	Instrument	Albums
JOHN BUNDRICK	K	(A
GLENN GIBSON	V	(A
TERRY WILSON	B	(A
RANDY DEHART	D	(A
JIMMY SMITH	G	(A

Album	Year	Label	Country	Number
(A) BLACKWELL	1970	ASTRO	us	9010

B125C OTIS BLACKWELL B125C

Member	Instrument	Albums
OTIS BLACKWELL	D	(A

Album	Year	Label	Country	Number
(A) THESE ARE MY SONGS	1978	INNER	US	1032

B125D HAL BLAINE B125D

Member	Instrument	Albums
HAL BLAINE	D	(ABC

Album	Year	Label	Country	Number
(A) DRUMS A GO GO	1966	DUNHILL	US	50002
(B) PSYCHEDELIC	1967	DUNHILL	US	50019
(C) HAVE FUN, PLAY DRUMS	196	DUNHILL	US	50035

B125E JOHN BLAIRE B125E

Member	Instrument	Albums
JOHN BLAIRE	V SIT	(ABC
GEORGIE COPPELA	V	(C
CLIFF CARTER	K	(C
GARY KING	B	(C
STEVE GADD	D	(C
RAY MANTILLA	PERC	(C
KIM CARLSON	V	(C
HIRAM BULLOCK	G	(C
HUGH McCRACKEN	HCA	(C
GORDON GRODY	V	(C
SUE EVANS	PERC	(C
IRENE CARA	V	(C
JOCELYN SHAW	V	(C

Album	Year	Label	Country	Number
(A) MYSTICAL SOUL	1971	A&R	US	7100 002
(B) SOUTHERN LOVE	1976	CBS	US	33950
(C) WE BELONG TOGETHER	1977	CTI	US	7 5004

B125F NORMAN BLAKE B125F

Member	Instrument	Albums
NORMAN BLAKE	G V	(ALL

Album	Year	Label	Country	Number
(A) HOME IN SULPHUR SPRINGS	19	ROUNDER	US	0012
(B) WHISKEY BEFORE BREAKFAST	19	ROUNDER	US	0063
(C) FIELDS OF NOVEMBER	19	FLYING FISH	US	004
(D) LIVE AT McCABES	19			
(E) BLACKBERRY BLOSSOM	19	FLYING FISH		005

B126 RONNEE BLAKLEY B126

RONNEE BLAKLEY K G V(ALL	(A) RONNEE BLAKLEY	1972 ELEKTRA US 75027
ROGER HAWKINS D (B	(B) WELCOME	1975 WB US 2890 UK K 56174
BARRY BECKETT K (B		
DAVID HOOD B (B	PETE CARR G (B	JIMMY JOHNSON G (B
REGGIE YOUNG G (B	EDDIE HINTON G (B	MUSCLE SHOALS HRNS (B
JOHNNY GIMBLE FDL (B	JOHN HUGHEY STEEL (B	BUDDY EMMONS STEEL(B
RANDY McCORMICK V (B	JERRY BRIDGES V (B	GERRY MASTERS B (B

B127 BOBBY BLAND B127

BOBBY BLAND V (ALL	(A) BAREFOOT ROCK AND YOU GOT ME	196 DUKE US X72
WITH	(B) LIKE ER RED HOT	196 DUKE US X73
MIKE OMARTIAN K (LMQN	(C) TWO STEPS FROM THE BLUES	196 DUKE US X74 VOCALION 160183
LARRY CARLTON G (LM	(D) HERES THE MAN	196 DUKE US X75 VOCALION 8041
ED GREENE D (LMQ	(E) CALL ON ME	196 DUKE US X77 VOCALION 8034
PAUL HUBINON HRNS (LM	(F) AINT NOTHIN' YOU CAN DO	196 DUKE US X78 VOCALION 8027
LEW McCREARY HRNS (M	(G) SOUL OF THE MAN	196 DUKE US X79
SID SHARP STRING(LMQ	( ) BEST OF BOBBY BLAND	1973 DUKE US X84
MAXINE WILLARD V (LMQ	( ) BEST OF VOL 2	19 DUKE US X86
JOHN KELSO HRNS (LM	(H) TOUCH OF THE BLUES	19 DUKE US X88 VOCALION 974
ERNIE WATTS HRNS (LMQ	(I) A PIECE OF GOLD	1969 ACTION UK ACLP6006
PETER CHRISTLIEB HRNS (M	(J) SPOTLIGHTING THE MAN	19 DUKE US X89
JULIA TILLMAN V (LMQ	(K) INTROSPECTIVE OF THE EARLY YEARS	19 DUKE US D92 ABC US 92/2
JOE SCOTT TPT (	(L) HIS CALIFORNIA ALBUM	1973 ABC UK ABCL5044 DUNHILL US 50163
PAT HARE G (	(M) DREAMER	1974 ABC UK ABCL5053 DUNHILL US 50169
SCOTT EDWARDS B (Q	(N) TOGETHER FOR THE FIRST TIME	1974 ABC UK ABCD605 DUNHILL US 50190
JAY GRAYDON G (Q	(N) TOGETHER FOR THE FIRST TIME	197 IMPULSE US
RAY PARKER G (Q	(O) TOGETHER AGAIN...LIVE	1976 IMPULSE AMPL 8027
LEE RITENOUR G (Q	(P) GET ON DOWN	1975 ABC UK ABCL5139 ABC US 895
STEVE BARRY PERC (Q	(Q) REFLECTIONS IN BLUE	1977 ABC UK ABCD5196 ABC US1018
CHUCK FINDLEY HRNS (LQ	(R) COME FLY WITH ME	1978 ABC UK ABCL5249 abc US1075
ORRIN WATERS V (Q	(S) GREATEST HITS (CASSETTE)	1979 fairway uk BBBC 1400
LUTHER WATERS V (Q	(T) I FEEL GOOD , I FEEL FINE	1979 MCA MCA US 3157
MICHAEL PRICE V (Q	(U) SWEET VIBRATIONS	1980 MCA UK 5145
DAN WALSH V (Q	(V) WOKE UP SCREAMING	1982 ACE UK CH41
DICK HYDE HRNS (L		
MEL BROWN G (L	DAVID COHEN G (L	MAX BENNETT B (L
BEN BENAY G (LM	DEAN PARKS G (LMQ	JUNIOR PARKER (A
WILTON FELDER B (LMQ	JIM HORN HRNS (MQ	TONY TERRAN HRNS (M
GINGER BLAKE V (LMQ	WAYNE BENNETT G (	B B KING G V (NO
CHUCK RAINEY B (Q	VICTOR FELDMAN PERC (Q	NINO TEMPO HRNS (Q
PHIL UPCHURCH B (U	CURTIS ROBINSON B (U	DAVID ERVIN SYN (U
WARREN HAYGOOD PERC (U	MONK HIGGINS PNO (U	KENNETH ELLIOTT D (U
BILLY McCOY PNO (U	GEORGE SMITH HCA (U	FREDDY ROBINSON G (U
ROGER WALLACE HRNS (U	GEORGE BOHANON TROM (U	SWEET SPIRIT V (UT
DON MYRICK SAX (U	FRED JACKSON HRNS (U	NOLAN SMITH HRNS (U
STEVE MADAIO HRNS (Q	ALSO SEE B B KING FOR LINE UP OF (N)	

B127A BLANKET OF SECRECY B127A

(A) WALLS HAVE EARS — 1982 F BEAT UK LP16

B128 BLAST B128

(A) BLAST — 1980 CBS US 36012

B129 CHARLIE BLEAK B129

CHARLIE BLEAK (A	(A) LET ME IN	1977 PIP US 6817

B129A SERGE BLENNER B129A

SERGE BLENNER (A	(A) LA VOGUE	1980 SKY 042

B130 LYNN BLESSING B130

LYNN BLESSING VIBES HCA (A	(A) SUNSET PAINTER	1969 EPIC US 26488
MEL TELFORD D (A		
WOLFGANG MELZ B (A	JOHN BECK G (A	ROBERT HIRTH G (A
SNEAKY PETE STEEL (A		

B131 CARLA BLEY B131

CARLA BLEY V K (ALL	(A) ESCALATOR OVER THE HILL	1972 JCOA EOTH 3
ROSEWELL RUDD TROM V(ADEFG	(A) ESCALATOR OVER THE HILL	1974 JCOA JT 4001
PERRY ROBINSON CLAR (A	(A) ESCALATOR OVER THE HILL	1974 BARCLAY 840050 1 2
GATO BARBIERI SAX (AB	(A) ESCALATOR OVER THE HILL	1974 JCOA US 1003 4 5
CHARLIE HADEN B V (AF	(B) TROPIC APPETITES	1974 VIRGIN JCOA WATT 1
MIKE MANTLER TPT PNO(ABCDEFGH	(C) 13/3/4	1975 VIRGIN WATT 3
PAUL MOTIAN D PERC(AB	(D) DINNER MUSIC	1977 VIRGIN WATT 6
BOB STEWART V TUBA(ACDEF	(D) DINNER MUSIC	1977 ECM 2313 106
KAREN MANTLER V GLOC(AF	(E) EUROPEAN TOUR	1977 VIRGIN WATT 8
JULIE TIPPETTS V (B	(E) EUROPEAN TOUR	1977 ECM 2313 108
HOWARD JOHNSON WIND (B	(F) MUSIQUE MECANIQUE	1979 WATT WATT 9
DAVID HOLLAND CELLO (B	(F) MUSIQUE MECANIQUE	1979 ECM 2313 109
TONY MARCUS VLN (B	(G) EUROPEAN TOUR LINE UP 78	
CARLOS WARD SAX (DH	(H) SOCIAL STUDIES	1981 WATT WATT 11
TONY DAGRADI WIND (H		
RICHARD TEE K (D	ERIC GALE G (D	CORNELL DUPREE G (D
GORDON EDWARDS B (D	STEVE GADD D (D	ELTON DEAN SAX (EG
GARY WINDO SAX (EF	JOHN CLARK HRNS (EF	TERRY ADAMS PNO (EF
HUGH HOPPER B (EG	ANDREW CYRILLE D (EG	STEVE SWALLOW B (FH
D. SHARPE D (FH	EUGENE SHADBOURNE G (F	SAM BROWN G (
RON McCLURE B (	DON CHERRY TPT PERC (A	JACK BRUCE V B (A
DON PRESTON SYN (A	JOHN McLAUGHLIN G (A	LINDA RONSTADT V (A
PAUL JONES V (A	ORCHESTRA & STRINGS (AC	GARY VOLENTE CLAR (H
JOE DALEY WIND (H	EARL McINTYRE HRNS (H	

B132 BLIFFERT B132

FRED BLIFFERT G V (A	(A) YOU'LL LIKE BLIFFERT	19 0 US 1

B133 BLINKY B133

(A) JUST WE TWO — 19 GORDY US 945

B134 BLIND FAITH B134

ERIC CLAPTON G V	(A) BLIND FAITH	1969 POLYDOR UK 583 059
STEVE WINWOOD K V	(A) BLIND FAITH	1969 RSO US 1 3016
RICK GRECH B V	(A) BLIND FAITH	1969 ATCO US 33304
GINGER BAKER D		

B134A BLISS BAND B134A

PAUL BLISS V K (A	(A) DINNER WITH RAOUL	1978 CBS US 35511
ANDY BROWN B V (A		
NIGEL ELLIOT D (A	ALAN PARK K (A	PHIL PALMER G V (A
MAUREEN McDONALD V (A	VENETTA FIELDS V (A	SHIRLEY MATTHEWS V (A
MIKE McDONALD V (A	KEITH KNUDSON V (A	JEFF BAXTER PROD G STEEL(A
GREG ADAMS HRNS (A	MICK GILLETTE HRNS (A	LENNY PICKETT HRNS (A
EMILLO CASTILLO HRNS (A	STEPHEN KUPKA HRNS (A	VICTOR FELDMAN PERC (A

B135 RORY BLOCK B135

RORY BLOCK V G (ALL	(A)RORY BLOCK	1975 RCA US 10733
WITH	(B) RORY BLOCK (I'M IN LOVE)	1976 BLUE GOOSE BG 2022
BILL PAYNE K (C	(C) INTOXICATION/ BITTER	1977 CHRYSALIS UK CHR 1157
ROLAND JOHN HINES B V (C	(D) YOU'RE THE ONE	1978 CHRYSALIS US CHR 1233
BRIAN LEONARD PERC (A	(E) HIGH HEELED BLUES	1982 ROUNDER US 3061
KEITH BENSON D (D		
BRIAN RUSSELL G (A	FRED LIPSIUS K SAX (A	PENTI GLAN D (A
DICK SMITH PERC (A	AL BRISCOE STEEL (A	DANNY WEISS G (A
PRAKASH JOHN B (A	MICHAEL FONFARA K (A	IAN GUENTHER FDL (A
SAM CLAYTON CONGA V(C	RICK SCHLOSSER D (C	FRED TACKETT G (C
JACK ASHFORD PERC (C	WILLIAM COLLETTE FLT (C	WILLIAM SMITH K (C
JIM HORN SAX (C	RITCHIE HAYWARD D V (C	PAUL STALLWORTH B (C
JOE PORCARO CONGA (C	REV JAMES CLEVELAND CHOIR (C	CINDY BULLENS V (C
ARTIE TRAUM G (B	ROLEY SALLEY B (B	PAT MURRAY CONGA(B
ERIC VALDINA D (B	ALAN SEIDLER PNO (B	KEN KOSEK FDL (B
PROF COTTON KENT K (D	VINCE FAY B (D	JAMES WILLIAMS B (D
LENNY PAKULA K (D	DENNIS HARRIS G (D	LARRY WASHINGTON PERC (D
RONNIE JAMES G (D	T J TINDALL G (D	JIMMY MAELEN PERC (D
GORDON TITCOMB STEEL (D	BOBBY ELI PERC G (D	GRANT MACAVOY D (D
BRUCE GRAY K (D	DEXTER WANSEL SYN (D	VINCE WARSAVAGE PERC (D
BARBARA INGRAM V (D	EVETTE BENTON V (D	CARLA BENSON V (D

B136 BLODWYN PIG B136

JACK LANCASTER WIND (AB	(A) AHEAD RINGS OUT	1969 ISLAND UK ILPS 9101
MICK ABRAHAMS G (AB	(A) AHEAD RINGS OUT	1969 A&M US AM 4210
ANDY PYLE B (AB	(B) GETTING TO THIS	1970 CHRYSALIS UK ILPS 9122
RON BERG D (AB	(B) GETTING TO THIS	1970 A&M US 4243
GRAHAM WALLER K (B		
PETER BANKS G (	CLIVE BUNKER D (	

B137 BLONDE ON BLONDE B137

GRAHAM DAVIS BANJ V G B (C	(A) CONTRASTS	1969 PYE UK NSPL18288
RICHARD JOHN B (B	(A) CONTRASTS	1969 JANUS US 3003
GARETH JOHNSON G (ABC	(B) REBIRTH	1970 EMBER UK NR 5049
DAVE THOMAS HCA B V G (BC	(C) REFLECTIONS ON A LIFE	1971 EMBER UK NR 5058
LES HICKS PERC D(ABC	(D) BLONDE ON BLONDE	1972 EMBER UK
KIP MELLA (C		
RICHARD HOPKINS B K (A	RALPH DENYER G V (A	

B138 (AMAZING)BLONDEL B138

TERRY WINCOTT V G K (ABCDEFGH	(A) AMAZING BLONDEL	1970 BELL UK SBLL 131
EDDIE BAIRD V G (ABCDEFGH	(B) EVENSONG	1970 ISLAND UK ILPS 9136
JIM CAPALDI D (C	(B) EVENSONG	1970 ISLAND US 9303
JOHN GLADWIN V G B (ABCD	(C) FANTASIA LINDUM	1971 ISLAND UK ILPS 9156 US 9310
WILLIAM MURRAY D (FG	(D) ENGLAND 72	1972 ISLAND UK ILPS 9205 US 9327
MICK FEAT G (FGH	(E) BLONDEL	1973 ISLAND UK ILPS 9257 US 9339
EDDIE JOBSON K VLN (F	(F) MULGRAVE STREET	1974 DJM DJF 20443 + DJLPS 443
ALAN SPENNER B (F	(G) INSPIRATION	1975 DJM DJF 20446 + DJLPS446
PAUL KOSSOFF G (F	(H) BAD DREAMS	1976 DJM DJLPS 472
SUE GLOVER V (EF	(H) BAD DREAMS	1976 DJM DJF 20472
SUNNY LESLIE V (EF	(I) LIVE IN TOKYO	1977 DJM 48089
SIMON KIRKE D (EF	(I) LIVE IN TOKYO	1977 DJM DJF 20503
JOHN RABBIT BUNDRICK K (F	(FG) MULGRAVE/INSPIRATION	197 DJM US 2239 701
STEVE WINWOOD B (E		
ADRIAN HOPKINS K (CE	BOZ BURRELL B (F	MICK RALPHS G (F
PAT DONALDSON B (F	PAUL RODGERS V (E	CHRIS KARAN PERC (B
ADAM SKEAPING VLN (B	DAVE SKINNER PNO (G	MEL COLLINS SAX (G
JACK LAROQUE (C	JOHN GILSTON D (H	

B139 BLONDIE B139

DEBBIE HARRY V (ALL	(A) BLONDIE	1976 PRIVATE STOCK PS 2023
CHRIS STEIN G (ALL	(A) BLONDIE	1976 PRIVATE STOCK PVLP 1017
CLEM BURKE D (ABCF456789DEG	(A) BLONDIE	1977 CHRYSALIS UK CHR 1165
JIMMY DESTRI K (ABCDEF789G	(A) BLONDIE	1978 PHONOGRAM FR 6307 616
GARY VALENTINE B (A67	(B) PLASTIC LETTERS	1978 CHRYSALIS UK CHR 1166
FRANK INFANTE B G (BCDE89FG	(B) PLASTIC LETTERS	1978 PHONOGRAM FR 6307 617
NIGEL HARRISON B (CDE9FG	(C) PARALLEL LINES	1978 CHRYSALIS UK CHR 1192
DALE POWERS V (BC	(C) PARALLEL LINES	1978 CHRYSALIS PIC DISC 5001
BILLY O'CONNOR D (123	(C) X OFFENDER	19 SONOPRESSE FR PS 69673
FRED SMITH B (1234	(D) EAT TO THE BEAT	1979 CHRYSALIS UK CDL 1225
JULIE V (1	(E) AUTO AMERICANS	1980 CHRYSALIS UK CDL 1290
ROBERT FRIPP G (C	(F) THE BEST OF BLONDIE	1981 CHRYSALIS UK CHR 1337
WAH WAH WATSON G (E	(G) THE HUNTER	1982 CHRYSALIS UK CHR 1384
JACKIE V (1	(1) AUTUMN 74 (2) OCT 74 JAN 75	(3) JAN 75 MAY 75 (4) MAY 75
IVAN KRAL G (2	(5) MAY 75 AUG 75 (6) AUT 75	(7) OCT 75 AUG 77 (8)AUG 77 (9) NOV 79
TISH V (2		
SNOOKIE V (2	LORNA LOFT V (D	DONNA DESTRI V (D
ELLIE GREENWICH V (D	MIKE CHAPMAN V (D	RANDY HENNES HCA (D
EMIL RICHARDS PERC (E	OLLIE BROWN PERC (E	TOM SCOTT SAX (E
MARK VOLMAN V (E	HOWARD KAYLAN V (E	RANDY HENNES HCA (D
ALEX ACUNA PERC (E	STEVE GOLDSTEIN K (E	RAY BROWN B (E
SCOTT LESSER PERC (E	THE 'B' GIRLS V (E	

BLONKER

B139A … B139A

Member	Instr	Albums
KAY JESSEN	V PERC	(A
THOMAS GRUTZMACHER	B PERC	(A
NICOLAS STALLARD		(A
HELGE TILLMAN		(AB
WOLFGANG SCHLUTER	VIBES	(B
FRANK FISCHIER	B	(B
DIETER GEIKE	G PERC	(AB
JOCHEN PETERSEN	SYN	(B
FRANK HIEBER	B	(B
PETER FRANKEN	PERC	(B

Album	Year	Label	Country	Number
(A) DIE ZEIT STEHT STILL	1979	BRAIN		0060 104
(B) WINDMILLS	1981	PHILIPS	GER	6435 125

BLOOD

B140 … B140

Album	Year	Label	Country	Number
(A) BLOOD	19	ENTERPRISE		ENTF 3002

BLOOD SWEAT & TEARS

B141 … B141

Member	Instr	Albums
AL KOOPER	K V	(AM
BOBBY COLOMBY	D	(ABCDEFGHIJKMZ
STEVE KATZ	V G	(ABCDEM
JIM FIELDER	B	(ABCDEFM
RANDY BRECKER	TPT	(AM
JERRY WEISS	TPT	(AM
DICK HALLIGAN	TROM	(ABCDM
FRED LIPSIUS	PNO SAX	(ABCDM
DAVID CLAYTON THOMAS	V	(BCDHIJKMZ
CHUCK WINFIELD	TPT	(BCDEFM
LEW SOLOFF	TPT	(BCDEFM
BOBBY DOYLE	V	(
JERRY FISCHER	V	(EG
JERRY LA CROIX	V	(G
TONY KLATKA	SAX	(GHIJKZ
LARRY WILLIS	K	(EFGHIJKZ
GEORGE WADENIUS	G	(EFGHI
DAVE BARGERON	TROM	(DEFGHIJKZ
DON HECKMAN	CLAR	(D
RON McCLURE	B	(GHJ
BILL TILLMAN	SAX	(GHIJKZ
JERRY HYMAN	TROM	(BM
ALAN RUBIN	TPT	(B
MIKE SMITH	CONGA	(D
LOU MARINI	WIND	(EF
JOE GIORGIANNI	TPT	(I
STEVE KAHN	G	(IJ
MIKE STERN	G	(IJKZ
DON ALIAS	PERC	(IJKZ
DANNY TRIPHAN	B	(JKZ
FOREST BATCHELL	TPT	(JKZ

Album	Year	Label	Country	Number
(A) CHILD IS FATHER TO THE MAN	1968	CBS	UK	63296
(A) CHILD IS FATHER TO THE MAN	1968	CBS	US	PC 9619
(A) THE FIRST ALBUM	1973	EMBASSY	UK	EMB 31028
(A) THE FIRST ALBUM	1977	EMBASSY	UK	EMB 31492
(B) BLOOD SWEAT & TEARS	1969	CBS	UK	63504
(B) BLOOD SWEAT & TEARS	1969	CBS	US	PC 9720
(C) THREE	1970	CBS	UK	64024
(C) THREE	1970	CBS	US	KC 30090
(D) FOUR	1971	CBS	UK	64355
(D) FOUR	1971	CBS	US	KC 30590
(E) NEW BLOOD	1972	CBS	UK	65252
(E) NEW BLOOD	1972	CBS	US	KC 31780
(F) NO SWEAT	1973	CBS	UK	65725
(F) NO SWEAT	1973	CBS	US	KC 32180
(G) MIRROR IMAGE	1974	CBS	UK	80153
(G) MIRROR IMAGE	1974	CBS	US	KC 32929
(H) NEW CITY	1975	CBS	UK	80784
(H) NEW CITY	1975	CBS	US	PC 33484
(I) IN CONCERT	1976	CBS NL 22006 SONY	JAP	139/140
(J) MORE THAN EVER	1976	CBS	UK	81465
(J) MORE THAN EVER	1976	CBS	US	PC 34233
(K) BRAND NEW DAY	1978	ABC	UK	ABCL 5234
(K) BRAND NEW DAY	1978	ABC	US	1015
(K) BRAND NEW DAY	1978	CARRERE	FR	68055
(BC) BLOOD SWEAT & TEARS/THREE (DBL)	1976	CBS	NL	22015
( ) GREATEST HITS	1972	CBS	US	PC 31170
( ) BLOOD SWEAT & TEARS	1978	HALLMARK		SHM 963
(M) CLASSIC B S T	1980	CBS		31824
(N) NUCLEAR BLUES	1980	MCA	UK	MCF 3061
(Z) 1976 JAPAN TOUR				

Member	Instr	Albums	Member	Instr	Albums	Member	Instr	Albums	Member	Instr	Albums
RON McCURDY	PERC	(K	JIMMY MEAULIN	PERC	(F	TOM MALONE	HRNS	(F	DAVE HENTSCHEL	SYN	(F
FRANK RICOTTI	PERC	(F	PAUL BUCKMASTER	SYN	(F	VALERIE SIMPSON	V	(F	STEVE TYRELL	PERC	(F
GARY KING	B	(J	RICHARD TEEE	K	(J	HUGH McCRACKEN	G	(J	ERIC WEISSBERG	BAN G	(J
BOB JAMES	K	(J	ERIC GALE	G	(J	JOHN FADDIS	TPT	(J	MARVIN STAMM	TPT	(J
DAVE TAYLOR	TROM	(J	ARNIE LAWRENCE	SAX	(J	DAVE FRIEDMAN	PERC	(J	SID WEINBERG	OBOE	(J
PATTI AUSTIN	V	(J	VIVIAN CHERRY	V	(J	LANI GROVES	V	(J	GWEN GUTHRIE	V	(J
YOLANDA McCULLOGH	V	(J	FRANK FLOYD	V	(J	WILLIAM EATON	V	(J	ZACHARY SANDERS	V	(J
CHAKA KHAN	V	(J	WILLIE SMITH	K V	(K	PETE JOLLY		(K	TOMMY MORGAN	HCA	(K
PAUL STALLWORTH	B	(K	PETER GRAVES	HRNS	(K	STU BLUMBERG	TPT	(K	TOM PETERSON	WIND	(K
ERNIE WATTS	HRNS	(K	JOHN ROSENBURG	TPT	(K	JOHN ALTSCHUL	HRNA	(K	JOHN GROSS	SAX	(K
JOHN MITCHELL	HRNS	(K	VANETTA FIELDS	V	(K	BRENDA BRYANT	V	(K	MIKE FINNIGAN	K	(K
CARL GRAVES	V	(K	TISH SMITH	V	(K	ROY HALEE	TPT	(K	BOB PAYNE		(K
GLEN GARRETT		(K	KING ERRISON		(K	RAY REED		(K			

BLOODROCK

B142 … B142

Member	Instr	Albums
STEVE HILL	K V	(ABCDEFG
ED GRUNDY	B V	(ABCDEFG
WARREN HAM	V WIND	(fg
RICK COBB	D PERC	(BCDEF
NICK TAYLOR	G V	(ABCDEFG
JIM RUTLEDGE	V D	(ABCDE
LEE PICKENS	G V	(ABCDE

Album	Year	Label	Country	Number
(A) BLOODROCK	1969	CAPITOL	US	ST 435
(B) BLOODROCK TWO	1970	CAPITOL	US	ST 491
(C) BLOODROCK THREE	1971	CAPITOL	US	EST 765
(D) LIVE	1972	CAPITOL	US	SVBB11038
(E) U S A	1971	CAPITOL	US	SM 645
(F) PASSAGE	1973	CAPITOL	US	SW 11109
(G) WHIRLWIND TONGUES	1973	CAPITOL	US	EST 11259
(H) BLOODROCK'N' ROLL	19	CAPITOL	US	SM 11417

BLOODSTONE

B143 … B143

Member	Instr	Albums
HARRY WILLIAMS	V PERC	(ABCD
CHARLES McCORMICK	B V	(ABCD
CHARLES LOVE	G V	(ABCD
WILLIS DRAFFEN	G	(ABCD
ROGER DURHAM	V PERC	(ABC
EDDIE SUMMERS	D	(A
HARRY WILKINS	G B	(C
DARRYL CLIFTON	D	(C
MARVIN WEBB		

Album	Year	Label	Country	Number
(A) BLOODSTONE	1972	DECCA	UK	TXS 110
(B) NATURAL HIGH	1973	DECCA	UK	SKL 5150
(B) NATURAL HIGH	1973	LONDON	US	620
(C) UNREAL	1974	DECCA	UK	SKL 5156
(C) UNREAL	1974	LONDON	US	634
(D) I NEED TIME	1974	DECCA	UK	SKL 5185
(D) I NEED TIME	1974	LONDON	US	647
(E) RIDDLE OF THE SPHINX	1975	DECCA	UK	SKL 5202
(E) RIDDLE OF THE SPHINX	1975	LONDON	US	654
(F) LULLABY OF BROADWAY	1976	DECCA	UK	SKL 5238
(G) TRAIN RIDE TO HOLLYWOOD	197	LONDON	US	665
(H) DO YOU WANNA DO A THING	197	LONDON	US	671
(J) DONT STOP	1979	TAMLA	UK	STML12097

MIKE BLOOMFIELD

B144 … B144

Member	Instr	Albums
MIKE BLOOMFIELD	K G V	(ALL
MARK NAFTALIN	K	(BCKMN
IRA KAMIN	K	(BCHLM
JOHN KAHN	B	(BCD
BOB JONES	D V	(BCJLKMN
DINO ANDINO	CONGA	(C
NOEL JEWKIS	SAX	(C
JOHN WILMETH	TPT	(C
JESSE ED DAVIS	G	(C
TAJ MAHAL	V	(C
NICK GRAVENITES	V	(BCHJK
AL KOOPER	K V G	(AD
STEPHEN STILLS	V G	(A

Album	Year	Label	Country	Number
(A) SUPER SESSION	1968	CBS	UK	63396
(A) SUPER SESSION	1968	CBS	US	CS 9701
(A) SUPER SESSION	1973	EMBASSY	UK	EMB 31029
(B) ITS NOT KILLING ME	1969	CBS	UK	63652
(C) LIVE AT BILL GRAHAMS FILLMORE WEST	1969	CBS	UK	63816
(C) LIVE AT BILL GRAHAMS FILLMORE WEST	1969	CBS	US	CS 9893
(D) LIVE ADVENTURES	1969	CBS	UK	66216
(E) TRY IT BEFORE YOU BUY IT	1973	CBS	US	PC 33173
(F) TRIUMVIRATE	1973	CBS	UK	65659
(F) TRIUMVIRATE	1973	XBS	US	CS 32172
(G) MILL VALLEY SESSION	1976	POLYDOR		
(H) IF YOU LOVE THOSE BLUES	1977	GUITAR PLAYER	US	3002
(H) IF YOU LOVE THOSE BLUES	1977	SONET	UK	SNTF 726

(CONTINUED)

B144

MIKE BLOOMFIELD (CONTINUED)

(J) ANALINE	1977	TAKOMA	US		1059
(J) ANALINE	1977	SONET	UK	SNTF	749
(J) ANALINE	1977	CBS	US	TRK	82516
(K) COUNT TALENT & THE ORIGINALS	1978	CLOUDS	US		
(L) MICHAEL BLOOMFIELD	1978	TAKOMA	US		1063
(M) BETWEEN THE HARD PLACE	1979	TAKAMO US 7070 LINE	GER		5110
(N) LIVING IN THE FAST LANE	1980	WATERHOUSE	US		11
(N) LIVING IN THE FAST LANE	1981	LINE	GER		5104
(O) LIVE IN ITALY	1980	MAMA BARLEY	IT		001
(P) CRUISIN' FOR BRUISIN'	1981	TAKOMA	US		7091
(R) GOSPEL DUETS	1981	KICKING MULE US/SONET	UK		164
(S) RED HOT & BLUES	1981		US		2328

CARLOS SANTANA	G	(D
DOUG KILMER	B	(HLM
DR. JOHN	PNO G	(F
CHRIS ETHRIDGE	B	(D
ERIC KRISS	K	(H
DAVE SHOREY	B V	(L
JAMES GORDON	HRNS	(F
BENNIE PARKS	PERC	(F
BARRY GOLDBERG	K	(M
JESSIE SMITH	V	(F
ROY RUBY	K	(B
RON STALLINGS	SAX	(BD
MARK ADAMS	HCA	(MN
MARCUS DOUBLEDAY	TPT	(B
DIANE TRIBUNO	V	(B
GEORGE BOHANON	TROM	(F
JOHN HAMMOND	V G HCA	(F
JEROME JUMONVILLE	HRNS	(F
MARK TEEL	SAX	(B
FRED STAEHLE	D	(F
GERALD OSHITA	SAX	(B
SKIP PROKOP	D	(D
TOM DONLINGER	D	(H
CRAIG KILBY	TROM	(L
MARGARET EDMONSON		(O
CARL SEVEREIOL	B	(N
HART McNEE	SAX	(P
CLAY COTTON	K	(KN
SOMA	B	(K
CHUCK BENNETT	TROM	(K
JERRY MARTINI	SAX	(K
ANDREW GOLDSTEIN	TROM	(K
SNOOKY FLOWERS	SAX	(C
ROBBIE MONTGOMERY	V	(F
THOMAS JEFFERSON KAYE	G V	(F
LORRAINE REBENNACK	B	(F
RICHARD SANTI	ACC	(B
FRED OLSEN	G	(B
ACE OF CUPS	V	(B
ELVIN BISHOP	G	(D
HART McNEE	SAX	(H
WOODY HARRIS		(RO
DERRICK WALKER	HCA	(P
HENRY ODEN	B	(P
KING PERKOFF	SAX	(P
DWIGHT DAILY	D	(N
RAY LOECKLE	SAX	(K
TED ASHFORD	K	(K
DENNIS MARCELLINO	SAX	(K
JOHN BOUDREAUX	PERC	(F
ROGER TROY	B	(HJKMN
RICHARD BLUE MITCHELL	HRNS	(F
MICHAEL MELFORD	MAND G V	(B
ANNA RIZZO	V	(JKN
RED RHODES	STEEL	(B
MARCIA ANN TAYLOR	V	(J
ROOSEVELT GOOK	K	(D
DAVE NEDITCH	B	(H
TREVES BLUES BAND		(O
GEORGE MARSH	D	(N
TOM RIZZO	D	(P
FRANK BINER	V	(N
MARCIA ANN TAYLOR	V	(K
CAL LEWISTON	TPT	(K
JACK BLADES	B	(K
MAX HESKETT	TPT	(K

B145

STEVE BLOOMFIELD

(A) ROCKABILLY ORIGINALS — 1978 CHARLY CR 30159

STEVE BLOOMFIELD G (

B145A

BLOOMSBURY PARK

(A) BLOOMSBURY PEOPLE — 1970 MGM US 4678

DING LORENZ	D	(A
DENNIS LANTING	G V	(A
JON WYDERKA	V PERC	(A
GREG JANICK	SAX K	(A
SIGMUND SNOPEK	K TROM	(A
PAUL DUJARDIN	B V TROM	(A

B145B

BLOONTZ

(A) BLOONTZ — 1973 EVOLUTION US 3020

TONY BRAUNAGEL	D	(A
ANDY CHAPMAN	V	(A
DAVID L KEALEY	G	(A
JIMMY DON	G	(A
LINDA LAWLEY	V	(A
MICHAEL JOHN MONTGOMERY	K	(A
STEVE RADNEY	G	(A
SHARON REDD	V	(A
TERRY WILSON	B G	(A
MARGARET DORN	V	(A
ZENOBIA	V	(A

B145C

BLOSSOMS

(A) THE BLOSSOMS — 1972 MGM LION LN 1007

B146

BLOSSOM TOES

(A) WE ARE EVER SO CLEAN	1967	MARMALADE	UK	607001
(B) IF ONLY FOR A MOMENT	1969	MARMALADE	UK	608010

BRIAN GODDING	G V K	(AB
BRIAN BELSHAW	B V	(AB
JIM CREGAN	G V	(AB
KEVIN WESTLAKE	D	(A
SEAN PHILLIPS	SITAR G	(B
BARRY REEVES	D PERC	(B
POLI PALMER	D	(B

B147

BLOW FLY

( ) ZODIAC PARTY	1978	WEIRD WORLD	2031
( ) BLOW FLY PARTY	1980	WEIRD WORLD	2034

B148

BLUE

(A) BLUE	1973	RSO	US		873
(A) BLUE	1973	RSO	UK	2394	105
(B) LIFE IN THE NAVY	1974	RSO	UK	2394	133
(C) ANOTHER NIGHT TIME FLIGHT	1977	ROCKET UK ROLL 7	US		2290
(D) FOOLS PARTY	1979	ROCKET	UK	TRAIN	4

IAN MACMILLAN	B G V	(ABCD
HUGH NICHOLSON	G V K	(ABCD
SMIGGY	G V	(B
TIMI DONALD	D V	(A
BEN KEITH	STEEL	(B
RAY COOPER	PERC	(C
CHARLIE SMITH	D	(CD
DAVID NICHOLSON	B K	(CD

B149

DAVID BLUE

(A) SINGER SONGWRITER (3 TRACKS)	1965	ELEKTRA			
(B) DAVID BLUE	1966	ELEKTRA	US	EKS	74003
(C) 23 DAYS IN SEPTEMBER	1968	REPRISE	US		6293
(D) ME	1970	REPRISE	US	RS	6375
(E) STORIES	1972	ASYLUM		SYL	9001
(E) STORIES	1972	ASYLUM			5052
(F) NICE BABY & THE ANGEL	1973	ASYLUM		SYL	9009
(G) COMIN' BACK FOR MORE	1975	ASYLUM		SYL	9025
(G) COMIN' BACK FOR MORE	1975	ASYLUM			1043
(H) CUPIDS ARROW	1976	ASYLUM UK K53056		SYL	1077

DAVID BLUE(COHEN)	G	(ALL
WITH		
BOB RAFKIN	B G	(EF
RUSS KUNKEL	D	(E
JAMES KARSTEIN	D	(E
DAVID LINDLEY	G VLN	(FH
JOHN BARBATA	D	(E
RY COODER	G	(E
MILT HOLLAND	PERC	(E
RALPH SCHUCKETT	K	(E
PETE JOLLY	ACC	(E
CHRIS ETHRIDGE	B	(EF
HARVEY BROOKS	B	(B
BUDDY SALZMAN	D	(B
GLENN FRAY	V	(F
GRAHAM NASH	G V K	(F
DANNY KOOTCH	G	(G
DAN PEEK	V	(G
BEN KEITH	STEEL	(G
JOHN GUERIN	D V	(G
KREAG COFFEY	HCA	(G
CAROL CARMICHAEL	V	(G
LEVON HELM	D	(H
AUBURN BARRELL JR	G	(H
BILL SCHWARTZ	V	(H
PATTIE BROOKS	V	(H
RITA COOLIDGE	V	(E
MONTE DUNN	G	(B
CHARLIE McCOY	HCA	(D
JENNIFER WARREN	V	(F
BEN BENAY	G	(G
ROBBIN FORD	G	(G
LARRY NASH	K	(G
MAX BENNETT	B	(G
DEWEY BUNNELL	V	(G
DICK HAMILTON	SYN	(G
KARIN LAMM	V	(G
MIKE BAIRD	D	(H
JESSE ED DAVIS	G	(H
JACKIE LOMAX	V	(H
PAUL HARRIS	K	(B
HERBERT LOVELLE	D	(B
TERRY ADAMS	CELLO	(F
DAVE MASON	G V	(F
LARRY CARLTON	G	(G
DON FELDER	G	(G
TOM HENSLEY	K	(G
RENIE PRESS	B	(G
BOB DYLAN	HCA	(G
JONI MITCHELL	V	(G
JERRY BECKLEY	V	(G
DUCK DUNN	B	(H
BARRY GOLDBERG	K	(H
PHYLLIS BROWN	V	(H

B149A BLUE ASH B149A

Member	Instrument	Albums
BILL BARTOLIN	V G	(AB
JIM KENDZOR	V	(AB
FRANK SECICH	V B	(AB
DAVID EVANS	D V	(A

Album	Year	Label	Country	Number
(A) NO MORE NO LESS	19	MERCURY		SRM 1 666
(B) FRONT PAGE NEWS	1978	PLAYBOY		34918

B149B BLUE ANGEL B149B

Member	Instrument	Albums
CYNDI LAUPEN	V	(A
JOHN TURI	K SAX	(A
LEE BROVITZ	B	(A
ROY HALEE	PROD	(A
JOHNNY MORELLI	D	(A
ARTHUR NEILSON	G	(A

Album	Year	Label	Country	Number
(A) BLUE ANGEL	1980	POLYDOR	UK	2391 486

B149C BLUE BAND B149C

Member	Instrument	Albums
JAN DAMEN	B	(A
HERMAN WILBRINK	G	(A
H J VOX	V K	(A
FRANS JONGMANS	G	(A
FRED VELTMAN	D	(A

Album	Year	Label	Country	Number
(A) SLITHERING	19	ARIOLA	NL	200 646 320

B150 BLUE CHEER B150

Member	Instrument	Albums
PAUL WHALEY	D	(BCE
RANDY HOLDEN	G	(C
DICK PETERSON	B V G	(ABCDE
GENE ESTES	PERC	(C
BRUCE'LEIGH'STEPHENS	G	(ABCDE
GENE ESTES		(
ERIC ALBRONDA	PROD	(A
BURNS KELLOGG	K	(BCDE
NORMAN MAYALL	D G	(DE
GARY YODER	G HCA V	(DE

Album	Year	Label	Country	Number
(A) VINCEBUS ERUPTUM	1968	PHILIPS		600 264
(A) VINCEBUS ERUPTUM	1967	PHILIPS 9001	UK	SBL7839
(B) OUTSIDE INSIDE	1968	PHILIPS		600 278
(B) OUTSIDE INSIDE	1968	PHILIPS		SBL 7860
(C) NEW IMPROVED	1969	PHILIPS		600 305
(C) NEW IMPROVED	1974	PHILIPS		SBL 7896
(C) NEW IMPROVED	1969	PHILIPS	GER	852 136
(D) BLUE CHEER	1969	PHILIPS		600 333
(D) BLUE CHEER	19	PHILIPS	GER	6336 001
(E) ORIGINAL HUMAN BEINGS	1970	PHILIPS 6336 004		600 347
(F) OH PLEASANT HOPE	19	PHILIPS		600 350

B150A BLUE GOOSE B150A

Member	Instrument	Albums
ALAN CULLAN	V G SYN	(A
SEAN LOCKE	D	(A
NICK SOUTH	B	(A
ALEXIS KORNER	V	(A
CHRIS PERRY	D	(A
MIKE TODMAN	G	(A
STEVE MARRIOTT	V	(A
NICK HOGARTH	K	(A
JOEY MOLLAND	V	(A

Album	Year	Label	Country	Number
(A) BLUE GOOSE	1975	ANCHOR		2005

B151 BLUE JAYS B151

Member	Instrument	Albums
JOHN LODGE	B V	(
JUSTIN HAYWARD	G V	(
GRAHAM DEACON	D	(
TOM TOMPKINS	CELLO	(
KIRK DUNCAN	PNO	(
JIM COCKNEY	VLN	(

Album	Year	Label	Country	Number
(A) THE BLUE JAYS	1975	THRESHOLD	UK	THS 1

B151A BLUE MAGIC B151A

Member	Instrument	Albums
WALTER SMITH	V	(E
VERNON SAWYER		(ABCD
RICHARD PRATT	V	(ABCDE
WENDELL SAWYER	B	(ABCD
KEITH BEATON	V	(ABCDE
TED MILLS	K	(ABCDE

Album	Year	Label	Country	Number
(A) BLUE MAGIC	19	ATCO US 7038	UK	K40532
(B) MAGIC OF THE BLUE	19	ATCO US 36103	UK	K50112
(C) 13 BLUE MAGIC LANE	19	ATCO US 36120	UK	K50181
(D) MYSTIC DRAGONS	19	ATCO	US	36140
(E) MESSAGE	19	ATCO	US	38104

B151B BLUE JUG BAND B151B

Member	Instrument	Albums
CLINT DELONG	G V	(A
ED RATZELOFF	V G	(A
BILL LITTLE	K	(A
RUFUS THIBODAUX	VLN	(A
BILL BURNETT	B	(A
RANDY SCRUGGS	G	(A
MAC PAUL WALKLEY	D	(A

Album	Year	Label	Country	Number
(A) BLUE JUG	1975	CAPRICORN		0158

B152 BLUE MINK B152

Member	Instrument	Albums
MADELINE BELL	V	(ALL
ROGER COOK	V	(ALL
BARRY MORGAN	D	(ALL
HERBIE FLOWERS	B	(ALL
ALAN PARKER	G	(ALL
ANN ODELL	K	(FGH
ROGER COULAM	K	(ABCDEFG
RAY COOPER	PERC	(FGH
ALLAN CLARKE	HCA	(D
DEREK WATKINS	TPT	(D

Album	Year	Label	Country	Number
(A) OUR WORLD	1970	PHILIPS	UK	6308 024
(B) MELTING POT	1970	PHILIPS	UK	SBL 1029
(B) MELTING POT	1970	PHILIPS	US	600 323
(C) LIVE AT THE TALK OF THE TOWN	1972	REGAL ZONOPHONE		SLRZ 1029
(D) A TIME OF CHANGE	1972	REGAL ZONOPHONE		SRZA 8507
(E) REAL MINK	1971	PHILIPS	US	600 339
( ) BEST OF BLUE MINK	1973	PHILIPS	UK	6382 077
(F) BLUE MINK	1973	MCA	US	332
(G) ONLY WHEN I LAUGH	1973	EMI	UK	EMA 756
(H) FRUITY	1974	EMI	UK	EMC 3021
(J) THE BEST OF BLUE MINK	1974	EMI	UK	EMC 3043
(K) HIT MAKING WORLD OF BLUE MINK	1975	DECCA	UK	SPA 437
(L) ATTENTION	1975	PHONOGRAM		6434 064

B152A BLUE MOUNTAIN EAGLE B152A

Member	Instrument	Albums
DAVID PRICE	G V	(A
RANDY FULLER	B G V	(A
BOB JONES	G V	(A
JOEY NEWMAN	G K V	(A
DON PONCHER	D V	(A

Album	Year	Label	Country	Number
(A) BLUE MOUNTAIN EAGLE	197	ATCO	US	33324
(B) SECOND	197	ATCO	US	

B153 BLUE NOTES B153

Member	Instrument	Albums
LOUIS MOHOLO	D	(AB
JOHNNY MBIZO DYAM	B	(AB
CHRIS McGREGOR	PNO	(AB
DUDU PUKWANA	SAX	(AB

Album	Year	Label	Country	Number
(A) BLUE NOTES FOR MONGEZI (DBL)	1977	OGUN		OGD 001/2
(B) BLUE NOTES IN CONCERT VOL1	1978	OGUN		OG 220

B154 BLUE OYSTER CULT B154

Member	Instrument	Albums
ERIC BLOOM	G V K	(ABCDEFGHJKL
ALLEN LANIER	K K V	(ABCDEFGHJKL
ALBERT BOUCHARD	D G V	(ABCDEFGHJKL
JOE BOUCHARD	B V G	(ABCDEFGHJKL
DONALD ROESER	G V K	(ABCDEFGHJKL
PATTI SMITH	V	(E
RANDY BRECKER	HRNS	(E
MARK RIVERA	SAX	(J
MICHAEL BRECKER	HRNS	(E
ELLEN FOLEY	V	(HJK
GENYA REVAN	V	(H
MICKEY RAPHAEL	HCA	(H
WENDY WEBB	V	(H
RICK DOWNEY	D	(L

Album	Year	Label	Country	Number
(A) BLUE OYSTER CULT	1973	CBS UK 64904	US	31063
(A) BLUE OYSTER CULT	1981	CBS	UK RI	32025
(B) TYRANNY & MUTATION	1974	CBS UK 65331	US	32107
(B) TYRANNY & MUTATION	1981	CBS	UK RI	32056
(C) SECRET TREATIES	1974	CBS UK 80103	US	32858
(C) SECRET TREATIES	1981	CBS	UK RI	32055
(D) ON YOUR FEET OR ON YOUR KNEES	1975	CBS UK 88116	US	33317
(E) AGENTS OF FORTUNE	1976	CBS UK 81385	US	34164
(F) SPECTRES	1977	CBS UK 86050	US	35019
(G) SOME ENCHANTED EVENING	1978	CBS UK 86074	US	35563
(H) MIRRORS	1979	CBS UK 86087	US	36009
(J) CULTOSAURUS ERECTUS	1980	CBS UK 86120	US	36550
(K) FIRE OF UNKNOWN ORIGIN	1981	CBS UK 85137	US	37389
(L) ETL	1982	CBS UK 22203		

(CONTINUED)

B154 **BLUE OYSTER CULT** (CONTINUED) B154

KARLA DEVITO V (JK — (EP) IN MY MOUTH OR ON THE GROUND — 1972 REICHSTAG US 1106
SANDY JEAN V (K
BILL CIVITELLA PERC (K — TONY CEDRONE PERC (K — SANDY PEARLMAN PROD (BCDE
MURRAY KRUGMAN PROD (BCDE — DAVID LUCAS PROD (E

B154A **BLUE STEEL** B154A

LEONARD ARNOLD G V (AB — (A) NO MORE LONELY NIGHTS — 1979 INFINITY INF9018 + INS2011
RICHARD BOWDEN G V (AB — NOTHING BUT TIME — 1981 ASYLUM US 6E308
HOWARD BURKE G V (AB
MARC DURAM B (AB — MICKEY McGEE D (A — REX CAUGHROM K (B
SKIP EDWARDS K (B — DON HENLEY V (B — KAREN BOWDEN V (B
DAVID DICKEY B V (B — JOHN HERRON K (B — MARIUS PENCZNER K (B
CLARENCE CLEMONS SAX (B — KRISTINE ARNOLD V (B — JANIS GILL V (B
MICHEAL HUEY D (AB

B154B **BLUES BAND** B154B

PAUL JONES V HCA (AB — (A) OFFICIAL BOOTLEG ALBUM — 1980 ARISTA BBBP 101
TOM McGUINNESS G (AB — (B) READY — 1980 ARISTA BB 2
HUGHIE FLINT D (AB
DAVE KELLY G V (AB — BOB HALL PNO (A — IAN STEWART PNO (B — GARY FLETCHER B (AB
GERAINT WATKINS PNO (B — ROCKIN' DOPSIE ACC (B — CHESTER ZENO PERC (B

B154C **BLUE RIVERS & THE MAROONS** B154C

(A) BLUE BEAT IN MY SOUL — 1967 COLUMBIA UK SX 6192

B154D **BLUE ROSE** B154D

TERRY FURLONG G (A — (A) BLUE ROSE — 1972 EPIC US 31252
DAVE THOMSON G B (A
STU PERRY D (A — JOHN URIBE B (A — DON PONCHER D (A

B154E **BLUE SHOUTERS** B154E

GEORGE J STEINMANN G HCA V(A — (A) LIVE AT KULTUR KARUSSELL — 19 BELLAPHON 33005
MAX GUGGER SAX V (A
ADI TOSETTO B (A — KLAUS FRIEDLI PNO (A — ANDRE BURI D (A

B155 **BLUES BROTHERS** B155

JOLIET JAKE BLUES V (ALL — (A) BRIEFCASE FULL OF BLUES — 1978 ATLANTIC UK K 50556
(JOHN BELUSHI) — (B) BLUES BROTHERS(SOUNDTRACK) — 1980 ATLANTIC US 16017 UK K 50715
ELWOOD BLUES HCA V (ALL — (C) MADE IN AMERICA — 1980 ATLANTIC US 16025 UK K 50768
(DAN AKROYD) — (D) BEST OF THE BLUES BROTHERS — 1981 ATLANTIC
PAUL SHAFFER K V (AC
STEVE CROPPER G (ABC — MATT MURPHY G (ABC — DONALD DUCK DUNN B (ABC
STEVE JORDAN D V (ABC — LOU MARINI SAX V(ABC — ALAN RUBIN TPT V(ABC
TOM SCOTT SAX V (AC — TOM MALONE HRS (ABC — MURPHY DUNNE K (BC
JEFF MIRONOV G (C — CAB CALLOWAY V (B — JAMES BROWN V (B
RAY CHARLES V (B — ARETHA FRANKLIN V (B — WILLIE HALL D (B
BRENDA CORBETT V (B — MARGARET BRANCH V (B — CAROLINE FRANKLIN V (B
PATTI AUSTIN V (B — VIVIAN CHERRY V (B — YOLLANDA McCULLOUGH V (B
REV JAMES CLEVELAND CHOIR (B — ELLIOTT RANDALL G (B — KEIV GINSBERG G (B
HIRAM BULLOCK G (B — LARRY WILLIS K (B — TERRY FRYER K (B
BILL PAYNE K (B — JOHN SPRINGER K (B — RICHARD T BEAR K (B
JOHN HASON K (B — ARTHUR DICKSON D (B — DAVID WESTON B (B
LEW DEL GATTO HRNS (B

B155A **BLUES DIMENSIONS** B155A

HELMIG VAN DER VEGT K (A — (A) BLUES DIMENSION — 1969 DECCA GERM ND254
RUDY VAN DIJK SAX (A
HERMAN DEINUM B (A — HANS LAFAILLE D (A — RIPKE (A

B155B **BLUES IMAGE** B155B

FRANK'SKIP' CONTE K (ABC — (A) BLUES IMAGE — 1969 ATCO US 33300
MIKE PINELLA G V (AB — (B) OPEN — 1970 ATCO US 33317
MALCOLM JONES B (ADC — (C) RED WHITE & BLUES IMAGE — 1970 ATCO US 33348
MANUEL BERTEMATTI D V (ABC — (C) RED WHITE & BLUES IMAGE — 1971 ATLANTIC UK 2400 120
JOE LALA PERC (ABC
DENNIS CORRELL V (BC — KENT HENRY G (C

B156 **BLUES INCORPORATED** B156

CYRIL DAVIES V HCA (— (A) BLUES INC/ALEXIS KORNER ALL STARS — 19 TRANSATLANTIC TRASAM 7
ALEXIS KORNER G V (
MICK JAGGER V HCA (— CHARLIE WATTS D (— IAN ARMITT K (
DICK HECKSTALL SMITH SAX (— JOHN PARKER (— RONNIE JONES (
JACK BRUCE B (— GRAHAM BOND K SAX (— GINGER BAKER D (

B157 **BLUES MAGOOS** B157

PEPPY THIELHEIM G V (ABCDEF — (A) BLUES MAGOOS — 1966 FONTANA STL 5402
RALPH SCALA V K (ABCD — (B) PSYCHEDELIC LOLLIPOP — 1966 MERCURY
RON GILBERT B (ABCD — (C) ELECTRIC COMIC BOOK — 1967 MERCURY
GEOFF DAKING D (ABCD — (D) BASIC BLUES MAGOOS — 1968 MERCURY US ST 61167
MIKE ESPOSITO G (BCDA — (E) NEVER GOING BACK TO GEORGIA — 1969 ABC US ABCS 697
JOHN LIELLO VIBES PERC (EF — (F) GULF COAST BOUND — 1970 ABC US ABCS 710
ERIC KAZ HCA V K (EF — (F) GULF COAST BOUND — 1972 PROBE US SPB 1024
RICHIE DICKON PERC (EF
ROGER EATON B V (E — HERB LOVELL D (E — DEAN EVANSON FLT (E
TITO CONGA (E — SOTO SAX (E — PEE WEE ELLIS PERC (F
COOKER LOPRESTI B (F — JIM PAYNE D (F — DADDY YA YA PERC (F

B158 **BLUES PROJECT** B158

AL KOOPER K (ABCG — (A) LIVE AT THE CAFE AU GO GO — 1966 VERVE FT 3000
STEVE KATZ G (AGBC — (B) PROJECTIONS — 1967 VERVE FTS 3008
TOMMY FLANDERS V (AEF — (B) PROJECTIONS — 1969 VERVE SVLP 6009
DANNY KALB G (ALL — (C) LIVE AT THE TOWN HALL — 1967 VERVE FTS 3025
ANDY KULBERG B (ABCDG — (D) PLANNED OBSOLESCENCE — 1968 VERVE FTS 3046
RAY BLUMENFIELD D (ABCDEFG — (E) LAZARUS — 1971 CAPITOL ST 872
RICHARD GREENE VLN (D — (F) BLUES PROJECT — 1972 CAPITOL EST 11017
DON KRETMAR SAX (DEF — (F) BLUES PROJECT — 197 MGM GAS 118
JOHN GREGORY G V (D — (G) REUNION IN CENTRAL PARK — 1973 MCA US 8003
DAVID COHEN G K (EF — ( ) BEST OF — 197 VERVE FTS 3069
BILL LUSSENDEN G (F — ( ) POP HISTORY — 19 POLYDOR 2625 020

(CONTINUED)

B158 (CONTINUED) B158

BLUES PROJECT

(Z) BLUES PROJECT 196 ELEKTRA US EKS 7264

JOHN KOERNER (Z
GEOFF MULDAUR (Z
DAVE RAY (Z
ERIC VON SCHMIDT (Z
JOHN SEBASTIAN (Z
IAN BUCHANAN (Z
TONY GLOVER (Z
DOUG POMEROY (Z
MARK SPOELSTRA (Z
FRITZ RICHMOND (Z
BOB (DYLAN) LANDY (Z

B159 B159

BLUESOLOGY

(A) RARE TRACKS(ONE TRACK) 1975 POLYDOR UK 2482 274

ELTON JOHN ORG
MARC CHARIG CORNET
ELTON DEAN SAX
PETE GAVIN D
PAT HIGGS TPT
REX BISHOP B
STUART BROWN V
FRED GANDY B
NEIL HUBBARD G
ALAN WALKER V
DAVE MURPHY SAX
MARSHA HUNT V
JOHN BALDRY V
MICK INKPEN D
JIMMY HOROWITZ K
CALEB QUAYE G
BERNIE HOLLAND G

B159A B159A

BLUESPLIZ

(A) EYES DON'T LIE 1979 Z 193

JORG FUNKE V HCA FLT(A
SIGGI SCHWARZ G (A
PIT ZAEPERNICK B (A
HARRY BERGER SAX (A
DIETER FUNKE D (A
ROMI SCHICKLE K (A

B160 B160

COLIN BLUNSTONE

(A) ONE YEAR 1971 EPIC UK 64557 US 30974
(B) ENNISMORE 1973 EPIC UK 65278 US 31994
(C) JOURNEY 1974 EPIC UK 65805 US 32962
(D) PLANES 1976 EPIC UK 81592
(E) NEVER EVEN THOUGHT 1978 EPIC UK 82835 RCA US 12903
(E) NEVER EVEN THOUGHT 1978 ROCKET SCAN 61328
(F) LATE NIGHTS IN SOHO 1979 ROCKET NL 9103 510

COLIN BLUNSTONE V G (ALL
PETE WINGFIELD K (BC
DEREK GRIFFITHS G (BC
JIM TOOMEY D (BC
ROBERT HENRIT D (B
BYRON LYEFOOR D (B
ROD ARGENT K (BCF
MIKE SNOW K G (B
PHIL DENNYS K (B
JIM RODFORD B (B
JOHN BEECHAM HRNS (C
KINGS SINGERS V (C
MIKE MORAN K (F
CLEM CLEMPSON G (F
MAURICE PERT PERC (F
RUSS BALLARD K G (B
MIKE COTTON HRNS (C
DUNCAN BROWNE G (C
TERRY POOLE D (BC
JOHN VERITY V (F
SIMON PHILLIPS D (F
JIMMY CHAMBERS V (F
STEVE BINGHAM B (B
NICK NEWELL HRNS (C
RICHARD KERR PNO (C
JOHN GIBLIN B (F
KATE KISSOON V (F
PAUL KOEGH G (F
STEVIE LANGE V (F

B160A B160A

BLURT

(A) FACTORY QUARTET (1 SIDE OF DBL) 198 FACTORY UK FACT24
(B) IN BERLIN 1981 ARMAGEDDON UK ARM 6

TED MILTON V SAX (AB
JAKE MILTON D V (AB
PETE CRISS G TROM(AB

B160B B160B

BO GRUMPUS

(A) BO GRUMPUS 1968
(B) BEFORE THE WAR 1968 ATCO US 33246

ED MOTTAU G (B
JIM COLEGROVE B G (B
FELIX PAPPALARDI K B G(B
JO HUTCHINSON G B K(B
N D SMART D (B
HERB LOVELLE D (B
RONNIE BLAKE D (B

B161 B161

BO STREET RUNNERS

(A) READY STEADY WIN (1 TRACK) 1964 DECCA UK LK 4634
(1) 1963

MICK FLEETWOOD D (A
TIM HINKLEY K (A
JOHN DOMINIC V (A1
MIKE PATTO V (A
DAVE CAMERON B (1
GARY THOMAS G (1
ROYSTON FRY K (1
GLYN THOMAS D (1

B161A B161A

BOA

(A) SCHIZIOD 1975 WOODEN NICKEL 0790

BEAU MAGGI G HCA V(A
THOMAS OBOMSAWIN G V (A
ROGER ALTHER D (A
ROBERT ZINNER G (A
ROGER KAHN K V (A
RONALD STOCKERT G V K (A
LEWIS MARK G (A
MARTIN HILL B V (A
DENNIS BELFIELD B V K (A
MICKEY McMEEL D V (A

B161B B161B

BOATZ

(A) BOATZ 1979 CAPRICORN US CPN 0222

THOM FLORA K V (A
GARY BAKER B V (A
PETE CARR G (A
STEVE NATHAN K (A
RICK POWELL D (A
ROGER CLARK D (A

B162 B162

BOB & EARL

(A) BOB & EARL 19 CRESTVIEW US 3055
(B) TOGETHER 19 JOY U JOYS 199
(C) BOB & EARL 1969 B&C U BCB 1
(D) HARLEM SHUFFLE 1971 JAYBOY 2004

BOB RELF V (ALL
EARL NELSON V (ALL

B163 B163

BOB & MARCIA

(A) YOUNG GIFTED & BLACK 1976 TROJAN TBL 122

BOB ANDY V (
MARCIA GRIFFITHS V (

B164 B164

BOBBIDAZZLER

(A) BOBBIDAZZLER 1978 RCA PL 12196
(A) BOBBIDAZZLER 1977 RCA US APLI 2196

GRANT GULLICKSON V (A
LANCE GULLICKSON V (A
JAMES DIVISEK D (A
GEORGE MARINELLI G (A
FRED DIVISEK (A
TONY PELUSO (A
BRIAN WHITCOMB K (A
PETE HENDERSON (A
STEVE PINKSTON (A
DENNIS BELFIELD B (A
JAY LEWIS G (A

B164A B164A

ROLAND BOCQUET

(A) PARADIA 19 COBRA GERM 60015

ROLAND BOCQUET K (A
DIDIER DUFRESNE B (A
MAXIME GOETZ G (A
GERARD GEOFFROY FLT (A

B165 B165

BODACIOUS

(A) BODACIOUS D F 1974 RCA US APLI02067
(A) BODACIOUS D F 1974 RCA UK SF 8391

MARTY BALIN G V (A
GREG DEWEY DAGREAZE D (A
VIC SMITH G (A
MARK RYAN B (A
CHARLIE HICKOX K (A

B165A BODAST

Member	Instrument	Albums
STEVE HOWE	G	(A
CLIVE MULDOON	G V	(A
BOBBY CLARKE	D	(A
DAVE CURTIS	B V	(A
CLIVE SKINNER	G V	(A

Album	Year	Label	Country	Catalogue
(A) BODAST TAPES(60's)	1981	CHERRY RED		BRED 12

B166 CURT BOETCHER

Member	Instrument	Albums
CURT BOETCHER	V K G	(A
WITH		
WEBB BURREL	V G K	(A
RIC DE LONG	B	(A
TESSIE	PERC	(A
RED RHODES	STEEL	(A
WAYNE YENTIS	SYN	(A
WILLIS MASONHEIMER	TUBA	(A
SKIP KONTE	K	(A
LES THORNTON	TUBA	(A

Album	Year	Label	Country	Catalogue
(A) THERE'S AN INNOCENT FACE	1973	ELEKTRA	US	EKS 75037

B166A BOGEY BOYS

Member	Instrument	Albums
JIMMY SMYTH	G	(AB
PAUL MORAN	D	(AB
DONALD NAGLE	B V	(AB
JOHN KEOGH	K	(A
LEO LYONS	PROD	(A

Album	Year	Label	Country	Catalogue
(A) FRIDAY NIGHT	1979	CHRYSALIS	UK	CHR 1241
(B) JIMMY DID IT	1980	CHRYSALIS	UK	CHR 1298

B166B BOFFALONGO

Member	Instrument	Albums
BASIL MATYCHAK	K V	(A
KEITH GINSBERG	G	(A
LARRY HOPPEN	B V	(A
RITCHIE	D	(A
WELLS KELLY	D	(

Album	Year	Label	Country	Catalogue
(A) BOFFALONGO	1969	UA	US	6726

B166C TIM BOGERT

Member	Instrument	Albums
TIM BOGERT		(A

Album	Year	Label	Country	Catalogue
(A) PROGRESSIONS	1981			

B168 MARC BOLAN & T REX

Member	Instrument	Albums
MARC BOLAN	G V	(ALL
WITH		
STEVE TOOK	D B PNO PERC	(ABC
MICKY FINN	PERC V	(69/75
TONY VISCONTI	PROD PNO	(BCDEF
JOHN PEEL	V	(AC
BILL LEGEND	D	(71/74
STEVE TURNER	B	(
STEVE CURRIE	B	(70/76
IAN McDONALD	SAX	(F
JACK GREEN	G	(73/75
PAT HALL	V	(73?75
GLORIA JONES	V	(73/76
DINO JONES	V	(75/77
TYRONE SCOTT	K V	(75/76
HERBIE FLOWERS	B	(76/77
TONY NEWMAN	D	(76/77
HOWARD KAYLAN	V	(FMS
MARK VOLMAN	V	(FMS
DAVY LUTTON	D	(74/76
MILLER ANDERSON	G	(
RICK WAKEMAN	K	(F
BURT COLLINS	HRNS	(F
LONNIE JORDAN		(S
DANNY THOMPSON		(S
B J COLE	STEEL	(S

Album	Year	Label	Country	Catalogue
(A) MY PEOPLE WERE FAIR	1968	REGAL ZONOPHONE	UK	SLRZ 1003
(B) PROPHET SEERS & SAGES	1968	REGAL ZONOPHONE	UK	SLRZ 1005
(AB) MY PEOPLE/PROPHET	1972	CUBE/FLY	UK	TOOFA 3
(C) UNICORN	1969	REGAL ZONOPHONE	UK	SLRZ 1007
(C) UNICORN	19	BLUE THUMB	US	
(D) BEARD OF STARS	1970	REGAL ZONOPHONE	UK	SLRZ 1013
(CD) UNICORN/BEARD OF STARS DBL	1972	CUBE	UK	TOOFA 9
(E) T REX	1970	FLY	UK	HIFLY 2
(F) ELECTRIC WARRIOR	1971	FLY	UK	HIFLY 6
( ) THE BEST OF T REX	1971	FLY	UK	TON 2
(G) BOLAN BOOGIE	1972	FLY	UK	HIFLY 8
(G) BOLAN BOOGIE	197	CUBE	UK	HIFLY 8
(J) RIDE A WHITE SWAN	1972	MFP	UK	MFP 5274
(K) HARD ON LOVE	1972	TRACK	UK	2406 101
(M) THE SLIDER	1972	EMI	UK	BLN 5001
(N) TANX	1972	EMI	UK	BLN 5002
( ) GREAT HITS	1972	EMI	UK	BLN 5003
(Q) ZINC ALLOY	1974	EMI	UK	BLNA 7751
(R) BEGINNING OF DOVES	1974	TRACK	UK	2410 201
(S) LIGHT OF LOVE	1974	CASABLANCA		NBLP 7005
(T) ZIP GUN	1975	EMI	UK	BLN 7752
(U) GET IT ON	1975	MFP	UK	90059
(V) FUTURISTIC DRAGON	1976	EMI	UK	BLN 5004
(W) DANDY IN THE UNDERWORLD	1977	EMI	UK	BLN 5005
(X) WORDS & MUSIC	1978	CUBE	UK	HIFLD 1
( ) GREATEST HITS VOL 1	1978	PICKWICK	UK	SHM 953
( ) T REX COLLECTION (DBL)	1978	PICKWICK	UK	PDA 044
( ) SOLID GOLD	1979	EMI	UK	NUT 5

B168A BOLD

Member	Instrument	Albums
TIM GRIFFIN	D V	(A
MICHAEL CHMURA	K	(A
ROBERT LAPALM	G V	(A
STEPHEN WALKER	B V	(A
DICK LAFRENIERE	G	(A

Album	Year	Label	Country	Catalogue
(A) BOLD	196	ABC	US	705

B169 TOMMY BOLIN

Member	Instrument	Albums
TOMMY BOLIN	G V K	(AB
STANLEY SHELDON	K	(A
DAVID FOSTER	K	(A
JEFF PORCARO	D	(A
PRAIRIE PRINCE	D	(A
PHIL COLLINS	PERC	(A
SAMMY ZIGUERON	PERC	(A
BOB BERGE	D	(A
BOBBYE HALL	PERC	(B
REGGIE McBRIDE	B V	(B
JAN HAMMER	K	(A
NARADA MICHAEL WALDEN	D	(A
RON FRANSEN	K	(A
MARK STEIN	K V	(B
DAVID SANBORN	SAX	(A
PAUL STALLWORTH	B	(A
BOBBY BERGE	D	(B
NORMA JEAN BELL	SAX PERC	(B

Album	Year	Label	Country	Catalogue
(A) TEASER	1975	ATLANTIC	UK	K 50208
(A) TEASER	1975	NEMPEROR US 436	RI	37534
(B) PRIVATE EYES	1976	CBS	UK	81612
(B) PRIVATE EYES	1976	CBS	US	C 34329

B169A MICHAEL BOLOTIN

Member	Instrument	Albums
MICHAEL BOLOTIN	V G	(AB
WILBUR BASCOMB	B	(A
PATRICK HENDERSON	PNO	(AB
JAN MULLANEY	ORG	(B
JAY MICHAELS	D	(B
SHARON LEE WILLIAMS	V	(B
DAVE SANBORN	SAX	(A
DENNY MOROUSE	SAX	(A
LANI GROVES	V	(A
WALT RICHMOND	K	(A
BILLY ELWORTHY	G	(B
PAPA JOHN CREACH	FDL	(B
RHONDA SILVER	V	(B
BERNARD PURDIE	D	(A
MARY McCREARY	V	(A
BARBARA MASSEY	V	(A
ANDY NEWMARK	D	(A
GARY FERRARO	B	(B
COLINA PHILLIPS	V	(B
WAYNE PERKINS		(A
JIM HORN	SAX	(A
MARCY LEVY	V	(A
FRED BOVA	G	(A
GEORGE STURTEVANT	FLT	(A

Album	Year	Label	Country	Catalogue
(A) MICHAEL BOLOTIN	1975	RCA UK SF 8451	US	APLI 0992
(B) EVERY DAY OF MY LIFE	1976	RCA	US	APLI 1550

B170 BONAROO

Member	Instrument	Albums
BILL CUOMO	K V	(A
MICHAEL HOSSACK	D PERC V	(A
ROBERT LICHTIG	B HRNS V	(A
MILT HOLLAND	PERC	(A
JERRY WEEMS	G V	(A
BOBBY WINKELMAN	G V	(A

Album	Year	Label	Country	Catalogue
(A) BONAROO	1974	WB	UK	K 56096

B171 GRAHAM BOND

Member	Instrument	Albums
GRAHAM BOND	K SAX V	(ALL
DICK HECKSTALL SMITH	SAX	(ABCJ
GINGER BAKER	D	(ABCJ
JOHN McLAUGHLIN	G	(C
JACK BRUCE	B	(ABCJ
DEREK FOLEY	G	(H
JON HISEMAN	D	(C
TERRY POOLE	G B	(E

Album	Year	Label	Country	Catalogue
(A) THE SOUND OF 65	1965	COLUMBIA	UK	33SX 1711
(B) THERE'S A BOND A BETWEEN US	1966	COLUMBIA	UK	33SX 1750
(C) SOLID BOND (DBL)	1970	WB UK 3001	UK	RI K 66004
(C) SOLID BOND	1970	WB	US	2555
(D) HOLY MAGICK	1971	VERTIGO	UK	6360 021
(D) HOLY MAGICK	1971	MERCURY	US	61327
(E) WE PUT OUR MAGICK ON YOU	1971	VERTIGO	UK	6360 042
(E) WE PUT OUR MAGICK ON YOU	1974	PHILIPS		SRMI 612

(CONTINUED)

B171 (CONTINUED) — GRAHAM BOND — B171

Record	Year	Label	Country	Number
(F) BOND IN AMERICA	1971	PHILIPS		6499200/1
(F) BOND IN AMERICA	1971	MERCURY	UK	6499200/1
(G) THIS IS GRAHAM BOND	1972	PHILLIPS		6382 010
(H) 2 HEADS ARE BETTER THAN ONE	1972	CHAPTER 1	UK	CHSR 813
(H) 2 HEADS ARE BETTER THAN ONE	1972	PATHE	FR	C064 93869
(J) BEGINNING OF JAZZ ROCK	1977	CHARLY		CR 30017
(K) MIGHTY GRAHAM BOND	1968	PULSAR		AR 10606
(L) LOVE IS THE LAW	1968	PULSAR		AR 10604
(M) FACES & PLACES VOL 4	19	BYG	FR	529 904
(1) INITIATION 1969 NO RECORDS				

Name	Instrument	Records
DIANE STEWART	V	(DE1LKH
HENRY WILLIAMS	G	(E
GASPAR LAWAL	PERC	(E
STEVE GREGORY	SAX	(E
JOHN WEATHERS	D	(E
VICTOR BROX	V	(D
ANNETTE BROX	V	(D
PETE BROWN		(H
ERICA BOND	V	(H
RIC GRECH	B	(D
STEVE YORK	B	(D
JOHN GROSS	SAX	(D
ALIKI ASHMAN	V	(D
KEITH BAILEY	D	(1D
JOHN MOORSHEAD	G	(D
EDDIE HOH	D	(K
RAY RUSSELL	G	(
SUE WOOLLEY	V	(H
MAX BENNETT	B	(K
NEIL HUBBARD	G	(
ALEX DMOCHOWSKI	B	(D
DAVE HOWARD	SAX	(1
KEVIN STACEY	G	(1D
JERRY SALISBURY	HRNS	(D
HARVEY MANDEL	G	(K
DELISLE HARPER	B V	(H
MICK WALKER	V PERC	(H
ALAN RUSHTON	D	(
BOB WESTON	G	(
PETE BAILEY	PERC	(D
DAVE USHER	WIND B V	(1
GODFREY McLEAN	D	(D
HAL BLAINE	D	(L
HARVEY BROOKS	K	(K
MICK HUTCHINSON	G	(H
DAVE SHEEHAN	D PERC	(L
DAVE QUINCEY	SAX	(

B171A — PETER BOND — B171A

Name	Instrument	Records
PETER BOND		(AB

Record	Year	Label	Country	Number
(A) ITS ALL RIGHT FOR SOME	1977	TRAILER		LER2108
(B) A DUCK ON HIS HEAD	1980	HIGHWAY		SHY 7012

B172A — GARY 'US' BONDS — B172A

Record	Year	Label	Country	Number
(A) DANCE TILL QUARTER TO THREE	19	LEGRAND	US	3001
(B) TWIST THE CALYPSO	19	LEGRAND	US	3002
(C) GREATEST HITS	19	LEGRAND	US	3003
(D) DEDICATION	1981	EMI	UK	3017
(E) ON THE LINE	1982	EMI	UK	3022

Name	Instrument	Records
GARY US BONDS	V	(ALL
J T BOWEN	SAX	(E
CLARENCE CLEMONS	SAX	(DE
JOE MARTIN	G V	(E
GEORGE RUIZ	B V	(E
BILL DERBY	G V	(E
DANNY FEDERICI	K	(DE
STEVE VAN ZANT	B G V	(DE
JOEY STANN	SAX V	(DE
BEN E KING	V	(D
CAROL SYLVAN	V	(D
LOUIE CONTE	G	(D
LA BAMBA	TROM	(D
MIKIE HARRIIS	V	(D
JOHN CLEMENTE	B	(D
ROB PARISSI	G	(D
ED MANION	SAX	(D
ELLI GREENWICH	V	(D
GARY TALLENT	B	(DE
BRUCE SPRINGSTEEN	G V	(D
MICHAEL SPENGLER	TPT	(D
BRANDA HILLIARD	V	(D
MIKE MICARA	D	(DE
ROY BITTAN	K	(DE
RICK GAZDA	V	(D
ULA HEDWIG	V	(D
MAX WEINBERG	D	(DE
RUSTY CLOUD	K	(DE
CHUCK JACKSON	V	(DE
CAROL WILLIAMS	V	(D

B173 — BONES — B173

Name	Instrument	Records
CASEY CUNNINGHAM	D	(A
JIMMY FARAGHER	SAX B V	(A
DANNY FARAGHER	HRS HCA K V	(A
GREG TORNQUIST	G V HCA	(A

Record	Year	Label	Number
(A) BONES	1972	SIGNPOST 8402	4251

B174 — BONEY M — B174

Record	Year	Label	Country	Number	Label	Country	Number
(A) TAKE THE HEAT OFF ME	1976	ATLANTIC	UK	K 50314	ATCO	US	36143
(B) LOVE FOR SALE	1977	ATLANTIC	UK	K 50385		US	19145
(C) NIGHT FLIGHT TO VENUS	1978	ATLANTIC	UK	K 50498	SIRE	US	6062
(D) OCEANS OF FANTASY	1979	ATLANTIC	UK	K 50610			

Name	Instrument	Records
MARCIA BARRETT	V	(CD
LIZ MITCHELL	V	(CD
OBBY FARRELL	V	(CD
MAIZIE WILLIAMS	V	(CD
WITH		
KEITH FORSEY	D	(CD
MATS BJORKLUND	G	(CD
FRANK FARIAN	V	(D
M CRETU	K	(D
LISA GRODANIER	SAX	(D
GEOFF STRADLING	TROM	(D
KARL BARTELMES	TPT	(D
GEORG DELAGALTE	TROM	(D
NICK WOODLAND	G	(CD
GARY UNWIN	B	(CD
PRECIOUS WILSON	V	(D
JIM POLIVKA	TPT	(D
BOBBY STERN	SAX	(D
ETIENNE CAP	TPT	(D
BENNY GEBAVER	SAX	(D
GEORG DELGALTE	TROM	(D
CHICO DE LOS REYES		(C
R BESSER	B	(D
SCOT NEWTON	TPT	(D
LANCE BURTON	SAX	(D
WALTER RAB	TPT	D(C
DINO SOLERA	WIND	(D

B174A — JUKE BOY BONNER — B174A

Name	Instrument	Records
JUKE BOY BONNER	HCA V G	(ALL
BRUCE LANGMAN	G V	(C
RON SKINNER	B	(C
MEL WRIGHT	D	(C
JOHN LEWIS	K	(C

Record	Year	Label	Country	Number
(A) I'M GOING BACK TO THE COUNTRY	1968	ARHOOLIE		F 1036
(B) THE STRUGGLE	19	ARHOOLIE		F 1045
(C) THINGS AINT RIGHT	1969	LIBERTY		83319
(D) LEGACY OF THE BLUES	19	SONET		SNTF 634
(D) LEGACY OF THE BLUES	19	GNP CRESCENDO	US	GNP 10015
(E) LOUISIANA BLUES	19	STORYVILLE		SLP 177
(F) ONE MAN TRIO	1979	FLYRIGHT		FLY 548

B174B — GRAHAM BONNET — B174B

Record	Year	Label	Country	Number
(A) GRAHAM BONNET	1977	RING O RECORDS	UK	2320 103
(B) LINE UP	1981	VERTIGO	UK	6302 151

Name	Instrument	Records
GRAHAM BONNET	V	(AB
MIKE GILES	D	(A
COZY POWELL	D	(B
DAVE MARKEE	B	(A
PIP WILLIAMS	G MAND	(A
STEVIE LANGE	V	(A
TERRY POPPLE	D	(A
GRAHAM PRESKETT	G	(A
GARY TWIGG	B	(B
KIRBY	G	(B
RICHARD PARFITT	G	(B
MEL COLLINS	SAX	(B
RUSS BALLARD	G	(B
CATHERINE HOWE	V	(A
JACQUIE SULLIVAN	V	(A
FRANK RICOTII	PERC	(A
COLIN GIBSON	B	(A
TONY HYMAS	K	(A
FRANCIS ROSSI	K G V	(B
IAN LYNN	K	(B
NEIL MURRAY	B	(B
MARTIN DITCHAM	PERC	(B
ANDY BOWN	K	(B
MICK MOODY	G	(AB
JOY YATES	V	(A
PETER ZORN	SAX	(A
KEN CRADDOCK	PNO	(A
BARDOT	V	(A
JOHN COOK	K	(B
CHRISSIE STEWART	B	(B
JON LORD	K	(B
ADRIAN LEE	K	(B

B174C — BONGO TEENS — B174C

Record	Year	Label	Country	Number
(A) BONGO TEENS	19	ORIGINAL SOUND	US	5009

B174D — BONGOS — B174D

Record	Year	Label	Country	Number
(A) THE BONGOS	1980	FETISH	UK	FET005

B174E — BONNEVILLES — B174E

Record	Year	Label	Country	Number
(A) MEET THE BONNEVILLES	196	DRUM BOY	US	1001

Name	Instrument	Records
BOBBIE MARKT	SAX V	(A
VINCE MAGNA	G	(A
WENDY COLBY	V	(A

B174F SEAN BONNIWELL'S MUSIC MACHINE B174F

Member	Instrument	Albums
SEAN BONNIWELL	V G	(AB
KIETH OLSEN	B V	(A
MARK LANDON	G	(A
DOUG RHODES	K V	(A
RON EAGER	G D	(A

Album	Year	Label	Country	Number
(A) BONNIWELL MUSIC MACHINE	1968	WB	US	1732
(B) TURN ON THE MUSIC MACHINE	1967	ORIGINAL SOUND	US	8875

B175 KARLA BONOFF B175

Member	Instrument	Albums
KARLA BONOFF	V K G	(ALL
WITH		
RUSS KUNKEL	D	(ABC
MARK JORDAN	K	(C
LEE SKLAR	B	(A
LINDA RONSTADT	V	(A
GREG LADANYI	PERC	(A
J D SOUTHER	V	(AC
DAN DUGMORE	STEEL	(A
DON HENLEY		(BC
DAVID LINDLEY		(B
BILL PAYNE	K	(C
IRA INGBER	G	(C
MICHAEL BOTTS	D	(A
JAI WINDING	PNO	(A
KENNY EDWARDS	G MAND B V	(AC
STEVE FORMAN	PERC	(ABC
WENDY WALDMAN	V	(A
GARTH HUDSON		(B
PHIL KENZIE	SAX	(C
DAVID SANBORN	SAX	(C
VICTOR FELDMSN	VIBES	(C
ANDREW GOLD	G K	(ABC
WADDY WACHTEL	G V	(AC
BROCK WALSH	V	(AC
GLENN FREY	V	(A
STRING SECTION		(B
DANNY KORTCHMAR		(BC
TIM SCHMIT	V	(C
DAVID WOLINSKI	SYN K	(C
JOE WALSH	G	(C

Album	Year	Label	Country	Number
(A) KARLA BONOFF	1977	CBS US 34672	UK	82455
(B) RESTLESS NIGHTS	1979	CBS US 35799	UK	83587
(C) WILD HEART OF THE YOUNG	1982	CBS US 37444		

B177 JACK BONUS B177

Member	Instrument	Albums
JACK BONUS	V G SAX FLT K	(A
TOM COSTER	K	(A
BRUCE CONTE	G	(A
ED BOGAS	VLN	(A
ANDY LIFLAND	D	(A
LORIN ROWAN	G	(A
BILLY WOLF	B	(A
STAN MONTEIRO	CLAR	(A
JACKIE KING	G	(A
STEVE TURRE	TROM	(A
FREDDIE ROULETTE	G	(A
STRING SECTION		(A
JON DETHERAGE	PNO	(A
CHRIS ROWAN	G	(A
GLENN CRONKHITE	D	(A
IVORY SMYLIE	CONGA	(A
BENNY VELARDE	PERC	(A
TONY SMITH	D	(A
JAMIE HOWELL	G	(A
SKIP OLSON	B	(A
DAVID DIADEM	MAND K	(A
EDDIE ADAMS	B	(A
JACK DORSEY	D	(A
KEN BALZELL	TPT	(A

Album	Year	Label	Country	Number
(A) JACK BONUS	1972	GRUNT		FTR 1005

B178 BONZO DOG DO DAH BAND B178

Member	Instrument	Albums
NEIL INNES	K B G V PROD	(ALL
VIVIAN STANSHALL	V TPT PROD	(ALL
ROGER RUSKIN SPEAR	SAX	(ALL
DAVE CLAGUE	B	(BEH
BUBS WHITE	G	(FH
RODNEY SLATER	SAX	(ABCDEH
TONY KAYE	K	(F
LEGS LARRY SMITH	D	(ALL
VERNON NOWELL	B BJO	(AEH
SAM SPOONS	PERC	(AEH
DENNIS COWAN	B V	(CDFH
DICK PARRY	WIND	(FH
ANDY ROBERTS	G	(FH
DAVE RICHARD	B	(FH
HUGHIE FLINT	D	(FH
GERRY BRON	PROD	(AB
GUS DUDGEON	PROD	(BC
BOB KERR	HRNS V	(AG
DAVE RICHARDS	B	(F
LEON WILLIAMS	TPT	(
JAMES CHAMBERS	WIND	(
SYD NICHOLLS	BJO	(
RAYMOND LEWITT	TUBA	(

Album	Year	Label	Country	Number
(A) GORILLA	1967	LIBERTY	UK	LBS 83056
((A) GORILLA	1970	SUNSET	UK	SLS 50160
(A) GORILLA	19	IMPERIAL	US	12370
(B) DOUGHNUT IN GRANNYS GREENHOUSE	1968	LIBERTY	UK	LBS 83158
(B) DOUGHNUT IN GRANNYS GREENHOUSE	1971	SUNSET	UK	SLS 50210
(C) TADPOLES	1969	LIBERTY	UK	LBS 83257
(C) TADPOLES	1969	LIBERTY	US	12445
(D) KEYNSHAM	1969	LIBERTY	UK	LBS 83290
(D) KEYNSHAM	1975	SUNSET	UK	SLS 50375
(D) KEYNSHAM	19	IMPERIAL	US	12457
(E) THE BEAST OF THE BONZOS (COMP)	1970	LIBERTY	UK	LBS 83332
(E) THE BEAST OF THE BONZOS (COMP)	19	UA	US	5517
(F) LETS MAKE UP & BE FRIENDLY	1972	UA	UK	UAS 29288
(F) LETS MAKE UP & BE FRIENDLY	1978	SUNSET	UK	SLS 50418
(C) URBAN SPACEMAN	1973	SUNSET	UK	SLS 50350
(C) URBAN SPACEMAN	197	IMPERIAL	US	12432
(H) HISTORY OF THE BONZOS (DBL)	1974	UA	UK	UAD60071/2
(H) HISTORY OF THE BONZOS (DBL)	1974	UA	US	LA 321 H

B179 JAMES BOOKER B179

Member	Instrument	Albums
JAMES BOOKER	PNO V	(AB

Album	Year	Label	Country	Number
(A) JUNCO PARTNERS	1976	ISLAND	UK	HELP 26
(B) NEW ORLEANS PIANO WIZZARD LIVE	1977	ROUNDER	US	2022

B180 BOOKER T & THE MG's B180

Member	Instrument	Albums
BOOKER T JONES	K G B	(ALL
WITH		
STEVE CROPPER	G	(
LOUIS STENBERG	D	(
AL JACKSON	D	(
DONALD DUCK DUNN	B	(
WILLIE HALL	D	(
DAVID T WALKER	G	(
JIM KELTNER	D	(
SAMMY CREASON	D	(
BOB GLAUB	B	(
ALEXANDER SMITH	B	(
BOBBYE HALL	PERC	(

Album	Year	Label	Country	Number
GREEN ONIONS	1962	LONDON UK		1640 354
GREEN ONIONS	1966	ATLANTIC	UK	587 033
GREEN ONIONS	1980	ATLANTIC	UK	K 40072
GREEN ONIONS	19	STAX	US	STAX 701
GREEN ONIONS	19	PICKWICK		SHM 3031
AND NOW	1966	STAX	UK	589 002
AND NOW	1966	STAX	US	STAX 711
AND NOW	19	ATLANTIC		7711
IN THE XMAS SPIRIT	19	STAX	US	STAX 715
HIP HUG HER	196	STAX	US	STAX 717
BACK TO BACK(WITH MARKEYS)	19	STAX	US	STAX 720
DOING OUR THING	1968	ATLANTIC	UK	2464 011
DOING OUR THING	1968	STAX	US	1040
DOING OUR THING	19	STAX	US	STAX 724
DOING OUR THING	19	ATLANTIC		7724
BEST OF	1968	ATLANTIC	UK	228 015
BEST OF	19	STAX	UK	2325 018
BEST OF	19	STAX	US	8202
BEST OF	1980	ATLANTIC	UK	K 50749
BEST OF	197	ATLANTIC	UK	K 40072
UPTIGHT	1968	STAX	UK	SXATS1005
UPTIGHT	1968	STAX	US	2006
SOUL LIMBO	1968	STAX	UK	SXATS1001
SOUL LIMBO	1968	STAX	UK	2325 001
SOUL LIMBO	19	STAX	US	2001
McLEMORE AVENUE	1970	STAX	UK	2326 016
McLEMORE AVENUE	1970	STAX	US	2027
McLEMORE AVENUE	1970	STAX		SXATS1031
BOOKER T SET	1970	STAX	UK	2326 012
BOOKER T SET	1970	STAX	UK	SXATS1015
BOOKER T SET	19	STAX	UK	2325 003
BOOKER T SET	19	STAX	US	STAX 2009
MELTING POT	1972	STAX	UK	2325 030
MELTING POT	1972	STAX	UK	STAX 1054
MELTING POT	197	STAX	US	STAX 2035

(CONTINUED)

B180 BOOKER T & THE MG's (CONTINUED) B180

Title	Year	Label	Country	Number
STAR COLLECTION	1973	WB		MID 30042
STAR COLLECTION	19	WB	UK	MID 20032
GREATEST HITS	1974	STAX	UK	STX 1017
GREATEST HITS	19	ATLANTIC	US	2033
GREATEST HITS	1974	STAX	UK	2362 002
MEMPHIS SOUND	1975	STAX	UK	STX 1037
UNION EXTENDED	1976	STAX	UK	STXS 2041
UNION EXTENDED	1976	STAX	UK	STX 1045
POP HISTORY	19	POLYDOR		2625 013
POP HISTORY	19	POLYDOR		2612 016
UNIVERSAL LANGUAGE	19	ASYLUM	US	7E 1093
UNIVERSAL LANGUAGE	19	ASYLUM	UK	K 53057
GET READY	19	ATLANTIC		UK228 004
TIME IS TIGHT (MARKEYS)	1979	STAX	UK	STAX 3007
SOUL DRESSING	19	STAX		USSTAX 705

B180A BOOKS B180A

Title	Year	Label	Country	Number
(A) EXPERTISE	1980	LOGO	UK	VOLUME 1

B180B BOOMERANG B180B

MARK STEIN K V (A
JAMES GALLUZI D (A
RICHARD RAMERIZ G (A
JO CASMIR B V (A

Title	Year	Label	Country	Number
(A) FIRST	19	RCA		LSP 4577

B181 BOOMTOWN RATS B181

BOB GELDOF V SAX (ALL
JOHNNIE FINGERS K V (ALL
GERRY COTT G (ABC
PETE BRIQUETTE B V (ABC
GERRY ROBERTS G V (ABC
SIMON CROWE D V (ABC
ANDY DUNCAN PERC (D
ALBE DONNELLY SAX (A
DAVE McCHALE SAX (A
TOM WINTER BOUZ (D

Title	Year	Label	Country	Number
(A) THE BOOMTOWN RATS	1977	ENSIGN		ENVY1
(A) THE BOOMTOWN RATS	1977	MERCURY	US	SRM 1188
(A) THE BOOMTOWN RATS	1977	MERCURY 6310950		9102 800
(B) TONIC FOR THE TROOPS	1978	ENSIGN ENVY3	CBS	US 35750
(B) TONIC FOR THE TROOPS	1978	MERCURY	GER	6310 954
(C) FINE ART OF SURFACING	1979	ENSIGN UK ROX 11		
(C) FINE ART OF SURFACING	1979	MERCURY	GER	6310 960
(D) MONDO BONGO	1980	MERCURY	UK	6359 042
(D) MONDO BONGO	1980	MERCURY	GER	6359 042

B181A BOONES FARM B181A

KENT SPRAGUE V PERC(A
GARY STOVALL G V (A
BRAD PALMER V B G (A
FRED DARLING D (A
MILT HOLLAND PERC (A

Title	Year	Label	Country	Number
(A) BOONES FARM	1972	COLUMBIA	US	31408

B181B BOOT B181B

MIKE MYCZ G V (AB
JIM O'BRECK D (AB
BRUCE KNOX G V (AB
DAN ELIASSEN V B (AB

Title	Year	Label	Country	Number
(A) BOOT	1972	AGAPE	US	2601
(B) TURN THE OTHER CHEEK	1977	GUINNESS	US	36002

B182 KEN BOOTHE B182

KEN BOOTHE V (ALL

Title	Year	Label	Country	Number
(A) BLACK GOLD & GREEN	19	TROJAN	UK	TRLS 58
(B) LETS GET IT ON	1974	TROJAN	UK	TRLS 83
(C) EVERYTHING I OWN	1974	TROJAN	UK	TRLS 95
(D) FREEDOM STREET	1975	TROJAN	UK	TRLS 120
(E) LIVE GOOD	1978	U A		LA 801
(F) 20 GREATEST REGGAE HITS	1979	CHARMERS		
(G) BLOOD BROTHERS	1978	TROJAN	UK	TRLS 148
(H) WHO GETS YOUR LOVE	1979	TROJAN	UK	TRLS 164

B182A BOOTS B182A

WERNER KRABBE V HCA (A
WILI GRUN ORG (A
BOB BRESSER B (A
HEINZ HOFF D (A
JOERG SCHULTE G (A

Title	Year	Label	Country	Number
(A) HERE ARE THE BOOTS	1966	TELEFUNKEN	GERM	SLE 14399

B183 BOOTSY'S RUBBER BAND B183

WILLIAM BOOTSY COLLINS GVB(ABC
WITH
PHELPS COLLINS B G (ABC
GARY SHIDER G (AB
MIKE HAMPTON G (AB
FRANKIE KASH WADDY D (ABC
BOOGIE D (A
GARY COOPER D V (ABC
CASPER B D G (ABC
RANDY BRECKER SAX (AB
BERNIE WORRELL K (AB
LESLYN BAILEY V (A
RICHARD GRIFFITHS HRNS (BC
FRED WESLEY TROM (ABC
RICK GARDNER TPT (ABC
SONNY TALBERT K (A
ROBERT JOHNSON V (ABC
GLEN GOINS G (B
MACEO PARKER SAX (ABC
MICHAEL BRECKER TPT (A
FREDRICK ALLEN K (A
JOEL JOHNSON K (BC
JEROME BRAILEY D (B

Title	Year	Label	Country	Number
(A) STRETCHIN OUT	1976	WB	UK	K56200
(A) STRETCHIN OUT	1976	WB	UK	B2920
(B) AAH...THE NAME IS BOOTSY BABY	1977	WB	UK	K 56302
(B) AAH...THE NAME IS BOOTSY BABY	1977	WB	US	2972
(C) PLAYER OF THE YEAR	1978	WB	UK	K56424
(C) PLAYER OF THE YEAR	1978	WB	US	K 3093
(D) THIS BOOT IS MADE FOR FONK'N	1979	WB	UK	K 56615

B183A BOPCATS B183A

Title	Year	Label	Country	Number
(A) ROCK'N'ROLL GRAFFITI	1980	MAGNUM FORCE		MFLP 001

B183B BORDERLINE B183B

JIM ROONEY G V (A
DAVID GARSHEN G V (A
JOHN GARSHEN G V (A
BILL MUNDI D (A
CAMPO MALAGVA K (A
KEN COSSECK FDL (A
BEN KEITH STEEL (A
JOHN SIMON K (A
DAVID SANBORN SAX (A
JIM COLGROVE B (A
DICK HARDLE K (A
VASSAR CLEMENTS FDL (A

Title	Year	Label	Country	Number
(A) SWEET DREAMS AND QUIET DESIRES	1972	AVALANCHE	US	LA016

B183C KEVIN BORICH EXPRESS B183C

KEVIN BORICH G V (A
TIM PARTRIDGE B (A
JOHN ANNAS D (A
JOHN WATSON D (A

Title	Year	Label	Country	Number
(A) LIVE	1979	AVENUE	US	L37139

B183D BOSS BROTHERS B183D

JON ASH K SYN V(A
STEVE WHALLEY G V (A
MIKE SMITH D (A
LENNI SAX (A
IAN WILSON G V K(A
JON LEVENSON G B (A
RITCHIE BRUNTON G (A
MELANIE HARROLD V (A
DAVID PETERS HCA (A

Title	Year	Label	Country	Number
(A) STALLING FOR TIME	1980	MERCURY	UK	9109 632

B184 — BOSTON — B184

Member	Inst	Records	Title	Year	Label	Country	Number
BARRY GOULDREAU	G PERC	(AB	(A) BOSTON	1976	EPIC UK EPC81622		RI 32038
TOM SCHOLZ	G K	(AB	(A) BOSTON	1976	EPIC	US	BL 34188
SIB HASHAIN	D	(AB	(B) DONT LOOK BACK	1978	EPIC UK EPC86057		RI 32048
BRADLEY DELP	V G	(AB	(B) DONT LOOK BACK	1978	EPIC	US	FE 35050
FRAN SHEEHAN	B PERC	(AB					
JIM MASDEA	D	(A					

B184A — BOSTON TEA PARTY — B184A

Member	Inst	Records	Title	Year	Label	Country	Number
RICHARD DE PERNA	B	(A	(A) THE BOSTON TEA PARTY	19	FLICKDISC	US	45000
ROBERT DE PERNA	K	(A					
TRAVIS FIELDS	V	(A					
DAVE NOVOGROSKI	D	(A					
MIKE STEVENS	G	(A					

B184B — SIMON BOSWELL — B184B

Member	Inst	Records	Title	Year	Label	Country	Number
SIMON BOSWELL		(A	(A) THE MIND PARASITES	1975	TRANSATLANTIC	UK	TRA 307

B185 — BOTHY BAND — B185

Member	Inst	Records	Title	Year	Label	Country	Number
TRIONA O'DONNELL	K V	(ABCD	(A) BOTHY BAND	1976	POLYDOR	UK	2383 379
PADDY KEENAN	PIPES	(ABCD	(A) BOTHY BAND	1976	MULLIGAN	IR	LUN 002
TOMMY PEOPLES	FDL	(C	(B) OLD HAG YOU HAVE KILLED ME	1976	MULLIGAN	IR	LUN 007
MATT MOLLOY	WIND	(ABCD	(B) OLD HAG YOU HAVE KILLED ME	1976	POLYDOR	UK	2383 417
DONAL LUNNY	G K	(ABCD	(C) OUT OF THE WIND	1977	POLYDOR	UK	2383 456
MICHAEL O'DONNELL	G	(ABCD	(C) OUT OF THE WIND	1977	MULLIGAN	IR	LUN
KEVIN BURKE	FDL	(D	(D) AFTER HOURS	1979	POLYDOR	UK	2383 530
PADDY GLACKIN	FDL	(AB	(D) AFTER HOURS	1979	MULLIGAN	IR	LUN 030
TONY McMAHON		(A					

B185A — BOULDER — B185A

Member	Inst	Records	Title	Year	Label	Country	Number
			(A) BOULDER	1979	ARISTA		

B185B — CHRISTIAN BOULE — B185B

Member	Inst	Records	Title	Year	Label	Country	Number
CHRISTIAN BOULE			( ) PHOTO MUSIC	19	POLYDOR		2473 086

B186 — DAVID BOWIE — B186

Member	Inst	Records	Title	Year	Label	Country	Number
DAVID BOWIE	V G SAX K	(ALL	(A) DAVID BOWIE(LOVE YOU TILL TUES)	1967	DERAM		SML 1007
			(A) DAVID BOWIE(TWO TRACK LESS)	1967	DERAM		18003
WITH			(A) THE WORLD OF DAVID BOWIE	1970	DECCA		SPA 58
CARLOS ALOMAR	G	(1LMOPRST	(B) MAN OF WORDS/ SPACE ODDITY	1969	PHILIPS	UK	SBL 7912
DENNIS DAVIES	PERC	(1LMOPRST	(B) MAN OF WORDS /SPACE ODDITY	1969	MERCURY	US	ST 61246
GEORGE MURRAY	B	(1MOPRST	(B) MAN OF WORDS /SPACE ODDITY	1969	RCA		LPS 4813
BRIAN ENO	K	(OPS	(C) MAN WHO SOLD THE WORLD	1970	RCA		LPS 4816
ROBERT FRIPP	G	(PT	(C) MAN WHO SOLD THE WORLD	1970	PHILIPS		461 006
SIMON HOUSE	VLN	(1RS	(C) MAN WHO SOLD THE WORLD	1971	MERCURY US 61325	UK	6338 041
ROGER POWELL	K	(1RS	(D) HUNKY DORY	1971	RCA US AFLI4623	UK	SF 8244
MICK RONSON	G	(CDEFG	(D) HUNKY DORY	197	RCA		443 041
STACEY HAYDEN	G	(	(E) RISE & FALL OF ZIGGY STARDUST	1972	RCA US AFLI4702	UK	SF 8287
MICK WAYNE	G	(B	(E) RISE & FALL OF ZIGGY STARDUST	1972	RCA		443 051
TIM RENWICK	G	(B	(F) ALADDIN SANE	1973	RCA		RS 1001
TONY VISCONTI	B WIND	(BCPT	(F) ALADDIN SANE	1973	RCA CPRS4543		AFLI 4852
HERBIE FLOWERS	B	(BJK	(F) ALADDIN SANE	1973	RCA		461 004
JOHN CAMBRIDGE	D	(B	(G) PIN UPS	1973	RCA AFLI0291		RS 1003
PAUL BUCKMASTER	CELLO	(B	(H) IMAGES 66 67	1973	LONDON US 628/9	UK	DPA3017/8
BENNY MARSHALL	HCA	(B	(J) DIAMOND DOGS	1974	RCA		APLI 0576
DIANE SUMLER	V	(L	(K) LIVE	1974	RCA		APL2 0771
LUTHER VANDROSS	V	(L	(L) YOUNG AMERICANS	1975	RCA US AFLI0998	UK	RS 1006
ROY YOUNG	PNO	(O	(M) STATION TO STATION	1976	RCA		APLI 1327
RICKY GARDINER	G	(O	(N) CHANGESONEBOWIE	1976	RCA AFLI1732		RS 1055
ANDY NEWMARK	D	(L	(O) LOW	1977	RCA		PL 12030
JOHN LENNON	V G	(L	(P) HEROES	1977	RCA		PB 1121
DAVID SANBORN	SAX	(LK	(P) HEROES	1977	RCA		AFLI 2522
LARRY WASHINGTON	PERC	(L	(P) HEROES	1977	RCA		PL 42373
TONY NEWMAN	D	(JK	( ) STARTING POINT	1977	LONDON		LC 50007
KEN FORDHAM	WIND	(FG	(Q) PETER & THE WOLF	1970	RCA		RL 12743
JUANITA FRANKLIN	V	(F	(R) STAGE	1978	RCA		PL 02913
AVA CHERRY	V	(L	(S) LODGER	1979	RCA AZLI 3254		BOW LP1
ALAN PARKER	G	(J	( ) GOLDEN DOUBLE	1979	RCA	JAP	SRA9503/4
MIKE GARSON	G	(JK	( ) BEST OF	1980	K TEL		NE 1111
ADRIAN BELEW	G	(1 RS	( )PROFILE	19	TELDEC	GERM	624009
ROBIN CLARK	V	(L	(T) SCARY MONSTERS	1980	RCA		BOW K2
SEAN MAYES	K	(RS	(T) SCARY MONSTERS	1980	RCA		PL 13647
KEITH CHRISTMAS	G	(B	( ) BEGINNINGS VOL 1	19	DERAM		
TERRY COX	D	(B	( ) BEGINNINGS VOL 2	19	DERAM		621680
RICK WAKEMAN	K	(BDE	(U) CHANGESTWOBOWIE	1981	RCA		AFLI4204
ANTONIA MAASS	V	(P	(V) ANOTHER FACE	1981	DECCA		TAP 17
MARY VISCONTI	V	(O	(1) 1978 TOUR BAND				
IGGY POP	V	(O					
MIKE KAMEN	K	(K					

Member	Inst	Records	Member	Inst	Records	Member	Inst	Records
RICHARD GRANDO	WIND	(K	GUI ANDRESINO	V	(K	WARREN PEACE	V	(KLM
WILLY WEEKS	B	(L	EARL SLICK	G	(KLM	EMIR KSASAN	B	(L
TREVOR BOLBER	B	(DEFG	MAC CORMACK	V	(FG	RALPH McDONALD	PERC	(L
LINDA LEWIS	V	(F	JOHN MAYER	K	(1	PABLO ROSARIO	PERC	(LK
ROY BITTAN	K	(MT	JEAN FINEBERG	V	(L	CHUCK HAMMER	G	(T
MICJ WOODMANSEY	D	(CDEF	ANTHONY HINTON	V	(L	JEAN MILLINGTON	V	(L
MICHAEL GARSON	K	(FGL	RALPH MACE	K	(C	AYNSLEY DUNBAR	D	(GJ
PETE TOWNSHEND	V	(T	MICHI HIROTA	V	(T	ANDY CLARK	SYN	(T
LYNN MAITLAND	V	(T	CHRIS PORTER	V	(T			

B187 — BOWLES BROTHERS BAND — B187

Member	Inst	Records	Title	Year	Label	Country	Number
BRIAN BOWLES	G V	(A	(A) ROGER BUYS A FRIDGE	1978	DECCA		TXS 127
RICHARD LEE	B	(A					

Member	Inst	Records	Member	Inst	Records	Member	Inst	Records
JULIAN SMEDLEY	G V VLN	(A	SUE JONES DAVIS	V	(A	RICHARD MARCANGELO	D	(A
CHARLES SEAWARD	FLT	(A	JONATHAN WADE	K	(A	COLIN FRECHTER	PNO	(A
CHRIS KARAN	PERC	(A	ROGER RETTIG	STEEL	(A			

B187A — JIMMY BOWEN — B187A

Member	Inst	Records	Title	Year	Label	Country	Number
JIMMY BOWEN	B V	(A	(A) JIMMY BOWEN	19	ROULETTE	US	25004
BUDDY KNOX	G	(A					
DAVE ALLDRED		(A					
DON LANIER		(A					

B188 ALAN BOWN SET B188

ALAN BOWN TPT (ALL — (A) LONDON SWINGS (½ LP) — 1966 PYE NPL 18121
WITH — (B) OUTWARD BOWN — 1967 VERVE US 3062 MGM US CUBLM 1
JOHN GOODSALL G (— (B) OUTWARD BOWN — 1967 MUSIC FACTORY UK M F 12000
JESS RODEN V (CD — (C) THE ALAN BOWN — 1968 DECCA SML 1049
ROBERT PALMER V (— (D) SECOND ALBUM — 1968 DERAM
DAVE GREEN SAX (— (D) SECOND ALBUM — 1968 MGM US
STAN HALDANE B V (BCE — (E) LISTEN — 1970 ISLAND 6339022 GER UK ILPS9131
PETE BURGESS G V (— (F) STRETCHIN' OUT — 1971 ISLAND ILPS 9163
VIC SWEENEY D (BCEF
DAVE LAWSON K (— TERRY STANNARD D (— JOHN ANTHONY HELLIWELL SAX (BCEF
GORDON NEVILLE V (EF — ANDY BROWN B V (F — JEFF BANNISTER K V (BCEF
TONY CATCHPOLE G (CEF — JOHN HEMMINGS TROM (C — MEL COLLINS PERC (E

B189 ANDY BOWN B189

ANDY BOWN G V (ALL — (A) GONE TO MY HEAD — 1972 MERCURY UK 6310 002
WITH — (A) GONE TO MY HEAD — 1972 MERCURY IMP SRM 1625
HAROLD FISHER PERC (D — (B) ANDY BOWN SWEET WILLIAM — 1973 G M GML 1001
FRANK RICOTTI D (D — (C) COME BACK ROMANCE — 1976 EMI EMC 3176
MO FOSTER B (D — (D) GOOD ADVICE — 1978 EMI EMC 3283
DAVE MARKEE B (D — (E) DROWNED IN TEXAS — 19 SONOPRESSE FR 06806605
GEOFF WESTLEY G (D
PHIL PALMER G (D — CHRIS NEILL V (D — DOMINIC BUGATTI V (D
FRANK MUSKER V (D — SHARAN CAMPBELL V (D — NICO RAMSDEN G (B
BARRY DE SOUZA D (B — CHRIS BELSHAW B (BA — B J COLE STEEL (B
GLEN LEFLEUR PERC (B — JIMMY HOROWITZ CELESTE (BA — SKAILA KANGA HARP (B
CAROLINE ATTARD V (AB — LESLEY DUNCAN V (AB — SUE GLOVER V (B
SUNNY LESLIE V (B — STRINGS (B — MARTIN JENNER G (C
CHRIS RAE G (C — TERRY SMITH G (C — TERRY STANNARD D (C
MICKY WALLER D (A — LIZA STRIKE V (A — PETER FRAMPTON V (A
JOHN MEALING K SYN (C — PETE ZORN SAX (C — CHAS CRONK B (C
PADDY McHUGH V (C — FRANK COLLINS V (C — DIANE BIRCH V (C
TOM ALLOM V (C — RAY JACKSON HCA (C — GLEN LEFLEUR D (C

B190 BOX TOPS B190

ALEX CHILTON G V (ALL — (A) THE LETTER NEON RAINBOW — 1968 STATESIDE UK SSL 10218
GARY TALLEY G (123 — (A) THE LETTER NEON RAINBOW — 1968 BELL US 6011
HAROLD CLOUD B (3 — (B) CRY LIKE A BABY — 1968 STATESIDE UK 105
BILL CUNNINGHAM K B (12 — (B) CRY LIKE A BABY — 1968 BELL US 6017
JOHN EVANS G K (1 — (C) NON STOP — 1968 BELL US 6023
RICK ALLEN B K (2 — ( ) SUPERHITS — 196 BELL US 6025
SWAIN SCHARFER K (3 — (E) DIMENSIONS — 1968 BELL US 6032
DANNY SMYTHE D (1 — ( ) THE BEST OF THE BOX TOPS — 1974 SOUNDS SUPERB UK SPR 90051
TOM BOGGS D (23

B191 BOXER B191

MIKE PATTO V K (ABC — (A) BELOW THE BELT — 1975 VIRGIN 27030 GER UK V2049
OLLIE HALSALL G K (AB — (A) BELOW THE BELT — 1975 VIRGIN US PZ 34115
KEITH ELLIS B (BA — (B) BLOODLETTING(NOT RELEASED UNTIL 1979 — 1976 VIRGIN UK V2073
TONY NEWMAN D (AB — (C) ABSOLUTELY — 1977 EPIC UK EPC 82151
CHRIS STAINTON K (CB — (C) ABSOLUTELY — 1977 EPIC US PE 34812
TIM BOGERT B V (C
ADRIAN FISHER G (C — EDDIE TUDURI D (C — BOZ BURRELL V (B
BOBBY TENCH V (B — TIN HINKLEY K (B — JEFF GLIXMAN PROD (C

B193 EDDIE BOYD B193

EDDIE BOYD V PNO (ALL — (A) FIVE LONG YEARS — 19 FONTANA STJL 905
WITH — (B) & HIS BLUES BAND — 1967 DECCA UK SKL 4872
PETER GREEN G (C — (C) 7936 SOUTH RHODES — 1968 BLUE HORIZON UK 7 63202
JOHN McVIE B (C — (C) 7936 SOUTH RHODES — 1968 EPIC US 26409
MICK FLEETWOOD D (C — (D) LIVE — 1968 STORYVILLE SLP 268
STOCKHOLM SLIM V (E — (E) LEGACY OF THE BLUES VOL 10 — 1974 SONET UK SNTF 670
ED THIGPEN D (E — (E) LEGACY OF THE BLUES VOL 10 — 1974 GNP US 10020
ROLF ALM B (E — (F) VACATION FROM THE BLUES — 1976 JEFFERSON SWED 601
LESTER JONES B 'F — (G) DUST MY BROOM — 19 LONDON US 554
CHRISTER ECKLUND SAX (E
PEPS PERSSON G HCA V(E — SAM LANGHORN G (F — RICO COLLINS SAX (F — WILLIE COBBS B HCA(F
BONES D (F — EDDIE KING MILTON G (F — CHINK EVANS D (F — DAYLIGHTERS V (F
ERNEST COTTON SAX (F — PERCY WALKER D (F — JIMMY CONLEY SAX (F — FRED BELOW D (F
ROBERT JR LOCKWOOD G (F — RONALD WILSON SAX (F — BOB CARTER B (F — SONNY ALLEN D (F
WILLIE JONES B (F — CHRISTINE KITRELL V (F — L C McKINLEY G (F — ALFRED ELKINS B (F
LOUIS MYERS G (F

B194 TERENCE BOYLAN B194

TERENCE BOYLAN G V (ALL — (A) ALIAS BOONA — 1969 VERVE FORECAST US FTS 3070
WITH — (B) TERENCE BOYLAN — 1977 ELEKTRA US 7E 1091
WALTER BECKER G B (A — (C) SUZY — 1980 ELEKTRA US 6E 201
DONALD FAGAN K V (AB
HERB LOVELLE D (A — JIMMY JOHNSON D (A — DARIUS DAVENPORT D (A — JIM GORDON D (BC
RUSS KUNKEL D (BC — JEFF PORCARO D (B — CHUCK RAINEY B (B — DAVID JACKSON B (B
LEE SKLAR B (BC — DEAN PARKS G (B — VICTOR FELDMAN PERC (BC — JAI WINDING K (BC
TIM SCHMIT V (BC — JOHN KLEMMER SAX (B — GARY FOSTER SAX (BC — WILTON FELDER B (B
DON HENLEY V (BC — BEN BENAY G (BC — MICKEY McGEE D (B — AL KOOPER ORG (B
DON EVANS G (B — DAVID PAICH K (B — BOB GLAUB B (B — STEVE LUKATHER G (B
DODIE PETIT V (B — JOHN GUERIN D (B — MAX BENNETT B (B — TOM KELLY V (B
DENNIS WHITTED D (C — WILL McFARLANE G B (C — JOHN HOLBROOK B (C — ED GREENE D (C
MICHAEL PORCARO B (C — MICHAEL OMARTIAN PERC (C — JEFF BAXTER G (C — LARRY CARLTON G (C
PAUL HARRIS PERC (C — JAY GRAYDON G (C — DON FELDER G (C — DAVID KEMPER D (C
CHEVY CHASE PERC (C — EMIL RICHARDS PERC (C — MIRANDA McGRATH V (C — ALMA BOYLAN V (C

B194A TOMMY BOYCE & BOBBY HART B194A

TOMMY BOYCE G V (A — (A) TEST PATTERNS — 19 A&M US SP 7126
BOBBY HART K V (A
LOUIE SHELTON G (A — WAYNE IRVIN G (A — LARRY TAYLOR B (A
GERRY McGEE G (A — BILLY LEWIS D (A

B195 GARY BOYLE B195

GARY BOYLE G (AB	(A) THE DANCER	1977 GULL 163305 GER UK GULP 1020
WITH	(B) ELECTRIC GLIDE	1978 GULL 148309 GER UK GULP 1028
ROBIN LUMLEY K (A	(C) STEP OUT	1980 INTERCORD GER 145 623
ROD ARGENT K (A	(C) STEP OUT	1981 PICK UP UK 80305
DONI HARVEY B (A		
SIMON PHILLIPS D (AB	ZOE KRONBERGER K (A	DAVE McCRAE K (A
STEVE SHONE B (A	JEFF SEOPARDI D (A	MAGGIE PERT V (A
MORRIS PERT PERC (A	ROBERT AHWAI G (B	PETE JACOBSON K (B
JOHN GIBLIN B (B	SIMON MORTON PERC (B	PHIL CHEN B (B
RICHARD BAILEY D (B	KENNY SHAW G (B	GARY MOORE G (B
PAUL BIRCHALL K (C	GARY CULSHAW B (C	GRAHAM DEAN D (C
JANNE SCHAFFER G (C	STEFAN NILSSON SYN (C	BJORN JASON LINDH FLT (C
JACOB ANDERSON PERC (C		

B196 THE BOYS B196

MATT DANGERFIELD V G (ABCD	(A) THE BOYS	1977 NEMS UK NELS 6001
CASINO STEEL PNO (ABC	(B) ALTERNATIVE CHARTBUSTERS	1978 NEMS UK NELS 6015
KID REID V B (ABCD	(C) TO HELL WITH THE BOYS	1978 SAFARI 8002 NL UK 1 2 BOYS
JACK BLACK D (ABCD	(D) BOYS ONLY	1980 SAFARI 8004 NL UK BOYS 4
JOHN PLAIN G (ABCD		

B196A BOYS NEXT DOOR B196A

NICK CAVE V K SAX(AB	(A) BOYS NEXT DOOR(EP)	19 MISSING LINK AUST LEP 3
TRACY PEW B CLAR (AB	(B) DOOR DOOR	1979 MUSHROOM AUST 36931
PHIL CALVERT D (AB		
ROWLAND HOWARD G SAX (AB	MICK HARVEY G K SYN B (AB	

B197 BOYZZ B197

MIKE TAFOYA G (A	(A) TOO WILD TO TAME	1978 EPIC UK EPC 82995
DIRTY DAN BUCK V PERC(A		
GIL PINI G V (A	ANATOLE HALINKOVICH K (A	KENT COOPER PERC V (A
DAVID ANGEL D (A	LOU DELGATTO SAX (A	LOU MARINI SAX (A
SAM BURTIS TROM (A	ALAN RUBIN TPT (A	

B197A BRAINBOX B197A

JAN AKKERMAN G K (A	(A) BRAINBOX	1971 CAPITOL IMP ST 596
HERMAN MEYER G (B	(A) BRAINBOX	1970 PARLOPHONE UK PCS 7094
ANDRE REYNEN B (A	(A) BRAINBOX	1970 IMPERIAL NL 054 24082
PIERRE VAN DER LINDEN (A	(B) BEST OF	1972
CASIMIERZ LUX V PERC(AB	(C) PARTS	19 HARVEST 056 24551
TOM BARIACHER FLT (A		
FRANS SMIT PERC (BC	JOHN SCHUURSMA (B	RUDI DE QUELJOE (B
ROBERT VERWEY B K (C	RON MEYJES G HCA (C	MICHAEL VON DIJK V FLT(C

B197B BRAINS B197B

TOM GRAY K V (A	(A) BRAINS	1980 MERCURY UK 6337103 US 1 3835
RICK PRICE G V (A	(B) ELECTRONIC EDEN	1981 MERCURY
BRYAN SMITHWICK B (A		
CHARLES WOLFF D V (A		

B197C BRAHMAN B197C

VICTOR STEWART V (A	(A) BRAHMAN	1971 MERCURY US 61348
ROBBIE KING K (A		
EDDIE PATTERSON G (A	DURIS MAXWELL V D (A	D LANZ (A

B197D SCOTT BRADFORD B197D

SCOTT BRADFORD K (A	(A) ROCK SLIDE	1969 PROBE US 4509
NATHAN DAVIS WIND (A		
STU MARTIN PERC (A	GUNTHER LENZ B (A	PHILIP CATHERINE G (A
JANET MORALES TPT (A	NICK KLETCHKOVSKY B (A	VINAGRE PERC (A

B197E BRIAN BRAIN B197E

MARTIN'BRIAN BRAIN'ATKINS V (A	(A) UNEXPECTED NOISES	1980 SECRET UK BRAIN 1
PETE JONES B V (A		
GEOFF SMYTH G V (A	JOHN MADDEN V (A	BOBBY SURGEONOR G SYN V B (A
BILLY K SAX (A	JOHN CATHERALL B (A	GARY SMALLMAN D (A

B197F BRAINCHILD B197F

BILL EDWARDS B V (A	(A) HEALING OF THE LUNITIC OWL	1970 A&M NL 979
BRIAN WILSHAW WIND (A		
HARVEY COLES B V (A	DAVE MULLER D (A	CHRIS JENNINGS K (A
LLOYD WILLIAMS TPT (A	IAN GOSS TROM (A	PAT STRACHAM TROM (A

B198 BRAINSTORM B198

	(A) STORMIN'	1977 RCA UK PL 12048
	(A) STORMIN'	197 CBS US 35327
	(b) JOURNEY TO THE NIGHT	1978 TABU
	(b) JOURNEY TO THE NIGHT	19 CBS US JZ 2048
	(C) FUNKY ENTERTAINMENT	1979 TABU UK TBU 83736

B198A BRAINSTORM B198A

EDDY VON OVERHEIDT K V (AB	(A) SMILE A WHILE	1972 SPIEGELEI GERM 28505
ROLAND SCHAEFFER G K (AB	(B) SECOND SMILE	1974 SPIEGELEI GERM 28596
JOACHIM KEINZER D (AB		
RAINER BODENSOHN B FLT V(AB	ENNO DERNOV G B (B	

B199 BRAINTICKET B199

JOEL VANDROOGENBROECK FLT K V (ABC	(A) PSYCHONAUT	19 BELLAPHON BLPS19104
ROLF HUG V G PERC(A	(B) COTTON WOOD HILL	1971 BELLAPHON GERM 19019
MARTIN SACHER B FLT (A	(C) CELESTRIAL SEA	1974 RCA SF 8398
BARNEY PALM D PERC(A		
JANE FREE V PERC(A	CAROLE MURIEL V (A	PETER GOOD VIBES (A
COSMO LAMPIS D (B	WOLFGANG PAAP PERC (B	DAWN MUIR V (B
HELLMUTH KELBE K (B	RON BAER G (B	WERNI PRAHLACH B (B

B199A BRAKES B199A

JOE FADIL G V (A	(A) FOR WHY YOU KICKA MY DONKEY	1979 MAGNET 624179 GER UK MAGL5029
KEITH WILSON G V (A		
JOHN BROWN D (A	BOB PENNY B (A	

B199B RANDALL BRAMBLETT B199B

Album	Year	Label	Country	Number
(A) THAT OTHER MILE	1975	POLYDOR	US	6045
(B) LIGHT OF THE NIGHT	1976	POLYDOR	US	6064

Musician	Instrument	Albums
RANDALL BRAMBLETT	K V G SAX	(AB
CHUCK LEAVELL	K	(A
SCOTT BOYER	G	(A
WILL LEE	B V	(A
HUGH McCRACKEN	G	(A
CHRIS PARKER	D	(A
BOB MANN	G	(A
TOMMY TALTON	G	(A
ANDY MUSEN	B	(A
PAUL HORNSBY	K	(A
RICK MAROTTA	D	(A
ERIC WEISSBERG	STEEL	(A
DAVID BROWN	B	(A
ELLIOTT RANDALL	G	(A
AL GORGONI	G	(A

B200 BONNIE BRAMLETT B200

Album	Year	Label	Country	Number
(A) SWEET BONNIE BRAMLETT	1973	CBS	UK	65001
(B) ITS TIME	1975	CAPRICORN	UK	2429 125
(B) ITS TIME	1975	CAPRICORN	US	0148
(C) LADY'S CHOICE	1976	CAPRICORN	UK	2429 145
(C) LADY'S CHOICE	1976	CAPRICORN	US	0169
(D) MEMORIES	1978	CAPRICORN	UK	2429 162
(D) MEMORIES	1978	CAPRICORN	US	0199

Musician	Instrument	Albums
BONNIE BRAMLETT	V	(ALL
WITH		
BARRY BECKETT	K	(C
DAVID HOOD	B	(C
JOHNNY SANDLIN	G	(C
ROGER HAWKINS	D	(C
TOMMY TALTON	G	(CB
HARVEY THOMPSON	HRNS	(C
RICHARD BETTS	G	(C
CHARLES ROSE	HRNS	(C
RICKY HIRSCH	G	(CB
GREGG ALLMAN	ORG	(CB
KENNY TIBBETTS	B PERC	(B
JAIMOE	CONGAS	(B
SHIRLEY MATTHEWS	V	(B
BIG BILL STEWART	D	(B
JOHNNY SANDLIN	G PERC	(B
CLYDIE KING	V	(B
JAY ARMENTROUT	D	(D
RANDALL BRAMBLETT	SAX	(CB
RON EADES	HRNS	(C
PAUL HORNSBY	K	(CB
DIANNE DAVIDSON	V	(C
JERRY THOMPSON	D	(B
EARL FORD	TROM	(B
DAVID BROWN	SAX	(B
BUTCH TRUCKS	CONGAS	(B
TOM RIDGEWAY	SYN	(B
HAROLD WILLIAMS	SAX	(B
ANITA BALL		(C
HARRISON CALLOWAY	HRNS	(C
CHUCK LEAVELL	PNO	(CB
JOE ENGLISH	D	(D
SCOTT BOYER	G	(BD
LAGATHA BECK-SMALLWOOD	V	(B
ROBERT MARTIN	K SAX	(D
EDDIE HINTON	G	(BD
LEO LABRANCHE	TPT	(B
JIMMY NAILS	G	(D

B201 DELANEY BRAMLETT B201

Album	Year	Label	Country	Number
(A) MOBIUS STRIP	19	CBS	US	KC 32420
(B) SOMETHINGS COMING	1972	CBS	UK	65131
(C) GIVING BIRTH TO A SONG	19	MGM	US	M3G 5011
(D) CLASS REUNION	1977	PRODIGAL	US	P7 10017
(D) CLASS REUNION	1977	PRODIGAL		PDL 2005

Musician	Instrument	Albums
DELANEY BRAMLETT	G V	(ALL
WITH		
SPIDER TAYLOR	G	(D
RANDY SHARP	G	(D
CHUCK RAINEY	B	(D
CHRIS ETHRIDGE	B	(D
RICK SUTHERLAND	K	(CD
JIM KELTNER	D	(D
JACKIE KELSO	HRNS	(D
CLYDIE KING	V	(BD
SUSIE ALLANSON	V	(D
STRINGS		(D
NICK VAN MAARTH	G	(C
RON GRAYSON	D PERC	(B
ROBERT WILSON	B	(B
JOE DAVIS	SAX	(B
GLORIA JONES	V	(B
BEN BENAY	G	(B
JIM HOBSON	K	(CD
CHUCK FINDLEY	HRNS	(D
DICK HYDE	HRNS	(D
SHIRLEY MATTHEWS	V	(BD
PAT ERICKSON	V	(D
JIM McGREW	G	(C
FRED RIVERA	B	(C
MILT HOLLAND	PERC	(B
DARRELL LEONARD	HRNS	(B
JIM GORDON	SAX	(B
BILLY PRESTON	K	(B
VANETTA FIELDS	V	(B
STU PERRY	D	(CD
OLLIE MITCHELL	HRNS	(D
QUITMAN DENNIS	HRNS	(D
MONALISA YOUNG	V	(D
PATTI QUATRO	V	(D
VICTOR PANTOJA	PERC	(C
COLE KESLER	HCA	(C
TIM HEDING	K	(B
LARRY SAVORE	HRNS	(B
JERRY JUMONVILLE	SAX	(B
JERRY McGEE	G	(B

B202 DELANEY & BONNIE BRAMLETT B202

Album	Year	Label	Country	Number
(A) HOME(67)	1969	STAX	US	2026
(A) HOME	1974	STAX	UK	2362 001
(B) ACCEPT NO SUBSTITUTE	1969	ELEKTRA	US	EKS 74039
(B) ACCEPT NO SUBSTITUTE	1969	APPLE	UK	SAPCOR 7
(B) ACCEPT NO SUBSTITUTE	1971	ELEKTRA	UK	K 42024
(C) ON TOUR	1970	ATLANTIC	UK	2400 013
(C) ON TOUR	1970	ATCO	US	33326
(C) ON TOUR	1971	ATLANTIC	UK	K 30030
(D) TO BONNIE FROM DELANEY	1970	ATLANTIC	UK	2400 029
(D) TO BONNIE FROM DELANEY	1970	ATCO	US	33341
(D) TO BONNIE FROM DELANEY	1971	ATLANTIC	UK	K
(E) MOTEL SHOT	1971	ATCO	US	33358
(F) COUNTRY LIFE	197	ATCO	US	33383
(G) GENESIS	1971	LONDON	UK	ZGL 113
(G) GENESIS	1971	CRECSENDO	US	2054
(H) TOGETHER	1972	CBS	UK	64959
(H) TOGETHER	1972	CBS	US	KC 31377
(I) BEST OF	1973	ATLANTIC	UK	K 40429

Musician	Instrument	Albums
DELANEY BRAMLETT	G V	(ALL
BONNIE BRAMLETT	V	(ALL
WITH		
BOOKER T JONES	K	(A
DONALD DUNN	B	(A
STEVE CROPPER	G	(A
AL JACKSON	D	(A
BEN BENAY	G	(DE
DUANE ALLMAN	G	(DE
JERRY JUMONVILLE	SAX	(D
FRANK MAYES	SAX	(D
DARRYL LEONARD	HRNS	(D
JIM GORDON	K	(D
KENNY GRADNEY	B	(DE
CHUCK MORGAN	D	(D
KING CURTIS	SAX	(D
CHARLIE FREEMAN	G	(D
BOBBY WHITLOCK	K V	(ABCD
TOM McCLURE	B	(D
JERRY SCHEFF	B	(D
RON TUTT	D	(D
ED LOGAN	SAX	(D
JACK HALE	TROM	(D
LITTLE RICHARD	PNO	(D
SNEAKY PETE KLEINOW	STEEL	(D
CARL RADLE	B	(BCE
BOBBY KEYS	SAX	(BCE
JERRY McGEE	G	(B
WILLIAM BELL	V	(A
BILLY PRESTON	K	(H
VANETTA FIELDS	V	(H
JOE COCKER	V	(E
BILLY STRANGE		(G
RITA COOLIDGE	V	(BC
SAMMY CREASON	D	(D
FLOYD NEWMAN	SAX	(D
SAM CLAYTON	CONGA	(D
MIKE UTLEY	PNO	(D
ERIC CLAPTON	G	(C
JIM GORDON	D	(C
GEORGE HARRISON	G	(
JIM KELTNER	D	(BE
EDDIE FLOYD	V	(A
EDDY KENDRICKS	V	(H
JOHN HARTFORD	BANJ	(E
BOBBY WOMACK	G	(H
JAMES BURTON	G	(G
TEX JOHNSON	CONGA	(C
ANDREW LOVE	SAX	(D
WAYNE JACKSON	TPT	(D
ALAN ESTES	PERC	(D
JIM DICKINSON	PNO	(D
DAVE MASON	G	(CE
JIM PRICE	HRNS	(BC
LEON RUSSELL	G K	(BEG
ISAAC HAYES	V	(A
GLEN CAMPBELL	G	(G
MERRY CLAYTON	V	(H
CLARENCE WHITE	G V	(E
AL CASEY	G	(G
HAL BLAINE	D	(G

B203 BRAND X B203

Album	Year	Label	Country	Number
(A) UNORTHODOX BEHAVIOUR	1976	CHARISMA	UK	CAS 1117 EURO 6369977
(B) MOROCCAN ROLL	1977	CHARISMA	UK	CAS 1126 EURO 9124010
(B) MOROCCAN ROLL	1977	PASSPORT	US	98022
(C) LIVE STOCK	1977	CHARISMA	UK	CLASS 5
(C) LIVE STOCK	1977	PASSPORT	US	9824
(D) MASQUES	1978	CHARISMA	UK	CAS 1138 EURO 9124030
(D) MASQUES	1978	PASSPORT	US	9829

Musician	Instrument	Albums
PERCY JONES	B	(ABCDEFG
ROBIN LUMLEY	K	(ABCFEG
JOHN GOODSALL	G	(ABCDFEG
PRESTON HEYMAN	D	(
PHIL COLLINS	PERC	(ABCFEG
JOE BLOCKER	PERC	(
MORRIS PERT	PERC	(BDFCE

(CONTINUED)

B203 BRAND X (CONTINUED) B203

Member	Instrument	Albums
KENWOOD DENNARD	D	(C
JACK LANCASTER	WIND	(A
CHUCK BURGI	D	(D
PETER ROBINSON	K	(FDEG
MIKE CLARKE	D	(FE
JOHN GIBLIN	B	(EFG
RAPHAEL RAVENSCROFT	SAX	(G
STEVEN SHORT	V D	(G

Album	Year	Label	Country	Number
(E) PRODUCT	1979	CHARISMA	UK	CAS 1147 EURO 9124045
(E) PRODUCT	1979	PASSPORT	US	9840
(F) DO THEY HURT	1980	CHARISMA	UK	CAS 1151 EURO 9124059
(G) IS THERE ANYTHING ABOUT	1982	CBS	UK	85967

B203A BRANDYWINE B203A

Member	Instrument	Albums
ALBERT MILLER	K V	(A
EDWARD STASIUM	G V	(A
CHIP MILES	D PERC	(A
SONNY SEALS	WIND	(A
MIKE CARUSE	B	(A
BILLY HOWELL	TROM	(A
CLIFF DAVIS	WIND	(A
PASQUALE SALERNE	TPT	(A

Album	Year	Label	Country	Number
(A) AGED	1970	BRUNSWICK	US	754171

B204 BRASS CONSTRUCTION B204

Member	Instrument	Albums
LARRY PAYTON	D	(
SANDY BILLUPS	V PERC	(
WAYNE PARRIS	TPT	(
WADE WILLIAMSON	B	(
MICHAEL GRUDGE	SAX	(
RANDY MILLER	V K	(
MORRIS PRICE	TPT	(
JESSE WARD	SAX	(
JOSEPH ARTHUR WONG	G	(

Album	Year	Label	Country	Number
(A) BRASS CONSTRUCTION	1976	UA	UK	UAS 29913
(A) BRASS CONSTRUCTION	1976	UA	US	LA 545G
(B) 2	1976	UA	UK	UAS 30016
(B) 2	1976	UA	US	LA 677G
(C) 3	1978	UA	UK	UAS 30124
(C) 3	1978	UA	US	LA 775H
(D) 4	1978	UA	UK	UAS 30210
(D) 4	1978	UA	US	LA 916H
(E) 5	1980	LIBERTY		
(F) 6	1981	LIBERTY		

B204A CHRIS BRAUN BAND B204A

Member	Instrument	Albums
CHRIS BRAUN	V	(AB
KLAUS MELCHERS	K	(B
BERND ADAM KEWITZ	G SAX	(B
JOCHEN BERNSTEIN	B	(B
PETER HAST	PERC	(B
ELMAR KROHN	D	(B
JIGGS WHIGHAM		(B

Album	Year	Label	Country	Number
(A) BOTH SIDES	1972			
(B) FOREIGN LADY	1974	PAN		87586

B205 RICHARD BRAUTIGAN B205

Member	Instrument	Albums
RICHARD BRAUTIGAN		

Album	Year	Label	Country	Number
(A) LISTENING TO	19	STRAIGHT		ST 424

B205A BRAVE BELT B205A

Member	Instrument	Albums
RANDY BACHMAN	G V	(AB
FRED TURNER	B V	(AB
ROBIN BACHMAN	D V	(B
CHAD ALLEN	K V	(A

Album	Year	Label	Country	Number
(A) BRAVE BELT	19	REPRISE	US	6447
(B) BRAVE BELT II	19	REPRISE	US	2057

B206 BREAD B206

Member	Instrument	Albums
DAVID GATES	G K V VLN	(ALL
LARRY KNECHTEL	K G B HCA	(DEFH
RON EDGAR	D	(A
JAMES GRIFFIN	K G V	(ABCDEFH
MIKE BOTTS	D	(BCDEFH
DEAN PARKS	G	(H
ROB ROYER	B	(ABCF
TOM SCOTT	WIND	(H
JIM GORDON	D	(A
MIKE BODDICKER	K	(H

Album	Year	Label	Country	Number
(A) BREAD	1969	ELEKTRA	UK	K 42029
(A) BREAD	1969	ELEKTRA	US	EKS 74044
(A) BREAD	1976	ELEKTRA	FR	22014
(B) ON THE WATER	1970	ELEKTRA	UK	K 42050
(B) ON THE WATER	1970	ELEKTRA	US	EKS 74076
(C) MANNA	1971	ELEKTRA	UK	K 52001
(C) MANNA	1971	ELEKTRA	US	EKS 74086
(C) MANNA	197	ELEKTRA	UK	K 42081
(D) BABY IM A WANT YOU	1972	ELEKTRA	UK	K 42100
(D) BABY IM A WANT YOU	1972	ELEKTRA	US	EKS 75015
(E) GUITAR MAN	1972	ELEKTRA	UK	K 52004
(E) GUITAR MAN	1972	ELEKTRA	US	EKS 75047
(F) BEST OF BREAD	1974	ELEKTRA	UK	K 42115
(F) BEST OF BREAD	1974	ELEKTRA	US	EKS 75076
(F) BEST OF BREAD	1974	ELEKTRA		EQ 5056
(G) BEST OF VOL 2	1974	ELEKTRA	UK	K 42161
(G) BEST OF VOL 2	1974	ELEKTRA	US	7E 1005
(H) LOST WITHOUT YOUR LOVE	1977	ELEKTRA	UK	K 52044
(H) LOST WITHOUT YOUR LOVE	1977	ELEKTRA	US	7E 1094
(I) SOUND OF BREAD	1977	ELEKTRA	UK	K 52062

B207 BREAD LOVE & DREAMS B207

Member	Instrument	Albums
ANGIE REW	V FLT	(ABC
DAVID McNIVEN	V K G	(ABC
CAROLYN DAVIS	G V	(ABC
DANNY THOMPSON	B	(C
TERRY COX	D	(C
DAVE RICHMOND	B	(C
JOHN ROMSEY	D	(
ALAN TRAJAN	K	(C

Album	Year	Label	Country	Number
(A) BREAD LOVE & DREAMS	1969	DECCA	UK	SKL 5008
(B) STRANGE TALE OF CAPTAIN SHANNON	1970	DECCA	UK	SKL 5048
(C) AMARYLLIS	1971	DECCA	UK	SKL 5081

B207A BREAKFAST SPECIAL B207A

Member	Instrument	Albums
RICHARD CROOKS	D	(A
ROGER MASON	B V	(A
ANDY STATMAN	SAX V MAN	(A
MARGUERITE CLARK	V	(A
JIM TOLLES	G	(A
TONY TRISCHKA	BJO STEEL	(A
KENNY KOSEK	FDL V	(A
STEVE BURGH	G	(A
JOE VAL		(A
STACY PHILLIPS	G TPT	(A
MOSHE SAVITSKY	G	(A

Album	Year	Label	Country	Number
(A) BREAKFAST SPECIAL	1976	ROUNDER	US	3012

B207B FRANCOIS BREANT B207B

Member	Instrument	Albums
FRANCOIS BREANT	K V	(AB
EMANUEL LACORDAIRE	D PERC	(B
JEAN MICHEL KAJDAN	G	(B
GUY KHALIFA	K V	(B
PASCAL ARROYO	B	(B
KLAUS BLASQUIZ	V	(B
FELIX BLANCHARD	K	(B
DIDIER LOCKWOOD	VLN	(B
LIZA DELUXE	V	(B
MICK MARTIN	G	(B
STELLA VANDER	V	(B

Album	Year	Label	Country	Number
(A) SONS OPTIQUES				
(B) VOYEUR EXTRA-LUCIDE	1979	BARCLAY	FR	BA215

B207C BREATHLESS B207C

Member	Instrument	Albums
MARK AVSEC	K V	(AB
BOB BENJAMIN	B	(AB
ALAN GREENE	G	(AB
JONAH KOSLEN	G V	(AB
RODNEY PSYKA	PERC	(AB
KEVIN VALENTINE	D	(AB

Album	Year	Label	Country	Number
(A) BREATHLESS	1979	EMI	UK	17013
(B) NOBODY LEAVES THIS SONG ALIVE	1980	EMI	UK	17041

B208 THE BRECKER BROTHERS B208

Member	Instrument	Albums
RANDY BRECKER	HRNS	(ALL
MICHAEL BRECKER	HRNS	(ALL
DAVE SANBORN	SAX	(AB
DON GROLNICK	K	(ABE
BOB MANN	G	(A
WILL LEE	B V	(AB

Album	Year	Label	Country	Number
(A) THE BRECKER BROTHERS	1975	ARISTA	UK	ARTY 103
(A) THE BRECKER BROTHERS	1975	ARISTA	US	AL 4037
(B) BACK TO BACK	1976	ARISTA	UK	ARTY 128
(B) BACK TO BACK	1976	ARISTA	US	AL 4061
(C) DONT STOP THE MUSIC	1977	ARISTA	UK	SPARTY 1007
(D) HEAVY METAL BE-BOP	1978	ARISTA	UK	SPART1070

(CONTINUED)

B208 (CONTINUED) THE BRECKER BROTHERS B208

(D) HEAVY METAL BE-BOP	1978	ARISTA US 4085	NL	202 113	
(E) DETENTE	1980	ARISTA US 4272	NL	202 380	
(F) STRAPHANGIN'	1981	ARISTA US 9550	NL	203 464	

HARVEY MASON	D	(A						
SAMMY FIGUEROA	PERC	(BD						
RAFAEL CRUZ	PERC	(BD						
TERRY BOZZIO	G	(D						
NEIL JASON	B V	(DE	PATTI AUSTIN	V	(B	DIANE SUMLER	V	(B
BARRY FINNERTY	G	(DF	RALPH MACDONALD	PERC	(ABE	ALLEE WILLIS	V	(B
KASH MONET	PERC	(D	JEFF SCHOEN	V	(D	ROY HERRING	V	(D
PAUL SCHAEFFER	K	(D	VICTORIA	TAMB	(D	ALLEN SCHWARZBERG	D	(D
STEVE KHAN	G	(B	CHRIS PARKER	D	(B	STEVE GADD	D	(BE
LEW DELGATTO	SAX	(B	DAVE FRIEDMAN	PERC	(B	LUTHER VANDROSS	V	(B
ROBIN CLARK	V	(B	D J ROGERS	V	(E	JEFF MIRANOV	G	(E
AIRTO	PERC	(E	HIRAM BULLOCK	G	(E	DAVID SPINOZZA	G	(E
PAULINHO DACOSTA	PERC	(E	MARK GRAY	K	(EF	MARCUS MILLER	B	(EF
STEVE JORDAN	D	(E	CARL CARLWELL	V	(E	RICHIE MORALES	D	(F

B208A RANDY BRECKER B208A

(A) SCORE	19	SOLID STATE	US	18051

RANDY BRECKER	HRNS	(A						
MICHAEL BRECKER	SAX	(A						
JERRY DODGION	FLT	(A	LARRY CORYELL	G	(A	HAL GALPER	K	(A
EDDIE GOMEZ	B	(A	CHUCK RAINEY	B	(A	MICKEY ROKER	D	(A
BERNARD PURDIE	D	(A						

B208B JOE BREEN B208B

(A) MORE THAN MEETS THE EYE	1978	VERTIGO	NL	6370 430

JOE BREEN	G V PERC	(A						
HENRY SPINETTI	D	(A						
MO FOSTER	B	(A	RICK HITCHCOCK	G	(A	ROGER GLOVER	K HCA	(A
DAVE MARKEE	B	(A	DAVE MACRAE	K	(A	LIZA STRIKE	V	(A
JOANNE STONE	V	(A	VICKY BROWN	V	(A	JOHN PERRY	B	(A
TONY HYMAS	K	(A	RAY GLYNN	SITAR G	(A	HUGH BURNS	G	(A
JON LORD	K SYN	(A	BARRY DESOUZA	D	(A	BOB BENHAM	G	(A

B208C BREEZE B208C

(A) ITS ONLY A MATTER OF TIME	19	ELECTROLA	EURO	064 82423

ED VAN TOOVENBURG	G V	(A						
FRED JANSEN	G V	(A						
BART VAN SCHOONHOVEN	G V	(A	HANS JANSEN	K	(A	LOUIS DOBEY	D	(A
PIET JAN BLAUW	PERC	(A	FREEK BERRIER	K	(A	JAN HOLLESTELLE	B	(A
CLAUS VAN MECHELEN	SAX	(A	ROB MEYN	PERC	(A			

B208D BRENDA & THE TABULATIONS B208D

(A) DRY YOUR EYES	19	DIONN	US	2000
(B) BRENDA & THE TABULATIONS	19	TOP & BOTTOM	US	100

B208E BRETHREN B208E

(A) BRETHREN	19	TIFFANY	US	0013
(B) MOMENT OF TRUTH	19	TIFFANY	US	0015

TOM COSGROVE	G V	(AB						
STU WOODS	B V	(AB						
RICK MAROTTA	D	(AB						
MIKE GARSEN	K	(AB	DR JOHN	K	(A	RUSTY YOUNG	STEEL	(A
PATRICK	PNO	(A	THE BLOSSOMS	V	(A	RALPH McDONALD	PERC	(B
BARRY ROGERS	TROM	(B	DAVE LIEBMAN	SAX	(B	MAERETHA STEWART	V	(B
ALBERTINE ROBINSON	V	(B	TASHA THOMAS	V	(B	MARILYN JACKSON	V	(B
ADRIENNE ALBERT	V	(B	AMANDA AMBROSE	V	(B			

B209 PAUL BRETT B209

(A) PAUL BRETT SAGE	1970	PYE UK NSPL18347 US	JANUS3026	
(B) JUBILATION FOUNDRY	1971	DAWN	UK	DNLS 3021
(C) SCHIZOPHRENIA	1972	DAWN	UK	DNLS 3032
(D) PAUL BRETT	1973	BRADLEY	UK	BRADL1001
(E) CLOCKS	1974	BRADLEYS	UK	BRADL1004
(F) PHOENIX FUTURE	1975	PHOENIX FUTURE	UK	
(G) EARTHBIRTH	1977	RCA	UK	PL 25080
(H) INTERLIFE	1978	RCA I2962 US	UK	PL 25149
(I) ECLIPSE	1979	RCA	UK	PL 25219
(J) GUITAR TREK	1980	RCA	UK	PL 25283

PAUL BRETT	G V	(ALL						
WITH								
NICKY HIGGINBOTTOM	WIND	(A						
DEREK AUSTIN	K	(H						
BOB VOICE	PERC	(A						
DICK DUFALL	B	(A						
MEL COLLINS	SAX	(H						
STEVE GREGORY	SAX	(H						
DAVID GRIFFITHS	B	(EH						
DELISLE HARPER	B	(H						
ROD COOMBES	D	(H						
TOM NICHOL	D	(IJ	DAVE OLNEY	B	(I	GRAHAM JARVIS	D	(I
ROB YOUNG	K	(I	CHRIS MERCER	SAX	(I	RAY WARLEIGH	SAX	(I
JOHNNY JOYCE	G	(I	ALAN TODD	G	(IJ	TOM NEWMAN	V	(I
DAVE WILLIAMS	B	(I	RICHARD HARVEY	K	(J	PAUL TOWNSHEND	B	(J
MIKE PIGGOTT	VLN G	(DE	NICK STERLING	CELLO	(D	DELISLE HARPER	B	(DH
ROB YOUNG	K FDL	(DI						

B209A BREWER & FARNER B209A

(A) MONUMENTAL FUNK	1974	QUADICO	US	QLP 7401

DON BREWER		(A
MARK FARNER		(A

B210 BREWER & SHIPLEY B210

(A) DOWN IN L A	1968	A&M	US	SP 4154
(B) WEEDS	1969	KAMA SUTRA	UK	2361 005
(B) WEEDS	1969	KAMA SUTRA	US	BS 2016
(C) TARKIO ROAD	1970	KAMA SUTRA	UK	2316 001
(C) TARKIO ROAD	1971	KAMA SUTRA	US	BS 2024
(C) TARKIO ROAD	19	KAMA SUTRA		2319 004
(D) SHAKE OFF THE DEMON	1972	KAMA SUTRA	US	BS 2039
(E) RURAL SPACE	1973	KAMA SUTRA	UK	2319 028
(E) RURAL SPACE	1973	KAMA SUTRA	US	BS 2058
(F) BREWER & SHIPLEY	1974	CAPITOL	US	ST 11261
(G) WELCOME TO RIDDLE BRIDGE	1975	CAPITOL	UK	EST 11402
(H) NOT FAR FROM FREE	1978	MERCURY	US	9100 044
( ) BEST OF	19	KAMA SUTRA	US	2-2613

MIKE BREWER	G V	(ALL						
TOM SHIPLEY	B V	(ALL						
WITH								
JERRY GARCIA	G	(C						
NICKY HOPKINS	K	(B						
MARK NAFTALIN	K	(BCDE						
RED RHODES	STEEL	(B						
BILLY MUNDI	D	(E						
PRAIRIE PRINCE	D	(E						
FRED BURTON	G	(CE						
JOHN KAHN	B	(BCDE						
LEON OAKLEY	CORNET	(E						
BILL VITT	D	(CE						
TURK MURPHY	TROM	(E						
PHIL HOWE	WIND	(E	JAMES MAIHACK	TUBA	(E	BUDDY CAGE	K	(E
MIKE LEECH	B	(G	NORBERT PUTNAM	B	(G	DAVID BRIGGS	K	(G
REGGIE YOUNG	G	(G	CHRIS LEUZINGER	G	(G	PAUL FRANKLIN	STEEL	(G
WELDON MYRICK	G	(G	KEN BUTTREY	D	(G	CHARLIE McCOY	HCA	(G
FARRELL MORRIS	PERC	(G	SHANE KEISTER	SYN	(G	CHARLES ROSE	HRNS	(G
RONNIE EADES	KRNS	(G	HARVEY THOMPSON	HRNS	(G	HARRISON CALLOWAY	HRNS	(G

(CONTINUED)

B210

BREWER & SHIPLEY (CONTINUED)

MARY HOLLADAY V (G
JIM MESSINA (A
JOHN CIPOLINA V (D
NOEL JEWEKS FLT (C
JOSE CHEPITO AREAS (D
FRED OLSEN G (B
REINOL ANDINO CONGA (B
DAVID LAFLAMME VLN (D
DOUG HAYWOOD B (F
BUDDY EMMONS STEEL (F
AL KOOPER ORG (F
RUSS KUNKEL D (F
GINGER HOLLADAY V (G
BOB JONES D (BC
SPENCER DRYDEN D (D
DIANE TRIBUNO V (C
ROBERT HUBERMAN B (B
PHIL FORD TABLA (B
LITTLE JOHN HARTEMAN D (D
JESSE ED DAVIS G (F
MICHAEL OMARTIAN PNO (F
BUD SHANK WIND (F
BILL PERKINS WIND (F
SNEAKY PETE KLEINOW STEEL (F
MIKE BLOOMFIELD G (B
NICK GRAVENITES V (BC
RICHARD GREENE VLN (B
DANNY COX V (C
IRA KAMIN K (B
APLLE JACK HCA (B
GLENN WALTERS D (D
GARY MALLABER D (F
JOHN BOYLAN K SYN(F
STEVE CASH HCA (F
LARRY KNIGHT G PERC(F

B211

BREWERS DROOP

(A) OPENING TIME 1972 RCA UK SF 8301

RON WATTS V PERC(A
STEVE DARRINGTON K HCA V (A
JOHN McKAY G V (A
PETE DUNCAN HRNS (A
BOB WALKER D PERC (A
DAVE GELLY SAX (A
MALCOLM BARRETT B VLN (A
JOHN WILLIAMS SAX (A

B212

BRICK

(A) GOOD HIGH 1976 BANG SHOT 003
(B) BRICK 1978 BANG SHOT 004
(C) STONEHEART 1979 BANG US 35969
(D) WAITING ON YOU 1980 BANG US 36262

JIMMY BROWN WIND V(AB
RAY RANSOM B V (AB
REGI HARGIS G V (AB
EDDIE IRONS K V (AB

B213

ALICIA BRIDGES

(A) ALICIA BRIDGES 1978 POLYDOR UK 2391 364
(B) PLAY IT AS IT LAYS 1979 POLYDOR US 6219

ALICIA BRIDGES V (AB
RANDY McCORMICK K (AB
TOM ROBB B (AB
ROY YEAGER D (A
STEVE BUCKINGHAM G (AB
ALAN FEINGOLD ORG (AB
VINNI O'NEAL V (A
LARRY BYRAM G (B
KEN BELL G (AB
MICKEY BUCKINS G PERC (AB
STEVE McRAY ORG (AB
KEITH'DOC'SAMUELS V (A
JAMES STROUD D (B
JOHN FRISTOE G V (AB
BERNADINE MITCHELL V (A
JAY SCOTT SAX (B

B214

DEE DEE BRIDGEWATER

(A) JUST FAMILY 1978 ELEKTRA UK K 52067
(A) JUST FAMILY 1978 ELEKTRA US 6E 119
(B) DEE DEE BRIDGEWATER 19 ATLANTIC US 18188

DEE DEE BRIDGEWATER V (AB
WITH
STANLEY CLARKE B (A
CHICK COREA K (A
GEORGE DUKE K (A
HARVEY MASON D (A
AIRTO MOREIRA PERC (A
ALPHONSO JOHNSON B (A
SCARLET RIVERA VLN (A
RAY GOMEZ G (A
DAVID T WALKER D (A

B216

MARC BRIERLEY

(A) HELLO 19 CBS UK 63835

MARC BRIERLEY

B216A

BRIGATI

(A) LOST IN THE WILDENESS 19 ELEKTRA US 7E 1074

EDDIE BRIGATI V (A
DAVID BRIGATI (A

B216B

ANN BRIGGS

(A) ANN BRIGGS 1971 TOPIC UK 12TS 207
(B) THE TIME HAS COME 1971 CBS UK 64612

ANN BRIGGS (AB

B216C

BRIAN BRIGGS

(A) BRAIN DAMAGE 1981 BEARSVILLE 6996

BRIAN BRIGGS ALL INST (A
RANDY VANWARMER V (A
SHANE FONTAYNE G (A
PATTY CAKES V (A
WILLIE WILCOX D (A
JOHNNY AVERAGE K (A
SUZY RONSON V (A
JOHN HOLBROOK PROD (A
RALPH CARNEY SAX (A
LOUIS ROLAND D (A
IAN KIMMET PROD (A

B217

BRIGHTWINTER

(A) A BAND FOR ALL SEASONS 1975 MYRR MYR 1030

B218

BRINSLEY SCHWARZ

(A) BRINSLEY SCHWARZ 1970 UA UK UAS 29111
(A) BRINSLEY SCHWARZ 1970 CAPITOL US SWBC11869
(B) DESPITE AT ALL 1970 LIBERTY UK LBG 83427
(C) SILVER PISTOL 1972 UA US 5566 UK UAS 29217
(D) NERVOUS ON THE ROAD 1972 UA US 5647 UK UAS 29374
(E) PLEASE DONT EVER CHANGE 1973 UA UK UAS 29489
(F) NEW FAVOURITES 1974 UA UK UAS 29641
(G) ORIGINAL GOLDEN GREATS 1974 UA UK USP 101
(H) 15 THOUGHTS OF BRINSLEY SCHWARZ 1978 UA UK UAK 30177

BRINSLEY SCHWARZ G V (ALL
NICK LOWE B V (ALL
BARRY LANDER K (
BOB ANDREWS K (ABCDEG
IAN GOMM G (CDEFG
PETER WHALE D (
BILLY RANKIN D (ABCDEFG
DAVE JACKSON SAX (B
JOHN WEIDER FDL (B
B J COLE STEEL (B
DAVE EDMUNDS V (F

B218A

BRITISH DISASTERS

(A) BREAKDOWN 197 ZED (EP)

B219

BRITISH LIONS

(A) THE BRITISH LIONS 1978 VERTIGO UK 9102 019
(B) TROUBLE WITH WOMEN 1980 CHERRY RED UK ARED 7

JOHN FIDDLER V G (AB
BUFFIN GRIFFIN D V (AB
OVEREND WATTS B (AB
RAY MAJOR G (AB
MORGAN FISHER K (AB
BRUCE IRVINE G (B

B219A

DAVID BROADSTREET

(A) DAVID BROADSTREET 1977 A&M CAN 9026
(B) DREAMING IN COLOUR 1978 A&M CAN 9032

DAVID BROADSTREET G V (AB
CARL KEESEE B V CLAR(AB
LANCE QUINN G (AB
JERRY MAROTTA D (A
JIM NEIL D V (B
CHRIS DADRICK ORG (B
BILL HUGHES V (B
BOB MANN G (AB
DOUG RILEY K (B
MATT ZIMBEL PERC (B
PETER PHILLIPS K (A
STEVE KENNEDY SAX (A
MICHAEL LEWIS V (B

B220

BROKEN GLASS

(A) BROKEN GLASS 1975 CAPITOL UK EST 11510

MILLER ANDERSON G V (A
STAN WEBB G V (A
ROBBIE BLUNT G (A
MAC POOLE D (A
ROB RAWLINSON B (A
TONY ASHTON K (A

B220A **BROKEN HOME** B220A

DICKEN V G (A (A) BROKEN HOME 1980 WB UK K 58148
PETE CROWTHER B K G(A
RONY WILLSON G V (A PETE BARNACLE D V (A RORY WILLSON (

B221 **DAVID BROMBERG** B221

DAVID BROMBERG V G (ALL (A) DAVID BROMBERG 1971 CBS US 31104 UK 64906
JODY STECHER MAND V(AB (B) DEMON IN DISGUISE 1972 CBS US 31753
STEVE BURGH B V (ABC (C) WANTED DEAD OR ALIVE 1974 CBS US 32717
DAVID NICHTERN K V (AB (D) MIDNIGHT ON THE WATER 1975 CBS US 33397 UK 80885
DAVID AMRAN HRNS (A (E) HOW LAT'LL YA PLAY TILL (DBL) 1976 FANTASY US 79007 UK 53
VASSAR CLEMENTS FDL (AJK (F) RECKLESS ABANDON 1977 FANTASY US 9540 UK 536
NORMAN BLAKE G (A (F) RECKLESS ABANDON 1977 MUSIDISC 5960
RANDY SCRUGGS B (A (G) BANDIT IN A BATHING SUIT 1978 FANTASY US 9555 UK 548
JERRY GARCIA G (BC (G) BANDIT IN A BATHING SUIT 1978 MUSIDISC 5966
PHIL LESH B (BC (H) MY OWN HOUSE 1978 FANTASY F 9572
NEIL ROSSI FDL (C ( ) BEST OF OUT OF THE BLUES 19 CBS US 34467
WILLOW SCARLET HCA (AB (J) HILLBILLY JAZZ VOL 1 1977 SONET UK SNTF721
ANDY STATMAN MAND SAX(BC (K) HILLBILLY JAZZ VOL 2 1977 SONET UK SNTF722
WINNIE WINSTON BANJO (C (L) MY OWN HOUSE 1979 FANTASY US 9572
GARTH HUDSON K (M (M) YOU SHOULD SEE 1980 FANTASY US 9590 UK WEA K58148
BILL KRUTZMANN D (B

TRACY NELSON V (BC JOE FERGUSON SAX (C HUNGRIA GARCIA PERC (C KEITH GODCHAUX K (BC
JEFF GUTCHEON K (CB JOEY HARRISON SCARBURY V(G TONY MARKELLIS B (C JOHN PAYNE WIND (C
JAY UNGAR FDL(CD JACK LEE V (BC ANDY McMAHON V (BC SWEET INSPIRATION V ((C
EVAN STOVER FDL(D BILLY NOVICK CLAR (D PAUL FLEISHER WIND (D BRIAN AHERN G (D
HUGH McDONALD B (DEF JESSE ED DAVIS G (D Dr JOHN PNO (DE JOE DARENSBEOURG CLAR(D
LYNDON UNGAR V (D LINDA RONSTADT V (D EMMYLOU HARRIS V (D HAIM SHTRUM V (D
RICHARD FEGY G FDL (DEFGHM BUDDY CAGE G (D ERNIE WATTS SAX (D BERNIE LEADON G (DE
BONNIE RAITT V (D JOHN HERALD V (D BRANTLEY KEARNS V (DE DOYLE LAWSON V (D
RICKY SKAGGS V (D RED RHODES STEEL(D BILL KREUTZMANN D (BC CURT LINBERG TROM(EFG
JOHN FIRMIN SAX(EFG GEORGE KINDLER FDL (EFGH HANK DE VITO STEEL(E HERB PEDERSEN V (EG
JIM ROTHERMEL WIND(E JANE SHARP V (E PHOEBE SNOW V (E STEVE MADAIO TPT (F
LANCE DICKERSON D (FG STEVE FORMAN PERC (F DANIEL MOORE V (F MATTHEW MOORE V (F
JIM PRICE V (F DARRELL LEONARD TPT (F BILL KURASCH (F BUDDY COLLETTE (F
PEGGY SANDVIG PNO(F DONNA GODCHAUX V (B DAVID SCHALLOCK B V (G MARTHA E WASH V (G
MARGARET REDMOND V (G MARILYN BRYANT V (G RUDY COPELAND PNO (G STEVE MOSLEY D V(ACE
RICHARD GRANDO SAX(A TUT TAYLOR MAND (A PETER ECKLUND HRNS (CDEFM KEN KOSEK FDL (B
TOM SHECHAN B (B JO ARMSTEAD V (B HILDA HARRIS V (B TASHA THOMAS V (B

B222 **BRONCO** B222

KEVIN GAMMOND G V (AB (A) COUNTRY HOME 1970 ISLAND US 9300 UK ILPS 9124
JESS RODEN V (AB (B) ACE OF SUNLIGHT 1971 ISLAND US 9309 UK ILPS 9161
ROBBIE BLUNT G V (AB (C) SMOKIN' MIXTURE 1973 POLYDOR UK 2383 215
JOHN PASTERNAK B (AB
PETE ROBINSON D (AB JEFF BANNISTER PNO (A CLIFFORD WARD V (A
IAN HUNTER K (B PAUL BENNETT V (B TREVOR LUCAS V (B
TERRY ALLEN ORG (B PAUL DAVENPORT PNO (B MICK RALPHS K (B

B223 **STANLEY BRONSTEIN** B223

STANLEY BRONSTEIN V SAX (AB (A) OUR ISLAND 19 MUSE US MR 5072
WITH (B) LIVING ON THE AVENUE 1976 MUSE MR 5113
DANNY SALZMAN K (B
DOROTHY TERRELL V (B STEVE TARSHIS G (B VAL BURKE B (B
ARNOLD RAMSEY D (B ANGEL JUSTINADO PERC (B DENNIS BELL K (B
LARRY ROSEN PERC (B TERRI BRONSTEIN V (B SHERROIL JENNINGS V (B
CLAUDETTE WASHINGTON V (B

B224 **BRONX CHEER** B224

TONY KNIGHT JUG PERC(AB (A) BARREL HOUSE PLAYER (EP) 1971 DAWN DNX 2522
JOHN REED G MAND (AB (B) GREATEST HITS 1972 DAWN DNLS 3034
BRIAN COOKMAN H HCA (AB
CHAS JOHNSON K (AB

B224A **HERMAN BROOD** B224A

HERMAN BROOD K V (ALL (A) THE FLASH & DANCE BAND 1975 UNIVERSE HOT 108 ARIOLA 200231
HANS LAFAILLE D (A (B) IN VITESSE 1975 REPRISE REPN54058
PAUL BAGMEIJER B (B (C) STREET (WITH WILD ROMANCE) 1977 AVES INT 146506 ARIOLA 28711
ROB TEN BOKUM G B V(B (D) SHPRITSZ (WITH WILD ROMANCE) 1978 AVES INT 146 503
HERMAN VAN BOEYEN D V (B (E) CHA CHA 1978 AVES INT 146 507
MARGRIET HILDE V (B (F) HERMAN BROOD & WILD ROMANCE 1979 ARIOLA ARL 5029
ROB VAN DONSELAAR K (B (G) GO NUTZ 1980 AVES INT 146 527
BIG JOHN HCA (B (H) SOUNDTRACK CHA CHA (5 TRACKS) 1980 CBS 70183
FERDIE KARMELK G HCA V(C (I) WAIT A MINUTE 1980 AVES INT 146 532
KIM FOWLEY (I (J) MODERN TIMES REVIVE 1981 ARIOLA GER 6635 NL 204206
AD SCHAAP SAX (J (K) IN A BAD MOOD 1980 ARIOLA US 50055
DAVID HOLLESTELLE K V (J
GERRIT VEEN B (C PETER WALRECHT D (C ELLEN PIEBES V (C RIA RUITER V (C
JAN AKKERMAN G (C FREDDIE CAVALLI B (DEGH ANI MEERMAN D (DEGHF DANNY LADEMACHER G(DEFGHJ
BERTUS BORGERS SAX (DEJ ROBERT JAN STIPS K (DJ MONIKA TJEN AKWOEI V (DE JOSEE VAN LERSEL V (DE
LENNY MACALUSO G (HG ERIC NELSON B (H ROGER GORDEN D (HG CRAIG KRAMPH D (HG
STEPHEN HINES K (HG PAGE PORRAZZO PERC (HG D'SRNEL PERSHING K (H RYAN UIYATE PERC (H
RICK KELLIS SAX (HG PETER BOOTSMAN G (J GEORGE KOOYMANS G (J BERT HANSEN HCA (J
GINO VAIN B (J JAN HOLLANDER SAX (J DEE DEE V (J RUUD VAN DIJK SAX (J
EDNA WRIGHT V (G DARLENE LOVE V (G CHUCK FRANCOUR V (G MARTIN OSTERWIJK TROM(J
FLOOR VAN ZUTPHEN (D PETER WALRECHY (J FREDDIE CAVALLI (J

B224B **GARY BROOKER** B224B

GARY BROOKER K V (A (A) NO MORE FEAR OF FLYING 1979 CHRYSALIS US UK 1224
TIM RENWICK G (A
BRUCE LYNCH B (A B J COLE STEEL (A DAVE MATTACKS D (A
CHRIS SMITH HCA (A STEPHANIE DESYKES V (A CLAIRE TORRY V (A
RICHARD MYHILL V (A DAVE REILLY V (A GONZALES HORNS (A

B224C BROOKLYN BRIDGE B224C

JOHNNY MAESTRO B V (ALL | (A) THE BROOKLYN BRIDGE 1968 BUDDAH US 5034
FRED FERRARA V G TPT(ABC | (B) THE SECOND BRIDGE 1969 BUDDAH US 5042
LES CAUCHI V PNO (ABC | (C) DAY IS DONE 1970 BUDDAH US 5065
MIKE GREGORIA V PNO (AB | (D) BRIDGE IN BLUE 1972 BUDDAH US 5107
JIMMY ROSICA B V G (ABC
TOMMY SULLIVAN SAX G V(ABC | CAROLYN WOOD(SULLIVAN) ORG (ABC | RICHIE MACIOCE G (ABC
ARTIE CANTANZARITA D TPT (ABC | SHELLY DAVIS K TPT (ABC | JOE RUVIO SAX V(ABC

B225 BROOKLYN DREAMS B225

JOE ESPOSITO G V (AB | (A) BROOKLYN DREAMS 1978 RCA XL 13047
EDDIE HOKENSON V PERC(AB | (B) SLEEPLESS NIGHTS 1979 RCA XL 13071
BRUCE SUDANO K V G (AB
WITH
ANDRE FISCHER (A | DENNIS BELFIELD B (A | VEYLER HILDERBRAND B (A | AL CINER (A
TONY D EISENBARGER (A | RON STOCKERT K (A | SNUFFY WALDEN G (A | SKIP KONTE K (A
JOE LALA PERC (A | DONNA SUMMER V (A | TONY MAIDEN G (A | MARK OLSON K (A
ED GREENE D (B | MIKE BAIRD D (B | CHUCK RAINEY B (B | SCOTT EDWARDS B (B
DAVID HUNGATE B (B | JAY GRAYDON G (B | THOM ROTELLA G (B | BOB ESTY PNO (B
JAI WINDING K (B | VICTOR FELDMAN PERC (B | DAN WYMAN SYN(B | LEE RITENOUR G (B
JERRY JUMONVILLE SAX (B | JERRY DOUCETTE G (B | GAIL LEVANT HARP(B | LEW SOLOFF TPT (B
BARRY ROGERS TROM (A | MICHAEL BRECKER SAX (B | LEW DELGATTO SAX (B | JERRY HEY TPT (B
STEVE MADAIO TPT (B | CHUCK FINDLEY TPT (B | GARY HERBIG SAX (B | JOHN KIP SAX (B
DAVID LUELL SAX (B | DICK HYDE TROM (B | BILL REICHENBACH TROM (B | STRINGS (B
VOCAL BACKING (B

B226 ELKIE BROOKS B226

ELKIE BROOKS V (ALL | (A) RICH MANS WOMAN 1975 A&M US 4556 UK AMLH64554
DAVID KEMPER D (A | (B) TWO DAYS AWAY 1977 A&M US 4631 UK AMLH68409
JEAN ROUSSEL K (CDB | (C) SHOOTING STAR 1978 A&M US 4695 UK AMLH64695
ELLIOTT RANDALL G (C | (D) LIVE & LEARN 1979 A&M UK AMLH68509
JERRY WHITMAN V (A | (E) PEARL 1981
NINO TEMPLE SAX (A
JERRY KNIGHT B (C | BEN BENAY G (AD | MAX BENNETT B (A | ANDY NEWMARK D (C
MIKE BODDIKER SYN (AD | ALAN ESTES PERC (A | PETE GAGE G (C | GENE ESTES PERC(A
JOHN GUERIN D (A | SIMON MORTON PERC (C | DAVID PAICH K (A | STAN FARBER V (A
JIM GILSTRAP V (AD | VENETTA FIELDS V (AD | GERRY GARRETT V (A | RON HICKLIN V (A
CLYDIE KING V (A | GENE MORFORD V (A | VERLENE ROGERS V (A | JOHN BARNES K (D
SCOTT EDWARDS B (D | JAMES GADSON D (D | HAL BLAINE D (D | MARLO HENDERSON G (D
TIM MAY G (D | SPENCER BEAN G (D | TOWER OF POWER HRNS (D | PAULINHO DA COSTA PERC(D
DARLENE LOVE V (D | ORRIN WATERS V (D | JULIA TILLMAN V (D | ED WATKINS B (D
MAGGIE HENRY V (D | ED GREENE D (D | PAUL WARREN G (D | CORKY HALE HARP(D
OLIVER LEIBER G PERC(D | MARCIA LEVY V (D | FRED TACKETT G (D | BRYAN GAROFALO B (D
LENNY PICKETT FLT (D | EDNA WRIGHT V (D | STEVE BURGH G (A | DENNIS KOVARIK B (A
STEVE YORK B (B | ISAAC GUILLORY G (B | TREVOR MORAIZ (B

B226A LONNIE BROOKS B226A

LONIE BROOKS G V (AB | (A) BROKE & HUNGRY 1969 US
CASEY JONES D (B | (B) BAYOU LIGHTNING 1979 SONET UK SNTF 798
BOB LEWIS G (B
ROB WATERS K (B | HARLAN TENSON B (B | BILLY BRANCH HCA (B

B227 PAUL BROOKS B227

PAUL BROOKS | ( ) STEPS FROM BEYOND 19 STATE ETAT 21

B227A TERRY BROOKS & STRANGE B227A

TERRY BROOKS G V (A | (A) TO EARTH WITH LOVE 1980 STAR PEOPLE SPR 005
JOHN KOTCH K (A
DONNIE CAPETTA B (A | JIM CHAPMAN D (A

B228 BROTHER BUNG B228

BOB PEARCE V G HCA (A | (A) BLUES CRUSADE (EP) 1968 AVENUE ARTISTS DEV 1055
BOB GORMAN G V (A
KEVIN FRANCIS B V (A | ROGER CHANTLER D (A

B228A BROTHER FOX & THE TAR BABY B228A

JOE SANTANGELO K (A | (A) BROTHER FOX & THE TAR BABY 1969 CAPITOL US 544 ORACLE CAN 703
RICHIE BARTLETT G (A
TOM BALLIVEAU B (A | BILL GARR D (A | STEVE HIGH V PERC (A
DAVE CHRISTIANSEN G (A

B228B BROTHER TO BROTHER B228B

(A) IN THE BOTTLE 1974 TURBO TU 7013

B228C BROTHERHOOD B228C

DRAKE LEVIN G V (AB | (A) BROTHERHOOD 1968 RCA US 4092
PHIL VOLK B V (AB | (B) BROTHERHOOD BROTHERHOOD 1969 RCA US 4228
MICHAEL SMITH D (A
GUY WEBSTER D (B

B229 BROTHERHOOD OF BREATH B229

CHRIS McGREGOR K (ALL | (A) BROTHERHOOD OF BREATH 1971 NEON NE 2
HARRY MILLER B (ALL | (B) BROTHERHOOD 1972 RCA SF8269
EVAN PARKER SAX (CD | (C) LIVE AT WILLISAU 1974 OGUN OG 100
NICK EVANS TROM (ABC | (D) PROCESSION 1978 OGUN OG 524
MONGEZI FEZA TPT (ABC
DUDU PUKWANA SAX (ALL | MIKE OSBORNE SAX (ABD | GARY WINDO SAX (BC
JOHNNY DYANNI B (D | MALCOLM GRIFFITHS TROM (AB | RADU MALFATTI TROM (CD
MARC CHARIG TPT (ALL | HARRY BECKETT TPT (ALL | RONNIE BEER WIND (A
ALAN SKIDMORE SAX (AB | JOHN SURMAN SAX (A | BRUCE GRANT WIND (D

B230 EDGAR BROUGHTON BAND(THE BROUGHTONS) B230

EDGAR BROUGHTON G V K B HCA(ALL | (A) WASA WASA 1969 HARVEST UK SHVL 757
STEVE BROUGHTON D V K B G (ALL | (A) WASA WASA 1969 EMI/HARVEST EURO 04083
ARTHUR GRANT G B V K (ABCDEFGH1 | (B) SING BROTHER SING 1970 HARVEST UK SHVL 772
JOHNNY VAN DERRICK VLN (C | (C) EDGAR BROUGHTON BAND 1971 HARVEST UK SHVL791 EURO 04774
VICTOR UNITT V G HCA K (CDE | (D) INSIDE OUT 1972 HARVEST UK SHTC 252
P HAROLD FATT V (C | (E) OORA 1973 HARVEST UK SHVL810 EURO 94260
DAVID BEDFORD PNO (CE | (F) BANDAGES 1975 NEMS UK NEL 6006
MIKE OLDFIELD MAND G HARP (CF | (G) PARLEZ VOUS ENGLISH 1979 BABYLON Z 80007
JOHN THOMAS G (FH | (H) LIVE HITS HARDER 1979 BB BB201009

(CONTINUED)

B230 (CONTINUED) EDGAR BROUGHTON BAND (The BROUGHTONS) B230

LEI ALOAH MEI V (F ( ) MASTERS OF ROCK 1975 EMI IC054 9548
PETE KNUDSEN K (F (X) BUNCH OF 45s 1975 HARVEST UK SHSM 2001
DUNCAN BRIDGEMAN K (1 (G) PARLEZ VOUS ENGLISH 1979 INFINITY INS 3027
DIGGER DAVIS G (F (1) BROUGHTONS 1979/80
MADELINE BELL V (E
DORIS TROY V (E LISA STRIKE V (E MAGGIE THOMAS V (E
RICHARD DE BASTION K V (G PETE TOLSEN G (G TOM NORDEN G V (G1
ALLAN SMITH SAX (G PETER HOPE EVANS HCA (G VICKI GAFFEE CELLO(G
SUSIE O'LIST V (G LOZ BROUGHTON V (G SHAZZI SCOOT V (G
SALLY BROUGHTON V (G ALI KIMBALL V (G TAMARA KIMBALL V (G
SHELLEY WATSON V (G KAY KARNERA V (G TERRY COTTAM G (H
PETER JENNER PROD (X TAMARA KARNERA V (G

B231 ARTHUR BROWN B231

ARTHUR BROWN V (ALL (A) THE CRAZY WORLD OF ARTHUR BROWN 1968 TRACK US 8190 UK 2407 012
VINCENT CRANE K (AG (A) THE CRAZY WORLD OF ARTHUR BROWN 1968 TRACK GER 184165 UK 613 005
DRACHEN THEAKER D (AEF (B) GALACTIC ZOO DOSSIER 1972 POLYDOR UK 2310 130
CARL PALMER D ((C) KINGDOM COME 1973 POLYDOR UK 2310 178
ANDY DALBY G (BCDEG (C) KINGDOM COME 19 TRACK· US GUD2003/4
KEITH TIPPETT K (E (D) THE JOURNEY 1973 POLYDOR UK 2310 254
McCULLOUGH K (F (D) THE JOURNEY 1974 PASSPORT US 98003
CHARLIE CHARLES D (E (E) DANCE 1974 GULL US 6/405 UK GULP 1008
LEE ROBINSON B (E (F) LOST EARS (PUDDLETOWN EXPRESS) 1976 GULL UK G 2003/4
PETE SOLLEY K (E (G) CHISHOLM IN MY BOSOM 1978 GULL UK GULP 1023
MALCOLM FLYNN PERC (E (H) FASTER THAN THE SPEED OF SOUND 1980 WEA NL 58088
BOBBIE McGHEE V (G
LLOYD PARKS B (E CHARLIE DUNBAR D (E THUNDERTHIGHS V (E
GEORGE KAHN SAX (E PAT LEWIS PERC (E JAMES MORGAN B (E
STEVE YORK B (E RANCHIE McCLEAN G (E ERROL NELSON K (E
PHIL SHUTT B (BCD MARTIN STEER D (BC MICHAEL HARRIS K (BC
SEAN NICHOLAS B (A DESMOND FISHER B (B JULIAN BROWN V (B
VICTOR PERAINO K (D DENNIS TAYLOR B (F GEORGE KHAN SAX (F
JOHN MARSHALL D (F ANDROID FUNNEL G (F RICK KULACK G (G
EUGENE DILEBERO G (G JOHN McBURNIE G (G ROBERT KIRBY K (G
DELISLE HARPER B (G CHAS CRONK B (G NORMAN WATTROY B (G
PHIL CRANHAM B (G STEVE HOLLY D (G JOHN LINGWOOD D (G
MORRIS PERT PERC (G ROBIN JAMES PERC (G TONY UTER PERC (GD
JACQUIE SULLIVAN V (G R J LANGE V (G

B231A BOBBY BROWN B231A

BOBBY BROWN MULTI (A (A) THE ENLIGHTENING BEAM OF AZONDA 1972 DESTINY US 4002

B232 BUSTER BROWN B232

BUSTER BROWN (A) RAISE A RUCKUS TONIGHT 1976 DJM DJM 22037
( ) NEW KING OF THE BLUES 19 FIRE US 102
( ) GET DOWN WITH BUSTER BROWN 19 SOUFLEC US 2014

B232A CHARLES BROWN B232A

CHARLES BROWN V (ALL (A) BLUES & BROWN 19 JEWEL US 5006
(B) DRIFTIN' BLUES 19 MAINSTREAM US368 US SCORE 4011
(C) CHARLES BROWN 1975 BULLDOG BDL 1001
(D) SUNNYLAND 1979 ROUTE 66 KIX5
( ) BALLADS 19 MAINSTREAM US 6035
( ) BOSS OF THE BLUES 19 MAINSTREAM 56007
( ) WILL GRIP YOUR HEART 19 KING US 878
( ) SINGS XMAS SONGS 19 KING US 775
( ) LEGEND 19 BLUESWAY US 6039

B233 CLARENCE 'GATEMOUTH' BROWN B233

CLARENCE GATEMOUTH BROWN HCA FDL(ALL(A)COLD STRANGE 1973 BLACK & BLUE 33096
LARRY SIEBERTH K (L (B) SINGS LOUIS JORDAN 1974 BLACK & BLUE 33053
WITH (C) GATES ON THE HEAT 1975 BARCLAY 80603
JACK McVEA SAX (E (D) DOWN SOUTH IN BAYOU COUNTRY 1975 BARCLAY 90002
GEORGE ALEXANDER TPT (E (E) SAN ANTONIO BALLBUSTER 1975 RED LIGHTNING RL 0010
WILMER SHAKESLINER SAX (E (E) SAN ANTONIO BALLBUSTER 1979 CHARLY CR 30169
GERALDINE CARELL V (D (F) BOGALUSA BOOGIE MAN 1976 BARCLAY 90035
LEON MEDICH B (G (G) BLACKJACK 1976 MUSIC IS MEDICINE 9002
BILL EVANS V (D (H) HOUSE OF THE BLUES VOL 3 19 BLUE STAR US 80603
CLARENCE GREEN PNO (E (J) THE BLUES AINT NOTHIN' 19 BLACK & BLUE 33033
GARY BARDWELL V (D (K) MAKIN' MUSIC(ROY CLARK) 1979 ABC UK MCF 3009
HAROLD EASTON D (E (LO ALRIGHT AGAIN 1981 ROUNDER US 2028
DAVID FENDER K (L
IRVIN REASON SAX (E CARL OWENS PNO (E DUKE BARKER D (E BILL HARVEY SAX (E
FRED FORD SAX (E JOHNNY PARKER B (E PLUMA DAVIS TROM (E JIMMY McCRACKLIN K(E
HENRY BOOZIER TPT (E JOE TOUSSAINT B (E SAN FRISCO JEFF D (E JOE SCOTT TPT (E
AL GREY TROM (E ALLEN CLARK SAX (E CARL LOTT B (E JOHNNY BOARD SAX (E
BOB LITTLE SAX (E PAUL MONDAY PNO (E RAY JOHNSON B (E ELLIS BARTES D (E
EMILE RUSSELL D (E NAT DOUGLAS G (E NATHAN WOODARD TPT (E DON BUZZARD STEEL(DG
RED LANE G (DL JIM EHINGER PNO (D JULIUS FARMER B (D DOUG MORGANO G (D
JACK HUFFMAN D (D DAVID CRAIG V (D CHARLIE GRESSETT V (D HOYT GARRICK V (D
ROD RODDY K (G DAVID PETERS D (G JEFF POLLARD G (G BOBBY CAMPO HRNS(G
MIET BUCKNER ORG (AB MICHAEL SILVA D (AB ARNETT COBB SAX (AB JAY MacSHANN PNO (A
ROLAND LOBLIGEOIS B (A PAUL GUNTHER D (A LLOYD HERRMAN SAX (L BILL SAMUEL SAX (L
ALVIN TYLER SAX (L JOE SUNSERI SAX (A STANTON DAVIS TPT (L JIM McMILLEN TROM(L

B233A DANNY JOE BROWN B233A

DANNY JOE BROWN V (A (A) DANNY JOE BROWN & BAND 1981 EPIC
BUZZY MEEKINS B (A
STEVE WHEELER G (A JOHN GALVIN K (A BOBBY INGRAM G (A
KENNY McVAY G (A JIMMY GLENN D (A

B234 **DENNIS BROWN** B234

Musician	Inst	Albums
DENNIS BROWN	V	(ABCD
HIPPY HARRY	V	(A
SLY DUNBAR	D	(D
LLOYD PARKS	B	(D
FRANKLYN WAUL	K	(D
CLIVE HUNT	TPT	(I
DANNY WALTERS	SAX	(I
DEAN FRASER	SAX	(I
SKULLY	PERC	(I
TAMLINS	V	(I
KEITH STIRLING	K	(I
VIN GORDON	TROM	(D
TOMMY McCOOK	SAX	(D
STICKY	PERC	(D
HERMAN MARQUIS	SAX	(D
STYLE SCOTT	D	(I
WILLIE LINDO	G	(I
ERROL NELSON	K	(D
BOBBY ELLIS	TPT	(D
ROBBIE SHAKESPEARE	G	(D
ROBERT XYN	K	(I
ANSEL COLLINS	K	(I
DAVID MADDEN	TPT	(I
HAROLD BUTLER	K	(D
ERIC LAMONT	G	(D
LENNOX GORDON	G	(D
GLADSTONE ANDERSON	K	(I
NOEL BAILEY	G	(I

Album	Year	Label	Country	Number
(A) MEETS HIPPY HARRY	19	GOLDEN AGE	UK	PIOLP 2
(B) SUPER HITS	19	TROJAN	UK	TRLS 57
(C) JUST DENNIS	1975	TROJAN	UK	TRLS 107
(D) VISIONS OF	1978	LIGHTNING	UK	LIP 7
(E) WESTBOUND TRAIN	1978	THIRD WORLD		TWS 934
(F) WORDS OF WISDOM	1979	LASER	UK	LASL 1
(G) LIVE IN MONTREUX	1979	LASER	UK	LASL 5
(H) WOLF & LEOPARDS	1979	EMI	UK	EMC 330
(I) SPELLBOUND	1980	LASER UK LASL8 NL WEA		82738
(J) JOSEPHS COAT OF MANY COLOURS	1980	LASER UK LASL6		

B235 **JAMES BROWN** B235

JAMES BROWN V (ALL

Album	Year	Label	Country	Number
AMAZING JAMES BROWN	196	KING	US	743
AT THE APOLLO	196	KING	US	826
AT THE APOLLO	196	LONDON	UK	HA 8184
AT THE APOLLO	196	POLYDOR	UK	583729/30
AT THE APOLLO	19	POLYDOR	U	2612 005
AT THE APOLLO	19	POLYDOR	UK	657 107
AT THE APOLLO	1975	POLYDOR		2482 184
AT THE APOLLO	19	POLYDOR		2659 011
PURE DYNAMITE	196	KING	US	883
PURE DYNAMITE	196	LONDON	UK	HA 8177
UNBEATABLE HITS	19	KING	US	919
UNBEATABLE HITS	196	LONDON	UK	HA 8203
PLEASE PLEASE	196	LONDON	UK	HA 8231
PLEASE PLEASE	196	KING	US	909
TOURS THE USA	1965	LONDON	UK	HA 8240
PAPAS GOT A BRAND NEW BAG	196	LONDON	UK	HA 8262
PAPAS GOT A BRAND NEW BAG	19	POLYDOR		657 001
PAPAS GOT A BRAND NEW BAG	196	KING	US	938
PAPAS GOT A BRAND NEW BAG	1966	PYE	UK	NPL 28099
PAPAS GOT A BRAND NEW BAG	19	POLYDOR	UK	2334 009
NIGHT TRAIN	196	POLYDOR	UK	657 106
GRITS & SOUL	1965	PHILIPS	UK	BL 7664
SHOWTIME	196	SMASH	US	MGS 27054
PLAYS JAMES BROWN	1966	PHILIPS		BL 7697
PLAYS RHYTHM & BLUES	19	PHILIPS	US	14575
PLAYS JAMES BROWN	1966	SMASH	US	MGS 27072
I GOT YOU	1966	PYE INT	UK	NPL 29074
I GOT YOU	1966	KING	US	946
ITS A MANS WORLD	1966	PYE INT	UK	NPL 28079
ITS A MANS WORLD	1966	POLYDOR		657 111
CHRISTMAS ALBUM	1966	PYE INT	UK	NPL 28097
RAW SOUL	196	POLYDOR		657 123
RAW SOUL	196	PYE INT	UK	NPL 28103
RAW SOUL	196	KING	US	1016
LIVE AT THE GARDEN	196	POLYDOR		658 041
LIVE AT THE GARDEN	196	PYE INT	UK	NPL 28104
COLD SWEAT	196	POLYDOR		658 043
PRESENTS HIS SHOW OF TOMORROW	19	POLYDOR		658 073
I CAN'T STAND MYSELF	196	POLYDOR		658 077
HANDFUL OF SOUL	1967	PHILIPS		SBL 7761
PLAYS THE REAL THING	1967	PHILIPS		SBL 7823
PLAYS THE REAL THING	1967	SMASH	US	67093
JAMES BROWN SHOW	1967			
22 GIANT HITS		SMASH	US	67109
PLAYS THE NEW BREED	1968	SMASH	US	MGS 27080
NOTHING BUT SOUL	1968	POLYDOR		658 101
I GOT A FEELING	196	POLYDOR		658 105
I GOT A FEELING	196	KING	US	1031
SOUL PARTY	19	POLYDOR		658 106
OUT OF SIGHT	1968			
SAY IT LOUD I'M BLACK & I'M PROUD	19	KING	US	1047
SAY IT LOUD I'M BLACK & I'M PROUD	19	POLYDOR	UK	583 741
GETTIN' DOWN TO IT	19	KING	US	1051
GETTIN' DOWN TO IT		POLYDOR		658 151
GETTIN' DOWN TO IT	19	POLYDOR	UK	583 742
THINKING ABOUT LITTLE WILLIE	19	KING	US	1038
REVOLUTION OF THE MIND	1972	POLYDOR US 25 3003	UK	2675034
THE POPCORN	19	KING	US	1055
THE POPCORN	19	POLYDOR		184 319
THE POPCORN	19	POLYDOR		658 172
GET ON THE GOOD FOOT	1973	POLYDOR		2675 054
GET ON THE GOOD FOOT	1973	POLYDOR		2659 018
GET ON THE GOOD FOOT	1973	POLYDOR	US	PD 23004
SOUL BROTHER No 1	1973	POLYDOR		
HOT PANTS	197	POLYDOR	US	PD 4054
ITS A MOTHER	19	POLYDOR		658 371
ITS A MOTHER	19	KING	US	1063
SLAUGHTERS BIG RIP OFF	1973	POLYDOR	UK	2391 084
SLAUGHTERS BIG RIP OFF	1973	POLYDOR		2490 119
AINT IT FUNKY	19	KING	US	1092
THERE IT IS	19	POLYDOR		2391 033
THERE IT IS	19	POLYDOR	US	PD 5028

(CONTINUED)

THE PAYBACK	1974	POLYDOR	UK	2659 030
THE PAYBACK	1974	POLYDOR	US	PD23007
THE PAYBACK		POLYDOR		2675 082
HELL	1974	POLYDOR	UK	2659 036
HELL	1974	POLYDOR	US	PD29001
HELL	1974	POLYDOR		2669 018
REALITY	1974	POLYDOR	UK	2391 164
REALITY	1974	POLYDOR		PD 6039
SOUL CLASSICS	1974	POLYDOR		2391 057
SOUL CLASSICS	1974	POLYDOR	US	PD 5401
BLACK CAESAR	1974	POLYDOR	UK	2490 117
MISTER DYNAMITE	197	POLYDOR		2357 004
THIS IS	19	PHILIPS		6336 210
SOUL ON TOP	19	POLYDOR	UK	2310 022
SOUL ON TOP	19	KING	US	KS 1100
IT'S A NEW DAY	197	POLYDOR	UK	2310 029
IT'S A NEW DAY	197	KING	US	1095
SHO IS FUNKY DOWN HERE	19	KING	US	1110
SHE IS FUNKY	197	POLYDOR	UK	2310 089
SUPER BAD	197	KING	US	KS 1127
SEX MACHINE	19	POLYDOR	UK	2625 004
SEX MACHINE	19	KING	US	71115
SEX MACHINE TODAY	1975	POLYDOR	UK	2391 175
SEX MACHINE TODAY	1975	POLYDOR	US	PD 6042
EVERYBODYS DOIN' THE HUSTLE	1975	POLYDOR	UK	2391 197
EVERYBODYS DOIN' THE HUSTLE	1975	POLYDOR	US	PD 6054
HOT	197	POLYDOR	US	PD 6059
SEX MACHINE LIVE	197	POLYDOR 9004	US	PD29004
SOUL CLASSICS VOL 2	1975	POLYDOR 5402	UK	2391 116
SOUL CLASSICS VOL 3	1975	POLYDOR	UK	2391 166
THE BEST OF JAMES BROWN	1975	POLYDOR	UK	2343 036
GET UP OFFA THING	1976	POLYDOR	UK	2391 228
GET UP OFFA THING	1976	POLYDOR	US	PD 6071
BODY HEAT	1976	POLYDOR US 6093	UK	2391 258
POP HISTORY	19	POLYDOR		2625 009
MUTHAS NATURE	1977	POLYDOR	UK	2391 300
MUTHAS NATURE	1977	POLYDOR	US	PD16111
SOLID GOLD	1977	POLYDOR	UK	2679 044
JAM 1980'S	1978	POLYDOR	UK	2391 343
JAM 1980'S	1978	POLYDOR	US	PD16140
TAKE A LOOK AT THOSE CAKES	197	POLYDOR	US	PD16181
TAKE A LOOK AT THOSE CAKES	1979	POLYDOR	UK	2391 384
ORIGINAL DISCO MAN	1979	POLYCOR US 6212	UK	2391 412
SOUL SYNDROME	1980	RCA PL25334		ALP 5006
PEOPLE	1980	POLYDOR US 6258		
HOT ON THE ONE	1980	POLYDOR US 6290		

B236 JOE BROWN B236

JOE BROWN	G V	(ALL
VICKI BROWN	V	(E
RAY GLYNN	G MAND	(E
PETE OAKMAN	B VLN	(E
DAVE HYNES	D	(E
JEFF PETERS	B V	(E
KIRK DUNCAN	PNO	(E

(A) PICTURE OF YOU	1962	GOLDEN GUINEA	UK	GGL 0146
(B) LIVE	1963	PICCADILLY	UK	NPL 38006
(C) HERE COMES JOE BROWN	196	GOLDEN GUINEA	UK	GGL 0231
(D) PICTURE OF JOE BROWN	19	ACE OF CLUBS	UK	ACL 1127
(E) BROWNS HOME BREW	1972	BELL	UK	BELLS 208
(F) TOGETHER	1974	VERTIGO	UK	6360 114
(G) JOE BROWN COLLECTION	1974	GOLDEN HOUR	UK	GH 583
(H) JOE BROWN LIVE	1977	POWER EXCHANGE	UK	PXLS 2002
(EP) HIT PARADE	196	PICCADILLY	UK	NEP 34025
(EP) ALL THINGS BRIGHT	196	PICCADILLY	UK	NEP 34026
(EP) A PICTURE OF YOU	1962	DECCA	UK	DFE 8500

B236A KEISA BROWN B236A

KEISA BROWN	V	(A	(A) KEISA BROWN ...LIVE	19	LITTLE STAR	US	1001

B236B MEL BROWN B236B

MEL BROWN	G	(AB
CLIFFORD COULTER	K	(C
JOHNNY CARSWELL	K	(C
MATTHEW KELLY	HCA	(C
BOB WEST	B	(C
GREG FERBER	D	(C

(A) BIG FOOT COUNTRY GIRL	19	IMPULSE		AS 9249
(B) IMPULSIVELY	19	IMPULSE	US	9266
(C) I'D RATHER SUCK MY THUMB	19	BLUE THUMB	US	9186

B237 PETE BROWN B237

(A) A MEAL YOU CAN SHAKE HANDS WITH	1969	HARVEST	UK	SHVL 752
(B) ART SCHOOL DANCE GOES ON FOREVER	1970	HARVEST	UK	SHVL 768
(C) THOUSANDS ON A RAFT	1970	HARVEST	UK	SHVL 782
(D) NOT FORGOTTEN ASSOCIATION	1973	DERAM	UK	SML 1103
(E) MY LAST BAND	1977	HARVEST	UK	SHSM 2017
(F) BACK TO FRONT LINE UP 1977				

(1) JAZZ POETRY GROUP 1966 (2) 1966/67 (B)&(C) PIBLIKO

PETE BROWN	V PERC LYRICS	(ALL
DICK HECKSTALL SMITH	SAX	(AE
JIM MULLEN	G B	(BCE
ROGER BRUNN	B	(BE
DAVE THOMPSON	D	(BCE
ROB TAIT	D	(ABCE
CHRIS SPEDDING	G	(AE
JOHN SURMAN	SAX	(1
PETE BAILEY	PERC	(AE
BIMBO ACOCK	SAX	(F
LYN MAKINELL	K	(F
DILL KATZ	B	(F
STEVE GLOVER	PERC B	(CE
JEFF CLYNE	B	(D
DEREK FOLEY	G	(D
HENRY LOWTHER	TPT	(D
PETER LEMUR		(1
VINCENT CRANE		(1
PHIL SEAMAN	D	(2
JEFF SEOPARDI	D	(F
ROGER BUTCH POTTER	B	(AE
BRIAN BREEZE	G	(E
JOHN WEATHERS	D	(E
IAN LYNN	K	(F
ED SPEVOCK	D	(D
MAX MIDDLETON	K	(D
RAY 'TAFF' WILLIAMS	G	(D
JACK LANCASTER	WIND	(D
ALAN JACKSON		(1
TONY ROBERTS		(2
HENRY LOWTHER	HRNS	(2
CHARLIE HART	K	(AE
PHIL RYAN	K	(E
BOB EMMINES		(
HELEN HARDY	V	(F
GEORGE KAHN] NISAR AHMED]	SAX	(AE
TONY HUDD	G	(D
VIV STANSHALL	TUBA	(D
RON RUBIN	B	(1
DANNY THOMPSON		(2
LAURIE ALLEN	D	(2

B238 RANDY BROWN B238

RANDY BROWN V (ALL — (A) WELCOME TO MY ROOM — 1978 PARACHUTE US 9005 RRL 1005
CHUCK BROOKS G (ABCD — (B) INTIMATELY — 1979 PARACHUTE RRL 2007
PAUL JACKSON G (B — (C) MIDNIGHT DESIRE — 1980 CHOCOLATE 2010
EDDIE WATKINS B (B — (D) RANDY — 1981 CHOCOLATE 2017
ELVIRA COLLINS PERC (B
EDDIE BROWN CONGA(A — PATTI BROOKS V (AB — BRENDA RUSSELL V (B
SHARON LEE V (B — JAMES GADSON (B — LARRY FARRON K (B
J MICHAEL DONIS PNO (B — KEITH BASS PNO (B — CARL HAMPTON PNO (A
BOB ZIMMITTI PERC (C — WAYNE STALLING K (A — BOBBY BRYANT TPT (C
GARY FERGUSON D (A — BILL GREEN SAX (C — ROGER HAWKINS D (C
WILLIE HALL D PERC(D — ROBERT RUSSELL B (D — HOMER BANKS PERC (D
SONNY SEALS SAX (D — BILL McFARLAND TROM (D

B239 RAY BROWN B239

RAY BROWN B (ALL — (A) SOMETHING FOR LESTER — 19 CONTEMPORARY US 7641
(B) BROWN'S BAG — 19 CONCORD JAZZ US 19

B240 ROY BROWN B240

ROY BROWN V (ALL — (A) HARD TIMES — 1973 BLUESWAY BLS 6056
WITH — (B) HARD LUCK BLUES — 19 STARDAY/KING KS 1130
FREDDIE HILL TPT (A — (C) BLUES ARE ALL BROWN — 19 BLUESWAY US BLS 6019
GARY COLEMAN PERC (A — (D) & WYNONIE HARRIS — 19 KING US 607
EARL PALMER D (A — (E) SINGS 24 HITS — 19 KING US 956
DON RANDI PNO (A — (F) GOOD ROCKING TONIGHT — 1978 ROUTE 66 US KIK 6
ARTHUR WRIGHT B (A — (G) CHEAPEST PRICE IN TOWN — 19 FAITH 91020
DENNIS BUDIMIR G (A — (H) LAUGHING BUT CRYING — 1978 ROUTE 66 KIX 2
JEFF KAPLAN G (A
MEL MOORE TPT (A — JOHN EWING TROM (A — JIM HORN SAX (A
JOHNNY WILLIAMS SAX (A — HERMAN RILEY SAX (A — JIMMY CARMICHAEL PNO (A
MEL BROWN G (A — CHARLES WRIGHT G (A — BOB WEST B (A
ABE MILES D (A — ALAN ESTES PERC (A — CLIFFORD SCOTT SAX (A
CAROL KAYE B (A — TONY TERRAN TPT (A — RICHARD LEITH TROM (A

B241 RUTH BROWN B241

RUTH BROWN V (ALL — (A) THE BEST OF RUTH BROWN — 19 ATLANTIC 8080
(B) MISS RHYTHM — 19 ATLANTIC 8026
(C) RUTH BROWN — 19 ATLANTIC 8004
(D) SUGAR BABE — 1976 PRESIDENT 1067

B242 SHIRLEY BROWN B242

SHIRLEY BROWN V (ALL — (A) WOMAN TO WOMAN — 1978 STAX UK STX3005 US TRUTH 4206
AL JACKSON D (A — (A) WOMAN TO WOMAN — 1980 STAX RI US 4135
DONALD DUNN B (AB — (B) SHIRLEY BROWN — 1977 ARISTA US 4129 UK SPARTY 1017
BOBBY MANUEL G (A — (C) FOR THE REAL FEELING — 1979 STAX UK STX3014 UA 4128
MARVELL THOMAS K (AB
LESTER SNELL K (ABC — MEMPHIS HORNS (AC — CHARLES SHALMERS SINGERS V (A
WILLIE HALL D (B — DONNO RHODES V (B — SANDRA RHODES V (B
D J ROGERS V (B — CARL MARSH SYN (C — DONALD O'CONNOR SYN (C
JIMMY McGHEE G (C — MICHAEL TOLLS G (C — RAY GRIFFIN B (C
BLAIR CUNNINGHAM D (C — TERRY JOHNSON PERC (C — MICHAEL BAIRD PERC (C
HOT BUTTERED SOUL V (C — MEMPHIS SYM ORCH (AC

B242A THE STANKY BROWN BAND B242A

JAMES BROWN K V (ABC — (A) STANKY BROWN — 1978 SIRE US SRIX 6053
RICHARD BUNKIEWICZ B (ABC — (B) OUR PLEASURE TO SERVE YOU — 1976 SIRE 7516
JERRY CORDASCO D (ABC — (C) IF THE LIGHT DONT GET YOU — 1977 SIRE US 7529
JEFFREY LEYNOR G (ABC
ALLAN ROSS SAX (BC — BOB MESSANO G V (A — JOHN ZANGRANDO WIND (A
JIMMY MILLER G (C — ELLIOTT RANDALL G (C — JIMMY MAELIN PERC (C
WERNER FRITZSCHING G (C — DAVID LASLEY V (C — LYNN PITNEY V (C
ARNOLD McCULLER V (C

B242B BROWN DUST B242B

VINNIE PARELO D (A — (A) BROWN DUST — 1972 FAMILY US 2701
FRANK RAMES SAX V(A
PAUL CISNEROS HRNS (A — LARRY NORAGER G (A — CARLES LONGORIA B V (A — GEORGE STANLEY SAX (A

B243 DUNCAN BROWNE B243

DUNCAN BROWNE G V (ALL — (A) GIVE ME TAKE YOU — 19 IMMEDIATE IMP Z12 52012
WITH — (A) GIVE ME TAKE YOU — 1968 IMMEDIATE UK IMSP 018
TONY HYMAS K (CD — (B) DUNCAN BROWNE — 1973 RAK UK SRKA 6754
JOHN GIBLIN B (CD — (C) WILD PLACES — 1978 LOGO UK 1007 US SIRE 6065
SIMON PHILLIPS D (CD — (D) STREETS OF FIRE — 1979 LOGO UK 1016 US SIRE 6080
DICK MORRISSEY SAX (D
JOHN BUNDRICK K (B — SUZI QUATRO V (B — ROBERT HENRIT D (B
JOHN CAMERON PNO (B — KEITH HODGE V (B — JIM RODFORD B (B
TONY CARR V (B

B244 JACKSON BROWNE B244

JACKSON BROWNE G V (ALL — (A) FIRST ALBUM (UNRELEASED) — 1967 ELEKTRA US
WITH — (B) JACKSON BROWNE — 1972 ASYLUM UK SYL9002 RI K 53022
RUSS KUNKEL D (CEFG — (B) JACKSON BROWNE — 1972 ASYLUM US SD 5051
JIM GORDON D (E — (C) FOR EVERYMAN — 1973 ASYLUM UK 4003 RI K 43003
CHUCK RAINEY B (E — (C) FOR EVERYMAN — 1973 ASYLUM US SD 5067
JOYCE EVERSON V (D — (D) LATE FOR THE SKY — 1974 ASYLUM UK SYL 9018 RI K 43007
BILL PAYNE K (CEG — (D) LATE FOR THE SKY — 1974 ASYLUM US 7E 1017
LOWELL GEORGE G (E — (E) THE PRETENDER — 1976 ASYLUM UK K53048 US 7E 1079
FRED TACKETT G (E — (F) RUNNING ON EMPTY — 1978 ASYLUM UK K53070 US 6E 1131
JOHN HALL G (E — (G) HOLD OUT — 1980 ASYLUM UK K52226 US 5E 511
MIKE UTLEY K (CE
JIM HORN HRNS (E — ALBERT LEE G (BE — LELAND SKLAR B (EF — ROY BITTAN PNO (E
ARTHUR GERST (E — JON LANDAU V PROD(E — BOB GLAUB B (EG — BONNIE RAITT V (CE
ROSEMARY BUTLER V (EFG — JEFF PORCARO D (E — GARY COLEMAN PERC (E — J D SOUTHER V (E
DON HENLEY V (CDE — CHUCK FINDLEY HRNS (E — DICK HYDE HRNS (E — QUITMAN DENNIS HRN(E
DAVID CROSBY V (BE — GRAHAM NASH V (E — MARK JORDAN K (— JOHN MAUCERN D (E

(CONTINUED)

B244 (CONTINUED) **JACKSON BROWNE** B244

BRYAN GAROFALO B (E DANNY KORTCHMAR G (FG DOUG HAYWOOD B V (CDFG SNEAKY PETE KLEINOW STEEL(BC
MICKY McGEE D (C JIM KELTNER D (C SPOONER OLDHAM ORG (C GARY MALLABER D (C
BETH FICHET V (D DAVID PAICH PNO (C ROCKADAY JOHNNIE PNO (C GLENN FREY V (C
JONI MITCHELL PNO (C WILTON FELDER B (C LARRY ZACK D (D JAI WINDING K (D
CLARENCE WHITE K (D DAVID JACKSON PNO (B JESSE ED DAVIS G (B JIM GORDON ORG(B
JIM FADDEN HCA (B DAVID CAMPBELL VLA (BE LEAH KUNKEL V (B DAVID LINDLEY G VLN(CDEFG
CRAIG DOERGE K (BEFG LEWIS F DAMIAN G V (E JOEL BERNSTEIN V (F ROBERT GUTIERREZ G V (E
DAN FOGELBERG V (D TERRY REID V (D PERRY LINDLEY V (D FRITZ RICHMOND JUG (D
JOE LALA PERC (G RICK MAROTTA D (G AL SCHMITT PROD (D

B245 **SEVERIN BROWNE** B245

SEVERIN BROWNE V PNO G (ALL
WITH
JOHN GUERIN D (A
EMORY GORDY B (A
SNEAKY PETE KLEINOW STEEL (A
RUSS KUNKEL D (B
RICHARD BENNETT G STEEL (AB
BOBBY TORRES PERC (B
DEAN WEBB MAND (B
BOBBI THOMAS V (B
STEVE LE FEVER B (A
BRUCE BUELL B (A

(A) SEVERIN BROWNE 1973 MOWEST US M774L
(B) NEW IMPROVED 1974 MOTOWN US 6 779
(B) LOVESONGS 1974 MOWEST UK MWS 7005

MERLE BREGANTE D (A
DAVID HUNGATE B (B
ALAN LINDGREN K SYN (AB
STEVE LEEDS SAX (B
JENNIFER WARREN V (B
JULES SHEAR V (B
RAY KELLY CELLO (A
KING ERRISON CONGAS (A

JEFF PORCARO D (B
DAVID PAICH ACC (B
JOE PORCARO PERC (B
ROBERT GRINNEDGE STDRUM (B
CAROL CARMICHAEL V (B
DENNIS CONWAY D (A
MAURY MANSEAU G (A

B246 **BROWNSVILLE STATION** B246

HENRY WEEK D V (CDGH
JIM BRUZZESE PERC (A
CUBBY KODA G HCA V(ABCDGH
MICHAEL LUTZ B G V K (ABCDGH
BRUCE NAZARIAN G K V (HG
TONY DRIGGINS B V (AB
T J CRONLEY D (A
PAT McCAFREY K (A
AL NALLI ACC (A
DAVID WECK D (B

(A) BROWNSVILLE STATION 19 PALLADIUM US 1004
(A) BROWNSVILLE STATION 19 PRIVATE STOCK US 2026
(B) A NIGHT ON THE TOWN 1972 BIG TREE US BTS 2010
(C) YEAH! 1973 BIG TREE US BT 2102
(D) SCHOOL PUNKS 1974 BIG TREE US 89500
(E) SMOKIN' IN THE BOYS ROOM 19 PHILIPS 6369 804
(F) MOTOR CITY CONNECTION 1975 BIG TREE 89510
(G) BROWNSVILLE STATION 1977 P STOCK US 2026 UK PVLP 1021
(H) AIR SPECIAL 1978 EPIC US 35606 UK EPC 83161

B246A **BROWNSTONE** B246A

BARBARA LOPEZ V (A
MICHAEL FRASS K V (A
DAVID P HOFFMAN G V (A
DOUGLAS WELBAUM G (A

(A) BROWNSTONE 19

SAMUEL JOHNSON D (A
STEVE SEIBERG B V (A

B247 **ANNETTE & VICTOR BROX** B247

VICTOR BROX V K (A
ANNETTE BROX V PERC(A
JEFF WALTERS WIND (A
CHARLENE COLLINS V 'A
LOUIS HUTCHINSON V (A
PAUL BURGESS PERC D(A
RAY RUSSELL G (A
JOHN PORTER G (A
BRIAN KEITH TROM V(A
JUNE LEWIS V (A

(A) ROLLIN' BACK 1974 SONET UK SNTF 663

GLEN CARTLIDGE G SAX (A
RAY WARLEIGH SAX (A
GORDON REED V (A
JOHN MOORSHEAD G (A
LARRY GANNON G (A
KEITH BAILEY D (A
GERALDINE CONNOR V (A
TOSH RYAN-CARTER SAX (A

HARVEY ROSE B V (A
BRUCE MITCHELL PERC (A
TONY MOSS B (A
ALEX DMOCHOWSKI B (A
PETE WAUGH G V (A
LOL CREME D (A
JOYCE HOBSON V (A
DAVE LOWARCH G (A

B248 **JACK BRUCE** B248

JACK BRUCE B V k (ALL
DICK HECKSTALL SMITH SAX (AB
CHRIS SPEDDING G (AC
JOHN McLAUGHLIN G (B
JON HISEMAN D (AB
JOHN MARSHALL D (AC
ART THEMEN SAX (A
HENRY LOWTHER HRNS (A
HARRY BECKETT HRNS (A
JOHN MUMFORD HRNS (A
MITCH MITCHELL D (C
LARRY CORYELL G (C
MIKE MANDEL K (C
GRAHAM BOND K (
MICK TAYLOR G (1
JIM GORDON D (D
SIMON PHILLIPS D (E
HUGH BURNS G (E
RONNIE LEAHY K (1
CLEM CLEMSON G (F
JIM KELTNER D (D
FELIX PAPPALARDI V PERC(A
TONY HYMAS K V (E
DAVID SANCIOUS K G (F
REG ISIDORE D (H

(A) SONGS FOR A TAYLOR 1969 POLYDOR UK 583 058
(A) SONGS FOR A TAYLOR 1969 ATCO US 33306
(A) SONGS FOR A TAYLOR 1969 POLYDOR GER 184 320
(B) THINGS WE LIKE 1970 POLYDOR UK 2343 033
(B) THINGS WE LIKE 1970 ATCO US 33349
(B) THINGS WE LIKE 1970 POLYDOR GER 2310 077
(C) HARMONY ROW 1971 POLYDOR UK 2310 107
(C) HARMONY ROW 1971 ATCO US 33365
(C) HARMONY ROW 1971 POLYDOR 2385 065
(D) OUT OF THE STORM 1974 POLYDOR UK 2394 143
(D) OUT OF THE STORM 1974 RSO 4805
(D) OUT OF THE STORM 1974 RSO 2479 123
(E) HOWS TRICKS 1977 RSO UK 2394 180
(E) HOWS TRICKS 1977 RSO US 1-3021
( ) POP GIANTS No. 14 (COMP) 19 BRUNSWICK IMP 2911 525
( ) AT HIS BEST (DBL) 1974 RSO 2659 024
( ) AT HIS BEST (DBL) 1972 POLYDOR US PD 3505
(1) JACK BRUCE BAND 1977
(F) IVE ALWAYS WANTED TO DO THIS 1980 EPIC UK 84672
(G) BRUCE LORDAN TROWER BLT 1981 CHRYSALIS 1324
(H) TRUCE 1982 CHRYSALIS 1352

CARLA BLEY K V (1
ROBIN TROWER G (GH
STEVE HUNTER G (1

BILLY COBHAM D (F
BILL LORDAN D (G
BRUCE GARY D (1

B249 **BILL BRUFORD** B249

BILL BRUFORD D (ALL
WITH
DAVE STEWART K (ABCD
JEFF BERLIN B (ABCD
ALLAN HOLDSWORTH G (AB
NEIL MURRAY B (A
ANNETTE PEACOCK V (A
JOHN GOODSALL G (A
JOHN CLARK G (CD
BARBARA GASKIN V (D

(A) FEELS GOOD TO ME 1978 POLYDOR US 6149 UK 2310 579
(A) FEELS GOOD TO ME 1978 POLYDOR 2302 075
(B) ONE OF A KIND 1979 POLYDOR US 6205 UK 2302 091
(B) ONE OF A KIND 1979 POLYDOR US POLD 5020
(C) BRUFORD TAPES 1980 POLYDOR BRUBOOT28
(D) GRADUALLY GOING TORNADO 1980 POLYDOR US 6261 UK EGLP 104

KENNY WHEELER HRNS (A
AMANDA PARSONS V (D

GEORGIE BORN CELLO (D

B250 BRUNNING HALL SUNFLOWER BLUES BAND B250

Album	Year	Label	No.
(A) BULLEN STREET BLUES	1968	SAGA	FID 2118
(B) SUNFLOWER BLUES BAND	196	GEMINI	GM 2010
(C) TRACKSIDE BLUES	1969	SAGA	EROS 8132

Member	Inst	LPs
BOB BRUNNING	B	(ABC
BIG SUNFLOWER(BOB HALL)	PNO	(ABC
MICK HALLS	G	(A
COLIN JORDAN	G	(AC
PETER FRENCH	V	(A
LEO MANNING	D	(B
STEVE RYE	HCA	(B
PETE BANHAM	D	(C
JEFF RUSSELL	D	(A
JO ANNE KELLY	V	(B
KEITH NELSON	BANJO	(B
PETER GREEN	G V	(C
PAT GROVER	V G	(B
JOHN O'LEARY	HCA	(B
BARRY GUARD	D	(B

B250A BRUSH ARBOR B250A

Album	Year	Label	Country	No.
(A) BRUSH ARBOR	1973	CAPITOL	US	11158
(B) BRUSH ARBOR II	1973	CAPITOL	US	11209
(C) PAGE ONE	1976	MONUMENT	US	6637
(D) STRAIGHT	1977	MONUMENT	US	7613

251

B251 PEABO BRYSON B251

Album	Year	Label	No.
(A) REACHING FOR THE SKY	1978	CAPITOL	EST 11729
(B) CROSSWINDS	1978	CAPITOL	ST 11875
(C) PARADISE	1980	CAPITOL	12-63

Member	Inst	LPs
PEABO BRYSON	V	(ALL
WITH		
PAUL LIBMAN	K	(A
SONNY SEALS	SAX	(A
TERRY FRYER	SYN	(A
ROSS TRAUT	G	(A
BOBBY CHRISTIAN	PERC	(A
LARRY BALL	B	(A
DAN LEAKE	G	(A
MORRIS JENNINGS	D	(A

B252 BUBBLE PUPPY B252

Album	Year
(A) BUBBLE PUPPY	19

Member	Inst	LPs
ROD PRINCE	G V	(A
TODD POTTER	G	(A
ROY COX	B	(A
M TAYLOR	D	(A

B253 ROY BUCHANAN B253

Album	Year	Label	Country	No.
(A) ROY BUCHANAN	1972	POLYDOR	UK	2391 042
(A) ROY BUCHANAN	1972	POLYDOR	US	PD 5033
(B) SECOND ALBUM	1973	POLYDOR	UK	2391 062
(B) SECOND ALBUM	1973	POLYDOR	US	PD 5046
(C) THATS WHAT I'M HERE FOR	1974	POLYDOR	UK	2391 114
(C) THATS WHAT I'M HERE FOR	1974	POLYDOR	US	PD 6020
(D) RESCUE ME	1975	POLYDOR	UK	2391 152
(E) LIVE STOCK	1975	POLYDOR	US	PD 6048
(F) A STREET CALLED STRAIGHT	1976	POLYDOR	UK	2391 233
(F) A STREET CALLED STRAIGHT	1976	ATLANTIC	US	SD 18170
(G) LOADING ZONE	1977	POLYDOR	UK	2391 295
(G) LOADING ZONE	1977	ATLANTIC	US	18138
(H) NOT ALONE	1978	ATLANTIC	US	SD 19170
( ) ROY BUCHANAN	1976	POLYDOR	UK	2482 275
( ) IN THE BEGINNING	19	POLYDOR	US	PD 6035
(K) MY BABA	1980	WATERHOUSE	US	12

Member	Inst	LPs
ROY BUCHANAN	G V	(ALL
WITH		
STEVE CROPPER	G	(G
DIVA GRAY	V	(G
RHETTA HUGHES	V	(G
LAURA WILLIAMS	V	(G
RON FOSTER	V	(G
RAY GOMEZ	G	(GH
STANLEY CLARKE	G	(G
NARADA MICHAEL WALDEN	D	(G
MALCOLM LUKENS	K	(GEF
JAN HAMMER	K	(G
SCOTT MUSMANNO	V	(G
DENNIS PARKER	B	(G
DAVID GARIBALDI	D	(G
DONALD DUCK DUNN	B	(G
JIM ROMEYN	SYN	(D
WILL LEE	B	(GF
DICK HEINTZE	K	(BAC
DON PAYNE	B	(B
BILLY PRICE	V	(CE
BILL SHEFFIELD	V	(D
BILL STEWART	D	(D
MIMI CASTILLO	SAX	(D
ED FREEMAN	K	(D
WILLIE WEEKS	B	(H
LUTHER VAN DROSS	V	(H
DAVIS LASLEY	V	(H
GORDON JACKSON	B	(K
DON BRUBECK	D	(K
TOM FLYE	PERC	(D
TEDDY IRWIN	G	(AB
CHUCK TILLEY	V	(AB
JOHN HARRISON	B V	(CEF
NEIL LARSEN	K	(D
GREG ADAMS	TPT	(D
MIC GILLETTE	HRNS	(D
VENETTA FIELDS	V	(D
ANDY NEWMARK	D	(FH
KRYSTAL DAVIS	V	(H
PETE VAN ALLEN	B	(A
BYRD FOSTER	D	(EFG
ARMANDO PERAZA	CONGA	(D
JERRY MERCER	D	(AB
NED DAVIS	D	(AB
ROBBIE MAGRUDER	D	(C
KENNY TIBBETTS	B	(D
LENNY PICKETT	SAX	(D
STEPHEN KUPKA	SAX	(D
CARLENE WILLIAMS	V	(D
GARY ST CLAIR	V	(H
ALFA ANDERSON	V	(H
PAUL JACOBS	K V	(K
RICHARD CROOK	D	(K

B254 BUCKACRE B254

Album	Year	Label	Country	No.
(A) MORNING COMES	1976	MCA	UK	MCF 2771
(A) MORNING COMES	1976	MCA	US	MCA 2218
(B) BUCKACRE	1978	MCA	US	MCA 2365

Member	Inst	LPs
ALAN THACKER	G FDL	(AB
DICK HALLEY	B BANJ	(AB
DICK VERUCCHI	D PERC	(AB
DARRELL DATA	STEEL G V	(AB
LES LOCKRIDGE	G	(A
DAVID ANSON	PNO K V	(B

B254A BUCKEYE B254A

Album	Year	Label / No.
(A) BUCKEYE	1979	POLYDOR US 6213 UK 2391 16

Member	Inst	LPs
RONN PRICE	V B G	(A
THOM FOWLE	G V	(A
GABRIEL KATONA	K V	(A
BEAVER PARKER	D PERC V	(A

B254B BUCKEYE POLITICIAN B254B

Album	Year	Label	No.
(A) LOOK AT ME NOW	1976	UTOPIA	US 1 1823

Member	Inst	LPs
L A	G V	(A
ROSCO	G V	(A
JAY	B V	(A
LONGDOG	K HCA HRNS	(A
BUZZARD	D V	(A
BOBBY	TPT K	(A

B254C LINDSEY BUCKINGHAM B254C

Album	Year	Label / No.
(A) LAW & ORDER	1981	MERCURY UK 6302 167 ASYLUM US 5E561

Member	Inst	LPs
LINDSEY BUCKINGHAM	G V	(A
MICK FLEETWOOD	D	(A
GEORGE HAWKINS	B	(A
CAROL HARRIS	V	(A
CHRISTINE McVIE	V	(A

B255 BUCKINGHAM NICKS B255

Album	Year	Label / No.
(A) BUCKINGHAM NICKS	1973	POLYDOR US PD5058 UK 2391 093
(1) PRE LP LINE UP 'FRITE' 1971		

Member	Inst	LPs
STEVIE NICKS	V	(A1
LINDSEY BUCKINGHAM	G V	(A1
GARY'HOPPY' HODGES	D	(A
JIM KELTNER	D	(A
MARK TULIN	B	(A
JORGE CALDERON	PERC	(A
BRIAN KANE	G	(1
JERRY SCHEFF	B	(A
RON TUTT	D	(A
MONTY STARK	SYN	(A
BOB GEARY	D	(1
ROBERT'WADDY'WACHTEL	G	(A
PEGGY SANDVIG	K	(A
XAVIER PACHECO	K V	(1
TOM CRIEFF	B	(

B255A BUCKINGHAMS B255A

Album	Year	Label	Country	No.
(A) KIND OF DRAG	1966	USA	US	107
(B) TIME & CHANGES	1967	CBS	US	2669
(C) PORTRAITS	1968	CBS	US	2798 9598
(D) IN ONE EAR & GONE TOMORROW	1968	CBS	US	9703
(E) GREATEST HITS	1969	CBS	US	9812
(F) MADE IN CHICAGO	1975	CBS	US	33333

Member	Inst	LPs
DENNY TUFANO	V	(
CARL GIAMMARESE	G	(
JON JON POULOS	D	(
NICK FORTUNE	B	(
MARTY GREBB	K	(
DENNIS MICCOLI	K	(

B256 TIM BUCKLEY B256

Musician	Instrument	Albums
TIM BUCKLEY	G V	(ALL
WITH		
LEE UNDERWOOD	G K	(ABCDEFGJ
VAN DYKE PARKS	PNO	(A
BILLY MUNDI	D	(A
JIMMY BOND	B	(B
DON RANDI	K	(B
BRIAN HARTZLER	G	(B
CARTER COLLINS	CONGAS	(BCDEG
JERRY YESTER	K	(B
JIMMY MADISON	D	(D
DAVID FRIEDMAN	PERC	(CD
JIM FIELDER	B	(ABJ
JOHN MILLER	B	(CD
EDDIE HOH	PERC	(B
DAVE GUARD	PERC	(B
BERNIE MYSIOR	B	(H
BUDDY HELM	D	(H
MARK TIERNAN	K	(HJ
JOE FALSIA	G	(HJG
JOHN FARSHA	G	(B
MIKE MELVOIN	PNO	(J
JESSE EHRLICH	CELLO	(J
ANTHONY TERRAN	HRNS	(J
VENETTA FIELDS	V	(JG
BUZZ GARDNER	HRNS	(F
KENNETH WATSON	PERC	(H
SHARON BEARD	V	(H
MARCIA WALDORF	V	(H
PAUL NORROS	SAX	(G
REINHOLD PRESS	B	(HG
CHUCK RAINEY	B	(JG
DAVID BLUEFIELD	K	(J
WILLIAM PETERSON	HRNS	(J
CLYDIE KING	V	(JG
BUNK GARDNER	HRNS	(F
ERIC DUMLER	HRNS	(H
LISA ROBERTS	V	(H
LARRY BUNKER	PERC	(H
EUGENE SIEGEL	SAX	(G
JERRY GOLDSTEIN	PERC	(G
EARL PALMER	D	(J
JIM HUGHART	B	(J
RICHARD NASH	HRNS	(J
SHIRLEY MATTHEWS	V	(J
MAURY BAKER	PERC	(F
FRED SELDON	FLT	(H
TOM SCOTT	SAX	(H
TERRY HARRINGTON	SAX	(J
KEVIN KELLY	PNO	(G
STRINGS		(G
KING ERRISON	PERC	(GHJ
CARY COLEMAN	PERC	(J
JOHNNY ROTELLA	HRNS	(J
JOHN BALKIN	B	(DEF
BOB RAFKIN	G	(H
MYRNA MATTHEWS	V	(H
DENNY RANDELL	K	(H
ED GREENE	D	(G
LORNA M WILLARD	V	(G
ALENA	DANCE	(G

Album	Year	Label	Country	Number
(A) TIM BUCKLEY	1966	ELEKTRA	US	EKS 74004
(A) TIM BUCKLEY	1971	ELEKTRA	UK	K 42010
(B) GOODBYE & HELLO	1967	ELEKTRA	US	EKS 7318
(B) GOODBYE & HELLO	1971	ELEKTRA	US	EKS 74028
(B) GOODBYE & HELLO	1971	ELEKTRA	UK	K 42070
(C) HAPPY SAD	1968	ELEKTRA	US	EKS 74045
(C) HAPPY SAD	1971	ELEKTRA	UK	K 42072
(D) BLUE AFTERNOON	1969	STRAIGHT	US	STS 1060
(D) BLUE AFTERNOON	1970	WB	US RI	WS 1842
(E) LORCA	1970	ELEKTRA	US	EKS 74074
(E) LORCA	1971	ELEKTRA	US	K42053
(F) STARSAILOR	1970	STRAIGHT	US	STS 1064
(F) STARSAILOR	1971	WB	US	WS 1881
(F) STARSAILOR	197	ELECTROLA	GERM	IC06292094
(G) GREETINGS FROM L A	1972	WB	US	BS 2631
(G) GREETINGS FROM L A	1972	WB	UK	K 46176
(H) SEFRONIA	1973	DISCREET	UK	K 49201
(H) SEFRONIA	1974	DISCREET	US	MS 2157
(J) LOOK AT THE FOOL	1974	DISCREET	UK	K 59204
(J) LOOK AT THE FOOL	1974	DISCREET	US	DS 2201

B257 BUCKWHEAT B257

Musician	Instrument	Albums
DUB CAMPBELL	G VLN	(ALL
MICHAEL BUCKY MOTHERMAN	K V	(ALL
RANDY JAMES	G	(A
MARK DURHAM	B	(ALL
RICK GILBERT	D	(C
SONNY RAY	D	(D
DEAN SMITH	G V	(D
DEBBIE CAMPBELL	G V	(BCD

Album	Year	Label	Number
(A) BUCKWHEAT	1971	LONDON US 595	UK SHU 8423
(B) MOVING ON	1972	LONDON US 609	UK SHU 8429
(C) CHARADE	1973	LONDON US 621	UK SHU 8444
(D) HOT TRACKS	1975	LONDON US 635	UK SHU 8470

B257A BUDDY ODOR STOP B257A

Musician	Instrument	Albums
PETER CALICHER	K	(A
MEIKE TOUW	V	(A
JAN CEESTANS	SAX	(A
RUUD BOS	HRNS	(A
BARNY HAY	V	(A
MAX MOLLINGER	D	(A
JOSEE IERSEL	V	(A
FRED LEEFLANG	HRNS	(A
GERHARD VAN DOOREN	B	(A
HUUB JANSSEN	PERC	(A
R J STIPS	K PROD	(A
BART TERLAAK	D	(A

Album	Year	Label	Country	Number
(A) BUDDY ODOR IS A GAS	1979	ARIOLA	UK	5045

B258 BUDGIE B258

Musician	Instrument	Albums
BURKE SHELLEY	B V	(ALL
TONY BOURGE	G V	(ABCDEFGHK
RAY PHILLIPS	D	(ABCHK
JOHN THOMAS	G	(FLM
PETE BOOT	D	(DH
STEVE WILLIAMS	D	(EFGHIJLM
ROB KENDRICK	G	(
MYF ISAAC	G	(
DUNCAN MACKAY	K	(M

Album	Year	Label	Country	Number
(A) BUDGIE	1971	MCA	UK	MKPS 2018
(A) BUDGIE	1974	MCA	UK	MCF 2506
(B) SQUAWK	1972	MCA	UK	MKPS 2023
(B) SQUAWK	1972	KAPP	US	3669
(B) SQUAWK	1974	MCA	UK	MCF 2502
(C) NEVER TURN YOUR BACK ON A FRIEND	1973	MCA	UK	MDKS 8010
(C) NEVER TURN YOUR BACK ON A FRIEND	1974	MCA	UK	MCG 3513
(D) IN FOR THE KILL	1974	MCA	UK	MCF 2546
(D) IN FOR THE KILL	1974	BARCLAY	FR	410026
(D) IN FOR THE KILL	1974	MCA	US	429
(E) BANDOLIER	1975	MCA	UK	MCF 2723
(E) BANDOLIER	1975	A&M	US	4618
(F) IF I WAS BRITANNIA I'D WAIVE...	1976	A&M	UK	AMLH68377
(F) IF I WAS BRITANNIA I'D WAIVE...	1976	A&M	US	4593
(G) IMPECKABLE	1978	A&M	UK	AMLH64675
(G) IMPECKABLE	1978	A&M	US	4675
(H) THE BEST OF	1976	MCA	UK	MCF 2766
(I) IF SWALLOWED DO NOT INDUCE VOMIT	1980	ACTIVE EP	UK	BUDGIE 1
(J) POWER SUPPLY	1980	ACTIVE	UK	ACTLP 1
(K) BEST OF	1981	CUBE	UK	HIFLY 36
(L) NIGHTFLIGHT	1981	RCA	UK	LP 6003
(M) DELIVER US FROM EVIL	1982	RCA	UK	RCALP 6054

B259 NORTON BUFFALO B259

Musician	Instrument	Albums
NORTON BUFFALO	V HCA PERC	(AB
WITH		
DAVE SHAPIRO	G MAND	(AB
FRED JONES	STEEL	(AB
KIRK HARWOOD	D	(AB
BYRON ALLRED	K	(AB
BOB McFEE	B	(AB
MICKEY HART	PERC	(AB
JOHN HOBBS	K	(B
GARY MALLABER	D	(B
GREG ADAMS	HRNS	(B
MIMI CASTILLO	HRNS	(B
STEVE KUPKA	HRNS	(B
PHIL RICHARDSON	VLN	(AB
TRAMAINE HAWKINS	V	(A
DAVID LADD	FLT	(AB
SEAN HOPPER	B	(A
FEDDIE SMITH	V	(A
JOE CHEMAY	B	(B
WILLIAM CHAMPLIN	V	(B
MICK GILLETTE	HRNS	(B
BOBBY KIMBALL	V	(B
GARY CRELLER	B	(AB
JOHN McFEE	G VLN STEEL	(AB
JOHN CIAMBOTTI	B	(A
LYNETTE HAWKINS	V	(A
STRING SECTION		(A
GREG DOUGLAS	G	(B
BOBBY BLACK	STEEL	(B
LENNY PICKETT	HRNS	(B
NICOLETTE LARSON	V	(B

Album	Year	Label	Country	Number
(A) LOVING IN THE VALLEY OF THE MOON	1977	CAPITOL	UK US	11625
(B) DESERT HORIZON	1978	CAPITOL	UK US	11847

B260 BUFFALO SPRINGFIELD B260

Musician	Instr	Albums	Album	Year	Label	Country	Number
NEIL YOUNG	G V HCA	(ALL	(A) BUFFALO SPRINGFIELD	1967	ATCO US 33200	UK	587 070
			(A) THE BEGINNING (REISSUE)	1973	ATLANTIC	UK RI	K30028
STEPHEN STILLS	G V K	(ALL	(B) BUFFALO SPRINGFIELD AGAIN	1967	ATCO	US	SD 33226
DEWEY MARTIN	D	(ALL	(B) BUFFALO SPRINGFIELD AGAIN	1968	ATLANTIC	UK	587 091
RICHIE FURAY	G V	(ABCEF	(B) BUFFALO SPRINGFIELD AGAIN	1971	ATLANTIC	UK	K 40014
BRUCE PALMER	B	(ABEF	(C) LAST TIME AROUND	1969	ATCO		228 024
KEN KOBLUN	B	(	(C) LAST TIME AROUND	1971	ATLANTIC	UK	K 40077
BOBBY WEST	B	(B	(C) LAST TIME AROUND	1969	ATCO	US	SD 33256
DOUG HASTINGS	G V	(A	(D) EXPECTING TO FLY	1970	ATLANTIC	UK	2462 012
JIM FIELDER	B	(A	(E) THE BEST OF/ RETROSPECTIVE	1969	ATCO	US	SD 33283
JIM MESSINA	B V	(CEF	(E) THE BEST OF/ RETROSPECTIVE	1972	ATLANTIC	UK	K 40071
CHARLIE CHIN	BANJO	(B	(E) THE BEST OF/ RETROSPECTIVE	1972	ATCO	US	SD 38105
JAMES BURTON	G	(B	(F) BUFFALO SPRINGFIELD (DBL)	1973	ATLANTIC	UK	K 70001
JACK NITZSCHE	K	(B	(F) BUFFALO SPRINGFIELD (DBL)	1973	ATCO	US	SD 2 806
DON RANDI	PNO	(B	( ) STAR COLLECTION	19	WEA MIDI	UK	K 30037

B261 JIMMY BUFFETT B261

Musician	Instr	Albums	Album	Year	Label	Country	Number
JIMMY BUFFETT	G V	(ALL	(A) DOWN TO EARTH	1972	BARNABY	US	Z 30093
WITH			(B) A WHITE SPORTS COAT & A PINK..	1973	PROBE	UK	SPB 1078
REGGIE YOUNG	G	(BCD	(B) A WHITE SPORTS COAT...	1973	DUNHILL	US	X 60150
LANNY FIEL	G	(ACGK	(B) A WHITE SPORTS COAT.....	1974	ABC	UK	ABCL 5036
DOYLE GRISHAM	STEEL	(BCDEO	(C) LIVING & DYING IN 3/4 TIME	1974	ABC	UK	ABCL 5047
TOMMY COGBILL	B	(CD	(C) LIVING & DYING IN 3/4 TIME	1974	DUNHILL	US	D 50132
MIKE UTLEY	K	(BCDFHIJLMO	(D) A.1.A	1975	ABC	UK	ABCL 5065
SAM CREASON	D	(BCDF	(D) A.1.A	1975	DUNHILL	US	D 50183
BRENDA BRYANT	V	(M	(E) RANCHO DELUXE (SOUNDTRACK)6TRACKS	1975	UA	US	LA 466G
GREG TAYLOR	HCA	(BCDFHIJLMO	(F) HAVANA DAYDREAMING	1976	ABC	US	ABCD 914
FARRELL MORRIS	PERC	(BCDFHIO	(F) HAVANA DAYDREAMING	1976	ABC	UK	ABCL 5148
DAVID BRYANT	V	(CDF	(G) HIGH CUMBERLAND JUBILEE(1972)	1976	BARNABY	US	BR 6014
DON GANT	V	(BCDF	(H) CHANGES IN LATITUDES	1977	ABC	UK	ABCL 5218
BUZZ CASON	V	(ABCDFGK	(H) CHANGES IN LATITUDES	1977	ABC	US	ABC 990
BERGEN WHITE	V	(CDFGK	(I) SON OF A SAILOR	1978	ABC	UK	ABCL 5242
BILL PUETT	HRNS	(CH	(I) SON OF A SAILOR	1978	ABC	US	ABC 1046
STEVE GOODMAN	G	(BDFI	(J) YOU HAD TO BE THERE (DBL)	1979	ABC		AK 1108/2
PAULETTE BROWN	V	(M	(J) YOU HAD TO BE THERE (DLE)	1979	MCA		MCDW 451
JAY SPELL	K	(IJL	(K) BEFORE THE SALT (A/G COMP)	1979	BARNABY	US	2BR 6019
DEBBIE McCALL	V	(IJMO	(M) VOLCANO	1979	MCA	US	5102
ROGER BARTLETT	G	(DFH	(M) VOLCANO	1979	MCA	UK	MCG 4005
PHILLIP FAJARDO	D	(E	(N) COCONUT TELEGRAPH	1981	MCA	US	5169
JOHNNY MONTEZUMA	PERC	(M	(O) SOMEWHERE OVER CHINA	1982	MCA		5287
DON DOUGLAS	BANJ	(M					

Musician	Instr	Albums	Musician	Instr	Albums	Musician	Instr	Albums	Musician	Instr	Albums
JERRY McGEE	G	(F	JOE OSBORN	B	(F	STEVE FORMAN	PERC	(M	JOHNNY GIMBLE	FDL	(F
GINGER HOLLADAY	V	(FI	ANITA BALL	V	(F	MUSCLE SHOALS HORNS		(F	HARRY DAILEY	B	(FHIJLMO
BARRY CHANCE	G	(J	MICHAEL GARDNER	D	(H	KENNY BUTTREY	D	(H	MIKE JEFFREY	G	(H
SHELLEY KURLAND	STRINGS	(H	RUSS KUNKEL	D	(M	ANDY McMAHON	K V	(M	STEVE SYKES	G V	(M
BARRY CHANCE	G	(JLM	NORBERT PUTNAM	B	(IMO	HARVEY THOMPSON	SAX	(I	JANIE FRICKE	V	(I
LEA JANE BERINATI	V	(I	PENNY NICHOLS	V	(I	LARRY LEE	V	(I	VANETTA FIELDS	V	(M
JAMES TAYLOR	G V	(M	JAMES ELMER	B	(M	TIM KREKEL	G	(IL	SHANE KEISTER	SYN	(B
PHIL ROYSTER	CONGAS	(B	ED WILLIAMS	B	(B	BOBBY THOMPSON	BANJ	(GK	PAUL TABET	D	(GK
RICK FIEL	B	(GK	SANDY GOODRUM	K	(GK	JACKIE DANGLER	PERC	(M	BILL JONES	REC	(M
DAVE LOGGINS	V	(MO	HUGH TAYLOR	V	(M	ALEX TAYLOR	V	(M	VASSAR CLEMENTS	FDL	(B
DON KLOETZE	V	(GK	TRAVIS TURK	D	(AK	KARL HIMMEL	D	(AK	BOB COOK	B G	(AK
DAVE HANEY	B	(AK	WILFRED TUILT	G	(M	JUAN CADIZ	V	(M	MARVIN GARDENS	PERC	(B
MATT'MATTY DREAD'BETTON	D	(O	JOSH LEO	G	(O	M L BENOIT	CONGA	(O	HANK DEVITO	STEEL	(O
FLORENCE WARNER	V	(O	CHRISTIAN BACCHELLIER	V	(O	DAVID LOGGINS	V	(O	FREDDY FISHSTICK	V	(O

B261A BUGGLES B261A

Musician	Instr	Albums	Album	Year	Label
TREVOR HORN	D V	(A	(A) THE AGE OF PLASTIC	1979	ATCO
GEOFFREY DOWNES	K	(A			

B262. BULL B262

Musician	Instr	Albums	Album / Musician	Year / Instr	Label / Albums	Country	Number
BARRY BULL GORDON	G B V	(A	(A) THIS IS BULL	1970	PARAMOUNT	US	PA 5028
ANDY MUSON	B	(A					
PAUL GRIFFIN	K	(A	HERB LOVELL D (A		CARLA CALDRWELL V (A		
HILDA HARRIS	V	(A	EILEEN GILBERT V (A		TASHA THOMAS V (A		
STRINGS		(A					

B262A BULLDOG BREED B262A

(A) MADE IN ENGLAND — 1970 — NOVA — UK — SDN 5

B262B BULLDOZER B262B

(A) BULLDOZER — 197 — RCA — FR — PL 37161

B262C BULLFROG B262C

Musician	Instr	Albums	Album	Year	Label	Number
SEBASTIAN LEITNER	G	(	(A) BULLFROG	1976	SKY	006 ANNUIT US 1003
GERD HOCH	V	(	(B) HIGH IN SPIRITS	1977	SKY	012
VINCENT TROST	B	(				
HARALD KALTENECKER	K	(	BRUNO PEROSA PERC (			

B262D SANDY BULL B262D

Musician	Instr	Albums	Album	Year	Label	Country	Number
SANDY BULL	MULTI	(ALL	(A) FANTASIES	19	VANGUARD	US	VSD 79119
BILLY HIGGINS	D	(AB	(B) INVENTIONS FOR GUITAR & BANJO	1965	VANGUARD	US	VSD 79191
DENNIS CHARLES	PERC	(C	(C) E PLURIBUS UNUM	1965	VANGUARD	US	VSD 6513
			(D) DEMOLITION DERBY	1972	VANGUARD	US	VSD 6578

B262E BULL ANGUS B262E

Musician	Instr	Albums	Album	Year	Label	Country	Number
GENO CHARLES	D	(A	(A) BULL ANGUS	19	MERCURY	US	SRM 1619
LARRY LAFALCE	G V	(A					
RON PICCOLO	K V	(A	DINO PAOLILLO G V (A		FRANKIE PREVITE V REC PERC(A		
LENNY VENDITTI	B	(A					

B262F BULLDOG B262F

Musician	Instr	Albums	Album	Year	Label	Country	Number
BILLY HOCHER	B V	(A	(A) BULLDOG	1972	MCA US 5370	UK MCF	2662
ERIC THORNGREN	G	(A	(A) BULLDOG	1972	MCA 510072	US DECCA	75370
JOHN TURK	K V	(A	(B) SMASHER	1974	BUDDAH		840 031
GENE CORNISH	G	(A	(B) SMASHER	197	BUDDAH US 5600	UK BDLP	4007
DINO DANELLI	D	(A					

B263 **CINDY BULLENS** B263

CINDY BULLENS V G (ALL — (A) DESIRE WIRE — 1978 UA US 933 UK UAG 30217
ROGER FREELAND B (A — (B) STEAL THE NIGHT — 1980 CASABLANCA 7185
JEFF MIRANOV G (A
MARK DOYLE G (AB — DAVID MANSFIELD G (A — LOU MARINI SAX (A
LANCE QUINN G (A — DANNY GATTON G (A — GEORGE YOUNG SAX (A
LEON PENDARVIS K (A — BILLY MERNIT K V (A — ROB MOUNSEY K (A
PAUL SCHAEFFER K (A — NEIL JASON B (A — BOB BABITT B (A
JERRY PETERSON SAX (A — JERRY MAROTTA D (A — ALLEN SCHWARZBERG D (A
KENNY BISCHEL SYN (A — JIMMY MAELEN PERC (A — JON JOYCE V (AB

B264 **BULLET** B264

HARRY LANG V G (A — (A) BULLET — 1977 pbr us 7003
PAUL GOODING K
STEVE THOMAS B V (— JOHN SHAW G V (— GRAHAM SPEARS D (

B264A **BULLSEYE** B264A

THOMAS FERRARA G V (A — (A) ON TARGET — 1979 CBS US 35973
ALAN CHILDS D (A
KEVIN CLOUGHERTY B V (A — MANNY DEMAGISTRIS G V (A — THOMAS GRAVES K V (A

B265 **BUMBLE BEE SLIM** B265

AMOS EASTON[BUMBLE BEE SLIM] — (A) EVERYBODY'S FISHING — 1977 MAGPIE PY 1808

B266 **THE BUNCH** B266

SANDY DENNY V (A — (A) THE BUNCH ROCK ON — 1972 ISLAND UK ILPS9189 US A&M4354
RICHARD THOMPSON G V (A
TREVOR LUCAS G V (A — ASHLEY HUTCHINGS V (A — GERRY CONWAY D (A
IAN WHITEMAN PNO (A — ROGER BALL SAX (A — LINDA PETERS V (A
TONY COX PNO (A — PAT DONALDSON B (A — DAVE MATTACKS D (A
MALCOLM DUNCAN SAX (A — MIKE ROSEN TPT (A

B266A **ROMAN BUNKA** B266A

ROMAN BUNKA G V K (A — (A) DEIN KOPF IST EIN SCHLAFENDES AUTO 1980 PRIVATE RELEASE F667342
GERALD LUCIANO HARTWIG B SITAR(A
FREDDY SETZ D PNO (A — SUN A YOON V (A — CHILLI BABA V (A

B267 **BUOYS** B267

CHRIS HANLON D (A — (A) THE BUOYS — 1971 WAND WNS 15 SCEPTRE 24001
BILL KELLY G FLT (A
CARL SIRACUSE G K (A — GERRY HLUDZIK B (A — FRAN BROZENA G K (A

B267A **WILBURN BURCHETTE** B267A

WILBURN BURCHETTE G (ALL — (A) OCCULT CONCERT — 1971 AMES US 7014
(B) OPENS THE SEVEN GATE — 1972 EBOS US 0001
(C) GUITAR GRIMOIRE — 1973 BURCHETTE US 001
(D) PSYCHIC MEDITATION MUSIC — 1974 BURCHETTE US 002
(E) MUSIC OF THE GODHEAD — 1975 BURCHETTE US 003
(F) TRANSCENDENTAL MUSIC — 1976 BURCHETTE US 004
(G) MIND STORM — 1977 BURCHETTE US 007

B268 **ERIC BURDON** B268

ERIC BURDON V (ALL — (A) GUILTY — 1971 UA UK UAG 29251
WITH — (A) GUILTY — 1971 MGM US SE 4791
JIMMY WITHERSPOON V (A — (B) SUN SECRETS — 1974 CAPITOL EST 11359
BOB MERCEREAU HCA (A — (C) STOP — 1975 CAPITOL EST 11426
LEE OSKAR HCA (A — (D) POP HISTORY(DBL) — 197 POLYDOR 2625 011
PAPA DEE ALLEN PERC (A — (E) STAR PORTRAIT(DBL) — 197 VERVE 2629 001
HAROLD BROWN D (A — (E) STAR PORTRAIT(DBL) — 197 MGM 2624 024
GEORGE SURANOVICH D (AC — (F) SURVIVOR — 1978 POLYDOR UK 2302 078
CHARLES MILLER SAX (A — (F) SURVIVOR — 1978 POLYDOR 2310 577
HOWARD SCOTT G (A — (1) 1978 MARCH TOUR
JOHN STERLING G (ACJ — (G) MADMAN — 1976 KARUSSELL GERM 2674 004
LONNIE JORDAN K (A — (H) DARKNESS DARKNESS — 1980 POLYDOR GER 2344 147
GLENN PENNISTON D (1H — (I) LAST DRIVE (FIRE DEPT) — 1980 ARIOLA EURO 202 800
TERRY RYAN K (AC — ( ) IN THE BEGINNING — 19 WAND US 690
SNUFFY WALDEN G (J — (J) COMEBACK (SOUNDTRACK) — 1982 LINE GER LLP 5202
B B DICKERSON B (A
GEOFF WHITEHORN G (F — ALVIN TAYLOR D (BCF — LARRY STEELE G (1
MORRIS WHEELOCK PERC (C — KIM KESTERSON B (AC — KENNY PARRY G (F
AALON BUTLER G (B — DELISLE HARPER B (1 — ZOOT MONEY K (F
DAVE DOVER D (F — RANDY RICE B (BC — RABBIT K (F
COLIN PINCOTT G (F — JUERGEN FRITZ K (F — ALEXIS KORNER G (F
FRANK DIETZ G (FI — STEFFI STEPHEN B (F — P P ARNOLD V (F
MAGGIE BELL V (F — VICKI BROWN V (F — BRIAN ROBERTSON G (H
BOBBY TENCH G (H — HENRY McCULLOGH G (H — CHRIS STEWART B (H
MICK WEAVER K (H — MEL COLLINS HRNS (H — JOHN PERRY V (H
JACKIE CARTER V (I — BERND GAERTIG G V (I — JEAN JACQUES KRAVETZ K (I
REGINALD WORTHY B (I — BERTRAM ENGEL D V K (I — NIPPY NOYA PERC (I
STEVE GOLDSTEIN K (J — LUIS CABEZA K (J — BILL McCUBBON B (J
TERRY WILSON B (J — TONY BRAUNAGLE D (J — TOM VIRGIL SAX (J
BOBBY MARTIN SAX (J — LYNN CAREY V (J — LISA SCOTT V (J
DEBI NEAL V (J — KATE MARKOVITZ V (J — JOYCE ANGAROLA V (J
HONEY BROWN V (J

B269 **SONNY BURGESS** B269

SONNY BURGESS (— (A) LEGENDARY SUN PERFORMERS — 19 CHARLY UK CR 30136
(B) OLD GANG — 1977 LAKE COUNTY LP 503
(EP)SONNY BURGESS(WE WANNA BOOGIE) — 19 CHARLY UK CEP 103

B269A **KEN BURIGAN** B269A

KEN BURGAN (A — (A) THE BIG WOW WOW STRAIN — 1974 BLUE THUMB US BTS 6016
GUS CONTOS (A
JOHN GIRTON (A — WILTON FELDER (A — HARVEY MASON (A
HILARY HAMBERG (A — PAUL HUMPHREY (A — MIKE SALTSBERG (A

B270 **KEVIN BURKE** B270

KEVIN BURKE FDL (— (A) IF THE CAT FITS — 1978 ROCKBURGH ROC 105
(A) IF THE CAT FITS — 1979 MULLIGAN LUN 021
(B) PROMENADE — 1979 MULLIGAN LUN 028

B271 **SOLOMON BURKE** B271

Musician	Inst.	Albums
SOLOMON BURKE	V	(ALL

	Title	Year	Label	Country	Cat. No.
( )	GREATEST	1963	LONDON	UK	HAK 8018
( )	GREATEST HITS	19	ATLANTIC		8067
( )	IF YOU NEED ME	19	ATLANTIC		8085
( )	ROCK'N'SOUL	1964	ATLANTIC		8096
( )	ROCK'N'SOUL	1964	ATLANTIC	UK	ATL 5009
( )	THE BEST OF	19	ATLANTIC		8109
( )	I WISH I KNEW	19	atlantic		88185
( )	KING OF ROCK'N' SOUL	1966	ATLANTIC	UK	590 004
( )	PROUD MARY	1969	BELL		SBLL 118
( )	PROUD MARY	1969	BELL	US	6033
( )	ELECTRONIC MAGNETISM	19	POLYDOR		2315 048
( )	ELECTRONIC MAGNETISM	19	MGM	US	4767
( )	HISTORY	1972	PRIDE	US	8131
( )	I HAVE A DREAM	1974	DUNHILL	US	50161
( )	MUSIC TO MAKE LOVE BY	1975	CHESS		9109 102
( )	WERE ALMOST HOME	19	mgm	us	4830
( )	MUSIC TO MAKE LOVE BY	197	CHESS	US	60042
( )	STAR COLLECTION	1975	ATLANTIC	UK	K 20064
( )	GET UP AND DO SOMETHING...	197	MGM		
( )	BACK TO MY ROOTS	19	CHESS	US	19002
( )	FROM THE HEART	1980	CHARLY	UK	CRB 1024

B271A **J J BURNEL** B271A

Musician	Inst.	Albums
J J BURNEL		(A

	Title	Year	Label	Country	Cat. No.
(A)	EUROMAN COMETH	1979	UA	GER	62557

B272 **BURLESQUE** B272

Musician	Inst.	Albums
IAN TRIMMER	SAX V	(AB
BILLY JENKINS	G V	(AB
STEVE PARR	K	(AB
STEVE HUGHES	B V	(AB
PAUL WARREN	D	(A
KEVIN CURRIE	D	(B

	Title	Year	Label	Country	Cat. No.
(A)	ACUPUNCTURE	1977	ARISTA		ARTY 151
(B)	BURLESQUE	1977	ARISTA	UK	SPARTY1028

B272A **DORSEY BURNETTE** B272A

Musician	Inst.	Albums
DORSEY BURNETTE	V	(A

	Title	Year	Label	Country	Cat. No.
(A)	DORSEY BURNETTE	1963	DOT US LONDON	UK	HAD 8050
(B)	TALL OAK TREE	1979	ERA	US	102
(C)	GREATEST HITS	196	ERA	US	800
(D)	HERE & NOW	1972	CAPITOL	US	11094
(E)	DORSEY BURNETTE	1973	CAPITOL	US	11219
(F)	COMIN' BACK (DBL)	197	TRIP	US	8506
(G)	DORSEY BURNETTE	197	BUCKBOARD	US	1024
(H)	BERTHA LOU DEVILS QUEEN	197	ZIRKON	CAN	104
(J)	THINGS I TREASURE	1977	CALLIOPE	US	7006
(K)	THE GOLDEN HITS	1979	GUSTO	US	0050

B272B **BILLY BURNETTE** B272B

Musician	Inst.	Albums
BILLY BURNETTE	G V	(ALL
EDDY ANDERSON	PERC	(C
HAYWOOD BISHOP	D	(C
CHRIS ETHRIDGE	B	(C
TOMMY COGBILL	B	(C
REGGIE YOUNG	G	(C
PHILLIP DONNELLY	G	(C
CHIPS MOMAN	G V	(C
RICHARD MAINEGRA	V	(C
KIMME GARDNER	B	(D
DAVID HOOD	B	(D
JIMMY JOHNSON	G	(E
RONNIE EADES	SAX	(E
AVA ALDRIDGE	V	(E
DAN PENN	V	(C
BOBBY EMMONS	K	(C
TONI WINE	V	(C
CHRIS BROSIUS	G V	(D
ROGER HAWKINS	D	(D
WAYNE PERKINS	G	(E
HARVEY THOMPSON	SAX	(E
CINDY RICHARDSON	V	(E
SHANE KEISTER	K	(C
JOHNNY CHRISTOPHER	G V	(C
JEFF WEST	V	(C
IAN WALLACE	D V	(D
BARRY BECKETT	K	(D
DUNCAN CAMERON	G	(E
PHILLIP HUMPHREY	SAX	(E
KIM MORRISON	V	(E

	Title	Year	Label	Country	Cat. No.
(A)	BILLY BURNETTE	1972	ENTRANCE	US	31228
(B)	BILLY BURNETTE	1979	POLYDOR	US	6187
(C)	BETWEEN FRIENDS	1979	POLYDOR	US	6242
(D)	BILLY BURNETTE	1980	CBS	US	36792
(E)	GIMME YOU	1981	CBS	US	37460

B273 **HANK C BURNETTE** B273

Musician	Inst.	Albums
HANK C BURNETTE	G V	(ALL

	Title	Year	Label	Country	Cat. No.
(A)	SPINNIN' ROCK BOOGIE	1974	SOUTHERN SOUND	UK	
(B)	DONT MESS WITH MY DUCKTAIL	1976	SONET	UK	SNTF 693
(C)	ROCKABILLY GASSEROONIE	1978	SONET	UK	SNTF 750
(D)	HOT LICKS & FANCY TRICKS	1979	SONET	UK	SNTF 792

B274 **JOHNNY BURNETTE** B274

Musician	Inst.	Albums
JOHNNY BURNETTE	G V	(ALL
DORSEY BURNETTE	B V	(
PAUL BURLISON	D	(

	Title	Year	Label	Country	Cat. No.
(A)	DREAMIN'	196	LONDON	UK	HAG 2306
(A)	DREAMIN'	196	LIBERTY	US	LRP 3183
(A)	DREAMIN'	19	SUNSET	UK	SLS 50007
(A)	DREAMIN'	19	SUNSET	US	SUS 6179
(B)	ROCK'N'ROLL TRIO	1956	CORAL 10"	UK	LVC 10041
(B)	ROCK'N'ROLL TRIO	1966	ACE OF HEARTS	UK	AH 120
(B)	ROCK'N'ROLL TRIO	1971	CORAL		CP 61
(B)	ROCK'N'ROLL TRIO	1974	CORAL MCA		CRLM 1043
(B)	ROCK'N'ROLL TRIO	1978	CORAL MCA		CDLM 8054
(C)	TEAR IT UP	1969	CORAL		CP 10
(C)	TEAR IT UP	1974	CORAL		CRLM 1022
(C)	TEAR IT UP	1975	MCA		COPS 6355
(C)	TEAR IT UP	1978	SOLID SMOKE	US	3001
( )	JOHNNY BURNETTE	196	LONDON		HAG 2349
( )	JOHNNY BURNETTE SINGS	196	LONDON		HAG 2375
( )	JOHNNY BURNETTE SINGS	196	LONDON		SAH 6175
( )	JOHNNY BURNETTE SINGS	196	LIBERTY	US	LST 7190
( )	JOHNNY BURNETTE SINGS MONO	196	LIBERTY	US	LRP 3190
( )	VERY BEST OF	19	UA	US	LA432
( )	BEST OF	19	SUNSET	CAN	SS 4028
( )	HITS & OTHER FAVOURITES	19	LIBERTY	UK	LBY 1006
( )	HITS & OTHER FAVOURITES	19	LIBERTY	US	LST 7206
( )	10th ANNIVERSARY ALBUM	1974	U A		UAS 29643
( )	10th ANNIVERSARY ALBUM	1978	SUNSET		SLS 50413
( )	STARS OF ROCK'N'ROLL VOL 1	1979	MCA	FR	410 074
( )	TOGETHER AGAIN	197	SOLID SMOKE	US	8005

B274A ROCKY BURNETTE B274A

Musician	Inst	Albums
ROCKY BURNETTE	V	(A
STEVE DEUTSH	B	(A
RON COLEMAN	G	(A
DAVE EDMUNDS	G	(A
JOHN HUNT	G	(A
BILLY WALKER	G	(A
JOHN HOBBS	K	(A
DENNIS DREITH	HRNS	(A
JIM SEITER	PERC	(A
RICK CROY	D	(A
MIKE PORTER	D	(A
STEVE TURNER	D	(A
CHRIS BROSIUS	G V	(A
RANDY STERN	K	(A
JOE RAMANO	HRNS	(A
BILLY GRAHAM	V	(A
BIFF DAWES	B	(A
BILL HOUSE	B PERC K	(A
CURTIS STONE	B	(A
BILLY BURNETTE	G	(A
MEL COLLINS	HRNS	(A
STANLEY BEHRENS	HCA	(A

Album	Year	Label
(A) SON OF ROCK'N'ROLL	1979	EMI US 17033 UK EMC 3323

B274B T BONE BURNETT B274B

Musician	Inst	Albums
T BONE BURNETT	G V	(A
DAVID MANSFIELD	G	(A
DAVID MINER	B	(A
STEVEN SOLES	V	(A
JUDE JOHNSON		(A
DAVID KEMPER	D	(A
BILLY SWAN	V	(A
STEPHEN BRUTON		(A
K O THOMAS	PNO	(A
JERRY McGEE	G	(A
GARY MONTGOMERY		(A

Album	Year	Label
(A) TRUTH DECAY	1980	CHRYSALIS CHR1317 LINE GER 5109

B275 BURNIN' RED IVANHOE B275

Musician	Inst	Albums
KIM MENZER	WIND VLN	(ACEFJ
OLE FICK	G V	(ACEFJ
KARSTEN VOGEL	SAX K	(ACEFJ
JESS STAEHR	B PERC	(CEFJ
BO THRIGE ANDERSEN	D	(ACEFJ
STEFFEN ANDERSON	B	(A
STEEN CLAESSON	G	(A
JOHN TCHICAI	SAX	(A
HUGH STEINMETZ	TPT	(A
MATS VINDING	B	(
CLAUS BOEHLING	G	(
KENNETH KNUDSON	K	(
TONY REEVES	PROD	(C
EDDIE LEE BEPPEAUX	PROD	(C

Album	Year	Label	Country	No.
(A) M144 DBL	1969	SONET	DK	SLPS1512/3
(B) KOKSI LADY (EP)	1969	SONET	DK	6092
(C) BURNIN' RED IVANHOE	1970	SONET	DK	SLPS 1522
(C) BURNIN' RED IVANHOE	1970	WB	UK	K 44062
(C) BURNIN' RED IVANHOE	1970	WB	DK	3013
(D) 6 ELEFANTSKOVCIKADEVISER	1971	SONET	DK	SLPS 1528
(E) WWW	1971	SONET	DK	ALSP 1530
(E) WWW	1971	DANDELION	UK	2310 145
(E) WWW	1980	TELDEC	GERM	
(F) MILEY SMILE	1972	SONET	DK	SLPA 1540
(F) MILEY SMILE	1972	TELEFUNKEN	GERM	SLE 14687
(F) MILEY SMILE	1980	TELDEC		
(G) RIGHT ON	1974	SONET	DK	SLPS 1549
(H) BURNIN' LIVE 1970-72 (CASSETTE)	1974	INSTANT		INS 2
(J) SHORTS	198	PICKUP		80304

B276 BURNING SPEAR B276

Musician	Inst	Albums
WINSTON RODNEY	V PERC	(ABCDEFGH
DELROY HINES	V	(AC
RUPERT WILLINGTON	V	(AC
PHILIP FULLWOOD	CONGA	(E
GEORGE LEE	SAX	(E
ANGUS GAYE	D	(EDH
CHINNA RANCHIE	G	(DH
EARL SMITH	G	(ACD
BRINSLEY FORDE	G	(EH
ROBBIE SHAKESPEARE	B	(ACDH
BOBBY ELLIS	TPT	(ACDEGH
COURTNEY HEMMINGS	K	(EH
DONALD GRIFFITHS	G	(E
GEORGE OBAN	B	(EH
LEROY WALLACE	D	(ACDH
WIRE LINDO	K	(DGH
NELSON MILLER	D	(G
JUNIOR MARVIN	G	(G
BERNARD HARVEY	K	(ACDH
DONALD GRIFFITHS	G	(EH
ASTON BARRETT	PERC B	(ACDGH
TYRONE DOWNIE	K	(ACG
EGBERT EVANS	HRNS	(G
HERMAN MARQUIS	SAX	(ACDGH
RICHARD HALL	SAX	(ACD
STICKY	PERC	(DH
DIRTY HARRY	HRNS	(H
TONY CHIN	G	(AC
CARLTON SAMUELS	FLT	(AC
ROOTS KINSLEY	G	(DH
RICO	HRNS	(H
SKULLY	PERC	(D
VIN GORDON	TROM	(ACDH

Album	Year	Label	Country	No.
(A) MARCUS GARVEY	1975	ISLAND		ILPS 9377
(B) MAN IN THE HILLS	1976	ISLAND		ILPS 9412
(C) GARVEY'S GHOST	1976	ISLAND/MANGO		ILPS 9382
(D) DRY & HEAVY	1977	ISLAND MANGO		MLPS 9431
(E) LIVE	1977	ISLAND		ILPS 9513
(E) LIVE	1977	PHONOGRAM	IMP	9101 680
(E) LIVE	1977	ISLAND	NL	200 511
(F) HARDER THAN THE REST	1979	ISLAND		ILPS 9567
(G) HAIL H.I.M.	1980	RADIC		RDC 2003
(H) SOCIAL LIVING	1980	STOP	UK	stop 1001
(J) LIVING DUB	1980	ISLAND	UK	ILPS 9556

B277 EDDIE GUITAR BURNS B277

Musician	Inst	Albums
EDDIE GUITAR BURNS	G V	(AB
WITH		
PAT GROVER	G	(A
BOB HALL	PNO	(AB
JOHN HUNT	D	(A
BOB WILSON	B G	(B
ERWIN HELFER	PNO	(A
JIMMY JEWELL	SAX	(A
ROGER HILL	G	(B
BOB BRUNNING	B	(A
DAVE GELLY	SAX	(A
PETER YORK	D	(B

Album	Year	Label	Country	No.
(A) BOTTLE UP & GO	1972	ACTION	UK	ACMP 100
(B) DETROIT BLACKBOTTOM	1975	BIG BEAR	UK	BEAR 7

B278 RANDY BURNS B278

Musician	Inst	Albums
RANDY BURNS	V G	(ALL
WITH		
BRUCE SAMUELS	V B	(DEF
MATT KASTNER	V G K	(DEF
JOHN O'LEARY	D	(D
A J MULHERN	V	(DEF
DAVID BROMBERG	G	(D
OZ	PNO	(D
BEN KEITH	STEEL	(E
DAVID MOHN	D PERC V	(EF
DAVID TWEEDY	K V	(F

Album	Year	Label	Country	No.
(A) OF LOVE & WAR	1966	E.S.P.		ESP 1039
(B) EVENING OF MAGICIAN	1968	E.S.P.		ESP 1089
(C) SONG FOR UNCERTAIN LADY	1970	E.S.P.		ESP 2007
(D) SKYDOG BAND	1971	MERCURY		SR 61329
(E) I'M A LOVER NOT A FOOL	1972	POLYDOR	US	PD 5039
(F) STILL ON OUR FEET	1973	POLYDOR	US	PD 5049

B278A PETER BURSCH & BROESELMASHINE B278A

Musician	Inst	Albums
PETER BURSCH	G V	(ALL
KLAUS DAPPER	WIND B	(BC
WILLI KISSMER	G V	(BC
MAHENDRA KAPADIA	PERC	(B
JAN FRIDE	D PERC	(B
MANI NEUMEIER	PERC	(B
GUNDI JOECKER	V	(C
ROLAND SCHAEFFER	B	(B
WALDO KARPENKIEL	D PERC	(C
MIKE GOSSEN	D PERC	(C

Album	Year	Label	Country	No.
(A) BROSELMASHINE	1971	PILZ	GER	
(B) PETER BURSCH UND DIE BROSELMASCHINE	76	XENOPHON	GER	161012
(C) I FEEL FINE	1978	SPIEGELEI	GER	160 610
(D) PETER BURSCH	1981	PLANE	GER	88264

B279 JAMES BURTON B279

Musician	Inst	Albums
JAMES BURTON	G V	(AB
RALPH MOONEY		(B

Album	Year	Label	Country	No.
(A) GUITAR SOUNDS OF JAMES BURTON	1971	A&M	UK	AMLS64293
(B) CORN PICKIN' & SLICK SLIDIN	196	CAPITOL	US	

B279A BUSH B279A

Musician	Inst	Albums
ROY KENNER	CONGAS V	(A
DOM TROIANO	G V	(A
PRAKASH JOHN	B V	(A
PENTTI J GLAN	D	(A

Album	Year	Label	Country	No.
(A) BUSH	1970	PROBE	UK	SPB 1012
(A) BUSH	1970	DUNHILL	US	50086

B280 KATE BUSH B280

Musician	Instr	Albums	Musician	Instr	Albums	Musician	Instr	Albums
KATE BUSH	V K	(ALL						
PRESTON HEYMAN	D	(C						
DEL PALMER	B	(BC						
BARRY DE SOUZA	D	(A						
DAVID PATON	B	(AB	IAN BAIRNSON	G	(ABC	DUNCAN MACKAY	K	(ABC
BRUCE LYNCH	B	(A	PAUL KEOGH	G	(A	ALAN PARKER	G	(A
ANDREW POWELL	K	(AB	ALAN SKIDMORE	SAX	(A	MORRIS PERT	PERC	(AC
PADDY BUSH	V HCA MAND	(ABC	CHARLIE MORGAN	D	(B	BRIAN BATH	G	(BC
FRANCIS MONKMAN	K	(B	RICHARD HARVEY	RECORDER	(B	STUART ELLIOTT	D	(ABC
JOHN GIBLIN	B	(C	MAX MIDDLETON	K	(C	ALAN MURPHY	G	(C
KEVIN BURKE	VLN	(C	GARY HURST	V	(C	ANDREW BRYANT	V	(C
MIKE MORAN	K	(C	ROY HARPER	V	(C	ROLAND	PERC	(C
MARTYN FORD ORCH		(C	ADAM SKEAPING	VLA	(C	JO SKEAPING	LIRONI	(C
LARRY FAST	K	(C						

Album	Year	Label		
(A) THE KICK INSIDE	1978	EMI US 11761	UK	EMC 3223
(B) LIONHEART	1978	EMI US 17008	UK	EMA 787
(C) NEVER FOR EVER	1980	EMI	UK	EMA 794

B280A BUSBOYS B280A

Musician	Instr	Albums	Musician	Instr	Albums	Musician	Instr	Albums
BRIAN O'NEAL	V K	(A						
VICTOR JOHNSON	G	(A						
KEVIN O'NEAL	B	(A	STEVE FELIX	D	(A	GUS LOUNDERMAN	V	(A

Album	Year	Label
(A) MINIMUM WAGE ROCK'N'ROLL	1980	ARISTA

B280B BILLY BUTLER B280B

Musician	Instr	Albums
BILLY BUTLER	V	(A

Album	Year	Label	Number
(A) RIGHT TRACK	19	OKEH	14115

B281 JERRY BUTLER B281

Musician	Instr	Albums
JERRY BUTLER	V	(ALL
WITH		
BETTY EVERETT	V	(*
THELMA HOUSTON	V	(+
JAMES GADSON	D	(R
JAMES JAMERSON	B	(R
H B BARNUM	K	(R
JOE SAMPLE	K	(R
DENNIS COFFEY	G	(R
DAVID T WALKER	G	(R
GENE ESTES	VIBES	(R
RICHARD EVANS	B	(S
MARVIN YANCY	K	(S
PHIL UPCHURCH	G	(S
BILLY BUTLER	G	(S
FRED WALKER	VIBES	(S
JIM SEALS	SAX	(S
KITTI HAYWARD SINGERS	V	(S
LEROY HUTSEN	V	(S
MATTIE BUTLER	V	(S
FRED CASH	V	(S
TENNISON STEPHENS	K V	(S
SOLA BOBROV	STR	(S

Album	Year	Label	Country	Number
HE WILL BREAK YOUR HEART	1963	STATESIDE	UK	SL 10032
HE WILL BREAK YOUR HEART	1963	VEE JAY	US	1029
FOLK SONGS	1963	STATESIDE	UK	SL 10050
FOLK SONGS	1963	VEE JAY	US	1057
THEY'RE DELICIOUS TOGETHER	19	VEE JAY	US	1099
THEY'RE DELICIOUS TOGETHER	19	JOY		JOYS 123
ALL TIME HITS	19	TRIP	US	8011
16 GREATEST HITS	19	TRIP	US	TOP16-45
JUST BEAUTIFUL	19	KENT	US	536
STARRING BETTY EVERETT	(*)19	TRADITION	US	2073
FOR YOUR PRECIOUS LOVE	19	JOY		JOY 104
LOVE ME	1968	JOY		JOYS 126
LOVE ME	1968	FONTANA	TL	5264
GIFT OF LOVE	1968	SUNSET	US	5216
ICE MAN COMETH	19	MERCURY	US	61198
JERRY BUTLER	19	PICKWICK	US	3202
STARRING	1969	TRADITION	US	2068
TOGETHER	19	BUDDAH	US	7507
VERY BEST	19	BUDDAH	US	4001
VERY BEST OF	19	UA	US	UASLA498
(R) POWER OF	1973	MERCURY	US	SRM1 689
(S) SWEET 16	1974	MERCURY	US	SRM11006
SUITE FOR A SINGLE GIRL	19	TAMLA	UK	STML12052
SUITE FOR A SINGLE GIRL	19	MOTOWN	US	M7878
IT ALL COMES OUT	19	TAMLA	UK	STML12073
IT ALL COMES OUT	19	MOTOWN	US	M7892
LOVE'S ON THE MENU	1976	TAMLA	UK	STML12032
LOVE'S ON THE MENU	1976	MOTOWN	US	M7850
THELMA HOUSTON & JERRY	(+)197	MOTOWN	US	M7887
THELMA HOUSTON & JERRY	(+)197	PATHE	FR	C066 99112
SPICE OF LIFE	1972	MERCURY		6338 102
SPICE OF LIFE	1972	MERCURY	US	2/7502
BEST OF	1972	MERCURY		6430 401
BEST OF	1972	MERCURY	US	61281
LOVE WE HAVE	1972	MERCURY		1/660
MR DREAM MERCHANT	19	MERCURY	US	20118
THE SOUL GOES ON	19	MERCURY	US	SR 61171
STUFF DREAMS ARE MADE OF	19	MERCURY		855 006
THE SAGITTARIUS MOVEMENT	19	MERCURY	US	SR 61347
MAKE IT EASY ON YOURSELF	1976	DJM		DJD 28027
MAKE IT EASY ON YOURSELF	197	JOY		JOY 171
GOLDEN HITS	19	MERCURY	US	61151
NOTHING SAYS I LOVE YOU	1978	PHILADELPHIA		PIR83810
NOTHING SAYS I LOVE YOU	1978	PHIL LA	US	35510
THEMLA HOUSTON & JERRY	1977	MOTOWN	UK	STML12063
TWO TO ONE	1978	MOTOWN	UK	STML12092
UP ON LOVE	1980	CHARLY		1005
BEST LOVE	1981	PHILLADELPHIA	US	36413

B282 PAUL BUTTERFIELD & THE BUTTERFIELD BLUES BAND B282

Musician	Instr	Albums
PAUL BUTTERFIELD	V HCA	(ALL
SAM LAY	D V	(ABM
JEROME ARNOLD	B	(ABCM
SMOKEY SMOTHERS	G	(A
ELVIN BISHOP	G V	(BCDEM
MIKE BLOOMFIELD	G	(BCM
BILLY DAVENPORT	D	(C
BUGSY MAUGH	B V	(DE
PHIL WILSON	D	(DEF
DAVE SANBORN	SAX	(DEFGHJL
KEITH JOHNSON	TPT	(DEF
GENE DINWIDDIE	SAX	(DEFGHJ
STEVE MADAIO	TPT	(FGH
BUZZY FEITEN	G V K	(F
ROD HICKS	V B	(FG
BIG BLACK	V PERC	(H
RALPH WASH	V G	(GH
DENNIS WHITTED	D V	(HJ
BOBBYE HALL	PERC	(H

Album	Year	Label	Country	Number
(A) OFFER YOU CANT REFUSE(1SIDE 1963)	1972	RED LIGHTNIN		R 008
(B) BUTTERFIELD BLUES BAND	1965	ELEKTRA	US	EKS 7294
(B) BUTTERFIELD BLUES BAND	1965	ELEKTRA	UK	K 42004
(B) BUTTERFIELD BLUES BAND	1975	MIDI		22004
(C) EAST WEST	1966	ELEKTRA	US	EKS 7315
(C) EAST WEST	197	ELEKTRA	UK	K 42006
(D) RESURRECTION OF PIGBOY CRABSHAW	19	ELEKTRA	UK US	74015
(D) RESURRECTION OF PIGBOY CRABSHAW	1971	ELEKTRA	UK	K 42017
(E) IN MY OWN DREAM	1968	ELEKTRA	UK US	EKS74025
(E) IN MY OWN DREAM	1976	ELEKTRA	UK	K 42042
(F) KEEP ON MOVING	1969	ELEKTRA	US	EKS 74053
(F) KEEP ON MOVING	1971	ELEKTRA	UK	K 42033
(G) LIVE	1970	ELEKTRA	US	7E 2001
(G) LIVE	1976	ELEKTRA	UK	K 62001
(H) SOMETIMES I JUST FEEL LIKE SMILIN'	1971	ELEKTRA	US	EKS 75013
(H) SOMETIMES I JUST FEEL LIKE SMILIN'	1971	ELEKTRA	UK	K 42095
(J) BETTER DAYS	1973	BEARSVILLE	US	BR 2119
(J) BETTER DAYS	1973	BEARSVILLE	UK	K 45515
(K) IT ALL COMES BACK	1974	BEARSVILLE	US	BR 2170

(CONTINUED)

GEORGE DAVIDSON D (GH (K) IT ALL COMES BACK 1974 BEARSVILLE UK K 45517
TREVOR LAWRENCE SAX (FH (L) PUT IT IN YOUR EAR 1975 BEARSVILLE US BR 6960
TED HARRIS PNO (FGH (L) PUT IT IN YOUR EAR 1976 BEARSVILLE UK K 55509
RONNIE BARRON K V (JK (M) WHATS SHAKIN' 19 ELEKTRA US EKS 4002
CHRISTOPHER PARKER D (JKL (M) WHATS SHAKIN' 1973 MIDI 22003
BOBBY CHARLES V (JK (N) GOLDEN BUTTER (BEST OF) 1972 ELEKTRA US 7E 2005
GEOFF MULDAUR V G VIBES (JK (N) GOLDEN BUTTER (BEST OF) 1972 ELEKTRA UK K 62011
AMOS GARRETT G (JK (EP) WITH JOHN MAYALL 196 DECCA UK DFE 8673
MARK NAFTALIN K (BCDEm (O) NORTH SOUTH 1981 WB US 6995
MARIA MULDAUR V (JK FRED BECKMAIER B (F J D PARRAN SAX (J BILLY RICH B (JK
HOWARD JOHNSON HRNS (JK SAM BURTIS TROM (J PETE ECKLUND TPT (J AL KOOPER ORG (E
CLYDIE KING V (GH VANETTA FIELDS V (GH OMA DRAKE V (GH MERRY CLAYTON V (GH
GARY BROCKS TROM (J JERRY RAGOVOY PNO (F STAN SHAFRAN TPT (J CHUCK RAINEY B (L
TIM DRUMMOND B (L JAMES JAMESON B (L GORDON EDWARDS B (L LEVON HELM D PERC(L
BERNARD PURDIE D (L STEVEN KROON D (L LLOYD MICHELS TPT (L IRVING MARKOWITZ TPT (L
AL DERISI TPT (L SONNY RUSSO TROM (L HENRY GLOVER K (L GARTH HUDSON K (L
RICHARD BELL K (L FRED CARTER G (L BEN KEITH G (L ERIC GALE G (L
JOHN HOLBROOK G (L NICK JAMESON G (L FRANK WEST SAX (L SELDON POWELL SAX (L
BABE CLARKE SAX (L MEL TAX SAX (L GAIL KANTOV V (L ERN DICKENS V (L
ANN SUTTON V (L EVANGELINE CARMICHAEL V(L LORNA WILLARD V (L JULIA TILLMAN V (L
ANDREA WILLIS V (L JEROME RICHARDSON SAX (L CLIFF SHANK SAX (L WILBUR SCHWARTZ SAX (L
GENE CIPRIANO SAX (L

B283 THE BUTTS BAND B283

JOHN DENSMORE D (AB (A) THE BUTTS BAND 1974 BLUE THUMB UK ILPS 9260
BOBBY KRIEGER G (AB (A) THE BUTTS BAND 1975 BLUE THUMB US 63
JESS RODEN V G (A (B) HEAR & NOW 1975 ABC UK ABCL 5117
PHIL CHEN B G (A (B) HEAR & NOW 1975 VOGUE FR 10042
ROY DAVIES K SYN(A (B) HEAR & NOW 1975 BLUE THUMB US BT 6018
ALLAN SHARP CONGA (A
MICK WEAVER K (A LARRY McDONALD CONGA (A MICHAEL STULL V G (B
MIKE BERKOWITZ D (B KARL RUCKNER B (B ALEX RICHMAN V K (B
BOBBYE HALL CONGAS(B

B283A BUX B283A

RALPH MORMAN V (A (A) WE CAME TO PLAY 1976 CAPITOL US 11459
PUNKY MEADOWS G (A
JAMES NEWLON G V (A ROCKY ISAAC D (A MICKEY JONES B (A
PAUL CHANSKY PNO (A

B284 BUZZCOCKS B284

HOWARD DEVOTO V (1 (1) SPIRAL SCRATCH (EP) 1977 NEW HORMONES UK ORG 1
PETE SHELLEY G V (AB1 (A) ANOTHER MUSIC IN A DIFFERENT KITCHEN 1977 UA UK UAG 30159
STEVE DIGGLE B G (AB (B) LOVE BITES 1978 UA UK UAG 30197
STEVE GARVEY B (AB (B) LOVE BITES 1978 SONOPRESSE FR 062 61897
GARTH SMITH B (B (C) DIFFERENT KINDS OF TENSION 1979 UA UK UAG30260 US A&M 009
JOHN MAHER D (AB1 (D) SINGLES GOING STEADY 1979 UA UK UAG30279 US A&M 001
(2) ARE EVERYTHING +5 (EP) 1981 IRS 9701

B284B BOBBY BYRD B284B

BOBBY BYRD (A (A) I NEED HELP 19 KING US 1119

B284C JOE BYRD & THE FIELD HIPPIES B284C

JOE BYRD K V SYN(A (A) THE AMERICAN METAPHYSICAL CIRCUS 1969 CBS US 7317
VICTORIA BOND V (A
SUSAN DE LANGE V (A GREGG KOVER D (A TOM SCOTT WIND (A
ED SHEFTEL TPT (A TED GREENE G (A JOHN CLAUDER D (A
DANA CHALBERG WIND (A FRED SELDEN WIND (A MEYER HIRSCH WIND (A
DON KERIAN TPT (A CHUCK BENNETT TROM (A RAY CAPPOCCHI HRNS (S

B285 BYRDS B285

ROGER McGUINN V G BANJO (ALL (A) EARLY FLIGHT (JET SET) 19 CBS ST 1014
GENE CLARK G V (ABCDOPQ (A) EARLY FLIGHT (JET SET) 19 TOGETHER SST 1001
MIKE CLARKE D (BCDEFGOP (B) PREFLYTE 1964 BUMBLE US GEXP 8001
CHRIS HILLMAN B V MAND (BCDEFGHOPQ(B) PREFLYTE 1972 CBS US KC 32183
DAVID CROSBY G V (ABCDEOP (B) PREFLYTE 19 ARIOLA HOLL 86468
KEVIN KELLEY D (HP (C) MR TAMBOURINE MAN 1965 CBS UK 62571
GRAM PARSONS G V (HPQ (C) MR TAMBOURINE MAN 1965 CBS US CS 9172
SNEAKY PETE KLEINOW STEEL (M (C) MR TAMBOURINE MAN 19 EMBASSY 31057
DOUG DILLARD G V ((C) MR TAMBOURINE MAN 19 EMBASSY 31503
CLARENCE WHITE G V (HJKLMNPR (D) TURN TURN TURN 1966 CBS UK 62652
JOHN YORK B (JKPR (D) TURN TURN TURN 1966 CBS US CS 9254
SKIP BATTIN B (LMNRP (D) TURN TURN TURN 19 EMBASSY 31526
GENE PARSONS D (JKLMNP (D) TURN TURN TURN 1976 EMBASSY UK 31257
JOHN GUERIN ((CD) MR TAMBOURINE/TURN TURN TURN 19 CBS 22018X2
EARL P BALL PNO (H (E) FIFTH DIMENSION 1966 CBS UK 62783
JIMMI SEITER PERC (M (E) FIFTH DIMENSION 1966 CBS US 9349
PAUL POLENA HRNS STRGS(M (F) YOUNGER THAN YESTERDAY 1967 CBS UK 62988
BYRON BERLINE FDL (M (F) YOUNGER THAN YESTERDAY 1967 CBS US CS 9442
LARRY KNECHTEL K (M ( ) GREATEST HITS 1967 CBS UK 63107
TERRY MELCHER PNO (M ( ) GREATEST HITS 196 CBS IMP 66298
( ) GREATEST HITS 19 CBS US 9516
JON CORNEAL D (H (G) NOTORIOUS BYRD BROTHERS 1968 CBS UK 63169
LLOYD GREEN STEEL (H (G) NOTORIOUS BYRD BROTHERS 1968 CBS US CS 9575
JAYDEE MANESS STEEL (H (H) SWEETHEART OF THE RODEO 1968 CBS UK 63353
JOHN HARTFORD BANJ G(H (H) SWEETHEART OF THE RODEO 1968 CBS US CS 9670
ROY M HUSKY B (H (H) SWEETHEART OF THE RODEO 19 EMBASSY EMB 31124
(GH) SWEETHEART / NOTORIOUS BYRD BROS 1976 CBS 22040
(J) DR BYRDS & MR HYDE 1969 CBS UK 63545
(J) DR BYRDS & MR HYDE 1969 CBS US CS 9755
(K) BALLAD OF EASY RIDER 1970 CBS UK 63795
(K) BALLAD OF EASY RIDER 1970 CBS US CS 9942
(L) UNTITLED (DBL) 1970 CBS UK 66253
(L) UNTITLED (DBL) 1970 CBS US G 30127

(CONTINUED)

B285

BYRDS (CONTINUED)

B285

Album	Year	Label	Country	No.
(M) BYRDMANIAX	1971	CBS	UK	64389
(M) BYRDMANIAX	1971	CBS	US	KC 30640
(N) FARTHER ALONG	1972	CBS	UK	KC 64676
(N) FARTHER ALONG	1972	CBS LE10215	US	KC 31050
( ) GREATEST HITS VOL 2	1972	CBS	UK	64650
( ) GREATEST HITS VOL 2	1972	CBS	US	PC 31795
(O) THE BYRDS	1973	ASYLUM	UK	SYLA 8754
(O) THE BYRDS	1973	ASYLUM	US	SD 5058
(O) THE BYRDS	19	WEA		K 53006
( ) HISTORY OF THE BYRDS	1973	CBS	UK	68242
( ) L A FULL CIRCLE	19	WEA	HOLL	23000
( ) L A FULL CIRCLE	19	MERCURY	US	SRM 11074
( ) GREATEST HITS VOL 3	19	CBS	UK	64966
( ) MR TAMBOURINE MAN(COMP DBL)	19	CBS	UK	66298
( ) MR TAMBOURINE MAN/TURN TURN	1975	CBS		33645
( ) SINGLES 1965 67	1980	CBS		31851
(P) PLAY DYLAN	1980	CBS US 36293	UK	31795
(Q) DOIN ALL RIGHT	1978	EXCITABLE	US	4506
(R) EASY RIDERS (69/70)	1981	PENGUIN	US	EGG FIVE

B286

DAVID BYRON

B286

Member	Instr	Albums
DAVID BYRON	V	(AB
LOU STONEBRIDGE	K	(A
DENNY BALL	B	(A
LEE KERSLAKE	D PERC	(A
STUART ELLIOTT	D	(B
LESTER FRY	PERC	(B
DANIEL BOONE	G K	(B
MATT LAMBERT	G V	(C
MICHAEL KENNY	V	(A
BARRY DE SOUZA	D	(B
PETE THOMPSON	PERC	(A
MICK BOX	G	(A
ROBERT SARZO	G	(A
BERNARD KENNY	G	(A
THOMMY PRICE	D V	(C
ALAN JONES	B	(B
JOEY VASTA	B V	(C
TOM MORRONGEILLO	G	(A

Album	Release
(A) TAKE NO PRISONERS	1975 BRONZE UK ILPS9342 US MERCURY1074
(B) BABY FACED KILLER	1978 ARISTA UK SPARTA 1077
(C) THIS DAY & AGE	1980 ARISTA US 4258

B286A

BYRON BAND

B286A

Member	Instr	Albums
DAVID BYRON	V	(A
ROBIN GEORGE	G	(A
MEL COLLINS	SAX	(A
JOHN SHEARER	D	(A
BOB JACKSON	K	(A
ROGER FLAVELLE	B	(A

Album	Year	Label	Country	No.
(A) ON THE ROCKS	1982	CREOLE	UK	CRX2

B287

BYSTANDERS

B287

Member	Instr	Albums
VIC OAKLEY	V	(1
RAY WILLIAMS	B	(1
JEFF JONES	D	(1
CLIVE JOHN	K V	(1
MICKEY JONES	G V	(1

(1) 1968

B288

BYZANTIUM

B288

Member	Instr	Albums
NICO RAMSDEN	G V	(A
CHAS JANKEL	G V	(AB
ROBIN LAMBLE	B V G	(AB
STEVE CORDUNER	D	(AB
DAVID HENTSCHEL	SYN	(B
ROBIN SYLVESTER	SYN	(B
MICK BARAKAN	G V	(B
JAMIE RUBINSTEIN	G V	(B
FRANK RICOTTI	PERC	(B
B J COLE	STEEL	(B

Album	Release
(A) BYZANTIUM	1972 A&M UK AMLS68104 US WB 2659
(B) SEASONS CHANGING	1972 A&M UK AMLH68163

C1

ROY C

C1

Member	Instr	Albums
ROY C	V	(AB

Album	Year	Label	No.
(A) SEX & SOUL	1975	MERCURY	9100 017
(B) MORE SAX & SOUL	19	MERCURY	6338 849

C1A

C C P P

C1A

Member	Instr	Albums
A CECCARELLI	D	(
M CHANTEREAU	PNO	(
C PADOVAN	B	(
SLIM PEZIN	G	(

Album	Year	Label	No.
(A) C.C.P.P.	19	FLAMOPHONE	2933 104

C2

C C S

C2

Member	Instr	Albums
ALEXIS KORNER	G V	(ALL
LES CONDON	TPT	(DA
PETER THORUP	V	(AD
JOHN CAMERON	PNO	(A
GREG BOWEN	TPT	(DA
TONY FISHER	TPT	(AD
HAROLD BECKETT	TPT	(AD
BILL LE SAGE	VIBES	(D
HENRY LOWTHER	TPT	(AD
KENNY WHEELER	TPT	(DA
DON LUSHER	TROM	(DA
HAROLD McNAIR	WIND	(DA
DANNY MOSS	WIND	(AD
ALAN PARKER	G	(DA
BARRY MORGAN	D	(DA
JOHN MARSHALL	TROM	(AD
BILL GELDARD	TROM	(DA
TONY COE	WIND	(AD
BOB EFFORD	WIND	(AD
HERBIE FLOWERS	B	(DA
TONY CARR	D	(DA
BRIAN PERRIN	TROM	(DA
NEIL SANDERS	HRNS	(DA
PETE KING	WIND	(AD
RON MOSS	WIND	(AD
SPIKE HEATLEY	B	(DA
JIM LAWLESS	PERC	(DA

Album	Year	Label	Country	No.
(A) C C S	1970	RAK UK SRKA 6751 US Z30559		
(A) C C S	19	CBS	GER	91783
(B) C C S 2	1972	RAK UK SRAK503	US	31569
(B) C C S 2	1972	RAK	GER	93232
(C) THE BEST BAND IN THE LAND	1973	RAK	UK	SRAK 304
(C) THE BEST BAND IN THE LAND	1973	RAK	GER	94611
(D) THE BEST OF C C S	1977	RAK	UK	SRAK 527
(D) THE BEST OF C C S	1977	RAK	GER	99020

C3

C M U

C3

Member	Instr	Albums
RICHARD JOSEPH	G V	(AB
LARRAINE ODELL	G	(AB
IAN HAMLETT	G	(A
LEARY HASSON	K	(AB
JAMES GORDON	G K V	(A
ROGER ODELL	D	(AB
STEVE COOK		(B
ED LEE	G B	(A

Album	Year	Label	Country	No.
(A) OPEN SPACES	1971	TRANSATLANTIC	UK	TRA 237
(B) SPACE CABARET	1972	TRANSATLANTIC	UK	TRA 259

C4

C O B (Clives Own Band)

C4

Member	Instr	Albums
CLIVE PALMER	BANJO V G	(AB
JOHN BIDWELL	BANJO K V	(AB
MICK BENNETT	PERC V K	(AB
RALPH McTELL	G D	(A
GENEVIEVE BAKER		(B
STEVE BONNETT	B	(A
DEMELZA VAL BAKER		(B
URSULA SMITH	CELLO	(A

Album	Year	Label	No.
(A) THE SPIRIT OF LOVE	1971	CBS	69010
(B) MOYSHE McSTIFF	1972	POLYDOR	2383 161

C4A

CABOOSE

C4A

Member	Instr	Albums
GARY JOHNS	V	(A
WALTER RAMSEY	K	(A
TOMMY CATHEY	B V	(A
PAT KARR	V	(A
JACKIE COOK	G	(A
JOEL WILLIAMS	PERC	(A

Album	Year	Label	Country	No.
(A) CABOOSE	19	ENTERPRISE	US	ENS 1015

C4B CABARET VOLTAIRE C4B

CHRISTOPHER R WATSON ELECT(AB
HAYDN BOYES-WESTON D (A
RICHARD KIRK G WIND(AB
STEPHEN MALLINDER B PERC V(AB
MICK ALLDAY D (D

(A) MIX UP 1979 ROUGH TRADE UK ROUGH 4
(B) LIVE AT YMCA 1980 ROUGH TRADE UK ROUGH 7
(C)VOICE OF AMERICA 1980 ROUGH TRADE UK ROUGH 11
(D) RED MECCA 19 ROUGH TRADE UK ROUGH 27
(D) RED MECCA 19 ROUGH TRADE GER 6435 117
( ) 3 CREPUSCULE TRACKS 1981 BRUITS BELG 018

C5 CACTUS C5

RUSTY DAY V (ABC
JIM McCARTY G (ABC
TIM BOGERT B (ABCD
CARMINE APPICE D (ABCD
PETER FRENCH V (D
DUANE HITCHINGS K (D
WERNER FRITZSCHINGS G (D
RON LEEJACK G (C
ALBHY GALUTEN PNO (C
DUANE HITCHINGS K (C

(A) CACTUS 1970 ATLANTIC UK 2400 020
(A) CACTUS 1970 ATCO US SD 33340
(B) ONE WAY OR ANOTHER 1971 ATLANTIC UK 2460 114
(B) ONE WAY OR ANOTHER 1971 ATCO US 33356
(B) ONE WAY OR ANOTHER 1972 ATLANTIC UK K 40216
(C) RESTRICTIONS 1972 ATLANTIC UK K40307
(C) RESTRICTIONS 1971 ATCO US SD 33377
(D) 'OT & SWEATY 1972 ATLANTIC UK K 50013
(D) 'OT & SWEATY 1972 ATCO US SD 7011

C5A CADETS C5A

(A) ROCKIN'N' REELIN' 19 CROWN US 5015
(B) THE CADETS 19 CROWN US 5370

C6 VINCE CADILLAC C6

VINCE CADILLAC G V (A
TRIGGER LYONS B (A
TIM FRANKS D (A
TONY TODD G (A
PAUL JENKINS G (A
PETE WINGFIELD K V (A
PETER LEMER PNO (A
DAVE EPPEL G (A
MIKE SMITH V (A
PAUL WESTWOOD B (A
BARRY MORGAN D (A
LARRY BARTLETT K (A
JOHN PORTER V (A
RICK HITCHCOCK G (A
BARRY DE SOUZA D (A

(A) MODERN BOY 1978 SATRIL UI SATL 4010

C6A CADILLACS C6A

(A) FABULOUS CADILLACS 19 JUBILEE US 1045
( ) CRAZY CADILLACS 19 JUBILEE US 1089
( ) TWISTING WITH 196 JUBILEE US 5009

C6B BRIAN CADD C6B

BRIAN CADD K V SYN(ALL
GEOFF FOX D (C
GUS FENWICK B (C
TONY NAYLOR G (C
CHARLIE GOULD G (C
ALAN HAWKIN G BAN (C
RUSS HAWKING G (C
MIKE BURKE STEEL (C
FRED OLBREI FDL (C
PHINEAS BROWNE STR (C
NIGEL OLSSON D (E
STEVE CROPPER G (E
MIKE PORCARO B (F
JEFF PORCARO D (F
RICHARD BENNETT G (F
JESSE ED DAVIS G (F
MARK T JORDAN K (F
OLIVER C BROWN PERC (F
JIM CONWAY HCA (C
PETER BEST V SYN (C
LYNN CASEY V (C
GARY COLEMAN PERC(E
RITCHIE ZITE G (EF
DAVID WINTOUR B (F
ALVIN TAYLOR D (F
DAVID KALISH G (F
J D MANESS STEEL(F
LARRY KNECHTEL K (F
JEFF HALES PERC (C
STEVE COONEY MAND (C
BILLY PAYNE K SYN (E
DEE MURRAY B (E
SNEAKY PETE STEEL (E
RICHIE HAYWARD D (F
STEVE BECKMEIER G (F
STEVE LUKATHER G (F
DAVEY JOHNSON MAND (F
MIKE MORAN K (F
MICK CONWAY JUG (C
IVAN HUTCHISON PNO (C
WILLIAM SMITH K SYN (E
BEN BENAY G BANJ (E
REGGIE McBRIDE B (F
DOUG LAVERY D (F
JOHN BELAND G (F
MICHAEL STEWART G (F
MIKE FINNIGAN K (F
JAY GRAYDON SYN (F

(A) BRIAN CADD 1973 CHELSEA US 10163 AUST BOOTLEG 023
(B) ? 1973
(C) MOONSHINE 1974 CHELSEA US 502 AUST BOOTLEG 044
(D) ? 1975
(E) WHITE ON WHITE 1975 CAPITOL US 11573
(F) YESTERDAYDREAMS 1978 CAPITOL US 11681

C7 CADO BELLE C7

COLIN TULLY SAX (BA
DAVY ROY D (AB
STUART MACKILLOP K (AB
GAVIN HODGSON B (AB
PADDY McHUGH V (A
MAGGIE REILLY V (AB
FRANK COLLINS V (A
ALAN DARBY G (AB

(A) CADO BELLE 1976 ANCHOR UK/US ANCL 2015
(B) CADO BELLE (EP) 1977 ANCHOR UK AN 1

C8 CAFE JACQUES C8

CHRISTOPHER THOMPSON G V (AB
MICHAEL OGLETREE D G (AB
COLIN NELSON B (AB
PETER VEITCH K (AB
GEOFFREY RICHARDSON G FLT(AB
JOHN PERRY B (AB
PHIL COLLINS PERC (AB

(A) ROUND THE BACK 1977 EPIC UK 82315 US 35294
(B) CAFE JACQUES INTERNATIONAL 1978 EPIC UK 83042 US 35697

C9 CAFE SOCIETY C9

RAPHAEL DOYLE G V (A
HEREWARD KAYE V PNO G (A
TOM ROBINSON V B G PNO(A
JIM FRANKS D (A
PAT DONALDSON B (A
JOHN GOSLING K (A
ROBIN WILLIAMS FDL (A
LOUIS STEWART G (A
MICK AVORY D (A
NICK SOUTH B (A
ROY DYKE D (A
JOHN BEECHAM HRNS (A
PHIL PALMER G (A

(A) CAFE SOCIETY 1975 KONK KONK 102

C9A JONATHAN CAIN BAND C9A

JONATHAN CAIN K V (A
JIMMY ARNOLD G V (A
TOMMY CAIN D (A
GARY RICHWINE B V (A
RALPH MACDONALD PERC (A
BOBBYE HALL PERC (A

(A) WINDY CITY BREAKDOWN 1977 BEARSVILLE US 6969

C10 CAJUN MOON C10

ALLAN TAYLOR G V (A
JOHN GILLASPIE K WIND(AB
BRIAN GOLBEY FDL G (AB
DIK CADBURY G V (B

(A) CAJUN MOON 1976 CHRYSALIS UK CHR 1116
(B) LATER LINE UP

C11 CAKE C11

BARBARA MORILLO V (AB
JANETTE JACOBS V (AB
ELEANOR BAROOSHIAN V (AB
MIKE MELVOIN ORG (
DAVID COHEN G (
MIKE DEASY G (
CAROL KAYE B (
LESLIE MILTON D (

(A) CAKE 1967 DECCA DL 74927
(A) CAKE 1968 MCA MUPS 303
(B) A SLICE OF CAKE 1968 DECCA DL 75039
(B) A SLICE OF CAKE 1969 MCA MUPS 390

C11A CALDARA C11A

JOHN ATKINS SYN K (A
TOBY SAKS CELLO (A

(A) A MOOG MASS 1972 KAMA SUTRA 2319 020

C11B JORGE CALDERON C11B

Album	Year	Label	Country	Number
(A) CITY MUSIC	1975	WB	US	BS 2904

Musician	Instr	Albums
JORGE CALDERON	V G	(A
WADDY WACHTEL	V G K	(A
HOPPY HODGES	D	(A
PAT RIZZO	HRNS	(A
TESSE COEN	PERC V	(A
JAMES GADSON	D	(A
RUSS TITELMAN	PERC	(A
BOBBY LYLE	K	(A
BOBBYE HALL	PERC	(A
WILLIE WEEKS	B	(A
STEVE MADAIO	HRNS	(A
YVONNE RANKIN	V	(A
VICTOR FELDMAN	PERC	(A
VALERIE CARTER	V	(A
JIM KELTNER	D	(A
MAYUTO	PERC	(A
WILLIAM SMITH	V K	(A
ANDY NEWMARK	D	(A
PAUL PAYDOS	PERC	(A
PAUL STALLWORTH	V	(A
NICK DE CARO	SYN	(A

C12 BOBBY CALDWELL C12

Album	Year	Label	Number
(A) BOBBY CALDWELL	1978	CLOUDS	8804
(A) BOBBY CALDWELL	1978	TKR (CBS)	83362
(B) CAT IN THE HAT	1980	TK UK 83386 US CLOUDS	8810

Musician	Instr	Albums
BOBBY CALDWELL	B G K SYN V	(AB
BRUCE EMODAMENT	K	(B
JOHN PAULUS	B	(B
ED GREENE	D	(AB
HAROLD SEAY	D	(AB
STEVE MEALY	G	(A
RICHIE VELASQUEZ	B	(A
JEFF KIEVET	HRNS	(B
ANDY NEWMARK	D	(B
GARY LINDSAY	CLAR	(B
JOE GALDO	D	(AB
ALFONS KETTNER	G	(A
MIKE LEWIS	SAX	(B
JERRY PEEL	HRN	(B
MARK COLBY	SAX	(B
BENNY LATIMORE	K	(A
GEORGE PERRY	B	(AB
CHRIS COLELESSOR	WIND	(B
JAMES MARSHALL	TROM	(B
HOLLIS BURRIDGE	HRNS	(B

C13 JOHN CALE C13

Album	Year	Label	Country	Number
(A) VINTAGE VIOLENCE	1970	CBS		64256
(A) VINTAGE VIOLENCE	1970	CBS	US	CS 1037
(B) CHURCH OF ANTHRAX	1971	CBS	UK	64259
(B) CHURCH OF ANTHRAX	1971	CBS	US	CS 30131
(C) ACADEMY OF PERIL	1972	REPRISE	UK	K 44212
(C) ACADEMY OF PERIL	1972	REPRISE	US	MS 2079
(D PARIS 1919	1973	REPRISE	UK	K 44239
(D) PARIS 1919	1973	REPISE	US	MS 2131
(E) FEAR	1974	ISLAND	UK/US	ILPS9301
(F) SLOW DAZZLE	1975	ISLAND	UK/US	ILPS9317
(G) HELEN OF TROY	1975	ISLAND	UK/US	ILPS9350
(G) HELEN OF TROY	1975	PHONOGRAM	EUR	9123 002
(H) GUTS	1977	PHONOGRAM	EUR	9101 672
(H) GUTS	1977	ISLAND	UK/US	ILPS9459
(J) JUNE 1 1974 (NICO ENO KEVIN AYERS)	1974	ISLAND	UK/US	ILPS9291
(K) SABOTAGE LIVE	1979	SPY	US	004
(L) HORI SOIT	1981	A&M	UK	64849
(EP) ANIMAL JUSTICE	1977	ILLEGAL	UK	IL003

Musician	Instr	Albums
JOHN CALE	VLA G K B V	(ALL
WITH		
TERRY RILEY	SAX K	(B
PHIL MANZANERA	G	(EF
BRIAN ENO	K	(EFGJ
NICO	V	(J
CHRIS SPEDDING	G	(FG
TIM DONALD	D	(FG
PAT DONALDSON	B	(FG
CHRIS THOMAS	K	(F
GERRY CONWAY	D	(F
GEOFF MULDAUR	V	(F
PHIL COLLINS	D	(G
OLLIE HALSALL	G	(J
JOHN RABBIT BUNDRICK	K	(J
ADAM MILLER	V	(BC
ARCHIE LEGGET	B	(EJ
KEVIN AYERS	B	(J
EDDIE SPARROW	D	(J
ROBERT WYATT	PERC	(J
MIKE OLDFIELD	G	(J
BRYN HAWORTH	G	(E
DOUG BRAWNE	D	(K
BOBBY GREGG	D	(B
R P O		(C
KEITH SMART	D	(FH
BARRY STJOHN	V	(H
MEREN STEIN	PROD	(A
JIM GORDON	K V	(L
JOHN GATCHELL	TPT	(L
LIZA STRIKE	V	(EJ
RICHARD THOMPSON	G	(E
JUDY NYLON	V	(E
GEORGE SCOTT	B	(K
RICHIE HAYWARD	D	(D
FRED SMITH	D	(EH
ANDY MACKAY	SAX	(FH
JOE BIDWELL	K V	(K
RON WOOD	G	(C
PETER MUNY	B V	(L
BOMBERETTES(MODETTES)	V	(L
IRENE CHANTER	V	(EJ
BRIAN TURRINGTON	B	(E
MICHAEL DESMARAIS	D	(E
HARVEY BROOKS	B	(A
LOWELL GEORGE	G	(D
TREVOR BURTON	B	(H
JOHN WOOD	SYN	(FH
DEERFRANCE	PERC V	(K
DEL NEWMAN	D	(C
ROBERT MEDICI	D V	(L
CHRIS THOMAS	PROD	(D
DOREEN CHANTER	V	(EJ
BOBBY COLOMBY	D	(B
MARK AARON	G	(K
SANDY KONIKOFF	D	(A
UCLA ORCH		(D
RAYMUND DUFFY	D	(H
TONY CARR	PERC	(H
JOHN McCLURE	PROD	(B
STURGIS NIKICLES	G V	(L

C14 J J CALE C14

Album	Year	Label	Country	Number
(A) NATURALLY	1971	A&M	UK	AMLS68105
(A) NATURALLY	1973	SHELTER	UK	ISA 5003
(A) NATURALLY	1971	SHELTER	US	8908
(A) NATURALLY	1972	CARRERE	FR	67614
(A) NATURALLY	1972	SHELTER US 2122		52009
(B) REALLY	1972	A&M	UK	AMLS68157
(B) REALLY	1972	SHELTER	UK	ISA 5002
(B) REALLY	1972	SHELTER US 8912		52015
(B) REALLY	1972	CARRERE	FR	67613
(C) OKIE	1972	A&M	UK	AMLS68261
(C) OKIE	1974	SHELTER	UK	ISA 5004
(C) OKIE	1974	SHELTER US 2107		
(C) OKIE	197	CARRERE	FR	67608
(D) TROUBADOUR	1976	SHELTER	UK	ISA 5011
(D) TROUBADOUR	1976	CARRERE	FR	67618
(D) TROUBADOUR	1976	SHELTER	US	52002
(E) No 5	1979	SHELTER	UK	ISA 5018
(E) No 5	1979	MCA	US	3163
(F) SHADES	1980	SHELTER	UK	ISA 5021
(F) SHADES	1980	MCA	US	5158
(G) GRASSHOPPER	1982	MERCURY	US	SRMI 4038

Musician	Instr	Albums
J J CALE	PNO B D G V	(ALL
WITH		
KARL HIMMEL	D	(ACDEFG
CHUCK BROWNING	G D	(AD
TIM DRUMMOND	D	(AC
CARL RADLE	B	(AE
NORBERT PUTNAM	B	(AB
BOB WILSON	PNO	(A
DAVID BRIGGS	K	(ABEFG
JERRY WHITEHURST	K	(AC
WELDON MYRICK	STEEL	(AC
BUDDY SPICHER	FDL	(A
SHORTY LAVENDER	FDL	(A
WALTER HAYNES	DOBRO	(A
MAC GAYDEN	G	(ABC
ED COLIS	HCA	(A
DIANE DAVIDSON	V	(A
ROGER HAWKINS	D	(B
DAVID HOOD	B	(B
BOBBY MOORE	B	(G
TONY MIGLIORI	PNO	(G
BILL KENNER	MAND	(E
PAUL DAVIS	G	(C
DON SHEFFIELD	TPT	(BE
FARRELL MORRIS	D VIBES	(BCDEG
BOB RAY	B	(B
JOE ZINKAN	B	(B
JIMMY KARSTEIN	D	(BDEFG
REG YOUNG	G	(CDFG
JOE OSBORN	B	(D
BUDDY EMMONS	STEEL	(D
GEORGE TIDWELL	TPT	(CDE
GARY PAXTON	V	(D
BEEGIE CRUZER	K	(C
PIG ROBBINS	K	(C
SHERRY PORTER	V	(E
LARRY BELL	K	(EF
EMORY GORDY	B	(F
RUSS KUNKEL	D	(F
JIM KELTNER	D	(F
GORDON SHRYCOCK	G	(F
MIKE LAWLER	SYN	(G
BARRY BECKETT	K	(B
BOB PHILLIPS	TPT	(B
BOBBY WOODS	K	(BD
ROBERT TARRANT	PERC	(B
JOSH GRAVES	DOBRO	(B
GARY GILMORE	B	(B
LLOYD GREEN	STEEL	(D
AUDIE ASHWORTH	PERC	(D
BILL RAFFENSPEGER	B	(D
DENNIS GOODE	TROM	(CDE
BILL PURSELL	K	(D
JOEL GREEN	B	(C
TERRY PERKINS	D	(C
STRING SECTION		(E
CAROL KAYE	B	(F
JAMES BURTON	G	(F
TOMMY TEDESCO	G	(F
GLEN D HARDIN	K	(F
DENNIS SOLEE	SAX	(FG
TERRY McMILLIAN	HCA	(G
JIMMY JOHNSON	G	(B
BILL HUMBLE	TROM	(B
KENNY BUTTREY	D	(BDEFG
JIMMY CAPPS	G	(B
VASSAR CLEMENTS	FDL	(B
BILL BOATMAN	G	(BDEFG
TOMMY COGBILL	B	(CDFG
DON TWEEDY	K	(D
J J ALLISON	PERC	(D
BILLY PUETT	SAX	(CD
MIKE LEECH	B	(C
JERRY SMITH	K	(C
BILLY COX	B	(E
TERRY WILLIAMS	HRNS	(E
BOBBY EMMONS	K	(FG
BILL PAYNE	PNO	(F
JOHNNY CHRISTOPHER	G	(FG
HAL BLAINE	D	(F
STEVE GIBSON	G	(G
ROBERT GREENIDGE	PERC	(G
JOAN SWEENEY	V	(B
NORMAN RAY	SAX	(B
GEORGE SOULE	D	(B
KOSSIE GARDNER	ORG	(B
CHARLIE McCOY	HCA	(B
CHARLES DUNGEY	B	(DG
HAROLD BRADLEY	G	(CDG
BUDDY HARMON	D	(DGE
GORDON PAYNE	G	(D
KENNY MALONE	D	(CD
RED SPIVEY	K	(C
GRADY MARTIN	G	(C
CHRISTINE LAKELAND	K V	(EFG
NICK RATHER	B	(EFG
MICHAEL RHODES	B	(F
LEON RUSSELL	PNO	(F
HAYWARD BISHOP	D	(F
GARY ALLEN	D	(FG
RAY EDENTON	G	(G
MARILYN DAVIS	V	(G

C15 CALICO C15

JERRY OATES G V (AB | (A) CALICO | 1975 UA US UALA 454
KEITH IMPELLITIER G V (AB | (B) CALICO 2 | 1976 UA US UALA 659
BULL MINOR D V (B
TOM MORREL STEEL (B | JOHN McCLURE K (B | MIKE REDDEN D (B
DAVE KIRBY G (B | KENNY MALONE D (A | BILL ROBERTSON D (B
JOE COPELAND G (A | JOE ALLEN B (A | BUDDY SPICHER FDL (B
LARRY HEATH B FDL V(A | HOWARD BARNARD STEEL B(A | JIMMY COLVARD G (A
LLOYD GREEN STEEL G(A | REGGIE YOUNG G (A | BOBBY THOMPSON G (A
CHUCK COCHRAN K (A | BOBBY WOOD K (A

C15A RANDY C15A

RANDY CALIFORNIA G V (AB | (A) KAPTAIN KOPTER & THE TWIRLY BIRDS | 1972 EPIC US 31755 UK EPC 65381
CHARLY BUNDY B (A | (A) KAPTAIN KOPTER & THE TWIRLY BIRDS | 1980 CBS UK RI 31829
TIM McGOVERN D (A | (B) EURO AMERICAN | 1982 LINE GER LLP5149
CASS(ED CASSIDY)STRANGE D(AB
NOEL(CLIT McTORIUS)REDDING B(A | LARRY KNIGHT B (AB | MITCH(HENRY MANCHOVITZ)MITCHELL D(A
CURLEY SMITH D (B | BRUCE GARY D (B | MARK ANDES B (B
JOHN LOCKE K (B | GEORGE VALUCK K V (B | JAY FERGUSON V (B
TOM HALL G (B | MATT ANDES G (B

C15B CALIFORNIA EARTHQUAKE C15B

BRIAN GRIFFIN ORG (A | (A) CALIFORNIA EARTHQUAKE | 1971 UA US UAS 6801
ROY SMITH V (A
JIM GORDON D (A | JOHN GUERIN (A | DENNIS POTTER (A
BILL CONNORS (A | MIKE BARROWMAN HRNS (A | JOEL PORTER HRNS (A
MAYO TIANA HRNS (A | JON CLARKE HRNS (A | DON ROBERTS HRNS (A

C16 MISSISSIPPI JOE CALLICOTT

MISSISSIPPI JOE CALLICOTT (| ( ) PRESENTING THE COUNTRY BLUES | 1972 BLUE HORIZON US 4606 UK863227

C17 TERRY CALLIER C17

TERRY CALLIER (ALL | (A) OCCASIONAL RAIN | 1972 CADET US 50007
MINNIE RIPERTON V (D | (B) WHAT COLOUR IS LOVE | 1974 CADET US 50019
SIDNEY BARNES V (D | (C) I JUST CANT HELP MYSELF | 1975 CADET US 50041
JYNEAN BELL V (D | (D) FIRE ON ICE | 1978 ELEKTRA US 6E143 UK K52096
ELLIE WILLIS V (D | (D) TURN ON YOUR LOVE | 1979 ELEKTRA US 189 UK K52140
CYNTHIA WHITE V (D
PHIL UPCHURCH G (D | W ROSS TRAUT G (D | DANNY LEAKE G (D
CHARLES FEARING G (D | LARRY WADE G (D | EDDIE HARRIS SAX (D
FRED JACKSON SAX (D | CHARLES OWEN SAX (D | CORINNE ALBRIGHT SAX (D
GARNETT BROWN TROM (D | GEORGE BOHANON TROM (D | STEVE MADAIO TPT (E
LARRY WADE G (E | ROBERT WHITE G (E | JIMMY CLEVELAND TROM (D
PAUL SERRANO TPT (D | KENNETH MASON TPT (D | EUGENE YOUNG TPT (D
REGINALD BURKE K (DE | MICHAEL BODDICKER SYN (D | SCOTT EDWARDS B (D
PAUL N HUMPHREY D (D | JAMES GADSON D (DE | FRED WALKER PERC (D
MORRIS JENNINGS PERC (D | SONNY BURKE K (E | EARL VAN DYKE K (E
KINI BURKE B (E | JAMES JAMERSON B (E | WAH WAH WATSON G (E
DAVID T WALKER G (E | OLIVER BROWN PERC (E | FRED WESLEY TROM (E
ERNIE WATTS SAX (E | GAIL LEVANT HARP (E | STRINGS (D

C18 ROBERT CALVERT C18

ROBERT CALVERT PERC V TPT (ABC | (A) CAPTAIN LOCKHEED & THE STARFIGHTERS 74 | UA US 1011 UK UAG 29507
PAUL RUDOLPH B G (AB | (B) LUCKY LEIF & THE LONGSHIPS | 1975 UA UK UAG 29852
SIMON KING D (A | (C) HYPE(SONGS OF TOM MAHLER) | 198 ASIDE UK IF 0311
NIK TURNER SAX (AC
LEMMY G B (A | ANDY ROBERTS G (B | DEL DETTMAR SYN (A
DAVE BROCK G (A | TWINK D (A | ARTHUR BROWN V (A
ADRIAN WAGNER K (A | VIV STANSHALL V (A | JIM CAPALDI V (A
TOM MITTELDORF V (A | RICHARD EALING V (A | SIMON HOUSE VLN (BC
MIKE NICHOLS D PERC | (B MICHAEL MOORCOCK BANJO(AC | SAL MAIDA B (B
BRIAN TURRINGTON PNO (

C19 CAMEL C19

PETER BARDENS K (ABCDEFG | (A) CAMEL | 1973 MCA MUPS473 UK MAPS 6477
ANDY LATIMER V G FLT (ABCDEFGHJ | (A) CAMEL | 1980 MCA NL 201 350
DOUG FERGUSON B (ABCDF | (A) CAMEL | 1974 MCA MCF2665 GER 900 095
ANDY WARD D PERC(ABCDEFGHJ | (B) MIRAGE | 1974 DERAM UK SML 1107
RICHARD SINCLAIR B V (EFG | (B) MIRAGE | 1974 DECCA 278135
COLIN BASS B V (HJ | (B) MIRAGE | 1974 JANUS US 7009
MEL COLLINS SAX (FGHJ | (C) SNOW GOOSE | 1975 DERAM UK SKLR 5207
DUNCAN MACKAY K (J | (C) SNOW GOOSE | 1975 DECCA 278136
JAN SCHELHAAS PNO (JH | (C) SNOW GOOSE | 1975 JANUS US 7016 NOVA GER 6 22250
CHRIS GREEN CELLO (J | (D) MOONMADNESS | 1976 DERAM UK TXSR 115
GASPAR LAWAL PERC (J | (D) MOONMADNESS | 1976 DECCA 278115 NOVA GER 6 22500
HERBIE FLOWERS TUBA (J | (D) MOONMADNESS | 1976 JANUS US 7024 JAP UA 1035
KIT WATKINS K FLT (H | (E) RAINDANCE | 1977 GAMA UK TXSR 124
PHIL COLLINS PERC (H | (E) RAINDANCE | 1977 DECCA 260015
RUPERT HINE V (H | (F) A LIVE RECORD(DBL) | 1978 DECCA UK DBCR7/8 NOVA GER28453
(G) BREATHLESS | 1978 DECCA UK TXSR 132
DAVID SINCLAIR K (F | (G) BREATHLESS | 1978 ARISTA US 4206
(G) BREATHLESS | 1978 NOVA GER 23570
(H) I CAN SEE YOUR HOUSE FROM HERE | 1979 DECCA UK TXSR 137
(H) I CAN SEE YOUR HOUSE FROM HERE | 1979 ARISTA US 4254
(H) I CAN SEE YOUR HOUSE FROM HERE | 1979 GAMA GER 24132
(J) NUDE | 1981 DECCA UK SKL 5323

C20 CAMEO C20

LARRY BLACKMON D (BCDEF | (A) CARDIAC ARREST | 1977 CASABLANCA UK CAL 2015
TOM CAMPBELL K (F | (A) CARDIAC ARREST | 1977 CHOCOLATE US 2003
GREGORY JOHNSON K V (BCDEF | (B) WE ALL KNOW WHO WE ARE | 1978 CASABLANCA CAL 2026
STEPHEN MOORE V (F | (B) WE ALL KNOW WHO WE ARE | 1978 CHOCOLATE US 2004
TOMI JENKINS V (BCDEF | (C) UGLY EGO | 1978 CASABLANCA CAL 2038
NATHAN LEFTENANT TPT (BCDEF | (D) SECRET OMEN | 1979 CASABLANCA CAL 2058
JERYL BRIGHT V TROM(F | (D) SECRET OMEN | 1979 CHOCOLATE US 2008
CHARLES SAMSON G (B | (E) CAMEOSIS | 1979 CHOCOLATE US 2011
ARNETT LEFTENANT SAX (BCDEF | (F) FEEL ME | 1980 CASABLANCA CAL 2016
ERIC DURHAM G (BC | (F) FEEL ME | 1980 CHOCOLATE US 2016
WAYNE COOPER V (BC | AARON MILLS G V (F
GARY DOW B (BC | ANTHONY COCKETT (C | ANTHONY LOCKETT G V (F
JOSE ROSSY PERC (F | ARTHUR YOUNG TPT (F | RANDY STERN K (F

C21 **JOHN CAMERON** C21

JOHN CAMERON PNO (AB — (A) COVER LOVER — 1967 COLUMBIA UK SCX 6116
DANNY THOMPSON B (B — (B) OFF CENTRE — 1969 DERAM UK SML 1044
TONY CARR D (B
HAROLD McNAIR SAX (B

C21A **JEFF CAMPBELL** C21A

JEFF CAMPBELL V G (A — (A) LIVE ON THE WIRE — 1979 ONEINE
DAVID JAUREQUI G (A
DAVID KOPPENHAUER G (A — BILLY LISKA B (A — KEVIN REDDING D (A
TONY TANNER PERC (A — DOUG FREEMAN G (A — CHARLIE G (A
ROB LIEBERMAN G (A — RICK STURBINS PNO (A — SUE RUEDA V (A

C21B **DICK CAMPBELL** C21B

DICK CAMPBELL G V (A — (A) SINGS WHERE ITS AT — 1965 MERCURY SR 61060
MICHAEL BLOOMFIELD G (A
JIMMY VINCENT G (A — PETER CETERA B (A — MARK NAFTALIN K (A
MARTY GREBB K TAMB(A — ARTIE SULLIVAN V TAMB(A — PAUL BUTTERFIELD HCA (A
BILLY HERMAN D (A — LARRY WRICE D (A — SAM LAY D (A

C22 **JUNIOR CAMPBELL** C22

JUNIOR CAMPBELL V (A — (A) SECOND TIME AROUND — 1974 DERAM UK SML 1106
(B) COLLECTION — 19 GALE 10" M501

C23 **PATRICK CAMPBELL-LYONS** C23

PATRICK CAMPBELL-LYONS (A — (A) ME & MY FRIEND — 1973 SOVEREIGN UK SVNA 7258
BOBBY HARRISON (A
PETER DENNIS (A — DANNY DEMON (A — SYLVIA SCHUSTER (A
BOB SARGEANT (A — JIM FRANK (A — CHOIRS V (A

C24 **ROBERT CAMPBESS** C24

ROBERT CAMPBESS (A — (A) LIVING IN THE SHADOW — 1977 DECCA UK SHL 5285

C24A **RAY CAMPI & THE ROCKABILLY REBELS** C24A

RAY CAMPI V (ALL — (A) ROCKABILLY LIVES — 197 ROLLIN' ROCK 004
(B) ROCKABILLY REBEL — 197 ROLLIN' ROCK 006
(C) EAGER BEAVER BOY — 1976 ROLLIN' ROCK 008
(D) ROCKABILLY ROCKET — 1977 ROLLIN' ROCK 013

C24B **CAMPO DI MARTE** C24B

ENRICA ROSA G K V(A — (A) CAMPO DI MARTE — 1973 UA ITALY 29497
MAURO SARTI D V FLT(A
ALFREDO BARDUCCI FLT K V(A — C FELICE MARCOVECCHIO D (A — PAUL RICHARD B V (A

C25 **CAN** C25

MALCOLM MOONEY V (ADGJ — (A) MONSTER MOVIE — 1969 UA UK UAS29094 GER 83342
JAKI LIEBEZEIT D (ABCDEFGHJKLMNQ — (B)TAGO MAGO DBL — 1971 UA UK UAD 60009/0
IRMIN SCHMIDT V K((ABCDEFGHKLJMNQ — (B) TAGO MAGO DBL — 1971 UA EURO 29211/2
MICHAEL KAROLI G VLN(ABCDEFGHJKLMNQ — (C) EGE BAMYASI — 1972 UA US 063 UK UAS 29414
HOLGER CZUKAY B (ABCDEFHKLGJ — (D) DEEP END (SOUNDTRACKS) — 1970 UA GER 83437 UK UAS 29283
KENJI'DAMO' SUZUKI V (BCDEKGJ — (E) FUTURE DAYS — 1973 UA US 213 UK UAS 29505
ROSKO GEE B (MNQ — (F) SOON OVER BABALUMA — 1974 UA US 343 UK UAG 29673
PETER GILMORE V (L — (G) LIMITED EDITION — 1974 UA UK USP 103
RENE TINNER V (L — (H) LANDED — 1975 VIRGIN UK V2041 HORZU GER29600
REEBOP KWAKU BAAH PERC (MNQ — (J) UNLIMITED EDITION (DBL) — 1976 CAROLINE UK CAD 3001
OLAF KUBLER SAX (HQ — (K) OPENER — 1976 SUNSET UK SLS 50400
(L) FLOW MOTION — 1976 VIRGIN UK V2071 HARVEST GER 31837
(L) FLOW MOTION — 1976 POLYDOR 2473 710
(M) SAW DELIGHT — 1977 VIRGIN UK V2079 HARVEST GER 32156
(M) SAW DELIGHT — 1977 POLYDOR 2473 712
(N) OUT OF REACH — 1978 LIGHTNING LIG4 PETERS INT 9024
(N) OUT OF REACH — 1978 HARVEST GER 32715
(O) CANNIBALISMS (COMP DBL) — 1978 UA UK UDM 105/6
(P) CLASSIC GERMAN ROCK SCENE — 19 SONOPRESSE FR 29772 /73
(Q) CAN — 1979 LASER UK LASL2 HARVEST GER 45099

C25A **CANDYMEN** C25A

JOHN RAINEY ADKINS G (AB — (A) THE CANDYMEN — 1967
RODNEY JUSTO V (AB — (B) BRING YOU CANDYPOWER — 1968 ABC US ABCS 633
DEAN DAUGHTRY K (AD
BILLY GILMORE B (AB — BOB NIX D (AB

C25B **CANIS MAJOR** C25B

JACQUELINE BODINEAD V (A — (A) BUTTERFLY QUEEN — 1980 GEM GEM 109
TONY BODINEAD G V (A
MICK GROVES G (A
SIMON COOPER B (A — JOHN PEPE K (A — GARY WISE D (A

C26 **CANNED HEAT** C26

BOB HITE V (ABCDGLMNEFJR — (A) CANNED HEAT — 1967 LIBERTY US LST 7526
HENRY VESTINE G (ABCDLMNJE — (A) CANNED HEAT — 1967 LIBERTY UK 83059
AL WILSON G V (ABCDGEFJ — (A) CANNED HEAT — 1972 U A UK UAG29304 SUNSET 50321
LARRY TAYLOR B (ABCDGEF — (B) BOOGIE WITH CANNED HEAT — 1968 LIBERTY UK LBS 83103
FRANK COOK D (EA — (B) BOOGIE WITH CANNED HEAT — 1968 LIBERTY US LST7541 RI 10105
FITO DE LA PARRA D (BCDGLMNFJ — (B) BOOGIE WITH CANNED HEAT — 197 UA UK UAG 29298
JAMES SHANE G (MN — (C) LIVING THE BLUES DBL — 1969 LIBERTY UK LDS 84001
ED BEYER K (MN — (C) LIVING THE BLUES DBL — 1968 LIBERTY 27200
RICHARD HITE B (MNR — (C) LIVING THE BLUES DBL — 1969 UA US 9955
HARVERY MANDEL G (GLF — (C) LIVING THE BLUES DBL — 19 UA 29258/9
JOEL SCOTT HILL V G (L — (D) HALLELUJAH — 1969 LIBERTY UK LBS 83239
ANTONIO BARRADA B (LJ — (D) HALLELUJAH — 1969 LIBERTY US LST 7618
CHRIS MORGAN G (— (E) VINTAGE HEAT — 1970 JANUS US JSL3009 GER 19021
GENE TAYLOR K (— (F) LIVE IN EUROPE — 1970 LIBERTY UK LBS 83333
STAN WEBB G (— (F) LIVE IN EUROPE — 1970 LIBERTY US 5509
MEMPHIS SLIM (K — (G) FUTURE BLUES — 1970 LIBERTY UK LBS 83364
JOHN LEE HOOKER V (J — (G) FUTURE BLUES — 1970 LIBERTY US LST 11002
SUNNYLAND SLIM PNO (B — (H) COOKBOOK — 1970 LIBERTY UK LBS 83303
MARK NAFTALIN K (D — (H) COOKBOOK — 1969 LIBERTY US LST11000 RI 10106
SKIP DIAMOND V (D — (H) COOKBOOK — 1975 SUNSET SLS 50377
ELLIOT INGBER V (D — (J) HOOKER & HEAT DBL — 1971 LIBERTY UK LPS 103/4
JAVIER BATISE V (D — (J) HOOKER & HEAT DBL — 1971 LIBERTY US 35002-1/2

(CONTINUED)

C26 (CONTINUED) CANNED HEAT C26

Personnel	Instr	
MIKE PACHECO	PERC	(D
ERNEST LANE	K	(DGL
DR JOHN	K	(G
LITTLE RICHARD	PNO	(L
CLIFFORD SOLOMON	SAX	(L
CHARLES LLOYD	FLT	(L
KEVIN BURTON	ORG	(L
RAY BUSHBAUM	PNO	(L
CLARA WARD SINGERS	V	(M
HARRISON CALLOWAY	TPT	(N
CHARLES ROSE	TROM	(N
RONNIE EADES	SAX	(N
HARVEY THOMPSON	SAX	

Album	Year	Label	Country	Number
(K) MEMPHIS HEAT	1971	BARCLAY		80607
( ) LIVE AT THE TOPANGA CORRAL	1971	WAND		693
( ) LIVE AT THE TOPANGA CORRAL	1976	DJM		DJS 26072
( ) LIVE AT THE TOPANGA CORRAL	197	PICKWICK		SPC 3364
( ) LIVE AT THE TOPANGA CORRAL	19	METROMOME		200 102
(L) HISTORICAL FIGURES	1972	UA	UK	UAG 29304
(L) HISTORICAL FIGURES	1972	UA	US	5557
( ) PORTRAIT VOL 1 & 2	19	UA		29320 /21
(M) NEW AGE	1973	UA	UK	UAS 29455
(M) NEW AGE	1973	UA	US	UALA 049F
(N) ONE MORE RIVER TO CROSS	1974	ATLANTIC	UK	K 50026
(N) ONE MORE RIVER TO CROSS	1974	ATLANTIC	US	SD 7289
(N) ONE MORE RIVER TO CROSS	1978	STRAND	GER	23683
(O) ROLLIN' & TUMBLIN'	1973	SUNSET		SLS 50321
(R) HUMAN CONDITION	197	SONET	UK	SNTF 783
(R) HUMAN CONDITION	197	TAKOMA	US	7066
( ) COLLAGE	19	SUNSET		SLS 50225
( ) CANNED HEAT	19	SUNSET	NL	60024/5
( ) COLLAGE	19	SUNSET	US	5298
( ) BEST OF	19	SCEPTER		18017
( ) MASTERS OF ROCK	19	UA	NL	92656
( ) ORIGINAL CANNED HEAT	19	SPRINGBOARD	US	SPB 4026
( ) BOOGIE WITH HOOKER & HEAT	19	SPRINGBOARD	US	TSX 3501
( ) BOOGIE WITH HOOKER & HEAT	19	MUSIDISC		ALB 202
( ) HISTORY OF	19	SONOPRESSE/UA		29862/63
( ) VERY BEST OF	19	UA		UASLA431E

C26A CANNED ROCK C26A

Personnel	Instr	
DOUGIE KENNARD	G SYN V	(AB
PETE BUCKBY	D PERC V	(AB
DON MAXWELL	B G V	(AB

Album	Year	Label	Country	Number
(A) KINETIC ENERGY	1978	CANNED ROCK	UK	CAN 002
(B) LIVE	1979	CANNED ROCK	UK	CAN 003

C27 ACE CANNON C27

Personnel	Instr	
ACE CANNON	SAX	(ALL

Album	Year	Label	Country	Number
( ) TUFF	186	HI	US	32007
( ) LOOKING BACK	1962	HI	US	32008
( ) MOANING SAX	1964	HI	US	32014
( ) ACES HIGH	1964	HI	US	32016
( ) GREAT SHOW TUNES	1964	HI	US	32019
( ) CHRISTMAS CHEER	1964	HI	US	32022
( ) LIVE	1965	HI	US	32025
( ) NASHVILLE HITS	1965	HI	US	32028
( ) SWEET & TUFF	1966	HI	US	32030
( ) MISTY SAX	1967	HI	US	32035
( ) MEMPHIS GOLDEN HITS	1968	HI	US	32040
( ) IN THE SPOTLIGHT	1969	HI	US	32046
( ) INCOMPARABLE SAX	197	HI	US	32048
( ) ACE OF SAX	1970	LONDON	UK	SHU 8407
( ) ACE OF SAX	1970	HI	US	32051
( ) HAPPY & MELLOW	1970	HI	US	32057
( ) COOL & SAXY	197	HI	US	32060
( ) BLOWING WILD	197	HI	US	32067
( ) COUNTRY CANNON	197	HI	US	32071
( ) BABY DONT GET HOOKED ON ME	1973	HI	US	SHL 32076
( ) COUNTRY COMFORT	197	LONDON	US	32080
( ) THAT MUSIC CITY FEELING	1974	HI	US	32086
( ) THAT MUSIC CITY FEELING	1974	LONDON	UK	SHU 8478
( ) SUPER SAX	1975	LONDON	US	32090
( ) VERY BEST OF ACE CANNON	1975	LONDON	UK	SHU 8486
( ) SAX MAN	1978	LONDON	US	HLP 8003

C28 FREDDY CANNON C28

Personnel	Instr	
FREDDY CANNON	V	(ALL

Album	Year	Label	Country	Number
( ) THE EXPLOSIVE FREDDY CANNON	1960	TOP RANK	UK	25 / 018
( ) THE EXPLOSIVE FREDDY CANNON	1960	SWAN	US	502
( ) THE EXPLOSIVE FREDDY CANNON	1976	SONIC		SON 007
( ) HAPPY SHADES OF BLUE	1962	TOP RANK	UK	35 / 106
( ) HAPPY SHADES OF BLUE	1962	SWAN	US	504
( ) FREDDY CANNON FAVOURITES	1961	TOP RANK	UK	35 / 113
( ) FREDDY CANNON FAVOURITES	1961	SWAN	US	505
( ) BANG ON	1963	STATESIDE	UK	SL 10013
( ) BANG ON	1963	SWAN	US	507
( ) STEPS OUT	1964	STATESIDE	UK	SL 10062
( ) STEPS OUT	1964	SWAN	US	511
( ) HITS	19	WB	US	WS 1544

C28A CANO C28A

Personnel	Instr	
MARCEL AYMAR	G V	(ABC
DAVID C BURT	G HCA	(ABC
MICHEL DASTI	D	(ABC
JOHN DEERR	B K TROM	(ABC
MICHEL KENDEL	K V B	(ABC
ANDRE PAIEMENT	G B V	(AB
KIM DESCHAMP	G	(B
FAMILLE ARMIN	STR	(C
ALISON REYNOLDS	SRT	(B
WASYL KOHUT	VLN MAN	(ABC
MERV DEERR	TROM	(A
MONIQUE PAIEMENT	V FLT	(BC
DAN ENGLERT	SAX	(C
JIMMY TANAKA	PERC	(A
RACHEL PAIEMENT	G V	(ABC
NICK AYOUB	CLAR	(A
MATT ZIMBEL	PERC	(C
RICK FRANCIS	G	(B

Album	Year	Label	Country	Number
(A) TOUS DANS L'MEME BATEAU	1976	A&M	CAN	9024
(B) AU NORD DE NOTRE VIE	1977	A&M	CAN	9028
(C) ECLIPSE	1978	A&M	CAN	9033

C29 CAPABILITY BROWN C29

Personnel	Instr	
TONY FERGUSON	V G B	(B
DAVE NEVIN	K V G B	(B
ROGER WILLIS	V D K	(B
GRAHAME WHITE	V K G	(B
KENNY ROWE	B V PERC	(B
JOE WILLIAMS	V PERC	(B

Album	Year	Label	Country	Number
(A) FROM SCRATCH	1972	CHARISMA	UK	CAS 1056
(B) VOICE	1973	CHARISMA	UK	CAS 1068
(C) LIAR	1976	CHARISMA	UK	CS5

C30 JIM CAPALDI C30

JIM CAPALDI V D (ALL | (A) OH HOW WE DANCED | 1972 ISLAND UK ILPS 9187
ROGER HAWKINS D (ABCE | (A) OH HOW WE DANCED | 1972 PHONOGRAM EURO 6896 015
DAVID HOOD B (ABCE | (B) WHALE MEAT AGAIN | 1974 ISLAND UK ILPS 9254
PETE CARR G (BCE | (B) WHALE MEAT AGAIN | 1974 PHONOGRAM EURO 9101 634
JIMMY JOHNSON G (ABCE | (C) SHORT CUT DRAW BLOOD | 1975 ISLAND UK ILPS 9336
BARRY BECKETT PNO (ABCE | (C) SHORT CUT DRAW BLOOD | 1975 PHONOGRAM EURO 6396 045
STEVE WINWOOD K B G (ABCE | (D) PLAY IT BY EAR | 1977 ISLAND UK ILPS 9497
MUSCLE SHOALS HRNS (ABC | (E) THE CONTENDER | 1978 POLYDOR UK 2383 490
RABBIT BUNDRICK K (BC | (F) DAUGHTER OF THE NIGHT | 1979 RSO US 1- 3037
JEAN ROUSSEL B K (BC | (G) ELECTRIC NIGHTS | 1979 POLYDOR UK 2383 534
POTATO SMITH V (B | (H) THE SWEET SMELL OF...SUCCESS | 1980 CARRERE UK CAL116 NL 67533
JOHN BARNES K (D
LAURENCE PEABODY V (B | CHRIS STAINTON K (B | REMI KABAKA PERC (BC | REBOP KWAKU BAAH PERC (ABC
RAY ALLEN SAX (CEGH | PHILIP CHEN B (C | JESS RODEN G (C | GERRY CONWAY D (C
ROSKO GEE B (CG | CHRIS SPEDDING G (C | PETER YARROW G (C | RICK GRECH B (A
PAUL KOSSOFF G (ACE | RICO RODRIGUES TROM (C | SUE GLOVER V (A | SUNNY LESLIE V (A
CHRIS WOOD WIND (AC | DAVE MASON HCA (A | JIM GORDON D (A | TREVOR BURTON B (A
MIKE KELLIE D (A | BOB GRIFFIN PNO (A | TREVOR MORAIS D (EG | ALAN SPENNER B (EGH
PETER BONAS G B (EGH | PHIL CAPALDI V PERC (EGH | RALPH RICHARDSON D (E | JACKIE McAULEY G (E
CHRIS PARREN K (EGH | ED GREENE D (E | DAVID SHIELDS B (E | CHUCK RAINEY K (E
RAY PARKER G (E | DEAN PARKS G (E | MEL COLLINS HRNS (H | ROB MASON D (H
BRENT FORBES B (H | MICK FEAT B (H | SIMON KIRKE D (G | PETER COX V (G
CHRIS STEWART B (B | BUBS WHITE G (B | DEREK QUINN PERC (B | GASPAR LAWAL PERC (B

C30A CAPITOL CITY ROCKETS C30A

JAMIE LYONS V (A | (A) CAPITOL CITY ROCKETS | 1973 ELEKTRA US 75059
ROBERT HILL G V (A
JERRY HERTIG D (A | MICHAEL WARNER G V (A | ERIC MOORE B (A

C30B CAPITOL LETTERS C30B

DANNY McKEN G V (A | (A) HEADLINE NEWS | 1979 GREENSLEVES
PAULINE SPENCER V (A
PAULETTE HAYDEN V (A | JUNIOR BROWN B (A | RODERICK HARVEY D (A
EARL LYNCH K V (A | GEORGE SCARLETT G (A | WENTY STEWART PERC (A

C30C CAPITOLS C30C

DANCE THE COOL JERK | 19 ATCO US 190
WE GOT A THING | 19 ATCO US 201

C31 CAPTAIN BEYOND C31

LARRY'RHINO'RHEINHART G (ABC | (A) CAPTAIN BEYOND | 1972 CAPRICORN UK K 47503
LEE DORMAN B V K (ABC | (A) CAPTAIN BEYOND | 1972 CAPRICORN US CP 0105
ROD EVANS V (AB | (B) SUFFICIENTLY BREATHLESS | 1973 CAPRICORN US CP 0115
BOBBY CALDWELL D V K (AC | (C) DAWN EXPLOSION | 1977 WB US BS 3047
GUILLE GARCIA PERC (B
MARTY RODRIGUEZ D (B | REESE WYNANS PNO (B | PAUL HORNSBY K (B
WILLY DAFFERN V (C

C32 CAPTAIN RUGELEYS BLUES BAND C32

CLIVE TIMPERLEE G (| (NO ALBUMS)
MARTIN LAMBLE D (

C33 GILBERT CARANHAC C33

GILBERT CARANHAC | (A) THE DOBRO | 1975 CHANT DU MONDE LDX 74508

C34 CARAVAN C34

RICHARD COUGHLAN D (ALL | (A) CARAVAN | 1968 VERVE 6011
PYE HASTINGS G V (ALL | (A) CARAVAN | 1968 MGM UK 2353 058
DAVE SINCLAIR K (ABCEFG145LZM | (A) CARAVAN | 1972 POLYDOR UK 2353 058
RICHARD SINCLAIR B (ABCD12M | (B) IF I COULD DO IT ALL OVER AGAIN... | 1970 DECCA UK SKL 5052
GEOFF RICHARDSON V G VLN (EFGK34567JZL | (B) IF I COULD DO IT ALL OVER AGAIN... | 1970 METRONOME FR MLP15 375
STEVE MILLER K (D2 | (B) IF I COULD DO IT ALL OVER AGAIN... | 1970 CARRERE FR 44002
BROTHER JAMES WIND (B | (B) IF I COULD DO IT ALL OVER AGAIN... | 1970 LONDON US PS 582
MIKE WEDGWOOD B (GK567JZ | (C) IN THE LAND OF THE GREY & PINK | 1971 DERAM UK SDL 1
JOHN G PERRY B V (EF4 | (C) IN THE LAND OF THE GREY & PINK | 1971 LONDON US 593 JAP LAX 1040
MEL COLLINS SAX (M | (C) IN THE LAND OF THE GREY & PINK | 19 MOTORS FR 2445 203
JIM HASTINGS WIND (CDE | (C) IN THE LAND OF THE GREY & PINK | 197 CARRERE FR 44007
DEREK AUSTIN K (3 | (D) WATERLOO LILY | 1972 DERAM UK SDL 8
STUART EVANS B (3 | (D) WATERLOO LILY | 1972 LONDON US PS 615
DEK MESSECAR B V (K7L | (D) WATERLOO LILY | 1980 VOGUE FR 6001 GER BRAIN 1010
JAN SCHELHAAS K (6JK | (E) FOR GIRLS WHO GROW PLUMP IN NIGHT | 1973 DERAM UK SKLR 12
DAVE GRINSTEAD PERC (C | (E) FOR GIRLS WHO GROW PLUMP IN NIGHT | 1973 LONDON US 627 JAP LAX 1041
FRANK RICOTTI PERC (E | (E) FOR GIRLS WHO GROW PLUMP IN NIGHT | 1980 VOGUE FR 6006
RUPERT HINE SYN (E | (F) & THE NEW SYMPHONIA | 1974 DERAM UK SKLR 1110
TONY COE WIND (E | (F) & THE NEW SYMPHONIA | 1974 LONDON US PS 650
TOMMY WHITTLE WIND (E | (F) & THE NEW SYMPHONIA | 1980 VOGUE FR 6008 GER BRAIN 1054
HARRY KLEIN WIND (E | (G) CUNNING STUNTS | 1975 DERAM UK SKLR 5210
PETE KING WIND (E | (G) CUNNING STUNTS | 1975 BTM BTM 5000
BARRY ROBINSON WIND (E | (G) CUNNING STUNTS | 197 RCA GER 26 21544
HENRY LOWTHER HRNS (E | (G) CUNNING STUNTS | 197 BTM BTM 1003
CHRIS PYNE TROM (E | (H) CANTERBURY TALES (DBL COMP) | 1976 DECCA UK DKLR81/82
JOHN BEECHAM TROM (E | (J) BLIND DOG AT ST DUNSTANS | 1976 BTM UK BTM1007 US ARISTA 4088
MIKE COTTON TPT (E | (K) BETTER BY FAR | 1977 ARISTA UK SPARTY 1008
DAVID HITCHCOCK PROD (EG | (K) BETTER BY FAR | 1977 ARISTA US AB 4134
JILL PRYOR V (E | (K) BETTER BY FAR | 1977 PATHE FR OC64 99089
PAUL BUCKMASTER CELL (E | (L) THE ALBUM | 1980 KINGDOM UK KVL 9003
VIVKI BROWN V (K | (L) THE ALBUM | 1980 KINGDOM NL 574015
FIONA HIBBERT HARP (K | (M) BACK TO FRONT | 1982 KINGDOM UK 5011
TONY VISCONTI REC (K | ( ) THIS IS CARAVAN | 19 BRAIN GERM 200164
( ) THE BEST OF | 1978 LONDON US 50011
(Z) THE BEST OF CARAVAN LIVE | 1980 KINGDOM FR 426002
( ) CARAVAN VOL1 | 19 POLYDOR 2445 202
( ) CARAVAN VOL2 | 19 POLYDOR 2445 203

C34A GUY CARAWAN C34A

GUY CARAWAN DULC (A | (A) THE TELLING TAKES ME HOME | 19 CUR NON US 722

C35 GLENN CARDIER C35

- GLENN CARDIER — (A) GLENN CARDIER — 1976 EMI UK EMC 3115

C35A CARGO C35A

- MIKE PROUDFOOT G (A — (A) SIMPLE THINGS — 1969 RINGSIDE RS 104
- NORM FOSTER D (A
- RAY PARKER ORG (A
- GARTH VAGAN B (A

C35B CARGOE C35B

- BILL PHILLIPS (— (A) CARGOE — 1972 ARDENT US ADS 2802
- TOMMY RICHARD (
- MAX WISLEY (
- TIM BENTON (

C35C CARILLO C35C

- (A) RINGS AROUND THE MOON — 1978 ATLANTIC US SD 19176
- (B) STREET OF DREAMS — 1979 ATLANTIC US 19235
- DAVID DONEN D (A
- KEVIN KEANE B V (A
- LUKE SPAGNUDO LYRICS(A
- FRANK CARILLO V G (A
- YVONNE ELLIMAN V (A
- JAN MULLANEY K V (A
- RICK SILECHIO G (A
- KRISTI BARTON V (A

C35D DAVE CARLSEN C35D

- (A) A PALE HORSE — 1973 SPARK UK SRLP 110
- DAVE CARLSEN (A
- KEITH MOON D (A
- HENRY McCULLOUGH G (A
- ROY ALLEN (A
- ROY HARRIS (A
- BERNIE O'GORMAN (A
- LES SAMSON (A
- NOEL REDDING B (A
- STEVE GREENE (A
- DICK PALMER (A
- KEN LAWS (A
- SPENCER DAVIS (A
- MIKE DAY (A
- BOB JELFS (A
- ALAN DICKENSON (A

C35E THUMBS CARLLILE C35E

- THUMBS CARLLILE G DOB (A — (A) ON HIS OWN — 19 GEMINI US 101

C36 LARRY CARLTON C36

- (A) SINGING PLAYING — 1973 BLUE THUMB US BST 46
- (B) LARRY CARLTON — 1978 WB UK K56548 US BSK3221
- (C) LIVE IN JAPAN — 1979 WB GER 56721 JAP P 10643
- (D) STRIKES TWICE — 1980 WB UK K56723 US BSK3380
- LARRY CARLTON G (ALL
- GREG MATHIESON K (BC
- JEFF PORCARO D (B
- PAULINHO DA COSTA PERC (BC
- WILLIAM'SMITTY' SMITH V (B
- ABE LABORIEL B (B
- GREG MATHIESON K (D
- TERRY TROTTER K (D
- ALAN ESTES PERC (A
- OMA DRAKE V (A
- JULIA TILLMAN V (A
- JOE SAMPLE K (A
- JOHN GUERIN D (A
- ROBERT POPWELL B (D
- DON FREEMAN K (D
- NEIL STUBENHAM B (C
- JIM GORDON D (A
- RON TUTT D (A
- MAXINE WILLARD V (A
- STIX HOOPER D (A
- REINIE PRESS B (A
- JOHN FERRARO D (DC
- BRIAN MANN K (D
- MICHAEL OMARTIAN K (A
- MICHAEL MILLS PERC (A
- JOE OSBORNE B (A
- WILTON FELDER B (A
- MAX BENNETT B (A
- CHRIS NELSON V (A

C37 CARMEN C37

- (A) FANDANGOS IN SPACE — 1973 REGAL ZONOPHONE UK SRZA 8518
- (A) FANDANGOS IN SPACE — 1973 DUNHILL US DP 50192
- (B) DANCING ON A COLD WIND — 1975 REGAL ZONOPHONE UK SLRZ1040
- (C) THE GYPSIES — 1976 MERCURY US SRM1 1047
- DAVID ALLEN G V (ABC
- ANGELA ALLEN V K (ABC
- ROBERTO AMARAL V PERC(ABC
- PAUL FENTON D (ABC
- JOHN GLASCOCK B V (ABC
- DAVID KATZ STR (B
- MARY VISCONTI V (B
- CHRIS KARAN PERC (B
- TONY VISCONTI WIND (B

C38 ERIC CARMEN C38

- (A) ERIC CARMEN — 1976 ARISTA UK ARTY 120 US 4057
- (B) BOATS AGAINST THE CURRENT — 1977 ARISTA UK SPARTY1015US 4124
- (C) CHANGE OF HEART — 1978 ARISTA UK SPART1068 US 4184
- (D) TONIGHT YOU'RE MINE — 1980 ARISTA UK SPART1134 US 9513
- ERIC CARMEN V K D (ALL
- JEFF PORCARO D (B
- ANDREW GOLD G V (B
- MICHAEL BODDIKER K (B
- TOMMY MORGAN HCA (C
- BRUCE JOHNSTON V (C
- RICHARD REISING G V (BCA
- JAI WINDING K (C
- DANIEL KORTCHMAR G (C
- CRAIG DOERGE K (C
- OLLIE BROWN PERC (B
- BRIAN RUSSELL V (C
- DAVE WINTOUR B (B
- GEORGE SIPL K V (A
- MICHAEL McBRIDE D V (A
- JOE CHEMAY V (C
- MIKE PORCARO B (C
- DONNY GERRARD V (C
- LEE SKLAR B (C
- JIM HORN SAX (B
- JOE PORCARO PERC (C
- BRENDA RUSSELL V (C
- GENE ESTES PERC (B
- STEVE KNILL B V (A
- JAMES NEWTON HOWARD SYN (C
- VALERIE CARTER V (C
- RUSS KUNKEL D (C
- RICHIE ZETO G (BC
- LAURA ALLEN V (C
- DAVID PAICH K (C
- SAMANTHA SANG V (C
- NIGEL OLSSON D (BC
- DWIGHT KRUEGER D (A
- BURTON CUMMINGS PNO (C
- BOBBY KEYS SAX (B
- TOM SCOTT SAX (B
- PAULINHO DA COSTA PERC(C
- FRED TACKETT G (C
- STEVE MADAIO TPT (B
- MIKE BOTTS D (C
- CURT BOETCHER V (C
- DAN HUDLICKA G V (A

C38A KIM CARNES C38A

- (A) REST ON ME — 1970 AMOS US 7016
- (B) KIM CARNES — 1975 A&M US 4548 UK 64548
- (C) SAILIN' — 1976 A&M US 4606 UK 64606
- (D) ST VINCENT'S COURT — 1979 EMI US 17004 UK 3001
- (E) ROMANCE DANCE — 1980 EMI US 17030 UK 3012
- (F) MISTAKES & IDENTITY — 1981 EMI US 17052 UK 3018
- (G) VOYEUR — 1982 EMI UK 3026
- KIM CARNES V PNO(ALL
- GLEN D HARDIN PNO (A
- LARRY MUHOBERAC K (A
- LARRY CARLTON G (A
- MIKE DEASY G (A
- JAMES BURTON G (A
- GIL ROGERS G (A
- DUANNE HITCHINGS SYN (G
- REINE PRESS B (AD
- MIKE SETTLE V (A
- DAVE ELLINGSON V G BJ(ABCDF
- DAVID FOSTER PNO (B
- JULIA TILLMAN V (BCEF
- BARRY BECKETT K (C
- BILL CUOMO K (DEFG
- MATT BETTON D (D
- GARY MONTGOMERY HCA (D
- BOBBY COCHRAN G (D
- BRIAN CADD V (D
- DAVID JACKSON B (D
- CRAIG KRAMPF D V (EFG
- MIKE THOMPSON K (E
- RAPHAEL RAVENSCROFT SAX(E
- STEVE GOLDSTEIN K (FG
- WADDY WACHTEL G V (FG
- WENDY WALDMAN V (F
- BILL PERRY B (A
- BROOKS HUNNICUTT V (A
- JIM KELTNER D (B
- STEVE FORMAN PERC (B
- MENTOR WILLIAMS V (B
- PETE CARR G DOB(C
- DAVID GRISMAN MAND V(C
- STEVE GEYER G MAN(DE
- DANIEL MOORE V (DF
- BOBBIE HALL PERC (D
- RICHIE HAYWARD D (D
- MATTHEW MOORE V (D
- MIKE PICCIRILLO G V (E
- DAVID HUNGATE B (E
- EDNA WRIGHT V (E
- BRIAN GAROFALO B V (FG
- DON FRANCISCO PERC (F
- ED GREENE D (A
- ETHAN GOYA V (A
- LELAND SKLAR B (BD
- MICHAEL UTLEY K SYN(B
- DAVID HOOD B (C
- JIMMY JOHNSON G (C
- BLACKIE SCHACKNER HCA (C
- JOHN BELAND G MAN(DE
- JERRY PETERSON SAX (DFG
- ETAN McELROY V (D
- RON BARRON ORG (D
- DARRELL LEONARD TPT (D
- SCOTT EDWARDS B (E
- KIN VASSEY V (E
- DARLENE LOVE V (E
- CRAIG HULL G V (FG
- M L BENOIT PERC (F
- DENNIS ST JOHN D (A
- DANNY TIMMS V (AD
- DEAN PARKES G (B
- MAXINE WILLARD V (BCEF
- ROGER HAWKINS D (C
- TOM ROADY PERC(C
- DOMINIC GENOVA B (D
- LARRY HIRSCH PERC(D
- VICTOR FELDMAN PERC(D
- TIM WEISBERG FLT (D
- JIM W GORDON ORG(D
- ERIC NELSON B (E
- PATRICK BOLEN V (E
- HERB PEDERSEN V (E
- JOEL PESKIN SAX(E
- JOSH LEO G V(FG
- DANNY KORTCHMAR G (F

C39 CARPENTERS C39

RICHARD CARPENTER K V (ALL | (A) CLOSE TO YOU | 1970 A&M | AMLS 998
KAREN CARPENTER D V (ALL | (A) CLOSE TO YOU | 1970 A&M | US 4271
JOE OSBORN B (ABDEM | (B) THE CARPENTERS | 1971 A&M | 6 3502
BOB MESSENGER B WIND(ABDEL | (C) TICKET TO RIDE | 1972 A&M | 6 4205
RON GORDON D (E | (C) TICKET TO RIDE | 1972 HAMLET | UK AMLP8001
DOUG STRAWN K WIND V(ABEL | (D) A SONG FOR YOU | 1972 A&M | 6 3511
JIM HORN WIND (AB | (E) NOW & THEN | 1973 A&M | 6 3519
HAL BLAINE D (ABDE | (F) THE SINGLES 69 73 | 1974 A&M | 6 3601
TIM WEISBERG FLT (D | (G) HORIZON | 1975 A&M | 6 4530
LOUIE SHELTON G (D | (H) A KIND OF HUSH | 1976 A&M | 6 4581
TONY PELUSO G B K V (DELM | (J) CARPENTER COLLECTION | 197 A&M | CARP 1000
RED RHODES STEEL (D | (K) LIVE IN JAPAN | 1975 A&M | GSW301/02
EARL DUMLER WIND (DEM | (L) LIVE AT THE PALLADIUM | 1977 A&M | 6 8403
NORM HERZBERG WIND (D | (M) PASSAGE | 1977 A&M | 6 4703
DANNY WOODHAMS B (A | (N) THE SINGLES 74 78 | 1978 A&M | 19748
CUBBY O'BRIEN D (L | (M) MADE IN AMERICA | 1980 A&M | US 3723
TOM SCOTT WIND (EM
GARY SIMS G (E | BUDDY EMMONS STEEL(E | JAYDEE MANESS STEEL(EM | PETE JOLLY PNO (M
DAVID LUELL SAX (M | KURT McGETTRICK SAX (M | JACKIE KELSO SAX (M | WALLY SNOW PERC(M
RAY PARKER G (M | CARLENA WILLIAMS V (M | BOBBY BRUCE FDL (M | TOM HENSLEY PNO (M
LEON RUSSELL PNO (M | LARRY MUHOBERAC PNO (M | RON TUTT D (M | TOMMY VIG PERC(M
JERRY STEINHOLTZ PERC (M | ED GREENE D (M | JULIA TILLMAN V (M | MAXINE WILLARD V (M
GAYLE LEVANT HARP (M | LARRY McNEALY BANJ (M | LEE RITENOUR G (M | VINCE CHARLES D (M

C39A PAUL CARRACK C39A

PAUL CARRACK V (A | (A) THE NIGHTBIRD | 1980 VERTIGO | 6359 016
RICHAR BAILEY D (A
ANDY NEWMARK D (A | JEFF SEOPARDIE D (A | ALAN SPENNER B (A
KUMA HARADA B (A | TIM RENWICK G (A | NEIL HUBBARD G (A
WINSTON DELANDRO G (A | NEVILLE MURRAY PERC (A | DYAN BIRCH V (A
ALAN BAM KING V (A | NOEL McCALLA V (A | MEL COLLINS HRNS (A
MARTIN DROVER HRNS (A | MALCOLM GRIFFITHS HRNS (A | GUY BARKER HRNS (A

C39B JOE 'KING' CARRASCO C39B

JOE'KING' CARRASCO V G (AB | (A) & THE EL MOLINO BAND | 1979 BIG BEAT | UK WIK 11
IKE RITTER (A | (B) JOE KING CARRASCO & THE CROWNS | 1980 STIFF | UK SEEZ 28
MIKE NAVARRO (B
KRIS CUMMINGS (B | BRAD KIZER (B | AUGIE MEYERS (A
ROCKY MORALES (A | ARTURO GONZALES (A

C39C CARPETTES C39C

NEIL THOMPSON G V (ABC | (A) CREAM OF THE YOUTH(EP) | 1978 SMALL WONDER | UK SMALL3
TIM WILDER D (ABC | (B) FRUSTRATION PARADISE | 1979 BEGGARS BANQUET | UK BEGA14
GEORGE MADDISON B (ABC | (C) FIGHT AMONGST YOURSELVES | 1980 BEGGARS BANQUET | UK BEGA21

C39D PETE CARR C39D

PETE CARR G V (ALL | (A) NOT A WORD ON IT | 1975 BIG TREE | US BT 89518
ROGER CLARK D (AB | (B) MULTIPLE FLASH | 1978 BIG TREE | US BT 76009
TIM HENSON K SYN (AB
CHUCK LEAVEL K (A | CLAYTON IVEY K (A | TOM ROADY PERC (A
LENNY LEBLANC B (A | HARVEY THOMPSON SAX (AB | BOB WRAY B (B
ROBERT BYRNE V (B | ROGER HAWKINS D (B | GARY BAKER B (B
STEVE NATHAN K (B | BUTCH LEADFORD B (B | RANDY McCORMICK K (B

C40 BARBARA CARROLL C40

BARBARA CARROLL PNO K (A | (A) FROM THE BEGINNING | 1977 UA | US UALA 778H
EUGENE BIANCO HARP (A | (A) FROM THE BEGINNING | 1978 UA | UK UAG 30168
IRWIN MARKOWITZ HRNS (A
MARVIN STAMM HRNS (A | JAY LEONHART B (A | STEVE GADD D (A
STEVE THORNTON PERC (A | RUSSELL GEORGE B (A | HUGH McCRACKEN G (A
BOB ROSE G (A | CRUSHER BENNETT PERC (A | GEORGE DEVENS VIBES(A
JAY BERLINER G (A | RICHARD DAVIS B (A | BILL LAVORGNA D (A
RON CARTER B (A

C40A JIM CARROLL C40A

JIM CARROLL V (A | (A) CATHOLIC BOY | 1980 ATCO | US 18132
BRIAN LINSLEY G (A
STEVE LINSLEY B (A | TERRELL WINN G (A | WAYNE WOODS D (A
ALLEN LANIER K (A | BOBBY KEYS SAX (A | AMY KANTNER V (A
JON TIVER G (A | SALLY V (A | NEON V (A
HILARY V (A | JANET V (A | LENNY KAYE G (A

C41 CARS C41

RIC OCASEK G V (ABCD | (A) THE CARS | 1978 ELEKTRA | UK K52088
ELLIOT EASTON G V (ABCD | (A) THE CARS | 1978 ELEKTRA | US 6E 135
DAVID ROBINSON D V (ABCD | (B) CANDY O | 1979 ELEKTRA | UK K 52148
BEN ORR(ORZECHOWSKI) B V (ABCD | (C) PANORAMA | 1980 ELEKTRA | UK K 52240
GREG HAWKES K V (ABCD | (D) SHAKE IT UP | 1981 ELEKTRA | US 5E 567
ROY THOMAS BAKER PROD (| (D) SHAKE IT UP | 1981 ELEKTRA | US K 52330

C41A CARSON C41A

BRODERICK SMITH V HCA (| (A) BLOWN | 19 HARVEST | UK SHVL 608
SLEEPY GREG LAWRIE G (| (B) ON THE AIR(LIVE) | 19 PATHE | FR 064 81774
IAN WINTER G (
GARY CLARKE B (| TONY LUNT D (

C42 CARLENE CARTER C42

CARLENE CARTER V G PNO(ALL | (A) CARLENE CARTER | 1978 WB US BSK3204 | UK K 56502
MARTIN BELMONT G (D | (B) TWO SIDES TO EVERY WOMAN | 1979 WB UK BSK3375
DAVE EDMUNDS G V (C | (C) MUSICAL SHAPES | 1980 F BEAT | UK XXLP3
ANDREW BODNAR B (A | (D) BLUE NUN | 1981 F BEAT | UK LP12
STEVE GOULDING D (A
BRINSLEY SCHWARZ G V (A | BOB ANDREWS K V (AB | CHRIS GOWER TROM (A | JOHN EARLE SAX (A
NICK LOWE B (ACD | GRAHAM PARKER G (A | TERRY WILLIAMS D (AC | RAY BEARIS SAX (A
DICK HANSON HRNS (A | KEVIN WELLS D (C | BILLY BREMNER G (CD | JOHN McFEE G (C
JOHN CIAMBOTTI B (C | SEAN HOPPER K (C | ROGER RETTIG STEEL(C | BETTY BRIGHT V (D
GINNY CLEE V (D | GLENN TILBROOK V (D | BOBBY IRWIN D (D | JAMES ELLER V B (D
MARTIN BELMONT G (D | HUGH GOWER G (D | JERRY MAROTTA D (B | ALAN SCHWARZBURG D (B

(CONTINUED)

C42 (CONTINUED)

CARLENE CARTER C42

BOB BABBIT B (B   HUGH McDONALD B (B   JEFF MIRONOU G (B   CHARLIE BROWN G (B
LANCE QUINN G (B   WERNER FRITZSCHING G (B   BOBBY BLAINE K (B   PAT REBILLOT K (B
PAUL SCHAFER K (B   ROB MOUNSEY K (B   CLARENCE CLEMMONS SAX (B   ROBERT LEE PATTON SAX (B
RANDY SINGER HENNES HCA(B   SUE EVANS PERC (B   ANN OBRIEN V (B   AL DOWNING V (D

C43

CLARENCE CARTER C43

Musician	Instr.		Record	Year	Label		Number
CLARENCE CARTER	V G K	(ALL	(A) THIS IS	1968	ATLANTIC	UK	588 152
KEN BALL	G	(J	(A) THIS IS	1968	ATLANTIC	US	SD 8192
CARL'FROG' WILLIAMS	G	(J	(B) THE DYNAMIC	1968	ATLANTIC	UK	588 172
STEVE NATHAN	K	(J	(B) THE DYNAMIC	1968	ATLANTIC	US	SD 8199
ROGER CLARK	D	(J	(C) TESTIFYIN'	1969	ATLANTIC	UK	588 191
BOB WRAY	B	(J	(C) TESTIFYIN'	1969	ATLANTIC	US	SD 8238
MICKEY BUCKIN	PERC	(J	(D) PATCHES	1970	ATLANTIC	UK	2400 027
DUNCAN CAMERON	STEEL	(J	(D) PATCHES	1970	ATLANTIC	US	SD 8267
MUSCLE SHOALS	HRNS	(J	(E) SIXTY MINUTES	1974	FAME		186
COLLETTE SIMPSON	V	(J	(F) REAL	1974	ABC	US	ABCD 833
MICHELLE MORGAN	V	(J	(F) REAL	1974	ANCHOR	UK	ABCL 5060
JERRY WALLACE	V	(J	(G) LONELINESS & TEMPTATION	1975	ABC	US	ABCD 896
CINDY RICHARDSON	V	(J	(H) HEART FULL OF SONG	1976	ABC	US	ABCD 943
PATRICIA COOLEY	V	(J	( ) THE BEST OF	1972	ATLANTIC US 8282		40245
			(J) IN PERSON	1981	VENTURE	US	1009

C44

RON CARTER C44

Musician	Instr.		Record	Year	Label		Number
RON CARTER	B	(ALL	(A) BLUES FARM	1973	CTI	US	6027
WITH			( ) ALL BLUES	1974	CTI	US	6037
BILLY COBHAM	D	(AJ	( ) ALONE TOGETHER	19	MILESTONE	US	904
BOB JAMES	K	(A	( ) MAGIC	19	PRESTIGE	US	24053
GENE BERTONCINI	G	(A	( ) OUT FRONT	19	PRESTIGE	US	7397
SAM BROWN	G	(A	( ) SPANISH BLUE	1975	CTI	US	6051
STEVE GADD	D	(G	(G) ANYTHING GOES	1975	KUDU		KU 25
JIMMY MADISON	D	(G	( ) WHERE	19	PRESTIGE	US	7843
BARRY ROGERS	TROM	(G	( ) UPTOWN CONVERSATION	197	EMBRYO		SD 521
ERIC GALE	G	(G	(J) YELLOW & GREEN	1976	CTI		63004
GEORGE DEVENS	PERC	(G	(J) YELLOW & GREEN	1976	CTI	US	6064
RALPH McDONALD	PERC	(AG	(K) PASTELS	1977	MILESTONE		9073
HUBERT LAWS	FLT	(AG	( ) SONG FOR YOU	1979	MILESTONE		9086
RANDY BRECKER	HRNS	(G	( ) PARADE	1979	MILESTONE		9088
HARVEY MASON	D	(K	(O) PATRAO	1980	MILESTONE		9099
ALAN RUBIN	HRNS	(G					

DON GROLNICK K (GJ   RICHARD TEE K (AG   CHET BAKER TPT (O
MICHAEL BRECKER HRNS (G   DAVE SANBORN SAX (G   PHIL WOODS SAX (G
PATTI AUSTIN V (G   MARILYN JACKSON V (G   MAERETHA STEWART V (G
KENNY BARRON PNO (JK   HARVEY MANDEL G (J   HUGH McCRACKEN G (JK
ARTHUR JENKINS PERC (G   DOM UM ROMAO PERC (J   BEN RILEY D (J
KENNY BARON PNO (O   JACK DEJOHNETTE D (O   EDISON MACHADO D (O
ALOISIO AGUIAR PNO (O   AMOURY TRISTAO G (O   NANA VASCONCELOS PERC (O

C45

VALERIE CARTER C45

Musician	Instr.		Record	Year	Label		Number
VALERIE CARTER	V	(ALL	(A) JUST A STONES THROW AWAY	1977	CBS	US	PC 34155
WITH			(A) JUST A STONES THROW AWAY	1977	CBS	UK	81958
BILL PAYNE		(A	(B) WILD CHILD	1978	CBS	US	JC 35084
LOWELL GEORGE	G	(A	(B) WILD CHILD	1978	CBS	UK	82556
JEFF PORCARO	D	(AB					

BOB GLAUB (A   FRED TACKETT G (AB   SAM CLAYTON PERC (A
CHARLES RAINEY B (AB   JOHN HALL (A   ERNIE WATTS SAX (A
TOM JANS (A   HERB PEDERSEN (A   MIKE UTLEY K (AB
JOHN SEBASTIAN (A   JACKSON BROWNE (A   OSCAR BRASHEAR HRNS (A
MIKE HARRIS (A   LOUIS SATTERFIELD (A   DON MYRICK SAX (AB
DAVID CAMPBELL (A   LARRY DUNN (A   AL McKAY (A
VERDINE WHITE B (AB   FRED WHITE (A   ANDREW WOOLFOLK (A
JERRY PETERS (A   SKIP SCARBOROUGH (A   GEORGE BOHANON (A
PAUL BARRERE (A   COLIN CAMERON (A   VICTOR FELDMAN PERC (B
DAVID HUNGATE B (B   STEVE LUKATHER G (B   JAMES NEWTON HOWARD K (B
STEVE PORCARO SYN (B   RAY PARKER G (B   JAY GRAYDON G (B
VINI PONCIA V (B   WENDY HAAS V (B   DAVID LASLEY V (B
TOMMY SAVIANO SAX (B   DAVEY JOHNSTONE G (B   LENNY CASTRO PERC (B
CHUCK FINDLEY HRNS (B   STEVE MADAIO HRNS (B   JIM HORN HRNS (B

C46

CARTER LEWIS & THE SOUTHERNERS C46

JOHN(JOHN SHAKESPEARE)CARTER V B G
KEN (KEN JAMES) LEWIS V K
JIMMY PAGE G   VIV PRINCE D

C47

MARTIN CARTHY C47

Musician	Instr.		Record	Year	Label	Number
MARTIN CARTHY	V G	(ALL	(A) MARTIN CARTHY	1965	FONTANA	STL 5269
WITH			(A) MARTIN CARTHY	1977	TOPIC	12TS 340
DAVE SWARBRICK	VLN	(ABCDEHI	(B) SECOND ALBUM	1966	FONTANA	STL 5362
MADDY PRIOR	V	(K	(B) SECOND ALBUM	1977	TOPIC	12TS 341
LEON ROSSELSON		(F	(C) BYKER HILL	196	FONTANA	STL 5434
			(C) BYKER HILL	1977	TOPIC	12TS 342
			(D) BUT TWO CAME BY	1968	FONTANA	STL 5477
			(D) BUT TWO CAME BY	1977	TOPIC	12TS 343
			(E) PRINCE HEATHEN	1969	FONTANA	STL 5529
			(E) PRINCE HEATHEN	1977	TOPIC	12TS 344
			(F) THE WORD IS	19	TRAILER	LER 3015
			(G) LANDFALL	1971	PHILIPS	6309 049
			(G) LANDFALL	1977	TOPIC	12TS 345
			(H) SELECTIONS	1971	PEGASUS	PEG 6
			(I) THIS IS MARTIN CARTHY	1972	PHILIPS	6282 022
			(J) SWEET WIVELSFIELD	1974	DERAM	SML 1111
			(K) SHEARWATER	1975	MOONCREST	CREST 25
			(K) SHEARWATER	197	PEGASUS	PEG 12
			(L) CROWN OF HORN	1976	TOPIC	12TS 300
			(M) BECAUSE ITS THERE	1979	TOPIC 12TS289 ROUNDER US	3031

C47A DAVE CARTWRIGHT C47A

Musician	Instrument	Album
DAVE CARTWRIGHT	V G K	(ALL
GARY TAYLOR	G B	(D
JIM GANNON	G	(D
DAVE MATTACKS	D	(D
PETE SOLLEY	K	(D
PETE WILSHIRE	STEEL	(D
ROY BABBINGTON	B	(B
BARRY DESOUZA	D	(B
MO FOSTER	B	(B
MARTIN JENNER	G	(D
MIKE MORAN	K	(B
TED TAYLOR	K	(B
RAY FENWICK	G	(B
TONY JACKSON	V	(D
CHRIS KARAN	D	(B
PAUL KOEGH	G	(B
GRAHAM PRESKOTT	VLN	(B

Album	Year	Label	Country	Number
(A) A LITTLE BIT OF GLORY	1972	TRANSATLANTIC		TRA 255
(B) BACK TO THE GARDEN	1973	TRANSATLANTIC	UK	TRA 267
(C) DONT LET YOUR FAMILY DOWN	1975	TRANSATLANTIC	UK	TRA 284
(D) MASQUERADE	1976	DJM	UK	DJF 20489

C47B CARTOON C47B

Musician	Instrument	Album
DEREK CREIGAN	G V	(A
MIKE ALLISON	G	(A
CHICK E COFFILS	D	(A
MO TROWERS	G	(A
JIMMY PAGE	G	(A

Album	Year	Label	Country	Number
(A) CARTOON	1969	ATLANTIC	UK	588 174

C48 CASABLANCA C48

Musician	Instrument	Album
BARRY CLARKE	V G	(A
DAVID COSTA	G V	(A
JUANITA FRANKLIN	V	(A
STEVE BINGHAM	B	(A
BRUCE ROWLAND	D	(A
GRAHAM PRESKETT	VLN	(A
LUIS JARDIM	PERC	(A
PHILIP CHEN	B	(A
ALIKI ASHMAN	V	(A
TERRY STANNARD	D	(A
TREVOR VALLIS	B	(A
JOHNNY WILSON	D	(A
PAUL VIGRASS	V	(A
BILLY LIVSEY	K	(A
LOL COXHILL	WIND	(A
NICK JUDD	K	(A
BIAS BOSHELL	B	(A
GARY OSBORNE	V	(A

Album	Year	Label	Country	Number
(A) CASABLANCA	1974	ROCKET		PIGL 7

C49 AL CASEY C49

Musician	Instrument	Album
AL CASEY	G	(ALL

Album	Year	Label	Country	Number
(A) SURFIN' HOOTENANY	1963	STACY	US	STM 100
(B) JUMPIN' WITH AL	1974	BLACK & BLUE		33056
(C) GUITAR ODYSSEY	1976	JAZZ ODYSSEY		JO 012

C50 JOHNNY CASH C50

JOHNNY CASH
WITH
JUNE CARTER CASH
THE CARTER FAMILY

Musician	Instrument	Musician	Instrument	Musician	Instrument	Musician	Instrument
HELEN CARTER	V						
CARLENE CARTER	V	ANITA CARTER	V	ROSANNE CASH	V	CINDY CASH	V
STATLER BROTHERS		KRIS KRISTOFFERSON	V	BILLY LEE RILEY	G	LARRY BUTLER	
LARRY GATLIN		JAN HOWARD		RON TUTT		REINIE PRESS	
DAVID FOSTER		LARRY MUHOBERAC		RON ELLIOTT		RY COODER	G
JAMES BURTON	G	RUSS TITELMAN		JERRY COLE		VICTOR FELDMAN	PERC
JOE PORCARO	PERC	GENE ESTES		NICK DE CARO		GENE CIPRIANO	SAX
REGGIE YOUNG		KENNY MALONE		HENRY STRZELECKI		SHANE KEISTER	K
TEDDY IRWIN		DAVID ALAN COE	V	JACKIE WARD	V	RON HICKLIN SINGERS	V
JIMMY CAPPS	G	ROSEY NIX	V	MARSHALL GRANT	B	JORDANAIRES	V
WES HOLLAND	D	BOB WOOTTON	G	CARL PERKINS	V	LUTHER PERKINS	G
CHARLIE McCOY	HCA	CHUCK COCHRAN		JOE ALLEN		EARL SCRUGGS	BANJO
OAKRIDGE BOYS	V	LARRY McCOY		RAY EDENTON		JERRY HENSLEY	G
JACK ROUTH	G	EARL BALL	PNO	MARK MORRIS	PERC	MICHAEL BACON	CELLO
SAM MULLINS	STRINGS	KATHLEEN BRIMM	V	RED LANE	G	BILL PURSELL	
TOMMY ALSUP	G	JACK CLEMENT	G	JACK HALE	HRNS	BOB LEWINS	HRNS
JOEL SONNIER	HCA	DENNIS GOODE	TROM	BILLY PUETT	WIND	WAYNE JACKSON	TPT
GENE LOWERY SINGERS	V	RICH SCHULMAN	V	JIMMY WILSON	PNO	JAMES VAN EATON	D
RODNEY CROWELL	V						

Album	Year	Label	Number
WITH HIS HOT & BLUE GUITAR	1957	SUN	SLP 1220
SONGS THAT MADE HIM FAMOUS	1958	SUN	US SLP1235
SONGS THAT MADE HIM FAMOUS	1967	LONDON	HAS 2157
FABULOUS JOHNNY CASH	1959	CBS	62042
GREATEST JOHNNY CASH	1959	SUN	US SLP1240
HYMNS BY JOHNNY CASH	1959	CBS	US CS8125
HYMNS BY JOHNNY CASH	1971	HALLMARK	SHM 739
SINGS HANK WILLIAMS	1960	SUN	US SLP1245
SINGS HANK WILLIAMS	196	LONDON	NZ HAM6195
SINGS HANK WILLIAMS	196	SUN	US 125
SONGS OF OUR SOIL	1959	CBS	US CS 8148
NOW THERE WAS A SONG	1960	PHILIPS	BBL 7358
NOW THERE WAS A SONG	1960	CBS	US CS 8254
NOW THERE WAS A SONG	1960	CBS	62028
RIDE THIS TRAIN	1960	CBS	62575
RIDE THIS TRAIN	1960	CBS	8255
NOW HERES JOHNNY CASH	1961	SUN	US SLP1255
RIDE THIS TRAIN	1960	CBS	US CS 8255
HYMNS FROM THE HEART	1962	CBS	US CS8522
ALL ABOARD THE BLUE TRAIN	1962	SUN	US SLP1270
SOUND OF JOHNNY CASH	1962	CBS	US CS 8602
BLOOD SWEAT & TEARS	1963	CBS	US CS 8730
BLOOD SWEAT & TEARS	1963	CBS	UK 65163
RING OF FIRE	1963	CBS	62171
RING OF FIRE	1963	CBS	US CS 8853
CHRISTMAS SPIRIT	1963	CBS	62284
KEEP ON THE SUNNYSIDE	1964	CBS	US CS 8952
I WALK THE LINE	1964	CBS	US CS8990
I WALK THE LINE	19	HILLTOP	US 6097
I WALK THE LINE	19	SUN	139
I WALK THE LINE	196	CBS	UK 62371
I WALK THE LINE	1974	CBS	70083
I WALK THE LINE	1974	HALLMARK	UK SHM 849
BITTER TEARS	1964	CBS	US 9048 UK62463
LORENA	1964	CBS	GERM 52705
COUNTRY ROUND UP	1964	FONTANA	301
ORIGINAL SUN SOUND OF J C	1964	SUN	US SLP1275
ORIGINAL SUN SOUND OF J C	1967	LONDON	HAS8220
ORANGE BLOSSOM SPECIAL	1965	CBS	62501
ORANGE BLOSSOM SPECIAL	1965	CBS	US CS 9109
TRUE WEST	1965	CBS	62538
TRUE WEST	1965	CBS	US C2S 838
MEAN AS HELL	1966	CBS	US CS 9246
TRUE WEST 2	196	CBS	62591
EVERYBODY LOVES A NUT	1966	CBS	62717
EVERYBODY LOVES A NUT	1966	CBS	US CS 9292
HAPPINESS IS YOU	1966	CBS	62760
GREATEST HITS	1967	CBS	63062
GREATEST HITS 1	1967	CBS	US CS 9478
CARRYIN' ON	1967	CBS	US9528 UK 63105
OLD GOLDEN THROAT	1968	CBS	63318
OLD GOLDEN THROAT	1975	CHARLY	CR 30005
THE HOLY LAND	1968	CBS	63428
THE HOLY LAND	196	CBS	US KCS9726
LEGENDS & LOVE SONGS	1968	CBS	CAN DS 363
MORE OLD GOLDEN THROAT	1969	CBS	63521
SINGING STORY TELLER	1969	SUN	US 115
SINGING STORY TELLER	19	BUCKBOARD	US BBS1021
JACKSON	1969	CBS	US CS 9528
FROM SEA TO SHINING SEA	1968	CBS	62972
AT FOLSOM PRISON	1968	CBS	63308
AT FOLSOM PRISON	1968	CBS	US CS 9639
AT SAN QUENTIN	1969	CBS	63629
AT SAN QUENTIN	19	CBS	28090/9
AT SAN QUENTIN	1969	CBS	US CS 9827
HELLO IM JOHNNY CASH	1969	CBS	US9943 uk 63796
WORLD OF JOHNNY CASH	1970	CBS	66237
WORLD OF JOHNNY CASH	1970	CBS	CG 29
HIS GREATEST HITS VOL 2	19	CBS	US 30887
JOHNNY CASH SHOW	1970	CBS	64089
ORIGINAL GOLDEN HITS 1	1970	SUN	6467 001
ORIGINAL GOLDEN HITS 1	19	SUN	US 100
ORIGINAL GOLDEN HITS 2	1970	SUN	6467 007
ORIGINAL GOLDEN HITS 2	19	SUN	US 101
THE GREAT JOHNNY CASH	1970	HALLMARK	SHM 696
ORIGINAL JOHNNY CASH	1970	CHARLY	CR 30113
LITTLE FAUSS & BIG HALSY	1970	CBS	70087
THE MAN & HIS WORLD	1971	SUN	6641 008
TRAINS & RIVERS	1971	SUN	6467012
TRAINS & RIVERS	197	SUN	US 104

(CONTINUED)

C50 (CONTINUED) JOHNNY CASH C50

Title	Year	Label / Catalogue
SHOWTIME	197	SUN US 106
GET RHYTHM	1971	SUN US105 6467 014
UNDERSTAND YOUR MAN	1971	HARMONY US 30916
A MAN IN BLACK	1971	CBS 64331
MAN IN BLACK	1971	CBS US 30550
THE LEGEND	197	SUN US 2 118
ROUGH CUT KING OF COUNTRY	197	SUN US 122
THE MAN THE WORLD HIS MUSIC	197	SUN US 126
PORTRAIT	197	CBS 64516
GIVE MY LOVE TO ROSE	1972	CBS US 31256
INTERNATIONAL SUPERSTAR	1972	CBS GERM 67284
A THING CALLED LOVE	1972	CBS 31332 64898
JOHNNY CASH	197	EMBASSY 31495
JOHNNY CASH	1974	EMBASSY 31039
SHOWTIME	197	SUN 6467 016
JOHNNY CASH SONG BOOK	1972	HARMONY US 31602
CHRISTMAS & THE CASH FAMILY	1972	CBS US 31764
ORIGINAL GOLDEN HITS 3	1972	SUN 6467 022
ORIGINAL GOLDEN HITS 3	197	SUN US 127
GOSPEL ROAD	1973	CBS US 32253
GOSPEL ROAD	1973	CBS UK 68243
SUNDAY MORNING COMING DOWN	197	CBS US 32240
MAGNIFICENT JOHNNY CASH	1972	HALLMARK SHM 777
COUNTRY & WESTERN SUPERSTAR	1973	CBS GERM 68224
AMERICA	1973	CBS 31645 65163
SUNDAY DOWN SOUTH	1973	SUN 119 US 6467024
ANY OLD WIND THAT BLOWS	1973	CBS 65431
ANY OLD WIND THAT BLOWS	197	CBS US KC32091
J CASH & HIS WOMAN	1973	CBS 65689
J CASH & HIS WOMAN	1973	CBS US KC32443
MIGHTY JOHNNY CASH	1973	HALLMARK SHM 804
FIVE FEET HIGH & RISING	1974	CBS US 32951
AT OSTERAKER PRISON	1974	CBS HOLL 65308
FOLSOM PRISON BLUES	1974	HALLMARK SHM 822
SOUND OF J CASH	197	EMBASSY 31081
BALLADS OF AMERICAN INDIANS	1974	HARMONY US 32388
BLUE TRAIN	197	SHARE US 5002
BLUE TRAIN	1979	SUN 141
UNKIE & JUICEHEAD	1974	CBS 80347
JUNKIE & JUICEHEAD	1974	CBS US 33086
ROUGH CUT KING	1974	SUN 6870 605
GENTLE GIANT OF COUNTRY	1974	SUN 6641 161
PRECIOUS MEMORIES	1976	CBS US 33087
RAGGED OLD FLAG	1974	CBS 80113
RAGGED OLD FLAG	1974	CBS US 32917
FOLSUM & SAN QUENTIN	1976	CBS DBL US 33639
JOHN R CASH	1974	CBS 33370 80634
RIDING THE RAILS	1975	CBS 88153
CHILDRENS ALBUM	1975	CBS US 32898
LOOK AT THEM BEANS	1975	CBS 81012
LOOK AT THEM BEANS	1975	CBS US 34193
I FORGOT TO REMEMBER	1975	HALLMARK SHM 884
BALLAD OF TEENAGE QUEEN	1975	HALLMARK SHM 862
STORY OF A BROKEN HEART	1976	HALLMARK SHM 897
KING OF COUNTRY	1975	MUSIDISC 174
SPOTLIGHT ON JOHNNY CASH	1975	SUN NL SPL01
COLLECTION	1976	PICKWICK PDA 005
DESTINATION VICTORIA STATION	1976	CBS US VS150
MAKING A LEGEND	1976	CHARLY 18051
JOHNNY CASH	19	PICKWICK US 2052
KINGS OF COUNTRY DBL	19	FESTIVAL US 174
SONGBOOK	19	CBS EUR51357
IN SWEDEN	1976	CBS 65308
STRAWBERRY CAKE	1976	CBS 34088 81211
ONE PIECE AT A TIME	1976	CBS 81416
ONE PIECE AT A TIME	1976	CBS US 34193
LAST GUNFIGHTER BALLAD	1977	CBS 81566
LAST GUNFIGHTER BALLAD	1977	CBS US 34314
THE RAMBLER	1977	CBS US 34833
THIS IS JOHNNY CASH	197	HARMONY US 11342
I WOULD LIKE TO SEE YOU	1978	CBS UNISSUED 82676
I WOULD LIKE TO SEE YOU	1978	CBS US 35313
GONE GIRL	1978	CBS 35646 83323
ANY OLD WIND	1978	CBS 32091
UNISSUED JOHNNY CASH	1878	BEAR FAM GER 15016
JOHNNY & JUNE	1978	BEAR FAM GER 15030
ITCHY FEET 20 FOOT TAPPERS	1978	CBS 10009
COLLECTION VOL 2	1978	PICKWICK PDA 033
RING OF FIRE	1979	HALLMARK SHM 998
SILVER	1979	CBS 36086
ROCK ISLAND LINE	19	HILLTOP US 6101
WITH JERRY LEE LEWIS	19	SUN US 125
THE BARON	19	CBS 37179
ROCKABILLY BLUES	19	CBS 36779
WALLS OF PRISONS	19	HARMONY 30138
GREATEST HITS VOL 3	1979	CBS US 35637
JOHNNY CASH TODAY	1978	K TEL CAN NC424
HOT'N'BLUE GUITAR RI	1980	CHARLY CRM 2013
BALLAD OF A TEENAGE QUEEN(EP)	1976	CHARLY

C51 CASHMAN (PISTILL) & WEST C51

Musician	Instr.	Albums
GENE PISTILL	G V	(AB
TERRY CASHMAN	V	(ALL
TOMMY WEST	V K G	(ALL
TOM MORGAN	HCA	(C
RAY POHLMAN	B	(CD
GARY KATZ	V	(C
MIKE OMARTIAN	K	(CD
JEFF BAXTER	STEEL	(CD
GARY COLEMAN	PERC	(CD
LOUIS SHELTON	G	(C
HUGH McCRACKEN	G	(B
JOE MACHO	B	(B
STEVE BARRI	PERC	(C
JIMMIE HASKELL	ACC	(CD
JIM GORDON	D	(CD
SAL DETROIA	G	(B
BOBBY GREGG	D	(B
BEN BENAY	HCA G	(CD
EDDIE LAMBERT	V	(D
AL GORGONI	G	(B
ARTIE KAPLAN	FLT	(B

Album	Year	Label / Catalogue
(A) CASHMAN PISTILL & WEST	1969	EMI UK EST 211
(B) BOUND TO HAPPEN(C P W)	19	ABC US 629
(C) SONG OR TWO	1972	DUNHILL US 50126 UK PROBE 6270
(D) MOONDOG SERENADE	1973	DUNHILL US DSX 50141
(D) MOONDOG SERENADE	1973	PROBE UK 6226 RI ABC 74 5058
(E) LIFESONG	1974	ABC UK ABCL 5058

C51A CASINO C51A

Album	Year	Label / Catalogue
(A) CASINO	1976	STATE ETAT 5
(A) CASINO	1976	MCA US 2191

C51B TERRY CASHMAN C51B

Musician	Instr.	Albums
TERRY CASHMAN	G V	(A
TOMMY WEST	K V	(A
HENRY GROSS	G	(A
DAVID SANBORN	SAX	(A
RICK MAROTTA	D	(A

Album	Year	Label / Catalogue
(A) TERRY CASHMAN	1976	LIFESONG US 6006

C51C CASIOPEA C51C

Musician	Instr.	Albums
ISSEI NORO	G K	(A
MINORU MUKAIYA	K	(A
TETSUO SAKURAI	G H	(A
AKIRA JIMBO	K B	(A

Album	Year	Label / Catalogue
(A) MINT JAMS	1982	ALFA ALF 85869

C52 JEAN PIERRE CASTELAIN C52

Musician	Instr.	Albums
JEAN PIERRE CASTELAIN	G	(ALL

Album	Year	Label / Catalogue
(A) DE MES YEUX VU	19	WEA 46155
(B) ALBERIA	19	WEA 46285
(C) LA SOURIS S'EN VA EN GUERRE	19	WEA 56188
(D) LE MIROIR DBL	19	WEA 86011

C52A DAVID CASTLE C52A

Musician	Instr.	Albums
DAVID CASTLE		(AB
ANDY BELLING	PNO	(A
CLARK GASSMAN	PNO	(A
CHUCK RAINEY	B	(AB
RICK SHLOSSER	D	(A
TREVOR VEITCH	G	(A
JIM HORN	SAX	(A
STEVE MADAIO	TPT	(A
JAMES L ROLLESTON	B	(B
STEVE FORMAN	PERC	(B
ABRAHAM LABORIEL	B	(A
BEN BENAY	G	(A
JAY GRAYDON	G	(A
WILLIAM PERKINS	SAX	(A
CHARLES FINDLEY	TPT	(A
PATRICK McCLURE	G	(B
DENNIS TREMBLY	B	(B
JAMES GADSON	D	(AB
LEE RITENOUR	G	(A
DOROTHY ASHBY	HARP	(A
BOBBYE HALL	PERC	(A
JERRY SOMMERS	D	(B
MIKE BODDICKER	SYN	(B

Album	Year	Label / Catalogue
(A) CASTLE IN THE SKY	1977	PARACHUTE US 9002 UK RRL2001
(B) LOVE YOU FOREVER	1979	PARACHUTE US 9015 UK RRL2009

C52B CASTON & MAJORS C52B

Musician	Instr.	Albums
LEONARD CASTON	V	(A
KATHY WAKEFIELD	V	(A
MATTIE LYRICKS	V	(A
TERRY McFADDIN	V	(A
ERROL SOBER	V	(A

Album	Year	Label / Catalogue
(A) CASTON & MAJORS	1974	MOTOWN US 6 814

C53 JIMMY CASTOR BUNCH C53

JIMMY CASTOR (ALL — ( ) ITS JUST BEGUN — 1972 RCA US 4640
GERRY THOMAS K (F — ( ) PHASE TWO — 1972 RCA US 4783
DOUGLAS GIBSON B (F — ( ) DIMENSION 3 — 1973 RCA APDI 0103
LANDON FRIDE CONGA (F — ( ) THE EVERYTHING MAN — 1974 ATLANTIC UK K 50052
ELLWOOD HENDERSON D (F — ( ) THE EVERYTHING MAN — 1973 RCA US 0313
JEFFREY GRIMES G (F — (F) SUPER SOUND — 1975 ATLANTIC UK K 50190
(F) SUPER SOUND — 1975 ATCO US SD 18150
( ) BUTT OF COURSE — 1975 ATLANTIC UK K 50120
( ) BUTT OF COURSE — 1975 ATCO US SD 18124
( ) E MAN GROOVIN — 1976 ATLANTIC UK K 50295
( ) E MAN GROOVIN — 1976 ATCO US SD 18186
( ) BEST OF — 1976 RCA US 0877
( ) HEY LEROY — 197 SMASH US MGS 27091
( ) MAXIMUM STIMULATION — 1977 ATLANTIC US SD 19111
( ) 'C' — 1980 LONG DISTANCE US 1201

C55 CASUALS C55

JOHN TEBB V ORG(A — (A) HOUR WORLD — 1969 DECCA UK SKL 5001
HOWARD NEWCOMB G (A
ALAN TAYLOR FL B V(A — BOB OBRIEN D (A — STEVE WALLACE B (
ROGER GREY D (— LLOYD COURTNEY D (

C55A CAT C55A

MIKE McQUEEN G (A — (A) CAT — 1970 RCA US 4267
PHIL MULHOLLAND D (A
GARY O'CONNOR G K (A — GRAHAM FIDLER B V (A — JIM CAMPBELL V (A

C56 CAT MOTHER C56

ROY MICHAELS B G V (ABCD — (A) THE STREET GIVETH — 1969 POLYDOR 184 300
MICHAEL EQUINE D G V (ABCD — (A) THE STREET GIVETH — 1969 POLYDOR 24 4001
LARRY PACKER G V (AB — (B) ALBION DOOWAH — 1970 POLYDOR 2425 021
BOB SMITH K D V (ABCD — (B) ALBION DOOWAH — 1970 POLYDOR 24 4023
CHARLIE CHIN BANJO G V (A — (C) LAST CHANCE DANCE — 1973 UA UAG 29481
JAY UNGAR G V (BC — (C) LAST CHANCE DANCE — 1973 POLYDOR 5042
PAUL JOHNSON G (B — (D) CAT MOTHER — 1974 BARCLAY 920 285
LYNDON LEE HARDY V (B — (D) CAT MOTHER — 1972 UA UAG 29313
CHARLIE HARCOURT (D — (D) CAT MOTHER — 1974 POLYDOR 24 5017
STEVE DAVIDSON PERC (DC
CHARLIE PRITCHARD G (— JOHN CHAMBERLAIN MAND (C — BUZZY LINHART VIBES (C
VELLA CAMERON V (C

C57 CATAPILLA C57

THIERRY RHEINHARDT WIND (A — (A) CATAPILLA — 1971 VERTIGO US 1006 UK 6360 029
ANNA MEEK V (AB — (B) CHANGES — 1972 VERTIGO 6360 074
HUGH EAGLESTONE SAX (A
ROBERT CALVERT SAX (AB — DAVE TAYLOR B (A — MALCOLM FRITH D (A
GRAHAM WILSON G (AB — BRYAN HANSON D (B — CARL WASSARD B (B
RALPH RAWLINSON K (B

C57A CATES GANG C57A

ERNIE CATE K V (AB — (A) WANTED — 1970 METROMEDIA US 1029
EARL CATE G V (AB — (B) COME BACK HOME — 1973 METROMEDIA US 1052
TERRY CAGLE (A
BILL WRIGHT B (A

C58 THE CATE BROTHERS C58

ERNIE CATE V K (ALL — (A) THE CATE BROTHERS — 1975 ASYLUM UK SYL 9030
EARL CATE V G (ALL — (A) THE CATE BROTHERS — 1975 ASYLUM US 7E 1050
NIGEL OLSSON D (A — (A) THE CATE BROTHERS — 1975 ASYLUM EURO 24 4001
ED GREENE D (A — (A) THE CATE BROTHERS — 1976 ASYLUM UK K 53019
LELAND SKLAR B (A — (B) IN ONE EYE — 1976 ASYLUM UK K 53049
SCOTT EDWARDS B (A — (B) IN ONE EYE — 1976 ASYLUM US 7E 1080
STEVE CROPPER G (AB — (C) THE CATE BROTHERS BAND — 1977 ASYLUM UK K 53064
MICHAEL BAIRD D (AB — (C) THE CATE BROTHERS BAND — 1977 ASYLUM US 7E 1116
KLAUS VOORMANN B (A — (D) FIRE ON THE TRACKS — 1979 ATLANTIC US SD 19240
DAVID FOSTER K (B — (D) FIRE ON THE TRACKS — 1979 ATLANTIC GERM ATL 50627
DONALD DUNN B (B
STEVE FORMAN PERC (B — GEORGE TERRY G (D — PAUL HARRIS K (D
TERRY CAGLE D V (BCD — ALBERT SINGLETON V (B — JAY GRAYDON K (B
JIM HORN SAX (B — BOBBY KEYS HRNS (B — SID SHARP VLN (B
BROOKS HUNNICUTT V (B — VERNA RICHARDSON V (B — LISA ROBERTS V (B
WILLIE HALL PERC (B — RON EOFF B (CD — JOE LALA PERC (CD
TIM SCHMIT V (C — STEVE MADAIO TPT (C — MARK UNDERWOOD TPT (C
JERRY JUMONVILLE SAX (C — JOHN PHILLIPS SAX (C — LINDA SMALL TROM (C
JOEL PESKIN SAX (C — KING ERRISON PERC (A — CARL MARCH SYN (A
MAXINE WILLARD V (A — JULIA TILLMAN V (A — GARY COLEMAN PERC (A
LEVON HELM D V (AD — WILLIAM SMITTY SMITH K (A — BOB GLAUB B (A

C58A CATFISH C58A

BOB HODGE V G K (AB — (A) GET DOWN — 1970 EPIC UK EPC 64006
MARK MANKO (A — (B) LIVE CATFISH — 1971 EPIC UK EPC 64408
HARRY PHILLIPS K (AB
JIMMY OPTNER (A — W R COOKE (A — DALLAS HODGE G (B
DENNIS CRANNER B (B — JIM DEMERS D (B — JOHN HILL PNO (B

C59 CATFISH HODGE C59

BOB 'CATFISH' HODGE V G K (ALL — (A) DYNASAURS & ALLEYCATS — 1974 EASTBOUND US 2008
DALLAS HODGE G (A — (B) SOAP OPERA'S — 1975 20th CENTURY W 202
LARRY ZACK D (B — (C) EYEWITNESS BLUES — 1979 ADELPHI AD 4113
CRISPIN CIOE SAX (A — (D) 'BOUT WITH THE BLUES — 1981 ADELPHI US
JOHN BADANJEK D (B
DENNIS KOVARIK B (B — DR JOHN K (B — WAYNE COOK K (B
SNEAKY PETE KLEINOW STEEL (B — BONNIE RAITT G (B — JAMES MONTGOMERY HARP (B
BOB SCARF WIND (B — COTTON KENT K (C — FREEBO V (C
JIM THACKERY G (C — JOHN LEE D (C — DUANE CAMPBELL B (C
DAVID NAMERDY G (C — JIMMY POWERS HCA (C — DIANA CRAWFORD V (C
DIXIE D BALLIN V (C — JAMES COTTON HCA (C — DOUG FAGAN SAX (C
JAMIE MACKINNON SAX (C — SAVOY BEARD SAX (C — GEORGE McWHIRTER TROM (C
BOB BABITCH PNO (A — WILLIAM LANDLESS B (A — AL WERNEKEN G (A
DAVE CHAMBERS D (A — JIM McCARTY G (A — CARTER THRELKELD TROM (A

C60			CATHARSIS	C60
PATRICK MOULIA	G K V	(ABCGHK	(A) CATHARSIS	19 DISCODIS FR AZSH 1025
CHARLIE EDDI	D	(ABCFGHKN	(A) CATHARSIS	19 SARAVAH 10025
YVES DE ROUBAIX	G V	(ABCGHKN	(B) CATHARSIS 2	19 DISCODIS FR AZSH 1035
ROLAND BOCQUET	K V	(ABCFGJK	(B) CATHARSIS 2	19 SARAVAH 10035
ALAIN GEOFFROY	K V	(ACGH	(C) CATHARSIS	19 EXPLOSIVE 558 004
CHARLOTTE	V VLN	(ACGK	(D) POP POEMS	19 528002
NILES BROWN	G VLN	(AG	(E) RIMBAUD C'EST TOI	19 PATHE FR 064 11473
CLAUDE	G SITAR	(F	(F) LE BOLERO DU VEAU DES DAMES	19 SONOPRESSE FR ST 69612
MICHEL	B	(F	(G) VOL 1 MASQ	19 FESTIVAL FR 650
			(H) VOL 2 LES CHEVRONS	19 FESTIVAL FR 651
			(J) 32 MARS	19 MUSIDISC FR 600507
			(J) 32 MARS	19 FESTIVAL FR 652
			(K) VOL 4 ILLUMINATIONS	19 FESTIVAL FR 655
			(L) VOL 5 LE BOLERO	19 FESTIVAL FR 676
			(M) VOL 6 ET S'AIMER	19 FESTIVAL FR 678
			(N) ET S'AIMER ET MOURIR	19 MUSIDISC FR FLD 678

C61			PHILIP CATHERINE	C61
PHILIP CATHERINE	G B K	(ALL	(A) STREAM	1972 WB FR 46049
LARRY CORYELL	G	(DE	(B) SEPTEMBER MAN	1974 WB GERM 46562
PALLE MIKKELBORG	TPT	(B	(C) GUITARS	1975 ATLANTIC UK K 50193
CHARLIE MANIANO	WIND	(BC	(D) TWIN HOUSE	1977 ATLANTIC UK K 50342
JOHN LEE	B	(BC	(E) SPLENDID	1978 ATLANTIC UK K 52086
GERRY BROWN	D	(BC	(F) BABEL	1980 ELEKTRA 52244
ROB FRANKEN	K	(C		
JASPER VAN HOF	K	(BC		

C61A			CATS (1)	C61A
DANNY WESTON	G	(A	(A) CATS	1980 ELEKTRA NL 52239 US 6E 275
DENNIS TILLI	B	(A		
FRED ZARRA	K SYN V	(A	MICHAEL CORR V (A	PETER KELTZ G (A
TOMMY STEWART	D V	(A		

C61B			CATS (2)	C61B
AL CAPPS		(A	(A) LOVE IN YOUR EYES	1979 FANTASY US 9447 EMI NL 25100
GORDON MARRON		(A		
REID DEILICH		(A	PIET VEERMAN (A	ARNOLD MUHREN (A
CEES VEERMAN		(A	BEN BENAY G (A	CRAIG FALL G (A
KING ERRISSON	PERC	(A	LARRY MUHOBERAC K (A	MICHAEL OMARTIAN K (A
TOM HENSLEY	K	(A	EARLE DUMLER WIND (A	BUDDY EMMONS STEEL (A
ROBERT HARDAWAY	K	(A	PAUL HUBINON TPT (A	CHARLES FINDLEY TPT (A
DALTON SMITH	TPT	(A	REINIE PRESS B (A	JOHN RAINES D (A
JOHN ROTELLA	SAX	(A		

C62			FELIX CAVALIERE	C62
FELIX CAVALIERE	V K	(AB	(A) FELIX	1974 BEARSVILLE US 6955
EARL FORD	TROM	(B	(B) DESTINY	1975 BEARSVILLE UK K55505 US 6958
ED LOGAN	SAX	(B	(C) CASTLES IN THE AIR	1979 EPIC 35990 UK 83817
EN BISCHEL	SYN	(B		
BUZZ FEITEN	G	(B	STEVE KHAN G (B	MERVIN BRONSON B (B
JACK SCARANGELLLA	D	(B	GEORGE YOUNG SAX (B	GAIL BOGGS V (B
RICK MAROTTA	D	(B	ALAN RUBIN TPT (B	WAYNE ANDRE SAX (A
JOE FARRELL	SAX	(B	TONY JIMINEZ PERC (B	DIANE SCANLON V (B
EDGAR MATTHEWS	TPT	(B	LAURA NYRO V (B	DARCY MILLER V (B
WILL LEE	B	(B	DINO DANELLI D (B	MICHAEL BRECKER SAX (B
DAVE SANBORN	SAX	(B	TOM MALONE TROM (B	JEFF SOUTHWORTH G (B
LESLIE WEST	G	(B	VICTOR MATTSON SAX (B	ELLIOT RANDALL G (B
EDDIE RIVERA	B	(B	NANCY O'NEILL V (B	

C62A			ANDRE CECCARELLI	C62A
ANDRE CECCARELLI	D	(A	(A) ANDRE CECCARELLI	19 SONOPRESSE FR 500 002
JANNIK TOP		(	(B) CECCARELLI	1979 INNER US 1057
HENRI GIORDANO		(A		
FRANCOIS JEANNEAU		(A	DIDIER LOCKWOOD (A	CHRISTIAN ESCOUDE (A
JEAN CLAUDE CHAVANAT			(A ALEX LIGERTWOOD (A	

C62B			CELEBRATION	C62B
RON ALTBACH	K	(A	(A) CELEBRATION	1978 PACIFIC ARTS US PAC7 122
CHARLES LLOYD	SAX	(A		
KIM CALKINS	D	(A	PAUL FAUERSO K V (A	DAVE ROBINSON V (A
TIM WESTON	G	(A	KEVIN BRANDON B (A	AL PERKINS G (A
MIKE LOVE	V	(A	WELLS KELLY (A	ED CARTER (A
GARY GRIFFIN	K	(	MIKE KOWALSKI D (	STEVE LEACH V (A
IRENE CATHAWAY	V	(A	LINDA MALLAH V (A	SUZANNE WALLACH V (A

C62C			CELLATRON & THE INVISIBLE	C62C
CELLUTRON	SYN K	(A	(A) REFLECTING ON THE FIRST WATCH	1978 GREEN MOUNTAIN US 4015
INDIANA STRAIGHT	G	(A		
SPACEBOY	SYN	(A	D TSIORBAS SYN (A	A TSIERBAS SYN V (A

C62D			CENTAURUS	C62D
JOEY BELFIORE	D	(A	(A) CENTAURUS	1978 AZRA US 61549
NICK PAINE	G	(A		
LOUIS MERLINO	V	(A	NICK COSTELLO B (A	

C63			CENTIPEDE	C63
JOHN MARSHALL	D	(A	(A) SEPTOBER ENERGY	1971 NEON NE9
TONY FENNELL	D	(A	(A) SEPTOBER ENERGY REISSUE	1974 RCA DPS 5042
ROBERT WYATT	D	(A		
BRIAN GODDING	G	(A	BRIAN BELSHAW B (A	MAGGIE NICHOLLS V (A
JULIE TIPPETT	V	(A	MIKE PATTO V (A	BOZ BURRELL V (A
MONGEZI FEZA	HRN	(A	ALAN SKIDMORE SAX (A	ROY BABBINGTON B (A
MARK CHARIG	CORNET	(A	LARRY STABBINS SAX (A	JILL LYONS B (A
MICK COLLINS	TPT	(A	GARY WINDO SAX (A	HARRY MILLER B (A
PETER PARKES	TPT	(A	BRIAN SMITH SAX (A	JEFF CLYNE B (A
ELTON DEAN	SAX	(A	DAVE WHITE SAX (A	DAVE MARKEE B (A
JAN STEEL	SAX	(A	KARL JENKINS SAX (A	KEITH TIPPETT PNO (A
IAN McDONALD	SAX	(A	JOHN WILLIAMS SAX (A	IAN CARR TPT (A
DUDU PUKWANA	SAX	(A	LARGE STRING SECTION (A	

C63A

CERTAIN RAT10

C63A

(A) TO EACH ... 19 FACTORY UK FACT 35

C63B

CERVELLO

C63B

(A) MELOS 1973 DISCHI RICORDI IT 6119

ANTONIO SPANGNOLO G B (A
GIULIO D'AMBROSIA WIND (A
GIANLUIGI DI FRANCE V FLT(A
CORRADO RUSTICI G V FLT (A
REMIGIO ESPOSITE D (A

C63C

CESAR

C63C

(A) CESAR 830 1975 FLYING DUTCHMAN US 0830

CESAR ASCARRUNZ PNO (A
MARK LEVINE PNO (A
MERL SANDERS PNO (A
JOE JAMMER G (A
MARTIN FIERRE SAX (A
STEVE MARCUS SAX (A
HAROLD MARTIN B (A
STEPHEN BUSFIELD G (A
HADLEY CALIMAN WIND (A
THOMAS RUTLEY B (A
JIM VINCENT G (A
JOSEPH ELLI JR TPT (A

C63D

PETER CETERA

C63D

(A) PETER CETERA 1981 FULL MOON FMH 3624

PETER CETERA G V (A
STEVE LUKATHER G (A
MICHAEL BODDICKER SYN (A
CHRIS PINNICK G (A
CRAIG HULL G (A
KENNY EDWARDS G (A
JOSH LEO G (A
RICH EAMES K (A
DAVID WOLINSKI SYN (A
MICHAEL BOTTS D (A
RICKY FATAAR D (A
MARK GOLDENBERG G (A
BOB GLAUB B (A
CRAIG DOERGE K (A
CARL WILSON G (A
WILLIAM SMITH K (A

C64

CHA LAWA

C64

(A) EXODUS DUB 1978 SKYNOTE

CHA LAWA (A

C64A

CHACALS DE BETHUNE

C64A

(A) LA MALEDICTION DES ROCKERS 197 BARCLAY FR 521194

C64B

CHAD & JEREMY

C64B

(A) BEFORE & AFTER 1964
(B) I DONT WANNA LOOSE YOU BABY 1965 EMBER 5031
(C) BEST OF 1967 EMBER 5036
(D) MORE 1966
(E) DISTANT SHORES 1966 CBS
(F) OF CABBAGES & KINGS 1967 CBS US 9471 2671
(G) THE ARK 1968 CBS US 9699

CHAD STUART G V (ALL
JEREMY CLYDE G V (ALL

C65

CHAIN

C65

(A) TWO OF A KIND 1973 MUSHROOM AUST 35017

JAMES MADISON G V (A
PHIL MANNING G (A
IAN CLYNE K (A
GREG LAWRIE G (A
GEORGE BEAUFORD HCA V (A
BARRY HARVEY D (A
BARRY SULLIVAN B (A
MAL CAPEWELL WIND (A

C66

CHAIN REACTION

C66

(A) INDEBTED TO YOU 1977 GULL GULP1021

C67

CHAIRMEN OF THE BOARD

C67

(A) CHAIRMEN OF THE BOARD 1970 INVICTUS UK SVT 1002
(A) CHAIRMEN OF THE BOARD 1970 INVICTUS US 7300
(B) IN SESSION 1971 INVICTUS UK SVT 1003
(B) IN SESSION 1971 INVICTUS US 7304
(C) BITTERSWEET 1972 INVICTUS UK SVT 1006
(D) GREATEST HITS 1973 INVICTUS UK SVT 1009
(E) SKIN I'M IN 1974 INVICTUS UK 65868
(E) SKIN I'M IN 1974 INVICTUS US 35526
(F) MEN ARE GETTING SCARCE 19 INVICTUS US 9801

GENERAL NORMAN JOHNSON V (
EDDIE CURTIS V (
HARRISON KENNEDY V (
DANNY WOODS V (

C68

CHALLENGERS

C68

(A) SURFBEAT 1963 STATESIDE UK SL 10030
(A) SURFBEAT 1963 VAULT US 100
(B) SURFING WITH THE CHALLENGERS 196 VAULT US 101
(C) TEENAGE FAIR 196 GNP US 2010
(D) MAN FROM UNCLE 196 GNP US 2018
(E) CALIFORNIA KICKS 196 GNP US 2025
(F) WIPE OUT 1967 VOCALION SAVN 8069
(F) WIPE OUT 1966 GNP US 2031
(G) 25 GREATEST HITS 1967 GNP US 609
(H) LIGHT MY FIRE 1969 GNP US 2045
(J) VANILLA FUNK 1970 GNP US 2056
(K) WHERE WERE YOU THE SUMMER OF 62 19 FANTASY US 9443
(L) BEST OF 1982 RHINO US RNLP 053

RICHARD DELVECCHIO(DELVY) D(ABF
GLENN GREY G (AB
JIM ROBERTS K (AB
RANDY NAVERT B (ABF
DON LANDIS G (AB
NICK HEFNER SAX (B
ED FOURNIER G (F
ART FISHER G (F

C68A

CATHY CHAMBERLAIN

C68A

(A) RAG'N ROLL REVUE 1976 BUDDAH US 5686
(B) RAG'N ROLL REVUE 1977 WB US 3032

CATHY CHAMBERLAIN V CONC(AB
FRED MOORE D V (AB
STU BROWN B HRNS(A
KAL DAVIS G (A
MARIA MULDAUR V FDL(A
JOHN MILLER B (A
KENNY DAVERN WIND (B
MILT HINTON B (B
ELLIOTT RANDALL G (B
RICHARD LOOK K V (AB
HARVEY BROOKS B (A
LOUIE MATCALF TPT (A
WARREN VACHE JR CORNET (B
JACK GALE TROM (B
NEIL JASON B (B
TONY PARENTI CLAR(A
BILLY FAIER BAN (A
LARRY PACKER STR (A
KASH MONET D (B
HOWARD JOHNSON D HRNS(B
DAVID BROMBERG G (B

C69

CHAMBERS BROTHERS

C69

(A) PEOPLE GET READY 1965 VAULT US 9003
(A) PEOPLE GET READY 1966 VOCALION UK SAVL 8058
(B) NOW 1966 VAULT US 115
(C) SHOUT 1968 VAULT US 120
(D) THE TIME HAS COME TODAY 1968 CBS US 9522
(D) THE TIME HAS COME TODAY 1968 DIRECTION UK 63407
(E) A NEW TIME A NEW DAY 1968 CBS US 9671
(E) A NEW TIME A NEW DAY 1968 DIRECTION UK 63451
(E) A NEW TIME A NEW DAY 1968 CBS US 33642
(F) LIVE AT FILLMORE EAST 1970 CBS US 20
(G) FEELING THE BLUES 1970 LIBERTY UK LBS83276
(G) FEELING THE BLUES 1970 VAULT US 128
(H) A NEW GENERATION 1971 CBS US 30032

LESTER CHAMBER V HCA (ALL
WILLIE CHAMBERS G V (ALL
GEORGE CHAMBERS B (ALL
JOE CHAMBERS G V (ALL
WITH
BRIAN KEENAN D (
STEVE CROPPER G (O

(CONTINUED)

C69 (CONTINUED)

CHAMBERS BROTHERS C69

Record	Year	Label	Country	No.
(H) A NEW GENERATION	1971	CBS	UK	64156
(I) OH MY GOD	1972	CBS	US	31158
(J) UNBONDED	1973	AVCO	US	11013
(K) LOVE PEACE & HAPPINESS	1974	CBS	US	KGP20
(K) LOVE PEACE & HAPPINESS	1974	CBS	UK	66228
(L) RIGHT MOVE	1975	AVCO	US	69003
( ) BEST OF	19	MUSIDISC	FR	6018
(DE) TIME HAS COME/NEW DAY DBL	19	CBS	US	33642
( ) THE BEST OF	19	FANTASY	US	24718
( ) GREATEST HITS	19	CBS US 30871	VAULT	135
(O) LIVE IN CONCERT ON MARS	1977	CHELSEA 548 ROXBURY		106

C69A CHAMELEON CHURCH C69A

TED NYERS G V (A
TONY SCHEUREN G B V(A
KYLE GARRAHAN V G K B(A
CHEVY CHASE V D K(A

(A) CHAMELEON CHURCH 1968 MGM 4574

C69B CHAMPAIGN C69B

PAULIE CARMAN V (A
RENA JONES V (A
ROCKY MAFFITT PERC (A
DANA WALDEN K (A
MICHAEL DAY K G (A
MICHAEL REED B (A
HOWARD REEDER G (A

(A) CHAMPAIGN 1981 CBS

C70 CHAMPION C70

GARY BELL V G (A
CLEM CLEMPSON G (A
DAMON BUTCHER K (A
JEFF RICH D (A
WILLIE BATH B (A
GEOFF BRITTON D (A

(A) CHAMPION 1978 EPIC US 35438 UK 83179

C70A BILL CHAMPLIN C70A

BILL CHAMPLIN V G K(A
KENNY LOGGINS PROD V(A
JOHN ROBINSON D (A
JON PIERCE B (A
ED GREENE D (A
LARRY TOLBERT D (A
VENNETTE GLOUD V (A
HUMBERT GATICA PERC (A
CHUCK FINDLEY TPT (A
BILL REICHENBACH TROM (A
CARMEN GRILLO V (A
JAMES NEWTON HOWARD STR (A
STEVE LUKATHER G (A
RICHARD PAGE V (A
ABRAHAM LABORIEL B (A
GARY HERBIG SAX (A
TOM SCOTT SAX (A
KIM HUTCHCROFT SAX (A
CHARLIE LOPER TROM (A
JEFF PORCARO D (A
DAVID FOSTER PROD SYN V D K(A
TOM KELLY V (A
PAUL LANI PERC (A
JAY GRAYDON G (A
JERRY HEY HRNS (A
GARY GRANT TPT (A
LARRY WILLIAMS SAX (A
TAMARA MATOESIAN V (A
LEE SKLAR B (A

(A) RUNAWAY 1981 ELEKTRA US 5E563

C71 CHAMPS C71

GLEN CAMPBELL G
CHUCK RIO SAX
BOBBY MORRIS B
DAVE BURGESS G
JIMMY SEALS SAX
DALE NORRIS G
DEAN BEARD PNO
GENE ALDEN D
VAN NORMAN B
DASH CROFTS D

Record	Year	Label	Country	No.
( ) EVERYBODY'S ROCKIN'	1960	CHALLENGE US 605		2500
( ) GO CHAMPS GO	196	LONDON	UK	HAH 2152
( ) GO CHAMPS GO	196	CHALLENGE	US	601
( ) GREAT DANCE HITS	196	LONDON	UK	HAH 2451
( ) GREAT DANCE HITS	196	CHALLENGE	US	613
( ) BEST OF THE CHAMPS	1977	LONDON	UK	ZGH 141
( ) PLAY ALL AMERICAN	19	CHALLENGE	US	2514
( ) PLAY JOSHUA LOGAN ALL AMERICAN	19	CHALLENGE	US	614

C72 GENE CHANDLER C72

GENE CHANDLER V (ALL
CLIFF DAVIS SAX (L
JONI BERLMON V (M
THERESA DAVIS V (M
RHONDA GRAISON V (M

Record	Year	Label	Country	No.
GENE CHANDLER	1967	CHECKER		3003
THERE WAS A TIME	197	MCA	UK	MUPS 367
THERE WAS A TIME	19	BRUNSWICK	US	754131
ALBUM	1974	JOY		JOYS 136
DUKE OF EARL	1976	DJM		DJB 26077
GET DOWN	19	20TH CENTURY	US	578
LIVE ON STAGE	19	ACTION		6010
WHEN YOU'RE No1	1979	20TH CENTERY	UK	598
SITUATION	1970	MERCURY	US	SR 61304
THE GIRL DONT CARE	19	BRUNSWICK	US	54124
TWO SIDES OF	19	BRUNSWICK	US	754149
(L)GET DOWN	19	20TH CENTURY	US	578
(M)GENE CHANDLER	1980	20TH CENTURY	US	605
JUST BE TRUE	1980	CHARLY	UK	1007
NOTHING CAN STOP ME (EP)	1980	CHARLY	UK	CTD 116

C72A CHANGO C72A

GEORGE TACKTIKES G V (A
REINEL ANDINE PERC V(A
PEPE GOMEZ D V (AB
MIKE CRUZ PERC V(B
THOMAS ALLETTO K V (A
MARTY GREBB SAX K(B
KEN WEISSMAN D (B
CHARLES ROOK G (B
BURLIN SPEAKES G B V (AB
MICHAEL BRITTON PERC (A

(A) CHANGO 1975 ABC US 872
(B) HONEY IS SWEETER THAN BLOOD 1976 MERCURY US 1103

C73 BRUCE CHANNEL C73

BRUCE CHANNELL V (ALL

HEY BABY 19 SMASH US 27008
GOIN BACK TO LOUISIANA 19 SONET SNT 301

C74 CHANTAYS C74

BRIAN CARMAN
BOB MARSHALL
WARREN WATERS
BOB WELCH
BOB SPICKARD

PIPELINE 1963 LONDON UK 8087 DOT US 25516
PIPELINE 1974 CONTOUR UK 2879 389

C74A CHANTELS C74A

WE ARE THE CHANTELS 19 END US 301
HERE'S OUR SONG AGAIN 19 END US 312

C75 CHANTERS SISTERS C75

DOREEN CHANTER K V (ALL
IRENE CHANTER K V (ALL
RAY WARLEIGH WIND (D
PETE WINGFIELD K (D
HENRY SPINETTI D (D
DAVE MARKEE B (D
RAY RUSSELL G (D
MICK MOODY G (D

Record	Year	Label	Country	No.
(A) BIRDS OF A FEATHER	1970	PAGE ONE	UK	POLS 027
(B) FIRST FLIGHT	1976	POLYDOR UK6075	UK	2383 382
(C) READY FOR LOVE	1978	SAFARI		LONG 3
(D) SHOULDER TO SHOULDER	1978	SAFARI		LONG 4

(CONTINUED)

C75 CHANTER SISTERS (CONTINUED) C75

Name	Instr	Albums
SIMON PHILLIPS	D	(D
RAY COOPER	PERC	(BD
MARTIN DROVER	WIND	(D
NEIL HUBBARD	G	(B
MIKE MORAN	K	(B
KENNY MALONE	D PERC	(C
JIMMY COUARD	G	(C
CHARLES COCHRAN	K	(C
RONNIE EADES	SAX	(C
JOHN GIBLIN	B	(D
HUGH BURNS	G	(BD
JIMMY CHAMBERS	V	(D
BARRY MORGAN	D	(B
JEFF DALY	SAX	(B
MIKE LEECH	B	(C
JOHNNY CHRISTOPHER	G	(C
HARVEY THOMPSON	HRNS	(C
GARY BROWN	SAX	(C
TONY HYMAS	CLAR PNO	(D
CHRIS MERCER	SAX	(D
TONY JACKSON	V	(D
HERBIE FLOWERS	B	(B
MADELINE BELL	V	(B
REGGIE YOUNG	G	(C
BOBBY WOODS	K	(C
HARRISON CALLAWAY	HRNS	(C

C76 HARRY CHAPIN C76

Name	Instr	Albums
HARRY CHAPIN	G V	(ALL
TIM SCOTT	CELLO	(CEGH
JOHN WALLACE	B V	(BCEGHKLFJ
PAUL LEKA	K	(CEG
JEANNE FRENCH	V	(C
BUDDY SALZMAN	D	(C
HOWIE FIELDS	D	(HGKLFJ
JOHN TROPEA	G	(EG
TOM CHAPIN	G BANJ	(GHLJ
STEVE CHAPIN	PNO V	(EGHFKLJ
ALLEN SCHWARZBERG	D	(EG
ED BEDNARSKI	CLAR	(EG

Album	Year	Label
(A) HEADS & TALES	1971	ELEKTRA US EKS75023 UK K42107
(B) SNIPER & OTHER LOVE SONGS	1972	ELEKTRA US EKS75042 UK K42125
(C) SHORT STORIES	1973	ELEKTRA US EKS75065 UK K42155
(D) VERITIES & BALDERDASH	1974	ELEKTRA US 7E 1012 UK K52007
(E) PORTRAIT GALLERY	1975	ELEKTRA US 7E 1041 UK K52023
(F) ON THE ROAD TO KINGDOM COME	1976	ELEKTRA US 7E 1082 UK K52040
(G) GREATEST STORIES LIVE	1976	ELEKTRA US 7E 2009 UK K62017
(H) DANCE BAND ON THE TITANIC	1977	ELEKTRA US 9E 301 UK K62021
(J) LIVING ROOM SUITE	1978	ELEKTRA US 6E 142 UK K52089
(K) LEGENDS OF THE LOST & FOUND	1979	ELEKTRA UK K62026
(L) SEQUEL	1980	BOADWALK US 36872 CBS UK 84996

Name	Instr	Albums
FRANK PORTO	ACC	(E
BOB SPRINGER	PERC	(EG
GEORGE SIMS	V	(EG
DAVE KONZIELA	V	(E
BOB SMITH		(EG
SUE WHITE	V	(EG
MARTY McCALL	V	(E
JIM KELTNER	D	(J
BILL PAYNE	K	(J
DAVID BURGEN	HCA	(J
TOM SMITH		(G
GEOFF PARKER	V	(E
BUD BRISBOIS	WIND	(E
GEORG BOHANON	WIND	(E
STEVE GADD	D	(H
ARTHUR JENKINS	PERC	(H
CRAIG MITCHELL	V	(H
JOHN QUAYLE	V	(H
BARBARA LINDQUIST	V	(H
DON PAYNE	B	(EG
MICHAEL MASTERS	CELLO	(CEG
CHUCK KIRKPATRICK	V	(L
DONNA RHODES	V	(L
CAROLYN DENNIS	V	(F
THE COWSILLS	V	(J
DONNA D REILLY	V	(H
KRIS KRISTOFFERSON	V	(E
ELLIOT RANDALL	G	(H
FRANK SIMMS	V	(E
PAUL GABRIEL		(EG
KATHY RAMOS	V	(EG
JACKIE WARD	V	(E
NEIL JASON	B	(J
ERNIE WATTS	SAX	(J
STEVE MADAIO	TPT	(J
TIM MOORE	K	(EG
JOAN FISHMAN	V	(E
JACKIE KELSO	WIND	(EJ
CHRISTINE FAITH	V	(G
NEIL JASON	B	(H
CHRIS WAITE	PERC	(H
THEODORE MARNEL	V	(H
ART KRAHULCK	V	(H
BERNIE KEISING	V	(H
BOBBY CARLIN	D	(C
RON PALMER	G V	(CEGH
HOWARD ALBERT	SYN	(L
RON EVANUIK	CELLO	(F
BOBBYE HALL	PERC	(F
DIXIE HUMMINGBIRDS	V	(J
ROB WHITEWHISTLE		(E
RITA COOLIDGE	V	(E
DOUG WALKER	G B	(GH
RON BACCHIOCCHI	PERC	(EG
JIMMY KEYES		(EG
KATHY PORTER	V	(F
CHERYL FERRIO	V	(G
LOU VOLPE	G	(J
DENNIS FRICK	WIND	(J
CHUCK FINDLEY	TPT	(J
SHEILA TURNER	V	(E
JUDI PARKER	V	(E
JAY MIGLIORI	WIND	(E
MARY MUNDY	V	(G
BUZZ BRAUNER	SAX	(H
VICTORIA	CONGA	(H
STEVE RANDALL	V	(H
BARBRA CARR	V	(H
STEVE CHAPIN	PNO V	(EGHKL
TOMI LEE BRADLEEY	V	(C
YVONNE CABLE	CELLO	(L
CHARLES CHALMERS	V	(L
DONNA FEIN	V	(F
BUZZ BRAUNER	REC	(F
KEN SMITH	PERC	(EG
BILLY SWAN	V	(E
DON PEAK	SYN	(E
SCOTT SPRAY		(EG
GENE BIANCO	HARP	(E
CAROLYN WILLIS	V	(E
JEFF GROSS	V	(EH
BOB COWSILL	G	(J
STEVE FORMAN	PERC	(J
GEORGE BOHANNON	TROM	(J
J FLOOD	V	(E
PAUL HUBINON	WIND	(E
JIM HORN	SAX	(E
BETSY WAGER	V	(G
HARRY DEVITO	TROM	(H
NANCY NEWMAN	V	(H
MARSH LYNN GOLDBERG	V	(H
MIKE SOLOMON	V	(H
DAVE ARMSTRONG	HCA	(C
KIM SCHOLES	CELLO	(HKJ
JOE LALA	PERC	(L
SANDRA RHODES	V	(L
MUFFY HENDRIX	V	(F
DICK HYDE	TROM	(J

C77 BLONDIE CHAPLIN C77

Name	Instr	Albums
BLONDIE CHAPLIN	V G B PERC	(A
RICKY FATAAR	D PERC	(A
DAVID MASON	PNO	(A
JOHN HARTMAN	PNO	(A
HOWARD TSUKAMOTO	B	(A
BRYAN GAROFALO	B	(A
KENNY GRADNEY	B	(A
MATTHEW MOORE	V	(A
RICHARD TEE	K	(A
STEVE LAWRENCE	SAX	(A
TOM BRAY	HRNS	(A
CLYDIE KING	V	(A
DANIEL MOORE	V	(A
RITA JEAN BODINE	V	(A
GARTH HUDSON	ACC	(A
KENNY WALTER	TROM	(A
CARLOS MUNOZ	ORG	(A
VANEETA FIELDS	V	(A
CAROL HOLMES	V	(A

Album	Year	Label
(A) BLONDIE CHAPLIN	1977	ASYLUM US 1095 UK K53062

C77A MARSHALL CHAPMAN C77A

Name	Instr	Albums
MARSHALL CHAPMAN	G V	(ALL
MIKE DESPAPAS	G	(BC
JEFF SMITH	G V	(BC
WILLIS BAILEY	D	(D
TOM COMET	B	(B
TERRY McMILLAN	PERC HCA	(C
BUDDY EMMONS	STEEL	(A
BILLY PUETT	HRNS	(A
LEA JANE BERINATI	V	(A
JAMES BURTON	G	(B
FRED NEWELL	G	(C
STEVE SCHAFFER	B	(C
REGGIE YOUNG	G	(A
JERRY CARRIGAN	D	(A
ANITA BALL	V	(A
AL KOOPER	K G B	(B
RON HICKLIN SINGERS	V	(B
MARY ANN KENNEDY	V	(C
JERRY KREEN	D	(C
TEDDY IRWIN	G	(A
HARGUS PIG ROBBINS	PNO	(A
GINGER HOLLADAY	V	(A
PHIL AABERG	PNO	(B
BILLY SANFORD	G	(C
PAM ROSE	V	(C
BOBBY EMMONS	K	(C
TED REYNOLDS	B	(A
YVONNE HODGES	V	(A
JANIE FRICKE	V	(A
DAVID WILCZEWSKI	SAX	(B
PETE DRAKE	STEEL	(C
ERNIE ROWELL	V	(C

Album	Year	Label
(A) ME I'M FEELIN FREE	1977	EPIC US 34422
(B) JADED VIRGIN	1978	EPIC US 35341
(C) MARSHALL	1979	EPIC US 36192

C78 MICHAEL CHAPMAN C78

Name	Instr	Albums
MICHAEL CHAPMAN	G K V	(ALL
WITH		
RAY LAIDLAW	D	(N
RICK KEMP	B	(ABCDEFGKM
BARRY MORGAN	D	(ABK
ANDY LATIMER	G	(HJ
DANNY THOMPSON		(A
CLEM CLEMPSON	G	(AK
NORMAN HAINES		(AK
ALEX DMOCHOWSKI	B	(AK
AYNSLEY DUNBAR	D	(AK
MICK RONSON	G	(ABJK
GUS DUDGEON		(B
PAUL BUCKMASTER	CELLO	(B
JOHNNY VAN DERRICK	VLN	(BCG
ANDRU CHAPMAN	V	(N
B J COLE	STEEL	(J
HAROLD FATT	G	(CK
PETE WINGFIELD	K	(J
PRELUDE	V	(F
JACK EMBLOW	ACC	(D
JOHN McBURNIE	V	(J
ALEX ATTERSON	PNO	(CE
LIZA STRIKE	V	(D
RICHIE DHARMA	D	(CK
PICK WITHERS	D	(DK
CLAUDETTE HOUCHEN	V	(D
VIV McAULIFFE	V	(J
RAY MARTINEZ	G	(DK
NEIL LANCASTER	V	(D

Album	Year	Label
(A) RAINMAKER	1969	HARVEST UK SHVL 755
(B) FULLY QUALIFIED SURVIVOR	1969	HARVEST US 816 UK SHVL 764
(B) FULLY QUALIFIED SURVIVOR	1979	CRIMINAL UK TAKE3
(C) WINDOW	1971	HARVEST UK SHVL 786
(D) WRECKED AGAIN	1971	HARVEST UK SHVL 798
(D) WRECKED AGAIN	1971	POLYDOR GERM 2310 192
(E) MILLSTONE GRIT	1973	HARVEST UK SML 1105
(F) DEAL GONE DOWN	1974	HARVEST UK SML 1114
(G) PLEASURES OF THE STREET	1975	NOVA GERM 622321
(H) SAVAGE AMUSEMENT	1976	GAMA DECCA UK SKLR 5242
(J) THE MAN WHO HATED MORNINGS	1977	DECCA UK SKLR 5290
(J) THE MAN WHO HATED MORNINGS	1978	CRIMINAL UK STEAL3
(K) LIVED HERE	1977	CUBE UK GNAT 1
(L) PLAYING GUITAR THE EASY WAY	1979	CRIMINAL UK STEAL2
(M) LIFE ON THE CEILING	1978	CRIMINAL US 7138 UK STEAL5
(N) LOOKING FOR ELEVEN	1980	CRIMINAL UK STEAL9
( ) LADY ON THE ROCKS	19	INTERCORD GER 126 309

(CONTINUED)

C78 (CONTINUED)

MICHAEL CHAPMAN C78

ALBERT HAMMOND V (D KEEF HARTLEY D (EGHJ NIGEL PEGRUM D (F MADDY PRIOR V (F
BRIDGET ST JOHN V (F PETER WOOD K (H LEO LE BLANC STEEL(H MUTT (GH
STEVIE V (GH FUZZ V (GH STEFFI STEFAN (G ACHIM REICHEL (G
PAUL SUTTON G (G ROD CLEMENTS B (JN ANDY ROBERTS G (HENRY McCULLOUGH G (
TIM RENWICK G (H PHIL PALMER G (M ANDY RICHARDS K (M DAVE MATTACKS D (M
DAVY WOOD K (N LESLEY DUNCAN V (M AL HODGE V (M

C79

ROGER CHAPMAN C79

ROGER CHAPMAN V (ALL (A) CHAPPO 1979 ARISTA UK SPART1083 LINE GER 5097
WITH (B) LIVE IN HAMBURG 1979 ACROBAT UK ACRO 6 LINE GER 5103
DAVE MARKEE B (A (C) MAIL ORDER MAGIC 1980 LINE GER 5080
BRIAN ODGERS B (A (D) HYENAS ONLY LAUGH FOR FUN 1981 LINE GER 5125
BILLY LIVSEY K (A (E) HE WAS SHE WAS....(DBL) 1982 LINE GER 6011
JOHN HALSEY D (C
LES BINKS D (C GEOFF WHITEHORN G (ABCDE MICK MOODY G (A HENRY SPINETTI D (A
SIMON MORTON PERC (A RAY COOPER PERC(A RON ASPERY SAX(A POLI PALMER SYN(ACDE
PETER HOPE EVANS HCA (A JOY YATES V (A VICKI BROWN V (A JIMMY CHAMBERS V (
GEORGE CHANDLER V (A MEL COLLINS SAX (B TIM HINKLEY K (BCDE JEROME RIMSON B V (BCD
JOHN WETTON B (C STRETCH D (BDE HELEN HARDY V (B KATHI O'DONOGHUE V (B
MITCH MITCHELL D (C STEVE SIMPSON VLN G (DE NICK PENTELOW SAX(DE ALAN COULTER D (D
BOZ BURRELL B (E

C80

CHARGE C80

ROSETTA HIGHTOWER V (A (A) CHARGE 1974 FRESH AIR 6308 900
LEE VANDERBILT V (A
MIKE WOODS G (A NEIL HUBBARD G (A ALAN SPENNER B (A
GODFREY MACLEAN D (A SMILEY DE JONNES PERC (A CHRIS STAINTON ORG (A
CHRIS MERCER SAX (A STEVE GREGORY SAS (A RON CARTHY TPT (A

C80A

MARK CHARIG C80A

MARK CHARIG TPT (A (A) PIPEDREAM 1977 OGUN OG710
KEITH TIPPETT K PERC V(A
ANN WINTER V (A

C80B

CHARIOT C80B

MICHAEL KOPLAN G V (A (A) CHARIOT 1968 NATIONAL GENERAL NG2003
LARRY GOULD B V
PUG BAKER D

C80C

CHARITY C80C

JEFF OXMAN V (A (A) NEW 1969 UNI 73061
BLOSSOMS V (A
WALT FLANNERY (A KENT HENRY G (A JAMES PETERS (A
JOHN CORTINAS (A

C81

CHARLATANS C81

DAN HICKS V D G (12 (A) THE CHARLATANS 1969 PHILIPS US 600 309
RICHARD OLSEN B (A123 (B) THE CHARLATANS 1979 GROUCHO IT MAR X
MICHAEL FERGUSON K (1 (1) 64 67 (2) 67 68 (C) 68 69
MIKE WILHELM V G (A123
PATRICK BOGERTY PNO (2 TERRY WILSON D (A23 DARRYL DEVORE K (A3
SAM LINDE D (1 GEORGE HUNTER V (12

C82

BOBBY CHARLES C82

BOBBY CHARLES(ROBERT GUIDRY)(A (A) BOBBY CHARLES 1972 BEARSVILLE US 2104 UK K45516
AMOS GARRETT G (A
DR JOHN K (A

C83

CHILI CHARLES C83

CHILLI CHARLES D V K (AB (A) BUSY CORNER 1974 VIRGIN UK V2009
DEL RICHARDSON G (AB (B) QUICKSTEP 1975 VIRGIN UK V2028
ROBERT BAILEY K (AB
JOE JAMMER G (B MEL COLLINS SAX (A GORDON SMITH G (A
FUZZY SAMUELS B (A PAT ARNOLD V (A KENNY COLE V (A
PHIL BECQUE B (A JEAN ROUSSEL B K (B BROTHER JAMES V (B
VICKY BUSISWE MHLONGO V (B GEORGE LARNYOH SAX (B EDDIE QUANSAH TPT (B
PETE VANDER PUIJE SAX (B JON PIRANA V (B SUZY SHUTE V (B

C84

RAY CHARLES C84

RAY CHARLES K V (ALL (EPs) HIT THE ROAD JACK 19 HMV 7EG 8729
I CANT STOP LOVING YOU 19 HMV 7EG 8781
BALLAD STYLE OF RAY CHARLES 19 HMV 7EG 8783
BALLAD STYLE OF RAY CHARLES 19 HMV GES 5864
SWINGING STYLE 19 HMV 7EG 8801
SWINGING STYLE 19 HMV GES 5871
BABY ITS COLD OUTSIDE 19 HMV 7EG 8807
TAKE THESE CHAINS 19 HMV 7EG 8812
BUSTED 19 HMV 7EG 8841
RAY CHARLES SINGS 19 HMV 7EG 8861

LPs

RAY CHARLES 1957 ATLANTIC 8006 IN PERSON 1960 ATLANTIC US 8039
RAY CHARLES (HALLELUJAH) 19 ATLANTIC UK 587056 IN PERSON 1960 LONDON UK 2284
THE GREAT R C 1958 ATLANTIC US 1259 GENIUS SINGS THE BLUES 1960 ATLANTIC 8052
THE GREAT R C 1958 LONDON UK 15134 GENIUS SINGS THE BLUES 1960 LONDON UK 15238
RAY CHARLES AT NEWPORT 1958 ATLANTIC 1289 DEDICATED TO YOU 1960 HMV UK 1362
RAY CHARLES AT NEWPORT 1958 LONDON UK 6008 DEDICATED TO YOU 1961 HMV UK 1449
RAY CHARLES AT NEWPORT 197 ATLANTIC UK K30032 DEDICATED TO YOU 1961 ABC UK 355
ORIGINAL RAY CHARLES 19 LONDON UK 8022 GENIUS+SOUL=JAZZ 1960 ATLANTIC A2
YES INDEED 1958 ATLANTIC 8025 GENIUS+SOUL=JAZZ 1961 HMV UK 1384
YES INDEED 1958 LONDON UK 2168 GENIUS+SOUL=JAZZ 1961 HMV UK 1475
WHAT'D I SAY 1959 ATLANTIC 8029 DO THE TWIST 196 ATLANTIC 8054
WHAT'D I SAY 1959 LONDON UK 2226 GENIUS HITS THE ROAD 196 ABC US 335
WHAT'D I SAY 19 ATLANTIC UK 588161 GENIUS HITS THE ROAD 1960 HMV UK 1387
WHAT'D I SAY 1971 ATLANTIC UK K40029 GENIUS HITS THE ROAD 1960 HMV UK 1320
GENIUS OF R C 1959 ATLANTIC 1312 & BETTY CARTER 1960 HMV UK 1520
RAY CHARLES 1959 XTRA 1103 & BETTY CARTER 1960 COLUMBIA 340742
SOUL BROTHERS 1959 LONDON UK 6030 & BETTY CARTER 196 ABC US 385
SOUL BROTHERS 19 ATLANTIC US 1279 & BETTY CARTER 196 HMV UK 1414
RAY CHARLES SEXTET 1960 LONDON UK 15178 MODERN SOUNDS IN C&W 196 HMV UK 1580
RAY CHARLES SEXTET 1960 ATLANTIC 1304 MODERN SOUNDS IN C&W 196 ABC US 410

(CONTINUED)

Title	Year	Label	Country	Number
MODERN SOUNDS IN C&W 2	196	HMV	UK	1613
MODERN SOUNDS IN C&W 2	196	ABC	US	435
SOUL MEETING(MILT JACKSON)	1962	ATLANTIC	US	1360
SOUL MEETING(MILT JACKSON)	197	ATLANTIC		K50234
SOUL MEETING(MILT JACKSON)	1963	LONDON	UK	8046
GREATEST HITS	1962	ABC	US	415
GREATEST HITS	196	HMV	UK	1482
GREATEST HITS	196	HMV	UK	1626
STORY VOL 1	1962	ATLANTIC		8063
STORY VOL 1	1962	LONDON	UK	8023
STORY VOL 2	1962	ATLANTIC		8064
STORY VOL 2	1962	LONDON	UK	8024
STORY VOL 3	1963	ATLANTIC		8083
GREAT HITS	1963	HMV	UK	1482
GREAT HITS	1963	ATLANTIC		7101
RECIPE FOR SOUL	1963	ABC	US	465
RECIPE FOR SOUL	1963	HMV	UK	1678
SWEET & SOUR TEARS	1963	ABC	US	480
SWEET & SOUR TEARS	1963	HMV	UK	1728
SWEET & SOUR TEARS	1963	HMV	UK	1537
C&W MEETS R&B	196	HMV	UK	1630
C&W MEETS R&B	196	HMV	UK	1914
STORY VOL 4	1964	ATLANTIC		8094
HAVE A SMILE WITH ME	1964	HMV	UK	1566
HAVE A SMILE WITH ME	1964	HMV	UK	1795
LIVE	196	ATLANTIC	US	2503
IN CONCERT	1965	HMV	UK	1872
IN CONCERT	1965	HMV	UK	1606
IN CONCERT	1965	ABC	US	500
TOGETHER AGAIN	1965	ABC	US	520
TOGETHER AGAIN	1965	HMV	UK	
SENSATIONAL	1965	SOCIETY		998
CINCINNATI KID	1965	MGM	US	SE4313
CRYING TIME	1966	HMV	UK	3533
CRYING TIME	1966	HMV	US	344
RAYS MOOD	1966	HMV	UK	3574
RAYS MOOD	1966	ABC	US	550
LISTEN	1967	HMV	UK	3630
LISTEN	1967	ABC	US	595
A MAN & HIS SOUL	1967	ABC		590
LE GRAND	196	ATLANTIC	FR	332030
IN THE HEAT OF THE NIGHT	1967	U A	US	5160
GREAT HITS (5LP SET)	19	LONGINES	US	95647
14 ORIGINAL HITS	19	STARDAY	US	K 5011
GREATEST HITS VOL 2	19	STATESIDE	UK	10241
LOVE COUNTRY STYLE	1969	PROBE		1015
LOVE COUNTRY STYLE	19	ABC		707
IM ALL YOURS BABY	1969	ABC		675
IM ALL YOURS BABY	1969	STATESIDE		10281
DOING HIS THING	1959	ABC	US	695
DOING HIS THING	1970	STATESIDE		10293
THE ARTISTRY OF	19	BARONET	US	111
3 OF A KIND	19	DESIGN	US	909
PORTRAIT OF RAY	1969	STATESIDE	UK	10269
PORTRAIT OF RAY	1969	ABC	US	625
MY KIND OF JAZZ	1970	TANGERINE		6495 001
FOCUS ON	1975	LONDON		F051/2
MY KIND OF JAZZ	1970	TANGERINE		TRCS1512
VOLCANIC ACTION	1971	PROBE		1039
VOLCANIC ACTION	1971	ABC	US	726
PRESENTS THE RAELETTES	1972	TANGERINE	US	1515
JAZZ NUMBER TWO	1973	TANGERINE	US	1516
MESSAGE FROM THE PEOPLE	1972	PROBE		1060
MESSAGE FROM THE PEOPLE	1972	ABC	US	755
25th ANNIVERSARY(DBL)	1972	ATLANTIC	UK	K60014
25th ANNIVERSARY(DBL)	1971	ABC	US	731
ORIGINAL RAY CHARLES	1972	BOULEVARD		4005
GENIUS IN CONCERT L A	1973	BLUESWAY		6053
ALLTIME GREAT C&W HITS	1973	PROBE	UK	108
THE FANTASTIC	19	MUSIDISC		ALB103
MEMORIES OF MOVIE FAN	19	ATLANTIC		SD 263
INCOMPARABLE	19	MUSIDISC		CV 964
STAR COLLECTION	1978	MIDI	FR	20015
BEST OF	19	POLYDOR		2472 044
THROUGH THE EYES OF LOVE	1973	PROBE	UK	1066
THROUGH THE EYES OF LOVE	1973	ABC	US	765
THE GREATEST HITS(5 LP SET)	1974	CROSSOVER		95647
COME LIVE WITH ME	1974	LONDON	UK	8467
ROCKIN WITH RAY	19	ARCH		358
COME LIVE WITH ME	1974	CROSSOVER		9000
WORLD OF RAY CHARLES VOL 2	1975	DECCA	UK	422
WORLD OF RAY CHARLES	1974	ARGO	UK	SPA361
LIVE IN JAPAN DBL	1975	CROSSOVER		535/6
RENAISSANCE	1975	LONDON	UK	8485
RENAISSANCE	1975	CROSSOVER		9005
MY KIND OF JAZZ VOL 3	1975	CROSSOVER		9007
THE GREAT R C	19	MUSIDISC		1232
HONEY HONEY	19	XTRA		1103
PORGY & BESS(CLEO LAINE)	1976	RCA	US	2 1831
PORGY & BESS(CLEO LAINE)	1976	LONDON		D 31/2
THE BEST OF	19	MCP	US	8029
RAY CHARLES	19	EVEREST	US	244
RAY CHARLES VOL2	19	EVEREST	US	292
RAY CHARLES	19	UPFRONT	US	UPF170
RAY CHARLES	19	UPFRONT	US	UPF192
TRUE TO LIFE	1977	LONDON		8509
TRUE TO LIFE	1977	ATLANTIC		19142
WHAT HAVE DONE TO THEIR SONG	1977	LONDON		ZGU 139
LOVE & PEACE	1978	LONDON		8519
BLUES	1978	EMBER	UK	CJS854
LOVE & PEACE	1978	ATCO		19199
FABULOUS RAY CHARLES	1978	MUSIDISC		CV1288
AIN'T IT SO	1979	LONDON	UK	SHL8537
SUPERDISC OF R C	1979	A&M		GXM9012
20 GOLDEN PIECES OF R C	1979	BULLDOG		BDL2012
BROTHER RAY	1980	ATLANTIC	US	19281

C84A RONNIE CHARLES C84A

RONNIE CHARLES (A
LOU REIZNER PROD (A
KEITH TIPPETT K (A
SPEEDY KEEN V (A
HERBIE FLOWERS B (A

(A) PRESTIDIGITION 1975 20CENTURY BT 491

C84B ROBERT CHARLEBOIS C84B

ROBERT CHARLEBOIS V (A
RICHARD PROVENCAL PERC (A
DANIEL HUBERT B (A
FRANK ZAPPA G (A
JEAN MARIE BENOIT K (A
MARCEL BEACHAMP K (A

(A) SWING CHARLEBOIS SWING 1977 RCA 6436

C85 CHARLIE C85

JOHN ANDERSON B V (ABCD
TERRY THOMAS G V (ABCD
STEVE GADD D PERC (ABCD
JULIAN COLBECK K (CD
EUGENE ORGAN G V (CD
GRAEME QUINTON-JONES K (A
MARTIN SMITH G V (A
SHEP LONSDALE D (D
VICTOR PAZ TPT (D
ARNIE LAWRENCE SAX (D
PHILLIP TODD FLT (D
LAWRENCE FELDMAN SAX (D
DAVID POTTS FLT (D
PETE THOMS TROM (D
RAY COOPER PERC (D

(A) FANTASY GIRLS 1976 POLYDOR UK 2382 373
(A) FANTASY GIRLS 1976 CBS US 34081
(B) NO SECOND CHANCE 1977 POLYDOR UK 2383 422
(B) NO SECOND CHANCE 1977 JANUS US 7032
(C) LINES 1978 POLYDOR UK 2383 487
(C) LINES 1978 JANUS UK 7036
(D) FIGHT DIRTY 1979 POLYDOR UK 2443 161 + 5017
(D) FIGHT DIRTY 1979 ARISTA US 4239

C86 CHARLIE & THE PEP BOYS C86

CHARLIE WOODS-PEARSON V (A
MICHAEL STERN G (A
ALAN ADKINS G (A
MICHAEL ZACK D (A
LEFTY POTOMAC K (A
BOBBY MANRIQUEZ G (A
MICHAEL S SAX (A
ROLF HANSON B (A
CRAIG RYAN TPT (A

(A) DADDY'S GIRL 1976 A&M UK AMLH64563 US 4563

C87 CHARLIE & THE WIDE BOYS C87

CHARLIE AINLEY V (AB
RICHARD WORTHY G (AB
GREG PHILLIPS V PERC (AB
NIGEL CHAPPELL B (AB
GUY EVANS D (AB
SIMON FRASER G (AB

(A) CHARLIE & THE WIDE BOYS (EP) 1974 ANCHOR ANCE 1007
(B) GREAT COUNTRY ROCKERS 1976 MFP ANCHOR 50293

C87A CHARLIE BOY C87A

CHARLIE NEWPORT G V (A
EDDY WILLIAMS B V (A
STEVE HODGES V (A
FRED LLOYD K (A
BRIAN ROPER D V (A
BRENDAN BONASS G (A
BILLY ROPER G STEEL V (A

(A) INTRODUCING CHARLIE BOY 19 RELEASE BRL 4076

C88 CHARTREUSE C88

PAUL JEFFREYS	B	
MILTON REAME-JAMES	K	
JEFF FAULKNER	G	
MALCOLM ASHMAN	D	
ROB ELLIOT	V	

C89 CHAS & DAVE C89

CHAS HODGES	V G K	(ALL
DAVE PEACOCK	B V FDL	(ALL
ALBERT LEE	G	(D
ERIC CLAPTON	G	(D
DAVE EDMUNDS	G	(D
MICKEY BURT	D	(ALL

(A) ONE FING 'N'ANUVVER	1975	RETREAT RT6004	NUT	NUT17
(B) CHAS & DAVE	1978	ROCKNEY		OCKNEY 1
(C) ROCKNEY	1978	EMI		EMC 3288
(D) DONT GIVE A MONKEYS	1979	EMI		
(E) MUSTN'T GRUMBLE	1981	ROCKNEY		909

C90 CHASE C90

BILL CHASE	TPT	(ABCD
ALAN WARE	TPT	(A
JERRY VAN BLAIR	TPT V	(A
PHIL PORTER	K	(A
DENNIS JOHNSON	B V	(A
ANGEL SOUTH	G V	(A
JAY SOLLENBERGER	TPT	(C
TED PIERCEFIELD	TPT V	(A
DARTANYAN BROWN	B V	(C
JAY BURRID	PERC	(A
TERRY RICHARDS	V	(A
WALLY YOHN	K	(C
JIM OATTS	TPT	(C
JOE MORRISSEY	TPT	(C
TOM GORDON	D	(C
JOHN EMMA	G	(C
JIM PETERIK	V	(C

(A) CHASE	1971	EPIC/CBS	UK	64544
(A) CHASE	197	EPIC	US	30472
(B) ENNEA	1972	EPIC/CBS	UK	64710
(B) ENNEA	1972	EPIC	US	31097
(C) PURE MUSIC	1974	EPIC	UK	80017
(C) PURE MUSIC	1974	EPIC	US	32572
(D) GET IT ON	197	EPIC	US	26297
(AB) CHASE/ENNEA	1976	EPIC	US	33737

C90A SAM CHATMON C90A

SAM CHATMON	G V	(AB

(A) THE MISSISSIPPI SHEIK	1974	BLUE GOOSE		2006
(B) SAM CHATMON	197	ROUNDER	US	2028

C90B CHINGA CHAVIN C90B

CHINGA CHAVIN	V	(A
BOB HARMANN	B	(A
FORREST BERRY	G V	(A

(A) COUNTRY PORN	1976	CHINGA		666

C92 CHEAP TRICK C92

RICK NIELSEN	G	(ABCDEFG
TOM PETERSSON	B	(ABCDEFG
ROBIN ZANDER	V	(ABCDEFG
BUN E CARLOS	D	(ABCDEFG
XENO	V	(
PETE COMITA	B	(
JAI WINDING	K	(E
TOM WERMAN	PROD	(E
JACK DOUGLAS	PROD	(G

(A) CHEAP TRICK	1977	EPIC US 34400 1980	UK	81917
(B) IN COLOR	1977	EPIC	UK	82214
(B) IN COLOR	1977	EPIC	US	34884
(C) HEAVEN TONIGHT	1978	EPIC	UK	82679
(C) HEAVEN TONIGHT	1978	EPIC	US	35312
(D) LIVE AT BUDOKAN	1978	EPIC	UK	86083
(D) LIVE AT BUDOKAN	1978	EPIC	US	35795
(E) DREAM POLICE	1979	EPIC US 33773	UK	85322
(F) ALL SHOOK UP	1980	EPIC US 36498	UK	86124
(G) FOUND ALL THE PARTS	1980	EPIC 10"	US	36453
(EP) OVER THE EDGE	19	EPIC	JAP	084P

C93 CHUBBY CHECKER C93

CHUBBY CHECKER	V	(ALL

CHEQUERED	19	LONDON	UK	SHZ 8419
TWIST	1962	COLUMBIA	UK	
DONT KNOCK THE TWIST	1962			
TWIST WITH	1962	PARKWAY	US	P7001
ITS PONY TIME	1962			
LETS TWIST AGAIN	1962	PARKWAY	US	P7004
YOUR TWIST PARTY	1962	PARKWAY	US	P7007
TWISTIN' AROUND THE WORLD	1962	PARKWAY	US	P7008
FOR TEEN TWISTERS ONLY	19	PARKWAY	US	P7009
TWISTIN' AROUND THE WORLD	1962	GOLDEN GUINEA	UK	GGL 0236
ALL THE HITS	1963	PARKWAY		P7014
LIMBO PARTY	1963	PARKWAY	US	P7020
BIGGEST HITS	1963			
LETS LIMBO SOME MORE	1963			
BEACH PARTY	1963			
TWIST IT UP	196			
CHUBBY CHECKER & BOBBY RYDELL	19	CAMEO		C1013
DISCOTHEQUE	19			
FOLK ALBUM	1964	PARKWAY		P7040
DOWN TO EARTH	1963	CAMEO		C1029
GOLDEN HITS	196	CAMEO	US	C1063
DANCIN' PARTY (EP)	1963	CAMEO		CPE 550
GREATEST HITS	1976	LONDON	UK	HAU 8492
GREATEST HITS	19	ABKCO		4219

C94 CHEECH & CHONG C94

RICHARD CHEECH MARIN		(ALL
THOMAS CHONG		(ALL
GEORGE HARRISON	G	(C
KLAUS VOORMANN	B	(C
JIM KARSTEN	D	(C
JIM KELTNER	D	(C
CAROLE KING	PNO	(C
NICKY HOPKINS	K	(C
TOM SCOTT	SAX	(C
DICK HYDE	HRNS	(C
WADDY WACHTEL	G	(G
STANLEY SHELDON	B	(G
BILLY PRESTON	ORG	(CG
PAUL HUBINON	HRNS	(C
RICK MAROTTA	D	(G
ANDY MUSON	B	(G
GEORGE BOHANNON	HRNS	(C
DANNY KORTMAR	G	(G
JAI WINDING	K	(G

(A) CHEECH & CHONG	1971	A&M UK AMLS67010	US WB 3250
(B) BIG BAMBU	1972	A&M UK AMLH67014	US WB 3251
(C) LOS COCHINOS	1973	ODE UK ODE77019	US WB 3252
(D) WEDDING ALBUM	1974	ODE UK ODE77025	US WB 3253
(E) SLEEPING BEAUTY	1976	ODE UK ODE77040	US WB 3254
(F) LETS MAKE UP A NEW DOPE DEAL	19	WB UK K56809	US WB 3391
(G) UP IN SMOKE	1978	WB	US 3249

C94A CHEFS C94A

(A) THE CHEFS	19	ATTRIX	UK	RB10

C95 CHELSEA C95

GENE OCTOBER	V G	(A
BRIAN JAMES	G	(A
BILLY IDOL	V	
JOHN TOWE	D	(
BOB JESSIE	B	(
JAMES STEVENSON	G V	(A
DAVE MARTIN	G V	(A
TONY JAMES	B	
MARTI STACEY	G	
GEOFF MYLES	B	(A
CHRIS BASHFORD	D V	(A
BOY CARIE	D	
GARY FORTUNE	D	
STEVE L JONES	D	
ROBIN	K	(A

(A) CHELSEA	1979	STEP FORWARD	UK	SFLP 2
(B) ALTERNATIVE HITS	1980	STEP FORWARD	UK	SFLP 5

C95A CHELSEA BEIGE C95A

Member	Instrument	Album
KENNY LEHMAN	WIND	(A
BILLY SCHWARTZ	G	(A
JOHN SCORZELLO	TPT	(A
STAFFORD L JAMES	B	(A
ALLAN SPRINGFIELD	V PNO	(A
CHRIS EFTHIMIAM	D	(A

Title	Year	Label	Country	Number
(A) MAMA MAMA LET YOUR SWEET BIRD SING	1971	EPIC	US	3041

C96 CHER C96

Member	Instrument	Album
CHER	V	(ALL
FRANK CAPP	D	(A
JESSE SAILES	D	(A
SHARKEY HALL	D	(A
HAROLD BATTISTE	PNO	(A
MIKE RUBINI	K	(A
BILL MARX	K	(A
LYLE RITZ	B	(A
CLIFF HILLS	B	(A
RENE HALL	B	(A
MEL POLLEN	B	(A
DON PEAKE	G	(A
BARNEY KESSEL	G	(A
STEVE MANN	G	(A
MONTE DUNN	G	(A
MIKE POST	G	(A
JEFF KAPLAN	G	(A
RANDY STEVLING	G	(A
JULIUS WECHTER	PERC	(A
GENE ESTES	PERC	(A
BRIAN STONE	PERC	(A
FRANK DEVITO	PERC	(A
MICHEL RUBINI	K	(O
JOE SAMPLE	K	(O
DEAN PARKS	G	(O
JEFF PORCARO	D	(O
DAVID PAICH	K	(O
TED DALE	K	(O

Title	Year	Label	Country	Number
(A) ALL I REALLY WANT TO DO	1965	LIBERTY	UK	SLBY 3058
(A) ALL I REALLY WANT TO DO	196	IMPERIAL	US	12292
SONNY SIDE OF CHER	1966	LIBERTY	UK	SLBY 3072
SONNY SIDE OF CHER	196	IMPERIAL	US	12301
CHER	1967	LIBERTY	UK	SLBY 3081
CHER	196	IMPERIAL	US	12320
WITH LOVE	1968	IMPERIAL	US	12358
BACKSTAGE	1968	IMPERIAL	US	12373
GOLDEN GREATS	1968			
3614 JACKSON HIGHWAY	19	ATCO	US	33298
CHER	1971	MCA	UK	MUPS 438
CHER	1974	MCA	UK	MCF 2508
CHER	1972	KAPP	US	5549
CHER(SUPERPAX 1)	19	UA	US	UXS 88
CHER(SUPERPAX 2)	19	UA	US	UXS 94
CHER	19	CBS	US	3649
SINGS THE HITS	19	SPRINGBOARD	US	4029
GREATEST HITS	19	SPRINGBOARD	US	4028
FOXY LADY	1972	MCA US 2019	MUPS	459
FOXY LADY	197	KAPP	US	KRS 5514
FOXY LADY	197	MCA	UK	MCF 2521
HITS OF CHER	1972	UA	UK	UAS 29317
(O)BITTERSWEET WHITE LIGHT	1973	MCA US 2101	UK	MUPS 484
(O)BITTERSWEET WHITE LIGHT	1974	MCA	UK	MCF 2511
HALF BREED	1974	MCA	UK	MCF 2501
HALF BREED	1974	MCA	US	2104
DARK LADY	1974	MCA	UK	MCF 2559
DARK LADY	1974	MCA	US	2113
STARS	1975	WB	US	2850
STARS	1975	WB	UK	K 56111
GOLDEN HITS	1975	SUNSET	UK	SLS 50378
GOLDEN HITS	19	UA	UK	UAS 29317
THIS IS CHER	197	SUNSET	US	5276
GREATEST HITS	1975	MCA	UK	MCF 2597
GREATEST HITS	197	MCA	US	2127
I'D RATHER BELIEVE IN YOU	1977	WB	US	BS 2898
I'D RATHER BELIEVE IN YOU	1977	WB	UK	K 56292
CHERISHED	1977	WB	US	S 3046
CHERISHED	1977	WB	UK	K 56401
TAKE ME HOME	19	CASABLANCA	US	7133
TAKE ME HOME	1979	CASABLANCA	UK	CAL 2047
PRISONER	1979	CASABLANCA		7184

C96A CHERUBIN C96A

Member	Instrument	Album
ANDY MARX	G V	(AB
BO BORN	K	(AB
PIT TREJA	PERC V	(AB
EBERHARD WILLHELM	D V	(AB
LUCY NEALE	V	(B
GARRY HUNWYN	B	(B
FRANK BAUM	STEEL	(A
THOR BALDURSON	K	(AB
KEITH FORSEY	D	(B
MICHAEL HODJERA	G V	(A
WOLFGANG GRUDE	WIND	(A
BLANDINE ANTONIO MARINHO	B V	(A
RAINER PIETSCH	V	(B
DIETER BAUER	B	(A

Title	Year	Label	Country	Number
(A) OUR SUNRISE	1974	UA	GER	29688
(B) CHERUB SAFETY MATCH	1975	UA	GER	29780

C96B CHEROKEE C96B

Member	Instrument	Album
CRAIG KRAMPF	D ACC	(A
DAVID DONALDSON	G HCA	(A
GEORGE DONALDSON	G SAX	(A
CHRIS HILLMAN	MAND B	(A
ROBERT DONALDSON	K V	(A
SNEAKY PET KLEINOW	STEEL	(A
TOM LATONDRE	TPT	(A
FLOYD 'GIB' GUILBEAU	VLN	(A

Title	Year	Label	Country	Number
(A) CHEROKEE	1971	ABC	US	719

C96C CHERRY PEOPLE C96C

Member	Instrument	Album
PUNKY MEADOWS	G	(A
ROCKY ISAAC	D	(A
CHRIS GRIMES		(A
DOUGY GRIMES	V	(A
JAN ZUKOWSKI	B	(A

Title	Year	Label	Country	Number
(A) THE CHERRY PEOPLE	19	HERITAGE	US	35000

C96D CHEVY C96D

Title	Year	Label	Country	Number
(A) CHEVY	1980	AVATAR	UK	AALP 5001

C97 CHEYNES C97

Member	Instrument
PETER BARDENS	K V
ROGER PEACOCK	V
PHIL SAWYER	G
MICK FLEETWOOD	D
EDDIE LYNCH	G
PETER HOLLIS	B

C98 CHI LITES C98

EUGENE RECORD
MARSHALL THOMPSON
ROBERT LESTER
CREADEL JONES

Title	Year	Label	Country	Number
GIVE IT AWAY	1968	MCA	UK	MUPS 397
GIVE IT AWAY	1968	BRUNSWICK	US	754152
I LIKE YOUR LOVIN	19	BRUNSWICK	US	754152
GIVE MORE POWER TO THE PEOPLE	1971	MCA	UK	MUPS 437
GIVE MORE POWER TO THE PEOPLE	1971	BRUNSWICK	US	754170
GIVE MORE POWER TO THE PEOPLE	1976	BRUNSWICK		BRLS 3011
A LONELY MAN	1972	MCA	UK	MUPS 457
A LONELY MAN	1972	BRUNSWICK	US	754179
A LONELY MAN	1976	BRUNSWICK		BRLS 3012
GREATEST HITS	1972	BRUNSWICK	UK	BRLS 3003
GREATEST HITS	1972	BRUNSWICK	US	754184
A LETTER TO MYSELF	1973	BRUNSWICK	UK	BRLS 3007
A LETTER TO MYSELF	1973	BRUNSWICK	US	754118
THE CHI LITES	1974	BRUNSWICK	UK	BRLS 3009
THE CHI LITES	1974	BRUNSWICK	US	754197
TOBY	1974	BRUNSWICK	UK	BRLS 3010
TOBY	1974	BRUNSWICK	US	754200

(CONTINUED)

C98 **CHI LITES** (CONTINUED) C98

Title	Year	Label	Country	Number
HALF A LOVE	1975	BRUNSWICK	UK	BRLS 3015
HALF A LOVE	1975	BRUNSWICK	US	754204
HALF A LOVE	1978	LONDON	UK	SHU 8521
HAPPY BEING LONELY	1976	MERCURY	UK	9100 027
HAPPY BEING LONELY	1976	MERCURY	US	SRM1 1118
VERY BEST OF THE CHI LITES	1976	BRUNSWICK	UK	BRLS 3023
CHILITETIME (COMP)	1976	LONDON	UK	SHU 8520
GREATEST HITS VOL 2	19	BRUNSWICK	US	754208
THE FANTASTIC CHI LITES	1977	MERCURY	UK	9100 041
THE FANTASTIC CHI LITES	1977	MERCURY	US	SRM1 1147
HEAVENLY BODY	1980	20TH CENTURY		619

C99 **CHIC** C99

Name	Instrument	Albums
NORMA JEAN	V	(A
BERNARD EDWARDS	V K	(ABC
DIVA GRAY	V	(ABC
LUCI MARTIN	V	(BC
VALERIE HAYWOOD	VLN	(
ALFA ANDERSON	V	(ABC
TONY THOMPSON	D	(ABC
DAVID LASLEY	V	(ABC
LUTHER VANDROSS	V	(ABC
ANDY SCHWARTZ	K	(ABC
JON FADDIS	HRNS	(ABC
KENNY LEHMAN	WIND	(A
GEORGE YOUNG	WIND	(A
MARIANNE CARROLL	VLN	(B
ELLEN SEELING	HRNS	(BC
NILE RODGERS	G	(ABC
RAYMOND JONES	K	(BC
BARRY ROGERS	TROM	(ABC
DAVID FRIEDMAN	PERC	(A
GLORIA AGOSTINI	HARP	(A
CHERYL HONG	VLN	(B
ALEX FOSTER	HRNS	(BC
ROBERT SABINO	K	(ABC
SAMMY FIGUEROA	PERC	(ABC
ROBIN CLARK	V	(A
TOM COPPOLA	K	(A
JOE ROSSY	PERC	(BC
KAREN MILNE	VLN	(B
JEAN FINEBERG	HRNS	(BC

Album	Year	Label	UK		US	
(A) CHIC	1978	ATLANTIC	UK	K50441	US	19153
(B) C'EST CHIC	1978	ATLANTIC	UK	K50565	US	19209
(C) RISQUE	1979	ATLANTIC	UK	K50634	US	16003
(D) GREATEST HITS	1979	ATLANTIC	UK	K50686	US	16011
(E) REAL PEOPLE	1980	ATLANTIC	UK	K50711	US	16016
(F) CHIC CHIC	1981	ATLANTIC				
(G) TAKE IT OFF	1981	ATLANTIC	UK	K50843	US	19323

C100 **CHICAGO** C100

Name	Instrument	Albums
PETER CETERA	B G V	(ALL
ROBERT LAMM	K V	(ALL
TERRY KATHBS	G V	(A'TO'L
JAMES PANKOW	TROM	(ALL
LEE LOUGHNANE	V PERC TPT	(ALL
WALTER PARAZEIDER	WIND	(ALL
DANIEL SERAPHINE	D	(ALL
LAUDIR DE OLIVEIRA	PERC	(ILMN
DONNIE DACUS	G	(MN
CARL WILSON	V	(L
DAVID WOLINSKI	SYN	(L
TIM CETERA	V	(L
CHAKA KHAN	V	(L
BLUE WEAVER	SYN	(M
MAYNARD FERGUSON	TPT	(N
AIRTO MOREIRA	PERC	(N

Album	Note	Year	Label	UK	US
(A) CHICAGO TRANSIT AUTHORITY	(DBL)	1968	CBS	UK 66221	US PG8
(B) CHICAGO	(DBL)	1970	CBS	UK 66233	US 2G24
(C) CHICAGO 3	(DBL)	1971	CBS	UK 66260	US 30110
(D) CHICAGO 4	(LIVE)	1971	CBS	UK 66405	US 30865
(E) CHICAGO 5		1972	CBS	UK 69018	US 31002
(F) CHICAGO 6		1973	CBS	UK 69041	US 32400
(G) CHICAGO 7	(DBL)	1974	CBS	UK 88015	US 32810
(H) CHICAGO 8		1975	CBS	UK 69130	US 33130
(I) GREATEST HITS		1975	CBS	UK 69222	US 33900
(J) LIVE IN JAPAN 1972		1975	CBS/SONY	JAP	SCPS31/32
(K) CHICAGO 10		1976	CBS	UK 86101	US 34260
(L) CHICAGO XI		1977	CBS	UK 86031	US 34860
(M) HOT STREETS		1978	CBS	UK 86069	US 35512
(N) No13		1979	CBS	UK 86093	US 36105
(O) CHICAGO XIV		1980	CBS	UK 86118	US 36517
(P) GREATEST HITS VOL 2		1981	CBS		US 37682
( ) AT CARNEGIE HALL 4 LP SET		19	CBS		
(Q) CHICAGO 16	CASSETTE	198	CBS	UK 499235	

C101 **CHICKEN SHACK** C101

Name	Instrument	Albums
STAN WEBB	G V	(ALL
CHRISTINE PERFECT	K V	(ABK
ANDY SYLVESTER	B	(ABCDK
DAVE BIDWELL	D	(ABCDK
BOB DAISLEY	B	(F
PAUL RAYMOND	V K	(CDK
JOHN GLASCOCK	B	(E
PAUL HANCOX	D	(E
CHRIS MERCER	SAX	(F
ED SPEVOCK	D	(H1J
STEVE YORK	B	(1J
ROBBIE BLUNT	G	(1HJ
DAVE WINTHROP	SAX	(1HJ
PAUL MARTINEZ	B	(H
ALAN ELLIS	TPT	(AK
DAVE WILKINSON	K	(G
ROB HULL	B	(G
ALAN POWELL	D	(G
TONY ASHTON	K	(FH
DON FEY	SAX	(B
BUD BEADLE	SAX	(B
ALISON YOUNG	V	(D
DICK HECKSTALL SMITH	SAX	(A
RODERICK LEE	TPT	(B
JOHNNY ALMOND	SAX	(AB
PAUL BUTLER	G V	(L
TERRY NOONAN	TPT	(B
STEVE GREGORY	SAX	(B
RIC LEE	D	(L
WALTER HORTON	HCA	(B
ALAN SCOTT	B	(L

Album	Note	Year	Label	Country	Number
(A) 40 BLUE FINGERS		1968	BLUE HORIZON	UK	7 63203
(B) O.K. KEN		1968	BLUE HORIZON	UK	7 63209
(C) 100 TON CHICKEN		1969	BLUE HORIZON	UK	7 63218
(D) ACCEPT		1970	BLUE HORIZON	UK	7 63861
(D) ACCEPT		1970	BLUE HORIZON	US	4809
(E) IMAGINATION LADY		1971	DERAM	UK	SDL5
(E) IMAGINATION LADY		1972	DERAM	US	18063
(F) UNLUCKY BOY		1973	DERAM	UK	SML1100
(F) UNLUCKY BOY		1973	LONDON	US	632
(G) GOODBYE	(LIVE)	1974	NOVA 6 21579	GER	SDL8008
(G) GOODBYE		1974	LANDON	JAP	LAX1035
(FG) STAN THE MAN	DBL	1977	NOVA	GER	6 28375
(H) THE CREEPER		1978	EURODISC		913 203
(H) THE CREEPER		1978	ARIOLA	GER	25891
(J) THATS THE WAY WE ARE		1978	SHARK	GER	148 501
(K) IN THE CAN	(COMP)	1980	CBS	UK	31811
(AB) GOLDEN ERA OF POP MUSIC	(DBL)	1977	CBS	UK	68252
(BC) GOLDEN ERA OF POP MUSIC	(DBL) 2	1977	CBS		68253
(EF) DOUBLE		1977	DERAM		3032/1-2
(L) CHICKEN SHACK		1979	GULL	UK	GULP 1034
(1) LIVE 78 GIG					
(M) ROADIES		1981	RCA		PL 25337

C102 **CHIEFTAINS** C102

Name	Instrument	Albums
PADDY MOLONEY	PIPES	(ALL
SEAN POTTS	WHISTLE	(ALL
SEAN KEANE	FDL	(BCDEFGHJK
MARTIN FAY	FDL	(ALL
MICK TUBRIDY	FLT	(ABCDEFGHJ
PEADAR MERCIER	BODHRAN	(BCDE
DEREK BELL	HARP	(EFGHJK
KEVEN CONNEFF	BODHRAN	(FHJ
RONNIE McSHANE	PERC	(EF
DOLORES KEANE	V	(F
MATT MOLLOY	FLT	(K
JOLYON JACKSON	CELLO	(K
RATHCOOLE PIPE BAND		(K
DAVID FALLON	BOD	(A
SEAN O'RIADA		(A

Album	Year	Label	Country	Number	Reissue
(A) CHIEFTAINS 1	1965	CLADDAGH	IRL	CC2	ISLAND 76 RI ILPS9364
(A) CHIEFTAINS 1	1978	CBS			RI 82986
(B) CHIEFTAINS 2	1969	CLADDAGH	IRL	CC7	ISLAND 76 RI ILPS9365
(B) CHIEFTAINS 2	1978	CBS			RI 82988
(C) CHIEFTAINS 3	1971	CLADDAGH	IRL	RRC10	ISLAND 76 RI ILPS9379
(C) CHIEFTAINS 3	1978	CBS			RI 82987
(D) CHIEFTAINS 4	1973	CLADDAGH	IRL	RRC14	ISLAND 76 RI ILPS9380
(D) CHIEFTAINS 4	1978	CBS			RI 82989
(E) CHIEFTAINS 5	1975	CLADDAGH	IRL	CC16	ISLAND 76 RI ILPS9334
(E) CHIEFTAINS 5	1978	CBS			RI 82991
(F) BONAPARTES RETREAT	1976	ISLAND	UK	ILPS9432	CBS 78 RI 82990
(G) LIVE	1977	ISLAND	UK	ILPS9501	CBS 78 RI 82985
(H) CHIEFTAINS 7	1978	CLADDAGH	IRL	CC24	
(H) CHIEFTAINS 7	1978	CBS	UK	82814	US 35612
(J) CHIEFTAINS 8	1979	CBS	UK	83262	
(K) BOIL THE BREAKFAST EARLY	1980	CBS	UK	84081	US 36401

C103 CHIFFONS C103

JUDY CRAIG V ((A) THE CHIFFONS 1963 LAURIE US 2018 UK STATESIDE 10040
BARBARA LEE V ((B) ONE FINE DAY 196 LAURIE US 2020
PATRICIA BENNET V ((C) SWEET TALKIN' GUY 1966 LAURIE US 2036 UK STATESIDE 10190
SYLVIA PETERSON V ((C) SWEET TALKIN' GUY 1972 LONDON UK ZGP 125
(D) SWEET TALKIN' 1972 PHASE 4 UK PFS4256
(E) EVERYTHING YOU ALWAYS WANTED TO HEAR19 LAURIE US 4001 UK 1001
(F) PICK HITS 1976 SONIC UK SON 005
(EP) THEY'RE SO FINE 19 STATESIDE UK SE1012

C103A CHILDREN C103A

(A) REBIRTH 19 ATCO US 33271

C103B CHIKKIN C103B

DAVID TONLINSON D V (A (A) WHICH CAME FIRST 1978 EGG CAN 3690
EDDY VALIQUETTE G V (A
GREG EVANS B V SYN(A

C103C DESMOND CHILD & ROUGE C103C

DESMOND CHILD K V (AB (A) DESMOND CHILD & ROUGE 1979 CAPITOL EST 11908
DAVID LANDAU G (A (B) RUNNERS IN THE NIGHT 1979 CAPITOL EST 11909
ALAN SCHWARTZBERG D (A
JERRY MAROTTA D (B JOHN SUSSWELL D (A NEIL JASON B (A JOHN SIEGLER B (AB
PAUL SHAFFER K (A RALPH SHUCKETT K (A JIMMY MEAULIN PERC (A RUBINS BASSINI PERC(A
ELLIOTT RANDALL G (A JEFF MIRANOFF G (A JOE CARO G (A JEFF LAYTON G (A
LARRY SALTZMAN G (A MARIA VIDAL V (AB RANDY COURTS K (B MYRIAN VALLE V (AB
BETTE SUSSMANN K (B DIANNE CRASSELLI V (AB G SMITH G (B

C105 CHILLI WILLI & THE RED HOT PEPPERS C105

MARTIN STONE G MAND(AB (A) KINGS OF THE ROBOT RHYTHM 1972 REVELATION UK REV 002
SNAKEFINGERS LITHMAN G (AB (B) BONGOS OVER BALHAM 1974 MOONCREST UK CREST 21
PETE THOMAS D (B (B) BONGOS OVER BALHAM 1974 NOVA GER 6 23101
BOB ANDREWS SAX K(AB
P C BAILEY BAN SAX G (B WILL STALLIBRASS HCA (B RED RHODES STEEL(B JO ANN KELLY V (AB
JACQUI McSHEE V (B SOPHIE ISRAEL V (B CAROL GRIMES V (B NICK LOWE B (A
BILLY RANKIN D (A ENGLISH JOHN FOX B (A BARRY EVERETT PERC (A DAVE VORHAUS SYN (A
PAUL RILEY B (B

C106 CHILLIWACK C106

BILL HENDERSON G V (ALL (A) CHILLIWACK 1971 LONDON UK SHU 8418 US 71040
HOWARD FROESE V G K((EF (B) CHILLIWACK 1971 A&M US 3509
CLAIRE LAWRENCE WIND K B(AB (C) ALL OVER YOU 1972 A&M US 4375
GKENN MILLER B V (ADEF (D) CHILLIWACK 1974 SIRE US 7506
ROSS TURNEY D (ABDEF (E) ROCKERBOX 1975 SIRE UK 9103 250 US 7511
JOAN HENDERSON V (C (F) DREAMS DREAMS DREAMS 1977 MUSHROOM US 5006
ROBBIE KING PNO (C (G) LIGHTS FROM THE VALLEY 1978 MUSHROOM US 5011
BOB BUCKLEY K (C (H) BREAKDOWN IN PARADISE 1980 MUSHROOM US 5016
JOHN ROLES G V (H (J) WANNA BE A STAR 1981 MILLENIUM BXL 17759
BRIAN MACLEOD D (H
AB BRYANT B (H

C106A ALEX CHILTON C106A

ALEX CHILTON PROD V (ALL (A) ONE DAY IN NEW YORK 1977 ORK 81978 TRIO JAP 2007
JON TIVEN PROS G V (A (B) LIKE FLIES ON SHERBET 1980 AURA UK 710
RICHARD ROSEBROUGH D (AB (C) BACHS BOTTOM 1981 LINE GER LP5081
RICH CLARK K V (A (1) 1980 TOUR BAND
TOMMY HOEN K V (A
DAVID BEAVER K (A KEN WOODLEY B (A THE COSSACKS (A LISA ALDRIDGE (B
LEE BAKER (B JIM DICKINSON PROD (B ROSS JOHNSON (B MIKE LADD (B
JIM LANCASTER (B SID SELRIDGE (B MATTHEW SELIGMANN B (1 MORRIS WINDSOR D (1
KNOX G (1 CHARLES BALL PROD (A

C106B CHIMO C106B

TONY COLLACOTT PNO (A (A) CHIMO 1971 EPIC US 30329
ROSS RABY ORG V(A
JOHN JOHNSON B V (A ANDY CREE D (A BREEN LEBOEUF V (A

C107 CHINA C107

DAVEY JOHNSTONE G (A (A) CHINA 1977 ROCKET UK ROLL 9
JAMES NEWTON HOWARD K (A
COOKER LOPRESTI B (A DENNIS CONWAY D (A JO PARTRIDGE G (ROGER POPE D (A
ELTON JOHN V (A KIKI DEE V (A CARMEN TWILLIE V (A CATHY COLLIER V (A
VENETTE GLOUD V (A SID POONYA PERC (A

C107A CHOCOLATE & CLAY C107A

GEORGE'CHOCOLATE' PERRY B(A (A) CHOCOLATE & CLAY 1977 cat us 2610
CLAY CROPPER G K (A
JOE MILLER SAX (A HAROLD SEAY D (A

C107B CHOCOLATE WATCHBAND C107B

GARY OSBORNE V (A (A) NO WAY OUT 1967 TOWER US 5096
(B) THE INNER MYSTIQUE 196 TOWER US 5106
(C) ONE STEP BEYOND 196 TOWER US 5153

C107C CHINESE PUZZLE C107C

DAVID RODENBLOOM G V (A (A) INSIDE OUTSIDE 1980 REBUS US 10 001
DAVID HOFSTRA B (A
JOHN MERNIT D (A

C107D CHOCLATE MILK C107D

(A) CHOCOLATE MILK 19 RCA US APLI 1399
(B) COMIN' 1977 RCA UK PL11830 US APLI 1830
(D) WE'RE ALL IN THIS TOGETHER 19 RCA US APLI 2331

C107E CHOPPER C107E

GEORGE LEGION G V (A (A) CHOPPER 1979 A&M US 4715
PETER BUNCH G V (A
BRAD SEIP D (A KIM BULLARD K V (A GERY LINK B V (A

C108 CHOPYN C108

ANN ODELL K V (A (A) GRAND SLAM 1975 JET UK LP 08
DENNY McCAFFREY V (A
RAY RUSSELL G V (A KLYDE McMULLIN G V (A SIMON PHILLIPS D (A SIMON COLCLOUGH V PERC(A

C108A **CHORDS** C108A

BRETT ASCOTT D (A — (A) SO FAR AWAY — 1980 POLYDOR UK POLS 1019 2383 575
CHRIS POPE G V (A — (A) SO FAR AWAY (DIFF TRACKS) — 1980 METRONOME GER 60 312
MARTIN MASON B V (A
BILLY HASSETT G V (A — MICK TALBOT PNO (A

C108B **RANDLE CHOWNING BAND** C108B

RANDLE CHOWNING V G HCA (A — (A) HEARTS ON FIRE — 1978 A&M US 4715
KEN SHEPHERD G V (A
LARRY VAN FLEET B V (A — LLOYD HICKS D V PERC(A — RICHARD TEE PNO V (A — BOB STEHL LYRICON(A
JASON LAMASTER G (A — PAUL LEKA K (A — KAT EPPLE FLT (A — RON BACCHIOCCHI K (A
STAN SWARTZ SAX K(A — RAY GANTEK STEEL(A — STEVEN GASPER ORG (A

C108C **CHRISMA** C108C

G DURINI D (A — (A) CHINESE RESTAURANT — 1977 POLYDOR IT 2448 060
E VEVEY G (A
MAURIZIO SYN (A — CHRISTINA D B K SYN(A

C108D **LOU CHRISTIE** C108D

LOU CHRISTIE V (ALL — (A) LOU CHRISTIE — 1963 ROULETTE US 25208
MADISON MASON G (J — (B) STRIKES BACK — 19 CE&CO US 1231
DON THOMAS G (J — (C) STRIKES AGAIN — 19 ROULETTE US 25332
TONY LEVIN B (J — (C) STRIKES AGAIN — 19 COLPIX US 4001
WALTER YOST B (J — (D) LIGHTNIN STRIKES — 19 MGM US 4360
BUDDY SALTZMAN D (J — (E) PAINTER OF HITS — 19 MGM US 4394
TONY ROMERO K (J — (F) LOU CHRISTIE & THE CLASSICS — 19 SPINERAMA US 173
PAUL PRESTOPINE BAN (J — (G) PAINT AMERICA LOVE — 19 BUDDAH US 5073
RUSSELL GEORGE FDL (J — (H) LOU CHRISTIE — 19 3 BROTHERS US 2000
LARRY PACKER FDL (J — (J) LOU CHRISTIE — 1974 CTI UK 24
MARC HAROWITZ STEEL(J
ERIC WEISSBERG STEEL (J

C109 **KEITH CHRISTMAS** C109

KEITH CHRISTMAS G V PERC(ALL — (A) STIMULUS — 1969 RCA SF 8059
WITH — (B) FABLE OF THE WINGS — 1970 B+C CAS 1015
PAT DONALDSON B (B — (C) PIGMY — 1971 B+C CAS 1041
GERRY CONWAY D (B — (D) BRIGHTER DAY — 1974 MANTICORE K 53503
BOB STEWART K (B — (E) STORIES FROM A HUMAN ZOO — 1976 ATLANTIC K 13515
ROGER POWELL D (B — (E) STORIES FROM A HUMAN ZOO — 1976 ATLANTIC UK K 53509
IAN WHITEMAN K (B — (F) KEITH CHRISTMAS — 19 POLYDOR 244 511
SHELAGH McDONALD V (B
ALAN SPENNER B (D — IAN WALLACE D (D — NEIL HUBBARD G (D — EDDIE MORDUE SAX (D
RAY WARLEIGH SAX (D — MEL COLLINS SAX (D — MALCOLM GRIFFITHS TROM (D — HENRY LOWTHER TPT (D
MARTIN DROVER TPT (D — DARRYL RUNSWICK B (D — IAN McDONALD K (D — PETE SOLLEY K (D
TOMMY REILLY HCA (D — SKAILA KANGA HCA (D — WILL WATSON HRNS (D — STEVE CROPPER G (E
SNUFFY WALDEN G (E — DAVID NICHTERN G (E — DONALD DUNN B (E — WILLIAM SMITH K (E
DAVID KEMPER D (E — PETER BERNSTEIN V SYN(E — WENDY WALDMAN V (E — DANIEL MOORE V (E
KEITH TIPPETT PNO (B — MIKE EVANS B (B

C109A **CHRISTOPHER** C109A

RICHARD AVITTS G (A — (A) CHRISTOPHER — 19 METROMEDIA 1024
DOUG WALDEN B (A
JOHN SIMPSON D (A — TERRANCE HAND D (A — DOUG TULL PERC (A — RON CRAMER PERC (A

C109B **CHRISTOPHER MILK** C109B

JOHN MENDELSOHN V D K(AB — (A) CHRISTOPHER MILK — 1971 UA US SP066
Mr TWISTER V (AB — (B) SOME PEOPLE WILL DRINK ANYTHING — 1972 REPRISE US 2111
THE KIDDO B V (AB
DONNY ALVARADO G V (A — G WHIZZ D (AB — RALPH OSWALD G SAX(AB

C110 **CHROME** C110

JOHN L CYBORG DATA (ACDE — (A) THE VISITATION — 1976 SIREN DE1000
DAMON EDGE V G K(ABCDE — (B) ALIEN SOUNDTRACKS — 1977 SIREN DE2200
GARRY SPAIN B G V(ABC — (C) HALF LIP MACHINE MOVES — 1979 SIREN DE 333
HELIOS CREED V G B(ABCDE — (D) RED EXPOSURE — 1980 BEGGARS BANQUET UK BEGA15
JOHN LAMBDIN G (B — (E) READ ONLY MEMORY(EP) — 1979 SIREN US 002 RED UK 12 002

C110A **CHRONICLE** C110A

NOBUO HOICHI B (C — (A) LIVE AT THE WHISKY A GO GO — 1975 EXPRESS JAP 72037
KEII SHIKAWA B V (C — (B) IMA WA TOKI NO SUBETE — 1975 EXPRESS JAP 72088
KENJI MISHIRO K V (C — (C) LIKE A MESSAGE FROM THE STORM — 1977 ALL EARS 11477
OSAMU TAKEDA D V (C

C111 **CHRYSALIS** C111

PAUL ALBUM B (A — (A) DEFINITION — 1968 MGM US 4547
J SPIDER BARBOUR V (A
RALPH KOTKOV K V (A — NANCY NAIN V (A — JOHN SABIN G (A
DAHAUD SHAAR D (A

C111A **CHUNKY NOVI & ERNIE** C111A

CHUNKY V K (A — (A) CHUNKY NOVI & ERNIE — 1976 REPRISE US 2146
NOVI VLN SYN K V (A — (A) CHUNKY NOVI & ERNIE — 1977 WB US 3030
ERNIE B V (A
RUSS KUNKEL D (A — STEVE FORMAN PERC (A — MILT HOLLAND PERC (A
BOBBYE HALL PERC (A — JIM COWGER WIND (A — IAN UNDERWOOD SYN WOOD(A
ELLEN LAZARES G (A — LEE RITENOUR G (A — TIRAN PORTER V (A
DOUG LIVINGSTON STEEL BAN (A — JAY GRAYDON G (A

C111B **THE CHURCH** C111B

STEVE KILBEY V K B (ABC — (A) OF SKIN & HEART — 1981 PARLOPHONE PCS 7583
NICK WARD D V (A — (B) THE CHURCH — 1982 CARRERE CAL 130
PETER KOPPES G (ABC — (C) BLURRED CRUSADE — 1982 CARRERE CAL 140
MARTY WILSON-PIPER G (ABC
BOB CLEARMOUNTAIN PROD (C — RICHARD PLOOG D (BC

C112 **CHICK CHURCHILL** C112

CHICK CHURCHILL K V (A — (A) YOU & ME — 1973 CHRYSALIS UK US CHR1051 GER 6307 525
LEO LYONS B (A
RIC LEE D (A — MARTIN BARRE G (A — BERNIE MARSDEN G (A
BILL JACKMAN SAX (A — COZY POWELL D (A — GARY PICKFORD HOPKINS V (A
ROGER HODGSON G B (A — RICK DAVIES D (A

C113

CHURLS

C113

Record	Year	Label	Country	Number
(A) THE CHURLS	196	A&M	US	4169
(B) SEND ME NO FLOWERS	196	A&M	US	4233

Member	Instrument	Records
BRAD FOWLES	D	(
HARRY SOUTHWORTH AMES	G	(
SAM HURRIE	G	(
JOHN BARR	B	(
BOB O'NEILL	V	(

C113A

CHUTE LIBRE

C113A

Record	Year	Label	Country	Number
(A) CHUTE LIBRE	19	PATHE		066 14359
(B) ALI BABA	19	PATHE		068 14522

Member	Instrument	Records
GILLES DOUIEB	B	(
OLIVIER HUTMAN	K	(
PATRICE CINILU	G	
MINO CINILU	PERC	(
PIERRE JEAN GIDEN	SAX	(
DENNIS BARBIER	FLT	(
ERIC LETOURNEUX	SAX	(A

C113B

CICHLIDS

C113B

Record	Year	Label	Country	Number
(A) BE TRUE TO YOUR SCHOOL	1980	BOLD	US	306

Member	Instrument	Records
DEBBIE MASCARO	G	(A
ALLAN PORTMAN	G	(A
SUSAN ROBINS	B K	(A
BOBBY TAK	D	(A

C113C

CIGARETTZ

C113C

Record	Year	Label	Country	Number
(A) CRAWL RITE OUTTA MY SKIN	1979	CANCER	UK	34794

C114

CIMARONS

C114

Record	Year	Label	Country	Number
(A) IN TIME	1974	TROJAN		TRLS 87
(B) ON THE ROCK	1976	VULCAN		VULA 501
(C) LIVE AT THE ROUNDHOUSE	1978	POLYDOR		2383 489
(D) MAKA	1978	POLYDOR		2383 512
(E) FREEDOM STREET	1980	VIRGIN	NL	203 092

Member	Instrument	Records
CARL LEVY	K G V	(BCD
FRANKLYN DUNN	B K V	(BCD
WINSTON REID	V PERC	(BCD
LOCKSLEY GICHIE	G V	(BCD
MAURICE ELLIS	D	(BCD

C115

CIRCUS (1)

C115

Record	Year	Label	Country	Number
(A) CIRCUS	1969	TRANSATLANTIC		TRA 207
(A) CIRCUS	1969	METRONOME		15 360
(B) LISTEN TO THE BAND	19	TRANSATLANTIC		
(C) CIRCUS	1977	PHASE 4	UK	4122

Member	Instrument	Records
PHILIP GOODHAND TAIT	K	(
MEL COLLINS	SAX	(A
IAN JELFS	G V	(A
CHRIS BURROWS	D	(A
ALAN BUNN		(
KEITH BLEASBY		(A
KIRK RIDDLE	B	(A

NB PREVIOUSLY THE STORMVILLE SHAKERS

C115A

CIRCUS (2)

C115A

Record	Year	Label	Country	Number
(A) CIRCUS	1974	HEMISPHERE	US	6679
(B) BAND 1975				

Member	Instrument	Records
RAY CYR	D PERC	(A
JIM ASH	D V PERC	(B
WAYNE KESTRASKI	B V	(AB
RANDY GLADOWSKI	G V	(AB
BRETT PETERSON	DOB G BAN V	(A
FRED OMERNIK	K V	(A

C116

CIRCUS MAXIMUS

C116

Record	Year	Label	Country	Number
(A) CIRCUS MAXIMUS	1967	VANGUARD		VSD 79260
(B) NEVERLAND REVISITED	1968	VANGUARD		VSD 79274

Member	Instrument	Records
BOB BRUNO	G V K	(AB
DAVID SCHERSTROM	D	(AB
GARY WHITE	B V	(AB
PETER TROUTNER	G V	(AB
JERRY JEFF WALKER	V G	(A

C116A

CITTA FRONTALE

C116A

Record	Year	Label	Country	Number
(A) EL TOR	1975	FONIT	IT	45

Member	Instrument	Records
ENZE AVITABILE	WIND	(A
MASSIMO GUARINE	D PERC	(A
RINE ZURZELE	B	(A
LINO VAIRETTI	G V HCA K	(A
GIANNI GUARRACINE	G SYN V	(A
PAOLO RAFFONE	K	(A

C117

CITY

C117

Record	Year	Label	Country	Number
(A) NOW THAT EVERYTHINGS BEEN SAID	1969	ODE	US	Z12 44012

Member	Instrument	Records
CAROLE KING	K V	(A
DANNY KORTCHMAR	G V	(A
JIM GORDON	D	(A
CHARLES LARKEY	B	(A

C117A

CITY

C117A

Record	Year	Label	Country	Number
(A) FIRST	1978	AMIGA	GDR	855586
(B) DREAMLAND	1980	POOL		624391

Member	Instrument	Records
GEORGI GOGOW	B G VLN	(AB
TONI KRAHL	V VLN	(AB
KLAUS SELMKE	D	(AB
FRITZ PUPPEL	G	(AB
PITTI	G	(B
RITCHIE	K	(B

C118

CITY BOY

C118

Record	Year	Label	Number	US Label	Number
(A) CITY BOY	1976	VERTIGO UK	6360 126	US MERCURY	1098
(B) DINNER AT THE RITZ	1976	VERTIGO UK	6360 136	US MERCURY	1121
(C) YOUNG MEN GONE WEST	1977	VERTIGO UK	6360 151	US MERCURY	1182
(C) YOUNG MEN GONE WEST	1977	PHONOGRAM			9102 018
(D) BOOK EARLY	1978	VERTIGO UK	9102 028	US MERCURY	13737
(E) DAY THE EARTH CAUGHT FIRE	1979	VERTIGO UK	9102 036		
(F) HEAD ARE ROLLING	1980	VERTIGO UK	6359 024	US ATLANTIC	19285

Member	Instrument	Records
LOL MASON	V	(ABCDEF
STEVE BROUGHTON	V G	(ABCDE
MAX THOMAS	V K	(ABCDEF
ETACHRA TRENCH	PNO	(B
R J LANGE	B	(BDE
B J COLE	STEEL	(B
ROGER KENT	D	(AB
ROY WARD	D	(DEF
DAVE JACKSON	SAX	(B
MIKE SLAMER	V	(ABCDEF
ALBIE DONNELLY	SAX	(C
GREG MATHIESON	K	(D
KENDAL STUBBS	B PERC	(E
DEREK KING	PNO	(E
VANDERGRAAF GENERATOR	V	(B
CHRIS DUNN	G B	(ABCDE
GEOFF TRISTRAM	CLAR	(C
MERLE ANGER	G	(D
HUEY LEWIS	HCA	(E
JACK HOLSTEIN	FDL	(B
TONY BRAUNAGEL	D	(C
FRANK RICOTTI	PERC	(C
ROY BABBINGTON	B	(D
TIM FRIESE-GREENE	SYN	(E

C118A

CITY LIGHTS

C118A

Record	Year	Label	Country	Number
(A) SILENT DANCING	1975	SIRE	US	7512

Member	Instrument	Records
LELAND BOBBE	D	(A
MARL ABEL	B V	(A
DON WILKINS	K V	(A
JOHN BERENZY	G V	(A

C118B

CITY WAITES

C118B

Record	Year	Label	Country	Number
(A) A GORGEOUS GALLERY OF GALLANT INVENTIONS	1974	EMI		EMC 3017
(B) CITY WAITES	1976	DECCA		SKL 5264

Member	Instrument	Records
ROD SKEAPING	VLN	(AB
JOE SKEAPING		(A
DOUG WOOTON		(AB
LUCIE FINCH		(AB
KEITH THOMPSON		(B

C119

CLANCY

C119

Record	Year	Label	Country	Number
(A) SERIOUSLY SPEAKING	1975	W B	UK	K 56103
(B) EVERYDAY	1975	W B	UK	K 56206

Member	Instrument	Records
DAVE SKINNER	K V	(AB
GASPAR LAWAL	PERC V	(AB
ERNIE GRAHAM	G V	(AB
DAVE VASCO	G V	(AB
JIM CUOMO	SAX	(AB
COLIN BASS	B V	(AB
BARRY FORD	D V	(AB
SAM MITCHELL	DOBRO	(B

CLANNAD

C120

Member	Instrument	Albums
MAIRE BRENNAN	HARP V	(ALL
PAUL BRENNAN	G V PERC FLT	(ALL
DONAL LUNNY	G PERC SYN	(B
CIARAN BRENNAN	B G V K	(ALL
ROBBIE BRENNAN	D	(B
PADRAIG DUGGAN	G V MAND	(ALL
JOHN WADHAM	D	(A
GRAINNE McMONAGLE	WHISTLE	(A
MICHAEL O'DOMHNAILL	G V	(B
PADRAIG O'DOMHNAILL	V	(B
NOEL DUGGAN	G V	(ALL
NICKY RYAN	V	(C
NEIL BUCKLEY	WIND	(F
EITHNE BRENNAN	K V PERC	(EF
PAT O'FARREL	G	(F
TRIONA O'DOMHNAILL	K	(B
NOEL BRIDGEMAN	D PERC	(F

	Title	Year	Label / Number
(A)	CLANNAD	1973	PHILIPS IR 6392 013
(B)	CLANNAD 2	1974	GAEL LINN IR 041 INTERCORD GER 160 058
(B)	CLANNAD 2	1974	SHANACHIE US 79007
(C)	DULAMAN	1976	GAEL LINN IR 058 INTERCORD GER 160 065
(C)	DULAMAN	1976	SHANACHIE US 79008
(D)	CLANNAD IN CONCERT	1978	OGHAM US IR 5001 INTERCORD GER 160 124
(E)	CRANN ULL	1980	TARA IR 3007 INTERCORD GER 160 153
(E)	CRANN ULL	1981	PHILIPS UK 6373 016
(F)	FUAIM	1982	TARA IR 3008

C121

ERIC CLAPTON

C121

Member	Instrument	Albums
ERIC CLAPTON	G V	(ALL
WITH		
CARL RADLE	B	(ABEFGJKLN
JAMIE OLDAKER	D	(EFGJKLN
DICK SIMS	K	(EFGJKLN
GEORGE TERRY	G	(EFGJKLN
YVONNE ELLIMAN	V	(EFJL
SERGIO RODRIGUEZ	PERC	(J
ALBHY GALUTEN	PNO	(EFJ
TOM BERNFELD	V	(E
RICK GRECH	B	(D
JIM KARSTEIN	D	(D
RONNIE WOOD	G	(DJ
STEVE WINWOOD	K V	(DB
BOBBY WHITLOCK	K V	(AB
GRAHAM LYLE	V	(N
JIM FOX	D	(E
SONNY CURTIS	V	(
ALBERT LEE	G	(O1P
LEON RUSSELL	PNO	(A
JIM GORDON	D	(AB
BENNY GALLAGHER	V	(N
HENRY SPINETTI	D	(O1P
CHRIS STAINTON	K	(O
DAVE MARKEE	B	(O1
JERRY ALLISON	V	(A
MARCY LEVY	V	(FGJKLN
GARY BROOKER	K	(1P
AL JACKSON	D	(E
PETE TOWNSHEND	G V	(D
CHRIS DREJA	G	(B
GINGER BAKER	D	(B
JIM PRICE	HRNS	(AB
JOHN McVIE	B	(B
BOBBY KEYS	SAX	(AB
LEON RUSSELL	PNO	(B
RICK DANKO	B	(J
RICHARD MANUEL	D	(J
WILTON SPEARS		(J
JESSE ED DAVIS	G	(J
LEVON HELM	D	(J
ROBBIE ROBERTSON	G K	(J
JOHN SIMON	K	(A
JIM CAPALDI	D	(D
JIM McCARTY	D	(B
PAUL JONES	HCA	(B
RITA COOLIDGE	V	(AB
JACK BRUCE	B V	(B
DAVE MASON	G	(B
DUANNE ALLMAN	G	(B
BOB ELLIS	TPT	(J
NAT JEFFERY		(J
DOMINIC LUMETTA		(J
TERRY DANKO	PERC	(J
RALPH MOSS	PERC	(J
SANDY CASTLE	V	(J
STEPHEN STILLS	G	(A
REBOP	PERC	(D
JOHN MAYALL	V K	(B
FELIX PAPPALARDI	K	(B
PAUL SAMWELL SMITH	B	(B
STEVE ANGELO	V	(B
TEX JOHNSON	PERC	(B
ED ANDERSON		(J
GEOFF HARRISON		(J
DICK LA PALM		(J
LARRY SAMUELS		(J
KONRAD KRAMER		(J
DREAD LEVER		(J
MICK TURNER		(J
MEL COLLINS	HRNS	(L
DELANEY BRAMLETT	G V	(AB
HUGHIE FLINT	D	(B
BONNIE BRAMLETT	V	(AB
KEITH RELF	V	(B
L'ANGELO MISTERIOSO	G	(B
KING CURTIS	SAX	(B
BOB DYLAN	V	(J
GARTH HUDSON	K SAX	(J
BILLY PRESTON	K	(J
BRAINS BRADLEY		(J
GEORGIE FAME	K	(J
CHRIS JAGGER	V	(J
WAH WAH WATSON	G	(J

	Title	Year	Label / Number
(A)	ERIC CLAPTON	1970	POLYDOR US PD13008 UK 2383 021
(A)	ERIC CLAPTON	1976	RSO UK 2394 186
(B)	HISTORY OF	1972	RSO 2659 012 RI 2671 107
(B)	HISTORY OF	197	ATCO US SD1 803
(B)	HISTORY OF	197	POLYDOR 2668 011
(C)	AT HIS BEST	1972	POLYDOR US 3503 UK 2659 025
(D)	RAINBOW CONCERT	1973	RSO US 877 UK 2394 116
(E)	461 OCEAN BOULEVARD	1974	RSO US 1 3023 UK 2479 118
(E)	461 OCEAN BOULEVARD	1974	RSO 4801
(F)	THERE'S ONE IN EVERY CROWD	1974	RSO US 4806 UK 2479 132
(G)	E C WAS HERE	1975	RSO EURO 2479154 UK 2394 160
(H)	BLUES WORLD OF E C	1975	DECCA UK SPA 387
(I)	THE BEST OF E C	1975	POLYDOR 2482 143
(J)	NO REASON TO CRY	1976	RSO US 1 3004 UK 2479 179
(L)	SLOWHAND	1977	RSO US 1 3030 UK 2479 201
(M)	CLAPTON	1978	RSO UK 2479 702
(N)	BACKLESS	1978	RSO US 1 3039 UK 2479 221
(N)	BACKLESS	1978	RSO EURO 2394 213 RSD 5001
(O)	JUST ONE NIGHT	1980	RSO 24202 UK 2479 240
( )	POP GIANTS	19	BRUNSWICK 2911 518
( )	POP HISTORY	19	POLYDOR 2668 001
( )	CLAPTON BECK & PAGE	1973	ELECTROLA 048 51780
( )	GREATEST HITS	1976	TELDEC GER 622282
( )	POP MUSIC	19	POLYDOR FR 2458 111
(P)	ANOTHER TICKET	1981	RSO US 1 3095 UK 2479 285
(Q)	ERIC CLAPTON 4 LP SET	1981	RSO NL 2658 276
(R)	STEPPIN OUT	1982	DECCA UK TAB21
(1)	1980 TOUR		

C122

DAVE CLARK FIVE

C122

Member	Instrument	Albums
DAVE CLARK	D V	(ALL
MIKE SMITH	K V	(ALL
LENNY DAVIDSON	G B	(ALL
RICK HUXLEY	G	(ALL
DENNIS PAYTON	SAX K	(ALL

	Title	Year	Label	Mono	Stereo
	A SESSION WITH	1963	COLUMBIA UK		33SX 1598
	A SESSION WITH	1968	M F P UK		MFP 1260
	GLAD ALL OVER	1964	EPIC	US MON LN24093	STER BN 26093
	AMERICAN TOUR	1964	EPIC	US MON LN24104	STER BN 26117
	RETURN	1964	EPIC	US MON LN24104	
	COAST TO COAST	1965	EPIC	US	STER BN 26128
	CATCH US IF YOU CAN	1965	COLUMBIA UK		SX 1756
	WILD WEEKEND	1965	EPIC	US MON LN24162	STER BN 26162
	I LIKE IT LIKE THAT	1966	EPIC		
	GREATEST HITS	1966	COLUMBIA UK		SX 6105
	GREATEST HITS	1966	EPIC	US	STER BN 26185
	TRY TO HARD	1966	EPIC	US MON LN24198	STER BN 26198
	SATISFIED WITH YOU	1966	EPIC	US MON LN24212	STER BN 26212
	MORE GREATEST HITS	1966	EPIC	US MON LN24221	STER BN 26221
	5 BY 5	1967	EPIC	US	
	YOU GOT WHAT IT TAKES	1967	EPIC	US	STER BN 26312
	EVERYBODY KNOWS	1968	COLUMBIA UK		SX 6207
	14 TITLES BY DAVE CLARK	1968	COLUMBIA UK		SCX 6309
	WEEKEND IN LONDON	1968	EPIC	US MON LN24139	STER BN 26139
	BEST OF	1970	STARLINE UK		SRS 5037
	IF SOMEBODY LOVES YOU(SOLO)	1971	COLUMBIA UK		SCX 6437
	GOOD OLD ROCK'N'ROLL	1971	STARLINE UK		SRS 5090
	GLAD ALL OVER	1975	EPIC US		33459
	GOOD OLD ROCK'N'ROLL	1975	MFP UK		MFP 90197
	BEST OF	197	EMI EURO	048 50737	
	25 THUMPING HITS	1978	POLYDOR UK		POLTV 7
	THE VERY BEST OF	19	MFP	EURO 96813/14	
	DAVE CLARK FIVE (DBL)	19	EPIC US		EG 30434
	BEAT BATTLE OF THE WORLD	19	GROOVEMASTER US		BR 140
	ACROSS CANADA	19	CAPITOL CAN		
	ON STAGE	19	CAPITOL CAN		
	OVER & OVER	19	CAPITOL CAN		
	INSTRUMENTAL ALBUM	1966	CAPITOL CAN	6162	
EPS	DAVE CLARK FIVE	1964	COLUMBIA UK	SEG 8289	
	HITS OF THE D CLARK FIVE	1964	COLUMBIA UK	SEG 8381	
	& FRIENDS	1972	COLUMBIA UK		SCX 6494

C122A

DEE CLARK

C122A

DEE CLARK (AB

(A) YOUR FRIENDS 1980 CHARLY UK CTD 115
(B) KEEP IT UP (EP) 1980 CHARLEY UK CRB 1010

C123

GENE CLARK

C123

GENE CLARK G V (ALL
LEON RUSSELL K (A
BUTCH TRUCKS D (F
RUSS KUNKEL D (F
MICHAEL UTLEY K (DFH
CRAIG DOERGE K (F
JOE LALA PERC (F
RICHARD GREENE VLN (F
CHRIS HILLMAN MAND (AF
TED MACHELL CELLO(F
JESSE ED DAVIS G (DF
BILL CUOMO K (F
JERRY McGEE G (FH
DANNY KOOTCH G (F
STEVE BRUTON G (F
CARLENA WILLIAMS V (F
DOUG DILLARD (ABH
BOBBYE HALL PERC (D
BILL RHEINHART G (A
MIKE CLARKE D (A
PEPPER WATKINS V (H
MATTHEW MOORE V (H
CLYDIE KING V (F
BUZZY FEITEN G (F
TIM SCHMIT V (F
EMMYLOU HARRIS V (H
GARY MALLABER D (D
CLARENCE WHITE G (A
SAMMY CREASON D (H
JOHN HARTFORD V (H
LELAND SKLAR B (F
RONNIE BARRON V (F
AL PERKINS G (H
BYRON BERLINE FDL (H
JOHN SELK G (D
GLEN CAMPBELL G (A
JIM FIELDER B (H
T JEFFERSON KAY PROD V (HF
CINDY BULLENS V (F
SHIRLEY MATTHEWS V (F
JEFF BAXTER G (H
CHRIS ETHRIDGE B (D
BEN SIDRAN K (D
JERRY COLE G (A
STEVE SOLES V (H
DANIEL MOORE V (H
VANETTA FIELDS V (F

(A) GENE CLARK & THE GOSDIN BROTHERS 1967 CBS US 9418 US CL2618
(B) FANTASTIC EXPEDITION 1969 A&M US 4159 UK AMLS 939
(C) THROUGH THE MORNING 1969 A&M US 4203 UK AMLS 966
(D) WHITE LIGHT 1972 A&M US 4292 UK AMLS64297
(D) WHITE LIGHT 1974 ARIOLA 88172
(E) ROAD MASTER 1973 ARIOLA 87584
(F) NO OTHER 1974 ASYLUM US 7E1016 UK SYL 9020
(F) NO OTHER 1974 ELEKTRA UK K53005
(G) KANSAS CITY SOUTHERN 1975 ARIOLA 86436
(H) TWO SIDES TO EVERY STORY 1977 RSO US 1 3011 UK 2394 176
( ) COLLECTORS CLASSICS 1976 CBS US 32998
( ) EARLY L A SESSIONS 1975 CBS US 31123
( ) GENE CLARK (COMP) 19 TOGETHER US ST 1001

C124

GUY CLARK

C124

GUY CLARK G V (ABC
MIKE LEECH B (AB
JERRY KROON D (ABC
JERRY CARRIGAN D (A
PHILLIP DONNELLY G (C
LARRIE LONDIN D (A
DICK FELLER G (A
DAVID BRIGGS K V (ABC
JOHNNY GIMBLE FDL (A
RODNEY CROWELL V (ABC
STEVE EARLE V (A
JACK HICKS BANJO (BC
JERRY JEFF WALKER G V (B
SUSANNA CLARK V (B
ALBERT LEE G (C
GORDON PAYNE V (C
DON BROOKS HCA (C
CHIP YOUNG G (A
JIM COLVARD G (A
CHUCK COCHRAN PNO (AB
BRIAN AHERN G (B
EMMYLOU HARRIS V (AB
SAMMI SMITH V (A
PETE GRANT STEEL(B
WAYLON JENNINGS G V (B
CHARLIE BUNDY V (B
B SPEARS B (C
BUCK WHITE MAND (C
STRING SECTION (C
PAT CARTER G V (A
REGGIE YOUNG G (A
SHANE KEISTER PNO (A
DANNY ROWLAND G V (B
GARY B WHITE V (A
STEVE KEITH FDL (B
CHRIS LAIRD PERC (B
CHIP MOMAN G (B
TRACY NELSON V (B
CHERYL WHITE V (C
SHARON HICKS V (C
STEVE GIBSON G (A
HAL RUGG DOB STEEL(A
LEA JANE BERINATI K V(ABC
MICKEY RAPHAEL HCA (AC
FLORENCE WARNER V (A
TOMMY WILLIAMS FDL (A
BYRON BACH CELLO (BC
NICOLETTE LARSON V (B
HOYT AXTON V (B
DON EVERLY V (C
FRANK DAVIS V (C

(A) OLD NUMBER ONE 1976 RCA APLI 1303
(B) TEXAS COOKIN' 1976 RCA US 1944 UK RS 1097
(C) GUY CLARK 1978 WB US 3241 UK K 56565
(D) SOUTH COAST OF TEXAS 1980 WB US 3381 UK K 56902

C124A

LOUIS CLARK

C124A

LOUIS CLARK K (A

(A) PER-SPEK-TIV 1979 JET UK LP218

C125

SANFORD CLARK

C125

SANFORD CLARK (ALL

( ) THEY CALL ME COUNTRY 19 EMBER CW 131
( ) MODERN ROMANCE 1975 DO JA US

C126

CLARK-HUTCHINSON

C126

ANDY CLARK V K (ABC
STEPHEN AMAZING B (AB
MICHAEL HUTCHINSON G (ABC
DEL COVERLY PERC (C

(A) A=MH² 1970 NOVA GER 6 22548 UK SDNR2
(A) A=MH² 1970 SIRE US 97021
(B) RETRIBUTION 1970 DERAM UK SML1076 GER NOVA 12014
(B) RETRIBUTION 1970 DERAM US 18055
(C) GESTALT 1971 DERAM UK SML 1090
(AB) A=MH²/RETRIBUTION 1973 TELDEC GERM SDM3015/ 2

C127

ALLAN CLARKE

C127

ALLAN CLARKE V (ALL
WITH
HERBIE FLOWERS B (AC
GARY BROOKER K (A
ROGER COULAM (A
JOE EGAN (A
JOE MORRETTI (A
B J COLE STEEL (C
ERIC DILLON (A
ALAN PARKER (A
TONY NEWMAN D V (B
LARRY BROWN PERC (E
MIKE PORCARO B (E
RANDY BISHOP G V (E
TONY NEWMAN D (C
LIZA STRIKE V (C
DEE MURRAY K V (AB
RAY GLYNN V G (BC
JAY GRAYDON G (E
ROBBIE BUCHANAN K (E
MIKE STATON STEEL(E
MIKE MORAN (C
MADELINE BELL V (C
MARGO NEWMAN V (B
STEVE KIPNER V (E
BEN BENAY G (E
DEAN WEBB MAND (E
DAVID WOLFER MAND (E
PETE ROBINSON K (C
KIRK DUNCAN K V (B
DAVID KEMPER D (E
TOM HENSLEY K (E
TONY BERG G (E
HERB PEDERSEN V (E
JOHN GUSTAFSON B (C

(A) MY REAL NAME IS 'AROLD 1972 RCA UK SF 8283
(B) HEADROOM 1973 EMI UK EMA 752
(C) ALLAN CLARKE 1974 EMI UK EMC 3041
(D) I'VE GOT TIME 1976 EMI UK EMC 3130
(D) I'VE GOT TIME 1976 ASYLUM US 7E 1056
(E) I WASN'T BORN YESTERDAY 1978 AURA UK AUL 704
(E) I WASN'T BORN YESTERDAY 1979 ATLANTIC US SD 19175
(F) LEGENDARY HEROS 1979 ELEKTRA UK 52224 US CURB 267

C128

JOHNNY CLARKE

C128

JOHNNY CLARKE

(A) ENTER INTO HIS GATES 1975 ATTACK ATLP 1015
(B) PUT IT ON 1975 VULCAN VULP 001
(C) ROCKERS TIME NOW 1976 VIRGIN V 2058
( ) AUTHORISED VERSIONS 1977 VIRGIN V 2076
( ) UP PARK CAMP 1977 JUSTICE JUS 001
( ) DONT STAY OUT LATE 1977 PARADISE PDL 001
( ) GIRL I LOVE YOU 1978 JUSTICE JUS 006
( ) SWEET CONVERSATION 1978 THIRD WORLD TWS 914
( ) KING OF THE ARENA 1978 THIRD WORLD TWS 932
( ) SATISFACTION 1979 THIRD WORLD TWSD 4

C129 STANLEY CLARKE C129

STANLEY CLARKE B PNO (ALL
BILLY COBHAM D (C
JEFF BECK G (BCDE
MILT HOLLAND PERC (C
CHICK COREA K (BC
CHARLES JOHNSON G (CF
GEORGE DUKE K SYN (BCEG
DAVID SANCIOUS G (BC
LENNY WHITE D (BC
SIMON PHILLIPS D (F
JON FADDIS TPT (ABC
LEW SOLOFF TPT (ABC
CARMINE APPICE D (D
TOM MALONE TROM (BC
JEFF BAXTER G (D
JAMES TINSLEY TPT (DE
ALFIE WILLIAMS SAX (DE
GERRY BROWN D (DEC
TONY WILLIAMS D (A
GARNET BROWN HRNS (A
JUANITA CURIEL (E
HARVEY MASON D (E
TOM SCOTT SAX (E
JOHN ROBINSON D (G
STRING SECTION (G

(A) STANLEY CLARKE 1974 NEMPEROR US 431 UK K50101
(A) STANLEY CLARKE RI 1980 EPIC US 36973 UK EMBASSY 32042
(B) JOURNEY TO LOVE 1975 NEMPEROR US 433 UK K50187
(B) JOURNEY TO LOVE RI 1980 EPIC US 36974 UK EMBASSY 32093
(C) SCHOOLDAYS 1976 NEMPEROR US 900 UK K50296
(C) SCHOOLDAYS RI 1980 EPIC US 36975 UK EMBASSY 32094
(D) MODERN MAN 1978 NEMPEROR US 35303 EPIC UK 82674
(E) I WANNA PLAY FOR YOU 1979 EPIC UK 88331
(F) ROCKS PEBBLES & SAND 1980 EPIC US 36506 UK 84342
(G) STANLEY CLARKE/GEORGE DUKE PROJECT 1981 EPIC US 36918 UK 84848
( ) CHILDREN OF FOREVER 1972 POLYDOR US PD 5531

PETER GORDON HRNS (ABC
JOHN CLARK HRNS (BC
JEFF PORCARO D (D
AL HARRISON TPT (DE
DALE DEVOE TROM (D
JOHN McLAUGHLIN G (BC
BILL CONNORS G (A
DARRYL BROWN (E
RONNIE FOSTER (E
GWEN OWENS V (E
STEVE BACH K (F
JERRY HEY TPT (G

ALAN RUBIN TPT (BC
EARL CHAPIN HRNS (BC
RAY GOMEZ G (CDE
DEE DEE BRIDGEWATER V (DE
MAXINE WILLARD V (D
STEVE GADD D (BCDE
AIRTO MOREIRA PERC (AE
CATHY CARSON (E
STAN GETZ SAX (E
LEE RITENOUR G (E
PHIL JOST K (E
GARY FOSTER WIND (G

DAVID TAYLOR TROM (ABC
WILMER WISE HRNS (BC
MICHAEL GARSON K (DE
BOBBY MALACH TPT (DE
JULIA TILLMAN V (D
JAN HAMMER K (A
JAMES BUFFINGTON HRNS (A
TODD COCHRAN K (E
FREDDIE HUBBARD (E
PETER ROBINSON K (E
MICHAEL BODDICKER SYN (G

C130 THE CLASH C130

TERRY CHIMES D (12A
KEITH LEVINE G (1
MICK JONES G V (123ABCD
JOE STRUMMER G V (123ABCD
NICKY HEADON D (3BCD
PAUL SIMONON B (123ABCD
BEN HEGART (D
MICKEY GALLAGHER K (D
TOMON DOGG V (D
MIKE DREAS V (D
ELLEN FOLEY (D

(A) THE CLASH 1977 CBS US 36060 UK 82000
(B) GIVE THEM ENOUGH ROPE 1978 CBS US 35543 UK 82341
(C) LONDON CALLING (DBL) 1979 CBS US 36328 UK CLASH3
(D) SANDINISTA (TRP) 1980 CBS US 37037 UK FSLN 1
(E) BLACK MARKET (10") 1980 EPIC US 36846
(F) PEARL HARBOUR 19 JAP
( ) COST OF LIVING (EP) 1979 CBS
(1) APR/SEP 1976 (2) SEP76/MARCH 77 (3) MAR77/>>

NORMAN WATTROY (D
DAVID PAYNE (D
J P NICHOLSON (D
RAY GASCOGNE (D

C131 CLASSIC NOUVEAUX C131

(A) NIGHT PEOPLE 1981 LIBERTY UK LBG30325 NL 83143
(A) CLASSIC NOUVEAUX (SAME TRACKS) 1981 LIBERTY US LT 1104

C132 CLASSICS IV C132

DENNIS YOST V (
JAMES COBB G (
WALLY EATON (
JOSEPH WILSON B (
KIM VENABLE D (
ALBURN BURRELL G (
DEAN DOUGHTRY G (
STEVE PULLIAS G (
MICHAEL HUEY D (

(A) SPOOKY 19 IMPERIAL US 12371
(B) MAMAS AND PAPAS SOUL TRAIN 19 IMPERIAL US 12407
(C) TRACES 19 IMPERIAL US 12429
( ) GOLDEN GREATS 19 IMPERIAL US 16000
( ) VERY BEST OF 19 UA US LA446
( ) DENNIS YOST & CLASSICS IV 19 M G M US 702

SAM ANDERSON SAX (
DANIEL RAMOS K (
WILLIAM GILMORE B (

C133 LEE CLAYTON C133

LEE CLAYTON HCA V G (ABC
COLIN CAMERON B (B
JIMMY DAY STEEL (B
PHILIP DONNELLY G (B1
CARLY SIMON V (A
DANNY LANE D (B
ANDY McMAHON K (B
REGGIE YOUNG G (A
RICHARD BOWEN G (A
BOBBY WOODS K (A
TIM DRUMMOND B (A
MICKY McGEE D (A
TONY NEWMAN D (1

(A) LEE CLAYTON 1973 MCA US 365
(B) BORDER AFFAIR 1978 CAPITOL NL85446 US ST 11751
(C) NAKED CHILD 1979 CAPITOL NL85880 US EST 11942
(D) THE DREAM GOES ON 1980 CAPITOL UK 12139
(1) 1979 TOUR

WAYNE JACKSON TPT (B
CHIP YOUNG G (A
LLOYS GREEN STEEL (A
SHANE KESTLER K (A
DENNIS LINDE B (A
BONNIE BRAMLETT V (A

ANDREW LOVE SAX (B
JOHN CHRISTOPHER G (A
ED BLACK STEEL (A
MIKE LEECH B (A
KENNY MALONE D (A
BILLY COX B (1

C134 MERRY CLAYTON C134

MERRY CLAYTON V (ALL
CAROLE KING PNO (B
GARY KING B (C
HUGH McCRACKEN G (C
DAVID SPINOZZA G (C
KEN ASHER K (C
BOB JAMES K (C
STEVE GADD D (C

(A) GIMME SHELTER 1970 A&M UK AMLS995 US ODE 77001
(B) MERRY CLAYTON 1971 A&M UK AMLS67012 US ODE 77012
(B) MERRY CLAYTON 197 EPIC US PE 34948
(C) KEEP YOUR EYE ON THE SPARROW 1975 ODE US 77030 US EPIC 34957
(D) CELEBRATION 197 ODE US X 77008
(E) EMOTION 1979 MCA US 3200

IDRIS MUHAMMED D (C

C135 PETER CLAYTON C135

PETER CLAYTON V (A
BLIND JOHN DAVIS PNO (A
RANSOM KNOWLING B (A

(A) PEARL HARBOUR BLUES (1 SIDE ONLY) 1970 RCA INT INT 1176

WILLIE LACEY G (A
ALFRED ELKINS B (A

C136 DAVID CLAYTON THOMAS C136

DAVID CLAYTON THOMAS V (ALL
WILLIAM D SMITH K (*
DOMENIC TROIANO G (*
PAUL STALLWORTH B (*
KENNETH RICE D (*
NEIL LEVANG BANJ (*
KEN MARCO G (*
CHUCK RAINEY B (*
GABRIEL MEKLER PNO (*

DAVID CLAYTON THOMAS 1969 DECCA DL 75146
DAVID CLAYTON THOMAS 1972 CBS US 31000
DAVID CLAYTON THOMAS 1972 CBS UK 65755
HARMONY JUNCTION 1973 RCA US UK SF 8381
(*) DAVID CLAYTON THOMAS 1973 RCA US APLI 0173
TEQUILA SUNRISE 1972 CBS US 31700 UK 65237
CLAYTON 19 ABC US 1104

MOUSE JOHNSON D (*
KING ERRISSON PERC (*

C136A CLEAR BLUE SKY C136A

JOHN SIMMONS G (A
MARK SHEATER B (A
KEN WHITE D (A

(A) CLEAR BLUE SKY 1971 VERTIGO UK 6360 013

C136B CLEAN LIVING C136B

ELLIOT SHERMAN K (A — (A) CLEAN LIVING — 1972 VANGUARD US 79318
ROBERT LAMOUNTAIN G V (AB — (B) MEADOWMUFFIN — 1973 VANGUARD US 79334
FRANK SHAW B V (AB
PAUL LAMBERT STEEL (AB — JEFFREY POTTER K PERC(B — TIM GRIFFIN D (AB
ROBERT LAPALM G (AB — NORMAN SCHELL G V (AB — K P BURKE HCA (A
AL ANDERSON G (AB — MIKE MANDEL PNO (B — TIM PITT G (B
GUILLAUME LAPALM FDL (B

C137 CLEARLIGHT C137

STEVE HILLAGE G (A — (A) CLEARLIGHT SYMPHONY — 1975 VIRGIN V 2029
DIDIER MALHERBE SAX (AD — (B) FOREVER BLOWING BUBBLES — 1975 VIRGIN V 2039
MARTIN ISAACS B (A — (C) LES CONTES DU SINGE FOU — 1976 ISADORA ISA 9009
CHRISTIAN BOULE G (ABD — (D) VISIONS — 1978 LTM FR 1005
JACKY BOULADOUX D PERC(D
GILBERT ARTMAN D PERC(AB — CYRILLE VERDEAUX K (ABCD — TIM BLAKE SYN (AC
FRANCOIS JEANNEAU WIND (B — BOB BOISADAN K (B — JOEL DUGRENOT B V (BC
JEAN CLAUDE AGOSTINI GFLT (B — CHRISTIAN STAPINOPOULOS D (B — BRUNO VERDEAUX SYN (B
BRIGITTE ROY V (B — FRANCIS MANDIN SYN (CD — YVES CHOUARD G (C
IAN BELLAMY V (C — DIDIER LOCKWOOD VLN (CD — SERGE AOUZI D PERC(C
DAVID CROSS VLN (A — GERARD GUSTIN V (D — PHILIPPE MELKONIAN B (D
LUC PLOUTON SYN (D — GERARD AUMONT V (D — PATRICK DEPAUMANOU SIT (D
MOHAMED TAHA PERC (D

C138 CLEAR LIGHT (US) C138

CLIFF DE YOUNG V (A — (A) CLEAR LIGHT — 1967 ELEKTRA US EKS 74011
DOUGLAS LUBAHN B (A
MICHAEL NEY D (A — BOB SEAL G (A — DALLAS TAYLOR D (A
RALPH SCHUCKETT K (A — DANNY KOOTCH G (

C138A EDDIE CLEARWATER C138A

EDDIE CLEARWATER (A — (A) EDDIE CLEARWATER — 1979 MCM FR 900 296

C138B VASSAR CLEMENTS C138B

VASSAR CLEMENTS (A — (A) VASSAR — 1981 FLYING FISH US FF232

C138C CLICKER C138C

STEVE TRACY B V (A — (A) CLICKER — 1973 HEMISPHERE US 5180
JERRY TRACY D V (A — (B) HARDE HAR HAR — 1975 CLICKER US 1975
MARK ERVERIST V (A
BOB SCMIDTKE G (A — DICK WIEGEL G V (A — CHRISTINE HESS V (A
LYNN McLAUGHLIN V (A — JEFF EISBERNER K (A

C139 JIMMY CLIFF C139

JIMMY CLIFF V (ALL — (A) HARD ROAD — 1967 ISLAND UK ILPS 962
WITH — (A) HARD ROAD — 1967 PHONOGRAM EUR 9101 675
JACKIE JACKSON B (E — (B) JIMMY CLIFF — 1969 TROJAN TRLS 16
WINSTON GRENNAN D (E — (B) JIMMY CLIFF — 1977 ISLAND UK ILPS 9414
RAD BRYAN G (E — (C) ANOTHER CYCLE — 1971 ISLAND UK ILPS9159 US 9202
HUX BROWN G (E — (D) HARDER THEY COME — 1972 ISLAND UK ILPS 9202
WINSTON WRIGHT ORG (E — (E) UNLIMITED — 1973 EMI UK EMA 757
GLADSTONE ANDERSON K (E — (E) UNLIMITED — 197 EMI FR 05404 US REPRISE 2147
LESLIE BUTLER K FLT (E — (F) STRUGGLING MAN — 1974 ISLAND UK ILPS 9235
HEPTONES V (E — (G) HOUSE OF EXILE — 1974 EMI UK EMC 3035
BOBBY ELLIS TPT (E — ( ) MUSIC MAKER — 1974 REPRISE US 2188
RITA MARLEY V (E — (H) BRAVE WARRIOR — 1975 EMI UK EMC 3078
JUDY MOWATT V (E — (H) BRAVE WARRIOR — 1975 PATHE FR 066 05873
NEVILLE GRANT V (E — (I) BEST OF JIMMY CLIFF — 1975 ISLAND UK ICD 6
BINGI BUNNY PERC (E — (J) FOLLOW MY MIND — 1976 REPRISE US 2218 UK K 54061
TOMMY McCOOK WIND (E — (K) GOODBYE YESTERDAY — 197 ISLAND IMP 85568
JEAN WATT V (E — (L) OH JAMAICA — 1976 EMI UK NUT 3 NL 06241
BOB TAYLOR V (E — (M) POP CHRONIK VOL 9 (DBL) — 1975 ISLAND IMP
DENSIL LAING PERC (E — (N) LIVE IN CONCERT — 1976 REPRISE US 2256 UK K 54086
RALSTON WEBB V (E — (O) WONDERFUL WORLD — 197 A&M US 4251
ZOOT SIMS (E — (P) GIVE THANX — 1978 WB US 3240 UK K 56558
RON WILSON WIND (E — ( ) SENSE OF DIRECTION — 197 SIRE US 7501
NORA DEAN V (E — ( ) CANT GET ENOUGH — 197 VEEP US VPS 16536
DONGO HERMAN PERC (E — (U) WONDERFUL WORLD — 197 ISLAND IMP 86488
STICKIE THOMPSON PERC (E — (P) I AM THE LIVING — 1980 WEA US 5153 UK 99089
TESFA McDONALD V (E — (Q) GIVE THE PEOPLE — 1981 WEA US 5153 UK 99160
GLENTON TAYLOR V (E
BARRY BECKETT K (C — ROGER HAWKINS D (C — DAVID HOOD B (C
JIMMY JOHNSON G (C — TIPPY ARMSTRONG G (C — JOSEPH HIGGS V (N
EDDIE HINTON G (C — ERNEST RANGLIN G (N — EARL 'BAGA'WALKER B (N
NOEL BAILEY G (N — SANTA D (N — ERNEST McCLEOD K (N

C139A BUZZ CLIFFORD C139A

BUZZ CLIFFORD V (— (A) BABY SITTIN' WITH BUZZ — 19 CBS US 8416 US 1616
(B) SEE YOUR WAY CLEAR — 1969 DOT US 25965

C139B DOUG CLIFFORD C139B

DOUG CLIFFORD (A — (A) DOUG'COSMO' CLIFFORD — 1972 FANTASY US 9411

C140 PAUL CLINCH & CHOYA C140

PAUL CLINCH V B G K(A — (A) LIVING LIKE A RICH MAN — 1976 BUDDAH US 5678
GARY GIES D (A
BRUCE LEY K V (A — DEBBIE SCHALL V STR (A — JOHN SHAND G SAX V (A
RICKY YORK V PERC(A — DAVE MORRISON G (A — DON PAVELING B (A
HAL GREER B (A — FRED MOLLIN G (A — WAYNE ST JOHN V (A
I GUENTHER FDL (A — G SEMKIW G (A

C140A CLIMAX C140A

SONNY GERACI V (A — (A) CLIMAX — 1972 ROCKY ROAD US RR 3506
JOE OSBORN B (A
STEVE LAFEVER B (A — REINIE PRESS B (A — JOE BELLAMY B (A
EARL PALMER D (A — JON GUTTMAN D PERC (A — JOHN RAINES D (A
WILT NIMS G (A — JOHN STEVENSON K (A — LARRY KNECHTEL K (A
NICK D'AMICO K (A — ALAN ESTES PERC (A — LARRY COX PERC (A
GORDON MacKINNON HRNS (A

C140B CLINIC C140B

Personnel	Recordings
GERRY MURPHY D (A	(A) NOW WE'RE EVEN 1973 ROULETTE US 3010
PHIL TRAINER B V (A	
PHIL RIGHAM G V (A	ALAN REEVES K SYN V(A

C140C CLOCK DVA C140C

Personnel	Recordings
CHARLIE COLLINS WIND (A	(A) THIRST 1981 FETISH UK 2002
ADI NEWTON V CLAR(A	( ) WHITE SOULS IN BLACK SUITS 19 CASS ONLY
ROGER QUAIL D (A	
TURNER B (A	PAUL WIDGER G (A

C141 CLIMAX BLUES BAND C141

Personnel	Recordings
ARTHUR WOOD K (ABCD	(A) CLIMAX CHICAGO BLUES BAND 1969 PARLOPHONE UK PCS 7069
GEORGE NEWSOME D (ABCD	(A) CLIMAX CHICAGO BLUES BAND 1970 SIRE US 4901 US SES 97013
PETE HAYCOCK V G (ALL	(B) PLAYS ON 1969 PARLOPHONE UK PCS 7084
COLIN COOPER SAX (ALL	(B) PLAYS ON 1970 SIRE US 6033 US SES 97023
RICHARD JONES K (BHJK	(C) A LOT OF BOTTLE 1970 HARVEST UK SHSP 4009
JOHN CUFFLEY D (EFJHGKLMN	(C) A LOT OF BOTTLE 19 SIRE US 6004 US 7518
DEREK HOLT B (ALL	(D) TIGHTLY KNIT 1971 HARVEST UK SHSP 4015
PETER FILLEUL K V (KL	(D) TIGHTLY KNIT 197 SIRE US 6008 US 7517
PETE RILEY PER (K	(E) RICH MAN 1972 HARVEST UK SHSP 4024
COLIN FAIRLEY V (K	(E) RICH MAN 197 SIRE US 7402
MADELINE BELL V (K	(F) FM/LIVE 1974 POLYDOR UK 2383 259
JOY YATES V (K	(F) FM/LIVE 197 SIRE US 6013 US 7411
LIZA STRIKE V (K	(G) SENSE OF DIRECTION 1974 POLYDOR UK 2883 291
HELEN CHAPPELLE V (K	(G) SENSE OF DIRECTION 1974 SIRE US SAS 7501
NICKY HOPKINS PNO (MN	(H) STAMP ALBUM 1975 B T M UK BTM 1004
GABRIEL KATONA SYN (M	(H) STAMP ALBUM 1975 SIRE US 6016
MAXINE WILLARD V (M	(H) STAMP ALBUM 19 SIRE US 7507
JULIA TILLMAN V (M	(I) 1969 72 1975 HARVEST UK SHSM 2003
CLYDENE JACKSON V (M	(J) GOLD PLATED 1976 B T M UK BTM 1009
JOHN RYAN PROD (M	(J) GOLD PLATED 197 SIRE US 7523
HUMPTY FARMER K (C	(K) SHINE ON 1978 WB UK K 56461 US SIRE 6056
BOB WALTERS TPT (G	(L) REAL TO REEL 1979 WB UK K56642 US 3334
DAVID CAMPBELL STGS (N	(M) FLYING THE FLAG 1980 WB UK K56871 US 3493
MICHAEL BODDICKER SYN (N	(N) LUCKY FOR SOME 1981 WB UK K56952 US 3623
GLENN HUGHES V (N	

C141A CLIQUE C141A

Personnel	Recordings
RANDY SHAW (A	(A) THE CLIQUE 197 WHITE WHALE US WW 7126
GARY ZEKLEY PROD (A	
SID (A	OSCAR (A DAVE (A

C141B CLOCKWORK C141B

(A) CLOCKWORK 19 GREEN BOTTLE US 1013

C142 CLOUDS C142

Personnel	Recordings
HARRY HUGHES D (AB	(A) SCRAPBOOK 1969 ISLAND UK ILPS 9100
IAN ELLIS G B V (AB	(A) UP ABOVE OUR HEADS 1969 DERAM US DES 18044
BILLY RITCHIE K B G V (AB	(B) WATERCOLOUR DAYS 1971 ISLAND UK ILPS 9151
	(B) WATERCOLOUR DAYS 1971 DERAM US DES 18058

C143 CLOUT C143

Personnel	Recordings
CINDI ALTER V (	(A) SUBSTITUTE 1978 CARRERE EMC 3279
INGE HERBST G V (	(B) CLOUT 1979 EPIC US 35617
BONES BRETTELL D (	(C) SIX OF THE BEST 1980 EPIC US 36350
JENNIE GARSON K (	(D) THREAT AND A PROMISE 1981 EMI UK 3363
SANDIE ROBBIE G V (	
LEE TOMLINSON B V (	

C144 CLOVER C144

Personnel	Recordings
JOHN McFEE VLN G V STEEL(ALL	(A) CLOVER 1970 FANTASY US 8395 LIBERTY UK 83340
JOHNNY CIAMBOTTI B V (ALL	(B) FOURTY NINER 1971 FANTASY US 8405 LIBERTY UK 83487
HUEY LOUIS HCA V (CDE	(C) CLOVER 1977 MERCURY US SRMI1169
SEAN HOPPER K V (CDE	(D) UNAVAILABLE 1977 VERTIGO UK 6360 145
ALEX CALL V G (ALL	(E) LOVE ON THE WIRE 1977 MERCURY US SRMI 3708 VERTIGO UK 6360 155
MICKY SHINE D V (CD	(AB) CHRONICLE (COMP AB) 1979 FANTASY UK FT550
ED BOGAS FDL (A	
TONY BRAUNAGEL D (E	MITCH HOWIE D (AB

C144A THE CLOVERS C144A

Personnel	Recordings
JOHN BUDDY BAILEY V (	(A) THE CLOVERS 19 ATLANTIC US 1248 US 8009
BILLY MITCHELL V (	(B) DANCE PARTY 19 ATLANTIC US 8034
BILL HARRIS G (	(C) IN CLOVER 19 UA US 3033 US POPLAR 1001
HAROLD LUCAS V (	(D) LOVE POTION No9 19 UA US 6099
MATTHEW McQUATER V (	(E) THE ORIGINAL LOVE POTION No9 19 GRAND PRIX US K428
HAROLD WINLEY V (	(F) THEIR GREATEST RECORDINGS 19 ATCO US SD33374
THOMAS WOODS V (	(EP) THE CLOVERS 19 ATLANTIC US 590
BILLY SHELTON V (	(EP) GOOD LOVIN' 19 ATLANTIC US 537
	(EP) ONE MINT JULEP 19 ATLANTIC US 504

C145 CLUSTER C145

Personnel	Recordings
HANS JOACHIM ROEDELIUS SYN(ALL	(A) KLOPFZEICHEN (KLUSTER) 1970 SCHWANN GER STUDIO511
DIETER MOEBIUS SYN(ALL	(B) ZWEI OSTEREI (KLUSTER) 1970 SCHWANN GER STUDIO512
CONRAD SCHNITZLER SYN(AB	(C) CLUSTER 1971 PHILIPS GER 6305 074
CONRAD PLANK (D	(D) CLUSTER 2 1972 BRAIN GER 1006 RI 0060 402
MICHAEL ROTHER G (E	(E) ZUCKERZEIT 1974 BRAIN GER 1065
HOLGER CZUKAY B (GH	(E) ZUCKERZEIT 1980 BRAIN UK 0040 116
BRIAN ENO SYN (GH	(F) SOWIESO 1976 RCA SKY GER 005
ASMUS TIETCHENS SYN (G	(G) CLUSTER & ENO 1977 RCA SKY GER 010
OKKO BEKKER G (G	(H) AFTER THE HEAT 1979 SKY GER 021
	(I) GROSSES WASSER 1979 SKY GER 027
	(J) CLUSTER 71 REISSUE OF(C) 1980 SKY GER 047
	(K) CURIOSUM 1981 SKY GER 063

C145A COAST ROAD DRIVE C145A

LES NICOL	G V	(A	(A) DELICIOUS & REFRESHING	1974	DERAM	UK	SML 1113
STEVE CHAPMAN	D	(A					
CHARLIE HARRISON	G B V	(A	STEVE KRIEGER G V (A	MICK WEAVER	K	(A	
NICKY HOPKINS	PNO	(A	CHRIS MERCER SAX (A	HENRY LOWTHER	TPT	(A	
CRAIG AUSTIN	V	(A					

C146 THE COASTERS C146

CARL GARDNER	V	THE COASTERS	19	ATCO	US	33101
BILLY GUY	V	COASTERS GREATEST HITS	19	ATCO	US	33111
BOBBY NUNN	V	COASTERS GREATEST HITS	19	LONDON	UK	HAE 2237
LEON HUGHES	V	ONE BY ONE	1961	ATCO	US	33123
YOUNG JESSIE	V	COASTIN' ALONG	1961	ATCO	US	33135
RONNIE BRIGHT	V	COASTIN' ALONG	1962	LONDON	UK	HAK 8033
RALPH HAMILTON	B	COASTIN' ALONG	19	ATLANTIC	UK	588 134
CORNEL GUNTER	V	GREATEST RECORDINGS	19	ATCO	US	33171
WILL'DUB' JONES	V	THATS ROCK 'N' ROLL	19	CLARION	US	605
JOE OLIVERA	PERC	ALL TIME GREATEST HITS	1967	ATLANTIC	UK	590 015
EARL CARROLL	V	THE EARLY YEARS	19	ATLANTIC	UK	K 30031
JIMMY NORMAN	V	ON BROADWAY	19	KING	US	1146
WITH		ON BROADWAY	1974	LONDON	UK	SHZ 8460
FRANCISCO POZO	PERC	16 GREATEST HITS	19	TRIP	US	TOP16/7
HARRY BREUER		WORLD FAMOUS COASTERS	1976	DJM	UK	DJM22053
PLAS JOHNSON	SAX	HUNGRY	19	JOY	UK	JOYS 189
KING CURTIS	SAX	20 GREAT ORIGINALS	1978	ATLANTIC	UK	K 30057
LLOYD TROTMAN	B	IT AINT SANITARY	19	TRIP	US	8028
BUDDY LUCAS	SAX HCA	EPS				
SELDON POWELL	SAX	ROCK'N'ROLL WITH	19	ATCO	US	4501
HAYWOOD HENRY	SAX	KEEP ROCKIN WITH	19	ATCO	US	4502
JIMMY POWELL	SAX	THE COASTERS	19	ATCO	US	4506
PAUL WILLIAMS	SAX	TOP HITS	19	ATCO	US	4507
NOBLE WATTS	SAX	COASTERS	19	LONDON	UK	REE 1203
MILT HINTON	B					

ALVA McCAIN	SAX	STEVE DOUGLAS	SAX	GRADY GAINES	SAX	CLIFFORD BURKS	SAX
BARNEY KESSEL	G	KENNY BURRELL	G	AL CAIOLA	G	ALAN HANLON	G
PHIL SPECTOR	G	CORNELL DUPREE	G	THOMAS PALMER	G	CARL LYNCH	G
EVERETT BARKSDALE	G	VINCENT BELL	G	AL GORGONI	G	BILLY BUTLER	G
MIMI ROMAN	G	BUCKY PIZZARELLI	G	JOE RICHARDSON	G	SONNY FORRIEST	G
GEORGE BARNES	G	RENE HALL	G	ART RYERSON	G	ADOLPH JACOBS	G
MICKEY BAKER	G	TONY MOTTOLA	G BAN	DON ARNONE	G	CLIFFTON BEST	G
ALVIN STOLLER	D	JOE MARSHALL	D	FRED BELOW	D	BUDDY SALZMAN	D
RAY LUCAS	D	PANAMA FRANCIS	D	GARY CHESTER	D	EMILE RUSSELL	D
BOB ROSENGARTEN	D	MELVIN POLLAN	D	DON LAMOND	D	ALFRED DREARES	D
JESSIE SAILES	D	WILLIE DIXON	B	MIKE STOLLER	PNO	RED SOLOMAN	TPT
WENDEL MARSHALL	B	LAMAR WRIGHT	TPT	JOE NEWMAN	TPT	BILL BERRY	TPT
BERT KEYES	PNO	BILL WINSTON	B	BOBBY DONALDSON	D	JAMES CLEVELAND	TROM
LEROY GLOVER	ORG	HORACE OTT	PNO	RUSS SAUNDERS	B	ELMON WRIGHT	TPT
GEORGE MATTHEWS	TROM	GEORGE STUBBS	PNO	JIMMY LEWIS	B	ART BUTLER	PNO
DUD BASCOMBE	TPT	HARRY DEVITO	TROM	AL LUCAS	B	OLSIE ROBINSON	B
GARY BELL		SANDY NELSON	D	JAMES DAVIDS		MICHAEL ADAMS	
LLEWELLYN KLASS		ABIE BAKER	B	JEWEL GRANT	B	ERNIE FREEMAN	PNO
EDDIE WILLIAMS	B	GEORGE DUVIVIER	B	PHIL KRAUS	PERC	WILL RODRIGUEZ	PERC
STICK EVANS	D						

C147 BILLY COBHAM C147

BILLY COBHAM	D PERC	(ALL	(A) SPECTRUM	1973	ATLANTIC	UK K40406	US 7268
TOMMY BOLIN	G	(A	(B) TOTAL ECLIPSE	1974	ATLANTIC	UK K50098	US 18121
LELAND SKLAR	B	(A	(C) CROSSWINDS	1974	ATLANTIC	UK K50037	US 7300
JIMMY OWENS	HRNS	(JA	(D) SHABAZZ	1975	ATLANTIC	UK K50147	US 18139
RON CARTER	B	(A	(E) A FUNKY THIDE OF SINGS	1975	ATLANTIC	UK K50189	US 18149
JOHN ABERCROMBIE	G	(BCD	(F) LIFE & TIMES	1976	ATLANTIC	UK K50253	US 18166
RANDY BRECKER	HRNS	(BCDEJ	(G) LIVE IN EUROPE	1976	ATLANTIC	UK K50316	US 19194
ALEX BLAKE	B	(BDE	(H) MAGIC	1977	CBS	UK 82277	
GLEN FERRIS	TROM	(BDE	(J) INNER CONFLICTS	1978	ATLANTIC		US 19174
JOHN SCOFIELD	G	(DEFGJ	(K) SIMPLICITY OF EXPRESSION	1978	CBS	UK 82967	
WALT FOWLER	TPT	(E	(L) A LIVE MUTHA FOR YA	1978	CBS	UK 82813	
LARRY SCHNEIDER	SAX	(E	(M) B C	1979	CBS	UK 83641	US 35993
TOM MALONE	TROM	(E	(N) THE BEST OF	1980	CBS	UK 84235	US 36400
STEVE KHAN	G	(LJ					

DAWILLI GONGA	K	(F	DOUG RAUCH	B	(F	ALAN ZAVOD	K	(F	PHIL BODNER	REEDS	B(F
AL BROWN	VIOLA	(F	KERMIT MOORE	CELLO	(F	GENE ORLOFF	VLN	(F	GARNETT BROWN	TROM	(CM
GEORGE DUKE	K V	(CGM	LEE PASTORA	PERC	(C	JOHN WILLIAMS	B	(C	ALFONSO JOHNSON	B V	(GL
TOM SCOTT	SAX	(L	JAN HAMMER	K	(A	JOE FARRELL	WIND	(A	JOHN TROPEA	G	(A
RAY BARRETO	PERC	(A	JOHN ABERCROMBIE	G	(BCD	MICHAEL BRECKER	HRNS	(BCDEJ	MILCHO LEVIEV	K	(BDE
JOACHIM KUHN	PNO	(H	PETE MAUNO	G	(H	MARK SOSKIN	K	(H	RANDY JACKSON	B	(H
ALVIN BATISTE	CLAR V	(H	SHEILA ESCOVEDO	CONG	(HJ	RUTH UNDERWOOD		(J	PETE ESCOVEDO	PERC V	(HJ
KATHLEEN KAAN	V	(H	DON GROLNICK	K	(J	JOSE NAJEIRA	PERC	(J	DAWILLI GONGO	K	(J
ERNIE WATTS	SAX	(JM	JULIAN PRIESTER	TROM	(J	JIM GILSTAP	V	(M	BOOBY LYLE	K	(M
NATHANIEL PHILLIPS	B	(M	VANCE TENORT	CONGA	(M	DONNA FEIN	V	(M	MERRY GREENE	V	(M
MUFFY HENDRIX	V	(M	JOE CROYLE	V	(M	MICHAEL WRIGHT	V	(M	WAYNE HENDERSON	TROM	(M
MICHAEL McGLAIRY	G	(M	ED REDDICK	B	(M	MIKI HOWERD	V	(M	AUGUST JOHNSON	V	(M
LOUIS PATTON	V	(M	ALEXANDRA BROWN	V	(M	JON JOYCE	V	(M	STEVE MADAIO	TPT	(M
OSCAR BRASHEAR	TPT	(M	ERNIE TACK	TROM	(M	PETER CHRISTLIEB	WIND	(M	BILL GREEN	WIND	(M
DAVID DUKE	HRNS	(M									

C147A COBRAA C147A

FRIEDEL AHRENS	K SYN	(A	(A) COBRAA	1974	ELECTROLA	GER 29507
BERND KLIEMT	D PERC	(A				
ROLF SONDERMANN	G B	(A	WOLFGANG HAUSMANN G (A	KLAUS SEBASTIAN G (A		

C148 COCHISE C148

B J COLE	STEEL G	(ABC	(A) COCHISE	1970	UA	UK	UAS	29117
MICK GRABHAM	G K V	(ABC	(B) SWALLOW TALES	1971	LIBERTY	UK		LBG83428
WILLIE WILSON	D	(AB	(B) SWALLOW TALES	1971	U A	US		5518
STEWART BROWN	V G	(AB	(C) SO FAR	1972	U A	UK	UAS	29286
RICK WILLS	B V	(ABC	(EP) SWALLOW TALES	1971	UA	US		SP 50
ROY OTEMRO	D	(C						
JOHN GILBERT	V	(CB	CALEB QUAYE PNO (B	STEVE MARRIOTT PNO V (B	NIGEL OLSSON V (B			
TIM RENWICK	G	(B	CAL BATCHELOR G (B					

C149 EDDIE COCHRAN C149

Personnel	Instr	Albums
EDDIE COCHRAN	D G V B	(ALL
GENE VINCENT	V	(*
JOE BROWN	G	(*

Title	Note	Year	Label	Country	Cat. No.
EDDIE COCHRAN		1960	LIBERTY	US	LST 7172
EDDIE COCHRAN		1960	LIBERTY	US	LRP 3172
CHERISHED MEMORIES		1962	LIBERTY		LBY 1109
CHERISHED MEMORIES		196	LIBERTY		LBS 83072
CHERISHED MEMORIES		1972	SUNSET	UK	SLS 50289
MEMORIAL ALBUM		1963	LIBERTY		LBY 1127
MEMORIAL ALBUM		19	LIBERTY		LBS 83009
MEMORIAL ALBUM		1960	LONDON	UK	HAG 2267
SINGING TO MY BABY		1963	LIBERTY		LBY 1158
SINGING TO MY BABY		19	LIBERTY	MONO	LRP 3061
SINGING TO MY BABY		1958	LONDON	UK	HAG 2093
SINGING TO MY BABY		1968	LIBERTY	UK	LBS 83152
MY WAY		1964	LIBERTY	US	LBY 1205
MY WAY		19	LIBERTY	UK	LBS 83104
NEVER TO BE FORGOTTEN		1963	LIBERTY	US	LRP 3220
SUMMERTIME BLUES		19	SUNSET	GERM	SLS 50094
SUMMERTIME BLUES		19	SUNSET	US	SUS 5123
SUMMERTIME BLUES		19	SUNSET MONO	US	SUM 1123
C'MON EVERYBODY		1970	SUNSET	UK	SLS 50155
10th ANNIVERSARY ALBUM		1970	LIBERTY	UK	LBS 83337
STORY VOL 1		1970	SONOPRESSE	FR	83430
STORY VOL 2		1970	SONOPRESSE	FR	83431
STORY VOL 3		1970	SONOPRESSE	FR	83432
STORY VOL 4		1970	SONOPRESSE	FR	83433
LEGENDARY		1971	U A	UK	UAS 29163
STORY VOL 5		1971	SONOPRESSE	FR	29167
LEGENDARY MASTERS	DBL	1972	UA	UK	60017/18
LEGENDARY MASTERS	DBL	1972	UA	US	9959
ON THE AIR	(*)	1972	UA	UK	UAS 29380
VERY BEST OF(15th ANNIVERSARY)		1975	UA	UK	UAG 29760
MANY SIDES OF		1975	ROCKSTAR		JGR 1001
LEGEND IN OUR TIME		1979	CHARLY		CR 30168
EDDIE COCHRAN	DBL	197	SUNSET		55003/4
VERY BEST OF		19	UA	US	LA 428E
A LEGEND IN OUR TIME		19	UNION PACIFIC	US	UP001
COFFRET	5 ALBUMS	19	UA	FR	25003/7
CREST SESSIONS		19	RAVE ON	FR	5001
SINGLES ALBUM		1979	UA	UK	UAK 30244
20th ANNIVERSARY ALBUM		1980	UA	UK	UCSP 20
MANY SIDES OF		1979	ROLLER COASTER		RSRLP1001
EPS					
NEVER TO BE FORGOTTEN		1962	LIBERTY	UK	LEP 2052
CHERISHED MEMORIES		19	LIBERTY	UK	LEP 2111
CHERISHED MEMORIES		1961	LONDON	UK	REG 1301
C'MON EVERYBODY		1959	LONDON	UK	REV 1214
C'MON EVERYBODY		19	LIBERTY	UK	LEP 2111
SOMETHIN' ELSE		1960	LONDON	UK	REV 1239
SOMETHIN' ELSE		1963	LIBERTY	UK	LEP 2122
CHERISHED MEMORIES OF EDDIE COCHRAN		1963	LIBERTY	UK	LEP 2123
EDDIES HITS		1960	LONDON	UK	REG 1262
EDDIES HITS		1963	LIBERTY	UK	LEP 2124
C'MON AGAIN		1964	LIBERTY	UK	LEP 2165
STOCKINGS N SHOES		1964	LIBERTY	UK	LEP 2180

C149A JACKIE LEE COCHRAN C149A

Personnel	Instr	Title	Year	Label	Country	Cat. No.
JACKIE LEE COCHRAN	V(A	(A) SWAMP FOX	19	ROLLIN ROCK	US	RR005

C150 WAYNE COCHRAN C150

Personnel	Instr	Albums
WAYNE COCHRAN	V	(ALL
ALLYN ROBINSON	D	(E
DENNIS WILSON	WIND	(E
HAROLD PIERCE	TPT	(E
SKIP WEISSER	TROM	(E
DON CARPON	TPT	(E
BUZZ TROY	TPT	(E
CHARLIE BRENT	G K	(E
BOB SCELLATO	TPT	(E
ARTIE GOLENIAK	B	(E
MICHAEL PALMIERI	SAX	(E
MIKE KATZ	TROM	(E
BOB BRAWN	TROM	(E
ROBERT GABLE	WIND	(E
RANDY EMERICK	SAX	(E

Title	Year	Label	Country	Cat. No.
(A) HIGH & RIDIN'	19	BETHLEHEM	US	10002
(B) ALIVE & WELL	19	KING	US	1116
(C) OLD KING GOLD	19	KING	US	16001
(D) WAYNE COCHRAN	19	CHESS	US	1519
(E) COCHRAN	19	EPIC	US	30989
(E) COCHRAN	19	EPIC	UK	64933

C151 BRUCE COCKBURN C151

Personnel	Instr	Albums
BRUCE COCKBURN	G DULC V	(ALL
ROBERT BOUCHER	B	(HIJ
PAT GODFREY	PNO V PERC	(I
BILL USHER	PERC V	(HI
RAY MACKAY	PIPES	(I
FRED STONE	HRNS	(H
BEVERLEY COPELAND	V	(J
BRENT TITCOMB	V	(J
BOB DISALLE	D	(HJ
GENE MARTYNEC	G	(J
MARTY NAGLER	V	(J
MICHAEL DONATO	B	(H
KATHY MOSES	WIND	(J
TOMMY GRAHAM	V	(J

Title	Note	Year	Label	Country	Cat. No.
(A) BRUCE COCKBURN		1970	TRUE NORTH	CAN	TN1
(A) BRUCE COCKBURN		1971	EPIC	US	30812
(B) HIGH WINDS WHITE SKY		1971	TRUE NORTH	CAN	TN3
(C) SUNWHEEL DANCE		1972	EPIC	UK	65187
(C) SUNWHEEL DANCE		1972	TRUE NORTH	CAN	TN7
(C) SUNWHEEL DANCE		1972	EPIC	US	31768
(D) NIGHT VISION		1973	TRUE NORTH	CAN	TN11
(E) HAND DANCING		197	TRUE NORTH	CAN	TN13
(F) SALT SUN AND TIME		1974	TRUE NORTH	CAN	TN16
(G) JOY WILL FIND A WAY		1975	TRUE NORTH	CAN	TN23
(H) IN THE FALLING DARK		197	TRUE NORTH	CAN	TN26
(H) IN THE FALLING DARK		197	ISLAND/TN	US	ILTA 9463
(I) CIRCLES IN THE STREAM	DBL	1977	ISLAND/TN	US	ILTA 9475
(J) FURTHER ADVENTURES		197	TRUE NORTH	CAN	TN33
(J) FURTHER ADVENTURES		197	ISLAND/TN	US	ILTA 9528
(K) DANCING IN THE DRAGONS JAW		1979	TRUE NORTH	CAN	TN37
(K) DANCING IN THE DRAGONS JAW		1979	MILLENNIUM	US UK	BXLI 7747
(L) HUMANS		1980	MILLENNIUM	US UK	FL1 7752
(M) RESUME		1981	MILLENNIUM	US UK	17757
(N) INNER CITY FRONT		1981	MILLENNIUM	US UK	17761

C151A

COCKNEY REJECTS

C151A

JEFFERSON 'STINKY TURNER V(ABCDE
VINCE RIORDAN B V (ABCDE
KEITH 'NIG' WARRINGTON D (ABCDE
MICK GEGGUS G V (ABCDE

(A) GREATEST HITS VOL 1	1980	ZONOPHONE	UK	101
(B) GREATEST HITS VOL 2	1980	ZONOPHONE	UK	102
(C) GREATEST HITS VOL 3	1981	ZONOPHONE	UK	ZEM 101
(D) THE POWER & THE GLORY	1981	ZONOPHONE	UK	105
(E) WILD ONES	1982	ZONOPHONE	UK	AKA 1

C151B

COCKRELL & SANTOS

C151B

BUD COCKRELL B V (A
PATTIE SANTOS V (A
ANGELO ROSSI G (A
JACO PASTORIUS G (A
AIRTO MOREIRA PERC (A
ERNIE WATTS SAX (A
MICHAEL SHELTON G (A
RON STOCKERT K (A
DAVID GARIBALDI PERC (A
FLORA PURIM V (A
JIM ANDERSON D (A
VICTOR FELDMAN PERC (A
STEVE MADAIO HRNS (A
ELMO PEELER K (A

(A) NEW BEGINNINGS	1978	A&M	US	SP 4712

C151C

CODE BLUE

C151C

DEAN CHAMBERLAIN G V (A
GARY TIBBS B V (A
RANDALL MARSH D V (A

(A) CODE BLUE	1981	WB US 3461	UK	K56868

C151D

DAVID ALLAN COE

C151D

DAVID ALLAN COE G V(ALL
SKEET PETTY D (L
WESLEY TAYLOR G (L
ALAN HICKS B (L
DALE SEIGFREID STEEL (L
PAM ROSE V (J
BARBARA SOUTH V (L
LINDA HARGROVE V (L

(A) PENITENTIARY BLUES	1968	SSS	US	9
(B) REQUIEM FOR A HARLEQUINN	1969	SSS	US	31
(C) MYSTERIOUS RHINESTONE COWBOY	1974	CBS	US	32942
(D) ONCE UPON A RHYME	1974	CBS UK 80908	US	33085
(E) LONG HAIRED REDNECK	1976	CBS	US	33916
(F) RIDES AGAIN	1977	CBS	US	34310
(G) TATTOO	1977	CBS	US	34870
(H) TEXAS MOON	1977	PLANTATION	US	507
(H) TEXAS MOON	1977	CHARLY	UK	CRL5006
(I) FAMILY ALBUM	1978	CBS	US	35306
(J) HUMAN EMOTIONS	1978	CBS	US	35535
(K) GREATEST HITS	1978	CBS	US	35627
(L) SPECTRUM SEVEN	1979	CBS	US	35789
(M) BUCKSTONE COUNTY PRISON	1979	COE	US	8095
(N) NOTHING SACRED	1979	COE	US	
(O) COMPASS POINT	1980	CBS	US	36277
(P) I'VE GOT SOMETHING TO SAY	1980	CBS	US	36489
(Q) INVICTUS	1981	CBS	US	36970
(R) ENCORE	1981	CBS	US	37352
(S) TENNESSEE WHISKEY	1981	CBS	US	37353

C152

PETER & CHRIS COE

C152

PETER COE (AB
CHRIS COE (AB
DAVE BLAND V (A
CLIVE WOOLF V (A
DOUG SHERRIFF V (A
STEVE ASHLEY V (A

(A) OPEN THE DOOR	1972	LEADER		LER 2077
(B) OUT OF THE SEASON	1976	LEADER		LER 2098
(C) GAME OF ALL FOURS	1979	HIGHWAY		SHY 7007

C152A

COEUR MAGIQUE

C152A

CLAUDE OLMOS G PERC(A
HARRY SEUR V (A
DIDIER LESSAGE D (A
LAURENT MURINO B PERC(A

(A) WANKAN TANKA	197	BYG	FR	529018

C153

DENNIS COFFEY & THE DETROIT GUITAR BAND

C153

DENNIS COFFEY G (ALL
WITH
ANDREW SMITH D (BC
BOB BABBITT B (BC
ERIC MORGANSEN K (BC
JACK ASHFORD PERC (BCD
EDDY BROWN PERC (C
EDDIE WILLIS G (G
RUDY ROBINSON PNO (G
GARY SCHUNK PNO (G
RODERICK CHANDLER B (G
LEE NATHAM D (G
LORENZO BROWN PERC (G
JOHN TRUDELL TPT (G
BRANDY V (G
MELVIN WAH WAH RAGIN G(D
CLARENCE McDONALD K (D
JOE CLAYTON CONGAS(D
BUD SHANK HRNS (D
VINCENT DEROSA HRNS (D
BOBBY BRYANT HRNS (D
MAURICE DAVIS TPT (G
JAMES BARNES PERC (B
ED GREENE D (D
MELVIN MELVOIN K (D
JAMES JAMERSON B (D
LLOYD HILDERBRAND HRNS(D
ARTHUR MAEBE HRNS (D
ERNIE WATTS HRNS (D
STU SANDERS TROM (G
TONY NEWTON B (B
JAMES GADSON D (D
STEPHANIE SPRUILL PERC (D
GARY COLEMAN VIBES(D
GENE CIPRIANO HRNS (D
GEORGE BOHANON HRNS (D
STRING SECTION (BD
LARRY NOZERO SAX (G
ART WRIGHT G (D
JOE SAMPLE K (D
KING ERRISON CONGAS(D
RONALD LANGINGER HRNS(D
CHUCK FINDLEY HRNS(D
DICK HYDE HRNS(D

(A) EVOLUTION	19	SUSSEX	US	7004
(A) EVOLUTION	19	A&M	UK	AMLS68035
(B) GOIN' FOR MYSELF	1972	SUSSEX	US	7010
(B) GOIN' FOR MYSELF	1972	A&M	UK	AMLS68072
(C) ELECTRIC COFFEY	1972	SUSSEX	US	7021
(D) INSTANT COFFEY	1974	SUSSEX	UK	8031
(E) DANCE PARTY	1974	SUSSEX	US	8152
(F) GETTIN' IT ON	1975	CARRERE	FR	67605
(G) BACK HOME	19	WESTBOUND	US	300
(G) BACK HOME	1977	ATLANTIC	UK	K 50371
(H) SWEET TASTE OF SIN	1978	WESTBOUND	US	6105
(J) FINGER LOOKIN' GOOD	19	WESTBOUND	US	212

C154

DAVID COHEN

C154

DAVID COHEN G (A

(A) HOW TO PLAY FOLK GUITAR	1976	KICKING MULE		SNKF 118

C155

JOE COCKER

C155

JOE COCKER V (ALL
WITH
ALAN SPENNER B (ACKF
NEIL HUBBARD G (FK
CHRIS STAINTON B K (ABCDKF
HENRY McCULLOUGH G (ABCGH
BRUCE ROWLAND D (AC
PAUL HUMPHREY D (BC
CAROL KAYE B (B
DAVID COHEN G (B
LAUDIR DE OLIVIRA PERC (B
CLEM CATTINI D (B
JIMMY PAGE G (B
ALBERT LEE G (BJ
B J WILSON D (B
MATTHEW FISHER ORG (B
STEVE WINWOOD K (B

(A) BACKING BANDS 1968/69 PRE RECORDS				
(B) WITH A LITTLE HELP FROM MY FRIEND	1969	REGAL ZONOPHONE		SLRZ 1006
(B) WITH A LITTLE HELP FROM MY FRIEND	19	A&M	US	AM 4182
(B) WITH A LITTLE HELP FROM MY FRIEND	19	POLYDOR	EURO	2326 015
(B) WITH A LITTLE HELP FROM MY FRIEND	1972	MFP		MFP 52757
(C) JOE COCKER	1969	REGAL ZONOPHONE	UK	SLRZ 1011
(C) JOE COCKER	197	A&M	US	AM 4224
(C) JOE COCKER	197	A&M	US	AM 4368
(C) JOE COCKER	197	CUBE POLYDOR	EURO	2326 018
(BC)WITH A LITTLE HELP/JOE COCKER	1972	FLY/CUBE		TOOFA 1/2
(D) MAD DOGS & ENGLISHMEN	1971	A&M	US/UK	AMLD 6002
(E) COCKER HAPPY	1971	FLY UK HIFLY3	EURO CUBE	2338009
(F) SOMETHING TO SAY	1973	CUBE UK HIFLY13	EURO	2338022
(G) I CAN STAND A LITTLE RAIN	1974	CUBE UK HIFLY18	EURO	2338027
(G) I CAN STAND A LITTLE RAIN	1974	A&M	US	AM 3633
(H) JAMAICA SAY YOU WILL	1975	CUBE UK HIFLY20	EURO	2326040
(H) JAMAICA SAY YOU WILL	1975	A&M	US	AM 4529

(CONTINUED)

C155 (CONTINUED) JOE COCKER C155

LEON RUSSELL V K G (CD (J) STINGRAY 1976 A&M US 4574 UK AMLH64574
SNEAKY PETE KLEINOW STEEL(C (K) LIVE IN L A 1976 CUBE UK HIFLY23 EURO 2326041
DON PRESTON G (D (L) LUXURY YOU CAN AFFORD 1978 ASYLUM US 6E145 UK K 53087
CARL RADLE B (D (L) LUXURY YOU CAN AFFORD 1978 ELEKTRA K 52092
JIM GORDON D (D ( ) JOE COCKER(BEST OF) 197 IMPACT FR 6886 554
JIM KELTNER D (DF ( ) GREATEST HITS 19 A&M US AM 4670
CHUCK BLACKWELL D PERC(D ( ) PLATINUM COLLECTION 1981 DAKOTA UK 1004
SANDY KONIKOFF PER (D
BOBBY TORRES PERC (D JIM PRICE V K HRNS(DGHK BOBBY KEYS SAX (DKL STU BLUMBERG TPT (G
STEVE MADAIO TPT (GH JIM HORN SAX (GHKF TREVOR LAWRENCE SAX (GH MAYO TIANA TROM(G
DAVID PAICH PNO (G RAY PARKER G (G RALPH HAMMER G (G DAVE McDANIEL B (GH
OLLIE BROWN D (G NICKY HOPKINS PNO (GH JAY GRAYDON G (G JEFF PORCARO D (G
RICHARD TEE K (GHL CORNELL DUPREE G (GHJL CHUCK RAINEY B (GHL BERNARD PURDIE D (GHL
CHRIS STEWART B (GH JIM KARSTEIN D (GHK JIMMY WEBB PNO (G PEGGY SANDVIG GH (GH
GREG MATHESON PNO (G RANDY NEWMAN PNO (G JEAN ROUSSEL ORG (H BEN BENAY G HCA(H
SID SHARP STRINGS(H DAN SAWYER G (H JOE CORRERO D (H DON PONCHER PERC(H
STEVE GADD D (JL GORDON EDWARDS B (J ERIC GALE G (J SAM RIVERS SAX (J
FLACO FALCON PERC (JKL ERIC CLAPTON G (J CLARENCE WHITE G (C ARTIE BUTLER PNO (B
TONY VISCONTE G (B MIKE KELLIE D (B TOMMY EYRE K (AB KENNY SLADE D (AB
MILT HOLLAND PERC (C BARRY BECKETT K (L CLIFF GOODWIN G (L HOWIE HERSH B (L
JOHN RILEY D (L GARY BROWN SAX (L HANK CRAWFORD SAX (L DAVID NEWMAN SAX (L
LEROY COOPER SAX (L MARCUS BELGRAVE TPT (L PHILIP GUILBEAU TPT (L RANDY McCORMICK K (L
JIMMY JOHNSON G (L GEORGE TERRY G (L DR JOHN K (L CLYDE KERR TPT (L
DONNY HATHAWAY K (L JOEY MURCIA G (L DAVID HOOD B (L ROGER HAWKINS D (L
LARRY BYROM G (L BILLY PRESTON K (L CHARLES ROSE HRNS (L WAYNE JACKSON HRNS (L
HARRISON CALLOWAY TPT (L RON EADES SAX (L HARVEY THOMPSON SAX (L PETE CARR G (L
ALLAN TOUSSAINT K PROD (L ALAN WHITE D (F RICK ALPHONSO TPT (F FRED SCERBO SAX (F
MILTON SLOANE SAX (F REEBOP BAHH PERC (F CONRAD ISADORE D (F RICK DANK B (L
ROSETTA HIGHTOWER V (B BRENDA HOLLOWAY V (B MERRY CLAYTON V (BCG PATRICE HOLLOWAY V (BC
MADELINE BELL V (B SUE GLOVER V (B SONNIE LESLIE V (B BONNIE BRAMLETT V (CJ
RITA COOLIDGE V (CD SHIRLEY MATTHEWS V (CGH CLAUDIA LENNEAR V (D DANIEL MOORE V (DGH
DONNA WEISS V (D PAMELA POLLAND V (D MATTHEW MOORE V (DH DONNA WASHBURN V (D
NICOLE BARCLAY V (D BOBBY JONES V (D CLYDIE KING B (GHL VANETTA FIELDS V (GH
CAROL STALLINGS V (H BUZZ CLIFFORD V (H JOANNE BELL V (H CYNTHIA BARCLAY V (H
LANI GROVES V (J DENIECE WILLIAMS V (J PHYLLIS LINDSAY V (J MAXINE WILLARD V (J
BRENDA WHITE V (J PATTI AUSTIN V (J GWEN GUTHRIE V (J VIOLA WILLS V (KF
BEVERLY GARDNER V (KF VIRGINIA AYERS V (KF GLORIA JONES V (F ANN LANG V (L
MONA LISA YOUNG V (L MITCH CHAKOUR G (L

C156 LEONARD COHEN C156

LEONARD COHEN V (ALL (A) SONGS OF LEONARD COHEN 1968 CBS UK 63241 US 9533
JENNIFER WARNES V (G (B) SONGS FROM A ROOM 1968 CBS UK 63587 US 9767
HAL BLAINE D (G (B) SONGS FROM A ROOM 1981 EMBASSY UK 32074
JIM KELTNER D (G (C) SONGS OF LOVE & HATE 1970 CBS UK 69004 US 30103
ART MUNSON G (G (D) LIVE SONGS 1973 CBS UK 65224 US 31724
DAVID KESSEL G (G (E) NEW SKIN FOR OLD CEREMONY 1974 CBS UK 69087 US 33167
DAVID ISAAC G (G (F) GREATEST HITS 1975 CBS UK 69161 US 34077
DAN KESSEL G K (G (G) DEATH OF A LADIES MAN 1977 CBS UK 86042 US WB 3125
JESSE ED DAVIS G (G (H) RECENT SONGS 1979 CBS UK 86097 US 36364
PHIL SPECTOR G K (G
CHARLES LOPER TROM (G RAY POHLMAN G B (G ALBERT PERKINS G (G PETE KLEINOW STEEL(G
PETE JOLLY K (G TOM HENSLEY K (G DON RANDI K (G BILL MAYS K (G
BARRY GOLDBERG K (G STEVE DOUGLAS WIND (G MIKE LANG K (G JACK REDMOND TROM (G
DEVRA ROBITAILLE SYN (G TERRY GIBBS PERC (G RAY NEOPOLITAN B (G EMIL RADOCCHIA PERC (G
GENE ESTES PERC (G BOB ZIMMITTI PERC (G BOBBY BRUCE FDL (G DON MENZA WIND (G
CONTE CANDOLI TPT (G JAY MIGLIORI SAX (G ALAN GINSBERG WIND (G BILLY DIEZ V (G
RONNEE BLAKELY V (G VENNETTE FIELDS V (G BRENDA BRYANT V (G GERRY GARRETT V (G
CLYDIE KING V (G LORNA WILLARD V (G JULIA TILLMAN V (GH ORNA DRAKE V (G
BOB DYLAN V (G JOHN BILEZIKJIAN G (H ABRAHAM LABORIEL B (H RANDY WALDMAN K (H
JENNIFER WARNES V (H STEVE MEADOR D (H CHARLES BECK B (H BILL GINN K (H
MITCH WATKINS G (H PAUL OSTERMEYER SAX (H STEPHANIE SPRUILL V (H MAXINE WILLARD V (H
JAMES GILSTRAP V (H ROGER ST KENERLY V (H JOHN MILLER B (H JOHN LISSAUER K (H
PABLO SANDOVAL TPT (H JOSE PEREZ TPT (H RICARDO GONZALEZ G (H FELIPE PEREZ (H
EVERADO SANDOVAL G (H GARTH HUDSON (H EARLE DUMLER OBOE (H

C156A COINCIDENCE C156A

JEAN-CLAUDE LLABADOR (A (A) COINCIDENCE 1977 DISQUES TROMBLAS FR RY1133
JEAN-PIERRE LLABADOR (A

C157 MARK COLBY C157

MARK COLBY SAX (A (A) SERPENTINE FIRE 1978 CBS UK 82668
ERIC GALE G (A (A) SERPENTINE FIRE 1978 CBS US 35298
STEVE KHAN G (A
BOB JAMES (A STEVE GADD D (A

C158 COLD BLOOD C158

CARL LEACH TPT (A (A) COLD BLOOD (FIRST BLOOD) 1970 SAN FRANCISCO US 200
RAUL MATUTE K (ABCDEF (A) COLD BLOOD (FIRST BLOOD) 1970 ATLANTIC UK 588 218
LARRY JONUTZ TPT (AB (B) SISYPHUS 1971 SAN FRANCISCO US 205
ROD ELLICOTT B (ABDE (B) SISYPHUS 1971 ATLANTIC UK 2400 102
FRANK J DAVIS D (A (C) FIRST TASTE OF SIN 1972 REPRISE US 2074
DANNY HULL SAX V(ABF (D) THRILLER 1973 REPRISE US 2130
DAVID PADRON TPT (A (E) LYDIA 1974 WB UK K56-47 US 2806
LYDIA PENSE V (ABCDEF (F) LYDIA PENSE & COLD BLOOD 1976 ABC UK 5172 US ABCD 917
SANDY McKEE D (B
LARRY FIELD G (AB MIC GILLETTE HRNS (AB JOSE CHEPITO AREAS PERC(B POINTER SISTERS V (BD
MIKE ANDREAS SAX (D RIGBY POWELL TPT (D MEL MARTIN SAX (D HOLLY TIGARD V(D
GAYLORD BIRCH D (DE BILL ATWOOD TPT FLT(D MAX HASKETT TPT V (DEF SKIP MESQUITE WIND V(D
BOB FERREIRA WIND (D MICHAEL SASAKI G (DEF TOMMY CATHEY B (E PAT OHARA TROM (D
PETER WELKER TPT (D JOE WILLIAMS D (E JOHN MEWBORN HRNS (D PAUL CANNON G (D
STEVE CROPPER G (E BENNY MAUPIN WIND (D MEMPHIS HORNS (E SMITH DOBSON PNO V(E
DANNY KOOTCH G (E BOBBYE HALL PERC (E DAVID LUELL SAX (E CHUCK BENNETT TROM(E
PAUL HUBINON TPT (E CHUCK FINDLEY TPT (E BOBBY SHEW TPT (E JIM HORN WIND(E
DON MENZA WIND (E PETER CHRISTLIEB WIND (E BROOKS HUNNICUTT V (E GWEN EDWARDS V (E
BRENDA GORDON V (E TISH SMITH V (E PAT COULTER V (E JERRY JONUTZ SAX (A
HARVEY HUGHES D (F DOMINGO BALINTON B (F SKIP KONTE SYN (F

C158A
COLD CHISEL
C158A

IAN MOSS G V (CDF
JIM BARNES V (CDF
DON WALKER K V (CDF
PHIL SMALL B V (CDF
STEVE PRESTWICH D V (CDF
JOE CAMILLERI SAX (D

(A) YOUR'E 13 1978 ELEKTRA EP 12001
(B) COLD CHISEL 1978 ELEKTRA
(C) BREAKFAST AT SWEETHEARTS 1979 ELEKTRA 90001
(D) EAST 1980 ELEKTRA 90003
(E) SWINGSHIFT 1981 ELEKTRA 90025
(F) CIRCUS ANIMALS 1982 POLYDOR POLS 1065

C159
COLD COMFORT
C159

DAVE PRICE V G K(A
DEREK SODEN V B G(A
NIGEL BAGGE V G (A
HENRY LOWTHER TPT (A
IAN BYRON D (A
GEOFF DALY SAX (A
ROD EDWARDS K VLN (A
CHRIS MERCER SAX (A
GRAHAM MATTHEWS PERC V(A

(A) IN THE CAN 1978 JET UK JET LP211

C159A
COLD FIRE
C159A

(A) TOO COLD 1981 CAPITOL 12096

C160
COLD STEEL
C160

DAVID LOVELACE K (A
GREG ATTAWAY V D (A
RICHARD BOWDEN G V (A
MIKE BOWDEN B V (A
SNEAKY PETE STEEL (A
GIB GUILBEAU FDL (A

(A) COLD STEEL 1974 ARIOLA IMP 87736

C160A
COLDWATER ARMY
C160A

BOBBY GOLDEN G V (A
KENNY GOLDEN B (A
RICKY HUGHES D (A
DALE MILLER SAX (A
BOB SPEARMAN K V (A
BOB GARRETT V TPT K(A
NICK JONES TPT V(A

(A) PEACE 1972 AGAPE US 2600

C161
B J COLE
C161

B J COLE STEEL G K (A
ROBERT KIRBY PNO (A
GRAHAM PRESKETT VLN (A
CRISPIAN STEEL PERKINS TPT(A
DANNY THOMPSON B (A
ANDY BABYNCHUK VLN (A
BRIAN HAWKINS VIOLA (A
TRISTRAM FRY PERC (A
LAURIE JELLYMAN D (A
MIKE GILES D (A
ROY GILLARD VLN (A
KEITH BAKER B (A
MICK AUDSLEY G V (A
FRANCIS MONKMAN K (A
SUE SHEPPARD CELLO(A

(A) NEW HOVERING DOG 1972 UA UK UAS 29418

C161A
JERRY COLE (& THE SPACEMEN)
C161A

JERRY COLE G

A GO GO GUITARS 19 CROWN US 539
OUTER LIMITS 19 CAPITOL US 2044
HOT ROD DANCE 19 CAPITOL US 2061
SURF AGE 19 CAPITOL US 2112

C161B
THE COLLECTORS
C161B

CLAIRE LAWRENCE WIND K HCA V(AB
GLENN MILLER B V (AB
ROSS TURNEY D (AB
BILL HENDERSON V G K(AB
NORM JEFFRIES VIBES(A
HOWIE VICKERS V (BA
JESSE ERLICH CELLO (A
LARRY KNECHTEL K (A

(A) THE COLLECTORS 1968 WB US WS 1746 MIDI 26008
(B) GRASS & WILD STRAWBERRIES 1968 WB US WS 1774 MIDI 26024

C161C
TONY COLE
C161C

TONY COLE G V (A
JOHN FARRAR G (A
TERRY BRITTEN G V (A
BARRIE GUARD D PERC(A
KEVIN PEEK G (A
HERBIE FLOWERS B (A
DAVE McCRAE K (A
SKAILA KANGA HARP (A
ALAN TARNEY B (A
BOB EFFORD REC (A
DAVE PERKIN B (A
WALLY SMITH TROM (A
TOM CAMPO B (A
JOHN BURDEN HRNS (A
BARRY MORGAN D (A
REINER SCHUELEIN REC (A
TIM KRAEMER CELLO(A
MIKE CLAYTON (A
RICK BUSCH HRNS (A
DAVID MACKAY V (A

(A) IF THE MUSIC STOPS 1972 20th CENT T 403

C161D
COLLAGE
C161D

DONNA (
JODIE (
JERRY (
RON (

(A) THE COLLAGE 1967 SMASH US 101

C161E
COLLECTIVE HORIZONTAL
C161E

(A) CRAP GAME (EP) 19 DOLMEN DO 1

C162
ALBERT COLLINS
C162

ALBERT COLLINS G V (ALL
WITH
LARRY BURTON G (G
JIM KELTNER D (F
BRIAN GAROFALO B (F
ALAN BATTS K (GH
A C REED SAX (GH
CASEY JONES D (G
CHUCK SMITH SAX (G
ARON BURTON B (G
MARVIN JACKSON G (H
JOHNNY GAYDEN B (H
PAUL HOWARD TPT (H
JERRY WILSON SAX (H
BILL McFARLAND TROM (H
HENRI FORD SAX (H
MAC REBENNACK K (F
MICHAEL ROSSO D (F
PETE CANDOLI TPT (F
PLAS JOHNSON SAX (F
BOB KNIGHT TROM (F
BILL SZYMCZYK V (F
JOE ZAGARINO K (F
JAMES DALLAM K (F
JIM HORN SAX (F
JAY MIGLIORI SAX (F
JUDY RODERICK V (F
LARRY DANIELS D (F
BUD BRISBOIS TPT (F
ERNIE WATTS SAX (F
LEW McCREARY TROM (F
BRENT WILLIAMSON V (F

(A) TRUCKIN 19 BLUE THUMB US B7S8
(B) COOL SOUND OF 19 I C F HALL US 8002
(C) LOVE CAN BE FOUND 1968 IMPERIAL US 12428
(C) LOVE CAN BE FOUND 19 LIBERTY UK 83238
(D) TRASH TALKIN' 1969 IMPERIAL US 12438
(E) COMPLEAT ALBERT COLLINS 19 IMPERIAL US 12445
(F) THERE'S GOTTA BE A CHANGE 19 TUMBLEWEED UK TW 3501
(F) THERE'S GOTTA BE A CHANGE 1971 TUMBLEWEED US TWS 103
(G) ICE PICKIN' 1978 SONET UK SNTF 707
(G) ICE PICKIN' 197 ALLIGATOR US 4713
(H) FROSTBITE 1980 SONET UK SNTF 837
(H) FROSTBITE 19 ALLIGATOR US
(J) ALIVE & COOL 197 RED LIGHTNIN UK RL 004
(K) FROZEN ALIVE 1981 SONET UK SNTF 874
(K) FROZEN ALIVE 1981 ALLIGATOR US 4725

C163
DAVE & ANSELL COLLINS
C163

DAVE COLLINS
ANSELL COLLINS

(A) DOUBLE BARREL 19 TROJAN TRL 162
(A) DOUBLE BARREL 19 BLUE THUMB US 2005
(B) IN THE GHETTO 1976 TROJAN TRLS 124

C164 # JUDY COLLINS C164

Musician	Instr.	Albums	Record	Year	Label	Country	Number
JUDY COLLINS	V G K	(ALL	(A)MAID OF CONSTANT SORROW	1962	ELEKTRA	US	EKS 7209
WITH			(A) MAID OF CONSTANT SORROW	1975	ELEKTRA	UK	K 52032
MICHAEL SAHL	K	(H	(B) GOLDEN APPLES OF THE SUN	1962	ELEKTRA	US	EKS 7222
STEPHEN STILLS	G	(H	(B) GOLDEN APPLES OF THE SUN	1975	ELEKTRA	UK	K
CHRIS ETHRIDGE	B	(H	(C) 3RD ALBUM	1964	ELEKTRA	US	EKS 7243
JAMES GORDON	D	(H	(C) 3RD ALBUM	19	CHANT DU MONTE	FR	4324
MICHAEL MELVOIN	K	(H	(D) CONCERT	1964	ELEKTRA	US	EKS 7280
JAMES BURTON	G	(H	(E) FIFTH ALBUM	1965	ELEKTRA	US	EKS 7300
BUDDY EMMONS	STEEL	(H	(E) FIFTH ALBUM	19	CHANT DU MONTE	FR	74333
VAN DYKE PARKS	K	(H	(F) WILD FLOWERS	1968	ELEKTRA	US	EKS 74012
FRED HELLERMAN	G	(A	(F) WILD FLOWERS	197	ELEKTRA	UK	K 42014
ERIK DARLING	BANJO	(A	(F) WILD FLOWERS	19	VOGUE	FR	217
WALTER RAIM	G BANJO	(BC	(G) IN MY LIFE	1967	ELEKTRA	US	EKS 74027
ROGER McGUINN	G BANJO	(C	(G) IN MY LIFE	197	ELEKTRA	UK	K 42009
BILL TAKAS	B	(CE	(G) IN MY LIFE	1968	ELEKTRA	US	7320
CHUCK ISRAELS	B CELLO	(DE	(G) IN MY LIFE	19	VOGUE	FR	155
STEVE MANDELL	G BANJO	(D	(H) WHO KNOWS WHERE THE TIME GOES	1969	ELEKTRA	US	EKS 74033
RICHARD FARINA	DULCIMER	(E	(H) WHO KNOWS WHERE THE TIME GOES	197	ELEKTRA	UK	K 42044
ERIC WEISSBERG	G V	(E	(H) WHO KNOWS WHERE THE TIME GOES	197	VOGUE	FR	322
JERRY DODGION	FLT	(E	( ) RECOLLECTIONS(BEST OF)	1969	ELEKTRA	US	74055
BOB SYLVESTER	CELLO	(E	( ) RECOLLECTIONS(BEST OF)	197	ELEKTRA	UK	K 42035
BILL LEE	B	(E	(I) BOTH SIDES NOW	1971	ELEKTRA US75030	UK	K 42098
JOHN SEBASTIAN	HCA	(E	(J) WHALES & NIGHTINGALES	1971	ELEKTRA US75010	UK	K 42059
DANNY KALB	G	(E	(K) LIVING	1972	ELEKTRA US75014	UK	K 42102
GEORGE MARGE	HRNS	(M	( ) COLOURS OF DAY (BEST OF)	1972	ELEKTRA	UK	75030
BILL SLAPIN	FLT	(M	( ) AMAZING GRACE (BEST OF)	1972	ELEKTRA	UK	K 42110
ROMEO PENQUE	FLT	(M	(L) TRUE STORIES & OTHER DREAMS	1973	ELEKTRA US75053	UK	K 42132
EMANUEL VARDI	VLA	(M	(M) JUDITH	1975	ELEKTRA US 1032	UK	K 52019
GENE ORLOFF	VLN	(M	(N) BREAD & ROSES	1976	ELEKTRA US 1076	UK	K 52039
KEN ASCHER	K	(M	(O) SO EARLY IN SPRING	1977	ELEKTRA US 6007	UK	K 62019
HUCH McCRACKEN	G	(M	(P) SAVE THE CHILDREN	197	WOMAN	US	W001
DAVID SPINOZZA	G	(M	( ) MOST BEAUTIFUL SONGS OF	1979	ELEKTRA	UK	K 62006
STEVE BURGH	G	(M	(R) HARD TIME FOR LOVERS	1979	ELEKTRA US6E171	UK	K 52121
STEVE GADD	D	(M	(S) RUNNING FOR MY LIFE	1980	ELEKTRA US6E253	UK	K 52205
TONY LEVIN	D	(M					

RALPH McDONALD	PERC	(M	KEN BISCHEL	SYN	(M	CHARLIE BROWN	G	(M	ERIC WEISSBERG	G	(M
PAT REBILLOT	K	(M	DON BROOKS	HCA	(M	SELDON POWELL	HRNS	(M	ARTHUR CLARKE	HRNS	(M
TONY STUDD	HRNS	(M	FRANK WESS	HRNS	(M	GARNETT BROWN	HRNS	(M	RANDY BRECKER	HRNS	(M
PAUL GRIFFIN	K	(M	STEVE GOODMAN	V	(M	DENVER COLLINS	V	(M	CISSY HOUSTON	V	(MR
SYLVIA SHEMWELL	V	(M	EUNICE PETERSON	V	(M	CORKY HALE	HARP	(M	DOMINIC CORTES	ACC	(M
JOEL KAYE	WIND	(M	BOB STEEN	WIND	(M	GEORGE RICCI	CELLO	(M	LES SCOTT	WIND	(M
JERRY SMITH	WIND	(M	SIDNEY WEINBERG	WIND	(M	LARRY WECHSLER	HRNS	(M	ALBERT RICHMOND	HRNS	(M
WAYNE ANDRE	TROM	(M	VINNIE FAMUELE	TROM	(M	THOMAS PEARSON	K	(M	ABE ROSEN	HARP	(M
CLIFF MORRIS	G	(M	HANK JARAMILLO	PERC	(M	JOHN BEAL	B	(M	CHARLIE McCRACKEN	CELLO	(M
KERMIT MOORE	CELLO	(M	DENNIS BUDIMIR	G	(R	LEE RITENOUR	G	(R	DAVID HUNGATE	B	(R
JAI WINDING	K	(R	JIM KELTNER	D	(R	DEAN PARKS	G	(R	MIKE LANG	K	(R
FRED TACKETT	G	(R	JEFF BAXTER	G STEEL	(R	DAVID WOLFERT	G	(R	NORTON BUFFALO	HCA	(R
MAERETHA STEWART	V	(R	HILDA HARRIS	V	(R	SID SHARP	STR	(R	HARRY BLUESTONE	STR	(R
VINCE DEROSA	HRNS	(R	DAVID DUKE	HRNS	(R	BOB HENDERSON	HRNS	(R	BILL LANE	HRNS	(R
LEW McCREARY	TROM	(R	DICK HYDE	TROM	(R	LOUISE DITULLIO	FLT	(R	SHERIDON STOKES	FLT	(R
CHARLES GOULD	WIND	(R	JACK MARSH	WIND	(R	JOHN ELLIS	WIND	(R	EARL DUMLER	WIND	(R
TED NASH	CLAR	(R	DICK SPENCER	CLAR	(R	JACK NIMITZ	CLAR	(R	GARRY COLEMAN	PERC	(R
LOU VOLPE	G	(S	WARREN DOZE	D	(S	BOB CRANSHAW	B	(S	TOM BARNEY	B	(S
BOB CHRISTIANSON	SYN	(S	THOMAS BOGOAN	V	(S	LESLIE DORSEY	V	(S	DAVID SMITH	V	(S
STEVE CLAYTON	V	(S	JUNE MAGRUDER	V	(S	HELEN MILES	V	(S	CHARLES MAGRUDER	V	(S
LENNY ROBERTS	V	(S	THOMAS TEXTOR	V	(S	STRING SECTION		(M			

C164A # PAUL COLLINS C164A

Musician	Instr.	Albums	Record	Year	Label	Country	Number
PAUL COLLINS	G V	(A	(A) PAUL COLLINS BEAT	1979	CBS	UK	83895
STEVEN HUFF	B V	(A					
LARRY WHITMAN	G V	(A	MICHAEL RUIZ D (A				

C164B # PHIL COLLINS C164B

Musician	Instr.	Albums	Record	Year	Release
PHIL COLLINS	D V K PERC	(AB	(A) FACE VALUE	1981	VIRGIN UK 2185 ATLANTIC US 16029
JOHN GIBLIN	B	(AB	(B) HELLO I MUST BE GOING	1982	VIRGIN UK 2252
DARYL STEURMER	G BAN	(AB			

STEPHEN BISHOP	V	(A	ALPHONSO JOHNSON	B	(A	DON MYRICK	SAX	(AB	LOUIS SATTERSFIELD	TROM	(AB
RAHMLEE MICHAEL DAVIS	TPT	(AB	MICHAEL HARRIS	TPT	(AB	JOE PARTRIDGE	G	(A	RONNIE SCOTT	SAX	(A
ERIC CLAPTON	G	(A	PETER ROBINSON	K	(AB	CHOIR		(A	MO FOSTER	B	(B

C165 # SHIRLEY COLLINS C165

Musician	Instr.	Albums	Record	Year	Label	Country	Number
SHIRLEY COLLINS	V G BANJO	(ALL	(A) FALSE TRUE LOVERS	1959	FOLKWAYS		FG3564
TONY ENGLE		(K	(B) FOLK ROOTS	1964	DECCA	UK	4652
PAUL NIEMAN	HRNS	(K	(C) THE SWEET PRIMEROSES	1967	TOPIC	UK	12TS 170
MICHAEL GREGORY	PERC	(K	(D) POWER OF THE TRUE LOVE KNOT	1968	POLYDOR	UK	583 025
DOLLY COLLINS	V	(EFGH	(E) ANTHEMS IN EDEN	1969	HARVEST	UK	SHVL 754
CHRIS HOGWOOD	K	(FJ	(F) LOVE DEATH & THE LADY	1970	HARVEST	UK	SHVL 771
ALLAN LUMSDEN	SACK	(FGJ	(G) NO ROSES	1971	PEGASUS UK PEG 7	US	ANTILLES7017
ADAM SKEAPING	VLN	(FJ	(G) NO ROSES	1974	MOONCREST	UK	CREST 11
ROD SKEAPING	VLN	(FJ	(H) ADIEU TO OLD ENGLAND	1974	TOPIC	UK	12T 238
ELEANOR SLOAN	REBEC	(F	(I) A FAVOURITE GARLAND (BEST OF)	1975	DECCA US 1017	UK	SML 1117
JOHN FORDHAM	REC	(FJ	(J) AMARANTH	1976	HARVEST	UK	SHSM2008
TERRY COX	PERC	(F	(K) FOR AS MANY AS WILL	1978	TOPIC	UK	12T 380
PETER WOOD	CONC	(F					

SIMON NICOL	V G	(GHJ	IAN WHITEMAN	PNO	(G	DAVE BLAND	CONC	(G	ASHLEY HUTCHINGS	B	(GJ
ROGER POWELL	D	(G	RICHARD THOMPSON	G	(G	LOL COXHILL	SAX	(G	ALAN CAVE	BASSOON	(G
TONY HALL	MEL	(G	DAVE MATTACKS	D	(GJ	JOHN KIRKPATRICK	ACC	(GJ	NIC JONES	V FDL	(G
BARRY DRANSFIELD	V FDL	(GK	TIM RENWICK	G	(G	FRANCIS BAINES	G	(G	COLIN ROSS	PIPES	(G
MADDY PRIOR	V	(G	LAL WATERSON	V	(G	ROYSTON WOOD	V	(G	STEVE MIGDEN	HRNS	(G
MIKE WATERSON	V	(G	GREGG BUTLER	SERP	(G	TREVOR CROZIER		(H	JOHN WATCHAM	CONC	(HJ
TERRY POTTER	HCA	(HJ	BILL MOLAN	V MEL	(H	GEOFF SINGLETON	V FDL	(H	JOHN HARRINGTON	V CONC	(H
IAN HOLDER	ACC	(H	BOB STEWART	PSALT	(H	ROGER SWALLOW	D	(H	JOHN RODD	CONC	(J
PAT DONALDSON	B	(H	ROGER BRENNER	SACK	(J	COLIN SHEEN	SACK	(J	PAUL BEER	SACK	(J
MARTIN NICHOLLS	SACK	(J	JOHN SOTHCOTT	VIELL	(G	DAVID MURROW	WIND	(J	STEVE ASHLEY	V	(J
RAY WORMAN	V	(J	JOHN MORGAN	V	(G	DAVID BUSBY	V	(J	MIKE CLIFTON	V	(J
DOTS DAULTREY	V	(J	STUART HOLLYER	V	(J	ROGER RIGDEN	V	(J	ADA TURNHAM	V	(J
OLIVER BROOKES	VLN	(J	MICHAEL LAIRD	CORNET	(J	RICHARD LEE	REC	(J	GILLIAN REID	BELL	(J
PHIL PICKETT	WIND	(K	DAVEY GRAHAM	G	(B						

C165A COLONEL BAGSHOT C165A

KEN PARRY G K V(A (A) OH! WHAT A LOVELY WAR 1971 CADET CONCEPT US 50010
DAVE DOVER B K V (A
BRIAN FARRELL G V (A TERRY McCUSKER D V (A

C166 COLOSSEUM C166

JON HISEMAN D (ALL (A) THOSE WHO ARE ABOUT TO DIE 1969 FONTANA UK STLS 5510
DICK HECKSTALL SMITH SAX (ALL (A) THOSE WHO ARE ABOUT TO DIE 1969 DUNHILL US 50062
TONY REEVES B (ABFD (B) VALENTYNE SUITE 1969 VERTIGO UK VO1 BRONZE HELP4
JAMES LITHERLAND G (ABDF (B) VALENTYNE SUITE 1 BRONZE UK BRNA 214
DAVE GREENSLADE K (ALL (C) DAUGHTER OF TIME 1970 VERTIGO UK 6360 017
MARK CLARKE B (CEF (C) DAUGHTER OF TIME 1970 DUNHILL US 50101
HARRY BECKETT TPT (C (D) GRASS IS GREENER(BEST OF) 1970 DUNHILL US 50079
DAVE CLEMPSON G (CEFD (E) LIVE 1971 BRONZE UK ICD 1
CHRIS FARLOWE V (CEF (E) LIVE 197 WB US 2XS 1942
LOUIS CENNAMO B (C (F) COLLECTORS COLOSSEUM 1971 BRONZE UK ILPS 9173
BARBARA THOMPSON WIND (BC (G) POP CHRONIK 1975 V012
DAVE GELLY SAX (B
JIM PHILLIP SAX (B DEREK WADWORTH TROM (C STRING SECTION (C
JIM ROCH G(PRE LP

C167 COLOSSEUM II C167

JON HISEMAN D (ABC (A) STRANGE NEW FLESH 1976 BRONZE UK ILPS 9356
NEIL MURRAY B (A (A) STRANGE NEW FLESH 1976 WB US 2016
JOHN CARY K ((B) ELECTRIC SAVAGE 1977 MCA UK MCF 2800
DON AIREY K (ABC (B) ELECTRIC SAVAGE 1977 MCA US 2293
MIKE STARR V (A (C) WARDANCE 1977 MCA UK MCF2817 UL RI 1603
GARY MOORE G (ABC (C) WARDANCE 1977 MCA US 2310
JOHN MOLE B (BC

C168 COLOURS C168

CARL RADLE B (A (A) COLOURS 19 DOT US 25854
CHUCK BLACKWELL D (A (B) ATMOSPHERE 19 DOT US 25935
GARY MONTGOMERY PNO (A (AB) COLOURS /ATMOSPHERE 19 PARAMOUNT US 81030
JACK DALTON G (A
ROB EDWARDS G (A

C168A P J COLT C168A

PJ COLT V (A (A) P J COLT 1976 POLYDOR UK 2489 011 US 244 043
FRANCISCO SERRANO B (A
JIM WILKINS D (A JEFF BAXTER G (A VALERIE ROBINSON V (A CYNTHIA OUTLAW V (A
GWEN ROGERS V (A ROSALIND ROGERS V (A ED COSTA K (A PEE WEE ELLIS HRNS (A
HANK CRAWFORD HRNS (A BARRY ROGERS HRNS (A JULIAN PRIESTER HRNS (A JOANNE BENNETT V (A
MONICA WILLIAMS V (A

C169 JESSI COLTER C169

JESSI COLTER V K (ALL (A) A COUNTRY STAR IS BORN 1970 RCA US LSP 4333
WITH (B) I'M JESSI COLTER 1975 CAPITOL US ST11363
WAYLON JENNINGS G V (BCDEF (C) JESSI 1975 CAPITOL US ST11477
JOHN LESLIE HUG G (D (D) DIAMOND IN THE ROUGH 1976 CAPITOL US ST11543
RITCHIE ALBRIGHT D (BCDEF (D) DIAMOND IN THE ROUGH 1976 CAPITOL US SM11822
SHERMAN HAYES B (CDEF (E) MIRRIAM 1977 CAPITOL US ST11583
RALPH MOONEY STEEL(BCDEF (F) THATS THE WAY A COWBOY ROCKS 1978 CAPITOL US ST11863
BILLY GRAHAM FDL MAND(D
CRAIG WARE HRNS (D ROBERT WARE HRNS (D TODD MILLER HRNS (D DON ROBERTSON K (D
BARNEY ROBERTSON K V (DEF CARTER ROBERTSON V (DEF JOHN BUCK WILKIN G (B REGGIE YOUNG G (BC
LARRY MUHOBERAC PNO (BC DUKE GOFF B (BC TOMMY COGBILL B (B WELDON MYRICK STEEL(B
JOHNNY GIMBLE FDL (BF JIM GORDON HRNS (BCE RANDY SCRUGGS G BANJ(C DICK HYDE TROM (BCE
MAC JOHNSON TPT (CE LARRY MURRAY DULC (C GORDON PAYNE G (EF G MERLIN DULC (E
JOHN CHRISTOPHER G (E GAYLE LEVANT HARP (E RANCE WASSON G (E FRED CARTER G (F
TONY JOE WHITE G HCA(F J J CALE G (F

C171 CHI COLTRANE C171

CHI COLTRANE V PERC K(ALL (A) CHI COLTRANE 1972 CBS US 31275 UK 65043
JIM GORDON D (BC (B) LET IT RIDE 1973 CBS US 32463 UK 65639
BARRY DE SOUZA D (B (C) ROAD TO TOMORROW 1977 TK 82501
JIM KELTNER D (D (D) SILK & STEEL 1981 CBS 85277
STEVE PARSONS D (B
CHRIS KARAN D (B KENNY EDWARDS B (C WILLIE WEEKS B (C LARRY KNECHTEL B (B
EMORY GORDY B (B KLAUS VOORMAN B (B CHRIS LAURENCE B (B MARK CIPOLA B (B
JOE PUERTA B (B BOBBYE HALL PERC (B PAUL BUCKMASTER SYN (B JOHN GUSTAFSON B (B
LEE RITENOUR G (B BEB BENAY G (BD LARRY BYROM G (B ALAN ESTES PERC (B
PAUL ESSARD CLAR (B MERRY CLAYTON V (B JEFF PORCARO D (C STEPHANIE SPRUILL V (B
CLYDIE KING V (C MICHAEL BOTTS D (C ABE LABORIEL B (C VICTOR FELDMAN PERC (C
GREG PRESTOPINO V (C JENNIFER WARNES V (C IAN UNDERWOOD SYN (C BRIAN RUSSELL V (C
JIM HORN HRNS (C CHUCK FINDLEY HRNS (C QUITMAN DENNIS HRNS (C

C172 COLWELL WINFIELD BLUES BAND C172

MIKE WINFIELD B (A (A) COLD WIND BLUES 1968 VERVE US 3056
BILL COLWELL G (A
MOOSE SORRENTO V (A CHUCK PURRO D (A JACK SHROER SAX (A
COLLIN TILTON WIND (A

C172A JEFFREY COMANOR C172A

JEFFREY COMANOR G V (AB (A) JEFFREY COMANOR 1975 EPIC US 32832
DON FELDER G (B (B) A RUMOR IN HIS OWN TIME 1976 EPIC US 34080
COLIN CAMERON B (B (C) SURE HOPE YOU LIKE IT 19 A&M US SP 4237
AL KOOPER ORG (B
DAVID GARLAND PNO (B GARY MALLABER D (B HUGH McCRACKEN G (B
TIM SCHMIT V (B RICHARD BELL (C DANNY COHEN (C
TOXEY FRENCH (C BONES HOWE (C GERY ILLINGSWORTH (C
LARRY KNECHTEL K (C JOE OSBORNE B (C RED RHODES STEEL (C
HOMER WILLIS (C

C172B COMFORTABLE CHAIR C172B

BERNIE SCHWARTZ V (A (A) THE COMFORTABLE CHAIR 1968 ODE 44005
BARBARA WALLACE V WIND(A
GENE EARFIN G (A TAD BACZEK K (A GARY DAVIS B G (A
GREG LEROY D (A JOHN DENSMORE PROD (A ROBBY KRIEGER PROD (A

C173 COMMANDER CODY & THE LOST PLANET AIRMEN C173

GEORGE FRAYNE	K V	(ALL	(A) LOST IN THE OZONE	1971	PARAMOUNT	US	PAR 6017
BILLY C FARLOW	HCA V	(ABCDEFG	(A) LOST IN THE OZONE	197	PARAMOUNT		SPFL 276
LANCE DICKERSON	D V	(ABCDEFG	(A) LOST IN THE OZONE	197	CARRERE	FR	68020
ANDY STEIN	FDL SAX	(ABCDEFG	(A) LOST IN THE OZONE	1976	ANCHOR	UK	ABC 5074
BILL KIRCHEN	G V	(ABCDEFG	(B) HOT LICKS COLD STEEL	1972	PARAMOUNT	US	PAS 6031
BRUCE BARLOW	B V	(ABCDEFGJ	(B) HOT LICKS COLD STEEL	197	PARAMOUNT		SPFL 281
BOBBY BLACK	STEEL V	(BCDFGJK	(B) HOT LICKS COLD STEEL	197	CARRERE	FR	68019
JOHN TICHY	G	(ABCDEF	(B) HOT LICKS COLD STEEL	1976	ANCHOR	UK	ABCL 5079
ERNIE HAGAR	STEEL	(E	(C) COUNTRY CASANOVA	1973	PARAMOUNT	US	PAS 6054
RICK HIGGINBOTHAM	G	(G	(C) COUNTRY CASANOVA	197	PARAMOUNT		SPFL 287
MIC GILLETTE	TPT	(EF	(C) COUNTRY CASANOVA	197	CARRERE	FR	68002
GREG ADAMS	TPT	(EF	(C) COUNTRY CASANOVA	1976	ANCHOR	UK	ABCL 5083
DAVID BROMBERG	G	(F	(D) LIVE DEEP IN THE HEART OF TEXAS	1974	PARAMOUNT	US	PAS 1017
HOYT AXTON	G V	(F	(D) LIVE DEEP IN THE HEART OF TEXAS	197	PARAMOUNT		SPFL 295
RONEE BLAKLEY	B V	(F	(D) LIVE DEEP IN THE HEART OF TEXAS	197	CARRERE	FR	68001
MIMI FARINA	B V	(F	(D) LIVE DEEP IN THE HEART OF TEXAS	1976	ANCHOR	UK	ABCL 5088
NORTON BUFFALO	HRNS V	(GK	(E) COMM' CODY HIS LOST PLANET AIRMEN	1975	WB	US	BS 2847
FRED MYER	D	(J	(E) COMM' CODY HIS LOST PLANET AIRMEN	1975	WB	UK	K 56108
DARIUS JAVAHER	G	(J	(F) TALES FROM THE OZONE	1975	WB	US	BS 2883
ROB GREER	B	(J	(F) TALES FROM THE OZONE	1975	WB	UK	K 56158
CISCO G	SAX	(J	(G) WEVE GOT A LIVE ONE HERE	1976	WB	US	BS 2939
CRAIG CHAQUICO	G	(J	(G) WEVE GOT A LIVE ONE HERE	1976	WB	UK	K 66043
RENEE ARMAND	V	(F	(H) MIDNIGHT MAN (CODY SOLO)	19	ARISTA	US	AB 4125
MARC EDELSTEIN	V	(F	(J) ROCK'N'ROLL AGAIN	1977	ARISTA	UK	SPART1018
NICOLETTE LARSON	V	(FJK	(J) ROCK'N'ROLL AGAIN	1977	ARISTA	US	AL 4135
GRAHAM BROAD	PERC	(J	(J) ROCK'N'ROLL AGAIN	1977	PATHE	FR	068 99251
DEBORAH ANDERSON	V	(F	(K) FLYING DREAMS	1978	ARISTA	UK	AB 4183
CHARRA PENNY	V	(J	(K) FLYING DREAMS	1978	ARISTA	US	SPART1067
TOM FLYE	PERC	(J					

KEVIN FARRELL	V	(F	SCOTT EDWARDS	B	(K	JEFF BAXTER	G	(K	NEIL LARSON	K	(K
JENNIFER WARNES	V	(K	ED GREENE	D	(K	BUZZ FEITON	G	(K	LEE MONTGOMERY	V	(K
ERNIE WATTS	SAX	(K	SHIRLEY MATTHEWS	V	(K	ABRAHAM LABORIEL	B	(K	RICHARD BOWDEN	G	(K
JOHN HUG H HARP K	D	(K	DAVID HUNGATE	B	(K	JOE ENGLISH	D	(K	VENETTA FIELDS	V	(K
CLYDIE KING	V	(K	DANNY GATTON	G	(K	DELANEY BRAMLETT	V	(K	STEVE BECKMEYER	G	(K
BUZZ BUCHANEN	PERC	(K	GARY COLEMAN	PERC	(K	WEST VIRGINIA CREEPER	STEEL	(A			

C173A THE COMMERCIALS C173A

LOYD GROSSMAN	G V	(A	(A) COMPARE & DECIDE	1980	EAT	US	EAT1
JOHN DEELP	B SYN	(A					
NEAL GROSSMAN	SYN	(A	GARY LONG	IAN DUCK	G	(A	

C174 COMMODORES C174

LIONEL RICHIE	(A) MACHINE GUN	1974	MOTOWN	US M7 798	UK STML11273
WILLIAM KING	(A) MACHINE GUN	1981	MOTOWN	US M5 121	UK 5002
WALTER ORANGE	(B) CAUGHT IN THE ACT	1975	MOTOWN	US M7 820	UK STML11286
RON LAPRAED	(C) HOT ON THE TRACKS	1976	MOWTOWN		UK STM 12031
MILAN WILLIAMS	(D) MOVIN ON	197	MOTOWN	US M7 848	UK STML12001
TOMMY McCLARY	(D) MOVIN ON	1981	MOTOWN	US M5 178	
	(E) ZOOM	1977	MOTOWN		UK STML12057
	(F) COMMODORES	197	MOTOWN	US M7 884	
	(G) LIVE	1978	MOTOWN	US M9 894	UK TMSP 6007
	(H) NATURAL HIGH	1978	MOTOWN	US M7 902	UK STML12087
	(I) GREATEST HITS	1978	MOTOWN	US M7 912	UK STML12100
	(J) MIDNIGHT MAGIC	1979	MOTOWN	US 926	UK STMA 8032
	(K) HEROS	1980	MOTOWN	US 939	UK STMA 8034
	(L) IN THE POCKET	1981	MOTOWN	US 995	UK STML12156
	(M) LOVE SONGS	1982	MOTOWN	US 1171	

C174A COMMON PEOPLE C174A

DANNY REBINETT	G V	(A	(A) OF THE PEOPLE BY THE PEOPLE FOR..	1969	CAPITOL	US	266
JOHN BARTLEY	G	(A					
JERRALD REBINETT	D	(A	MICHAEL McCARTHY	B	(A		

C174B COMSAT ANGELS C174B

MIC GLAISHER	D	(ABC	(A) WAITING FOR AN MIRACLE	1980	POLYDOR	UK	2383 578
STEPHEN FELLOWS	G V	(ABC	(B) COMSAT ANGELS	19	METRONOME	GER	60357
KEVIN BACON	B	(ABC	(EP) EYE OF THE LENS +3	1981	METRONOME	GER	930 031
ANDY PEAKE	K V	(ABC	(C) SLEEP NO MORE	1981	POLYDOR	UK	POLS 1038

C174C BOBBY COMSTOCK C174C

BOBBY COMSTOCK	V	(A	(A) BOBBY COMSTOCK	19	ASCOT	US	13026

C174D COMPANYIA ELECTRICA DHARMA C174D

ESTEVE FORTUNY	G	(AB	(A) DIUMENGE	1975	ZELESTE EDIGSA	FR	2018
JORDI SOLEY	K	(AB	(B) L'OUCEMBALLA	1976	ZELESTE EDIGSA	FR	2026
JEAN FORTUNY	SAX	(AB					
CARLES VIDAL	B	(AB	JOSEP FOTUNY	D	(AB		

C175 COMUS C175

ROGER WOOTTON	G V	(AB	(A) FIRST UTTERANCE			1971 DAWN	UK	DNLS 3019
BOBBIE WATSON	V PERC	(AB	(B) TO KEEP FROM CRYING			1974 VIRGIN	UK	V 2018
COLIN PEARSON	VLN	(A						
ROB YOUNG	PERC	(A	KEITH HALE	K	(B	ANDY HELLABY	B	(B
LINDSAY COOPER	WIND	(B	GORDON CAXON	D	(B	PHIL BARRY	PERC	(B
DIDIER MALHERBE	SAX	(B	TIM KRAEMER	CELLO	(B			

C175B CONGO ASHANTE ROY C175B

(A) SIGN OF THE STAR 1981 CHARISMA UK PREX 8 NL6302 147

C176 CONGO C176

(A) HEART OF THE CONGO	1978	BLACK ART		
(B) CONGO	1979	CBS		83796

C176A CONGRESS OF WONDERS C176A

(A) REVOLTING	19	FANTASY	US	7016

C176B ARTHUR CONLEY C176B

ARTHUR CONLEY	V	(ALL	( ) SWEET SOUL MUSIC	19	ATCO	US	33215
			( ) SHAKE RATTLE & ROLL	19	ATCO	US	33220
			( ) SOUL DIRECTION	19	ATCO	US	33243
			( ) MORE SWEET SOUL	19	ATCO	US	33276

C176C CONTINIUM C176C

Member	Instr.	Albums
YOEL SCHWARCZ	G HCA	(A
HARVEY TROUPE	D	(AB
TIM RICE	K	(B
PETER BILLAM	B G	(AB

Album	Year	Label	Country	No.
(A) CONTINIUM	1970	RCA	US	8157
(B) AUTUMN GRASS	1971	RCA	US	8196

C177 BILLY CONNOLLY C177

BILLY CONNOLY

Album		Year	Label	Country	No.
LIVE		1972	TRANSATLANTIC	UK	TRA 258
LIVE	RI	1981	TRANSATLANTIC	UK	TRS 103
SOLO CONCERT		1974	TRANSATLANTIC	UK	TRA 279
WORDS & MUSIC		1975	TRANSATLANTIC	UK	TRASAM 32
COP YER WHACK FOR THIS		1974	POLYDOR	UK	2383 310
GET RIGHT INTAE HIM		1975	POLYDOR	UK	2383 368
ATLANTIC BRIDGE		1977	POLYDOR	UK	2383 419
RAW MEAT FROM THE BALCONY		1977	POLYDOR	UK	2383 464
BILLY CONNOLLY		1977	HALLMARK	UK	SHM 927
B C COLLECTION		1978	PICKWICK		PDA 035
THE BIG YIN		1976	TRANSATLANTIC	UK	TRASAM 38
GOLDEN GIFT BOX		1976	TRANSATLANTIC	UK	GAR1
ANTHOLOGY		1978	TRANSATLANTIC	UK	MTRA 2008
RIOUTOUS ASSEMBLY		1979	POLYDOR	UK	2383 543

C177A ROBERT CONNOLLY C177A

Member	Instr.	Albums
ROBERT CONNOLLY	G B K	(A
GREG McILVEEN	D	(A
DAVE BEATLY	G	(A
HOWIE STRUTT	V	(A
PETER CROLLY	B V FLT	(A
SHEILA WILLICK	V	(A
FRANK RUSSELL	D	(A
SANDRA WILLICK	V	(A

Album	Year	Label	Country	No.
(A) PLATEAU	1978	TUBE		TSH 352

C177B BILL CONNORS C177B

Member	Instr.	Albums
BILL CONNORS	G	(AB
JAN GARAREK	SAX	(B
GARY PEACOCK	B	(B
JACK DEDOHNETTE	D	(B

Album	Year	Label	Country	No.
(A) THEME TO THE GUARDIAN	1975	ECM		1057
(B) OF MIST & MELTING	1978	ECM		1120

C177C CONTOURS C177C

Member	Instr.	Albums
BILLY GORDON		
JOE BILLINGSLEA		
SYLVESTER POTTS		
BILLY HOGGS		
HUBERT JOHNSON		
HUEY DAVIS	G	

Album	Year	Label	Country	No.
(A) DO YOU LOVE ME	19	GORDY	US	901
(B) BABY HIT & RUN	1974	M F P	UK	50054

C177D CONTORTIONS C177D

Member	Instr.	Albums
JAMES CHANCE/WHITE	V K SAX	(ALL
GINGER LEE	D	(CD
RICHARD HARRISON	D	(C
DON CHRISTENSEN	G	(D
VIVIENNE DICK	VLN	(D
AL MACDOWELL	B	(C
FRED WELLS	G	(C
GEORGE SCOTT	B	(D
PAT PLACE	V	(D
BOB QUINE	G	(D
PATRICK GEOFFROIS	G	(C
LYDIA LUNCH	G	(D
ADELE BERTEI	PNO	(D
JODY HARRIS	V	(D
LORENZO WYCHE	TPT	(C
RAY MANTILLA	PERC	(D
PAUL COLIN	SAX	(D
CHRISTIAN HOFFMAN	PNO	(D

Album	Year	Label	Country	No.
(A) BUY	1979	ZE	CAN	33002
(B) SECOND CHANCE	1980	PVC	US	7918
(C) LIVE AUX BAINS DOUCHES	1980	INVISIBLE	FR	10008
(D) JAMES WHITE & THE BLACKS	1980	ZE	GER	202 452

C178 CONTRABAND C178

Member	Instr.	Albums
MAE McKENNA	G V	(A
PETER CAIRNEY	G B	(A
JOHN MARTIN	VLN	(A
BILLY JOHNSON	B	(A
ALEC BAIRD	D G	(A
GEORGE JOHNSON	MAND K KG	(A

Album	Year	Label	Country	No.
(A) CONTRABAND	1974	TRANSATLANTIC	UK	TRA 278

C178A CONTRABAND (US) C178A

Member	Instr.	Albums
DAVID PRITCHARD	G	(A
CHARLES ORENA	WIND	(A
PETE ROBINSON	K	(A
BRUCE CALE	B VLN	(A
BRIAN MOFFATT	D PERC	(A

Album	Year	Label	Country	No.
(A) TIME & SPACE	1971	EPIC	US	30814

C178B CONTRABAND (AUSTR) C178B

Member	Instr.	Albums
MARK EVANS	B V	(A
GRAHAM KENNEDY	G V	(A
PETER McFARLANE	D V	(A
KERRIE BIDDELL	V	(A
OWEN ORFORD	V	(A
RALPH WHITE	HRNS	(A
CHRIS JONES	G	(A

Album	Year	Label	Country	No.
(A) NOTHING TO HIDE	1978	PORTRAIT	US	35450

C179 RY COODER C179

Album	Year	Label	US	UK
(A) RY COODER	1971	REPRISE	US 6402	UK K44093
(B) INTO THE PURPLE VALLEY	1972	REPRISE	US 2052	UK K44142
(C) BOOMERS STORY	1972	REPRISE	US 2117	UK K44224
(D) PARADISE & LUNCH	1974	REPRISE	US 2179	UK K44260
(E) CHICKEN SKIN MUSIC	1976	REPRISE	US 2254	UK K54083
(F) SHOWTIME	1977	WB	US 3059	UK K56386
(G) JAZZ	1978	WB	US 3197	UK K56488
(H) BOP TILL YOU DROP	1979	WB	US 3358	UK K56691
(I) BORDERLINE	1980	WB	US 3489	UK K56864
(J) LONG RIDERS(SOUNDTRACK)	1980	WB	US 3448	UK K56826
(K) THE SLIDE AREA	1982	WB	US 3651	
(1) NOV 1980 TOUR(UK)				

Member	Instr.	Albums
RY COODER	G V B MAND	(ALL
JIM KELTNER	D	(BCDEHIJK
MILT HOLLAND	PERC	(ABCDEFHJ
ROGER HAWKINS	D	(C
CHARLES LAWING	CLAR	(C
RANDY NEWMAN	PNO	(C
GEORGE BOHANON	HRNS	(BCEGJ
ATTA ISAACS	G	(E
TOMMY McCLURE	B	(C
GENE FINNEY	HCA	(C
CHUCK RAINEY	B	(K
SLEEPY JOHN ESTES	G V	(C
JIM DICKINSON	PROD PNO	(BCJK

Member	Instr.	Albums	Member	Instr.	Albums	Member	Instr.	Albums	Member	Instr.	Albums
ISAAC GARCIA	D	(F	HENRY BIG RED OJEDA	B	(EF	FRANK VILLAREAL	SAX	(F	ELDRIDGE KING	V	(F
BOBBY KING	V	(1DEFHIK	TERRY EVANS	V	(EF	PAT RIZZO	SAX	(EFG	JESSE PONCE	BANJO	(F
EARL HINES	PNO	(DG	RITCHIE HAYWARD	D	(A	ROY ESTRADA	B	(A	JOHN BARBEDA		(A
MAX BENNETT	B	(A	BOBBY BRUCE		(A	GEORGE McCURN	V	(D	WALTER COOK	V	(D
RICHARD JONES	V	(D	KARL RUSSELL	V	(D	TOM PEDRINI	B	(G	RANDY ALLCROFT	TROM	(G
DAVID SHERR	CLAR	(G	HARVEY PITTEL	WIND	(G	TOM COLLIER	PERC	(G	BARBARA STARKEY	K	(G
CHUCK DOMANICO	B	(G	MARIO GUARNERI	CORNET	(G	RED CALLENDER	B TUBA	(DEG	MARK STEVENS	D	(G
DAVID LINDLEY	G MAND	(GHJ	CHRIS ETHRIDGE	B	(ABCED	FRITZ RICHMOND	B	(B	JERRY JUMONVILLE	HRNS	(B
JOE DAVIS	HRNS	(B	IKE WILLIAMS	HRNS	(B	JOHN CRAVIOTTO	D	(B	VAN DYKE PARKS	PROD K	(AB
GLORIA JONES	V	(AB	DONNA WASHBURN	V	(B	DONNA WEISS	V	(B	CLAUDIA LENNEAR	V	(B
SIMON PICO PAYNE	V	(G	BILL JOHNSON	V	(DG	JIMMY ADAMS	V	(GH	CHUCK BERGHOFFER	B	(G
WILLIE SCHWARTZ	CLAR	(G	BILL HOOD	SAX	(G	JOHN RODBY	K	(G	FRED JACKSON	SAX	(E
STUART BROTMAN	CYMB	(G	OSCAR BRASHEAR	CORNET	(DEGJ	CLIFF GIVENS	V	(EGH	RUSS TITELMAN	PROD B V	(DE
BENNY POWELL	TROM	(E	GABBY PAHINUI	STEEL	(E	RONNIE BARRON	K	(DH	HERMAN JOHNSON	V	(EHK
JOHN DUKE	B	(D	PLAS JOHNSON	SAX	(D	GENE MUMFORD	V	(D	RANDY LORENZO	V	(H
TIM DRUMMOND	B	(HIK	PATRICK HENDERSON	K	(H	PICO PAYNE	V	(HJ	GREG PRESTOPINO	V	(H

(CONTINUED)

C179 (CONTINUED) RY COODER C179

FLACO JIMINEZ	ACC	(EF	CHAKA KHAN	V	(H	GEORGE McFADDEN	V	(HK	GEORGE PIERRE	PERC	(IJK
REGGIE McBRIDE	B	(HIK	WILLIAM D SMITH	K V	(IK	JOHN HIATT	G V	(IK	JESSE HARMS	SYN	(I1
WILLIE GREEN	V	(1IK	CURT BOUTERSE	DULC	(J	BILL BRYSON	B	(J	TOM SAUBER	BAN G	(J
MITCH GREENHILL	G V	(J	JOE CHAMBERS	V	(J	JIM KEACH	V	(J	LESTER CHAMBERS	V	(J
HARRY CAREY JRN	V	(J	DAN PENN	V	(C	DARRELL VERDUSCO	D	(1	JAMES ROLLESTON	B	(1
JOSEPH BYRD	PROD	(G	LENNY WARONKER	PROD	(ABCD	PICO PAYNE	V	(G	BOBBY BAKER	V	(K
KAZU MATSUI		(K	NICK DECARO	SRT	(K						

C179A SAM COOKE C179A

COOKES TOUR	1960	RCA		2221
HITS OF THE 50s	1960	RCA	US	2236
ONE & ONLY	196	RCA	US	2264
SAM COOKE	19	CAMDEN	US	2433
SAM COOKE	196	RCA	US	2293
MY KIND OF BLUES	1961	RCA	US	2392
GOLDEN SOUND	19	TRIP	US	28030
TWISTIN THE NIGHT AWAY	1961	RCA	US	2555
TWISTIN THE NIGHT AWAY	1976	STARCALL	UK	1034
BEST OF SAM COOKE VOL1	1962	RCA	US	2625
MR SOUL	1962	RCA	US	2673
3 GREAT GUYS(ANKA SEDAKA)	196	RCA	US	2720
NIGHT BEAT	1963	RCA	US	2709
SOUL STIRRERS	1964	SAR	US	105
SOUL STIRRERS	1964	LONDON		
AINT THAT GOOD NEWS	1964	RCA	US	2899
AINT THAT GOOD NEWS	1964	SPECIALTY		2115
GOSPEL SOUL OF SAM COOKE	196	SPECIALTY	US	2116
2 SIDES	19	SPECIALTY	US	2119
2 SIDES	1971	SONET	UK	SNTF5009
GOSPEL SOUL VOL 2	196	SPECIALTY	US	2128
AT THE COPA	1964	RCA	US	2970
ORIGINAL SOUL STIRRERS	196	SPECIALTY	US	2137
THATS HEAVEN TO ME	196	SPECIALTY	US	2146
GOLDEN SOUND	196	TRIP	US	8030
16 GREATEST HITS	196	TRIP	US	15 2
SHAKE	1965	RCA	US	3367
BEST OF VOL 2	1965	RCA	US	3373
SAMS SONGS	196	FAMOUS	US	502
ONLY SIXTEEN	196	FAMOUS	US	505
SO WONDERFUL	196	FAMOUS	US	508
YOU SEND ME	196	FAMOUS	US	509
YOU SEND ME	19	CAMDEN US		ACL10445
CHA CHA CHA	196	FAMOUS	US	512
RIGHT ON	196	CHERIE	US	1001
TRY A LITTLE LOVE	1965	RCA	US	3435
HIT KIT	196	KEEN	US	86101
I THANK GOD	196	KEEN	US	86103
SAM COOKE	196	KEEN	US	2001
ENCORE	196	KEEN	US	2003
TRIBUTE TO THE LADY	196	KEEN	US	2004
ENCORE VOL 2	196	KEEN	US	2008
WONDERFUL WORLD(50s)	1966	IMMEDIATE	UK	IMLP002
WONDERFUL WORLD(50s	1966	KEEN	US	86106
UNFORGETTABLE SAM COOKE	1966	RCA	US	3517
UNFORGETTABLE SAM COOKE	196	CAMDEN	US	2610
MAN WHO INVENTED SOUL	1968	RCA	US	3991
GOLDEN AGE	196	RCA	UK	1054
THE LATE SAM COOKE	1969	RCA INT	UK	INT1080
THIS IS SAM COOKE	1971	RCA	UK	2007
THIS IS SAM COOKE	197	RCA	US	6027
SINGS BILLIE HOLIDAY	1976	STARCALL	UK	1030
SINGS BILLIE HOLIDAY	197	UPFRONT	US	160
INTERPRETS BILLIE HOLIDAY	19	RCA		APL10899
INTERPRETS BILLIE HOLIDAY	1976	RCA	UK	HY1030
FOREVER	1976	RCA		7194
ANOTHER SATURDAY NIGHT	19	RCA	US	4375
WHEN I FALL IN LOVE	1979	NUT	UK	NUTM23

C179B CALVIN COOL & THE SURF KNOBS C179B

CALVIN COOL	(A) THE SURFERS BEAT	19	CHARTER	US	103

C179C DOUG COOK BAND C179C

DOUG COOK	(A	(A) LATE NIGHT BAR FIGHTS	1978	ROCKING HORSE	US	5520

C179D ROGER COOK C179D

ROGER COOK	V	(ALL	(A) STUDY	1970	COLUMBIA UK SCX 6388
LES HURDLE	B	(B	(B) MEANWHILE BACK AT THE WORLD	1972	REGAL ZONO UK8508 US KAMASUTRA 2056
JIMMY HOROWITZ	FLT K	(B	(C) MINSTREL IN FLIGHT	1973	REGAL ZONO UK1935 US KAMASUTRA 2069
VICKI BROWN	V	(B	(D) ALRIGHT	1976	POLYDOR UK 2383357 US WB 2909
LIZA STRIKE	V	(B			

ROSETTA HIGHTOWER	V	(B	LESLEY DUNCAN	V	(B	NEIL LANCASTER	V	(B	TONY BURROWS	V	(B
JOHNNY GOODWIN	V	(B	ALAN BRANSCOMBE	SAX	(B	BARRY DESOUZA	D	(B	ALAN PARKER	G	(B
CHRIS SPEDDING	G	(BC	CALEB QUAYE	G	(B	MIKE EGAN	G	(B	TONY NEWMAN	D	(C
HERBIE FLOWER	B	(CD	RAY COOPER	PERC	(C	BRIAN PARRISH	G	(C	FRANK RENSHAW	G V	(C
TONY KELLY	G	(C	PAUL YOUNG	V	(C	B J COLE	STEEL	(C	PETE ROBINSON	K	(C
DAVE WILKINSON	ORG	(C	HUGH BURNS	G	(D	RAY GLYNN	G	(D	JOHNNY CHRISTOPHER	G	(D
REGGIE YOUNG	G	(D	MARY HOPEFINGER	HARP	(D	DENNIS GOOD	TROM	(D	GEORGE TIDWELL	TPT	(D
JILL HUTTON	V	(D	SANDY MASON	V	(D	MADELINE BELL	V	(D	DOREEN CHANTER	V	(D
IRENE CHANTER	V	(D	SAM LORBER	V	(D	RICHARD BRANNON	V	(D	RICHARD LEIGH	V	(D
KENNY MALONE	D	(D	BARRY MORGAN	D	(D	JOE ALLEN	B	(D	BILLY PUETT	WIND	(D
BOBBY WOOD	K	(D	CHARLES COCHRAN	K	(D	MIKE MORAN	K	(D			

C180 RITA COOLIDGE C180

RITA COOLIDGE V (ALL (A) RITA COOLIDGE 1971 A&M US 4291 UK AMLS 2015
WITH (B) NICE FEELIN' 1971 A&M US 4325 UK AMLS64325
LEON RUSSELL K (A (C) LADY'S NOT FOR SALE 1972 A&M US 4370 UK AMLS64370
DANIEL TIMMS V (F (C) LADY'S NOT FOR SALE 1981 M F P UK 50500
SPOONER OLDHAM K (A (D) FALL INTO SPRING 1974 A&M US 3627 UK AMLS63627
CLARENCE WHITE G (A (E) ITS ONLY LOVE 1975 A&M US 4531 UK AMLS64531
MARC BENNO G (ABC (F) ANYTIME ANYWHERE 1977 A&M US 4616 UK AMLH64616
CHRIS ETHRIDGE B (A (G) LOVE ME AGAIN 1978 A&M US 4699 UK AMLH64699
JIM KELTNER D (ACH (H) SATISFIED 1979 A&M US 4781 UK AMLH64781
FRED TACKETT G (HI (I) HEARTBREAK RADIO 1981 A&M US 3727 UK AMLK63727
STEPHEN STILLS G (A ( ) GREATEST HITS(VERY BEST OF) 1980 A&M US 4836 UK AMLH68520
BOOKER T JONES B K(ACDEFGH (FH) ANYTIME/SATISFIED 1980 A&M CASS UK CAM CR5
BOBBY WOMACK G (A
DONALD DUNN B (A BOBBYE HALL PERC(ADEF LARRY LEE V (G JERRY McGEE G (ACDEFG
PLAS JOHNSON SAX (A RY COODER G (A FUZZY SAMUELS B (A JIM HORN SAX (AC
JOHN KELSO SAX (A DON MENZA SAX (A CLIFFORD SCOTT SAX (A PETER CHRISTLIEB (A
GEORGE BOHANON HRNS (A LEW McCREARY TROM (A ERNIE TACK TROM (A JACK REDMAN TROM (A
DICK HYDE TROM (A OLLIVER MITCHELL HRNS (A CHUCK FINDLEY TPT (A AL AARONS TPT (A
DALTON SMITH HRNS (A VINCE DE ROSA HRNS (A BILL HENSHAW HRNS (A ARTHUR MAEBE HRNS (A
DAVID DUKE HRNS (A CLYDIE KING V (AEF VANETTA FIELDS V (AF SHIRLEY MATTHEWS V(ACEF
PRISCILLA COOLIDGE V (ACDH DONNA WEISS V (AC GRAHAM NASH V (A BOB SEGARINI V (A
RANDY BISHOP V (A MIKE UTLEY K (BCDCEFGHI CARL RADLE B (C AL PERKINS G (CE
RUSS KUNKEL D (DI JAY GRAYDON G (G JIM HAAS V (G STEPHEN BRUTON V G (GH
BERNIE LEADON G (C LEE SKLAR B (CDEF AL KOOPER G (C JOHN SEBASTIAN HCA (C
CHARLIE FREEMAN G (BC TOMMY McCLURE B (BCH SAMMY CREASON D (BCDEFH SNEAKY PETE STEEL(C
BROOKS HUNNICUTT V (DE JENNIFER WARNES V (DE PETSYE POWELL V (E STEVE FORMAN PERC (G
MAXINE WILLARD V (CG KRIS KRISTOFFERSON V (C BARBARA CARROLL PNO (E CHUCK DOMANICO B (E
COLIN BAILEY D (E MIKE BAIRD D (FG DENNIS BELFIELD B (G JULIA TILLMAN V (G
ORRIN WATERS V (G LUTHER WATERS V (G CORY WELLS V (G DEAN PARKS G (DFHI
BOB GLAUB B (HI DOROTHY ASHBY HARP (H JOHN SEITER V (H MICHAEL McDONALD V (H
RICHIE CANNATA HRNS (H DONNY GARRARD V (H RITA JEAN BODINE V (D LINDA DILLARD V (D
KEN EDWARDS V (DI ANDREW GOLD G K PER V (DID DANIEL TIMMS V (F GAYLE LEVANT HARP (F
JEFF PORCARO D (I WADDY WACHTEL G (I NICOLETTE LARSON V (I BILL PAYNES K (I
LENNY CASTRO V (I KIM CARNES V (F BROCK WALSH V (I MAUREEN McDONALD V (I
MIKE BOTTS D (I J D SOUTHER V (I WILLIAM SMITH V (I GIB GUILBEAU FDL (D
GEOFF LEVIN G (D DAVID CAMPBELL STR (DI NICK DE CARO ACC (BDI RUSTY YOUNG STEEL(B
HERB PEDERSEN BAN (D MILT HOLLAND PERC (D DON BROOKS HCA (B

C182 ALICE COOPER C182

[ALICE COOPER V (ALL (1) SPIDERS (2) EARWIGS(EARLY GROUPS)
VINCENT FURNIER] (A) PRETTIES FOR YOU 1969 STRAIGHT US STS1051 WB 1840
GLEN BUXTON G (123ABCDEFGH (B) EASY ACTION 1969 STRAIGHT US 1061 WB 1845
MICHAEL BRUCE K G(123ABCDEFGH (AB)SCOOLDAYS(PRETTIES/EASY ACTION 1973 STRAIGHT UK K 66021
STEVE HUNTER G (FJKLM (C) LOVE IT TO DEATH 1971 STRAIGHT STS 1065
PRAKASH JOHN B (JLM (C) LOVE IT TO DEATH 1971 WB US 1883 UK K 46177
JOSEF CHIROWSKI K (JL (C) LOVE IT TO DEATH 197 MIDI 20633
DICK WAGNER G (EFGJKLMOR (D) KILLER 1971 WB GER 46121 UK K 56005
NEAL SMITH D (123ABCDEFGH (D) KILLER 1971 WB US 2567
DENNIS DUNAWAY B (123ABCDEFGH (E) SCHOOLS OUT 1972 WB US 2623 UK K 56007
DAVID BRIGGS PNO (B (F) BILLION DOLLAR BABIES 1973 WB US 2685 UK K 56013
JULIA TILLMAN V (L (G) MUSCLE OF LOVE 1974 WB US 2748 UK K 56018
ALLEN SCHWARZBERG D (KL (H) GREATEST HITS 1974 WB US 3107 UK K 56043
AL McMILLAN PNO (KL (J) WELCOME TO MY NIGHTMARE 1975 ANCHOR UK 2011 CARRERE FR 68051
AL KOOPER K (L (J) WELCOME TO MY NIGHTMARE 1975 ATLANTIC US 19130
DAVEY JOHNSTONE G (OP (K) GOES TO HELL 1976 WB US 2896 UK K 56171
TONY LEVIN B (JKL (L) LACE & WHISKEY 1977 WB US 3027 UK K 56365
JIM KELTNER D (O (M) ALICE COOPER SHOW 1977 WB US 3138 UK K 56439
DONOVAN G (F (N) ALICE COOPER 19 CHARTERLINE CTR 46177
JOHNNY BADANJEK D (J (O) FROM THE INSIDE 1978 WB US 3263 UK K 56577
REGGIE VINCENT G V (E (P) FLUSH THE FASHION 1980 WB US 3436 UK K 56805
SHARON LEE WILLIAMS V(K (Q) SPECIAL FORCES 1981 WB US 3581 UK K 56927
JAN UVENA D (R (R) ZIPPER CATCHES SKIN 1982 WB UK K 57021
CRAIG KRAMPF D (R (S) LIVE IN TORONTO 1982 WB
COLINA PHILLIPS V (K
DENNY VOSBURGH V (K JIM GANNON V (K BILL MISENER V (K JIM MAELEN PERC(K
JOHN TROPEA G (K MICHAEL SHERMAN V (K SHAUN JACKSON V (K SHEP GORDON V (K
LAUREL WARD V (K DENNIS CONWAY D (P JOHN LOPRESTI B (P PENTTI GLAN D (JM
FRED MANDEL K (MP VANETTA FIELDS V (L LORNA WILLARD V (L ERNIE WATTS SAX (L
JIM GORDON D (KL RICK NIELSEN G (O BOB BABBITT B (LK BOB EZRIN PROD K V (DJKL
GERRY LYONS V (J STU DAY V (G DAVE LIBERT V (FG RONNIE SPECTOR V (G
NONA HENDRYX V (G MICK MASHBIR G (G LIZA MINNELLI V (G SARAH DASH V (G
POINTER SISTERS V (G DENNIS FERRANTE V (G MARK VOLMAN V (P HOWARD KAYLAN V (P
RICKY TIERNEY V (P KEITH ALLISON V (P MIKE PINERA G (QR DUANE HITCHINGS G (QR
DANNY JOHNSON G (Q CRAIG KRAMPF D (Q ERIK SCOTT B (Q JOHN TATUM (1
JOHN SPEAR (1 JOHN NITZINGER G (R BILLY STEELE G (R

C182 A D B COOPER C182A

D B COOPER V (ABC (A) EVERY MAN A KING 1980 BLUE CELLAR US 001
JON CHAPMAN D (C (B) BUY AMERICAN 1980 WB UK K 56831 US 3444
MICHAEL TOWERS G V (C (C) DANGEROUS CURVES 1981 WB US 3544
BOB IRVING K (C
ROGER HEATH G (C ROBBY SCHARF B (C

C183 MIKE COOPER C183

MIKE COOPER V (ALL (A) INVERTED WORLD 1968 MATCHBOX SDM 159
WITH (B) OH REALLY 1969 PYE UK NSPL18281 US JANUS3004
ALAN COOK K ((C) DO I KNOW YOU 1970 DAWN UK NLS 3005 US JANUS3021
TIM RICHARDSON PERC ((D) TROUT STEEL 1970 DAWN UK DNLS 3011
LES CALVERT BASS ((E) PLACES I KNOW 1971 DAWN UK DNLS 3026
STEFAN GROSSMAN G (D (F) MACHINE GUN COMPANY 1972 DAWN UK DNLS 3031
THE HERON V (D (G) LIFE & DEATH IN PARADISE 1974 FRESH AIR UK 6370 500
ALAN SKIDMORE SAX (D

(CONTINUED)

C183 (CONTINUED)

MIKE COOPER C183

JOHN TAYLOR PNO (D
BILL BOAZMAN G (D
ROY BABBINGTON B (D
HARRY MILLER DBL B (CG
LOUIS MUHOLO D (G
ALAN GOWER PNO (G
GERRY FIELDS VLN (D
MIKE OSBORNE WIND (DG
NICK PICKETT VLN (D
IAN A ANDERSON (A
COLIN BOYD B (G
TERRY EVERETT SYN (G
ALAN JACKSON D (D
GEOFF HAWKINS WIND (D
POOR LITTLE ANN V (C
TERRY CLARKE G V (G
IAN FOSTER D (G

C183A COOPER BROTHERS C183A

(A) THE DREAM NEVER DIES 1978 CAPRICORN US 0206 UK 2429 171

BRIAN COOPER B V (A
RICHARD COOPER G V (A
TERRY KING STEEL V (A
GLEN BELL D V (A
KEITH JOLLIMORE SAX (A
LENNY SOLOMON STRINGS(A
DON BREGG V (A
DARRYL ALGUIRE PERC V (A
GLOVES McGUINTY PNO (A
CHARLIE ROBERTSON FLT (A
AL SERWA K V (A
JOHN SAUNDERS BANJO(A
AL BRISCOE DOBRO(A
STEVE HOLLINGWORTH D V (A

C184 JOHN COOPER-CLARKE C184

(A) DISGUISE IN LOVE 1978 CBS UK 83132
(B) OU EST LA MAISON DE FROMAGE 197 EPIC US
(B) OU EST LA MAISON DE FROMAGE 197 RABID UK NOZE1
(C) WALKING BACK TO HAPPINESS(LIVE) 1979 CBS 10" UK JCC1
(D) SNAP CRACKLE BOP 1980 EPIC UK 84083
(E) ME & MY BIG MOUTH 1981 EPIC UK 84979

JOHN COOPER CLARKE V (ALL
PAUL BURGESS D (AD
LYN OAKLEY G (DA
BILL NELSON G (AD
PETE SHELLEY G (AD
STEVE HOPKINS K (AD
MARTIN HANNETT B (AD
JOHN SCOTT G (AD
DAVE HASSELL (D
TREVOR SPENCER (D
STEPHANIE FORMULA V (D
KARL BURNS (D
TOBY (D

C184A GREG COPELAND C184A

(A) REVENGE WILL COME 1982 GEFFEN US 2010

GREG COPELAND V (A
IAN WALLACE D (A
BOB GLAUB B (A
JACKSON BROWNE G (A
DANNY KORTCHMAR G (A
JIM EHRINGER K (A
RICK VITO G (A
BILLY PAYNE K SYN(A

C184B COPPERPENNY C184B

(A) COPPERHEAD 1970 RCA US LSP 4291

RICH WAMIL V B K G(A
KEN HOLLIS V (A
BERT HAMER D V (A
LAVERNE McDONALD G V (A
PAUL REIBLING B V (A

C185 COPPERHEAD C185

(A) COPPERHEAD 1973 CBS UK 65715 US 32250
(A) COPPERHEAD 1980 CBS NL 84483

JOHN CIPOLLINA G (A
GARY PHILIPPET V G K (A
JIM McPHERSON V G B (A
HUTCH HUTCHINSON V B (A
DAVID WEBER D (A

C185A JOHN COPPIN C185A

(A) NO GOING BACK 1979 ROLA R002

JOHN COPPIN V G K (A
PHIL BEER VLN G V (A
TONY BENNETT G V (A
MICK DOLAN G (A
REGINE CANDER V (A
DIK CADBURY V (A
MICK CANDLER D (A
BIMBO ACOCK SAX (A
GILLY ELKINS V (A
STEVE HUTT B V (A
ANTHONY HEAD V (A
GILLY DARBEY V (A

C185B PHIL CORDELL C185B

(A) BORN AGAIN 1977 PRODIGAL PDL 2006

PHIL CORDELL G B (A
BARRY DE SOUZA D (A
CHRIS HUNT D (A
PAUL KENDRICK B V (A
REV STOCKDALE K (A
DOREEN CHANTER V (A
JIMMY HELMS V (A
CHAS O'BRIEN D (A
DAVE MARKEE D (A
MADELINE BELL V (A
LIZA STRIKE V (A
TONY BURROWS V (A
RAY FENWICK G (A
LENNIE WATTS K (A
R & J STONE V (A
GEORGE CHANDLER V (A
WESLEY McGOOGAN SAX (A

C185C CORNELLS C185C

(A) BEACH BOUND 196 GAREX US LPGA 100

C185D CORONARIAS DAN C185D

(1) 1969 71 (2) 71 72 (3) 73+
(A) BREATHE 1971 PARLOPHONE EUR MOCK 1018
(B) VISITOR 1975 STEEPLECHASE SCS 1032

KENNETH KNUDSEN K (AB123
CLAUS BOHLING G (3B
OLE STREENBERG D (B23
PETER FRIIS NIELSEN B (123AB
CLAUS BOJE D (A1

C185E JERRY CORBETTA C185E

(A) JERRY CORBETTA 1978 WB US 3230

JERRY CORBETTA K V (A
MIKE BAIRD D (A
MIKE PORCARO B (A
CINDY BULLENS V (A
JIM HAAS V (A
JAY GRAYDON G (A
JON JOYCE V (A
BOB WEBBER G (A
GREG MATHIESON PNO (A
RUSTY BUCHANAN B (A
MYREN POLLOCK D (A

C185F MIKE CORBETT & JAY HIRSH C185F

(A) MIKE CORBETT & JAY HIRSH 1972 ATCO US 33361

MIKE CORBETT FLT PERC (A
JAY HIRSH (A
HUGH McCRACKEN G (A
SCOT McCRACKEN V (A
PAUL GRIFFIN K (A
AL ROGERS D (A
MICHAELLE PROSKY V (A
JOHN SIOMOS D (A
CHRISTIE THOMPSON K (A
ERIC WEISBERG STEEL (A
JANET SAPADIN V (A
JODI McCRACKEN V (A
LEO WARRINGTON HRNS (A
RUSSELL GEORGE FDL (A
MARIA BRAY V (A

C185G CORBIN / HANNER C185G

(A) FOR THE SAKE OF THE SONG 1981 ALFA US 10003

C185H CORPORATION C185H

(A) THE CORPORATION 1969 CAPITOL US 175
(B) GET ON OUR SWING 19 AGE OF AQUARIUS US 4150
(C) HASSELS IN MY MIND 19 AGE OF AQUARIUS US 4250

KENNETH BERDOLL B V (A
JOHN KONDOS G V K FLT (A
NICHOLAS KONDOS D V (A
GERARD SMITH G V (A
PATRICK McCARTHY K TROM(A
DANIEL PEIL V (A

C185J HUGH CORNWALL/ ROBERT WILLIAMS C185J

(A) NOSFERATU 1979 LIBERTY UK UAG 30251

HUGH CORNWALL G B V (A
ROBERT WILLIAMS D B V SYN (A
A N RUSSIAN V (A
IAN UNDERWOOD SAX SYN (A
DAVID WALLDROOP G (A
MARK MOTHERBAUGH SYN V (A
BOB MOTHERSBAUGH G V (A

CHICK COREA	K	(ALL	(A) TONES FOR JOANS BONES	1968	VORTEX IMP 2004
FLORA PLURIM	V PERC	(INj	(A) TONES FOR JOANS BONES	1978	ATLANTIC UK K50302
AIRTO MOREIRA	D PERC	(INTj	(B) IS	1969	SOLID STATE US 18055
JOE FARRELL	WIND	(AJNThj	(C) NOW HE SINGS	1969	SOLID STATE US 7011
STANLEY CLARKE	B	(JKONTUWahj	(D) SONG OF THE SINGING	1971	BLUENOTE US 84353 RI 78 40030
ANTHONY BRAXTON	WIND	(Tf	(E) COREA	19	BLUENOTE 39542
DAVE HOLLAND	B	(DFTf	(F) ARC	1971	ECM 1009
BARRY ALTSCHUL	D	(DFT	(G) PIANO IMPROVISATIONS	1972	ECM 1014
BILL CONNORS	G	(K	(H) CRYSTAL SILENCE	1972	ECM 1024
LENNY WHITE	D	(KOUWh	(I) LIGHT AS A FEATHER	1972	POLYDOR US 5525 uk 2310 247
BENNY MAUPIN		(BQ	(I) LIGHT AS A FEATHER	1981	POLYDOR RI 2482 497
AL DIMEOLA	G	(OUWh	(J) CHILDREN OF FOREVER	1972	POLYDOR UK 2310 267
GAYLE MORAN	V	(Yah	(K) HYMN OF THE SEVENTH GALAXY	1972	POLYDOR US 5536 UK 2310 286
STEVE GADD	D	(ah	(K) HYMN OF THE SEVENTH GALAXY	1972	POLYDOR EURO 2302 028
EDDIE GOMEZ	B	(Y	(L) PIANO IMPROVISATIONS 2	1972	ECM 1020
ANTHONY JACKSON	B	(Y	(M) BLISS	1973	MUSE 5011
BILL WATRONS	TROM	(Y	(N) RETURN TO FOREVER	1972	ECM 1022
WAYNE ANDRE	TROM	(Y	(O) WHERE HAVE I KNOWN YOU BEFORE	1974	POLYDOR US 6509 UK 2310 354
DANNY CAHN	TPT	(Y	(O) WHERE HAVE I KNOWN YOU BEFORE	197	POLYDOR EURO 2302 030 2482502
BOB MILLIKAN	TPT	(Y	(P) ROUND TRIP	1974	EPIC UK 65559
JOHN GATCHELL	TPT	(Y	(Q) SUNDANCE	1974	PEOPLE UK 09 US G MERCHANT2202
JEAN LUC PONTE	VLN	(a	(R) INNER SPACE	1974	ATLANTIC US 2305 uk K60081
DON ALIAS	PERC	(aj	(S) WITH UNDERSTANDING	1975	MUSE 5083
JOHN THOMAS	TPT	(a	(T) LIVE IN NEW YORK 74	1975	OXFORD US 3005
JOHN ROSENBURG	TPT	(a	(U) NO MYSTERY	1975	POLYDOR US 6512 UK 2310 378
RON MOSS	TPT	(a	(V) CAPTAIN MARVEL	1975	VERVE 2304 225
NARADA MICHAEL WALDEN	D	(a	(W) ROMANTIC WARRIOR	1976	CBS US 34076 UK 81221
WOODY SHAW	TPT	(A	(X) CIRCLING IN	1976	BLUENOTE BLNAD 472
STEVE SWALLOW	B	(A	(Y) LEPRECHAUN	1976	POLYDOR UK 2391 217
JOE CHAMBERS	D	(A	(Z) MUSIC MAGIC	1977	CBS US 81959
GERRY BROWN	D	(	(a) MY SPANISH HEART	1977	POLYDOR UK 2672 031
PETE LE ROCCO	D	(M	(b) MAD HATTER	1978	POLYDOR US 16130 uk 2490 114
STAN GETZ	SAX	(V	(c) LIVE	1978	CBS UK 82808
SADAO WATANABE		(P	(d) SECRET AGENT	1979	POLYDOR UK 2391 381
STUART BLUMBERG	TPT	(A	(e) DELPHI VOL 1	1979	POLYDOR UK 2490 150
HERBIE HANCOCK	K	(g	(f)CIRCLES PARIS CONCERT (DBL)	197	ECM 1018/19
JIM PUGH	TROM	(h	(g) COREA HANCOCK	1979	POLYDOR UK 2672 049
LAUDIR DE OLIVEIRA	PERC	(j	(h) BEST OF RETURN TO FOREVER	1980	CBS UK 84292
HUBERT LAWS	FLT	(j	(j) TAP STEP	1980	WB US 3425 UK K 56801
BUNNY BRUNEL	B	(j	(k) 3 QUARTETS	1981	WB U 3552 UK K 56908
TOM BRECHTLEIN	D	(j	(m) BLISS	1981	MUSE 5011
AL VIZZUTTI	TPT	(j	(n) CHICK & LIONEL	1982	GATEWAY UK 7005
JAMIE FAUNT	B	(j			
JOE HENDERSON	SAX	(j	STRING SECTION (aY		LIONEL HAMPTON VIBES (n
JOHN GILMORE	SAX	(m	WALTER BOOKER B (m		PETE LA ROCA D (m

C186A DAVE'BABY' CORTEZ C186A

DAVE'BABY' CORTEZ	ORG	(ALL	RINKY DINK	19	CHESS US 1473
			ORGAN SHINDIG	19	ROULETTE US 25298
			GOLDEN HITS	1964	LONDON UK HAU 8142
			MUSIC AROUND THE CLOCK	19	CLOCK US CX201
			IN ORBIT WITH	19	ROULETTE US 25328
			HAPPY ORGAN	19	RCA US 2099
			FABULOUS ORGAN	19	METRO US 550
			& JERRYS HOUSE ROCKERS	19	CROWN US 357
			DAVE BABY CORTEZ	19	CLOCK US 331

C187 CORTINAS C187

JEREMY VALENTINE	V	(A	(A) TRUE ROMANCES	1978	CBS UK 82831
MIKE FEWINGS	G	(A			
NICK SHEPPARD	G	(A	DEXTER DALWOOD B (A		DAN SWAM D (A

C189 LARRY CORYELL C189

LARRY CORYELL	K G SYN B	(ALL	(A) FREE SPIRIT	1967	ABC 062 90593
BILLY COBHAM	D	(DJN	(B) LADY CORYELL	1969	VANGUARD VSD 6509+19051 MUSIDISC 23017
CHICK COREA	K	(DJN	(C) CORYELL	1969	VANGUARD VSD 6547 19059 MUSIDISC 23020
JACK BRUCE	B	(	(D) SPACES	1970	VANGUARD VSD 6558 79345 MUSIDISC 23002
WILL LEE	B	(N	(D) SPACES	1974	VANGUARD 6359 005
JOHN MARSHALL	D	(	(E) FAIRYLAND	1971	FLYING DUTCHMAN 51500 MEGA US 607
MICHAEL LAWRENCE	TPT	(DNOXY	(E) FAIRYLAND	1972	PHILIPS 6369 411
MIROSLAV VITOUS		(BN	(F) AT THE VILLAGE GATE	1971	VANGUARD VSD 6573 MUSIDISC 23024
JOHN LEE	B	(OQUY	(G) BAREFOOT BOY	1972	FLYING DUTCHMAN 10139 PHILIPS 6369 407
MIKE MANDEL	K	(CGHIJNOPQXY	(H) OFFERING	1972	VANGUARD 79319 MUSIDISC 23001
ALPHONSE MOUZON	PERC	(JORUXYN	(I) THE REAL GREAT ESCAPE	1973	VANGUARD 79329 MUSIDISC 23019
STEVE KHAN	G	(OQNV	(J) INTRODUCING 11TH HOUSE	1974	VANGUARD 79342
PHILIP CATHERINE	G	(STU	(K) ESSENTIAL	1975	VANGUARD VSD 75/76
TAWATHA AGEE	V	(U	(L) RESTFUL MIND	1975	VANGUARD 79353 MUSIDISC 23013
DANNY TRIFAN	B	(JRXN	(M) THE OTHER SIDE OF	1975	VANGUARD 79360
MICHAEL BRECKER	HRNS	(IQW	(N) PLANET END	1976	VANGUARD 79367 MUSIDISC 23022
MERVIN BRONSON	B	(FCHIJ	(O) LEVEL ONE	1976	ARISTA US 4025 UK ARTY 113
HARRY WILKINSON	D	(FGIJ	(P) BASICS (68/69)	1976	VANGUARD 79375
JULIE CORYELL	V	(FI	(Q) ASPECTS	1976	ARISTA US 4077 UK ARTY 133
MITCH MITCHELL	D	(	(R) LION & THE RAM	1976	ARISTA US 4108 UK ARTY 154
JIM PEPPER	SAX	(AC	(S) TWIN HOUSE	1976	ATLANTIC UK K50342
CHRIS HILLS	B	(A	(T) SPLENDID	1976	ELEKTRA UK K52086
BOB MOSES	D	(AB	(U) BACK TOGETHER AGAIN	1977	ATLANTIC US 18220 UK K50382
CHIP BAKER	G	(A	(V) TWO FOR THE ROAD	1977	ARISTA UK SPART1050
RON CARTER	B	(CP	(W) DIFFERENCE	1978	EGG EURO 900 558
BERNARD PURDIE	D	(CEP	(X) AT MONTREUX(74)	1978	VANGUARD 79410
STEVE HAAS	D	(P	(Y) LIVE IN EUROPE	1978	LC IMP IC1
RAY MANTILLA	PERC	(Pc	(Z) STANDING OVATION	1978	MOOD 22888 ARISTA UK 3024
TERUMASA HINO	TPT	(Q	(a) EUROPEAN IMPRESSIONS	1978	ARISTA US 3005
MTUME	PERC	(Q	(b) BETTER THAN LIVE	1978	DIRECT DD109
DAVID SANBORN	SAX	(QW	(c) RETURN	1979	VANGUARD 79426

(CONTINUED)

C189 LARRY CORYELL (CONTINUED) C189

DANNY TOAN G (QR — (d) FREE SMILE 1979 ARISTA US
ARTHUR RHAMES G (W — (e)TRIBUTARIES 1980 NOVIS US 3017
GLEN MOORE B (W — (f) LARRY CORYELL 1982 BOLERO 33850
STEVE GADD D (W
CHERYL ALAXANDER V (U — RANDY BRECKER HRNS (JQ — CHUCK RAINEY B (CEP — GERRY BROWN D (Q
TONY WILLIAMS D (W — DON GROLNICK K (W — L SUBRUMANIUM VLN (Z — LAWRENCE KILLIAN CONGA(G
STEVE MARCUS SAX (GHI — ROY HAYNES D (G — ALBERT STINSON B (C — JIM GARRISON B (B
ELVIN JONES D (B — JOE BECK SYN G B (Rc — MICHEL URBANIAK VLN (R — RALPH TOWNER G (L
COLIN WALCOTT CONGA (L — GLEN MOORE B (L — JOHN McLAUGHLIN G (DN — DARIUS BRUBECK PNO (c
CHRIS BRUBECK B (c — DAN BRUBECK D (c — JOACHIM KUHN PNO (T — JOHN SCOFIELD G (e

C190 COS C190

BOB DARSCH D (A — (A) VIVA BOMMA 1976 IBC BEL 23605
MARC MOULIN SYN (A — (B) SWISS CHALET 19 IBC NL 23902
DENIS VAN HECKE CELLO (A
PHILIPPE ABLAERT D (B — PASCALE SON V OBOE (AB — ALAIN GOUTIER B (AB
DANIEL SCHELL G FLT (A — MARC HOLLANDER K (A — GUY LONNEUX D (B
PIPOU PITOU PERC (A — JIB HAESEVEETS PERC (A — CHARLES LOOS K (B
MUTSARI B (B

C191 COSMIC EYE C191

AMANCIO D'SILVA G (A — (A) DREAM SEQUENCE 1972 REGALZONOPHONE UK SLRZ 1030
V JASANI SIT (A
JOHN MAYER VLN (A — RAY SWINFIELD FLT (A — DAVE GROSSMAN FLT (A
C TAYLOR FLT (A — ALAN BRANSCOMBE SAX (A — TONI CAMPO B (A
KESHAV SATHE TABLA (A — D WRIGHT D (A

C192 COSMIC JOKERS C192

DIETER DIERKS — (A) COSMIC JOKERS 1974 METRONOME KM 58008
JURGEN DOLLASE — (B) PLANET SIT IN 1974 METRONOME KM 58013
MANUEL GOETTSCHING
HARALD GROSSKOPF — KLAUS SCHULZE — STERNEN MADCHEN GILLE

C192A COSMIC SOUNDS C192A

PAUL BEAVER SYN ELEC(A — (A) THE ZODIAC 1967 ELEKTRA EKS 74009
CYRUS FARYAR V (A

C193 ELVIS COSTELLO C193

ELVIS COSTELLO G V (ALL — (A) MY AIM IS TRUE 1977 STIFF JAP 6581 UK SEEZ 3
JOHN McFEE G V (AFGJ — (A) MY AIM IS TRUE 1977 CBS US 35037 BARCLAY FR 940566
HUEY LOUIS HCA V (AFG — (B) THIS YEARS MODEL 1978 RADAR JAP 10538 UK RAD 3
JOHNNY CIAMBOTTI B V (AFG — (B) THIS YEARS MODEL 1978 CBS US 35331 SMASH SWED SLEPT2
DAVE EDMUNDS V (FG — (B) THIS YEARS MODEL 1981 F BEAT UK XXLP4
SEAN HOPPER K V (AFG — (C) ARMED FORCES 1979 RADAR JAP 10627 UK RAD14
ALEX CALL G V (AFG — (C) ARMED FORCES 1979 CBS US 35709 SMASH SWED SLEPT5
STEVE GOULDING D (G — (C) ARMED FORCES 1981 F BEAT UK XXLP5
MICKY SHINE D V (AFG — (D) LIVE AT MOCAMBO 1978 CBS CAN PROMO
STEVE MASON (NAIVE) K (BCFGHJK — (E) GET HAPPY 1980 F BEAT UK XXLP 1
NICK LOWE B V (1FGJ — (E) GET HAPPY 1980 CBS US 36347 SMASH SWED SLEPT7
BRUCE THOMAS B (BCEFGHJK — (F) TAKING LIBERTIES 1980 CBS US 36839
ANDREW BODMAR B (G — (G) 10 BLOODY MARYS (CASS) 1980 F BEAT UK XXC6
PETER THOMAS D (BCDEFGHJK — (H) TRUST 1981 F BEAT UK XXLP 11 EURO WEA58260
GLENN TILBROOK V (F — (H) TRUST 1981 CBS US 37051
MARTIN BELMONT G (F — (J) ALMOST BLUE 1981 F BEAT UK XXLP13 EURO WEA58392
NASHVILLE STRINGS (J — (J) ALMOST BLUE 1981 CBS US 37562
NASHVILLE SINGERS (J — (K) IMPERIAL BALLROOM 1982 CBS US 38157
BILLY SHERRILL PROD (J — (EP)HIGH FIDELITY 1980 F BEAT UK XX3
TOMMY MILLER VLN (J

C194 GENE COTTON C194

GENE COTTON G V (ALL — (A) GRAY OF THE MORNING 1974 MYRRH US MST 6511
WITH — (B) LIBERTY 1974 MYRRH US MST 6524
PETE WADE G (BA — (C) FOR ALL THE YOUNG WRITERS 1976 ABC US AB 933
BILLY SANFORD G (AB — (D) RAIN ON 1976 ABC UK ABCL5213 US AB 983
JOHNNY CHRISTOPHER G (BC — (E) SAVE THE DANCER 1978 ARIOLA US50031 UK ARL 5015
SANDY COTTON FLT (B — (E) SAVE THE DANCER 1978 EMI INT INS 3018
CHARLIE McCOY HCA (B — (F) NO STRINGS ATTACHED 1979 ARIOLA US 50070
JACK WILLIAMS B (ABCDF — (G) ECLIPSE OF THE BLUE MOON 1981 KNOLL US 1001
KENNY BUTTREY D (ABCF
SHANE KEISTER K SYN(DF — JIM COLVARD G (C — RON OATES K (D — LARRIE LONDIN D (D
KENNY MALONE D (D — JOE OSBORN B (C — TED REYNOLDS B (D — STEVE GIBSON B G MAND(CDF
FARRELL MORRIS PERC (DF — DIANNE DARLING SYN PERC V(F — MARC SPEER G STEELV(F — TOMMY WELLS D (F
JAMES OWMBY K SAX V(F — MIKE JOYCE B V (F — BOBBY OGDIN K SYN(F — BUDDY SKIPPER SYN (F
MIKE LAWLER SYN (F — GUNNAR SCRIVENOR AUTOHARP(F — DOYLE GRISHAM STEEL(F — BILL JONES SAX (F
BOBBY THOMPSON G BANJ(C — CHARLIE CRINO PNO (A — JOE ALLEN B (A — JERRY CARRIGAN D (A
WELDON MYRICK STEEL(A — JERRY WASLEY B (A — BEEGIE CRUSER K (A

C195 JAMES COTTON BLUES BAND C195

JAMES COTTON V HCA(ALL — (A) JAMES COTTON BLUES BAND 1967 VERVE FVS9507 US 3023
WITH — (B) PURE COTTON 1968 VERVE FVS9512 US 3038
MATT MURPHY G (EFG — (C) COTTON IN YOUR EARS 1968 VERVE US 3060
JAMES BOOKER PNO (— (D) CUT YOU LOOSE 1968 VANGUARD 19035 79283
BOB ANDERSON B (— (E) TAKING CARE OF BUSINESS 19 CAPITOL SM814
ALBERT GIANQUINTO PNO (— (F) 100% COTTON 1974 BUDDAH BDS5620
FRANCIS CLAY D (— (G) HIGH ENERGY 1978 BUDDAH 5650 BDLP 4048
MARTIN FIERRO SAX (D — (H) LIVE & ON THE MOVE 1977 BUDDAH 5661
MIKE FENDER TPT (D
EDDIE ADAMS B (D — JOE RODRIGUEZ D (D — LITTLE BO SAX (F — CHARLES CALMESE B (FG
KENNY JOHNSON D (FH — LENNY KING SAX (F — PHIL JEKANOWSKI PNO (F — JAMES COOK G (D
MIKE BLOOMFIELD G (E — TODD RUNDGREN PERC G V (E — DOMENIC TROIANO G (E — JOHNNY WINTER G (E
MARK KLINGMAN V K (E — RALPH SCHUCKETT PNO (E — STU WOODS B V (D — RITCHIE HAYWARD D (E
JOEL BISHOP OBRIEN D (E — N D SMART D V (E — TOM COSGROVE V (E — CISSY HOUSTON V (E
VENERIT SIMMS V (E — RONELLE STAFFORD V (E — DEIRDRE TUCK V (E — GENE DINWIDDIE HRNS(E
TREVOR LAWRENCE HRNS (D — DAVE SANBORN HRNS (E — STEVE MADAIO HRNS (E — LUTHER TUCKER G (
WAYNE TALBERT K (D — ALLEN TOUSSAINT K (G — STEVE HUGHES G (G — TEDDY ROYAL G (G
CLYDE KERR TPT (G — SHAVIS SHERRIFF SAX (G — ALVIN THOMAS SAX (G — LON PRICE SAX(G
NANCEE SEHORN FLT (G — MIKE ZAITCHIK K (H — GEORGE T GREGORY III (H

C195A COTTONWOOD C195A
GARY ROWLES (A (A) CAMARADERIE 1971 ABC US ABC 729
RICK ALLEN (A
DAVID WEYER (A DOUG PHILLIPS (A DAVID FARRELL (A

C195B COTTONWOOD SOUTH C195B
(A) COTTONWOOD SOUTH 19 CBS US 33009

C195C COUCHIS C195C
CHRIS COUCHIS G V D (AB (A) COUCHIS 1979 WB US 3289
PAT COUCHIS G V (AB (B) NASTY HARDWARE 1980 WB UK K56829 US 3420
MIKE COUCHIS D V (AB
HOWARD MESSER B V (AB CHAS CARLSON K V (AB

C196 JOHNNY COUGAR C196
JOHNNY COUGAR MELLENCAMP (ALL (A) CHESTNUT ST INCIDENT 1977 MCA US 2225
MIKE BOYER G (A (B) BIOGRAPHY 1978 RIVA RVLP6
JIMMY HOROWITZ (C (C) JOHNNY COUGAR 1979 RIVA RVLP9
ROBERT FRANK B (BC (D) NOTHING MATTER'S & WHAT IF IT DID 1980 RIVA RVLP10
TOM KNOWLES D (BC (E) NIGHT DANCIN' 1980 RIVA US 7401
JOHN SMITH (C
ANDY MACKAY SAX (B LARRY CRANE G (BC MIKE RANCHIE G (AC
BRIAN BEC VAR (C JOE LALA PERC (C PAUL HARRIS K (C
BLUE WEAVER K (C MIKE LEWIS (C RICHARD KELLY G (A
DAVID PARMAN G (A MICK RONSON G (A MICHAEL KAMEN K (A
STEVE LINDEMAN K (A TOM WINCE K (A BILLY BERGMAN D (A
JERRY DEUPREE D (A HILLY MICHAELS D (A WAYNE HALL SAX (A
KIRK BUTLER SYN PERC (A DAVID MANSFIELD STEEL MAND VLN(A

C197 DENNIS COULSON C197
DENNIS COULSON (A) DENNIS COULSON 1973 ELEKTRA 75067 US K 42148

C198 CLIFFORD COULTER C198
CLIFFORD COULTER K V G (ALL (A) EAST SIDE SAN JOSE 1971 IMPULSE US 9197
JOHN TURK TPT (AB (B) DO IT NOW WORRY ABOUT IT LATER 1872 IMPULSE US 9216
CORNELIUS BUMPUS SAX (A (C) BETTER PART OF ME 1980 CBS US 35786
GINO LANDRY SAX (A
MEL BROWN G (AB JERRY PEREZ G (A JIMMY CALHOUN B (AB
JOE PROVOST D (A BILLY INGRAM D (A RON BECK D (B
RAY MacCARTY G (B HARRY EDISON TPT (B BILL PERKINS SAX (B
MARSHALL ROYAL SAX (B PLAS JOHNSON SAX (B JIMMY CLEVELAND TROM (B
WILLIE RUFF HRNS (B SONNY GLAZE G (B LUCY WILKINS V (B
MARLENE WILKINS V (B DONNIE ROGERS V (B SHANNE COULTER V (B

C199 COUNT BISHOPS C199
JOHNNY GUITAR G V (ABCD (A) THE COUNT BISHOPS"GOOD GEAR" 1977 DYNAMITE HOLL 33001
PAUL BALBI D (ABCD (B) COUNT BISHOPS 1977 CHISWICK UK WIK1
STEVE LEWINS B (AB (C) LIVE 12" 1978 CHISWICK UK CH7
ZEN DEFLEUR HIEROWSKI G V(ABCD (C) LIVE 10" 1978 CHISWICK UK CHT7
MIKE SPENCER V ((C) LIVE 12" 1979 CHISWICK RIUK CWK 3006
DAVE TICE V (BCD (C) LIVE 10" 1979 CHISWICK UK CWM 2001
PAT McMULLEN B (CD (D) CROSSCUT(BISHOPS) 1979 CHISWICK UK CWK 3009
JULIAN HOLLAND PNO (BD (E) SPEEDBALL 1979 CHISWICK EP UK SW1
RUAN O'LOCHLAIN HRNS (D
NOEL NORRIS HRNS (D

C199A COUNT FIVE C199A
KENN ELLNER V HCA 'A (A) PSYCHOTIC REACTION 1966 DOUBLE SHOT US DSM 1001
SEAN BYRNE G (A
JOHN MICHALSKI G (A ROY CHANEY B (A CRAIG ATKINSON D (A

C199B COUNTS C199B
LEROY EMANUEL G V (B (A) IT'S WHATS UP THAT COUNTS 1972 WESTBOUND US 2011
MOSE DAVIS K V (B (B) LOVE SIGN 1973 AWARE US 2002
DEMO CATES WIND V(B (C) FUNK PUMP 1975 AWARE US 2006
ANDREAU GIBSONT D V (B (D) LOVE SIGNS 197 GRC US 2002

C199C COUNTRY COOKING C199C
RUSS BARENBERG G MAND(ALL (A) COUNTRY COOKING 1971 ROUNDER US 006
KENNY KOSEK FDL K (ALL (B) FRANK WAKEFIELD WITH C C 1972 ROUNDER US 007
JOHN MILLER B G (ALL (C) BARREL OF FUN 1973 ROUNDER US 033
HARRY GILMORE MAND (A
TONY TRISCHKA BAN STEEL(ALL PETER WERNICK BAN (ALL FRANK WAKEFIELD G MAND (B
ANDY STATMAN MAND (C NONDI LEONARD V (BC

C200 COUNTRY GAZZETTE C200
BYRON BERLINE FDL V (ABCDELK (A) TRAITOR IN OUR MIDST 1972 U A US 5596 UK UAG 29404
ROGER BUSH B V (ABCDELM (B) LIVE IN AMSTERDAM 1972 BUMBLE GEXD 301
ALAN MUNDE BANJ V(ALL (C) DONT GIVE UP YOUR DAY JOB 1973 U A US 090 UK UAS 29491
KENNY WERTZ G V (ABCDEHL (D) BLUEGRASS SPECIAL 1973 ARIOLA 86 501HT
HERB PEDERSEN V G (AC (E) BANJO SANDWICH 197 ARIOLA NL 27239
SKIP CONOVER DOBRO (AFK (F) LIVE 1975 TRANSATLANTIC UK TRA 291
CHRIS SMITH G (A (F) LIVE 1975 ARIOLA NL 88558
CLARENCE WHITE G (C (G) MILESTONES 1975 EMI INT COPS7418D1/2
AL PERKINS STEEL (CH (H) SUNNY SIDE OF THE MOUNTAIN 1976 TRANSATLANTIC UK TRA 318
ROLAND WHITE (FHKMN (J) OUT TO LUNCH 197 FLYING FISH US FF027
LEE SKLAR B (C (K) WHAT A WAY TO EARN A LIVING 1977 TRANSATLANTIC UK TRA 347
DAVE FERGUSON FDL (HM (K) WHAT A WAY TO EARN A LIVING 1977 RIDGE US 008
BILL BRYSON B V (K (L) FROM THE BEGINNING 1978 SUNSET UK SNS 50414
RICHARD GREENE FDL (K (M) ALL THIS AND MONEY TOO 1979 RIDGE RUNNER US RRR 017
MIKE RICHEY G (KMN (AC)TRAITOR/DONT GIVE UP 19 UA 184 52064/5
MICHAEL ANDERSON B V (MN (N) AMERICAN & CLEAN 1981 FLYING FISH US 252
JOE CARR G V (MN
TOMMY SPURLOCK STEEL(M MIKE McCARTY D (M MICHAEL J DOHONEY D (M
SAM BUSH FDL (N DATTRELL NORRIS D (N

C201 PIERRE COURBOIS C201
PIERRE COURBOIS D (A (A) ASSOCIATION 1970 MUNICH 6802634
JASPER VANTHOF PNO (A
SIGGI BUSCH B (A PETER KRIJNEN B (A TOTO BLANKE G (A

C201A DAVID COURTNEY C201A

DAVID COURTNEY V PNO (A — (A) FIRST DAY — 1975 EMI UK EMC3094 US UA LA 553G
BARRY MORGAN D (A
BRIAN ODGERS B (A — STEVE GAY PNO (A — PAUL KEOGH G (A — ALAN PARKER G (A
SKAILA KANGA HARP (A — TONY BURROWS V (A — MIKE MORAN K (A — BARRY DE SOUZA D (A
ANDREW POWELL B K (A — FRANCIS MONKMAN SYN K(A — JEAN ROUSSEL PNO (A — RUSS BALLARD G (A
FRANK RICOTTI PERC (A — BRUCE LYNCH B (A — AIXA COURTNEY V (A — JANE POWELL V (A
B J COLE STEEL G(A — MORRIS PERT PERC (A — ALF DUKES FLEXATONE(A — PILOT V (A
RICHARD HARVEY WIND (A — BERNARD THOMAS WIND (A — DAVE GILMOUR G (A — ENGLISH CORALE V (A

C202 DAVE COUSINS C202

DAVE COUSINS PER V G PNO(AB — (A) TWO WEEKS LAST SUMMER — 1972 A&M UK AMLS68118
ROGER GLOVER B (A — (B) OLD SCHOOL SONGS — 1980 O SCHOOL UK 1 US PVC 8901
TOM ALLOM ORG (A
MILLER ANDERSON G (A — DAVE LAMBERT G (A — JON HISEMAN D (A — RICK WAKEMAN K (A
LAMPOON (A — KIDDINGTON COSSACKS (A — ROBERT KIRBY WIND (A — BRIAN WILLOUGHBY G(B

C203 DON COVAY C203

DON COVAY V (ALL — (A) MERCY — 1964 ATLANTIC US 8104
WITH — (B) SEE SAW — 1966 ATLANTIC US 8120
JOE RICHARDSON G V (C — (C) HOUSE OF BLUE LIGHT — 1969 ATLANTIC US 8237
MARGARET WILLIAMS G V (C — (C) HOUSE OF BLUE LIGHT — 1969 ATLANTIC UK K 50225
JOHN HAMMOND HCA G (C — (D) DIFFERENT STROKES — 1970 JANUS US 3038
BUTCH VALENTINE B (C — (E) SUPERDUDE — 1973 MERCURY UK 6338 211
DANNY JONES D (C — (E) SUPERDUDE — 1973 MERCURY US SRM1 653
JERRY JEMMOTT B (CF — (F) HOT BLOOD — 1975 MERCURY UK 9100 010
CHARLES OTIS D (C — (G) TRAVELLIN' IN HEAVY TRAFFIC — 1976 PHILAD INT PIR 81492
SREDNI VOLLNER HCA (F — (G) TRAVELLIN' IN HEAVY TRAFFIC — 1976 PHILAD INT 33957
TONY VON COVAY (F — ( ) COUNTRY FUNK — 19 POLYDOR 2482 018
RODNEY BEYTHAM K (F
BILLY CADIEUX G (F — LEMON JEFFERSON (D — DENNIS HARRIS G (G — NEIL LARSEN K (G
ROLAND CHAMBERS G (G — T J TINDALL G (G — MICHAEL FOREMAN B (G — RON KERSEY K (G
LARRY WASHINGTON CONGA(G — CHARLES COLLINS D (G — KARL CHAMBERS D (G — BARBARA INGRAM V (G
CARLA BENSON V (G — EVETTE BENTON V (G

C203A COVEN C203A

JINX DAWSON V (C — (A) WITCHCRAFT — 1970 MERCURY US 61239
CHRISTOPHER NIELSEN G V (C — (B) COVEN — 19 MGM US 4801
JOHN HOBBS K (C — (C) BLOOD ON THE SNOW — 1974 BUDDAH 5614 BDLH 5011
OZ OSBORNE B (C
STEVE ROSS D (C — FRANK SMITH SAX (C — ALAN ESTES CONGA(C

C204 DAVID COVERDALE & WHITESNAKE C204

DAVID COVERDALE V (ALL — (A) WHITESNAKE — 1977 PURPLE UK TPS 3509
MICK MOODY G (ABCDEFGHIJ — (A) WHITESNAKE — 1977 VOGUE FR 20257
SIMON PHILLIPS D (A — (B) NORTHWINDS — 1978 PURPLE UK TPS 3513
TIM HINKLEY K (A — (C) TROUBLE — 1978 SUNBURST INS 3022
HELEN CHAPPELLE V (A — (C) TROUBLE — 1980 UA US 937 UK 30305
RON ASPERY SAX (AB — (D) SNAKEBITE (EP) — 1978 SUNBURST INEP 751
DELISLE HARPER B (A — (E) SNAKEBITE (LP) — 1978 SUNBURST NL 61290 US/UA 915
ROGER GLOVER K B PERC (AB — (F) LOVEHUNTER — 1979 UA US 981 UK UAG 30264
DAVID DOWLE D (CDEFI — (G) LIVE IN THE HEART OF THE CITY — 1980 UA SNAKE 1
BERNIE MARSDEN G (CDFGHIJ — (H) READY & WILLING — 1980 UA UAG 30302
BRIAN JOHNSTON K (— (I) LIVE AT HAMMERSMITH — 1978 SUNBURST 1288
DOREEN CHANTER V (B — (J) COME AN' GET IT — 1981 LIBERTY UK LBG 3023
IREENE CHANTER V (B
NEIL MURRAY B (CDEFGHJI — JON LORD K (CH — BARRY ST JOHN V (A
IAN PAICE D (EFGHIJ — PETE SOLLEY K (D — ALAN SPENNER B (B
TONY NEWMAN D (B — LEE BRILLEAUX HCA (B — HENRY LOWTHER HRNS (B
MALCOLM GRIFFITHS TROM (B — GRAHAM PRESKETT K (B — LIZA STRIKE V (AB

C205 JOEY COVINGTON C205

JOEY COVINGTON D V (A — (A) FAT FANDAGO — 1973 GRUNT BFL1 0149
PATRICK CRAIG K (A
STEVE MIDNITE G (A — JACK PRENDERGAST B (A

C206 JULIE COVINGTON C206

JULIE COVINGTON V (AB — (A) BEAUTIFUL CHANGES — 1971 COLUMBIA UK SCX 6466
RICHARD THOMPSON G (B — (B) JULIE COVINGTON — 1978 VIRGIN UK V 2107
NEIL LARSEN K (B
WILLIE WEEKS B (B — RAY COOPER PERC (B — JOHN KIRKPATRICK ACC (B — TREVOR LUCAS G (B
SIMON NICOL G (B — CHRIS SPEDDING G (B — RUSS TITELMAN G (B — STEVE WINWOOD K (B
ANDY FAIRWEATHER LOW V (B — IAN MATTHEWS V (B — GARY TRAVERS V (B — GREG PRESTOPINO V (B
PLAS JOHNSON SAX (B — ANDY NEWMARK D (B — JOHN CALE K (B

C207 COWBOY C207

SCOTT BOYER G (ALL — (A) REACH FOR THE SKY — 1971 ATLANTIC UK 2466 022
JOHNNY SANDLIN B (CD — (A) REACH FOR THE SKY — 1970 CAPRICORN US 33351
TOMMY TALTON G V (ALL — (B) 5'LL GET YOU TEN — 1972 ATLANTIC UK K 40312
BILL SYEWART D (CD — (B) 5'LL GET YOU TEN — 1971 CAPRICORN US 864
BILL PILLMORE K G V (A — (AB) WHY QUIT WHEN YOU'RE LOSING — 1975 CAPRICORN US 2CX 0121
TOMM WYNN D PERC(A — (C) BOYER & TALTON — 1975 CAPRICORN US 0127
GEORGE CLARK B V (AB — (D) HAPPY TO BE ALIVE — 1976 CAPRICORN US 0167
PETE KOWALKE G V (AB — (E) COWBOY — 1977 CAPRICORN US 0194
DUANE ALLMAN G DOBRO(B
CHUCK LEAVELL PNO (BCD — CHARLIE HAYWARD B (C — PAUL HORNSBY K (C — JIMMY NALLS G (C
RANDALL BRAMBLETT SAX V(CE — DAVID BROWN SAX V(C — DONNA HALL V (C — TOY CALDWELL G (C
DREW LOMBAR BANJ (C — JAIMOE PERC (CE — JOHN HUGHEY G (C — ELLA BROWN V (C
JOYCE KNIGHT V (C — BONNIE BRAMLETT V (D — CHIP CONDON K V (E — CHIP MILLER D PERC(E
ARCH PEARSON B V (E — TOPPER PRICE HCA (E — HAROLD WILLIAMS SAX (E

C207A COWBOYS INTERNATIONAL C207A

TERRY CHIMES D (A — (A) THE ORIGINAL SIN — 1979 VIRGIN UK V2136 US 13138
KEN LOCKE V (A
JIMMY HUGHES B (A — EVAN CHARLES PNO (A — RICK JACKS G (A — KEITH LEVINE G (A

C207B STANLEY COWELL C207B

STANLEY COWELL (A — (A) NEW WORLD — 1981 GALAXY GXY 5131

C208 BILLY COX C208

BILLY COX B (A — (A) NITRO FUNCTION — 1971 PYE UK NSPL25158
CHAR VINNEDGE G (A
ROBERT TARRANT D (A

C208A DANNY COX C208A

DANNY COX G V (AB — (A) BIRTH ANNOUNCEMENT — 1969 TOGETHER US ST1011
RICHARD RUSHER G (A — (B) DANNY COX — 1971 DUNHILL US 50114
DOUG RHODEN B (A — (C) FEEL SO GOOD — 197 CASABLANCA ? ?
JOHN KAHN B (B
MERL SANDERS K (B — RED RHODES STEEL(A — PAT SHANAHAN D (A — STEVE LEFEVER B (A
BILL VITT D (B — JOSE CHEPITO AREAS PERC(B — TIM BARNES G (B — WALTER HAWKINS V (B
LYNNETTE HAWKINS V (B — TRAMAINE HAWKINS V (B — SKIP MESQUITE WIND (B — STEVE KUPKA SAX (B
EMILIO CASTILLO SAX (B — MIC GILLETTE TPT (B — GREG ADAMS WIND (B

C208B MICK COX C208B

MICK COX G V PERC(A — (A) MICK COX BAND — 1973 CAPITOL ST11175
TONY O'MALLEY V (A
MICK WEAVER K (A — PETE ARNESON K (A — CHRIS STEWART B (A — ANDREW STEELE D (A
ALAN SKIDMORE SAX (A

C209 LOL COXHILL C209

LOL COXHILL SAX (ALL — (A) EAR OF THE BEHOLDER — 1971 DANDELION 69001 8008
STEVEN MILLER PNO (C — (A) EAR OF THE BEHOLDER — 1971 AMPEX US 10132
DAVID BEDFORD ORG (A — (B) TOVERBAL SWEET — 1972 MUSHROOM 150MR 23
MIKE OLDFIELD G (A — (C) COXHILL MILLER — 1973 CAROLINE UK C1503
ROBERT WYATT PERC V(AD — (D) STORY SO FAR...OH REALLY ½LP — 1974 CAROLINE UK C1507
PIERRE COURBOIS D (AB — (E) LOL COXHILL & WELFARE STATE — 1975 CAROLINE UK C1514
JASPER VANT HOF PNO (AB — (F) FLEAS IN THE CUSTARD — 1975 CAROLINE UK C1515
PIP PYLE PERC(C — (G) DIVERSE — 1976 OGUN OG 510
RICHARD SINCLAIR B (C — (H) THE JOY OF PARANOIA — 1978 OGUN OG 525
PHIL MILLER G (AD — (I) MOOT — 1978 ICTUS 0008
LAURIE ALLEN CYMB(CD — (J) LID — 1978 ICTUS 0011
ARCHIE LEGGETT BASS(CD — (K) MURDER IN THE AIR (EP) — 1978 CHILTERN SOUND CS 100
KEVIN AYERS G (AD — (L) DIGSWELL DUETS — 1979 RANDOM RADAR RRR 005
JOHN FOX SAX (E — (M) SLOW MUSIC — 1980 PIPE PIPE 1
MORGAN FISHER G B K V (M
LOU GLANDFIELD TROM(E — PHIL MINTON TROM (E — COLIN WOOD CELLO(EG — TED SPEIGHT G (A
CATHY KIDDLE CLAR(E — STEVE GUMBLEY PERC (E — PENNY GLANFIELD PERC (E — WARNER VEN WELY V (E
JANE DURRANT SAX (E — PETER KIDDLE WHIST(E — JOHN CHAPMAN WHIST(E — LIZ LOCKHART FLT(E
SUE FOX V (E — DIANA DAVIES ORG (E — BORIS HOWARTH VLN G(E — MICK AUDSLEY V (F
KEN ELLIS V (F — G F FITZGERALD G (F — DAVE GREEN B (G — ANDREA CEMTAZZO D (I
JOHN MITCHELL D (G — MICHAEL GARRICK PNO (H — PAUL MITCHELL DAVIDSON B (H — KEN SHAW G (H
VERYAN WESTON PNO (H — RICHARD WRIGHT G (H

C210 KEVIN COYNE C210

KEVIN COYNE V G (ALL — (A) CASE HISTORY — 1972 DANDELION 2310 228
WITH — (B) MARJORY RAZORBLADE — 1973 VIRGIN EURO 87742 UK VD 2501
GORDON SMITH G (BCDK — (C) BLAME IT ON THE NIGHT — 1974 VIRGIN UK V2012
JEAN ROUSSEL K (BK — (D) MATCHING HEAD & FEET — 1975 VIRGIN EURO 88919 UK V2033
TONY COUSINS B (BCK — (E) HEARTBURN — 1976 VIRGIN EURO 27265 UK V2047
CHILI CHARLES D (BCK — (F) IN LIVING BLACK & WHITE (DBL) — 1976 VIRGIN UK VD2505
STEVE VERROCA PERC K(BK — (F) IN LIVING BLACK & WHITE (DBL) — 1976 POLYDOR EUR 2676 710
RUAN O'LOCHLAINN SAX G K(CK — (G) DYNAMITE DAZE — 1978 VIRGIN UK V2095
FI TRENCH K (C — (G) DYNAMITE DAZE — 1978 POLYDOR EUR 2933 746
RICK DODD SAX (C — (H) MILLIONAIRES & TEDDY BEARS — 1978 VIRGIN EURO 200215 UK V2110
TERRY SLADE D (C — (I) BEAUTIFUL EXTREMES — 1978 VIRGIN UK V2527
ARCHIE LEGGET B (DK — (J) BABBLE — 1979 VIRGIN EURO 200596 UK V2128
PETER WOOLF D (DEFK — (K) LETS HAVE A PARTY — 19 VIRGIN EURO 89800
TIM PENN K (DK — (L) BURSTING BUBBLES — 1980 VIRGIN EURO 201654 UK V2151
ANDY SUMMERS G (DEFK — (M) SANITY STOMP — 1980 VIRGIN EURO 301427 UK V3504
LISA STRIKE V (C — (N) BOXED SET — 1980 BUTT BOX1
JOANNE WILLIAMS V (C — (O) POINTING THE FINGER — 1981 CHERRY RED UK RED23
BARRY ST JOHN V (C
ZOOT MONEY K V(EFGJ — STEVE THOMPSON B (EF — BOB WARD G (HJM — PAUL WICKENS K (GHJM
VIC SWEENEY D (GHJL — AL JAMES B (GHJM — DAGMAR KRAUSE V (J — MICK SWEENEY G (A
NICK CUDWORTH G (A — DAVE CLAGUE G (AB — MALCOLM HEALEY K (B — TIM RICE K (G
JERRY DECADE K (J — BRIAN GODDING G (LMO — CHRIS HUNTER SAX (L — PAUL FOX G (M
DAVE RUFFY D (M — GARY BARNACLE SAX (M — ROBERT WYATT G V K(M — DAVE SHEEN D V (O
STEVE LAMB B (O — STEVE BULL K (O — SEGS B (M

C211 CRABBY APPLETON C211

MICHAEL FENNELLY G V (AB — (A) CRABBY APPLETON — 1970 ELEKTRA EKS 74067
PHIL JONES D (AB — (B) ROTTEN TO THE CORE — 1971 ELEKTRA EKS 74106
CASEY FOUTZ K (AB
FLACO FALCON PERC (AB — HANK HARVEY B (AB — DAVID GRISMAN MAND (B
BYRON BERLINE FDL (B — CLYDIE KING V (B — OMA DRAKE V (B
JESSICA SMITH V (B — DON GALLUCCI PROD (A

C212 CRACK THE SKY C212

JOHN PALUMBO K V (ABCEFG — (A) CRACK THE SKY — 1975 LIFESONG 6000
RICK WITKOWSKI G (ABCDEF — (A) CRACK THE SKY (RI) — 197 LIFESONG US 34994
JIM GRIFFITHS G V (ABCDEF — (B) ANIMAL NOTES — 1976 LIFESONG 6005
JOE MACRE B V (ABCDEF — (B) ANIMAL NOTES (RI) — 197 LIFESONG US 34996
JOEY D'AMICO D V (ABCDEF — (C) SAFETY IN NUMBERS — 1978 LIFESONG 6015
GARY LEE CHAPPELL V (CDE — (C) SAFETY IN NUMBERS (RI) — 19 LIFESONG US 35041
ROB STEVENS K (C — (D) LIVE SKY — 1978 LIFESONG 35620
CAREY ZIEGLER B (G — (E) WHITE MUSIC — 1980 LIFESONG 8028
JOHN TRACEY D (G — (F) CLASSIC CRACK — 1980 LIFESONG 8029
VINCE DEPAUL K (DEG — (G) PHOTOFLAMINGO — 1981 LIFESONG 8133
MICHAEL TAYLOR G K (G

C212A CRACKERS C212A

STEVE ALMAAS B V (A — (A) THE CRACKERS 1980 TWIN TONE US TTR 8122
KAREN INDIANA G V (A
JAY PECK D V (A

C212B CRAMPS C212B

BRYAN GREGORY G (AB — (A) GREATEST HITS (EP) 1979 ILLEGAL UK ILS 12013
CONGO POWERS G (C — (B) SONGS THE LORD TAUGHT US 1980 ILLEGAL UK 005 US IRS 007
IVY RUHRSCHACH V (ABC — (C) PSYCHEDLIC JUNGLE 1981 ILLEGAL UK 009 US IRS 10016
LUX INTERIOR B (ABC
NICK KNOX D (ABC — BOOKER C K (B — ALEX CHILTON PROD (B

C212C CRAMPLE C212C

ARMIN CHRISTOPH V K SYN(A — (A) RIGHT IN TIME 1980 ? GER 91155
UWE HOFFMEISTER V SAX (A
MARKUS MAYER B (A — WOLFGANG D (A — GUNTER KREMPL G (A
HANS PRITACHET TPT PERC(A — EBERHARD STOIBER G V (A

C213 CRACKIN' C213

PETER BUNETTA D (BC — (A)CRACKIN 1975 POLYDOR UK2391 187 US 6044
JERRY MARTINI SAX (A — (B) MAKINGS OF A DREAM 1977 WB US BS2989
RICK CHUDACOFF B (ABC — (C) CRACKIN 1977 WB US BS3123
ARNO LUCAS V PERC(ABC — (D) SPECIAL TOUCH 1978 WB US 3235
LESLIE O SMITH V PERC(ABC
GT CLINTON K (ABC — BOB BORDY G (BC — LESTER ABRAMS V K (ABC
BRIAN RAY G (C — GENE DINWIDDIE HRNS (BC — VICTOR FELDMAN PERC (B
MILT HOLLAND PERC (B — DAVID SANBORN HRNS (B — STEVE MADAIO HRNS (C
CHUCK FINDLEY HRNS (C — JACKIE KELSO HRNS (C — FRED SELDON STRGS(C
MICHAEL OMARTIAN K (C — STEMSY HUNTER SAX (C — CHEPITO AREAS PERC (A

C213A CRASS C213A

STEVE IGNORANT V — (A) STATION OF CRASS (DBL) 1979 CRASS 52 1984
PENNY RIMBAUD D (A — (B) FEEDING THE 5000 1980 CRASS
EVE LIBERTINE V (A — (C) PENIS ENVY 1981 CRASS 321984/1
JOY DE VIVRE V K G (A
N A PALMER G V (A — PETE WRIGHT V B (A — PHIL FREE G V (A

C213B CRAVATS C213B

ROB DALLAWAY G V (A — (A) IN TOYTOWN 1980 SMALL WONDER UK CRAVAT1
DAVE BENNETT D (A
THE SHEND B V (A — RICHARD LONDON(SVOR NAAN) SAX(A

C213C THE CRAWDADDYS C213C

STEVE POTTERF G V HCA(A — (A) CRAWDADDY EXPRESS 1979 VOX/BOMP US 200001 UK 28541
MARK ZADERNOWSKI B (A — (A) CRAWDADDY EXPRESS 1980 LINE GER LLP 5012
RON SILVA G V (A — (B) STILL STEAMIN' 1980 LINE GER LSLP 4005
DAN McCAIN D (A

C213D HANK CRAWFORD C213D

HANK CRAWFORD SAX (ALL — (A) MORE SOUL 1961 ATLANTIC US 1356
MILT TURNER (AG — (B) SOUL CLINIC 1961 ATLANTIC US 1372
DAVID NEWMAN SAX (ABCI — (C) FROM THE HEART 1962 ATLANTIC US 1387
JOHN DUKE B (R — (D) SOUL FROM THE BALLAD 1963 ATLANTIC US 1405
CARL LETT JR D (R — (E) TRUE BLUE 1964 ATLANTIC US 1423
SONNY FORRIEST (CE — (F) DIG THESE BLUES 1965 ATLANTIC US 1436
MARTY PAICH (D — (G) AFTER HOURS 1967 ATLANTIC US 1455
WENDELL HARRISON (G — (H) Mr BLUES 1967 ATLANTIC US 1470
JOE NEWMAN (I — (I) DOUBLE CROSS 1968 ATLANTIC US 1503
JACK McDUFF (I — (J) Mr SOUL PLAYS LADY SOUL 19 ATLANTIC US 1523
RICHARD TEE K (LMN — (K) HELP ME MAKE IT THROUGH THE NIGHT 19 KUDU US 06
BOB CRANSHAW B (L — (L) WILDFLOWER 1973 KUDU US 15
IDRIS MUHAMMAD D (LM — (M) DONT YOU WOORY 'BOUT A THING 1974 KUDU US 19
JOE BECK G (L — (N) I HEAR A SYMPHONY 1975 KUDU US 26
BOB JAMES K (M — (O) HANK CRAWFORDS BACK 19 KUDU US 33
GARY KING B (MN — (P) TICO RICO 19 KUDU US 35
HUGH McCRACKEN G (M — (Q) CAJUN SUNRISE 19 KUDU US 39
RALPH McDONALD PERC (MN — (R) 1959 LINE UP
JOE FARRELL WIND (M
ERIC GALE G (N — BERNARD PURDIE D (N — PHIL BODNER WIND (M — PEPPER ADAMS SAX (M
RANDY BRECKER TPT (M — JON FADDIS TPT (M — ALAN RUBIN TPT (LM — ROMEE PENQUE SAX (M
BERNIE GLOW TPT (L — MARVIN STAMM TPT (L — WAYNE ANDRE TROM (L — TONY STUDD TROM (L
PAUL FAULISE TROM (L — JIMMY BUFFINGTON HRNS (L — BROOKS TILLOTSON HRNS (L — BILL EATON V (L
RANDY PEYTON V (L — HILDA HARRIS V (L — MAERETHA STEWART V (L

C213E RANDY CRAWFORD C213E

RANDY CRAWFORD V (ALL — (A) EVERYTHING MUST CHANGE 1976 WB UK K56328 US 2975
JEROME RICHARDSON SAX (A — (B) MISS RANDY CRAWFORD 1977 WB UK K56882 US 3083
DICK SPENCER SAX (A — (C) RAW SILK 1978 WB UK K56592 US 3283
RAY PIZZI WIND (A — (D) NOW WE MAY BEGIN 1980 WB UK K56791 US 3421
LEW TABAKIN WIND (A — (E) SECRET COMBINATION 1981 WB UK K56904 US 3541
BILL HOOD WIND (A — (F) WINDSONG 1982 WB UK K57011
MICHAEL SEMBELLO G (F
BOBBY BRYANT HRNS (A — SNOOKY YOUNG HRNS (A — BILL BERRY HRNS (A — BUDDY CHILDERS HRNS(A
JACK RAINES HRNS (A — DICK NASH HRNS (A — BRITT WOODMAN HRNS (A — GARNET BROWN TROM(A
MAURICE SPEARS TROM (A — DON GRUSIN PNO (AC — JOHN WILLIAMS B (A — RALP HUMPHREY D (A
MUNDELL LOWE G (A — JOE SAMPLE K (AD — ROBERT POPWELL B (A — JAMES GADSON D (AC
LARRY CARLTON G (A — JAY GRAYDON G (A — RALPH MACDONALD PERC (A — ERIC GALE G (A
HUGH McCRACKEN G (A — ANTHONY JACKSON B (A — RICK MAROTTA D (AC — PAT REBILLOT K (A
DEAN PARKS G (ADEF — HAROLD VICK SAX (A — HUGH MASEKELA HRNS (A — RANDY McCORMICK K (B
KEN BELL G (B — LARRY BYROM G (B — ROGER CLARK D (B — BOB WRAY B (B
HARRISON CALLAWAY HRNS (B — RONNIE EADES HRNS (B — DENNIS GOOD HRNS (B — HARVEY THOMPSON HRNS(B
BILL PUETT FLT (B — MAXINE WILLARD V (BD — JULIA TILLMAN V (BD — PAT HENDERSON V (B
DONNA RHODES V (B — SANDRA CHALMERS V (B — GREG POREE G (C — ABRAHAM LABORIEL B (CDE
LEON PENDARVIS PNO (CEF — JOHN TROPEA G (C — WILL LEE B (C — JOE PORCARO PERC (C
WILLIAM D SMITH K (C — PHYLLIS STJAMES V (C — ROLAND BAUTISTA G (D — TIM MAY G (D
DAVID T WALKER G (D — WILTON FELDER B SAX(D — STIX HOOPER D (D — MIKE BAIRD D (D
PAULINHO DACOSTA PERC (D — EDDIE BROWN PERC (D — OSCAR BRASHEAR TPT (D — GWEN OWENS V (D
MELVIN FRANKLIN V (D — JEFF PORCARO D (EF — STEVE LUKATHER G (EF — LENNY CASTRO PERC(EF
ROBBEN FORD G (E — ERNIE WATTS FLT (E — NEIL LARSEN K (E — LARRY WILLIAMS HRNS(EF
BILL REICHENBACH HRNS (E — GARY HERBIG HRNS (EF — JIM HORN HRNS (EF — CHUCK FINDLEY HRNS(E

(CONTINUED

C213E RANDY CRAWFORD (CONTINUED) C213E

TOMMY LIPUMA PROD (EF BUZZY FEITEN G (F DAVID SANBORN SAX (F GARY GRANT HRNS(F
LEW McCREARY HRN (F PAUL JACKSON G (F RICHARD PAGE V (F CARMEN TWIDLIE V (F
LPAULETTE BROWN V (F STEVEN GEORGE V (F BILL CHAMPLIN V (F MARTY WALSH G (F
NEIL STUBENHAUS B (F JERRY HEY HRN (F CHARLES LOPER HRNS (F ROBBIE BUCHANAN SYN(F
STRING SECTION (B

C214 CRAWLER C214

TONY CARR PERC (A (A) CRAWLER 1977 EPIC US 34900 UK EPC 82083
TERRY WILSON SLESSER V (AB (B) SNAKE RATTLE & ROLL 1979 EPIC US 35482 UK EPC 82965
TERRY WILSON B V (AB
TONY BRAUNAGEL D V (AB JOHN BUNDRICK K (AB TED BUNTING SAX (A
CHRIS WOOD FLT (A STEVIE LANGE V (A GEOFF WHITEHORN G (A

C214A PEE WEE CRAYTON C214A

PEE WEE CRAYTON PEE WEE CRAYTON 1975 BULLDOG BDL 1004
PEE WEE CRAYTON 197 CROWN US CLPS 5175
THINGS WE USED TO DO 1976 VANGUARD US VSD 6566
THINGS WE USED TO DO 197 CHARLY UK CR 30014
BLUE GUITAR GENIUS VOL 1 (10") 19 ACE UK 10CH 23

C214B ROBERT CRAY BAND C214B

ROBERT CRAY G V (A (A) WHO'S BEEN TALKIN' 1980 TOMATO US 7041
CURTIS SALADO HCA V (A
RICHARD COUSINS B (A DAVE OLSON D (A

C214C CRAZE C214C

(A) SPARTANS 1980 HARVEST UK SHSP 4114

C215 CRAZY CAVAN & THE RHYTHM ROCKERS C215

CRAZY CAVAN GROGAN V (* CRAZY RHYTHM 19 ROCKHOUSE 7510
LYNDON NEEDS G (* ROCKABILITY 1976 CHARLY UK CR 5001
TERRY WALLEY G (* ROCKABILITY 1976 POLYDOR 2445 210
GRAHAM PRICE B (IS STILL ALIVE 19 CHARLY UK CR 5002
MICK COFFEY D (* IS STILL ALIVE 19 POLYDOR 2445 211
STEVE VINCENT B (* OUR OWN WAY OF ROCKIN' 1977 CHARLY UK CR 5004
GERAINT WATKINS K (* OUR OWN WAY OF ROCKIN' 1977 POLYDOR 2933 214
LIVE AT THE RAINBOW 1978 CHARLY UK CR 30139
CRAZY RHYTHM 19 CHARLY UK CR 30156
RED HOT 'N' ROCKABILLY 1979 CHARLY UK CR 30174
(*) MR COOL 1979 CHARLY UK CR 31203
ROCKABILLY IN PARIS 1981 MAGNUM FORCE UK 003
(EP) BOPPIN & SHAKIN 1978 CHARLY UK CEP 118

C215A CRAZY ELEPHANT C215A

LARRY ALUFER K V (A (A) CRAZY ELEPHANT 19 BELL US 6034
BOB AVERY D (A
RONNIE BRETONE B (A KENNY COHEN K SAX V (A HAL HING V (A

C216 CRAZY HORSE C216

BILLY TALBOT B (ALL (A) CRAZY HORSE 1971 REPRISE US RSLP 6438
RICK CURTIS G V (C7 (A) CRAZY HORSE 1980 REPRISE RI GERM REP 24026
RALPH MOLINA D (ALL (A) CRAZY HORSE 1972 REPRISE UK K 44114
DANNY WHITTEN G V (A123456 (B) LOOSE 1972 REPRISE US MS 2059
BOBBY NOTKOFF VLN (CD1234 (B) LOOSE 1972 REPRISE UK K 44171
LEON WHITSELL G V (1 (C) AT CROOKED CREEK 1973 EPIC US KE 31710
GEORGE WHITSELL G V (B17 (C) AT CROOKED CREEK 1973 EPIC UK EPC 65223
NILS LOFGREN G V (A4568 (D) CRAZY MOON 1978 RCA AFL1 3054
JACK NITZSCHE K (A6
GREG LEROY G V (BCD67 (1) 1962 68 ROCKETS
JOHN BLANTON K (B67 (2) 69 +NEIL YOUNG LP(EVERYBODY)
MICHAEL CURTIS G K V (CD7 (3) 1969
BEN KEITH STEEL (8 (4) 1969 70
FRANK SAMPEDRO G (D9 (5) MID 70 + NEIL YOUNG LP(GOLDRUSH)
PACHECO CONGA (C (6) JULY70 DEC71
SNEAKY PETE KLEINOW STEEL (C (7) 1972 73
PATTI MOAN V (C (8) LATE 73 + NEIL YOUNG LPs(TONIGHTS +ON THE BEACH)
STEVE LAWRENCE SAX (D (9) FEB 75 + NEIL YOUNG LP (ZUMA)
KIRBY PNO (D
NEIL YOUNG G V (D2589 RY COODER G (A GIB GUILBEAU FDL (A
BARRY GOLDBERG K (D TOM BRAY TPT (D JOEL TEPP HCA (B
JAY GRAYDON G (D KENNY WALTER TROM (D MICHAEL KOWALSKI D (D

C217 PAPA JOHN CREACH C217

PAPA JOHN CREACH VLN V(ALL (A) PAPA JOHN CREACH 1971 GRUNT FTR 1003
BIG JOE TURNER V (B (B) FILTHY 1972 GRUNT FTR 1009
HARMONICA FATS HCA (B (C) ZULU (PLAYING MY FIDDLE FOR YOU 1974 GRUNT BFL1 0418
CARL BYRD D (B (D) IM THE FIDDLE MAN 1975 BUDDAH UK 4039 US 5649
JACK CASADY B (AB (E) ROCK FATHER 1976 BUDDAH US 5660 FR VOGUE 60007
JOHN PARKER K (BE (F) THE CAT & FIDDLE 1977 DJM DJM11 DJF 20515
SAM WILLIAMS B (B (G) INPHASION 1978 DJM DJM18 UK DJF 20545
HENRY COKER TROM(B
SAMMY PIAZZA D (AB JOHN EWING TROM (B BLUE MITCHELL TPT (B JOE LANE DAVIS SAX(B
JERRY JUMONVILLE SAX (B MAURICE SIMON SAX (B MAXINE WILLARD V (B VANETTA FIELDS V (B
SHIRLEY MATTHEWS V (B MARTI McCALL V (B LUTHER WATERS V (B ORRIN WATERS V (B
GREG ADAMS TPT (A JACK BONUS SAX (A JOHN CIPOLLINA G (A JOEY COVINGTON D (A
MIC GILLETTE TROM(A MIKE LIPSKIN K (A PETE SEARS B (A GRACE SLICK V (
STAN MONTEIRO CLAR(A BOB WILSON G (A NICK BLACK PNO (A BRUCE CONTE G (A
DOUGLAS RAUCH B (A STEVE HABERMAN K (FG BRIAN TILFORD B V (EFG MARK LEON D V(E(FG
JOE BRASLER G (FG REID KING V G (FG TONY SMITH D (A CARLOS SANTANA G (A
ART HILLERY PNO (A PAUL KANTNER G (A BOBBY HAYES B (A AL STAEHELY V (F
SCOTT CUSHNIE K (F BOB ZIMMITTI D (G JOHNNY GUITAR WATSON G (G CHARLIE DANIELS FDL (G
DR JOHN K (G DAVID LAFLAMME FDL (G RUFUS ANDERSON G (A DAVID BROWN B (A
JERRY GARCIA G (A GREGG ROLIE ORG (A KEVIN MOORE G (BE JORMA KAUKONEN G (AB
HOLDEN RAPHAEL PERC(BC DAVID BROWN B (A TRACY RICHARDSON V (F RACHEL OLDFIELD V (F
ROY SCIACCA V (F ERNESTINE GOLDSTEIN V (G

C218 CREAM C218

ERIC CLAPTON G V (ALL
JACK BRUCE HCA K B V (ALL
GINGER BAKER D V (ALL
FELIX PAPPALARDI B K VLA PROD G(*

Title	Year	Label	Country	Number
FRESH CREAM	1966	REACTION	UK	594 001
FRESH CREAM	1966	ATCO	US	33206
FRESH CREAM	1966	POLYDOR	GERM	623 031
FRESH CREAM	197	RSO	US	1 3009
FRESH CREAM	1978	RSO	GER	2479 180
FULL CREAM	1966	REACTION	UK	2447 010
DISRAELI GEARS	1967	REACTION	UK	594 003
DISRAELI GEARS	1967	POLYDOR	GERM	184 105
DISRAELI GEARS	1967	ATCO	US	33232
DISRAELI GEARS	19	POLYDOR	UK	2442 114
DISRAELI GEARS	197	RSO	US	1 3010
DISRAELI GEARS	197	RSO		2394 129
WHEELS OF FIRE (DBL)*	1968	POLYDOR	UK	583 031/2
WHEELS OF FIRE (DBL)*	1968	ATCO	US	2/700
WHEELS OF FIRE (DBL)*	1972	POLYDOR	UK	2612 001
WHEELS OF FIRE (DBL)*	1972	POLYDOR		2658 110
WHEELS OF FIRE (DBL)*	197	RSO	US	2 3802
WHEELS OF FIRE (DBL)*	19	RSO		2671 109
WHEELS OF FIRE(STUDIO)*	1968	POLYDOR	UK	583 033
WHEELS OF FIRE (LIVE)	1968	POLYDOR	UK	583 040
GOODBYE	1969	POLYDOR	UK	583 053
GOODBYE	1969	ATCO	US	7001
GOODBYE	1969	POLYDOR	GERM	184 203
BEST OF CREAM	1969	POLYDOR	UK	583 060
BEST OF CREAM	1969	POLYDOR	GERM	184 298
BEST OF CREAM (DBL)	19	RSO	FR	2675 087
I FEEL FREE	1969	KARUSSELL	GERM	2499 002
BEST OF (DBL)	1969	KARUSSELL	GERM	2499 010
SWLABR	19	KARUSSELL	GERM	2499 013
ROCK SENSATION	1969	KARUSSELL	GERM	2499 112
CREAM LIVE	1970	POLYDOR	UK	2383 016
CREAM LIVE	1970	ATCO	US	33328
CREAM LIVE	197	RSO	US	1 3014
CREAM LIVE 2	1972	POLYDOR	UK	2383 119
CREAM LIVE 2	197	RSO	US	1 3015
CREAM LIVE 2	1972	ATCO	US	7005
OFF THE TOP	1972	POLYDOR	US	5529
HEAVY CREAM	1973	POLYDOR	UK	2659 022
HEAVY CREAM	1973	POLYDOR	US	3502
CREAM	1975	POLYDOR	UK	2384 067
PORTRAIT OF CREAM	1975	POLYDOR	UK	2482 142
THE BEST VOL 2	1975	POLYDOR	UK	2675 087
POP GIANTS	19	BRUNSWICK		2911 528
BEST OF CREAM LIVE	19	POLYDOR		2674 018
POP HISTORY	197	POLYDOR		2675 014
CREAM VOL 2	1978	RSO	UK	2479 701
EARLY CREAM	19	SPRINGBOARD	US	4037
BEST	19	ATCO	US	33291
CREAM (6LPS)	1981	POLYDOR	NL	2658 142

C219 CREATION C219

JACK JONES D (ABC
KENNY PICKETT V (ABC
EDDIE PHILLIPS G (ABC
BOB GARNER B (ABC

Title	Year	Label	Country	Number
(A) WE ARE THE PAINTERMEN	1967	SONET DK		SLPS 1251
(A) WE ARE THE PAINTERMEN	1970	SONET RI	DK	1933
(A) WE ARE THE PAINTERMEN	1967	HIT TON	GERM	340 037
(B) BEST OF CREATION	1968	POP GERM		ZS 10 168
(C) 1966 67 CREATION	1973	CHARISMA	UK	CS8
( ) SUPER ROCK	19	TOSHIBA	US	95016
( ) THIS IS CREATION	19	TOSHIBA	US	95024
( ) CREATION	1975	ATCO	US	7041

C219A CREATION REBEL C219A

Title	Year	Label	Number
(A) STARSHIP AFRICA	1980	4D RHYTHMS	4DLP 1
(B) PSYCHOTIC JUNKANOO	1981	STATIK	9994

C219B CREATIVE ROCK C219B

HEIKO STEINSIEK D PERC(AB
M M MAASS B G K V (AB
APOSTOLOS PAPANIKOLAOU G(B
RUDIGER STREMMEL SAX V(AB HUBERTUS KREUTNER TPT V(AB RAINER ERBEL V (AB KLAUS WEBER G PERC(A
GUNTER SCHMEIDE G B (A

Title	Year	Label	Number
(A) GORILLA	1973	BRAIN	1017
(B) LADY PIG	1974	BRAIN	1061

C220 CREATIVE SOURCE C220

MELVIN RAGIN G (B
RAY PARKER G (B
JAMES JAMESON B (B
KENNETH RICE D (B
CLARENCE McDONALD K (B
SKIP SCARBOROUGH K (B
BOBBYE HALL PERC (B
MIKE STOKES K (B
CARL AUSTIN STINGS(B
RALPH TERRANA SYN (B JOHN TRADEL HRNS (B

Title	Year	Label	Country	Number
(A) CREATIVE SOURCE	1974	SUSSEX		LPSX6
(A) CREATIVE SOURCE	1974	SUSSEX	US	8027
(B) MIGRATION	1974	SUSSEX		LPSX7
(B) MIGRATION	1974	SUSSEX	US	8035
(C) PASS THE FEELING ON	1976	POLYDOR		2391 196
(C) PASS THE FEELING ON	1976	POLYDOR	US	6052
(D) CONSIDER THE SOURCE	1976	POLYDOR		2391 221
(D) CONSIDER THE SOURCE	1976	POLYDOR	US	6065

C220A CREATURES C220A

Title	Year	Label	Country	Number
MONSTER RALLY	19	RCA	US	1923

C220B CREDIBILITY GAP C220B

Title	Year	Label	Country	Number
A GREAT GIFT IDEA	1973	REPRISE	US	2154

MICHAEL McKEAN G V (
LOWELL GEORGE G (
RON ELLIOTT G (RICHARD HAYWARD D (HARVEY MASON PERC (
MILT HOLLAND PERC (JOE PORCARO PERC (KENNY GRADNEY B (
RAY POHLMAN B (DAVID HERSCHER B (HARRY SHEARER K V (
MARK LEVINE K (NICK DECARO K (TOMMY MORGAN HCA (
PENNY NICHOLS V (RICHARD BEEBE V (DAVID LANDER V (

C220C CREED C220C

Title	Year	Label	Country	Number
(A) CREED	1980	ASYLUM	US	146

C221 CREEDENCE CLEARWATER REVIVAL C221

TOM FOGERTY G V (ALL
JOHN FOGERTY G V (ALL
STU COOK D (ALL
DOUG CLIFFORD B (ALL

Title	Year	FANTASY UK	FANTASY US	LIBERTY UK	MUSIDISC FR
(A) CREEDENCE CLEARWATER REVIVAL	1969	506	8382	83259	6049
(B) BAYOU COUNTY	1969	507	8387	83261	6048
(C) GREEN RIVER	1969	504	8393	83273	6047
(D) WILLIE & THE POOR BOYS	1970	503	8397	83338	6046
(E) COSMOS FACTORY	1970	502	8402	83388	6043
(F) PENDULUM	1971	508	8410	83400	6042
(G) MARDI GRAS	1972	505	9404		6036
(H) CREEDENCE GOLD	1973	501	8402		6029
(H) CREEDENCE GOLD	197		9418	NL MFP 58089	
(I) MORE CREEDENCE GOLD	1973	512	9430		6019
(J) LIVE IN EUROPE	1974	520	FCCR 1		6009
(K) MASTERS OF ROCK	1975	EMI IMP	SC054		
(L) CHRONICLE	1976	528	FCCR 2		235
(L) CHRONICLE	1978	FESTIVAL ALB 235 IMP			
(M) LIVE AT THE ALBERT HALL (70)	1981	FANTASY US 4501 NL 614 173			
(AB) C C R/ BAYOU COUNTRY	1978	FANTASY SWE CCR68			
(CD) GREEN RIVER/WILLIE	1978	FANTASY SWE CCR69			
(EF) COSMOS/PENDULUM	1978	FANTASY SWE CCR70			

(CONTINUED)

C221 **CREEDENCE CLEARWATER REVIVAL** (CONTINUED) C221

( ) LIVE IN GERMANY 197 FANTASY GER 15200
( ) 20 GREATEST HITS 19 FANTASY 558
( ) CREEDENCE COUNTRY 1981 MFP 4509
(EP) C C R 1981 FANTASY NL 64441

C221A **CREEPY JOHN THOMAS** C221A

CREEPY JOHN THOMAS G V (A — (A) CREEPY JOHN THOMAS 1969 RCA UK SF 8061
PAUL ROGERS V (A
ANDY MARX B V (A — HELMUT POHL D (A

C222 **LOL CREME & KEVIN GODLEY** C222

LOL CREME G B V K PERC (ALL — (A) CONSEQUENCES 1977 MERCURY CONS017 6641658
KEVIN GODLEY D V PERC B K(ALL — (A) CONSEQUENCES 1977 MERCURY US SRM31700
PHIL MANZANERA G (D — (B) "L" 1978 MERCURY UK9109611 US POLYDOR 6177
JONATHAN HANDELSMAN SAX (B — (C) MUSIC FROM CONSEQUENCES 1978 MERCURY 9109 615
ANDY MACKAY SAX (B — (D) FREEZE FRAME 1979 POLYDOR UK 2442 166 +5027 US 6257
PAUL GAMBACCINI V (B — (E) ISMISM 1981 POLYDOR UK 2442 193 +5043
PAUL McCARTNEY V (D

C222A **CRESCENDOS** C222A

DALE WARD V (A — (A) OH JULIE 196 GUEST STAR US 1453

C222B **MARSHALL CRENSHAW** C222B

MARSHALL CRENSHAW G V PROD(A — (A) MARSHALL CRENSHAW 1982 WB US 3673 UK K57010
CHRIS DONATO B V (A
MICHAEL OSBORNE PERC (A — ROBERT CRENSHAW D V (A — TONY GARNIER B (A
RICHARD GOTTEHRER PROD (A

C223 **CRESSIDA** C223

ANGUS CULLEN V G (AB — (A) CRESSIDA 1970 VERTIGO V07
PETER JENNINGS K (AB — (B) ASYLUM 1971 VERTIGO 6360 025
KEVIN McCARTHY B (AB
IAIN CLARK D (AB — HAROLD McNAIR FLT (B — JOHN CULLEY * G (B
*SAME PERSON?? — JOHN HEYWORTH * G (A

C223A **CRESTS** C223A

JOHNNY MAESTRO V (— CRESTS SING 19 POST US 3000
JAY CARTER V (— CRESTS SING ALL BIGGIES 19 COED US 901
HARROLD TORRES V (— BEST OF THE CRESTS 19 COED US 904
TOMMY GOUGH V (

C223B **CRETONES** C223B

STEVE BEERS D (A — (A) SNAP SNAP 1981 PLANET P15
PETER BERNSTEIN B V (A
MARK GOLDENBERG G V (A — STEVE LEONARD K (A — PHIL KANZIE SAX (A

C224 **CRICKETS** C224

BUDDY HOLLY G V (A — (A) CHIRPIN CRICKETS 1958 CORAL UK LVA 9081
JERRY ALLISON D (ALL — (A) CHIRPIN CRICKETS 1969 CORAL UK CP 20
LARRY WELBORN B (— (A) CHIRPIN CRICKETS 1974 MCA UK CRLM 1023
NIKI SULLIVAN G (A — (A) CHIRPIN CRICKETS 1975 MCA UK CDLM 8035
JOE MAULDIN B (ALL — (A) CHIRPIN CRICKETS 19 BRUNSWICK US 54038
JERRY NAYLOR — (A) CHIRPIN CRICKETS 19 BRUNSWICK US 71036
GLEN D HARDIN G K — (B) BOBBY VEE MEETS THE CRICKETS 196 LIBERTY UK SLBY 1086
SONNY CURTIS G V (— (B) BOBBY VEE MEETS THE CRICKETS 1974 SUNSET UK SLS 50357
RICK GRECH B (JK — (C) IN STYLE WITH 196 CORAL UK LVA 9142
BOBBY VEE V (B — (C) IN STYLE WITH 196 CORAL 57320
ALBERT LEE G (JK — (D) CALIFORNIA SUN 19 LIBERTY US 7372
NICKY HOPKINS K (— (E) SOMETHING OLD SOMETHING NEW ... 19 LIBERTY UK SLBY 1120
BOB MONTGOMERY PROD (K — (E) SOMETHING OLD SOMETHING NEW 19 LIBERTY US 7272
CAROL MONTGOMERY V (K — (F) WE GOTTA GET TOGETHER 19 LIBERTY US 55742
STEVE KRIKORIAN V HCA (JK — (G) ROCKIN 50s ROCK'N'ROLL 1971 CBS UK 64301
NICK VANMAARTII G V (JK — (G) ROCKIN 50s ROCK'N'ROLL 1971 BARNABY US 30268
(H) ROCK REFLECTIONS 1971 SUNSET UK SLS 50207
(I) BUBBLEGUM, POP , BALLADS & BOOGIE 1973 PHILIPS UK 6308 149
(J) REMNANTS 1973 VERTIGO 1020 NL 6360 104
(J) REMNANTS 1973 MERCURY US 1 695
(K) LONG WAY FROM LUBBOCK 1974 MERCURY UK 6310 007
(L) BACK IN STYLE 1975 M C A UK MCFM 2710

EPS

STRAIGHT NO STRINGS 19 LIBERTY UK SLEP 2094
THE CRICKETS 19 CORAL US 81192
CHIRPING CRICKETS 19 BRUNSWICK US 71036
SOUND OF THE CRICKETS 19 BRUNSWICK US 71038
BOBBY VEE & THE CRICKETS 19 LIBERTY UK LEP 2084
A FOREVER KIND OF LOVE 19 LIBERTY UK LEP 2089
BOBBY VEE MEETS THE CRICKETS 19 LIBERTY UK LEP 2116
BOBBY VEE MEETS THE CRICKETS 2 19 LIBERTY UK LEP 2149
COME ON 19 LIBERTY UK LEP 2173

C225 **CRISIS** C225

TONY WAKEFIELD B (A — (A) NO TOWN HALL (EP) 1979 C A G UK
DOUG PEARCE G (A — (B) HYMNS OF FAITH (EP) 1980 ADRCOR UK
LESTER JONES G (A
INSECT ROBIN D (A — PHRAZER V (A

C226 **CRISPY AMBULANCE** C226

(A) UNSIGHTLY & SERENE (EP) 1980 FACTORY 10" UK FAC 32
(B) LIVE ON HOY AUGUST NIGHT (EP) 1981 FACTORY 12" BELG FACBN 4

C227 **PETE CRISS** C227

PETE CRISS D V (ABC — (A) PETE CRISS 1978 CASABLANCA NBLP 7122
STEVE LUKATHER G (ABC — (B) OUT OF CONTROL 1980 CASABLANCA NBLP 7240
(B) OUT OF CONTROL 1980 MERCURY UK 6302 065
(D) LET ME ROCK YOU 1981 MERCURY UK 6302 194

C227A **CRISTINA** C227A

CRISTINA MONET V (A — (A) CRISTINA 1980 ZE UK ILPS 7004
CAROL COLEMAN B (A
MICKEY MARTINEZ D (A — DUANE ROGERS G (A — BERNARD HAVEN K (A
RALPH SHUCKETT K (A — MILTON CARDONS PERC (A

C227B **CRITICAL MASS** C227B
(A) ITS WHATS INSIDE THAT COUNTS 19 MCA US 3260

C228 **CRITTERS** C228
CHRIS DARWAY AUTOHARP (( ) TOUCH'N GO WITH THE CRITTERS 196 PROJECT 3 US PB 4001
KENNY GORKA B (( ) THE CRITTERS 1966 PROJECT 3 US PB 4002
BOB SPINELLA K (( ) YOUNGER GIRL 1966 KAPP US 1485
JIM RYAN G (( ) YOUNGER GIRL 1966 KAPP US STEREO 3485
JEFF PELOSI D (

C229 **JIM CROCE** C229
JIM CROCE G V (ALL (A) CROCE 19 CAPITOL US ST315
INGRID CROCE (AI (B) YOU DONT MESS AROUND WITH JIM 1971 VERTIGO UK 6360700 US ABC 756
GARY CHESTER D (BC (B) YOU DONT MESS AROUND WITH JIM RI 19 COMMAND US 40006 LIFESONG US 34993
H J BOYLE G (B (B) YOU DONT MESS AROUND WITH JIM RI 1981 ROADRUNNER 9996
ELLIE GREENWICH V (BCD (C) LIFE & TIMES 1973 VERTIGO UK 6360 701 US ABC 769
TASHA THOMAS V (BCD (C) LIFE & TIMES 197 COMMAND US 40007 LIFESONG US 35008
JOE MACHO B (BCD (C) LIFE & TIMES 1981 ROADRUNNER 9997
TERRY CASHMAN V (BC (D) I GOT A NAME 1973 VERTIGO UK 6360 703 US ABC 797
JIM RYAN B (B (D) I GOT A NAME 197 COMMAND US 40008 LIFESONG US 35009
MAURY MUEHLEISEN G V (BCD (D) I GOT A NAME 1981 ROADRUNNER 9998
TOMMY WEST K V B (BCD (E) PHOTOGRAPHS & MEMORIES 1975 LIFESONG UK 500 US ABC 835
ALAN ROLNICK G V (CD (E) PHOTOGRAPHS & MEMORIES 197 COMMAND US 40020 LIFESONG US 35010
KENNY ASCHER ORG (C (F) THE FACES I'VE BEEN 1975 LIFESONG UK US ELSDP900
RICK MAROTTA D (D (G) JIM CROCE COLLECTION 197 TEE VEE US TVLP77024
STEVE GADD D (D (H) TIME IN A BOTTLE 197 LIFESONG US 35000
MARTY NELSON V (D (I) ANOTHER DAY 1977 PICKWICK US 3332
TERENCE MINOGUE STR V(D (J) BAD DAB LEROY BROWN 1979 LIFESONG US 35571
ERIC WEISSBERG FDL (C (K) ZIJN GROOTSHE SUCCESSEN (NL) 19 ROADRUNNER NL 9999
MICHAEL KAMEN SYN (CD (L) HIS GREATEST SONGS 1980 K TEL UK NE 1059
GEORGE DEVENS PERC (D
STU WOODS B (D BOBBY MATOS PERC (D LEROY BROWN V (D

C229A **CROCODILES** C229A
(A) NEW WAVE GOODBYE 1981 AURA UK AUL 716

C229B **CROMAGNON ORGASM** C229B
(A) CROMAGNON ORGASM 1969 ESP US 2001

C229C **CROME SYRCUS** C229C
LEE GRAHAM B V FLT(A (A) THE LOVE CYCLE 196 COMMAND RS 925
DICK POWELL K V HCA(A
ROD PILLOUD D (A TED SHREFFLER K (A JOHN GABORIT G (A

C230 **ANDREW CRONSHAW** C230
ANDREW CRONSHAW G ZITHER(ALL (A) A IS FOR ANDREW 1974 TRANSATLANTIC UK XTRA 1139
MARTIN SIMPSON G (C (B) EARTHED IN CLOUD VALLEY 1977 TRAILER UK LER 2104
RIC SAUNDERS VLN (C (C) WADE IN THE FLOOD 1978 TRANSATLANTIC UK LTRA 508
JOHN GILLESPIE K (C
HOLLY TANNEN DULC (C RICK KEMP B (C

C230A **CROOKS** C230A
DINO DEAN V G K(A (A) JUST RELEASED 1980 BLUEPRINT UK 5002
CHRIS BRODERICK B V (A
JIM FINGERS G V (A MICHAEL SPARROW D (A SIMON BOSWELL K (A

C231 **STEVE CROPPER** C231
STEVE CROPPER G (ALL (A) WITH A LITTLE HELP FROM MY FRIENDS1971 STAX UK SXATS1008
WITH (A) WITH A LITTLE HELP FROM MY FRIENDS1971 VOLT US VOS 6006
ALBERT KING G (B (B)JAMMED TOGETHER 1971 STAX UK STX 3009
POP STAPLES G (B (C) PLAYING MY THANG 1980 MCA US 5171
DUCK DUNN B (C (D) NIGHT AFTER NIGHT 1982 MCA US 5340
JERRY HAY TPT (C
RAYFORD GRIFFIN D (D NEAL STUBENHAUS B (C RICK SCHLOSSER D (C CRAIG KRAMPF D (C
WILLY HALL D (C DAVID PAICH K (C ANDREW LOVE HRNS (C JIM HORN HRNS(CD
JACK HALE TROM (C DAN FERGUSON G (C STEVE FOREMAN PERC (CD JOHN JARVIS K (C
KRON SYN (C TREVOR VEITCH G (C WILLIAM D SMITH K (CD BILL PAYNE K (C
BOBBY KIMBALL V (CD BRUCE ROBB V (DC JOE ROBB V (C STEVE ROBB V (C
ROGER HAWKINS D (D SCOTT EDWARDS B (D DAVID HOOD B (D CLAYTON IVEY K (D
BARRY BECKETT K (D RUSSELL FARENTE K (D CHARLES FEARING G (D JIM JOHNSON G (D
WAYNE PERKINS G (D JEFF BAXTER G (D CHUCK FINDLEY HRNS (D JULIA TILLMAN V (D
MAXINE WILLARD V (D CLYDENE JACKSON V (D TIM SCMIDT V (D BURTON CUMMINGS V (D
BONNIE BRAMLETT V (D

C232 **DAVID CROSBY** C232
DAVID CROSBY G V (A (A) IF I COULD ONLY REMEMBER MY NAME 1971 ATLANTIC UK 2401 005 K40320
GRAHAM NASH G V (A (A) IF I COULD ONLY REMEMBER MY NAME 1971 ATLANTIC US 7203
BILL KREUTZMANN (A
PHIL LESH G (A DAVID FREIBERG (A ETHAN CROSBY (A MICKEY HART (A
HENRY DILTZ (A LAURA ALLEN (A PAUL KANTNER (A JERRY GARCIA (A
MICHAEL SHRIEVE (A JACK CASADY (A JORMA KAUKONEN (A GRACE SLICK (A
GREGG ROLIE (A JONI MITCHELL (A GARY BURDEN (A STEPHEN BARNCARD (A
ROBERT HAMMER (A DAVID GEFFEN (A RONALD STONE (A ELLIOT ROBERTS (A
NEIL YOUNG (

C233 **CROSBY & NASH** C233
DAVID CROSBY G V (ALL (A) CROSBY & NASH 1972 ATLANTIC UK K50011 US 7220
GRAHAM NASH G V K(ALL (B) WIND ON THE WATER 1975 POLYDOR UK 2310 428
TIM DRUMMOND B (BCDE (B) WIND ON THE WATER 1975 POLYDOR EUR 2302 038
DANNY KORTCHMAR B G (ABCDE (B) WIND ON THE WATER 1975 ABC US 902 MCA RI 37007
CRAIG KINLERS G (C (C) WHISTLE DOWN THE WIRE 1976 POLYDOR UK 2310 468
DAVID LINDLEY VLN G(BCDE1 (C) WHISTLE DOWN THE WIRE 1976 ABC US 956
CRAIG DOERGE K (ABCDE1 (D) LIVE 1977 POLYDOR UK 2310 565
JOEL BERNSTEIN G (BC (D) LIVE 1977 ABC US 1042
BEN KEITH G (BC (E) BEST OF 1978 POLYDOR UK 2310 626 RI 2482490
RUSS KUNKEL D (ABCDE (E) BEST OF 1977 ABC US 1102
STAN SZELESTE K (BC (1) 1976 BRITISH TOUR
LEE SKLAR B (ABCE
BILL KREUTZMANN D (AE LEAH KUNKEL V (E JERRY GARCIA G STEEL(AE JACKSON BROWNE (BE
JOHN BARBATA D (AE JONI MITCHELL V (E JAMES TAYLOR V (BCE CAROLE KING K (BCE
GREG REEVES B (A CHRIS ETHRIDGE K (A DAVE MASON G (A PHIL LESH B (A
LEVON HELM D (B ARTHUR MAEBE HRN (A DAVID DUKE HRN (A GEORGE PRICE HRN (A
DANA AFRICA FLT (A LAURA ALLEN ZITHER(C

C234 CROSBY STILLS & NASH (& YOUNG) C234

DAVID CROSBY G V (ABCDE1234FG (A) CROSBY STILLS & NASH 1969 ATLANTIC UK 588 189 RI K40033
GRAHAM NASH G V (ABCDE1234FG (A) CROSBY STILLS & NASH 1969 ATLANTIC US 8229
NEIL YOUNG G V (BCD234 (B) DEJA VU 1970 ATLANTIC UK 2401 001 RI K50001
STEPHEN STILLS B G V K(ABCDE1234FG (B) DEJA VU 1970 ATLANTIC US 7200 RI 19118
CALVIN SAMUELS B (C2 (C) FOUR WAY STREET 1972 ATLANTIC UK 2657 007 RI K60003
JOE LALA PERC (4G (C) FOUR WAY STREET 1972 ATLANTIC US 2/902
TIM DRUMMOND B (4E (D) SO FAR 1974 ATLANTIC UK K50023
RUSS KUNKEL D (4EG (D) SO FAR 1974 ATLANTIC US 18100
JERRY GARCIA STEEL(B (E) C S N 1977 ATLANTIC US19104 UK K50369
DALLAS TAYLOR D (AB12 (F) REPLAY 1980 ATLANTIC US 16082 UK K50766
TIM SCHMIDT V (G (G) DAYLIGHT AGAIN 1982 ATLANTIC US 19360 UK K50896
JOHN SEBASTIAN HCA (B (1) 1968/1969 (2) 1969/70 (3) 1970 (4) 1974/75
GREG REEVES B (B2
JOHN BARBATA D (C3 CRAIG DOERGE K (EG GEORGE PERRY B (EG JOE VITALE D K FLT (EG
JIMMY HASLIP B (EG RAY BARRETTO PERC (E TIM DRUMMOND B (E GERALD JOHNSON B (E
MIKE FINNIGAN K (E MICHAEL STERGIS G V (G WAYNE GOODWIN FDL (G LEE SKLAR B (G
GERRY TOLMAN G (G ROBERLEIGH BERNHART CELLO(G ERNIE EKHART CELLO (G BOB GLAUB B (G
JOEL BERNSTEIN G (G RICHARD T BEAR K (G DEAN PARKS G (G JAY FERGUSON K (G
MIGUEL MARTINEZ CELLO(G ART GARFUNKEL V (G

C234A CROSS COUNTRY C234A

JAY SIEGEL V PERC(A (A) CROSS COUNTRY 1973 ATLANTIC UK K 40516
MITCH MARGO V PERC K G (A (A) CROSS COUNTRY 1973 ATCO US SD 7024
BOB MANN G (A
PHIL MARGO V PERC(A AL GORGONE G (A HUGH McCRACKEN G (A JERRY FRIEDMAN G (A
LOREN KOREVEC G (A ERIC WEISSBERG STEEL(A RICK McGRATH STEEL (A KIRK HAMILTON B (A
STU WOODS B (A GREG WALKER B (A ALLEN SCHWARZBERG D (A JIM MAELEN PERC(A
GEORGE DEVENS PERC (A MAX HOLLANDER STRINGS(A

C234B CROSSFIRE C234B

(A) EAST OF WHERE 1981 HEADFIRST US 9704

C234C CROSSFIRES C234C

HOWARD KAYLAN SAX V(A (A) CROSSFIRES 1981 RHINO US 019
MARK VOLMAN SAX V(A
AL NICHOL G V (A DON MURRAY D (A CHUCK PORTZ B (A JIM TUCKER G (A
TOM STANTON G (A TERRY HAND D (A

C234D CHRISTOPHER CROSS C234D

CHRISTOPHER CROSS G V (A (A) CHRISTOPHER CROSS 1979 WB US 3383 UK K56789
TOMMY TAYLOR D (A (B) ANOTHER PAGE 1983 WB
ANDY SALMON B (A
DON ROBERTS SAX (A MICHAEL OMARTIAN SYN K V(A STORMIE OMARTIAN V (A JAY GRAYDON G (A
LENNY CASTRO PERC (A NICOLETTE LARSON V (A ROB MEURER K SYN(A MYRNA MATTHEWS V (A
MARTY McCALL V (A VICTOR FELDMAN PERC (A CHUCK FINDLEY HRNS (A VALERIE CARTER V (A
MICHAEL McDONALD V (A LARRY CARLTON G (A DON HENLEY V (A J D SOUTHER V (A
ERIC JOHNSON G (A TOMAS RAMIREZ SAX (A JIM HORN SAX (A JACKIE KELSO SAX (A
LEW McCREARY TROM (A

C234E KEITH CROSS & PETER ROSS C234E

KEITH CROSS G V (A (A) BORED CIVILIANS 1972 DECCA UK SKL 5129
PETER ROSS G V (A
SID GARDNER (A JENNY MASON (A BILLY RANKIN (A CHRIS STEWART B (A
PETER ARNESSON (A STEVE CHAPMAN (A JIMMY HASTINGS (A DEE MURRAY (A
TONY SHARP (A TONY CARR (A BRIAN COLE (A NICK LOWE (A
LEA NICHOLSON (A

C235 CROW C235

DAVE WAGNER V (ABCDE (A) CROW MUSIC 1969 AMARET 5001
DICK WIEGAND G (ABCD (A) CROW MUSIC 1969 STATESIDE UK SSL 10301
LARRY WIEGAND B (ABCD (B) CROW BY CROW 1970 AMARET 1970 5006
KINK MIDDLEMIST K (ABCD (B) CROW BY CROW 1970 STATESIDE UK SSL 10310
DENNY CASSWELL D V (BCD (C) MOSAIC 1981 AMARET US 5009
BROOKS HUNNICUTT V (B (D) BEST OF 1972 AMARET US 5012
MAXINE WILLARD V (B (E) DAVID WAGNER,CROW 1972 AMARET US 5-13
JULIA TILLMAN V (B
MARK'CHICO' PEREZ PERC (B JIM GORDON D (E JOHN GUERIN (E LARRY BROWN (E
BOBBYE HALL PERC (E JOE OSEBORNE (E MIKE DEASY (E DON PEAKE (E
DEAN PARKS G (E MICHAEL OMARTIAN (E JACKIE KELSO (E BUD BRISBOIS (E
BUDDY CHILDERS (E OLLIE MITCHELL (E RON HICKLIN (E STAN FARBER (E
GENE MORFORD (E

C236 CROWBAR C236

SONNIE BERNARDI D (ABCDEF (A) OFFICIAL MUSIC(KING BISCUIT BOY) 1970 PARAMOUNT US PAS 5030
JOZEF CHIROWSKI FLT PERC K(ABCDEF (B) BAD MANORS 1970 CAPITOL SBA 16004
JOHN 'GHETTO'GIBBARD G V(ABCDEF (B) BAD MANORS 1971 PARAMOUNT UK SPLA 272
KELLY JAY K V (ABCDEF (B) BAD MANORS 1971 PARAMOUNT US PAR 6007
ROLAND GREENWAY B V (ABCDEF (C) LARGER THAN LIFE 1971 PARAMOUNT SPLA 7002
RHEAL LANTHIER G V (ABCDE (D) HEAVY DUTY 1972 DAFFODIL AUST DDL 34665
RAY FENNELL PERC (C (D) HEAVY DUTY 1973 PARAMOUNT SPFL 283
SKIP PROKOP PERC (C (E) CROWBAR 1973 EPIC UK 80046
LEIGH ROBINSON PERC (C (E) CROWBAR 1973 EPIC US KE 32746
KING BISCUIT BOY V (B (F) CROWBAR CLASSICS 1972 CAPITOL 16030
BOB BRYDEN V (B
RITCHIE YORK PERC (B BRUCE FLYNN HRNS (C BRIAN LE BLANC HRNS (C STEVE KENNEDY HRNS K(BC
BRUCE CASSIDY HRNS (B GREG MUDRY HRNS (C KEITH JOLLIMORE HRNS (C HOWARD SHORE HRNS (C
PETE SIMPSON HRNS (C LARRY GREEN HRNS (C MICHAEL BRECKER HRNS (E THE ROCK (E
PAUL PRESTOPINO (E RANDY BRECKER HRNS (E STEVE HUNTER G (E SNEAKY PETE KLEINOW STEEL(E
HUGH McCRACKEN G (E WADE MARCUS (E JAY MESSINA (E ED SPRIGG (E
JOHN PEARSON (E TERRY BERRY CHOIR V (BC LARRY SMITH (E JANEY DICKENSON V (D
BARRY TALLMAN HRNS (D DAVID DOBBS HRNS (D JEAN PIERRE GALIPEAU HRNS(D

C236A CROWD C236A

(A) A WORLD APART 1981 POSHBOY US 108

C236B J D CROWE & THE NEW SOUTH C236B

J D CROWE BAN V (A (A) THE NEW SOUTH 19 ROUNDER US 0044
TONY RICE G V (A
RICKY SKAGGS MAND FDL(A BOBBY SLONE B (A JERRY DOUGLAS DOB G(A

C237 RODNEY CROWELL C237

RODNEY CROWELL GV (A — (A) AINT LIVING LONG LIKE THIS 1978 WB US BSK3228 UK K 56564
LARRY LONDIN D (BC — (B) BUT WHAT WILL THE NEIGHBORS THINK 1980 WB US BSK3407 GERM 56776
EMORY GORDY B (ABC — (C) RODNEY CROWELL 1981 WB US BSK3587 UK K 56934
ALBERT LEE G V PNO (ABC
JAMES BURTON G DOBRO(A — AMOS GARRETT G (AB — RY COODER G (A — JOHN WARE D (A
HAL BLAINE D (A — JIM KELTNER D (A — EMMYLOU HARRIS V G (A — MAC REBENNACK K (A
RICKY SKAGGS FDL V(A — BYRON BERLINE FDL (A — BRIAN AHERN G PERC(A — GLEN D HARDIN PNO (A
JERRY JUMONVILLE HRNS (A — RICHARD GREENE STRINGS(A — HANK DEVITO STEEL (ABC — MICKEY RAPHAEL HCA (A
NICOLETTE LARSON V (A — WILLIE NELSON V (A — LARRY WILLOUGHBY V (ABC — DONIVAN COWART V (A
TOM SAUBER BANJO(A — TONY BROWN V (BC — FRANK RECKARD G (B — STEVE WOOD K V (B
DON WHALEY V (B — CRAIG LEON PNO FLT(B — TOWER OF POWER HRNS (B — BOOKER T JONES K (C
RICHARD BENNETT G (C — PHIL KENZIE SAX (C — ROSEMARY BUTLER V (C — VINCE GILL G V (C
ROSANNE CASH V (C — BILL LAMB HRNS (C

C238 CROWFOOT C238

RUSSELL DASHIELL G K B V (AB — (A) CROWFOOT 1970 PARAMOUNT US 265
SAM McGUIRE G V (B — (B) FIND THE SUN 1971 ABC US ABCS745 UK PROBE 1042
DON FRANCISCO D PERC V (B
RICK JAEGER D (A

C239 ARTHUR 'BIG BOY' CRUDUP C239

ARTHUR'BIG BOY' CRUDUP (ALL — (A) LOOK ON YONDERS WALL 1968 DELMARK DS 614
RANSOM KNOWLING B (AC — (B) MEAN OLE FRISCO 1969 TRIP US 7501
EDWARD EL G (AC — (B) MEAN OLE FRISCO 1969 BLUE HORIZON UK 763855
DAVE MYERS B (AC — (C) CRUDUPS MOOD 1970 DELMARK DS 621
LAWRENCE 'JUDGE' RILEY D(AC — (D) FATHER OF ROCK'N'ROLL 1971 RCA UK RD 8224
WILLIE DIXON B (C — (D) FATHER OF ROCK'N'ROLL 1971 RCA US 573
(E) ROEBUCK MAN 1974 LIBERTY UK UAS 29092
(F) THATS ALL RIGHT MAMA 1976 DJM UK 22025
HARPIN' ON IT 197 POLYDOR 2941 001
ARTHUR BIG BOY CRUDUP 19 FIRE US 103

C240 R CRUMB & THE CHEAP SUIT SERENADERS C240

R CRUMB BANJO(AB — (A) CHEAP SUIT SERENADERS VOL 1 1974 BLUE GOOSE BG 2014
ROBERT ARMSTRONG G (AB — (B) CHEAP SUIT SERENADERS VOL 2 1976 BLUE GOOSE BG 2019
ALLAN DODGE FDL MAND(AB — (C) CHEAP SUIT SERENADERS VOL 3 1978 BLUE GOOSE BG 2025
TERRY ZWIGOFF CELLO (AB

C241 CRUSADERS C241

WILTON FELDER SAX (ALL — FREEDOM SOUND 1961 PACIFIC JAZZ PJ 27
LOOKING AHEAD 1962 PACIFIC JAZZ PJ 43
JOE SAMPLE K (ALL — AT THE LIGHTHOUSE 1963 PACIFIC JAZZ PJ 57
TOUGH TALK 1963 PACIFIC JAZZ PJ 58
LARRY CARLTON G (ABCDEFGHIN — HEAT WAVE 1965 PACIFIC JAZZ PJ 87
STIX HOOPER D (ABCDEFGHIJKLNY — CHILE CON SOUL 1966 PACIFIC JAZZ PJ 20092
LIGHTHOUSE 66 1966 PACIFIC JAZZ PJ 20098
WAYNE HENDERSON TROM (ABCDEFGY — TALK THAT TALK 1966 PACIFIC JAZZ pj 20106
ROY GAINES G (— FESTIVAL JAZZ 1967 PACIFIC JAZZ PJ 20115
JIMMY BOND B (Y — LIGHTHOUSE 68 1968 PACIFIC JAZZ PJ 20131
JOE PASS G (Y — UH HAH 1968 PACIFIC JAZZ PJ 20175
MONK MONTGOMERY B (Y — POWERHOUSE 1969 PACIFIC JAZZ PJ 20136
LARRY GOSKIN (— LIGHTHOUSE 69 1969 PACIFIC JAZZ PJ 20165
BILLY ROGERS G (JK — BEST OF THE JAZZ CRUSADERS 1969 PACIFIC JAZZ PJ 20175
POPS POPWELL B (GHIJ — GIVE PEACE A CHANCE 19 LIBERTY LIB11005
ARTHUR ADAMS G (ABCGHK — (Y) YOUNG RABBITS 1976 BLUE NOTE UK BND4028 BNLA 530
MAX BENNETT B (C — OLD SOX NEW SHOES 19 CHISA 804
DAVID T WALKER G (ABN — OLD SOX NEW SHOES 1971 RARE EARTH SRE 3001
DEAN PARKS G (JHLN — PASS THE PLATE 19 CHISA 807
PAULINHO DA COSTA PERC (JHLNK — HOLLY WOOD 1973 MOWEST 118
ROLAN BAUTISTA G (JHLK — HOLLYWOOD 1973 MOWEST 7004
CHUCK RAINEY B (A — AT THEIR BEST 19 MOWEST 796
BILL WITHERS V (L — (A) CRUSADERS (DBL) 1971 ABC US ABCD 609
RANDY CRAWFORD V (K — (A) CRUSADERS (DBL) 1971 BLUE THUMB US BTS6001 UK ILPS 9218
VICTOR GASKIN B (Y — (B) SECOND CRUSADE (DBL) 1972 ABC ABCD 610 BTS 7000
LEROY VINNEGAR B (Y — (C) UNSUNG HEROES 1973 ABC ABCL 5180 BLUE THUMB BTS 6007
CHARLES WILLIAMS B (Y — (D) SCRATCH 1975 ABC ABCL 5181 BLUE THUMB BTS 6010
BOBBY HAYNES B (Y — (E) SOUTHERN COMFORT (DBL) 1975 ABC ABCD 607 BLUE THUMB BT 9002
CLARE FISCHER K (Y — (F) CHAIN REACTION 1975 ABC ABCL 5144 BLUE THUMB BT 6022
JOE COCKER V (N — (F) CHAIN REACTION 1981 MCA US 37146
CARLOS VIDAL CONG (Y — (G) THOSE SOUTHERN KNIGHTS 1976 ABC ABCL 5164 BLUE THUMB BTS 6024
BARRY FINNERTY G (NK — (G) THOSE SOUTHER KNIGHTS 1981 MCA US 37147
RALPH MACDONALD PERC (H — (H) FREE AS THE WIND 1977 ABC ABCL 5226 BLUE THUMB BT 6029
REGGIE YOUNG G (N — (H) FREE AS THE WIND 1981 MCA US 37073
ALPHONSO JOHNSON B (LK — (I) BEST OF THE CRUSADERS(DBL) 1976 ABC ABCD 612 BLUE THUMB BT 6027
STEVE GIBDON G (N — (I) BEST OF THE CRUSADERS(DBL) 1981 MCA US 26006 UK MCLD 602
BOB MANN G (L — (J) IMAGES 1978 ABC ABCL 5250 BLUE THUMB BT 6030
JON GOIN G (N — (J) IMAGES 1981 MCA UK 1625
HUBERT LAWS FLT (Y — (K) STREET LIFE 1979 MCA UK MCF 3008
AL McKIBBON B (Y — (L) RHAPSODY & BLUES 1980 MCA UK MCG 4010
HUNGRIA GARCIA PERC (Y — (M) ONGAKU KAI/LIVE IN JAPAN 1981 CRUSADERS US 16002
PHIL UPCHURCH G (L — (N) STANDING TALL 1981 MCA UK 3122 US 5254
JAMES JAMERSON B (K — (O) ROYAL JAM 1982 MCA UK 455
SHEILA ESCOVEDO PERC (L
ABRAHAM LABORIEL B (L — RALF RICKERT TPT (L — MARCUS MILLER B (N
LOUIS JOHNSON B (N — BILLY PRESTON K (N — MAXINE WILLARD V (N
JULIA TILLMAN V (N — STEPHANIE SPRUILL V (N — ROBERT OBRYAN TPT (K
OSCAR BRASHEAR TPT (K — JEROME RICHARDSON SAX (K — BILL GREEN SAX (K
GARNETT BROWN TROM (K — PAUL M JACKSON G (K

(NOTE) RECORDS BEFORE (A) ARE BY THE JAZZ CRUSADERS

C241A CRYAN SHAMES C241A

Member	Instr.	Records	Album	Year	Label	Country / No.
JIM FAIRS	G B FLT	(AB	(A) A SCRATCH IN THE SKY	1967	CBS	US 2786
DENNIS CONROY	D	(AB	(A) A SCRATCH IN THE SKY	1967	CBS	US 9586
TOM DOODY	V	(AB	(B) SUGAR & SPICE	1966	CBS	US 2589 9389
LENNY KERLEY	G B V	(A	(C) SYNTHESIS	1968	CBS	US 9719
ISAAC GUILLORY	B G K	(A				
J C HOOKE	PERC V	(A	JIM PILSTER TAMB (B		JERRY STONE G (B	
DAVE PURPLE	K B	(B				

C241B CRYSTAL MANSION C241B

Member	Instr.	Records	Album	Year	Label	Country / No.
ERIC FAULKNER	V	(A	(A) CRYSTAL MANSION FEATURING J CASWELL	19	CAPITOL	US SKAO 227
JOHNNY CASWELL	V PNO	(A	(B) CRYSTAL MANSION	1971	RARE EARTH	US R540L
JERRY MARLOW	B	(A				
RONNIE GENTILE	G B	(A	RICKEY MORLEY D (A		DAVE WHITE PNO V (A	
SAN ROTA	K	(	MARIO SANCHEZ V PERC (		BILL CRAWFORD B (	

C241C THE CRY C241C

Member	Instr.	Records	Album	Year	Label	Country / No.
ROBBO MACPHERSON	K V	(A	(A) THE CRY	1980	RCA	0368
GARY SCROTTON	G	(A				
KIMALL FOX	V	(A	BILL WADE D (A		BRIAN WHITTY B (A	

C241D CRY FREEDOM C241D

Member	Instr.	Records	Album	Year	Label	Country / No.
GERHARD BILLMAN	K SYN	(ABC	(A) VOLCANO	1976	?	GER 66 21313
DIETER URBASSIK	SAX	(A	(B) SUNNY DAY	1979	ERLKONIG	GER 148 408
RUDI MADSIUS	G V	(ABC	(C) NOBODY'S FOOL	1980	ERLKONIG	GER 148 416
KLAUS KUKLA	B	(A				
HELMUT KORBER	B	(BC	KLAUS BRAUN D (ABC		JAMES T DURHAM SAX PERC(BC	
OLDERS FRENZEL	PERC	(C				

C241E CRYERS C241E

Album	Year	Label	Country / No.
(A) CRYERS	1979	MERCURY	US 3734
(B) TELL ME YOUR DREAMS	1980	MERCURY	US 3785

C241F CRYSTAL GRASS C241F

Album	Year	Label	Country / No.
(A) CRYSTAL WORLD	1974	POLYDOR	US PD6516 UK 2391 185

C242 CRYSTALS C242

Member	Instr.	Records	Album	Year	Label	Country / No.
MARY THOMAS	V	(	WALL OF SOUND VOL3 THE CRYSTALS	1975	PHIL SPECTOR	2307 006
DEE DEE KENNIEBREW	V	(	HES A REBEL	196	LONDON 8120 PHILLES	4001
LALA BROOKS	V	(	TWIST UPTOWN	196	PHILLES	4000
BARBARA ALSTON	V	(	GREATEST HITS	196	PHILLES	4003
VICKI ALSTON	V	(				
PAT WRIGHT	V	(				

C242A CUBAN HEELS C242A

Member	Instr.	Records	Album	Year	Label	Country / No.
LUURIE CUFFE		(A	(A) WORK OUR WAY TO HEAVEN	1981	VIRGIN UK2210	GER 204064
NICK CLARK		(A				
JOHN MILARKY		(A				
ALI MACKENZIE		(A				

C243 CUBY & THE BLIZZARDS C243

Member	Instr.	Records	Album	Year	Label	Country / No.
HARRY'CUBY'MUSKEE	PROD V HCA	(ALL	(A) DESOLATION	1966	PHILIPS	UK SBL7874 NL 6440 309RI
EELCO GELLING	G	(ABDGHIKMQ	(B) WITH REGARDS FROM GROLLO	1967	PHILIPS	NL 6343 227 6440 310RI
HANS KINDS	G	(AFMBQ	(B) WITH REGARDS FROM GROLLO	1967	PHILIPS	855 040
WILLY MIDDEL	B	(ABDFMQ	(B) GROETEN UIT GROLLO	1967	PHILIPS	9286 131
HENK HILBRANDIE	PNO	(AQ	(C) TRIPPIN'THRU' A MIDNIGHT BLUES	1967	PHILIPS	NL 6343 228
EDDIE BOYD	PNO	(D	(D) PRAISE THE BLUES	1968	PHILIPS	NL 6440 308RI
HERMAN BROOD	K V	(BCSFGMOPQ	(D) PRAISE THE BLUES	1968	PHILIPS	US 665 033
JAAP VAN EIK	B	(CDFGPQ	(E) SOUL	1968		
DICK BEEKMAN	D	(CFGPQ	(F) BEST OF (66 68)	1968	PHILIPS	NL 6677 023
EDWARD NINCK BLOK	TPT	(C	(G) LIVE	1968	PHILIPS	NL 6440 091 6440 307RI
ROEL HEMMES	SAX	(C	(G) LIVE	1968	PHILIPS	US 600 307
JEUNE MEINEMA	SAX	(C	(H) APPLEKNOCKERS FLOPHOUSE	1969	PHILIPS	UK SBL 7918
ALEXIS KORNER	G V	(G	(H) APPLEKNOCKERS FLOPHOUSE	1969	PHILIPS	NL 849 0167
HELMIG VANDER VEGT	K	(HIKLPQ	(I) TOO BLIND TO SEE	1969	PHILIPS RI	NL 6440 312
HERMAN DEINUM	B	(BHIKLPQ	(I) TOO BLIND TO SEE	1969	PHILIPS	NL 6413 002
BAS MUNNINKSNA	WIND	(I	(J) KING OF THE WORLD	1970	PHILIPS	NL 6314 002
RUDI VAN DIJK	SAX	(I	(J) KING OF THE WORLD	1970	PHILIPS	US 600 331
FRANK NUYENS	G	(NO	(K) SIMPLE MAN	1971	PHILIPS	6413 014
LOURENS LEEUW	B	(NO	(K) SIMPLE MAN	1971	PHILIPS	NL 6440 306
HERMAN VAN BOEYEN	D	(N	(L) SOMETIMES	1972	PHILIPS	6413 026
GEORGE KOOYMANS	G V	(N	(L) SOMETIMES	1972	PHILIPS	NL 6440 311
ROBERT JAN STIPS	K	(N	(M) AFSCHEIDSCONCERT	1974	PHILIPS	NL 6343 229
EGON JANSEB	PERC	(N	(N) RED WHITE BLUE	1975	POLYDOR	NL 2925 034
MELS BOL	D	(O	(N) RED WHITE BLUE	1975	VERTIGO	NL 6360 631
MAGGIE McNEAL	V	(O	(O) KID BLUE	1976	CNR	NL 660 002
JAN GROENONK	D	(R	(O) KID BLUE	1976	INTERCORD	GER 145 604
MARGRIET ESHUIS	V	(O	(P) OLD TIMES GOOD TIMES	1977	PHILIPS	NL 6416 111
NEPPY NOYA	PERC	(O	(Q) FORGOTTEN TAPES	1977	PHILIPS	NL 6401 107
JAN SCHUURMAN	PERC	(O	(R) LOVE VENDETTA(HARRY MUSKEE BAND)	1977	NEGRAM	NL NN3
ROB HOEKE	PNO	(P	(S) LIVE FEATURING HERMAN BROOD	1979	MELODY EXPRESS	NL ME1
MARTIN VAN DIJK	PNO	(R				
BERNARD PEINKE	G	(R	PIET VAN BLAUW D (R		HANS WATERMAN D (AQ	
HANS LAFAILLE	D	(HIKQ				

C243A RON CUCCIA C243A

Member	Instr.	Records	Album	Year	Label	Country / No.
RON CUCCIA		(A	(A) MUSIC FROM THE BIG APPLE	1981	ARMAGEDDON	UK 10 US OBLIQUE 10

C243B CUDDLY TOYS C243B

Album	Year	Label	Country / No.
(A) GUILLOTINE THEATRE	1980	FRESH	UK LP 1
(EP) CUDDLY TOYS	1981	FRESH	
(B) TRAILS & LOSSES	1981	?	

C243C CULPEPER C243C

Member	Instr.	Records	Album	Year	Label	Country / No.
GARY CY NICKLIN	G V PERC	(AB	(A) CULPEPER'S ORCHARD	1971	POLYDOR	GER 2380 006
NIELS HENDRIKSEN	G K V	(A	(B) ALL DRESSED UP & NOWHERE TO GO	1977	SONET	SLP 1558
MICHAEL FRILE	B K FLT	(A				
RODGER BARKER	D	(A	TOM MCEWAN D (B		TOM PUGGAARD-MULLER G (B	

C244 **CULT** C244

THE MAIL MUST GO THROUGH 19 STARBURST US SLT 500

C245 **CULTURE** C245

JOSEPH HILL V (ABCDE (A) 2 7S CLASH 1978 LIGHTNING UK LIP1
KENNETH LLOYD DAYES V (ABCDE (B) AFRICA STAND ALONE 1978 APRIL ADI 735
ALBERT WALKER V (ABCDE (C) HARDER THAN THE REST 1978 FRO'T LINE UK FL1016
ROBBIE SHAKESPEARE B (ACD (D) CUMBOLO 1979 FRONT LINE UK FL1040
ANSEL COLLINS K (CD (E) INTERNATIONAL HERB 1979 FRONT LINE UK FL1047
EARL WIRE LINDO K (CD (F) BALDHEAD BRIDGE 1980 LASER UK LASL 7
WILLIE LINDO G (CD (G) VITAL SECTION 1981 VIRGIN UK V 1001
RANCHIE G (CD ( ) CULTURE 1981 JOE GIBBS US 6038
SLY DUNBAR D (ACD
STICKY PERC (ACD DAVID MADDEN TPT (CD VIN GORDON TROM (ACD ERROL NELSON K(A
CEDRIC BROOKS SAX (CD ERIC LAMONT G (A FELIX HEADLEY SAX (CD LENNOX GORDON G (A
LLOYD PARKS B (A HERMAN MARQUIS SAX (A FRANKLIN WAUL K (A BOBBY ELLIS TPT(A
TOMMY McCOOK SAX (A KEN PALEY V (D MICHAEL RICHARD D (D RADCLIFFE BRYAN G (D
HAROLD BUTLER K (D CLIVE HUNT SAX (D

C246 **BURTON CUMMINGS** C246

BURTON CUMMINGS K V (ALL (A) BURTON CUMMINGS 1976 PORTRAIT UK 81573 US 34261
DICK WAGNER G (C (B) MY OWN WAY TO ROCK 1977 PORTRAIT UK 82012 US 34698
RANDY BACHMAN G V (BC (C) DREAM OF A CHILD 1978 PORTRAIT UK 82962 US 35481
TREVOR LAWRENCE SAX (B (D) SWEET SWEET 1981 ALFA US 11007
IAN GARDINER B (BC
JIM GORDON D (C JEFF BAXTER G (C BOBBY KING V (B E L KING V (B
RICK SCHLOSSER D (BC TERRY EVANS V (B PHYLLIS ST JAMES PERC (BC STEVE MADAIO HRNS(C
BECKY LOPEZ V (C VANETTA FIELDS V (C PLAS JOHNSON SAX (C SHIRLEY MATTHEWS V (C
JIMMY PHILLIPS K SYN(BC JEFF PORCARO D (BC JIM HORN SAX (BC DANNY WEIS G (B
LENNY CASTRO PERC (B RAY PARKER G (B SCOTT EDWARDS B (B OLLIE E BROWN D (B

C247 **RICK CUNHA** C247

RICK CUNHA G V (AB (A) CUNHA SONGS 1973 GRC US GA 5004
JERRY CARRIGAN D (A (B) MOVING PICTURES 1977 CBS US 33697
TOMMY COGBILL B (A
JOE OSBORN B (A BILL CUNNINGHAM (A LARRY MUHOBERAC (A REGGIE YOUNG G (A
LARRY CARLTON G (A JEFF GILKENSON (A DON BROOKS HCA (A DAVID BRIGGS K (A
JOHN GUERIN (A WAYLON JENNINGS (A CATES SISTERS (A WELDON MYRICK (A
GARY SCRUGGS (A NASHVILLE EDITION (A DAVID DAWSON (A RANDY SCRUGGS (A
STEVE NORMAN (A DONNA WEISS (A DONNA WASHBURN (A

C247A **CURE** C247A

ROBERT SMITH G (ABCD (A) THREE IMAGINARY BOYS 1979 FICTION UK FIX001
MATHIEU HARTLEY K (B (B) SEVENTEEN SECONDS 1980 FICTION UK FIX004
LAURENCE TOLHURST D (ABCD (C) BOYS DONT CRY 1980 FICTION UK FIX005 US PVC 7916
SIMON GALLUP B (B (D) FAITH 1981 FICTION UK FIX006 US 2383 605
MICHAEL DEMPSEY B (ACD (BD) HAPPILY EVER AFTER (DBL) 1981 A&M US 6020
CHRIS PARRY K (CD
MIKE HEDGES PROD (B

C247B **CURFEW** C247B

(A) LET THERE BE DARK 19 UA US 6746

C247C **CURLY CURVE** C247C

MARTIN KNADEN G (A (A) CURLY CURVE 1974 BRAIN GER 1040
KURT HERKENBERG B V (A
CHRIS AXEL KLOBER K (A HANNO BRUHN G V (A HANS WALLBAUM D (A

C247D **PAT CUPP & HIS FLYING SAUCERS** C247D

PAT CUPP (A (A) MODERN ROCKABILLY 1981 ACE 10" CH 32

C248 **CHERIE CURRIE** C248

CHERIE CURRIE V (A (A) BEAUTY'S ONLY SKIN DEEP 197 MERCURY
MARIE CURRIE K V (A
STEPHAN T (G V (A SAL MAIDA B (A MIKE BAIRD D (A WILLIE ORNELAS D (A
MOOSE McCAINS B V (A BILLY THOMAS D (A THOM ROTELLA G (A DAN FERGUSON G (A
DAVID HUNGATE B (A

C248A **CHERIE & MARIE CURRIE** C248A

CHERIE CURRIE V (A (A) MESSIN' WITH THE BOYS 1980 CAPITOL ST 12022
MARIE CURRIE V (A
MIKE BAIRD D (A MIKE PORCARO B (A STEVE LUKATHER G (A JOEY BRASLER G (A
JAI WINDING K SYN(A TREVOR VEITCH G (A BOBBY KIMBALL V (A BILL CHAMPLIN V (A
TOM KELLY V (A MICHAEL BODDICKER SYN (A TOM WERMAN TAMB (A KEITH LANDRY V (A
TOM FUNDERBUNK V (A BILLY BIZEAU G (A WADDY WACHTEL G (A JON PIERCE B (A
MIKE LANDAU G (A

C249 **TIM CURRY** C249

TIM CURRY V (ABC (A) READ MY LIPS 1978 A&M US 4717 UK AMLH64717
DICK WAGNER G (B (B) FEARLESS 1979 A&M US 4773 UK AMLH64773
MICHAEL KAMEN K (B (C) SIMPLICITY 1981 A&M US 4830 UK AMLH64830
BOB BABITT B (B
JIN MAELEN PERC (B CHARLES COLLINS D (B DAVID LASLEY V (B ARNOLD McCULLER V (B
ULA HEDWIG V (B BOB KULICK G (B BETTE SUSSMAN K (B MICHAEL TSCHUDIN SYN(B
DAVE SANBORN SAX (B ALLEN SCHWARZBERG D (B

C250 **LITTLE JOE CURTIS** C250

LITTLE JOE CURTIS V (A (A) LITTLE JOE CURTIS 19 MARBLE ARCH MAL 772
(B) SOUL 19 ALSTON 5082

C250A **MAC CURTIS** C250A

MAC CURTIS V (ALL (A) GOOD ROCKIN TOMORROW 19 ROLLIN ROCK US LP007
(B) RUFFABILLY 19 ROLLIN ROCK US LP002
(C) SUNSHINE MAN 19 EPIC US 26419
(D) ROCKABILLY KINGS 1974 POLYDOR UK 2310 293
(E) ROCKIN' MOTHER 1979 RADAR UK RAD22

C250B **SONNY CURTIS** C250B

SONNY CURTIS G V (ALL (A) BEATLE HITS FLAMENCO STYLE GUITAR 1964 IMPERIAL US 12276
(B) 1ST OF SONNY CURTIS 1968 VIVA US V 36012
(c) SONNY CURTIS STYLE 1969 VIVA US V 36021
(D) SONNY CURTIS 1979 ELEKTRA US UK 6E227
(E) LOVE IS ALL AROUND 1980 ELEKTRA US 6E283

C250C **CURTISS A** C250C

CURTISS A V (A — (A) COURTESY — 1980 TWIN TONE US 8015
TOM BURNEVIK SAX (A
DALE STRENGTH G V (A — DAVE AHL D (A — MARK GOLDSTEIN K (A
FRANK BERRY G (A — BILLY STEINER HCA (A — BOB STRENGTH V (A
RENALDO TORO B (A — BART HAZLETT D (A — BUZZ BARKER G (A

C251 **CURVED AIR** C251

SONJA KRISTINA V (ABCDEFG — (A) AIR CONDITIONING — 1970 WB US 1903 UK K 56004
FLORIAN PILKINGTON MIKSA D(ABCE — (A) AIR CONDITIONING — 1970 WB PIC DISC 3012
FRANCIS MONKMAN K (ABCE — (B) SECOND ALBUM — 1971 WB US 1951 UK K 46092
DARYL WAY VLN (ABCEFG — (C) PHANTASMAGORIA — 1972 WB US 2628 UK K 46158
KIRBY G (D — (D) AIR CUT — 1973 WB UK K 46224
JIM RUSSELL PERC (D — (E) LIVE — 1975 DECCA UKSML119 US BTM 5001
STEWART COPELAND D (FG — (F) MIDNIGHT WIRE — 1975 BTM UK BTM 1005
MIKE JACQUES G (FG — (G) AIRBORNE — 1976 BTM UK BTM 1008
PHILIP KOHN B G (E — ( ) BEST OF — 1976 WB K 36015
TONY REEVES B (G — ( ) CURVED AIR — 197 MIDI UK 20021
HENRY LOWTHER HRNS (G
COLIN CALDWELL PERC (C — ALEX RICHARDSON K (— JEAN AKERS PERC (C
MAL LINWOOD ROSE PERC (C — STEVE SAUNDERS TROM (C — DAVID PARKER TROM (C
ALAN GOUT TROM (C — CHRIS PYNE TROM (C — FRANK RICOTTI PERC (CG
JACK EMBLOW ACC (G — BOB SARGEANT K (G — ANNIE STEWART FLT (C
CRISPIAN STEEL PERKINS TPT(C — JIM WATSON TPT (C — PAUL KOSH TPT (C
GEORGE PARNABY TPT (C — JOHN PERRY B (F — PETER WOOD K (F
DEREK DAMAIN V (F — ROBIN LUMLEY PNO (G — ALAN SKIDMORE SAX (G
IAN EYRE B (AB — MIKE WEDGEWOOD B (CD

C251A **CURVES** C251A

(A) CURVES — 1981 LIBERTY US LT 1111

C251B **IAN CUSSICK** C251B

IAN CUSSICK B V (A — (A) IAN CUSSICK — 1978 METRONOME GER 60101
PETER FRANKEN D (A
PETER WEIHE G (A — CLAUS KRUSE K (A — LEMMY LEMBRECHT PERC (A
SIGURD SCHMIDT G (A — WOLFGANG SCHLUTER PERC (A — GARY L TODD B (A

C252 **IVOR CUTLER** C252

IVOR CUTLER V K (ALL — WHO TORE YOUR TROUSERS — 19 DECCA LK 4405
LUDO — 19 DECCA
DANDRUFF — 1974 VIRGIN V 2021
VELVET DONKEY — 1975 VIRGIN V 2037
JAMMY SMEARS — 1976 VIRGIN V 2065
LIFE IN A SCOTCH SITTING ROOM — 1978 HARVEST SHSP4084

C253 **CYANIDE** C253

BOB DE VRIES V (A — (A) CYANIDE — 1978 PYE UK NSPL18554
DAVE STEWART G (A
DAVE THOMPSON B (A — MICK STEWART D (A

C253A **JOHN L CYBORG** C253A

JOHN L CYBORG SYNS (A — (A) SATORI & THE FLOWER TRAVELLING BAND 198 GTR CAN 9230 1005
AKISI YAMANAKA V (A
MASANI WADA D (A — HIDEKI SHIMA G (A — SHIGEYUKI KOBAYASHI B (A

C254 **CYMANDE** C254

RAY KING V PERC(A — (A) CYMANDE — 1973 JANUS US JSL 3044
PETER SERREO SAX (A — (A) CYMANDE — 1973 ALASKA ALKA 100
MIKE ROSE WIND PERC (A — (B) SECOND TIME AROUND — 1973 JANUS US JLS 3054
PABLO GONSALES CONGA (A — (C) PROMISED HEIGHTS — 1974 CONTEMPO CLP 508
SAM KELLY D (A
JOEY DEE V PERC(A — DEREK GIBBS SAX (A — STEVE SCIPIO B (A
PATRICK PATTERSON G (A

C254A **CYMARRON** C254A

(A) RINGS — 1971 ENTERPRISE US 30962

C254B **CYMBELINES** C254B

(A) CYMBELINES (EP) — 19 TORCH UK TOR07

C255 **CYRKLE** C255

TOM DAWES SITAR G B (AB — (A) RED RUBBER BALL — 1966 CBS MONO US 2544
MICHAEL LOSEKAMP K (AB — (A) RED RUBBER BALL — 1966 CBS STEREO 9344
MARTY FRIED D PERC(AB — (B) NEON — 1967 CBS MONO US 2632
DON DANNEMAN G (AB — (B) NEON — 1967 CBS STEREO 2977
BOBBY GREGG PERC (B — (B) NEON — 1967 CBS UK 62977
BUDDY SALZMAN PERC (B
JOHN SIMON K (B — RAY BARRETTO PERC (B

C255A **CYRUS** C255A

(A) CYRUS — 1971 ELEKTRA US 74105

C256 **HOLGER CZUKAY** C256

HOLGER CZUKAY V G K SYN(AB — (A) MOVIES — 1979 HARVEST EUR 45754
JAKI LIEBEZEIT D (AB — (A) MOVIES — 1979 EMI UK EMC 3319
MICHAEL KAROLI G (A — (B) ON THE WAY TO THE PEAK OF NORMAL — 19 WELT GER 46400
IRMIN SCHMIDT PNO (A
REBOP KWAKU BAAH PERC (A — JAH WOBBLE B (B

C257 **CZUKAY, WOBBLE & LIEBEZEIT** C257

HOLGER CZUKAY G K HRNS(A — (A) 4 TITLE EP — 1981 EMI GER 64419

D1 **D C NIGHTHAWKS** D1

(A) THE D C NIGHTHAWKS — 1980 MERCURY 6337 111

D1A **D F K BAND** D1A

LES DUDEK G (AB — (A) SPECIAL TOUR SAMPLER — 1978 CBS US AS430
MIKE FINNIGAN K (AB — (B) DFK BAND — 1979 CBS US 35770
JIM KRUEGER G (AB
MAX GRONENTHAL K (AB — TREY THOMPSON B (AB — MIKE HOSSACK D (A
BILL MEEKER D (AB — BOBBYE HALL PERC (B — JAMES NEWTON HOWARD K (B

D1B DMZ D1B

RICK CORACCIO B (A — (A) DMZ — 1978 SIRE SRK 6051
PAUL MURPHY D (A — (1) 1976
JAY RASSLER G (A1
PETER GREENBERG G (A1 — DAVE ROBINSON D (1 — MONO MANN V K PERC(1
MIKE LEWIS B (1

D1C DBs D1C

PETER HOLSAPPLE G V (AB — (A) STANDS FOR DECIBELS — 1981 ALBION UK 105
CHRIS STAMEY G V (AB — (B) REPERCUSSION — 1981 ALBION CASS 109
WILL RIGBY D (AB
GENE HOLDER B (AB — JOHN EARLE SAX (B — ANDY CLARK K (B
DICK HANSEN TPT (B — CHRIS GOWER TROM (B — ALAN BETROCK PROD(A
SCOTT LITT PROD (B

D1D D V C D1D

JOHN BOLIN D (A — (A) DVC — 1981 ALFA US AAB 11005
MAX PADILLA B V (A
JOHN BARTLE G V (A — ROB FOREST G V (A

D2 MICHAEL D'ABO D2

MICHAEL D'ABO V K (ALL — (A) D'ABO — 1970 UNI 6369 601
WITH — (A) D'ABO — 1970 MCA MAPS 2040
GRAHAM NASH V (C — (B) DOWN AT RACHEL'S PLACE — 1972 A&M US 4363 UK AMLH68097
DENNY SEIWELL (C — (B) DOWN AT RACHEL'S PLACE — 1972 RCA FR SP 4346
MIKE BLOOMFIELD G (C — (C) BROKEN RAINBOWS — 1974 A&M US 3634 UK AMLH63634
TEDDY IRWIN (C — (D) SMITH & D'ABO — 1976 CBS uk 81583
RAB NOAKES (C — (1) TOURING BAND 1971 ??
JACK LANCASTER SAX (D — (E) GULLIVERS TRAVELS — 19 INSTANT INLP 003
TONY V (A
GARY TAYLOR B (C — MARK NAFTALIN K (C — JORDANAIRES V (C
BOBBY THOMPSON (C — BEN KEITH (C — MO FOSTER B (B1
GRANT SERPELL D (B1 — JIMMY ROBERTSON ACC (B — MIKE MORAN K (B
MIKE JOPP G (B1 — JOHN KONGOS G (B — RAY COOPER PERC (B
LYN DOBSON HCA FLT SAX(B — MIKE LENTIN G (B — KEITH CHRISTIE TROM (B
ALBERT LEE G (A — CHRIS SPEDDING G (A — PAT DONALDSON B (A
ROY BABBINGTON B (A — GERRY CONWAY D (B — JOHN MARSHALL D (A
MATTHEW HCA (A — LEW WARBURTON STRINGS — MIKE LEANDER STRING(A
SUE GLOVER V (A — SUNNY LESLIE V (A — DORIS TROY V (A
NANETTE V (A — HUGH V (A — JOHN NEIL V (A

D3 PAULINHO DACOSTA D3

PAULINHO DACOSTA PERC V(A — (A) AGORA — 1977 POLYDOR UK 2335 747
(B) HAPPY PEOPLE — 1979 POLYDOR UK 2312 102

D4 DADA D4

ELKIE BROOKS V (A — (A) DADA — 1970 ATCO 2400 030
ROBERT PALMER V (
PAUL KORDA V (A — JIMMY CHAMBERS V PERC (A — MARTYN HARRYMAN D (A
ERNIE LAUCHLAN HRNS (A — PETE GAGE G B (A — BARRY DUGGAN WIND (A
STEVE YORK B (— DON SHINN K (A — MALCOLM CAPEWELL WIND (A

D4A DADDY COOL D4A

ROSS WILSON HCA G V (ABC — (A) DADDY COOL — 1971 REPRISE US 6471
ROSS HANNAFORD G V (ABC — (B) TEENAGE HEAVEN — 1972 REPRISE US 2088
WAYNE DUNCAN B V (ABC — (C) LIVE — 1972 WIZARD US 202
GARY YOUNG D V (ABC
IAN WINTERS G (BC — DAVE BROWN WIND (A — ROBIE PORTER K STEEL(A
JERRY NOONE SAX K (B

D5 DADDY LONGLEGS D5

KURT PALOMAKI B V CLAR (ABC — (A) DADDY LONGLEGS — 1970 WB UK 3004
CLIFF CARRISON D (ABCD — (B) OAKDOWN FARM — 1971 VERTIGO UK 6360 038
STEVE HAYTON G V (AC — (C) THREE MUSICIANS — 1972 POLYDOR UK 2371 261
MOE ARMSTRONG V (A — (D) SHIFTING SANDS — 1972 POLYDOR UK 2371 323
STEVE MILLER K (AC
IVAN CHANDLER K (C — GARY NORTON HOLDERMAN G V (BD — PETER ARNESEN K (BC

D5A PATTI DAHLSTROM D5A

PATTI DAHLSTROM V (ABCD — (A) THE WAY I AM — 1973 20th CENTURY US T 421
LARRY KNECHTEL K (BC — (A) THE WAY I AM — 1973 20th CENTURY CAN 9209 421
MICHAEL UTLEY K (B — (B) YOUR PLACE OR MINE — 1975 20th CENTURY US T 461
ANDY CAHAN K (B — (C) LIVIN' IT THRU' — 1976 20th CENTURY US T 521
GEORGE CLINTON K (B
JACK CONRAD B (BC — DAVID HUNGATE B (B — KLAUS VOORMANN B (B
DAVID KEMPER D (B — GARY MALLABER D (B — JIM KELTNER D (B
DEAN PARKS G (B — AL STAEHELY G (B — ART MUNSON G (B
FRED TACKETT G (B — STEVE CROPPER G (B — JAY GRAYDON G (B
AL CASEY G (B — DAVID LINDLEY BANJ FDL G (B — NICK DE CARO ACC (B
JIM HORN HRNS (BC — CHUCK FINDLEY HRNS (BC — JACKIE KELSO HRNS (BC
LON VAN EATON HRNS (B

D5B DON DAILEY D5B

DON DAILEY (A — (A) SURF STOMPIN' — 19 CROWN US CST 314

D5C DAKOTA D5C

JERRY HLUDZIK G V (A — (A) DAKOTA — 1980 CBS US 36261
BILL KELLY G V (A
JEFF MITCHELL K V (A — BILL McHALE B V (A — LOU COSSA K V (A

D6 DAKOTAS D6

ROBIN McDONALD G (— (A) MEET THE DAKOTAS (EP) — 196 PARLOPHONE GEP 888
MIKE MAXFIELD G
RAY JONES B — TONY MANSFIELD D

D6A WES DAKUS & THE REBELS D6A

WES DAKUS — WES DAKUS REBELS — 19 KAPP US 3536
WES DAKUS ALBUM — 19 CAPITOL US 6120

D6B DALEK I D6B

ALAN GILL V SYN B(A — (A) COMPASS — 1980 BACK DOOR UK OPEN1
DAVE HUGHES (A
CHRIS HUGHES B (A — HUGH JONES D (A — DAVE BATES V (A

D6C

EARL DALEY

D6C

EARL '16' DALEY (A
(A) REGGAE SOUND 1981 DREAD AT CONTROL DCLP3

D7

MICHAEL D'ALBUQUERQUE

D7

MICHAEL D'ALBUQUERQUE G V K(AB
FRANK RICOTTI PERC SAX(AB
OLLIE HALSALL G V K (A
GORDON BECK K (A
B J COLE STEEL (A
CHRIS PINE TROM (A
DAVID KATZ STR (A
ALAN SKIDMORE SAX (A

(A) WE MAY BE CATTLE BUT WEVE ALL GOT NAMES 1974 RCA UK SF 8383
(B) STALKING THE SLEEPER 1976 WB UK K 56276

CHRIS LAWRENCE B (A
GERRY CONWAY D (A
JOHN UCKERIDGE TPT (A
ROBIN SYLVESTER B (A
BRIAN BENNETT D (A
STAN SALZMAN SAX (A
HENRY LOWTHER TPT (A
JOHN TAYLOR K (A

D7A

DALLAS COUNTY

D7A

(A) DALLAS COUNTY 19 ENTERPRISE US 1011

D8

KATHY DALTON

D8

KATHY DALTON V (A
WITH
LOWELL GEORGE G V (A
PAUL BARRERE G (A
BILL PAYNE K (A
VAN DYKE PARKS PNO V(A
LOULIE JEAN NORMAN V (A
TONY MARTIN V (A
LARRY WILSON HRNS (A
STAN AYEROFF G (A

(A) AMAZING 1973 DISCREET UK K59202 US DS2168
(A) BOOGIE BANDS & ONE NIGHT STANDS 1974 DISCREET US DS2208
(ONE TRACK DIFFERENT)

SAM CLAYTON PERC (A
SNEAKY PETE STEEL(A
BILLY HINSCHE V (A
VANILLA GRITS V (A
JIMMY REED HRNS (A
KENNY GRADNEY B (A
CLYDIE KING V (A
CARL WILSON V (A
JOHN RAYFORD HRNS (A
JAY MIGLIORI HRNS (A
RICHIE HAYWARD D (A
JIMMY GILSTRAP V (A
JEAN JUDSON V (A
GABRIEL FLEMMING HRNS(A
ERIC HORD G (A

D8A

DALTON BROTHERS

D8A

SCOTT ENGEL V (A
JOHN'MAUS' STEWART V

I ONLY CAME TO DANCE 1964 TOWER UST5026

D9

ROGER DALTREY

D9

ROGER DALTREY V (ALL
WITH
RUSS BALLARD V G (AB
PADDY McHUGH V (B
DYAN BIRCH V (B
FRANK COLLINS V (B
DAVE WINTOUR B (AB
PHILIP GOODHAND TAIT PNO(B
CLEM CLEMPSON G (B
HENRY SPINETTI D (B
ALAN BROWN (B
DAVE ARBUS VLN (A
JOHN ENTWISTLE B (CE
ROD ARGENT K (C
JOHN PERRY V (C
DAVE MATTACKS D (E
BILLY NICHOLS G (E
RON ASPERY FLT (E

(A) DALTREY 1973 TRACK UK 2406 207
(A) DALTREY 1973 POLYDOR 2409 202
(A) DALTREY 1973 MCA US 328 RI 37052
(B) RIDE A ROCK HORSE 1975 POLYDOR UK 2442 135
(B) RIDE A ROCK HORSE 1975 MCA US 2147 RI 37030
(C) ONE OF THE BOYS 1977 POLYDOR UK 2441 146
(C) ONE OF THE BOYS 1977 MCA US 2271 RI 37031
(D) BEST OF 1981 POLYDOR UK 2490 162
(E) McVICAR(SOUNDTRACK) 19 POLYDOR GER 2303 102 US 6284

STEWART FRANCIS D (B
B J COLE STEEL (A
STUART TOSH D (C
PHIL KENZIE SAX (C
STUART CALVER V (C
HERBIE FLOWERS B (E
KEN FREEMAN K SYN (E
DAVE COURTNEY PNO (A
ROY YOUNG BAND HRNS (A
JIMMY McCULLOCH G (C
JIMMY JEWELL SAX (C
KENNY JONES D (E
DAVE MARKEE B (E
FRANK RICOTTI PERC (E
BOB HENRIT D (A
BRIAN ODGERS B (C
PAUL KEOGH G (C
TONY RIVERS V (C
STUART ELLIOTT D (E
RICKY HITCHCOCK G (E
TONY CARR PERC (E

D9A

DAMNATION

D9A

ADAM BLESSING V (ABC
JIM QUINN G V PERC(ABC
BOB KAFAMASZ G V (ABC
RAY BENICK B (ABC
BILL SCHWARK D (ABC
KEN CONSTABLE (A

(A)WHICH IS THE JUSTICE 1971 UA US UAS 5533
(B) SECOND DAMNATION 19 UA US UAS 6773
(C) THE DAMNATION OF ADAM BLESSING 19 UA US UAS 6738

D10

DAMNED

D10

DAVE VANIAN V (ABCD
BRIAN JAMES G V (AB
CAPTAIN (RAY BURNS)SENSIBLE GB(ABCD
RAT SCABIES(CHRIS MILLAR)D (ABCD
PAUL GREY B (D
NICK LOWE PROD(A
ROBERT 'LU'EDMUNDS G (B
ROMAN JUGG K (

(A) DAMNED DAMNED DAMNED 1977 STIFF UK SEEZ1
(B) MUSIC FOR PLEASURE 1977 STIFF UK SEEZ5
(C) MACHINE GUN ETIQUETTE 1979 CHISWICK UK CWK 3011
(D) THE BLACK ALBUM 1980 CHISWICK UK 3015 IRS NL 70012
(E) BEST OF 1981 ACE UK DAM1

LOL COXHILL SAX (B
JOHN MOSS D (
ALGY WARD B (C

D10A

DANCE BAND

D10A

LOU STONEBRIDGE V G (A
STEVE VANDELLER G (A
ROB TOWNSEND D (A
DICK HANSON TPT (A

(A) FANCY FOOTWORK 1980 DOUBLE D UK DDLP1

STEVE MULLENS B (A
JOHN IRISH EARLE SAX (A
PETER HOPE EVANS HCA (A

D10B

THE DANCE

D10B

(A) IN LUST 1981 STATIK UK LP 3

D11

DANDO SHAFT

D11

MARTIN JENKINS V MAND VLN(ABCD
POLLY BOLTON V (BCD
DAVE COOPER G V (ABCD
KEVIN DEMPSEY G V B(ABCD
TED KAY PERC(ABCD
ROGER BULLEN B (AB
PAUL DUNMALL SAX (D
ROD CLEMENTS B (D

(A) AN EVENING WITH DANDO SHAFT 1970 YOUNGBLOOD UK SSYB6
(A) AN EVENING WITH DANDO SHAFT 1970 DECCA US 75217
(B) DANDO SHAFT 1971 NEON UK NE5
(C) LANTALOON 1972 RCA UK SF 8256
(D) KINGDOM 1977 RUBBER UK RUB 034

TOMMY KEARTON K (D
DANNY THOMPSON B (D
JON STEVENS D (D

D11A

BARBARA DANE

D11A

BARBABRA DANE V (AB

(A)& THE CHAMBERS BROTHERS 19 FOLKWAYS US 2468
(B) SINGS THE BLUES 19 FOLKWAYS US 2471

D11B

RODNEY DANGERFIELD

D11B

RODNEY DANGERFIELD (AB

(A) NO RESPECT 1980 CASABLANCA US 7229
(B) THE LOSER 1980 RHINO US 012

D12 CHARLIE DANIELS D12

Musician	Instr	Albums
CHARLIE DANIELS	G FDL V	(ALL
WITH		
JOEL DIGREGORIO	K V	(ABCDEFGHIJKL1
EARL 'TE JOHN' GRIGSBY	B V	(ABC
JEFF 'WOLFMAN' MYER	D	(AB
BUDDY DAVIS	D	(CD
FRED EDWARDS	D	(CDEFGHI*JKL1
HOLLADAY SISTERS	V	(C
TIM DRUMMOND	B	(B
MYLON LEFEVRE	V PERC	(*
BILLY COX	B	(BD
KARL HIMMEL	D	(B
BOB WILSON	K	(B
BEN KEITH	STEEL	(B
JERRY CORBITT	V G	(B
BARRY BAINES	G V	(D
GARY ALLEN	D	(DE
MARK FITZGERALD	B V	(DE
LEA JANE BERINATI	V	(DK
TED REYNOLDS		(D
CHARLIE HAYWARD	B	(FGHIJ*1KL
DICKIE BETTS	G	(E*
TOY CALDWELL	G STEEL	(FGI*
JAMES MARSHALL	D	(1KL
MARIE CAIN		(D
TOM CRAIN	G V	(FGHI*KL
PAUL HORNSBY	K	(FG
DON MURRAY	D	(FGHI
SHARON VAUGHN		(D
BANJO BANJO	G	(E
DOUG GRAY	V PERC	(*
CHUCK LEAVELL	PNO	(*
GARY PEACEMAKER	D	(*
JAIMIE NICHOLS	PERC	(E*
JAI JOHANNY JOHANSON	D	(FG
JERRY EUBANKS	SAX	(*
JIMMY HALL	HCA	(*
RONNIE STONEMAN	BANJO	(*
GEORGE McCORKLE	G	(I*
TOM CALDWELL	B	(*
PAUL RIDDLE	D	(*
DAVID BROWN	B	(*

Album	Year	Label		Country	No.
(A) TE JOHN, GREASE & WOLFMAN	1970	KAMA SUTRA		US	2060
(A) TE JOHN, GREASE & WOLFMAN	1978	EPIC	RI	SU	34665
(B) CHARLIE DANIELS	1970	CAPITOL US ST11414	RI		8116039
(C) HONEY IN THE ROCK	1970	KAMA SUTRA		US	2071
(D) WAY DOWN YONDER	1970	KAMA SUTRA		US	2076
(D) WHISKEY	1977	EPIC	RI	US	34664
(E) FIRE ON THE MOUNTAIN	1975	KAMA SUTRA		US	2603
(E) FIRE ON THE MOUNTAIN	1975	KAMA SUTRA		UK	7007
(E) FIRE ON THE MOUNTAIN	1979	EPIC	RI	US	34365
(E) FIRE ON THE MOUNTAIN	1981	EMBASSY		UK RI	31830
(F) NIGHTRIDER	1975	KAMA SUTRA		US	2607
(F) NIGHTRIDER	1975	KAMA SUTRA		UK	7009
(F) NIGHTRIDER	197	EPIC		US	34402
(G) SADDLE TRAMP	1976	EPIC		UK	81335
(G) SADDLE TRAMP	1976	EPIC		US	34150
(H) UNEASY RIDER	197	EPIC		US	34369
(I) HIGH & LONESOME	1977	EPIC		US	34377
(I) HIGH & LONESOME	1977	EPIC		UK	81666
(J) MIDNIGHT WIND	1977	EPIC		US	34970
( ) ESSENTIAL CHARLIE DANIELS	197	KAMA SUTRA		US	2/2612
(*) VOLUNTEERS JAM	1976	CAPRICORN		UK	2429 143
( ) VOLUNTEERS JAM 3/4	1978	EPIC		US	E2 35368
( ) VOLUNTEERS JAM (EP)	197	KAMA SUTRA		US	EP10
(1) NOV 1979 GIG					
(K) MILLION MILE REFLECTIONS	1979	EPIC US 35751		UK	83446
(L) FULL MOON	1980	EPIC US 36571		UK	84461
( ) VOLUNTEERS JAM VI	1980	EPIC		UK	22107

(*) NOT STRICTLY CHARLIE DANIELS ALBUMS BUT HES ON EVERY TRACK.

D12A PHIL DANIELS & THE CROSS D12A

Musician	Instr	Albums
PHIL DANIELS	G V	(A
JOHN McWILLIAMS	D	(A
BARRY NEIL	B	(A
PETER HUGODALY	K	(A

Album	Year	Label	Country	No.
(A) PHIL DANIELS & THE CROSS	1980	RCA	UK	PL 25259

D13 RICK DANKO D13

Musician	Instr	Albums
RICK DANKO	B G	(A
WITH		
DENNY SEIWELL	D	(A
TERRY DANKO	D	(A
LEWIS BUSTOS	HRNS	(A
GERRY BECKLEY	V G	(A
WALT RICHMOND	PNO	(A
ERIC CLAPTON	G	(A
GEORGE WEBER	ORG	(A
GARTH HUDSON	ACC	(A
LEVON HELM	V	(A
ROCKY MORALES	HRNS	(A
JIM ATKINSON	G	(A
RON WOOD	G	(A
KEN LAUBER	PNO	(A
CHARLIE McBURNEY	HRNS	(A
ROBBIE ROBERTSON	G	(A
DOUG SAHM	G	(A
BLONDIE CHAPLIN	G B	(A
TIM DRUMMOND	B	(A
JIM PRICE	HRNS	(A
RICHARD MANUEL	K	(A
MICHAEL DE TEMPLE	G	(A
ROB FRABONI	PERC	(A
WAYNE NEUENDORF	V	(A
JIM GORDON	K HRNS	(A
JOE LALA	PERC	(A
DAVID PAICH	K	(A

Album	Year	Label	Country	No.
(A) RICK DANKO	1978	ARISTA	UK	SPARTY1037
(A) RICK DANKO	1977	ARISTA US 4141	EURO	63173

D14 DANNY & THE JUNIORS D14

DANNY RAPP
DAVE WHITE
BILL CARLUCCI
FRANK MAFFEI
JOE TERRANOVA

Album	Year	Label	Country	No.
( ) ROCK AND ROLL IS HERE TO STAY	19	SINGULAR	US	569

D14A BOBBY DARIN D14A

BOBBY DARIN V (ALL

Album	Year	US Label	US No.	UK Label	UK STEREO	UK MONO
BOBBY DARIN	195	ATCO	33102	LONDON		HAE 2140
THATS ALL	195	ATCO	33104	LONDON		HAE 2172
THIS IS	1959	ATCO	33115	LONDON	SAH 6067	HAE 2235
AT THE COPA	19	ATCO	33122	LONDON	SAH 6103	HAE 2291
FOR TEENAGERS ONLY	19	ATCO	1001	LONDON		HAE 2311
TWO OF A KIND	196	ATCO	33124	LONDON		HAK 2363
25TH DAY OF DECEMBER	1961	ATCO	33123			
BOBBY DARIN STORY	196	ATCO	33131	LONDON		HAK 2372
LOVE SWINGS	196	ATCO	33134	LONDON	SAHK 6193	HAK 2394
TWIST WITH	1962	ATCO	33138			
SINGS RAY CHARLES	1962	ATCO	33140	LONDON	SAHK 6243	HAK 2456
THINGS & OTHER THINGS	196	ATCO	33148	LONDON		HAK 8030
ITS YOU OR NO ONE	196	ATCO	33124	LONDON		HAK 8192
OH LOOK AT ME NOW	196	CAPITOL	1791			1791
EARTHY	196	CAPITOL	1826			
YOU'RE THE REASON	1963	CAPITOL	1866			
18 YELLOW ROSES	196	CAPITOL	1942			
GOLDEN FOLK HITS	1964	CAPITOL	2007			
HELLO DOLLY	1964	CAPITOL	2194			
VENICE BLUE	1965	CAPITOL	2322			
BEST OF	196	CAPITOL	2571			
I WANNA BE AROUND	196	CAPITOL	2322			
SHADOW OF YOUR SMILE	19	ATLANTIC	8121	ATLANTIC	588 014	
DR DOOLITTLE	196	ATLANTIC	8154			
IF I WERE A CARPENTER	196	ATLANTIC	8135	ATLANTIC	588 051	
WINNERS	196	ATLANTIC	33167	ATLANTIC	ATL5014	
STORY	196	ATLANTIC	33187	ATLANTIC		587 065
IN A BROADWAY BAG	196	ATLANTIC	8126	ATLANTIC	588 020	
SOMETHING SPECIAL	196			ATLANTIC		587 073
GREATEST MOMENTS	196			ATLANTIC		K40547
BOBBY DARIN	1973	MOTOWN	8 753			
1936/73	1975	MOTOWN	813			
BOBBY DARIN	19	DIRECTION	1936			
COMMITMENT	19	DIRECTION	1937			

D14B **DARK DAY** D14B

ROBIN LEE CRUTCHFIELD V K PERC(A (A) EXTERMINATING ANGELS 1980 LUST US JMB 229
PHIL KLINE G SYN B (A
BARRY FRIAR D (A STEVEN BROWN SAX (A MYSTERY WOMAN V (A

D14C **DARK STAR** D14C

RIK STAINES K V (A (A) DARK STAR 1981 AVATAR AALP 5003
DAVE HARRISON G V (A
BOB KEY G V (A MARK OSELAND G V (A STEVE ATKINS D V (A

D15 **DARLING** D15

ALICE SPRINGS V (A (A) PUT IT DOWN TO EXPERIENCE 1979 CHARISMA US 2204 UK CAS 1144
MICK HOWARD B (A
PAUL VARLEY D (A HAL LINDES G (A

D16 **JENNY DARREN** D16

JENNY DARREN V (ABC (A) CITY LIGHTS 1977 DJM UK DJF20497
CLIFF WADE G B V(ABC (B) JENNY DARREN 1978 DJM UK DJF20523
GEOFF GILL PERC V(ABC (C) QUEEN OF FOOLS 1978 DJM UK DJF20547
WILL MALONE PNO V(A (D) JENNY DARREN 1980 DJM UK DJF20569 NL 64122
STUART BUCKLEY SAX (C
BRIAN JONES SAX (A TONY SPATH (A MIKE ASHCROFT G (BEAU CHEMIN K (
COLIN ELLAR B (KELLY CONOVER D (LEE PATRICK G V (BC DES TONGUE B (BC

D17 **CHRIS DARROW** D17

CHRIS DARROW BAN G V MAND VLN(ALL (A) CHRIS DARROW 1973 UA UK UAG29453 US UALA 048
WITH (B) UNDER MY OWN DISGUISE 1974 UA UK UAG29634 US UALA 242
CALEB QUAYE PNO G(A (C) FRETLESS 1979 PACIFIC ARTS US PAC7 132
CLIVE CHAMAN B (A (D) ARTIST PROOF 1978 FANTASY US 9403
ROGER POPE D (A (E) SOUTHERN CALIFORNIA DRIVE 1980 LINE GER 5060
DAVID JONES PERC (C (F) EYE OF THE STORM 1981 TAKOMA US 7092
TITO LLOYD PERC (C
STEVE CAHILL G V AUTOHARP(AC EARL DANN G (A SONNY BINNS K (A TREVOR WHITE B (A
DANNY SMITH D (A DAVE PEGG B (A DAVE MATTACKS D (A ALAN STIVELL HARP FLT (A
DOLLY COLLINS K (A ALAN LUMSDEN SACK (A RODERICK SKEAPING VLA (A JOSEPH SKEAPING REBEC(A
THERESA CAUDLE WIND (A ANDREW VANDER BEEK HRNS(A RANDY STERLING B (C JOHN RUSSELL D (C
LOREN NEWKIRK PNO (C STEVEN DARROW PERC (C JERRY WALLER TPT K (C BOB SIGGINS V STEEL(C
MAX BUDA HCA (C ROBB STRANDLUND G V (C FRANK RECKARD G (C STEVE MORK HRNS (C
CINDY EDWARDS V (C CORKY CARROLL V (C EARL SHAKELFORD V (C GREG PRESTOPINO V (C
BABATUNDE OLATUNJI CONGA(C

D17A **PHIL D'ARROW** D17A

PHIL D'ARROW G V (A (A) SUB ZERO 1980 POLYDOR US PD6271
ROGER MURDOCK D (A
BILL COMMAROTA K V (A JOSEPH JAMES G (A BRIAN STANLEY B (A KATHERINE PHOENIX V (A
SAMMY FIGUEROA PERC (A JAMES E MONROE SAX (A JON PARIS HCA (A CURTIS FIELDS SAX(A

D18 **DARTS** D18

HORATIO HORNBLOWER SAX (AB (A) DARTS 1977 MAGNET UK MAg 5020 US UA 1977
GEORGE CURRIE G (AB (B) EVERYBODY PLAYS DARTS 1978 MAGNET UK MAG 5022
GRIFF FENDER V (AB ( ) AMAZING DARTS 1978 MAGNET 062 61889
JOHN DUMMER D (AB ( ) AMAZING DARTS 1978 K TEL UK DLP 7901
DEN HEGARTY V (AB (C) DART ATTACK 1979 MAGNET UK MAGL5030 US 63186
RITA RAY V (AB ( ) GREATEST HITS 1980 MAGNET UK MAGL 5037
THUMP THOMPSON B (AB ( ) DARTS 1980 US 6250
MIKE DEACON K (( ) DOUBLE TOP 1981 HALLMARK SHM 3087
HAMMY HOWELL K (AB
BOB FISH V (AB
KENNY EDWARDS V (DAVE KELLY G (

D18A **DARTS(US)** D18A

( ) HOLLYWOOD DRAG 19 DELFI US DFST 1244

D18B **RUSSELL DASHIELL** D18B

RUSSELL DASHIELL V G K PERC(A (A) ELEVATOR 1978 EPIC UK 82637 US 35074
STU COOK B (A
DOUG CLIFFORD D (A JOHN TANNER PNO (A

D18C **DAS DRITTE OHR** D18C

UDO WOLF V HCA (A (A) BLUE & BOOGIE 19 FUR OHNE POLITUR FR 7701
HELMUT MEYER B (A
TOM SCHRADER G V (A FERDI PETERS D (A

D19 **DAUGHTERS OF THE ALBION** D19

GREG DEMPSEY (A (A) DAUGHTERS OF THE ALBION 1968 FONTANA 67586
KATHLEEN YESSE (A (A) " " " 1968 FONTANA NL 887806 UK STL 5486

D19A **WOLFGANG DAUNER** D19A

WOLFGANG DAUNER K FLT (ALL (A) DREAM TALK 1964
EBERHARD WEBER B CELLO(DGHKM (B) FREE ACTION 1967
FRED BRACEFUL D (HKLMNQ (C) PSALMUS SPEI 1969
ROLAND WITTICH D (KGM (D) FUR 1969 CALIG GER 30603
SIGFRIED SCHWAB G (KM (E) OLMELS 1970
LARRY CORYELL G (L (F) BEO BACH TUNGEN 1970
GUNTER LENZ B (L (G) MUSIC ZOUNDS 1970 MPS GER 15270
JON HISEMAN D (L (H) OUTPUT 1970 ECM 1006
RICHARD KETTERER V (L (J) DAUNER SATO 1971
JURGEN SCHMIDT-OEHM VLN FLT(N (K) ET CETERA 1971 INTERCORD GER 26001
MATHIES THUROW B (N (L) KHIRSH 1972 MPS GER 2 121 432
LACA KOVACEV D (N (M) RISCHKAS SOUL 1972 BRAIN GER 1016
ZBIGNIEW SEIFERT V SAX (P (N) ET CETERA LIVE 1973 MPS GER 2 921 754
HANS KOLLER SAX (P (O) THIS IS 1974 BRAIN GER 200 150
ABELHARD ROIDINGER B (P (P) KUNSTKOPFINFIANER 1974 MPS GER 2 122 019
JANUS STEFANSKI D (P (Q) GIRL FROM MARTINIQUE 19 ECM 1008
ROBIN KENYETTA (Q (R) CHANGES 1979 MOOD GER 23333
ARILD ANDERSON (Q

D20 **DAVE DEE, DOZY, BEAKY, MICK , & TITCH** D20

DAVE DEE(HARMAN) V (ALL DAVE DEE, DOZY, BEAKY, MICK & TITCH 1966 FONTONA STL 5350
TREVOR'DOZY' DAVIES B (IF MUSIC BE THE FOOD OF LOVE 1966 FONTANA STL 5388
JOHN'BEAKY' DYMOND G D (IF MUSIC BE THE FOOD OF LOVE 1967 FONTANA 858 030
MICHAEL'MICK' WILSON D (GOLDEN HITS 1967 FONTANA STL 5441
IAN 'TITCH' AMEY G (WHATS IN A NAME 1967 FONTANA 858 000
PETER LUCAS G (

(CONTINUED)

D20 (CONTINUED) DAVE DEE, DOZY, BEAKY, MICK , & TITCH D20

PETER LUCAS G (IF NO ONE SANG 1968 FONTANA 886 478
IF NO ONE SANG 1968 FONTANA STL 5471
GREATEST HITS 1968 FONTANA SFL 13002
TOGETHER 1969 FONTANA 701 751
TOGETHER 1969 FONTANA SFL 13173
LEGEND OF 1969 FONTANA SFL 13063
FRESH AIR 1970 PHILIPS 6308 029
ATTENTION 19 FONTANA 6438 058
GREATEST HITS 1971 PHILIPS 6382 018
GREATEST HITS 19 FONTANA US 67567
GREATEST HITS 19 FONTANA US 27567
GREATEST HITS 1976 PHILIPS UK SON =!%

D20A DAVEY & THE BADMEN D20A

WANTED 19 KRW US 63 054

D20B DAVID & JONATHAN D20B

DAVID (A) MICHELE 19 CAPITOL T2473
JONATHAN

D21 DIANNE DAVIDSON D21

DIANNE DAVIDSON V G (AB (A) BABY 1971 JANUS us 3031
WITH (B) BACKWOODS WOMAN 1972 JANUS UK 6310 209 US 3043
MAC GAYDEN G V (ABC (C) MOUNTAIN MAMA 1972 JANUS US 3048
JOHN HARRIS PNO (BC
TIM DRUMMOND B (ABC KARL HIMMEL D (BC KENNETH BUTTREY D (AC KENNY MALONE D (C
WELDON MYRICK STEEL(BC RUTH PFAU VIOLA(C BRENT DAVIDSON STEEL DRUM(C ANITA BALL G V (C
TRACY NELSON V (BC CHARLIE McCOY G B (AB BOBBY THOMPSON K (B VASSAR CLEMENTS FDL (B
BUDDY SPICHER FDL (B LAUREL CANYON V (B JANIS SIEGEL V (B JOHN DRUMMOND G (A
DR JOHN HARRIS K (A LINDA RONSTADT V (A PHIL ROYSTER CONGA (B HONEY COMBS V (B

D22 ALUN DAVIES D22

ALUN DAVIES V G (A (A) DAYDO 1972 CBS US 31469 UK 65108
JEREMY TAYLOR G (A
CAT STEVENS K (A CHARLIE GAINSFORD BANJO(A GERRY CONWAY D (A CHRIS LAURENCE B (A
JEAN ROUSSEL K (A LARRY STEELE B (A HARVEY BURNS D (A

D23 CYRIL DAVIES D23

CYRIL DAVIES HCA V(A (A) THE LEGENDARY CYRIL DAVIES 1957 PRIVATE PRESSING UK
WITH (A) THE LEGENDARY CYRIL DAVIES 1970 FOLKLORE UK FLEUT 9
ALEXIS KORNER V G (A (EP) THE SOUND OF DAVIES 19 PYE INT UK NEP 44025
LISA TURNER V BANJ(A ( ) CYRIL DAVIES 19 ACE OF CLUBS UK ACL 1130
MIKE COLLINS PERC (A
TERRY PLANT B (A JEFF BRADFORD G MAND(A REG TURNER JUG (A

D23A RON DAVIES D23A

RON DAVIES G (AB (A) SILENT SONG THROUGH THE LAND 1970 A&M UK AMLS 933
MIKE DEASY G (A (B) I DONT BELIEVE IT 1980 FIRST AMERICAN 7714
DIMITRI CALLAS G (A
MIKE LANG PNO (A LARRY KNECHTEL ORG (A CHAD STUART B (A JIM KELTNER D (A
VICKI DAVIES V (A LEON RUSSELL PNO (A DOUG DILLARD BANJO (A BYRON BERLINE MAND(A
MERRY CLAYTON V (A CLYDIE KING V (A VANETTA FIELDS V (A

D24 BETTY DAVIS D24

BETTY DAVIS V (ALL (A) BETTY DAVIS 1973 JUST SUNSHINE JSS5
WITH (B) THEY SAY IM DIFFERENT 1974 JUST SUNSHINE US JSS 3500
GREGG ERRICO D (A (B) THEY SAY IM DIFFERENT 1974 POLYDOR UK 2933 402
HERSHALL KENNEDY K V (AB (C) NASTY GAL 1975 ISLAND UK ILPS 9329
VICTOR PANTOJA PERC (AB
DOUG RODRIGUES G (A NEAL SCHON G (A BUDDY MILES G (B MERL SAUNDERS K (A
LARRY GRAHAM B (A RICHARD KERMODE K (A DOUG RAUCH B (A PETE SEARS PNO (A
GREG ADAMS HRNS (A SKIP MESQUITE SAX (A MIC GILLETTE TROM (A JULES BROUSSARD SAX (A
POINTER SISTERS V (A KATHI McDONALD V (A PATRYCE BANKS V (A WILLY SPARKS D V (AB
LARRY JOHNSON B (BC FRED MILLS K V (B CARLOS MORALES G V (B NICKY NEAL D V (B
ERROL BENNETT PERC (B JAMES ALLEN SMITH K (B DEBBIE BURRELL V (B ELAINE CLARK V (B
TRUDY PERKINS V (B MARY JONES V (B TONY VAUGHN K V (B CORDELL DUDLEY V G (B
PETE ESCOVEDO PERC (B MIKE CLARKE D (B JIMMY GODWIN G (B SYLVESTER V (A
ANNIE SAMPSON V (A

D25 EDDIE DAVIS D25

EDDIE DAVIS LIVE AT MINTONS 1964 STATESIDE UK SL 10102
JOHNNY GRIFFIN SAX (LIVE AT MINTONS 196 PRESTIGE US 7309
SHIRLEY SCOTT K (COOKBOOK 1974 PRESTIGE PR 24039
LEAPIN' ON LENNOX 1976 BLACK'N'BLUE 33072
TOUGHESS TENORS 1976 MILESTONES M 47135
EDDIE LOCKJAW DAVIS 1976 MAHOLNY 558 104

D25A FRANK DAVIS D25A

FRANK DAVIS METAMORPHOSIS (UNRELEASED)

D26 JESSE ED DAVIS D26

JESSE ED DAVIS G V (ALL (A) JESSE ED DAVIS 1971 ATCO US 33346 UK 2400106
ALBHY GALUTEN PNO (B (B) ULULU 1972 ATCO US 33382 UK ATLANTIC K40329
LEON RUSSELL PNO (AB (C) KEEP ON COMING 1973 EPIC US 32133 UK CBS 65649
LARRY KNECHTEL K (AB
DONALD DUNN B (B BILLY RICH B (AB ARNOLD ROSENTHAL B (B JIM KELTNER D (B
MAXINE WILLARD V (A GRAM PARSONS V (AB MERRY CLAYTON V (AB VANETTA FIELDS V (AB
CLYDIE KING V (AB CHUCK KIRKPATRICK V (B CHARLES CHALMERS SINGERS(B ERIC CLAPTON G (A
JOEL SCOTT HILL G (A LARRY PIERCE K (A BEN SIDRAN K (A JOHN SIMON K (A
STEVE THOMPSON B (A CHUCK BLACKWELL D (A STEVE MITCHELL D (A BRUCE ROWLAND D (A
ALAN WHITE D (A PATT DALEY PERC (A SANDY KONIKOFF PERC (A JACKIE LOMAX PERC(A
PETE WADINGTON PERC (A JOHNNIE WARE PERC (A ALAN YOSHIDA PERC (A JIM GORDON HRNS(A
JERRY JUMONVILLE HRNS (A DARRELL LEONARD HRNS (A FRANK MAYES HRNS (A NIKKI BARCLAY V (A
BOBBY JONES V (A GLORIA JONES V (A MAC REBANNACK PNO (B STAN SZELESTE PNO (B

Musician	Instrument	
MILES DAVIS	TPT	(ALL
WITH		
WAYNE HENDERSON	TROM	(
JOE ZAWINUL		(
TONY WILLIAMS	D	(
HERBIE HANCOCK	K	(
KEITH JARRETT	K	(
JOHN McLAUGHLIN	G	(
CHICK COREA	K	(
LARRY CORYELL	G	(
GEORGE PAULIS	K	(
AL FOSTER	D	(
T M STEVENS	B	(
MASUBUMBI KIKUCHI	K	(
WAYNE SHORTER	SAX	(
DAVE HOLLAND	B	(
RON CARTER	B	(
JOHN COLTRANE	SAX	(
DIZZY GILLESPIE	TPT	(
CHARLIE PARKER	SAX	(
GIL EVANS		(
CANNONBALL ADDERLEY	SAX	(
TADD DAMERON	PNO	(
RED GARLAND	K	(
OSCAR PETERSON	KB	(
PAUL CHAMBERS	B	(
PHILLY J JONES	D	(
MILT JACKSON	VIBES	(
THELONIUS MONK	PNO	(
PERCY HEATH	B	(
KENNY CLARKE	D	(
CHARLES MINGUS	PNO B	(
MAX ROACH	D	(
JOHN LEWIS	PNO	(
SONNY ROLLINS	SAX	(
HORACE SILVER	PNO	(
ART BLAKEY	D	(
WYNTON KELLY	PNO	(
BILL EVANS	PNO	(
JIMMY COBB	D	(
VICTOR FELDMAN	PNO	(
GEORGE COLEMAN	SAX	(
FRANK BUTLER	D	(
HANK MOBLEY	SAX	(
BOB DOROUGH	V	(
GEORGE BENSON	G	(
LENNY WHITE	D	(
BENNY MAUPIN	CLAR	(
JIM RILEY	PERC	(
JACK DEJOHNETTE	D	(
HARVEY BROOKS	B	(
CHARLES ALIAS	D	(
LARRY YOUNG	PNO	(
STEVE GROSSMAN	SAX	(
BILLY COBHAM	D	(
MICHAEL HENDERSON	B	(
AIRTO MOREIRA	PERC	(
GARY BARTZ	SAX	(
HERMETO PASCAL	PNO	(
KHAUL BALAKRISHNA	SITAR	(
REGGIE LUCAS	G	(
SEAK LAWSON	ORG	(
MTUME	PERC	(
BADAL ROY	TAB	(
CARLOS GARNETT	SAX	(
BIHARI SHARMA	SITAR	(
LONNIE SMITH	D	(
WILLIAM HART	D	(
SONNY FORTUNE	WIND	(
HAROLD WILLIAMS JR	K SITAR	(
DAVID LIEBMSN	FLT	(
PETE CASEY	G	(
DOMINIQUE GAUMONT	G	(
CEDRIC LAWSON	PNO	(
JOHN STOBBLEFIELD	SAX	(
BERNARD PURDIE	D	(
CORNEL DUPREE	G	(
WALLY CHAMBERS	HCA	(
ELVIN JONES	D	(
BUSTER WILLIAMS	B	(
JOE BECK	B	(
DAVE SCHILDKRAUT	SAX	(
J J JOHNSON	TROM	(
LUCKY THOMPSON	SAX	(
SAMMY FIGUEROA	PERC	(
BILL EVANS	SAX	(
MARCUS MILLER	B	(
BARRY FINERTY	G	(
MIKE STERN	G	(
RANDY HALL	SYN V	(
ROBERT IRVINE	K	(
FELTON CREWS	B	(
VINCENT WILBURN	D	(

Title	Year	Label	No.	Label	No.
MUSSINGS OF MILES	1955	PRESTIGE	US 7007		
MILES	1955	PRESTIGE	US 7014		
BAGS GROOVE	195	PRESTIGE	US 24012		
COOKIN	195	PRESTIGE	24053		
RELAXIN'	195				
MILES DAVIS DBL	195	PRESTIGE	24001		
SOULIN	195				
WORKIN'	195	PRESTIGE	7166		
STEAMIN'	195	PRESTIGE	7200		
WORKIN' & STEAMIN'	1974	PRESTIGE	US 24034		
ODYSSEY	19	PRESTIGE	US 7540		
MODERN JAZZ GIANTS	19	PRESTIGE	US 7650		
CONSEPTION	19	PRESTIGE	US 7744		
MILES AHEAD	19	PRESTIGE	US 7822		
OLEO	19	PRESTIGE	US 7847		
WALKIN'	195	PRESTIGE	US 7608		
KIND OF BLUE	1959	CBS	US 8163		UK 62066
PORGY & BESS	1959	CBS	US 8085		UK 62108
SKETCHES OF SPAIN	1959	CBS	US 8271		UK 62327
ROUND ABOUT MIDNIGHT	1962	CBS	US 8649		UK 62323
FRIDAY AT THE BLACKHAWK	19	CBS			UK 62306
FRIDAY AT THE NIGHTHAWK VOL2	19	CBS			UK 62307
IN PERSON AT THE BLACKHAWK	19	CBS	US C2S 820(DBL)		
MILESTONES	1959	CBS	US 9428		UK 62308
MILES & MONK AT NEWPORT	19	CBS	US 8978		UK 62389
SOMEDAY MY PRINCE WILL COME	1962	CBS	US 8465		UK 62104
AT CARNEGIE HALL	19	CBS	US 8612		
SEVEN STEPS TO HEAVEN	19	CBS	US 8851		UK 62170
QUIET NIGHTS	1964	CBS	US 8906		
IN EUROPE	1964	CBS	US 8983	EMBASSY	UK 31103
MY FUNNY VALENTINE	1965	CBS	US 9106		UK 62510
FOUR & MORE	1966	CBS	US 9253		UK 62655
MILES AT ANTIBES	19	CBS			UK 62390
MILES AHEAD	19	CBS	US 8633		UK 62496
FACETS	19	CBS			UK 62637
IN BERLIN	19	CBS			UK 62976
TRUMPET GIANTS	1964	NEWJAZZ S	8296	STATESIDE	UK 10103
PLAYS RICHARD RODGERS	1964			STATESIDE	UK 10111
PLAYS RICHARD RODGERS	1976	PRESTIGE	US 7332	CBS	UK 88029
ESP	1965	CBS	US 9150		UK 62577
PLAYS FOR LOVERS	1966	PRESTIGE	US 7352	STATESIDE	UK 10168
GREATEST HITS	1966	PRESTIGE	US 7457		
MILES SMILES	1967	CBS	US 9401		UK 62933
THE SORCERER	1967	CBS	US 9532		UK 63097
NEFERTITI	1968	CBS	US 9594		UK 63248
MILES IN THE SKY	1968	CBS	US 9628		UK 63352
AT NEWPORT	19	CBS			UK 63417
FILLES OF KILIMANJARO	1968	CBS	US 9750		UK 63551
GREATEST HITS	1969	CBS			UK 63620
IN A SILENT WAY	1969	CBS	US 9857		UK 63630
BITCHES BREW	1970	CBS	US PG26		UK 66236
BITCHES BREW	197	CBS			30997
LIVE AT THE FILLMORE(DBL)	1971	CBS			UK 66257
JACK JOHNSON(SOUNDTRACK)	1971	CBS	US 30455		UK 70089
LIVE EVIL(DBL)	1972	CBS	US 30954		UK 67219
ON THE CORNER	1973	CBS	US 31906		UK 65246
IN CONCERT(DBL)	1973	CBS			UK 68222
ESSENTIAL MILES DAVIS	1973	CBS			UK 66310
AT NEWPORT	197	CBS			UK 66417
TALLEST TREES(DBL)	1973	PRESTIGE			24012
COLLECTORS ITEMS (DBL)	1973	PRESTIGE			24022
BASIC MILES	197	CBS	US 32025		UK 65343
JAZZ AT THE PLAZA	1974	CBS	US 32470		UK 65778
BIG FUN	1974	CBS	US 32866		UK 88024
BLACK BEAUTY	1974	CBS			
GET UP WITH IT	1974		33236		UK 88092
CLASSICS (DBL)	1975	CBS			UK 88138
AGHARTA (DBL)	1975	CBS	US 33967		UK 88159
BIRD & MILES	1975	DJM	DJB26062		DJML 062
EARLY MILES	1975	PRESTIGE	US 7674		UK PR7674
MILES DAVIS	1975	BLUENOTE			81501/2
ALL STARS	1976	BEPPO			BEP 502
AT THE BIRDLAND	1976	BEPPO			BEP 501
DAVIS PARKER GILLESPIE	1976	VOGUE			VKD5529
GREEN HAZE	1976	PRESTIGE			24064
WATER BABIES	1977	CBS	US 34396		
DIRECTIONS	197	CBS			UK 88514
WITH JOHN COLTRANE	197	CBS			UK 88029
TUNE UP	19	PRESTIGE	PRESTIGE 24077		
WITH LEE KOWITZ,TEDDY CHARLES	197	EZZTHETIC	7013		
PARIS FESTIVAL	197	CBS			
PRE BIRTH OF THE COOL	197	JAZZLIVE	BLJ 8003		
AT BIRDLAND	197	JAZZLIVE	BLJ 8023		
STAN GETZ & MILES DAVIS	197	KINGS OF JAZZ			KLJ 20013
& JOHN COLTRANE	197	UNIQUE JAZZ	UJ 19		
ARCHIVES OF JAZZ VOL 3	19	PATHE			FR 062 95819
BIRTH OF THE COOL	19	CAPITOL			40678
BLUE HAZE	19	PRESTIGE			054 10134
COMPLETE BIRTH OF THE COOL	19	PATHE			FR 062 80798
DIG	19	PRESTIGE			24054
MILES OF JAZZ	19	TRIP			5015
SOMETHING ELSE	19	CBS			81595
LIVE AT THE PLUGGED NICKEL	19	CBS			

(CONTINUED)

D27 MILES DAVIS D27

LEE KONITZ SAX (PONGAEA 19 CBS
SAL MOSCA PNO (JAZZ TRACK 19 CBS US 1268
BILLY BAHER G (MOUNTAINS IN THE SKY 19 ATCO US SD1622
ARNOLD FISHKIN B (CIRCLE IN THE ROUND 1979 CBS US 36278
JIMMY RANEY G (THE MAN WITH HORN 1981 CBS US 36790
DICK MINESON B (
ED SHAUGHNESSY D (TEDDY CHARLES VIBES(JAMES MOODY SAX (KAI WINDING TROM (
JUNIOR COLLINS HRNS (GERRY MULLIGAN SAX (AL HAIG PNO (JOE SCHULMAN B(
SANDY SIEGELSTEIN HRNS (NELSON BOYD B (GUNTHER SCHULLER HRNS (AL McKIBBON B(
MIKE ZWERIN (JOHN LEWIS (KENNEYH HAGOLD (BREW MOORE (
GENE RAMAY B (STAN GETZ SAX (BILL EVANS PNO (PAUL CHAMBERS B(
ART TAYLOR D (BILL BARBER TUBA (DANNY BANK CLAR (JIMMY BUFFINGTON HRNS(
RONEO PENQUE WIND (

D27A PAUL DAVIS D27A

PAUL DAVIS V (ALL (A) LITTLE BIT OF P D 197 BANG US 223
JIMMY JOHNSON G (D (B) PAUL DAVIS 1974 BANG US 226
DAVID HOOD B (D (C) RIDE 'EM COWBOY 1975 BANG US 401
BARRY BECKETT K (D (D) SOUTHERN TRACKS & FANTASIES 1976 BANG US 405
ROGER HAWKINS D (D (E) SINGER OF SONGS 1977 BANG US 410 UK SHOT 002
BARRY BAILEY G (C (F) PAUL DAVIS 1980 BANG US 36094
CHARLIE OWEN STEEL (C (G) COOL NIGHT 1981 ARISTA US 9578
TOM ROBB B (C
CHRIS ETHRIDGE B (C ROY YEAGER D (C AUBURN BURRELL G (C

D27B SANDY DAVIS D27B

PAUL 'SANDY' DAVIS V G K B D(AB (A) INSIDE EVERY FAT MAN 1974 EMI UK EMC 3029
PETER SKELLERN PNO (A (B) BACK ON MY FEET AGAIN 1975 EMI UK EMC 3070
ALAN CAWDEROY G (A
MARTIN BRILEY G (AB ANDREW PRYCE JACKMAN K (A GORDON HUNTE G (B
DELISLE HARPER B (B ROY DAVIES K (B STEVE FERRONE D (B
CHRIS MERCER SAX (B AVERAGE WHITE BAND V (B

D28 SPENCER DAVIS D28

SPENCER DAVIS G V (ALL (A) EVERY LITTLE BIT HURTS 1965 WING UK WL 1165
MUFF WINWOOD G V B(ABCDEFGHIKNO (A) THEIR FIRST LP 1965 SONET SW1401 FONTANA TL 5242
STEVE WINWOOD K G V(ABCDEFGHIKNO (A) THEIR FIRST LP 19 ISLAND RI GER 201658
PETER YORK D (ABCDEFGHIJKLMNO (B) SECOND ALBUM 1966 FONTANA UK TL 5295
EDDIE HARDIN K (JLM (C) AUTUMN 66 1966 FONTANA UK STL 5359
PHIL SAWYER G (1967 (D) GIMME SOME LOVIN' 1967 UA US 3578
RAY FENWICK G (JLM1 (D) GIMME SOME LOVIN' 1967 UA US 6578
NIGEL OLSSON D (69/70 (E) I'M A MAN 1967 UA US 3589
DEE MURRAY B (68/70 (E) I'M A MAN 1967 UA US 6589
GARY COOPER G (L (F) THE BEST OF SPENCER DAVIS 1967 ISLAND UK ILPS 9070
CHARLIE McCRACKEN B (LM (G) VERY BEST OF 1968 UA US 443E
TONY COE CLAR (M (H) HERE WE GO ROUND THE MULBERY BUSH 1968 UA UK SULP1186 FR RI 29637
BRIAN DEXTER ACC (M (I) GREATEST HITS 1968 UA US 3461
MARTYN FORD HRNS (M (I) GREATEST HITS 1968 UA US 6641
DORIS TROY V (M (J) WITH THEIR NEW FACE ON 1968 UA US 6652
LIZA STRIKE V (M (J) WITH THEIR NEW FACE ON 1968 UA 1192
RUBY JAMES V (M (J) LETS DANCE WITH 19 SUNSET GERM 50141
DAVE HYNES D (68/69 (K) HEAVIES 1969 UA US 6691
TRAFFIC (H (L) GLUGGO 1973 VERTIGO UK 6360088 GER6360102
ANDY ELLISON (H (L) GLUGGO 1973 VERTIGO US 1015
PETER JAMESON (X (M) LIVING ON A BACK STREET 1974 VERTIGO UK 6360 105
SNEAKY PETE STEEL (Y (M) LIVING ON A BACK STREET 197 VERTIGO UK 6499 978 US 1021
LARRY KNECHTEL K (YX (N) GIMME SOME LOVIN' 1973 ISLAND GER 85897ZT
KENNY SALMON ORG (A (O) SOMEBODY HELP ME 1973 ISLAND GER 85925 ET
TRET FURE G (Y ( )POP CHRONIK (DBL) 1975 ISLAND IMP VOL4
ANDY WAY B (Y ( ) POP CHRONIK (DBL) 1977 ISLAND IMP 87213
GIB GILBEAUX FDL (Y ( ) SPENCER DAVIS GROUP 19 SONET GP 9916
LEE SKLAR B (Y ( ) BEST OF 19 SONET GP 9992
CHUCK FINDLEY HRNS (Y (EP) SPENCER DAVIS KEEP ON RUNNING 1978 ISLAND UK 1EP10
ERNIE WATTS SAX (Y (EP) EVERY LITTLE BIT HURTS 1965 FONTANA UK
GEORGE BOHANNON TROM (Y (EP) YOU PUT THE HURT ON ME 1965 FONTANA UK TF17444
HARRY EDISON TPT (Y (EP) SITTIN' & THINKIN' 1966 FONTANA UK TF17463
BARRY HESSEL (X (X) ITS BEEN SO LONG (S DAVIS SOLO) 1971 UA 34416 UK UAS 29177
(X) ITS BEEN SO LONG 1971 MEDIARTS US 4111
RICHARD LANDIS (X (Y) MOUSETRAP (S DAVIS SOLO) 1972 UA UK UAS 29361
(Z) NOSTALGIA VOL 2 197 UA FR 29629

D29 BRIAN DAVISON D29

BRIAN DAVISON D V (A (A) EVERY WHICH WAY 1970 CHARISMA UK CAS1021 MERCURY US 61340
GRAHAM BELL V K (A
GEOFF PEACH WIND (A ALAN CARTWRIGHT B (A JOHN HEDLEY G (A

D29A TIM DAWE D29A

TIM DAWE G V (A (A) PENROD 1970 STRAIGHT US S1058
ARNIE GOODMAN K (A
CHRIS KEBECK G (A DON PARRISH B (A CLAUDE MATHIS D (A

D29B DAWN PATROL D29B

DAWN V (A (A) DAWN PATROL (EP) 198 DINOSAUR DD005
STEVE (A
REBECCA B V (A NEON IAN G V (A

D30 JIMMY DAWKINS D30

JIMMY DAWKINS G V (ALL (A) TRANSATLANTIC 770 1972 BLUE HORIZON UK
WITH (A) TRANSATLANTIC 770 1975 CONTEMPO CLP 513
JOE JAMMER G (A (A) TRANSATLANTIC 770 1978 SONET SNTF 758
ROSA DOTSON V (A (A) TRANSATLANTIC 770 197 EXCELLO US 8024
BOB BRUNNING B (A (B) FAST FINGERS 19 DELMARK DS 623
CECIL MOSS TPT (A (C) ALL FOR BUSINESS 1971 DELMARK DS 634
MIKE VERNON PERC (A (D) BLISTERING 1977 DELMARK US 641
PETE WINGFIELD K (A (E) I WANT TO KNOW 1977 MCM IMP 900 290
TONY STEVENS B (A (F) COME BACK BABY 19 MCM FR 900 295
BILLY GRAHAM TROM (A (G) TRIBUTE TO ORANGE 1971 BLACK & BLUE 33538
(CONTINUED)

D30 JIMMY DAWKINS (CONTINUED) D30

NOVELLE WILLIAMS V K (A
REG ISADORE D (A — A G'BUBBLES' WHITE G (A — ANDREW'BIG VOICE' ODOM V (C
OTIS RUSH G (C — JIM CONLEY SAX (C — SONNY THOMPSON PNO (C
ERNEST GATEWOOD B (C — ROBERT CROWDER D (C — CHARLES HICKS D (C
CLARENCE 'GATEMOUTH' BROWN G(G — COUSIN JOE PNO (G — MAC THOMPSON B (G
TED HARVEY D (G — VELMA SMITH V (A — CHRIS MERCER SAX (A
DICK PARRY SAX (A

D30A BOBBY DAY D30A

BOBBY DAY V (A — (A) ROCKIN' ROBIN — 19 CLASS US LP 5002

D30B DAY BLINDNESS D30B

DAVE MITCHELL V D (A — (A) DAY BLINDNESS — 19 STUDIO 10 DBX 101
GARY PIHL G V (A
FELIX BRIA V B K (A

D31 DAY OF THE PHOENIX D31

HANS LAURIDSEN V (AB — (A) WIDE OPEN N WAY — 1970 SONET SLPS 1510
ERIK RASMUSSEN B V (A — (A) WIDE OPEN N WAY — 197 GREENWICH UK GSLPR1002
HENRIK FRIIS NIELSEN D (AB — (B) THE NEIGHBOUR'S SON — 1972 SONET SLPS 1541
KARSTEN LYNG G (AB — (B) THE NEIGHBOUR'S SON — 197 CHAPTER ONE UK CNSR 812
OLE PREHN G V (AB
KENNETH KNUDSEN PNO (A — PETER FRIIS NIELSEN B (A — TONY REEVES B (B

D31A DAYLIGHT D31A

MIKE SILVER G V (A — (A) DAYLIGHT — 1971 RCA UK SF 8194
STEVE HATTON G MAND V (A
CHRISSIE QUAYE G (A — TONY CARR D (A — SPIKE HEATLEY B (A
LYN DOBSON WIND (A

D31B STU DAYE D31B

STU DAYE (A — (A) FREE PARKING — 1976 CBS US 33936

D31C DAYSHIFT D31C

(A) LIVING IN THE UK (EP) — 1980 WOT WOT1

D31D DAYTON D31D

(A) CUTIE PIE — 1981 LIBERTY US LT 1093

D32 DEAD BOYS D32

STIV BATORS V (AB — (A) YOUNG LOUD & SNOTTY — 1977 SIRE UK 9103 329
JOHNNY BLITZ D (AB — (A) YOUNG LOUD & SNOTTY — 1978 SIRE UK SRK 6038
CHEETAH CHROME G (AB — (B) WE HAVE COME FOR YOUR CHILDREN — 1978 SIRE UK SRK 6054
JIMMY ZERO G (AB — (B) WE HAVE COME FOR YOUR CHILDREN — 1978 SIRE GER 28 387
JEFF MAGNUM B (AB
FELIX PAPPALARDI V (B — JOEY RAMONE V (B — DEE DEE RAMONE V (B

D33 DEAD FINGERS TALK D33

BOBO PHOENIX V (A — (A) STORM THE REALITY STUDIOS — 1978 PYE UK NSPH 24
ANDY LINKLATER B (A
JEFF PARSONS G (A — TONY CARTER D (A

D33A DEAD KENNEDYS D33A

EAST BOY RAY G (A — (A) FRESH FRUIT FOR ROTTING VEGETABLES 1980 CHERRY REDUK RED10 FAULTY US70014
TED D (A — (EP) CALIFORNIA — 198 FAST UK FAST12
KLAUS FLOURIDE B V (A
JELLO BIAFRA V (A — PAUL ROESSLER K (A — NINOTCHKA K (A
ROCKY MOUNTAIN ARSENAL CHOIR(A

D33B DEAD SEA FRUIT D33B

DAVE'BEANO'LASHMAR G V (A — (A) DEAD SEA FRUIT — 1967 CAMP UK 603001
CLIVE KENNEDY V (A
CHRISTOPHER HALL B G V (A — JOHN TOWNSEND PERC V (A — SI CLIFFORD K (A

D33C DEADLY EARNEST & THE HONKY TONK HEROES D33C

(A) DEADLY EARNEST — 1979 PACIFIC ARTS 7134+ WHEELER 80

D33D DEADLY NIGHTSHADES D33D

HELEN HOOKE G V FDL K SYN (AB — (A) THE DEADLY NIGHTSHADES — 1975 RCA US BPL1 0955
ANNE BOWEN G V PERC(AB — (B) F & W — 1976 RCA US BPL1 1370
PAMELA BRANDT V B (AB

D33E DEAF AIDS D33E

CRAIG WAITES (A — (A) HEROES EP — 1980 CONSPIRACY UK CONS 1 12
JOHN O'ROURKE (A
GRAHAM HOGGARD (A — TERRY GAMWELL (A

D34 DEAF SCHOOL D34

TIM WHITTAKER D (BC — (A) DONT STOP THE WORLD — 1975 WB UK K 56364
ENRICO CADILLAC V (ABC — (B) SECOND HONEYMOON — 1976 WB UK K 56280
CLIVE LANGER G (ABC — (AB) DONT STOP/2ND HONEYMOON — 197 WB US 2LS 3011
MAX RIPPLE K (ABC — (C) ENGLISH BOYS WORKING GIRLS — 1978 WB UK K 56450
ERIC SHARK V (CB — (C) ENGLISH BOYS WORKING GIRLS — 197 WB US 3169
BETTE BRIGHT V (ABC
PAUL PILNICK G B ACC (B — IAN RITCHIE SAX (BC — STEVE LINDSEY B (BC

D34B TONE DEAF & THE IDIOTS D34B

TONE DEAF V (A — (A) CATASTROPHE ROCK — 1979 BLUE ANGEL UK BLISS 1
BEAN HOWARD G V (A
LEW KNEE B V (A — HARRY 'DEAD' TREES D V (A — NIGEL BROMLEY D (A
BUNK DOGGER G V (A — ROGER WYATT G (A

D34C CHRISTOPHER DEAN D34C

CHRISTOPHER DEAN (— (A) IMAGES — 197 MAINSTREAM US 302

D35 ELTON DEAN D35

ELTON DEAN SAX (ALL — (A) ELTON DEAN — 1971 CBS UK 64539
PHIL HOWARD D (A — (B) THEY ALL BE ON THIS OLD ROAD — 1977 OGUN OG 410
MARK CHARIG CORNET(A — (C) CRUEL BUT FAIR — 1977 COMPENDIUM NOR FID 4
NEVILLE WHITEHEAD B (A — (D) EL SKID — 1978 VINYL VS 103
MIKE RATLEDGE K (A — (E) ROGUE ELEMENTS — 1978 OGUN UK OG 527
ROY BABBINGTON B (A — (F) CHEQUE IS IN THE POST — 1977 OGUN UK OG 610
ALAN SKIDMORE (D — (G) NINESENSE — 1977 OGUN UK OG 900
HUGH HOPPER B (CE — (H) HAPPY DAYS — 1978 OGUN UK OG 910
KEITH TIPPETT PNO (CB
JOE GALLIVAN (CF — CHRIS LAURENCE B (BD — JOHN MARSHALL D (D
KENNY WHEELER TPT (F — LOUIS MOHOLO D (B

D35A **DEBRIS** D35A

(A) DEBRIS 19 STATIC DISPOSAL PIG0000

D36 **CHRIS DE BURGH** D36

CHRIS DE BURGH G V (ALL (A FAR BEYOND THESE CASTLE WALLS 1975 A&M US 4516 UK AMLH68284
RAY JACKSON MAND/HCA (A (B) SPANISH TRAIN & OTHER STORIES 1975 A&M US 4568 UK AMLH68343
CHRIS LAURENCE B (AB (C) AT THE END OF A PERFECT DAY 1977 A&M US 4647 UK AMLH64647
LIZA STRIKE V (A (D) CRUSADER 1979 A&M US 4746 UK AMLH64746
JOY YATES V (A (E) EASTERN WIND 1980 A&M US 4815 UK AMLH64815
KEN FREEMAN SYN (AB (F) BEST MOVES 1981 A&M UK AMLH68532
MADELINE BELL V (A (G) THE GETAWAY 1982 A&M UK AMLH68549
RUPERT HINE SYN (G
TONY REEVES B (B CHRIS MERCER SAX (B MICK EVE SAX (B IAN BAIRNSON G (B
DAVID PATON B (D STUART ELLIOTT D (D MIKE MORAN K (D ANDREW POWELL PNO (D
BARRY DE SOUZA D (AB BRIAN ODGERS B (A LENNOX LAINGTON PERC (AB RONNIE LEAHY K (A
RAY GLYNN G (AB B J COLE STEEL (A TONY HYMAS K (B PHILIP GOODHAND TAIT K(AB
TIM WYNVEEN G V (E GLENN MORROW K (E AL MARNIE B V (E JEFF PHILLIPS D (E
JOHN HELLIWELL SAX (E DICK SMITH PERC (E ERIC ROBERTSON K (E LISA DELBELLO V (E
COLLEENA PHILLIPS V (E SHARON LEE WILLIAMS V (E DAVID HENTSCHEL SYN (B PHIL PALMER G (G
JOHN GIBLIN B (G STEVE NEGUS D (G DAVID CADDICK PNO (G

D36A **MIKE DEASY** D36A

MIKE DEASY V G K B(A (A) LETTERS TO MY MIND 1973 CAPITOL US 1170
JIM GORDON D (A
JIM KELTNER D (A
LEE SKLAR B (A JERRY SCHEFF B (A MAX BENNETT B (A MIKE MELVOIN K (A
LARRY KNECHTEL K (A JAY DEE MANESS STEEL(A ART MANSON G (A GARY COLEMAN PERC(A
JIM HORN HRNS (A CHUCK FINDLEY HRNS (A JACKIE KELSO HRNS (A OLLIE MITCHELL HRNS(A
PAUL HUBINON HRNS (A SLYDE HYDE HRNS (A LEW McCREARY HRNS (A PLAS JOHNSON HRNS(A
VANETTA FIELDS V (A KATHY DEASY V (A ANNIE HENING V (A STEVE ADLER V (A
KATH WARD V (A CHARLES MERRIAM V (A TRIS JONS V (A MICHAEL CLOUGH V (A

D37 **DECAMERON** D37

DAVE BELL G B (ABCDE (A) DECAMERON 1973 VERTIGO UK 6360 097
DIK CADBURY B G V(BCDE (B) MAMMOTH SPECIAL 1974 MOONCREST UK CREST 19
JOHNNY COPPIN G K (ABCDE (C) THIRD LIGHT 1975 TRANSATLANTIC UK TRA 304
AL FENN HCA G B (ABCDE (D) BEYOND THE LIGHT 1975 MOONCREST UK CREST 28
GEOFF MARCH K V SAX(ABCDE (E) TOMORROWS PANTOMIME 1976 TRANSATLANTIC UK TRA 325
JOHN HALSEY D (BC
FRANK RICOTTI PERC (B JOHN MEALING K (C DUDU PUKWANA PERC (B MONGEZI FEZA PERC(B
MIKE WINFIELD HRNS (C GASPAR LAWAL PERC (B SHAMSI SARUMI PERC (B BOB CRITCHLEY D (E
ANDY ROBERTS G (A B J COLE STEEL (A IAN WHITMAN K (A TIMI DONALD D (A

D37A **DECEMBERS CHILDREN** D37A

DECEMBERS CHILDREN 19 MAINSTREAM US 6128

D37B **DECCENNIUM** D37B

GER BRANDS D (AB (A) SONG OF SAD TIMES 1974 NR 501
FRITS VAN UDEN ORG V(A (B) HIGHWAY SONG 1980 KILLROY NL 19923
JACQUE KESSELS G V (AB

D37C **DEDRINGER** D37C

J J HOYLE V (A (A) DIRECT LINE 1981 DINDISC UK DID 7
LEE FLAXINGTON B V K (A (B) MAXINE (DBL) 1982 DINDISC UK DID 11
NEIL HUDSON G (A KENNY JONES D (A AL SCOTT G (A

D38 **DE DANANN** D38

ALEC FINN ((A) DE DANANN 1977 DECCA UK SKL 5287
FRANKIE GAVIN ((B) MIST COVERED MOUNTAIN 1980 GAELLIN IR CEF 087
DOLORES KEANE (
JOHNNY McDONAGH (CHARLIE PIGGOTT (JOHNNY MOYNIHAN (TIM LYONS (
JACKIE DALLY (

D38A **JOEY DEE & THE STARLIGHTERS** D38A

JOEY DEE V (ALL PEPPERMINT TWISTERS 196 SCEPTER US 503
CARLTON LATIMORE K SAX(DOIN' THE TWIST 196 ROULETTE US RS25166
WILLIE DAVIS D V (HEY LETS TWIST 196 ROULETTE US RS25168
LARRY VERNIERI V (ALL THE WORLD IS TWISTIN' 196 ROULETTE US RS25171
DAVID BRIGATI V SAX(BACK AT THE PEPPERMINT LOUNGE 196 ROULETTE US RS25173
JIMI HENDRIX G (1 TWO TICKETS TO PARIS 196 ROULETTE US RS25182
JOEY DEE (SOLO) 19 ROULETTE US RS25197
DANCE DANCE DANCE (SOLO) 19 ROULETTE US RS25221
(1) LIVE 1966

D38B **GRAHAM DEE** D38B

GRAHAM DEE G V (A (A) SOMETHIN' ELSE 197 PYE UK NSPL 18570
FRANK RICOTTI PERC (A
RAY WARLEIGH WIND (A RICHY HITCOCK G (A SIMON MORTON PERC (A FRANK GIBSON D (A
JEAN GILBERT V (A PAUL HART K VLN (A LAWRENCE JUBER G (A KEVIN PEEK G (A
PAUL WESTWARD B (A GARRY TRAVERS V (A JOY YATES V (A

D39 **KIKI DEE** D39

KIKI DEE V (ALL (A) I'M KIKI DEE 1968 FONTANA UK STL 5455
BIAS BOSHELL K (GDJK (B) GREAT EXPECTATIONS 1970 TAMLA US TS303 UK STM 11158
ROGER POPE D (D (C) LOVING & FREE 1973 ROCKET US 3040 UK PIGL 5
JO PARTRIDGE G (D (C) LOVING & FREE 1973 MCA US 395
BRIAN HOLLAWAY G (G (D) IVE GOT THE MUSIC IN ME 1974 ROCKET US 3042 UK PIGL 10
ANDY DALBY G (G (D) IVE GOT THE MUSIC IN ME 1974 MCA US 458
B J COLE STEEL(CD (E) KIKI DEE 1974 SOUNDS SUPERB UK SPR 90030
ROGER BALL SAX (C (F) PATTERNS 1974 PHILIPS UK 6382 079
DAVEY JOHNSTONE G (CG (F) PATTERNS 1974 LIBERTY US LST 763
NIGEL OLSSON D (C (G) KIKI DEE 1977 ROCKET US 2257 UK ROLA 3
DOREEN CHANTER V (C (H) STAY WITH ME 1979 ROCKET US 3011 UK TRAIN 3
DAVE MATTACKS D (C (I) GREATEST HITS 1980 WARWICK UK WW 5092
DEE MURRAY B (CG (J) PERFECT TIMING 1981 ARIOLA UK 5050 US RCA 14180
KAY GARNER V (CD
PAUL KEOGH G (C JIMMY HALL K (C IRENE CHANTER V (CD JIM RYAN G (C
JOHN McBERNIE G (GERRY CONWAY D (C ELTON JOHN K (C LESLEY DUNCAN V (C
RONNIE LEAHY K (C LIZA STRIKE V (C PETE CLARKE D (D MIKE DEACON K (D

(CONTINUED)

D39 KIKI DEE (CONTINUED) D39

CISSY HOUSTON V (D — JOSHIE ARMSTEAD V (D — MAERETHA STEWART V (D — BARRY MORGAN PERC(D
JEFF TITMUS PERC (D — CLIVE FRANKS V (D — STUART EPPS V (D — BARRY ST JOHN V (D
BILLY LAWRIE V (D — PAUL VIGRASS V (D — GARY OSBORNE V (D — PHIL CURTIS B (DG
MELVIN GALE PERC (G — HUGH McDOWELL CELLO(G — RAY COOPER PERC (G — DAVID SANBORN HRNS(G
MICHAEL BRECKER HRNS (G — RANDY BRECKER HRNS (G — R & J STONE V (G — SUNNY LESLIE V (G
STEVE HOLLY D (GJ — JAMES NEWTON HOWARD (G — RICHARD TANDY SYN (G — TONY BURROWS V (G
BOB JENKINS D (J — GARY TWIGG B (J — FRANK RICOTTI PERC (J — PIP WILLIAMS G (J
PATRICK MORAZ K (J

D39A DEEP D39A

PSYCHEDELIC MOODS 196 PARKWAY US 7051

D39B DEEP FEELING (1) D39B

JOHN POLI PALMER VIBES(A
GORDON JACKSON G V (A
LUTHER GROSVENOR G V (A
JIM CAPALDI D V (A
DAVE MASON B V (A

(A) ROCK GENERATION VOL 8(2 TRACKS) 1971 BYG FR 529708

D39C DEEP FEELING (2) D39C

JOHN SWAIL'GUY DARRELL' V(A
DEREK ELSON K (A
MARTIN JENNER G V (A
DAVID GREEN B V FLT(A

(A) DEEP FEELING 1971 DJM DJLPS419

D39E DEEP FREEZE D39E

SHERRIE LAWRENCE PNO (A
ALAN JENKINS G B CLAR(A
GRAHAM SUMMERS D (A
ERICA STOCK PERC (A
MICK BUNNAGE V (A

(A) MY GERANIUMS ARE BULLETPROOF 1979 MOLE EMBARKING UK MOLE1

D40 DEEP PURPLE D40

JON LORD K (ALL
IAN PAICE D (ALL
RITCHIE BLACKMORE G [(ABCDEFGHIJ (KLNOPQST*VW
NICK SIMPER B (ABC*SIT
ROD EVANS V (ABCTSI
ROGER GLOVER B (DEFGHIJNOQ*STW
IAN GILLAN V (DEFGHIJNOQ*STW
DAVID COVERDALE V (KLMPRW
GLEN HUGHES B (KLMPRTW
TOMMY BOLIN G (MRT
$ RANDY CALIFORNIA G

$ REPLACED BLACKMORE IN US 1 NIGHT

(A) SHADES OF DEEP PURPLE 1968 PARLOPHONE UK PCS 7055
(A) SHADES OF DEEP PURPLE 1977 HARVEST UK AHSM 2016
(A) SHADES OF DEEP PURPLE 19 PATHE FR 066 04175
(A) SHADES OF DEEP PURPLE 1968 TETRAGRAMMATON US 102
(B) BOOK OF TALIESYN 1969 HARVEST UK SHVL 751
(B) BOOK OF TALIESYN 196 TETRAGRAMMATON US 107
(B) BOOK OF TALIESYN 19 PATHE FR 066 04000
(C) DEEP PURPLE 1969 HARVEST UK SHVL 759
(C) DEEP PURPLE 19 TETRAGRAMMATON US 119
(C) DEEP PURPLE 19 PATHE FR 066 90505
(D) CONCERTO FOR GROUP & ORCHESTRA 1970 HARVEST UK SHVL 767
(D) CONCERTO FOR GROUP & ORCHESTRA 1970 PATHE FR 90749 US WB 1860
(E) DEEP PURPLE IN ROCK 1970 HARVEST UK SHVL777 US WB 1877
(F) FIREBALL 1971 HARVEST UK SHVL793 US WB 2564
(G) MACHINE HEAD 1972 PURPLE UK TPSA 7504
(G) MACHINE HEAD 1972 PATHE FR 83261 US WB 2607
(H) MADE IN JAPAN 1972 PURPLE UK TPSP351 US 2701
(H) LIVE IN JAPAN 197 PURPLE 55067
(I) BEST OF 1972 SCEPTER US 18010
(J) WHO DO WE THINK WE ARE 1973 PURPLE UK TPSA7508 US WB 2678
(J) WHO DO WE THINK WE ARE 1973 PATHE FR 066 94140
(K) BURN 1974 PURPLE UK TPS3505 US WB 2766
(L) STORMBRINGER 1974 PURPLE UK TPS 3508
(L) STORMBRINGER 197 PATHE FR 96004 US WB 2832
(*) Mk 1 & 2 1974 PURPLE FR 188 94865
(M) COME TASTE THE BAND 1975 PURPLE UK TPSA 7515
(M) COME TASTE THE BAND 1975 PATHE FR 97044 US WB 2895
(N) 24 CARAT PURPLE 1975 PURPLE UK TPSM2002 FR 96424
(O) PURPLE PASSAGES 1972 WB US 2644
(P) MADE IN EUROPE 1976 PURPLE UK TPSA 7517
(P) MADE IN EUROPE 197 PATHE FR 98181 US WB 2995
(Q) POWER HOUSE 1977 PURPLE UK TPS3510 FR 60072
(R) LAST CONCERT IN JAPAN 1977 PURPLE UK P 10370
(S) THE SINGLES A's & B's 1978 HARVEST UK SHSM 2026
(T) WHEN WE ROCK WE ROCK 1978 WB US 3223
(V) DEEP PURPLE Mk 2 SINGLES 1979 PURPLE UK TPS 3514
(W) DEEPEST PUPLE 1980 HARVEST UK EMITV25 US 3486
(X) IN CONCERT (DDL) 1980 HARVEST UK SHDW412
(EP) NEW LIVE & RARE 1978 PURPLE UK PUR 137

D40A DEEP SIX D40A

( ) DEEP SIX 19 LIBERTY US LRP 3475

D40B DEF LEPPARD D40B

STEVE CLARK G (ABC
RICK SAVAGE B (ABC
PETE WILLIS G (ABC
RICK ALLEN D (ABC
JOE ELLIOTT V (ABC

(A) GETCHA ROCKS OFF (EP) 1979 BLUDGEON 001 RI VERTIGO 6059240
(B) ON THROUGH THE NIGHT 1980 VERTIGO UK 9102040 US MERCURY 3828
(C) HIGH & DRY 1981 VERTIGO UK 6359045 US MERCURY 4021

D40C DEFENDERS D40C

( ) PLAY THE BIG ONES(WILD WEEK END) 19 WORLD PACIFIC US WP 1810
( ) DRAG BEAT 19 DEL FI US DFLP 1242

D40D JACK DeJOHNETTE D40D

JACK DeJOHNETTE D G K SYN (ALL
JOHN ABERCROMBIE G (GHJK
GARY PEACOCK (I
KEITH JARRETT PNO (EI
MIROSLAV VITOUS B (
EDDIE GOMEZ B (K
LESTER BOWIE TPT (K
ALEX FOSTER SAX (J
MIKE RICHMOND B (GJ
WARREN BERNHARDT K (G
JOHN PURCELL WIND (N
CHICO FREEMAN WIND (N
PETER WARREN B (N

(A) THE DE JOHNETTE COMPLEX 1968 MILESTONE 9022
(B) HAVE YOU HEARD 19 MILESTONE 9029
(C) SORCERY 19 MILESTONE 9061
(C) SORCERY 19 PRESTIGE 10081
(D) COSMIC CHICKEN 1975 PRESTIGE 10094
(E) RUTS AND DAITYA 1975 ECM 1021
(F) GATE WAY 1975 ECM 1061
(G) UNTITLED 1976 ECM ECM 1074
(H) PICTURES 1977 ECM ECM 1079
(I) TALES OF ANOTHER 1977 ECM 1101
(J) NEW RAGS 1977 ECM ECM 1103
(K) NEW DIRECTION 1978 ECM ECM 1128
(L) SPECIAL EDITIONS 1980 ECM 1152
(M) NEW DIRECTIONS IN EUROPE 1980 ECM 1157
(N) TIN CAN ALLEY 1980 ECM 1189

D40E DEFUNKT D40E

Album	Year	Label	Country	Number
(A) DEFUNKT	1981	HANNIBAL	UK	1301

D41 DESMOND DEKKER D41

Member	Instr	
DESMOND DEKKER	V	(ALL
WITH		
BARRY HOWARD	V	
SAMMY JONES	V	

Album	Year	Label	Country	Number
(A) ISRAELITES	1975	CACTUS		CTLP 111
(A) ISRAELITES	19	UNI	US	73059
(B) DOUBLE DEKKER	1973	TROJAN		TRLD 401
(C) YOU CAN GET IT	1970	TROJAN		TRL 146
(D) SWEET 16 HITS	1978	TROJAN	UK	TRLS 154
( ) THIS IS	1969	TROJAN		TTL4
( ) BLACK & DEKKER	1980	STIFF	UK	SEEZ 26
( ) COMPASS POINTS	1981	STIFF	UK	SEEZ 36

D41A DELEGATES D41A

Album	Year	Label	Country	Number
(A) THE DELEGATES	197	MILESTONE	US	100

D42 DELFONICS D42

Member	Instr	
WILLIAM HART	V	(ALL
WILBERT HART	V	(ALL
RANDY CAIN	V	(
RITCHIE DANIELS	V	(
MAJOR FARRIS	V	(
BRUCE PETERSON	V	(

Album	Year	Label	Country	Number
(A) LA MEANS I LOVE YOU	1968	BELL UK SBLL106	US	1150
(B) SOUND OF SEXY SOUL	1969	BELL UK SBLL121	US	1151
(C) DELFONICS	1971	BELL	UK	SBLL 137
(D) SUPER HITS	1972	BELL	UK	BELLS 204
(D) SUPER HITS	197	PHILLY GROOVE	US	1152
(E) TELL ME THIS IS A DREAM	1973	BELL UK BELLS217	US	1154
(F) ALIVE & KICKING	1974	BELL UK BELLS245	US	1501
(G) LET IT BE ME	1975	SOUNDS SUPERB	UK	SPR 90078
( ) DIDN'T I BLOW YOUR MIND	19	PHILLIES		1153

D43 DEL VIKINGS D43

Member	Instr	
NORMAN WRIGHT	V	(
CORINTHIAN JOHNSON	V	(
DONALD BAKUS	V	(
DAVID LERCHEY	V	(
CLARENCE E QUICK	V	(

Album	Year	Label	Country	Number
COME GO WITH ME	19	DOT	US	DLP 3695
COME GO WITH ME	19	LUNAVERSE	US	LP 1000
COME GO WITH ME	19	CONTOUR	UK	2870 388
AND THE SONNETS	19	CROWN	US	CLP 5368
NEWIES & OLDIES	19	FEE BEE	US	205
SWINGING SINGING RECORD SESSION	19	MERCURY	US	MG 20353
THEY SING THEY SWING	19	MERCURY	US	MG 20314
(EPS)				
COME GO WITH US	19	DOT	US	DEP 1058
DEL VIKINGS	19	MERCURY	US	MEP 35A
THEY SING THEY SWING	19	MERCURY	US	EP1 3362

D43A DELIVERANCE D43A

Album	Year	Label	Country	Number
(A) TIGHTROPE	1979	GLOBAL		0063 215

Member	Instr	
DAVE McSPARREN	B	(A
JACQUES BELZING	G	(A
DANNY JANZ	V	(A
KEN JANZ	V	(A
SCOTT NEWTON	TPT	(A
GUY ROELLINGER	B	(A
ELMER LOUIS	PERC	(A
BOBBY STERN	SAX	(A
PAUL JANZ	V	(A
LEE HARPER	TPT	(A
HORST MULLER	PROD	(A

D44 DELLS D44

Member	Instr	
MARVIN JOHNSON	V	(
CHUCK BARKSDALE	V	(
VERNE ALLISON	V	(
JOHNNY CARTER	V	(
MIKE McGILL	V	(
JOHNNY FUNCHES	V	(

Album	Year	Label	Country	Number
THERE IS	19	CADET	US	804
GREATEST HITS	19	CADET	US	824
MUSICAL MENU	19	CADET	US	822
LOVE IS BLUE	1969	CADET	US	829
LIKE IT IS	19	CADET	US	837
FREEDOM MEANS	197	CADET	US	50004
SING DIONNE WARWICK	19	CADET	US	50017
SWEET AS FUNK CAN BE	1974	CADET	US	50021
GREATEST HITS	1974	CADET	US	50036
GIVE YOUR BABY	1974	CADET	US	50037
DELLS	1974	CADET	US	50046
CORNERED DBL	1977	DJM	UK	DJD 28032
BEST OF	1973	CHECKER	US	6467 303
MIGHTY MIGHTY	1975	CHESS US 60030	UK	9109 100
WE GOT TO GET TOGETHER	1975	CADET	US	6044
OH WHAT A NITE	19	VEE JAY	US	1010
OH WHAT A NIGHT	19	JOY UK JOYS186	US	BUDDAH5053
NO WAY BACK	19	MERCURY	US	SRM 11084
ITS NOT UNUSUAL	19	VEEJAY	US	1141
FACE TO FACE	19	ABC	US	AA 1113
LOVE CONNECTION	1978	mERCURY	US	SRM1 3711
THEY SAID IT COULN'T BE DONE BUT WE DID		MERCURY	US	SRM1 1145
NEW BEGINNINGS	1978	ABC	US	1100
I TOUCHED A DREAM	1980	20TH CENT	UK	T 618
WHATEVER TURNS YOU ON	1981	20th CENT		T 633
(EP) STAY IN MY CORNER	1980	CHARLY		CTD 110

D44A DELMORE BROTHERS D44A

Album	Year	Label	Country	Number
(A) BEST	19	KING	US	1C90

D44B DELTA CROSS BAND D44B

Member	Instr	
BILLY CROSS	G V	(A
TROELE JENSEN	G K V	(A
PREBEN FEDDERSEN	D	(A
SOREN ENGEL	B HRN	(A
SVEND ASMUSSEN	HRNS	(A
BOB CURLAN	HRNS	(A
ANNE GRETHE	HRNS	(A
JORGEN LANG	HRNS	(A

Album	Year	Label	Country	Number
(A) RAVE ON	1979	MEDLEY	EURO	6031
(B) UP FRONT	198	ARIOLA	GER	203 942

D45 DELTA FIVE D45

Album	Year	Label	Country	Number
(A) SEE THE WHIRL	1981	PRE	UK	PREX 6

D45A DEMIAN D45A

Member	Instr	
ROD PRINCE		
ROY COX	B V	(A
TODD POLTER	G V	(A
DAVID FORE	D	(A

Album	Year	Label	Country	Number
(A) DEMIAN	1971	ABC	US	718

D45B DEMIAN D45B

Album	Year	Label	Country	Number
(A) ROCK STAR FARM	19	STARBURST		ARC 3301

D45C MAX DEMIAN BAND D45C

Member	Instr	
PAUL ROSE	G V	(A
KIRT PENNEBAKER	B V	(A
JIM LEFEVRE	K G V	(A
DANIEL HOWE	G K V	(A
PETE SIEGEL	D	(A

Album	Year	Label	Country	Number
(A) TAKE IT TOO THE MAX	1979	RCA		PL 13273

D45D **DELUXE BLUES BAND** D45D

(A) LIVE AT HALF MOON PUTNEY 1981 HOT BOX UK HOT1

D46 **DEMICK & ARMSTRONG** D46

HERBIE ARMSTRONG V G (AB | (A) LITTLE WILLIE RAMBLE | 1971 MAM UK MAM 1001
ROD DEMICK V G STEEL HCA(AB | (B) LOOKING THROUGH | 1972 A&M 2504 UK AMLH68098
WITH
GORDON SMITH G V (AB | HENRY SPINETTI D PERC (B | TONY KNIGHT D (A
DAVID WATKINS PNO (A | ALICE PEPPER V (| SUE GLOVER V
SUNNY LESLIE V (| KAY GARNER V (

D46A **DEMICS** D46A

JIMMY WEATHERSTONE D (AB | (A) TALKS CHEAP (EP) | 1979 READY CAN RR001
LAIN ATKINSON B (AB | (B) THE DEMICS | 1980 INTERCAN CAN IC 1010
ROB BRENT G (A
STEVE KOCH (B | TOM TRUMUTH K (B | KEITH WHITTAKER V (AB
STEVE KOCH (B

D46B **DEMON** D46B

DAVE HILL V (| (A) NIGHT OF A DEMON | 1981 CARRERE UK CAL 126
MAL SPOONER G (| (B) THE UNEXPECTED GUEST | 1982 CARRERE UK CAL 129
LES HUNT G (
CHRIS ELLIS B (| JOHN WRIGHT D (

D47 **DEMON FUZZ** D47

SMOKEY ADAMS V (A | (A) AFREAKA | 1971 JANUS US JLS 3029
STEVEN JOHN D (A | (A) AFREAKA | 1971 DAWN UK DNLS 3013
RAY RHODES K (A | (EP) I PUT A SPELL ON YOU | 1970 DAWN UK DNX 2504
SLEEPY JACK JOSEPH B (A
W RAPHAEL JOSEPH G (A | CLARENCE BROOMS CROSDALE TROM (A | PADDY COREA WIND (A
AYINDE FOLARON CONGA (A

D48 **DEMON THOR** D48

TOMMY'DEMON'FORTMAN V (AB | (A) ANNO 1972 | 1974 UA UK UAS 29393
STEPHEN NUESCH K (B | (B) WRITTEN IN THE SKY | 1974 UA UK UAS 29496
GEFF HARRISON V (
VEIT MARCUS K (| CLAUDE THOMAN D (B | PETER BISCHOF V (B
OLIVER FREYTAG V (B | GEFF HARRISON V (B

D48A **DEMONS** D48A

MARTIN RAPPOPORT D PERC(A | (A) DEMONS | 1977 MERCURY US SRM1 1164
MARTIN BUTLER G (A
ELIOT KIDD G V PERC(A | ROBBIE TWYFORD B V (A | BOB JONES G V (A
LIZA BURNS V (A | CRAIG LEON PROD K(A

D49 **SANDY DENNY** D49

SANDY DENNY V (ALL | (A) ALL OUR OWN WORK | 1968 PICKWICK UK SHM 813
TONY HOOPER G V (A | (B) FOTHERINGAY | 1970 ISLAND UK ILPS9125 US A&M4269
DAVE COUSINS G V K(A | (C) SANDY DENNY | 1970 SAGA UK 8153
RON CHESTERMAN B (A | (C) SANDY DENNY | 1977 NOVA GERM 6 22968AK
KEN GUDMAND D (A | (C) SANDY DENNY (*) | 1978 MOONCREST UK CREST 28
TREVOR LUCAS G V (BDF | (D) NORTHSTAR GRASS MAN & THE RAVENS | 1971 ISLAND UK ILPS9165 US A&M4317
GERRY CONWAY D (BDF | (E) SANDY | 1972 ISLAND UK ILPS9207 US A&M4371
LINDA (THOMPSON) PETERS V(BE | (F) LIKE AN OLD FASHIONED WALTZ | 1973 ISLAND UK ILPS9258 US 9340
IAN WHITEMAN K (D | (G) RENDEZVOUS | 1977 ISLAND UK ILPS 9433
TONY REEVES B (D | (*) HAS 1 TRACK EXTRA
BARRY DRANSFIELD V (D
ROBIN DRANSFIELD V (D | ROYSTON WOOD V (D | ROGER POWELL D (D | LADYBIRDS V (G
BUDDY EMMONS STEEL(D | TIMI DONALD D (EG | DAVE SWARBRICK VLN (E | JERRY DONAHUE G V (BDFG
SNEAKY PETE KLEINOW STEEL(E | RABBIT BUNDRICK K (EFG | DAVE PEGG B (FG | DAVE MATTACKS D (FG
DANNY THOMPSON B (F | ALAN SKIDMORE (F | PAT DONALDSON B V(BDEFG | RICHARD THOMPSON G V (DEFG
IAN ARMIT B (F | JEAN ROUSSEL K (F | DIZ DISLEY G (F | STEVE WINWOOD K (G
JUNIOR MARVIN G (G | BROTHER JAMES G (G | JIMMY HAINES (G | FRANK RICOTTI G (G
JOHN GILLASPIE (G | DICK CUTHELL (G | BILLIE LIVSEY K (G | BOB WESTON G (G
JESS RODEN V (G | SUE GLOVER V (G | SUNNY LESLIE V (G | KAY GARNER V (G
CLAIRE TORRY V (G | BENNIE GALLAGHER V (G | GRAHAM LYLE V (G

D50 **DEODATO** D50

EUMIR DEODATO K (ALL | (A) PRELUDE | 1973 CTI CTL 10 US 6021
RON CARTER B (AB | (B) DEODATO 2 | 1973 CTI CTL 17 US 6029
STANLEY CLARKE B (AB | (C) IN CONCERT | 1974 CTI CTL 21 US 6041
BILLY COBHAM D (ABD | (D) WHIRLWINDS | 1974 MCA UK MCG3518 US 410
AIRTO MOREIRA PERC (AC | (E) VERY TOGETHER | 1976 MCA UK MCG2774 US 2219
JOHN FROSK (A | (E) VERY TOGETHER | 19 BARCLAY FR 414004
RUBENS BASSINI PER (BD | (F) LOVE ISLAND | 1978 WB UK K56416 US BSK 3132
MARVIN STAMM TPT (ABD | (G) ARTISTRY | 1975 MCA MCF2587 US 457
GARNETT BROWN TROM (AB | (H) FIRST CUCKOO | 1975 MCA MCF 2728 US 491
WAYNE ANDRE TROM (ABF | (H) FIRST CUCKOO | 197 BARCLAY FR 410039
GEORGE STRAKEY TROM (A | (I) 2001 | 1972 CTI CTI 7081
MARKY MARKOWITZ TPT (A | (J) NIGHT CRUISER | 1980 WB US BSK3467 GERM 56848
BILL WATRONS TROM (A | (K) KNIGHTS OF FANTASY | 1979 WB US 3321
PAUL FAULISE HRNS (A
JOE SHEPLEY TPT (AB | BILL BUFFINGTON HRN(ABDF | JOHN TROPEA G(ABCED | PETER GORDON HRNS (A
JOHN GUILING B (BD | GERRY CHAMBERLAIN TROM(F | TONY LEVIN B (D | HUBERT LAWS FLT (AB
PHIL BODNER WIND (AD | GEORGE MARGE WIND (ABD | ROMEO PENQUE WIND(ABDF | BURT COLLINS HRNS (B
JAY BERLINER G (A | RICK MAROTTA D (BF | GILMORE DEGAP PERC (BD | RAY BARRETTO CONGA(A
JON FADDIS HRNS (BD | VICTOR PAZ HRNS (BD | ALAN RUBIN HRNS (BD | TONY STUDD HRNS (B
BROOKS TILLOTSON HRNS (BFD | JOE TEMPERLEY HRNS (BD | LARRY CARLTON G (F | RAY GOMEZ G (FJ
POPS POPWELL B (F | HARVEY MASON D (F | JIMMY MAELEN PERC (FJ | CHARLIE CONRAD PERC (F
VICTOR FELDMAN PERC (F | RAY ARMANDO PERC (F | JOE CORRERO D (F | AL McKAY G (F
VERDINE WHITE B (F | PHILIP BAILEY PERC (F | GORDON EDWARDS B (F | JERRY DODGION FLT (F
JOEL KAYE FLT (F | WALLY KANE FLT (F | JOHN GATCHELL TPT (F | RANDY BRECKER TPT (F
BOB MILLIKAN TPT (F | SAM BURTIS TROM (DF | TONY PRICE TUBA (DF | NICK REMO D (D
JOHN ECKERT TPT (D | LARRY SPENCER TPT (D | URBIE GREEN TROM (D | ARTIE KAPLAN WIND (D
GARY GRANGER B (J | STEPHEN DANIELS PERC (J | GEORGE PARRISH G (J | PLATINUM HOOK V (J
SERGIO DIAS G (J | DAVID BRAVO K (J | SKIPP INGRAM B (J | VICTOR JONES G (J
RONALD BELL SAX (J | KEITH O'QUINN TROM (J | HARVEY ESTRIN FLT (J | LOU MARINI SAX (J
STRING SECTION (DJ

D50A DEPECHE MODE D50A

(A) SPEAK & SPELL 1981 MUTE UK STUMM 5

D51 DEPRESSIONS D51

(A) THE DEPRESSIONS 1978 BARN UK 2314 105
(B) IF YOU KNOW WHAT I MEAN(AS D Ps) 1978 BARN UK 2314 107

'AMMER SMITH G (A
RICO THE KNIFE G (A
DAVE BARNARD B V (AB
KROBAR GARVEY D (AB
ERIC WRIGHT G V (B
TONY MAYBERRY G V (B

D51A LOUIS DEPRESTIGE D51A

(A) LE MONDE EST ROCK 1980 MOTORS FR 77017

LOUIS DEPRESTIGE G (A
FRANCOIS AUGER D (A
DOMINIQUE PERRIER PNO (A
PATRICK JOUASSIN G (A
GEORGE RODI SYN (A
ALAIN HATOT SAX (A

D51B ROBERT DERBY D51B

(A) I'M NORMAL 1980 CATCHALOT US 111

ROBERT DERBY (A

D52 DEREK & THE DOMINOES D52

(A) LAYLA & OTHER ASSORTED LOVE SONGS 1971 ATCO US SD2 704
(A) LAYLA & OTHER ASSORTED LOVE SONGS 1971 POLYDOR GER 2625 005
(A) LAYLA & OTHER ASSORTED LOVE SONGS 1977 RSO US 3801 UK 2671 110
(A) LAYLA & OTHER ASSORTED LOVE SONGS 1977 RSO US 3801
(A) LAYLA & OTHER ASSORTED LOVE SONGS 197 POLYDOR 2612 014
(B) LIVE IN CONCERT 1973 POLYDOR UK 2659 020
(B) LIVE IN CONCERT 1973 POLYDOR GER 2671 101
(B) LIVE IN CONCERT 197 RSO US SO 28800

ERIC CLAPTON G V (AB
CARL RADLE B (AB
BOBBY WHITLOCK K (AB
JIM GORDON D (AB
DAVE MASON G V (LIVE
DUANE ALLMAN G (A

D53 RICK DERRINGER D53

(A) ALL AMERICAN BOY 1973 BLUE SKY US 32481 UK EPC 65831
(B) SPRING FEVER 1975 BLUE SKY US 33423 UK SKY 80733
(C) DERRINGER 1976 BLUE SKY US 34181 UK SKY 81458
(D) SWEET EVIL 1977 BLUE SKY US 34470 UK SKY 81847
(E) LIVE 1977 BLUE SKY US 34848 UK SKY 82130
(F) IF YOU WEREN'T SO ROMANTIC 1978 BLUE SKY US 35075 UK SKY 82464
(G) GUITARS & WOMEN 197 BLUE SKY US 36092 UK SKY 83746
(H) FACE TO FACE 1980 BLUE SKY US 36551 UK SKY 84462
(I) LIVE IN CLEVELAND 1977 BLUE SKY US PRO265

RICK DERRINGER G V (ALL
VINNY APPICE D (CDEI
DANNY JOHNSON G (CDEI
KENNY AARONSON B (CDEFGI
MYRON GROMBACHER D (FG
TASHA THOMAS V (C
MAERETHA STEWART V (C
NEIL GERALDO PNO (G
JIMMY WILCOX D V (H
BENJY KING K V (H
ROGER POWELL SYN (G
BOBBY CALDWELL D (AB
PAUL HARRIS SYN K(A
DAN HARTMAN V (BF
TASHA THOMAS V (A
TOOTS THIELMAN HCA (B
JOHNNY WINTER G (B
DONNIE KISSELBACH B V (H
LANI GROVES V (A
EDGAR WINTER SAX SYN K V(AB
DORIS STILL V (B
JOE WALSH G (A
JOHN SIEGLER B (B
MARK CUNNINGHAM G (F
KASIM SULTON B V (G
CARL HALL V (A
JOHN SIOMOS D (B
DAVID JOHANSEN HCA (B
JOE VITALE D (A
ALLEN NICHOLS V (B
TODD RUNDGREN V (G
KENNY PASSERELLI B (A
PAUL PRESTOPINO MAND V(B
JOE LALA PERC(A
DAVID BROMBERG G (A
CHICK COREA SYN(B

D53A MICHAEL DESBARRES D53A

(A) I'M ONLY HUMAN 1980 DREAMLAND US 15001 UK 2394 279

MICHAEL DESBARRES G V(A
PAUL DELPH K V(A
NIGEL HARRISON B (A
JOHN GOODSALL G (A
RIC PARNELL D V (A

D53B DESERTERS D53B

(A) THE DESERTERS 1981 CAPITOL US ST 12164

D53C JACKIE DESHANNON D53C

(A) JACKIE DESHANNON 1963 LIBERTY US 7320
(B) THIS IS 196 IMPERIAL US 12286
(C) YOU WON'T FORGET ME 196 IMPERIAL US 12294
(D) IN THE WIND 196 IMPERIAL US 12296
(E) BREAKING IT UP 1965 LIBERTY US 7390
(F) ARE YOU READY FOR THIS 196 IMPERIAL US 12328
(G) NEW IMAGE 196 IMPERIAL US 12344
(H) FOR YOU 196 IMPERIAL US 12352
(I) ME ABOUT YOU 196 IMPERIAL US 12386
(J) WHAT THE WORLD NEEDS NOW 1965 IMPERIAL US 12404
(K) LAUREL CANYON 196 IMPERIAL US 12415
(L) C'MON LIVE A LITTLE 1967 LIBERTY US 7430
(M) LONELY GIRL 1968 SUNSET US 5225
(N) PUT A LITTLE LOVE IN YOUR HEART 1969 IMPERIAL US 12442
(O) TO BE FREE 1970 IMPERIAL US 12453
(P) SONGS 1971 CAPITOL US ST 772
(Q) JACKIE 1972 ATLANTIC US 7231
(R) YOUR BABY IS A LADY 1973 ATLANTIC US 7303
(S) NEW ARRANGEMENT 1975 CBS US 33500
(T) YOU'RE ONLY THE DANCER 1977 AMHERST US 1010
( ) JACKIE DE SHANNON 19 SUNSET US 5322
( ) THE VERY BEST OF 19 UA US LA434
( ) HERES JACKIE 19 SUNSET US 1029

JACKIE DESHANNON V G(ALL
RON TUTT D (S
LARRY KNECHTEL K SYN(S
JOHN KHAN B (S
MIKE DEASY G (SP
WADDY WACHTEL G (S
JESSE ED DAVIS G (S
MICHAEL STEWART G (S
JOE CLAYTON PERC (S
LAURA CREAMER V (S
BOB CLAIR FLT (S
MARK CREAMER V (S
SUSAN STEWART V (S
KENNY RANKIN G (S
BRIAN WILSON V (S
MARILYN WILSON V (S
RANDY EDELMAN V (SP
PETER MARSHALL B (S
GARY DALTON G (S
BUDDY EMMONS STEEL (S
LEE SKLAR B (S
BARRY FASMAN SYN (S
VICTOR FELDMAN VIBES (S
DANNY KOTCH G (P
DICK ROSSMINI G (P
JERRY JUMONVILLE SAX (P
CHARLES CHALMERS V (Q
CISSY HOUSTON V (Q
RENELLE STAFFORD V (Q
JOHN CHRISTOPHER G (Q
RUSS TITLEMAN G (K
BISHOP HEYWOOD D (Q
BARRY WHITE V (K
JOHN STEWART XYLO (Q
ARIF MARDIN ACC (Q
BRYAN GAROFALO B (P
CLYDIE KING V (P
SANDRA RHODES V (Q
DEIDRE TUCK V (Q
REGGIE YOUNG G (Q
HAROLD BATTISTE PNO (K
MIKE LEACH B (Q
PAUL HUMPHREY D (K
DENZIL LAING G (Q
DON McALLISTER V (K
SEYCHELLES SINGERS V (S
RUSS KUNKEL D (P
ALBHY GALUTEN K (Q
DONNA RHOADS V (Q
VANETTA FIELDS V (P
MAC REBBENACK PNO (K
BOBBY WOODS PNO (Q
CRAIG TARWATER B (K
LARRY McDONALD PERC (Q
BRENDA DAVIES V (K
BWIA SUNSET BAND (Q

D54 ANDY DESMOND D54

(A) LIVING ON A SHOE STRING 1975 KONK KONK 103
(B) ANDY DESMOND 1978 ARIOLA ARL 5001

ANDY DESMOND V G (AB
RON LAWRENCE B (AB
NICK TREVISICK D (B
TOM KING V G (B
DYAN BIRCH V (B
KEITH NELSON BANJO(B
BARRY ST JOHN V (B
MICK WEAVER K (B
FRANK COLLINS V (B
DEBI DOSS HCA (B
DAVE MARKEE B (B
LOZ NETTO G (B
BONNIE WILKINSON V (B
JACK EMBLOW ACC (B
TERRY JONES HRNS (B
PAUL CARTWRIGHT PERC(AB
NICKY PAYN HCA SAX (B
IAN LYNN SYN V (B
GRAHAM COLLYER G (B

(CONTINUED)

D54 **ANDY DESMOND** (CONTINUED) D54

NOEL McCALLA V (B GRAHAME SMITH VLN (B SHIRLEY RODEN V (AB IAIN WHITMORE V (B
LUCY KLEE V (B GINNY KLEE V (B NEIL McBAIN D (A EDDY SPENCE K (A
PHIL PALMER G (A RICK LLOYD MAND G (A RICHARD GARRETT V (A PAMELA TRAVIS V (A
ALAN HOLMES WIND (A JOHN GOSLING K (A DAVE DAVIES G V (A

D54A **DESPARADOS** D54A

(A) THE DESPARADOS 1981 CHARISMA UK CLASS11

D55 **DESPERATE BYCYCLES** D55

DANNY WIGLEY V K (A
NICKY STEPHENS B HCA (A
DAN ELECTRO G (A JEFF TITLEY D (A

(A) REMORSE CODE 1980 REFILL UK RR6

D56A **JIMMY DESTRI** D56A

JIMMY DESTRI G V (A
CLEM BURKE D (A
JOHN SIEGLER B (A TOMMY MORRONGIELLO G (A EARL SLICK G (A CARLOS ALOMAR G V(A
MICHAEL KAMEN K V (A CHRIS STEIN G HCA(A DONNA DESTRI V (A DEBBIE HARRY V (A
SASHA KAMEN V (A JOEY WILSON V (A

(A) HEART ON A WALL 1981 CHRYSALIS CHR 1368

D56B **JIMMY DESTRY & DESTINY** D56B

JIMMY DESTRY (A

(A) GIRLS ROCK'N' ROLL & CARS 1980 MILLENIUM 7753

D57 **DETECTIVE** D57

BOBBY PICKETT B (ABC
TONY KAYE K (ABC
MICHAEL DES BARRES V (ABC
JON HYDE D V (ABC
MICHAEL MONARCH G (ABC

(A) DETECTIVE 1977 SWANSONG US SS8417 UK 59405
(B) IT TAKES ONE TO KNOW ONE 1978 SWANSONG US SS8504 UK 59406
(C) LIVE 1978 SWANSONG US LAAS 002

D57A **DETERGENTS** D57A

(A) THE MANY FACES OF THE DETERGENTS 19 ROULETTE US 25308

D57B **DETONATORS** D57B

(A) NEED YOU LOVE EP 197 LOCAL LP1

D57C **DETROIT EMERALDS** D57C

ABE TILLMAN V (ALL
JAMES MITCHELL V (ALL
IVORY TILLMAN V (ALL

(A) YOU WANT IT YOU GET IT 1972 JANUS UK 6310 207
(B) ABE JAMES & IVORY 1973 WESTBOUND UK 6309 101
(C) LET'S GET TOGETHER 1978 ATLANTIC UK K 50452
(D) FEEL THE NEED 1977 WESTBOUND UK K 50372

D57D **DEUTSCH AMERIKANISCHE FREUNDSCHAFT(D A F)** D57D

ROBERT GORL D (BCD
W SPELMANS G SYN V(B
GABI DELGADOOLOPEZ V (BCD
C HAAS B SAX SYN(B

(A) EIN PRODUKT DAR D.A.F. 19
(B) DIE KLEINEN UND DIE BOSEN 1980 MUTE STUMM1
(C) ALLES IST GUT 1981 VIRGIN UK V2202 GER 203 644
(D) GOLD UND LIEBE 1981 VIRGIN UK 2218 GER 204 165

D57E **HARI DEUTER** D57E

HARI DEUTER (A

(A) SILENCE IS THE ANSWER 1981 KUCKUCK 049/050

D58 **DEVIANTS** D58

MICK FARREN V (AB
SID BISHOP (A1
DUNCAN SANDERSON (A1C
RUSS HUNTER D (AB1C
M J McDONNELL (A
DENNIS HUGHES (A
PAUL RUDOLPH G (AC
STEPHEN SPARKES (A
DICK HECKSTALL SMITH SAX (A
GEORGE (A
PETE BROWN (A TONY FERGUSON (A JIMMY ASHWORTH (A
KARL DALLAS (A ANDREW JOHNS (A CORD REES B G V(A

(A) DISPOSABLE 1968 STABLE UK SLP 7001
(A) DISPOSABLE 1969 SIRE US 97005
(B) PTOOFF 1969 UNDERGROUND IMPRESARIOS IMP1
(B) PTOOFF 1969 SIRE US 97001
(B) PTOOFF 1969 DECCA UK SKLR 4993
(C) DEVIANTS 1969 TRANSATLANTIC UK TRA 204
(C) DEVIANTS 1978 LOGO UK MOGO 4001
(C) No3 197- SIRE US 97016
( ) SCREWED UP(EP) 19 STIFF UK LAST 4

D58A **DEVILS ANVIL** D58A

(A) HARD ROCK FROM THE MIDDLE EAST 19 CBS US 9464

D58B **KARLA DEVITO** D58B

KARLA DEVITO (A

(A) IS THIS A COOL WORLD OR WHAT 1981 EPIC US 37014 UK 84841

D59 **DEVO** D59

MARK MOTHERSBAUGH G V K(ALL
BOB MOTHERSBAUGH G V (ALL
BOB CASALE G K V(ALL
GERALD CALE K V (ALL
ALAN MYERS D (ALL
BRIAN ENO PROD (A

(A) Q.ARE WE NOT MEN A. WE ARE DEVO 1978 VIRGIN UK 2106 US WB BSK 3239
(B) DUTY NOW FOR THE FUTURE 1979 VIRGIN UK 2115 US WB BSK 3337
(C) FREEDOM OF CHOICE 1980 VIRGIN UK 2162 US WB BSK 3435
(D) DEVO LIVE(MINI LP) 1981 VIRGIN UKOVED1 US WB BSK 3584
(E) NEW TRADITIONALISTS 1981 VIRGIN UK 2191 US WB BSK 3595

D59A **DEXY'S MIDNIGHT RUNNERS** D59A

KEVIN ROWLAND V (
GROCK D (
PETE WILLIAMS B (STEVE SPOONER HRNS (J B HRNS (
JIMMY PATERSON HRNS (

(A) SEARCHING FOR THE YOUNG SOUL REBELS 1980 PARLOPHONE UK PCS 7213

D59B **CLIFF DE YOUNG** D59B

CLIFF DE YOUNG V (A
JOE OSBORN B (A
VICTOR FELDMAN PERC (A DENNIS BUDIMIR G (A BEN BENAY G (A
LARRY MUHOBERAC PNO (A BROOKS HUNNICUTT V (A NORMAN KURBAN PNO V(A
DAVID KEMPER D (A DAVID HUNGATE B (A ART MUNSON G (A
GEORGE BOHANON TROM (A OSCAR BRASHEAR TPT (A JACKIE KELSO SAX (A
VALERIE CARTER V (A

(A) CLIFF DE YOUNG 1975 MCA US 432

D59C **DIAMOND** D59C

(A) DIAMOND 1974 PARAMOUNT US 1021

D59D **DHARMA BLUES BAND** D59D

MIKE KING K (A
JOHN HILLARY G V (A
GARY COMPTON HCA (A

(A) DHARMA BLUES 1969 MAJOR MINOR SMCP5017

D60 DYAN DIAMOND D60

DYAN DIAMOND V G (A — (A) IN THE DARK 1978 MCA US 3053 UK MCF 2875
CRAIG MAGEE G (A
JERRY ACKERMAN B (A — JOSEPH FITZGERALD K (A — RANDY WHELPLEY D (A
CHRIS DARROW G MAND(A

D61 DIAMOND HEAD D61

SEAN HARRIS G V (AB — (A) LIGHTNING & THE NATIONS 198 FAN CLUB ONLY?
BRIAN TATLER G (AB — (B) LIVING ON BORROWED TIME 1982 MCA UK DH1001
COLIN KIMBERLEY B (AB — (EP) DIAMOND LIGHTS 19
DUNCAN SCOTT D (AB — (EP) FOUR CUTS 1982 MCA UK DH101

D61A DIAMOND REO D61A

NORM NARDINI G B V(A — (A) DIAMOND REO 1975 BIG TREE US 89507
BOB McKEAG G V (A
ROB JONES D V (A — FRANK JOHNS D V (A

D62 THE DIAMONDS D62

DAVE SOMERVILLE V (AB — POP HITS 19 WING CAN 12178
MIKE DOUGLAS V (B — AMERICA'S No 1 SINGING STYLISTS 19 MERCURY US MG 20309
JOHN FELTON V (B — MEET PETE RUGOLO 19 MERCURY US MG 20368
EVAN FISHER V (B — OLD WEST 19 MERCURY US MG 60159
BILL REED V (A — STROLL 19 MERCURY US EP 13390
TED KOWALSKI V (Z — DIAMONDS 19 BRUNSWICK US EP 71031
PHIL LEAVITT V (A — (A) 1955/58 (B) 1959>

D63 MANU DIBANGO D63

MANU DIBANGO SAX PERC V K(ALL — (A) SOUL MAKOSSA 1972 ATLANTIC US 7267
JOBY JOBS D (A — (B) OBOSO 1973 LONDON UK SH 8451
ROBBIE SHAKESPEARE B (J — (C) MAKOSSA MAN 1974 ATLANTIC US 7276
MALEKANI GERRY G (A — (D) MAKOSSA MUSIC 1975 CREOLE UK CRLP 503
VAL DOUGLAS B (J — (E) MANU 76 1976 DECCA FR 362 001
GEOFF CHUNG B G K (J — (F) SUPER KUMBA 1976 DECCA FR 360 052
CLYDE BULLARD B (J — (G) AFROVISION 1976 DECCA UK SKLR 5296
SLY DUNBAR D (J — (G) AFROVISION 1978 ISLAND US 9526
MIKEY BOO RICHARDS D (J — (H) A L'OLYMPIA DBL 1978 FIESTA FR 360 099/100
CRUSHER BENNETT PERC (J — (I) SUN EXPLOSION 1978 DECCA UK SKLR 5303
STICKY PERC (J — (J) GONE CLEAR 1980 ISLAND UK ILPS 9539
MIKEY MAO CHUNG G (J — (K) ABASSADOR 1981 ISLAND UK ILPS 9658
WILLIE LINDO G (J
ANSEL COLLINS K (J — BARRY ROGERS TROM (J — LOU MARINI SAX (J — RANDY BRECKER TPT (J
JON FADDIS TPT (J — ED BYRNE TROM (J — WAYNE ARMOND G (J — PETER ASHBOURNE K (J
MIKE LAWRENCE TPT (J — ROBBIE LYN K (J — CLIVE HUNT K (J — GWEN GUTHRIE V (J
YOLLANDA McCULLOUGH V (J — BRENDA WHITE V (J — YVONNE LEWIS V (J — FRANK FLOYD V (J
JOCELYN BROWN V (J — LONG MANFRED B 'AC — PATRICE GALAS PNO (C — SLIM PEZIN G (C
HARRY GATIBELZA ORG (C — LUCIEN DOBAT D (C — FREEDY N'KOUNKOU PERC (C — MANU RODANET (AC
FREDDY MARS PERC (A — PIERRE ZOGO G (A — GEORGES ARVANITAS PNO (A — JERRY MALEKANY G (C
PHILIPPE NEVEU B (C — CLAUDE VAMUR D (C

D63A DICK & DEE DEE D63A

DICK ST JOHN V (— YOUNG & IN LOVE 19 WB US 1500
DEE DEE SPERLING V (— TURN AROUND 19 WB US 1538
THOU SHALT NOT STEAL 19 WB US 1586
SONGS WEVE SUNG 19 WB US 1623
TELL ME 19 LIBERTY US 7236

D63B DICKEY DOO & THE DONTS D63B

GERRY'DICKEY DOO'GRANAHAN V(— ( ) THE MADISON 196 UA US UAS 6094
JERRY GRANT V (— ( ) TEEN SCENE 196 UA US UAS 6097
HARVEY DAVIS V (
AL WAYS V (— RAY GANGI V (

D63C TOM DICKIE & DESIRES D63C

TOM DICKIE G V (A — (A) COMPETION 1981 MERCURY US 14918 EURO 6337 168
MICHAEL ROY G V (A
MICKY CURRY D (A — JON MACEY B V (A — GARY CORBETT K (A
RONNIE BELL PERC (A — JOE MARTINO G (A

D64 DICKIES D64

LEONARD PHILIPS K V (AB — (A) THE INCREDIBLE SHRINKING DICKIES 1979 A&M UK AMLH64742
STAN LEE G V (AB — (B) DAWN OF THE DICKIES 1979 A&M UK AMLE68510
BILLY CLUB V B (AB
KARLOS KABALLERO D (AB — CHUCK WAGON K G (AB — BONITA BUTTER V (A
JOHN HEULETT PROD (B

D64A JAMES LUTHER DICKINSON D64A

JAMES LUTHER DICKENSON (A — (A) DIXIE FRIED 19 ATLANTIC US 8299

D65 DICTATORS D65

HANDSOME DICK MANITOBA V (ABC — (A) GO GIRL CRAZY 1975 EPIC US 33348 UK 80767
ANDY SHERNOFF B K V (ABC — (B) MANIFEST DESTINY 1977 ASYLUM US 7E1109 UK 53061
SCOTT KEMPER G (— (C) BLOOD BROTHERS 1978 ASYLUM US 147 UK K53083
ROSS FUNICELLO G V (ABC — (D) LIVE,FUCK 'EM IF THEY CANT TAKE 1981 REACH OUT US 102
RITCHIE TEETER D V (BC
MARK MENDOZA B (B — STU BOY KING D (A — SCOTT'TOP TEN' KEMPER G (A
PETRONIUS WOOCS K (B — MURRAY KRUGMANN PROD (ABC
SANDY PEARLMAN PROD (ABC — ALAN GLOVER K (A

D66 BO DIDDLEY D66

BO DIDDLEY'ELIAS McDANIELS' G V(ALL
JEROME GREEN MARACAS
OTIS SPANN PNO (— BILLY BOY ARNOLD HCA (— FRANK KIRKLAND D (— THE DUCHESS G (
CHUCK BERRY G (— HOWLIN' WOLF V HCA(* — MUDDY WATERS G V (* — COOKIE VEE V (X
RICHARD EVANS B (X — CLIFFORD DAVIS SAX (X — WILLIE HENDERSON SAX (X — GENE BARGE SAX (X
STEVE GALLOWAY TROM (X — FRANK GORDON TPT (X — MURRAY WATSON TPT (X — ARTHUR HOYLE TPT (X
PHILIP UPCHURCH G (X — GERALD SIMS G (X — TENNYSON STEPHENS PNO (X — DERF REKLAW RAHEEM CONGA(X
ROBERT CROWDER D (X — BRIAN GRICE D (X — MARY ANN STEWART V (X — MARYLYN HAYWOOD V (X
VIVIAN HARRELL V (X — ROY WOOD B (X — EDDIE HARDIN ORG (X — RAY FENWICK G (X
KEITH SMART D (X — CHARLES GRIMAR CONGA(X — NIGEL GRAINGE PERC (X — GREGORY TAYLOR V (X
CHARISE TAYLOR V (X — JUANITA BUCKNER V (X — CRYSTAL BRAKE V (X — ANGELA SMITH V (X
LYNN MOORE V (X — TOM THOMPSON G (Z — RICHARD DAVIS B (Z — ED O'DONNELL D (Z

(CONTINUED)

SHUGGIE OTIS	G	(Z	DAVE ARCHULETTA	ORG	(Z	TERRY GOTTLIEB	B	(Z	JOHNNY OTIS	D	(Z
CARMINE APPICE	D	(V	TIM BOGERT	B	(V	BILLY JOEL	K	(V	ALBERT LEE	G	(V
ROGER McGUINN	G	(V	DANIEL MOORE	V	(V	TED NEELEY	V	(V	ELVIN BISHOP	G	(V
JOE COCKER	V	(V	CARKY LAING	PERC	(V	ALVIN LEE	G	(V	KEITH MOON	D	(V
MATTHEW MOORE	V	(V	LESLIE WEST	G	(V	JOHN TROPEA	G	(Z	CARL LYNCH	G	(Z
ERNEST HAYES	K	(Z	WILBUR BASCOMB	B	(Z	JIMMY JOHNSON	D	(Z	MONTEGO JOE	PERC	(Z
ESMOND EDWARDS	PERC	(Z	JOE NEWMAN	TPT	(Z	JOHN BELLO	TPT	(Z	MARVIN STAMM	TPT	(Z
JON FADDIS	TPT	(Z	IRWIN MARKOWITZ	TPT	(Z	HARRY DIVITO	TROM	(Z	GARNETT BROWN	TROM	(Z
DOMICK GRAVINE	TROM	(Z	WILLIS JACKSON	SAX	(Z	JOHN LEONE	SAX	(Z	TONY PRICE	TUBA	(Z
MICHAEL PICKETT	HCA	(Z	GENE BIANCO		(Z	J R BAILEY	V	(Z	KEN WILLIAMS	V	(Z
MELVIN KENT	V	(Z									

HAVE GUITAR WILL TRAVEL	196	CHECKER	US		2974
IN THE SPOTLIGHT	196	CHECKER	US		2976
IN THE SPOTLIGHT	1964	PYE	UK	NPL	28034
IS A GUNSLINGER	1963	PYE INT	UK		280
IS A GUNSLINGER	196	CHECKER	US		2977
A LOVER	196	CHECKER	US		2980
IS A TWISTER	196	CHECKER	US		2982
BO DIDDLEY	1963	PYE	UK		28026
BO DIDDLEY	196	CHESS	UK		704
BO DIDDLEY	196	CHECKER	US		2984
BO DIDDLEY	196	CHECKER	US		1431
BO DIDDLEY RIDES AGAIN	1963	PYE	UK		28029
BEACH PARTY	1963	PYE	UK		28032
(**)TWO GREAT GUITARS	1964	PYE	UK		28047
(**)TWO GREAT GUITARS	1964	CHECKER	US		2991
HEY GOOD LOOKING	1964	CHESS	UK	CRL	4002
BO DIDDLEY & COMPANY	196	CHECKER	US		2985
SURFIN' WITH BO DIDDLEY	196	CHECKER	US		2987
SURFIN' WITH BO DIDDLEY	196	MARBLE ARCH	UK	MAL	751
ROAD RUNNER	196	CHECKER	US		2988
16 ALL TIME HITS	1964	PYE INT	UK		28049
16 ALL TIME HITS	196	CHECKER	US		2989
LET ME PASS	1965	CHESS	UK	CRL	4507
HEY BO DIDDLEY	196	PYE	UK		28025
HEY BO DIDDLEY	1967	GOLDEN GUINEA	UK		GGO358
HEY BO DIDDLEY	1968	MARBLE ARCH	UK		MAL814
HEY BO DIDDLEY	196	CHECKER	US		2992
500% MORE MAN	196	CHECKER	US		2996
ORIGINATOR	196	CHECKER	US		3001
GO BO DIDDLEY	196	CHECKER	US		3006
GO BO DIDDLEY	196	CHECKER	US		1436
GO BO DIDDLEY	1959	LONDON	UK	HAM	2230
BOSS MAN	196	CHECKER	US		3007
(*) SUPER BLUES BAND	1968	CHECKER	US		3010
BLACK GLADIATOR	196	CHECKER	US		3013
BLACK GLADIATOR	196	CHECKER	US		50004
(X) LONDON SESSIONS	1972	CHECKER	UK	6499	476
(X) LONDON SESSIONS	197	CHESS	US		50029
GOT ANOTHER BAG OF TRICKS	1973	CHECKER	UK	6467	304
GOT ANOTHER BAG OF TRICKS	1973	CHESS	US		2CH60005
GOLDEN DECADE	1973	CHESS	UK	6310	123
ANOTHER DIMENSION	1975	CHESS	US		50001
(V) 20thANNIVERSARY	1976	RCA			1042
(V) 20thANNIVERSARY	1976	RCA		APLI	1225
(W) WHERE IT ALL BEGAN	197	CHESS	US		50016
(Z) BIG BAD BO	197	CHECKER	US		50047
I'M A MAN(DBL)	1977	M F	US		202/2
CHESS MASTER	1981	CHESS	UK		4003
EPS					
CHUCK & BO	1963	PYE	UK	NEP	44009
HEY BO DIDDLEY	1963	PYE	UK	NEP	44014
THE STORY OF BO DIDDLEY	1964	PYE	UK	NEP	44019
IS A LUMBERJACK	1964	PYE		NEP	44031
DIDDLING	1964	PYE	UK	NEP	44036
IM A MAN	1965	CHESS	UK	CRE	6008
ROOSTER STEW	1966	CHESS	UK	CRE	6023
BO DIDDLEY	19	CHESS	US		5125

D66A

DIESEL

D66A

ROB VUNDERLINK G V (A
MARK BOON G V (A
FRANK PAPENDRECHT B V (A
PIM KOOPMAN D K V(A

(A) WATTS IN A TANK 1980 REGENCY 19315 POLYDOR 2925 092

D66B

DIESEL SMOKE

D66B

(A) DIESEL SMOKE 1963 STARDAY US 250

D66C

DIESTELMANN

D66C

STEFAN DIESTELMANN G V (A
BERND KLEINOW HCA (A
DIETRICH PETZOLD V (A
MEMPHIS SLIM PNO V (A
RUDIGER PHILLIP B (A
VOLKER SCHLOTT (A
WOLFGANG FIEDLER PNO (A

(A) FOLK BLUES BAND 19 AMIGA 855633

D66D

DIF JUZ

D66D

(A) HUREMICS 1981 4AD UK BAD 109

D67

DIGA RHYTHM BAND

D67

MICKEY HART	D	(A						
JIM LOVELESS	PERC	(A						
RAY SPIEGEL	PERC	(A						
JOY SCHULMAN	PERC	(A	ZAKIR HUSSAIN	PERC	(A	PETER CARMICHAEL	PERC	(A
ARSHAD SYED	PERC	(A	JORDAN AMARANTHA	PERC	(A	VINCE DELEACHO	PERC	(A
TOR DIETRICHSON	PERC	(A	ASHIM CHAUDHURI	PERC	(A			

(A) DIGA RHYTHM BAND 1976 UA ROUND UK UAS 29975
(A) DIGA RHYTHM BAND 1976 UA ROUND US RXLA 600G

D68 RICHARD DIGANCE D68

Member	Instr	Albums
RICHARD DIGANCE	G V	(ALL
JOHN O'CONNOR	G V	(ACF
BARRIEMORE BARLOW	D V	(F
RICK KEMP	B V	(F
DOUG MORTER	G V	(CDF
MIKE LEWIS	K	(F
DAVE COOKE	PNO	(C
ENGLISH TAPESTRY	V	(D
PETER CURTIS	B K	(C
ALAN BROOKS	D	(C
MICHAEL CHAPMAN	G	(D
DIK CADBURY	B V	(D
MIKE BIEVENEU	PNO	(D

Album	Year	Label	Country	Number
(A) PISCES	1971	TRAILER	UK	LER 2025
(B) IN CONCERT 74	1976	TRANSATLANTIC	UK	TRASAM 35
(C) ENGLANDS GREEN & PLEASANT LAND	1974	TRANSATLANTIC	UK	TRA 277
(D) HOW THE WEST WAS LOST	1975	TRANSATLANTIC	UK	TRA 289
(E) TREADING THE BOARDS	1975	TRANSATLANTIC	UK	TRA 306
(F) LIVE AT QUEEN ELIZABETH HALL	1978	CHRYSALIS	UK	CHR 1187
(G) COMMERCIAL ROAD	1979	CHRYSALIS	UK	CHR 1262
( ) RICHARD DIGENCE	1975	MERCURY	US	1 1042

Member	Instr	Albums
PHIL MILNER	B V	(D
MARTIN JENKINS	BANJO FDL	(D
GERRY MORRIS	B	(D
JOHN REDPATH	D	(D
NIGEL PEGRUM	PERC	(D
ALEX ATTERSON	V HARMONIUM	(D
PAUL RODRIGUEZ	K	(D

D68B DOUG DILLARD D68B

Member	Instr	Albums
DOUG DILLARD	BANJO G	(ALL
BERNIE LEADON	G	(A
ANDY BELLING	K	(ABC
MILT HOLLAND	PERC	(A
RED MITCHELL	B	(A
GENE CLARK	HCA	(A
DON BECK	G	(A
SKIP CONOVER	G	(E
DAN CRARY		(D
MARK SORGER		(D
VASSAR CLEMENTS	FDL	(C
JOHN RAINES	D	(CD
BUDDY EMMONS	STEEL	(BC
RICK RUSKIN	G	(C
BYRON BERLINE	FDL	(BDE
BILLY RAY LATHAM	G	(B
DONNA WASHBURN	V	(CD
JOE OSBORNE	B	(C

Album	Year	Label	Country	Number
(A) THE BANJO ALBUM	1969	TOGETHER	US	1003
(B) DUELLING BANJOS	1973	20th CENTURY	US	T 409
(C) DOUGLAS FLINT DILLARD	1974	20th CENTURY	US	T 426
(D) HEAVEN	1979	FLYING FISH	US	FF086
(E) JACKRABBIT	1980	FLYING FISH	US	208

Member	Instr	Albums
JOHN HARTFORD	FDL	(A
SAM BUSH	MAND	(E
JEFF GILKINSON	B	(DB
ROD DILLARD	G V	(CDB
RAY PACK	G V	(E
MARK DAWSON	HCA	(C
DOUG BOUNSALL	G	(D
DAVID JACKSON	B	(B
SNEAKY PETE KLEINOW	STEEL	(C
LINDA DILLARD	V	(CD
PEPPER WATKINS	V	(C
HERB PEDERSEN	GV	(C
BILL BRYSON	B	(E
PAUL BREIDENBACH	G	(E
JOHN HOBBS		(D
COLIN CAMERON	B	(C
PAUL YORK	D	(CDB
DICK ROSINI	G	(EB
BILLY CONSTABLE	G	(DE
COLIN CAMERON	B	(B
RON STARR	SAX	(C
RICK CUNHA	G	(B
DAVID JACKSON	B	(CD

D69 DILLARD & CLARK D69

Member	Instr	Albums
DOUG DILLARD	BANJO G	(ALL
GENE CLARK	G V	(ALL
DAVID JACKSON	B V	(ABC
BERNIE LEADON	G V	(AC
JON CORNEAL	D	(BC
BYRON BERLINE	FDL	(BC
MICHAEL CLARK	D	(A
DON BECK	G HCA	(AC
DONNA WASHBURN	V G	(BC
CHRIS HILLMAN	MAND	(C

Album	Year	Label	Country	Number
(A) FANTASTIC EXPEDITION	1968	A&M	US	AMLS 939
(A) FANTASTIC EXPEDITION	1975	A&M	US	SP 4158
(B) THROUGH THE MORNING	1969	A&M	UK	AML 966
(B) THROUGH THE MORNING	1975	A&M	US	SP 4203
(C) GENE CLARK & DOUG DILLARD	1975	ARIOLA		86027
(D) KANSAS CITY SOUTHERN	1975	ARIOLA		86436
( ) GRASS ROOTS (½ ALBUM ½BURRITOES)	1972	MAYFAIR	UK	AMLB51038

Member	Instr	Albums
ANDY BELLING	K	(C
SNEAKY PETE	STEEL	(C

D70 DILLARD HARTFORD DILLARD D70

Member	Instr	Albums
DOUG DILLARD	BAN	(ABCD
ROD DILLARD	G V	(AD
JOHN HARTFORD		(AD
SAM BUSH	MAND	(A
AMOS GARRETT	G	(D
IM COLVARD	G	(A
HARGUS ROBBINS	PNO	(A
KENNY MALONE	D	(A
PHIL AABERG	K	(D
SAMM BENNETT	CONGA	(D
GINGER BLAKE	V	(D

Album	Year	Label	Country	Number
(A) DILLARD HARTFORD DILLARD	1977	SONET	UK	SNTF 730
(B) GLITTER GLASS	1977	FLYING FISH	US	FF036
(C) DILLARD HARTFORD DILLARD	19	FLYING FISH	US	036
(D) PERMANENT WAVE	1980	FLYING FISH	US	233

Member	Instr	Albums
BUDDY EMMONS	STEEL	(A
HENRY STRZELECKI	B	(A
BENNY MARTIN	V	(A
MAC CRIDIN	B	(D
GREG SELKER	MARIMBA	(D
LAURA CREAMER	V	(D
PEPPER WATKINS	G	(A
JEFF GILKENSON	HCA	(A
MICHAEL MELFORD	MAND	(AD
SCOTT MATHELOS	D	(D
LINDA DILLARD	V	(D

D71 THE DILLARDS D71

Member	Instr	Albums
DOUG DILLARD	BAN G	(ABCM
ROD DILLARD	G	(ABCDEFGJLKM
DEAN WEBB	MAND	(ABCDEFGJLKM
MITCH JAYNE	B V	(ABCDEFGM
HERB PEDERSEN	BANJO	(DELKM
ANDREW BELLING	K	(G
COLIN CAMERON	B	(G
JOHN HARTFORD	FDL	(GM
BUCK GRAVES	DOBRO G	(G
DON GALLESE	PERC	(G
BUDDY EMMONS	STEEL	(D
JOE OSBORNE	B	(D
TOXEY FRENCH	D	(D
JIM GORDON	D	(D
JOHN RAINES	D	(G
JEFF GILKENSON	B V	(JKLM
JEFF SILVERMAN	G	(J
BILLY RAY LATHAM	G	(FGL
DOUG BOUNSALL	G V	(LKM
HOMER DILLARD SNR	FDL V	(M
HOMER DILLARD JR	ACC	(M
MARK SORGER		(K
EARL DILLARD	BAN	(M

Album	Year	Label	Country	Number
(A) BACK PORCH BLUE GRASS	1963	ELEKTRA	US	EKS 7232
(B) LIVE ALMOST	1964	ELEKTRA	US	EKS 7265
(C) PICKIN' & FIDDLIN'	1965	ELEKTRA	US	EKS 7285
(D) WHEATSHEAF SUITE	1968	ELEKTRA US 74035	UK	K 42045
(E) COPPERFIELDS	1970	ELEKTRA US 74054	UK	K 42034
(F) ROOTS & BRANCHES	1972	UA UK UAS29366	US	ANTHEM 5091
(G) TRIBUTE TO THE AMERICAN DUCK	1973	UA UK UAS29516	US	POPPY 175
(H) BEST OF THE DILLARDS	1976	ELEKTRA	UK	K 52035
(J) Vs THE INCREDIBLE L A TIME MACHINE	77	SONET	UK	SNTF 743
(J) Vs THE INCREDIBLE L A TIME MACHINE	77	FLYING FISH	US	FF040
(K) DECADE WALTZ	1979	FLYING FISH	US	FF082
(L) MOUNTAIN ROCK	1980	CRYSTAL CLEAR		5007
(M) HOMECOMING & FAMILY REUNION	1980	FLYING FISH	US	215

Member	Instr	Albums
IRV DUGAN	G	(G
DOUG HAYWOOD	B V	(J
GABRIEL KATONA	K	(J
PAUL YORK	D	(EFGJLK
RAY PARKS	FDL	(LK
BILL BRYSON	B	(M
EMORY GORDY	B	(K
EARLING DILLARD	G	(M
LINDA DILLARD	V	(GM
JOEY SCARBURY	V	(J
BYRON BERLINE	FDL	(CE
GARY ITRI	B	(G
RICHARD GODFREY	D	(M
GLENN HARDIN	K	(K
BRIAN DILLARD	TAMB	(M
CHUCK FLORE		(K

D71A DILLINGER D71A

Member	Instr	Albums
DILLINGER		(ALL
SLY DUNBAR	D	(A
EARL CHINNA SMITH	G	(A
ASTON BARRETT	B	(A
STICKY	PERC	(A
TOMMY McCOOK	HRNS	(A
NOEL BENBOW	D	(A
VIN GORDON	HRNS	(A
TRINITY	V	(A
BOBBY ELLIS	HRNS	(A
CLINT EASTWOOD	V	(I

Album	Year	Label	Country	Number
(A) CB 200	1975	MANGO	US	9385
(B) BIONIC DREAD	1977	MANGO/ISLAND		9455
(C) TALKING BLUES	1977	MAGNUM		DEAD 1001
(D) TOP RANKING	1977	THIRD WORLD		919
(E) ANSWER ME QUESTION	1978	THIRD WORLD		928
(F) MARIJUANA MY BRAIN	1978	JAMAICA SOUND		002
(G) LIVE AT THE MUSIC MACHINE	1978	JAMAICA SOUNS		004
(H) BABYLON FEVER	19	UA	US	795
(I) LIVE IN LONDON	1981	ECHO	UK	020
(J) CORNBREAD	1981	ECHO	UK	021
(K) BADDER THAN THEM	1981	A&M	UK	AMLH68528

D71B DIMEOLA, McLAUGHLIN , DELUCIA D71B

AL DIMEOLA	G	(A	(A) FRIDAY NIGHT IN SAN FRANCISCO	1980	PHILIPS GER 302137 CBS UK 84962
JOHN McLAUGHLIN	G	(A			
PACO DELUCIA	G	(A			

D71C DILLMAN BAND D71C

PAT FREDERICK	V VLN	(A	(A) LOVIN THE NIGHT AWAY				1981	RCA
DANNY FLAHERTY	D V	(A						
STEVE SOLMONSON	G V	(A	STEVE SEAMANS	STEEL	(A	DIK SHOPTEAU	B	(A

D72 AL DIMEOLA D72

AL DIMEOLA	G	(ALL	(A) LAND OF MIDNIGHT SUN				1976	CBS US 34074		UK	81220
PETER CANNAROZZI	K	(D	(A) LAND OF MIDNIGHT SUN				1981	EMBASSY RI		UK	32027
MINGO LEWIS	PERC K	(ABCDE	(B) ELEGANT GYPSY				1977	CBS US 34461		UK	81845
STEVE GADD	D	(ABCDE	(C) CASINO				1978	CBS US 35277		UK	82645
ANTHONY JACKSON	B	(ABCDE	(D) SPLENDIDO HOTEL				1979	CBS US 36270		UK	88468
PHILLIPE SAISSE	K	(DE1	(E) ELECTRIC RENDEZVOUS				1982	CBS		UK	85431
ROBBIE GONZALES	D	(1D	(1) 1978 UK TOUR								
CHICK COREA	K	(AD									
LENNY WHITE	D	(AB	BARRY MILES	K	(AC	EDDIE COLON	PERRC	(CD1	STANLEY CLARKE	B	(A
JAN HAMMER	K	(BDE	PATTI BIYAKAS	V	(A	PACO DE LUCIA	G	(BE	ALPHONSE MOUZON	D	(A
JACO PASTORIUS	B	(A	WILODEK GULGOWSKI	K	(1	LES PAUL	G	(D	TIM LANDERS	B	(D1

D72A MICHAEL DINNER D72A

MICHAEL DINNER	G V	(AB	(A) PRETENDER				1974	FANTASY		US	9454
WADDY WACHTEL	G V	(B	(B) TOM THUMB				1976	FANTASY UK 3006		US	9512
DAVID FOSTER	K	(B									
BILL CHAMPLIN	K V	(B	LAURA ALLEN	V	(B	CHUCK FINDLEY	TPT	(B	LENNY PICKETT	SAX	(B
GARY ROWLES	V	(B	DEE MURRAY	B V	(B	NIGEL OLSSON	D V	(B	TIM SMITH(TIM SCHMIT)?	V	(B
ALAN ESTES	PERC	(B	DICK HYDE	TROM	(B	RICHIE HAYWARD	V	(B	BOB WARFORD	G	(A
ED BLACK	STEEL	(A	JOHN BOYLAN	K	(A	MIKE BOWDEN	B	(A	MICKEY McGEE	D	(A
SNEAKY PETE	STEEL	(A	DON FELDER	G	(A	MICK UTLEY	ORG	(A	GAIL DAVIES	V	(A
RUSS KUNKEL	D	(A	LINDA RONSTADT	V	(A	DOUG HAYWOOD	V	(A	HERB PEDERSEN	V	(A
ROBERT GRINNEDGE	STEELDRUM	(A	MILT HOLLAND	PERC	(A	ANDREW GOLD	PNO	(A	GARY MALLABER	D	(A
LARRY KNECHTEL	PNO	(A	RONEE BLAKLEY	V	(A	NICK DE CARO	ACC	(A			

D72B DINGOES D72B

BRODERICK SMITH	V HCA	(AB	(A) FIVE TIMES THE SUN				1977	A&M US 4636		UK	AMLH64636
CHRIS STOCKLEY	G	(A	(B) ORPHANS OF THE STORM				1979	A&M US 4733		AUST	36721
KERRYN TOLHURST	G MAND	(AB									
JOHN DU BOIS	B	(AB	JOHN LEE	D	(AB	NICKY HOPKINS	PNO	(A	GARTH HUDSON	K	(A
ANDREW HARDIN	G V	(B	HOLLY SHERWOOD	V	(B	CHERRI GRASSO	V	(B	JAMES McLAIN	V	(A
SMIGGY	V	(B									

D73 DIODES D73

PAUL ROBINSON	V	(ABC	(A) THE DIODES	1978	CBS	NL	82681
JOHN CATTO	G	(ABC	(B) RELEASED	1978	EPIC	CAN	80002
IAN McKAY	B V K	(ABC	(C) ACTION/REACTION	1980	ORIENT	CAN	001
JOHN HAMILTON	D V K SAX	(AB					
MIKE LENGYELL	D V	(BC					

D74 DION & THE BELMONTS D74

DION DI MUCCI	V	(ALL	PRESENTING DION & THE BELMONTS	196	LAURIE	US	2002
FRED MILANO	V	(	DION ALONE	196	LAURIE	US	2004
ANGELO D'ALEO	V	(	TOPPERMOST VOL 1	1960	TOP RANK	UK	25/027
CARLO MASTRANGELO	V	(	WISH UPON A STAR	196	LAURIE	US	2006
RON FRANGIPANE	PNO	(S	RUNAROUND SUE	196	LAURIE	US	2009
JOE MACK	B	(S	RUNAROUND SUE	196	HMV	UK	CLP 1539
AL ROGERS	D	(S	LOVERS WHO WONDER	196	LAURIE	US	2012
SAL DITROIA	G	(S	LOVERS WHO WONDER	196	STATESIDE	UK	SL 10034
GEORGE DEVENS	PERC	(S	DIONS GREATEST HITS	196	LAURIE	US	2013
DAVE BROMBERG	G	(S	LOVE CAME TO ME	196	LAURIE	US	2015
SELDON POWELL	SAX	(S	TOGETHER WITH BELMONTS	196	LAURIE	US	2016
MIKE OMARTIAN	K V	(*	SONGS TO SANDY	1966	LAURIE	US	2017
LEE SKLAR	B	(*	15 MILLION SELLERS	1966	LAURIE	US	2019
DAVID KEMPER	D	(*	MORE GREATEST HITS DION	19	LAURIE	US	2022
DEAN PARKS	G	(*	RUBY BABY	1963	CBS	US	2010
BEN BENAY	G	(*	DONNA THE PRIMA DONNA	19	CBS	US	2107
VICTOR FELDMAN	PERC	(*	DONNA THE PRIMA DONNA	19	CBS	US	8907
GARY COLEMAN	PERC	(*	WONDER WHERE IM BOUND	19	CBS	US	9773
STEVE BARRI	PERC	(*	TOGETHER AGAIN	1967	ABC	US	599
CHUCK FINDLEY	TPT	(*	TOGETHER AGAIN	1967	HMV	UK	CSD 3618
STEVE MADAIO	TPT	(*	TOGETHER AGAIN	19	B+C	UK	CAS 1007
NINO TEMPO	SAX	(*	DION	1969	LONDON	UK	SHP 8390
ERNIE WATTS	SAX	(*	DION	196	LAURIE	US	2047
STEVE DOUGLAS	SAX	(*	SIT DOWN OLD FRIEND	1970	WB	US	WS 1826
DICK HYDE	TROM	(*	YOU'RE NOT ALONE	1971	WB	US	WS 1872
SID SHARP	STRINGS	(*	(S)SANCTUARY	1972	WB	US	WS 1945
PHIL EVERLY	V	(*	(S)SANCTUARY	1972	WB	UK	K 46122
ORRIN WATERS	V	(*	SUITE FOR LATE SUMMER	1972	WB US 2642	UK	K 46199
ANN WHITE	V	(*	LIVE AT MADISON SQUARE GARDENS 1972	1972	WB	US	2664
LUTHER WATERS	V	(*	REUNION	1973	WB US 2664	UK	K 46208
CAROLYN WILLIS	V	(*	BORN TO BE WITH YOU	1975	PHILLES	UK	2307 002
KERRY CHATER	V	(*	BORN TO BE WITH YOU	197	PHIL SPECTOR	US	002
MYRNA MATTHEWS	V	(*	(*) STREET HEART	1976	WB	UK	K 56279
JIM HAAS	V	(*	(*) STREET HEART	197	WB	US	BS 2954
STORMIE OMARTIAN	V	(*	PICK OF THE RADIO GOOD GUYS VOL 1	1976	SONIC	UK	SON ?
			PICK OF THE RADIO GOOD GUYS VOL 2	197	SONIC	UK	SON 004
			PICK OF THE RADIO GOOD GUYS VOL 3	197	SONIC	UK	SON 019
			RETURN OF THE WANDERER	1978	LIFESONG	US	35356
			60 HITS BOX SET	19	LAURIE	US	SLP 6000
			DOOWOP	19	PICKWICK	US	VSP 3521
			EVERYTHING YOU WANTED TO HEAR BY DION	19	LAURIE	US	4002
			20 HITS	19		US	ENY 8
			DIONS GREATEST HITS	1973	CBS	US	31942
			OLDIES BUT GOODIES	1979	TELDEC	GER	623646
			REUNION	1981	WB	UK	K26049
			INSIDE JOB	1981	STRINGDAY	UK	4006

D75 DIRE STRAITS D75

Member	Instrument	Albums
MARK KNOPFLER	G V	(ALL
DAVID KNOPFLER	G V	(AB
JOHN ILLSLEY	B V	(AB1CD
PICK WITHERS	D	(AB1CD
B BEAR	K	(B
HAL LINDES	G	(1
ALAN CLARK	K	(1
MIKE MAINIERI	VIBES	(D
ROY BITTAN	K	(C
ED WALSH	SYN	(D

Record	Year	Label / Catalogue
(A) DIRE STRAITS	1978	VERTIGO UK 9102 021 US WB 3266
(B) COMMUNIQUE	1979	VERTIGO UK 9102 031 US WB 3330
(C) MAKING MOVIES	1980	VERTIGO UK 6359 034 US WB 3480
(1) 1980 TOUR		
(D) LOVE OVER GOLD	1982	VERTIGO UK 6359 109

D75A DIRECTIONS D75A

Record	Year	Label	Country	Catalogue
(A) THREE BANDS TONIGHT(EP)	1979	TORCH	UK	TOR004

D76 DIRTY ANGELS D76

Member	Instrument	Albums
CHARLIE KARP	V G	(AB
DAVID HULL	K B V MANS	(AB
GEORGE MAHER	G	(AB
JIMMY MAHER	D V	(AB
JACK KRAFT	K	(B
JOAN ELLINGTON	V	(B
RICHARD GOTTEHRER	K V	(A
PAT ELLINGTON	V	(B
DICKY SIMMONS	HCA	(B
ARTIE KAPLAN	SAX	(A
JUDY ELLINGTON	V	(B
MONTEGO JOE	PERC	(B

Record	Year	Label / Catalogue
(A) KISS TOMORROW GOODBYE	1977	PRIVATE STOCK UK 1019 US 2020
(B) DIRTY ANGELS	1978	A&M US 4716

D77 DIRTY BLUES BAND D77

Member	Instrument	Albums
ROD PIAZZA	V HCA	(AB
GLEN ROSS CAMPBELL	G	(A
ROBERT SANDELL	STEEL	(A
PAT MALONE	K	(AB
LES MORRISON	B	(A
JOHN MILLIKEN	D	(A
GREGG ANDERSON	B	(B
FREDDIE HILL	TPT	(B
DAVE MITER	D	(B
JIMMY FORREST	SAX	(B
RICK LUNETTA	G	(B
WILLIE GREEN	SAX	(B

Record	Year	Label	Country	Catalogue
(A) DIRTY BLUES BAND	1967	BLUESWAY	US	BLS 6010
(A) DIRTY BLUES BAND	196	STATESIDE	UK	SSL 10234
(B) STONE DIRT	1969	BLUESWAY	US	BLS 6020
(B) STONE DIRT	1969	STATESIDE	UK	SSL 10268

D77A DIRTY DOG D77A

Record	Year	Label	Country	Catalogue
(A) LET GO OF MY HAND	1977	LIGHTNING	UK	GIL 511

D77B DIRTY DOGS D77B

Record	Year	Label	Country	Catalogue
(A) 7 LIVES FOR ROCK'N'ROLL	1979	CBS	UK	83929

D77C DIRTY JOHNS HOT DOG STAND D77C

Record	Year	Label	Country	Catalogue
(A) RETURN FROM THE DEAD	19	AMSTERDAM	US	12004

D77D DIRTY LOOKS D77D

Member	Instrument	Albums
PATRICK BARNES	G V	(A
MARCO SIN	B V	(A
PETER PARKER	D V	(A
CHARLIE GIORDANA	K	(A

Record	Year	Label / Catalogue
(A) DIRTY LOOKS	1980	STIFF UK SEEZ22 US 36434
(B) TURN IT UP	1981	STIFF UK SEEZ 38

D78 DIRTY TRICKS D78

Member	Instrument	Albums
TERRY HORBURY	B	(ABC
ANDY BEIRNE	D	(C
KENNY STEWART	V	(ABC
JOHN FRASER BINNIE	G K	(ABC
JOHN LEE	D	(A

Record	Year	Label / Catalogue
(A) DIRTY TRICKS	1975	POLYDOR UK 2383 351
(B) NIGHT MAN	1976	POLYDOR US 16082 UK 2383 398
(C) HIT & RUN	1977	POLYDOR US 16104 UK 2383 466

D78A DIXIE CUPS D78A

Record	Year	Label	Country	Catalogue
(A) CHAPEL OF LOVE	1964	REDBIRD	US	20100
(B) IKO IKO	196	REDBIRD	US	20103
(C) RIDIN' HIGH	196	PARAMOUNT	US	525
(D) TEENAGE ANGUISH VOL1	197	CHARLY	UK	CRM 2004

D78B DISCHARGE D78B

Record	Year	Label	Country	Catalogue
(A) DECONTROL(EP)	1980	CLAY	UK	CLAY5
(B) REALITIES OF WAR(EP)	19	CLAY	UK	
(C) FIGHT BACK (EP)	1980	CLAY	UK	

D78C DISLOCATED DANCE D78C

Record	Year	Label	Country	Catalogue
(A) SLIP THAT DISC	1981	NEW HORMONES	UK	ORG10

D78D DISTRACTIONS D78D

Member	Instrument	Albums
MIKE FINNEY	V	(A
STEVE PERRIN	G	(A
PIP NICHOLLS	PNO	(A
ADRIAN WRIGHT	G K	(A
ALEC SIDEBOTTOM	D	(A

Record	Year	Label	Country	Catalogue
(A) YOU'RE NOT GOING OUT DRESSED LIKE THAT	1979	TJM (EP)	UK	TJM2
(B) NOBODY'S PERFECT	1980	ISLAND	UK	ILPS9604

D78E DIVERSIONS D87E

Member	Instrument	Albums
LENE LOVICH	V SAX	(A
GLENN CARTLIDGE	G	(A
JEFFREY RAY SMITH	K	(A
GREG SHEEHAN	D	(A
DAVE QUINN	B	(A
STEVE SAXON	SAX	(A
LES CHAPPELL	G	(A
MIKE VERNON	PROD	(A

Record	Year	Label
(A) SOUL SURVIVORS	1977	POLYDOR(NOT RELEASED)

D78F DIXIE BELLES D78F

Record	Year	Label / Catalogue
(A) DOWN AT PAPA JOES	1964	SAVAGE STAGE US 7 UK LONDON8152

D79 DIXIE DREGS (The DREGS) D79

Member	Instrument	Albums
ROD MORGENSTEIN	D	(ABCDEF
ANDY WEST	B	(ABCDEF
ALLEN SLOAN	VLN	(ABCDE
STEVE MORSE	G	(ABCDEF
STEVE DAVIDOWSKI	K	(A
MARK PARRISH	K	(BC
T LAVITZ	K	(DEF
PATRICK SIMMONS	V	(F
STEVE HOWE	G	(F
ALEX LIGERTWOOD	V	(F

Record	Year	Label / Catalogue
(A) FREE FALL	1977	CAPRICORN US 0189 UK 2429 154
(B) WHAT IF	1978	CAPRICORN US 0203 UK 2429 165
(C) NIGHT OF LIVING DREGS	1979	CAPRICORN US 216 UK 2429 181
(D) DREGS OF THE EARTH	1980	ARISTA US 9528 NL 202 207
(E) UNSUNG HEROES (DREGS)	1981	ARISTA US 9548 NL 203 630
(F) INDUSTRY STANDARD (DREGS)	1982	ARISTA US 9588 GER 204 559

D79A ERROL DIXON D79A

Member	Instrument	Albums
ERROL DIXON		(A

Record	Year	Label	Country	Catalogue
(A) BLUES IN A POT	19	LONDON	US	PS550

D80 FLOYD DIXON D80

Member	Instrument	Albums
FLOYD DIXON		(ALL

Record	Year	Label	Country	Catalogue
(A) OPPORTUNITY BLUES	1978	ROUTE 66		KIX1
(B) ROCKIN' THIS JOINT TONITE	1978	JSP	UK	1002
(C) HOUSTON JUMP	1979	ROUTE 66	SWED	KIX11

D80A WILLIE DIXON D80A

Member	Instrument	Albums
WILLIE DIXON	B V	(ALL
MEMPHIS SLIM	PNO	(AE

Record	Year	Label	Country	Catalogue
(A) WILLIES BLUES	19	PRESTIGE	US	1003
(B) I AM THE BLUES	1976	CBS	US	9987
(C) AUX TROIS MAILOTS	19	POLYDOR	US	658148
(D) CATALYST	19	PATHE	FR	064 9603
(D) CATALYST	1976	OVATION	UK	1433

(CONTINUED)

D80A WILLIE DIXON (CONTINUED) D80A

(E) AT THE VILLAGE GATE 19
(F) WHAT HAPPENED TO MY BLUES 1978 OVATION QD 1441
(G) EARTHQUAKE & HURRICANE 19 SPOONFUL US
(H) EVERY WHICH WAY 19 VERVE US 3007
(J) SONGS 19 FOLKWAYS US 2385

D81 LYN DOBSON D81

LYN DOBSON (A) JAM SANDWICH 1974 FRESH AIR 6370 501

D81A DOC HOLLIDAY D81A

BRUCE BROOKSHIRE G V (A (A) RIDES AGAIN 1982 A&M UK AMLH64882
EDDIE STONE K V (A
JOHN SAMUELSON B V (A RICK SKELTON G V (A HERMAN NIXON D (A
BOB BROOKSHIRE HCA (A TOM ALLOM K PERC V(A ERNEST C CHARLES V (A

D82 DR ALIMANTADO D82

GREGORY ISAACS V (A (A) BEST DRESSED CHICKEN IN TOWN 1978 GREENSLEEVES UK GREL1
HORACE ANDY V (A (B) SONS OF THUNDER 1981 GREENSLEEVES UK GREL22
JACKIE EDWARDS V (A
JAH WOOSH V (A JIMMY RADWELL V (A DROPPY V (A

D83 DR BUZZARD'S ORIGINAL SAVANNAH BAND D83

CORY DAYE V (AB (A) DR BUZZARD'S ORIGINAL SAVANNAH BAND 1976 RCA RS 1072 US APLI 1504
AUGUST DARNELL V B (AB (B) DR BUZZARD MEETS KING PENETT 1978 RCA APLI 2402
ANDY HERNANDEZ ACC PERC(AB (C) GOES TO WASHINGTON 1980 ELEKTRA US 218
MICKEY SEVILLA D (AB
SANDY LINGER PROD (A PAULINHO DA COSTA PERC (B SUSANDRA MINSKY V (B
DON ARMANDO BONILLA PERC (A STONY BROWDER V G K (AB

D83A DR DOPO JAM D83A

K POMMER K G V (A (A) FAT DOGS & DANISHMEN 1974 ZEBRA DENM 2949 012
J KNUDSEN G (A
S SNITKER HRNS (A A GAARDMAN WIND (A J NORDAL TROM (A
B C LAUSEN D G VIBES (A E WEISGARD D PERC (A V HANSEN B (A
LARS BISGAARD V (A BORGE LYSHOLMORTENSEN V (A BIRGIT SMIDT V (A
BIRGITE HOLM SORENSEN V (A

D84 DR FEELGOOD D84

LEE BRILLEAUX V G HCA(ALL (A) DOWN BY THE JETTY 1975 UA UK UAS 29727
JOHN B SPARKS B (ALL (B) MALPRACTICE 1975 UA UK UAS 29880
FIGURE MARTIN D (ALL (B) MALPRACTICE 1975 CBS US 34098
WILKO JOHNSON G V (ABCD (C) STUPIDITY 1976 UA UK UAS 29990
HENRY McCULLOUGH G (1 (D) SNEAKIN' SUSPICION 1977 UA UK UAS 30075
JOHN MAYO G (EFGHJ (D) SNEAKIN' SUSPICION 1977 CBS US 34806
TIM HINKLEY K (D (E) BE SEEING YOU 1977 UA UK UAS 30123
BOB ANDREWS K SAX (AB (F) PRIVATE PRACTICE 1978 UA UK UAG 30184
BRINSLEY SCHWARZ SAX (A (G) AS IT HAPPENS 1979 UA UK UAS 30239
(H) LET IT ROLL 1979 UA UK UAS 30269
(J) CASE OF SHAKES 1980 UA UK 30311 US STIFF USE 12
(K) ON THE JOB 1981 LIBERTY UK LBG 30328
(L) CASEBOOK 1981 LIBERTY UK LBG 30341
(M) FAST WOMEN & SLOW HORSES 1982 CHISWICK UK TOSS 4
(1) 1977 TOUR

D85 DR HOOK & THE MEDICINE SHOW D85

RAY SAWYER V G (ALL (A) DR HOOK & THE MEDICINE SHOW 1971 CBS US 30898
(A) DR HOOK & THE MEDICINE SHOW 1971 CBS UK 65754
DENNIS LOCORRIERE V G (ALL (B) SLOPPY SECONDS 1972 CBS US 31622
(B) SLOPPY SECONDS 1972 CBS UK 65132
WILLIAM FRANCIS K (ALL (C) BELLY UP 1973 CBS US 32270
(C) BELLY UP 1973 CBS UK 65560
RICHARD ELSWIT G (B>P (D) FRIED FACE 1974 CBS UK 80372
GEORGE CUMMINGS STEEL (ABCD (E) BALLAD OF LUCY JORDAN 1975 CBS UK 80114
JANCE GARFAT B (B>O (F) BANKRUPT 1976 CAPITOL 11397
JOHN DAVID D (ABCD (G) A LITTLE BIT MORE 1976 CAPITOL 11522
JOHN WOLTERS D (EFGHIJKLNOP (H) MAKIN' LOVE & MUSIC 1977 CAPITOL 11632
BOB HENKE (EFGHIJK (I) STREET PEOPLE 197 CBS US 32920
ROD SMARR G (MOP (J) REVISITED 197 CBS US 34147
BILL EMERSON G (C (K) PLEASURE & PAIN 1978 CAPITOL 11859
EDWARD ADAMS B (C ( ) SYLVIAS MOTHER 1977 EMBASSY UK 31458
JOCK SCHROER HRNS (C ( ) BEST OF 197 CBS US 34147
JULES BROUSSARD HRNS (C ( ) BEST OF (DBL) 1980 CBS 22102
JOHN WILMETH HRNS (C (L) GREATEST HITS 1980 CAPITOL 26037
FOREST BUCHTEL HRNS (C (M) RISING 1980 MERCURY 6302 076
TOMMY WILLIAMS FDL (C (N) SOMETIMES YOU WIN 1990 CAPITOL 12023
SHERRY FOX V (C (O) LIVE IN THE UK 1981 CAPITOL 26706
ELLEN SCHROER V (C (P) PLAYERS IN THE DARK 1982 MERCURY MERS 002
NANCY PARIS V (C

D86 DR JOHN D86

Dr JOHN(MAC REBENNACK) K V (ALL (A) DrJOHN AND HIS NEW ORLEANS CONG 19 ACE US 2020
WITH (B) GRIS GRIS 1968 ATLANTIC GER 30045 UK 588 147
ERIC CLAPTON G (E (B) GRIS GRIS 1968 ATCO US 33234
SHIRLEY GOODMAN V (EF (B) GRIS GRIS 1972 ATLANTIC UK K 40168
RONNIE BARRON V K (EFLT (C) BABYLON 1969 ATLANTIC UK 228 018
VICTOR BROX HRNS K(E (C) BABYLON 1969 ATCO US 33270
P P ARNOLD V (E (D) REMEDIES 1970 ATLANTIC UK 2400 015
DORIS TROY V (E (D) REMEDIES 1970 ATCO US 33316
STEVE YORK B (E (E) SUN MOON & HERBS 1971 ATLANTIC UK 2400 161
CALVIN SAMUELS PERC (E (E) SUN MOON & HERBS 1971 ATCO US 33362
GRAHAM BOND SAX (E (E) SUN MOON & HERBS 1971 ATLANTIC UK K 40250
JIM PRICE TPT (E (F) GUMBO 1972 ATLANTIC UK K 40384
JOHN BOUDREAUX D (ELA (F) GUMBO 1972 ATCO US 7006
TAMMY LYNN V (EFLT (G) IN THE RIGHT PLACE 1973 ATLANTIC UK K 50017
ALVIN BISHOP ROBINSON G (FLT (G) IN THE RIGHT PLACE 1973 ATCO US 7018
ROBBIE MONTGOMERY V (FJL (H) TRIUMVIRATE(BLOOMFIELD HAMMOND) 1974 CBS US 32172 UK 65659
TOMMY FERRONNE G (E (J) DESITIVELY BONAROO 1974 ATLANTIC UK K 50035
RAY DRAPER TUBA V(E (J) DESITIVELY BONAROO 1974 ATCO US 7043

(CONTINUED)

D86 (CONTINUED) **DR JOHN** D86

FRED STAEHLE D PERC(EFT | (K) CUT ME WHILE I'M HOT 1975 DJM UK DJM22019 DJSLM 019
MICK JAGGER V (E | (L) HOLLYWOOD KNOW THY NAME 1975 UA UK UAG 29902
JONI JONZ FLT (E | (L) HOLLYWOOD KNOW THY NAME 1975 UA US UALA 552
KEN TERROADE FLT (E | (M) ONE NIGHT LATE 19 KARATE US 5402
CHRIS MERCER SAX (E | (N) Dr JOHN SUPERPAH 19 TRIP US 3507
WALTER DAVIS PNO (E | (O) ZU ZU MAN 19 TRIP US 9518
BOBBY WHITLOCK V (E | (O) Dr JOHN 19 SPRINGBOARD US 4018
JIM GORDON PERC (E | (Q) 16 GREATEST HITS 19 TRIP US TOP 16/1
JESSIE BOYCE B (E | (R) CITY LIGHTS 1978 HORIZON US AMLJ 732
WAYNE JACKSON HRNS (E | ( ) ANYTIME ,ANYPLACE 19 BAROMETER US BRM67001
BOB EZRIN K V (L | ( ) MARDI GRAS 19 ATLANTIC 40554
ROGER HOPPS TPT (E | ( ) NITE TRIPPER AT HIS BEST 1975 RARE BID 8014
FREEMAN BROWN PERC (E | (T) TANGO PALACE 1979 HORIZON US 740
ANDREW LOVE SAX (E
BOBBY KEYS SAX (E | CARL RADLE B (E | JULIUS FARNER B (L | JACK HALE TROM(E
ED LOGAN SAX (E | JAMES MITCHEL SAX (E | RON JOHNSON B (E | ED HOERNER TPT (E
JERRY JUMONVILLE SAX (E | MELVIN LASTIE CORN(F | SIDNEY GEORGE SAX HCA (F | LEE ALLEN SAX (F
DAVID LASTIE SAX (F | MOE BECHAMIN SAX V(F | HAROLD BATTISTE WIND (F | KEN KLIMAK G (F
JIMMY CALHOUN B (F | RICHARD WASHINGTON PERC(F | JESSIE SMITH V (FJ | ALLEN TOUSSAINT K (GJ
DAVID SPINOZZA G (G | RALPH McDONALD PERC(G | GARY BROWN SAX (GJ | LEO NOCENTELLI G (GJ
ARTHUR NEVILLE K (GJ | GEORGE PORTER B (GJ | JOSEPH MODELISTE D (GJ | STEVE HUNTER G (L
THE METERS (J | MARK COLBY WIND(J | WHIT SIDENER SAX (J | KEN FAULK HRNS(J
PETER GRAVES HRNS (J | JOHNNY BADANJEK D (L | LEROY COOPER SAX (L | ERNIE WATTS SAX (L
CHAUNCEY WELSH TROM (L | BOBBY TORRES CONGA (L | VENETTA FIELDS V (L | WARREN LUENING TPT (L
JAMES SMITTY SMITH G (L | CLIFFORD SOLOMON SAX (L | KENNY ASCHER K (L | TOMMY VIG PERC(L
STEVE GADD D (RT | WILL LEE B (R | RICHARD TEE K (R | HUGH McCRACKEN G (RT
JOHN TROPEA G (R | ARTHUR JENKINS PERC(R | POO PAH DOO PERC (A | ? DITMUS PERC(A
? MANN G (A | BATTISTE OF SCORPIO B (A | ? McLEAN MAND (A | ? BOLDEN FLT (A
DIDO (A | ? RONYARDS (A | ?CHINA (A | GONCY O'LEARY (A
SHIRLEY LAVEAUX (A | ? DURDEN (A | PLAS JOHNSON WIND (AT | WEST BROWNING (A
JEAN FREUNX (A | JOHN GUMBO (A | CECILIA LA FAVORITE (A | KARLA LE JEAN (A
ALVIN 'RED' TYLER SAX (A | HUEY SMITH PNO (A | FRANKIE FORD V (A | ROLAND STONE V (A
ABRAHAM LABORIEL B (T | HERMAN ERNEST D PERC(T | ANDRE FISCHER D (T | PAULINHO DACOSTA PERC(T
NEIL LARSEN PERC (T | CHARLIE MILLER HRNS(T | OSCAR BRASHEAR HRNS (T | WARREN LUENING HRNS(T
BENNY POWELL TROM (T | HERMAN RILEY SAX (T | JACKIE KELSO WIND (T | GARY HERBIG SAX (T
TOMMY JOHNSON TUBA (T | LARRY WILLIAMS WIND(T | KIM HUTCHCROFT SAX (T | STEPHANIE ? (A
THERESA (A

D86A **DR K's BLUES BAND** D86A

GEOFF KRIVIT G B (A | (A) DR K'S BLUES BAND 1968 WORLD PACIFIC US 21903
ROGER ROLT G (A | (A) DR K'S BLUES BAND 1968 SPARK UK 101
DR K(RICHARD KAY) PNO (A
HAROLD VICKERS B (A | ERIC PEACHEY D (A | MICK HASSE V HCA (A

D86B **DR KOCK VENTILATOR** D86B

DR KOCK G (A | (A) DR KOCK VENTILATOR 1980 REFLEKTOR GER 0060272
KLAUS BLUMENTHAL K (A
CHRIS CHAOS K (A | ALFRED E WAGNER SAX (A | SCHMITT MARTIN B (A

D87 **DR MARIGOLDS PRESCRIPTION** D87

DAVE MORRIS D (| (A) PICTURES OF LIFE 1969 MARBLE ARCH UK MALS 1222
FRED RADLEY G V (| (B) HELLO GIRL 1973 SANTA PONSA UK PNL 501
ALAN FRENCH K (
BILL FRENCH B (

D87A **DR MIX & THE REMIX** D87A

ERIC DEBRIS V (B | (A) PSYCHEDELIC DESERT 19 CELLULIOD (EP) CEL 6585
PAT VINCENT G V (B | (B) WALL OF NOISE 19 ROUGH TRADE ROUGH 6
CHARLIE H K G D V(B

D87B **DR STRUT** D87B

DAVID WOODFORD WIND (AB | (A) DR STRUT 1979 MOTOWN US 924 UK STML 12120
KEVIN BASSINSON K (AB | (B) STRUTTIN' 1980 MOTOWN US 931 UK ATML 12432
TIM WESTON G (AB
PETER FREIBERGEL B (AB | CLAUDE PEPPER D (AB | EVERETT BRYSON PERC (A

D88 **DR STRANGELY STRANGE** D88

TIM GOULDING V K (B | (A) KIP OF THE SERENES 1969 ISLAND UK ILPS 9106
TIM BOOTH V G (B | (B) HEAVY PETTING 1970 VERTIGO UK 6360 009
IVAN PAWLE V B K (B
JOHNNY MOYNIHAN BAZ (B | DAVE MATTACKS D (B | GARY MOORE G (B
JAY MYRDAL GLOCK (B | HEATHER WOOD V (B | ANDY IRVINE MAND (B
LINUS PERC (B | JOHANNA V K (B | ANNIE CHRISTMAS V K (B
BRENDAN SHIELS B (B

D88A **DR WEST'S MEDICINE SHOW & JUNK BAND** D88A

NORMAN GREENBAUM V (A | (A) THE EGGPLANT THAT ATE CHICAGO 19 GREGEOR US 001
BONNIE WALLACH G V (A
JACK CARRINGTON G PERC V(A | EVAN ENGBER PERC (A

D88B **DR 'Z'** D88B

KEITH KEYES K V (A | (A) THREE PARTS TO MY SOUL 1971 VERTIGO UK 6360 048
ROB WATSON B (A
BOB WATKINS D (A

D89 **DOCTORS OF MADNESS** D89

DAVE VANIAN V (2 | (1) 1978 (2) 1978 APRIL (3) MAY 1978>
RICHARD'KID' STRANGE G V (ABCD123 | (A) LATE NIGHT MOVIES 1976 POLYDOR UK 2383 378
COLIN'STONER' BROWN B (123ABCD | (B) FIGMENTS OF EMANCIPATION 1976 POLYDOR UK 2383 403
PETER DILEMMA D (ABC123D | (C) SONS OF SURVIVAL 1978 POLYDOR UK 2383 472
JILL MACKINTOSH V (B | (D) DOCTORS OF MADNESS 1978 UA US 871
URBAN BLITZ G VLN (ABC | (E) REVISIONISM 1981 POLYDOR UK 2478 146
CLAIRE TORRY V (B
STEPHANIE DE SYKES V (B

D90 **DODGERS** D90

JOHN WILSON G B V (A | (A) LOVE ON THE REBOUND 1978 POLYDOR UK 2391 379
ROGER LOMAS G B V (A | (A) LOVE ON THE REBOUND 1978 POLYDOR US PD1 6174
BOB JACKSON K V G (A | (A) LOVE ON THE REBOUND 1978 POLYDOR UK 2383 513
PAUL HOOPER D V (A

D90A **ERNIE K DOE** D90A

ERNIE K DOE V (A | (A) ERNIE K DOE | 1972 JANUS US 3030

D91 **DOG SOLDIER** D91

KEEF HARTLEY D (A | (A) DOG SOLDIER | 1975 UA US UALA405 UK UAS 29769
MILLER ANDERSON G V (A1 | (1) LATER LINE UP
PAUL BLISS B (A1
MEL SIMPSON K (A1 | DEREK GRIFFITHS G (A1 | ERIC DILLON D (1

D92 **BUNK DOGGER** D92

BUNK DOGGER V G SYN (AB | (A) FIRST OFFENCE | 1978 RCA UK PL 25138
ANDY ROBERTS G (A | (B) GREAT DETECTIVE | 1980 RCA UK PL 25298
JIMMY JEWELL SAX (A
LESLEY DUNCAN V (A | TONY BURROWS V (A | DAVE QUINN B V (B
PETE WINGFIELD K (A | ALAN HODGE G (AB | IAN WILSON G (A
NACHUM HEIMAN ACC (A | RUSSELL STONE V (A | TOM WILDY SAX (AB
PHIL CURTIS B (A | JOHN ATKINSON B (A | MARY CARROLL V (A
FRANK RICOTTI PERC (A | LUIS JARDIM PERC (A | ALUN EDEN D (AB
TONY COX PNO (A | GERRY CONWAY D (A | RICKY WORTHY G V (B
STEVE THUNDER B V (B | LESLEY DUNCAN V (B | JOHN WOOLLAMS SAX (B
FOXY D (B | STEVE HENDERSON PERC (B | BARRIE GUARD PERC (B
ANDY ROBERTS G (B | BILLY LIVSEY K (B | GAYLE CUNNINGHAM V (B
GEOFF WESTLEY PNO (B | TREVOR HARGREAVES HRNS (B

D93 **DOGGEREL BANK** D93

WILLIAM BEALBY WRIGHT V (AB | (A) SILVER FACES | 1973 CHARISMA UK CAS 1079
SUSAN BAKER VLN MAND HCA (AB | (B) MISTER SKILLICORN DANCES | 1975 CHARISMA UK CAS 1102
GARY BOYLE G (AB
ANDREW STEELE D (A | TONY CAMPO B (A | RAY COOPER PERC (A
JIM PARKER K (AB | TOM PARKER K (AB | RICHARD MORCOMBE G (B
DAVE OLNEY B (B | MARTIN FRY TUBA (B | JONATHAN ADAMS V (B
JOE CASTALDINI BASSOON (B | TINA CHARLES V (B | CLAIRE TORRY V (B
MARTIN JAY V (B

D93A **DOGFEET** D93A

TREVOR POVEY G V (A | (A) DOGFEET | 1970 REFLECTION REFL 8
ALAN PEAVE G V (A
DUCK PERRY D (A | DAVE NICHOLS B (A | ANDREW CAMERON MILLAR PROD (A

D93B **BILL DOGGETT** D93B

BILL DOGGETT ORG (ALL | WOW | 1965 HMV UK CLP1884 US ABC 507
HONKY TONK | 19 CBS US 1814
PRELUDE TP THE BLUES | 19 CBS US 1942
FINGERTIPS | 19 CBS US 2082
HONKY TONK | 19 HARMONY US 11237
MOONDUST | 19 KING US 502
HOT DOGGETT | 19 KING US 514
AS YOU DESIRE | 19 KING US 523
EVERYBODY DANCE THE HONKY TONK | 19 KING US 531
DAME DREAMING | 19 KING US 532
A SALUTE TO ELLINGTON | 19 KING US 533
DOGGETT BEAT FOR DANCING FEET | 19 KING US 557
CANDLE GLOW | 19 KING US 563
SWINGIN' EASY | 19 KING US 582
DANCE AWHILE | 19 KING US 585
CHRISTMAS SONGS | 19 KING US 600
HOLD IT | 19 POWER US 269 US KING 609
HIGH & WIDE | 19 KING US 633
BIG CITY DANCE PARTY | 19 KING US 641
ON TOUR | 19 KING US 667
FOR REMINISCENT LOVERS | 19 KING US 706
BACK AGAIN WITH MORE | 19 KING US 723
MANY MOODS | 19 KING US 778
PLAYS AMERICAN SONGS | 19 KING US 830
IMPRESSIONS | 19 KING US 868
THE BEST OF | 19 KING US 908
BONANZA OF 24 HIT SONGS | 19 KING US 959
HONKY TONK POPCORN | 19 KING US 1078
THE NEARNESS OF YOU | 19 KING US 1097
RAM BUNK SHUSH | 19 KING US 1101
SENTIMENTAL MOOD | 19 KING US 1104
SOFT | 19 KING US 1108
HONKY TONK A LA MOD | 19 ROULETTE US 25330
3046 PEOPLE DANCED TILL 4am | 19 W B US 1404
THE BAND WITH THE BEAT | 19 W B US 1421
SWINGS | 19 WB US 1452
PRESENTS | 1977 WHOS 21002
16 BANDSTAND FAV'S | 19 STAR 3-23
MIDNIGHT SLOWS 9 | 1981 BLACK & BLUE 33145

D93C **DOGS** D93C

? HUGHES B (B | (A) DOGS | 1979 PHILIPS CAN 9120 412
DOMINIQUE G V (B | (B) WALKING SHADOWS | 1980 PHILIPS FR 6313 058
MICHEL D (B

D93D **DOGWATCH** D93D

ROY WEARD V (A | (A) LIVE | 1979 BRIDGEHOUSE UK 002
ROGER GLYNN G (A
NICK SACK D (A | TONY MORLEY B V (A | LINDA KELSEY K (A
JOHN TRELAWNEY VLN TROM (A

D93E **DANE DOHERTY** D93E

DANE DOHERTY V (A | (A) DANE DOHERTY | 1978 CBS US 34278

D93F DENNY DOHERTY D93F

Member	Instr		Title		Year	Label	Country	No.
DENNY DOHERTY	V G	(AB	(A) WHAT'CHA GONNA DO		1971	DUNHILL	US	50096
EDDY FISCHER	G	(A	(B) WAITING FOR A SONG		1973	EMBER	UK	5080
RUSS KUNKEL	D	(A						

BRIAN GAROFALO	B	(A	GABE LAPANO	K V	(A	ERIC HORD	G SIT	(A
BARRY McGUIRE	G HCA	(A	BUDDY EMMONS	STEEL	(A	JIMMIE HASKELL	ACC	(A
BILL SZYMCZYK	PERC	(A						

D93G KLAUS DOLDINGER D93G

Member	Instr		Title			Year	Label	No.
KLAUS DOLDINGER	SAX	(A	(A) BLUES HAPPENING			19	WORLD PACIFIC	20167
INGFRIED HOFFMAN	PNO	(A						
HELMUT KANDELBURGER	B	(A	CEES SEE	D	(A			

D93H DON DOKKEN D93H

Member	Instr		Title			Year	Label	Country	No.
DON DOKKEN	G V	(A	(A) BREAKIN' THE CHAINS			1982	CARRERE	UK	CAL 136
JUAN CROCIER	B V	(A							
GEORGE LYNCH	G	(A	MICK BROWN	D V	(A				

D94 DOLL D94

Member	Instr		Title					
MARION VALENTINE	V G	(A	(A) LISTEN TO THE SILENCE			1979 BEGGARS BANQUET UK BEGA12 NL 660055		
DENNIS HAINES	K	(A						
JAMES WEST-ORAM	G	(A	CHRISTOPHER YIANNI	B	(A	PAUL TURNER	D	(A

D95 DOLL BY DOLL D95

Member	Instr		Title		Year	Label	Country	No.
JACKIE LEVEN	V G	(ABC	(A) REMEMBER		1979	AUTOMATIC	K	56618
JO SHAW	V G K	(ABC	(B) GYPSY BLOOD		1979	AUTOMATIC	K	56755
TONY WAITE	V B	(BC	(C) DOLL BY DOLL		1981	MAGNET UK 5039	UK	5269
ROBIN SPREAFICO	B	(A	(D) DXD	(EP)	1981	MAGNET	NL	64587
DAVID McINTOSH	V D	(ABC	(E) GRAND PASSION		1982	MAGNET	UK	5047
GRAHAM PRESKETT	VLN K	(B						

B J COLE	STEEL G	(B	GEOFF WESTLEY	PNO	(C	SHELLEY MORRIS	PERC	(C
NINA SPENCER		(C	ROD BEDDALL	ACC	(C	PETE GIBSON	HCA	(C
TOM NEWMAN		(C	FIONA PRENDERGAST		(C	SUSIE O'LIST	V	(C

D95A DOLPHIN D95A

Member	Instr		Title			Year	Label	No.
ROY DAVIES	K	(A	(A) GOODBYE			1977	PRIVATE STOCK	PVLP 1055
GERRY CONWAY	D	(A	(B) MOLECULES			1980	GALE	LP 02
JOHN GIBLIN	B	(A						
JIMMY JEWELL	SAX	(A	ROGER CHURCHYARD	VLN	(A	PAUL CARMAN	B BANJO V	(A
GLEN LEFLEUR	D	(B	DAVE ROSE	SYN	(B	PRESTON HEYMAN	D	(B

D95B DOME D95B

Member	Instr		Title			Year	Label	Country	No.
B C GILBERT	V B G D PERC	(ABC	(A) DOME1			1980	DOME	UK	DOME1
G LEWIS	V B G SYN PERC	(ABC	(B) DOME 2			1980	DOME	UK	DOME2
ERIC RADCLIFFE	G	(C	(C) DOME 3			1981	DOME	UK	DOME3
D O MILLER	SAX	(C							
NISSELL MILS	V PERC	(C	PETER PRICE	D	(C				

D96 FATS DOMINO D96

ANTOINE 'FATS' DOMINO PNO V(ALL

WITH

LEE ALLEN	SAX	DAVE BARTHOLOMEW	TPT	SMOKEY JOHNSON	D	JOE HARRIS	SAX
HERB HARDESTY	SAX	ALVIN RED TYLER	SAX	CLARENCE HALL	SAX	ERNEST McLEEN	G
FRANK FIELDS	B	EARL PALMER	D	WENDEL DUCONGE	SAX	ROBERT BUDDY HAGANS	SAX
WALTER NELSON	G	BILLY DIAMOND	B	CORNELIUS COLEMAN	D	HARRISON VERRETT	G
JUSTIN ADAMS	G	CHARLES WILLIAMS	D	WALDRON JOSEPH	TROM	CLARENCE FORD	SAX
ROY MONTRELL	G	JIMMY DAVIS	B	FREDRICK KEMP	SAX	FRED SHEPPARD	SAX
WALTER LASTIE	D	WALTER KIMBLE	SAX	ROGER HAYWARD LOUIS	SAX	DAVID DOUGLAS	B
MORRIS SIMON	SAX	THOMAS JOHNSON	TPT	CARLTON MACWILLIAMS	B	JOSEPH JOHNSON	D

LP's

Title	Year	US	US	US RI	UK		UK
CARRY ON ROCKIN	19	IMPERIAL	9004		LONDON		2041
ROCK AND ROLLIN'	19	IMPERIAL	9009	12387	LONDON		2028
THIS IS FATS DOMINO	1956	IMPERIAL	9028	12389	LONDON		2073
HERE STANDS FATS DOMINO	1957	IMPERIAL	9038	12390	LONDON		2052
THIS IS FATS	1958	IMPERIAL	9040	12391	LONDON		2087
FABULOUS MR D	1958	IMPERIAL	9055	12394	LONDON		2135
FATS DOMINO SWINGS	19	IMPERIAL	9062	12091			
LETS PLAY FATS DOMINO	1959	IMPERIAL	9065		LONDON		2223
FATS DOMINO SINGS	1960	IMPERIAL	9103	12103			
A LOT OF DOMINO'S	1960	IMPERIAL	9127	12066	LONDON		2312
I MISS YOU SO	1961	IMPERIAL	9138	12398	LONDON		2364
LET THE 4 WINDS BLOW	1961	IMPERIAL	9153	12073	LONDON		2420
WHAT A PARTY	1961	IMPERIAL	9164		LONDON		2426
TWISTIN' THE STOMP	1962	IMPERIAL	9170		LONDON		2447
JUST DOMINO	1963	IMPERIAL	9206		LONDON		8039
LETS DANCE	1963	IMPERIAL	9239				
HERE HE COMES AGAIN	1963	IMPERIAL	9248				
WALKING TO NEW ORLEANS	1963	IMPERIAL	9227	12227	LONDON		8084
HERE COMES FATS	1963	ABC	455		HMV		1690
FATS ON FIRE	1963	ABC	479		HMV		1740
GETAWAY WITH FATS	1966	ABC	510		HMV		1821
FANTASTIC FATS	196	ABC			STATESIDE		10240
FATS DOMINO	196	SUNSET	5103				
AINT THAT A SHAME	19	SUNSET	5130				
WHEN IM WALKING	19	HARMONY	11343				
BIG ROCK SOUNDS	19	SUNSET	1011				
GOLDEN GREATS	19	LIBERTY	8668				
STOMPIN'	1967	SUNSET	5158				
WHEN MY DREAMBOAT	19	PICKWICK	3165				
FATS DOMINO	19	GRAND AWARD	267				
FATS DOMINO	19	EVEREST	280				
TROUBLE IN MIND	196	SUNSET	5200				
FATS IS BACK	1968	REPRISE	6304		VALIANT		107
FATS	1970	REPRISE	6439				
MILLION SELLERS	1962	IMPERIAL	9195	12195	LIBERTY	3303	83023
MILLION SELLERS VOL 2	19				LIBERTY	3046	83024
MILLION SELLERS VOL 3	19				LIBERTY		83101

(CONTINUED)

	Year	US	US	UK	UK
FAT SOUND	19			LIBERTY	83142
'65	1965	MERCURY	20070(M) 62039		
VERY BEST OF	19	UA	223 380	LIBERTY	83331
SOUTHWIND USA	19	MERCURY	21065 (M)61065(S)		
RARE DOMINO'S	19			LIBERTY	83174
30 HITS	19	UA	104		
COOKING WITH FATS	1966	UA	122	UA	60061/2
BE MY GUEST	1971			SUNSET	50252
RARE DOMINOS VOL 2	1972			UA	29152
LEGENDARY MASTERS (DBL)	1972	UA	9958	UA	60015/6
PLAY IT AGAIN FATS	1973			UA	29467
LIVE IN LAS VEGAS	1973			PHILIPS	6336 217
LIVE AT MONTREUX	1974			ATLANTIC	K 50107
FATS DOMINO STORY (DBL)	1974			LIBERTY	83456/7
LIVE IN NEW YORK	1976			PHILIPS	6336 275
20 GREATEST HITS	1976			UA	29967
STAR COLLECTION	19			WB MIDI	MD2 4006
BLUEBERRY HILL	19	PICKWICK	3111		
MY BLUE HEAVEN	19	PICKWICK	3295		
STORY VOL1	1977			UA	30067
STORY VOL2	1977			UA	30068
STORY VOL 3	1977			UA	30069
STORY VOL 4	1977			UA	30070
STORY VOL 5	1977			UA	30117
STORY VOL 6	1977			UA	30118
LIVE IN EUROPE	1978			UA	30121
SLEEPING ON THE JOB	1979	POLYDOR	PD 3215	SONET	SNTF 793
GOLDEN GREATS	1979			HAMMER	HMR 9002
WHEM IN WALKING	1979	CBS	35996		
EP's					
BLUES FOR LOVE	196			LONDON	1022
BLUES FOR LOVE 2	196			LONDON	1062
FATS	196			LONDON	1073
HERE COMES FATS	196			LONDON	1079
HERE COMES FATS	196			LONDON	1080
CARRY ON ROCKIN'	19			LONDON	1115
CARRY ON ROCKIN' 2	19			LONDON	1116
BLUES FOR LOVE 3	19			LONDON	1117
BLUES FOR LOVE 4	19			LONDON	1121
HERE COMES FATS 3	19			LONDON	1138
THE ROCKIN Mr D	19			LONDON	1206
THE ROCKIN Mr D	19			LONDON	1207
BE MY GUEST	19			LONDON	1261
THE ROCKIN Mr D 3	19			LONDON	1265
WHAT A PARTY	19			LONDON	1340
RED SAILS IN THE SUNSET	19			HMV	7EG 8862

D97 DON & DEWEY D97

DON 'SUGARCANE' HARRIS VLN(AB — (A) DON & DEWEY — 19 SPECIALTY UK SNTF 5006
DEWEY TERRY K V (AB — (B) THEY'RE ROCKIN TILL MIDNIGHT — 19 SPECIALTY US SPS 2131
PLAS JOHNSON SAX
JACKIE KELSO SAX (— RENE HALL B (— EARL PALMER D (
PETE SMITH B (— SONNY GILLETTE D (

D97A LOU DONALDSON D97A

LOU DONALDSON SAX (AB — (A) SASSY SOUL STREET — 1973 BLUE NOTE US 109
HORRACE OTT PNO (AB — (B) SWEET LOU — 1974 BLUE NOTE US 259
DAVID SPINOZZA G (AB
JIMMY YOUNG D (B — PAUL GRIFFIN K (AB — JOHN TROPEA G (A — ERNIE ROYAL TPT (B
JOE SHEPLEY TPT (B — DANNY MOORE TPT (B — GARNETT BROWN TROM (B — SELDON POWELL WIND(B
ARTHUR CLARKE WIND (B — BUDDY LUCAS HCA (B — CORNELL DUPREE G (B — HUGH McCRACKEN G (B
WILBUR BASCOMBE B (B — BERNARD PURDIE D (B — BARBARA MASSEY V (B — HILDA HARRIS V (B
EILEEN GILBERT V (B — CARL WILLIAMS V (B — WILLIAM SAMPLE V (B — BILL DAVIS V (B
ERIC FIGUEUOA V (B

D97B PETER DONATO D97B

PETER DONATO (A — (A) PETER DONATO — 1974 CAPITOL CAN 6423
MICHAEL HEYDON (A
DENNIS PENDRITH B (A — BARRY KEANE D (A — BERT HERMISTON SAX (A — DAVID McLEY (A
BRUCE PENNYCOOK (A — JAMES ATKINSON (A — ERIC ROGERTSON K (A — JANIS CRAMER (A
RUSS LITTLE TROM (A — MOE KOFFMAN HRNS (A — BOB VAN EVERA (A

D98 RAL DONNER D98

RAL DONNER V (ALL

		Year	Label		No.
( )	TAKIN CARE OF BUSINESS	196	GONE	US	5012
( )	TAKIN CARE OF BUSINESS VOL1	19	RONDO	US	RLP 22436
( )	TAKIN CARE OF BUSINESS VOL2	19	RONDO	US	RLP 22437
( )	ELVIS SCRAPBOOK	1977	GONE US		5033
( )	YOU DONT KNOW WHAT YOU GOT	1978	PYE UK		NSPL28269

D99 DONOVAN D99

DONOVAN LEITCH V G HCA (ALL
WITH
LESLEY DUNCAN V (QL
SUZI QUATRO V (Q
VALERIE CARRINGTON V (Q
JILL UTTING V (Q
NICK CURTIS V (Q
CARY WILSON V (Q
GAYNOR STEWART V (Q
JULIE FORSYTHE V (Q
LESLYE ASH V (Q
JOHN McCARTHY V (Q
LESLIE FYSON V (Q

		Year	Label		No.
(A)	WHAT'S BIN DID	1965	PYE	UK	NPL 18117
(A)	WHAT'S BIN DID	1968	MARBLE ARCH	UK	MAL 795
(B)	CATCH THE WIND	1965	HICKORY	US	123
(B)	CATCH THE WIND	1971	HALLMARK	UK	HMA 200
(C)	FAIRYTALE	1965	PYE	UK	NLP 18128
(C)	FAIRYTALE	1965	HICKORY	US	127
(C)	SONGS FOR SUNSHINE (1 DIFF TRACK)	1965	PYE	UK	2053
(C)	FAIRYTALE	1969	MARBLE ARCH	UK	MAL 867
(D)	SUNSHINE SUPERMAN	1967	PYE	UK	NPL 18181
(D)	SUNSHINE SUPERMAN	1966	EPIC	US	BN 26217
(E)	THE REAL DONOVAN	1966	HICKORY	US	LP 135
(F)	MELLOW YELLOW	1967	EPIC	US	BN 26239
(G)	FOR LITTLE ONES	1967	EPIC	US	BN 26350

(CONTINUED)

Musician	Instr	Albums
CHRIS SPEDDING	V	(Q
COZY POWELL	D	(Q
ALAN WHITE	D	(Q
CLIVE CHAMAN	B	(Q
DENNIS WALL	B	(Q
PHIL CHEN	B	(Q
JOHN BUNDRICK	K	(Q
BOBBY KEYS	SAX	(Q
JIM HORN	SAX	(Q
PETE HALLING	VLN	(Q
JACK EMBLOW	ACC	(Q
TONY CARR	PERC	(GJLQ
RONNIE LEAHY	K	(V
NICK SOUTH	B	(V
COLIN ALLEN	D	(V
ISAAC GUILLORY	G	(V
JOHNNY CHRISTOPHER	G	(T
DAVID BRIGGS	K	(T
HARVEY THOMPSON	HRNS	(T
HARRISON CALLOWAY	HRNS	(T
BEN CAULEY	HRNS	(T
CHARLIE ROSE	HRNS	(T
RONNIE EADES	HRNS	(T
BUFFY ST MARIE	V	(T
LEA JANE BERINATI	V	(T
GINGER HOLLADAY	V	(T
DAVID HUNGATE	B	(U
MARY HOLLADAY	V	(T
FLORENCE WARNER	V	(T
BYRON WARNER	V	(T
WILTON FELDER	B	(U
KLAUS VOORMANN	B	(U
LELAND SKLAR	B	(U
JIM KELTNER	D	(U
DOUG DAVIS	CELLO	(U
TOM SCOTT	WIND	(U
DAVID FOSTER	K	(U
EMIL RICHARDS	PERC	(U
BOBBYE HALL	PERC	(U
CHUCK FINDLEY	HRNS	(U
PHILIP DONNELLY	G	(U
JESSE ED DAVIS	G	(U
LEW McCREARY	HRNS	(U
B J COOK	V	(U
DONNY GERRARD	V	(U

Album	Title	Year	Label	Country	Number
(H)	WEAR YOUR LOVE LIKE HEAVEN	1967	EPIC	US	BN 26349
(I)	UNIVERSAL SOLDIER	1967	MARBLE ARCH	UK	MAL 718
(J)	IN CONCERT	1968	PYE	UK	NSPL18237
(J)	IN CONCERT	1968	EPIC	US	BN 26386
(DJ)	IN CONCERT/SUNSHINE SUPERMAN(DBL)	19	EPIC	US	33734
(K)	HURDY GURDY MAN	1968	EPIC	US	BN 26420
(L)	BARABAJAGAL	1968	EPIC	US	BN 26481
(KL)	HURDY GURDY/BARABAJAGAL(DBL)	19	EPIC	US	33731
(M)	A GIFT FROM A FLOWER TO A GARDEN	1968	PYE (DBL)	UK	NSPL20000
(M)	A GIFT FROM A FLOWER TO A GARDEN	1968	EPIC(DBL)	US	B2N 171
(N)	LIKE IT IS	1968	HICKORY	US	143
( )	GREATEST HITS	1969	PYE	UK	NSPL18283
( )	GREATEST HITS	1969	EPIC	US	BN 26836
( )	GREATEST HITS	19	EPIC	US	26439
( )	BEST OF DONOVAN	19	HICKORY	US	149
( )	DONOVAN P LEITCH	19	JANUS	US	3022
( )	WORLD OF DONOVAN	1969	MARBLE ARCH	UK	MAL 1168
( )	WORLD OF DONOVAN	19	EPIC		66289
( )	WORLD OF DONOVAN	19	EPIC		64494/5
( )	WORLD OF DONOVAN	19	EPIC	US	31210
(O)	OPEN ROAD	1970	DAWN	UK	DNLS 3009
(O)	OPEN ROAD	1970	EPIC	US	30125
( )	GOLDEN HOUR	1971	PYE	UK	GH 506
(P)	H M S DONOVAN (DBL)	1971	DAWN	UK	DNLD 4001
( )	COLOURS	1972	HALLMARK	UK	HMA 241
(Q)	COSMIC WHEELS	1973	EPIC US 32156	UK	65450
(R)	ESSENCE TO ESSENCE	1973	EPIC US 32800	UK	69050
(S)	LIVE IN JAPAN	1973	EPIC SONY		ECPM 25
(T)	7 TEASE	1974	EPIC US 33245	UK	69104
(T)	7 TEASE	1974	EPIC	NL	80531
( )	DONOVAN	1974	JOKER	IT	13730
( )	DONOVAN	197	ARISTA	US	4143
( )	DONOVAN	19	VOGUE	FR	687
(U)	SLOW DOWN WORLD	1976	EPIC US 33945	UK	86011
(U)	SLOW DOWN WORLD	1976	EPIC	NL	81371
(V)	DONOVAN	1977	RAK EURO 9929	UK	SRAK 528
(W)	DONOVAN FILE	1977	PYE	UK	FILD 004
( )	TROUBADOUR	19	MODE	IMP	MD 9034
( )	HEAR ME NOW	19	JANUS	US	3025
( )	HISTORY OF POP	1976	PYE	US	502
( )	SPOTLIGHT	1981	PRT	UK	1017
( )	4 SHADES 4 lps	19	PYE	UK	11PP 102

Musician	Instr	Albums	Musician	Instr	Albums	Musician	Instr	Albums	Musician	Instr	Albums
ED WHITTING	V	(U	JENNETTE CLINGER	V	(U	STACY JO CLINGER	V	(U	ALLAN DELORY	V	(U
RON HICKLIN	V	(U	JENNIFER HICKLIN	V	(U	SUSIE IVES	V	(U	JOHN MERLINO	V	(U
MAXINE WILLARD	V	(U	JULIA TILLMAN	V	(U	CLIFF BARTON	B	(HM	JACK BRUCE	B	(HM
MIKE O'NEIL	K	(HMO	KEITH WEBB	D	(HM	CANDY JOHN CARR	PERC	(GHMO	HAROLD McNAIR	FLT	(GHJLM
MIKE CARR	VIBES	(HM	ERIC LEESE	G	(HM	BRIAN LOCKING	B	(AB	SKIP ALLEN	D	(AB
GYPSY DAVE	KAZOO	(AB	DANNY THOMPSON	B	(L	ALAN HAWKSHAW	PNO	(L	MADELINE BELL	V	(L
JEFF BECK	G	(L	KEN BALDOCK	B	(GM	RON WOOD	G	(L	ROD STEWART	V	(L
NICKY HOPKINS	K	(L	AYNSLEY DUNBAR	D	(L	MIKE THOMPSON	V G	(O	JOHN PAUL JONES	K	(F
SHAWN PHILLIPS	G	(C	JOHN CAMERON	K	(F						

D100 LONNIE DONEGAN D100

LONNIE DONEGAN BANJ V G (ALL

WITH

Musician	Instr	Albums
DENNY WRIGHT	G	(A
MICKY ASHMAN	B	(A
NICK NICHOLLS	D	(A
DAVE WINTOUR	B	(T
RAY COOPER	PERC	(T
HENRY SPINETTI	D	(T
RINGO STARR	D	(T
NICKY HOPKINS	K	(T
BRUCE GARY	D	(T
GARY BROOKER	K	(T
FRANK GIBSON	D	(T
PETE WINGFIELD	K	(T
JIM KELTNER	D	(T
ALAN JONES	B	(T
KLAUS VOORMANN	B	(T
MICK RALPHS	G B	(T
PETER JAMESON	G	(T
RORY GALLAGHER	G	(T
ROGER McKEW	G B	(T
ALBERT LEE	G	(T
PETER BANKS	G	(T
BRIAN MAY	G	(T
RON WOOD	G	(T
LEO SAYER	HCA V	(T
ZOOT MONEY	PNO	(T
ELTON JOHN	PNO	(T
WILLIAM D SMITH	ORG	(T
COLIN FAIRLEY	D	(T
MICHELLE PHILLIPS	V	(T
REV JAMES CLEVELAND	PNO	(T

Album	Title	Year	Label	Country	Number
(A)	SHOWCASE	1956	PYE NIXA	UK	NPT 19012
(A)	SHOWCASE	1968	MARBLE ARCH	UK	MAL 797
(B)	LONNIE	1958	PYE NIXA	UK	NPT 19027
(C)	TOPS WITH LONNIE	1957	PYE	UK	NPL 18034
(D)	RIDES AGAIN	1959	PYE	UK	NPL 18043
(D)	RIDES AGAIN	1969	MARBLE ARCH	UK	MAL 1153
(E)	MORE TOPS WITH LONNIE	1961	PYE	UK	NPL 18063
(F)	SING HALLELUJAH	1962	PYE	UK	NPL 18073
(F)	SING HALLELUJAH	19	ABC	US	433
(G)	GOLDEN AGE OF DONEGAN	1962	GOLDEN GUINEA	UK	GGL 0135
(G)	GOLDEN AGE OF DONEGAN	1965	MARBLE ARCH	UK	MAL 636
(H)	GOLDEN AGE OF DONEGAN VOL 2	1963	GOLDEN GUINEA	UK	GGL 0170
(H)	GOLDEN AGE OF DONEGAN VOL 2	1967	MARBLE ARCH	UK	MAL 698
(I)	FOLK ALBUM	1965	PYE	UK	NPL 18126
(I)	FOLK ALBUM	1967	GOLDEN GUINEA	UK	GGL 0382
(J)	AN ENGLISHMAN SINGS AMERICAN FOLK	19	MERCURY	US	20229
( )	HITS OF LONNIE DONEGAN	1978	MFP	UK	50389
(K)	LONNIE POPS	19	DECCA	UK	SKL 5068
(L)	GOLDEN HOUR	197	PYE	UK	GH 514
(M)	GOLDEN HOUR VOL2	1973	PYE	UK	GH 564
(N)	GREATEST HITS	19	RONCO	UK	RTL 2017
(O)	MY OLD MANS A DUSTMAN	1971	HALLMARK	UK	HMA 204
(P)	LONNIE DONEGAN	19	HALLMARK	UK	HMA 252
(Q)	LONNIE DONEGAN	19	DOT	US	3394
(R)	SKIFFLE FOLK MUSIC	19	ATLANTIC	US	8038
(S)	LONNIE DONEGAN FILE (DBL)	1977	PYE	UK	FILD 0111/2
(T)	PUTTIN' ON THE STYLE	1977	CHRYSALIS	UK	CHR 1158
(T)	PUTTIN' ON THE STYLE	1977	UA	US	UALA 827
(T)	PUTTIN' ON THE STYLE	197	PHONOGRAM	EUR	6367 618
(U)	SUNDOWN	1978	CHRYSALIS	UK	CHR 1205

D101 DOOBIE BROTHERS D101

JOHN HARTMAN D (ABCDEFH*J (A) DOOBIE BROTHERS 1971 WB US 1919 UK K 46090
TOM JOHNSTON G V (ABCDEFH*J (B) TOULOUSE STREET 1973 WB US 2634 UK K 46183
DAVE SHOGREN K B V (A (C) THE CAPTAIN & ME 1974 WB US 2694 UK K 46217
PAT SIMMONS G V (ABCDEFGHJK (D) WHAT WERE ONCE VICES 1974 WB US 2750 UK K 56026
MICHAEL HOSSACK D (BCD (E) STAMPEDE 1975 WB US 2835 UK K 56094
TIRAN PORTER B V (BCDEFGHJK (F) TAKING IT TO THE STREETS 1976 WB US 2899 UK K 56196
KEITH KNUDSEN D V (DEFGHJK (G) BEST OF 1976 WB US 2978 UK K 56308
JEFF BAXTER G STEEL (CDEFGHJ (H) LIVING ON THE FAULT LINE 1977 WB US 3045 UK K 56383
BILL PAYNE K (CDEJ (J) MINUTE BY MINUTE 1979 WB US 3193 UK K 56486
MILT HOLLAND PERC (D ( ) STAR COLLECTION 1974 MIDI 26022
MIKE McDONALD K V (FGHJK (K) ONE STEP CLOSER 1980 WB US 3452 UK K 56824
BOBBY LAKIND CONGA (FHJK (*) 1970 LINE UP NO ALBUMS
MARIA MULDAUR V (EF ( ) BEST OF THE DOOBIES 1980 WB US 3112
WAYNE JACKSON HRNS (DF ( ) BEST OF VOL 2 1981 WB US 3612 UK K 56956
ANDREW LOVE HRNS (DF
NOVI VLA (D JAMES MITCHELL HRNS (DF LEWIS COLLINS HRNS (F JACK HALE TROM (DF
RITCHIE HAYWARD D (F JESSE BUTLER ORG (F DAN ARMSTRONG SITAR (H NORTON BUFFALO HCA (H
VICTOR FELDMAN PERC (EH ROSEMARY BUTLER V (H MAUREEN McDONALD V (H RY COODER G (E
KARL HIMMEL D (E BOBBYE HALL PERC (E SHIRLEY MATTHEWS V (E VANETTA FIELDS V (E
JESSICA SMITH V (E CONTE CONDOLI TPT (E PETE CONDOLI TPT (E EDDIE GUZMAN PERC (D
ARLO GUTHRIE HCA (D WILLIE WEEKS B (TED TEMPLEMAN PERC (K JOEL PESKIN SAX (K
CHRISTOPHER THOMPSON V (K LEE THOMBERG TPT (K PAT HENDERSON K (K BYRON BERLINE FDL (K
NICOLETTE LARSEN V (JK BEN CAULEY TPT (J CHET McCRACKEN D (K JIMMY HASKELL STR (K
JERRY JUMONVILLE SAX (K BILL ARMSTRONG TPT (K HERB PEDERSEN BAN (J JAMES BOOKER PNO (D
LESTER ABRAMS PNO (J JOHN McFEE G V (K CORNELIUS BUMPUS SAX V (K

D102 DOOMED D102

DAVE VANIAN (A) NO RECORDS
RAT SCABIES
CAPT SENSIBLE HENRI BADOWSKI

D102A DOOR & THE WINDOW D102A

(A) FIRST EP 19 NB UK NB 1
(B) SECOND EP 19 NB UK NB 2
(C) DETAILED TWANG (LIM EDITION) 19 NB UK NB 5

D103 THE DOORS D103

JIM MORRISON V (ABCDEFGJMNO (A) THE DOORS 1967 ELEKTRA US UK 74007
RAY MANZAREK K V (ALL (A) THE DOORS 1971 ELEKTRA UK K 42012
ROBBIE KRIEGER G (ALL (B) STRANGE DAYS 1968 ELEKTRA US UK 74014
JOHN DENSMORE D (ALL (B) STRANGE DAYS 1971 ELEKTRA UK K42016 RI 22008
DOUGLAS LUBAHN B (BCDN (C) WAITING FOR THE SUN 1968 ELEKTRA US 74024
HARVEY BROOKS B (DN (C) WAITING FOR THE SUN 1971 ELEKTRA UK K 42041
JERRY SCHEFF B (GHMN (D) SOFT PARADE 1969 ELEKTRA US 75005
MARC BENNO G (GN (D) SOFT PARADE 1971 ELEKTRA UK 42079
CURTIS AMY SAX (DN (E) MORRISON HOTEL 1970 ELEKTRA US 75007
GEORGE BOHANON TROM (D (E) MORRISON HOTEL 1971 ELEKTRA UK K 42080
CHAMP WEBB HRNS (D (F) ABSOLUTELY LIVE (DBL) 1970 ELEKTRA US 2 9002
JESSE McREYNOLDS MAND (D (F) ABSOLUTELY LIVE (DBL) 1971 ELEKTRA UK K 62005
JIMMY BUCHANAN FDL (D (G) LA WOMAN 1971 ELEKTRA US 75011
REINOL ANDINO PERC (D (G) LA WOMAN 1971 ELEKTRA UK K 42090
KERRY MAGNESS B (C (H) OTHER VOICES 1971 ELEKTRA US 75017
LEROY VINEGAR B (C (H) OTHER VOICES 1971 ELEKTRA UK K 42104
RAY NEAPOLITAN B (EH (J) WEIRD SCENES INSIDE THE GOLDMINE 1971 ELEKTRA (DBL) US 2 6001
LONNIE MACK B (EN (J) WEIRD SCENES INSIDE THE GOLDMINE 1971 ELEKTRA (DBL) UK K 62009
G PUGLESE (J SEBASTIAN) HCA (E (K) DOORS 13 197 ELEKTRA US 74079
JACK CONRAD B (HL (K) DOORS 13 1971 ELEKTRA UK K 42062
WILLIE RUFF B (H (L) FULL CIRCLE 1972 ELEKTRA US 75038
FRANCISCO AQUABELLA PERC (H (L) FULL CIRCLE 1972 ELEKTRA UK K 42116
EMIL RICHARDS PERC (H (M) AN AMERICAN PRAYER 1978 ELEKTRA US 5E502
WOLFGANG MELTZ B (H (M) AN AMERICAN PRAYER 1978 ELEKTRA UK K 52111
CHRIS ETHRIDGE B (L ( ) GREATEST HITS 1980 ELEKTRA US 515 uk 52254
CHARLES LARKEY B (L ( ) BEST OF 1974 ELEKTRA US EQ 5035
BOBBYE HALL PERC (L ( ) BEST OF 1974 ELEKTRA UK K 42143
CHARLES LLOYD WIND (L ( ) STAR COLLECTION 1975 MIDI UK 22001
LELAND SKLAR B (L ( ) STAR COLLECTION 2 1975 MIDI UK 22019
CHICO BATERA PERC (L (AB) DOORS /STRANGE DAYS (DBL) 1975 ELEKTRA GERM 621013
CLYDIE KING V (L
VANETTA FIELDS V (L MELISSA MACKAY V (L BOB GLAUB B (M
JOHN SEBASTIAN HCA (N JOHN HARVEY (M FRANK LUSCIANDRO (M
PAUL ROTHCHILD PROD (ABCDEFGHM BRUCE BOTNICK PROD (M REIND ANDINA PERC (M
ARTHUR BARROW SYN (M

D104 CHARLIE DORE D104

CHARLIE DORE V (AB (A) WHERE TO NOW 1979 ISLAND UK ILPS 9559
ALAN TARNEY G K B V (A (B) LISTEN 1981 CHRYSALIS UK CHR 1225
TREVOR SPENCER D (A
MEL COLLINS SAX (A GARY TAYLOR B V (A CLIFF HALL K (A DALE SELLARS G (A
REGGIE YOUNG G (A SONNY CURTIS G (A JULIAN LITTMAN G MAND V (A BOBBY WOOD K (A
DAVID BRIGGS K (A TOMMY COGBILL B (A MIKE LEECH B (A JERRY CARRIGAN D (A
KARL HIMMEL D (A CHARLIE McCOY HCA (A LARRY SASSER STEEL (A JERRY ROBERTS ACC (A
FARRELL MORRIS PERC (A SHELLY KURLAND STR (A ROY CHRISTIANSEN STR (A JOHNNY CHRISTOPHER V (A
JEFF PORCARO D (B STEVE LUKATHER G (B MIKE PORCARO B (B ROBBIE BUCHANAN K SYN (B
STEWART LEVINE PROD (B

D105 RAY DORSET D105

RAY DORSET G V (A (A) COLD BLUE EXCURSION 1972 DAWN UK DNLS 3033
MIKE McNAUGHT PNO (A
DAVE MARKEE B (A MIKE TRAVIS D (A JOE RUSH PERC (A SUNNY LESLIE V (A
SUE GLOVER V (A COLIN EARL (A JOHN GODFREY B (A

D106 LEE DORSEY D106

LEE DORSEY V (ALL — (A) LEE DORSEY — 1966 AMY US 8010 UK STATESIDE 10177
ALLEN TOUSSAINT PNO (— (B) NEW LEE DORSEY — 1966 AMY US 8011 UK STATESIDE 10192
CHARLES WILLIAMS D (— (C) YES WE CAN — 1970 POLYDOR 2482 280 + 2489 006
ROY MONTRELL G (— (C) YES WE CAN — 1970 POLYDOR GERM 244042
NAT PERILLAT SAX (— (D) GREATEST HITS — 19 SUE /ISLAND UK ILP924
( ) GREATEST HITS — 1974 SOUNDS SUPERB UK SPR 90045
( ) BEST OF — 19 STARLINE UK SRS 5023
( ) NIGHT PEOPLE — 1978 ABC US 1048
( ) GONNA BE FUNKY — 1980 CHARLY UK CRB 1001
( ) WORKING IN A COALMINE — 1980 CHARLY EP UK CTD 101

D106A DOUCETTE D106A

JERRY DOUCETTE V G B(A — (A) MAMA LET HIM PLAY — 19 MUSHROOM US 5009
DURIS MAXWELL D K (A — (B) THE DOUC IS LOOSE — 1979 MERCURY GER 9124 410
DONNIE CUMMINGS B (A
MARK OLSON K (A IRA HIRSCHEL SYN (PETER HOORELBEKE D (A

D106B EARLE DOUD D106B

EARLE DOUD V PERC(ALL — (A) LYNDON JOHNSONS LONELY HEARTS CLUB BAND — 19 ATCO US SD33230
ALEN ROBIN — (B) HONEST TO GOD WE REALLY MEANT IT — 19 BRUNSWICK US 754201
(C) WELCOME TO L B J RANCH — 19 CAPITOL US 2423

D106C STEVE DOUGLAS & THE REBEL ROUSERS D106C

STEVE DOUGLAS (A — (A) TWIST — 19 CROWN US 5254

D106D DOVELLS D106D

LEN BARRY V (— (A) BRISTOL STOMP — 1961 PARKWAY US 7006
JERRY SUMMERS V (— (B) ALL THE HITS — 1962 PARKWAY US 7010
MIKE DENNIS V (— (C) FOR YOUR HULLY GULLY PARTY — 1962 PARKWAY US 7020
ARNIE SATIN V (— (D) YOU CANT SIT DOWN — 1962 PARKWAY US 7025
DANNY BROOKS V (— (E) BIGGEST HITS — 196 WYNCOTE US 9114
(F) DISCOTHEQUE — 19 WYNCOTE US 9052
(G) CAMEO PARKWAY SESSIONS — 1979 LONDON UK HAU 8515

D106E KENNY DOSS D106E

KENNY DOSS (A — (A) MOVIN ON A FEELING — 1980 BEARSVILLE 202224

D106F DOUG & THE SLUGS D106F

DOUG BENNETT G V (A — (A) COGNAC & BOLOGNA — 1981 RCA US AFL 13387
SIMON KENDALL K (A
JOHN BURTON G V (WALLY WATSON D (A RICHARD BAKER G (A STEVE BOSLEY B (A

D106G DANNY DOUMA D106G

DANNY DOUMA G V (A — (A) NIGHT EYES — 1979 WB US 3326
PETER FRIEBERGER B (A
TODD SHARP G (A ERIC CLAPTON G (A JOHN McVIE B (A AMOS GARRETT G (A
LINDSEY BUCKINGHAM G (A MICHELLE GRUSKA V (A CLAUDE PEPPER D (A NICK VAN MAARTH G V(A
JAY GRUSKA K (A MICK FLEETWOOD D (A CHRISTINE McVIE K V (A DAVID WOODFORD SAX(A
GARTH HUDSON ACC (A

D107 BRENTON DOWE D107

BRENTON DOWE V (A — (A) BUILD ME UP — 19 TROJAN UK TRLS 76

D107A JOHN DOWIE D107A

JOHN DOWIE (A — (A) ANOTHER CLOSE SHAVE — 1977 VIRGIN UK VEP 1004

D108 BOB DOWNES D108

BOB DOWNES V WIND(ALL — (A) DREAM JOURNEY — 1970 PHILIPS SBL 7922
CHRIS SPEDDING G (ABC — (B) ELECTRIC CITY — 1970 VERTIGO UK 6360 005
RAY RUSSELL G (BCF — (C) DEEP DOWN HEAVY — 1970 M F P UK MFP 1412
PETER BILLAM G (C — (D) DIVERSIONS — 1974 OPENIUM BDOM 001
ROBERT COCKBURN V (C — (E) EPISODE AT 4 AM — 1974 OPENIUM BDOM 002
DEREK HOGG D (AC — (F) HELLS ANGELS — 1975 OPENIUM BDOM 003
JOHN STEVENS D (AF — (G) OPEN MUSIC — 19
ALAN RUSHTON D (BC
HARRY MILLER B (ABCF LAURIE ALLEN D (C DAVE BROOKS SAX (BF HERBIE FLOWERS B (BF
DARRYL RUNSWICK B (B DENNIS SMITH D (ABDF JIM GREGORY FLT (A CLEM CATTINI D (B
DOM FAY SAX (BF NIGEL CARTER TPT (AB KENNY WHEELER TPT (B BUD PARKES HRNS (B
HAROLD BECKETT HRNS (BF IAN CARR HRNS (B ROBIN JONES PERC (B JOHN WARREN SAX (A
CHRIS PYNE TROM (A BUTCH HUDSON TPT (A LAURIE BAKER SYN (DF WENDY BENKA FLT PER (E
TONY ROBERTS SAX (F CLIVE STEVENS SAX (A HENRY LOWTHER TPT (AF BARRY GUY B (DF
JEFF CLYNE B (DF MARC CHARIG TPT (F

D109 DOWNLINER SECT D109

DON CRAINE V (ALL — (A) THE SECT — 1964 COLUMBIA UK 33SX 1658
PAUL TITLER HCA V (D — (A) THE SECT — 1977 CHARLY GER 3014 UK CR 30122
KEITH GRANT V B (ALL — (B) THE COUNTRY SECT — 1965 COLUMBIA UK 33SX 1745
TERRY GIBSON G (ALL — (B) THE COUNTRY SECT — 1979 CHARLY GER 3021 UK CR 30137
JOHN SUTTON D (ABC — (C) THE ROCK SECTS IN — 1966 COLUMBIA UK SCX 6028
PIP HARVEY V (— (C) THE ROCK SECTS IN — 1978 CHARLY GER 3035 UK CR 30140
JOHN PAUL JONES PNO (— (D) SHOWBIZ — 1979 SKY GER 301 UK RAW RWLP106
MICHAEL SUTTON PERC D(— (E) THE DOWNLINERS SECT — 19 HMV SWED SGLP 534
RAY SONE HCA (A — (EP) NITE AT GT NEWPORT STREET — 1964 RBC UK 001
PAUL HOLM D (DE — (EP) SECT SING SICK SONGS — 1965 COLUMBIA UK SEG 8438
(EP) SHOWBIZ — 1979 SKY GER 103
(EP) I WANT MY BABY BACK — 1978 CHARLY UK CEP 119

D109A DOWNTRIP D109A

JEAN PAUL GOSSENS V (A — (A) DOWNTOWN — 1979 PHILIPS NL 6410 976
PAUL VANDER GOOSSENS V (A
JOHN HASTRY B (A JOS CUISSET G (A

D109B LAMONT DOZIER D109B

LAMONT DOZIER V (ALL — (A) OUT HERE ON MY OWN — 1974 ABC US 804
(B) BLACK BACH — 1975 ABC US 839
(C) LOVE & BEAUTY — 1975 INVICTUS US 33134
(D) RIGHT THERE — 1976 WB US 2929
(E) PEDDLIN' — 1977 WB US 3039
(F) BITTERSWEET — 1979 WB UK K56594
(G) WORKING ON YOU — 1981 ARC US 37129

D110 **PETER DOYLE** D110

PETER DOYLE G V (A | (A) SKIN DEEP | 1977 RCA PL 25113
ALAN TARNEY V G B K (A
GEOFF WHITEHORN G (A | PAUL KEOGH SLIDE (A | TREVOR SPENCER D (A
SIMON PHILLIPS D (A | B J COLE STEEL (A | TONY HYMAS K (A
MAC TONTOH TPT (A | JOY YATES V (A | JEAN GILBERT V (A
VAL STOKES V (A

D110A **DRAGON** D110A

NEIL STORY D (| ( ) SCENTED GARDENS FOR THE BLIND | 19 PHONOGRAM 6360 903
IVAN THOMPSON K (| ( ) SAME OLD BLUES | 19 PORTRAIT 32636
MARC HUNTER V (| ( ) RUNNING FREE | 1977 CBS UK 33005
ROBERT TAYLOR G V (| ( ) DRAGON | 1977 PORTRAIT UK PRT 82636
KERRY JACOBSON D (
PAUL HEWSON K V ((| TODD HUNTER B V (

D110B **DRAGONFLY** D110B

(A) ALMOST ABANDONED | 1974 RETREAT UK 6002 US METROMEDIA ?

D111 **NICK DRAKE** D111

NICK DRAKE V G PNO (ALL | (A) FIVE LEAVES LEFT | 19 ANTILLES US AN 7010
DORIS TROY V (B | (A) FIVE LEAVES LEFT | 1969 ISLAND UK ILPS 9105
PAUL HARRIS PNO (AB | (B) BRYTER LAYTER | 1970 ISLAND UK ILPS 9134
RICHARD THOMPSON G (AB | (B) BRYTER LAYTER | 1977 ANTILLES US AN 7028
DANNY THOMPSON B (AD | (C) PINK MOON | 1972 ISLAND US 9318 UK ILPS 9184
ROCKY DZIDZORNU PERC (AD | (ABC)FRUIT TREE(+ EXTRA TRACKS) | 1979 ISLAND UK NDSP 100
CLARE LOWTHER CELLO (AD | (D) NICK DRAKE | 19 ISLAND US ILPS 9307
TRISTAN FRY D VIBES(A
DAVE PEGG B (BD | DAVE MATTACKS D (B | RAY WARLEIGH SAX (B
ED CARTER B (B | MIKE KOWALSKI D (BD | LYN DOBSON FLT (B
JOHN CALE VLA K (BD | CHRIS McGREGOR V (B | P P ARNOLD V (B

D112 **PETE DRAKE** D112

PETE DRAKE STEEL (ALL | FOREVER | 1964 SMASH US SRS 67053
PETE DRAKE & HIS TALKING GUITAR | 19 MOUTAIN DEW US S 7042
AMAZING | 19 STARDAY US 319
THE HITS I PLAYED ON | 1969 AMBASSADORE US S 98061
PLAYS ALL TIME COUNTRY FAVOURITES | 19 HOLLYWOOD US HLP 506
STEEL AWAY | 1973 CANAAN UK CGS 8502
PETE DRAKE SHOW | 19 STOP US 1011
FABULOUS STEEL GUITAR | 19 STARDAY US 180

D112A **DRAMATIS** D112A

CHRIS PAYNE K V (A | (A) FOR FUTURE REFERENCE | 1981 ROCKET UK TRAIN 18
DENNIS HAINES K V (A
RUSSELL BELL G (A | CEDRIC SHARPLEY D (A

D113 **THE DRANSFIELDS** D113

ROBIN DRANSFIELD V G (ABDEG | (A) ROUT OF THE BLUES | 1970 TRAILER UK LER 2011
BARRY DRANSFIELD V G FDL (ABCDEF | (B) LORD OF ALL I BEHOLD | 1971 TRAILER UK LER 2026
BRIAN HARRISON D (D | (C) BARRY DRANSFIELD | 1972 POLYDOR UK 2383 160
CHARLIE SMITH V B K (D | (D) THE FIDDLERS DREAM | 1976 TRANSATLANTIC UK TRA 322
(E) POPULAR TO CONTRARY BELIEF | 1977 FREE REED UK FRR 018
(F) BOWIN' & SCRAPIN' | 1978 TRANSATLANTIC UK TRA 386
(G) TIDEWAVE | 1981 TOPIC UK 12TS 414

D113A **MIKEY DREAD** D113A

MIKEY DREAD V (AB | (A) DREAD AT THE CONTOLS | 1979 TROJAN UK TRLS 178
EARL"BAGGA" WALKER B (A | (B) WORLD WAR THREE | 1980 DREAD AT THE CONTROLS TNT 1
ROBBIE SHAKESPEARE B (A
FRANKLYN WAUL K (A | SLY DUNBAR D (A | LARRY"HORSE MOUTH"WALLACE D (A
SANTA D (A | EARL"CHINNA"SMITH G (A | RAD"DOUGGIE"BRYAN G (A
BOO PEE BROWN G (A | WINSTON BROWN G (A | AUGUSTO PABLO K (A
ANSEL COLLINS PNO (A | STICKY PERC (A | SKULLY PERC (AB
LATTY GOURZONG PERC (A | FRANKLYN"BLUBBER"WAUL SYN (A | VIN GORDON TROM (A
FELIX"DEADLEY" HEADLEY WIND(AB | GLADSTONE ANDERSON PNO (A | ERROL"FLABBA"HOLT B (B
LINCOLN"STYLE"HOLT D (B | NOEL"SOWELL"BAILEY G (B | BONGO HERMAN PERC (B
ANTHONY"STEELIE"NELSON ORG(B | EDI FITZROY V (B | EARL SIXTEEN V (B
MICHAEL CAMPBELL V (B | WALTY BURNETT V (B

D114 **DREAM** D114

DEKE LEONARD G V (A | (A) 1967/ 68 NO ALBUMS
MARTIN ACE G V (A
WES REYNOLDS B (A | TERRY WILLIAMS D (A

D115 **DREAMS** D115

JEFF KENT K G V (A1 | (1) 1969 (2) LATER LINE UPS
DOUG LUBAHN B V (A1 | (A) DREAMS | 1970 CBS US 30225 UK 64203
MARK WHITTAKER D (1 | (B) IMAGINE MY SUPRISE | 1971 CBS US 30960 UK 64597
RANDY BRECKER HRNS (AB
MICHAEL BRECKER HRNS (AB | BILLY COBHAM D (AB | JOHN ABERCROMBIE G (A
BOB MANN G WIND V (B | EDWARD VERNON V (AB | WILL LEE B (B
BARRY ROGERS TROM (AB | DON GROLNICK K (B | STEVE CROPPER G (B
TONI TORRENCE V (B | ANGEL ALLENDE CONGA (A | ALLEN SCHWARZBERG D (2
STEVE GADD D (2 | CHUCK RAINEY B (2

D116 **DRIFTERS** D116

CLYDE McPHATTER V (| ( ) CLYDE McPHATTER & THE DRIFTERS | 1958 ATLANTIC US 8003
BEN E KING V (| ( ) ROCKIN' & DRIFTIN' | 1958 ATLANTICO US 8022
DAVID BAUGHN V (| ( ) DRIFTERS GREATEST HITS | 1960 ATLANTIC US 8041
ELSBERRY HOBBS V (| ( ) SAVE THE LAST DANCE FOR ME | 1962 ATLANTIC US 8059
RUDY LEWIS V (| ( ) SAVE THE LAST DANCE FOR ME | 1962 ATLANTIC UK 587 063
BILLY LEWIS V (| ( ) I'LL TAKE YOU WHERE THE MUSIC'S.. | 1965 ATLANTIC US 8113
CLYDE BROWN V (| ( ) I'LL TAKE YOU WHERE THE MUSIC'S.. | 1965 ATLANTIC UK 587 061
DIONNE WARWICK V (| ( ) I'LL TAKE YOU WHERE THE MUSIC'S.. | 1971 ATLANTIC UK RI K40009
JO BLUNT V (| ( ) GOLDEN HITS | 1966 ATLANTIC US 8153
( ) GOLDEN HITS | 1966 ATLANTIC UK 588 013
( ) GOLDEN HITS | 1972 ATLANTIC UK K40018

(CONTINUED)

D116 (CONTINUED) DRIFTERS D116

Member	Inst	
DEE DEE WARWICK	V	(
CISSY HOUSTON	V	(
DORIS TROY	V	(
JIMMY OLIVER	G	(
TOMMY EVANS	V	(
CHARLES HUGHES	V	(
ANDREW THRASHER	V	(
BOBBY HENDRICKS	V	(
JOHNNY MOORE	V	(
BILL PINKNEY	V	(
GERHARD THRASHER	V	(
CHARLIE THOMAS	V	(
DOC GREEN	V	(

	Title	Year	Label	Country	No.
( )	THE DRIFTERS	197	ATLANTIC	UK	K40412
( )	STAR COLLECTION	197	MIDI	UK	20027
( )	THE DRIFTERS NOW	1973	BELL	US	219
( )	LOVE GAMES	1975	BELL UK BELLS246	US	246
( )	THERE GOES MY FIRST LOVE	1975	BELL UK BELLS280	US	260
( )	24 ORIGINAL HITS	1975	ATLANTIC	UK	K60106
( )	THE DRIFTERS STORY	1975	ATLANTIC	UK	K40565
( )	SAVE THE LAST DANCE	1975	SOUNDS SUPERB	UK	SPR 90083
( )	EVERY NIGHT IS SATURDAY NIGHT	1976	ARISTA		AB 4140
( )	UP ON THE ROOF	1963	ATLANTIC	US	8073
( )	UP ON THE ROOF	1963	ATLANTIC	UK	588 160
( )	OUR BIGGEST HITS	196	ATLANTIC	US	8093
( )	OUR BIGGEST HITS	196	ATLANTIC	UK	587 038
( )	UNDER THE BOARDWALK	1964	ATLANTIC	US	8099
( )	GOOD LIFE	1965	ATLANTIC	US	8103
( )	GREATEST RECORDINGS	19	ATCO	US	33375

D117 DRIFTWOOD D117

Member	Inst	
NEIL ALFORD	G V	(A
NICK HARRISON	G V HCA	(A
NEIL HARRISON	K V	(A

	Title	Year	Label	Country	No.
( )	DRIFTWOOD	1970	DECCA	UK	SKL 5069

D118 JULIE DRISCOLL D118

Member	Inst	
JULIE DRISCOLL (TIPPETS)	V	(ALL
WITH		
KEITH TIPPETT	K	(A
CHRIS SPEDDING	G B	(A
BOB DOWNES	FLT	(A
JEFF CLYNE	B	(A
ELTON DEAN	SAX	(AC
KARL JENKINS	OBOE	(A
DEREK WADSWORTH	TROM	(A
JIM CREGAN	G	(A
HARRY MILLER	B	(C
NICK EVANS	TROM	(AC
BUD PARKES	TPT	(A
BRIAN GODDING	V G	(AC
BARRY REEVES	D	(A
LOUIS MOHOLO	D	(C
TREVOR TOMKINS	D	(A
STAN SULZMANN	SAX	(A
BRIAN BELSHAW	B V	(CA
MARC CHARIG	HRNS	(AC

	Title	Year	Label	Country	No.
(A)	JULIE DRISCOLL	1971	POLYDOR		2480 074
(A)	JULIE DRISCOLL	1971	POLYDOR	GER	2383 077
(B)	STARPORTRAIT	197	POLYDOR		2625 008
(C)	SUNSET GLOW	1976	UTOPIA		UTS 601
(D)	JULIE DRISCOLL	19	SPRINGBOARD	US	SPB 4043

D119 DRIVER D119

Member	Inst	
PETER GLIDEMAN	G V	(A
DENNIS COATS	B V	(A
STEVE ROXFORD	D	(A

	Title	Year	Label	Country	No.
(A)	NO ACCIDENTS	1977	A&M	US	4545

D120 DRONES D120

Member	Inst	
M J DRONE	V G	(A
PETE PURRFECT	D	(
STEVE CUNDALL	B	(
SIMON HUMPHREY	PROD	(A
GUS CALLENDER	G	(
P LAMBERT HOWELLS	D	(A

	Title	Year	Label	Country	No.
(A)	FURTHER TEMPTATIONS	1977	VALER	UK	VLRP1

D120A DRUG ADDIX D120A

	Title	Year	Label	Country	No.
(A)	FROM NEW ADDINGTON(EP)	1978	CHISWICK	UK	SW 39

D120B JOE DROUKAS D120B

Member	Inst	
JOE DROUKAS		(A

	Title	Year	Label	Country	No.
(A)	SHADOWBOXING	1975	SOUTHWIND	US	6400

D121 DRUICK & LORANGE D121

Member
DWIGHT DRUICK
KIRK LORANGE

	Title	Year	Label	Country	No.
(A)	DRUICK & LORANGE	1974	GOODEAR		EARLH5001

D122 DRUID D122

Member	Inst	
NEIL BREWER	B	(AB
ANDREW McCRORIE SHAND	K	(AB
CEDRIC SHARPLEY	D PERC	(AB
DANE	G V	(AB

	Title	Year	Label	Country	No.
(A)	TOWARDS THE SUN	1975	EMI	UK	EMC 3081
(B)	FLUID DRUID	1976	EMI	UK	EMC 3128

D122A DRUIDS OF STONEHENGE D122A

	Title	Year	Label	Country	No.
(A)	CREATION	19	UNI	US	73004

D122B DRY CITY SCAT BAND D122B

	Title	Year	Label	Country	No.
( )	DRY CITY SCAT BAND	19	ELEKTRA	US	7292

D122C DUCKS D122C

Member	Inst	
BRUCE BRYMEN	D V	(A
KENT HOUSEMAN	G V	(A
DENNIS LANIGAN	V K SAX FLT	(A
DONALD LUTHER	B V	(A
JIM GORDON	D	(A

	Title	Year	Label	Country	No.
(A)	DUCKS	1973	JUST SUNSHINE	US	JSS6

D123 DUCKS DELUXE D123

Member	Inst	
SEAN TYLA	G V K	(ABCDE12
MARTIN BELMONT	G	(ABCDE12
NICK GARVEY	B HCA	(AB1
TIM ROPER	D	(ABC1
BOB ANDREWS	K V	(AE
GEORGE LARNYOH	SAX	(A
PETER VANDER PUIJE	SAX	(A
EDDIE QUANSAH	TPT	(A
BILLY RANKIN	D	(2E
NICK LOWE	G	(E
LEE BRILLEAUX	V	(E
DAVE EDMUNDS	G	(BD
BRINSLEY SCHWARZ	G V	(2E
MARTIN STONE		(E
ANDY McMASTERS	K V	(1
MICK GROOM	B	(2CE
KEN WHALEY		(

	Title	Year	Label	Country	No.
(A)	DUCKS DELUXE	1974	RCA		PI 5008
(B)	TAXI TO THE TERMINAL ZONE	1974	RCA	UK	SF 8402
(C)	JUMPIN' (EP)	1975	SKYDOG		005
(D)	DONT MIND ROCKIN' (COMPILATION)	1978	RCA US 3025	PL	25132
(1) 1974 (2) FINAL LINE UP 1975					
(E)	LAST NIGHT OF A PUB ROCK BAND(DBL)	1979	DYNAMITE	NL	3303

D124 LES DUDEK D124

Member	Inst	
LES DUDEK	G V	(ALL
WITH		
JEFF PORCARO	D	(ABC
MARL HUDSON	V	(D
GERALD JOHNSON	B	(ABC
DAVID PAICH	K	(ABC
JERI STEVENS	V	(A
MYRNA MATTHEWS	V	(A
CHUCK RAINEY	B	(AB
MAILTO CORREA	CONGA	(A
ALAN FEINGOLD	K	(B
DAVID SANCIOUS	K	(B
SHIRLEY MATTHEWS	V	(B
PAT MURPHY	PERC	(BC
GARY MALLABER	D	(C
MAXINE GREEN	V	(A
JIM HUGHART	B	(A
DAVID HUNGATE	B	(A
BOZ SCAGGS	V	(A
GLEN CHRONCHITE	PERC	(A
JOACHIM YOUNG	K	(B
TONY WILLIAMS	D	(B
CLYDIE KING	V	(B
JIM KRUEGER	G	(C
JACK BRUCE	V	(C
PEPPER SWENSON	V	(A
CAROLYN WILLIS	V	(A
REBECCA LOUIS	V	(AB
DAVID FOSTER	K	(A
JIM KELTNER	D	(C
TED STRAON	K	(B
KEVIN CALHOUN	PERC	(B
REYMONDO	PERC	(B
MIKE FINNIGAN	K V	(CD
ROBERT 'POPS' POPSWELL	B	(BC

	Title	Year	Label	No.
(A)	LES DUDEK	1976	CBS US 33702	UK 81380
(B)	SAY NO MORE	1977	CBS US 34397	UK 81758
(C)	GHOST TOWN PARADE	1978	CBS US 35088	UK 82562
(D)	GYPSY RIDE	1981	CBS US 36798	NL 84611

D124 LES DUDEK (CONTINUED) **D124**

MAX GRONENTHAL K V (CD — CARMINE APPICE D (C — TOM SCOTT LYRICON (A
JERRY KNIGHT V (D — PETER SCHLESS K (D — TREY THOMPSON B (D
MAX NOLAND B (D — JAMES NEWTON HOWARD K (D — GARY FERGUSON D (D
CLIFF NEWTON G V (D — MARK STEIN SYN (D

D125 DUDES **D125**

BRIAN GREENWAY G V (A — (A) WERE NO ANGELS — 1975 CBS US 33577
DAVID HENMAN G V (A — (EP) WANNA DANCE — 19 CBS US 156
WAYNE CULLEN D V (A
BOB SEGARINI G V (A — RITCHIE HENMAN D V (A — KOOTCH TROCHIM B V (A

D125A DUFFO **D125A**

DUFFO V (AB — (A) DUFFO — 1979 BEGGARS BANQUET UK BEGA5
TIM WHEATLEY B (C — (A) DUFFO — 1979 BEGGARS BANQUET GER 146512
MIKE HOWLETT B (A — (B) THE DISAPPEARING BOY — 1980 PVK UK PVK 2 NL DURECO 66012
NICHOLAS COLA PNO (AB — (C) BOB THE BIRDMAN — 1981 PVK UK DUF1 FR 2801
DAVID HERZOG G (A
PETER DOBSON D (AB — ROB ADAMS D (C — DICK MIDDLETON G (C
LEW SEVARINI KOWICZ K SYN(B — CHRIS PASKALEDES B (B — TIM GRAPPELLI VLN (B
JIMMY PURSEY V (B — BRIAN ARMSTEAD (

D125B DUESENBERG **D125B**

(A) CHAPTER IV — 1981 VERTIGO NL 6435077

D126 DUFFY **D126**

DUFFY (AB — (A) SCRUFFY DUFFY — 1973 CHAPTER ONE UK CHSR 814
(B) JUST IN CASE YOU'RE INTERESTED — 19 ARIOLA 85846

D126A LARS DUGGAN **D126A**

LARS DUGGAN (A — (A) FROM THE LAKE STUDIOS — 1980 PHILO PH 9002

D126B DORIS DUKE **D126B**

DORIS DUKE V (AB — (A) IM A LOSER — 19 CANYON 7704 CONTEMPO 101
PAUL HORNSBY K (A — (B) LEGEND IN HER OWN TIME — 19 MANKIND 200
JERRY WILLLIAMS K (AB
ROBERT POPWELL B (AB — JESSE CARR G (AB — JASPER GUARINO D (B — CHARLIE CHALMERS V (B
SANDRA RHODES V (B — DONNA RHODES V (B — JEANIE GREEN V (B — JOHNNY SANDLIN (A
CHUCK LEAVELL K (B

D127 GEORGE DUKE **D127**

GEORGE DUKE K V (ALL — (A) GEORGE DUKE QUINTET — 19 MPS 68233
JEROME RICHARDSON WIND (Q — (B) SAVE THE COUNTRY(1969) — 1978 LIBERTY 11004 PICKWICK 3588
JOHN HEARD B (ABCEF — (C) GEORGE DUKE (1969) — 1978 PACIFIC JAZZ UK 891
DAVID SIMMONS TPT (A — (D) LIVE IN L A — 1971 SUNSET 50232
GEORGE WALKER D (A — (E) FEEL — 1974 MPS US 25355 GER 212 23124
JAY GRAYDON G (BC — (F) FACES IN REFLECTION — 1975 MPS US 22018
ERNIE WATTS SAX (BC — (G) I LOVE THE BLUES — 1975 MPS US 25671 GER 5071
RICHARD BERK D (BCQ — (H) THE AURA WILL PREVAIL — 1975 BASF US 25613 GER 5064
ERNIE TACK TROM (BC — (I) LIBERATED FANTASIES — 1976 BASF GER 22835
JAY DAVERSA TPT (BC — (J) LIVE IN EUROPE — 1976 ATLANTIC US 18194 UK K50316
CHARLES FINDLEY TPT (BC — (K) FROM ME TO YOU — 1977 EPIC US 34469 UK 81850
GLENN FERRIS TROM (BC — (L) REACH FOR IT — 1977 EPIC US 34883 UK 82216
LEON NDUGU CHANCLER D PERC(EFGHIK — (M) DONT LET GO — 1978 EPIC US 35366 UK 82821
AIRTO MOREIRA PERC (EGHI — (N) FOLLOW THAT RAINBOW — 1979 EPIC US 35701 UK 83336
JOHNNY GUITAR WATSON G (G — (O) MASTER OF THE GAME — 1979 EPIC US 36263 UK 83951
FLORA PURIM V (EGNO — (P) BRAZILIAN LOVE AFFAIR — 1980 EPIC US 36483 UK 84311
FRANK ZAPPA G (E — (Q) INNER SOURCE — 19 MPS 88031/2
TOM FOWLER B (G — (R) POLYRHYTHM — 19 LISTENING HOUSE 91003
LEE RITENOUR G (G
BYRON MILLER B (GKNO — GEORGE JOHNSON G (GI — DARYL STUERMER G (GI — EMIL RICHARDS PERC (G
JOHN WITTENBERG VLN (G — JANET FERGUSONHOFF V (GI — LUIS GASCA TPT (Q — ARMANDA PERAZA PERC (Q
RUTH UNDERWOOD PERC (GI — BRUCE FOWLER TROM (G — ALPHONSO JOHNSON B (HJS — SYLVIA ST JAMES V (H
KATHY WOEHRLE V (H — GEE JANZEN V (H — EMBAMBA B (I — NAPOLEON MURPHY BROCK V (INO
DAVID AMARO G (I — RASHID DUKE V (I — BILLY COBHAM D (J — JOHN SCOFIELD G (J
STANLEY CLARKE B (K — MIKE SEMBELLO G (K — DIANE REEVES V (K — MAXINE WILLARD V (K
JULIA TILLMAN V (K — JESSICA SMITH V (K — RICKY LAWSON D (NO — CHARLES JOHNSON G (N
SHEILA ESCOVEDO PERC (NO — LYNN JAMES V (NO — JOSIE JAMES V (NO — ROLAND BAUTISTA (O
GARY GRANT (O — GARY HERBIG SAX (O — JERRY HEY HRNS (O — DAVID MYLES (O
RAY OBIEDO G (O — BILL REICHENBACH TROM (O — FRED WASHINGTON (O — JOHN HERD B (Q
JAMES LEARY (Q — PETE MAGANINI D (R — DAVE YOUNG B (R — DON MENZA (R

D127A DUKE & THE DRIVERS **D127A**

RHINESTONE MUDFLAPS V SAX (AB — (A) CRUISIN' — 19 ABC US 911
MAD MISSISSIPPI BUFFALO V K(AB (TOM SWIFT) — (B) ROLLIN ON — 1975 ABC US 942
SAM DELUXE G V (AB — CADILLAC JACK G V (AB — BOBBY BLUE SKY D V (B
DR FEELGOOD FUNK D V (A — KOKO DEE B V (AB — EDDIE KRAMER PROD (A

D127B DUKE JUPITER **D127B**

GEORGE BARAJAS B V (ALL — (A) SWEET CHEEKS — 1978 MERCURY 9110 064
DON MARACLE G (ALL — (B) TASTE THE NIGHT — 1979 MERCURY US SRM 13756
GREG WALKER G V (ALL — (C) BAND IN BLUE — 1980 MERCURY US SRMI 3815
MARSHALL STYLER K V (ALL
DAVID HANLON D PERC(BC — YVONNE M LEWIS V (B — JANET WRIGHT V (B
DIVA GRAY V (B — CHUCK LEAVELL K (A — STEVE KATZ HCA (C
EARL JETTY D (A — JAI JOHANNY JOHANSON PERC (A — RANDALL BRAMBLETT SAX (A
HAROLD WILLIAMS HRNS (A — RONNIE EADES HRNS (A — HARVEY THOMPSON HRNS (A
HARRISON CALLOWAY HRNS (A — DENNIS GOOD HRNS (A

D127C THE DUKES **D127C**

MILLER ANDERSON G V (A12 — (A) THE DUKES — 1979 WB US BSK 3376 UK K56710
RONNIE LEAHY K (A12 — (1) 1979 (2) 1980
JIMMY McCULLOCH G V (A1
CHARLIE TUMAHAI B V (A12 — STUART ELLIOTT D (A — BARRY DE SOUZA D (A
MORRIS PERT PERC (A — GREG JACKMAN D (A — MICK GRABHAM G (2
NICK TREVISICK D (12

D127D **DULCIMER** D127D

JEM NORTH B PERC(A — (A) DULCIMER 1971 NEPENTHA 6437 003
DAVE EVES G HCA REC(A
PETE HODGE G DULC(A — RICHARD DODD V (A

D128 **JOHN DUMMER** D128

JOHN DUMMER D (ALL — (A) CABAL 1969 MERCURY UK SMCL20136
BOB HALL PNO (AB — (B) JOHN DUMMERS BLUES BAND 1969 MERCURY UK SMCL20167
DAVE KELLY G V (ABH12E — (B) JOHN DUMMERS BLUES BAND 1969 MERCURY NZ MCY138166
ADRIAN PIETRYGA G (2BDHAC — (C) FAMOUS MUSIC BAND 1970 PHILIPS UK 6382 040
CHRIS TRENGROVE SAX (C — (C) FAMOUS MUSIC BAND 1970 FONTANA GER 6309 008
IAIN THOPSON B V (AB12DHC — (D) BLUE 1972 VERTIGO UK 6360 055
NICK PICKETT V VLN G K (1BCDE — (E) THIS IS(COMP) 1972 PHILIPS 6382 039
KINGSLEY WARD PNO (H — (F) TRY ME ONE MORE TIME (COMP) 197 PHILIPS UK 6382 040
MIKE EVANS VLN (H — (G) VOL 2 (COMP) 1973 PHILIPS 6382 083
JO ANN KELLY V (ABH1 — (H) OOBLEEDOOBLEEJUBILEE 1973 VERTIGO UK 6360 083
MIKE COOPER G (1 — (H) OOBLEEDOOBLEEJUBILEE 1974 MERCURY 2360 083
ELLIOTT JACKSON (1 — (1) 1968 (2) 1969
ROGER BROWN V (H
KEITH TILLMAN B (A — TONY McPHEE G V (AE — JOHN O'LEARY HCA (A1
STEVE MILLER PNO (A — JOHN FAIRWEATHER HARMONIUM(C

D129 **AYNSLEY DUNBAR** D129

AYNSLEY DUNBAR D (ALL — (A) AYNSLEY DUNBAR RETALIATION 1969 BLUE THUMB US BTS 4
VICTOR BROX HRNS K G V (ABCD1 — (A) AYNSLEY DUNBAR RETALIATION 1968 LIBERTY UK LBL 83154
JOHN MOORSHEAD G V (ABCD1 — (A) AYNSLEY DUNBAR RETALIATION 19 BYG FR 529501
ALEX DMOCHOWSKI B (ABCD — (B) DOCTOR DUNBARS PRESCRIPTION 1969 LIBERTY UK LBS 83223
TOMMY EYRE K (CE — (B) DOCTOR DUNBARS PRESCRIPTION 1969 BLUE THUMB US BTS 6
PETER GREEN G (— (B) DOCTOR DUNBARS PRESCRIPTION 1969 BYG FR 529504
ANNETTE BROX V (D — (C) TO MUM FROM AYNSLEY & THE BOYS 1969 LIBERTY UK LBS 83223
KEITH TILLMAN B (1 — (C) TO MUM FROM AYNSLEY & THE BOYS 19 BYG FR 529506
CHARLES GREETHAM WIND (E — (C) RETALIATION 1976 BLUE THUMB US BTS 14
PAUL WILLIAMS B (E — (D) REMAINS TO BE HEARD 1970 LIBERTY UK LBS 83316
PETER FRIEDBERG (E — (E) REMAINS TO BE HEARD 1970 BYG FR 529506
PAT HICKS TPT (E — (E) BLUE WHALE 1970 WB UK K 46062
IVAN ZAGNI G (E — (E) BLUE WHALE RI 1978 CHARLY GER 3038 UK CR 30142
NORMAN LEPPARD SAX (E — ( ) CLASSIC BRITISH ROCK 19 SONOPRESSE FR 2978889
ROGER SUTTON B (E — ( ) JOY TO THE WORLD 19 CAPITOL US SMAS 788
EDWARDS REAY-SMITH TROM (E — (1)1967 LINE UP
JACK BRUCE (— ( ) HISTORY OF BRITISH BLUES(COMP) 1973 SIRE 3701
ROD STEWART V (?

D130 **SLY DUNBAR** D130

SLY DUNBAR D (AB — (A) SIMPLE SLY MAN 1978 FRONT LINE UK 1008
ROBBIE SHAKESPEARE B (B — (B) SLY WICKED & SLICK 1979 FRONT LINE UK 1042
MIKEY CHUNG K G B(B
ANSEL COLLINS K (B — KEITH STERLING K (B — RAD BRYAN G (B — ROBERT LYN K (B
DEAN FRASER SAX (B — TOMMY McCOOK SAX (B — VIN GORDON TROM (B — HERMAN MARQUIS SAX(B
ELNATHAN BRACKENRIDGE TPT(B — BERES HAMMOND V (B — CALMAN SCOTT V (B — TAMLINS V (B
TOUTER V (B — STICKY PERC (B — SCULLY PERC (B — BARNABAS PERC(B

D131 **LESLEY DUNCAN** D131

LESLEY DUNCAN V G MAND (ALL — (A) SING CHILDREN SING 1971 CBS UK 64202
WITH — (B) EARTH MOTHER 1972 CBS UK 64807
ELTON JOHN PNO (A — (C) EVERYTHING CHANGES 1974 GM UK GML 1007
TERRY COX D (A — (D) MOONBATHING 1975 GM UK GML 1017 US MCA 2207
TRISTAN FRY PERC (A — (E) MAYBE IT'S LOST 1977 GM UK GML 1019 US MCA 2274
TONI CAMPO B (A
JOE MORETTI G (A — RAY COOPER PERC (A — DAVID KATZ STR (A — CHRIS SPEDDING G BOUZ (ABDE
BOB COHEN G (C — LARRY STEELE B (C — LIZA STRIKE V (CD — JIMMY HOROWITZ K (ABCDE
SUE GLOVER V (C — ANDY BOWN B (BC — PETER FRAMPTON G (C — PETE DENNIS B (DE
GLEN LEFLEUR D (DE — BARRY DE SOUZA D (BC — JOANNA NEWMAN V (D — DEREK GROSSMITH WIND(D
JACK ROTHSTEIN STR (B — ROBERT AHWAI G (E — NICO RAMSDEN G V (E — ALAN MURPHY G (E
BOBBY KEYS SAX (E — LAURIE ANDREW V (E — JOHN PERRY V (E — MADELINE BELL V (E

D132 **DAVID DUNDAS** D132

DAVID DUNDAS V K (AB — (A) DAVID DUNDAS 1977 CHRYSALIS UK CHR 1141
WITH — (B) VERTICAL HOLD 1978 CHRYSALIS UK CHR 1197
ALAN TARNEY B (B
GERRY CONWAY D (B — GRAHAM PRESKETT K MAND V(B — FRANK RICOTTI PERC (B — KEN FRIEDMAN SYN(B
JIMMY JEWELL SAX (B — RON ASPERY SAX (B — DOREEN CHANTER V (B — JOHN GREEN HRNS(B
IRENE CHANTER V (B — RICKY HITCHCOCK G (B — EDDIE HOWELL V (B

D132A **KEVIN DUNN** D132A

KEVIN DUNN (A — (A) THE JUDGEMENT OF PARIS 1981 ARMAGGEDON UK ARM3
DEBBI HEIDEL (A
LEONORE THOMPSON (A — TERRY COBURN (A

D132B **CORNELL DUPREE** D132B

CORNELL DUPREE G (A — (A) TEASIN' 1975 ATLANTIC UK K50071 US 7311
RICHARD TEE K (A
CHUCK RAINEY B (A — BERNARD PURDIE D (A — RALPH McDONALD PERC (A
PAUL GRIFFIN K (A — GEORGE STUBBS K (A — DAVID NEWMAN SAX (A
JOE FARRELL SAX (A — SELDON POWELL SAX (A — ERNIE ROYAL TPT (A
JOE NEWMAN TPT (A — GARNETT BROWN TROM (A — MARK MEYERSON PROD (A
MICHAEL CUSCUNA PROD (A — TREVOR KOEHLER SAX (A — JON FADDIS TPT (A

D133 **CHAMPION JACK DUPREE** D133

CHAMPION JACK DUPREE V K D (ALL
WITH — SINGS THE BLUES 19 KING US 735
MICKEY BAKER G (EFJ — CHAMPION JACK DUPREE 19 STORYVILLE SLP 107
HAL SINGER SAX (J — CHAMPION JACK DUPREE 19 EVEREST US 217
MICHEL CARRAS ORG (M — BLUES FOR EVERYONE 19 KING STARDAY US KS 1084
LARRY MARTIN G (ML — (A)CHAMPION JACK DUPREE 19 STORYVILLE SLP 824
PAUL PECHANAERT G (M — PLAYS & SINGS THE BLUES 19 STORYVILLE SLP 145
ZOX B (LM — BEST OF THE BLUES 19 STORYVILLE SLP 151
JACQUES MAHIEUX D (LM — BARREL HOUSE BLUES 19 STORYVILLE SLP 155
RICHARD STUDT VLN (H — CHAMPION JACK DUPREE 19 STORYVILLE SLP 161
REG COLE VLN (H — BOOGIE BLUES & BARRELHOUSE BLUES 19 STORYVILLE SLP 183
— PIANO BLUES VOL 2 19 STORYVILLE SLP 187

(CONTINUED)

D133 CHAMPION JACK DUPREE (CONTINUED) D133

Musician	Instr	Rec
PETER OXER	VLN	(H
TERRY NOONAN	HRNS	(H
BUD PARKES	HRNS	(H
ALAN SKIDMORE	SAX	(H
LES WINGFIELD	SAX	(H
JIM CHESTER	SAX	(H
WALLACE TRING	B	(H
MIKE VERNON	PERC	(H
BIG CHIEF DRUMSTICK	D PERC	(H
CHRISTOPHER TURNER	HCA	(G
STAN WEBB	G	(G
MICK TAYLOR	G	(H3
EDUARDO GIVEZANO	B	(H
HARRIS DUNDEE	D	(G
PAUL KOSSOFF	G	(12G
STUART BROOKS	B	(12G
SIMON KIRKE	D	(12G
GARY THAIN	B	(3
KEEF HARTLEY	D	(3
DUSTER BENNETT	HCA	(3G
HORST LANGE	G	(A
MOGENS SEIDELIN	B	(A
KING CURTIS	SAX	(N

(1) 1968 APRIL
(2) 1968 LIVE BAND
(3) 1969 SESSION

Title	Year	Label	Country	Number
JACK DUPREE	19	STORYVILLE		SLP 193
JACK DUPREE	19	STORYVILLE		SLP 194
BLUES IN EUROPE	19	STORYVILLE		SLP 214
CHAMPION JACK DUPREE	19	STORYVILLE		SLP 216
FROM NEW ORLEANS TO CHICAGO	1966	DECCA	UK	LK 4747
FROM NEW ORLEANS TO CHICAGO	196	LONDON	US	553
(E)& HIS BLUES BAND	1967	DECCA	UK	SKL 4871
BLUES FROM THE GUTTER	196	ATCO	US	8019
BLUES FROM THE GUTTER	1975	ATLANTIC	UK	K 40526
CHAMPION OF THE BLUES	19	ATLANTIC	US	8056
(F)ANTHOLOGIE DU BLUES	1968	VOGUE	FR	CLVLX 271
(G)WHEN YOU FEEL THE FEELING	1968	BLUE HORIZON	UK	763206
(G) WHEN YOU FEEL THE FEELING	1968	CBS	US	7702
(H)SCOOBY DOOBY DOO	1969	BLUE HORIZON	UK	763214
HEAVY BLUES	1969	SIRE	US	97010
NATURAL & SOULFUL BLUES	196	ATLANTIC	US	8045
CHAMPION OF THE BLUES	196	ATLANTIC	US	8056
TRICKS	19	GNP		10001
(J)IM HAPPY TO BE FREE	1971	GNP		10005
CHAMPION JACK DUPREE	1971	FESTIVAL		FLD 653
INCREDIBLE	1970	SONET		SNTF 614
LEGACY OF THE BLUES VOL 3	197	GNP		10013
LEGACY OF THE BLUES VOL 3	1972	SONET	UK	SNTF 626
(N) BLUES FROM MONTREUX	19	ATCO	US	1637
(N) BLUES FROM MONTREUX	1972	ATLANTIC	UK	K 40434
CHAMPION JACK	1972	BLUE HORIZON	US	4610
WALKING BLUES	19	KING	US	1084
LOWDOWN BLUES	19	CONTINENTAL		16002
CHAMPION JACK DUPREE	19	OKEH	US	14103
WOMAN BLUES	19	FOLKWAYS		3825
TROUBLE TROUBLE	19	MUSIDISC	FR	ST 21001
FINE & MELLOW	19	MUSIDISC	FR	ST 21009
HAMBURG SESSIONS	1974	HAPPYBIRD		HAPB 5011
BLUES OF C J DUPREE	1976	STORYVILLE		SLP 240
(L)SHAKESPEARE SAYS	1976	SARAVAH		SH 10065
(M)1977	1977	ISADORA		ISL 6405

D133A ROBBIE DUPREE D133A

Musician	Instr	Rec
ROBBIE DUPREE	V HCA PERC	(AB
BILL ELLIOTT	SYN K	(AB
ROBERT PALMER	G	(A
RICK CUDACOFF	K B	(AB
BILL LABOUNTY	K V	(AB
BOB BORDY	G	(A
ALAN ESTES	PERC	(A
ARNO LUCAS	PERC V	(AB
JOE LALA'	PERC	(B
LEE THORNBURG	TPT	(B
BILL McWHIRTER	TROM	(B
PETER BUNETTA	D PERC	(AB
BRIAN RAY	G	(AB
JERRY PETERSON	SAX	(AB
KAL DAVID	SITAR V	(AB
MATTHEW WEINER	V	(AB
DAVID ANDERSON	V	(B
DARREL LEONARD	TPT	(B
MIGUEL RIVERA	PERC	(A
DENNIS HERRING	G	(AB
MICHAEL BODDICKER	SYN	(AB
LESLIE SMITH	V	(AB
JOE TURANO	V	(AB
DAVID WOODFORD	HRNS	(B
BILL ARMSTRONG	TPT	(B

(A) ROBBIE DUPREE — 1980 ELEKTRA US 6E273 UK K52235
(B) STREET CORNER HEROES — 1981 ELEKTRA US 6E344 UK K52290

D134 SIMON DUPREE & THE BIG SOUND D134

Musician	Instr	Rec
DEREK SHULMAN	V	(
PHIL SHULMAN	SAX	(A
RAY SHULMAN	B G V	(A
PETER O'FLAHERTY	B	(A
GEARY KENWORTHY		(
TONY RANSLEY	D	(A
ERIC HINE		(
MARTIN SMITH	D	(

(A) WITHOUT RESERVATIONS — 1967 PARLOPHONE UK PCS 7029
(A) WITHOUT RESERVATIONS — 1967 CAPITOL US T 5097

D134A VAN DUREN D134A

Musician	Instr	Rec
VAN DUREN	G K B SYN V	(AB
HILLY MICHAELS	D	(A
DOUG SNYDER	PERC	(A
JON TIVEN	G SAX	(A

(A) STARING AT THE CEILING — 1978 LONDON UK SHY8530 US BIGSOUND3816
(B) ARE YOU SERIOUS — 1978 US BIGSOUND 019

D134B DURAN DURAN D134B

Musician	Instr	Rec
SIMON LE BON	V	(AB
JOHN TAYLOR		(AB
NICK RHODES		(AB
ROGER TAYLOR		(AB
ANDY TAYLOR		(AB

(A) DURAN DURAN — 1981 EMI UK EMC3372 US HARVEST 12158
(B) RIO — 1982 EMI UK EMC3411

D135 TERRY DURHAM D135

TERRY DURHAM
WITH

Musician	Instr	Rec
EVAN PARKER	SAX	(A
CHRIS KARAN	D	(A
ALAN PARKER	G	(A
JOHN COLEMAN	PNO	(A

(A) CRYSTAL TELEPHONE — 1969 DERAM UK SML 1042

D135A DUROCS D135A

Musician	Instr	Rec
RON NAGLE	V K	(A
SCOT MATTHEWS	D B G K SAX	(A
LARRY REID	V	(A
STEVE DOUGLAS	SAX	(A
ERIC STEIN	SYN	(A
MAURICE GRIDLIN	ACC	(A
PHIL AABERG	K B SYN	(A
LARRY BLACKSHIRE	VIBES	(A
JOHN BLAKELEY	G B	(A
CHRIS RICHIE	G	(A

(A) DUROCS — 1979 CAPITOL US 11981

D136 DURUTTI COLUMN D136

Musician	Instr	Rec
TONY BOWERS	B G	(
VINNIE RILEY	G K	(ABC
DAVE ROWBOTHAM	G B	(
CHRIS JOYCE	D	(
PHIL RAYNHAM	V	(
TOLY	D	(A
BRUCE MITCHELL	PERC	(C
PETE CROOKS	B	(A

(A) RETURN OF DURUTTI COLUMN — 1980 FACTORY UK FAC14
(B) 2 TRIANGLES — 1981 FACTORY BEL 10
(C) LC — 1981 FACTORY UK FACT 44

D137 IAN DURY & THE BLOCKHEADS D137

	DATE	LABEL	US	UK	OTHER
(A) NEW BOOTS & PANTIES	1977	STIFF	US 0002	UK SEEZ4	
(B) DO IT YOURSELF	1979	STIFF	US 36104	UK SEEZ14	
(C) LAUGHTER	1980	STIFF	US 36998	UK SEEZ30	
(D) LORD UPMINSTER	1981	POLYDOR	US 16337	UK 5042	NL 2383 617
(E) JUKE BOX JURY	1981	STIFF		UK SEEZ41	

IAN DURY	V	(ALL	MICK GALLAGHER	K	(BC	JOHN TURNBULL	G	(BC
CHARLEY CHARLES	D	(ABC	ROBBIE SHAKESPEARE	B	(D	DON CHERRY	TPT	(D
NORMAN WATT ROY	B	(ABC	IVOR RAYMOND	STR	(C	TYRONE DOWARE		(D
CHAZ JANKEL	G K	(ABD						
DAVEY PAYNE	SAX	(ABC						
EDWARD SPEIGHT	G	(A						
GEOFF CASTLE	K	(A						
SLY DUNBAR	D	(D						
RAY COOPER	PERC	(C						
WILKO JOHNSON	G V	(C						

D138 DUST D138

RICHIE WISE	G V	(AB	
MARC BELL	D	(A	
KENNY AARONSON	B STEEL G	(AB	

	DATE	LABEL		
(A) DUST	19	POLYDOR	UK 2319 014	US MYRRH6504
(A) DUST	19	KAMA SUTRA	US	KSBS 2041
(B) HARD ATTACK	19	KAMA SUTRA	US	KSBS 2059

D138A DUSTY CHAPS D138A

	DATE	LABEL		
(A), HONKY TONK MUSIC	197	CAPITOL	US	11614
(B) DOMINO JOE	197	CAPITOL	US	11755

D139 BOB DYLAN D139

BOB DYLAN HCA V G (ALL

WITH

ROBBIE ROBERTSON	G V	(GKOPR	RICK DANKO	B V VLN	(GKOPR	LEVON HELM	D V MAND	(KOPR	RICHARD MANUEL	K V D	(GKOPR
GARTH HUDSON	K SAX	(GKOPR	AL KOOPER	G K HRNS	(KLGFN	CHARLIE McCOY	G HCA	(GHJKF	KENNY BUTTREY	D	(GHJKN
JOHNNY CASH	V	(J	JIM KELTNER	D	(MXY	EMMYLOU HARRIS	V	(S	MICK RONSON	G	(T
ROGER McGUINN	G	(M	PETE DRAKE	STEEL	(HJKN	CHARLIE DANIELS	B G	(JKLN	NORMAN BLAKE		(JKN
BOB WILSON		(JK	TONY BROWN	B	(Q	BUDDY CAGE	STEEL	(Q	PAUL GRIFFIN	K	(EFQ
ERIC WEISSBERG	BAN	(Q	DELIVERANCE		(Q	STEVEN SOLES	VG	(STUV	ALAN PASQUA	K	(UV
CAROLYN DENNIS	V	(UWXY	WAYNE MOSS	G V	(G	BILLY CROSS	G	(UV	JERRY SCHEFF	B	(U
IAN WALLACE	D	(U	JO ANN HARRIS	V	(U	DAVID MANSFIELD	MAND G	(TUV	STEVE DOUGLAS	SAX	(UVY
BOBBYE HALL	PERC	(U	HELENA SPRINGS	V	(UW	JOAN BAEZ	G V	(	PAUL BUTTERFIELD	HCA	(
JESSE ED DAVIS	G	(	FRED KATZ	CELLO	(M	DAVID BROMBERG	G	(KLN	BILLY DAVENPORT	D	(
ROB STONER	B	(STV	ALBERT W BUTLER		(K	RINGO STARR	D	(Y	RONNIE BLAKLEY	V	(S
FRED CARTER		(KN	MARK NAFTALIN		(	LUTHER RIX	PERC	(S	MARVIN D CHANTRY	VIOLA	(K
MIKE BLOOMFIELD	G	(F	HOWARD WYETH	D PNO	(ST	RON CORNELIUS	G	(KLN	BILLY PRESTON	K	(
GARY BURKE	D	(T	DOTTIE DILLARD	V	(K	ELVIN BISHOP	G	(	SCARLET RIVERA	VLN	(ST
DELORES EDGIN		(KN	LEON RUSSELL	K	(	TED MICHEL	CELLO	(M	SOLIE J FOTT		(K
JEROME ARNOLD		(	DOM CORTESE	MAND	(S	BUBBA FOLLER	G	(KN	KLAUS VOORMANN	B	(
GEORGE BARNES	B	(B	DENNIS A GOODE	TROM	(K	SAM LAY	D	(	DICK WELLSTOOD	PNO	(B
EMANUEL GREEN	VLN	(K	GEORGE HARRISON	G V	(	HERB LOVELL	D	(B	HILDA HARRIS	V	(KLN
ERIC CLAPTON	G	(S	HOWIE COLLINS	G	(B	FREDRICK HILL	TPT	(K	BYRON BERLINE	FDL	(M
LEONARD GASKIN	B	(B	KARL HIMMEL	D	(K	TERRY PAUL	B	(M	BRUCE LANGHORNE	G	(BME
LILIAN HUNT		(K	BRENDA PATTERSON	V	(M	BYRON BACH	VLN	(K	MARTIN KATAHN	V	(K
CARL FORTINA	K	(M	BRENTON BANKS	VLN SYN	(K	DOUG KERSHAW	VLN	(K	GARY FOSTER	WIND	(M
GEORGE BINKLEY	VLN	(K	MILLIE KIRKHAM		(KN	MARTHA McCRORY	CELLO	(K	BARRY McDONALD		(K
SHELDON KURLAND	VLN	(K	OLIVER MITCHELL	TPT	(K	CAROL MONTGOMERY		(KN	BOB MOORE	B	(KN
GENE A MULLINS		(K	JUNE PAGE	V	(KN	REX PEER		(K	GARY VAN OSDALE	VIOLA	(K
BILL PURSELL		(KN	ALBERTINE ROBERTSON	V	(KLN	ALVIN ROGERS	D	(KN	FRANK C SMITH		(K
MAERETHA STEWART	V	(KLONPR	ANTHONY FERRON		(K	STU WOODS	B	(KN	STEVE MADAIO	TPT	(U
HAPPY TRAUM	B G V BANJ	(*	HARVEY BROOKS	B	(FL	BUZZY FEITEN	G	(L	RUSS KUNKEL	D	(LMN
BILL MUNDI	D	(L	BOOKER T JONES	B	(M	CAROL HUNTER	G V	(M	DONNA WEISS	V	(M
PRISCILLA JONES	V	(M	VINCENT BELL	BAZ	(S	T BONE BURNETT	G PNO	(T	JOE SOUTH		(G
HENRY STRZELECKI	B	(G	BILL ATKINS	K	(G	JERRY KENNEDY	G	(G	HARGUS ROBBINS	K	(G
HARVEY GOLDSTEIN	B	(F	NEIL YOUNG	G V	(+	BEN KEITH	STEEL	(+	JOLLY ROGER	BAN	(M
AL GORGONI	G	(E	KEN RANKIN	G	(E	JOHN SEBASTIAN	B	(E	JOHN BOONE	B	(E
BOBBY GREGG	D	(E	FRANK OWENS	PNO	(EF	JOE MACHO	B	(E	WILLIAM LEE	B	(E
JOHN HAMMOND JR	G	(E	RUSS SAVAKUS	B	(F	MICKEY JONES	D	(G	FRED FOSTER	G	(K
BARRY CORNFIELD	G	(Q	RICHARD CROOKS	G	(Q	CHARLIE BROWN	G	(Q	KEN ODEGUARD	G	(Q
CHRIS WEBER	G	(Q	BILL PRESTON	B	(Q	GREG INHOFER	K	(Q	BILL BERG	D	(Q
LUTHER RIX	CONGA	(S	DEBBIE DYE	V	(V	MARK KNOPFLER	G	(W	BARRY BECKETT	K PERC	(W
TIM DRUMMOND	B	(WXY	PICK WITHERS	D	(W	MUSCLE SHOALS HORNS		(W	MICKEY BUCKINS	PERC	(W
REGINA HAVIS	V	(WX	FRED TACKETT	G	(XY	SPOONER OLDHAM	K	(X	TERRY YOUNG	K	(X
CLYDIE KING	V	(XY	MONA LISA YOUNG	V	(X	REGINA McCRORY	V	(Y	MADELYN QUEBEC	V	(Y
STEVE RIPLEY	G	(Y	CARL PICKHARDT	PNO	(Y	BENMONT TENCH	K	(Y	DANNY KORTCHMAR	G	(Y
WILLIAM SMITH	ORG	(Y	DONALD DUCK DUNN	B	(Y	RON WOOD	G	(Y	BOB NEUWIRTH	G	(
RAMBLIN JACK ELLIOTT	G	(	JERRY GARCIA	G	(	CARLOS SANTANA	G	(			

LP's

	DATE	US	STEREO	MONO	JAPAN		UK	
(A) BOB DYLAN	1962	CBS	8579	1779	CBS SONY	25AP 268	CBS	62022
(A) BOB DYLAN							RI EMBASSY	32001
(B) FREEWHEELIN' BOB DYLAN	1963	CBS	8786	1986	CBS SONY	25AP 269	CBS	62193
(C) TIMES THEY ARE A CHANGIN'	1964	CBS	8905	2105	CBS SONY	25AP 270	CBS	62251
(D) ANOTHER SIDE OF BOB DYLAN	1964	CBS	8993	2193	CBS SONY	25AP 271	CBS	62429
(E) BRINGING IT ALL BACK HOME	1965	CBS	9128	2328	CBS SONY	25AP 272	CBS	62515
(F) HIGHWAY 61 REVISITED	1965	CBS	9189	2389	CBS SONY	25AP 273	CBS	62572
(G) BLONDE ON BLONDE (DBL)	1966	CBS	C2S841	C2841	CBS SONY	40 AP 274/5	CBS	66012
(H) JOHN WESLEY HARDING	1968	CBS	9604	2804	CBS SONY	25AP 277	CBS	63252
(J) NASHVILLE SKYLINE	1969	CBS	9825		CBS SONY	25AP 278	CBS	63601
(K) SELF PORTRAIT (DBL)	1970	CBS	30050		CBS SONY	40AP279/80	CBS	66250
(L) NEW MORNING	1970	CBS	30290		CBS SONY	25AP 281	CBS	69001
(M) PAT GARRETT & BILLY THE KID	1973	CBS	32460		CBS SONY	25AP 284	CBS	69042
(N) DYLAN	1973	CBS	32747		CBS SONY	25AP 285	CBS	69049
(O) PLANET WAVES	1974	ASYLUM	7E1003				ISLAND	ILPS9261
(P) BEFORE THE FLOOD (DBL)	1974	ASYLUM	AB 201				ISLAND	IBD 1
(Q) BLOOD ON THE TRACKS	1974	CBS	33235		CBS SONY	25AP 286	CBS	69097
(R) BASEMENT TAPES (DBL)	1975	CBS	33682		CBS SONY	40AP287/8	CBS	88147
(S) DESIRE	1976	CBS	33893		CBS SONY	25AP 289	CBS	86003
(T) HARD RAIN	1976	CBS	34349		CBS SONY	25AP 290	CBS	86016
(U) STREET LEGAL	1978	CBS	35453		CBS SONY	25AP 1099	CBS	86067
(V) AT BUDOKAN (DBL)	1978	CBS	36067		CBS SONY	40AP 2200	CBS	96004
(W) SLOW TRAIN COMING	1979	CBS	36120				CBS	86095
(X) SAVED	1980	CBS	36553				CBS	UK 83113
(Y) SHOT OF LOVE	1981	CBS	37496				CBS	85178

(CONTINUED)

D139 **BOB DYLAN** (CONTINUED) D139

( ) GREATEST HITS	1967	CBS 9463	2663	CBS SONY 25AP 276		CBS	62847
( ) GREATEST HITS VOL 2	19	CBS 31120				CBS	62911
( ) GREATEST HITS VOL 3	19	CBS				CBS	63111
(*) MORE GREATEST HITS (DBL)	1972	CBS				CBS	67239
( ) NOBODY SINGS LIKE BOB DYLAN	19	CBS				CBS	62694
( ) 11 YEARS IN THE LIFE OF BOB DYLAN	197	CBS		SOPI 11/12			
(+) S N A C K	1975	VIBRATOR 160					
( ) BOB DYLAN	197	JOKER ITALY T63					
( ) BROADSIDE BALLADS	19	BROADSIDE BR301					
( ) BROADSIDE REUNION	1972	FOLKWAYS 5315					
( ) NEWPORT BROADSIDE	1964	VANGUARD 79144				FONTANA	6038
( ) EVENING CONCERTS AT NEWPORT	1964	VANGUARD 79148				FONTANA	6138
( ) TRIBUTE TO WOODY GUTHRIE	19					CBS	64861
( ) WE SHALL OVERCOME	1964	FOLKWAYS	5592				
( ) MASTERPIECES(TPL)	197	CBS AUSTRALIA	220502				
(EP) I WANT YOU	19	CBS	43683			CBS	6051
(EP) ONE TOO MANY MORNINGS	1965	CBS				CBS	6070
(EP) Mr TAMBOURINE MAN	1966					CBS	

D140 **DYNAMIC ROCKERS** D140

(A) THE DYNAMIC ROCKERS — 1980 DURECO — NL 44019

D141 **DYNAMIC SUPERIORS** D141

(A) GIVE	1977	MOTOWN	US	879
(B) PURE PLEASURE	1977	MOTOWN	US	841
(C) YOU NAME IT	1977	MOTOWN	US	875

D142 **DYNASTY** D142

(A) YOUR PIECE OF THE ROCK	1980	SOLAR	UK 3398
(B) ADVENTURES IN THE LAND OF MUSIC	1980	SOLAR	UK 3576

D143 **DZYAN** D143

JOCHEN LEUSCHNER V PERC(A	(A) DZYAN	1972	ARONDA	10006
REINHARD KARWATKY B (ABC	(B) TIME MACHINE	1973	BACILLUS	19161
GERD EHRMANN SAX (A	(C) ELECTRIC SILENCE	1975	BACILLUS	19202
HARRY KRAMER G (A				

LUDWIG BRAUM D PERC(A — EDDY MARRON G (BC — PETER GIGER D (BC

E1 **EAGLE** E1

WAYNE ULAKY B (A — (A) COME UNDER NANEY'S TENT — 19 JANUS US JLS 3011
JOHN WRIGHT V (A
ROBERT RHODES K HRNS (A — J JAMES G V (A

E2 **EAGLES** E2

						UK	UK
				US			
RANDY MEISNER V B G(ABCDE	(A) THE EAGLES	1972	ASYLUM	5054	SYTC101 +	K 53009
GLENN FREY V G (ABCDEFG	(B) DESPARADO	1973	ASYLUM	5068	SYLA9011+	K 53008
DON HENLEY D V (ABCDEFG	(C) ON THE BORDER	1974	ASYLUM	7E1004	SYL9016 +	K 43005
BERNIE LEADON G V BAN(ABCD	(D) ON OF THESE NIGHTS	1975	ASYLUM	7E1039	SYLA 8759+	K 53014
DON FELDER G V (CDEFG	(E) HOTEL CALIFORNIA	1976	ASYLUM	7E1084 RI 103		K 53051
JOE WALSH G V (EFG	(F) THE LONG RUN	1979	ASYLUM	6 508		K 52181
TIM SCHMIT B V (FG	(G) EAGLES LIVE	1980	ASYLUM	705		K 62032
J D SOUTHER V G (G	( ) GREATEST HITS	1975	ASYLUM	6E105		K 53017
JOE VITALE K D (G						

PHIL KENZIE SAX (G	VINCE MELAMED K (G	JAGE JACKSON G (G
ALBHY GALUTEN SYN (D	JIM ED NORMAN PNO (D	DAVID SANBORN SAX (F
AL PERKINS STEEL (C	DAVID BROMBERG FDL (D	JIMMY BUFFET V (F

E3 **BOBBY EAGLESHAM** E3

BOBBY EAGLESHAM G V (A — (A) BOBBY EAGLESHAM — 1974 XTRA UK XTRA 1137
SID CAIRNS B (A

E3A **SNOOKS EAGLIN** E3A

SNOOKS EAGLIN G V (ALL	(A) NEW ORLEANS STREET SINGER	19	FOLKWAYS	US	2476
ELLIS MARSHAL PNO (C	(B) LEGACY VOL2	19	GNP	US	10012
CLARENCE FORD SAX (C	(C) DOWN YONDER	1978	SONET	UK	SNTF 752
GEORGE FRENCH D (C					
BOB FRENCH D (C					

E3B **RICHARD EARL** E3B

RICHARD EARL (A — (A) EGG STORE ILK — 1981 PILOT UK PILOT1

E3C **EARLY BIRD** E3C

ALBERT VELD (A — (A) FLY AWAY — 1980 KILLROY NL 16963
HENDRIK WARINGA (A
KARINA HENSON-KLOK (A — MEINE BRUINSMA (A — LEO ROODHOF (A
HARRY ZIJLSTRA (A

E3D **EARLY FROST** E3D

(A) EARLY FROST — 1978 VANGUARD US 79392

E4 **EARTH & FIRE** E4

JERNEY KAAGMAN V (ALL	(A) EARTH & FIRE	1971	NEPENTHAL	NL 6437 004	POLYDOR NL 2441011
GERARD KOERTS V FLT VIBES K(ALL	(A) EARTH & FIRE	197	REDBULLET	US 3000	
HANS ZIECH B (ABCG	(B) SONG OF MARCHING CHILDREN	197	POLYDOR	NL 2925 003	
THEO HURTS G B (DE	(B) MEMORIES	1975	POLYDOR	GER 2310 209	
CHRIS KOERTS G V (ABCD	(C) ATLANTIS	1973	POLYDOR	NL 2419 059	NL 2925013
TON VANDER KLEIJ D V (ALL	(C) ATLANTIS	1975	POLYDOR	GER 2310 262	
BERT RUITER B (EG	(D) TO THE WORLD A FUTURE	1975	POLYDOR	NL 2925 033	2374121
RONNIE MAYES G (G	(E) GATE TO INFINITY	1977	POLYDOR	NL 2925 065	
AD TAMBOER D (G	(F) REALITY FILLS FANTASY	1979	VERTIGO	NL 6413 501	
	(G) ANDROMEDA GIRL	1981	VERTIGO	NL 6399 271	
	( ) SUPERSTARSHINE VOL1 COMP	19	POLYDOR	NL 2419 029	
	( ) ROCK SENSATION	19	POLYDOR	GER 2499 109	
	( ) BEST OF	1975	POLYDOR	NL 2491 004	
	( ) BEST OF	1979	POLYDOR	NL 2426 012	
	( ) THE STORY OF	1976	POLYDOR	NL 2925 044	
	( ) THE HITS OF	1980	ORION	NL	
	( ) GREATEST HITS	1980	POLYDOR	NL2475 206	

E5 EARTH OPERA E5

Album	Year	Label / Catalogue
(A) EARTH OPERA	1968	ELEKTRA 74016
(B) THE GREAT AMERICAN EAGLE TRAGEDY	1969	ELEKTRA 74038

Name	Instr	Albums
PETER ROWAN	V SAX G	(AB
DAVID GRISMAN	K SAX	(AB
JOHN NAGY	B	(AB
BILL STEVENSON	K	(A
PAUL DILLON	D G V	(AB
RICHARD GRANDO	SAX	(B
JACK BONUS	WIND	(B
BILL KEITH	STEEL	(B
DAVE HOROWITZ	K	(B
HERB BUSHLER	B	(B
BILL MUNDI	PERC	(A
JOHN CALE	G V	(B
BOB ZACHARY	PERC	(B

E6 EARTH QUAKE E6

Album	Year	Label / Catalogue
(A) EARTHQUAKE	1971	A&M US SP 4308
(B) WHY DO YOU TRY ME	1972	A&M US 4337
(C) EARTHQUAKE LIVE	1975	U A UK UAS 29853
(C) ROCKIN' THE WORLD	1975	BESERKLEY US0045 RI 34752
(C) ROCKIN' THE WORLD	197	BESERKLEY GER 23356
(C) ROCKIN' THE WORLD	1978	BESERKLEY UK BSERK 3
(D) 8.5	197	BESERKLEY US 0047 RI 34754
(D) 8.5	1976	BESERKLEY UK BSERK5
(E) LEVELED	197	BESERKLEY US 0054 RI 34801
(E) LEVELED	1977	BESERKLEY UK BSERK7 GER 23311
(F) 2 YEARS IN A PADDED CELL	1979	BESERKLEY US 10065

Name	Instr	Albums
ROBBIE DUNBAR	G V	(ALL
JOHN DOUKAS	V PNO	(ALL
STAN MILLER	B V	(ALL
STEVE NELSON	D	(ALL
GARY PHILLIPS	G V	(CDE
PETE SEARS	K	(B
LENNY PICKETT	SAX	(B
CHUCK FINDLEY	TPT	(B
JIM HORN	SAX	(B
MATTHEW KAUFMAN	PROD	(C

E7 EARTH WIND & FIRE E7

Album	Year	Label / Catalogue
(A) EARTH WIND & FIRE	1971	WB US 1905
(B) THE NEED OF LOVE	1972	WB US 1958
(C) ANOTHER TIME	1972	WB US 2798
(D) LAST DAYS & TIME	1973	CBS US 31702 UK 65208
(D) LAST DAYS & TIME	1979	EMBASSY UK 31761
(E) HEAD TO THE SKY	1973	CBS US 32194 UK 65604
(E) HEAD TO THE SKY	1981	EMBASSY UK 32017
(F) OPEN YOUR EYES	1974	CBS US 32712 UK 65844
(F) OPEN YOUR EYES	1981	EMBASSY UK 32033
(G) THATS THE WAY OF THE WORLD	1975	CBS US 33280 UK 80575
(G) THATS THE WAY OF THE WORLD	1981	EMBASSY UK 32054
(H) GRATITUDE	1975	CBS US 33694 UK 88160
(J) SPIRIT	1977	CBS US 34241 UK 81451
(K) ALL AND ALL	1978	CBS US 34905 UK 86051
(L) BEST OF VOL 1	1978	CBS US 35647 UK 83284
(M) I AM	1979	CBS US 35730 UK 86084
(N) FACES (DBL)	1980	CBS US 36795 UK 88498
(O) EARTH WIND & FIRE (TRIPLE BOX)GJK	1979	CBS UK 66350
(EP) SING A SONG(PROMO EP)	1977	CBS EWF1
(P) RAISE	1981	CBS US 37548 UK 85272

Name	Instr	Albums
MAURICE WHITE	D V	(ALL
VERDINE WHITE	B V	(FKMDNPJ
FRED WHITE	D PERC	(KMNPJ
ANDY WOOLFOLK	WIND	(FKMNPJ
DICK HYDE	TROM	(PJ
PHILIP BAILEY	V PERC	(FKMNDPJ
LEW McCREARY	TROM	(PJ
RONALD BATTISTA	G	(DP
CHARLES LOPER	TROM	(PJ
LARRY DUNN	K SYN	(DFMKNPJ
GARY GRANT	TPT	(P
RON WAYNE LAWS	WIND	(D
RALPH JOHNSON	D PERC	(FKMDNPJ
AL McKAY	G PERC	(FKMNDJ
JOHNNY GRAHAM	G	(FKMNPJ
DAVID FOSTER	K	(MNP
EDDIE DEL BARRIO	PNO	(KM
MARLO HENDERSON	G	(MNP
SKIP SCARBOROUGH	PERC	(K
BELOYD TAYLOR	G	(P
PAULINHO DA COSTA	PERC	(KMNP
DONALD MYRICK	SAX	(KMPJ
RAHMLEE DAVIS	TPT	(MNP
BILLY MYERS	K	(MP
STEVE PORCARO	SYN	(M
WANDA HUTCHINSON	V	(M
OSCAR BRASHEAR	TPT	(MDNPJ
HERMAN RILEY	SAX	(M
BARBARA KORN	HRNS	(M
STEVE MADAIO	TPT	(MNJ
SIDNEY MULDREW	HRN	(M
WAYNE VAUGHN	K	(P
CHUCK FINDLEY	TPT	(PNJ
GARRY GLEN	K	(N
FRED WESLEY	TROM	(N
JOHN JOHNSON	TUBA	(N
JERRY PETERS	K	(NJ
VINCENT DEROSA	HON	(N
LOUIS SATTERFIELD	TROM	(KMNPJ
JESSICA CLEAVES	V	(D
SHEILA WHITT	V	(M
JEANETTE HAWES	V	(M
ELMER BROWN	TPT	(M
FRED JACKSON	SAX	(MN
JEROME RICHARDSON	SAX	(M
DOROTHY ASHBY	HARP	(MJ
GEORGE BOHANON	TROM	(MNPJ
RICHARD PERISSI	HRNS	(M
MICHAEL BODDICKER	K	(P
80 PIECES STRING SEC		(N
NOLAN SMITH	TPT	(N
ARTHUR MAEBE	HRN	(NJ
REGGIE ANDREWS		(D
GARY GRANT	TPT	(N
GEORGE PRICE	HRN	(N
MICHAEL HARRIS	TPT	(KMNPJ
STEVE LUKATHER	G	(MN
BENJAMIN POWELL	TROM	(M
BILL REICHENBACH	TROM	(MNP
MAURICE SPEARS	TROM	(M
BOBBY BRYANT	TPT	(MDN
JERRY HEY	TPT	(MNP
RICHARD LEPORE	PERC	(M
GARNETT BROWN	TROM	(M
MARILYN ROBINSON	HRN	(MNJP
LARRY HULL	TPT	(P
HARVEY MASON	PERC	(J
JEFF CLAYTON	TROM	(N
ALAN ROBINSON	HRN	(N
MARTIN YARBOUGH		(D
LAWRENCE WILLIAMS	WIND	(N
TOM JOHNSON	HRNS	(J

E7B EARTHQUIRE E7B

Album	Year	Label / Catalogue
(A) EARTHQUIRE	1972	NATURAL RESOURCES NR 106L

Name	Instr	Albums
TATA VEGA	V	(A
GREG MATHESON	K	(A
MARK KOFSTEIN	WIND	(A
JIM VARLEY	D	(A
BRIE BRANDT	V	(A
BOB CROSBY	WIND	(A
MIKE GORFAINE	V	(A
LAURIE ANNE BALL	V	(A
CHARLIE STEPHENS	B	(A

E7C EARTHSTAR E7C

Album	Year	Label / Catalogue
(A) FRENCH SKYLINE	1979	SKY SKY 031
(B) ATOM KRAFT ? NEIN DANKE	1981	SKY 051

Name	Instr	Albums
DENNIS REA	G	(AB
TIM FINNEGAN	FLT	(A
CRAIG WUEST	K	(AB
NORMAN PEACH	B	(A
DIRK SCHMALENBACH	SITAR	(A
RAINER BOHM	VLN	(B
JOHN BUNKFELDT	HCA	(B
DARYL TRIVIERI	VLN	(AB
LOUIS DEPONTE	TAPES	(B
CHRISTOPHER LAGEMANN	CELLO	(B
MARTY BURDETTE	G	(B
MARLA THOMSON	HRNS	(A
DAN ZONGRONE	PNO	(B
MELANIE LOIRE	PERC	(B

E7D CHRIS EAST E7D

Album	Year	Label / Catalogue
(A) HOTEL IN THE COUNTRY	1978	GTO UK GTLP 034

Name	Instr	Albums
CHRIS EAST	G	(A
MO WITHAM	G B	(A
PAUL THOMPSON	D	(A
B J COLE	STEEL	(A
KEVIN MORRIS	D	(A
ALAN HAWKSHAW	K	(A
IAN GIBSONS		(K

E8 EAST OF EDEN E8

Album	Year	Label / Catalogue
(A) MERCATOR PROJECTED	1969	DERAM US 18023 UK SML 1038
(B) SNAFU	1970	DERAM US 18043 UK SML 1050
(AB)SNAFU/MERCATOR	1975	DERAM UK SDM3013 1/2
(C) EAST OF EDEN	1971	HARVEST US 806 UK SHVL 792
(D) NEW LEAF	1971	HARVEST UK SHVL 796
(E) WORLD OF (COMP)	1971	DECCA UKSPA34+SPA157
(F) HERE WE GO AGAIN	1976	EMI EURO 062 98065
(G) MASTERS OF ROCK (COMP)	1975	EMI EURO 062 95117
(H) THINGS COMP AB	1976	NOVA GER 628367
(I) JIG A JIG	197	DECCA 210006
(J) ANOTHER EDEN	1975	EMI GER 97101
(K) IT'S THE CLIMATE	1976	EMI GER 61810
(L) SILVER PARK	1978	EMI GER 62639

Name	Instr	Albums
DAVE ARBUS	WIND VLN	(12ABCEGDJ
RON CAINES	V SAX	(12ABE
PETER FILLEUL	K	(F
DAVE DUFORT	D	(AE
STEVE YORK	B	(AE
ANDY SNEDDON	B	(12BE
JEFF ALLEN	D	(2DEFGJKL
JOE O'DONNELL	VLN	(J
DAVID JACKS	B	(CEFGDKL
JIM ROCHE	G	(CDH
DAVE WELLER	SAX	(DFKL
LES DAVIDSON		(FKL
GEOFF NICHOLSON	G V	(ABE12

(CONTINUED)

E8 EAST OF EDEN (CONTINUED) E8

GEOFF BRITTON D (BE1 — (1) 1969 (2) 1970
BARRY ST JOHN V (K
BIMBO ACOCK (K — THEO THUNDER (K — GARTH WATT ROY (J
DYL KATTS B (KL — MARTIN FISHER (J — BRENDA LYNN (K
DAVE ROSE (K — GEORGE HOWDEN (K

E8A EAST SIDE KIDS E8A

DAVE POTTER — (A) TIGER & THE LAMB 19 UNI 73032
JOE MADRID V (A
DAVID DOUD G (A — MIKE DOUD B (A

E8B CLINT EASTWOOD E8B

CLINT EASTWOOD V (A — (A) SEX EDUCATION 1980 GREENSLEEVES UK GREL11

E9 EASY STREET E9

PETER MARSH G (AB — (A)EASY STREET 1976 POLYDOR UK 2383 415
KEN NICOL G (AB — (B) UNDER THE GLASS 1977 POLYDOR UK 2383 444
JIM HALL B (AB — (B) UNDER THE GLASS 1977 CAPRICORN US 0184
KEVIN SAVIGAR K (B
JOHN WALTERS SAX (A — PETE ZORN B SAX (A — CHRISTOPHER PNO (A
RICHARD BURGESS D (AB — ROD ARGENT K (A — DICK PEARCE HRNS (A
PETER THOMS HRNS (A — ROGER WILLIAMS HRNS (A — KENNY KING HRNS (A

E10 EASYBEATS E10

GEORGE YOUNG G V (CG — (A) FRIDAY ON MY MIND 1967 UA US UAS 6588
DICK DIAMONDE B (CG — (B) GOOD FRIDAY 1967 UA UK SULP 1167
HARRY VANDA G V (CG — (B) GOOD FRIDAY 1967 UA US UA 29627
STEVE WRIGHT V (CG — (C) FALLING OFF THE EDGE OF THE WORLD 1968 UA US UAS 6667
GORDON FLEET D (CG — (D) VIGIL 1968 UA UK SULP 1199
TONY CAHILL D (— (E) FRIENDS 1970 POLYDOR UK 2482 010
(F) ABSOLUTE ANTHOLOGY (DBL) 19 AUST
(G) NOSTALGIA 19 UA FR 29627
(H) THE SHAME JUST DRAINED 1978 ALBERT 026

E11 EATER E11

ANDY BLADE V (A — (A) THE ALBUM 1977 THE LABEL UK TLRLP 001
BRIAN CHEVETTE G (A — (B) GET YER YO YO'S OUT(EP LIVE) 1978 THE LABEL UK TLR 007
IAN WOODCOCK B (A
DEE GENERATE D (A

E11A EBERSON. GRAF. HOVENSJO. CHRISTENSEN E11A

JON EBERSON G (A — (A) BLOW OUT 1977 COMPENDIUM NOR FID 10
HAKON GRAF K (A
SVEINUNG HOVENSJO B (A — JOHN CHRISTENSEN D (A — MIKI NDOYE CONGA (A
FRODE HOLM (

E11B ECHO & THE BUNNYMEN E11B

WILL SARGEANT G (ABC — (A) CROCODILES 1980 KOROVA UK KODE1 US SIRE 6096
IAN McCULLON G V (C — (B) SHINE SO HARD 1981 KOROVA UK ECHO1 NL WEA 28223
LES PATTERSON B (C — (C) HEAVEN UP HERE 1981 KOROVA UK KODE3US SIRE 3569
LESLIE PENNY WIND (C — (EP) A PROMISE 1981 KOROVA UK 15T
PETER DE FREITAS D (C
HUGH JONES PROD (C

E12 ECLECTION E12

KERRILEE MALE V (A — (A) ECLECTION 1968 ELEKTRA EKS 74023
MICHAEL ROSEN V G TPT(A
TREVOR LUCAS G V (A — GERRY CONWAY D V (A — GEORG HULTGREEN V G (A
DORRIS HENDERSON V (— POLI PALMER V VIBES(— MICK WOODS D (
KEVIN WESTLAKE PERC G(— GARY BOYLE G (— ERIC JOHNS G (

E12A ECLIPSE E12A

PIERRE GAUTHIER K V (A — (A) NIGHT & DAY 1977 CASABLANCA US NBLP7097
JESSE OTTEN G V (A
MIKE DINARDO D PERC(A — CLAUDE LAFERRIERE B G (A

E13 EDDIE & THE HOT RODS E13

BARRY MASTERS V (ABCDE — (E) LIVE AT THE MARQUEE (EP) 1976 ISLAND UK IEP 2
DAVE HIGGS G K (ABCDE — (B) TEENAGE DEPRESSION 1976 ISLAND UK ILPS 9457
STEVE NICOL D (ABCDE — (B) TEENAGE DEPRESSION 1976 PHONOGRAM EURO 9101 671
PAUL GRAY B (ABCDE — (C) LIFE ON THE LINE 1977 ISLAND US/UKILPS9509
GRAEME DOUGLAS G V K (CD — (C) LIFE ON THE LINE 1977 PHONOGRAM EURO 9123 025
AL KOOPER K G V (E — (EP) AT THE SOUND OF SPEED 1977 ISLAND IEP5
RUFUS JENKINS ACC (E — (D) THRILLER 1979 ISLAND UK ILPS 9563
MARTIN AUBREY V (E — (E) FISH & CHIPS 1980 EMI UK 3344 US 17037
KEITH COTTON V (E
PATTI HELD V (E — GEORGE PAGE V (E

E13A EDDIE BOY BAND E13A

JOSH LEO G V (A — (A) EDDIE BOY BAND 1975 MCA US 2153 UK MAPS 8150+MCF 2735
MARK GOLDENBERG V G K (A
TIM WALKOE B V (A — JOHN PARUDO K V (A — DAVID WOLINSKI SYN (A
DENNIS EBERT D PERC(A — JON CARSON G (A — MIKE LERNER D PERC(A
DICK CAINE G (A

E14 DUANE EDDY E14

DUANE EDDY G
WITH
AL CASEY B G — LARRY KNECHTEL K — STEVE DOUGLAS SAX — IKE CLANTON B
BUDDY WHEELER B — BOB TAYLOR D — CORKY CASEY G — JIM HORN SAX
DON OWEN G — JIMMY TROXEL D — BEN DEMOTTO V

HAVE TWANGY GUITAR WILL TRAVEL	1958	JAMIE	US	3000	LONDON UK (M) HAW 2160
ESPECIALLY FOR YOU	1958	JAMIE	US	3006	LONDON UK (M) HAW 2191 (S) SAHW 6045
TWANGS THE THANG	1959	JAMIE	US	3009	LONDON UK (M) HAW2236 (S) SAHW 6068
SONGS FOR OUR HERITAGE	1960	JAMIE	US	3011	LONDON UK (M) HAW 2285 (S) SAHW 6119
1,000,000 DOLLARS OF TWANG	1961	JAMIE	US	3014	LONDON UK (M) HAW 2325
GIRLS GIRLS GIRLS	1961	JAMIE	US	3019	LONDON UK (M) HAW 2373 (S) SAHW 6173
1,000,000 DOLLARS OF TWANG	1964	JAMIE	US	3021	LONDON UK (M) HAW 2435
TWISTIN' & TWANGIN'	1962	RCA	US	LSP2525	
TWANGY GUITAR SILKY STRINGS	1962	RCA	US	LSP2576	RI CAMDEN CDS 1072

(CONTINUED)

E14 (CONTINUED) DUANE EDDY E14

Title	Year	Label	Country	No.	Label	Country	No.
TWISTIN'	196	JAMIE	US	3022			
SURFIN'	1964	JAMIE	US	3024			
IN PERSON	196	JAMIE	US	3025			
16 GREATEST HITS	196	JAMIE	US	3026			
DANCE WITH THE GUITAR MAN	1963	RCA	US	LSP2648			
PURE GOLD	19	RCA	US	ANL2671			
TWANGS A COUNTRY SONG	1963	RCA	US	LSP2681	RCA	UK	SF 7560
TWANGIN' UP A STORM	1963	RCA	US	LSP 2700	RCA	UK	RD 7568
LONELY GUITAR	1964	RCA	US	LSP2798			
WATERSKIING	196	RCA	US	LSP2918			
TWANGIN' GOLDEN HITS	196	RCA	US	LSP2993	RCA INT	UK	INT 1057
DUANE A GO GO	1965	COLPIX	US	PXL490			
DUANE DOES DYLAN	1965	COLPIX	US	PXL494			
TWANGSVILLE	1965	RCA	US	LSP3432			
BEST OF	1965	RCA	US	LSP3477	CAMDEN	UK	CDS 1109
BIGGEST TWANG OF ALL	1966	REPRISE	US	6218	VALIANT	UK	VS 108
ROARIN' TWANGIES	1967	REPRISE	US	6240			
MOVIN' & GROOVIN'	1970				LONDON	UK	ZGW 105
MOVIN' & GROOVIN'	1980	LONDON	NL	6399093			
LEGEND OF ROCK	1974				DERAM		DLL5033/4
LEGEND OF ROCK 2	1974				TELDEC	GER	LS 3259
LEGEND OF ROCK 3 RARE ITEMS	1974				LONDON		LS 3281
YESTERDAYS POP SCENE	1975				TELEFUNKEN	AF	622002
GUITAR MAN	1975				GTO		GTLP 002
GUITAR MAN	197				HALLMARK		947
VINTAGE YEARS	1975	SIRE	US	3707/2			
PURE GOLD	1978	RCA	US	2671			
DUANE EDDY	1979				RCA UKAPL		12671
GREATEST HITS	1979				RONCO	UK	RTL 2035
OLDIES BUT GOODIES	1979				TELDEC	GERM	623647
DUANE EDDY COLLECTION	1978				PICKWICK	UK	PDA 043
20 TERRIFIC TWANGIES	1980				RCA INT		5056

(EPS)

Title	Year	Label	Country	No.
MOVIN' & GROOVIN'	19	JAMIE	US	JEP 100
YEP	19	JAMIE	US	JEP 300
DETOUR	19	JAMIE	US	JEP 301
SHAZAM	19	JAMIE	US	JEP 303
BECAUSE THEY'RE YOUNG	19	JAMIE	US	JEP 304

E15 RANDY EDELMAN E15

Album	Year	Label	Country	No.
(A) RANDY EDELMAN	1972	SUNFLOWER	US	5005
(B) LAUGHTER & TEARS	1973	LION	US	1012
(C) PRIME CUTS	1976	20TH CENT	US UK	448
(D) FAIRWELL FAIRBANKS	1976	20th CENT		494
(E) IF LOVE IS REAL	1977	20th CENT		542
(E) IF LOVE IS REAL	1977	ARISTA	US	4139
(F) UPTOWN UPTEMPO	1979	20th CENT		601
(G) YOU'RE THE ONE	1979	20th CENT		581
(G) YOU'RE THE ONE	1979	ARISTA	US	4210

Member	Inst	Albums	Member	Inst	Albums	Member	Inst	Albums
RANDY EDELMAN	K V	(ALL						
NIGEL OLSSON	D V	(DEG						
REINIE PRESS	B	(D						
GARY COLEMAN	PERC	(D						
DEAN PARKS	G	(DEG						
LEE RITENOUR	G	(D						
AL KOOPER	G	(D						
JEFF PORCARO	D	(E						
LEE SKLAR	B	(EG						
TOMMY VIG	PERC	(E						
STEVE CROPPER	G	(D	ART MUNSON	G	(D	BEN BENAY	G	(DG
ANDREW GOLD	G	(D	DEE MURRAY	V	(ED	JIMMY HAAS	V	(DE
TOM BAHLER	V	(D	MELISSA MANCHESTER	V	(D	JACKIE DeSHANNON	V	(D
VINI PONCIA	V	(D	VICTOR FELDMAN	PERC	(E	DOUG MASEK	SAX	(E
JOHN JOYCE	V	(E	JOHN GUERIN	D	(B	LYLE RITZ	B	(BG
JAY GRAYDON	G	(G	MIKE PORCARO	B	(G	MATTHEW McCAWLEY	SYN	(G
RICK MAROTTA	D	(G	FRED MOLLIN	PERC	(G	DAVID PAICH	K	(G
ERICA GOODMAN	HARP	(G	NICK BAIRD	D	(G			

E16 EDENS CHILDREN E16

Member	Inst	Albums	Album	Year	Label	Country	No.
RICHARD SCHAMACH	G	(AB	(A) EDENS CHILDREN	1968	ABC	US	ABCS 624
JIMMY STURMAN	D	(AB	(A) EDENS CHILDREN	1968	STATESIDE	UK	SSL 10235
LARRY KILEY	B	(AB	(B) SURE LOOKS REAL	1969	ABC	US	ABCS 652

E17 EDGE E17

Member	Inst	Albums	Album	Year	Label	Country	No.
JOHN MOSS	D	(A	(A) SQUARE ONE	1980	HURRICANE	UK	FLAK102 NL 55019
LU EDMUNDS	G	(A	(B) EDGE	1981	CASABLANCA		7214
GAVIN POVEY	K	(A					
GLYN HAVARD	B	(A					

E17A EDGE 2 E17A

Album	Year	Label	No.
(A) UNEASY PEACE	1975	INTERN	NSPL 41037

E18 GRAEME EDGE E18

Album	Year	Label	Country	No.	Label	Country	No.
(A) KICK OFF YOUR MUDDY BOOTS	1974	THRESHOLD	UK US	THS15	NOVA	GER	22281
(B) PARADISE BALLROOM	1977	DECCA	UK	TXS 121	NOVA	GER	23087
(B) PARADISE BALLROOM	1977	LONDON	US	PS 686			

Member	Inst	Albums	Member	Inst	Albums	Member	Inst	Albums
GRAEME EDGE	D V	(AB						
ADRIAN GURVITZ	G V K	(AB						
PAUL GURVITZ	B V	(AB						
MICK GALLAGHER	K	(A						
BRIAN PARRISH	V	(B	RAY THOMAS	V	(A	SUNNY LESLIE	V	(A
RUBY JAMES	V	(A	NICKY JAMES	V	(A	LESLEY DUNCAN	V	(A
BARRY ST JOHN	V	(A	JOANNE WILLIAMS	V	(A	GINGER BAKER	D	(A
ANN ODELL	K	(B	TONY HYMAS	K	(B	BLUE WEAVER	K	(B
REBOP	PERC	(B	LAWRIE McMILLAN	HRNS	(B	B J COLE	STEEL	(B
BILL EASLEY	HRNS	(B	KEN SPAIN	HRNS	(B	BEN CAULEY	HRNS	(B
EDGAR MATTHEWS	HRNS	(B						

E18A EDISON ELECTRIC BAND E18A

Album	Year	Label	Country	No.
(A) BLESS YOU, DR WOODWARD	1970	COTILION	US	SD 9022

Member	Inst	Albums	Member	Inst	Albums	Member	Inst	Albums
DAN'FREEBO'FRIEDBERG	G B	(A						
T J TINDALL	G V	(A						
MARK JORDAN	K G	(A	RIP STOCK	V D	(A	MICHAEL ZIEGLER	G	(A
NORMAN PRIDE	CONGA	(A	BROOKMEAD MUMBLE CHOIR	V	(A			

E18B EDITION SPECIALE E18B

Member	Inst	Albums	Album	Year	Label	Country	No.
ANN BALLISTER	K	(	ALLEE DES TILLEULS	19	SONOPRESSE	FR	UAS 29965
MIMI LORENZINI	G V	(	ALIQUANTE	19	RCA	PL	37069
JOSQUIN TURENNE	B G V	(					
J J BOUCHET D'ANGELY	D	(					

E18C EDITH NYLON E18C

MYLENE KHASKI V SYN (A — (A) EDITH NYLON 1979 CBS CAN 90571
KARL MORMET B (A
ALBERT T D (A — CHRISTOPHE BOUTIN G (A — ZAKO G (A

E19 DAVE EDMUNDS (& ROCKPILE) E19

DAVE EDMUNDS G K V B PROD(ALL
MICKEY GEE G (HJ — (A) ROCKPILE 1971 REGAL ZONOPHONE UK SLRZ 1026
B J COLE STEEL (A — (A) ROCKPILE 1972 MAM US MAM3 EURO EMI 93282
ANDY FAIRWEATHER LOW G (A — (B) STARDUST (SOUNDTRACK 1 SIDE)(DBL) 1974 RONCO UK RG2009/10
BILLY RANKIN D (D — (C) SUBTLE AS A FLYING MALLET 1975 ROCKFIELD UK RRL 101
STEVE GOULDING D (D — (C) SUBTLE AS A FLYING MALLET 1978 RCA UK PL 25129 RI INTS 5131
PAUL RILEY B (D — (C) SUBTLE AS A FLYING MALLET 1975 RCA US APL15003 GER 21505
GERRY HOGAN STEEL (E — (D) GET IT 1977 SWANSONG UK 59404 US 8418
PETE KELLY PNO (E — (E) TRACKS ON WAX 1978 SWANSONG UK 59407 US 8505
IAN GOMM G V (C — (F) REPEAT WHEN NECESSARY 1979 SWANSONG UK 59409 US 8507
PICK WITHERS D (C — (G) SECONDS OF PLEASURE(ROCKPILE) 1980 F BEAT UK XXLP7 GER 58218
ALBERT LEE G (FJ — (H) TWANGIN' 1981 SWANSONG UK 59411 US 16034
BOB ANDREWS K (CD — (I) BEST OF 1981 SWANSONG US 8510
BILLY RANKIN D V (C — (J) D E 7 1982 ARISTA GER 204508
NICK LOWE PROD B V (CDEFGH — ( ) COLLEGE RADIO PRESENTS (PROMO) 198 SWANSONG PR 230
JOHN WILLIAMS B (H
BILLY BREMNER G V(CDEFGH — TERRY WILLIAMS D (ACDEFGH — BRINSLEY SCHWARZ G (C
STRAY CATS (H — HUGHIE LEWIS HCA (F — ROGER BECHINAN PNO (F
CHESTERFIELD KINGS HCA (H — DAVE PEACOCK B (J — BOBBY IRWIN D (J
NEIL KING TPT (J — LIAM GRUNDY PNO (J — DAVE CHARLES D (J
JOHN DAVID B (J — GERAINT WATKINS K (J — DICK HANSON TPT (J
JOHN'IRISH' EARLE SAX (J

E19A EDWARD BEAR E19A

( ) EDWARD BEAR 19 PENNYFARTHING UK PELS 532

E19B EDWARD BEAR E19B

LARRY EVOY D V (BD — (A) BEARINGS 1969 CAPITOL US SKAO 426
DANNY MARKS G V BAN(B — (B) ECLPSE 1970 CAPITOL CAN 6349 US 580
GENE MARTYNEC SYN (D — (C) EDWARD BEAR 197 CAPITOL US ST 11157
PAUL WELDON K B V (B — (D) CLOSE YOUR EYES 1973 CAPITOL CAN SMAS11192
ROGER ELLIS G V (D
BOB KENDALL K V (D — DENNY DEPORTER G V (D — RANDY GULLIVER K V (D
BILL LOOP B V (D — TIM WYNVEER G V (D

E19C JACKIE EDWARDS E19C

JACKIE EDWARDS V (ALL — ( ) STAND UP FOR JESUS 1964 ISLAND UK ILP 912
( ) COME ON HOME 1965 ISLAND UK ILP 931
( ) THE BEST OF 1966 ISLAND UK ILP 936
( ) PLEDGING MY LOVE 1966 ISLAND UK ILP 941
( ) BY DEMAND 1966 ISLAND UK ILP 940
( ) PREMATURE GOLDEN SANDS 1967 ISLAND UK ILP 960
( ) PUT YOUR TEARS AWAY 19 VEEP US PS 16533
( ) I DO LOVE YOU 1972 TROJAN UK TRL 47
( ) DO YOU BELIEVE IN LOVE 1976 KLIK UK KLP 9009
( ) BEFORE THE NEXT TEARDROP 1977 THIRD WORLD TWS 928
( ) LET'S FALL IN LOVE 1978 THIRD WORLD TDWD 3
( ) COME TO ME SOFTLY 1979 THIRD WORLD TDWD 10

E19D JANG EDWARDS E19D

JANG EDWARDS (AB — (A) CLOWN POWER 19 ARIOLA NL 202 144
(B) LIVE IN EUROPE 19 POLYDOR NL 2925 113

E20 JONATHAN EDWARDS E20

JONATHAN EDWARDS B G HCA V(ALL — (A) JONATHAN EDWARDS 1971 CAPRICORN US 821
STUART SCHULMAN B VLN K(ABCD — (A) JONATHAN EDWARDS 1971 ATLANTIC UK K 40282
BILL KEITH STEEL BANJO (ABCD — (B) HONKY TONK STARDUST COWBOY 1972 ATCO US SD 7015
BILL ELLIOTT PNO ORG(CD — (C) HAVE A GOOD TIME FOR ME 1973 ATCO US SD 7036
GEORGE GRANTHAM D V (C — (D) LUCKY DAY 1974 ATCO US SD 36104
R DAVIES B (C — (E) ROCKIN' CHAIR 1976 REPRISE US 2238
DAVID BROMBERG G MAND DOBRO(C — (F) SAILBOAT 1977 WB US BS 3020
AL ANDERSON G (D
ERIC LILLEQUIST G V (ABD — DEAN ADRIAN PERC (BD — BOB CHOUINARD D (D
DAVE CONRAD B (D — JOHN WARE D (EF — GLEN D HARDIN PNO (EF
JAMES BURTON G (E — HANK DE VITO STEEL (EF — EMORY GORDY B MAND(EF
EMMYLOU HARRIS V G (EF — JEFF LABES K (A — RICHARD ADELMAN D (AB
CHANDLER TRAVIS MARACAS(B — BILL PAYNE PNO (E — BRIAN AHERN G (EF
RODNEY CROWELL G (EF — BYRON BERLINE FDL (E — HERB PEDERSEN BANJ V(EF
DAVID GRISMAN MAND (E — DIANNE BROOKS V (EF — LYNNIE (DALL) EDWARDS V (DE
MIKE AULDRIDGE DOBRO (F — ALBERT LEE G MAND (F

E20A STONEY EDWARDS E20A

STONEY EDWARDS V (AB — (A) MISSISSIPPI, YOU'RE ON MY MIND 197 CAPITOL 11401
GEORGE KIRIAKIS G (B — (B) BLACKBIRD 1976 CAPITOL 11499
JOHN PLATANIA G (B
CRAZY JOE RENDA K (B — PHIL TRIMBLE FDL (B — DON BROOKS HCA (B
DAVID KAPELL B (B — BEAU SEGAL D (B — DAVID MANSFIELD K STEEL G (B
CHIP TAYLOR G (B

E21 EDWARDS HAND E21

ROY EDWARDS K V (ABC — (A) EDWARDS HAND 1969 GRT US 10005
ROGER HAND G V (ABC — (B) STRANDED 1971 RCA UK SF 8154
JAMES LITHERLAND G (B — (C) RAINSHINE 1973 REGAL ZONOPHONE UK SRZA 8513
JOHN WETTON B (B
CLEM CATTINI D (B

E21A EELA CRAIG E21A

HUBERT BOGNERMAYR K V (A	(A) ONE NITER	1976 VERTIGO 6360 635
HUBERT SCHNAUER K (	(B) HATS OF GLASS	1977 VERTIGO 6360 638
HARALD ZUSCHRADER K G (	(C) MISSA UNIVERSALIS	1978 PHILIPS 6360 639
WILL ORTHOFER V (	(D) ONE NIGHTER	1981 ARIOLA NL 202 311
FRITZ RUDELBERGER G K V (		
GERHARD ENGLISCH B PERC(	FRANK HUEBER D (	

E21B EFENDI'S GARDEN E21B

CURTIS EFENDI V (A	(A) EFENDI'S GARDEN	19 BABYLON GER 80004
FRANK MEIER B (A		
WOLFGANG KRANTZ K G (A	WOLFGANG SCHREINER D PERC (A	KLAUS HESS G (A
HEINZ ALBERDING SAX (A		

E22 JOE EGAN E22

JOE EGAN G V (A	(A) OUT OF NOWHERE	1979 ARIOLA US 50064 UK ARL 5021
HENRY SPINETTI D (A	(B) M A P	1981 ARIOLA UK ARL 5052
DAVE MARKEE B (A		
BILLY LIVSEY K (A	PAUL PILNICK G (A	PHIL PALMER G (A
ALAN PARKER G (A	CHARLES SPITTERI PERC (A	BENNY GALLAGHER ACC (A
GRAHAM LYLE MAND (A	SYLVIA V (A	JOY YATES V (A
VICKY BROWN V (A	GEORGE CHANDLER V (A	JIMMY ELLIS V (A

E23 WALTER EGAN E23

WALTER EGAN V (ALL	(A) FUNDAMENTAL ROLL	1977 POLYDOR UK 2310 614
WITH	(A) FUNDAMENTAL ROLL	1977 UA UK UAG 30032
ANNIE McCLOONE V (BCD	(A) FUNDAMENTAL ROLL	1977 CBS US 34679
TOM MONCRIEFF G V (BCD	(B) NOT SHY	1978 CBS US 35077
LINDSEY BUCKINGHAM G (ABCD	(B) NOT SHY	1978 POLYDOR UK 2310 609
MICK FLEETWOOD D (B	(C) HI FI	1979 CBS US 35796
EARL SHAKLEFORD V PERC(BCD	(D) THE LAST STROLL	1981 EDGE UK HOG 3 US CBS 36513
JOHN SELK B V G (ABCD		
MIKE HUEY D PERC(BCD	STEVE HAGUE K V (B	STEVIE NICKS V (BA
DEAN TORRANCE V (B	JOHN ZAMBETTI V (BCD	SKIP EDWARDS K G V(CD
LEE KIX D V (D	DEKE LEONARD G V (D	JEAN ANNE CHAPMAN V (D
EARLE MANKEY PROD (D	GARY ROWLES V (A	DENNID MANSFIELD D (A
BILL CUOMO K (A	JOHN WARE D (A	

E24 EGG E24

HUGH MONTGOMERY CAMPBELL K(ABC	(A) EGG	1970 NOVA SDN 14
DAVE STEWART K (ABC	(A) EGG	1970 DERAM US 18039
CLIVE BROOKS D (ABC	(B) POLITE FORCE	1970 DERAM UK SML 1074
ANN ROSENTHAL V (C	(B) POLITE FORCE	1970 DERAM US 18056
AMANDA PARSONS V (C	(C) CIVIL SURFACE	1974 CAROLINE UK C 1510
STEVE HILLAGE G (C		
BARBARA GASKIN V (C	JEREMY BAINES FLT (C	LINDSAY COOPER WIND (C
TIM HODGKINSON CLAR (C	HENRY LOWTHER TPT (B	MIKE DAVIS TPT (B
BOB DOWNES SAX (B	TONY ROBERTS SAX (B	MAURICE CAMBRIDGE CLAR (C
STEPHEN SOLLOWAY FLT (B	CHRIS PALMER WIND (B	

E24A EGGS OVER EASY E24A

AUSTIN DELONE K G V (A	(A) GOOD'N' CHEAP	1972 A&M US 4366
BRIEN HOPKINS K B G V(A		
JACK OHARA G B HCA V(A	BILL FRANZ D (A	

E24B EGO E24B

	(A) ON THE ROCKS	1981 JUPITER NL 624692

E24C EIGHT O ONE (801) E24C

PHIL MANZANERA G V (A	(A) 801 LIVE	1976 ISLAND UK ILPS 9444 US POLYDOR6178
BRIAN ENO K (A	(A) 801 LIVE	1977 POLYDOR RI UK 2302 044
LLOYD WATSON G (A		
FRANCIS MONKMAN K (A	BILL MACCORMICK B (A	SIMON PHILLIPS D (A

E25 EIGHTEEN CARAT GOLD E25

KLAUS EBERTS G	( ) ALL BUMM	1974 UA UK UAS29559 TELEFUNKEN NL624853
JURG EVERS G (		
LOTHER MEID B (	KEITH FORSEY D (	

E25A ALF EMIL EIK E25A

ALF EMIL EIK D G V K B (A	(A) JOYS AND BREATH OF ETERNITY	1979 RVEST NOR 37377
IRIS REUTZ V (A		
ANNE ENGH V (A	SVEND UNDSETH WIND (A	JOHN ERIK HOLTAN PNO (A

E26 EIRE APPARENT E26

MICHAEL COX G (A	(A) SUNRISE	1969 BUDDAH 203 021 US 5031
DAVE LUTTON D (A	(B) ROCK'N'ROLL BAND	19 POLYDOR
ERNIE GRAHAM B (A		
JIMI HENDRIX G (A	CHRIS STEWART B (A	HENRY McCULLOUGH G (
NOEL REDDING B (A	ROBERT WYATT D (A	MITCH MITCHELL D (A
TERRY TAYLOR G V (	VIC BRIGGS PNO (A	PETE TOLSON G (A

E27 EKSEPTION E27

RICK VAN DER LINDEN K (ABCDEJKLP	(A) EKSEPTION	1969 PHILIPS NL 873 003
REIN VAN DER BROEK HRNS (ALL	(A) EKSEPTION	1970 PHILIPS UK 6314 005
PETER DE LEEUWE D V (ACDEAOP	(A) EKSEPTION	1970 PHILIPS 600 344
COR DEKKER B (ADEGOBC	(B) BEGGAR JULIA'S TIME TRIP	1969 PHILIPS 6314001 US 600 348
DICK REMELINK WIND (BCDEOP	(C) 3	1972 PHILIPS 6423 005
PETER VOOGT D (G	(D) 00.04	1971 PHILIPS 6423 019
JAN VANNIK WIND (	(E) EKSEPTION 5	1972 PHILIPS 6423 042
DENNIS WHITBREAD D (B	(E) EKSEPTION 5	197 PHILIPS US 700 002
TONY VASSA SAX (OP	( ) BEST OF	197 PHILIPS 6423 053
STEVE ALLEN V (BP	(F) TRINITY	1973 PHILIPS NL 6423 056
ROB KRUISMAN WIND G V (AP	(G) NEW FORMULA	1974 BINGO 6413 501
HANS JENSEN K (G	(H) CLASSICS IN POP	197 PHILIPS 6423 079
HUIB VAN KAMPEN G SAX (AP	(I) MIND MIRROR	1975 PHILIPS NL 6423 082
TONY VOS SAX (O	(J) CLASSICS	1975 PHILIPS 6410 044
MICHEL VAN DIJK V PERC(B	(K) REFLECTION SERIES	1976 PHILIPS NL 6428 111
LINDA VAN DYCK V (B	(L) GREATEST HITS	197 PHILIPS 6677 025
	(M) BACK TO THE CLASSICS	197 POLYDOR 2393 167

(CONTINUED)

E27 EKSEPTION (CONTINUED) E27

(N) LA CINQUIEME 197 PHILIPS 6440 217
(O) EKSPETION 78 1978 MERCURY NL 665 081
(P) SENSATIONAL 19 PHILIPS 928 857
(Q) DANCE MACABRE 1981 ARIOLA 203 629
(R) GREATEST HITS 1982 PHILIPS NL 6423 490

E28 ELASTIC BAND E28

ANDY SCOTT (A) EXPANSIONS ON LIFE 1969 NOVA SND 6
DAVE SCOTT
TED YEADON SEAN JENKINS

E29 DONNIE ELBERT E29

DONNIE ELBERT V (ALL
( ) ROOTS OF DONNIE ELBERT 1973 EMBER UK EMB 3421
( ) STOP IN THE NAME OF LOVE 1976 D J M UK 22014 US TRIP 9524
( ) WHERE DID OUR LOVE GO 19 ALL PLATINUM US 3007
( ) DONNIE ELBERT SINGS 19 KING US 629
( ) HAVE I SINNED 19 DELUXE US DLP 12003
( ) DANCING THE NIGHT AWAY 1978 ALL PLATINUM US 3019

E30 EL CHICANO E30

BOBBY ESPINOSA K V (CDEFGJ
MICKEY LESPRON G (CDEFGJ
ENRIQUE BAEZA PERC (CDEFGJ
DANNY LAMONT D (C
HECTOR REGALADO D PERC(CDEG
BRIAN MAGNESS B (E
JERRY SALAS G V (DEG
EDDIE RODRIGUEZ D PERC(E
SHERRY WILLIAMS V (DJ
FREDDIE SANCHEZ B V (C
JOHN DE LUNA D (CJ
MAX GARDUNE G V PERC(C
STEVE SALAS V (C
JAMES ESPINOZA B (D
DANNY LAMONT D (D
CRUZ BACA V (D
JOESEPH PERREIRA B SYN V(J
DICK HENDERSON B (D
DAVID BATTEAU V (J
JERRY ANGELO WIND (J
BOBBY LOYA TPT (D
MARK GREEN SYN (J

(A) VIVA TIRADO 1970 MCA US 548 KAPP US 3632
(B) REVOLUTION 1971 MCA UK MCA 2654 KAPP US 3640
(C) CELEBRATION 1972 MCA UK MUPS456 KAPP US 3663
(C) CELEBRATION 1974 MCA UK MCA 2659
(D) EL CHICANO 1973 MCA UK MUPS 445 MCA US 312
(D) EL CHICANO 1974 MCA UK MCA 69
(E) CINCO 1974 MCA UK MAPS7262MCA US 401
(E) CINCO 1974 MCA US MCF 2556
(F) LOOK OF LOVE 197 MUSIDISC CU 1183
(G) PYRAMID OF LOVE & FRIENDS 1975 MCA US 2150
(H) THE BEST OF EVERYTHING 1975 MCA US 437
(J) THIS IS EL CHICANO 1976 SHADYBROOK US 33005

E31 EL COCO E31

W MICHAEL LEWIS K SAX (ABC
LAURIN RINDER V D SAX (ABC
JOE BELLAMY B (A
JOHN HUNT G (A
HARRY KIM TPT (ABC
JACK WEBER G (A
MARSHA THACKER V (AB
MERRIA ROSS V (ABC
BILL HENDERSON VLN (B
MIKE JACOBSEN CELLO (B
SHAMSI SARUMI PERC (C
DOUG RICHARDSON WIND (ABC
CHRIS BOCCHINO V (A
ADRIENNE WILLIAMS V (AB
PAT POWDRILL V (A
PAM TOMPKINS VLN (B
DAVID STOUT TROM (C
ALEX BROWN V (C
DAVE CAHOUN PNO (A
JERRI BOCCHINO V (A
KATHY NIXON V (A
CLEO KENNEDY V (B
JIMBO ROSS VIOLA(B
BOB ETOLL G (C
MORTONETTE JENKINS V (C

(A) LET'S GET IT TOGETHER 1976 PYE UK NSPL28229
(B) COCOMOTION 1978 PYE UK NSPL28237
(C) DANCING IN PARADISE 1978 PYE UK NSPL28268

E31A COON ELDER BAND E31A

COON ELDER G V (A
BRENDA PATTERSON V (A
PHIL BLACK G FDL V(A
BILL MARSHALL D PERC V(A
MARK SALLINGS WIND HCA V(A
ROCKY BERETTA B (A

(A) THE COON ELDER BAND 1977 MERCURY US SRM11140

E31B ELDERS E31B

(A) LOOKING FOR THE ANSWER 1972 AUDIO FIDELITY 6247

E31C FRANKIE ELDORADO E31C

FRANKIE ELDORADO V PERC(A
MARK ROCKET D K (A
THOMAS MORRANGELO V PERC(A
JOE MAURI G (A
JACK LESLIE SYN (A
KASIM SULTAN B (A

(A) FRANKIE ELDORADO 1980 EPIC UK 84128 US 36291

E31D ELECTRA E31D

RAINER UEBEL K SYN (A
WOLFGANG RIEDEL B (A
PETER LUDEWIG D (A
GISBERT KORENG G (A
BERND AUST WIND (A
MANUEL V SENDEN V K PERC(

(A) ADAPTIONEN 19 AMIGA GER 855501
(B) 3 19 AMIGA GER 855762

E31E ELECTRA FIVE E31E

TOM FERRARA G V (A
TOM GRAVES K (A
ALAN CHILDS D (A
KELVYN HALLIFAX G V (A
MIKE TOMASIO B V (A

(A) PICTURE 1981 TELDEC GER 24949

E31F ELECTRIC BANANA E31F

PHIL MAY G B V(ALL
DICK TAYLOR G B V(ABCG
SKIP ALLAN D V (A
JOHN POVEY K D (ABCDFG
WALLY ALLEN WALLER G B V(ABCG
PETER TOLSON G B (DF
GORDON EDWARDS V G B (DF
TWINK(JOHN ALDER) D (G
MICKY FINN G (F
BRIAN JOHNSON K (F
BILLY LOVEDAY MAND (F
CHICO GREENWOOD D (F

(A) ELECTRIC BANANA 1967 DE WOLFE UK 3040
(B) MORE ELECTRIC BANANA 1968 DE WOLFE UK 3069
(C) EVEN MORE ELECTRIC BANANA 1969 DE WOLFE UK 3123
(D) HOT LICKS 1973 DE WOLFE UK 3284
(E) RETURN OF THE ELECTRIC BANANA 1979 DE WOLFE UK 3381
(F) ELECTRIC BANANA THE 70's 1979 BUTT UK NOTT001
(G) ELECTRIC BANANA THE 60's 1980 BUTT UK NOTT003

E32 WAYNE/JAYNE COUNTY & THE ELECTRIC CHAIRS E32

WAYNE/JAYNE COUNTY V (ABCDEFG
GREG VAN COOK G (B
VAL HALLER B (BCD
J J JOHNSON D (BCD
JOOLS HOLLAND K (B
ELLIOT MICHAELS G (DG
HENRI PADOVANI G (CDEF
DAVID CUNNINGHAM SYN (D
SHARON C HCA (B
DARRYL WAY VLN (C
SAMMY MINELLI D (F
MORGAN FISHER K (C
PETER JORDAN B (F

(A) EP THE ELECTRIC CHAIRS 1977 ILLEGAL UK IL002
(B) ELECTRIC CHAIRS 1978 SAFARI UK LONG1 GER 26308
(B) ELECTRIC CHAIRS 1978 SAFARI UK SPA 20308
(C) STORM THE GATES OF HEAVEN 1978 SAFARI UK GOOD1 GER 61847
(D) THINGS YOUR MOTHER NEVER TOLD 1979 SAFARI UK GOOD2 GER 62853
(E) EP BLATANTLY OFFENSIVE 1978 SAFARI UK WC 2
(F) MAN ENOUGH TO BE A WOMAN 1978 SAFARI GER 61986
(G) R'N'R RESERUCTION LIVE 1980 SAFARI UK LIVE 1

E33 ELECTRIC FLAG E33

Member	Instruments	Albums
NICK GRAVENITES	V G	(ABCD
MIKE BLOOMFIELD	G V	(ACD
BUDDY MILES	D V	(ABCD
BARRY GOLDBERG	K	(ACD
HARVEY BROOKS	G B V	(ABD
HERBIE RICH	SAX K G V	(ABD
MARCUS DOUBLEDAY	TPT	(ABD
STEMSY HUNTER	V SAX	(AB
PETER STRAZZA	SAX	(A
SIVUCA	G	(A
MIKE FONFARA	K	(A
JOHN COURT	V PERC	(A
JOE CHURCH	PERC	(A
JOHN SIMON	PNO	(B
VIRGIL GONSALVES	WIND	(B
NICK MARRERO	PERC	(C
RICHIE HAVENS	PERC	(A
PAUL BEAVER	K	(A
HOSHAL WRIGHT	G	(B
GEORGE TERRY	G	(C
RICHARD NEWELL	HCA	(C
ALBHY GALUTEN	K	(C
ROGER TROY	B	(BC
TERRY CLEMENTS	SAX	(B
BARRY BECKETT	K	(C
RICHARD TEE	K	(C

Album	Year	Label	Country	Number
(A) A LONG TIME COMIN'	1968	CBS	UK	63294
(A) A LONG TIME COMIN'	1968	CBS	US	CS 9597
(A) A LONG TIME COMIN'	1974	EMBASSY	UK RI	31061
(B) ELECTRIC FLAG	1969	CBS	UK	63462
(B) ELECTRIC FLAG	1969	CBS	US	CS 9714
(C) THE BAND KEPT PLAYING	1974	ATLANTIC	UK	K 50090
(C) THE BAND KEPT PLAYING	1974	ATLANTIC	US	18112
(D) THE BEST OF	1971	CBS US 10169	US	30422
(D) THE BEST OF	1971	CBS	UK	64337
(E) THE TRIP SOUNDTRACK	19	SIDEWALK		ST 5908

E34 ELECTRIC LIGHT ORCHESTRA E34

Member	Instruments	Albums
ROY WOOD	G V	(A
RICK PRICE		(
JEFF LYNNE	SYN K G V	(ALL
BEV BEVAN	D V	(ALL
RICHARD TANDY	SYN V K	(B>R
MICHAEL D'ALBUQUERQUE	B V	(BCDEFG
MIKE EDWARDS	CELLO	(BCDEFG
COLIN WALKER	CELLO	(B
WILF GIBSON	VLN	(B
HUGH McDOWELL	CELLO	(EFGHIJK
MIK KAMINSKI	VLN	(CDEFGHIJ
MELVYN GALE	CELLO	(FGHIJK
KELLY GROUCUTT	B	(FGIJKNPQR
BILL HUNT	HRNS	(A
STEVE WOOLAM	VLN	(A
TED BLIGHT	CELLO	(CD
SANDI	V	(R
GHISLAINE	V	(R

Album	Year	Label	Country	Number
(A) ELECTRIC LIGHT ORCHESTRA	1971	HARVEST	UK	SHVL 797
(A) ELECTRIC LIGHT ORCHESTRA	197	SONOPRESSE	FR	69670
(A) ELECTRIC LIGHT ORCHESTRA	197	UA	US	5573
(A) NO ANSWER(RI OF(A)	1978	JET	US	35524
(A) NO ANSWER(RI OF (A)	1972	UA	US	UALA 040
(B) ELO 2	1973	HARVEST	UK	SHVL 806
(B) ELO 2 RI	1978	JET US 35533	US	LA040
(B) ELO 2	197	SONOPRESSE	FR	69671
(C) ON THE THIRD DAY	1973	WB	UK	K 56021
(C) ON THE THIRD DAY	197	SONOPRESSE	FR	30091
(C) ON THE THIRD DAY	1978	JET UK LP202	US	35525
(C) ON THE THIRD DAY	1973	UA	US	UALA 188
(D) SHOWDOWN	1974	HARVEST	UK	SHSP 4037
(E) THE NIGHT THE LIGHTS WENT IN	1974	WB	UK	K 56058
(E) THE NIGHT THE LIGHTS WENT IN	197	UA	US	UALA 318
(F) FACE THE MUSIC	1975	JET	UK	LP 11
(F) FACE THE MUSIC	1978	JET	UK	LP 201
(F) FACE THE MUSIC	197	SONOPRESSE	FR	30034
(F) FACE THE MUSIC	1975	UA	US	UALA 546
(F) FACE THE MUSIC	197	POLYDOR	GREECE	2310 414
(F) FACE THE MUSIC	1978	JET	US	35526
(G) ELDORADO	1975	WB	UK	K 56090
(G) ELDORADO	197	SONOPRESSE	FR	30092
(G) ELDORADO	1978	JET UK LP203	US	35526
(G) ELDORADO	1975	UA	US	UALA 339
(H) OLE' ELO	1976	JET	UK	LP 19
(H) OLE' ELO	1978	JET	US	35528
(H) OLE' ELO	1978	JET	NL	LP 903
(H) OLE' ELO	1976	UA	US	UALA 630
(J) NEW WORLD RECORD	1976	JET	UK	30034
(J) NEW WORLD RECORD	1977	UA	US	UALA 679
(J) NEW WORLD RECORD	1978	JET UK LP200	US	35529
(J) NEW WORLD RECORD	197	SONOPRESSE	FR	30017
(K) OUT OF THE BLUE	1977	JET	UK	UAR 100
(K) OUT OF THE BLUE	1978	JET		DP 400
(K) OUT OF THE BLUE	1978	JET	US	35530
(K) OUT OF THE BLUE	1978	JET	US	JTLA 823
(L) THE LIGHT SHINES ON	1977	HARVEST	UK	SHSM 2015
(M) THE LIGHT SHINES ON VOL2	1979	HARVEST	UK	SHSM 2027
(N) DISCOVERY	1979	JET		LX500
(N) DISCOVERY	1979	JET	US	35769
(N) DISCOVERY	1979	CBS SONY	JAP	25AP 1600
(O) GREATEST HITS	1979	JET	UK	LX525
(O) GREATEST HITS	1979	JET	US	36310
(P) XANADU (SOUNDTRACK)	1980	JET	UK	526
(P) XANADU	1980	MCA	US	6100
(Q) BOX OF THEIR BEST	1980	JET	US	36966
(R) TIME	1981	JET	UK	236
(R) TIME	1981	JET	US	37371
(EP) E L O	1978	JET		EL01

E34A ELECTRIC SANDWICH E34A

Member	Instruments	Albums
JORG OHLERT	G K	(A
KLAUS LORMANN	B	(A
JOCHEN CARTHAUS	V SAX	(A
WOLF FABIAN	D	(A
DAVID AXELROD		(D

Album	Year	Label	Country	Number
(A) ELECTRIC SANDWICH	1973			

E34B ELECTRIC SUN E34B

Member	Instruments	Albums
ULI ROTH	G	(AB
CLIVE EDWARDS	D	(AB
ULE RIGEN	B	(AB

Album	Year	Label	Country	Number
(A) EARTHQUAKE	1979	BRAIN	GER	0060 196
(B) FIREWIND	1979	BRAIN		6410

E34C ELEKTRICS E34C

Album	Year	Label	Country	Number
(A) CURRENT EVENTS	1981	CAPITOL		12093
(B) STATE SHOCK	1981	CAPITOL		12162

E34D THE ELECTRIC TOILET E34D

Member	Instruments	Albums
DAVE HALL	G V	(A
MONT ?		(A
? RAISIN		(A
? WILLARD		(A

Album	Year	Label	Country	Number
(A) IN THE HANDS OF KARMA	1970	NASCO	US	NASCO 9004

E35 ELECTRIC PRUNES E35

JIM LOWE AUTOHARP V G (AB | (A) ELECTRIC PRUNES | 1967 REPRISE US RLP 6248
JOHN HERREN K (CDE | (A) ELECTRIC PRUNES | 1967 REPRISE GER 24033
MARK TULIN B (AB | (B) UNDERGROUND | 1967 REPRISE US RLP 6262
KEN WILLIAMS G (AB | (C) MASS IN F MINOR | 1968 REPRISE US RLP 6275
PRESTON RITTER D (A | (C) MASS IN F MINOR | 1972 REPRISE UK K 34003
WEASEL SPAGNOLA G (AB | (C) MASS IN F MINOR | 197 MIDI UK 24010
DAVE HASSINGER PROD (AB | (C) MASS IN F MINOR | 1980 REPRISE NL 44057
RON MORGAN G (CDE | (D) RELEASE OF AN OATH | 1968 REPRISE US RLP 6316
MARK KINCAID G V (CDE | (E) JUST GOOD OLD ROCK'N'ROLL | 1969 REPRISE US RSLP 6342
RICHARD WHETSTONE D G V (CDE
BRETT WADE B V FLT (CDE | QUINT D (B

E35A ELECTRIC STRING BAND E35A

DENNY LAINE V G (
ANDY LEIGH B V (
VIV PRINCE D (| JOHN STEIN VLN (| CLIVE GILLINSON CELLO (
ANGUS ANDERSON VLN (| HAFLIDR HALYNISSON CELLO (

E35B ELECTROPHON E35B

BURT ALCANTARA (A | (A) ZYGOAT | 1974 POLYDOR 2383 270
( ) FURTHER THOUGHTS ON THE CLASSICS | 1977 POLYDOR 2482 335

E35C BIG MOJO ELEM E35C

BIG MOJO ELEM V B (A | (A) MOJO BOOGIE | 1978 MCM FR 900303
FRED BELOW D (A
WAYNE BENNETT G (A | WILLIE JAMES LYONS G (A

E36 ELEPHANT E36

DICK GLASS V G (AB | (A) ELEPHANT | 1973 CAPITOL SMAS11154
RUSS KUNKEL D (A | (B) THE ELEPHANT | 1974 MOONWATCHER US 20001
CHARLES LARKEY B (A
GEOFF LEVIN G (AB | AMBROSE CAMPBELL PERC (A | HAROLD COWART B (B
RONALD ZEIGLER D (B

E37 ELEPHANTS MEMORY E37

RICK FRANK D V (ABCDE | (A) ELEPHANTS MEMORY | 1969 BUDDAH 5033
STAN BRONSTEIN V SAX (ABCDE | (A) ELEPHANTS MEMORY | 1969 BUDDAH 203 022
GARY VAN SCYOC B V (ABCDE | (B) MIDNIGHT COWBOY (SOUNDTRACK) | 1969 BUDDAH 5038
WAYNE TEX GABRIEL G V (D | (C) TAKE IT TO THE STREETS | 1971 METRONOME MD 1052
JOHN LENNON V G K PERC (D | (C) TAKE IT TO THE STREETS | 1971 METRONOME 1035
CHRIS ROBISON V K G (E | (D) ELEPHANTS MEMORY | 1972 APPLE US SMAS 3389
ADAM IPPOLITO K TPT V (D | (D) ELEPHANTS MEMORY | 1972 APPLE SAPCOR.22
THUNDERTHIGHS V (E | (E) ANGELS FOREVER | 1974 POLYDOR 2383 260
TERRY & THE PIRATES V (E | (E) ANGELS FOREVER | 1974 RCA APLI 0569
YOKO ONO V (D
MARTHA VELEZ V (D
HILDA HARRIS V (D | KEITH JOHNSON TPT (D | DAVID PEEL V (D
TONI WINE V (D | LINDA NOVEMBER V (D | MYRON YULES V (D
JON SACHS G V (D | JOHN WARD B (| RICHARD SUSSMAN K (

E37A ELEVATORS E37A

TOM MYERS K (A | (A) FRONTLINE | 1980 ARISTA US 4270
JOHN CLARK G (A
JERRY ELLIS B (A | ZONDER KENNEDY G (A | WILLIAM BENJAMIN D (A

E38 ELF E38

RONNIE JAMES DIO]SAME V B(ABC | (A) ELF | 19 EPIC US 31789
RON PADAVONA | (B) CAROLINA COUNTRY BALL | 1974 PURPLE UK TPSA 3506
MICKEY LEE SOULE K G (ABC | (B) L A /59 | 1974 MGM US M3G 4974
GARY DRISCOLL D (ABC | (C) TRYING TO BURN THE SUN | 1975 MGM US M3G 4994
DAVE FEINSTEIN G (A
GRAIG GRUBER B (BC | STEVE EDWARDS G (BC | MARK NAUSEEF PERC (C
CHRIS PYNE TROM (B | HENRY LOWTHER TPT (B | HELEN CHAPPELL V (B
LIZA STRIKE V (B | BARRY ST JOHN V (B

E38A ELIAS HULK E38A

PETER THOPE V (A | (A) ELIAS HULK UNCHAINED | 1970 YOUNGBLOOD US SSYB 8
GRANVILLE FRAZER G (A
NEIL TATUM G (A | JAMES HAINES B (A | BERNARD JAMES D (A

E39 ELIZABETH E39

STEVE WEINGARTEN G ORG (A | (A) ELIZABETH | 1968 VANGUARD UK SVRL 19010 US VSD6501
JIM DAHME V FLT G(A
BOB PATTERSON G V (A | STEVE BRUNO B K (A | HANK RANSOME D G B(A

E40 YVONNE ELLIMAN E40

YVONNE ELLIMAN V (ALL | (A) I DON'T KNOW HOW TO LOVE HIM | 1972 POLYDOR 2383141 US DECCA 75341
WITH | (B) FOOD OF LOVE | 1973 PURPLE UK TPS 3504
DAVID SPINOZZA G (A | (B) FOOD OF LOVE | 1973 MCA US 356
HUGH McCRACKEN G (A | (C) RISING SUN | 1975 RSO UK 2393 149 US 4808
STU WOODS B (A | (D) LOVE ME | 1977 RSO US 3018 UK 2394 182
RICK MAROTTA D (A | (E) NIGHT FLIGHT | 1978 RSO US 3031 UK 2394 197
MICHAEL OMARTIAN K (F | (F) YVONNE | 1979 RSO US 3038 UK RS 16
JIM KELTNER D (FE
JEFF PORCARO D (F | STEVE CROPPER G (FE | JAY GRAYDON G (F | RICHIE ZETO G (F
MARTY WALSH G (F | DAVEY JOHNSTONE G SITA(EF | MIKE PORCARO B (F | LEE RITENOUR G (F
VICTOR FELDMAN PERC (F | PAUL STALLWORTH B (FE | STEVE BARRI PERC (F | LEE SKLAR B (FE
JIM HORN WIND (FE | BUELL NEIDLINGER B (F | MAXINE WILLARD V (FE | DAVID PAICH K (F
JULIA TILLMAN V (F | TOM SNOW K (F | JIM HAAS V (F | TOM CANNING K (F
JON JOYCE V (F | BILL PAYNE K (F | STAN FARBER V (F | CRAIG DOERGE K (FE
JOHN HENRY KURTZ V (F | DR JOHN K V (F | GARY COLEMAN PERC (DEF | JOE PORCARO PERC(F
FRED STAEHLE PERC (F | CHUCK FINDLEY HRNS (FE | ERIC CARMEN V K (EF | JACKIE KELSO HRNS(EF
MATTHEW MOORE V (F | KATHY COLLIER V (FE | CARMEN TWILLIE V (EF | VENNETTE GLOUD V (EF
MIKE BAIRD D (E | SONNY BURKE K (E | BOB BOWLES G (ED | JAMES GADSON D (ED
JAMES NEWTON HOWARD K (E | LOWELL GEORGE G (E | RITCHIE HAYWARD D (E | WILLIAM SMITH K (E
STEVE HUNTER G (E | RUSS KUNKEL D (E | KIKI DEE V (E | DANNY KORTCHMAR G (E
BABOO PIERRE PERC (E | DONNY GERRARD V (E | DEAN PARKES G (E | PAULINHO DA COSTA PERC(ED
SCOTT EDWARDS B (ED | HENRY KAPONO V (E | BOB ZIMITTI PERC (DE | DEE MURRAY B (E

(CONTINUED)

E40 (CONTINUED)

YVONNE ELLIMAN

E40

MARTI McCALL V (E FRED PERREN SYN (ED BEN BENAY G (E CECILIO RODRIGUEZ V (E
BRUCE EPSTEIN G (A FRANK CARILLO G (C MARK WARNER G (A PETER GORDON HRNS(A
RALPH MacDONALD PERC (A GARY STARBUCK G (D JOHN BARNES K PERC(D PETER ROBINSON K (A
ALAN WEIGHALL B (A KENNY ASCHER K (A LOUIS STEWART G (A BRUCE ROWLAND D (A
GEORGE BUTCHER PNO (A GEORGE YOUNG FLT (A

E41

MARC ELLINGTON

E41

MARC ELLINGTON V G BAGPIPES(ALL (A) MARC ELLINGTON 1969 PHILIPS UK SBL7883 US APMEX 10131
WITH (B) RAINS/ REINS OF CHANGE 1971 B&C UK CAS 1033
KAREN ELLINGTON V (ABC (C) A QUESTION OF ROADS 1972 PHILIPS UK 6308 120
RICHARD THOMPSON G (ABE (D) RESTORATION 1972 PHILIPS UK 6308 143
DAVE PEGG B (B (E) MARC TIME 1972 XTRA UK XTRA 1154
CHRIS HILLMAN V MAND(B
DAVE MATTACKS D (BDE IAN MATTHEWS V (BD SNEAKY PETE KLEINOW STEEL(B TONY COX K (BDE
MIKE DIEGHAN G BANJO(BCD PAT DONALDSON B (BDE GERRY CONWAY D (BE GORDON HUNTLEY B (AB
RAY DUFFY D (BC SANDY DENNY V (B FRITZ FRYER V (B STEVE RYE HCA (B
MICK FRENCH VLN(B RICK ROBERTS V (B GERRY FIELD VLN (B TIM RENWICK G (C
BRUCE THOMAS B (C ANDY LEIGH B (C JOHN WILSON D (C DAVE RICHARDS B PNO(CDE
ANDY ROBERTS G K(CDE ERIC ELLINGTON V (C JERRY DONAHUE G (DE DAVE PEACOCK B (D
DAVE HEPBURN B (D TIMI DONALD D (DE BARRY DE SOUZA D (D PHIL CHESTERTON D (D
TOM PARKER PNO(D ZOOT MONEY PNO(D DOLLY COLLINS PNO (D BOB RONGA G (D
SIMON NICOL G (ACE PHIL PICKETT G (D RAY WARLEIGH SAX (D IAN WHITEMAN K (DE
SUE DRAHEIM VLN(D MAC KISSOON V (DE SANDY ROBERTSON G (E LONGDANCER V (D
KATHY KISSOON V (DE ROGER SWALLOW D (AE LINDA THOMPSON V (E B J COLE STEEL(E
STEVE ASHLEY HCA(E REG POWELL K (A JAMIE OGILVY FORBES PIPES(D MARK GRIFFITHS B (AB

E42

CASS ELLIOT

E42

CASS ELLIOT V (ALL (A) CASS ELLIOT 1968 RCA US LSP 4619
DAVE MASON G V(F (B) DREAM A LITTLE DREAM 1968 DUNHILL US 50040
HARVEY BROOKS (B (B) DREAM A LITTLE DREAM 1968 STATESIDE UK 5004
JAMES BURTON G (B (C) BUBBLE GUM LEMONADE & SOMETHING 1969 DUNHILL US 50055
CYRUS FARYAR (B (C) BUBBLE GUM LEMONADE & SOMETHING 1969 STATESIDE UK 5014
JIM GORDON D (B (D) MAKE YOUR OWN MUSIC 19 DUNHILL US 50071
STEPHEN STILLS G V(B (E) MAMA'S BIG ONES 1971 PROBE UK SPB1020 RI ABC 5011
JOHN SIMON (B (E) MAMA'S BIG ONES 1974 DUNHILL US 50093
DON RANDI PNO(A (F) DAVE MASON & CASS ELLIOT 1971 PROBE UK SPB6259 US BTHUMB8825
JOHN GUERIN D (A (G) ROAD IS NO PLACE FOR A LADY 1974 RCA US LSA 3194 UK SF 8306
LOUIE SHELTON G (A (G) ROAD IS NO PLACE FOR A LADY 1972 RCA US 4753
AL CASEY G (A (H) DON'T CALL ME MAMA ANYMORE 1974 RCA UK APLI 0303
JULES GREENBERG VIBES(A
BRUCE JOHNSTON K V(A CAROL KAYE B (A REGGIE COLSON PERC (A LARRY CARLTON G (A
DENNIS BUDIMIR G (A EDWIN CARTER G (A CARL FORTINA K (A JOE OSBORN B (A
ED GREENE D (A MICHAEL LANG PNO(A EDWARD KUSBY TROM (A GROVER MITCHELL TROM (A
MAURICE TROM(A WILLIAM ANDERSON TPT(A GINO BOZZACCO TPT (A MOACIR SANTOS SAX (A
JACK NIMITZ SAX(A JERGME RICHARDSON SAX(A JAN GASSMAN V (A BENNY COLSON V (A
CLARK BURROUGHS V (A MARILYN MESSINA V (A CARL WILSON V (A CLYDIE KING V (A
SHIRLEY MATTHEWS V (A VENETTA FIELDS V (A

E43

COLONEL ELLIOT

E43

COLONEL ELLIOT (A) INTERSTELLA REGGAE DRIVE 1974 RHINO SRNP 9001

E44

DAVE ELLIOTT

E44

DAVID ELLIOTT G V B(AB (A) DAVID ELLIOTT 1972 ATLANTIC UK K 40374
CALEB QUAYE G PNO (A (A) SOLID GROUND 1973 ATLANTIC UK K 40527
DEE MURRAY B (A
NIGEL OLSSON D (A CHRIS KARAN D (AB DAVE MATTACKS D (A
FRANCIS MONKMAN K (A ROY O TEMRO D (A MICK GRABHAM G (AB
RICK WILLS B (A ALBERT LEE G (A JOHN PERRY B (B
B J COLE STEEL (AB GASPER LAWAL CONGAS (B TERRY STANNARD D (B
DAVID HOOD B (B ROGER HAWKINS D (B BARRY BECKETT K (B
PETE CARR DOB (B JIMMY JOHNSON G (B

E45

RON ELLIOTT

E45

RON ELLIOTT G V (A (A) CANDELESTICK MAKER 19 WB WS 1833
MARC McCLURE G V (A
CHRIS ETHRIDGE B (A DENNIS DRAGON D (A BUD SHANK FLT (A
SAL VALENTINO TAMB (A DAN LEVITT G V (A RY COODER G (A
LYLE RITZ B (A PAUL HUMPHREY D (A

E46

ELLIS

E46

STEVE ELLIS V (AB (A) RIDING ON THE CREST OF A SLUMP 1972 EPIC US 31945 UK 64878
ZOOT MONEY K V (AB (B) WHY NOT? 1973 EPIC UK 65650
ANDY GEE G (AB
DAVE LUTTON D (AB COLIN ALLEN D PERC (B GARY FARR HCA (
JIM LEVERTON B (A MAGGIE BELL V (AB MICK WEAVER K (
NICK SOUTH B (B JULIE TIPPETTS V (B ROGER CHAPMAN V (B
MIKE PATTO V (B MAGGIE NICHOLLS V (B

E47

DAVE ELLIS

E47

DAVE ELLIS G (A (A) ALBUM 1973 SONET UK SNTF 646
GORDON GILTRAP G (A

E48

MATTHEW ELLIS

E48

MATTHEW ELLIS V G K (ALL (A) MATTHEW ELLIS 1971 REGAL ZONOPHONE UK SRZA 8501
CHRIS SPEDDING g (B (B) AM I 1971 REGAL ZONOPHONE UK SRZA 8505
TONI CAMPO B (B
CLEM CATTINI D (B BARRY MORGAN D (B CHRIS WALKER K (B REX MORRIS SAX (B
PAUL SCHERMAN VLN (B TOMMY REILLY HCA (B SUNNY LESLIE V (B KAY GARNER V (B
LESLEY DUNCAN V (B

E49

PEE WEE ELLIS

E49

PEE WEE ELLIS SAX K V PERC(A (A) HOME IN THE COUNTRY 1977 SAVOY IMP SJL 3301
ROLAND HANNA K (A
JON SCHOLLE G (A JEFF BERLIN B (A IDRIS MUHAMMAD D (A JIMMY STRASSBURG D (A
JUMMA SANTOS CONGA (A CHARLOTTE CROSSLEY V (A LILLIAN TYNES V (A CHARLES BROWN G (A
ANTHONY JACKSON B (A BABATUNDE CONGA (A GORDON EDWARDS B (A MELANIE JORDIN V (A
JOHN GATCHELL TPT (A BARRY ROGERS TROM (A ERNIE HAYES K (A CORNELL DUPREE G (A
ERIC GALE G (A BERNARD PURDIE D (A RAY MANTILLA PERC (A LEON THOMAS V (A
LANI GROVES V (A WAYMON REED TPT (A GEORGE BENSON G (A CHRIS PARKER D (A
VIVIAN CHERRY V (A DWAIN JONES V (A DAVE LIEBMAN SAX (A ELEANA STEINBERG V (A

E49A LORRAINE ELLISON E49A

Member	Instr	Albums	Record	Year	Label	Catalogue
LORRAINE ELLISON	V	(ALL	(A) HEART & SOUL/STAY WITH ME	1970	WB	US 1821 UK K46037
RICK JAEGER	D	(B	(B) LORRAINE ELLISON	1974	WB	US 2780
MARC JORDON	K	(B	(C) BEST OF PHILADELPHIAS QUEEN	1976	WB	UK K 56230
TOM RUTLEY		(B				
WILTON FELDER	B	(B	KENNY GRADNEY B (B		ARTHUR ADAMS G (B	

E50 ELMER GANTY'S VELVET OPERA E50

Member	Instr	Albums	Record	Year	Label	Catalogue
ELMER GANTRY	V G	(AB	(A) ELMER GANTRY'S VELVET OPERA	1968	DIRECTION	UK 863300 US EPIC 26415
COLIN FORSTER	G	(A	(B) 1968 LIVE LINE UP			
JOHN FORD	B	(AB				
RICHARD HUDSON	D	(AB	PAUL BRETT G (B			

E50A ELOY E50A

Member	Instr	Albums	Record	Year	Label	Catalogue
FRANK BORNEMANN	V G	(ALL	(A) INSIDE	1973	ELECTROLA	GERM 29479
KLAUS PETER MATZIOL	V B	(DJK	(A) INSIDE	1973	JANUS	US 3062
FRITZ RANDOW	D G	(ABK	(B) FLOATING	1974	ELECTROLA	GERM 29521
HANNES ARKONA	G K	(JK	(B) FLOATING	1974	JANUS	US 7018
DETLER SCHMIDTCHEN	K SYN	(D	(C) POWER & THE PASSION	1975	ELECTROLA	GERM 29602
JURGEN ROSENTHAL	D	(D	(D) DAWN	1976	ELECTROLA	GERM 31787
MANFRED WIECLORKE	K G V	(AB	(E) OCEAN	1977	ELECTROLA	GERM 32596
WOLFGANG STOCKER	B	(B	(F) SILENT CRIES AND MIGHTY ECHOES	1978	ELECTROLA	GERM 45269
LUITJEN JANSSEN	B	(B	(G) LIVE	1978	ELECTROLA	GERM 32934
HANNES FOLBERTH	K	(JK	(H) COLOURS	1980	ELECTROLA	GERM 064 45936
JIM McGILLIVRAY	D	(J	(J) PLANETS	1982	HEAVY METAL	HM LP1
			(K) TIME TO TURN	1982	ELECTROLA	GER 46548

E50B ELUSION E50B

Record	Year	Label	Catalogue
(A) ALL TOYS BREAK	1981	ATLANTIC	US 16040

E51 JOE ELY E51

Member	Instr	Albums	Record	Year	Label	Catalogue
JOE ELY	G V	(ALL	(A) JOE ELY	1977	MCA	US 2242 UK MCF 2808
WITH			(A) JOE ELY	1981	MCA RI	1604
LLOYD MAINES	STEEL V	(BCE	(B) HONKY TONK MASQUERADE	1978	MCA	US 2333 UK MCF 2832
JESSE TAYLOR	G V	(BCE	(C) DOWN IN THE DRAG	1979	MCA	US 3080 UK MCG 3532
GREGG WRIGHT	B V	(BC	(D) LIVE SHOTS	1980	MCA	US 5262 UK MCF 3064
STEVE KEETON	D	(BC	(E) MUSTA NOTTA GOTTA LOTTA	1981	MCA	US 5183 UK MCA 3099
PONTI BONE	K	(BCE				
SMOKEY JOE MILLER	SAX	(E	CHIP YOUNG G (B		SHANE KEISTER K (B	
FARRELL MORRIS	PERC	(B	ED CIZARD SAX (C		RICHARD BOWDEN FDL (C	
DAVID MASON	K	(C	DINK THOMAS WHISTLE(C		PETER WEST V (C	
LEA JANE BERINATI	V	(B	GINGER HOLLADAY V (B		LISA SILVER V (B	
BUTCH HANCOCK	V	(B	MICHAEL BROVSKY PROD (E		MICHAEL ROBBERSON B (E	
ROBERT MARQUAM	D	(E	REESE WYNAMS K (E		JAMES FENNER PERC (E	
MARK HALLMAN	V	(E	JUDY PRICE V (E			

E52 EMBRYO E52

Member	Instr	Albums	Record	Year	Label	Catalogue
CHRISTIAN BURCHARD	V D K	(ALL	(A)OPAL	1970	OHR	GERM OMM 56003
EDGAR HOFFMANN	VLN V WIND	(12ABCD	(B) EMBRYO'S RACHE	1971	LIBERTY	GERM UAS 29239
MAL WALDRON	K	(DE	(C) FATHER SON HOLY GHOST	1972	LIBERTY	GER UAS 29344
JOHN KELLY	G V	(1A	(D) STEIGAUS	1973	BRAIN	GERM 1023
UWE MULLRICH	B	(2	(E) ROCK SESSION	1973	BRAIN	GERM 1036
ROMAN BUNKA	G V CLAR	(2BDGH	(E) ROCK SESSION	197	BRAIN	201190
RALPH FISCHER	B V	(1A	(F) THIS IS EMBRYO	1974	BRAIN	GER 200152
JIMMY JACKSON	K	(DE	(G) WE KEEP ON	1974	BASF	US/ GERM 21865/1
SIEGFRIED SCHWAB	G	(CE	(H) SURFIN'	1975	BASF	US/ GER 22385/3
JORG EVERS	B	(E	(J) EMBRYO LIVE	1976	TRIKONT	0003
BETTSY ALLEN	V	(A	( ) CLASSIC GERMAN ROCK SCENE	1975	UA	GER UAS 29774
ROBERTO DETREE		(A	(1) 1969 (2) 1977			
DIETER MIEKAUTSCH	K	(G				
UWE MULLRICH	B	(D	FRANZ BONTGEN V (B		HERMAN BREUKERK (B	
DAVE KING	D FLT V	(DE	HOLGER TRULZSH PERC (A		HANSI FISCHER FLT PERC(B	
CHARLIE MARIANO	WIND	(GH	LOTHER MEID (1		ALFRED JONES (	
JORG EVERS		(	KLAUS GOTZNER (		MULLAH STILETTI (	
MARIA ARCHER		(	BUTZE FISCHER (		MICHAEL WEHEMEYER (	

E52A EMERGENCY E52A

Member	Instr	Albums	Record	Year	Label	Catalogue
HANUS BERKA	WIND PERC	(ABCDE	(A) EMERGENCY	1971	CBS	GER 64381
JOHN REDPATH	D	(D	(B) ENTERANCE	1972	CBS	GER 64928
FRANK DIEZ	G B	(DE	(C) GET TO THE COUNTRY	1973	BRAIN	GER 1037
HANS STOER	G B	(D	(D) GOLD ROCK	1973	BRAIN	GER 201104
PETER BISCHOF	B	(CD	(E) NO COMPROMISE	1974	BRAIN	GER 1052
RICHARD PALMERJAMES	G	(D				
MARTIN HARRISON		(D	ELMAR SCHMIDT D (		RALF TOURSEL K SYN(	
UDO LIDENBERG	D PERC	(A	JIRO MATOUSEK K (A		OTTO BEZLOJA B (A	
BARRIE NEWBY	G	(A	REDDY V PERC(A		DUSKO GOYKOVIC TPT (A	
RICHARD PALMER-JAMES	G	(C	VEIT MARVOS K (C		BERND KNAAK D (C	
YERZY ZIEMBROWSKI	B	(C				

E52B BILLY THE KID EMERSON E52B

Member	Instr	Albums	Member	Instr	Albums	Member	Instr	Albums	Member	Instr	Albums
BILLY THE KID EMERSON	V PNO	(A	(A) LITTLE HEALTHY THING			19 CHARLY			UK CR 30187		
EUGENE FOX	SAX	(A									
OLIVER SAIN	SAX	(A	IKE TURNER	G	(A	JESSE KNIGHT	B	(A	CHARLES SMITH	TPT	(A
MOSES REED	SAX	(A	CALVIN NEWBORN	G	(A	ROBERT PRINDELL	D	(A	WILLIE SIMS	D	(A
BOBBY FIELD	SAX	(A	LUTHER TAYLOR	SAX	(A	JEWEL BRISCOE	SAX	(A	KENNETH BANKS	B	(A
RAYMOND HILL	SAX	(A	BENNY MOORE	SAX	(A	ELVEN PARR	G	(A	PHINEAS NEWBORN	D	(A

E52C KEITH EMERSON E52C

Member	Instr	Albums	Record	Year	Label	Catalogue
KEITH EMERSON	K	(AB	(A) INFERNO(SOUNDTRACK)	1980	ARIOLA	NL 202079 WB UK K50753
FRANK SCULLY	D	(AB	(B) NIGHTHAWKS	1981	MCA	NL 203 453 UK MCF 3107
KENDAL STUBBS	B	(AB				
NEIL SYMONETTE	D	(B	TRISTAM FRY PERC (B		JEROME RICHARDSON SAX (B	
GREG BOWEN	TPT	(B	PAULETTE McWILLIAMS V (B		STRINGS & ORCH (AB	

E53 EMERSON LAKE & PALMER E53

Musician	Inst	Albums	Album	Year	Label	Country	Number
KEITH EMERSON	K	(ALL	(A) EMERSON LAKE & PALMER	1970	ISLAND	UK	ILPS 9132
GREG LAKE	PROD B G V	(ALL	(A) EMERSON LAKE & PALMER	1973	MANTICORE	UK	K 43503
CARL PALMER	D	(ALL	(A) EMERSON LAKE & PALMER	1970	COTILLION	US	9040
WITH			(A) EMERSON LAKE & PALMER	197	MANTICORE	US	19120
LONDON SYMPHONY ORCH		(GH	(A) EMERSON LAKE & PALMER	197	ARIOLA	GERM	87 224ET
JOE WALSH	G	(G	(B) TARKUS	1971	ISLAND	UK	ILPS 9155
ORCH DE L'OPERA DE PARIS		(GH	(B) TARKUS	1973	MANTICORE	UK	K 43504
JAMES BLADES	PERC	(G	(B) TARKUS	1971	COTILLION	US	9900
			(B) TARKUS	197	MANTICORE	US	19121
			(B) TARKUS	197	ORRIZONTE	IT	8214
			(B) TARKUS	197	ARIOLA	GERM	87225XOT
			(C) PICTURES AT AN EXHIBITION	1971	ISLAND	UK	HELP1
			(C) PICTURES AT AN EXHIBITION	1973	MANTICORE	UK	K 33501
			(C) PICTURES AT AN EXHIBITION	197	MANTICORE	US	66666
			(C) PICTURES AT AN EXHIBITION	197	MANTICORE	US	19122
			(C) PICTURES AT AN EXHIBITION	197	ARIOLA	GERM	87 226,ET
			(C) PICTURES AT AN EXHIBITION	1981	MOBILE	US	031
			(D) TRILOGY	1972	ISLAND	UK	ILPS 9186
			(D) TRILOGY	1973	MANTICORE	UK	K 43505
			(D) TRILOGY	1972	COTILLION	US	9903
			(D) TRILOGY	197	MANTICORE	US	19123
			(D) TRILOGY	197	ARIOLA	GERM	87 227XOT
			(E) BRAIN SALAD SURGERY	1973	MANTICORE	UK	K 53501
			(E) BRAIN SALAD SURGERY	1973	MANTICORE	US	66669
			(E) BRAIN SALAD SURGERY	197	ATLANTIC	US	19124
			(E) BRAIN SALAD SURGERY	197	ARIOLA	GERM	87 302XOT
			(F) WELCOME MY FRIENDS	1974	MANTICORE	UK	K 63500
			(F) WELCOME MY FRIENDS	1974	MANTICORE	US	MC3 200
			(F) WELCOME MY FRIENDS	197	ARIOLA	GERM	88 150XET
			(G) WORKS	1977	MANTICORE	UK	K 80009
			(G) WORKS	1977	ATLANTIC	US	SD2 7000
			(G) WORKS	197	ARIOLA	GERM	28 614XDU
			(H) WORKS VOL 2	1977	ATLANTIC	UK	K 50422
			(H) WORKS VOL 2	1977	ATLANTIC	US	19147
			(H) WORKS VOL 2	197	ARIOLA	GERM	25 553XOT
			(J) LOVE BEACH	1978	ATLANTIC	UK	K 50552
			(J) LOVE BEACH	1978	ATLANTIC	US	19211
			(J) LOVE BEACH	1978	ARIOLA	GERM	200249320
			(K) IN CONCERT	1979	ATLANTIC	UK	K 50757
			(K) IN CONCERT	1979	ATLANTIC	US	19255
			(L) BEST OF	1980	ATLANTIC	US	19283
			(L) BEST OF	1980	ATLANTIC	UK	K 50652

E53A EMIGRE E53A

Musician	Inst	Albums	Album	Year	Label	Country	Number
WILLI MORRISON	G V	(A	(A) EMIGRE	1979	CHRYSALIS	US	CHR 1228
IAN GUENTHER	VLN	(A					
BARRY KEANE	D	(A	JOHN SHAND G (A		MITCHELL LEWIS G (A		
CHRIS VICKERY	B	(A	BRUCE LEY K (A		DICK SMITH PERC (A		
JIM CAMPBELL	V	(A					
BOB BONNELL	V	(A	GEORGE SEMKIW PROD (A				

E53B BOBBY EMMONS E53B

Musician	Inst	Albums	Album	Year	Label	Country	Number
BOBBY EMMONS	K	(A	(A) BLUES WITH A BEAT AND AN ORGAN	19	HI	US	32024

E54 BUDDY EMMONS E54

Musician	Inst	Albums	Album	Year	Label	Country	Number
BUDDY EMMONS	STEEL	(ALL	(A) 2 ACES BACK TO BACK(I SIDE)	1971	K ARK	US	K6028
BUDDY SPICHER	FDL	(E	(B) EMMONS GUITAR INC	197	EMMONS	US	
LENNY BREAU		(	(C) STEEL GUITAR	1975	FLYING FISH	UK	SNTF 708
JOHNNY GIMBLE	FDL	(C	(C) STEEL GUITAR	1975	FLYING FISH	US	FF 007
BUNKY KEELS	PNO	(C	(D) SINGS BOB WILLS	1976	FLYING	UK	SNTF 706
BUD LOGAN	B	(C	(D) SINGS BOB WILLS	1977	FLYING FISH	US	FF 017
MICHAEL MILFORD	MAND	(C	(E) BUDDIES	1977	FLYING FISH	US	FF 041
LEON RHODES	G	(C	(E) BUDDIES	1977	FLYING FISH	UK	SNTF 741
KARL HIMMEL	D	(C	(F) EMMONS LIVE VOL 1	197	MIDLAND	US	ISGC1
MIKE LEECH	B	(C	(G) EMMONS LIVE VOL 2	197	MIDLAND	US	ISGC2
KENNY MALONE	D	(C	(H) MINORS ALOUD	1979	FLYING FISH	US	FF 088
RON OATES	PNO	(C	(H) MINORS ALOUD	1979	FLYING FISH	UK	SNTF 799
DALE SELLERS	G	(C					

E55 EMOTIONS E55

Musician	Inst	Albums	Album	Year	Label	Country	Number
JEANETTE HAWES	V	(E	(A) SO I CAN LOVE YOU	1970	VOLT 4110	US	6008
SHEILA HUTCHINSON	V	(EFG	(B) SONGS OF LOVE	19	VOLT	US	6921
WANDA HUTCHINSON	V	(EFG	(C) UNTOUCHED	1972	VOLT 4112	US	6015
PAMELA	V	(F	(D) CHRONICLE	19	STAX	US	4121
THERESA DAVIS	V	(G	(E) FLOWERS	1976	CBS US 34163	UK	81639
VERDINE WHITE	B	(EFH	(F) REJOICE	1977	CBS US 34762	UK	82065
LARRY DUNN	K	(EF	(G) SUNSHINE	1977	STAX US 4100	UK	3003
AL McKAY	G	(EFH	(H) SUNBEAM	1978	CBS US 35385	UK	82864
JOE HUTCHINSON	G	(E	(J) BEST OF	1979	STAX US 4121	UK	3008
BAR KAYS		(C	(K) COME INTO OUR WORLD	1980	CBS US 36149	UK	83483
MICHAEL HARRIS	TPT	(EH	(L) CHRONICLE	1980	STAX	NL	62752
SOUL SPACEMEN		(C	(M) NEW AFFAIR	1981	CBS US 37456	UK	85172
FRED WHITE	D	(EFH					

Musician	Inst	Albums	Musician	Inst	Albums	Musician	Inst	Albums	Musician	Inst	Albums
WILLIE HALL	D	(G	DON MYRICK	D	(EFH	OSCAR BRASHEAR	TPT	(EFH	RICHARD BROWN	SAX	(E
DAVID SHIELDS	B	(F	JAMES GADSON	D	(F	MAURICE WHITE	D	(FH	JERRY PETERS	K	(F
PAULINHO DACOSTA	PERC	(FH	SKIP SCARBOROUGH	K	(FH	MARLO HENDERSON	G	(FH	CLARENCE McDONALD	K	(F
LOUIS SATTERFIELD	TROM	(EFH	MICHAEL TOLES	G	(G	BOBBY MANUEL	G	(G	MARVELL THOMAS	K	(G
LESTER SNARE	K	(G	RONNIE WILLIAMS	K	(G	EARL THOMAS	B	(G	DONALD DUCK DUNN	B	(G
AL JACKSON	D	(G	TERRY MARSHALL	K	(H	CHARLES HOSCH	B	(H	BARBARA KORN	HRNS	(H
ALAN ROBINSON	HRNS	(H	MARILYN ROBINSON	HRNS	(H	GEORGE PATTERSON	SAX	(H	GARY GRAINGER	B	(H
KEITH HENDERSON	G	(H	JON LIND	G	(H	DOUZELL DAVIS	D	(H	EARL DE ROVEN	PERC	(H
CHUCK FINDLEY	HRNS	(H	GEORGE BOHANON	TROM	(H	MAURICE SPEARS	TROM	(H	SID MULDROW	HRNS	(H
GALE ROBINSON	HRNS	(H									

E55A **EMPEROR** E55A

JOE ALEXANDER G V (A — (A) EMPEROR — 1977 PRIVATE STOCK 2029
JOE MARQUES B V (A
MIKE LOBETT K V (A — STEVE WATTS D V (A — RANDY BUDIHAS D V (A

E56 **END** E56

DAVE BROWN B V (A — (A) INTROSPECTION — 1969 DECCA UK SKL5015 US LONDON 505
TERRY TAYLOR G (A
NICK GRAHAM K V (A — HUGH ATTWOOL D (A — COLIN GRFFIN STEEL V(A
BILL WYMAN B (A — CHARLIE WATTS D (A — NICKY HOPKINS K (A

E56A **ENGLAND** E56A

MARTIN HENDERSON B V (A — (A) GARDEN SHED — 1977 ARISTA UK ARTY 153
FRANC HOLLAND G V (A
ROBERT WEBB K V (A — JODE LEIGH B V (A

E56B **ENGERLING BLUES BAND** E56B

WOLFRAM BODAG K V HCA(A — (A) ENGERLIND BLUES — 197 AMIGA GER 855 597
JENS SALEH B (A
MICHA ARNOLD B (A — HEINER WITTE G (A — BERND KUHNERT G (A
GOTTFRIED KLIER SAX (A — RAINER LOJEWSKI D (A

E57 **ENGLAND DAN & JOHN FORD COLEY** E57

ENGLAND DAN SEALS V G (ALL — (A) ENGLAND DAN & JOHN FORD COLEY — 197 A&M US 4305 UK AMLS64305
JOHN FORD COLEY V G K (ALL — (B) FABLES — 197 A&M US 4350 UK AMLS64350
WITH — (C) I HEAR MUSIC — 1976 A&M US 4616 UK AMLH64613
BOBBY THOMPSON G BAN (DEF — (D) NIGHTS ARE FOREVER — 1976 BIG TREE US 89517 UK K 50297
JOHNNY CHRISTOPHER G(F — (E) DOWDY FERRY ROAD — 197 BIG TREE US 76000 UK K 50362
STEVE GIBSON G MAND(FDEG — (F) SOMETHINGS DONT COME EASY — 1978 BIG TREE US 70006 UK K 50470
LEE RITENOUR G (G — (G) DR HECKLE & MR JIVE — 1979 BIG TREE US 76015 UK K 50602
GINGER HOLLADAY V (D — (H) BEST OF — 1980 BIG TREE US 76018
LARRY LONDIN D (DDE — (I) JUST TELL ME IF YOU LOVE ME — 1980 BIG TREE US
STEVE LUKATHER G (G
DAN FERGUSON G (G — WAH WAH WATSON G (G — DOYLE GRISHAM STEEL (FD — JACK WILLIAMS B (F
JOE OSBORN B (FDCE — WILTON FELDER B (G — DEE MURRAY B (G — DAN GORMAN D (G
JOHN LELAND B (G — LEE SKLAR B (G — SHANE KEISTER K (FG — JOEY CARBONE PNO (G
BOBBY EMMONS ORG (F — GREG PHILLINGANES PNO (G — MICHAEL BODDIKER SYN (G — STEVE PORCARO SYN (G
MICHAEL VERNACCHIO K(G — BILL PAYNE SYN (G — FARRELL MORRIS PERC (F — CYNDI REYNOLDS HARP(F
MIKE MILLER SAX (F — BILLY PUETT WIND(FDE — GUNNAR SCRIVENER AUTOHARP(F — HARRISON CALLOWAY HRNS(F
HARVEY THOMPSON HRNS(F — RONNIE EADES HRNS(F — DENNIS GOODE HRNS (FDE — SHELLEY KURLAND STR(F
LISA SILVER V (FDE — SHERI KRAMER V (FD — DIANE TIDWELL V (FDE — VICKI LEHNING V (F
DENISE PERALTA V (F — STEVE FORMAN PERC(G — ERNIE WATTS SAX (G — GARY MALLABER D (G
RALPH HUMPHREY D (G — JEFF PORCARO D (G — RICHIE ZETO G (G — JIM GILSTRAP V (G
JAI WINDING PNO (G — LESLIE BULKIN V (G — KELLY BULKIN V (G — OVID STEVENS G (G
ED GREENE D (G — BUBBA KEITH HCA (G — GARY TORPS G)G — TED REYNOLDS B (D
KYLE LEHNING B (D — SHANE KEISTER K (DE — JIM SEALS G FDL (DE — GEORGE CUNNINGHAM TPT(D
DON DHEFFIELD TPT (D — DENIS SOLEE WIND(D — JANIE FRICKIE V (D — RUSS KUNKEL D (B
LARRY MOHOBERAC K (B — JACK CONRAD B (B — CLARENCE McDONALD K (BC — MAX BENNETT B (BC
JOHN GUERIN D (B — BOBBIE HALL PERC (B — MARTY PAICH STR (B — JEFF PORCARO D (C
DAVID HUGATE B (C — MARK STEVENS PERC(C — WENDY SUITS V (E — REINEE PRESS B (B
LOUIE SHELTON G B SIT(BC — JIM GORDON D (BC — HAL BLAINE D (B — PAUL HUMPHREY D (B
LARRY KNECHTEL K (B — DON RANDI K (B — RON TUTT D (C — DAVID PAICH K (C
ALLAN ESTES PERC(C — TOMMY MORGAN HCA (C — DOYLE GRISHAM STEEL (DE — GEORGE TIDWELL TPT(E
BUDDY SKIPPER WIND(E

E58 **THE ENID** E58

ROBERT GODFREY K (ABCD — (A) THE ENID — 1976 BUK UK BULP 2014 US 52001
FRANCIS LICKERISH G (ABCD — (A) IN THE REGION OF THE STARS — 1977 EMI INS3005 BUK GER 6 22929
STEPHEN STEWART G (ABCD — (B) AERIE FAERIE NONSENSE — 1977 EMI INS3012
GLEN TALLETT B K HRNS(A — (B) AERIE FAERIE NONSENSE — 1977 BELLAPHON GER 44005
DAVID STOREY D (BC — (C) TOUCH ME — 1979 PYE UK N6PH10593
CHARLIE ELSTON K (B — (D) SIX PIECES — 1979 PYE UK N 116
TERRY PACK (BC — (E) RHAPSODY IN ROCK — 1980 PYE UK 18619
WILLAIM GILMOUR K (CD — (NB) SOME OF ABOVE HAVE BEEN REISSUED ON THE ENID LABEL
TONY FREER HRNS (C
MARTIN RUSSELL K B (D — ROBBIE DOBSON D (AD

E59 **BRIAN ENO** E59

BRIAN ENO V K SYN (ALL — (A) NO PUSSYFOOTIN' — 1973 ISLAND UK HELP16 US ANTILLES7001
WITH — (A) NO PUSSYFOOTIN' — 197 PHONOGRAM EURO 9101 629
ROBERT FRIPP G (ABEFHJ — (B) HERE COME THE WARM JETS — 1973 ISLAND UK ILPS9268 GER 87665
KURT SCHWITTERS V (H — (B) HERE COME THE WARM JETS — 1974 PHONOGRAM EURO 6396 032
FREDDIE SMITH D (D — (C) JUNE IST 1974 — 1974 ISLAND UK ILPS 9291
SHIRLEY WILLIAMS PERC (H — (D) TAKING TIGER MOUNTAIN BY STRATEGY — 1974 ISLAND UK US ILPS 9309
JAKI LIEBEZEIT D (H — (D) TAKING TIGER MOUNTAIN BY STRATEGY — 197 POLYDOR UK 2302 068
RHELL DAVIES PERC (H — (D) TAKING TIGER MOUNTAIN BY STRATEGY — 197 ISLAND US 1-3001
PAUL RUDOLPH G (BEHJ — (E) ANOTHER GREEN WORLD — 1974 ISLAND UK US ILPS 9351
FRED FRITH G (HJ — (E) ANOTHER GREEN WORLD — 1974 POLYDOR UK 2302 069
PERCY JONES B (EHJ — (F) EVENING STAR — 1975 ISLAND UK HELP22 US ANTILLES7018
BILL McCORMICK B (HJB — (G) DISCREET MUSIC — 1975 OBSCURE UK OB 4 US ANTILLES7030
PHIL COLLINS PERC (HJDE — (H) BEFORE & AFTER SCIENCE — 1977 POLYDOR UK 2302 071
DAVE MATTACKS PERC (HJ — (H) BEFORE & AFTER SCIENCE — 1977 POLYDOR EURO 2310 547 2344 087
ROD MELVIN K (EJ — (H) BEFORE & AFTER SCIENCE — 1977 ISLAND US 9478
ANDY FRASER B (H — (J) MUSIC FOR FILMS — 1978 POLYDOR UK 2310 623
JOACHIM ROEDELIUS K (HK — (K) AFTER THE HEAT — 1978 SKY GER 021
MOBI MOEBIUS K (HK — (L) MUSIC FOR AIRPORTS — 1979 AMBIENT UK 001 US PVC 7908
BRIAN TURRINGTON B (DEH — (M) POSSIBLE MUSIC — 1980 EDITIONS EGED7
RABBIT BUNDRICK K (C — (N) THE PLATEAUX OF MIRRORS — 1980 EDITIONS EGAMB 002
EDDIE SPARROW D (C — (O) FOURTH WORLD — 1980 EG UK EGED 7
MIKE OLDFIELD G (C — (P) MY LIFE IN THE BUSH — 1981 EG UK EGED 48 US SIRE 6093
JOHN CALE VIOLA K(CE — (Q) EMPTY LANDSCAPES — 1981
OLLIE HALSALL G PNO(C — (R) ON LAND — 1982 EG UK EGED 20
ARCHIE LEGGET B (C
KEVIN AYERS B (C — ROBERT WYATT PERC(CDL — NICO V HARMONIUM(C — JOHN HASSEL (M
HAROLD BUDD (N — INGE ZEININGER V (L — NICK JUDD K (B — ANDY MACKAY SAX K(BD
PHIL MANZANERA G (BD — SWEETFEED V (B — CHRIS THOMAS B (B — LLOYD WATSON G (B
PAUL THOMPSON PERC (B — MARTY SIMON PERC(B — SIMON KING PERC (B — JOHN WETTON B (B
BUSTA CHERRY JONES B (B — CHRIS SPEDDING G (B — CHRISTA FAST V (L — CHRISTINE GOMEZ V (L

(CONTINUED)

E59 (CONTINUED)

BRIAN ENO

E59

PORTSMOUTH SINFONIA		(D
DAVID BYRNE		(P
DENNIS KEELEY		(P
STEVE SCALES	SONGA	(P
SAMIRA TEWFIK	V	(P
BILL LASWELL	B	(R
POLLY ELTES	V	(D
DAVID VAN TIEGHAM	D	(P
MINGO LEWIS	PERC	(P
BUSTA JONES	B	(P
MICHAEL BEINHORN	SYN	(R
JON HASSELL	TPT	(R
SIMPLISTICS	V	(D
JOHN COOKSOY	D	(P
PRAIRIE PRINCE	D	(P
TIM WRIGHT	B	(P
MICHAEL BROOKS	G	(R
RANDI & PYRAMIDS	V	(D
CHRIS FRANTZ	D	(P
JESSE ROSSY	G	(P
DUNYA YUSIN	V	(P
AXEL GROS	G	(R

E60

JOHN ENTWISTLE

E60

JOHN ENTWISTLE	B V K	(ALL
GRAHAM DEACON	D PERC	(CD
TONY ASHTON	PNO	(CD
JIM RYAN	G	(D
HOWIE CASEY	SAX	(CD
JIMMY McCULLOCH	G	(B
DAVE CASWELL	TPT	(D
JOHN MUMFORD	TROM	(D
DICK PARRY	SAX	(D
DOREEN CHANTER	V	(D
BRYAN WILLIAMS	TROM K	(CB
IRENE CHANTER	V	(D
MIKE WEDGEWOOD	G	(D
EDDIE JOBSON	K	(D
NEIL SHEPPARD	K	(B
ALAN ROSS	G	(C
PETER FRAMPTON	G	(B
NEIL INNES	PERC(	(B
DAVE LAYSTON	G	(A
JOE VITALE	D K FLT	(F
JOHN MEALING	PNO	(D
LADYBIRDS	V	(C
JERRY SHIRLEY	D	(A
KEITH MOON	PERC	(B
JOHN WEIDER	VON	(B
BILLY NICHOLLS	V	(F
JUANITA FRANKLIN	V	(D
ROD COOBES	D	(B
VIV STANSHALL	PERC	(B
CYRANO	G	(A
JOE WALSH	G K SYN	(F

(A) SMASH YOUR HEAD	1971	TRACK UK 2406 005
(A) SMASH YOUR HEAD	1971	MCA US 2024 GER POLYDOR 2480033
(A) SMASH YOUR HEAD (DIFF MIX)	1971	DECCA US 79183
(B) WHISTLE RHYMES	1972	TRACK UK 2406 104
(B) WHISTLE RHYMES	197	DECCA US79190 US MCA 2027
(B) WHISTLE RHYMES	1972	POLYDOR GER 2480 202
(C) RIGOR MORTIS SETS IN	1973	TRACK UK 2406 106
(C) RIGOR MORTIS SETS IN	1972	MCA US 321
(D) MAD DOG	1975	TRACK UK TX 5114
(D) MAD DOG	197	MCA US 2129 GER NOVA 622212
(D) MAD DOG	197	LONDON JAP LAX 1034
(E) BACKTRACK 14 (THE OX)	1971	TRACK UK 2407 014
(F) TOO LATE THE HERO	1981	WEA UK 99179 US ATCO 38142

E60A

EON

E60A

EON	1976	SCEPTER US 5122
EON	1977	ARIOLA US 50038

E60B

EPITAPH

E60B

CLIFF JACKSON	G V	(C
KLAUS WALZ	G	(C
BERND KOLBE	B	(C
BILLY SHAW	ORG	(C
ACHIM WIELERT	D	(C
FRED KAZ	PNO	(C

(A) EPITAPH	1971	
(B) STOP LOOK LISTEN	1972	
(C) OUTSIDE THE LAW	1974	BRAIN 22 1311 BILLINGSGATE US 1009
(D) SEE YOU IN ALASKA	1980	BRAIN NL 760 274
(E) LIVE	1981	BRAIN 50038

E61

EPISODE SIX

E61

(1) 1965 (2) 1965/7 (3) 1967 (4) 1967/8

SHEILA CARTER DIMMOCK	K V	(1234
GRAHAM CARTER DIMMOCK	G V	(1234
TONY LANDER	G V	(1234
ANDY ROSS	V G	(1
ROGER GLOVER	B V	(1234
HARVEY SHIELD	D V	(12
JOHN KERRISON	D	(3
IAN GILLAN	V	(234
MICK UNDERWOOD	D	(4

E61A

PRESTON EPPS

E61A

BONGOLA	19	TOP RANK US RM 349
BONGO ROCK	1959	ORIGINAL SOUND US 1001
SURFIN' BONGOS	19	ORIGINAL SOUND US 5009M+8872S
BONGO	1966	ORIGINAL SOUND US 8851

E61B

EPSILON

E61B

MICHAEL WINZKOWSKI	G V	(ABC
HARTMUT PFANNMULLER	D PERC	(ABC
WALTER ORTEL	K	(AB
MICHAEL ERTL	B	(AB
CURT CRESS	D PERC	(B
JOHAN DAANSEN	G K V	(C
CHRISTIAN FELKE	FLT	(B
PETE BENDER	V	(B
HIENRICH MOHN	G	(C
RAINER MARS	G V	(B

(A) EPSILON	1971	BELLAPHON GER BLPS19070
(B) MOVE ON	197	BELLAPHON GER BLPS19078
(C) EPSILON OFF	1974	PHILIPS GER 6305 216

E62

EQUALS

E62

DERVIN GORDON	V	(1234
DAVE MARTIN	G	(CD
LINCOLN GORDON	G	(1234
EDDIE GRANT	G	(1
PAT LLOYD	G	(1234
JOHN HALL	D	(123
JIMMY HAYNES	G	(B
NEIL McBAIN	D	(4

(1) 1966 (2) 1971
(3) 19673 (4) 1975

UNEQUALLED	1967	PRESIDENT PTL 1006
UNEQUALLED	196	LAURIE US 2045
EQUAL SENSATION	1968	PRESIDENT PTL 1015
SENSATIONAL EQUALS	1968	PRESIDENT PTLS 1020
EQUALS SUPREME	1968	PRESIDENT PTLS 1025
BABY COME BACK	1968	RCA US LSP 4078
EQUALS STRIKE BACK	1969	PRESIDENT PTLS 1030
BEST OF THE EQUALS	1969	PRESIDENT PTLS 1050
BEST OF THE EQUALS	1969	JOY PRESIDENT JOYS 137
AT THE TOP	1970	PRESIDENT PTLS 1038
EQUALS ROCK AROUND THE CLOCK	1974	PRESIDENT PTLS 1054
GREATEST HITS	1974	M F P UK MFP 50153
DOIN' THE 45's	1975	RHAPSODY RHAS 9017
BORN YA	1976	MERCURY UK 9109 601
MYSTIC SYNSTER	1978	ICE UK ICEL 1002

E62A

ERGO SUM

E62A

LIONEL LEDISSEZ	V	(
JEAN GUERIN	K	(
MAX TOUAT	B	(
BRUTUS	D	(
ROLAND MEYNET	VLN	(
MICHEL LEONARDI	G	(

(A) MEXICO	19	THELEME FR 6332 500

E62B

ROKY ERICKSON & THE ALIENS

E62B

ROKY ERICKSON	G V	(AB
DUANE ASLAKSEN	G	(AB
BILL MILLER	AUTOHARP	(AB
JEFF SUTTON	D	(B
BRIAN MARNELL	V	(A
SCOTT MATTHEWS	D	(A
BOBBY GORMAN	B	(
FUZZ FURIOSO	D	(AB
STU COOK	B	(B
STEVE BURGESS	B	(AB
LINK DAVIS	ORG	(A
ANDRE LEWIS	SYN K	(AB

(A) ROKY ERICKSON & THE ALIENS	1980	CBS UK 84463
(B) THE EVIL ONE	1981	415 US 415A

E62C

EQUATORS

E62C

(A) HOT	1981	STIFF UK SEEZ 35

E63 EROC E63

JOACHIM H EHRIG K SYN G D VLN (ABCD
CARLOS BOTTICH G (C
KASI KLASSEN B V HCA(C
VOLKER KAHRS K (C
WOLFGANG JAEGER B (C
GERD KUHN G V (C
BERNHARD UHLEMANN B V (C
STEPFAN DANIELAK G V (C
EDD HUBER B (C

(A) EROC 1975 BRIAN EURO 1069
(A) EROC 1977 BRAIN UK 201 109
(B) ZWEI 1976 BRAIN 006 0007
(C) 3 (RECORDED 1969 79) 1979 BRAIN 0060 197

E63A KING ERRISSON E63A

KING ERRISSON PERC (
WITH
PRESTON LOVE WIND (A
FREDDIE HILL TPT (A
JACK WALRATH TPT (A
GEORGE BOHANON TROM (A
CLARENCE McDONALD PNO (A
DAVID T WALKER G (A
CHARLES CLARK V (C
PAMELA VINCENT V (C
BENNY PARKS D (A
JYMM YOUNG PNO (A
WILTON FELDER B (A
CLEVELAND HORNE V (C
CYNTHIA DOUGLAS V (C
WASHINGTON RUCKER D (A
CALVIN KEYS G (A
BILL UPCHURCH B (A
DONNA DAVIS V (C
MAURICE SPEARS TROM (A

(A)THE KING ARRIVES 197 CANYON US 7703
(B) MAGIC MAN 197 WESTBOUND US 224
(C) L A BOUND 1977 WESTBOUND US WT 307
(C) L A BOUND 1977 WEA 50426

E64 ERUPTION E64

(A) ERUPTION 1978 ATLANTIC US 50033 UK K 50454
(B) LEAVE A LIGHT 1979 ATLANTIC UK K 50595
(C) FIGHT FIGHT FIGHT 1980 HANSA NL 201 716
(D) BEST OF 1981 HANSA NL 203 490

E64A ESCORTS E64A

(A) 3 DOWN 4 TO GO 1973 ALIGATOR US 9106

E65 COKE ESCOVEDO E65

COKE ESCOVEDO PERC (ALL
WITH
ERROL KNOWLES V (B
FRANK MERCURIO K (B
GLEN SYMMONDS D (B
JOE HENDERSON SAX (B
MARG PHILLIPS B (B
GABOR SZABO G (B
ABEL ZAPATE G (B

(A) COKE 1975 MERCURY US SRM1 1041
(B) COMIN' AT YA 197 MERCURY US SRM1 1085
(C) DISCO FANTASY 1977 MERCURY US SRM1 1132

E66 ESPERANTO ROCK ORCHESTRA E66

RAYMOND VINCENT VLN (ABC
TONY MALISAN D (ABC
GINO MALISAN B (ABC
TONY HARRIS VIOLA (ABC
BRUNO LIBERT K V (AB
TIMOTHY KRAEMER CELLO (ABC
BRIGETTE DU DOIT V (ABC
KIM MOORE V (C
KEITH CHRISTMAS V (B
GLEN SHORROCK V (ABC
JANICE SLATOR V (A
GODFREY SALMON VLN V (ABC
BRIAN HOLLAWAY G (AB
ROGER MEAKIN G (C

(A) ESPERANTO ROCK ORCHESTRA 1973 A&M US 4399 UK AMLH68175
(B) DANSE MACABRE 1974 A&M US 3624 UK AMLH63624
(C) LAST TANGO 1975 A&M US 4524 UK AMLH68294

E66A ESSENTIAL LOGIC E66A

RICH TEA (A
LORA LOGIC (A
ASHLEY BUFF (A
MARK TURNER (A
DAVE WRIGHT (A

(A) BEAT RHYTHM NEWS 1979 ROUGH TRADE UK ROUGH 5

E67 SLEEPY JOHN ESTES E67

SLEEPY JOHN ESTES G V (ALL
WITH
HAMMIE NIXON HCA (ABDCI
YANK RACHELL G (BD
ED WILKENSON B (AD
RANSOM KNOWLING B (D
SUNNYLAND SLIM PNO (F
JIMMY DAWKINS G (F
ODIE PAYNE D (F
CAREY BELL HCA (F
EARL HOOKER B (F
JOE HARPER B (F
MIKE BLOOMFIELD G (B
JOHN'KNOCKY' PARKER PNO (A

(A) LEGEND OF 1963 DELMARK DL 603
(A) LEGEND OF 19 TRIO JAP PA 6212
(B) BROKE & HUNGRY 19 DELMARK DL 608
(C) IN EUROPE 1966 DELMARK DL 611
(D) BROWNSVILLE BLUES 1965 DELMARK DL 613
(E) ELECTRIC SLEEP 19 DELMARK DL 619
(F) 1929 1940 1967 FOLKWAYS RF8
(G) DOWN SOUTH BLUES 1974 MCA 510 091
(H) SLEEPY JOHN ESTES 19 COLLECTORS CLASSICS CC.24
(I) & HAMMIE NIXON 19 STORYVILLE SLP 172

E67A ETERNITYS CHILDREN E67A

(A) ETERNITYS CHILDREN 19 TOWER US ST 5223

E67B ETHEL THE FROG E67B

(A) ETHEL THE FROG 1980 EMI UK EMC 3329

E68 ETHIOPIANS E68

(A) WOMAN CAPTURE MAN 1970 TROJAN TBL 112
(B) SLAVE CALL 1977 THIRD WORLD TWS 15

E69 CHRIS ETHRIDGE E69

CHRIS ETHRIDGE B V (A
JOEL SCOTT HILL G V (A
JOHN BARBATA D (A

(A) L A GETAWAY 1971 ATLANTIC US 33357 UK K 40310

E69A ETRON FOU LELOUBLAN E69A

GUIGOU CHENEVIER D (AB1234
JEAN BAPTISTE MOULU K (1
MOREY B (1
CHRIS(EULALIE RYNAT)CHANET SAX(123A
FERDINAND RICHARD B (34AB
FRANCIS'PICHENETTE' GRAND SAX(B4
JEAN PIERRE GRASSET G (B
MICHAEL GREZES (B

(A) BATELAGES 1976 GRATTE CIEL FR CIEL 2001
(B) LES TROIS FOUS PERDEGAGNENT 1978 9H17 RECORDS FR 7001
(B) LES TROIS FOUS PERDEGAGNENT 197 TAPIOCA TP 10020
(1) 1971 (2) 1972 (3) 1973 (4) 1977
(C) LIVE IN AMERICA 1981

E69B EUPHONIOUS WAIL E69B

BART LIBBY K (A
STEVE TRACY G V (A
GARY VIOLESTTI B V (A
SUZANNA REY V (A
DOUG HOFFMANN D (A

(A) EUPHONIOUS WAIL 19 KAPP US 3668

E69C EUPHORIA E69C

(A) EUPHORIA 19 HERITAGE US HTS35,005

E69D EUCLID BEACH BAND E69D

(A) EUCLID BEACH BAND 1981 CLEVELAND INT US 35619

CHRIS EVANS (A (A) STONEHENGE 1980 WEA 58092
DAVE HANSELMANN (A

E70 EVEN DOZEN JUG BAND E70

MARIA D'AMATO(MULDAUR) V (A (A) EVEN DOZEN JUG BAND 1964 ELEKTRA US EKS 7246
STEVE KATZ G V (A (A) JUG BAND SONGS OF SOUTHERN MOUNTAINS LEGACY US LEG 119
PETE SIEGEL G V (A
JOHN SEBASTIAN G V (A JOSHUA RIFKIN PNO (A STEFAN GROSSMAN G V (A

E71 BETTY EVERETT E71

BETTY EVERETT V (ALL (A) THERE'LL COME A TIME 1974 MCA UK MCF 2676
JOE SAMPLE K (B (A) THERE'LL COME A TIME 197 UNI US 73048 UNLS 109
GENE PAGE K (B (B) HAPPY ENDINGS 1975 FANTASY FT 524
GARY COLEMAN PERC (B (B) HAPPY ENDINGS 1975 FANTASY US 9480
RAY PARKER G (B (C) ITS IN HIS KISS 19 JOY JOYS 106
DEAN PARKS G (B (C) ITS IN HIS KISS 1976 DJM DJM 22042
MELVIN WAH WAH RAGIN G (B (D) THEY'RE DELICIOUS TOGETHER 197 JOYS 123 VEEJAY 1099
DAVID T WALKER G (B (E) BETTY EVERETT STARRING 197 TRADITION US 2073
SCOTT EDWARDS B (B (F) & KETTY LESTER 19 GRAND PRIX US K 125
KETTY LESTER V (F ( ) LOVE RHYMES 1973 FANTASY 9447
BOBBYE HALL PERC (B ( ) HOT TO HOLD 1980 CHARLY UK CRB 1006
CAROLYN WILLIS V (B ( ) BETTY EVERETT 1968 SUNSET 5220
ED GREENE D (B ( ) TOGETHER 19 BUDDAH US 7507
MARTI McCALL V (B ( ) YOU'RE NO GOOD 19 VEEJAY 1077
EDNA WRIGHT V (B ( ) VERY BEST OF 19 VEEJAY 1122
JACKIE WARD V (B ( ) GETTING MIGHTY CROWDED 1980 CHARLY US CTD 1011
JERRY BUTLER V (B

E71A EVERGREEN BLUES BAND E71A

MANNY ESPARZA V (A (A) 7 DO ELEVEN 19 MERCURY US SR 61157
KEN WALTHER TROM (A
RICK BARRIO G (A SAM LOMBADO D (A JOE McSWEYN B (A
STEVE LAWRENCE K (A TOM BRAY TPT (A

E72 EVERGREEN BLUESHOES E72

SKIP BATTIN B V (A (A) THE BALLAD OF EVERGREEN BLUESHOES 1969 LONDON UK SHU 8399
LANNY MATHIJSSEN G (A (A) THE BALLAD OF EVERGREEN BLUESHOES 1969 AMOS US 7002
AL ROSENBERG G (A
KEN KLEIST K (A CHESTER McCRACKEN D (A

E72A EVERY MOTHERS SON E72A

BRUCE MILNER K (A (A) EVERY MOTHER'S SON 19 MGM US SE 4471
DENNIS LARDEN V G BANJO (A (B) BACK 1968 MGM US SE 4504
LARRY LARDEN G V (A
CHRISTOPHER AUGUSTINE D (A SCHUYLER LARSEN B (A DON KERR B (

E73 DON EVERLY E73

DON EVERLY G V (ALL (A) DON EVERLY 1971 ODE US 77005 A&M UK 2007
JEAN ROUSSEL B (B (B) SUNSET TOWERS 1974 ODE US/UK 77023
BUDDY EMMONS STEEL(BC (C) BROTHER JUKE BOX 1977 DJM UK 20501
PETE GAVIN D PERC(B (C) BROTHER JUKE BOX 1977 HICKORY US 44003
ALBERT LEE G B K(B
JOE OSBORN B (BC RAY SMITH G (B LANI GROVES V (B JUNE WILLIAMS V (B
SHIRLEY BREWER V (B STEPHANIE SPRUILL V (B JESSICA CLEAVES V (B CYNTHIA BULLENS V (B
REGGIE YOUNG G (C JOHN LEE CHRISTOPER G (C JERRY STEMBRIDGE G (C LOUIS NUNLEY V (C
BOBBY R WOOD PNO (C MICHAEL LEECH B (C KENNY MALONE D (C LEA JANE BERINATI V (C
JANIE FRICKE V (C GINGER HOLLADAY V (C BOBBY HARDEN V (C J ALAN MOORE V K STR(C
DAVID VANDERPOOL STR(C MARILYN SMITH STR (C PAUL YANDELL G (C TONY MIGLIORE PNO(C
RALPH GALLANT D (C THOMAS MARTIN G (C HARGUS ROBBINS PNO (C JEANINE WALKER V (C
WILLIAM WRIGHT V (C DOROTHY DILLARD V (C

E74 PHIL EVERLY E74

PHIL EVERLY V G (ALL (A) STAR SPANGLED SPRINGER 1973 RCA UK SF 8370
WITH (A) STAR SPANGLED SPRINGER 1973 RCA US APLI 0092
WARREN ZEVON G K (AC (B) NOTHINGS TOO GOOD FOR MY BABY 1974 PYE UK NSPL18448
JAMES BURTON G (A (B) PHILS DINER 197 PYE US 12104
DUANE EDDY G (A (C) MYSTIC LINE 1975 PYE UK NSPL18473
DONNIE LANIER G (A (C) MYSTIC LINE 1975 PYE US 12121
NEIL LEVANG G (A (D) PHIL EVERLY (LIVING ALONE) 1979 ELEKTRA US 6E213
JOE MORETTI G (B (E) PHIL EVERLY 1983 CAPITOL UK
KENNY CLAYTON PNO (B
SAMMY McCUE G K STEEL(A DEAN PARKS G (A BUDDY EMMONS STEEL (A JAY DEE MANESS STEEL(A
REINIE PRESS B (A LYLE RITZ B (A JOHN GUERIN D (A EARL PALMER D (A
VICTOR FELDMAN PERC (A JIM HORN SAX (A MARTIN KERSHAW G (C FOGGY LITTLE G (BC
FRANK McDONALD B (C RONNIE VERRELL D (C CLEM CATTINI D (C RICHARD BENNETT G (A
BARRY MORGAN D (B TONY CAMPO B (B

E75 THE EVERLY BROTHERS E75

DON EVERLY G V (ALL (EP)
PHIL EVERLY G V (ALL THE EVERLY BROTHERS 1958 CADENCE US CEP104 LONDON UK 1113
WITH THE EVERLY BROTHERS 2 1958 CADENCE US CEP105 LONDON UK 1148
CHET ATKINS G (* THE EVERLY BROTHERS 3 1958 CADENCE US CEP107 LONDON UK 1149
PAUL YANDELL G (* THE EVERLY BROTHERS 4 1959 CADENCE US CEP111 LONDON UK 1174
DALE SELLERS G (* THE EVERLY BROTHERS 5 1960 CADENCE US CEP118 LONDON UK 1229
PETE WADE G (* THE EVERLY BROTHERS 6 1961 CADENCE US CEP121 LONDON UK 1311
BOBBY THOMPSON G BANJ(* SONGS OUR DADDY TAUGHT US 1959 CADENCE US CEP108 LONDON UK 1195
WELDON MYRICK STEEL (* SONGS OUR DADDY TAUGHT US 1959 CADENCE US CEP109 LONDON UK 1196
HAROLD RUGG STEEL (* SONGS OUR DADDY TAUGHT US 1959 CADENCE US CEP110 LONDON UK 1197
HARGUS ROBBINS PNO (* ROCKIN WITH 1960 CADENCE MINI LP US CLLP 333
DAVID BRIGGS PNO (* ROCKIN WITH 1960 CADENCE MINI LP US CLLP 334
STEVE SCHAFFER B (* ESPECIALLY FOR YOU 1961 CADENCE US CEP1381/1 WB UK 6034
RALPH GALLANT ESPECIALLY FOR YOU 1961 CADENCE US CEP1381/2
LARRY LONDIN] D (* ITS EVERLY TIME 1961 WB ED 1381/1 WB UK 6056
JOHNNY GIMBLE FDL MAN(* BOTH SIDES OF AN EVENING(FOR DANCING) 1963 WB ED 1418/1 UK 6115
DELANEY BRAMLETT G V (S BOTH SIDES OF AN EVENING(FOR DREAMING)1964 WB UK 6117
JEFF KENT G V (S BOTH SIDES OF AN EVENING(FOR FUN) 1965 WB UK 6138
DENNIS LINDE G (S FOR EVERLY YOURS 1962 WB UK 6049
(CONTINUED)

GEOFF MULDAUR G (S
WAYNE PERKINS G (S
JOHN SEBASTIAN G HCA V(S
WADDY WACHTEL G (S
DANNY WEISS G (S
CLARENCE WHITE G (S
RY COODER G (S
BUDDY EMMONS G (S
JERRY McGEE G (S
SPOONER OLDHAN K (S
WARREN ZEVON K (S
JOHN BARBATA D (S
JIM GORDON D (S
RUSS KUNKEL D (S
GEORGE BOHANNON HRNS (S
TOMMY JOHNSON HRNS (S
JIMMY HASKEL STR (S
BONNIE BRAMLETT V (S
DAVID CROSBY V (S
DOUG LEBAHN V (S
GRAHAM NASH V (S
CHRIS ETHRIDGE B (S

(EP)EVERLY BROTHERS(MUSKRAT+2 19 WB US 5501
A DATE WITH VOL1 1963 WB UK 6107
A DATE WITH VOL2 1963 WB UK 6109
INSTANT PARTY 1 1963 WB UK 6111
INSTANT PARTY 2 1963 WB UK 6113
GREAT COUNTRY HITS 1 1964 WB UK 6128
GREAT COUNTRY HITS 2 1964 WB UK 6131
GREAT COUNTRY HITS 3 1964 WB UK 6132
THE PRICE OF LOVE 1965 WB UK WEP604
ROCK'N'SOUL 1965 WB UK WEP608
ROCK'N'SOUL 1965 WB UK WEP609
LOVE IS STRANGE 1966 WB UK WEP610
PEOPLE GET READY 1966 WB UK WEp612
WHAT AM I LIVING FOR 1966 WB UK WEP618
LEAVE MY GIRL ALONE 1967 WB UK WEP622
SOMEBODY HELP ME 1967 WB UK WEP623
THE EVERLY BROTHERS 1971 WB UK K16124
THE EVERLY BROTHERS 1972 WB UK K 16209
(LP)
THE EVERLY BROTHERS 1958 LONDON UK HA A 2081
THE EVERLY BROTHERS 1958 CADENCE US CLP 3003
SONGS OUR DADDY TAUGHT US 1958 LONDON UK 2150
SONGS OUR DADDY TAUGHT US 1958 CADENCE US CLP 3016
SONGS OUR DADDY TAUGHT US 1975 PHILIPS 6467 500
FOLK SONGS BY THE EVERLY BROTHERS RI 19 CADENCE (M)CLP3059 (S) 25059
THEIR BEST 1959 CADENCE US CLP 3025
FABULOUS STYLE OF THE EVERLY BROTHERS 1960 CADENCE US CLP3040 (S) 25040
FABULOUS STYLE OF THE EVERLY BROTHERS 1960 LONDON UK 2266
ITS EVERLY TIME 1960 WB US 1381
ITS EVERLY TIME 1960 WB UK(M)4012 (S) 8012
A DATE WITH THE EVERLY BROTHERS 1960 WB US 1395
A DATE WITH THE EVERLY BROTHERS 1960 WB UK(M)4028 (S) 8028
BOTH SIDES OF AN EVENING 1961 WB US 1418
BOTH SIDES OF AN EVENING 1961 WB UK(M)4052 (S) 8052
INSTANT PARTY 1962 WB US 1430
INSTANT PARTY 1962 WB UK(M)4061 (S) 8061
GOLDEN HITS 1962 WB 1471
GOLDEN HITS 1962 WB UK 8108
CATHYS CLOWN(GOLDEN HITS) 1980 PICKWICK 3030
GOLDEN HITS 1971 WB UK RI 1471
GOLDEN HITS 1971 WB UK RI K 46005
CHRISTMAS WITH 1962 WB US 1483 UK 8116
CHRISTMAS WITH 1969 HARMONY US 11350
15 HITS 1962 CADENCE US CLP3062 (S) 25062
SING GREAT COUNTRY HITS 1963 WB US 1513 UK 8138
VERY BEST OF 1965 WB US 1554 UK 0163
VERY BEST OF 1972 WB UK K46008
ROCK'N'SOUL 1965 WB US 1578 UK 8171
ROCK'N'SOUL 1965 WB RI UK 1578
GONE GONE GONE 1965 WB US 1585 UK 8169
GONE GONE GONE 1965 WB RI UK 1585
GONE GONE GONE 1970 VALIANT UK VS 109
BEAT & SOUL 1965 WB US 1605 UK 1605
IN OUR IMAGE 1965 WB US 1620 UK 1620
TWO YANKS IN ENGLAND 1965 WB US 1646 UK 1646
HIT SOUNDS OF 1967 WB us 1676 UK 1676
THE EVERLY BROTHERS SING 1967 WB US 1708 UK 1708
ROOTS 1968 WB US 1752 UK 1752
ROOTS 1971 WB UK RI K 46128
ROOTS 1973 WB UK RI K36002
WAKE UP LITTLE SUSIE 1969 HARMONY US 11304
CHAINED TO A MEMORY 1970 HARMONY US 11388
THE EVERLY BROTHERS SHOW (DBL) 1970 WB US 1858 UK 1858
THE EVERLY BROTHERS SHOW (DBL) 1971 WB UK RI K 66003
MOST BEAUTIFUL SONGS 1973 WB UK 66016
ORIGINAL GREATEST HITS (DBL) 1970 BARNABY US 6006 UK CBS 66255
END OF AN ERA (DBL) 1970 BARNABY US 30260 UK CBS 66259
(S) STORIES WE COULD TELL 1972 RCA US 4620 UK SF 8270
(S) STORIES WE COULD TELL 1974 RCA INT 1474
(S) THE EVERLY BROTHERS 1975 CAMDEN UK 1142
HISTORY OF THE EVERLY BROTHERS 1972 BARNABY US 15008
(*)PASS THE CHICKEN 1973 RCA US 4781 UK SF 8332
(*)EXCITING EVERLY BROS(PASS THE CHICKEN)1975 CAMDEN RI CDS 1136
FABULOUS 50s TREASURY 1974 JANUS 6310 300
EVERLYS 1975 RCA 7507
WALK RIGHT BACK 1975 WB UK K 56168
BYE BYE EVERLYS 1975 MIDI 66032
NEW ALBUM 1977 WB UK K 56415
EVERLY BROTHERS 197 GTE US GTR 7702
ORIGINAL HITS 197 MUSIDISC 256
20 SUPERHITS 197 TELDEC GERM AP6 23484
LIVING LEGENDS 1977 WARWICK UK WW 5027
GREATEST HITS 1 1978 BARNBY US 4004
GREATEST HITS 2 1978 BARNABY US 4005
GREATEST HITS 3 1978 BARNABY US 4006
GREATEST HITS COLLECTION DBL 1979 PICKWICK US 063
THE EVERLY BROTHERS (PROFILE) 19 TELDEC GER 6 24003
ROCK'N'ROLL FOREVER 1981 WB UK 26003
THE EVERLY BROTHERS 1981 WB UK 26010

E76 **EVERYONE** E76

ANDY ROBERTS G V VLN (A — (A) EVERYONE 1971 B&C UK CAS 1028
BOB SARGEANT G V K HCA(A — (A) ANDY ROBERT WITH EVERYONE 1971 AMPEX US 10117
JOHN PEARSON D(A
DAVE RICHARDS VB K (A JOHN PORTER G (A

E76A **EXCITERS** E76A

BRENDA REID V (— (A) TELL HIM 19 UA US MONO 3264 US STER 6264
CAROL JOHNSON V (— (B) EXCITERS 19 ROULETTE US 25326
LILIAN WALKER V (— (C) CAVIAR & CHITLINS 19 RCA US LSP 4211
HERBERT ROONEY V (— (D) BLACK BEAUTY 19 TODAY US TLP 1001

E76B **EX** E76B

(A) DISTURBING DOMESTIC PEACE 1980 VERRECORD NL 005

E76C **EXHIBIT A** E76C

(A) NO ELEPHANTS THIS SIDE OF WATFORD GAP(EP)19 IRRELEVANT WAMBAT

E77 **EXILE** E77

J P PENNINGTON G V (BCD — (A) EXILE 1973 WOODEN NICKEL US 1020
JIMMY STOKEY V (BC — (B) MIXED EMOTIONS 1978 RAK UK SRAK 533 WB US 3205
BUZZ CORNELISON K V (BC — (C) ALL THERE IS 1979 RAK UK SRAK 535 WB US 3323
MARLON HARGIS K V (BCD — (D) STAGE PASS 1979 RCA US 3087
SONNY LEMAIRE B V (BCD — (E) DONT LEAVE ME THIS WAY 1981 WB US 3437
STEVE GOETMAN D (BCD — (F) HEART & SOUL 1982 WB US 3588
SUE RICHMAN V (C
RUSTY BUCHANAN V (C LYNDA LAWLEY V (C ANDREA ROBINSON V (B DANNY WILLIAMS V B(B
LEY TAYLOR G V (D MACK GRAY K V (D

E77A **EXILED** E77A

SVOLTA V (A — (A) EXILED 1980 RCA PL 25297
SEICO BROTHERS V (A
LESLEY DUNCAN V (A TERRY CASSIDY V (A DAN McCAFFERTY V (A FRANCIS ROSSI V (A
BERNIE FROST V (A COLIN BLUNSTONE V (A NIGEL MARTINEZ D (A STUART ELLIOTT D (A
PAUL THOMPSON D (A DELISLE HARPER B (A JOHN GIBLIN B (A ANDY PASK B (A
JOE JAMMER G (A PAUL KEOGH G (A RAY RUSSELL G (A MITCH DALTON G (A
LAWRENCE JUBER G (A STEVE COE K (A DAVE LAWSON K (A ROBIN LUMLEY K (A
CHRIS PARREN K (A CRAIG PRUESS K (A TOMMY EYRE K (A LUIS JARDIM PERC(A
JOHN EARLE SAX (A ROBERT POWELL NARRATIVE(A

E77B **EXMAGMA** E77B

FRED BRACEFUL D PERC(A — (A) GOLDBALL 1974 DISJUUCTA FR 000 00009
ANDY GOLDNER G B SAX(A
THOMAS BALLUFF K TPT WIND(A

E77C **EXPERIMENTS WITH ICE** E77C

DAVID JIGGENS K (A — (A) EXPERIMENTS WITH ICE 1981 UNITED DARIES UK EX001
ROBIN KNAPP D (A
NICKY PATRIACHAEOS G V SYN(A PHIL ROSE B (A

E77D **EXPRESSO** E77D

(A) PROMISES & TIES 1981 WEA 58303

E77E **EXPLOITED** E77E

WATTIE V (A — (A) PUNKS NOT DEAD 1981 SECRET UK SEC 1
BIG JOHN G V (A
GARY B V (A DRU STIX D V (A CAROLE V (A HAVI V (A

E78 **EXUMA** E78

EXUMA G V PERC(ALL — (A) EXUMA 19 BARCLAY 920 208
YOGI BEN MAUSEL V PERC (— ( ) EXUMA 1973 BARCLAY 920 291
O'NEIL GUIMUNGIE SAX V (— ( ) EXUMA 19 VERTIGO 6338 018
KESTER SMITH D (— ( ) EXUMA II 1973 MERCURY US 61314
BARON SAMEDI PERC(— ( ) SNAKE 19 POLYDOR 2319016 KAMA SUT US 2052
R WISE G (— ( ) REINCARNATION 19 POLYDOR 2319 026
KENNY AARONSON D (— ( ) REINCARNATION 1973 KAMA SUTRA US 2062
PAUL CARPENTER K (— ( ) LIFE 1974 KAMA SUTRA US 2074
F GUMBS D (— ( ) THE OBEAH MAN 19 MERCURY US 61265
( ) DO WAH NANNY 1973 KAMA SUTRA US 2040
( ) PENNY SAUSAGE 1980 INAGUA US 999

E78A **EYELESS IN GAZA** E78A

MARTYN BATES V ALL (AB — (A) PHOTOGRAPHS AS MEMORIES 1980 CHERRY RED UK BRED 13
PETE BECKER V ALL (AB — (A) CAUGHT IN THE FLUX 1981 CHERRY RED UK BRED 18

E78B **TIM EYERMANN & EAST COAST OFFERING** E78B

TIM EYERMANN WIND (A — (A) ALOHA 1980 INNER CITY US 1095
PHIL McCUSKER G (A
WADE MATTHEWS B (A BRUCE HARRISON K (A JOHN MOLO D (A LOUIS SCHERR K (A

E79 **EYES** E79

NEIL MERRYWEATHER B V (A — (A) RADICAL GENES 1980 RCA NL 44019
KEN SPENCE G SAX (A
CEES MEERMAN D (A MICHAEL WILLIS G (A

E80 **EYES OF BLUE** E80

GARY PICKFORD HOPKINS V (B1 — (A) CROSSROADS OF TIME 1968 MERCURY US 61184 UK 20134
JOHN WEATHERS F (B — (A) CROSSROADS OF TIME 1968 MERCURY NL 134 087
RITCHIE FRANCIS G (B1 — (B) IN FIELDS OF ARDATH 1969 MERCURY US 61220 UK 20164
WYNDHAM REES D (1 — (B) IN FIELDS OF ARDATH 1969 MERCURY NL 134 224
R BENNETT B (B — (1) 1967
PHIL RYAN K (AB1
RAY WILLIAMS B (1

FI **F B I** F1

BONNIE WILKENSON V (A — (A) F B I 1976 GOODEARTH UK GDS 802
ROOT JACKSON V (A
JOANE BLACK V (A HERSCHEL HOLDER PERC (A LLOYD SMITH HRNS (A

F1A **F M** F1A

BEN MINK VLN G V(CD — (A) F M 19
MARTIN DEKER D (BCD — (B) BLACL NOISE 1979 PASSPORT US 7007 NL WEA 58198
CAMERON HAWKINS V SYN B(D — (C) SURVEILLANCE 1980 PASSPORT US 2001 NL WEA 58197
NASH THE SLASH VLN V (B — (D) CITY OF FEAR 1981 PASSPORT US 6004 UK LOGO 1031

F2

F WORD

F2

DUTCH SCHULTZ D (A — (A) F WORD LIKE IT OR NOT 1978 PBS US 101
RICK L RICK V (A
DIM WANKER G (A — STEVE EFFETE B (A

F2A

FABIAN

F2A

FABIAN V (ALL
( ) HOLD THAT TIGER 19 CHANCELLOR US 5003
( ) FABULOUS FABIAN 19 CHANCELLOR US 5005
( ) GOOD OLD SUMMERTIME 19 CHANCELLOR US 5012
( ) ROCKIN' HOT 19 CHANCELLOR US 5019
( ) 16 GREATEST HITS 19 CHANCELLOR US 5024
( ) 16 GREATEST HITS 1974 ABC US 806
( ) 16 GREATEST HITS 19 TRIP US TOP 1620
( ) VERY BEST OF FABIAN 19 UA US UA LA 449
( ) FACADE 19 CHANCELLOR US 68902
( ) FABIAN 1974 EMI NL 95031

F2B

FABLE

F2B

PETER GAOLBY G V MAND (A — (A) FABLE 1973 MAGNET UK MAG 5002
PAUL ROBBINS K B V (A
PETER MACKIE B V (A — KEITH TULLY D PERC(A — MAC BAILEY G (A

F3

FABULOUS POODLES

F3

TONY DE MEUR G V (ABCD — (A) FABULOUS POODLES 1977 PYE UK NSPL18530
BOBBY VALENTINO VLN (ABCD — (B) UNSUITABLE 1978 PYE UK NSPH 25
RICHIE ROBERTSON B (ABCD — (C) THINK PINK 1979 BLUEPRINT UK BLUP 5001
CHRIS SKORNIA K (C — (C) THINK PINK 1979 EPIC US 36256
BRYN B BURROWS D (ABCD — (D) MIRROR STARS 1979 EPIC US 35666
JOHN PARSONS (C
IAN TRIMMER SAX (C — MARY ANN MORGENTHALER V (C

F3A

FABULOUS RHINESTONES

F3A

MARTY GREBB SAX K V G (AB — (A) THE FABULOUS RHINESTONES 1972 JUST SUNSHINE US JS1
HARVEY BROOKS B V (ABC — (B) FREEWHEELIN' 1973 JUST SUNSHINE US JSS9
KAL DAVID G V (ABC — (C) THE RHINESTONES 1975 JUST SUNSHINE US
TERRY EATON SAX (B
GREG THOMAS D (AB — BOB LEINBACK K HRNS (C — ARTIE FUNARO G V (C
DAVE SANBORN SAX (B — REINOL ISAAC ANDINO CONGA (AB — RANDY BRECKER HRNS (B
MICHAEL BRECKER HRNS (B — BARRY ROGERS TROM (B — DENNIS WHITTED D (B
JEAN'TOOTS' THIELEMANS HCA(B — TITO PUENTE PERC (B — KAT McCORD V (B
ERIC PARKER D (C

F3B

FABULOUS THUNDERBIRDS

F3B

JIMMY VAUGHAN G (ABCD — (A) FABULOUS THUNDERBIRDS 1979 CHRYSALIS UK CHR 1250
DENNY BRUCE PROD (ABC — (A) FABULOUS THUNDERBIRDS 1979 TAKOMA US 7068
KIM WILSON V HCA (ABCD — (B) WHATS THE WORD 1980 CHRYSALIS UK US CHR 1287
KEITH FERGUSON B (ABCD — (C) BUTT ROCKIN 1981 CHRYSALIS UK US CHR 1319
NICK LOWE PROD (D — (D) T BIRD RHYTHM 1982 CHRYSALIS UK US CHR 1395
MIKE BUCK D (AB
FRAN CHRISTINA D PERC(BC — AL COPLEY PNO (C — DOUG JAMES SAX (C
GREG PICOLO SAX (C — ANSON FUNDERBURGH G (C

F3C

FACE DANCER

F3C

SCOTT McGINN B SYN V(AB — (A) THIS WORLD 1979 CAPITOL EST 11934
JEFF ADAMS G (AB — (B) ABOUT FACE 1980 CAPITOL EST 12082
BILLY TRAINOR D (AB
MICHAEL MILSAP K V (B — CAREY KRESS (A — DAVID UTTER G V (A

F4

FACES

F4

RONNIE LANE B (ABCDE — (A) FIRST STEP 1970 WB US UK K 46053
IAN MACLAGAN K (ABCDE — (B) LONG PLAYER 1971 WB US 1892 UK K 46064
KENNY JONES D (ABCDE — (C) A NODS AS GOOD AS A WINK 1972 WB US 2574 UK K 56006
ROD STEWART V (ABCDE — (D) OOH LA LA 1973 WB US 2665 UK K 56011
RON WOOD G (ABCDE — (E) OVERTURE /COAST TO COAST 1974 MERCURY US 1 697 UK 9100 011
TETSU YAMAUCHI B (E — (AB) FIRST STEP/LONG PLAYER 1977 WB UK K 66027
BOBBY KEYS SAX (B — ( ) BEST OF 1977 RIVA UK RVLP.3
HARRY BECKETT TPT (B — ( ) SNAKES & LADDERS (BEST OF) 1976 WB US2897 UK K 56172
( ) ROD STEWART & THE FACES 19 SPRINGBOARD US 4030
(EP) STAY WITH ME 1977 RIVA RIVA8

F4A

FAD GADGET

F4A

FAD GADGET V SYN WIND(A — (A) FIRESIDE FAVOURITES 1980 MUTE UK STUMM 3
ERIC RADCLIFFE G B BAN (AB — (B) INCONTINENT 1981 MUTE UK STUMM 6 GER 146802
JOHN FRYER PERC (AB
NICK CASH D V ACC (AB — DANIEL MILLER PERC SYN (AB — PHIL WAUQUAIRE B (A
PETER BAHNER G B (B — DAVID SIMMONDS PER SYN V (B — BIJI FROST V (B
ANNE CLIFT V (B — ROBERT GOTOBED D (B

F4B

FACTORY

F4B

YVES MATRAT V (AB — (A) BLACK STAMP 1977 COBRA FR 37010
DENIS FUSI (A — (B) CACHE TA JOIE 1979 PATHE FR 14828
LAHMI "PUCE" SAIBI G (AB
FOURMI B (A — BAPS D (A — RIDO BAYONNE B PERC (A
HERVE DUCLOS K (B — ALAIN GUILLARD (B — YVES GUILLARD (B
ARIANE CADDIER V (B — ELISABETH WIENER V (B

F4C

DONALD FAGEN

F4C

DONALD FAGEN K V HRNS(A — (A) THE NIGHTFLY 1982 WB UK 923696
GREG PHILLINGANES K SYN(A
ROB MOUNSEY SYN HEN(A — ROGER NICHOLS PERC (A — JEFF PORCARO D (A — DEAN PARKS G(A
CHUCK RAINEY B (A — MICHAEL OMARTIAN K (A — MARCUS MILLER B (A — ABE LABORIEL B (A
STEVE JORDON D (A — LESLIE MILLER V (A — RANDY BRECKER TPT(A — MICHAEL BRECKER SAX (A
DAVE BARGERON TROM (A — ZACK SANDERS V (A — GORDON GRODY V (A — DAVE TOFANI SAX (A
VALERIE SIMPSON V (A — LARRY CARLTON G (A — ED GREEN D (A — STEVE KAHN G (A
WILL LEE B (A — GARY KATZ PROD (A — HUGH McCRACKEN G HCA (A — STARZ VANDERLOCKET PERC(A
ANTHONY JACKSON B (A — RON CUBER SAX (A — FRANK FLOYD V (A — RICK DERRINGER G (A

F4D

RICHARD FAGAN

F4D

RICHARD FAGAN (A — (A) RICHARD FAGAN 1980 MERCURY US 3811

JOHN FAHEY

JOHN FAHEY	G (ALL	JOHN FAHEY	1966	US VANGUARD VSD 79259	
WITH		TRANSFIGURATION OF BLIND JOE DEATH	1967	US TAKOMA 9015	UK 19 SONET SNTF 607
JAY FERGUSON	K (Y	TRANSFIGURATION OF BLIND JOE DEATH	1970	US TAKOMA 1002	UK 19 SONET SNTF 774
MARK ANDES	B (Y	TRANSFIGURATION OF BLIND JOE DEATH	19	US RIVER RB1	UK TRANSATLANTIC TRA173
MATT ANDES	G (Y	DEATH CHANTS & BREAKDOWNS	1968	US TAKOMA 1003	UK 1969 SONET SNTF 608
KEVIN KELLEY	D (Y	(Y)YELLOW PRINCESS	1968	US VANGUARD VSD 79293	UK 19 SVRL 19033
WOODROW MANN	G (O	REQUIA	19	VANGUARD	UK SVRL 19055
JACK FEIERMAN	TPT V(O	DANCE OF DEATH	196	US TAKOMA 1004	
ALLAN REUSS	G BANJO(O	GREAT SAN BERNADINO BIRTHDAY PARTY	196	US TAKOMA 1008	
JOE DARENSBOURG	CLAR(O	DAYS HAVE GONE BY	1967	US TAKOMA 1014	
IRA WESTLEY	TUBA(O	VOICE OF THE TURTLE	1968	US TAKOMA 1019	
JOHN ROTELLA	SAX(O	NEW POSSIBILITY	19	US TAKOMA 1020	
BRITT WOODMAN	TROM(O	FARE FORWARD VOYAGERS	1974	US TAKOMA 1035	UK 1974 SONET SNTF 656
DICK CARY	PNO (O	FAHEY, LEO KOTTKE , PETER LANG	19	US TAKOMA 1040	UK 197 SONET SNTF 675
NICK FATOOL	D (O	(O)OLD FASHIONED LOVE	1975	US TAKOMA 1043	UK 1975 SONET SNTF 688
BOBBY BRUCE	V VLN(O	CHRISTMAS ALBUM	19	US TAKOMA 1045	UK 1976 SONET SNTF 702
		BEST OF 1959 77	1977	US TAKOMA 1058	UK 197 SONET SNTF 733
		OF RIVERS & RELIGION	1972	US REPRISE 2089	UK 197 REPRISE K 44213
		AFTER THE BALL	1973	US REPRISE 2145	UK 197 REPRISE K 44246
		FAHEY,KELLY ,MANN,MILLER,SEIDLER	19	US BLUE GOOSE BG 2009	
		ESSENTIAL JOHN FAHEY	1979	VANGUARD VSD 55/56	
		VISITS WASHINGTON DC	1980	US TAKOMA 7069	
		YES JESUS LOVES ME	1980	US TAKOMA 7085	
		LIVE IN TASMANIA	1981	US TAKOMA 7089	UK SONET SNTF 861

FAIRFIELD PARLOUR

F5A F5A

PETER DALTREY	V K (A	(A) FROM HOME TO HOME	1970	VERTIGO	UK 6360 001
EDDY PUMER	V K G(A				
STEVE CLARK	B FLT(A	DAN BRIDGMAN V D (A	DVAID SYMONDS	PROD (A	

FAIRPORT CONVENTION

F6 F6

(A) 1966(ETHNIC SHUFFLE ORCH)
(B) 1967 SPRING (1 GIG)
(C) 1967 JULY NOV
(D) 1967 NOV/MAY 1968
(E) 1968 MAY/FEB 1969
(F) 1969 FEB/JUNE 1969
MOTORWAY ACCIDENT KILLED
MARTIN LAMBLE.
(G) 1969 SEPT/NOV
(H) 1969 DEC/JAN1971
(i) 1971 JAN/DEC
(J) 1971 DEC RAINBOW GIG
(K) 1971 DEC/FEB 1972
(L) 1972 FEB /JUNE
(M) 1972 JUNE/AUTUMN. RECORDED
MANOR ALBUM NOT RELEASED.
(N) 1972 AUTUMN/SUMMER 1973
(O) 1973 SUMMER/MARCH 1974
(P) 1974 MARCH/ JAN 1975
(Q) 1975 JAN/FEB
(R) 1975 FEB /DEC
(S) 1976 JAN/FEB
(T) 1976 MARCH
(U) 1976 MARCH
(V) 1976 APRIL/SEPT. SHORTENED
NAME TO 'FAIRPORT'.
(W) 1976 SEPT/AUG 1979 RESTORED
NAME TO 'FAIRPORT CONVENTION'
(X) 1979 AUG GROUP ABANDONED
APART FROM ANNUAL REUNIONS

N.B. (13) MARKED
"FOR RADIO USE ONLY" ALSO USED
AS A PRIZE IN N.M.E. COMPETITION.

(1) FAIRPORT CONVENTION	1968	POLYDOR	UK	583 035
(1) FAIRPORT CONVENTION	1968	COTILLION	US	SD 9024
(1) FAIRPORT CONVENTION	1975	POLYDOR RI	UK	2384 047
(1) FAIRPORT CONVENTION	197	POLYDOR	EURO	2383 355
(1) FAIRPORT CONVENTION	197	POLYDOR	NL	2485 211
(2) WHAT WE DID ON OUR HOLIDAYS	1969	ISLAND	UK	ILPS 9092
(2) WHAT WE DID ON OUR HOLIDAYS	19	ARIOLA		88 183XAT
(2) FAIRPORT CONVENTION	1969	A&M	US	4185
(3) UNHALFBRICKING	1969	ISLAND	UK	ILPS 9102
(3) UNHALFBRICKING	1976	ISLAND	IT	8088
(3) UNHALFBRICKING	19	A&M	US	4206
(4) LIEGE AND LIEF	1969	ISLAND	UK	ILPS 9115
(4) LIEGE AND LIEF	19	A&M	US	4257
(5) FULL HOUSE	1970	ISLAND	UK	ILPS 9130
(5) FULL HOUSE	1970	A&M	US	4265
(6) ANGEL DELIGHT	1971	ISLAND	UK	ILPS 9162
(6) ANGEL DELIGHT	1976	ISLAND	IT	8338
(6) ANGEL DELIGHT	1971	A&M	US	4319
(7) BABBACOMBE LEE	1971	ISLAND	UK	ILPS 9176
(7) BABBACOMBE LEE	1971	A&M	US	4333
(7) BABBACOMBE LEE	1980	ISALND	NL	200 572
(8) HISTORY OF (DBL)	1972	ISLAND	UK	ICD 4
(8) HISTORY OF (DBL)	197	PHONOGRAM	EURO	6405 004
(9) ROSIE	1973	ISLAND	UK	ILPS 9208
(9) ROSIE	197	ISLAND	GER	88106
(9) ROSIE	1973	A&M	US	4386
(10) FAIRPORT NINE	1973	ISLAND	UK	ILPS 9246
(10) FAIRPORT NINE	1973	A&M	US	4407
(10) FAIRPORT NINE	197	A&M	US	3603
(11) FAIRPORT LIVE A MOVEABLE FEAST	1974	ISLAND US	UK	ILPS 9285
(12) RISING FOR THE MOON	1975	ISLAND US	UK	ILPS 9313
(13) FAIRPORT CONVENTION(TOUR SAMPLER)	1975	ISLAND	UK	ISS2
(14) GOTTLE O' GEER	1976	ISLAND	UK	ILPS 9389
(14) GOTTLE O' GEER	1976	PHONOGRAM	EURO	9101 665
(15) CHRONICLES	1976	A&M	US	3530
(16) LIVE AT L A TROUBADOUR	1976	ISLAND	UK	HELP 28
(17) HEYDAY (CASSETTE ONLY)	1976			
(18) BONNY BUNCH OF ROSES	1977	VERTIGO	UK	9102 015
(18) BONNY BUNCH OF ROSES	1977	PHONOGRAM	EURO	6360 152
(19) TIPPLERS TALES	1978	VERTIGO	UK	9102 022
(20) FAREWELL FAREWELL	1979	SIMONS	UK	GAMA 1
(20) FAREWELL FAREWELL	1979	WOODWORM	UK	BEAR22

DAVE SWARBRICK VLN V MAN (GHiJKLMNOPQRSTUVWX3.4.5.6.7.8.9.10.11.12.13.14.15.16.17.18.19.20.
DAVE PEGG B V (HiJKLMNOPQRSTUVWX 5.6.7.8.9.10.11.12.13.14.15.16.17.18.19.20.
SIMON NICOL V G (ABCDEFGHiJWX 1.2.3.4.5.6.7.8.13.14.15.16.17.18.19.20.
DAVE MATTACKS D (GHiJKOPN 4.5.6.7.8.9.10.11.12.13.15.16.
RICHARD THOMPSON V G(ABCDEFGHJ 1.2.3.4.5.8.9.13.15.16.17.
ASHLEY HUTCHINGS B V (ABCDEFG 1.2.3.4.8.13.15.17.
SANDY DENNY V G PNO(EFGJPQR 2.3.4.8.9.11.12.13.15.17.
JERRY DONAHUE G V(NOPQR 9.10.11.12.13.15.
TREVOR LUCAS V G PERC (NOPQR 3.8.9.10.11.12.13.15.
BRUCE ROWLAND D (RSTUVWX 12.13.14.18.19.20.
MARTIN LAMBLE D VLN (CDEF 1.2.3.8.13.15.17.
IAN MATTHEWS V PERC(DE 1.2.3.8.13.17.
JUDY DYBLE V AUTOHARP (BCD1
IAN FRATER D (B
MARC ELLINGTON V (3
A L LLOYD V (7
PHILIP STIRLING WALL V (7
DAVID REA V G BANJO (M
BOB BRADY K V (UV 14.

BENNY GALLAGHER V G ACC (14.
ROGER BURRIDGE V VLN (TUV 14.
TIMI DONALD D (9
ROGER HILL G V (KL
LINDA THOMPSON V (9.13.15.

TONY COX PNO (15.
PAT DONALDSON B (15.
IAN WHITEMAN PNO (15.
IAN WILSON V (14.
ERIC JOHNS G (14.
HENRY LOWTHER HRNS (14.
JIMMY JEWELL SAX (14.
NICK JUDD PNO (14.
GRAHAM LYLE V G ACC (14
MARTIN CARTHY G (14.
CLARE LOWTHER CELLO(1.2.8.
DAN AR BRAS G (V
PAUL WARREN D (Q
GERRY CONWAY D (9.13.15.
TOM FARNELL D (LM
RALPH McTELL G (9

F7 ANDY FAIRWEATHER LOW F7

Personnel			Albums	Year	Label		
ANDY FAIRWEATHER LOW	G V	(ALL	(A) BEGINNING FROM AN END(FAIRWEATHER	1971	NEON	UK US	NE1
WITH			(B) SPIDER JIVING	1974	A&M US 3646	UK	AMLH68263
HENRY McCULLOUGH	G	(B	(C) LA BOOGA ROOGA	1975	A&M US 4542	UK	AMLH68328
MARK NAFTALIN	K	(B	(D) BE BOP & HOLLA	1976	A&M US 4602	UK	AMLH64602
MICK WEAVER	K	(BD	(E) ANDY FAIRWEATHER LOW (COMP)	1976	RCA		HY 1033
BLUE WEAVER	K	(A	(F) MEGA SHEBANG	1980	WB US BSK3450	UK	K 56820
CHRISSY STEWART	B	(B					

DENNY SEIWELL	D	(B	JOHN KAHN	G	(B	JIMMY JEWELL	SAX	(C	CHARLIE McCOY	HCA	(B
WELDON MYRICK	STEEL	(B	BUDDY SPICHER	FDL	(B	VASSAR CLEMENTS	FDL	(B	BOBBY THOMPSON	BANJ	(B
LEA JANE BERINATI	V	(B	MEMPHIS HORNS		(B	JOHN DAVID	B V	(CDF	B J COLE	STEEL	(ACD
GERRY RAFFERTY	V	(C	JOE EGAN	V	(C	EDDIE THORNTON	TPT	(CD	STEVE GREGORY	HRNS	(CDF
BUD BEADLE	SAX	(CDF	NEIL JONES	G	(A	CLIVE TAYLOR	B	(A	GEORGIE FAME	K	(CD
BENNY GALLAGHER	V	(C	GRAHAM LYLE	V	(C	DAVE MATTACKS	D	(C	BRUCE ROWLAND	D	(C
BERNIE LEADON	G	(CD	DOREEN CHANTER	V	(C	IRENE CHANTER	V	(C	BARRY ST JOHN	V	(C
LIZA STRIKE	V	(C	JOANNE WILLIAMS	V	(C	HENRY SPINETTI	D	(DF	KENNY BUTTREY	D	(B
MARY HOLLADAY	V	(B	GINGER HOLLADAY	V	(B	DIANE DAVIDSON	V	(B	DENNIS BRYON	D	(A
JULIAN DIGGLE	PERC	(D	RABBIT BUNDRICK	K	(CD	KENNY JONES	D	(CD	TUNJI OMOSHETI	PERC	(D
MALCOLM GRIFFITHS	TROM	(D	MARTIN DROVER	TPT	(D	GLYN JOHNS	PERC	(D	BRYN HAWORTH	G	(D
BUD PARKES	TPT	(A	TERRY NOONAN		(A	DEREK WADSWORTH	HRNS	(F	DAVE CHARLES	B	(F
LINCOLN CARR	D	(F	GERAINT WATKINS	K	(F	MICKEY GEE	G	(F	GEORGE CHISHOLM	HRNS	(F
MEL COLLINS	SAX	(F									

F7A FAITHFUL BREATH F7A

Personnel			Albums	Year	Label		
HEINZ MIKUS	G V	(A	(A) FADING BEAUTY	1973	CADE	GER	10002
MANFRED VON BUTTLAR	K	(ABC	(B) BACK ON MY HILL	1980	SKY		SKY 038
HORST STABENOW	B	(AB	(C) ROCK LIONS	1981			
JURGEN WERITZ	D	(AB					
RENATE HEEMANN	V	(A					

F7B ADAM FAITH F7B

Personnel			Albums	Year	Label		
ADAM FAITH	V	(ALL	(A) ADAM	196	PARLOPHONE	UK PCS 3010	PMC 1120
RUSS BALLARD	G K	(HJ	(B) BEAT GIRL	196	COLUMBIA	UK	33SX 1125
JOHN BARRY		(B	(C) ADAM FAITH	196	PARLOPHONE	UK PCS 3025	PMC 1162
BOB HENRIT	D	(HJ	(D) FROM ADAM WITH LOVE	196	PARLOPHONE	UK PCS 3038	PMC 1192
PETE SALT	G	(HJ	(E) FOR YOU	106	PARLOPHONE	UK	PMC 1213
MOD ROGAN	B	(H	(F) ON THE MOVE	196	PARLOPHONE	UK	PMC 1228
CHRIS ANDREWS	V	(H	(G) FAITH ALIVE	196	PARLOPHONE	UK	PMC 1249
DAVE WINTOUR	B	(J	(H) THE TWO BEST SIDES OF ADAM FAITH	196	EMI	UK	NUT 16
DAVE COURTNEY	PNO	(J	(J) I SURVIVE	1976	WB US 2791	UK	K 56054
MARTIN BIRCH	G	(J	(K) BEST OF	1974	STARLINE	UK	SRS 5067
RICHIE BLACKMORE	G	(J	(EP)				
MIM	ACC	(J	(ADAMS HIT PARADE	196	PARLOPHONE	UK	GEP 8811
ROYSTON WILLOCK	SAX	(J	ADAM No1	196	PARLOPHONE	UK SGE 2014	GEP 8824
			ADAM No2	196	PARLOPHONE	UK SGE 2015	GEP 8828
			ADAM No3	196	PARLOPHONE	UK SGE 2018	GEP 8831
			BEAT GIRL	196	COLUMBIA	UK SEG 8138	
			ADAM'S HIT PARADE No 2	196	PARLOPHONE	UK	GEP 8841
			ADAM FAITH No1	196	PARLOPHONE	UK	GEP 8851
			ADAM FAITH No2	196	PARLOPHONE	UK	GEP 8852
			ADAM FAITH No3	196	PARLOPHONE	UK	GEP 8854
			ADAMS HIT PARADE No3	196	PARLOPHONE	UK	GEP 8862
			LATEST HITS	196	PARLOPHONE	UK	GEP 8877
			TOP OF THE POPS	196	PARLOPHONE	UK	GEP 8893
			FOR YOU ADAM	196	PARLOPHONE	UK	GEP 8904
			A MESSAGE FROM ADAM	196	PARLOPHONE	UK	GEP 8929
			SONGS AND THINGS	196	PARLOPHONE	UK	GEP 8939

F7C FAITH BAND F7C

Personnel			Albums	Year	Label		
CARL STORIE	V HCA	(BC	(A) FAITH	1973	BROWN BAG	US	BB 085
DAVID BENNETT	G	(BC	(B) ROCK'N' ROMANCE	1978	MERCURY		
JOHN CASCELLA	K SAX V	(BC	(C) FACE TO FACE	1979	MERCURY	US	3770
MARK CAWLEY	B V	(BC	(D) VITAL SIGNS	197)	MERCURY	US	
DAVID BARNES	D	(BC					

F8 MARIANNE FAITHFULL F8

Personnel			Albums	Year	Label		
MARIANNE FAITHFULL	V	(ALL	(A) COME MY WAY	1965	DECCA	UK LK 4688	
WITH			(B) MARIANNE FAITHFULL	1965	DECCA	UK LK 4689	US LONDON 3423
THE GREASE BAND		(*	(C) GO AWAY FROM MY WORLD	1965			US LONDON 3452
JOE MAVERTY		(KL	(D) NORTH COUNTRY MAID	1966	DECCA	UK LK 4778	
BARRY REYNOLDS		(KL	(E) FAITHFULL FOREVER	1966			US LONDON 3482
STEVE YORK	B	(KL	(F) LOVE IN A MIST	1967	DECCA	UK LK 4854	
TERRY STANNARD		(KL	(G) GREATEST HITS	196	DECCA	UK LK	US LONDON 3547
FRANKIE COLLINS	V	(KL	(H) WORLD OF	1969	DECCA	UK SPA 17	
JULIAN DIGGLE		(L	(*I) DREAMIN' MY DREAMS	1976	NEMS	UK NEL 6007	
MARTIN DROVER		(L	(*J) FAITHLESS	1978	NEMS	UK NEL 6012	
DENNIS HAINES		(L	(K) BROKEN ENGLISH	1979	ISLAND	UK+US	ILPS 9570
NEIL HUBBARD	G	(L	( ) AS TEARS GO BY (COMP)	1981	DECCA	UK TAB 13	
JIM LEVERTON		(	(L) DANGEROUS ACQUANTANCES	1981	ISLAND	UK	ILPS 9648
ISABELLA DULANEY		(K	(EP) MARIANNE FAITHFULL	1965	DECCA	UK DFE 8624	
FUZZY SAMUELS	B	(L					

DIANE SPENNER		(L	CHRIS STAINTON	K	(L	PICKFORD SYKES		(L
PETER VEITCH		(L	STEVE WINWOOD		(KL	TONY CALDER	PROD	(AB
MARK MILLER MUNDAY	PROD	(K	DIANE BIRCH		(K	MORRIS PERT	PERC	(K
JIM CUOMO		(K	GUY HUMPHRIES		(K	DARRYL WAY		(K

F8A BILLY FALCON F8A

Personnel			Albums	Year	Label		
BILLY FALCON	G V	(ABC	(A) BILLY FALCONS BURNING ROSE	1978	PHILIPS	UK	9103 450
RICHIE MEADE	V	(A	(A) BILLY FALCONS BURNING ROSE	1978	MANHATTAN	US	832
MICHAEL VISAGGIO	K FLT V	(A	(B) IMPROPER ATTIRE	1979	UA	US	967
RICK ZOLLO	G V	(A	(C) FALCON AROUND	1980	MCA US 3238	UK	MCF 3065
BILLY MILNE	D V	(A					
GLENN EICHLER	B HCA	(A	GREG MEADE V (A		PAGE TO THE WIND CHOIR(A		

F8B

RODERICK FALCONER

F8B

RODERICK FALCONER SYN V G(AB (A) NEW NATION 1976 UA US 651 UK UAG 29992
HIRAM BINGHAM B (A (B) VICTORY IN ROCK CITY 1977 UA US 777 UK UAG 30100
MIKE KELLIE D (A
MIKE JAPP G (AB MATTHEW FISHER K (A BRUCE GARY D (B
REGGIE McBRIDE B (B BRIE HOWARD V (B WENDY HAAS V (B
JIMMIE GREENSPOON K (B PATTI QUATRO V (B PETER IVERS PROD (B

F8C

TAV FALCO'S PANTHER BURNS

F8C

TAV FALCO G V (A (A) BEHIND THE MAGNOLIA CURTAIN 1982 FRENZI 400 ROUGH TRADE 16
ALEC CHILTON G D (A
JIM DUCKWORTH G D (A RON MILLER B (A TATE COUNTY DRUM COROS (A

F8D

FALCKENSTEIN

F8D

MONIKA MARIE DOMIN G V (A (A) FALCKENSTEIN 1979 NATURE GER 60 179
WENDELIN WERNER G (A
JOACHIM LUHRMANN D PERC(A PETER LOWNER B (A MICK FRANKE G (A
THOMAS KAGERMANN VLN G(A

F9

FALCONS

F9

1950s EARLY 60S
JOE STUBBS V
MACK RICE V LANCE FINNIE V WILLIE SCHOFIELD V EDDIE FLOYD V WILSON PICKETT V

F10

FALL

F10

KARL BURNS D (345ABCDEFG (A) LIVES AT THE WITCH TRIALS 1979 STEP ORWARD UK 1 US A&M SP003
MARK SMITH V (12345ABCDEFG (B) DRAGNET 1979 STEP FORWARD SFLP 4
ERIC B (4 (C) TOTALES TURNS 1980 ROUGH TRADE UK ROUGH10
MIKE LEIGH D (BCDE (D) GROTESQUE 1980 ROUGH TRADE UK ROUGH18
YVONNE PAWCETT K (AE (E) SLATES 1981 ROUGH TRADE UK RT073
STEVE HANLEY B (5BCDEFG (F) EARLY YEARS (1977/1979 1981 STEP FORWARD UK SFLP 6
PAUL HANLEY G D (G (G) HEX EDUCATION 1982 LINE GER LLP 5194
MARTIN BRAMAH G (A1234 (1) 1976 (2) 1977 (3) 1978 (4) 1978 (5) 1979
UNA BAINES K (234
JONNIE BROWN B (3 TONY FRIEL B (12E MARC RILEY G B(A5BCDEFG
CRAIG SCANLON G (5BCDFG KAY CARROLL V PERC (G

F11

FALL MOUNTAIN

F11

JIM KATZIN VLN (A (A) EARLY FALL 1979 PARACHUTE P 009
BOB OSTERTAG SYN (A
NED ROTHENBERG WIND (A RICHARD ROGERS PNO (A DAVID WILES PERC (A

F11A

FALLENROCK

F11A

LARRY KEITH (A) WATCH FOR FALLENROCK 1974 CAPRICORN US 0143 UK 2429 122
STEVE PIPPIN
RAFE VAN HOY

F12

FAMILY

F12

ROGER CHAPMAN V HCA (ALL (A) MUSIC IN A DOLLS HOUSE 1968 REPRISE UK/US 6312
CHARLIE WHITNEY G (ALL (A) MUSIC IN A DOLLS HOUSE 1971 REPRISE RI UK K44057 GER 24018
ROB TOWNSEND D (ALL (B) FAMILY ENTERTAINMENT 1969 REPRISE UK/US 6340
JIM KING WIND V(ABH (B) FAMILY ENTERTAINMENT 1971 REPRISE UK RI K 44069
JOHN WEIDER B V (CDHJ (C) A SONG FOR ME 1970 REPRISE US 6384
(C) A SONG FOR ME 1970 REPRISE UK 9001
POLI PALMER K VIBES(CDEFHJ (C) A SONG FOR ME 1971 REPRISE UK RI K 44104
JOHN WETTON B V (EF (D) ANYWAY 1970 REPRISE UK 9005
RICK GRECH B V VLN (ABHJ (D) ANYWAY 1971 REPRISE UK RI K 54002
JIM CREGAN G B (G (D) ANYWAY 1970 UA US 5527
TONY ASHTON K (G (E) FEARLESS 1971 REPRISE UK K 54003
CHARLIE McCRACKEN G (G (E) FEARLESS 1971 UA US 5562
PETER HOPE EVANS (G (F) BANDSTAND 1972 REPRISE UK K 54006
ROY DYKE (G (F) BANDSTAND 1972 UA US 5644
LADBROKE HORNS (E (G) ITS ONLY A MOVIE 1973 RAFT UK RA 58501
DAVE MASON PROD (A (G) ITS ONLY A MOVIE 1973 UA US UALA 181
JIMMY MILLER PROD (A (H) OLD SONGS NEW SONGS 1971 REPRISE US 6413 UK K 34001
GEORGE CHKIANTZ PROD (E (J) BEST OF FAMILY 1974 REPRISE UK K 54023

F13

FAMILY DOGG

F13

STEVE ROWLAND ((A) A WAY OF LIFE 1969 BELL SP 22122
ALBERT HAMMOND G V (B (B) VIEW FROM ROWLANDS HEAD 1972 POLYDOR UK 2318 061
MIKE HAZELWOOD (B (B) VIEW FROM ROWLANDS HEAD 197 BUDDAH US BDS 5100
JIMMY PAGE G (A
JOHN PAUL JONES (CHRISTINE HOLMES B (IRENE SHERR V (B GARY TAYLOR B V (B
ANDREW STEEL E D (B ALAN PARKER G (B B J COLE DOB G (B BARRY MORGAN D (B
LIZA STRIKE V (B DORIS TROY V (B MIKE MORGAN K (B CHRIS SPEDDING G (B
MADELINE BELL V (B PHIL DENNYS PNO (B TONY CARR PERC (B SUE LYNN V (B
PAT ARNOLD V (B CLAIRE TORRY V (B

F13A

FAMILY TREE

F13A

BOB SEGARINI G V (A (A) MISS BUTTERS 1968 RCA US LSP 3955
VANN SCATER (A
MICHAEL DURE (A BILL TROCHIM B (A JIMMY DE COCQ G K (A

F13B

FAMILY FODDER

F13B

ALIG G K B SAX(ABC (A) SUNDAY GIRLS EP 1980 FRESH UK 9
MARTIN B G V(BC (B) MONKEY BANANA KITCHEN 1980 FRESH UK LP3
NINA V (B (C) SCHIZOPHRENIA PARTY EP 198 FRESH UK 37
FELIX K VLN V(B
DOMINIQUE V (B RICK D PERC(B IAN K V HCA(B MICK B PERC(B
CHARLES D G V(B JUDY V (B NARESH V (B GRAHEME CELLO (B
MARK PERC (B MIKE G (B IAN HILL V PERC (C BAT SMITH PERC (C
GRAHAM PAINTING V G B(C LYNN ALICE V (B

F14 GEORGIE FAME (& THE BLUE FLAMES) F14

Musician	Inst	Albums	Title	Year	Label	Country	No.
GEORGIE FAME(CLIVE POWELL)	K V	(ALL	(A) R& B AT THE FLAMINGO	1964	COLUMBIA	UK	SX 1599
WITH			(B) FAME AT LAST	1964	COLUMBIA	UK	33SX 1638
COLIN GREEN	G	(CDR1	(C) SWEET THING	1966	COLUMBIA	UK	SX 6043
TED MAKINS	B	(	(D) SOUND VENTURE	1966	COLUMBIA	UK	SX 6076
GEORGE KISH	G	(G	( ) YEH YEH	1966	IMPERIAL	US	12282
JOHN McLAUGHLIN	G	(G	( ) GET AWAY	1966	IMPERIAL	US	12331
RED PREECE	D	(	(E) HALL OF FAME	1967	COLUMBIA	UK	SX 6120
AL WATSON	SAX	(	(F) TWO FACES OF FAME	1967	CBS	UK	63018
CLIFF BARTON	B	(C	(G) THIRD FACE OF FAME	1968	CBS	UK	63293
PHIL BATES	B	(DFG	(H) SEVENTH SON	1969	CBS	uk	63786
RICK BROWN	B	(F	(J) GEORGIE FAME	1969	STARLINE	UK	SRS 5002
FRANK CLARKE	B	(G	(K) DOES HIS OWN THING WITH STRINGS	1970	CBS	UK	63650
RONNIE SEABROOK	B	(G	(L) GOING HOME	1971	CBS	UK	64350
JEFF CLYNE	B	(F	(M) FAME & PRICE	1971	CBS	UK	64392
JOHN MITCHELL	D	(C	(N) ALL ME OWN WORK	1972	REPRISE	UK	K 44183
PHIL SEAMAN	D	(D	(O) FAME AGAIN	1972	STARLINE	UK	SRS. 5107
BILL EYDEN	D	(DFG	(P) BALLAD OF BONNIE & CLYDE	1973	EMBASSY UK 31033 EPIC	US	26368
HUGHIE FLINT	D	(F	(Q) GEORGIE FAME	1974	ISLAND	UK	ILPS 9293
HAYDEN JACKSON	D	(G	(R) RIGHT NOW	1979	PYE	UK	NSLP18600
SPEEDY ACQUAYE	D	(CRS	(S) THATS WHAT FRIENDS ARE FOR	1979	PYE	UK	N 119
J SCOTT	D	(F	(T) CLOSING THE GAP	1980	PICCADILLY	UK	N 137
JIM MULLEN	G	(S	(1) 1969 LIVE BAND				
TONY OXLEY	D	(F	(U) IN HOGLAND	1981	BALD EAGLE	UK	BELP 181
ANNIE ROSS	V	(U					

Musician	Inst	Albums	Musician	Inst	Albums	Musician	Inst	Albums	Musician	Inst	Albums
TERRY SMITH	G	(GR	ARTHUR GREENSLADE	K	(G	GORDON BECK	K	(DFG	ERNIE SHEARS	G	(G
STAN TRACY	K	(D	PETER COE	SAX	(C	GLEN HUGHES	SAX	(C	ROY WILCOX	SAX	(D
RAY WARLEIGH	SAX	(DR	RONNIE SCOTT	SAX	(DFG	TUBBY HAYES	SAX	(D	HARRY KLEIN	SAX	(DFG
ALAN BRANSCOMBE	SAX	(DF	TONY COE	SAX	(DFG	DICK MORRISSEY	SAX	(DFS	LYN DOBSON	SAX	(F
TOMMY WHITTLE	SAX	(G	ART ELLEFSON	SAX	(G	CYRIL REUBENS	SAX	(G	JOHNNY MARSHALL	SAX	(FG
PETER KING	SAX	(F	ED THORNTON	TPT	(CFST	GREG BOWEN	TPT	(DFG	BERT COURTLEY	TPT	(D
IAN HAMMER	TPT	(DFGS	JIMMY DEUCHER	TPT	(D	LES CONDON	TPT	(DGH	KENNY WHEELER	TPT	(DF
TONY FISHER	TPT	(D	DEREK WATKINS	TPT	(FG	DEREK HEALEY	TPT	(G	ALBERT HALL	TPT	(G
BOB HAUGHEY	TPT	(G	KEITH CHRISTIE	TROM	(DF	ALAN PARKER	G	(RS	CHRIS SMITH	TROM	(DF
KEN GOLDE	TROM	(D	GIB WALLACE	TROM	(DFG	DEREK WADSWORTH	TROM	(F	MORRIS PLATT	TROM	(G
BERNIE HOLLAND	G	(R	BRIAN ODGERS	B	(RS1	BARRY MORGAN	D	(RS	HENRY LOWTHER	TPT	(R
STEVE GREGORY	SAX	(SR	MALCOLM GRIFFITHS	TROM	(RS	FRANK RICOTTI	PERC SAX	(1	ALAN SKIDMORE	SAX	(1
JOHN WARREN	SAX	(1	HAROLD BECKETT	TPT	(1	CHRIS PYNE	TROM	(1	HARVEY BURNS	D	(1
HENRY SPINETTI	D	(S	MIKE DAVIS	TPT	(S	BRIAN SMITH	WIND	(S	REGGAE PHILHARMONIC ORCH		(T
JAMES LASCELLES	HRNS	(T	GUARDIAN ANGELS	V	(T	JACKIE SHARP	SAX	(D			

F15 FAMOUS JUG BAND F15

Musician	Inst	Albums	Title	Year	Label	Country	No.
JILL JOHNSON	V G	(AB	(A) SUNSHINE POSSIBILITIES	1969	LIBERTY	UK	LBS 83263
PETE BERRYMAN	G V	(AB	(B) CHAMELEON	1970	LIBERTY	UK	LBS 83355
CLIVE PALMER	G V	(A					
HENRY VIII BARTLETT	V JUG	(AB					

F16 FANCY F16

Musician	Inst	Albums	Title	Year	Label	Country	No.
RAY FENWICK	G	(C	(A) FANCY MEETING YOU HERE	19	POISON RING	US	2238
MO FOSTER	B	(CB	(B) WILD THING	1974	ATLANTIC	UK	K 51502
LES BINKS	D	(CB	(B) WILD THING	1974	BIG TREE	US	89502
ANNIE KAVANAGH	V	(CB	(C) SOMETHING TO REMEMBER	1975	ARISTA	US	ARTY 102
MARLON	G V	(B	(D) TURNS YOU ON	1976	RCA	US	APLI 1482

F16A (NICK SIMPERS) FANDANGO F16A

Musician	Inst	Albums	Title	Year	Label	Country	No.
NICK SIMPER	B	(AB	(A) SLIPSTREAMING	1979	GULL	UK	GULP 1033
PETE PARKS	G	(AB	(B) FUTURE TIMES	1980	SHARK	GER	148 506
JIM PROOPS	V	(AB					
RON PENNEY	D	(A	NEIL McARTHUR ORG (A				

F16B FANDANGO F16B

Musician	Inst	Albums	Title	Year	Label	Country	No.
JOE LYN TURNER	G V	(ALL	(A) FANDANGO	1978	RCA	US	
RICK BLAKEMORE	G	(ALL	(B) LAST KISS	1979	RCA	US	
BOB DANYLS	B	(ALL	(C) ONE NIGHT STAND	1979	RCA	US	
ABE SPELLER	D	(ALL	(D) CADILLAC	1980	RCA	US	AFLI 3591

F17 FANIA ALL STARS F17

Musician	Inst	Albums	Title	Year	Label	Country	No.
JOHNNY PACHECO	FLT PERC	(CDEHJ	(A) LIVE AT THE RED GARTER	1968	FANIA	US	355
STEVE WINWOOD	G	(K	(B) LIVE AT THE RED GARTER 2	1968	FANIA	US	364
RAY BARRETTO	PERC	(CDEHJ	(C) LIVE AT THE CHEETA VOL 1	1971	FANIA	US	415
BOBBY VALENTIN	B	(CDEHJ	(D) LIVE AT THE CHEETA VOL 2	1973	FANIA	US	416
NIKKY MARRERO	PERC	(CDEHJ	(E) LATIN SOUL ROCK	1973	FANIA	US	470
ROBERTO ROENA	PERC	(CDEHJ	(F) SALSA	1975	ISLAND	UK	HELP 20
PAPO LUCCA	PNO	(K	(G) FANIA ALL STARS	1975	ISLAND	UK	ILPS 9331
WILLIE COLON	TROM	(CDEHJ	(H) SALSA LIVE	1976	ISLAND	UK	HELP 21
LARRY HARLOW	K	(CDEHJ	(H) LIVE AT YANKEE STADIUM VOL1	1976	FANIA	US	476
RICHARD RAY	K	(CDEHJ	(J) LIVE AT YANKEE STADIUM VOL2	1976	FANIA	US	477
MONGO SANTAMARIA	PERC	(EHJ	(K) DELICATE & JUMPY	1976	ISLAND	UK	ILPS 9447
CELIA CRUZ	V	(HJ	(K) DELICATE & JUMPY	1976	CBS	US	34283
JUSTO BETANCOURT	V	(HJ	(L) RHYTHM	1977	CBS	US	34711
SANTOS COLON	V	(CDEHJ	(H) SPANISH FEVER	1978	CBS	US	35336
BOBBY CRUZ	V	(CDEHJ	(N) CROSSOVER	1979	CBS	US	36109
CHEO FELICIANO	V	(CDEHJ					

Musician	Inst	Albums	Musician	Inst	Albums	Musician	Inst	Albums
PETE RODRIGUEZ	V	(CDEHJ	LEWIS KAHN	TROM	(EHJ	HECTOR LAVOE	V	(CDEHJ
RAY MALANALDO	TPT	(EHJ	BARRY ROGERS	TROM	(CDEHJ	ISMAEL MIRANDA	V	(CDEHJ
LUIS ORTIZ	TPT	(EHJ	YOMO TORO	TRES	(CDEHJ	ISHMAEL QUINTANA	V	(HJ
VICTOR PAZ	TPT	(EHJ	LOU SOLOFF	TPT	(E	BILLY COBHAM	D	(E
JAN HAMMER	K	(E	JORGE SANTANA	G	(E	MANU DIBANGO	SAX	(EJ
ROBERTO RODRIGUEZ	TPT	(CD	HECTOR ZARZUELA	TPT	(CD	RARRY SPENCER	TPT	(CD
RENALDO JORGE	TROM	(CD	ORESTES VILATO	PERC	(CD	ADALBERTO SANTIAGO	V	(CD

F18 FANNY F18

JEAN MILLINGTON G B V (ABCDE12 — (A) FANNY 1970 REPRISE US 6416 UK 6416
JUNE MILLINGTON G V (ABCD2 — (B) CHARITY BALL 1971 REPRISE US 6456 UK K44144
NICOLE BARCLAY K V (ABCDE — (C) FANNY HILL 1972 REPRISE US 2058 UK K44174
ALICE DE BUHR D V (E1 — (D) MOTHERS PRIDE 1973 REPRISE US 2137 UK K44233
PATTI QUATRO B (E1 — (E) ROCK'N'ROLL SURVIVORS 1975 CASABLANCA US 7007 UK 4001
BRIE HOWARD D (E2 — (E) ROCK'N'ROLL SURVIVORS 19 PATHE FR 064 96062
CAM DAVIES D (1 — (1) 1974 (2) 1975
BOBBY KEYS SAX (C
JIM PRICE WIND (C — JAMES NEWTON HOWARD K (E

F18A FANNY ADAMS F18A

TED TOI B (A — (A) FANNY ADAMS 1971 KAPP US 3644
VINCE MELANEY G (A
DOUG PARKINSON G (A — JOHNNY DICK D (A

F18B FANTASTIC BAGGIES F18B

PHIL SLOAN (A — (A) TELL 'EM I'M SURFIN' 196 IMPERIAL US 12270
STEVE BARRI (A

F18C FANTASY F18C

DAVID REED B V (A — (A) PAINT A PICTURE 1973 POLYDOR 2383 246
PAUL LAWRENCE G V (A
DAVID MATCALFE K V (A — PETER JAMES G V (A — JON WEBSTER D V (A

F19 RICHARD & MIMI FARINA F19

MIMI FARINA V (ALL — (A) RICHARD & MIMI FARINA 1965 VVANGUARD 79174
RICHARD FARINA V (ABCDE — (B) CELEBRATIONS FOR A GREY DAY 1965 FONTANA 6060 VANGUARD VSD 79281
RUSS KUNKEL D (F — (C) REFLECTIONS IN A CRYSTAL WIND 1965 FONTANA 6075 VANGUARD VSD 79204
TOM JANS V (F — (D) MEMORIES 1968 VANGUARD19047 VSD 79263
JOAN BAEZ G V (D — (E) RICHARD FARINA 1968 VANGUARD VSD 79281
RUSS SAVAKUS B (D — (F) MIMI FARINA & TOM JANS 1971 A&M US 4310 UK AMLS64310
BRUCE LANGHORNE G (D — ( ) THE BEST OF RICHARD & MIMI FARINA 70 VANGUARD VSD 21/2
CHARLES SMALL PNO (D
AL ROGERS D (D — JOHN HAMMOND HCA (D — FRITZ RICHMOND B (D
KYLE GRAHAN HCA (D — EMIL RICHARDS PERC (F — GRADY MARTIN G (D
CRAIG DOERGE K (F — LEE SKLAR B (F — EDGAR LUSTGARTEN PPNO (F
SNEAKY PETE STEEL (F
JIM KELTNER D (F — (RICHARD DIED 1966,MIMI IS JOAN BAEZ SISTER)

F19A FAR CRY F19A

JERE WHITING V HCA (A — (A) FAR CRY 19 VANGUARD US VSD 6510 UK SVRL 19041
PAUL LENART G (A
DICK MARTIN SAX PERC(A — DAVID PERRY G V (A — LARRY LUDDECKE K (A
SEAN HUTCHINSON B (A — VICTOR McGILL D PERC (A

F20 FAR CRY (2) F20

PETER THAN V (A — (A) THE MORE THE BETTER 1980 CBS US 36286
PHIL GALDSTON K V (A

F20A FAR EAST FAMILY BAND F20A

FUMIO MIYASHTA V G K SYN (— (A) NEPPORJIN 1975 VERTIGO 6370 850
HIROHITO FUKUSHIMA G V (— (B) THE CAVE DOWN TO EARTH 1975 MULAND CD 7139M
YUJIN HARADA D PERC(— (C) PARALLEL WORLD 1976 MULAND LQ 7002M
AKIRA FUKAKUSA B (— (D) TENKEYIN 1977 ALL EARS US 11479

F20B DON FARDON F20B

DON FARDON V (A — (A) LAMENT OF THE CHEROKEE 1968 GNP US 2044
(B) IVE PAID MY DUES 1970 DECCA US 75225
(C) RELEASED 1970 YOUNGBLOOD US YB13

F20C LEE FARDON F20C

LEE FARDON (A — (A) STORIES OF ADVENTURE 1981 AURA AUL 713

F21 CHRIS FARLOWE F21

CHRIS FARLOWE V (ALL — (A) CHRIS FARLOWE & THE THUNDERBIRDS 1966 COLUMBIA UK SCX 6034
ALBERT LEE G (AB — (B) STORMY MONDAY 1966 M F P UK MFP 1186
IAN HAGUE D (— (B) CHRIS FARLOWE & THE THUNDERBIRDS 1978 CHARLY UK CR 30021
DAVE GREENSLADE K (— (C) OUT OF TIME 1966 IMMEDIATE Z12 52010
BRUCE WADDELL B (H — (C) OUT OF TIME 1976 IMMEDIATE UK RI IML 1002
PAT DONALDSON B (J — (C) GREATEST HITS 1977 IMMEDIATE UK IML 2002
RICKY CHARMAN B (— (D) 14 THINGS TO THINK ABOUT 1966 IMMEDIATE UK IMLP 005
PAUL CARSON SAX (— (E) THE ART OF CHRIS FARLOWE 1966 IMMEDIATE UK IMLP 006
CARL PALMER D (— (F) THE BEST OF CHRIS FARLOWE 1968 IMMEDIATE UK IMCP 010
PETE SHELLEY D (— (G) THE LAST GOODBYE 1969 IMMEDIATE UK IMLP 021
STEVE HAMMOND G (H — (H) FROM HERE TO MAMA ROSA 1970 POLYDOR UK 2425 029
JOANNE WILLIAMS V (J — (H) FROM HERE TO MAMA ROSA 1970 POLYDOR US 20 4041
COLIN DAVY D (H — (J) CHRIS FARLOWE BAND LIVE 1975 POLYDOR UK 2460 259
PETER ROBINSON K (H — (K) OUT OF TIME/PAINT IT BLACK 1976 CHARLY UK CR 300020
PAUL BUCKMASTER CELLO (H — (C) GREATEST HITS 1977 IMMEDIATE UK IML 2002
JEAN ROUSSEL K (J — ( ) PAINT IT BLACK 19 IMMEDIATE SHZEL 9
GERRY CONWAY D (J — (EP) AIR TRAVEL 19 DECCA UK DFE 8665
CHRIS MERCER SAX (J — (EP) FARLOWE IN THE MIDNIGHT HOUR 19 IMMEDIATE UK IMEP 001
MADELINE BELL V (J — (EP) HITS 19 IMMEDIATE UK IMEP 004
RON CARTHY HRNS (J — (EP) THE IMMEDIATE CATALOGUE 19 VIRGIN UK SV 102

F22 MARK FARNER F22

MARK FARNER G V (AB — (A) MARK FARNER 1978 ATLANTIC US 18232 UK K50419
PHIL AABERG K (A — (B) NO FRILLS 1979 ATLANTIC US 19196
ANDY NEWMARK D (B
BOB BABITT B (A — BOB KULICK G (A — AL WOTTON D (A
JIM MAELEN PERC (A — DICK WAGNER G (A — RICKY FARNER V (A
DENNIS BALLINGER V (AB — KAREN LAWSON V (B

F22A FARQUAHR F22A

BARNSWALLOW FARQUAHR G V (AB — (A) FABULOUS FARQUAHR 19 VERVE FORECAST FTS 3053
HUMMINGBIRD FARQUAHR G V (AB — (B) FARQUAHR970 ELEKTRA US EKS 74083
CONDOR FARQUAHR G V (AB
FLAMINGO FARQUAHR G V (AB — JERRY RAGOVOY K (B — GARY CHESTER D (B
ERIC WEISSBERG BANJO (B — JOE MACK B (B — LOU MAURO (B

F23 GARY FARR F23

GARY FARR V G (ALL — (A) TAKE SOMETHING WITH YOU 1969 MARMALADE UK 608 013
MIKE STEPHENS G (A — (B) STRANGE FRUIT 1971 CBS UK 64138
ROGER POWELL D (A — (C) ADDRESSED TO THE CENSORS OF LOVE 1973 ATCO US SD 7034
IAN WHITEMAN WIND K(A — (D) LONDON 1964/65 1977 CHARLY UK CR 300015
ANDY LEIGH B (A — (E) ROCK GENERATION VOL 7 (1 SIDE) 19 BYG FR 529 707
MARTIN STONE G (A
BRIAN BELSHAW B (A — NICK JONES PERC (A — RICHARD THOMPSON G (B — VINCE WETHERALL G (D
MICHAEL EVANS B (A — ANDY McKECHNIE G (D — STU PARKS B (D — BRIAN WALKELEY D (D
ANDY STEELE D (D — HARVEY THOMPSON WIND(C — MIKE LEWIS WIND (C — RONNIE EADES SAX (C
HARRISON CALLOWAY TPT(C — BEN CAULEY TPT (C — CHARLES ROSE TROM (C — GEORGE TERRY G (C
JIMMY JOHNSON G (C — PETE CARR G (C — BARRY BECKETT K (C — DAVID HOOD B (C
GERRY MASTERS B (C — ROGER HAWKINS D (C

F23A JOHN FARRAR F23A

JOHN FARRAR G V K (A — (A) JOHN FARRAR 1980 CBS UK 84324 US 36475
MICHAEL BOTTS D (A
TOM SNOW PNO (A — ED GREENE D (A — MICHAEL BODDICKER SYN (A
MICHAEL PORCARO B (A — DAVID McDANIELS B (A

F24 MICK FARREN F24

MICK FARREN V (AB — (A) CARNIVOROUS CIRCUS(MONA) 1970 TRANSATLANTIC UK TRA 212
WILKO JOHNSON G (B — (B) VAMPIRES STOLE MY LUNCH MONEY 1978 LOGO UK LOGO 1010
ALAN POWELL D (B
WILL STALLIBRASS HCA(B — ANDY COLQUHOUN B (B — CHRISSIE HYNDE V (B — SONJA KRISTINA V (B
SUSIE V (B — MARIA V (B — TWINK D (A — STEVE TOOK B (A
VICTOR BROX K (A — PETE ILLINGWORTH (— FRANK NEWBOLD (A — JOHN GUSTAFSON B (A
STEVE HAMMOND G (A — PAUL BUCKMASTER CELLO(A

F24A FASHION F24A

DIK PERC HCA V(A — (A) PRODUCT PERFECT 1979 FASHION UK FML1 US IRS 002
LUKE G V (A
MULLIGAN B SYN V (A

F25 FAST F25

PAUL ZONE (A — (A) THE FAST FOR SALE 1980 RECCA 2000
MIKI ZONE (A
ARMAND ZONE (— PETER HOFFMAN (— TOMMIE MODNIL (— JOE POLISENO (A
LOUIS BOVA (A

F26 FAST BUCK F26

DAVID KERR CLEMSON (— (A) FAST BUCK 1976 JET UK JETLP 16
ANDREW LOCKE (
MIKE BARON (— EDWIN HAMILTON (— MIKE HOUGH (— JAMIE PEARCE (— STEPHEN FORREST (

F26A FAST LANE F26A

(A) FAST LANE EP 19 ACE UK 006

F27 FAT F27

PETER NEWLAND V HCA (A — (A) FAT 1970 RCA LPS 4368 LSA3009
JAMES KAMINSKI G V (A
MICHAEL BENSON G (A — GUY DE VITO V (A — WILLIAM BENJAMIN D V (A

F27A FAT CITY F27A

WILLIAM DANOFF G V (AB — (A) REINCARNATION 1969 PROBE US CPLI 4508
TAFFY DANOFF V (AB — (B) WELCOME TO FAT CITY 19 PARAMOUNT US 6308
EVERETT BARKSDALE B (A
JIM PARKER G (AB — TED SOMMER D (A — HUBERT LAWS FLT (A
DAVE APPEL G (A — MARGARET ROSE HARP (A — BOB JAMES K (A
ARTIE TRAUM G (A — BERNARD PURDIE D (A — RONNIE ZITO D (A
HOWARD COLLINS G (A — BUCKY PIZZARELLI G BAN (A — ERNIE HAYES K (A
RICHARD GREENE VLN (B — ERIC WEISSBERG STEEL (B — DICK WEISSMAN BAN (B
FRANK OWENS K (B — CLIVE STEVENS FLT (B — CHRIS SARANDON V (B
SUE SARANDON V (B — TIMMY JEROME V (B — ELIZABETH LINDSAY V (B

F27B FAT CHANCE F27B

FAT CHANCE 1972 RCA US 4626

F28 FAT MAN RIDDIN SECTION F28

(A) ISRAEL TAFARI 1978 TOP RANKING UK

F29 FAT MATTRESS F29

NOEL REDDING G B V (A1 — (A) FAT MATTRESS 1969 POLYDOR UK 583 056 ATCO US 33309
STEVE HAMMOND G (2 — (B) FAT MATTRESS 2 1970 POLYDOR UK 2383 025 ATCO US 33347
NEIL LANDON V (12A — (1) 1969 (2)1970
JIM LEVERTON K B V (12A
ERIC DILLON D (12A — CHRIS WOOD FLT (A — MICK WEAVER K (

F29A FAUN F29A

(A) FAUN 19 GREGAR US GG 7000

F29B FATAL MICROBES F29B

(A) MEET THE POISON GIRLS 1979 SMALL WONDER UK WEENY 3

F29C FAT WATER F29C

(A) FAT WATER 19 MGM US 4660

F30 FAUST F30

WERNER DIERMAIER (ABC — (A) FAUST 1971 POLYDOR UK 2310 142
JEAN HERVE PERON (ABC — (A) FAUST 1979 RECOMMENDED RR1
RUDOLF SOSSNA (ABC — (B) SO FAR 1972 POLYDOR UK 2310 196
TONY CONRAD (C — (B) SO FAR 1972 RECOMMENDED RR2
HANS JOACHIM IRMLER (AB — (C) OUTSIDE DREAM SYNDICATE 1973 CAROLINE UK C1501
GUNTHER WUSTHOFF (AB — (D) FAUST 4 1973 VIRGIN UK V2004 GER 87739
ARMULF MEIFERT (A — (E) FAUST TAPES 1973 VIRGIN UK VC501
UWE NETTLEBECK PROD (— (F) FAUST TAPES 198 RECOMMENDED UK RR6
(G) CASABLANCA MOON 198 RECOMMENDED UK RR5

F30A BILL FAY F30A

BILL FAY V PNO (AB — (A) BILL FAY — 1970 DERAM NOVA SDN..12
GEORGE BIRD B (A — (B) TIME OF LAST PERSECUTION — 1971 DERAM SML1079
JOHN MARSHALL D (A
TREVOR TAYLOR D (A — RICHARD MILLS G (A — RAY RUSSELL G (A
ALAN RUSHTON D (B — DARYL RUNSWICK B (B — TONY ROBERTS WIND (B
NICK EVANS TROM (B — BUD PARKES TPT (B

F30B FEAR ITSELF F30B

(A) FEAR ITSELF — 19 DOT US DLP 25942

F30C FAY RAY F30C

OWEN HUGHES D (A — (A) FAY RAY — 1982 WEA GER 99188
JOHN LOVERING G (A
SHEILA McCARTNEY V L PERC(A — JEFF TAYLOD WIND ACC(A — TONY TRAVIS B V (A

F31 CHARLIE FEATHERS F31

CHARLIE FEATHERS G V (ALL — (A) ROCKABILLY KING — 1974 POLYDOR UK 2310 293
QUINTON CLAUCH G (C — (B) CHARLIE FEATHERS (EP)GONE GONE — 1977 CHARLY UK CEP 116
BILL CANTRELLI FDL (C — (C) ROCKABILLY MAN — 1978 CHARLY UK CR 30161
STAN KESTER STEEL (C — ( ) GOOD ROCKIN' TONIGHT — 19 BARRELHOUSE US BH 03
BILL BLACK B (C — ( ) LIVE IN MEMPHIS TENNESSEE — 197 BARRELHOUSE US BH.06
JEFF TODD B (C — ( ) THAT ROCKABILLY CAT — 1979 BARRELHOUSE US BH014
BILLY RILEY B (C — ( ) CHARLIE FEATHERS VOL 1 — 1979 FEATHERS US FR101
MARCUS VAN STORY B (C — ( ) CHARLIE FEATHERS VOL 2 — 1979 FEATHERS US FR102
BUBBA FEATHERS G (C — ( ) ROCK'N'ROLL — 19 STAR US
MACK SELF V (C
JIMMY VAN EATON D (C — JACK SMITH D (C — WILLIAM DIEHL B (C — BRAD SUGGS G (C

F32 DR FEELGOOD F32

WILLIAM 'DR FEELGOOD' PERRYMAN (ALL — ( ) R& B WITH DR FEELGOOD(EP) — 196 COLUMBIA UK SEG 8310
AKA PIANO RED — ( ) PERCUSSIVE PIANO — 19 EUPHONIC US 1212
( ) JUMPIN' THE BOOGIE — 19 US 1 2821
( ) PIANO RED — 19 BLACK LION BLP 30171

F32A FEELIES F32A

BILL MILLION PERC G V(A — (A) CRAZY RHYTHMS — 1980 STIFF UK SEEZ 20
KEITH CLAYTON D B V (A
GLENN MERCER G V D (A — ANTON FIER D (A

F33 WILTON FELDER F33

WILTON FELDER HRNS B(AB — (A) WE ALL HAVE A STAR — 1978 ABC UK ABCL5265 US MCA 1109
DEAN PARKS G (B — (B) INHERIT THE WIND — 1980 MCA UK MCG 4013 US MCA 5144
ARTHUR ADAMS G (B
ROLAND BAUTISTA G (B — JOE SAMPLE K SYN (B — ABRAHAM LABORIEL B (B — NDUGU CHANCLER D (B
RICKY LAWSON D (B — PAULINHO DA COSTA PERC (B — BOBBY WOMACK V (B — MERRY CLAYTON V (B
PAT POWDRILL V (B — GWEN EVANS V (B — GERRY GARRETT V (B — ALEX BROWN V (B
JIM GILSTRAP V (B — ZEDRIC TURNBOUGH V (B — AUGIE JOHNSON V (B

F34 VICTOR FELDMAN F34

VICTOR FELDMAN PERC PNO VIBES(ALL — (A) ROCKAVIBABE — 1977 DJM UK DJM 22058
JOHN GUERIN D (A — ( ) SUITE 16 — 19 C3541
TOM SCOTT SAX (AY — ( ) THE ARRIVAL OF VICTOR FELDMAN — 1958 CONTEMPORARY S7549 + LAC 12172
CHUCK DOMANICO B (A — ( ) LATINSVILLE — 1960 COMTEMPORARY LAC 580
TERRY GIBBS (* — (D) ARTFUL DODGER — 1976 CONCORD JAZZ US .38
LARRY BUNKER (* — (*) VIBES TO THE POWER OF 3 — 1960 TOP RANK UK 30 007
JACK SHELDON (D — (*) VIBES TO THE POWER OF 3 — 19 INTERLUDE US
( ) IN MY POCKET(DIRECT CUT) — 1978 COHEARANT US CER 1001
(Y) YOUR SMILE — 1975 CHOICE US 1005

F35 JULIE FELIX F35

JULIE FELIX V G (ALL — (A) JULIE FELIX — 1964 DECCA UK SKL 4626
WITH — (B) SINGS DYLAN & GUTHRIE — 1965 DECCA UK LK 4683
STEVE HAYTON G V (P — (C) 2ND ALBUM — 1965 DECCA UK LK 4724
DANNY THOMPSON B (P — (D) 3RD ALBUM — 1967 DECCA UK LK 4820
BILLY STEVENS HCA (P — (E) CHANGES — 1966 FONTANA UK TL/STL 5368
KESH SATHIE TABLA (P — (F) FLOWERS — 1967 FONTANA UK TL/STL 5437
TED LAZER ACC (P — (F) FLOWERS — 1974 CONTOUR UK 6870 507
(G) THIS WORLD GOES ROUND & ROUND — 1968 FONTANA UK TL/STL 5473
(H) THE WORLD OF JULIE FELIX — 1969 DECCA UK SPA 6
(I) GOING TO THE ZOO — 1969 DECCA SFL 13117
(J) THE WORLD OF VOL 2 — 1970 DECCA UK SPA 76
(K) THIS IS JULIE FELIX — 1970 PHILIPS UK 6382 019
(L) CLOTHO'S WEB — 1972 RAK US 31609 UK SRKA 6752
(M) THIS IS JULIE FELIX VOL 2 — 1974 PHILIPS UK 6382 049
(N) LIGHTNING — 1974 EMI UK EMC 3030
(O) LONDON PALLADIUM — 1974 RCA LSP 6021
(P) HOT CHOCOLATA — 1979 GULL UK GULP 1032

F35A DICK FELLER F35A

DICK FELLER V (ALL — ( ) NO WORDS ON ME — 1974 ASYLUM US CM1
CHARLIE McCOY HCA (— ( ) SOME DAYS ARE DIAMONDS — 1975 ASYLUM US 7E 1044
JOHNNY GIMBLE FDL (— ( ) THEN I WROTE — 1973 UA US 094 349
PETE DRAKE STEEL (

F35B NARVEL FELTS F35B

NARVEL FELTS V (ALL — (A) DRIFT AWAY — 19 CINNAMON US 5000
( ) RECONSIDER ME — 1975 DOT US DOSD 2025
( ) GREATEST HITS — 19 DOT US DOSD 2036
( ) NARVEL THE MARVEL — 1976 DOT US 2033
( ) THIS TIME — 1976 HI US 32098
( ) DOIN WHAT I LIKE — 1977 DOT US 2065
( ) TOUCH OF FELTS — 1977 DOT US 2070

F35C FENDERMEN F35C

JIM SUNDQUIST (A — ( ) MULE SKINNER BLUES — 196 SOMA US MG 1240
PHIL HUMPHREY (A

F36 MICHAEL FENNELLY F36

MICHAEL FENNELLY G V (ALL (A) LANE CHANGER 1974 EPIC UK 80230 US 32703
CASEY FOUTZ K (A (B) STRANGERS BED 1975 MERCURY US 1-1043
NICK NEWELL SAX(A
JIM RODFORD B (A ROBERT HENRIT D (A HENRY SPINETTI D (A DAVE WINTOUR B (A
MIKE COTTON TPT(A JOHN BEECHAM TROM (A ALAN HOLMES SAX (A ROD ARGENT V (A
RUSS BALLARD V (A GASPAR LAWAL PERC (A MIKE GILES D (A

F37 SHANE FENTON & THE FENTONES F37

SHANE FENTON V (A (A) GOOD ROCKIN TONIGHT 1974 CONTOUR UK 2870 409
(BERNARD JEWRY) IM A MOODY GUY EP 1977 EMI UK 2696
(LATER ALVIN STARDUST)

F38 RAY FENWICK F38

RAY FENWICK G V (A (A) KEEP AMERICA BEAUTIFUL 1971 DECCA UK SKL 5090
CALEB QUAYE G (A
DEE MURRAY B (A (A NIGEL OLSSON D (A PETE YORK D (A
EDDIE HARDIN K (A ROGER POPE D (A

F38A FERGUS F38A

FERGUS G V (A (A) FERGUS 1978 RONDERCREST ROND LP1

F39 JAY FERGUSON F39

JAY FERGUSON K V(ALL (A) ALL ALONE IN THE END ZONE 1976 ASYLUM US 1063 UK K53040
JOE WALSH G (ABCDE (B) THUNDER ISLAND 1977 ASYLUM US 1115 UK K53066
JOE VITALE D PERC (AC (C) REAL LIFE AINT THIS WAY 1979 ASYLUM US 6E 158 UK K53086
JOEY MURCIA G (AB (D) TERMS & CONDITIONS 1980 CAPITAL US 12083
MARK ANDES B (E (E) WHITE NOISE 1982 CAPITOL US 12196
GEORGE PERRY B V(A
JOE LALA PERC(A STAN SKIPPER D (AC TONY BATTAGLIA B (BCD ED BROWN B (B
HAROLD COWART B (B BILL SZYMCZYK PERC PROD)BC BOB WEBB G (BCDE ROBBIE ALBERT K (D
DAVID WHITE B V(D CURLY SMITH D (DC HARRY STINSON V (D JIM HORN SAX (D
TERRY NELSON PERC(D JUAN PEREZ PERC (C COL CLESSER SAX (C MARK COLBY SAX (C
SCOTT CHAMBERS B (C MIKE HAMILTON G (E TRIS IMBODEN D (E TOM KELLY V (E
RANDY CALIFORNIA G (E KEVIN VALENTINE D (E TOM FERGUSON VLN (E DAVID TOLEGIAN HRNS (E

F40 ANDY FERNBACH F40

ANDY FERNBACH G V (A1 (A) IF YOU MISS YOUR CONNEXION 1969 LIBERTY UK LBS 83233
DAVE FERNBACH K (A (1) 1969 BAND CALLED CONNEXION
PETE CRUICKSHANK B (A
KEN PUSTELNIK D (A CHRIS ELVIN HCA (A J D FANGER G (A1 BOB ROWE B (1
PHILLIP CROWTHER D (1

F40A AL FERRIER & HIS BOPPIN' BILLIES F40A

AL FERRIER (A) BIRTH OF ROCKABILLY 19 GOLDSTAR US
(B) SOUND OF ROCKABILLY 19 SHOWTIME US 1000
(C) BOPPIN' TONIGHT 1977 FLYRIGHT UK LP525

F41 FERRIS WHEEL F41

MICHAEL SNOW V K G (AB (A) CANT BREAK THE HABIT 1967 PYE UK NPL 18203
LINDA LEWIS V (AB (B) FERRIS WHEEL 1970 POLYDOR UK 588 066
DAVID SWEETNAM/FORD SAX (AB
GEORGE SWEETNAM/FORD B V(AB DENNIS ELLIOTT D (AB TERRY EDMUNDS G (B BERNIE HOLLAND G (B
DIANA FERREZ V (A MICKY LISTON (A KEITH ANTHONY (A

F42 BRIAN FERRY F42

BRIAN FERRY V PNO (ALL (A) THESE FOOLISH THINGS 1973 ISLAND UK ILPS9249 ATLANTIC US 7304
WITH (A) THESE FOOLISH THINGS 1977 POLYDOR RI2302 046 2310 507
ROBBIE MONTGOMERY V (A (A) THESE FOOLISH THINGS 1973 ISLAND GER 87266
ANN ODELL V (1 (B) ANOTHER TIME ANOTHER PLACE 1974 ISLAND UK ILPS9284 ATLANTIC US18113
CHRIS SPEDDING G (CD1 (B) ANOTHER TIME ANOTHER PLACE 1977 POLYDOR RI 2302 047 2310 508
ANGELETTES V (A (B) ANOTHER TIME ANOTHER PLACE 1974 ISLAND GER 86067
JOHN WETTON B (BCD1 (C) LET'S STICK TOGETHER 1976 ISLAND UK ILPS9367 ATLANTIC US18187
PHIL MANZANERA G (ACD1 (C) LET'S STICK TOGETHER 1977 POLYDOR RI 2302 045 2310 045
JESSIE DAVIS V (A (C) LETS STICK TOGETHER 1976 ISLAND GER 27953
DYAN BIRCH V (D1 (D) IN YOUR MIND 1977 POLYDOR RI 2302 055 ATLANTIC US18216
PADDY McHUGH V (D1C (E) BRIDE STRIPPED BARE 1978 POLYDOR POLD 5003 ATLANTIC US19205
MALCOLM DUNCAN SAX (A (E) BRIDE STRIPPED BARE 1978 POLYDOR NL 2344 110
FRANK COLLINS V (D1 (EP) PRICE OF LOVE 1976 ISLAND UK IEP 1
PAUL THOMPSON D (ABCD1 (1) 1977 LIVE TOUR
MARTIN DROVER HRNS (BCD1
NEIL HUBBARD G (CED ALAN SPENNER G (E WADDY WACHTEL K G (E RICK MAROTTA D (E
CHRIS MERCER SAX (BCD MEL COLLINS SAX (CD EDDIE JOBSON VLN K (AC MORRIS PERT PERC(BC
JOHN GUSTAFSON B (C RICK WILLS B (C JOHN PORTER G B (ABCD DAVID O'LIST G (BC
HENRY LOWTHER HRNS (BA RUAN OLOCHLAINN SAX (BA CHRIS PYNE TROM (B TONY CARR (B
TONY CHARLES (B PAUL KOSH (B GEOFF DALEY (B BOB EFFORD (B
MALCOLM GRIFFITHS (B JIMMY HASTINGS (B JOHN PUNTER D (AB ALF REECE (B
PETER ROBINSON (B RONNIE ROSS (B BRUCE ROWLAND (B STEVE SAUNDERS (B
ALAN SKIDMORE (B WINSTONE STONE (B DAVID SKINNER PNO (AD VICKI BROWN V (BC
RAY COOPER PERC (D MARK WARNER (B JACQUIE SULLIVAN V (DC HELEN CHAPPELLE V (BCD
DOREEN CHANTER V (DC PRESTON HAYWARD (D BARRY ST JOHN V (B LIZA STRIKE V (B
DON CIRILO V (B ROGER BALL SAX (A MARTHA WALKER V (C

F43 FEVERTREE F43

E E WOLFE B (ABCD (A) FEVER TREE 1968 UNI UK UNLS 102 US 73024
JOHN TUTTLE PERC(ABCD (A) FEVER TREE 19 MCA RI US 551 NL EMI 99191
ROB LANDES WIND K (ABCD (B) ANOTHER TIME ANOTHER PLACE 1968 UNI US 73040 UK MCA MUPS 347
DENNIS KELLER V (ABCD (C) CREATION 19 UNI US 73067
MICHAEL G (ABCD (D) FOR SALE 1970 AMPEX US A 10113
KEVIN KELLEY D (D
GRANT JOHNSON K (D HAL BLAINE D (D DAVID COHEN G (D WALT MESCAL G (D
JOE OSBORNE B (D LARRY KNECHTAL K (D

F43A KAREL FIALKA F43A

KAREL FIALKA V SYN (A (A) STILL LIFE 1980 BLUEPRINT U BULP 5003
ROBERT LANGRIDGE K (A
MARTIN DEEGAN D (A HAMTONES V (A ANDY BROWN B (A DEREK TULLOCH SAX (A

F44 **FIELDS** F44

GRAHAM FIELD K (A | (A) FIELDS | 1971 CBS UK 69009 US EPIC 31154
ALAN BARRY G V B SYN(A
ANDY McCULLOCH D (A FRANK FARRELL B (

F44A **FIELDS (2)** F44A

STEVE LAGAN D (A | (A) FIELDS | 1969 UNI US 73050
PATRICK BURKE B (A
RICHARD FORTUNATO G(A

F44B **FIFTY FOOT HOSE** F44B

CORK MARCHESCHI (AB | (A) CAULDRON | 1968 LIMELIGHT 86062
DAVID BLOSSOM G (AB | (B) I'VE PAID MY DUES | 1970 DECCA 75225
LARRY EVANS G V (AB
KIM KIMSEY D (AB TERRY HUNSLEY B (AB NANCY BLOSSOM V (AB

F44C **FIFTH AVENUE BAND** F44C

KENNY ALTMAN G B (A | (A) FIFTH AVENUE BAND | 1969 REPRISE RSLP 6369
JERRY BURNHAM B FLT(A
PETER GALLWAY G V (A PETE HEYWOOD D (A JON LIND V (A MURRAY WEINSTOCK K (A

F45 **FINCH** F45

JOOP VAN NIMWEGEN G (CD | (A) FINCH | 19
AD WAMMES K (D | (B) BEYOND EXPLOSION | 19
HANS BASBOOM D (D | (C) GLORY OF THE INNER FORCE | 1975 ATCO US 36124
PETER VINK B (CD | (D) GALLEON OF PASSION | 1977 ROCKBURGH UK ROC 103
BEER KLAASSE D (CD
CLEEM DETETMEIJER K (CD

F45A **FINE WINE** F45A

BOB MOSLEY B V (A | (A) FINEWINE | 1976 POLYDOR GER 2310 438
JERRY MILLER G V (A
MICHAEL BEEN G V (A JOHN CRAVIOTTA D (A

F46 **PETER FINGER** F46

PETER FINGER G (ALL | (A) DETLEF & FINGER | 197 KICKING MULE UK 104
(B) BOTTLENECK GUITAR SOLOS | 1975 KICKING MULE UK 105 US 116
(C) ACCOUSTIC ROCK GUITAR | 1977 KICKING MULE UK 144 US 149

F47 **FINGERPRINTZ** F47

JIMME O'NEIL G V (ABCD | (A) THE VERY DAB | 1979 VIRGIN UK 2119 GER 201 048
CHA BURNZ G V (ABCD | (B) DISTINGUISHING MARKS | 1980 VIRGIN UK 2170 GER 202 284
KENNY ALTON B V (ABCD | (B) DISTINGUISHING MARKS | 1980 VIRGIN US 13136
BOB SCHILLING D (ABC | (C) DANCING WITH MYSELF 12" EP | 1979 VIRGIN UK 23512
STEP LANG V (C | (D) BEAT NOIR | 1981 VIRGIN UK 2201
BOGDAN WICZLING (D
STEVE KING K (D SADIE THE CAT V (D RON FRANCOIS B (D DON SNOW K (D
KRZYSTOF KAFKA ACC (D JOHN EARLE SAX (D DICK HANSON TPT (D

F48 **MIKE FINNIGAN** F48

MIKE FINNIGAN B V (AB | (A) MIKE FINNIGAN | 1976 WB US 2944 UK K56257
ROGER HAWKINS D (A | (B) BLACK & WHITE | 1978 CBS US 35258
DAVID HOOD B (B
BARRY BECKETT K (A PETE CARR G (A JIMMY JOHNSON G (A AMOS GARRETT G (B
TOM ROADY PERC (A JOHNNY GIMBLE FDL (A TEX WEX PERC (A HARRISON CALLOWAY HRNS(A
RON EADES SAX (A CHARLES ROSE TROM (A PEE WEE ERWIN TPT (A BUDDY MORROW TROM(A
BOB WILBUR CLAR (A DON BUTTERFIELD TUBA (A ED SAUTER STR (A STAMPS QUARTET V (A
FRANCES BARNETTE V (A PRISCILLA THOMAS V (A JACKIE DIXON V (A SUZY STORM V (A
BARBARA WYRICK V (A AVA ALDRIDGE V (A JAMES GRIFFIN V (A MARIA MULDAUR V (A

F48A **FINNIGAN & WOOD** F48A

MIKE FINNIGAN V K HCA(A | (A) CRAZED HIPSTERS | 1972 BLUE THUMB US BTS .35
JERRY WOOD V G (A
DON CLAREY D (A RAY BAGBY D (A DAVE GATES B (A RAY LOECKLIE SAX (A

F48B **FIRE** F48B

DAVID LAMBERT V G K(A | (A) MAGIC SHOEMAKER | 1970 PYE UK NSPL18343
BOB VOICE D V (A
DICK DUFALL B V (A

F48C **FIRE ESCAPE** F48C

HANK LEVINE PROD (A | ( ) PSYCHOTIC REACTION | 19 GNP CRESENDO US 2034
LARRY GOLDBERG (

F48D **FIRE & RAIN** F48D

(A) FIRE & RAIN | 1973 MERCURY US 1 654

F48E **FIRE ENGINES** F48E

RUSSELL BURN G (A | (A) LUBRICATE YOUR LIVING ROOM | 1980 ACCESSORY UK ACC001
DAVID HENDERSON G V (A | (B) AUFGELADEN UND BEREIT FUR ACTION | 1981 FAST GER
GRAHAM MAIN B (A
MURRAY SLADE G (A

F48F **FIREBALLET** F48F

JIM COMO V D PERC(AB | (A) NIGHT ON BALD MOUNTAIN | 1975 PASSPORT US 98010
BRYAN HOWE K V SAX(AB | (B) TWO TOO | 1976 PASSPORT US 98016
RYCHE CHLANDA G V MAN(AB
MARTIN BIGLIN G B (AB FRANK PETTO K SYN V(AB IAN McDONALD WIND(A JOHN ZANGRADO WIND (B
BRIAN CUOMO K (B MARY ELLEN DURKA V (B IRENE CONRAD V (B JUDY ELLINGTON V (B
JOAN ELLINGTON V (B PAT ELLINGTON V (B ALPHONSE ROCQUE PEC (B

F49 **FIREBALLS** F49

JIMMY GILMER K (| (A) VAQUERO | 1961 TOP RANKUK35 105 US(M)343(S)643
GEORGE TOMSCO G (| ( ) TORQUAY | 1963 DOT US 25512
STAN LARK B (| ( ) SUGAR SHACK | 196 DOT US 25545
ERIC BUDD D (| ( ) FIREWATER | 196 DOT US 25856
( ) SUGER SHACKERS | 19 CROWN US
( ) JIMMY GILMER & FIREBALLS | 19 CROWN US 5376
( ) HERE WE ARE | 19 WARWICK US W2042
( ) BOTTLE OF WINE | 1968 STATESIDEUK10237 US ATCO 33239
( ) COME ON REACT | 1969 LONDON UK 8396 US ATCO 33275
( ) CAMPUSOLOGY | 19 DOT US

F50 FIREFALL F50

RICK ROBERTS G V (ABCDEF — (A) FIREFALL — 1976 ATLANTIC US 18174 UK K 50260
MIKE CLARKE D (ABCDF — (B) LUNA SEA — 1977 ATLANTIC US 19101 UK K 50355
MARK ANDES B (ABCDF — (C) ELAN — 1978 ATLANTIC US 19183 UK K 50494
JOCK BARTLEY G (ABCDEF — (D) UNDERTOW — 1980 ATLANTIC US 16006 UK K 50665
LARRY BURNETT V G (ABCDEF — (E) CLOUDS ACROSS THE SUN — 1981 ATLANTIC US 16024 UK K 50767
DAVID MUSE K WIND(ABCDEF — (F) BEST OF — 1981 ATLANTIC US 19316 UK K 50839
PETER GRAVES TROM (A
WHIT SIDENER SAX (A — ANDREW LOVE SAX (B — KEN FAULK TPT (A — WAYNE JACKSON HRNS (A
JACK HALE TROM (A — LEWIS COLLINS SAX (B — JAMES MITCHELL SAX (B — CLYDIE KING V (B
VANETTA FIELDS V (B — SHIRLEY MATTHEWS V (B — JOE LALA PERC(B — FLACO PADRON PERC(B
ALAN ESTES PERC(B — SKIP EDWARDS PNO (B — TIM SCHMIT V (B — JERRY AIELLO ORG(B
LAURA TAYLOR V (C — STEVE FOREMAN PERC (C — JIM KELTNER D (C — TRIS IMBODEN D (EF
TOM KELLY V (D — CHRISTOPHER DENNIS PERC(D — SANDRA RHODES V (D — DONNA RHODES V (D
CHARLIE CHALMERS V (D — GEORGE HAWKINS B V (EF — PAUL HARRIS K (D — ANDY NEWMARK D (D
BILL PAYNE K (D — DAVID MUSEL WIND K(EF — LISA MENZO V (EF — MARY ANN KENNEDY V(E
FARRELL MORRIS PERC(E — KYLE LEHNING K (E — PAM ROSE V (E

F50A FIREFLIES F50A

RITCHIE ADAMS — ( ) YOU WERE MINE — 19 TAURUS US 1002
LEE REYNOLDS
JOHNNY VISCELLI — PAUL GIACOLONE

F50B FIREPOINT F50B

BOB HALL K (A — (A) FIREPOINT — 1969 SPARK UK SRLM 2003
MIKE COOPER G (A
SAM MITCHELL G (A — DAVE KELLY G (A — DUFFY POWER HCA (A — TOM ROBINSON
GERALD HARP (

F51 FIRESIGN THEATRE F51

DAVID OSSMAN V PERC(ALL — (A) WAITING FOR THE ELECTRICIAN OR SOMEONE — 1968 CBS UK 65129 US 9518
PHILIP AUSTIN G K V (ALL — (B) HOW TO BE IN TWO PLACES AT ONCE — 1969 CBS UK 65130 US 9884
PHILIP PROCTOR VLN V FLT (ALL — (C)DONT CRUSH THAT DWARF HAND ME THE PLIERS — 1972 CBS US 30102
PETER BERGMAN SAX V G B (ALL — (D) I THINK WERE ALL BOZOS ON THIS BUS — 1972 CBS US 30737
DAVID GRIMM ORG (B — (E) DEAR FRIENDS DBL — 1972 CBS US 31099
THE GRATEFULL BOOGIES K(B — (F) NOT INSANE OR ANY THING YOU WANT — 1972 CBS US 31585
WILLIAM F MAAOCH (B — (G) IN THE NEXT WORLD YOU'RE ON YOUR OWN — 1972 CBS US 31383 RI 33475
CATHE COZZI (B — (H) TV OR NOT TV — 1973 CBS US 32199
ANNA LEE AUSTIN (B — (J) THE TALE OF THE GIANT RAT OF SUMATRA — 1974 CBS US 32370
JANE DANSIE V (B — (L) EVERYTHING YOU KNOW IS WRONG — 1975 CBS US 33141
ELIZABETH PLUMB V (B — (M) FORWARD INTO THE PAST — 1977 CBS US 34391
JOHN KINICK V (B — (N) JUST FOLKS — 197 BUTTERFLY US 001
CATHLEEN O'MARA V (B — (O) FIRESIGN WORLD — 197 WRMB US 512
THE ANDROID SISTERS V (B — (P) NICK DANGER THE CASE OF THE MISSING SHOE — 1979 RHINO US 506
LITTLE BUBBLES SAX (B — (Q) FIGHTING CLOWNS — 1980 RHINO US 018
AMBIENTS NOYES CHORAL V(B
OONA ELLIOTT V (C — C D TAYLOR G (F — MICHAEL GWYNNE D FLT(F — BO MAY SAX (F
CYRUS FARYAR B (FH — RICHARD PARKER K (Q — JEFF BAXTER G (Q — ED ROSCETTI D (Q
JOHN MITCHELL SAX (T — DICK SPENCER WIND (Q — RICHARD COOPER TPT (Q

F51A FIRST AID F51A

ALAN WORMALD G V (A — (A) NOSTRADAMUS — 1977 DECCA UK TXS 117
KEITH PARKINSON K (
DAVE FREEMAN PERC (A — NORRIE TENNENT B (A

F53 FIRST CLASS F53

CHAS MILLS V (— ( ) FIRST CLASS — 1974 UK 53109 US UK UKAL 1008
TONY BURROWS V (— ( ) S S T — 1976 UK UK UKAL 1022
JOHN CARTER V (— ( ) GOING FIRST CLASS — 1978 ALL PALTINUM US 3018
DEL JOHN V (— ( ) FIRST CLASS — 1981 SUGARHILL US 255
SPENCER JAMES G V (
EDDIE RICHARDS D V (
ROBIN SHAW B V (— CLIVE BARRETT K V (

F54 WILD MAN FISCHER F54

LARRY 'WILD MAN' FISCHER V(ALL — (A) AN EVENING WITH WILD MAN FISCHER — 1970 REPRISE 6332 BIZARRE 6332
DON BUCHANAN G (B — (B) WILDMANIA — 1977 RHINO RNLP 001
JOE STODDARD D (B
STUART DEAL B (B — LEONARD SAMARTINO G V A(B — SANDRA SAMARTINO V (B
FRANK ZAPPA PERC (A — ART TRIPP PERC (A — KIM FOWLEY (A
RODNEY BINGENHEIMER (A — G T O's (A

F54A FISCHER Z F54A

JOHN WATTS G V (ABC — (A) WORD SALAD — 1979 UA US 975 UK UAG 30232
STEVE SKOLNIK K V (AB — (B) GOING DEAF FOR A LIVING — 1980 UA US 1048 UK UAG 30295
STEVE LIDDLE D PERC(ABC — (C) RED SKIES OVER PARADISE — 1981 LIBERTY NL83100 UK UAG 30326
DAVID GRAHAM B (ABC — (EP) OVER GERMANY — 1981 LIBERTY GER 83101

F55 FISHBAUGH FISHBAUGH ZORN F55

GARY FISHBAUGH V G PERC (A — (A) FISHBAUGH FISHBAUGH & ZORN — 1972 CBS UK 64783
PAULA FISHBAUGH V PNO PERC(A
PETE ZORN V B G WIND PERC(A — RICK WEST G (A — BRIAN DALY G (A
JUNIOR CAMPBELL G K (A — STUART COWELL G (A — TERRY COX D (A
RAYMOND DUFFY D (A — REG GUEST K (A — GORDON HUNTLEY STEEL(A
GRAHAM PRESKETT VLN (A — MIKE STONE PERC (A

F55A SONNY FISHER F55A

SONNY FISHER (A — (A) TEXAS ROCKABILLY 10" — 19 ACE UK 10CH14

F56 MATTHEW FISHER F56

MATTHEW FISHER PERC V K G HCA(ABC — (A) JOURNEYS END — 1973 RCA UK SF8380 APLI 0195
GEOFF SWETTENHAM D (A — (B) I'LL BE THERE — 1974 RCA APLI 0325
MICK HAWKSWORTH B (A — (C) MATTHEW FISHER — 1980 VERTIGO UK 9198652 US A&M4801
BOBBY HARRISON V (A — (D) STRANGE DAYS — 1981 MERCURY NL 6302 108
TONY BURROWS V (A
JOHN CARTER V (A — MIKE JAPP G (B — ALAN COULTER D PERC (B — STEVE BINGHAM B (BC
JIM RYAN B G(B — JAMES FRANK D (B — DAVE MATTACKS D (C — HENRY SPINETTI D (C
BARRY DE SOUZA D (C — DILL KATZ B (C — PAUL WESTWOOD B (C — TIM RENWICK G (C
MICK GRABHAM G (C — JIM DEWAR V (C — PETE ZORN V (C — JOHN VERITY V (C
ROD ARGENT V (C — KEN LEWIS V (B

F56A FIST F56A

HARRY HILL D (A — (A) TURN HELL ON 1980 MCA UK MCF 3082
KEITH SATCHFIELD G V (A — (B) HOT SPIKES 1981 A&M US 4823
JOHN WYLIE B V (A
DAVE IRWIN G V (A

F56B PATRIK FITZGERALD F56B

PATRIK FITZGERALD V (ALL — (A) SAFETY PIN STUCK IN MY HEART EP 1978 SMALL WONDER UK SMALL4
(B) PARANOID WARD EP 1979 SMALL WONDER UK WEENY1
(C) BACK STREET BOYS EP 1979 SMALL WONDER UK SMALL6

F57 G F FITZGERALD F57

G F FITZGERALD G B K V (A — (A) MOUSEPROOF 1970 UNI UNLS 115
ALAN PLACE G (A
ROD HERMAN G (A — B J COLE STEEL (A — RIK KENTON B (A
IAN ANDREWS B (A — GEOFF LEIGH SAX (A — SAM GOPAL TABLA (A
TED TETLAN D (A — TONY TURNBULL D (A

F57A FIVE AMERICANS F57A

( ) I SEE THE LIGHT 19 ABNAK US 8503
( ) WESTERN UNION 19 ABNAK US 2067
( ) PROGRESSIONS 19 ABNAK US 2069
( ) NOW & THEN 19 ABNAK US 2071

F57B FIVE BY FIVE F57B

(A) NEXT EXIT 1968 PAULA US LPS 2202

F58 FIVE DOLLAR SHOES F58

GREGG DIAMOND D V (A — (A) FIVE DOLLAR SHOES 1972 NEIGHBORHOOD UK NH 3001
TOM GRAVES K V (A
JIM GREGORY B V (A — MIKE MILLIUS V HCA (A — SCOTT WOODY G V (A

F59 FIVE HAND REEL F59

BOBBY EAGLESHAM V G (ABCD — (A) FIVE HAND REEL 1976 RUBBER 019 RCA PL 25065
DICK GAUGHAN G V (ABC — (B) FOR A' THAT 1977 RCA PL 25066
TOM HICKLAND K VLN V (ABCD — (C) EARL O'MORAY 1978 RCA PL 25150
BARRY LYONS PERC B K (ABCD — (D) BUNCH OF FIVES 1979 TOPIC 12TS 406
DAVE TULLOCH D (ABCD — (E) NOTHING BUT THE BEST 1980 RCA UK 25267
SAM BRACKEN V G (D

F59A FIVE MAN ELECTRICAL BAND F59A

LES EMMERSON G V (— ( ) FIVE MAN ELECTRICAL BAND 1969 CAPITOL US ST165
BRIAN RADING V B (— ( ) FIVE MAN ELECTRICAL BAND 19 PICKWICK US SPC 3289
RICK BELANGER D V (— ( ) COMING OF AGE 197 LIONEL 1101
TEDDY GEROW SAX K V(— ( ) GOODBYE & BUTTERFLIES 19 LIONEL 1100 US MGM 4725
MIKE BELANGER V PERC(— ( ) SWEET PARADISE 19 LIONEL 1009
( ) FIND THE ONE 1972 LIONEL US

F59B FIVE ROYALES F59B

LOWMAN PAULING V (— ( ) DEDICATED TO YOU 19 KING 580
CLARENCE PAULING V (— ( ) FIVE ROYALES 19 KING 678
JOHNNY MOORE V (— ( ) ALL TIME HITS 19 KING 955
OBEDIAH CARTER V (— ( ) ROCKIN' 19 APOLLO 488
JOHNNY TANNER V (

F59C FIVE OR SIX F59C

(A) POLAR EXPOSURE 1981 CHERRY RED UK CHERRY23

F59D FIVE SPECIAL F59D

(A) SPECIAL EDITION 1980 ELEKTRA US 270 K52230

F60 ROBERTA FLACK F60

ROBERTA FLACK V PNO(ALL — (A) FIRST TAKE 1969 ATLANTIC US 8230 UK588 204
WITH — (A) FIRST TAKE 1971 ATLANTIC RI UK K40040
JOHN PIZZARELLI G (A — (B) CHAPTER TWO 1970 ATLANTIC US 1569 UK 2400 023
RON CARTER B (A — (B) CHAPTER TWO 1971 ATLANTIC RI UK K40097
RAY LUCAS D (A — (C) QUIET FIRE 1971 ATLANTIC US 1594 UK K40297
FRANK WESS SAX (A — (D) & DONNIE HATHAWAY 1972 ATLANTIC US 7716 UK K40380
SELDON POWELL SAX (A — (E) KILLING ME SOFTLY 1973 ATLANTIC US 7271
BENNIE POWELL TROM (A — (E) KILLING ME SOFTLY 1973 ATLANTIC US 19154 UK K50021
JOE NEWMAN TPT (A — (F) FEEL LIKE MAKIN LOVE 1975 ATLANTIC US 18131 UK K50049
JIMMY NOTTINGHAM TPT (A — (G) BLUE LIGHTS IN THE BASEMENT 1977 ATLANTIC US 19149 UK K50440
REGGIE LUCAS G (GHJ — (H) ROBERTA FLACK 1978 ATLANTIC US 19186 UK K50495
HOWARD KING D V (GHJ — (J) FEATURING DONNIE HATHAWAY 1980 ATLANTIC US 16013 UK K50696
JIM GILSTRAP V (G — (K) LIVE & MORE 1981 ATLANTIC US 2/7004
DAVID SPINOZZA G (GH
HARRY WHITTAKER K (GHJ — (AB) FIRST TAKE / CHAPTER TWO 1975 ATLANTIC RI UK K60062
RONNIE FOSTER K (GHJ — ( ) FIRST TIME I SAW YOU 19 PICKWICK SHM 3022
DAVE CAREY PERC (GH
GARY KING PERC (G — DON GROLNICK K (G — PAUL GRIFFIN K (GH — MICHAEL KAMEN OBOE (G
ROB MOUNSEY K (GH — LEON PENDARVISK V (GH — GWEN GUTHRIE V (GHJ — ANTHONY JACKSON B (GHJ
BRENDA WHITE V (GHJ — BASIL FEARRINGTON B (GHJ — WILL LEE B (GH — LANI GROVES V (GH
JIMMY MAELEN PERC (G — STEVE GADD D (GH — JIMMY WONG D (G — IDRIS MUHAMMAD D (G
ALLEN SCHWARZBERG D (G — MTUME PERC (GH — ERROL BENNETT PERC (GHJ — DONNY HATHAWAY V PNO(DJ
EUGENE McDANIELS V (G — ZACK SANDERS V (GH — HIRAM BULLOCK G (HJ — CLIFF MORRIS G (H
MONTY ALEXANDER K (H — HOWARD SCHNEIDER K (H — BRIAN ALLSOP B (H — ULLLANDA McCULLOUGH V (H
ELEANORE MILLS V (J — JOCELYN SHAW V (J — ERIC MERCURY V (J — ED WALSH SYN (J
HUBERT EAVES SYN (J — STEVE FERRONE D (H — GARY MURE D (H — WARREN CHIASSON PERC (H
ANGELO DIBRACCIO SAX (H — LARRY ALEXANDER PERC (H — SHERRY WILSON FLT (H — FRANK LLOYD V (H
LUTHER VANDROSS V (HJ — YVONNE LEWIS V (GH — TOMMY SMITH V (H — ELURIEL BARFIELD B (J
RAY JONES K (J — RAY CHEW K (J — HUGH McCRACKEN G (GH — JEFF MIRONOV G (GHJ
JOHN TROPEA G (GJ — DENIECE WILLIAMS V (G

F60A FLAME F60A

JIMMY CRESPO G (A — (A) QUEEN OF THE NEIGHBOURHOOD 1977 RCA PL 12160
FRANK RUBY G (A — (B) FLAME 1978 RCA US 2690
MARGE RAYMOND V (A

F60B FLAIRCK F60B

( ) GEVECHT MET DE ENGEI 1980 POLYDOR NL 2925 097
( ) VARIATIONS ON A LADY 1980 POLYDOR NL 2480 508
( ) LIVE IN AMSTERDAM DBL 1980 POLYDOR NL 2646 103

F61 FLAMIN' GROOVIES F61

CYRIL JORDAN G V (123ABDEGJK — (A) SNEAKERS 10" LP 1969 SNAZZ US 2371
GEORGE ALEXANDER B (123ABCEGJK — (A) SNEAKERS 10" LP 1975 SKYDOG US FGG 803
TIM LYNCH G (ABDE — (B) SUPER NAZZ 1970 EPIC US 26487
DANNY MIHM D (12ABDE — (D) FLAMINGO 1971 KAMA SUTRA US KSBS 2021
RON GRECO D (— (D) THIS IS (FLAMINGO) 1975 METRONOME EURO 201 707
JAMES FARRELL G (23G — (E) TEENAGE HEAD 1971 KAMA SUTRA US KSBS 2031
CHRIS WILSON G V (23GJK — (DE)FLAMINGO/HEAD 1976 KAMA SUTRA UK KSMD101/1
JEAN CHARLES COSTA V(E — (DE)COLLECTORS ITEMS (HEAD/FLAMINGO 1976 KAMA SUTRA 940 106/7
JIM DICKINSON PNO (E — (DE) FLAMIN' GROOVIES DBL 19 POLYDOR UK 2683 003
TERRY RAE D (— (F) GREASE (EP) 197 SKYDOG US 66001
DAVID WRIGHT D (3KGJ — (G) SHAKE SOME ACTION 1976 SIRE UK 9103 251
MIKE WILHELM G (KJ — (G) SHAKE SOME ACTION 197 SIRE US 7521 GER 26464
ROY A LONEY V (1ABDE — (G) SHAKE SOME ACTION 197 PHILIPS EURO 6370 804
STEPHEN GOLDMAN PROS (B — (H) MORE GREASE(EP) 19 SKYDOG US 66002 FR FG13
RICHARD ROBINSON PROD (DE — (I) STILL SHAKIN' 1976 BUDDAH US 5683
DAVE EDMUNDS G PROD(GJ — (I) STILL SHAKIN' 1976 PHILIPS EURO 940541
KANN BERG V (E — (J) NOW 1978 SIRE US 6059 UK 7059
R MELTZER V (— (J) NOW 1978 SIRE 9103 333
ROGER BECHINAN PROD (K — (J) NOW 1978 SIRE 7222 103
(K) JUMPIN IN THE NIGHT 1979 SIRE UK SRK 6067
(EP) SLOW DEATH 197 UA UK 406
(EP) SHAKE SOME ACTION 197 SIRE UK 6198 086
(EP) ABSOLUTELY SWEET MARY 197 SIRE UK SIR 4018
(EP) FEEL A WHOLE LOT BETTER 1978 SIRE UK 6078 619

F61A FLAMIN' OH'S F61A

ROBERT WILKINSON G V (A — (A) FLAMIN' OH'S 1980 FAT CITY US 2504
BOB MEIDE PNO (A
JODY RAY B (A — JOSAF H BEHREND K V (A

F62 FLAMING YOUTH F62

RONNIE CARYL B (A — (A) ARK 2 19 UNI 73075
GORDON SMITH G (A — (A) ARK 2 1969 FONTANA UK STL 5533
PHIL COLLINS D (A
BRIAN CHATTON K (A

F62A TOMMY FLANDERS F62A

TOMMY FLANDERS V (A — (A) THE MOONSTONE 1969 VERVE US 3075 UK SVLP 6020
JERRY SCHEFF (A
BRUCE LANGHORN (A — DICK ROSMINI (A — MICHAEL BOTTS (A — DENNIS McCARTHY (A

F63 FLASH F63

TONY KAYE K (A — (A) FLASH 1972 SOVEREIGN UK SVNA 7251 US CAPITOL 11040
PETER BANKS BAN G V SYN (ABC — (B) FLASH IN THE CAN 1972 SOVEREIGN UK SVNA 7255 US CAPITOL 11115
COLIN CARTER V D (ABC — (C) OUT OF OUR HANDS 1973 SOVEREIGN UK SVNA 7260 US CAPITOL 11218
RAY BENNETT K B G V SYN(ABC — (C) OUT OF OUR HANDS 1973 SOVEREIGN IMP XHVL 1026
MIKE HOUGH D PERC (ABC

F64 FLASH CADILLAC F64

FLASH CADILLAC GV (ABCD — (A) FLASH CADILLAC & THE CONTINENTAL 1973 EPIC US 31787 UK 65438
WARREN'BUTCH'KNIGHT B V(ABC — (B) NO FACE LIKE CHROME 1974 EPIC US 32488 UK 65870
SAM McFADIN G V (A — (C) SONS OF BEACHES 1975 PRIVATE STOCK US 2003
WALLY STEWART D (C — (C) SONS OF BEACHES 1975 PRIVATE STOCK UK 1002 +2012
ANGELO MOE K V (A C — (D) ROCK'N'ROLL FOREVER 19 EPIC US 33465
GEORGE ROBINSON SAX (A
JOHN MASION D V (A — LINN PHILLIPS G V (— TOXEY FRENCH PROD (C — SPIDER BEMENT SAX (C

F65 FLASH FEARLESS F65

ELKIE BROOKS V (A — (A) FLASH FEARLESS Vs THE ZORG WOMEN 1975 CHRYSALIS UK CHR 1081
FRANKIE MILLER (US) V (A
ALICE COOPER V (A — JAMES DEWAR V (A — JIM DANDY V (A — KAY GARNER V (A
MADDY PRIOR V (A — DOREEN CHANTER V (A — LESLEY DUNCAN V (A — KEITH MOON V (A
THUNDERTHIGHS V (A — JOHN ENTWISTLE V B (A — MICK GRABHAM G (A — CARMINE APPICE D (A
NICKY HOPKINS K (A — MIKE DEACON K (A — GRAHAM DEACON PERC (A — ROBERT JOHNSON G (A
JOHN WEIDER G (A — BILL BRUFORD D (A — JUSTIN HAYWARD G (A — JIM FRANK HCA (A
EDDIE JOBSON K VLN(A — STEVE PETTICAN G (A — CHICK CHURCHILL K (A — HOWIE CASEY SAX (A
JILL MACKINTOSH V (A — KIRK DUNCAN PNO (A — KENNEY JONES D (A

F65A FLASH AND THE PAN F65A

GEORGE YOUNG SYN V(AB — (A) FLASH AND THE PAN 1979 ENSIGN UK ENVY6 US EPIC 36018
HARRY VANDA G V (AB — (A) FLASH AND THE PAN 1979 MERCURY EURO 6310 956
WARREN MORGAN PNO (B — (B) LIGHTS IN THE NIGHT 1980 ENSIGN UK ENVY13 US EPIC 36432
RAY ARNOTT D (B — (B) LIGHTS IN THE NIGHT 1980 MERCURY EURO 6359 012
LES KARSKI B (B

F65B STEVE FLASHMAN F65B

STEVE FLASHMAN G K V(AB — (A) FREEFALL 1980 KINGSWAY UK KMR313
(B) SIGNWRITER 1981 KINGSWAY UK KMB349

F65C FLASHMAN F65C

(A) FLASHMAN 1979 VANGUARD US VSD79403

F65D FLATLANDERS F65D

JIMMY GILMORE G V (A — (A) ONE MORE ROAD(1972 REC) 1980 CHARLY UK CR 30189
JOE ELY G V (A
BUTCH HANCOCK V (A — TOMMY HANCOCK FDL (A — SYLVESTER RICE B (A — STEVE WESSON SAW?(A

F65E FLAVIUM F65E

(A) NO KIDDING 1980 POLYDOR NL 2925 096
(B) FLAVIUM LIVE 1980 POLYDOR NL 2925 170
(C) BEST OF 1980 ELF NL 9586

F65F MICK FLEETWOOD F65F

MICK FLEETWOOD G PERC V(A (A) THE VISITOR 1981 RCA US AFLI 4080 UK 5044
GEORGE HAWKINS V B K G(A
PETER GREEN G V (A LORD TIKI PERC(A TODD SHARP G (A GEORGE HARRISON G V(A
IAN BAIRNSON G (A MIKE MORAN SYN (A EBALI GBIKO ENSEMBLE (A ACCRO R C CHOIR V(A
ADJO & SUPERBRAINS (A GHANA FOLKLORE GROUP (A

F66 FLEETWOOD MAC F66

MICK FLEETWOOD D (ALL (A) FLEETWOOD MAC 1968 BLUE HORIZON UK 7 63200 US EPIC 26402
JOHN McVIE B (ALL (A) FLEETWOOD MAC 1973 EMBASSY 31036 + 31494
CHRISTINE McVIE V K(BGHJKLMNOPQR XY (B) MR WONDERFULL 1968 BLUE HORIZON UK 7 63205
PETER GREEN G V (ABCDEGWXYZV (C) BLUES JAM AT CHESS 1969 BLUE HORIZON US 3801 UK 7 66227
JEREMY SPENCER G V (ABCDEFGXYZV (C) FLEETWOOD MAC IN CHICAGO 1969 SIRE US 3715+2XS 6009
BOB BRUNNING B (A (D) THEN PLAY ON 1969 REPRISE US 6368 UK MIDI24001
BOB WELCH G V (HKLMJ (D) THEN PLAY ON 1970 REPRISE UK K 44103
STEVE GREGORY SAX (B (E) PIOUS BIRD OF GOOD OMEN 1969 BLUE HORIZON (COMP) UK 7 63215
RAY LINDSAY G (RQ (E) PIOUS BIRD OF GOOD OMEN 1981 EMBASSY UK 32050
JOHNNY ALMOND SAX (B (F) KILN HOUSE 1970 REPRISE US 6408 UK 9004 + K 54001
ROLAND VAUGHAN SAX (B (G) ORIGINAL FLEETWOOD MAC 1971 SIRE US 6045 UK CBS 63875
DUSTER BENNETT HCA (B (H) FUTURE GAMES 1971 REPRISE UUS6465 UK K 44153
DAVE HOWARD SAX (B (J) BARE TREES 1972 REPRISE US 2080+2278 UK K 44181
DANNY KIRWAN V (CDEFHXV (K) PENGUIN 1973 REPRISE US 2138 UK K 44235
BOB WESTON G (LK (L) MYSTERY TO ME 1973 REPRISE US 2158+2279 UK K 44248
MARTIN BIRCH G (L (M) HEROES ARE HARD TO FIND 1974 REPRISE US 2196 UK K 54026
DAVE WALKER HCA V(K (N) FLEETWOOD MAC 1975 REPRISE US 2225 +2281 UK K 54043
STEVE NYE K (K (O) RUMOURS 1977 WB US 3010 UK K 56344
RALPH RICHARDSON PERC (K (P) TUSK DBL 1980 WB US 3350 UK K 66088
RUSSEL VALDEZ PERC (K (Q) LIVE DBL 1980 WB US 3500 UK K 66097
FRED TOTESANT PERC (K (R) MIRAGE 1982 WB US 23607
WADDY WACHTEL G (N
STEVE NICKS V (NOPQR (U) ENGLISH ROSE 1969 EPIC US26446 75 RI 33740 UK CBS 22025
LINDSEY BUCKINGHAM G V(NOPQR (V) BLACK MAGIC WOMAN 197 EPIC US 30632 UK 31798
OTIS SPANN PNO (C (W) GREATEST HITS 1971 CBS UK CBS 69011
WILLLIE DIXON B (C (X) VINTAGE YEARS 1975 SIRE 3706+ 6006 UK CBS 88227
WALTER HORTON HCA (C (Y) ALBATROSS 1977 EMBASSY UK 31569
GUITAR BUDDY G (C (Z) MAN OF THE WORLD 1978 CBS UK 83110
HONEYBOY EDWARDS G (C ( ) BEST OF 1978 REPRISE UK K 44138
SP LEARY D (C ( ) BLACK MAGIC WOMAN 1980 EMBASSY UK 31798
SNEAKY PETE STEEL(M
J T BROWN V SAX(C EDDIE BOYD V PNO (E TONY TORARO PERC (Q JEFFREY SOVA K (Q

F66A JOY FLEMING F66A

JOY FLEMING V (ALL (A) JOY FLEMING 1973 INTERCORD 26011/7
GARY UNWIN B (ABC (B) LIVE 1974 ATLANTIC 40566
KEITH FORSEY D (ABC (C) THIS IS MY LIFE 1974 ATLANTIC 50056
RALF NOWY FLT (ABC
THOR BALDURSSON K (BC DON ANDERSON PERC (B SYLVESTER LEVAY K (ABC PAUL VINCENT G (ABC
BERNIE PROCK PERC (A RALPH SIEGEL K (A MARTIN HARRISON D (B VICTOR BEHRENS TPT (C
ANDY MARX G (A

F66B FLESH EATERS F66B

(A) NO QUESTIONS ASKED 1980 UPSETTER US 34
(B) A MINUTE TO PRAY A SECOND TO DIE 1981 INITIAL IRC 007

F66C FLESHTONES F66C

PETER ZAREMBA V K HCA(A (A) BLAST OFF 1982 ROIR CASS A107
KEITH STRONG G V (A
JAN MAREK PAKULSKI B V (A LENNY CALDERONE D V (A ALAN VEGA V (A MARTY THAU PROD (A

F66D ROBERT FLEISCHMAN F66D

ROBERT FLEISCHMAN (A (A) A PERFECT STRANGER 1979 ARISTA US 4220

F67 FLICKS F67

TOMMY WILLIS G (A (A) GO FOR THE EFFECT 1979 ARIOLA ARL 5024
JOHN BUTLER G V (A
DAVE SMITH D V (A JOHNNY KAPP G V (A LEE STRZELCZYK B (A

F67A FLIGHT F67A

(A) FLIGHT 1976 CAPITOL US 11458
(B) INCREDIBLE 1976 CAPITOL US 11536

F67B FLINT F67B

DON BREWER D V (A (A) FLINT 1979 CBS
MEL SCHACHER B G V(A
CRAIG FROST K (A BILLY ELWORTHY G V (A

F68 FLO & EDDIE F68

FLO(MARK VOLMAN) V (ALL (A) PHLORESCENT LEECH & EDDIE 1972 REPRISE US 2097 UK K44201
EDDIE (HOWARD KAYLAN)V(ALL (B) FLO & EDDIE 1973 REPRISE US 2141 UK K44234
JIM PONS B (AB (C) IMMORAL ILLEGAL & FATTENING 1974 CBS US 33554
AYNSLEY DUNBAR D (ABC (D) MOVING TARGETS 1976 CBS US 33262 UK 81509
GARY ROWLES G (AB (E) ROCK STEADY WITH FLO & EDDIE 1981 EPIPHANY US ELP 4010
DON PRESTON K (A
DANNY KOOTCH G (C LEE SKLAR B (C IAN UNDERWOOD K (C JOHN HERREN K (B
LYNN BLESSING (A CLAUDE WILLIAMS (A ERIC SCOTT B (C ANDY CAHAN D K (CE
PHILL REED G (C EARL CHINNA SMITH G(E AUGUSTOS PABLO K (E LEASLIE BUTLER K (E
ASTON BARRETT B (E SANTA DAVIS D (E STICKY THOMPSON PERC (E ALBERT WING SAX (E
JIMMY'SENYA' HAYNES B (E PHIL RAMOCAN K (E ARNOLD BRACKENRIDGE HRNS(E ELNATHAN BRACKENRIDGE HRNS(E
ENROY GRANT SAX (E NAMBO TROM (E DEAN FRAZIER SAX (E WALT FOWLER TROM (E

F69 FLOATING BRIDGE F69

RICK DANGEL G (A (A) FLOATING BRIDGE 1969 LIBERTY UK LPS 83271
JOE JOHANSEN G (A (A) BROUGHT UP WRONG 1970 VAULT US 124
JOE JOHNSON B (A
MIKE MARINELLI D (A

F69A FLOATING HOUSE BAND F69A

(A) FLOATING HOUSE BAND 1972 TAKOMA US 1029

F69B FLOATING OPERA F69B

STEVE WELKOM G (A — (A) THE FLOATING OPERA 1971 EMBRYO US 730
JOHN NEMEROVSKI PNO (A
CAROL LEES K (A GARY MUNCE B (A ARTIE ALINKOFF D (A

F69C FLOCK OF SEAGULLS F69C

A SCORE D (A — (A) A FLOCK OF SEAGULLS 1982 ARISTA US 6600
M SCORE V G K(A
P REYNOLDS G (A F MAUDSLEY B V (A

F70 FLOCK F70

JERRY GOODMAN VLN (AB — (A) FLOCK 1969 CBS US 9911 UK 63733
FELIX PAPPALRDI V (C — (A) FLOCK 1981 EMBASSY RI UK 31910
FRED GLICKSTEIN G V (ABC — (B) DINOSAUR SWAMPS 1971 CBS US30007 UK 64055
JAMES L HIRSEN K V (C — (C) INSIDE OUT 1975 MERCURY US 11035 UK 9100 016
JERRY SMITH B V (ABC — (AB) FLOCK (DBL) 1972 CBS NL 67278
RON KARPMAN D V (ABC
MIKE ZYDOWSKY VLN (C RICK CANOFF SAX (AB TOM WEBB (AB FRANK POSA (A

F70A FLOH DE COLOGNE F70A

BRITTA BATTRUSCHAT (A — (A) VIETNAM 1968 PLANE 33101
HANSI FRANCHI D (ABC — (B) FLIESSBANDBABYS BEAT SHOW 1970 OHR GER OMM556000
DIETER KLEMM V (ABCD — (C) ROCKOPER PROFITGEIER LIVE 1971 OHR GER OMM556010
MARKUS SCHMIDT G K (ABCD — (D) GEYER SYMPHONIE 1973 OHR GER OMM556033
DICK STADTLER B (ABCD — (E) LUCKY STREIK LIVE 1973 OHR GER OMM556029
GERD WOLLSCHON V (ABCD — (F) MUMIEN 1974 PLANE 99201
DIETER SUVERKRUP (A
THEO KONIG (D

F70B HERBIE FLOWERS F70B

HERBIE FLOWERS B (AB — (A) PLANT LIFE 1975 PHILIPS 9109 204
JACK COLLIER B (A — (B) A LITTLE POTTY 1980 NOTE NTS 216
TONY NEWMAN D (A
RONNIE VERRELL D (A ANDY WHITE D (A MARK SINGER D (A FRANK RICOTTI PERC (A
RAY COOPER PERC (A CHRIS SPEDDING G(A ALAN PARKER G (A BRYAN DALY G (A
JACK EMBLOW ACC (A DAVID SNELL HARP (A ALBERT HALL HRNS(A GREG BOWEN HRNS (A
ALAN DOWNEY HRNS (A TED BARKER HRNS (A DUNCAN LAMONT HRNS(A F GABARRO CELLO(A
W DEMONT CELLO(A JOANNE WILLIAMS V(A MADELINE BELL V (A KAY GARNER V (A
GILLIAN LINDSAY V (A SUE CHAPMAN V (A CATHERINE FAULKNER V (A GEORGE FENTON V (A
ROSSETTA HIGHTOWER V(A EDDIE LESTER V (A NICK CURTIS V (A FRANK HOLMES V (A
TONY MANSELL V (A

F71 FLOW F71

JOHN WINTER SAXK (A — (A) FLOW 1970 CTI US 1003
DON FELDER G (A
CHUCK NEWCOMB V B (A MIKE BARNETT D (A ED SHAUGHNESSY PERC (A ANGEL ALLENDE PERC (A
JOHNNY PACHECO PERC (A

F71A FLOWER TRAVELLING BAND F71A

JOE YAMANAKA V HCA(BCDE — (A) CHALLENGE (as 'THE FLOWERS' 1969 CBS JAP 10063
GEORGE WADE D (ALL — (B) ANYWHERE 1970 PHILIPS JAP 8507
HIDKI ISHIMA G (BCDE — (C) SATORI 1971 ATLANTIC JAP 8056
JUN KOZUKI G B (BCDE — (D) MADE IN JAPAN 1972 ATLANTIC JAP 8187
YUCA UCHIDA V PERC(AB — (E) MADE UP DBL 1973 ATLANTIC JAP 5073/74
REMI ASOH V (A
KATSUHIKO KOBAYASHI STEEL(A KEN HASHIMOTO B (A

F72 EDDIE FLOYD F72

EDDIE FLOYD V (ALL — ( ) KNOCK ON WOOD 1967 ATCO UK 228 014
ISAAC HAYES V (X — ( ) KNOCK ON WOOD 1967 STAX US 714
DAVID PORTER V (X — ( ) NEVER FOUND A GIRL 19 STAX US 2002
JOHNNIE TAYLOR V (X — ( ) RARE STAMPS 19P GTAX US9 2011
BOOKER T JONES G K B(X — ( ) YOU'VE GOT TO HAVE EDDIE 197 POLYDOR UK 2363010 US STAX2017
AL JACKSON D (X — ( ) CALIFORIA GIRL 19 STAX US 2029
( ) DOWN TO EARTH 19 STAX US 2041
( ) THINK ABOUT IT 19 ATCO US 7023
( ) SOUL STREET 1974 STAX US 5512 UK 1002
( ) BABY LAY YOUR HEAD 1975 STAX US 3016
( ) EXPERIENCE 1977 MALACO 6352
(X) CHRONICLE 1978 STAX US 4122 UK 7005

F73 FLYING ACES F73

MARTIN ACE G B V(AB — (A) 1975 (B) 1977
GEORGINA ACE G B V(AB
RICHARD TREECE G (B MICK GIBBON D (B

F74 FLYING BURRITO BROTHERS F74

CHRIS ETHRIDGE K B V(AFE — (A) GILDED PALACE OF SIN 1969 A&M US 4175 UK 931
CHRIS HILLMAN G V B (ABCDEKO — (B) BURRITO DELUXE 1970 A&M US 4258 UK 983
JON CORNEAL D (AE — (C) FLYING BURRITO BROTHERS 1971 A&M US 4295 UK 64295
GRAM PARSONS G V MAND (ABEFKO — (D) LAST OF THE RED HOT BURRITOS 1971 A&M US 4343 UK 64343
PETE KLEINOW STEEL(ABCEFJKMOPK — (E) CLOSE UP THE HONKY TONKS (COMP) 1974 A&M US 3631 UK 63631
BERNIE LEADON G V (BCDEKO — (F) FLYING AGAIN 1975 CBS US 33817 UK 61984
RICK ROBERTS G V (CDEHLO — (G) HOT BURRITO 1975 ARIOLA US 9379 NL 85272
MIKE CLARKE D (BCDEKO — (H) LIVE IN AMSTERDAM 1975 BUMBLE US 301 ARIOLA NL 86439
BYRON BERLINE FDL (ABDELK — (H) LIVE IN AMSTERDAM 1975 PHONOGRAM 6641 144
ROGER BUSH B (DHL — (J) AIRBORNE 1976 CBS US 34222 UK 81433
KENNY WERTZ G V (DEHL — (K) SLEEPLESS NIGHTS 1976 A&M US 4578 UK 64578
AL PERKINS D (DEK — (L) BLUEGRASS SPECIAL 19 ARIOLA NL 86501
ALAN MUNDE G V (HL — (M) LIVE FROM TOKYO 1978 REGENCY US 79001
HERB PEDERSEN G V (EOK — (M) CLOSE ENCOUNTERS TO THE WEST COAST 78 BETTERDAYS JAP Yx 7218
ERIC DALTON G (HL — (N) POP CHRONIK (DBL) 19 ARIOLA NL 89136
DON BECK STEEL(HL — (O) HONKY TONK HEAVEN (DBL) 19 ARIOLA NL 87585
JAMES BURTON G (K — (P) HEARTS ON THE LINE 1980 CURB US 37004
SKIP BATTIN B (JMP
GENE PARSONS D (FJ EDDIE HOH D (AE SAM GOLDSTEIN D (AE POPEYE PHILLIPS D (AE
SPOONER OLDHAM K (F GIB GUILBEAU G FDL(FJMP JOEL SCOTT HILL G V (FJ ED PONDER D (
LEON RUSSELL PNO (BE LEOPOLD CARBAJAL ACC(B FRANK BLANCO PERC (B TOMMY JOHNSON HRNS(B

(CONTINUED)

F74 (CONTINUED) FLYING BURRITO BROTHERS F74

BUDDY CHILDERS HRNS (B   GREG HARRIS G BAN V(M   GENE CLARK V (EO   JOHN BELAND G V (P
RON TUTT D (K   EARL BALL PNO (C   BOB GIBSON G (C   MIKE DEASY G (C
STEVIE WONDER K (J   JIMMI SEITER PERC(J   LUIS CABAZA K (J   JAMIE FAUNT B (J
WARREN PEMBERTON D (J   MICK McGEE D (P   KIM CARNES V (P   CHARLES HARWOOD K (P
MARK HUDSON (P   ALAN ESTES (P   TOM HENSLEY (P   RON KRASINSKI (P
JOHN HOBBS (P   DOLLY PARTON V (P   DAVID WHEATLEY (P   GLEN D HARDIN PNO (K
HENRY LEWY PROD (B   JIM DICKSON PROD (B   EMORY GORDY B (K

F74A FLYING CIRCUS F74A

(A) PREPARED IN PEACE 1970 CAPITOL US ST11147 HARVEST UK SHSP4010

F74B FLYING ISLAND F74B

JEFF BOVA K TPT((A) FLYING ISLAND 19 VANGUARD US 79359
RAY SMITH G ((B) ANOTHER KIND OF SPACE 1976 vANGUARD US 79368
BILL BARON D (
FAITH FRAIOLI VLN (THOM PREL B (A

F74C FLYING LIZARDS F74C

PATTI PALLADIN V (B   (A) FLYING LIZARDS 1980 VIRGIN US 13137 UK V2150
STEVE BERESFORD K G B(A   (A) FLYING LIZARDS 1980 VIRGIN GER 201426
JJ JOHNSON D PERC(B   (B) FOURTH WALL 1981 VIRGIN UK V2190
DAVID CUNNINGHAM G VLN K V(B   (B) FOURTH WALL 1981 VIRGIN GER 203204
PETER GORDON SAX (B
ROBERT FRIPP G (B   GARETH SAGER SAX (B   JULIAN MARSHALL K V (B   CHERYL LEWIS V (B
V HALLER B (B   MICHAEL NYMAN PNO (B   LUCY SKEAPING (B   NICK HAYLEY (B
BEN GROVE B (B   EDWARD PILLINGER K (B   RORY ALLAM K (B   ANNE BARNARD HRN (B
STEVE SAUNDERS TROM (B   KEITH THOMPSON SAX (B

F74D FLYING MACHINE F74D

TONY NEWMAN G (A   (A) DOWN TO EARTH 19 PYE NSPL 18328
STUART COLEMAN B V (A
STEVE JONES G V (A   PAUL WILKINSON D V (A

F75 FLYING SAUCERS F75

SANDY FORD G V (A   (A) KEEP ON COMING 1978 ALASKA UK 101 CHARLY UK CR30207
NIGGSY OWEN G   (B) SOME LIKE IT HOT 1981 EMI UK EMC3366
PETE PRITCHARD B ((EP) BALLAD OF JOHNNY RED 19 CHARLY UK CEP121
ROLLIN' DANNY D (

F75A FLYING SAUCERS F75A

( ) WATERGATE 19 IX CHAINS US 9000

F75B FLYING SQUAD F75B

IAN MUIR G (A   (A) FLYING SQUAD 1978 EPIC UK 82875
MONTY McMONAGLE G (A
GEORGE CROSSAN B K V(A   ALEX CALDER G V (A   JIM KELLY D (A

F75C FLYIN' SPIDERZ F75C

GUUS G V (A   (A) FLYIN' SPIDERZ 1977 EMI NL 25725
AAD B V (A   (B) LET IT CRAWL 1977 EMI GER 26049
KOOS G V (AB
HENRI D PERC V(AB
JOHN B V (B   APPIE BAARS SAX (B

F76 FLYS F76

NEIL O'CONNOR G V K(AB   (A) WAIKIKI BEACH REFUGEES 1978 EMI UK EMC 3249
DAVID FREEMAN G V (AB   (B) OWN 1979 EMI UK EMC 3316
JOE HUGHES B (AB   (EP) BUNCH OF FIVES 1977 ZAMA UK BSS 209
PETE KING D (A
GRAHAM DEACON D (B   VANCE ANDERSON V PERC(A   MIKE FINESILVER V PERC(A   WILLY BARRETT FDL(A
LYNN DOBSON SAX (A   KEN FREEMAN SYN STR(A

F77 FOCUS F77

THIJS VAN LEER FLT SYN K V(ABCDEFGHI   (A) IN & OUT OF FOCUS 1971 POLYDOR UK 2344 003 US SIRE 97027
(A) IN AND OUT OF FOCUS 197 RI US SIRE 7404
JAN AKKERMANN G PERC (ABCDEFG   (B) MOVING WAVES 1971 BLUE HORIZON UK 2931 002
(B) MOVING WAVES 1971 POLYDOR UK RI 2931 002 US SIRE 7401
HANS ERIC CLEUVER D(AE   (C) FOCUS THREE 1972 POLYDOR UK 2659 016 US SIRE 3901
MARTIN DRESDEN B(AE   (D) AT THE RAINBOW 1973 POLYDOR UK 2443 118 US SIRE 7408
PIERRE VAN DER LINDEN D(BCEF   (E) HAMBURGER CONCERTO 1974 POLYDOR UK 2442 124 US ATCO 36100
CYRIL HAVERMANS B(B   (F) SHIP OF MEMORIES 1974 HARVEST UK SHSP4068 US SIRE 7531
BERT RUITER PERC B(CDEFG   (G) MOTHER FOCUS 1975 POLYDOR UK 2302 036 US ATCO 36117
COLIN ALLEN PERC D(EFG   (G) MOTHER FOCUS 197 POLYDOR ABCR 266 2310 408
DAVID KEMPER D(FG   (H) FOCUS 1975 POLYDOR UK 2384 070
PHILIP CATHERINE G(I   (I) FOCUS CON PROBY 1978 HARVEST IS 11721 IMP EMI 064 25713
STEVE SMITH D(I   (J) DUTCH MASTERS 19 US SIRE 7505
P J PROBY V(I   ( ) MASTERS OF ROCK 1975 EMI 054 25130
EEF ALBERS G(I
MIKE VERNON PROD (BCDE   HUBERT TEREGGEN PROD(AG

F78 DAN FOGELBERG F78

DAN FOGELBERG V K G(ALL   (A) HOME FREE 1973 CBS US 31751 UK 81 31847
WITH   (B) SOUVENIRS 1975 EPIC US 33137 UK 80623
NORBERT PUTNAM B (ABCD   (C) CAPTURED ANGEL 1975 EPIC US 34499 UK 69189
DON HENLEY V (BDE   (D) NETHERLANDS 1977 EPIC US 34185 UK 81574
KENNY BUTTREY D (ADF   (E) TWIN SONS OF DIFFERENT MOTHERS 1978 EPIC US 35339 UK 82774
JOE WALSH G (BD   (F) PHEONIX 1980 EPIC US 35634 UK 83317
GAYLE LEVANT HARP (F   (G) THE INNOCENT AGE 1981 EPIC US·37393 88533
FRANK MAROCCO ACC (D
WELDON MYRICK STEEL G (A   BUDDY SPICHER FDL (A   GLENN FREY V (B   DAVID BRIGGS PNO (A
GLEN SPREEN STRINGS(A   RUSS KUNKEL D (BCD   FARRELL MORRIS PERC (A   AL PERKINS STEEL(BC
JOE VITALE D (D   JOHN DAVID SOUTHER V (DC   JOE LALA PERC (CDE   TIM WEISBERG FLT (DE
JOHN STRONACH PERC (D   HOT DAMN BROTHERS V (C   KENNY PASSARELLI B (B   GRAHAM NASH V (B
JIMMY HASKELL ACC (B   PAUL HARRIS K (F   BRYAN GAROFALO G (B   NEIL LARSEN K (E
BOBBYE HALL PERC (E   ANDY NEWMARK D (E   WILLIE WEEKS B (E   JIM KELTNER D (E
EARL DUMLER HRNS (E   DAVID BREINENTHAL BASSOON(E   JOHN HUG G (E   ANN MASON STOCKTON HARP(E
JOHN ELLIS OBOE (E   VINCENT DE ROSA HRNS(E   GARY COLEMAN PERC (E   FLORENCE WARNER V (E
RANDY MEISNER V (B   JODY BOYER V (B   MARIE OUHRABKA V (B   MIKE UTLEY K (F
GERRY BECKLEY G (B   JODY LINSCOTT CONGA(F   MARTY LEWIS PERC (F   TOM SCOTT SAX (F
JERRY HEY HRNS (F

F79 JOHN FOGERTY F79

JOHN FOGERTY G V (ALL (A) BLUE RIDGE RANGERS 1973 FANTASY UKFT511 US 9415
(B) JOHN FOGERTY 1975 FANTASY UKFT526
(B) JOHN FOGERTY 1975 ASYLUM US7E 1046
(C) HOODOO 1976 ASYLUM US 7E1081

F80 TOM FOGERTY F80

TOM FOGERTY G V (ALL (A) TOM FOGERTY 1972 FANTASY US 9407
STU COOK B G V SYN (C (B) EXCALIBUR 1973 FANTASY US 9413
DOUG CLIFFORD D V (C (C) ZEPHYR NATIONAL 1974 FANTASY US 9448
J C FOGERTY G V (C (D) MYOPIA 1975 FNTASY US 9469
MERL SAUNDERS K V (AB (E) DEAL IT OUT 1981 FANTASY US 9611
JOHN KAHN B (AB
JERRY GARCIA G (B BILL VITT D PERC (AB RUSS GARY G V (AD BILLY MUNDI PERC (A
ROGER COLLINS V (A TOM PHILLIPS G (C GARY POTTERTON G (C STEPHEN MILLER K(D
STEPHEN FUNK K (C JEFF NERELL STEEL DR(C REV RON STALLINGS SAX (C JOHN BLAKELEY G(E
GREG DOUGLAS G (E BILL SWARTZ G (E JOHN ALLAIR K SYN(E MARC RUSSO K(E
MARK ISHAM K (E PEEWEE ELLIS SAX (E TOM LILIENTHAL B (E DAVID HAYES B V(E
JEFF MYER D (E SCOTT MORRIS D (E DANNY KOPELSON V (E MARK SPRINGER V(E
JEANIE TRACY V (E LILLIAN,NETTA & JO=THE STOVELLS V(D

F81 FOGHAT F81

ROD PRICE V DOBRO G (ABCDEFGHJK (A) FOGHAT 1972 BEARSVILLE US 2077 UK K45503
DAVE PEVERETT V G (ABCDEFGHJKL (B) FOGHAT ROCK'N'ROLL 1973 BEARSVILLE US 2136 UK K 45514
NICK JAMESON K G B V (E (C) ENERGISED 1974 BEARSVILLE US 6950 UK K 55500
ROGER EARL D (ABCDEFGHJKL (D) ROCK'N'ROLL OUTLAWS 1974 BEARSVILLE US 6956 UK K 55502
TONY STEVENS B (ABCD (E) FOOL FOR THE CITY 1975 BEARSVILLE US 6959 UK K 55507
CRAIG MACGREGOR B (FGHJKL (F) NIGHT SHIFT 1977 BEARSVILLE US 6962 UK K 55511
DAVE EDMUNDS G (A (G) LIVE 1977 BEARSVILLE US 6971 UK K 55518
TODD RUNDGREN (A (H) STONE BLUE 1978 BEARSVILLE US 6977
JOHN WILLIAMS (A (J) BOOGIE MOTEL 1979 BEARSVILLE US 6990
ANDY FAIRWEATHER LOW V(A (K) TIGHT SHOES 1980 BEARSVILLE US 6999 UK ILPS9637
ALTO REED SAX (K (K) TIGHT SHOES 1980 BEARSVILLE EURO 202457
ERIK CARTWRIGHT B (L (L) GIRLS TO CHAT,BOYS TO BOUNCE 1981 BEARSVILLE US 3578 EURO 203917
JIMMY AMBROSIA K (K
COLIN EARL K (K

F81A ELLEN FOLEY F81A

ELLEN FOLEY V (A (A) NIGHT OUT 1979 EPIC UK 83718
KERRYN TOLHURST G (A (B) SPIRIT OF ST LOUIS 1981 EPIC US 36984 UK 84809
IAN HUNTER K V PERC (A
TOM MANDEL K (A HILLY MICHAELS D (A MARTIN BRILEY B (A RORY DODD V (A
MICK RONSON G V K PERC(A

F81B FOODBAND F81B

WOLF MAAHN V G (A (A) FOODBAND 1979 ELECTRIC TRIX10
AXEL MANRICO HEILHECKER G V(A
MATHIAS KEUL B K V (A JUMPY ZERLETT K V (A JAN DIX D V (A WOLFGANG BULLMEYER B(A
LYN DOBSON SAX (A ZWIEBEL B (A PACO SAVAL V (A MIDNIGHT HANDCLAP SEC V(A

F81C THE FOOL F81C

SEEMON POSTHUMA (A (A) FOOL 1969 MERCURY US 61178 UK 20138
MARIJKE KOGER (A
JOSJE LEEGER (A BARRY FINCH (A

F81D THE FOOLS F81D

RICK BARTLETT G (B (A) SOLD OUT 1980 EMI US 17024 UK AML 3008
DOUG FORMAN B (B (B) HEAVY MENTAL 1981 EMI US 17046
CHRIS PEDRICK D (B
STACEY PEDRICK G (B MIKE GIRARD V (B

F82 FOOLS GOLD F82

TOM KELLY V G B(AB (A) FOOLS GOLD 1976 ARISTA US 5500 UK ARTY 131
DENNY HENSON G V (AB (B) MR LUCKY 1977 CBS US 34828 UK 82148
DOUG LIVINGSTON G K (AB
RON GRINEL D (A KEITH OLSON PERC (A TOM SCOTT SAX (B ANDREW GOLD G (B
DAN FOGELBERG STEEL(B DAVID FOSTER K (B DON FELDER G MAND(B COLIN TULLY SAX (B
MIKE PORCARO B (B JEFF PORCARO D (D JOE WALSH G (B DUNCAN CAMERON G V(B
DAVID PAICH K (B BILL CHAMPLIN K (B WADDY WACHTEL G (B MEL COLLINS SAX(B

F83 FOOT IN COLD WATER F83

BOB HORNE K (AC (A) A FOOT IN COLD WATER 1972 DAFFODIL CAN 16012
HUGHIE LEGGAT B G V(AC (B) SECOND FOOT IN COLD WATER 1973 DAFFODIL CAN 16028
ALEX MACHIN V (AC (C) OR ALL AROUND US 1974 ELEKTRA US 7 1025
PAUL NAUMANN G B (AC (C) A FOOT IN COLD WATER 1974 ELEKTRA UK 52011
DANNY TAYLOR D V (AC (D) BREAKING THROUGH 1976 ANTHEM CAN 1 1008

F83A STEVE FORBERT F83A

STEVE FORBERT HCA G V (ALL (A) ALIVE ON ARRIVAL 1978 NEMPEROR US 35538 UK EPIC 83308
SID McGINNIS G (D (A) ALIVE ON ARRIVAL 1980 EMBASSY UK 32053
STEVE BURGH G (AD (B) JACKRABBIT SLIM 1979 NEMPEROR US 36191 UK EPIC 83879
BARRY LAZAROWITZ D (ACD (C) LITTLE STEVIE ORBIT 1980 NEMPEROR US 36595 UK EPIC 84501
HUGH McDONALD G B (ACD (D) STEVE FORBERT 1982 NEMPEROR US 37434
CLAY BARNES G (D
ROBBIE KONDOR K (ACD HARVEY SHAPIRO STEEL (A DAVID SANBORN SAX (AD BRIAN TORFF B(A
BOBBY OGDIN PNO (B PAUL ERRICO K (BC JOHN GOIN G (B GUNNAR GELLOTE D(B
BOB WRAY B (B ALAN FREEDMAN G (B JACK WILLIAMS B (B ROGER CLARK D(B
JERRY BRIDGES B (B BILL JONES SAX (BC MIKE LEECH B (B RON KELLER TPT(B
DENNIS GOODE TROM (A AVA ALDRIDGE V (B CINDY RICHARDSON V (B MARIE TOMLINSON V(B
SHANE FONTAYNE G (C KEN KOSEK FDL (C BOBBY LLOYD HICKS D (C LARRY CAMPBELL STEEL(D
LENNY PICKETT SAX (D CHUCK WILSON SAX (D GORDON STOKER V (D DWAYNE WEST V (D
NEIL MATTHEWS V (D RAY WALKER V (D YVONNE LEWIS V (D LARITA GASKINS V (D
CHRISTINE WILSHIRE V (D RORY DODD V (D ERIC TROYER V (D PETER ECKLUND HRNS(D
CRIS CIOE SAX (D JOSH SHNEIDER SAX (D ROGER ROSENBERG SAX (D JOE HELLENY TROM (D

F83B FRANKIE FORD F83B

FRANKIE FORD V (ALL (A) ON A SEA CRUISE 19 ACE US 1005
(B) FRANKIE FORD 19 BRIARMEADE US 5002
(EP) BEST OF 19 ACE US EP 105

F83C FORCE 10 F83C

GRIFF STEVENS V SAX(A — (A) FORCE 10 — 1981 WB UK K56932 US 3557
LARRY TUTTLE B V (A
RICK WHITE K V (A — THOMAS BRIGHTON G V (A — JEFF SWISSTACK D (A

F83D JIM FORD F83D

JIM FORD (A — (A) HARLAN COUNTY — 19 WHITE WHALE US 1002

F83E NEAL FORD & THE FANATICS F83E

NEAL FORD V (A — (A) NEAL FORD & THE FANATICS — 19 HICKORY US LPS141
JON PARELES G V (A
W JOHNSON B (A — LAMIER GREIG K (A — JOHN CRAWLEY D (A

F83F ROBBEN FORD F83F

ROBBEN FORD G V (A — (A) THE INSIDE STORY — 1981 ATLANTIC US 16999
ROLAND K (A
RUSSELL FERANTES K (A — JIMMY HASLICK B (A — RICK LAWSON D PERC(A

F84 FOREIGNER F84

MICK JONES K V G (ABCD — (A) FOREIGNER — 1977 ATLANTIC US 18215 UK K50356
IAN McDONALD K G D V (ABC — (B) DOUBLE VISION — 1978 ATLANTIC US 19999 UK K50476
LOU GRAMM V (ABCD — (C) HEAD GAMES — 1979 ATLANTIC US 29999 UK K50651
TOM DOLBY SYN (D — (D) '4' — 1981 ATLANTIC US 16999 UK K50796
DENNIS ELLIOTT D (ABCD — (EP) FEELS LIKE THE FIRST TIME — 1978 ATLANTIC UK K11086
AL GREENWOOD SYN K(ABC
ED GAGLIARDI V B (AB — IAN LLOYD V (BD — MUTT LANGE V (D — BOB MAYO K (D
RICK WILLS G V (D — MARK RIVERS SAX (D — HUGH McCRACKEN G (D — JUNIOR WALKER SAX (D
LARRY FAST SYN (D — MICHAEL FONFARA K (D

F85 FOREST F85

MARTIN WELHAM G V K PERC(AB — (A) FOREST — 1969 HARVEST UK SHVL 760
DEREK ALLENBY K V HCA PERC(AB — (B) FULL CIRCLE — 1970 HARVEST SHVL 784
HADRIAN WELAHM G K V HCA PERC(AB
GORDON HUNTLEY STEEL (B

F85A FOREVER MORE F85A

STEWART FRANCIS D V (AB — (A) YOURS FOREVER MORE — 1970 RCA US LSP 4272 UK SF8016
ALAN GORIE K B (AB — (B) WORDS ON BLACK PLASTIC — 1971 RCA US LSP 4435 UK 3015
ONNIE MAIR G V B(AB
MICK TRAVIS G (AB

F85B DAVID FORMAN F85B

DAVID FORMAN — (A) DAVID FORMAN — 1976 ARISTA US 4084

F85C FORMERLY FAT HARRY F85C

PHIL GREENBERG V G (A — (A) FORMERLY FAT HARRY — 1971 HARVEST UK SHSP 4016
GARY PETERSON V G K PERC(A — (A) FORMERLY FAT HARRY — 1971 CAPITOL US 877
BRUCE BARTHOL B (A
LAURIE ALLEN D (A — NISAR AHMAD GEORGE KHAN SAX (A

F86 SHARON FORRESTER F86

SHARON FORRESTER V (A — (A) SHARON — 1974 ASHANTI SHAN105+ VULCAN
GEOFFREY CHUNG K V G(A
ROBERT BAILEY K (A — PHIL CHEN B (A — RICHARD BAILEY D (A — WINSTON DELANDRO G (A
ALLAN SHARP PERC (A — DEL RICHARDSON HCA (A — MIKE MORAN K (A — HENRY LOWTHER TPT (A
RON CARTHY TPT (A — RAY WARLEIGH HRNS (A — GRAHAM PRESKETT MAND (A — VAL DOUGLAS B (A
MICHAEL RICHARDS D (A — ROBERT LYN PNO (A — EARL LINDO K (A — MALCOLM GRIFFITHS TROM(A
CHRIS MERCER SAX (A — MEL COLLINS SAX (A — MARTIN DROVER TPT (A — MARTYN FORD HRNS (A
38 PIECE ORCHESTRA (A — NINE BACKING SINGERS (A

F86A FORT MUDGE MEMORIAL DUMP F86A

CAROLINE STRATTON (A — (A) FORT MUDGE MEMORIAL DUMP — 197 MERCURY 61256
DAN KEADY (A
JAMES DEPTULA (A — DAVID AMARAL (A — RICHARD CLERICI (A

F86B FORTRESS F86B

DONNY VOSBURGH D (A — (A) HAND IN THE TILL — 1981 ATLANTIC US 19282 UK K50782
ERIC TURNER G (A
JIM WEST V (A — CHARLES SAUZA B (A

F87 FORTUNES F87

BARRY PRITCHARD G V (— (A) FORTUNES — 1965 DECCA LK 4736
DAVID CARR K (— (B) FORTUNES — 1972 CAPITOL ST 21891
ROD ALLEN B (— (C) REMEMBER ING THE FORTUNES — 1976 DECCA REM2
ANDY BROWN D (— ( ) HERE COMES THAT RAINY DAY — 1973 CAPITOL 809
GLEN DALE G V (— ( ) STORM IN A TEACUP — 1972 CAPITOL 11041
SHEL McCRAE (

F88 FOSTER BROTHERS F88

GRAHAM FOSTER G V SYN(A — (A) ON THE LINE — 1977 ROCKET UK ROLL10
MALCOLM FOSTER G V (A
EDDIE WILLIAMS D PERC(A — ROB McINTOSH V K (A — PETE WINGFIELD K (A — STEVE GREGORY HRNS (A
BUD BEADLE SAX (A — GEORGE CHISHOLM TPT (A — MALCOLM GRIFFITHS TROM (A

F88A RONNIE FOSTER F88A

RONNIE FOSTER V K (AB — (A)CHESHIRE CAT — 1975 BLUE NOTE US LA425
DENNIS DAVIS D (AB — (B) LOVE SATELLITE — 1978 CBS UK 83037
LEON CHANCLER PERC (B
ALPHONSO JOHNSON B (B — PAULINHO DA COSTA PERC(B — HARVEY MASON D (B — BYRON MILLER B (B
JERRY PETERS V PNO (B — STEVE WONDER D (B — ROY AYERS VIBES (B — JOE BECK G (A
GEORGE BENSON G (A — WILLIAM ALLEN B (A — GARY KING B (A — JAMES MTUME PERC(A

F89 FOTHERINGAY F89

SANDY DENNY V (A — (A) FOTHERINGAY — 1970 ISLAND UK ILPS9125 US A&M4269
TREVOR LUCAS G (A
JERRY DONAHUE G (A — PAT DONALDSON B (A — GERRY CONWAY D (A — LINDA THOMPSON V (A
TOD LLOYD V (A

F90 FOTOMAKER F90

WALLY BRYSON G V (A — (A) FOTOMAKER — 1978 ATLANTIC US 19165 UK K50450
GENE CORNISH B V (A — (B) VIS A VIS — 1978 ATLANTIC US 19208
DINO DANELLI D (A — (C) TRANSFER STATION — 1979 ATLANTIC US 19246
LEX MARCHESI G V (A
FRANKIE VINCI K V (A — EDDIE KRAMER PROD (A

F90A FOUNDATIONS F90A

Member	Inst		Title	Year	Label	Country	No.
CLEM CURTIS	V	(A	(A) FROM THE FOUNDATIONS	1967	PYE	UK	NPL 18206
COLIN YOUNG	V	(D	(A) BABY NOW THAT IVE FOUND YOU	1967	UNI	US	73016
ALAN WARNER	G	(AD	(B) ROCKING THE FOUNDATION	1968	PYE	UK	NPL 18227
ERIC ALLENDALE	TROM	(AD	(C) BUILD ME UP BUTTERCUP	1968	UNI	US	73043
TONY GOMEZ	ORG	(AD	(D) DIGGING THE FOUNDATIONS	1969	PYE	UK	NPL 18290
TIM HARRIS	D	(AD	(D) DIGGING THE FOUNDATIONS	1969	UNI	US	73058
PETER MACBETH	B	(AD	( ) THE FOUNDATIONS	1968	MARBLE ARCH	UK	MALS11571
PAT BURKE	WIND	(AD	(EP) ITS ALL RIGHT	1968	PYE	UK	NEP 24297
MIKE ELLIOTT	SAX	(A	( ) GOLDEN HOUR	1973	PYE	UK	GH574
			( ) ROCK FROM BRITAIN VOL 2	1979	MODE	US	9040

F90B FOUR HUNDRED & FIFTY ONE DEGREES (451°) F90B

Member	Inst		Title	Year	Label	Country	No.
DAN LOWE	G	(A	(A) 451°	1981	INTERCORD		1009
HAL WHITFORD	V	(A					
BRAD STECKEL	G V	(A					
JIM CLENCH	B V	(A					
STEVE NELSON	D	(A					

F90C FOUR OUT OF FIVE DOCTORS F90C

Member	Inst		Title	Year	Label	Country	No.
JEFF SEVERSON	V G K	(A	(A) 4 OUT OF 5 DOCTORS	1980	NEMPEROR	US	36575
CAL EVERETT	B V	(A					
GEORGE PITTAWAY	G V	(A					
TOM BALLEW	D V	(A					
PATRICE CARROLL	V	(A					
JEFF KIRK	WIND	(A					

F91 FRANKIE VALLI & THE FOUR SEASONS F91

Member	Inst		Title	Year	Label	US	UK	UK No.
FRANKIE VALLI	V	(XSV	SHERRY	1963	VEE JAY	US 1053	UK STATESIDE	10033
TOMMY DEVITO			GREETINGS	1963	VEE JAY	US 1055	UK STATESIDE	10051
NICK DEVITO			BIG GIRLS	1963	VEE JAY	US 1056		
NICK MASSI			AINT THAT A SHAME	1963	VEE JAY	US 1059	UK STATESIDE	10042
BOB GAUDIO	K V	(SV	STAY	1964	VEE JAY	US 1082		
JOEY LONG			GOLDEN HITS	196	VEE JAY	US 1088		
GERRY POLCI	D V	(XSV	WE LOVE GIRLS	196	VEE JAY	US 1121		
DON CICCIONE	B	(XSV	LIVE ON STAGE	196	VEE JAY	US 1154		
LEE SHAPIRO	K	(SV	DAWN	1964	PHILIPS	US 600124		BL 7621
JOHN PAIVA	G V	(SV	BORN TO WANDER	1964	PHILIPS	US 600129		BL 7611
JERRY CORBETTA	K V	(X	RAG DOLL	1964	PHILIPS	US 600146		BL 7643
LARRY LINGLE	G V	(X	SING BIG HITS	1965	PHILIPS	US 600150		BL 7687
REX ROBINSON	K	(X	ENTERTAIN YOU	1965	PHILIPS	US 600164		BL 7663
ROBBY ROBINSON	K	(X	BIG HITS BY BACHARACH,DAVID & DYLAN		PHILIPS	US 600193		
RICHARD GARCIA	PERC	(X	GOLD VAULT HITS	1965	PHILIPS	US 600196		BL 7719
TOBEE TYLER	V	(X	WORKING MY WAY BACK TO YOU	1965	PHILIPS	US 600201		BL 7699
TONY WALTHERS	V	(X	2ND VAULT	196	PHILIPS	US 600221		
			LOOKING BACK	196	PHILIPS	US 600222		BL 7752
			CHRISTMAS ALBUM	1966	PHILIPS	US 600223		BL 7753
			NEW GOLD HITS	196	PHILIPS	US 600243		
			GENUINE IMITATION LIFE GAZETTE	1968	PHILIPS	US 600290		
			HALF & HALF	196	PHILIPS	US 600341		
			EDIZIONE D'ORO	1969	PHILIPS	US 2 6501	UK	6640 002
			SEASONED HITS	1968	FONTANA		UK	SFJL 952
			BIG ONES	1971	PHILIPS		UK	6336 208
			CHAMELEON	1972	MOWEST	US 108	UK	MWAS 5501
			CHAMELEON	1975	MOWEST		UK RI	MWS 7006
			GOLD	1975	PRIVATE STOCK			
			OUR DAY WILL COME	1975	PRIVATE STOCK			
			CLOSE TO YOU	1975	PRIVATE STOCK		UK	PVLP 1001
			FALLEN ANGEL	1975	PRIVATE STOCK		UK	PVLP 1005
			(S)WHO LOVES YOU	1975	WB	US 2900	UK	K 56179
			INSIDE STORY	1976	MOWEST		UK	MWS 7007
			STORY	1976	PRIVATE STOCK	US 7000		
			(V) HELICON	1977	WB	US 3016	UK	K 56350
			FRANKIE VALLI IS THE WORD	1978	WB	US		
			(X) REUNITED	1981	WB	US 3497	UK	K 66098
			GREATEST HITS	1976	K TEL		UK	952
			GREATEST HITS 4 ALBUM SET	19	LONGINES	US 95883		
			BROTHERHOOD OF MAN (EP)	19	PICKWICK	US 3223 + SEARS US 609		
			GENUINE IMITATION LIFE GAZETTE	19	PHILIPS	US 2704		
			FOUR SEASONS SING	19	VEE JAY	US 902		
			PEANUTS	19	VEE JAY	US 901		

F92 FOUR TOPS F92

Member	Inst		Title	Year	Label	US	UK	UK No.
LEVI STUBBS	V	(ALL	(A)FOUR TOPS	1965	TAMLA MOTOWN	US 622	UK	STML11010
RENALDO BENSON	V	(ALL	(B)SECOND ALBUM	1966	TAMLA MOTOWN	US 647	UK	STML 11021
LAWRENCE PAYTON	V	(ALL	(B)SECOND ALBUM	199	TAMLA MOTOWN		UK RI	STMR9007
ABDUL FAKIR	V	(ALL	ON TOP	1966	TAMLA MOTOWN	US 634	UK	STML 11037
WITH			LIVE	1967	TAMLA MOTOWN	US 654	UK	STML 11041
ED GREENE	D	(*SU	REACH OUT	1967	TAMLA MOTOWN	US 660	UK	STML 11056
MAX BENNETT	B	(*	ON BROADWAY	1967	TAMLA MOTOWN	US 657	UK	STML 11046
WILTON FELDER	B	(*QRSU	GREATEST HITS	1968	TAMLA MOTOWN	US 662	UK	STML 11061
BEN BENAY	G	(*RSU	YESTERDAYS DREAM	1969	TAMLA MOTOWN	US 669	UK	STML 11087
DAVID T WALKER	G	(*R	FOUR TOPS NOW	1969	TAMLA MOTOWN	US 675	UK	STML 11113
LEE RITENOUR	G	(*	SOUL SPIN	1970	TAMLA MOTOWN	US 695	UK	STML 11138
DEAN PARKS	G	(*SU	STILL WATERS RUN DEEP	1970	TAMLA MOTOWN	US 704	UK	STML 11149
JAY GRAYDON	G	(*	CHANGING TIMES	1971	TAMLA MOTOWN	US 721	UK	STML 11173
MICHAEL OMARTIAN	K	(*RSU	MAGNIFICENT SEVEN	1971	TAMLA MOTOWN		UK	STML 11179
CLIFFORD CARTER	K	(*UV	RETURN OF THE MAGNIFICENT SEVEN	71	TAMLA MOTWON		UK	STML 11192
VICTOR FELDMAN	PERC	(*Q	GREATEST HITS VOL 2	1971	TAMLA MOTOWN	US 740	UK	STML 11195
KING ERRISSON	PERC	(*QRSU	DYNAMITE (SUPREMES)	1972	TAMLA MOTOWN	US 745	UK	STML 11203
ERNIE WATTS	HRNS	(*U	(P)NATURE PLANNED IT	1972	TAMLA MOTOWN	US 748	UK	STML 11206
CHUCK FINDLEY	HRNS	(*	BEST OF	197	TAMLA MOTOWN	US 764		
PAUL HUBINON	HRNS	(*	(Q) KEEPER OF THE CASTLE	1972	DUNHILL	US 50129 PROBE	UK	SPB 1064
JACKIE KELSO	HRNS	(*	(Q) KEEPER OF THE CASTLE RI	1974	ABC	UK ABCL5023 1976 MFP	UK	50253
LEW McCREARY	HRNS	(*	FOUR TOPS STORY	1973	TAMLA MOTOWN		UK	TMSP 1124
FRED SELDON	HRNS	(*	(R) MAIN STREET PEOPLE	1973	DUNHILL	US 50144 PROBE	UK	SPBA 6277
SID SHARP	STRINGS	(*	(R) MAIN STREET PEOPLE	1974	ABC		UK	ABCL 5037
GINGER BLAKE	V	(*	(S) MEETING OF THE MINDS	1974	DUNHILL	US 50166 PROBE	UK	SPBA 6283
LEONARD CASTON	K	(P	(S) MEETING OF THE MINDS	1974	ABC		UK	ABCL 5046

(CONTINUED)

F92 (CONTINUED) FOUR TOPS F92

Title	Year	Label			
SHAFT IN AFRICA(SOUNDTRACK)	1974	PROBE	UK SBP1077	ANCHOR UK	ABCL 5035
(U)LIVE IN CONCERT	1974	DUNHILL	US 50188	ANCHOR UK	ABCL 5062
(*) NIGHT LIGHTS HARMONY	1974	ABC	US 862	ANCHOR UK	ABCL 5130
SUPER HITS	1976	TAMLA MOTOWN		UK	STML 8028
(W)CATFISH	1976	ABC	US 968	UK	ABCL 5197
MILESTONES	1977	EMI		UK	50207/8
ANTHOLOGY	197	TAMLA MOTOWN	US M9809		
MOTOWN SPECIAL	1977	TAMLA MOTOWN		UK	STMX 6004
SHOW MUST GO ON	1977	ABC	US 1014	ANCHOR UK	ABCL 5223
(Z) AT THE TOP	1978	ABC		UK	ABCL 5262
ITS ALL IN THE GAME	1979	MFP		UK	50416
REACH OUT 20 GOLDEN GREATS	1981	TAMLA MOTOWN		UK	EMTV 26
TONIGHT	1981	CASABLANCA	US 7258		
(EP) FOUR TOPS HITS	1967	TAMLA MOTOWN		UK	TMA 2018

ANDREW SMITH D (P
EDDIE BONGO BROWN PERC(PV
EDDIE WILLIS G (PV
JAMES JAMERSON B (P
LARRY CARLTON G (QRS
JOE SMITH G (QTV
CHIP CRAWFORD K (QR
JIMMIE HASKELL SYN (Q
MICHAEL WOFFORD K (R
SCOTT EDWARDS B (S
RAY PARKER G (S
JEROME RICHARSON HRNS (U
SIHAB SHIHAB HRNS (U
JULIUS BROOKS HRNS (U
CHARLES LOPER HRNS (U
MAURICE SPEAR HRNS (U
GENE ESTES PERC U
EUGENE YOUNG HRNS (U
DENNIS COFFEY G (PV
DAVID COHEN G (Q
BRIAN POTTER PERC (QR
JOE GUASTELLA G (V
GREG COLES B (V
BRUCE GRAY K (Z
KEITH BENSON D (Z
MARION CHILDERS HRNS (U
LAWRENCE PAYTON K (V
MELVIN RAGIN G (P
RICHARD BENNETT G (Q
STEVE BARRI PERC (S
ROBERT WHITE G (V
DAVE PENNEY PERC (V
LARRY WASHINGTON PERC (Z
HENRI SMITH PERC (Z
HERMAN RILEY HRNS (U
RICHARD ALLEN D (P
PAUL HUMPHREY D (QR
DENNIS LAMBERT K (QRS
RICHARD BUDSON K (V
URIEL JONES D (V
NORMAN HARRIS G (Z
T J TINDALL G (Z
STRINGS (VZ
GEORGE BOHANON HRNS(U
JACK ASHFORD PERC (P
RONNIE BROWN B (Q
GARY COLEMAN PERC (QRS
EARL VAN DYKE K (V
JOHNNY TRUDELL HRNS(V
EDWARD MOORE G (Z
CARETON H KENT K (Z

F93 FOURMOST F93

BRIAN O'HARA G V (A
MIKE MILLWARD G V (A
BILLY HATTON B (A
DAVE LOVELADY D (

Title	Year	Label			
(A) FIRST & FOURMOST	1965	PARLOPHONE	UK	PMC	1259
(EP)FOURMOST SOUND	1964	PARLOPHONE	UK	GEP	8892
(EP)FOURMOST	1964	PARLOPHONE	UK	GEP	8917

F94 KIM FOWLEY F94

KIM FOWLEY V K (ALL
MIKE ALLSUP G (D
EDDIE HOH PERC (D
MARS BONFIRE G (DGP
JIMMY GREENSPOON K (D
JOE SCHERMIE B (D
ORVILLE RHODES STEEL(G
WAYNE TABERT K (D
CARMAN RIALE B (D
BEN BENAY G (DG
JOE TORRES PERC (D
PETE SEARS B K (GP
WARREN KLEIN G (G
DRACHEN THEAKER D (GP
KERRY SCOTT G VIBES(IP
GLEN TURNER G V PERC(IP
CHARLIE McCRACKEN B(IP
TONY MAC D PERC(IP
TONY MARSH PNO (IP
JUSTIN CHEEN PERC (IP
PETER MOSS BAN HCA K VLN(IP
CARLOS BERNAL (P
RON BURNS PERC (IP
MADELINE BELL V (IP
CHRIS DARROW (P
RON CHARLES V (IP
PETER LION (P
TORNADO TURNER (P
JOHN ELSTAR HCA (IP
JIM MOON D (P

Title	Year	Label / Numbers
(A) LOVE IS ALIVE AND WELL	1967	TOWER US DT 5080
(B) IN THE UNDERGROUND	1968	
(C) BORN TO BE WILD	1968	IMPERIAL US LP 12413
(D) OUTRAGEOUS	1969	IMPERIAL US LP 12423
(E) GOOD CLEAN FUN	1969	IMPERIAL US LP 12443
(F) THE DAY THE EARTH STOOD STILL	1970	MNW SWED MNWL 7P
(G) I'M BAD	1972	CAPITOL US ST11075 GER 81208
(H) OUTLAW SUPERMAN (NOT RELEASED	1971	RCA US
(I) INTERNATIONAL HEROES	1973	CAPITOL US ST11159 GER 81385
(J) SUNSET BOULEVARD	1978	ILLEGAL UK 002 US PVC 7906
(K) AUTOMATIC	197	CAPITOL 11248
(L) LIVING IN THE STREETS	1977	SONET UK SNTF 755
(M) ANIMAL GOD OF THE STREETS	1979	CAPITOL 24636
(N) LEGENDARY DOG DUKE SESSIONS	19	B F D BFD 5012
(O) SNAKE DOCUMENT MASQUERADE	1979	ISLAND ILPS 9572 EURO 201217
(O) SNAKE DOCUMENT MASQUERADE	1979	ANTILLES US 7075
(P) VISIONS OF THE FUTURE	19	CAPITOL 24626
( ) VAMPIRES FROM OUTER SPACE	19	BOMP US 40050

F95 FOX F95

NOOSHA FOX V (AB
HERBIE ARMSTRONG G V (A
KENNY YOUNG G V (A
GARY TAYLOR B V (A
JIM FRANK D PERC V (A
PETE SOLLEY K V (A
JIM GANNON G V (A

Title	Year	Label / Numbers
(A) FOX	1975	GTO UK GTLP001 ARIOLA US50001
(A) TALES OF ILLUSION	1975	GTO UK GTLP 006
(C) BLUE HOTEL	1977	GTO UK GTLP 020

F95A THE FOX F95A

STEVE BRAYNE G (A
WINSTON WEATHERILL G SITAR(A
TIM REEVES D (A
DAVID WINDCROSS B PNO(A
ALEX LANE K (A

Title	Year	Label / Numbers
(A) FOR FOX SAKE	1970	FONTANA UK 6309 007

F96 FOXX F96

Title	Year	Label / Numbers
(A) REVOLT OF EMILY YOUNG	1971	MCA UK MUPS419 US DECCA 75193

F97 INEZ & CHARLES FOXX F97

CHARLES FOXX V (ALL
INEZ FOXX V (ALL
WITH
WILLIE HALL V (C
DEBORAH MANNING V (C
BENNY MABONE V (C
WILLIAM BROWN V (C
JOYCE THARP V (C
WILLIAM MURPHY B (C
LESTER SNELL K (C
CHARLES PITT G (C
MARVEL THOMAS K (C
BOBBY MANUEL G (C
MICHAEL TOLES G (C

Title	Year	Label / Numbers
(A) MOCKINGBIRD	1964	SUE US 1027 UK ILP911
(A) MOCKINGBIRD	1969	UA 29025
(B) INEZ & CHARLES FOXX	196	SUE US 1037 LONDON UK 8241
(C) AT MEMPHIS	1973	VOLT US 6022
(D) COME BY HERE	1968	DYNAMO 8000 DIRECTION UK863085
(E) GREATEST HITS	19	DYNAMO 8002 PYE UK 4406
( ) HITS	1968	DIRECTION UK 863281

F97A JOHN FOXX F97A

JOHN FOXX G D SYN(ALL
JOHN BAKER SYN (A
JAKE DURANT B (AB
GARETH JAMES PERC (B
DUNCAN BRIDGEMAN B (B
JO DVORNIAK B (B
PHILIP ROBERTS D (B

Title	Year	Label / Numbers
(A) METAMATIC	1980	VIRGIN UK V2146
(B) THE GARDEN	1981	VIRGIN UK V2194 GER 204 096
(C) JOHN FOXX(COMP)	1981	VIRGIN CAN

F98 FOXY F98

CARL DRIGGS V PERC(A
ISH LEDESMA G V (A
ARNOLD PASEIRO B (A
RICHIE PUENTE PERC K(A
WAYNE THALER VIBES(A
CHARLIE MURCIANO K V WIND(A
BONAROO HORNS HRNS (A
JOE CALDO D V (A
WILDFLOWER V (A
PETER BROWN B (A

Title	Year	Label / Numbers
(A) GET OFF	1978	TK TKR 82544
(B) HOT NUMBERS	1979	TK UK TKR 83353

F99 GARLAND FRADY F99

GARLAND FRADY (A) PURE COUNTRY 1973 COUNTRYSIDE US CS101

F99A RENZO FRAESE F99A

RENZO FRAESE K SYN(A (A) FILALMENTE 1978 PYE UK NSPL28267
BOB DAUGHERTY B (A
DAVE WILLIAMS B (A CHET McCRACKEN D (A DOUG RICHARDSON PERC (A SANFORD RICHMOND PERC(A
DALTON SMITH TPT (A BOB PAYNE TROM (A DAVE ROBERTS HRNS (A ANDY MACKINTOSH WIND(A
JOE IZEN G V (A BILL LAMB TPT (A LOU KORELL HRNS (A LON NORMAN TROM(A
STEVE KRAVITZ WIND (A PHIL AYLING WIND (A TOM JUSTIN G (A BILL STAPLETON TPT(A
JOE KRUGER HRNS (A ERNIE CARLSON TROM (A HOWARD FALLMAN WIND (A DOUG WINTZ TROM(A
DON RADER TPT (A

F100 PETER FRAMPTON F100

PETER FRAMPTON G V B K(ALL (A) WIND OF CHANGE 1972 A&M US 4348 UK AMLS68099
RICK WILLS B V (BC (B) FRAMPTONS CAMEL 1973 A&M US 4389 UK AMLH68150
MICK GALLAGHER K (B (C) SOMETHINGS HAPPENING 1974 A&M US 3619 UK AMLH63619
MIKE KELLIE D (A (D) FRAMPTON 1975 A&M US 4512 UK AMLH64512
JOHN SIOMOS D (BDEF (E) COMES ALIVE 1975 A&M US 3703 UK AMLG63703
ANDY BOWN K (AD (F) I'M IN YOU 1977 A&M US 4704 UK AMLK64704
BOB MAYO V K G(EFG (G) WHERE I SHOULD BE 1979 A&M US 3710 UK AMLK63710
STANLEY SHELDON B (EFG (H) BREAKING ALL THE RULES 1981 A&M US 3722 UK AMLK63722
MARK GOLDENBERG V G K(A (J) THE ART OF CONTROL 1982 A&M UK AMLH64905
STEVIE WONDER HCA (F
JAMIE OLDACKER D (G FRANK CARILLO G V PERC(AB POLI PALMER VIBES (D RITCHIE HAYWARD PERC(F
JOHN HEADLEY DOWN D (C NICKY HOPKINS PNO (C STEVE FORMAN PERC (G CHRIS KARAN PERC(A
FRANK RICOTTI PERC (A MICKEY JONES G (A RINGO STARR D (F JOE VITALE V (G
STEVE CROPPER G (G DONALD DUNN B (G DAVID ALLEN DUKE HRNS (G JIM PRICE HRNS(A
KLAUS VOORMANN B (A TOWER OF POWER HRNS (G ED MANTELEONE G (H STEVE LUKATHER G (H
JEFF PORCARO D (H JOHN REGAN B (HJ WATERS FAMILY V (G HARRY STINSON D(J
IAN LLOYD V (J EDDIE KRAMER V (J JOHN DWORKOW V (J

F101 RITCHIE FRANCIS F101

RITCHIE FRANCIS PNO V(A (A) SONGBIRD 1971 PEGASUS UK PEG 1+ INTERCORD 26006-7U
MIKE KELLIE D (A
BARRY MORGAN D (A WILL MALONE D (A PHIL CURTIS B (A JOHN ROSTILL B (A
TAFF WILLIAMS G (A JIM SULLIVAN G (A

F101A BOB FRANK F101A

BOB FRANK G V (A (A) BOB FRANK 19 VANGUARD US 6582

F101B STANLEY FRANK F101B

STANLEY FRANK G K V PERC(A (A) PLAY TILL IT HURTS 1980 A&M AMLH 64828
PAUL HANNAH D (A
BILL WADE D (A ANTON EVANS B V (A WOODY WEST G V (A MARK RUTTER ORG (A
DAVE WILCZEWSKI SAX (A DOC FINGERS PNO (A ROBIN CABLE PROD (A

F101C FRANKE AND THE KNOCKOUTS F101C

FRANKE PREVITE V (A (A) FRANKE AND THE KNOCKOUTS 1981 MILLENIUM LP5026 BXL17755
BILLY ELWORTHY G (A
BLAKE LEVINSON K (A LEIGH FOXX B (A CLAUDE LEHENAFF D (A TOMMY AYERS K SYN V(A
CHARLIE DOMINICI V (A JIMMY MAELEN PERC (A BROOKLYN DREAMS V (A

F101D FRANKFURT CITY BLUES BAND F101D

ANDREUS AUGUST V G K(AB (A) ...IS IN TOWN 1979 TRION CASS GER 7901
MANFRED HAEDER G (AB (B) SECOND STEP 1979 MOONSHINE CASS GER 5001
TSCHO THOMAS SCHILLING B(AB
GEORGE VIEL D (AB BERNARD DILL HCA G (AB ACHIM FAHR SAX(AB HELMUT SCHICK HRN(B
CONNY KELLER V (B DORIS TANGEL V (B THOMAS GOERTEN PERC(B LOTHAR KRELL K (B
EVA MITTMANN G (B

F102 FRANKIE & JOHNNY F102

FRANK RUBY G V (A (A) SWEETHEART SMPLER 1973 WB US 2675
JOHN PAUL FETTA B V (A
DARRY DAILEY G (A EDDIE BARBATO G (A AL KOOPER GK (A J R COBB G (A
DEAN DAUGHTRY K (A ROBERT NIX D (A MIKE GATELY V (A

F103 ARETHA FRANKLIN F103

ARETHA FRANKLIN PNO V (ALL ARETHA 1961 CBS US 8412 FONTANA UK TFL5173
WITH ELECTRIFYING 1962 CBS US 8561
CORNELL DUPREE G (* TENDER,MOVING & SWINGING 1962 CBS US 8676
JACK CAVARI G (* LAUGHING ON THE OUTSIDE 1963 CBS US 8897
TOM HANLON G (* UNFORGETTABLE 1964 CBS US 8963
RICHARD TEE K (* SONGS OF FAITH 1964 CHECKER US 10009 ATLANTIC UK'67 588066
KEN ASCHER K (* RUNNING OUT OF FOOLS 1964 CBS US 9081
PAUL GRIFFIN K (* YEAH 1965 CBS US 9151 UK 62556
VAN McCOY V K (* SOUL SISTER 1966 CBS US 9321 UK 62744
GORDON EDWARDS B (* QUEEN OF SOUL 196 HARMONY US 11274 CBS UK 52562
BRIAN ALLSOP B (* TAKE IT LIKE YOU GIVE IT 1967 CBS US 9429 UK 62969
CHRIS PARKER D (* LEE CROSS 1967 CBS UK 63160
CRUSHER BENNETT PERC (* GREATEST HITS 1967 CBS US 9473 UK 64536
GEORGE DEVENS PERC (* TAKE A LOOK 1967 CBS US 9554 UK 63269
KEN BISCHEL SYN (* I NEVER LOVED A MAN 1967 ATLANTIC US 8139 UK 588 066
DESTRY V (* I NEVER LOVED A MAN 1972 ATLANTIC UK K 40134
ZULEMA CUSSEAUX V (* ONCE IN A LIFETIME 196 HARMONY US 11349
ALBERT BAILEY V (* GREATEST HITS 1960/65 196 HARMONY US 30606
BRENDA HILLIARD V (* ARETHA ARRIVES 1967 ATLANTIC US 8150 1972 UK K 40157
JEROME JACKSON V (* GREATEST HITS VOL 2 1968 CBS US 9601+31355 UK 63064
RICHARD HARRIS V (* LADY SOUL 1968 ATLANTIC US 8176 UK 588 099
PETE MARSHALL V (* LADY SOUL 1972 ATLANTIC UK RI K40016
CAROLYN FRANKLIN V (* ARETHA NOW 1968 ATLANTIC US 8186 UK 588 114
SHARON BROWN V (* LIVE AT PARIS OLYMPIA 1968 ATLANTIC US 8207 UK 588 149
PAT WILLIAMSON V (* LIVE AT PARIS OLYMPIA 1972 ATLANTIC UK K49924
CURTIS MAYFIELD G (Z BEST OF 1968 ATLANTIC US 8305
GARY THOMPSON G (Z SOUL 69 1969 ATLANTIC US 8212 UK 588 163
DONNEL HAGAN D (Z TODAY I SING THE BLUES 1969 CBS US 9956
ALFONZO SURRET V (Z SOFT & BEAUTIFUL 196 CBS US 9776
DICKI LINTON V (Z ARETHA GOLD 1969 ATLANTIC US 8227 UK 588 192
RICH TUFO K (Z ARETHA GOLD 1972 ATLANTIC UK K 40036
JOSEPH SCOTT B (Z SATISFACTION 19 ATLANTIC US 8215

(CONTINUED)

F103 (CONTINUED) **ARETHA FRANKLIN** F103

HENRY GIBSON PERC (Z
MATTIE BUTLER V (Z
DERNESE HEARD V (Z

Title	Year	Label	US			No.
I SAY A LITTLE PRAYER	1969	ATLANTIC			UK	2464 002
THIS GIRLS IN LOVE WITH YOU	1970	ATLANTIC	US 8248		UK	2400 004
SPIRITS IN THE DARK	1970	ATLANTIC	US 8265	1972	UK	K 40095
DONT PLAY THAT SONG	1970	ATLANTIC			UK	2400 021
LIVE AT FILLMORE WEST	1971	ATLANTIC	US 7205		UK	2400 136
LIVE AT FILLMORE WEST	1972	ATLANTIC			UK	K 40222
YOUNG GIFTED & BLACK	1971	ATLANTIC	US 7213		UK	2400 188
YOUNG GIFTED & BLACK	1972	ATLANTIC			UK	K 40323
ARETHAS GREATEST HITS	1971	ATLANTIC	US 8295		UK	K 40279
AMAZING GRACE	1972	ATLANTIC	US 2 906		UK	K 60023
HEY HEY NOW	1973	ATLANTIC	US 7265		UK	K 40504
COLLECTION	1973	MIDI			UK	30035
FIRST 12 SIDES	1973	CBS	US 31953	EMBASSY	UK	31006
LET ME INTO YOUR LIFE	1974	ATLANTIC	US 7292		UK	K 50031
WITH EVERY THING I FEEL IN ME	1975	ATLANTIC	US 18116		UK	K 50093
TWO ORIGINALS	1975	ATLANTIC			UK	K 80007
YOU	1975	ATLANTIC	US 18151		IL	K 50159
SPARKLE	1976	ATLANTIC	US 18176		UK	K 56248
TEN YEARS OF GOLD	1976	ATLANTIC	US 18204		UK	K 50326
SWEET PASSION	1977	ATLANTIC	US 19102		UK	K 50368
MOST BEAUTIFUL SONGS	1977	ATLANTIC	US		UK	K 60030
(Z) ALMIGHTY FIRE	1978	ATLANTIC	US 19161		UK	K 50445
STAR COLLECTION	1978	MIDI			UK	K 20017
STAR COLLECTION 2	1978	MIDI			UK	K 20079
(*) LA DIVA	1979	ATLANTIC	US 19248		UK	K 50637
ARETHA	1980	ARISTA			UK	SPART 1147
LOVE ALL THE HURT AWAY	1981	ARISTA			UK	SPART 1170
GREATEST HITS	1982	ATLANTIC			UK	K 40279
JUMP TO IT	1982	ARISTA			GER	204 742

F103A **CAROLYN FRANKLIN** F103A

CAROLYN FRANKLIN V (ALL

Title	Year	Label			No.
(A) BABY DYNAMITE	1969	RCA	US		LSP 4160
( ) I'D RATHER BE LONELY	1975	RCA	US		LSP 4411
( ) CAROLYN FRANKLIN	1976	RCA		UK	APLI 0420
( ) CHAIN REACTION	19	RCA		US	LPS 4317
( ) FIRST TIME I CRIED	19	JOY		UK	JOYS 180

F103B **ERMA FRANKLIN** F103B

ERMA FRANKLIN V (

Title	Year	Label		No.
(A) SOUL SISTER	1975	BRUNSWICK		754147
( ) HER NAME IS ERMA	19	EPIC	US	3824

F103C **RODNEY FRANKLIN** F103C

Title	Year	Label	US		No.
(A) YOU'LL NEVER KNOW	1980	CBS	US 36122	UK	83812
(B) RODNEY FRANKLIN	1980	CBS	US 36747	UK	84528
(C) ENDLESS	1981	CBS	US 37154	UK	84945

RODNEY FRANKLIN K B V (AB
VINCENT SPAULDING G (AB
HAROLD FOREMAN B (A
IAN UNDERWOOD SYN (A
TONY ST JAMES D (AB
RANDY MERRITT D (A
LISA ROBERTS V (A
DAVID LUELL HRNS (B
BOBBY BRYANT HRNS (B
DENNIS BUDIMIR G (B
ERNIE WATTS SAX (B
KENNETH NASH PERC (A
PAUL JACKSON B (A
BROOKS HUNNICUTT V (A
SEAWIND HRNS (A
PAULINHO DA COSTA PERC (B
DAVID SHIELDS B (B
LEONARD GIBBS PERC (B
DEAN HOLZKAMP WIND(a
RAY PIZZI CLAR(A
AUDREY FRANKLIN V (A
PHIL UPCHURCH G (B
MARTI McCALL V (B
JEFF PORCARO D (B
DON MYRICK SAX (B
MEL MARTIN WIND (A
PHYLLIS ST JAMES V(AB
OSCAR BRASHEAR HRNS(B
NATHAN EAST B(B
CARMEN TWILLIE V)B
VICTOR FELDMAN PERC(B
FREDDIE HUBBARD HRNS(B

F103D **MICHAEL FRANKS** F103D

Title	Year	Label	US		No.
(A) MICHAEL FRANKS	1973	BRUT		US	6005
(B) THE ART OF TEA	1976	REPRISE		US	2230
(C) SLEEPING GYPSY	1977	WB	US 3004	UK	K 56346
(D) BURCHFIELD NINES	197	WB	US 3167		
(E) TIGER IN THE RAIN	1979	WB	US 3294	UK	K 56612
(F) ONE BAD HABIT	1980	WB	US 3427	UK	K 56814
(G) LIVE	1981	WB			56922
(H) OBJECTS OF DESIRE	1982	WB	US 3642	UK	K 56975

MICHAEL FRANKS (ALL
JOE SAMPLE K (C
WILTON FELDER (C
JOHN GUERIN (C
LARRY CARLTON G (C
RICK ZUNIGAR (F
DAVID SANBORN (C
MICHAEL BRECKER HRNS (C
LARRY BUNKER (C
RAY ARMANDO (C
DENNIS BELFIELD (F
EDDIE GOMEZ (F
RICK MAROTTA D (F
DAVID SPINOZZA G (F
LARRY BUNKER PERC (
CAROLE KAYE B (A
JOAO PALMA (C
LENNY CASTRO (F
DON GROLNICK K (F
HUGH McCRACKEN G (F
TENNISON STEPHENS (F
WENDY WALDMAN V DULC(
JOAO DONATO (C
ANDRE FISHER (F
JERRY HEY HRNS (F
GEORGE SOPUCH (F
TOM SCOTT SAX (
ED GREENE D (
HELIO DELMIRO (C
ERIC GALE G (F
NEIL JASON B (F
LARRY WILLIAMS (F
LOUIE SHELTON G (
JERRY McGEE G (

F103E **FRANTIC** F103E

Title	Year	Label		No.
(A) FRANTIC	19	LIZARD	US	20103

F103F **FRANZ** F103F

MICK HANNES G (AB
STEFAN JOSEFUS D (AB
PETER JOSEFUS B V (AB
WERNER BECKER K (B

Title	Year	Label		No.
(A) SENSEMANN	1972	RUHR	GER	007
(B) ROCK IN DEUTSCH	1973	ZEBRA	GER	2949 014

F104 **ANDY FRASER** F104

ANDY FRASER B V (AB1
NICK JUDD K (A1
KIM TURNER D (A
FRANKIE MILLER V (1
HENRY McCULLOUGH G (1
MIKE KELLIE D (1

Title	Year	Label		No.
(A) ANDY FRASER BAND	1975	CBS	UK	80731
(B) IN YOUR EYES	1975	CBS	UK	81027
(1) 1974 MILLER FRASER BAND				

F104A **FRATERNITY OF MAN** F104A

ELLIOT INGBER G (AB
WARREN KLEIN G SITAR (AB
RICHIE HAYWARD D V (AB
MARTIN KIBBEE B (AB
LAWRENCE WAGNER G V (AB

Title	Year	Label		No.
(A) THE FRATERNITY OF MAN	19	ABC	US	ABCS 647
(B) GET IT ON	19	DOT	US	25955

F105 JOHN FRED & HIS PLAYBOYS F105

Member	Inst.	Records
JOHN FRED	V HCA	(ALL
ANDREW BERNARD	SAX	(
RONNIE GOODSON	TPT	(
CHARLIE SPIN	TPT	(
JIMMY O'ROURKE	G	(
HAROLD COWART	B	(
TOMMY DE GENERES	ORG	(
JOE MICELY	D	(

Record	Year	Label	Country	No.
(A) JOHN FRED & HIS PLAYBOYS	1968	PAULA	US	2191
(B) 34.40 OF JOHN FRED	196	PAULA	US	2193
(C) AGNES ENGLISH	19	PAULA	US	2197
(C) JUDY IN DISGUISE	19	PAULA	US	
(D) PERMANENTLY STATED	1968	PAULA	US	2201
(E) LOVE IN MY SOUL	19	UNI	US	73077

F105A FRED BANANA COMBO F105A

Member	Inst.	Records
NICOLLE MEYER	D V	(AB
BILL BROWN	B V	(AB
GODFREY TOLLMAN	G B V	(AB
DIZZY FISCHER	TROM	(B
PETER RUEBSAM	PIPES	(B
HORDT GLAESKER	K	(B
CHRIS BOLLMANN	HRNS	(B
GERD POSNY	D SAX	(A
KAI WOLF	D	(A
RAY McENTHUN	D	(A
THE ORDINAIRES	V	(A

Record	Year	Label	Country	No.
(A) FRED BANANA COMBO	1980	ARIOLA	GER	201722
(B) THE INCREDIBLE FRED BANANA COMBO	1981	GEEBEEDEE	GER	0647

F106 FREDDIE & THE DREAMERS F106

Member	Inst.	Records
FREDDIE GARRITY	V	(ALL
ROY CREWSDON	G	(
PETE BIRRELL	D	(
BERNIE DWYER	D	(
DEREK QUINN	G	(

Record	Year	Label	Country	No.
FREDDIE & THE DREAMERS	1963	COLUMBIA	UK	33SX 1577
YOU WERE MADE FOR ME	1964	COLUMBIA	UK	33SX 1663
SING ALONG	1965	COLUMBIA	UK	SX 1785
IN DISNEYLAND	1966	COLUMBIA	UK	SCX 6069
FREDDIE & THE DREAMERS	1966	MERCURY	US	61017
DO THE FREDDIE	196	MERCURY	US	61026
SEASIDE SWINGERS	1966	MERCURY	US	61031
FRANTIC FREDDIE	196	MERCURY	US	61053
FUN LOVIN'	196	MERCURY	US	61061
KING FREDDIE & DREAMING KINIGHTS	1967	COLUMBIA	UK	SX 6177
I'M TELLING YOU	19	TOWER	UK	5003
OLIVER IN OVERWORLD	1970	STARLINE	UK	SRS 5019
BEST OF	1977	EMI UK NUT11 US CAPITOL		11896
EPo				
IF YOU MAKE A FOOL	1963	COLUMBIA	UK	SEG 8275
CRAZY WORLD	1964	COLUMBIA	UK	SEG 8287
YOU WERE MADE FOR ME	1964	COLUMBIA	UK	SEG 8302
FREDDIE & THE DREAMERS	1965	COLUMBIA	UK	SEG 8323
READY FREDDIE GO	1965	COLUMBIA	UK	SEG 8403
JUST FOR YOU	196	COLUMBIA	UK	SEG 8349
FREDDY GARRITY	1974	BUSSTOP		BUS 5002
I'M TELLING YOU NOW	1977	EMI	UK	2694

F107 BILL FREDERICKS F107

Member	Inst.	Records
BILL FREDERICKS		

Record	Year	Label	Country	No.
(A) LOVE WITH YOU	1978	POLYDOR	UK	2382 470

F108 FREE F108

Member	Inst.	Records
PAUL RODGERS	V	(ABCDEGH13456
PAUL KOSSOFF	G	(ABCDEFGH1235
ANDY FRASER	B	(ABCDEG13
SIMON KIRKE	D	(ABCDEFGH123456
TETSU YAMAUCHI	B	(FH2456
RABBIT BUNDRICK	K	(FH2456
SNUFFY WALDEN	G	(H
WENDEL RICHARDSON	G	(6
B J COLE	STEEL	(F
STEVE MILLER	PNO	(A
REBOP	PERC	(H

(1) 1968/71 (2) MAY71/JAN72
(3) 71 /72 (4) JUL72/SEP72
(5) SEPT 72 (6) JAN73/JUNE73

Record	Year	Release	Release
(A) TONS OF SOBS	1969	A&M US 4198	UK ISLAND ILPS 9089
(B) FREE	1969	A&M US 4204	UK ISLAND ILPS 9104
(C) FIRE & WATER	1970	A&M US 4268	UK ISLAND ILPS 9120
(C) FIRE & WATER	1970	ISLAND GER 6339007	RI EURO 200 563
(D) HIGHWAY	1970	A&M US 4287	UK ISLAND ILPS 9138
(D) HIGHWAY	1970	ISLAND GER 6339028	
(E) LIVE	1971	A&M US 4306	UK ISLAND ILPS 9160
(F) KOSSOFF,KIRKE,TETSU & RABBIT	1971		UK ISLAND ILPS 9188
(G) FREE AT LAST	1972	A&M US 4349	UK ISLAND ILPS 9192
(G) FREE AT LAST	1972	ISLAND GER 86171	
(H) HEARTBREAKER	1972	ISLAND US 9324	UK ILPS 9217
(H) HEARTBREAKER	19	ISLAND RI EURO	200 561
(J) THE FREE STORY (DBL)	1973		UK ISLAND ISLD4
(K) BEST OF FREE	1975	A&M US 3663	
(L) FREE & EASY ROUGH READY	1976		UK ISLAND ILPS 9453
(M) POP CHRONIK (DBL)	1977		EURO ISLAND 89236
(EP) ALL RIGHT NOW	1978	ISLAND UK IEP 6	

F108A FREE BEER F108A

Member	Inst.	Records
SANDY ALLEN	V G B	(ABC
MICHAEL PACKER	V G B	(ABC
CALEB POTTER	V G PERC	(ABC
NED ALBRIGHT	PNO	(A
RICHARD CROOKS	D	(A
BRENDAN HARKIN	G V	(A
JON HARRIS	HCA	(A
ERIC WEISSBERG	FDL DOB	(A
JERRY MAROTTA	D	(B
HUGH McCRACKEN	G	(C
CHRISTOPHER PARKER	D	(C
JOE X DUBE	D	(A
PATTIE DARDY HARKIN	V	(A
BERNARD PURDIE	D	(A
DANIEL BEN ZEBULON	PERC	(AB
DAN DALEY	STEEL	(A
STEVE KHAN	G	(C
STU WOODS	B	(C
LARRY GONSKY	K SYN	(A
JACK JENNINGS	PERC	(A
RONNIE RENNINGER	G	(A
MARKY MARKOWITZ	HRNS	(A
WERNER FRITZSCHING	G	(B
KEN ASCHER	K	(C
RICHARD HARBERT	PNO	(A
GEORGE MARGE	SAX	(A
PAUL SCHWARZ	D	(A
BOB MINTZER	SAX	(A
RALPH SCHUCKETT	K	(BC
WILL LEE	B	(C

Record	Year	Label	Country	No.
(A) FREE BEER	1975	COUTIWIND	US	SWS 6402
(B) HIGHWAY ROBBERY	1976	RCA		APLI 1733
(C) NOUVEAU CHAPEAU	1977	RCA		APLI 2072

F109 FREE CREEK F109

Member	Inst.	Records
TODD RUNDGREN	G	(A
ROY MARKOWITZ	D	(A
MOOGY KLINGMAN	ORG	(A
STU WOODS	B	(A
LEW SOLOFF	TPT	(A
ERIC CLAPTON	G	(A
DELANEY BRAMLETT	G	(A
ELLIOTT RANDALL	G	(A
MAERETHA STEWART	V	(A
JACK WILKINS	G	(A
FITO DE LA PARRA	D	(A
CAROL HUNTER	G	(A
RICHARD CROOKS	D	(A
HARRY HALL	TPT	(A
TIMMY HARRISON	V	(A
LEW DELGATTO	TROM	(A
ALAN RUBIN	TPT	(A
KEITH EMERSON	ORG	(A
CHRIS WOOD	FLT	(A
RED RHODES	STEEL	(A
HILDA HARRIS	V	(A
JIMMY GREENSPOON	K	(A
BILLY CHESBORO	CONGA	(A
RICHARD DAVIS	B	(A
TOMMY COSGROVE	V	(A
LINDA RONSTADT	V	(A
ERIC MERCURY	V	(A
BOBBY KELLER	TROM	(A
BILL CHASE	TPT	(A
MITCH MITCHELL	D	(A
JOE FARRELL	FLT	(A
JOHN LONDON	B	(A
VALERIE SIMPSON	V	(A
LARRY TAYLOR	B	(A
EARLE DOUD	V CONGA	(A
DOCTOR JOHN	PNO	(A
DOUGIE RODRIGUEZ	G	(A
BERNIE LEADON	G	(A
BOB SMITH	ORG	(A
MECO MONARDO	TROM	(A
BUZZY FEITEN	G	(A
CHUCK RAINEY	B	(A
TOM MALONE	TROM	(A
JOHN WARE	D	(A
HARVEY MANDEL	G	(A
LARRY PACKER	VLN	(A
DIDYMUS	PERC	(A
KING COOL	G	(A
BOBBY DEAN	TROM	(A
CHRIS DARROW	VLN	(A
GERI MILLER	V	(A

Record	Year	Label	Country	No.
(A) MUSIC FROM FREE CREEK	1973	CHARISMA	UK	CADS 101
(A) SUMMIT MEETING	1976	CHARISMA		CS3

F109A

FREE SPIRIT

F109A

LARRY CORYELL G (A — (A) OUT OF SIGHT & SOUND 19 ABC US 593
JIM PEPPER SAX (A
CHRIS HILL B V (A — CHIP BAKER G (A — BOB MOSES D (A

F110

FREEDOM

F110

BOBBY HARRISON V D (ALL — (A) FREEDOM 1970 PROBE UK SPBA 6252
STEVE JOLLY G (ALL — (B) AT LAST 1970 METRONOME UK MLP 15371
PETER DENNIS V B K(ALL — (C) THROUGH THE YEARS 1971 COTILLION US SD 9048
ROGER SAUNDERS V G K(ALL — (D) FREEDOM 1971 VERTIGO UK 6360 049
(E) IS MORE THAN A WORD 1972 VERTIGO UK 6360 072

F110A

BOBBY FREEMAN

F110A

BOBBY FREEMAN V (ALL — (A) DO YOU WANNNA DANCE 1958 JOSIE US 1086
(B) C'MON & SWIM 1964 AUTUMN US 102
(C) GET IN THE SWIM 1959 JOSIE US 4007
(D) TWIST WITH 19 JUBILEE US 5010
(E) LOVABLE SIDE OF 1960 KING US 930

F110B

FREEPORT

F110B

CRAIG HOLT G V (A — (A) FREEPORT 1969 MAINSTREAM US 6130
KEVIN RALEIGH K V (A
ROGER LEWIS G V (A — BILL STALLING D V (A — DENNIS STADNEY G (A

F110C

FREEWAY

F110C

JOHN HOBBS K B G (A — (A) FREEWAY 1979 DECCA UK TXS 131
J D MANESS STEEL(A
TERRY MELCHER V PNO(A — MEL COLLINS SAX (A — RICKY FATAAR D PERC(A — JIM SEITER PERC (A

F111

ACE FREHLEY

F111

ACE FREHLEY V B G SYN (A — (A) ACE FREHLEY 1978 CASABLANCA UK/US NBLP 7121
ANTON FIG D (A
WILL LEE B (A — CARL TALLARICO D (A — LARRY KELLY V (A — DAVID LASLEY V (A
BILL SCHENIMAN V (A — SUSAN COLLINS V (A

F112

FRESH

F112

MILO MARTIN B (A — (A) GET FRESH 1977 MCA US 2241 UK MCF 2797
BILL PRATT V (A — (B) FRESH - FELLIN' FRESH 1978 PRODIGAL US 10024
FRED ALLEN D (A — (C) OMNIVERSE 1979 PRODIGAL US 10028
ELAINE MAYO G (A
PAUL MARSHALL G (A — DAVID KAFFINETTI K(A

F113

FRESH

F113

BOB GORMAN G V (AB — (A) FRESH OUT OF BORSTAL 1970 RCA US 4328 UK 8122
KEVIN FRANCIS B V (AB — (B) FRESH TODAY 1971 RCA US 3027
ROGER CHANTLER D (AB

F113A

FRESH START

F113A

(A) FRESH START 1975 DUNHILL US 50175

F113B

FRESHIES

F113B

(EP) BAISER 19 RAZZ UK EP1
(EP) STRAIGHT IN AT No 2 197 RAZZ UK EP2
(EP) WRAP UP THE ROCKETS 1980 MCA UK MCAT 693

F114

FRESHLY LAYED BAND

F114

TIM HOLT G V (A — (A) A LOW VOLUME(200??) CASSETTE RELEASED BY THE GROUP THEMSELVES
BOB PENDRY G V (A
RICHARD FURTER B (A — NICK BUCKLER D (A — ROGER HUNT V (A

F114A

GLENN FREY

F114A

GLENN FREY G V K B SYN(A — (A) NO FUN ALOUD 1982 ASYLUM US 60129
MICHAEL HUEY D (A
JOHN ROBINSON D (A — ROGER HAWKINS D (A — BRTAN GAROFALO B (A — BOB GLAUB B (A
ROBERTO PINON B (A — DAVID HOOD B (A — JOSH LEO G (A — DAN KORTCHMAR G (A
DUNCAN CAMERON G (A — DAVID WOLINSKI SYN (A — "HAWK" K (A — ALLAN BLAZEK K (A
AL GARTH SAX (A — ERNIE WATTS SAX (A — JIM HORN SAX (A — BILL BERGMAN SAX (A
JIM COILE SAX (A — GREG SMITH SAX (A — HARVEY THOMPSON SAX (A — RONNIE EADES SAX (A
JIM ED NORMAN STR (A — LEE THORNBURG TPT (A — JOHN BERRY TPT (A — MARCY LEVY V (A
TOM KELLY V (A — BILL CHAMPLIN V (A — OREN WATERS V (A — JULIA TILLMAN V (A
MAXINE WILLARD V (A

F114B

JAMES FREUD

F114B

JAMES FREUD V (A — (A) BREAKING SILENCE 1980 MUSHROOM AUST 37309
ROGER MASON V SYN K(A
MICK PRAGUE B (A — TOMMY HOSIE D (A — PETER COOK G V (A

F115

DEAN FRIEDMAN

F115

DEAN FRIEDMAN G K V(AB — (A) AN FRIEDMAN 1978 LIFESONG US 35001 UK 6008
DON SARLIN G V (B — (B) WELL WELL SAID THE ROCKING CHAIR 1978 LIFESONG UK 6019
JONNY MANN B (B
BILL WARD D (B — GEORGE YOUNG SAX (B — ANDY GOLDMARK V (B — HOLLY SHERWOOD V (B
JIM RYAN V (B — MARK RIVERA SAX V (B — JOSEPH SHEPLEY TPT (B — DAVID TAYLOR TROM (B
DENISE MARSA V (B — STU NUNNERY V (B — ROB STEVENS VIBES (B — MICHELE LAMB V (B
LORRAINE REBIDAS V (B — TONY LEVIN B (B — RON McCLURE B (B

F116

KINKY FRIEDMAN

F116

KINKY FRIEDMAN V (ALL — (A) SOLD AMERICAN 1974 VANGUARD US 79333
JIM ATKINSON G (C — (B) KINKY FRIEDMAN 1975 ABC US 829 UK ANCHOR 5134
T BONE BURNETT G (C — (C) LASSO FROM EL PASO 1976 EPIC US 34304 81640
MICK RONSON G (C
TOM CULPEPPER G (C — BILL HAM G (C — LEVON HELM G (C — RON WOOD G (C
STEVE SOLES G (C — ERIC CLAPTON DOBRO(C — MICHAEL DE TEMPO G (C — BRIAN CLARKE B (C
TERRY DANKO B (C — ROB STONER B (C — IRA WILKES B (C — MAJOR BOLES D (C
GARY BURKE D (C — TEDDY JACK EDDY D (C — RICHARD MANUEL D (C — DARRELL NORRIS D (C
HOWIE WYETH D (C — DR JOHN K (C — KEN LAUBER K (C — JEWFORD SHELBY K (C
RED YOUNG K (C — DAVID MANSFIELD STEEL(A — RUSTY YOUNG STEEL(C — SNAKEBITE JACOBS HRNS(C
ROGER McGUINN BANJO(C — AL GARTH FDL (C — FRENCHIE BOURKE FDL (C — RINGO STARR V (C
TERRY BALIN V (C — RICK DANKO B V (C — RONNIE HAWKINS V (C — ROSCOE WEST V (C

F117 BRIAN FRIEL F117

BRIAN FRIEL V G (ABC — (A) BRIAN JOSEPH FRIEL 1974 DAWN UK 3054
COLIN PINCOTT G (B — (A) ASHES & MATCHSTICKS 1976 PYE US 12102
DELISLE HARPER B (B — (B) ARRIVEDERCI ARDROSSAN 1975 DAWN UK 3064
MICK DEVONPORT G (B
TIM RENWICK G (B — ANDY ROBERTS G (B — ARTHUR RODMAN G (B — ZOOT MONEY K (AB
CRAIG PRUESS K(B — PAUL FRANCIS D (B — BILLY LAWRIE V (A — PAUL VIGRASS V (AB
STEVE THOMPSON B (A — GARY OSBORNE V (A — COLIN ALLEN D (A — THE PHANTOM G (A
B J COLE STEEL(A — MAGS McGLINT V (A

F118 TERRY FRIEND F118

TERRY FRIEND — (A) COME THE DAY 1978 TRAMP

F119 FRIENDS F119

MARC COHEN SAX (A — (A) FRIENDS 1975 CAROLINE UK C1511
CLINT HOUSTON B (A
JOHN ABERCROMBIE G (A — JEFF WILLIAMS D (A

F119A FRIENDSHIP F119A

ALEX ACUNA D (A — (A) FRIENDSHIP 1979 ELEKTRA US 6E 241 UK K52185
ERNIE WATTS WIND (A
DAVE GRUSIN K (A — ABRAHAM LABORIEL B (A — LEE RITENOUR G (A

F120 FRIJID PINK F120

TOM BEAUDRY B (ALL — (A) FRIJID PINK 1970 DERAM UK 1062 US PARROT 71033
RICH STEVERS D (ALL — (B) DEFROSTED 1970 DERAM UK 1077 US PARROT 71041
GARY THOMPSON G (ALL — (C) EARTH OMEN 1973 LIONEL US 1004
KELLY GREEN V (— (D) IN THE BEGINNING 1973 TELDEC GER 621 681
(E) ALL PINK INSIDE 1975 FANTASY US 9464

F120A FRINGE BENEFIT F120A

JOHN JONES G V (A — (A) FRINGE BENEFIT 1977 CAPRICORN US CP 0183
CHRIS HAINES B (A
DAVE GRAY G (A — STEVEN LAURIE D (A — MIKE MORAN K (A

F121 ROBERT FRIPP F121

ROBERT FRIPP G (ALL — (A) NO PUSSY FOOTIN' 1972 ISLAND UK HELP16 US ANTILLES 7007
BRIAN ENO K (ABC — (A) NO PUSSY FOOTIN' 1977 POLYDOR EG UK 2343 095
BARRY ANDREWS K (C — (B) EVENING STAR 1975 ISLAND UK HELP22 US ANTILLES 7018
PETER HAMMILL V (C — (B) EVENING STAR 1977 ISLAND GER 89867 EG UK 2343094
PHIL COLLINS D PERC(C — (C) EXPOSURE 1979 EG UK EGLP 101 GER 2302 092
PETER GABRIEL V (C — (C) EXPOSURE 1979 POLYDOR US 6201
MICHAEL WALDEN D (C — (D) GOD SAVE THE QUEEN/MANNERS 1980 EG UK EGLP 105 GER 2302 098
DARYL HALL V (C — (D) GOD SAVE THE QUEEN/MANNERS 1980 POLYDOR US 6288
TERRE ROCHE V (C — (E) FRIPPERTRONICS/LET THE POWER FALL 1981 EG UK EGED 10 GER 2311 073
TONY LEVIN B (C
DAVID BYRNE V (D — PAUL DISKIN D (D — BUSTA CHERRY JONES B (D

F122 LORRAINE FRISAURA F122

LORRAINE FRISAURA V G(A — (A) BE HAPPY FOR ME 1976 RCA PL 13034
STEVE KHAN G (A
DON GROLNICK K (A — MICHAEL BRECKER HRNS (A — MERLE MILLER V (A — ERIN DICKINS V (A
WILLIAM F LEE B (A — MIKE MANDEL SYN (A — GAIL KANTOR V (A — CHRIS HILLS D (A
MTUME PERC (A — KAY T OSLIN V (A

F122A FRISKY F122A

(A) FRISKY 1980 VANGUARD US 79430

F123 FRED FRITH F123

FRED FRITH SYN G B K D (ALL — (A) GUITAR SOLS 1974 CAROLINE UK C1508
DEREK BAILEY (B — (B) GUITAR SOLOS 2 1976 CAROLINE UK C1518
HANS REICHEL (B — (C) GUITAR SOLOS 3 1979 RIFT RIFT1
HASSE BRUNIUSSON HRNS (E — (D) WITH FRIENDS LIKE THIS 1979 METALANGUAGE 107
HENRY KAISER (C — (E) GRAVITY 1980 RALPH US 8057
G F FITZGERALD (B — (F) SPEECHLESS 1981 RALPH US 8106
CHIP HANDY (C
PETER CUSACK (C — DAVEY WILLIAMS (C — KEITH ROWE (C — EUGENE CHADBOURNE (C
AKIRA HIJIMA (C — EINO HAAPALA G MAND (E — LARS HOLLMER K ACC(E — CHRIS CUTLER PERC (E
OLIVIA BUYNHOOGHE PERC(E — MARC HOLLANDER WIND (E — TINA CURRAN B WIND(E — CATHERINE JAUNIAUX PERC(E
FRANK WUYTS PERC D(E — MICHEL BERKMANS PERC (E — STORM V (F — ETIENNE CONOD PERC(E
DENIS VAN HECKE PERC (E — VERONIQUE VINCENT PERC (E — ASHA SWANSON V (EF — FRED MAHER D (F
DAVE NEWHOSE SAX K(F — BILLY SWAN B (E — PAUL SEARS D (E — GUIGON CHEVENIER D SAX(F
MARGOT MATHIEU SAX V(F — FERDINAND RICHARD B V (F — JO THIRION K (F — TOM SCOTT SAX (E
ROGER PARSONS PIPES(F — BILL LASWELL B (F — STEVE BUCHANAN SAX (F — GEORGE CARTWRIGHT SAX (F
MARS WILLIAMS SAX (F

F123A DONNIE FRITTS F123A

DONNIE FRITTS V PNO(A — (A) PRONE TO LEAN 1974 ATLANTIC US SD 18117
PETE CARR G DOB(A
JIMMY JOHNSON G (A — EDDIE HINTON G HCA(A — BARRY BECKETT K VIBES(A — MIKE UTLEY ORG(A
DAVID HOOD B (A — ROGER HAWKINS D (A — SAMMY CREASON D (A — JERRY McGEE G (A
TONY JOE WHITE G B V(A — JERRY MASTERS B (A — SPOONER OLDHAM VIBES (A — MICKEY RAPHAEL HARP(A

F124 EDGAR FROESE F124

EDGAR FROESE MULTI INST(ALL — (A) AQUA 1974 VIRGIN US 13111 UK V2016
KLAUS KRIEGER D (C — (B) EPSILON IN MALAYSIAN PALE 1975 VIVGIN UK V2040
(C) AGES 1977 VIRGIN UK V2507
CHRIS FRANK SYN (A — (D) MACULA TRANSFER 19 IMP
GUNTHER BRONSCHEN (A — (E) STUNT MAN 1979 VIRGIN UK V2139
(F) ELECTRONIC DREAMS 197 BRAIN GER 0040 148

F125 WYNDER K FROG F125

WYNDER K FROG(MICK WEAVER) K (ALL — (A) SUNSHINE SUPER FROG 1967 ISLAND UK ILPS 944
CHRIS MERCER SAX (BC — (B) OUT OF THE FRYING PAN 1968 UA US 6695 UK ISLANDILPS 9082
REBOP PERC (B — (C) INTO THE FIRE 1970 UA US 6740
NEIL HUBBARD G (BC
ALAN SPENNER B (BC — BRUCE ROWLAND D (BC — DICK HECKSTALL SMITH SAX(B — HENRY LOWTHER HRNS (B
ROCKY DZIZORDNU PERC (C — SHAWN PHILLIPS G V (C

F126 RAYMOND FROGGATT F126

RAYMOND FROGGATT V (ABCD — (A) VOICE AND WRITING OF — 1969 POLYDOR UK 583 044
LOUIS CLARK K (A — (B) BLEACH — 1972 BELL UK BELLS 207
LEONARD ABLETHORPE D (A — (C) ROGUES & THIEVES — 1974 REPRISE UK K 44257
HARTLEY CAIN G (A — (D) SOUTHERN FRIED FROG — 1978 JET UK JATLP 209
JOHN FIDDY B (A — (E) CONVERSATIONS — 1979 JET US 35729
JORDANAIRES V (D
BILLY SANFORD G (D — PETE DRAKE STEEL (D — BUDDY HARMON D (D — LARRY BUTLER PNO (D
JAMES CAPPS G (D — TOMMY ALSUP B (D

F126A FROGGIE BEAVER F126A

JOHN TROIA V (A — (A) FROM THE POND — 19 FROGGIE BEAVER US 7301
JOHN FISCHER V G B(A
ED STASZKO K V (A — RICK BROWN D V(A — CHRIS STOVALL VIBES (A — MIKE McKEEN PERC (A

F127 FROGMORTON F127

MIKE SMITH G V (A — (A) FROGMORTON AT LAST — 1976 PHILIPS UK 6308 261
LUCY SHARPE G PERC V (A
CHRIS TULLOCH K MAND V(A — DAVE HARDY ACC PERC(A — BILL LYNN B (A — TERRY NEWBURY D (A

F127A FRANK FROST F127A

FRANK FROST (A — (A) HEY BOSS MAN — 1980 CHARLY UK CRM 2011

F128 STEVEN FROMHOLZ F128

STEVEN FROMHOLZ G V (ALL — (A) FROMMOX — 1969 PROBE US CPLP45115
JOHN BEAL B (A — (B) HOW LONG IS THE ROAD TO KENTUCKY — 1973 NOT RELEASED
DON BROOKS HCA (A — (C) A RUMOR IN MY TIME — 1976 CAPITOL US 11521
BOB JAMES PNO (A — (D) FROLICKING IN THE MYTH — 1977 CAPITOL US 11611
OMAR CLAY D (A — (E) MUSIC FROM OUTLAW BLUES(3SONGS) — 1977 CAPITOL US 11691
EVERETT BARKSDALE B (A — (F) JUS' PLAYIN' ALONG — 1978 LONE STAR US L4601
ERIC WEISSBERG FDL G STEEL B(A — (G) FROMHOLZ LIVE — 1979 FELICITY RECORDS US FR001
KENNY ALTMAN B (A
GARY BARRY (C — RANDY BEAVERS (A — BILL BROWDER (C — MICHAEL CAMPBELL (C
DOUG DILLARD BANJO G(CE — DONNY DOLAN D PERC (C — KELLY DUNN K SYN (C — DAVE FERGUSON K (C
PAUL HARRIS PNO (C — ROGER HARRIS (C — JOHN INMON G V (C — MICHAEL JEFFREY G (C
FRED KRC D PERC (C — ROBERT LIVINGSTON G B V (C — REX LUDWICK (C — WILLIE NELSON V (C
GARY NUNN G K B V SYN (C — JODY PAYNE (C — GARY PELFRY (C — JOE PORCARO PERC (C
MICKEY RAPHAEL HCA (C — RED RHODES STEEL (CD — JOHN SEBASTIAN G V (C — BEE SPEARS B (C
B W STEVENSON G V (C — CASSELL WEBB V (C — KIRK BRUNER D (D — MIKE McKINNEY B V(D
STEVE FORMAN PERC (D — JIM SCHULMAN PERC G V(D — STANLEY SCHWARTZ PNO (D — LARRY NYE G (D
JOE RENZETTI G (D — JAY GRAYDON G (D — JOHN BARNES K SYN (D — DAVID LUELL SAX (D
ANDY MUSON B (D — JIM KELTNER D (E — JEFF BAXTER G (E — ROBBEN FORD G(E
GEORGE CLINTON PNO (E — ARNIE MOORE B (E — RICHARD GREENE FDL (E — J J WALKER PERC (E
MARK DAWSON HCA (E — PETE GRANT STEEL (E — BAMBI ROBERTS K (E

F129A FROST F129A

DICK WAGNER G V (ABC — (A) FROST MUSIC — 19 VANGUARD US 6520
DON HARTMAN G V (ABC — (B) ROCK'N' ROLL MUSIC — 19 VANGUARD US 6541
GERDY GARRIS D K V (ABC — (C) THROUGH THE EYES OF LOVE — 19 VANGUARD US 6556
BOB RIGGS D (ABC

F130A FRUMPY F130A

CARSTEN BOHN B PERC(ABCDE — (A) ALL WILL BE CHANGED — 1970 VERTIGO 6305 067
KARL HEINZ SCHOTT B(ABCDE — (B) FRUMPY 2 — 19 VERTIGO 6305 098
RAINER BAUMANN G STEEL (BCDE — (C) BY THE WAY — 19 VERTIGO 6360 604
ERWIN KANIA K(C — (C) BY THE WAY — 1974 BILLINGSGATE BG 1003
INGA RUMPF V G (ABCDE — (D) LIVE — 19 VERTIGO 6623 022
JEAN JACQUES KRAVETZ K(ABCDE — (E) ATTENTION — 19 FONTANA 6434 163

F131 FRUUP F131

PETER FARELLY B G V(ABCD — (A) FUTURE LEGENDS — 1973 DAWN UK DNLS 3053
STEPHEN HOUSTON K OBOE V(ABC — (B) PRINCE OF HEAVENS EYES — 1974 DAWN UK DNLH 2
MARTIN FOYE D PERC(ABCD — (C) SEVEN SECRETS — 1974 DAWN UK DNLS 3058
VINCE McCUSKER G V (ABCD — (D) MODERN MASQUERADES — 1975 DAWN UK DNLS 3070
JOHN MASON K (D
IAN McDONALD SAX (D

F132 FUCHIA F132

TONY DURANT G V (A — (A) FUCHSIA — 1971 PEGASUS PEG 8
MADELINE BLAND CELLO K V(A
MICHAEL GREGORY D (A — VANESSA HALL-SMITH VLN V(A — JANET ROGERS VLN V (A — MICHAEL DAY B (A

F132A FUGITIVES F132A

(A) FUGITIVES AT DAVES HIDEOUT — 19 HIDEOUT US HLP 1001

F132B FUHRS & FROHLING F132B

GERD FUHRS D SYN V(AB — (A) AMMERLAND — 1978 BRAIN GER 60 105
HEINZ FROHLING G V PERC(AB — (B) STRINGS — 1979 BRAIN GER 60 223
JAN GROENING D (B — (C) DIARY — 1981 BRAIN GER 60 333
DETLEF WIEDEKE B D V(B
KOOS BLOESMA PERC(B

F133 FUGS F133

ED SANDERS V (CEDFG — (A) FIRST ALBUM — 1965 ESP US 1018 UK FONTANA 5513
JIM PEPPER FLT (G — (A) FIRST ALBUM — 1965 ESP EXPLOSIVE FR 538114
KEN WEAVER V D (ACEDGF — (B) THE FUGS(KILL FOR PEACE) — 1966 ESP US 1028
DAN HAMBURG G (G — (B) THE FUGS — 1966 ESP EXPLOSIVE FR 538115
PETER STAMPFEL G BAN HCA (ABC — (B) THE FUGS — 1970 FONTANA UK STL 5524
TULI KUPFERBERG V PERC(ABCDEFGH — (C) VIRGIN FUGS — 1966 ESP US 1028 UK FONTANA 5501
JULIUS WATKINS HRNS (F — (C) VIRGIN FUGS — 1966 ESP EXPLOSIVE FR 538116
KEN PINE G V (EDGF — (D) TENDERNESS JUNCTION — 1966 TRANSATLANTIC UK TRA 180
CHARLES LARKEY B (EDGF — (D) TENDERNESS JUNCTION — 1968 REPRISE US 6280
BOB MASON D (EF — (E) IT CRAWLED INTO MY HAND HONEST — 196 TRANSATLANTIC UK TRA 181
BETSY KLEIN (— (E) IT CRAWLED INTO MY HAND HONEST — 19 REPRISE US 6305
PETE KEARNEY (— (F) GOLDEN FILTH — 1968 REPRISE US 6396
LU CRABTREE (ABC — (G) BELLE OF AVENUE A — 1969 REPRISE US 6359
STEVE WEBER G (ABC — (H) FUGS 4 ROUNDERS SCORE — 1975 ESP US 2018
VINNY LEARY G (ABC
JOHN ANDERSON B V (ACB — DOUG FRANKLIN V (E — JENNIFER BROWN V (E — EARL BAKER V (E
KENNETH BATES V (E — BILL WOLF B (— LESLIE DORSEY V (E — BOB DOROUGH V (E
BARBARA CALABRIA V (E — MARLYS TRUNKHILL V (E — BOB HANSON V (E — JAMES JARVIS B (E
ALLEN GINSBERG V HCA(D — DANNY KORTCHMAR G (ED — MARETTA GREER V (D — CARL LYNCH G (F
RICHARD LEE K (— HOWARD JOHNSON HRNS(F

F133A FULL MOON F133A

LUCAS AMOR VLN (AB — (A) MOON FOOLS 1976 FULL MOON FM001
JOHANNES LUTTICK G V (AB — (B) NOTHING VENTURED NOTHING GAINED 1977 FULL MOON FM002
NORMAN HASSALL PERC (A
BERT KLEYN D PERC(B — MAX BRUNET G SYN (AB — GERARD AMMERLAAN B STRINGS(AB

F133B BOBBY FULLER FOUR F133B

BOBBY FULLER (ALL — (A) I FOUGHT THE LAW 196 MUSTANG US 901
JIM REESE (— (A) I FOUGHT THE LAW 1981 LINE GER 5133
RANDY FULLER (— (B) K R L A KING OF THE WHEELS 196 MUSTANG US 900
WAYNE QUIRICO (— (B) K R L A KING OF THE WHEELS 1981 LINE GER 5146
(C) CIVIL DEFENSE 19 ? US
(D) MEMORIAL ALBUM 1966 PRESIDENT US 1003

F134 LOWELL FULSON F134

LOWELL FULSON G V (ALL — (A) BLUES MASTERS (DBL) 1977 CHESS UK US 205
TOMMY CATHEY (E — (B) HUNG DOWN HEAD 19 CHESS US 408
STEVE CROPPER G (E — (C) IN A HEAVY BAG 1972 POLYDOR UK 2384038 US JEWEL5003
AL JACKSON D (E — (D) LOWELL FULSON (EARLY RECORDINGS) 1975 ARHOOLIE US 2003
MARVELL THOMAS (E — (E) THE OL' BLUES SINGER 1975 JET UK LP9 GRANITE US 1006
MICHAEL TOLES (E — (F) SOUL 19 KENT US 516 UNITED US 7737
BEN BENAY G (E — (G) TRAMP 19 KENT US 520 UNITED US 7741
REINIE PRESS (E — (H) NOW 19 KENT US 531 UNITED US 7752
MIKE HENDERSON (E — (J) LETS GO GET STONED 19 KENT US 558 UNITED US 7768
DONALD MENZA (E — (K) IVE GOT THE BLUES 1973 JEWEL US 5009
DALTON SMITH (E — (L) EVERYDAY I HAVE THE BLUES 19 NASHVILLE US 2030
LEONARD MALARSKY (E — (M) LOWELL FULSON 19 KENT US 5020
JULIA TILLMAN V (E — (N) SAN FRANCISCO BLUES 19 VOGUE FR 512508
CARL LAMAGNA (E — (O) MAN OF MOTION 1980 CHARLY UK CRB 1018
BILLY AADNOT B (A — (P) LOVEMAKER 1978 BIG TOWN 1008
EDDIE CHAMBLEE SAX (EAB
RAY KELLEY (E — MAXINE WILLARD V (E — JOHN KELSO HRNS (E — BUD BRISBOIS (E
LOU McCREARY (E — THOMAS SHEPARD (E — CAROLYN WILLIS V (E — BOBBYE HALL PERC(E
JAMES GETZOFF (E — HARRY WESTONE (E — LOU KLASS (E — MURRAY ADLER (E
BONNIE DOUGLAS (E — GARETH NUTTYCOMBE (E — SAM BOGHOSSIAN (E — JAN KELLEY (E
HARRY BLUESTONE (E — EARL BROWN SAX (AEBN — LLOYD GLENN PNO (ABEN — ELDRIDE McCARTHY PNO(N
BIG DAD B (N — RUFUS J RUSSELL PNO (N — ARTHUR ROBINSON N (N — ASAL CARSON D (N
ELLIS SOLOMON PNO (N — RALPH HAMILTON B (E — BOB HARVEY D (N — ROGER HAWKINS D (C
EDDIE HINTON G (C — BARRY BECKETT K (C — DAVID HOOD B (C — ROBERT SIMS D (A
LOUIS WILLIAMS SAX (A — JIM WYNN SAX (A

F135 FUMBLE F135

DES HENLY G V (B — (A) FUMBLE 1972 SOVEREIGN UK SVNA7254 US 11125
DAVE CHRISTOPHER G V (B — (B) POETRY IN LOTION 1974 RCA UK SF 8403 US 5082
SEAN MAYES V PNO(B
MARIO FERRARI B V (B — BARRY PIKE D (B

F135A FUN & GAMES F135A

(A) ELEPHANT CANDY 19 UNI US 73042

F135B FUNERAL F135B

MIKE MARTT G V (A — (A) FUNERAL 1981 AZRA (EP)
MATT DORSETT G (A
JOHN NEFF B (A — D THUM D (A

F136 FUNGUS F136

FRED PIEK G V (A — (A) LIEF ENDE LEID 1975 NEGRAM NL NR 115
BOB DEKENGA K (A
KOOS PAKVIS B V (A — LOUIS DEBIJ D (A — RENS VANDER ZALM VLN G(A — SIDO MARTENS G(A

F136A FUNK FACTORY F136A

(A) FUNK FACTORY 1976 ATCO US 36116

F137 FUNKADELIC F137

GARY SHIDER G V (FK — (A) FUNKADELIC 1970 WESTBOUND US 216 PYE UK 28137
MIKE HAMPTON G (K — (B) FREE YOUR MIND YOUR ASS WILL FOLLOW 71 WESTBOUND US 2001 PYE UK 28144
BOBBY LAVIS G (K — (C) MAGGOT BRAIN 1971 WESTBOUND US 2007 UK6310200
WALTER MORRISON K SYN(K — (D) COSMIC SLOP 1973 WESTBOUND US 2022
BERNARD WORRELL K V (KF — (E) AMERICA EATS ITS YOUNG 1973 WESTBOUND US 2020
TYRONE LAMPKIN D (FK — (F) STANDING ON THE VERGE OF TIME 19 WESTBOUND US 208
BOOTSY COLLINS D (K — (G) LETS TAKE IT TO THE STAGE 1975 WESTBOUND US 215
JEROME BRAILEY D (K — (G) LETS TAKE IT TO THE STAGE 1975 20TH CENTURY UK 215
JIMMY CALHOUN B (F — (H) GREATEST HITS 1975 WESTBOUND US 1004
LARRY FRATANGELO D (K — (I) TALES OF KIDD FUNKADELIC 197 WESTBOUND US 227
RAYMOND DAVIS V (KF — (J) HARDCORE JOLLIES 1978 WB US 2973 UK K56299
LYNN MABRY V (K — (K) ONE NATION UNDER A GROOVE 1978 WB US 3209 UK K56539
RON FORD V (K — ( ) BEST OF THE EARLY YEARS 197 WESTBOUND US 303
DAWN SILVA V (K — (M) UNCLE JAM WANTS YOU 1979 WB US 3371 UK K56539
LEON PATILLO PNO (F — (N) ELECTRONIC SPANKING OF BABIES 1980 WB US 3482 UK K56874
GARY BRONSON D (F — (O) CONNECTIONS & DISCONNECTIONS 1981 LAX US 37987
RON BRYLOWSKI G (F
DEBBIE WRIGHT V (K — GARY SHIDE V (K — JEANETTE WASHINGTON V (K — MULLIN FRANKLIN V (K
CORDELL MOSSON V B (KF — GEORGE CLINTON V (KF — GRADY THOMAS V (KF — CALVIN SIMON V PERC(K
CLARENCE HASKINS V (F — R FULWOOD V PERC (F

F137A FUNKY COMMUNICATION COMMITTEE F137A

(A) BABY I WANT YOU 1979 FREE FLIGHT US AHLI 3405

F138 FUNKY KINGS F138

JACK TEMPCHIN V G HCA(A — (A) FUNKY KINGS 1976 ARISTA US AL 4078
RICHARD STEKOL V G PNO(A
JULES SHEAR G V(A — FRANK COTINOLA D (A — BILL BODINE B V (A — GREG LEISZ G STEEL V (A
MIKE FINNIGAN V K(A — BARRY BECKETT PNO (A — KATY MOFFATT V (A

F139 RICHIE FURAY F139

RICHIE FURAY V G (ALL — (A) I'VE GOT A REASON — 1976 ASYLUM US 7E1067 UK K 53043
JAY TRUAX B V (A — (B) DANCE A LITTLE — 1978 ASYLUM US 6E115 UK K 53074
JOHN MEHLER D (AB — (C) I STILL HAVE DREAMS — 1981 ASYLUM US 6E213
TOM STIPE K V (A
MICHAEL OMARTIAN K V (A — STORMIE OMARTIAN V (A — AL PERKINS G (AB — STEVE CROPPER G (A
ANN WADE V (A — MYRNA MATTHEWS V (A — CAROLYN WILLIS V (AB — AL MacDOUGALL PERC(A
DON BARBER BANJO(A — BILLY BATSTONE B V (BC — GABRIEL KATONA K (B — JIM MASON PERC(B
WILLIAM SMITH K (C — DAN DUGMORE G (C — VIRGIL BECKHAM G V (B — JIM HORN HRNS(B
TIM SCHMIDT V (BC — JIM LOILLE HRNS (B — DAVID CASSIDY V (B — JACK REDMAN HRNS(B
CRAIG FULLER V (C — JIM MESSINA G (B — CHUCK FINDLEY HRNS (B — ED COBB V (B
STEVE MADAIO HRNS (B — CHRIS HILLMAN V (B — VICTOR FELDMAN PERC (B — GEORGE GRANTHAM V(B
RUSTY YOUNG STEEL(B — TOM KUBIS HRNS(B — RANDY MEISNER V (C — RUSS KUNKEL D (C
ROSEMARY BUTLER V (C — LEE SKLAR B (C — VANETTA FIELDS V (C — WADDY WACHTEL G (C
J D SOUTHER V (C

F140 BILLY FURY F140

BILLY FURY V (ALL — (A) THE SOUND OF FURY 10" — 1960 DECCA UK (RI 1981) LF 1329
JOE BROWN G (A — (B) BILLY FURY — 1960 ACE OF CLUBS UK ACL 1047
ARTHUR GREENSLADE K (A — (C) HALFWAY TO PARADISE — 1961 ACE OF CLUBS UK ACL 1083
(D) BILLY — 1963 DECCA UK LK 4533
(E) WE WANT BILLY — 1963 DECCA UK SKL 4548
(F) BEST OF — 1967 ACE OF CLUBS UK ACL 1229
( ) WORLD OF — 1972 DECCA UK SAA 108
( ) THE BILLY FURY STORY DBL — 1977 DECCA UK DPA 3033
( ) GOLDEN YEARS — 1979 K TEL UK NE 1020

F140A FUSE F140A

RICK NIELSEN G K (A — (A) FUSE — 1968 EPIC US 26502
CRAIG MEYERS G (A
CHIP GREENMAN D (A — JOE SUNDBERG V (A — TOM PETERSON B (A

F140B FUSION ORCHESTRA F140B

COLIN DAWSON G (A — (A) SKELETON IN ARMOUR — 1973 EMI UK EMA 758
DAVE BELL D (A
JILL SAWARD G SYN FLT V (A — STEN LAND G SYN PERC HCA(A — DAVE COWELL B HCA(A

F140C FUSE ONE F140C

(A) FUSE ONE — 1981 CTI UK 2406 012 US 9003

F140D FUSION F140D

REG WEBB K V (A — (A) TILL I HEAR FROM YOU — 1980 TELEPHONE TEL 101
NICK KERSHAW G V (A
ALAN CLARKE D (A — KENN ELSON B (A

F140E FUTURE FLIGHT F140E

(A) FUTURE FLIGHT — 1981 CAPITOL US 12154

F141 FUZZY DUCK F141

MIKE HAWKSWORTH B (1 — (A) FUZZY DUCK — 1971 MAM UK MAM 1005
PAUL FRANCIS D (1 — (1) POST LP LINE UP DIFFERENT GUITARIST ON LP
GARTH WATT ROY G V (1
ROY SHARLAND ORG (1

F142 FYNN McCOOL F142

CHRIS STONE G V (A — (A) FYNN McCOOL — 1970 RCA UK SF 8112
MICK CARTER D (A
ALAN ESCOMBE B (A — MICK FOWLER K V (A

G1 JOHNNY G G1

JOHNNY G G V (A — (A) G SHARP G NATURAL — 1979 BEGGARS BANQUET UK BEGA 6
GRAHAM HINE G (A — (B) G BEAT — 1980 BEGGARS BANQUET UK BEGA16
TAFFY DAVIES K (A — (C) WATER INTO WINE — 1981 BEGGARS BANQUET UK BEGA30
PAUL HUGHES B V (B
KEITH TRUSSELL (A — JOHN RANDALL D PERC(A — CHAS AMBLER V (AB — MALCOLM BENNETT B (A
CHRIS GOWER TROM (A — DICK HANSON HRNS (A — RAY BEAVIS SAX (A — JOHN EARLE SAX (A
DAVE BELLOTTI (A — ANGUS GAYE D (A — TERRY BARKHAM B (A — NICK HOWELL D (A
STEVE LILLYWHITE B (A — NICK GLENNIE SMITH PNO (A — MARK HOLLIS V (A — JOHN SPENCER (A
JOHN EVERY HCA (B — BRETT V (B — FIN V (B

G1A G FORCE G1A

GARY MOORE G K V(A — (A) G FORCE — 1980 JET UK JETLP 229
MARK NAUSEEF D PERC(A
WILLIE DEE B K V(A — TONY NEWTON V (A

G1B GABRIEL G1B

FRANK BUTORAC G V (A — (A) THIS STAR ON EVERY HEEL — 1975 ABC US ABCD 885
MICHAEL KINDER D PERC(A — (B) SWEET RELEASE — 1976 ABC US AB 972
STACY CHRISTENSON K V (A — (C) GABRIEL — 1978 EPIC US 35454
GARY RUHL B (A
TERRY LAUBER G STEEL V (A — MARK PENNICK CONGA(A

G1C BB GABOR G1C

B B GABOR — (A) BB GABOR — 1980 BLUEPRINT UK 5004

G2 PETER GABRIEL G2

PETER GABRIEL V K (ALL — (A) PETER GABRIEL — 1977 CHARISMA UK CDS 4006
ALLEN SCHWARZBERG D (A — (A) PETER GABRIEL — 1977 PHONOGRAM EURO 9103 115
TONY LEVIN B V (ABC — (A) PETER GABRIEL — 1977 ATCO US 36147
JIM MAELEN G (A — (B) PETER GABRIEL — 1978 CHARISMA UK CAS 4013
STEVE HUNTER G (A — (B) PETER GABRIEL — 1978 ATLANTIC US 19181
ROBERT FRIPP G (ABC — (B) PETER GABRIEL — 1978 PHONOGRAM EURO 9103 123
DAVID RHODES V (C — (B) PETER GABRIEL — 1978 CHARISMA GER)!"$ 025
JOSEF WAGNER G (— (C) PETER GABRIEL — 1980 CHARISMA UK CAS 4019
JERRY MAROTTA V D (BC — (C) PETER GABRIEL — 1980 MERCURY US 3848
SIDNEY McGINNIS G V (B — (C) PETER GABRIEL — 1980 CHARISMA GER 9124 054
LARRY FAST SYN (ABC
TIM CAPELLO SAX (B — BAYETE K (B — ROY BITTAN K (B — GEORGE MARGE RECORDERS(B
JOSEF CHIROWSKI K (A — JOHN GIBLIN B (C — PAUL WELLER V (C — DAVE GREGORY V (C
KATE BUSH V (C — PHIL COLLINS D (C

G2A GABRIEL BONDAGE G2A

REX BUNDY G V ((A) ANOTHER TRIP TO EARTH 1978 DHARMA US 808
TONY STRAM B V (
L JAMES BIERACKI G MAND V(RON SCHWARTZ K SYN(BILL WISNIEWSKI WIND V (NOEL LEVITT D V (

G2B GADGETS G2B

? TUCKER (A (A) GADGETREE 1980 FINAL SOLUTION UK 001
? JOHNSON (A (B) LOVE CURIOSITY FRECKLES & DOUBT 1980 FINAL SOLUTION UK 002
? HYDE (A

G2C GAFFA G2C

(A) NEITHER USE NOR ORNAMENT 19 GAFFA ZZZZ001

G3 GAGS G3

GERRY MacLOUGHLIN G (A (A) DEATH IN BUZZARD GULCH 1978 GAG
BREN GORE K V (A
JOHN KELLY B (A NIGEL COATMAN D (A

G3A GALACTIC SUPERMARKET G3A

GILLE (A) GALACTIC SUPERMARKET 1974 KOMISCHE KM 58010
ROSI
DIETER DIERKS (JURGEN DOLLASE (A MANUEL GOETTSCHING (HARALD GROSSKOPF (
KLAUS SCHULZE (

G3B ARLYN GALE G3B

ARLYN GALE G V (A (A) BACK TO THE MIDWEST NIGHT 1978 ABC UK ABCL 5261
ALONA TUSEL K SYN(A
OMAR HAKIM D V (A IVAN ELLIS B (A STEVE CAVARETTA G (A

G4 ERIC GALE G4

ERIC GALE G (ALL (A) FORECAST 1973 KUDU US 11 UK KUL .8
BOB JAMES K (B (B) GINSENG WOMAN 1977 CBS US 34421 UK 82958
RICHARD TEE K (BD (C) MULTIPLICATION 1978 CBS US 34938 UK 82283
ANTHONY JACKSON B (BD (D) PART OF YOU 1979 CBS US 35715
HARVEY MASON D (D (E) TOUCH OF SILK 1980 CBS US 36570 UK 84509
STEVE GADD D (BD (F) BEST OF 1980 CBS US 36363 UK 84201
RALPH MACDONALD PERC (BD
GROVER WASHINGTON SAX (BDE ALLEN TOUSSAINT K (E ROBERT DABON K (E GARY KING B (B
ANDREW SMITH D (B GEORGE YOUNG SAX (B GARY BROWN SAX (E ARTHUR BLYTHE SAX (E
HAROLD VICK SAX (E WAYNE ANDRE TROM (B DAVE TAYLOR TROM (B LOU SOLOFF TPT (B
BILL EATON V (B ZACK SANDERS V (B RAY SIMPSON V (B FRANK FLOYD V (B
VIVIAN CHERRY V (B LANI GROVES V (B PATTI AUSTIN V (B RANDY BRECKER TPT (B
ALAN RUBIN TPT (B JON FADDIS TPT (B EDDIE DANIELS SAX (B MICHAEL BRECKER SAX (B
CHARLES EARLAND K (E IDRIS MUHAMMAD D (DE KENNETH WILLIAMS PERC (E JAMES BLACK D (E
DAVID BARARD B (E BERNADETTE RANDLE PNO (D NEIL JASON B (D DAVE CRUSIN PNO (D

G4A GALE FORCE G4A

(A) GALE FORCE 1978 FANTSAY US 9527
(B) TIRO 1978 FANTASY US 9551

G5 RORY GALLAGHER G5

RORY GALLAGHER G V (ALL (A) RORY GALLAGHER 1971 POLYDOR UK 2383 044
(A) RORY GALLAGHER 1971 ATLANTIC US 33368
(A) RORY GALLAGHER 198 CHRYSALIS CHR 1258
GERRY McAVOY B (ABCDEFGHIJKLMNO (A) RORY GALLAGHER 1975 POLYDOR UK 2384 066
WILGAR CAMPBELL D (ABCJLZ (B) DEUCE 1971 POLYDOR UK 2383 076
(B) DEUCE 1971 ATLANTIC US 7004
(B) DEUCE 198 CHRYSALIS CHR 1254
(B) DEUCE 19 CHRYSALIS NL 511 254
ROD DeATH D (EDFJK (C) LIVE IN EUROPE 1972 POLYDOR US 5513 UK 2383 112
(C) LIVE IN EUROPE 19 CHRYSALIS NL 202 647
LOU MARTIN K (EDFJKZ (D) BLUEPRINT 1973 POLYDOR US 5522 UK 2383 189
(D) BLUEPRINT 198 CHRYSALIS CHR 1253
TED McKENNA D (MNO (E) TATTOO 1973 POLYDOR US 5539 UK 2383 230
(E) TATTOO 198 CHRYSALIS CHR 1259
VINCENT CRANE K (A (F) IRISH TOUR 1974 1974 POLYDOR US 9501 UK 2659 031
(F) IRISH TOUR 1974 1974 POLYDOR GER 2679 030
BOB ANDREWS K (P (G) IN THE BEGINNING 1974 EMERALD GEM UK GES1 101
RICHARD McCRACKEN B (ZY (G) IN THE BEGINNING 197 SPRINGBOARD US 4056
JOHN WILSON D (ZY (H) AGAINST THE GRAIN 1975 CHRYSALIS UK/US CHR 1098
RAY BEAVIS SAX (P (H) AGAINST THE GRAIN 1975 POLYDOR EURO 6307 563
DICK PARRY SAX (P (I) SINNER ....& SAINT 197 POLYDOR US 6510 2383 315
BRENDAN ONEIL D (P (J) THE STORY SO FAR 1975 POLYDOR US 6519 UK 2383 376
ERIC KITTERINGHAM B (G (K) CALLING CARD 1976 CHRYSALIS UK/US CHE 1124
NORMAN DAMERY D (G (K) CALLING CARD 1976 PHONOGRAM EURO 6307 586
(L) THE BEST YEARS 1976 POLYDOR 2664 303
(M) PHOTO FINISH 1978 CHRYSALIS UK CHR 1170
(M) PHOTO FINISH 1978 CHRYSALIS GER 6307 620
(N) TOP PRIORITY 1979 CHRYSALIS UK/USCHR 1235
(N) TOP PRIORITY 1979 CHRYSALIS NL 511 235
(O) STAGE STRUCK 1980 CHRYSALIS UK/US CHR 1280
(O) STAGE STRUCK 1980 CHRYSALIS GER 202 884
( ) LIVE TRACKS FROM (C) (F) 1977 POLYDOR 2384 079
(P) JINX 1982 CHRYSALIS UK CHR 1359
(P) JINX 1982 MERCURY US SRM1 4051
(W) TAKE IT EAST BABY 1976 SPRINGBOARD US 4056
(X) RORY GALLAGHER 1980 HALLMARK UK 3041
(Y) FIRST & BEST 19 BELLAPHON GER 29385
(Z) STORY OF R G 197 POLYDOR GER 2664 377

G6 GALLAGHER & LYLE G6

BENNY GALLAGHER G V (ALL (A) GALLAGHER & LYLE 1972 CAPITOL US 11016 UK 21906
GRAHAM LYLE G V (ALL (A) GALLAGHER & LYLE 1972 A&M UK AMLS68125
WITH (B) WILLIE & THER LAP DOG 1973 A&M US 4384 UK AMLH68148
JIMMY JEWELL SAX (1DEF (C) SEEDS 1973 A&M US 4425 UK AMLS68207
JOHN MUMFORD HRN (1EF (D) LAST COWBOY 1974 A&M US 3665 UK AMLS68273
IAIN RAE K (1F (E) BREAKAWAY 1976 A&M US 4566 UK AMLH68348
ALAN HORNALL B (12EFG (F) LOVE ON THE AIRWAVES 1976 A&M US 4620 UK AMLH64620
CHRIS STEWART B (A (F) LOVE ON THE AIRWAVES 1981 MFP UK RI 50497
RAY DUFFY D (12EFG (G) SHOWDOWN 1978 A&M US 4675 UK AMLH68461
BILLY LIVSEY K (2DEG (H) LONESOME NO MORE 1979 MERCURY UK 9109 628
STEVE GREGORY WIND (2 (I) BEST OF 1980 WARWICK UK WW 5080
PAUL NIEMAN TROM (2 (1) 1977 TOUR (2) 1978 TOUR
PHIL RYAN K (2 (EG) BREAKAWAY/SHOWDOWN 1981 A&M CASS CR6
BRYN HAWORTH G (2
PETE TOWNSHEND HCA (B RAY COOPER PERC (G BRUCE ROWLAND D PERC(ABD HUGHIE FLINT D (B
JIM HORN SAX (G

G7 GALLIARD G7

RICHARD PANNELL G ((A) STRANGE PLEASURE 1969 NOVA UK SDN4
GEOFF BROWN V ((B) NEW DAWN 1970 DERAM UK SML 1075
ANDREW ABBOTT B (
LESLIE PODRAZA D (JOHN SMITH WIND (DAVE CASWELL WIND (

G7A GAMBLER G7A

NATHAN SHAFFER V G (A (A) TEENAGE MAGIC 1979 LIBERTY AML 3005
WARREN MAYS G V (A (B) LOVE AND OTHER CRIMES 1980 U A AML 3010 EMIUS 17017
DEL BRECKENFELD B V (A
CHUCK SCHWARTZ D (A BRUCE BRECKENFELD K V (A

G7B GAMMA G7B

RONNIE MONTROSE G (CA (A) 1 1980 ELEKTRA US 6E 129 UK K 52163
JIM ALCIVAR SYN (A (B) 2 1980 ELEKTRA US 6E 228 UK K 52245
DAVEY PATTISON V (CA (C) 3 1980 ELEKTRA US 60034
ALAN FITZGERALD B (A
SKIP GILLETTE PERC (A MITCHELL FROMM K (C DENNY CARMASSI D (C GLENN LEITSCH B (C

G7C GANG OF FOUR G7C

JOHN KING V (A (A) ENTERTAINMENT 1979 EMI UK EMC 3313 US WB 3446
ANDY GILL G (A (B) SOLID GOLD 1981 EMI UK EMC 3364 US WB 3565
HUGO BURNHAM D (A (EP) GANG OF FOUR 1981 MINI UK 3494
DAVE ALLEN B (A

G7D GANGSTERS G7D

RICHARD HOLGARTH G V (A (A) GANSTERS 1979 STORTBEAT BEAT2
BILL MEADOWS G V (A
TERRY HANDS D (A MARTIN HOLDEN B (A STEVE HORTON K (A

G7E GAME G7E

CHUCK FITZPATRICK G V B(B (A) GAME 19 EVOLUTION US 2021
GEORGE TERRY G B (B (B) LONG HOT SUMMER 19 EVOLUTION US 3008
SCOTT KIRKPATRICK D TPT(B
EDDIE KEATING B V (B LES LUHRING K VIBES V(B

G8 CECIL GANT G8

CECIL GANT PNO V(ALL (A) INCOMPARABLE 19 SOUND US 601
(B) ROCK LITTLE BABY 1974 FLYRIGHT UK 4710
(C) CECIL BOOGIE 1976 FLYRIGHT UK 4714
(D) KILLER DILLER BOOGIE 1979 MAGPIE UK PY1816

G9 JERRY GARCIA G9

JERRY GARCIA G V (ALL (A) GARCIA 1972 WB US 2582 UK K46139
HOWARD WALES K (B (B) HOOTEROLL 1972 DOUGLAS US 30859 69013
JOHN KAHN B (BCEF (C) LIVE AT THE KEYSTONE 1973 FANTASY 79002
CURLY COOKE G (B (D) GARCIA 1974 GARCIA/ROUND 59301 102
BILL VITT D (BC (E) REFLECTIONS 1976 UA/ROUND US LA565 UK 29921
MICHAEL MARINELLI D (B (F) CATS UNDER THE STARS 1978 ARISTA UK SPART1053 US AB4160
KEN BALZALL TPT (B
MARTIN FIERRO WIND (B KEITH GODCHAUX V K (FE DONNA GODCHAUX V K (FE BRIAN GODCHAUX VLN (F
CANDY GODCHAUX VLN (F RON TUTT D (FE MERL SANDERS K (FC MARIA MULDAUR V (FD
STEVE SCHUSTER WIND (F BOB WEIR G (E PHIL LESH B (E BILL KREUTZMANN D (AE
MICKEY HART D (E NICKY HOPKINS K (E LARRY KNECHTEL PNO (E LARRY CARLTON G (A
MICHAEL O'MARTIAN K (D BOBBYE HALL PERC (D RICHARD GREENE VLN (D CLYDIE KING V (D
BEN BENAY G (D AMOS GARRETT G (D MERRY CLAYTON V (D TERRY ADAMS CELLO(D
ROBERT HUNTER G (A

G10 ART GARFUNKEL G10

ART GARFUNKEL V (ALL (A) ANGEL CLARE 1973 CBS US 31474 UK 69021
JAMES GILSTRAP V (D (A) ANGEL CLARE 1981 EMBASSY UK 32076
LARRY CARLTON G (A (B) BREAKAWAY 1975 CBS US 33700 UK 86002
DEAN PARKS G (AF (C) WATERMARK 1977 CBS US 34975 UK 86054
STEVE CROPPER G (B (D) FATE FOR BREAKFAST 1979 CBS US 35780 UK 86082
MAX BENNETT B (B (E) ART GARFULKEL 1979 CBS TRIPLE UK 66351
LON VAN EATON G (B (F) SISSORS CUT 1981 CBS US 37392 UK 85259
MAXINE ANDERSON V (D
LOUIE SHELTON G (ABD MIKE OMARTIAN K (A JIM GORDON D (A JOE CLAYTON PERC (B
PETE CARR G (BCF LARRY KNECHTEL K (ABDF RUSS KUNKEL D (BF TOM ROADY PERC (C
PAUL SIMON G V(ABCF BRUCE JOHNSTON PNO (B DENNY SEIWELL D (B THOMAS LA TONDRE PERC (C
JIMMY JOHNSON G (C BILL PAYNE K (BC JIM KELTNER D (B CRAIG KRAMPF PERC (C
HUGH McCRACKEN G (DC NICKY HOPKINS K (B RICK SCHLOSSER D (BC TOMMY VIG VIBES(CF
ANDREW GOLD G V (BF JIMMY WEBB K (CF JOHN GUERIN D (B DEREK BELL HARP (C
STEPHEN BISHOP G V (BCD RICHARD TEE K (CD ROGER HAWKINS D (BC MICHAEL TUBRIDY FLT (C
JOE OSBORN B (ABCF BARRY BECKETT PNO (BC STEVE GADD D (CD SEAN KEANE FDL (C
LEE SKLAR B (B JOHN JARVIS PNO V (BF HAL BLAINE D (A PADDY MOLONEY WIND (C
KLAUS VOORMANN B (B PAUL DESMOND SAX (C RALPH McDONALD PERC (C JOE FARRELL WIND (C
DAVID HOOD B (B MARTIN FAY FDL (C GRAHAM NASH V (B DAVID CROSBY V (BC
REINIE PRESS B (B TONI TENNILLE V (B JAN JOYCE V (B JAY CLAYTON V (B
TONY LEVIN B (CF SHELLEY HIRSCH V (C ED HASSELBRINK V (C FRED FARELL V (C
(CONTINUED)

G10 **ART GARFUNKEL** (CONTINUED) G10

CAROL FLAMM V (C ALEXANDRA STAVROU V (C JAMES TAYLOR V (C BOB DOROUGH V (C
LEAH KUNKEL V (CDF RICHIE ZITO G (D MICHAEL BAIRD D (D NEIL JOHNSON B (D
MICHAEL BRECKER SAX (DF BOB MOUNSEY STR (D PENNY NICHOLS V (D LYLE FORMAN PERC (D
CHRIS SPEDDING G (D LES HURDLE B (D EDWIN ROXBURGH B (D JEFFREY STATON G V (DF
MICHAEL BODDICKER SYN (F LISA GARBER V (F GRAHAM LYLE G (F RICK MAROTTA D (F
LEWIS SOLOFF HRNS (F CAROLYLN DENNIS V (D LARRY ROLANDS G (D DENNIS BELFIELD B (D
ALAN ESTES PERC (D DEL NEWMAN STR (DF CRUSHER BENNET PERC (DF ALESSI BROTHERS V (D
TOM SCOTT SAX (D SIMON PHILLIPS D (D ROLAND HARKER G (D ROY MORGAN D (D
RAY COOPER PERC (D LEE RITENOUR G (D DAVID CAMPBELL STR (F SCOTT CHAMBERS B (F
RICK SCHLOSSER D (F MICHAEL STATON G (F MARK FRIEDMAN REC (A JIMMY HASKELL STR (A
JJ CALE G (A JERRY GARCIA G (A CARL RADLE B (A JULES BROUSSARD SAX (A
JORGE MILCHBERG PERC (A MILT HOLLAND PERC (A SALLY STEVENS V (A ERNIE FREEMAN STR (A
PETER MATZ STR (A FRED CARTER G (A TOMMY TEDESCO MAND (A JACK SHROER SAX (A
DOROTHY MORRISON V (A ST MARYS CHOIR V (A LYLE HARPER B (D NEIL JASON B (D
OKLAHMA UNI CHORALE (C

G10A **GARRISON & VAN DYKE** G10A

MICHAEL GARRISON V (A (A) GARRISON & VAN DYKE 1979 ATCO US 38119
RINUS VAN DYKE G B K HCA(A
SHELL SHELLEKENS D (A EELCO GELLING G (A DANNY LADEMACHER G (A KOKO KAUWSOLEA PERC (A

G10B **AMOS GARRETT** G10B

AMOS GARRETT G V UKE(A (A) GO GO CAT GO 1980 WATERFRONT UK 006
MAC DRIDLIK B (A
BILL SLAIS SAX (A MICHAEL MILFORD MAND (A DARYL COLEY V (A KYLE WRIGHT V (A
PHIL AABERG K SYN(A SCOTT MATTHEWS D PERC(A HIROSHI SATO SYN (A DAVE BERGEN HCA (A
LARRY ROBERSON V (A

G10C **MICHAEL GARRISON** G10C

MICHAEL GARRISON V (A (A) IN THE REGIONS OF SUN RETURN 1979 ARIOLA 202 864

G11 **GARUDA** G11

TONY COE WIND (A (A) GARUDA 1977 EMI UK EMC 3174
JEFF DALEY WIND (A
HENRY LOWTHER HRNS (A DAVE HORTER TROM (A ZACK LAWRENCE K (A TONI CAMPO B G (A
BARRY MORGAN D (A HAROLD FISHER D (A FRANK RICOTTI PERC (A

G11A **GAS** G11A

(A) EMOTIONAL WARFARE 1981 POLYDOR UK POLE 1052

G11B **GAS MASK** G11B

ENRICO RAVA TPT (A (A) THEIR FIRST ALBUM 1970 TONSIL US 4001
BOBBY OSBOURNE V (A
DAVID GROSS WIND (A NICK OLIVA K (A RAY BROOKS B (A RICHARD GRANDO WIND(A
BILL DAVIDSON G (A JAMES STRASSBURG D (A

G11C **GAS WORKS** G11C

JOHN BROWN V G B(A (A) GAS WORKS 1973 REGAL ZONOPHONE UK SRLZ1026
MICK DRAPER VLN MAN HCA (A

G11D **GASKIN** G11D

(A) END OF THE WORLD 1981 RONDELET ABOUT4

G12 **GASOLIN** G12

FRANZ BECKERLEE G K SYN V (ALL (A) ANGAENDE LONE (EP) 1970 SONET T 7259
WILI JONSSON B K V (ALL (B) GASOLIN 1971 CBS 64685
KIM LARSEN G V (ALL (C) GASOLIN 2 1972 CBS 65229
TOM BAILEY G ((D) GASOLIN 3 1973 CBS 65798
TOM McEWAN D ((E) GASOLIN 1974 CBS UK 80099
NIELS HARRIT SAX (E (F) STAKKELS JIM (LAST JIM) 1974 CBS 80549 UK 80470
BJORN UGLEBJERG D (A (G) GAS 5 1975 CBS 80993
SOREN BERLEV D (ALL (H) LIVE SADAN DBL 1976 CBS 88207
KLAUS AGERSCHOU K (M (J) LEMON (US GASOLIN) 1976 CBS US 34149 UK 81436
FELIX PAPPARDI B G K (N (K) EFTER ENDNU EN DAG 1976 CBS 81630
(L) GOR DET NOGET 1977 CBS 82378
(M) KILLIN' TIME 1978 CBS 82900
(N) LIVE IN EUROPE 1978 CBS 83240
(O) SUPERMIX 1980 CBS 84154

G12A **GASOLINE BAND** G12A

BRIAN BEVAN G V (A (A) THE GASOLINE BAND 1972 CUBE UK HI FLY9
GEORGE THOMPSON B (A
FRED SCHWARTZ K (A JEROME JOHNSON TROM (A MAJOR WILBURN SAX (A CHARLES BOWEN SAX (A
RONALD PHILLIPS TPT (A JIM DVORAK TPT (A WILLIAM GOFFIGAN D (A JOE OGE PERC(A

G13 **GASS** G13

BOB TENCH B V (A (A) GASS 1979 POLYDOR UK 2383 022
GODFREY McLEAN D (A
ERROL McLEAN PERC (FRANK CLARK K (HUMPHREY OKAN SAX (ALAN ROSKAMS G (
DELISLE HARPER B PERC(A MICHAEL PIGGOTT VLN (A DEREK AUSTIN K (A PETER GREEN G (A
MEL COLLINS PROD (A

G14 **DAVID GATES** G14

DAVID GATES V G (ALL (A) FIRST ALBUM 1973 ELEKTRA US 75066 UK K 42150
MIKE BOTTS (ACE (B) NEVER LET HER GO 1975 ELEKTRA US 1028 UK K 52012
LARRY CARLTON G (AC (C) GOODBYE GIRL 1978 ELEKTRA US 6E148 UK K 52091
JAMES GETZOFF STRING(A (D) SONGBOOK 197 ELEKTRA US 6002
RUSS KUNKEL D (ACE (E) FALLING IN LOVE AGAIN 1980 ELEKTRA US 251 UK K 52206
JOHN GUERIN D (A (F) TAKE ME NOW 1081 ARISTA US 9563 UK SPART1175
DAVID LINDLEY FDL (E
JIM GORDON D (AC JIM HORN SAX (ACE LARRY KNECHTEL K (ACE LOUIE SHELTON G (A
HUDLEY HOCKENSMITH G (EF ROBIN WILLIAMSON (E DEAN PARKS G (C DAN DUGMORE STEEL(CE
DAVID MINOR G (E

G15 **GATOR CREEK** G15

ALLAN BEUTLER WIND (A (A) GATOR CREEK 1970 MERCURY 6338 085
DEE BARTON V K (A
MIKE DEASY G V (A RAY NEAPOLITAN B (A MERRY CLAYTON V (A LOUIE SHELTON V (A
CHUCK FINDLEY TPT (A NICK CEROLI D (A LARRY KNECHTEL G (A VANETTA FIELDS V (A
MIKE OMARTIAN K (A KATHY DEASY V PERC (A KENNY LOGGINS G V (A GENE PELLO D (A
CLYDIE KING V (A LOUIS GASCA TPT (A JOHN BANISTER K (A

G15A GATE G15A

MANOS TSANGARIS D G (AB — (A) LIVE — 1977 BRAIN GER 60 043
ANGELOS TSANGARIS K B (AB — (B) RED LIGHT SISTER — 1978 BRAIN GER 60 093
MARTIN KOHMSTEDT G (AB
MANFRED SCHROPFER G B V(A — HORST KAMP V PERC (AB — LOTHAR KRELL K (B — STAFAN LANG PERC(B
OLIVER PETRY SYN (B

G16 MAC GAYDEN G16

MAC GAYDEN V G BANJO MAND(ALL — (A) McGAVOCK GAYDEN — 1973 EMI UK EMA 760
BILL CHEATHAM G (C — (B) SKYBOAT — 1976 ABC US 927 UK ABCL 5169
VIC MASTRIANNI D (C — (C) HYMN TO THE SEEKER — 1976 ABC US 960
MIKE MILLER WIND V(CB
BILL AIKENS K (C — NELSON M PADRON PERC (C — BUZZ CASON V (CB — RANDY MEISNER V (C
ANITA BALL V (C — KEN BUTTREY D (A — PHILLIP ROYSTER CONGA(A — KARL HIMMEL PERC (AB
BOB JOHNSTON HCA (A — JAMES MOON V (A — CHARLES MYERS V (A — PAUL EASLEY V (A
JAMES CLEMMONS V (A — JIM ALTHOUSE B (B — JAMI NICHOLS SONGA(B — PETER KEEBLE (B
QUITMAN DENNIS SAX (B — ANDY MvMAHAN K (B — JACK LEE B (B — WASUNT PUNDANT TABLA (B
KRISTY KARSON V (B — BOBBY OGDIN K (B — JACL WILLIAMS B (B — DANNY SPERRY CELLO V(B
CINDY REYNOLDS HARP (B — TAMMY CASON V (B — KIM GAYDEN V (B — VIVKIE HATNIE V (B
JANIE FRICKE V (B — GINGER HOLLADAY V (B — ROBERT KNIGHT V (B — FARRELL MORRIS PERC(B
STEVE GIBSON G (B — TOMMY COGBILL B (B — JERRY CARRIGAN D (B

G17 MARVIN GAYE G17

MARVIN GAYE V K D(ALL — SOULFUL MOOD — 1961 TAMLA US 221 THAT STUBBORN KINDA
WITH — FELLOW 1963 TAMLA US 239
KIM WESTON V — LIVE ON STAGE — 1963 TAMLA US 242
DIANA ROSS V — WHEN I'M ALONE I CRY — 1964 TAMLA US 251
TAMMY TERRELL V — GREATEST HITS — 1964 TAMLA US 252
MARY WELLS V — HOW SWEET IT IS — 1964 TAMLA US 258 UK STML11004
RAYMOND CROSSLEY K (Z — HOW SWEET IT IS — 1973 MFP UK 90006
GORDON BANKS G (Z — HOW SWEET IT IS — 1979 MFP UK 50423
CURTIS NOLEN G (Z — HELLO BROADWAY — 1964 TAMLA US 259 UK STML11015
ROBERT AHWAI G (Z — TOGETHER (MARY WELLS) — 1964 TAMLA US 613 STATESIDE UK 10097
SUNSHIP PERC (Z — MARVIN GAYE — 1964 STATESIDE UK 10100
JOE MAYO PERC (Z — TRIBUTE TO NAT KING COLE — 1965 TAMLA US 261 UK STML11022
NOLAN SMITH TPT (Z — MOODS OF MARVIN GAYE — 1966 TAMLA US 266 UK STML11033
GEORGE SHAW TPT (Z — TAKE TWO — 1966 TAMLA US 270 UK STML11049
KENNY MASON TPT (Z — UNITED (TAMMY TERRELL) — 1966 TAMLA US 277 UK STML11062
RAY BROWN TPT (Z — GREATEST HITS — 196 TAMLA UK STML11065
FRANK BLAIR D B (Z — YOU'RE ALL I NEED TO GET BY — 1968 TAMLA US 284 UK STML11084
BUGSY WILCOX D (Z — IN THE GROOVE — 1968 TAMLA US 285 UK STML11091
NIGEL MARTINEZ D (Z — M.P.G. — 1969 TAMLA US 292 UK STML11119
ELMIRA COLLINS VIBES(Z — & HIS GIRLS(TERRELL WELLS KIM WESTON) — 1969 TAMLA US 293 UK STML11123
GARY JONES PERC (Z — EASY — 1969 TAMLA US 294 UK STML11132
FLEECY JOE JAMES PERC (Z — THATS THE WAY LOVE IS — 1969 TAMLA US 299 UK STML11136
SIDNEY MULDREW HRNS (Z — SUPERHITS — 19 TAMLA US 300
RAPHAEL RAVENSCROFT SAX(Z — GREATEST HITS — 1970 TAMLA US 302 UK STML11153
FRANK BATES (Z — WHATS GOING ON — 1971 TAMLA US 310 UK STML11190
LEE KENTLE (Z — HITS OF MARVIN GAYE — 1972 TAMLA UK STML11201
WILTON FELDER B (S — TROUBLED MAN (SOUNDTRACK) — 1972 TAMLA US 322 UK STML11225
JAMES JAMERSON B (ST — (S) LETS GET IT ON — 1973 TAMLA US 329 UK STMA 8013
EDDIE BROWN D (S — MARVIN ' DIANA — 1974 TAMLA US 803 UK STMA 8015
BOBBYE HALL PERC (S — (T) LIVE — 1974 TAMLA US 333 UK STML 8018
MELVIN RAGIN G (S — ANTHOLOGY — 1974 TAMLA US 790/1 UK TMSP 1128
PAUL HUMPHRIES D (S — I WANT YOU — 1976 TAMLA US 342 UK STML12025
URIEL JONES D (S — THE BEST OF — 1976 TAMLA US 348 UK STML12042
LOUIS SHELTON G (S — LIVE AT LONDON PALLADIUM — 1977 TAMLA US 352 UK TMSP 6006
DAVID T WALKER G (ST — HERE MY DEAR — 1978 TAMLA US 364 UK TMSP 6008
ROBERT WHITE G (S — LOVE MAN (WITHDRAWN)??? — 1979 TAMLA US 369 UK STML12126
EDDIE WILLIS G (S — EARLY 1961/64 — 1980 TAMLA US UK STML 9004
EMIL RICHARDS PERC (S — (Z) IN OUR LIFETIME — 1981 TAMLA UK STML12149
MARVIN JENKINS PNO (S — (EP)
JOE SAMPLE PNO (ST — MARVIN GAYE — 1966 TAMLA UK TME 2016
VICTOR FELDMAN VIBES(S — ORIGINALS FROM — 1967 TAMLA UK TME 2019
ED GREEN D (T
RAY PARKER G (T
JOHN ARNOLD PERC (T
JOE CLAYTON CONGA(T — JAMES GETZOFF SRT (T — JACK SHULMAN STR (T — PAUL HUBINON TPT(T
GEORGE BOHANON TROM (T — ERNIE WATTS SAX (T — WILLIAM GREEN SAX (T — ERIC DOLEN V (T
CHARLES BURNS V (T — DWIGHT OWENS V (T — MICHAEL TORRENCE V (T — WALLY COX V (T

G17A GAYLADDS G17A

(A) UNDERSTANDING — 1979 BALLISTIC UK UAG30236

G17B GEARS G17B

(A) ROCKIN' AT GROUND ZERO — 1980 PLAYGEMS US 6471

G18 RON GEESIN G18

RON GEESIN V K SYN BANJO(ALL — (A) THE BODY — 1970 HARVEST UK SHSP 4008 SW751
ROGER WATERS (A — (B) ELECTROSOUND — 197 KPM 1102
(C) AS HE STANDS — 197 GEESIN UK RON 28
(D) PATRUNS — 197 GEESIN UK RON 31
(E) RIGHT THROUGH — 197 GEESIN UK RON 323

G19 J GEILS BAND G19

J GEILS G (ALL — (A) J GEILS BAND — 1971 ATLANTIC US 8275 UK K 40108
PETER WOLF V (ALL — (B) MORNING AFTER — 1972 ATLANTIC US 8297 UK K 40293
SETH JUSTMAN K V (ALL — (AB) J GEILS /MORNING AFTER — 1975 ATLANTIC UK K 60061
MAGIC DICK TPT HCA (ALL — (C) LIVE FULL HOUSE — 1972 ATLANTIC US 7241 UK K 40426
DANNY KLEIN B (ALL — (D) BLOODSHOT — 1973 ATLANTIC US 7260 UK K 40479
STEPHEN BLADD D V (ALL — (E) LADIES INVITED — 1974 ATLANTIC US 7286 UK K 40536
BARBARA INGRAM V (J — (F) NIGHTMARES — 1974 ATLANTIC US 18107 UK K 50073
EVETTE BENTON V (J — (G) HOT LINE — 1975 ATLANTIC US 18147 UK K 50175
HARRIET THARPE V (J — (H) BLOW YOUR FACE OUT — 1976 ATLANTIC US 2/507 UK K 60115
LUTHER VANDROSS V (JN — (J) MONKEY ISLAND — 1977 ATLANTIC US 19130 UK K 50381
G DIANE SUMLER V (J — (K) SANCTUARY — 1978 EMI US 17006 UK AMS 2004
MICHELLE COBBS V (J — (L) LOVE STINKS — 1980 EMI US 17016 UK AML 3004

(CONTINUED)

G19 J GEILS BAND (CONTINUED) G19

THERESA REED V (J — (M) BEST OF — 1980 ATLANTIC US 19284 NL 50762
GEORGE YOUNG HRNS (N — (N) FREEZE FRAME — 1981 EMI US 17062 UK 3020
LOU MARINI HRNS (N
MICHAEL BRECKER HRNS (J — RON CUBER SAX (JN — LEW DEL GATTO SAX (J — FRANK VICARI SAX (J
RANDY BRECKER HRNS (JN — ALAN RUBIN TPT (JN — LEW SOLOFF TPT (J — JUKE JOINT JIMMY G (H
TOM MALONE HRNS (N — KENNY WILLIAMS V (N — TAWATHA AGEE V (N — CISSY HOUSTON V (JN
FONZI THORNTON V (N — GEOFFREY HASLEM PROD (A — BRAD SHAPIRO PROD (A — BILL SZYMEZYK PROD(EF
SETH JUSTMAN PROD (L

G20 GENERATION X G20

BILLY IDOL G V (ALL — (A) GENERATION X — 1978 CHRYSALIS UK/US 1169 GER6307623
BOB ANDREWS G V (AB1 — (B) VALLEY OF THE DOLLS — 1979 CHRYSALIS UK/US 1193 NL 511193
TONY JAMES B (ABC1 — (C) KISS ME DEADLY — 1981 CHRYSALIS UK 1327 NL 203259
JOHN TAOWE D (1 — (1) 1976/77
MARK LAFF D (AB
TERRY C CHIMES D (C — JOHN McGEOGH G (C — JAMES STEVENSON G (C — STEVE JONES G (C

G21 GENESIS G21

JOHN MAYHEW D (AB — (A) FROM GENESIS TO REVELATION — 1969 US LONDON 643 UK DECCA 4990
ANTHONY PHILLIPS G (AB — (A) IN THE BEGINNING — 1974 US LONDON 50006 UK DECCA 4990
TONY BANKS K (ALL — (B) TRESPASS — 1970 US ABC'74 816 UK CHARISMA CAS 1020
(B) TRESPASS — 1970 US IMPULSE 9295
MIKE RUTHERFORD G B (ALL — (C) NURSERY CRYME — 1971 US/UK CHARISMA CAS 1052
(C) NURSERY CRYME — 1971 PHILIPS GER 6369916
PETER GABRIEL V FLT PERC(ABCDEFG — (BC) TRESPASS/NURSERY CRYME — 1975 US/uK CHARISMA CGS 102
PHIL COLLINS D PERC V(CDEFGHJKLMN12o — (D) FOXTROT — 1972 US/UK CHARISMA CAS 1058
(CD) NURSERY/FOXTROT — 1976 CHARISMA US 2701 RI BUDDAH US 5659
STEVE HACKETT G B (CDEFGHJKL — (E) SELLING ENGLAND BY THE POUND — 1973 CHARISMA US 6060 UK CAS 1074
(E) SELLING ENGLAND BY THE POUND — 1973 CHARISMA GER 6369 944
BILL BRUFORD D PERC(K — (DE)FOXTROT /SELLING ENGLAND — 1975 UK CHARISMA CGS 103
CHESTER THOMPSON D PERC(12 K — (F) LIVE — 1973 CHARISMA US 1066 UK CLASS 1
(F) LIVE — 1973 CHARISMA GER 6499 593
DARYL STUERMER G (12 — (G) THE LAMB LIES DOWN ON BROADWAY — 1974 US ATCO 2401 UK CHARISMA CGS 101
(G) THE LAMB LIES DOWN ON BROADWAY — 1974 CHARISMA GER 6641 226
CHRIS STEWART D (* — (H) TRICK OF THE TAIL — 1976 US ATCO 36129 UK CHARISMA CDS 4001
(H) TRICK OF THE TAIL — 1976 CHARISMA GER 6369 974
DAVID HITCHCOCK PROD (B — (H) TRICK OF THE TAIL — 19 US ATCO RI 38101
JIM SILVER D (* — (J) WIND & WUTHERING — 1977 US ATCO 36144 UK CHARISMA CDS 4005
EARTH WIND & FIRE HRNS (O — (J) WIND & WUTHERING — 197 US ATCO RI 38100
DAVE HENTSCHEL V (N — (K) SECONDS OUT — 1977 ATLANTIC 20002 UK CHARISMA GE 2001
(K) SECONDS OUT — 1977 CHARISMA GER 6641 697
(L) SPOT THE PIGEON (EP) — 1977 ATLANTIC US 1800 UK CHARISMA GEN 001
(M) AND THEN THERE WERE THREE — 1978 ATLANTIC 19173 UK CHARISMA CDS 4010
(M) AND THEN THERE WERE THREE — 1978 CHARISMA GER 9124 024
(N) DUKE — 1980 ATLANTIC 16014 UK CHARISMA BRA 101
(N) DUKE — 1980 CHARISMA GER 9124 053
(O) ABACAB — 1981 ATLANTIC US 19313 UK CHARISMA CBR102
(O) ABACAB — 1981 VERTIGO NL 6302 162
( ) ROCK ROOTS — 1975 UK DECCA ROOTS.1
( ) REFLECTION — 1975 FONTANA 9299 515
( ) THE BEST OF — 1976 US BUDDAH 56592
( ) STORY OF GENESIS — 1978 JAP FLYOVER 10061/2
(1) 1978 TOUR (2) 1980 TOUR (*) PRE RECORDING MUSICIANS

G21A GENOCIDE G21A

(A) GENOCIDE — 1979 SAFARI UK SAP 2

G21B AX GENRICH G21B

AX GENRICH G V B (A — (A) HIGHDELBERG — 1975 HAPPY BIRD GER 5015
JAN FRIDE D (A
MANI NEUMEIER D PERC(A — HELMUTH HATTLER B V (A — DIETER MOEBIUS SYN (A — ACHIM ROEDELIUS PNO(A
PETER WOLFBRANDT V G PERC(A

G22 GENTLE GIANT G22

PHIL SHULMAN SAX (ABCD — (A) GENTLE GIANT — 1970 UK VERTIGO 6360 020
DEREK SHULMAN V G B (ALL — (B) ACQUIRING THE TASTE — 1971 US VERTIGO 1005 UK VERTIGO 6360 041
RAY SHULMAN V B VLN PERC(ALL — (C) THREE FRIENDS — 1972 US CBS 31649 UK VERTIGO 6360 070
(AC)THREE FRIENDS/GENTLE GIANT — 1972 GER VERTIGO 6685 016
KERRY MINNEAR K V (ALL — (D) OCTOPUS — 1973 US CBS 32022 UK VERTIGO 6360 080
GARY GREEN G V (ALL — (E) IN A GLASS HOUSE — 1973 GER VERTIGO 6366100 UK WWA WWA 002
MARTIN SMITH D (AB — (F) THE POWER & THE GLORY — 1974 US CAPITOL 11337 UK W W A WWA 010
CLAIRE DENIZ CELLO (A — (F) THE POWER & THE GLORY — 1976 US CAPITOL 16044
JOHN WEATHERS D V (DEFGHJKLMNO — (G) FREE HAND — 1975 US CAPITOL 11428 UK CHRYSALIS 1093
(G) FREE HAND — 197 US CAPITOL 16048
MIKE VICKERS SYN (D — (H) A GIANT STEP (DBL) (COMP) — 1975 UK VERTIGO 6641 334
MARTIN RUSHENT SYN (D — (J) INTERVIEW — 1976 US CAPITOL 11532 UK CHRYSALIS 1115
TONY VISCONTI PROD (A — (J) INTERVIEW — 19 US CAPITOL 16047
CHRIS THOMAS SYN (B — (K) PLAYING THE FOOL (LIVE DBL) — 1976 US CAPITOL 11592 UK CHRYSALIS 1133
(K) PLAYING THE FOOL (LIVE DBL) — 1976 GER CHRYSALIS 6641 579
PAUL KOSH TPT (B — (L) THE MISSING PIECE — 1977 US CAPITOL 11696 UK CHRYSALIS 1152
(L) THE MISSING PIECE — 1977 GER CHRYSALIS 6307 604
MALCOLM MORTIMER D (— (M) PRETENTIOUS DBL(COMP) — 1977 UK VERTIGO 6641 629
(N) GIANT FOR A DAY — 1978 US CAPITOL 11813 UK CHRYSALIS 1186
(O) CIVILIAN — 1980 US CBS 36341 UK CHRYSALIS 1285
(O) CIVILIAN — 1980 NL CHRYSALIS 511 285
( ) GREATEST HITS — 1981 PHILIPS 6381 045

G22A GENTLEHOOD G22A

HAL BLAINE D (A — (A) GENTLEHOOD — 19 CBS US 32032
JOE OSBORNE B (A
GENE PELLO D (A — DANN MATHER B (A — JANET LAING VLA (A — PHIL SAWYER PNO (A
KATHI GRANDE V (A

G22B GENTRYS G22B

LARRY RASPBERRY V (A — (A) KEEP ON DANCING — 1965 MGM US 4336
BRUCE BOWLES V (— (B) TIME — 1966 MGM US 4346
LARRY WALL D (— (C)GENTRYS — 1970 SUN US 117
JIMMY HART V (
PAT NEAL B (— JIMMY JOHNSON TPT (— BOBBY FISHER G (

G22C **RON GEODERT** G22C

RON GEODERT K V (A — (A) BREAKING ALL THE RULES — 1980 POLYDOR 6265

JERRT RUNYAN G (A

RIFF WEST B (A — JACK WEST D (A — JOHN ANTONY K (A

G23 **GEORDIE** G23

BRIAN JOHNSON V (A — (A) HOPE YOU LIKE IT — 1973 EMI UK EMC 3001

TOM HILL B (— (B) MASTERS OF ROCK — 1974 EMI UK 054 95689

BRIAN GIBSON D (— (C) DONT BE FOOLED BY THE NAME — 1974 EMI UK EMA 764

VIC MALCOLM G (— (D) SAVE THE WORLD — 1976 EMI UK EMC 3134

(E) FEATURING B JOHNSON — 1981 REDBUS UK RBMP 5001

G24 **LOWELL GEORGE** G24

LOWELL GEORGE G V (A — (A) THANKS I'LL EAT IT HERE — 1979 WB US 3194 UK K 56487

JIM GORDON D (A

JIM KELTNER D (A — JIM PRICE HRNS (A — MIKE BAIRD D (A — DARRELL LEONARD HRNS(A

CHUCK RAINEY B (A — FRED TACKETT G (A — BILL PAYNE K (A — DAVID FOSTER K (A

JIMMY GREENSPOON PNO (A — JEFF PORCARO D (A — BONNIE RAITT V (A — CHILLI CHARLES D (A

DENNIS BELFIELD B (A — GORDON DE WITTE K (A — JAMES HOWARD K (A — NICKY HOPKINS K (A

PAUL STALLWORTH B (A — JERRY JUMONVILLE HRNS (A — STEVE BRUTON G (A — DEAN PARKS G (A

FLOYD SNEED D (A — ROBERTO GUTIERREZ (A — LUIS DAMIAN G (A — RICHIE HAYWARD D (A

HERB PEDERSEN V (A — J D SOUTHER V (A — MAXINE WATERS V (A — BOBBY BRUCE FDL (A

PEGGY SANDVIG (A — BRUCE PAULSON (A — MAXAYN LEWIS V (A — JOEL PESKIN SAX (A

JOHN PHILLIPS SAX (A

G24A **GERMS** G24A

DARBY CRASH V (A — (A) G I — 1979 SLASH US SR103

LORNA B (A — (B) THE DECLINE (VAR ARTIST) — 1980 SLASH US SR105

DON D (A

PAT G (A

G25 **GERONIMO BLACK** G25

JIMMY CARL BLACK D (AB — (A) GERONIMO BLACK — 1972 UNI 127 1974 MCA MCF 2683

TJAY CANTRELLI G (AB — (B) WELCOME BACK GERONIMO BLACK — 19 HELIOS US 704

DENNY WALLEY G (AB

BUNK GARDNER WIND (AB — ANDY CAHAN K (AB — TOM LEAVEY B (AB — BUZZ GARDNER (AB

DON PRESTON K (B — RAY COLLINS V (B — MEATBALL D (B — JOE LALA PERC (B

JAMES HARMON HARP (B — JERRY McGEE G (B — MURRAY ROMAN V (A — KEITH OLSON V (A

STRING SECTION (A

G25A **DENNY GERRARD** G25A

DENNY GERRARD (A — (A) SINISTER MORNING — 1970 DERAM NOVA SDN10

TONY HILL G (A

SIMON HOUSE VLN (A — PETER PAVLI B (A — ROGER HADDEN D (A

G26 **GERRY & THE PACEMAKERS** G26

GERRY MARSDEN G V (ALL — HOW DO YOU DO IT — 1963 COLUMBIA 1546(M) SCX 3492(S)

FREDDIE MARSDEN D (ALL — FERRY ACROSS THE MERSEY — 1964 COLUMBIA SCX3544 US UA3387

LES McGUIRE B V (ALL — DONT LET THE SUN CATCH YOU CRYING — 196 LAURIE US 2027

LES CHADWICK PNO (ALL — SECOND ALBUM (US) — 196 LAURIE US 2037

I'LL BE THERE — 196 LAURIE US 2030

GREATEST HITS — 196 LAURIE US 2031

GIRL ON A SWING — 196 LAURIE US 2037

BEST OF — 1977 EMI UK NUT 1o CAPITOL US 11898

EPS

HOW DO YOU DO IT 19663 COLUMBIA SEG 8257 — YOU'LL NEVER WALK ALONE 1964 COLUMBIA SEG8295

I'M THE ONE 1964 COLUMBIA SEG 8311 — DONT LET THE SUN 1964 COLUMBIA SEG8346

IT'S GONNA BE ALL RIGHT1964 COLUMBIA SEG 8367 — GERRY IN CALIFORNIA 1964 COLUMBIA SEG8388

FERRY ACROSS THE MERSEY1965 COLUMBIA SEG 8397 — RIP IT UP 1965 COLUMBIA SEG8426

G26A **RENEE GEYER BAND** G26A

RENNE GEYER V (ALL — (A) IT'S A MAN'S WORLD — 1974 RCA UK SF8450 AUST MVP1 0024

MARK PUNCH G V (BE1 — (B) READY TO DEAL — 1975 RCA AUST VPL1 0105

GREG TELL D (BC — (C) REALLY REALLY LOVE ME — 1976 RCA AUST VPL1 0120

MAL LOGAN K (BCDE1 — (D) MOVING ALONG — 1977 RCA AUST VPL1 0140

RUSSELL SMITH TPT (BC — (E) BLUES LICENSE — 1978 RCA AUST VPL1 0214

TONY BUCHANAN WIND (BE1 — (1) 1977 TOUR BAND

BARRY SULLIVAN B (B

TWEED HARRIS K (A — GARRY HYDE PERC (A — JULIE McKENNA V (A — WENDY REECE V (A

BOBBY BRIGHT V (A — MIKE BRADY V (A — BRUCE SANDELL SAX (C — MIGUEL CARRANZA TROM(C

OTIS KEVINAGH V (C — DOUGLAS WILLIAMS V (C — STANLEY BROWN V (C — PHIL LAWSON B (1

RUSSEL DUNLOP D (1 — JOHN PUGH G (C — ERNIE WATTS SAX (d — NICA REJTO FLT (D

CHARLES VEAL STRING(D — JACK ASHFORD PERC (D — REG BURKE PNO (D — HARRY BOOKER K (D

STEPHEN BECKMEIER G (D — FREDERICK LEWIS PERC (D — JAMES JAMERSON B (D — RAY E PARKER G (D

JERRY PETERS K (D — GREGG POREE G (D — RAYMOND POUNDS D (D — NATHAN WATTS B (D

VENETTA FIELDS V (D — PAT HENDERSON B (D — SHIRLEY MATTHEWS V (D — TIEMEYER McCAIN V (D

OTIS STOKES V (D — FRANK WILSON V (D — KEVIN BORICH G (E — JOHN ANNUS D (E

TIM PARTRIDGE B (E — JOHN WATSON D (E — KERRI BIDELL V (E — RON KING HCA(E

TIM PIPER G (E — STEVE HOPES D (E

G26B **GIANT CRAB** G26B

E RNIE OROSCO V G (A — (A) A GIANT CRAB COMES FORTH — 1968 UNI US 73037

RAY OROSCO B K (A — (B) COOL IT HELIOS — 196 UNI US 73057

RUBEN OROSCO B D SAX(A

DENNIS FRICIA D HRNS (A — KENNY FRICIA K HRNS VIBES(A

G26C **GIANTS** G26C

KARL RUCKER B (A — (A) THANKS FOR THE MUSIC — 1976 CASABLANCA US NBLP 7027

JOHN COHEN V (A

JOHN PLATANIA G V (A — LAURIE COHEN V (A — BRUCE GARY B PERC (A — RON ELLIOTT G (A

G26D **GIANTS 2** G26D

GREG ERRICO D SYN(A — (A) GIANTS — 1978 MCA UK MCF 3058

CARLOS SANTANA G (A — ( ) GIANTS — 1980 MCA US 3188

HERBIE HANCOCK PNO (A

LEE OSKAR HCA (A — NEAL SCHON G (A — MIKE CARABELLO K (A — BIANCA THORNTON-ODEN V(A

COKE ESCOVEDO V (A — GREGG ROLLIE K (A — CHEPITO AREAS PERC (A — RICO REYES PERC (A

DOUG RAUCH B (A — MIKE GARCIA VIBES (A — WENDY HAAS K V (A — GENE WASHINGTON V (A

JODY MOREING V (A — VICTOR PANTOJA CONG (A — ROBERT VEGA B (A — DOUG RODRIGUEZ G (A

FREDDIE POOL V (A — LINDA TILLERY V (A

G27 STEVE GIBBONS G27

STEVE GIBBONS G V (ALL (A) SHORT STORIES 1971 WIZARD UK SWZA 5501
TREVOR BURTON B V G(BCDEFGH (B) ANY ROAD UP 1976 MCA US 2183 POLYDOR UK 2383 381
BOB WILSON G K V(BCDEF (C) ROLLING ON 1977 MCA US 2243 POLYDOR UK 2383 433
DAVE CARROLL G (BCDEF (D) CAUGHT IN THE ACT 1977 MCA US 2305 POLYDOR UK 2478 112
CHRIS BARBER TPT (H (D) CAUGHT IN THE ACT 1977 POLYDOR EURO 2460 276
BOB LAMB D (BCDEF (E) DOWN IN THE BUNKER 1978 POLYDOR US 6154 UK 2391.358
MIKE COTTON TPT (H (E) DOWN IN THE BUNKER 1978 POLYDOR EURO 2383 502
GARY WRIGHT K (A (G) STREET PARADE 1980 RCA US 6293 UK LP 5005
MIKE KELLIE D (A (H) SAINTS & SINNERS 1981 RCA UK PL25387
P J WRIGHT V G K(H
DORIS TROY V (A PAT DONALDSON B (A MADELINE BELL V (A JERRY DONAHUE G (A
JIMMY MILLER PERC (A GREG RIDLEY B (A HUGH McCRACKEN G (A NICK PENTELOW SAX(EH
TONY VISCONTI SYN B(A LONDON SYMPHONY ORCH (E HARRY RIX D V (G BILL PAUL SAX (G
GINGER JOHNSON PERC (A IAN WHITEMAN PNO (A LARRY FALLON WIND (A ALAN WHITE PERC FLT (A
GERRY CONWAY STEEL(A ROCKY DZIDZORNU PERC (A JOHNNY VAN DERRICK (A CLAIRE DENIZ CELLO(A
BILL POVEY CLAR (A DEREK WOOD B V (H ALAN WICKETT D V (H AL SHACKLOCK K (H
GERAINT WATKINS K ACC(H

G28 GIFT G28

UWE PATZKE B V (AB (A) GIFT 1972 TELEFUNKEN 14680
RAINER BAUR G (AB (B) BLUE APPLE 1974 NOVA GER 8002
HELMUT TREICHEL G (A
HERMANN LANGE D PERC(AB DIETER ALTARER G V (B DIETER FREI K SYN(B

G29 NICK GILDER G29

NICK GILDER V (ABCD (A) YOU KNOW WHO YOU ARE 1977 CHRYSALIS UK CHR 1147
JAMES McCULLOCH G (ABCD (B) CITY NIGHT 1978 CHRYSALIS UK CHR 1202
JAMES HERNDON K SYN G V(BCD (C) FREQUENCY 1979 CHRYSALIS UK CHR 1219
ERIC NELSON B V (ABCD (D) ROCK AMERICA 1980 CASABLANCA UK 7243 EURO 6302066
STEVE KALTER K (A
CRAIG KRAMPF D PERC V (BC CHET McCRACKEN D (A KEN MANSFIELD PROD (D JIMMY HUNTER D (D

G29A GILES GILES & FRIPP G29A

MIKE GILES D (A (A) CHEERFUL INSANITY 1968 DERAM SML 1022 UK SPA 423
PETER GILES B (A
ROBERT FRIPP G (A JUDY DYBLE V (CLIFF HARDIE TOM (A T BARKER TROM (A
THE BREAKAWAYS V (A STRING SECTION (A NICKY HOPKINS K (A MIKE HILL K (A

G30 GILGAMESH G30

PHIL LEE G (AB (A) GILGAMESH 1975 CAROLINE UK CA 2007
ALAN GOWEN K (AB (B) ANOTHER FINE TUNE YOU'VE GOT ME INTO 1978 CHARLY UK CRL 5009
JEFF CLYNE B (A
MICHAEL TRAVIS D (A HUGH HOPPER B (B AMANDA PARSONS V (A TREVOR TOMKINS D (B

G30A GILA G30A

CONNY VEIT SYN G V (A (A) GILA 1971 BASF GER 20 21109/6
DANIEL ALLUNO D PERC(A (B) BURY MY HEART AT WOUNDED KNEE 1973 WB GER 46234
FRITZ SCHEYHING G K (A
SABINE MERBACH V (B WALTER WIEDERKEHR B (A FLORIAN FRICKE K (B DANIEL FIECHELSCHER D(B

G31 IAN GILLAN G31

IAN GILLAN V (ALL (A) CHILD IN TIME 1976 OYSTER UK 2490 136 US 1602
MARK NAUSEEF D PERC(ABCDEF (A) CHILD IN TIME 1976 POLYDOR UK ACBR 261
JOHN GUSTAFSON B V (ABCDEF (B) CLEAR AIR TURBULANCE 1977 ISLAND UK ILPS 9500
RAY FENWICK G V (ABCDEF (C) SCARABUS 1977 ISLAND UK ILPS9511 US ANTILLES 7066
BERNIE TORME G (HJKLM (D) LIVE AT BUDOKAN VOL 1 1978 EAST WPRLD JAP 81112
COLIN TOWNS K(BCDEFGHIJKLM (E) LIVE AT BUDOKAN VOL 2 1978 EAST WORLD JAP 81113
MICK UNDERWOOD D (HJKLM (F) LIVE AT BUDOKAN (DBL) (DE) 1978 EAST WORLD JAP
JANICK GERS G (M (G) GILLAN 1978 EAST WORLD JAP 8112-
MIKE MORAN K (A (H) MR UNIVERSE (DIFF) 1979 INTERFUSION AUST 37135
STEVE BYRD D (GJ (J) MR UNIVERSE 1979 ACROBAT UK ACRO 3
PHIL KENZIE SAX (B (K) GLORY ROAD 1980 VIRGIN US 13146 UK V 2171
LIAM GENOCKEY D (GJ (K) FOR GILLAN FANS ONLY FREE WITH ABOVE UK VDJ32
JOHN HUCKRIDGE TPT (B (L) FUTURE SHOCK 1981 VIRGIN UK V 2196
DEREK HEALEY TPT (B (M) DOUBLE TROUBLE 1981 VIRGIN UK VGD 3506
MALCOLM GRIFFITHS TROM (B (EP) NO LAUGHING IN HEAVEN 1981 VIRGIN UK VS 425
MARTIN FRITH SAX (B
ROGER GLOVER SYN V(A STEVE TOWNES K (JOHN McCOY B(GHJKLM PETER BARNACLE D (

G32 DANA GILLESPIE G32

DANA GILLESPIE V G SYN(ABC1 (A) BOX OF SURPRISES 1969 DECCA UK SKL 5012
BRIAN ODGERS B (B (A) FOOLISH SEASONS 1969 LONDON US 540
DAVE WINTOUR B (B (B) WERE'NT BORN A MAN 1973 RCA UK/us APLI0354
PAT DONALDSON B (B (C) AIN'T GONNA PLAY NO SECOND FIDDLE 1974 RCA UK/US APLI0682
MIKE MORAN K (B (1) 1978 TOUR
PAUL KEOGH G (B CHRIS RAY G (B RONNIE LEAHY K (B RAY GLYNN G (B
JIM RYAN G (B RICK WAKEMAN K (B BARRY DE SOUZA D)B TERRY COX D (B
BOBBY KEYS SAX (B RAY COOPER PERC (B FRANK RICOTTI PERC (B ROSETTA HIGHTOWER V (B
LIZA STRIKE V (B JOANNE WILLIAMS V (B JOHN HAWKEN K (1 JOHN KNIGHTSBRIDGE G(1
BARBARA SPITZ G (1 NEIL KORNER B (1 JOHN BARKER D (1 TONY HALL SAX(1
JOHN PORTER G (C BRYN HAWORTH G (C DAVE SKINNER K (C PHIL CHEN B (C
BOB WESTON G (C SIMON PHILLIPS D (C MEL COLLINS SAX (C ROBIN SYLVESTER B (C
EDDIE JOBSON SYN VLN(C JOHN TURNBULL G (C MICK GALLAGHER PNO (C JODY LINSCOTT CONGA(C
RABBIT BUNDRICK K (B FRANK COLLINS V (C DYAN BIRCH V (C PADDY McHUGH V (C
MALCOLM DUNCAN HRNS (C ROGER BALL HRNS (C HENRY LOWTHER HRNS (C

G33 STEVE GILLETTE G33

STEVE GILLETTE (A) STEVE GILLETTE 1967 VANGUARD US VSD79251
(B) ALONE 1980 SIERRA US 1001

G33A MICKEY GILLEY G33A

MICKEY GILLEY (AB (A) THATS ALL THAT MATTERS TO ME 1980 EPIC UK 84391
(JERRY LEE LEWIS COUSIN) (B) DOWN THE LINE 1981 CHARLY UK 30192

G34 DAVE GILMOUR G34

DAVE GILMOUR G V (A — (A) DAVID GILMOUR — 1978 US CBS 35388 UK HARVEST SHVL817
MICK WEAVER K (A
WILLIE WILSON D (A RICK WILLS B (A

G35 GORDON GILTRAP G35

GORDON GILTRAP G (ALL — (A) TESTAMENT OF TIME — 1971 MCA MKPS 2020 + MCF 2688
CLIVE BUNKER D (E — (B) GILTRAP — 1973 PHILIPS 6308 175
JOHN G PERRY B (CE — (C) VISIONARY — 1976 ELECTRIC UK TRIX.2
ROD EDWARDS K V (EC — (D) PERILOUS JOURNEY — 1977 ELECTRIC UK TRIX.4
ROGER HAND G V (E — (E) FEAR OF THE DARK — 1978 ELECTRIC UK TRIX.7
EDDIE SPENCE K (— (F) PEACOCK PARTY — 1980 PVK UK GIL 1
RIC SANDERS VLN (F — (G) EARLY DAYS — 1968 ALLEGRO UK 4052
IAN MOSLEY D (F
SIMON PHILLIPS D (EC GRAHAM PRESKETT VLN (E SHIRLEY RODEN V (E RICHARD HARVEY RECORDER(EF
TONY CARR PERC (E JOHN BAILEY G (C BIMBO ACOCK WIND (F JOHN GUSTAFSON B (F
MORRIS PERT PERC (F

G35A GINA X PERFORMANCE G35A

G IN A KIKOINE V (A — (A) GINA X PERFORMANCE — 1979 EMI UK EMC 3314
ZEUS B HELD K (A — (B) X TRA ORDINAIRE — 1980 EMI UK EMC 3336
LASZLO CXIGANY D (A
HEINZ TREWER SYN (A MARTIN HAMBERG SYN (A

G35B GIPSY LOVE G35B

CHARLY RATZER G V (A — (A) GIPSY LOVE — 197 BASF GER 21115
KURT HAUENSTEIN B V K(A
GEORG DOGGETTE V (A PETER WOLF K (A JANO STOJKA D (A RICHARD SCHONHERZ K (A

G36 GINHOUSE G36

GEOFF SHARKEY G V (A — (A) GINHOUSE — 1971 B&C UK CAS 1031
STEWART BURLISON B V (A
DAVE WHITAKER D (A

G36A GIRL G36A

SIMON LAFFY G (AB — (A) SHEER GREED — 1980 JET US 36490 UK JETLP224
GERRY LAFFY B V (AB — (B) WASTED YOUTH — 1982 JET UK JETLP238
PHILIP LEWIS V (AB
PHIL COLLEN G (AB DAVE GAYNOR G (A PETE BARNACLE G (B

G37 GIRLS SCHOOL G37

ENID WILLIAMS B V (A — (A) DEMOLITION — 1980 BRONZE UK BRONX 525
KELLY JOHNSON G V (A — (B) HIT & RUN — 1981 BRONZE GER 203 556
KIM McAULIFFE G V (A — (C) WILDLIFE EP — 198
DENISE DUFORT D (A
KIM WESTON B V (

G37A GIRLS AT OUR BEST G37A

JUDY EVANS V (A — (A) PLEASURE — 1981 HAPPY BIRTHDAY UK RULP 1
JAMES ALAN G V (A
D CARL HARPER D 'A GERARD SWIFT B V (A ROD JOHNSON D (A ALAN WAKEMAN CLAR(A
DAVE FISHEL K (A THOMAS DOLBY SYN (A LAWRENCE DIANA PROD (A

G38 GIRLS TOGETHER OUTRAGEOUSLY G38

MISS PAMELA V (A — (A) PERMANENT DAMAGE — 1969 STRAIGHT UK STS 1059
MISS MERCY V (A
MISS CHRISTINE V (A MISS CINDERELLA V (A MISS SANDRA V (A JIMMY CARL BLACK D (A
ROY ASTRADA B (A IAN UNDERWOOD K (A CRAIG DOERGE K (A JEFF BECK G (A
NICKY HOPKINS K (A ROD STEWART V (A FRANK ZAPPA TAMB (A DON PRESTON SYN(A

G38A GLACIER G38A

(A) FROM SEA TO SKY 19 — MERCURY US MG 20895

G38B GLAD G38B

(A) FEELIN' GLAD — 19 ABC US 665

G38C GIZMO G38C

STEVE WISE D (A — (A) JUST LIKE MASTER BATES — 1979 ACE 001
MAURICE MEMMOTT K VLN(AB — (B) VICTIMS — 1981 CLEEP'N'EAT 1
DAVE RADFORD G V (AB
BRIAN GOULD SYN K(AB GRAME QUINTON JONES G (B

G39 GLADIATORS G39

CLINTON FEARON B V (ABCDE — (A) TRENCH TOWN MIX UP — 197 VIRGIN UK V 2062
ALBERT GRIFFITHS V G (ABCDE — (B) PROVERBIAL REGGAE — 1978 FRONT LINE UK FL1002
LLOYD PARKS B (AC — (C) NATURALITY — 1978 FRONT LINE UK FL1035
GALLIMORE SUTHERLAND V G(ABCDE — (D) SWEET SO TILL — 1979 FRONT LINE UK FL1048
SCULLY PERC (C — (E) GLADIATORS — 1980 VIRGIN UK V 2161
ANSEL COLLINS K (Bd
STICKIE THOMPSON PERC (BCD EARL LINDO K (B SLY DUNBAR D (B PABLO BLACK K (D
RICHARD ACE K (D EARL BAGGA B (D BONGO HERMAN PERC (D SKY JUICE PERC (D
TOMMY McCOOK WIND (D HEADLEY BENNETT HRNS (D LEROY WALLACE D (CD ERNEST RANGLIN G (D
JIMMY BECKMAN HCA (D SOJIE PERC (D BOBBY ELLIS HRNS (D RANCHIE McLEAN G (C
WINSTON WRIGHT K (C ANGUS GAYE D (E EDDIE GRANT K G (E DONALD BENJAMIN G (E
TONY ZAP EDMUNDS K (E TONY KING K (E MARK JAMES B (E COACH HOUSE HORNS (E

G40 GLADSTONE G40

H L VOELKER V (BA — (A) GLADSTONE — 1972 PROBE UK SPBA6264 ABC US751
DOUG RHONE G V (BA — (B) LOOKIN' FOR A SMILE — 1973 ABC US ABCX 778
JERRY SCHEFF B (BA
RON TUTT D (AB RANDY FOUTS K (BA BOBBY TUTTLE STEEL(B MICK RAPHAEL HCA (B
ROBIN BRIANS V PERC(BA DAVID STANLEY B (B PAUL LEIM D (B GARY CRAPSTER D (B
LARRY WHITE DOBRO(BA A D WASHINGTON CONG (B LYNN GROOM K (B TOM RUSSELL V (B
DALE BAKER V (B DAHRILL RHONE B (A MICHAEL RABON G (A ALAN ESTES CONGA(A
GARRY MOORE BAN (A

G41 GLASS FAMILY G41

RALPH PARRETT G V (A — (A) A ELECTRIC BAND — 1967 WB US 1776
DAVID CAPILOUTO K B (A
GARY GREEN D PERC(A

G41A GLASS MOON G41A

(A) GLASS MOON 1980 RADIO UK 2003

G42 GLASS PRISM G42

(A) ON JOY & SORROW 1970 RCA US LSP 4270
( ) POE THROUGH THE GLASS PRISM 1969 RCA US LSP 4201

G43 GLASSHARP G43

PHIL KEAGGY G V (A — (A) GLASSHARP 1972 MCA UK MUPS431 US DECCA 75261
JOHN SFERRA D V G(A — (B) SYNERGY 1972 MCA UK MUPS449 US DECCA 75306
DAN PECCHIO B V (A — (C) IT MAKES ME GLAD 1973 MCA UK MUPS470 US DECCA 5358

G44 GLASSHOUSE G44

(A) THANKS I NEEDED THAT 19 INVICTUS US T9810

G45 GLENCOE G45

GRAHAM MAITLAND K V (AB — (A) GLENCOE 1972 EPIC US 31901 UK 65207
NORMAN WATT ROY B V (AB — (B) THE SPIRIT OF GLENCOE 1973 EPIC us 32353 UK 65717
STEWART FRANCIS D (AB
JOHN TURNBULL G V (AB GERALD JOHNSON B (B KOFI AYIVOR PERC (B BEN SIDRAN K (B

G46 GLOBAL VILLAGE TRUCKING COMPANY G46

JON OWEN G V (AB — (A) GREASY TRUCKER LIVE AT DINGWALLS 1973 GREASY TRUCKERS UK GT 4997
JOHN McKENZIE B (AB — (B) GLOBAL VILLAGE TRUCKING COMPANY 1976 CAROLINE UK C 1516
JIMMY LASCELLES K (AB
SIMON STEWART D (AB MIKE MEDORA HCA G V (AB PETE KIRTLEY G V (B CAROMAY DIXON V (B
JIM CUOMO SAX (B JEREMY LASCELLES PERC (B MONICA GARELTS V (B

G47 GLOBE UNITY G47

ENRICO PAVA TPT (G — (A) LIVE IN WUPPERTAL 1973 FMP 0160
MANFRED SCHAF HRNS (G — (B) EVIDENCE 1976 FMP 0220
PETER BROTZMANN — (C) INTO THE VALLEY 1976 FMP 0270
EVAN PARKER — (D) PEARLS 1977 FMP 0380
KENNY WHEELER HRNS (G — (E) JAHRMARKET 1977 POTORCH JWB3
TONY BRAXTON — (F) IMPROVISATIONS 1978 JAPO 60021
GERK DUDEK SAX (G — (G) COMPOSITIONS 1979 JAPO 60027
MICHEL PILZ CLAR (G
BOB STEWART HRNS (G BUSCHI NIEBERGALL B (G PAUL LOVENS D (G ALBERT MANGELSDORFF TROM (G
ALEXANDER V SCHLIPPENBACH (G GRUNKI CHRISTMANN TROM(G PUAL RUTHERFORD TROM (G STEVE LACY SAX (G
EVAN PARKER S SAX (G

G48 GLORIA MUNDI G48

EDDIE MAELON V (AB — (A) I INDIVIDUAL 1978 RCA UK PL 25157
MIKE NICHOLLS D (AB — (B) WORD IS OUT 1979 RCA UK PL 25244
SUNSHINE K V (AB
BEETHOVEN G (A KIRBY G (B CC SAX (AB NIGEL ROSS SCOTT B (B
ICE B (A

G48A GLORY G48A

(A) A MEST MUSIC 1969 TEXAS REVOLUTION US 69

G49 JOHN GLOVER G49

JOHN GLOVER G V (A — (A) MIDNIGHT OVER ENGLAND 1978 ELECTRIC UK TRIX9
PETE VAN HOOKE D (A
PAUL WESTWOOD B (A JOHN MEALING K (A STEVE O'DONNELL K (A PETER ARNESEN PNO (A
TONY HICKS G (A JOHN IRISH EARLE SAX (A STEVE GREGORY WIND (A GEOFF RICHARDSON VLA (A
COLIN JENNINGS PERC (A DICK HANSON TPT (A JACQUIE SULLIVAN V (A JOY YATES V (A
B J COLE STEEL(A ROGER SAUNDERS G (A

G50 ROGER GLOVER G50

ROGER GLOVER B V (AB — (A) BUTTERFLY BALL 1974 PURPLE UK TPSA 7514
SIMON PHILLIPS D (B — (A) BUTTERFLY BALL(ROGER GLOVER) 1974 OYSTER US 1605
GRAHAM PRESKETT VLN (B — (B) ELEMENTS 1978 OYSTER US 1637 UK POLYDOR 2391 306
RONNIE ASPERY WIND (b
MICKY LEE SOULE K V (AB MARTIN BIRCH (B LIZA STRIKE V (AB HELEN CHAPPELLE V (AB
EDDIE HARDIN K SYN(A LES BINKS D (A RAY FENWICK G (A MO FOSTER B (A
MIKE MORAN K (A BARRY ST JOHN V (A JUDY KUHL V (A KAY GARNER V (A
JOANNE WILLIAMS V (A ANN ODELL PNO (A MIKE GILES D (A NIGEL WATSON SAX (A
EDDIE JOBSON VLN (A JACK EMBLOW ACC (A CHRIS KARAN TABLA(A ROBIN THOMPSON BASSOON (A
GLENN HUGHES V (A NEIL LANCASTER V (A JOHN GOODISON V (A DAVID COVERDALE V (A
RONNIE DIO V (A

G51 SUE GLOVER G51

SUE GLOVER V (A — (A) SOLO 1976 DJM DJF 20469 + DJLPS 469
EDDIE BAIRD (A
TONY BRAUNAGEL D (A IRENE CHANTER V (A DOREEN CHANTER V (A MICK FEAT B (A
PAUL KOSSOFF G (A DAVE MATTACKS D (A RABBIT BUNDRICK K (A TONY WILLIAMS D (A
TERRY WILSON B (A SUNNY LESLIE V (A

G51A GLAXO BABIES G51A

ROB CHAPMAN V (C — (A) THIS IS YOUR LIFE (EP) 1979 HEARTBEAT 12PULSE3
DAN CATSIS G V (C — (B) NINE MONTHS TO THE DISCO 1980 HEARTBEAT HB2
TONY WRAFTERS SAX (C — (C) PUT ME ON THE GUEST LIST 1980 HEARTBEAT HB3
TOM NICHOLS B V (C
GEOFF ALSOPP D (C CHARLES LLEWELLYN D (C

G51B GNAGS G51B

HENNING STAERK D PER(B — (A)
JENS J NEILSEN D PRC(B — (B) BURHONS 1979 GENLYD LP114
PETER AG NIELSEN B V (B — (C) INTERCITY 1980 GENLYD LP122
IVAN SORENSEN K G SYN(B
JACOB RIIS-OLSEN G V (B PER FROST G SYN K V(B

G52 GNIDROLOG G52

STEWART GOLDRING G (AB — (A) IN SPITE OF HARRY'S TOENAIL 1971 RCA UK SF8261
COLIN GOLDRING G V SAX (AB — (B) LADY LAKE 1972 RCA UK SF8322
NIGEL PEGRUM D FLT OBOE(B
JOHN EARLE V WIND(B PETER COWLING B CELLO(B CHARLOTTE FENDRICH PNO (B

G52A GOBLIN G52A

CLAUDO SIMONETTI K (A — (A) SUSPIRIA(SOUNDTRACK) 1979 EMI UK 3222
MASSIMO MORANTE G V (A
FABIO PIGNATELLI B G PERC V(A AGNOSTINO MARANGOLA D V (A

G52B GO GOS G52B

CHARLOTTE CAFFEY G K V(A — (A) BEAUTY & THE BEAT — 1981 IRS 70021
BELINDA CARLISLE V (A — (B) VACATION — 1982 IRS 70031
GINA SCHOCK D PERC(
KATHY VALENTINE B V (A — JANE WIEDLIN G V (

G53 KEITH & DONNA GODCHAUX G53

KEITH GODCHAUX K V ((A — (A) KEITH & DONNA GODCHAUX — 1975 ROUND UK/US RX 104
DONNA GODCHAUX V (A
JERRY GARCIA G V (A — BRIAN GODCHAUX VLN (A — JOHN KAHN B (A — DENNY SEIWELL D (A
MERL SAUNDERS ORG (A — JIM BRERETON D (A — CHRISSY STEWART B (A — BERNARD PURDIE D (A
BILL WOLF B (A

G53A GODDO G53A

GREG GODOVITZ V B (ALL — (A) GODDO — 1976 POLYDOR 2424 901
GINO SCARPELLI G (BD — (B) WHO CARES — 1978 POLYDOR 2424 902
DOUG INGLIS D (BD — (C) AN ACT OF GODDO — 1979 POLYDOR 2424 189
ROSEMARIE TEDESCO PNO (B — (D) LIGHUE — 1981 ATTIC 1107
PETER SCHENKMAN CELLO(B
DR JOHN BJARNASON HCA (B — MARTIN MELHUISH G (B — PAUL IRVINE SAX (B

G53B STEVE GODDARD G53B

STEVE GODDARD G V K(A — (A) WAITING FOR GODDARD — 1981 KINSWAY UK KMR 310

G54 ROBERT JOHN GODFREY G54

ROBERT JOHN GODFREY (A — (A) FALL OF HYPERION — 1974 CHARISMA UK CAS 1084

G55 GODIEGO G55

YUKIHIDE TAKEKAWA G (A — (A) WATER MARGIN — 1978 SATRIL UK SATL 4009
MICKIE YOSHINO K (A — (B) ROAD OF BROODY CLAP — 197 UK
TAKAMI ASANO G (A — (C) MONKEY — 1980 BBC UK 384
TAKAHIKO ISHIKAWA G (A
MEGUNI SAKAMOTO V (A — JUNKO KAMIMURA V (A — STEVE FOX B (A — RYOJI ASANO D (A
YUJIN HARADA D (A

G56 GODS G56

KEN HENSLEY K G V PERC (ABC1 — (A) GENESIS — 1968 COLUMBIA UK SCX 6286
LEE KERSLAKE D (ABC1 — (B) TO SAMUEL A SON — 1970 COLUMBIA UK SCX 6372
JOE KONAS G V (ABC1 — (C) GODS — 1976 HARVEST UK SHSM 2011
JOHN GLASCOCK B V (ABC — (1) PRE LP LINE UP
GREG LAKE B V (1

G57 THE GODZ G57

ERIC MOORE B V (AB — (A) GODZ — 1978 MILLENNIUM 8003 + RCA XL13051
GLEN CATALINE D V (AB — (B) NOTHING IS SACRED — 1979 CASABLANCA 7134 + RCA XL13072
MARK CHATFIELD G V (AB
BOB HILL G K V(AB

G58 THE GODZ G58

PAUL THORNTON D (ABCD — (A) CONTACT HIGH — 1967 ESP US 1037 NL FONTANA 858108
JAY DILLON K (ABD — (B) GODZ TWO — 1968 ESP US 1047 RI BASE IT 1077
LARRY KESSLER G VLN(ABCD — (B) GODZ TWO — 1969 FONTANA UK STL5512
JIM McCARTHY G V (ABCD — (C) THIRD TESTAMENT — 19 ESP US 1077
CHARLES CAZALET G (D — (D) GODZHUNHEIT — 19 ESP US 2017
MORTY KALB (C
THE GREAT PAHENE PNO (D — HERB ABRAMSON (C — BILLY PAYNE D (D — BOB UNGER B (D
SMOKEY HEAD G (D — JIMMY NORWOOD G (D — LESLIE FRADKIN G B V(D — PATTIE THORNTON V (D
U E GLASS G (D — GEORGE CAMERON D V (D — BOB GALLAGHER G (D — ROBERT FRIEDMAN B (D
GIOVANNI ROSARIO D (D

G58A GERRY GOFFIN G58A

GERRY GOFFIN — (A) IT AINT EXACTLY ENTERTAINMENT — 19 ADELPHI US 4102

G59 HERBIE GOINS G59

HERBIE GOINS — (A) No ONE IN YOUR HEART — 1967 PARLOPHONE UK PMC 7026

G60 ANDREW GOLD G60

ANDREW GOLD G V K B D(ALL — (A) ANDREW GOLD — 1975 ASYLUM US 7E 1047 UK SYL 9028
KENNY EDWARDS G VB(ABDC — (A) ANDREW GOLD — 1975 ASYLUM UK K 53020
DON FRANCISCO V (A — (B) WHAT'S WRONG WITH THIS PICTURE — 1976 ASYLUM US 7E 1086 UK K 53052
GENE GARFIN V D (A — (C) ALL THIS & HEAVEN TOO — 1978 ASYLUM US 6E 116 UK K 53072
MIKE BOTTS D (ABD — (D) WHIRLWIND — 1980 ASYLUM US 6E 264 UK K 52219
LINDA RONSTADT V (AB
TREVOR LAWRENCE HRNS (A — BOBBY KEYS HRNS (A — PETER BERNSTEIN B (A — DAVID KEMPER D (A
DAN DUGMORE G STEEL (A — BROCK WALSH K V (BDC — WADDY WACHTEL G (BDC — RUSS KUNKEL D (BC
LEE SKLAR B (BC — DONALD MENZA SAX (B — DANNY KORTCHMAR G (B — PETER ASHER V PERC(B
VAL GARAY V (B — TESSE COEN PERC (B — CLARENCE McDONALD K (B — BRYAN GAROFALO B (D
RICK MAROTTA D (DC — DON GROLNICK K (D — ERNIE WATTS SAX (C — JEFF PORCARO D (C
MARK SAFAN V (C — BEAU SEGAL D (C — J D SOUTHER V (C — STIX AKIMBO PERC(C
JENNIFER WARNES V (C — BRAD PALMER B (C

G60A JIM GOLD G60A

JIM GOLD V (ALL — (A) JIM GOLD & GALLERY — 1976 WESTBOUND US 225
JOHN STEVENSON B V (C — (B) I CANT FACE — 1977 TABU US 1 2308
DAVE THOMPSON K (C — (C) HOMETOWN HERO — 1978 TABU US 35520
MIKE EVERSOLE G (C
DAVE EVERSOLE B STEEL V(C — SCOTT THOMPSON D (C — MIKE IRISH G MAND(C

G61 BARRY GOLDBERG G61

BARRY GOLDBERG V G K (ALL — (A) CHICAGO ANTHOLOGY — 1966 TOGETHER US ST1024
DAVID HOOD B (HJK — (B) BLOWING MY MIND — 1966 EPIC US 26199
ROGER HAWKINS D (J — (C) REUNION — 1968 BUDDAH US 5012
PETE CARR G V (J — (D) TWO JEWS BLUES — 1969 BUDDAH US 5029
JIMMY JOHNSON G (EJ — (D) TWO JEWS BLUES — 1969 BUDDAH UK 203 020
EDDIE HINTON G (DHJ — (E) STREETMAN — 1970 BUDDAH US 5051
RULE YARBOROUGH BANJO(J — (F) BARRY GOLDBERG AND — 1972 RECORD MAN US CR5105
HARVEY THOMPSON WIND (J — (G) IVAR AVENUE REUNION(N MERRYWEATHER) — 197 RCA US LSP 4442
WAYNE HILL TPT (J — (H) BLAST FROM MY PAST — 1974 BUDDAH US 5081
ARTHUR JENKINS PERC (J — (H) BLAST FROM MY PAST — 1974 POLYDOR UK 2318 938
TEX BERNFELD V (J — (J) BARRY GOLDBERG — 1974 ATCO US 7040
MARGARET BRANCH V (J — (K) &FRIENDS RECORDED LIVE — 1976 BUDDAH US 5684

(CONTINUED)

G61 BARRY GOLDBERG (CONTINUED) G61

GEORGE TERRY G (J
AL LESTER FDL (J BARRY BECKETT K (J JIMMY EVANS CONGA(J RONNIE EADES SAX (J
HARRISON CALLOWAY TPT (J CHARLES ROSE TROM (J RALPH MACDONALD PERC (J BOB DYLAN V PERC(J
JERRY WEXLER PERC (J TOM BERNFIELD V (J BRENDA BRYANT V (J PAT SMITH V (J
MIKE BLOOMFIELD G (DFHK DANNY WHITTED G (H DUANE ALLMAN G (DH HARVEY MANDEL G(ABCDFHK
MARKEYS HRNS (H DON McCALLISTER B (CDH PETE STRAZZA SAX (H CHARLIE MUSSELWHITE HCA(ABCDGHK
NETTIE'MAMA' GOLDBERG K(CH EDDY HOH D (CDK RON WOODS PERC (C RONALD MINSKY PERC(C
SOULVILLE HORNS (D GREAT G HRNS(D NEIL MERRYWEATHER B (GK LYNN CAREY V (G
JOHN RICHARDSON G (G ROBIN BOERS D (G RON RUBY B (AB BOBBY JONES G (A
VINNIE BELL G (K MAURICE McKINLEY D (B BILLY BUTLER G (E ERIC GALE G (E
JERRY JEMMOTT B (E BOBBY GREGG D (E

G61A STU GOLDBERG G61A

STU GOLDBERG K (A (A) SOLOS/DUOS/TRIO 1978 MPS GER 61400
LARRY CORYELL G (A
L SUBRAMANIAM VLN (A

G62 GOLDBRIARS G62

(A) GOLDBRIARS 19 EPIC US BN 26087
(B) STRAIGHT AHEAD 19 EPIC US BN 26114

G62A GOLDEN DAWN G62A

TOM RAMSEY ((A) POWER PLANT 1967 INTERNATIONAL ARTISTS US IA 4
GEORGE KINNEY (
BILL HALLMARK (BOBBY RECTOR (A BIRD (

G62B JOHN GOLDING G62B

JOHN GOLDING G V (A (A) PHOTOGRAPHS 1974 ATLANTIC UK K50085
GEORGE VAN RISTELL MAND(A
DAVE DODDINGTON G DULC(A JIMMY JEWELL SAX (A PETE COSKER B (A PAUL GARRETT K (A
PAUL MIDDLETON B STEEL(A RODGER NARRWAY PERC (A PETE SAGE VLN (A ROY WEBBER V (A

G64 GOLDEN EARRING G64

GEORGE KOOYMANS G V (ALL (A) JUST EARRING 1964 POLYDOR NL 736 007
RINUS GERRITSEN B K (ALL (B) WINTER HARVEST 196 CAPITOL US 2823 POLYDOR NL 736 068
BARRY HAY V FLT(C>W (C) MIRACLE MIRROR 196 CAPITOL US 164 POLYDOR NL 1236 283 + 2459 330
ROBERT JAN STIPS K (MNQTV (D) ON THE DOUBLE 196 POLYDOR NL 2653 001 +2236 823/4
CESAR ZUIDERWIJK D (C>W (E) EIGHT MILES HIGH 1969 MAJ/MIN UKSM 65 POLYDOR NL 1656 015 UK 658 900
TONY BRITNEL SAX (TV (E) EIGHT MILES HIGH 1969 POLYDOR GER 184 356 ATLANTIC US 8244
EELCO GELLING G (LPQSFM (F) GOLDEN EARRING 197 CAPITOL US11315 POLYDOR 2499 009 + 2482 329
PAT PAAY V (LQ (F) GOLDEN EARRING 197 DWARF US 200 POLYDOR GER 2488 308
BERTUS BORGERS SAX (FLMN (G) SING MY SONG 197 KARUSSELL GER 2499 009
KEVIN NANCE K (S (H) SEVEN TEARS 1971 POLYDOR 2344 008 UK 2310 135
LANI GROVES V (ST (I) TOGETHER 1972 POLYDOR NL 2925 009 UK 2310 210
JIM MAELEN PERC (ST (J) BEST OF 1973 KARUSSELL 2499053 POLYDOR 2459 259
JOHN ZANGRANDO SAX (ST (K) HEARING EARRING 1973 TRACK UK 2406109
JOAP EGGERMONT D (ABCDE (L) MOONTAN 1974 MCA US 2354 POLYDOR UK 2310 288
NEPPIE NOYA PERC (Q (L) MOONTAN 1973 MCA US 396 TRACK UK 2406 112
FRANS KRASSENBURG V (ABC (M) SWITCH 1975 MCA US 2139 POLYDOR UK 2310 381
SIEB WARNER D PERC(E (M) SWITCH 1975 TRACK UK 2406117
JOHN LEGRAND HCA (U (N) TO THE HILT 1976 MCA US 2183 POLYDOR 2430 330
CHRIS MERCER SAX (N (O) MAD LOVE 1977 MCA US 2254
PETER DE PONDE G (AB (P) LIVE (DBL) 1977 POLYDOR 2625 034
(Q) CONTRABAND 1977 POLYDOR 2344 059 UK 2310 491
(R) STORY 1977 POLYDOR 2664 372
(S) POTRAIT OF 1977 POLYDOR EURO 2482 192
(T) GRAB IT FOR A SECOND 1979 POLYDOR UK 2310 639
(U) NO PROMISES 1979 POLYDOR US 6223
(V) PRISONER OF THE NIGHT1980 POLYDOR NL 2344 161
(V) LONG BLOND ANIMAL 1980 POLYDOR US 1 6303
(W) 2ND LIVE 1981 POLYDOR 2335 222VERTIGO 2625 042

G64A GOLIATH G64A

JOSEPH ROSBOTHAM WIND(A (A) GOLIATH 1970 CBS UK 64229 US ABC702
MALCOLM GRUNDY G (A
LINDA ROTHWELL V (A JOHN WILLIAMSON B (A ERIC EASTMAN D PERC(A

G64B GOLLIWOGS G64B

JOHN FOGERTY G V (A (A) GOLLIWOGS(PRECREEDENCE) 1975 FANTASY US F9474 FAN 5996
TOM FOGERTY G V (A
STU COOK B (A DOUG CLIFFORD D (A

G64C RAY GOMEZ G64C

RAY GOMEZ G V K B PERC (A (A) VOLUME 1980 CBS US 36243 UK 84134
CHRIS PALARO K VIBES(A
JIMMY HASLIP B (A WILL LEE B (A GREG MANN (A NARADA MICHAEL WALDEN D(A
RONNIE ST GERMAIN (A RANDY BRECKER TPT (A MICHAEL BRECKER SAX (A GEORGE YOUNG SAX (A
SAMMY FIGUEROA CONGA(A RAFAEL CRUZ PERC (A DIVA GRAY V (A ULLANDA McCULLOUGH V (A
LANI GROVES V (A DAVID SANCIOUS K (A

G65 IAN GOMM G65

IAN GOMM V G (AB (A) GOMM WITH THE WIND]SAME 1978 STIFF US 36103 ALBION UK DAI1
HERBIE FLOWERS B (AB (A) SUMMER HOLIDAY 1978 ALBION UK ALBG 100
CHRIS PARREN K (AB (B) WHAT A BLOW 1980 STIFF US 36433 ALBION UK 102
BARRY DE SOUZA D (AB
RAY TAFF WILLIAMS G V (B ROD DEMICK B V (B NICK GLENNIE SMITH K V (B B J COLE STEEL (B
ALAN COULTER D V (B MARTIN RUSHENT V (B MALCOLM MORLEY K (B RAPHAEL RAVENSCROFTBRASS(B

G66 GONG G66

FRANCIS MOSE B (DG (A) MAGICK BROTHER 1970 BYG FR 5293 305 GER METRONOME MLP 15372
DI BOND STEWART D (M (A) MAGICK BROTHER 1977 AFFINITY UK AFF 4
CHRISTIAN TITSCH G B (BCDEJ (B) CAMEMBERT ELECTRIQUE 1971 BYG FR 529353 1974 CAROLINE UK 1052
DELMELZA PERC (O (B) CAMEMBERT ELECTRIQUE 197 VIRGIN UK VG502
IDIER MALHERBE WIND(ABCDEFGHIJLN (C) CONTINENTAL CIRCUS 1971 PHILIPS 6332 330
DAEVID ALLEN G V (CDEFIJ (D)THE FLYING TEAPOT 1973 VIRGIN UK 2002 + BYG FR 529027
GILLI SMYTH V (ABCDEFIJ (E) ANGELS EGG 1973 VIRGIN UK 2007
PIP PYLE D (BC (F) YOU 1974 VIRGIN UK 2019 GER 88424
CHARLES HAYWARD D (A (G) SHAMAL 1976 VIRGIN UK 2046 US 34156 GER VIRGIN 28423
LAURIE ALLEN D (E (H) GAZEUSE 1977 VIRGIN UK 2074 + POLYDOR 2473 711
BOB TAIT D (I (I) LIVE ETC 1977 VIRGIN UK 3501 POLYDOR 2676 723
STEVE HILLAGE G (DEFGIJ (J) GONG EST MORT DBL 1977 TAPIOCA 10002/3 LTM 1003/4
TIM BLAKE K (DEFIJ (K) EXPRESSO 2 1978 VIRGIN UK 2099 POLYDOR 2473 742
RACHID HOUARI D (AD (K) EXPRESSO 1980 ARISTA US 4204 VIRGIN GER 25856
MIKE HOWLETT B V (DFGIJ (L) DOWNWIND 1979 ARISTA UK 1080 US 4219 NL 62272
BILL BRUFORD D ((M) TIME IS THE KEY 1979 ARISTA UK SPART 1105 US 4255
BRIAN DAVISON D ((N) P MOERLENS GONG LIVE 1979 ARISTA UK SPART 1130 NL 202 205
MIREILLE BAUER PERC (EGHILK (O) LEAVE T OPEN 1981 ARISTA NL 202 955
PIERRE MOERLEN D (EFGHIKLMNO
PATRICE LEMOINE K (GI JORGE PINCHEVSKY VLN (G EARL FREEMAN (A SANDY COLLEY (G
DARRYL WAY VLN (LKM FRANCOIS CHAUSSE PERC(LKNO ALLAN HOLDSWORTH G(HLKM MICK TAYLOR G (LK
HANNY ROWE B (LKMNO MIKE OLDFIELD G B (LN BENOIT MOERLEN PERC(HKLN STEVE WINWOOD K (L
MAC POOLE D (ROSS RECORD G (L MINO CINELON PERC(H DIETER GEWISSLER (A
BURTON GREEN (A JAMSIN (A MIQUETTE GIRAUDY V K(GI FRANCIS BACON (D
DIDIER LOCKWOOD VLN (L FRANCOIS COUSSE CONGA(LK BON LOZAGA (KMNO PERE CUSHION DE D (J
MISTER T BEING B (J TERRY OLDFIELD FLT (L JOE KIRBY B (M PETE LEMER K (M
NICO RAMSDEN G (M CHARLES MARIANO SAX (O BRIAN HOLLOWAY G (O PHIL NEWELL PROD (I
JOHN WALTERS PROD (I BARE PHILLIPS B (A PIERRE LATTES PROD (D SIMON HEYWORTH PROD (F

G67 GONZALEZ G67

MICK EVE SAX (ABCDE (A) GONZALEZ 1974 EMI UK EMC 3046
BUD BEADLE SAX (ABCDE (B) OUR ONLY WEAPON IS OUR MUSIC 1975 EMI UK EMC 3100
RON CARTHY TPT (ABCDE (B) OUR ONLY WEAPON IS OUR MUSIC 197 CAPITOL US ST 11644
ROY DAVIES K (ABCDE (C) HAVEN'T STOPPED DANCIN' 1979 CAPITOL US 11855 SIDEWALK UK2001
STEVE GREGORY SAX (ABCE (D) MOVE IT TO THE MUSIC 1979 CAPITOL US 11995 SIDEWALK UK2003
GORDON HUNTE G (ABCE (E) SHIPWRECKED(SOME TRACKS AS C) 1977 CAPITOL US SW 11855
SERGIO CASTILO D (D (F) WATCH YOU STEP 1980 CAPITOL 12103
CHRIS MERCER SAX (ABCDE
BOBBY STIGNAC D (BCDE COLIN JACAS TROM (CDE STEVE WALLER G V (CE GEORGE CHANDLER V (A
JOHN GIBLIN B (CE DE LISLE HARPER B (A GLEN LE FLEUR D (AB PRESTON HEYMAN D (B
ALLAN SHARPE PERC (AB RICHARD BAILEY D (ACE LENNY ZAKATEK G (BCE BOBBY JOHN PERC(A
LINDA TAYLOR V (CDE MARTIN DROVER HRNS (CDE LARRY STEELE B (B ROBERT AHWAI G (B
KEN FREEMAN SYN (B MALCOLM GRIFFITHS TROM(B LANCE DIXON SYN (B GODFREY McLEAN PERC(B
VIOLA WILLS V (B ALAN MARSHALL V (D TIM CANSFIELD V G (D HUGH BULLEN B (D

G67A GOOD MISSIONARIES G67A

MARK PERRY G K V(A (A) FIRE FROM HEAVEN 1979 DEPTFORD FUN CITY UK DLP 04
GILLIAN HANNA V REC(A
DAVE GEORGE G FLT V(A DENNIS BURNS B (A HENRY BADOWSKI D SAX (A GLYN COLLINS FLT (A
PAUL REEKIE B (A SOOZE V (A

G68 GOOD OLD BOYS G68

PATRICK CAMPBELL B (AB (A) PISTOL PACKIN' MAMA 1976 UA UK UAS 29951 US ROUND LA57G
DAVID NELSON G V (AB (B) BLUEGRASS 1978 FLYING FISH US FF 049
DON RENO DAN V(AB
FRANK WAKEFIELD MAND V(AB CHUBBY WISE FDL (AB

G69 GOOD RATS G69

JOE FRANCO D (BCDEFG (A) GOOD RATS 1968 KAPP US 3580
LENNY KOTKE B (BCDEFG (A) TASTY 1974 WB US 2813 RI 78 RAT CITY8002
PEPPI MARCHELLO V (BCDEFG (C) RAT CITY IN BLUE 1976 PLATINUM US RCR 8001
MICKEY MARCHELLO G V (BCDEFG (C) RAT CITY IN BLUE 1976 PHILIPS 6310 625
TOM JULIANO SAX (D (D) RATS TO RICHES 1978 RADAR UK RAD5 PATHE FR 606<5
BRIAN CUOMO PNO (DE (D) RATS TO RICHES 1978 PASSPORT US 9825 NL 062
HOWARD KAYLAN V (D (E) BIRTH COMES TO US ALL 1979 PASSPORT US 9830
MARK VOLMAN V (D (F) LIVE AT LAST 1980 RAT CITY 998 PASSPORT NL 68032
JOHN GATTO K G(BCDEF (G) GREAT AMERICAN MUSIC 1981 RAT CITY 8003 LOGO UK 1027
MANFRED MANN K (E
RICHARD TEE K (E JOHN TROPEA G (E JIMMY MAELIN PERC(E JANIS PENDANVIS V (E
JOSHIE ARMSTEAD V (E ZEPHRYN V (E JOE ZANGRANDO FLT (E MEL COLLINS SAX (E
PETER WOODS K (E LARRY FAST SYN (E STEPHEN GALFAS K (E MAX MIDDLETON K (E
JOHN GATTI WIND K(F SCHUYLER DEALE B (G BRUCE KULICK G (G

G70 GOOD THUNDER G70

JAMES CAHOON LINDSAY V PERC(A (A) GOOD THUNDER 1972 ELEKTRA UK K 42123 US EKS 75041
JOHN DESAUTELS D (A
DAVID HANSON G V (A BILL RHODES B (A WAYNE COOK K(A

G70A GOOD GUYS G70A

(A) SIDEWALK SURFING 19 GNP CRESCENDO US 2001

G71 PHILLIP GOODHAND TAIT G71

PHILLIP GOODHAND TAIT K V(ALL (A) REHEARSAL 1971 DJM UK DJLPS 411
ANDY LATIMER G (B (B) I'LL WRITE A SONG 1971 DJM UK DJLPS 416
DOUG FERGUSON B (B (C) SONGFALL 1972 DJM UK DJLPS 425
ANDY WARD D (B (D) PHILIP GOODHAND TAIT 1973 DJM UK DJLPS 432
(D) PHILIP GOODHAND TAIT 1973 20TH CENTURY US 424
(E) JINGLE JANGLE MAN 1975 DJM UK DJLPS 453
(F) OCEANS AWAY 1976 CHRYSALIS UK CHR 1113
(G) TEACHING AN OLD DOG 1977 CHRYSALIS UK CHR 1146
(H) GOOD OLD PHIL'S 1980 GUNDOG GUN LP1

G71A GOODIES G71A

BILL ODDIE V PERC(ALL (A) THE GOODIES LP 1976 BRADLEYS UK BRAOL 1012

TIM BROOKE-TAYLOR V (ALL (B) NOTHING TO DO WITH US 1976 ISLAND UK ilps9452

GRAEME GARDEN V (ALL

DAVE McRAE K (B JEFF SEOPARDIE D (B BILLY KRISTIAN B (B CHRIS RAE G (B

RAY FLACK G (B BERNIE HOLLAND G (B DEREK WATKINS TPT (B HENRY LOWTHER TPT (B

JOHN HUCKRIDGE TPT (B PAUL COSH TPT (B CHRIS PYNE TROM (B GEOFF WRIGHT TROM(B

RON ASPREY SAX (B GEOFF DAILEY SAX (B TONY CARR D (B ALAN PARKER G (B

BRIAN ODGES B (B GRAHAM PRESCOTT FDL (B JOY YATES V (B JACQUIE SULLIVAN V (B

STEVIE LANGE V (B RUSSELL STONE V (B CHAS MILLS V (B TONY BURROWS V (B

CHARLIE DORE V (B DAVID KATZ STR (B

G71B GOODNESS G71B

(A) GOODNESS 1977 AUDIO FIDELITY US 6284

G71C GOODNESS & MERCY G71C

DAVE TALISMAN V (A (A) GOODNESS & MERCY 19 MGM US SE 4730

PETER MARTIN K V (A

JOE BELLAMY B V (A RIC MILLER D (A ELVIS DITTA PERC (A JOHN TROMBATORE G (A

HARRY KIM TPT (A JERRY GRANT SAX (A STEVE DAVIS TROM (A

G72 STEVE GOODMAN G72

STEVE GOODMAN G V (ALL (A) STEVE GOODMAN 1971 BUDDAH US BDS 5096

DONNIE FRITTS ORG (A (A) STEVE GOODMAN 1972 BUDDAH US BDLH 5007

NORBERT PUTNAM B (A (B) SOMEBODY ELSE'S TROUBLE 1973 BUDDAH UK4019 US 5121

DAVID BRIGGS PNO (A (C) JESSIE'S JIG & OTHER FAVOURITES 1975 ASYLUM UK SYL 9017

CHARLIE McCOY HCA (A (C) JESSIE'S JIG & OTHER FAVOURITES 1975 ASYLUM UK K53025 US 7E 1037

BILLY SANFORD G BAN(A (D) WORDS WE CAN DANCE TO 1976 ASYLUM UK K53038 US 7E 1061

BUCKY WILKIN G (A (E) THE ESSENTIAL (AB) 1975 BUDDAH US 5665

BEN KEITH STEEL(A (F) SAY IT IN PRIVATE 1977 ASYLUM UK K53067 US 7E 1118

BRIAN RAY G (J (G) HIGH & OUTSIDE 1979 ASYLUM US 174

JEFF BAXTER G (J (H) GATHERING 1980 MOUNTAIN RAILWAY US 670

AMOS GARRETT G (J (J) HOT SPOT 1980 ASYLUM US 297

BILL ELLIOTT K (J

STEPHEN BRUNTON PERC (A GRADY MARTIN (A VASSAR CLEMENTS FDL (A PETE WADE G (A

GEORGE TIDWELL TPT (A WILLIAM PUETT CLAR (A GENE MULLINS TROM (A DENNIS GOODE TROM(A

MARTHA McCRORY CELLO(A STEVE BURGH G (BCD STEVE MOSLEY D (BD SID SIMS B (D

SAUL BROUDY HCA (D WINNIE WINSTON BAN STEEL(DC JEFF GUTCHEON K (BCD BILL SWOFFORD V (DC

HUGH McDONALD B (BCD RUAN MacKINNON V (DC DIANE HOLMES V (DC MARK GAFFNEY V (D

JIM ROTHERMEL SAX (DJ PETER ECKLUND CLAR (D JETHRO BURNS MAND (DC KENNY KOSEK FDL (D

LEW LONDON DOBRO(D TOM RADTKE TIMBALES (D JOHN FRIGO B VLN(D BOBBY ROSSI ACC (D

KEN BUTTREY PERC (A RICK CHUDACOFF B (J PETER BUNETTA D (J ARNO LUCAS PERC(J

MATTHEW WERNER V (J ALAN ESTES PERC (J BILL LABAMTY V (J PHOEBE SNOW V (J

JACK McGANN G ACC(B HUGH McCRACKEN G (B EDDIE BRIGATI V (B DAVID NEWMAN SAX (B

WILLIE BRIDGES SAX (B MARK HOROWITZ G BAN(B JERRY BARNHAM FLT (B ARIF MARDIN PNO (B

DAVID BRIGATI V (B CHARLES McCRACKEN CELLO(B LARRY PACKER FDL (B DAVID BROMBERG G MAND(B

ROBERT THOMAS PNO V(B MARIA MULDAUR V (B SHELDON PLOTKIN D PERC(C VASSAR CLEMENTS FDL (C

JOHN BURNS G (C ABBY NEWTON CELLO (C VIEN BLOOM WIND (C TED BOGAN G (C

HOWARD ARMSTRONG FDL (C BONNIE KOLAC V (C SAUL BROUDY HCA (C JACK THE BEAR TPT (C

CARL MARTIN MAND V(C

G72A GOOSE CREEK SYMPHONY G72A

RITCHIE HART V G (A (A) GOOSE CREEK SYMPHONY 19 CAPITOL US M444

PAUL HOWARD G V (A (B) WORDS OF EARNEST 1972 CAPITOL EST 11044

BOB HENKE G K V(A (C) WELCOME TO GOOSE CREEK 1973 CAPITOL US 690

ELLIS SCHWEID FDL ((D) DO YOUR THING 1974 CBS US 32918

DENNIS KENMORE D (

DAVE BIRKETT B (A MIKE McFADDEN G (A CHARLES GEARHART G (B PAUL SPRADLIN G (B

JIM TOLLES VLN (B FRED VLN (B FROGGY B (B FLASH D (B

WILLARD G (B RANDALL SAX (B HAROLD SAX (B PAT MOORE B (

CHRIS MOSTERT SAX (

G73 SAM GOPAL G73

SAM GOPAL PERC (AB (A) SAM GOPAL 1969 STABLE UK SLE 8001

IAN 'LEMMY'WILLIS G V (AB (B) ESCALATOR

ROGER DIELIA G (AB

PHIL DUKE B (AB SUNNY LESLIE V (A SUE GLOVER V (A

G73A GORDIAN KNOT G73A

PAT KINCADE G V (A (A) TONES 1968 VERVE US V6 5062

DULIN COMMODORE LANCASTER D(A

J D LOBUE K V (A LELAND RUSSELL B V(A JAMES WEATHERLY G V (A

G73B JIM GORDON G73B

JIM GORDON (A (A) PLAYS HEAVY 19 CREAM US 9007

G74 ROBERT GORDON G74

ROBERT GORDON V (ALL (A) ROBERT GORDON & LINK WRAY 1977 PRIVATE STOCK PVLP1027+PS 2030

JORDANAIRES V (B (A) ROBERT GORDON & LINK WRAY 19 RCA RI 3296

LINK WRAY G (AB (B) FRESH FISH SPECIAL 1978 PRIVATE STOCK PVLP1038+ 7008

CHRIS SPEDDING G (C (B) FRESH FISH SPECIAL 19 RCA RI 3299

HOWIE WYETH D (ABC (C) ROCK BILLY BOOGIE 1979 RCA APLI 3294

ROB STONER B PNO(ABC (D) LIVE AT DJ PARADISE BOSTON 197 RCA 3411

CHARLIE MESSING G (A (E) BAD BOY 1980 RCA 3523

RICHARD GOTTEHRER PNO (A (G) ARE YOU GONNA BE THE ONE 1980 RCA UK 5033 us 3773

BILLY CROSS G (AB

TERRY VERNON V (C PAUL EVANS V (C MARTIN NELSON V (C ROBIN GREAN V (C

G75 GORILLAS G75

ALAN BUTLER B (A (A) MESSAGE TO THE WORLD 1978 RAW UK RWLP 103

GARY ANDERSON D (A

JESSE HECTOR G V (A

G76 GOSPEL OAK G76

JOHN RAPP G (A (A) GOSPEL OAK 1970 UNI UNLS 113

BOB DEGATE G V (A

KERRY GAINES D (A MATTHEW KELLY HCA G(A GORDON HUNTLEY STEEL (A

G76A GRAHAM GOULDMAN G76A

GRAHAM GOULDMAN G V B G(AB (A) GRAHAM GOULDMAN THING 1978 RCA LSP3954
RICK FENN G V (B (B) ANIMALYMPICS 1980 MERCURY UK 9109630 A&M US4810
DUNCAN MACKAY K (B
PAUL BURGESS D (B STUART TOSH V (B MIKE TIMONY ACC (B

G76B GOTHAM G76B

GOTHAM 1978 DREAM US 3501

G76C BARRY GOUDREAU G76C

BARRY GOUDREAU G V (A (A) BARRY GOUDREAU 1980 PORTAIT US 36542 UK 84449
JESSE ERLICH CELLO(A
JOY LYLE VLN (A SID SHARP VLN (A DAVID SCHWARTZ VLA (A

G76D GOTHIC HORIZON G76D

ANDY DESMOND V G B(AB (A) THE JASON LODGE POETRY BOOK 1979 ARGO
RICHARD GARRETT V (AB (B) TOMORROW IS ANOTHER DAY 1972 ARGO UK ZDA 150

G77 MICK GRABHAM G77

MICK GRABHAM G V (A (A) MICK THE LAD 1972 U A UK UAS 29341
NIGEL OLSSON D (A
MIKE STOREY PNO (A DICK PARRY SAX (A CALEB QUAYE G (A

G77A GRACIOUS G77A

PAUL DAVIS G V (A (A) GRACIOUS! 1970 VERTIGO UK 6360 002 CAPITOL US 602
MARTIN KITCAT K (A (B) THIS IS 1972 PHILIPS UK 6382 004
ALAN COWDEROY G V (A
TIM WHEATLEY B (A ROBERT LIPSON D (A

G77B GRADUATE G77B

CURT SMITH B V (A (A) ACTING MY AGE 1980 PRECISION UK PART 001
STEVE BUCK K FLT(A
ANDY MARSDEN D (A ROLAND ORZABAL G V (A JOHN BAKER G V (A

G77C GRAFFITI G77C

GEORGE STRUNZ G (A (A) GRAFFITI 1968 ABC US ABCS 663
JOHN ST JOHN G (A
RICHIE BLAKIN D (A STEVE BENDEROTH K B (A TONY TAYLOR V (A

G77D GRACE G77D

(A) GRACE 1981 MCA UK MCF 3102

G78 DAVEY GRAHAM G78

DAVEY GRAHAM G V (ALL (A) GUITAR PLAYER 1963 GOLDEN GUINEA UK GGL 0224
WITH (B) FOLK ROOTS NEW ROUTES 1964 DECCA UK LK4652 RI RIGHTEOUS001
SHIRLEY COLLINS BANJO(B (C) FOLK BLUES & BEYOND 1965 DECCA UK LK 4649
EDDIE TRIPP B (G (D) MIDNIGHT MAN 1966 DECCA UK LK 4780
TONY KINSEY D (G (E) LARGE AS LIFE & TWICE AS NATURAL 1968 DECCA UK SKL 4969
KESHAU SATHE TABLA(G (F) HAT 1969 DECCA UK SKL 5011
(G) GODINGTON BOUNDARY 1970 PRESIDENT PTLS 1039
(H) 3/4 AD 19 TOPIC UK TOP 70
(I) HOLLY KALEIDOSCOPE 1970 DECCA UK SKL 5056
(J) COMPLETE GUITARIST 1978 KICKING MULE UK SNKF 138
(K) DANCE FOR TWO PEOPLE 1979 KICKING MULE UK SNKF 158

G79 ERNIE GRAHAM G79

ERNIE GRAHAM G V (A (A) ERNIE GRAHAM 1971 LIBERTY UK LBS 83485
BOB ANDREWS G V K(A
C CUNNINGHAM VLN (A J EICHLER V (A IAN GOMM G V (A NICK LOWE B V (A
MALCOLM MORLEY G V (A BILLY RANKIN D (A BRINSLEY SCHWARZ G (A RICHARD TREECE G (A
DAVE CHARLES D V (A KEN WHALEY B (A

G79A LARRY GRAHAM G79A

LARRY GRAHAM B D G K V (ALL (A) STAR WALK 1979 WB US 3322
ERIC DANIELS K V (B (B) ONE IN A MILLION 1980 WB US 3447 NL 56843
WILTON RABB G V (B (C) JUST BE MY LADY 1981 WB UK 56909
TINA GRAHAM V (B

G79B TOMMY GRAHAM G79B

TOMMY GRAHAM G SITAR (A (A) PLANET EARTH 1972 CAPITOL EAST21956
SKIP BECKWITH B (A
JOSH COLLINS D (A RON BULLY D (A EUGENE AMARO FLT (A MIKE LEWIS PNO (A
BILLY SPEER PNO (A BUDDY CAGE STEEL (A KATHY MOSES FLT (A MILES WILKINSON (A
JENNY BABOOLA TAMB (A BRIAN AHERN G (A

G80 GRAHAM CENTRAL STATION G80

LARRY GRAHAM V B G (ALL (A) GRAHAM CENTRAL STATION 1974 WB UK K 46286 US 2763
PATRYCE BANKS D V (ABD (B) RELEASE YOURSELF 1974 WB UK K 56062 US 2814
HERSHALL KENNEDY WIND (ABDE (C) AINT NO BOUT ADOUT IT 1975 WB UK K 56147 US 2875
WILLIE SPARKS D (AB (D) MIRROR 1976 WB UK K 56235 US 2937
DAVID VEGA G (ABDE (E) NOW DO U WANNA DANCE 1977 WB UK K 56359 US 3041
ROBERT SAM K V (ABDE (F) MY RADIO SURE SOUNDS GOOD 1978 WB US 3175
MILT HOLLAND PERC (A
LENNY WILLIAMS V (A FREDDIE STONE G (A GAYLORD BIRCH D (DE GAIL MULDROW G V (E
GREG ADAMS HRNS (D EMILIO CASTILLO HRNS (D MICK GILLETTE HRNS (D STEVE KUPKA HRNS(D
LENNY PICKETT HRNS (D

G80A BILLY GRAMMER G80A

BILLY GRAMMER G V (A (A) TRAVELLIN' ON 1959 MONUMENT US 4000

G80B GRAND FUNK RAILROAD G80B

MARK FARNER K G V HCA(ALL (A) ON TIME 1969 CAPITOL EURO 80249 EST 307
MEL SCHACHER V B(A>M (B) GRAND FUNK 1970 CAPITOL EURO 80357 EST 406
DON BREWER D V (ALL (C) CLOSER TO HOME 1970 CAPITOL EURO 80456 EST 471
CRAIG FROST K V (LK (D) LIVE 1971 CAPITOL UK ESTDW1/2 EST 633
TODD RUNDGREN G (K (E) SURVIVAL 1971 CAPITOL EURO 80783 ESW 764
FRANK ZAPPA G (P (F) E PLURIBUS FUNK 1972 CAPITOL EAS 853
DENNIS BELLINGER V B (R (G) MARK,DON & MEL 1969 71(COMP) 1972 CAPITOL UK ESTSP10 11042
DOUG KERSHAW FDL (H (H) PHOENIX 1973 CAPITOL 11099
(J) WE'RE JUST AN AMERICAN BAND 1973 CAPITOL EURO 81469 11207
(K) SHININ' ON 1974 CAPITOL 11278
(L) MASTERS OF ROCK (COMP) 1975 EMI 054 81479 EMI 81580
(M) ALL THE GIRLS IN THE WORL BEWARE 1975 CAPITOL 11356

(CONTINUED)

G80B **GRAND FUNK RAILROAD** (CONTINUED) G80B

(N) CAUGHT IN THE ACT (DBL) 1975 CAPITOL UK ESTSP 15 11445
(O) BORN TO DIE 1976 CAPITOL EURO 82107 11482
(P) GOOD SINGING, GOOD PLAYING 1976 EMI UK 1503 MCA US 2216
(Q) HITS (COMP) 1977 CAPITOL US 12010 11579
(R) GRAND FUNK LIVES 1981 WEA UK 99191

G81 **GRAND HOTEL** G81

COL CAMPSIE V (A — (A) DO NOT DISTURB 1979 CBS UK 83134
IVAN PENFOLD G K V(A
ROB GREEN G V (A MEL COLLINS SAX (A GEORGE McFARLANE B K V(A GRAHAM BROAD D PERC(A
DANNY McINTOSH G (A NICKY GRAHAM STRINGS (A

G81A **GRAND PRIX** G81A

PHIL LANZON K V (AB — (A) GRAND PRIX 1980 RCA UK PL 25321
MICHAEL O'DONAGHUE G V (AB — (B) THERE FOR NONE TO SEE 1982 RCA UK RCALP6027
RALPH HOOD B V (AB ANDY BEIRNE D PERC(AB BERNIE SHAW V (A ROBIN McAULEY V (B

G81B **GRANNY'S INTENTION** G81B

PAT NASH D (A — (A) HONEST INJUN 1970 DERAM UK SML 1060
PETE CUMMINGS B FLT (A
JOHN RYAN K (A JOHNNY DUHAN V (A JOHNNY HOCKEDY G MAND(A

G81C **GRANATI BROTHERS** G81C

BERNIE GRANATI K V (A — (A) G FORCE 1979 A&M US 4748
RICKY GRANATI D V (A
JOEY GRANATI K B V(A DAVID GRANATI G B V(A TONY LEE BONOMO D V (A

G81D **GRANFALLOON** G81D

(A) LASER PACE 197 TAKOMA US 9021

G81E **GRANDMOTHERS** G81E

JIMMY CARL BLACK V (ALL — (A)ANTHOLOGY OF PREVIOUSLY UNRELEASED MATERIAL 1980 RHINO US 302 LINE GER 5101
DON PRESTON K (ALL — (B)OFFICIAL GRANDMOTHERS FAN CLUB TALK ALBUM 1981 PANDA 001
ELLIOT INGBER G (ALL — (C)LOOKING UP GRANNY'S DRESS 1982 RHINO US 004 LINE GER 5106
BUNK GARDNER WIND (ALL
BUZZ GARDNER HRNS (ALL JAMES SHERWOOD SAX (ALL RAY COLLINS V (C TOM FOWLER B VLN (C
CHRIS PARLATA D (A TJAY CONTRELLI WIND (AC JOHN BALKIN (A IRA INGBER PERC (AC
RAW MILK D (A CHRISTY RUNDQUIST SYN (A ANDY CAHAN D (AC DENNY WALLEY G (A
TOM LEAVEY B (AC EMIL RICHARDS PERC (A ERIC LINDERMAN PNO (A DAVE PARLATA G B (A
JOHNNY DYRE HARP (A KEITH OLSEN D (A MEATBALL D (A RICHIE HAYWARD D (A
SANDY REINER D (A PHIL DAVIS SYN (A WALT FOWLER TPT K V(C LARRY TAYLOR B (A
LIL' JOHNNY G (A PAUL HUFF (C DON K MATIC TROM (C JOHN LASONIO B (C
DAVID TRENT D PERC(C DANNY NEWMARK K (C SID THE KID SAX (C DUSTY WAKEMAN B (C
STEELFINGER G (C TOM BROWN G (C FRANK SARKIN SAX (C FRANK ZAPPA D (C

G81F **EDDIE GRANT** G81F

EDDIE GRANT (ALL — (A) WALKING ON SUNSHINE 1979 ICE UK 4 EPIC US 36244
(B) LOVE IN EXILE 1980 ICE UK 19 EPIC US 36522
(C) CANT GET ENOUGH 1981 ICE UK 21

G82 **GRAPEFRUIT** G82

GEOFF SWETTENHAM D (AB — (A) DEEP WATER 1969 RCA US LSP4215 ST 8030
GEORGE ALEXANDER B (AB — (B) AROUND GRAPEFRUIT 1969 DUNHILL US 50050
JOHN PERRY G (AB — (B) AROUND GRAPEFRUIT 1969 STATESIDE UK SSL 5008
PETE SWETTENHAM G (B
BOB HALE (MICK FOWLER (

G83 **GRASS ROOTS** G83

JOEL LARSON D (J — (A) GRASS ROOTS 19 HAVEN US 9204
BONES HOWE PERC (B — (B) WHERE WERE YOU WHEN I NEEDED YOU 19 DUNHILL US 50011
WARREN ENTNER G (ABCDEFGHI — (C) LETS LIVE FOR TODAY 19 DUNHILL US 50020
ROB GRILL V (ABCDEFGHI — (D) FEELINGS 19 DUNHILL US 50027
VIRGIL WEBER (J — (E) GOLDEN GRASS 1969 DUNHILL US 50047
REED KAILING (J — (F) LOVIN' THING 1969 DUNHILL US 50052
ERIK MICHAEL COONCE D (ABCDEFGH — (G) LEAVING IT BEHIND 1969 DUNHILL US 50067
CREED BRATTON G (ABCDEF — (G) LEAVING IT BEHIND 1969 STATESIDE UK SSL 5012
DENNIS PROVISOR V (— (H) MORE GOLDEN GRASS 1970 DUNHILL US 50087
TERRY FURLONG G (— (I) 16 GREATEST HITS 1971 DUNHILL US 50107
LARRY KNECHTEL K (B — (J) MOVE ALONG 1972 DUNHILL US 50112
JOE OSBORNE G (B — (K) A LOT OF MILEAGE 197 DUNHILL US 50137
BOBBY RAY G (B
P F SLOAN G (B

G84 **GRATEFUL DEAD** G84

JERRY GARCIA G V(A11 — (A) GRATEFUL DEAD 1967 WB US 1689
ROD'PIGPEN'McKERNAN K V(ABCDEFGHI — (B) ANTHEM FOR THE SUN 1968 WB US 1749 UK K 46021
(AB) GRATEFUL/ANTHEM 1976 WB GER 66040
BOB WEIR G (ALL — (C) AOXOMOXOA 1969 WB US 1790 UK K 46027
PHIL LESH B V (ALL — (D) LIVE/DEAD(DBL) 1970 WB US 1830 UK K 66002
MICKEY HART D (BCDFPRTUVW — (E) WORKINGMANS DEAD 1970 WB US 1869 UK K 46049
BILL KREUTZMANN D (ALL — (F) AMERICAN BEAUTY 1971 WB US 1893 UK K 46074
(F) AMERICAN BEAUTY 1980 MOBILE US 014
TOM CONSTANTEN K (CD — (G) GRATEFUL DEAD LIVE(DBL) 1971 WB US 1935 UK K 66009
ROBERT HUNTER (EFGHPT — (H) EUROPE 72 (TRIPLE) 1972 WB US 3X2662 UK K 66019
KEITH GODCHAUX K (HPRTUV — (I) VINTAGE DEAD 1972 POLYDOR UK 2310 172
DONNA GODCHAUX V (HPRTUV — (I) VINTAGE DEAD 197 SUNFLOWER US SNF 5001
DAVE NELSON (EF — (J) HISTORY OF(BEARS CHOICE) 1973 WB US 2721 UK K 46246
DAVE TORBERT B (F — ( ) HISTORY OF 197 PRIDE US 0016
DAVE GRISMAN MAND(F — (L) HISTORIC DEAD 197 POLYDOR UK 2310 171
BRENT MYDLAND (UVW — (IL) POP HISTORY 1972 POLYDOR 2612 019 GER 2335 059
HOWARD WALES K (F — ( ) HISTORIC DEAD 197 SUNFLOWER US 5004
NED LAGIN K (F — (M) WAKE OF THE FLOOD 1973 G DEAD US 01 UK K 49301
MERL SAUNDERS K (G — (M) WAKE OF THE FLOOD 1976 UA UK RI 29903
JOHN DAWSON G V (— (N) FROM MARS HOTEL 1974 G DEAD US 102 UK K 59302
BOB MATTHEWS G V (— (N) FROM MARS HOTEL 1976 UA UK RI29904 GER 63826
STEVEN SCHUSTER (P — (MN) WAKE /MARS HOTEL 1977 UA UK UDM103/4
BILL ATWOOD TPT (MN — (O) SKELETONS FROM THE CLOSET 1974 WB US 2764 UK K 56024
VASSAR CLEMENTS VLN(MN — (P) BLUES FOR ALLAH 1975 G DEAD US 494 UK UAS 29895
PAT OHARA TROM (MN — (Q) STEAL YOUR FACE(DBL) 1976 G DEAD US 62 UK UAD60131/2
JOE ELLIS TPT (MN — (R) TERRAPIN STATION 1977 ARISTA US 7001 UK 1016

(CONTINUED)

G84 (CONTINUED)

GRATEFUL DEAD G84

MARTIN FIERRO SAX (MN
SARAH FULCHER V (MN
MATTHEW KELLY HCA (MNT
DOUG SAHM G(MN
BENNY VELARDES PERC(MN
JORDAN AMARANTHA PERC (T
FRANK MORIN SAX (MN

(S) WHAT A LONG STRANGE TRIP(COMP)1978 WB US 3091 UK K 66073
(T) SHAKEDOWN STREET 1978 ARISTA US 4198 UK ARTY159 GER 62101
(U) GO TO HEAVEN 1980 ARISTA US 9508 UK 1115
(V) RECKONING 1981 ARISTA US 8604 UK DARTY GER 301 621
(W) DEAD SET LIVE 1981 ARISTA UK ARTY 11 GER 301738

G84A

NICK GRAVENITES G84A

NICK GRAVENITES G V (ALL
PETE SEARS B K (C
JOEY COVINGTON D (C
HUEY LOUIS HCA (C
MIKE BLOOMFIELD G (AD
GREG DOUGLAS G (C WILLY TROST G (C ROGER TROY B V (C JOHN CIPOLLINA G (C
MARLA HUNT V (C DIANE HURST V (C JOB JONES D (A MARK NAFTALIN PNO (A
DINO ANDINO CONGA(A IRA KAMIN ORG (A JOHN KAHN B (AD JOHN WILMETH TPT (A
NOEL JENKINS SAX (A GERALD OSHITA SAX (A MERL SAUNDERS ORG (D PAUL BUTTERFIELD HCA(D
MARIA MULDAUR V (D

(A) MY LABORS 1969 CBS US 9899 UK 63818
(B) JUNKYARD IN MALIBU 1980 LINE GERM 6 24264
(C) BLUE STAR 1980 LINE GERM LLP 5039
(D) STEEL YARD BLUES(SOUNDTRACK) 1973 LIBERTY US 352662

G84B

GRAUZONE G84B

MARTIN EICHER G B V(A
MARCO REPETTO D G V(A
STEPHAN EICHER G V B K(A ERIENNE CONOD PNO (A

(A) GRAUZONE 1981 OFF COURSE GER 46 500

G85

GRAVY TRAIN G85

NORMAN BARRETT V G (ABCD
BARRY DAVENPORT D (AB
J D HUGHES WIND K V (ABCD
LES WILLIAMS B V (ABCD
GEORGE LYNON G (D
PETE SOLLEY SYN (D MARY ZINOVIEFF SYN VLN(D

(A) GRAVY TRAIN 1970 VERTIGO UK 6360 023
(B) BALLAD OF A PEACEFUL MAN 1971 VERTIGO UK 6360 051
(C) SECOND BIRTH 1973 DAWN UK DNLS 3046
(D) STAIRCASE TO THE DAY 1974 DAWN UK DNLH 1

G85A

DOBIE GRAY G85A

DOBIE GRAY V (ALL
DAVID BRIGGS K (ABC
MIKE LEECH B (ABC
KENNY MALONE D (ABC
TROY SEALS G (ABC
REGGIE YOUNG G BAN(ABC
WELDON MYRICK STEEL(A
BUDDY SPICHER FDL (AB MENTOR WILLIAMS G (A CHARLIE McCOY HCA (B TOMMY COGBILL B (C
LONNIE MACK G (C NORBERT PUTNAM B (C HERSHEL WIGINTON B V (C HARVEY THOMPSON HRNS(C
BEN CAULEY HRNS (C CHARLES ROSE HRNS (C HARRISON CALLOWAY HRNS (C RONNIE EADES HRNS(C
RANDY McCORMICK K (EF ROGER CLARK D (EF LARRY BYROM G (EF KEN BELL G (EF
BOB WRAY B (EF MICKEY BUCKINS PERC (E LENNY LEBLANC V (EF EDDIE STRUZICK V (EF
THOM FLORA V (E STEVE NATHAN K (EF OWEN HALE D (F JIMMY ENGLISH G (F
WALT ALDRIDGE G (F RALPH EZELL B (F DANNY KIRSCH SAX (F CHUCK GODWIN FLT (F
CHALMERS DAVIS K (F MARK GRAY K V (F DONNA RHODES V (F CHARLIE CHALMERS V (F
SANDRA RHODES V (F

(A) DRIFT AWAY 1973 DECCA US 7 5397
(B) LOVING ARMS 1973 MCA US 371
(C) HEY DIXIE 1974 MCA US 449
(D) NEW RAY OF SUNSHINE 197 CAPRICORN US 0163
(E) MIDNIGHT DIAMOND 1978 INFINITY US 9001
(F) DOBIE GRAY 1979 INFINITY US 9016

G86

GREASE BAND G86

HENRY McCULLOUGH G (AB
MICK WEAVER K (B
ALAN SPENNER B (AB
BRUCE ROWLAND D (AB
NEIL HUBBARD G (AB
CHRIS STAINTON K (B TERRY STANNARD D (B MEL COLLINS SAX (B TOMMY EYRE K (
JOHN WEATHERS D (

(A) THE GREASE BAND 1971 HARVEST UK SHVL790 SHELTER US 8904
(A) THE GREASE BAND 1981 LINE RI GER LLP 5005
(B) AMAZING GREASE 1975 GOODEAR UK 2902 RI CHARLY 30166
(B) AMAZING GREASE 1981 LINE RI GER LLP 5008

G86A

GREAT BEAR G86A

(A) GREAT BEAR 1971 WAND UK WNS8
(A) GREAT BEAR 197 SCEPTER US SPS 585

G86B

GREAT BUILDINGS G86B

DANNY WILDE G V K(A
RICHARD SANFORD D PERC(A
PHILLIP SOLEM G V (A IAN AINSWORTH B K V(A

(A) APART FROM THE CROWD 1981 CBS US 36920

G87

GREAT JONES G87

BILLY CADIEUX G (A
GARY KOLLARUS D (A
DAVID TOLMIE B (A JEFF GUTCHEON K (A MERRY CLAYTON V (A VANETTA FIELDS V (A
CLYDIE KING V (A

(A) ALL BOWED DOWN 197 TONSIL US T 4002

G87A

GREAT METROLPOLITAN STEAM BAND G87A

(A) GREAT METROPOLITAN STEAM BAND 1969 MCA UK MUPS 403 + MAPS 2162

G88

GREAT SOCIETY G88

GRACE SLICK V (AB
PETER VANDERGELD B (B
JERRY SLICK D (B
DARBY SLICK G (B
DAVID MINOR G (B

(A) GREAT SOCIETY 196 CBS US 30459 UK 63476
(A) GREAT SOCIETY 197 EMBASSY UK 31800
(B) CONSPICUOUS ONLY IN ITS ABSENCE 1968 CBS US 9624
(C) HOW IT WAS 1968 CBS US 9702 30461
(D) SOMEBODY TO LOVE 19 HARMONY US 30391
(ABC) COLLECTORS ITEM 19 CBS US 30459

G89

GREATEST SHOW ON EARTH G89

COLIN HORTON JENNINGS V G D(AB
GARTH WATT ROY VG (AB
NORMAN WATT ROY V B (AB
MIKE DEACON K (AB
RON PRUDENCE CONGA D(AB DICK HANSON HRNS (AB TEX PHILPOTTS SAX (IAN AITCHISON SAX (

(A) HORIZONS 1970 HARVEST UK SHVL769 GER 04310
(B) THE GOING'S EASY 1970 HARVEST UK SHVL783 GER 04570
(AB) GREATEST SHOW ON EARTH 1975 HARVEST UK SHSM 2004

G90

JOHN GREAVES & PETER BLEGVAD G90

JOHN GREAVES B V K PERC(A
PETER BLEGVAD V G SAX(A
LISA HERMAN V (A ANDREW CYRILLE D PERC(A MIKE MANTLER HRNS (A CARLA BLEY V SAX(A
MICHAEL LEVINE VLN V(A VITO RENDACE WIND (A APRIL LANG V (A DANA JOHNSON V (A
BORIS KINBERG CLAVE (A

(A) KEW RHONE 1977 VIRGIN UK V2082 US 34758

G91 **RICK GRECH** G91

RICK GRECH B VLN V(A (A) THE LAST FIVE YEARS(COMP) 1973 RSO US 876 UK 2394 111

G91A **GREEN** G91A

GARY CASEBEER K HRNS V(A (A) GREEN 1969 ATCO UK 33282
RICHARD GARDZINA K V HRNS(A
WILSON FISHER V HCA(A JOHN MARTIN K V (A JAMES NEEL V K WIND (A BOBBY BLOOD HRNS (A

G92 **AL GREEN** G92

AL GREEN V (ALL (A) BACK UP TRAIN 19 HOT LINE US 1500
WAYNE JACKSON TPT (H (B) GREEN IS BLUES 1970 HI US 32055
ANDREW LOVE SAX (H (C) GETS NEXT TO YOU 1971 HI US 32062 LONDON UK 8424
ED LOGAN SAX (H (D) LETS STAY TOGETHER 1972 HI US 32070 LONDON UK 8430
JAMES MITCHELL SAX (H (E) I'M STILL IN LOVE WITH YOU 1972 HI US 32074 LONDON UK 8443
JACK HALE TROM (H (F) CALL ME 1973 HI US 32077 LONDON UK 8457
HOWARD GRIMES D PERC(H (G) LIVING FOR YOU 1974 HI US 32082 LONDON UK 8464
LEROY HODGES B (H (H) EXPLORES YOUR MIND 1974 HI US 32087 LONDON UK 8479
CHARLES HODGES K (H (I) AL GREEN IS LOVE 1975 HI US 32092 LONDON UK 8488
TEENIE HODGES G (H (J) FULL OF FIRE 1976 HI US 32097 LONDON UK 8493
ARCHIE TURNER PNO (H (K) HAVE A GOOD TIME 1976 HI US LONDON UK 8505
MICHAEL ALLEN PNO (H (L) BELLE ALBUM 1977 HI US 6004 CREAM UK 6004
MEMPHIS STRINGS (H (M) TRUTH & TIME 1978 HI US 6009
REUBEN FAIRFAX B (L (N) CREAM OF 1980 CREAM US HLP101
JAMES BASS G (L ( )=AL GREEN 19 BELL US 6076
MARGARET FOXWORTH V (L ( ) GREATEST HITS 1981 TELDEC GER 622217
LINDA JONES V (L ( ) HITS VOL 2 1979 HI US 32105
HARVEY JONES V (L ( ) TOKYO LIVE 1981 HI UK 5001
LEON THOMAS K (L ( ) HIGHWAY TO HEAVEN 1981 MYRRH US 6661
DARRYL NEELY HRNS (L
JOHNNY BROLIN K (L FRED JORDAN TPT K (L JOHN TONEY D (L RON ECHOLS SAX (L
ROB PAYNE PERC (L ARDIS HARDIN D (L BUDDY JARRETT SAX (L

G92A **BUNKY GREEN** G92A

BUNKY GREEN (ALL (A) THE LATINIZATION OF.. 19 CADET US LP 780
(B) TESTIFYIN' TIME 19 CADET US LP 753
(C) PLAYING FOR KEEPS 19 CADET US LP 766

G92B **DANNY GREEN** G92B

DANNY GREEN G V (A (A) NIGHT DOG 1978 ABC UK ABCL5259 MCA US 1085
DON BARRETT B (A
GINO ZIMMERMAN G (A CARSON WHITSETT K (A KAREN TAYLOR V (A JOE HARDY V (A
JAMES STROUD D PERC(A ED FORESMAN B V (A WALTER POLK D (A JUDY RODMAN V (A
JERRY McKINNEY HRNS (A DR JOHN PNO (A WILLIAM C BROWN V (A DUNCAN SISTERS V (A
JOE MULHERIN HRNS (A MIKE PLUNKETT K (A

G92C **IAN GREEN** G92C

IAN GREEN (A (A) REVELATION 1970 CBS UK 63840
ROSSETTA HIGHTOWER V (A
MADELINE BELL V (A

G92D **JACK GREEN** G92D

JACK GREEN G B V(AB (A) HUMANESQUE 1980 RCA RCAALP 5004 APL1 3639
RICHIE BLACKMORE G (A (B) REVERSE LOGIC 1981 RCA AFLI 4122
BRIAN CHATTON K (AB
MEL COLLINS SAX (AB ANDY DALBY G (AB IAN ELLIS B (AB SIMON FOX D (B
MAC POOLE D (A PETE TOLSON G (AB GEORGE SERGHI (B

G94 **PETER GREEN** G94

PETER GREEN G V (ALL (A) THE END OF THE GAME 1970 REPRISE UK RSLP9006+RI K44106
ZOOT MONEY PNO (A (A) THE END OF THE GAME 1970 REPRISE US 6434
GODFREY MACLEAN D (AB (B) IN THE SKIES 1979 PVK UK 101 LOTUS EURO 4063
JEFF DALY SAX (D (B) IN THE SKIES 1979 CREOLE GER 6 23793
NICK BUCK K (A (C) LITTLE DREAMER 1980 PVK UK 102 LOTUS EURO 4090
MO FOSTER SAX (D (C) LITTLE DREAMER 1980 CREOLE GER 6 24300
ALEX DMOCHOWSKI B (A (D) WHATCHA DONNA DO? 1981 PVK UK PET 1 NL POLYDOR 2925119
JOHN EDWARDS B (CE (E) BLUE GUITAR 1981 CREOLE CRX 5
KUMA HARADA B (BCE
REG ISADORE D (B RON JOHNSON G (CDE PAUL WESTWOOD B (CDE DAVE WILKEY PNO (C E
SNOWY WHITE G (BE LENNOX LAINGTON D ((DE PETER BARDENS K (BE ROY SHIPSTON K (CDE
PETER VERNON KELL PNO (CE DAVE MATTACKS D (CDE MORRIS PERT PERC (CE CAROL INGRAM V (CE
PAM DOUGLAS V (CE

G95 **GREEN BULLFROG** G95

RICHIE BLACKMORE G (A (A) GREEN BULLFROG 19 MCA MKPS 2021 RI 74 MCF 2689
ALBERT LEE G (A (A) GREEN BULLFROG 19 ECY STREET 16 DECCA 75269
ROGER GLOVER B (A
IAN PAICE D (A BIG JIM SULLIVAN G (A CHAS HODGES B (A ROD ALEXANDER G (A
MATTHEW FISHER K (A TONY ASHTON K (A EARL JORDON V (A

G96 **NORMAN GREENBAUM** G96

NORMAN GREENBAUM V G K (ALL (A) SPIRIT IN THE SKY 1969 REPRISE US 6365
DAN HICKS PERC (B (B) BACK HOME AGAIN 1972 REPRISE US 6422
DAN PAIK MAND (B (C) PETALUMA 1973 REPRISE US 2084
STEVE BUSFIELD G (B
LYNN ELDER (B RUSSEL DASHIELL G (BA BILL DOUGLAS B (B DOUG KILLMER B (BA
NORMAN MAYELL D (BA JOHN McFEE STEEL(B BILL MEEKER D (B STOVAL SISTERS V (B
WILLIAM TRUCKAWAY SYN (BA ROBBIE ROBINSON G (A CHUCK PETERSON (A DAN PADIRIS (A
JOHN COPPOLA (A BILL SABATINI (A

G96A **JEANIE GREENE** G96A

JEANIE GREENE K V (A (A) MARY CALLED JEANNIE GREENE 1971 ELEKTRA 74103
MARLIN GREENE B (A
ROGER HAWKINS D (A BARRY BECKETT K (A WAYNE PERKINS G SIT(A LEO LEBLANC STEEL (A
CLAUDIA LENNEAR V (A MARY PEDERSON V (A CHRIS ETHRIDGE B (A TIM SCHMIT V (A
DAVID HOOD B (A LARRY NICHOLSON G (A JIMMY JOHNSON G (A

G96B **MARLIN GREENE** G96B

MARLIN GREENE G V (A (A) TIPTOE PAST THE DRAGON 1972 ELEKTRA UK K 42111
WAYNE PERKINS G (A
LARRY NICHOLSON G (A EDDIE HINTON G (A ROGER HAWKINS D (A FRED PROUTY D (A
LOU MULLENIX D (A BARRY BECKETT K (A CHUCK LEAVELL K (A JERRY MASTERS B (A
DAVID HOOD B (A LEO LE BLANC STEEL(A JEANIE GREENE PNO (A CASEY KELLY G (A

G96C **MIKE GREENE** G96C

MIKE GREENE V K WIND (AB (A) PALE PALE MOON 1975 GENERAL REC 10013
RANDE POWELL D (AB (B) MIDNIGHT MIRAGE 1976 MERCURY US SRM1 1100
DAVID MICHAEL G (AB
MIKE HOLBROOK B (AB NEIL LARSEN K (A CARLOS MARTINEZ PERC (A GURU VIR PERC (A
DEAN BROTHERS V (A SKIP LANE STR (B FARRELL MORRIS PERC (B

G97 **GREENSLADE** G97

DAVE GREENSLADE K (ABCD (A) GREENSLADE 1973 WB UK K 46207+ PHILIPS 6325 500
TONY REEVES B (ABC (B) BEDSIDE MANNERS ARE EXTRA 1973 WB UK K 46259+
DAVE LAWSON K (ABCD (C) SPYGLASS GUEST 1974 WB UK K 56055+ MERCURY US 1015
ANDY McCULLOCH D (ABCD (D) TIME & TIDE 1975 WB UK K 56126+ MERCURY US 1025
ANDY ROBERTS G (C (D) TIME & TIDE 1975 VERTIGO EURO 6370 113
MARTIN BRILEY G B (D
DAVE CLEMPSON G (C GRAHAME SMITH VLN (C MICK ROGERS G V (BARRY MORGAN PERF (D
JILL MACKINTOSH V (D DAVE MARKEE B (ANN SIMMONS V (D TREVERVA MALE CHOIR (D
JEREMY ENSOR EFFECTS (C GREG JACKMAN EFFECTS(C

G97A **DAVE GREENSLADE** G97A

DAVE GREENSLADE K (AB (A) CACTUS CHOIR 1976 WB UK K 5630&
TONY REEVES B (A (B) PENTATEUCH OF THE COSMOGONY(DBL) 1979 EMI UK EMC3321/2
SIMON PHILLIPS D (A
JOHN PERRY B (A STEVE GOULD V (A BILL JACKMAN WIND (A MICK GRABHAM G (A
JOHN LIGERTWOOD PERC (B PHIL COLLINS PERC (B

G97B **ELLIE GREENWICH** G97B

ELLIE GREENWICH V (A (A) LET IT BE WRITTEN,LET IT BE SUNG 1973 MGM VC5091 2315 243
RICK MAROTTA D (A
STEVE GADD D (A AL ROGERS D (A RUSSELL GEORGE B (A CHARLIE BROWN G (A
VINNIE BELL G (A ERIC WEISSBERG G (A SAL DITROIA G (A JOHN ABBOTT G (A
STEVE FLEDMAN K (A ARTIE BUTLER K (A STEVE TUNANGER PERC (A

G98 **MICK GREENWOOD** G98

MICK GREENWOOD V G K(ABC (A) LIVING GAME 1971 MCA UK 8003+RI MCA 74 MCG 3520
JIMMY HELMS V (B (A) LIVING GAME 1971 DECCA US 75318
JERRY DONAHUE G V (AB (B) TO FRIENDS 1972 MCA UK 2026+RI MCA UK MCF 8692
DORIS TROY V (B (B) TO FRIENDS 1972 MCA US 307
TONY COX K V (AB (C) MIDNIGHT DREAMER 1974 WB UK K56059
PAT DONALDSON B (A
GERRY CONWAY D (A LYN DOBSON WIND SITAR(A DAVE PEGG B (A ANDY SMITH BANJO (A
CHRISTINE QUAILE V (A DUDU PUKWANA SAX (A KARL JENKINS SAX (A BUD PARKES TPT (A
DEREK WADSWORTH TROM (A NED BALEN PERC (A BARRY DE SOUZA D (A DAVE PEACOCK B V VLN (B
BARRY ST JOHN V (B

G99 **NICK GREENWOOD** G99

NICK GREENWOOD (A (A) COLD CUTS 1972 KINGDOM UK KVLP 9002

G100 **GREEZY WHEELS** G100

CLEVE HATTERSLEY V G (AB (A) JUST LOVE DEM 'OL GREEZY WHEELS 1975 LONDON US PS 657
LISSA HATTERSLEY G V (AB (B) RADIO RADIALS 1976 LONDON US 667 UK SHU 8497
MARY EGAN FDL (AB
PAT PANKRATZ G (AB TONY AIROLDI G (AB MIKE PUGH B (AB TONY LAIER D (AB
MADRILLE WILSON CONGA(AB JIMMY DAY STEEL (A ALFRED ROBERTS PERC (A RILEY OSBORNE PERC(A

G100A **ZAINE GRIFF** G100A

ZAINE GRIFF SYN (A (A) ASHES & DIAMONDS 1980 AUTOMATIC US 34834 UK K56834
ANDY DUNCAN D (A
STEVE BOLTON G (A ANDY CLARK K (A TONY VISCONTI B V PERC(A HANS ZIMMER SYN (A

G101 **GRIFFIN** G101

GRAHAM BELL V (1 (1) 1969
ALAN WHITE D (1
COLIN GIBSON B (1 PETE KIRTLEY G (1 KEN CRADDOCK K (1

G101A **JAMES GRIFFIN** G101A

JAMES GRIFFIN G V (A (A) JAMES GRIFFIN 1978 POLYDOR UK 2391 274
DAVID PAICH K (A (B) EAGLE 197 POLYDOR US 6018
DAVE BUDAMEYER B (A ( ) BREAKING UP IS EASY 1974 POLYDOR UK 2391 113
JIM GORDON D (A
JACK HALE TROM (A DEAN PARKS G (A JIM HORN HRNS (A LARRY KNECHTEL B(A
MIKE BOTTS D (A CAROL CARMICHAEL V (A DAVID GATES D (A JOE LAMANO B (A
ED LOGAN SAX (A BARRY BURTON G (A ANDREW LOVE SAX (A JAMES MITCHELL SAX (A
WAYNE JACKSON HRNS (A

G101B **ROB GRILL** G101B

ROB GRILL V (A (A) UPROOTED 1979 MERCURY 9111 055 US SRM1 3798
ROBBIE BUCHANAN K (A
STEVE HUNTER G (A JOHN McVIE B (A MICK FLEETWOOD D (A MARK LEONARD B (A
LINDSEY BUCKINGHAM G (A MIKE HUEY D (A DENNIS PROVISOR K (A ANNIE McCLOONE V (A
DONNIE GERRARD V (A BILL CHAMPLIN V (A JAY GRUSKA V (A CARL GRAVES V (A
KATHY COLLIER V (A BRIAN NAUGHTON G (A

G102 **CAROLE GRIMES** G102

CAROL GRIMES V (ALL (A) FOOLS MEETING(WITH DELIVERY) 1970 B+C CAS 1023 PHILIPS GER 6369 004
STEVE MILLER PNO (A (B) WARM BLOOD 1974 CAROLINE UK CA 2001
ROY BABBINGTON B (A (C) CAROLE GRIMES 1976 DECCA UK SKLR5258
GARY TWIGG B (2 (C) CAROLE GRIMES 1979 CHARLY UK CR 30164
PHIL MILLER G (A (1) MAY 1978 TOUR
PIP PYLE D (A (2) 1980 F.A. RECORDING IN SWEDEN
LOL COXHILL SAX (A (C) CAROLE GRIMES 1979 CHARLY 30164
TONY HICKS D (2
BOB WILSON K (B RON CORNELIUS G (BC MAC GAYDEN G (B KENNY BUTTREY D (B
TOMMY COGBILL B (B KARL HIMMEL D (B GRAHAM BELL HCA V(B SAM MITCHELL G (B
RABBIT BUNDRICK K (B TOMMY EYRE K (B ARCHIE LEGGET V (B JESS RODEN V (B
ROGER BALL SAX (B MALCOLM DUNCAN SAX (B HENRY LOWTHER TPT (B JOHN McKENZIE B (1
NIGEL WATSON D (1 COLIN FLETCHER G (1 ANDY WINFIELD G (1 TINO TURVILLE K (1
MICHAEL BRECKER HRNS (C MEMPHIS HRNS (C WESTETTES V (C GINGER HOLLADAY V (C
MARY HOLLADAY V (C BOB MANUEL G (C BUDDY DAVIES G (C HUGH McCRACKEN G (C
NEIL HUBBARD G (C DONALD DUNN B (C JOE DAVIES B (C WILLIE HALL D (C
LLOYD PERRATA D (C BOBBY EMMONS PNO (C JAY SPELL PNO (C BOB CLAIRE HRNS PNO (C
FREDERICK KNIGHT (C OLLIE MALLARD K V (2 PETE KIRTLEY G V (2

G103 GRIMMS G103

NEIL INNES G K V(ABC (A) GRIMMS 1973 ISLAND UK HELP1 US ANTILLES 7012
ROGER McGOUGH V (ABC (B) ROCKING DUCK 1973 ISLAND UK ILPS 9248
JOHN GORMAN V (ABC (C) SLEEPERS 1976 D J M UK DJLPS 470
ANDY ROBERTS G (BC
DAVE RICHARDS B V (BC JOHN MEGGINSON B V K(ABC OLLIE HALSALL G V (B ZOOT MONEY K (AC
MIKE McGEAR V (AB GERRY CONWAY D (B ADRIAN HENRI V (A BRIAN PATTEN V(AB
TIMI DONALD D (C MIKE GILES D (A

G104 GRINDERSWITCH G104

DRU LOMBAR G V (ABCDE (A) HONEST TO GOODNESS 1974 CAPRICORN US CP 0135
STEPHEN MILLER K V (CDE (B) MACON TRACKS 1975 CAPRICORN US CP 0150
LARRY HOWARD G V (ABCD (C) PULLIN' TOGETHER 1977 CAPRICORN UK2429 144 US CP 0173
JOE DAN PETTY B V (ABCDE (D) REDWING 1977 ATCO US 36152
RICK BURNETT D (ABCDE (E) GRINDERSWITCH 1981
PAUL HORNSBY K (ABE
CHARLIE DANIELS FDL (B JIMMY HALL HCA (C JEROME JOSEPH CONGA(C DICKIE BETTS G (A
JAIMOE JOHNANNY CONGAS(A

G105 GRINGO G105

JOHN G PERRY B V (A (A) GRINGO 1971 MCA US 75314 UK MKPS 2017
CATHY SYNGE V (
SIMON BYRNE D V (HENRY MARSH G K V(CASEY V (A

G106 GROBSCHNITT G106

JOACHIM H EHRIG(EROC)D V SYN(ALL (A) GROBSCHNITT 1972 BRAIN 1008
AXEL HARLOS(FELIX) D PERC (A (B) BALLERMANN 1974 BRIAN 2/1050 BRAIN 0021 050
STEFAN DANIELAK(WILDSCHWEIN) G V(ALL (C) JUMBO ENGLISH LYRICS 1975 BRAIN 1076
BERNARD UHLEMANN(BAER) B FLR PERC(AB (C) JUMBO GERMAN LYRICS 1976 BRAIN 1081
GERD KUHN (LUPO) G V (ALL (D) ROCKPOMMELS LAND 1977 BRAIN 0060 041
HERMANN QUETTING(QUECKSILBER)K PERC(A (E) SOLAR MUSIC LIVE 1978 BRAIN 0060 139
WOLFGANG JAEGER(PEPE) B (CDEFG (F) MERRY GO ROUND 1979 BRAIN 0060 224
VOLKER KAHRS(MIST) K V (BCDEFG (G) VOLLE MOLLE 1980 BRAIN 0060 291
MILLA KAPOLLKE B (HJ (H) ILLEGAL 1981 BRAIN 0060 510
TONY MOFF MOLLO V (J (J) RAZZIA 1982 BRAIN 0060 510

G106A MAX GRONENTHAL G106A

MAX GRONENTHAL K V (AB (A) WHISTLING IN THE DARK 1979 CHRYSALIS UK/us CHR1231
BILLY MEEKER D (A (B) MAX 1980 CHRYSALIS UK/US CHR1278
TREY THOMPSON B (A
TIMMY GOODMAN G (A WILL McFARLANE G (A MICHAEL O'NEILL G (A JAMES N HOWARD SYN (A
ROCKE GRACE V (A KENNY LOGGINS V (A GERARD McMAHON V (A MICHAEL McDONALD V (A
PATRICK SIMMONS V (A RICKY FATAAR D PERC V G(B JERRY WILSON B V (B RICK BEILKE G V (B
RENEE GEYER V (B MIKE FINNIGAN V (B MARCY LEVY V (B RUSTY ANDERSON G (B

G107 GROOTNA G107

ANNA RIZZO V (A (A) GROOTNA 1972 CBS US 31033
KELLY BRYAN B (A
SLIM CHANCE G (A GREG DEWEY DA GREASE D (A RICHARD SUSMAN PNO (A VIC SMITH G (A
JACK BONUS SAX (A TERRY ADAMS STR (A CAROL GARNETT STR (A MICHAEL LAFFERTY TROM(A
BENNET FRIEDMAN CLAR (A

G108 WINSTON GROOVY G108

WINSTON GROOVY (A (A) PRESENTING WINSTON GROOVY 1974 TROJAN UK TRLS 88
(B) WINSTON GROOVY 1978 LIGHTNING UK PIL 6

G109 HENRY GROSS G109

HENRY GROSS V G (ALL (A) HENRY GROSS 1969 ABC US ABCX 747
JERRY McGEE G (A (B) PLUG ME INTO SOMETHING 1970 A&M US 4502 UK AMLS 64502
CARL WILSON V (B (C) HENRY GROSS 1974 A&M US 4426 UK AMLH 64416
RICKY FATAAR V (B (D) SHOW ME THE STAGE 197 LIFESONG US 6016 RI 35002
CARLOS MUNOZ V (B (E) RELEASE 1976 LIFESONG 6002 RI 34995
TERRY CASHMAN V (BE (E) LOVE IS THE STUFF 197 LIFESONG 35280
TOMMY WEST V (BCE
STEVE GADD D (CE WARREN NICHOLS B (BE PHIL AABERG K (BE ALLEN SCHWARZBERG D (BE
ANN E SUTTON V (BE MICHAEL KAMEN SYN (BC MARTY NELSON V (BCE RICHIE SCHMIERER V (B
TASHA THOMAS V (BCE DAVE SANBORN SAX (E ELLIE GREENWICH V (E HUGH McCRACKEN G (E
GEORGE DEVENS PERC (CE BUCKY PIZZARELLI G (E LARRY PACKER FDL (E MIKE CORBETT V (E
STU WOODS B (C ARNIE LAWRENCE FLT (C TYRONE BABBOZZA V (C JOE MACHO B (C
ERIC WEISSBERG VLN (C RONDO RAPPONE V (C ZELDA GROSS V (C EUGENE BIANCO HARP (C
JIM KELTNER D (A MAX BENNETT B (A SNEAKY PETE STEEL(A SPOONER OLDHAM PNO (A
PAUL HARRIS K (A WILTON FELDER B (A STRINGS (A

G109A HARALD GROSSKOPF G109A

HARALD GROSSKOPF (A) SYNTHESIST 1980 SKY GER 043

G110 STEFAN GROSSMAN G110

STEFAN GROSSMAN G (ALL (A) YAZOO BASIN BOOGIE 1970 TRANSATLANTIC UK TRA 217
WITH (A) YAZOO BASIN BOOGIE 197 KICKING MULE UK SNKF 134
DANNY KALB (U (A) YAZOO BASIN BOOGIE 1975 KICKING MULE US 102
PAUL ROWAN HCA (Q (B) RAGTIME COWBOY JEW 1970 TRANSATLANTIC UK TRA 223
EDDIE HOUSE V (Q (C) HOW TO PLAY BLUES 1971 TRANSATLANTIC UK XTRA 1113
JO ANN KELLY V (Q (C) HOW TO PLAY BLUES 197 KICKING MULE US 109 UK SNKF 150
PAT DONALDOSN B (B (C) HOW TO PLAY BLUES 1971 ELEKTRA US 324
MIKE COOPER G (KQ (D) THOSE PLEASANT DAYS 1971 TRANSATLANTIC UK TRA 246
SAM MITCHELL G (QT (E) HOT DOGS 1972 TRANSATLANTIC UK TRA 257
DUCK BAKER G (TU (E) HOT DOGS 197 KICKING MULE US 131
TONY ROBERTS WIND (U (F) GRAMERCY PARK SHEIK 1972 SONET UK SNTF 627
JOHN RENBOURN G (RT (G) ANN MOLLY'S MURRAY FARM 1973 SONET UK SNTF 640
RORY BLOCK G (C (H) LIVE 1973 TRANSATLANTIC UK TRA 264
GERRY DONAHUE G (B (I) MEMPHIS JELLYROLL 1973 TRANSATLANTIC UK TRA 274
TREVOR LUCAS G (B (I) MEMPHIS JELLYROLL 1973 KICKING MULE US 118
LINDA PETER V (B (J) FINGER PICKIN' 1974 TRANSATLANTIC UK XTRA 1138
GERRY CONWAY D (B (K) BOTTLENECK SERENADE 1975 TRANSATLANTIC UK TRA 293
PETER BARDENS K (B (K) BOTTLENECK SERENADE 1975 KICKING MULE US 121
BERNIE HOLLAND G (B (L) HOW TO PLAY RAGTIME GUITAR 1975 TRANSATLANTIC UK XTRA 1151
TODD LLOYD V (B (M) MY CREOLE BELLE 1976 TRANSATLANTIC UK TRA 326
RICHARD THOMPSON G (D (N) ACOUSTIC MUSIC FOR BODY & SOUL 1976 KICKING MULE US 105
DANNY THOMPSON B (D (O) BOX SET (TRIPLE) 1977 TRANSATLANTIC UK GRS 6

(CONTINUED)

G110 (CONTINUED) — STEFAN GROSSMAN — G110

HARVEY BURNS D (D | (P) HOW TO PLAY RAGTIME | 197 KICKING MULE US 115
THE KAERNES V (D | (Q) COUNTRY BLUES GUITAR | 1977 KICKING MULE UK SNKF 129
ALAN WHITE D (E | (Q) COUNTRY BLUES GUITAR | 1977 KICKING MULE US 145
BIG JIM SULLIVAN G (E | (R) AND JOHN RENBOURN | 1978 KICKING MULE UK SNKF 139
HOWRD BUZZ FEITEN G (W | (R) AND JOHN RENBOURN | 197 KICKING MULE US 152
BARRY FINNERTY G (W | (S) HOW TO PLAY BLUES VOL2 | 197 KICKING MULE 148
ONAJE ALLEN GUMBS K (W | (T) UNDER THE VOLCANO | 1979 KICKING MULE UK SNKF 161
MASABUNI KIKUCHI K (W | (U) THUNDER ON THE RUN | 1980 KICKING MULE UK SNKF 170
MARK EGAN B (W | (V) CROSSCURRENTS | 19 COTILLION US SD 9007
MARCUS MILLER B (W | (W) PERSPECTIVE | 1979 ATLANTIC US 19230
STEVE JORDON D (W
VICTOR LEWIS D (W RAPHAEL CRUZ PERC(W SAMMY FIGUEROA CONGA(W LENNY WHITE D (W

G111 LUTHER GROSVENOR G111

LUTHER GROSVENOR B G V (A | (A) UNDER OPEN SKIES | 1971 ISLAND ILPS 9168
MIKE KELLIE D (A
JOHN HAWKEN PNO (A JIM CAPALDI V (A MICK RALPHS V (A MIKE GILES D (A
TREVOR BURTON B (A TREVOR LUCAS V (A PAUL BENNETT V (A

G111A < GROUP 87 G111A

(A) FIRST | 1980 CBS 84397

G111B GROUP THERAPY G111B

(A) YOU'RE IN NEED OF... | 19 PHILIPS UK SBL 7883

G112 GROUNDHOGS G112

TONY McPHEE G B SYN V (All | (A) SCRATCHING THE SURFACE | 1968 LIBERTY UK LBS 83199
PETER CRUICKSHANK B (ABCDEFGH | (A) SCRATCHING THE SURFACE | 197 WORLD PACIFIC US 21892
DAVE BOORMAN D (| (B) BLUES OBITUARY | 1969 LIBERTY UK 83253
BOB HALL PNO (| (B) BLUES OBITUARY | 196 IMPERIAL US 12452
KEN PUSTELNIK D (ABCDEH | (C) THANK CHRIST FOR THE BOMB | 1970 LIBERTY UK 83295 US 7644
STEVE RYE HCA (A | (C) THANK CHRIST FOR THE BOMB | 1975 SUNSET UK 50376
DAVE WELLBELOVED G (KL | (D) SPLIT | 1971 LIBERTY UK 83401 US UA5513
(D) SPLIT | 19 UA RI 1017
MARTIN KENT B (KL | (E) LIVE AT LEEDS | 1971 (LTD ED? OR BOOT?)
MICK COOK D (KL | (F) WHO WILL SAVE THE WORLD | 1972 UA UK 29237 US UA5570
CLIVE BROOKS D (GH | (G) HOGWASH | 1972 UA UK 29419 US UA 008
RICK ADAMS G (K | (H) SOLID | 1974 WWA UK 004
(I) GOT TO GET ENOUGH | 1972 TURBO US 7005
(J) BEST OF 1969 72 | 1974 UA UK 60063/4
(K) CROSSCUT SAW | 1976 UA UK 29917 US LA 603
(L) BLACK DIAMOND | 1976 UA UK 29994 US LA 680
( ) JOHN LEE HOOKER,JOHN MAYALL | 19 CLEVE US 82871
(BF) BLUES ORBITUARY/WHO WILL SAVE | 1975 UA GER 29794/95 DBL

G112A GROWL G112A

MICK SMALL G (A | (A) GROWL | 1974 DISCREET US DS 2209
DENNIS RODRIGUEZ V (A
RICHARD MANUPUTI V (A DANNY McBRIDE D (A HARRY BRENDER BRANDIS G V(A GENO LUCERO B (A

G112B GROW UP G112B

STEVEN WESTWOOD D (A | (A) THE BEST THING | 1979 OBJECT UK OBJ005
BILLY JOHN McDONALD D V(A
JOHN BISSET-SMITH G B K V(A ROGER BLACKBURN G B (A RICHARD WESTWOOD WIND (A ANN BISSET-SMITH V (A

G112C GROWING CONCERN G112C

RALPH WILLIAMS D (A | (A) GROWING CONCERN | 196 MAINSTREAM US 6108
PETE GUERINO G V (A
RALPH TOMS G (A JOHN PEDLEY B (A DON PASSAGLIA K V (A BONNIE McDONALD V (A
MARY GARSTKI V (A

G112D JACK GRUNSKY G112D

JACK GRUNSKY V G K(ALL | (A) MY SHIP | 1969
MIKE ROSEN K (B | (B) TORONTO | 1970
ANNETTE BROX V (B | (C) BUFFALO BRAIN | 1971 KUCKUCK 2375 007
MICK TAYLOR G (B | (D) NEWBORN MAN | 1972 KUCKUCK 2375 011
ALEXIS KORNER G (B | (E) JACK GRUNSKY | 1972 KUCKUCK 2375 015
THEO BINA G B (CDE
ULRIKE BISCOFF (C FRANK DIEZ G (D OLDERS FRENZEL D (CD MUCK GROH (C
SONNY HENNINIG K (CD TOMMY ROEDER B (CD GEORGE MEYER FLT (CD ERNST SCHULTZ (E
WALTER SCHNEIDER B (D GUNTHER STORCH D (E JIMMY WOODE (E THOMAS HOLM (E

G113 GRUPPO SPORTIVO G113

HANS VANDENBURG G V (ABC | (A) 10 MISTAKES | 1977 ARIOLA NL 25464+1978 EPIC UK 82793
ANN MARTIN (C | (A) 10 MISTAKES | 1978 SIRE US 6066 BELLAPHON GER 2548
MAX MOLLINGER D (ABC | (B) BACK TO 78 | 1978 ARIOLA NL 26472 EPIC UK 83263
ERIC WEHRMEYER B (ABC | (C) COPY COPY | 1980 ARIOLA EURO 202 327
MARTIN BAKKER G V (C | (EP) RARE TRACKS | 1977 POLYDOR 2454 120
PETER CALICHER K (ABC
EDWIN THEUERZEIT TPT (C JOSEE VAN IERSEL V (AB MEIKE TOUW V (AB JANKEES TANS SAX (B
ROB KRUISMAN HRNS (B REIN VANDER BROEK HRNS (B MAARTEN VAN NORDEN HRNS (B JAN DE LIGT SAX (C
LAURENS DE JONGE SAX (C

G113A DAVE GRUSIN G113A

DAVE GRUSIN K (AB | (A) MOUNTAIN DANCE | 1980 ARISTA 5010
STANLET TURRENTINE (B | (A) A FLIP OF THE COIN | 1980 MANHATTAN UK 5008
HARVEY MASON D (A
MARCUS MILLER B (A JEFF MIRONOV G (A ED WALSH SYN (A IAN UNDERWOOD SYN (A
RUBENS BASSINI PERC (A

G114 GRYPHON G114

BRIAN GULLAND REC HRNS (ALL | (A) GRYPHON | 1973 TRANSATLANTIC UK TRA 262
RICHARD HARVEY WIND HRNS(ALL | (B) MIDNIGHT MUSHRUMPS | 1974 TRANSATLANTIC UK TRA 282
GRAEME TAYLOR G (ABCD | (C) RED QUEEN TO GRYPHON 3 | 1974 TRANSATLANTIC UK TRA 287
DAVID OBERLE PERC (ALL | (C) RED QUEEN TO GRYPHON 3 | 197 ARISTA US 4018 BRAIN GER 1071
MALCOLM BENNETT (CD | (D) RAINDANCE | 1975 TRANSATLANTIC UK TRA 302
BOB FOSTER G (E | (E) TREASON | 1977 HARVEST UK SHSP 4063
ALEX BAIRD D (E
JON DAVIE B (E PHILIP NESTOR B (BC PETER AIREY G (GRAEME GULLAND G (A
DAVID BRIAN PERC (A RICHARD BRIAN K (A PETE REDDING G B (BC ERNEST HART K (A

G115 GUESS WHO G115

BURTON CUMMINGS V K (ALL — ( ) SHAKIN ALL OVER — 1968 SCEPTER US 533+ SPRINGBAORD4022
GARRY PETERSON D (A>V — (A) GUESS WHO — 19 MGM US 4654
RANDY BACHMAN G V (ABCDE — (B) PLAY THE GUESS WHO — 1976 PIP US 6804
CHAD ALLEN V (R — (C) WHEATFIELD SOUL — 1969 RCA US LSP 4141 ANLI 1171
(C) WHEATFIELD SOUL — 1969 RCA UK SF 8037
JIM KALE B (CDEFGHIOPSW — (D) CANNED WHEAT — 1969 RCA US LSP 4157 RI ANLI 0986
KURT WINTER G (FGHIJKLPS — (E) AMERICAN WOMAN — 1970 RCA US LSP 4266 UK SF 8107
GREG LESKIW G (FGHOPS — (F) SHARE THE LAND — 1970 RCA US LSP 4359 UK SF 8153
BILLY WALLACE B (JKLMNOPS — (G) SO LONG BANNATYNE — 1971 RCA US LSP 4574 UK SF 8216
DOMENIC TROIANO G (NM — (H) ROCKIN' — 1972 RCA US LSP 4602 UK SF 8269
DON McDOUGAL G (IJKLW — (H) ROCKIN' — 1978 RCA ANLI 2683
ALLAN McDOUGALL V (W — (I) LIVE AT THE PARAMOUNT — 1972 RCA US LSP 4779 UK SF 8329
DAVID PARASZ HRNS (W — (J) TEN — 1973 RCA US APLI 0130
DAVID INGLIS G (W — (K) ARTIFICIAL PARADISE — 1973 RCA US LSP 4830 UK SF 8349
VANCE MASTERS V D (W — (L) ROAD FOOD — 1974 RCA US APLI 0405
(M) FLAVOURS — 1975 RCA US APLI 0636 UK SF 8399
(N) POWER IN THE MUSIC — 1975 RCA US APLI 0995 UK RS 1017
(O) BEST OF THE GUESS WHO — 1971 RCA US LSPX 1004 UK AFLI2594
(P) BEST OF VOL 2 — 1974 RCA US APLI 0269
(Q) GREATEST — 19 RCA US APLI 2253
(R) BORN IN CANADA — 1976 WAND 691
(S) HISTORY OF — 1973 PRIDE 0012
(T) WILD ONE — 19 PICKWICK US 3246
(U) GUESS WHO — 19 PICKWICK US 3240
(W) ALL THIS FOR A SONG — 1979 AQUARIUS US 3246 HILLTAK 19299

G116 GIB GUILBEAU G116

GIB GUILBEAU FDL (ALL — GIB GUILBEAU — 1973 ALSHIRE US AS 209
CAJUN COUNTRY — 197 ALSHIRE US S 5121
CAJUN COUNTRY — 1975 ARIOLA 87147
TOE TAPPIN' MUSIC — 1979 SHILOH US 4085

G116A ISAAC GUILLORY G116A

ISAAC GUILLORY G V B K (A — (A) ISAAC GUILLORY — 1974 ATLANTIC US 7307 UK 40521
SAM GOPAL TABLAS(A — (B) SOLO — 1980 CBS NL 84568
JIM CAREY D (A
FRED GANDY B (A — MOX HCA (A — JIM COLE B V (A — CATHY HALL FLT (A
JIM FAIRS G DULC (A — JOHNSE HOLT G (A — PETE GAVIN D (A — ROGER POPE D (A

G116B GUITAR SLIM G116B

JAMES(GUITAR SLIM) STEPHENSON G V(ALL — (A) THINGS I USED TO DO — 19 SPECIALTY US 2120
ALSO USED NAME GUITAR SLIM GREEN — (B) STONE DOWN BLUES — 19 UNITED US 7764
(C) GREENSBORO ROUNDER — 1977 FLYRIGHT UK LP 538
( ) CAROLINA BLUES — 19 ARHOOLIE US 2005

G116C GUILLOTINE G116C

CAROL BREVAL (A — (A) GUILLOTINE — 19 AMPEX US 10122
JOE TREVSONNO (A
PAUL MORIN (A — JEAN MORIN (A — PAUL DALONZO (A — ANDRE MORIN (A
FRANCOIS (A — PIERRE NADEAU (A — ROBERT TURMEL (A

G117 GULLIVER G117

DARYL HALL K V (A — (A) GULLIVER — 1969 ELEKTRA US 74070+1970 UK 2410006
JIM HELMER D (A
TIM MOORE G V (A — TOM SELLERS B K (A

G117A GUN G117A

ADRIAN CURTIS(GURVITZ) G (AB — (A) GUN — 1968 CBS US 26468 + UK 63552
PAUL CURTIS(GURVITZ) B (AB — (B) GUNSIGHT — 1969 CBS US 26551 + UK 62683
LOUIS FARRELL D (A
PETER DUNTON D (— TIM MYCROFT (

G117B GUN CLUB G117B

WARD DOTSON G V (A — (A) FIRE OF LOVE — 1981 NEW ROSE ROSE8
JEFFREY LEE PIERCE G V (A
ROB RITTER B (A — TERRY GRAHAM D (A — TITO LARNIA VLN (A — LOIS GRAHAM V (A

G117C GUNHILL ROAD G117C

GLENN LEOPOLD V G K(A — (A) GUNHILL ROAD — 19 KAMA SUTRA US KSBS 2061
STEVEN GOLDRICH V PNO(A
GIL ROMAN G V (A — KENNY ROGERS B V (A — LARRY BROWN D (A — BILL PERRY B (A
JIM RYAN B (A — ANDY NEWMARK D (A — PAUL COTTON G (A — GENE LORENZO K (A
GEORGE GRANTHAM D (A — REINIE PRESS B (A — DENNIS LEPRI G (A

G119 ARTHUR GUNTER G119

ARTHUR GUNTER — (A) BLACK & BLUES — 19 CONTEMPO UK119+EXCELLO US 8017
(B) BLUES AFTER HOURS — 19 BLUE HORIZON 2431 012

G120 GURU GURU G120

MANI NEUMEIER PROD D K (ALL — (A) UFO — 1970 OHR GER 556005
ULI TREPTE B (ABC — (B) HINTEN — 1971 OHR GER 556027
AX GENRICH G (ABCDEG — (C) KAN GURU — 1972 BRAIN GER 1007
SEPP JANDRISITS G (GHI — (D) GURU GURU — 197 BRAIN 1025
TOMMY GOLDSCHMIDT PERC (GHI — (E) DONT CALL US WE CALL YOU — 1973 ATLANTIC 50022
JAN FRIDE K (G — (F) DANCE OF THE FLAMES — 1974 ATLANTIC UK K50044
INGO BISCHOF K (GHIK — (G) MANI UND SEINE FREUNDE — 1975 ATLANTIC GER K50157
MOEBI MOEBIUS K (G — (H) TANGO FANGO — 1976 BRAIN GER 1089
JOACHIM RODELIUS K (G — (I) GLOBETROTTER — 1977 BRAIN 0060 039
JOGI KARPENTIEL B (GHI — (J) LIVE DBL — 1978 BRAIN GER 0080 018
GERD DUDECK WIND (G — (K) HEYDU — 1979 BRAIN 0060 187
HELMUT HATTLER B (GI — ( ) THIS IS (COMP) — 1973 BRAIN GER 200 145
PETER WOLBRANDT G (G — ( ) DER ELEKTROLURCH (COMP (DBL) — 1974 BRAIN GER 2 1057
CHAMPION JACK DUPREE K (G
CHRISTA FAST (G — PETER KUHMSTEDT B (ILK — ROLAND SCHAEFFER SYN G(HIJK — HOUSCHANG NEJADEPOUR G(F
CONNY PLANK G K (CDG — HANS HARTMANN B (EF — GERALD LUCIANO HARTWIG B(K — MICHAEL PITZ CLAR(
KARLA VON SINNEN B (K — BUTZE FISCHER D PERC(K — BRUNO SCHABB B (D — LARRY CONGA (I
DIETER BORNSCHLRGEL G (J

G120A ADRIAN GURVITZ G120A

ADRIAN GURVITZ G V (A — (A) SWEET VENDETTA 1979 JET US 35782 UK JETLP 220
JOE PORCARO PERC (A — (B) IL ASSASSINO 1980 JET UK JETLP 226
JEFF PORCARO D (A
ED GREENE D (A RICK SCHLOSSER D (A DAVID HUNGATE G (A DAVID SHIELDS B (A
FRED TACKETT G (A STEVE PORCARO K (A DAVID PAICH PNO (A STEVE LEEDS SAX FLT(A
DICK HYDE TROM (A CHUCK FINDLEY TPT (A STEVE MADAIO TPT (A JERRY HEY TPT (A
EARL LON PRICE SAX (A PAUL GURVITZ V (AB

G121 ARLO GUTHRIE G121

ARLO GUTHRIE G V (ALL — (A) ALICES RESTAURANT 1967 REPRISE US 6267 UK K44045
KEVIN BURKE FDL (H — (B) ARLO 1968 REPRISE US 6299 UK K44052
JIM KELTNER D (HI — (C) RUNNING DOWN THE ROAD 1969 REPRISE US 6346 UK K44071
BOB GLAUB B (HK — (D) WASHINGTON COUNTY 1970 REPRISE US 6411 UK K44099
JESSE ED DAVIS G (HI — (E) ALICES RESTRAURANT (SOUNDTRACK) 1969 UA US 5195 UK 29061
JIM GORDON K (HI — (F) ARLO GUTHRIE (COMP) 1972 CHARTER LINE IT 24003
GEORGE BOHANON HRNS (H — (G) HOBOES LULLABYE 1972 REPRISE US 2060 UK K44169
DICK HYDE TROM (H — (H) LAST OF THE BROOKLYN COWBOYS 1973 REPRISE US 2142 UK K44236
GENE COE HRNS (H — (I) ARLO GUTHRIE 1974 REPRISE US 2183 UK K54019
NICK DECARO ACC (HIK — (J) TOGETHER (DBL) LIVE) 1975 REPRISE US 2214 UK K64023
JERRY WIGGINS D (H — (K) AMIGO 1975 REPRISE US 2239 UK K54077
DOYLE SINGER B MAND(H — (L) THE BEST OF 1977 WB US 3117 UK K56431
STAN FREE K (B — (M) ONE NIGHT 1978 WB US 3232
PETE SEEGER G V (J — (N) OUTLASTING THE BLUES 1978 WB US 3336 UK K56658
DON RICH G FDL(H — ( ) STAR COLLECTION 197 MIDI UK 4003
BOB ARKIN B (B — (P) POWER OF LOVE 1981 WB US 3558 UK K56910
BUDDY ALAN G (H
BOB MORRIS G (H JIM SHAW PNO (H DON CHRISTLIEB WIND (H BUDDY COLLETTE CLAR (H
JERRY BRIGHTMAN STEEL (H WILLIAM GREEN OBOE (H ERNIE WATTS FLT (H LEE SKLAR B (H
RY COODER G (HI JOHN PILLA G (HIN GENE PARSONS D (H THAD MAXWELL B (H
DOUG DILLARD BANJO(HI GIB GUILBEAU FDL (H CLARENCE WHITE G (H GRADY MARTIN G (H
RICHARD HAYWARD D (H CHUCK RAINEY B (H MIKE UTLEY ORG (H JESSIE SMITH V (HI
CLYDIE KING V (HI VANETTA FIELDS V (H GENE MERLINO V (H THURLE RAVENSCROFT V (H
ROBERT TEBOW V (H BILL COLE V (H TERRY A LA BERRY (N STEVE IDE (N
DAVID GROVER (N DAN VELIKA (N CAROL IDE (N ED SHAUGHNESSY D (B
LINDA RONSTADT V (K STRINGS (N BYRONE BERLINE FDL (L ROGER BUSH B (L
BUDDY EMMONS STEEL(L CHRIS ETHRIDGE B (L WILTON FELDER B (L DARRYL HARDY V (L
MILT HOLLAND PERC (LK MARTY McCALL V (L SPOONER OLDHAM PNO (L GREG PRESTOPINO G K (L
SOUTHERN CAL COMM CHOIR(L LEAH KUNKEL K V (K RUSS KUNKEL D (K WADDY WATCHELL G (K
JAI WINDING K (K GAYLE LEVANT HARP (K RICK JAEGER D (K BILLY GREEN G (K
DAVID GROVER G BAN(MN CAROL IDE G (MN STEVE IDE G TROM(MN DON VELIKA B (K
TERRY ALA BERRY D (MN PETER ADAMS STEEL(N JOHN SAVER K (N JOHN CULPO ACC (N
RON SLOAN HCA (N

G122 BUDDY GUY G122

BUDDY GUY G V (ALL — (A) HOODOO MAN BLUES 1966 DELMARK 612
JUNIOR WELLS HCA V(JKM — (B) ITS MY LIFE BABY 1966 VANGUARD VSD 79231
ERIC CLAPTON G (J — (C) COMING AT YOU 1968 VANGUARD SVRL19001 VSD 79262
DR JOHN PNO (J — (D) A MAN AND HIS BLUES 1968 VANGUARD SVRL19002 VSD 79272
J GEILS BAND (J — (E) I LEFT MY BLUES IN SAN FRANCISCO 1968 CHESS 1527 BELLAPHON 4069
LONNIE TAYLOR D (DH — (F) BLUES TODAY 1968 VANGUARD SVRL 19004
MIKE UTLEY K (J — (G) THIS IS BUDDY GUY 196 VANGUARD SVRL 19008 VSD 79290
TIM KAIHATSU G (GH — (H) HOT & COOL 1979 VANGUARD VSD 79290
JACK MYERS D (DHJKLM — (I) HOLD THAT PLANE 1972 VANGUARD VSD 79323
GLENWAY McTEER D (GH — (J) & JUNIOR WELLS PLAY THE BLUES 1972 ATLANTIC K 40240
NORMAN SPILLER TPT (GH — (K) I WAS WALKING THROUGH THE WOODS 19 CHESS LP 409
BOBBY FIELD SAX (DGH — (L) IN THE BEGINNING(58/64) 1971 RED LIGHTNING RL 001
JUNIOR MANCE PNO (H — (M) GOT TO USE YOUR HEAD 1979 BLUES BALL 2005
GARY BARTZ SAX (HI — (N) DOLLAR DONE FELL 1980 JSP 1009
MARK JORDAN K (I — (EP) CRAZY MUSIC 1965 CHESS CRE 6004
LEROY STEWART B (J — (EP) WITH THE BLUES 1965 CHESS CRE 6009
BARRY ALTSCHUL D (IJ — ( ) BUDDY & THE JUNIORS 19 BLUE THUMB 8820
BILL WYMAN B (O — (O) DRINKIN' TNT SMOKIN' DYNAMITE 1981 RED LIGHTNIN' UK 0034
PINETOP PERKINS PNO (O — (P) BREAKIN' OUT 1981 JSP UK 1017
TERRY TAYLOR V (O
JUKE JOINT JIMMY (J LESLIE CRAWFORD SAX (GH SETH JUSTMAN PNO (J GEORGE ALEXANDER TPT(GH
J W WILLIAMS B (N ERNEST JOHNSON B (HM WAYNE BENNETT G (DG AL DUNCAN D (M
CLIFTON JAMES D (M ROBERT NIGHTHAWK G (M FRED BELOW D (DKLHM SONNY BOY WILLIAMSON HCA(LM
FREEBO B (I ROOSEVELT SHAW D (J CARL RADLE B (JL STEPHEN BLADD D (J
MAGIC DICK HCA (J LAFAYETTE LEAKE PNO (MKL A C REED SAX (GHIJ PHILIP GUY G (HJN
JESSE LEWIS D (HI OTIS SPANN PNO(DHKLM AARON CORTHEN SAX (DH PHIL THOMAS D (LM
DAVID RIP STOCK D (I BILL FOLWELL B (I JIM GORDON D (J DANNY KLEIN B (J
GERRY GIBSON SAX (KLM BOB NEELY SAX (LM MACK EASTER B (L OTIS RUSH G (L
WILLIE DIXON B (L ODIE PAYNE D (L DONALD HANKINS SAX(DHLM SONNY TURNER TPT(LM
MURRAY WATSON TPT (LM ABE LOCKE SAX (LM LEFTY BATES G (LM LITTLE PHIL SMITH G (N
RAY ALLISON D (N DALLAS TAYLOR D (O

G122A DENNY GUY G122A

DENNY GUY V (A — (A) DENNY GUY 1972 DAY BREAK US DR 2008
RANDALL ATON B (A
JOHN MILLIKEN D (A JAMES JEFFERS G (A THOMAS GUY G (A EMPERADOR ATON D (A

G123 GWENDAL G123

BRUNO BARRE VLN (AB — (A) GWENDAL 1974 PATHE FR 064 12725
JEAN MARIE RENARD G (AB — (B) GWENDAL 2 1975 PATHE FR 064 13075
YOUENN LEBERRE WIND (AB
PATRICE GRUPALLO MAND PERC(AB ROGER SCHAUB B G (AB

G124 GYPSY G124

ROBIN PIZER G V (AB — (A) GYPSY 1971 UA UK UAS 29155
MOTH SMITH D (AB — (B) BRENDA & THE RATTLESNAKE 1972 UA UK UAS 29420
ROD READ G V (A
DAVID McCARTHY B V (AB JOHN KNAPP V G K (AB RAY MARTINEZ G V (B RAY COOPER PERC (B

H1 H P LOVECRAFT H1

GEORGE EDWARDS	V G B(AB	(A) H P LOVECRAFT	1967 PHILIPS BL 7830+6336210+600252
DAVE MICHAELS	K V (AB	(B) H P LOVECRAFT2	1968 PHILIPS SBL7872+6336213+600279
TONY CAVALLARI	V G (AB		
JERRY McGEORGE	V B (A	MICHAEL TEGZA V D (AB JEFF BOYAN	B (B LEN DRUSS HRNS(A
RALPH CRAIG	TROM (A	HERB WEISS TROM (A CLYDE BACHAND	TUBA (A BILL TRAUB WIND(A
EDDIE HIGGINS	VIBES(A	PAUL TERVELT HRNS (A JACK HENNINGBAUM	HRNS (A

H2 HABIBIYYA H2

ROGER POWELL	(A	(A) IF MAN BUT KNEW	1972 ISLAND US 9305 UK HELP 7
IAN WHITEMAN	(A		
MIKE EVANS	(A		

H2A HACKAMORE BRICK H2A

CHICK NEWMAN	(A	(A) ONE KISS LEADS TO ANOTHER	1970 KAMA SUTRA US 2025
ROBBIE BIEGE	(A		
BOB ROMAN	(A	TOMMY MOONLIG (A	

H3 HACKENSACK H3

PAUL MARTINEZ	B (A	(A) UP THE HARDWAY	1971 POLYDOR 2383 263
RAY SMITH	G (A		
NICKY MOORE	V (A	SIMON FOX D (A	

H4 STEVE HACKETT H4

STEVE HACKETT	V G K(ALL	(A) VOYAGE OF THE ACOLYTE	1975 CHARISMA UK CAS1111 US 1176
PHIL COLLINS	D V (A	(A) VOYAGE OF THE ACOLYTE	1975 CHARISMA EURO 9103106 GER 6369970
JOHN HACKETT	FLT K(ABC1EF	(B) PLEASE DONT TOUCH	1978 CHARISMA UK CAS4012 US 1112
JOHN ACOCK	K (AB	(B) PLEASE DONT TOUCH	1978 CHARISMA EURO 9103122
MIKE RUTHERFORD	B (A	(C) SPECTRAL MORNINGS	1979 CHARISMA UK CDS4017 US 1223
KIM POOR	V (F	(C) SPECTRAL MORNINGS	1979 CHARISMA GER 9124 039
SALLY OLDFIELD	V (A	(D) DEFECTORS	1980 CHARISMA UK CDS4018 US 3103
NICK MANUS	K (CDEF	(D) DEFECTORS	1980 CHARISMA GER 9124 058
GRAHAME SMITH	VLN (B	(E) CLOCKS EP	1979 CHARIAMA UK 34112
TOM FOWLER	B (B	(F) CURED	1981 CHARISMA UK CDS4021 EPIC US 37632
JAMES BRADLEY	PERC (B	(F) CURED	1981 CHARISMA GER 6302 153
PETER HICKS	V (1CE	(1) 1978 TOUR	
DIK CADBURY	B (1CE		
ROBIN MILLER	WIND (A	NIGEL WARREN-GREEN CELLO(A PERCY JONES	B (A JOHN GUSTAFSON B (A
RANDY CRAWFORD	V (B	RICHIE HAVENS V PERC(B STEVE WALSH	V (B DAVE LEBOLT K (B
JOHN SHEARER	D (C1E	HUGH MALLOY CELLO(B CHESTER THOMPSON	PERC(B PHIL EHART PERC(B

H5 SAMMY HAGAR H5

SAMMY HAGAR	G V (ALL	(A) NINE ON A TEN SCALE	1976 CAPITOL EST 11489
JERRY SHIRLEY	D (A	(A) NINE ON A TEN SCALE	1981 GREENLIGHT 2017
BILL CHURCH	B (ABCDEFGH	(B) SAMMY HAGAR	1977 CAPITOL EST 11599
MARK JORDAN	K (E	(B) SAMMY HAGAR	1981 GREENLIGHT 2007
ALAN FITZGERALD	K (ABCDG	(C) MUSICAL CHAIRS	1978 CAPITOL UK EST 11706
STEVE DOUGLAS	SAX (E	(C) MUSICAL CHAIRS	1981 GREENLIGHT 2021
DENNIS CARMASSI	D (CD	(D) ALL NIGHT LONG(LIVE)	1978 CAPITOL UK EST 11812
SCOTT QUICK	G (A	(E) STREET MACHINE	1979 CAPITOL UK EST 11983
JIM HODDER	D (A	(F) DANGER ZONE	1979 CAPITOL UK EST 12069
AYNSLEY DUNBAR	D (A	(G) LOUD & CLEAR (COMP)	1980 CAPITOL UK EST 25330
DALLAS TAYLOR	D (A	(H) STANDING HAMPTON	1981 GEFFEN 85456
DAVID LAUSER	D (H		
VANETTA FIELDS	V (A	SHIRLEY MATTHEWS V (A MAXAYN LEWIS	V (A WIZARD STAN K (A
JOE CRANE	K (A	DAVID LEWARK G (B JOHN BLAKELEY	G (A MIC GILLETTE HRNS(A
GREG ADAMS	HRNS (A	EMILIO CASTILLO HRNS (A STEVE KUPKA	HRNS (A LENNY PICKETT HRNS(A
SCOTT MATTHEWS	D (B	GARY PIHL G (ALL CHUCK RUFT	D V (EF NEAL SCHON G (EF
STEVE PERRY	V (F	GEOFF WORKMAN K (F	

H5A NINA HAGEN BAND H5A

NINA HAGEN	V (	(A) NINA HAGEN BAND	1978 CBS UK 83136
REINHOLD HEIL	K V (AB	(B) UNBEHAGEN	1979 CBS UK 84159
HERWIG MITTEREGGER	D V (AB	(C) NINA HAGEN BAND 10"	1980 CBS US 36817
BERNNARD POTSCHKA	G V (AB		
MANNE PRAEKER	B G V(AB		

H5B HAIR H5B

PETER ROINAES	D (A	(A) PIECE	1970 COLUMBIA SCX 6452
ALLEN SORENSEN	B (A		
BENNY DYHR	G (A	PADDY GYTHFELDT K G (A	

H5C THE HAGERS H5C

JIM HAGER	(A	(A) THE HAGERS	1974 ELEKTRA US 7E 1021
JOHN HAGER	(A		
PETE JOLLIE	K (A	SNEAKY PETE STEEL(A JOHN GUERIN	D (A RON TUTT D (A
LYLE RITZ	D (A	CAROL KAYE B (A JAMES BURTON	G (A BEN BENAY G (A
AL CASEY	G (A	JOHN MORRELL G (A	

H5D JERRY HAHN H5D

JERRY HAHN	G BAN V(AB	(A) JERRY HAHN'S BROTHHOOD	19 CBS US 1044
GEORGE MARSH	D (AB	(B) MOSES	19
MIKE FINNIGAN	K HCA V(A		
CLYDE GRAVES	B (A	MEL GRAVES B (B MERL SAUNDERS	K SYN(B

H6 BILL HALEY H6

BILL HALEY	G V (	EPS				
RUDY POMPELLI	SAX (	DIM DIM THE LIGHTS	1955	BRUNSWICK	UK	9129
FRANCIS BEECHER	G (	ROCK'N'ROLL	1955	LONDON	UK	1031
JOHN GRANDE	K (	LIVE IT UP 1	1956	LONDON	UK	1049
BILLY WILLIAMSON	STEEL(	LIVE IT UP 2	1956	LONDON	UK	1050
AL REX	B (	ROCK'N'ROLL	1956	BRUNSWICK	UK	9214
DON RAYMOND	D (	ROCK AROUND THE CLOCK	1956	BRUNSWICK	UK	9250
		LIVE IT UP 3	1956	LONDON	UK	1058
		ROCK 'N'ROLL STAGE SHOW 1	1956	BRUNSWICK	UK	9278
		ROCK'N'ROLL STAGE SHOW 2	1956	BRUNSWICK	UK	9279
		ROCK'N'ROLL STAGE SHOW 3	1956	BRUNSWICK	UK	9280
		ROCKIN THE OLDIES 1	1958	BRUNSWICK	UK	9349
		ROCKIN' THE OLDIES	1958	BRUNSWICK	UK	9350
		ROCKIN THE OLDIES	1958	BRUNSWICK	UK	9351

(CONTINUED)

BILL HALEY

Title	Year	Label	Country	Prefix	No.
EPS					
ROCKIN AROUND THE WORLD	1959	BRUNSWICK	UK		9446
BILL HALEY & HIS COMETS	1959	BRUNSWICK	UK		9459
HALEY & HIS COMETS	1960	WB	UK		6001
HALEY'S JUKE BOX	1961	WB	UK		6025
BILL HALEY	1964	WB	UK		6133
BILL HALEY 2	1964	WB	UK		6136
LPs					
LIVE IT UP 10"	1955	LONDON	UK		1042
BILL HALEY & THE COMETS	19	DECCA	US		2670
" " " "	19	WB	US		1378
HALEYS JUKE BOX	1960	WB	US		1391
SHAKE RATTLE & ROLL 10"	19	DECCA	US		5560
ROCK AROUND THE CLOCK	1956	BRUNSWICK	UK		8117
" " " "	1956	DECCA	US		8225
" " " "	1970	HALLMARK	UK	SHM	668
" " " "	1971	CORAL			CP 55
" " " "	1974	CORAL		CDL	8017
" " " "	1974	CORAL	UK	CRLM	1039
" " " "	1961	ACE OF HEARTS	UK	AH	13
" " " "	1981	WB	UK	K	26007
ROCK 'N' ROLL STAGE SHOW	1956	DECCA	US		8345
" " " " "	1956	BRUNSWICK	UK		8139
TWISTING KNIGHTS	1962	ROULETTE	US		25174
" "	1962	COLUMBIA	UK	33sx	1460
ROCKIN' THE OLDIES	1957	BRUNSWICK	UK		8219
" " "	1962	ACE OF HEARTS	UK	AH	35
" " "	19	DECCA	US		8569
ROCKIN' AROUND THE WORLD	19	DECCA	US		8692
ROCKIN' THE JOINT 10"	1957	DECCA	US		8775
" " "	1957	BRUNSWICK	UK		8268
" " " " "	1964	GOLDEN GUINEA	UK		0282
" " " " "	1966	MARBLE ARCH	UK		817
" " " " "	1979	ROLLERCOASTER	UK		2002
" " " "	1957	LONDON	US	HAF	2037
CHICKS	1964	ACE OF HEARTS	UK	AH	66
"	1959	BRUNSWICK	UK	STA	3011
"	1959	DECCA	US		8821
HE DIGS ROCK'N'ROLL	19	DECCA	US		8315
STRICTLY INSTRUMENTAL	1960	BRUNSWICK	UK	LAT	8326
" " "	196	DECCA	US		8964
GREATEST HITS	1968	MCA	US		161
ON STAGE	1970	HALLMARK	UK	SHM	694
ROCK'N'ROLL	19	GNP	US		2077
ROCK AROUND THE COUNTRY	1971	SONET	UK	SNTF	623
" " " "	197	GNP CRESCENDO	US		2097
" " " "	1974	HALLMARK	UK	SHM	837
GOLDEN KING OF ROCK'N'ROLL	1972	HALLMARK	UK	SHM	773
KING OF ROCK	1973	EMBER	UK	EMB	3396
" "	197	ALSHIRE	US		5313
BILL HALEY & THE COMETS	19	VALIANT	UK	VS	103
RIP IT UP	19	MCA	UK	MUPS	318
Mr ROCK'N'ROLL	19	EMBER	UK	EMB	3401
TRAVELLING BAND	19	JANUS	US		3035
RAZZLE DAZZLE	19	JANUS	US		7003
ROCK 'N' ROLL DANCE PARTY	19	SUMMERSET	US		4600
ROCK WITH	19	TRANSWORLD	US		202
JUST ROCK'N'ROLL MUSIC	1973	SONET	UK	SNTF	645
KING OF ROCK'N'ROLL MUSIC	1973	MUSIDISC		ALB	137
LIVE IN LONDON 74	1974	ATLANTIC	UK	K	51501
RARE ITEMS	1975	MCA			COPS72741/2
SCRAPBOOK	19	KAMA SUTRA			2014
ROCK	19	ESSEX	US		202
COLLECTIONS	1976	PICKWICK		PDA	006
ROCK ROCK ROCK	1975	MUSIDISC		CV	1072
GOLDEN HITS	1974	MCA	UK	MCF	2555
" "	197	DECCA	US		7211
R O C K	1976	SONET	UK	SNTF	710
ARMCHAIR ROCK'N'ROLL	1978	MCA	UK	MCF	2838
GOLDEN COUNTY ORIGINS	1978	GRASS ROOTS			1001
20 GOLDEN PIECES OF	1979	BULLDOG	UK	BDL	2002
EVERYONE CAN ROCK'N'ROLL	1979	SONET	UK	SNTF	808
TRIBUTE TO BILL	1981	MCA	UK	MCF	3105
ROCK'N'ROLL REVIVAL	1981	WB	US		1831
ROCK'N'ROLL FOREVER	1981	WB	UK	K	40555

H6A

HALF JAPANESE

H6A

(A) HALF JAPANESES (BOX SET) 19 ARMAGEDDON UK ABOX1
(B) LOUD 1981 ARMAGEDDON UK ARM7

H7

HALFBREED

H7

MICK WHITTAKER V (A — (A) HALFBREED 1975 U A UK UAG 29877
TOM FARRIER G (A
JIM LOWERY K (A GEOFF HUTCHINSON D (A FRANKIE GIBBON B (A

H7A

DARYL HALL

H7A

DARYL HALL V K (A — (A) SACRED SONGS 1980 RCA UK US 3573
ROBERT FRIPP G (A
KENNY PASSARELLI B (A ROGER POPE D (A CALEB QUAYE G (A CHARLIE DRACHEN SAX(A
DAVID KENT V (A

H7B

BOBBYE HALL

H7B

BOBBYE HALL(PORTER) V PERC(A — (A) BODY LANGUAGE FOR LOVERS 1977 20TH CENTURY US 534

H7C

CAROL HALL

H7C

CAROL HALL (AB (A) IF I BE YOUR LADY 19 ELEKTRA UK 74078
(B) BEADS & FEATHERS 19 ELEKTRA UK 75018

H7D

JIMMY HALL

H7D

JIMMY HALL V HCA SAX PERC(AB (A) TOUCH YOU 1980 EPIC US 36516
JACK HALL B V (A (B) CADILLAC TRACKS 1982 EPIC US 37701
GUNNAR GELOTTE D PERC(A
BONNIE BRAMLETT V (A MIKE DUKE PNO (A MIKE EUBANK PNO (A SHELLY KURLAND STR (A
FARRELL MORRIS PERC (A GREG TAYLOR HCA (A NORBERT PUTNAM STR (A DONNA HALL V (A
ANITA HALL V (A STEVE BRANTLEY V (A DAVE LOGGINS V (A LARRY BERWALD G (AB
JON GOIN G (AB KENNY MINS G (B BILL SANFORD G (B LARRY BYROM G (B
RANDY McCORMICK K (B MIKE HANNA K (B SHANE KEISTER K (AB BOB WRAY B (B
JAMES TSROUD D (B KENNY MALONE PERC (B HARRISON CALLOWAY HRNS (B RONNIE EADES HRNS(B
CHARLES ROSE HRNS (B HARVEY THOMPSON HRNS (B ROGER BISSELL HRNS (B QUITMAN DENNIS HRNS(B
RON KELLER HRNS (B DENIS SOLEE HRNS (B GEORGE TIDWELL HRNS (AB

H7E

JOE HALL

H7E

JOE HALL V G HCA PERC(A (A) JOE HALL & THE CONTINENTAL DRIFT 1978 POSTERITY CAN 13009
TONY QUARRINGTON G K PERC(A
PAUL QUARRINGTON B V (A GEORGE DOBO K G (A MARTIN WORTHY D (A STEVE HUTT SAX (A
PETER STRYNIAK VLN (A ART JANSEN VLA (A JOEY QUARRINGTON B (A

H8

JOHN HALL

H8

JOHN HALL G V (ALL (A ACTION 1973 CBS US 1043
WELLS KELLY D (A)B) JOHN HALL 1978 ASYLUM US 6E 117 UK K 53075
MICHAEL BRECKER HRNS (B (C) POWER 1979 CBS US 35790
PAUL HARRIS K (A (D) DOUBLE OR NOTHING 1979 A&M US 4760
RICHARD GREENE VLN (A (E) ALL OF THE ABOVE 1981 EMI AM US 17058
LYNN PITNEY V (BC
GARLAND JEFFREYS V (B JOEL TEPP HCA (B JERRY LAWSON V (B CHUCK RAINEY B (B
STEVE GADD D (B JOE SAMPLE K (B JIMMY HAYES V (B BILL PAYNE K (B
SONNY BURKE K (B DAVID LASLEY V (B ARNOLD McCULLER V (B TUBO V (B
ED GREENE D (B PHILIP BALLOU V (BC DAVID SANBORN SAX (B DAVID HUNGATE B (B
JAMES TAYLOR V (BC CARLY SIMON V (B WILTON FELDER V (B MILT HOLLAND PERC(B
DAVID PAICH PNO (B LOWELL GEORGE G V (B JAY OTIS WASHINGTON V (B BONNIE RAITT V B(B
JOSEPH RUSSELL V (B JOHN SEBASTIAN G HCA(A ELLIOTT ZIGMUND D (A JIM COLGROVE B (A
HARVEY BROOKS B (A SHARON ALEXANDER V (A BOB LEINBACH K V (E JODY LINACOTT PERC(C
LOUIS LEVIN K (C JOHN POUSETTE DART V (A TONY LEVIN B (C CARLY SIMON V (C
ERIC PARKER D (CE DAVID SCHWARTZ B (C BRYAN CUMMINGS SAX G(C JOHN TROY V (CE
MICHAEL MARNION VIBES(C

H8A

LANI HALL

H8A

LANI HALL V (ALL (A) SUNDOWN LADY 1974 A&M US 4359 UK AMLS64359
CHARLES LOPER TROM (C (B) HELLO ITS ME 1975 A&M US 4508 UK AMLS64508
LEW McCREARY TROM (C (C) SWEETBIRD 1977 A&M US 4617 UK AMLH64647
TONY TERRAN TPT (C (D) DOUBLE OR NOTHING 1979 A&M US 4670 UK AMLH64670
JOHN PISANO G (B (E) BLUSH 1981 A&M US 4829
PAPITO HERNANDEZ B (B
STEVE SCHAEFFER D (B CLARENCE McDONALD K (B VINCE CHARLES PERC(B
LARRY CARLTON G (BC BOB FINDLEY TPT (B WILTON FELDER B (B MARK STEVENS D (B
PETE JOLLY ACC (B HERB ALPERT TPT PNO (BC JIM HUGHART B (B MICHEL COLOMBIER B (BC
EMIL RICHARDS PERC (B JULIUS WECHTER PERC (B DAVE FRISHBERG PNO (B BOB EDMONDSON TROM(B
MIKE MELVOIN PNO (B JIM GORDON D (B ERNIE McDANIELS B (B NICK CEROLI D (B
JOHN AUDINO TPT (C BOBBY SHEW TPT (C LEE RITENOUR G (C DENNIS BUDIMIR G (C
CHUCK DOMANICO B (CD STAN CLARKE B (C JIM KELTNER D (C MILT HOLLAND PERC(C
MICHAEL BODDICKER SYN (C GAYLE LEVANT HARP (C DAVID DUKE HRNS (C NEIL LARSEN K (D
BUZZ FEITEN G (D PETER DONALD D (D MANOLO BADRENA PERC (D JERRY KNIGHT B (D
LERRY TOLBERT D (D VINCENT DEROSA HRNS (C ROBERT HENDERSON HRNS (C EARL DUMLER OBOE(C
LANNY MORGAN WIND (C CLIFFORD SHANK FLT (C JEROME RICHARDSON FLT (C STRING SECTION (C

H9

HALL & OATES

H9

DARYL HALL K V G(ALL (A) WHOLE OATES 1972 ATLANTIC US 7242 UK 76 K50306
JOHN OATES G V K(ALL (B) ABANDONED LUNCHEONETTE 1973 ATLANTIC US 7269 UK K40534
CHRIS BOND G K (BDEG (B) ABANDONED LUNCHEONETTE 197 ATLANTIC RIUS 19139
TOM SCOTT SAX (EG (C) WAR BABIES 1974 ATLANTIC US 18109 UK K50008
GARY COLEMAN PERC (DEG (D) HALL & OATES 1975 RCA APLI1144 UK RI 80 INTS 5010
GORDON EDWARDS B (B (E) BIGGER THAN BOTH OF US 1976 RCA APLI1467 UK RI 81 INTS 5088
LELAND SKLAR B (DEG (F) NO GOODBYES 1977 ATLANTIC US 18213 UK K50347
JIM GORDON D (DE (F) NO GOODBYES 197 RCA RI US/UK I/2802
ED GREENE D (DE (G) BEAUTY ON A BACK STREET 1977 RCA US/UK I/2300
EDDIE ZYNE D ((H) ALONG THE RED LEDGE 1978 RCA US/UK I/2894
DAVE KENT K V (JH (I) PAST TIME BEHIND 1977 CHELSEA US 547
TODD SHARP G ((J) LIVE TIME 1978 RCA US/UK I/2802
STEPHEN DEAN B ((K) X STATIC 1979 RCA US/UK I/3494
JIM GETZOFF K (E (L) VOICES 1980 RCA US/UK I/3646
TOM HENSLEY PNO (E (M) PRIVATE EYE 1981 RCA AFLI4028 UK RCALP6001
TODD RUNDGREN G (C (N) H^2O 1982 RCA UK RCALP6056
TOM WOLK B (N
ROGER POPE D (HJ DON YORK K (C JOHN SIEGLER B (C JOHN WILCOX D (C
MIKE McCARTY B (A JIM HELMER D (A HUGH McCRACKEN G (B BERNARD PURDIE D (B
RALPH McDONALD PERC (B LARRY PACKER FDL (B JOE FARRELL SAX (B RICK MAROTTA D (B
RICHARD TEE K (B GLORIA AGOSTINI HARP (B JOHN BLAIR VLN (B CLARENCE McDONALD K (D
SCOTT EDWARDS B (DEG STEVE GELSAND G B (B JERRY RICKS G (B PANCHO MORALES D (B
PAT REBILLOT K PERC (B MARK HORWITZ BANJO (B MARVIN STAMM HRNS (B MIKE BAIRD D (D
C O B SYN (SANDY ALLEN V (D JEFF PORCARO D (G TONI MOTTOLA V (G
GAIL BOGGS V (C KENNY PASSARELLI B (JHK CALEB QUAYE G (JH RALPH SCHUCKETT K (K1
CHARLES DE CHANT K V(HJKMN YOGI HORTON D (K NEIL JASON B (K WERNER FRITZSCHING G(K
STEVE LOVE G (K GEORGE BITZER (H ROBERT FRIPP G (H JAY GRAYDON G (HK
RICK NIELSON G (H DICK WAGNER (H JOHN SIEGLER B (KLM CHUCK BURGI D (LM
LARRY FAST SYN (M RAY GOMEZ G (M DAVID FOSTER K (HK STEVE LUKATHER G (H
GEORGE HARRISON G (H STEVE PORCARO (H LES THOMPSON (H G E SMITH (KLMN
JERRY MAROTTA D (KLM JEFF SOUTHWORTH G (LM MIKE KLVANA SYN (L MICKET CURRY D (M
JIMMY MAELIN PERC (MK JOHN JARRETT V (M

H9A FERGUS HAMBLETON H9A

FERGUS HAMBLETON V K G B SAX(A (A) ALL THE RIGHT NOISES 1971 CAPITOL CAN ST 6370
GREG HAMBLETON V (A
ALVIN FALL HRNS (A JACK TAYLOR HRNS (A STAN THERIAULT B (A PAUL CLINCH D (A
STRINGS

H9B PETER MICHAEL HAMEL H9B

PETER MICHAEL HAMEL K(AB (A) HAMEL 1972 VERTIGO GER 6641 055
ANATOL ARKUS ((B) VOICE OF SILENCE 1973 VERTIGO GER 6360 613

H10 CHICO HAMILTON H10

CHICO HAMILTON PERC D(ALL (A) PASSIN' THRU 1963 IMPULSE AS 29
BILL PAYNE PNO (I (B) MAN FROM TWO WORLDS 1964 IMPULSE AS 59
LOWELL GEORGE G (I (C) CHIC CHIC CHICO 1965 IMPULSE AS 82
KENNY GRADNEY B (I (D) EL CHICO 1966 IMPULSE AS 9102
GEORGE BOHANON TROM (K ( ) FURTHER ADVENTURES OF EL CHICO 1966 IMPULSE AS 9114
PAUL BARRERE G (I (E) THE DEALER 1967 IMPULSE AS 9130
STU GARDNER K (I (F) BEST OF 1975 IMPULSE AS 9174
SAM CLAYTON D (I (G) HIS GREAT HITS 19 IMPULSE AS9213/2
JERRY AIELLO K (I (H) WITH GERRY MULLIGAN 19 FANTASY 8082
ERIC DOLPHY WIND (K (I) CHICO THE MASTER 1973 STAX/ENTERPRISE ENS 7501
DENNIS BUDIMIR G (K (J) MONTREUX FESTIVAL 1975 STAX STX 1029
CHARLES LLOYD SAX (K (K) THAT'S JAZZ 1976 WB UK K 56239
ALBERT STINSON B (K ( ) HEAD HUNTER 1969 SOLID US 18050
WYATT RUTHER G (K ( ) & PLAYERS 1976 BLUE NOTE 622
GABOR SZABO G (K ( ) PEREGRINATIONS 1976 BLUE NOTE 520
NATHAN GERSHMAN CELLO(K ( ) CAT WALK 1976 MERCURY 1163

H10A HAMILTON, JOE FRANK (& REYNOLDS) H10A

DAN HAMILTON G V (ALL (A) HAMILTON JOE FRANK & REYNOLDS 1970
JOE FRANK CAROLLO B V (ALL (B) DON'T PULL YOUR LOVE OUT 1971 ABC US 3555
JOE CARRERO D (ALL (C) HALWAY SYMPHONY 1972 ABC US
ALAN DENNISON K V (DE (D) FALLIN' IN LOVE 1975 PLAYBOY US 407
TOMMY REYNOLDS V FLT G(ABC (E) LOVE & CONVERSATION 1976 PLAYBOY US 414

H11 CLAIRE HAMILL H11

CLAIRE HAMILL V G K(ALL (A) ONE HOUSE LEFT STANDING 1971 ISLAND US 9316 UK ILPS9182
JOHN MARTYN G (A (B) OCTOBER 1973 ISLAND UK ILPS9225
PAUL BUCKMASTER CELLO(A (C) STAGE DOOR JOHNNIES 1974 KONK UK 101
DAVID LINDLEY G (A (D) ABRACADABRA 1975 KONK UK 104
JOHN HAWKEN K (A
RAY WARLEIGH FLT (A JACK EMBLOW ACC (A JOHN PIGNEGNY HRNS (A AUBREY JOHNSON OBOE(A
PHIL BATES B (A TERRY REID G V (A SIMON KIRKE D (A TETSU YAMAUCHI B (A
RABBIT BUNDRICK K (A WAYNE PERKINS G V (B JEAN ROUSSEL K (B TIM SMITH G V (B
STEVE SMITH K V (B CHRIS LAURENCE B (B ALAN WHITE D (B GERRY CONWAY D (B
PAT DONALDSON B (B HENRY SPINETTI PERC (B NICK SOUTH B (C PHILIP CHEN B (CD
PAUL WESTWOOD B (C DAVE ROWEBERRY K (C TIM HINKLEY K (C JIM FRANKS D (C
CLEM CATTINI D (C NEIL McBAIN D (C PHIL PALMER G (CD DIZ DISLEY G (C
ROY NEVE G (C LAURIE BROWN TPT (C ALAN HOLMES FLT (C JOHN HARTMANN K (D
GARY RAY D (D MEL COLLINS SAX (D DOREEN CHANTER V (D VICKY BROWN V (D
TOM ROBINSON V (D RAPHAEL DOYLE V (D HEREWARD KAYE V (D ALEX WELSH BAND (A

H11A HAMILTON FACE BAND H11A

LENNY LAKS V (A (A) AIN'T GOT NO TIME 1970 BELL US 6042 UK SBLL132
RUTH UNDERWOOD D (A
STEVEN MARGOSHES PNO (A RONNIE SELDIN G (A ALAN COOPER B (A

H12 JAN HAMMER H12

JAN HAMMER K (ALL (A) LIKE CHILDREN 1974 ATLANTIC UK K 50092 US NEMPEROR 430
JERRY GOODMAN VLN (A (B) FIRST SEVEN DAYS 1975 ATLANTIC UK K 50184 US NEMPEROR 432
JEFF BECK G (E (C) OH YEAH 1976 NEMPEROR UK K 50276 US 437
STEVE KINDLER VLN G(BCG (D) MAKE LOVE 1976 BASF GERM 20688
FERNANDO SAUNDERS B V (CHG (E) LIVE WITH JEFF BECK 1977 CBS UK 86025 US EPIC 34433
TONY SMITH D V (CHG (F) TIMELESS 197 US ECM 1047
DAVID EARLE JOHNSON PERC(B (G) MELODIES 1979 EPIC UK 82405 US NEMPEROR35003
COLIN HODGKINSON V (H (H) BLACK SHEEP 1979 ASYLUM UK K 53089 US ASYLUM 6E173
BOB CHRISTIANSON V (H
GREGG GEYA CARTER V (H

H12A HAMMER H12A

JACK O'BRIEN G (A (A) HAMMER 1971 SANFRANCISCO US SD 203
NORMAN LANDSBERG K (A
JOHN DEROBERTS V (A RICHIE McBRIDE B (A JOHN GUERIN D (A

H12B HAMMERSMITH H12B

(A) HAMMERSMITH 197 MERCURY US SRM11040
(B) IT'S FOR YOU 197 MERCURY US SRM11102

H13 PETER HAMMILL H13

PETER HAMMILL V G K(ALL (A) FOOLS MATE 1972 CHARISMA US/UK CAS1037 NL 9199 190
GUY EVANS D (ABCDEFL (B) CHAMELEON IN THE SHADOW 1973 CHARISMA US/UK CAS1067 NL 9124 051
DAVID JACKSON SAX (ABCEGJKL (C) THE SILENT CORNER 1974 CHARISMA US/UK CAS1083 NL 9198 771
HUGH BANTON K (ABCE (D) IN CAMERA 1974 CHARISMA US?UK CAS1089 NL 9198 770
NIC POTTER B (ABF (E) NADIRS LAST CHANCE 1975 CHARISMA US/UK CAS1099 NL 9198 772
PAUL WHITHEAD D (AD (F) OVER 1977 CHARISMA US/UK CAS1125 NL 9124 008
RANDY CALIFORNIA G (C (G) FUTURE NOW 1978 CHARISMA UK CAS1137 US 2202
GRAHAME SMITH VLN (FJG (H) VISION(COMP) 1978 GTR US 9211 1016
CHRIS SMITH PERC V (D (J) P H 7 1979 CHARISMA UK CAS1146 US 2205
ROD CLEMENTS B VLN(A (J) P H 7 1979 CHARISMA GER 9124 044
ROBERT FRIPP G (A (K) BLACK BOX 1980 MERCURY EURO 6302 067
MARTIN POTTINGER D (A (L) SITTING TARGETS 1981 VIRGIN UK 2205 GER MERCURY 6203 130
RAY JACKSON HCA MAND (A ( ) BETWEEN CONTEMPLATION 19 AURAL US 5067
PAUL WHITEHEAD D (A
DAVID FERGUSON SYN (K PHIL HARRISON SYN (L MORRIS PERT PERC(L DAVID HENTSCHEL SYN (D

H14 ALBERT HAMMOND H14

ALBERT HAMMOND G V (ALL (A) IT NEVER RAINS IN SOUTHERN CALIFORNIA 1973 MUM US 31905 UK 65320
MIKE OMARTIAN K (B (B) FREE ELECTRIC BAND 1973 MUM US 32267 UK 65554
JIM GORDON D (B (C) ALBERT HAMMOND 1974 MUM US 32834 UK 80026
JOE OSBORN B (B (D) 99 MILES FROM LA 1975 EPIC 80961
JAY LEWIS G (B (E) WHEN I NEED YOU 1977 EPIC 81983
LARRY CARLTON G (B (F) GREATEST HITS 1978 EMBASSY 31643
CAROL CARMICHAEL V (B (G) YOUR WORLD IS MY WORLD 1980 CBS US 36964 UK 84824
SID SHARP STRING(B

H14A LAWRENCE HAMMOND H14A

LAWRENCE HAMMOND G K V(A (A) COYOTES DREAM 1976 TAKOMA 1047
ALAN McSHANE D (A
BILL WEINGARDEN STEEL(A BYRON BERLINE FDL (A LENI ISAACS FLT (A LEROY DEWEY D (A
DAVID ROBINSON G (A 2 BUTTON GREENE PERC (A JAMES LOUIS PARBER G (A

H15 JOHN HAMMOND H15

JOHN HAMMOND HCA G V (ALL (A) JOHN HAMMOND 1963 VANGUARD US 2148
BILLY BUTLER G (BEQ (B) BIG CITY BLUES 1964 VANGUARD US VSD 79153
JAMES SPRUILL G (BEQ (B) BIG CITY BLUES 1964 FONTANA UK TFL 6046
JIMMY LEWIS B (BCEFQ (C) SO MANY ROADS 1965 VANGUARD US VSD 79178
BOBBY DONALDSON D (BEQ (C) SO MANY ROADS 1965 FONTANA UK TFL 6059
CHARLIE MUSSELWHITE HCA(CEQ (D) COUNTRY BLUES 1965 VANGUARD US VSD 79198
JAIME R ROBERTSON G (CEFQ (E) MIRRORS 1968 VANGUARD US VSD 79245
LEVON HELM D (CEQ (F) I CAN TELL 1968 ATLANTIC US SD 8152
MIKE BLOOMFIELD G PNO (CEQL (G) SOONER OR LATER 1968 ATLANTIC US SD 8206
DR JOHN K (O (H) SOUTHERN FRIED 1970 ATLANTIC US SD 8251
BILLY NICHOLS B (K (K) SOURCE POINT 1971 CBS US 30458 UK 64365
EDDIE HINTON G PNO(R (L) LITTLE BIG MAN (SOUNDTRACK) 197 CBS US 30545
RANDALL BRAMBLETT K (R (M) WHEN I NEED 197 CBS US 30549
KENNY BUTTREY D (R (N) I'M SATISFIED 1972 CBS UK 65051
TOMMY COGBILL B (R (O) TRIUMVIRATE 1973 CBS UK 65659
SPOONER OLDHAM PNO (R (P) SPIRITUALS TO SWING 19 VANGUARD VRS8523/4
LEONARD FEATHER G (F (Q) BEST OF (SOUTHERN FRIED) 1974 VANGUARD VSD 11/2
ROGER HAWKINS D (R (R) CANT BEAT THE KID 1975 CAPRICORN US CP 0153
RICK DANKO B (F (S) MY SPANISH ALBUM 19 CAYTRONICS US 1493
BILL WYMAN B (F (T) JOHN HAMMOND SOLO 197 VANGUARD US VSD 79380
JAN ZUKOWSKI B (V (U) FOOTWORK 197 VANGUARD US VSD 79400
JIMMY THACKERY G (V (V) HOT TRACKS 197 VANGUARD US VSD 79424
MARK WEINER HCA (V (W) MILEAGE 1979 SONET UK SNTF835 US ROUNDER3032
PETE RAYUSA D (V
ERIC 'GARTH' HUDSON ORG(CEQ CHARLES OTIS D (FKW BOB MONTALTO PNO (W ROBBIE KONDOR PNO (W
SHERMAN HOLMES B (W SEE MIKE BLOOMFIELD ENTRY FOR FULL LINE UP ON(O)

H15A HANGMEN H15A

(A) BITTER SWEET 19 MONUMENT US MLP 8077

H15B HANK THE KNIFE H15B

(A) BEST OF 1980 MFP NL 58095
(B) CRAZY GUITAR 1980 MERCURY NL 6423 343

H16 HANNIBAL H16

ALEX BOYCE V (A (A) HANNIBAL 1970 B&C UK CAS 1022
BILL HUNT K HRNS(A
ADRIAN INGRAM G (A JACK GRIFFITHS B (A JOHN PARKES D (A

H16A RANDY HANSEN H16A

RANDY HANSEN G V (A (A) RANDY HANSEN 1980 CAPITOL EST 12119
SCOTT ROSBURG B V (A
CHARLES TAPP D V (A

H16B HANS A PLAST H16B

(A) HANS A PLAST 1978 LLAVA 79 449

H17 JUNIOR HANSON H17

JUNIOR HANSON G V (AB (A) NOW HEAR THIS 1973 MANTICORE US 66670 UK K43507
JEAN ROUSSEL K (A (B) MAGIC DRAGON 1974 MANTICORE US MC 66672
CLIVE CHAMAN B (A
CONRAD ISADORE D (A LISLE HARPER B (A REBOP KWAKU BAAH PERC (A JIMMY THOMAS V (A
KEN CUMBERBATCH PNO (A CHRIS WOOD FLT (A BOB TENCH G V (A GODFREY MACLEAN D V(A
NEIL MURRAY B (B BROTHER JAMES PERC (B GLEN LEFLEUR D (B ANDRE LEWIS K (B
MARLO HENDERSON G (B CASSANDRA V (B

H18 BO HANSSON H18

BO HANSSON G K B (ALL (A) LORD OF THE RINGS 1972 PVC US 7907 CHARISMA UK 1059
RUNE CARLSSON D (ABC (B) MAGICIANS HAT 1973 CHARISMA UK 1073 US 6062
GUNNAR BERGSTEN WIND (ABC (C) ATTIC THOUGHTS 1975 SIRE US 7525 CHARISMA UK 1113
STEN BERGMAN FLT (ABC (D) WATERSHIP DOWN 1977 SIRE US 6044 CHARISMA UK 1132
KENNY HAKANSSON B G (BCD
ROLF SCHERRER G (BC BOBO STENSSON K (B OWE GUSTAVSSON B (B PELLE EKMAN D (B
GORAN FREESE SAX (B BILL OHRSTROM CONGA(B GORAN LAGERBERG B G (CD THOMAS NETZLER B (CD
MATS GLENNGARD VLN (C BO SKOGLUND D (D TORBJORN EKLUND FLT (D FREDRIK NOREN D (D
PONTUS OLSSON PNO (D

H18A HANSSON & KARLSSON H18A

BO HANSSON ORG (AB (A) SWEDISH UNDERGROUND 1967 POLYDOR 184 196
JAN KARLSSON D (AB (B) GOLD (COMPILATION) 19 KARUSSELL 2468 009

H18B HANUMAN H18B

AOLF-RUDIGER UHLIG K V (A (A) HANUMAN 1972 KUCKUCK GER 2375 012
JORG HAHNFELD B (A
PETER BARTH WIND (A THOMAS HOLM D (A

H19 HERBIE HANCOCK

Musician	Instr	Albums	Album	Year	Label	US/Other	UK
HERBIE HANCOCK	K V	(ALL	(A) TAKIN' OFF	1963	BLUENOTE		84109
EDDIE HENDERSON	TRP PERC	(JLOd	(B) MY POINT OF VIEW	1963	BLUENOTE		84126
BILLY HART	D PERC	(JLQ	(C) INVENTIONS & DIMENSIONS	196	BLUENOTE		84147
JULIAN PRIESTER	TROM	(JLd	(D) EMPYREAN ISLES	1964	BLUENOTE		84175
BUSTER WILLIAMS	B PERC	(JLQd	(E) HERBIE HANCOCK	1964	BLUENOTE		84190
BENNY MAUPIN	WIND PERC	(JLMNdhlm	(F) MAIDEN VOYAGE	1966	BLUENOTE	US 40020	84195
JACO PASTORIUS	B	(L	(G) SPEAK LIKE A CHILD	1968	BLUENOTE	40025	84279
PATRICK GLEASON	SYN	(L	(H) PRISONER	19	BLUNOTE		84321
VICTOR PONTOJA	CONGA	(L	(I) THE BEST OF	19	BLUNOTE	US 33199	80546
CANDY LOVE	V	(L	(J) MWANDISHI	1971	WB	US 1898	UK K46077
SANDRA STEVENS	V	(L	(K) CROSSING	1972	WB	US 2617	UK K46164
DELTA HORNE	V	(L	(L) SEXTANT	1972	CBS	US 33212	UK 65582
VICTOR DOMAGALSKI	V	(L	(M) HEAD HUNTERS	1974	CBS	US 32731	UK 65928
SCOTT BEACH	V	(L	(N) THRUST	1974	CBS	US 32965	UK 80193
RON CARTER	B	(Gcde	(O) TREASURE CHEST	1974	WB	US 2/2807	
TONY WILLIAMS	D	(cde	(P) BLOW UP (SOUNDTRACK) VAR ARTIST)	197	MGM	US 4447	
FREDDIE HUBBARD	TPT	(d	(Q) FAT ALBERT ROTUNDA	1974	WB	US 1834	UK K46039
WAYNE SHORTER	SAX	(d	(R) DEATH WISH	1975	CBS	US 33199	UK 80546
WAH WAH WATSON	G	(Xdehmn	(S) MAN CHILD	1975	CBS	US 33812	uk 69185
RAY PARKER	B	(Xdmnh	(T) LIVE IN JAPAN (DBL)	1975	CBS/SONY	JAP 98/99	
JOHNNY COLES	HRNS	(Qe	(U) SUCCOTASH	1975	BLUENOTE	US LA152	
PAUL JACKSON	B	(MYdelm	(V) WATER BABIES	197	CBS		UK 81741
FREDDIE WASHINGTON	B	(eh	(W) HANCOCK	1975	BLUENOTE	US LA399	
SHEILA ESCOVEDO	V	(e	(X) SECRETS	1976	CBS	US 34280	UK 81591
JAMES LEVI		(Xdh	(Y) KAWAIDA	1976	DJM		UK 22008
KENNETH NASH	PERC	(Xdm	(Z) LIVE UNDER THE SKY	1976	CBS/SONY	JAP 1037/875	
LEON CHANCLER	D	(Jom	(b) FLOOD	1977	cbs		
JOSE AREAS	PERC	(J	(c) HERBIE HANCOCK TRIO	1977	CBS	JAP 25AP650	
RONNIE MONTROSE	G	'J	(d) V S O P	1977	CBS	US 34976	UK 88235
GARNETT BROWN	TROM	(Q	(e) QUINTET	1977	CBS		UK 88273
TOOTIE HEATH	D	(Q	(f) SUNLIGHT	1978	CBS	US 34906	UK 82240
HARVEY MASON	D	(Mo	(g) TEMPEST IN THE COLOSSEUM	1978	CBS/SONY	JAP 40AP771/2	
ALPHONSE MOUSON	D	(nlh	(h) FEETS DONT FAIL ME NOW	1979	CBS	US 35764	UK 83491
BILL SUMMERS	PERC	(Mhlmo	(j) AN EVENING WITH	1979	CBS		UK 88329
BYRON MILLER	B	(ml	(k IN CONCERT(DUETS)	1979	CBS	US 35663	
BYRON DAVIS	PERC	(h	(l) DIRECT STEP	1979	CBS/SONY	JAP 30AP1032	
DON KERR	V	(Xm	(m) BEST OF	1979	CBS		UK 84106
BILL CHAMPLIN	V	(n	(n) MONSTER	1980	CBS		UK 84237
RANDY HANSEN	G	(n	(o) MR HANDS	1980	CBS		UK 84638
LUTHER WATERS	V	(hmn	(p) HANCOCK ALLEY	1980	MANHATTAN		UK 5021
OREN WATERS	V	(HMN	(q) MAGIC WINDOWS	1981	CBS		UK 85144
MICHAEL CLARK	D	(m					
EDDIE WATKINS	B	(hm					

Musician	Instr	Albums	Musician	Instr	Albums	Musician	Instr	Albums	Musician	Instr	Albums
GREG WALKER	V	(n	FRED DOBBS	V	(Xm	WEBSTER LEWIS	K	(lh	GAVIN CHRISTOPHER	V	(n
MAXINE WILLARD	V	(hmn	JULIA TILLMAN	V	(Xmn	CHICK COREA	K	(k	COKE ESCOVEDO	PERC	(hm
RAUL RAKOW	PERC	(m	ART BALDACCI	V	(Xm	FREDDIE WASHINGTON	B	(n	JERRY DODGION		(G
CARLOS SANTANA	G	(n	JAMES GADSON	D	(Xm	PETER PHILLIPS	TROM	(G	THAD JONES	HRNS	(G
MICKEY ROKER	D	(G	CHRIS MANCINI	V	(Xm	RAY OBIEDO	G	(lhm			

H19A HAPPY THE MAN H19A

Musician	Instr	Albums	Album	Year	Label	US	UK
KIT WATKINS	SYN K	(AB	(A) HAPPY THE MAN	1976	ARISTA	US 4120	UK SPART1057
MICK BECK	PERC	(A	(B) CRAFTY HANDS	1978	ARISTA	US 4181	
RICK KENNELL	B	(AB					
STANLEY WHITAKER	G V	(AB					

FRANK WYATT WIND K V (AB RON RIDDLE D PERC(B

H19B HAPSHASH & COLOURED COAT H19B

Musician	Instr	Albums	Album	Year	Label	Country	No.
TONY McPHEE	G V	(AB	(A) HAPSHASH & COLOURED COAT	1967	MINIT	US	40001
GUY STEVENS		(A	(B) WESTERN FLYER	1969	LIBERTY	UK	83212
MICHAEL RAMSDEN	V	(B	(B) WESTERN FLYER	1969	IMPERIAL	US	LP 12430
ANDY RENTON	D	(B	(C) HUMAN HOST & THE HEAVY METAL KIDS	19	LIBERTY	UK	40001
MICHAEL MAYHEW	G	(A					
[HEAVY METAL KIDS MICKEY FINN]	PERC	(B					

EDDIE TRIOO B (AB FREDDIE BALLERINI VLN(AB MIKE BATT K (AB

H19C HARDCAKE SPECIAL H19C

Musician	Instr	Albums	Album	Year	Label	Country	No.
ANDY KIRNBERGER	G K	(A	(A) HARDCAKE SPECIAL	1974	BRAIN	GERM	1060
REINHART BOPP	G V	(					
RON SCHEEPMAKER	K	(A					

JOCHEN LEUSCHNER G (A GUNTER BOPP B V (A HANS HARBRECHT D (A

H20 HARCOURTS HEROS H20

Musician	Instr	Albums	Album
CHARLIE HARCOURT	G V	(A	(A) 1977 LINE UP
RAY JACKSON	V	(A	
MARTIN CRAGGS	SAX PERC	(A	

COLIN MASON D (A BARRY SPENCE B V (A LES DODDS G (A

H20A HARD ROAD H20A

Musician	Instr	Albums	Album	Year	Label	Country	No.
JOHN SPENCER	G	(A	(A) NO PROBLEM	1979	GOODSTUFF	UK	LP1002
KRIS GRAY	G V	(A					
HEANOR HUCKNALL	B	(A					

RORY O'CARROLL (A

H21 HARD STUFF H21

Musician	Instr	Albums	Album	Year	Label
JOHN GUSTAFSON	B	(A	(A) BULLET PROOF	1972	PURPLE UK 7505 MERCURY US 663
JOHN CANN	G	(A	(B) BOLEX DEMENTIA	1973	PURPLE UK 7507
PAUL HAMMOND	D	(			

H22 EDDIE HARDIN H22

Musician	Instr	Albums	Album	Year	Label	Country	No.
EDDIE HARDIN	V K	(A	(A)YOU CANT TEACH AN OLD DOG NEW TRICKS	1977	ATTIC	UK	LAT 1023
LIZA STRIKE	V	(A	( ) HOME IS WHERE YOU FIND IT	1972	DECCA	UK	TXS 106
HENRY SPINETTI	D	(A					
IAN PAICE	D	(AB					
BARRY DE SOUZA	D	(A					
DEE MURRAY	B	(AB					
PETE YORK	D	(B					

Musician	Instr	Albums	Musician	Instr	Albums	Musician	Instr	Albums
B J COLE	STEEL	(A	MO FOSTER	B	(A	HELEN CHAPELLE	V	(A
ROGER GLOVER	PERC V	(A	DORIS TROY	V	(A	RAY FLEMING	G V	(A
BOBBY KEYS	SAX	(B	JIM PRICE	HRNS	(B	RAY FENWICK	G V	(B

H23 TIM HARDIN H23

Musician	Instr.	Albums	Album	Year / Label / Catalogue
TIM HARDIN	K V G	(ALL	(A) TIM HARDIN 1	1966 VERVE UK 5018 US 3004 GER 9501
WARREN BERNHARDT	K	(F	(B) TIM HARDIN 2	1967 VERVE UK 6002 US 3022
BOB COHEN	G	(K	(C) THIS IS TIM HARDIN	1967 ATCO UK 588 082 US 33210
GARY KLAIN	K	(F	(D) LIVE IN CONCERT	1968 VERVE UK 6010 US 3049
DONALD McDONALD	D	(F	(E) TIM HARDIN 4	1969 VERVE UK 6016 US 3064
MONTE DUNN	G	(F	(F) SUITE FOR SUSAN MOORE & DAMIAN	1970 CBS UK 63571 US 9787
KEITH	TPT	(F	(G) THE BEST OF	1970 VERVE UK 2317003 US 3078
DAVID	SAX	(F	(H) BIRD ON A WIRE	1970 CBS UK 64335 US 30551
BUZZ	CELESTE	(F	(I) PAINTED HEAD	1973 CBS UK 65209 US 31764
ANDY BOWN	B	(K	(J) ARCHETYPES	1973 MGM US 4952
PHILIPE	CONGA	(F	(K) NINE	1974 ANTILLES US 7023 GM UK 1004
WALTER YOST	B	(A	(K) NINE	1974 PHILIPS GER 6370 105
JOHN MEALING	K	(K	(AB) TIM HARDIN 1&2	1974 VERVE UK 2683 048
EARL PALMER	D	(A	(L) STATE OF GRACE	1981 CBS US 37164
BOB BUSHWELL	B	(A		

Musician	Instr.	Albums	Musician	Instr.	Albums	Musician	Instr.	Albums	Musician	Instr.	Albums
MIKE DRISCOLL	D	(K	JIMMY HOROWITZ	K	(K	PETER FRAMPTON	G	(K	LESLEY DUNCAN	V	(K
LIZA STRIKE	V	(K	MADELINE BELL	V	(K	SUSAN GLOVER	V	(K	DAVID KATZ	STRINGS	(K
JOHN SEBASTIAN	HCA	(A	GARY BURTON	VIBES	(A	PHIL KRAUSS	VIBES	(A	BUDDY SALZMAN	D	(A

H24 HARDIN & YORK H24

Musician	Instr.	Albums	Album	Year / Label / Catalogue
EDDIE HARDIN	K V	(ALL	(A) TOMORROW TODAY	1969 BELL US 6043 UK SBLL 125
PETER YORK	D	(ALL	(B) WORLDS SMALLEST BIG BAND	1970 BELL UK SBLL 136
HERBIE FLOWERS	B	(A	(C) FOR THE WORLD	1971 LONDON US 602 DECCA UK SKL 5095
MIKE HURST	G	(A	(AB)POP HISTORY	1972 POLYDOR 2625 021
MEL THORPE	HRNS	(AE	(D) AIN'T NO BREEZE	197 PHONOGRAM 6360 622
VIC FLICK	G	(A	(E) HARDIN & NEW YORK	1981 TELDEC GER 6 24595
ROGER MENNS	K SYN	(E		
STEVE RICHARDSON	B V	(E		

H25 HARDMEAT H25

Musician	Instr.	Albums	Album	Year / Label / Catalogue
MICK CARLESS	D PERC	(A	(A) HARDMEAT	1970 WB WS 1852
MICK DOLAN	G HCA V	(AB	(B) THROUGH A WINDOW	1970 WB WS 3008 US UK WS 1879
STEVE DOLAN	B G V	(AB		

Musician	Instr.	Albums	Musician	Instr.	Albums	Musician	Instr.	Albums	Musician	Instr.	Albums
IAN WHITEMAN	PNO FLT	(A	BRUCE HOWARD	PNO	(A	PETE WESTBROOK	FLT	(B	PHIL JUMP	K	(B

H26 LINDA HARGROVE H26

Musician	Instr.	Albums	Album	Year / Label / Catalogue
LINDA HARGROVE	G V	(ALL	(A) MUSIC IS YOUR MISTRESS	1973 ELEKTRA US EKS 75063
BUDDY HARMON	D	(BA	(B) BLUE JEAN COUNTRY QUEEN	1974 ELEKTRA US 7E1013
KENNY MALONE	D	(B	(C) LOVE,YOU'RE THE TEACHER	1975 CAPITOL US ST 11463
JERRY CARRIGAN	D	(BA	(D) JUST LIKE YOU	1976 CAPITOL US ST 11564
BOB MOORE	B	(BA	(E) IMPRESSIONS	1977 CAPITOL US ST 11685
TOMMY COGBILL	B	(B		

Musician	Instr.	Albums	Musician	Instr.	Albums	Musician	Instr.	Albums	Musician	Instr.	Albums
LARRY BUTLER	PNO	(B	HARGUS'PIG'ROBBINS	PNO	(AB	BOBBY WOOD	PNO	(B	PETE DRAKE	STEEL	(AB
BOBBY BLACK	STEEL	(B	PETE WADE	G	(B	JIMMY CAPPS	G	(B	DAVE KIRBY	G	(AB
REGGIE YOUNG	G	(B	RONNIE LIGHT	G	(B	LARRY BLACK	G	(B	GRADY MARTIN	G	(AB
JIMMY COLVARD	G	(BA	BUDDY SPICHER	FDL	(B	BOBBY THOMPSON	BANJO	(BA	MARY HOLLADAY	V	(B
GINGER HOLLADAY	V	(B	LEA JANE BERINATI	V	(B	JERRY SMITH	PNO	(A	JOE ALLEN	B	(A
MELBA MONTGOMERY	V	(A	GARY S PAXTON SINGERS		(A	CHIP YOUNG	G	(A	JACK SOLOMAM	G	(A
EARL BALL	K	(A	HENRY STRZELECKI	B	(A	ANITA GROUP SINGERS		(A	KARL HIMMEL	D	(A
HAROLD BRADLEY	G	(A	SHELLEY KURLAND STRINGS		(A						

H26A STEVE HARLEY & COCKNEY REBEL H26A

Musician	Instr.	Albums	Album	Year / Label / Catalogue
STEVE HARLEY	V	(ALL	(A) THE HUMAN MENAGERIE	1974 EMI US 11294 UK EMA 759
STUART ELLIOTT	D	(ABEDFGHKL1	(B) PSYCHOMODO	1974 EMI US 11330 UK EMC 3033
JEAN PAUL CROCKER	VLN	(ABEFK	(C) BEST YEARS OF OUR LIVES	1975 EMI US 11394 UK EMC 3068
PAUL JEFFREYS	B	(ABFK	(D) TIMELESS FLIGHT	1976 EMI US 11500 UK EMA 775
MILTON REAME JAMES	K	(ABFK	(E) LOVE IS A PRIMA DONNA	1976 EMI US 11596 UK EMC 3156
JIM CREGAN	G V	(ECFKD	(F) A CLOSER LOOK	1976 EMI US 11456
GEORGE FORD	B	(CEFGHKD	(G) FACE TO FACE	1977 EMI US 11661 UK EMSP 320
DUNCAN MACKAY	K	(CEFGKHD	(H) HOBO WITH A GRIN	1978 EMI US !!''= UK EMC 3254
LINDSAY ELLIOTT	PERC	(DEGK1	(J) CANDIDATE	1979 EMI UK EMC 3311
JO PARTRIDGE	G	(EK1	(K)BEST OF STEVE HARLEY & COCKNEY R	1980 EMI UK EMC 3345
STUART CALVER	V	(G	(1) 1979 OCT CONCERT LINE UP	
TONY RIVERS	V	(G		

Musician	Instr.	Albums	Musician	Instr.	Albums	Musician	Instr.	Albums	Musician	Instr.	Albums
JOHN PERRY	V	(G	BILL PAYNE	PNO	(K	BOBBY KIMBALL	V	(K	JIMMY HOROWITZ	K	(1
BOB GLAUB	B	(K	GREG POREE	G	(K	BILL CHAMPLIN	V	(K	TOMMY KELLY	V	(K
JOHN GIBLIN	B	(1	NICO RAMSDEN	G	(1	LINDA LEWIS	V	(C	YVONNE KEELY	V	(CDH
TINA CHARLES	V	(C	MARTIN JAY	V	(C	LIZA STRIKE	V	(CD	BARRY ST JOHN	V	(D
PATRICIA PAAY	V	(D	JOY YATES	V	(D	MADELINE BELL	V	(D	GEORGE FORD	V	(D
PETER CLARKE	V	(D	LEROY WIGGINS	V	(D	LARRY STEEL	V	(D			

H26B HARLIS H26B

Musician	Instr.	Albums	Album	Year / Label / Catalogue
CHARLY MAUCHER	B V	(AB	(A) HARLIS	1975 SKY 001
WERNER LOHR	D V	(AB	(B) NIGHT MEETS THE DAY	1976 SKY 008
WOLFGANG KRANTZ	G	(AB		
ARNDT SCHULZ	G	(AB		

H26C HARLEQUINN H26C

Musician	Instr.	Albums	Album	Year / Label / Catalogue
GEORGE BELANGER	V	(A	(A) LOVE CRIMES	1981 A&M
GARY GOLDEN	K V G	(A		

Musician	Instr.	Albums	Musician	Instr.	Albums	Musician	Instr.	Albums
RAPLH JANES	B	(A	GLEN WILLOWS	G V	(A	DAVID BUDZAK	D V	(A

H27 HARMONIA H27

Musician	Instr.	Albums	Album	Year / Label / Catalogue
DIETER MOEBIUS	K V	(AB	(A) HARMONIA	1973 BRAIN 1044
JOACHIM ROEDELIUS	K V	(AB	(B) DE LUXE	1975 BRAIN 1073
MICHAEL ROTHER	K G V	(AB	( ) DINO	197 BRAIN GER 0040 116
MANI NEUMEIER	D PERC	(B		

H28 HARMONIUM H28

Album	Year / Label / Catalogue
(A) L'HEPTADE	19 CBS 88234

H29 ROY HARPER H29

ROY HARPER G V B K SYN(ALL (A) SOPHISTICATED BEGGAR 1967 STRIKE JHL 105
BILL BRUFORD D (J (A) SOPHISTICATED BEGGAR 1970 YOUNGBLOOD SYB.7
HENRY McCULLOUGH G (K (A) SOPHISTICATED BEGGAR 1972 BIRTH RAB.3 1977 BIGBEN 502
KEITH MOON D ((B) COME OUT FIGHTING GHENGIS SMITH 1967 CBS UK 63184
DAVE COCHRAN (JK (C) FOLKJOKEOPUS 1969 LIBERTY UK LBS 83231
JIMMY PAGE G (RFH (C) FOLKJOKEOPUS 1975 SUNSET UK SLS 50373
JOHN HALSEY D (K (C) FOLKJOKEOPUS 19 WORLD PACIFIC US 21888
RONNIE LANE G B (K (D) FLAT BAROQUE & BERSERK 1970 HARVEST US 418 UK SHVL 776
BRIAN HODGES B (RF (D) FLAT BAROQUE & BERSERK 1978 CHRYSALIS US 1160
DAVE LAWSON K (KQ (E) STORMCOCK 1971 HARVEST UK SHVL 789
LAURIE ALLEN D (BF (E) STORMCOCK 1978 CHRYSALIS US 1161
CHRIS SPEDDING G (J (F) LIFE MASK 1973 HARVEST UK SHVL 808
IAN ANDERSON FLT (H (F) LIFE MASK 1978 CHRYSALIS US 1162
ANDY ROBERTS G (KQ (G) VALENTINE 1974 HARVEST UK SHSP 4027
KEITH EMERSON K (D (G) VALENTINE 1974 PATHE FR 062 05531
TONY CARR D (RF (G) VALENTINE 1978 CHRYSALIS US 1163
BRIAN DAVISON D (DR (H) FLASHES FROM THE ARCHIVES 1974 HARVEST UK SHDW 405
LEE JACKSON B (D (H) FLASHES FROM THE ARCHIVES 197 PATHE FR 162 05736
RAY WARLEIGH WIND (JR (H) FLASHES FROM THE ARCHIVES 1978 CHRYSALIS US 1164
WINGS (K (J) WHEN AN OLD CRICKETER 1975 CHRYSALIS US 1105
TONY VISCONTI RECORDER(D (J) H Q 1975 HARVEST UK SHSP 4046
STEVE BROUGHTON K G V(KJRQ (J) HQ 1975 PATHE FR 066 05883
B J COLE STEEL(KQ (K) BULLINAMINGVASE 1977 HARVEST UK SHSP 4060
HERBIE FLOWERS B (K (K) BULLINAMINGVASE 1977 PATHE FR 068 06336
RUSS B (C (K) ONE OF THOSE DAYS IN ENGLAND 1977 CHRYSALIS US 1138
BRIAN GOFF (K (L) COMMERCIAL BREAK 1977 HARVEST UK SHSP 4077
PERCY JONES B (K (M) THE EARLY YEARS 1977 EMBASSY UK 31544
JIMMY McCULLOCH G (K (N) ROY HARPER 70/75 1978 HARVEST UK SHSM 2025
DAVID BEDFORD K (EGJQ (Q) UNKNOWN SOLDIER 1980 HARVEST UK SHVL 820
MOX (C (R) LIFE MASK 1981
CLEM D (C (K) AFTER LEGAL ACTION(FEB 1979) ONE TRACK REMOVED
NICKY PNO (C
JOHN PAUL JONES B (J SKAILA KANGA (A ALVIN LEE G (K MAX MIDDLETON K (K
DAVE PLOWMAN (K DAVID GILMOUR (JQ JANE (C S FLAVIUS MERCURIUS (E
GRIMETHORPE COLLIERY BAND(J SARA POZZO (Q JIM CUOMO (Q HAYDN BENDALL (Q
NEIL JASON (Q WILL LEE (Q DAVE SCANCE (Q SAL DiTROIA (Q
TONY LEVI (Q DON GROLNICK (Q HUGH BURNS (Q TIM DONALD (Q
JIM BAIN (Q ANDY NEWMARK (Q JIMMY MAELIN (Q PETE WINGFIELD K (Q
GEORGE CONSTANTINO (Q JO PARTRIDGE (Q KATE BUSH V (Q

H30 HARPERS BIZARRE H30

TED TEMPLEMAN G V (ABCDE (A) FEELIN' GROOVY 1967 WB US WS 1693
DICK SCOPPETTONE G (ABCDEF (B) ANYTHING GOES 1967 WB US WS 1716
EDDIE JAMES G (ABCDEF (C) SECRET LIFE OF HARPERS BIZARRE 1968 WB US WS 1739
JOHN PETERSON D (ABCDE (D) HARPERS BIZARRE 4 1969 WB US WS 1784
DICK YOUNT B (ABCDEF (E) BEST OF 1974 WB UK K56044
VAN DYKE PARKS PNO (E (F) AS TIME GOES BY 1976 FOREST BAY CO US 7545

H31 SLIM HARPO H31

SLIM HARPO V HCA G(DIED 1970)ALL (A) A LONG DRINK OF THE BLUES 1965 STATESIDE UK SL 10135
GUITAR GABLE G (DF (B) HE KNEW THE BLUES 19 BLUE HORIZON UK 763844
WARREN STORM D (F (B) HE KNEW THE BLUES 19 EXCELLO US 8013
FATS PERRODIN B (DF (B) HE KNEW THE BLUES 1978 SONET UK SNTF 769
JERRY WEST D (D (C) TIP ON IN 19 PRESIDENT US PTS 1017
BOBBY McBRIDE B (F (C) TIP ON IN 19 EXCELLO US 8008
JAMES JOHNSON G (D (D) TRIGGER FINGER 1971 BLUE HORIZON UK 2431 013
SAMMY K BROWN D (D (E) BLUES HANGOVER 1976 FLYRIGHT UK LP 520
RUDOLPH RICHARD G (D (F) GOT LOVE IF YOU WANT IT 1980 FLYRIGHT UK FLY 558
GEESE AUGUST B (D (G) BABY SCRATCH MY BACK 19 EXCELLO US 8005
CLARENCE ETIENNE D (F (H) RAINING IN MY HEART 19 EXCELLO US 8003
AUSTIN BROUSSARD D (F (I) THE BEST OF 19 EXCELLO US 8010
AL FOREMAN G (F
MERTON THIBODEAUX PNO (F RUFUS THIBODEAUX B (F

H31A GEORGE HARRASMENT H31A

GEORGE HARRASMENT (A (A) MASAI SLEEP WALKING 19 BLACK NOISE UK 12 6
MICHELLE (A
L VOAG B (A THE HOMOSEXUALS (A ZOE (A VIDA (A

H32 CAREY BELL HARRINGTON H32

CAREY BELL HARRINGTON V HCA(AB (A) BLUES HARP 19 DELMARK DS 622
DAVE MYERS B (B (B) LAST NIGHT 1973 BLUESWAY BLS 6079
WILLIE SMITH D (B
EDDIE TAYLOR G (B JOE PERKINS K (B

H33 DERRICK HARRIOTT H33

DERRICK HARRIOTT (ALL (A) UNDERTAKER 19 TROJAN TBL 114
(B) PSYCHEDELIC TRAIN 19 TROJAN TBL 141
(C) REGGAE HITS 1975 TROJAN TRLS 116

H34 DON 'SUGARCANE' HARRIS H34

DON SUGARCANE HARRIS V FDL(ALL (A) KEEP ON DRIVING 19 MUSIDISC 15060 + MPS 68027
VOLKER KRIEGEL G (AFGI (B) FIDDLER ON THE ROCK 1970 BASF878 POLYDOR 20878
TERJE RYPDAL G (C (B) FIDDLER ON THE ROCK 19 MUSIDISC 15062 + MPS 68028
NEVILLE WHITEHEAD B (C (C) GOT THE BLUES 19 POLYDOR 21283
ROBERT WYATT (C (C) GOT THE BLUES 19 MUSIDISC 15079 + MPS 68029
PAUL LAGOS D (BDEJ (D) CUPFUL OF DREAMS 1973 POLYDOR 21792
HARVEY MANDEL G (BDJ (D) CUPFUL OF DREAMS 1973 BASF US MPS 68030
LARRY TAYLOR B (BD (E) I'M YOUR CASE 19 MPS 21912 MPS 68031
JOHNNY OTIS (H (F) FLASHIN' TIME 19 SONOPRESSE 60204 MPS 68032
SHUGGIE OTIS G B (H (G) SUGARCANE 1971 EPIC US 26524 + 30027
CLIFTON EDDIE D (E (H) DON'SUGARCANE 'HARRIS 1970 EPIC 26286
DEWEY TERRY K (EDFI (I) KEY STOP 19 BASF MPS 68032
JAMES BRADSHAW G (E (J) CHOICE CUTS 1972 EPIC US 31401
RANDY RESNICK G (EDJ (K) NEW VIOLIN SUMMIT 1971 METRONOME 22720
RICHARD APLANALP SAX (E JEAN LUC PONTE FDL (K MICHAEL URBANIAK VLN (K
BILL SPRAGUE TPT (E DALNE VAIL V (E ELSIE LEWIS V (E TONY OXLEY D (A
WOLFGANG DAUNER K (C GUNTER LENZ (FI TODD CANADY (FI VICTOR CONTE B (DJ

H35 EMMYLOU HARRIS H35

EMMYLOU HARRIS V G (ALL (A) GLIDING BIRD 1969 JUBILEE US JGS 0031
BEN KEITH STEEL(BCG (A) GLIDING BIRD 1979 PYE UK PKL 5577
BYRON BERLINE FDL MAND (BC (A) GLIDING BIRD 19 AMOS US 12052
JAMES BURTON G (BCDEGL (B) PIECES OF THE SKY 1975 REPRISE US 2213 UK K 54037
GLEN D HARDIN K (BCDEGL (B) PIECES OF THE SKY 197 WB RI US 2284
EMORY GORDY B (CDEGLK (C) ELITE HOTEL 1976 REPRISE US 2236 UK K 54060
JOHN WARE D (CDEGLK (D) LUXURY LINER 1977 REPRISE US 2998
HANK DE VITO STEEL(CDEGL (D) LUXURY LINER 1977 WB US 3115 UK K 56334
RODNEY CROWELL G V (CDEGL (E) 1/4 MOON IN A TEN CENT TOWN 1978 WB US 3141 UK K 56443
ALBERT LEE G V (DEGLK (F) PROFILE (COMP) 1978 WB US 3258 UK K 56570
RAY POHLMAN B (B (G) BLUE KENTUCKY GIRL 1979 WB UK K 56627
RON TUTT D (BCG (H) CHRISTMAS ALBUM(LIGHT IN THE STABLE)79 WB US 3484
HERB PEDERSEN G BANJ V (BCD1 (J) HER BEST SONGS 1980 K TEL UK NE 1058
DON EVERLY V (G (K) ROSES IN THE SNOW 1980 WB US 3422 UK K 56796
BERNIE LEADON V G BANJ (BC (L) EVANGELINE 1981 WB US 3508 UK K 56880
BRIAN AHERN B G(BCDEGLK
RICK CUNHA G (BCD RICHARD GREENE FDL (B FAYSSOUX STARLING V (BCDEG BILL PAYNE K (BC
BRUCE ARCHER G (AB TOM GUIDERA B (B DANNY PENDLETON STEEL(B RICKY SKAGGS FDL MAND(BDGLK
DUKE BARDWELL B (BG AMOS GARRETT G (BCL MARK CUFF D (B LINDA RONSTADT V (BCGLK
DIANNE BROOKS V (CDE JOHN STARLING V (C JONATHAN EDWARDS V (C MIKE AULDRIDGE G (CD
DOLLY PARTON V (DGLK NICOLETTE LARSON V (DE MICK RAPHAEL HCA(CDEGL CHERYL WARREN V (GL
FRANK RICKARD G (L TONY RICE G V (LK SHARON WHITE V (LK DON JOHNSON K V(L
DAVID BRIGGS K (L HAL BLAINE F (L BRYAN BOWERS AHARP(K BUCK WHITE K V (K
TONY BROWN K (GL MIKE BOWDEN B (GL LINCOLN DAVIS ACC (G TANYA TUCKER V (G
SHARON HICKS V (G CRAIG SAFAN STR (L JERRY DOUGLAS DOB G(LK WAYLON JENNINGS V (L
BARRY TASHIAN V (L LARRIE LONDIN D (L STEVE FISHELL DOB G(L MAC REBBENACK K (L
LYNN LANGHAM SYN (L WILLIE NELSON G (K JOHNNY CASH V (K

H35A HI TIDE HARRIS H35A

HI TIDE HARRIS V G (AB (A) CELEBRATING WITH HI TIDE HARRIS 1978 RCA JAP RVL 8031
JUNJI YAMAGISHI G (A (B) GENTLEMANS BLUES 197 RCA JAP RVL
OSAMU ISHIDA G (A
SHINJI SHIOTSUGU G (A TADASHI KOBORI B (A YU FUJII B (A TERUO MATSUMOTO D (A
CHARLES SHIMIZU K (A YASUHARU NAKANISHI K (A TATSURO KONDO K (A SHUICHI CHINO K (A
RYUICHIRO SENOO HCA (A TETSU NAKAMURA SAX (A JUNICHI KANEKAZI TPT (A ICHIRO ARAI HRNS (A

H35B GENE HARRIS H35B

GENE HARRIS G V (A (A) ASTRAL SIGNAL 1974 BLUENOTE US LA 313
HARVEY MASON D (A
JERRY PETERS K V (A CHUCK RAINEY B (A JOHN ROWEN G (A DAVID T WALKER G (A
KEG JOHNSON V (A JIM SIFFLETT HRNS (A GEORGE BOHANNON HRNS (A OSCAR BRASHEAR HRNS(A
SIDNEY MULDROW HRNS (A ERNIE WATTS HRNS (A MAXINE WILLARD WATERS V (A JULIA TILLMAN WATERS V(A
OREN WATERS V (A TRISHA CHAMBERLAIN V (A LYNN MACK V (A

H36 JET HARRIS H36

JET HARRIS B (A (A) REMEMBERING 1976 DECCA UK REM.1
TONY MEEHAN D (A

H36A JOHNNY HARRIS H36A

JOHNNY HARRIS (A (A) ALL TO BRING YOU MORNING 1973 WB UK K56185
JON ANDERSON V (A
STEVE HOWE G (A

H37 SHAKEY JAKE HARRIS H37

SHAKEY JAKE HARRIS HCA V(ABC (A) FURTHER ON UP THE ROAD 1969 LIBERTY UK 83217
JOHN MAYALL G K (B (A) FURTHER ON UP THE ROAD 19 WORLD PACIFIC US 21886
KENNY COURTNEY HCA (A (B) THE DEVIL'S HARMONICA 1972 POLYDOR US 5014 UK 2391 015
ELLIOT INGBER G (B (C) GOOD TIMES 19 BLUESVILLE US 1008
PHIL PARKER D (B (D) MOUTH HARP BLUES 19 BLUESVILLE US 1027
WANDERING JOHN PNO (A
LUTHER ALLISON G (A ROBERT MOJO ELEM B (A SUNNYLAND SLIM PNO (A DENNY BRUCE PERC(A
FRANCIS CLAY D (A STEVE CUMMINS PERC (A FREDDY ROBINSON G (B LARRY TAYLOR B (B
RON SELICO D (B

H37A SHAUN HARRIS H37A

SHAUN HARRIS G V B(A (A) SHAUN HARRIS 1973 CAPITOL ST 11168
DAN HARRIS G V (A
BEN BENAY G (A DEAN PARKS G (A BOBBY PHILLIPS G (A HAL BLAINE D (A
JIM GORDON D (A JOHN GUERIN D (A JOHANNA HARRIS K (A LARRY KNECHTEL K (A
MICHAEL OMARTIAN K (A CAROL KAYE B (A JOE OSBORN B (A BRUCE JOHNSTON V (A

H37B BILLY HARRISON H37B

BILLY HARRISON V G (A (A) BILLY WHO?; 1980 VAGABOND GERM VRLP 8 80001
NIELS TABY D (A
PETER URBAN K (A MARTIN TIEFENSEE B (A HANNES BAUER G (A RAINER BAUMANN G (A

H37C WYNONIE HARRIS H37C

WYNONIE HARRIS G V (A (A) GOOD ROCKIN' BLUES 19 KING US 1086

H38 DON HARRISON BAND H38

DON HARRISON V G (ABC (A) DON HARRISON BAND 1976 ATLANTIC US 18171 UK K 50263
STU COOK B V (ABC (B) RED HOT 1976 ATLANTIC US 18208 UK K 50340
DOUG CLIFFORD D V (ABC (C) NOT FAR FROM FREE 1977 MERCURY US SRM11185 UK9100 044
RUSSELL DASHIELL G V (ABC
JOHN TANNER K (B MICHAEL CARROLL B (C JEFF MORROW K (C JOEL PESKIN SAX (C
GARY GOSSETT D (C KAREN FRIEDMAN V (C NOVI NOVAG VILA (C DAN STICKLER G (C
PAT MATA V (C MEMPHIS HRNS (A

H38A GEFF HARRISON H38A

GEFF HARRISON V (A (A) TOGETHER 19 JUPITER 25595
PETER OEHLER G V (A
ALAN WROE B V (A ASTOR ASTOR D V (A CHRIS KLOBER K V (A

H39 GEORGE HARRISON H39

GEORGE HARRISON G V (ALL (A) WONDERWALL 1968 APPLE FR 90490 US 3350 UK SAPCOR 1
ERIC CLAPTON G (CDFK (B) ELECTRONIC SOUNDS 1969 APPLE US 3358 UK ZAPPLE2
JESSE ED DAVIS G (DG (C) ALL THINGS MUST PASS 1971 APPLE STCH639+PATHE FR 040789
RINGO STARR D (CDFE (D) CONCERT FOR BANGLA DESH 1972 APPLE STCX3385
JIM KELTNER D (DFEG (E) LIVING IN A MATERIAL WORLD 1973 APPLE PAS10006 US 3410
KLAUS VOORMANN B (CDFEG (F) DARK HORSE 1974 APPPLE PAS 10008 US 3418
BILLY PRESTON K (CDFGH (F) DARK HORSE 1974 PATHE FR 068 05774
RICHARD TEE K (GH (F) DARK HORSE 1980 M F P UK 50510
LEON RUSSELL K B V(DG (G) EXTRA TEXTURE 1975 APPLE PAS 10009 US 3420
STEVE WINWOOD K V (K (G) EXTRA TEXTURE 1975 PATHE FR 068 05952
WILLIE WEEKS B (FKGH (H) 33 1/3 1976 DARK HORSE K 56319+ US DH3005
ANDY NEWMARK D (FKG (J) BEST OF 1976 PARLOPHONE UK 10011
GARY WRIGHT K (CFEGH (J) BEST OF 1976 PATHE FR 068 06249
MICK JONES G (F (J) BEST OF 1976 CAPITOL US 11578
DEREK TAYLOR (G (J) BEST OF 1981 M F P UK 50523
CHUCK FINDLEY HRNS (FG (K) GEORGE HARRISON 1979 DARK HORSE K 56562+ US 3255
ALI AKBAR KHAN (D (L) SOMEWHERE IN ENGLAND 1981 DARK HORSE US 3492 UK 56870
DERREK VAN EATON V (F
ROGER KELLAWAY PNO (F NICKY HOPKINS PNO (FEG DAVE MASON G V (C JIM PRICE (C
BOBBY KEYS SAX (C GINGER BAKER D (C RON WOOD G (F JIM HORN FLT (FEDG
ROBBEN FORD G (F PATTI HARRISON V (F TOM SCOTT SAX (FG LON VAN EATON V (F
EMIL RICHARDS PREC(FGHK MAX BENNETT B (F ALAN WHITE D (C ALVIN LEE G (F
JOHN GUERIN D (F PAUL STALLWORTH B (G LEGS LARRY SMITH V (G NORM KINNEY PERC (G
GAYLE LEVANY HARP (K JIM GORDON D (EG ZAKIR HASSIEN TABLA(E CARL RADLE B (DG
ALLA RAKAN TABLA(D BOB DYLAN V HCA (D DON PRESTON V (D RAVI SHANKAR SITAR (D
KAMBLA RAVARTY PERC (D PETER HAM G (D JOHN BARNHAM STR (E DAVID FOSTER K (GH
PETER SELLERS (G DON AIRALI (G DENNIS KILLEEN (G ALVIN TAYLOR D (H
ERIC IDLE (G CHUCK TRAMELL (G

H39A JERRY HARRISON H39A

JERRY HARRISON V G B K(A (A) THE RED AND BLACK 1981 SIRE UK SRK 3631
YOGI HORTON D (A
JOHN COOKSEY D (A STEVE SCALES D PERC(A GEORGE NURRAY B (A TINKER BARFIELD B (A
BERNIE WORRELL K (A ADRIAN BELOW G (A NONA HENDRYX V (A DOLETTE McDONALD V (A
KOKO MAE EVANS G (A DAVE JERDEN PROD (A

H40 MIKE HARRISON H40

MIKE HARRISON V K HCA (ABC (A) MIKE HARRISON 1971 ISLAND US 9313 UK ILPS 9170
KEN IVERSON D V (A (B) SMOKESTACK LIGHTNING 1972 ISLAND US 9321 UK ILPS 9209
PETER BATEY B (A (C) RAINBOW RIDER 1975 GOODEAR UK 7002+SONOPRESSE37007
NORBERT PUTNAM B (C (C) RAINBOW RIDER 1975 ISLAND US 9359
IAN HERBERT G V K(A
FRANK KENYON G V (A ARTHUR BELCHER SAX (A PETER CARR G (B JIMMY JOHNSON G (B
WAYNE PERKINS G (B LUTHER GROSVENOR G (B BARRY BECKETT K (B CLAYTON IVEY K (B
DAVID HOOD B (B HARRISON CALLOWAY TPT (B MIKE STACEY TPT (B HARVEY THOMPSON SAX (B
RONNIE EADES SAX (B CHARLES ROSE TROM (B MORGAN FISHER K (C KENNY BUTTREY D (C
MICKY JONES G (C BOB COHEN G (C WAYNE JACKSON HRNS (C KIRK LORANGE G (C
MEMPHIS HRNS (C 20TH CENTURY SINGERS (C CORONA STAGE SCHOOL V(C

H40A NEIL HARRISON H40A

NEIL HARRISON V K G (A (A) ALL DRESSED UP WITH NOWHERE TO GO 1974 DERAM SML 1115
JULI LANDO V (A
ADE COOKE G SYN(A ROB WRIGHT G V (A MIKE FREEMAN B (A JOHN MEYDAM D PERC(A
GRAHAM PRESCETT B K HCA(A B J COLE STEEL(A PIP WILLIAMS G (A PAUL KEOUGH G (A
JOHN RICHARDSON D (A JIM LAWLESS PERC (A CHRIS LAWRENCE B (A PAUL NIEMAN TROM(A
RICK KENTON K (A KEITH WHITING PROD (A

H41 WILBERT HARRISON H41

WILBERT HARRISON V G (ALL (A) LETS WORK TOGETHER 1969 SUE US 8801 LONDON UK SH8415
(B) BATTLE OF THE GIANTS(1 SIDE) 1962 JOY JOYS191
(C) KANSAS CITY 19 SPHERE US 7000
(D) WILBERT HARRISON 1972 BUDDAH US 5092
(E) SOUL FOOD MAN 19 CHELSEA US 523
(F) ANYTHING YOU WANT 19 WET SOUL US 1001
(G) SHOOT YOU FULL OF LOVE 19 JUGGERNAUT US 8803

H42 MELANIE HARROLD H42

MELANIE HARROLD V (AB (A) FANCY THAT(AS JOANNA CARLIN) 1977 DJM DJF 20508
JERRY DONAHUE G (A (B) BLUE ANGEL 1979 DJM DJF 20550
PAT DONALDSON B (A
JOHNNY VAN DERRICK VLN (A TOMMY EYRE K (A BOB HIRSCHMAN TROM (A HENRY SPINETTI D (A
GLEN LE FLEUR D (A PETE ZORN SAX FLT (A KEITH NELSON BANJO(A PETE SOLLEY K (A
MICK MOODY G (A MARTIN JAY V (A GRAHAME SMITH FDL (B JULIAN LITTMAN G (B
PAUL DI VINCI V (B RICHARD BRUNTON G (B BILL SKEAT K FLT(B SIMON MORTON PERC(B
MALCOLM GRIFFITHS TROM (B BETSY COOKE V (B ALBERT WING SAX (B LIAM GENOCKEY D (B
GARY TAYLOR B (B

H42A DEBBIE HARRY H42A

DEBBIE HARRY V (A (A) KOO KOO 1981 CHRYSALIS 1347 GER 203810
NILE RODGERS G V (A
BERNARD EDWARDS B (A ROBERT SABINO K (A TONY THOMPSON D (A RAYMOND JONES K (A
CHRIS STEIN G (A VINCENT DE ROSA HRNS (A RAY MALDONADO HRNS (A SAMMY FIGUEROA PERC(A
MANUEL BADRENA PERC (A ROGER SQUITERO PERC (A SPUD & PU DEVO V (A GORDON GORDY V (A
FONZI THORNTON V (A CHUCK MARTIN (A

H43 HARSH REALITY H43

MARK GRIFFITHS G (A (A) HEAVEN & HELL 1969 PHILIPS SBL 7891
CARL BARNWELL G (A
ROGER SWALLOW D (A CLIFF JENKINS (A STEVE MILLER (A

H44 BILLY HART H44

BILLY HART (A (A) ENCHANCE 1978 HORIZON AMLJ 725

H45 MICKEY HART H45

MICKEY HART D V (A — (A) ROLLING THUNDER — 1972 WB US 2635 UK K 46182
STEPHEN STILLS G V (A
JOHN CIPOLLINA G (A — JERRY GARCIA G (A — CARMELO GARCIA TIMBALES (A — BOB WEIR G V (A
STEVE SHUSTER FLT (A — BARRY MELTON G (A — BILL CHAMPLIN K (A — ALLA RAKHA (A
TOWER OF POWER HRNS (A — DAVID FREIBERG K G V B(A — ROBBIE STOKES G (A — GRACE SLICK V (A
PHIL LESH V (A — MIKE HINTON MARIMBA (A — ZAKIR HUSSAIN TABLA(A — SAM ANDREW G (A
PAUL KANTNER V (A — GREG ERRICO D (A — TERRY HAGGERTY B (A — NANCY HINTON MARIMBA(A

H46 MIKE HART H46

MIKE HART G V (AB — (A) MIKE HART BLEEDS — 1970 DANDELION UK 63756
NEIL FORD G K (A — (B) BASHER CHALKY PONGO & ME — 1972 POLYDOR UK 2310 211
JAN SCHELLHAS K (A
DAVE PAULL B (A — JOHN SKORSKY D (A — RICK SANDERS G (A — ANDY DONALDSON HCA (A
VIVIAN STANSHALL V REC(B — MORAY SLADEN BAN (B — ROBIN PARK K (B — ED JONES B (B
JOHN RAMSEY D V (B — DAVE MURRICANE K (B — JOHN COMMING V (B — BOB HAMILTON V (B
MIKE HARRIGAN V (B — TONY HAYGARTH V (B — DEREK O'CONNOR V (B — JOHN SHRAPNEL V (B

H47 TIM HART H47

TIM HART G V (A — (A) TIM HART — 1979 CHRYSALIS UK CHR1218 GER 6307658
RICK KEMP B (A
NIGEL PEGRUM D (A — VIC EMERSON SYN (A — STEWART GOLDRING K (A — ASHLEY MULFORD G (A
MADDY PRIOR V (A — STEVE BROOMHEAD G (A — DES TONGUE B (A — PETE GLENNON B (A
DAVE HASSEL PERC (A — ALAN FAWKES WIND (A

H48 TIM HART & MADDY PRIOR H48

TIM HART G V (ALL — (A) FOLK SONGS OF OLDE ENGLAND 1 — 1968 B&C TEPEE105
MADDY PRIOR V (ALL — (A) FOLK SONGS OF OLDE ENGLAND 1 — 19 ADRHYTHM ARP 53
ANDY IRVINE MAND (C — (A) FOLK SONGS OF OLDE ENGLAND 1 — 1974 MOONCREST CREST 23
JOHN RYAN B (C — (B) FOLK SONGS OF OLDE ENGLAND 2 — 19 ADRHYTHM ARP 54
GERRY CONWAY D (C — (B) FOLK SONGS OF OLDE ENGLAND 2 — 1976 MOONCREST CREST 26
PAT DONALDSON B (C — (B) FOLK SONGS OF OLDE ENGLAND 2 — 1968 TE PEE
(C) SUMMER SOLSTICE — 1972 B&C CAS 1035
(C) SUMMER SOLSTICE — 1974 MOONCREST CREST 12

H49 JOHN HARTFORD H49

JOHN HARTFORD G FDL BAN(ALL — (A) LOOKS AT LIFE — 1967 RCA US LSP 3687
BENNY MARTIN FDL (KM — (B) EARTHWORDS & MUSIC — 1967 RCA US LSP 3796
KENNY MALONE D (KM — (C) THE LOVE ALBUM — 1968 RCA US LSP 3884
DALTON DILLINGHAM B (K — (D) HOUSING PROJECT — 1968 RCA US LSP 3998
ROY HUSKY JR B (MK — (E) GENTLE ON MY MIND — 1968 RCA US LSP 4068
JIMMY COLVARD G (MK — (F) JOHN HARTFORD — 1969 RCA US LSP 4156
DALE SELLERS G (K — (G) IRON MOUNTAIN DEPOT — 1970 RCA US LSP 4337
DAVID BRIGGS K (KM — (H) AERO PLAIN — 1971 WB US 1916
BUDDY EMMONS STEEL(KM — (I) MORNING BUGLE — 1972 WB US 2651
SAM BUSH V MAND(KM — (J) MARK TWANG — 1976 FLYING FISH US FF 020
MAC WISEMAN V (K — (J) MARK TWANG — 1976 SONET UK SNTF 700
LARRIE LONDIN D (M — (K) NOBODY KNOWS WHAT YOU DO — 1976 FLYING FISH US FF 028
CURLY SECKLER V (M — (K) NOBODY KNOWS WHAT YOU DO — 1977 SONET UK SNTF 727
HENRY STRZELECKI B (M — (L) DILLARD HARTFORD DILLARD (*) — 1977 FLYING FISH US FF 036
PIG ROBBINS PNO (M — (L) DILLARD HARTFORD DILLARD (*) — 1977 SONET UK SNTF 730
JACK GREENE V (N — (M) ALL IN THE NAME OF LOVE — 1977 FLYING FISH US FF 044
JEANNIE ELLEY V (N — (M) ALL IN THE NAME OF LOVE — 1978 SONET UK SNTF 747
DIANE TIDWELL V (N — (N) HEADING DOWN INTO THE MYSTERY BELOW 78 FLYING FISH US FF 063
BILLY RAY REYNOLDS V (N — (O) SLUMBERIN' ON THE CUMBERLAND — 1979 FLYING FISH US FF 095
LISA SILVER V (N — (P) YOU AND ME AT HOME — 1981 FLYING FISH US 228
PAT BURTON (A
(*) FULL LINE UP IN DILLARD HARTFORD DILLARD ENTRY)

H50 KEEF HARTLEY H50

KEEF HARTLEY D (ALL — (A) HALFBREED — 1969 DERAM UK SML 1037 US 18024
MILLER ANDERSON G V (ABCDE — (B) BATTLE OF N W 6 — 1970 DERAM UK SML 1054 US 18035
PETER DINES K (AD — (C) THE TIME IS NEAR — 1970 DERAM UK SML 1071 US 18047
SPIT JAMES G (AB — (D) OVERDOG — 1971 DERAM UK DSL 2 US 18057
GARY THAIN B (ABCDEF — (E) LITTLE BIG BAND — 1971 DERAM UK SDL 4
HENRY LOWTHER VLN TPT(ABC — (F) SEVENTY SECOND BRAVE — 1972 DERAM UK SDL 9 US 18065
HARRY BECKETT TPT (ABE — (G) LANCASHIRE HUSTLER — 1973 DERAM UK SDL 13 US 18070
LYN DOBSON WIND (ABE — (H) THE BEST OF (DBL) — 1974 DERAM UK DPA 3011/2
CHRIS MERCER SAX (ABEF — (I) THROUGHOUT THE YEARS (DBL) — 197 LONDON US 2 6001
MICK WEAVER K (BDFG
RAY WARLEIGH FLT (B — MICK TAYLOR G (B — MIKE DAVIS TPT (BE — DAVE CASWELL TPT (CD
LYLE JENKINS SAX (CD — BARBARA THOMPSON WIND (BE — STUART WICKS K (C — DEL ROLL PERC(C
JOHNNY ALMOND FLT (D — JON HISEMAN D (D — INGRID THOMAS V (D — JOAN KNIGHTON V (D
VALERIE CHARRINGTON V (D — PETE WINGFIELD K V (F — JUNIOR KERR G V (FG — NICK NEWELL WIND (F
JESS RODEN V (G — JEAN ROUSSEL K (G — PHIL CHEN B (G — PETE GAGE G (G
ELKIE BROOKS V (G — ROBERT PALMER V (G — JIMMY JEWELL SAX (BC — PETE YORK PERC(E
DEREK AUSTIN K (E — ROGER WADE SAX (E — MIKE ROSEN TPT (E — TERRY NOONAN TPT (E
MARTIN DROVER TPT (E — DANNY ALLMARK TROM (E — DEREK WADSWORTH TROM (E — JOHN MAYALL V (A

H51 DAN HARTMAN H51

DAN HARTMAN V K G B (ALL — (A) IMAGES — 1976 BLUE SKY US 34322
EDGAR WINTER HRNS (ABC — (B) INSTANT REPLAY — 1978 BLUE SKY US 35641 UK 83265
HILLY MICHAELS D (BC — (C) RELIGHT MY FIRE — 1979 BLUE SKY US 36302 UK 84073
BLANCHE NAPOLEON V (BC
G E SMITH G (BC — LARRY WASHINGTON CONGA(BC — VINNIE CUSANO G V (B — JOHN WILCOX D (A
JOHN SIEGLER B (A — RONNIE MONTROSE G (A — RICK DERRINGER G (A — CARL HARTMAN (A
CLARENCE CLEMONS SAX (A — REVELATION V (A — TOM STROHMAN FLT (A — RANDY BRECKER HRNS(A
GEORGE YOUNG HRNS (A — TONY POGANO HRNS (A — LARRY SADLER D (A — JOE ABBONDANZA B (A
JIMMY MAELEN PERC (C — STEVIE WONDER HCA (C — PHIL HOUGHTON CONGA(C — LOLEATTA HOLLOWAY V (C
BRIAN BRAKE D (C — CRAIG PEYTON VIBES(C — OOGAH BUNCH V (C — SCHOOLHOUSE KIDS V (C

H52 ALEX HARVEY H52

ALEX HARVEY G V (ALL — (A) ALEX HARVEY SOUL BAND — 1964 POLYDOR 237624 KARUSSEL GER 635 049
ZAL CLEMINSON G (EFGHIJKLMO — (B) THE BLUES — 1964 POLYDOR 5LPHM237641
CHRIS GLEN B (EFGHIJKLMO — (C) ROMAN WALL BLUES — 1969 FONTANA UK STL 5534
MICKEY KEENE G (C — (D) JOKER IS WILD — 1972 METRONOME GER 15429
LESLIE HARVEY G (C — (D) THIS IS — 19 METRONOME RI GER 2001
HUGH McKENNA K (EFGHIJKLM — (E) FRAMED — 1972 VERTIGO UK 6360 081
TED McKENNA D (EFGHIJKLMO — (F) NEXT — 1974 VERTIGO US 1017 UK 6360 103
TOMMY EYRE K (1OR — (G) IMPOSSIBLE DREAM — 1974 VERTIGO US 2000 UK 6360 112
PHIL KENZIE SAX (E — (H) TOMORROW BELONGS TO ME — 1975 VERTIGO US 2004 UK 6360 120
BUD BEADLE SAX (E — (I) LIVE — 1975 ATLANTIC US18184 VERTIGO UK6360 122
DAVID BATCHELOR V (F — (J) PENTHOUSE TAPES — 1975 VERTIGO EURO 9103 205 UK 9102 007
VICKI SILVA V (G — (K) STORIES — 1976 MOUNTAIN UK TOPS 112
VICKY BROWN V (H — (L) BIG HITS & CLOSE SHAVES — 1977 VERTIGO UK 6360 147
LIZA STRIKE V (H — (M) FOURPLAY — 1977 MOUNTAIN 4 UK TOPC5006
BARRY ST JOHN V (H — (N) PRESENTS THE LOCK NESS MONSTER 1977 K TEL NE 984
B J COLE STEEL(I — (O) ROCK DRILL — 1978 MOUNTAIN UK TOPS 114
SIMON CHATTERTON D (1R — (P) VAMBO ROOLS — 197 VERTIGO EURO 6370422
MATTHEW CANG G (1R — (Q) COLLECTORS ITEMS — 1980 MOUNTAIN UK TOPS 129
DON WELLER SAX (1R — (R) MAFIA STOLE MY GUITAR — 1979 RCA UK PL 25257
GORDON SELLARS B (1R — (1) LIVE LINE UP
MAURICE COCKERILL K (C — ( ) ATTENTION — 19 FONTANA GER 9199 091
PETER WOLFE D (C
BUD PARKS TPT (C — DEREK WATKINS TPT (C — ASHTON TOOTLE WIND (C — LAURIE BAKER B ELEC(C

H52A ALEXANDER HARVEY H52A

ALEXANDER HARVEY V (ALL — (A) ALEX HARVEY — 1971 CAPITOL US 789
CRAIG DOERGE PNO (A — (B) SOUVENIRS — 1973 CAPITOL US EST 11128
PETE SEARS K B (B — (C) ALEXANDER — 1974
HONEY COMBS V (A — (D) PRESHUS CHILD — 197 KAMA SUTRA US KSBS 2618
AYNSLEY DUNBAR D (B — (E) PURPLE CRUSH — 1978 BUDDAH US 5696
JOHN HOBBS PNO (A
DAVID JACKSON B (A — DENNIS ST JOHN D (AB — KEN VASSEY G (A — DANNY ROWLAND G (A
RANDY STERLING B G (A — AL PERKINS STEEL (A — KENNY ROGERS V (A — CAROL CARMICHAEL V (A
LARRY CANSLER STRING(A — VANGIE CARMICHAEL V (A — JOHN HARRIS PNO (A — KENNETH BUTTREY D (A
MAC GAYDEN G (A — WELDON MYRICK STEEL(A — WAYNE MOSS G (A — BROOKS HUNNICUTT V (A
KIM GARNES V (A — DAVID ELLINGTON V (A — BUDDY SPICHER VLN (A — JOE ALLEN B (A
JIMMY ISBELL D (A — KEN MALONE D (A — JOHN DARNALL G (A — BOBBY THOMPSON G (A
TRACY NELSON V (A — DIANNE DAVIDSON V (D — NEIL SCHON G (B — ROBBIE MONTGOMERY V (B
RUSSEL DASHIELL G (B — BRUCE GARY D (B — STEVE LEFEVER B (B — EMORY GORDY B (B
VANETTA FIELDS V (B — RICHARD BENNETT G (B — BETTY GOUCHE V (B — DELORES PATTERSON V (B
DENISE ERWIN V (B — CLYDIE KING V (B — SHIRLEY MATTEWS V (B

H53 RICHARD HARVEY H53

RICHARD HARVEY WIND (A — (A) DIVISION ON A GROUND — 1975 TRANSATLANTIC TRA 292

H54 GORDON HASKELL H54

GORDON HASKELL G V (AB — (A) SAIL IN MY BOAT — 1969 CBS UK 63741
JOHN WETTON B K V(B — (B) IT IS AND IT ISN'T — 1974 ATLANTIC US 33378 UK K40311
DAVE KAFFINETTI K (B
BILL ATKINSON D (B — ALAN BARRY G (B — ARIF MARDIN K (B — DAVID SPINOZZA G (B
NEAL ROSENGARDEN PNO (B — EDDIE BRIGATI V (B — DAVID BRIGATI V (B

H55 ANNIE HASLAM H55

ANNIE HASLAM V (A — (A) ANNIE IN WONDERLAND — 1978 SIRE US 6046 WB UK K 56453
JON CAMP G B (A
DAVE DONOVAN D (A — LOUIS CLARK SYN (A — ROY WOOD G B K D WIND(A

H55A HASSLES H55A

JOHN EDWARD DIZEK V PERC(AB — (A) HASSLES — 19 US US UAS 6631
BILLY JOSEPH JOEL V K(AB — (B) HOUR OF THE WOLF — 19 UA US UAS 6699
HOWARD ARTHUR BLAUVELT B(A
JONATHAN SMALL D (AB — RICHARD McKENNER G (A

H55B TORU HATANO H55B

TORU HATANO ALL INST(A — (A) LOVE FOR YOU — 1976 MULAND LX 7024M

H56 GEORGE HATCHER H56

GEORGE HATCHER V (ABC — (A) DRY RUN — 1976 UA UK UAG 29997
JOHN THOMAS G (ABC — (B) HAVE BAND WILL TRAVEL(10") — 1977 UA UK EXP 100
STEVE WREN K (ABC — (C) TALKIN' TURKEY — 1977 UA UK UAS 30090
JAMES MORGAM G (D — (D) RICH GIRL — 1978 SHARK GER 148 502
HARRIS JOANNOU B V (ABC
PHIL SWAN G (ABC — TERRY SLADE D (ABC — JOHN McFEE STEEL (C — HUEY LOUIS HCA (C
TONY CARR PERC (C — DYAN BIRCH V (C — FRANK COLLINS V (C — PADDY McHUGH V (C
PETE GOSHING G (D — GERAINT WATKINS K (D — RENATE MAUERER V (D — CLAUDIA SCHWARZ V (D
GITTA WALTHER V (D — VIC YOUNG B (D — MAC POOLE D (D

H56A HATE H56A

JAMES LACEY G (A — (A) HATE KILLS — 1970 FAMOUS US 5752
LEONARD GRAHAM B (A
ALAN PRATT D (A — NEIL BRUCE K (A — ROBERT MUNRO V (A

H57 HATFIELD & THE NORTH H57

RICHARD SINCLAIR B V (AB — (A) HATFIELD & THE NORTH — 1974 VIRGIN UK V2008
PIP PYLE D (AB — (B) THE ROTTERS CLUB — 1975 VIRGIN UK V2030
STEVE MILLER K (— (C) AFTERS — 1979 VIRGIN UK VR5
PHIL MILLER G (AB
DAVID SINCLAIR K (— DAVE STEWART K (AB — AMANDA PARSONS V (AB — BARBARA GASKIN V (AB
ANN ROSENTHAL V (AB — GEOFF LEIGH WIND (A — JEREMY BAINES WIND (A — ROBERT WYATT V D(A
JIMMY HASTINGS WIND (B — MONT CAMPBELL HRNS (B — LINDSAY COOPER WIND (B — TIM HODGKINSON CLAR(B

H57A HELMUT HATTLER H57A

HELMUT HATTLER B V (A — (A) BASEBALL — 1977 EMI GER 32523
INGO BIRSCHOF K (A
PETER WOLFBRANDT G (A — TRUC SSERC D (A — GERD DUDEK SAX (A — ANDY GOLDNER V (A
NOPS NOPPENEY VLA (A — JAN FRIDE D (A — JOEY ALBRECHT G (A — ROLAND SCHAEFFER SAX(A
ELMER LOUIS PERC (A

H58 DONNIE HATHAWAY H58

DONNIE HATHAWAY V (ALL — (A) EVERYTHING IS EVERYTHING — 1970 ATLANTIC US 33332 UK 2465 019
ROBERTA FLACK V (DF — (A) EVERYTHING IS EVERYTHING — 1971 ATLANTIC UK K40063
ERIC GALE G (F — (B) DONNIE HATHAWAY — 1970 ATLANTIC US 33360 UK 503 068
DAVID SPINOZZA G (F — (B) DONNIE HATHAWAY — 1971 ATLANTIC US UK K40241
CORNELL DUPREE G (BFC — (C) LIVE — 1972 ATLANTIC US 33386 UK K40369
PHIL UPCHURCH B G (FCB — (D) FLACK & HATHAWAY — 197 ATLANTIC UK K40380
MIKE HOWARD G (FC — (E) EXTENSION OF MAN — 1973 ATLANTIC US 7029 UK K40487
KEITH LOVING G (F — (F) BEST OF — 1980 ATLANTIC US 38107 UK K50525
DAVE SANBORN WIND (F — (G) IN PERFORMANCE — 1980 ATLANTIC US 19278 UK K50742
HERB SMITH B (F
CHUCK RAINEY B (FB — DEREK GRAVES B (F — BERNARD PURDIE D (F — STEVE NOVOSEL B (FB
WILLIE WEEKS B (FC — BILLY COBHAM F (F — AL JACKSON D (FB — MORRIS JENNINGS D (F
FRED WHITE D (FC — RAY LUCAS D (F — BILLY JOHNSON D (F — RALPH McDONALD PERC(F
EARL DEROUEN PERC (FC — JACK JENNINGS PERC (FB — LEONARD GIBBS PERC (F — JOE GENTLE WIND(F
KING CURTIS SAX (FB — I STONE V (B — L TYNES V (B — CISSY HOUSTON V (B
SYLVIA SHEMWELL V (B — DEIDRE TUCK V (B — J R BAILEY V (B — MYRNA SUMMERS V (B
S WHITE V (B — JOE NEWMAN TPT (B — MYRNA SMITH V (B — JUDY CLAY V (B
SAMMY TURNER V (B — RONALD BRIGHT V (B — THE INTERDENOMINATIONAL SINGERS V(B

H58A HAVE MERCY H58A

STEVE BAKER G V HCA(A — (A) BOODLAM — 1977 ANTAGON 3209
BRIAN BARNETT V G DOB(A
DICK BIRD V G DOB(A — JON ECHOLLS V HCA PERC(A — HENRY HEGGEN V HCA PERC(A — RORY McLEOD V HCA PERC(A

H59 RICHIE HAVENS H59

RICHIE HAVENS G V SITAR(ALL — (A) RICHIE HAVENS RECORD — 1965 TRANSATLANTIC 199UK US DOUGLAS 779
JERRY FRIEDMAN G (L — (B) ELECTRIC HAVENS — 1966 TRANSATLANTIC 187 US DOUGLAS 780
ERIC WEISSBERG STEEL(L — (C) MIXED BAG — 1967 VERVE UK 2317002 US MGM 4698
ERIC OXENDINE B (JLK — (D) SOMETHING ELSE AGAIN — 1968 VERVE UK 2317030 US VERVE 3034
ARNIE MOORE B (E — (D) SOMETHING ELSE AGAIN — 1968 MGM US 4699
PAUL WILLIAMS G (CDEJLOK — (E) RICHARD D HAVENS 1983 — 1969 VERVE UK 2620001 US VERVE 3047
CARTER COLLINS CONGA(E — (E) RICHARD D HAVENS 1983 — 1969 MGM US 4700
DANIEL BEN ZEBULON D (DEL — (F) STONEHENGE — 1970 POLYDOR UK 2317004 US STORMY FOREST 6001
PAUL HOFFERT ORG (L — (G) A STATE OF MIND — 1971 VERVE UK 2304050
BILLIE MITCHELL G (L — (H) ALARM CLOCK — 1971 POLYDOR UK 2310080 US STORMY FOREST 6005
WARREN BERNHARDT K (DE — (J) GREAT BLIND DEGREE — 1972 POLYDOR UK 2480049 US STORMY FOREST 6016
JEREMY STEIG FLT (DE — (K) LIVE ON STAGE — 1972 POLYDOR UK 2659015 US STORMY FOREST 6012
DONALD MACDONALD D (DE — (L) PORTFOLIO — 1973 POLYDOR UK 2480166 US STORMY FOREST 6013
EDDIE GOMEZ B (D — (M) MIXED BAG 2 — 1974 POLYDOR UK 2310356 US STORMY FOREST 6201
DON PAYNE B (D — (N) END OF THE BEGINNING — 1976 A&M UK AMLH64598 US A&M 4598
ADRIAN GUILLERY G (D — (O) MIRACE — 1977 A&M UK AMLH64641 US A&M 4641
JOHN BLAIR VLN (D — (P) RICHIE HAVENS — 19 POLYDOR UK 2482273
SKIP PROKOP D (DE — (Q) POP HISTORY — 197 POLYDOR UK 2612017
DARRYL JOHNSON G K (ON — (R) CONNECTIONS — 1980 ELEKTRA US 242 NL 52186
JUMM FAIRS B (E
HERMAN ERNEST D (ON — TONY BROUSSARD B (O — DAVID LEBOLT K (O — WILLIAM SMITTY SMITH K V (O
TOM SCOTT WIND (O — GARY COLEMAN PERC (O — DUITCH HELMER V (O — CHRISTOPHER BOND G (O
DENNY GERRARD B (F — EMILE LATIMER CONGA(JK — BOB MARGOULEFF SYN (J — MALCOLM CECIL SYN (J
PAUL HARRIS K (C — HARVEY BROOKS B (C — BILL LAVORGNA D (C — HOWARD COLLINS G (C
JOE PRICE PERC (C — JOHN ORD K (E — BRAD CAMPBELL B (E — KEN LAUBER K (E
TEDDY IRWIN G (E — WELDON MYRICK STEEL(E — CAROL HUNTER B (F — BRUCE LANGHORNE G (E
COLLIN WALCOTT SITAR(E — CHARLIE SMALL K (E — STEVE STILLS B (E — MARK ROTH (E
BOB CHASE PERC (E — DIANE COMINS HARP (E — CHARLES HOWALL V (E — JOEY OLIVER K (N
TESSIE COEN PERC (N — BRENDA RUSSELL V (N — JULIA TILLMAN V (N — MIKE BAIRD D (N
DUCK DUNN B (N — DANNY MOORE V (N — WILLIAM SMITH K V (N — JEFF BAXTER G (N
BRIAN RUSSELL V (N — DIANNE BROOKS V (N — BOOKER T JONES K (N — STEVE CROPPER G (N
MATT MOORE V (N

H60 CYRIL HAVERMANNS H60

CYRIL HAVERMANS V G B(AB — (A) CYRIL — 1973 MGM 2315 261 + MGM SE 4926
PIERRE VANDER LINDEN D(A — (B) MIND WAVE — 1974 MGM 2315 311
THIJS VAN LEER K FLT(A
JACKIE WARD V (A — ANDREA WILLIS V (A — MAXINE WILLARD V (A — CHUCK DOMANICO B (A
EMIL RICHARDS PERC (A — BOBBY BRUCE VLN (A — JOHN D'ANDREA PERC (AB — HERMAN DEINUM B PERC(B
RUDY DE QUELJOU G (B — HANS LAFAILLE PERC (B — CAROLYN WILLIS V (A

H61 DALE HAWKINS H61

DALE HAWKINS V (ALL — ( ) LETS TWIST AT THE PEPPERMINT LOUNGE 196 ROULETTE US 25175
JAMES BURTON G (— ( ) DALE HAWKINS 19 CHESS 703
( ) SUSIE Q 19 CHECKER UK6467310
( ) SUSIE Q 1958 CHESS US 1429
( ) LA MEMPHIS & TYLER TEXAS 1970 BELL US 6036

H62 RONNIE HAWKINS H62

RONNIE HAWKINS V (ALL — (A) RONNIE HAWKINS — 1959 ROULETTE US R25078
KING BISCUIT BOY HCA (J — (B) Mr DYNAMO — 1960 ROULETTE US R25102
BYRON BACH STR (L — (B) Mr DYNAMO — 1960 COLUMBIA UK SX 1238
ROBBIE ROBERTSON G (G — (C) FOLK BALLADS — 1960 COLUMBIA UK SX33 1295
BARRY BECKETT K (J — (C) FOLK BALLADS — 1960 ROULETTE US R25120
SCOTT CUSHNIE K (J — (D) SINGS HANK WILLIAMS — 1961 ROULETTE US R25137
DUANE ALLMAN G (J — (E) SINGS HANK WILLIAMS — 19 GRAND PRIX SWED GP 9970
EDDIE HINTON G (J — (F) THE BEST OF — 1963 ROULETTE US R25255
JIMMY JOHNSON G (J — (F) THE BEST OF(EITH THE BAND) — 19 ROULETTE US SR42045
DAVID HOOD B (J — (G) MOJO MAN — 1964 ROULETTE US R25390
ROGER HAWKINS D (J — (H) RRRRACKET TIME — 1965 WLW CAN WLW101
JAMES COTTON HCA (H — (H) RRRRACKET TIME — 1980 CHARLY UK CR 30180
LEVON HELM D (ABCDGH — (I) RONNIE HAWKINS — 1968 YORKVILLE US YVS 33002
FRED CARTER G (HL — (I) HAWK IN WINTER(REISSUE OF ABOVE) — 1976 POLYDOR CAN 2424 121

(CONTINUED)

H62 (CONTINUED) RONNIE HAWKINS H62

DAVE KIRBY G (L (J) RONNIE HAWKINS 1970 COTILLION US SD 9019
JERRY CARRIGAN D (L (J) RONNIE HAWKINS 1970 ATLANTIC UK 2400 009
DAVID BRIGGS ORG (L (K) THE HAWK 1971 COTILLION US SD 9039
BOOTS RANDOLPH SAX (L (L) ROCK & ROLL RESURRECTION 1972 MONUMENT US KZ 31330
DON SHEFFIELD TPT (L (L) ROCK & ROLL RESURRECTION 1972 MONUMENT UK 65122
DAVID DARLING STRINGS(L (M) GIANT OF ROCK'N'ROLL 1974 MONUMENT US KZ 32940
JAMES CASON V (L (N) ROCKIN 197 MODE FR MO 9028
MARY HOLLADAY V (L (N) ROCKIN 1977 PYE UK NSPL28238
TIM DRUMMOND B (L (O) THE HAWK 1979 UA US LA968 UK UAG 30283
STAN SZELESTE PNO (LO (LM) GIANT /RESURRECTION 1976 MONUMENT US 33855
RAY PAULMAN G (AB ( ) ARKANSAS ROCKPILE 196 ROULETTE US 1003
CHARLIE McCOY HCA (L (EP) ROCKIN' WITH RONNIE 196 COLUMBIA UK ESG 7792
NORMAN RAY SAX ((L (EP) ROCKIN' WITH RONNIE 2 196 COLUMBIA UK ESG 7795
MARVIN CHANTRY STRINGS(L
JUNE PAGE V (L GINGER HOLLADAY V (L GRADY MARTIN G (L KENNETH BUTTREY D (L
FARRELL MORRIS PERC (L PETE DRAKE STEEL(L BILL PUETT SAX (L GARY VANOSDALE STRINGS(L
D BERGEN WHITE V (L JEANNIE GREENE V (A KEITH ALLISON V G B (O JAMES BURTON G (O
WADDY WACHTEL G (O DEE MURRAY B (O JERRY SOMMERS D (O RICK SSHLOSSER D (O
GARTH HUDSON ACC SYN (O GABRIEL KATONA SYN (O CARL MATHERS FDL (O JERRY PETERSON SAX (O
PAUL BUTTERFIELD HCA (O RYELAND ALLISON PERC (O BOBBY LAKIND CONGAS(O BROOKS HUNNICUTT V (O
LISA ROBERTS V (O PHYLLIS ST JAMES V (O TERRY DANKO V (O JAMES G EVANS B (B

H63 SCREAMING JAY HAWKINS H63

JALACY 'JAY' HAWKINS V(ALL (A) AT HOME WITH 1957 EPIC US 3448
GINNY HAWKINS V (F (B) THE NIGHT & DAY OF 19 PLANET US 1001
RED PRYSOCK SAX (H (C) A NITE AT THE FORBIDDEN CITY 19 SOUND OF HAWAII US 50158
TINY GRIMES G (H (D) WHAT THAT IS 1969 PHILIPS US 600319
LEROY KIRKLAND BAND (H (E) SCREAMIN' JAY HAWKINS 1970 PHILIPS US 600336
TEDDY McRAE ORCHESTRA (H (F) PORTRAIT OF A MAN & HIS WOMAN 1972 HOT LINE US 10024
SAMMY LOWE'S ORCHESTRA (H (G) I PUT A SPELL ON YOU 1969 EPIC US 26457
WALTER YOUNG ORCHESTRA (H (H) SCREAMIN' THE BLUES 1979 RED LIGHTNING UK RL0025
GRAHAM BOND K (
EARL PALMER D (D PLAS JOHNSON SAX (D LYLE RITZ B (D MIKE ANTHONY G BAN(D
EDDIE HOH D (D RON JOHNSON B (D ERNEST McLEAN BAN (D HERB ELLIS G (D
BILLY WATKINS SINGERS V(D CARL GOTTLIEB V (D CHRISTOPHER ROSS V (D SAL VALENTINO V (D
DEIRDRE LA PORTE V (D TOM REID V (D THEA MARCUS V (D

H63A THE HAWKS H63A

DAVE HEARN K V (A (A) THE HAWKS 1980 CBS US 36922
LARRY ADAMS D (A
FRANK WIEWEL B V (A KIRK KAUFFMAN G V (A DAVE STEEN G V (A

H64 HAWKWIND & HAWKLORDS H64

DAVE BROCK HCA V G V K(ABCDEFGHJKLPQ(A) HAWKWIND 1970 LIBERTY US 5519 UK LBA 83348
TIM BLAKE K (PQ (A) HAWKWIND 1980 LIBERTY RI UK 1012
NIK TURNER V SAX(ABCDEFGHJ (A) HAWKWIND 1975 SUNSET UK SLS 50374
TERRY OLLIS D (ABJG (B) IN SEARCH IN SPACE 1971 U A US 5567 UK UAG 29202
DAVE ANDERSON B (J (C) DOREMI FARSOLATIDO 1972 U A US LA 001 UK UAG 29364
BOB CALVERT (DHJKLG (D) SPACE RITUAL 1973 U A US LA 120 UK UAD600378
DIKMIK K (ABCDJG (E) HALL OF THE MOUNTAIN GRILL 1974 U A US 328 UK UAG 29672
HENRY LOWTHER TPT (L (E) HALL OF THE MOUNTAIN GRILL 1981 LIBERTY RI
ADRIAN SHAW B (K (F) WARRIOR ON THE EDGE OF TIME 1975 U A UK UAG 29766
MARTIN GRIFFIN D (L (F) WARRIOR ON THE EDGE OF TIME 1975 ATLANTIC US 36 115
LLOYD LANGTON G (AJPQG (G) ROAD HAWKS 1976 U A US 624 UK UAK 29919
IAN'LEMMY' KILMISTER B G V(CDEFJ (H) ASTOUNDING SOUNDS 1976 CHARISMA UK CDS 4004
SIMON KING D (CDEFHJKLPG (J) MASTERS OF THE UNIVERSE 1977 U A UK UAG 30025
DEL DETTMAR K (BCDEJG (K) QUARK STRANGENESS & CHARM 1977 CHARISMA US 4008 US SIRE 6047
SIMON HOUSE K (EFHJKL (L) 25 YEARS (HAWKLORDS) 1978 CHARISMA US 2203 UK CDS 4014
PAUL RUDOLPH B (H (M) HAWKWIND(ROCKFILE) 197 LIBERTY UK LBR 1012
ALAN POWELL D (FHG (N) PXR 5 1979 CHARISMA UK CDS 4016
JOHN HARRISON B (AJG (O) REPEAT PERFORMANCE (COMP) 1980 CHARISMA UK BG2
MICHAEL MOORCOCK V (F (P) LIVE 79 1980 BRONZE UK BRON 527
HARVEY BAINSBRIDGE B V (LOP (Q) LEVITATION 1980 BRONZE UK BRON 530
LES McCLURE B (L (R) SONIC ATTACK 1981 BRONZE
STEVE SWINDELLS K V (L

H65 BRYN HAWORTH H65

BRYN HAWORTH G V (ALL (A) LET THE DAYS GO BY 1974 ISLAND UK ILPS 9287
BRUCE ROWLAND D (AB (B) SUNNY SIDE OF THE STREET 1975 ISLAND UK ILPS 9332
TERRY STANNARD D (AB (C) GRAND ARRIVAL 1978 A&M UK AMLH68462
FRAN BYRNE D (1 (D) KEEP THE BALL ROLLING 1979 A&M UK AMLH68507
STU CALVER V (D (E) GAP 1980 CHAPEL UK 8004
BUGS PEMBERTON D (A (1) 1978 TOUR
KARL HIMMEL D (C
BUDDY HARMON D (C ALAN SPENNER B (AB CHRIS STAINTON K (BD BUDDY EMMONS G (C
DAVE MATTACKS D (B JOHN COWAN B (C RABBIT BUNDRICK K (A JIM MULLEN G (B
KEVIN KELLEY D (A DAVE PEGG B (B PETE WINGFIELD K (ABD JOHN PORTER G (A
JERRY CARRIGAN D (C PAT DONALDSON B (B TONY O'MALLEY K (B BILLY SANFORD G (C
HENRY SPINETTI D (D FREEBO B (A MICK WEAVER K (1 HAROLD BRADLEY G (C
DAVE SWARBRICK FDL (B GORDON HASKELL B (A BOBBY WOOD K (C BAM KING G (1
SHELLEY KURLAND STRINGS(C JESSIE BOYCE B (C RON OATES K (C RONNY LIGHT G (C
COURTNEY JOHNSON BANJO(C TEX COMER B (1 PIG ROBBINS K (C CURTIS BURCH G (C
ALAN MUNDE BANJO(B JOE OSBORN B (C GRAHAM MAITLAND K (A TERRY HELLYER TROM (D
FARRELL MORRIS PERC (C NICK RATHER B (C BILLY PUETT SAX (C DENNIS GOODE TROM (C
SAM BUSH MAND (C TOMMY COGBILL B (C ANDREW LOVE SAX (C GEORGE TIDWELL TPT(C
SIMON MORTON PNO (D DAVE MARKEE B (D MEL COLLINS SAX (ABD WAYNE JACKSON TPT(C
IMPERIALS V (C MADELINE BELL V (B STEVE GREGORY SAX FLT (D MARTIN DROVER TPT(D
LEE VANDERBILT V (B JOANNE WILLIAMS V (B BUD BEADLE SAX (D PADDY McHUGH V (B
FRANK COLLINS V (B MARY HOLLADAY V (C GINGER HOLLODAY V (C JIM CUOMO SAX (D
DYAN BIRCH V (B DON EVERLY V (C CLIFF RICHARD V (D JOHN PERRY V (D
TONY RIVERS V (D

H65A ISAAC HAYES H65A

ISAAC HAYES K V (ALL (A) PRESENTING 1967 ENTERPRISE US 13 100
LESTER SNELL K (FMN (A) IN THE BEGINNING 1972 ATLANTIC US 1599
WILLIE HALL D (FMN (B) HOT BUTTERED SOUL 1969 ENTERPRISE US 1001 RI STAX 5002
RONALD HUDSON B (F (C) ISAAC HAYES MOVEMENT 1970 ENTERPRISE US 1010
MICHAEL TOLES G (FMN (D) TO BE CONTINUED 1970 ENTERPRISE US 1014 RI 4133
ANTHONY SHINAULT G MN (E) SHAFT 1971 ENTERPRISE US 2 5002
WILLIE COLE D (MN (F) BLACK MOSES 1972 ENTERPRISE US 5003
TOMMY WILLIAMS SAX (MN (G) AT SAHARA TAHOE 1973 ENTERPRISE US 5005
LEWIS COLLINS SAX (M (H) JOY 1973 ENTERPRISE US 5007
BILL EASLEY SAX (MN (I) TOUGH GUYS 1974 ENTERPRISE US 7504
WILLIAM TAYLOR TPT (MN (J) TRUCK TURNER 1974 ENTERPRISE US 7507
RICHARD DOLPH HRN (MN (K) CHOCOLATE CHIP 1975 ABC US 874
JOHNNY DAVIS TPT (M (L) DISCO CONNECTION 1975 ABC US 923
BILL FLORES TROM (M (M) GROOVE A THON 1976 ABC US 925
GARY RUSSELL TROM (MN (N) JUICY FRUIT 1976 SBC US 953
KIM PALUMU G (N (O) A MAN AND A WOMAN 1977 ABC US 966/2
KEN SPAIN TROM (N (P) HOT BED 1977 STAX US 4102
CHARLE SPITTS G (FMN (Q) NEW HORIZON 1978 POLYDOR US 6120
GARY JONES PERC (F (R) FOR SAKE OF LOVE 1979 POLYDOR US 6146
SIDNEY KIRK PNO (FMN (S) DONT LET GO 1980 POLYDOR US 6224
WILLIAM VAUGHN G (M (T) AND ONCE AGAIN 1980 POLYDOR US 6269
ERROLL THOMAS B (NM (U) ENTERPRISE GREATEST HITS 1980 STAX UK 88003
JIMMY THOMPSON PERC (MN (V) LIFETIME THING 1981 POLYDOR UK 2311 074
DARNELL SMITH SAX (MN
EMERSON ABLE SAX (MN
FLOYD NEWMAN SAX (MN BEN CAULEY TPT (MN BRYANT MUNCH HRNS (MN EDGAR MATTHEWS TPT (MN
JACKIE THOMAS TROM (MN JAZZMO PERC (N DEREK GALBREITH B (N NICK VERGOS HRN (N

H65B HAYSTACKS BALBOA H65B

MARK MAYO (A (A) HAYSTACK BALBOA 1970 POLYDOR US 24 4032 GER 2425 032
MARK POLITT (A
BRUCE SCOTT (A DEBORAH MAYO (A MARK BABABI (A LARRY WEST (A
LLOYD LANDESMAN (A

H66 JUSTIN HAYWARD H66

JUSTIN HAYWARD G V (AB (A) SONGWRITER 1977 DERAM US 18073 DECCA UK SDL 15
AJ WEBBER (A (B) NIGHT FLIGHT 1980 DERAM US 4801 DECCA UK TXS 138
KEN FREEMAN (A
CLEM CATTINI D (A TERRY ROWLEY (A PETE MORGAN (A MEL GALLEY G (A
DAVE HOLLAND (A DAVID SNELL HARP (A

H66A TONY HAZZARD H66A

TONY HAZZARD G V (ALL (A) TONY HAZZARD SINGS 1969 CBS U 63608
B J COLE STEEL(BC (B) LOUDWATER HOUSE 1971 BRONZE UK ILPS 9174
CHRIS SPEDDING G (B (C) WAS THAT ALRIGHT THEN 1973 bronze UK ILPS 9222
ROY O'TEMRO D (B
CHRIS SLADE D (B CLEM CLEMPSON G (B CALEB QUAYE G (B TONI CAMPO B (BC
MIKE BATT PNO (B DAVE GREENSLADE K (BC LAGHTY AMAO CONGAS(B RAY COOPER PERC(BC
SUE GLOVER V (B SUNNY LESLIE V (B LESLEY DUNCAN V (B KAY GARNER V (B
JACKIE LEE V (B RUSSELL STONE V (B RICHARD BARNES V (B ROGER McKEW G (C
MICK WEAVER PNO (C TEX MARSH D (C GLENN LEFLEUR D (C HELEN SCOTT V (C
TONY CHARLES STEEL BAND(C

H67 HAZZARD & BARNES H67

TONY HAZZARD G (A (A) HAZZARD & BARNES 1977 WB US 4670 UK k56233
RICHARD BARNES G (A
HERBIE FLOWERS B (A BARRY DE SOUZA D (A TONY HYMAS K (A ROGER McKEW G BAN(A
PETER SWETTENHAM K (A JACK EMBLOW ACC (A JOHNNY VAN DERRICK FDL (A CHRIS NEILL HCA (A
TONY ASHTON K (A DAVE LAWSON SYN (A FRANK RICOTTI PERC (A LESLEY DUNCAN V (A
LIZA STRIKE V (A +HRNS & STRINGS (A

H68 EDDIE HAZEL H68

EDDIE HAZEL (A (A) GAMES, DAMES & GUITAR THANGS 1977 WB US BS 3058
(B) SUGAR DONT YOU KNOW 1979 AUDIOFILE US 137
(C) TAKE YOUR SHOES OFF 1979 MONMOUTH US 7075

H69 HEAD H69

BILL KYLE D (ABC (A) F F T 1973 SRT 72254
HOWARD COPLAND SAX (AB (B) RED DWARF 1975 CANNON UK 5970
CHARLES ALEXANDER G (AB (C) BLACKPOOL COOL 1978 HEAD HSLP 330
JOHN DAVIES TPT K(ABC
GORDON CRUICKSHANK SAX (C LACHLAN McCOLL G (C GRAHAM MINCE B (ABC

H69A HEAD (US) H69A

(A) HEAD 19 BUDDAH BDS 5062

H70 MURRAY HEAD H70

MURRAY HEAD G V (ALL (A) NIGEL LIVED 1973 CBS US 31947 UK 65503
BOB WESTON G V (B (B) SAY IT AINT SO 1975 ISLAND FR 9101 655 UK ILPS 9347
BRIAN BROCKLEHURST B (B (B) SAY IT AINT SO 1975 A&M US 4558
GINNY CLEE V PERC(E (C) BETWEEN US 1979 PHILIPS GER 9198 177
ALUN DAVIES G V (B (D) JOKES/VOICES 1980 MERCURY NL 6313 045
GEOFF RICHARDSON G VLA(E (E) FIND THE CROWD 1981 MERCURY FR 6313 179
JIM CREGAN G (B
BRUCE LYNCH B (B
TONY KAYE PNO (B GLENN LE FLEUR D (B PAM KEEVIL V (B JOHN ALTMAN CLAR(B
ARTHUR WATTS B (B LIZA STRIKE V (B PETE THOMPSON D (B BROTHER JAMES CONGA(B
CHILLI CHARLES PERC (B MICKY FINN G (B NICKY SOUTH B (B SIMON PHILLIPS D (B
P J CROTTY WIND (B BILLY DAY K (B MORRIS PERT PERC (B BRIAN JOHNSTON K (B
CHAS JANKEL K (B ANN O'DELL K (B GERRY CONWAY D (B SUE LYNCH V (B
ANTHONY HEAD V (B VICKY BROWN V (B GRAHAM PRESKETT MAND (B TROPIC ISLES STEEL BAND(B
NOEL NORRIS TPT (B MARK WARNER G (A CLIVE CHAMAN B (A DAVE WINTOUR B (A
PETER GILES B (A MIKE GILES D (A COZY POWELL D (A BARRY DESOUZA D (A
PETE ROBINSON K (A FIACHRA TRENCH K (A TONY COE SAX (A JIMMY HASTINGS SAX (A
TOMMY WHITTLE SAX (A JIM CHESTER SAX (A CHRIS MERCER SAX (AD CHRIS NEIL HCA (A

(CONTINUED)

H70 (CONTINUED) MURRAY HEAD H70

SUE GLOVER V (A SUNNY LESLIE V (A KAY GARNER V (A FRIENDLY SISTERS V (A
FRANK RICOTTI PERC (A RAY COOPER PERC (A SPIKE HEATLEY B (A JOHN DONNELLY HRNS(A
HENRY LOWTHER HRNS (A DAVE CHAMAN HRNS (A MARTIN FRY HRNS (A RALPH HO HRN (A
JAMES HARPHAM REC (A NICK DECARO ACC (A SKAILA KANGA HARP (A CHRIS KARAM TABLA (A
MIGUEL BARADOS STEEL DRUM(A JACK ROTHSTEIN VLN (A MIKE RENNIE VLN (A PETE VEITCH K VLN (E
PHIL PALMER G (E ALAN SPENNER B (E TREVOR MORIAS D (CE BOB WESTON G (C
JOHN PERRY B (C JEFF BECK G (D

H71 HEAD EAST H71

ROGER BOYD K V (ABCDEFG (A) FLAT AS A PANCAKE 1975 A&M US 4537 UK AMLH64537
DAN BIRNEY B V (ABCDE (B) GET YOURSELF UP 1976 A&M US 4579 UK AMLH64579
MIKE SOMERVILLE G V (ABCDE (C) GETTIN' LUCKY 1977 A&M US 4624 UK AMLH64624
JOHN SCHLITT V (ABCDE (D) HEAD EAST 1978 A&M US 46680 UK AMLH64680
STEVE HUSTON D V (ABCDE (E) LIVE (DBL) 1979 A&M US 6007 UK AML 66007
RICHARD PODOLOR G (C (F) A DIFFERENT KIND OF CRAZY 1980 A&M US 4795
STAN GILL ORG (E (G) US1 1980 A&M US 4826
KEN KRUEGER V (G
DEDE TOWNSEND G (G FLOYD BROWN D (G STEVE HUTTON D V (FG TONY GATES G V (FG
MACK BOATMAN V (FG DAN ODUM V PERC(FG JIMMY GREEN SAX (G JESSE HENDERSON D (G
CHRIS HARWOOD G (G

H71A HEADBOYS H71A

LOU LEWIS G V (A (A) HEADBOYS 1980 RSO US 3968 GER 2394 244 UK 13
GEORGE BOYTER B V (A
CALUM MALCOLM K V (A DAVY ROSS D V (A ROBIN MORTON PERC (A ALY BAIN FDL (A
BOB HEATLIE SAX (A

H71B HEAD MACHINE H71B

(A) ORGASM 19 VOGUE 522

H71C HEADBANK H71C

EDDIE COLTON B (A (A) LETTIN EVERYTHING GO 1981 MADDOG 106077
DINO FASANO V (A
SIMON GANNETT K (A EDDIE WISCONSIN G (A ANDY RUBBO D (A

H72 HEADHUNTERS H72

BENNIE MAUPIN WIND V(DF (A) HEADHUNTERS 1973 CBS US 32731
MICHAEL CLARK D (F (B) THRUST 1974 CBS US 32965
PAUL JACKSON B V (F (C) DEATH WISH 1974 CBS US 33199
OBSIDIKTION BLACKBYRD]G B V(F (D) SURVIVAL OF THE FITTEST 1975 ARISTA US 4038 UK ARTY 116
DWAYNE McKNIGHT (E) MAN CHILD 1976 CBS US 33812
PAUL PORTYEN K V (F (F) STRAIGHT FROM THE GATE 1977 ARISTA US 4146 UK APART1048
DERRICK YOUMAN V (F
BILL SUMMERS PERC(F

H73 HEADSTONE H73

MARK ASHTON G V (AB (A) BAD HABITS 1974 EMI UK EMA766 US DUNHILL 50176
STEVE BOLTON G (AB (B) HEADSTONE 1975 EMI UK EMC 3073
PHILIP CHEN B (A (B) HEADSTONE 19 20TH CENTURY US T483
CHILLI CHARLES D (A
JOE O'DONNELL VLN G(AB STEVE GOULD V (A SPARKIE V (A JUANITA FRANKLIN V(AB
CARL DOUGLAS V (A TONY LUKYN SYN (A DAVE KAFFINETTI K (A PETER VAN HOOKE D (B
JEROME RIMSON B (B

H74 HEADS HANDS & FEET H74

ALBERT LEE G V (ABC (A) HEADS HANDS & FEET 1971 CAPITOL US 608 UK ISLAND ILPS9149
PETE GAVIN D V (ABC (B) TRACKS 1972 CAPITOL US11051 UK ISLAND ILPS 9185
CHAS HODGES B G FDL V (ABC (C) OLD SOLDIERS NEVER DIE 1973 ATLANTIC US 7025 UK K40465
MIKE O'NEIL K (A
RAY SMITH B G V(BAC JERRY DONAHUE V (BC RAY OSBORNE V (B BARRY ST JOHN V (B
LINDA THOMPSON V (C GERRY HOGAN STEEL (B LINDA LEWIS V (C NORMA WINSTONE V (C
JIM DONNELLY V (C DAVE SWARBRICK V (C JACKIE LYNTON V (C PAM SUILICON V (C
SYLVIA KING V (C ELTON DEAN SAX (A TONY COLTON V (ABC

H75 HEART H75

NANCY WILSON V G (ALL (A) DREAMBOAT ANNIE 1976 MUSHROOM US 5005 ARISTA UK ARTY139
ANN WILSON K V (ALL (B) LITTLE QUEEN 1977 PORTRAIT US 34799 UK 82075
MICHAEL DEROSIER D (ABCDEFGH (C) MAGAZINE 1978 MUSHROOM US 5008 ARISTA UK 1024
HOWARD LEESE G K SYN (ABCDEFGH (D) DOG AND BUTTERFLY 1978 PORTRAIT US 35555 UK 83080
STEVE FOSSEN B PERC(ABCDEFGH (E) BEBE LE STRANGE 1980 EPIC US 36371 UK 84135
ROGER FISHER STEEL G (ABCDG (F) GREATEST HITS LIVE 1981 UK 84829
KAT HENDRIKSE D (A (G) GREATEST HITS LIVE (DBL) 1980 EPIC US 36888
BRIAN NEWCOMBE B (A (H) PRIVATE AUDITION 1982 EPIC US 38049
DURIS MAXWELL D (A
ROB DEANS K SYN(A MIKE FLICKER PERC (A DAVE WILSON D (A ROY AYOTTE PERC (A
GEOFF FOUBERT BANJO(A SUE ENNIS G V (E CHRISSY SHEFTS G (E LYNN WILSON/KEAGLE V (BH
GARY HUMPHREY V (E DON WILHELM V (E TOWER OF POWER HRNS(E SEAL DUNNINGTON V (E
LENNY PICKETT HRNS (EFG GREG ADAMS HRNS (EFG STEVE KUPKA HRNS(E MIC GILLETTE HRNS (EFG
EMILIO CASTILIO HRNS (EFG

H76 HEARTBREAKERS H76

JOHNNY THUNDERS G V (AB (A) L.A.M.F. 1977 TRACK 2400 218
JERRY NOLAN V D (A (B) LIVE AT MAX'S KANSAS CITY 1979 BEGGARS BANQUET BEGA9
WALTER LURE G (AB
RICHARD HELL B V (A BILLY RATH B (AB TY STYX D (B PETE CRAWLEY PROD (B
SPEEDY KEEN PROD (A DANIEL SECUNDA PROD(A

H77 HEARTS & FLOWERS H77

DAVE LAWSON V AUTOHARP (AB (A) NOW IS THE TIME 1967 CAPITOL US ST 2762
LARRY MURRAY G V (AB (B) OF OLD HORSES,KIDS & FORGOTTEN 1968 CAPITOL US ST 2868
RICK CUNHA G V (AB
BERNIE LEADON G (B DAVID JACKSON B (

H78 HEARTSFIELD H78

ARTIE BALDACCI D SYN K V(ABCD (A) HEARTSFIELD 1973 MERCURY US SRM1 688
GREG BIELA B V (ABCD (B) WONDER OF IT ALL 1974 MERCURY US SRM1 1003
FRED DOBBS G BAN V (ABCD (C) FOOLISH PLEASURES 1975 MERCURY US SRM1 1034
J C HARTSFIELD G MAN FDL V(ABCD (D) HEARTSFIELD COLLECTORS ITEM 1977 CBS US 34456
PHIL LUCAFO G STEEL V(ABCD
PERRY CORDELL JORDAN G V(ABCD
FLACO FALCON PERC (A TOM GEVING SAX PNO (AC BRIAN PRICE FDL (C CHEPITO AREAS PERC (C
KURT McGETTRICK HRNS (D TED ASHFORD PNO (D TERRY ADAMS CELLO(D JACK KRAMMER TPT (B
BILL DINWIDDIE TROM (B BRANDON LEAVITT PERC (B

H78A HEARTWOOD H78A

BYRON PAUL G V (A (A) NOTHING FANCY 1975 GRC US GA 10008
CARTER MINOR V HCA PERC(A
T M HILDEBRANDT G V (A JOE McGLOHON STEEL SAX(A BUDDY BLACKMAN BANJO(A JERRY JOSEPH CONGA (A
BILL BUTLER V G K(A DAVID BLACKMAN MAND (A ROBERT HUDSON V B (A PAUL HORNSBY K (A
DAVIS CAUSEY G (A GARY JOHNSON V B (A

H79 HEAT H79

JEFF FORMOSA D ((A) HEAT 1980 MCA US 3225
JEFF LI B G (
DWYTT DAYAN V D (ALVIN ROBERTSON D (TALLY TALIOFERRO G (

H80 HEATERS H80

MERCY BERMUNDEZ V SAX((A) THE HEATERS 1978 ARIOLA 50032
MAGGIE CONNELL K ((B) ENERGY TRANSFER 1980 CBS US 36486 UK 84454
MISSY CONNELL B V (

H81 HEATWAVE H81

JOHNNY WILDER V CONGA(ABCD (A) TOO HOT TOO HANDLE 1976 GTO UK GTLP 013 EPIC US 34761
ROD TEMPERTON K (ABC (B) CENTRAL HEATING 1978 GTO UK GTLP 027 EPIC US 35260
KEITH WILDER V (ABD (C) HOT PROPERTY 1979 GTO UK GTLP 039 EPIC US 35970
J D NICHOLAS V (D (D) CANDLES 1980 GTO UK GTLP 047 EPIC US 36873
MARIO MANTESE B (AB
ERIC JOHNS G (AB ERNEST BERGER D (ABD ROY CARTER B PNO (A CALVIN DUKE K (D
DEREK BRAMBLE D (D WILLIAM L JONES G V (D

H82 HEAVEN & EARTH H82

(A) HEAVEN & EARTH 1978 MERCURY US 3722
(B) FANTASY 1979 MERCURY US 3763

H82A HEAVEN 17 H82A

GLENN GREGORY V (A (A) PENTHOUSE & PAVEMENT 1981 VIRGIN UK V2208 GER 204 017
IAN CRAIG MARSH SYN SAX (A
MARTIN WARE K SYN V (A JOHN WILSON G B SYN(A JOSIE JAMES V (A STEVE TRAVELL PNO (A
BOYS OF BUDDAH HRNS (A

H83 HEAVEN H83

TERRY SCOTT V G K(A (A) BRASS ROCK 1 (DBL) 1971 CBS UK 66293
EDDI HARNETT G V (A
JOHN JAMES GORDON V B (A VIC GLOVER D (A DAVE GAUTREY HRNS (A BUTCH HUDSON HRNS(A
DAVID HORLER TROM K(A RAY KING HRNS (A DEREK SOMERVILLE HRNS (A

H84 HEAVY JELLY H84

JOHN MOORSHEAD G (ABCDEFG JIM CAPALDI D (BC STEVE THOMPSON B (GF CHRIS WOOD WIND (BC
ALEX DMOCHOWSKI B (ABCDE JACKIE LOMAX V G(CDEFG DAVEY LUTTON D (G BARRY JENKINS D (D
BRUCE ROWLAND D (EF ROCKY (A CARLO LITTLE D (A

(A) EARLY 1969 (B) 1969 (C) JULY 1969 (D) JAN 1970 (E) MARCH 1970 (F) MID 1970 (G) LATE 1970.

(NB) THE HEAVY JELLY ON THE ISLAND SAMPLER(NICE ENOUGH TO EAT'(I KEEP SINGING THAT SAME OLD SONG) WAS REALLY SKIP BIFFERTY. THE NAME HEAVY JELLY BEGAN AS A REVIEW HOAX BUT WAS REGISTERED BY JOHN CURD OF HEAD RECORDS AND APPLIES TO THE LINE UPS HERE.
ONE SINGLE 'CHEWN IN/TIME OUT' ON HEAD 4001. AN ALBUM WAS PREPARED BUT WAS NOT RELEASED. ALSO A SESSION FOR THE B.B.C. WAS RECORDED MID 1970.

H85 HEAVY METAL KIDS H85

GARY HOLTON V (AB12 (A) HEAVY METAL KIDS 1974 ATLANTIC US 7047 UK K50047
RONNIE THOMAS B V (AB12 (B) ANVIL CHORUS 1975 ATLANTIC UK K50143
KEITH BOYCE D (ABC12 (C) KITSCH 1977 RAK UK SRAK 323
JOHN SINCLAIR K V (1 (1) 1976 (2) 1977/78
BARRY PAUL G V (12
JAY WILLIAMS (2 MICKEY WALLER G (A DANNY PEYRONEL K V (AB PHIL KENZIE SAX (B
MADELINE BELL V (B IRENE CHANTER V (B DOREEN CHANTER V (B COSMO G (2

H86 DICK HECKSTALL SMITH H86

DICK HECKSTALL SMITH SAX(A (A) A STORY ENDED 1972 BRONZE UK ILPS 9196 US WB 2650
PAUL WILLIAMS V (A
CALEB QUAYE G (A DAVE GREENSLADE K (A JON HISEMAN D (A MARK CLARKE B (A
GORDON BECK PNO (A CHRIS SPEDDING G (A ROB TAIT D (A GRAHAM BOND K V (A
CHRIS FARLOWE V (A

H86A DASHIELL HEDAYAT H86A

DASHIELL HEDAYAT G V K(AB (A) MELMOTH LA DEVANTURE DES IVRESSES 1969 ARION FR 30 T079
RICHARD RAUX WIND (A (B) OBSOLETE 1971 SHANDAR FR 10009 CBS UK 83512
ROBERT BALESTER D (A
JOSE B FADLA G (A DIDIER DE ST JORES K (A DAEVID ALLEN G (B WILLIAM BURROUGHS V(B
DIDIER MALHERBE WIND (B PIP PYLE G D (B GILLI SMYTH V (B CHRISTIAN TRITSCH G B(B
SAM WYATT V (B

H87 HEDGEHOG PIE H87

MARGI LUCKLEY V 'BC (A) HIS ROUND 1972 RUBBER UK RUB 002
JED GRIMES G (BCD (B) HEDGEHOG PIE 1975 RUBBER UK RUB 009
MARTIN JENKINS V MAND VLN(BC (C) GREEN LADY 1975 RUBBER UK RUB 014
STU LUCKLEY V B (BC (D) JUST ACT NORNAL 1978 RUBBER UK RUB 024
DIK D (C (EP) WONDERFUL LEGEND OF LAMBTON 1977 RUBBER UK TUB 12
WALTER FAIRBAIRN G (D
TONY CAPSTICK (A TOM DUFFY B (D DAVE BURLAND (D MICHAEL DOONAM FLT (BCD
PHIL MURRAY B (

H87A HEE BEE GEE BEES H87A

(A) 439 GOLDEN GREATS 1981 HEEBEEGEEBEE TWITS 101

H87B HEINSIGHT H87B

(A) THE GREAT WHITE 1978 churchill us 67233

H88 HEINZ H88

(A) TRIBUTE TO EDDIE 1964 DECCA UK LK 4599
(B) REMEMBERING 1977 DECCA UK REM.7

H89 ZEUS B HELD H89

ZEUS B HELD (A) ZEUS AMUSEMENT 1978 BRAIN 0060 120

H89A HELDON H89A

RICHARD PINHAS G K (ALL (A) ELECTRONIC GORILLA 1974 DISJUNCTA 000 001
PATRICK GAUTHIER K SYN(ACDEFJ (A) ELECTRONIC GORILLA 1979 COBRA 37019
GEORGES GRUNBLATT SYN K(ABC (B) ALLEZ TEIA 1975 DISJUNCTA 000 002
PIERROT ROUSSEL B (A (C) ITS ALWAYS ROCK AND ROLL 1975 DISJUNCTA 000 006/7
COCO ROUSSEL PERC (AD (D) AGNETA NILSSON 1976 URUS 000 011
GILLES DELEUZE V (A (E) UN REVE SANS CONSEQUENCE SPECIALE 1976 COBRA 60008 37002
ALAIN BELLAICHE G (BD (F) INTERFACE 1976 COBRA 37013
KLAUS BLASQUIZ V (J (G) A DREAM WITH OUT 1978 INNER 1021
JANIK TOP B (E (H) HELDON IV 1979 AURAL US 5001
ALAIN RENAUD G (ABC (J) STAND BY 1979 EGG 900 578
JEAN MY TRUONG D (C
GILBERT ARTMAN D (C ARIEL KALMA K (C PHILIBERT ROSSI SYN (D MICHEL ETTORI G (D
GERARD PREVOST B (D FRANCOIS AUGER D PERC(EFJ DIDIER BATARD B (EJC
AURORE V (C

H89B ERWIN HELFER H89B

ERWIN HELFER PNO (A (A) BOOGIE PIANO CHICAGO SYTLE 1976 BIG BEAR BEAR 11

H89C HELIX H89C

BRAIN DOERNER D V (A (A) BREAKING LOOSE 1979 HANDS 101
BRENT DOERNER G (A (B) WHITE LACE & LEATHER 1981
PAUL HACKMAN G (A
BRAIN VOLLMER V (A KEITH ZURBRIGG B (A

H90 RICHARD HELL H90

RICHARD HELL B V (ALL (A) BLANK GENERATION 1976 STIFF UK BUY7
MARC BELL D (B1 (B) BLANK GENERATION 1977 SIRE US 6037 UK 9103 327
IVAN JULIAN G (B1 (1) MAY 1978
ROBERT QUINE G (B1
JERRY ANTONIUS K B (1 FRANK MAURO D (1

H91 HELL PREACHERS H91

RUMOURED TO BE (A) SUPREME PSYCHEDELIC UNDERGROUND 1968 MARBLE ARCH UK MAS 1169
RITCHIE BLACKMORE G
JON LORD K IAN PAICE D IN PRE DEEP PURPLE DAYS BUT ALWAYS DENIED BY THEM ALL.

H91A HELLFIELD H91A

RICK LAMB K G V(A (A) HELLFIELD 1979 EPIC US 36005
MITCH HELLFIELD D G V(A (B) NIGHT MUSIC 1979 EPIC UK 80028
JAMIE LARSEN B V (A
DICK SMITH D (A DAVE HOVEY G (A

H91B HELLO PEOPLE H91B

N D SMART D V (A (A) THE HANDSOME DEVILS 1974 DUNHILL US 50184
LAURENCE TASSE (A (B) BRICKS 19 ABC US 883
ROBERT SEDITA (A (C) THE HELLO PEOPLE 19 PHILIPS PHS 600165
GREGORY GEDDES (A (D) FUSION 19 PHILIPS PHS 600276
(E) HAVE YOU SEEN THE LIGHT 19 MEDIARTS US 41/8

H92 LEVON HELM H92

LEVON HELM D V (AB (A) LEVON HELM & THE RCO ALL STARS 1977 ABC US 1017 UK ABCL 5236
PAUL BUTTERFIELD HCA (A (B) LEVON HELM 1978 ABC US 1089
FRED CARTER G (AC (C) AMERICAN SON 1980 MCA US 5120
HAROLD ROBBINS K (C
DONALD DUNN B (A STEVE CROPPER G (AB BOOKER T JONES K (A JOHN FLAMINGO V (A
JEANETTE BAKER V (A ROBBIE ROBERTSON G (A GARTH HUDSON ACC (A CHARLES MILLER SAX (A
ALAN RUBIN TPT (AB LOU MARINI SAX (AB WILLIE HALL D (B TOM MALONE TROM(B
HOWARD JOHNSON HRNS (AB ROGER HAWKINS D (B DR JOHN K G (A EMMARETTA MARKS V (A
BARRY BECKETT K (B RANDY McCORMICK K (B ERNIE CATE V (B DAN FERGUSON G (B
LARRY BYROM G (B EARL CATE V (B JIMMY JOHNSON G (B SCOTT EDWARDS B (B
DAVID HOOD B (B LOU DEL GATTO SAX (B MARY BERRY V (B BOBBY OGDEN K (C
BILLY SANFORD G (C HENRY STRZELECKI B (C JERRY CARRIGAN D (C MITCH HUMPHRIES K (C
STEVE SCHAFFER B (C BUDDY EMMONS STEEL(C JERRY SHOOK K (C STEVE GIBSON G (C
KENNY BUTTREY D (C BUSTER PHILIPS D (C CLIFFORD ROBERTSON K (C BEEGIE ADAIR K (C
BUZZ CASON V (C TODD CERNEY V (C

H92A HELMET BOY H92A

(A) HELMET BOY 1980 ELEKTRA US 280 uk K 52249

H93 HELP YOURSELF H93

MALCOLM MORLEY G V (ABCDE (A) HELP YOURSELF 1971 LIBERTY US 5583 UK 83484
RICHARD TREECE G V (ABCDE (B) STRANGE AFFAIR 1972 U A US 5591 UK UAS 29287
KEN WHALEY B (ADE (C) BEWARE OF THE SHADOW 1972 U A US 079 UK UAS 29413
DAVE CHARLES D V (ABCDE (D) RETURN OF KEN WHALEY 1973 U A UK UAS 29487
PAUL BURTON B G (BCDE (E) HAPPY DAYS 1973 U A UK FREE1
MARTIN ACE V B (E (DE) RETURN/HAPPY DAYS 1973 U A UK UDG 4001
GEORGINA ACE V G (E
VIV MORRIS G V (E ERNIE GRAHAM V G (B JOJO GLEMSER G (B

H94 HEMLOCK H94

MILLER ANDERSON G V (A (A) HEMLOCK 1973 DERAM UK SML 1102
JIM LEVERTON B V (A
ERIC DILLON D (A MICK WEAVER K (A PETER DINES K G V(A CHRIS MERCER SAX (A
PETE WILLSHER STEEL(A CHRIS STEWART V (A

H94A BUGS HENDERSON H94A

BUGS HENDERSON G V (A (A) AT LAST 1978 ARMADILLO US ARLP78
RON THOMPSON D (A
ROBERT CHITWOOD B (A

H95 DORRIS HENDERSON H95

Musician	Instr.	Albums
DORRIS HENDERSON	ACC V	(ABC
JOHN RENBOURN	G	(AB
TIM WALKER	G	(B
DANNY THOMPSON	B	(B

	Title	Year	Label	Country	No.
(A)	THERE YOU GO	1965	COLUMBIA	UK	SX 6001
(B)	WATCH THE STARS	1967	FONTANA	UK	STL 5385
(C)	ROTTERDAM BLUES(EP)	196	SHR	NL	VR 108

H96 WAYNE HENDERSON H96

Musician	Instr.	Albums
WAYNE HENDERSON	TROM	(AB
RONNIE LAWS	SAX	(A
DEBORAH SHOTLOW	V	(A
ALEXANDRA BROWN	V	(A
AUGIE JOHNSON	V	(A
BOBBY LYLE	K	(A
ROLAND BAUTISTA	G	(A
STEVEN GUITIERREZ	D	(A
DON BECK	B	(A
MARLON McLAIN	G	(A
NATHANIEL PHILLIPS	B	(A
BRUCE CARTER	D	(A
VANCE TENORT	PERC	(A
DEAN GANT	SYN	(A
VICTOR FELDMAN	PERC	(A
JAY GRAYDON	G	(A
GEORGE DEL BARRIO	K	(A
GEORGE BOHANON	TROM	(A
DONALD COOKE	TROM	(A
JOHN ERVIN	WIND	(A
EARL DUMLER	OBOE	(A
JACK MARSH	WIND	(A
OSCAR BRASHEAR	TPT	(A
STEVE MADAIO	TPT	(A
DAVE GROVER	TPT	(A
BOB GREVE	WIND	(A
CHUCK BROOKE	WIND	(A
SYLVIA ST JAMES	V	(A
SAUNDRA ALEXANDER	V	(A
JIM GILSTRAP	V	(A
MYRNA MATTHEWS	V	(A
SYREETA WRIGHT	V	(A

	Title	Year	Label / No.
(A)	LIVING ON A DREAM	1978	POLYDOR US 16145 UK 2391 343
(B)	FREEDOM SOUNDS	19	ATLANTIC US 1512
( )	AT BIG DADDY'S PLACE	1977	ABC US
( )	STEP INTO YOUR LIFE	1978	POLYDOR POLS 1004 UK 2391 380
( )	EMPHASISED	1979	POLYDOR

H97 EDDIE HENDERSON H97

Musician	Instr.	Albums
EDDIE HENDERSON	HRNS	(ALL
PATRICE RUSHEN	B K	(E
GEORGE CABLES	K	(E
CHARLES MIMMS	K	(E
MTUME	K V PERC	(E
LEE RITENOUR	G	(E
AL McKAY	G	(E
MANI BOYD	WIND	(E
CONNIE HENDERSON	WIND	(E
JULIAN PRIESTER	TROM	(E
PHILIP BAILEY	V PERC	(E
HOWARD KING	D	(E
PAUL JACKSON	B	(E
SKIP DRINKWATER	PERC	(E
DIANE REEVES	V	(E

	Title	Year	Label / No.
(A)	INSIDE OUT	1974	CAPRICORN US CP0122 UK 2429 106
(A)	INSIDE OUT	1974	CAPRICORN UK K 57504
(B)	REALIZATION	1974	CAPRICORN US CP0118 UK K 57505
(C)	SUNBURST	1975	BLUENOTE BNLA 464
(D)	HERITAGE	197	BLUENOTE BNLA 636
(E)	COMIN' THROUGH	1977	CAPITOL EST 11671
(F)	MAHAL	1978	CAPITOL EST 11846
(G)	RUNNING TO YOUR LOVE	1979	TOWER EST 11984

H98 MICHAEL HENDERSON H98

Musician	Instr.	Albums
MICHAEL HENDERSON	V B K	(ALL
ROZ RYAN	V	(E
ELI FONTAINE	SAX	(E
KATHY KOSINS	V	(E
SHEILA HORNE	V	(E
CAROL HALL	V	(E
JEANETTE McFRUDER	V	(E
VENNA KEITH	V	(E
RANDALL JACOBS	G PNO	(E
RAY PARKER	G	(E
OLLIE E BROWN	D	(E
CORY HEATH	D	(E
BOBBY FRANKLIN	D	(E
CHERYL NORTON	V	(E
ERIK WALLACE	D	(E
RON PANGBORN	D	(E
ERNESTRO WILSON	K	(E
GARY NESTER	K	(E
MANON SAULSBY	K	(E
SYLVESTER RIVERS	PNO	(E
MICHAEL IACOPELLI	SYN	(E
LORENZO BROWN	PERC	(E
MIGUEL FUENTES	PERC	(E

	Title	Year	Label / No.
(A)	SOLID	1976	BUDDAH BDS5662
(B)	GOIN' PLACES	1977	BUDDAH BDLH 5018
(C)	IN THE NIGHT TIME	1978	BUDDAH BDLH 4055
(D)	DO IT ALL	1979	BUDDAH US 5719 UK BDLP 4062
(E)	WIDE RECEIVER	1980	BUDDAH US 6004 UK BDLP 4065

H99 JIMI HENDRIX H99

Musician	Instr.	Albums
JIMI HENDRIX	G V	(ALL
NOEL REDDING	B	(ABCDIMN
MITCH MITCHELL	D	(ABCDHIKLMNU
BILLY COX	B	(GHIJKLNOU
JACK CASADY	B	(
BUDDY MILES	D	(FLWU
AL KOOPER	K	(D
JIM MORRISON	V HCA	(W
JIM McCARTY	G	(W
ROLAND ROBINSON	B	(U
LARRY YOUNG	K	(U
LARRY LEE	G	(U
STEVE WINWOOD	K	(H
JEFF MIRANOV	G	(OS
ALLEN SCHWARZBERG	D	(OS
LANCE QUINN	G	(S
JIMMY MAELEN	PERC	(OS
MAERETHA STEWART	V	(S
HILDA HARRIS	V	(S
VIVIAN CHERRY	V	(OS
BUDDY LUCAS	HCA	(S
CHRIS WOOD	WIND	(H
LINDA NOVEMBER	V	(O
JUMA EDWARDS	PERC	(I
RONETTES	V	(I
GHETTO FIGHTERS	V	(HI
EMERETTA MARKS	V	(H
BUZZY LINHART	VIBES	(H
BARBARA MASSEY	V	(O
JOHNNY WINTER	G	(W
RANDY HOBBS	B	(W
RANDY ZEHRINGER	D	(W
BOB BABITT	B	(OS
LONNIE YOUNGBLOOD	V SAX	(A
HERMAN HITSON		(
DAVE MASON	G	(D
ROCKY DZIDZORNU	PERC	(
CURTIS McTEARA	B	(
RONNETTES	V	(T
CURTIS KNIGHT		(
MIKE EPHON	K	(
LEE MOSES	G	(
MICHAEL WATSON	G	(
NURTE EDMONDS	K	(
JEANETTE JACOBS	V	(D
EDDIE KRAMER	V	(N
KEN WEAVER	V	(N
STEVE STILLS	PNO	(H

	Title	Year	Label	Country	No.
(A)	ARE YOU EXPERIENCED	1967	TRACK		2407 004
(A)	" " "	1967	POLYDOR	GER	184 085
(A)	" " "	1970	BACKTRACK		2407 010
(A)	" " "	19	REPRISE	US	RS6261
(A)	" " "	19	TRACK		612 001
(B)	AXIS BOLD AS LOVE	1967	REPRISE	US	RS6281
(B)	" " " "	1967	TRACK	UK	2407 011
(B)	" " " "	19	POLYDOR	GER	184 110
(B)	" " " "	19	TRACK	GER	239 000
(AB)	ARE YOU/AXIS	19	POLYDOR		2383 031
(C)	SMASH HITS	1968	REPRISE	US	MS2025
(C)	" "	1968	TRACK	UK	613 004
(C)	" "	1973	POLYDOR	UK	ACD 219
(C)	" "	1968	POLYDOR	GER	184 138
(D)	ELECTRIC LADYLAND(DBL)	1968	TRACK	UK	2657 001
(D)	" "	1968	REPRISE	US	2RS 6307
(D)	" "	1968	POLYDOR	GER	2612 002
(D)	" "	197	POLYDOR	UK	2657 012
(D)	" "	19	BARCLAY	FR	80583/4
(D)	" " PT1	1968	TRACK	UK	613 010
(D)	" " PT1	1974	POLYDOR	UK	2310 271
(D)	" " PT2	1968	TRACK	UK	613 017
(D)	" " PT2	1968	POLYDOR	UK	2310 272
(E)	ELECTRIC HENDRIX*****	1968	TRACK	UK	2856 002
(F)	MONTEREY	1970	REPRISE	UK	K40430
(F)	" "	1970	REPRISE	US	MS 2029
(G)	BAND OF GYPSYS	1970	TRACK	UK	2406 002
(G)	" " "	1970	CAPITOL	US	STA0472
(G)	" " "	1970	BARCLAY	FR	92922
(G)	" " "	1974	POLYDOR	UK	2480 005
(H)	CRY OF LOVE	1971	POLYDOR	UK	2302 023
(H)	" " "	1971	BARCLAY	FR	80433
(H)	" " "	1971	REPRISE	US	RS 2034
(H)	" " "	197	POLYDOR		2406 002
(H)	" " "	197	POLYDOR		2408 101
(I)	RAINBOW BRIDGE	1971	REPRISE	UK	K44159
(I)	" "	1971	REPRISE	US	RS 2040
(J)	ISLE OF WIGHT	1971	BARCLAY	FR	80462
(J)	" " "	1971	POLYDOR	UK	2302 016
(K)	IN THE WEST	1972	POLYDOR	UK	2302 018
(K)	" " "	1972	BARCLAY	FR	80448
(K)	" " "	1972	REPRISE	US	RS 2049
(L)	WAR HEROES	1973	POLYDOR	UK	2302 020
(L)	" "	1973	BARCLAY	FR	80448
(L)	" "	1973	REPRISE	US	RS 2103
(M)	JIMI HENDRIX(COMP)	1973	REPRISE	UK	K64017
(N)	LOOSE ENDS	1973	POLYDOR	UK	2310 301
(N)	" "	1973	BARCLAY	FR	80491

(CONTINUED)

PAUL CARUSO	HCA	(H
LITTLE RICHARD	V K	(
DEWEY TERRY	G	(
DON SUGARCANE HARRIS	VLN	(
EDDIE BROWN	D	(
MIKE FINNIGAN	B	(D
FREDDIE SMITH	SAX	(D
LARRY FAUCETTE	CONGA	(D
GARY LEEDS		(B
ROY WOOD	V	(B
TREVOR BURTON	V	(B
GRAHAM NASH		(B
MIKE MANDEL	PNO	(D

***** THIS ALBUM WITHDRAWN BEFORE PUBLIC RELEASE A FEW DJ COPIES CAN BE BOUGHT.

(O) CRASH LANDING	1975	POLYDOR UK	2310 398
(O) " " "	1975	REPRISE US	RS 2204
(P) JIMI HENDRIX(SPECIAL)	1975	POLYDOR UK	2343 080
(Q) JIMI HENDRIX 2(COMP)	1975	POLYDOR UK	2343 086
(R) LEGACY (COMP)	1971	POLYDOR UK	MP9357/8
(S) MIDNIGHT LIGHTNING	1976	POLYDOR UK	2310 415
(S) " "	197	POLYDOR	2302 039
(S) " "	1976	REPRISE US	RS 2229
(T) THE ESSENTIAL	1978	POLYDOR UK	2612 034
(T) THE ESSENTIAL	1978	REPRISE US	2245
(U) 9 TO THE UNIVERSE	1980	POLYDOR	POLS1023
(U) " " " "	1980	POLYDOR UK	2344 155
(U) " " " "	1980	REPRISE US	2299
(V) STONE FREE	1981	POLYDOR UK	2343 114
(W) WOKE UP THIS MORNING	1980	RED LIGHTNIN'	0015
(W) SKY HIGH(BOOTLEG ?)	1972	SKYDOG	SGSH20/7378
(W) SKY HIGH(BOOTLEG ?)	197	KUSTOM	SJSH 1
(X) ESSENTIAL II	1979	REPRISE US	2293
(X) ESSENTIAL II	1979	POLYDOR UK	2311 014
( ) BOX SET 13 LP	1980	POLYDOR UK	2625 040
( ) BOX SET 13 LP	1980	POLYDOR NL	2625 038
( ) LEGENDARY	1980	POLYDOR NL	2490 156
( ) CONCERTS	1	1982	
JIMI HENDRIX	1968	SAGA	6307
AT HIS BEST 1	1972	SAGA	6313
AT HIS BEST 2	1972	SAGA	6314
AT HIS BEST 3	1972	SAGA	6315
LOOKING BACK	1974	EMBER	EMB3428
EXPERIENCE (SOUNDTRACK)	1971	EMBER	NR 5057
EXPERIENCE (SOUNDTRACK)	1971	VOGUE	30148
EXPERIENCE (SOUNDTRACK)	1978	MODE	9011
MORE EXPERIENCE	197	EMBER	NR 5061
MORE EXPERIENCE	1972	VOGUE	782
MORE EXPERIENCE	1972	BULLDOG	BDL4003
JIMI HENDRIX	197	TRIP	3505
JIMI HENDRIX	197	TRIP	3509
ROOTS OF HENDRIX	197	TRIP	9501
IN THE BEGINNING	1973	EMBER	NR 5068
IN THE BEGINNING	197	SHOUT	502
IN THE BEGINNING	197	T NECK US	3007
THE EARLY YEARS	19	MFP	
BIRTH OF SUCCESS	1970	MFP	50053
FRIENDS(LITTLE RICHARD)	1977	EMBER	EMB3434
JIMI HENDRIX	1973	BOULEVARD	41060
JIMI HENDRIX VOL1	1973	PAN	6313
JIMI HENDRIX VOL2	1973	PAN	6314
JIMI HENDRIX VOL3	1973	PAN	6315
HENDRIX 66	197	ENTERPRISE	1030
VERY BEST OF	1975	UA	LA 505
FOR REAL	1976	DJM	DJLMD8011
THE BEST OF	19	MUSIDISC	CV 1208
RARE HENDRIX	1975	ENTERPRISE	3000
RARE HENDRIX	1981	AUDIO FIDELITY	1016
RARE HENDRIX	1975	EXPLOSIVE	558002
RARE HENDRIX	1973	TRIP US	9500
HENDRIX STORY	197	WB	K64017
SUPER HENDRIX	197	MUSIDISC	1354
ETERNAL	197	HALLMARK	732
IN CONCERT	197	SPRINGBOARD	4031
THE WILD ONE	1973	HALLMARK	SHM 791
GET THAT FEELING(C KNIGHT)	1968	LONDON	SH 8349
GET THAT FEELING	1968	CAPITOL US	2856
JIMI HENDRIX	19	BELLAPHON	1552
FACE & PLACE	19	BYG FR	529912
VOODOO CHILE	19	KARUSSEL GER	2999012
STAR PORTRAIT	19	KARUSSEL GER	2672002
BEFORE THE DELUGE	19	EMI	50780
JIM	19	PICKWICK	3528
STRANGE THING	1968	LONDON	SH 8369
BACKTRACK 4(1 SIDE)	19	TRACK	2407 004
BACKTRACK 5(1 SIDE)	19	TRACK	2407 005
GENIUS OF HENDRIX	1978	FESTIVAL	ALB 204
STAR PORTRAIT	197	POLYDOR	2672 002
POP HISTORY	197	POLYDOR	2675 013
JIMI HENDRIX	19	SPRINGBOARD	4010
HIGH LIVE & DIRTY	19	NUTMEG US	1001
COSMIC TURN AROUND	19	AUDIO FIDELITY	1002
TOGETHER	19	PICKWICK US	3347
FREE SPIRIT	19	ACCORD US	7101
BEFORE LONDON	1981	ACCORD US	7101
SUPER PACK	19	TRIP US	3509
GENIUS	19	TRIP US	9523
ROOTS OF ROCK	19	EVEREST US	296
GREATEST SEESIONS	1980	SAAR IT	2506
MOODS	19	TRIP US	9512
2 GREAT EXPERIENCES	1971	PLATINUM UK	6004
2 GREAT EXPERIENCES	1971	MAPLE US	6004
DAY TRIPPER	19	QUALITY	1814
LIVE VOL1	19	STATESIDE	SL155
WHAT'D I SAY	1972	M F P UK	5278

GET THAT FEELING 19 FLASHING US 659
FLASHING 1968 CAPITOL US 2894
LAST NIGHT 19 ALSTAN GER 201016
SECOND TIME AROUND 19 ALSTAN GER 201018
MR PITIFUL 19 ALSTAN GER 201019
WELCOME HOME 19 ALSTAN GER 201020
HUSH NOW 19 ALSTAN GER 201021

H99A SONNY HENNIG H99A

FRANK DIEZ G (A (A) TRANENGAS 1971 KUCKUCK GER 237 5008
WALTI SCHNEIDER B (A
GUNTHER STORCH D (A TOMMI ROEDER SAX (A ERNST SCHULTZ G (A ELKART RAHN B (A

H99B HENRICH & HOCHSTETTER H99B

CHRISTIAN HOCHSTETTER G SIT(A (A) HENRICH & HOCHSTETTER 19 PHILIPS GER 6305 149
UDO HENRICH G V (A
DAGMAR DECKERS V (A HANS ESSERS HCA (A PETE SMITH D PERC (A RALPH KLEINE-TELBE B (A

H100 PIERRE HENRY H100

PIERRE HENRY K SYN(A (A) MESSE DE LIVERPOOL 19 PHILIPS 6510 001
(LINE UP FOR (B) SEE SPOOKY TOOTH (B) CEREMONY (WITH SPOOKY TOOTH) 1969 ISLAND UK ILPS9107
(C) MESSE POUR LE TEMPS 19 PHILIPS 836 893

H101 HENRY COW H101

TIM HODGKINSON SAX K V (ALL (A) LEGEND 1973 VIRGIN US 13107 UK V 2005
ROBERT WYATT V (DE (A) LEGEND 1973 VIRGIN GER 87738
FRED FRITH G VLN K (ALL (B) UNREST 1974 VIRGIN UK V 2011
JOHN GREAVES B PNO(ABCD (C) IN PRAISE OF LEARNING 1975 VIRGIN UK V 2027
PETER BLEGVAD G V CLAR(C (D) CONCERTS 1976 CAROLINE UK CAD 3002
CHRIS CUTLER V (ALL (D) CONCERTS 1978 COMPENDIUM FIDARO 1
ANTHONY MOORE K (C (E) WESTERN CULTURE 1978 BROADCAST BC 1
LINDSAY COOPER WIND (ABCDE
GEOFF LEIGH SAX (CA MONGEZI FEZA TPT (C DAGMAR KRAUSE (ACD GEORGIE BORN B (BE
ANNEMARIE ROELOFS TROM (E LOL COXHILL (B HENK WELIEVRED (B D J PERRY (B
JACK BALCHIN (B MIKE OLDFIELD (B CHARLES FLETCHER (B

H102 HENSKE YESTER H102

JUDY HENSKE V (AB (A) FAREWELL ALDEBARAN 1969 STRAIGHT GER 90928 UK STS 1052
ZAL YANOVSKY PROD (A (A) FAREWELL ALDEBARAN 1969 RERPISE US 6388
JERRY YESTER G B V(AB (B) ROSEBUD 1971 REPRISE RS 6426
GRAIG DOERGE K V (B
JOHN SEITER D V (B DAVID VAUGHT B (B RAY BROWN B (B BUDDY EMMONS STEEL(B
BARRY ZWEIG G (B MIKE DEASY G (B

H103 JUDY HENSKE H103

JUDY HENSKE V (ALL (A) JUDY HENSKE 1963 ELEKTRA EKS 7231
JOHN FORSAY G (BC (B) HIGH FLYING BIRD 1964 ELEKTRA EKS 7241
TOM TEDESCO G (C (C) DEATH DEFYING 1965 REPRISE UK RS 6203
JIMMY BOND B (A (D) A LITTLE BIT OF SUNSHINE 1965 MERCURY US SR 61010
JOHN EWING TROM (A

H104 KEN HENSLEY H104

KEN HENSLEY V G K(AB (A) PROUD WORDS ON A DUSTY SHELF 1973 BRONZE UK ILPS 9223+RI BRON 223
B J COLE STEEL(B (A) PROUD WORDS ON A DUSTY SHELF 1973 MERCURY US 1 661
DAVE PAUL B(A (B) EAGER TO PLEASE 1975 BRONZE UK ILPS 9307+RI BRON 307
GARY THAIN B(A (B) EAGER TO PLEASE 197 WB US 2863
LEE KERSLAKE D(A (C) FREE SPIRIT 1980 BRONZE UK 533
MARK CLARKE B(B
BUGS PEMBERTON D(B

H105 HEPTONES H105

EARL MORGAN G V (D (A) HEPTONES & FRIENDS 1972 TROJAN TBL 183
LEROY SIBBLES B V (D (B) NIGHTFOOD 1976 ISLAND ILPS 9381
BARRY LLEWELLYN V ((C) COOL RASTA 1976 TROJAN TRLS 128
WILLIE LINDO G (D (D) PARTY TIME 1977 ISLAND ISPS 9456
PHILL G (D (E) IN LOVE WITH YOU 1978 UA LA 805
R WILLIAM G (D (F) BETTER DAYS 1978 THIRD WORLD TDWD 1
SKULLY PERC (D (F) BETTER DAYS 1981 MERCURY 6302 037
DAVID MADDEN HRNS (D (G) HEPTONES & FRIENDS VOL 2 197 ATTACK ATLP 1001
GLEN DA COSTA HRNS (D (H) GOOD LIFE 1979 GREENSLEEVES GREL 6
VIN GORDON HRNS (D (J) KING OF MY TOWN 1980 MERCURY 9103 565
BORIS GARDINER B (D
KEITH STERLING PNO (D WINSTON WRIGHT K (D MIKEY BOO D (D

H106 HERD H106

PETER FRAMPTON G V (A (A) PARADISE LOST 1968 FONTANA UK STL 5458
ANDY BOWN K (A (B) LOOKIN' THRU YOU 1968 FONTANA US 67579
GARY TAYLOR B (A (C) NOSTALGIA 1972 BUMBLE US GEMP 5001
ANDREW STEELE D (
RIC ROTHWELL D (HENRY SPINETTI D (TONY CHAPMAN D (TERRY CLARKE G (
LEWIS RICH V (MICK UNDERWOOD D (LOUIS CENNAMO B (

H107 HERE & NOW H107

STEFFY SHARPSTRING G V(ABC (A) WHAT YOU SEE (½ LP WITH A'TV)1 178 DEPTFORD FUN CITY DLP 02
GAVIN DA BLITZ K SYN V(ABC (B) GIVE & TAKE 1978 CHARLY UK NOW 1
KEITH DAMISSILEBASS B V(ABC (C) ALL OVER THE SHOW 1979 CHARLY UK NOW 2
KIF KIF LE BATTER D G V (AB (EP) A DOG IN HELL 1978 CHARLY UK CEP 122
SUZE DA BLOOZ V (AB
ANNE WOMBAT V (AB ROB BOUGIE D (C BERNIE ELLIOTT G (C

H108 HERMANS HERMITS

PETER NOONE V G K(ALL
DEREK LECKENBY G V (KEITH HOPWOOD G V (KARL GREEN B V (BARRY WHITWAM D (
FRANK RENSHAW G (CHRIS FINLEY G (DAVE BARROW (

Title	Year	Label	Country	Number
HERMANS HERMITS	1965	COLUMBIA	UK	33SX1727
HERMANS HERMITS	1965	MGM	US	4382
HERMANS HERMITS	1965	COLUMBIA	GERM	C 73994
HERMANS HERMITS	196	H M V	SW	SGLP 532
HERMANS HERMITS	197	M F P	AUST	A 8148
HERMANS HERMITS	1968	REGAL	UK	SREG1117
THE BEST OF	1965	COLUMBIA	UK	SCXC 27
THE BEST OF	1965	MGM	US	SE 4315
HERMANS HERMITS HITS	1965	COLUMBIA	GERM	C 74030
BRITISH GOGO (ANIMALS)	1965	MGM	US	SE 4306
INTRODUCING	1965	MGM	US	SE 4282
INTRODUCING	1965	ODEON	JAP	7282
ON TOUR	1965	MGM	US	SE 4295
WHEN THE BOYS MEET THE GIRL	65	MGM	US	SE 4334
WHEN THE BOYS MEET THE GIRL	65	MGM	UK	8006
BOTH SIDES OF	1966	COLUMBIA	UK	SX 6084
BOTH SIDES OF	1966	MGM	US	SE 4386
AGAIN	1966	COLUMBIA	GERM	SMC74150
LUCKY 13	1966	COLUMBIA	GERM	SMC74232
HOLD ON(SOUNDTRACK)	1966	MGM	US	SE 4342
BEST OF VOL 2	1966	MGM	US	SE 4416
BEST OF VOL 2	1966	COLUMBIA	UK	SCX 32
THERE'S A KIND OF HUSH	1967	COLUMBIA	UK	SCX 6174
THERE'S A KIND OF HUSH	1967	COLUMBIA	UK	SCXC 34
THERE'S A KIND OF HUSH	1967	MGM	US	SE 4438
X15	1967	COLUMBIA	GERM	SMC74317
BLAZE	1967	MGM	US	SE 4478
BLAZE	1967	COLUMBIA	UK	SCX 35
MRS BROWN (SOUNDTRACK)	1968	COLUMBIA	UK	SCX 6303
MRS BROWN (SOUNDTRACK)	1968	MGM	US	SE 4548
BEST OF VOL 3	1968	MGM	US	SE 4505
THE BEST OF UK	1969	COLUMBIA	UK	SCX 6332
THE MOST OF	1972	M F P	UK	MFP 5216
MOST OF VOL 2	1973	M F P	UK	MFP50008
XX THEIR GREATEST HITS	1973	ABKOC	US	AB 4227
20 GREATEST HITS	1977	K TEL	UK	NE 1001
GREATEST HITS	1980	CRYSATAL	GER	50727
A WHALE OF A TALE (HERMITS)		RCA NOT RELEASED		
ROCK'N'ROLL PARTY	1969	MGM NOT RELEASED		
ROCK'N'ROLL BEST	1977	RAK	JAP	90062
VERY BEST OF	1980	MFP	GER	97206
(EP) HERMANIA	1965	COLUMBIA		SEG 8380
(EP)MRS BROWN	1965	COLUMBIA		SEG 8440
(EP) HITS	1965	COLUMBIA		SEG 8442
(EP) A MUST TO AVOID	1965	COLUMBIA		SEG 8477
(EP) HOLD ON	1966	COLUMBIA		SEG 8503
(EP) DANDY	1966	COLUMBIA		SEG 8520
(EP) LONDON LOOK	1968	YARDLEY (PROMO)		SLE15

H108A HERO

JEFF JONES D (B
MARK HOULE B (B
NEIL CITRONS G V (B
CUT HOULE K V (B SCOTT PHARES V (B

(A) HERO 1977 MERCURY US 1137
(B) BOYS WILL BE BOYS 1978 20 CENTURY US 573

H108B HEROES

(A) BORDER RAIDERS 1980 POLYDOR US 6254 NL 2442 171

H109 HERON

ROY APPS V G K(B
STEVE JONES K (B
TONY POOK V PERC(B
GERALD T MOORE V G K(B MIKE FINESILVER B (B TERRY GITTINS D (B MIKE COOPER G V (B
WILLIE BOAZMAN G V (B

(A) HERON 1970 DAWN UK DNLS 3010
(B) TWICE AS NICE 1972 DAWN UK DNLS 3025

H110 MIKE HERON

MIKE HERON G G K (ABC
DUDU PUKWANA SAX (A
MALCOLM LE MAISTRE C(AB
SIMON NICOL G (A
BETSY COOK V (D
DAVE PEGG B (A
JOE BOYD PROD(A

(A) SMILING MEN WITH BAD REPUTATIONS 1971 ISLAND UK ILPS9146 GER 85381
(A) SMILING MEN WITH BAD REPUTATIONS 197 ELEKTRA US EKS74093
(B) MIKE HERONS REPUTATION 1975 NEIGHBOURHOOD UK NBH 80637
(C) DIAMOND OF DREAM 1977 BRONZE UK ILPS9460+RI BRON460
(C) DIAMOND OF DREAM 1977 BRONZE GER 28571
(D) MIKE HERON 1980 CASABLANCA US 7186

MIKE KOWALSKI D (A RICHARD THOMPSON G (AB GERRY CONWAY D (A SUE GLOVER V (A
SUNNY LESLIE V (A LIZA STRIKE V (A VEMU MUKUNDA (A MOHANA LAKSHMIPATHY (A
VSHAILENDRA (A P R MONEY (A HEATHER WOOD V (A DR STRANGELY STRANGE V(A
PAT DONALDSON B (A TONY COX SYN (A FRANK USHER G (C DAVID SAMS K (C
MIKE TOMICH B (C JOHN GILSTON D (CB SUSIE WATSON-TAYLOR V (CB DAVID BARKER K (C
PETE TOWNSHEND G (A* JOHN ENTWISTLE B (A* KEITH MOON D (A* KRYSIA KOCJAN V (CB
ROSE SIMPSON B (A DAVE MATTACKS D (A JOHN CALE B G K V VLN (A GRAHAM FORBES G (B
TIM HINKLEY K (B AMIN MONAMMED B (B RON LEAHY K (B ULF RONQUIST G (B
BARRY HARWOOD G (B JOHN MULKEY B (B ROY YEAGER PERC (B EDDIE JOBSON VLN (B
ROBIN WILLIAMSON V WHIS(B MELANIE V (B LINDA THOMPSON V (B BENNY KING PERC (B
DUNCAN BROWNE G (B JOE BAVIN B V K (D STEVE LIPSON G V (D DON WELLER SAX (D
JOHN GORDON B (D PETE WINGFIELD K (D HUGH MURPHY PNO (D LIAM GENOCKEY D (D
RICHARD HARVEY WIND (D MEL COLLINS SAX (D FRANK USHER (D FRANK RICOTTI PERC(D
GRAHAM PRESKETT VLN (D NIK ROWLEY STR (D RICHARD BRUNTON G (D PHIL BODGER V (D

*CREDITS ON ALBUM AS TOMMY & THE BIJOUX

H111 GARTH HEWITT

GARTH HEWITT G V (ALL
GRAHAM JARVIS D PERC(A
DAVE WINTOUR B (A
JO PARTRIDGE G (A
MIKE MORAN K (A
KEVIN PEEK G (A
CLIFF RICHARD V (AE
DAVE LAWSON K (A

(A) THE LION & THE RAM 1973 MYRRH MYR1001
(B) I NEVER KNEW LIFE 1974 MYRRH MYR1017
(C) LOVE SONGS T THE EARTH 1976 MYRRH MYR1051
(D) I'M GRATEFUL 1979 MYRRH MYR1078
(E) DID HE JUMP OR DID HE FALL 1979 PATCH UK WOOF1001
(F) UNDER THE INFLUENCE 1981 MARSHALL ART 1002
(G) BEST OF 1980 MYRRH 1093

ADRIAN LEE SYN (A BRYN HAWORTH G (AF PETE WILLSHER STEEL(F VICKI BROWN V (F
TOM BLADES G (F JAN PULSFORD K V (F LUIS JARDIN PERC (F RON ASPERY SAX(F
NETWORK 3 V (F STEVE BRUCE D (F BOB HADDRELL K (F ROB BURNS B (B
CLIFF HALL K (B LAURA WARMUN V (B

H111A JOHN HIATT

JOHN HIATT VG (ALL
JON PARIS B G (C
DOUG YANKUS G (C
BRUCE GARY D (C
B J WILSON D (C
GERRY CONWAY D (C

(A) HANGING ROUND THE OBSERVATORY 197 EPIC US
(B) OVERCOATS 1975 EPIC US 33190
(C) SLUG LINE 1979 MCA US 3088 UK MCF3005
(D) TWO BIT MONSTERS 1980 MCA US 5123 UK MCF3078
(E) ALL OF A SUDDEN 1982 GEFFEN US 2009

JESSE HARMS K V (E THOM MOONEY D (C TODD COCHRAN K (C ETAN McELROY PNO V(C
VEYER HILDEBRAND B (C HOWARD EPSTEIN (D SHANE KEISTER (D DARYL VERDUSCO V D (DE
JAMES ROLLESTON B V (E

H111B JIMMY HIBBERT H111B

JIMMY HIBBERT PERC (A — (A) HEAVY DUTY — 1980 LOGO UK LOGO 1021 NL 63871
MANFRED MANN SYN (A
GEOFF WHITEHORN G V (A — PAT KING B V (A — JOHN LINGWOOD D V (A — GRAHAM PRESKETT SYN (A
ED CROSS V (A — LAURIE CATHAM V PERC(A — DAVE PHEE V (A — STEVE WALLER V (A
STEVE BOLTON V (A

H111C HIFI H111C

LARRY BERRIDGE G V K(AB — (A) TOWNS & BARS — 1980 WEA GER 58105
BYRON CONTOSTAULOS B V (AB — (B) SING SONG — 1981 WEA GER 58270
STEVE GOODWIN PERC (B
TERRY JENKINS G V (AB — STEVE JONES D PERC(A — HERBERT BOHME V (B — JACKSON CONGAS(B

H111D HI TEK H111D

(A) HI TEK — 1981 ORIGINAL ORA105

H111E HI TENSION H111E

PAUL PHILLIPS G (A — (A) HI TENTION — 1978 ISLAND UK ILPS 9564
PAUL McLEAN G (A
DAVID PHILIPS K (A — KEN JOSEPH B (A — DAVID REID D (A — LEROY WILLIAMS CONGA(A
JEFFREY GUISHARD PERC (A — PATRICK McLEAN SAX (A

H112 DAN HICKS & HIS HOT LICKS H112

DAN HICKS V G HCA (ALL — (A) ORIGINAL RECORDINGS — 1969 EPIC US 26464
JON WEBER G (A — (B) WHERES THE MONEY — 1971 BLUE THUMB US BTS29
SID PAGE V VIOLA(ABCDF — (C) STRIKING IT RICH — 1972 BLUE THUMB US 36 UK ILPS 9204
SHERRY SNOW V (A — (D) LAST TRAIN TO HICKSVILLE — 1973 BLUE THUMB US 51 RI US MCA 671
CHRISTINA GANCHER V K (A — (E) HEY GOOD LOOKIN' — 1975 WB UK K 56157
JAIME LEOPOLD VLN B(ABCD — (F) IT HAPPENED ONE BITE — 1978 WB US BSK 3158
MARYANN PRICE V PERC(BCDF
NAOMI EISENBERG V VLN PERC(BCD — JOHN L GIRTON G (CDF — GERRY STEINHOLTZ D PERC(F — BOB SCOTT D (D
MICHAEL FRANKS BANJO(F — LYLE RITZ B (F — CLARENCE McDONALD K (F — BILL DICKENSON B (F
JOHN PISANO G (F — RICHARD BORD D PERC(E

H113 JOE HIGGS H113

JOE HIGGS (A — (A) LIFE OF CONTRADICTION — 1976 VULCAN GROL 508
(B) UNITY IS POWER — 1979 ISLAND ILPS 9535

H113A HIGH INERGY H113A

(A) HIGH INERGY — 1981 MOTOWN UK STML12157

H113B HIGH COTTON H113B

(A) HIGH COTTON — 1975 ISLAND US 9395

H114 HIGH COUNTRY H114

(A) HIGH COUNTRY — 19 RACOON US 1937 UK 7
(B) DREAMS — 19 RACOON US 2608

H114A HIGHWIND H114A

(A) HIGHWIND — 1979 EMI UK INS 3025

H115 HIGH TIDE H115

TONY HILL G (AB — (A) SEA SHANTIES — 1969 LIBERTY US 7638 UK LBS 83264
SIMON HOUSE VLN (AB — (B) HIGH TIDE — 1970 LIBERTY UK LBS 83294
PETER PAVLI B (AB
ROGER HADDEN D (AB

H116 HIGHWAY H116

DARYL BRAITHWAITE V (A — (A) HIGHWAY 1 — 1979 EPIC UK 83760
GARTH PORTER K V (A
TONY MITCHELL B V (A — HARVEY JAMES G V (A — ALAN SANDON D (A — JIM HORN SAX (A
DAVID FOSTER SYN (A — JAY LEWIS G SIT(A — BILL CUOMO K (A — STEVE FORMAN PERC(A
MICHAEL BODDICKER SYN (A — CARMEN TWILLIE V (A — VENNETTE GLOUD V (A — SHARON ROBINSON V(A

H116A HIGHWAY (UK) H116A

RAY MINHINNIT G V (AB — (A) HIGHWAY — 1974 EMI UK EMA 3019
JIM HALL K V (AB — (B) SMOKING AT THE EDGE — 197 EMI UK EMA 770
JOHN GORDON B G V(AB
JON ELSTAR V HCA PERC(AB — IAN BYRON D V (AB

H116B HIGHWAY ROBBERY H116B

DON FRANCISCO D V (A — (A) FOR LOVE OR MONEY — 1972 RCA US LSP 4735
MICHAEL STEVENS G V (A
JOHN LIVINGSTON TUNISON B V(A

H116C ROSSETTA HIGHTOWER H116C

ROSSETTA HIGHTOWER V (A — (A) HIGHTOWER — 1971 CBS UK 64201
HENRY McCULLOUGH G (A
RICK GRECH B (A — KEN CRADDOCK K (A — GORDON BECK K (A — JIM PRICE TPT (A
BOBBY KEYS SAX (A — COLIN GREEN G (A — HAROLD McNAIR WIND(A — HENRY LOWTHER TPT(A
BRUCE ROWLANDS D (A

H117 DAN HILL H117

DAN HILL G V (ALL — (A) DAN HILL — 1976 20th CENTURY BTH 500
LARRY LONDIN D (BC — (B) HOLD ON — 197 20th CENTURY BTH 526
RICK HOMME B (ABC — (C) LONGER FUSE — 1978 20th CENTURY BTH 8005+BT 547
DON POTTER V G (ABC — (D) FROZEN IN THE NIGHT — 1978 20th CENTURY BT 558
JOHN CAPEK K (BC — (E) IF DREAMS HAD WINGS — 1980 EPIC US 36411 UK 84273
FRED MOLLIN G V (ABC — (F) BEST OF — 1980 20TH CENTURY 614
MATTHEW McAULEY V K (ABC — (G) PARTIAL SURRENDER — 1981 EPIC
CATHY SMITH V (B
BOB MANN G (BC
BRIAN RUSSELL G (AB — BOBBY OGDIN PNO (C — BEN MINK MAND (C — ERICA GOODMAN HARP(C
TOM SZCZESNIAK B (ABC — JORN ANDERSEN D (BC — DENNIS PENDRITH B (C — RON LAURIE CELLO B(C
BOB BOUCHER B (B — BRIAN LEONARD D (A — BARRY KEANE D (A — STEPHANIE TAYLOR V (C
ERIC ROBINSON K (ABC

H117A JESSE HILL H117A

JESSIE HILL V (A — (A) NATURALY — 197 BLUE THUMB US BTS31
DAVE LASTIE (A
BUCK BLACK (A — SHINE ROBINSON (A

H118 ROY HILL H118

ROY HILL V (A12 (A) ROY HILL 1978 ARISTA UK SPART1034
MIKE TAYLOR K (12 (1) 1978 (2) 1979
JAMIE WEST ORHAM G (1
STEVE SHONE B (1 COLIN WILKINSON D (1 JOHN KNIGHTSBRIDGE G (2 CHAS CRONK B (2
PETE ACOCK WIND (2 PETE THOMAS WIND (2 TONY FERNANDEZ D (2

H119 STEVE HILLAGE H119

STEVE HILLAGE G SYN V (ALL (A) FISH RISING 1975 ATLANTIC US 13118 VIRGIN UK V2031
MIQUETTE GIRAUDY K (BCDEFGA (B) "L" 1975 ATLANTIS US 18205 VIRGIN UK V2066
PIERRE MOERLEN PERC (A (B) "L" 1975 VIRGIN GER 28023
DON CHERRY HRNS (B (C) MOTOVATION RADIO 1977 ATLANTIC US 19144 VIRGIN UK V2777
MIKE HOWLETT B (A (C) MOTOVATION RADIO 1977 VIRGIN GER 25469
ROGER POWELL K (B (D) GREEN 1978 VIRGIN GER 25875 UK V2098
JOHN WILCOX D (B (E) LIVE HERALD (DBL) 1978 VIRGIN GER 200 273 UK 3502
KASIM SULTON B (B (F) OPEN 1979 VIRGIN UK V2135
LARRY KARUSH PERC(B (G) RAINBOW DOME MUSICK 1979 VIRGIN EURO 2445301 UK VR1
SONJA MALKINE K (B ( ) AURA 1980 AURA US 1 GER 202 799
LINDSAY COOPER WIND (A
COLIN BASS B (E PHILIP HODGE K (E BASIL BROOKS K (E JAHIB PERC (E
CHRISTIAN BOULE G (EA CLIVE BUNKER D (E CURTIS ROBERTSON B (DE JOE BLOCKER D (BCDE
CHUCK BYNUM K G (JOHN McKENZIE B (E ANDY ANDERSON D (DEF DAVE STEWART G V (F
JEAN PHILIPPE RYKIEL SYN(F REG McBRIDE B (C MALCOLM CECIL SYN (C DAVE STEWART SYN (AFG
PAUL FRANCIS B (F TIM BLAKE SYN (A DIDIER MALHERBE WIND(A GILLI SMYTH V (A
NICK MASON D (D RUPERT ATWILL (G

H120 CHRIS HILLMAN H120

CHRIS HILLMAN G V B(ALL (A) CHRIS HILLMAN 1974 TOG 1012
LARRY SIMS B V (C (B) SLIPPIN' AWAY 1976 ASYLUM US 7E 1062 UK K 53041
AL GARTH SAX FDL(C (C) CLEAR SAILIN' 1977 ASYLUM US 7E 1104 UK K 53060
MEREL BREGANTE D (C
FUZZY SAMUELS B (RICHARD MARS G V (BC SKIP EDWARDS K SYN STE(C JOHN BRENNEN G (C
JOE LALA PERC (BC JIM GORDON D (B PAUL HARRIS K (B GEORGE TERRY G (B
STEVE CROPPER G (B TIM SCHMIT V (BC HERB PEDERSEN V (B MARK VOLMAN V (B
HOWARD KAYLAN V (B JIM FIELDER B (B RUSS KUNKEL D (B LEE SKLAR B (B
AL PERKINS STEEL(B ALBHY GALUTEN SYN (B DONNIE DACUS G (B RICK ROBERTS V (B
DONALD DUNN B (B SAM BROUSSARD G (B DAVID GARIBALDI D (B HOWARD ALBERT PERC(B
IVORY JOE HARRIS K (B BYRON BERLINE V FDL(B BERNIE LEADON G V (B JOCK BARTLEY G (C
MICHAEL CLARKE TAMB (C BOBBY LAKIND PERC (C RON ALBERT PROD(C HOWARD ALBERT PROD (B

H121 RUPERT HINE H121

RUPERT HINE G V HCA (AB (A) PICK UP A BONE 1971 PURPLE US 879 UK TPSA 7502
SIMON JEFFES G (A (B) UNFINISHED PICTURE 1973 PURPLE UK TPSA 7509
DAVID MACIVER G (A (C) IMMUNITY 1981 A&M US 4858 UK AMLH68519
BARRY DE SOUZA D (A
PETER ROBINSON K (A PETE MORGAN B (A TERRY COX D (A CLIVE HICKS G (A
RAUL MAYORA PERC (A ERIC FORD G (A JOE MORETTI G (A STEVE HAMMOND G BAN(A
PAUL BUCKMASTER CELLO(A EDDIE MORDUE WIND (A ROY WILCOX WIND (A ROGER GLOVER PERC(A
GEOFF RICHARDSON VLA (A PHIL COLLINS PERC (C PHIL PALMER G (C OLLIE W TAYLOR WIND(C
MARIANNE FAITHFULL V (C TREVOR MORAIS D PERC(C

H122 JUSTIN HINES H122

JUSTIN HINES V (AB (A) JEZEBEL 1976 ISLAND UK ILPS 9416
(B) JUST IN TIME 1979 MANGO UK MLPS 9532

H122A MARCIA HINES H122A

MARCIA HINES V (A (A) OOH CHILD 1980 LOGO UK LOGO 1023
MIKE PORCARO B (A
DAVID HUNGATE B (A LEE RITENOUR G (A TIM MAY G (A FRED TACKETT G (A
ROBBIE PORTER PERC (A RICK SPRINGFIELD G (A BOB MACK G (A PAUL SABY G (A
WILLIE ORNELAS D (A ED GREENE D (A STEVE FORMAN PERC (A JAI WINDING K (A
AL CAPPS K (A TERRY YOUNG K (A JULIUS WECHTER PERC (A BOB CONTI PERC (A
CARL FRIBERG PERC (A

H123 HINKLEYS HERO'S H123

TIM HINKLEY K (12 PICK UP BAND WHICH FORMS FROM TIME TO TIME FOR ODD GIGS PERSONNEL VARIES
MIKE PATTO V (1 (1) 1976/JAN 77
BOZ BURRELL B (12 (2) JULY 1980
HENRY McCULLOUGH D (12
POLI PALMER VIBES(12 CHARLIE WHITNEY G (1 BRIAN ROBERTSON G (1 MICK RALPHS G (1
JOHN HALSEY D (12 BERNIE HOLLAND G (1 BOB TENCH G V (1 ROGER CHAPMAN V (12
STEVE SIMPSON G (2 MITCH MITCHELL D (12 MEL COLLINS SAX (12 JIM CREGAN G (1
ERIC BURDON V (1 KIKI DEE V (2

H123A HIROSHIMA H123A

(A) HIROSHIMA 19 ARISTA US 4252

H124 HITCH HIKERS H124

(A) HITCH HIKERS 1977 ABC ABCL 5209

H124A HITMEN H124A

BEN WATKINS G V (A (A) AIM FOR THE FEET 1980 URGENT UK ZIP84888 CBS US 36874
PETE GLENISTER G V (A
NEIL BROCKBANK B (A STAN SHAW K (A MIKE GAFFEY D V (A

H124B ROBYN HITCHCOCK H124B

ROBYN HITCHCOCK V K B G (A (A) BLACK SNAKE DIAMOND ROLE 1981 ARMAGEDDON UK ARM4
MORRIS WINDSOR D V (A
GARY BARNACLE SAX (A MATTHEW SELIGMANN B (A VINCE ELY D (A KIMBERLEY REW G (A
KNOX G (A ROBB APPLETON V (A HOWIE GILBERT V (A TOM DOLBY SYN(A

H125 HOBO H125

STUART HARRISON V G (A (A) HOBO 1976 ROCKFIELD UAS 29909
COLIN DUGGAN V G (A
JOHN MORRIS V G (A PAUL COBBOLD B K (A STEVE BULL D (A ROGER DAVIES V (A

H125A TOMMY HOEHN H125A

TOMMY HOEHN V K G(A (A) LOSING YOU TO SLEEP 1978 LONDON US 719 UK SHU 8536
GENE NUNEZ G B (A
JOHN HAMPTON D PERC(A KEITH YOUNG B (A

H125B **HOELDERLIN** H125B

JOACHIM GRUMBKOW G K (AF — (A) HOELDERLIN TRAUM — 1972
CHRISTIAN GRUMBKOW G V (AF — (B) HOELDERLIN — 1975 SPIEGELEI GER 160601
NANNY DE RUIG V (A — (C) CLOWN & CLOUDS — 1976 SPIEGELEI GER 160607
CHRISTOPH NOPPENEY WIND(A — (D) RARE BIRDS — 1977 SPIEGELEI GER 160608
PETER KASEBERG B G V(A — (E) HOELDERLIN LIVE — 1978 SPEGELEI GER 160602
MICHAEL BRUCHMANN D (A — (F) NEW FACES — 1979 SPEGELEI GER 145605
PETER BURSCH SIT (A
MIKE HELLBACK TABLA(A WALTER WESTRUPP FLT (A HANS BAR B V (F EDWARD SCHICKE D PERC(F
TOMMY LONE K G V(F RUDIGER ELZE G (F

H126 **MICHAEL HOENIG** H126

MICHAEL HOENIG K SYN(A — (A) DEPARTURE FROM THE NORTHERN WASTELAND 1978 WB US BSK3152 UK K56464
LUTZ ULBRICH G (A
MICKY DUWE V (A USCHI V (A

H126A **HOG HEAVEN** H126A

PETER LUCIA D V (A — (A) HOG HEAVEN — 1971 ROULETTE US 42057
MIKE VALE B V (A
RON ROSMAN K V (A EDDIE GRAY G (A

H127 **SILAS HOGAN** H127

SILAS HOGAN — (A) TROUBLE AT HOME — 19 CONTEMPO CRM 117
(A) TROUBLE AT HOME — 1971 BLUE HORIZON 2431 008

H128 **SMOKEY HOGG** H128

SMOKEY HOGG — (A) SINGS THE BLUES — 19 EMBER EMB 3405
(B) JOHN LEE HOOKER,LIGHTNING HOPKINS 1973 SPECIALTY SNTF 5013
(C) U BETTER WATCH THAT JIVE — 1974 SPECIALTY SNTF 5018
( ) SMOKEY HOGG — 19 TIME US 6
( ) ORG FOLK BLUES — 19 UNITED US 7745
( ) ORG FOLK BLUES — 19 KENT US 5024
( ) SINGS — 19 CROWN US 5226

H128A **HOGS HEAD** H128A

COLIN DAVIDSON G V (A — (A) ROCKIN(IN THE COUNTRY — 1979 ROLLERCOASTER ROLL 2003
D G ELVIN G (A
KEN CLEAVE G (A DAVID VAUGHAN HCA (A JERRY ALLSFORD FDL (A DAVE HATFIELD B (A
RICHIE BULL BAN PROD(A

H129 **HOKUS POKE** H129

CLIVE BLENKHORN G V (A — (A) EARTH HARMONY — 1972 VERTIGO UK 6360 064
SMITH CAMPBELL B (A
ROGER CLARKE G STEEL(A JOHNNIE MILES D (A

H129A **HOKUS POKUS** H129A

MICHAEL MONARCH (— (A) HOKUS POKUS — 19
JON HYDE (
SCOTT THURSTON (BILLLY CIOFFI (DANNY GORMAN (

H129B **RANDOM HOLD** H129B

RANDOM HOLD V (ABC — (A) RANDOM HOLD (EP) — 1979 POLYDOR UK RHX 1
DAVE FERGUSON K (AB — (B) THE VIEW FROM HERE — 1980 POLYDOR POLS1015 2383 564
DAVID RHODES G (AB — (C) ETCETERAVILLE — 1980 PASSPORT US 9847
BILL MACCORMICK B (AB
PETER PHIPPS D (AB DAVID LEECH D (SIMON AINLEY G V (

H130 **RAM JAM HOLDER** H130

RAM JAM HOLDER (ALL — (A) BOOTLEG BLUES — 1974 BEACON BEA 17
(B) BLACK LONDON BLUES — 1974 BEACON BEA 2
(C) YOU SIMPLY ARE — 1975 FRESH AIR 9299 470

H131 **ALLAN HOLDSWORTH** H131

ALLAN HOLDSWORTH G (A — (A) VELVET DARKNESS — 1977 CTI 6068
ALPHONSE JOHNSON B (A
ALAN PASQUE K (A NARADA MICHAEL WALDEN D (A

H131A **MARC HOLLANDER** H131A

MARC HOLLANDER K CLAR SAX(A — (A) ONZE DANSES POUR COMBATTRE LA MIGRAINE1977 KAMIKAZE KAM1
PAOLO RADONI G (A
JEANNOT GILLIS VLN (A VINCENT KENIS ACC (A CATHERINE JAUNIAUX V (A LUCY GRAUMAN V (A
CHRIS JORIS K SAX(A DAVID LEE SCHLOSS SAX (A

H131B **HOLLANDER** H131B

(A) SIDE KICKS — 1980 CBS 84567

H131C **JOOLS HOLLAND** H131C

JOOLS HOLLAND V K (A — (A) AND THE MILLIONAIRES — 1981 A&M UK AMLH 68534

H131D **BRENDA HOLLOWAY** H131D

BRENDA HOLLOWAY V (ALL — (A) EVERY LITTLE BIT HURTS — 19 TAMLA US 257
(B) ARTISTY OF — 19 TAMLA UK STML11083

H132 **THE HOLLIES** H132

TONY HICKS G (ALL — (A) STAY WITH THE HOLLIES — 1964 PARLOPHONE UK (S)3054 (M) 1220
(A) STAY WITH THE HOLLIES — 1964 WORLD RECORDS 1035
ALLAN CLARKE V (ABCDEFGHIJX — (B) IN THE HOLLIES STYLE — 1965 PARLOPHONE UK (M) 1235
TERRY SYLVESTER G V (X — (C) HERE I GO — 1965 IMPERIAL US 12265
MICHAEL RICKFORS B (— (D) HEAR HERE — 1965 IMPERIAL US 12299
GRAHAM NASH G/V (ABCDEFGHIJ — (E) THE HOLLIES — 1965 PARLOPHONE UK (M) 1261
DON RATHBONE D (— (E) THE HOLLIES — 1965 IMPERIAL US 12312
ERIC HAYDOCK B (— (F) WOULD YOU BELIEVE — 1966 PARLOPHONE UK 7008
BOBBY ELLIOTT D (X — (G) FOR CERTAIN BECAUSE — 1966 PARLOPHONE UK 7011
BERNIE CALVERT B (X — (H) EVOLUTION — 1967 EPIC US 26315 PARLOPHONE UK7022
(H) EVOLUTION — 1978 PARLOPHONE UK RI 7175
PETE WINGFIELD K (XYZ — (I) BUTTERFLY — 1967 PARLOPHONE UK 7039
PETER ARNESEN K (YZ — (I) BUTTERFLY — 1978 PARLOPHONE UK RI 7177
JIMMY JEWELL SAX (Y — (J) HOLLIES GREATEST — 1968 EPIC US 32061 PARLOPHONE UK7057
TONY COE SAX (Y — (J) HOLLIES GREATEST — 19 ODEON SM074 236
REG BROOKS HRNS (Z — ( ) KING MIDAS — 1968 EPIC US 26344
SOL AMARFIO CONGA(Y — ( ) SING DYLAN — 1969 EPIC US 26447 PARLOPHONE UK7078
HOWIE CASEY HRNS (Z — ( ) SING HOLLIES — 1969 PARLOPHONE UK 7092
DON HARPER VLN (Z — ( ) GREATEST HITS — 1969 IMPERIAL US 12350
DAVE CASWELL HRNS (Z — ( ) MOVING FINGER — 196 EPIC US 30255
RON ASPERY HRNS (Z — (E) REFLECTION — 1969 STARLINE UK SRS 5008

(CONTINUED)

	Title	Release
( )	HE AINT HEAVY	1970 EPIC US 26538
( )	CONFESSIONS OF THE MIND	1970 PARLOPHONE UK 7116+RI 1978 7178
( )	BUS STOP	19 IMPERIAL US 12330
( )	BUS STOP	19 EMIDISC EURO 048 50732
( )	DISTANT LIGHT	1971 EPIC US 30958 PARLOPHONE 10005
( )	STOP STOP STOP	1971 IMPERIAL US 12339 STARLINE 5088
( )	ROMANY	1972 EPIC US 31992 POLYDOR 2383 144
(H)	HOLLIES	1972 M F P UK 5252
( )	GREATEST HITS VOL 2	1972 PARLOPHONE 7148
( )	GREATEST HITS VOL 2	1974 BOVEMA EURO 054 05432
( )	THE HOLLIES	1974 EPIC US 32574 POLYDOR 2383 262
(f)	I CANT LET GO	1974 M F P 50094
( )	ANOTHER NIGHT	1975 EPIC US 33387 POLYDOR 2441 128
( )	HISTORY OF THE HOLLIES DBL	1975 EMI EMSP 650
( )	WRITE ON	1976 POLYDOR 2442 141
( )	RUSSIAN ROULETTE	1976 POLYDOR 2382 421
( )	VINTAGE RARE	19 WRC US 979
( )	VERY BEST OF	1975 UA US LA 329
( )	POP CHRONIK	19 POLYDOR GERM
(X)	LIVE HITS	1977 POLYDOR UK2383 428+GERM2374 123
( )	BEST OF THE HOLLIES	1978 PARLOPHONE UK 7174
( )	THE OTHER SIDE OF	1978 PARLOPHONE UK 7176
( )	20 GOLDEN GREATS	1978 EMI UK EMTV 11
(Y)	CRAZY STEAL	1978 E½IC US 35334 POLYDOR 2383 474
( )	DOUBLE SEVEN O FOUR	1979 POLYDOR UK 2442 160
(Z)	HOLLIES SING HOLLY	1980 POLYDOR UK POLTV 12
( )	THE AIR THAT I BREATH	1980 POLYDOR UK 2384 115
( )	LONG COOL WOMAN	1980 MFP UK 50450
( )	THE BEST OF THE HOLLIES EPS	19 PARLOPHONE UK PMC 7174
( )	THE BEST OF THE HOLLIES EPS RI	19 EMI UK NUT 30
( )	THE OTHER SIDE OF THE HOLLIES	19 PARLOPHONE UK PMC 7186

EPS

	Title	Release
( )	ROCKIN ROBIN	19 PARLOPHONE UK GEP 8909
( )	JUST ONE LOOK	19 PARLOPHONE UK GEP 8911
( )	HERE I GO AGAIN	19 PARLOPHONE UK GEP 8915
( )	WERE THROUGH	19 PARLOPHONE UK GEP 8927
( )	IN THE HOLLIES STYLE	19 PARLOPHONE UK GEP 8934
( )	I'M ALIVE	19 PARLOPHONE UK GEP 8942
( )	I CANT LET GO	19 PARLOPHONE UK GEP 89

H132A LAURIE HOLLOWAY H132A

LAURIE HOLLOWAY K (A
DAVE MARKEE B (A
HUGH BURNS G (A — NORMA WINSTONE V (A — JOHN GIRVAN G (A — BARRY MORGAN D (A

(A) CUMULUS — 1979 HOBO H0503

H133 LOLEATTA HOLLOWAY H133

LOLEATTA HOLLOWAY V (A					
EARL YOUNG D (A					
MADELINE STRICKLAND V (A					
SCOTTY MILLER D (A	STEVE GADD D (A	JIMMY WILLIAMS B (A	RAYMOND EARL B (A		
GORDON EDWARDS B (A	NORMAN HARRIS G (A	T J TINDALL G (A	EDWARD MOORE G (A		
DENNIS RICHARDSON K (A	MIKKI FARROW V (A	CORNELL DUPREE G (A	ERIC GALE G (A		
KIM MILLER G (A	BUNNY SIGLER K (A	RON KERSEY K (A	BRUCE GARY K (A		
JIMMY SIGLER K (A	RICHARD TEE K (A	GEORGE BUSSEY K (A	RON TYSON V (A		
LARRY WASHINGTON CONGA(A	JAMES WALKER CONGA (A	EMANUEL WILLIAMS CONGA(A	BUNNY HARRIS PERC(A		
MOTO PERC (A	CARLA BENSON V (A	EVETTE BENTON V (A	BARBARA INGRAM V (A		

(A) QUEEN OF THE NIGHT — 1978 SALSOUL UK1509 GOLDMINE US 9501
( ) LOLAETTA — 1977 SALSOUL UK5513 GOLDMINE US 9504
( ) LOVE SENSATION — 1980 GOLDMINE US 9506

H133A HOLLY & THE ITALIENS H133A

HOLLY VINCENT V (A

(A) THE RIGHT TO BE ITALIan — 1981 VIRGIN UK 2186 US 37359 EURO 203 434

H134 BUDDY HOLLY H134

BUDDY HOLLY G V(ALL			
BOB MONTGOMERY (			
TOMMY ALSUP G (	JERRY ALLISON D (	NIKI SULLIVAN G (	JOE MAULDIN B(
SONNY CURTIS G FDL(	LERRY WELBORN B (	GRADY MARTIN G (	FARIS COURSEY D (
RAMONA TOLLETT V (	BILL PICKERING V (	BOB LATHAM V (	NORMAN PETTY K (
BOB LINVILLE V (	DAVID BIGHAM V (	PANAMA FRANCIS D (	BO CLARKE D (
WAYLON JENNINGS V (	PHIL EVERLY V (	DON GUESS B (	BOOTS RANDOLPH SAX(
OWEN BRADLEY PNO (	GARY TOLLETT V (	JOHN PICKERING V (	VI PRTTY V (
G W KENDALL PNO (	RAY RUSH V (	RAY RUSH V (	SAM TAYLOR SAX(
HELEN WAY SINGERS V (	GEORGE ATWOOD B (	KING CURTIS SAX (	LOU GIORDANO V (

Title	Release	Title	Release
CHIRPIN CRICKETS	1957 BRUNSWICK US 54038	GREATEST HITS	1967 ACE OF HEARTS AH148
CHIRPIN CRICKETS	1958 CORAL UK 9081	GREATEST HITS	1969 CORAL UK CP8
CHIRPIN CRICKETS	1969 CORAL UK CP 20	GREATEST HITS	1974 MCA UK CDLM 8007
CHIRPIN CRICKETS	1975 MCA UK CD 8035	GREATEST HITS	1974 CORAL UK CRLM 1001
BUDDY HOLLY	1958 CORAL UK 9085	GREATEST HITS	1974 CORAL UK CRL 1005
BUDDY HOLLY	19 CORAL US 57210	GREATEST HITS 2	1970 CORAL UK CPS 47
BUDDY HOLLY	1975 MCA UK CP 8034	LISTEN TO ME	1968 MCA UK MUPS 312
BUDDY HOLLY STORY	1959 CORAL UK 9105	LISTEN TO ME	1974 MCA UK MCF 2613
BUDDY HOLLY STORY	19 CORAL US 57279	THE GREAT BUDDY HOLLY	196 CORAL US 57492
BUDDY HOLLY STORY	19 CORAL US 81182	THE GREAT BUDDY HOLLY	196 VOCALION UA VL 3811
BUDDY HOLLY STORY 2	1960 CORAL UK 9127	RAVE ON	1968 MCA UK MUPS 313
BUDDY HOLLY STORY 2	196 CORAL US 57326	RAVE ON	1974 MCA UK MCF 2614
THAT'LL BE THE DAY	1961 ACE OF HEARTS AH3	RAVE ON	1975 M F P UK 50176
THAT'LL BE THE DAY	1974 CORAL UK CP 24	BROWN EYED HANDSOME MAN	1968 MCA UK MUPS 314
THAT'LL BE THE DAY	197 DECCA US 8707	BROWN EYED HANDSOME MAN	1974 MCA UK MCF 2615
THAT'LL BE THE DAY	1974 CORAL UK CRL1024	HE'S THE ONE	1968 MCA UK MUPS 315
REMINISCING	1963 CORAL UK LVA 9212	TRUE LOVE WAYS	1968 MCA UK MUPS 319
REMINISCING	1963 CORAL US 57426	TRUE LOVE WAYS	1974 MCA UK MCF 2616
REMINISCING	1974 MCA UK MCF2615	WISHIN'	1968 MCA UK MUPS 320
SHOWCASE	1964 CORAL UK LVA 9222	GIANT	1969 MCA UK MUPS 371
SHOWCASE	1964 CORAL US 57450	GIANT	196 CORAL US 57504
HOLLY IN THE HILLS	1965 CORAL UK LVA 9227	GIANT	1974 MCA UK MCF 2625
HOLLY IN THE HILLS	1965 CORAL US 57463	REMEMBER	1971 CORAL UK CPS 71
BEST OF	1966 CORAL US CXB 8	REMEMBER	1974 CORAL UK CRL 1087
		GOOD ROCKIN'	1971 VOCALION US 73923

(CONTINUED)

H134 BUDDY HOLLY (CONTINUED) H134

ROCK'N'ROLL COLLECTION 1972 MCA 2 4009
ROCK'N'ROLL COLLECTION 1972 DECCA US DSXE 7207
LEGEND 1974 MCA UK CDMSP 802
COMPLETE B H (9LP SET) 1974 MCA UK COPS 7100H1/9
NASHVILLE SESSIONS 1975 MCA UK CDLM 8038
STORY 1975 WORLD RECORDS 301/5
PORTRAIT IN MUSIC 1975 TELDEC EURO 4408
PORTRAIT IN MUSIC (DBL) 1975 CORAL UK 5616/7
WESTERN & BOP 1978 MCA UK CDLM 8055
20 GREATEST HITS 1978 MCA UK CMTV8
20 GOLDEN GREATS 19 MCA UK 3040
BUDDY HOLLY (6LP SET) 1979 CORAL CDMSP 807
BUDDY HOLLY LIVES 1978 MCA EMTV 8
BUDDY HOLLY STORY 1979 WARWICK WW 5064
BUDDY HOLLY 1980 PICKWICK UK 3070
ROCK ON WITH BUDDY HOLLY 1980 M F P UK 54495

E Ps
LISTEN TO ME 1958 CORAL UK 2002
SOUND OF THE CRICKETS 1958 CORAL UK 2003
RAVE ON 1958 CORAL UK 2005
ITS SO EASY 1959 CORAL UK 2014
HEARTBEAT 1959 CORAL UK 2015
IT DOESN'T MATTER ANY MORE 1959 CORAL UK 2032
BUDDY HOLLY 1 1959 BRUNSWICK UK 9456
BUDDY HOLLY 2 1959 BRUNSWICK UK 9457
LATE GREAT 1960 CORAL UK 2044
4 MORE 1960 CORAL UK 2060
THAT'LL BE THE DAY 1960 CORAL UK 2062
BY REQUEST 1964 CORAL UK 2065
TEX MEX SOUND 1964 CORAL UK 2066
WISHING 1964 CORAL UK 2067
SHOWCASE 1965 CORAL UK 2068
SHOWCASE 2 1965 CORAL UK 2069
SINGS 1965 CORAL UK 2070

H134A HOLLYWOOD ARGYLES H134A

GARY PAXTON V (
BOBBY REY V (
TED MARSH V (GARY WEBB D (DEANY WEAVER G (TED WINTERS B (A

(A) ALLEY OOP 196 LUTE US L9001

H135 HOLLYWOOD BRATS H135

ANDREW MATHESON V (AB
EUNON BRADY G (AB
WAYNE MANOR B (AB
LOUIS SPARKS D (AB CASINO STEEL G V K (AB

(A) GROWN UP WRONG 1975 US
(B) HOLLYWOOD BRATS (RECORDED 73) 1980 CHERRY RED UK ARED 6

H135A HOLLYWOOD STARS H135A

TERRY RAE V D (A
RUBEN DE FUENTES G (A
BOBBY DRIER D (A MARK ANTHONY V G (A NICKY HOPKINS PNO (A MICHAEL RUMMANS B (A
STEVE DeLACY G (A OLLIVER E BROWN CONGA(A

(A) HOLLYWOOD STARS 1977 ARISTA AL4119

H135B HOLLYWOOD FATS BAND H135B

HOLLYWOOD FATS G (A
FRED KAPLAN PNO (A
LARRY TAYLOR B (A AL BLAKE V HCA (A RICHARD INNES D (A

(A) HOLLYWOOD FATS BAND 1979 PBR 7008

H136 JAKE HOLMES H136

JAKE HOLMES G K V(ALL
TED IRWIN G (A
WELDON MYRICK STEEL(A
DAVID BRIGGS PNO (A
KENNY BUTTREY D (A

(A) JAKE HOLMES 1969 POLYDOR UK 583 578
(B) SO CLOSE SO VERY FAR TO GO 1970 POLYDOR UK 2425036 US 244 034
(C) HOW MUCH TIME 1972 CBS US 30996 UK 64905
( ) ABOVE GROUND SOUND OF JAKE HOLMES 19 TOWER US ST 5079

H136A NICK HOLMES H136A

NICK HOLMES G V (A
DONALD McDONALD D (A
TONY LEVIN B (A MICHAEL MAINIERI K VIBES(A HUGH McCRACKEN G (A DAVID BROMBERG DOB (A
JON PIERSON V (A DAVID SPINNOZA G (A RANDY BRECKER HRNS (A JEREMY STEIS FLT (A

(A) THE SOULFUL CROONER 1973 JUST SUNSHINE US JSS 3

H137 RUPERT HOLMES H137

RUPERT HOLMES V K SYN (ALL
DEAN BAILIN G (F
BENNY GRAMM D PERC(F
ALAN SCHWARZBERG D (C
JOHN CARUSO B (F
CHRISSY FAITH V (F
PHIL BUDHOS PNO (F
SETH GLASSMAN B (F
JIMMIE YOUNG D (C
JIMMY MAELEN PERC (C WILBUR BASCOMB B (C WILL LEE B (C JOE MACK B (C
STEVE KHAN G (C ELLIOTT RANDALL G (C HILDA HARRIS V (C CARTER CATHEART K (C
PAT REBILLOT K (C MICHAEL BRECKER SAX (C RANDY BRECKER HRNS (C MEL DAVIS TPT (C
MARVIN STAMM TPT (C PETER GORDON HRNS (C VIVISN CHERRY V (C LANI GROVES V (C
MAERETHA STEWART V (C

(A) RUPERT HOLMES 1975 EPIC UK 80942 US 33443
(B) WIDESCREEN 1975 EPIC UK 80323 US 32864
(C) PURSUIT OF HAPPINESS 1978 PRIVATE STOCK UK1034 US 7006K
(C) PURSUIT OF HAPPINESS 1980 MCA RI US 3241
(D) SINGLES 197 EPIC US 34283
(E) PARTNERS IN CRIME 1979 MCA UK MCF3051 INFINITY US 9020
(F) ADVENTURE 1980 MCA UK MCF3088 MCA US 5129
(G) FULL CIRCLE 1981 ELEKTRA US 560 UK K52328

H137A HOLOCAUST H137A

(A) THE NIGHTCOMERS 1981 PHOENIX UK PSLP1

H137B GARY HOLTON & CASINO STEEL H137B

GARY HOLTON V (AB
CASINO STEEL (PNO (AB
GEIR WADE (
BARD SVENDSEN (BARD FREDRIKSEN (CARL H WAADELAND (IVAR GAFSETH (
J P WEST (EUNAN BRADY (JOHN CHIVERS (GUNNAR BERG (
BJORN NESSJOE (SEXY BERIT (TRONDHEIM SYM ORCH (

(A) GARY HOLTON & CASINO STEEL 1981 POLYDOR SCAN 2382 124
(B) PART 2 1982 POLYDOR SCAN 2382 130

H138 ROOSEVELT HOLTS H138

ROOSEVELT HOLTS G V (

(A) PRESENTING THE COUNTRY BLUES 19 BLUE HORIZON UK 763201+US 7704
(B) AND HIS FRIENDS 1974 ARHOOLIE US 1057

H138A HOLY MACKEREL H138A

PAUL H WILLIAMS V (A
GEORGE HILLER G K V (A
RALPH WILLIAMS G V (A JEREMIAH SCHEFF B V (A MIKE CANNON D V (A CYNTHIA FITZPATRICK FLT(A

(A) HOLY MACKEREL 1968 REPRISE US 6311

H139 HOLY MODAL ROUNDERS H139

JOHN WESLEY ANNIS D (
ASTEVE WEBER G V (A
RICHARD TYLER PNO (
SAM SHEPARD D (A
PETER STAMPFEL FDL BANJ V(A
ROBIN REMAILLY (
MICHAEL HURLEY (
LUKE FAUST (
KEN CRABTREE K (A
ANTONIA V (A
BARBARA V (A WENDY V (A

(A) INDIAN WAR HOOP 1967 ESP US 1068
(B) MORAY EELS EAT 1968 ELEKTRA US 74026
(C) HOLY MODAL ROUNDERS 1968 PRESTIGE US 7720
(D) HOLY MODAL ROUNDERS 2 1968 PRESTIGE US 7410
(E) GOOD TASTE IS TIMELESS 1969 METROMEDIA US 740
(F) STAMPFEL & WEBER (COMP DBL) 1972 FANTASY US 24711
(G) ALLEGED IN THEIR OWN TIME 1975 ROUNDER US 3004
(H) LAST ROUND 1979 ALDELPHI US 1030
(I) HOLY MODAL ROUNDERS 19 TRANSATLANTIC UK 7451

H139A HOLY MOSES H139A

BILLY BATSON K V (A (A) HOLY MOSES 1971 RCA UK SF 8204 US LSP4523
DAVID VITTEK G BV(A
TEDDY SPEDEDS G V (A MARTY DAVID B SAX V(A CHRISTOPHER PARKER PERC(A

H139B HOMBRES H139B

JOHN W HUNTER D (A (A) LET IT OUT 19 VERVE US 3036
JERRY LEE MASTERS B (A
GARY W McEWEN G (A B B CUNNINGHAM K (A

H140 HOME H140

LAURIE WISEFIELD G V (ABC (A) PAUSE FOR A HOARSE HORSE 197 EPIC US 31146 UK 64365
MICK STUBBS K V G(ABC (B) HOME 1972 CBS UK 64752
CLIFF WILLIAMS B V (ABC (C) ALCHEMIST 1973 CBS UK 65550
MICK COOK V D (ABC
JIMMY ANDERSON K (C DAVID SKILLIN LYRICS (C WILL WEIDER FDL (A CLIVE JOHN K (A

H141 HOMETOWN BAND H141

SHARI ULRICH V VLN FLT (AB (A) FLYING 1976 A&M US 4605 UK AMLH 64605
CLAIRE LAWRENCE WIND (AB (B) HOMETOWN BAND 1977 A&M US 4671
GEOFF EYRE D V (AB
ROBBIE KING K V (AB DOUG EDWARDS K B V G(AB EDWARD PATTERSON G V (B

H142 HONEY BOY H142

(A) SWEET CHERRIES 1974 CACTUS CTLP 101
(B) A TASTE OF HONEY 1975 CACTUS CTLP 105
(C) LOVERS 1977 THIRD WORLD TWLP 108
(D) STRANGE THOUGHTS 1977 TROJAN TRLS 125
(E) DARK END OF THE STREET 1978 DIAMOND DMLP 402
(F) ARISE 1981 DIAMOND UK DMLP 403

H143 HONEYBUS H143

PETER DELLO V ((A) STORY 1970 DERAM UK SML 1056
JIM KELLY G V (A
RAY CANE V G K V (A PETE KIRCHER (COLIN HARE V G B (A

H143A HONEYCOMBS H143A

HONEY LANTREE D V (A (A) ALL SYSTEMS GO 1965 PYE UK NPL 18132
DENIS D'ELL V HCA(A
MARTIN MURRAY G (A ALAN WARD G (A JOHN LANTREE B (A

H144 HONEYDEW H144

(A) HONEYDEW 1971 ARGO ZFB 15

H144A HONK H144A

(A) HONK 1974 20TH CENT 406
(B) HONK 1975 EPIC US 33094

H145 HONKY H145

RAY OTHEN V PERC(A (A) HONKY 1978 CREOLE UK CRLP513
BOB WHITE D (A
TREVOR CUMMINS G (A CLIFF BARKS B (A MALCOLM BAGGOTT SAX (A CLARK NEWTON SAX (A
RON TAYLOR SAX (

H146 HOODOO RHYTHM DEVILS H146

JOHN REWIND G (ABC (A) BARBEQUE OF THE DEVILLE 197 BLUE THUMB US BTS 42
JOE CRANE V (ABCE (B) RACK JOBBERS BLUES 1972 CAPITOL US ST 842
BOB PLUMES G (C (C) WHAT THE KIDS WANT 1973 BLUE THUMB BTS 57+VOGUE FR 10029
GLENN WALTERS PERC V (ABCE (D) SAFE IN THEIR HOMES 1976 FANTASY 9522+WORLD JAZZ 9201
DEXTER C PLATES B (ABC (E) ALL KIDDING ASIDE 1978 FANTASY FTC 540 + F 9543
SKIP MESQUITE SAX (( ) TOO HOT TO HANDLE 1973
JEROME D (C
BOB WRAY B (E MUSCLE SHOALS HRNS (E CLAYTON IVEY K (E BARBARA WYRICK V (E
ROGER CLARK D (E LARRY BYROM G (E SUZY STORM V (E TOM ROADY PERC(E
MARTIN FIERRO HRNS (B MEL MARTIN HRNS (B BOOTS HUGHSTON HRNS (B MIC GILLETTE HRNS(B
CHESTER CRILL HCA (B POINTER SISTERS V (B

H146A HOOK H146A

BOBBY ARLIN G (AB (A) THE HOOK WILL GRAB YOU 19 UNI US 73023
LEE 'BUDDY' SKLAR B (AB (B) HOOKED 19 UNI US 73038
DENNIS PROVISOR K (A
DALE LOYALE D (A CRAIG BOYD D (B

H147 EARL HOOKER H147

EARL HOOKER G (ALL (A) DON'T HAVE TO WORRY 1969 BLUESWAY US 6032
REGGIE BOYD G (J (B) SWEET BLACK ANGEL 1970 BLUE HORIZON UK 763850
JOHNNY'BIG MOOSE'WALKER K V(JJ (B) SWEET BLACK ANGEL 1970 BLUE THUMB US BT8812
LILLIAN OFFITT V (J (C) THERES A FUNGUS 1972 RED LIGHTNING UK RL 009
RICK ALLEN V (J (D) DO YOU REMEMBER 1973 BLUESWAY US BLS6072
A C REED V (J (E) 2 BUGS & A ROACH 1975 ARHOOLIE F 1044
STEVE MILLER PNO V(G (G) HOOKER & STEVE 1975 ARHOOLIE US F 1051
LOUIS MYERS HCA (G (H) FIRST & LAST 1975 ARHOOLIE US F 1066
GENO SKAGGS B V (AG (J) LEADING BRAND 1977 RED LIGHTNING UK RL 0018
BOBBY JOHNSON D (G (K) THE LAST OF THE GREAT EARL HOOKER 1977 ANTILLES US 7024
ROOSEVELT SHAW D (A (L) THE GENIUS 197 CUCU US 3400
ANDREW OLDHAM V (A (M) MEMORIAL ALBUM 19 BLUE FLAME 102
JEFFREY M CARP HCA (A (N) IF YOU MISS HIM 19 BLUESWAY US 6038
PAUL ASBELL G (A (O) BLUE GUITAR 1981 P VINE JAP 9015

H148 HOOKFOOT H148

CALEB QUAYE G V K(ALL (A) HOOKFOOT 1971 DJM UK DJLPS413 US A&M 4316
DAVE GLOVER B (ABE (B) GOOD TIMES A COMIN' 1972 A&M US SP4338 UKDJM DJLPS 422
IAN DUCK HCA V(ALL (C) COMMUNICATIONS 1973 DJM UK DJLPS428 US A&M 4380
ROGER POPE D V (ALL (D) ROARING 1974 DJM UK DJLPS435 US A&M 3608
PETER ROSS HCA V(AE (E) HEADLINES (DBL)(COMP) 1975 DJM DJLPS28013+ DJLMD 8013
FREDDY GANDY B V (CDE
BOB KULICK G V (BE

H149 MARSHALL HOOKS & CO H149

MARSHALL HOOKS G V (A — (A) MARSHALL HOOKS & CO 1970 BLUE HORIZON 2431 003
JOHN GOINES D (A
RON SIMPKINS K (A JIM SUARD B (A

H150 JOHN LEE HOOKER H150

JOHN LEE HOOKER V (ALL
ROBERT HOOKER K (DH
CLIFF COULTER K (DH BENNY ROWE G (DH LUTHER TUCKER G (DEH GINO SKAGGS B (DBH
RON BECK D (DH KEN SWANK D (DEH CHARLIE MUSSELWHITE HCA(D CHUCK GRIMMELL D (DH
MICHAEL WHITE VLN (DH MARK NAFTALIN K (DH PAUL WOOD G (DH MEL BROWN G (DH
RAY McCARTY G (DH ELVIN BISHOP G (DH VAN MORRISON V (DH EDDIE KIRKLAND G (J
MEMPHIS SLIM PNO (A JIMMY REED V G (AK ALAN WILSON G HCA PNO (C HENRY VESTINE G (C
ANTONIO BARRADA B (C ADOLFO DE LA PARRA D (C EDDIE TAYLOR G (K GEORGE WASHINGTON B(K
TOM WHITEHEAD D (K OTIS FINCH SAX (K QUINN WILSON B (K FRANKIE BRADFORD PNO (K
EVERETT McCRARY B (K RICHARD JOHNSON D (K JOE HUNTER PNO (K EARL PHILLIPS D (K
OSCAR BRASHEAR HRNS (H GEORGE BOHANON TROM (H JOHN KLEMMER SAX (H DON MENZA SAX (H
STEVE MILLER PNO (H DON SUGARCANE HARRIS VLN(H JOHN KAHN B (H MARTI McCALL V (H
BLINKY WILLIAMS V (H OMA DRAKE V (H TONY McPHEE G (G GROUNDHOGS (G
CHARLIE GRIMES G (E LEX SILVER B (E EARL HOOKER G (B PAUL ASBELL G (B
JOHNNY WALKER K (B JEFFREY CARP HCA (B ROOSEVELT SHAW D (B

HOUSE OF THE BLUES 1960 CHESS US 1454
HOUSE OF THE BLUES 19 MARBLE ARCH 663
PLAYS & SINGS THE BLUES 1961 CHESS US 1454
TUPELO BLUES 1962 RIVERSIDE 673020
FOLKLORE OF JOHN L HOOKER 1962 STATESIDE UK 10014
FOLKLORE OF JOHN L HOOKER 1962 VEE JAY US 1033
FOLKLORE 19 JOY JOYS133
(A) PREACHIN THE BLUES 1964 STATESIDE UK 10053
(A) BIG SOUL 1964 VEE JAY US 1088
(A) BIG SOUL 19 JOY JOYS147
I WANT TO SHOUT THE BLUES 1964 STATESIDE UK 10074
I WANT TO SHOUT THE BLUES 1964 VEE JAY US 1066
SEVEN NIGHTS 1966
IT SERVES YOU RIGHT 1966 HMV UK CSD3542
IT SERVES YOU RIGHT 1966 IMPULSE US 9103
LIVE AT CAFE AU GO GO 1966 HMV UK CSD3612
LIVE AT CAFE AU GO GO 1973 BLUESWAY BLS6002
REAL FOLK BLUES 1968 CHESS US 1508
REAL FOLK BLUES 19 TRADITIONAL US 2089
URBAN BLUES 1968 STATESIDE 10246
URBAN BLUES 1973 BLUESWAY BLS6012
(B) IF YOU MISS 'IM 1969 BLUESWAY BLS6038
SIMPLY THE TRUTH 1969 STATESIDE 10280
SIMPLY THE TRUTH 1969 BLUESWAY US BLS6023
I'M JOHN LEE HOOKER 196 JOY JOYS101
I'M JOHN LEE HOOKER 19 VEE JAY VJLP1007
BURNIN' 196 JOY JOYS124
BURNIN' 19 VEE JAY 1043
TRAVELLIN' 19 JOY JOYS129
TRAVELLIN' 19 VEE JAY 1023
CONCERT AT NEWPORT 196 JOY JOYS142
CONCERT AT NEWPORT 196 VEE JAY 1078
IN PERSON 196 JOY JOYS152
BEST OF 196 JOY JOYS156
BEST OF 196 VEE JAY 1049
THATS WHERE ITS AT 1970 STAX 2362 017
THATS WHERE ITS AT 197 STAX US 2013
THATS WHERE ITS AT 19 STAX RI US 4343
FOLK BLUES 19 CROWN US CLP5295
MOANIN' & STOMPIN THE BLUES KING US SK 1085
I FEEL GOOD 1972 JEWEL US 5005
NO FRIEND AROUND 1970 RED LIGHTNIN' RL 003
DRIFTIN THE BLUES 19 UNITED US 7710
THE BLUES 19 UNITED US 7725
FOLK BLUES 19 UNITED US 7729
GREAT BLUES SOUNDS 19 UNITED US 7731
IN THE MOOD 19 UPFRONT US 104
IS HE REALY THE WORLDS GREAT VEE JAY US 8502
VERY BEST OF 19 BUDDAH US 4002
BIG RED BLUES 19 BUDDAH US 7506
GOING DOWN HIGHWAY 51 19 SPECIALTY US 2127
BURNIN HELL 19 RIVERSIDE
THATS MY STORY 19 RIVERSIDE 321
FOLK BLUES 19 RIVERSIDE 838
HOOKED ON BLUES 19 ARC FOLK 347
BLUES MEN 19 BATTLE US 6113
HOW LONG BLUES 19 BATTLE US 114
SINGS THE BLUES 19 CROWN US 5232
BLUES 19 CROWN US 5157
SINGS THE BLUES 19 KING US 727
FRIEND AROUND 1979 CHARLY UK CR30170
NO FRIEND AROUND 1970 RED LIGHTNIN' RL 003
NO FRIEND AROUND 1979 CHARLY UK CR30170
COAST TO COAST 1971 U A 29235
COAST TO COAST 1971 U A US 5512
(C) HOOKER & HEAT 1971 LIBERTY UK 103/4
(C) HOOKER & HEAT 19 TRIP US 3501
(C) HOOKER & HEAT 1971 U A US 3500/2
WHISKEY & WIMMEN 19 TRIP US X 9504
REAL BLUES 19 TRADITION US 2089
BOOGIE CHILLIN' 1971 FANTASY US 24706
ENDLESS BOOGIE 1971 PROBE UK SPB1034
ENDLESS BOOGIE 1971 ABC US 720
(D) NEVER GET OUT OF BLUES1972 PROBE UK SPB1057
(D) NEVER GET OUT OF BLUES1972 ABC US 736
(E) LIVE AT SOLEDAD PRISON 72 ABC UK 716
DETROIT SPECIAL 197 ATLANTIC UK K40405
DETROIT SPECIAL 197 ATLANTIC US 7228
SLIMS STOMP 197 POLYDOR UK 2310256
JOHN LEE HOOKER 19 XTRA XTRA114
JOHN LEE HOOKER 19 EVEREST US 222
JOHN LEE HOOKER 19 KENT US 525
JOHN LEE HOOKER 1963 GALAXY (US 8201
JOHN LEE HOOKER 1966 VERVE US 3003
JOHN LEE HOOKER 19 ARCHIVE US 222
GREATEST HITS 19 KENT US 559
JOHN LEE HOOKER 1975 NEW WORLD NW 6003
(F) DUSTY ROAD (DBL) 19 BELLAPHON BLS 5523
(G) DON'T WANT NOBODY 19 INTERCORD 128607
KABUKI WUKI 1973 BLUESWAY BLS6052
(H)BORN IN MISSISSIPPI 1973 ABC ABCX 768
MADMAN BLUES 19 CHESS US 68011
JOHN LEE VOL 1 1973 GREENBOTTLE GN4002
THE BLUES 197 MUSIDISC AM 6078
LIVE AT SUGAR HILL 19 MUSIDISC AM 6094
LIVE AT SUGAR HILL 19 US GALAXY 8205
I WANNA DANCE ALL NIGHT 19 MUSIDISC AM 6101
LIVING WITH BLUES 19 MUSIDISC CV 955
KING OF FOLK BLUES 19 MUSIDISC AM 6074
GREAT BLUES SOUND OF 19 MUSIDISC AM 6077
BLACK R&B 1975 MUSIDISC ALB 186
(J) MAD MAN BLUES 1973 CHECKER 6467 305
(J) MAD MAN BLUES 197 CHESS US 2 60011
BEST OF 1974 CRESCENDO 210007
FREE BEER & CHICKEN 1974 ABC ABCL 5059
FREE BEER & CHICKEN 1974 ABC US 838
ALONE 1974 SPECIALTY SNTF 5005
ALONE 197 SPECIALTY US 2125
ALONE 1980 LABOR US 4
DONT TURN ME FROM YOUR DOOR 74 ATLANTIC UK K40507
DONT TURN ME FROM YOUR DOOR 74 ATCO US SD33151
BIG MACEO MERRIWEATHER 19 FORTUNE US 3002
BLUES BEFORE SUNRISE 1976 BULLDOG 1011
(K) DIMPLES 1977 DJM DJD 28026
BLACK SNAKE 1978 FANTASY US 24722
LIVE 1978 LUNARZ LZS 2008
THE CREAM (DBL) 1978 TOMATO US 2 7009
THIS IS HIP 1980 CHARLY 1004
SITTIN HERE THINKING 1980 MUSE US 5205
EVERYBODY ROCKIN' 1980 CHARLY UK CRB1014

H150A STIX HOOPER H150A

STIX HOOPER D (A — (A) WORLD WITHIN 1979 MCA MCF3042 UK US 3180
ALPHONSO JOHNSON B (A
BOBBY HUTCHERSON PERC (A PAULINHO DA COSTA PERC V(A DEAN PARKS G (A BARRY FINNERTY G (A
ROLAND BAUTISTA G (A KIM HUTCHCROFT HRNS (A LARRY WILLIAMS HRNS (A JERRY HEY HRNS(A
OSAMU KITAJIMA KOTO (A KAZU MATSUI PERC (A TODD COCHRAN SYN (A FRANK MAROCCO MUSETTE(A

H150B HOOVER H150B

(A) HOOVER 1969 EPIC US 26537

H150C **HOPE** H150C

(A) HOPE 1973 A&M US 4329

H151 **MARY HOPKIN** H151

MARY HOPKIN V G HCA (ALL
KEVIN PEEK G (B
BRIAN DALY G (B
RALPH McTELL G (B
TERRY WEIL CELLO(B
DAVE COUSINS G BAN(B
CLIVE ANSTEE CELLO(B DANNY THOMPSON B (B TONY VISCONTI V (B

(A) POSTCARD 1969 APPLE SW 3351 US UK SAPCOR 5
(B) EARTH SONG 1971 APPLE SW 3381 US UK SAPCOR 21
(C) THOSE WERE THE DAYS 1972 APPLE SW 3395 US UK SAPCOR 23
(D) WELSH WORLD OF (RECORDED 1968) 1979 DECCA UK SPA 546
(E) KIDNAPPED 19 AIR US 1042

H152 **LIGHTNIN' HOPKINS** H152

SAM LIGHTNIN' HOPKINS G V(ALL
EARL PALMER D (
JIMMY BOND B (

CALIFORNIA MUDSLIDE 19 VOLT US 129
KEEPS ON RAININ' 19 SUPERSCOPE US 047
LIGHTNING STRIKES 1963 STATESIDE UK 10031
LIGHTNING STRIKES 196 VERVE 5014
LIGHTNING STRIKES 196 TRADITION US 2013
KIGHTNING STRIKES 19 VEE JAY US 1044
LIGHTNING STRIKES 19 MAYFAIR 4000
LIGHTNING STRIKES 19 JOY 5115
COFFEE HOUSE BLUES 19 JOY 5175
BLUES HOOT 1964 STATESIDE 10076
BLUES HOOT 196 HORIZON US 1617
HOOTIN' THE BLUES 1965 STATESIDE UK 10110
HOOTIN' THE BLUES 196 PRESTIGE US 14021
HOOTIN' THE BLUES 196 PRESTIGE 7806
DOWN HOME BLUES 1965 STATESIDE UK 10155
DOWN HOME BLUES 1965 PRESTIGE US 1086
& SPIDER KILPATRICK 196 ARHOOLIE F1011
& BARBARA DANE 1965 ARHOOLIE F1022
TEXAS BLUES MAN 1965 ARHOOLIE F1034
LIGHTNIN' HOPKINS 1966 SAGA ERO8001
THE BLUES 1969 ACE OF HEARTS 183
LIGHTNIN' VOL 1 1970 POPPY 11000
LIGHTNIN' 197 POPPY US 60002
IN NEW YORK 19 BARNABY US 30247
SHAKE IT BABY 19 VOGUE 891
BLUES UNDERGROUND 19 "D" 8000
LIGHTNIN' HOPKINS VOL 1 19 TIME US
LETS WORK AWHILE 1971 BLUE HORIZON 2431005
EARTH BLUES 19 UA 40006
FAST LIFE WOMAN 19 VERVE US 8453
SINGS THE BLUES 19 CROWN US 5224
AT HIS NATURAL BEST 19 RHAPSODY US RHAP8
FREE FORM PATTERNS 19 INT ARTISTS AT6
BURNIN' IN L A 19 FONTANA 688 801ZL
BLUE BIRD BLUES 19 FONTANA 688 803ZL
AUTOBIOGRAPHY 1960 TRADITION 1040
BEST 19 TRADITION 2056
GREATEST HITS 19 PRESTIGE 7592
BEST OF TEXAS BLUES BAND 19 PRESTIGE 7714
DOUBLE BLUES 19 FANTAGE 24702
GOIN' AWAY 19 PRESTIGE 1073
HIS GREATEST HITS 19 BLUESVILLE US 1084
AND THE BLUES 19 IMPERIAL US 12211
AND THE BLUES 19 HERALD US 1012
FREEFORM PATTERNS 19 INT ART US 6
ORIGINAL FOLK BLUES 19 KENT US 525
LEGEND IN HIS OWN TIME 19 KENT US 9008
SOUTHERN MEETING 19 KIMBERLEY US 2017
BLUES IN MY BOTTLE 19 XTRA UK 5036
FIRST MEETING 1964 WORLD US 1817
GOTTA MOVE YOUR BABY 19 PRESTIGE US 7831
SOMETHING BLUE 19 VERVE US 3013
SINGS THE BLUES 19 CROWN US 5224
IN TOWN 19 FOLKART US 5003
AT THE BIRD LOUNGE 19 GUEST STAR 1459
LIGHTNING HOPKINS 19 GUEST STAR 1909
COUNTRY BLUES 1960 TRADITION 1035
LAST OF THE GREAT BLUES 19 TIME US 70004
MOJO HAND 19 FIRE US 104
ON STAGE 19 IMPERIAL US 9180
SOUL BLUES 19 PRESTIGE US 7377
LIGHTNIN' HOPKINS 19 TRIP 8015
LIGHTNIN' HOPKIN 19 ARCHIVES 241
GOTTA MOVE YOUR BABY 19 PRESTIGE 7831
LIGHTNIN HOPKINS 19 HORIZON US 1617
REALLY THE BLUES 19 MUSIDISC AM 6080
PENITENTIARY BLUES 19 CHANT DU MONDE 53822
LIGHTNIN' HOPKINS 19 PATHE FR 40005
LIGHTNIN' HOPKINS 19 VOGUE 68130
LIGHTNIN' HOPKINS 19 TRIUMPH 240036
& JOHN LEE HOOKER 19 STORYVILLE SLP 174
ROOTS OF 19 XTRA XTRA 1127
ROOTS OF 19 FOLKWAYS US 31011
ROOTS OF 19 VERVE 5003
ROOSTER CROWED IN ENGLAND 19 77 LA 12/200
LEGACY OF THE BLUES 19 SPECIALTY SNTF 672
LEGACY OF THE BLUES 19 GNP US 10022
LONESOME LIGHTNIN' 1972 CARNIVAL 2941005
BLUE LIGHTNIN' 197 JEWEL 5000
BLUE LIGHTNIN' 197 DISCODIS 155 505
TALKING SOME SENSE 197 JEWEL 5001
TALKING SOME SENSE 197 PATHE FR C240842
GREAT ELECTRIC SHOW 1973 MUSIDISC FR AM013/4
GREAT ELECTRIC SHOW 197 JEWEL US 5002
DIRTY BLUES 1973 MAINSTREAM MSL1001
DIRTY BLUES 197 MAINSTREAM US 326
THE BLUES 1974 MAINSTREAM MSL1020
THE BLUES 197 MAINSTREAM US 311
THE BLUES 197 PRESTIGE US 7811
LOWDOWN DIRTY BLUES 1975 MAINSTREAM MSL1031
LOWDOWN DIRTY BLUES 1975 MAINSTREAM US 405
IN BERKELEY 1975 ARHOOLIE F1063
EARLY RECORDINGS 1975 ARHOOLIE F2007
EARLY RECORDINGS 2 1975 ARHOOLIE F2010
LEGEND IN HIS OWN TIME 1976 BLUE ANTHOLOGY 5608
ALL THEM BLUES 1976 DJM 28016
KING OF DOWLING STREET 19 PATHE 83254
GOT TO MOVE YOU BABY 19 XTRA UK 5044

H153 **NICKY HOPKINS** H153

NICKY HOPKINS K (ALL

(A) REVOLUTIONARY PIANO 1966 CBS UK 62679
(B) TIN MAN WAS A DREAMER 1973 CBS US 32074 UK 65416
(C) NO MORE CHANGES 1975 MERCURY US SRM1 1028

H154 **HUGH HOPPER** H154

HUGH HOPPER B PNO(ALL
JOHN MARSHALL D (A
PYE HASTINGS G (A
LOL COXHILL SAX (A
GARY WINDO SAX (AC
MALCOLM GRIFFITHS TROM (A
NICK EVANS TROM (A
ELTON DEAN SAX (BCDE KEITH TIPPETT PNO (B JOE GALLIVAN D SYN(B MARK CHARIG CORNET(C
FRANK ROBERTS PNO (C DAVE STEWART ORG (C MIKE TRAVIS D (CE RICHARD BRUNTON G (C
NIGEL MORRIS D (C ALAN GOWAN ORG (D SHEEN (D JEAN PIERRE CAROLFI K (E
JEAN PIERRE WEILLER B (E

(A) 1984 1973 CBS UK 65466
(A) 1984 1980 ATMOSPHERE US IRI 5010
(B) CRUEL BUT FAIR 1976 COMPENDIUM FIDARDO 4
(C) HOPPER TUNITY BOX 1977 COMPENDIUM FIDARDO 7
(D) ROUGE ELEMENT 197 OGUN OG 527
(E) MONSTER BAND 1979 ATMOSPHERE IRI 5003

H155 **HOPSCOTCH** H155

ONNIE McINTYRE V G (A
STEWART FRANCIS D (A
GRAHAM MAITLAND K (A ALAN GORRIE V B (A

(A) 1967

H155A **HORDE CATALYTIQUE POUR LA FIN** H155A

RICHARD ACCART WIND (A
FRANCKY BOURLIER HARP VIBES(A
JACQUES FASSOLA B BAN G(A GIL STERG D PERC (A

(A) GESTATION SONORE 1971 FUTURA FR SON 003

H155B JIM HORN H155B

JIM HORN FLT SAX(AB (A) THROUGH THE EYE 1972 SHELTER US 8906
(B) JIM'S HORN 1973 SHELTER US 8918

H156 PAUL HORN H156

PAUL HORN HORNS(ALL (A) IN KASHMIR 19 LIBERTY 83084
JIM KELTNER D (J (B) INSIDE 1969 EPIC US 26466 UK 65201
ABRAHAM LABORIEL B (J (C) INSIDE TWO 19 EPIC US 31600
DEAN PARKS G (J (D) VISIONS 1974 EPIC US 32837
ERNIE WATTS SA (J (E) SPECIAL EDITION 1974 ISLAND UK ISLD 6
JIM HORN SAX (J (F) PAUL HORN & NEXUS 1976 EPIC UK 69219
CHARLES LOPER HRNS (J (G) IN INDIA (1967) 1976 BLUENOTE UK BNLAD 519
CHUCK FINDLEY HRNS (J (H) ALTURA 1977 EPIC US 34231
OSCAR BRASHEAR HRNS (J (J) DREAM MACHINE 1978 MUSHROOM 5010
MIKE MELVION K SYN (J (K) CONCERT ENSEMBLE 19 OVATION US 1405
JOE SAMPLE K SYN(JD
CLARK SPANGLER K (J LALO SCHIFRIN K SYN(J EMIL RICHARDS PERC (J PAULINHO DACOSTA PERC(J
ROBIN HORN PERC (J LYN BLESSING VIBES(E ART JOHNSON G (E DAVE PARLATO B (E
BART HALL D (E TOM SCOTT K? (D JOHN GUERIN D (D MAX BENNETT B (D
LARRY CARLTON G (D ROGER JOHNSON G (D RUBENS BASSINI PERC (D JONI MITCHELL V K(D
CARMEN KNEDDY V (D KATHY COLLIER V (D

H157 JIMMY BO HORNE H157

JIMMY BO HORNE V (A (A) DANCE ACROSS THE FLOOR 1978 TK TKR82533
HARRY CASEY K (A (B) BEST OF 1980 TK TKR83391
SNOOPY DEAN G (A
MIKE LEWIS SAX (A ROBERT JOHNSON D (A RONALD ZIEGLER D (A RICHARD FINCH B (A
WHIT SIDENER SAX (A VINNIE TANNO TPT (A KEN FAULK TPT (A FERMIN GOYTISLO PERC(A
JEROME SMITH G (A

H157A HORSE H157A

ROD ROACH G (A (A) HORSE 1970 RCA GER 10308 UK SF8109
COLIN STANDRING B (A
RIC PARNELL D (A ADRIAN HAWKINS V (A

H157B HORSES H157B

(A) HORSES 19 WHITE WHALE US WW 7121

H157C HORSESHOE H157C

ARTO BORG G (A (A) FIRST KICK 19 BASF GERM 20 25727.4
TIMO JUUTI B PERC(A
HANS RANTIO D PERC V (A ARI TALKAMO V G PNO(A

H158 HORSLIPS H158

EAMONN CARR D V (ABDEFGHIJKL (A) HAPPY TO MEET 1973 OATS M003
CHARLES O'CONNOR VLN (ABCDEFGHIJKL (A) HAPPY TO MEET 197 ATLANTIC GER 20119
DECLAN SINNOTT G (J (A) HAPPY TO MEET 197 ATCO US 7030
GUS GUEST G (J (A) HAPPY TO MEET 1978 DJM UK DJF 20544
JIM LOCKHART FLT VLN K (ABCDEFGHIJKL (B) THE TAIN 1973 OATS M005
BARRY DEVLIN V B (ABCDEFGHIJKL (B) THE TAIN 197 ATLANTIC GER 50034
DEC O'DOHERTY PNO (K (B) THE TAIN 197 ATCO US 7039
JOHN FEAN V G (ABCDEFGHIJKL (B) THE TAIN 1978 DJM UK DJF 20543
STEVE KATZ TAMB (K (C) DANCEHALL SWEETHEARTS 1974 OATS M007
(C) DANCEHALL SWEETHEARTS 1974 RCA APL10709
(D) UNFORTUNATE CUP OF TEA 1975 OATS M008
(D) UNFORTUNATE CUP OF TEA 1975 RCA SF 8432
(E) DRIVE THE COLD WINTER AWAY 1976 OATS M009
(F) HORSLIPS 1976 OATS M0010
(G) CELTIC SYMPHONY/BOOK OF INVASIONS 1977 DJM DJM10 US UK DJF 20498
(H) ALIENS 1977 DJM DJM16 US UK DJF 20519
(H) ALIENS 1977 ATLANTIC GER 64202
(I) TRACKS FROM THE VAULTS 1978 OATS M0013
(J) MAN WHO BUILT AMERICA 1979 DJM DJM20 US UK DJF 20546
(K) SHORT STORIES -TALL TALES 1980 MERCURY US 3809 UK 9100 070
(L) THE BELFAST GIGS 1980 OATS UK M0020
(L) THE BELFAST GIGS 1980 MERCURY US 3842

H159 WALTER HORTON H159

WALTER HORTON V HCA(ALL (A) SOUL OF BLUES HARMONICA 1964 ARGO US 4037
ROBERT NIGHTHAWK G (B (B) AN OFFER YOU CANT REFUSE(1SIDE) 1972 RED LIGHTNIN' UK RL008
JIMMY DE BERRY G (C (C) COTTON PATCH HOTFOOTS (1SIDE) 1973 POLYDOR 2383 200
WILLIE NIX D (C (D) AND HOT COTTAGE 1974 EXTRA 1135
CAREY BELL HARRINGTON HCA(E (E) WITH CAREY BELL 1972 ALLIGATOR 4702+UK SONET SNTF677
EDDIE TAYLOR G (E (F) FINE CUTS 19 BLIND PIG US 006
JOE HARPER B (E (G) SOUTHERN COMFORT 19 SIRE 97011
BUDDY GUY G (A (H) LITTLE BOY BLUE 1980 JSP UK 1019
BOBBY BUSTER ORG (A
JACK MYERS B (A WILLIE SMITH D (A FRANK SWAN D (E LEFT HAND FRANK G (H
RONNIE HORVATH G (H OLA DIXON D (H MICHAEL WARD B (H

H159A HOT CHOCOLATE H159A

ERROL BROWN V (ALL (A) CICERO PARK 1974 RAK UK SRAK 507
PAT OLIVE B ((B) HOT CHOCOLATE 1975 RAK UK SRAK 516
LARRY FERGUSON K ((C) MAN TO MAN 1976
TONY CONNOR D ((D) 20 GREATEST HITS 1976 RAK UK SRAK 524
HARVEY HINSLEY G ((E) EVERY 1's A WINNER 1978 RAK UK SRAK 531
TONY WILSON B V ((F) GOING THROUGH THE MOTIONS 1979 RAK UK SRAK 536
(G) CLASS 1980 RAK UK SRAK 536
(H) 20 HOTTEST HITS 1980 EMI UK EMTV 22

H160 HOT DOGS H160

BILL RENNIE V (A (A) SAY WHAT YOU MEAN 1973 ARDENT ADS 2805
GREG REDING PNO G V(A
TERRY MANNING G (A JACK HOLDER G (A ROBERT JOHNSON G (A FRED PROUTY D (A
STEVE HOLT D (A RICHARD ROSEBROUGH D (A STEVE SMITH K (A CARGOE V (A

H161 HOT TUNA H161

JORMA KAUKONEN G V (ALL (A) HOT TUNA 1970 RCA UK SF 8125 US LSP 4353
JACK CASADY B V (ALL (B) FIRST PULL UP(ELECTRIC)LIVE 1971 RCA US LSP 4550
WILL SCARLETT HCA (AB (C) BURGERS 1972 GRUNT UK 1004 US 0921 GER 2591
PAPA CREACH V VLN(CB (D) PHOSPHORESCENT RAT 1974 GRUNT UK US BFLI 0348
JOEY COVINGTON D ((E) AMERICA'S CHOICE 1975 GRUNT UK FTR2003 US BFLI 0820
SAMMY PIAZZA D V (CDB (F) YELLOW FEVER 1975 GRUNT US BLFI 1238
NIKKI BUCK K SYN(CFGH (G) HOPPKORV 1976 GRUNT UK FTR2006 US BFLI 1920
BOB STEELER D (EFGH (H) DOUBLE DOSE (DBL LIVE) 1977 GRUNT UK FL02545 US CYL 22545
JOHN SHERMAN G (FG (I) FINAL VINYL 1979 GRUNT UK FL13357
MARTY BALIN G (
PAUL ZEIGLER G (DAVE CROSBY V (C RICHARD TALBOTT V G (C KAREN TOBIN V (G
ANDREW NARVELL PERC (D

H162 HOT VULTURES H162

IAN A ANDERSON G V (AB (A) CARRION ON 1976 RED RAG UK RRR 005
MAGGIE HOLLAND B V (AB (B) EAST ST SHAKES 1978 RED RAG UK RRR 015
MARTIN SIMPSON G BAN(B
RAGGY FARMER PERC V(B DAVE GRIFFITHS VLN MAND(A AL JONES G (A JOHN PILGRIM PERC(A
DAVE PEABODY HCA (A SIMON MAYOR FDL MAND(B HILARY JONES V (B

H162A HOTEL H162A

TOMMY CALTON G V (AB (A) HOTEL 1979 MCA US 3158 UK MCF 3036
MARC PHILLIPS K V (AB (B) HALFMOON SILVER 1980 MCA US 5113
MICHAEL REID G V (AB
GEORGE CREASMAN B V (AB LEE BARGERON K V (AB MICHAEL CADENHEAD D PERC(AB FARRELL MORRIS PERC (A
SHANE KEISTER SYN (AB JOHN NUCKOLS D (A

H163 HOTLEGS H163

ERIC STEWART G B V(ABC (A) THINK SCHOOL STINKS 1971 PHILIPS 6308 057+ 6308 047
KEVIN GODLEY D V (ABC (A) THINK SCHOOL STINKS 1971 CAPITOL US ST 378
LOL CREME G B K V (ABC (B) SONGS 197 PHILIPS 6308 080
BAZ BARKER VLN (C (C) YOU DIDN'T LIKE IT 1976 SONIC SON 009
GRAHAM GOULDMAN B (C
MIKE TIMONEY ORG (C

H164 THE HOURGLASS H164

GREGG ALLMAN K V (ALL (A) HOURGLASS 1968 LIBERTY US 7536 UK LBL 83219
PAUL HORNSBY K (A (B) POWER OF LOVE 19 LIBERTY US 7555
DUANE ALLMAN G (ALL (AB) HOURGLASS (DBL) 1973 UA US 013G2 UK USD 303/4
JESSE WILLARD CARR (
MABRON McKINNEY (JOHNNY SANDLIN (PETE CARR B (A

H164A DIXON HOUSE BAND H164A

DIXON HOUSE K V (A (A) FIGHTING ALONE 1979 INFINITY INS 2006
CHRISSY SHEFTS G (A
HOWARD LEESE G (A CHUCK GARDNER G (A JAMES KENFIELD B (A FRED ZEUFELDT B(A

H164B BEE HOUSTON H164B

BEE HOUSTON G V (A (A) BEE HOUSTON 19 ARHOOLIE US 1050

H164C CISSY HOUSTON H164C

CISSY HOUSTON V (ALL (A) CISSY HOUSTON 1971 JANUS UK 6310 205
RICK MAROTTA D (B (B) CISSY HOUSTON 1977 PRIVATE STOCK UK PVLP 1030
STEVE JORDAN D (B (C) THINK IT OVER 1978 PRIVATE STOCK UK PVLP 1044
LEON PENDARVIS K (B (D) STEP ASIDE FOR A LADY !)(= EMI UK EMC 3327
RICHARD TEE K (B
DONNY HARPER B (BC BOB BABBIT B (B LANCE QUINN G (B VOICES OF HOPE V (B
ARNOLD McCULLER V (B YOLANDA McCULLOUGH V(B DAVID LASLEY V (B MAERETHA STEWART V (B
KEN WILLIAMS V (B WHITNEY HOUSTON V (C ALVIN FIELDS V (C LANI GROVES V (C
ALLEN SCHWARZBERG D (CD FRANCISCO CENTENO B (CD JEFF MIRANOV G (BCD ROB MOUNSEY K (BCD
RUBENS BASSINI PERC (BCD LUTHER VAN DROSS V (D WILL LEE B (BD STEVE LOVE G (D
GERALD CHAMBERLAIN TROM(D RONNIE CUBER SAX (D JOHN GATCHELL TPT (D JOCELYN BROWN V (D
JERRY NNIEWOOD WIND (D ELTESA WEATHERSBY V (D STRINGS (D BEVERLY INGRAM V (C

H165 HOUSESHAKERS H165

(A) DEMOLITION ROCK 1974 CONTOUR UK 2870 160

H166 CHUCK HOWARD H166

CHUCK HOWARD V (A (A) CHUCK HOWARD 1977 CREAM US CR1005
KEN PARK D (A
JERRY COLE G (A BEN BENAY G (A ROB WALSH G (A DAVE McDANIELS B (A
MARK GIBBONS K (A RAY PIZZI WIND (A JONATHAN LEE HCA (A JEFF TWEED V (A
JOHN NICOLS V (A

H167 CATHERINE HOWE H167

CATHERINE HOWE V K (ALL (A) HARRY 1975 RCA LPI 5091 + SF 8407
PETER BOITA D (C (B) SILENT MOTHER NATURE 1976 RCA RS 1041
ALAN PARKER G (C (C) DRAGONFLY DAYS 1977 ARIOLA ARL 5013
CHRIS REA G (C (EP) TRUTH OF THE MATTER 1977 RCA PE 5004
FOGGY LITTLE G (C
PAUL KEOGH G (C LES HURDLE B (C MELT KINGTON B (C CHRIS KARAN PERC (C
RICHARD HEWSON SYN (C DAVID HANCOCK HRNS (C PETE WINGFIELD K (C DICK HOLMES K (C

H168 STEVE HOWE H168

STEVE HOWE G V B K SYN PERC(AB (A) BEGINNINGS 1977 ATLANTIC US 18514 UK K 50151
PATRICK MORAZ K (AB (B) STEVE HOWE ALBUM 1979 ATLANTIC US 19243 UK K 50621
ALAN WHITE D (AB (C) THE BODAST TAPES 1980 CHERRY RED UK RED12
DAVID OBERLE D (A
JOHN MECK VIOLA(A PATRICK HALLING VLN (A WILLIAM REID VLN (A PETER HALLING CELLO (A
CHRIS LAURENCE B (A JAMES GREGORY FLT (A MALCOLM BENNETT FLT (A BUD BEADLE SAX (A
SIDNEY SUTCLIFFE OBOE (A BILL BRUFORD D (AB MICK EVE SAX (A GWYN BROOKE BASSOON (A
COLIN GIBSON B (A RONNIE LEAHY K (B CLIVE BUNKER D (B CLAIRE HAMILL V (B
GRAHAM PRESKETT VLN (B
GRAEME TAYLOR G (A

* SEE 'BODAST' FOR LINE UP OF (C)

H169 EDDIE HOWELL H169

EDDIE HOWELL G V K(A (A) GRAMOPHONE RECORD 1975 WB UK K 56154
PHIL COLLINS D (A
JOHN GOODSALL G (A PERCY JONES B (A GARY MOORE G (A ROBIN LUMLEY K (A
JACK LANCASTER WIND (A GASPAR LAWAL PERC (A TONY SADLER G (A CHARMING LEMMINGS PERC(A
DAVID MINNS V (A MARTIN KITCAT V (A JEROME RIMSON B (A

H169A REUBEN HOWELL H169A

RUEBEN HOWELL V (A (A) REUBEN HOWELL 1973 MOTOWN US 771
CLAYTON IVEY K G PERC(A
GEORGE SOULE B V (A KEN BELL G (A CHARLES CHALMERS STR V(A HARRISON CALLOWAY HRNS (A
HARVEY THOMPSON SAX (A TERRY WOODFORD V (A SANDRA RHODES V (A PHILLIP MITCHELL V (A
LAURA STRUZICK V (A JIMMY EVANS B PERC (A PETE CARR G (A MIKE LEWIS STR (A
BEN CAULEY HRNS (A RONNIE EADES SAX (A CHARLES ROSE TROM (A SUE RICHARDS V (A
DONNA RHODES V (A JEANNIE GREENE V (A

H170 HOWLIN' WOLF H170

HOWLIN' WOLF(CHESTER BURNETT)V G HCA (A) MOANING IN THE MOONLIGHT 1964 CHESS UK 4006 US 1434
HUBERT SUMLIN G (MNPQUVWZY (A) " " " " 196 MARBLE ARCH UK MAL 665
WILLIE JOHNSON G (EFQSTUWX (A) EVIL 196 CHESS US 1540
WILLIE DIXON B (QUVWY (B) POOR BOY 1965 CHESS UK CRL4508
SAM LAY D (UVXY (C) REAL FOLK BLUES 1966 CHESS US 1502
HOSEA LEE KENNARD PNO (QTUVWXY (D) BIG CITY BLUES 1966 EMBER UK 3370 UNITED US 7717
EARL PHILLIPS G D (QTUVXYW (E) CITY BLUES 19 UNITED US 7717 + US CUSTOM 2055
JODY WILLIAMS G (QXYW (F) ORIGINAL FOLK BLUES 19 UNITED US 7747 + US KENT 526
SP LEARY D (NUVXY (G) SINGS THE BLUES 19 CROWN US 5240
FRED BELOW D (NWX (H) MORE REAL FOLK BLUES 1967 CHESS US 1512
IKE TURNER PNO (EFSTWVX (I) SUPER SUPER BLUES BAND 1968 CHECKER UK 3010 + US CHESS 4537
HENRY GRAY PNO (VWY (J) THE HOWLIN' WOLF ALBUM 1969 CADET UK LPS319+US CHESS 4543
WILLIE STEEL D (EFQSTVWX (K) AKA CHESTER BURNETT 1974 CHESS US 60016
JAMES COTTON HCA (TVW (L) MESSAGE TO THE YOUNG 1971 CHESS UK 6310108 +US CHESS 50002
JOHNNY JONES PNO (UVY (M) LONDON SESSIONS 1971 ROLLSTONES 49101 +US CHESS 60008
J T BROWN SAX (UXY (N) LIVE & COOKIN' AT ALICES REVISITED1972 CHESS US 50015
BILLY DOBKINS SAX (TUV (O) BACK DOOR WOLF 1973 CHESS US 50045 GER 9287 008
OTIS SMOTHERS G (TUWX (P) LONDON REVISITED 1974 CHESS US 60026
DON HANKINS SAX (UY (Q) BLUES MASTERS 1977 CHESS UK 2ACBM 201
JUNIOR BLACKMAN D (XY (R) SAM'S BLUES 197 CHARLY UK CR 30102
BUDDY GUY G (V (S) LEGENDARY SUN PERFORMERS 197 CHARLY UK CR 30134
WILLIE WILLIAMS D (WX (T) HEART LIKE A RAILROAD STEEL 19 BLUES BALL US 2001
L D McGHEE G (VYU (U) CANT PUT ME OUT 19 BLUES BALL US 2002
LAYFAYETTE LEAKE PNO (MU (V) FROM EARLY TO LATE 19 BLUE NIGHT BN 0731667
DAVE MYERS B (N (W) GOIN' BACK HOME 19 SYNDICATE CHAPTER US SC 003
JEROME ARNOLD (X (X) HOWLIN' WOLF 19 PYTHON US PLP KM 13
ALBERT LUANDREW PNO (N (Y) CHANGIN MY WAY 1977 CHESS CHV 418
OTIS SPANN PNO (Q (Q) CHESS MASTERS 1981 CHESS UK 4004
IAN STEWART PNO (M
BRYCE ROBERSON G (L SONNY THOMPSON PNO (L ALFRED ELKINS B (UT ERIC CLAPTON G (M
STEVE WINWOOD K (M BILL WYMAN B (MP CHARLIE WATTS D (MP JEFFREY M CARP HCA(MP
KLAUS VOORMAN B (M JOHN SIMON K (M PHIL UPCHURCH B (MJ DENNIS LANSING HRNS(M
DONALD MYRICK FLT (J GENE BARGE HRNS (J JOE MILLER HRNS (M JORDON SANDKE HRNS(M
MORRIS JENNINGS D (J ROLAND FAULKNER G (J JOHN STOCKLIN G (L TYRONE SMITH D (L
LOUIS SATTERFIELD B (J MUDDY WATERS G V (I PETE COSEY G (J BOB CROWDER D (L
ALBERT WILLIAMS PNO (Q JOHN JERIMIAH ORG (L BO DIDDLEY G V (I JIMMY ROGERS G (Y
ABE LOCKE SAX (WY LV WILLIAMS B (U ERNIE SHAW SAX (U ANDREW PALMER B (Y
ARNOLD ROGERS SAX (Y ADOLPH DOLLINS SAX (W ERNIE SHAW SAX (U

H171 LINDA HOYLE H171

LINDA HOYLE V (A (A) PIECES OF ME 1971 VERTIGO UK 6360 060
CHRIS SPEDDING G (A
JOHN MARSHALL D (A JEFF CLYNE B (A KARL JENKINS OCBE K (A COLIN PURBROOK PNO(A

H171A HUB H171A

(A) HUB 1975 CAPITOL US 11439

H171B HUBBLE BUBBLE H171B

ALAN VON BUR G V (AB (A) HUBBLE BUBBLE 198 SINUS BEL 120 330 036
DANNY JOAN G V (B (B) FAKING 198 SINUS BEL 120 330 045
ROGER JUNIOR D V (A
DEE MASSART B V (A JERRY D (B J L U BOAT B (B LIPSTICK D (B

H172 KEITH HUDSON H172

KEITH HUDSON (A) TOUCH OF FREEDOM 1975 ATRA 1001
SLY DUNBAR D (C (B) TOO EXPENSIVE 1976 VIRGIN UK V 2056
ERIC CLARKE D (C (C) RASTA COMMUNICATIONS 1978 JOINT JT0003
ROBBIE SHAKESPEARE G (C (D) RASTA COMMUNICATION 1979 GREENSLEVES UK GREL 5
EARL SMITH G (C
RANCHIE McLEAN B G (C DONALD GITS G (C PAGET KING K V (C TONY BROTHER PERC (C
STICKMAN V (C LAZA STRIKE V (C THEO BECKFORD K (C TARZAN NELSON K (C
KEITH STIRLING K (C WILLY BARRETT G (C KEN ELLIOT K (C

H172A HUDSON BROTHERS H172A

BILL HUDSON G V (ALL (A) HUDSON 197 PLAYBOY US PB 102
MARK HUDSON G V (ALL (B) HOLLYWOOD SITUATION 1974 CASABLANCA US 9008 UK 4002
BRETT HUDSON V B (ALL (C) TOTALLY OUT OF CONTROL 1975 MCA US 406 JAP ROCKET 80363
CRAIG KRAMPF D (B (D) BA FA 1975 ROCKET US PIG2169
PHIL REED G (B (E) HUDSON 1977 PLAYBOY US 34734
MIKE PARKER K (B (F) PEOPLE LIKE US 1978 ARISTA US
BARRY PULMAN SYN (B (G) HUDSON BROTHERS 1978 FIRST AMERICAN US 7708
(H) TRUTH ABOUT US 1979 ARISTA US 4199

H173 HUDSON FORD H173

RICHARD HUDSON V G PERC (ABCD (A) NICKELODEON 1973 A&M US 3616 UK AMLH 68208
JOHN FORD G B (ABCD (B) FREE SPIRIT 1974 A&M US 3652 UK AMLH 68274
KEN LAWS D (D (C) WORLDS COLLIDE 1975 A&M US 4535 UK AMLH 64535
BRENT FORBES B (D (D) DAYLIGHT 1977 CBS UK 82027
CHRIS PARREN K (D
DAVE MARKEE B (D IAN BAIRNSON G (D GRAHAM PRESKETT VLN K(D MARTIN DROVER TPT (D
RAY RUSSELL G (D

H173A LEON HUFF H173A

LEON HUFF (A — (A) HERE TO CREATE MUSIC — 1980 PHILADELPHIA US 36758 UK 84530

H174 HUG H174

MIKE HUGG V K (A — (A) NEON DREAM — 1975 POLYDOR UK 2383 330
RON TELEMACQUE D V (A
MARCUS JAMES D V (A JOHN KNIGHTSBRIDGE G V (A

H175 MIKE HUGG H175

MIKE HUGG V K (AB — (A) SOMEWHERE — 1972 POLYDOR UK 2383 140
MICKY WALLER D (AB — (B) STRESS & STRAIN — 1973 POLYDOR UK 2383 213
KIM GARDNER B (B
DAVE KING G (AB SONNY CORBETT HRNS (B DAVID HEATH HADFIELD G (B EDDIE GRANT G (B
LYN DOBSON HRNS (B PAUL WESTWOOD B (B KEVIN PEEK G (AB ELTON DEAN SAX(AB
IAN CARR HRNS (B TONY RIVERS K V (B ANDY BOWN B (A TOM McGUINESS G (A
LIZA STRIKE V (A JUDITH POWELL V (A ALAN TARNEY B (A BRIAN HUGG V (A
MANFRED MANN ORG (A TWEED HARRIS STRINGS(A ROGER POPE D (A BARRY ST JOHN V (A
GRAHAM PRESKETT B (A TERRY BRITTEN G (A CALEB QUAYE G (A MICK ROGERS G (A
HENRY SPINETTI D (A GERRY BECKLEY G (A

H176 GLENN HUGHES H176

GLENN HUGHES V G B K(A — (A) PLAY ME OUT — SAFARI 1977 LONG2 +1978 6/23085
MEL GALLEY G (A
BILL BOWMAN G (A PAT TRAVERS G (A DAVE HOLLAND D (A TERRY ROWLEY PNO (A
ROBERT BAILEY PNO (A RON ASPERY SAX (A HENRY LOWTHER TPT (A MARK NAUSEEF PERC(A
LIZA STRIKE V (A JOY WRIGHT V (A HELEN CHAPPELLE V (A

H176A JIMMY HUGHES H176A

JIMMY HUGHES (A — (A) A SHOT OF RHYTHM & BLUES — 1980 CHARLY CTD 103

H177 ALAN HULL H177

ALAN HULL V G PERC K (ABC — (A) PIPEDREAM — 1973 CHARISMA UK CAS 1069
KEN CRADDOCK G V K PERC(ABC — (B) SQUIRE — 1975 WB US WS4587 UK K 56121
COLIN GIBSON B PERC(ABC — (C) PHANTOMS — 1979 ROCKET UK TRAIN 6
RAY LAIDLAW D (ABC
MICK MOODY G (B LESLEY DUNCAN V (BC JOHN TURNBULL G (A RAY JACKSON HCA MAND (AB
BRIAN CHATTON K (B JO NEWMAN V (BC DAVE BROOKS SAX (A TERRY POPPLE D (B
ALBERT LEE G (B JEAN ROUSSEL K (B PETER KIRTLEY G (C STEVE GREGORY HRNS(C
BUB BEADLE HRNS (C LIZA STRIKE V (C RAB NOAKES V (C

H178 HUMAN BEAST H178

GILLIES BUCHAN G V (A — ( ) HUMAN BEAST — 1970 DECCA UK SKL 5053
EDWARD JONES B V (A
JOHN ROMSEY D (A DAVID McNIVEN CLAR (A

H178A HUMAN LEAGUE H178A

IAN CRAIG MARSH SYN V(AB — (A) REPRODUCTION — 1979 VIRGIN UK V 2133
PHILIP OAKLEY SYN V(ALL — (B) TRAVELOGUE — 1980 VIRGIN UK V 2160
MARTIN WARE SYN V(AB — (C) DARE — 1981 VIRIGN UK V 2192
PHILIP ADRIAN WRIGHT SYN(ABC — (EP)THE DIGNITY OF LABOUR — 1979 FAST UK V F 1
JO CALLIS SYN (C
IAN BURDEN SYN (C JOANNE CATHEDRALL V (C SUSANNE SULLEY V (C COLIN THURSTON PROD (A
MARTIN RUSHANT PROD (C

H178B HUMAN SEXUAL RESPONSE H178B

(A) FIGURE 14 — 1980 DONT FALL OF THE MOUNTAIN UK 1
(A) FIGURE 14 — 1980 PASSPORT US 9851
(B) IN A ROMAN MOOD — 1981 UK K11

H179 HUMBLE PIE H179

STEVE MARRIOTT G V K HCA(ALL — (A) AS SAFE AS YESTERDAY IS — 1969 IMMEDIATE US 101 UK IMSP025
PETER FRAMPTON G V (ABCDELKMN — (B) TOWN & COUNTRY — 1969 IMMEDIATE UK IMSP027
JERRY SHIRLEY D (ALL — (B) TOWN & COUNTRY — 1978 CHARLY UK CR 300016
GREG RIDLEY B (ABCDEFGHJKLMN — (C) HUMBLE PIE — 1970 A&M US 4270 UK AMLS 986
DAVE CLEMPSON G (FGHJN — (D) ROCK ON — 1971 A&M US 4301 UK AMLS 2013
B J COLE STEEL(CDGN — (E) ROCKIN' AT FILLMORE (DBL) — 1971 A&M US 3506 UK AMLH 63506
WILLIE WILSON D (C — (F) SMOKIN' — 1972 A&M US 4342 UK AMLS 64342
ALEXIS KORNER V (DF — (G) EAT IT — 1973 A&M US 3701 UK AMLS 6004
BOBBY KEYS SAX (D — (H) THUNDERBOX — 1974 A&M US 3611 UK AMLH 63611
DORIS TROY V (DF — (J) STREET RATS — 1975 A&M US 4514 UK AMLS 68282
P P ARNOLD V (D — (K) CRUST OF(COMP) — 1975 EMI IMP C048 50720
CLAUDIA LENNEAR V (D — (L) BACK HOME AGAIN — 1976 IMMEDIATE UK IML 1005
MADELINE BELL V (F — (M) GREATEST HITS(COMP) — 1977 IMMEDIATE UK IML 2005
STEPHEN STILLS (F — (N) POP CHRONIK (COMP) — 19 A&M IMP 88771
RICKY WILLS (F — (O) FAMOUS POP GROUPS OF THE 60s(+NICE 19 MFP GERM 14694319/2
SYDNEY GEORGE SAX (GN — (P) ON TO VICTORY — 1980 JET UK 231 US ATLANTIC 38122
BILLIE BARNUM V (GHN — (AB) LOST & FOUND (DBL) — 1973 A&M US 3513
MAXINE DIXON V (Q — (AB) LOST & FOUND (DBL) — 1975 CHARLY GER CR 3002
TIM HINKLEY K (J — (Q) GO FOR THE THROAT — 1981 ATLANTIC UK 38131
BOB TENCH G V (PQ — (D+) SHINE ON — 1971 CLUB GER 92982
DANA KRAL V (Q
ROBYN BECK V (Q ANTHONY JONES B V (PQ LYN DOBSON WIND (ALM CLYDIE KING V (GN
CARLENA WILLIAMS V (H VANETTA FIELDS V (GHN MEL COLLINS HRNS (HJ GLYNN JOHNS PROD(D

H180 HUMBLEBUMS H180

BILLY CONNOLLY V G (ABC — (A) FIRST COLLECTION.... — 1969 TRANSATLANTIC UK TRA 186
TAM HARVEY V G MAND (A — (B) HUMBLEBUMS — 1969 TRANSATLANTIC UK TRA 201
RONNIE RAE B (A — (B) HUMBLEBUMS — 1969 LIBERTY US 7636
GERRY RAFFERTY G V (BC — (C) OPEN UP THE DOOR — 1970 TRANSATLANTIC UK TRA 218
BERNIE HOLLAND G (C — (C) OPEN UP THE DOOR — 1970 LIBERTY US 7656
TERRY COX D (C — (ABC) THE COMPLETE.. — 1974 TRANSATLANTIC UK TRAT288
JIMMY TAGFORD (C — ( ) HUMBLEBUM — 1981 TRANSATLANTIC UK TRS 107
BARRY DRANSFIELD FDL (C
REG GUEST (C

H181 **HUMMINGBIRD** H181

BOB TENCH G V (ABC (A) HUMMINGBIRD 1975 A&M US 4536 UK AMLS 68292
MAX MIDDLETON K (ABC (B) WE CANT GO ON MEETING LIKE THIS 1976 A&M US 4595 UK AMLH 68383
CLIVE CHAMAN B (ABC (C).DIAMOND NIGHTS 1977 A&M US 4661 UK AMLH 64661
BERNIE HOLLAND G (AB
BERNARD PURDIE D (BC ROBERT AHWAI G (BC CONRAD ISADORE D (A JIM HORN WIND (C
QUITMAN DENNIS HRNS (C CHUCK FINDLEY HRNS (C AIRTO MOREIRA PERC (C PANCHO MORALES PERC(C
VANETTA FIELDS V (C MAXINE WILLARD V (C JULIA TILLMAN V (C STEPHANIE SPRUILL V(C
PAULETTE McWILLIAMS V (C LISA FREEMAN ROBERTS V (C LINDA LEWIS V (A SANDRA ISADORE V (A
GODFREY MACCLEAN CONGA(A MADELINE BELL V (B JOANNE WILLIAMS V (B LIZA STRIKE V (B

H182 **HUNGRY CHUCK** H182

PETER ECKLUND WIND (A (A) HUNGRY CHUCK 1972 BEARSVILLE BR 2071
N D SMART V D (A
JIM COLGROVE B G V(A BEN KEITH STEEL(A AMOS GARRETT G TROM V(A JEFFREY GUTCHEON K V(A

H183 **HUNGRY WOLF** H183

ALAN HAWKSHAW K (A (A) HUNGRY WOLF 1970 PHILIPS 6308 009
ALAN PARKER G (A
CLEM CATTINI D (A BOBBY HAUGHEY TPT (A DEREK WATKINS TPT (A HERBIE FLOWERS B (A
PETER LEE STIRLING V (A TONY FISHER TPT (A CLIFF HARDY TROM (A KEN GOULDIE TROM (A
JOHNNIE EDWARDS TROM (A

H183A **HUNT** H183A

PAUL DICKINSON G V (AB (A) HUNT 1975 CAN
PAUL KERSEY D 'AB (B) BACK ON THE HUNT 1980 VISA 7013 US UK LOGO 1028
BRIAN GAGREN B V K G (AB

H184 **MARSHA HUNT** H184

MARSHA HUNT V (A (A) WOMAN CHILD 1971 TRACK UK 2410 101 GERM 2383081
(A) ATTENTION WOMAN CHILD) 1974 FONTANA GERM RI

H184A **HUNTER** H184A

LES HUNT G V (A (A) ROCK ON 1978 PATHE FR 068 61882
LES CRITCHLOW D (A
P G CORNELL VLN TROM K(A NICK EGAN B (A CHRIS ELLIS K (A

H184B **CHRIS HUNTER** H184B

(A) EARLY DAYS 1981 ORIGINAL UK ORA 104

H185 **IAN HUNTER** H185

IAN HUNTER G V (ALL (A) IAN HUNTER 1975 CBS US 33480 UK 80710
EARL SLICK G (C (B) ALL AMERICAN ALIEN BOY 1976 CBS US 34142 UK 81310
MICK RONSON G V (ABDEFG (C) OVERNIGHT ANGELS 1977 CBS US 34721 UK 81993
ROB RAWLINSON B (C (D) SHADES OF (COMP DBL) 1978 CBS US 36251 UK 88476
CURLY SMITH D (C (E) YOU'RE NEVER ALONE WITH A SCHIZO' 1979 CHRYSALIS UK CHR 1214
PETER OXENDALE K (C (F) LIVE WELCOME TO THE CLUB(DBL) 1980 CHRYSALIS US 1269 UK CJT6
DENNIS ELLIOTT D (AC (G) SHORT BACK & SIDES 1981 CHRYSALIS CHR1326
JOHN HOLBROOK B (G
AYNSLEY DUNBAR D (B PETER ARNESEN K (A DAVID SANBORN SAX (B FREDDIE MERCURY V (B
CHRIS STAINTON K (B GEOFF APPLEBY B HCA V (A BRIAN MAY V (B ROGER TAYLOR V (B
MILLER ANDERSON V (CG ROY BAKER PERC (C LEM LUBIN V (C ROY BITTAN K (E
GARRY TALLENT B (E MAX WEINBERG D (E JOHN CALE K (F GEORGE YOUNG SAX (E
LEW DEL GATTO SAX (E ELLEN FOLEY V (EFG RORY DODD V (E ERIC BLOOM V (E
ERIC PARKER D V (FG MARTIN BRILEY B V (FG TOMMY MORRONGIELLO G B V(FG TOMMY MANDEL K V(FG
GEORGE MEYER K V (FG SUSIE RONSON V (F BO SEGARINI V (B JOHN GUSTAFSON B (A
PACO PASTORIOUS G B (B MOTT THE HOOPLE (D GARY WEEMS G (D DOMINIC CORTESE SAX (B
CORNELL DUPREE G (B DON ALIAS PERC (B ARNIE LAWRENCE CLAR (B DAVE BARGENN TROM (B
LEW SOLOFF TPT (B ANN SUTTON V (B MICK BARAKEN G (G TODD RUNDGRAN B V (G
ROGER POWELL V (G GARY WINDO SAX (G WELLS KELLY D (G MICK JONES G V (G
TOPPER HEADON D (G TYMON DOGG VLN (G

H186 **ROBERT HUNTER** H186

ROBERT HUNTER V G (ABC (A) TALES OF GREAT RUM RUNNERS 1974 ROUND RX 101
MICKEY HART D (AB (D) TIGER ROSE 1975 ROUND RX 105
BARRY MELTON G (A (C) JACK O' ROSES 1980 DARK STAR DSLP 8001
JERRY GARCIA G K SYN(AB
DAVID FREIBERG B K SYN(AB PETER ALBIN B (A KEITH GODCHAUX K (A DONNA GODCHAUX V (AB
STEVEN SCHUSTER SAX (A SNOOKY FLOWERS SAX (A MARIO CIPOLLINA (A BRUCE GAPINSKI (A
MILT FARROW (A JOHN FAREY (A DAVID KESSNER (A RAY SCOTT (A
JEFF SLATTERY (A RANDALL SMITH (A BILL STEELE (A HADI EL SADOON TPT(A
RODNEY ALBIN V FDL(A T WILL CLAIRE V (A MAUREEN AYLETT SPOONS(A BUDDY CAGE STEEL (A
RICKY SHUBB BANJ (A MARKEE SHUBB MAND (A ROBBIE STOKES G (A JAMIE PARIS (A
PETE SEARS B K (AB CHRISTIE BOURNE PERC (A DAVE TORBERT B (B B D SHOT D (B
DAVID GRISMAN MAND (B

H187 **STEVE HUNTER** H187

STEVE HUNTER G V (A (A) SWEPT AWAY 1977 ATCO US SD 36148
PRAKASH JOHN B (A
JIM GORDON D (A BOB EZRIN K PERC V (A JIM MAELEN PERC (A JOSEF CHIROWSKI K (A
C EZRIN B (A CAROL POPE V (A JOANNE BROOKS V (A TONY D'AMICO V (A

H188 **HUNTER MUSKETT** H188

DANNY THOMPSON B (A (A) EVERYTIME YOU MOVE 1970 DECCA NOVA SND 20
DOUG MORTER G V (AB (B) HUNTER / MUSKETT 1973 BRADLEYS BRADL 1003
CHRIS GEORGE G HCA V(AB
TERRY HISCOCK G K V(AB MIKE GILES D (B KEN FREEMAN SYN (B JIM McCARTY PERC (B
ROGER TREVIT B V PER(B

H189 **MICHAEL HURLEY** H189

MICHAEL HURLEY G V FDL(ABC (A) ARMCHAIRBOOGIE 1971 WB US WS 1915
JEFFREY FREDERICKS V PERC(B (B) HAVE MOICY 1976 ROUNDER US 3010
ROBERT IWASKIEWICZ G V B(BC (C) LONG JOURNEY 19 ROUNDER US 3011
ROBERT NICKSON D (BC ( ) HI FI SHOCK UPTOWN 19 RACCOON US 2625
PAUL PRESTI G V (B ( ) SNOCKGRASS 1980 ROUNDER US 3043
DAVE REISCH B V (BC ( ) FIRST SONGS 19 FOLK US 3581
ROBIN REMAILY V FDL MAND(B
PETER STAMPFEL V BAN FDL(BC JOHN NAGY MAND (B MORGAN HUBER B PNO(C DEREK SEMLER B V (C
ROB HYKYS STEEL(C AL ZANZLER TPT (C ELVIN WOODS FDL (C CHRISTOPHER L'ESTRANG G (C
MEDULLA V (C JOHN KEYES V (C

H190 HURRIGANES H190

REMU AALTONEN D V (CDEF — (A) ROCK & ROLL ALL NIGHT LONG — 19 LOVE SW LRLP 84
CISSE HAKKINEN B V (CDEF — (B) ROAD RUNNER — 19 LOVE SW LRLP 117
RICHARD STANLEY F (F — (C) CRAZY DAYS — 1975 LOVE SW 141 SONET 3018
ILE KALLIO G (C — (D) HOT WHEELS — 19 LOVE SW LRLP 206
(E) HURRIGANES — 1977 SONET FR STA 20311 UK SNTF 732
(F) USE NO HOOKS — 1978 SONET FRSTA20345UK SNTF754
(F) ISUGU WAY — 1977 LOVE SCAN LRLP250
(G) STRANDED IN THE JUNGLE — 1978 SONET SLP 3039
(H) 16 GOLDEN GREATS — 1977 LOVE SCAN LRLP 230

H192 PHIL HURTT H192

PHIL HURTT V PNO(AB — (A) GIVING IT BACK — 1978 FANTASY US 9552 F 546
EVETTE BENTON V (AB — (B) P H FACTOR — 1979 FANTASY US 9582 FT 561
BARBARA INGRAM V (AB
CARLA BENSON V (AB — BABBS STEWART V (A — RICHIE ROME K (A — GREG POREE G (A
DAVID WILLIAMS G (A — GREG MIDDLETON B (A — LARRY TOLBERT D (A — SHONDON AKIEM PERC(A
CARL HELM V (B — RON TYSON V (B — ANN S CLARK PNO (B — LARRY WASHINGTON PERC(B
MIGUEL FUENTES PERC (B

H193 HUSTLER H193

TONY BEARD D (A — (A) HIGH STREET — 1974 A&M US 4504 UK AMLS 68276
HENRY SPINETTI D (B — (B) PLAY LOUD — 1975 A&M US 4556 UK AMLH 33001
STEVE HAYNES V (AB
MICKEY LLEWELYN G V (AB — KENNY DAUGHTERS K (AB — KENNY LYONS B V (AB

H193A HUSTLER (2) H193A

(A) JUKEBOX QUEEN — 19 REFINED UK RR1

H193B WILLIE HUTCH H193B

WILLIE HUTCH G V (ALL — (A) FULLY EXPOSED — 1973 MOTOWN US 784 UK STML11247
LAWRENCE DICKENS B (A — (B) FOXY BROWN — 1975 MOTOWN UK STML11269
TOMMY MYLES WIND (A — (C) MARK OF THE BEAST — 1975 MOTOWN UK STML11280
KING ERRISON PERC (A — (D) ODE TO MY LADY — 1975 MOTOWN UK STML12015
JOE SAMPLE PNO (A
ALAN ESTES PERC (A — JULIA TILLMAN V (A — OREN WATERS V (A — MILTON HAYES V (A
TIM LAWSON G (A — FRED WHITE D (A — SAM CLAYTON CONGA(A — GENE ESTES PERC(A
MAXINE WILLARD V (A — CAROL WILLIS V (A — RICHARD HUTCH V (A — DENNIS ALBERT V (A

H194 ASHLEY HUTCHINGS H194

ASHLEY HUTCHINGS V B (ALL — (A) MORRIS ON — 1972 ISLAND UK HELP 5
RICHARD THOMPSON G V (A — (B) COMPLEAT DANCING MASTER — 1974 ISLAND UK HELP 17 US ANTILLES7003
BARRY DRANSFIELD G V VLN(A — (C) RATTLEBONE & PLOUGHJACK — 1976 ISLAND UK HELP24
JOHN KIRKPATRICK V ACC(AB — (D) SON OF MORRIS ON — 1976 HARVEST UK SHSM 2012
DAVE MATTACKS D (ABD — (E) KICKIN' UP THE SAWDUST — 1977 HARVEST UK SHSP 4073
SHIRLEY COLLINS V (AD
BERT CLEAVER PIPE (AB — PHIL PICKETT WIND (BD — SIMON NICOL G)BD — ROGER SWALLOW D (B
ROD SKEAPING VLN (B — JEREMY MONTAGU PERC (B — SUE HARRIS OBOE (B — RICHARD HARVEY CLAR(B
ADAM SKEAPING VLN (B — ALAN LUMSDEN SERPENT (B — TERRY POTTER HCA (BE — DAVE KETTLEWELL WIND(B
ALAN WARD CELLO(B — FANNY WARLOCK SPINET (B — PETER KNIGHT VLN (B — RAY WARLEIGH SAX (B
FRANCIS BAINES VLN (B — ELIZABETH BAINES VLN (B — LONI PATT VLN (B — PETER VEL VLN (B
JOHN WATCHAM CONC (D — MICHAEL GREGORY D PERC (DE — MARTIN CARTHY G (D — JOHN TAMS CONC V (DE
JAMES PLESTER VLN (D — JOHN RODD CONC (DE — IAN CUTLER VLN (D — BOB CANN MELODEON (E
JIMMY COOPER DULC (E — MICHAEL HEBBERT CONC K(E — PETER BULLOCK WIND SYN (E — GRAEME TAYLOR G (E

H194A J B HUTTO H194A

J B HUTTO V G (ALL — (A) HAWKSQUAT — 1973 DELMARK US DS 617
BREWER PHILLIPS G V (C — (B) SLIDEWINDER — 1974 DELMARK US DS 636
MARK HARRIS B (C — (C) LIVE VOLUME ONE — 1977 CHARLY UK CR 30182
TED HARVEY D (C — (D) BLUES FOR FONESSA — 1979 AMUGO AMLP 823
MIKE ALLEN PNO (C — (E) LIVE AT SANDY'S JAZZ REVUE — 1979 BARON 101
SUNNYLAND SLIM PNO (A — (F) MASTER OF MODERN BLUES — 19 TESTAMENT US 2213

H194B HYBRID KIDS H194B

LOL COXHILL SAX (B — (A) A COLLECTION OF CLASSIC MUTANTS — 1980 CHERRY RED UK ARED 5
MORGAN FISHER K (AB — (B) CLAWS — 1980 CHERRY RED UK BRED 11
MAGGIE NICHOLS V (B
JOEL CUTRARA (B — IAIN MONEY V (A — CHRIS ROSS V (B — VALERIE ROSS V (B

H195 HYDRA H195

WAYNE BRUCE V K (AB — (A) HYDRA — 1974 CAPRICORN US 0130 UK 2429120
SPENCER KIRKPATRICK G (AB — (B) LAND OF MONEY — 1975 CAPRICORN US 0157 UK 2429130
ORVILLE DAVIS B (AB — (C) ROCK THE WORLD — 1977 CAPRICORN US 6096
STEVE PACE D (AB
DAN TURBEVILLE K (A — RANDALL BRAMBLETT SAX (A — WILL BOULWARE K (B — EARL FORD TROM(A
JOHNNY SANDLIN PERC (B — OSCAR JACKSON SAX (A — TODD LOGAN TPT (A — CHUCK LEAVELL K (B
BILL STEWART PERC (B

H196 HYDRAVION H196

PHILIPPE BESOMBES K G V(A — (A) HYDRAVION — 1978 SONET UK SNTF766 GER DECCA 69068
PIERRE BATTAILLET D (A
DOMINIQUE ESNAULT D (A — PATRICK VERBEKE G (A — COOKY RHINOSCEROS G (A — CHRIS SAINT ROCK B (A
CHRISTIAN WERBROUCK EFFECT(A

H197 PHYLLIS HYMAN H197

PHYLLIS HYMAN (ALL — (A) PHYLLIS HYMAN — 1977 BUDDAH US 5681 BDLP 4046
(B) SING A SONG — 1979 BUDDAH BDLP 4058
(C) SOMEWHERE — 1979 ARISTA US 4202
(D) YOU KNOW HOW TO LOVE ME — 1980 ARISTA US 9509 UK 1114
(E) CANT WE FALL IN LOVE — 1981 ARISTA UK SPART 1154

H198 HYPSTRZ H198

ERNEST BATSON G (A — (A) HYPSTRIZATION — 1980 LINE GERM 5093 US VOXX 200003
RANDY WIESS B (A
BILL BATSON V (A — JOHN HAGA D (A

I1 I DON'T CARE I1

GARY BOGGESS K SYN(A — (A) ASK ANYONE — 1976 BUDDAH KSBS 2617
FRANK PELLINE G K V(A
PETER KNAPP HRNS V(A — JOSE ORTIZ D V (A — TIM GRAZIANO B (A — PAUL McDONALD WIND(A
FRANK BONZIE V (A — DOUG THOMAS V (A

I1A

I ROY

I1A

I ROY REED		(ALL
ROBBIE SHAKESPEARE	B	(I
LEROY WALLACE	D	(I
EARL LINDO	K	(I
EARL SMITH	G	(I
CARLTON DAVIS	D	(I
SCIENTIST	PERC	(I
SCULLY	PERC	(I
PABLO BLACK	SYN	(I

(A) PRESENTING I ROY	19	TROJAN		TRLS 63
(B) HELL & SORROW	19	TROJAN		TRLS 71
(C) I ROY	1974	TROJAN		TRLS 91
(D) VERSIONS GALORE	19	TROJAN		TBL 161
(E) DREAD BALDHEAD	1976	KLIK		KLP 9020
(F) CRISUS TIME	1976	CAROLINE	UK	CA 2011
(G) CANT CONQUER RASTA	1977	JUSTICE		JUSTLP 008
(H) MUSICAL SHARK ATTACK	1977	VIRGIN	UK	V 2075
(I) HEART OF A LION	1978	FRONT LINE	UK	FL 1001
(J) TEN COMMANDMENTS	1978	FRONT LINE	UK	FL 1028
(K) DREADLOCKS IN JAMAICA	1978	LOVE & LIVE		05
(L) GODFATHER	1978	THIRD WORLD		930
(M) THE GENERAL (DBL)	1978	FRONT LINE	UK	FLD6002
(N) WORLD ON FIRE	1978	FRONT LINE	UK	FL 1033
(O) CANCER	1979	FRONT LINE	UK	4001
(P) WHAP'N BAP'N	1980	VIRGIN	UK	2164
(Q) MANY MOODS	1981	TROJAN	UK	TRLS91

I2

JANIS IAN

I2

JANIS IAN G V (ALL
AL ROGERS D (D
WILL LEE B (A
JEFF MIRANOV G (A
B BUSHNELL B (D
DICK HYMAN ORG (D
HUGH McCRACKEN G (D
MARVIN STAMM VLN (D
STU SCHARF G (D
STEVE GADD D (AM
RALPH CASALE G (D
TONY STUD TROM (DA
WAYNE ANDRE TROM (A
BERNIE GLOW TPT (D
RAY ALONGE HRNS (D
GEORGE YOUNG SAX (A
BRAD SPINNEY PERC (D
GENE ORLOFF VLN (DA
HAROLD COLETTA VIOLA(DA
GEORGE RICCI CELLO(DFG
CLAIRE BAY V (HJA
PHIL BODNER WIND (FGH
LARRY HARLOW K (H
BUCKY PIZZARELLI G (H
JOE FARRELL SAX (D
AARON ROSAND VLN (D
SAL DE TROIA G (AGM
RUSSELL GEORGE B (G
PHOEBE SNOW V (H
BURT COLLINS TPT (G
MIKE MAINIERI VIBES(M
RON GETMAN G (M
LES HURDLE B (M
STEPHANIE SPRUILL V (M
SCOTT ZITO G (M
ALLAN SCHWARZBERG D (M
LANI GROVES V (M
GONZALO FERNANDEZ (H
ODETTA (H
STU WOODS B (HJ
ROMEO PENQUE SAX (DFH
JULES SCHACTER VLN (D
JOE MARK B (A
BUDDY SALZMAN D (A
RAY BECKENSTEIN WIND (F
RUBENS BASSINI CONGA(J
RICHARD CROOKS D (M
STEVE LOVE G (M
STEVE MADAIO TPT (M
LISA ROBERTS V (M
MATS BJOERKLUND G (M
NEIL JASON B (M
DINO SOLERA SAX (M
RON FRANGIPANE STR(K
JEFF LAYTON G (HJ
RICHARD DAVIS B (AFGH
MANNY GREEN VLN (D
ARTIE BUTLER K (A
ARTIE KAPLAN FLT (A
ALAN RAPH TROM (G
JOE SHEPLEY HRNS (F
PHIL KRAUS PERC (J
JIM MAELEN PERC (MA
GARY HERBIG SAX (M
KEITH FORSEY D (M
FRANK OWENS K (M
GORDON GRODY V (M
JOE D'ELIA (M
GLORIA AGOSTINI HARP (M
AL GORGONI G(AGH
BARRY LAZAROWITZ PERC(FGHJ
JOE MALIN VLN (D
VINNIE BELL G (A
KEN KOSEK FDL (G
JESSE LEVY STRINGS(H
DON PAYNE B (G
CLARENCE CLEMONS SAX(M
JOHN CROWDER B V (M
CHICK COREA PNO (M
HAROLD FACTERMEYER K(M
BOB KULICK G (M
FRANK FLOYD V (M
JOCELYN BROWN V (M

(A) JANIS IAN	1967	VERVE FORECAST	US	FTS3017
(A) JANIS IAN	1976	POLYDOR		PD 6058
(A) JANIS IAN	1967	POLYDOR GER 2391 202 RI		9506
(A) JANIS IAN	1982	VERVE	UK RI	2482 572
(B) FOR ALL THE SEASONS	1968	VERVE	US	FTS3024
(C) SECRET LIFE OF EDDIE FINK	1968	VERVE	US	FTS3048
(D) WHO REALLY CARES	1969	VERVE MGS 1850	US	FTS3063
(E) PRESENT COMPANY	1971	CAPITOL SM683		VMP 1014
(F) STARS	1974	CBS US 32857	UK	80224
(F) STARS	1981	CBS	UK RI	32049
(G) BETWEEN THE LINES	1975	CBS US 33394	UK	80635
(H) AFTERTONES	1975	CBS US 33919	UK	69220
(H) AFTERTONES	1981	CBS	UK RI	32018
(J) MIRACLE ROW	1977	CBS US 34440	UK	81879
(K) JANIS IAN	1978	CBS US 35325	UK	82700
(L) JANIS IAN (COMP)	1978	CBS JAP		26AP 1327
(M) NIGHT RAINS	1979	CBS US 36139	UK	83802
(N) BEST OF	1980	CBS	UK	84711
(O) MY FAVOURITES	1980	CBS NL		84188
(P) RESTLESS EYES	1981	CBS US 37360	UK	85040

I3

IAN & SYLVIA

I3

IAN TYSON G V (ALL)
SYLVIA TYSON AUTOHARP V(ALL
MONTE DUNN G (D
RUSS SAVAKUS B (D
AMOS GARRETT G (R
BUDDY CAGE STEEL(R
N D SMART D (R
KEN KALMUSKY B (R
DAVID BRIGGS PNO (R

(A) IAN & SYLVIA	1962	VANGUARD US 79215		+ VSD 2113
(B) FOUR STRONG WINDS	1964	VANGUARD		VSD 2149
(C) NORTHERN JOURNEY	1964	VANGUARD		VSD 79154
(D) EARLY MORNING RAIN	1965	VANGUARD US 79175 FONTANA		TF6053
(E) PLAY ONE MORE	1966	VANGUARD		VSD 79215
(F) SO MUCH DREAMING	1967	VANGUARD		VSD 79241
(G) NASHVILLE	1968	VANGUARD		VSD 79284
(H) FULL CIRCLE	1968	MGM		4550
(I) BEST OF	1968	VANGUARD UK SVRL19004		VSD 79269
(J) IAN & SYLVIA (GREATEST HITS)	19	VANGUARD		VSD 5/6
(K) BEST OF	19	CBS US 32516	UK	64634
(L) LOVIN' SOUND	19	POLYDOR 2353 063 US MGM		4388
( ) OL'OEN(SOLO IAN)	19	A&M		SP 9017
( ) WOMANS WORLD (SOLO SYLVIA)	19	CAPITOL		ST 11434
( ) ONE JUMP AHEAD OF THE DEVIL(IAN)	1979	BOOT	CAN	BOS 7189
( ) YOU WERE ON MY MIND	19	CBS	US	31337
( ) GREATEST HITS	19	VANGUARD		23/4
( ) IAN & SYLVIA	1971	CBS	US	30736
(R) GREAT SPECKLED BIRD	19	AMPEX	US	10103

I3A

JIMMY IBBOTSON

I3A

JIMMY IBBOTSON G V (A
LARRY THOMPSON D (A
STEVE SYKES G (A
STAN ROGERS HRNS (A
DIK DARNELL PNO (A
PAM ADDINGTON GRAZIER V(A
JOHN MACY STEEL(A
RENE ULIBARRI V (A
ALBERT CAMPBELL K (A
PAM MARTIN V (A
PAUL VASTOLA SYN (A
MIKE MARTIN V (A
GERARD McMAHON K (A
RAY BONNEVILLE HCA (A
HILLIARD WILSON B (A
PHILIP McLOURD SAX (A

(A) NITTY GRITTY IBBOTSON	1977	FIRST AMERICAN	US	7718

I4

ICE

I4

JOHN CARTER (
STEVE TURNER B (
GLYN JAMES (
LYNTON NAIFE K (
GRANT SERPELL D (

(A) ICE	1974	PASSPORT	US	10075
(B) IMPORT/EXPORT	1975	PASSPORT	US	10096

I5

ICEBREAKERS

I5

(A) PLANET MARS DUB	1978	FRONT LINE	UK	FL 1010

I5A ICEHOUSE I5A

IVA DAVIES G V (A (A) ICE HOUSE 1981 CHRYSALIS GER 203 845 UK 1350
KEITH WELSH B V (A
GEOFF OAKES SAX (A JOHN LLOYD D V (A ANTHONY SNITH K V (A IAN MOSS G (A
MICHAEL HOSTE K (A

I5B IDEAL I5B

F J KRUGER G V (A (A) IDEAL 1980 IC GERM 80004
ANNETTE K V (A
ULI DENKER B V (A HANS BEHRENDT D V (A

I6 IDES OF MARCH I6

JOHN LARSON TPT (A (A) VEHICLE 1970 WB US WS1863
RAY HERR G B V(A (B) COMMON BOND 1971 WB US WS1896
JAMES PETERIK G V (ABCD (C) WORLD WOVEN 1972 RCA US LSP 4812
LARRY MILLAS G B FLT V (ABCD (D) MIDNIGHT OIL 1973 RCA US APLI 0143
MIKE BORCH D VIBES (ABCD
BOB BERGLAND B V (ABCD CHUCK SOUMAR PERC HCA V(ABCD DAVE ARELLANO K (D RUSTY YOUNG STEEL/DOB(D

I7 IDLE RACE I7

JEFF LYNE G V (1AB (A) BIRTHDAY PARTY 1968 LIBERTY US 7603 UK LBS 83132
GREG MASTERS B (1ABC (A) BIRTHDAY PARTY 1976 SUNSET UK SLS 50381
DAVE WALKER (C (B) IDLE RACE 1969 LIBERTY UK LBS 83221
BOB WILSON ((C) TIME IS 1971 REGAL ZONOPHONE SLRZ 1017
BOB LAMB ((D) IMPOSTERS OF LIFE MAGAZINE 1974 DAFFODIL CAN 10046
RITCHIE WALKER ((E) ON WITH THE SHOW 1973 SUNSET UK SLS 50354
DAVE PRITCHARD G (1ABC (1) 1967
MIKE HOPKINS (C
ROGER SPENCER D (1ABC

I7A BILLY IDOL I7A

BILLY IDOL V (A (A) BILLY IDOL 1982 CHRYSALIS UK CHr1377

I8 IF I8

TERRY SMITH G (ABCDI (A) IF 1970 CAPITOL US 539 UK ISLAND ILPS 9129
DICK MORRISSEY SAX (ALL (B) IF2 1970 CAPITOL US 676 UK ISLAND ILPS 9137
JOHN MEALING K (ABCDI (C) IF3 1971 CAPITOL US 820 UK U A UAG 29158
JIM RICHARDSON B (ABCDI (D) IF4 1972 UK U A UAG 29315
DENNIS ELLIOTT F (ABCDI (E) NOT JUST A BUNCH OF PRETTY.. 1974 CAPITOL US 11299 UK GULL GULP 1004
J W HODGKINSON (ABCDI (F) TEA BREAK IS OVER 1975 CAPITOL US 11344 UK GULL GULP 1007
DAVE QUINCY SAX (ABCDI (G) THIS IS IF 1973 BRAIN 201 005
DAVE GREENSLADE K ((H) GOLDROCK 1974 BRAIN 201 103
DAVE WINTOUR B (I (I) WATERFALL 1971 METROMEDIA IMP 1057
CLIFF DAVIS V D SYN (EHIFJ (J) DOUBLE DIAMOND 1973 METROMEDIA 1 0174
WALT MONAGHAN V B (EHIF
FI TRENCH K (J KURT PALOMAKI PERC (J PETE ARNESEN K (J GEOFF WHITEHORN G (EHIF
GABRIEL MAGNO K (EFHI STEVE ROSENTHAL G V (J CARLOS MARTINEZ PERC (F

I9 IGGINBOTTOM'S WRENCH I9

ALLAN HOLDSWORTH G V (A (A) IGGINBOTTOM'S WRENCH 1969 DERAM UK SML1051
DAVE FREEMAN D (A
STEVE ROBINSON G V (A MICK SKELLY B (A

I 10 IGGY POP & THE STOOGES I10

IGGY POP V (ALL (A) THE STOOGES 1969 ELEKTRA US EKS74051 UK K 42032
SCOTT THURSTON B V G K(EGHJ (B) FUN HOUSE 1970 ELEKTRA UK K 42055
SCOTT ASHETON D (ACEBL (C) RAW POWER 1973 CBS US 32111 UK 65586
FRED SONIC SMITH G ((C) RAW POWER 1977 EMBASSY UK 31464
TONY SALES B (FGH (D) IDIOT 1976 RCA PL12275
RICKY GARDINER G (FH (E) METALLIC K O 1976 SKYDOG US IMP1015
GARY RASMUSSEN B ((F) LUST FOR LIFE 1977 RCA PL12488
HUNT SALES D (FGH (G) KILL CITY 1978 BOMP US 4001 RADAR UK K56467+RAD2
DAVID BOWIE PNO V(FH (H) T V EYE 1978 RCA PL12796
STACEY HAYDEN G (H (J) NEW VALUES 1979 ARISTA US 4237 UK APART1092
ROBERT DUPREE G (M (J) NEW VALUES 1979 ARISTA GER 62 699
DAVE ALEXANDER B (AB (K) SOLDIER 1980 ARISTA US 4259 UK SPART1117
STEVE TRANIO B (G (L) NO FUN (COMP) 1980 ELEKTRA US EF 7095 UK K 52234
JAMES WILLIAMSON G V (CEGJ (M) PARTY 1981 ARISTA GER 203 806 UK SPART1158
RON ASHETON V B G(ACE (N) ZOMBIE BIRDHOUSE 1982 ANIMAL UK CHR1399
CARLOS ALOMAR G V (F (EP) JESUS LOVES THE STOOGIES 1977 LINE GER 3006
GAYNIA V (G
BRIAN GLASCOCK D (G
JOHN HARDEN SAX (GJ DAVE BROCK STRINGS (J GLEN MATLOCK G V(K IVAN KRAL K G (KM
STEVE NEW (K BARRY ANDREWS (K EARL SHAKELFORD V (J ALFONO SISTERS V (J
KLAUS KRUGER D (JK JACKIE CLARK B (J DOUGLAS BROWNE D (M MICHAEL PAGE B (M

I11 IGUANA I11

BRUCE ROBERTS G V (A (A) IGUANA 1974 POLYDOR UK 2383 108 US LION 1011
PETE HUNT D (A
JOHN CARTWRIGHT B (A RON TAYLOR SAX (A CHRIS GOWER TROM (A DON SHINN PNO (A

I11A IHRE KINDER I11A

SONNY HENNIG V G K(ALL (A) IHRE KINDER 1969 PHILIPS GER 844393
WALTI SCHNEIDER G V B(ABF (B) LEERE HANDE 1970 KUCKUCK GER 237 5001
JUDITH BRIGGER V PERC(A (C) 2375004 1970 KUCKUCK GER 237 5004
OLDHAM FRENZEL D (ABCDE (D) WERDOHL 1971 KUCKUCK GER 237 5013
MUCK GROL G (ABE (E) POP HISTORY VOL 24 19 POLYDOR GER 2634 018
GEORGIE MEYER V FLT(ABCDE (F) ANFANG OHNE ENDE 1972 KUCKUCK GER 237 5016
ERNST SCHULTZ V FLT(BCDE
TOMMI ROEDER B SAX(CDE WOLF STUMM G (F GUNTHER STORCH D (F

I12 IJAHMAN I12

IJAHMAN V G(AB (A) HAILE I HYMN 1978 ISLAND ILPS 9521
JONI G (A (B) ARE WE A WARRIOR 1979 ISLAND ILPS 9557
BO PEE G (A
WILLIE LINDO G (A EARL SMITH G (A DEL RICHARDSON G (A GEOFFREY CHUNG K G (A
STEVE WINWOOD K (A EARL LINDO K (A ERROL NELSON PNO (A ROBERT LYN PNO (A
OSSIE HIBBERT PNO (A VAL DOUGLAS B (A ROBBIE SHAKESPEARE B (A LLOYD PARKS B (A
MICKY RICHARDS D (A SLY DUNBAR D (A BOBBY ELLIS TPT (A HERMAN MARQUIS SAX (A
RICHARD HALL SAX (A EDDIE BLAIR HRN (A ADRIAN BRETT WIND (A ALAN BEEVER FLT (A
HI HO SILVER PERC (A SONS OF NEGUS PERC(A GROCO PERC (A

I12A **ILLINOIS SPEED PRESS** I12A
PAUL COTTON G V (AB — (A) ILLINOIS SPEED PRESS 1969 CBS US 9792 UK 63691
FRED PAGE D (A — (B) DUO 1970 CBS US 9976
MICHAEL ANTHONY K (A
KAL DAVID G V (AB ROB LEWINE B (A

I12B **ILLUSION (US)** I12B
MIKE RICCIARDELLA D (ALL — (A) ILLLUSION 1969 STEED US 37033 UK SLPD531
RICHIE CERNIGLIA G (ALL — (B) TOGETHER 19 STEED US 37005
CHUCK ADLER B (ALL — (C) IF IT'S SO 19 STEED US 37006
MIKE MANISCALCO G K(ALL
JOHN VINCI V (ALL

I13 **ILLUSION** I13
JANE RELF V (AB — (A) OUT OF THE MIST 1977 ISLAND ILPS9489 GER 28663
JIM McCARTY G V (AB — (B) ILLUSION 1978 ISLAND ILPS 9519
JOHN HAWKEN K (AB
EDDIE McNEIL D (AB LOUIS CENNAMO B (AB JOHN KNIGHTSBRIDGE G (A PAUL SAMWELL SMITH V(B

I13A **ILLUSTRATION** I13A
BILL LEDSTER V (A — (A) ILLUSTRATION 1970 PYE INTERNATIONAL NSPL28140
JOHN RANGER K (A — (A) ILLUSTRATION 1970 JANUS US 3010
BENOIT HARINEN TPT (A
GARY BEATTIE G (A NORMAN BURGESS SAX (A ROGER HOMEFIELD TPT (A RICHARD TERRY B (A
DONALD SANDERS SAX (A CLAUDE RAY D (A

I13B **IMAN CALIFATO INDEPENDIENTE** I13B
KIKO GUERRERO D (A — (A) CAMUNO DEL AGUILA 19 CBS SPAIN S84277
MARCOS MANTERO K (A
MANUEL RODRIGUES G V (A URBANO MORALES B (A

I13C **IMPALAS** I13C
JOE FRAZIER V (— (A) SORRY(I RAN ALL THE WAY HOME) 19 CUB US 8003
TONY CARLUCCI V (
LENNY RENDA V (RICHIE WAGNER V (A

I13D **ILMO SMOKEHOUSE** I13D
KEITH RAND G (A — (A) ILMO SMOKEHOUSE 19
FREDDIE TIEKEN SAX V(A
GERRY GABEL K FLT V(A DENNIS TIEKEN D V (A

I14 **IMPERIALS** I14
TIME TO GET IT TOGETHER 1974 KEY KL 012
FOLLOW MAN WITH MUSIC 1974 KEY KL 025
THE IMPERIALS NOW 19 IMPACT US HWS1990
WHO'S GONNA LOVE ME 1978 POWER EXCHANGE PXL 029
HEED TO CALL 1979 DAYSPRING 4003
SAIL ON 1978 DAYSPRING UK DAY4001
PRIORITY 1981 DAYSPRING 4005
ONE MORE SONG 1982 DAYSPRING 4004

I14A **IMPROVED SOUND LIMITED** I14A
JOHNNY FICKERT V SAX(B — (A) IMPROVED SOUND LIMITED 1971
AXEL LINSTADT G V K(B — (B) CATCH A SINGING BIRD 1973 CBS 65619
ULI RUPPERT B (B
ROLF GROSCHNER D (B FRANK BAUM STEEL (B RALF NOWY SAX (B

I15 **IMPRESSIONS** I15
JERRY BUTLER V — THE IMPRESSIONS 1963 ABC US 450
CURTIS MAYFIELD V — NEVER ENDING IMPRESSIONS 1963 ABC US 468 HMV UK CLP 1743
SAMUEL GOODEN V — KEEP ON PUSHING 1964 ABC US 493
FRED CASH V — PEOPLE GET READY 1965 ABC US 505
LEROY HUGHES V — GREATEST HITS 1965 ABC US 515
REG TORAIN V — ONE BY ONE 1965 ABC US 523
RALPH JOHNSON V — BIG 16 1965 HMV UK (M) CLP 1935 (S)CSD1642
RIDIN' HIGH 1966 ABC US 545 UK HMV CSD3548
FABULOUS IMPRESSIONS 1967 ABC US 606 UK HMV CSD3631
WE'RE ON A WINNER 1968 ABC US 635 UK STATESIDE 10239
THIS IS MY COUNTRY 1968 CURTOM US 8001
YOUNG MOD'S FORGOTTEN STORY 1969 CURTOM US 8003 UK POLYDOR 2359 003
BEST IMPRESSIONS 196 CURTOM US 8004
BIG 16 VOL 2 1969 UK STATESIDE 10279
AMEN 196 UK POLYDOR 2359 009
BEST OF 19 ABC US 654
VERSATILE 19 ABC US 668
CHECK OUT YOUR MIND 197 CURTOM US 8006 UK POLYDOR 2318 017
TIMES HAVE CHANGED 1972 CURTOM US 8012 UK POLYDOR 2310 059
16 GREATEST HITS 197 ABC US 727
EARLY YEARS 1973 UK PROBE GTSP 201
PREACHER MAN 1973 CURTOM US 8016
FINALLY GOT MYSELF TOGETHER 1974 CURTOM US 8019 UK BUDDAH 4003
FIRST IMPRESSIONS 1975 CURTOM US 0103 UK K 56143
FIRST IMPRESSIONS 1979 RSO RI RSS 009
BIG 16 RI 1975 ABC UK ABCL5104
SOONER OR LATER 1975 CURTOM US 5003
FOR YOUR PRECIOUS LOVE 1976 VEE JAY US1075 UK DJM DJB26086
FOR YOUR PRECIOUS LOVE 197 JOY JOYS104
IT'S ABOUT TIME 1976 COTILLION US 9912
ORIGINALS (DBL) 1976 ABC US 303
LOVING POWER 1976 CURTOM US 5009 UK K 56211
VINTAGE YEARS 197 SIRE US 3717
THREE THE HARD WAY 197 CURTOM US 8602
COLLECTION 197 ABC US 30009
COME TO MY PARTY 197 20TH CENTURY 596
FANS THE FIRE 1981 20TH CENTURY 624
LOVING POWER 19 RSO US RSS 10

I15B **IN TRANSIT** I15B
(A) IN TRANSIT 1980 RCA US 3607

I15C INCREDIBLE BONGO BAND I15C

(A) BONGO ROCK 1973 PRIDE US 028 UK DJM 76 20452
(B) RETURN OF 1974 PRIDE US 6010

I15D INCREDIBLE HOG I15D

KEN GORDON G HCA V(A (A) VOLUME ONE 1973 ? ?
JIM HOLMES B V (A
TONY AWIN D (A

I16 INCREDIBLE STRING BAND I16

ROBIN WILLIAMSON G V K VLN+(ALL (A) INCREDIBLE STRING BAND 1966 ELEKTRA EKS 7322
MIKE HERON K G V B HCA FLT+(ALL (B) THE 5000 SPIRITS 1967 ELEKTRA EKS 74010+RI K 42001
CLIVE PALMER V G BANJO (A (C) HANGMANS BEAUTIFUL DAUGHTER 1968 ELEKTRA EKS 74021+RI K 42002
ROSE SIMPSON B PERC(CDEGJFH (D) THE BIG HUGE 1968 ELEKTRA EKS 74037+RI K 42022
LICORICE McKECHNIE VLN K(BCDGFHJK (E) WEE TAM 1968 ELEKTRA EKS 74036+RI K 42021
MALCOLM LeMAISTRE V K B+(KLMN (F) CHANGING HORSES 1969 ELEKTRA EKS 74057+RI K 42037
GERALD DOTT CLAR K (LM (G) I LOOKED UP 1970 ELEKTRA EKS 74061+RI K 42046
GREG HEAT SITAR(H (G) I LOOKED UP 1970 ELEKTRA UK 2460 002
JOHN GILSTON D ((H) 'U' 1970 ELEKTRA EKS 7E2003 K62002
STAN LEE B V STEEL (KMN (I) RELICS OF I S B 1970 ELEKTRA K62008+ K 42060
WALTER GRUNDY HCA (K (I) RELICS OF I S B 1970 ELEKTRA US7E2004
GRAHAM FORBES G (N (J) BE GLAD FOR THE SONG 1970 ISLAND ILPS 9140
MIKE TOMICH ((K) LIQUID ACROBAT 1971 ISLAND GER 85749 UK ILPS 9172
DAVID BARKER ((K) LIQUID ACROBAT 1971 ELEKTRA US 74112
IVAN PAWLER K (F (L) EARTH SPAN 1972 ISLAND UK ILPS 9211
JACK INGRAM V D (MN (M) NO RUINOUS FEUD 1973 ISLAND UK ILPS 9229
JANET SHANKMAN V (H (M) NO RUINOUS FEUD 1973 REPRISE US 2139
DANNY THOMPSON B (BN (N) HARD ROPE & SILKEN TWINE 1974 ISLAND UK ILPS 9270
JOHN GIMBRI FLT (G (N) HARD ROPE & SILKEN TWINE 1974 REPRISE US 2198
JOHN HOPKINS PNO (B (O) SEASONS THEY CHANGE 1976 ISLAND UK ISLD 9
SUSIE WATSON TAYLOR FLT(M
B J WILSON D (M STAN SCHNIER B V (M ALUN EDEN D (M JANET WILLIAMSON FLT (M
SOMA SITAR TAMBOURA (B GERRY CONWAY D (K JOE BOYD PROD (B DAVE MATTACKS D (G
PETER GRANT BAN (H

I17 INCREDIBLES I17

(A) HEART & SOUL 1974 CONTEMPO CLP 512
(A) HEART & SOUL 19 AUDIO ARTS AAS 7000

I17A INDIAN SUMMER I17A

BOB JACKSON K V (A (A) INDIAN SUMMER 1971 NEON NE 3
COLIN WILLIAMS G V (A
PAUL HOOPER D PERC V (A MALCOLM HARKER B VIBES V (A

I17B INDUSTRIALS I17B

DANNY STAG V G K B (A (A) INDUSTRIALS 1980 EPIC UK 84399
J B FRANK V G K D (A
JAN MACKENZIE V (A MIKE BOLT V G K(A CALVIN TEARDROP B (A CYCLOPS D (A

I17C INFERNAL BLUES MACHINE I17C

WARREN RAY V (A (A) INFERNAL BLUES MACHINE 1976 LONDON US 666 UK SHU 8496
GREG MIDDLETON B (A
MIKE CAVANAUGH K (A GREGG PARKER G (A

I17D INDIGO I17D

(A) INDIGO 1977 WB US 2991

I18 INFA RIOT I18

(A) STILL OUT OF ORDER 1982 SECRET UK SEC 7

I18A INMATES I18A

PETER GUNN G V (AB (A) FIRST OFFENCE 1979 RADAR UK 25 GER 56743 US POLYDOR6241
BILL HURLEY V (AB (B) SHOT IN THE DARK 1980 RADAR UK 28 US POLYDOR6302
BEN DONNELLY B (AB
TONY OLIVER G V (AB LAURIE GARMAN HCA (A JOHN BULL D (A EDDIE D (A
JOHN EARLE SAX (A DICK HANSON TPT (A RAY BEAVIS SAX (A GAVIN POVEY K (A
JIM RUSSELL D V (AB VIC MAILE PROD (AB

I19 INNER CIRCLE I19

ROGER LEWIS G ((A) ROCK THE BOAT 1974 TROJAN TRLS 93
JACOB MILLER ((B) BLAME IT ON THE SUN 1975 TROJAN TRLS 114
BERNARD 'TOUTER' HARVEY K((C) REGGAE THING 1976 CAPITOL EST 11574
IAN LEWIS B ((D) READY FOR THE WORLD 1977 CAPITOL EST 11664
LESTER ADDERLEY G V ((E) KILLER DUB 1978 TOP RANKING 8364 182
CALVIN McKENZIE D ((F) EVERYTHING IS GREAT 1979 ISLAND ILPS 9558
CHARLES FARQUHARSON K ((G) NEW AGE MUSIC 1980 ISLAND ILPS 9608
EVERALD 'BLACKSPY' JAHSON PERC((H) SOMETHING SO GOOD 1982 CARRERE CAL 143
JOE ORTIZ (

I19A INNER CITY UNIT I19A

NIK TURNER V SAX(AB (A) PASS OUT 1980 RIDDLE RID 002
TREN THOMS G V (AB (B) MAXIMUM EFFECT 1981 AVATAR AALP 5004
DEAD FRED V K (AB (C) PUNKADELIC 1982 FLICKKNIFE SHARP 103
BAZ MAGNETO B V (A
MICK STUPP D (A DINO FERARI D (B CAPTAIN SENSIBLE G (B BILL BOSTON HRN (B
MAX WALL V (B

I19B INNER LIFE I19B

(A) I'M CAUGHT 1980 PRELUDE US 12175

I19C INNER SOUND OF THE ID I19C

(A) THE INNER SOUND OF THE ID 1967 RCA US LSP 3805

I20 NEIL INNES I20

NEIL INNES G V HCA K (ABCD (A) LUCKY PLANET (WORLD) 1970 LIBERTY LBG 83419
IAN WALLACE D (A (B) HOW SWEET TO BE AN IDIOT 1973 U A UAG 29492
ROGER McKEW G (A (C) RUTLAND TIMES 1976 BBC REB 233
ROGER ROWAN B (A (D) TAKING OFF 1977 ARISTA SPARTY1004
JOHN HALSEY D (CD (E) INNES BOOK OF RECORDS 1979 POLYDOR 2383 556
TIMMI DONALD D (D (F) NEIL INNES A GO GO 1980 LIBERTY UK LBR 1018
ROGER SWALLOW D (C
JON FIELD CONGA(D BRIAN HODGSON B (CD ALAN JAMES B (D BILLY BREMNER G (CD
ROGER RETTIG G STEEL(CD JOHN MEGGINSON K (D JULIAN SMEDLEY VLN V(D KEITH NELSON BANJO(D
WILLIE FAHEY WIND (D BRIAN BOWLES V (D SUE JONES DAVIS V (D GERRY CONWAY D (B

(CONTINUED)

I20 **NEIL INNES** (CONTINUED) I20

ANDY ROBERTS G (BC MIKE KELLIE D (B DAVE RICHARDS B (BC OLLIE HALSALL G (B
ERIC IDLE V (C DAVE BALLBY V (C STUART ELLIOTT D (E PETE VAN HOOK D (E
BRUCE LYNCH B (E HARVEY WESTON B (E BILLY LIVESY K (E BRIAN HOLLOWAY G (E
RICHARD BRUNTON G (E MITCH DALTON G (E BRIAN LEMON PNO (E JOHN MUMFORD TROM(E
SHARON CAMPBELL V (E YVONNE KEELEY V (E ANNIE KAVANAGH V (E PAUL TRAVIS V (E
KENNY DUKAYNE V (E GARY TRAVERS V (E HENRY LOWTHER TPT (E DIGBY FAIRWEATHER TPT(E
MARTIN DROVER TPT (E DAVE SPENCE TPT (E PAUL NIEMAN TROM (E PETE STRANGE TROM (E
BILL SKEAT SAX (E RANDY COLVILLE SAX (E TOMMY WHITTLE SAX (E KEITH GEMMELL SAX (E
PAT KYLE SAX (E

I21 **INSECT TRUST** I21

LUKE FAUST HCA G V (AB (A) INSECT TRUST 1968 CAPITOL US SKAO 109
TREVOR KOEHLER WIND D (AB (B) HOBOKEN SATURDAY NIGHT 1970 ATCO US SD 33313
ROBERT PALMER WIND (AB
NANCY JEFFRIES V (AB BILL BARTH G STEEL(AB HUGH McCRACKEN G (AB ELVIN JONES D (B
BERNARD PURDIE D (AB BUDDY SOUTHMAN D (A CHARLES NEALY D (B DONALD McDONALD D (B
WILLIAM FOLWELL B TPT(B JOE MACHO B (B BOB BUSHNELL B (B CHARLIE MACEY G B(B
WARREN GARDNER TPT (B RALPH CASALE G (B

I21A **INSTRUCTIONS** I21A

OWEN SMITH V (A (A) INSTRUCTIONS 1980 QUALITY CAN 2067
MARTIN WALL K (A
PETER CROLLY B (A REGAN MYERS K (A ALAN WEBSTER D (A DAVE BEATTY G (A
DOMENIC TROIANO G (A LARRY V (A JANET WILLIAMSON V (A KIMBERLEY JOHNSTON V (A

I22 **INTERGALACTIC TOURING BAND** I22

DAVID SCANCE G (A (A) INTER GALACTIC TOURING BAND 1977 CHARISMA UK CDS 4009
BRIAN CUOMO K (A
STEVE BARTH V (A ROD ARGENT V (A PETER SABEL B (A LARRY FAST K SYN(A
RYCHE CHLANDA G (A PERCY JONES B (A DAVE COUSINS V (A JEFFREY LEYNOR V (A
JIM CUOMO V (A MR SNIPS V (A JOHN TROPEA G (A MARGE RAYMOND V (A
PAUL MARCHETTI PERC (A FRANCIS ROSSI V (A ANNIE HASLAM V (A JOEL KRATZ V (A
ANTHONY PHILLIPS G (A FRANK PRESCOD B (A DAVID BEDFORD (A MIGHTY JOE YOUNG (A
FRANK D'AGOSTINO (A CLARENCE CLEMONS SAX (A RICK PARFITT (A ARTHUR BROWN (A
MEATLOAF V (A BEN E KING V (A WILL MALONE (A

I23 **INTERNATIONAL SUBMARINE BAND** I23

GRAM PARSONS G V (A (A) SAFE AT HOME 1968 LHI US LHIS12001 SHILOH RI 4087
BOB BUCHANAN G V (A
IAN DUNLOP B (A JOHN NUESE G (A JON CORNEAL D (A JAYDEE MANESS STEEL (A
EARL BALL PNO (A

I23A **INTERVIEW** I23A

JEFF STARRS V (AB (A) BIG OCEANS 1979 VIRGIN US 13131 UK V2123
PETE ALLERHAND G V K(AB (B) SNAKES & LADDERS 1980 VIRGIN US 13141 UK V2157
ALAN BRAIN G V (AB
MANNY ELIAS D (AB PHIL CROWTHER B (A MARLIS DUNKLAN V (B PETE WINGFIELD K (B

I23B **INVISIBLE MANS BAND** I23B

(A) INVISIBLE MANS BAND 1980 ISLAND UK ILPS 9537

I23C **INVADERS** I23C

SOO LUCAS V (A (A) TEST CARD 1980 POLYDOR UK 2383 589

I23D **IONA** I23D

MICHAEL STOREY V K HCA(A (A) CUCKOO 1978 SILVERSCALES KOO 13913
JAMES LASCELLES K V (A
DAVE SHEEN D V (A JOHN McKENZIE B (A PETE KIRTLEY G (A COLIN GIBSON B (A
DARRYL LEE QUE PERC (A KUMA HARADA B (A JOHN PORTER G B (A

I23E **DONNIE IRIS (& THE CRUISERS)** I23E

DONNIE IRIS G V (AB (A) BACK ON THE STREETS 1980 MCA US 3272
MARK AVSEC K (A (B) KING COOL 1981 MCA
MARTY LEE G (A
ALBRITTON McLAIN D (A KEVIN VALENTINE B V (A KENNY BLAKE (A

I24 **IRON BUTTERFLY** I24

RON BUSHY D (ABCDEFH (A) HEAVY 1967 ATCO US 33227 US 2465 015
MAXINE WILLARD V (F (A) HEAVY 1973 ATLANTIC GER 20050
DOUG INGLE K V (ABCDEH (B) IN A GADDA DA VIDA 1968 ATCO US 33250 UK 588 116
JERRY PENROD ((B) IN A GADDA DA VIDA 196 ATCO UK K40022 FR WE341
DANNY WEIS ((C) BALL 1969 ATLANTIC US 33280 UK 228 011
DARRYL DELOACH ((D) LIVE 1970 ATLANTIC US 33318 UK 2400 014
DENIECE WILLIAMS V (F (D) LIVE 1970 ATLANTIC GER 20095 UK RI K40086
ERIC BRANN G V (BCFGHD (E) METAMORPHOSIS 1970 ATLANTIC US 33339 UK 2401 003
MIKE PINERA G (E (F) METAMORPHOSIS 1972 ATLANTIC UK K 40294
LARRY RHEINHART G (E (F) SUN & STEEL 1975 MCA US 2164 UK MCF 2738
PHIL KRAMER B (FG (F) SUN & STEEL 1975 MCA IMP 32869
HOWARD REITZES K (G (G) SCORCHING BEAUTY 1975 MCA US 465 UK MCF 2694
LEE DORMAN B (BCDEH ( ) EVOLUTION (BEST OF) 1970 ATLANTIC US 33369 UK K 40298
BILL DEMARTINES K V (F ( ) STAR COLLECTION 1973 ATLANTIC 30038 + 20021
RICHARD PODOLOR G SITAR(E (CE) BALL METAMORPHOSIS (DBL) 1975 ATLANTIC UK K 80003
BILL COOPER G (E
JEROME JUMMONVILLE HRNS(F JULIA TILLMAN V (F

I24A **IRON CITY HOUSEROCKERS** I24A

JOE E GRUSHECKLY G V (ABC (A) LOVES SO TOUGH 1979 MCA UK MCF 3031
NED E RANKIN D (ABC (B) HAVE A GOOD TIME 1980 MCA US 5111
GIL SNYDER K (ABC (C) BLOOD ON THE BRICKS 1981 MCA US 5252
BILLY CROSS G (A
RICHARD REISING V (A SUSAN LYNCH V (A RODNEY PSYKA V (A MARC REISMAN HCA (ABC
PAUL GLANZ PNO (A ART NADINI B (ABC GARY SCALESE G (A DENNY MARTIN ACC (A
TAMPA LANN V (A EDDIE BRITT G V (BC TOMMY MANDEL K (B MICK RONSON K MAND(B
JOEY MISCULIN ACC (B IAN HUNTER G V K (B ROY MARTIN V (B ELLEN FOLEY V (B
STEVE CROPPER G (C JIM HORN SAX (C STEVE FORMAN PERC (C STEVE MADIAO TPT (C

I25 IRON MAIDEN I25

PAUL DI'ANNO V (ABCD — (A) IRON MAIDEN 1980 EMI UK EMC3330 US HARVEST 12094
DAVE MURRAY G (ABCD — (B) KILLERS 1981 EMI UK EMC3357 US HARVEST 12141
ADRIAN SMITH G (BCD — (C) SOUNDHOUSE TAPES 1979 ROCKHARD ROK1
STEVE HARRIS B V (ABCD — (D) MAIDEN IN JAPAN 1981
DENNIS STRATTON G V (AC — (E) NUMBER OF THE BEATS 1982 EMI UK EMC3400
CLIVE BURR D (ABD
BRUCE DICKINSON V (E

I25A IRONHORSE I25A

RANDY BACHMAN G SYN V (AB — (A) IRONHORSE 1979 SCOTTI BROS US 7103 UK K 50598
TOM SPARKS G V (AB — (B) EVERYTHING IS GREY 1980 SCOTTI BROS US 7108 UK K 50730
JOHN PIERCE B (A
MIKE BAIRD D (A FRANK LUDWIG V K (B RON FOOS B (B CHRIS LEIGHTON D (B
MAVIS McCAULEY V (A BARRY ALLEN V (A

I25B WELDON IRVINE I25B

WELDON IRVINE K SAX V(A — (A) COSMIC VORTEX 1974 RCA US APL10703
NALO V (A
BOB CRANSHAW B (A WESLEY WATSON D (A HENRY GRATH G (A NAPOLEON REVELS PERC (A
BUD JOHNSON CONGAS(A JIMMY OWENS TPT (A ROY ROMAN TPT (A BILL BARNWELL FLT (A
GENE JEFFERSON SAX (A OJULEBA V (A GORDON EDWARDS B (A JIM YOUNG D (A
CORNELL DUPREE G (A EVERETT HOLLINS TPT (A GEORGE MURRAY B (A LENNY WHITE D (A
JOE CARO G (A CHIPPER LYLES D (A

I26 GREGORY ISAACS I26

GREGORY ISAACS (ALL — ( ) IN PERSON 1975 TROJAN RI 82 TRLS 102
SLY DUNBAR (— ( ) ALL I HAVE IS LOVE 1976 TROJAN TRLS 121
ROBBIE SHAKESPEARE (— ( ) COOL RULER 1978 FRONT LINE UK FL 1020
( ) BEST OF 1978 CHANNEL GO 30
RADICS (— ( ) LONELY LOVER 1980 PRE/CHARISMA 001
( ) SOON FORWARD 1979 FRONT LINE UK FL 1044
() FOR EVERYONE 1980 SUCCESS 102
( ) THE EARLY YEARS 1981 TROJAN UK TRLS!)&
( ) MORE GREGORY 1981 POE UK PREX9
( ) EXTRA CLASSICS 1981 ECHO UK 1003
( ) ALL I HAVE IS LOVE 1982 TROJAN UK TRLS121
( ) NIGHT NURSE 1982 ISLAND UK ILPS 9721

I26A ISHMAEL I26A

PETER 'ISHMAEL' SMALE G V(ALL — (A) CHARGE OF THE LIGHT BRIGADE 1980 KINGSWAY UK 335
DEREK MOON K SYN (B — (B) LAND OF HOPE & GLORIES 1981 KINGSWAY UK 340
NEIL COSTELLO G (B — (C) IF YOU CANT SHOUT'SAVED' 19 KINGSWAY UK DOVE60
LES MOIR B (B
TIM SMALE B (B CHAS O'BRIAN D (B

I27 ISIS I27

CAROL MACDONALD G V (AB — (A) ISIS 1974 BUDDAH BDS5605 + BDLP 4002
GINGER BIANCO D (AB — (B) AIN'T NO BACKIN' UP NOW 1975 BUDDAH BDS5626
STELLA BASS B (AB
LIBERTY MATA PERC (AB JEANIE FINEBERG WIND (AB LOLLIE BIENENFIELD TROM V(A JUNE MILLINGTON G (B
EDITH DANKOWITZ WIND V(B ELLEN SEELING TPT (B RENATE FERRIER G (B LEWIS SOLOFF TPT(B
MARGO LEWIS K V (B LAUREN DRAPER HRNS (A SUZI GHEZZI G (A

I28 ISLEY BROTHERS I28

RUDOLPH ISLEY V (ALL — SHOUT 1959 RCA US LSP 2156
RONALD ISLEY V (ALL — TWIST & SHOUT 1962 WAND US 653 UK DJM 76 2628
KELLY ISLEY V (ALL — TWISTING & SHOUTING 196 UA US 6313 UK UA ULP 1064
MARVIN ISLEY B (ABCDEFGH — TAKE SOME TIME OUT 1966 T NECK US 552 UK MARBLEARCH 894
ERNIE ISLEY G D (ABCDEFGH — THIS OLD HEART OF MINE 1966 TAMLA US 269 UK STML 11034
JIMI HENDRIX G (* — THIS OLD HEART OF MINE 1981 MOTOWN UK RI STMS 5026
CHRIS JASPER K (ABCDEFGH — SOUL ON THE ROCKS 1966 TAMLA US 275
TAMLA MOTOWN PRESENTS 1967 TAMLA US 37080
ROCKY DZIDZORNU CONGA(A — DOIN' THEIR THING 1969 TAMLA US 287 UK SUNSET 5257
TRUMAN THOMAS K (A — IT'S OUR THING 1969 TNECK US 3001
GEORGE MORELAND D (A — THE BROTHERS ISLEY 1969 TNECK US 3002 UK STATESIDE10300
LIVE AT YANKEE STADIUM 1970 TNECK US 3004
GET INTO SOMETHING 1970 TNECK US 3006
(*) IN THE BEGINNING 1970 TNECK US 3007
GIVING IT BACK 1971 TNECK US 3008
ROCK ON BROTHER 1971 RCA CAMDEN US 0126
BROTHER BROTHER BROTHER 1972 TNECK US 3009
LIVE 197 TNECK US 3010
GREATEST HITS 197 TNECK US 3011 UK STARLINE 5043
ROCK AROUND THE CLOCK 19 CAMDEN US ACL10861
(A)THREE + THREE 1973 TNECK US 32453 UK EPIC 65740
BEST OF 19 BUDDAH US 2 5652
VERY BEST OF 19 UA US LA 500G
LIVE IT UP 1974 TNECK US 33070 UK EPIC 80317
(B)THE HEAT IS ON 1975 TNECK US 33536 UK EPIC 69139
(C)HARVEST FOR THE WORLD 1976 TNECK US 33809 UK EPIC 81268
SUPER HITS 1976 UK TAMLA STMA8024
(D) GO FOR YOUR GUNS 1977 TNECK US 34432 UK EPIC 86027
(E)FOREVER GOLD (COMP) 1977 TNECK US 34452 UK EPIC 86040
(F) SHOWDOWN 1978 TNECK US 34930 UK EPIC 86039
TIMELESS 1978 TNECK US 36650 UK EPIC 88327
(G) WINNER TAKES ALL 1979 TNECK US 36077 UK EPIC 88460
(H) GO ALL THE WAY 1980 TNECK US 36035 UK EPIC 65740
INSIDE YOU 1981 UK EPIC 85252
GRAND SLAM 1981 TNECK US 37080 UK EPIC 84914
SUPER HITS 1981 MOTOWN UK STMA 8024
THE REAL DEAL 1982 TNECK US UK EPIC 85790
SOUL SHOUT 19? PICKWICK CAN 3331
AND MARVIN & JOHNNY 19 CROWN US 643

I29 ISOTOPE I29

GARY BOYLE G (ABCD (A) ISOTOPE 1974 POLYDOR FR 2933 701 UK GULL 1002
BRIAN MILLER K (A (B) ILLUSION 1974 POLYDOR FR 2933 704 UK GULL 1006
(B) ILLUSION 1974 US GULL 402
JEFF CLYNE B (A (C) DEEP END 1976 UK GULL 1017
LAURENCE SCOTT K (BC (D) BEST OF 1978 UK GULL 1024
HUGH HOPPER B (BC
ZOE KRONBERGER K V (C FRANK ROBERTS K (C NIGEL MORRIS D (ABC AUREO DE SOUZA D (
DAN K BROWN B (C MORRIS PERT PERC (C NEVILLE WHITEHEAD B (C

I30 ISRAEL VIBRATION I30

(A) SAME SONG 1978 TOP RANKING IMP+HARVEST UK SHSP4099

I31 ITS A BEAUTIFUL DAY I31

DAVID LAFLAMME F FLT VLN V(ALL (A) ITS A BEAUTIFUL DAY 1968 CBS US 9768 UK 63722
DON WALDROP HRNS (E (A) ITS A BEAUTIFUL DAY 1980 CBS UK RI 83787
LINDA LA FLAMME K (A (A) ITS A BEAUTIFUL DAY 196 ALLIED PRODUCTION (PROMO) 364
PATTI SANTOS V PERC(ABCDE (B) MARRYING MAIDEN 1970 CBS US 1058 UK 64065
GREG BLOCH VLN MAND (E (B) MARRYING MAIDEN 1980 CBS NL RI 83905 UK RI 82 32132
BILL GREGORY G (CDE (C) CHOICE QUALITY STUFF 1971 CBS US 30734 UK 64314
JERRY GARCIA G BAN(B (C) CHOICE QUALITY STUFF 1980 CBS NL RI 83904
TOM FOWLER B (CD (D) LIVE AT CARNEGIE HALL 1972 CBS US 31338 UK 64929
HAL WAGENET G V (ABC (D) LIVE AT CARNEGIE HALL 1979 CBS NL RI 83907
MITCHELL HOLMAN HCA V B(ABC (E) TODAY 1973 CBS US 32181 UK 65483
RICHARD OLSEN CLAR (B (E) TODAY 1980 CBS NL RI 83908
ROLF STUART FLT (C (F) 1001 NIGHTS 1974 CBS US 32660 UK 65812
BUD COCKRELL B V (E (F) 1001 NIGHTS 1982 CBS UK RI 32133
JOSE AREAS PERC (C
FRED WEBB K V (BCDE VAL FUENTES D V(ABCDE COKE ESCOVEDO PERC (C SID PAGE VLN (BC
BRUCE STEINBERG HCA (AC VAN HUGHES TROM(C BILL ATWOOD TPT (C ROBERT FERREIRA SAX (C
CHARLES PETERSON SAX (C GREGG ROLIE K (C

I32 PETER IVERS BAND I32

PETER IVERS V HCA (A (A) TERMINAL LOVE 1974 WB US 2804
ALICE DE BUHR D (A
BUELL NEDLINGER B (A PAUL LENART G (A MARTY KRYSTALL SAX (A KATHY APPLEBY VLN (A
BEN BENAY G (A DAVID COHEN G (A ELLIOT INGBER G (A BILLY OSBORNE PERC(A
SHIRLEY MATTHEWS V (A MARTI McCALL V (A LISA ROBERTS V (A ANDRA WILLIS V (A
JACKIE WARD V (A DEAN ROD V (A

I33 THE IVEYS I33

RON WOOD G (A (A) MAYBE TOMORROW 1969 APPLE SAPCOR 8
PETE HAM V G (A
TOM EVANS B V (A MIKE GIBBONS D (A

I34 IVORY I34

KENNY THOMURE (A (A) IVORY 1968 TETRAGRAMMATON US 104
MIKE McCAULEY (A
CHRIS CHRISTMAN V (A

J1 J.A.L.N J1

(A) LIFE IS A FIGHT 1976 MAGNET MAG 5017
(B) JUST ANOTHER LONELY NIGHT 1977 MAGNET MAG 5018
(C) MOVIN' CITY HIGH 1978 MAGNET MAG 5023
(EP) NOTHING EVER COMES THAT EASY 1977 MAGNET MAG 901

J1A J.B.s J1A

(A) FOOD FOR THOUGHT 1972 PEOPLE US 5601 POLYDOR UK 2391 034
(B) DAMN RIGHT I AM SOMEBODY 1974 PEOPLE US 6602 POLYDOR UK 2391 125

J2 J J BAND J2

GARCIA MORALES D V (A (A) J J BAND 1971 CBS UK 64396
FRANCIS WEYER G V (A
GUY DELO K TPT(A RALPH BENATAR WIND (A MIKE LOVELL HRNS (A YVAN DE SOUTER B V (A
BRUNO CASTELLUCCI D V (A DOUGLAS LUCAS HRNS (A JEAN CLAUDE CLEMENT SAX (A

J2A J.P. J2A

JAN PIET DEN TEX (A (A) HEARTBEAT 1980 BUBBLE NL 202 852
MICHIEL JANSEN G (A
JAAP VENDERSLUYS B (A KEES MEERMAN D (A WILLEM ENNES K (A

J3 J.S.D. BAND J3

DES COFFIELD MAND G K V(ABCD (A) COUNTRY OF THE BLIND 1971 REGAL ZONOPHONE UK SLRZ 1018
SEAN O'ROURKE G V FDL (ABCD (B) TAKE OFF YOUR HEAD(VAR ART) 1972 RUBBER UK RUB 001
JIM DIVERS B CELLO V (ABCD (C) J S D BAND 1972 FLY UK HIFLY11 CUBE GER 07269
CHUCK FLEMING FDL MAND(DA (D) TRAVELLING DAYS 1973 CUBE UK HIFLY14 GER 26608/9
COLIN FINN D (CDA
LINDSAY SCOTT VLN V(C

J4 JABULA J4

VICKY BUSISWE MHLONGO V(A (A) JABULA 1975 CAROLINE UK CA 2004
GRAHAM MORGAN D (AB (B) THUNDER INTO OUR HEARTS 1976 CAROLINE UK CA 2009
KEN ELY SAX (AB (C) IN AMSTERDAM 1979 JABULA JBL2003
MADUMETJA RANKU G PERC(AB
EDDI QUANSAH TPT (A WILLIE CHEETHAM PERC V(A GEORGE LARNYOH WIND (A JEAN ROUSSEL K (A
SEBOTHANE BAHULA PERC (AB SPARTACUS R B (B MIKE ROSE FLT (B MAUREEN KOTO LEMBEDE V(A
FRANK ROBERTS K (B BOB HOWSE WIND (B JIM CHAMBERS V (B DUDU PUKWANA SAX (AB
PETER VANDER PUIJE SAX (A MOGOTSI MOTHLE B V (AB NICK EVANS TROM (B JIM DVORAK TPT (B
JIM THOMAS V (B

J4A ALAN JACK CIVILIZATION J4A

ALAN JACK K V (A (A) BLUESY MIND 19 BYG 529011
CLAUDE OLMOS G V (A
RICHARD FONTAINE B V (A JEAN FALISSARD D V (A

J4B JACK KNIFE J4B

JOHN WETTON B V K(A (A) I WISH YOU WOULD 1979 POLYDOR UK POLS1010 GER 2302 094
RICHARD PALMER-JAMES G (A
JOHN HUTCHESON K V (A CURT CRESS D PERC(A PETER BISCHOF V (A MICHAEL LOHMANN SAX (A
KRISTIAN SCHULZE K (A

J5 JACK THE LAD J5

RAY LAIDLAW D V (ABC (A) JACK THE LAD 1974 CHARISMA UK CAS 1085
PHIL MURRAY B V (BCD (B) OLD STRAIGHT TRACK 1974 CHARISMA UK CAS 1094
BILLY MITCHELL G V (ABCD (C) ROUGH DIAMONDS 1975 CHARISMA UK CAS 1110
WALTER FAIRBAIRN G V (BCD (D) JACKPOT 1976 UA UK UAS 29999
RAY JACKSON HCA (CD ( ) ITS JACK 1975 ASYLUM US 1014
TOM ALLOM (D
MADDY PRIOR V (A TOMMY EYRE K (A CHRIS MERCER HRNS (D JOHN KIRKPATRICK ACC (C
JIMMY WRIGHTSON CONC (A STEVE GREGORY HRNS (D ROD CLEMENTS (A ANDY BOWN K (D
BUD BEADLE HRNS (D SIMON COWE G V (AB

J6 BRIAN JACKSON J6

BRIAN JACKSON (ALL (A) ITS YOUR WORLD 1976 ARISTA UK DARTY1
(B) SECRETS 1978 ARISTA UK SPARTY 1073
(C) WINTER IN AMERICA 19 STRAT EAST US 19742

J6A BULLMOOSE JACKSON J6A

BULLMOOSE JACKSON (A (A) SINGS HIS HITS 19 AUDIO LAB US 12RY

J7 CHARLES JACKSON J7

CHARLES JACKSON V (AB (A) PASSIONATE BREEZES 1978 CAPITOL 11775
BRUCE CONTE G (B (B) GONNA GETCHA LOVE 1979 TOWER EST 12002
MICHAEL McGLOIRY G (B
COLEMAN HEAD G (B VICTOR CONTE B (B JERRY KNIGHT B V (B JULIA TILLMAN V (B
MELVIN BRITT V (B WELTON GITE B (B HARVEY HUGHES D (B DENNIS DAVIS D (B
GAVIN CHRISTOPHER K V (B GREG LEVIAS K (B MAXINE WILLARD V (B JUDY JONES V (B
NATE GINSBERG K (B CHESTER THOMPSON K (B RONNIE FOSTER K (B ROBERT THE ROOK HCA(B
SYLVIA COX V (B LUTHER WATERS V (B

J8 J J JACKSON J8

J J JACKSON V K PERC(ALL (A) WITH THE GREATEST LITTLE SOUL BAND 1967 STRIKE UK 104
DICK MORRISSEY SAX (BC (B) THE GREATEST LITTLE SOUL BAND 1969 MCA UK SKA100
TERRY SMITH G (BC (C) J J JACKSONS DILEMMA 1971 RCA UK SF8093 US PERCEPTION 3
ROY EDWARDS TPT (BC
JOHN MARSHALL SAX (B STU HAMMER TPT (B RICO RODIGUEZ TROM (B BRIAN HENDERSON K (B
JEFF WHITTAKER CONGA(A LARRY STEELE B (BC BILL EGDEN D (B RONNY STEPHENSON D (B
TERRY JENKINS D (B IAN HAGUE D (C CHRIS PARREN K (C JOHN BENNETT TROM(C
GEORGE JONES TPT (C DAVE QUINCY SAX (C JEFF McCARTHY B (C GEORGE BARKER TPT (C
DICK PARRY SAX (C

J9 GORDON JACKSON J9

GORDON JACKSON G V SITAR(A (A) THINKING BACK 1969 MARMALADE UK 608 012
(NOT THE ACTOR)
REMI KABAKA PERC (A STEVE WINWOOD B K (A POLI PALMER V K (A JIM CAPALDI V (A
LUTHER GROSVENOR V (A ROCKY DZIDZORNU PERC (A RICK GRECH B (A CHRIS WOOD WIND (A
JULIE DRISCOLL V (A DAVE MASON B (A ROB BLUNT SITAR G (A JIM KING SAX (A
REG KING V (A

J9A LEE JACKSON J9A

LEE JACKSON G V (A (A) LONELY GIRL 197
CAREY BELL HCA (A
PHIL UPCHURCH B (A BRIAN GRICE D (A GERALD SIMS G (A BRAD FIELD K (A

J10 JOE JACKSON J10

JOE JACKSON V K HCA (ALL (A) LOOK SHARP 1979 A&M US 4743 UK AMLH 64743
PETE THOMAS SAX (D (A) LOOK SHARP 1982 RI A&M AMID120
GARY SANFORD G (ABC (A) LOOK SHARP (10" DOUBLE) 1979 A&M US SP 3666
GRAHAM MABY B (ABC (B) I'M THE MAN 1979 A&M US 4794 UK AMLH 64794
DAVE HOUGHTON D (ABC (C) BEAT CRAZY 1980 A&M US 4837 UK AMLH 64837
DAVID KERSHENBAUM PROD (AB (D) JUMPIN' JIVE 1981 A&M UK AMLH 68530
RAUL OLIVERIA TPT (D (E) NIGHT & DAY 1982 A&M UK AMLH 64609
NICK WELDON PNO (D
DAVE BITELLI WIND (D LARRY TOLFREE D (D

J10A MICK JACKSON J10A

MICK JACKSON V (A (A) MICK JACKSON 1979 ATLANTIC UK K 50605
KEITH FORSEY D (A
CURT CRESS PERC (A MATS BJOERKLUND G (A GUNTHER GEBAUER B (A SYLVESTER LEVAY K ‹(A
PATRICIA SHOKLEY V (A TIM TOUCHTON V (A ERIK THONER V (A GABOR CRISTIF TPT (A
GUISEPPE SOLERA SAX (A GEOFF BASTOW K (A PATRICK GAMMON K V (A MAX GREGOR K (A
KRISTIAN SCHULZE SYN (A TOOTS THIELEMANS HCA (A VICTORIA MILES V (A JERRY RIX V (A
WOLFGANG EMPERHOFF V (A BOBBY STERN SAX (A BENNY GEBAUER SAX (A HERMANN BREUER TROM(A

J10B MICHAEL JACKSON J10B

MICHAEL JACKSON V (ALL (A) GOT TO BE THERE 1972 MOTOWN US 747 UK STML 11205
GREG PHILLINGANES K (J (A) GOT TO BE THERE 1981 MOTOWN RI UK STMS 5005
BILL WOLFER K (J (B) BEN 1973 MOTOWN US 755 UK STML 11220
MICHAEL BODDICKER K (J (B) BEN 1981 MOTOWN RI UK STMA 5008
DAVID WILLIAMS G (J (C) MUSIC & ME 1974 MOTOWN US 767
LOUIS JOHNSON B (J (D) FOREVER 1975 MOTOWN US 825 UK STMA 8002
PAULINHO DACOSTA PERC (J (E) BEST OF M JACKSON 1975 MOTOWN UK STML12005 RI STMR9009
JERRY HEY TPT (J (F) OFF THE WALL 1979 EPIC US 35745 UK 83468
GARY GRANT TPT (J (G) SUPERSTAR 1980 MOTOWN US 107
LARRY WILLIAMS WIND (J (H) ONE DAY IN YOUR LIFE 1981 MOTOWN UK STMC 12158
EDDIE VAN HALEN G (J (J) THRILLER 1982 EPIC UK 85930
JULIA WATERS V (J
BILL REICHENBACH TROM (J MAXINE WATERS V (J OREN WATERS V (J JAMES INGRAM K V (J
BUNNY HULL V (J BECKY LOPEZ V (J DAVID PAICH SYN K(J STEVE PORCARO SYN (J
NDUGO CHANCLER D (J DAVID FOSTER SYN (J DEAN PARKS G (J STEVE LUKATHER B G(J
JEFF PORCARO D (J VINCENT PRICE V (J ROD TEMPERTON SYN (J BRIAN BANKS SYN (J
TOM BAHLER K (J GREG SMITH K (J PAUL JACKSON G (J HOWARD WEWETT V (J
JANET JACKSON V (J LATOYA JACKSON V (J

J11 MILLIE JACKSON J11

Musician	Inst	Albums	Album	Release
MILLIE JACKSON	V	(ALL	(A) MILLIE JACKSON	1972 POLYDOR UK 2391 025 US SPRING 5703
JIMMY JOHNSON	G	(DEJFKMLP	(B) IT HURTS SO GOOD	1972 POLYDOR UK 2391 091 US SPRING 5706
PETE CARR	G	(EFK	(C) MILLIE	197 US SPRING 6701
BARRY BECKETT	K	(DFJKML	(D) CAUGHT UP	197 POLYDOR UK 2391 147 US SPRING 6703
DAVID HOOD	B	(DFJKMLP	(E) STILL CAUGHT UP	197 POLYDOR UK 2391 183 US SPRING 6708
ROGER HAWKINS	D	(DEJFKMLP	(F) FREE & IN LOVE	197 POLYDOR UK 2391 215 US SPRING 6709
BRAD SHAPIRO	PERC	(D	(G) BEST OF	1976 POLYDOR UK 2391 247
TOM ROADY	PERC	(DEJFKML	(H) LOVINGLY YOURS	197 POLYDOR UK 2391 252 US SPRING 6712
CHARLES CHALMERS	V	(EF	(J) FEELIN' BITCHY	1977 POLYDOR UK 2391 301 US SPRING 6715
SANDY RHODES	V	(EF	(K) GET IT OUTCHA SYSTEM	1978 POLYDOR UK 2391 336 US SPRING 6719
DONNA RHODES	V	(EF	(L) ROYAL RAPPIN'S	1979 POLYDOR UK 2480 516
ISAAC HAYES		(L	(M) MOMENTS PLEASURE	1979 POLYDOR UK 2391 395 US SPRING 6722
KEN BELL	G	(JFP	(O) LIVE	1980 US SPRING 6725
SPIDERMAN HARRISON	V	(JK	(P) FOR MEN ONLY	1980 POLYDOR UK 2391 460
MARY LOU VAN DE PITTE	V	(K	(Q) I HAD TO SAY IT	1980 POLYDOR UK 2391 495
RANDY McCORMICK		(MLP	(R) LIVE & OUTRAGEOUS	1982 POLYDOR UK 2391 540
MICKY BUCKINS		(P		

Musician	Inst	Albums	Musician	Inst	Albums	Musician	Inst	Albums	Musician	Inst	Albums
RON EADES	HRNS	(FP	CYNTHIA DOUGLAS		(K	THE MOMENTS	V	(H	HARRISON CALLOWAY	HRNS	(FP
DONNA DAVIS	V	(K	STEVE MELTON		(K	HARVEY THOMPSON	HRNS	(FP	SHELDON KIRKLAND	STRINGS	(K
BRANDYE	V	(JHML	TIM HENSON	K	(J	PAM VINCENT	V	(K	CHARLES ROSE	HRNS	(F
LARRY BYROM	G	(JML	MIKE MEYERS		(K	BEN CAULEY	HRNS	(P	CLAYTON IVEY		(LMP
JANE FRICKE	V	(E									

J13 WANDA JACKSON J13

Musician	Inst	Albums	Album	Year	Label	Country	Number
WANDA JACKSON	V	(ALL	ROCKIN WITH WANDA	1960	CAPITOL	US	TS 1384
BILLY SANFORD	G	(*	ROCKIN WITH WANDA	1977	CAPITOL	UK	CAPS 1007
RAY EDENTON	G	(*	RIGHT OR WRONG	1061	CAPITOL	US	ST 1596
RUSSELL HICKS	G	(*	WONDERFUL WANDA	1962	CAPITOL	US	ST 1776
JERRY SHOOK	G	(*	THERE'S A PARTY GOING ON	19	CAPITOL	US	ST 1511
JAMES CAPPS	G	(*	WANDA JACKSON	19	CAPITOL	US	T 1041
WELDON MYRICK	STEEL	(*	LOVE ME FOREVER	19	CAPITOL	US	ST 1911
CHARLIE McCOY	HCA	(*	I GOT TO SING	19	CAPITOL	US	ST 669
JERRY SMITH	PNO	(*	2 SIDES OF WANDA	19	CAPITOL	US	ST 2030
JACK WILLIAMS	B	(*	WANDA JACKSON	19	PICKWICK	UK	2053
HENRY STRZELECKI	B	(*	BLUES IN MY HEART	19	CAPITOL	US	ST 2306
KENNY MALONE	D	(*	SINGS COUNTRY SONGS	1966	CAPITOL	US	ST 2438
JERRY CARRIGAN	D	(*	COUNTRY MUSIC HALL OF FAME	1967	CAPITOL	US	ST 2606
FARRELL MORRIS	PERC	(*	YOU'LL HAVE MY LOVE	19	CAPITOL	US	ST 2812
DELORES EDGIN	V	(*	CREAM OF THE CROP	1969	CAPITOL	US	ST 2976
JUNE PAGE	V	(*	BEST OF	19	CAPITOL	US	ST 2883
BERGEN WHITE	V	(*	BEST OF	19	CAPITOL	UK	ST 11166
HURSHAL WIGGINTON	V	(*	A PORTRAIT OF	1970	CAPITOL	US	ST 21530
JOSEPH BABCOCK	V	(*	A WOMAN LIVES TO LOVE	1970	CAPITOL	US	ST 554
			COUNTRY	1970	CAPITOL	US	ST 434
			PRAISE THE LORD	1972	CAPITOL	US	ST 11023
			PIONEERS OF ROCK	1972	STARLINE	UK	SRS 5120
			COUNTRY KEEPSAKES	1973	CAPITOL	US	ST 11161
			I WOULD'NT WANT YOU ANY OTHER WAY	1973	CAPITOL	US	ST 11096
			COUNTRY CLASSICS	1973	CAPITOL	EURO	5C 052 81215
			WHEN IT'S TIME TO FALL IN LOVE AGAIN	1974	CAPITOL	US	ST 6513
			COUNTRY GOSPEL	1974	WORD US (UK82)		WST 9514
			NOW I HAVE EVERYTHING	1975	MYRRH US 6533		MYR 1021
			MAKE ME A CHILD AGAIN	1976	MYRRH		MYR 1043
			MY TESTAMENT	1982	WORD		9617
			(*)I'LL STILL LOVE YOU	1976	DJM	UK	DJF 20493
			LEAVE MY BABY	19	HILLTOP	US	JS 6074
			PLEASE HELP ME I'M FALLING	19	HILLTOP	US	JS 6058
			WE'LL SING IN SUNSHINE	19	HILLTOP	US	JS 6116
			BY THE TIME I GET TO PHOENIX	19	HILLTOP	US	JS 6123
			TEARS AT GRAND OLE OPRY	19	HILLTOP	US	JS 6184
			NOBODY'S DARLIN'	19	VOCALION	US	VL 73861
			CLOSER TO JESUS	1978	WORD	(UK82)	WST 9580
			ROCK'N'ROLL HISTORY	1979	CAPITOL	US	U38 82098
			GREATEST HITS	1979	CAPITOL	US	134 53025/6

J14 JACKSON HEIGHTS J14

Musician	Inst	Albums	Album	Year	Label	Country	Number
LEE JACKSON	B V G	(ABCD	(A) KING PROGRESS	1970	CHARISMA	UK	CAS 1018
CHARLIE HARCOURT	G K V	(A	(A) KING PROGRESS	197	MERCURY	US	SR 61331
TOMMY SLOANE	D	(A	(B) 5TH AVENUE BUS	1972	VERTIGO	UK	6360 067
MARIO ENRIQUE	B	(A	(C) RAGAMUFFINS FOOL	1973	VERTIGO	UK	6360 077
COVARRURAS TAPIA		(A	(C) JACKSON HEIGHTS	1973	VERVE	US	V6 5089
PATRICK MORAZ	K	(	(D) BUMP & GRIND	1973	VERTIGO	UK	6360 092
MIKE GILES	D	(BCD					

Musician	Inst	Albums	Musician	Inst	Albums	Musician	Inst	Albums	Musician	Inst	Albums
BRIAN CHATTON	K V	(BCD	JOHN McBURNIE	G V K	(BCD	TONY CONNOR		(C	LAWRIE WRIGHT	PNO	(B
DAVE WATTS	PNO	(B	IAN WALLACE	D	(D	ROGER McKEW	G	(D	JOHNNY VAN DERRICK	FDL	(D
BILLY BELL	BANJO	(D	CHRIS LAURENCE	B	(D	JOHNNY TOOGOOD	SAX	(C	RACE McCLEOD	D	(C
MO FLETCHER	B	(C	MOX	HCA	(C	KEITH HARRIS	BANJO	(C	OLI OLIVER	FDL	(C
LAURIE JAY	D	(C									

J14A JACKSON HIGHWAY J14A

Musician	Inst	Albums	Album	Year	Label	Country	Number
DENNIS GULLEY	V G K	(A	(A) JACKSON HIGHWAY	1980	CAPITOL	US	ST 12044
BRITT MEACHAM	G V	(A					

Musician	Inst	Albums	Musician	Inst	Albums	Musician	Inst	Albums	Musician	Inst	Albums
TOMMY PATERSON	K V	(A	RUSSELL GULLEY	B V	(A	RONNIE VANCE	D V	(A	ROGER HAWKINS	D	(A
DAVID HOOD	B	(A	JIMMY JOHNSON	G	(A	RANDY McCORMICK	K	(A	RICKY MEDLOCKE	D	(A
GREG T WALKER		(A	DUNCAN CAMERON		(A						

J15 THE JACKSONS J15

Musician	Inst	Albums	Album	Year	Label	Country	Number
MICHAEL JACKSON	V	(	I WANT YOU BACK	1969	TAMLA US		
JACKIE JACKSON	V	(	DIANA ROSS PRESENTS	1970	TAMLA US 700	UK	STML 11142
TITO JACKSON	V	(	A B C	1970	TAMLA US 709	UK	STML 11156
BILL CROSBY		(	A B C	1982	TAMLA	UK RI	STMS 5068
JERMAINE JACKSON	V	(	CHRISTMAS ALBUM	1970	TAMLA	UK	STML 11168
MARLON JACKSON	V	(	THIRD ALBUM	1971	TAMLA US 718	UK	STML 11174
TOMMY SMOTHERS		(	THIRD ALBUM	1982	TAMLA	UK RI	STMS 5037

(CONTINUED)

J15 (CONTINUED) **THE JACKSONS** J15

RANDY JACKSON V (MAYBE TOMORROW 1971 TAMLA US 735 UK STML 11188
ROSEY GRIER (GREATEST HITS 1972 TAMLA US 741 UK STML 11212
JON MOFFETT D (GREATEST HITS 1982 TAMLA UK RI STMS 5032
DAVID WILLIAMS G (LOOKIN' THROUGH WINDOWS 1972 TAMLA US 750 UK STML 11214
MICHAEL McKINNEY B (SKYWRITER 1973 TAMLA US 761 UK STML 11231
BILL WOLFER K (DANCING MACHINE 1973 TAMLA US 780 UK STML 11275
WESLEY PHILLIPS HRNS (GET IT TOGETHER 1973 TAMLA US 783 UK STML 11243
GLORIS GRIMES HRNS (MOVING VIBRATIONS 1975 TAMLA US 829 UK STML 11290
JACKSONS 1976 EPIC US 34229 UK 86009
JACKSONS 1982 EPIC UK RI 32101
MOTOWN SPECIAL 1977 TAMLA UK STMX 6006
ANTHOLOGY 1977 TAMLA US M7868 UK TMSM 6004
JOYFUL JUKEBOX MUSIC 1977 TAMLA US 865 UK STML 12046
GOIN' PLACES 1977 EPIC US 34835 UK 86035
DESTINY 1978 EPIC US 35520 UK 83200
ZIP A DEE DOO DAH 1979 MFP UK 50418
20 GOLDEN GREATS 1979 TAMLA UK STML 12121
JACKSON 5 19 PICKWICK US 2080
TRIUMPH 1980 EPIC US 36424 UK 86112
LIVE (DBL) 198 EPIC UK 88562

J15A **DALE JACOBS** J15A

DALE JACOBS K (A (A) COBRA 1979 EPIC US 36100 UK 83761
JOEL WADE B (A
BRETT WADE G (A JIM VALLANCE D (A JIM McGILLEVRAY PERC(A DOUG LOUIE K (A
WAYNE KOSAK WIND (A LOU HOOVER D (A TOM LAVIN G (A BRIAN HARRISON B (A
KAT HENDRIKSE D (A DOUG CUTHBERT D (A RALPH DYCK VIBES(A

J15B **JADD FAIR** J15B

(A) ZOMBIES OF MORA TAM 1980 ARMAGEDDON UK AEP 003

J16 **JADE WARRIOR** J16

TONY DUHIG G B K(ALL (A) JADE WARRIOR 1971 VERTIGO US 1007 UK 6360 033
JON FIELD PERC G K FLT(ALL (B) RELEASED 1971 VERTIGO US 1009 UK 6360 062
COLERIDGE GOODE B (DF (C) AUTUMNS DREAM 1972 VERTIGO US 1012 UK 6360 079
GLYN HAVARD B G V(ABC (D) FLOATING WORLD 1974 ISLAND US /UK ILPS 9290
DAVID DUHIG G (CDE (E) WAVES 1975 ISLAND US /UK ILPS 9318
ALAN PRICE D (BC (F) KITES 1976 ISLAND US /UK ILPS 9393
SKAILA KANKA HARP(DG (G) WAY OF THE SUN 1978 ISLAND UK ILPS9552 US ANTILES7068
CHRIS KARAN D (D (H) REFLECTIONS (COMP) 1980 BUTT BUTT 001
GRAHAM DEACON D (D
MARTHA MDENGE V (D STEVE WINWOOD K (E CLODAGH SIMMON V (F ROGER BRYSON PNO (F
JOE O'DONNELL VLN (F GOWAN TURNBULL SAX (FG DAVE CONNERS WIND (B GRAHAM MORGAN D (FGE
DEBBIE HALL VLN (F GEOFF WESTLEY PNO (F JOHN DENTITH D (G DICK CUTHELL HRNS(G
PETE GIBSON HRNS (F WILLIE PERC (F FRED FRITH VLA (F BILL SMITH B (G

J16A **JAGS** J16A

NICK WATKINSON G V (ABC (A) BACK OF MY HAND (EP) 1979 ISLAND UK 12SWIP6501
JOHN ALDER G V (ABC (B) EVENING STANDARD 1980 ISLAND UK ILPS9603 EURO 201 291
ALEX BAIRD D (ABC (C) NO TIE LIKE A PRESENT 1981 ISLAND UK ILPS9655 EURO 203 379
STEVE PRUDENCE B V (AB
CHRIS HUNTER HRNS (B GUY BARKER HRNS (B MICHAEL COTTON B V (C PADDY O'TOOLE K (C

J16B **CHRIS JAGGER** J16B

CHRIS JAGGER V K FLT(AB (A) CHRIS JAGGER 1973 G M UK GML1003
ROGER EARLE D (A (B) THE ADVENTURES OF VALENTINE VOX...1974 ASYLUM US 7E1009
JOHN URIBE B V G(A
DAVID PIERCE G K (AB BOBBY KEYS SAX (A MICK JAGGER V (A MICHAEL OMARTIAN K (A
DON PONCHER D PERC(A OLIVER TOBIAS V (A PAT VEGAS B (A PAT ARNOLD V (A
ELAINE V (A CLAUDIA LENNEAR V (A BOB DENT CELLO(A DIANE PERC(A
BOB GRIFFITH B (A IAN STEWART PNO (A MIKE KELLIE D (A BRIAN BELSHAW B (A
KEVIN WESTLAKE G (A DAVE FARREL B (A PICK WITHERS D (B ANDY BOWN B V (B
JOHN MEALING K (B BOB COHEN G (B JIM RYAN G (B CHRIS STAINTON K (B
BUSTER CHERRY JONES B (B NEIL HUBBARD G (B TERRY STANARD D (B PETER FRAMPTON G (B
PETE SEARS B (B MICKY WALLER D (B STEVE DARRINGTON ACC (B JOHN ROUSSEAU K WIND(B
DAVE EDMUNDS G (B ALAN SPENNER B (B STEVE SMITH V PERC(B

J16C **JAGGERZ** J16C

JIMMY ROSS HRNS B V(A (A) WE WENT TO DIFFERENT SCHOOLS 1970 KAMA SUTRA US 2017
BENNY FAIELLA G BV (A
DOMINIC LERACE G B V(A THOM DAVIS K HRN (A BILLY MAYBRAY B D V (A JIM PUGLINRO D V (

J17 **JAGUAR** J17

ROY HOWELL G MAND B (A (A) JAGUAR 1977 RCA APLI 2420
ED FORESMAN B V (A
WALTER POLK D PERC(A RANDY COPELAND B (A DREW HAYS V PERC(A PAT TAYLOR G V (A
DOUG MAYO K PERC(A BEVERLEY BAXTER V (A

J17A **JAH LION** J17A

JAH LION (A (A) COLUMBIA COLL 1976 ISLAND/MANGO UK/US ILPS 386

J17B **JAH LLOYD** J17B

JAH LLOYD V (AB (A) THE HUMBLE ONE 1978 FRONT LINE UK 1005
SLY DUNBAR D (B (B) BLACK MOSES 1979 FRONT LINE UK 1031
ROBBIE SHAKESPEARE B (B
ANSEL COLLINS K (B BOBBY KALPHAT PNO (B ERIC LAMONT G (B RAD BRYAN G (B
STICKY THOMPSON PERC (B HUNTLEY FLT (B

J17C **JAH STITCH** J17C

JAH STITCH V (ALL (A) MY PRECIOUS LOCKS 1978 CANCER 002
CARLTON'SANTA' DAVIS D(BC (B) NO DREAD CAN'T DEAD 19 THIRD WORLD 401
ROBBIE SHAKESPEARE B(BC (C) WATCH YOUR STEP YOUTH MAN 1979 THIRD WORLD 701
LLOYD PARKS B (BC
TOUTER HARVEY K (BC TARZAN K PREC(BC SKULLY PERC (BC EARL SMITH G (BC
TONY CHINN G (BC AUSSIE'NOGO' HERBERT K(BC JOHNNIE CLARKE PNO (BC BARNABAS PERC (BC
DOPEPEA G (BC ANSEL COLLINS K (BC SLY DUNBAR D (BC

J17D JAH THOMAS J17D

JAH THOMAS V (AL — (A) STOP YU LOAFIN — 1978 GREENSLEVES UK GREL3
DUGGIE G (A — (B) DANCE HALL STYLE — 1980 DADDY KOOL P16
SLY DUNBAR D (A
BARNABAS PERC (A — RANCHIE B (A — SKULLEY PERC (A — STICKY PERC (A
TOUTER HARVEY K (A — ROBBIE SHAKESPEARE B (A — ANSEL COLLINS K (A

J17E JAH WOOSH J17E

JAH WOOSH (ALL — (A) THE WORLD MARIJUANA TOUR — 1977 CARIB GEMS
ERROL NELSON (D — (B) LICK HIM WITH THE DUSTBIN — 1977 KAB
TARZAN (G — (C) JAH WOOSH — 1974 CACTUS CTLP 103
TOUTER HARVEY D (G — (D) JAH JAH DEY DEY — 1976 CACTUS CTLP 116
FULLY B (G — (E) DREADLOCK AFFAIR — 1976 TROJAN TRLS 113
RANCHIE B (G — (F) PSALMS OF WISDOM — 1977 BLACKWAX LP2
STICKY PERC (G — (G) RELIGIOUS DREAD — 1979 TROJAN TRLS 157
CHINNA G (G

J18 JAKE & THE FAMILY JEWELS J18

JAKE(ALLAN JACOBS) V G (AB — (A) JAKE & THE FAMILY JEWELS — 1970 POLYDOR US 24 4029 UK 2425 027
MIKE ROSA D (AB — (B) BIG MOOSE CALLS HIS BABBY — 1971 POLYDOR US 5024
JEREMIAH BURNHAM FLT B V(A
ROB ROTHSTEIN B (B — DAN MANSOLINO K V (A — DANIEL BEN ZEBULON PERC(A — KENNY PINE G V(A
KATHLEEN WHELEN PERC (A — VITO JACOBS G V (A — MYLES ARONOWITZ JEWSHARP(A — JON LIND G V(A
JIM STARSES G (A — BOB SMITH PNO (A — PERRY ROBINSON CLAR(A — LARRY PACKER FDL(A
CHARLIE CHIN BANJ (A — DON BROOKS HCA (A — BUZZY LINHART V (A — BUNKY ROCHELLE SKINNER V(A
DANNY MANSELINO K (B

J19 THE JAM J19

PAUL WELLER G V (ALL — (A) IN THE CITY — 1977 POLYDOR US 6110 UK 2383 447
RICK BUCKLER D (ALL — (B) THIS IS THE MODERN WORLD — 1977 POLYDOR US 6129 UK 2383 475
BRUCE FOXTON B V (ALL — (C) ALL MOD CONS — 1978 POLYDOR US 6118 UK 2442 155
MICK TALBOT PNO (D — (C) ALL MOD CONS — 1978 POLYDOR UK POLD 5008
STEVE RUDI SAX (D — (D) SETTING SONS — 1979 POLYDOR US 6249 UK5018 2442 168
(E) SOUND AFFECTS — 1980 POLYDOR US 6315 UK5035
(F) THE GIFT — 1982 POLYDOR UK 5055
(AB) IN THE CITY/MODERN WORLD — 1980 POLYDOR UK 2683 074
(EP) THE JAM — 1981 POLYDOR

J20 BOB JAMES J20

BOB JAMES K (ALL — ( ) BOB JAMES TRIO — 1965 ESP US 1009
RON TOOLEY TPT (L — (A) ONE — 1975 CTI 6043
LUTHER VANDROSS V (L — (A) ONE — 1981 CBS UK 84820
GARY KING B (ABCDEFGHIKL — (B) TWO — 1975 CTI 6057
BABI KLOYD V (L — (B) TWO — 1981 CBS UK 84821
STEVE GADD D (ABDEFIK — (C) THREE — 1976 CTI 6063
MILT GRAYSON V (L — (C) THREE — 1981 CBS UK 84822
RALPH McDONALD PERC (ABCDEFGHIKL — (D) FOUR — 1977 CTI 7074
JOHN ROBINSON D (L — (D) FOUR — 1981 CBS UK 84823
GROVER WASHINGTON SAX (ACEHIL — (E) HEADS — 1977 CBS US 34896 UK 02271
JON FADDIS HRNS (ACEHIKL — (F) TOUCHDOWN — 1978 CBS US 35594 UK 83175
LEW SOLOFF TPT (ABCDEI — (G) ONE ON ONE — 1979 CBS US 36241 UK 83931
WAYNE ANDRE TROM (ABCEIK — (H) 'H' — 1980 CBS US 36422 UK 84238
EDDIE DANIELS WIND (BCDEHIL — (I) BEST OF — 1978 CTI UK 630.34
GEORGE MARGE WIND (ADEHIGL — (J) EXPLOSIONS — 1975 ESP US 1009
ROMEO PENQUE WIND (ADHIG — (K) LUCKY SEVEN — 1979 CBS US 36056 UK 83729
ERIC GALE G (BCDEGIKL — (L) SIGN OF THE TIMES — 1981 CBS UK 85181
ARTHUR JENKINS PERC (BI — (M) ALL AROUND THE TOWN — 1981 CBS UK 88509
HUBERT LAWS FLY (BCDEI — (N) HANDS DOWN — 1982 CBS UK 85848
RANDY BRECKER HRNS (BEHIK
MARVIN STAMM TPT (ABCI — DANNY CAHN TPT (H — MICHAEL LAWRENCE TPT (HKL — IDRIS MUHAMMAD D (AEHK
RICHIE RESNICOFF G (ABIK — ERIC WEISSBERG STEEL(AI — DAVE FRIEDMAN VIBES(AI — HUGH McCRACKEN HCA(ACI
THAD JONES HRNS (AI — VICTOR PAZ TPT (ABI — ALAN RUBIN TPT (ABI — PAUL FAULISE TROM (AHI
JACK GALE TROM (AFI — ALAN RAPH TROM (AI — ANDREW SMITH D (BI — JOHN FROSK HRNS(BCDEI
JIMMY BUFFINGTON HRNS (BEIGK — PETER GORDON HRNS (BIEK — AL RICHMOND HRNS (BI — EDDIE BERT TROM (BI
TOM MITCHELL TROM (BEI — TONY STUDD TROM (BI — PATTI AUSTIN V (DEIKL — FRANK FLOYD V (IBL
LANI GROVES V (BEI — ZACHARY SANDERS V (BI — SIDNEY WEINBERG WIND (DI — EARL KLUGH G (FG
BARRY ROGERS TROM (H — LIBERTY DE VITO D (BI — DAVID BROWN G (H — HIRAM BULLOCK G (HFK
BUDDY WILLIAMS D (HL — HARVEY MASON D (CGI — ANDY NEWMARK D (CE — WILL LEE B (CE
JEFF MIRANOV G (CE — JERRY DODGION FLT (CHI — DAVE BARGERON HRNS (CI — DAVE TAYLOR TROM (CEIKL
GLORIA AGOSTINI HARP (CEI — ART FARMER HRNS (DI — JOHN GATCHELL TPT (D — JIM PUGH TROM (HL
DOUG STEGMEYER B (H — LEONARD GIBBS PERC (HL — AIRTO MOREIRA PERC (HL — BRUCE DUNLAP G (HL
MICHAEL MAINERI VIBES(E — DAVE SANBORN SAX (EFK — VIVIAN CHERRY V (EL — GWEN GUTHRIE V (E
ALLEN SCHWARZBERG D (E — ALPHONSO JOHNSON B (E — STEVE KHAN G (EKL — JEFF LAYTON G (E
BROOKS TILLOTSON HRNS (E — PHIL BODNER WIND (EHGL — MICHAEL BRECKER SAX (EK — GERRY NIEWOOD WIND (E
RON CARTER B (FG — NEIL JASON B (GK — MONGO SANTAMARIA (F — JIMMY MAELIN PERC (K
RICK MAROTTA D (L — WALLY KANE WIND (GL — JAY BECKENSTEIN SAX (L — MARCUS MILLER B (L
MAJOR HOLLEY B (L — CASEY CYSCK V (L — HILLARY JAMES V (L — YVONNE LEWIS V (L
WHIT SIDENER WIND (L

J21 ELMORE JAMES J21

ELMORE JAMES G V (ALL — (A) TOUGH — 197 BLUE HORIZON UK 7 63204
JOHN BRIM (AK — (B) TO KNOW A MAN — 1969 BLUE HORIZON UK 7 66230
JOHNNY JONES PNO (DELMN — (C) LEGEND OF — 1970 UA UK UAS 29109
HOMESICK JAMES WILLIAMSON(E — (D) COTTON PATCH(1 SIDE) — 1973 POLYDOR UK 2383 200
J T BROWN SAX (DELMN — (E) ALL THEM BLUES — 1975 DJM UK DJLMD 8008
ODIE PAYNE D (DE L — (F) RESURRECTION OF ELMORE JAMES — 1976 BLUES ANTHOLOGY UK AB 5610
BOYD ATKINS SAX (D — (F) RESURRECTION OF ELMORE JAMES — 197 KENT US 9010
IKE TURNER PNO (D — (G) LEGEND OF ELMORE JAMES — 1976 BLUES ANTHOLOGY UK AB 5601
JAMES PARR TPT (D — (G) THE LEGEND OF ELMORE JAMES — 1976 KENT US 9001 UNITED US 7778
MAXWELL DAVIS SAX (D — (H) BEST OF — 19 SUE UK ILP 918
JEWELL GRANT SAX (D — (J) MEMORIAL ALBUM — 19 SUE UK ILP 927
JESSE SAILES D (D — (K) WHOSE MUDDY SHOES — 19 CHESS 1537 RI UK 82 2007
EDDIE TAYLOR G (M — (L) THE BLUES IN MY HEART — 19 CUSTOM US 1054 UNITED US 7716
WILLARD McDANIEL (— (M) STREET TALKIN' — 19 MUSE MR 5087
BUSHY HEAD PNO (B — (N) DUST MY BLUES — 19 GLOBE VIP 5004M
CHUCK HAMILTON (— (O) ELMORE JAMES — 19 KENT US 522

(CONTINUED)

J21 (CONTINUED) ELMORE JAMES J21

(P) HISTORY OF VOL 1 1975 TRIP US 8007
(Q) HISTORY OF VOL 2 19 TRIP US 9511
(R) ONE WAY OUT 1980 CHARLY UK CRB 1008
(S) SKY IS CRYING 19 SPHERE SOUND US 7002
(T) SCREAMING BLUES 19 HARLEM HIT PARADE 5014
(U) BLUES MASTERS VOL 1 19 BLUE HORIZON US 46021
(V) I NEED YOU 19 SPHERE SOUND US 7008
( ) ELMORE JAMES 19 BELL US 6037
( ) BLUES AFTER HOURS 19 CROWN US 5168
( ) ORIGINAL FOLK BLUES 19 KENT US 522 US UNITED 7743
( ) THE GREAT ELMORE JAMES 19 UPFRONT US 122
( ) GOT TO MOVE 1981 CHARLY UK CRB 1017
( ) BEST OF 1981 ACE UK CH31

J22 ETTA JAMES J22

ETTA JAMES V (ALL — AT LAST 1961 CADET US 4003
WITH — SECOND TIME AROUND 1961 CADET US 4011
JEFF PORCARO D (* — ETTA JAMES 1963 CADET US 4013
CHUCK RAINEY B (* — SINGS FOR LOVERS 1963 CADET US 4018
LARRY CARLTON G (* — TOP TEN 1963 CADET US 4025
CORNELL DUPREE G (* — ROCKS THE HOUSE 1963 CADET US 4032
BRIAN RAY G (* — QUEEN OF SOUL 1965 CADET US 4040
RICHARD TEE K (* — CALL MY NAME 196 CADET US 4055
KEITH JOHNSON PNO (* — (X)TELL MAMA 1969 CADET US 802
ALEXANDER HAMILTON V (* — (X)TELL MAMA 1969 CHESS CRL 4536
MERRY CLAYTON V (* — FUNK 1970 CADET US
JOYCE AUSTIN V (* — MISS ETTA JAMES 19 CROWN US CLP 5209
GILBERT IVEY V (* — BEST OF 19 CROWN US CLP 5234
REUBEN FRANKLIN V (* — TWIST WITH 19 CROWN US CLP 5250
HENRY JACKSON V (* — GOLDEN DECADE 1972 CHESS UK 6310 126
THE SNAKES V (* — ETTA JAMES 1973 CHESS 50042
TOM ROADY PERC (* — COME A LITTLE CLOSER 1974 CHESS 60029
RICK SCHLOSSER D (* — ETTA IS BETTA THAN EVAH 1975 CHESS 19003
JIM HORN SAX (* — PEACHES 1973 CHESS 2CH 60004
RON STOCKERT K (* — LOOSERS WEEPERS 1974 CADET US 847
CARL BANKS ORG (X — SINGS 19 UNITED US 7712
BARRY BECKETT ORG (X — BEST OF 19 UNITED US 7727
CHARLES CHALMERS V (X — (*) DEEP IN THE NIGHT 1978 WB US BSK 3156 UK K 56492
GEORGE DAVIS K (X — CHESS MASTERS 1981 CHESS UK 2000
ROGER HAWKINS D (X — GOOD ROCKIN MAMA 1981 ACE UK CH33
DAVID HOOD B (X
JIMMY RAY JENKINS G (X — ALBERT LOWE G (X — GENE MILLER TPT (X — JAMES MITCHELL SAX (X
FLOYD NEWMAN SAX (X — DEWEY L OLDHAM K (X — MARVELL THOMAS PNO (X — AARON VARNELL SAX (X
ALIMASH SHANANDA PERC (* — STEVE CROPPER G (* — PLAS JOHNSON SAX (*

J23 GARY JAMES J23

GARY JAMES — (A) THIRDS 19 ABC DUNHILL US ABCX 721

J24 JIMMY JAMES & THE VAGABONDS J24

JIMMY JAMES V (ABC — (A) NEW RELIGION 1966 PICCADILLY NPL 38027
COUNT MILLER V (A — (B) OPEN UP YOUR SOUL 1968 PYE NSPL 18231
WALLACE WILSON G (A — (C) THIS IS JIMMY JAMES 1968 MARBLE ARCH MAL 823
RUPERT BALGOBIN D (A — (D) LONDON SWINGS (1SIDE) 1968 PYE NSPL 18156
NAT FREDERICK SAX (A — (E) YOU DONT STAND A CHANCE 1975 PYE US 12111 UK NSPL 18457
PHIL CHEN B (A — (F) NOW 1976 PYE NSPL 18495
PAT GRAVESEND SAX (— (G) COME SOFTLY TO ME 19 ATCO US SD33222
ARTHUR REGIS ORG (— (H) LIFE 1977 CASABLANCA US 7054
CARL NOEL ORG (A — (J) DANCIN' TILL DAWN 1979 PYE UK N101
MILTON JAMES SAX (A — (K) GOLDEN HOUR 1979 PYE GH 679

J25 JOHN JAMES J25

JOHN JAMES G V (ALL — (A) MORNING BRINGS THE LIGHT 1970 TRANSATLANTIC UK TRA 219
PETE BERRYMAN G (C — (B) JOHN JAMES 1971 TRANSATLANTIC UK TRA 242
JOHN RENBOURN G (DEF — (C) SKY IN MY PIE 1972 TRANSATLANTIC UK TRA 250
CHRIS BILLINGS G (F — (D) HEAD IN THE CLOUDS 1975 TRANSATLANTIC UK TRA 305
DUCK BAKER G (E — (E) DESCRIPTIVE GUITAR INSTRUMENTALS 1977 KICKING MULE UK 128 US 143
(F) IN CONCERT 1978 KICKING MULE UK SNKF 136

J26 KEEF JAMES J26

KEEF JAMES (A — (A) ONE TREE OR ANOTHER 1973 RARE EARTH US 539 UKSRE 3007

J27 NICKY JAMES J27

NICKY JAMES V PERC G (ABC — (A) NICKY JAMES 1971 PHILIPS 6308 069
KIRK DUNCAN PNO V (AC — (B) EVERY HOME SHOULD HAVE ONE 1973 THRESHOLD UK THS 10
MIKE WEDGWOOD B V (AC — (C) THUNDERTHROAT 1976 THRESHOLD UK THS 19
GRAHAM DEACON D (AC
LYNDON GREEN G (C — RAY GLYNN G (AC — RAY THOMAS FLT (C — GERRY HOFF V (C
DAVID KATZ STRINGS (C — NASHVILLE KATZ STRINGS(C — JUSTIN HAYWARD G (C — MOX FLT HCA (C
B J COLE STEEL(C — ALAN FELDMAN K (C — BROTHER FATAAR B (C — CHICO GREENWOOD D (C
BARRY MARTIN WIND V(C — JOHN WEIDER G VLN (C — MAGGIE CAIRNES V (C — HIROSHI KATO G (C
IRENE CHANTER V (C — DOREEN CHAMTER V (C

J28 RICK JAMES J28

RICK JAMES (A — (A) COME GET IT 1978 MOTOWN UK STML12085
STONE CITY BAND — ( ) BUSTIN' OUT OF L SEVEN 1979 MOTOWN UK STML12104 GORDY US 894
( ) FIRE IT UP 1979 MOTOWN UK STML12128 GORDY US 990
( ) 3 TIMES IN LOVE 1980 GORDY US 995
( ) GARDEN OF LOVE 1981 MOTOWN UK STML12141
( ) STREET SONGS 1981 MOTOWN UK STML12153
( ) THROWING DOWN 1981 MOTOWN UK STML12167

J29 SKIP JAMES J29

SKIP JAMES G V (ALL — A TRIBUTE 19 BIOGRAPH BLP 12016
THIS OLD WORLD 1974 BIOGRAPH BLP 12027
EARLY RECORDINGS 19 BIOGRAPH BLP 12029
THEY SANG THE BLUES 19 HISTORICAL HLP 22
SKIP JAMES TODAY 1965 VANGUARD SVRL 19001+VSD 79219
DEVIL GOT MY WOMEN 1968 VANGUARD VSD 79273
GREATEST OF THE DELTA BLUES SINGERS 19 MELODEON US 7321
GREATEST OF THE DELTA BLUES SINGERS 19 STORYVILLE GER 670185
I'M SO GLAD 1978 VANGUARD VPD 20001

J30 TOMMY JAMES & THE SHONDELLS J30

Musician	Inst	Albums	Title	Release
TOMMY JAMES	V	(ALL	(A) HANKY PANKY	1966 ROULETTE US 25336
RONNIE ROSMAN	K	(K	(B) ITS ONLY LOVE	196 ROULETTE US 25344
PETER LUCIA	D	(K	(C) I THINK WE'RE ALONE NOW	196 ROULETTE US 25353
MIKE VALE	B	(K	(D) SOMETHING SPECIAL	196 ROULETTE US 25355 42005
EDDIE GRAY	G	(K	(E) GETTING TOGETHER	196 ROULETTE US 25357
PETE DRAKE	STEEL	(N	(F) MONY MONY	1968 ROULETTE US 25012
DALE SELLERS	G	(N	(G) CRIMSON & CLOVER	1969 ROULETTE US 42023
DAVE KIRBY	G	(N	(H) CELLOPHANE SYMPHONY	1969 ROULETTE US 42030
LINDA HARGROVE	G	(N	(J) BEST OF	1970 ROULETTE US 42040
RAY EDENTON	G	(N	(K) TRAVELIN'	1970 ROULETTE US 42044
HARGUS ROBBINS	K	(N	(L) TOMMY JAMES	197 ROULETTE US 42051
GEORGE RICHEY	K	(N	(M) CHRISTIAN OF THE WORLD	1972 ROULETTE US 3001 42062
BUDDY HARMON	D	(N	(N) MY HEAD,MY BED & MY RED GUITAR	1973 ROULETTE US 3007 UK 2432 005
D J FONTANA	D	(N	(O) AT THE SATURDAY HOP	19 LOUISIANNE US
RUSS LESLIE	D	(N	(P) IN TOUCH	19 FANTASY US 9509
BOB KING	B	(N	(Q) MIDNIGHT RIDER	1979 FANTASY US 9532
BUDDY SPICHER	FDL	(N	(R) 20 GENUINE US CHARTBUSTERS	1977 PYE UK NSPL28260
NASHVILLE EDITION	V	(N	(S) 3 TIMES IN LOVE	1980 RCA US 7748
CHARLIE McCOY	HCA	(N	(T) EASY TO LOVE	1980 MILLENIUM US 7758

J31 JAMES GANG J31

Musician	Inst	Albums	Title	Release
JIM FOX	D V	(ABCDEFHJLMEGH	(A) YER ALBUM	1969 STATESIDE UK 10295 ABC US 688
DALE PETERS	B V	(BCDFGHLME	(A) YER ALBUM	1969 BLUESWAY US 6034
GLENN SCHWARTZ	G	(	(B) JAMES GANG RIDES AGAIN	1970 PROBE UK 6253 ABC US 711
TOM KRISS	B	(A	(B) JAMES GANG RIDES AGAIN	1970 ABC UK 5009 MCA GERM 52075
DOMENIC TROIANO	G	(EF	(C) THIRDS	1971 PROBE UK 038 ABC US 721
ROY KENNER	V	(EHJF	(D) LIVE IN CONCERT	1971 PROBE UK 1045 ABC US 733
TOMMY BOLIN	G	(HJ	(D) LIVE IN CONCERT	1974 ABC UK 5016
BUBBA KEITH	G V	(L	(E) STRAIGHT SHOOTER	1972 PROBE UK 1056 ABC US 741
RICHARD SHACK	G	(I	(F) PASSIN' THROUGH	1972 PROBE UK 1065 ABC US 760
ALBHY GALUTEN	K	(J	(G) BEST OF	1972 PROBE UK 1070 ABC US 774
RUSTY YOUNG	STEEL	(B	(G) BEST OF	1973 ABC UK 5027 MCA US 1615
SHELLY KURLAND	VLN	(E	(H) BANG	1973 ATLANTIC UK K50028 ATCO US ')£)
DAVID BRIGGS	ORG	(LF	(I) GOLD RECORD	1973 ABC EURO 68303
TOM DOWD	K	(L	(J) MIAMI	1974 ATLANTIC UK K50068 US 36102
KEN HAMANN	SYN	(L	(K) 16 GREATEST HITS	1974 ABC US 801/2
GEORGE RICCI	CELLO	(L	(L) NEWBORN	1975 ATLANTIC UK K50148 US 36112
DONNY BROOKS	HCA	(L	(M) JESSE COME HOME	1976 ATCO US 36141
AL PERKINS	STEEL	(L	(N) LAST RIDE	1976 ATCO
BOB WEBB	V G	(M		
PHIL GIALLOMARDO	K V	(M		
JOE WALSH	G V	(ABCD		
FLACO PADRON	PERC	(M		
CHARLIE McCOY	HCA	(F		
WELDON MYRICK	STEEL	(F		
WILLIAM SMITH	K	(F		
CRAIG SAPPHIN	STR	(F		

J32 NICK JAMESON J32

Musician	Inst	Albums	Title	Release
NICK JAMESON	V G B K D	(A	(A) ALREADY FREE	1977 BEARSVILLE US 6972 UK K 55519
ERIC PARKER	D	(A		
PAUL BUTTERFIELD	HCA	(A		

J33 JAMESTOWN SHEIKS J33

Title	Release
(A) JAMESTOWN SHEIKS	19 CHAPTER ONE UK CMS 1001

J33A JAMME J33A

Musician	Albums	Title	Release
D ADEY	(A	(A) JAMME	197 DUNHILL US 50072
K ADEY	(A		
P DOWNEY	(A		

J34 JOE JAMMER J34

Musician	Inst	Albums	Title	Release
JOE JAMMER	G V	(A	(A) BAD NEWS	1973 REGAL ZONOPHONE UK SRZA 8515
TONY STEVENS	B	(A		
REG ISADORE	D	(A		
SAPPHO KORNER	V	(A		
JEAN ROUSSEL	K	(A		
CHRIS MERCER	HRNS	(A		
DANNY LEWINSON	V	(A		

J35 JAMMING WITH EDWARD J35

Musician	Inst	Albums	Title	Release
MICK JAGGER	V	(A	(A) JAMMING WITH EDWARD	1972 ROLLING STONES COC 39100
NICKY HOPKINS	K	(A		
RY COODER	G	(A		
BILL WYMAN	B	(A		
CHARLIE WATTS	D	(A		

J36 JAN & DEAN J36

Musician	Inst	Albums	Title	Release
JAN BERRY	V	(ALL	GOLDEN HITS	1962 LIBERTY US (M) 3248 (S)7248
DEAN TORRENCE	V	(ALL	GOLDEN HITS	1962 LIBERTY UK LBY 1279
WITH			TAKE LINDA SURFIN'	1963 LIBERTY US (M) 3294 (S)7294
HAL BLAINE	D	(*	(*) SURF CITY	1963 LIBERTY US (M) 3314 (S)7314
RAY POHLMAN		(*	(*) SURF CITY	1963 LIBERTY UK LBY 1163
LEON RUSSELL	K	(*	DRAG CITY	1963 LIBERTY US (M) 3339 (S)7339
LARRY KNECHTEL	B	(*	DEAD MANS CURVE/NEW GIRL IN SCHOOL	1964 LIBERTY US (M) 3361 (S)7361
STEVE DOUGLAS	SAX	(*	RIDE THE WILD SURF	1964 LIBERTY US (M) 3368 (S)7368
			RIDE THE WILD SURF	1981 GREENLIGHT UK 2011
TOMMY TEDESCO	G	(*	LITTLE OLD LADY FROM PASADENA	1964 LIBERTY US (M) 3377 (S)7377
BILL PITMAN		(*	COMMAND PERFORMANCE	1965 LIBERTY US (M) 3403 (S)7403
BILLY STRANGE		(*	GOLDEN HITS VOL 2	1965 LIBERTY US (M) 3417 (S)7417
GLEN CAMPBELL	G V	(*	FOLK & ROLL	1965 LIBERTY US (M) 3431 (S)7431
			FILET OF SOUL	1966 LIBERTY US (M) 3441 (S)7441
			MEET BATMAN	1966 LIBERTY US (M) 3444 (S)7444
			POPSICLE	1966 LIBERTY US (M) 3458 (S)7458
			GOLDEN HITS VOL 3	1966 LIBERTY US (M) 3460 (S)7460
			SAVE FOR A RAINY DAY	1967 J &D US JDS101 + CBS US 9461
			JAN & DEAN	1968 SUNSET US (M) 1156 (S)5156
			JAN & DEAN	1968 SUNSET UK 50001
			LEGENDARY MASTERS	1971 UA UAS 9961
			REMEMBER (EP)	1973 UA US REM401
			VERY BEST OF	19 SUNSET UK 50165
			GOTTA TAKE THAT ONE LAST RIDE	1974 UA US UALA 341H2
			JAN & DEAN (DBL)	197 SUNSET NL 12860020/1
			20 ROCK'N'ROLL HITS	1979 UA SWED ROCK10
			STORY	1980 CREOLE UK PAST 1 US KTEL502
			DEAD MANS CURVE	1980 UA US 10011
			BEST	1981 LIBERTY US 10115

J36A JAN & LORRAINE J36A

JAN HENDIN G K V(A (A) GYPSY PEOPLE 1969 ABC US 691
LORRAINE LEFEVRE V G (A
KAESHAW SATHE TABLA(A CLEM CATTINI D (A BRIAN ODGERS B (A NAZIR JAIR AZBHOY TAM (A
TERRY COX PERC (A ROAD MINFIELD PERC (A

J37 JAN DUKES DE GREY J37

DEREK NOY G TPT TROM(B (A) SORCERERS 1970 NOVA UK SDN 8
DENIS CONLAN D (B (B) MICE & RATS IN THE LOFT 1971 TRANSATLANTIC UK TRA234
MICHAEL BAIRSTOW WIND(B

J38 JANE J38

BERND PULST V (A (A) JANE TOGETHER 1972 BRAIN GER 1 002
KLAUS HESS G V (ABCDEFGHJK (B) HERE WE ARE 1973 BRAIN GER 1 032
WERNER NADOLNY K FLT(AB (C) JANE 3 1974 BRAIN GER 1048 CAPITOL US 11425
CHARLY MAUCHER B V (AC (D) LADY JANE 1975 BRAIN GER 1 066
PETER PANKA D V (ABCDEFGHJK (E) FIRE, WATER , EARTH & WIND 1975 BRAIN GER 1 084
MARTIN HESSE B (DEFGHJK (F) LIVE 1976 BRAIN GER 0080 001/2
GOTTFRIED JANKO K V (D (G) BETWEEN HEAVEN & HELL 1977 BRAIN GER 0060055
WOLFGANG KRANTZ G PNO(BC (H) AGE OF MADNESS 1978 BRAIN GER 60124 LOGO UK 1005
DIETER DIERKS SYN (B (J) SIGN No NINE 1979 BRAIN GER 0060 218
PEDJA V STR(K (K) JANE 1981 BRAIN GER 0060 354
MIRAIM KALENBERG V (B
ARIANE GOTTBERG V (B BRIGITTE BLUNCK V (B ANGELIKA WINKLER V (B PETER HEINEMANN V (B
GUNTER KORBER V (B WERNER ADOLUNG (E MANFRED WIECZORKE K V (FG A ZCCHENKER HARP (G

J38A LU JANIS J38A

LU JANIS V K (A (A) OR DURVS 1978 INPHASION 3900
AL CINER G (A
JOEY BRASLER G (A PHIL REED G (A DENNIS BELFIELD V B (A BUTCH RILLERA D (A
BOBBY RUFFINO D (A CRAIG KRAMPF D (A ROY BRAVERMAN K (A BECKY LEWIS V (A
VINCE POULOS EFFECTS (A SILKY MAYER G (A

J38B JANUARY J38B

JANUARY TYME K V PERC(A (A) FIRST TIME FROM MEMPHIS 19 ENTERPRISE US 1004
ALLEN COOLEY D V (A
STEVE CIANTRO B (A WILLIAM BRANCACCIO G K V(A ANTHINY IZZO G V (A

J39 CHAS JANKEL J39

CHAS JANKEL V K PERC G (A (A) CHAS JANKEL 1980 A&M US 4862 UK AMLH 68518
PETER VAN HOOKE D (A (B) CHASANOVA 1981 A&M US UK AMLH 68533
CHRIS WARWICK SYN (A
MARK ISHAM TPT SAX SYN(A KUMA HARADA B (A CHRIS HUNTER SAX (A PAUL WESTWOOD B (A

J39A JANUS J39A

(A) GRAVEDIGGER 1974 ELECTROLA IC062 29433

J39B NOEL JANUS J39B

NOEL JANUS (A (A) HEROES OF THE WORLD 1977 DJM UK DJF 20509
KIRBY G (A
JEFF RICH D (A STEVE EMERY B (A JOHN COOK K SYN(A

J40 JAPAN J40

DAVID SYLVIAN V G (ABCDEF (A) ADOLESCENT SEX 1978 ARIOLA US 50037 UK AHAL 8004
(A) ADOLESCENT SEX 1978 HANSA GER 26091
MICK KARN B V (ABCDEF (B) OBSCURE ALTERNATIVES 1979 ARIOLA US 50047 UK AHAL 8007
(B) OBSCURE ALTERNATIVES 1979 HANSA GER 200 166
STEVE JANSEN D V (ABCDEF (C) QUIET LIFE 1979 ARIOLA AHAL 8011
(C) QUIET LIFE 1979 HANSA GER 201 261
(C) QUIET LIFE 1982 FAME UK 3037
ROB DEAN G V (ABC (D) GENTLEMEN TAKE POLAROIDS 1980 VIRGIN UK V 2180
RICHARD BARBIERI K V (ABCDEF (E) ASSEMBLAGE 1981 ARISTA UK HANLP1
RAY SINGER V (AB (F) TIN DRUM 1981 VIRGIN UK V 2209
SIMON HOUSE VLN (F (EP) LIVE IN JAPAN 1980 HANSA GER 600242
YUKA FUJII V (F

J41 BERT JANSCH J41

BERT JANSCH G V PNO(ALL (A) BERT JANSCH 1965 TRANSATLANTIC UK TRA 125
JAY LACY G (NM (B) IT DON'T BOTHER ME 1965 TRANSATLANTIC TRA 132
JIM BAKER G V (N (C) JACK ORION 1966 TRANSATLANTIC UK TRA 143
DON WHALEY B V (N (C) JACK ORION 196 VANGUARD US VSD 6544
ERNIE McDANIELS B (N (D) BERT & JOHN RENBOURN 1966 TRANSATLANTIC UK TRA 144
DAVID HUNGATE B HRNS(N (E) LUCKY THIRTEEN 1966 VANGUARD VSD79212
DANNY R LANE D (NM (F) NICOLA 1967 TRANSATLANTIC UK TRA 157
TRIS IMBODEN D (N (G) BIRTHDAY BLUES 1968 TRANSATLANTIC UK TRA 179
RED RHODES STEEL(M (G) BIRTHDAY BLUES 1968 REPRISE US 6343
ROBERT GREENIDGE D (N (H) STEPPING STONES 1969 VANGUARD US 6506 UK VSD79292
CRAIG BULHER HNRS (N (I) SAMPLER 1969 TRANSATLANTIC UK TRASAM 10
DARREL LEONARD HRNS (N (J) ROSEMARY LANE 1971 TRANSATLANTIC UK TRA 235
DUFFY POWER HCA (G (J) ROSEMARY LANE 1971 REPRISE US 6455
JIM GORDON HRNS (N (K) BOX OF LOVE (COMP) 1972 TRANSATLANTIC UK TRASAM 27
BILL SMITH K (N (L) MOONSHINE 1973 REPRISE US 2129 UK K44225
DAVID BARRY K (N (M) L.A. TURNAROUND 1974 CHARISMA UK CAS 1090
GEORGE SEYMOUR K (N (N) SANTA BARBARA HONEYMOON 1975 CHARISMA UK CAS 1107
RAY WARLEIGH FLT (KG (A) EARLY BERT 1976 XTRA UK XTRA 1163
BETH FICHET V (N (B) EARLY BERT VOL 2 1976 XTRA UK XTRA 1164
RON McGUIRE V (N (F) EARLY BERT VOL 3 1976 XTRA UK XTRA 1165
STEVE WOOD V (N (J) EARLY BERT VOL 4 1977 XTRA UK XTRA 1170
MICHAEL NESMITH G (M (O) A RARE CONUNDRUM 1977 CHARISMA UK CAS 1127
TERRY COX D (G (O) A RARE CONUNDRUM 1977 KICKING MULE US 302
RALPH McTELL HCA (OL (P) ANTHOLOGY 1978 TRANSATLANTIC UK MTRA 2007
DAVE BAINBRIDGE K (O (Q) AVOCET 1979 CHARISMA UK CLASS 6
PICK WITHERS D (O (R) 13 DOWN 1980 KICKING MULE US 309 UK 162
ROD CLEMENTS G B MAND (O (S) BEST OF 1980 KICKING MULE 334
DANNY THOMPSON B (GLQ (T) HEARTBREAK 1982 LOGO UK 1035
MIKE PIGGOTT VLN (O
JOHN RENBOURN G (BCDKH
NIGEL PORTMAN SMITH B K(LUCE LANGRIDGE D (JACQUI McSHE V (MARTIN JENKINS FLT VLN MAND(KQ
TONY VISCONTE B (L MARY VISCONTE V (L DAVE MATTACKS D (L SKAILA KANDA HARP (L
ALI BAIN FDL (L LAURIE ALLAN D (L RICHARD ADENEY FLT (L THEA KING CLAR (L
MARILYN SANSON CELLO(L GARY BOYLE G (L DANNY RICHMOND D (L MIKE COHEN PNO (M
KLAUS VOORMANN B (M JESSE ED DAVIS G(M BYRON BERLINE FDL (M

J42 JEAN MICHEL JARRE J42

JEAN MICHEL JARRE K SYN(ALL — (A) OXYGENE — 1977 POLYDOR US 6112 UK 2310 555
(B) EQUINOXE — 1978 POLYDOR US 6175 UK POLD 5007
(B) EQUINOXE — 1978 POLYDOR EURO 2310 636
(C) MAGNETIC FIELDS — 1981 POLYDOR US 6325 UK POLS 1033
(D) CONCERTS IN CHINA — 1982 POLYDOR UK PODV 3

J43 AL JARREAU J43

AL JARREAU V (ALL — (A) WE GOT BY — 1975 WB US 2224 UK K 54045
TOM CANNING K (AB — (B) GLOW — 1976 WB US 2248 UK K 54073
JOE CORRERO D (AB — (C) LOOK TO THE RAINBOW(DBL) LIVE) — 197 WB US 3052 UK K 66059
WILTIN FELDER B (B — (D) ALL FLY HOME — 1979 WB US 3229 UK K 56546
LARRY CARLTON G (B — (E) THIS TIME — 1980 WB US 3434 UK K 56804
LARRY NASH K (B — (F) BREAKING AWAY — 1981 WB UK K 56957
JOE SAMPLE PNO (B
LARRY BUNKER VIBES(A STEVE FORMAN PERC (B RALPH MACDONALD PER (B DAVE GRUSIN K (A
WILLIE WEEKS B (B PAUL STALLWORTH B (AB ABE LABORIEL B (E GREG MATHIESON K SYN(E
MICHAEL OMARTIAN SYN (E RALPH HUMPHREY D (E CARLOS VEGA D (E STEVE GADD D (E
TOM CANNING PNO (E DAVID FOSTER PNO (E LARRY WILLIAMS PNO (E GEORGE DUKE PNO (E
JAY GRAYDON G (E OSCAR NEVES G (E DEAN PARKS G (E EARL KLUGH G (E
JERRY HEY HRNS (E CHUCK FINDLEY HRNS (E BILL REICHENBACH TROM (E LON PRICE SAX (E
LES THOMPSON HCA (E ARTHUR ADAMS G (A

J43A JASPER J43A

STEVE RADFORD G (A — (A) LIBERATION — 1969 SPARK SRLP 103
ALAN FELDMAN K (A
JON TAYLOR B (A NICK PAYN V HCA FLT(A CHICO GREENWOOD D (A

J43B JASPER WRATH J43B

MICHAEL SOLDAN (A — (A) JASPER WRATH — 19 MGM US SNF5003
CHRISTOPHER HAWKE (A
ROBERT GENNETTE (A PHILLIP STOLTIE (A

J44 JAY & THE AMERICANS J44

JAY BLACK V (ALL — (A) SHE CRIED — 1962 UA US 6222
KENNY VANCE (— (B) AT THE CAFE WHA — 1963 UA US 6300
SANDY YAGUDA (— (C) COME A LITTLE BIT CLOSER — 1965 UA US 6407
MARTY SANDERS (— (D) BLOCKBUSTERS — 1965 UA US 6417
WALTER BECKER B G (— (E) GREATEST HITS VOL 1 — 1965 UA US 6453
DONALD FAGEN K (— (F) SUNDAY & ME — 1966 UA US 6474
HOWIE KANE G (— (G) LIVING ABOVE YOUR HEAD — 1966 US US 6534
JAY TRAYNOR V (A — (H) GREATEST HITS VOL 2 — 1967 UA US 6555
(J) TRY SOME OF THIS — 1967 UA US 6562
(K) SAND OF TIME — 1969 UA US 6671
(L) WAX MUSEUM VOL 1 — 1970 UA US 6719
(M) WAX MUSEUM VOL 2 — 197 UA US 6751
(N) VERY BEST OF(COMP) — 1975 UA UK LBR1000 US> UALA 357
(O) CAPTURE THE MOMENT — 19 UA US 6762
( ) EARLY AMERICAN HITS — 19 SUNSET US 5278
( )GOOD TIMES — 19 SUNSET US 1001
( ) GREATEST HITS — 1980 UA US 1010

J45 JAZZ ROCK EXPERIENCE J45

(A) JAZZ ROCK EXPERIENCE — 1970 NOVA SDN 19

J45A JEBADIAH J45A

(A) ROCK'N'SOUL — 1978 EPIC US 35592 NL KILLROY 19912

J46 JEFFERSON AIRPLANE & STARSHIP J46

PAUL KANTNER G V (ABCDEFGHJKLMNOPQRSTV — (A) JEFFERSON AIRPLANE TAKES OFF — 1966 RCA US LSP 3584 UK SF 8195
(A) JEFFERSON AIRPLANE TAKES OFF — 1974 RCA INTERNATIONAL INT 1476
JORMA KAUKONEN G V (ABCDEFGHJKLP — (B) SURREALISTIC PILLOW**** — 1967 RCA US LSP 3766 UK SF 7889
(B) SURREALISTIC PILLOW**** — 1975 RCA YLI3738 RI 81 UK INTS5030
MARTY DALIN G V (ABCDEFJLMNOPQR — (C) AFTER BATHING AT BAXTERS — 1967 RCA US LSO 1511 UK SF 7926
(C) AFTER BATHING AT BAXTERS — 197 RCA AFLI 4545
SIGNE ANDERSON V (ALP — (D) CROWN OF CREATION — 1968 RCA US LSP 4058 UK SF 7976
SKIP SPENCE D (ALP — (E) BLESS ITS POINTED LITTLE HEAD — 1969 RCA US LSP 4133 UK SF 8019
SPENCER DRYDEN D (BCDEFJLP — (E) BLESS ITS POINTED LITTLE HEAD — 197 TELDEC GR 3012 +RCA AFLI 4133
BOB HARVEY D (— (F) VOLUNTEERS — 1969 RCA US LSP 4238 UK SF 8076
JACK CASADY B (ABCDEFGHJKLP — (G) BARK — 1971 GRUNT FTR 1001
GRACE SLICK K V (BCDEFGHJKLMNOPQV — (H) LONG JOHN SILVER — 1972 GRUNT FTR 1007
JOEY COVINGTON D (FGHL — (J) THE WORST OF (COMP) — 1970 RCA US LSP 4459 UK SF 8164
JERRY GARCIA G (FL — (K) 30 SECONDS OVER WINTERLAND — 1973 GRUNT BFLI 0147
PAPA JOHN CREACH VLN V(GHKMNR — (L) EARLY FLIGHT — 1974 GRUNT APLI 0437
JOHN HAMMOND HCA (LF — (M) DRAGONFLY — 1974 GRUNT BFLI 0717
NICKY HOPKINS K (F — (N) RED OCTOPUS — 1975 GRUNT FTR 2002 BFLI 0999
JOHN BARBATA D (HKMNOQR — (N) RED OCTOPUS — 1980 GRUNT US RI 3660
SAMMY PIAZZA D (H — (O) SPITFIRE — 1976 GRUNT BFLI 1557
DAVID FREIBERG V (KMNOQRSV — (P) FLIGHT LOG — 1977 RCA US LSP 3766 UK SF 7889
IRV COX SAX (N — (P) FLIGHT LOG — 1976 GRUNT US/UK 1255
PETER KAUKONEN B (— (Q) EARTH — 1978 GRUNT US/UK 2515
BOBBYE HALL PERC (N — (R) GOLD (COMP) — 1979 GRUNT US/UK 13247
CRAIG CHAQUICO G (MNOQRSV — (S) FREEDOM AT POINT ZERO — 1979 GRUNT US/UK 13452
PETER SEARS B K (MNOQRSV — (T) BEST OF — 1980 RCA INT US 42727 UK 5030
AYNSLEY DUNBAR D (SV — (AB) SURREALISTIC AIRPLANE (DBL) — 19
MICKEY THOMAS V (SV — (DF) CROWN/VOLUNTEERS — 1980 RCA NL 43302
DAVID CROSBY V (F — ( ) ELEPHANT MOUNTAIN — 1975 GRUNT US 4510
STEVE STILLS ORG (F — (V) MODERN TIMES — 1980 GRUNT US 3848 UK 3050 RI INT5027
RICK JARRARD PROD (B AL SCHMITT PROD (F MARY GANNON V (F MARILYN HUNT V (F
DEANE HURSH V (F DENISE JEWKES V (F BILL LANDER V (G MATTHEW KATZ PROD(A
TOMMY OLIVER PROD (A

J48 GARLAND JEFFREYS

Musician	Instr	Albums	Album	Release
GARLAND JEFFREYS	PERC G V	(ALL	(A) GARLAND JEFFREYS	1973 ATLANTIC US SD 7253
STEVE GADD	D	(BC	(B) GHOST WRITER	1977 A&M US 4629 UK AMLH 64629
DON GROLNICK	K	(BC	(C) ONE EYED JACK	1978 A&M US 4681 UK AMLH 64681
DR JOHN	K	(ABC	(D) AMERICAN BOY & GIRL	1979 A&M US 4778 UK AMLH 64778
JEFF MIRANOV	G	(C	(E) ESCAPE ARTIST	1980 EPIC US 36983 UK 84808
RICHARD TRIFAN	K	(C	(F) ROCK'N' ROLL ADULT	1982 EPIC 85307
DAVID SANBORN	SAX	(BC		

Musician	Instr	Albums	Musician	Instr	Albums	Musician	Instr	Albums	Musician	Instr	Albums
LUTHER VANDROSS	V	(C	HUGH McCRACKEN	G HCA	(BC	G E SMITH	G B	(E	ANDREW BODNER	B	(E
MICHAEL BRECKER	SAX	(BCE	PHOEBE SNOW	V	(C	PAUL PRESTOPINO	MAND	(D	DAVID SPINOZZA	K G	(BC
RANDY BRECKER	TPT	(BCE	DAVID LASLEY	V	(BC	ALAN FREEDMAN	G	(ABDE	PAT AUSTIN	V	(A
DAVID BROMBERG	DOBRO	(A	DONALD BROOKS	HCA	(A	HUX BROWN	G	(A	LORI BURTON	V	(A
GEOFFREY CHUNG	G	(A	RICHARD DAVIS	B	(A	WINSTON GRENNAN	D	(A	PAUL GRIFFIN	K	(A
NEVILLE HINDS	ORG	(A	JACKIE JACKSON	B	(A	JIMMY JOHNSON	D	(A	DENZIL LAING	PERC	(A
RALPH MACDONALD	PERC	(A	MIKE MAINIERI	VIBES	(A	ADAM MILLER	V	(A	DAVID NEWMAN	SAX	(A
CHRIS OSBORNE	G	(A	LARRY PACKER	VLA VLN	(A	THE PERSUASIONS	V	(A	BERNARD PURDIE	D	(A
CHUCK RAINEY	B	(A	ALBERTINE ROBINSON	V	(A	JOHN SIMON	PNO	(A	MAERETHA STEWART	V	(A
WINSTON WRIGHT	PNO	(A	ANTHONY JACKSON	B	(BC	RUBENS BASSINI	PERC	(B	ARNOLD McCULLER	V	(B
JAMES TAYLOR	V	(B	JOHN BOUDREAUX	D	(B	PHIL MESSINA	TROM	(B	SUGARBEAR	G	(B
DANNY CAHN	TPT	(B	LYNNE PITNEY	V	(B	AL COHN	SAX	(B	LEON PENDARVIS	K	(B
DAVID PEEL	V	(B	BURT COLLINS	TPT	(B	ROBERT ATHAS	G B	(D	TIMMY CAPELLO	K SAX V	(D
ANTON FIG	D	(D	RAFAEL GOLDFIELD	B	(D	RORY DODD	V	(D	ERIC TROYER	V	(D
HERB ALPERT	TPT	(D	MICHAEL CUSCUNA	PROD	(A	STEVE GOULDING	D	(E	DANNY FREDERICI	K ACC	(E
ROY BITTAN	PNO	(E	LINTON KWESI JOHNSON	V	(E	ARTY FUNERO	G K	(E	LARRY FAST	SYN	(E
ADRIAN BELEW	G	(E	ROBERT ATHAS	G	(E	EARL LINDO	ORG	(E	JIMMY MAELIN	PERC	(E
LOU REED	V	(E	DIANE GRASSELLI	V	(E	MYRIAM VALLE	V	(E	MARIA VIDAL	V	(E
BOB CLEARMOUNTAIN	V	(E	JOHN KPIAYE	G	(E	EATON BLAKE	B	(E	DENNIS BOVELL	K G	(E
WEBSTER JOHNSON	K PERC	(E	ERROL MELBOURNE	D	(E	SEYOUM NET FA	MEL	(E	PATRICK TENYRE	HRNS	(E
AUGUSTOS TENYRE	HRNS	(E									

J49 JELLY J49

Musician	Instr	Albums	Album	Release
FRED BLIFFERT	V	(A	(A) TRUE STORY	1977 ASYLUM US 7E 1096
JESSE ROE	V	(A		
AMY MADIGAN	V	(A		

J49A JELLY BEANS J49A

(A) JELLY BEANS — 1976 BAAL UK 89002

J50 JELLYBREAD J50

Musician	Instr	Albums	Album	Release
PAUL BUTLER	G V	(ABC	(A) FIRST SLICE	1969 BLUE HORIZON US 4801 UK 7 63853
PETE WINGFIELD	K V	(AB	(B) 65 PARKWAY	1970 BLUE HORIZON 2431 002
JOHN BEST	B	(ABC	(C) BACK TO BEGIN AGAIN	1972 BLUE HORIZON 2931 004
CHRIS WATERS	D	(AB		
RICK HAYWARD	G	(C	KENNY LAMB D PERC (C	

J51 JELLYROLL J51

Musician	Instr	Albums	Album	Release
BOB THRONE	TROM	(A	(A) JELLYROLL	1971 MCA UK MUPS 420 + US KAPP 3626
LES ASCH	SAX	(A		
DAVE PARKINSON	SAX	(A	TIM HEDDING K (A ED SETGER G (A ROGER TROY B (A	
STU PERRY	D	(A		

J52 JOHNNY JENKINS J52

Musician	Instr	Albums	Album	Release
JOHNNY JENKINS	V G HCA	(A	(A) TON TON MACOUTE	1970 ATLANTIC UK 2400 033+ RI K40105
DUANE ALLMAN	G	(A	(A) TON TON MACOUTE	1970 ATCO US SD 33331+ FR 503056
PETE CARR	G	(A	(B) TON TON MACOUTE	1974 CARRI US RI 0136
PAUL HORNSBY	G K	(A		

Musician	Instr	Albums	Musician	Instr	Albums	Musician	Instr	Albums	Musician	Instr	Albums
ROBERT 'POPS' POPWELL	B	(A	BERRY OAKLEY	B	(A	BUTCH TRUCKS	D	(A	ELLA BROWN	V	(A
JOHNNY SANDLIN	D	(A	JAI JOHANNY JOHANSON	PERC	(A	EDDIE HINTON	PERC	(A	JOHNNY WYKER	PERC	(A
TIPPY ARMSTRONG	PERC	(A	SOUTHERN COMFORT	V	(A						

J52A BILL JENNINGS J52A

Musician	Instr	Albums	Album	Release
BILL JENNINGS		(A	(A) GUITAR MOODS	19 KING US KEP 342

J53 WAYLON JENNINGS J53

Musician	Instr	Albums	Album	Release
WAYLON JENNINGS	G V	(ALL	FOLK COUNTRY	1965 RCA US LSP 3523
BILLY SANFORD	G	(OM	LEAVIN TOWN	1966 RCA US LSP 3620
DALE SELLERS	G	(O	NASHVILLE REBEL	1966 RCA US LSP 3736
REGGIE YOUNG	G	(OPZX	SINGS OL' HARLAN	1966 RCA US LSP 3660
GERRY GROPP	G	(O	JEWELS	1969 RCA US LSP 4085
EDDIE HINTON	G	(O	LOVE OF THE COMMON PEOPLE	1967 RCA US LSP 3825
BILLY REYNOLDS	G	(OQMUS	HANGIN' ON	1968 RCA US LSP 3918
RANDY SCRUGGS	G	(OQS	ONLY THE GREATEST	1968 RCA UK SF 8003 US LSP 4023
LARRY WHITMORE	G	(OPQUS	COUNTRY FOLK	1969 RCA US LSP 4180
STEVE YOUNG	G	(O	JUST TO SATISFY YOU	1969 RCA US LSP 4137
RALPH MOONEY	STEEL G	(OPMSTUXZ	WAYLON JENNINGS	1969 VOCALION US VL 73873
JOE ALLEN	B	(OQ	BEST OF	1970 RCA UK LSA 3000 US LSP 4341
BEE SPEARS	B	(OZ	WAYLON	1970 RCA US LSP 4260
HENRY STRZELECKI	B	(OM	SINGER OF SAD SONGS	1970 RCA UK LSA 3025 US LSP 4418
TOMMY WILLIAMS		(O	SINGER OF SAD SONGS	1980 RCA INT UK INTS5020
BYRON BACH	CELLO	(	DONT THINK TWICE	1969 A&M US S 4238
MARTHA McCRORY	CELLO	(O	COUNTRY STYLE OF	1970 A&M AMLB 1006
DAVID BRIGGS	PNO	(O	THE TAKER	1970 RCA US LSP 4487
ANDY McMAHON	ORG	(OQ	THE ONE & ONLY WAYLON	1967 CAMDEN CAS 2183
DON BROOKS	HCA	(OPZ	CEDARTOWN GEORGIA	1970 RCA UK LSA 3053 US LSP 4567
WILLIE ACKERMAN	D	(O	(M)LADIES LOVE OUTLAWS	1971 RCA UK LSA 3142 US LSP 4751
RICHIE ALBRIGHT	D	(OPQSTUXZ	GOOD HEARTED WOMAN	1972 RCA US LSP 4647
BUDDY HARMON	D	(OM	HEARTACHES BY THE NUMBER	1972 CAMDEN CAS 2556
FRED NEWELL	G	(PQ	LONESOME ON'RY & MEAN	1972 RCA US LSP 4854
WILLIE NELSON	V B	(P	(O) HONKY TONK HEROES	1973 RCA US APL1 0240
JESSI COLTER	K	(P	RUBY DONT TAKE YOUR LOVE TO TOWN	1973 CAMDEN CAS 2608
DEE MOELLING	K	(P	(P) THIS TIME	1974 RCA US APL0539
DUKE GOFF	B	(OPQSTU	(Q) RAMBLING MAN	1974 RCA UK LSA 3136 US APL1 0734
KYLE LEHMING	K TPT	(OPQ	NED KELLY	1975 U A US UALA 3066
CHARLIE McCOY	HCA	(S	OUTLAWS	1976 RCA UK RS 1078 US APL1 1321
ROGER CRABTREE	HCA	(QSU	(S)DREAMING MY DREAMS	1975 RCA UK LSA 3247US APL1 1062
CHARLES LOCHRAN	PNO	(S	(T)ARE YOU READY FOR COUNTRY	1976 RCA UK RS 1067 US APL1 1816
MERLE WATSON	G	(S	ARE YOU READY FOR THE COUNTRY	1981 RCA UK 3663
JOHN WILKIN	G	(MRS	(U)LIVE	1976 RCA UK PL 11108 US APL1 1108

(CONTINUED)

J53 WAYLON JENNINGS (CONTINUED) J53

JOE PALLEN G (S MACKINTOSH & TJ (SOUNDTRACK) 1976 RCA US APL1 1520
JIMMY COLVARD G (S HITS OF 1977 RCA UK PL 42211
KENNY MALONE D (S (X)OL' WAYLON 1977 RCA UK PL 12317 US APL1 2317
BUDDY SPICHER FDL (S WAYLON & WILLIE 1978 RCA UK PL 12686 US APL1 2686
STRING SECTION (S (Z) I'VE ALWAYS BEEN CRAZY 1978 RCA UK PL 12959 US APL1 2959
DAVE KIRBY G (MQ WAYLON AT JDs 1978 BEAR FAMILY GERM JD 1001
BUNKY KEELS PNO (Q A SOUVENIR OF ARIZONA 19 LJR 114
LARRIE LONDIN D (MQ ONLY DADDY THAT'LL WALK THE LINE 19 RCA ACLI 0306
THOMAS JACKSON FDL (Q DARK SIDE OF FAME 19 RCA ACLI 7019
LEON RHODES B (Q GREATEST HITS OF WAYLON 1979 RCA UK PL 13378
CARL GAY G (Q WHAT GOES AROUND 1979 RCA UK PL 13493
SHERMAN HAYES B (Q EARLY YEARS 1979 CORAL CDL 8501
JOHN LESLIE HUG G (T WAYLON MUSIC 1980 RCA UK PL 43166
BARNEY ROBERTSON PNO/V(T MUSIC MAN 1980 RCA US 3602
GRAHAM NASH V (T GREATEST HITS 1981 RCA UK LP 3031
JIM GORDON HRNS (T LEATHER & LACE 1981 RCA UK LP 3931
MAURICE SPEARS HRNS (T BLACK ON BLACK 1982 RCA UK 3072
MACK JOHNSON HRNS (T
CARTER ROBERTSON V (TXZ
GORDON PAYNE V (ZX RANCE WASSON V (TXZ JERRY STEMBRIDGE G (M FRED CARTER (Z
TONY JOE WHITE (Z STAN REECE (Z CLIFF ROBERTSON K (XZ JOHNNY GIMBLE G (S
KENNY BUTTREY D (M NORBERT PUTNAM B (M HARGUS 'PIG' ROBBINS PNO(M JIM PIERCE PNO (M
JOHN CHRISTOPHER G (X BOBBY DYSON B (N BILLY GRAHAM FDL (T DON ROBERTSON (T
BOBBY THOMPSON G (Q QRICK POWELL SYN (M

J53A JENSON INTERCEPTOR J53A

CHARLOTTE WIEBE K V (A (A) JENSON INTERCEPTOR 1980 HOUSE OF LORDS 1002
DOUG JENSON G V (A
KENNY JENSON K (A ALBERT BLAINE D (A JOHN FYNN D (A

J54 JEREMY & THE SATYRS J54

JEREMY STEIG FLT (A (A) JEREMY & THE SATYRS 1968 REPRISE US RS 6282
DONALD McDONALD D (A
EDDIE GOMEZ B (A ADRIAN GUILLERY G (A WARREN B BERNHARDT K (A

J55 JERICHO J55

ROBB HUXLEY G (AB (A) JUNKIES MONKEYS AND DONKEYS 1971 A&M UK AMLH 68050
AMI TRIEBICH D (AB (B) JERICHO 1972 A&M UK AMLS 68079
DANNY SHOSHAN V (AB
MICHAEL GABRIELLOV B (AB HAIM ROMANO G (AB

J56 JERONIMO J56

RINGO FUNK D V (A (A) TIME RIDE 1972 BELLAPHON BLPS 19095
MICHAEL KOCH G V K(A
GUNNAR SCHAEFER V B G(A DIETER DIERKS V (A PETER HAUKE V (A

J56A JACK JERSEY J56A

JACK JERSEY (A (A) FOREVER 19 EMI IMP 064 25560

J56B JERUSALEM J56B

LINDEN WILLIAMS V (A (A) JERUSALEM 1972 DERAM UK SDL 6
BOB COOK G (A
BILL HAYDEN G (A PAUL DEAN B (A RAY SPARROW D (A

J57 JET J57

DAVY O'LIST G (A (A) JET 1975 CBS UK 80699
CHRIS TOWNSON D (A
PETER OXENDALE K (A MARTIN GORDON B (A ANDY ELLISON V (A

J58 JETHRO TULL J58

IAN ANDERSON FLT G V (ALL (A) THIS WAS JETHRO TULL 1968 ISLAND UK ILPS 9085
CLIVE BUNKER D (ABCDE (A) " " " " 1973 CHRYSALIS UK CHR 1041
MICK ABRAHAMS G (AE (A) " " " " 1969 REPRISE US 6336
GLEN CORNICK B (ABCE (A) " " " " 197 PHONOGRAM EURO 6307 517
JEFFREY HAMMOND HAMMOND B(DEFHGJ (B) STAND UP 1969 ISLAND UK ILPS 9103
MARTIN BARRE G (1BCDEFGHJKLMNOPQRS(B) " " 1973 CHRYSALIS UK CHR 1042
ANGELA ALLEN V (K (B) " " 1973 CHRYSALIS GER 202 057
TONY IOMMI G ((B) " " 197 REPRISE US 6360
BARRIEMORE BARLOW D (1FHMOPQGJK (B) " " 197 PHONOGRAM EURO 6307 519
JOHN EVAN K (1CDEFGHJMPOQ (C) BENEFIT 1970 ISLAND UK ILPS 9123
JOHN GLASCOCK B (MOPQK (C) " " 1973 CHRYSALIS UK CHR 1043
STRING SECTION (J (C) " " 1973 ISLAND GER 6339 009
HARRY HUGHES D ((C) " " 197 REPRISE US 6400
DAVID PALMER K (1MOPQHJ (C) " " 197 PHONOGRAM EURO 6307 516
TONY WILLIAMS B (1M (D) AQUALUNG 1971 ISLAND UK ILPS 9145
FRANCIS WILSON V (Q (D) " " 1973 CHRYSALIS UK CHR 1044
DAVE PEGG B (RS (D) " " 197 REPRISE US 2035
MARK CRAWEY D (R (D) " " 197 PHONOGRAM EURO 6307 515
EDDIE JOBSON K VLN(R (E) LIVING IN THE PAST 1972 CHRYSALIS UK CJT1
DAVY OLIST G ((E) " " " " 197 CHRYSALIS US 1035
STEVE CROPPER G (D (E) " " " " 197 CHRYSALIS US 2106
DARRYL WAY VLN (D (F) THICK AS A BRICK 1972 CHRYSALIS UK CHR 1003
JAMES ANDERSON (R (F) " " " " 197 REPRISE US 2071
MADDY PRIOR V (K (F) " " " " 197 PHONOGRAM EURO 6307 502
TERRY ELLIS PROD (AB (G) PASSION PLAY 1973 CHRYSALIS UK CHR 1040
PETER JOHN VETTES K V (S (G) " " 197 PHONOGRAM EURO 6307 518
GERRY CONWAY D (S (H) WAR CHILD 1974 CHRYSALIS US+UK CHR 1067
(H) " " 197 PHONOGRAM EURO 6307 537
(J) MINSTREL IN THE GALLERY 1975 CHRYSALIS US+UK CHR 1082
(J) " " " " 197 PHONOGRAM EURO 6307 559
(K) TOO OLD TO ROCK'N'ROLL 1976 CHRYSALIS US+UK CHR 1111
(K) " " " " 197 PHONOGRAM EURO 6307 572
(L) THE BEST OF JETHRO TULL 1976 CHRYSALIS UK CHR 1078
(M) SONGS FROM THE WOOD 1977 CHRYSALIS US+UK CHR 1132
(M) " " " " 197 PHONOGRAM EURO 6307 591
(N) REPEAT (BEST OF VOL 2) 1977 CHRYSALIS UK CHR1135 GER 6307611
(O) HEAVY HORSES 1978 CHRYSALIS US+UK CHR 1175
(O) " " 197 PHONOGRAM EURO 6307 622

(CONTINUED)

J58 (CONTINUED)

JETHRO TULL J58

(P) LIVE BURSTING OUT 1978 CHRYSALIS US 21201 UK CJT4
(Q) STORMWATCH 1979 CHRYSALIS UK CDL1238 GER 6307670
(R) "A" 1980 CHRYSALIS UK CDL1301 GER 202834
(S) BROADSWORD & BEAST 1982 CHRYSALIS CDL 1380
(1) LIVE TV SHOW VIA SATELLITE
(EP) LIFE IS A LONG SONG 1971 CHRYSALIS UK WIP 6106
(EP) RING OUT SOLSTICE BELLS 1976 CHRYSALIS UK CPX2

J58A

JETS (UK) J58A

BOBBY COTTON V B (AB — (A) JETS 1981 EMI UK 3356
TONY COTTON V D (AB — (A) JETS 1982 FAME RI UK 3036
RAY COTTON G V (AB — (B) 100% COTTON 1982 EMI UK 3399
JOHNNY PARIS SAX (A
DAVEY PAYNE SAX (A MICK GALLAGHER K (A

J59

JETS J59

(A) ROCK'N'ROLL MUSIC 1974 SEVEN SUN SBLP 100

J59A

JOAN JETT J59A

JOAN JETT V (ALL — (A) JOAN JETT 1980 ARIOLA ARL 5058
(B) BAD REPUTAION 1981 BOARDWALK US 37065 EPIC UK 85045
(B) I LOVE ROCK 'N' ROLL 1982 BOARDWALK US 33245 EPIC UK 85686

J60

JIMMY JEWELL J60

JIMMY JEWELL SAX (AB — (A) I'M AMAZED 1977 AFFINITY AFF2
JOHN MUMFORD TROM (AB — (B) FROM THE FIRST TIME I MET YOU 1978 AFFINITY AFF5
BILLY LIVSEY PNO (AB
RICHARD BRUNTON G (AB STEVE BINGHAM B (AB RAY DUFFY D (AB

J61

JIG SAW J61

DES DYER V D (A — (A) SKY HIGH 1975 SPLASH 1001
CLIVE SCOTT K V (A — (B) JIGSAW 1977
BARRIE BERNARD B (A
TONY CAMPBELL G (A

J62

JIVA J62

MICHAEL LANNING G V (A — (A) JIVA 1975 DARK HORSE/A&M UK AMLH 22003
JAMES STRAUSS B V (A
THOMAS HILTON G V (A MICHAEL REED D PERC(A

J63

JIVE BUREAUX J63

TONY MESSENGER G V HCA (A — (A) STICK IT 1978 GULL UK GULP 1025
SHAM V (A
TIM MATTHEWMAN B V (A BOB WILSON K (A IAN STEPHENSON PERC (A JOE SLYTHE D (A
ROGER QUESTED PERC (A SUE GLOVER V (A SUNNY LESLIE V (A J STONE V (A
GARY WINDO SAX (A HARRY BECKETT TPT (A NICK EVANS TROM (A BARRY MORGAN PERC (A
FRANK RICOTTI VIBES(A

J64

JO JO GUNNE J64

MARK ANDES B V (A — (A) JO JO GUNNE 1972 ASYLUM US SD 5053 UK SYLA 8752
JOHN STRONACH PROD (D — (A) JO JO GUNNE 1976 ASYLUM UK RI K53034
JAY FERGUSON K V (ABCD — (B) BITE DOWN HARD 1973 ASYLUM US SD 5065 UK SYL 9005
MATT ANDES G V (ABC — (C) JUMPIN' THE GUNNE 1973 ASYLUM US 5071 UK SYL 9015
CURLY SMITH D (ABCD — (D) SO...WHERE'S THE SHOW 1974 ASYLUM US 7E 1022 UK SYL 9019
JIMMIE RANDALL B (BCD
JOHN STAEHELY G V (D

J64A

JO JO ZEP & THE FALCONS J64A

JOE CAMILLERI SAX V(ALL — (A) DON'T WASTE IT 1976 EMI AUSTRALIA 062 61153
JEFF BURSTIN G (ALL — (B) WHIP IT OUT 1977 OZ AUSTRALIA OZS 1004
JOHN POWER B V (ALL — (C) SO YOUNG 1978 OZ " " OZS 1002
GARY YOUNG D (ALL — (D) LIVE IN CONCERT 1978 OZ " " OZS 1013
TONY FAEHSE G (BCDEFGH — (E) SCREAMING TARGETS 1979 MUSHROOM UK K99094 US CBS 36442
WILBUR WILDE SAX (BCDEFGH — (F) JO JO ZEP & THE FALCONS 1979 ROCKBURGH UK ROC 108
WAYNE BURT G V (ABEFG — (G) TAKIN' THE WRAPS OFF (DBL) 1979 ROCKBURGH UK ROCD 110
ROSS WILSON PROD (G — (H) HATS OFF, STEP LIVELY 1980 MUSHROOM UK K37321

J65

JO MAMA J65

BOB WILLIAMS TPT (A — (A) JO MAMA(O SOLE MIO) 1971 ATLANTIC US SD 8269 UK 2400 129
MICHAEL DUBKIN SAX (A — (B) J IS FOR JUMP 1971 ATLANTIC US SD 8288 UK 2400 174
OLLIE MITCHELL TPT (A
MAYO TIANA TROM (A ABIGALE HANESS V (AB CHARLES LARKEY B (AB CAROLE KING V (B
JOEL BISHOP-O'BRIEN D (AB RALPH SCHUCKETT K V (AB DANNY KOOTCH G V (AB

J65A

JOBRIATH J65A

BARDEN JOBRIATH (AB — (A) JOBRIATH 1973 BARCLAY FR 80514 ELEKTRA US 75070
STEVE LOVE G (— (B) CREATURES OF THE STREET 1974 ELEKTRA US 7E 1010
ANDY MUSON B (
JOHN SIOMOS D (

J66

JO'BURG HAWK J66

BRAHAM MALBERBE G PERC(A — (A) JO'BURG HAWK 1973 CHARISMA UK CAS 1064
JULIAN LAXTON G (A
DAVE ORNELLAS V (A LES GOODE B (A SPOOK KAHN G (A IVOR BACK D (A
BILLY KNIGHT PERC V(A AUDREY MOTAUNG PERC V(A PETE KUBHAKA PERC V(A

J66A

J JOCKO J66A

J JOCKO — (A) THAT'S THE SONG 19 KAMA SUTRA US KSBS 2604

J67

JODY GRIND J67

TIM HINKLEY K V (AB — (A) ONE STEP ON 1969 UA US UAS 6774
PETE GAVIN D (B — (A) ONE STEP ON 1969 TRANSATLANTIC UK TRA 210
BARRY WILSON D (A — (B) FAR CANAL 1970 TRANSATLANTIC UK TRA 221
IVAN ZAGNI G (A — (B) FAR CANAL 1970 METRONOME EURO MLP15 388
BERNIE HOLLAND G (B
LOUIS CENNAMO B (A

J69 BILLY JOEL J69

BILLY JOEL V K (ALL (A) COLD SPRING HARBOUR 1972 PHONOGRAM 6269 150 US FAMILY 2700
RICHIE CANNATA K WIND(EF (B) PIANOMAN 1973 CBS US 32544 JAP 25AP952 UK 80719
PHIL RAMONE PROD (G (B) PIANOMAN 1981 CBS RI UK 32002
LIBERTY DEVITO D (DEFGH (C) STREET LIFE SERENADE 1975 CBS US 33146 JAP 25AP1078 UK 80766
HIRAM BULLOCK G (E (C) STREET LIFE SERENADE 1981 CBS RI UK 32035
DOUG STEGMEYER B (DEFGH (D) TURNSTILES 1976 CBS US 33848 JAP 25AP953 UK 81195
PHIL WOODS SAX (E (D) TURNSTILES 1981 CBS RI UK 32057
RUSSEL JAVORS G (DGH (E) STRANGER 1977 CBS US 34987 JAP 25AP843 UK 82311
STEVE KHAN G (FE (F) 52nd STREET 1978 CBS US 35609 JAP 25AP1152 UK 83181
HOWIE EMERSON G (D (G) GLASSHOUSES 1980 CBS US 36384 UK 86108
JAMES SMITH G (D (H) SONGS IN THE ATTIC 1981 CBS US 37461 UK 85273
DEAN PARKS G (B (DEF) BOX SET 1980 CBS UK 66356
RON TUTT D (BC
ERIC WEISSBERG BANJ (B LAURA CREAMER V (B LARRY CARLTON G (B WILTON FELDER K (BC
RHYS CLARK D (B FRED HEILBRUN BANJO(B MARK CREAMER V (B RICHARD BENNETT G (ABC
EMORY GORDY B (ABC MIKE OMARTIAN ACC (B BILLY ARMSTRONG FDL (B SUSAN STEWARD V (B
LARRY KNECHTEL B (C TOM WHITEHORSE STEEL(C GARY DALTON G (C MINGO LEWIS PERC (D
JOE CLAYTON CONGA(C MIKE DEASY G (C ROJ RATHOR G (C AL HERTZBERG G (C
DON EVANS G (C ART MUNSON G (C MICHAEL STEWART G (C WILLIAM SMITH K (C
FREDDIE HUBBARD TPT (F MIKE MAINIERI PERC (F ZACK SANDERS V (F MILT GRAYSON V (F
RAY SIMPSON V (F GEORGE MARGE RECORDER(F DAVID SPINOZZA G (F DONNIE DACUS V (F
PETER CETERA V (F DAVID FRIEDMAN PERC (F RALPH MACDONALD PERC (FE ERIC GALE G (F
FRANK FLOYD V (F BABI FLOYD V (F HUGH McCRACKEN G (EF RICHAR TEE ORG (E
LANI GROVES V (E PATTI AUSTIN V (E STEVE BURGH G (E DOMINIC CORTESE ACC (E
PHOEBE SNOW V (E GWEN GUTHRIE V (E DAVID BROWN G (E

J70 DAVID JOHANSEN J70

DAVID JOHANSEN V K (AB (A) DAVID JOHANSEN 1978 BLUE SKY US 34926 UK 82335
JOHNNY RAO G (A (B) IN STYLE 1979 BLUE SKY US 36082 UK 83745
THOMAS TRASK G (A (C) HERE COMES THE NIGHT 1981 BLUE SKY US 36589 UK 84504
BUZ VERNO B (A
SARA DASH V (A SCARLET RIVERA VLN (A STAN BRONSTEIN HRNS (A TONY MACHINE PERC (A
FELIX CAVALIERE ORG (A BOBBIE BLAIN ORG (A NONA HENDRYX V (A JOE PERRY K (A
FRANKIEN LAROCKA D (A

J70A ANDREW JOHN J70A

ANDREW JOHN V G B K D WIND(A (A) THE MACHINE STOPS 1972 CBS UK 64835
MIKE WOODS G B (A
CLIVE SARSTEDT B (A RIC LEE D (A CARSTEN SMEDEGAARD D (A

J71 CLIVE JOHN J71

CLIVE JOHN(CLINT SPACE)G K V(A (A) YOU ALWAYS KNOW WHERE YOU STAND WITH A BUZZARD 1975 UA UK UAS 29733
MARTIN ACE B (A
DAVE CHARLES D (A TOMMY RILEY D (A PHIL RYAN K (A BRIAN BREEZE G (A
ANDY FAIRWEATHER LOW G V(A PETE HURLEY B (A JOHN WILLIAMS V (A TED CROOK HCA (A

J72 ELTON JOHN J72

ELTON JOHN V K (ALL (A) EMPTY SKY 1969 MCA US 2130 UK DJM DJLPS 403
STEVE WRATHER G (R (A) EMPTY SKY 19 MCA RI US 3008 RI UK 80 22086
CALEB QUAYE G (ABCFMO (B) ELTON JOHN 1970 UNI US 93090 UK DJM DJF 20406
DAVID PAICH K (R (B) ELTON JOHN 1970 MCA US 3000 RI 37067 RI UK 22087
DAVEY JOHNSTONE G (FGHJKMO (C) TUMBLEWEED CONNECTION 1970 UNI US 73096 UK DJM DJLPS410
STEVE LUKATHER G (RQ (C) TUMBLEWEED CONNECTION 19 MCA RI US 3001 UK RI DJM 22088
TIM SCHMIT V (R (D) 17.11.70 1971 UNI US 93105 UK DJM DJLPS 414
FRANK CLARK G (B (D) 17.11.70 1971 MCA US 2015+3002
COLIN GREEN G (B (E) FRIENDS 1971 PARAMOUNT 6004 + SPFL 269
GLEN FREY V (R (F) MADMAN ACROSS THE WATER 1971 UNI US 93120 UK DJM DJH 20420
CLIVE HICKS G (B (F) MADMAN ACROSS THE WATER 1971 MCA US 3003 RI
ROLAND HARKER G (B (G) HONKY CHATEAU 1972 MCA US 3004 UK DJM DJLPH 423
DON HENLEY V (R (G) HONKY CHATEAU 19 MCA RI US 37063 UK RI UK 22090
ALAN PARKER G (F (H) DONT SHOOT ME, I'M ONLY THE PIANO'1973 MCA US 3005 UK DJM DJLPH 427
RICHIA CARNATA SAX (R (H) DONT SHOOT ME, I'M ONLY THE PIANO 19 MCA US 2100 US RI 37113
MAX GROENTHAL V (RS (H) DONT SHOOT ME, I'M ONLY THE PIANO 1981 DJM UK RI 22091
LES THATCHER G (F (J) GOODBYE YELLOW BRICK ROAD 1973 MCA US 2/10003 UK DJM LP 1001
CHRIS SPEDDING G (F (J) GOODBYE YELLOW BRICK ROAD 1976 UK DJM DJE29001
TIM RENWICK G (PT (K) CARIBOU 1974 MCA US 3006 UK DJM DJLH 439
PAT SIMMONS V (Q (K) CARIBOU 197 MCA US RI 37065 UK 2116
LARRY HALL WIND (R (K) CARIBOU 1980 DJM UK RI 22092
B J COLE STEEL(F (L) CAPTAIN FANTASTIC 1974 MCA US 3009 UK DJM DJLPX 1
CLIVE FRANKS PERC (R (L) CAPTAIN FANTASTIC 19 MCA US RI 2142 + 81 RI 37066
ALLAN TAYLOR D (RS (L) CAPTAIN FANTASTIC 1981 UK DJM RI 22094
RICHIE ZITO G (RST (M) ROCK OF THE WESTIES 1975 MCA US 3010 UK DJM DJLPH 464
BILL CHAMPLIN V (RS (M) ROCK OF THE WESTIES 19 MCA US 2163 US RI 80 621
JERRY HEY WIND (R (M) ROCK OF THE WESTIES 1980 DJM UK RI 22093
TONY MURRAY B (A (N) HERE & THERE 1976 MCA US 2197 UK DJM DJH 20473
DAVE RICHMOND B (B (O) BLUE MOVES 1976 MCA US211004 UK ROCKET ROLL12
CHUCK FINDLEY HRNS (R (O) BLUE MOVES 197 ROCKET UK ROSP1
LES HURDLE B (B (P) SINGLE MAN 1978 MCA US 3065 UK ROCKET TRAIN 1
VICTOR FELDMAN PERC (RS (P) SINGLE MAN 1978 ROCKET EURO 9103 500
BRIAN ODGERS B (F (Q) VICTIM OF LOVE 1979 ROCKET EURO 9103 509 UK HISPD125
HERBIE FLOWERS B (F (R) 21 AT 33 1980 ROCKET EURO 9103 511+UK HISPD126
CHRIS LAURENCE B (F (S) THE FOX 1981 ROCKET EURO 6302 106 UK TRAIN 16
DEE MURRAY B (CFGHJKRST (S) THE FOX 1981 GEFFEN US 2002
JIM HORN SAX (RS (T) JUMP UP 1982 GEFFEN US
BILL REICHENBACH TROM (R
VENNETTE GLOUD V (RS ( ) GREATEST HITS 1974 MCA US 2128 3007 UK DJM 442
KENNY PASSARELLI B (MO ( ) POP CHRONIK 1975 DJM EURO VOL7
DAVID GLOVER B (GF ( ) GREATEST HITS 1977 MCA UA 3027 UK DJM 20520
ALAN WEIGHELL B (B ( ) LIVE COLLECTION (DBL) 1979 PICKWICK US PDA 047
BARRY MORGAN D (BF ( ) LIVE (NEW YORK 1970) 1978 HALLMARK UK SHM 942
TERRY COX D (BF ( ) LONDON & NEW YORK 1978 HALLMARK UK SHM 966
ROGER POPE D (ACFMO ( ) LADY SAMANTHA (COMP) 1980 UK DJM 22085
STEVE HOLLY D (PT ( ) VERY BEST OF 1980 K TEL UK NE 1094
DENNIS LOPEZ PERC (B (EP) FOUR FROM FOUR EYES 1977 UK DJM 18001
RAY COOPER PERC (FGJKMO ( ) GREATEST HITS 1&2 DBL 1981 UK DJM DJLP1

(CONTINUED)

NIGEL OLSSON D(ACFGHJKRS
JAN JOYCE V (O GENE MORFORD V (O BRIAN DEE K (BD DIANA LEWIS SYN (EF
RICK WAKEMAN K (F DAVID HENTSCHEL K (GJK CHESTER THOMPSON K (K JAMES NEWTON HOWARD K (MO1
JACK EMBLOW ACC (F CARL FORTINA ACC (O MARTYN FORD ORCHESTRA (O DON FAY WIND (A
LEROY GOMEZ SAX (J STEVE KUPKA SAX (K EMILIO CASTILLO SAX (K MIC GILLETTE HRNS (K
GREG ADAMS HRNS (K RANDY BRECKER HRNS (O MICHAEL BRECKER HRNS (O BARRY ROGERS HRNS (O
DAVID SANBORN HRNS (O LENNY PICKETT WIND (K LESLEY DUNCAN V (BCF TONY HAZZARD V (BG
BARRY ST JOHN V (F TERRY STEELE V (F SHIRLEY MATTHEWS V (K CARL WILSON V (K
BILLY HINSCHE V (K ANN ORSON V (M JOE CHEMAY V (O CINDY BULLENS V (O
CURT BOETCHER V (O KAY GARNER V (B ROGER COOK V (BF LIZA STRIKE V (FG
KIKI DEE V (JM JESSIE MAY SMITH V (K BRUCE JOHNSTON V (KO LABELLE V (M
DAVID CROSBY V (O CLARK BURROUGHS V (O RON HICKLIN V (O CORNERSTONE CHIOR V (O
JACQUES BOLOGNESI TROM (G IVAN JULIAN TPT (G JEAN LOUIS CHAUTEMPS SAX(G ALAIN HATOT SAX (G
JEAN LUC PONTY VLN (G LEGS LARRY SMITH (G LARRY STEELE V (G GUS DUDGEON V WHISTLE(G
TEX NAVARRA PERC (B IAN DUCK HCA (C SKAILA KANGA HARP (B GRAHAM VICKERY HCA (A
PAUL BUCKMASTER CELLO(B GENE PAGE STR (O MICHAEL HURWITZ CELLO(O MADELINE BELL V (BG
TONY BURROWS V (BF SUE GLOVER V (F SUNNY LESLIE V (F CLYDIE KING V (K
DUSTY SPRINGFIELD V (K TONI TENNILLE V (KO CLIVE FRANKS V (MP GRAHAM NASH V (O
CARMAN TWILLEY V (R LENNIE CASTRO PERC (R STEPHANIE SPRUILL V (QRS BYRON BERLINE FDL (R
GARY OSBORNE V (T PETE TOWNSHEND G (T JEFF PORCARO D (T KEITH FORSEY D (Q
MARCUS MILLER B (Q CRAIG SNYDER G (Q TIM CANSFIELD G (Q THOR BALDURSSON K (Q
ROY DAVIES K (Q PAULINHO DACOSTA PERC (Q JULIA TILLMAN V (Q MAXINE WILLARD V (Q
MIKE McDONALD V (Q TAMARA MATOESIAN V (S REGGIE McBRIDE B (S RONALD BAKER V (S
CHUCK CISSEL V (S GARY OSBORNE V (S MICKEY RAPHAEL HCA (S JAMES GILSTRAP V (S
JOHN LEHMAN V (S CARL CARWELL V (S ROY GALLOWAY V (S OREN WATERS V (S
CLARENCE FORD V (S

J73 JOHNNY LITTLE JOHN J73

JOHNNY LITTLE JOHN G V(ALL (A) JOHNNY LITTLE JOHN & CHICAGO BLUES BAND 197 ARHOOLIE F 1043
DAVE MYERS B (B (B) FUNKY FROM CHICAGO 1973 BLUESWAY BL 6069
EDDIE TAYLOR G (B (C) JOHNNY LITTLE JOHN 197 MCM FR 900 300
FRED BELOW D (B
MONROE JONES G (A ALVIN NICHOLS B (A ROBERT PULLIAM SAX (A WILLIE YOUNG SAX (A
BOOKER SIDGROVE D (A

J73A ROBERT JOHN J73A

ROBERT JOHN V (ALL (A) ON THE WAY UP 1971 HARMONY US 31353
GEORGE TOBIN V (B (B) ROBERT JOHN 1979 EMI AMERICA AML 3003
ED GREENE D (B (C) BACK ON THE STREET 1980 EMI UK 3014 US 17027
HAL BLAINE D (B
H LEE WOLEN D PERC(B SCOTT EDWARDS B (B DAVID SHIELDS B (B DENNIS BELFIELD B (B
MIKE PICCIRILLO G V (B BILL NEALE G (B STEWART LEVIN K (B MIKE THOMPSON K (B
EDNA WRIGHT V (B DARLENE LOVE V (B GEORGE TOBIN V (B

J74 JOHNNY & THE HURRICANES J74

JOHNNY PARIS SAX (JOHNNY & HURRICANES 1960 WARWICK US W2007
PAUL TESLUK ORG (STORMSVILLE 1960 WARWICK US W2010 +LONDON UK 2269
DAVE YORKO G (BIG SOUND 1960 LONDON HAX 2322 BIG TOP US 1302
LIONEL MATTICE B (BEATNIK FLY 19 TWIRL US 5002
DON STACZEK D (BEST OF 19 BIRCHMOUNT US 565
BILL SAVICH D (RED RIVER ROCK 196 LONDON UK HA 2227
TONY KAYE D (PROFILE 19 TELDEC GERM 624008
LIVE AT THE STAR CLUB HAMBURG 196 ATILA US 1030
(EP)REMEMBER 1973 UA REM 401
VERY BEST OF 1975 CONTEMPO CRMD 1002
LEGEND OF ROCK VOL 1 (DBL) 19 LONDON DP628 329
LEGEND OF ROCK VOL 2 (DBL) 19 LONDON DP628 318
(EP) JOHNNY & THE HURRICANES 19 WARWICK US 700
JOHNNY & THE HURRICANES 1981 LONDON UK TAB 32

J74A JOHNNY & THE JAILBIRDS J74A

(A) OUT ON BAIL 19 CHARLY UK CR 30184

J75 JOHNS CHILDREN J75

ANDY ELLISON V (A (A) ORGASM 19 WHITE WHALE US WW 7128
MARC BOLAN G V ((A) THE LEGENDARY ORGASM ALBUM(+TRACKS)1982 CHERRY RED UK BRED31
JOHN HEWLETT B (A
CHRIS TOWNSON D (A

J75A ALPHONSO JOHNSON J75A

ALPHONSO JOHNSON B V (AB (A) MOONSHADOWS 1976 EPIC US 34118
DAWILLI GONGA K V (A (B) YESTERDAYS DREAMS 1976 EPIC US 34364
PATRICE RUSHEN K (AB (C) SPELLBOUND 1978 EPIC US 34369 UK 82197
GEORGE BOHANON TROM (B ( ) BEST OF 1980 EPIC US 36521
CHRIS BOND G (A
IAN UNDERWOOD K (AB FLORA PURIM V (AB BENNIE MAUPIN WIND (A NARADA MICHAEL WALDEN D K(A
LEON CHANCLER D (A BLACKBIRD McKNIGHT G (A ALEJANDRO ACUNA PERC (A AIRTO MOREIRA PERC (A
GARY BARTZ SAX (A ALPHONSE MOUZON K (A GROVER WASHINGTON SAX (B RAY GOMEZ G (B
LEE RITENOUR G (AB MARK JORDAN KRG (B DAVID FOSTER ORG (B RUTH UNDERWOOD PERC (B
CHESTER THOMPSON D (B MIKE CLARK G (B SHEILA ESCOVEDO PERC (B GARNETT BROWN TROM (B
JON LUCIEN V (B PHILIP BAILEY V (B DIANE REEVES V (B ERNIE WATTS SAX (B
ERNIE FIELDS SAX (B CHUCK FINDLEY TPT (B GARY GRANT HRNS (B

J75B BOB JOHNSON & PETER KNIGHT J75B

BOB JOHNSON (A (A) KING OF ELFLAND'S DAUGHTER 1977 CHRYSALIS UK CHR1137
PETER KNIGHT (A
CHRISTOPHER LEE V (A MARY HOPKIN V (A FRANKIE MILLER V (A ALEXIS KORNER V (A
P P ARNOLD V (A DEREK BRIMSTONE V (A CHRIS FARLOWE V (A

J76 DAVID EARLE JOHNSON J76

DAVID EARL JOHNSON (A (A) TIME IS FREE 1978 VANGUARD VSD 79401
JAN HAMMER K (A

J77 JIMMY JOHNSON J77

JIMMY JOHNSON (AB (A) JIMMY JOHNSON & LUTHER JOHNSON 1977 MCM 900 294
LUTHER JOHNSON G (A (B) JIMMY JOHNSON 1978 MCM 900 302
(C) JOHNSONS WHEELS 1980 DELMARK UK 644

J78 LARRY JOHNSON J78

Personnel	Inst	Albums	Title	Year	Label	Country	No.
LARRY JOHNSON	G V	(ALL	(A) PRESENTING THE COUNTRY BLUES	1970	BLUE HORIZON		7 63851
			(B) COUNTRY BLUES	197	BIOGRAGHICAL	US	BLP 12028
JOHN PAUL HAMMOND		(B	(C) FAST & FUNKY	19	BLUE GOOSE		BG 2001

J78A LINTON KWESI JOHNSON J78A

Personnel	Inst	Albums	Title	Year	Label	Country	No.
LINTON KWESI JOHNSON	V	(ALL	(A) FORCES OF VICTORY	1979	ISLAND	UK	ILPS 9566
			(B) BASS CULTURE	1980	ISLAND	UK	ILPS 9605
			(c) L K J IN DUB	1980	ISLAND	UK	ILPS 9650
			(D) BEST OF	1980	EPIC	US 36521	
			(E) DREAD BEAT & BLOOD	1981	VIRGIN	UK	1002

J79 LONNIE JOHNSON J79

Personnel	Inst	Albums	Title	Year	Label	Country	No.
LONNIE JOHNSONG	K VLN	(ALL	(A)LONNIE JOHNSON	1974	STORYVILLE		SLP 162
ELMER SNOWDEN	G	(	LONNIE JOHNSON	19	COLLECTORS CLASSICS		CC 30
VICTORIA SPIVEY	V	(	BLUES GUITAR VOL 2	1970	PARLOPHONE		PMC 7106
OTIS SPANN	PNO	(K	ANOTHER NIGHT TO CRY	19	BLUESVILLE	US	1062
JOHN HUGHES	PNO	(K	TOMORROW NIGHT	196	STARDAY/KING SK1083+ GD		5039X
ROY COULTER	B	(K	MR JOHNSONS BLUES	197	MAMUSH		3807
ALLEN SMITH	PNO	(K	BLUES & BALLADS	19	PRESTIGE	US	1011
MONTE MORRISON	B	(K	BLUES BY LONNIE JOHNSON	19	PRESTIGE	US	1007
HERMAN SMITH	PNO	(K	IDLE HOURS	19	PRESTIGE	US	1044
JAMES JOHNSON	G	(T	WOMAN BLUES(AS VICTORIA SPIVEY)	19	PRESTIGE	US	1054
JACK ERBY	PNO	(T	(K)LONESOME ROAD	19	KING	US	520
LAZY HARRIS	G	(T	SINGS 24 12 BAR BLUES	19	KING	US	958
PORTER GRAINGER	PNO	(T	LOSING GAME	19	PRESTIGE	US	1024
JOSHUA ALTHEIMER	PNO	(S	(S) BLUEBIRS No 13	19	RCA		PM 42390
ALFRED ELKINS	B	(S	(T) WOKE UP THIS MORNING	1980	ORIGINAL JAZZ		OJL 23
LIL ARMSTRONG	PNO	(S					
BLIND JOHN DAVIS	PNO	(S					
ANDREW HARRIS	B	(S					

J79A LUTHER 'GEORGIA BOY SNAKE' JOHNSON J79A

Personnel	Inst	Albums	Title	Year	Label	Country	No.
LUTHER JOHNSON	G V	(ABC	(A) WITH THE MUDDY WATERS BLUES BAND	1969	TRANSATLANTIC	UK	TRA 188
GEORGE 'MOJO' BUFORD	HCA	(A	(A) WITH THE MUDDY WATERS BLUES BAND	1969	DOUGLAS	US	SD 781
MUDDY WATERS	G	(A	(B) BORN IN GEORGIA	1974	BLACK & BLUE	FR	33503
OTIS SPANN	PNO	(A	(C) ON THE ROAD AGAIN	1976	BLACK & BLUE	FR	33509
SAMMY LAWHORN	G	(A	( ) COME ON HOME	19	DOUGLAS	US	SD 789
FRANCIS CLAY	D	(A	( ) LUTHER JOHNSON	1975	MUSE	US	5021

J80 ROBERT JOHNSON J80

Personnel	Inst	Albums	Title	Year	Label	Country	No.
ROBERT JOHNSON	G V	(ALL	KING OF THE DELTA BLUES SINGERS	1966	CBS US CL1654	UK	62456
			KING OF THE DELTA BLUES SINGERS VOL 2	1970	CBS US 30034	UK	64102
			LEGACY	19	CBS US 33904		

J81 ROBERT JOHNSON J81

Personnel	Inst	Albums	Title	Year	Label	Country	No.
ROBERT JOHNSON	G V	(AB	(A) CLOSE PERSONAL FRIENDS	1979	ENSIGN UK ENVY4 INFINITY		9000
DAVID COCHRAN	V B D	(AB	(B) MEMPHIS DEMOS	1980	ENSIGN		ENRJ 12
BLAIR CUNNINGHAM	V D	(AB					

J82 WILKO JOHNSON & SOLID SENDERS J82

Personnel	Inst	Albums	Title	Year	Label	Country	No.
WILKO JOHNSON	G V	(A	(A) SOLID SENDERS	1978	VIRGIN	UK	V 2105
JOHN POTTER	K	(A	(A) LIVE (FREE WITH V 2105)	1978	VIRGIN	UK	VDJ 26
STEVE LEWINS	B	(A	(B) ICE ON THE MOTORWAY	1981	FRESH	UK	LP 4
MICKEY GALLAGHER	K	(B					
ALAN PLATT	D	(A					
ALEX BINES	D	(B					
DAVE BROOKS	SAX	(A					
JOHN DENTON	PNO	(A					
RUSSELL STRUTHER	B	(B					

J83 BROTHERS JOHNSON J83

Title	Year	Label	Country	No.
(A) LOOK OUT FOR NO 1	1976	A&M	UK	AMLH 64567
(B) RIGHT ON TIME	1977	A&M	UK	AMLH 64644
(C) BLAM	1978	A&M	UK	AMLH 64714
(D) LIGHT UP THE NIGHT	1980	A&M	UK	AMLK 62716
(E) WINNERS	1981	A&M	UK	AMLK 63724

J84 ADRIENNE JOHNSTON J84

Personnel	Inst	Albums	Title	Year	Label	Country	No.
ADRIENNE JOHNSTON	V	(A	(A) ADRIENNE JOHNSTON OF THE JOHNSTONS	1975	RCA	UK	SF 8416
DON FRASER	PNO	(A					
PAT DONALDSON	B	(A					
MICHAEL HURWITZ	CELLO	(A					
WILF GIBSON	VLN	(A					
JOHN HORNET	HRNS	(A					
BARRY MORGAN	D	(A					
BARRY CASTLE	HRNS	(A					
HOWARD DAVIS	VLN	(A					
FRANK RYECROFT	HRNS	(A					
GERRY CONWAY	D	(A					
CHRIS ANDREETY	V	(A					
GEORGE ROBERTSON	VLA	(A					
MIRIAM KEOGH	HARP	(A					
GREG BARON	CELLO	(A					
TOM MADDEN	V	(A					
CLIVE ANSTEE	CELLO	(A					
SIMON NICOL	G	(A					

J85 BRUCE JOHNSTON J85

Personnel	Inst	Albums	Title	Year	Label	Country	No.
BRUCE JOHNSTON	G V	(ABC	(A) SURFIN' PAJAMA PARTY	196	DELFI	US	634
			(B) SURFIN' AROUND THE WORLD	196	CBS US 2057 +		8857
			(C) GOING PUBLIC	1977	CBS US 34459	UK	81854

J85A TOM JOHNSTON J85A

Personnel	Inst	Albums	Title	Year	Label	Country	No.
TOM JOHNSTON	V G	(A	(A) EVERYTHING YOU'VE HEARD IS TRUE	1979	WB	US BSK 3304	UK K 56632
JIM KELTNER	D	(A	(B) STILL FEELS GOOD TO ME	1981	WB	US BSK 3527	
TOWER OF POWER	HRNS	(A					
RICK SCHLOSSER	D	(A					
BOB GLAUB	B	(A					
DAVID PAICH	K	(A					
TED TEMPLEMAN	V	(A					
JERRY JUMONVILLE	SAX	(A					
STEVE KUPKA	HRNS	(A					
DAVID GARIBALDI	D	(A					
RICK CHUDACOFF	B	(A					
MARK JORDAN	K	(A					
ANDREW LOVE	SAX	(A					
JACK HALE	HRNS	(A					
MIC GILLETTE	HRNS	(A					
KEITH KNUDSEN	D	(A					
PAUL BARRERE	G	(A					
MICHAEL McDONALD	K	(A					
LEWIS COLLINS	HRNS	(A					
LENNY PICKETT	HRNS	(A					
GREG ADAMS	HRNS	(A					
PAUL STALLWORTH	B	(A					
BILL PAYNE	K	(A					
NICOLETTE LARSON	V	(A					
BEN CAULEY	HRNS	(A					
EMILIO CASTILLO	HRNS	(A					

J86 DAVEY JOHNSTONE J86

Personnel	Inst	Albums	Title	Year	Label	Country	No.
DAVEY JOHNSTONE	G V	(A	(A) SMILING FACE	1973	ROCKET UK PIGL2 RI		ROLA 2
DAVE HENTSCHEL	SYN	(A	(A) SMILING FACE	1973	MCA	US	340
JOAN ARMATRADING	PNO	(A					
GUS DUDGEON	PERC	(A					
CHRIS LAURENCE	B	(A					
JO PARTRIDGE	G	(A					
DI JOHNSTONE	V	(A					
B J COLE	STEEL	(A					
MICHAEL HINTON	TPT	(A					
CHRIS KARAN	TABLA	(A					
ELTON JOHN	HCA	(A					
MOHAMMED AMIR	HCA	(A					
GRAHAM MORGAN	D	(A					
RAY COOPER	PERC	(A					
NIGEL OLSSON	D	(A					
RICK BATEMAN	HCA	(A					
MICK FLYNN	WHISTLE	(A					
DEE MURRAY	B	(A					
DEL NIEWMAN	SAX	(A					

J86A JOLLIVER ARKANSAW J86A

Personnel	Inst	Albums	Title	Year	Label	Country	No.
LESLIE WEST	G	(A	(A) HOME	1969	BELL	US	119
FELIX PAPPALARDI		(A					

J87 JOLT J87

JIM DOAK B V (A (A) JOLT 1978 POLYDOR UK 2383 504

ROBERT COLLINS G V (A

IAIN SHEDDEN D (A

J87A JON & THE NIGHTRIDERS J87A

JON BLAIR G (AB (A) SURF BEAT '80 1980 VOXX US 200002 LINE GER LLP5088

DAVE WRONSKI G (B (A) SURF BEAT 1981 CHARLY UK CR30213

DDIE B GIANNI G (A (B) LIVE AT THE WHISKY 1981 VOXX US 200005 LINE GER LLP5118

NIKI SYXX B (AB

DUSTY WATSON D (AB

J87B JON & VANGELIS J87B

JON ANDERSON V (AB (A) SHORT STORIES 1980 POLYDOR UK 5030 US 6072

VANGELIS K SYN (AB (B) FRIENDS OF MR CAIRO 1981 POLYDOR UK 5039 US 6326

RAPHAEL PRESTON G (B

DAVID COKER V (B SALLY GRACE V (B DICK MORRISEY WIND (B CAROL KENYON V (B

CLAIR HAMILL V (B

J88 JONAH J88

ROBERT GENGO G V (A (A) JONAH 1974 20TH CENT T 456

MICHAEL GREGORIO PERC V(A

VINCENT LA FATA G V (A JOE GENGO PERC (A DON GROLNICK ORG (A BOB MANN G (A

EDDIE BRIGATI PERC (A TOMMY WEST K (A TONY SANTARELLA B (A MIKE BRECKER SAX (A

ALLEN SCHWARZBERG D (A

J88A BOOKER T JONES J88A

BOOKER T JONES K V (A (A) TRY AND LOVE AGAIN 1978 A&M UK AM 64720

PATRICIA HENDERSON V (A (B) THE BEST OF YOU 1980 A&M US 4798 UK AMLK 64789

JAY GRAYDON G (A

DENNIS BELFIELD B (A MIKE BAIRD D (A MIKE UTLEY K (A JIM GILSTRAP V (A

JOHN LEHMAN V (A MARLENA TETER V (A

J89 BRIAN JONES J89

BRIAN JONES (A (A) PRESENTS THE PIPES OF PAN AT JOUJOUKA 1971 ROLLING STONES COC 49100

J89A BUSTA JONES J89A

BUSTA JONES (A (A) BUSTA JONES 19 SPRING US 6728

J89B CASEY JONES & THE GOVERNORS J89B

CASEY JONES V (AB (A) DONT HA HA 1964 GOLDEN 12 106

ROGER HOOK G (AB (B) SECOND ALBUM 1965 GOLDEN 12 108

DAVID COLEMAN G (AB

JIM REDFORD B (AB PETER RICHARDS D (AB

J90 CHRISTOPHER JONES J90

CHRISTOPHER JONES (A (A) NO MORE RANGE TO ROAM 1978 TRANSATLANTIC UK TRA 503

MICK LINNARD G B (A

PICK WITHERS D (A GERALD MOORE G (A JEFFREY JONES HCA G K(A

J91 CURTIS JONES J91

CURTIS JONES PNO V(AB (A) NOW RESIDENT IN EUROPE 1968 BLUE HORIZON UK 7 63207

BRIAN BROCKLEHURST B(A (B) TROUBLE BLUES 19 PRESTIGE US 1022

DOUGIE WRIGHT D (A (C) LONESOME BEDROOM BLUES 1979 DELMARK DL 605

ALEXIS KORNER G (

J91A GLORIA JONES J91A

GLORIA JONES V (AB (A) WINDSTORM 1977 CAPITOL 11854 SIDEWALK 1002

DAN FERGUSON G (A (A) WINDSTORM 1979 EMI RI UK EMC3291

ROBERT WHITE (A (B) GLORIA JONES 1978 MOTOWN US 790

LAWRENCE HILL V (A

DARRYL MOORE (A PAUL HUMPHREY D (A OMA DRAKE V (A T YOUNG V (A

M YOUNG V (A RAY PARKER G (A JOE SAMPLE K (A SCOTT EDWARDS B (A

JACK ASHFORD PERC (A EDDIE BROWN (A JAMES GADSON D (A EMANUEL GREEN VLN (A

SYLVESTER RIVERS K (A WAH WAH WATSON G (A TIM MAY (A RON COLEMAN (A

GARY COLEMAN PERC (A J SINGLETON V (A JOE GREEN V (A JESSE KIRKLAND V (A

SHARON MINGUS V (A NANIS NORMAN V (A

J92 GRACE JONES J92

GRACE JONES V (ALL (A) PORTFOLIO 1977 ISLAND UK ILPS 9470

JOHN DAVIS K (B (B) FAME 1978 ISLAND UK ILPS 9525

PIGGY PIGERINO VLN (B (C) MUSIC 1979 ISLAND UK ILPS 9538

JIMMY WALKER PERC (B (D) WARM LEATHERETTE 1980 ISLAND UK ILPS 9592

LARRY WASHINGTON PERC (AB (E) NIGHT CLUBBING 1981 ISLAND UK ILPS 9624

CRAIG SNYDER G (B

JIMMY WILLIAMS B (B CARLA BENSON V (AB SWEETHEARTS OF SIGMA V(AB BARBARA INGRAM V (AB

EVETTE BENTON V (AB ALLAN SCHWARZBERG D (A WILBUR BASCOMB B (A LANCE QUINN G (A

CLIFF MORRIS G (A BOBBY ELI G (A CARLTON KENT (A RON KERSEY K (A

VINCE MONTANA VIBES(A MOTO TAMB (B DON RENALDO STR(AB KEITH BENSON D (B

SLY DUNBAR D (D ROBBIE SHAKESPEARE B (D BARRY REYNOLDS G (D MICHAEL CHUNG G (D

WALLY BADAROU K (D STICKY THOMPSON PERC (D

J92A JOHNNY JONES J92A

JOHNNY JONES K V (A (A) LIVE IN CHICAGO 1979 ALLIGATOR US 4717 SONET UK 821

BILLY BOY ARNOLD V HCA(A

J92B LINDA JONES J92B

LINDA JONES V (A (A) YOUR PRECIOUS LOVE 19 TURBO 7007

J93 MICKEY JONES BAND J93

MICKY JONES G V (

TWEKE LEWIS G (

STEVE DIXON D (STEVE GURL K (A ALAN McKENNA B (

J93A NIGEL MAZLYN JONES J93A

NIGEL MAZLYN JONES G V(A (A) SHIP TO SHORE 1976 ISLE OF LIGHT IOL 666/1

(B) SENTINEL 1978 AVADA AVA 105

J93B PAUL JONES J93B

PAUL JONES V G HCA(ALL (A) MY WAY 1966 HMV UK CLP 3586

(B) PRIVILEGE 1966 HMV UK CLP 3523

(C) LOVE ME LOVE MY FRIENDS 1967 HMV UK CSD 3602

(D) CRUCIFIX IN A HORSESHOE 1971 VERTIGO UK 6360 059 LONDON US605

(E) SINGS PRIVILEGE & OTHERS 19 CAPITOL US ST 2795

(F) HITS & BLUES 1980 ONE UP UK 2231

J93C

RICKIE LEE JONES

J93C

RICKIE LEE JONES G K V PERC(AB (A) RICKIE LEE JONES 1979 WB US BSK 3296 UK K 56628
STEVE GADD D (AB (B) PIRATES 1981 WB US 3432 UK K 56816
JERRY HEY HRNS (B
ANDY NEWMARK D (A VICTOR FELDMAN PERC K D(AB MARK STEVENS D PERC(A JEFF PORCARO D (A
TOM SCOTT HRNS (A ARNO LUCAS V (AB MATTHEW WIENER V (A WILLIE WEEKS B (A
RED CALLENDER B (A BUZZY FEITEN G (AB FRED TACKETT G (A NEIL LARSEN K (AB
CHUCK FINDLEY HRNS (A LESLIE SMITH V (AB MICHAEL McDONALD V (A RANDY KERBER K (AB
RALPH GRIERSON K (A DR JOHN K (A RANDY NEWMAN SYN (A MICHAEL BODDICKER SYN(AB
ERNIE WATTS HRNS (A JOE TORANO V (AB NICK DE CARO ACC (A CHUCK RAINEY B (B
ART RODRIGUEZ D (B DEAN PARKS G (B STEVE LUKATHER G (B DAVID KALISH G (B
RUSSELL FERRANTE K (B CLARENCE McDONALD K (B LENNY CASTRO PERC (B DONALD FAGEN SYN (B
ROB MOUNSEY SYN (B RANDY BRECKER TPT (B DAVID SANBORN SAX (B SAL BERNARDI HCA V(B

J93D

JONESES

J93D

HAROLD TAYLOR V SAX (A (A) KEEPIN' UP WITH THE JONES 1974 MERCURY US 1021
REGGIE NOBLE SAX (A
GLENN DORSEY B (A WENDELL NOBLE SAX (A SAM WHITE SAX (A RICHARD TEE K (A
PAUL GRIFFIN K (A CORNELL DUPREE G (A CARL LYNCH G (A LEE VALENTINE G (A
WILBUR BASCOMBE B (A WARREN SMITH PERC(A BILL LA VORGNA D (A STEVE GADD D (A
RICK MAROTTA D (A DODDIE LONDIN D (A ALAN SCHWARZBERG D (A SAL SCHLINGER HRNS(A
CRAWFORD PERRY D (A RICHARD PRATT CONGA(A RALPH McDONALD CONGA(A SELDON POWELL HRNS(A
JON FADDIS HRNS (A ERNIE ROYAL HRNS (A GARNETT BROWN HRNS (A DANNY MOORE HRNS (A
GEORGE COLEMAN HRNS (A HELENE MILES V (A ADRIENNE ALBERT V (A MAERETHA ALBERT V (A

J94

JONESY

J94

ALAN BOWN TPT PERC(BC (A) NO ALTERNATIVE 1972 DAWN UK DNLS 3042
PLUG THOMAS D V (BC (B) KEEPING UP 1973 DAWN UK DNLS 3048
JAMIE KALETH K V (ABC (C) GROWING 1973 DAWN UK DNLS 3055
JOHN EVAN JONES G V (ABC1 (1) JONESY 1978
GYPSY JONES G V (BC
JACK JONES (1 MORRIS PERT PERC (C PAUL STARK (1 DAVID PAULL B V (A
JIM PAYNE D (A PHIL CLARKE (1 KEN ELLIOT SYN (C CLIVE LONIE (1
BERNIE HAGLEY SAX (C

J94A

JOOK

J94A

(A) WATCH YOUR STEP(EP) 197 CHISWICK UK SW30

J95

JANIS JOPLIN

J95

JANIS JOPLIN G V (ALL (A) I GOT DEM OL' KOZMIC BLUES AGAIN 1969 CBS US 9913 UK 63546
BRAD CAMPBELL B (ABCF (B) PEARL 1971 CBS US 30322 UK 64188
CLARK PIERSON D (BCF (C) IN CONCERT (DBL) 1972 CBS US 31160 UK 67241
KEN PEARSON ORG (BCF (D) GREATEST HITS 1973 CBS US 32168 UK 65470
DAVE GETZ D (CF (D) GREATEST HITS 1982 CBS UK RI32190
JOHN TILL G (BCF (E) JANIS (SOUNDTRACK)(DBL) 1974 CBS US 33345 UK 88115
RICHARD BELL PNO (BCF (F) ANTHOLOGY (DBL) 1980 CBS US 88492 UK 22101
SANDRA CROUCH TAMB (B (G) JANIS JOPLIN 19 SUPRAPHON IMP 1 13 2215
BOBBYE HALL PERC (B
BOBBY WOMACK G (B VINCE MITCHELL V (B PHIL BADELLA V (B JOHN COOKE V (B
SAM ANDREW G V (ACF RICHARD KERMODE K (AF GABRIEL MEKLER K (AF MAURY BAKER D (A
LONNIE CASTILLE D (AF SNOOKY FLOWERS SAX (AF TERRY CLEMENTS SAX (AF LUIS GASCA TPT (AF
JAMES GURLEY G (CF PETER ALBIN B (CF

J96

LONNIE JORDAN

J96

LONNIE JORDAN K B D V(A (A) DIFFERENT MOODS OF ME 1978 MCA US 2329 UK Mcg 3526
EUGENE PALMER V (A
DAROLD MATHEW V (A MOSES WHEELOCK PERC (A CAMEO ROSS V (A LARRY BROWN G (A
ANDY SHAPHIN SYN (A TOM LETONDRE TPT (A JOE ROBB SAX (A SUSAN BUCKNER V (A
DEBORAH PRATT V (A LEM TAYLOR V (A MILTON MYRICK V (A DOUGLAS PARKS V (A
DAWN PARKS V (A MICHAEL PARKS V (A GREGORY PARKS V (A CAROL WILSON V (A
KEVIN FARMER V (A KIMBERLY FARMER V (A ROBIN PARKS V (A

J97

LOUIS JORDAN

J97

LOUIS JORDAN V SAX(ALL (A) SOMEBODY UP THERE LIKES ME 19 WING US 16126+MERCURY US 20242
SHUGGIE OTIS G B K(I (B) GREATEST HITS 19 MCA US 274 + DECCA US 75033
JOHNNY OTIS D PNO(I (C) LOUIS JORDAN VOL 1 19 DECCA US 2029
IRV COX SAX (I (D) LOUIS JORDAN VOL 2 19 DECCA US A645
BOB MITCHELL TPT (I (E) MAN WERE WAILIN' 19 MERCURY US 20331
CHRIS BARBER (N (F) & HIS TYMPANI FIVE 19 JAZZ CLUB US 123+ PERFORMANCE3001
BUD JOHNSON ((G) HALLELUJAH 1964 TANGERINE 1503
ERNIE ROYAL ((H) LET THE GOOD TIMES ROLL 1970 CORAL CP 59 +CP 54 + CRLM 1042
JIMMY CLEVELAND ((H) LET THE GOOD TIMES ROLL 19 DECCA US 8551
SAM TAYLOR ((I) GREAT RHYTHM & BLUES 1973 BULLDOG RI 82 BDL 1000
TEDDY EDWARDS SAX ((J) BEST OF 1975 MCA US 2 4079 +UK MCFM 2715
(K) I BELIEVE IN MUSIC 1975 BLACK & BLUE 33059
(L) CHOO CHOO CH BOOGIE 1975 PHILIPS 6336 246
( ) CHOO CHOO CH BOOGIE 1982 MFP 50557
(M) IN MEMORIAM 1975 MCA PCO 7837
(M) IN MEMORIAM 1975 CORAL 622175
(N) LOUIS JORDAN SWINGS 1976 BLACK LION BLP 30175
(O) & HIS ORCHESTRA 1976 M C A PCO 8332
(P) COLLATES 1979 SWINGHOUSE UK SWH2
(Q) JUMPIN' STUFF 1981 RARITIES 46
(R) BEST OF 1981 MCA MCL 1631

J98

JORDANAIRES

J98

HOYT HAWKINS V (1 WE'D LIKE TO TEACH THE WORLD TO SING 1972 EMBER UK CW 141
NIAL MATTHEWS V (1 SPOTLIGHT ON THE JORDANAIRES 19 CAPITOL US ST 1742
LOVIS NUNLEY V (1 BIG COUNTRY HITS 19 CBS US 9258
GORDON STOKER V (1 MONSTER MAKERS 19 STOP US 10010
CHURCH IN THE WILDWOOD 19 VOCALION US 73854
THE JORDANAIRES 19 CBS US
(1)1978

J98A

JOSEFUS

J98A

DOUG TULL PERC (A (A) JOEFUS 19 MAINSTREAM US 6127
PETE BAILEY V HCA(A
RAY TURNER B (A DAVE MITCHELL G (A

J98B JOWE HEAD J98B

(A) PINCER MOVEMENT 1981 HEDONICS HEDON5 UK

J99 JOURNEY J99

GREGG ROLIE G V (ABCDEFGHJ (A) JOURNEY 1975 CBS US 33388 UK 80724
NEAL SCHON G (ALL (B) LOOK INTO THE FUTURE 1976 CBS US 33904 UK 69203
JONATHAN CAIN K G V(K (B) LOOK INTO THE FUTURE 198 CBS UK 32102
AYNSLEY DUNBAR D (ABCDF (C) NEXT 1977 CBS US 34311 UK 81554
GEORGE TICKNER G (AF (D) INFINITY 1978 CBS US 34912 UK 82244
ROSS VALORY B (ALL (E) EVOLUTION 1979 CBS US 35797 UK 83566
ROBERT FLEISHMAN V ((F) IN THE BEGINNING(DBL) (COMP) 1979 CBS US 36324 22073
STEVE PERRY V (DEGHJK (G) DEPARTURE 1980 CBS US 36339 UK 84101
STEVE SMITH D (EGHJK (H) DREAM AFTER DREAM 1980 CBS JAP 27AP1950
(J) ESCAPE 1981 CBS US 37406 UK 85138
(K) CAPTURED 1981 CBS US 37016 UK 88525
(L) TRON (SOUNDTRACK Part) 1982 CBS UK 85669

J99A JOY DIVISION J99A

IAN CURTIS V (ABC (A) UNKNOWN PLEASURES 1979 FACTORY UK FACT 10
BERNARD ALBRECHT G K (ABC (B) CLOSER 1980 FACTORY GER 60361 UK FACT 25
PETER HOOK B (ABC (C) STILL (DBL) 1981 FACTORY UK FACT 40
STEVE MORRIS D (ABC

J100 JOY OF COOKING J100

TONI BROWN V K G(ABC (A) JOY OF COOKING 1970 CAPITOL EST 661
TERRY GARTHWAITE V G (ABC (B) CLOSER TO THE GROUND 1971 CAPITOL EST 828
FRITZ KASTEN D SAX(ABC (C) CASTLES 1972 CAPITOL EST 11050
JEFF NEIGHBOR B TROM (BC
RON WILSON PERC HCA (ABC JIM HORN SAX (C DAVID GARTHWAITE B G (A

J100A JOY UNLIMITED J100A

KLAUS NAGEL G FLT(AB (A) OVERGROUND 1970 PILZ GER
ROLAND HECK K (ABCD (B) SCHMETTERLINGE 1971 PILZ GER 20 21090/1
HANS HERKENNE PERC (ABCD (C) REFLECTIONS 1973 BASF GER 20 21686/1
ALBIN METZ B TPT(ABCD (D) MINNE 1975 BASF GER 12 22 331/0
DIETER KINDL G (AB
JOY FLEMING V (A HANS LINGENFELDER G (D JOSCHI DINIER G B V (D KEN TRAYLOR G (C
GERD KOTHE FLT (D

J101 JUBAL J101

DENNIS LINDE G V (A (A) JUBAL 1972 ELEKTRA US 75033

J101A JUDAS JUMP J101A

ALAN JONES WIND (A (A)SCORCH 1970 PARLOPHONE UK PAS 10001
ANDT BOWN K G (A (A) SCORCH 1972 PRIDE US 0003
CHARLIE HARRISON B (A
HENRY SPINETTI D (A TREVOR WILLIAMS G (A ADRIAN WILLIAMS V (A

J102 JUDAS PRIEST J102

K K DOWNING G (ALL (A) ROCKA ROLLA 1974 GULL UK GULP1005 VISA 7001
GLEN TIPTON G (ALL (B) SAD WINGS OF DESTINY 1976 GULL UK GULP 1015
ROB HALFORD V (ALL (B) SAD WINGS OF DESTINY 1976 JANUS US 7019 OVATION RI 1751
IAN HILL B (ALL (C) SIN AFTER SIN 1977 CBS US 34587 UK 82008
JOHN HINCH D (AD (D) THE BEST OF 1978 GULL UK GULP 1026
ALAN MOORE D (BD (E) STAINED CLASS 1978 CBS US 35296 UK 82430
SIMON PHILLIPS D (C (F) KILLING MACHINE 1978 CBS UK 83135
(F) KILLING MACHINE 1982 CBS UK 32218
LES BINKS D (FG (G) UNLEASHED IN THE EAST 1979 CBS US 36179 UK 83852
DAVE HOLLAND D (HK (H) BRITISH STEEL 1980 CBS US 36443 UK 84160
(J) POINT OF ENTRY 1981 CBS US 37052 UK 84834
(K) SCREAMING TO VENGENCE 1982 CBS UK 85941
(CEF) BOX SET 1980 CBS UK 66357

J102A JUDD J102A

TAT MEAGER D (A (A) JUDD 1970 PENNY FARTHING UK PEL 504
ROGER FLAVELL B (A
ROGER McKEW G (A MARK WIRTZ K (A SUE GLOVER V (A SUNNY LESLIE V (A
DORIS TROY V (A MADELINE BELL V (A

J103 JUDE J103

ROBIN TROWER G (
FRANKIE MILLER V (
JIMMY DEWAR B (CLIVE BUNKER D (

J104 JUDGE DREAD J104

JUDGE DREAD (A) DREADMANIA 1973 TROJAN TRLS 60
(B) WORKING CLASS 'ERO 1974 TROJAN TRLS 100
(C) BEDTIME STORIES 1975 CACTUS CTLP 1130
(D) LAST OF THE SKINHEADS 1976 CACTUS CTLP 123
(E) BEST OF 1976 KLIK KLP 9008
( ) 40 BIG ONES 1980 CREOLE UK BIG 1
(EP) JAMAICA JERK 1977 CACTUS CT 98

J104A JUDITH NYLON J104A

ERIC VANDER BRINK G V (A (A) THIS IS FEEDBACK 1980 LINK NL 80002
BOB BARNEVELD B (A
RENE VAN BARNEVELD G(A JOS SMULDERS D V (A MARCUS NIJSSEN PNO (A HAROLD SCHELLINCK SYN (A

J104B JUICE J104B

(A) DOMESTIC REGGAE 1981 FULL CIRCLE UK 8002

J104C JUICE ON THE LOOSE J104C

RON KAVANA G V (A (A) JUICE ON THE LOOSE 1981 JUICE UK JJOS1 LINE GER LLP5151
FRAN BYRNE D (A
BAM KING G V B(A CHARLIE HART B V K(A NICK PENTELOW SAX (A GERAINT WATKINS K (A
ED DEANE G (A PETER THOMS TROM (A MARTIN DROVER TPT (A CRAIG MACKIE K (A
TWINKI V (A

J104D JUICY GROOVE J104D

RAINBOW NEAL G V (A (A) FIRST TASTE 1978 PAYOLA US
MERCURY FLYER G (A
MARS BONFIRE G (A MAGIC MARKER B (A THUNDERCLOUD D (A VICTORIA REID V (A
RON BUSHY D (A LARRY LAZAR B (A GARY MORELL D (A

J105 JUICY LUCY J105

RAY OWEN V (A (A) JUICY LUCY 1969 VERTIGO UK 847 901 US ATCO 33367
ROD COMBES D (BC (A) JUICY LUCY 1969 BRONZE GER 26323
GLENN CAMPBELL V G (ABC (B) LIE BACK & ENJOY IT 1970 VERTIGO UK 6360014 US ATCO 33345
PAUL WILLIAMS V K PERC (BCD (B) LIE BACK & ENJOY IT 1970 BRONZE GER 200 411
CHRIS MERCER SAX K(ABC (C) GET A WIFF A THIS 1971 BRONZE UK ILPS9157 US ATCO 33367
NEIL HUBBARD G (A (D) PIECES 1972 POLYDOR UK 2310 160
KEITH ELLIS B (AB (E) BEST OF 19 ISLAND EURO 85814 BRONZE GER25842
PETE DOBSON D (A
MICK WEAVER K (D IAN McLAGAN K (D REMI KABAKA PERC (A JEAN ROUSSEL K (D
RON BERG D (D LOUGHTY AMAO PERC (A ANDY PYLE B (D JIM LEVERTON B (C
MICK MOODY G (BCD

J105A JULES & THE POLAR BEARS J105A

JULES SHEAR G V (AB (A) GOT NO BREEDING 1978 CBS US 35601
JIM GORDON D (A (A) PHONETICS/FENETIKS 1979 CBS US 36138 UK 83865
RICHARD BREDICE G (AB
STEPHEN HAGUE K SYN(AB DAVID BEEBE D (AB DAVID WHITE B (B KENNY ALTMAN B (B
LARRY HIRSCH PERC (A JERRY PETERSON SAX (A JERRY JUMONVILLE SAX (A MIKE HENDERSON SAX (A
LEE THORNBERG TPT (A DARRELL LEONARD TPT (A BILL EDWARDS TROM (A MARK UNDERWOOD TPT (A
JAY PRUITT TPT (A SKIP WIESNER TROM (A LINDA SMALL TROM (A

J105B JULVERNE J105B

PIERRE COULON FLT (AB (A) A NEUF 19 CRAMMED DISCS CRA 274
MICHEL DURET CLAR (A (B) COULONNEUX 19 IBC/EMI 058 99069
MICHEL BERCKMANS BASSOON(A
JEAN PAUL LAURENT PNO (AB CHARLES LOOS PNO (A BAUDOUIN DEHAYE VIBES(A JOSE BEDEUR B (A
DENIS VAN ECKE CELLO(AB JEAN FRANCOIS LACROIX SAX(A JEANNOT GILLIS VLN (AB MICHEL DAYEZ G (B
RICHARD ROUSSELET TPT (B ANNE DENIS VLN (B JEAN COULON TROM (B

J105C JUKIN' BONE J105C

JOE WHITING V (A (A) WAY DOWN EAST 1972 RCA US LSP 4768
MARK DOYLE G K V(A
GEORGE EGOSARIAN G (A JOHN DEMASO B PERC V(A DANNY COWARD D PERC(A KEVIN SHWARYK D (A

J105D JULY J105D

TOM NEWMAN V (A (A) JULY 1968 MAJOR MINOR SMLP 29
CHRIS JACKSON K (A
TONY DUHIG G (A JON FIELD FL (A ALAN JAMES B (A

J106 JUMBO J106

(A) CITY GIRLS 1978 PYE INT UK 28234

J107 JUNCO PARTNERS J107

RONNIE BARKER (1 (A) JUNCO PARTNERS 197 BARCLAY FR 920193
JOHN WOODS D (1BA (B) JUNCO PARTNERS 1971 PHILIPS 6308 032
DAVE SPROAT B (1BA (1) 1978 REFORMED
KENNY BARKER G (1
BOB SARGEANT K V (BA NEIL PERRY SAX (1 MAV LANDERS V (1 CHARLES HARCOURT G (AB

J108 JUNIORS EYES J108

MICK WAYNE ((A) JUNIOR'S EYES 196 A&M US SP 4189
JOHN REDFERN ((B) BATTERSEA POWER STATION 1969 REGAL ZONOPHONE UK SLRZ 1008
STEVE CHAPMAN (
GROM KELLY (TIM RENWICK G (JOHN CAMBRIDGE (

J109 JUNKYARD ANGELS J109

KEN IVERSON D V (A (A) APPEARED ON MIKE HARRISON LP 1971 ISLAND UK ILPS 9170
PETER BATEY B (A
IAN HERBERT G V K(A FRANK KENYON G V (A

J110 MICKEY JUPP J110

MICKEY JUPP G V K(ABC (A) JUPPANESE 1978 STIFF GER 6.23055 UK SEEZ 10
ROBIN TROWER G (B (A) JUPPANESE 1980 LINE GER 5095
DAVE EDMUNDS G V (A (B) LEGEND (COMP OF 'LEGEND'TRACKS) 1978 STIFF GER 6 23442 UK GET 2
BILLY BREMNER G (A (C) LONG DISTANCE ROMANCER 1979 CHRYSALIS GER 6307 686 UK CHR1261
TONY VISCONTI (B (C) LONG DISTANCE ROMANCER 1080 LINE GER 5099
SANDY ROBERTSON (B (D) OXFORD 1980 LINE GER 5083
IAN DUCK G HCA(D (E) SOME PEOPLE CANT DANCE 1982 A&M UK AMLH 68535 GER LINE 5148
NICK LOWE B (A (1) 1975 BAND
TERRY WILLIAMS D (A
GARY BROOKER K (AB BRUCE LYNCH B (A CHRIS SPEDDING G (A DAVE MATTACKS D (A
MO WITHAM G (B BOB CLOUTER D (B1D BILL FIFIELD D (B CHRIS EAST G (B
STEVE GEERE B (B NIGEL DUNBAR D (B CHRIS COPPING B (B B J WILSON D (B
TIM RENWICK G (B MICK MOODY G (B COLIN GIBSON B (B HENRY SPINETTI D (B
JIMMY JEWELL SAX (B PETE SOLLEY PROD PNO (B GLEN LE FLEUR PERC (B KEVIN GODLEY D V (C
GARY TIBBS B (C LOL CREME G V (C ANDY MACKAY SAX (C PETRINA LORDAN V (C
ERIN LORDAN V (C JOHN PUGH SAX (1 BOB FISH V (1 COLIN MAXWELL D (1
PETE ZEAR G (1 JOY SARNEY V (1 PAUL MITCHELL B (1 FRANK MEAD SAX (1
PETE THE HAT V (1 RON TELEMACQUE D (JOHN GORDON B (MICK GRABHAM G (
DAVE BRONZE B (D

J111 BILL JUSTIS J111

BILL JUSTIS SAX (RAUNCHY & OTHER GUITAR INSTRUMENTALS 1974 SUN UK 6467 010
SID MANKER G (RAUNCHY 19 SUN US 109
ENCHANTED SEA 1972 HARMONY US 31189
SOLID & RAUNCHY 19 PHILIPS INTERNATIONAL US 1950

J112 JUSTWATER J112

GUSKIN MARTIN D (A (A) THE RIFF 1977 BRANDED 2027
TOM KORBA B (A
MITCHELL DANCIK V G (A DANNY RUBIN G (A

J112A JUSTINE J112A

JOHN McBURNIE G (A (A) JUSTINE 1970 UNI UK UNLS 111
VALERIE COPE V PERC(A
LAURIE STYVERS V (A KEITH TROWSDALE G V (A JERRY HOVELL B (A CHRIS GIBB D (A

J113

PATRICK JUVET

PATRICK JUVET V K (ALL — (A) PARIS BY NIGHT — 1977 BARCLAY 90098
SONNY BURKE K (A — (B) PATRICK JUVET — 1978 CASABLANCA US 7107 UK CAL 2028
HENRY DAVIS B (A — (C) LADY NIGHT — 1979 CASABLANCA CAL 2049
SCOTT EDWARDS B (A — (D) STILL ALIVE — 1980 BARCLAY 96112
JIM GORDON D (A — (E) I LOVE AMERICA — 19 BARCLAY 91003
JAMES GADSON D (A
ED GREENE D (A — GARY COLEMAN PERC(A — KEITH FORSEY D (D — BARRY FINNERTY G (C
PARKER G (A — LEE RITENOUR G (AD — ERNIE WATTS HRNS (A — JIM HORN SAX (A
MIKE BODDIKER K (AD — K SCHAEFFER STRINGS (A — GEORGES RODI SYN (A — RUSSELL DABNEY D (AC
ALFONSO CAREY B (BC — JIMMY LEE G (BC — ROGER LEE G (BC — NATHANIEL WHITE K (B
ERROL BENNETT CONGA(B — M GRILLO PERC (B — PHIL KRAUS PERC (B — BABATUNDE OLATUNJI PERC(B
GEORGE DEVENS PERC (B — JEFF BAXTER G (D — TOM POLITE PNO (C — NATHANIEL WICKIE K (C
JIMMY MAELEN PERC (C — TREVOR WHITEHEAD PERC (C — TREVOR VEITCH G (D — LES HURDLE B (D
THOR BALDURRSON K (D

K1

K C & THE SUNSHINE BAND

HARRY WAYNE 'KC'CASEY K(ALL — (A) DO IT GOOD — 1974 JAYBOY JSL 9 + US TK 500
ROBERT JOHNSON D (GH — (A) DO IT GOOD — 197 TK UK TK 82505 + US TK 600
RICHARD FINCH B D (GH — (B) K C & THE SUNSHINE BAND — 1975 JAYBOY JSL 9 + US TK 603
JEROME SMITH G (GH — (C) SOUND OF SUNSHINE — 1975 US TK 604
FERMIN GOYTISOLO PERC (GH — (D) PART THREE — 1977 TK UK TK 82507 + US TK 605
MIKE LEWIS SAX (G — (E) THE BEST OF — 197 JAYBOY UK JSB 101
VINNIE TANNO TPT (G — (F) I LIKE TO DO IT — 1977 PRESIDENT JRE 500
KEN FAULK TPT (G — (G) WHO DO YA LOVE — 1978 TK UK TK 86100 + US TK 607
WHIT SIDENER SAX (G — (H) DO YOU WANNA PARTY — 1979 TK UK 83369
BEVERLEY CHAMPION V (G — (I) GREATEST HITS — 1980 TK UK 83385
JEANETTE WILLIAMS V (G — (J) SPACE CADET — 1980 TK UK
(K) THE PAINTER — 1981 EPIC UK 85219

K1A

JOSEF K

JOSEF K (A — (A) ONLY FUN IN TOWN — 1981 POSTCARD UK 811

K2

K G B

RAY KENNEDY V (AB — (A) K G B — 1976 MCA UK MCF 2749 US 2166
MIKE BLOOMFIELD G (A — (B) MOTION — 1976 MCA UK MCF 2773 US 2221
RICK GRECH B (A
CARMINE APPICE D (AB — BARRY GOLDBERG K (AB — BEN SCHULTZ G (B — GREG SUTTON B (B

K3

KAJANUS / PICKETT

GEORG KAJANUS (A — (A) HI HO SILVER — 1973 SIGNPOST UK SGZ500 MCA US 304
PHIL PICKETT (A

K3A

HARRY KAKOULLI

HARRY KAKOULLI V B SYN G D(A — (A) EVEN WHEN I'M NOT — 1980 OVAL UK OVLP 505
GARRELL REDFEARN SYN (A
NIGEL SHARPE G (A — NICK ROBBINS D (A

K3B ****

KAK

DELMER C PATTEN G V (A — (A) KAK — 19 EPIC US 26423
GARY L YODEN G V (A
JOSEPH DAMRELL B SIT(A — CHRISTOPHER LOCKHEED D K V(A

K4

KALA

JOHNNIE MILES D V (A — (A) KALA — 1973 BRADLEYS UK BRADL 1002
PERRY SINCLAIR G V (A
SID GARDNER B V (A — DAVE CODLING G V (A — DAVE SKINNER PNO (A — PAUL BENNETT V (A
LES NICOL G V (A — JACK STEVENSON PERC (A — PETER ARNESEN PNO (A — SHIVA JONES V K (A
CAROL GRIMES V (A — JOHN BARHAM CELLO (A

K5

KALEIDOSCOPE

PETE DALTREY K (— (A) TANGERINE DREAM — 1967 FONTANA UK TL 5448
EDDIE PUMER G (— (B) FAINTLY BLOWING — 1969 FONTANA UK STL 5491
DANNY BRIDGMAN F (
STEVE CLARK B (

K6

KALEIDOSCOPE(US)

FENRUS EPP VLN K(ABCDE **** — (A) SIDE TRIPS — 1967 EPIC US 26304
JOHN VIDICAN PERC (AB — (B) BEACON FROM MARS — 1968 EPIC US 26333
SOLOMON FELDTHOUSE G V (ABCDE — (C) INCREDIBLE KALEIDOSCOPE — 1969 EPIC US 26467
DAVID LINDLEY VLN G V(ABCD — (D) BERNICE — 1970 CBS UK 64005 US 26508
CHRIS DARROW FDL G V (ABE — (E) WHEN SCOPES COLLIDE — 1976 ISLAND UK ILPS 9462
STUART BROTMAN B V (CDE — (E) WHEN SCOPES COLLIDE — 1976 PACIFIC ARTS US 102
PAUL LAGOS D V (CDE — (F) BROTHER MARY (ZABRISKIE POINT — 19 POLYDOR 2315 002
RICHARD APLAN FLT (
JEFF KAPLAN G V (D — BARRY FRIEDMAN PROD (A — PETE MADLIN G (B — JOHN WARE D (E
RON JOHNSON B (D — DE PARIS LETANTE G (E
****CONNIE CRILL/MAX BUDA/TEMPLETON PARCELY ARE ALL FENRUS EPP

K6A

KALEIDOSKOP

HARDY WRIEDEN V (A — (A) 100% LIVE — 1982 ROCKFARM ROLP 8101
HANNO BONSDORF G (A
NORBERT WESCH G V (A — GUNTER BLENDERMANN B (A — DIETER SCHMIDT D (A

K6B

KALYAN

(A) ALL THE WAY LIVE — 1980 RCA 3514

K7

AMORY KANE

AMORY KANE G V (AB — (A) MEMORIES OF TIME UNWOUND — 1968 MCA UK MUPS 348
DAVE PEGG B (B — (B) JUST TO BE THERE — 1970 CBS UK 63849
NED BALEN D (B

K8

KANGAROO

JOHN HALL B (A — (A) KANGAROO — 1968 ? US
TEDDY SPELEOD G (A
N D SMART II D (A — BARBARA KEITH V (A

K9 KANSAS K9

PHIL EHART D (ABCDE (A) MASQUE 1975 KIRSHNER US 33806
STEVE WALSH K V (ABCDE (B) KANSAS 1975 KIRSHNER US 32817 UK 80174
ROBBIE STEINHARDT VLN V(ABCDE (C) SONG FOR AMERICA 1976 KIRSHNER US 33385 UK 80740
DAVE HOPE B (ABCDE (D) LEFTOVERTURE 1976 KIRSHNER US 34224 UK 81728
RICH WILLIAMS G (ABCDE (E) POINT OF KNOW RETURN 1977 KIRSHNER US 34929 UK 82234
KERRY LIVGREN G K (ABCDE (F) TWO FOR THE SHOW 1978 KIRSHNER US 35560 UK 88318
(G) MONOLITH 1979 KIRSHNER US 36008 UK 83644
(H)AUDIO VISIONS 1980 KIRSHNER US 36588 UK 84500

K10 PAUL KANTNER K10

PAUL KANTNER G V (ABC (A) ITS A FRESH WIND THAT BLOWS .... 1970 RCA US LPS 4448 UK SF 8163
GRACE SLICK K V (ABC (B) SUNFIGHTER 1971 GRUNT FTR 1002
DAVID FREIBERG V (AC (C) BARON VON TOLLBOOTH 1973 GRUNT BFLI 0148
JACK CASADY B (ABC
POINTER SISTERS V (C PAPA JOHN CREACH VLN (BC JOHN BARBATA D (C CRAIG CHAQUICO G (C
MICKEY HART D (AC PETER KAUKONEN G (A PHIL SAWYER (AB BILL KREUTZMANN D (A
CHRIS ETHRIDGE B (C DAVID CROSBY V G (ABC JORMA KAUKONEN G (ABC RON DUDLEY (A
JOEY COVINGTON D PERC(AB BILL THOMPSON (A JERRY GARCIA G BAN(ABC JACK TRAYLOR V (C
HARVEY BROOKS B (A GRAHAM NASH V PERC(AB SPENCER DRYDEN (B

K10A KARAT K10A

BERD ROMER G ((A) FIRST 19 AMIGA GER 855573
HERBERT DREILICH V ((B) UBER SIEBEN BRUCKEN 19 AMIGA GER 855695
HENNING PROTZMANN B ((C) SCHWANENKONIG 19 AMIGA GER 855770
ULRICH ED SWILLMS V K (
MICHAEL SCHWADT D (

K10B JURGEN KARG K10B

JURGEN KARG ((A) ELEKTRONISCHE MYTHEN 1976 MOOD 23 555

K10C BILLY KARLOFF K10C

BILLY KARLOFF V (ALL (A) THE MANIAC 1978 JUPITER GER 26373
CHRIS PYE G V (A (B) LET YOUR FINGERS DO THE TALKING 1981 WB 56894
JULIAN G (A
ED DUANE B (A PEDRO ORTIZ D V (A PAUL JELLIMAN G (B NEIL HAY G V (A
GLEN BUGLASS B (B DOLPHIN TAYLOR D V(B CHUCK LEAVELL PNO (B STEVE NATHAN SYN (B
RICK KURTZ G (B

K10D KAROLINE K10D

SERGE TAFINI V (A (A) KAROLINE 1980 WEA NL 58141
JEFF CASTALDI G V (A
VINCENT CASTALDI B V (A DANIEL APROSIO PERC V(A

K10E CHRIS KARRER K10E

CHRIS KARRER G V SAX(A (A) CHRIS KARRER 1980 VINYL GER 6 24328
CURT CRESS D (A
GEORGE INCHL K (A GERRARD CARBONNEL B (A JORG EVERS G B V (A

K11 KARTHARGO K11

JOEY ALBRECHT V G (ABCDE (A) KARTHARGO 1971 BASF GERM 2021/185/1
GLENN CORNICK B (C (B) SECOND STEP 1973 BASF US 217 80 GERM 2021/180/1
INGO BISCHOF K V (ABCDE (C) ROCK'N'ROLL TESTAMENT 1974 BELLAPHON GERM BLPS 19201
TOMMY GOLDSCHMIDT D (ABCDE (D) LIVE AT THE ROXY 1976 BELLAPHON GERM BDA 7506
NORBERT LEHEMANN D (B (E) LIVE 1976 BELLAPHON GERM B 15190
KONNI BOMMARIUS D (C
GERALD HARTWIG B V PERC(ABD WOLFGANG BROCK D PERC (A RINGO FUNK D (D REINHARD BOPP G V (D
VICKI BROWN V (C BARRY ST JOHN V (C JOANNE WILLIAMS V (C TOM CUNNINGHAM V (C

K11A NICK KATZMAN K11A

NICK KATZMAN G V (ALL (A) MISSISSIPPI RIVER BOTTOM BLUES 1975 KICKING MULE US !!!
RAY GOLDSTEIN G (B (B) SPARKLING RAGTIME & HARDBITTEN BLUES80 KICKING MULE US 167
TERRY GARTHWAITE V(AB

K12 JORMA KAUKONEN K12

JORMA KAUKONEN G V (ALL (A) QUAH 1975 GRUNT US BLFI 0209
TOM HOBSON V (A (B) JORMA 1979 RCA 13446
DENNY DEGORIO B (C (C) BARBECUE KING 1980 RCA 13727
JOHN STENCH D (C
HILARY STENCH B (C MIKE BUTERA SAX (C LARRY WHITMAN V (C STEVE HUFF V (C

K13 PETER KAUKONEN K13

PETER KAUKONEN G V (A (A) BLACK KANGAROO 1971 GRUNT US FTR 1006
SHELLEY SILVERMAN D (A
TERRY ADAMS CELLO(A DIANE EARL V (A LARRY WEISBERG B (A NICK BUCK K (A
PETER MARSHALL B (A MARK RYAN B (A JOEY COVINGTON D V (A

K13A RYO KAWASAKI K13A

RYO KAWASAKI G (AB (A) JUICE 19 RCA US 1855
ALEX BLAKE B (B (B) NATURES REVENGE 1978 MPS 61332
BUDDY WILLIAMS D (B
DAVE LIEBMAN SAX (B TOM COSTER K (A

K14 JOHN KAY K14

JOHN KAY V G HCA (ALL (A) FORGOTTEN SONGS & UNSUNG HEROES 1972 DUNHILL US 50120 UK PROBE 1054
KENT HENRY G (AB (B) MY SPORTIN' LIFE 1973 DUNHILL US 50147 UK PROBE 8011
GEORGE BIONDO B (AB (B) MY SPORTIN' LIFE 1973 UK PROBE 6274
PENTTI GLAN D (AB (C) ALL IN GOOD TIME 1978 MERCURY US 1 3715 UK 9110 054
HUGH SULLIVAN K (AB (D) JOHN KAY & SPARROW 19 CBS UK 63564
LARRY KNECHTEL K (B
BILL COOPER B (B ALAN O'DAY K (B DANNY KORTCHMAR G (B RUSS KUNKEL D (B
LEE SKLAR B (B MIKE UTLEY PNO (B DARRYL DRAGON K (B RICHARD PODOLOR K MAND(B
SHIRLEY MATTHEWS V (B GLORIA JONES V (B VANETTA FIELDS V (B STAN FARBER V (B
GENE MORFORD V (B JOAN SLIWIN V (A MARSHA TEMMER V (A ALEXANDRA SLIWIN V (A

K16 KAYAK K16

CEES VAN LEEUWEN B (AB — (A) SEE SEE THE SUN — 1973 HARVEST UK SHSP4033 US 11305 NL 24933
TON SCHERPENZEEL K (ABCDEFGHI — (B) KAYAK — 1974 HARVEST UK SHSP4036 NL 24993
MAX WERNER V D K((ABCDEFGHI — (C) THE LAST ENCORE — 19
JOHAN SLAGER G (ABCDEFGH — (D) ROYAL BED BOUNCER — 1975 VERTIGO UK 6360 530 US JANUS7023
PIM KOOPMAN D (ABD — (D) ROYAL BED BOUNCER — 1975 EMI N 0625271
CHARLES SCHOUTEN D (e — (E) STARLIGHT DANCER — 1977 VERTIGO UK 6360 856 US JANUS7034
BERT VELDKAMP B (DI — (F) THE BEST OF — 1978 EMI NL 25828
THEO DEJONG B (E — (G) PHANTOM OF THE NIGHT — 1978 VERTIGO NL 6413 507 US JANUS7039
GERRIT JAN LEENDERS V (A — (H) PERISCOPE LIFE — 1980 VERTIGO EURO 6413 960 MERCURY US SRM13824
ERNST REIZIGER CELLO(A — (I) MERLIN — 1981 VERTIGO EURO 6399 115
GINNY BUSCH VLN (A
MARTIN KOEMAN VLN (A — RIJN PETER DE KLERK (A — EDWARD REEKERS V (GHI — IRENE LINDERS V (HGI
JIM PRICE HRNS (H — KATHERINE LAPHORN V (GHI — PETER SCHERPENZEEL B (GHI — LEE THORNBURG HRNS(H
JIM GORDON SAX (H — JACK LANCASTER PROD (E — G PERLEE BARRELORGAN (A — REIN VANDER BROCK WIND(I
BENNY BEHR STR (I

K16A THOMAS JEFFERSON KAYE K16A

THOMAS JEFFERSON KAYE G V(AB — (A) THOMAS JEFFERSON KAYE — 1973 PROBE UK SPB 1074
MICHAEL OMARTIAN K (B — (B) FIRST GRADE — 1974 DUNHILL US 50142 ABC UK ABCL5048
DONALD FAGEN K (AB
WALTER BECKER B (AB — JOE OSBORNE B (B — JIM GORDON D (B — VIC FELDMAN PERC (AB
RICK DERRINGER G (AB — DEAN PARKS G (B — RICHIE FURAY V (B — TIM SCHMIT V (B
JEFF BAXTER G (AB — DUSTY SPRINGFIELD V (B — CLYDIE KING V (AB — SHIRLEY MATTHEWS V (AB
JIM MASON V (B — JIMMY HASKEL HRNS (B — RICK SLOSSEN D (A — JOE FRANK CORROLA B (A
TOM SALISBURY PNO (A — RANDY HOBBS B (A — VENETTA FIELDS V (A — DAVID PALMER V (A
DOROTHY MORRISON V (A — DIANE MORRISON V (A — CHRIS WILLIAMSON V (A — MARK SPRINGER V (A
MICKI ST CLAIR V (A

K17 ERIC KAZ K17

ERIC KAZ V G K HCA SYN (ABC — (A) IF YOU'RE LONELY — 1972 ATLANTIC UK K 40468 US SD 7246
BOB BABITT B (B — (B) CUL DE SAC — 1973 ATLANTIC US SD 7290
PAUL BARRERE G (B — (C) FULLER/KAZ — 1978 CBS US 35324
MALCOLM CECIL SYN (B
GORDON EDWARDS B (B — BOOKER T JONES HRNS K G(B — JOHN KELSO HRNS (B — JIM KELTNER D (B
RAY LUCAS D (B — TIM MOORE V (B — BERNARD PURDIE D (B — JEROME RICHARDSON SAX (B
ROCKY DZIDZORNU PERC (B — SNEAKY PETE KLEINOW STEEL(B — DAVID T WALKER G (B — CRAIG FULLER G V (C
DAN DUGMORE G (C — LEE SKLAR B (C — RUSS KUNKEL D PERC(C — CRAIG DOERGE K (C
DON GROLNICK K (C — STEVE LUKATHER G (C — CHARLES VEAL VLN (C — ROLLICE DALE VLA (C
DENNIS KARMAZYN CELLO(C — LEAH KUNKEL V (C — LEO SAYER V (C — JAMES NEWTON HOWARD K (C

K19 LINDA KEEL K19

LINDA KEEL V (A — (A) LADY ROCK'N'ROLL — 1978 PYE UK NSPL 28273
JACKY CHALARD B (A
PATRICK VERBEC G (A — MOREAU SERRI G (A — JEAN PIERRE PREVOTAT D (A — JEAN YVES D'ANGELO K (A
ROLLY HCA (A — RENE MORIZURE SAX (A — PIERROT PLOQUIN TPT(A — FREDDY OMEZIAN TPT(A
ERIC BAMI V (A

K20 JOHN 'SPEEDY' KEEN K20

JOHN'SPEEDY'KEEN V G K D(AB — (A) PREVIOUS CONVICTIONS — 1971 TRACK UK 2406 105 US MCA 331
JIMMY McCULLOCH G (B — (B) Y' KNOW WOT I MEAN — 1975 ISLAND UK ILPS 9338
DAVE McDOUGALL K (
BUTCH SANDFORD G (B — TERRY WILSON B (B — EMANUEL RENTZOS K (B — TONY BRAUNAGEL D (B
RABBIT BUNDRICK K (B — B J COLE STEEL(B — PETER VANDER PUIJE HRNS (B — LIZA STRIKE V (B
GEORGE LEE HRNS (B — EDDIE QUANSAH HRNS (B

K21 ACE KEFFORD K21

ACE KEFFORD B (1 — (1) ACE KEFFORD STAND 1969
COZY POWELL D (1
DAVE BALL G (1 — DENNIS BALL (1

K21A KEITH K21A

DAVID JIMINEZ G (A — (A) THE ADVENTURES OD KEITH — 1969 RCA US LSP 4143
JOE COYLE G (A
DAVE FIEBRT B (A — RICK FOX D (A

K22 CASEY KELLY K22

CASEY KELLY V G HCA (AB — (A) CASEY KELLY — 1972 ELEKTRA US 75040 UK K 42121
LEE SKLAR B (A — (B) FOR SALE — 197 ELEKTRA
RUSS KUNKEL D (A
CRAIG DOERGE K (A — SNEAKY PETE KLEINOW STEEL(A — AL GARTH FDL (A — DANNY COHEN ACC (A
JIM MESSINA G (A

K22A DAVE KELLY K22A

DAVE KELLY G V PERC(ALL — (A) KEEPS IT IN THE FAMILY — 1969 MERCURY UK 20151
STEVE GURL K (DE — (B) DAVE KELLY — 1971 MERCURY UK 6310 001
BOB HALL PNO (ABDE — (C) SURVIVORS — 1979 APPALOOSA ITALY AP 001
PAUL JONES HCA (DE — (D) WILLING — 1979 APPALOOSA ITALY AP 003
GARY FLETCHER B (DE — (E) FEELS RIGHT — 1981 COOLKING UK CKLP1
JO ANN KELLY V (AB
ANDY RYGA G V (A — KEITH TILLMAN B (A — PETER GEE G (A — BOB BRUNNING B (B
ALAN HAWKSHAW K (B — BARRY GUARD D (B — RANDY JONES D (B — STEVE RYE HCA(B
ALAN PARKER G (B — HERBIE FLOWERS B (B — CLEM CATTINI D (B — JOHN ALTMAN WIND(B
JOHNNY DEAN PERC (B — KENNY WHEELER HRN (B — PETER SNELL HARP (B — TOM McGUINNESS G B (E
LOU STONEBRIDGE K V (E — ROY MORGAN D (E — GRAHAM PRESKETT VLN (E — KEITH NELSON BJO (E
JOHN EARLE SAX (E — STEVE BENNETT V (E

K23 JO ANN KELLY K23

JO ANN KELLY G V (ABCD — (A) SAME THING ON THEIR MINDS — 1971 SUNSET UK SLS 50209
JOHN FAHEY G (B — (B) WITH FAHEY,MANN & MILLER — 1972 BLUE GOOSE US 2009
ALAN SEIDLER (B — (C) JO ANN KELLY — 1969 CBS UK 63841 US EPIC 26491
WOODY MANN (B — (D) DO IT — 1976 RED RAG RRR 006
PETE EMERY (D
TONY McPHEE G V (A — JOHN MILLER G V (A

K24 JONATHAN KELLY K24

JONATHAN KELLY V G K D(ALL — (A) JONATHAN KELLY 1970 PARLOPHONE UK PCS 7114
BRIAN GASCOIGNE MARIM (E — (B) TWICE AROUND THE HOUSES 1972 RCA UK SF 8262
MARK GRIFFITHS B (C — (C) WAIT TILL THEY CHANGE THE BACKDROP 73 RCA UK SF 8353
ROY BABBINGTON B (C — (D) WAITING ON YOU 1974 RCA UK LPL 15022
RAY DUFFY D (C — (E) TWO DAYS IN WINTER 1865 RCA UK SF 8415
PETER WOOD K (BC
THUNDERTHIGHS V (C — BARRY DESOUZA D (C — BRUCE THOMAS B (C — WILLIE WILSON D (C
TIM RENWICK G FLT V (BC — IAIN SUTHERLAND V (C — GAVIN SUTHERLAND V (C — MICHAEL OLIVER D (C
LENNOX JAMES PERC (C — LUCIANO BRAVO D (C — KEN SCOTT PERC (C — TREVOR WILLIAMS B (D
CHAS JANKEL G (D — DAVE SHEEN D (DE — SNOWY WHITE G (D — LARRY STEELE D (B
GERRY CONWAY D (B — RICK KEMP B (B — HARVEY BURNS D (B — DONAL LUNNY G (B
DAVE BALL G (B — JIM TOOMEY D (B — BYRON LYEFOOT D (B — JERRY DONAHUE G (B
KUMA HARADA B G PERC(E — DARRYL LEE QUE CONGA(E — PIZZA QUARTET (E

K25 TONY KELLY K25

TONY KELLY G V (A — (A) BRING ME BACK 1972 POLYDOR UK 2383 123
PAUL MILLINS K (A
JACK MILLS G (A — KEITH EVANS B (A — CODY PERC HCA(A — TERRY STANNARD D PERC (A
CLAUDIA LENNEAR V (A — KATHI MacDONALD V (A — LINDA NOVEMBER V (A — HELEN MILES V (A
HILDA HARRIS V (A

K26 EDDIE KENDRICKS K26

EDDIE KENDRICKS V (ALL — (A) ALL BY MYSELF 1971 TAMLA US 309 UK STML 11186
(B) PEOPLE HOLD ON 1973 TAMLA US 315 UK STML 11213
(C) EDDIE HENDRICKS 1973 TAMLA US 327 UK STML 11245
(D) BOOGIE DOWN 1974 TAMLA US 330 UK STML 11266
(E) FOR YOU 1975 TAMLA US 335 UK STMA 8020
(F) THE HIT MAN 1975 TAMLA US 338 UK STML 12001
(G) HE'S A FRIEND 1976 TAMLA US 343 UK STML 12016
(H) GOING UP IN SMOKE 1976 TAMLA US 346 UK STML 12043
(J) SLICK 1977 TAMLA US 356 UK STML 12071
(K) AT HIS BEST 1978 TAMLA US 354 UK STML 12080
(L) VINTAGE 78 1978 ARISTA US 4170 UK SPART 1040
(M) SOMETHING MORE 1981 ARISTA US 4250
(N) LOVE KEYS 1981 ATLANTIC UK K 50779

K26A GRAHAM KENDRICK K26A

GRAHAM KENDRICK G V (AB — (A) FIGHTER 1980 KINGSWAY DOVE 55
DAVE McSPARFAN D (B
SPUD SPURLING B (B — LES MOIR B (B — ANDY BILLUPS G (B — NEIL COSTELLO G (B
CHRIS EATON PNO (B — BASIL MEADE K V (B — JOHN PANTRY SYN (B — MAXINE SIMPSON V (B

K26B RAY KENNEDY K26B

RAY KENNEDY V (A — (A) RAY KENNEDY 19 CBS US 36395

K27 CHRIS KENNER K27

CHRIS KENNER V (A — (A) LAND OF A THOUSAND DANCES 1963 ATLANTIC US SD 8117

K27A KENNY & THE KASUALS K27A

KENNY DANIELS V G HCA B(ABC — (A) IMPACT 1965 MARK US
TOMMY NICHOLS B (B — (B) LIVE AT THE STUDIO CLUB 1966 MARK US MARK 5000
LEE LIGHTFOOT B (AB
DAVID BLACKLEY D (AB — PAUL ROACH K (AB — JERRY SMITH G (AC — ROSEBUD B (C
WALLY WILSON K (C — GREGG DANIEL B (C — RON MASON K PERC(C — MAX BALL SAX (C
JACK MORGAN G (C — KARL TOMORROW K (C — TONY VINSEY VLN (C — CAIN SISTERS V (C

K28 KENSINGTON MARKET K28

ALEX DAROU B (— (A) KENSINGTON MARKET, AVENUE ROAD 1968 WB US WS 1754
LUKE GIBSON V (— (B) AARDVARK 1969 WB US
GENE MARTYNEC V G PNO(
KEITH McKIE G V (— JIMMY WATSON D (

K28A KLARK KENT K28A

KLARK'STEWART COPELAND'KENT — (A) KLARK KENT 10" 1980 A&M UK AMLE68511 IRS US 70600

K28B PAUL KENT K28B

PAUL KENT V K (AB — (A) P C KENT 1970 RCA UK SF 8083
DAVID RICHARDS V G K(A — (B) PAUL KENT 1971 B&C UK CAS 1044
GAVIN WATSON V G B(AB
JOHN WARD D (A — PAT DONALDSON B (B — TIM RENWICK G (B — TONY REEVES B (B
KATHY KISSOON V (B — MIKE LONDON V (B — GERRY CONWAY D (B — RAY WARLEIGH WIND (B
ROGER POWELL D (B — CHRIS TURNER HCA (B — MAC KISSOON V (A — ANDY ROBERTS G (B

K29 KENTUCKY COLONELS K29

CLARENCE WHITE G V (ALL — (A) NEW SOUND OF BLUEGRASS 1963 BRIAR US M109
ROLAND WHITE V MAND(BCDEFGH — (B) APPALACHIAN SWING 1964 WORLD PACIFIC US 1821
BILLY LEE LATHAM BAN ABCDEF — (B) KENTUCKY COLONELS 1974 UA RI 29514 US ROUNDER 0070
ERIC WHITE B (EFG — (C) LIVING IN THE PAST (1961/65) 1975 BRIAR US 4202
LEROY MACK DOB (ABC — (D) LIVE IN L.A. WITH SCOTTY STONEMAN 1975 BRIAR US 4206
DENIS MORRIS G (EG — (E) KENTUCKY COLONELS (1965) 1977 ROUNDER US 070
BOBBY SLONE FDL (ABC — (F) CLARENCE WHITE & KENTUCKY COLONELS1980 ROUNDER US 098
SCOTT STONEMAN FDL (CDE — (G) KENTUCKY COLONELS 66 1978 SHILOH US 4084
BOB WARFORD BAN (EFG — (H) THE WHITE BROTHERS LIVE IN SWEDEN 1979 ROUNDER US 073
ROGER BUSH B V (ABCDEF
BOBBY CRANE FDL (G — ALAN MUNDE BAN (H

K29A WOODY KERN K29A

JOHN SANDERSON WIND VLN(A — (A) THE AWFUL DISCOSURES OF MARIA MONK 1967 PYE UK NSPL 18273
RICK KENTON K (A
MIKE WHEAT B (A — STEVE HARRIS D (A

K29B SARAH KERNOCHAN K29B

SARAH KERNOCHAN V PNO(AB — (A) HOUSE OF PAIN 1973 RCA US 10343
BOB MANN G (A — (B) BEAT AROUND THE BUSH 1974 RCA US 10671
JOE BECK G (A
JOE COCUZZO PERC (A — VINNIE BELL G (A — TONY LEVIN B (A — LYN CHRISTIE B (A
RALPH SCHUCKETT K (A — TOM KEENE K (B — ROBERT WACHTEL G (B — EARL PALMER D (B
LYLE RITZ B (B — DAN DUGMORE STEEL(B — LINCOLN MAYORGA K (B — BOB JAMES K (B
ED SUMMERLIN SYN (B — PETER JAMESON G (B — RON TUTT D (B — PAUL HUMPHREY D (B
MIKE DEASY G (B — BOB BRUCE FDL (B — FRANK MAROCCO ACC (B

K30 **DOUG KERSHAW** K30

DOUG KERSHAW G V (ALL (A) THE CAJUN WAY 1969 WB US WS 1820
JOHN CHRISTOPHER G (EF (B) SPANISH MOSS 1970 WB US WS 1861
JIMMY COLVARD G (E (C) DOUG KERSHAW 1971 WB US WS 1906
TROY SEALS G (E (D) SWAMP GRASS 1972 WB US BS 2581
BUDDY KILLEN PERC (E (E) DEVILS ELBOW 1972 WB UK K 46196 US BS 2649
WILLIE ACKERMAN D (E (F) DOUGLAS JAMES KERSHAW 1973 WB UK K 46264 US BS 2725
STU BASORE STEEL(E (G) MAMA KERSHAWS BOY 1974 WB US BS 2793
CURLY CHALKER STEEL(E (H) ALIVE & KICKIN' 1975 WB US BS 2851
BOBBY EMMONS K (EF (I) RAGIN' CAJUN 1976 WB US BS 2910
BOBBY WOOD K (EF (J) FLIP FLOP FLY 1977 WB US BS 3025
KARL HIMMEL D (E (K) LOUISIANA MAN 1978 WB US BS 3166
JOE ALLEN B (EF (L) LOUISIANA CAJUN COUNTRY 1979 STARFLITE US 2003
JERRY CARRIGAN D (E (A) M) INSTANT HERO 1981 SCOTTI BROS US 37428
HARRISON CALLOWAY TPT (J
CHARLIE McCOY HCA (E TOMMY COGBILL B (E KENNY MALONE D (EF JORDANAIRES V (EF
CHIP MOMAN G (F RICHARD MAINEGRA G V (F REGGIE YOUNG G (F MIKE LEECH B (F
LARRIE LONDIN D (F DON SHEFFIELD TPT (F DWAYNE WEST V (F GORDON STOKER V (F
RAY WALKER V (F HOYT HAWKINS V (F DOTTIE DELEONIBUS V (F BILL STEWART D (J
MARTY VADALABENE D (J CALVIN ARLINE B (J MAX PAUL SCHWENNSEN G V (J JOHNNY SANDLIN G (J
JIMMY NALLS G (J ELVIN BISHOP G (J NEIL URPEN K (J JOHN HUGHEY STEEL(J
BONNIE BRAMLETT V (J RONNIE EADES SAX (J CHARLES ROSE TROM (J PETE PENDRAS G (J
AL KAATZ G (J DR JOHN K (J ANNIE ROSE DEARMAS V (J RANDALL BRAMBLETT SAX(J
HARVEY THOMPSON SAX (J

K31 **RUSTY KERSHAW** K31

RUSTY KERSHAW (A (A) CAJUN IN BLUES COUNTRY 1970 COTILLION US SD 9030

K32 **RUSTY & DOUG KERSHAW** K32

DOUG KERSHAW FDL V(ABC (A) LOUISIANA MAN 1971 LONDON UK LGE 114
RUSTY KERSHAW G V (ABC (B) LOUISIANA MAN 1976 DJM UK DJB 26080
TOMMY JACKSON FDL (B (C) CAJUN COUNTRY ROCKERS 1979 BEAR FAMILY GERM BRX 15036
HOWARD JOHNSON G (B
CHET ATKINS G (B EDDIE HILL G (B HAROLD RAY BRADLEY G (B HANK GARLAND G (B
RAY EDENTON G (B FLOYD CHANCE B (B WOODY WOODHAMS B (B ERNIE NEWTON B (B
JIMMY DAY STEEL(B BOB FOSTER STEEL (B PETE DRAKE STEEL(B CHARLES THERIOT STEEL(B
LOUIS FOURNERAT STEEL(B FLOYD CRAMER PNO (B WILEY BARKDULL PNO V(B MARK H HARMAN D (B
CAROLEE COOPER V (B

K32A **KESTREL** K32A

DAVE BLACK G V (A (A) KESTREL 1975 CUBE HIFLY 19
JOHN COOK G V SYN (A
DAVID WHITAKER D PERC(A FENWICK MOIR B (A TOM KNOWLES V (A

K32B **KEY** K32B

VOLKER LANGEFELD V(MULTI INST)A (A) FIT ME IN 1978 ELECTROLA EURO IC 064 45137
ALAN WARREN D (A

K32C **KEW A GO GO PARTY** K32C

KEES MAAS (A (A) LIFE IS LIKE A PENGUIN 1980 IDIOTEN NL 7777
WILLEM WISSELIWK (A
JOHAN VISSER G B (A FRED BONTHUIS D (A

K33 **KEY LARGO** K33

PAT McAULIFFE V (A (A) KEY LARGO 1970 BLUE HORIZON UK 7 63859
LAURENCE GARMAN HCA (A
BOB SAVAGE K (A LAURIE SANFORD G (A TOM STEAD B (A KENNY LAMB D (A

K33A **TROYCE KEY & JJ MALONE & THE RHYTHM ROCKERS** K33A

TROYCE KEY (A (A) I'VE GOTTA NEW CAR 1980 RED LIGHTNIN' UK 0028
J J MALONE (A

K34 **BOBBY KEYS** K34

BOBBY KEYS SAX (A (A) BOBBY KEYS 1972 WB UK K46141
JIM PRICE HRN K(A
JIM GORDON D (A RINGO STARR D (A CORKY LAING D (A JACK BRUCE B (A
CARL RADLE B (A FELIX PAPPALRDI B (A KLAUS VOORMANN B (A MIKE UTLEY K (A
NICKY HOPKINS K (A JOHN URIBE G (A DAVE MASON G (A LESLIE WEST G (A
CHARLIE FREEMAN G (A GEORGE HARRISON G (A

K34A **KEYS** K34A

(A) THE KEYS ALBUM 1981 A&M US 4868 UK AMLH 68526

K35 **KHAN** K35

STEVE HILLAGE G (12A (A) SPACE SHANTY 1972 BRAIN GER UK DERAM SDLR11
ERIC PEACHEY D (12A (A) SPACE SHANTY 1978 PVC US 7902
NICK GREENWOOD B (A1 (1) APRIL 1971 JULY 1972 (B) JULY 1972 NOV 1972
NIGEL SMITH B (2
DICK HENNINGHAM K (1 DAVE STEWART K (2A

K36 **CHAKA KHAN** K36

CHAKA KHAN V (A (A) CHAKA 1978 WB US BSK 3245 UK K56560
RICHARD TEE K (AC (B) NAUGHTY 1980 WB US BSK 3385 UK K56713
KERMIT MOORE CELLO(A (C) WHAT CHA GONNA DO FOR ME 1981 WB US 3526 UK K56888
TERRI GONZALES V (A
STEVE FERRONE D (AC PHIL UPCHURCH G (A HAMISH STUART G V (AC WILL LEE B V (A
ANTHONY JACKSON B (AC BROOK TILLOTSON HRNS (A JIM BUFFINGTON HRNS (A ARTHUR JENKINS K (A
ONNIE McINTYRE G (A MARK STEVENS B V (AC SAMMY FIGUEROA CONGA(A TONY MAIDEN G (A
RICHARD BOCK CELLO(A CISSY HOUSTON V (A DAVID LASLEY V (A RANDY BRECKER TPT (AC
GEORGE YOUNG SAX 'A MICHAEL BRECKER SAX (AC GENE BIANCO HARP (A ALAN GORRIE V (A
GEORGE BENSON V (A RAFAEL CRUZ CONGA(A DAVID SANBORN SAX (A JOHN CLARK HRNS (A
PAUL FAULISE TROM (A JESSE LEVY CELLO(A BARRY ROGERS TROM (A RONNIE CUBER SAX (A
LEON PENDARVIS K (A RICK MAROTTA D (A CORNELL DUPREE G (A KEN BISCHEL SYN (A
EDDIE DANIELS FLT (A PHIL BODNER FLT (A GEORGE MARGE FLT (A AIRTO MOREIRA PERC (A
ANDREW KASTNER G (A LARRY WILLIAMS K SAX(C DAVID WILLIAMS G (C GREG PHILLINGANES K (C
MIKE SEMBELLO G (C RAY POUNDS D (C PAULINHO DA COSTA PERC (C DIZZY GILLESPIE TPT (C
HERBIE HANCOCK K (C RONNIE FOSTER K (C ABRAHAM LABORIEL B (C CASEY SCHELIERELL D(C
CHRUSHER BENNETT PERC (C JERRY HEY TPT (C DAVID RICHARDS SYN (C HIRAM BULLOCK G (C

K37 STEVE KHAN K37

STEVE KHAN G (ALL (A) TIGHTROPE 1978 CBS US 34857 UK 82230
JEFF MIRANOV G (C (B) BLUE MAN 1978 CBS US 35539 UK 83146
WILL LEE B (C (C) ARROWS 1979 CBS US 36129
CRUSHER BENNETT PERC (C (D) BEST OF 1980 CBS US 36406 UK 84234
DAVID SANBORN SAX (C
ROB MOUNSEY SYN (C ELLIOT SCHEINER PROD(C DON GROLNICK K (C STEVE GADD D (C
RANDY BRECKER HRNS(C MICHAEL BRECKER HRNS (C RICK MAROTTA D (C

K38 KID CREOLE & THE COCONUTS K38

AUGUST DARNELL B V (AB (A) OFF THE COAST OF ME 1980 ISLAND UK 7012 ANTILLES US 7078
BROOKSIE WELLS V (A (B) FRESH FRUIT IN FOREIGN PLACES 1981 ISLAND UK 7014 SIRE US 3534
LOURDES COTTO V (A (B) FRESH FRUIT IN FOREIGN PLACES 1981 ISLAND EURO 203 805
ADRIANA KAEGI V (AB (C) TROPICAL GANSTERS 1982 ISLAND UK 7016
FONDA RAE V (A
PETER SCHOTT PNO (AB FRANZ KRAUNS G (A COATIMUNDI VIBES (AB ANDREW LLOYD PERC(AB
WINSTON GRENNAN D (AB TOMMY BROWDER B (A MARC MAZUR (B CAROL COLMAN (B
YOGI HORTON (B LORI EASTSIDE (B STEVE KROON (B CHERYL POIERER V (B
DON ARNONE (B DAVE CHARLES (B DOMINICK CORTESE (B SAL GALLINA (B
SATN BROWDER K (A FREDDIE HARRIS (B MICKEY SEVILLA D (A SUGAR COATED ANDY (A
SAM TURNER (B JILL JAFFE'S STR (B DON ARMANDO BONILLA V (A
RONNIE RODGERS SYN (A GICHY DAN V (A FREDDIE HARRIS D (AB JAY ATOYALL G (A
MIA MARTINEZ V (A DURCH ROBINSON (B DON HAMILTON (B BEVERLY BROWN (B
ANGELINA DE LA LANA (B ARROLL CORUN (B RUBIN BASSINI (B CHARLES LAGROND HRNS (B

K39 JOHNNY KIDD & THE PIRATES K39

JOHNNY KIDD(FRED HEATH) V(ALL (A) SHAKIN' ALL OVER 1971 STARLINE UK SRS 5100
ALAN CADDY G (12 (B) YOUR CHEATIN' HEART 197 PATHE IMP 2C062 04731
TOMMY DOCHERTY G (1 (C) MEMORIAL ALBUM 197 PATH IMP 2C062 04422
JOHNNY GORDON B (1 (D) BEST OF 1978 EMI UK NUT M12
CLEM CATTINI D (1 (EP) PLEASE DONT TOUCH 1960 HMV UK 7EG 8628
KEN McKAY D (2 (EP) I'LL NEVER GET OVER YOU 1963 HMV UK 7EG 8834
BRIAN GREGG B (2 (1) 1958/9 (2) 1959 (3) 1962 (4) 1962/65
JOE MORETTI G (2 (5) 1965 (6) 1966 (7) 1966 (8) 1966/67
THUNDERCLAP JONES PNO (2
JOHNNY PATTO G (3 JOHNNY SPENCER B (345 FRANK FARLEY D (345 MICK GREEN G (345
JOHN WEIDER G (5 ROGER TRUTH D (678 NICK SIMPER B (678 JOHNNY CARROL ORG (8
RAY SOAPER ORG (6 MICKY STEWART G (678

K40 GREG KIHN K40

GREG KIHN G V (ALL (A) GREG KIHN 1976 BESERKLEY US 0046 UK BSERK 4 GER 623358
STEVE WRIGHT B V (ABCDEFGH (B) GREG KIHN AGAIN 1977 BESERKLEY US 0052 UK BSREK 8 GER 623467
LARRY LYNCH D V (ABCDEGH (C) NEXT OF KIHN 1978 BESERKLEY US 0056 UK BSERK13
ROBBIE DUNBAR V K G(A (D) GREG KIHN /RUBINOOS LIVE 1978 BESERKLEY UK GIG1
DAVE CARPENDER G V (BCDEGH (E) WITH THE NAKED EYE 1979 BESERKLEY US 10063 UKBSERK20 GER 623865
GARY PHILLIPS K V (AGH (F) POWERLINES 1980 BESERKLEY UK BSERK20
MARK JORDAN K (A (G) GLASSHOUSE ROCK 1980 BESERKLEY US 10068 GER 624361
JOHN DOUKAS K (A (H) ROCKIHNROLL BAND 1980 BESERKLEY US 10069 UK 85213

K41 KILBURN & THE HIGH ROADS K41

IAN DURY V (A (A) HANDSOME 1975 DAWN UK DNLS 3065
KEITH LUCAS G (A (A) HANDSOME 1977 PYE UK NSPL 18541
DAVEY PAYNE SAX (A (B) WOT A BUNCH 1978 WB UK K 56513
RODERICK MELVIN PNO (A (EP) KILBURN & THE HIGH ROADS 19 BONAPARTE UK BONE1
CHARLES SINCLAIR B (A
CLAIRE TORRY (A MARIO GIBBINGS (A CLYDE DIAS (A MATTHEW EMMANUEL (A
DAVID NEWTON ROHOMAN D (A PETE WILLSHER (A LES THATCHER (A DAVE MATTACKS D (A
JON FIELD (A ROD KING (A MARTIN JAY (A TONY CHARLES (A
TREVOR CUMBERBATCH (A TINA CHARLES V (A

K42 KILLERS K42

SUCHARD THITTICHAI G (A (A) KILLER 1978 ARIOLA ARL 5003
JOHN CLAY G V (A
TONY MAYBERRY B (A STUART GREEN D (A PHIL KENZIE SAX (A

K43 KILLING FLOOR K43

MICK CLARKE ((A) KILLING FLOOR 1970 SPARK SRLP 102+1973 SRLM 2004
BILL THORNYCROFT ((A) KILLING FLOOR 1970 SIRE US 97019
STU McDONALD ((A) KILLING FLOOR 1970 PINK ELEPHANT 855 009
BAS SMITH ((B) OUT OF URANUS 197 PENNY FARTHING UK PELS 511
LOU MARTIN (

K43A KILLING JOKE K43A

JAZZ COLEMAN K V (A (A) KILLING JOKE 1980 EG UK 5 45 US EDITIONS 109
PIG YOUTH B V (A (B) WHATS THID FOR... 1981 EG UK 550 US EDITIONS 111
PAUL D (A (B) WHATS THIS FOR... 1981 POLYDOR NL 2302 109
GEORDIE G (A

K43B KILO K43B

(A) KILO 1979 STAX US 4125

K44A KIND HEARTS & ENGLISH K44A

TONY BIRD V ((A) A WISH FOR A SEASON 1976 DJM UK DJF 20490
JOHN TIPPET G PNO((B) BEACHCOMBER 1977 DJM UK DJM 20512
PAUL KEOGH G (
LEE FOTHERGILL G (PAUL BIRCHIL G (FRANK MacDONALD B (KEVIN WELLS D (
DOUGLAS KEAN SYN (

K44B KIN PING MEH K44B

KALLE WEBER D (BC (A) KIN PING MEH 1971
TORSTEN HERZOG B V (B (B) KIN PING MEH 2 1972 ZEBRA GER 2944 005
FRIEDER SCHMITT K V (BCD (C) KIN PING MEH 3 1973 ZEBRA GER 2949 011
WILLIE WAGNER G V (A (D) VIRTUES & SINS 1974 NOVA GER 6/22015
WERNER STEPHAN G V)BC
ULI GROSS G (BC GERHARD MROZECK (BCD ALAN WROE B (CD GEFF HARRISON V (CD
CHARLY WEBER D (D JEAN JACQUES KRAVETZ K (D

KINDRED

GLORIA GAIONE	V	(AB				(A) KINDRED	19			
MARTY RODGERS	V	(AB				(B) NEXT OF KIN	19	WB	US	2640
BOBBY COCHRAN	G V	(AB								
BERNIE MYSIOR	B	(AB	DAVID BLUEFIELD	K	(AB	RON GRINEL PERC (A	OLIVER BROWN CONGA (A			
JIMMY ERICKSON	PERC	(B								

B B KING

B B KING	G V PNO	(ALL				(A)LIVE AT THE REGAL	1975	ABC	US	ABCS 724
KENNY SANDS	TPT	(A	HENRY BOOZIER	TPT	(A	(A) " " "	1965	ABC	US	ABCD 509
PLUMA DAVIS	TROM	(A	LAWRENCE BURDINE	SAX	(A	(A) " " "	1965	HMV	UK	
JOHNNY BOARD	SAX	(A	BARNEY HUBERT	SAX	(ADFH	(B) BLUES ON TOP OF BLUES	1967	BLUESWAY	US	BLS 6011
MILLARD LEE	PNO	(A	MAYALL YORK	B	(A	(B) " " "	1968	STATESIDE	UK	10238
SONNY FREEMAN	D	(ADFHI	JOHN BROWNING	TPT	(DF	(B) " " "	19	ABC	US	ABC 709
BROOKER WALKER	SAX	(DL	RON LEVY	SYN PNO	(DFLHI	(C) INDIANOLA MISSISSIPPI	1970	PROBE	UK	SPB 6255
ALEXIS KORNER	G	(E	RINGO STARR	D	(E	(C) " " "	197	ABC	US	713
JIM PRICE	HRNS	(E	BOBBY KEYS	HRNS	(E	(D) LIVE AT COOK COUNTY	1971	PROBE	UK	SPB 1032
GARY WRIGHT	K	(E	KLAUS VOORMANN	B	(E	(D) " " "	197	ABC	US	723
DUSTER BENNETT	HCA	(E	STEVE MARRIOTT	G	(E	(E) B B KING IN LONDON	1971	PROBE	UK	SPB 1041
GREG RIDLEY		(E	JERRY SHIRLEY		(E	(E) " " "	197	ABC	UK	ABC 5015
PETE WINGFIELD	K	(E	PAUL BUTLER		(E	(E) " " "	197	ABC	US	730
JOHN BEST		(E	JIM GORDON	D	(E	(F) L A MIDNIGHT	1972	PROBE	UK	SPB 1051
BILL PERKINS		(E	OLLIE MITCHELL		(E	(F) " " "	1977	ABC		743
CHUCK FINDLEY	HRNS	(EJ	JIM KELTNER	D	(E	(G) FRIENDS	1974	ABC	UK	ABCL5051
MAC REBENNNACK	PNO	(E	JOHN URIBE		(E	(G) " " "	1977	ABC	US	AB 825
BARRY FORD		(E	RICK WRIGHT		(E	(H) TOGETHER	1974	DUNHILL	US	751096
DAVID SPINOZZA		(E	CARL HALL		(E	(H) " "	1974	ANCHOR	UK	ABCD 605
JOE SAMPLE	K	(J	WILTON FELDER	SAX	(J	(I) GUESS WHO	1973	PROBE	UK	1063
STIX HOOPER	D	(J	POPS POPWELL	B	(J	(I) " "	1973	ABC	US	759
DR RAGOVOY		(E	JOSHIE ARMSTEAD	V	(E	(I) " "	197	ABC		5021
TASHA THOMAS	V	(E	CAROLE KING	PNO	(C	(J) MIDNIGHT BELIEVER	1978	ABC	UK	ABCL5246
BRYAN GAROFALO	B	(CF	RUSS KUNKEL	D	(C	(K) KINGSIZE	1977	ABC	US	977
LEON RUSSELL	PNO	(C	JOE WALSH	G	(FC	(K) KINGSIZE	1977	EMI	EUROIC	95148
PAUL HARRIS	K	(FC	HUGH McCRACKEN	G	(C	(L) LUCILLE TALKS BACK	1975	ABC	UK	5149
JERRY JEMMOTT	B	(CI	HERB LOVELL	D	(C	(L) LUCILLE TALKS BACK	197	ABC	US	898
SHIRLEY MATTHEWS	V	(C	MERRY CLAYTON	V	(C	(M) NOW APPEARING AT O'MISS	80	MCA		MCA28016
CLYDIE KING	V	(C	VANETTA FIELDS	V	(C	(N) TO KNOW YOU IS TO LOVE	1973	PROBE	UK	1083
BOBBY BRYANT	TPT	(FK	PLAS JOHNSON	SAX	(F	(N) " " "	1973	ABC	US	5083
BOB MORIN	D	(F	MEL BROWN	G	(FH	(N) " " "	1974	ABC	US	794
JOHN TURK	ORG	(F	EARL PALMER	D	(F	(O) TAKE IT HOME	1979	MCA	US	3151
RONNIE BAKER	B	(GN	ELLI TARKESTY	G	(GN	(P) MUST BE A BETTER WORLD	1981	MCA	UK	3095
WILL BOULWARE	K	(G	VINCE MONTANA	VIBES	(GN	B B KING STORY	1968	BLUE HORIZON		7 63216
MEMPHIS HRNS	HRNS	(GN	MELVIN JACKSON		(H	B B KING STORY VOL 2	1969	BLUE HORIZON		7 63226
CATO WALKER		(H	CHARLES POLK		(H	LIVE & WELL	1970	STATESIDE	UK	10297
THEODORE ARTHUR		(H	JOSEPH HARDIN		(H	" "	1973	BLUESWAY	US	BLS6031
DEAN PARKS	G	(J	ROLAND BAUTISTA	G	(J	" "	19	ABC	US	819
KURT McGETTRICK	SAX	(J	LUTHER WATERS	V	(J	COMPLETELY WELL	1970	STATESIDE	UK	10299
JULIA TILLMAN	V	(J	RED CALLENDER	TUBA	(F	" " "	19	ABC		868
JESSE ED DAVIS	G	(F	STEVIE WONDER	K	(N	" " "	1974	BLUESWAY	US	BLS6037
CLIFF COULTER	K PERC	(F	RANDY WOLFE	G	(F	" " "	19	NEW WORLD		NW6005
SANDY KONIKOFF	PERC	(F	DERYLL INMAN	G	(G	BACK IN THE ALLEY	1973	BLUESWAY	US	6050
ROLAND CHAMBERS	G	(GN	RON KERSEY	K	(G	" " "	1977	ABC	US	878
ANDREW LOVE	SAX	(G	DON RENALDO STRINGS		(G	GREATEST HITS	1973	PROBE	UK	1069
BEN BENAY	G	(H	BOBBY FORTE	SAX	(HLI	GREATEST HITS VOL 1	19	UNITED	US	7766
TOMMY PUNKSON		(H	THEODORE REYNOLDS		(H	" " "	19	KENT	US	552
ALFRED THOMAS		(H	JAMES GADSON	D	(J	LUCILLE	1969	STATESIDE	UK	10272
GEORGE BOHANON	HRNS	(J	GARY HERBIG	FLT	(J	" "	1973	BLUESWAY	US	6016
ORRIN WATERS	V	(J	MAXINE WILLARD	V	(J	" "	1977	ABC	US	712
RED HOLLOWAY	SAX	(F	VICTOR FELDMAN	PERC K	(F	MR BLUES	19	ABC	US	456
EARL TURBINTON	SAXI	(FI	TAJ MAHAL	HCA G	(F	BEST OF	1973	ABC		5026
RON BROWN	B	(F	EARL YOUNG	D	(GN	" "	19	ABC		767
NORMAN HARRIS	G	(GN	DAVE CRAWFORD	K	(GN	" "	1981	MCA	UK	1612
LARRY WASHINGTON	PERC	(GN	WAYNE JACKSON	TPT	(GN	B B KING	19	NEW WORLD		6004
PHILADELPHIA STRINGS		(GN	MILTON HOPKINS	G	(KHLI	B B KING VOL 2	19	NEW WORLD		6006
EDWARD ROWE	HRNS	(HLI	HAROLD POTIER JR		(H	CLASSIC REVISITED	1977	ABC	US	724
LEO PENN		(H	MICHAEL OMARTIAN	K	(H	SOUL OF B B KING	19	FESTIVAL		532
STEVE MADAIO	TPT	(JI	QUITMAN DENNIS	HRNS	(J	" " "	19	KENT	US	5-16
ABE MOST	CLAR	(J	LEE RITENOUR	G	(K	" " "	19	KENT	US	516
JAMES TONEY	ORG	(KL	RONNIE BARRON	ORG	(K	" " "	19	CUSTOM	US	2052
SONNY BURKE	K	(K	JOE TURNER	B	(K	" " "	19	CUSTOM	US	1052
SCOTT EDWARDS	B	(K	JOHN STARKS	D	(KL	" " "	19	UNITED	US	7714
ED GREENE	D	(K	EARL NASH	PERC	(K	BLUES IS KING	19	ABC	US	704
EDDIE BROWN	PERC	(K	AL AARONS	TPT	(K	" " "	196	HMV	UK	3608
ROY POPER	TPT	(K	GARNETT BROWN	TROM	(KI	" " "	19	BLUESWAY	US	6001
JIMMY FORREST	SAX	(K	FRED JACKSON	WIND	(K	CONFESSIN' THE BLUES	19	ABC	US	528
ERNIE WATTS	SAX	(K	JEROME RICHARDSON	SAX	(K	" " "	19	HMV	UK	3514
JOE LIGON	V	(K	JOHNNY MARTIN	V	(K	THE ELECTRIC B B KING	1977	ABC	US	813
ELMEO FRANKLIN	V	(K	RICHARD WALLACE	V	(K	" " "	19	ABC	US	1061
CALVIN OWENS	TPT	(M	CALEP EMPHREY	D	(M	" " "	1969	STATESIDE	UK	10284
EDGAR SYNIGAL	SAX	(M	LEONARD GILL	G	(M	" " "	1969	BLUESWAY	US	6022
STEVE SHERARD	TROM	(M	HILTON JOSEPH	SAX	(M	KING OF THE BLUES	1976	M F P	UK	50259
PHIL BLACKMAN	K	(M	JOHN WILLIE COOK	TPT	(M	" " "	19	CROWN	US	5167
JON JONES	G	(M	NANA VASCONCELOS	PERC	(M	" " "	19	UNITED	US	7730
RUDY AIKELS	B	(L	MARCUS BARNETT	PERC	(L	TOGETHER AGAIN	1976	IMPULSE		8027
JOSEPH BURTON	TROM	(LI	JESS DANIELS	G	(L	" "	1976	IMPULSE	US	9317
HERBERT HARDESTY	SAX	(L	RUSSELL JACKSON	B	(M	TAKE A SWING WITH ME	19	BLUE HORIZON		2431 004
WILBERT FREEMAN	B	(DFMHI	EDDIE MILLER	WIND	(J	B B KING ANTHOLOGY	1976	ABC		5611
DAVID SANBORN	SAX	(I	LOUIS HUBERT	SAX	(I	" " "	19	KENT	US	9011
GENE DINWIDDIE	SAX	(I	CORNELL DUPREE	G	(I	FEELING THEY CALL THE BLUES	19	TRIO	JAP	PA 6220
FRANK OWENS	PNO	(I	BERNARD PURDIE	D	(I	FEELING THEY CALL VOL2	19	TRIO	JAP	PA 6221
ERNIE ROYAL	TPT	(I	TREVOR LAWRENCE	SAX	(I	B B KING LIVE	19	KENT	US	565
HOWARD JOHNSON	SAX	(I	RON KERSEY	K	(N	LIVE	19	KENT	US	515
CHARLIE MANN	K V	(N	ANDREW LOVE	HRNS	(N	LIVE	19	UNITED	US	7771

(CONTINUED)

K45 B B KING (CONTINUED) K45

Title	Year	Label	Country	No.
ON STAGE LIVE	19	UNITED	US	7736
ON STAGE LIVE	19	KENT	US	5015
SING SPIRITUALS	19	CROWN	US	5119
SWING LOW	19	UNITED	US	7721
BETTER THAN EVER	19	KENT	US	561
BOSS OF THE BLUES	19	KENT	US	529
BOSS OF THE BLUES	19	UNITED	US	7750
DOING MY THING LORD	19	KENT	US	563
FROM THE BEGINNING	19	KENT	US	533
INCREDIBLE SOUL OF	19	KENT	US	539
INCREDIBLE SOUL OF	19	UNITED	US	7756
B B KING STORY	19	JOKER	ITALY	3727
SINGIN' THE BLUES	19	CROWN	US	5020
SINGIN' THE BLUES	19	UNITED	US	7726
MORE	19	CROWN	US	5230
MY KIND OF BLUES	19	CROWN	US	5188
MY KIND OF BLUES	19	UNITED	US	7724
SPANISH HARLEM	19	ATCO	US	33133
THE BLUES	19	CROWN	US	5063
THE BLUES	19	UNITED	US	7732
ROCK ME BABY	19	KENT	US	5012
ROCK ME BABY	19	UNITED	US	7733
TWIST WITH B B KING	19	CROWN	US	5248
LET ME LOVE YOU	19	KENT	US	513
LET ME LOVE YOU	19	UNITED	US	7734
ORIGINAL SWEET 16	19	KENT	US	568
ORIGINAL SWEET 16	19	UNITED	US	7773
PURE SOUL	19	KENT	US	517
THE JUNGLE	19	KENT	US	521
THE JUNGLE	19	UNITED	US	7742
TURN ON WITH B B KING	19	KENT	US	548
TURN ON WITH B B KING	19	UNITED	US	7763
UNDERGROUND BLUES	19	KENT	US	535
9 X 9.5	19	UNITED	US	7788
WAILS	19	CROWN	US	5115
WAILS	19	CROWN	US	147
BLUE FOR ME	19	UNITED	US	7708
BLUE FOR ME	19	CUSTOM	US	2046
BLUES IN MY HEART	19	CROWN	US	309
EASY LISTENING BLUES	19	CROWN	US	5286
EASY LISTENING BLUES	19	UNITED	US	7705
GREAT B B KING	19	CROWN	US	5143
THE GREAT	19	UNITED	US	7728
HEART FULL OF BLUES	19	UNITED	US	7703
I LOVE YOU SO	19	CUSTOM	US	2049
I LOVE YOU SO	19	UNITED	US	7711

K46 ALBERT KING K46

Musician	Instr.	Albums
ALBERT KING	G V	(ALL
DONALD 'DUCK' DUNN	B	(FHO
STEVE CROPPER	G	(F
AL JACKSON	D	(EFCO
JIM KELTNER	D	(H
ROGER HAWKINS	D	(H
WILLIE HALL	D	(O
EDDIE WILLIS	G	(R
JAMES GADSON	D	(L
DAVID HOOD	B	(H
EARL THOMAS	B	(O
HENRY DAVIS	B	(L
CHUCK RAINEY	B	(L
JESSE ED DAVIS	G	(H
TIPPY ARMSTRONG	G	(H
WAYNE PERKINS	G	(H
MICHAEL TOLES	G	(H
VERNON BURCH	G	(O
BOBBY MANUEL	G	(O
WAH WAH WATSON	G	(L
BILLY FENDER	G	(L
GREG POREE	G	(L
RONALD WRIGHT	D	(R
LESTER SNELL	K	(O
GLEN GOINS	G	(R
JOE SAMPLE	K	(L
JEANIE ARNOLD	V	(L
BERT DECOTEAUX	K	(L
MEMPHIS HORNS		(O
WILLIAM C BROWN	V	(O
RUDY ROBINSON	K	(R
DWAYNE LOMAX	D	(R
JOHN FRAGA	B	(R
FRED WESLEY	HRNS	(R
SANDY KONIKOFF	PERC	(H
OTIS RUSH	G V	(P
JEANNE GREENE	V	(H
BARRY BECKETT	K	(H
MAXINE WILLARD	V	(L
ANTHONY WILLIS	B	(R
BARBARA HUBY	PERC	(R
JAMES McCARTY	G	(R
KING ERRISSON	PERC	(L
JOHN GALLIE	K	(H
LANI GROVES	V	(L
MARVELL THOMAS	K	(O
DEE IRVIN	V	(L
AARON WILLIS	G	(R
LARRY FRATANGELO	PERC	(R
DENNIS ROBBINS	G	(R
DENIECE WILLIAMS	V	(L
WINSTON STEWART	K	(O
JULIA TILLMAN	V	(L
JERRY PETERS	K	(L
MOUNT ZION SINGERS	V	(H
RAY TINI JR	G	(R
BRANDYE	V	(R
JOHN BADANJEK	D	(R

Album	Release
(A) THE BIG BLUES	1962 KING US 852
(B) TRAVELLING TO CALIFORNIA	1967 KING US K1060
(B) TRAVELLING TO CALIFORNIA	1967 POLYDOR UK 2343 026
(C) BORN UNDER A BAD SIGN	1967 STAX/ATLANTIC US 7723
(D) KING OF THE BLUES GUITAR	1968 ATLANTIC UK 588 173 US SD8213
(D) KING OF THE BLUES GUITAR	197 ATLANTIC UK RI K40494
(E) LIVE WIRE BLUES POWER	1968 STAX US 2003 UK 1002
(E) LIVE WIRE BLUES POWER	1980 STAX US RI 4128
(F) DOES THE KINGS THING	1968 STAX US 2015 UK 1017
(G) YEARS GONE BY	1969 STAX US 2010 UK 1022
(H) LOVEJOY	1971 STAX US 2040 UK 2325
(I) I'LL PLAY THE BLUES FOR YOU	1972 STAX US 3009 UK 1019
(I) I'LL PLAY THE BLUES FOR YOU	197 POLYDOR UK 2325089
(J) I WANNA GET FUNKY	1974 STAX US 5505 UK 1003
(K) MONTREUX FESTIVAL	197 STAX US 5520
(L) TRUCKLOAD OF LOVIN'	1976 UTOPIA US 1 1387 UK UTS 602
(M) LIVE (DBL)	1977 UTOPIA US 2 2205
(N) ALBERT	1977 UTOPIA US 1 1731
(O) THE PINCH	1978 STAX US 4101 UK 3001
(P) DOOR TO DOOR	19 CHESS 1538
(Q) CHRONICLE (1 SIDE)	1979 STAX US 4123
(R) KING ALBERT	1977 TOMATO US 6002
(S) ALBERT LIVE	1979 TOMATO US 7009
(T) NEW ORLEANS HEAT	1979 TOMATO US 7022

K47 BEN E KING K47

Musician	Instr.	Albums
BEN E KING	V	(ALL
GWEN GUTHRIE	V	(I
JEFF MIRANOV	G	(OI
KEN HATFIELD	G	(O
KEN KIRKLAND	K	(O
JIMMY YOUNG	D	(O
BEN E KING JR	B	(O
MARCUS MILLER	B	(O
SAMMY FIGUEROA	PERC	(O
YVONNE LEWIS	V	(O
JANET PENDARVIS	V	(O
RICKY WILLIAMS	K	(I
CRYSTAL DAVIS	V	(O
DEIRDRE TUCK-COREL	V	(O
RODNEY PHELPS	G	(O
KEVIN DOUGLAS	B	(O
JERRY FRIEDMAN	G	(I
CARLOS ALOMAR	G	(I
RICARDO WILLIAMS	D	(O
JAMES DRUMGOLE	TPT	(O
BERT DE COTEAUX	K	(I
PHIL KRAUS	PERC	(I
YVONNE GUTHRIE	V	(I
KATHY ALSON	V	(G
JOHN BRIGANTI	D	(G
EMMANUEL REDDING	D	(O
RONNELLE STAFFORD	V	(O
BOB BABBIT	B	(I
TED SOMMERS	PERC	(I
BRENDA GUTHRIE	V	(I
LESLIE ZIMEI	V	(G
CARE SCICKLER	G	(G
TYRONE WILLIAMS	K	(O
JAMILLAR MUHAMMAD	V	(O
JERRY JEMMOTT	B	(I
JACK JENNINGS	PERC	(I
LANI GROVES	V	(I
RONNIE CANGRO	D	(F
MIKE MATTIA	K	(G
GREGORY McCOY	K	(O
DEREK SMITH	K	(I
GEORGE DEVENS	PERC	(I
CARLOS MARTIN	CONGA	(I
LYNN WEIPPERT	V	(G
DON OLSEN	B	(F

Album	Release
(A) WHAT IS SOUL	196 ATCO UK 587 072
(B) SPANISH HARLEM	1961 ATCO US 33133 UK 590 000
(C) SINGS FOR SOULFUL LOVERS	1962 ATCO US 33137 UK LONDON 8026
(D) DONT PLAY THAT SONG	1962 ATCO US 33142 UK LONDON 8012
(E) GREATEST HITS	1964 ATCO US 33165 UK 2464 010
(F) SEVEN LETTERS	1965 ATCO US 33174
(G) BEGINNING OF IT ALL	1971 MANDALA US 3007 UK CBS 64570
(H) ROUGH EDGES	197 MAXWELL US 88001 UK CREWE 203
(I) SUPERNATURAL THING	1975 ATLANTIC US 18132 UK K50118
(J) BEN E KING STORY	1975 ATLANTIC UK K50139
(K) I HAD A LOVE	1976 ATLANTIC US 18169 UK K50264
(L) BENNY & US (A W B)	1977 ATLANTIC US 19105 UK K50384
(M) LET ME LIVE IN YOUR LIFE	1978 ATLANTIC US 19200 UK K50527
(N) STAR COLLECTION	197 MIDI GERM 20040
(O) MUSIC TRANCE	1980 ATLANTIC US 19269 UK K50713
(P) STREET TOUGH	1980 ATLANTIC US 19300 UK K50787
(Q) YOUNG BOY BLUES	19 CLARION US 606

K47A BOBBY KING K47A

Musician	Albums	Album	Release
BOBBY KING	(A	(A) CHASER	197 MCM FR 900 292

K48 CAROLE KING K48

CAROLE KING G PNO V (ALL — (A) NOW THAT EVERYTHINGS BEEN SAID 1969 ODE Z1244 012(BY GROUP CITY)
RALPH SCHUCKETT K (BCDL — (B) WRITER 1970 ODE US 77006 US RI EPIC 34944
CHARLES LARKEY B (BCDEFGLN — (B) WRITER 1970 A&M UK AMLS 996
DANNY KOOTCH G V (BCDEFGIL — (C) TAPESTRY 1972 ODE US 77009 US RI EPIC 34956
JAMES TAYLOR G V (BCDIL — (C) TAPESTRY 197 A&M UK 2025 UK RI EPIC 82308
BOBBYE HALL PERC (DEFL — (D) MUSIC 197 ODE US 77013 US RI EPIC 34949
THERESA CALDERONE PERC (DL — (D) MUSIC 197 A&M UK AMLH 67013
ABIGALE HANESS V (BDG — (E) RHYMES & REASONS 1972 ODE 77016 US RI EPIC 34950
MERRY CLAYTON V (CDL — (F) FANTASY 1973 ODE 77018 US RI EPIC 34962
WILLIAM GREEN WIND (DL — (G) WRAP AROUND JOY 1974 ODE 77024 US RI EPIC 34953
WILLIAM COLLETTE WIND (DL — (H) REALLY ROSIE 1975 ODE 77027 US RI EPIC 34955
ERNIE WATTS WIND (DEFGJKL — (I) THOROUGHBRED 1976 ODE 77034 US RI EPIC 34963
DEBORAH NORTH V (N — (I) THOROUGHBRED 1980 EMBASSY UK RI 31841
PLAS JOHNSON WIND (DL — (J) SIMPLE THINGS 1977 CAPITOL 11667
MIKE ALTSCHUL WIND (DFG — (K) WELCOME HOME 1978 CAPITOL 11785
OSCAR BRASHEAR WIND (DJ — (L) GREATEST HITS 1978 ODE 86043 US EPIC 34967
CURTIS AMY WIND (CDFL — (M) TOUCH THE SKY 1979 CAPITOL 11953
OSCAR FORD JR V (N — (N) PEARLS 1980 CAPITOL 12073
DON KNAUB TROM (N
BILL INN STR (N — MARK MANISCALE BAN (N — ERIC JOHNSON G (N — STEVE MEADOR D (N
GLORIA HINES V (N — LYDIA NORTH V (N — MICHAEL MUNDAY TROM (N — BOBBY MEYER TPT (N
RAY CRISARA TPT (N — BETTY WHITLOCK FDL (N — CHRISTOPHER GROSS G (N — RICK EVERS PERC(K
GEORGIA KELLY HARP (K — ANNE GOLIA TAMB (K — BOB HARRINGTON DULC (K — ANN WHITE V (K
HARVEY MASON D (EFL — DAVID T WALKER G (DEL — RED RHODES STEEL(E — HARRY EDISON HRNS (E
ROBERT BRYANT HRNS (E — GEORGE BOHANON TROM(EFGJKL — CHARLIE LOPER TROM (EL — DICK HYDE TROM (FGL
OLLIE MITCHELL HRNS (F — CHUCK FINDLEY TPT (FGL — ALBERT AARONS TPT (EL — TOM SCOTT SAX (FGJL
ANDY NEWMARK D (GL — DEAN PARKS G (GL — FRED JACKSON HRNS (G — GENE COE HRNS (G
JIM HORN SAX (G — EDDIE KENDRICKS SINGERS(F — LOUISE GOFFIN V (GJL — SHERRY GOFFIN V (GLJ
WADDY WACHTEL G (IL — RUSS KUNKEL D (CIL — LEE SKLAR B (LI — RALPH MACDONALD PERC(IL
DAVID CROSBY V (I — GRAHAM NASH V (I — J D SOUTHER V (I — ROBERT McENTEE V G K(JK
MARK HALLMAN G V K(JKMN — ROB GALLOWAY B (KJ — MICHAEL WOOTEN D (JK — MIGUEL RIVERA PERC (JKM
RICHARD HARDY WIND(JKMN — CLARK SPANGLER SYN (JK — NOLAN SMITH HRNS (JK — MAURICE SPEARS TROM (J
TERRY HARRINGTON SAX (J — JOEL O'BRIEN D (CL — PENN STEINBERG B (C — JULIA TILLMAN V (BL
JOHN FISCHBACK SYN (B — DOLORES HALL V (B — LEO LEBLANC G V (M — REESE WYNANS K (MN
FRED KRC D V (M — DAVE PERKINS G V (M — BOBBY RAMBO G V (M — TOMAS RAMIREZ WIND V(MN
STEPHANIE SPRUILL V (K — ALEXANDRA BROWN V (K — STRING SECTION (CEFK

K49 CLYDIE KING K49

CLYDIE KING V (A — (A) BROWN SUGAR 1974 POLYDOR UK 2310 231

K49A DENNY KING K49A

DENNY KING G V B(A — (A) EVIL WIND IS BLOWING 1973
ALEX ST CLAIR G B TPT(A
JESSE BRIONES B (A — GREG HAMPTON D (A — AL CARR CONGA (A — DOUGLAS MOON HCA (A
PETE DOLAN FLT (A

K49B DON KING K49B

DON KING (AB — (A) LONELY HOTEL 19 EPIC US 36469
(B) WHIRLWIND 19 EPIC US 37105

K50 EARL KING K50

EARL KING (AB — (A) NEW ORLEANS ROCK'N'ROLL 1978 SONET UK SNTF 719
(B) EARL KING 19 VIVID JAP 1012

K51 FREDDIE KING K51

FREDDIE KING G V (ALL — (A) FREDDIE KING SINGS 196 KING US 762
SONNY THOMPSON PNO (ABCDE — (B) LETS HIDEAWAY & DANCEAWAY 196 KING US 773
CLIFFORD SCOTT SAX (ABCDE — (C) GIRL BOY GIRL 196 KING US 777
GENE REDD SAX (ABCDE — (D) BOSSA NOVA & BLUES 196 KING US 821
FRED JORDAN G (ABC — (E) FREDDIE KING GOES SURFIN' 196 KING US 856
WILLIAM WILLIS B (ABCDE — (F) BONANZA OF INSTRUMENTALS 196 KING US 928
BENNY TURNER B (F — (G) VOCALS & INSTUMENTALS 196 KING US 964
PHILIP PAUL D (ABC — (H) HIDEAWAY 196 KING US 1059+ 1977 RI STARDAY 5033
BUD BEADLE SAX (PRT — (I) KING OF R&B VOL 2 1969 POLYDOR UK 2343 009
RON CARTHY TPT (PRT — (J) IS A BLUES MASTER 1969 ATLANTIC UK 588 186 + RI K 40496
ROY DAVIES K (PRT — (J) IS A BLUES MASTER 1969 COTILLION US SD9004
MICK EVE SAX (PRT — (K) HIS EARLY YEARS 197 POLYDOR UK 2343 047
STEVE FERRONE D (PRT — (L) MY FEELING FOR THE BLUES 1970 COTILLION US SD9016
STEVE GREGORY SAX (PRT — (L) MY FEELING FOR THE BLUES 1975 ATLANTIC UK RI K 40947
DELISLE HARPER B (PRT — (M) GETTING READY 1971 A&M UK AMLS65004 US SHELTER 8905
CHRIS MERCER SAX (PRT — (N) TEXAS CANNONBALL 1972 A&M UK AMLS68113 US SHELTER 8905
BOB TENCH G V (PRT — (O) WOMAN ACROSS THE WATER 1973 A&M UK AMLS68919 US SHELTER 8919
MIKE VERNON PERC (RT — (P) BURGLAR 1974 RSO UK 2394 140 US RSO 4803
PETE WINGFIELD K (PRT — (Q) BEST OF FREDDIE KING 1974 A&M UK AMLS68313 US SHELTER 2140
LONNIE MACK G (F — (Q) BEST OF FREDDIE KING 1974 SHELTER US 52021
BRIAN AUGER ORG (p — (R) LARGER THAN LIFE 1975 RSO UK 2394 163 US RSO 4811
MISTY BROWNING V (P — (S) ORIGINAL HITS 1977 STARDAY/KING US 5012
P P ARNOLD V (P — (T) 1934 TO 1976 1977 RSO UK 2394 192 US RSO 1 3025
VIE V (P — (U) REST OF FREDDIE KING 1976 ISLAND UK ISA 5001
ERIC CLAPTON G V (PT — (V) 17 HITS 1978 KING US 5012
JOHN THOMAS TPT (R
JAMIE OLDAKER D (PT — CARL RADLE B (OPNT — DICK SIMS K (PT — GEORGE TERRY G (PT
SERGIO PASTORA PERC (T — MELVIN JONES ORG (T — LOUIS STEPHENS PNO (RT — KING CURTIS SAX (L
JERRY JEMMOTT B (L — ERNIE ROYAL TPT (L — FRANK WESS SAX (L — JOHN GALLIE K (MN
DON PRESTON G V(MNO — CLAUDIA LENNEAR V (M — SONNY BURKE K (R — JIM KELTNER D (O
HENRY DAVIS B (R — JIM GORDON K SAX (R — ANDREW JONES G (R — MIKE O'NEILL G (N
BENNY TURNER B (RT — KENNY PASSARELLI B (T — ROBERT WILSON B (R — WILLIE BRIDGES SAX (L
GEORGE COLEMAN SAX (L — TREVOR LAWRENCE SAX (L — KENNY RICE D (L — CHUCK BLACKWELL D(MNO
JIM GORDON D (N — LEON RUSSELL K (MNO — KATHI McDONALD V (M — SAM CLAYTON PERC(N
O'NEILL TWINS V (O — BIG JOHN ETHOMASSIE D (R — ALVIN HEMPHILL K (R — DARRYL LEONARD TPT (R
MELVIN WAH WAH RAGIN G (R — K O THOMAS PNO (R — SAM WYLE G (T — CHARLES ROBINSON D(T
MARTIN BANKS TPT (L — CORNELL DUPREE G (L — HUGH McCRACKEN HCA (L — GEORGE STUBBS PNO (L
DONALD DUCK DUNN B (MN — AL JACKSON D (N — JOEY COOPER V (M — CHARLES MYERS D (MR
JOE DAVIS SAX (R — REV PAT HENDERSON K (O — JAMES GADSON D (R — JERRY JUMONVILLE SAX(R
DAVID NEWMAN SAX (R — JOHN THOMAS TPT (R

K52 REG KING K52

REG KING G V (A — (A) REG KING — 1971 UA UK UAS 29157
MICK EVANS B (A
ROGER POWELL D (A — IAN WHITEMAN K B FLT (A — BRIAN GODDING G V (A — DORIS TROY V (A
PETER DALE V (A — NICK JONES PERC (A — MARTIN STONE G (A — BRIAN BELSHAW B V(A
PETER SWALES V (A — BRENDA FRENCH V (A — ALAN KING G (A — KEVIN WESTLAKE D G(A
DICK THOMAS D (A — FRANK FARRELL B (A — JO WRIGHT G (A — GEORGE BARKER TPT(A
PAUL NIEMAN TROM (A — BARRY JENKINS D (A — MICK TAYLOR G (A — BRIAN AUGER K (A
DANNY McCULLOCH B (A — ELTON DEAN SAX (A — MARK CHARIG TPT (A — STEVE WINWOOD K (A

K53 KING BISCUIT BOY K53

KING BISCUIT BOY HCA G V(ALL — (A) GOOD UNS — 1971 PARAMOUNT US PAS 6023+SPFA 7001
(RICHARD NEWELL) — (A) GOOD UNS — 19 DAFFODIL IMP 934 505
LARRY ATAMANUIK D (AB — (B) OFFICIAL MUSIC — 1971 PARAMOUNT US PAS 5030+SPFL 270
ROLY GREENWAY B (AB — (C) KING BISCUIT BOY — 1974 EPIC US 32891
SONNIE BERNARDI D (A
DIANNE BROOKS V (A — BRIAN RUSSELL V (A — RHONDA SILVER V (A — RICK BELL K (AB
RHEAL LANTHIER G (AB — KELLY JAY K (AB — STEVE KENNEDY HRNS (AB — SLIDE TALLMAN HRNS(A
ALLEN TOUSSAINT PROD K V(C — ARTHUR NEVILLE K (C — LEO NOCENTELLI G (C — GEORGE PORTER JR B (C
JOSEPH MODELISTE D (C — ALFRED ROBERTS CONGA(C — CLYDE KERR JR HRNS (C — LESTER CALISTE HRNS(C
CARL BLOUIN HRNS (C — ALVIN THOMAS HRNS (C — JOAN HARMON V (C — DR JOHN G (C
DANNY McBRIDE G (C — JOHN GIBBARD G (B — DOUG RILEY K (B — MOE KOFFMAN HRNS)B
GREGG MUDRI HRNS (B

K54 KING CRIMSON K54

ROBERT FRIPP G K (ALL — (A) IN THE COURT OF THE CRIMSON KING 1969 ISLAND UK ILPS9111
MIKE GILES D (ABK — (A) IN THE COURT OF THE CRIMSON KING 1969 ATLANTIC US 8245 +RI SD19155
GREG LAKE B V (AB — (A) IN THE COURT OF THE CRIMSON KING 1969 POLYDOR UK 2302 057 +FR 2310 516
IAN McDONALD FLT K (AHK — (B) IN THE WAKE OF POSEIDON 1970 ISLAND UK ILPS9127 +US ATLANTIC 8266
MEL COLLINS SAX (BCDEH — (B) IN THE WAKE OF POSEIDON 197 POLYDOR UK 2302 058 +FR 2310 517
PETE SINFIELD LYRICS (ABCDE — (C) LIZARDS 1970 ISLAND UK ILPS9141 +US ATLANTIC 8278
PETE GILES B (BK — (C) LIZARDS 197 POLYDOR UK 2302 059 +FR 2310 518
TONY LEVIN B (M — (C) LIZARDS 1977 POLYDOR GER 2344 071
GORDON HASKELL B V (BC — (D) ISLANDS 1971 ISLAND UK ILPS9175 +US ATLANTIC 7212
ANDY McCULLOCH D (C — (D) ISLANDS 1971 POLYDOR UK 2302 060 +FR 2310 519
BOZ BURRELL B V (DE — (E) EARTHBOUND 1972 ISLAND UK HELP 6
IAN WALLACE D V (DE — (E) EARTHBOUND 1977 POLYDOR UK 2343 092 +FR 2344 074
BILL BRUFORD D (FGHJM — (F) LARKS TONGUES IN ASPIC 1973 ISLAND UK ILPS9230 +US ATLANTIC 7263
JOHN WETTON B (FGHJ — (F) LARKS TONGUES IN ASPIC 1977 POLYDOR UK 2302 061 +FR 2310 520
DAVID CROSS VLN K(FGHJ — (G) STARLESS & BIBLE BLACK 1974 ISLAND UK ILPS9275 +US ATLANTIC 7298
KEITH TIPPETT K (BCD — (G) STARLESS & BIBLE BLACK 1977 POLYDOR UK 2302 065 +FR 2310 521
ADRIAN BELEW G V (M — (G) STARLESS & BIBLE BLACK 1977 POLYDOR GER 2459 348
OBIN MILLER WIND (CDH — (H) RED 1974 ISLAND UK ILPS9308 +US ATLANTIC 18110
MARK CHARIG CORNET(CDH — (H) RED 1977 POLYDOR UK 2302 066 +FR 2310 522
HARRY MILLER B (D — (J) U S A 1975 ISLAND UK ILPS9316 +US ATLANTIC 18136
JON ANDERSON V (C — (J) U S A 1977 POLYDOR UK 2302 067 +FR 2310 523
JAMIE MUIR PERC (F — (J) U S A 1977 POLYDOR GER 2344 075
NICK EVANS TROM (C — (K) YOUNG PERSONS GUIDE TO K C DBL 1975 ISLAND UK ISLD 7 GER 89497
EDDIE JOBSON K VLN(J — (K) YOUNG PERSONS GUIDE TO K C 1977 POLYDOR UK 2612 036 +FR 2625 035
PAULINA LUCAS V (D — (L) GREATEST 197 PHONOGRAM FR 6641 356
TONY LEVIN B V (M — (M) DISCIPLINE 1981 EG UK EGLP49 GER 2302 112 US WB BSK3429

K55 KING CURTIS K55

KING CURTIS SAX (ALL — HAVE TENOR WILL BLOW — 1959 ATCO US 33113
(CURTIS OUSLEY) — SAX IN MOTION — 1963 US RI CAMDEN 2242
WILLIE BRIDGES SAX (L — SOUL SERENADE — 1964 CAPITOL US 2095
MELVIN LASTIE CORNET(L — PLAYS HITS OF SAM COOKE — 1965 US
CHARLES RAINEY B (L — THAT LOVIN' FEELIN' — 1966 ATCO US 33189
CORNELL DUPREE G (L — (L) LIVE AT SMALLS PARADISE — 1966 ATCO US 33198 UK ATLANTIC K30029
PAUL GRIFFIN PNO (L — PLAYS GREAT MEMPHIS HITS — 1967 ATCO US 33211 UK ATLANTIC 588 067
RAY LUCAS D (L — KINGSIZE SOUL — 1967 ATCO US 33231 UK ATLANTIC 587 043
NOBLE KNIGHTS (S — SWEET SOUL — 1968 ATCO US 33247 UK ATLANTIC 588 115
SHIRELLES V (E — BEST OF KING CURTIS — 1968 ATCO US 33266+US PRESTIGE 7709
BEST OF KING CURTIS — 19 ATLANTIC UK 228 002 + K40067
CHAMPION JACK DUPREE V K(B — INSTANT GROOVE — 1968 ATCO US 33293 UK ATLANTIC 228027
ONE MORE TIME(BEST OF) — 196 PRESTIGE US 7775
GET READY — 196 ATCO US 33338
LIVE AT FILLMORE — 19 ATCO US 33359 UK ATLANTIC K40214
EVERYBODY'S TALKIN' — 19 ATCO US 33385 UK ATLANTIC K40360
(E) ETERNALLY SOUL — 1970 WAND WNS4
(S) SOUL SERENADE — 1972 EMBER SPE 6600
MR SOUL — 1972 EMBER SPE 6607
(B) BLUES AT MONTREUX — 197 ATLANTIC US 1637 UK K40430
SOUL TWIST — 19 ENJOY US 2001
SOUL TIME — 19 UPFRONT US UPF 157
KING SOUL — 19 PRESTIGE US 7789
SOUL MEETING — 19 PRESTIGE US 7833
JAZZ GROOVE — 1974 PRESTIGE US 24033
STAR COLLECTION — 1974 ATLANTIC UK K30049
SAX ROCK — 1976 MUSIDISC EURO CV 1334

K56 KING EARL BOOGIE BAND K56

COLIN EARL (A — (A) TROUBLE AT MILL — 1972 DAWN DNLS 3040
PAUL KING (A
DAVE LAMBERT G (A — RUSSELL JOHN BROWN D (A — JOE RUSH PERC (A

K57 KING HARRY K57

HAROLD KING D (A — (A) DIVIDED WE STAND — 1977 EMI UK EMC 3188 US CAPITOL 11753
JOHN DICKERSON K V (A
ALAN BOWERY G B V(A — TINO LICINIO G B V (A

K58 KING HARVEST K58

Member	Inst.	Records
PETER CETERA		(B
MIKE LOVE		(B
CARL WILSON		(B
LANCE HOPPEN	B V	(A
RON ALTBACK	K	(B
TONY CAHILL	B	(B
WELLS KELLY	D	(A
ROD NOVAK	SAX	(B
SHERMAN KELLY	K	(B
DAVID ROBINSON	V B HCA	(B
BOBBY FIGUERA	D	(B
EDDIE TULEJA	G	(B
DAVID MONTGOMERY	D	(B

Record	Year / Label
(A) DANCING IN THE MOONLIGHT	1973 PYE UK NSPL28174 US PERCEPTION36
(B) KINGHARVEST	1975 A&M US SP 4540

K59 KING OF HEARTS K59

Member	Inst.	Records
ROBERT FITOUSSI	V	(A
MARC TOBALY	V G	(A
ELLIOTT RANDALL	G	(A
JAI WINDING	K	(A
JEFF LAYTON	G	(A
LEE SKLAR	B	(A
PAUL GRIFFIN	ORG	(A
RICHARD LANDIS	PROD	(A
STEVE PORCARO	K	(A
MICHAEL BRAUN	D	(A
TONY WELLS	V	(A
IVAN ELIAS	B	(A
MARTY NELSON	V	(A
STU WOODS	B	(A
PEPPI CASTRO	B	(A
LENNY ROBERTS	V	(A
DAVID BROWN	G	(A
JON JOYCE	V	(A
RICK SCHLOSSER	D	(A
DEAN KRAUS	K	(A
JIM HAAS	V	(A
JIM MAELEN	PERC	(A
LOREN FARBER	V	(A

Record	Year / Label
(A) CLOSE BUT NO GUITAR	1978 CAPITOL 11873

K59A KING PEACH K59A

Member	Inst.	Records
DONNIE McCUTCHEON	B V	(A
JOE COPELAND	G V	(A
DANNY HAYNES	K V	(A
RANDY DEHART	D V	(A

Record	Year / Label
(A) FAIR WARNING	1981 FLYING HIGH US 6504

K59B KINGBEES K59B

Member	Inst.	Records
JANIE JONES	G V	(AB
REX ROBERTS	D	(AB
MICHAEL RUMMANS	B	(AB

Record	Year / Label
(A) KINGBEES	1980 RSO
(B) THE BIG ROCK	1981 RSO

K60 KINGFISH K60

Member	Inst.	Records
DAVE TORBERT	V B	(ABC
MATTHEW KELLY	V G	(ABC
BOB WEIR	G	(AB
ROBBY HODINOTT	G	(AB
CHRIS HEROLD	D	(AB
BARRY FLASH	PNO	(A
DAVE PEPPER	D V	(AC
JOE ENGLISH	D	(C
MICHAEL O'NEILL	G V	(C
JOHN HUG	G	(C
BOB HOGINS	K V	(C
JOHNNY SANDLIN	B	(C

Record	Year / Label
(A) KINGFISH	1976 ROUND US LA 564 UK UAG 29922
(B) LIVE & KICKIN'	1977 JET US LA 732 UK UAG 30080
(C) TRIDENT	1978 JET US 35479 UK JETLP 215

K60A KINGS K60A

Member	Inst.	Records
ARYAN ZERO	G V	(AB
DAVID DIAMOND	B V	(AB
SONNY KEYES	K	(AB
MAX STYLES	D	(AB
BOB EZRIN	PNO	(B

Record	Year / Label
(A) THE KINGS ARE HERE	1980 ELEKTRA US 6E274 UK K 52250
(B) AMAZON BEACH	1981 ELEKTRA US 5E543

K60B KINGSMEN K60B

Record	Year / Label
(A) IN PERSON	1963 WAND 657
(B) VOLUME II	1964 WAND 659 PYE INT UK 28054
(C) VOLUME III	196 WAND 662
(D) ON CAMPUS	196 WAND 670
(E) 16 GREAT HITS	1966 WAND 674
(F) BEST OF	1972 SCEPTOR 18002

K61 KINKS K61

Member	Inst.	Records
RAY DAVIES	V G	(ALL
DAVE DAVIES	G V	(ALL
MICK AVORY	D	(ALL
PETER QUAIFE	B	(ABCDEFGHIJKL
JOHN DALTON	B	(OPRSTUVYbcfh
JOHN GOSLING	K	(PRSVYjbcfh6
ALAN HOLMES	HRNS	(VYbcf
LAURIE BROWN	HRNS	(Ybc
JOHN BEECHAM	HRNS	(VYbc
ANDY PYLE	B	(hj
JIM RODFORD	B	(ns
GORDON EDWARDS	K	(
NICK TREVISIK	D	(j
RON LAWRENCE	B	(j
PAMELA TRAVIS	V	(Yc
SHIRLEY RODEN	V	(c
LYNDSEY MOORE	V	(c
JUNE RITCHIE	V	(c
NICK NEWELL	K SAX	(fn
LEE PAVEY	V	(Y
KRYSIA KOCJAN	V	(Y
MIKE COTTON	TPT	(SV
SUE BROWN	V	(Y
DAVEY JONES	WIND	(V
LEWIS RICH	V	(Y
IAN GIBBONS	K	(n
SHEL TALMY	PROD	(K
A GIRTON	V	(b

Record	Year / Label
(A) THE KINKS	1964 PYE UK NPL 18096(M) 83021(S)
(B) YOU REALLY GOT ME	1965 REPRISE US 6143
(C) KINKSIZE	1965 REPRISE US 6158
(D) KINDA KINKS	1965 PYE UK NPL 18112 REPRISE US 6173
(D) KINDA KINKS	1969 MARBLE ARCH UK MAL1100
(E) KINKS KINGDOM	1966 REPRISE US 6184
(F) KINKS KONTROVERSY	1966 PYE UK NPL 18131 REPRISE US 6197
(G) KINKS GREATEST HITS	1966 REPRISE US 6217
(H) FACE TO FACE	1966 PYE UK NPL 18149 REPRISE US 6228
(I) THE KINKS (COMP)	1966 GOLDEN GUINEA UK GGL0357
(J) WELL RESPECTED KINKS	1966 MARBLE ARCH UK MAL 612
(K) LIVE AT KELVIN HALL	1967 PYE UK NSPL18191 REPRISE US 6260
(L) SOMETHING ELSE	1967 PYE UK NSPL18193 REPRISE US 6279
(M) SUNNY AFTERNOON (COMP)	1967 MARBLE ARCH UK MAL 716
(N) VILLAGE GREEN PRESERVATION SOC	1968 PYE UK NSPL18233 REPRISE US 6327
(O) ARTHUR OR DECLINE OF BRITISH EMP	1969 PYE UK NSPL18317 REPRISE US 6366
(P) KINKS PART 1 (LOLA Vs POWERMAN	1970 PYE UK NSPL18359 REPRISE US 6423
(Q) THE KINKS (COMP DBL)	1970 PYE UK NPL 18326
(R) PERCY (SOUNDTRACK)	1971 PYE UK NSPL18365
(S) MUSWELL HILLBILLIES	1971 RCA UK SF 8423 US LSP4644
(T) GOLDEN HOUR	1971 PYE UK GH 501
(U) LOLA	1971 HALLMARK UK HMA 201
(V) EVERYBODY'S IN SHOWBIZ	1972 RCA UK DPS 2035 US 6065
(W) KINK KRONIKLES	1972 REPRISE US 6454
(X) GREAT LOST KINKS ALBUM	1973 REPRISE US 2127
(Y) PRESERVATION ACT 1	1973 RCA UK SF 8392 US LPL5002
(Z) ALL THE GOOD TIMES	1973 PYE UK
(a) GOLDEN HOUR VOL 2	1973 PYE UK GH 558
(b) PRESERVATION ACT 2	1974 RCA UK 5040 US CPL5040
(c) SOAP OPERA	1975 RCA UK SF 8411 US LPI5081
(d) POP CHRONIK	1975 PYE VOL1
(e) CELLULOID HEROES (COMP)	1976 RCA UK RS 1059 US LPI1743
(f) SCHOOLBOYS IN DISGRACE	1976 RCA UK RS 1028 US FLI5102
(g) KINKS (FILE DBL)	1977 PYE UK FILD 001-1/2
(h) SLEEPWALKER	1977 ARISTA UK 1002 US AL 4106
(i) ALL THE GOOD TIMES	197 PYE UK ILPP 100/4
(j) MISFITS	1978 ARISTA UK 1055 US AL 4167
(k) 20 GOLDEN GREATS	1978 RONCO UK RPL2031
(m) LOW BUDGET	1979 ARISTA UK 1099 US AB 4240
(n) ONE FOR THE ROAD (LIVE DBL)	1980 ARISTA UK DARTY6
(o) YOU REALLY GOT ME (COMP)	1980 PYE UK NSPL18615 FR MODE 9017
(p) ALL DAY & ALL OF THE NIGHT	19 FR MODE 9054
(q) KINKS COLLECTION	1980 HALLMARK UK 072
(r) 2ND TIME AROUND	1980 RCA US 3520
(s) SPOTLIGHT	1981 PRT UK 1009
(t) GIVE THE PEOPLE WHAT THEY WANT	1981 ARISTA US 3549 UK SPARTY1171
(u) 100 MINUTES (CASSETTE)	1982 PRT UK ZCTON 102

(CONTINUED)

(EPS)
KINKSIZE HITS 1964 PYE UK NEP 24203
KWIETKINKS 1965 PYE UK NEP 24221
FOUR TIMES FOUR 1965 PYE UK NEP 24228
KINKSIZE SESSION 1966 PYE UK NEP 24200
DEDICATED KINKS 1966 PYE UK NEP 24258

K61A STEVE KIPNER K61A

STEVE KIPNER (A — (A) KNOCK DOWN THE WALLS 1980 E+ELTRA US 202

K62 KIPPINGTON LODGE K62

BARRY LANDERMAN K V — 1965/69
BOB ANDREWS K V
NICK LOWE B V — BRINSLEY SCHWARZ G V — PETER WHALE D

K63 KIRBY K63

KIRBY G (A — (A) COMPOSITION 1978 HOT WAX HW2
FRAN BYRNE D (A
IAN PAICE D (A — STEVE EMERY B (A — JOHN COOK K (A — CHRIS FLETCHER PERC(A
ROBIN JAMES PERC (A — NIGEL WATSON G (A — TONY RIVERS V (A — STUART CALVER V (A
JOHN PERRY V (A — MICK EVE HRNS (A — NORMAN NEWELL HRNS (A — BUD BEADLE HRNS (A
COLIN JACAS HRNS (A — MIKE BAILEY HRNS (A — RON ASPERY SAX (A

K64 BASIL KIRCHIN K64

BASIL KIRCHIN (AB
(A) A WORLD WITHIN WORLDS 1971 COLUMBIA UK SCX 6463
(B) WORLDS WITHIN WORLDS 3/4 1974 ISLAND UK HELP18

K64A RICHARD H KIRK K64A

RICHARD H KIRK (A — (A) DISPOSABLE ½ TRUTHS 1981 INDUSTRIAL CASS 34

K64C JOHN KIRKBRIDE K64C

JOHN KIRKBRIDE V G (A — (A) TRACKS 1976 EMI/SONGBIRD GER 31138
HERMAN VAN DER VLAG STEEL G (A
JAN THEELEN K (A — NICO VERHOEVEN B (A — MITCH CAHNEN D (A — JOKE VAN HOUT V (A
MARIETTE VIEVERMANNS V(A

K65 JOHN KIRKPATRICK & SUE HARRIS K65

JOHN KIRKPATRICK K WIND V(ABCDEFG
SUE HARRIS WIND DULC V (ABCDEFG
TONY ROSE WIND V(A
MARTIN BRINSFORD V (F
BERI CROWE V (A
ROB LENNOX V (A
ANGELA McNEILL V (A
FI FRASER V (F
TERRY ROBINSON V (A — DAVE WIGHT V (A — DENIS SHEEHAN V (A — AGNES MIRREN G (A
ASHLEY HUTCHINGS B (A — PENNIE HARRIS DULC (E — TUFTY SMITH MELOD(E — DEREK PEARSE BAN PERC(EF
GEOFF HARRIS G (E — STEWART GOLDRING G (F — ALAN HARRIS BAN (F — BILL CADDICK G (F
COLIN GOLDRING B (F — NIGEL PEGRUM D (F

(A) JUMP AT THE SUN 1972 TRAILER LER 2033
(B) ROSE OF BRITAINS ISLE 1974 TOPIC 12TS 247
(C) AMONG THE ATTRACTIONS...... 1976 TOPIC 12TS 295
(D) PLAIN CAPERS 1976 FREE REED FRR 010
(E) SHREDS & PATCHES 1977 TOPIC 12TS 355
(F) GOING SPARE 1978 FREE REED FRR 030
(G) FACING THE MUSIC 1980 TOPIC 12TS 408

K66 DANNY KIRWAN K66

DANNY KIRWAN V G (ALL
GEOFF BRITTON D (A
JIM RUSSELL D (A
ANDY SYLVESTER B (A
PAUL RAYMOND K (A
JOHN COOK PNO (BC — TEX COMER B (C — STUART CALVER V (C — JOHN PERRY V (C
STEVE EMERY B (B — KIRBY G (C — FRAN BYRNE D (C — KEVIN KITCHEN K (C
DANA GILLESPIE V (C — JEFF RICH D (B — BOB WESTON G (C — TONY RIVERS V (C
CHRIS FLETCHER PERC (C

(A) SECOND CHAPTER 1975 DJM UK DJLPS 454 US DJM 1
(B) MIDNIGHT IN SAN JUAN 1976 DJM UK DJF 20481
(C) HELLO THERE BIG BOY 1979 DJM UK DJF 20555 US DJM 22
(B) DANNY KIRWAN 1971 DJM US DJM 9

K67 KISS K67

ACE FREHLEY G (ALL
PAUL STANLEY G (ALL
GENE SIMMONS B (ALL
PETE CRISS D (A>N
BRUCE FOSTER PNO (A
ERIC CARR D (O

(A) KISS 1975 CASABLANCA US 7001 UK CBC 4003
(A) KISS 1977 CASABLANCA UK RI CAL 2006
(B) HOTTER THAN HELL 1974 CASABLANCA US 7006 UK 77 CAL 7007
(C) DRESSED TO KILL 1975 CASABLANCA US 7016 UK CBC 4004
(C) DRESSED TO KILL 1977 CASABLANCA UK RI CAL 2008
(D) ALIVE 197 CASABLANCA US 7020 UK RI CAS 5001
(E) DESTROYER 1976 CASABLANCA US 7025 UK 77 CAL 2009
(F) THE ORIGINALS 197 CASABLANCA US 7032
(G) ROCK'N'ROLL OVER 197 CASABLANCA US 7037 UK 77 CAL 2001
(H) LOVE GUN 197 CASABLANCA US 7057 UK 77 CAL 2027
(J) ALIVE 2 1978 CASABLANCA US 7076 UK CAL 5004
(K) DOUBLE PLATINUM (DBL) 1978 CASABLANCA US 7100-2 UKCALD5005
(L) DYNASTY 1979 CASABLANCA US 7152 UK CALH2051
(M) UNMASKED 1980 MERCURY US 7225 UK 6302 032
(N) THE BEST OF THE SOLO ALBUMS 1981 CASABLANCA UK 6302 060
(O) MUSIC FROM THE ELDER 1981 CASABLANCA UK 6302 163
(P) ROCK'N'ROLL OVER 1982 CASABLANCA UK 6399 060

K67A KITE K67A

(A) KITE 19 SOLENT SS 050

K67B THE KITCHEN CINQ K67B

(A) EVERYTHING BUT ..... 19 L H I US 12000

K67C KITTYHAWK K67C

(A) KITTYHAWK 19 EMI US 17029
(B) RACE FOR THE OASIS 19 EMI US 17053

K67D KIX K67D

DONNIE PURNELL B (A — (A) KIX 1981 ATLANTIC US
JIMMY CHALFANT D (A
STEVE WHITEMAN V (A — RONNIE YOUNKINS G (A — BRIAN FORSYTHE G (A

K68 KLAATU K68

(A) KLAATU 1976 CAPITOL 11542
(B) HOPE 1977 CAPITOL 11633
(C) SIR ARMY SUIT 1978 CAPITOL 11836
(D) ENDANGERED SPECIES 1980 CAPITOL 12080

K68A KLEER K68A

WOODY CUNNINGHAM D V (ABC — (A) I LOVE TO DANCE — 1979 ATLANTIC US SD 19237 UK K50614
MELANIE MOORE (C — (B) WINNERS — 1980 ATLANTIC US 19262
RICHARD LEE G (ABC — (C) LICENSE TO DREAM — 1981 ATLANTIC US SD 19288
YVETTE FLOWERS (C
PAUL CRUTCHFIELD PERC V(ABC NORMAN DURHAM B V (ABC ISABELLE COLES V (AC RANDY BRECKER HRNS (A
MARVIN STAMM HRNS (A TERRY DOLPHIN PNO (AC RICHARD CUMMINGS K (A ANGEL NATER PERC (A
LOUISE FISCHER V (A ERIC ROHRBAUGH (C

K68C SNEAKY PETE KLEINOW K68C

SNEAKY PETE STEEL(AB — (A) SNEAKY PETE — 1979 CHILOH SLP 4086
GENE PARSONS D (A — (B) COLD STEEL — 19 ARIOLA 87736
MICKEY McGEE D (A
ED PONDER D (A GREG HARRIS G (A BOBBY COCKRAN G (A SKIP BATTIN B (A
JAMIE FAUNT B (A CONNIE WILLIAMS V (A CHARLIE HARWOOD PNO (A GIB GUILBEAU V FDL(A
R BOWDEN G (B D LOVELACE PNO (B GREG ATTAWAY V D (B M A BOWDEN B (B

K68D MARK KLINGMAN K68D

MARK 'MOOGY' KLINGMAN K V (A — (A) MARK MOOGY KLINGMAN — 197 CAPITOL ST11072
RALPH SCHUCKETT (A
JOHNNY SIOMOS D (A JOHNNY SEIGLER B (A JOEL BISHOP O'BIEN MAN(A DOUG RODRIGUEZ G (A
PETE LABARBA VIBES(A COLIN WILCOX HRNS (A TERRY EATON HRNS (A KEITH JOHNSON HRNS(A
MARK ROSENGARTEN CONGA(A AMOS GARRETT G (A TODD RUNDGREN G K (A N D SMART D (A
STU WOODS B (A TOMMY COSGROVE G (A RICK DERRINGER G (A BEN KEITH STEEL DOBR(A
ROBBIE KOGEL G (A BUZZY LINHART (A RICHARD COREY FDL (A JOHNNY MILLER B (A

K68E KLYMAXX K68E

LORENA PORTER V (A — (A) NEVER UNDERESTIMATE THE POWER... — 1981 SOLAR S21 52304

K69 EARL KLUGH K69

EARL KLUGH G (ALL — (A) EARL KLUGH — 1976 BLUENOTE US LA 596
GREG PHILLINGANES K (E — (B) LIVING INSIDE YOUR LOVE — 1977 UA UK UAG 20009 BLUENOTE US 667
CHARLES MEEKS B (E — (C) FINGER PAINTING — 1977 UA UK UAG 20011 BLUENOTE US 737
RALPH MACDONALD PERC (E — (D) MAGIC IN YOUR EYES — 1978 UA UK UAG 30171 US 877
VICTOR LEWIS D (E — (E) HEART STRING — 1979 UA UK UAG 30233 US 942
PHIL UPCHURCH G (E — (F) DREAM COME TRUE — 1980 UA UK UAG 30092 LIBERTY US 1026
GLORIA AGOSTINI HARP (G — (G) LATE NIGHT GUITAR — 1980 UA UK UAG 30332 LIBERTY US 1079
DR GIBBS PERC (G — (H) CRAZY FOR YOU — 1981 LIBERTY UK 30329
DAVID SPINOZZA G (G
PHIL BODNER WIND (G WALTER KANE WIND (G DAVID FRIEDMAN PERC (G JOSEPH SHEPLEY TPT (G
SAM BURTIS TROM (G JOSE MADERA PERC (G LEWIS PEAR B (G JACK KULOWITCH B (G
JAY ELFENBEIN B (G RON CUBER SAX (G KEN ASCHER PNO (G MICHAEL COLLAZO PERC(G
GINO BIONDO B (G MARCUS MILLER B (G JOHN GATCHELL TPT (G DAVID TOFANI SAX (G

K69A THE KNACK K69A

DOUG FIEGER G (ABC — (A) GET THE KNACK — 1979 CAPITOL 11948
BERTON AVERRE G (ABC — (B) BUT THE LITTLE GIRLS UNDERSTAND — 1980 CAPITOL 12045
BRUCE GARY D (ABC — (C) ROUND TRIP — 1981 CAPITOL
PRESCOTT NILES B (ABC

K69B KNICKERBOCKERS K69B

JOHN CHARLES B (— (A) LLOYD THAXTON PRESENTS... — 196 CHALLENGE US 12664
BEAU CHARLES G (— (B) JERK & TWINE — 196 CHALLENGE US 621 RI GER LINE5082
BUDDY RANDALL SAX (— (C) LIES — 1966 CHALLENGE US 622 LONDON UK 8294
JIMMY WALKER D (A — (C) LIES — 198 LINE GER 5056
(D) STICK WITH US — 198 LINE GER 5155

K70 CURTIS KNIGHT K70

CURTIS KNIGHT G V (ALL — (A) DOWN THE VILLAGE — 19 PARAMOUNT US5023
JIMI HENDRIX G (BCD — (B) GET THAT FEELING — 1968 LONDON UK SH 8349 DECCA US195002
EDDIE CLARKE G (E — (C) STRANGE THINGS — 1968 LONDON UK SH 8369 DECCA US185005
NICKY HOPKINS K (E — (D) THE WILD ONE — 1973 HALLMARK UK 791
CHRIS PERRY PERC (E — (E) SECOND COMING — 1974 DAWN UK DNLS3060
JOHN WEIR B (E

K71 JEAN KNIGHT K71

JEAN KNIGHT — (A) Mr BIG STUFF — 1977 STAX US ST2045 UK STX 1004

K72 GLADYS KNIGHT & THE PIPS K72

GLADYS KNIGHT V (ALL — EVERYBODY NEEDS LOVE — 1967 SOUL US 706 TAMLA UK STML 11058
WITH — FEELIN BLUESY — 1968 SOUL US 707
THE PIPS — TASTIEST HITS — 1968 BELL US 6013
MERALD KNIGHT V (— SILK & SOUL — 1969 SOUL US 711 TAMLA UK STML 11100
BRENDAN KNIGHT V (— NITTY GRITTY — 1970 SOUL US 713 TAMLA UK STML 11135
WILLIAM GUEST V (— GREATEST HITS — 1970 SOUL US 723 TAMLA UK STML 11148
ELENOR GUEST V (— ALL IN A KNIGHTS WORK — 197 SOUL US 730
EDWARD PATTEN V (— IF I WERE YOUR WOMAN — 1971 SOUL US 731 TAMLA UK STML 11187
DEAN PARKS G (X — STANDING OVATION — 1972 SOUL US 736 TAMLA UK STML 11208
DAVID T WALKER G (X — HELP ME MAKE IT THROUGH THE NIGHT — 1973 TAMLA UK STML 11226
BOB BABBITT B (X — NEITHER ONE OF US — 1973 SOUL US 737 TAMLA UK STML 11230
REINI PRESS B (X — ALL I NEED IS TIME — 1974 SOUL US '39 TAMLA UK STML 11264
JOE SAMPLE K (X — ANTHOLOGY — 1974 TAMLA US 792 UK TMSP 1127
VICTOR FELDMAN PERC (X — GLADYS KNIGHT & THE PIPS — 1974 HALLMARK UK SHM 833
PLAS JOHNSON HRNS (X — IMAGINATION — 1974 BUDDAH US 5141 UK BDLP 4005
DAVID LUELL HRNS (X — CLAUDINE — 1974 BUDDAH US 5602 UK BDLP 4010
GARY GRANT TPT (X — I FEEL A SONG — 197 BUDDAH US 5612 UK BDLP 4030
RANDY ALOSCROFT TROM (X — 2ND ANNIVERSARY — 1975 BUDDAH US 5639 UK BDLP 4038
JIM GILTRAP V (X — 2ND ANNIVERSARY — 1975 BUDDAH UK 2318 111
DAN FERGUSON G (X — KNIGHT TIME — 1975 SOUL US 741 TAMLA UK STML 11279
DAVID HUNGATE B (X — A LITTLE KNIGHT MUSIC — 1975 SOUL US 744 TAMLA UK STML 12013
BOB GLOUB B (X — BEST OF — 1975 STAX UK STX 1042
DAVID FOSTER PNO (X — GLADYS KNIGHT & THE PIPS — 1975 DJM UK DJMLD 8010
ED GREENE D (X — SUPER HITS — 1976 TAMLA UK STMA 8026
JIM HORN HRNS (X — PIPE DREAMS — 1976 BUDDAH US 5676 UK BDLP 5017
MIKE ALTSCHUL HRNS (X — TAKE ME IN YOUR ARMS — 1976 MFP UK 50304
RAY PIZZI HRNS (X — STILL TOGETHER — 1977 BUDDAH US 5689 UK BDLP 5014
GENE GOE TPT (X — BEST OF — 1977 BUDDAH UK BDLP 5013
BILL WATROUS TROM (X — BLESS THIS HOUSE — 1978 BUDDAH US 5651 UK BDLP 4050
GLADYS KNIGHT — 1979 CBS UK 83341
(X) MISS GLADYS KNIGHT — 1979 BUDDAH US 5714 UK BDLP 4056
(X) MISS GLADYS KNIGHT — 1979 BUDDAH GER 6 23694

(CONTINUED)

K72 GLADYS KNIGHT & THE PIPS (CONTINUED) K72

LETTER FULL OF TEARS 19 FURY US 1003
VERY BEST OF 19 UA US LA503
EARLY HITS 19 SPRINGBOARD US 4035
HOW DO YOU SAY GOODBYE 19 SPRINGBOARD US 4050
BEST OF 19 MODE FR 9021
GLADYS KNIGHT & THE PIPS 19 TRIP US 3500
" " " " " 19 UP FRONT US 130
" " " " " 19 UP FRONT US 185
" " " " " 19 SPHERE SOUND US 7006
" " " " " 19 MAXX US 3000
20 GOLDEN GREATS 1979 MOTOWN UK STML 12122
30 GREATEST HITS 1979 K TEL UK NE1004
MEMORIES 1979 BUDDAH BLD 2004
A TOUCH OF LOVE 1980 K TEL UK 1090
SPOTLIGHT 1980 PRT UK 1006
ABOUT LOVE 1980 CBS US 36387 UK 84178
TAKE ME BACK 1980 MANHATTAN UK 5000
NIGHTFUL 1980 MANHATTAN UK 5001
FIRST SHOT 1980 MANHATTAN UK 5002
FUNKY 1980 MANHATTAN UK 5003
I HEARD IT THROUGH THE GRAPVINE 19 PICKWICK US 3534
POW 19 PICKWICK US 3374
GOLDEN HITS 19 FIRST RECORD US 1001

K73 REGGIE KNIGHTON K73

REGGIE KNIGHTON G V (AB
BRIAN RAY G (B
GLENN SYMMONDS D (B
JOHN STAEHELY G (B KURTIS TEEL B (B GEOFF WORKMAN STRINGS(B JON LIND V (B
RICHARD HOVEY V (B

(A) REGGIE KNIGHTON 1977 CBS US 34685
(B) REGGIE KNIGHTON BAND 1978 CBS US 35286 UK 82627

K74 BUDDY KNOX K74

BUDDY KNOX G V (ALL
DON LANIER G (
DAVE ALLDRED D (
JIMMY BOWEN B (

BUDDY KNOX 1957 ROULETTE US 25003
BUDDY KNOX & JIMMY BOWEN(1 SIDE EACH 19 ROULETTE US 25048
BUDDY KNOX 19 POINT US 201
BUDDY KNOX IN NASHVILLE 19 POINT US 289
GOLDEN HITS 196 LIBERTY US LST 7251
GYPSY MAN 1970 U A US UAS 6689
ROCK REFLECTIONS 1971 SUNSET UK SLS 50206
BUDDY KNOX ROCKS 1973 SWEETWATER CAN SW 1001
PARTY DOLL 1978 PYE INT UK NSPL28243
FOUR ROCK LEGENDS (8 TRACKS) 1978 HARVEST HERITAGE UK SHSM 2024

K75 KRYSIA KOCJAN K75

KRYSIA KOCJAN G V (A
STEVE HAYTON G (A
JERRY DONAHUE G (A RABBIT BUNDRICK K (A ALAN SHEARER VLV (A JOHN McLEVY TPT (A
ROY SIDWELL SAX (A DAVE PEGG B (A RAY COOPER PERC(A ROGER CHURCHYARD VLN (A
DAVE SHARMAN TROM (A DAVE MATTACKS D (A MOX FLT (A TONY COE CLAR (A
HARRY KLEIN SAX (A

(A) KRYSIA 1974 RCA UK LPLI 5052

K75A JOHN KOERNER K75A

'SPIDER' JOHN KOERNER (ALL
WILLIE MURPHY (D

(A) MUSIC IS JUST A BUNCH OF NOTES 19 SWEETJANE US SJL 5872
(B) SONGS LIKE THEY USED TO 19 SWEETJANE US 1074
(C) SPIDER BLUES 19 ELEKTRA US 7290
(D) RUNNING JUMPING STANDING STILL 19 ELEKTRA US 74041 UK K42026

K75B KOERNER,RAY & GLOVER K75B

JOHN KOERNER G (ALL
DAVE RAY G (ALL
TONY GLOVER HCA (ALL

(A) BLUES RAGS & HOLLERS 19 ELEKTRA US 240
(B) GOOD OLD KOERNER, RAY & GLOVER 19 MILL CITY US MCR 172
(C) LOTS MORE BLUES RAGS & HOLLERS 19 ELEKTRA US 7267
(D) RETURN OF KOERNER ,RAY & GLOVER 19 ELEKTRA US 7305

K76 KOKOMO K76

TONY O'MALLEY V K (ABC
PADDY McHUGH V (ABC
DYAN BIRCH V (ABC
FRANK COLLINS V (ABC
MEL COLLINS SAX (ABC TERRY STANNARD D (A JIM MULLEN G (A ALAN SPENNER V B (ABC
JOHN SUSSEWELL D (B NEIL HUBBARD G (ABC JODY LINCOTT PERC(C STEVE BERRY TROM (C
TONY BEARD D (C JAMES MACK K (C BOB WESSBERG PERC(C BOBBY LEWIS TPT (C
PAUL HOWARD TPT 'C FRANK TESUINSKY TROM (C PAT FERRERI G (C TERRY FRYER SYN (C

(A) KOKOMO 1975 CBS US 33442 UK 80670
(B) RISE & SHINE 1975 CBS US 34031 UK 69229
(C) KOKOMO 1982 CBS UK 85604

K76A MARTIN KOLBE UND RALF ILLENBERGER K76A

MARTIN KOLBE (AB
RALF ILLENBERGER (AB

(A) COLOURING THE LEAVES 19 MOOD 23 700
(B) WAVES 1980 MOOD 22 900

K76B KOLLEKTIV K76B

JURGEN KARPENKIEL B (A
JURGEN HAUIX G (A
WALDERMAR KARPENKIEL D(A KLAUS DAPPER WIND (A

(A) KOLLEKTIV 1973 BRIAN GER 1034

K77 BONNIE KOLOC K77

BONNIE KOLOC G V (ALL
NORMAN CHRISTIAN D (ABC
RON SCROGGIN G HCA B V (ABC
STU HEISS G (A
PHIL UPCHURCH B G (AB
ALLEN BARCUS PNO (AB
SID SIMMS B (A
TREVOR VEITCH G DOB(B

(A) AFTER ALL THIS TIME 1971 LONDON UK 8432 OVATION US 14 21
(B) HOLD ON TO ME 1972 LONDON UK 8440 OVATION US 14 26
(C) BONNIE KOLOC 1973 OVATION US 14 29
(D) YOU'RE GONNA LOVE YOURSELF 1974 OVATION US 14 38
(E) CLOSE UP 1976 EPIC US 34184
(F) WILD RECLUSE 1978 EPIC US 35254
(G) AT HER BEST 1977 OVATION US 1701

BOB LEWIS G (B BOBBY CHRISTIAN PERC (BC PHIL THOMAS CONGA(B WALLY PILLICH B (B
CHUCK DE MEYER K V (C JONATHAN PEARTHREE G V(C HAROLD KRITZ B (C DAVID VAN DELINDER G (C
LONNIE KNIGHT G (C DANNY LONG PNO (C DAVID BRIGGS PNO (D MIKE LEECH B (D
NORBERT PUTNAM B (D HENRY STRZELECKI B (D REGGIE YOUNG G (D JOHNNY CHRISTOPHER G (D
BILLY SANFORD G (D JIMMY COLVARD G (D PETE WADE G (D STEVE GOODMAN G (DE
KENNY MALONE D (D LARRY LONDIN D (D JERRY CARRIGAN D (D FARRELL MORRIS PERC (D
RUSTY YOUNG STEEL(E DAVID LINDLEY G (E PAUL HARRIS K (E BRYAN GAROFALO B (E
GARY MALLABER D (E GUILLE GARCIA CONGA(E PHILIP DONNELLY G (E JAI WINDING PNO(E
DONNIE FRITTS PNO (E CHUCK DOMANICO B (E CORKY SIEGEL HCA (E MIKE CAMPBELL G (E
DON MENZA WIND (E RAY NEOPOLITAN B (E

K77A KOMINTERN K77A

SERGE CATTALANO D (A (A) LE BAL DU RAT MORT 1971 HARVEST PATHE FR 2C 062 11774
RICHARD AUBERT VLN (A
OLIVIER ZDRZALIK B G V (A FRANCIS LEMONNIER SAX V(A MICHEL MUSAC G (A PASCAL CHASSIN G (A

K78 JOHN KONGOS K78

JOHN KONGOS V G PERC (AB (A) CONFUSIONS ABOUT GOLDFISH 1969 JANUS US 3032 DAWN UK DNLS 3002
CALEB QUAYE G (B (B) JOHN KONGOS 1971 ELEKTRA US 75019 FLY UK HIFLY 7
DAVE GLOVER B (B
ROGER POPE D (B RAY COOPER PERC (B MIKE NOBLE PERC(B DAVID CHAMBERS HRNS (B
LOL COXHILL SAX (B MIKE MORAN K (B RALPH McTELL G (B GUS DUDGEON PERC(B
SUE GLOVER V (B SUNNY LESLIE V (B CLAIRE DENIZ CELLO(B

K79 KOOBAS K79

ROY MORRIS (A (A) KOOBAS 1969 COLUMBIA UK SCX 6291
STU LEATHERWOOD (A
KEITH ELLIS B (A TONY O'RILEY (A

K80 KOOL & THE GANG K80

ROBERT 'KOOL' BELL B V(ALL (A) KOOL & THE GANG 19 DE LITE US 2003
CHARLES'CLAYDES'SMITH G V(OQRCF (B) MUSIC IS THE MESSAGE 19 DE LITE US 2011 POLYDOR 2347 004
GEORGE BROWN D V K(OQRCF (C) LIVE AT THE SEX MACHINE 19 DELITE US 2008 POLYDOR 2343 083
ROBERT MICKENS TPT V(OQRCF (D) BEST 19 DE LITE US 2009
OTHA NASH V HRNS(O (E) LIVE AT PJs 19 DE LITE US 2010
DENNIS THOMAS WIND K V (OQRCF (F) GOOD TIMES 19 DE LITE US 2012
RON'KHALIS BAYYAN'BELL WIND K V(OQRCF(G) WILD & PEACEFUL 1974 DE LITE US 2013 POLYDOR UK 2310 299
DONAL BOYCE V (O (H) LIGHT OF WORLDS 1974 DE LITE US 2014 POLYDOR UK 2310 357
KEVIN LASSITER K V (O (J) GREATEST HITS 1975 DE LITE US 2015 POLYDOR UK 2310 401
RENEE CONNEL V (O (K) SPIRIT OF THE BOOGIE 1975 DE LITE US 2016 POLYDOR UK 2310 416
ARTHUR CAPEHART TPT (O (L) LOVE & UNDERSTANDING 1976 DE LITE US 2018 POLYDOR UK 2310 441
BEVERLEY OWENS V (O (M) BEHIND THE EYES 197 POLYDOR
CYNTHIA HUGGINS V (OQ (N) OPEN SESAME 197 DE LITE US 2025
M.F.S.B. STRINGS (O (O) THE FORCE 1977 DE LITE US 9501 MERCURY 6372 700
JOAN MOTLEY V (OQ (P) SPIN THEIR TOP HITS 1978 DE LITE US 9507
CHRIS ALBERT TPT (Q (Q) LADIES NIGHT 1979 DE LITE US 9513 UK 6372 763
JON FADDIS TPT (Q (R) CELEBRATE 1980 DE LITE US 9518 UK 6359 029
EARL TOON K V (RQ ( ) KOOL JAZZ 1975 DE LITE US 4001
DIANE CAMERON V (Q (T) EVERYBODYS DANCIN' 1979 DE LITE US 9509
CEDRIC TOON V (RQ (U) SOMETHING SPECIAL 1981 DELITE UK DSR 001
KEVIN BELL K (R
JAMES J T TAYLOR V (QR MEEKAEEL MUHAMMAD V (R ADAM IPPOLITO K (RQ EUMIR DEODATO K (Q
CLIFF ADAMS TROM (Q STRINGS (F SHARON MOE HRN(F BILLY BROWN HRN (F
ASSUNTA DELL AQUILA HARP(F RICKY WESTFIELD K (CF

K81 AL KOOPER K81

AL KOOPER K G V(ALL (A) SUPER SESSION 1969 CBS US 9701 UK 63396
MIKE BLOOMFIELD G (ACL (A) SUPER SESSION 1973 EMBASSY RI UK 31029
STEPHEN STILLS G (AL (B) I STAND ALONE 1969 CBS US 9718 UK 63538
HARVEY BROOKS B (AGL (C) LIVE ADVENTURES (DBL) 1969 CBS US PG6 UK 66216
EDDIE HOH D (AL (D) YOU NEVER KNOW WHO YOUR FRIENDS...1969 CBS US 9855 UK 63651
BARRY GOLDBERG K (AL (E) KOOPER SESSIONS 1970 CBS US 9951 UK 63797
SHUGGIE OTIS G (EL (F) EASY DOES IT 1970 CBS US 30031 UK 66252
WELLS KELLY D (EGL (G) LANDLORD 1971 U A UK 29120
STU WOODS B (ELF (H) NEW YORK CITY 1971 CBS US 30506 UK 64340
MARK KLINGMAN K (E (J) POSSIBLE PROJECTION OF FUTURE 1972 CBS US 31159 UK 64208
CARLOS SANTANA G (C (K) NAKED SONGS 1973 CBS US 31793 UK 65193
RALPH CASALE G (D (L) AL'S BIG DEAL(UNCLAIMED FREIGHT)DBL)1975 CBS US 33169 UK 88093
ERIC GALE G (DG (N) ACT LIKE NOTHINGS WRONG 1976 UA UK 30020
ERNIE HAYES K (D (O) AL KOOPER & STEVE KATZ 19 VERVE UK 2304010
PAUL GRIFFIN K (D
FRANK OWENS K (DG CHUCK RAINEY B (DG JERRY JEMMOTT B (D JOHN MILLER B (DGF
BERNARD PURDIE D (D AL RODGERS G D (DFG BERNIE GLOW TPT (DG ERNIE ROYAL TPT(D
MARVIN STAMM TPT (DG RAY DESIO TROM (D JIMMY KNEPPER TROM (D BILL WATRONS TROM(D
TONY STUDD TROM (D GEORGE YOUNG SAX (DG SOL SCHLINGER SAX (D SELDON POWELL SAX (D
JOE FARRELL SAX (DG MANNY GREEN VLN (D JERRY KUSHNICK STRINGS(D STAN POLLEY STRINGS(D
AARON SCHECTER STRING(D HILDA HARRIS V (DEL CONNIE ZIMET V (D ALBERTINE ROBERTSON V(DELK
MIKE GATELY V (DJK ROBERT JOHN V (DJK LOU CHRISTIE V (D CHARLIE CALELLO V(D
MAERETHA STEWART V((GLK LORRAINE ELLISON V (G STAPLES SINGERS V (G JOHN HALL G(G
PHIL BODNER WIND (G PAUL HARRIS PNO (G JOE BECK G (G STEVE KATZ G(LO
FRED LIPSIUS SAX (LF BOBBY COLOMBY D V (FL JERRY WEISS HRNS (L RANDY BRECKER HRNS(L
DICK HALLIGAN HRNS (L JIM FIELDER B (L AL GORGONI G (L JOHN SIMON PNO (L
VALERIE SIMPSON V (LE MELBA MOORE V (L BOB DYLAN G V (L RON CORNELIUS G(L
CHARLIE DANIELS G B (BLF RUSS KUNKEL D (L JOHN KAHN B (LC SKIP PROKOP D(L
PAUL SIMON V (LC J R COBB G (LK BARRY BAILEY G (LK DEAN DAUGHTRY PNO(LK
PAUL GODDARD B (L ROBERT NIX D (LK EILEEN GILBERT V (LK LINDA NOVEMBER V(LK
TASHA THOMAS V (LK PATTI AUSTIN V (LK JERRY KENNEDY G (LB WAYNE MOSS G (LBF
CHARLIE McCOY HCA (BFL KENNY BUTTREY D (LBF RICK MAROTTA D (LF HERBIE FLOWERS B (LHJ
KEN SCOTT (L BLOSSOMS V (LBF DON ELLIS HRNS (B ELVIN BISHOP G (B
STEVEN MILLER K (B DAVE BROWN B (B JOE OSBORNE B (F LYLE RITZ B (F
STU SCHAFF G (FJ KEITH ALLISON G (F FREDDIE WELLER G (F LOUIE SHELTON G (FH
TOMMY TEDESCO G (F TOM COSGROVE G (F DAVID BROMBERG STEEL(F PETE DRAKE STEEL(F
EARL PALMER STEEL(F MILT HOLLAND PERC (F GEORGE DEVENS PERC (F LARRY KNECHTEL K (F
CALEB QUAYE G (H SNEAKY PETE STEEL(H CAROL KAYE B (H BOBBY WEST B (HJ
BOBBIE HALL PERC (HJ ROGER POPE D (H PAUL HUMPRHIES D (HJ RITA COOLIDGE V (H
VANETTA FIELDS V (HJ CLYDIE KING V (HJ DONNA WEISS V (H JULIA TILLMAN V (H
DOROTHY MORRISSON V (H CLAUDIA LENNEAR V (HJ EDNA WRIGHT V (HJ LORNA WILLARD V (H
EDNA WOODS V (H MAXINE WILLARD V (H ROBBIE MONTGOMERY V (H JESSIE SMITH V (H
ROBERT JOHN V (H MIKE GATELY V (H JAY SEIGAL V (H ALAN PARKER G (J
BARRY MORGAN D (J LINDA LEWIS V (J OMA DRAKE V (J CHARLIE BROWN G (K
JOHN PAUL FETTA B (J PAUL GODDARD B (J JUNIOR HANLEY D (J RICHARD GREEN FDL (J
MARUGA PERC (J

K82 PAUL KORDA K82

PAUL KORDA V K G(A (A) PASSING STRANGER 1971 MAM MAM AS 1003
ALAN GORRIE B K G V(A
ROB TAIT D (A ONNIE McINTYRE G (A RAY RUSSELL G (A DORIS TROY V (A
MADELINE BELL V (A NANETTE NEWMAN V (A ANDY ROBERTS G (A CHRIS SPEDDING G (A
JONATHAN COUDRILLE K (A MIKE STOREY K (A

K83 KORGIS K83

ANDY DAVIS V K D MAND (A (A) THE KORGIS 1979 RIALTO UK TENOR 101 US WB 3349
JAMES WARREN V B (A (B) DUMB WAITERS 1980 RIALTO UK TENOR 104 US ASYLUM290
PHIL HARRISON K PERC(A (C) STICKT GEORGE 1981 RIALTO UK ALTO 103
GLENN TOOMEY K (A
DAVID LORD K (A BILL BIRKS D (A AL POWELL D (A STUART GORDON VLNMAND(A
KEITH WARMINGTON HCA (A KENNY LACEY PERC (A JO MULLEY V (A JO POMEROY V (A

K84 ALEXIS KORNER K84

ALEXIS KORNER G V (ALL
ERIC CLAPTON G (V
ZOOT MONEY K (HNPQV
CHRIS FARLOWE V (V
IAN STEWART V (VY
PAUL JONES V (V
ART THEMAN WIND (CHDRV
MEL COLLINS HRNS (NOPQV
DICK MORRISSEY SAX (VT
DICK HECKSTALL SMITH SAX(DHMVX
JOHN SURMAN SAX (MVI
MIKE ZWERIN TROM (V
COLIN HODGKINSON B (IMPQSTV
STU SPEAR (V
JIMMY LITHERLAND G (V
GUS JOHNSON (V
IAN WALLACE D (NOPQ
BOZ BURRELL B (NOPQ
STEVE MARRIOTT ORG (NS
DAVE CASTLE WIND (CHR
HERBIE GOINS V (CHMR
RON EDGEWORTH K (CHR
DANNY THOMPSON B (CEHM
BARRY HOWTEN D (CHR
CYRIL DAVIES HCA V(CMX
KEITH SCOTT PNO (MA
COLIN BOWDEN D (M
DAVE STEVENS PNO (M
CHARLIE WATTS D (MY
JACK BRUCE B (MXY
TERRY COX D (ME
CHRIS PYNE TROM PNO (MEI
RAY WARLEIGH SAX (MI
DAVE HOLLAND B (M
ALAN SKIDMORE SAX (ME
GINGER BAKER D (MX

(A) R & B AT THE MARQUEE 1962 ACE OF CLUBS UK ACL 1130
(A) R & B AT THE MARQUEE 196 DECCA 846039
(B) AT THE CAVERN 1964 ORIOLE UK
(C) RED HOT FROM ALEX 1964 TRANSATLANTIC UK TRA 117
(D) BLUES INC 1965 ACE OF CLUBS UK ACL 1187
(D) BLUES INC 196 DECCA GER 419
(E) BLUES INC 1967 POLYDOR UK 236 206
(F) I WONDER WHO 1967 FONTANA UK STL5381
(G) NEW GENERATION OF BLUES 1968 SONET SLP 64
(G) NEW GENERATION OF BLUES 1968 LIBERTY LBS 83147
(G) NEW GENERATION OF BLUES 1968 PHILIPS 6401 901
(H) ALEXIS KORNERS ALL STARS BLUES INC 69 TRANSATLANTIC UK TRASAM 7
(I) BOTH SIDES 1969 METRONOME MLP 15364
(J) THE NEW CHURCH 1970 METRONOME
(K) ALEXIS 1971 RAK UK SRAK 501
(L) WHATS THAT SOUND I HEAR 1971 SUNSET UK SLS 50245
(M) BOOTLEG HIM 1972 RAK UK SRAKSP 51 US WB 1966
(N) ACCIDENTALLY BORN IN NEW ORLEANS 1973 TRANSATLANTIC UK TRA 269
(N) ACCIDENTALLY BORN IN NEW ORLEANS 1973 WB US 2647
(N) THE ACCIDENTAL BAND 1973 BRAIN GER 1022
(O) SNAPE LIVE ON TOUR 1974 BRAIN 2/ 1039
(P) ALEXIS KORNER 1974 POLYDOR GER 2374 109
(Q) MR BLUES 1974 TOADSTOOL 35434
(R) BLUES INC 1974 JUST SUNSHINE US JUST13
(S) GET OFF MY CLOUD 1975 CBS US 33427 UK 69155
(T) JUST EASY 1978 INTERCORD INT 60099
(U) ME (DIRECT CUT) 1979 JETON 100 3305
(V) THE PARTY LP 1980 INTERCORD GER 170 000
(W) TELL 1980 TELDEC GER 623075
(X) PROFILE 1981 TELDEC GER 624425
(Y) ROCKETT 88 1981 ATLANTIC 50776
(Z) THE ORIGINAL 1980 TRANSATLANTIC NL 44014
(a) WHITE & BLUE 1980 BLUE SILVER FR 3008

GRAHAM BOND SAX (MX JOHNNY PARKER PNO (MXD NIGEL STANGER SAX (M BRIAN SMITH SAX (M
PETER THORUP V G(MNOPQI PAUL RODGERS V (MI ANNETTE BROX V (MI ANDY FRASER B (MI
LOL COXHILL SAX (M JOHN MARSHALL D (MI MALCOLM GRIFFITHS TROM(M HAROLD BECKETT TPT(IQPM
HENRY LOWTHER TPT (MI VICTOR BROX PNO TPT V(M ROBERT PLANT V HCA(M STEVE MILLER PNO (MG
PETER FENSOME V (M ROY BABBINGTON B (M CHRIS McGREGOR PNO (M LARRY POWER G (M
JACK BROOKS D (M JOHN CAMERON K (MP ALAN PARKER G (M HERBIE FLOWERS B (M
BARRY MORGAN D (M TONY CARR D (MQP SPIKE HEATLEY B (AMX JIM LAWLESS PERC(M
BILL LESAGE PERC (M HAROLD McNAIR FLT (M TONY COE WIND (M PETE KING WIND(M
DANNY MOSS WIND (M BOB EFFORD WIND (M RON ROSS WIND (M NEIL SANDERS HRNS(M
KENNY WHEELER TPT (MI GREG BOWEN TPT (M TONY FISHER TPT (M LES CONDON TPT (M
DON LUSHER TROM (M JOHN MARSHALL TROM(M BRIAN PERRIN TROM (M BILL GELDARD TROM(M
SAPPHO GILLETT KORNER V(JSTV GRAHAM BURBRIDGE D (A LONG JOHN BALDRY V (AX MIKE SCOTT (D
PHIL SEAMAN D (D MIKE PATTO PNO (QP ELTON DEAN SAX (QP NICK EVANS TROM (QP
CAROL MORGAN V (Q RON ASPERY SAX (QP RICK MISHLEN V (Q EDDIE MORDUE SAX (QP
DUSTER BENNETT HCA (QP PADDY McHUGH V (S DYANE BIRCH V (S MORRIS PERT PERC(S
GEORGE CALDWELL PERC (S JASON CAINE PERC (S TONY O MALLEY PNO (S NICKY HOPKINS PNO (S
TERRY STANNARD D (S RICK WILLS D (S ALAN SPENNER D (S PETER FRAMPTON G(S
GASPAR LAWAL PERC (O DUFFY POWER HCA (EV TIM HINKLEY P(ONPQ NEIL HUBBARD G(S
KEITH RICHARD G (S NEIL FORD G (T GEORGE GREEN PNO (Y COLIN SMITH TPT (Y
FRANK COLLINS V (S IRENE CHANTER V (S SUNNY LESLIE V (S LISA STRIKE V(S
BARRY ST JOHN V (S JOANNE WILLIAMS V (S JIM DIAMOND V (T DAVE WINTOUR B (T
HENRY SPINETTI D (T GRAHAM DEAKIN D (T GRAHAM BROAD D (T MICK WEAVER K (T
RICHIE ZITO G (T PETER WARD G (T DANNY McKINTOSH G (T RONNIE JONES V (X
JIM BRAY B (X MIKE COLLINS PERC (X CHRIS CAPON B (X DAVE STEVENS PNO (X
HAL SINGER SAX (Y JOHN PICARD TROM (Y DON WELLER SAX (Y

K84A ARTIE KORNFELDS TREE K84A

TONY LEVIN B (A (A) A TIME TO REMEMBER 1970 DUNHILL 50092 UK PROBE SPB 1022
HUGH McCRACKEN G (A
FRANK HARRIS K (A MIKE MENICCI PERC (A DONALD McDONLD D (A

K84B KORONA K84B

BRUCE BLACKMAN K V (A (A) KORONA 1980 UA US 1020
BOB GAUTHLER G V (A

K85 KORPS K85

(A) HELLO WORLD 1979 LIMP IMP 1002

K86 DANNY KORTCHMAR K86

DANNY KORTCHMAR G V (A (A) KOOTCH 1973 WB US BS 2711
WILLIAM SMITH K (A (B) INNUENDO 1980 ASYLUM US 250 NL 52207
CRAIG DOERGE K (A
JIM HORN WIND (A DOUG RICHARDSON SAX (A ABIGALE HANESS V (A DAVID KEMPER D (B
BOB GLAUB B (B LOUISE GOFFIN V (B DAVID LASBY V (B JIM KELTNER D (B
LEE SKLAR B (B WADDY WACHTEL G V (B MICHAEL BODDICKER SYN (B KENNY EDWARDS B (B
JULES SHEAR V (B ARNOLD McCULLER V (B RICK MAROTTA PERC (B PAUL STALLWORTH B(B

K86A TONY KOSINEC K86A

TONY KOSINEC G V (A — (A) PROCESSES 19 CBS US 9832
SKIP PROKOP D (A
PAUL HOFFERT K (A HARVEY BROOKS B (A RALPH COLE G (A PATTI LABELLE V (A
BLUEBELLES V (A

K87 PAUL KOSSOFF K87

PAUL KOSSOFF G (AB — (A) BACK STREET CRAWLER 1973 ISLAND UK/US ILPS 9264
ALAN WHITE D (A — (B) KOSS (COMP DBL) 1977 DJM US 300 UK 29002
EDDIE QUANSAH HRNS (B — (C) THE HUNTER 1981 STREET TIMES UK STLP 001
RABBIT BUNDRICK K (AB
ALAN SPENNER B (A JEAN ROUSSEL K (A JESS RODEN V (A TETSU YAMAUCHI B (AB
SIMON KIRKE D (AB JOHN MARTYN G (AB PAUL RODGERS V (AB ANDY FRASER B (AB
CONRAD ISADORE D (A CLIVE CHAMAN B (A TREVOR BURTON B (A DAVID HOOD B (B
ROGER HAWKINS D (B BARRY BECKETT K (B PETE CARR G (B JIMMY JOHNSON G (B
MIKE KELLIE D (B DAVID ELLIOTT PNO (B TONY BRAUNAGEL D (B TERRY WILSON B (B
MIKE MONTGOMERY PNO (B PETER COX V (B JIM CAPALDI V (B SUE GLOVER V (B
EDDIE BAIRD G K V(B TERRY WINCOTT G V (B WILLY MURRAY D (B SUNNY LESLIE D (B
MICK FEAT B (B TERRY WILSON SLESSER V (B GEORGE LARNYOH HRNS (B PETER VANDER PUIJE HRNS(B
EDDIE QUANSAH HRNS (B

K88 LEO KOTTKE K88

LEO KOTTKE G (ALL — (A) CIRCLE AROUND THE SUN 1970 SYMPOSIUM 2001
MIKE JOHNSON G (G — (B) MUDLARK 1971 CAPITOL 682
BILL BERG PERC (FGI — (C) LEO KOTTKE 6 & 12 STRING GUITAR 1972 SONET UK SNTF 629 TAKOMA US1024
BILL PETERSON B (FGI — (D) GREENHOUSE 1973 CAPITOL 11000
BILL BARBER SYN (FGI — (E) MY FEET ARE SMILING 1973 CAPITOL 11164
CAL HAND STEEL(FG — (F) ICE WATER 1974 CAPITOL 11262
HERB PILHOFER PNO (G — (G) DREAMS & ALL THAT STUFF 1974 CAPITOL 11335
JOHN FAHEY G PROD(BH — (H) LEO KOTTKE,JOHN FAHEY & PETER LANG1974 SONET UK SNTF 675
JACK SMITH PNO (GI — (I) CHEWING PINE 1975 CAPITOL 11446
ROY ESTRADA B (B — (J) BEST OF 1976 CAPITOL UK CAPS1003
PAUL LAGOS D (B — (K) LEO KOTTKE 1976 CHRYSALIS UK CHR 1106
WAYNE MOSS B (B — (L) BURNT LIPS 1978 CHRYSALIS UK CHR 1191
PETER LANG G (H — (L) BURNT LIPS 1978 CHRYSALIS EURO 6307 631
KEN BUTTREY D (BO — (M) THE BEST 1978 CAPITOL US 11867 UK ESTSP 21
JOHN HARRIS PNO (BO — (N) LEO KOTTKE 1971/76 1976 CAPITOL 11576
MIKE LEECH B (O — (O) BALANCE 1979 CHRYSALIS UK CHR 1234
BOBBY OGDIN PNO (O — (P) LIVE IN EUROPE 1980 CHRYSALIS UK CHR 1284
LARRY TAYLOR B (B — (Q) GUITAR MUSIC 1981 CHRYSALIS UK CHR 1328
KIM FOWLEY V (B
DENNY BRUCE PROD (BDEFIL KERRY FAHEY PROD (H PAT SMITH B (B JEFFREY KAPLAN PNO (B

K89 KRAAN K89

PETER WOLBRANDT G V (ABCDEFGH — (A) WINTHRUP 1972 SPIEGELEI 28523/9
HELLMUT HATTLER B (ABCDEFGH — (B) KRAAN 1973 SPIEGELEI 28778/9
JAN FRIDE D (ABCDEF — (C) ANDY NOGGER 1975 GULL UK 1009 PASSPORT US 98006
JOHANNES PAPPERT SAX (ABCDE — (D) KRAAN LIVE 1975 GULL UK 2001/2
INGO BISCHOF K (EFGH — (D) KRAAN LIVE 1975 SPIEGELEI 26440/8
TOMMY GOLDSCHMIDT PERC (F — (E) LET IT OUT 1975 GULL UK 1013 PASSPORT US 98015
UDO DAHMEN D (G — (E) LET IT OUT 1975 SPIEGELEI 24548/1
(F) WIEDERHOREN 1977 HARVEST ELECTROLA GER 064 32110
(G) FLYDAY 1978 HARVEST ELECTROLA 064 45210
(H) TOURNEE 1980 EMI GER 064 45931

K90 KRACKER K90

KARL DRIGGS V PERC(B — (A) LA FAMILIA 1972 DUNHILL US 50134
BOBBY KEYS SAX (B — (B) KRACKER BRAND 1973 ROLLING STONES COC 49102
CHUCK FRANCOUR K V (B — (B) KRACKER BRAND 1973 DUNHILL US 50154
VICTOR ANGULO G V (B — (C) ROCKIN THE NATION 1980 PS US 0001
CARLOS GARCIA B V (B
ARTHUR CASADO D (B MALCOLM CECIL SYN(B ROBERT MARGOULEFF SYN(B

K91 KRACQ K91

(A) CIRCUMVISION 1978 UAP 003

K92 KRAFTWERK K92

RALF HUTTER V K D(ABCDEFGHIJK — (A) KRAFTWERK 1 1971 PHILIPS 6305 058
FLORIAN SCHNEIDER D K(ABCDEFGHIJK — (B) KRAFTWERK 2 1972 PHILIPS 6305 117
KLAUS ROEDER VLN G(E — (AB) KRAFTWERK DBL 1973 VERTIGO UK 6641 077
WOLFGANG FLUR PERC(EFGHIJK — (D) RALF & FLORIAN 1973 VERTIGO UK 6360 616
FLAK KUEBLER (J — (D) RALF & FLORIAN 1973 WB US 2006
MARTIN TEWIS (J — (E) AUTOBAHN 1974 VERTIGO US 2003 UK 6360 620
CAROL MARTIN (J — (E) AUTOBAHN 1974 MERCURY US 1 3704
KARL BARTOS PERC(FGHIJK — (F) RADIOACTIVITY 1975 CAPITOL 11457
CONRAD PLANK PROD (C — (G) EXCELLER 8 1975 VERTIGO UK 6360 629
BOB KRASNOW (J — (H) TRANS EUROPE EXPRESS 1977 CAPITOL 11603
MARVIN KATZ (J — (I) MAN MACHINE 1978 CAPITOL 11728
IAN FLOOKS (J — (J) COMPUTOR WORLD 1980 EMI UK 3776 US WB 3549
DOREEN D'AGOSTINO (J — (K) ELECTROKINETIK 1981 VERTIGO UK 6449 066
TOM LANIK (J
TAKESHI SHIKVRA (J

K93 BILLY J KRAMER & THE DAKOTAS K93

BILLY J KRAMER V (ALL — LISTEN TO 1963 PARLOPHONE UK (M) 1209 (S) 3047
MIKE MAXFIELD G (— I'LL KEEP YOU SATISFIED 196 IMPERIAL US (M) 9273 (S)12273
ROBIN McDONALD G (— LITTLE CHILDREN 196 IMPERIAL US (M) 9287 (S)12267
RAY JONES B (— TRAINS BOATS & PLANES 196 IMPERIAL US (M) 9291 (S)12291
TONY MANSFIELD D (— THE BEST OF 1977 EMI UK NUT 9 US CAPITOL 11897
(EP) HITS 1963 PARLOPHONE UK GEP 8885
(EP) I'LL KEEP YOU SATISFIED 1964 PARLOPHONE UK GEP 8895
(EP) LITTLE CHILDREN 1964 PARLOPHONE UK GEP 8907
(EP) FROM A WINDOW 1964 PARLOPHONE UK GEP 8921
(EP) PLAYS FROM THE STATES 1965 PARLOPHONE UK GEP 8928

K93A BERNIE KRAUSE K93A

BERNIE KRAUSE (A — (A) CITADELS 1981 TAKOMA US 7074

K93B JEAN JACQUES KRAVETZ K93B

JEAN JACQUES KRAVETZ K (A (A) KRAVETZ 1972 VERTIGO 6360 605

UDO LINDENBERG D V (A

THOMAS KRETZSCHMER G(A CARL G STEPHAN B (A INGA RUMPF V (A ROGER HOOK G (A

K94 KRAZY KAT K94

GRAHAME WHITE G V (AB (A) CHINA SEA 1976 MOUNTAIN TOPC 5004

TONY FERGUSON G V (AB (B) TROUBLED AIR 1977 MOUNTAIN TOPC 5009

ROGER BRADLEY-WILLIS D(AB

RAY LEWIS B V (AB HENRY MACDONALD K V (AB

K94A ROBBIE KRIEGER K94A

ROBBIE KRIEGER G V K(A (A) ..AND FRIENDS 1977 BLUE NOTE LA 664

ED GREENE D (A

REGGIE McBRIDE B (A RON STOCKERT K (A SAL MARQUEZ HRNS K (A JOCK ELLIS TROM (A

JOEL PESKIN SAX (A BRUCE GARY D (A KENNY WILD B (A GREG MATHESON ORG (A

SHARON ROBINSON V (A AFREEKA TREES V (A JIMMY SMITH ORG (A JOHN DENSMORE D (A

STU GOLDBERG SYN K(A PERICO CONGA(A EDDIE TALAMANTES TIMBS(A GARY BARONE TPT (A

BOB GLAUB B (A

K94B SONJA KRISTINA K94B

SONJA KRISTINA V (A (A) SONJA KRISTINA 1980 CHOPPER CHOPE5

LIAM GENOCKEY D (A

ALFIE AGIUS B (A STEVE BYRD G (A COLIN TOWNS FLT K (A GASPAR LAWAL PERC (A

NIGEL GRAY SYN (A DARRYL WAY VLN (A ALEXANDER SKEAPING K(A LAWRENCE JUBER G (A

IAIN DUNNET SYN (A DAVE SMITH B (A TONY HENDRICKS D (A BOB BARNETT G (A

DAVID WALKER K (A BRIAN DEVITO B (A PETER VAN HOOKE D (A DAVE OLNEY B (A

IAN MILNE K (A PETE ACOCK SAX (A TONY CARR PERC (A CORONA STAGE SCHOOL V(A

K94C VOLKER KRIEGEL K94C

VOLKER KRIEGEL G SIT (ALL (A) SPECTRUM 1971 MPS GER 21/20874/5

JOHN TAYLOR K (ABC (B) MISSING LINK 1972 MPS GER 3321431/1

CECS SEE PERC (ABC (C) LIFT 1973 MPS GER 2121753/1

ALBERT MANGELSDORFF (B (D) MILD MANIAC 1974 MPS GER 2122020/6

HEINZ SAUER SAX (B

JOHN MARSHALL D (B ZBIGNIEW SEIFERT VLN (C JOE NAY D (D PETER TRUNK B CELLO(A

PETER BAUMEISTER D (A ALAN SKIDMORE SAX (B EBERHARD WEBER B (BCD STAN SULZMANN WIND (C

RAINER BRUNINGHAUS K (D PETER GIGER PERC (D

K95 KRIS KRISTOFFERSON K95

KRIS KRISTOFFERSON V G (ALL (A) KRISTOFFERSON 1970 MONUMENT UK 5042

WITH (A) HELP ME MAKE IT THROUGH THE NIGHT 1980 EMBASSY UK 31839

JERRY KENNEDY G (ACD (A) ME & BOBBY McGEE(RI) 1973 MONUMENT UK 64631 US 30817

NORBERT PUTNAM B (CE (B) CISCO PETE 197 CBS US 9154

JERRY CARRIGAN D (CD (C) SILVER TONGUED DEVIL & I 1971 MONUMENT UK 64636 US 30679

DAVID BRIGGS K (CE (D) BORDER LORD 1972 MONUMENT UK 64963 US 31302

JERRY SHOOK G (CED (E) JESUS WAS A CAPRICORN 1973 MONUMENT UK 65391 US 31909

NORMAN BLAKE G (C (F) SPOOKY LADY'S SIDESHOW 1974 MONUMENT UK 69074 US 32914

BOBBY DYSON B (C (G) WHO'S TO BLESS & WHO'S TO BLAME 1975 MONUMENT UK 69158 US 33379

CHARLIE McCOY HCA K(CD (H) SURREAL THING 1976 MONUMENT UK 81496 US 35254

FARRELL MORRIS PERC (CD (J) SONGS OF KRISTOFFERSON 1977 MONUMENT UK 82002 US 34254

BILLY SWAN B V (CDEGH (K) A STAR IS BORN (SOUNDTRACK) 1977 CBS UK 86021

CHRIS GANTRY G (C (L) EASTER ISLAND 1978 MONUMENT UK 86056 US 35310

DONNIE FRITTS K V (CDG (M) MR SHAKE HANDS 1979 CBS US 36135

JERRY SHOOK G (D (N) TO THE BONE 1981 CBS UK 84818 US 36885

RITA COOLIDGE V (CDFHG

LARRY GATLIN V (E BENNY WHITEHEAD V (E RANDY CULLERS V (E ALAN RUSH V (E

TERRY DEARMORE V (E ALLEN WALD V (H TERRY PAUL V (HGD GARY BUSEY V (H

KENNY BUTTREY D (ED ANDY NEWMARK D (E JOSH GRAVES G (E JERRY McGEE G V(FH

LEE SKLAR B (FHG BARBARA STREISLAND V (K SAMMY CREASON D (FHG BOBBYE HALL PERC(FG

JIM HORN SAX (F JACKIE KELSO SAX (F CHUCK FINDLEY TPT (F DICK HYDE TROM(F

HERB PEDERSEN V (FHG LARRY MURRAY V (F JOHN BELAND V (F BOBBY NEUWIRTH V (F

CLYDIE KING V (HG SHIRLEY MATTHEWS V (H BYRON BERLINE V (H JACK SKINNER V (H

CHARLES CHALMERS V (E SANDRA CHALMERS V (E DONNA RHODES V (E D BERGEN WHITE V (E

JAMES E CASON V (E JUNE PAGE V (E JORDANAIRES V (E RAYMOND WALKER V (E

HOYT HAWKINS V (E JOHN HARRIS K (E GORDON STOKER V (E DON GANT V (E

MILDRED KIRKHAM V (F STEPHEN BRUTON G V (ED DENNIS LINDE G (ED TOM COGBILL B (E

MAC GAYDEN G (E CHIP YOUNG G (E JOHN BUCK WILKIN G (ED JAMES COLVARD G (E

GRADY MARTIN G (E FRED CARTER G (E JOHN L CHRISTOPHER G (E WELDON MYRICK STEEL(E

MIKE UTLEY K V (EG BOBBY WOOD K (E BOBBY EMMONS K (E PETE DRAKE STEEL(D

TOMMY JACKSON FDL (D BENNY WHITEHEAD (D FRED TACKETT G (G NICK DECARO ACC (G

MENTOR WILLIAMS V (G WARREN OATES V (G

K96 KRIS KRISTOFFERSON & RITA COOLIDGE K96

KRIS KRISTOFFERSON V (ABC (A) FULL MOON 1973 A&M US 4403 UK AMLH64403

RITA COOLIDGE V (ABC (B) BREAKAWAY 1974 MONUMENT US 33278 UK 80547

STEPHEN BRUTON G V (AC (C) NATURAL ACT 1978 A&M US 4690 UK AMLH64690

CHIP YOUNG G (B

JIM COLVARD G (B JOHN L CHRISTOPHER G (B JERRY SHOOK G (B WELDON MYRICK STEEL(B

MIKE UTLEY K (ABC BOBBY WOOD K (B BOBBY EMMONS K (B TOMMY COGBILL B (B

JOSH GRAVES G (A JERRY McGEE G (AC LEE SKLAR B (A SAMMY CREASON D (ABC

BOBBYE HALL PERC (A TERRY PAUL V (A GENE CHRISMAN D (B BUDDY SPICHER FDL (B

REGGIE YOUNG G (B RAY EDENTON G (B SHANE KEISTER K (B FARRELL MORRIS PERC (B

CHARLIE McCOY HCA (B RON EADES HRNS (B HARRISON CALLOWAY HRNS(B CHARLES ROSE HRNS (B

DON SHEFFIELD HRNS (B DAVID BROMBERG G (A NICK DE CARO (A DAVID SMITH (A

GARY SCRUGGS (A RANDY SCRUGGS (A VASSAR CLEMENTS FDL (A BOOKER T JONES K (A

HERB ALPERT TPT (A BILLY SWAN V (C DONNIE FRITTS K (C JERRY JUMONVILLE SAX(C

DENNIS BELFIELD B (C

K96A KROKUS K96A

MARC STORACE V (AB (A) METAL RENDEZVOUS 1980 ARIOLA ARL 5056

TOMMY KIEFFER G V (AB (B) HARDWARE 1981 ARIOLA UK ARL5064 GER 203322

FERNANDO VON ARB G V (AB (C) PAINKILLER 1981 MERCURY NL 6326 800

CHRIS VON ROHR B V (AB

FREDDY STEADY D V (AB JUERG NAEGELI K V (A

K96B **JIM KRUEGER** K96B

JIM KRUEGER (A   (A) SWEET SALVATION   1978 CBS US 35295

K96C **KROKODIL** K96C

TERRY STEVENS G B V(ABEF   (A) KROKODIL   1969 LIBERTY LBS 83306
HERDY HEPP K VLN(ABF   (B) SWAMP   1970 LIBERTY LBS 83417
DUDE DURST PERC D(ABEF   (AB) CLASSIC GERMAN ROCK SCENE   197 UA GER DBL UAS 29776/77
MOJO WEIDELI FLT HCA (ABEF   (C)
WALTY ANSELMO B V SIT(ABEF   (D) MUSIC
RAINER MARZ G (F   (E) GETTING UP FOR THE MORNING   1972 BELLAPHON GER 19117
VEIT FEIDEN K VIBES(F   (F) SWEAT & SWIM   1973 BELLAPHON GER 7502

K97 **DAVID KUBINEC** K97

DAVID KUBINEC G V PNO (A   (A) SOME THINGS NEVER CHANGE   1978 A&M US 4766 UK AMLH68501
CHRIS SPEDDING G (A
JIM BAIN B (A   JOHN CALE K (A   OLLIE HALSALL G (A   ALAN MACLEOD PIPES (A
TIMI DONALD D (A   PAT DONALDSON B (A

K98 **JOACHIM KUHN** K98

JOACHIM KUHN K (ALL   (A) BOLD IS WONDERFUL   19 MPS 15239
PHILIP CATHERINE G (L   (B) CINEMASCOPE   1976 MPS BASF 2122270 5
JOHN LEE B (L   (C) IMPRESSION OF NEW YORK   19 IMPULSE 9158
GERRY BROWN D (L   (D) INTERCHANGE   19 MPS 21328 5
ZBIGNIEW SEIFERT VLN (L   (E) PARIS IS WONDERFUL   19 BYG 529 346
CURT CRESS D (L   (F) PIANO   1971 MPS BASF 2121330 7
ROLF KUHN (CK   (G) SOLOS   1974 FUTURA GER 18
PETER WARREN (J   (H) SOUNDS OF FEELING   19 BYG 519 317
DANIEL HUSSAIN (J   (J) THIS WAY OUT   19 BASF 2921752 3
GERD DUDEK (J   (K) TRANSFIGURATION   19 MPS 15118
JAN AKKERMAN G (O   (L) SPRING FEVER   1977 ATLANTIC US 1695 UK K50280
(M) CHARISMA   19 ATLANTIC K50352
(N) MONDAY MORNING   19 ELECTROLA SHZE 909B
(O) SUNSHOWER   1978 ATLANTIC US 19193

K99 **STEVE KUHN** K99

STEVE KUHN PNO (ALL   (A) CHILDHOOD IS FOREVER   1969 BYG 529136
JACK DEJOHNNETTE D (B   (B) TRANCE   1974 ECM 1052
SUE EVANS PERC (B   (C) ECSTASY   1974 ECM 1058
STEVE SWALLOW B (B   (D) RAINDROPS   1975 MUSE US 5106
HARVEY SCHWARZ B (EFH   (E) MOTILITY   1977 ECM 1094
MICHAEL SMITH D (E   (F) NON FICTION   1978 ECM 1124
STEVE SLAGLE WIND (EF   (G) WATCH WHAT HAPPENS   19 MPS 15193
BOB MOSES D (FH   (H) PLAYGROUND   197 ECM 1059
SHEILA JORDAN V (H

K99A **LEAH KUNKEL** K99A

LEAH KUNKEL V K(AB   (A) LEAH KUNKEL   1979 CBS US 35778
RUSS KUNKEL D (A   (B) I RUN WITH TROUBLE   1980 CBS US 36398
LELEAND SKLAR B (A
DANNY KORTCHMAR G (A   JIM HORN FLT (A   STEVEN BISHOP G (A   DAN DUGMORE G (A
ROSEMARY BUTLER V (A   ANDREW GOLD G (A   JACKSON BROWNE V (A   DOUG LIVINGSTONE G(A
MIKE PORCARO B (B   JEFF PORCARO D (B   GRAHAM NASH V (B   STEPHEN BISHOP G (B
JOHN GUERIN D (B   MATT MURPHY K STR(AB   PENNY NICHOLS V (B   PAMELA STANLEY V (B
DAVID HUNGATE B (B   BERNARD FLEISCHER FLT (B   BOBBY SHEW HRN (B   WILLIAM SMITH K V (B
DAVID DUKE HRNS (B   CRAIG DOERGE PNO (B   JOHN JARVIS PNO (B   STEVE LUKATHER G (AB
LENNY CASTRO PERC (B   TOM SCOTT SAX (B   STEVE FOREMAN PERC (B   IAN FAIRBAIRN-SMITH V(B
JAMES LEE STANLEY V (B   PAUL FANERSO K (B   MITCH HOLDER G (B   JAMES SELF HRNS(B
ERNEST CARLSON TROM (B   DAVID LASLEY V (B   HARLAN COLLINS V (B   RONALD LEONARD (B

K99B **TOLI KUPPERBERG** K99B

TULI KUPPERBERG (A   (A) NO DEPOSIT NO RETURN   19 ESP US 1035

K100 **KURSAAL FLYERS** K100

PAUL SHUTTLEWORTH V (ALL   (A) CHOCS AWAY   1975 UK UK UKAL1011 UK 2330 101
BOB ANDREWS SAX (B   (A) CHOCS AWAY   1975 UK EURO 2330 106
RICHIE BULL B V (ALL   (B) GREAT ARTISTE   1975 UK UK UKAL1018
GRAEME DOUGLAS G (ABC   (C) GOLDEN MILE   1976 CBS UK 81622
VIC COLLINS G V STEEL (ALL   (D) FIVE LIVE KURSAALS   1977 CBS UK 82253
WILL BIRCH D (ALL
BARRY MARTIN G V (D   DIGBY FAIRWETHER TPT (B   BRINSLEY SCHWARZ SAX (B

K100A **KWAME** K100A

(A) FOLLOW I   1980 POLYDOR US 6310

K101 **JIM KWESKIN** K101

JIM KWESKIN G V (ALL   (A) UNBLUSHING BRASSINESS   1963 VANGUARD VSD 2158
MARIA(D'AMATO) MULDAUR V(FB   (B) JUG BAND MUSIC   1965 VANGUARD VSD 79163
GEOFF MULDAUR G V (FB   (C) RELAX YOUR MIND   1966 VANGUARD VSD 79188
BILL KEITH BAN STEEL(FB   (D) SEE REVERSE SIDE FOR TITLE   1966 VANGUARD VSD 79234 FONTANA 6080
MEL LYMAN HCA (B   (E) JUMP FOR JOY   1967 VANGUARD VSD 79243
FRITZ RICHMOND B (FB   (F) GARDEN OF JOY   1967 REPRISE US 6266
RICHARD GREENE FDL (F   (G) BEST OF   1968 VANGUARD VSD 79270
REX RAKISH V PERC(B   (H) WHATEVER HAPPENED TO THOSE DAYS   1968 VANGUARD VAS 79278
BRUNO WOLF V (B   (J) AMERICAN AVIATOR   1969 REPRISE US 6353
(K) GREATEST HITS(DBL)   1970 VANGUARD VSD 13/14
(L) JIM KWESKIN'S AMERICA   1971 REPRISE US 6464
(M) JIM KWESKIN   1978 MOUNTAIN RAILROAD MR 52780
(N) LIVES AGAIN   1978 MOUNTAIN RAILROAD MR 52782
(O) SIDE BY SIDE   1980 MOUNTAIN RAILROAD US 52790
(P) SWING ON A STAR   1980 MOUNTAIN RAILROAD US 52793

K102 **KWICK** K102

(A) KWICK   1981 EMI US 17025

L1 **L A EXPRESS** L1

DAVID LUELL SAX (AB (A) L A EXPRESS 1976 CARIBOU US 33940 UK 81267
ROBBEN FORD G (A (B) SHADOW PLAY 1976 CARIBOU US 34355 UK 81671
VICTOR FELDMAN PERC K (AB
PETER MAUNU G (B MAX BENNETT B (AB JOHN GUERIN D K (AB JONI MITCHELL V (B
PAULETTE McWILLIAMS V (B

L1A **L A JETS** L1A

KAREN LAWRENCE V (A (A) L A JETS 1976 RCA US APLI 1547
HARLIN McNEES G V (A
RON CINDRICH B (A JOHN DESAUTELS D (A SILVER HANSON G (A WAYNE COOK K(A
JAMES LINDSEY PERC (A

L1B **L A BOPPERS** L1B

(A) L A BOPPERS 1980 MERCURY US 3816
(B) BOP TIME 1981 MERCURY US 4006

L2 **L T D** L2

BILLY OSBORNE K (C (A) LOVE TOGETHERNESS & DEVOTION 197 A&M US 3602
JEFF OSBORNE D V (C (B) GITTIN' DOWN 1975 A&M US 3660 UK AMLS63660
HENRY DAVIS B V (C (C) LOVE TO THE WORLD 1976 A&M US 4589 UK AMLH64589
JIMMIE DAVIS K V (C (D) SOMETHING TO LOVE 1977 A&M US 4646 UK AMLH64646
ROBERT SANTIEL PERC (C (E) TOGETHERNESS 1978 A&M US 4705 UK AMLH64705
JOHN McGEE G (C (F) DEVOTION 1979 A&M US 4771 AMLH64771
ABRAHAM MILLER SAX V(C (G) SHINE ON 1980 A&M US 4819 UK AMLH64819
CARLE VICKERS HRNS (C
LORENZO CARNEGIE SAX (C JAKE RILEY TROM(C TOBY WYNN SAX (C

L2A **JOAN LA BARBARA** L2A

JOAN LA BARBARA V (A (A) VOICE IS THE ORIGINAL INSTRUMENT 1976 WIZARD US RVW 2266

L3 **SLEEPY LA BEEF** L3

SLEEPY LA BEEF G V (ALL (A) BULLS NIGHT OUT 1976 SUN US 130
TERRY DUNCAN PNO (E (B) EARLY RARE & ROCKIN 19 BARON US 102
LONNIE SEABOLT B (E (B) EARLY RARE & ROCKIN 1979 CHARLY RI UK CR 30181
CLETE CHAPMAN D (E (C) WESTERN GOLD 1977 SUN US 138
BUCKY MEADOWS G ORG(E (D) ROCKABILLY 77 1977 SUN US 1004
CLIFF PARKER G (E (E) BEEFY ROCKABILLY 1978 CHARLY UK CR 30145
GORDON TERRY FDL (E (F) DOWN HOME ROCKABILLY 1979 CHARLY UK CR 30172
(F) DOWN HOME ROCKABILLY 197 SUN US 1014
RUFUS THIBODEAUX FDL (E (G) ROCKABILLY HEAVYWEIGHT 1979 CHARLY UK CRL 5017
(H) SLEEPY LA BEEF & FRIENDS(10") 1979 ACE 10 CH16
(J) SLEEPY LABEEF 1981 SONET UK SNTF843
(EP) TORE UP 1978 CHARLY UK CEP 123

L4 **LABELLE** L4

PATTI LABELLE V (ALL (A) OVER THE RAINBOW(BLUEBELLS) 196 ATLANTIC US SD8119
SARAH DASH V (HAJ (B) DREAMER 1967 ATLANTIC US 8147
NONA HENDRYX V (HAJ (C) LA BELLE 1971 WB US 1943
ALLEN TOUSSAINT K (H (D) MOON SHADOWS 1972 WB US 2618
JAMES ELLISON K (H (E) MERRY CHRISTMAS 19 MISTLETOE US 1204
JAMES BOOKER K (H (F) PRESSURE COOKIN' 1974 RCA US LSA 3223 UK APLI0205
HERMAN ERNEST D (H (G) NIGHT BIRDS 197 EPIC US 33075
GEORGE PORTER B (H (H) PHOENIX 1975 EPIC US 33579 UK 69167
CARMINE ROJAS B (H (J) C'EST LA VIE 1975 DJM UK DJSL 050
LEO NOCENTELLI G (H (K) CHAMELEON 1976 EPIC US 34189 UK 81422
TEDDY ROYAL G (H (L) PATTI LABELLE 1977 EPIC US 34847 UK 82226
LON PRICE WIND (H (M) EARLY HITS 19 TRIP US 800 9525
JOHN LONGO TPT (H (N) TASTY (PATTI SOLO) 197 EPIC US 35335
CINDY BIRDSONG V (AJ (O) ITS ALL RIGHT WITH ME 1979 EPIC US 35772 UK 83524
EDWARD BATTS G (H (P) GREATEST HITS 19 TRIP US 8000
JEFFREY SHANNON PERC (H ( ) THE APPOLLO PRESENTS THE BLUEBELLS19 NEWTOWN US 631
JIM MOORE WIND (H ( ) SLEIGHBELLS RING 19 NEWTOWN US 632
LESTER CALISTE TROM (H ( ) ON STAGE 19 PARKWAY US 7043
STEVE HUGHES G (H ( ) LIVE AT THE APPOLLO 19 UPFRONT US 129
STEVE HOWARD HRNS (H ( ) PATTI LABELLE (SOLO) 19 EPIC US 34847
CARL BLOUIN SAX (H ( ) ALRIGHT WITH ME 19 EPIC US 35772
( ) RELEASED 1980 EPIC US 36381 UK 84190
( ) GONNA TAKE A MIRACLE 19 CBS US 30987

L4A **JERRY LACROIX** L4A

JERRY LACROIX V (A (A) SECOND COMING 1974 MERCURY US SRM 1 701
LAUREL ANNE MASSE V (A (A) LA CROIX 1972 EPIC US 31555
DAVID SPINOZZA G (A
JOHNNY WINTER G (A BOB MANN G (A EDGAR WINTER K (A JERRY FRIEDMAN G (A
BOB ROSE G (A HUGH McCRACKEN G (A STU WOODS B (A JOHN TROPEA G (A
PAUL GRIFFIN K (A RICK MAROTTA D (A RALPH MACDONALD PERC (A TASHA THOMAS V (A
CARL HALL V (A HILDA HARRIS V (A CHARLOTTE GILBERT V (A RALPH SCHUCKETT K (A
RICHARD CROOKS D (A RANDY BRECKER HRNS(A ROBERT MILLIKAN HRNS (A DAVID SANBORN HRNS(A
LEW DELGATTO HRNS (A JAMES MAELIN PERC (A RICK DERRINGER G (A GAIL KANTOR V (A
MERLE MILLER V (A

L4B **LADEMACHER** L4B

DANNY LADEMACHER G V (A (A) INNER SLEEVE 1981 ARIOLA NL 203 383
ROGER WOLLAERT D (A
JAAP VAN DER SLUYS B V(A EMILE DEN TEX V (A

L5 **LA DUSSELDORF** L5

KLAUS DINGER G V (AB (A) LA DUSSELDORF 1976 DECCA UK SKLR3252 NOVA GER 22550
THOMAS DINGER PERC V (AB (A) LA DUSSELDORF 1978 RADAR UK RAD 7
HANS LAMPE PERC SYN K(AB (B) VIVA 1978 RADAR UK RAD10 STRAND GER 23626
NIKOLAUS VAN RHEIN K (AB (C) INDIVIDUELLOS 1980 TELDEC GER 24524
HARALD KONIETZKO B (AB
ANDREAS SCHELL PNO (B

L5A **LADY JUNE** L5A

LADY JUNE V (A (A) LINGUISTIC LEPROSY 1974 CAROLINE UK C1509
KEVIN AYERS G B SYN(A
BRIAN ENO K G V(A KIM SOLOMON PNO (A DAVID VORHAUS (A MARTHA V (A
PIP PYLE D (A JAKOB KLAASE PNO (A

L6 LAFAYETTE AFRO ROCK BAND L6

(A) SOUL MAKOSSA 1973 MUSIDISC FR CV1269
(B) MALIK 19 AMERICA 30AM6137

L7 DENNY LAINE L7

DENNY LAINE G K V(ABC (A) AAH LAINE 1973 WIZARD US 2190 UK 2001
PAUL McCARTNEY V B G D K(BC (B) HOLLY DAYS 1976 CAPITOL US 11588 UK EMI781
LINDA McCARTNEY K V (B (C) JAPANESE TEARS 1980 SCRATCH UK 5001
JOHN MOORSHEAD G (A
STEVE THOMPSON B (A MACEY McCREARY V (A PHOEBE LAOB V (A COLIN ALLEN D (A
JO JO LAINE V (C STEVE HOLLY D V (C BUDDY EMMONS STEEL(C THADIUS RICHARDS FLT(C
LAWRENCE JUBER G (C GORDON SELLAR (C ANDY RICHARDS (C MIKE PIGGOTT (C
HOWIE CASEY SAX (C DENNY SEIWELL D (C HENRY McCULLOUGH G (C

L8 DAVID LAFLAMME L8

DAVID LAFLAMME V VLN(AB (A) WHITE BIRD 1977 AMHERST us AMH 1007
MITCHELL FROOM K TPT VIBES(AB (B) INSIDE OUT 1978 AMHERST US AMH 1012
JAMES RALSTON G (AB
DOUG KILMER D (AB MICHAEL BAIRD D (B DOMINIQUE DELLACROIX (AB PETER MILIO D (AB
MITCHELL HOLMAN B (A TOM MARKEN D (A JEFF DAMBRAU BANJO(A ROGER GLENN FLT (A
CARL TASSI PERC (A GREG ADAMS HRNS (A MIC GILLETE HRNS (A EMILIO CASTILLO SAX(A
LENNY PICKETT SAX (A STEVE KUPKA SAX (A

L9 CORKY LAING L9

CORKY LAING V D G(A (A) MAKIN' IT ON THE STREET 1977 ELEKTRA US 7E 1097
CLYDIE KING V (A
PETE CARR G (A NEIL LARSEN K (A HARVEY THOMPSON HRNS (A RANDALL BRAMBLETT HRNS(A
VANETTA FIELDS V (A TOMMY TALTON G (A CHARLES ROSE HRNS (A FRANK VICARI HRNS (A
SHIRLEY MATTHEWS V (A CALVIN ARLINE B (A RON EADES HRNS (A HARRISON CALLOWAY HRNS(A
MIKE MONTGOMERY K (DONNY KRIETER B (BOB KULICK G (TUPPER LIENICE PNO (

L9A GREG LAKE L9A

GREG LAKE G V (A (A) GREG LAKE 1981 CHRYSALIS CHR 1357
TOMMY EYRE K (A
BILL CUOMO K (A GREG MATHIESON K (A GARY MOORE G (A STEVE LUKATHER G (A
DEAN PARKS G (A SNUFFY WALDEN G (A TRISTIAN MARGETTS B (A DAVID HUNGATE B (A
TED McKENNA D (A MICHAEL GILES D (A JODE LEIGH D (A JEFF PORCARO D (A
CLARENCE CLEMONS SAX (A WILLIE COCHRANE PIPES(A DAVID MILNER PIPES(A

L10 LAKE L10

JAMES HOPKINS-HARRISON V(ABC (A) LAKE 1976 CBS US 34763 UK 81661
DEITER AHRENDT D V (ABC (B) LAKE 2 1978 CBS US 35289 UK 82651
GEOFF PEACEY G K V(ABC (C) PARADISE ISLAND 1979 CBS US 35817 UK 83480
ALEX CONTI G V (ABC (D) OUCH 1980 CBS US 37083 84310
CARL WILSON (B
DETLEF PETERSEN K V (BC MARTIN TIEFENSEE B (ABC OTTO WAALKEN CONGA(C JAMES WILLIAM GUERCIO(B

L10A LAKESIDE L10A

FRED ALEXANDER D (C (A) LAKESIDE 197 ABC US AB 999
NORMAN BEAVERS K (C (B) SHOT OF LOVE 1979 RCA UK 12937
MARVIN CRAIG B (C (C) ROUGH RIDERS 1979 SOLAR US 3490 UK 13490
FRED LEWIS PERC (C (D) FANTASTIC VOYAGE 1980 SOLAR US BXL13720
TIEMEYER McCAIN PERC V(C
MARK A WOOD K V (C THOMAS SHELBY V (C STEPHEN SHOCKLEY G K (C OTIS STOKES K B GV(C

L10B LAMB L10B

BARBARA MAURITZ G V K(ALL (A) A SIGN OF CHANGE 1970 CBS NL 63954
BOB SWANSON G BAN(ALL (B) CROSS BETWEEN 1971 WB US 1920
BILL DOUGLASS B (AB (C) BRING OUT THE SUN 1971 WB US 1952
DAVID LITURIN WIND SYN(A
WALTER RAPAPORT (A DIVA GOODFRIEND-KOVEN FLT(A ED BOGAS VLA (ABC ROBERT HUBBARD HRNS(A
DOUGLAS BLUMENSTOCK CELLO(A TOM SALISBURY K(C RICHARD SCLOSSER D (C MARK SPRINGER G (C
JOHN McFEE STEEL(C MICHAEL PRENDERGRASS G(C ED JANG (B EDDIE LEE CHARLTON D(C
CLYDE FLOWERS B (C WARREN GALE TPT (C DWIGHT HALL TPT (C MEL MARTIN SAX (C
CHARLES PETERSON SAX (C BILL ATTWOOD TPT (BC ELLEN DESSIER (B PATRICK GLEASON SYN(C
JOHN VIERA SYN (C VINCE DELGRADO TABLA (C LAWRENCE DUCKLES (B LEONARD LASHER B (C
MYRON MU HRNS (C STEPHEN FURRE TROM (C DAVID HAYES B (BC JERRY GARCIA (B
STEVIE LANGE V (A JUNIOR MARVIN G (A

L11 KEVIN LAMB L11

KEVIN LAMB G V (A (A) SAILIN' DOWN THE YEARS 1978 ARISTA US AB 4166 UK SPART1026
STEVE GOULD G (A
MICK FEAT B (A BILLY LIVSEY K (A DAVID DOWLE D (A RAY COOPER PERC (A
ANDY SUMMERS G (A B J COLE STEEL(A GEOFF DALY SAX (A CHRIS THOMPSON V (A

L12 DAVE LAMBERT L12

DAVE LAMBERT G V (A (A) FRAMED 1979 POLYDOR PD 1 6193 UK 2391 391
JOHN ENTWISTLE B (A
RICHARD BENNETT G (A LEE SKLAR B (A TOM HENSLEY K (A LARRY BROWN PERC(A
DENNY SEIWELL D (A ROBBIE BUCHANAN PNO (A

L12A LAMBRETTAS L12A

JEZ BIRD G V (A (A) BEAT BOYS IN THE JET AGE 1980 ROCKET US PIG 3257 UK TRAIN 10
DOUG SANDERS G V (A (A) BEAT BOYS IN THE JET AGE 1980 PHONOGRAM NL 6302 034
MARK ELLIS B (A (B) AMBIENCE 1981 ROCKET UK TRAIN 14
PAUL WINCER PERC (A
DICK HANSON HRNS (A PETE THOMS HRNS (A RONNIE ASPERY HRNS(A MARTIN DOBSON HRNS (A

L12B LAMBERT & NUTTYCOMBE L12B

DENNIS LAMBERT G V (A (A) AS YOU WILL 19 20TH CENT US 415
CRAIG NUTTYCOMBE G V (A
WADDY WACHTEL G (A HOPPY HODGES D (A PEGGY SANDVIG K (A JOE LAMANNO B (A
GAIL LEVANT HARP PERC(A LEE ALLEN SAX (A LINDSEY BUCKINGHAM G (A DOMENIC TROIANO G(A
WILLIE WEEKS BV (A JORGE CALDERON V (A TESSIE COHEN V (A

L13 ROBERT LAMM L13

ROBERT LAMM (A (A) SKINNY BOY 1975 CBS US 33095 UK 80359
TERRY KATH G B (A
ROSS SALOMONE D (A JAMES VINCENT G (A ALAN DE CARLO G (A POINTER SISTERS V (A
GUILLE GARCIA PERC (A STRING SECTION (A WILLIAM COLLETTE WIND (A

L14 LAMONT CRANSTON BAND L14

PAT HAYES HCA (A (A) LAMONT CRANSTON BAND 19 SHADOW US 3346
LARRY HAYES G V (A (B) SPECIALS 19 SHADOW US 3348
JIM NOVAK D (E (C) EL CEE NOTES 19 WATERHOUSE US 6
RICK O'DELL SAX (E (D) UP FROM THE ALLEY 19 WATERHOUSE US 10
JIM GREENWELL SAX (E (E) SHAKEDOWN 1981 WATERHOUSE US 15
TERRY GRANT B (E
CHARLIE BINGHAM G (E BRUCE McCABE K V (E STEVE KILBRIDE K G (E TOM HEINIG B (E
DAVE SALISBURY G (A MIKE NELSON TROM (E

L15 JACK LANCASTER L15

JACK LANCASTER WIND (AB (A) MARSCAPE 1976 RSO US 3020 UK 2394 170
ROBIN LUMLEY K (A (B) WILD CONNECTIONS 1979 ACROBAT UK ACRO 2
RICK VAN DER LINDEN K (B
JOHN GOODSALL G (A SIMON JEFFES KOTO (A PERCY JONES B (A BERNIE FROST V (A
PHIL COLLINS D (A MORRIS PERT PERC (A BARRY MORGAN D (B

L15A ROBIN LANE & THE CHARTBUSTERS L15A

ROBIN LANE V (ABC (A) 5 LIVE EP 1980 WB US MINI 3494
LEROY RADCLIFFE G V (ABC (B) ROBIN LANE & THE CHARTBUSTERS 1980 WB EURO 56813 US 3424
ASA BREBNER G V (ABC (C) IMITATION LIFE 1981 WB US 3537
SCOTT BAERENWALD B V (ABC
TIM JACKSON D (ABC PETER WOOD K (C

L16 LANDSCAPE L16

JOHN WALTERS WIND K(AB (A) LANDSCAPE 1979 RCA UK PL 25248 RI 81 3034
RICHARD BURGESS D (Ab (B) FROM THE TEAROOMS OF MARS 1981 RCA UK PL 25328 RI 81 5003
ANDY(CAPT WHORLIX)PASK B(AB (C) MANHATTEN BOOGIE WOOGIE 1982 RCA UK LP 6037
CHRIS HEATON K(B
PETER THOMAS TROM (AB

L16A RONNIE LANE & SLIM CHANCE L16A

RONNIE LANE V B G(ALL (A) ANYMORE FOR ANYMORE 1974 GM GMI 1017 US + UK 1024
CHARLIE HART VLN K(BC (B) RONNIE LANE'S SLIM CHANCE 1975 ISLAND UK ILPS 9321 US A&M 3638
BRIAN BELSHAW B (BC (C) ONE FOR THE ROAD 1976 ISLAND UK ILPS 9366
COLIN DAVY D (C (D) SEE ME 1979 GEM UK GEM107
STEVE SIMPSON G K (BC
RUAN O'LOCHLAINN SAX (B KEVIN WESTLAKE G (A KEN SLAVEN FDL (A GLEN LEFLEUR D (B
BENNY GALLAGHER G B ACC(A BILLY LIVSEY K (A THE TANNERS V (A BRUCE ROWLAND D (A
GRAHAM LYLE G BAN MAND (A STEVE BINGHAM B (A JIMMY JEWELL SAX (A

L16B PETER LANG L16B

PETER LANG G V (ALL (A) LYCURGUS 19 FLYING FISH US FF014
JOHN BOBLETT TROM (C (B) THE THING AT THE NURSERY WINDOW 19 TAKOMA US 1034
MARK BRUNNER TPT (C (C) BACK TO THE WALL 1978 WATERHOUSE US 7
JEFF DAYTON STEEL(C
BRAD GRAPP D (C JAMES HAUCK MARACAS (C GARY LOPAC B (C JIM PRICE VLN (C
TED UNSETH SAX (C PRUDENCE JOHNSON V (C TOM LIEBERMAN V (C TIM SPARKS V (C

L16C CLIVE LANGER & THE BOXES L16C

CLIVE LANGER G V (AB (A) I WANT THE WHOLE WORLD 1978 RADAR UK RDR 2
BUDGIE B D (A (B) SPLASH 1980 F BEAT UK XXLP2
STEVE ALLEN V (AB
BETTE BRIGHT V (AB BEN BARSON K (AB JAMES ELLER B (B MARTIN HUGHES D (B
RUMOUR BRASS HRNS (B ALAN WINSTANLEY PROD (B WILL STALLIBRASS (B IAN BROWDIE (B
ALAN JONES (B PAUL RILEY (B ELVIS COSTELLO (B

L16D HIP LANKCHAN L16D

HIP LANKCHAN G V (A (A) I AM ON MY WAY 197 MCM FR 900299
JIMMIE MILLER G (A
ERNEST GATEWOOD B (A TYRONE CENTURY D (A

L16E LA PERVERSITA L16E

HAMILTON BARCLAY D V (A (A) LA PERVERSITA 1979 INVISIBLE FR 10005
JEANNE FOLY V (A
LAY JEAME G V (A HENRY KAISER G (A JACK KASPIER V (A MEDOR MADER G B (A
MARTIN MESONIER G (A JOHN SINDLER VLN (A HECTOR ZAZU PNO (A

L17 LARD FREE L17

GILBERT ARTMAN D K (ABC (A) LARD FREE 1973 VAMP FR VP 59500
PHILIPPE BOLLIET SAX (A (B) I'M AROUND ABOUT MIDNIGHT 1975 VAMP FR VP 59502
FRANCOIS MATIVET G (A (C) LARD FREE 1977 COBRA FR 37007
HERVE EYHANI B SYN(A
RICHARD PINHAS G SYN(B JEAN JACQUES MIETTE B (A ALAIN AUDAT SYN SAX(B ANTOINE DUVERNET WIND(B
XAVIER BAULLERET G (C YVES LANES SYN (C JEAN PIERRE THIRAUT CLAR (C

L17A LARRY & THE MOVERS L17A

LARRY G V K(A (A) THE BEST OF LARRY & THE MOVERS 1981 LINE GER 5094
IAN CUSSICK B V (A
PETER (A WERNER BECKER K (A HANS UWE REINERS SAX (A JOACHIM WITT V (A

L18 NEIL LARSEN L18

NEIL LARSEN K (AB (A) JUNGLE FEVER 1978 HORIZON AMLJ733 + 3116
BUZZ FEITEN G (AB (B) HIGH GEAR 1979 HORIZON 738 + 3117
LARRY WILLIAMS WIND (A
RALPH MACDONALD PERC (A JERRY HEY HRNS (A WILLIE WEEKS B (A MICHAEL BRECKER HRNS(AB
ANDY NEWMARK D (A RICKIE LEE JONES V (B ABRAHAM LABORIEL B (B LENNY CASTRO V (B
STEVE GADD D (B TOMMY LIPUMA PROD (B PAULINHO DACOSTA PERC (B JOE FARRELL FLT (B

L18A LARSEN/ FEITEN BAND L18A

NEIL LARSEN K (A (A) LARSEN/FEITEN BAND 1980 WB nl 56849 US BSK 3468
BUZZ FEITEN G (A
WILLIE WEEKS B (A KIM HUTCHCROFT SAX (A LENNY CASTRO V PERC(A ART RODRIGUEZ D (A
BILL REICHENBACH HRNS (A LARRY WILLIAMS SAX (A

L18B KIM LARSON L18B

KIM LARSON G V (A (A) SITTING ON A TIME BOMB 1982 EPIC US 37677
RICK BLAKEMORE (A
JOE DELIA (A ABE SPELLER (A DENNIS ESPANTMAN (A

L19 NICOLETTE LARSON L19

NICOLETTE LARSON V G PERC(ALL (A) NICOLETTE 1978 WB US BSK 3243 UK K56569
BILL PAYNE K (AC (B) IN THE NICK OF TIME 1979 WB US BSK 3370 UK K56750
JAMES BURTON G (A (C) RADIOLAND 1980 WB US BSK 3502 UK K56878
BOB GLAUB B (AC
PAUL BARRERE G (AC HERB PEDERSEN V G (A RICK SCHLOSSER D (AC MARK JORDAN K (A
DAVID KALISH G (A ANDREW LOVE SAX (A PLAS JOHNSON FLT (A TED TEMPLEMAN V (AC
JIM HORN HRNS (A CHUCK FINDLEY HRNS (A STEVE MADAIO HRNS (A VALERIE CARTER V (A
MIKE McDONALD V (A LINDA RONSTADT V (AC KLAUS VOORMANN B (AC FRED TACKETT G (AC
ALBERT LEE MAND (A PATRICK SIMMONS G (AC KEITH KNUDSEN D (C TIRAN PORTER B (C
JOHN McFEE G (C ANDREW KASTNER G (C DOUG LIVINGSTONE K (C MARK JORDAN K (C
BOBBY LAKIND PERC (C MAUREEN McDONALD V (C JERRY JUMONVILLE SAX (C GENE MEROS SAX (C
LEE THORNBURG TPT (C

L19A D C LARUE L19A

D C LARUE (ALL (A) CATHEDRALS 19 PYRAMID US 9003
(B) TEN DANCE 19 PYRAMID US 9006
(C) CONFESSIONS 19 CASABLANCA US 7098
(D) FORCES OF THE NIGHT 1980 CASABLANCA US 7160
(E) STAR BABY 1981 CASABLANCA US 7247

L20 LA SEINE L20

TOM SEUFERT G V (A (A) LIKE THE RIVER 1976 ARIOLA UK AAA752 US 50008
DON WHALEY B (A
TRIS IMBODEN D (A STEVE HAGUE K (A BOB EASTON G SYN (A MARK CREAMER V (A
LAURA CREAMER V (A

L21 LASO L21

FRANK OWENS K (A (A) LASO 1977 MCA US 2247 UK MCF 2804
GORDON EDWARDS B (A
ALLEN SCHWARZBERG D (A GEORGE DEVENS VIBES(A EUGENE BIANCO HARP (A GERRY CHAMBERLAIN TROM(A
RAY CADLE G)A JOE BATAAN PNO (A ADRIAN ALBERT V (A MAERETHA STEWART V (A
HILDA HARRIS V (A JIM MAELEN CONGA (A PETER QUINTERO CONGA(A BOB PORCELLI SAX (A
LOU MARINI WIND (A LEW SOLOFF TPT (A VICTOR PAZ TPT (A BARRY ROGERS TROM (A
LOUIE DEVIS B (A JULIAN LLANOS V (A JOCELYN SHAW V (A BIG B V (A

L21A LAST L21A

JOE NOLTE G V (A (A) L A EXPLOSION 1979 BOMP US 4004 LONDON UK SHZ8540
MIKE NOLTE V (A
DAVID NOLTE B V (A VITUS MATARE K FLT (A JACK REYNOLDS D (A

L21B LAST NIKEL L21B

LENNY McDANIEL B V (A (A) THE LAST NIKEL 19 MAINSTREAM US 6122
WALLY McDANIEL K (A
ROGER BERTRAND G (A MIKE SCORSONE SAX (A GORDON SCHUMERT TPT (A CLAY MUSACCHIA TROM(A
JERRY ROUSELLE D (A

L21C LAST TOUCH L21C

LADIES OF GREY 1981 ZILCH RIEN 3

L22 THE LAST POETS L22

ALAFIA PUDIM V (THE LAST POETS 1970 DOUGLAS US 30811
OMAR BEN HASSEN V (THIS IS MADNESS 1971 DOUGLAS UK 69012 US 30583
NILIJAH PERC (CHASTISEMENT 1972 BLUE THUMB US 539
ABIO DUN OYEWOLE V (RIGHT ON 19 JUGGERNAUT US 8802
SULIAMAN EL HADI V (THE REVOLUTION WILL NOT BE TELEVISED 197
JAZZOETRY 197
DELIGHTS OF THE GARDEN 19 CASABLANCA US 7501

L22A LAST WORDS L22A

JOHNNY IOMBARDO V (A (A) LAST WORDS 1968 ATCO US SD 33235
MIKE BYRNES G (A
STEVE SECHAK K (A RICKY COOK D (A

L22B LAST WORDS (2) L22B

MALCOLM BAXTER V (A (A) THE LAST WORDS 1980 ARMAGEDDON UK ARM2
ANDY GROOME G (A
JOHN DUNN D (A RICKY LEIGH KENDALL B (A STEVE BERESFORD K (A DICK NIGHTDOCTOR SAX(A

L23 LATE SHOW L23

BILL CLIFT G V (A (A) SNAP 1979 DECCA UK TXS134
DAVE HEAD G V (A
MIKE JELLY G V VLN(A TIM JOYCE B V (A NIX F PLONK K (A BRUIZER CLIVE (A
DON WELLER SAX (A GEORGE CHISHOLM TPT (A MALCOLM GRIFFITHS TROM(A ALAN PRICE G (

L23A LAUGHING CLOWNS L23A

ROBERT FARRELL SAX (A (A) LAUGHING CLOWNS 1980 MISSING LINK AUS MLB001
DAN WALLACE-CRABBE K (A
BEN WALLACE-CRABBE B (A JEFFREY WEGENER D PER(A EDMUND KUEPPER G V (A

L23B LAUGHING HANDS L23B

(A) DOG PHOTOS 1980 ADHESIVE UK 2

L23C LAURIE & THE SIGHS L23C

LAURIE BEECHMAN V (A (A) LAURIE & THE SIGHS 1980 ATLANTIC US 19268 GER 50706
TONY SALINAS G (A
DAVID WOFFORF B (A DEMO RAY AGCAOLI D (A DEREK FOX K (A

L24 LATIMORE L24

BENNY LATIMORE PNO (ABC (A) LATIMORE 1974 PRESIDENT UK 1058 GLADES US6502
FREDDIE SCOTT D (A (B) IT AIN'T WHERE YOU BEEN 1977 TK UK XL14034 GLADES US7509
VAN OLANDER D (A (C) LATIMORE 3 1977 PRESIDENT UK 1065 GLADES US7505
BOBBY RADELOFF D (A (D) MORE MORE MORE 19 GLADES US6503
BETTY WRIGHT V (A (E) DIG A LITTLE DEEPER 19 GLADES US7515
MIKE LEWIS FLT (A
RON BOGDON B (A GWEN McCRAE V (A AL KOOPER K (A JOEY MURCIA G (A
GEORGE McCRAE V (A

L24A LAUGHING DOGS L24A

MOE POTTS D V (A (A) LAUGHING DOGS 1979 CBS 36033 UK 83807
RONNIE CARLE B HCA V(A (B) LAUGHING DOGS MEET THEIR MAKER 1980 CBS 36429 UK 84328
CARTER CATHCART K G V(A
JAMES LEONARD G V (A

L24B LAVA L24B

THOMAS KARRENBACH K V (A — (A) TEARS ARE GOING HOME — 1973 BRAIN GER 1031
STEFAN OSTERTAG G V (A
JURGEN KRAAZ G B FLT B K(A — CHRISTIAN OSTERTAG B (A — ARCHER WEAVER D HCA V(A — PETER MOSES PERC(A

L24C LAVA (2) L24C

TOR VISTER V (A — (A) CRUSIN' — 1981 POLDOR 2382 120
ROLF GRAF B (A
SIGURD KOHN SAX (A — MARCUS MILLER G (A — PER HILLESTAD PERC (A — TERJE BAKKO V (A
SIDSEL ENDRESEN V (A — JAN ERIK AASLAND V (A — PER KALSTAD K (A — SVEIN DAG HAUGE G (A
NINA ASKELAND V (A

L25 LAVENDER HILL MOB L25

NICKY CRIGENO V B (A — (A) LAVENDER HILL MOB — 1977 UA UK UAS30043
RONNY JONES G V (A
GERRY HARDY V WIND(A — HECTOR JACOB G V (A — CHUCK CHANDLER K V (A — VITO FIORY D (A

L25A BETTY LAVETTE L25A

BETTY LAVETTE V (A — (A) EASIER TO SAY (THAN DO) — 1980 CHARLY UK CTD107

L26 LAW L26

TOM POOL D (A — (A) LAW — 1975 GRC US GA10017
RONNIE LEE CUNNINGHAM K V(AB — (B) BREAKIN' IT — 1977 MCA US 2240 UK 2785
STEVE ACKER G V (AB — (C) HOLD ON TO IT — 1978 MCA US 2306
JOHN McIVERS B (AB
JOE LALA PERC (A — ALBHY GALUTEN SYN (A — MEMPHIS HRNS (A — STEVE LAWRENCE D V (B
ROY KENNER V (B — JOEY MURCIA G (B — MIAMI HRNS (B — BILL COLANTONE PERC(B
FLACO PADRON PERC (B

L26A DOMINIQUE LAWARLEE L26A

DOMINIQUE LAWARLEE K (ALL — (A) INFINITUDES — 197 WALRUS WLS001
MARC HOLLANDER PNO (C — (B) LE CHOIX DU TITRE EST UN FAUX — 1977 WALRUS WLS003
CHARLES LOOS PNO (C — (C) TRACES — 1978 WALRUS WLS004
(D) BRINS D'HERBE — 1978 WALRUS WLS005
(E) VIS A VIS — 1979 WALRUS WLS006

L26B CLAIRE LAWRENCE L26B

CLAIRE LAWRENCE V WIND(A — (A) LEAVING YOU FREE — 1973 HAIDA CAN HL5103
JIM GORDON D (A
MAX BENNETT B (A — LARRY CARLTON G (A — DEAN PARKS G (A — BRETT WADE G (A
CLARENCE McDONALD PNO (A — RON TUTT D (A — LOUIS SHELTON G (A — KATHY STACK V (A
STEPHANIE SPRUILL V (A — BEVERLEY JACKSON V (A — LISA ROBERTS V (A — STRING SECTION (A

L26C LAWLER & COBB L26C

(A) MEN FROM NOWHERE — 1981 ASYLUM US 279

L27 BILLY LAWRIE L27

BILLY LAWRIE V (A — (A) SHIP IMAGINATION — 1973 RCA UK SF8395
RONNIE LEAHY K (A
JIMMY McCULLOCH G (A — COLIN ALLEN D (A — TIM RENWICK G (A — STEVE THOMPSON B (A
WILLIE WILSON D (A — BRUCE THOMAS B (A — GARY OSBORNE G V (A — PAUL VIGRASS V (A
ROGER BALL HRNS (A — MALCOLM DUNCAN HRNS (A — RAY COOPER PERC (A — LULU V (A
LIZA STRIKE V (A — MAGGIE BELL V (A — KIM GARDNER B (A — KENNY JONES D (A
BARRY CLARKE G (A — LUIS JARDIM PERC (A — JUANITA FRANKLIN V (A — PETER WOOD K (A
LES HARVEY G (A — JOHN COLEMAN PNO (A — JO PARTRIDGE G (A

L28 RONNIE LAWS L28

RONNIE LAWS V (ALL — (A) PRESSURE SENSITIVE — 1975 BLUENOTE 452 UK 76 UAG20002
MARLOW THE MAGICIAN G (B — (B) FEVER — 1976 UA US 628 UAG20007
NATHANIEL PHILLIPS B (BD — (C) FLAME — 1978 UA UAG30204
BRUCE CARTER D (B — (D) EVERY GENERATION — 1980 LIBERTY US LT 1001 UA UAG30289
DONALD HEPBURN K (B
MICHAEL HEPBURN K (B — BRUCE SMITH PERC (B — BOBBY LYLE K (BD — STEVE GUITIERREZ D(AB
WILTON FELDER B (AB — TONY BEN CONGA(B — STRING SECTION (BD — ELOISE LAWS V (D
ALEXANDRA BROWN V (D — JEAN THOMPSON V (D — MIKE HOWARD V (D — DOROTHY ASHBY HARP(D
PAT KELLY G (D — BARNABY FINCH SYN (D — LARRY DUNN (CD — RONNIE FOSTER (D
HUBERT LAWS (D — PATRICE RUSHEN (D — JOE SAMPLE K (AD — PHILIP BAILEY (C
ROLAND BAUTISTA (AC — JOHN W ROWIN G (A — CLINT MOSLEY B (A — MICHAEL WILLARS D(A
MIKE CAVANAUGH K (A — JERRY PETERS K (A — JOE CLAYTON PERC (A

L28A LAZARUS L28A

SHELBY SINGLETON (A — (A) LAZARUS — 1970 AMAZON US AM 1001
STEVE McNICOL (A — (A) LAZARUS — 197 BEARSVILLE US 2004
THOMAS BOMBACI (A — (B) FOOLS PARADISE — 1974 BEARSVILLE US 2135
RAYMOND CICHON (A
RONALD STABLINI (A — TONY BERTOLLOTTI (

L29 KEN LAZARUS L29

KEN LAZARUS V (ALL — REGGAE SCORCHERS — 1970 LONDON UK ZGJ102
REGGAE GREAT HITS VOL1 — 1970 LONDON UK ZGJ107
REGGAE GREAT HITS VOL 2 — 1970 LONDON UK ZGJ108

L30 LAZY RACER L30

TIM RENWICK G V (AB — (A) LAZY RACER — 1979 A&M US 4768 UK AMLH64768
HENRY SPINETTI D (AB — (B) FORMULA 2 — 1980 A&M US 4808 UK AMLH64808
DAVE MARKEE B (A
TIM GORMAN V K (AB — BILL LAMB G V (AB — KELLY HARLAND V (AB — PAT DONALDSON D (B

L31 BERNIE LEADON & MICHAEL GEORGIADES L31

BERNIE LEADON G V BAN(A — (A) NATURAL PROGRESSION — 1977 ASYLUM US 7E1107 UK K53063
MICHAEL GEORGIADES G V (A
BRYAN GAROFALO B (A — DAVID KEMPER D (A — STEVE GOLDSTEIN K (A — BOBBYE HALL PERC(A
IRVING AZOFF V (A — JOHN BANDINI BRENNAN G(A — ED SILVERS V (A — JOE SMITH V (A
BARON STEWART V (A

L32 LEAFHOUND L32

(A) GROWERS OF MUSHROOMS — 1971 DECCA UK SKLR 5094
(A) GROWERS OF MUSHROOMS — 1971 TELEFUNKEN GER 14604

L32A LEAGUE OF GENTLEMEN L32A

ROBERT FRIPP G (A — (A) LEAGUE OF GENTLEMEN — 1981 EG UK EGED9 GER 2315 215
BARRY ANDREWS K (A — (A) LEAGUE OF GENTLEMEN — 1981 POLYDOR US 16317
JOHNNY TOOBAD D (A
SARAH LEE B (A

L33 LEATHER COATED MINDS L33

J J CALE G (A — (A) TRIP DOWN SUNSET STRIP 19 FONTANA UK 5412 VIVA US 36003

L33A LEATHER NUN L33A

(A) SLOW DEATH (EP) 19 INDUSTRIAL IR 0006

L34 LEAVES L34

JIM PONS B V (AB — (A) HEY JOE 1966 MIRA US 3005 RI LINE GER 5144
BILL RHEINHART (A — (B) ALL THE GOOD THAT'S HAPPENING 1967 CAPITOL US ST 2638
JOHN BECK G V (
BOBBY ARLIN G V (TOM RAY D (ROBERT REINER (

L34A LENNIE LEBLANC L34A

LENNIE LEBLANC G V (ALL — (A) LENNY LEBLANC 1976 BIG TREE US 89515
PETE CARR G (A — (B) HOUND DOG MAN 1977 BIG TREE US 76003
BUTCH LEADFORD B (A — (C) BREAKTHROUGH 1980 CAPITOL
ROGER CLARK D (A
EDDIE STRUZICK V (A LAURA STRUZICK V (A HARVEY THOMPSON SAX (A JIMMY EVANS D (A
RANDY McCORMICK PNO (A STEVE HERBERT D (A

L35 LEBLANC & CARR L35

LENNIE LEBLANC G V (AB — (A) MIDNIGHT LIGHT 1978 BIG TREE US 89521 UK K50474
PETE CARR G V (AB — (B) LIVE FROM THE ATLANTIC STUDIOS 1978 BIG TREE US 003
BUTCH LEADFORD B (A
BOB WRAY B (A RANDY McCORMICK K (A TIM HENSON K (A CLAYTON IVEY K (A
ROBERT BYRNE G (A RICK POWELL D (B STEVE NATHAN K (B LEON SHERRILL G (B
THOM FLORA K (B GARY BAKER B V (B

L36 LED ZEPPELIN L36

JIMMY PAGE G (ALL — (A) LED ZEPPELIN 1968 ATLANTIC US 8216 UK 588171
ROBERT PLANT V HCA(ALL — (A) LED ZEPPELIN 1971 ATLANTIC US 19126 UK K40031
JOHN BONHAM D (ALL — (B) LED ZEPPELIN 2 1969 ATLANTIC US 8236 UK 588198
JOHN PAUL JONES B K (ALL — (B) LED ZEPPELIN 2 1971 ATLANTIC US 19127 UK K40037
WITH — (C) LED ZEPPELIN 3 1970 ATLANTIC US 7201 UK2401002
VIRAM JASANI TABLAS(A — (C) LED ZEPPELIN 3 1971 ATLANTIC US 19128 UK K50002
SANDY DENNY V (D — (D) LED ZEPPELIN 4 1971 ATLANTIC US 7208 UK2401012
(D) LED ZEPPELIN 4 1971 ATLANTIC UK K50008
(E) HOUSES OF THE HOLY 1973 ATLANTIC US 7255 UK K50014
(F) PHYSICAL GRAFFITI 1975 SWANSONG US SS2 200 UK K89400
(G) PRESENCE 1976 ATCO US 7255
(G) PRESENCE 1976 SWANSONG US SS 8416 UK K59402
(H) THE SONG REMAINS THE SAME 1976 SWANSONG US SS2 201 UK K89402
(I) LIVE 197 JOKER ITALY SM3721
(J) IN THROUGH THE OUT DOOR 1979 SWANSONG US 16002 UK K59410

L36A ALBERT LEE L36A

ALBERT LEE V G K MAND(A — (A) HIDING 1979 A&M US 4750 UK AMLH64750 NL 271
JOHN WARE D (A
EMORY GORDY B (A HANK DEVITO STEEL V (A GLEN D HARDIN PNO (A RICKY SKAGGS V FDL(A
EMMYLOU HARRIS V (A MICKEY RAPHAEL HCA (A BRIAN AHERN G (A DON EVERLY V (A
PETE GAVIN D (A DAVE PEACOCK B (A CHAS HODGES PNO (A BRUCE GARY D (A
BUDDY EMMONS STEEL(A GERRY CONWAY D (A PAT DONALDSON B (A JERRY JUMONVILLE HRNS(A
RODNEY CROWELL V (A DONIVAN COWART V (A

L37 ALVIN LEE L37

ALVIN LEE G V (ALL — (A) ROAD TO FREEDOM 1973 CHRYSALIS UK 1054 US CBS 32729
MYLON LEFEVRE G V PERC(A — (B) IN FLIGHT (DBL) 1974 CHRYSALIS UK 1069 US CBS 33187
STEVE WINWOOD K (A — (C) PUMP IRON 1975 CHRYSALIS UK 1094 US CBS 33796
JIM CAPALDI D (A — (D) LET IT ROCK 1978 CHRYSALIS UK 1190
MICK HAWKSWORTH B (EF — (E) ROCKET FUEL 1978 POLYDOR UK 2344 103 RSO US 3033
REBOP BAAH PERC (A — (F) RIDE ON 1979 POLYDOR UK 2310 678 RSO US 3049
CHRIS STAINTON K (H — (G) FREE FALL 1980 AVATAR UK AALP5002
MIKE PATTO V (A — (H) RX5 1981 ATLANTIC US 19306
TIM HINKLEY K (ABC
GEORGE HARRISON G (A RON WOOD G B D(A MICK FLEETWOOD G (A PETER THOMS TROM(G
ANDY STEIN FDL (A IAN WALLACE D (ABC BOBBY BLACK STEEL(A BOZ BURRELL B (AC
MEL COLLINS SAX (A ALAN SPENNER B (B NEIL HUBBARD G (B DYAN BIRCH V (B
FRANK COLLINS V (B PADDY McHUGH V (B BRYSON GRAHAM D (C JACK LANCASTER HRNS (C
HAROLD BURGON K (C RONNIE LEAHY K (C STEVE THOMPSON B (C BROTHER JAMES PERC(C
RON BERG D (C ANDY PYLE B (C COLIN GIBSON B (C STEVE GOULD G V (GH
MICK FEAT B V (GH TOM COMPTON D PERC (EFGH DEREK AUSTIN K (GH AL KOOPER ORG (G
RAPHAEL RAVENSCROFT SAX(G BERNIE CLARKE K (E MICK WEAVER K (E

L38 ARTHUR LEE L38

ARTHUR LEE G V (A — (A) VINDICATOR 1972 A&M US 4356 UK AMLS64356
DON PONCHER D (A — (B) ARTHUR LEE 1981 BEGGARS BANQUET UK BEGA 26
CHARLES KARP G (A — (B) ARTHUR LEE 1981 LINE GER LLP5120
DAVID HULL B (A
CRAIG TARWATER G (A FRANK FAYAD B (A CLARENCE McDONALD K (A

L39 BRENDA LEE L39

TITLE	YEAR	LABEL	COUNTRY	NO.	TITLE	YEAR	LABEL	COUNTRY	NO.
BRENDA LEE	1960	DECCA	US	74039	THATS ALL	1962	BRUNSWICK	UK STA	8516
GRANDMA WHAT GREAT SONGS		BRUNSWICK	UK LAT	8319	ALL ALONE AM I	1962	DECCA	US	74370
" " "	"	DECCA	US	78873	" " "	1962	BRUNSWICK	UK STA	8530
MISS DYNAMITE	196	BRUNSWICK	UK LAT	8347	LOVE YOU	1963	ACE OF HEARTS	UK	AH59
THIS IS BRENDA LEE	1961	BRUNSWICK	UK LAT	8360	LET ME SING	1964	DECCA	US	74439
" " "	1961	DECCA	US	74082	" "	1964	BRUNSWICK	UK STA	8548
EMMOTIONS	1961	DECCA	US	74104	BY REQUEST	1964	DECCA	US	74509
" "	1961	BRUNSWICK	UK LAT	8376	" "	1964	BRUNSWICK	UK STA	8576
" "	1961	BRUNSWICK	UK STA	3044	MERRY CHRISTMAS	1964	DECCA	US	74583
ALL THE WAY	1961	DECCA	US	74176	" " "	1964	BRUNSWICK	UK STA	8590
" "	1961	BRUNSWICK	UK LAT	8383	TOP TEEN HITS	1965	DECCA	US	74626
" "	1961	BRUNSWICK	UK STA	3048	" " "	1965	BRUNSWICK	UK STA	8603
SINCERELY	1961	DECCA	US	74216	VERSATILE	1965	DECCA	US	74661
" "	1961	BRUNSWICK	UK LAT	8396	"	1965	BRUNSWICK	UK STA	8614
" "	1961	BRUNSWICK	UK STA	3056	TOO MANY RIVERS	1965	DECCA	US	74684
" "	197	MCA	US	477	" " "	1965	BRUNSWICK	UK STA	8622
THAT'S ALL	1962	DECCA	US	74326	BYE BYE BLUES	1966	DECCA	US	74755
					" " "	1966	BRUNSWICK	UK STA	8649

(CONTINUED)

Title	Year	Label	Country	Cat. No.
10 GOLDEN YEARS	1966	DECCA	US	74757
" " "	19	MCA	US	107
COMING ON STRONG	1967	DECCA	US	74825
" " "	1967	BRUNSWICK	UK	8672
REFLECTIONS IN BLUE	1967	DECCA	US	74941
" " "	19	MCA	UK	MUPS 306
CALL ME BRENDA	196	MCA	UK	MUPS 321
GOOD LIFE	196	MCA	UK	MUPS 322
HERE'S BRENDA LEE	1967	VOCALION	US	VL 7 3795
LET IT BE ME	19	VOCALION	US	VL 7 3890
" " "	19	CORAL	US	CB 20044
FOR THE FIRST TIME	1968	MCA	UK	MUPS 332
" " "	196	DECCA	US	74955
JOHNNY ONE TIME	1969	DECCA	US	75111
" " "	1970	MCA	UK	MUPS 396
" " "	1974	MCA	UK	MCF 2633
MEMPHIS PORTRAIT	1970	DECCA	US	75232
" " "	1971	MCA	UK	MUPS 423
" " "	1974	MCA	UK	MCF 2519
MISS DYNAMITE	1979	MCA	FR	414030
A WHOLE LOTTA	1972	MCA	UK	MUPS 460
" "	1974	MCA	UK	MCF 2660
BRENDA	197	MCA	US	305
"	1973	MCA	UK	MUPS 485
"	1974	MCA	UK	MCF 2507
BRENDA LEE STORY	1974	MCA	UK	MCDW 428
" " "	197	DECCA	US	74012
NEW SUNRISE	1974	MCA	US	373
" "	1974	MCA	UK	MCF 2527
NOW	1975	MCA	US	433
"	1975	MCA	UK	MCF 2593
SINCERELY	1975	MCA	US	477
" "	1975	MCA	UK	MCF 2709
FUNNY HOW TIME SLIPS	1975	SOUNDS SUPERB	UK	90067
LITTLE MISS DYNAMITE	1976	MCA	UK	MCF 2729
LET IT BE ME	19	VOCALION	US	73840
L A SESSION	1977	MCA	UK	MCF 2783
" "	1977	MCA	US	2233
LEGENDS OF ROCK (DBL)	19	CORAL	US	61141/2
LITTLE MISS DYNAMITE	1980	WARWICK		WW 5083

L39A BYRON LEE & THE DRAGONAIRES L39A

BYRON LEE (ALL

Title	Year	Label	Country	Cat. No.
SOUNDS OF JAMAICA	19	TOWER HALL	US	LP 006
REGGAE	19	TROJAN		TRLS 18
REGGAE SPLASH DOWN	19	TROJAN		TRL 28
REGGAE HOT COOL EASY	19	TROJAN		TRLS 40
REGGAE BLASH OFF	19	TROJAN		TBL 110
REGGAE FEVER	1974	POLYDOR		2460 229
DISCO REGGAE	1975	MERCURY	US	SRMI 1063
MIDAS TOUCH	1975	DRAGON		DRLS 5006
& MIGHTY SPARROW	1976	DYNAMIC		DYLP 3002
THIS IS CARNIVAL	1976	DYNAMIC		DYLP 3006
REGGAE INTERNATIONAL	1976	DYNAMIC		DYLP 3008
ART OF MAS	1977	DYNAMIC		DYLS 1002
BYRON LEE & THE DRAGONAIRES	19	JAD	US	JAS 1004
MORE CARNIVAL	1978	DYNAMIC		DYLP 3012
CARNIVAL EXPERIENCE	1979	DYNAMIC		DYLP 3014
JAMAICA'S GOLDEN HITS VOL 1	1979	STATE		ETMP 14
JAMAICA'S GOLDEN HITS VOL 2	1979	STATE		ETMP 17
DANCE THE SKY	19	B M N		BLP 004
JUMP UP	19	ATCO	US	33 182
REGGAE BLAST OFF	1980	TROJAN	UK	110
SOUL SKA	1981	ECHO	UK	1001

L40 FREDDY FINGERS LEE L40

FREDDY FINGERS LEE (AB

Title	Year	Label	Country	Cat. No.
(A) FREDDY FINGERS LEE	1978	CHARLY		CR 30160
(B) OL' ONE EYE IS BACK	1979	CHARLY		CR 30178

L41 JOHN LEE & GERRY BROWN L41

JOHN LEE K B PERC (ABC
GERRY BROWN D PERC(ABC
PHILIP CATHERINE G (B
EEF ALBERS G (BC
ERIC TAGG K (B | JASPER VANT HOF K (B | ROB FRANKEN K (AB | MIKE MANDEL K (B
WAH WAH WATSON G (B | DARRYL THOMPSON G (C | PALLE MIKKELBORG TPT PERC(C | KENNETH KNUDSEN K (C
BOBBY MALACH SAX (C | REGGIE LUCAS G (A | RAY GOMEZ G (A | HUBERT EAVES K (A
MTUME V PERC (A | TAWATHA AGEE V (A | RANDY BRECKER HRNS (A | MICHAEL BRECKER SAX(A
DAVID SANBORN SAX (A | BARRY ROGERS TROM (A | HAROLD WILLIAMS K (A | IAN UNDERWOOD SYN (A
DONALD SMITH V (A | C P ALEXANDER V (A | JON FADDIS TPT (A | ERNIE WATTS SAX (A
GARY BARTZ SAX (A | RON CUBER SAX (A

Title	Year	Label	Country	Cat. No.
(A) STILL CAN'T SAY ENOUGH	1976	BLUENOTE	US	BNLA 701
(B) MANGO SUNRISE	1976	BLUENOTE	US	BNLA 541 UK 20004
(C) CHASER	1979	CBS	US	36212

L42 RANDY LEE L42

RANDY LEE V (A
PETE DRAKE STEEL(A
LARRY SASSER STEEL(A | JERRY CARRIGAN D (A | PIG RODDINS PNO (A | JAMES M JOHNSON G (A
DON TWEEDY HRNS (A | GEORGE CUNNINGHAM HRNS (A | WENDELLYN SUITS V (A | TOMMY COGBILL B (A
KENNY BUTTREY D (A | EARL BALL PNO (A | JIMMY COLVARD G (A | BOB PHILLIPS HRNS (A
LEA JANE BERINATI V (A | GARY S PAXTON SINGERS (A | HOYET HENRY B (A | KEN MALONE D (A
JACK SOLOMAN G (A | BILLY SANFORD G (A | LOUIS BROWN HRNS (A | SHARON VAUGHN V (A

Title	Year	Label	Country	Cat. No.
(A) SOAKIN' WITH TEARS	1974	ELEKTRA	US	EKS 75081

L42A LEE RIDERS L42A

ROBERT LEE G V (A
MIKE O'CONNOR K (A
MATT PRESBY G (A | MIKE REILLY B V (A | ROY OTEMRO D PERC G (A | B J COLE STEEL (A

Title	Year	Label	Country	Cat. No.
(A) LEE RIDERS	1972	UA		UAS 29312

L42B THOMAS LEER & ROBERT RENTAL L42B

THOMAS LEER V SYN G (A
ROBERT RENTAL V G SYN B(A

Title	Year	Label	Country	Cat. No.
(A) THE BRIDGE	1979	INDUSTRIAL	UK	1R0007

L42C THOMAS LEER L42C

THOMAS LEER V ANST (A

Title	Year	Label	Country	Cat. No.
(A) CONTRADICTIONS	1982	CHERRY RED		RED 26

L43 JOHN LEES L43

JOHN LEES (A
SKIP ALLEN D (A
ROD ARGENT K (A
ERIC STEWART G (A | WALLY WALLER B (A | KEVIN GODLEY (A | GORDON EDWARDS PNO(A
REX MORRISON SAX (A

Title	Year	Label	Country	Cat. No.
(A) A MAJOR FANCY	1973	HARVEST	UK	SHVL 811
(A) A MAJOR FANCY	1977	HARVEST RI	UK	SHSM 2018

L44 MYLON LEFEVRE

MYLON LEFEVRE G V (ALL (A) MYLON 1971 ATLANITC 2400 104 L44
PIERCE LEFEVRE (CE (A) MYLON 197 COTILLION US SD 9026
AUBURN BURRELL G (AB (B) OVER THE INFLUENCE 1972 CBS US 31472
ALVIN LEE G V (D (C) PIERCE & MYLON LEFEVRE 1972 CANAAN UK CAS 9673
J P LAUZON G (B (D) ROAD TO FREEDOM 1973 CHRYSALIS UK CHR 1054
MARTY SIMON D (B (E) LEFEVRES GREATEST HITS 197 STARDAY US SD 3006
LESLIE WEST G (B (F) WEAK AT THE KNEES 1977 WB US 3070 UK K56407
DR JOHN K (B (G) RUSTLER 1978 WB US 3216
TINA BLOUNT V (B (H) ROCK'N'ROLL RESURRECTION 1980 MERCURY US 3799
TOM ROBB B (B
SHRILEY MATTHEWS V (A CLYDIE KING V (A ALLEN TOUSSAINT K (B BARRY BAILEY G (AB
RENAY GARVIN V (B LESTER LANGDALE K (B RICHARD PENNIMAN V (B STEVE SANDERS V (B
PAT CUMMINGS V (B KIM VENABLE D (A DEAN DAUGHTRY K (A RON GRAYBEAL B (A
MERRY CLAYTON V (A VANETTA FIELDS V (A ** FOR FULL LINE UP OF D SEE ALVIN LEE ENTRY

L45 LEFT BANKE

RICK BRAND G BAN(A (A) WALK AWAY RENEE 1967 PHILIPS SBL 7773 L45
STEVE MARTIN V (AB (A) WALK AWAY RENEE 1967 SMASH US (M)27088 (S) 67088
TOM FINN B (AB (B) TOO 1969 SMASH US (S) 67113
MIKE BROWN K (A
GEORGE CAMERON D (AB HARRY LOOKOSKY PROD (A

L45A LEGAL WEAPON

KAT V (A (A) NO SORROW (EP) 1981 ARSENAL UK LW68 L45A
PATRICIA B V (A
CHARLIE VARTAHIAN D (A BRIAN HANSEN G (A

L45B JOHNNY LEGEND & THE SKULLCAPS

JOHNNY LEGEND (A (A) ROCKABILLY RUMBLE 1981 RONDELET UK ABOUT 1002 L45B

L46 LEGEND

MICKEY JUPP G K V(ALL (A) LEGEND 1969 BELL UK SBLL 115 L46
NIGEL DUNBAR D (A (A) LEGEND 1969 BELL US 6027
STEVE GEARE B V (A (B) RED BOOT ALBUM 1971 VERTIGO UK 6360 019
CHRIS EAST G V (A (C) MOONSHINE 1972 VERTIGO UK 6360 063
MO WITHAM G (BCD (D) MICKEY JUPPS LEGEND (COMP) 1978 STIFF UK GET2
JOHN BOBIN B (BCD
BILL FIFIELD D (B BOB CLOUTER D (C BARNEY JAMES D (TIM RENWICK G (D
MICK MOODY G (D COLIN GIBSON B (D HENRY SPINETTI D (D JIMMY JEWELL SAX (D
PETE SOLLEY K (D GARY BROOKER PNO (D CHRIS COPPING B (D B J WILSON D (D
GLEN LEFLEUR D (D

L47 LEGOVER

RAPHAEL RAVENSCROFT WIND(A (A) WAIT TILL NIGHTTIME 1978 SMACK UK SL1001 L47
DAVID ULM PERC V(A
LINDSAY SCOTT VLN V (A SEAN BYRNE G V (A DAVE ROSE K (A MICKEY FEAT B (A
DEREK AUSTIN K (A DELISLE HARPER B (A PHIL CHEN B (A THEODORE THUNDER D(A
GLEN LEFLEUR D (A JOHN DENTITH D V (A BILL SKEAT WIND (A ALAN BOWN TPT(A
GEORGE HOWDEN TROM (A MICK PACE HCA (A JOHN WELLS V (A

L47A LEGS DIAMOND

MIKE PRINCE K V ((A) FIRE POWER 1978 CREAM US 1010 L47A
JEFF POOLE D ((B) LEGS DIAMOND 1978 MERCURY US 1136
MICHAEL DIAMOND B ((C) A DIAMOND IS A HARD ROCK 1979 MERCURY US 1191
RICK SANFORD V FLT(
ROGER ROMEO G V (

L47B PETER LEICH

PETER LEICH G (A (A) JUMPT STREET 1981 JAZZ HOUSE 7001 L47B
GEORGE McFETRIDGE K (A
NEIL SWOINSON B (A TERRY CLARKE D (A

L47C LEINEMANN

GOTTFRIED BOTTGER K (ALL (A) LEINEMANN'S HONKY TONK 1971 BASF GER 060 L47C
JORN SEELENMEYER G BAN V(ALL (B) PIANO SKIFFLE ROCK 1972 PHILIPS GER 630 5141
JURGEN BAHRS G V HCA(ALL (C) LAST TRAIN TO SAN FERNANDO 1973 PHILIPS GER 630 5185
ULRICH SALM B (ALL (D) LONNIE DONEGAN MEETS LEINEMANN 1974 PHILIPS GER 630 5227
ULF KRUGER PERC (ALL (E) DAS IST LEINEMANN 1975 PHILIPS GER 630 5224
LONNIE DONEGAN G V (D
PETER HESSLEIN G (D BERRY SAARLOUIS G V (D BOLLE BURMEISTER G (E JURGEN MAASS G(E
WILLIAM SIMPSON G (E FRANK REINKE G (E KARL ALLOUT G (E DIETER ARENDT D (E
WOLF SCHMIDTZ (D LORENZ WESTPHAL VLN V(DE BARRY REEVES D (D CHRIS HERRMANN HRN(D

L48 ANDY LEIGH

ANDY LEIGH B V G K PERC(A (A) MAGICIAN 1970 POLYDOR UK 2343 034 L48
BRYN HAWORTH G (A (A) MAGICIAN 197 SIRE US SES97025
KEVIN WESTLAKE D V (A
REG KING K V(A GORDON JACKSON SITAR(A GARY FARR HCA G(A MIKE KELLIE D (A
BRIAN GODDING G (A TONY PRIESTLAND WIND(A GARY WRIGHT K (A

L48A LEMON KITTENS

KARL BLAKE G V (A (A) WE BUY A HAMMER FOR DADDY 1980 UNITED DAIRIES UK UD02 L48A
DANIELLE DAX SAX (A
MIKE BARNES D (A IAN STURGESS B (A

L48B JO LEMAIRE & FLOUZE

JO LEMAIRE V (ALL (A) JO LEMAIRE & FLOUZE 1979 ROCKET UK TRAIN 11 L48B
PHILIPPE DEPREUX D (AB (A) JO LEMAIRE & FLOUZE 1979 VERTIGO EURO 9198 448
DANIEL FRANCOIS G (AB (B) PRECIOUS TIME 1980 VERTIGO EURO 6299 102
ATTILIO BORTOLIN C+AR G(A
GIOVANNE BORTOLIN K SAX SYN(AB MARC SANTKIN B(A ALAIN PIRE G (B FERDINAND PHILIPPOT B(B
MARC HEROUET (A PETRICK GERARD (A OSCAR DENAYER (A WINNY NUYENS (A

L49 LEMON PIPERS

BILL ALBAUGH D (A (A) GREEN TAMBOURINE 1968 BUDDAH UK 2349 006 L49
REG NAVE ORG (A (B) JUNGLE MARMALADE 1968 BUDDAH US BDS 5016
BILL BARTLETT G (A
STEVE WALMSLEY B (A IVAN BROWNE G V (A PAUL LENKA PROD (A

L49A LENINGRAD SANDWICH

MIKE LENINGRAD V (A (A) GO EAST 1980 UP 3001 L49A
JOHNNY LENINGRAD G (A
D LENINGRAD B (A CHARLIE HONGKOMG D (A

L50 CLAUDIA LENNEAR L50

CLAUDIA LENNEAR	V	(A	(A) PHEW	1973	WB	US BS2654	UK K 46204
RY COODER	G	(A					

JOHN CRAVIOTTO D (A	JIM DICKINSON G K (A	CHARLES GRIMES G (A	MILT HOLLAND PERC (A
MIKE UTLEY K (A	DICK HYDE TROM (A	JIM KELTNER D (A	RICK LITTLEFIELD G (A
LEW McCREARY TROM (A	SPOONER OLDHAM K (A	WILLIAM SMITH K (A	ARTHUR ADAMS G (A
HAROLD BATTISTE JR SAX (A	TESSIE CALDERON CONGA(A	GENE CIPRIANO SAX (A	MARLINE GREENE G (A
PAUL HUBINON TPT (A	WARREN LUENING JR TPT (A	DON MENZA WIND (A	CHUCK RAINEY B (A
ALLEN TOUSSAINT K V (A			

L51 JOHN LENNON & YOKO ONO L51

JOHN LENNON	G K V	(ALL	(A) TWO VIRGINS	1968	APPLE	US 5001	UK SAPCOR 2
YOKO ONO	V WIND	(ALL?	(B) LIFE WITH THE LIONS	1969	APPLE	US 3357	UK ZAPPLE 01
KLAUS VOORMANN	B	(DEFHJNO	(C) WEDDING ALBUM	1969	APPLE	US 3361	UK SAPCOR 11
STEVE BRENDELL	B	(H	(D) LIVE PEACE IN TORONTO	1969	APPLE	US 3362	UK CORE 2001
ALAN WHITE	D	(DEFHJ	(E) PLASTIC ONO BAND	1970	APPLE	US 3372	UK SAPCOR 17
GEORGE HARRISON	G	(HJ	(F) PLASTIC ONO BAND	1971	APPLE		UK PCS 7124
NICKY HOPKINS	K	(HJN	(H) IMAGINE	1971	APPLE	US 3379	UK PAS 10004
TED TURNER	G	(H	(J) SOMETIME IN NEW YORK CITY	1972	APPLE	US 3392	UK PCSP 7161
ROD LINTON	G	(H	(K) MIND GAMES	1973	APPLE	US 3414	UK PCS 7165
JOSE FELICIANO	G	(O	(K) MIND GAMES	1980	MFP		UK 50509
JOHN TOUT		(H	(L) APPROXIMATELY INFINITE UNIVERSE	1973	APPLE		UK SAPDO1001
JIM KELTNER	D	(HJKNO	(M) FEELING THE SPACE	1973	APPLE		UK SAPCOR 26
JOHN BARHAM	K	(H	(N) WALLS & BRIDGES	1974	APPLE	US 3416	UK PCTC 253
JIM GORDON	D	(H	(O) ROCK'ROLL	1975	APPLE	US 3419	UK PCS 7169
LEON RUSSELL	K	(O	(O) ROCK'ROLL	1975	APPLE	GER 05834	
KING CURTIS	SAX	(H	( ) SINGS ROCK'ROLL (ROOTS)	1975	ADAM	US 8018	
TOM EVANS	G	(H	(P) SHAVED FISH	1975	APPLE	US 3421	UK PCS 7173
JOEY MOLLAND	G	(H	(Q) DOUBLE FANTASY	1980	GEFFEN	US 2001	UK K 99131
NINO TEMPO	SAX	(O	( ) BOX SET(8 LP SET)(DHEKNOJP)	1981	PARLOPHONE		UK JLB8
MIKE PINDER	PERC	(H					

KEN ASCHER K (KNO	GORDON EDWARDS B (K	RICK MAROTTA D (K	MICHAEL BRECKER SAX(K
SNEAKY PETE STEEL(K	JESSE ED DAVIS G (NO	ERIC CLAPTON G (DJ	RINGO STARR D (EF
JULIAN LENNON D (N	FRANK ZAPPA G V (J	MARK VOLMAN V (J	HOWARD KAYLAN V (J
JIM PONS B V (J	STAN BRONSTEIN SAX (JL	DON PRESTON SYN (J	RICHARD FRANK D (JL
IAN UNDERWOOD WIND K V(J	BOB HARRIS K V (J	ADAM IPPOLITO K (JL	WAYNE GABRIEL G (JL
BOBBY KEYS SAX (JNO	GARY VAN SCYOC B (JL	AYNSLEY DUNBAR D (J	BILLY PRESTON K (JE
KEITH MOON D (J	JOHN LA BOSCA PNO (J	ARTHUR JENKINS PERC (NO	EDDIE MOTTAU G (NO
ELTON JOHN K V (N	LORI BURTON V (N	MAY PANG V (N	HARRY NILSSON V (N
STEVE MADAIO HRNS (N	HOWARD JOHNSON HRNS (N	RON APREA HRNS (N	FRANK VICARI HRNS(N
DAVID SPINOZZA G (K	PHIL SPECTOR PNO (E	DENNIS MOROUSE HRNS (O	FRANK VICARI HRNS(O
PETER JAMESON (O	JOE TEMTERLEY (O	STEVE CROPPER G (O	HAL BLAINE D (O
JEFF BARRY (O	BARRY MANN (O	EARL SLICK G (Q	TONY LEVIN B (Q
ANDY NEWMARK D (Q	ED WALSH K (Q	CASSANDRA WOOTEN V (Q	JACK ERIC TROYER V (Q
ROBERT GREENRIDGE PERC (Q	RANDY STEIN CONC(Q	GRANT HUNGERFORD HRNS (Q	SELDON POWELL HRNS (Q
ROGER ROSENBERG HRNS (Q	RONALD TOOLEY HRNS (Q	HUGH McCRACKEN G (Q	GEORGE SMALL K (Q
ARTHUR JENKINS PERC (Q	MICHAELLE SIMPSON V (Q	CHERYL MASON V (Q	BENNY CUMMINGS SINGERS V(Q
MATTHEW CUNNINGHAM DULC(Q	HOWARD JOHNSON HRNS (Q	JOHN PARRAN HRNS (Q	GEORGE OPALISKY HRNS(Q
DAVID TOFANI HRNS (Q			

L51A LENNY & SQUIGGY L51A

(A) LENNY & THE SQUIGTONES	1980	CASABLANCA	UK	7149

L52 J B LENOIR L52

J B LENOIR	G V	(ALL	(A) CRUSADE	1970	POLYDOR	UK	2482 014
ALEX ATKINS	SAX	(BC	(B) NATURAL MAN	19	CHESS	US	410
ERNEST COTTON	SAX	(BC	(C) BLUESMASTER	1976	CHESS		2A CMB208
JOE MONTGOMERY	PNO	(BC	(D) ALABAMA BLUES	1979	L+R		42 001
LORENZO SMITH	SAX	(BC	(E) DOWN IN MISSISSIPPI	1980	L+R		42 012
ALFRED WALLACE	D	(BCF	(F) THE TAY MAY CLUB	1980	FLYRIGHT	UK	FLY 564
WILLIE DIXON	D	(ABCDE					

FRED BELOW D (DAE	LEROY FOSTER G (BC	J T BROWN SAX (F	AL GAVIN D (BC
SUNNYLAND SLIM PNO (BCF			

L52B KLAUS LENZ BAND L52B

KLAUS LENZ			(A) WIEGENLIED	1978	VINYL	UK	VS001

L53 DEKE LEONARD L53

DEKE LEONARD	G K V	(ALL	(A) ICEBERG	1973	UA	US LA150	UK UAG 29464
MARTIN RUSHANT	PROD V	(C	(A) ICEBERG	1980	LIBERTY ROCKFILE		UK LBR 1042
MARTIN ACE	B	(ABC	(B) KAMIKAZE	1974	UA	US 306	UK UAG 29544
DAVE CHARLES	PROD D V	(ABC	(C) BEFORE YOUR VERY EYES	1981	UA		UK UAG 30240
MICKY JONES	G	(AB					

PAUL BURTON B V (A	VICKY SILVER V (C	DOREEN CHANTER V (C	KENNY MOORE V (C
TOMMY RILEY D (AB	BEAU ADAMS D (A	RICHARD TREECE G (A	DAVE PHILIPS VLN (A
BRIAN BREEZE G (B	KEITH HODGE D (B	LINCOLN CARR B G (B	KEN WHALEY B (B
TERRY WILLIAMS D V (BC	BYRON BERLINE FDL (AB	BILLY HAYNES V (C	JAN STEVENS (C
VIRGINIA PECK (C	JOHN McKENZIE B (C	BILLY BREMNER V (C	MALCOLM MORLEY K V(C
ANTON MATTHEWS V (C	DAVE EDMUNDS V (C	RON FRANCOIS B (C	CHRIS PARREN K (C
LENNY MACALUSO G (C	CHRIS MERCER SAX (C	RON ASPERY SAX (C	MARTIN DROVER TPT (C

L54 LEOPARD L54

(A) KANSAS CITY SLICKERS	1978	MOON	IMP

L54A LE ORME L54A

ANTONIO PAGLIUCA	K	(ABCDEFGHJ	(A) COLLAGE	1971	PHILIPS	6323 007
ALDO TAGLIAPIETRA	B V G	(ABCDEFGHJ	(B) UOMO DI PEZZA	1972	PHILIPS	6323 013
MIKI DEI ROSSI	PERC	(ABCDEFGHJ	(C) FELONA & SERONA	1973	PHILIPS	6323 023
GERMANO SERAFIN	G	(GHJ	(C) FELONA & SERONA	1973	CHARISMA	CAS 1072
TOLO MORTON	G V	(G	(D) IN CONCERT	1974	PHILIPS	6323 028
			(E) CONTRAPPUNTI	1974	PHILIPS	6323 035
			(F) BEYOND LENG	1975	COSMOS	PILP 9008
			(G) SMOGMAGICA	1975	PHILIPS	6323 041
			(H) VERITA NASCOSTE	1976	PHILIPS	6323 045
			(J) STORIA O LEGGANDA	1977	PHILIPS	6323 052
			(K) FLORIAN	1979	PHILIPS	6323 086
			(L) PICCOLA RAPSODIE DELL APE	1980	PHILIPS	6323 102

L55 **LE PAMPLEMOUSSE** L55

W MICHAEL LEWIS K (AB — (A) LE SPANK — 1978 PYE NSPL28244
LAURIN RINDER D V (AB — (B) SWEET MAGIC — 1978 AV AVLP 501
MORTONETTE JENKINS V(B — (C) PLANET OF LOVE — 1980 AV 6080
DAVE WILLIAMS B (AB
GIL KARSON B (A SHIRLEY JONES V (A BRENDA JONES V (A VALORIE JONES V (A
DOUG RICHARDSON SAX (AB HARRY KIM TPT (AB JEFF SIGMAN B (B DAVID STOUT TROM (A
ALEX BROWN V (B PATTI HALL V (B

L56 **LE ROUX** L56

JEFF POLLARD G V (ABC — (A) LOUISIANA'S LE ROUX — 1978 CAPITOL 11734
LEON MEDICA B (ABC — (B) KEEP THE FIRE BURNIN' — 1979 CAPITOL 11926
DAVID PETERS D (ABC — (C) UP — 1980 CAPITOL 12092
BOBBY CAMPO D V (ABC
TONY HABELDON G (ABC RON RODDY K (ABC

L56A **MIKE LESLEY**

MIKE LESLEY — (A) MIKE LESLEY — 1976 BIG TREE 89516 L56A

L56B **SUNNY LESLIE** L56B

SUNNY LESLIE V (A — (A) DOCTORS ORDERS — 1974 CBS 80219

L56C **LESLIE, KELLY & JOHN FORD COLEY** L56C

LESLIE BULKIN V (A — (A) LESLIE, KELLY & JOHN FORD COLEY — 1981 A&M UK AMLH 64841
KELLY BULKIN V (A
JOHN FORD COLEY V K (A VAN DUNSON (A HARVEY MASON D (A PAULINHO DACOSTA PERC(A
DASH CROFTS V (A DAVID FOSTER K (A STEVE LUKATHER G (A JEREMY LUBBOCK STR HRN(A

L57 **LES VARIATIONS** L57

ROBERT FITOUSSI G V (A — (A) CAFE DE PARIS — 1975 BUDDAH BDS5625
JACQUES GRANDE B (A — ( ) TAKE IT OR LEAVE IT — 1974 PATHE FR 064 12628
JACKY BITTON D PERC V (A — (B) MOROCCAN ROLL — 1974 BUDDAH BDS5601
MARC TOBALY G V (A
MAURICE MAIMOUN VLN (A JIM MORRIS K V (A PATRICK ADAMS STRINGS (A JIM MAELEN PERC (A
MICHAEL MONTGOMERY K (A PHIL BATES (A GARY DORN (A MICHAEL WENDROFF V (A

L57A **LEVI & THE RIPCORDS** L57A

LEVI DEXTER V (A — (A) CAT FIGHT (EP) — 1980 GUN
DANNY B HARVEY G (A
JIMMY REED G (A DAVE CURRY B (A PAT BROWN D (A

L57B **LEVEL 42** L57B

PHIL GOULD D (A — (A) LEVEL 42 — 1981 POLYDOR UK POLS 1036
MIKE LINDUP K V (A — (B) STRATEGY — 1981 ELITE UK LEVLP1
BOON GOULD G SAX(A
MARK KING B V (A

L57C **LEVIATHAN** L57C

SHOF BEAVERS (A — (A) LEVIATHAN — 197 MACH AMA US 12501
WAIN BRADLEY (A
PETER RICHARDSON (A JOHN SADLER (A DON SWEARINGEN (A GRADY TRIMBLE (A

L58 **LEVITT McCLURE** L58

DAN LEVITT (A — (A) LIVING IN THE COUNTRY — 19 CASABLANCA WS 1807
DOUG McCLURE (A

L58A **BARRINGTON LEVY** L58A

BARRINGTON LEVY (All — (A) ENGLISHMAN — 1979 GREENSLEVES GREL 9
ERROL'FLABBA'HOLT B (C — (B) BOUNTY HUNTER — 1979 JAH LIFE
CARLTON 'SANTA' DAVIS D(C — (C) ROBIN HOOD — 1980 GREENSLEEVES GREL 14
GLADSTONE ANDERSON K (C — (D) SHINE I GAL — 1980 ECHO 1039
ANSEL COLLINS K (C
ERIC LAMONT G (C EARL SMITH G (C CHRISTOPHER BLAKE PERC(C HEADLEY BENNETT TROM(C
BOBBY ELLIS TPT (C

L58B **O'DONEL LEVY** L58B

O'DONEL LEVY G (ALL — (A) SIMBA — 1973 GROOVEMERCHANT US 526
JON FADDIS TPT (AB — (B) DAWN OF A NEW DAY — 1974 GROOVEMERCHANT US 518
ERNIE ROYAL TPT (A — (C) EVERYTHING I DO GONNA BE FUNKY — 1974 GROOVEMERCHANT US 535
LEW SOLOFF TPT (AD — (D) WINDOWS — 1976 GROOVEMERCHANT US 3313
DAVID E SMITH WIND (D
JIMMY WILSON TPT (D ALETA GREENE V (D STAFFORD LEVY D (D GARY GRAINGER B (D
CHARLES COVINGTON K SYN(BD LEW DELGATTO WIND (D GEORGE YOUNG WIND (D RANDY BRECKER TPT(D
BARRY ROGERS TROM (D JOE RANDAZZO TROM (D BURT COLLINS TPT (AB CECIL BRIDGEWATER HRN(AB
BILL WATROUS TROM (AB EDDIE DANIELS WIND (A WARREN BERNHARDT K (A TONY LEVIN B (A
STEVE GADD D (A JIM MADISON PERC (A CHESTER THOMPSON D (B GEORGE RUSSEL B (B
MARVIN STAMM TPT (B WAYNE ANDRE TROM (B EDDIE BURT TROM (B JUDD WATKINS V PERC(C
HUGH WALKER D (C STRINGS (D

L59 **JONA LEWIE** L59

JONA LEWIE K V D G PNO (AB — (A) ON THE OTHER HAND THERE'S A FIST — 1978 STIFF US USE8 UK SEEZ 8
MALCOLM MORTIMER D (A — (A) ON THE OTHER HAND THERE'S A FIST — 1980 STIFF UK RI (DIFF TRACKS)
DORRIS HENDERSON V (A — (B) ALIAS JONA LEWIE — 1980 SONET UK SNTF 794
CLIVE CHAPPEL G B (A
TIM BRANSTON G (A MALCOLM HINE G (A JOHN RANDALL PERC (A KEITH TRUSSELL PERC (A
ROB CAROL D (A MICK SMYTHE D (A KEN BUTCHER SAX (A HELEN ROBINSON V (A
CATHY CLELAND V (A DENNIS BOVELL V (A DICK HANSON TPT (A JOHN EARLE SAX (A
JOHN STONE PNO (A MIKE DAY V (A

L60 **DAVE LEWIS** L60

DAVE LEWIS G K (ABC — (A) FROM TIME TO TIME — 1976 POLYDOR UK 2383 420
PRESTON HEYMAN D (B — (B) A COLLECTION OF HIS SHORT DREAMS — 1978 POLYDOR UK 2383 522
FELIX KRISH B (B — (C) THE LATE SHOW — 1978 POLYDOR UK 2383 493
STEVE BRANTLEY B V PERC(B
BRUCE DEES G V (B JAMIE BRANTLEY G (B ANDY MACMAHON K V (B MAGGIE RYDER V (B

L61 FURRY LEWIS L61

Musician	Inst		Album	Year	Label	Country	Number
FURRY LEWIS	G V		PRESENTING THE COUNTRY BLUES	1969	BLUE HORIZON		763228
			IN MEMPHIS	1970	MATCHBOX		SDR 190
			FURRY LEWIS	1971	XTRA		XTRA 1116
			FABULOUS FURRY LEWIS	19	SOUTHLAND	US	3
			FURRY LEWIS BAND	19	FOLKWAYS		3823
			BEALE STREET BLUES	19	BARCLAY	FR	920 352
			FOURTH & BEALE	19	BARCLAY	FR	80602
			& FRED McDOWELL	19	BIOGRAPH		BLP12017
			IN HIS PRIME	19	YAZOO		L 1050
			BLUES MASTERS VOL 5	19	BLUE HORIZON	US	BM 4605
			HOUSE OF BLUES VOL 2	19	BLUE STAR	FR	80 602
			ON THE ROAD AGAIN	1969	ADELPHI		1007
			BACK ON MY FEET AGAIN	19	PRESTIGE	US	7810
			BACK ON MY FEET AGAIN	197	BLUESWAY	US	1036
			SHAKE 'EM ON DOWN	19	FANTASY	US	24703
			LIVE AT THE GAS LIGHT	19	AMPEX		A10140
			WHEN I LAY MY BURDEN DOWN	19	BIOGRAPH	US	12017
			DONE CHANGED MY MIND	19	BLUESVILLE	US	1037

L61A HUEY LEWIS & THE NEWS L61A

Musician	Inst		Album	Year	Label	Country	Number
HUEY LEWIS	V	(AB	(A) HUEY LEWIS & THE NEWS	1980	CHRYSALIS		CHR 1292
CHRIS HAYES	G V	(AB	(B) PICTURE THIS	1982	CHRYSALIS		CHR 1340
SEAN HOPPER	K V	(AB					
MARIO CIPOLLINA	B	(AB					

BILL GIBSON D V (AB JOHNNY COLLA G SAX V(AB TOWER OF POWER HRNS(B

L61B GARY LEWIS & THE PLAYBOYS L61B

Musician	Inst		Album	Year	Label	Country	Number
GARY LEWIS	G V	(ALL	(A) THIS DIAMOND RING	1965	LIBERTY	US	7408
BOBBY KEYS	SAX	(L	(B) A SESSION WITH	1965	LIBERTY	US	7419
BILL BOATMAN	D	(L	(C) EVERYBODY LOVES A CLOWN	1965	LIBERTY	US	7428
ARNOLD ROSENTHAL	B	(L	(D) SHES JUST MY STYLE	1966	LIBERTY	US	7435
CHARLIE CAREY	G	(L	(E) HITS AGAIN	1966	LIBERTY	US	7452
JOHN GALLIE	K	(L	(F) GOLDEN GREATS	1966	LIBERTY	US	7468
GEORGE BOHANON	TROM	(L	(G) PAINT ME A PICTURE	1967	LIBERTY	US	7487
JIM PRICE	HRNS	(L	(H) NEW DIRECTIONS	1967	LIBERTY	US	7519
JOHN L WEST	K	(P	(I) NOW	1968	LIBERTY	US	7893
AL RAMSAY	G	(P	(J) MORE GOLDEN GREATS	1968	LIBERTY	US	7867
DAVE COSTELL	G	(P	(K) RHYTHM OF THE RAIN	1969	LIBERTY	US	7623
DAVE WALKER	G	(P	(L) I'M ON THE RIGHT ROAD NOW	1969	LIBERTY	US	7633
			(M) PLAYBOYS	196	SUNSET	US	5168
			(N) RHYTHM	1969	SUNSET	US	5262
			(O) AT THEIR BEST	19	SUNSET	US	1026
			(P) 20 GOLDEN GREATS	1979	LIBERTY	UK	LBR1005

L61C GRAHAM LEWIS & BRUCE GILBERT L61C

Musician	Inst		Album	Year	Label	Country	Number
GRAHAM LEWIS		(A	(A) DOME	1980	ROUGH TRADE	UK	DOME1
BRUCE GILBERT		(A	(B) 3R4	1980	4AD	UK	CAD16

L61D JIMMY LEWIS & THE CHECKERS L61D

Musician	Inst		Album	Year	Label	Country	Number
JIMMY LEWIS	G V	(A	(A) YEAH RIGHT	1980	BOMP	US	BLP 4014
JERRY NAIJEH	D V	(A					
ODY NEWTON	G	(A					
MIKE CAMPBELL	G	(A					

DOUGLAS NELSON B V (A MARTY DAVICH K (A BENIMONT TENCH K (A
GORDON SHRYOCK PROD (A NOAH SHARK PROD (A

L62 LEW LEWIS & REFORMER L62

Musician	Inst		Album	Year	Label	Country	Number
LEW LEWIS	V HCA	(A	(A) SAVE THE WAIL	1979	STIFF	UK	SEEZ 16
PETE ZEAR	G	(1	(1) 1977 LIVE (2) 1979 REFORMER				
LEE GREEN	G	(1					
JOHNNY OCEAN	B	(1					
BUZZ BARWELL	D	(2A					

BOB CLOUTER D (1 JOHNNY SQUIRREL B (2A RICK TAYLOR G (2A
GAVIN POVEY PNO (A

L63 LINDA LEWIS L63

Musician	Inst		Album	Year	Label	Country	Number
LINDA LEWIS	V G	(ALL	(A) SAY NO MORE	1971	REPRISE	UK	K44130
CHRIS SPEDDING	G	(A	(B) LARK**	1972	REPRISE US 2120	UK	K44208
RAY COOPER	PERC	(A	(C) FATHOMS DEEP	1973	REPRISE US 2172 RAFT	UK	48501
SHAWN PHILLIPS	G	(A	(D) NOT A LITTLE GIRL ANYMORE	1975	ARISTA US 4047	UK	ARTY 109
IAN McDONALD	FLT	(A	(E) WOMAN OVERBOARD	1977	ARISTA	UK	SPARTY1003
MIKE EGAN	G	(A	( ) HEART STRINGS	1974	REPRISE US 2192		
SKAILA KANGA	HARP	(A	(F) HACIENDA VIEW	1970	ARIOLA	UK	ARL 5033
FIACHRA TRENCH	K	(A	(1) 1975 OCT GIG				
LOUIS CENNAMO	B	(A					

**TWO VERSIONS WITH SLIGHTLY DIFFERENT TRACKS

Musician	Inst		Musician	Inst		Musician	Inst		Musician	Inst	
TONY CAMPO	B	(A	GEORGE FORD	B	(A	TERRY COX	D	(A	PETE GAVIN	D	(A
JIMMY HOROWITZ	K	(A	JIM CREGAN	G V	(BCDE1	EMILE LATIMER	PERC	(B	PAT DONALDSON	B	(B
GERRY CONWAY	D	(BD	JEAN ROUSSEL	K	(BDE	ERIC OXENDINE	B	(B	POLI PALMER	FLT VIBES	(BC
PAUL WILLIAMS	G	(B	MICK EVE	SAX	(BC	BOB TENCH	G	(C	MAX MIDDLETON	K	(CDE
CLIVE CHAMAN	B	(CD	CONRAD ISADORE	D	(C	ROBERT AHWAI	G	(CD	PHIL CHEN	B	(CDE1
RICHARD BAILEY	D	(CDE	ALLAN SHARPE	PERC	(C	DANNY THOMPSON	B	(C	LARRY STEELE	PERC	(C
STEVE GREGORY	WIND K	(CDE1	RON CARTHY	TPT	(C	CHRIS MERCER	SAX	(C	ANNA PEACOCK	V	(DE
DEREK SMITH	K	(DE	JEFF MIRANOV	G	(DE	JERRY FRIEDMAN	G	(DE	LANCE QUINN	G	(DE
BOB BABITT	B	(DE	PHIL KRAUS	PERC	(DE	TED SOMMERS	PERC	(DE	JACK JENNINGS	PERC	(DE
CARLOS MARTIN	PERC	(DE	DUNCAN McKAY	K	(D	CAPABILITY BROWN	V	(D	TOWER OF POWER	HRNS	(D
DOMINO	V	(D1	DARRYL LEE QUE	PERC	(DE1	LENNY PICKETT	FLT	(D	BERNIE HOLLAND	G	(D
LOWELL GEORGE	G	(D	LISA STRIKE	V	(DE	SNOWY WHITE	B	(DE	GEOFF SEOPARDI	D	(1
DEREK AUSTIN	K	(E1	CLYDE TOVAL	B	(E	ALEX BROWN	V	(E	HERMAN ERNEST	D	(E
JIM GILSTRAP	V	(E	KIM JOSEPH	PERC	(E	PAUL BATISTE	G	(E	TONY RIVERS	V	(E
WALTER HARRIS	G	(E	STU CALVER	V	(E	JAMES BOOKER	K	(E	JOHN PERRY	V	(E
ALLEN TOUSSAINT	K	(E	TIM RENWICK	G	(E	WINSTON DELANDRO	G	(E	BARRY ST JOHN	V	(E
VICKY BROWN	V	(E	ALUN DAVIES	G	(E	WILLIE WEEKS	B	(E	PETER HOPE-EVANS	HCA	(E
OLLIE BROWN	D	(E	BOB BARTON	V	(E	BOBBYE HALL	PERC	(E	RAY PARKER	G	(E
JUNE D WILLIAMS	V	(E									

JERRY LEE LEWIS	PNO V	(ALL
LEO LODNER	G	(N
ROLAND JANES	G	(N
JIMMY VAN EATON	D	(N
BILLY RILEY	G B	(N
JACK CLEMENTS	B	(
OTIS JETT	D	(
J W BROWN	D	(
SCOTTY MOORE	G	(N
HANK GARLAND	G	(
KEN LOVELACE	G	(
ROBBY BROWN	D	(
JOEL SHUMAKER	B	(
DELANEY BRAMLETT	G V	(L
ALBERT LEE	G	(L
GARY WRIGHT	K	(L
PETER FRAMPTON	G V	(L
ANDY BROWN	K	(L
TONY ASHTON	K	(L
KENNY JONES	D	(L
KLAUS VOORMANN	B	(L
RORY GALLAGHER	G	(L
MIKE KELLIE	D	(L
BRAD SUGGS	G	(N
CLIFF ACRED	B	(N
CHARLIE RICH	PNO	(N
JEFF DAVIS	D	(N
ALBERT JACKSON	B	(N
R W McGHEE	D	(N
HERMAN HAWKINS	B	(N
GEORGE WEBB	G	(N
WILLIAM RAY FELTS	ORG	(N
MORRIS TARRANT	D	(N
BUDDY HARMAN	B	(N
FLOYD CHANCE	B	(N
LITTLE JOHNNY DEMPSEY	G	(N
CARL PERKINS	G V	(
JOHNNY CASH	V	(
LINDA GAIL	V	(

JERRY LEE LEWIS	196	LONDON	UK	HAS2138	SUN	US	1230
GREATEST	196				SUN	US	1265
JERRY LEE LEWIS VOL 2	196	LONDON	UK	HAS2440			
WHOLE LOTTA SHAKIN' GOIN' ON	196	LONDON	UK	HAS8251			
BREATHLESS	196	LONDON	UK	HAS8323			
GOLDEN HITS	1964	PHILIPS	UK	SBL7622+	SMASH	US	67040
LIVE AT THE STAR CLUB HAMBURG	1964	PHILIPS	UK	SBL7646			
GREATEST LIVE SHOW ON EARTH	1964	PHILIPS	UK	SBL7650	SMASH	US	67056
RETURN OF ROCK	1963				WING	US	16340
RETURN OF ROCK	1967	PHILIPS	UK	SBL7668	SMASH	US	67063
COUNTRY SONGS FOR CITY FOLKS	1965	PHILIPS	UK	SBL7688	SMASH	US	67071
MEMPHIS BEAT	196	PHILIPS	UK	SBL7706	SMASH	US	67079
BY REQUEST	1967	PHILIPS	UK	SBL7746	SMASH	US	67086
SOUL MY WAY	196	PHILIPS	US	20117	SMASH	US	67097
ANOTHER PLACE ANOTHER TIME	1968	MERCURY	UK	21011	SMASH	US	67104
SHE STILL COMES AROUND	1969	MERCURY	UK	20147	SMASH	US	67112
COUNTRY HITS	1969	DBL			SMASH	US	67117/8
TOGETHER (LINDA GAIL)	1969	PHILIPS	UK	20172	SMASH	US	67126
SHE EVEN WOKE ME UP TO SAY G'BYE	1970				SMASH	US	67128
BEST OF	196				SMASH	US	67131
I'M ON FIRE	1969	MERCURY	UK	20156			
COUNTRY MUSIC HALL OF FAME	19	MERCURY	UK	20157			
COUNTRY MUSIC HALL OF FAME 2	19	MERCURY	UK	20158			
BEST OF	1970	MERCURY	UK	6338014			
ORIGINAL GOLDEN HITS	1970	SUN	UK	6467002	SUN	US	102
THERE MUST BE MORE TO LOVE	1971	MERCURY	UK	6338043		US	61323
ORIGINAL GOLDEN HITS VOL 2	1970	SUN	UK	6467008	SUN	US	103
ROCKIN RHYTHM & BLUES	1971	SUN	UK	6467017	SUN	US	107
GOLDEN CREAM OF COUNTRY	1971	SUN	UK	6467011	SUN	US	108
TASTE OF COUNTRY	1971	SUN	UK	6467015	SUN	US	114
MEMPHIS ROCK'N'ROLL	197				SUN	US	116
SUNDAY DOWN SOUTH(JOHNNY CASH)	1971	SUN	UK	6467024	SUN	US	119
MEMPHIS COUNTRY	1971				SUN	US	120
OLD TYME COUNTRY MUSIC	1971	SUN	UK	6464020	SUN	US	121
MONSTERS	1971	SUN	UK	6467019	SUN	US	124
SINGS WITH HANK WILLIAMS	1971	SUN	UK	6467018	SUN	US	125
IN LOVING MEMORIES	1971				MERCURY	US	61338
ORIGINAL GOLDEN HITS VOL3	1972	SUN	UK	6467023	SUN	US	128
ROCKIN' UP A STORM	1972	SUN (DBL)	UK	6641162			
THE KILLER ROCKS ON	1972	MERCURY	UK	6338088		US	1/637
WOULD YOU TAKE ANOTHER CHANCE	1972	MERCURY	UK	6338071		US	61346
WOULD YOU TAKE ANOTHER CHANCE	1975	CONTOUR	UK	6870620			
ROCKIN'	1972	MERCURY	UK	6336300			
LIVE AT THE INTERNATIONAL	1973	MERCURY	UK	6338148		US	61278
WHO'S GONNA PLAY THE OLD PIANO	1973				MERCURY	US	61366
SOLID GOLD ROCK'N'ROLL VOL 2	197				MERCURY	US	61372
SOMETIMES A MEMORY AINT ENOUGH	1973				MERCURY	US	1 677
(L) LONDON SESSION	1973	MERCURY	UK	6672008	MERCURY	US	2 803
TOUCHING HOME	1973	MERCURY				US	61343
1 40 COUNTRY	1974				MERCURY	US	1 710
COUNTRY STYLE	197	MERCURY	UK	6851001			
ROCKIN' & FREE	1974	SUN	UK	6467029			
FAN CLUB CHOICE	1974	MERCURY	UK	6338496			
SOUTHERN ROOTS	1974	MERCURY	UK	6338452		US	1/690
WHOLE LOTTA SHAKIN	1978	IMPACT	UK	6995 401			
JERRY LEE LEWIS	197	IMPACT	UK	6886402			
FOR LOVERS ONLY	19	CAMDEN				US	9030
ROLL OVER BEETHOVEN	19	HILLTOP				US	6110
SUNSTROKE(CARL PERKINS)	1974	EMBER	UK	NR 5038			
RARE VOL1	1975	CHARLY	UK	CR30006			
RARE VOL2	1975	CHARLY	UK	CR30007			
24 ORIGINAL HITS	1975	MUSIDISC	FR	ALB 170			
BOOGIE WOOGIE COUNTRY MAN	1975				MERCURY	US	1 1030
ORIGINAL SUPER ROCK	1975	MUSIDISC	FR	ALB 184			
I'M A ROCKER	1975	MERCURY	UK	6338602			
ODD MAN IN	197				MERCURY	US	1 1064
EXPLOSIVE	19	CONTOUR	UK	6870533			
GOOD ROCKIN' TONIGHT	1975	HALLMARK	UK	SHM 867			
COUNTRY CLASS	1976				MERCURY	US	1 1109
GOLDEN HITS	1976	PHILIPS	INT	6336245			
& HIS PUMPING PIANO	1975	CHARLY	UK	CR30002			
THE ORIGINAL	1976	CHARLY	UK	CR30111			
NUGGETS	1977	CHARLY	UK	CR30121			
(N)NUGGETS VOL 2	1977	CHARLY	UK	CR30129			
COUNTRY MEMORIES	1977				MERCURY	US	1 5004
BEST OF VOL 2	1978				MERCURY	US	1 5006
KEEPS ON ROCKIN'	1978				MERCURY	US	1 5010
BACK TO BACK	1978	MERCURY	UK	6641869			
SHAKIN' JERRY LEE	1978	ARCADE	UK	ADEP 34			
ESSENTIAL JERRY LEE LEWIS	1978	CHARLY	UK	CRM2001			
JERRY LEE LEWIS	1978	IMPACT		6995401			
JERRY LEE LEWIS	1978	FESTIVAL		ALB 233			
DUETS	1978	CHARLY	UK	SUN1002			
20 GREATEST HITS	1979	ARCADE	FR	FR18			
COLLECTORS EDITION	19	SUN	NL	NY6			
JERRY LEE LEWIS	1979	ELEKTRA	UK	K52132			
FROM THE VAULTS OF SUN	19	STARDAY				US	PO 247
HIGH HEELED SNEAKERS	19				PICKWICK	US	3224
ROLL OVER BEETHOVEN	19				PICKWICK	US	6110
RURAL ROUTE No1	19				PICKWICK	US	6120
COLLECTION	19	PICKWICK	UK	PDA 007			
BREATHLESS(DBL)	19				PICKWICK	US	2055
BEST OF J L L	19				TRIP DBL	US	8501

L64 JERRY LEE LEWIS (CONTINUED) L64

Title	Year	UK	US
GREAT BALLS OF FIRE	19	HALLMARK UK SHM 823	
WHOLE LOTTA SHAKIN'	19	HALLMARK UK SHM 851	
DRINKIN' WINE SPO DEE O DEE	19		PICKWICK US 3344
GOT YOU ON MY MIND	19	FONTANA UK SFJL964	
JERRY LEE LEWIS	1979	ELEKTRA UK K52132	ELEKTRA US 6E 184
JERRY LEE LEWIS	19		EVEREST US 298
GREATEST HITS VOL1	19	IMPACT 6886402	
GREATEST HITS VOL2	19	IMPACT 6886408	
LIVE AT THE STAR CLUB HAMBURG	1980	PHILIPS UK 6336 634	
JERRY LEE'S GREATEST	1980	CHARLY CRM 2008	
WHEN TWO WORLDS COLLIDE	1980	ELEKTRA UK K52113	US 254
& FRIENDS (DUETS)	1980	SUN UK 1002	US 1018
KILLER COUNTRY	1980	ELEKTRA UK K52246	US 291
COUNTRY MEMORIES	1981	MERCURY	US 5004
BEST OF COUNTRY HALL OF FAME	1981	MERCURY UK 6463 085	
GREAT BALLS OF FIRE	1982	CHARLY UK CFM 516	
PUMPIN' PIANO CAT	1982	CHARLY UK CFM 514	
TRIO PLUS	1980	CHARLY UK SUN 1004	
(EPs)			
JERRY LEE LEWIS VOL 1	195	LONDON UK RES 1140	
JERRY LEE LEWIS VOL 2	195	LONDON UK RES 1186	
JERRY LEE LEWIS VOL 3	195	LONDON UK RES 1187	
JERRY LEE LEWIS VOL 4	195	LONDON UK RES 1296	
JERRY LEE LEWIS VOL 5	195	LONDON UK RES 1336	
JERRY LEE LEWIS VOL 6	195	LONDON UK RES 1351	
4 MORE FROM JERRY LEE	19	LONDON UK RES 1378	
COUNTRY STYLE	19	PHILIPS UK 12599	
LEWIS BOOGIE	1976	CHARLY UK CEP 105	

L65 RAMSEY LEWIS L65

Musician	Instr		Title	Year	UK	US	No.
RAMSEY LEWIS	K	(ALL	AN HOUR WITH	1959		US CADET	645
ELDEE YOUNG	B	( ]TRIO	STRETCHIN OUT	1962		US CADET	665
ISAAC HOLT	D	(	MORE MUSIC FROM SOUL	1962		US CADET	680
JON LIND	V	(R	NEVER ON SUNDAY	1962		US CADET	686
MAURICE WHITE	V	(R	SOUND OF CHRISTMAS	1964		US CADET	693
PAULINHO DACOSTA	PERC	(R	SOUND OF SPRING	1964		US CADET	693
FRED WHITE	PERC	(R	POT LUCK	1964		US CADET	715
DON MYRICK	SAX	(R	BAREFOOT SUNDAY BLUES	1964		US CADET	723
LOUIS SATTERFIELD	TROM	(R	BACK TO THE BLUES	196		US CADET	732
DERF REKLAW RAHEEM	PERC V	(O	AT THE BOHEMIAN CAVERNS	1965	PYE UK NJL55	US CADET	741
BYRON GREGORY	G	(OQ	MORE SOUNDS OF CHRISTMAS	1965	CHESS UK 4504	US CADET	745
TERRY FRYER	K	(OQ	CHOICE	1965	CHESS US 4518	US CADET	755
RON HARRIS	B	(OQ	THE IN CROWD	1965	CHESS UK 4511	US CADET	757
KEITH HOWARD	D	(O	HANG ON RAMSEY	1966	CHESS UK 4517	US CADET	761
JIMMY BRYANT	K V	(O	SWINGIN'	1966		US CADET	771
RAHM LEE	HRNS	(OR	WADE IN THE WATER	1966	CHESS UK 4522	US CADET	774
MICHAEL DAVIS	V TPT	(OR	GOIN' LATIN	1967	CHESS UK 4528	US CADET	790
MIKE McGLOIRY	G	(Q	MOVIE ALBUM	1967	CHESS UK 4531	US CADET	782
ED REDDICK	B	(Q	DANCIN' IN THE STREET	1968	CHESS UK 4533	US CADET	794
JAMES GADSON	D	(QR	RAMSEY LEWIS TRIO	1968		US CADET	796
VANCE TENORT	PERC	(Q	UP POPS RAMSEY	1968	CHESS UK 4535	US CADET	799
ALEXANDRA BROWN	V	(Q	MAIDEN VOYAGE	1968	CHESS UK 4539	US CADET	811
JIM GILSTRAP	V	(Q	MOTHER NATURES SON	1969	CHESS UK 4545	US CADET	821
STEPHANIE SPRUILL	V	(Q	(K) UPENDO NI PAMOJA	197	CBS UK 64718	US CBS	31096
ANGELA WINBUSH	V	(Q	BACK TO THE ROOTS	1971	CHESS UK 6310 106	US CADET	60001
ALLEN TOUSSAINT	K	(R	ANOTHER VOYAGE	197		US CADET	827
HERMAN V ERNEST	D	(R	PIANO PLAYER	197		US CADET	836
WARREN WEINBERG	V	(R	INSIDE	197		US CADET	60018
JOHN REASONS	K G	(Q	BEST OF	1972	CHESS UK 6310 114	US CADET	839
SAM HENRY	G	(R	THEM CHANGES	197		US CADET	844
BOBBY LYLE	K	(Q	TOBACCO ROAD	1972	CHESS UK 6310 124		
MORRIS JENNINGS	D	(KLMQ	(L) FUNKY SERENITY	1973	CBS UK 65307	US	32030
KEITH CARTER	V	(Q	GREATEST HITS	1973	CBS UK 65759	US	32490
CYNTHIA HARRELL	V	(Q	GROOVER	1974	CHESS UK 6467 305	US CADET	50020
KITTY HAYWOOD	V	(Q	(M) SOLAR WIND	1974	CBS UK 80083	US	32897
VIVIAN HAYWOOD	V	(Q	DON'T IT FEEL GOOD	1975	CBS UK 81006	US	33800
KENNETH WILLIAMS	PERC	(R	SUN GODDESS	1975	CBS UK 80677	US	33194
LEO NOCENTELLI	G	(R	SOLID IVORY	1975	CHESS UK 6641 328	US CADET	50058
AVID BARARD	B	(R	LIVE IN TOKYO	1975		US CADET	SMS7501
ZURI RAHEEM	V	(O	SALONGO	1976	CBS UK 81406	US	34173
DARLENE KOLDENHOVEN	V	(Q	(O) LOVE NOTES	1977	CBS UK 82024	US	34696
PAT FERRARI	G	(Q	(P) TEQUILA MOCKING BIRD	1977	CBS UK 83270	US	35018
LARRY DUNN	K	(R	LEGACY	1978	CBS UK 82964		
AL McKAY	G	(R	(Q) RAMSEY	1979	CBS UK 83584	US	35815
BYRON MILLER	B	(R	(R) ROUTES	1980	CBS UK 84243		
LEON CHANCLER	D	(R	DOWN TO EARTH	19		US MERCURY	36150
KENNY BURKE	B	(R	3 PEICE SUITE	1981	CBS UK 84980		
ROLAND BAUTISTA	G	(R	BEST OF	1981	CBS UK 84911		
CLEVELAND EATON	B	(KLM					
ED GREENE	PERC VLN	(L					
STEVE CROPPER	G	(M					

L66 SMILEY LEWIS L66

Musician	Instr		Title	Year	UK	US
SMILEY LEWIS	V	(ALL	SHAME SHAME SHAME	1970	LIBERTY UK LBS 83308	
			I HEAR YOU KNOCKING	1978	UA UK UAS 30167	US IMPERIAL 9141
			THE BELLS ARE RINGING	1978	UA UK UAS 30186	

L66A WEBSTER LEWIS L66A

Musician	Instr		Title	Year	UK
WEBSTER LEWIS	K V	(A	(A) 8 FOR THE 80's	1980	EPIC UK EPC 84283
JAMES GADSON	D	(A			

Musician	Instr		Musician	Instr		Musician	Instr		Musician	Instr	
NATHANIEL WATTS	B	(A	PAUL JACKSON	G	(A	WAH WAH WATSON	G	(A	TOWER OF POWER	HRNS	(A
OSCAR BRASHEAR	HRNS	(A	D J ROGERS	V	(A	SYLVIA COX	V	(A	CHERYL PITTS	B	(A
JOHNNY BAKER	V	(A	BOBBY BRYANT	HRNS	(A	GARNETT BROWN	HRNS	(A	BENNY POWELL	HRNS	(A
BILL GREEN	HRNS	(A	HERBIE HANCOCK	K	(A	CARMEN TWILLIE	V	(A	YOLANDA HOWARD	V	(A
VENETTE GLOUD	V	(A	JUDITH JONES	V	(A	BILL CHAMPLIN	V	(A			

L66B LEYDEN ZAR L66B

PASCAL MAILLOUX K V (A — (A) LEYDEN ZAR — 1981 A&M
SERGE GRATTON D PERC(A
BRIAN WILSON G V (A — JACQUES NOEL G (A — PAUL GRONDIN B V (A

L66C LIAISONS DANGEREUSES L66C

BEATE BARTEL (A — (A) LIAISONS DANGEREUSES — 1981 TIS GER 22433
CHRIS HAAS (A
KRISTINE GEINEAU V (A — JOANNA V (A

L67 LIAR L67

CLIVE BROOKS D (AB — (A) STRAIGHT FROM THE HIP — 1977 DECCA UK SKL 5275
DAVE BURTON G (AB — (B) SET THE WORLD ON FIRE — 1979 BEARSVILLE US 6982 UK K 55524
PAUL TRAVIS G (AB
STEVE MANN G K (AB — DAVID TAYLOR B (AB

L67A LIBRA L67A

LIBRA — 1976 MOTOWN US M 847
WINTER DAYS NIGHTMARE — 1976 MOTOWN US M 864

L67B DAVID LIEBMAN L67B

DAVID LIEBMAN SAX (ALL — (A) DRUM ODE — 1975 EMC US 1046
JOHN ABERCROMBIE D (A — (B) LOOKHOUSE FARM — 1975 EMC US 1039
JEFF BERLIN B (F — (C) FATHER TIME — 1976 ENJA GER 2056
AL FOSTER D (F — (D) SWEET HANDS — 1977 HORIZON US SP 702
RICHARD BEIRACH PNO (AEF — (E) FORGOTTEN FANTASIES — 1977 HORIZON US SP 709
LINK CHAMBERLAND G (F — (F) LIGHT'N UP PLEASE — 1977 HORIZON US SP 721
PEE WEE ELLIS PNO (F — (G) IF ONLY THEY KNEW — 1980 TIMELESS 151
SONNY BROWN PERC (F
CHRIS HAYES G (F — TONY SAUNDERS B (F — JIMMY STRASSBURG D (F — JUMMA SANTOS CONGAS(F
LEON THOMAS V (F — HAROLD WILLIAMS K (F — JOHN SCOFIELD G (G — RON McLURE B (G
ADAM NUSSBAUM D (G — RICHIE BEIRACH K (A — GENE PERLA B (A — JEFF WILLIAMS D (A
BOB MOSES D (A — PATATO VALDEZ PERC (A — STEVE SATTAN PERC (A — BARRY ALTSCHUL PERC(A
BADAL ROY TABLA(A — COLIN WALCOTT TABLA(A — RAY ARMANDO PERC (A — ELEANA STEINBERG V(A
TERUMASA HINO HRN (G

L68 LIEUTENANT PIGEON L68

ROBWOODWARD (— (A) MOULDY OLD MUSIC — 1973 DECCA UK SKL 5154
NIGEL FLETCHER (— (B) PIGEON PIE — 1974 DECCA UK SKL 5174
Mrs FLETCHER (— (C) PIGEON PARTY — 1974 DECCA UK SKL 5196
STEVE JOHNSON B (

L68A LIFE L68A

ROGER COTTON K V (A — (A) LIFE AFTER DEATH — 1974 POLYDOR 2383 295
IAN GIBBONS K FLT(A
RICHARD THORPE B V (A — PAUL THORPE D V(A

L68B LIFE(US) L68B

GEORGE TERRY G V (A — (A) LIFE — 1981 ELEKTRA US 6E 339
KITTY WOODSON V (A
JAMIE OLDAKER D (A — GEORGE BITZER K (A — JOEY MURCIA G (A — HAROLD COWART B (A
RON ZIEGLER D (A

L69 LIFESTYLE L69

JERRY JAY FERGUSON K V (A — (A) LIFESTYLE — 1977 MCA UK MCF 2809 US 2246
JOHNNY MATHIS V (A
WADE 'HOLMES' DAVIS V (A — SHEDRICK SWEET V (A — RICHIE ROME K (A — DENNIS HARRIS G (A
GEORGE BERG SAX (A — JON FADDIS TPT (A — CHARLES LEE V (A — MICHAEL FOREMAN B (A
LARRY WASHINGTON CONGA(A — ARTHUR CLARKE SAX (A — VICTOR PAZ TPT (A — MEL DAVIS TPT(A
PAUL GRIFFIN K (A — CHARLES COLLINS D (A — RICHARD DAVIS B (A — BILLY JACKSON PERC(A
ROMEO PENQUE SAX (A — BUDDY TERRY SAX (A — JANICE ROBINSON TROM (A — STRING SECTION (A

L70 (TONY WILLIAMS) LIFETIME L70

TONY WILLIAMS D (ALL — (A) LIFETIME — 1965 BLUENOTE 84180
( ) SPRING — 1966 BLUENOTE UK 84216
JACK BRUCE B (CF — (B) EMERGENCY — 1969 POLYDOR 583 574 US 25/3001
JOHN McLAUGHLIN G (BCF — (B) EMERGENCY — 197 POLYDOR 2673 002
ALLAN HOLDSWORTH G (HG — (C) TURN IT OVER — 1970 POLYDOR UK 2425019 US 244021
ALAN PASQUA K (HG — (D) EGO — 197o POLYDOR 2425 070 ++ 2440 065
TONY NEWTON B V (HG — (E) THE OLD BUMS RUSH — 1972 POLYDOR 2391 052 US 5040
RON CARTER B CELLO (D — (F) LIFETIME — 1975 POLYDOR 2482 179
KHALID(LARRY YOUNG)YASIN ORG(BDF — (G) BELIEVE IT — 1976 CBS UK 69201 US 33836
TOM DUNBAR G (D — (H) MILLION DOLLAR LEGS — 1976 CBS UK 81510 US 34263
DON ALIAS PERC (D — (J) LIFETIME — 1978 BLUENOTE 40018
WARREN SMITH PERC (D — (K) JOY OF FLYING — 1979 CBS UK 83338

L70A LIFT L70A

WERTEHR LOHSE D V (A — (A) FIRST — 1977 AMIGA GER 855550
MICHAEL HEUBACH K SYN(AB — (B) MEERESFAHRT — 1979 AMIGA GER 855638
TILL PATZER WIND V(AB
WOLFGANG SCHEFFLER K SYN(AB — HENRY PACHOLSKI V (AB — GERHARD ZACHER B V (AB — FRANK ENDRICK MOLL D (B

L71 JOE & JIMMY LIGGINS L71

JOE LIGGINS (AB — (A) JOE LIGGINS — 1975 BULLDOG BDL 1005
JIMMY LIGGINS (AB — (B) JOE & JIMMY LIGGINS — 1976 SONET UK SNTF5020

L71A LIGHT L71A

JIM ARMSTRONG G (A — (A) LIGHT — 1977 MINT MINT11
ALBERT MILLS B V (A
BRIAN SCOTT K FLT V (A — GEORGE O'HARA G V (A — BERTIE MACDONALD D (A

L71B LIGHT OF THE WORLD L71B

NEVILLE McKRIETH G V (A — (A) ROUND TRIP — 1980 ENSIGN UK ENVY14 US MERCURY 3819
PATRYCEBANKS V (A — ( ) LIGHT OF THE WORLD — 1979 ENSIGN UK ENVY 7
PAUL WILLIAMS B V (A — ( ) THE BEST REMIXED — 1981 MERCURY 6350 062
PETER HINDS K (A
AUGIE JOHNSON V (A — EVERTON McCALLA D (A — GANIYU BELLO PERC V(A — NATHANIEL AUGUSTIN TROM(A
CANUTE WELLINGTON HRNS V(A — DAVID BAPTISTE WIND V(A — WAYNE HENDERSON TROM (A — BOBBY LYLE PNO(A
VICTOR FELDMAN VIBES(A — MIKI HOWARD TPT (A — STEVE MADAIO TPT (A — JOHN ERVIN TROM (A
CHUCK BROOKE SAX (A — BOB GREAVES SAX (A — VANCE TENORT PERC (A — STEVE BECKMEIER G (A
GREG PRECLES HRNS (A — MEL GAYNOR D (A — STRING SECTION (A

L72 GORDON LIGHTFOOT L72

GORDON LIGHTFOOT G PNO V(ALL | (A) LIGHTFOOT | 1966 UA US 6487
TERRY CLEMENTS G (JLMNORSV | (B) WAY I FEEL | 1967 UA US 6587SUNSET UK 50231
RICK HAYNES B (HJLMNORSVK | (C) LIGHTFOOT | 1968
PEE WEE CHARLES STEEL(NORSV | (D) DID SHE MENTION MY NAME | 1968 US US 6649 UK SULP 1199
BARRY KEANE D (LORSV | (E) BACK HERE ON EARTH | 1969 UA US 6672 UK SULP 1239
GENE MARTYNEC SYN (MR | (F) EARLY LIGHTFOOT | 1969 UA UK UAS 29012
JIM GORDON D (MNOR | (G) SUNDAY CONCERT | 1969 UA US 6714 UK UAS 29040
RED SHEA G (HJLMNOSBK | (H) SIT DOWN YOUNG STRANGER | 1970 REPRISE US 6392 UK K 44091
DAVID BROWN PERC (LK | (J) DON QUIXOTE | 1972 REPRISE US 2056 UK K 44166
JOHN STOCKFISH B (BMNO | (K) SUMMERSIDE OF LIFE | 1971 REPRISE US 2037 UK K 44132
CATHERINE SMITH V (M | (L) OLD DANS RECORDS | 1972 REPRISE US 2116 UK K 44219
BRUCE GOOD AUTOHARP (LOV | (M) SUNDOWN | 1974 REPRISE US 2177 UK K 44258
NICK DE CARO ACC (LMNOV | (N) COLD ON THE SHOULDER | 1975 REPRISE US 2206 UK K 54033
MILT HOLLAND PERC (MNO | (O) GORD'S GOLD | 1975 REPRISE US 2237 UK K 64033
JACK ZAZA WIND (NS | (P) VERY BEST OF | 1975 UA US LA445EMI 5C 05096474
SUSIE McCUNE V (N | (Q) EARLY MORNING RAIN | 1976 SUNSET UK SLS 50398
TOM SZCZESNIAK B (S | (R) SUMMERTIME DREAM | 1976 REPRISE US 2246 UK K 54067
LARRY GOOD BAN (LO | (S) ENDLESS WIRE | 1978 WB US 3149 UK K 56444
MITCH CLARKE BASSOON (S | (T) CLASSIC LIGHTFOOT | 19 UA UK UAS 5510
OLLIE STRONG STEEL(LO | (U) GORDON LIGHTFOOT HUDBA A SLOVA | 19 SUPRAPHON
DOUG RILEY PNO (S | (V) DREAM STREET ROSE | 1980 WB US 3426 UK K 56802
DAVID BROMBERG G (L | (JK) 2 ORIGINALS OF GORDON LIGHTFOOT | 19 REPRISE UK K 64022
JUNIOR HUSKY B (OK | (W) BEST | 19 UA US 6754
PIG ROBBINS PNO (OK | (X) SUNDOWN | 1980 MOBILE US 018
LENNY CASTRO PERC (V | (Y) THE BEST OF | 1981 REPRISE UK K 56915
BOB GLAUB B (V
KEN BUTTREY D (BKO | GAYLE LEVANT HARP (V | CHARLIE McCOY HARM (BKO | MICHAEL OMARTIAN K (V
HERB PEDERSEN BAN (V | JACKIE WARD V (N | CHIP YOUNG G (K | HENRY STRZELECKI B (K
BUDDY HARMON D (K | JIMMY ISBELL D (N | VASSAR CLEMENTS FDL (K | JERRY SHOOK G (K
RY COODER G (H | VAN DYKE PARKS HCA (H | JOHN SEBASTIAN G HCA(H | FARRELL MORRIS PERC(K
JAMES ROLLESTON B (K | GORDON STOKER V (K | NEAL MATTHEWS V (K | HOYT HAWKINS V (K
RAY WALKER V (K | LAVERNA MOORE V (K | MILDRED KIRKHAM V (K

L73 PAPA GEORGE LIGHTFOOT L73

PAPA GEORGE LIGHTFOOT V HCA(ALL | (A) RURAL BLUES VOL 2 | 19 LIBERTY UK LBL 83214
CARSON WHITSETT PNO (B | (B) NATCHEZ TRACE | 1969 LIBERTY UK LBS 83353
RON JOHNSON B (B | (B) NATCHEZ TRACE | 1969 VAULT US 130
JERRY PUCKETT G (B
TOMMY TATE D (B

L74 LIGHTHOUSE L74

SKIP PROKOP G D V(ABCDEFGHJK | (A) LIGHTHOUSE | 1969 RCA US LSP4173
PAUL HOFFERT K (ABCDEG | (B) PEACING IT ALL TOGETHER | 1970 RCA US LSP4225 UK SF 8121
RALPH COLE G V (ABCDEFGHJK | (C) SUITE FEELING | 1970 RCA US LSP4241 UK SF 8103
DON DINOVO VLA (ABCDEFGHJK | (D) ONE FINE MORNING | 1971 EVOLUTION US 3007
DICK ARMIN CELLO(BCDEGJK | (D) ONE FINE MORNING | 1971 VERTIGO UK 6342010
LOUIS YACKNIN B (DEG | (E) THOUGHTS OF MOVING ON | 197 EVOLUTION US 3010
KEITH JOLIMORE WIND V(DE | (E) THOUGHTS OF MOVING ON | 197 VERTIGO UK 6342011
LARRY SMITH TROM V (DEGJ | (F) LIVE | 197 EVOLUTION US 3014
HOWARD SHORE SAX (BCDGAE | (G) SUNNY DAYS | 1972 EVOLUTION US 3016
DALE HILLARY SAX V(JK | (G) SUNNY DAYS | 1972 MOONCREST UK CREST 2
RICK STEPTON TROM (JK | (H) ONE FINE LIGHT | 1972 RCA US 6047
PAUL ARMIN VLN (BC | (J) CAN FEEL IT | 1974 POLYDOR US PD 5056 UK 2391088
PAUL ADAMSON TPT (C | (K) GOOD DAY | 19 POLYDOR US 6028 UK 2391133
ARNIE CHYCOSKI TPT (BA | (L) BEST OF | 19 JANUS US JXS7025
JOHN CAPON TROM (B
PETE PANTALUK TPT (D | JOHN NASLEN TPT (GJ | PINKY DAUVIN V (ABC | MYRON MOSKALYK VLN(C
BRUCE CASSIDY TPT (BC | BOB McBRIDE PERC V (DGE | ALAN WILMOT B (GJ | GRANT FULLERTON B V(ABC
LES SNIDER CELLO(ADC | RUSS LITTLE TROM (ABC | MIKE MALONE TPT (E | FREDDY STONE TPT (A
IAN GUENTHER VLN (A | DON WHITTON CELLO(A | TERRY WILKINS B V (K | BILLY KING D (K
SAM SEE K (K

L75 LIGHTNIN' SLIM L75

LIGHTNIN' SLIM(OTIS HICK G V (ALL | (A) ROOSTER BLUES | 196 EXCELLO US 8000
PETE WINGFIELD K (E | (A) ROOSTER BLUES | 196 BLUE HORIZON UK 7 63863
LAURIE GARMAN HCA (E | (B) BELL RINGER | 196 EXCELLO US 8004
RICK HAYWARD G (E | (C) HIGH & LOW DOWN | 196 EXCELLO US 8018
PAUL BUTLER G (E | (C) HIGH & LOW DOWN | 197 CONTEMPO CRM118
KENNY LAMB D (E | (C) HIGH & LOW DOWN | 1978 SONET UK SNTF 770
JOHN BEST B (E | (D) A LONG DRINK OF BLUES(1 SIDE) | 1964 EMI UK SL10135
DICK PARRY SAX (E | (E) LONDON GUMBO | 1972BLUE HORIZON UK 2931 005
WILL THAKE HCA (E | (E) LONDON GUMBO | 1975 CONTEMPO UK CLP514 US EXCELLO 8023
CECIL MOSS TPT (E | (E) LONDON GUMBO | 1978 SONET UK SNTF 757
MIKE VERNON G D (E | (F) THE EARLY YEARS | 1977 FLYRIGHT CLP 524
ROGER BROOKS TROM (E | (G) TRIP TO CHICAGO | 1978 FLYRIGHT CLP 533
LAZY LESTER HCA (A
WARREN STORM D (AB | AL FOREMAN G (B | BOBBY McBRIDE G (B | KATIE WEBSTER PNO (B
AUSTIN BROUSSARD D (B | RUFUS THIBODEAUX B (B | JESSE CARR G (C | CLAYTON IVEY K (C
STACY GOSS HRNS (C | MIKE STOUGH HRNS (C | SONNY ROYAL HRNS (C | CHARLES ROSE HRNS(C
FRED PROUDLY D (C | BOB WARY B (C | TIPPY ARMSTRONG HCA (C

L75A LILAC ANGELS L75A

JOE STICK G K V(A | (A) I'M NOT AFRAID TO SAY YES | 1973 DINGERLAND 0949 0211
NAPPES RAPIERSKY D (A
DET SILVERSTEIN B V (A | HORREX G V (A

L76 LILIENTAL L76

(A) LILIENTAL | 19 BRAIN 0060 117

L76A LIMELIGHT L76A

MIKE SCRIMSHAW V B G K(A | (A) LIMELIGHT | 1980 FUTURE EARTH FER 008
GLENN SCRIMSHAW G K V (A
PAT COLEMAN D V (A

L76B **LIMEY** L76B

BRIAN ENGEL G V (AB (A) LIMEY 1976 RCA UK SF 8463
JOHN KNIGHTSBRIDGE G (B (B) SILVER EAGLE 1977 RCA PL 25032
PAUL KEOGH G (B
GARTH WATT-ROY G (B TOM WILLIS G (B ALAN SPENNER B (B BOB HENRIT D (B
JIM RODFORD B (B TOMMY EYRE K FLT(B DAVE BOWKER B (AB IAN KEWLEY K (AB
ROBIN LE MESURIER G (AB MAC McINERNEY D PERC(A B J COLE STEEL (A PETER GATTEN PROD(A
STEPHANIE DE SYKES V (A CLAIRE TORREY V (A SUE VANNER V (A

L76C **PHILAMORE LINCOLN** L76C

PHILAMORE LINCOLN V (A (A) NORTH WIND BLEW SOUTH 19 EPIC US 26497
THE YARDBIRDS (A

L77 **DENNIS LINDE** L77

DENNIS LINDE B G V D K(ALL (A) LINDE MANOR 1970 INTREPID US IT 74004
WAYNE MOSS G B (AB (B) DENNIS LINDE 1973 ELEKTRA US 75062 UK K42149
DOODLES LANCASTER D (A (C) TRAPPED IN THE SUBURBS 1974 ASYLUM US 1011 ELEKTRA UK K52013
BERGEN WHITE HRNS (A (D) SURFACE NOISE (NOT RELEASED) 197 MONUMENT
BUDDY SPICHER STRINGS (ABE (E) UNDER THE EYE 1977 MONUMENT US MG 7608
FARRELL MORRIS PERC (AC
JERRY SMITH K (A BENNY WHITEHEAD HRN V(B RANDY CULLERS D B G V(BCE TERRY DEARMORE G V (B
BOBBY OGDIN FDL K FLT (BCE ALAN RUSH V G BANJO (BCE ROBERT GALBRAITH K V(BC LLOYD GREEN STEEL(BC
CHIP YOUNG V (BC BILLY SWAN V (B JOHN HARRIS K (B KENNY MALONE D (B
WELDON MYRICK STEEL(B BOBBY THOMPSON BANJ (E RUSS HICKS STEEL(B RON EADES SAX (C
HARRISON CALLOWAY HRNS(C JOHNNY CHRISTOPHER G (C JIMMY COLVARD G (C BOBBY EMMONS K (CE
HURSHAL WIGGINTON V (C SHANE KEISTER SYN K(E JERRY CARRIGAN D (E THOMAS CAIN PNO (E
MAC GAYDEN G (E MARY HOLLADAY V (E GINGER HOLLADAY V (E

L78 **UDO LINDENBERG** L78

UDO LINDENBERG V D PERC(ALL (A) LINDENBERG 1971 TELEFUNKEN GERM SLE14637
THOMAS KRETSCHMER G (HBCD (B) DAUMEN IM WIND 1972 TELEFUNKEN GER 14679
KARL ALLAUT G (HCD (C) ALLES KLAR AUF DER ANDREA DORIA 1973 TELEFUNKEN GERM SLE14719
HELMUT FRANKE G (ABDH (D) BALL POMPOS 1974 TELEFUNKEN GERM SLE14790
STEFFI STEPHAN B (ABCDH (E) VOTAN WAHNWITZ 1975 TELEFUNKEN GERM 6 22223
GOTTFRIED BOTTGER K ((CDH (F) DAS SIND DIE HERRN VOM ANDERN STERN 76 TELEFUNKEN GERM 6 22460
JEAN JACQUES KRAVETZ K (HCD (G) SISTER KING KONG 1976 TELEFUNKEN GERM 6 22609
KEITH FORSEY D PERC(HD (H) NO PANIC 1976 DECCA UK TXSR116
DIETER AHRENDT D PERC (HD
LONZO WESTPHAL VLN (HD PETER HERBOLZHEIMER HRNS(BD BOLLE BURMEISTER SAX (D RAINER REGEL SAX (D
PETER HESSLEIN G (C OLAF KUBLER SAX (D CHRIS HERRMANN TPT(D GIGO SEELENMEYER BAN (D
BACKI BACKHAUSEN D (D WOLFGANG SCHMITZ HRNS (B ANDY MARK G (A ROGER HOOK G (B
MICHAEL NAURA K (B RALE OBERPICHLER V (B JO KISSTEN ACC (B JOHNNY MULLER (B
RAINER RUBINK BANJ(B

L79 **BJORN JAYSON LINDH** L79

BJORN JAYSON LINDH FLT(AB (A) JAYSON LINDH 1977 ATLANTIC UK K50337
ERNIE WATTS SAX (A (B) DAY AT THE SURFACE 1980 SONET UK SNTF 833
NAGI EL HABASHI CELLO(B ( ) RAMADAM 19 METRONOME US 3000
DON GRUSIN PNO (A ( ) COUS COUS 19 METRONOME US 3001
LEE RITENOUR G (A ( ) SISSEL 19 METRONOME US 3002
KEN WILD B (A
JOE LALA PERC (A LARS CARLSSON SAX (A JIM JOHNSON G (A TOM ROADY PERF (A
BERTIL LOVGREN TPT (A JANNE KLING WIND (A JIM GILSTRAP V (A AUGIE JOHNSON V (A
JAN KOHLIN TPT (A ULF ADAKER TPT (A ULF ANDERSSON SAX (A JOHAN STENGARD SAX(A
BARRY BECKETT K (A DAVID HOOD B (A LARS OLOF KYNDEL K (A SVEN LARSSON TROM(A
PETER SUNDELL PERC (B PETE ROBINSON K (B GEORGE WADENIUS B (B OKAY TEMIZ PERC(B
JAN BANDEL VLN (B LENNART ABERG SAX (B JON CHRISTENSEN D (B JANNE SCHAFFER G (AB
STEFAN BROLUND B (AB MALANDO GASSAMA D (AB MATS GLENNGARD VLN (A AKE ERIKSSON D (A
KEN BELL G (A ROGER HAWKINS D (A AMERICO BELLOTTO TPT (A LARS OLOFSSON TROM(A
JOE CORRERO D (A

L79A **DAVID LINDLEY** L79A

DAVID LINDLEY V G B FDL(AB (A) EL RAYO 1981 ASYLUM UK K52283 US 5E524
IAN WALLACE D (AB (B) WIN THIS RECORD 1982 ASYLUM US 60178
WILLIAM SMITTY SMITH K (AB
BOOKER T JONES K (B BILL PAYNE K (A JORGE CALDERON V (AB CURT BOUTERSE DULC(A
RUS BABOO V PERC(A BOB GLAUB B (A JACKSON BROWNE V (A REGGIE McBRIDE B (A
GARTH HUDSON K (A BERNIE LARSEN V G B(B

L80 **LINDISFARNE** L80

ALAN HULL V B K G(ALL (A) NICELY OUT OF TUNE 1970 CHARISMA UK CAS1025 US ELEKTRA 74099
ROD CLEMENTS V G K (ABCDHIJK (B) FOG ON THE TYNE 1971 CHARISMA UK CAS1050 US ELEKTRA 75021
RAY JACKSON V G MAND(ABCDEFGHIJK (C) DINGLY DELL 1972 CHARISMA UK CAS1057 US ELEKTRA 75043
SIMON COWE V G MAND(ABCDGHIJK (D) LINDISFARNE LIVE 1973 CHARISMA UK CLASS 2
RAY LAIDLAW D (ABCDGHIJK (E) ROLL ON RUBY 1973 CHARISMA UK CAS1076 US ELEKTRA 75077
PAUL NICHOLS D (EF (F) HAPPY DAZE 1974 WB UK K56070 US ASYLUM 7018
TOM DUFFY B (EF (G) FINEST HITS 1975 CHARISMA UK CAS1108
KEN CRADDOCK K G (EF (H) LADY ELEANOR 1976 PICKWICK SHM 919
CHARLIE HARCOURT G (EF (I) BACK & FOURTH 1978 MERCURY UK 9109609 US ATCO 38108
BUD BEADLE HRNS (F (J) MAGIC IN THE AIR 1978 MERCURY UK 6641877
STEVE GREGORY HRNS (F (K) THE NEWS 1979 MERCURY UK 9109626
FRANK RICOTTI PERC (K ( ) THE SINGLES ALBUM 1981 CHARISMA UK BG5
PETE WINGFIELD PERC (K
NICK ROWLEY HRNS(K STRING SECTION (K

L80A **LINER** L80A

TOM FARMER V B (A (A) LINER 1979 ATLANTIC US 38113 UK K50553
EDDIE GOLGA G V (A
ARIF MASDIN SYN (A IAN LYNN K (A MEL COLLINS SAX (A DICK MORRISSEY SAX (A
KEN BISCHEL K (A MARVIN STAMM TPT (A JON FADDIS TPT (A GEORGE YOUNG SAX (A
FRANK VICARI SAX (A CISSY HOUSTON V (A BARRY ROGERS TROM (A RONNIE CUBER SAX (A
MAERETHA STEWART V (A BEVERLEY INGRAM V (A

L80B **LINES** L80B

RICHARD CONNING V (AB (A) COOL SNAP (EP) 1980 RED
NIKOLAS CASH D (AB (B) THE LINES (EP) 198 RED RL12005
JO 40 B (AB
MICK LINEHAM G (AB

L80C BUZZY LINHART L80C

BUZZY LINHART G V D K (ALL | (A) BUZZY 1969 PHILIPS UK SBL 7885
BIG JIM SULLIVAN SITAR(A | (B) MUSIC 1971 BUDDAH UK 2318 028 US ELEUTHERA 3601
KESHAV SATHE TABLA(A | (C) THE TIME TO LIVE IS NOW 1971 KAMA SUTRA UK 2319 011
RAY 'TAFF' WILLIAMS G (A | (D) BUZZY 1972 KAMA SUTRA UK 2319 024 US 2053
RITCHIE FRANCIS B (A | (E) THE BEST OF 19 KAMA SUTRA US 2615
PHIL RYAN K (A | (F) PUSSYCATS CAN GO FAR 1974 ATLANTIC UK K50046
JOHN WEATHERS D (A
DOUGLAS RAUCH B G (B DOUG RODRIGUES G PERC(B JOHN SIOMOS D (B DAVID BROMBERG G (B
MARK KLINGMAN K (BD LUTHER RIX D (CD BILL TAKAS B V(C JEANNIE LINHART C (C
KEN ASHER K (C JEFF BAXTER G STEEL (C PETER PONZOL WIND(D DANNY TRIFAN B V K PERC (C
PETER PLANSKY TAMB (D BARRY BECKETT K (F ROGER HAWKINS PERC(F PETE CARR G (F
JIMMY JOHNSON G (F DAVID HOOD B (F JERRY MASTERS B (F HARRISON CALLOWAY TPT (F
BEN CAULEY TPT (F CHARLES ROSE TROM (F RONNIE EADES SAX(F CHARLIE CHALMERS SAX (F
KIRBY CAMPBELL CLAR (F BARRY GOLDBERG K (F FRANK TABINO (F HERBIE MANN PERC?(F
PERRY BARBER V (F BARNABY BYE V (F CAROLE BAYER SAGER V(F PETER ALLEN V (F
JORDON KAPLAN DRUNK(F FLORENCE STATE UNI CHOR V(F

L81 LINN COUNTY L81

SNAKE McANDREW D (AB | (A) PROUD FLESH SOOTHSEER 1968 MERCURY UK 20142 US 61181
DINO LONG B (AB | (B) FEVER SHOT 1969 MERCURY UK 20165 US 61218
FRED WALK SITAR G (AB | (C) TILL THE BREAK OF DAWN 1970 PHILIPS US 600326
LARRY EASTER WIND (AB
STEPHEN MILLER V ORG(AB

L81A LION L81A

STEVE WEBB G V (A | (A) RUNNING ALL NIGHT 1980 A&M US 4755 UK AMLH64755
ROBIN LE MESURIER G (A
GARY FARR V (A ERIC DILLON D (A STEVE HUMPHREYS B (A JOHN SINCLAIR K V (A

L81B LINX L81B

DAVE GRANT V PERC(AB | (A) INTUITION 1981 CHRYSALIS UK CHR 1332
SKETCH B (AB | (B) GO AHEAD 1981 CHRYSALIS UK CHR 1358
BOB CARTER K G PERC(A
ANDY DUNCAN D PERC(A LARRY TOLFREE D (SPIKE EDNEY K G HRN(CHRIS HUNTER SAX (
J J BELLE G (JUNIOR GISCOMBE V (CANUTE EDWARDS G (A

L82 LIPS L82

(A) LIPS 1979 NEMPOER US 35621

L82A LIPS INC L82A

CYNTHIA JOHNSON V (ABC | (A) MOUTH TO MOUTH 1980 CASABLANCA UK NBLP 7197
IVAN RAFOWITZ K SYN(CA | (B) PUCKER UP 1980 CASABLANCA UK NBLP 7242
STEVEN GREENBERG K SYN (AC | (C) DESIGNER MUSIC 1981 CASABLANCA NBLP 7262
SCOTT JONES K V (C
ROGER DUMAS SYN (CA BOBBY SCHNITZER G (C TERRY GRANT B (AC BOBBY VANDELL D (C
MELANIE ROSALES V (C ANDRE CYMONE V (C ROCKIE ROBBINS V (C TOM RIOPELLE G (A
DAVID RIVKIN G (A DALE MENDENHAL HRNS (A JACK GILLESPIE HRNS(A RICHARD JORGENSEN HRNS(A
DANA GREENBERG V (A JOYCE LEPINSKY V (A STRINGS (A

L82B LIQUID SMOKE L82B

SANDY PANTALEO V (A | (A) LIQUID SMOKE 1969 AVCO 33005
VINCE FERSAK G (A
MIKE ARCHELETA B (A CHAS KIMBRELL D (A BENNY NINMANN K (A

L82C LITTER L82C

JIM KANE B SYN(AB | (A) DISTORTIONS 196 WARICK US 671
DENNY WAITE V K (B | (B) $100. FINE 196 HEXAGON US 681
TOM CAPLAN G (B | (C) EMERGE 1969 PROBE 4504
MARK GALLAGHER V (C
TOM MURRAY D (BC DAN RINALDI G V (BC RAY MELINA G V (C

L83 BOOKER LITTLE L83

BOOKER LITTLE TPT (A | (A) THE LEGENDARY QUARTET ALBUM 1977 ISLAND UK ILPS 9454
TOMMY FLANAGAN PNO (A
WYNTON KELLY PNO (A SCOTT LA FARO B (A ROY HAYNES D (A

L83A KEN LITTLE L83A

KEN LITTLE V (A | (A) SOLO 1973 DHARMA US 801
OAK SHULTZ K (A
GORDY JOHNSON D (A RON RAMELLI K HCA V (A FRANK MUSTARI G (A DANNY MARTIN B (A
NORMAN WAGNER G (A SUGARCANE HARRIS VLN V(A JOHN CAMELOT K (A RICK MACOWSKI D (A
DETROIT JR PNO (A HUBERT SUMLIN G (A JOE PARENTI D (A

L84 MARIE LITTLE L84

MARIE LITTLE V (AB | (A) FACTORY GIRL 1972 ARGO FB 19
ROBIN DRANSFIELD (A | (B) MARIE LITTLE 1973 LEADER LER2084
BARRY DRANSFIELD (A
SMILEY MOSES G (A DAVE MOSES B RECORDER(A

L85 LITTLE ANTHONY & THE IMPERIALS L85

ANTHONY GOURDINE V (| (A) OUT OF SIGHT OUT OF MIND 1969 UA US 6720 RI LIBERTY 10117
CLARENCE COLLINS (| (B) FOREVER YOURS 19 ROULETTE US 42007
TRACY LORD (| (C) GREATEST HITS 19 ROULETTE US 25292
ERNEST WRIGHT (| (D) GOIN' OUT OF MY HEAD 1965 DCP US 6808 VEEP US 16511
NAT ROGERS (| (E) ON A NEW STREET 1974 AVCO US 11012
SAM STRAIN (| (F) WE ARE THE IMPERIALS 19 END US 303
(G) SHADES OF THE 40's 19 END US 311
(H) I'M ON THE OUTSIDE LOOKIN' IN 1964 DCP US 3801
(I) PAYIN' OUR DUES 1967 VEEP US 16513
(J) REFLECTIONS 1967 VEEP US 16514
(K) SING THEIR HITS 19 FORUM US 9107
(L) MOVIE GRABBERS 19 VEEP US 16516
(M) BEST OFVOL 1 196 VEEP US 16512
(N) BEST OF VOL 2 196 VEEP US 15519
( ) HITS OF 19 PICKWICK US 3029
( ) LITTLE ANTHONY & IMPERIALS 1970 SUNSET US 5287
( ) ON THE OUTSIDE 19 DCP US 3801 VEEP US 16510
( ) VERY BEST OF 19 UA US LA 255
(EP) REMEMBER 1976 UA UK REM 405

L86 LITTLE BEAVER L86

WILLIE' LITTLE BEAVER'HALE G V(ABC (A) LITTLE BEAVER 1974 PRESIDENT PTLS1060
RON BAGDON B (AB (B) PARTY DOWN 1975 PRESIDENT PTLS1063
EDMUND COLLINS B (A (C) BLACK RHAPSODY 19 CAT CAT 1602
FREDDIE SCOTT D (A
ROBERT FERGUSON D (AB BENNY LATIMORE K (AB GEORGE PERRY B (B NELSON PADRON B (B
TIMMY THOMAS K (B GLEN HOLMES PERC (B WILLIE CLARKE PERC (B BETTY WRIGHT V (B

L86A LITTLE BO BITCH L86A

DERMOT MOUGHAN K (A (A) LITTLE BO BITCH 1979 COBRA CBR1002 EMI 062 07160
BOB WAINWRIGHT B (A
STEVE CARROLL G (A TERRY REECE D (A TONY WATSON V (A

L87 LITTLE BOB STORY L87

BOB PIAZZA V (ABCDEF (A) OFF THE RAILS 1977 CHISWICK UK WIK6 GER 67052
GUY GREMY G (ABCDE (B) LITTLE BOB STORY 1978 CRYPTO FR ZAL6415
DOMINIQUE GUILLON G (AB (EP) I'M CRYING 1977 CHISWICK UK SW7
DOMINIQUE QUERTIER D (ABC (C) HIGH TIME 1977 ARCANE FR 913 076
DOMINIQUE LELAN B (ABCDEF (D) COME ON SEE ME 1978 RCA FR PL 37217
SEAN TYLA G (A (E) LIVE +EP 1979 RCA FR PL 37360
VICO REBIBO D V (DEF (F) LIGHT OF MY TOWN 1980 RCA FR PL 37412
SERGE HENDRIX G V (DE
DOMINIQUE COMONT K V (F JOHN EARL SAX (F LOUP DURET G V HCA(F

L87A LITTLE BOY BLUES L87A

MARC COPLAN V (A (A) IN THE WOODLAND OF WEIR 196 FONTANA US 67578
BILL MOONEY D (A
PETER POLLACK G (A RAY LEVIN K B FLT(A BASIL ACCOLADE CLAR (A

L88 LITTLE EVA L88

LITTLE EVA V (ALL (A) LLLLLOCOMOTION 1962 DIMENSION US 6000
(A) LLLLLOCOMOTION 1963 LONDON UKHAU8036
(A) LOCOMOTION 1972 LONDON UKSHU8437

L89 LITTLE FEAT L89

LOWELL GEORGE G V (ALL (A) LITTLE FEAT 1971 WB US WS 1890 UK K46072
RITCHIE HAYWARD D V (ALL (B) SAILIN' SHOES 1972 WB US BS 2600 UK K46156
RY COODER G (A (C) DIXIE CHICKEN 1973 WB US BS 2686 UK K46200
PAUL BARRERE G V (CDEFGH (D) FEATS DONT FAIL ME NOW 1974 WB US BS 2784 UK K56030
SAM CLAYTON V PERC (CDEFGH (E) LAST RECORD ALBUM 1976 WB US BS 2884 UK K56156
KEN GRADNEY B (CDEFGH (F) TIME LOVES A HERO 1977 WB US BS 3015 UK K56349
BILL PAYNE K V PERC (ALL (G) WAITING FOR COLUMBUS(DBL LIVE) 1978 WB US 2 3140 UK K66075
ROY ESTRADA B V (AB (H) DOWN ON THE FARM 1979 WB US HS 3345 UK K56667
JEFF BAXTER G (F (AC)TWO ORIGINALS 1975 WB UK K66038
FRED TACKETT G (ACFH (J) HOY HOY 1981 WB UK K66100
MICK TAYLOR G (C
PAT SIMMONS G V (F MIKE McDONALD V (F GREG ADAMS TPT (FG EMILIO CASTILLO SAX (AFG
MIC GILLETTE HRNS (AFG STEVE KUPKA SAX (AFG LENNIE PICKETT SAX (AFG ELLIOT INGBER (AG
DEBBIE LINDSEY V (BC EMMYLOU HARRIS V (D JOHN HALL G (E DAVID LINDLEY (H
RUSS TITELMAN PROD PNO (AB MILT HOLLAND PERC (BC FRAN TATE V (DE VALERIE CARTER V (E
JULIA TILLMAN V (H JERRY JUMONVILLE (H SNEAKY PETE STEEL(ABCH RON ELLIOTT G (B
BONNIE RAITT V (DHC FRAN PAYNE V (H EARL PALMER (H MAXINE WILLARD V (H
ROBBEN FORD (H ROSEMARY BUTLER V (H DAN SMITH (H LUTHER WATERS V (H
ORRIN WATERS V (H LEE THORNBERG (H STEPHANIE SPRUILLE V (C TED TEMPLEMAN PROD(B
BONNIE BRAMLETT V (C TRETT FURE V (C GLORIA JONES V (C MALCOLM CECIL SYN(C
DAN HUNTER V (C

L89A LITTLE FREE ROCK L89A

PETER ILLINWORTH G V (A (A) LITTLE FREE ROCK 1969 TRANSATLANTIC UK TRA 608
PAUL VARLEY D (A
FRANK NEWBOLD B V PERC(A

L90 LITTLE MILTON L90

LITTLE MILTON CAMPBELL G V(ALL (A) WERE GONNA MAKE IT 19 CHECKER US 2995
BOBBY MANUEL G (F (B) SINGS BIG BLUES 1968 CHECKER US 3002
LESTER SNELL PNO (F (C) GRITS & GROCERIES 1969 CHESS UK 4552 CHECKER US 3011
MICHAEL TOLES G (F (D) IF WALLS COULD TALK 1969 CHECKER US 3012
WILLIAM MURPHY B (F (E) FRIEND OF MINE 19 GLADES US 7508
DAVID WEATHERSPOON B (F (F) BLUES & SOUL 1974 STAX UK STX1013 US 5514
WILLIE HALL D (F (G) GOLDEN DECADE 1974 PHONOGRAM 6310 120
MEMPHIS HRNS (F (H) MONTREUX FESTIVAL 1974 STAX UK STX 1029
LAWRENCE TAYLOR SAX (J (J) RAISE A LITTLE SAND 1975 RED LIGHTNIN' UK RL 0011
EUGENE TURNER PNO (J (K) BLUES MASTERS 1976 CHESS 2A CMB204
JERRY WALKER D (J (L) SAMS BLUES 1976 CHARLY UK CR 30102
LARRY PROTO TPT (J (M) WAITIN' FOR 1973 STAX UK SAS 3012
FONTELLA BASS PNO (J (N) GREATEST HITS 1973 CHESS CH 50113
C W TATE SAX (J (O) CHRONICLE 1979 STAX UK STX 4123
CLEOPHUS ROBINSON B (J
IKE TURNER PNO (J OLIVER SAIN SAX (J LONNIE HAYES D (J VERN HARRELL SAX (J
JESSE KNIGHT B (J JAMES CARR SAX (J

L91 LITTLE RICHARD L91

LITTLE RICHARD (PENNIMAN)PNO V(ALL HERE'S LITTLE RICHARD 1958 SPECIALTY US 2100 UK LONDON 2055
WITH LITTLE RICHARD 2 1958 SPECIALTY US 2103 UK LONDON 2126
JIMI HENDRIX G V (* THE FABULOUS 1959 SPECIALTY US 2104 UK LONDON 2193
BIGGEST HITS 196 SPECIALTY US 2111
GREATEST HITS 196 SPECIALTY US 2113
WELL ALRIGHT 1959 SPECIALTY US 2136
SINGS GOSPEL 1964 STATESIDE UK SL10054
LITTLE RICHARD IS BACK 196 JOY US 100
LITTLE RICHARD IS BACK 196 FONTANA UK TL5235
LITTLE RICHARD IS BACK 196 VEEJAY US 1107
LITTLE RICHARDS GREATEST HITS 1964 JOY US 107
MR BIG 196 JOY US 195
RIP IT UP 196 JOY US 260
SLIPPIN' & SLIDIN' 196 JOY US 270
GREAT HITS 196 UK FONTANA 5314
ITS REAL 196 UK FONTANA 13010
LITTLE RICHARD STORY 196 JOY US 5003/4
COMING HOME 1964 CORAL US 757446 UK LVA9220
SINGS FREEDOM SONGS 1963 CROWN US 5362

(CONTINUED)

L91

LITTLE RICHARD (CONTINUED)

L91

Title	Year	Label	US	Other
GREATEST HITS LIVE	19	MODERN	US 100	
KING OF GOSPEL SONGS	1965	MERCURY	US 12288	
WILD & FRANTIC	1965	MODERN	US 103	
WILD & FRANTIC	19	UNITED	US 7777	
THE EXPLOSIVE	1967	OKEH	US 14117	UK COLUMBIA 6136
GREATEST HITS LIVE	19	OKEH	US 14121	
& ROY ORBISON	1970	RCA		UK CDS 1077
THE RILL THING	1971	REPRISE	US 6406	
KING OF ROCK 'N' ROLL	1971	REPRISE	US 6462	UK K 44156
SECOND COMING	1971	REPRISE	US 2107	UK K 44204
THE GREAT ONES	197			UK MFP 50096
GREATEST HITS	1972	TRIP	US 8013	
ALL TIME HITS	1972	SONET		UK SNTF 5000
ROCK HARD ROCK HEAVY	1972	SONET		UK SNTF 5001
THE ORIGINAL	1972	SONET		UK SNTF 5011
LITTLE RICHARD SINGS	19	20TH CENTURY	5010	
LITTLE RICHARD	19	KAMA SUTRA	US 2023	
LITTLE RICHARD	19	BUDDAH	US 7501	
BEST OF	19	SCEPTER	US 18020	
RECORDED LIVE	19	EMBASSY		UK 31065
THE INCREDIBLE	19	CONTOUR		UK 2870 150
YOU CANT KEEP A GOOD MAN DOWN	1972	UNION PACIFIC		UK UP 003
SINGS SPIRITUALS	19	UNITED	US 7723	
GREATEST HITS	19	UNITED	US 7775	
RIGHT NOW	19	UNITED	US 7791	
THE BEST OF	19	UPFRONT	US 123	
KEEP A KNOCKIN	19	RHAPSODY	US 9013	
EVERY HOUR WITH	1970	CAMDEN	US 2430	
KING OF GOSPEL SINGERS	19	WING	US 12288	
CLAP YOUR HANDS	19	SPINORAMA	US S 119	
BIG HITS	19	GNP		US 9033
THE ONE & ONLY	1974	POLYDOR		UK 2482 440
STAR COLLECTION	1975	REPRISE		UK K24009
THE VERY BEST OF	1975	UA	US LA4976	
DOLLARS DOLLARS & MORE DOLLARS	1975	CHARLY		UK CR 30009
CAST A LONG SHADOW	197	EPIC		UK 66285
LITTLE RICHARD	197	EPIC	US 26260	
GREATEST HITS	197	EPIC	US 24257	UK EMBASY 31504
& SISTER ROSETTA THARPE	19	MARBLE ARCH		UK MALS1319
(*) FRIENDS FROM THE BEGINNING	197	EMBER		UK EMB 3434
GOOD GOLLY MISS MOLLY	19	HALLMARK		UK SHM 858
22 ORIGINAL HITS	1977	WARWICK		UK WW5034
20 ORIGINAL HITS	1976	SPECIALTY		UK SNTF5017
NOW	1977	CREOLE		CRLP 510
GREATEST HITS	1980	SPECIALTY		UK SNTF 5028
GEORGIA PEACH	1980	CHARLY		UK CR 30190
MODERN SIDES 10"	1981	ACE		UK CH38
ROCK'N'ROLL FOREVER	19	REPRISE		UK K24031
(EP)				
HERE'S LITTLE RICHARD	195	SPECIALTY	US	SEP 400
" " " " 2	195	SPECIALTY	US	SEP 401
" " " " 3	195	SPECIALTY	US	SEP 402
LITTLE RICHARD 1	195	SPECIALTY	US	SEP 403
" " " 2	195	SPECIALTY	US	SEP 404
" " " 3	195	SPECIALTY	US	SEP 405
ROCKS	19	RCA	US	CAE 446
LITTLE RICHARD	19	RCA CAMDEN	US	CAE 4111
LONG TALL SALLY	1977	SPECIALTY	UK	SONE 1
LITTLE RICHARD	19	SPECIALTY	UK	SON 5016

L92

LITTLE RIVER BAND

L92

Member	Inst	Albums
GRAHAM GOBLE	G V	(ABCDEFGHJK
DAVID BRIGGS	G	(BCDEFGHJK
GLENN SHORROCK	HCA V	(ABCDEFGHJK
GEORGE McARDLE	B	(BCD
DEREK PELLICCI	D	(ABCDEFGHJK
BEEB BIRTLES	G	(ABCDEFGHJK
WAYNE NELSON	B V	(K
RICK FORMOSA	G	(AC
IAN MASON	PNO	(AC
COL LAUGHNAN	SAX	(A
PETER SULLIVAN	PNO	(C
TONY BUCHANAN	SAX	(C
EDDIE DENTON		(C
BILL COUMO	K	(K
ROGER McLACHLAN	B	(A
GRAHAM LYALL	FLT	(C
STEPHEN COONEY	MAND	(A
PETER JONES	PNO	(AK
GARY HYDE	PERC	(A
GEOFF SKEWES	K	(A

Album	Year	Label	Release
(A) LITTLE RIVER BAND	1975	EMI	UK EMC3144 US CAPITOL 11512
(B) AFTER HOURS	1976	EMI	UK EMC2546 US CAPITOL 16072
(C) DIAMANTINA COCKTAIL	1977	EMI	UK EMC3187 US CAPITOL 11645
(D) SLEEPER CATCHER	1978	EMI	UK EMA 786 US CAPITOL 11782
(E) IT'S A LONG WAY THERE	1978	EMIIMP	064 82516
(F) FIRST UNDER THE WIRE	1979	CAPITOL	11954
(G) BEGINNINGS	1979	CAPITOL	16141
(H) BACKSTAGE PASS	1980	CAPITOL	12061
(J) BEGINNINGS	1980	CAPITOL	16142
(K) TIME EXPOSURE	1981	CAPITOL	GER 40042 12163

L92A

LITTLE SONNY

L92A

LITTLE 'LITTLE SONNY'ARRON G G HCA(AB

Album	Year	Label	Country	No.
(A) NEW KING OF BLUES HARMONICA	197	ENTERPRISE	US	1005
(B) BLACK N BLUE	197	ENTERPRISE	US	1018

L93

LITTLE TINA & FLIGHT 56

L93

Album	Year	Label	Country	No.
(A) THIS GIRL GONNA ROCK	1978	CHARLY	UK	CR 30155

L94

LITTLE WALTER

L94

Member	Inst	Albums
LITTLE WALTER JACOBS	HCA	A(ALL
LOUIS MYERS	G	(AGHLMNJ
DAVE MYERS	G	(AGHLMNJ
WILLIE DIXON	B	(AGHLMNJ
FRED BELOW	D	(AGHLMNJ
ROBERT LOCKWOOD	G	(GHLMNJ
FRED ROBINSON	G	(AGHLMNJ
OTIS SPANN	PNO	(AGHLMNJ
MUDDY WATERS	G	(AGLMNJ
GEORGE HUNTER	D	(AGHLMNJ
LUTHER TUCKER	G	(AGHLMNJ
JIMMY LEE ROBINSON	G	(G

Album	Year	Label	Release
(A) LITTLE WALTER	1964	PYE INT	UK NPL 28043
(A) LITTLE WALTER	1968	MARBLE ARCH	UK RI MAL 815
(B) SUPER BLUES	1967	CHESS	UK CRL 4529
(C) BEST	196	CHESS	US 1428 +CHECKER 3004
(D) BOSS OF BLUES HARMONICA	196	CHESS	US 60014
(E) BLUES MASTERS	196	CHESS	UK 2A CBM 202
(F) HATE TO SEE YOU GO	19	CHESS	US 1535
(G) & HIS JUKES	19	PYTHON	US PLPKM 20
(H) QUARTER TO TWELVE	1970	RED LIGHTNIN'	UK RL 002
(J) THUNDERBIRD	1971	SYNDICATE CHAPTER	SC 004
(K) CONFESSIN' THE BLUES	1976	CHESS	US 416 EURO CH 50043
(L) BLUE & LONESOME	19	ROI DU BLUES	CAN 33 2007

(CONTINUED)

L94 (CONTINUED) LITTLE WALTER L94

LEONARD CASTON G (GJ (M) SOUTHERN FEELING 19 ROI DU BLUES CAN 33 2012
BILL STEPNEY D (G (N) BLUE MIDNIGHT 19 ROI DU BLUES CAN 33 2017
THE CORONETS V (M (O) CHESS MASTERS 1981 CHESS CXMD 4002
BO DIDDLEY G (G
JIMMY ROGERS G (L ELGIN EVANSIDE D (L HENRY GRAY PNO (L ANDREW STEPHENSON B (M
JARRETT GIBSON SAX (MH JACK MYERS B (MN J T BROWN SAX (N FRANCIS CLAY D (M
LAFAYETTE LEAKE PNO (MN AL DUNCAN D (MN PAT HARE G (M BUDDY GUY G (MN
BILLY EMERSON K (MN ERNEST 'BIG' CRAWFORD B (N

L94A LITTLE WILLIE LITTLEFIELD L94A

LITTLE WILLIE LITTLEFIELD (A) LITTLE WILLIE LITTLEFIELD VOL 1(10") 1980 ACE 10CH 24
(B) IT'S MIDNIGHT 19 ROUTE 66 SWED KIX 10
(C) LITTLE WILLIE LITTLEFIELD (10"0 1981 ACE 10CH 34

L94B LIVERPOOL EXPRESS L94B

BILLY KINSLEY B (A (A) TRACKS 1976 WB UK K56281
TONY COATES G V (A
DEREK CASHIN D (A ROGER CRAIG K (A

L95 LIVERPOOL SCENE L95

ANDY ROBERTS G V (ABCDEF1 (A) INCREDIBLE NEW LIVERPOOL SCENE 1967 CBS 63045 UK EPIC US BN 26336
ADRIAN HENRI V (ABCDEF1 (B) AMAZING ADVENTURES OF 1968 RCA US LSP4189 UK SF 7995
MIKE EVANS V SAX(BCDE1 (C) BREAD ON THE NIGHT 1969 RCA US LSP4267 UK SF 8057
MIKE HART V G (BE1 (D) ST ADRIAN & CO 1970 RCA UK SF 8100
PERCY JONES B HCA(BCDE (E) HEIRLOON 1970 RCA UK SF 8134
BRIAN DODSON D (BCDE (F) RECOLLECTIONS 1972 CHARISMA UK CS 3
PETE CLARKE (E (1) 1974 REFORM
ROGER McGOUGH V (A
TOM KEMPINSKI V (E DAVE RICHARDS B (1 MIKE KELLIE D (1 FRANK GARRETT (E
KARL JENKINS SAX (D IAN CARR TPT (D JOHN MUMFORD TROM (D IAN WHITMAN K (D

L95A LIVE WIRE L95A

GERMAN GONZALES D V (ABC (A) PICK IT UP 1979 A&M US 4793 UK AMLH 64793
MIKE EDWARDS V G (ABC (B) NO FRIGHT 1980 A&M US 4814 UK AMLH 64814
JEREMY MEEK B V (ABc (C) CHANGES MADE 1981 A&M UA 4856 UK AMLH 68502
CHRIS CUTLER G V (A
SIMON BOSWELL G K V(BC JOHN IRISH EARLE SAX (C

L95B LIVIN' BLUES L95B

NICKO CHRISTIANSEN V G SAX(ABCDE (A) HELLS SESSION 1969 PHILIPS NL 6440 315
TED OBERG G (ABCDEFG (B) WANG DANG DOODLE 1970 PHILIPS 6440 125
JOHN LA GRAND HCA (ABCDE (C) BAMBOOZLE 1971 PHILIPS 6413 024
HENK SMITSKAMP B K (AF (D) ROCKIN' AT THE TWEEDMILL 1972 PHILIPS GER 6423 052
CESAR ZUIDERWIJK D (A (E) RAM JAM JOSEY 1973 ARIOLA GER 88525
RUUD VAN BUUREN B (BCDE (F) LIVE '75 1975 ARIOLA 89243
DICK BEEKMAN D (B (G) BLUE BREEZE 1976 ARIOLA NL 28430
ARJEAN KAMMINGA D (D
PETE WINGFIELD PNO (DE MIKE VERNON V (D KENNY LAMB D (E JOHN FREDRIKSZ V (FG
COR VAN DER BEEK D (F ANDRE REIJNEN B (G JACOB VAN HEININGEN D (G MARGRIET ESHUYS V (G
MAGGIE McNEAL V (G MARTIN AGTERBERG K (G JONNY LE JEUNE D (D

L95C KERRY LIVGREN L95C

KERRY LIVGREN K G B D V(A (A) SEEDS OF CHANGE 1980 KIRCHNER US 36567 UK 84453
STEVE WALSH V (A
BARRIEMORE BARLOW D (A PHIL EHART D (A PAUL GODDARD B (A BOBBY CAMPO HRNS/PERC(A
JEFF POLLARD V (A MYLON LEFEVRE V (A RONNIE JAMES DIO V (A JOEY JELL V (A
DARRYL KUTZ HCA (A JOHN THOMPSON D (A BARY GILBERT B (A DONNA WILLIAMS V (A
DAVE PACK V (A DAVY MOIRE V (A VICTORIA LIVGREN V (A STEVE VENEZIA V (A
ROBBIE STEINHARDT VLN (A BRAD AARON V (A JOHN FRISTOE V (A

L96 DANDY LIVINGSTONE L96

DANDY LIVINGSTONE (ALL (A) RETURNS 19 TROJAN TRL 2
(B) DANDY LIVINGSTONE 19 TROJAN TRL 45
(C) MORNING SIDE OF THE MOUNTAIN 19 TROJAN TBL 118
(D) CONSCIOUS 19 MOONCREST CREST 5
(E) SOUTH AFRICAN EXPERIENCE 1978 NIGHT OWL NORLP 1001

L97 CHARLES LLOYD L97

CHARLES LLOYD WIND (ALL (A) MOONMAN 1972 MCA MUPS 421 UK+1974 UK MCF 2643
MIKE LOVE (E (B) LOVE IN 19 ATLANTIC US SD 1481
CARL WILSON (E (C) IN EUROPE 19 ATLANTIC US SD 1500
AL JARDINE (E (D) SOUNDTRACK 19 ATLANTIC US SD 1519
ROGER McGUINN (E (E) WAVES 1972 A&M US SP 3044

L98 IAN LLOYD L98

IAN LLOYD V PROD(AB (A) IAN LLOYD 1976 POLYDOR US 1 6066
JIM VALLANCE (BC (B) GOOSE BUMPS 1979 SCOTTI BROS UK K50655 US SB 7104
STEVE BUSLOWE (B (C) 3 WC 1980 SCOTTI BROS UK K50770 US 7110
STEVE LOVE G (A
JIMMY CRESPO (B MICK JONES G V (ABC LOU GRAMM (B DENNIS ELLIOTT (B
RICK OCASEK (B BENJAMIN ORR (B JIMMY MAELEN PERC (AB DAVID SINCLAIR (B
MICHAEL BRECKER HRNS (B LINDSAY MITCHELL (B LARRY FAST (B GREGG DIAMOND PROD D (AC
IAN McDONALD SAX (A JAMES GREGSON B (A KENNETH BICHEL K (A DAVE BYRON V (A
BRAN ADAMS G (C NANCY NASH V (C THE ALIENS (C BRUCE FAIRBAIRN V (C

L98A RICHARD LLOYD E98A

RICHARD LLOYD G V PNO HCA(A (A) ALCHEMY 1979 ELEKTRA UK K52196
MATTHEW MACKENZIE G PNO V(A
JIM MASTRO G (A FRED SMITH B V (A VINNY DENUNZIO D V (A MICHAEL YOUNG G SYN(A

L99 ANDREW LLOYD WEBBER L99

ANDREW LLOYD WEBBER (A (A) VARIATIONS 1977 MCA UK MCF 2824
DON AIREY K (A
ROD ARGENT K (A GARY MOORE G (A JON HISEMAN D (A BARBARA THOMPSON WIND (A
JOHN MOLE B (A JULIAN LLOYD WEBBER CELLO(A

L100 LOADING ZONE L100

LINDA TILLERY V B D HCA(A (A) LOADING ZONE 1968 RCA US LSP 3959
PAUL FAUERSO V K (A (B) ONE FOR ALL 19 UMBRELLA US 101
PETER SHAPIRO G (A
TODD ANDERSON WIND K(A PAT O'HARA TROM (A STEVE DOWLER G (A BOB KRIDLE B (A
GEORGE NEWCOM D (A

L100A

LOCAL HEROES
L100A

KEVIN ARMSTRONG V G (A   (A) DRIP DRY ZONE   1980 OVAL UK OVLP 504
KIM BARTI D (A
MATTHEW SELIGMAN B (A

L100B

KEN LOCKE
L100B

KEN LOCKE V K SYN SAX(A   (A) THE IMPOSSIBLE   1981 VIRGIN UK V2187
JIM KERR V (A
BOBBY COLLINS V (A   SUSIE O'LIST V (A   STEVIE SHEARS G (A   JOHN McGEOCH G (A
JO DWORNIAK B (A   LEE ROBERTSON B (A   JOHN DOYLE D (A   PRESTON HEYMAN D (A
PAUL SIMON D (A   NASH THE SLASH VLN (A

L101

GERRY LOCKRAN
L101

GERRY LOCKRAN V (ALL   (A) HOLD ON I'M COMING   1967 PLANET PLL 1002
KIRK LORANGE G V (D   (B) THE ESSENTIAL   1969 SPARK SRLP104
NEIL HUBBARD G (DC   (C) WUN   1972 POLYDOR 2383 122
HENRY McCULLOUGH G (DC   (D) RAGS TO GLADRAGS   1976 DECCA UK SKLR5257
ISRAEL ZACUTO G (D   (E) BLUES VENDETTA   19 WAVERLEY ZLP 2091
CHRIS STEWART B (DC   (1) BLUES BAND 1968
BRUCE ROWLAND D (D
MEL COLLINS SAX (D   CLIFF AUNGIER (1   PHIL CHEN B (D   LOUIE MARTIN PERC (D
DWIGHT DRUICK V (D   HARVEY BURNS D (1   TERRY STANNARD D (D   PETE WINGFIELD PNO (D
JOHNNY PARKER PNO (1   BRIAN HOPKINS (1   RON WOOD G (C   ANDY PYLE G (C
JUNIOR HANSON G (C   RON BERG SAX (C   CLIFF AUNGIER (C   JEAN ROUSSEL K (C
NICK PEARSON K (C   MICK RALPHS G (C   BRUCE ROWLANDS D (C   CHRIS MERCER SAX (C

L102

ROBERT LOCKWOOD
L102

ROBERT 'JUNIOR'LOCKWOOD G V(ALL   (A) STEADY ROLLIN' MAN   1976 DELMARK 630
GENE SCHWARTZ B (DF   (B) COUNTRY BLUES CLASSICS   19 BLUES CLASSICS 7
GEORGE COOK D (D   (C) LONESOME ROAD BLUES   19 YAZOO 1038
MAURICE REEDUS SAX (DF   (D) CONTRASTS   1974 TRIX 330 7
LOUIS MYERS G HCA(F   (E) BLUES LIVE   1975 ADVENT US 2807 ,TRIO JAP 6024
DAVE MYERS B (E   (F) DOES 12   1976 TRIX 331 7
FRED BELOW D (E   (G) HANGIN' ON   19 ROUNDER US 2023
MARK HAHN G (F
JIMMY JONES D (F   JOHNNY SHINES G V (G

L103

LOCOMOTIV GT
L103

TAMAS BARTA G V HCA (A   (A) LOCOMOTIV GT   1974 ABC ABCX 811 +EPIC UK80229
JOSEPH LAUX D (A   (B) ALL ABOARD   1975 ABC US 860
GABOR PRESSER K V (A
THOMAS SOMLO B V SAX VLN(A   JACK BRUCE HCA (A   JIMMY MILLER PERC (A

L104

LOCOMOTIVE
L104

MICK HINCKS B V (A   (A) WE ARE EVERYTHING YOU SEE   1969 PARLOPHONE UK PCS 7093
MIKE TAYLOR TPT (A
NORMAN HAINES K V (A   CHRIS WOOD WIND (A   BILL MADGE SAX (A   BOB LAMB D (A
HENRY LOWTHER TPT (A   DICK HECKSTAL SMITH SAX(A   LYNN DOBSON SAX (A   CHRIS MERCER SAX (A

L104A

LOCOMOTIVE (US)
L104A

(A) LOCOMOTIVE   19 MGM US SE4653

L104B

LOCOMOTIVE KREUZBERG
L104B

ANDREAS BRAUER V K SYN(AB   (A) KOLLEGE KLATT   1972 PLANE GER 99 101
VOLKER HIEMANN G V (AB   (B) JAMES BLOND   1973 PLANE GER 99 103
UWE HOLZ V D HCA(AB   (C) FETLE JAHRE   1975 PLANE GER 99 104
FRANZ POWALLA B V (A
KARL HEINZ SCHERFLING V(AB   MANFRED PRAEKER V B G (B

L105

LOCUST
L105

(A) PLAYGUE   1977 ANNUIT COEPTIS AC1004

L105A

LOCUST (2)
L105A

PHIL SPINELLI V PERC(A   (A) ALPHA WAVES(LOCUST)   1976 BUK 6 22930 UK BULP 2001
PETE BONAS G (A
CHRIS PARREN K (A   RAY ALLEN SAX V PER(A   BRENT FORBES B (A   JOHN DILLON D (A
(UK EDITION NOT RELEASED???)

L106

JOHN LODGE
L106

JOHN LODGE V G (A   (A) NATURAL AVENUE   1977 DECCA UK TXS 120 LONDON US 603
KENNEY JONES (A
BRIAN ROGERS (A   MEL COLLINS SAX (A   JOHN RICHARDSON (A   STEVE SIMPSON (A
CHRIS SPEDDING G (A   MARTIN DOBSON (A   ALAN WILLIAMS (A   MICK WEAVER (A
JIMMY JEWELL WIND (A   GARY OSBORNE (A   BILLY LAWRIE (A

L107

NILS LOFGREN & GRIN
L107

NILS LOFGREN G VK(ALL   (A) GRIN   1971 EPIC UK 64272 US SPINDIZZY 30321
JERRY PETERSON SAX (M   (A) GRIN   1980 EMBASSY UK 31770
BOB BERBERICH D V (ABCDL   (B) ONE PLUS ONE   1972 EPIC UK 64652 US SPINDIZZY 31038
BOB GORDON B V (ABCDL   (C) ALL OUT   1972 EPIC UK 65166
TOM LOFGREN G V (CDFGHJKL1   (D) GONE CRAZY   1975 A&M UK 64415 US A&M SP4415
REV PAT HENDERSON K (HJ   (E) NILS LOFGREN   1975 A&M UK 64509 US A&M SP4509
WORNELL JONES B V (EFHJ   (F) CRY TOUGH   1976 A&M UK 64573 US A&M SP4573
KATHI McDONALD V (CL   (G) BACK IT UP(AUTHORIZED BOOTLEG)   1975 A&M US A&M SP8362
AYNSLEY DUNBAR D (EF   (H) I CAME TO DANCE   1977 A&M UK 64628 US A&M SP4628
STU GARDNER V (E   (J) NIGHT AFTER NIGHT   1977 A&M UK 69439 US A&M SP3707
CHUCK RAINEY B (F   (K) NILS   1979 A&M UK 64756 US A&M SP4756
JIM GORDON D (F   (L) NILS LOFGREN & GRIN   1979 CBS US 31770
BOB EZRIN PERC V K (K   (AB) GRIN/ONE PLUS ONE   1976 CBS UK 88204
DOUG RILEY ORG (K   (1) LIVE TOUR 1975 LINE UP
EMIL RICHARDS PERC (F   (M) NIGHT FADES AWAY   1981 MCA UK MCF 3121
AL KOOPER K (FG
CHUCK FINDLEY HRN (M   RON HICKLIN SINGERS (F   P P ARNOLD V (F   CLAUDIA LENNEAR V (F
BUDDY MILES V (F   RALPH MOLINA V (F   MIKE ZACK D (1G   BOBBYE HALL PERC (D
PAUL STALLWORTH B (F   SCOTT BALL B (F1G   DAVID PLATSHON D (J   ANDY NEWMARK D (H
HOLDEN RAPHAEL PERC (F   GRAHAM NASH V (B   CLYDIE KING V (D   SHIRLEY MATTHEWS V (D
MERRY CLAYTON V (D   ALLEN SCHWARZBERG D (K   JODY LINSCOTT PERC (K   DAVID SANBORN SAX (K
STU DAYE G V (K   BOB BABITT B (K   JEFF BAXTER G PROD(M   NICKY HOPKINS K (M
RITCHIE HAYWARD (M   JEFF PORCARO D (M   ED GREENE D (M   DAVID HUNGATE B (M
NEIL STUBENHAUS B (M   ELLIOTT RANDALL G (M   BILLY TALBOT V (F   TREVOR VEITCH G (M
GREG MATHIESON K (M   NEIL JASON B (M   DEL SHANNON V (M   FABULOUS ROBBS V (M
ELLEN SNORTLAND V (M   MIGHTY CLOUD OF LOS SCUMBO(M

L108 DAVE LOGGINS L108

DAVE LOGGINS G V (ALL — (A) PERSONAL BELONGINGS 1972 VANGUARD UK VSD 6580
JERRY CARRIGAN D (B — (B) APPRENTICE 1974 EPIC US 32833 UK 80622
JOHN GUERIN D (B — (C) COUNTRY SUITE 1976 EPIC US 33946
KENNY MALONE D (BCD — (D) ONE WAY TICKET TO PARADISE 1977 EPIC US 34713
NORBERT PUTNAM B (BA — (E) DAVID LOGGINS 1977 EPIC US 35972
WILLIAM SMITH PNO (B
BILLY SANFORD G (BA BYRON BACH CELLO(B FARRELL MORRIS PERC (B JOHN RAINES D(B
LEE SKLAR B (B DAVID BRIGGS PNO (AB MIKE NOBLE G (BC AL DELEONIBUS ACC(B
LARRY LONDIN D (B SHANE KEISTER K (B STEVE GIBSON G (BD MAC GAYDEN FDL G (BC
WELDON MYRICK STEEL(BC GREG JOHNSON HCA V (C LENNY KERLEY G (C SHERRY KRAMER V (CD
BOB GELOFFE V (C BERGEN WHITE V (CD CRAIG LINK V (C YVONE HODGES V (D
BUZZ CASON V (D JOHN CHRISTOPHER G (D JOHNNY GIMBLE FDL (D GAIL WHITFIELD SAX(D
POP BOTTLE B (D REGGIE YOUNG G (D JIM ISABELL D (A CHARLIE McCOY HCAK(A
GLENN KENNER G V (A JERRY CRUTCHFIELD K V (A RANDOLF GOODRUM K SYN(CD JACK WILLIAMS B (CD
BILLY SANFORD G (C BEN PEDIGOE BAN (C LISA SILVER FDL (C DIANE TIDWELL V (CD
JIM SALESTROM V (C

L109 KENNY LOGGINS L109

KENNY LOGGINS G V (ALL — (A) CELEBRATE ME HOME 1977 CBS US 34655 UK 81882
ROBBEN FORD G (A — (B) NIGHTWATCH 1978 CBS US 35387 UK 82865
STEVE GADD D (A — (C) KEEP THE FIRE 1979 CBS US 36172 UK 83869
LAUDIR DE OLIVEIRA PERC(A — (D) ALIVE(DBL) 1980 CBS US 36378 UK 88500
ERIC GALE G (A
GEORGE HAWKINS B V(ABCD VINCE DENHAM WIND V (ABCD MIKE HAMILTON G V (BCD BRIAN MANN K V(D
TRIS IMBODEN D HCA(BCD JON CLARKE WIND PERC(ABCD STEVE WOOD V (D RICHARD STEKOL V (C
MIKE McDONALD V (C GWEN GUTHRIE V (A STEVE NICKS V (B PATTI AUSTIN V)A
HUGH McCRACKEN G (A TOMMY TEDESCO MAND(A RICHARD TEE K (A BOB JAMES K (A
STEVE FORMAN PERC (A HIRAM BULLOCK G (A DEAN PARKS G (A LANI GROVES V (A
STEVE KHAN G (A RALPH McDONALD D (A HARVEY MASON D (A LEE RITENOUR G (A
MICHAEL JACKSON V (C MICHAEL BRECKER SAX (C FRED TACKETT G (C MILT HOLLAND PERC(C
RICHARD PAGE V (C JEFF BOUCHARD V (C PAULINHO DACOSTA PERC (D MARK WITTENBERG G (D
ALBHY GALUTEN STR (D

L110 LOGGINS & MESSINA L110

KENNY LOGGINS G V (ALL — (A) SITTIN' IN 1971 CBS US 31044 UK 64902
JIM MESSINA G B V(ALL — (B) LOGGINS & MESSINA 1972 CBS US 31748 UK 65194
LARRY SIMS B (ALL — (C) FULL SAIL 1973 CBS US 32540 UK 65775
AL GARTH HRNS FDL (ALL — (D) ON STAGE 1974 CBS US 33848 UK 88014
MEREL BREGANTE D (ALL — (E) MOTHERLODE 1975 CBS US 33175 UK 80431
JON CLARKE HRNS (ALL — (F) SO FINE 1975 CBS US 33810 UK 69169
MIKE OMARTIAN K (ABCHK — (G) NATIVE SONS 1976 CBS US 33578 UK 69227
JACK LENZ FLT (J — (H) BEST OF FRIENDS 1977 CBS US 34388 UK 81692
VINCE DENHAM SAX (JFGK — (J) FINALE 1978 CBS US 34167 UK 88205
DON ROBERTS SAX (JEFGK — (K) BEST OF 1980 EMBASSY UK 31826
RICHARD GREENE VLN (JFGK
STEVE FORMAN PERC(JFGK WOODY CHRISMAN G (J GEORGE HAWKINS B V (J DOUG LIVINGSTON K (J
WILLIE ORNELAS D (J ED SANFORD V (GK MARTY PAICH STR (GK MIKE RUBIN PNO (FGK
DAVID PAICH K (EK RUSTY YOUNG G (B VICTOR FELDMAN PERC(EGK STEVE STILLS V (B
DAVID WALLACE SYN (EK CHRIS BROOKS KOTO (EK MURRAY MacLEOD V (GK JOHN TOWNSEND V (GK
MILT HOLLAND PERC(ABCDEFGHK VINCE CHARLES D (C

L110A LOGIC SYSTEM L110A

(A) LOGIC 1981 EMI UK EMC 3375

L110B LOLLIPOP SHOPPE L110B

FRED COLE V (A — (A) JUST COLOUR 1967 UNI UK 73019
RON BUZZEL G V (A
ED BOWEN G V (A BOB ATKINS B (A TIM ROCKSON D (A JOHN THE GREEK K (A
CARL FORTINA ACC(A

L111 JACKIE LOMAX L111

JACKIE LOMAX G V — (A) IS THIS WHAT YOU WANT 1969 APPLE US 3354 UK SAPCOR 6
(AKA RICK RED STREAK) — (B) HOME IS IN MY HEAD 1971 WB US 1914 UK K 46091
JOHN BARHAM (A — (C) THREE 1972 WB US 2591 UK K 46151
HAL BLAINE D (A — (D) LIVIN' FOR LOVIN' 1976 CAPITOL 11558
ALAN BRANSCOMBE (A — (E) DID YOU EVER 1977 CAPITOL 11668
ERIC CLAPTON G (A
PETE CLARKE (A NICKY HOPKINS K (A BISHOP O'BRIEN (A RINGO STARR D V (A
BRYN HAWORTH G V (B PAUL GRIFFIN K (B LINDA NOVEMBER V (B BILLY RICH B (C
ROBBIE ROBERTSON G (C RICHARD MANUEL (C RON STOCKERT K V (DE STEVE BECKMAIER G (D
HARVEY MASON D (D IAN MATTHEWS V (D GEORGE HARRISON G (A LARRY KNECHTEL (A
TONY NEWMAN (A KLAUS VOORMANN B (A BUGS PEMBERTON D (BDE EDDIE BRIGATI V (B
SELDON POWELL SAX (B MAERETHA STEWART V (B JOHN HALL G (C LEVON HELM V D (C
MARTY GREBB SAX (D WILLIAM D SMITH K (D MARTY DAVID B (DE CHRISTOPHER PARKER D (D
DON WHALEY V (D SPIKE HEATLEY (A PAUL McCARTNEY (A JOE OSBORN (A
ISRAEL ZACUTO G (B TOMMY CACCETTA B (B DAVID BRIGATI V (B HELENE W MILES V (B
BERNARD PURDIE D (C RICK DANKO (C GARTH HUDSON (C JIMMY ROBERTS SAX (DE
RANDY ZACUTO G (D RITCHIE HAYWARD D (D JOE CORRERO D (D AL STAEHELY V (D
ANDRE FISCHER D (E AL CINER G (E MAX MIDDLETON SYN (E GENE DINWIDDIE WIND(E
DEBORAH LINDSEY V (E STEVE MADAIO TPT (E JIM PRICE TROM (E PAT MURPHY PERC(E
BROOKS HUNNICUTT V (E LISA FREEMAN ROBERTS V (E

L112 LOMAX ALLIANCE L112

JACKIE LOMAX V G (— NO ALBUMS
BUGS PEMBERTON D (
TOM CACCETTA B (JOHN CANNING G (C

L113 LONDON L113

RIFF REGAN V (A — (A) ANIMAL GAMES 1978 MCA MCF 2823
STEVE VOICE B (A — (B) LONDON (EP) 1977 MCA MCA 319
JOHN MOSS D (A
DAVE WIGHT G (A

L113A LONE GROOVER L113A

(A) WHO CARES (EP) 1978 CHARLY UK CEP 124

L114 LONE STAR L114

KEN DRISCOLL V (A — (A) LONE STAR 1976 CBS US 34475 UK CBS 81545
TONY SMITH G (AB — (B) FIRING ON ALL SIX 1977 CBS US 34937 UK CBS 82213
PAUL CHAPMAN G (AB
PETE HURLEY B (AB DIXIE LEE D (AB RICK WORSNOP K (AB JOHN SLOMAN V (B

L115 LONESOME SUNDOWN L115

LONESOME SUNDOWN (CORNELIUS GREEN) V G (AB — (A) LONESOME LONELY BLUES 1970 EXCELLO US 8012
(A) LONESOME LONELY BLUES 1970 BLUE HORIZON UK 7 63864
LIONEL PREVO SAX (A — (B) BEEN GONE TOO LONG 1979 JOLIET US 6002
AUSTIN BROUSSARD D (A
KATIE WEBSTER PNO (A MERT THIBODEAUX PNO (A LAZY LESTER HCA (A DEE DEE GRADNIER HCA(A
BOBBY McBRIDE B (A RUFUS THIBODEAUX B (A WARREN STORM D (A

L115A ROY LONEY & THE PHANTOM MOVERS L115A

ROY LONEY V (ABC — (A) PHANTOM TRACKS (EP) 1980 SOLID SMOKE 9002
DANNY MIHM D (A — ( ) OUT AFTER DARK 1979 SOLID SMOKE US 9001
JAMES FERRELL G (A — (C) CONTENTS UNDER PRESSURE 1981 WAR BRIDE UK 9003
MAURICE TANI B (AC
LARRY LEA G (AC MOREY GOLDSTEIN SAX (C JOHN REWIND G PERC(C JOHNNY SURRELL D (C
NICK BUCK K (C JOHN KALDOR GV (C RAFAEL MARTINES PERC (C

L115B LONG TALL ERNIE L115B

(A) DO YOU REMEMBER 197 POLYDOR GER 2417 113

L116 LONGBRANCH PENNYWHISTLE L116

J D SOUTHER G V (A — (A) LONGBRANCH PENNYWHISTLE 1970 AMOS US AAS 7007
GLENN FREY G V (A
JAMES BURTON G (A RY COODER G (A JIM GORDON D (A BUDDY EMMONS STEEL(A
LARRY KNECHTEL PNO (A JOE OSBORN B (A DOUG KERSHAW G V (A

L117 LONGDANCER L117

MATT IRVING K G V(B — (A) IF IT WAS SO SIMPLE 1973 ROCKET PIGL 1 US MCA 339
STEVE SPROXTON G V (AB — (B) TRAILER FOR A GOOD LIFE 1974 ROCKET PIGL 6
BRIAN HARRISON G B V(AB
DAVE STEWART G B V(AB CHARLIE SMITH D V (B JIMMY HALL PNO (A ROGER POWELL D(A
VIRAM JASANI SITAR(B TOMMY McCARTHY PIPES(B POPART STRINGS (B KAI OLSSON G V (A
BOB RONGA B (A ANDY ROBERTS DULC (A KESH SATHIE PERC (B BONES V (B
DAVE MATTACKS F (A TONY ASHTON K (A DEL NEWMAN K (B JUDD PROCTOR BANJ(B
CHARLES YOUNG CHOIR (B

L117A LONG HELLO L117A

(A) LONG HELLO 1979 BUTT NOTT 002
(B) LONG HELLO VOL 2 1981 BUTT NOTT 004

L118 PROFESSOR LONGHAIR L118

PROFESSOR LONGHAIR V PNO(ALL — (A) NEW ORLEANS PIANO 1972 ATLANTIC US 7225 UK K 40402
LEE ALLEN SAX (A — (A) NEW ORLEANS PIANO 197 PIONEER JAP P4582A
RED TYLER SAX (A — (B) ROCK'N' ROLL GUMBO 1975 BARCLAY 80606 RI IMS 81
EDGAR BLANCHARD B (A — (C) LIVE ON THE QUEEN MARY 1978 HARVEST UK SHSP 4086
EARL PALMER D (A — (D) CRAWFISH FIESTA 1980 SONET UK SNTF 830
ROBERT PARKER SAX (A — (D) CRAWFISH FIESTA 1980 ALLIGATOR US AL 4718
DAVID LEE WATSON B (D
CHARLIE BURBECK SAX (A AL MILLER D (A JOHN WOODROW D (A DR JOHN G (D
ANDY KASLOW SAX (D TONY DAGRADI SAX (D JOHN VIDACOVICH D (D JIM MOORE SAX(D
ALFRED ROBERTS CONGA(D

L119 WILBERT LONGMIRE L119

WILBERT LONGMIRE G V (ABC — (A) SUNNY SIDE UP 1978 CBS UK 82845
BOB JAMES K (ABC — (B) CHAMPAGNE 1979 CBS UK 83257
DAVE SANBORN SAX (A — (C) WITH ALL MY LOVE 1980 CBS US 36342 UK 84155
ERIC GALE G (AB
HARVEY MASON D (AB RICHARD TEE K (AB RANDY BRECKER TPT (B JON FADDIS TPT (B
WAYNE ANDRE TROM (BC RON CUBER SAX (B EDDIE DANIELS FLT (BC GORDON GRODY V (B
STEVE KHAN G (C GILMORE DIGAP PERC (C PETER GORDON HRNS (C GLORIA AGOSTINI HARP(C
JOCELYN SHAW V (C GARY KING B (BC JIM MAELEN PERC (BC IDRIS MUHAMMAD D (B
LEWIS SOLOFF TPT (B MIKE LAWRENCE TPT (BC PAUL FAULISE TROM (B GEORGE MARGE WIND(BC
PHIL BODNER FLT (BC LANI GROVES V (BC BARRY MILES K (C MARVIN STAMM HRNS(C
JIM BUFFINGTON HRNS (C BABBI B FLOYD V (C EARL McINTYRE TROM (B BARRY ROGERS TROM(B
MICHAEL BRECKER SAX (B GEORGE YOUNG SAX (B DIVA GRAY V (BC ZACK SANDERS V (BC
BUDDY WILLIAMS D (C DAVE TAYLOR HRNS (C FRANK FLOYD V (C

L119B LOOKING GLASS L119B

ELLIOT LURIE G V (AB — (A) LOOKING GLASS 1972 EPIC US 31320 UK EPC 65041
LARRY GONSKY K V (AB — (B) SUBWAY SERENADE 1973 EPIC US 32167
PIET SWEVAL B V (AB
JEFF GROB D (A BARBARA MASSEY V (A CAROLYN DAVIS V (A TASHA THOMAS V (A
SELDON POWELL SAX (B RALPH MACDONALD PERC (B JOE DUBE PERC (B MAXINE DIXON V (B
NANCY NALENCE V (B NANCY FARRELL V (B STEVE VON SCHREIBER V (B

L119C JEFF LORBER FUSION L119C

JEFF LORBER K (ALL — (A) SOFT SPACE 197 INNER CITY US IC1056
TERRY LAYNE WIND (A — (B) WATER SIGN 1979 ARISTA US AB4234
LESTER McFARLAND B (A — (C) WIZARD ISLAND 1980 ARISTA US AL9516
DENNIS BRADFORD D (ABC — (D) GALAXIAN 1981 ARISTA
FREDDY HUBBARD HRNS (B
RON YOUNG PERC (A DANNY WILSON B (BC DOUG LEWIS G (B KENNY GORELICK WIND (C
CHICK COREA K (AC JOE FARRELL SAX (AB DENNIS SPRINGER SAX (B JAY KODER G (BC
PAULINHO DA COSTA PERC (C BRUCE SMITH PERC (AB DEAN REICHERT G (A

L120 JON LORD L120

JON LORD K (ALL — (A) GEMINI SUITE 1971 PURPLE UK TPSA7501
TONY ASHTON K V (AB — (B) WINDOWS 1974 PURPLE UK TPSA7513
DAVID COVERDALE V (B — (C) SARABANDE 1976 PURPLE UK TPSA 7516
RAY FENWICK G (B
GLENN HUGHES V G B(B EBERHARD SCHOENER K (B ROGER GLOVER B (A ALBERT LEE G (A
PETE YORK D (BC YVONNE ELLIMAN V (A IAN PAICE D (A ORCHESTRAS (BC
PAUL KARASS B (C MARK NAUSEEL PERC (C ANDY SUMMERS G (C

L121 LORDS L121

ULLI GUNTHER V (— (A) BLACK & WHITE 1965 COLUMBIA GER 83859
KLAUS PETER LIETZ G (— (B) THE LORDS II 1966 COLUMBIA GER 84013
RAINER PETRY G (— (C) SOME FOLKS 1967 COLUMBIA
BERND ZAMULA B (— (D) GOOD SIDE OF JUNE 1968 COLUMBIA GER 74244
PETER DONATH D (— (E) ULLEOGAMAXBE 1969 COLUMBIA GER 74343
KNUD KUNTZE B (— (F) SHAKIN' ALL OVER '70 1970 COLUMBIA GER 28478
HEINZ HEGEMANN B (— (G) INSIDE OUT 1971 COLUMBIA GER 28887
(H) BEST OF 1971 COLUMBIA GER 29783
(I) THE LORDS (COMP) 1972 M F P 5142
(J) THE LORDS 1974 COLUMBIA GER 31972
(K) THE BEST OF 1964/71 (COMP) 19 COLUMBIA GER 64871

L121A LOST & FOUND L121A

JAMES HARRELL (A — (A) EVERYBODY'S HERE 1976 INTERNATIONAL ARTISTS IALP3
PETE BLACK (A
JIMMY FROST (A STEVE WEBB (A

L121B LOS BRAVOS L121B

(A) LOS BRAVOS 1966 PRESS 83003
(B) BRING A LITTLE LOVIN' 1968 PARROT US 71021
(C) BLACK IS BLACK (COMP) 1974 DECCA GER 21670

L121C LOSEKES BLUES BAND L121C

FALK STEHR V HCA(AB — (A) BEST WISHES 19 BLIND MAN WAM 780064
BERNIE RINGE V HCA SAX(AB — (B) RED HOT MAMA 19 BLIND MAN 062506
KALLE WEBER G (AB
HERBERT WEBER D (AB UWE BRUCHHAUSER PNO (AB THOMAS PLOG B (AB

L122 LOST GONZO BAND L122

GARY NUNN PNO V B G (A — (A) LOST GONZO BAND 1975 MCA UK MCF 2727 US MCA 487
ROBERT LIVINGTON B K V(B — (B) THRILLS 1976 MCA US MCA2232
JOHN INMON G V (B — (C) SIGNS OF LIFE 1978 CAPITOL US 11788
KELLY DUNN SYN K(B
DONNY DOLAN D PERC(B

L122A LOTHAR & THE HAND PEOPLE L122A

JOHN EMELIN V EFFECTS(A — (A) PRESENTING LOTHAR & THE HAND PEOPLE 1968 CAPITOL US 2997
KIM KING G SYN (A — (B) SPACE HYMN 19 CAPITOL US 247
TOM FLYE D (A
PAUL CONLEY K (A RUSTY FORD B (A

L123 J D LOUDERMILK L123

J D LOUDERMILK — LANGUAGE OF LOVE 196 RCA US LSP 2434
12 SIDES OF 196 RCA US LSP 2539
SINGS A BIZARRE COLLECTION 1966 RCA UK RD7890 US LSP 3497
SURBURBAN ATTITUDES 1967 RCA US LSP 3807
COUNTRY LOVE SONGS 1968 RCA US LSP 4040
THE OPEN MIND OF J D LOUDERMILK 1969 RCA US LSP 4097
ELLOREE VOL 1 1971 WB UK K46124 US 1922
BEST OF 1973 RCA US LSA 3159
ENCORES 1975 RCA US LSA 3220
JUST PASSING THROUGH 1978 MIM US MIMLP9009

L124 LOUDSPEAKERS L124

RICHIE RAE D (A — (A) LOUDSPEAKERS 1978 EBONY UK EBY 1004
CHRIS THOMAS G V (A
IAN GAIR K V (A BRIAN ENGEL V (A BRENDAN WALSH B G (A

L125 JOE HILL LOUIS L125

JOE HILL LOUIS G V HCA(A — (A) BLUE IN THE MORNING 1973 POLYDOR 2383 214
WILLIE NIX D V (A
BILLY 'RED' LOVE PNO (A WILLIE JOHNSON G (A

L126 LOUISIANA RED L126

IVERSON'LOUISIANA RED'MINTER G V(ALL — (A) SEVENTH SON 1963 CARNIVAL RI 2941 002
BILL DICEY HCA (C — (A) LOW DOWN BACK PORCH BLUES 196 ROULETTE US 25200
TOMMY TUCKER PNO (C — (C) SINGS THE BLUES 1972 ATLANTIC UK K40436 US 33389
DAVE'BABY 'CORTEZ ORG (C — (D) SWEET BLOOD CALL 1975 BLUE LABOR US BL 104
ROBERT BANKS PNO (C — (E) DEAD STRAY DOG 1976 BLUE LABOR US BL 107
NAPOLEON ALLEN G (C — (F) RED FUNK & BLUE 1978 BLACK PANTHER UK BP1001
EARL WILLIAMS D (C — (G) NEW YORK BLUES 1979 L&R 42 002
PAUL MARTINEZ B (C — (H) KING BEE 1979 JSP 1006
KEN MIMMS G (C — (J) REALITY BLUES 1980 L&R 42 011
SUGAR BLUES HCA (F — ( ) LOUSIANA RED 19 FORUM 9100
DICK BUNN B (C
DON COOK PNO (C JIM EVANS D (C BOB MALENKY G (C LEONARD GASKIN B (C
SID BARNES D (C ELAINE MONK V (G VIVIAN MINTER V (G HUBERT SUMLIN G (J
SUNNYLAND SLIM PNO (J BOB STROGER B (J ODIE PAYNE D (J CAREY BELL HARRINGTON HCA(J

L128 LOVE L128

ARTHUR LEE PROD G V (ABCDEFG — (A) LOVE 1966 ELEKTRA EKS 74001
JOHN ECHOLS G (ABCE — (B) DA CAPO 1967 ELEKTRA UK K42011 EKS 74005
BRYAN MACLEAN G V (ABCE — (C) FOREVER CHANGES 1967 ELEKTRA UK K42015 EKS 74013
KEN FORSSI B (ABCE — (D) FOUR SAIL 1969 ELEKTRA UK K42030 EKS 74049
ALBAN PFISTERER D (ABE — (E) LOVE REVISTITED 1970 ELEKTRA 2469 009 EKS 74058
DON CONKA D (— (E) LOVE REVISITED 1971 ELEKTRA UK K42091
MICHAEL STUART PERC (BC — (F) OUT HERE 1969 BLUE THUMB US BTS 9000
TJAY CANTRELLI PERC (B — (F) OUT HERE 1969 HARVEST UK SHDW 3/4
JAY DONNELLAN G (DF — (G) FALSE START 1970 BLUE THUMB US BTS 8822
FRANK FAYAD B (DFG — (G) FALSE START 1970 HARVEST UK SHVL 787
GEORGE SURANOVICH D (DFG — (H) LOVE MASTERS 1972 ELEKTRA UK K32002
GARY ROWLES G (FG — (J) REEL TO REAL 1974 RSO 2394 145 US 4804
NOONEY RICKETT G V (G — (K) BEST OF 1980 RHINO US 800
JIMI HENDRIX G (G — (L) LOVE LIVE 1981 LINE GER 5153
DRACHEN THEAKER D (DF
JOEY BLOCKER D (J SHERWOOD AKUNA B (J ROBERT ROZELLE B (J MELVAN WHITTINGTON G (J
BUZZY FEITEN G (J JOEY DEAGUERO VIBES(J VANETTA FIELDS V (J CLIFFORD SOLOMON HRNS (J
WILBER BROWN HRNS (J PAUL MARTIN G (F JIM HOBSON K (F JOHN STIRLING G (J
ART FOX G (J BOBBY LYLE K (J CARLENE WILLIAMS V (J JOHN CLAUDER HRNS(J
ALAN DE VILLE HRNS (J HERMAN McCORMICK CONGA(J HARVEY MANDEL G (J GARY BELL SYN(J
JESSIE SMITH V (J FRED CARTER HRNS (J BILLY SPRAGUE HRNS (J PAUL ROTHCHILD PROD (B
BRUCE BOTNICK PROD (C

L128A CLAYTON LOVE L128A

CLAYTON LOVE V PNO(A (A) COME ON HOME BLUES(10") 197 RED LIGHTNING RL0029
SID WALLACE V (A
EUGENE WASHINGTON D (A GEORGE BRAZIER B (A NAT RIGGINS G (A

L129 MIKE LOVE L129

MIKE LOVE V (A (A) CELEBRATION 197
CHARLES LLOYD WIND (A
RON ALTBACH PNO V(A ED CARTER G (A DAVE ROBINSON B (A WELLS KELLY G (A
MIKE KOWALSKI D (A GARY GRIFFIN K (A

L129A LOVE AFFAIR L129A

LYNTON GUEST K (A (A) EVERLASTING 19
MICK JACKSON B (AB (B) NEW DAY 1970 CBS UK 64109
MAURICE BACON D (AB (C) GOLDEN ERA OF POP MUSIC 1973 CBS UK 68255
REX BRAYLEY G (B
MORGAN FISHER K (A AUGUSTE EADON V FLT(A STEVE ELLIS V (A

L130 LOVE COMMITTEE L130

NORMAN FRAZIER V (A (A) LAW & ORDER 1978 SALSOUL UK 1506 GOLDMINE US9500
CARLA BENSON V (A (A) LOVE COMMITEE 1970 ELECTRIC US 3233
LARRY RICHARDSON V (A
JOE FREEMAN V (A RON TYSON V PERC(A EARL YOUNG D (A KEITH BENSON D (A
RON BAKER B (A JIMMY WILLIAMS B (A NORMAN HARRIS G (A BOBBY ELI G (A
ROLAND CHAMBERS G (A T J TINDALL G (A EDDIE MOORE G (A RON KERSEY K (A
COTTON KENT K (A BRUCE GRAY K (A T G CONWAY K (A BRUCE HAWES K (A
LARRY WASHINGTON CONGAS(A ALLAN FELDER PERC (A DON RENALDO STRINGS (A EVETTE BENTON V (A
BARBARA INGRAM V (A

L130A LOVECRAFT L130A

MICHAEL TEGZA D V (AB (A) VALLEY OF THE MOON 1970 REPRISE 6419
LALOMIE WASHBURN V PERC(B (B) WE LOVE YOU WHOEVER YOU ARE 1975 MERCURY US SRMI 1031
FRANK CAPEK G (B
JORGE RODRIGUEZ G (B CRAIG GIGSTAD B (B GEORGE AGOSTO PERC (B MARK JUSTIN K SYN(B
JIM DONLINGER (A MICHAEL BEEN (A MARTY GREBB (A

L130B LOVERBOY L130B

MIKE RENO V (AB (A) LOVERBOY 1980 CBS UK 84798 US 36762
PAUL DEAN G V (AB (B) GET LUCKY 1981 CBS US 37638
MATT FRENETTE D (AB
DOUG JOHNSON K (AB SCOTT SMITH B (AB NANCY NASH V (B

L130C LOVE SCULPTURE L130C

DAVE EDMUNDS G V (ALL (A) BLUES HELPING 1968 PARLOPHONE UK 7059 US RARE 505
TERRY WILLIAMS D (D (B) FORMS & FEELINGS 1969 PARLOPHONE UK 7090 US PARROT 71035
B J COLE STEEL(D (B) FORMS & FEELINGS 1969 ODEOM GER 90637
JOHN WILLIAMS B V K(AB (C) CLASSIC TRACKS 1974 ONE UP 2047
PETE KERR (B (D) ROCKERS 197 PARLOPHONE UK EURO 99546/7
MIKE FINESILVER (B (E) SINGLES 1980 HARVEST UK 2032
BOB JONES D V (ABD (F) DAVE EDMUNDS & LOVE SCULPTURE 198 EMI EURO 05637
ANDY FAIRWETHER LOW G(D

L131 LENE LOVICH L131

LENE LOVICH V SAX(AB (A) STATELESS 1978 STIFF US 36102 UK SEEZ 7
LES CHAPPELL G (AB (B) FLEX 1979 STIFF US 36308 UK SEEZ 19
MARK CHAPLIN B V (B (B) FLEX 1979 STIFF GER 6 24228
JUSTIN HILDRETH D (B
DEAN KLAVETT K V (B NICK PLYTAS K (AB CHRIS JUDGE-SMITH V (B JEFF SMITH SYN (A
BOBBI IRWIN D (A RON FRANCOIS B (A

L132 LOVING AWARENESS L132

CHARLEY CHARLES D (A (A) LOVING AWARENESS 1976 MORE LOVE ML 001
NORMAN WATT-ROY B (A
MICK GALLAGHER K (A JOHN TURNBULL G (A

L133 LOVING SPOONFUL L133

JOHN SEBASTIAN G V (ALL (A) DO YOU BELIEVE IN MAGIC 1965 PYE UK 28069 KAMA SUTRA US 8050
ZAL YANOVSKY V G (ABCDEF (B) DAYDREAMS 1966 PYE UK 28078 KAMA SUTRA US 8051
JOE BUTLER D (ABCDEF (C) WHATS UP TIGER LILY[SOUNDTRACK] 1966 KAMA SUTRA US 8053
STEVE BOONE B (ABCDEF (D) HUMS 1966 KAMA SUTRA UK 401 US 8054
JERRY YESTER G ((D) HUMS 196 KAMA SUTRA GERM 2319 034
GLEN COVE D ((E) BEST OF VOL 1 1967 KAMA SUTRA UK 403 US 2608
WOODY ALLEN (C (E) BEST OF VOL 1 1967 KAMA SUTRA GERM 620004 US 8056
ERIK JACOBSEN PROD (A (F) YOU'RE A BIG BOY NOW 1967 KAMA SUTRA UK 402 US 8058
JOEL WISSERT PROD (G (G) EVERYTHING PLAYING 1967 KAMA SUTRA UK 404 US 8061
HENRY DILTZ CLAR (D (G) EVERYTHING PLAYING 1967 KAMA SUTRA GERM 620006
LARRY HANKIN (D (H) BEST OF VOL 2 1968 KAMA SUTRA UK 405 US 8064
(H) BEST OF VOL 2 1968 KAMA SUTRA GERM 620007
(J) REVELATION REVOLUTION '69 1969 KAMA SUTRA UK 406 US 8073
(K) THE VERY BEST OF (COMP) 19 KAMA SUTRA US 2013
(L) GREATEST HITS 1970 KAMA SUTRA 2361 002
(M) POP HISTORY (DBL) 19 POLYDOR 2625 010
(AG)MORE GOLDEN SPOONFUL 1974 KAMA SUTRA KSMD 9002
(AG)MORE GOLDEN SPOONFUL 1974 KAMA SUTRA 2683 042
( ) BEST OF 196 MARBLE ARCH UK MAL1115
( ) BEST OF VOL 2 196 MARBLE ARCH UK MAL1116
( ) JOHN SEBASTIAN SONGBOOK 1967 KAMA SUTRA US 2011 G
( ) JOHN SEBASTIAN SONGBOOK 1967 BUDDAH GER 623133
( ) ONCE UPON A TIME 19 KAMA SUTRA US 2029
( ) RUN WITH YOU 196 KAMA SUTRA 8073
( ) 24 KARAT HITS 1968 KAMA SUTRA 750
(BC) DAYDREAM/TIGER LILY 19 KAMA SUTRA UK 2683 034
(O) GOLDEN HOUR 1975 PYE UK GH 838
(P) THE GREAT YEARS 19 MODE FR MD 9022
(Q) LOVING SPOONFUL 19 PROFILE GERM 624 018
(R) FILE 1977 PYE UK FILD009
( ) GREAT YEARS 1980 VOGUE NL 9022

(CONTINUED)

L133 (CONTINUED)

LOVING SPOONFUL

L133

(EPs)

Title	Year	Label	Number
DID YOU EVER	1966	KAMA SUTRA	KEP 300
JUG BAND MUSIC	1966	KAMA SUTRA	KEP 301
SUMMER IN THE CITY	1966	KAMA SUTRA	KEP 302
DAY BLUES	1967	KAMA SUTRA	KEP 303
NASHVILLE CATS	1967	KAMA SUTRA	KEP 304
LOVING YOU	1967	KAMA SUTRA	KEP 305
SOMETHING IN THE NIGHT	1967	KAMA SUTRA	KEP 306

L134

LOW NUMBERS

L134

HAROLD BRONSON V (A — (A) TWIST AGAIN WITH THE LOW NUMBERS 1978 RHINO RNLP 004
LOUIS MAXFIELD G (A
DAVE DENNARD B (A — DAVID SCHNEIDER D (A — MARK LEVITON (A — PAGE PORRAZZO (A
MICK ROSEN (A — PETER DEAL (A — STUART DEAL (A — STEVE ROSEN (A
DON BUCHANAN (A — ROB LAMPL (A — DON KRAIG (A — BARRY SQUIRE (A

L135

NICK LOWE

L135

NICK LOWE B V G(ALL — (A) JESUS OF COOL 1978 RADAR UK RAD 1 + RADAR K56466
DAVE EDMUNDS G (AB — (A) PURE POP FOR NOW PEOPLE 1978 CBS US 35329 SCAN SMASH SLEPT1
BILLY BREMNER G (ABC — (B) LABOUR OF LUST 1979 RADAR UK RAD21 GER RADAR 56676
TERRY WILLIAMS D (ABC — (B) LABOUR OF LUST 1979 CBS US 36087 SCAN SMASH SLEPT6
MARTIN BELMONT G (C — (C) NICK THE KNIFE 1982 F BEAT UK XXLP14
NEIL KING K (C
STEVE NIEVE K (C — PAUL CARRACK K (C — HUEY LEWIS HCA (C — BOB ANDREWS K (C
BOB IRWIN D V (C — ALDO BOCCA G (C — CARLENE CARTER/LOWE V(C — BEN BARSON K (C
JAMES ELLER B (C

L136

HENRY LOWTHER

L136

HENRY LOWTHER HRNS VLN(A — (A) CHILD SONG 1970 DERAM UK SML 1070
TONY ROBERTS WIND (A
MIKE McNAUGHT K (A — DARYL RUNSWICK B (A — MIKE TRAVIS D (A — JIMMY JEWELL SAX (A
NEIL SLAVEN PERC (A

L136A

SHARALEE LUCAS

L136A

SHARALEE LUCAS V (A — (A) DAUGHTER OF MUSIC 1978 GREENTREE R3520
FARRELL MORRIS PERC (A
SHANE KEISTER K (A — LARRY LONDIN D (A — JOE OSBORN B (A — BOBBY THOMPSON G BAN(A
STEVE GIBSON G (A — JOHN THOMPSON G (A — JACK WILLIAMS B (A — BUDDY SKIPPER SAX (A
CINDY REYNOLDS HARP(A — BOBBY TAYLOR HRNS (A — KATHY THOMPSON V (A — BOB FARRELL V (A

L137

TREVOR LUCAS

L137

TREVOR LUCAS V G (A — (A) OVERLANDER 1966 REALITY RY1002
ALF EDWARDS CONC (A
CYRIL HARLING FDL (A — GEORGE GIBBS B (A

L138

LUCIFER

L138

(A) BIG GUN 19 LLP 1
(B) EXIT 19 LLP 2
(C) MARGRIET 19 EMI IMP 064 25655
(D) BLACK MASS 19 UNI US 73111
(E) LUCIFER 19 INVICTUS US 7309

L139

LUCIFERS FRIEND

L139

PETER HECHT K (ABCDEFGH — (A) LUCIFERS FRIEND 1971 PHILIPS GER 6305 068
DIETER HORNS B V (ABCDEFGH — (A) LUCIFERS FRIEND 1973 BILLINGSGATE US 1002
JOHN LAWTON V (ABCDEH — (B) WHERE GROUPIES KILLED THE BLUES 1972 PASSPORT US 98008
PETER VAN ASLEN V (F — (B) WHERE GROUPIES KILLED THE BLUES 1973 VERTIGO GER 6360 602
JOACHIM RIETENBACH D (ABC — (C) I'M JUST A ROCK'N'ROLL SINGER 1974 BILLINGSGATE US 1008
PETER HESSLEIN G V (ABCDEFGH — (C) I'M JUST A ROCK'N'ROLL SINGER 1974 VERTIGO GER 6360 611
BOB LANESE TPT (CD — (D) BANQUET 1975 PASSPORT US 98012
HERB GELLER WIND (CD — (D) BANQUET 1975 VERTIGO GER 6360 618
HERBERT BORNHOLDT PERC V(CDEFGH — (E) MIND EXPLODING 1976 VERTIGO GER 6360 633
KARL HERMANN LUER WIND (E — (E) MIND EXPLODING 1976 +JANUS US 7030
DRIAN ASKEW K V (GH — (F) GOOD TIME WARRIOR 1978 ELEKTRA 63 159
MIKE STARRS V (FG — (F) GOOD TIME WARRIOR 1978 ELEKTRA GER 52081
(G) SNEAK ME IN 1980 ELEKTRA GERM 52203 US 265
(H) MEAN MACHINE 1981

L139A

LUDUS

L139A

(A) THE VISIT (EP) 19 NEW HORMONE ORG 4
(B) PICK POCKET 1981 NEW HORMONES CASS CAT1

L140

LULU

L140

LULU(MARIE LAWRIE V (ALL — (A) SOMETHING TO SHOUT ABOUT 1965 DECCA UK LK 4719
JIM DEWAR B (— (B) LULU 1967 ACE OF CLUBS UK ACL 1232
ROSS NELSON (— (C) TO SIR WITH LOVE 1967 EPIC US 26339 FONTANA UK 5446
ALEC BELL (— (D) ITS LULU 1970 EPIC US 26536
JIMMY SMITH (— (E) LOVE LOVES TO LOVE LULU 1967 COLUMBIA UK SCX 6201
TONY TIERNEY (— (F) LULU'S ALBUM 1969 COLUMBIA UK SCX 6365
DAVID MILLER (— (G) WORLD OF LULU 1969 DECCA UK SPA 8
DUANE ALLMAN G (J — (H) WORLD OF LULU 1969 DECCA UK SPA 94
MAX BENNETT (M — (J NEW ROUTES 1970 ATLANTIC US 33310 UK 228031
JOE OSBORN B (M — (K) MELODY FAIR 1970 ATLANTIC US 33330 UK 2400 017
LOUIE SHELTON (M — (M) MAKE BELIEVE WORLD 1973 CHELSEA US 0144
DEAN PARKS G (M — ( ) LULU 19 PICKWICK US 3237
HAL BLAINE D (M — ( ) TO LOVE SOMEBODY 19 HARMONY US 30449
BOB HARDAWAY (M — ( ) FROM LULU WITH LOVE 19 PARROT US 71016
JEROME RICHARDSON (M — (P) DONT TAKE LOVE FOR GRANTED 1979 ROCKET UK TRAIN8 US 3073
TOM SCOTT WIND (M — ( ) BOY 19 EPIC US 26396
SLYDE HYDE TROM (M — ( ) VERY BEST OF 1980 WARWICK UK 5097
CHUCK FINDLEY TPT (M
VICTOR FELDMAN PERC (M — GARY COLEMAN PERC (M — MICHAEL O'MARTIAN K (M — TOM HENSLEY (M
DAN PEAKE (M

L141 BOB LUMAN L141

BOB LUMAN G V (ALL | LETS THINK ABOUT LIVING | 1960 | WB | | WS1396
AINT GOT TIME | 1968 | EPIC | | 26393
COME ON HOME | 1969 | EPIC | | 26463
GETTING BACK TO NORNA | 1970 | EPIC | | 26541
IS IT ANY WONDER THAT I LOVE YOU | 197 | EPIC | US | 30617
A CHAIN DONT TAKE TO ME | 19 | EPIC LE10187 | | 30923
LIVIN LOVIN SOUNDS | 1971 | LONDON UK ZGE115 US HSP 124006
WHEN YOU SAY LOVE | 1972 | EPIC | | 31375
LONELY WOMEN MAKE GOOD LOVERS | 1972 | EPIC | US | 31746
BOB LUMAN | 1973 | HARMONY | US | 32006
NEITHER ONE OF US | 1973 | EPIC | US | 32192
GREATEST HITS | 1974 | EPIC | US | 32759
RED CADILLAC & BLACK MUSTACHE | 197 | EPIC | US | 33177
STILL LOVING YOU | 1974 | HICKORY | US | 4508
WHEN YOU SAY LOVE/LONELY WOMEN (DBL) | 197 | EPIC | US | 33755
A SATISFIED MIND | 1976 | EPIC | US | 33942
ALIVE & WELL | 1977 | EPIC | US | 34445
BOB LUMAN ROCKS | 1977 | DJM | UK | DJM 22057
THE PAY PHONE | 1978 | POLYDOR | US | PDI6135
THE ROCKER | 1979 | BEAR FAMILY | GERM | 15037
MORE OF THE ROCKER | 1979 | BEAR FAMILY | GERM | 15039

L141A LYDIA LUNCH L141A

PAT IRWIN (| (A) QUEEN OF SIAM | 1980 | ZE US 33006
JACK RUBY (
DOUG BROWNE (ROBERT QUINE (

L142 LURKERS L142

PETE STRIDE G (ABC | (A) FULHAM FALL OUT | 1978 | BEGGARS BANQUET | UK | BEG2
HOWARD WALL V (ABC | (B) GODS LONELY MEN | 1979 | BEGGARS BANQUET | UK | BEGA8
MANIC ESSO D (ABC | (C) GREATEST HITS LAST WILL & TESTAMENT 80 | BEGGARS BANQUET | UK | BOPA2
NIGEL MOORE B (ABC | (EP) SHADOW | 1979 | BEGGARS BANQUET | UK | BACK1
KYM BRADSHAW B (| (EP) I DONT NEED TO TELL HER | 1979 | BEGGARS BANQUET | UK | BACK3
PETE EDWARDS V HCA(A
JOHN PLAIN G (C ARTURO BASSICK B (C

L142A WILLIAM LYALL L142A

WILLIAM LYALL V PERC K SYN(A | (A) SOLO CASTING | 1976 | EMI | UK | EMA 780
PHIL CHEN B (A
RONNIE LEAHY PNO (A PHIL COLLINS D (A DAVID PATON G (A ROBERT AHWAI G (A
IAN BAIRNSON G (A PATATO CONGA(A CHRIS MERCER SAX (A TERRY WALSH BAN (A
FRANK MUSKER V (A DICK TATE PERC (A DOMINIC BUGATTI G (A BARRY DESOUZA D (A
JACK EMBLOW ACC (A PAUL BUCKMASTER CELLO(A RAY RUSSELL G (M

L143 BOBBY LYLE L143

BOBBY LYLE K V (A | (A) NEW WARRIOR | 1978 CAPITOL/TOWER | 11809
WAYNE HENDERSON PERC V(A | (B) NIGHT FIRE | 1980 CAPITOL | 11956
ANGELA WINDUSH V (A
NATHANIEL PHILLIPS B (A HARVEY MASON D (A STEPHANIE SPRUILL V (A JOE BLOCKER PERC (A
RON BANKS V (A JIM GILSTRAP V (A VANCE TENORT V (A ALEXANDRA BROWN V (A
MIKE BODDIKER SYN (A PAULINHO DA COSTA PERC (A GREGORY MATTA V (A DAVID T WALKER G (A
MARTINETTE JENKINS V (A SUNSHIP PERC (A ROLAND BAUTISTA G (A AUGIE JOHNSON V (A
STRING SECTION (A

L144 FRANKIE LYMON & THE TEENAGERS L144

FRANKIE LYMON V (ALL | (A) WHY DO FOOLS FALL IN LOVE | 1956 GEE US + UK PYE 1978 28251
( ) TEENAGERS | 195 GEE US 701
SHERMAN GARNES (| (B) ROCK'N' ROLL PARTY | 19 | GUEST STAR | US | GS 1406
JOE NEGRONI (| (C) AT THE LONDON PALLADIUM | 19 | ROULETTE | US | R 25013
HERMAN SANTIAGO (| (D) GREATEST HITS | 19 | ROULETTE | US | R 25250
JIMMY MERCHANT (| (EP) FRANKIE LYMON WITH THE TEENAGERS 19 | SONET | DK | SXP 3025
(EP)AT THE LONDON PALLADIUM | 19 | ROULETTE | US | EPR 1304

L144A BARBARA LYNN L144A

BARBARA LYNN V (A | (A) HERE IS | 1976 OVAL | UK | OVLM5002
( ) YOU'LL LOOSE A GOOD THING | 19 JAMIE | US 3023

L144B PHIL LYNOTT L144B

PHIL LYNOTT V B (AB | (A) SOLO IN SOHO | 1980 | VERTIGO UK 9102038 US WB 3405
TONY CHARLES D (A | (B) THE PHILIP LYNOTT ALBUM | 1982 | VERTIGO UK 6359 117
BRIAN DOWNEY D (A
BOBBY BENBERG D (A SCOTT GORHAM G (A SNOWY WHITE G (A MARK KNOPFLER G (A
FLACHRA TRENCH STR (A ANDY DUNCAN PERC (A HUEY LEWIS HCA (A JEROME RIMSON B (A
JIMMY BAIN K SYN(A MIDGE URE SYN (A BILLY CURRIE SYN (A MARK NAUSEEF D (A
GARY MOORE G (A

L145 JACKIE LYNTON L145

JACKIE LYNTON V (ALL | (A) THE JACKIE LYNTON ALBUM | 1974 | WWA | WWA 012
TONY LEACH V PNO(B | (B) JACKIE LYNTON BAND (DBL) | 1980 | SCRATCH | SCRL 5002
GRAHAME WHITE G V (B
GREG TERRY-SHORT D V (B KIRK RIDDLE B (B

L145A WILLIE JAMES LYONS L145A

WILLIE JAMES LYONS G (A | (A) W J LYONS & W KENT GHETTO | 197 | MCM | FR | 900 291
WILLLIE KENT (A

L146 LYNYRD SKYNYRD L146

RONNIE VAN ZANT V (ALL | (A) PRONOUNCED LEHNERD SKINNERD | 1974 MCA US 363 NL 201 US RI 3019
STEVE GAINES G (EF | (A) " " " " " | 1974 MCA UK 3502 FR BARCLAY 410010
GARY ROSSINGTON G (ALL | (B) SECOND HELPING | 1974 MCA US 413 US RI 3020
ALLEN COLLINS G (ALL | (B) " " " | 1974 MCA UK 2547 FR BARCLAY 410020
LEON WILKESON B (ALL | (C) NUTHIN' FANCY | 1975 MCA US 2137 US RI 3021
BILLY POWELL K (ALL | (C) " " " | 1975 MCA UK 2700 FR BARCLAY 410042
ARTIMUS PYLE D (ECDF | (D) GIMME BACK MY BULLETS | 1976 MCA US 2170 US RI 3022
CASSIE GAINES V (EGF | (D) " " " " | 1976 MCA UK 2744 FR BARCLAY 410048
JO BILLINGSLEY V (EGF | (E) ONE MORE FROM THE ROAD | 1976 MCA US 2/8001 RI 801
LESLIE HAWKINS V (EGF | (E) " " " " | 1976 MCA UK 279 FR BARCLAY410060/1
SAM McPHERSON HCA (E | (F) STREET SURVIVORS | 1977 MCA US 3029
JIMMY JOHNSON G (G | (F) " " " " | 1977 MCA UK 3525 FR BARCLAY 511002
DAVID FOSTER K (C | (F) " " " " | 1982 MCA UK RI MCL 1694

L146 (CONTINUED) LYNYRD SKYNYRD L146

RICKY MEDLOCKE D (GF — (G) SKYNYRDS FIRST & LAST — 1978 MCA US 3047 UK 3529 UK RI 1627
RANDY McCORMICK K (G — (H) GOLD & PLATINUM BAND (DBL) — 1979 MCA US 11008 UK MCSP 308
BOBBY KEYS SAX (B — (H) GOLD & PLATINUM (DBL) — 1982 MCA UK RI MCDW 456
MERRY CLAYTON V (B — (EP) DOWN SOUTH JUKIN' — 1978 MCA UK MCEP 101
TREVOR LAWRENCE SAX (B
ED KING G (ABCFG — ROOSEVELT GOOK B K V(A — BOBBYE HALL PERC (AC — WAYNE PERKINS G (G
GREG WALKER B (GF — TIM SMITH V (GF — MIKE PORTER D (B — STEVE MADAIO TPT(B
ROBERT BURNS D (ABG — ROBERT NIX D (A — STEVE KATZ HCA (A — RON EADES SAX (GF
GIMMER NICHOLS G (G — CLYDIE KING V (B

M1 M C 5 M1

ROB TYNER HCA V(ABC — (A) KICK OUT THE JAMS — 1969 ELEKTRA US 74042 UK 1977 K42027
FRED SMITH V K G HCA (ABC — (B) BACK IN THE USA — 1970 ATLANTIC US 8247 UK 2400 016
MIKE DAVIS B V (ABC — (B) BACK IN THE USA — 1977 ATLANTIC UK K50346
DENNIS THOMPSON D V (ABC — (C) HIGH TIME — 1971 ATLANTIC US 8285 UK K40223
WAYNE KRAMER G V K(ABC
PETE KELLY K (B
CHARLES MOORE HRN V(C — JOANNE HILL V (C — BRENDAN KNIGHT V (C — MERLENE DRISCOLL V (C
DAVID OVERSTEAK TUBA (C — LARRY HORTON TROM (C — BOBBY WAYNE DERMINER PERC(C — BUTCH O'BRIEN PERC (C
LEON HENDERSON SAX (C — RICK FERRETTI SAX (C — SKIP KNAPP ORG (C — KINKI LE PEW PERC (C
DAN BULLOCK TROM (C — BOB SEGER PERC (C — SCOTT MORGAN PERC (C — TERRY TRABANDT PERC (C
DAVE HELLER PERC (C — DAVE MORGAN PERC (C — ELLIS DEE PERC (C — DANNY JORDAN K (B

M1A 'M' M1A

ROBIN SCOTT G V (AB — (A) NEW YORK, LONDON ,PARIS ,MUNICH — 1979 MCA US 6084 UK MCF3046
PHILIP GOULD D (AB — (A) NEW YORK, LONDON, PARIS, MUNICH — 1979 MCA GER 62147 NL 201268
WALLY BADAROU SYN K(A — (B) OFFICIAL SECRETS ACT — 1980 SIRE US 6099 MCA UK MCF3085
MARK KING G B D(B — (B) OFFICIAL SECRETS ACT — 1980 MCA NL 203071
JULIAN SCOTT B (AB
DEIRDRIE COSTELLO V (B — DAVID VORHAUS SYN (B — GARY BARNACLE WIND (AB — PADDY KEENAN PIPES(B
BRIGIT VINCHON V (AB — DENIS BLACKHAM V (B — MOG AHERNE V (B — JOHN KEOGH V (B
BILLY BROWN V (B — DES SMITH V (B

M2 M.F.S.B. M2

DEXTER WANSEL K (J — (A) M.F.S.B. — 1973 T S O P UK 65903 US 32046
JAMES HERB SMITH G (J — (B) T S O P — 1974 T S O P UK 80154
LARRY MOORE B (J — (C) LOVE IS THE MESSAGE — 197 T S O P US 32707
EVAN SOLOT TPT (J — (D) UNIVERSAL LOVE — 1975 T S O P UK 80410 US 33158
LARRY McKENNA SAX (J — (E) PHILADELPHIA FREEDOM — 1976 T S O P UK 69206 US 33845
CLIFFORD RUDD D (J — (F) SUMMERTIME — 1976 T S O P UK 81459 US 34238
MIGUEL FUENTES PERC (J — (G) END OF PHASE ONE — 1978 T S O P UK 81889 US 34658
EVETTE BENTON V (J — (H) M F S B & GAMBLE HUFF ORCHESTRA — 1978 T S O P UK 83010
JOHN L USRY K (J — (J) MYSTERIES OF THE WORLD — 1980 T S O P UK 84251
DENNIS HARRIS G (J
DON RENALDO VLN (J — ZAHMU V (J — CARLTON KENT K (J — DAVID CRUSE PERC (J
MARC RUBIN G (J — ALPHONSO CAREY B (J — QUINTON JOSEPH D (J — STEVE GOLD K (J
DERRICK GRAVES B (J — BILLY JOHNSON D (J — CARLA BENSON V (J — BARBARA INGRAM V (J
LENNY PAKULA K (J — STEVE GREEN B (J — BOB MALACH SAX (J — JOEL BRYANT K (J
JOHN R FAITH FLT (J — LEON HUFF K (J

M3 THE M Gs M3

DONALD DUNN B (A — (A) THE M Gs — 1973 STAX STS 3024
AL JACKSON D (A
BOBBY MANUEL G (A — CARSON WHITSETT K (A

M3A M P G M3A

STEVE CAREY K V (A — (A) M P G — 1981
KIM SMITH G V (A
DAVID MIKEAL G V (A — MICHAEL BOLT D V (A — STEVE LOCKLIN B V (A

M4 MX 80 SOUND M4

BRUCE ANDERSON G (ABC — (A) HARD ATTACK — 1977 ISLAND GER 25539 UK ILPS9529
RICH STIM G K (ABC — (B) OUT OF THE TUNNEL — 1980 RALPH US 8002
DALE SOPHIEA B (ABC — (C) CROWD CONTROL — 1981 RALPH US 8102
JEFF ARMOUR D (A
DAVE MAHONEY D (ABC

M4A MABEL M4A

PETER NILSSON G K (A — (A) ANOTHER FINE MESS — 1977 POLYDOR 2380 050
MIKE KRAMP G (A
ANDY LARSSON G B (A — CHRIS HAVE D (A

M5 WILLIE MABON M5

WILLIE MABON V PNO(ALL — (A) THE COMEBACK — 196 AMERICA AM 6126
MICKEY BAKER G (D — (B) CHICAGO 63 — 1963 AMERICA AM 6136
DAN ARMSTRONG B (D — (C) WILLIE MABON — 19 CHESS US 1439
PETE YORK D (D — (D) COMEBACK — 1973 BIG BEAR BEAR 9
DYAN BIRCH V (D — (E) COLD CHILLY WOMAN — 1975 BLACK & BLUE 33501
COLIN SMITH TPT (D — (F) SHAKE THAT THING — 1975 BLACK & BLUE 33506
BILL WARREN D (EG — (G) SINGS "I DONT KNOW" — 1976 ANTILLES US
ERNEST SUTTON B (AE — (H) CHICAGO BLUES SESSION — 1979 L & R 42 003
JIMMY ROGERS G (F
LOUIS MYERS G (F — DAVE MYERS B (F — FRED BELOW D (F — FRANK COLLINS V (D
JOHNNY BARNES SAX (D — PADDIE McHUGH V (D — EDDY TULEJA G (A — TONY CAHILL D (A
CLIFTON JAMES D (B — WILLIE HUDSON G (B — AL DUNCAN D (B — EARL CROSSLEY SAX (
JOHNNIE CAMERON SAX (B — BILLY THE KID EMERSON K(B — JIMMY RICHARDS B (G — MALCOLM SIMMONS HCA (G
MIGHTY JOE YOUNG G (G — EUGENE PEARSON G (G — HUBERT SUMLIN G (H — EDDIE TAYLOR G (H
AARON BURTON B (H — CASEY JONES D (H

M6 JACKIE McAULEY M6

JACKIE McAULEY V G K(A — (A) JACKIE McAULEY — 1971 DAWN UK DNLS3023 PYE US 3300
MIKE McNAUGHT K (A
HENRY LOWTHER VLN HRNS (A — MIKE TRAVIS D (A — TONY ROBERTS FLT (A — ROY BABBINGTON B (A
PETE HOSSEL JUG (A

M7 DAN McCAFFERTY M7

DAN McCAFFERTY V (A — (A) DAN McCAFFERTY — 1975 MOUNTAIN UK TOPS108 US AM4553
MANNY CHARLTON G (A
HUGH McKENNA K (A — CHRIS MERCER SAX (A — HELEN CHAPPELLE V (A — JOHN PERRY V (A
ZAL CLEMINSON G (A — TED McKENNA D (A — LIZA STRIKE V (A — JOANNE WILLIAMS V (A
ROGER GLOVER B (A — GRAHAM PRESKETT VLN (A — BARRY ST JOHN V (A — TONY RIVERS V (A

M7A NOEL McCALLA M7A

NOEL McCALLA V PERC(A — (A) NIGHT TIME EMOTION — 1979 EPIC UK 83838
TREVOR RABIN G K B(A
PRESTON HEYMAN D (A — NICK PAYN SAX (A — TONY BEARD D (A — VICKI BROWN V (A
CHRIS THOMPSON V (A — DOUG BAINBRIDGE SAX (A — MEL COLLINS SAX (A — JOHN McKENZIE B (A
GRAHAM BROAD D (A — STEVIE LANGE V (A

M8 JIM McCARTHY M8

JIM McCARTHY (A — (A) GUIDE ME TO YOUR LOVE — 1974 ESP US ESP 3008

M9 PAUL McCARTNEY & WINGS M9

PAUL McCARTNEY B V G K (ALL — (A) McCARTNEY — 1970 APPLE UK 7102 US 3363
(A) McCARTNEY — 1979 CBS RI US 36478
LINDA McCARTNEY K V (ALL — (B) RAM — 1971 APPLE UK 10003 US 3375
(B) RAM — 1979 CBS RI US 36479
DENNY LAINE G V K(CDEFGHJKLO — (C) WILD LIFE — 1971 APPLE UK 7142 US 3386
DENNY SEIWELL D (BCD — (D) RED ROSE SPEEDWAY — 1972 APPLE UK 251 US 3409
HENRY McCULLOUGH G (D — (E) BAND ON THE RUN — 1974 APPLE UK 10007 US 3415
JIMMY McCULLOCH G (FGHJ — (E) BAND ON THE RUN — 1974 EMI EURO 05503 US CAPITOL 11901
GEOFF BRITTON D (F — (F) VENUS & MARS — 1975 EMI UK 254 US CAPITOL 11419
JOE ENGLISH D (GHJF — (G) WINGS AT THE SPEED OF SOUND — 1976 EMI UK 10010 US CAPITOL 11525
DAVE MASON G (F — (H) WINGS OVER AMERICA — 1976 EMI UK 720 US CAPITOL 11593
AFRO PERC (F — (J) LONDON TOWN — 1978 EMI UK 10012 US CAPITOL 11777
TONY DORSEY TROM (HG — (K) WINGS GREATEST — 1978 EMI UK 256
HUGH McCRACKEN G (B — (L) BACK TO THE EGG — 1979 PARLOPHONE UK 257 US CBS 36057
THADEUS RICHARD WIND (HG — (M) McCARTNEY 11 — 1980 PARLOPHONE UK 258 US CBS 36511
DAVID SPINOZZA G (B — (N) McCARTNEY INTERVIEW — 1981 EMI UK CHAT1
STEVE HOWARD HRNS (HG — (O) TUG OF WAR — 1982 PARLOPHONE UK 259 US CBS 37642
ALLEN TOUSSAINT K (F
HOWIE CASEY SAX (EH — TOM SCOTT SAX (F — ERIC STEWART G V (O — CARL PERKINS G (O
CAMPBELL MALONY D (O — STEVE GADD D (O — RINGO STARR D (O — ADRIAN SHEPARD D (O
DAVE MATTACKS D (O — GEORGE MARTIN PNO (O — STANLEY CLARKE B (O — STEVIE WONDER V K SYN D(O
ADRIAN BRETT PIPES(O — ANDY McKAY LYRICON(O — JACK ROTHSTEIN VLN (O — BERNARD PARTRIDGE VLN(O
IAN JEWEL VLA (O — KEITH HARVEY CLO (O — JACK BRYMER CLAR (O — STEVE HOLLY D (L
REMI KABAKA PERC (E — LAWRENCE JUBER G (L

M9A BILLY EARL McCLELLAN M9A

BILLY McCLELLAN (A — (A) VERY EARLY — 1978 LECAM 505
(B) ZERO HIND SIGHT — 1981 ELEKTRA US 258

M10 DELBERT McCLINTON M10

DELBERT McCLINTON (ALL — (A) DELBERT & GLEN — 1972 CLEAN US CN6010598
GLEN CLARK (AB — (B) SUBJECT TO CHANGE — 1973 CLEAN US CN6020598
ROGER HAWKINS D (IJ — (C) VICTIM OF LIFE'S CIRCUMSTANCES — 1975 ABC US AB 907
DAVID HOOD B (IJ — (D) GENUINE COWHIDE — 1976 ABC US ABC 959
BARRY BECKETT K (IJ — (E) LOVE RUSTLER — 1977 ABC UK ABCL5217 US AB 991
JIMMY JOHNSON G (IJ — (F) SECOND WIND — 1978 CAPRICORN US CP 0201
BONNIE BRAMLETT V (IJ — (G) VERY EARLY DELBERT McCLINTON — 1978 LECAM US LCS 404A
WAYNE PERKINS G (IJ — (H) KEEPER OF THE FLAME — 1979 CAPRICORN US CP 0223
HARRISON CALLOWAY HRNS (IJ — (I) JEALOUS KIND — 1980 CAPITOL 12115
BILLY SANDERS G (IJ — (J) PLAIN FROM THE HEART — 1981 CAPITOL 12188
ROBERT HARWELL SAX (IJ
AVA AULDRIDGE V (J — LENNY LEBLANC V (IJ — BEN CAULEY TPT (J — LARRY LANGE B (J
REESE WYMANS K (JI — HARVEY THOMPSON HRNS (JI — RONNIE EADES HRNS (IJ — CINDY RICHARDSON V (J
JOHN JARVIS PNO (J — CHARLES ROSE TROM (JI — BARRY FROST D (J — JAMES PENNEBAKER G (J
ERNIE DURAWA PERC (J — RANDY McCORMICK K (I — ROBERT BYRNE V (I — EDDIE STRUZICK V (I
MARY BETH McCLMORE V (I — BOB KRUSEN PERC (I — DICK COOPER PERC (I

M10A MARC McCLURE M10A

MARC McCLURE G PERC K V(A — (A) MARC McCLURE — 1972 CAPITOL US 11113
DAVID VAUGHT B (A
DENNIS DRAGON D (A — CHARLES FINDLEY TROM (A — JOHN SEITER D (A — CHRIS DARROW MAND(A
SPOONER OLDHAM K (A — JIM HORN SAX (A — ROBIN BATTEAU VLN (A — BILL PLUMMER B (A
VINCE DEROSA HRN (A — RON ELLIOTT G (A — DAN LEVITT G BAN(A

M10B DAVID McCLUSKY M10B

DAVID McCLUSKY V (A — (A) A LONG TIME COMING — 1978 GRT 9230 1081
JOHN JARVIS K (A
STEVE LUKATHER G (A — ANDY NEWMARK D (A — BOBBY KIMBALL V (A — FRED MOLLIN V G(A
TOM SZCZESNIAK B (A — BOB MANN G (A — BRIAN RUSSELL G (A — DAN DUGMORE G (A
ERNIE WATTS SAX (A — JIMMY FARAGNER V (A — BOB DISALLE D (A — JIM WYNVEEN G (A
RACHEL PALEMENT (A — LEE SKLAR B (A — JIM HORN SAX (A — MATTHEW McCAULEY V (A
DOUG RILEY K (A — JORN ANDERSEN D (A — JOHN CAPEK K (A — MIKE PORCARO B (A
JEFF PORCARO D (A — HERB PEDERSEN V (A — BOB BOUCHER B (A — JON GOLDSMITH K STR(A

M10C KIRSTY MacCOLL M10C

KIRSTY MacCOLL V (A — (A) DESPERATE CHARACTER — 1981 POLYDOR POLS 1035
LU G (A
BILLY BREMNER G (A — MALCOLM MORLEY G (A — PHIL RAMBOW G (A — NICK 'BAZZA'LOWE PROD G(A
GLYN HAVARD B (A — PAUL RILEY B (A — GAVIN POVEY K (A — LEE PARTISS D (A
BEN MANDELSON FDL (A — LEW LEWIS HCA (A — JOHN EARLE SAX (A — RAY BEAVIS SAX (A
CHRIS GOWER TROM (A — DICK HANSON TPT (A

M11 CHARLIE McCOY M11

CHARLIE McCOY HCA V(ALL — (A) HARPIN' THE BLUES — 1970 MONUMENT UK 69204 US 33802
JIM ISBELL D (FAJK — (A) HARPIN' THE BLUES — 197 MONUMENT US 6629
KENNETH BUTTREY D (AFJK — (B) CHARLIE McCOY — 1972 MONUMENT UK 5034 US 31910
JERRY WHITE D (FA — (B) CHARLIE McCOY — 197 MONUMENT US 6624
KENNY MALONE PERC (AF — (C) REAL McCOY — 1972 MONUMENT US 6623 US 31329
SI EDWARDS PERC (FAJK — (D) GOOD TIME CHARLIE — 1973 MONUMENT US 6625 US 32215
FARRELL MORRIS VIBES(FAJK — (E) FASTEST HARP IN THE SOUTH — 1973 MONUMENT US 6626 US 32749
BUDDY SKIPPER K V CLAR (FAJ — (F) NASHVILLE HIT MAN — 1974 MONUMENT UK 80115 US 6627
GEORGE BINKLEY VLN (F — (G) CHARLIE MY BOY — 1975 MONUMENT US 6628 US 33384
RUSS HICKS STEEL V G (FAJK — (H) CHRISTMAS ALBUM — 197 MONUMENT US 6645 US 33176

(CONTINUED)

M11 (CONTINUED) M11

CHARLIE McCOY

BUDDY SPICHER	FDL	(AF	(I) GREATEST HITS	197 MONUMENT	US	7622
BRENTON BANKS	VLN	(F	(J) PLAY IT AGAIN CHARLIE	197 MONUMENT UK 81559	US	6630
LENNIE HAIGHT	VLN	(F	(K) COUNTRY COOKIN'	1977 MONUMENT UK 82444	US	7612
BERGEN WHITE	V	(F	(L) STONE FOX CHASE	1977 MONUMENT	UK	81886
WENDY SUITS	V	(F	(M) APPALACHIAN FEVER	1979 MONUMENT UK 83516	US	7632
LARRY BUTLER	PNO	(F				

DON SMITH	B	(AFJK	LEON RHODES	B G	(F	JOHNNY GIMBLE	FDL	(FK	BTRON BACH	CELLO	(F			
BOBBY THOMPSON	G BAN	(AFJK	RAY EDENTON	G	(AFJK	HAROLD BRADLEY	G	(FAJK	JIM COLVARD	G	(AF			
JOSH GRAVES	DOBRO	(FAJK	CARL GORODETZKY	VLN	(F	GARY VANOSDALE	VLA	(F	PIG ROBBINS	PNO	(AFJK			
BILLY LINNEMAN	B	(FJ	JOE ZINKAN	B	(F	BOBBY DYSON	B	(FA	STEPHANIE WOOLF	VLN	(F			
MARTHA McCRORY	CELLO	(F	DAVE KIRBY	G	(FJ	CHIP YOUNG	G	(F	BILLY SANFORD	G	(F			
JIMMY WILKERSON	G	(FA	SHELDON KURLAND	VLN	(F	CAROL MONTGOMERY	V	(F	MARVIN CHANTRY	VIOLA	(F			
JOHN PROBST	PNO	(FA	WAYNE MOSS	B	AFJK	JOHNNY JOHNSON	B	(FA	HAL RUGG	STEEL	(F			
STEVE SMITH	VLN	(F	TOMMY ALSUP	G	(F	TERRY DEARMORE	G	(AFJK	FRED NEWELL	G	(FJ			
DALE SELLERS	G	(FA	WELDON MYRICK	STEEL	(FAJK									

M12 M12

VAN McCOY

VAN McCOY	V PNO	(ALL	( ) SOUL IMPROVISATIONS	1972 BUDDAH	US	5103
			(A) DISCO BABY	1975 AVCO	UK	9109 004
ALBERT BAILEY	V	(E	(B) DISCO KID	1975 AVCO	UK	9109 007
DESTRY	V	(E	(C) THE REAL McCOY	1976 H&L	UK	9109 009
ZULEMA	V	(E	(D) THE HUSTLE	1976 H&L	US	69016
BRENDA HILLIARD	V	(E	(E) MY FAVOURITE FANTASY	1978 MCA UK MCF 2843	US	3036
DIANE WILSON	V	(E	(F) LONELY DANCER	19 MCA	US	3071
BERNIE GLOW	TPT	(E	(G) DANCIN'	19 SSS	US	33
URBIE GREEN	TROM	(E	(H) FROM DISCO TO LOVE	19 BUDDAH US 5648	FR MODE	9026
MICKEY GRAVINE	TROM	(E	(J) SWEET RHYTHM	1979 H&L		6467 651
PHIL BODNER	FLT	(E				

BOB ADAMS	D	(E	SKIP FENSELL	K	(E	DAVID CAREY	PERC	(E	ARTHUR JENKINS	PNO	(E
CHARLIE KIPPS	G	(E	CORNELL DUPREE	G	(E	STEVE GADD	D	(E	LEON PENDARVIS	K	(E
PRISCILLA BASKERVILLE	V	(E	MEL DAVIS	TPT	(E	WAYNE ANDRE	TROM	(E	TOM MALONE	TROM	(E
JIM BUFFINGTON	HRNS	(E	DENNIS RICHEY	G D	(E	JAMES FUNCHES	B	(E	PAT REBILLOT	PNO	(E
BERT JONES	G	(E	GORDON EDWARDS	B	(E	RICHARD TEE	PNO	(E	JOHN TROPEA	G	(E
MIKE MAINIERI	PERC	(E	JON FADDIS	TPT	(E	VICTOR PAZ	TPT	(E	BOB ALEXANDER	TROM	(E
PAUL FAULISE	TROM	(E	BROOKS TILLOTSON	HRNS	(E	ARTHUR LISI	K	(E	JON WARE	PERC	(E
STEVE JORDAN	D	(E	CRUSHER BENNETT	PERC	(E	CHRIS PARKER	D	(E	GEORGE DEVENS	PERC	(E
HUGH McCRACKEN	G	(E									

M13 M13

McCOYS

RICK DERRINGER	G V	(ALL	(A) HANG ON SLOOPY	1965 BANG US 212	JOY	JOYS 196
RANDY ZEHRINGER	D	(ALL	(A) HANG ON SLOOPY	196 IMMEDIATE	UK	IMLP 001
RANDY HOBBS	B	(ALL	(B) YOU MAKE ME FEEL SO GOOD	1966 BANG	US	213
BOBBY PETERSON	K	(ALL	(C) INFINITE McCOYS	1968 MERCURY US 21128	US	61163
PETE DRAKE	STEEL	(D	(D) HUMAN BALL	1968 MERCURY	US	61207
DICK HALLIGAN	TROM	(C	(EP) McCOYS	1966 IMMEDIATE	UK	MEP002
FRED LIPSIUS	SAX	(C	(EP) McCOYS 2	196 IMMEDIATE	UK	MEP003
RANDY BRECKER	TPT	(C				
JERRY WEISS	TPT	(C				

M13A M13A

JIMMY McCRACKLIN

JIMMY McCRACKLIN	PNO V	(ALL	MY ANSWER	19 IMPERIAL	US	LP 12306
DAVID BLUNSTON	PNO	(	EVERYNIGHT EVERYDAY	19 IMPERIAL	US	LP 12285
JOHN HENRY	B	(	THINK	19 IMPERIAL	US	LP 12297
ALRAY KIDD	D	(	I JUST GOTTA KNOW	19 IMPERIAL	US	LP 12219
ROBERT KELTON	G	(	JIMMY McCRACKLIN SINGS	19 CHESS	US	LP 1464
LITTLE RED	D	(	LETS GET TOGETHER	19 MINIT	US	LP 24011
JOE CONWRIGHT	SAX	(	NEW SOUL OF	19 IMPERIAL	US	LP 12316
CHARLES SUTTER	SAX	(	(H) TWIST WITH	19 CROWN US CLP5244	US CUSTOM	2057
LAFAYETTE THOMAS	G	(H	ROCKIN' MAN	19 ROUTE 66	SWED	KIX 12
SAN FRISCO JEFF	D	(	AND HIS BLUESBLASTERS	1981 ACE		CH 28
JOHNNY PARKER	SAX	(	BEST OF	19 MINIT	US	24009
			YESTERDAY IS GONE	1972 STAX	US	2047
			SINGER MAN	19 MINIT	US	24017
			MY ROCKIN SOUL	19 UNITED	US	7719

M14 M14

MARY McCREARY

MARY McCREARY	V	(AB	(A) JEZEBEL	1973 SHELTER		US 2110
			(B) BUTTERFLIES IN HEAVEN	1975 MCA	US	347

M15 M15

HENRY McCULLOUGH

HENRY McCULLOUGH	G V	(A	(A) MIND YOUR OWN BUSINESS	1975 DARK HORSE	UK	AMLH22005
ALAN SPENNER	B	(A				

STEVE CHAPMAN	D	(A	MICK WEAVER	K	(A	JOHN HALSEY	D	(A	LLOYD SMITH	SAX	(A
NEIL HUBBARD	G	(A	CHARLIE HARRISON	B	(A	TIM HINKLEY	K	(A	FRANKIE MILLER	V	(A
LIONEL KINGHAM	SAX	(A	BRUCE ROWLAND	D	(A	JIM LEVERTON	B	(A	JOE O'DONNELL	VLN	(A
HERSCHEL HOLDER	TPT	(A	JOHN JANSEN	PROD	(A						

M15A M15A

LENNIE McDONALD

LENNIE McDONALD	G V	(A	(A) HARD ROAD	1975 ARISTA	UK	ARTY 117
ALAN TARNEY	B	(A				

MIKE GILES	D	(A	CLIFF HALL		(A	CHRIS RAINBOW	PERC V	(A	MIKE BARKER	G	(A
RAY JACKSON	HCA	(A	WILF GIBSON	VLN	(A	DARRELL RUNSWICK	B STR	(A	DENNIS LOPEZ	PERC	(A
MEL COLLINS	SAX	(A	GORDON HUNTLEY	STEEL	(A	KOKOMO SINGERS		(A	LONDON CHAMBER CHOIR		(A

M16 M16

KATHI McDONALD

KATHI McDONALD	V	(A	(A) INSANE ASYLUM	1974 CAPITOL	US	ST 11224
NILS LOFGREN	G	(A				

PETE SEARS	G B K	(A	BOBBYE HALL	PERC	(A	RONNIE MONTROSE	G	(A	GREG DOUGLAS	G	(A
NEAL SCHON	G	(A	MARK UNOBSKI	G	(A	PAPA JOHN CREACH	FDL	(A	JIM McPHERSON	B	(A
JOHN CIPPOLLINA	G	(A	GARY PHILIPPET	G	(A	BOOTS HOUSTON	HRNS	(A	AYNSLEY DUNBAR	D	(A
TOWER OF POWER	HRNS	(A	SLY STONE	V	(A	POINTER SISTERS	V	(A			

M16A MICHAEL McDONALD M16A

MICHAEL McDONALD K V (A — (A) IF THATS WHAT IT TAKES — 1982 WB US 23703
STEVE GADD D (A
JEFF PORCARO D (A WILLIE WEEKS B (A LOUIS JOHNSON B (A MIKE PORCARO B (A
DEAN PARKS G (A STEVE LUKATHER G (A ROBBEN FORD G (A EDGAR WINTER SAX (A
TOM SCOTT SAX (A LENNY CASTRO PERC (A BOBBY LAKIND PERC (A PAULINHO DACOSTA PERC(A
TED TEMPLEMAN PERC (A GREG PHILLINGANES K (A MICHAEL O'MARTIAN K (A ED SANFORD V (A
MAUREEN McDONALD V (A KENNY LOGGINS V (A AMY HOLLAND V (A MICHAEL BODDICKER SYN(A

M17 RALPH MACDONALD M17

RALPH MACDONALD PERC (ALL — (A) SOUND OF A DRUM — 1976 MARLIN US 2202+ XL XL14030
GROVER WASHINGTON JR SAX(ABC — (B) THE PATH — 1978 MARLIN UA 2210+ TK TKR82515
CHUCK RAINEY B (AB — (C) COUNTERPOINT — 1979 TK UK TKR83373
ERIC GALE G B (ABC
RICHARD TEE PNO (ABC ARTHUR JENKINS K (ABC DAVID FRIEDMAN VIBES(AB CLINTON THOBOURNE CLAR(AB
JOE FARRELL HRNS (A JIMMY OWENS HRNS (A PATTI AUSTIN V (AB RAYMOND SIMPSON V (A
RICK MAROTTA D (AB WILLIAM EATON V (A NICHOLAS MARRERO PERC (AB URIAS FRITZ BOTTLE(A
SELDON POWELL HRNS (A VERGIL JONES HRNS (A ZACHARY SANDERS V (AC GWEN GUTHRIE V (AB
JEAN THIELEMANS HCA (AB BOB JAMES SYN (AB WILLIAM SALTER B (AB HAROLD VICK HRNS (AC
KIANE ZAWADI HRNS (A VIVIAN CHERRY V (A FRANK FLOYD V (AC STEVE GADD D (BC
HARVEY MASON D (C ROBERT GREENIDGE PERC (C MICHAEL BRECKER HRNS (CB RANDY BRECKER HRNS (CB
BARRY ROGERS HRNS (CB JOE BROWN B PERC (C WILL LEE B (CB TOM SCOTT WIND (C
JON FADDIS HRNS (C RON CUBER HRNS (C DAVE SANBORN HRNS (CB KEN WILLIAMS V (C
HOWARD JOHNSON HRNS (C TOM MALONE HRNS (C STRING SECTION (ABC

M18 COUNTRY JOE McDONALD & THE FISH M18

JOE McDONALD G HCA C G(ALL — (A) ELECTRIC MUSIC FOR THE MIND — 1967 VANGUARD US VSD 79244 UK SVRL19026
JOHN LEHMAN V (W — (A) ELECTRIC MUSIC FOR THE MIND — 1967 FONTANA UK STFL 6081
BARRY MELTON G (ABCGIXb — (B) I FEEL LIKE I'M FIXIN TO DIE — 1967 VANGUARD US VSD 79266 UK SVRL19029
DAVID COHEN K (ABCIXb — (B) I FEEL LIKE I'M FIXIN TO DIE — 1967 FONTANA UK STFL 6087
BRUCE BARTHOL B HCA(ABCQIXb — (C) TOGETHER — 1968 VANGUARD US VSD 79277 UK SVRL19006
CHICKEN HIRSH D (ABIJX — (D) HERE WE ARE AGAIN — 1969 VANGUARD US VSD79299 UK STVL19048
DAVID GETZ D (M — (E) THINKING OF WOODY GUTHRIE — 1969 VANGUARD US VSD 6546 UK VRL 19057
PETER ALBIN B (M — ( ) GREATEST HITS — 1969 VANGUARD US VSD 6545 UK SVRL19058
JEFF PORCARO D (W — (F) TONIGHT I'M SINGING FOR YOU — 1970 VANGUARD US VSD 6557 UK 6359 004
MIKE PORCARO B (W — (G) C J FISH — 1970 VANGUARD US VSD 6555 UK 6359 002
MAC CRIDLIN B (WZ — (H) QUIET DAY IN CLICHY — 1971 SONET UK SNTF 622
STEVE MADAIO HRNS (QWX — (I) FROM ASHBURY TO WOODSTOCK (DBL) — 1971 VANGUARD VSD 27/28
JAY GRAYDON G (WZ — (J) HOLD ON ITS COMING — 1971 VANGUARD US VSD 79314
JOHN BLAKELEY G (WQZ — (K) WAR WAR WAR — 1971 VANGUARD US VSD 79315
DAVID FOSTER K (W — (L) INCEDIBLE LIVE — 1972 VANGUARD US VSD 79316
BILL CUOMO K (W — (M) PARIS SESSIONS — 1973 VANGUARD US VSD 79328
MICHAEL BODDIKER K (W — (O) THE BEST OF — 1973 VANGUARD US VSD 79000 UK SVRL19058
CHILI CHARLES D (W — (P) COUNTRY JOE — 1975 VANGUARD US VSD 79348
STEPHANIE SPRUILL V (W — (Q) PARADISE WITH AN OCEAN VIEW — 1975 FANTASY US 9495 UK FTA 3002
CARL SHRAGER (b — (Q) PARADISE WITH AN OCEAN VIEW — 1975 BELLAPHON GER 19225
MARTI McCALL V (W — (R) THE ESSENTIAL (DBL) — 1976 VANGUARD VSD 85/86
LISA ROBERTS V (W — (T) LOVE IS A FIRE — 1976 FANTASY US 9511 UK FTA 3005
JAN JOYCE V (W — (U) GOLDEN HOUR — 1977 PYE UK GH 865
JIM GILSTRAP V (QW — (V) GOODBYE BLUES — 1977 FANTASY US 9525 UK FT 529
PETE WALSH V B (VWZ — (W) ROCK'N'ROLL FROM PLANET EARTH — 1978 FANTASY US 9544 UK FT 539
BILL STEEL (b — (W) ROCK'N'ROLL FROM PLANET EARTH — 1978 BELLAPHON GER 2553
ROGER KENERLY SAINT V (W — (X) REUNION — 1977 FANTASY US 9530
PAUL ARMSTRONG PERC (b — (X) REUNION — 1977 BELLAPHON GER 2534
ANDREA ROBINSON V (W — (Y) TRIBUTE TO WOODY — 19 WB US 2W 3007
CHUCK FINDLEY HRNS (W — (Z) LEISURE SUITE — 1979 FANTASY US 9586 UK FT 565
JOHN MITCHELL HRNS (W — (a) ON MY OWN — 1980 RAG BABY US 147 406
TREVOR LAWRENCE HRNS (QW — (b) COLLECTORS ITEM(FIRST 3 EPs) — 1980 RAG BABY UK 1008
MIKE BEARDSLEE V (b — (c) EARLY YEARS — 1981 PICCADILLY US 33091
JOHN GUNNING D (b
NACHO DEWEY HCA (b SAROD ASHISH KHAN TAMB (W GREG DEWEY D (GJIb DOUG METZNER B (GI
MARK KAPNER K (GI DAVID HAYES B (QZ PETER MILIO D (QV TED ASHFORD K (QV
STEVE GABOURY PNO (Q VANETTA FIELDS V (Q SALLY STEVENS V (Q MARLEENA JETTER V (Q
SID SHARP STRING(Q PHIL MARSH G (MQ BOBBY KEYS SAX (QX CARLENA WILLIAMS V (Q
MAXINE ANDERSON V (Q AUGIE JOHNSON V (Q RON MARABUTO D (Q JOHNNY ROTELLA SAX (Q
SHIRLEY MATTHEWS V (Q MICHAEL IRWIN V (Q GERALD GARRETT V (Q RICHARD CORSELLO G (Z
SCOTT LAWRENCE PNO (Z GREG DOUGLAS G (Z JIM HOBSON PNO (Z HERB JIMMERSON SYN (Z
TIP WIRRICK G (Z CHUCK DAY G (Z VIC SMITH B (bJ DAHUD SHAAR D (Z
BOB KINGSON B (Z JEFFREY MEYER D (Z MICHAEL HERBICK D (Z KELVIN DIXON D (Z
PERSUASIONS V (Z FISCHLERS V (Z BILL COLLINS V (Z DANIEL GUNNIP V (Z
BOBBI VANDERVOORT V (Z DAVID GUNNIP V (Z SEBASTIAN CONG(M JOHN REWIND G (Mb
DIANE RASCONIA V (Z DAVID BROMBERG G (V JERRY CORBITT V (V NATHAN RUBIN VLN (V
MALVINA REYNOLDS V (V BILL SUMMERS PERC (V MARTY BALIN V (V ANNE RIZZO STEEL V (VMb
TERRY ADAMS CELLO(V DOROTHY MISKOWITZ V PNO(M TUCKI BAILEY WIND (M JOHN VIERRA SYN (M
RICHARD SUSSMAN K (bJ PETER KRUG G V (b PAUL ARMSTRONG REC (I CARVEL BASS G (I
PEREGRINE PICKLE B (I MARK RYAN B (I JOHN FRANCIS GUNNING D (I ROBIN McDONALD PERC(I
GRADY MARTIN G SIT (EF ALEX DMOCHOWSKI B (J SPENCER DAVIS G V HCA(J RAY EDENTON G (EF
NORBERT PUTNAM B (EF HAROLD BRADLEY G B (EF HARGUS ROBBINS PNO (EF BUDDY HARMON D (EF
THE JORDANARIRES V (F PHIL KAFFEL PERC V (JOHN FULLER HARP (V NICK BUCK PNO(J
ROCKHEAD G (J ED BOGAS VLN (J JOHN HUG G (T SIDI SIDDY D (J
ERIC WEISSBERG B (J JOHN BLAKELEY G (T JAYDEE MANESS STEEL(T DAVID HAYES (T
RALPH WASH G (T TED ASHFORD (T JIM GORDON D (T JIM ED NORMAN PNO (T
MAGGI PAYNE WIND (V CARL PEDERSEN VLN (V JOHN OTIS CONGA(X SAM CHARTERS JUG (X
JIM PRICE HRNS (X

M19 SHELAGH McDONALD M19

SHELAGH McDONALD G V K(AB — (A) SHELAGH McDONALD — 1970 B & C CAS 1019
JOHN RYAN B (B — (B) STARGAZER — 1971 B & C CAS 1043
DANNY THOMPSON B (B
KEITH CHRISTMAS G (AB HARVEY BURNS D (B RAY WARLEIGH SAX (B IAN WHITEMAN K (AB
DAVE RICHARDS B (B KATHY KISSOON V (B MAC KISSOON V (B MIKE LONDON V (B
RICHARD THOMPSON G (B DAVE MATTACKS D (B PAT DONALDSON B (AB ANDY ROBERTS G (A
ROGER POWELL D (A KEITH TIPPETT PNO (A GERRY CONWAY D (A MIKE EVANS B (A
GORDON HUNTLEY STEEL(A TRISTAN FRY VIBES(A

M20 ## McDONALD & GILES M20

IAN McDONALD K SAX(A — (A) McDONALD & GILES — 1970 ISLAND UK ILPS 9126
MIKE GILES D (A — (A) McDONALD & GILES — 1977 POLYDOR UK 2302 070
MICHAEL BLAKESLEY TROM (A — (A) McDONALD & GILES — 197 COTILLION US 9042
PETER GILES B (A
STEVE WINWOOD (A STRINGS (A

M20A ## MACEO M20A

(A) US 1974 PEOPLE US PE6601 UK POLYDOR 2391122

M21 ## KATE & ANNA McGARRIGLE M21

KATE McGARRIGLE K V G BAN(ALL — (A) KATE & ANNA McGARRIGLE — 1975 WB US BS2862 UK K 56218
ANNA McGARRIGLE V K BAN(ALL — (B) DANCER WITH BRUISED KNEES — 1977 WB US BS3014 UK K 56356
TONY LEVIN B (AC — (C) PRONTO MONTO — 1978 WB US BS3248 UK K 56561
STEPHEN GADD D (ABC — (D) KATE & ANNA McGARRIGLE — 1980 ISLAND UK 9654
TREVOR LAWRENCE G (A
DAVID SPINOZZA G (AC GREG PRESTOPINO G V K(A BOBBY KEYS SAX (A TONY RICE G (A
JOEL TEPP CLAR HCA (A DAVID GRISMAN MAND (A RED CALLENDER B (A AMOS GARRETT G (A
JANIE McGARRIGLE-DOW V K(AB PETER WELDON V HCA BAN(ABC DANE LANKEN V (ABC CHAIM TANNENBAUM V G HCA(ABC
JAY UNGAR FDL (AB FLOYD GILBEAU FDL (A ANDREW GOLD G (A DENSIL LANG PERC(A
PLAS JOHNSON WIND (A RUSS KUNKEL D (A NICK DECARO ACC (A DIMMY DIMBUSTER PERC(A
SCOT LANG G (A JOHN CALE K (A MIKE VISCIGLIA B (B GRADY TATE D (BC
TOMMY MORGAN HCA (B RICHARD DAVIS B (B PAT DONALDSON B (BC DAVE MATTACKS D (B
KENNY PEARSON K (BC WARREN SMITH PERC (B RON DOLEMAN VLN (B SUSAN EVANS PERC(BC
GORDIE FLEMING ACC (B GILLES LOSIER B (B ANDREW COWAN G (B GEORGE BOHANON HRNS(AB
LOWELL GEORGE G (A HUGH McCRACKEN G V (B JEFF MIRANOV G (C JERRY DONAHUE G (C
GEORGE YOUNG CLAR (C BOB GLAUB B (C VICTOR FELDMAN PERC (C BRYAN CUMMING SAX (C
GEORGE DEVENS PERC (C BERNARD PURDIE D (C GORDON EDWARDS B (C JOHN SCHOLLE G (C
MICHAEL MOORE B (C FREEBO TUBA (C DAVID NICHTERN B (C DAVID WOODFORD SAX (C
KEN KOSEK FDL (C GARY MALLABER D (C GARY MURE (MICHAEL SMALL V (A

M22 ## MISSISSIPPI FRED McDOWELL M22

MISSISSIPPI FRED McDOWELL G V(ALL — (A) MISSISSIPPI DELTA BLUES — 1964 ARHOOLIE US F1021
MIKE RUSSO G (E — (A) MISSISSIPPI DELTA BLUES — 19 POLYDOR UK 2460 193
JOHN KAHN B (E — (B) MY HOME IS IN THE DELTA — 1964 TESTAMENT US 2208
BOB JONES D (E — (C) AMAZING GRACE — 1964 TESTAMENT US 2219
FANNIE DAVIS (— (D) MISSISSIPPI DELTA BLUES VOL 2 — 1966 ARHOOLIE US F 1027
MILES PRATCHER (— (E) & HIS BLUES BOYS — 19 ARHOOLIE US F 1046
ANNIE MAE McDOWELL V (ABC — (F) LONDON 1 — 1970 TRANSATLANTIC UK TRA 194
(F) LONDON 1 — 1970 SIRE US 97018
ELI GREEN V (D — ( ) LONDON 2 — 19 TRANSATLANTIC UK TRA 203
( ) LONG WAY FROM HOME — 19 CBS UK 63735 MILESTONE US 93003
( ) & FURRY LEWIS — 19 BIOGRAPH BLP 12017
( ) KEEP YOUR LAMP TRIMMED — 19 ARHOOLIE US F1068
( ) I DONT PLAY NO ROCK'N' ROLL — 19 CAPITOL US 409
( ) 1904 72 — 1974 XTRA UK XTRA 1136
( ) MISSISSIPPI FRED McDOWELL — 19 EVEREST US 253
( ) LIVE IN NEW YORK — 19 OBLIVION US OBL1
( ) SOMEBODY KEEPS CALLIN' ME — 19 ANTILLES US 7022
( ) MISSISSIPPI FRED McDOWELL — 19 ARC FOLK US 253
( ) BLUES ROLL ON — 19 ATLANTIC US 590025
( ) GOING DOWN SOUTH — 1970 POLYDOR US 2365

M23 ## MIKE McGEAR M23

MIKE McGEAR V (AB — (A) WOMAN — 1972 ISLAND UK ILPS 9191
ZOOT MONEY K (A — (B) McGEAR — 1974 WB US 2825 UK K 56051
JOHN MEGGINSON K (A
NORMAN YARDLEY HCA (A CHRIS PYNE HRNS (A MALCOLM DUNCAN HRNS (A PAUL KORDA V (A
GINGER JOHNSON PERC (A DENNY LAINE G V (B PADDY MOLONEY PIPES(B ANDY ROBERTS G (A
DAVE RICHARDS B (A GERRY CONWAY D (AB CENTIPEDE STRINGS (A CECIL MOSS HRNS(A
MIKE ROSEN HRNS (A ROGER BALL HRNS (A TONY COE SAX (AB ALAN GORRIE V (A
STEVE GOULD V (A BRIAN AUGER K (A LINDA McCARTNEY V K (B JIMMY McCULLOCH G (B
BRIAN JONES SAX (B DENNY SEIWELL D (B

M24 ## DONNA McGHEE M24

DONNA McGHEE (A — (A) MAKE IT LAST FOREVER — 1978 ANCHOR UK ANCL 2027

M25 ## ROGER McGOUGH M25

ROGER McGOUGH V (A — (A) A SUMMER WITH MONIKA — 1978 ISLAND UK ILPS 9551
PAT DONALDSON B (A
JOHN MEGGINSON K (A DAVE OLNEY B (A TIMI DONALD D (A JACK EMBLOW ACC (A
DAVE LAWSON SYN (A ZOOT MONEY K (A ANDY ROBERTS G (A

M25A ## BAT McGRATH M25A

BAT McGRATH (ABC — (A) ANTRODUCING — 19 EPIC US 26499
(B) FROM THE BLUE EAGLE — 1977 AMHERST US 1005
DON ETHAN POTTER G (— (C) THE SPY — 1978 AMHERST US 1011

M26 ## JIMMY McGRIFF M26

JIMMY McGRIFF ORG(ALL — (A) CHERRY — 196 SOLID STATE US SM 17006
ERIC GALE G (A — (B) THE BIG BAND — 1968 SOLID STATE US LAS 1800
ALLAN SCHWARZBERG D (R — ( ) BAG FULL OF SOUL — 196 SOLID STATE US 18002
GRADY TATE D (A — (C) ELECTRIC FUNK — 19 BLUENOTE US BST 84350
MILT HINTON B (A — (D) SOMETHING TO LISTEN TO — 19 BLUENOTE US BST 84364
EVERETT BARKSDALE G (A — (E) BLACK PEARL — 19 BLUENOTE US BST 84374
GROOVE HOLMES K (KP — (F) GOOD THING DONT HAPPEN.... — 1973 GROOVEMERCHANT US GM 2205
O'DONEL LEVY G (K — (G) GROOVE GREASE — 19 GROOVEMERCHANT US GM 503
GEORGE FREEMAN G (K — (H) BLACK & BLUES — 19 GROOVEMERCHANT US GM 2203
BERNARD PURDIE D (K — (H) BLACK & BLUES — 19 PEOPLE PLEO 501
LARRY FRAZIER (I — (I) ORGAN & BLUES BAND — 1968 SOLID STATE US 18052
BUB ASHTON (I — () BAG FULL OF BLUES — 1968 SOLID STATE US 18017
BOBBY CRANSHAW B (N — ( ) IVE GOT A NEW WOMAN — 1968 SOLID STATE US 18030
RICHARD MITCHELL (I — ( ) HONEY — 1968 SOLID STATE US 18036
DON TURNER (I — ( ) THINGS TO COME — 1969 SOLID STATE US 18060
LAWRENCE KILLIAN PERC (N — ( ) WORM — 1969 SOLID STATE US 18045
KWASI JAYOURBA CONGA(K — (J) FLYDUDE — 1974 GROOVEMERCHANT US GM 509
ERNEST JONES SYN (N — (J) FLYDUDE — 1974 PEOPLE PLEO 14
LEO JOHNSON SAX (N — (K) COME TOGETHER — 1974 GROOVEMERCHANT US GM 520
JIMMY PONDER G (RSN — (K) COME TOGETHER — 1974 PEOPLE PLEO 16
JESSE MORRISON SAX (N — (L) LETS STAY TOGETHER — 1974 PEOPLE PLEO 19

M26 (CONTINUED) **JIMMY McGRIFF** M26

FATS THEVS (I — (L) LETS STAY TOGETHER — 1974 GROOVEMERCHANT US 5000
JOE THOMAS SAX (N — (M) IF YOU'RE READY — 1974 PEOPLE PLEO 23
JESSE KIRKPATRICK (I — (M) IF YOU'RE READY — 1974 GROOVEMERCHANT US 529
RALPH BYRD G (N — (N) STUMP JUICE — 1975 GROOVEMERCHANT US GM 3309
ANDREW McCLOUD B (N — (O) FLYIN' TIME — 19 GROOVEMERCHANT US GM 4403
JR PARKER (F — ( ) MAIN SQUEEZE — 1976 GROOVEMERCHANT US 534
HANK CRAWFORD SAX (S — ( ) MEAN MACHINE — 1976 GROOVEMERCHANT US 3311
NEIL JASON B (S — (P) GIANT OF THE ORGAN — 19 GROOVEMERCHANT US GM 3300
JEFF MIRANOV G (S — (Q) SUPA COOKIN' — 19 GROOVEMERCHANT US GM 4409
BARRY MILES K (S — (R) TAIL GUNNER — 1977 L R C LRC 9316
JIMMY YOUNG D (RS — (S) OUTSIDE LOOKIN' IN — 1978 L R C LRC 9330
RON ZITO D (RS
PAT REBILLOT K (RS — FRANCISCO CENTENO B (R — JERRY FRIEDMAN G (R — JIMMY MAELEN PERC (RS
LEW DELGATTO HRNS (RS — EDDIE DANIELS HRNS (RS — GEORGE YOUNG HRNS (R — ALAN RUBIN HRNS (R
RANDY BRECKER HRNS (R — JACK FROSK HRNS (R — MARVIN STAMM HRNS (R — JOE SHEPLEY HRNS (R
DAVE TAYLOR HRNS (R — DOMINIC MENARDO HRNS (R — BARRY ROGERS HRNS (R — JOE RANDAZZO HRNS (R
PAUL GRIFFIN K (R — RALPH SCHUCKETT K (R — BOB BABITT B (RS — WILL LEE B (R
LANCE QUINN G (RS — RUBENS BASSINI PERC (R — AL DOWNING V (R — DENISE WOOTEN V (R
PATRICIA JOHNSON V (R

M27 **ROGER McGUINN** M27

ROGER McGUINN G V B(ALL — (A) ROGER McGUINN — 1973 CBS US 31946 UK 65274
BUDDY EMMONS STEEL(A — (B) PEACE ON YOU — 1974 CBS US 32956 UK 80171
BRUCE JOHNSTON PNO (A — (C) ROGER McGUINN & HIS BAND — 1975 CBS US 33341 UK 80877
DAVID CROSBY G V (A — (D) CARDIFF ROSE — 1976 CBS US 34154 UK 81369
JOHN GUERIN D (A — (E) THUNDERBYRDS — 1977 CBS US 34656 UK 81883
DAVID VAUGHT B (A — (1) THUNDERBYRDS 1976 (2) UK TOUR 1974 AUG
LELAND SKLAR B (AB
JIM GORDON D (A — JERRY COLE G (A — CHRIS ETHRIDGE B (A — SPOONER OLDHAM K (A
SPANKY McFARLANE V (A — HAL BLAINE D (A — BOB DYLAN HCA (A — CHRIS HILLMAN B (A
MICHAEL CLARKE D (A — CHARLES LLOYD SAX (A — GENE CLARK V (A — JIMMY JOYCE CHILDRENS CHOIR(A
RICK VITO G (E — GREG THOMAS D (E — CHARLIE HARRISON B (E — MICK RONSON G V K(D
ROB STONER B V (D — HOWIE WYETH D (D — TIM SCHMIT V (D — RICHARD BOWDEN (2
JAMES SMITH G (1 — MARTY GREBB K (E — JANIS OLIVER V (E — DAVID MANSFIELD G K (D
KIM HUTCHCROFT SAX (D — GREG ATTAWAY (2C — DAVID LOVELACE (2C — STEVE LOVE B (2C
BRUCE BARLOW B (1E — LANCE DICKERSON D (1 — TOM SCOTT SAX (E — JENNIFER O'NEILL V (E
KRISTINE OLIVER V (E — STEVE FORMAN PERC (E — JOHN BOYLAN PROD (C — RUSS KUNKEL D (B
PAUL HARRIS K (B — DONNIE DACUS G V (B — DAN FOGELBERG G V (B — AL PERKINS STEEL(B
AL KOOPER K G (B — MARK VOLMAN V (B — HOWARD KAYLAN V (B

M28 **McGUINN HILLMAN /CLARK** M28

ROGER McGUINN G V (ABC — (A) McGUINN,HILLMAN & CLARK — 1979 CAPITOL 11910
CHRIS HILLMAN V G B(ABC — (B) CITY — 1980 CAPITOL EURO 86075 12043
GENE CLARK V (AB — (C) McGUINN , HILLMAN — 1980 CAPITOL EURO 86237 US 12108
JOE LALA PERC (AC
DONNA RHODES V (A — GREG THOMAS D (A — PAUL HARRIS K (A — SANDRA CHALMERS V (A
GEORGE TERRY G (A — JOHN SAMBARATO G V (ABC — CHARLES CHALMERS V (A — SCOTT KIRKPATRICK D V(BC
CHUCK CRANE G (B — SKIP EDWARDS K STEEL (B — WAYNE PERKINS G (C — BARRY BECKETT K (C

M29 **McGUINNESS FLINT** M29

TOM McGUINNESS G B V(ABCDEF — (A) McGUINNESS FLINT — 1971 CAPITOL US SMAS625 UK EST 22625
HUGH FLINT D V (ABCDEF — (B) HAPPY BIRTHDAY RUTHIE BABY — 1971 CAPITOL ST 22794
DENNIS COULSON K G V(ABC — (C) LO & BEHOLD — 1972 DJM UK DJLPS 424 SIRE US SAS 7405
BENNY GALLAGHER V G (AB — (D) RAINBOW — 1973 BRONZE UK ILPS 9244 UK RI 87330
GRAHAM LYLE V G (AB — (E) CEST LA VIE — 1974 BRONZE UK ILPS 9302
DIXIE DEAN V B K(CDE — (F) GREATEST HITS — 197 SOUNDS SUPERB UK SPR 80537
LOU STONEBRIDGE HCA G V K(DE
JIM EVANS STEEL FDL G (DE — PAUL RUTHERFORD HRNS (AC — NICKY HOPKINS K (B — JOHN MUMFORD (B
JIMMY JEWELL SAX (B — MIKE HUGG K (C — HARRY BECKETT TPT (C

M30 **BARRY McGUIRE** M30

BARRY McGUIRE V G B(ALL — (A) EVE OF DESTRUCTION — 1965 DUNHILL US 50003 UK ABC ABCL 5110
MICHAEL CLARKE D (D — (A) EVE OF DESTRUCTION — 19 RCA UK RD 7751
ERIC HORD G V (D — (B) THIS PRECIOUS TIME — 1966 DUNHILL US 50005 UK
CHRIS HILLMAN B (D — (C) WORLDS LAST PRIVATE CITIZEN — 1968 DUNHILL US 50033
BERNIE LEADON G (D — (D) BARRY McGUIRE & THE DOCTOR — 1971 ODE US 77004 UK A&M AMLS 2008
ROCKIE HILTON G (D — (E) SEEDS — 1974 MYRRH US 6519 UK MYRRH 1006
BILLY MUNDI D (D — (F) NARNIA — 1974 MYRRH UK 1007
BYRON BERLINE FDL (D — (G) LIGHTEN UP — 1975 MYRRH US 6531 UK MYRRH 1020
SNEAKY PETE KLEINOW STEEL(D — (H) TO THE BRIDE — 1976 MYRRH US 6548 UK MYRRH 1044
RILEY WILDFLOWER B (D — (I) EVE OF DESTRUCTION MAN — 197 EMBER UK EMB 3362
NICKY WOODS PERC (D — (J) C'MON ALONG — 1976 SPARROW UK BIRD 105
MERLE BOATMAN D (D — (K) HAPPY ROADS — 19 DJM UK DJM 22071
LARRY KNECHTAL B (A — (L) HAVE YOU HEARD — 1976 SPARROW BIRD 3+ BIRD 111
HAL BLAINE D (A — (M) COSMIC COWBOY — 1979 SPARROW UK BIRD 117
STEVE BARRI PERC (A — ( ) INSIDE OUT — 1980 SPARROW 112
P F SLOAN G (A — (N) JUBILATION — 19 MYRRH US 6555
TOMMY TEDESCO G (A — (O) JUBILATION TOO — 19 MYRRH US 6568
LEW ADLER PROD (A — (P) BARRY McGUIRE ALBUM — 19 HORIZON US 1636 US MIRA US 3000
(Q) FINER THAN GOLD — 1981 SPARROW 132

M30A **MACHIAVEL** M30A

MARIO GUCCIO V (A — (A) MECHANICAL MOONBEAMS — 1978 EMI HARVEST EURO 064 23805
ROLAND DE GREEF B (A — (B) NEW LINES — 1980 HARVEST EURO 064 23980
MARC YSAYE D V (A
ALBERT LETECHEUR K (A — JEAN PAUL DEVAUBE G (A

M30B **MACHINES** M30B

(EP) MACHINES — 19 WAX EAR1

M31A **ELLEN McILWAINE** M31A

ELLEN McILWAINE G V (ABC — (A) HONKY TONK ANGEL — 19 POYLDOR US 5021
DON PAYNE B (B — (B) WE THE PEOPLE — 19 POLYDOR US 5044
DON MOORE B (A — (C) THE REAL ELLEN McILWAINE — 19 KOT'AI US 3306
JIMMY MADISON D (B
JERRY MERCER D (B — COLIN TILTON SAX (A — CANDIDO CONGA(A

M31B JIMMIE MACK M31B

JIMMIE MACK (AB — (A) JIMMIE MACK 19 BIG TREE US 76007
(B) ON THE CORNER 1979 BIG TREE US 76014

M32 LONNIE MACK M32

LONNIE MACK G V (ALL — (A) THE WHAM OF THE MEMPHIS MAN 1964 FRATERNITY US 1014
WAYNE BULLOCK K B (AF — (A) THE WHAM " " " " 1967 PRESIDENT US PTL 1004
TRUMAN FIELDS K (A — (A) FOR COLLECTORS ONLY (THE WHAM) 1970 ELEKTRA US EKS74077
RON GRAYSON D (AC — (A) THE WHAM 1973 ELEKTRA UK K 42056
MARV LIEBERMAN SAX (A — (B) GLAD I'M IN THE BAND 1969 ELEKTRA US 74040 UK K 42025
IRV RUSSOTTO SAX (A — (C) WHATEVER'S RIGHT 1969 ELEKTRA US 74050 UK K 42031
BILL JONES B (A — (D) THE HILLS OF INDIANA 1972 ELEKTRA US 74102 UK K 42097
DAVID BYRD K (AC — (E) HOME AT LAST 1977 CAPITOL US 11619
TIM DRUMMOND B (CFD — (F) LONNIE MACK WITH PISMO 1978 CAPITOL US 11703
IAN WALLACE D (F
TROY SEALS V (FD — DAVID LINDLEY G (F — BEN KEITH STEEL(F — DAVID BRIGGS K (FD
BILLY McINTOSH (F — STAN SZELESTE K (F — TERRY ADAMS CELLO(F — GRAHAM NASH V (F
TIMOTHY HEDDING ORG (C — DENZIL RICE PNO (C — JERRY LOVE D (C — RUSTY YORK HCA(C
JACK BRICKLES HCA (C — ROY CHRISTIANSEN CELLO(C — SHIRLEY MATTHEWS SINGERS(C — Mt ZION SINGERS V (D
DON NIX SAX (D — BUDDY SPIKER FDL (D — ROGER HAWKINS D (D — BARRY BECKETT K (D
WAYNE PERKINS G (D — KENNY BUTTREY D (D — NORBERT PUTNAM B (D — LLOYD GREEN STEEL(D

M33 WARNER MACK M33

WARNER MACK G V (ALL — (A) GOLDEN COUNTRY HITS 1963 LONDON UK SHU 8025
LLOYD GREEN STEEL(J — (B) DRIFTING APART 1968 BRUNSWICK UK 8684 US DECCA 74883
(C) THE COUNTRY TOUCH 196 US DECCA 74766
(D) MANY COUNTRY MOODS 196 US DECCA 74995
(E) THE CONTRY BEAT OF WARNER MACK 1969 US DECCA 75092
(F) WARNER MACK VOL 1 196 US KAPP 8002
(G) WARMER MACK VOL 2 196 US KAPP 8025
(H) I'LL STILL BE MISSING YOU 1970 US DECCA 75165
(I) LOVE HUNGRY 1970 US DECCA 75219
(J) YOU MAKE ME FEEL LIKE A MAN 1971 US DECCA 75272
(K) GREAT COUNTRY 197 US MCA 20001
(L) THE BEST OF THE BEST 1979 US GUSTO 0042

M34 ANDY MACKAY M34

ANDY MACKAY WIND K SYN(AB — (A) IN SEARCH OF EDDIE RIFF 1974 ISLAND UK ILPS9278
PHIL MANZANERA G (AB — (A) IN SEARCH OF EDDIE RIFF 1977 POLYDOR UK 2302064
JOHN PORTER B (A — (B) RESOLVING CONTRADICTIONS 1978 BRONZE UK BRON 510 NL 26448
JOHN GUSTAFSON B (A
LLOYD WATSON G (A — ROGER GLOVER B (A — PAUL THOMPSON D (AB — EDDIE JOBSON VLN K(A
BRIAN CHATTON K (A — BRUCE ROWLAND D (A — SADIE MACKENZIE VLN (A — JANE RIFF VLN (A
MO FOSTER B (B — TONY STEVENS B (B — PETER VAN HOOKE D (B — TIM WHEATER FLT (B
CHRIS PARREN K (B — GAVIN WRIGHT VLN (B — MICHAEL LAIRD TPT (B — RAY RUSSELL G (B

M35 DUNCAN MACKAY M35

DUNCAN MACKAY K (AB — (A) SCORE 1977 EMI UK EMC 3168
STEVE HARLEY V (A — (B) VISA 1980 EDGE UK HOG 2
JOHN WETTON B (A
CLIVE CHAMAN B (A — ANDY McCULLOCH D PERC(A — MEL COLLINS WIND (A — YVONNE KEELY V (A
SIMON PHILLIPS D (B — ALAN JONES (B

M35A FREDDIE McKAY M35A

FREDDIE McKAY (A — (A) CREATION 1979 PLANT MUSIC PLAN1003

M36 JOANNE MACKELL M36

JOANNE MACKELL V (A — (A) JOANNE MACKELL 1978 UA UK UAG 30180
JOE FALSIA G PERC(A
JAMES BURTON G (A — STEVE CROPPER G (A — PETER JAMESON G (A — AUBURN BARRY G (A
JIMMY GREENSPOON K (A — JAI WINDING K (A — WAYNE COOK K (A — BARRY GOLDBERG K (A
MICHAEL HUEY D (A — ED GREEN D (A — DONALD DUCK DUNN B (A — BOB GLAUB B (A
EMORY GORDY B (A — DIANNE BROOKS V (A — MARTHA REEVES V (A — JULIA WATERS V (A
BARBARA BENNETT V (A — MILES WILKINSON V (A

M36A RABBIT MACKAY M36A

RABBIT MACKAY G HCA K V(A — (A) BUG CLOTH 1968 MCA UK MUPS 351
MIKE FLEMING G V (A
BOB THOMPSON D (A — JOHN RAINES D (A — DAVID SUEYEREES K V (A — JOHN PILLA G (A
REJI PEKAR G (A — BILL ST PIERRE FLT (A — WALK KUNNECKE FLT (A — HARRY HELLINGS TPT (A

M37 MCKENDREE SPRING M37

FRAN McKENDREE V B G K(ALL — (A) McKENDREE SPRING 1969 DECCA US75104 MCA 277
FRED HOLMAN B V (CD — (B) SECOND THOUGHTS 1970 DECCA US75230
MICHAEL DREYFUSS VLN K(ABCDEFG — (C) SECOND THOUGHTS 1971 MCA UK MUPS 433 RI 74 MCF 2651
MARTIN SLUTSKY G (ABCDEFG — (C) THREE 1972 MCA UK MUPS 454 RI 74 MCF 2658
HANK DEVITO STEEL(D — (C) THREE 1972 MCA US MCA 44 DECCA US 75332
ANDY NEWMARK D (CD — (D) TRACKS 1973 MCA UK MUPS 476 RI 74 MCF 2666
RAUN MACKINNON K (CD — (D) TRACKS 197 DECCA US 75385
ARTIE KAPLAN SAX (D — (E) SPRING SUITE 1973 MCA US 370
DAVID WOODS G (D — (F) GET ME TO THE COUNTRY 1975 DAWN UK DNLS3076 US PYE 12108
JO ANN VENT V (D — (G) TOO YOUNG TO FEEL THIS OLD 1976 US PYE 12124
BOB HIPWELL V (D
JOHN MONTGOMERY V (D — CARSON MICHAELS D V (EG — CHRISTOPHER BISHOP B V K(EFG — VALERIE ROSA V (F
HOWARD WYETH K (F — CHILLI CHARLES PERC (F — BOBBY GREGG D (C — ELLEN KEARNEY V (C
JERRY BURNHAM FLT (C — RUSSELL GEORGE B (C — JOHN DEVOE V (C — SUZANNE FRENCH V (C
WARREN BERNHARDT K (G — LARRY TUCKER B (AB — ADAM MITCHELL K SYN HCA(B

M38 MAE McKENNA M38

MAE McKENNA V (ABC — (A) MAE McKENNA 1975 TRANSATLANTIC UK TRA297 PYE US 12117
TREVOR SPENCER D (A — (B) EVERYTHING THAT TOUCHES ME 1976 TRANSATLANTIC UK TRA 321
MARTIN BRILEY G B (A — (C) WALK ON WATER 1977 TRANSATLANTIC UK TRA 345
GRAHAM PRESKETT B (A
B J COLE STEEL(A — SKAILA KANGA HARP (A — ISAAC GUILLORY G (BC — ELLIOT RANDALL G(BC
RONNIE LEAHY K (BC — PETE WILLSHER STEEL(BC — TIMI DONALD D (B — PAT DONALDSON B(B
RITCHIE GOLD V (B — PETE WINGFIELD K (C — JOHN GIBLIN B (C — GLEN LEFLEUR D(C
COLIN BLUNSTONE V (C — ROD ARGENT V (C — ALAN JAMES B (C — GERRY CONWAY D(C
MORRIS PERT PERC (C

M39 McKENNA MENDELSON MAINLINE M39

MIKE McKENNA G (ABC (A) STINK 1969 LIBERTY UK LBS 83251
JOE MENDELSON G V K HCA(ABC (B) NO SUBSTITUTE 1975 TAURUS CAN TR 103
TONY VOLASCO D (AC (C) CANADA OUR HOME & NATIVE LAND 19
MIKE HARRISON B (A
ADAM MITCHELL MAND V PERC(B T TOTH VLN (B JØRN ANDERSEN PERC (B EDWARD PURDIE K (B
ZEKE SHEPPARD B MAND (C

M39A SCOTT McKENZIE M39A

SCOTT McKENZIE V (AB (A) VOICE OF SCOTT McKENZIE 1967 ODE US 44002
(B) STAINED GLASS MORNING 1970 ODE US 77007
(C) SAN FRANCISCO 19 EMBASSY UK 31077

M39B IAN MCLAGAN M39B

IAN McLAGAN V K G(AB (A) TROUBLEMAKER 1979 MERCURY US SRM 13786
GEOFF WORKMAN PROD (A (B) BUMP IN THE NIGHT 1981 MERCURY US 4007
JOHNNY LEE SCHELL G V (A
RON WOOD G (A KEITH RICHARDS G (A JIM KELTNER D (A RINGO STARR D (A
JOSEPH MODELISTE D (A PAUL STALLWORTH B (A STANLEY CLARKE B (A FLAP WORKMAN ACC(A
BOBBY KEYS HRNS (A RON WOOD V HRNS(A STEVE MADAIO HRNS (A JAIME SEGEL V (A

M39C MURRAY McLAUCHLAN M39C

MURRAY McLAUCHLAN G K HCA V(A (A) HARD ROCK TOWN 1977 TRUE NORTH US 9466
JØRN ANDERSEN D V (A
DENNIS PENDRITH B V (A BEN MINK FDL V (A GENE MARTYNEC G (A RONNEY ABRAMSON V (A
KETHRYN MOSES FLT (A

M40 JOHN McLAUGHLIN & THE MAHAVISHNU ORCHESTRA M40

JOHN McLAUGHLIN G (ALL (A) EXTRAPOLATION 1969 MARMALADE UK 608007 RI70 2343 012
TONY OXLEY D (A (A) EXTRAPOLATION 1972 POLYDOR UK 2310018+ PD6074 US 5510
BRIAN ODGERS B (A (B) MY GOALS BEYOND 1971 DOUGLAS UK 69014 US CBS 30766
JOHN SURMAN SAX (AE (C) DEVOTION 1971 DOUGLAS UK 65075 US 31568 NL 64537
JERRY GOODMAN VLN (BCDFMH (D) INNER MOUNTING FLAME 1971 CBS UK 64717 US CBS 31067
BILLY COBHAM D (BDFGMH (E) WHERE FORTUNE SMILES 1972 DAWN UK DNLS3018
JAN HAMMER K (DFGH (F) BIRDS OF FIRE 1973 CBS UK 65321 US 31996
JEAN LUC PONTY VLN (IJ (G) LOVE DEVOTION & SURRENDER 1973 CBS UK 59037 US 32034
RICK LAIRD B (DFH (H) BETWEEN NOTHINGNESS & ETERNITY 1974 CBS UK 69046 US 32766
CARLOS SANTANA G (G (I) APOCALYPSE 1974 CBS UK 69076 US 32957
TONY WILLIAMS D (ML (J) VISIONS OF THE EMERALD BEYOND 1975 CBS UK 69108 US 33411
MILES DAVIS TPT ((K) INNER WORLDS 1976 CBS UK 69216 US 33908
JACK BRUCE B (ML (L) IN RETROSPECT(DBL) 1976 POLYDOR UK 2675 091 GER 2679 027
CHICK COREA K (M (M) ELECTRIC GUITARIST 1978 CBS UK 82702
STANLEY CLARKE B (M (N) ELECTRIC DREAMS (ONE TRUTH BAND) 1979 CBS UK 83256 US 35785
ALPHONSO JOHNSON (M (O) BEST OF MAHAVISHNU ORCHESTRA 1980 CBS UK 84232 US 36394
PATRICE RUSHEN V (M (P) BEST OF JOHN McLAUGHLIN 1980 CBS UK 84455 US 36355
DAVID SANBORN SAX (M (1) ONE TRUTH BAND 1978 LIVE
FERNANDO SAUNDERS B (1 (Q) EXTRAPOLATION 1981 POLYDOR UK 2310 018
DAVE LIEBMAN SAX (B (R) BELLO HORIZONTE 1981 WB UK K99185
BUDDY MILES D (C
MARSHA WESTBROOK VLA (I LARRY YOUNG K (CGL BILLY RICH B (C STU GOLDBERG K (K1
ANTHONY ALLEN SMITH D (1 L SHANKAR VLN PERC (1 ARMANDO PERAZA CONGA(G DON ALIAS D (G
DOUG RAUCH B (FG MINGO LEWIS PERC (G RALPH ARMSTRONG B (KJI GAYLE MORAN K (JI
NARADA MICHAEL WALDEN D(JKI STU MARTIN (E STEVE KINDLER VLN (J DAVE HOLLAND D (E
KARL BERGER (E CAROL SHIRE VLN (IJ PHILLIP HIRSCHI CELLO(IJ BOB KNAPP WIND(J
AIRTO MOREIRA PERC (B CHARLIE HAYDEN B (B MAHALAKSHMI SITAR(B BADAL ROY PERC(B
KATIA LA BEQUE PNO K(R FRANCOIS COUTURIER SYN (R JEAN PAUL CELEA B (R TOMMY CAMPBELL D (R
FRANCOIS JEANNEAU SAX (R JEAN PIERRE DROUET PERC(R STEVE SHEMAN PERC (R AUGUSTIN DUMAY VLN (R
PACO DE LUCIA G (R

M41 DON McLEAN M41

DON McLEAN G V (ALL (A) TAPESTRY 1972 UA UK UAS 29350 US 5522
GEORGE RICCI CELLO(A (B) AMERICAN PIE 1972 UA UK UAS 29285 US 5535
PAUL GRIFFIN K (D (B) AMERICAN PIE 1981 GREENLIGHT UK RI 2004
RALPH MACDONALD PERC(DC (C) DON McLEAN 1972 UA UK UAS 29399 US 5651
DON BROOKS HCA (DC (D) PLAYIN' FAVOURITES 1973 UA UK UAS 29528 US LA161 G
DICK HYMAN PNO (DC (E) HOMELESS BROTHER 1974 UA UK UAG 29646 US LA315 G
WARREN BERNHARDT PNO (DBC (F) SOLO (LIVE DBL) 1976 UA UK UAD 60139/40 US LA652H2
TONY LEVIN B (DC (G) PRIME TIME 1977 EMI UK INS 3011 ARISTA US 4149
ED TRICKETT DULC (DC (H) CHAIN LIGHTNING 1979 EMI UK INS 3025 CASABLANCA US7173
BUZZY FEITEN G (DC (J) VERY BEST OF 1980 UA UK UAG 30314
CHRIS PARKER D (DC
NEIL LARSEN K (DC RUSS SAVAKUS VLN (DC BOB ROTHSTEIN B V(DBC YUSEF LATEEF (E
KENNY VANCE (E BOB MOORE G (H KEN ASCHER K (G PAT REBILLOT K (G
JOHN FARRELL G (G ROBBIE STONER V B (G HOWIE WYETH K V(G DAVE SANBORN SAX(G
RONA WYETH V (G CHRISTINE FAITH V (G ANGELA HOWELL V (G GENE ORLOFF STRING (GE
RUBENS BASSINI PERC (G DOM CORTESE ACC (G BILLY SANFORD G (H JAMES CAPPS G (H
JOSEPH CHRISMAN D (H JORDANAIRES V (H RAY EDENTON G (H PETE DRAKE STEEL (H
TOMMY ALSUP G (H EDDY ANDERSON D (H PIG ROBBINS PNO(H CHUCK COCHRAN PNO(H
BOBBY WOOD K (H JERRY CARRIGAN D (H PERSUASIONS V (E RAY COLCORD K (B
MIKE MARIERI PERC (B CHUCK GREEN (C ANDREW SMITH D (E DAVID SPINOZZA G (E
WILLIE WEEKS B (E GEORGE BARROW SAX (E CHARLES FAWLKES SAX(E DANNY MOORE TPT (E
CISSY HOUSTON V (E DEIDRE TUCK V (E NED ALBRIGHT V (E WALLY KING WIND(E
JONATHAN DORN TUBA (E JOEL DORN V (E ARLENE MARTELL V (E MARLENE VERPLANCK V(E
GEORGE DUVIVIER B (E RICHARD TEE K (E ARTHUR JENKINS K (E HUGH McCRACKEN G (E
SELDON POWELL SAX (E CHARLES WILLIAMS SAX (E GARNETT BROWN TROM(E JOESEPH WILDER TPT (E
RENNELLE STAFFORD V (E STEVEN SOLES V (E PETE SEEGER V (E JAMES BUFFINGTON HRN (E
BILLY SLAPIN WIND (E LINDA NOVEMBER V (E HELENE MILES V (E JERRY TEIFFER (E
BROOKS TILLOTSEN HRN (E GEORGE MARGE WIND (E JERRY LAWSON V (E JIMMY HAYES V (E
HERBERT RHOAD V (E PETER GORDON HRNS (E RAY ALONGE HRN (E NORMA HOLMES V (E
SWEET JOE RUSSELL V (E W C DANIELS V (E WILLIS JACKSON SAX (E RAY MARKOWITZ D (B
RAY COLCORD K (B

M41A SANDY McLELLAND & THE BACKLINE M41A

SANDY McLELLAND V (A (A) SANDY McLELLAND & THE BACKLINE 1979 MERCURY UK 9109 620
DAVID BATES PERC (A (B) McLELLAND 1981 ACTION UK AL 1000
PAUL KAMOWSKI G (A
ROBIN RANKIN K (A ANDY HAMILTON SAX (A ROBERT PATERSON B (A PETER COE D (A
MARK KNOPFLER G (A JIM MULLEN G (A DICK HANSON HRNS (A JOHN EARLE HRNS(A
CHRIS GOWER TROM (A RAY BEAVIS HRNS (A FRANK COLLINS V (A DYAN BIRCH V (A
COLLETTE WILKINSON V (A ANDY LUNN PERC (A JON ASTLEY PERRC(A

M41B ANDREW McMAHON M41B

Musician	Instrument	On
ANDREW'BLUEBLOOD' McMAHON		(A

Album	Year	Label	Country	No.
(A) GO GET MY BABY	1978	MCM	FR	900 301

M41C OSCAR McLOLLIE & HIS HONEY JUMPERS M41C

Album	Year	Label	Country	No.
(A) ROLL HOT ROD ROLL	1981	ACE	UK	10CH27

M42 HAROLD McNAIR M42

Musician	Instrument	On
HAROLD McNAIR	FLT	(ALL
RICK GRECH	B	(B
KEITH TIPPETT	PNO	(B
BILL LESAGE	PNO	(AC
TONY CARR	D	(ABC
SPIKE HEATLEY	B	(AC
COLIN GREEN	G	(B
ALAN BRANSCOMBE	ORG	(B
TERRY COX	D	(B
DANNY THOMPSON	B	(B

Album	Year	Label	Country	No.
(A) HAROLD McNAIR	1968	RCA	UK	SF 7969
(B) THE FENCE	1970	B&C	UK	CAS 1016
(C) HAROLD McNAIR(A) DIFF TRACK 1)	1971	B&C	UK	CAS 1045
(D) AFFECTION FINK	19	ISLAND	UK	
(E) FLUTE & NUT	19	RCA	UK	INTS1096

M42A MACONDO M42A

Musician	Instrument	On
ALBERT HERNADNEZ	G V	(A
MAX UBALLEZ	G V	(A
FRED RAMIREZ	K VIBES	(A
RON CHRETIN	B	(A
FRANK MARTINEZ	D	(A
LEE PASTORE	PERC	(A
EDDIE CAICEDO	PERC	(A

Album	Year	Label	Country	No.
(A) MACONDO	1972	ATLANTIC	US	SD 7234

M42B BIG JAY McNEELY M42B

Musician	Instrument	On
BIG JAY McNEELY		(AB

Album	Year	Label	Country	No.
(A) BIG JAY IN 3D	19	KING	US	650
(B) LIVE AT CISCO'S	19	WB	US	1523

M43 CLYDE McPHATTER M43

Musician	Instrument	On
CLYDE McPHATTER	V	(ALL

Album	Year	Label	Country	No.
CLYDE McPHATTER & THE DRIFTERS	195	ATLANTIC	US	SD 8003
LOVE BALLADS	1958	ATLANTIC	US	SD 8024
CLYDE	1959	ATLANTIC	US	SD 8031
BEST OF CLYDE McPHATTER	1963	ATLANTIC	US	SD 8077
TA TA	19	MERCURY	US	(M)20597 (S) 60252
GOLDEN BLUES HITS	19	MERCURY	US	(M)20665 (S) 60665
LOVER PLEASE	19	MERCURY	US	(M)20711 (S) 60711
RHYTHM & SOUL	19	MERCURY	US	(M)20750 (S) 60750
GREATEST HITS	1963	MERCURY	US	(M)20783 (S) 60783
SONGS OF THE BIG CITY	1964	MERCURY	US	(M)20902 (S) 60902
LIVE AT THE APOLLO	1964	MERCURY	US	(M)20915 (S) 60915
MAY I SING FOR YOU	1966	MERCURY	US	(M)12224 (S) 16224
LETS START OVER	19	MGM	US	3775
GREATEST HITS	19	MGM	US	3866
WITH BILLY WARD & THE DOMINOES	19	KING	US	559
18 ORIGINAL HITS	19	KING	US	5006
WELCOME HOME	1971	MCA	UK	MCPS 418 RI 74 MCF2642
WELCOME HOME	19	DECCA	US	75231
A TRIBUTE TO CLYDE McPHATTER	19	ATLANTIC	UK	K30033

M44 TONY McPHEE M44

Musician	Instrument	On
TONY McPHEE	G K V	(ALL
JO ANN KELLY	V G	(ABC
GROUNDHOGS		(B
BRETT MARVIN & THUNDERBOLTS		(B

Album	Year	Label	Country	No.
(A) ME & THE DEVIL	1968	LIBERTY	UK	LBS83190
(B) I ASKED FOR WATER(VAR ARTIST)	1969	LIBERTY	UK	LBS83252 US 12455
(C) SAME THING ON THEIR MINDS	1971	SUNSET	UK	SLS50209
(D) TWO SIDES OF	1973	WWA	UK	WWA 001

(***) C FEATURES TRACKS FROM A+B

M45 RALPH McTELL M45

Musician	Instrument	On
RALPH McTELL	G V	(ALL
MIKE PIGGOTT	FDL	(1GH
NIGEL SMITH	K	(1
DAVE PEGG	B	(1HL
DAVE MATTACKS	D	(1G
BRIAN BROCKLEHURST	B	(C
FOLK WEAVERS	V	(C
HENRY VIII	JUG	(ABC
PETE BERRYMAN	G	(ABH
ROD CLEMENTS	B	(HL
GOLDRUSHERS	V	(H
DANNY THOMPSON	B	(GHL
DANNY LANE	D	(H
BOB KERR	SAX	(H
JERRY DONAHUE	G	(H
WIZZ JONES	G	(G
BOB STRAWBRIDGE	MAND	(L
WHISPERING MICK	PERC	(AB
ANDY CRONSHAW	ZITHER	(H
STEVE BONNETT	MAND	(G
SANDY SPENCER	CELLO	(H
GERRY CONWAY	D	(G
GRAHAM PRESKETT	K	(L
KEN GOLD	V	(L
JOHN KONGOS	V	(G
ALAN HARRIS	PERC	(H
BERT JANSCH	G	(G
PETER SWETTENHAM	K	(L
JOHN PERRY	V	(L
RABBIT BUNDRICK	K	(H
ROD EDWARDS	PNO	(H
PICK WITHERS	D	(L
SAMMY MITCHELL	DOB	(L
JOHN MARTYN	V	(L
LINDSAY SCOTT	VLN	(G
MADDY PRIOR	V	(H
JON STEVENS	D	(L
TONY RIVERS	V	(L
McGANN	G	(A

Album	Year	Label	Country	No.
(A) 8 FRAMES A SECOND	1968	TRANSATLANTIC	UK	TRA 165
(B) SPIRAL STAIRCASE	1969	TRANSATLANTIC	UK	TRA 177
(C) MY SIDE OF YOUR WINDOW	1969	TRANSATLANTIC	UK	TRA 209
(D) REVISITED	1970	TRANSATLANTIC	UK	TRA 227
(E) YOU WELL MEANING BROUGHT ME HERE	1971	FAMOUS 5753	UK	+ ABC ABCL 5084
(F) NOT TILL TOMORROW	1972	REPRISE US 2121	UK	K44210
(G) EASY	1973	REPRISE	UK	K54013
(H) STREETS	1975	WB	UK	K56105
(I) STREETS OF LONDON	1975	TRANSATLANTIC	UK	TRASAM34
(K) STAR COLLECTION	1975	MIDI		MID26030
(L) RIGHT SIDE UP	1976	WB	UK	K56296
(M) COLLECTION	1977	TRANSATLANTIC	UK	TRASAM39
(N) RALPH,ALBERT,SYDNEY	1977	WB	UK	K56399
(O) MAGINOT WALTZ (EP)	1977	WB	UK	K17008
(P) RALPH McTELL	1978	PICKWICK		SHM 962
(Q) SLIDE AWAY THE SCREEN	1979	WB	UK	K56599
(R) EASY	1979	KICKING MULE	US	303
(S) LIVE	1979	FANTASY	US	571

M45A DAVID McWILLIAMS M45A

Musician	Instrument	On
DAVID McWILLIAMS	G V	(ALL

Album	Year	Label	Country	No.
(A) DAYS OF PEARLY SPENCER	1971	STARLINE	UK	SRS5075
(B) LORD OFFALY	1972	DAWN	UK	DNLS3039 PYE US 3302
(C) BEGGAR & THE PRIEST	1973	DAWN	UK	DNLS3047
(D) LIVING JUST A STATE OF MIND	1974	DAWN	UK	DNLS3059
(E) DAVID McWILLIAMS	1977	EMI	UK	EMC 3169

M45B MAD MAGAZINE M45B

Album	Year	Label	Country	No.
(A) MAD TWISTS ROCK'N'ROLL	19	BIG TOP	US	1305
(B) FINK ALONG WITH MAD	19	BIG TOP	US	1206

M45C MADE IN SWEDEN M45C

Musician	Instrument	On
GEORGE WADENIUS	G V	(ALL
TOMMY BORGUDD	D	(ABCDE
BO HAGGSTROM	B	(ABCDE
TOMMY KORBERG	V	(G
PEKKA POHJOLA	B	(G
VESA AALTONEN	D	(G
WLODEK GULGOWSKI	K	(G
PETER SUNDELL	D	(

Album	Year	Label	Country	No.
(A) MADE IN SWEDEN	1969	SONET		SLP71
(B) SNAKES IN A HOLE	1969	SONET		SLP2504
(C) LIVE AT THE GOLDEN CIRCLE	1970	SONET		SLP2506
(D) MADE IN ENGLAND	1970	SONET		SLP2512
(E) MAD RIVER	1971	SONET	UK	SNTF 621
(F) THE BEST OF	19	GRAND PRIX		9997
(G) WHERE DO WE BEGIN	1976	POLYDOR		2480 358

M45D **MADISON DYKE** M45D

JURGEN BAUMANN G K SYN V(A (A) ZEITMASCHINE 1988 RACKET GER 15.001
BURKHARD RITTLER V FLT (A
ANDREAS NEDDE G V (A ROBERT KRAUSE B (A BURKHARD ENGEL D (A

M46 **MAD RIVER** M46

TOM MANNING V (ALL (A) MAD RIVER 1968 CAPITOL ST2985 RI GER 85882
DAVID ROBINSON G (ALL (B) PARADISE BAR & GRILL 1969 CAPITOL ST 185
RICK BOCHNER G (ALL (EP) MAD RIVER 1967 WEE 10021
LAURIE HAMMOND B V K(ALL
GREG DEWEY D HCA V(ALL JERRY CORBITT STEEL(B RON WILSON PERC (B BANANA STEEL (B

M46A **MADNESS** M46A

MIKE BARSON HCA PERC K(ABC (A) ONE STEP BEYOND 1979 STIFF UK 17 GER 624174 US SIRE 6085
CHRIS FOREMAN G (ABC (B) ABSOLUTELY 1980 STIFF UK 29 GER 624511 US SIRE 6094
GRAHAM 'SUGGS'McPHERSON V PERC(ABC (C) MADNESS 7 1981 STIFF UK 39 US SIRE
MARK BEDFORD B (ABC
LEE THOMPSON SAX V(ABC DAN WOODGATE D (ABC CHAS SMASH TPT V(ABC

M46B **JIMMY MAELEN** M46B

JIMMY MAELEN PERC V(A (A) BEATS WORKIN' 1980 CBS US 36319 UK 84211
NEIL JASON V (A
FRANK MAELEN V (A RANDY BRECKER TPT (A BARRY ROGERS TROM(A ELLIOT RANDALL G (A
LANI GROVES V (A IRENE CARA V (A STEVE LOVE HRNS (A ROBIN BECK V (A
VICKI SUE ROBINSON V (A ANNIE SUTTON V (A LUTHER VANDROSS V (A GEORGE YOUNG SAX(A
JOHN TROPEA G (A ROB MOUNSEY K (A PAT REBILLOT K (A JOHN LONGO TPT(A
LEW SOLOFF TPT (A KEN ASCHER K (A ALLEN SCHWARZBERG D (A PAUL SHAFFER K (A
RONNIE CUBER SAX (A LAWRENCE FELDMAN SAX (A

M46C **MADURA** M46C

ALAN DE CARLO G V (A (A) MADURA 1971 CBS US 30794
ROSS SOLOMONE D V (A
HAWK WOLINSKI K V (A

M47 **MAGAZINE** M47

HOWARD DEVITO V G (ALL (A) REAL LIFE 1978 VIRGIN UK V2100 GER 26190
BARRY ADAMSON B V (ABCDE (B) SECONDHAND DAYLIGHT 1979 VIRGIN UK V2121 GER 200385
DAVE FORMULA K (ABCDE (C) CORRECT USE OF SOAP 1980 VIRGIN UK V2156 GER 202116 US INT 13144
MARTIN JACKSON D (A (D) PLAY LIVE 1980 VIRGIN UK V2184 US INT 70015
SUPER MAGS V (B (E) MAGIC MURDER & THE WEATHER 1981 VIRGIN UK V2200 GER 203776 US INT 70020
JOHN McGEOCH G K SAX (ABC (EP) SWEETHEART CONTRACT 1980 VIRGIN 368
JOHN DOYLE D (BCDE (EP) ABOUT THE WETHER 1981 IRS US 70404
LAURA TERESA V (CE
ROBIN SIMON G (D RAY SHELL V (E BEN MENDELSON G VLN(E

M47A **MAGIC** M47A

(A) MAGIC 1972 RARE EARTH US 527

M47B **MAGIC LANTERNS** M47B

JIMMY BILSBURY PNO V(A (A) SHAME SHAME 1969 ATLANTIC US 8217
BEV BEVERAGE G V (A
PETER GARNER G V (A MIKE 'OZ' OSBORNE B V (A HARRY PAUL WARD D V (A

M47C **MAGIC MIXTURE** M47C

JIM THOMAS G V (A (A) THIS IS 1968 SAGA FID 2125
STAN CURTIS ORG (A
MELVYN HACKER B (A JACK COLLINS D (A

M48 **MAGIC SAM** M48

MAGIC SAM MAGHETT G V (ALL (A) MAGIC SAM 1937/69 1970 BLUE HORIZON UK 763223
LITTLE BRO MONTGOMERY K(ADE (B) BLACK MAGIC 19 DELMARK DS 620 JAP TRIO PA 6216
MACK THOMPSON B (ABCDEF (C) WEST SIDE SOUL 19 DELMARK DS 615 JAP TRIO PA 6214
WILLIE DIXON B (ADE (D) MAGIC ROCKER 1980 FLYRIGHT UK FL 561
BILLY STEPNEY D (ABE (E) OTIS RUSH & MAGIC SAM 1980 FLYRIGHT UK FL 562
EDDIE SHAW SAX (B (F) LATE GREAT MAGIC SAM 1980 L&R 42014
LAFAYETTE LEAKE PNO (B (G) BLUES MASTERS VOL 3 19 BLUE HORIZON US BN 4603
MIGHTY JOE YOUNG G (BC
ODIE PAYNE D (ABCDE SHAKEY JAKE HARRIS V (ADE SYL JOHNSON B (ADE HARRY BURRAGE PNO (ADE
STOCKHOLM SLIM PNO (C ERNEST JOHNSON B (C ROBERT ST JULIEN D (EF BOYD ATKINS SAX (
JOHNNY JONES PNO (ODELL CAMPBELL B (E S P LEARY D (FOUR DUCHESSES V (
AMMONS SISTERS V (

M48A **MAGIC SAND** M48A

(A) MAGIC SAND 1970 UNI US 73094

M48B **MAGIC SLIM** M48B

MAGIC SLIM G V (ALL (A) BORN UNDER A BAD SIGN 197 MCM FR 900 298
JUNIOR PETTIS G (A (B) VOL 2 197 MCM FR 900 305
NICK HOLT B (A (C) LIVE AT THE ZOO BAR 1980 CANDY APPLE US
DOUGLAS HOLT D (A

M48C **MAGITS** M48C

(A(FULLY COHERENT (EP) 19 OUTER HIMALAYAN ?

M49 **MAGMA** M49

CHRISTIAN VANDER D PERC V K(ALL (A) MAGMA (DBL) 1970 PHILIPS 63595 001/2
JANNIK TOP B (CDF (B) 1001 CENTIGRADE 1971 PHILIPS 9101 286 + 6397 031
KLAUS BLASQUIZ V PERC(ABCDEFH (C) KOHN TARKOSZ 1974 A&M US 3650 UK AMLH68260
TEDDY LASRY WIND (ABD (C) KOHN TARKOSZ 1974 VERTIGO EURO 6325 750
JEAN LUC VANDERLIER K (D (D) MEKANIK DESTRUKTIW KOMMANDOH 1974 A&M US 4397 UK AMLH64397
RENE GARBES CLAR V(D (D) MEKANIK DESTRUKTIW KOMMANDOH 197 VERTIGO EURO 6499 729 LTM 100
CLAUDE OLMOS G (D (E) LIVE (DBL) 1975 UTOPIA US CYL21245 + SPC 0002
BENOIT WIDEMANN K (HDEF (F) UDU WUDU 1976 TOMATO 6001 RCA FPLA 7332
TONY RUSSO TPT (H (F) UDU WUDU 1976 UTOPIA US 1 1730
BERNARD PAGANOTTI B (FE (G) EDITS 1977 TAPIOCA
DOM REINHARDT V (D (H) ATTAHK 197 WEA EURO 913213 TOMATO US 7021
LOUIS SARKISSIAN SAX (BC (I) RETROSPECTIVE VOL 1 19 RCA
LUCILLE CULLAZ V (F (J) RETROSPECTIVE VOL 2 19 RCA
MURIEL STREISFELD V (D
GABRIEL FEDEROW G (E LIZA DELUXE V (F DIDIER LOCKWOOD VLN (E JEAN POL ASSELINE K (E
STELLA VANDER V (CDEFH EVELYNE RAZYMOVSKI V (D MURIEL STREIFELD V (D LOUIS TOESCA TPT(B
CLAUD ENGEL G V (A FRANCIS MOZE B (AB FRANCOIS CAHEN K (AB JEFF SEFFER SAX(B
ALAIN HATOT FLT (F PATRICK GAUTHIER K (F PIERRE DU TOUR TPT (F RICHARD RAUX WIND (A
ALAIN CHARLERY TPT (C GERLAD BIKAILO K (C MICHEL GRAILLIER K (CF BRIAN GODDING G (C
MICHELLE SANTHIER V (LAURENT THIBAULT PROD (AH ROLAND HULDA PROD (B GIORGIO GOMELSKY PROD(CDEF
DORIS REINHARDT V (D MICHELE SAULNIER V (D JACQUES BOLOGNESI TROM (H CATHERINE SZPIRA V (F

M50 MAGNA CARTA M50

Member	Inst	Albums	Title	Year	Label / Catalogue
CHRIS SIMPSON	G V	(ALL	(A) MAGNA CARTA	1969	MERCURY SMCL20166
DAVEY JOHNSTONE	G V	(BEFH	(B) SEASONS	1970	VERTIGO 6360003 US DUNHILL 50091
GLEN STUART	V	(ABEFGH	(C) TIMES OF CHANGE	197	FONTANA NL 6438 080
LYELL TRANTER		(AB	(D) BEST OF MAGNA CARTA	197	VERTIGO NL 9107 100
STAN GORDON	G V	(GH	(D) BEST OF MAGNA CATRA	197	VERTIGO NL RI 9199 737
BARRY MORGAN	D	(B	(E) SONGS FRON WASTIES ORCHARD	1971	VERTIGO UK 6360 040
TONY CARR	D	(ABH	(F) IN CONCERT	1972	VERTIGO UK 6360 068
TONY VISCONTI	B PERC	(BE	(G) LORD OF THE AGES	1973	VERTIGO UK 6360 093
SPIKE HEATLEY	B	(B	(H) MARTINS CAFE	197	VERTIGO NL 6360 146
RICK WAKEMAN	K	(BE	(J) PUTTING IT BACK TOGETHER	1976	POLYDOR 2321 012 GTO GTLP 012
PICK WITHERS	D	(J	(J) PUTTING IT BACK TOGETHER	1976	ARIOLA US 50014
ALASTAIR ANDERSON		(E	(K) TOOK A LONG TIME	197	GTO 2321 112
RON CHESTERMAN		(E	(L) SPOTLIGHT ON	1977	PHILIPS 6625 031
GUS DUDGEON		(E	(M) PRISONERS ON THE LINE	1978	PHILIPS 9109 229
CHRIS LAURENCE		(E	(N) LIVE IB BERGEN 8/10/78	1978	FONTANA NL 6438 080
DANNY THOMPSON	B	(AEG	(O) NO TRUTH IN THE RUMOUR	1979	ARIOLA NL 201 176
CHRIS KARAN	D	(J			

FRANK HODGES	PERC	(A	PETER WILLISON	CELLO	(B	DAVE ARTHUR		(E	HEATHER CORBETT		(E
HOOKFOOT		(E	NIC POTTER		(E	TIM RENWICK	RECORDER	(B	DEREK GROSSMITH	FLT	(B
TONI ARTHUR		(C	JOHNNY VAN DERRICK		(E	HAROLD McNAIR	FLT	(A	DAVE MARKEE	B	(M
GRAHAM SMITH	B V HCA	(H	LES CYRCLE	D	(M	HENNIE BEKKER	K	(M	MIKE FINDLEY	G	(M
DAVE BARKER		(	TOMMY HOY		(MJ	NIGEL SMITH	ACC	(MJ	LEE ABBOT		(O
ROBIN THYNE		(M	TOM McCONVILLE		(O	GEORGE MORRIS		(	AL FENN		(
ROY BABBINGTON	B	(M	ROBIN ELLIS	V	(M	EMIL ZJHBZ	V	(M	CHRIS KARAN		(C
GRAHAM STUART		(	GORDON HUNTLEY	STEEL	(G	B J COLE	STEEL	(M	DAVE MATTACKS	D	(H
JOHN MEALING	K	(H									

M51A THE MAGNIFICENTS M51A

(A) DANCING WITH T M 19 VARIETON 1282

M52 MAGNUM M52

Member	Inst	Albums	Title	Year	Label / Catalogue
TONY CLARKIN	G V	(ABC	(A) KINGDOM OF MADNESS	1978	JET US 35811 UK LP 210
RICHARD BAILEY	K V FLT	(ABC	(B) MAGNUM 2	1979	JET UK LP 222
BOB CATLEY	G V	(ABC	(C) MARAUDER	1980	JET UK LP 230
KEX GORIN	D	(ABC	(D) CHASE THE DRAGON	1981	JET UK LP 235
COLIN LOWE	B V	(ABC			

M53 TAJ MAHAL M53

Member	Inst	Albums	Title	Year	Label / Catalogue
TAJ MAHAL	G V HCA BANJ	(ALL	(A) TAJ MAHAL	1967	DIRECTION UK 863279
RY COODER	G	(A	(A) TAJ MAHAL	1967	CBS US (M) 2779 (S) 9579
JESSE ED DAVIS	G	(ABCE	(B) NATCH'L BLUES	1978	DIRECTION UK 863397 US CBS 9698
JAMES THOMAS	B	(A	(C) GIANT STEP/DE OLE FOLKS (DBL)	1969	CBS UK 866226 US CBS 18
SANFORD KONIKOFF	D	(A	(D) THE REAL THING (DBL)	1971	CBS UK 66288 US CBS 30619
BILL BOATMAN	G	(A	(E) HAPPY JUST TO BE LIKE I AM	1971	CBS UK 64447 US CBS 30767
GARY GILMORE	B	(ABC	(F) RECYCLING THE BLUES	1972	CBS UK 65090 US CBS 31605
EARL LINDO	K	(JK	(G) THE SOUNDER(SOUNDTRACK)	1972	CBS 70123
CHUCK BLACKWELL	D	(ABC	(H) OOH SO GOOD 'N' BLUES	1973	CBS UK 65814 US CBS 32600
AL KOOPER	K	(B	(I) MO ROOTS	1974	CBS UK 80346 US CBS 33051
EARL PALMER	D	(B	(J) MUSIC KEEPS ME TOGETHER	1975	CBS UK 80972 US CBS 33801
JAMES CHARLES OTEY	D	(E	(K) SATISFIED N TICKLED TOO	1976	CBS UK 81346 US CBS 34103
JOHN SIMON	K	(ED	(L) ANTHOLOGY VOL 1 1966/76	1976	CBS US CBS 34466
BILL RICH	B	(EIJDPQO	(M) MUSIC FUH YA	1977	WB UK K56324 US 2994
HOSHAL WRIGHT	G	(EIJK	(N) BROTHERS	1977	WB US 3024
ROCKY DZIDZORNU	PERC	(EDIJMNKO	(O) EVOLUTION	1978	WB US 3094
HOWARD JOHNSON	HRNS	(EDF	(P) & INTERNATIONAL RHYTHM BAND LIVE	1979	CRYSTAL CLEAR(DIRECT) CCX 5011
BOB STEWART	HRNS	(ED	(Q) & INTERNATIONAL RHYTHM BAND	1980	MAGNET MAGL 5035
ANDY NARELL	STEEL DRUM	(E	(R) GOING HOME (COMP)	1980	CBS 31844
MERL SAUNDERS	K	(H	(S) THE BLUES	19	CBS 63279
DAVID COLMAN	G	(E	(T) THE BEST OF	19	CBS US 36528
SAM LIGHTNIN HOPKINS		(G			

CLAUDIA LENNEAR	V	(IN	LARRY McDONALD	PERC K	(MNJKO	BISMARK FRANCO	PERC	(M	JONI HAASTRUP	V	(M
RASHAIDA NIROBE	V	(M	JOSEPH DALEY	HRNS	(DE	EARL MacINTYRE	HRNS	(DE	KESTER SMITH	PERC	(IJKMNOPQ
RUDY COSTA	WIND	((MNJKOPQ	ASTON BARRETT	K	(I	CAROLE FREDERICKS	V	(JKMIO	TOMMY HENDERSON	V	(I
MERRY CLAYTON	V	(I	ROBERT GREENIDGE	D V	(MNOPQ	RAY FIZPATRICK	B G KV	(MNJK	INSHIRAH MAHAL	V	(M
MONA RAM	V	(M	YVONNE FIMBRES	V	(M	ALISON MILLS	V	(N	JOHN HALL	G	(D
GREG THOMAS	D	(D	JUMMA SANTOS	PERC	(PQ	ELLA JAMERSON	V	(PQ	GERI JOHNSON	V	(PQ
BIANCA ODEN	V	(PQ	VERLIN SANDLES	V	(PQ	OLA MARIE TYLER	V	(PQ	CAREY WILLIAMS	V	(PQ
POINTER SISTERS	V	(F	JO BAKER	V	(JK	ANNIE SWAMPSON	V	(JK	ROB MOUNSEY	K	(O
LEON PENDARVIS	K	(O	BOB BABBITT	B	(O	MARY MURE	D	(O	ERROLL BENNETT	PERC	(O
RAFFAEL RAMIREZ	CONGA	(K	JOHN TROPEA	G	(O	JANICE GADSDEN	V	(O	JOSHIE ARMSTEAD	V	(O
BILLY BARNES	V	(O	WAYNE GARFIELD	V	(O	CLAUDIA SIEFER	V	(O	MARK ISHAM	TPT	(
ZANE WOODSWORTH	TPT	(	CHARLES McCARTHY	SAX	(	STEPHEN KELLER	SAX	(	CARL LARKIN	G	(K
JOACHIM YOUNG	K	(K	DON MOORS	VIBES	(K	SAM COX	D	(K	JOHN TURK	K	(K
STAN MULELLAND	B	(K	RICK MYERS	SAX	(K	GORDON FOWLEY	TROM	(K	FRITZ HEILBRON	TROM	(K
CLIFF MORRIS	G	(O	WILL LEE	B	(O	DAVE CAREY	PERC	(O	STEVE JORDON	D	(O
BARRY FINERTY	G	(O	VIRGIL JONES	TPT	(O	DENNY MOORE	TPT	(O	DENNY MAROUSE	TROM	(O
JOHN ZANGRANDO	SAX	(O	ALAN RAPH	TROM	(O	SELDON POWELL	SAX	(O			

M54 MAHOGANY RUSH M54

Member	Inst	Albums	Title	Year	Label / Catalogue
FRANK MARINO	G VK	(ALL	(A) CHILD OF THE NOVELTY	1975	20TH CENTURY US T 451
PAUL HARWOOD	B	(ALL	(B) MAXOOM	1975	20TH CENTURY US T 463
JIMMY AYOUB	D	(ALL	(C) STRANGE UNIVERSE	1975	20TH CENTURY US T 482
NANETTE WORKMAN	V	(G	(D) MAHOGANY RUSH Iv	1976	CBS UK 81417 US 34190
VINCE MARINO	G	(H	(E) WORLD ANTHEM	1977	CBS UK 81978 US 34677
PHIL BEA	K	(E	(F) LIVE	1978	CBS UK 82625 US 35257
			(G) TALES OF THE UNEXPECTED	1979	CBS UK 83494 US 35753
			(H) WHATS NEXT	1980	CBS UK 83897 US 36204
			(I) POWER OF ROCK'N'ROLL	1981	CBS UK 84969

M54A MAILER MACKENZIE BAND M54A

Member	Inst	Albums	Title	Year
KID VAN ETTINGER	G	(A	(A) MAILER MACKENZIE BAND	19
PAUL VAN MELZEN	B	(A		
JAAP MOSSEL	D	(A	FOORT VERBRUGGE V HCA(A	

M55 **MAINHORSE** M55

PATRICK MORAZ K (A — (A) MAINHORSE — 1971 POLYDOR UK 2383049+VISA IMP 1001
PETER COCKETT G VLN V(A
BRYSON GRAHAM D (A JEAN RISTON B CELLO V(A

M55A **MIKE MAINIERI** M55A

MIKE MAINIERI VIBES(A — (A) JOURNEY THRU AN ELECTRIC TUBE — 1969 UA UAS 29051
JEREMY STEIG FLT (A
JOE BECK G (A SALLY WARING V (A SAM BROWN G (A WARREN BERNHARDT PNO (A
DONALD MACDONALD D (A HAL TAYLOR B (A CHUCK RAINEY B (A

M55B **MAINLAND** M55B

LES PAYNE G V (A — (A) EXPOSURE — 1979 CHRISTY MUSIC AMCL 0200
ANDY NYE V K (A
ADE WALKER B (A JAKE JACOBS G (A

M56 **MAJOR LANCE** M56

MAJOR LANCE (ALL
RHYTHM OF — 19 OKEH UK 33SX 1728
GREATEST HITS — 1973 CONTEMPO COLP 1001
BEST OF — 1976 EPIC UK 81519
LIVE AT THE TORCH — 1977 CONTEMPO CLP 523
NOW ARRIVING — 1978 TAMLA UK STMC 12094

M57 **MAJOR SURGERY** M57

JIM ROCHE G (A — (A) FIRST CUT — 1977 NEXT NEXT 1
DON WELLER SAX (A
TONY MARSH D (A BRUCE COLLCUT B (A

M57A **MALACHI** M57A

MALACHI G (A — (A) CHEVROLET — 19 VERVE ?
STEVE CUNNINGHAM (A

M57B **MALICORNE** M57B

LAURENT VERCAMBE VLN K V(ABCDEH — (A) MALICORNE — 1974 HEXAGONE FR 883002 GER ANTIGON 3220
HUGHES DE COURSON G B V (ABCDEH — (B) MALICORNE TWO — 197 HEXAGONE FR 883004 GER ANTIGON 3221
GABRIEL YACOUB G V (ABCDEFGH — (C) ALMANACH — 1976 HEXIGONE FR 883007
MARIE YACOUB V DULC (ABCDEFGH — (D) MALICORNE IV — 197 HEXAGONE FR 883015 GER ANTIGON 3223
OLIVER ZDRZALIK B K V(CDEFGH — (E) QUINTESSENCE — 1977 HEXAGONE FR 883018 GER ANTIGON 3224
BRIAN GULLAND HRN V K(h — (F) L(EX TRAORDI NAIZE — 1978 BALLON FR 13006
ANDRE PROULX FLT (H — (G) L'EXTRAORDINAIRE TOUR DE'FRANCE — 1978 BALLON FR 13003
DOM REGER STR V(H — (H) EN PUBLIC A MONTREAL — 1979 BALLON FR 13010
PATRICK LEMERCIER FDL G V(H — (J) BESHAIRE — 1979 BALLON FR 13012
JEAN ARNOUX D (H
NIC KINSEY PROD (ABCE

M57C **MALIBOOZ** M57C

JOHN ZAMBETI G V (A — (A) MALIBOOZ RULE — 1981 RALPH US
WALTER EGAN G B V(A
TOM RUDE G B (A SCOTT MONAHAN K (A LEE KIX D (A TED ZAMBETTI D (A

M58 **MALLARD** M58

BILL HARKLEROAD G (AB — (A) MALLARD — 1976 VIRGIN UK V 2045
MARK BOSTON G V B(AB — (B) IN A DIFFERENT CLIMATE — 1977 VIRGIN US 34489 UK V 2077
ARTIE TRIPP D (A
SAM GALPIN V k (AB BARRY MORGAN PERC (A JOHN THOMAS K V (B GEORGE DRAGGOTA D (B
JOHN JAMES K (RABBIT BUNDRICK K (A JOHN McFEE STEEL(B

M59 **MALO** M59

JORGE SANTANA G (ALL — (A) MALO — 1972 WB US BS 2584 UK K46142
RON SMITH HRNS (CD — (B) DOS — 1972 WB US BS 2652 UK K46179
WILLIE G V (D — (C) EVOLUTION — 1973 WB US BS 2702 UK K46221
TONY SMITH PERC V(CD — (D) ASCENSION — 1974 WB US BS 2769 UK K56033
FRANCISCO AQUABELLA PERC V(BCD
STEVE SHERARD TROM (CD MIKE FUGATE TPT (D ABEL ZARATE G (A RICHARD SPREMICH D (AB
ROY MURRAY HRNS (A ARCELIO GARCIA V PERC (ABC FORREST BUCHTEP TPT (BC RICK QUINTANAL D (B
RON DEMASI K V (CD LUIS GASCA TPT (A PAUL REKOW PERC (B COKE ESCOVEDO PERC (A
CARLOS FEDERICO PNO (C AL ZULAICA PNO (C JOHN WATSON V (B PABLO TELLEZ B PERC (ALL
RICHARD KERMODE K (AB LEO ROSALES PERC (B VICTOR PANTOJA PERC (A RICHARD BEAN V PERC (A
HADLEY CALIMAN WIND (B GEORGE BERMUDEZ CONGA(B BILL ATWOOD TPT (B MIKE HEATHMAN TROM (B
JOSE SANTANA VLN (B TOM POOLE TPT (B ALEX RODRIGUEZ TPT (B

M60 **MAMA LION** M60

LYNN CAREY V (AB — (A) MAMA LION — 1972 PHILIPS 6369 153 US FANTASY 2702
NEIL MERRYWEATHER V B (AB
COFFI HALL D (AB RICK GAXIOLA G (A JIM HOWARD K V (AB ALAN HUTTZ G (B
ED MIKENAS B (B BOB ROSE G (B

M61 **MAMA'S & THE PAPA'S** M61

CASS ELLIOT V (ALL
MICHELLE GILLIAM PHILLIPS(ALL
JOHN PHILLIPS V (ALL
DENNY DOHERTY V (ALL

HAL BLAINE D (
LARRY KNECHTEL K (X
JOE OSBORN B (X
FAST EDDIE D (X
ERIC HORDE G (X

IF YOU CAN BELIEVE YOUR EYES — 1966 DUNHILL US 50006 UK RCA RD 7803
CASS,JOHN,MICHELLE & DENNY — 1966 DUNHILL US 50010 UK RCA SF 7834
DELIVER — 1967 DUNHILL US 50014 UK RCA SF 7880
BOOK OF SONGS — 196 DUNHILL US 50022
FAREWELL TO 1ST GOLDEN ERA — 1968 DUNHILL US 50025
PAPAS & MAMAS — 1968 DUNHILL US 50031 UK RCA SF 7960
GOLDEN ERA VOL 2 — 1968 DUNHILL US 50038 UK STATESIDE 5002
HITS OF GOLD — 1969 ABC (74) 5003 UK STATESIDE 5007
16 OF THE GREATEST — 19 DUNHILL US 50064
A GATHERING OF FLOWERS — 1970 DUNHILL US 50073 UK PROBE 1003/4
(X) MONTEREY INTERNATIONAL POP FESTIVAL — 1971 DUNHILL US 50100
PEOPLE LIKE US — 1972 DUNHILL US 50106 UK PROBE 1048
PEOPLE LIKE US — 1974 RI UK ABC ABCL5017
20 GOLDEN HITS — 1972 DUNHILL US 50145 UK PROBE 200
20 GOLDEN HITS — 1974 RI UK ABC ABCL 604
BIGGEST HITS — 197 PICKWICK 2076
MONDAY MONDAY — 1973 PICKWICK US 3380 UK MFP 90025
CALIFORNIA — 1974 PICKWICK US 3357 UK MFP 90050
BEST OF — 1977 ARCADE UK
20 GREATEST HITS — 1980 MFP UK 50493

M62 MAMAS PRIDE M62

DON LISTON G V (AB (A) MAMAS PRIDE 1976 ATLANTIC US 36122 UK K 50197
PAT LISTON G V (AB (B) UPTOWN..LOWDOWN 1977 ATLANTIC US 36146 UK K 50348
MAX BAKER K (AB
KEVIN SANDERS (AB JOE TUREK B V (AB DICKIE STETTENPOHL B V (B FRANK GAGLIANO K SYN (A
JOE LALA PERC (B JIM MASON HRNS (B DENNIS DREITH HRNS (B PAUL WILLETT K V (B
JERRY JUMONVILLE HRNS (B

M63 MAN M63

MICKY JONES G V (ALL (A) REVELATION 1969 PYE UK 18275
CLIVE JOHN G K V(ABCDFGJ (B) 2OZ OF PLASTIC WITH A HOLE 1969 PYE GER 88003 DAWN UK 3003
DEKE LEONARD G V(ABCSEGJKLMNOP (C) MAN 1970 LIBERTY UK 83464 US 9803
TERRY WILLIAMS D V (CDEFHJKLMOPN (C) MAN 1970 1976 SUNSET RI UK 50380
JEFF JONES D (ABG (D) DO YOU LIKE IT HERE,ARE YOU... 1971 LIBERTY US 1032 UK UA 29236
RAY WILLIAMS B (ABG (E) LIVE AT THE PADGET ROOMS PENARTH 1972 UA UK USP 100
MARTIN ACE B G V(CDEJMP (F) BE GOOD TO YOURSELF... 1972 UA US LA 077 UK US 29417
TWEKE LEWIS G (H (G) GOLDEN HOUR(COMP FROM A &B) 1973 PYE UK GH 569
WILL YOUATT B V (FHJ (H) BACK INTO THE FUTURE(DBL) 1973 UA US 170 GER 29547 UK 60053/4
PHIL RYAN K V (FHJNO (J) CHRISTMAS AT THE PATTI(10" DBL) 1973 UA UK UDX205/6
KEN WHALEY B (KL (K) RHINOS, WINOS & LUNATICS 1974 UA US LA 247 UK 29631
MALCOLM MORLEY K G V(JK (L) SLOW MOTION 1974 UA US LA 345 UK 29675
JOHN McKENZIE B V (NO (M) MAXIMUM DARKNESS 1975 UA UK 29872
JOHN CIPOLLINA G (M (N) THE WELSH CONNECTION 1976 MCA US 2190 UK MCF2753 GER 6 22481
DAVE CHARLES (J (O) ALL'S WELL THAT ENDS WELL 1977 MCA GER 62098 UK MCF 2815
GEORGINA ACE B (J (P) ALSO APPEARED ON GREASY TRUCKERS 1972 UA Uk UDX203/4 GER GAMMA 3265
PLUM HOLLIS V (J (EP) BANANAS 1976 UA UK REM 408
DAVE EDMUNDS G V (J (Z) GOLDEN HOUR OF MAN 1973 PYE UK GH 567
VIC MAILE PROD (H
MICKEY GEE G (J B J COLE STEEL(J STAN PHIFER V (J SEAN TYLA G V(J
RICHARD TREECE G (J PAUL BURTON B (J MARTIN BELMONT G V (J TIM ROPER D (J
NICK GARVEY B (J RAY THOMAS BAKER PROD (K

M64 MANASSAS M64

STEPHEN STILLS G V K(AB (A) MANASSAS (DBL) 1972 ATLANTIC US 2/903 UK K60021
AL PERKINS STEEL(AB (B) DOWN THE ROAD 1973 ATLANTIC US 7250 UK K40440
PAUL HARRIS K (AB
ROGER BUSH B (A JOE LALA PERC (AB KENNY PASSARELLI B V (JOE WALSH G (B
DALLAS TAYLOR D (AB BOBBY WHITLOCK K V (B SYDNEY GEORGE FLT (AB CALVIN SAMUELS B (AB
JERRY AIELLO ORG (AB CHARLIE GRIMES G (B CHRIS HILLMAN B G V(AB GUILLE GARCIA PERC(B
LACHY ESPINOL PERC (B PAT ARNOLD V (B BILL WYMAN B (A BYRON BERLINE FDL (A

M65 MANCHILD M65

ANTHONY JOHNSON B (A (A) POWER & LOVE 1977 CHINA TOWN US LA765 UK UA 30134
KENNY EDMONDS G V (A (B) FEEL THE PHUFF 19 CHINA TOWN US LA 872
DARYL SIMMONS PERC V(A
FLASH FERRELL V (A ROBERT PARSON D (A CHUCKIE BUSH K(A REGGIE GRIFFIN SAX G(A

M65A MELISSA MANCHESTER M65A

MELISSA MANCHESTER V K (ALL (A) HOME TO MYSELF 1974 ARISTA US 4006 UK BELL 233
ALLAN SCHWARZBERG D (A (B) BRIGHT EYES 1974 ARISTA US 4011
GEORGE DEVENS PERC (A (C) MELISSA 1975 ARISTA US 4031 UK ARTY104
BOB MANN V G BAN(A (D) BETTER DAYS & HAPPY ENDINGS 1977 ARISTA US 4067 UK ARTY125
JOHN STROLL PNO (A (E) HELP IS ON THE WAY 1977 ARISTA US 4095 UK ARTY147
CORKY HALE HARP (A (F) SINGIN' 1977 ARISTA US 4136
DAVID MANCHESTER BASSOON(AJ (G) DONT CRY OUT LOUD 1978 ARISTA US 4186
CHRIS DEDRICK K (A (H) MELISSA MANCHESTER 1978 ARISTA US 9506
ANDY MUSON B (A (J) FOR THE WORKING GIRL 1980 ARISTA US 9533
JOHN LOPRESTI B V (ACDE
DAVE APPELL G (A MICHAEL JOHNSON G (A HANK MEDROSS PERC (A JAMES NEWTON HOWARD K (CEF
DAVID WOLFERT G SIT(CDE KIRK BRUNER V D TROM (CDE KING ERRISON PERC (C STEVE MADAIO TPT (CDG
JOHN ROTELLA SAX (C DAVID LASLEY V (C DON DIEGO GOJU PERC (C STANLEY SCHWARTZ SAX K(EFG
DAVID SPINOZZA G (F SID McGINNIS G (F TONY LEVIN B (F DON GROLNICK K (F
VINI POCIA V (CEF TREVOR LAWRENCE SAX (C LEW McCREARY TROM (CFG GENE DINWIDDIE SAX (C
ARNOLD McCULLER V (C MORTON K SALT PERC (C LENNY CASTRO PERC V(DEFG JEFF MIRONOV G (F
WILL LEE B (F STEVE GADD D (F TOM SAVIANO WIND (EFG ANDREW MACKINTOSH SAX (EF
LES WORTH POTTO FLT (F WENDY HAAS V (F CLAUDIA CAGAN V (FG FARAGHER BROTHERS V (F
JOE BEAN ESPOSITO V (E DOUG WINTZ HRN (E DICK HYDE TROM (EG DAVID T WALKER G (G
JAMES GADSON D V (G RICHARD TEE K (G GENE PAGE STR (G HARRY BLUESTONE VLN (G
DENNIS BUDIMIR G (G JIM KELTNER D (G SONNY BURKE SYN (G CHUCK FINDLEY TPT (G
TOMMY MORGAN HCA (G JAY GRAYDON G (G JAMES STROUD D (J TOM ROBB B (J
ALAN FEINGOLD SYN (J TOMMY COOPER GLOCK(J STEVE BUCKINGHAM G (J DON HENLEY V (J
CHARLES CHALMERS V (J PAUL DAVIS V (J ED SEAY V (J BERNADINE MITCHELL V (J
BARRY FASMAN STR HRN(J RICH FELTO TPT (EF GEORGE BOHANON TROM (F MICHAEL CARNAHAN WIND (FG
BRIE HOWARD V (CEF GAIL KANTOR V (F JOHN VASTANO G V (E GARY COLEMAN VIBES (E
BILL PETERSEN HRN (E DICK NASH HRN (E CHUCK RAINEY B (G GREG PHILLANGANES PNO (G
LEON WARE V (G LEE RITENOUR G (G DAVID BLUMBERG STR (G DAVID HUNGATE B (G
BILL PAYNE PNO (G MICHAEL BODDICKER SYN (G DAVID LUELL SAX (G ART RODRIGUEZ D (G
ED GREENE D (G LARRY BYROM G (J RANDY McCORMICK K (J AVTAR SINGH KHALSA VIBES (J
BETH COOPER HRNS (J BEABO BRYSON V (J SANDRA RHODES V (J DONNA RHODES V (J
STEVE CARLISLE V (J KATHLEEN JACKSON V (J PATTI ALLINSON V (J STEVEN CAGAN STR HRN(J
STEVE NELSON V (E SUNDRAY TUCKER V (E CHARITY McCRARY V (E LINDA McCRARY V (E
THERESA HENDRICKS V (E BETTY JONES V (E JAN E JONES V (E BRENDA L GOOCH V (E

M66 MANDALA M66

GEORGE OLLIVER V (A (A) SOUL CRUSADE 1968 ATLANTIC US SD 8184
DOMENIC TROIANO G (A
HUGH SULLIVAN K (A ROY KENNER V (A JOEY CHIROWSKI K (A DON ELLIOTT B (A
WHITEY GLAN D (A

M67 MANDALABAND M67

DAVID DURANT V (A | (A) MANDALABAND 1975 CHRYSALIS UK CHR 1095
ASHLEY MULFORD G (A | (B) THE EYE OF WENDOR 1978 CHRYSALIS UK CHR 1181
JOHN STIMPSON B G (A
TONY CRESSWELL D (A | VIC EMERSON K (A | RITCHIE CLOSE PNO (B | DAVY ROHL PNO (B
KIM TURNER G D (B | MEL PRITCHARD D (B | GRAHAM GOULDMAN B (B | PETE GLENNON B (B
ALF TRAMONTIN B (B | NOEL REDDING B (B | LES HOLROYD B (B | STEVE BROOMHEAD G (B
JIMMY McDONNELL G (B | JOHN LEES G (B | MADDY PRIOR V (B | MARK GILBANKS TPT (B
ANDY CROMPTON TROM (B | MIKE CARLTON TROM (B | ERIC STEWART V (B | TONY SPATH OBOE(B
JOHN GILSTON PERC (B | GERRY MURPHY PIPES(B | RICHARD SCOTT RECOD(B | MICKY PURTON HRNS(B
RUSSELL HAYWARD HRNS (B | PAUL BRYAN FARR HRNS (B | ANDY WARDAUGH TPT (B | MARTIN LAWRENCE PERC(B
DAVID HASSALL PERC (B | PHIL CHAPMAN WIND (B | JOHN TURNER K (B | STEWART WOLSTENHOLME K(B
NORMAN BARRETT G (B | GERALD BROWN SINGERS V (B | DAVE GORTON TROM (B | KEVIN GODLEY V (B
PAUL YOUNG V (B | JUSTIN HAYWARD V (B | LOL CREME V (B | IAN WILSON V (B
FRIDAY BROWN V (B | GILLY ROHL V (B | FIONA PARKER V (B

M68 HARVEY MANDEL M68

HARVEY MANDEL G (ALL | (A) CRISTO REDENTOR 1968 PHILIPS UK SBL 7873 RI 70 6336009
PETE DRAKE STEEL(A | (A) CRISTO REDENTOR 1968 PHILIPS US 600281
KENNY BUTTREY D (A | (B) RIGHTEOUS 1969 PHILIPS UK SBL 7904 US 600306
BOB MOORE B (A | (C) GAMES GUITARS PLAY 1970 PHILIPS UK SBL 7915 US 600325
HARGUS ROBBINS K (A | (D) BABY BATTER 1971 DAWN UK DNLS3015 US JANUS 3017
LARRY TAYLOR B (CEGD | (E) ELECTRONIC PROGRESS(SAME AS D??) 1971 BELLAPHON GER 15182 JANUS NL 61701
GRAHAM BOND K (A | (F)GET OFF IN CHICAGO 1972 LONDON UK SHO 8426 US OVATION1415
EDDIE HOH D (ABC | (G) THE SNAKE 1972 JANUS UK 6310 210 US 3037
RICHARD MARTIN V (H | (G) THE SNAKE 1972 BELLAPHON GER 19170
CHIP MARTIN G (A | (H) SHANGRENADE 1973 JANUS UK 6499 831 US 3047
BOB JONES G (AB | (J) FEEL THE SOUND OF 1974 JANUS US 3067
CATHERINE GOTTHOFER HARP(A | (K) BEST OF 1975 JANUS US 7014
BARRY GOLDBERG K (A
ARMANDO PERAZA CONGA(A | CAROLYN WILLIS V (A | JACQUELINE MAY ALLEN V(A | STEVE MILLER K (A
CARTER COLLINS CONGA(A | DUANE HITCHINGS K (B | ART STAVRO B (AB | LARRY EASTER SAX (A
JULIA TILLMAN V (A | FREDDIE FOX V (F | VICKI HUBLEY V (F | G E STINSON G (F
NORM WAGNER G (F | DAVE COOK K (F | IRA KART K (F | DON CODY B (F
PETER MILIO D (F | KEN LITTLE B V (F | BOBBY DAVIS D (F | JUDY ROBERTS K V (F
JOHN BISHOP G (F | NICK TOUNTAS B (F | RUSTY JONES D (F | PHIL JOHNSON D (F
EARL PALMER D (BG | BUDDY CHILDERS TPT (B | JOHN AUDINO TPT (B | STAN FISHELSON TPT (B
OLLIE MITCHELL TPT (B | LEW McCREARY TROM (B | MIKE BARONE TROM (B | PETE MYERS TROM (B
DICK LEITH TROM (B | ERNIE WATTS SAX (B | PLAS JOHNSON SAX (B | BILL PERKINS SAX (B
GENE CIPRIANO SAX (B | JACK NIMITZ SAX (B | PETE JOLLY K (B | BOB WEST B (B
HOWARD ROBERTS G (B | VICTOR FELDMAN PERC (B | NICK DECARO K (A | CHARLIE MUSSELWHITE HCA (A
CRAIG RASBAND B (F | COLEMAN HEAD G (HJ | PAUL LAGOS D (DGHJ | VICTOR CONTE G (GHJ
BOBBY LYLE K (| BOBBY NOTKOFF STR (H | FRED ROULETTE STEEL(GH | DON 'SUGARCANE'HARRIS VLN(GH
HOWARD WALES K (ED | BIG BLACK CONGA (ED | MIKE MELVOIN K (ED | COLIN BAILEY D (E
EMIL RICHARDS PERC (ED | JOE PORCARO PERC (ED | SANDRA CROUCH TAMB (ED | RUSSEL DASHIEL G V K(C
ALDOLFO DELA PERRA D (G | CHUCK DOMANICP B (G | ANTONIO DELA BARREDA B (G | RANDY RESNICK G (G
JIM TAYLOR PNO (G | KEVIN BURTON K (G | CHARLES LLOYD FLT (G | RAY LESTER B (JH
MARK SKYER G V (JH | DANNY KELLER D (JH

M69 MIKE MANDEL M69

MIKE MANDEL K (A | (A) SKY MUSIC 1978 VANGUARD VSD 79409
DAVE SANBORN SAX (A
GARY ANDERSON SAX (A | DARRYL THOMPSON G (A | BURT KHAN G (A | WILBUR BASCOMB B (A
JOHN LEE B (A | CHRISTOPHER PARKER D (A | GERRY BROWN D (A | CRUSHER BENNETT PERC(A
CHRIS HILLS PERC (A | JON FADDIS HRNS (A | LOU SOLOFF HRNS (A | DAVE TAYLOR HRNS(A
GEORGE YOUNG SAX (A | ALEX FOSTER SAX (A | BARRY ROGERS TROM (A | LOU MARINI SAX (A

M70 MANDRAKE MEMORIAL M70

KEVIN LALLY D (ABC | (A) MANDRAKE MEMORIAL 1968 US POPPY 40002
RANDY MONACO V B (ABC | (B) MEDIUM 1969 RCA UK SF 8028 US POPPY 40003
CRAIG ANDERTON G (ABC | (C) PUZZLE 1970 POPPY UK 11003 US POPPY 40006
MICHAEL KAC K V (AB

M71 MANDRAKE PADDLESTEAMER M71

MARC BRIERLEY (A | (A) 1969 LINE UP
BRIAN MARTIN (A
PAUL RIBB (A | JOHN WHITEHEAD (A | PAUL WHITEHEAD (A

M72 MANDRILL M72

CARLOS WILSON SAX V(ALL | (A) MANDRILL 1970 POLYDOR UK 2489 028 US 24 4050
CLAUDE CAVE K V (ALL | (B) MANDRILL IS 1972 POLUDOR UK 2391 030 US 5025
ANDRE LOCKE D V (F | (C) COMPOSITE TRUTH 19 POLYDOR UK 2391 061 US 5043
BRIAN ALLSOP B V (FE | (D) JUST OUTSIDE OF TOWN 1973 POLYDOR UK 2391 092 US 5049
TOMMY TRUJILLO G V (F | (E) BEST OF 19 POLYDOR UK 2391 186 US 6047
RICK WILSON SAX (ALL | (F) SOLID 1975 UA UK UAG29786 US UA LA408
LOU WILSON TPT PERC V(ALL | (G) BEAST FROM THE EAST 1976 UA UK UAS29920 US UA LA577
CHARLES WILSON HRNS PERC V(F | (H) MANDRILLAND 197& POLYDOR UK 2672 023 US 9002
CHARLES PADRO D PERC V(| (J) WE ARE ONE 1978 ARISTA UK SPART1035 US 4144
FUDGIE KAE B (BDH | (K) NEW WORLD 1978 ARISTA UK ARTY 162 US 4195
OMAR MESA G PERC V(ABD | (L) GREATEST 19 ARISTA US 7000
BUNDIE CENAS B PERC (A | (M) GETTING IN THE MOOD 1980 ARISTA US 9527
CHARLES PADRO D PERC(AB
NEFTALI SANTIAGO D PERC(H | DOUG RODRIGUES G V (H

M73 MANDRE M73

ANDRE LEWIS MANDRE (| (A) MANDRE 1977 MOTOWN UK STML23062 US 882
(B) MANDRE 2 1978 MOTOWN UK STML12084 US 7900

M74 GAP MANGIONE M74

GAP MANGIONE K (ALL | (A) GAP MANGIONE 1977 A&M US 4621
DAN SAWYER SAX (B | (B) SUITE LADY 1978 A&M UK AMLH 64694
LARRY CARLTON G (B | (C) DANCIN 1979 A&M US 4762
POPS POPWELL B (B
GREG MATHESON PNO (B | ABRAHAM LABORIEL B (B | RALPH HUMPHREY D (B | JEFF PORCARO PERC (B
CHUCK FINDLEY TPT (B | PETER DONALD D (B | VINCENT DE ROSA HRNS(B | JOE PORCARO PERC (B
BILL REICHENBACH TROM (B

MANHATTAN TRANSFER

Musician	Inst	On	Album	Release
TIM HAUSER	V	(ABCDEFGH	(A) JUKIN'	1971 CAPITOL US 778 E ST 11405
MICKEY ROKER	D	(A	(A) MANHATTAN TRANSFER	1978 MFP RI UK 50387
ERIN DICKINS	V	(A	(B) MANHATTAN TRANSFER	1975 ATLANTIC US 18133 UK K50138
PAT ROSALIA	V	(A	(C) COMING OUT	1976 ATLANTIC US 18183 UK K50291
MARTY NELSON	V CLAR	(A	(D) PASTICHE	1978 ATLANTIC US 19163 UK K50444
ALAN PAUL	V	(BCDEFGH	(E) LIVE	1978 MOBILE US 22 ATLANTIC UK K50540
LAUREL MASSE	V	(BCDE	(F) EXTENSIONS	1979 ATLANTIC US 19258 UK K50674
JANIS SIEGEL	V	(BCDEGH	(G) MECCA FOR MODERNS	1981 ATLANTIC US 16036 UK K50789
CHERYL BENTYNE	V	(FG	(H) BEST OF	1981 ATLANTIC
GENE PISTILLI	V G	(A		

JOHN MAYER PNO (D	NORBERT PUTNAM B (A	MIKE ROD SAX (B	KENNY BUTTREY D (A
TOMMY WEST K (A	MURRAY WEINSTOCK K (B	DAVID BRIGGS K (A	GARY CHESTER D (A
JERRY FRIEDMAN G (B	GEORGE EDWARDS STEEL(A	HAYWOOD HENRY SAX (A	RICHARD TEE K (B
BUDDY SPICHER FDL (A	IRA NEWBORN G (BCD	MICHAEL BRECKER SAX (BC	ADAM MITCHELL G (A
DON GROLNICK K (BD	JERRY DODGION SAX (AB	RANDY BRECKER TPT (BCD	ANDY MUSON B(BCD
DANIEL BEN ZEBULON PERC(B	AL GIBBONS SAX (A	ROY MARKOWITZ D (BC	ZOOT SIMS SAX (B
EARL WILLIAMS D (A	PAUL FAULISE TROM (B	SELDON POWELL WIND (B	BOB BUSHNELL B (A
MICKEY GRAVINE TROM (B	LEW DELGATTO SAX (BD	BIG AL WILLIAMS K (A	QUENTIN JACKSON TROM(B
MEL DAVIS TPT (B	LEW TABACKIN SAX (A	ALAN RAPH TROM (B	JON FADDIS TPT (B
FRANK BEROWSKI SAX (A	PHIL BODNER SAX (B	BOB McCOY TPT (B	BURT COLLINS TPT (A
GEORGE DORSEY SAX (B	MARKY MARKOWITZ TPT (BD	GARNETT BROWN TROM (AB	HARVEY ESTRIN SAX (B
MARVIN STAMM TPT (BD	WAYNE ANDRE TROM (ABD	DAVE SANBORN SAX (B	ALAN RUBIN TPT(BD
SABER G (A	FRANK VICARI SAX (B	GEORGE YOUNG SAX (B	RON CARTER B (A
WALLY KANE WIND (B	PAUL GRIFFIN K (C	BOBBYE HALL PERC (CD	RINGO STARR D (C
MAC REBENNACK K (C	DOUG THORNGREN PERC (C	JIM GORDON D (CD	JOHN BARNES PNO (CD
BEN BENAY G (CD	STEVE PAIETTA ACC (C	JAY MIGLIORI SAX (C	RICK SCHLOSSER D (C
CLARENCE McDONALD PNO (C	RALPH MACDONALD PERC (C	JACKIE KELSO SAX (C	JIM NELSON D (C
BILL PAYNE PNO (C	ROGER STEINMAN PNO (C	ARTHUR JENKINS PNO (C	NICK MARRERO PERC(C
JOHN RODRIGUEZ PERC (CD	DAVID KEMPER D (C	BOB BOWLES G (C	JIM KELTNER D (C
JOHN RODRIGUEZ PERC (CD	DAVID KEMPER D (C	BOB BOWLES G (C	JIM KELTNER D (C
DAVID FRISHBERG K (C	JOHN GIMBLE FDL (D	AL COHN SAX (D	JIMMY GUFFRIE SAX (D
DAVID TAYLOR TROM (D	STU WOODS B (D	ART RODRIGUEZ D (D	DICK FRANK G (D
TOMMY VIG PERC (D	LEE KONITZ SAX (D	HURBIE GREEN TROM (D	STEVE GADD D(DG
BUDDY EMMONS STEEL(D	PETE WADE G (D	CHARLIE McCOY HCA (D	SHORTY LAVENDER FDL (D
BRITT WOODMAN TROM (D	DAVID WALLACE K (D	LARRY EMERINE PERC (D	STEVEN SCHAFFER D (D
MIKE BODDIKER K (DFG	DAVID FRISHBERG K (D	MIKE MELVOIN K (D	JEANNE ASHBY HARP (D
JEFF PORCARO D (DF	SCOTT EDWARDS B (D	DAVID FOSTER K (DFG	JAY GRAYDON G SYN(DFG
VICTOR FELDMAN PERC K(DG	MICHAEL OMARTIAN K (DF	WILLIE HALL D (D	DUCK DUNN B (D
BOOKER T JONES K (D	STEVE CROPPER G (D	TOM HENSLEY K (D	PETER JOHNSON D (D
WAYNE JOHNSON G (D	MICHAEL SCHNOEBELEN B (D	DON ROBERTS WIND (DFG	GENE PAGE STR (D
RALPH HUMPHREY D (F	DAVID HUNGATE B (F	RICHIE COLE SAX (FG	GREG MATHIESON K SYN(FG
JIMMY WYBLE G (F	IAN UNDERWOOD SYN (F	CHUCK DOMANICO B (F	BILL MAYS PNO (F
STEVE LUKATHER G (FG	JAI WINDING PNO (F	PAULINHO DA COSTA PERC (F	ABRAHAM LABORIEL B (FG
ALEX ACUNA D (FG	DEAN PARKS G (FG	MIKE BAIRD D (G	JERRY HEY TPT)G
TOM SCOTT HRNS (G	ANDY NOVELL D (G	YARON GERSHOVSKY PNO (G	AL VIOLA G (G
MILCHO LEVIEV K (G	JON HENDRICKS V (G	STEVE GEORGE SYN (G	

M76

MANHATTANS

M76

Album	Year	Label	Country	Cat	Country	Cat
DEDICATED	19	CARNIVAL			US	201
FOR YOU & YOURS	19	CARNIVAL			US	202
WITH THESE HANDS	19				US DELUXE	12000
MILLION TO ONE	1972	LONDON	UK	SHB 8449	US DELUXE	12004
THERE'S NO ME WITHOUT YOU	19	CBS			US	32444
THATS HOW MUCH I LOVE YOU	19	CBS			US	33064
MANHATTANS	1976	CBS	UK	81513	US	33820
I WANNA BE YOUR EVERYTHING	1976	DJM	UK	26084		
IT FEELS SO GOOD	1978	CBS	UK	84828	US	34450
THERE'S NO GOOD IN GOODBYE	1978	CBS	UK	82567	US	35252
LOVE TALK	1979	CBS	UK	83342	US	35693
AFTER MIDNIGHT	1980	CBS	UK	84223	US	36411
BEST OF	1980	EMBASSY	UK	31806		
GREATEST HITS	1980	CBS			US	36861

M76A

MANIACS

M76A

Musician	Inst	On	Album	Release
RAY BOOSTER	G V	(A	(A) MANIACS	197 BLUBBER LIPS GER 803
MANNY MANIAC	B V	(A		
CHARLIE ENDURE	D	(A		
JOHN ROOTBEER	G	(A		

M77

CARL MANN

M77

Musician	Inst	On	Album	Year	Label	Country	Cat
CARL MANN	G V	(ALL	(A) LIKE MANN	1959	PHILIPS INT	US	PLP1960
			(B) CARL MANN	19	SONET	SWED	SPO 13
			(C) LEGENDARY SUN PERFORMERS	1977	CHARLY	UK	CR 30130
			(D) GONNA ROCK'N' ROLL TONIGHT	1978	CHARLY	UK	CR 5008
			(EP) CARL MANN	1977	CHARLY	UK	CEP 114
			( ) LIKE MANN	1980	CHARLY	UK	CRM 2006

M78

HERBIE MANN

M78

Musician	Inst	On	Album	Year	Label	UK	US
HERBIE MANN	FLT	ALL	WITH JOAO GILBERTO & ANTONIO JOBIM	19	ATLANTIC		US SD 8105
BILL EVANS	PNO	(N	THE COMMON GROUND	1961	ATLANTIC		US SD 1343
CHUCK ISRAELS	B	(N	THIS IS MY BELOVED	19	ATLANTIC		US SD 1367
PAUL MOTIAN	D	(N	FAMILY OF MANN	19	ATLANTIC		US SD 1371
CHICK GANIMIAN		(I	AT THE VILLAGE GATE	1962	ATLANTIC	UK 599 054	US SD 1380
ROY AYERS	VIBES	(IM	RIGHT NOW	19	ATLANTIC		US SD 1384
BRUNO CARR	D	(IM	DO THE BOSSA NOVA	19	ATLANTIC		US SD 1397
REGGIE WORKMAN	B	(I	RETURN TO THE VILLAGE GATE	19	ATLANTIC		US SD 1407
CARLOS VALDES	PERC	(IL	(L)LIVE AT NEWPORT	1963	ATLANTIC		US SD 1413
THOMAS KAZANAN	PERC	(I	LATIN FEVER	1964	ATLANTIC		US SD 1422
GERALDINE SWEE	PERC	(I	(N)NIRVANA	1964	ATLANTIC	UK K 50238	US SD 1426
JIMMY OWENS	TPT	(I	MY KINDA GROOVE	196	ATLANTIC		US SD 1433
JULIAN PRIESTER	SAX	(I	THE SMELL OF THE CROWD,ROAR OF G PAINT	196	ATLANTIC		US SD 1437
JOE ORANGE	SAX	(I	STANDING OVATION AT NEWPORT	196	ATLANTIC		US SD 1445
MOHAMED ELEKLAD	ZITHER	(I	TODAY	196	ATLANTIC		US SD 1454
ATTILA ZOLLER	G	(IL	MONDAY NIGHT AT THE VILLAGE GATE	196	ATLANTIC		US SD 1462
RICHARD DAVIS	B	(I	OUR MANN FLUTE	196	ATLANTIC		US SD 1464

(CONTINUED)

HERBIE MANN

M78

Personnel	Instr.	Title	Year	Label	Issue
GLORIA AGOSTINI	HARP (I	NEW MANN AT NEWPORT	196	ATLANTIC	US SD 1471
DAVE PIKE	VIBES(L	(I)IMPRESSIONS OF THE MIDDLE EAST	1967	ATLANTIC	US SD 1475
DON FRIEDMAN	PNO (L	BEAT GOES ON	196	ATLANTIC	US SD 1483
BEN TUETHE	B (L	STRING ALBUM	196	ATLANTIC	US SD 1490
BOB THOMAS	D (L	WAILING DERVISHES	196	ATLANTIC	US SD 1497
WILLIE BOBO	PERC (L	(U) MEMPHIS UNDERGROUND	1969	ATLANTIC	UK 588 200 US SD 1522
MELVIN LASTIE	HRNS (M	(U) MEMPHIS UNDERGROUND	197	ATLANTIC	UK K 40038 RI UK K50520
IKE WILLIAMS	HRNS (M	LIVE AT THE WHISKY	196	ATLANTIC	US SD 1536
GEORGE BOHANAN	TROM (M	BEST OF	19	ATLANTIC	US SD 1544
AL VESCOVO	G (M	TURTLE BAY	19	ATLANTIC	UK K 50020 US SD 1642
JOHN BARNES	K (M	GLORY OF LOVE	1969	A&M	UK AMLS 944 US 3003
DARREL CLAYBORN	B (M	EVOLUTIONOF MANN	19	ATLANTIC	UK K 60020 US SD 2 300
RICHARD WATERS	D (M	BEST OF	19	PRESTIGE	US 7432
VICTOR PANTOJA	PERC (M	BIG BOSS MAN	19	CBS	US 1068
LARRY CORYELL	G (M	ET TU FLUTE	19	VERVE	68821
REGGIE YOUNG	G (M	LATIN MANN	19	CSP	US JCS 9188
BOBBY EMMONS	K (M	MANN IN SWEDEN	19	PRESTIGE	US 7659
BOBBY WOOD	K (M	SUPER MANN	1973	TRIP	US 5031
MICK LEECH	B (M	WITH FLOOT TO BOOT	19	SPRINGBOARD	US 4055
GENE CHRISTMAN	D (M	CONCERTO GROSSO IN D BLUES	196	ATLANTIC	UK 2465005
ERIS WEISSBERG	G (M	STONE FLUTE	19	ATLANTIC	UK 2465088 US EMBRYO 520
SONNY SHARROCK	G (M	MUSCLE SHOALS NITTY GRITTY	19	ATLANTIC	UK 2400022 UK RI K40096
CHARLIE BROWN	G (M	MUSCLE SHOALS NITTY GRITTY	19	EMBRYO	US SD 526
MIROSLAV VITOUS	B (M	(M)MEMPHIS TWO STEP	1971	EMBRYO	US SD 531
RON CARTER	B (M	(P)PUSH PUSH	1971	EMBRYO	US SD 532
RICHIE RESNICOFF	G (M	(P)PUSH PUSH	1971	ATLANTIC	UK 2400191 UK RI K40283
PAT REBILLOT	K (G	BRAZIL BLUES	197	UA	UK UAS 5631US 5638
SAM BROWN	G (G	MISSISSIPPI GAMBLER	1974	ATLANTIC	UK K 40385 US 1610
TONY LEVIN	B (G	HOLD ON IM COMING	197	ATLANTIC	UK K 40467 US 1632
STEVE GADD	D (G	LET ME TELL YOU	1974	MILESTONE	ML 47010
MINURO MURAOKA	(G	(O)LONDON UNDERGROUND	1974	ATLANTIC	UK K 50032 US SD 1648
MODERN SHOMYO STUDY GROUP	(G	REGGAE	1974	ATLANTIC	UK K 50053 US SD 1655
ONO GAGAKU SOCIETY	(G	STAR COLLECTION	1975	MIDI	UK K 20018
DUANE ALLMAN	G (P	DISCOTHEQUE	1975	ATLANTIC	UK K 50128 US SD 1670
CORNELL DUPREE	G (P	WATER BED	1975	ATLANTIC	UK K 50174 US SD 1676
BERNARD PURDIE	D (P	(G) GAGAKU & BEYOND	1976	FINNADAR	SR 9014
JERRY JEMMOTT	B (P	SURPRISES	19	ATCO	US 1682
AL JACKSON	D (P	BIRD IN A SILVER CAGE	1977	ATLANTIC	UK K 50338 US SD 18209
GENE BIANCO	HARP (P	BRASIL	1978	ATLANTIC	UK
RICHARD TEE	K (P				

CHUCK RAINEY	B (P	RALPH MACDONALD	PERC (P	DONALD DUNN	B (P	RAY BARRETTO	PERC (
BABATHNDE OLATUNJI	PERC(	RAY MANTILLA	PERC (	ARMANDO PERAZA	PERC (	MICK TAYLOR	G (O
ALBERT LEE	G (O	PAT REBILLOT	K (O	FUZZY SAMUELS	B (O	AL GORRY	B (O
AYNSLEY DUNBAR	D (O	ROBBIE McINTOSH	D (O	IAN McDONALD	SAX)O	STEPHANE GRAPPELLI	VLN (O

M79

MICHAEL MANTLER

M79

Personnel	Instr.	Title	Year	Label	Issue
MICHAEL MANTLER	TPT (ALL	(A) JAZZ COMPOSERS ORCHESTRA	1974	VIRGIN	UK JD 3001
DON CHERRY	HRNS (AB	(B) NO ANSWER	1974	VIRGIN	UK WATT 2
STEVE LACY	SAX (A	(C) 13 3/4	1975	VIRGIN	UK WATT 3
AL GIBBONS	SAX (A	(D) THE HAPLESS CHILD	1976	VIRGIN	UK WATT 4
GENE HULL	SAX (A	(E) SILENCE	1976	VIRGIN	UK WATT 5
BOB DONOVAN	SAX (A	(F) MOVIES	1978	VIRGIN	UK WATT 7
LEW TABACKIN	SAX (A				

GEORGE BARROW	SAX (A	CHARLES DAVIS	SAX (A	LLOYD MICHAELS	HRNS (A	RANDY BRECKER	HRNS(A
BOB NORTHERN	HRNS)A	JULIUS WATKINS	HRNS (A	JIMMY KNEPPER	TROM (A	JACK JEFFERS	TROM(A
STEPHEN FURTADO	(A	HOWARD JOHNSON	TUBA (A	EDDIE GOMEZ	B (A	STEVE SWALLOW	B (ADF
CARLA BLEY	K V(ALL	KENT CARTER	B (A	BEAVER HARRIS	D (A	RON CARTER	B (A
ROSWELL RUDD	TROM (A	RICHARD DAVIS	B (A	PHAROAH SANDERS	SAX (A	CHARLIE HADEN	B (A
CECIL TAYLOR	PNO (A	REGGIE WORKMAN	B (A	JIMMY LYONS	SAX (A	ANDREW CYRILLE	D (A
BOB CUNNINGHAM	B (A	LARRY CORYELL	G (A	REGGIE JOHNSON	B (A	STEVE MARCUS	SAX (A
ALAN SILVA	B (A	FRANK WESS	SAX (A	JACK BRUCE	B V (AB	ROBERT WYATT	V (DE
JACK DEJOHNETTE	D (D	TERJE RYPDAL	G (D	KEVIN COYNE	V (C	CHRIS SPEDDING	G (E
RON McCLURE	B (E	CLARE MAHER	CELLO (E	TONY WILLIAMS	D (F		

M80

MANFRED MANN

M80

Personnel	Instr.	Title	Year	UK	US / other
MANFRED MANN	K SYN V(ALL	(A)MANFRED MANN ALBUM	1964		US ASCOT 16015
MIKE HUGG	D (ABCDEFGHIJKLMO37	(B) FIVE FACES OF MANFRED MANN	1964	HMV CLP 1731	US ASCOT 16018
MIKE VICKERS	SAX (ABCD3I	(C) MANN MADE	1964	HMV CLP 1911/1628	US ASCOT 16024
DAVE RICHMOND	B (GI	(C) MANN MADE	1969	STARLINE	UK SRS 5007
PAUL JONES	V (ABCDHI3	(D) MY LITTLE RED BOOK OF WINNERS	1965		US ASCOT 16021
TOM McGUINNESS	B G(ABCDEFGHIJK37	(E) MANN MADE HITS	1966	HMV CLP 3559	
JACK BRUCE	B (3I	(F) PRETTY FLAMINGO	1966		US UA 6549
MIKE D'ABO	V (GK37	(G) AS IS	1966	FONTANA STL 5377	
BERNIE LIVING	WIND (NO	(H) GREATEST HITS	1966		US UA 6551
STEVE YORK	B (NO	(I) SOUL OF MANN	1967	HMV CLP 3594	US CAPITOL 6199
CRAIG COLLINGE	D (NO	(J) UP THE JUNCTION	1968	FONTANA STL 5460	UK 6852 005
SONNY CORBETT	TPT (NO	(K) MIGHTY GARVEY	1968	FONTANA STL 5470	
IAN FENBY	(N	(L) WHAT A MAN	1968	FONTANA SFL13003	
HAROLD BECKETT	TPT (N	(M) MIGHTY QUINN	1968		US MERCURY 61168
DAVID COXHILL	SAX (NO	(N) CHAPTER THREE	1969	VERTIGO UK V03	US POLYDOR 4013
DEREK WADSWORTH	(GK	(O) CHAPTER THREE VOL 2	1970	VERTIGO UK 6360 012	
CHRIS PYNE	(N	(P) THIS IS MANFRED MANN	1971	PHILIPS UK 6382 020	
DAVE QUINCY	(N	(Q) EARTH BAND	1972	PHILIPS UK 6308 086	US POLYDOR 5015
PHIL KENZIE	(N	(Q) EARTH BAND	1977	BRONZE UK BRON 252	
DAVE POTTER	(N	(R) GLORIFIED MAGNIFIED	1972	PHILIPS UK 6308 125	US POLYDOR 5031
GEOFF DRISCOLL	(N	(R) GLORIFIED MAGNIFIED	1977	BRONZE UK BRON 257	
NICK EVANS	(N	(S) MESSIN'	1973	PHILIPS UK 6360 087	RI 77 BRONZE 261
MADELINE BELL	V (N	(T) GET YOUR ROCKS OFF	1973		US POLYDOR 5050
SUNNY LESLIE	V (N	(U) SOLAR FIRE	1973	BRONZE UK ILPS9265	US POLYDOR 6019
SUE GLOVER	V (N	(U) SOLAR FIRE	1977	BRONZE UK BRON 265	GER 28778
BRIAN HUGG	G (NO	(V) THE GOOD EARTH	1974	BRONZE UK ILPS9306	US WB BS 2826
DAVE BROOKS	SAX (O	(V) THE GOOD EARTH	1977	BRONZE UK BRON 306	GER 88369
CLIVE STEVENS	SAX (O	(W) NIGHTINGALES & BOMBERS	1975	BRONZE UK ILPS9337	US WB BS 2877

(CONTINUED)

M80 (CONTINUED) MANFRED MANN M80

GERRY FIELDS FDL (0 — (W) NIGHTINGALES & BOMBERS 1977 BRONZE UK BRON 337 GER 89059
CONRAD ISADORE D (0 — (X) ROARING SILENCE 1976 BRONZE UK ILPS9357 US WB BS 3055
ANDY McCULLOCH D (0 — (X) ROARING SILENCE 1977 BRONZE UK BRON 357
COLIN PATTENDEN B (QRSUVWZX — (Y) THE BEST OF MANFRED MANN 1977 EMI UK NUT 7
CHRIS SLADE D (QRSUVWZ1X — (Z) THE EARTH BAND 1971 /73 1977 VERTIGO UK 9199 107 GER 200 367
MICK ROGERS G V (QRSUVWZ24X — (1) WATCH 1978 BRONZE UK BRON 507 US WB BS 3157
DAVE FLETT G (X1 — (2) ANGEL STATION 1979 BRONZE UK BRON 516 US WB 3302
LIZA STRIKE V (S — (3) SEMI DETATCHED SUBURBAN 1979 EMI UK EMTV 19
RUBY JAMES V (SW — (4) CHANCE 1980 BRONZE UK BRON 529 GER 202 970 US Wb 3498
GRAHAM ELLIOTT CELLO(W — (5) THE BEST OF MANFRED MANN 197 CAPITOL US 11688
MARTHA SMITH V (W — (6) THE BEST OF MANFRED MANN 197 JANUS US 3064
VICKY SILVA V (1 — (7) ONE WAY 1968 FONTANA NL 858037
STEVE WALLER G V (24 — (8) ATTENTION (COMP) 19 FONTANA GER 6438 063
ANTHONY MOORE G K (12 — (9) MANNERISMS 1976 SONIC SON 016
DAVID BOSWELL-BROWN CELLO(W — (10) ATTENTION VOL 2 197
DAVID CULPAN RECORDER(X — (11) HISTORY OF BRIT POP VOL 6 19 EMI NL 05020
BARBARA THOMPSON SAX (X4 — (12) REMEMBER THE GOLDEN YEARS DBL 19 EMI GER 06532/33
KLAUS VOORMANN B (GK7 — (EP) GROOVIN' WITH 1964 HMV UK 7EG8876
CHRIS THOMPSON G V (X124 — (EP) MANFRED MANN 1964 HMV UK 7EG8848
IRENE CHANTER V (1X — (EP) INSTRUMENTAL ASSASSINATION 1967 FONTANA UK TE 17473
KIM GOODY V (2 — (EP) INSTUMENTAL ASYLUM 1966 HMV UK 7EG8949
JIM O'NEILL G (2 — (EP) THE ONE IN THE MIDDLE 1965 HMV UK 7EG8908
DOREEN CHANTER V (W1X — (EP) THERE'S NO LIVING WITHOUT 1965 HMV UK 7EG8922
DAVID MILLMAN STRINGS (WX — (EP) MACHINES 1966 HMV UK 7EG8942
TONY ROWELL RECORDER(X — (EP) AS WAS 1966 HMV UK 7EG8962
PAT KING B (124
LAURIE BAKER (W
STEVIE LANGE V (1
GEOFF BRITTON D (2
DYAN BIRCH V (24 — MARGARET WOOD RECORDER(X — CHRIS WARREN-GREEN VLN (W — NIGEL WARREN-GREEN CELLO(W
JOHN LINGWOOD D (4 — TREVOR RABIN G (4 — SUSANNE LYNCH V (X — LYN DOBSON SAX (I
HENRY LOWTHER TPT (I — GRAHAM PRESKETT VLN (4 — ROBBIE McINTOSH G (4 — GEOFF WHITEHORN G (4
WILLY FINLAYSON V (4 — PETER MARSH V (4 — CAROL STOCKER V (4

M80A MANTRA M80A

(A) MANTRA 1981 CASABLANCA NBPL 7256

M81 PHIL MANZANERA M81

PHIL MANZANERA G V K(ALL — (A) DIAMOND HEAD 1975 ISLAND ILPS 9315 US ATC036113
SIMON PHILLIPS D PERC(BC — (A) DIAMOND HEAD 1975 ISLAND GER 88 750
BRIAN ENO K (AB — (A) DIAMOND HEAD 1977 POLYDOR UK RI 2302 062
BILL MACCORMICK B (ABC — (B) LISTEN NOW 1977 POLYDOR UK 2302 074
IAN McDONALD PIPES(A — (C) K SCOPE 1978 POLYDOR UK 2302 083 US 6147
PAUL THOMPSON D (AC — (D) PRIMITIVE GUITARS 1981 EDITIONS UK EGED14
SONNY AXPAN PERC (A
CHYKE MADU PERC (A — DOREEN CHANTER V (A — JOHN WETTON PERC (AC — DAVE SKINNER K V (C
ROBERT WYATT (A — BRIAN TURRINGTON B (A — ANDY MACKAY WIND (A — EDDIE JOBSON K VLN(AB
DANNY HEIBS PERC (A — CHARLES HAYWARD PERC (A — DAVE JARRETT K (A — LOL CREME V GISMO(BC
KEVIN GODLEY V PERC(BC — SIMON AINLEY G V (BC — MAL COLLINS SAX (BC — BILLY LIVSEY K WIND(B
IAN MacCORMICK V (B — DAVE MATTACKS D (B — FRANCIS MONKMAN SYN (BC — EDDIE RAYNER K SYN (BC
JOHN WHITE TUBA (B — RHETT DAVIES K (B — ALAN LEE V (B — TIN FINN V (BC
NEAL FINN (C

M82 RAY MANZAREK M82

RAY MANZAREK K V (ABC — (A) THE GOLDEN SCARAB 1975 MERCURY UK 6398 007 US SRMI 703
LARRY CARLTON G (A — (B) THE WHOLE THING STARTED WITH R'N'R1975 MERCURY UK 6338 552 US SRMI1014
JERRY SCHEFF B (A — (C) NITE CITY 1977 20TH CENTURY US 528
TONY WILLIAMS D (A
TONY SALES (C — STEVE FORMAN PERC (AB — NIGEL HARRISON (C — HUNT SALES D (C
MAILTO CORREA PERC (A — OSCAR BRASHEAR TPT (A — MARK PINES G (B — MILT HOLLAND PERC(A
GARY MALLABER D PERC (B — MIKE FENNELLY G (B — TIM DOWNS D (A — ERNIE WATTS SAX (A
NOAH JONES V (C — PAUL WARREN G V (C — MARK VOLMAN V (B — HOWARD KAYLAN V (B
JOE WALSH G (B — GEORGE SEGAL BANJO(B — JOHN KLEMMER SAX (B — PAUL DAVIS PERC(B
PATTI SMITH V (B

M82A JOE MAPHIS M82A

JOE MAPHIS G (ALL — (A) GUITARATION GAP 1972 CHART US 1042
(B) DIM LIGHTS THICK SMOKE 1978 CHM US 6224
(C) GRASS & JAZZ 1978 CHM US 6215
(D) BOOGIE WOOGIE FLAT TOP 1979 CHM US 6239

M83 MIKE MARAN M83

MIKE MARAN (A — (A) FAIR WARNING 1971 BRONZE ILPS 9221
KENNY WHEELER TPT (A
BUTCH HUDSON TPT (A — HENRY LOWTHER TPT (A — CHRIS PYNE TROM (A — DAVE HORLER TROM (A
GEOFF PEERKINS TROM (A — ALAN SKIDMORE SAX (A — STAN SULZMAN SAX (A — BARBARA THOMPSON WIND (A
ROY BABBINGTON B (A — FRANK RICOTTI PERC (A — DAVE MATTACKS D (A — DAVE MacRAE K (A
TONY ASHTON K (A — JOHN MARSON HCA (A — GERRY BRON PROD (A — STRING SEC (A

M83A MARCUS HOOK ROLL BAND M83A

HARRY VANDA (A — (A) MARCUS HOOK ROLL BAND 1973 CAPITOL US 11991
GEORGE YOUNG (A

M84 MARCUS M84

MARCUS MALONE V (A — (A) MARCUS 1978 UA UK UAS 30000 US UA LA 668
GENE BLOCH G (A
RANDALL DAVID G (A — TIM BOGERT B (A — JACK WEBER G (A — DANDY HOLMES D (A

M84A BENNY MARDONES M84A

BENNY MARDONES V (ALL — (A) THANK GOD FOR GIRLS 1978 PRIVATE STOCK US PS 7007
MICK RONSON G (A — (A) NEVER RUN 1980 POLYDOR US 6263
JERRY SHIRLEY D (A — (C) TOO MUCH TO LOOSE 1981 POLYDOR US
MIKE NEVILLE B (A
HAYDEN WAYNE K V (A — RON FRANGIPANE K (A — JOEY STANN SAX (A — MERLE MILLER V (A
KIMBERLEY CARLSON V (A — D L BYRON V (A — SANDY GENNARO D (B — RON BLOOM G (B
BOBBY MASSANO G (B — KINNY LANDRUM K (B — LEIGH FOXX B (B

M84B MARIAH M84B

(A) MARIAH 197 UA US UALA 493

M84C JON MARK M84C

JON MARK G V (A (A) SONGS FOR A FRIEND 1975 CBS US 33339
TOMMY EYRE K (A
SALLI TERRI V (A RON CARTER B (A LARRY KNECHTEL B (A HAL BLAINE D (A
DONALD REINBERG TPT (A GAYLE LEVANT HARP (A VICTOR FELDMAN PERC (A ANDREW NARELL STEEL D(A
PATRICK GLEASON SYN (A

M84D CHARLIE MARIANO M84D

CHARLIE MARIANO WIND (A (A) HELEN OF TREES 1976 MPS BASF 22941
ZBIGNIEW SEIFERT VLN³ (A
JAN HAMMER K (A JACK BRUCE B (A JOHN MARSHALL D (A NIPPY NOYA PERC (A

M84E MARIE ET LES GARCONS M84E

(A) MARIE ET LES GARCONS 1080 ZE FR 2 6564

M84F FRANK MARINO M84F

FRANK MARINO G V SYN (AB (A) POWER OF ROCK'N'ROLL 1981 CBS US 37099

M85 THE MARKEYS M85

STEVE CROPPER G ((A) THE MARKEYS 1961 ATLANTIC US 8055
DONALD DUCK DUNN B ((B) DO THE POPEYE 1962 ATLANTIC US 8062
TERRY JOHNSON D ((C) GREAT MEMPHIS SOUND 1965 STAX US 707 UK ATLANTIC587024
AL JACKSON D ((D) BACK TO BACK 196 STAX US 720
PACK AXTON SAX ((E) DAMIFIKNEW 1969 COTILLION US SD 9014
DON NIX SAX ((F) MEMPHIS HORNS 1970 COTILLION US 9014
BOOMER T JONES ORG ((G) MEMPHIS EXPERIENCE 1970 STAX US 2036
WAYNE JACKSON TPT ((H) HIGH ON MUSIC 1976 RCA US 1056
ANDREW LOVE SAX ((I) MELLOW JELLY 19 ATLANTIC UK 587 135
ISAAC HAYES PNO (
JERRY LEE SMITH K (FLOYD NEWMAN SAX (

M86 MARK ALMOND M86

JON MARK V G B PERC (ALL (A) MARK ALMOND 1971 HARVEST UK SHSP 4011 US BLUETHUMB BTS 27
JOHN ALMOND SAX V PERC (ALL (A) MARK ALMOND 1971 HARVEST GER 92200
TOMMY TEDESCO MAND (H (B) MARK ALMOND 2 1972 BLUE THUMB US BT 32
TOMMY EYRE K G PERC (AB (C) RISING 1972 HARVEST UK SHVL 809 US CBS 31917
JOHN LEFTWICH B (H (C) RISING 1972 NOVA GER 6 22365
ROGER SUTTON G V PERC (AB (D) MARK ALMOND 73 1973 NOVA GERM 628448 US CBS 32486
BOBBY VEGA B (H (D) MARK ALMOND 73 1974 KUCKUCK GER 2375 027
JOHN TROPEA G (F (E) TO THE HEART 1976 ABC UK ABCL 5183 US ABC ABCD 945
LEON PENDARVIS K (F (F) OTHER PEOPLES ROOMS 1978 HORIZON UK AMLJ 730 US A&M AM 730
MARK CRANNY D (H (G) BEST OF 1980 KILLROY GER 19955
BILL BERG D (H (H) TUESDAY IN NEW YORK 1980 LINE GER LLP5040
RALPH MACDONALD PERC (F
DANNY RICHMOND D (BC JEFF CONDON FLT V(C KEN CRADDOCK K V G(C COLIN GIBSON B V PERC(C
WILL LEE B (F LARRY WILLIAMS SYN (F STEVE GADD D (F JERRY HEY HRNS (F
JEANNIE McLAINE PERC V(H JAY LEWIS G (H LARRY KNECHTEL K (H JIM SALARGIE PNO (H
CARLOS RIOS G (G MARK ROSS SYN K (GH DAVE MAROTTA B (GH ROBERTO PATTACIA D (G
BILLY COBHAM D (E WOLFGANG MELZ B (E MILT HOLLAND PERC(E JOCK ELLIS TROM (E
TOMMY EYRE K (E JIM GORDON D (E GREG BLOCH VLN (E GARY BARONE HRNS (E

M86A BOB MARKLEY M86A

BOB MARKLEY (A (A) MARKLEY 1969 FORWARD US STF 1007
SHAUN HARRIS (
DAN HARRIS (MICHAEL LLOYD (

M87 ALAIN MARKUSFELD M87

ALAIN MARKUSFELD G V (ALL (A) LE DESERT NOIR 1978 EGG 900 528
JOEL DUGRENEST B ((B) PLATOCK 1978 EGG 900 556
LAURENT THIBAULT K ((C) LE MONDE EN ETAGES 19 BARCLAY 920 179
DOMINIQUE FRANCARD SYN((D) LE SON TOMBE DU CIEL 19 BARCLAY 920 327
GERA FRENZI D ((E) CONTEMPORUS 1979 EGG 900 581 US VISA 7012

M88 BOB MARLEY M88

BOB MARLEY G V (ALL (A) SOUL REBEL 1971 TROJAN TBL 126
PETER TOSH (BDN (B) CATCH A FIRE 1972 ISLAND UK ILPS 9241
BUNNY LIVINGSTONE (BDN (C) AFRICAN HERBSMAN 1973 TROJAN TRL 62
EARL LINDO K (DFQS (D) BURNIN' 1973 ISLAND UK ILPS 9256
JUNIOR BRAITHWAITE ((E) RASTA REVOLUTION 1974 TROJAN UK TRLS 89
BEVERLEY KELSO ((F) NATTY DREAD 1975 ISLAND UK ILPS 9281
CARLTON BARRETT D (BDFJPTQSGK (G) LIVE 1975 ISLAND UK ILPS 9376
ASTON BARRETT G B (BDFJPTQSGK (H) JAH LIVE 1975 ISLAND UK IDJ 8
AL ANDERSON G (FJTQSG (J) RASTA MAN VIBRATION 1976 ISLAND UK ILPS 9383
BERNARD HARVEY K (FG (K) EXODUS 1977 ISLAND UK ILPS 9498
TYRONE DOWNIE K (QSK (L) BIRTH OF A LEGEND 1977 EPIC UK 82066
ALVIN PATTERSON PERC (FJPQSGK (M) BIRTH OF A LEGEND (DBL) 1977 CALLA CAS 1240
CHINNA SMITH G (J (N) EARLY MUSIC 1977 EMBASSY UK 31584
JUDY MOWATT V (FJPQSGK (O) REFLECTION 1977 FONTANA FR
MARCIA GRIFFITH V (FJPTQSGK (P) KAYA 1978 ISLAND UK ILPS9517
RITA MARLEY V (FJPQSGK (Q) BABYLON BY BUS (DBL) 1978 ISLAND UK ILPD 11
JUNIOR MARVIN G (FPQSK (R) BOB MARLEY & THE WAILERS 1979 HAMMER MHR 9006
DONALD KINSLEY G (J (S) SURVIVAL 1979 ISLAND UK ILPS9542
WAYNE PERKINS G (B (T) UPRISING 1980 ISLAND UK ILPS9596
RABBIT BUNDRICK K (B (U) IN THE BEGINNING 1979 PSYCHO PLP 6002
WINSTON RILEY K (B ( ) BIRTH OF A LEGEND 1980 EMBASSY UK 31815
( ) SOUL SHAKEDOWN 19 ESP NL 165837

M88A RITA MARLEY M88A

RITA MARLEY V (A (A) RITA MARLEY 1980 TRIDENT TLP 001

M89 MARMALADE M89

PAT FAIRLEY B (E (A) THERE'S A LOT OF IT ABOUT 1968 CBS UK 63414
JUNIOR CAMPBELL G (E (B) BEST OF 1969 CBS US 26553 UK SPB36
DEAN FORD G HCA V (EF (C) REFLECTIONS 1970 LONDON US 575 UK DECCA SKL5047
GRAHAM KNIGHT B V (EFH (D) SONGS 1971 DECCA UK SKL5111
ALAN WHITEHEAD D (EH (E) OB LA DI 1973 EMBASSY UK EMB31032
MIKE JAPP G V K(F (F) OUR HOUSE IS ROCKING 1974 EMI UK EMC 3047
DOUGLAS HENDERSON D (F (G) THE WORLD OF MARMALADE 1976 DECCA UK SPA 470
JOE BREEN B (F (H) ONLY LIGHT ON MY HORIZON NOW 1977 TARGET UK TGS 501
HOWIE CASEY HRNS (F (I) DOING IT ALL FOR YOU 1979 SKY LP1
SANDY NEWMAN G K V(H (J) BACK ON THE ROAD(69/72) 1981 DECCA UK TAB 19
GARTH WATT ROY G V (H

M89A STEVE MARRIOTT M89A

STEVE MARRIOTT G V (A — (A) MARRIOTT — 1976 A&M US 4572 UK AMLH64572
GREG RIDLEY B V (A
IAN WALLACE D (A — MICKEY FINN G (A — DAVID FOSTER K (A — DENNIS KOVARIK B (A
BEN BENAY G (A — MIKE BAIRD D (A — RED RHODES STEEL (A — ALAN ESTES CONGA (A
ERNIE WATTS SAX (A — DAVID SPINOZZA G (A — MAXINE WILLARD V (A — VANETTA FIELDS V (A
CARLEENA WILLIAMS V (A

M90 JOHNNY MARS M90

JOHNNY MARS HCA V (AB — (A) BLUES FROM MARS — 1972 POLYDOR UK 2460 168
BOB HALL PNO MAND (A — (B) OAKLAND BOOGIE — 1976 BIG BEAR UK BEAR 12
BOB BRUNNING B (A — (C) MIGHTY MARS — 1980 JSP UK 1023
BOOGIE WOOGIE RED V (A
PAT GROVER G (A — BABY BOY WARREN V (A — JOHN HUNT D (A

M90A BERNIE MARSDEN M90A

BERNIE MARSDEN G V (AB — (A) ABOUT TIME TOO — 1979 PARLOPHONE UK PCS 7215
DON AIREY K (A — (B) LOOK AT ME NOW — 1980 PARLOPHONE UK PCS 7217
JACK BRUCE B (A
IAN PAICE D (A — TONY RIVERS V (A — COZY POWELL D (A — NEIL MURRAY B (A
SIMON PHILLIPS D (A — DOREEN CHANTNER V (A — IRENE CHANTNER V (A — JON LORD K (A
ALAN CARVELL V (A — STUART CALVER V (A

M91 MARSEILLE M91

PAUL DALE V (AB — (A) RED WHITE & SLIGHTLY BLUE — 1978 MOUNTAIN UK TOPC5012
NEIL BUCHANAN G (AB — (B) MARSEILLE — 1979 MOUNTAIN UK TOPS 125 US RCA 3631
ANDY CHARTERS G (AB
STEVE DINWOODIE B (AB — KEITH KNOWLES D (AB

M92 MARSHALL/HAIN M92

(A) FREE RIDE — 1978 HARVEST UK SHSP 4087

M92A KEITH MARSHALL M92A

KEITH MARSHALL (A — (A) KEITH MARSHALL — 1981 ARRIVAL UK SPIN 1

M93 MARSHALL TUCKER M93

TOY CALDWELL G V (ABCDEFGHIJ — (A) MARSHALL TUCKER BAND — 1973 CAPRICORN US 0112 UK 2429 114
TOMMY CALDWELL B V (ABCDEFGHIJ — (A) MARSHALL TUCKER BAND — 197 CAPRICORN UK RI K 47509
GEORGE McCORKLE G (ABCDEFGHIJKLM — (B) A NEW LIFE — 1974 CAPRICORN US 0124 UK 2429 101
JERRY EUBANKS SAX (ABCDEFGHIJKLM — (B) A NEW LIFE — 1974 CAPRICORN UK K 57501
PAUL RIDDLE D (ABCDEFGHIJKLM — (C) SEARCHIN' FOR A RAINBOW — 1975 CAPRICORN US 0161 UK 2429 129
DOUG GRAY G V (ABCDEFGHIJKLM — (D) WHERE WE ALL BELONG — 1975 CAPRICORN US 0145 UK 2659 042
PAUL HORNSBY K (ABCF — (E) LONG HARD RIDE — 1976 CAPRICORN US 0170 UK 2429 140
CHARLIE DANIELS FDL (BCEFL — (F) CAROLINA DREAMS — 1977 CAPRICORN US 0180 UK 2476 130
JOHN McEUEN BANJO (E — (G) TOGETHER FOREVER — 1978 CAPRICORN US 0205 UK 2476 139
JEROME JOSEPH PERC (CE — (H) GREATEST HITS — 1978 CAPRICORN US 0214
RICHARD BETTS G (C — (I) BEST OF — 1978 CAPRICORN UK 2429 190
CHUCK LEAVELL K (CFJ — (J) RUNNING LIKE THE WIND — 1979 WB US 3317 UK K 56621
AL McDONALD MAND (C — (K) TENTH — 1980 WB US 3410 UK K 56778
FRANKLIN WILKIE HRNS (LM — (L) DEDICATED — 1981 WB US 3525
NORTON BUFFALO HCA (L — (M) TUCKERIZED — 1982 WB US 3684
EARL FORD HRNS (B
LEO LABRANCHE HRNS (C — JAIMOE JOHANSON CONGA (FAB — BUDDY THORNTON (A — FRED WISE FDL (A
DONNA HALL V (A — ERNESTINE JONES V (A — ELLA BROWN V (A — OSCAR JACKSON SAX (A
SAM DIXON TPT (A — STEVE MADAIO HRNS (J — GARY GRANT HRNS (J — DAVID LUELL HRNS (J
GARY HERBIG HRNS (J — BILL REICHENBACH HRNS (J — TODD LOGAN HRNS (B — RONNIE GODFREY K (M
YOLANDA McCULLOUGH V (M — SARAH DASH V (M — KRYSTAL DAVIS V (M

M94 JOHN MARTYN M94

JOHN MARTYN G V K HCA (ALL — (A) LONDON CONVERSATION — 1967 ISLAND UK ILPS 952
HAROLD McNAIR FLT (B — (B) THE TUMBLER — 1968 ISLAND UK ILPS 9091
BEVERLEY MARTYN V G (CDEH — (C) STORMBRINGER — 1970 ISLAND UK ILPS 9113 US WB 1854
PAUL HARRIS K (CD — (D) THE ROAD TO RUIN — 1970 ISLAND UK ILPS 9133 US WB 1882
HARVEY BROOKS B (C — (E) BLESS THE WEATHER — 1971 ISLAND UK ILPS 9167 US 9311
LEVON HELM D (C — (F) SOLID AIR — 1973 ISLAND UK ILPS 9226 US 9325
WELLS KELLY D (D — (G) INSIDE OUT — 1973 ISLAND UK ILPS 9253 US 9335
BILLY MUNDI D (C — (H) SUNDAYS CHILD — 1975 ISLAND UK ILPS 9296 US 9296
HERBIE LOVELL D (C — (J) SO FAR SO GOOD — 1976 ISLAND UK ILPS 9484 US 9484
JOHN SIMON K (C — (K) LIVE AT LEEDS — 1975 ISLAND UK ILPS 9343
MIKE KOWALSKI D (D — (L) ONE WORLD — 1977 ISLAND UK ILPS 9492
ROCKY DZIDZORNU PERC (D — (M) GRACE & DANGER — 1980 ISLAND UK ILPS 9560
DAVE PEGG B (DLF — (N) GLORIOUS FOOL — 1981 WEA UK K 99178
DAVE MATTACKS D (F
ALAN SPENNER B (D — DANNY THOMPSON B (DEGHLF — LYN DOBSON FLT (D — RAY WARLEIGH SAX (D
STEVE WINWOOD K B (GL — REMI KABAKA PERC (G — CHRIS STEWART (G — CHRIS WOOD WIND (G
KESH SATHIE TABLA (GHL — BOBBY KEYS SAX (G — LIAM GENOCHEY D (H — TONY BRAUNAGEL D (H
TERRY WILSON B (H — AL ANDERSON B (H — RABBIT BUNDRICK K (HF — DUDU PUKWANA SAX (D
JON FIELD FLT (L — TRISTRAN FRY PERC (LF — GEORGE LEE SAX (L — NEIL MURRAY B (L
ANDY NEWMARK D (L — MORRIS PERT PERC (L — RICO RODRIGUES TROM (L — HANSFORD ROWE B (L
BRUCE ROWLAND D (L — JON STEVENS D (L — PAUL WHEELER G (B — DAVE MOSES B (B
TONY REEVES B (E — IAN WHITEMAN K (E — SMILEY DE JONNES PERC (E — RICHARD THOMPSON G (EF
ROGER POWELL D (E — PHIL COLLINS PROD D V (MN — TOMMY EYRE K (M — JOHN GIBLIN B (M
DAVE LAWSON SYN (M — TONY COE SAX (F — SIMON NICOL (F — SUE DRAHEIM VLN (F
SPEEDY ACQUAYE PERC (F

M95 MARSUPILAMI M95

DAVE LAVEROCK G (AB — (A) MARSUPILAMI — 1970 TRANSATLANTIC UK TRA 213
LEARY HASSON K (AB — (B) ARENA — 1971 TRANSATLANTIC UK TRA 230
FRED HASSON V HCA (AB
MIKE FOURACRE D (AB — JESSICA STANLEY-CLARKE FLT V (AB — RICHARD LATHAN HICKS B (AB — BOB WEST V (B
PETER BARDENS PERC (B — MANDY RIEDELBANCH WIND (B

M95A MARTHA & THE MUFFINS M95A

MARTHA JOHNSON V K (ABC — (A) METROMUSIC — 1980 DINDISC UK DID1 GER VIRGIN 202178
MARTHA LADLY K V TROM (AB — (B) TRANCE & DANCE — 1980 DINDISC UK DID5 GER VIRGIN 202837
ANDY HAAS SAX (ABC — (C) THIS IS THE ICE AGE — 1981 DINDISC GER 204181
CARL FINKLE B (AB
MARK GANE G (ABC — TIM GANE D (ABC — MIKE HOWLETT (A — JOCELYNE LANOIS B PERC (C
DANIEL LANOIS PERC V (C — NICK GANE (C — ANDY CONDON (C — SANDY HORNE V (C
GORDON DEPPE V (C — ALYX SKRIABOW V (C — GEORGE AXON PERC (C — CORINNE PLOMISH V (C
GLEN SCHELLENBERG PNO (C

M95B **DEWEY MARTIN** M95B

DEWEY MARTIN D V (A (A) DEWEY MARTIN & MEDICINE BALL 19 UNI US 73088
BILL DARNELL G (A
PETE BRADSTREET PNO (A BUDDY EMMONS STEEL(A RANDY FULLER G V (A STEVEN LEFEVER B (A
HARVEY KAGEN B (A TERRY GREGG B V (A

M95C **MIKE MARTIN** M95C

MIKE MARTIN (A (A) ON THE ROAD 1979 FLYRIGHT FLY 301

M95D **VINCE MARTIN** M95D

VINCE MARTIN G V K(A (A) VINCE MARTIN 1973 CAPITOL US 11181
DUKE BARDWELL B (A
JEFF COMANOR G (A CHRIS DARROW G K FDL(A VENETTA FIELDS V (A SIDNEY GEORGE SAX (A
BUDDY HELM D (A ERIC HORD G (A CLYDIE KING V (A CHARLES LARKEY B (A
VAN DYKE PARKS (A JOHN SEBASTIAN HCA (A KELLY SHANAHAN D (A HANK WILLIAMS V (A

M95E **VINCE MARTIN & FRED NEIL** M95E

VINCE MARTIN G V (A (A) TEAR DOWN THE WALLS 196 ELEKTRA US EKL248
FED NEIL G V (A
FELIX PAPPALARDI B HCA(A JOHN SEBASTIAN HCA G(A

M96 **MOON MARTIN** M96

JOHN 'MOON'MARTIN G V (ALL (A) SHOTS FROM A COLD NIGHTMARE 1979 CAPITOL UK/US 11787 GER 85513
HOWIE WYETH D (B (B) ESCAPE FROM DOMINATION 1979 CAPITOL UK/US 11933 GER 85944
GARY VALENTINE B (AX (C) STREET FEVER 1980 CAPITOL UK/US 12099
CRAIG LEON K (AC (D) MYSTERY TICKET 1982 CAPITOL US 12200
PHIL SEYMOUR D V (A (X) EP(VICTIMS OF ROMANCE +4 1978 CAPITOL UK 16076
DANY WYNN D (D
MICHAEL BOTTS D (D SUSAN HALL PERC (A CHARLIE MERRIAM V (A WILLIE ALEXANDER PNO (A
JIM LEITH V (A JUDE COLE V (BC DENNIS CROY B (BC RICK CROY D (BC
JEFF FARGUS K V (C STEVE DOUGLAS SAX (C DANA FERRIS G (C ROBERT WRIGHT V (C
P ROBINSON V (C P MAROSHEK V (C S HESS V (C ROB STONER B (B
BOB BABBETTE B (D PETER BERNSTEIN B (D MARK CHRISTIAN G (D ANDREW GOLD G (D
CHRIS BROSIUS G V (D JACK WALDMAN K (D GENE TAYLOR K (D JEFF FARGUS K (D
BILL ELLIOTT K (D JOHN HOBBS K (D BILL HOUSE V (D

M96A **HIRTH MARTINEZ** M96A

HIRTH MARTINEZ (AB (A) HIRTH FROM EARTH 19 WB US B 2867
(B) BIG BRIGHT STREET 19 WB UK K56400 US B 3031

M97 **NIGEL MARTINEZ** M97

NIGEL MARTINEZ (A (A) BETTER THINGS TO COME 1978 STATE UK ETAT 17

M98 **MARVELETTES** M98

WANDA YOUNG V ((A)PLEASE MR POSTMAN 1961 TAMLA US TS 228
KATHERIN SCHAFFNER V ((B) MARVELETTES SING 196 TAMLA US TS 229
ANN BOGAN V ((C) PLAYBOY 1963 TAMLA US TS 231
GLADYS HORTON V ((D) MARVELOUS MARVELETTES 1963 TAMLA US TS 237 UK 65 STML11008
GEORGEANNA TILLMAN V ((E) LIVE ON STAGE 196 TAMLA US TS 243
KATHY ANDERSON V ((F) GREATEST HITS 196 TAMLA US TS 253
JUANITA COWART V ((G) MARVELETTES 1967 TAMLA US TS 274 UK 67 STML11052
(H) SOPHISTICATED SOUL 1968 TAMLA US TS 286 UK 69 STML11090
(I) IN FULL BLOOM 1970 TAMLA US TS 288 UK STML11145
(J) RETURN OF THE MARVELETTES 197 TAMLA US TS 305
(K) BEST OF 1975 TAMLA UK STML11258
(L) ANTHOLOGY 197 TAMLA US M7 827

M99 **BRETT MARVIN & THE THUNDERBOLTS** M99

GRAHAM HINE G V (AB (A) BRETT MARVIN & THE THUNDERBOLTS 1970 SONET UK SNTF 616 METRONOME 15380
DAVE ARNOT D (A (B) 12 INCHES OF 1971 SONET UK SNTF 619
JIM PITTS G V HCA (AB (C) BEST OF FRIENDS 1971 SONET UK SNTF 620
PETE GIBSON PERC V TROM(AB (D) ALIAS TERRY DACTYL 1972 SONET UK SNTF 630
JOHN LEWIS K V (AB (E) TEN LEGGED FRIEND 1973 SONET UK SNTF 651
KEITH TRUSSELL PERC (AB (F) BRETT MARVIN 19 BARCLAY FR 920 242
BIG JOHN RANDALL PERC (AB
DAVE ELLIS G (B

M100 **HANK MARVIN & (MARVIN WELCH & FARRAH)** M100

HANK MARVIN G V B(ALL (A) HANK MARVIN 1969 COLUMBIA UK SCX 6352
BRUCE WELCH G V (BCD (B) MARVIN WELCH & FARRAR 1971 REGAL ZONO UK 8502 US CAPITOL 760
JOHN FARRAR G V B(BCD (B) MARVIN WELCH & FARRAR 1971 EMI NL 04715
FRANK RICOTTI PERC (E (C) SECOND OPINION 1971 REGAL ZONO UK 8504 US SIRE 7403
HERBIE FLOWERS B (E (C) SECOND OPINION 1971 EMI GER 04894
BRIAN BENNETT D PERC(CD (D) MARVIN & FARRAR 1973 EMI UK EMA 755 US CAPITOL11403
DAVE RICHMOND B (C (E) GUITAR SYNDICATE 1977 EMI UK EMC3215
AL HAWKSHAW K (C
JOHNNY VAN DERRICK FDL (C OLIVIA NEWTON JOHN REC (D TREVOR SPENCER D PERC(D ALAN TARNEY B (D
ALAN PARKER G (E KEVIN PEEK G (E PAUL KEOGH G (E ALAN SPARKES G (E
LES THATCHER G (E VIC FLICK G (E COLIN GREEN G (E RICKIE HITCHCOCK G (E
CHRIS REA (E CLEM CATTINI D (E

M100A **MARZ & EPERJESSY** M100A

(A) MARZ & EPERJESSY 1971 BELLAPHON BLPS19072

M100B **CAROLYNE MAS** M100B

CAROLYNE MAS (AB (A) CAROLYNE MAS 1979 MERCURY UK 9100 068 US 3783
CRISPIN CIDE SAX (B (B) HOLD ON 1980 MERCURY UK 6337 105 US 3841
DAVID LANDAU G (B (C) MODERN DREAM 1981 MERCURY US 4022
CHARLIE GIORDANO K (B
BOBBY CHOUINARD D (B

M100C **MASCARA** M100C

(A) DESOLATED WORLD (EP) 19 OPTIMISTIC OPT 006

M100D **MASHMAKHAN** M100D

PIERRE SENECAL K WIND G V(AB (A) MASHMAKHAN 1969 CBS US 30 365
RAYBURN BLAKE G V (AB (B) THE FAMILY 197 EPIC US 30813
BRIAN EDWARDS B V (AB
JERRY MERCER D V (AB

M100E MASKED MARAUDERS M100E

(A) THE MASKED MARAUDERS 1969 REPRISE US 6378

**REPORTED BY ROLLING STONE MAGAZINE THAT BOB DYLAN, LENNON & McCARTNEY GEORGE HARRISON AND MICK JAGGER WAS INCLUDED IN THE LINE UP BUT WAS IN FACT 'THE GOODLINESS & CLEANLINESS SKIFFLE BAND' DOING IMITATIONS OF THEM

M100F JIMMIE LEE MASLON M100F

JIMMIE LEE MASLON		(A	(A) YOUR WILDCAT WAYS	1981 RONDELET ABOUT 1003

M101 DAVE MASON M101

DAVE MASON	G V	(ALL	(A) ALONE TOGETHER	1970 HARVEST UK SHTC251 UK ABC 197 5191
LEON RUSSELL	K	(A	(A) ALONE TOGETHER	1975 BLUE THUMB US BTS 29 + BT 8819
JIM CAPALDI	D	(A	(B) DAVE MASON & CASS ELLIOT	1971 PROBE UK 6259 US BLUE THUMB 8825
JOHN SIMON		(A	(C) HEADKEEPER	1072 BLUE THUMB UK ILPS9203 US BTS 34
JIM KELTNER	D	(A	(C) HEADKEEPER	1973 ABC RI UK ABCL5189
JIM GORDON	D	(AF	(D) IS ALIVE	1972 BLUE THUMB US BTS 54
CHRIS ETHRIDGE		(A	(E) SCRAPBOOK	1972 ISLAND UK ICD 5
CARL RADLE	B	(A	(F) IT'S LIKE YOU NEVER LEFT	1974 CBS US 31721 UK 65258
LARRY KNECHTEL		(A	(G) BEST OF	1974 BLUE THUMB US BTSD6013
MICK DE TEMPLE		(A	(H) DAVE MASON	1975 CBS US 33096 UK 80360
JOHN BARBATA	D	(A	(J) SPLIT COCONUT	1975 CBS US 33698 UK 69163
DELANEY BRAMLETT	G V	(A	(K) AT HIS BEST	1975 ABC US TD880 UK ABCL5122
BONNIE BRAMLETT	V	(A	(L) CERTIFIED LIVE	1976 CBS US 34174 UK 88293
CLAUDIA LENNEAR	V	(A	(M) LET IT FLOW	1977 CBS US 34680 UK 81984
RITA COOLIDGE	V	(AC	(N) MARIPOSA DE ORO	1978 CBS US 35285 UK 82625
GERRY BECKLEY	V	(N	(O) VERY BEST OF	1979 BLUE THUMB 6032
JACK STORTI		(A	(P) OLD CREST ON A NEW WAVE	1980 CBS US 36144 UK 83828
JERRY WILLIAMS	G	(N	(Q) BEST OF	1981 CBS US 37089
LOU COOPER		(A		

CASS ELLIOT	V	(B	MIKE COOLIDGE		(A	MARK JORDAN	K	(CJ	BOB NORWOOD		(A
LONNIE TURNER	B	(CF	RICK JAEGER	D	(CFHJPN	FELIX FLACO FALCON	PERC	(C	SPENCER DAVIS	V	(C
GRAHAM NASH	V G	(CJN	KATHY McDONALD	V	(C	JIM KRUEGER	G	(HJLMPN	CHUCK RAINEY	B	(F
ROCKY DZIDZORNU	PERC	(F	MAXINE WILLARD	V	(F	CLYDIE KING	V	(F	JULIA TILLMAN	V	(F
KATHLEEN SAROYAN	V	(F	SON OF HARRY	G	(F	CHARLES FLETCHER	B	(F	GREG REEVES	B	(F
JOHN BATDORF	V	(F	STEVE MADAIO	HRNS	(F	DENNIS MOROUSE	HRNS	(F	NORMA BELL	HRNS	(F
STEVIE WONDER	HCA	(F	NASTYEE		(F	MIKE FINNIGAN	K V	(HLMPN	BOB GLAUB	B	(HNP
GARY BARONE	HRNS	(H	JERRY JUMONVILLE	HRNS	(H	JOCK ELLIS	HRNS	(H	SAL MARQUEZ	HRNS	(H
TIM WEISBERG	FLT	(H	EMIL RICHARDS	PERC	(J	DAVID CROSBY	V	(J	GERALD JOHNSON		(LJMN
JAI WINDING	K	(J	MANHATTAN TRANSFER	V	(J	DON PRESTON		(A	STEPHEN STILLS	V	(MN
YVONNE ELLIMAN	V	(M	ERNIE WATTS	SAX	(MN	BOBBYE HALL	PERC	(M	BROOKS HUNNICUTT	V	(M
VERNA RICHARDSON	V	(M	KAREN PATTERSON	V	(M	BRYAN GAROFALO	B	(B	RUSS KUNKEL	D PERC	(B
PAUL HARRIS	K	(B	MICHAEL JACKSON	V	(P	RAY REVIS	PERC	(P	MARK STEIN	K V	(NP
RON GREENE	PERC	(N	JEFF PORCARO	D	(N	JOHN SAMBARATO	V	(N	JOE WISSERT PROD		(P

M102 HARVEY MASON M102

HARVEY MASON	D	(ALL	(A) MARCHING IN THE STREETS	1976 ARISTA US 4054
JAN HAMMER	K	(B	(B) EARTHMOVER	1976 ARISTA US 4096
GREG ADAMS	HRNS	(C	(C) FUNK IN A MASON JAR	1977 ARISTA US 4157 UK SPART 1049
DOROTHY ASHBY		(C	(D) GROOVIN' YOU	1979 ARISTA US 4227 UK ARTY 166
STANLEY BANKS	B	(C	(E) WORLD CLASS	1981 ARISTA US 4283
WILFREDOWILSON		(D		

GEORGE BENSON	G V	(C	EMILIO CASTILLO	HRNS	(C	MERRY CLAYTON	V	(C	JORGE DALTO	K	(C
BOB JAMES	K	(CD	KENNY MASON	TPT	(CD	AL McKAY	G	(C	RAY PARKER	G	(CD
MIKE PORCARO	B	(CD	TOM SCOTT	HRNS	(C	TOWER OF POWER	HRNS	(C	CHARLES VEAL	VLN	(CD
MAXINE WILLARD	V	(AB	VANETTA FIELDS	V	(C	CHUCK FINDLEY	HRNS	(C	DAVID FOSTER	B	(CD
RONNIE FOSTER	K	(CD	MIC GILLETTE	HRNS	(C	LOUIS JOHNSON	B	(C	MARVIN MASON		(C
PAULETTE McWILLIAMS	V	(C	JERRY PETERS	K	(ACD	LEE RITENOUR	G	(ACD	IAN UNDERWOOD		(C
DAVID T WALKER	G	(C	BILL WATRONS	TROM	(C	LARRY WILLIAMS	WIND	(C	BILL CHAMPLIN	V	(D
TONY DUMAS		(C	GARY GRANT	HRNS	(C	JAY GRAYDON	G	(CD	DAVE GRUSIN	K	(AC
JERRY HEY	HRNS	(C	KIM HUTCHCROFT	V	(C	DICK HYDE	HRNS	(C	ANTHONY JACKSON	B	(C
HOPPY MASON		(CD	RALPH McDONALD	PERC	(CD	DAVID PAICH	K	(C	LENNY PICKETT	HRNS	(C
SEAWIND	HRNS	(C	STEPHANIE SPRUILL	V	(CD	PHIL UPCHURCH	G	(CD	JULIA TILLMAN	V	(AC
NATE WATTS	B	(C	ART WILSON		(C	PETER CHAIKIN		(D	SHEILA ESCOVEDO		(D
JAMES GILSTRAP	V	(AD	BUNNY HULL		(D	ROGER ST KENNERLY	V	(D	PHIL MOORE		(D
RICHARD TEE	K	(D	JERRY WHITMAN	V	(D	JAI WINDING	PNO	(D	JIM HAAS	V	(D
NEIL JASON	V B	(D	STEVE LUKATHER	G	(D	DAVID SHIELDS	B	(D	RANDY WALDMAN		(D
DAVID WILLIAMS	D	(D	BOB WERTZ		(DA	RON HICKLIN		(D	MORRIS PAUL KENNEDY		(D
BILL MEYERS		(D	DAVID SPINOZZA	D	(D	WAH WAH WATSON	G	(D	CHUCK RAINEY	B	(A
OSCAR BRASHEAR	TPT	(A	ERNIE WATTS	SAX	(A	GEORGE BOHANNON	TROM	(A	BLUE MITCHELL	TPT	(A
RANDY CRAWFORD	V	(A	HUBERT LAWS	FLT	(A	HERBIE HANCOCK	K	(A	PAUL JACKSON	B	(A
BENNY MAUPIN	SAX	(A	FRANK ROSOLINO	TROM	(A	MELVIN RAGIN	G	(A	BOBBY BRYANT	TPT	(A

M102A JAE MASON M102A

JAE MASON		(A	(A) CROSSROADS	196 BUDDAH US BDS5604
			(B) TENDERMAN	196 BUDDAH US BDS5640

M102B MASON - PROFFIT M102B

JOHN TALBOT	G V	(ALL	(A) MASON PROFFIT WANTED	1969 HAPPY TIGER US 1009
TERRY TALBOT	G V	(ALL	(B) MOVING TOWARDS HAPPINESS	1970 HAPPY TIGER US 1019
TIM AYERS	B	(ALL	(AB) COME & GONE (DBL)	1974 WB US 2746 RI LINE GER 8002
BRUCE KURNOW	K HCA	(DE	(C) LAST NIGHT I HAD STRANGEST DREAM	1971 AMPEX US 10138
BYRON BERLINE	VLN	(	(D) ROCKFISH CROSSING	1972 WB US 2657 RI LINE GER 5065
BILL CUNNINGHAM	FDL G V	(E	(E) BAREBACK RIDER	1973 WB US 2704 RI LINE GER 5061
ART NASH	D	(ALL		
RON SCHUETTER	G V	(ABC		

RICK DWETT	PNO	(A	JOHN FRIGO	FDL	(A	KINKY SCHNITZNER	G	(E
TOM RADTRE	PERC	(E						

M102C MASON,WOOD,CAPALDI & FROG M102C

DAVE MASON	G B V	(A	CHRIS WOOD	WIND	(A	JIM CAPALDI	D V	(A	MICK WEAVER	K	(A

M102D MASQUERADERS M102D

(A) EVERYBODY WANNA LIVE ON 1976 ABC US ABCD921

(B) LOVE ANONYMOUS 1977 ABC UK ABCL5222 US ABC 962

M102E NICK MASON M102E

NICK MASON (A — (A) FICTITIOUS SPORTS — 1981 HARVEST UK SHSP4116 CBS US 37307
ROBERT WYATT V (A — (A) FICTITIOUS SPORTS — 1981 CBS US 37307
KAREN KRAFT V (A
CHRIS SPEDDING G (A — CARLA BLEY K (A — GARY WINDO WIND (A — GARY VALENTINE TROM V(A
MIKE MANTLER TPT (A — HOWARD JOHNSON TUBA (A — STEVE SWALLOW B (A — TERRY ADAMS K HCA(A
CARLOS WARD V (A — D SHARP V (A — EARL McINTYRE V (A — VINCENT CHANCEY V (A

M102F MASSACRE M102F

FRED FRITH G V K(A — (A) KILLING TIME — 1981 CELLULOID FR 6597 GER 802 272
FRED MAHER D (A
BILL LASWELL TPT (A

M103 MASS PRODUCTION M103

(A) WELCOME TO OUR WORLD — 1977 COTILLION UK K 50331 US SD9910
(B) BELIEVE — 1977 COTILLION UK K 50400 US SD9918
(C) THREE MILES HIGH — 1978 COTILLION UK K 50510 US SD5205
(D) IN THE PUREST FORM — 1979 COTILLION UK K 50601 US SD5211
(E) MASTERPIECE — 1980 COTILLION US 5218
(F) GIRLS ALRIGHT WITH ME — 1980 WHITFIELD US 3389
(G) TURN UP THE MUSIC — 1981 COTILLION UK K 50784
(H) IN A CITY GROOVE — 1982 COTILLION UK K 50877

M103A MASTERS M103A

JIMMY BERICK G V (A — (A) MASTERS OF THE AIRWAVES — 1974 EPIC UK X598 US 33060
RANDY RAND B G (A
DAVE RADA D V (A — JON FLAK V (A

M103B MASTERS APPRENTICES M103B

DOUG FORD G V (AB — (A) MASTERS APPRENTICES — 197
JAMES KEAYS V (A — (B) A TOAST TO PANAMA RED — 197
COLIN BURGESS D V (
GLENN WHEATLEY B V (A

M105 MATCHBOX M105

BOB BURGOS D (— (A) SETTIN' THE WOODS ON FIRE — 1978 CHISWICK UK WIK 10
GRAHAM FENTON V (— (B) RIDERS IN THE SKY — 1978 CHARLY UK CR 30157
FRED POKE B (— (C) MATCHBOX — 1979 MAGNET UK MAGL5031
GORDON WATERS G V (— (D) MIDNIGHT DYNAMO — 1980 MAGNET US 5036
STEVE BLOOMFIELD G MAND(
JIMMY REDHEAD D (

M105A MATERIAL M105A

FRED MAHER F D (BC — (A) TEMPORARY MUSIC — 19
MICHAEL BEINHORN K SYN (BC — (B) TEMPORARY MUSIC 2 — 1980 RED 12 008
BILL LASWELL B (BC — (C) TEMPORARY MUSIC (COMP) — 198 CELLULOID FR 6576
CLIFF CULTRERI G (C
DON DAVIS SAX (C

M106 MATCHING MOLE M106

ROBERT WYATT D V (AB — (A) MATCHING MOLE — 1972 CBS UK 64850
PHIL MILLER K G (AB — (B) LITTLE RED RECORD — 1973 CBS US 32148 UK 65260
BILL MACCORMICK B (AB
DAVE MACRAE K (AB — ENO SYN (B — DAVE SINCLAIR K (A — DAVE GALE V (B
RUBY CRYSTAL V (B — LITTLE HONEST INJUN V (B

M106A ANDREW MATHESON M106A

ANDREW MATHESON V (A — (A) MONTEREY SHOES — 1979 ARIOLA ARL 5025
PETE KIRCHER D (A
ANDY PASK B (A — RAPHAEL RAVENSCROFT SAX (A — TOMMY EYRE K (A — NIGEL JENKINS G (A
EUNON S BRADY G (A — HOWIE CASEY SAX (A — BILL STREET HRNS (A

M106B MATRIX M106B

NICK ZESSES (A — (A) MATRIX — 1972 RARE EARTH US R542L
DINO FEKARIS (A
TOM BAIRD (A

M106C MATRIX (2) M106C

LARRY DARLING HRNS SYN V(A — (A) THE WIZARD — 1978 WB US 3260
KURT DIETRICH HRNS SYN V(A
MIKE HALE HRNS D V(A — JOHN HARMAN K PERC (A — JOHN KIRCHBERGER WIND (A — BRAD McDOUGAL HRNS V(A
MIKE MURPHY D PERC(A — JEFF PIETRANGELO HRNS PERC(A

M107 DAVE MATTHEWS M107

DAVE MATTHEWS K (AB — (A) SHOOGIE WANNA BOOGIE — 1976 KUDU KU 30
DON GROLNICK K (A — (B) DUNE — 1977 CTI 5005
ANDY NEWMARK D (AB
BARRY MILES K (A — JERRY FRIEDMAN G (A — STEVE KHAN G (A — ANTHONY JACKSON B (A
SUE EVANS PERC (AB — RANDY BRECKER TPT (AB — JON FADDIS TPT (AB — MICHAEL BRECKER SAX (A
RON CUBER SAX (A — BURT COLLINS TPT (AB — ALAN RUBIN TPT (A — JOE SHEPLEY TPT (AB
TOM MALONE TROM (AB — SAM BURTIS TROM (AB — DAVE TAYLOR TROM (AB — PATTI AUSTIN V (A
VIVIAN CHERRY V (A — GWEN GUTHRIE V (A — JIM BUFFINGTON HRNS (A — PETER GORDON HRNS(A
JOE FARRELL SAX (A — FRED WESLEY TROM (A — LANCE QUINN G (A — JOHN TROPEA G (A
CARLOS MARTIN PERC (A — KEN ASCHER K (A — WILL LEE B (A — NICKY MARRERO PERC(A
PAT REBILLOT K (A — JEFF BERLIN B (A — CLIFF CARTER K (B — MARK EGAN B (B
GARY KING B (B — JIM BOSBY HRNS (B — JOHN GATCHELL HRNS (B — LEW SOLOFF HRNS(B
STEVE GADD D (B — HIRAM BULLOCK G (B — ERIC GALE G (B — GORDON GOTTLIEB PERC(B
WAYNE ANDRE TROM (B — GERRY CHAMBERLAIN TROM (B — DAVID SANBORN SAX (B — GROVER WASHINGTON SAX(B
LEW DEL GATTO WIND (B — DAVID TOFANI WIND (B — GOOGIE COPPOLA V (B — SANFORD ALLEN STRINGS(B

M108 IAN MATTHEWS & MATTHEWS SOUTHERN COMFORT M108

IAN MATTHEWS G V (ALL (A) MATTHEWS SOUTHERN COMFORT 1970 UNI UNLS108 MCA UK MAPS 1641
ROGER COULAM K (AC (A) " " " " 1974 MCA RI MCF2675 US DECCA 75191
SIMON NICOL G (A (B) SECOND SPRING 1970 UNI UNLS112 MCA UK MAPS 2038
ANDY LEIGH B V (BC (B) " " " 1974 MCA RI MCF2677 US DECCA 75242
CARL BARNWELL G V (BC3 (B) " " " 197 UNI FR 6369 600
KEITH NELSON BANJO(C (C) LATER THAT SAME YEAR 1970 MCA MKPS2015 MAPS3976
CAL BATCHELOR G (E (C) " " " " 1974 MCA MCF2686
BRUCE THOMAS B (E (C) " " " " DIFF TRACKS 197 DECCA US 75264 PICKWICK CAN 3698
BILLY GRAHAM B FDL(FG (D) IF YOU SAW THROUGH MY EYES 1971 VERTIGO US VEL1002 UK 6360 034
MICHAEL NESMITH G (F (E) TIGERS WILL SURVIVE 1972 VERTIGO US VEL1010 UK 6360 056
BYRON BERLINE FDL (F (E) " " " " (POP LEGEND) 1980 VERTIGO NL 9199 139
JEFF BAXTER G (G (F) VALLEY HI 1973 ELEKTRA US EKS75061 UK K42144
DANNY WEIS G (G (G) SOME DAYS YOU EAT THE BEAR.... 1974 ELEKTRA US EKS75078 UK K42160
B J COLE STEEL(G (H) JOURNEYS FROM GOSPEL OAK 1974 MOONCREST UK CREST18
JERRY DONAHUE G (H (H) " " " " 1979 BOULEVARD BD 3009
MIKE PORTER D (J (J) GO FOR BROKE 1976 CBS US 34102 UK 81316
KENNY EDWARDS B (J (K) HIT & RUN 1977 CBS US 34671 UK 81930
PETER WOOD K (J (L) STEALIN' HOME 1978 ROCKBURGH UK ROC106
SHANE KEISTER K (J (L) " " " 1978 MUSHROOM MRS 5012
MUSCLE SHOALS HRNS (J (M) SIAMESE FRIENDS 1979 ROCKBURGH UK ROC107
BONNIE MURRAY V (K (N) SHAKE IT (12" EP) 1978 ROCKBURGH UK ROCS209
MICK WEAVER K (1M (O) SPOT OF INTERFERENCE 1980 ROCKBURGH US 3092 UK 2383582
PETE WINGFIELD K (LN ( ) BEST OF MATTHEWS SOUTHERN COMFORT 1975 MCA NL 201362 UK MCF2574
SIMON MORTON PERC (LMN (1) 1978 TOUR (2) 1979 FEB TOUR (3) 1970 LIVE
BOB METZGER G (2MO (P) DISCREET REPEAT (DBL) 1979 ROCKBURGH UK 109
WOLFE J FLYWHEEL ACC (E (ABC) 1 2 3 TOO GOOD DBL 1970 MCA GER MAPS 7290D1/2
GERRY CONWAY D (AD
ASHLEY HUTCHINGS B (A
RICHARD THOMPSON G (AD GORDON HUNTLEY STEEL(ABC3 PETE WILLSHER G (A DOLLY COLLINS K (A
POLI PALMER FKT (A RAY DUFFY D (BC MARK GRIFFITHS B G V(123BCMO TOM PALEY BAN (B
ROGER CHURCHYARD FDL (B MARTIN JENKINS MAND (B TRISTRAM FRY VIBES(C PAT DONALDSON B (DH
TIM RENWICK G (DE ANDY ROBERTS G (DEGH SANDY DENNY K V (D TIMI DONALD D (EGH
WILLIE WILSON D (E IAN WHITEMAN K (E BOB RONGA K B (E RAY WARLEIGH SAX (E
DANNY LANE D (FG JAY LACY G (FGJK BOBBY WARFORD G (FG RED RHODES STEEL(F
DAVID BARRY K (FG WILLIE LEACOX D (G DAVID DICKEY B (G MICHAEL FONFARA K (G
STEVE GILLETTE G (G JOEL TEPP HCA G (12GJM LYN DOBSON SAX (G AL GARTH SAX (G
DAVID LINDLEY STEEL(G TRIS IMBODEN D (JK KENNY BUTTREY D (J DON WHALEY B (JK
NORBERT PUTNAM B (J MIKE LEECH B (J STEVE WOOD K (J DAVID BRIGGS K (J
GLEN SPREEN K (J REG YOUNG G (J HARRY ROBINSON G (J STEVE HOOKS WIND(K
CHARLIE HARWOOD K V (K PHIL PALMER G (1LN JIM RUSSELL D (1LMN BRYN HAWORTH G MAND(LN
RICK KEMP B (LN MEL COLLINS SAX (LMN DUFFY POWER HCA (L PETER WATKINS B (3
ROGER SWALLOW D (3 CRAIG BUHLER SAX (M DAVE WINTOUR B (O ROBERT HENRIT D (O
KEITH TIPPETT K (D MARC ELLINGTON PERC (A

M108A MILT MATTHEWS INC M108A

MILT MATTHEWS (A (A) MILT MATTHEWS INC 1971 EMBER NR 5056
NORMAN HARRISON K (A
RANDY B WINGY G (A TOMMY BYRD D (A CARL MATTHEWS B (A

M109 MATUMBI M109

DENNIS BOVELL V G K(BC (A) BEST OF MATUMBI 1977 TROJAN TRLS 145
BEVIN FAGAN B V (ABC (B) SEVEN SEALS 1978 HARVEST SHSP 4090
EUTON JONES PERC (ABC (C) POINT OF VIEW 1979 M R RDC 2001 US EMI 17034
GLAISTER VENN V (ABC (D) AH WHO SEH ? GO GO DEH! 197 RAMA R
EATON BLAKE B (ABC
LLOYD DONALDSON D (ABC WEBSTER JOHNSON K V (ABC PATRICK TENYUE HRNS (C HENRY TENYUE HRNS (C
NICK STRAKER K (C ANDY G (C JULIO FINN HCA (C

M109A CHARLIE MAUCHER M109A

CHARLIE MAUCHER V G B(A (A) PERFORMANCE 1980 CM GER 1111
ULI BOTTCHER G (A
WOLFGANG KRANTZ K (A PETER PANKA D PERC(A

M109B MAUDS M109B

J ROGERS (A (A) HOLD ON 1967 MERCURY 61135
B WINTER (A
F FUSCALDO (A T CONIGLIO (A P WEINBERG (A

M110 BENNIE MAUPIN M110

BENNIE MAUPIN SAX (ALL (A) THE JEWEL IN THE LOTUS 1975 ECM ECM1043
(B) MOONSCAPES 1978 MERCURY
(C) SLOW TRAFFIC TO THE RIGHT 197 MERCURY US SRMI1148
(D) AKMANAC 1978 IMPROVISING IAI373851

M111 JOHN MAYALL & THE BLUESBREAKERS M111

JOHN MAYALL G V HCA K (ALL (A) JOHN MAYAL PLAYS JOHN MAYALL 1964 DECCA UK LK 4680
JOHN McVIE B (ABCDLOak (B) BLUESBREAKERS 1965 DECCA UK SLK4804 US LONDON PS492
KEITH TILLMAN B (GH (B) BLUESBREAKERS 1965 DECCA GER SLK 16547
MICK FLEETWOOD D (LO (C) A HARD ROAD 1967 DECCA UK SKL4853 US LONDON PS502
PETE WARD D (A (C) A HARD ROAD 196 DECCA GER SLK 16490
HENRY LOWTHER TPT (LJOa (BC) BLUESBREAKERS/HARD ROAD(DBL) 19 DECCA GER 3027
CHRIS MERCER SAX (DGHOa (D) CRUSADE 1967 DECCA UK SKL4890 US LONDON PS529
HUGHIE FLINT D (BCDLal (D) CRUSADE 196 GER SLK 16499
JON HISEMAN D (Ja (E) BLUES ALONE 1967 ACE UK SCL1243 US LONDON PS534
ERIC CLAPTON G (BOXdp (F) RAW BLUES 1967 ACE UK SCL1220 US LONDON PS543
DICK HECKSTALL SMITH SAX(GHJOa (EP)WITH PAUL BUTTERFIELD 1967 DECCA UK DFE8673
JIMMY McCULLOCH G (3 (G) DIARY OF A BAND VOL 1 1968 DECCA UK SKL4918 GER SLK 16543
PAUL WILLIAMS B (Oa (H) DIARY OF A BAND VOL 2 1968 DECCA UK SKL4919
COLIN ALLEN D (K (GH) DIARY OF A BAND VOL 1/2 1970 US LONDON PS570
JOHNNY ALMOND SAX (BCPQOXk (I) BLUES GIANT 1968 DECCA IMP 3117
ALEX DMOCHOWSKI B (k (J) BARE WIRES 1968 DECCA UK SKL4945 US LONDON PS537
HARVEY MANDEL G (RXY (J) BARE WIRES 1968 DECCA GER SLK 16558
PAUL LAGOS D (X (K) LAUREL CANYON 1969 DECCA UK SKL4972 US LONDON PS545
AYNSLEY DUNBAR D (CLOa (K) LAUREL CANYON 196 DECCA GER SLK16573 GER NOVA 6 21413
BERNIE WATSON G (OLa (L) SO MANY ROADS 1969 DECCA GER SLK16590 GER RI 6835 132
ANDY FRASER B ((M) LIVE 1969 DECCA GER SLK 16615

(CONTINUED)

JOHN MAYALL & THE BLUESBREAKERS

Musician	Inst	Albums		Title	Release
KEEF HATYLEY	D	(GHOEXabce3	(N)	BEST OF JOHN MAYALL	1969 DECCA GER SLK 16632
ROGER DEAN	G	(ALOa	(O)	LOOKING BACK	1970 DECCA UK SKL5010 US LONDON PS562
JACK BRUCE	B	(O1	(O)	LOOKING BACK (DIFF TRACKS)	1969 DECCA GER 3104 1/2
MICK TAYLOR	G	(DGHJKOQXad	(P)	TURNING POINT	1970 POLYDOR UK 583 571 US PD 4004
TONY REEVES	B	(Ja	(P)	TURNING POINT	1982 POLYDOR RI UK 2485 222 GER 2459 355
RIP KANT	HRNS	(DO	(Q)	EMPTY ROOMS	1970 POLYDOR UK 583 580 US 4010
JEFF KRIBBETT	G	(1	(Q)	EMPTY ROOMS	19 POLYDOR GER 2425 051
PETER GREEN	G	(CLOadK	(PQ)	TURNING POINT/EMPTY ROOMS	1974 POLYDOR UK 2683 039
STEVE THOMPSON	B	(KPQX6nr	(R)	USA UNION	1970 POLYDOR UK 2425 020 US 4022
JON MARK	ACC G	(PQk	(S)	LIVE IN EUROPE	1970 LONDON US PS589
LARRY TAYLOR	B	(RWXZbghik3Qm	(T)	WORLD OF VOL1	1970 DECCA UK SPA 47
DON SUGARCANE HARRIS	VLN	(RXehik	(U)	WORLD OF VOL2	1971 DECCA UK SPA 138
JERRY McGEE	G	(WX	(V)	DOWN THE LINE	1972 LONDON US PS618/9
BLUE MITCHELL	TPT	(Zbek	(W)	MEMORIES	1971 POLYDOR UK 2425 085 US 5012
CLIFFORD SOLOMON	SAX	(Zb	(X)	BACK TO THE ROOTS	1971 POLYDOR UK 2657 005 US 3002
RON SELICO	D	(Z	(X)	BACK TO THE ROOTS	1971 POLYDOR FR 2673 003
FREDDY ROBINSON	G V	(Zbe	(Y)	BEYOND THE TURNING POINT	1971 POLYDOR UK 2483 016
VICTOR GASKIN	B	(be	(Z)	JAZZ BLUES FUSION	1972 POLYDOR UK 2425 103 US PD 5027
RED HOLLOWAY	SAX	(egkm	(Z)	JAZZ BLUES UNION	19 POLYDOR GER 2391 032
ERNIE WATTS	SAX	(b	(a)	THROUGH THE YEARS	1971 DECCA UK SKL5086 US LONDON PS600/1
CHARLES OWENS	SAX	(b	(b)	MOVING ON	1973 POLYDOR UK 2391 047 US PD 5036
HIGHTIDE HARRIS	G	(g	(c)	BEST OF	197 POLYDOR US PD 23006
SOKO RICHARDSON	D	(ghik56nrv	(d)	JOHN MAYALL PROFILE	197 TELDEC GER 624010
RANDY RESNICK	G	(g	(e)	TEN YEARS ARE GONE	1973 POLYDOR UK 2683 036 US PD 3005
DEE McKINNIE	V	(hik	(f)	STAR PORTAIT	1973 POLYDOR IMP 2675019
NOLAN SMITH	TPT	(4m	(f)	POP HISTORY	1973 POLYDOR IMP 2675017
ANN PATERSON	WIND	(4mn	(g)	LATEST EDITION	1975 POLYDOR UK 2391 141 US PD 6030
JIMMY ROBERTS	SAX	(4m	(h)	NEW YEAR NEW BAND NEW COMPANY	1975 ABC UK ABCL5115 US 6019
BILL LAMB	TPT	(4m	(i)	NOTICE TO APPEAR	1975 ABC UK ABCL5142 US ABCD 926
WARREN BRYANT	PERC	(4m	(i)	NOTICE TO APPEAR	1975 ABC GER 25237
DAVID LI	SAX	(4m	(j)	JOHN MAYALL	1976 POLYDOR UK 2482 272
FRANK WILSON	D	(4m	(k)	BANQUET IN BLUES	1976 UK UK ABCL5187 US ABCD 958
EDMOND LEE	B	(5	(m)	LOTS OF PEOPLE	1977 ABC UK ABCL5126 US ABCD 992
BRAD THOELKE	TROM	(tn	(n)	A HARD CORE PACKAGE	1977 ABC US ABCD 1039
JESSE ED DAVIS	G	(	(p)	PRIMAL SOLOS	1977 LONDON US LC 50003
ALLAN TOUSSAINT	K	(i	( )	HIGHLIGHTS	1977 POLYDOR GER 2674 013
RICK VITO	G	(hikt	(q)	BLUES ROOTS	1978 DECCA UK ROOTS 8
JAY SPELL	K	(hikm	(r)	LAST OF THE BRITISH BLUES	1978 ABC US ABCD 1086
LARRY BLOUIN	SAX	(i	(s)	BOTTOM LINE	1979 DJM UK DJF20556 US 23 GER 64216
LON PRICE	WIND	(i	(t)	NO MORE INTERVIEWS	1979 DJM UK DJF20564 US 29 GER 63537
NICK MESSINA	TPT	(i	(v)	ROAD SHOW BLUES	1981 DJM GER 64231
HERMAN ERNEST	D	(i	( )	BLUESBREAKERS BOX SET (12LP)	1981 TELDEC GER 30122
JAMES CARROLL BOOKER	K	(i	( )	ROOM TO MOVE	19 MEDIUM 2486041
TONY BROUSSARD	B	(i		(1) 1969 (2) 1971 (3)1971 (4) 1977	(5) 1977
KIM JOSEPH	CONGA	(i			
STEVE HUGHES	G	(i			

Musician	Inst	Albums	Musician	Inst	Albums	Musician	Inst	Albums	Musician	Inst	Albums
ALAN SKIDMORE	SAX	(BO	DENNIS HEALEY	TPT	(BO	BUCK CLARK	PERC	(k	BENNY POWELL	TROM	(k
RONNIE BARRON	K V	(kt	RON McCURDY	D	(k	DOUG BARE	K	(k	MIKE COOLEY	G	(k
LENNY McDANIEL	B	(k	PHIL DESPOMMIER	D	(k	NOVI NOVAG	VLA	(k	PAT SMITH	V	(m
PEPPER WATKINS	V	(s4mnr	JAMES SMITH	G	(56	LEON PENDARVIS	K	(s	BOB BABITT	B	(s
FRANCISCO CENTENO	B	(s	JEFF MIRANOV	G	(s	SIDNEY McGINNIS	G	(s	JOHN TROPEA	G	(s
STEVE JORDAN	D	(s	ERROL BENNETT	PERC	(s	ARTHUR JENKINS	PERC	(s	ROB MOUNSEY	K	(s
JON FADDIS	HRNS	(s	VERGIL JONES	HRNS	(s	STEVE FORMAN	PERC	(s	LEE HOLDRIDGE	STRING	(s
CHERYL LYNN	V	(s	DELBERT LANGSTON	V	(s	ALAN RAPH	TROM	(s	HOWARD JOHNSON	HRNS	(s
VIVIAN CHERRY	V	(s	ULLANDA McCULLOUGH	V	(s	GORDON EDWARDS	B	(s	JANICE PENDARVIS	V	(s
CORNELL DUPREE	G	(s	JEFF LAYTON	G	(s	PAUL SCHAEFFER	K	(s	RUBENS BASSINI	PERC	(s
ALEJANDRO ACUNA	PERC	(s	JOHN JARVIS	K	(s	JEFF PORCARO	D	(s	STEVE LUKATHER	G	(s
BEN BENAY	G	(s	RANDY BRECKER	HRNS	(s	MICHAEL BRECKER	HRNS	(s	RON CUBER	WIND	(s
LEW SOLOFF	TPT	(s	BERNARD KRAUSE	SYN	(s	DAVID SHIELDS	B	(s	TIM DRUMMOND	B	(s
LEE RITENOUR	G	(s	NIGEL STANGER	SAX	(AL	MARTIN HART	D	(LOa	NICK NEWELL	SAX	(L
MAGGIE PARKER	V	(t	JAMES QUILL SMITH	G	(nrtv	CHRIS CAMERON	K	(t	CHRISTIAAN MOSTERT	WIND	)t
ANGUS THOMAS	B	(t	RUBIN ALVAREZ	D	(t	BECKIE BURNS	V	(mnil	BUDDY McDANIELS	SAX	(th
GEORGE SHAW	TPT	(t	RAY WARLEIGH	WIND	(C	TONY McPHEE	G	(O	MALCOLM POOL	B	(O
BILL SHORTT	PERC	(O	JACK DUPREE	V	(O	NIGEL STANGER	SAX	(O	GARY ROWLES		(m
CLIFF ERVIN	TPT	(n	BUDDY McDANIEL	SAX	(n	JODY LINCOTT	PERC	(n	JIM PRICE	TROM	(n
TREVOR LAURENCE	SAX	(n	STEVE MADAIO	TPT	(n	MARILYN SCOTT	V	(nr	MINDY MICKEL	V	(n
EDNA RICHARDSON	V	(n	MARTY GWYNN	V	(r	DONNA WASHBURN	V	(r	MAUREEN	V	(r
COLLEEN	V	(r	JUDY BROWN	V	(r	KEVIN McCORMICK	B	(v	MAGGIE PARKER	V PERC	(v

M111A

MAX

M111A

(A) MAX — 1980 CHRYSALIS UK CHR 1278

M112

MAX WEBSTER

M112

Musician	Inst	Albums		Title	Release
DAVE MYLES	B V	(DE	(A)	MAX WEBSTER	1975 ANTHEM CAN ANR 1006
KIM MITCHELL	G V	(DE	(B)	HIGH CLASS & BORROWED SHOES	1977 ANTHEM CAN ANR 1007 MERCURY US1160
TERRY WATKINSON	K V	(ED	(C)	MUTINY UP MY SLEEVE	1978 CAPITOL 11776
GARY McCRACKEN	D V	(DE	(D)	MILLION VACATIONS	1979 CAPITOL 11937
			(E)	LIVE MAGNETIC AIR	1979 CAPITOL 12042
			(F)	UNIVERSAL JUVENILES	1980 MERCURY UK 6337 144 US SRM13855
			(G)	HANGOVER	1977 MERCURY US 1131

M113

MAXFIELD PARRISH

M113

Musician	Inst	Albums	Musician	Inst	Albums	Musician	Inst	Albums	Musician	Inst	Albums
DAVID BIASOTTI		(A	(A) IT'S A CINCH TO GIVE LEGS.... 1972 CURNON US CNL 721								
PERRIN MUIR		(A									
DAVID McCLELLAN		(A	RANDY GROENKE		(A	CHRIS DARROW	G	(A	DAVID LINDLEY	FDL V	(A
BERNIE LEADON	G	(A	JOHN LONDON	B	(A	JOHN WARE	D	(A	CHESTER CRILL		(A

M114A

PHIL MAY

M114A

Musician	Inst	Albums	Musician	Inst	Albums	Musician	Inst	Albums	Musician	Inst	Albums
PHIL MAY	V	(A	(A) PHIL MAY & THE FALLEN ANGELS 1978 PHILIPS NL 6410 969								
WALLY WALLER	B V	(A									
CHICO GREENWOOD	D	(A	BILLY LOVELADY	G	(A	ED DEAN	G	(A	BRIAN JOHNSTON	K	(
MICKEY FINN	G	(A	JACK JOHNSTON	K	(A	JOHN POVEY	V	(A	JOHN PORTER	G	(A
FRAN BYRNE	D	(A	L SHANKA	VLN	(A						

M114B MAY BLITZ M114B

Member	Role	Title	Release
TONY NEWMAN	VIBES D(AB1	(A) MAY BLITZ	1970 VERTIGO UK 6360007 US PARAMOUNT 5020
REID HUDSON	B V (AB	(B) SECOND OF MAY	1971 VERTIGO UK 6360037
JAMES BLACK	G V (AB1	(1) 1969 LINE UP	
TERRY POOLE	B (1		
KEITH BAKER	D (1		

M115 CURTIS MAYFIELD M115

Member	Role	Title	Release
CURTIS MAYFIELD	V (ALL	EARLY YEARS	1973 PROBE UK GTSP 201 UK ABC ABCD780
WENDELL STEWART	D (S	SWEET EXORCIST	1974 BUDDAH BDLH 5001 RI UK 2318 099
TOM FERRONE	G (S	SWEET EXORCIST	1976 CURTOM US 8601 UK K 56284
TIM TOBIAS	K (S	ROOTS	1974 BUDDAH BDLH 5006 UK 2318 045
RICH TUFO	K (S	ROOTS	1976 CURTOM US 8009 UKRI K 56249
KEN BURKE	B (S	CURTIS	1974 BUDDAH BDLH 5005 UK 2318 015
JOE SCOTT	B (S	CURTIS	1976 CURTOM US 8005 UK K 56252
ROSS TRAUT	G (S	BACK TO THE WORLD	1974 BUDDAH BDLH 5008 UKRI K 56251
TONY CARPENTER	PERC (S	BACK TO THE WORLD	197 CURTOM US 8015
SONNY SEALS	HRNS (S	IN CHICAGO LIVE	1974 BUDDAH BDLH 5009
LEN DRUSS	HRNS (S	IN CHICAGO LIVE	1976 CURTOM US 8018 UK K 56250
ART HOYLE	HRNS (S	SHORT EYES	197 CURTOM US 5017
PAUL HOWARD	HRNS (S	DO IT ALL NIGHT	197 CURTOM US 5022
DALE CLEVENGER	HRNS (S	MOVE ON UP	1974 BUDDAH BDLP 4015
BILL PORTER	HRNS (S	SUPERFLY	1974 BUDDAH BDLH 4018
ROBERT LUSTREA	HRNS (S	SUPERFLY	197 RSO US RSS5 UK 2394 233
GILL ASKEY	HRNS (S	GOT TO FIND A WAY	1974 BUDDAH BDLP 4029 CURTOM US 8604
		AMERICA TODAY	1974 BUDDAH BDLP 4033 CURTOM US 5001
		GIVE GET TAKE HAVE	1976 BUDDAH BDLP 4042 CURTOM US 5007
		CURTIS LIVE	1974 BUDDAH BDLD 2001 CURTOM UK K66047
		CURTIS LIVE	197 CURTIM US 8008
		NEVER SAY YOU CANT SURVIVE	1977 CURTOM CU 5013 UK K56352
		HEARTBEAT	1979 CURTOM US 3053
		(S)SOMETHING TO BELIEVE IN	1980 CURTOM UK 2393 271 US 3077

M116 PERCY MAYFIELD M116

Member	Role	Title	Release
PERCY MAYFIELD	V PNO(ALL	(A) PERCY MAYFIELD	1969 TANGERINE UK TRC 1505
		(B) BOUGHT BLUES	1969 TANGERINE US TRS 1510
		(C) TIGHTROPE	1969 BRUNSWICK 754145
		(D) SINGS	1970 RCA VICTOR US 4269
		(E) WEAKNESS IS A THING CALLED MAN	1970 RCA VICTOR US 4444
		(F) BLUES & THEN SOME	1971 RCA VICTOR US 4558
		(G) THE INCREDIBLE	1972 SPECIALTY US 5010 UK SNTF 5010
		(H) BEST OF	197 SPECIALTY US 2126

M117 MAZE M117

Member	Role	Title	Release
FRANKIE BEVERLY	(	(A) ARMAGEDDON	197 MTA US MTS 5012
		(B) MAZE	1977 CAPITOL 11607
		(C) GOLDEN TIME OF DAY	1978 CAPITOL 11710
		(D) INSPIRATION	1980 CAPITOL 11912
		(E) JOY AND PAIN	1980 CAPITOL 12087

M118 MEAL TICKET M118

Member	Role	Title	Release
CHRIS HUNT	D PERC (AB	(A) CODE OF THE ROAD	1977 EMI UK INS 3008
JACK BRAND	B V (AB	(B) THREE TIMES A DAY	1978 EMI UK INS 3010
RAY FLACKE	G V (AB	(C) TAKEAWAY	1978 LOGO UK 1008
STEVE SIMPSON FDL	G V (ABC		
RICK JONES	K V (ABC	KEITH NELSON BANJO(BC DAVE PIERCE (	WILLY FINLAYSON G V K(ABC
DON WELLER	SAX (B	ALAN COULTER D (C ROD DEMICK	B (C

M119 MEAN STREET DEALERS M119

Member	Role	Title	Release
MARK BRISTOW	G (A	(A) BENT NEEDLES	1979 MEAN ST DEALERS MSD 001
NIGEL DARVILLS	K (A	(A) BENT NEEDLES	1979 GRADUATE GRAD LP1
JAMES LANGSTON	V (A		
JIM SIMPSON	D (A	BOB BOUCHER B (A	

M120 MEATLOAF M120

Member	Role	Title	Release
MEATLOAF	V (ABC	(A) STONEY & MEATLOAF	1971 RARE EARTH SRE3005 PRODIGAL 62172
KARLA DEVITO	V (	(A) MEATLOAF(FEATURING STONEY)	1979 PRODIGAL US 10029 UK PDL 2010
ED KING	G (	(B) BAT OUT OF HELL	1978 EPIC US 44974 UK 82419
TODD RUNDGREN K G V	(B	(C) DEADRINGER	1981 EPIC US 36007 UK 83645
JIM STEINMAN K SONGS	(BC		
ELLEN FOLEY	(		
ROY BITAN	K (ABC	KASIM SULTON B V (AB ROGER POWELL	SYN (B JOHN WILCOX D(B
EDGAR WINTER	SAX (B	MARVIN LEE V (B MAX WEINBERG	D (BC RORY DODD V (BC
DAVEY JOHNSTONE	G (C	STEVE BUSLOWE B (C LIBERTY DEVITTO	D (C LARRY FAST SYN(C
JIMMY MAELEN	PERC (C	LESLIE LOAF V (C JOE DE ANGELIS	G (C NICKY HOPKINS K (C
YMMIJ NELEAM	PERC (C	ALAN RUBIN HRNS (C LOU MARINI	HRNS (C LOU DELGATTO HRNS(C
TOM MALONE	HRNS (C	CHER V (C TED NEELEY	V (C ALLEN NICHOLLS V (C
ERIC TROYER	V (C	RHONDA COULET V (C	

M121 MEDICINE HEAD M121

Member	Role	Title	Release
JOHN FIDDLER	G V (ALL	(A) NEW BOTTLES OLD MEDICINE	1970 DANDELION UK 63757
PETER HOPE EVANS HCA V	(ABDEFG	(B) HEAVY ON THE DRUM	1971 DANDELION DAN 8005 K 49005
KEITH RELF	B V (C	(C) DARK SIDE OF THE MOON	1971 DANDELION UK 2310 166
JOHN DAVIES	D (C	(D) ONE & ONE IS ONE	1972 POLYDOR US 5532 UK 2310 248
ROB TOWNSEND	D (E	(E) THRU A FIVE	1974 POLYDOR UK 2383 272
ROGER SAUNDERS	G (E	(F) MEDICINE HEAD (COMP)	1975 POLYDOR UK 2384 069
IAN SAINTY	B (	(G) TWO MAN BAND	1976 BARN UK 2314 102
CHARLIE McCRACKEN	B (	( ) POP HISTORY VOL XXV	1973 POLYDOR 2625 026
GEORGE FORD	B V (E	( ) BEST OF	1981 VERTIGO UK 2485 204
TONY ASHTON	K (DE		
CLIVE THACKER	D (D	ROY DYKE D (D PAT DONALDSON	B (D MIKE LIBER G (D
BRIAN PARRISH	G (D		

M121A MEDIUM MEDIUM M121A

Member	Role	Title	Release
		(A) THE GLITTERHOUSE	1981 CHERRY RED UK BRED19 GER 148 202

M122 MEDITATIONS M122

(A) WAKE UP 1978 THIRD WORLD TWS 929

M122A BILL MEDLEY M122A

BILL MEDLEY
100% BILL MEDLEY 1968 MGM US 4583 UK 8091
SOFT & SOULFUL 1969 MGM US 4603
GONE 1970 MGM US 4741
SOMEONE IS STANDING OUTSIDE 1970 MGM US 4640
NOBODY KNOWS 1970 MGM US 4702
A SONG FOR YOU 1972 A&M US 3505 UK AMLH 63505
WINGS 19 A&M US 3506
SMILE 1973 A&M US 3517
SWEET THUNDER 1980 LIBERTY US 1024 UK LT 1097

M123 RANDY MEISNER M123

RANDY MEISNER G V(ALL — (A) RANDY MEISNER 1978 ASYLUM US 6E140 UK K53079
PATRICK SHANAHAN D (A — (B) ONE MORE SONG 1980 EPIC US 36748 UK 84531
STEVE EDWARDS G (A — (C) RANDY MEISNER 1982 EPIC US 38121
DANNY CARMASSI D (C
KERRY MORRIS B (A — JOHN HOBBS PNO (A — JERRY SWALLOW G (A — TITA KERPAN V (A
BYRON BERLINE FDL (A — DONNY ULLSTROM V (A — ERNIE WATTS SAX (A — ALAN BRACKETT V (A
GEOFFREY LEIB PNO (A — RICHIE WALKER V (A — J D SOUTHER V (A — BILL LAMB V (A
DAVID CASSIDY V (A — DON FRANCISCO PERC V(B — CRAIG HULL STEEL(B — BRYAN GAROFALO B (B
CRAIG KRAMPF D (B — STERLING SMITH K (BC — WENDY WALDMAN G V (B — BILL CUOMO SYN (B
MICHAEL JACOBSON SAX (B — KIM CARNES V (B — DON HENLEY V (B — GLENN FREY V (B
JOHN COREY G K V(C — TOM ERAK B (C — MITCHELL FROOM SYN (C — NICKY HOPKINS K (C
DIXON HOUSE K V (C — PHIL KENZIE SAX (C — HOWARD LEESE G V SYN(C — MARCY LEVY V (C
BRIAN SMITH G (C — ANN WILSON V (C — NANCY WILSON V (C — TOWER OF POWER HRNS (C

M124 MEKONS M124

JON LANGFORD D (— (A) THE QUALITY OF MERCY IS NOT 1979 VIRGIN UK V 2143
ROSS ALLEN B (— (B) MEKONS 1980 RED RHINO UK 1
ANDY CARRIGAN V (
MARK WHITE V (— KEVIN LYCETT G (— TOM GREENHALGH G (

M125 MELANIE M125

MELANIE SAFKA V (ALL — (A) BORN TO BE 1969 BUDDAH 203 019 BDLH 5002
RON FRANGIPANE K (GJDO — (B) AFFECTIONATELY 1969 BUDDAH 203 028 BDLP 4016
JOE MACK B (G — (C) CANDLES IN THE RAIN 1970 BUDDAH 2318 009 BDLP 5003
SAL DE TROIA G (GJVD — (C) CANDLES IN THE RAIN 1970 BUDDAH GER 2318006 US 5060
ERIC WEISSBERG FDL (G — (D) LEFTOVER WINE 1970 BUDDAH 2318 011 BDLH 5004
BARRY MORGAN D (C — (D) LEFTOVER WINE 1970 BUDDAH GER 623142 US 5066
VINNIE BELL G (G — (E) ALL THE RIGHT NOISES 1971 BUDDAH 2319 034
HUGH McCRACKEN G (GJU — (F) GARDEN IN THE CITY 1972 BUDDAH 2318 054 BDLP 4017
GEORGE DEVENS D (GD — (F) GARDEN IN THE CITY 1972 BUDDAH US 5095
BUDDY SALZMAN D (G — (G) GOOD BOOK 1971 BUDDAH 2322 001 BDLH 5010
GEORGE MARCH WIND (G — (G) GOOD BOOK 197 BUDDAH US 5006 MODE FR MD9024
DAVE SANBORN SAX (U — (H) GATHER ME 1971 NEIGHBORHOOD US 4700 BUDDAH 4022
RANDY BRECKER HRNS (U — (I) FOUR SIDES OF (COMP DBL) 1974 BUDDAH UK BDLD 2002 US 9505
MICHAEL BRECKER HRNS (U — (J) STONEGROUND WORDS 1972 NEIGHBORHOOD US 47005 UK NHTC 251
RICHARD TEE K (U — (J) STONEGROUND WORDS 1975 ABC RI UK ABCL 5077
WILL LEE B (U — (K) AT CARNEGIE HALL 1973 NEIGHBORHOOD US 49001 UK NHSP 301
CHRIS PARKER D (U — (K) AT CARNEGIE HALL 1975 ABC RI UK ABCL 606
JOHNNY PACHECO CONGA(J — (L) VERY BEST OF 1974 BUDDAH UK BDLP 4001
BILL KEITH STEEL(J — (M) PLEASE LOVE ME 1974 BUDDAH US 5132 UK BDLP 4021
DON PAYNE B (J — (N) MADRUGADA 1974 NEIGHBORHOOD US 48001 UK NH 3003
CHUCK DOMANICO B (J — (N) MADRUGADA 1975 ANCHOR UK ABCL 5085
ROGER KELLAWAY PNO (J — (O) AS I SEE IT NOW 1975 NEIGHBORHOOD US 3000 UK NBH 80636
DONALD McDONALD D (J — (P) SUNSET & OTHER BEGINNINGS 1975 NEIGHBORHOOD US 3001 UK NBH 69168
MEL LEWIS D (J — (Q) FROM THE BEGINNING (COMP) 1975 ABC US 879 UK ABLC 5124
RICHARD DAVIS B (JU — (R) PROFILE (COMP) 197 TELDEC GER 624022
ROBBIE GEORGIA (W — (S) GOLDEN HOUR (COMP) 1977 PYE UK GH 861
BOB LEONE (W — (T) BEST OF (COMP) 197 BUDDAH US 5664 UK BDLP 5705
MARY McCAFFREY V (W — (U) PHONOGENIC 1978 MIDSONG US 3033 MCA UK MCF 8033
LOUIS CABAZA (W — (V) PHOTOGRAPH 1979 ATLANTIC US 18190
TONY DATTAGLIA (W — (W) BALLROOM STREETS 1979 RCA XL 03073 US TOMATO 9003
STAN KIPPER D (W — ( ) MELANIE 19 BUDDAH US 5041
ALAN PARKER G (C
ALAN HACKSHAW K (C — HAROLD McNAIR FLT (C — RICO REYES CONGA (C — EDWIN HAWKINS K (C
HERBIE FLOWERS B (C — AL GORGONI G (D — JOSEPH MACHO B (— GREG DIAMOND D (D
ART KAPLAN WIND (D — ROY YEAGER D PERC V (O — JOHN MULKEY B V (O — BARRY HARWOOD G STEEL V(O
FRANK FRANCO G (O — STEVE FELDMAN K V (O — JOHN SHANE KEISTER K (O — SY MANN PNO (O
CLIFF NIVISON V (O — GEORGE MARGE WIND(O — GENE BIANCO HARP (O — TOOTS THIELEMANS HCA (O
GEORGE RICCI CELLO(O — HARRY WIMMER CELLO (O — SUSIE WATSON TAYLOR V (O — MIKE HERON V G (O
ROBIN WILLIAMSON (O — DAVE DORAN G V (V — DEAN PARKS G (V — LOUIS SHELTON G (V
DAVID PAICH K (V — JIM DRENNAN K (V — JAY WOLFE B V (V — JERRY SCHEFF B (V
DAVID JACKSON B (V — JIM GORDON D (V — JEFF PORCARO D (V — JOHN GUERIN D (V
MILT HOLLAND PERC (V — VICTOR FELDMAN PERC (V — ANGELO MAUCERI PERC V(V — CAROL PARKS V (V
DENNY BELL V (V — ART PEPPER SAX (V — RICHAR GREENE VLN (V — DAVID CAMPBELL VLA (V

M125A TERRY MELCHER M125A

TERRY MELCHER V K (ALL — (A) TERRY MELCHER 1974 REPRISE US MS 2185 UK k54016
JIM KELTNER D (A — (B) ROYAL FLUSH 1976 RCA US 0948
DORIS DAY V (A
HAL BLAINE D (A — MICHAEL CLARKE D (A — JOE OSBORN B (A — CHRIS HILLMAN B (A
CLARENCE WHITE G (A — RY COODER G (A — MIKE DEASY G (A — TONY MARTIN JR G (A
SNEAKY PETE STEEL(A — J D MANESS STEEL(A — LARRY KNECHTEL K (A — SPOONER OLDHAM K (A
JIM HORN HRNS (A — SLYDE HYDE HRNS (A — CHUCK FINDLEY HRNS (A — JACKIE KELSO HRNS(A
JIMMIE HASKELL STRING(A — BRUCE JOHNSTON V (A — SPANKY MACFARLANE V (A

M126 BARRY MELTON M126

Musician	Instr.	Albums
BARRY MELTON	G V	(ALL
DONNIE HATHAWAY	PNO	(A
PHIL UPCHURCH	B	(A
JAY LEVY	K V	(B
RICK DEY	B V	(B
JIM BOYES	V	(D
TONY DEY	D	(B
MORRIS JENNINGS	D	(A
KEN WHALEY	B	(C
PAUL COBBOLD	B	(D
HEATHER BRADY	V	(D
BOB FLURIE	B V	(E
DAVE CHARLES	D	(C
ROB PIZER	G	(D
MOTH SMITH	D	(D
GERALD SIMS	G	(A
ROBERT HOGINS	K V	(E
TOMMY EYRE	K	(C
BOB FLURIE	G	(D
BOB HOGINS	PNO	(D
HAROLD ACEVES	D V	(E
RAY MARTINEZ	G	(CD
ELMO SHROPSHIRE	BAN	(D
DAVE BRADY	V	(D
BILL ASHLEE	B V	(E

Album	Year	Label	Catalogue
(A) BRIGHT SUN IS SHINING	1970	VANGUARD	US VSD 6551
(B) MELTON,LEVY & THE DEY BROTHERS	1972	CBS	US 31279
(C) THE FISH	1975	UA	UK UAS 29908
(D) WE ARE LIKE THE OCEAN	1977	MUSIC IS MEDICINE	US MIM 9007
(E) LEVEL WITH ME	1979	RAG BABY	US 1004 GER 85001
(E) LEVEL WITH ME	198	MUSIC IS MEDICINE	US 9014

M127 MEMBERS M127

Musician	Instr.	Albums
NICKY TESCO	V	(AB
NIGEL BENNETT	G V	(AB
CHRIS PAYNE	B V	(AB
ADRIAN LILLYWHITE	D PERC	(AB
JEAN CARROLL	G V	(AB
STEVE 'RUD' THOMPSON	SAX	(A
RUPERT HINE	K	(B
JOE JACKSON	PNO	(B
ALBE DONNELLY	SAX	(B
DICK CUTHELL	HRNS	(B
RICO RODRIGUES	TROM	(B

Album	Year	Label	Catalogue
(A) AT THE CHELSEA NIGHTCLUB	1979	VIRGIN	UK V2120 GER 200 480
(B) 1980 THE CHOICE IS YOURS	1980	VIRGIN	UK V 2153 GER 202 099

M128 MEMPHIS BEND M128

Musician	Instr.	Albums
MICKY GEE	G V	(A
LINCOLN CARR	B	(A
TOM RILEY	D V	(A
MICK WEAVER	K	(A
JOHN JENKINS	PNO	(A
B J COLE	STEEL	(A
JOHN DAVID	B	(A

Album	Year	Label	Catalogue
(A) GOOD ROCKIN TONITE	1977	UA	UK UAS 30036

M129 MEMPHIS SLIM M129

Musician	Instr.	Albums
MEMPHIS 'PETER CHATMAN'SLIM	PNO V	(ALL
CHRIS SPEDDING	G	(B
PETER GREEN	G	(B
DUSTER BENNETT	HCA	(B
PETE WINGFIELD	K	(B
LARRY STEELE	B	(B
CONRAD ISADORE	D	(B
ROOSEVELT SYKES	K G	(N
BUDDY GUY	G	(NS
JUNIOR WELLS	HCA	(N
PHILIP GUY	G	(N
ERNEST JOHNSON	B	(N
ROOSEVELT SHAW	D	(N
A C REED	SAX	(N
JIMMY CONLEY	SAX	(N
ALEXIS KORNER	G	(CF
STAN GRIEG	D	(CF
LEROY BATCHELOR	B	(M
ALFRED ELKINS	B	(M

Album	Year	Label	Catalogue
ALL THEM BLUES	1976	DJM	DJD 28012
AT LAUSANNE	1974	MUSIDISC	EURO CV 1289
AT THE GATE OF HORN	19	BARNABY	US 31291 JOY UK 143
AT THE GATE OF HORN	19	VEE JAY	1012
AT THE VILLAGE GATE	19	FOLKWAYS	US 2386
BAD LUCK & TROUBLE	1972	CBS	US 31291 UK 67248
BLUE MEMPHIS	1971	BARCLAY	FR 920214 US WB1899
BLUES IN EUROPE	19	STORYVILLE	SLP 188
BLUES IN EUROPE	19	STORYVILLE	SLP 214
BLUES IS EVERYWHERE	19	GNP CRESCENDO	US 10002
BLUES MAN	1975	MUSIDISC	FR ALB187
BORN WITH BLUES	1972	JEWEL	US 5004
BOOGIE WOOGIE	1978	FESTIVAL	ALB247
BROKEN SOUL BLUES	19	UA	US LA 3137
BABY PLEASE COME HOME	19	BATTLE	US 6122
BLUES EVERY WHICH WAY	19	VERVE	US 3007
BLUE PORTRAIT	19	SCEPTER	US 536
BLUES & WOMEN	1981	ISABEL	FR 900 506
CHICAGO BLUES	19	FOLKWAYS	US 3536 UK XTRA 1085
CLASSICAL AMERICAN BLUES	1973	BARCLAY	FR 920 407
CHICAGO BOOGIE	1976	BLACK LION	BLP 30196
() FRISCO BAY BLUES	1960	FONTANA	UK 688 315
FATTENIN FROGS FOR SNAKES	1976	MELODISC	MLPS12149
FAVOURITE BLUES	19	FOLKWAYS	US 2387
GREAT MEMPHIS SLIM	19	AMERICA	AM 6076
GOIN' BACK TO TENNESSEE	1975	BARCLAY	FR 90034
HONKY TONK SOUND	19	FOLK	US 3535
HOUSE OF THE BLUES VOL1	19	BLUE STAR	FR 80601
HOUSE OF THE BLUES VOL 7	19	BLUE STAR	FR 80607
JUST BLUES	19	PRESTIGE	US 1018
LEGACY OF THE BLUES	1973	GNP CRESCENDO	US 10017
LEGACY OF THE BLUES	1973	SONET	UK SNTF 647
LIVE	1974	STORYVILLE	UK SLP 219
LEGEND OF THE BLUES VOL 2	19	BEACON	BEAS 6
LONESOME BLUES	19	SPINERAMA	US 149
MEMPHIS SLIM	19	B&B	33002
MEMPHIS SLIM	19	ARC FOLK	US 215
MEMPHIS SLIM	19	BARNABY	US 31241
MEMPHIS SLIM	19	STORYVILLE	UK SLP 118
MEMPHIS SLIM	19	BARCLAY	FR 920214
MEMPHIS SLIM	1974	AMERICA	AM 6130
MEMPHIS SLIM	19	KING	US 885
MEMPHIS SLIM	19	EVEREST	US 215
MEMPHIS SLIM	19	CHESS	US 1455
MEMPHIS SLIM	19	BLACK & WHITE	FR 730 581
MEMPHIS SLIM (BLUEBIRD No 3)	19	RCA	FXMI 7215
MEMPHIS SLIM VOL 2	19	EVEREST	US 286
MEMPHIS SLIM & MATTHEW MURPHY	1974	BLACK & BLUE	33 002
MEMPHIS SLIM & WILLIE DIXON(PARIS)	19	BATTLE	US 6122
MEMPHIS SLIM & WILLIE DIXON	19	FOLKWAYS	US 2385
MEMPHIS SLIM & S BOY WILLIAMSON	19	GNP CRESCENDO	US GNP10003
MEMPHIS SLIM STORY	19	VOGUE	LD 58330
MAMPHIS HEAT	1981	IMS	1080 607
MESSIN' AROUND WITH THE BLUES	19	KING	US 1082
MOTHER EARTH	1972	BUDDAH	BDS 7505
NO STRAIN	19	PRESTIGE	US 1031
OLD TIMES NEW TIMES	1972	BARCLAY	FR 920332 3
PIANO BLUES	19	STORYVILLE	UK SLP 168
RAINING THE BLUES	19	FANTASY	US 24705
REAL FOLK BLUES	19	CHESS	US 1510
REAL HONKY TONK	19	FOLKWAYS	US 3535
REAL BOOGIE WOOGIE	19	FOLKWAYS	3523
RIGHT NOW	19	TRIP	US 8025
ROCK ME BABY	1975	BLACK LION	2460 155
SELF PORTRAIT	19	SCEPTER	US 535
STEADY ROLLIN BLUES	19	PRESTIGE	US 1075

M129 **MEMPHIS SLIM** (CONTINUED) M129

SOUL BLUES 1933 EMBER UK 3422
(S)SOUTH SIDE REUNION 1975 BARCLAY FR 80501
(S)SOUTH SIDE REUNION 19 WB US 2646
USA 19 CANDID US 9024
WORLDS FOREMOST BLUES SINGER 19 STRAND US 1046
WILLIES BLUES 19 PRESTIGE US 1003

M130 **MEMPHIS HORNS** M130

WAYNE JACKSON HRNS (ALL (A) MEMPHIS HORNS 197 COTILLION US 9014
ROGER HOPPS HRNS ((B) HIGH ON MUSIC 1976 RCA UK 1056 US 1355
ANDREW LOVE HRNS (C (C) GET UP & DANCE 1977 RCA US 2198
ED LOGAN SAX ((D) MEMPHIS HORNS BAND 2 1979 RCA US 2643
JACK HALE TROM (C (E) WELCOME TO 1979 RCA US 3221
JAMES MITCHELL SAX (C
LEWIS COLLINS SAX (C CLARENCE McDONALD K (C JAMES GADSON D (C MARLO HENDERSON G (C
DAVID SHIELDS B (C JAY GRAYDON G (C BOBBY EATON B (C PATRICK MOTEN SYN(C
PAULINHO DACOSTA PERC (C

M130A **MEN AT WORK** M130A

COLIN HAY G V (A (A) BUSINESS AS USUAL 1982 CBS US 37978
RON STRYKERT G V (A (B) CARGO 1983 CBS
JERRY SPEISER D V (A GREG HAM WIND K V(A JOHN REES B V (A

M131 **MENAGE A TROIS** M131

GREG MOORE G (A (A) MANAGE A TROIS 1980 ARIOLA NL 200 148
EDDIE WATKINS B (A
LARRY TOLBERT D (A PAULINHO DACOSTA PERC (A MICHAEL DOVE K SYN(A SYLVIA COX V (A
CARL ANDERSON V (A CAROLYN DENNIS V (A ROY GALLOWAY V (A KAY McNEELY V (A
HELENA SPRINGS V (A AFREEKA TRESS V (A

M131A **ANDY MENDELSON** M131A

ANDY MENDELSON V K G B(A (A) ANDY MENDELSON 1978 ARISTA US 4207
RICHARD MENDELSON D (A
FRANK DE FONDA D (A DAVID SHAPIRO B (A GAIL HEIDEMAN V (A GWEN OWENS V (A
GREG HAWKES WIND (A TOM SCOTT WIND (A JOE FARRELL SAX (A ERNIE WATTS SAX (A
ANDY PRATT V (A MARY HASLIM V (A LAURA CREAMER V (A

M132 **JOE MENDELSON** M132

JOE MENDELSON V G B D K(AB (A) MR MIDDLE OF THE ROAD 19 NOBADY 9230 1027
(B) SOPHISTO JOE MENDELSON 19 TAURUS

M132A **THE MENTAL** M132A

(A) GOD FOR A DAY 19 KAMIKAZE

M132B **MENTAL AS ANYTHING** M132B

MARTIN PLAZA G V (A (A) MENTAL AS ANYTHING 1980 VIRGIN UK 2148 EURO 201 435
GREEDY SMITH V K HCA(A
REG MOMBASSA G V (A WAYNE DELISLE D (A PETER O'DOHERTY B V (A

M132C **MEPHISTOPHELES** M132C

FRED TACKETT G K TPT V(A (A) IN FRUSTRATION 19 REPRISE US 6355
STEVEN SIMONE G V (A
BOB SILLER G V (A GORDON GRANT K (A SKIP MOSHER B FLT(A DARYL BURCH D (A
DAVID HASSINGER PROD(A

M132D **ERIC MERCURY** M132D

ERIC MERCURY V (A (A) ERIC MERCURY 19 MERCURY US SRM 1 1026
WILLIAM SMITH K (AB (B) FUNKY SOUNDS NURTURED IN FERTILE SOIL 197 ENTERPRISE US 1020
JIM JOHNSON B (B
JAY MITTHAUER D (A PAUL STALLWORTH B (A DANNY KORTCHMAR G (A GARY COLEMAN PERC (A
LARRY VON NASH SYN (A JIM KELTNER D (A DENNIS COFFEY G (A JESSE ED DAVIS G (A
DAVID FOSTER PNO (A KLAUS VOORMANN B (A ED BROWN B (A WADDY WACHTEL G (A
DAVID PAICH K (A ERIC JOHNSON D (A BOBBY KEYS HRNS (A TREVOR LAWRENCE PERC(A
JEFF BAXTER STEEL(A DOUG RICHARDSON HRNS (A SONNY BURKE K (A PAT MURPHY CONGA(A
GARY HODGES D (A VERNON BERCH G (A LON VAN EATON G (A GARY DELORME G (A
LYNDA LAWRENCE V (A VANETTA FIELDS V (A CARLINA WILLIAMS V (A SID SHARP STR (A
PAUL CANNON G (B STEVE CROPPER G (B JAY SPELL K (B MEMPHIS HRNS (B

M132E **BILLY MERNIT** M132E

BILLY MERNIT V K (A (A) SPECIAL DELIVERY 1973 ELEKTRA US EKS 75054
JOHN SEITER D (A
PETER KLIMES G (A DAVID VAUGHT B (A

M133 **MERGER** M133

BARRY FORD G V WIND(A1 (A) EXILES IN BABYLON 1977 SUNSTAR SUN 1001
IVOR STEADMAN B (A1 (B) ARMAGEDDON TIME 1980 EMERGENCY UK 010
WINSTON BENNETT G V (A12 (1) 1978 (2) LATE 1978
RAS DANJUMA G (2
MIKE OSEI D (12 EVER WELLINGTON B (2 TONY OSEI K (12 FAR I PERC(2
MICHAEL DAN K V (A ADETOKUMBO ILLORIN G (A JIMMY THOMAS V PERC(A EUNICE GREEN V (A
PAM NESTOR V (A STRECKER CATIOUS V (A

M134 **MAX MERRITT & THE METEORS** M134

MAX MERRITT G V (ALL (A) A LITTLE CLOSER 1975 ARISTA UK ARTY 108
STEWART SPEER D (AB (B) OUT OF THE BLUES 1976 ARISTA UK ARTY 134
LANCE DIXON K SAX V(B (C) KEEPING IN TOUCH 1978 POLYDOR UK 2383 514
JOHN GOURD G (B
BARRY DUGGAN WIND V(A RAY COOPER PERC (A DEL NEWMAN PROD (A DAVE McRAE K (A
B J COLE STEEL(A

M134A **MERRY GO ROUND** M134A

EMIT RHODES G K V(A (A) YOU'RE VERY LONELY WOMAN 1967 A&M US 4132
BILL RHINEHARDT G V (A
GARY KATO B V (A JOEL LARSON D V (A

M135 NEIL MERRYWEATHER M135

NEIL MERRYWEATHER B G V(ALL (A) NEIL MERRYWEATHER & THE BOERS 19 KENT US KST 546
MICHAEL WILLIS G (EC (B) WORD OF MOUTH 1969 CAPITOL US STBB 278
TIM McGOVERN D (EC (C) IVAR AVENUE REUNION 1970 RCA US LPS 4442
ED GEMONT SYN (E (D) VACUUM CLEANER 1971 RCA UK SF 8210 US LSP 4485
STEVE MILLER G V (B (E) SPACE RANGERS 1974 MERCURY UK 9100008 US SRMI 1007
BARRY GOLDBERG K (B (F) KRYPTONITE 1975 MERCURY US SRMI 1024
DAVE MASON G (B (*C) SEE BARRY GOLDBERG FOR C
BARRY GOLDBERG (C
CHARLIE MUSSELWHITE HCA(B HOWARD ROBERTS G (B DAVE BURT G V (B SIDNEY GEORGE HRNS (D
COFFI HALL D (BD EDWARD ROTH FDL FLT K(BD KAL DAVID G (D HUEY SULLIVAN PNO (D
ROBIN BOERS D (AD J J VELKER K (D JOHN RICHARDSON G (DA LYNN CAREY V (D
JAMIE HERNDON K G (CE JIM TAYLOR PNO (E

M136 MERSEYBEATS M136

TONY CRANE G V (A (A) MERSEYBEATS 1964 FONTANA UK TL 5210
AARON WILLIAMS G V (A (B) MERSEYBEATS 1965 WING WL 1163
BILLY KINSLEY B V (A (C) ENGLANDS BEST SELLERS 19 ARC INTERNATIONAL US ARC 834
JOHN BANKS D (A (EP) MERSEYBEATS 1964 FONTANA UK TE 17423
JOHN GUSTAFSON B ((EP) ON STAGE 1964 FONTANA UK TE 17422
BOB GARDNER B ((EP) WISHIN' & HOPIN' 1964 FONTANA UK TE 17432

M136A MERTON PARKAS M136A

MICK TALBOT PNO V(A (A) FACE IN THE CROWD 1979 BEGGARS BANQUET UK BEGA 11 GER 146523
DANNY TALBOT G V (A
SIMON SMITH D (A NEIL HURRELL B V (A

M136B MESSAGE M136B

ALLAN MURDOCH G (ABCDEFG (A) THE DAWN ANEW IS COMING 197 BELLAPHON GER BLPS19081
TOM McGUIGAN V WIND SYN(ABCD (B) FROM BOOKS AND DREAMS 1973 BELLAPHON GER BLPS19159
HORST STACHELHAUS B (ABCD (C) MESSAGE 1975 NOVA GER 622213 DECCA UKSKLR5213
GERHARD SCHABER PERC V(A (D) SYNAPSE 1976 NOVA GER 622523
ALLAN'TAFF' FREEMAN SYN V(AE (E) ASTRAL JOURNEYS 1978 BRAIN GER 0060 165
BILLY TABBERT G V (A (F) USING THE HEAD 1977 BRAIN GER 0060 078
GUNTHER KLINGER D (B (G) MILES OF SMILES 1980 INTERCORD GER 145 609
MANFRED VON BOHR D PERC(CD
TONY GREAVES WIND (D SAMMY KUNIG V SAX PERC(E PETER SCHMIDT D PERC(E FRITZ GROGER G PERC(E
JEANETTE MACLEOD V (E MANFRED KNEIL VIBES(E REINER NAGEL B K (E UTE NAGEL V (E
HELMUT FICHTNER K (F EMIL WIRTH B (F DAVID HANSELMANN V (F TOMMY WAHL D PERC(F
HERB GELLER SAX (F LAWRENCE ELAM TPT (F WOLFGANG AHLERS TROM(F RAB ? PERC(B
VOLKER KUNSCHER SYN K(G PIT LOW K SYN(G WERNER PERC (ANGELIKA HANSCHEN V(F
GABI BOROWSKI V (F TINY HAGEN HARP (THOMAS'CHUCK' TSCHESCHNER B(G

M136C JIM MESSINA M136C

JIM MESSINA V G (ALL (A) JIM MESSINA & THE JESTERS 196 AUDIO FIDELITY 7037 RI THIMBLE3
BILL BECKMAN G (A (B) OASIS 1979 CBS US 36140 UK 83803
RON HOUSE G (A (C) MESSINA 1981 WB US 3559 GER 56911
JIM SHOLSTEDT B (A
DAVE ARCHULETA SAX (A LARRY CUNDIEFF D (A WAYNE NELSON B V (B CRAIG THOMAS WIND (BC
MILT HOLLAND PERC (B TONY MORENO D (B JIM STUDER V K SYN(BC JEFF ELLIOTT HRNS (B
MICHAEL BRADY B V (C JOE PORCARO PERC(C NEIL LARSEN K (C DAVID GRISMAN MAND (C
SILVIA WOODS HARP (C PAULINE WILSON V (C JANNIE LITTLEPAGE V (C JEFF PORCARO D (C
VICTOR FELDMAN PERC (C TOM HENSLEY K (C JERRY HEY HRNS (C CHUCK FINDLEY HRMS (C
DAROL ANGER VLN (C JIM HOCHANADLE WIND (C ALAN THORNHILL V (C

M136D METAL URBAIN M136D

(A) LES HOMMES MORT EST DANGEREUX 1981 BYZANTEEN 8101

M137 METABOLIST M137

ANTON LOACH K ((A) METABOLIST (EP) 19 DROMM DR01
MALCOLM LANE G ((B) HANSTEN KLORK 19 DROMM DR02
SIMON MILLWARD B (JED KINGSFORD D (

M137A METEORS M137A

HUGO SINZHEIMER V (AB (A) TEENAGE HEART 1979 EMI UK EMC3315 NL 26235
FERDINAND BAKKER G V (AB (A) TEENAGE HEART 1979 PASSPORT US 7911
JOHN VEE B (A (B) HUNGER 1980 HARVEST NL 26540 ARIOLA GER 203140
AKE DANIALSON K (AB
ERIC DE ZWAAN G V (A JOB TARENSKEEN V D SAX(A KIM HAWORTH D (B GERRIT VEEN B (B
MIKE OTTE (B FREDDY CAVALLI B (B MONICA V (B MARJAN V (B
FLOOR V (B

M138 THE METERS M138

ART NEVILLE K (ABCDEFGHI (A) THE METERS 1971 JOSIE US 4010
CYRIL NEVILLE PERC (FGHI (B) LOOK KA PY PY 1972 JOSIE US 4011
LEO NOCENTELLI G V (ABCDEFHIG (C) CABBAGE ALLEY 1972 REPRISE UK K33242 US MS 2076
GEORGE PORTER B (ABCDEFGHI (D) REJUVENATION 1974 REPRISE UK K54027 US MS 2200
JOE MODELISTE D (EFHIABCDG (E) CISSY STRUT 1974 ISLAND UK ILPS9250
EARL KING V (H (E) SECOND LINE STRUT 1980 CHARLY RI CRB 1009
KURT McGETTRICK SAX (I (F) FIRE ON THE BAYOU 1975 REPRISE UK K54044 US MS 2228
SWAMP TABERNACLE CHOIR (I (G) BEST OF THE METERS 1975 REPRISE UK K54076
( ) BEST OF THE METERS 1975 VIRGO SV12002
(H) TRICK BAG 1976 REPRISE UK K54078 US MS 2252
(I) NEW DIRECTION 1977 WB UK K56378 US MS 3042
(J) GOOD OLD FUNKY MUSIC 1979 PYE UK PKL5578
(EP) LOOK KA PY PY 1980 CHARLY UK CTD 113

M138A PAT METHENY M138A

PAT METHENY G B (ALL (A) BRIGHT SIZE LIFE 1975 ECM 1073
JACO PASTORIUS B (A (B) WATERCOLOURS 1977 ECM 1097
BOB MOSES D (A (C) PAT METHENY GROUP 1978 ECM 1114
LYLE MAYS K (BCEG (D) NEW CHAUTAUQUA 1978 ECM 1131
EBERHARD WEBER B (B (E) AMERICAN GARAGE 1979 ECM 1155
DAN GOTTLIEB D (BCE (F) 80 81 1980 ECM
MARK EGAN B (CE (G) AS WICHITA FALLS SO FALLS WICHITA 1980 ECM 1190
NANA VASCONCELES D V (G
MICHAEL BRECKER SAX (F JACK DEJOHNETTE D (F CHARLIE HADEN B (F

M138B METHOD ACTORS M138B
(A) RHYTHMS OF YOU 1981 ARMAGEDDON UK 12005

M139 METHOD M139
MICK BRASSINGTON V (A (A) METHOD 1976 UK UK UKAL1020
JOHN HUGHES G (A

M139A METHUSALEM M139A
BUBU HIFIKER D V (A (A) FOR OUR FRIENDS 1979 METHUSALEM METH7901
ANDY SABER G V (A
RICK HOCHULI B V (A FERNANDO PALENCIAS G V (A ROBY WURGLER G V (A MARCO RAUBER K (A

M139B METHUSELAH M139B
JOHN GLADWIN V VIBES(A (A) MATTHEW MARK LUKE & JOHN 19 ELEKTRA US EKS 74052
TERRY WINCOTT G V (A
CRAIG AUSTIN B V (A LESLIE NICOL G V (A M J BRADLEY D (A

M140 METRO M140
SEAN LYONS G (AB (A) METRO 1977 TRANSATLANTIC UK TRAG340 US SIRE 6041
PETER GODWIN V SAX SYN(AB (B) NEW LOVE 1979 EMI UK EMC 3295
DUNCAN BROWNE V G K B (A (C) FUTURE IMPACT 1980 EMI UK EMC 3334
JOHN LAFORGE D (B
JOHN GIBLIN B (A SIMON PHILLIPS D (A GRAHAM PRESKETT VLN (A BARRY HUSBAND V (A
TONY ADAMS B V (B COLIN WIGHT G (B

M140A METROPOLIS M140A
UTE KANNENBERG V PERC(A (A) METROPOLIS 1974 PAN 87439
THOMAS HILDEBRAND D (A
HELMUT BINZER G (A MICHAEL WESTPHAL B (A MICHAEL DUWE G V (A

M141 AUGIE MEYER M141
AUGIE MEYER K G V(ALL (A) YOU AINT ROLLIN YOUR ROLL 1973 PARAMOUNT US 6065
DOUG SAHM (E (B) WESTERN HEAD MUSIC CO 1973 POLYDOR US 24 4069
JIM LOVING B (B (C) LIVE AT THE LONGNECK 197 TEXAS US 1002
HARVEY KAGEN B (B (D) CALIFORNIa BLUES 1974 PARAMOUNT US
BOB RAFKIN G (B (E) FINALLY IN LIGHTS 1977 TEXAS US TRC1005 SONET UK SNTF303
DAVID PRICE G (B
B J JONES G (B DON POUNCHER D (B STEVE ZWIERN D (B JOHN PEREZ D (B
MORY BAKER D (B CAROL MEYER V (B SANDIE JONES V (B

M141A FREDDI MEYER M141A
FREDDI MEYER (A (A) FREDDI MEYER 19 BARN NARB 002

M141B MI SEX M141B
STEVE GILPIN V (A (A) COMPUTOR GAMES 1980 CBS US 36349 UK 84157
DON MARTIN V B (A (B) SPACE RACE 1980 CBS US 36744 UK 84446
KEVIN STANTON G V (A
MURRAY BURNS K V (A RICHARD HODGKINSON D (A

M142 STEPHEN MICUS M142
STEPHEN MICUS (A) ARCHAIC CONCERTS 1976 CAROLINE UK C 1517
(B) IMPLOSIONS 1977 JAPO 60017

M143 GORDON MICHAELS M143
GORDON MICHAELS V G K (A (A) STARGAZER 1979 HORIZON US SP 737
HUGH McCRACKEN G HCA(A
RICK MAROTTA D (A TONY LEVIN B (A RICHARD TEE K (A MIKE MAINIERI PERC(A
GEORGE YOUNG FLT (A ED WALSH SYN (A DAVID SANBORN SAX (A GEORGE MARGE WIND(A
LISA GILKYSON V (A ARTHUR JENKINS PERC (A BILL BROWN HRNS (A LINDA REDDWOLF V (A

M143A HILLY MICHAELS M143A
HILLY MICHAELS D G K(AB (A) CALLING ALL GIRLS 1980 WB US 3431 UK K 56837
DAN HARTMAN K B G(AB (B) LUMIA 1981 WB US 3566
JIMMY McALLISTER G (A
G E SMITH G (A MORGAN WALKER K (AB BILLY CROSS G V (A GREG HAWKS G (A
T MANDYE K (A GEORGE YOUNG (A ELLIOTT RANDALL G (D RICK DERRINGER G (D
LARRY RUSSELL B (B TOM MANDEL K (B JEFF BOVA K (B

M144 LEE MICHAELS M144
LEE MICHAELS V B K(ALL (A) CARNIVAL OF LIFE 1968 A&M US 4140
KEITH KNUDSEN D (GH (B) RECITAL 1969 A&M UK AMLS 928 US 4152
JOEL CHRISTIE B (G (C) LEE MICHAELS 1969 A&M UK AMLS 936 US 4199
DRAKE LEVIN G (GBD (D) BARREL 1970 A&M UK AMLS 991 US 4249
NORMA KINNEY PERC (E (E) FIFTH 1971 A&M UK AMLS64302 US 4302
RICHARD MADRID PERC (E (F) LIVE 1972 ARIOLA 86725 US A&M 3518
HENRY LEWY PERC (E (G) SPACE & FIRST TAKES 1972 A&M UK AMLS64336 US 4336
JOEL LARSEN SAX (E (H) NICE DAY FOR SOMETHING 1973 CBS UK 65651 US 32275
BARTHOLOMEW SMITH-FROST D(CDF (J) TAILFACE 1974 CBS UK US 32846
MURRAY CLAYTON ((K) SATURN RINGS 197 ABC US ABCD684
FRANK DAVIS D (B
JOHN BARBATA D (B LARRY KNECHTAL B (B

M145 MAX MIDDLETON & ROBERT AHWAI M145
MAX MIDDLETON K (A (A) ANOTHER SLEEPER 1979 HARVEST SHSP 4103
ROBERT AHWAI G (A
RICHARD BAILEY D (A KUMA HARADA B (A DARRYL LEE QUE PERC (A STEVE GREGORY WIND (A
BUD BEADLE WIND (A GEORGE CHISHOLM TPT (A TREVOR BARBER TPT (A CHRIS RAINBOW V (A
LINDA TAYLOR V (A CHRISTIE THOMPSON V (A

M146 MIDNIGHT OIL M146
ROB HIRST D V (A (A) HEAD INJURIES 1979 POWDER WORKS AUST MLF 322
PETER GARRETT V (A
JAMES MOGINIE G K (A ANDREW JAMES B V (A MARTIN POTSEY G (A

M146A MIDNIGHT RAGS M146A
PAUL ROLAND (A) WEREWOLF OF LONDON 1980 ARMAGEDDON UK ARM1

M146B MIDNIGHT FLYER M146B
MAGGIE BELL V (AB (A) MIDNIGHT FLYER 1981 SWANSONG US 8509
ANTHONY GLYNNE G (AB (B) EP ROCK'N'ROLL PARTY 1981 SWANSONG US
TONY STEVENS B V (AB
DAVID DOWLE D (AB JOHN COOK K (AB CHRIS PARREN K (B

M146C MIDNIGHT STAR M146C

BELINDA LIPSCOMB V (A (A) THE BEGINNING 1980 RCA US 3491 UK SOLA 2
REGINALD CALLOWAY V HRNS(A (B) STANDING TOGETHER 1981 SOLAR UK K 52305
VINCENT CALLOWAY HRNS(A
JEFF COOPER G (A BO WATSON K V (A HARVEY MASON PERC (A BILL REICHENBACH HRNS (A
GEORGE BOHANON HRNS (A WILLIAM COLLETTE HRNS (A JEROME RICHARDSON WIND (A KENNETH GANT B V (A
WILLIAM SIMMONS V SAX(A MICHAEL BODDICKER K (A KENNY MASON HRNS (A JERRY HEY HRNS (A
OSCAR BRASHEAR HRNS (A DAVID DUKE HRNS (A

M147 MIDNIGHT SUN M147

BENT HESSELMANN WIND (ABCD (A) RAINBOW BAND 1970 SONET SLPS 1523
NIELS BRONDSTED K (ABCD (A) RAINBOW BAND (DIFF VOCALS) 1971 SONET SLPS1523A
CARSTEN SMEDGAARD D (ABCD (B) MIDNIGHT SUN 1972 MCA MKPS 2019
PEER FROST G (ABC (C) WALKING CIRCLES 1972 SONET SLPS 1536 UK MCA MKPS 2024
BO STIEF B (ABC (D) MIDNIGHT DREAM 1974 SONET SLPS 1547
LARS BISGAARD V (A
HANS LAURIDSEN V (C JENS ELBØL B (D TOM HEATH G (D ALLAN MORTENSEN V (B

M148 MIGHTY BABY M148

PETE WATSON G (1 (A) MIGHTY BABY 1969 HEAD UK HDLS6002 US 025
MIKE EVANS B (12345A (B) A JUG OF LOVE 1971 BLUE HORIZON UK 2931 001
ROGER POWELL D (12345A (1) 1963 (2) ACTION 1966 (3) ACTION (4) ACTION (5) 1968 71
REG KING V (123
ALAN 'BAM 'KING G (12345A IAN WHITEMAN V WIND K(245A MARTIN STONE G (345A

M149 MIGHTY DIAMONDS M149

DONALD SHAW V (BCDEF (A) RIGHT TIME 1976 VIRGIN US 34235 UK V 2052
FIZTROY SIMPSON V (BCDEF (B) ICE ON FIRE 1977 VIRGIN US 34235 UK V 2078
LLOYD FERGUSON V (BCDEF (C) PLANET EARTH 1978 VIRGIN UK V 2102
DWIGHT RICHARDS D (B (D) STAND UP 1978 CHANNEL ONE
KENNETH WILLIAMS PERC (B (E) DEEPER ROOTS 1979 FRONT LINE UK FLD 6001
STEVE HUGHES G (B (F) TELL ME WHAT'S WRONG 1980 J&J US
HERMAN MARQUIS SAX (CF
DAVE BARARD B (B ROBERT DABON PNO (B CLYDE KERR JNR TPT (B JOHN LONGO TPT (B
ALVIN THOMAS SAX (B MICHAEL PIERCE SAX (B CARL BLOUIN SAX (B THEODORE ROYAL G (B
WARDELL QUEZERGUE K (B RAYMOND JONES PNO (B ISAAC BOLDEN PNO (B CARLTON DAVIS D (B
EARL CHINNA SMITH G (B SLY DUNBAR D (CF STICKY PERC (CF TOMMY McCOOK SAX (CF

M149A MIGHTY FLEA M149A

GENE'MIGHTY FLEA'CONNERS V TROM(A (A) LET THE GOOD TIMES ROLL 1973 BIG BEAR 19 + POLYDOR79 2460185

M149B MIGHTY SPARROW M149B

(A) PEACE & LOVE 1979 TROJAN UK TRLS 159

M150 MIGIL FIVE M150

(A) MOCKINGBIRD HILL 1964 PYE UK NPL 18093
(B) COME DANCE WITH 1969 JOY JOYS 138

M150A MIKE, SLOT & BUMPER M150A

(A) AMAZIN' R&B (EP) 1979 BLUEPORT BLU3

M151 BUDDY MILES M151

BUDDY MILES V D G K B (ALL (A) EXPRESSWAY TO YOUR SKULL 1968 MERCURY US SR61196 UK SMCL 20137
HERBIE RICH ORG SAX (A (B) ELECTRIC CHURCH 1969 MERCURY US SR61222 UK SMCL 20163
JIM McCARTY G (ABC (C) THEM CHANGES 1970 MERCURY US SR61280 UK 6338 016
BILL RICH B (A (D) WE GOT TO LIVE TOGETHER 1970 MERCURY US SR61313 UK 6338 028
RON WOODS D (A (E) MESSAGE TO THE PEOPLE 1970 MERCURY US SRM1608 UK 6338 048
TERRENCE CLEMENTS SAX (A (F) LIVE 1971 MERCURY US SRM7500 UK 6641 033
MARCUS DOUBLEDAY TPT (A (G) WITH CARLOS SANTANA 1972 CBS US 31308 UK 65142
VIRGIL GONSALVES WIND (A (H) CHAPTER VII 1973 CBS US 32048 UK 65406
BILL McPHERSON WIND (AD (J) BOOGER BEAR 1973 CBS US 32694 UK 65820
DUANE HITCHINGS ORG (BCH (K) ALL THE FACES OF BUDDY MILES1974 EPIC US 33089 UK 80349
TOBIE WYNN SAX (BC (L) MORE MILES PER GALLON 1975 CASABLANCA US 7019 UK 4006
JAMES TATUM SAX (BC (M) BICENTENNIAL GATHERING 1976 CASABLANCA US 7024
BOBBY ROCK SAX (B (N) SNEAK ATTACK 1981 ATLANTIC UK K60156
PETER CARTER TPT (BC
TOM HALL TPT (BCF BOB PARKINS ORG (C WALLY ROSSUNOLO G (C BILLY COX B (C
ROBERT PITTMAN SAX (C TEDDY BLANDIN TPT (C CHARLIE KARP G (CDEF BOB HOGINS K TROM (CDF
ROBIN McBRIDE K (C ANDRE LEWIS ORG (CDEH MARLO HENDERSON G (CDEH DAVID HULL B (CDEF
LEE ALLEN SAX (CD PHIL WOOD HRNS (CD MARK WILLIAMS WIND(CD ROLAND ROBINSON B (CJ
FRED ALLEN PERC (DE JOE PORTER TPT (D DICK GABRIEL SAX (D MICHAEL FUGATE TPT (E
HANK REDD SAX (EF STEMSY HUNTER SAX (EFL DONNIE BECK ORG (FJM ADRIAN CURTIS G V (H
RON JOHNSON B (H ROBERT HOGGINS G V (H RICHARD APLANALP SAX (H BILLY SPRAGUE HRNS(H
DAVID DHALSTON HRNS (H DENISE PANTOS MILES D (H WILLIE BOBO PERC (H VICTOR PANTOJA CONGA(H
JAMES BRADSHAW G (H PAUL GURVITZ(CURTIS) V (H STEVE BUSHFIELD G (J BOB FERREIRA SAX (J
PAT O'HARA TROM (J PETER WALKER TPT (J BILL ATWOOD TPT (J MINGO LEWIS PERC(J
JERRY PETERS K (K CLARENCE McDONALD K (K JAMES JAMERSON B (K EDWARD GREENE D (K
KEN HAWKINS G (K, RAY PARKER G (K MELVIN RAGIN G (K JOE CLAYTON PERC (K
GENE ESTES PERC (K ERNIE WATTS SAX (K BEN SCHULTZ G K (LM BOBBY BERGE D (LM
STEVE LAWRENCE SAX (LM KEN WALTER TROM (LM TOM BRAY TPT (LM PAUL CACRA TPT (LM
STEVIE WONDER K (L AL BROWN D (L JOHN MALLER D (M DANNY HULL SAX (M
RON PERRY B (M BOYD ALBRITTON G (M DICKIE BETTS G (M

M152 JOHN MILES M152

JOHN MILES G V K(ALL (A) REBEL 1976 DECCA UK SKL 5231 US LONDON 669
BOB MARSHALL B (ABCDE (B) STRANGER IN THE CITY 1976 DECCA UK TXS 118 US LONDON 682
BARRY BLACK D (ABCDE (C) ZARAGON 1978 DECCA UK TXS 126 US ARISTA4176
GARY MOBERLEY K (B (D) MMMMPH 1979 DECCA UK TXSR 135
BRIAN CHATTON K (DE (E) SYMPATHY 1980 US ARISTA4261
ORCHESTRA (DE (F) HIGH MILES 1981 EMI UK EMC 3374

M153 MILESTONES M153

BEATRIX NEUNDLINGER FLT V(B (A) MILESTONES 1971
CHRISTIAN KOLONOVITS K B V(B (B) EMIGRATION 1973 CBS UK 65738
GUNTHER GROSSLERCHER G V (B
NORBERT NIEDERMAYER B G V(B CHRI VANDER SCHYT D (B

M154 **MILK & COOKIES** M154

IAN NORTH K G (A (A) MILK & COOKIES 1977 ISLAND UK ILPS 9320

JUSTIN STRAUSS V (A

SAL MAIDA B (A MIKE RUIZ D (A JIM GREGORY B (MUFF WINWOOD PROD(A

M155 **MILKWOOD** M155

BEN ORR ((A) MILKWOOD 1972 PARAMOUNT US 6046

RICHARD OCASEK ((B) HOW'S THE WEATHER 19 PARAMOUNT US

M156 **MILLENIUM** M156

CURT BOETCHER V (A (A) BEGIN 1968 CBS US CS 9663

MICHAEL FENNELLY G V (A

LEE MALLORY (A JOE STEC (A RED RHODES STEEL(A DOUG RHODES (A

KEITH OLSEN (A PAT SHANAHAN (A RON EDGAR (A DOUG DILLARD (A

JIM RYAN (A

M157 **FRANKIE MILLER** M157

FRANKIE MILLER V G (ALL (A) ONCE IN A BLUE MOON 1973 CHRYSALIS UK/US CHR1036

ALLEN TOUSSAINT K (B (B) HIGH LIFE 1974 CHRYSALIS UK/US CHR1052

JOE WILSON G (B (C) THE ROCK 1975 CHRYSALIS UK/US CHR 1088

BOB ANDREWS K V (A (D) FULL HOUSE 1977 CHRYSALIS UK/US CHR 1128

BRINSLEY SCHWARZ G (A (E) DOUBLE TROUBLE 1978 CHRYSALIS UK/US CHR 1174

BILLY RANKIN D (A (F) FALLING IN LOVE/PERFECT FIT 1979 CHRYSALIS UK/US CHR 1220

JOE OSBORN B (G (F) FALLING IN LOVE/PERFECT FIT 1979 CHRYSALIS EURO 6307 652

IAN GOMM G (A (G) EASY MONEY 1980 CHRYSALIS UK/US CHR 1268

NICK LOWE B V (A (EP) JEALOUS GUY 1977 CHRYSALIS UK CHS 2184

TOM ROBB B (B (1) FEB 1978 TOUR (2) MARCH 1978 TOUR

MIKE HUEY D (B (3) MAY 1978 TOUR (4) SEPT 1978 TOUR

G C COLEMAN D (B

AUBURN BURRELL G (B BARRY BAILEY G (B LESTER CALISTE TROM (B CLYDE KERR JR TROM(B

GARY BROWN SAX (B JOHN LONGO TPT (B ALVIN THOMAS SAX (B HENRY McCULLOUGH G (C

MICK WEAVER K (C CHRIS STEWART B(CDF123 STU PERRY D (C RAY MINHINNIT G (D

JAMES HALL K (D GRAHAM DEACON D (D KAREN LAWRENCE V (E HUGH BURNS G (3

FRAN BYRNE D (F4 RICHARD SUPA V (E STEPHEN TYLER V HCA(E MARTIN DROVER TPT (E12

CHRIS MERCER SAX (E123 PAUL CARRACK K V(EF12 B J WILSON D (E123 RAY RUSSELL G (E2

MICK MOODY G (1 LANI GROVES V (E ERIC TROYER V (E CHRIS SLADE D (F

TEX COMER B (F4 DAVE WINTOUR B (F BARRIE GUARD PERC (F TIM RENWICK G (F

ED DEAN G (F4 TERRY BRITTEN G (F STEVE SIMPSON G (F4 LINDA TAYLOR V (F

RON ASPERY HRNS (F CHRIS HALL K (F CHRIS SPEDDING G (D RABBIT K (D

GARY BROOKER K V (D MEMPHIS HORNS HRNS (D LARRY LONDIN D PERC(G REG YOUNG G (G

BOBBY THOMPSON G (G

M158 **JACOB MILLER** M158

JACOB MILLER (A (A) DREAD DREAD 1978 UA US UALA 806

( ) WANTED 1979

( ) TENEMENT STEPS 1980 ISLAND NL 201 087

( ) JACOB KILLER MILLER 1980 ISLAND NL 201 088

( ) MIXED UP MOODS 1980 ISLAND NL 202 883

M158A **STEPHEN MILLER (UK)** M158A

STEPHEN MILLER K (AB (A) MILLER & COXHILL 1974 CAROLINE UK C 1503

LOL COXHILL WIND (A (B) STORY SO FAR 1974 CAROLINE UK C 1507

LAURIE ALLEN PERC (B

M158B **STEPHEN MILLER (US)** M158B

STEPHEN MILLER K V (A (A) STEPHEN MILLER 197 MERCURY US

FRED WALK G (A

LARRY EASTER WIND (A CLARK PIERSON D (A DINO LONG B (A ELVIN BISHOP G (A

APPLE JACK HCA (A JOHN CHAMBERS D (A KIP MAERCKLIN B (A

M159 **STEVE MILLER BAND** M159

STEVE MILLER HCA SYN G K V(ALL (A) CHILDREN OF THE FUTURE 1968 CAPITOL 718 RI US 2920

LONNIE TURNER B G(13456ABCDEHIJK (B) SAILOR 1969 CAPITOL 719 RI US 2984

TIM DAVIS B (12ABCDE (AB) LIVING IN USA(DBL) 1973 CAPITOL 717 EURO 197/98

JAMES COOKE G (1EJK (C) BRAVE NEW WORLD 1969 CAPITOL 184 EURO 80117

JIM PETERMAN K (AB (D) YOUR SAVING GRACE 1970 CAPITOL 331 EURO 80277

BOZ SCAGGS G V (AB (E) NUMBER FIVE 1970 CAPITOL 436 EURO 80570

BEN SIDRAN K (CDEG (F) ROCK LOVE 1971 CAPITOL 748 EURO 80962

NICKY HOPKINS K (CDE (G) RECALL THE BEGINNING 1972 CAPITOL 11022 EURO 81099

JIMMY MILLER G (E (H) THE JOKER 1973 CAPITOL 11235 EURO 81514

BOBBY THOMPSON B (E (J) FLY LIKE AN EAGLE 1976 MERCURY UK 9286177 US CAPITOL11497

KENNY LEE LEWIS G (M (J) FLY LIKE AN EAGLE 1976 MERCURY EURO 6303 925

BOBBY WINKLEMAN B (2 (K) BOOK OF DREAMS 1977 MERCURY UK 9286455 US CAPITOL11630

JOHN MASSARO G (M (K) BOOK OF DREAMS 1977 MERCURY EURO 6303 926

ROSS VALORY B (F (L) CIRCLE OF LOVE 1981 MERCURY UK 6302 061 US CAPITOL12121

JOHN KING D (45H (M) ABRACADABRA 1982 US CAPITOL12216

( ) REVOLUTION(QUICKSILVER,MOTHER EARTH)1968 UA UK 29069 US UA UAS5185

JACK KING D (FG3 ( ) TRIPLE SET(QUICKSILVER,BAND) 19 CAPITOL STCR 288

GERALD JOHNSON B (345GHLM ( ) ANTHOLOGY 1973 CAPITOL UK ESTSP12 US 11114

JIM KELTNER D (G ( ) BEST OF 1973 HORVU EURO SHZE 901

DICKY THOMPSON K (345GH ( ) MASTERS OF ROCK 1974 EMI EURO 054 81583

GARY MALLABER D (GJKLM ( ) PROFILES 1974 EMI EURO 81581

LES DUDEK G (6JK ( ) THE LEGEND 1975 CAPITOL VMP 1008

DOUG CLIFFORD D (6 ( ) ADVENTURES OF A SPACE COWBOY 1975 CAPITOL EURO 81645

NORTON BUFFALO V HCA(K ( ) BEST OF 1968 73 1977 CAPITOL EST 24058

DAVID DENNY G (K ( ) GREATEST HITS 1974/78 1978 MERCURY UK 9199916 US CAPITOL11822

BYRON ALLRED K (KLM

JOHN McFEE G (J (1) NOV 1966 (2) NOV 1969/70 (3) JAN 1972

JOACHIM YOUNG K (KJ (4) MAR 1972 (5) OCT 1972 (6) JULY 1975

BUD BILLINGS TPT (E

KENNY JOHNSON D (JK SNEAKY PETE KLEINOW STEEL(H GREG DOUGLAS G (K BUDDY SPICHER FDL (E

JAMES COTTON HCA (J ROGER CLARK D (34G CHARLIE McCOY HCA (E WAYNE MOSS G B (E

LEE MICHAELS K (E JIMMY TILLMAN D (E CHARLIE CALMESE B (K BOB GLAUB B (K

JESSE ED DAVIS G (G PAUL McCARTNEY B D V(C GLYN JOHNS G V PERC(

M160 **MILLINGTON** M160

JEAN MILLINGTON B V (A (A) LADIES ON THE STAGE 1978 UA US LA 821 UK UAG 30158
JUNE MILLINGTON G V (A
LEO ADAMIAN D V (A TONY RAMOS V (A IRENE CARA V (A VICKI RANDLE V (A
FAITH FUSILLO V (A GORDON GRODY V (A CHRIS WILLIAMSON V (A FLEMING WILLIAMS V (A
TOM SCOTT WIND (A DEBBY GABER G (A SNEAKY PETE STEEL(A RALPH SCHUCKETT K (A
COLLEEN STEWART K (A TOM SELLERS K (A MARGO LEWIS V (A ED GREENE D (A
SCOTT EDWARDS B (A BRIE HOWARD V (A ROLAND ROZZELLE K (A LARRY CARLTON G (A
KENNY NEMIROFF K (A GARY COLEMAN PERC (A JUNE ADAMIAN V (A BRYAN PARRIS D (A
ELLEN SHIPLEY V (A NEGRA V (A LEE RITENOUR G (A DEAN PARKS G (A
CHRISTOPHER BOND G (A EARL SLICK G (A

M160A **MARIO MILLO** M160A

MARIO MILLO V G K B D (A (A) EPIC III 19 AUST
MARK KENNEDY D (A
JACKIE ORSZACZKY B (A COS RUSSO K (A LAURA CHISLETT FLT (A SAFANYA V (A
GERG TELL D (A PETER KENNY K (A DAVID GLYDE SAX (A

M161 **GARNET MIMMS** M161

GARNET MIMMS V (ALL WARM & SOUL 1966 UA UK ULP 1145
WITH REMEMBER (EP) 1973 UA UK REM 403
SAM BELL V (HAS IT ALL 1978 ARISTA US 4153 UK SPART1032
ZOLA PEARNELL V (AS LONG AS I HAVE YOU 1964 UA US UAS 6396
CHARLES BOYER V (CRY BABY 1963 UA US UAS 6305
I'LL TAKE GOOD CARE OF YOU 1966 UA US UAS 6498

M162 **(WAYNE FONTANA) & THE MINDBENDER** M162

WAYNE FONTANA V ((A) WAYNE FONTANA & THE MINDBENDERS 1965 FONTANA UK TL 5230
ERIC STEWART G V ((A) WFATM(SAME AS ABOVE +3 TRACKS) 1967 FONTANA SPEC SFL 13106
(A) WFATM(SAME AS A +2 TRACKS) 1967 WING WL 1166
BOB LAND B ((B) ERIC RICK WAYNE BOB 1966 FONTANA UK TL 5257
RICK ROTHWELL D ((C) WAYNE ONE(WAYNE SOLO) 196 FONTANA UK STL 5351
PAUL HANCOX D ((D) THE MINDBENDERS 1966 FONTANA UK 5324 RI SFL 13045
GRAHAM GOULDMAN G ((E) WITH WOMAN IN MIND 1967 FONTANA UK STL 5403
JAMES O'NEIL G ((F) A GROOVY KIND OF LOVE 1967 FONTANA US(M) 27554 (S) 67554
( ) TO SIR WITH LOVE(ON SOUNDTRACK) 1967 FONTANA UK STL 5446

M162A **LINCOLN SUGAR MINOTT** M162A

LINCOLN 'SUGAR' MINOTT (AB (A) BLACK ROOTS 1980 ISLAND UK/US 9591
(B) GIVE THE PEOPLE 1980 BALLISTIC UK 30310

M162B **MINT TATTOO** M162B

BRUCE STEPHENS G V (A (A) MINT TATTOO 1 DOT US 25918
BURNS KELLOGG B K V(A
GREGG THOMAS D (A

M163 **MINK DEVILLE** M163

WILLY DE VILLE V G (ALL (A) MINK DEVILLE 1977 CAPITOL UK/US 11631
BOBBY LEONARDS K (AB (B) RETURN TO MAGENTA 1978 CAPITOL UK/US 11780
VAL HERON V (A (C) LE CHAT BLEU 1980 CAPITOL US 11955 GER 86086 UK25390
RUBIN SIQUENZA B SAX(AB (D) COUP DE GRACE 1981 CAPITOL
LOUIE ERLANGER G V (ABC
THOMAS R ALLEN D (A STEVE DOUGLAS PROD SAX (BC RITCH COLBERT K (KENNY MARGOLIS K V (C
JACKIE KELSO SAX (B DR JOHN PNO (B DAVID FORMAN V (B LEON DOUGLAS V (B
MIKE JOHNSON V (A MAX BOWMAN V (AB JAKE V (C JERRY SCHEFF B D (C
RON TUTT D (C EVE MOON V (C

M163A **MIRAGE** M163A

GEORGE KHAN SAX FLT(A (A) NOW YOU SEE IT 1977 COMPENDIUM NORWAY FIDARO 9
BRIAN GODDING G (A
STEVE COOK B (A DAVE SHEEN D (A

M163B **STEVE MIRO & THE EYES** M163B

STEVE MIRO V G (A (A) RUDE INTRUSIONS 1980 OBJECT OBJ008
JIMMY CARTER B V (A (B) SECOND SENTENCE 1981 OBJECT OBJ015
BRIAN MARTIN D V (A
DUNCAN PRESTBURY K V (A STEVE SOLAMAR HCA (A FREDRICK BURROWS TPT (A

M163C **MISFITS** M163C

GLENN DANZIG (A (A) BEWARE(EP) 1979 CHERRY RED UK PLP9
MR JIM D (A
JERRY ONLY (A BOBBY STEELE (A JOEY IMAGE (A

M163D **MISSION OF BURMA** M163D

CLINT CONLEY B VG (A (A) SIGNALS CALLS & MARCHES (EP) 19 ACE OF HEARTS CAN 1006
ROGER MILLER G V (A
PETER PRESCOTT D V (A MARTIN SWOPE TAPE (A

M163E **MISSUS BEASTLY** M163E

JURGEN BENZ WIND PERC(A (A) MISSUS BEASTLY 19 NOVA GER 6 22030
FRIEDEMANN JOSCH WIND (A
NORBERT DOMLING G B (A LUTZ OLDEMEIER D (A DIETER MIEKAUTSCH K (A

M164 **MR BIG** M164

JEFF DICKEN HCA B G V (AB (A) SWEET SILENCE 1975 EMI UK EMC 3101
PETE CROWTHER G B (AB (B) MR BIG 1977 EMI UK EMC 3171
EDDIE CARTER G V (B
VINCE CHAULK V D (AB JOHN MARTER D V (JOHN BURNIP D (A IAN BLUNSDON K (A
JOHN PUNTER SYN (A ROBERT HIRSCHMAN B TROM(A

M165 **MR BLOE** M165

(A) GROOVIN WITH MR BLOE 1973 SILVERLINE 036 + DJM 1974 DJLPS409

M165A **Mr FLOOD'S PARTY** M165A

JAY HIRSH (A (A) MR FLOODS PARTY 1969 COTILLION US 9003
MIKE CORBETT (A
FRED TESCANO (A RICK MIRAGE (A TOM CASTAHNARA (A MARCEL THOMPSON (A

M166 **MR FOX** M166

BOB PEGG V G B K (AB — (A) MR FOX — 1970 TRANSATLANTIC UK TRA226
CAROLE PEGG V FDL(AB — (B) THE GYPSY — 1971 TRANSATLANTIC UK TRA236
ALUN EVANS D (AB — (AB THE COMPLETE MR FOX — 1975 TRANSATLANTIC UK TRA303
BARRY LYONS B DULC (AB
ANDREW MASSEY CELLO(A JOHN MYATT WIND(A RICHIE BULL B BANJ(GRIDLEY TABERNACLE ORCH (B
NICK STRUTT MULTI(

M166A **MISTERS** M166A

BERT DECORTE G V (A — (A) CHANGE PARTNERS — 1978 ARIOLA GER 200 229
LUC'LEWIS' VAN RUMST G V(A — (B) SNAKING OUT FROM THE DARK — 1980 POLYDOR FR 2427 931
KLAUS WAGNER B (A
ROY HARLINGTON D (A PIETRO LACIRIGNOLA SAX (A DANNY BODDIN PNO (A FRANK TOMMELEIN V (B
PAUL COWBELL (B

M167 **MISTRESS** M167

CHARLIE WILLIAMS G V (A — (A) MISTRESS — 1979 RSO US 13059 RSS 14
DAVID BROWN B (A
KENNY HOPKINS G V (A DANNY CHAUNCEY G V (A MIKE UTLEY K (A DOUG DILLARD BAN (A
CHRIS PAULSEN D (A JOHN McFEE STEEL(A RICK CLARK V (A GREG DOUGLAS G (
DAVE WALKER V (SKIP OLSON B (

M167A **MISTY IN ROOTS** M167A

(A) LIVE AT COUNTER EUROVISION — 1980 PEOPLE UNITE PU003
(B) WISE & FOOLISH — 1981 PEOPLE UNITE PU101

M168 **MISTUNDERSTOOD** M168

GLEN FERNANDO CAMPBELL STEEL(AB — (A)MISTUNDERSTOOD 1966 1967 (B) 1969
TONY HILL G V (A
GREG TREADWAY G V (A RICK BROWN V (A STEVE WHITING B (A RICK MOE D (A
STEVE HOARD V (B DAVY O'LIST G (B NIC POTTER B (B CHRIS MERCER SAX(B
NEIL HUBBARD G (B GUY EVANS D (B

M169 **BLUE MITCHELL** M169

BLUE MITCHELL HRNS (A

Title	Year	Label	Country	No.
THING TO DO	19	BLUENOTE		BST 84178
BRING IT HOME TO ME	19	BLUENOTE		BST 84228
BOSS HORN	19	BLUENOTE		BST 84257
HEADS UP	19	BLUENOTE		BST 84272
COLLISION IN BLACK	19	BLUENOTE		BST 84300
BANTU VILLAGE	19	BLUENOTE		BST 84324
BLUE MITCHELL	1972	MAINSTREAM	US	315
VITAL	197	MAINSTREAM	US	343
BLUE'S BLUE	197	MAINSTREAM	US	374
GRAFFITI BLUES	1974	MAINSTREAM	US 400	MSL 1026
MANY SHADES OF BLUE	1975	MAINSTREAM	US 402	MSL 1028
STRATO SONIC	1975	RCA	US 1109	
FUNKTION	1976	RCA	US 1493	

M169A **IAN MITCHELL BAND** M169A

IAN MITCHELL V G K B (A — (A) LONELY NIGHTS — 1979 WB UK K 58070
JON JAY B V G(A
NICKY DIAMOND K V (A PAUL JACKSON G K V(A LINDSAY SIMON HONEY D V K(A

M170 **JONI MITCHELL** M170

Title	Year	Label	US	UK
(A) JONI MITCHELL	1968	REPRISE	US 6293	UK K 44051
(B) CLOUDS	1969	RERPISE	US 6341	UK K 44070
(C) LADIES OF THE CANYON	1970	REPRISE	US 6376	UK K 44085
(D) BLUE	1971	REPRISE	US 2038	UK K 44128
(E) FOR THE ROSES	1972	ASYLUM	US 5057	UK SYLA 8753
(E) FOR THE ROSES	1975	ASYLUM	RI	UK K 53007
(F) COURT & SPARK	1974	ASYLUM	US 7E1001	UK SYLA 8756
(F) COURT & SPARK	1975	ASYLUM	RI	UK K 53002
(G) MILES OF AISLES	1974	ASYLUM	US 202	UK SYSP 902
(G) MILES OF AISLES	1975	ASYLUM	RI	UK K 63001
(H) HISSING OF SUMMER LAWNS	1975	ASYLUM	US 7E1051	UK SYLA 8763
(H) HISSING OF SUMMER LAWNS	1975	ASYLUM	RI	UK K 53018
(J) HEJIRA	1976	ASYLUM	US 7E1087	UK K 53053
(K) DON JUANS RECKLESS DAUGHTER	1977	ASYLUM	US 101	UK K 63003
(L) MINGUS	1979	ASYLUM	US 5E505	UK K 53091
(M) SHADOWS & LIGHT (DBL)(BEST OF)	1980	ASYLUM	US 704	UK 62030
(N) WILD THINGS RUN FAST	1982	GEFFEN		UK 25102

JONI MITCHELL V G K(ALL
TOM SCOTT WIND (EJFG
WILTON FELDER B (EFH
RUSS KUNKEL D (DE
BOBBYE HALL PERC (EJK
GRAHAM NASH V HCA(EFH
JAMES BURTON G (E
STEPHEN STILLS G B (ABDE
JAMES TAYLOR G V (DHN
SNEAKY PETE KLEINOW STEEL(D
JOHN GUERIN D (FGHJKN
MAX BENNETT B (FGHJ
JIM HUGHART B (F
MILT HOLLAND PERC (CF
CHUCK FINDLEY TPT (FJH
JOE SAMPLE K (FH
STEVE LUKATHER G (N
DAVID CROSBY V (FH
SUSAN WEBB V (F WAYNE PERKINS G (F DENNIS BUDIMIR G (F ROBBIE ROBERTSON G (F
JOSE FELICIANO G (F ROBBEN FORD G (GH JEFF BAXTER G (H CHEECH & CHONG V (F
VICTOR FELDMAN PERC K (FJN BUD SHANK WIND (H JACO PASTORIUS B (JKLM NEIL YOUNG HCA (J
ABE MOST CLAR (J CHUCK DOMANICO B (J TERESSA ADAMS CELLO(C PAUL HORN WIND(C
JIM HORN SAX (C SASKATUNES V (C WAYNE SHORTER SAX (KLN HERBIE HANCOCK K (L
PETER ERSKINE D (L DON ALIAS CONGA(LKM EMIL RICHARDS PERC (L MANOLO BADRENA PERC(K
AIRTO MOREIRA PERC (K GLENN FREY V (K LYLE MAYS K (M PERSUASIONS V (M
LARRY CARLTON G (FHJKN MICHELE COLOMBIER PNO (K ALEJANDRO ACUNA PERC (K CHAKA KHAN V (K
J D SOUTHER V (K PAT METHENY G (M MICHAEL BRECKER SAX (M LEE KEEFER (M
LARRY NASH PNO (G CHARLIE MINGUS V (L VINNIE COLAIUTA D (N LIONEL RICHIE V (N
HOWARD KINNEY V (N RUSSELL FERRANTE SYN (N KENNY RANKIN V (N SKIP COTTRELL V (N
LARRY KLEIN B (N LARRY WILLIAMS K SAX(N CHARLES VALENTINO V (N MIKE LANDAU G (N
ROBERT DE LA GARZA V (N KIM HUTCHCROFT SAX (N

M171 **SAM MITCHELL** M171

SAM MITCHELL G V (AB — (A) BOTTLENECK & SLIDE GUITAR — 1978 KICKING MULE SNKF 121
(B) FOLLOW YOU DOWN — 1978 KICKING MULE SNKF 147

M172 **WILLIE MITCHELL** M172

WILLIE MITCHELL TPT (ALL
MICHAEL TOLES G K (K
AL JACKSON D (
CHARLES HODGES K (G
JAMES MITCHELL SAX (G
LEROY HODGES B (G
HOWARD GRIMES D (G
MABON HODGES G (G

Title	Year	Label / No.
(A) ITS WHATS HAPPENING	196	HI US 32007
(B) HOLD IT	1964	HI US 32021
(C) HIT SOUND	196	HI US 32034
(D) SOUL SERENADE	1968	HI US 32039 UK LONDON SHU 8365
(E) LIVE	1968	HI US 32042 UK LONDON SHU 8368
(F) SOLID SOUL	1969	HI US 32045 UK LONDON SHU 8372
(G) ON TOP	1969	HI US 32048 UK LONDON SHU 8388
(H) SOUL BAG	1970	HI US 32050 UK LONDON SHU 8408
(I) ROBINS NEST	197	HI US 32058
(J) BEST OF	19	HI US 32068
(K) LISTEN DANCE	1981	BEARSVILLE US BRK 3520

M173 HANK MIZELL M173

HANK MIZELL G V (ALL (A) JUNGLE ROCK 1976 CHARLY UK CRL 5000
JIMMY DEMPSEY G (A (EP) HIGHER 1977 CHARLY UK CEP 115
JAMES BOBO G (A
LEO JACKSON G (A BILL COLLINS D (A JERRY KROON D (A EDDIE B (A
JACK ROSS B (A D J FONTANA D (A BOB DEAN (A BILL HUMBLE B (A
ALAN MOORE PNO SAX (A

M173A MO DETTES M173A

(A) STORY SO FAR 1980 DERAM UK SML 1120

M174 MOBY GRAPE M174

PETER LEWIS G (ABCDEFGH (A) MOBY GRAPE 1967 CBS US CS 9498(S) CL 2698 (M)
JOEL SCOTT HILL V ((A) MOBY GRAPE 196 CBS US 30392 UK 63090
KENT DUNBAR D ((B) WOW 1968 CBS US 9613 UK 63271
BOB MOSLEY B (ABCEF (B) WOW/GRAPE JAM (FREE LP WITH WOW) 1968 CBS US cxs3 UK 66209
SKIP SPENCE G D (ABEFH (C) MOBY GRAPE 69 1969 CBS US 9696 UK 63430
BOB NEWKIRK D ((D) TRULY FINE CITIZEN 1970 CBS US 9912 UK 63698
DON STEVENSON G D (ABCDEF (E) 20 GRANITE CREEK 1972 REPRISE US 6460 UK K 44152
JERRY MILLER G (ABEFCDH (F) GREAT GRAPE 1974 CBS US 31098 UK 64743
BOB MOORE B (D (G) BEST OF 1976 CBS EURO 53371
GORDON STEVENS VLN G(E (H) GRAPE LIVE 1979 ESCAPE IMP ESAIA
ANDY NARELL PERC (E ( ) OMAHA 1971 HARMONY US 30392
DAVID RUBINSTEIN PNO PERC(E
JEFFREY COHEN B (E CORNELIUS BUMPUS SAXK(H JOHN OXENDINE D (H CHRISTIAN POWELL B (H
TOMMY SPURLOCK G (DANNY TIMMS K (FRANK RECARD G V (JEFF BLACKBURN G V (
JOHN CRAVIOTTA D (

M175 MODELS M175

CLIFF FOX G V ((A) YES WITH MY BADY 1980 WINFIELD US 3642
MARCO PIRRONI G (
MICK ALLEN B (TERRY DAY D (

M175A MODERATES M175A

BOB CARR G (A (A) FETISHES (EP) 19 OPEN EYE OE1001
TOM GOULD G (A
PHIL ALLEN D (A HEIDI KURE V (A BRADY K V (A MARTIN COOPER B (A
BOB MORTEN SAX (A

M175B MODERN MAN M175B

DANNY MITCHELL G SYN(A (A) CONCRETE SCHEME 1980 MAM LP 5001
JIM COOK V (A
MIKE MORAN B (A ALI McLEOD G (A COLIN KING D V (A

M175C MODERNAIRES M175C

PHILLIP BRADLEY G V SYN(A (A) WAY OF LIVING 1980 ILLUMINATED UK JAMS 3
DAVID BAYNTON POWER D V(A
HUGH HUGHES B K V(A LEA MINSHULL WINS V (A

M175D MODERN ENGLISH M175D

STEPHEN WALKER K (A (A) MESH & LACE 1981 4AD UK CAD105
MICK CONROY B V (A
RICHARD BROWN D (A GARY McDOWELL G V (A ROBBIE GREY V (A

M175E MODERN EON M175E

BOB WAKELIN SYN V PERC(A (A) FICTION TALES 1981 DINDISC UK DID11
CLIFF HEWITT D PERC(A
DANNY HAMPSON B (A TIM LEVER G SAX(A ALIX G V K HRN(A

M175F MOEBIUS & PLANK M175F

DIETER MOEBIUS K SYN (A (A) RASTAKRAUT 1980 SKY 039
CONNIE PLANK K SYN (A

M176 MOGUL THRASH M176

JAMES LITHERLAND G (A (A) MOGUL THRASH 1971 RCA UK SF 8156
JOHN WETTON B (A
BILL HARRISON D (A ROGER BALL SAX (A MAL DUNCAN SAX (A MIKE ROSEN TPT (A

M177 ESSRA MOHAWK M177

ESSRA(SANDY HURVITZ)MOHAWK K V(ALL (A) SANDYS ALBUM IS HERE AT LAST 1969 VERVE US V6 5064
JIM PEPPER SAX (A (B) PRIMORDIAL LOVERS 1970 REPRISE US RS 6377
LARRY CARLTON G (C (C) ESSRA MOHAWK 1975 MOONCREST UK CREST24 US ASYLUM1023
TOM SELLERS K B G(C (D) ESSRA 1977 PRIVATE STOCK PS 2024 + PVLP 1016
WILTON FELDER B (V
DENNIS PARKER B (C KING ERRISSON PERC (C ED GREENE D (C GENE ESTES PERC (C
ZITRO D (C GENE PELLO D (C KENNY JENKINS FLT (C SKIP SWITZER D (C
DEAN PARKS G (C TOM HENSLEY K (C ERIC GALE G (D JONATHAN KALB G (D
DAVID STONE G (D SONNY BURKE K (D RICHARD DAVIS B (D ANDY NEWMARK D (D
BERNARD PURDIE D (D HOWIE WYETH D (D PAUL GRIFFIN K (D JERRY RAGOVOY K (D
JEREMY STEIG FLT (AD DAVID LASLEY V (D ULA HEDWIG V (D ARNOLD McCULLER V (D
IAN UNDERWOOD (A RHETTA HUGHES V (D

M177A MOLKIE COLE M177A

BOB STEINMETZ K SAX(A (A) MOLKIE COLE 1977 JANUS US 7031
TIMOTHY COLE D (A
PHILIP JAMES G (A PAUL POPE G (A PAT COLE B (A JAMES M TESTA HCA (A

M178 MOJO HANNAH M178

MIKE STEWART G V (A (A) SIX DAYS ON THE ROAD 1972 KINGDOM UK KVL 9001
PAUL MACCULLUM B V (A
MIKE FUDGE MAND VLN (A CHRIS HUNT D (A JOE GILLINGHAM K (A

M178A MOLLY HATCHET M178A

DUANE ROLAND G (ABCD (A) MOLLY HATCHET 1978 EPIC US 35347 UK 83250
DAVE HLUBEK G (ABCD (B) FLIRTIN' WITH DISASTER 1979 EPIC US 36110 UK 83791
STEVE HOLLAND G (ABCD (C) BEATIN' THE ODDS 1980 CBS US 36572 UK 84471
BRUCE CRUMP D (ABCD (D) TAKE NO PRISONERS 1981 EPIC US 37480 UK 85296
JIMMY FARRAR V (CD
BANNER THOMAS B (ABCD DANNY JOE BROWN V (AB JAI WINDING K (D PAULINHO DACOSTA PERC(D
TOM WERMAN PERC (D BABY JEAN V (A TOWER OF POWER HRNS (D BABY JEAN V (D
MINDY STERLING V (D LAURIE BONO V (D KATY SAGAL V (D

M178B **MOMS APPLE PIE** M178B

TONY GIGLIOTTI V (A (A) MUSIC 1973 BROWN BAG US BB LA 073
BOB FIORINO V (A (B) MOMS APPLE PIE 1973 BROWN BAG US 14200
BOB MILLER G (A
DAVE MAZZOCHI K V (A JOE AHLADIS G (A PAT AULIZIA D (A GREG YOCHMAN B (A
ROGER FORCE WIND (A BOB PINTA TPT (A FRED MARZULLA TROM (A

M178C **MONEY** M178C

LARRY PHILLIPS B V (A (A) FIRST INVESTMENT 1979 GULL UK GULP1031
DAVID WEST-MULLEN VPERC(A
JOHN OVERTON G V (A TONY BODEN D PERC V (A CHRIS TSANGARIDES K (A

M178D **MOLOCH** M178D

LEE BAKER G V (A (A) MOLOCH 19 ENTERPRISE ENS 1002
PHILLIP DURHAM D V (A
FRED NICHOLSON ORG(A STEVE SPEAR B (A GENE WILKINS V (A

M179 **EDDIE MONEY** M179

EDDIE MONEY V K SAX(ABC (A) EDDIE MONEY 1977 CBS US 34909 UK 82434
JIMMY LYON G (ABC (B) LIFE IS FOR THE TAKING 1978 CBS US 35598 UK 83159
GARY MALLABER D (ABC (C) PLAYING FOR KEEPS 1980 CBS US 36514 UK 84371
LONNIE TURNER B (ABC
GENE PARDUE D (A POPS POPWELL B (A ALAN PASQUA K (AB EMILIO CASTILLO HRNS(C
STEVE KUPKA HRNS (C MAUREEN McCORMICK V (C RANDY NICHOLS K (ABC FREDDIE WEBB K (A
KEVIN CALHOUN PERC (A TOM SCOTT SAX (AB JO BAKER V (A MYRNA MATTHEWS V (C
JULIA TILLMAN V (C MARTI McCALL V (C VALERIE CARTER V (C DAVID LEWARK G (C
JOHN NELSON G (C GREG DOUGLAS G (C BOB GLAUB C (C KENNY LEWIS B (C
NICKY HOPKINS K (B LLOYD CHIATE G (B JOHN WHITNEY G (B DAVE DANZA D (B
GREGORY PHILLINGANES K (B DAVID LINDLEY G (B TIM SHERIDAN B (B STEVE PORCARO SYN (B
DARRELL VERDUSCO V (B K WINBUSH V (B

M180 **ZOOT MONEY** M180

ZOOT MONEY K V (ALL (A) IT SHOULD HAVE BEEN ME 1965 COLUMBIA UK SX 1734
PAUL WILLIAMS B V (2BE (B) ZOOT 1966 COLUMBIA UK SCX 6075
COLIN ALLEN D (12BE (C) TRANSITION 1968 DIRECTION UK 863231
NICK NEWELL SAX (23BE (D) WELCOME TO MY HEAD 1969 CAPITOL US 318
ANDY SUMMERS G (12BE (E) ALL HAPPENING AT KLOOKS KLEEK 19 EPIC US 24241
CLIVE BURROWS SAX (2 (F) ZOOT MONEY 1970 POLYDOR UK 2482 019
PAT DONALDSON B (1 (G) MR MONEY 1980 MAGIC MOON LUNE 1
BARRY WILSON D (4 (1) DANTALIONS CHARIOT (2) BIG ROLL BAND
JOHNNY ALMOND SAX (BE (3) MUSIC BAND 1969 (4) MUSIC BAND
BERNIE BYRNES D (3
JOHN DEAN B (4 MIKE COTTON TPT (3 JOHN BEECHAM TROM (3 LEN LUBIN B (3
MICK MOODY G (34 JIM GORDON D (D DAVID COHEN (D LYLE RITZ (D
DON PEAKE (D MIKE RUBINI (D GARY COLEMAN PERC (D JIMMY GETZOFF VLN(D
VINCE DEROSA HRNS (D BILL HENSHAS HRNS (D ART MAEBE HRNS (D HENRY SIGISMONTI HRNS(D

M180A **MONGREL** M180A

ROBERT BRADY K V (A (A) GET YOUR TEETH INTO THIS 1973 POLYDOR UK 2383 182
STUART SCOTT G (A
RICK PRICE D (A KEITH SMART D (A CHARLIE GRIMA PERC (A MEGAN DAVIES B (A
TOM FARNELL D (A ROGER HILL G (A

M180B **MEREDETH MONK** M180B

MEREDITH MONK V ORG (A (A) KEY 1977 LOVELY MUSIC US LML 1051
DANIEL IRA SVERDLIK (A
DICK HIGGINS (A COLLIN WALCOTT (A LANNY HARRISON (A MARK MONSTERMAKER (A

M180C **FRANCIS MONKMAN** M180C

FRANCIS MONKMAN (A (A) ENERGISM 1980 WEA NL 58133

M181 **THE MONKEES** M181

DAVY JONES V (ALL THE MONKEES 19 RCA UK SF7844 COLGEMS US 101
MICKEY DOLENZ G D V K(ALL MORE OF THE MONKEES 19 RCA UK SF7868 COLGEMS US 102
PETER TORK G B V(ALL EX* (C)HEADQUARTERS 1967 RCA UK SF7886 COLGEMS US 103
MICHAEL NESMITH G V (ALL EX * (D)PISCES,AQUARIUS, CAPRICORN & JONES 1967 RCA UK SF 7912 COLGEMS US 104
THE BIRDS THE BEES & THE MONKEES 1968 RCA UK SF7948 COLGEMS US 109
TOMMY BOYCE PROD (* INSTANT REPLAY 1969 RCA UK SF8016 COLGEMS US 113
BOBBY HART PROD (* GREATEST HITS 1969 COLGEMS US 115
BILL MARTIN K (D CHANGES 1970 COLGEMS US 119
EDDIE HOH D (D HEAD 1969 RCA UK SF8015 COLGEMS US 5008
KIM COPLI D (D GOLDEN HITS 19 COLGEMS US 329
CHIP DOUGLAS K B PROD(D BARREL FULL OF MONKEES 1970 COLGEMS US 1001
FAITHLING HATFIELD PROD(D THE MONKEES (DBL) 19 LAURIE HOUSE US 8009
PAUL BEAVER SYN (D THE MONKEES 1973 SOUNDS SUPERB UK 90032
DOUG DILLARD BANJ (D RE FOCUS 19 BELL US 6081
VINCE DEROSA HRNS (C GREATEST HITS 19 ARISTA GERM 201115
FRED SEYKORA CELLO(C GREATEST HITS 19 ARISTA 4089
MONKEES PRESENT 19 COLGEMS US 117
MONKEES 1973 MFP UK 90032
(*)JONES DOLENZ BOYCE & HART 1976 CAPITOL 11513
40 TIMELESS HITS 1980 EMI UK

M181A **MONKS (1960s)** M181A

GARY BURGER G (A (A) BLACK MONK TIME 1966 POLYDOR UK 2417129
LARRY CLARK ORG (A
EDDIE SHAW B (A ROGER JOHNSTON D (A

M181B **MONKS(1979)** M181B

JOHN FORD (A (A) BAD HABITS 1979 EMI UK EMC 3309
RICHARD HUDSON (A
TERRY CASSIDY (A

M181C **MONOCHROME SET** M181C

LESTER SQUARE G V (AB (A) STRANGE BOUTIQUE 1980 DINDISC UK DID4
BID V G (AB (B) LOVE ZOMBIES 1980 DINDISC UK DID8
ANDY WARREN B V (AB
J D HANEY D V (AB BOB SARGEANT K V (A ALVIN CLARK K (B TONY POTTS (B

M181D **MONROE** M181D

STEVE BUTLER V (A (A) MONROE 1980 POLYDOR UK 2383 597
GARY SHARPE G (A
PETE HUMPHRIES G (A JAN TAYLOR B (A STEVE GIBSON D (A

M182 MONTAGE M182

Personnel	Inst	Albums	Title	Release
BOB STEURER	V	(A	(A MONTAGE	1969 LAURIE US SLP 2049
VANCE CHAPMAN	D V	(A	(B) HOT PARTS	19 KAMA SUTRA US 2054
MIKE SMYTH	G V	(A		
LANCE CORNELIUS	B V	(A	MICHAEL BROWN K (A	

M182A MONTE CAZAZZA M182A

Personnel	Inst	Albums	Title	Release
			(A) SOMETHING FOR NOBODY (EP)	19 INDUSTRIAL IR 0010

M183 CHRIS MONTEZ M183

Personnel	Inst	Albums	Title	Release
CHRIS MONTEZ	V	(ALL	THE MORE I SEE YOU	1966 PYE UK NPL23080 MAYFAIR AMLB1011
			THE MORE I SEE YOU	19 A&M US 4115
			TIME AFTER TIME	1967 PYE UK NSPL28187 HAMLET AMLP8006
			TIME AFTER TIME	19 A&M US 4120
			FOOLIN' AROUND	1967 A&M US 4128 UK AML 906
			WATCH WHAT HAPPENED	1968 A&M US 4157 UK AML 925
			LETS DANCE	19 CBS UK 65408 LONDON UK HAU8079
			LETS DANCE	19 MONOGRAM US 100 M F P UK 50122

M184 JAMES MONTGOMERY BAND M184

Personnel	Inst	Albums	Title	Release
JAMES MONTGOMERY	V HCA	(ALL	(A) FIRST TIME OUT	1974 CAPRICORN US CP 0120
BARRY WASHINGTON	PERC	(A	(B) HIGH ROLLER	1974 CAPRICORN US CP 0142
BILLY MATHER	B V	(AB	(C) JAMES MONTGOMERY BAND	1977 ISLAND UK ILPS9419 US ANTILLES 7059
PETER MALICK	G V STEEL	(AB	(D) DUCK FEVER	1979 WATERHOUSE US 5
DAVE CASE	K V	(AB		
CHUCK PURRO	D V	(AB	PETER BELL G V (AB SKIP DRINKWATER PROD (A	

M185 LITTLE BROTHER MONTGOMERY M185

Personnel	Inst	Albums	Title	Release
EURREAL MONTGOMERY	V PNO	(ALL	LITTLE BROTHER MONTGOMERY	1960 DECCA UK LK 4664
LEE COLLINS	TPT	(	LITTLE BROTHER MONTGOMERY	1960 COLUMBIA UK 33SX 1289
OLIVER ALCORN	WIND	(	TASTY BLUES	1960 BLUESVILLE US 1012 PRESTIGE 7807
ERNEST CRAWFORD	B	(	AFTER HOURS BLUES	19 BIOGRAPH BLP 12010
JEROME SMITH	D	(	& SUNNYLAND SLIM	19 77 LA 1211
ALEXIS KORNER	G	(	FARRO STREET JIVE	19 XTRA XTRA1115 FOLKWAYS 31014
LAYFAYETTE THOMAS	G	(	1972	1972 MATCHBOX SDM 223
JULIAN EULL	B	(	DEEP SOUTH PIANO	1975 STORYVILLE SLP 228
KEN COLYER	TPT	(	1930/69	1971 MATCHBOX SDR 213
JACK FALCON	B	(	NO SPECIAL RIDER	19 ADELPHI US 1003
ROB GUTHRIE		(	BLUES	19 FOLKWAY US 3527
LONNIE JOHNSON	G	(	SPIRITUALS	19 FOLKWAYS US 31042
SONNY GREER	D	(	SOUTH SIDE BLUES	19 REV US 403
MAMA YANCEY		(	TISHOMINGO BLUES	1980 JSP 1015
			LITTLE BROTHER MONTGOMERY	19 COLLECTORS CLASSICS US CC 35
			LITTLE BROTHER MONTGOMERY	19 DELMARK US 610

M187 MONTROSE M187

Personnel	Inst	Albums	Title	Release
RONNIE MONTROSE	G	(ALL	(A) MONTROSE	1973 WB US 2740 UK K46276
BOB JAMES	V	(CD	(B) PAPER MONEY	1974 WB US 2823 UK K56069
JIM ALCIVAR	K	(CDE	(C) WB PRESENTS	1975 WB US 2892 UK K56170
ALAN FITZGERALD	B	(BCE	(D) JUMP ON IT	1976 WB US 2963 UK K56291
DENNY CARMASSI	D	(ABCD	(E) OPEN FIRE (RONNIE)	1978 WB US 3134 UK K56451
BILL CHURCH	B	(A		
SAMMY HAGAR	V	(AB	MARK JORDAN K (B NICK DE CARO K (B	NOVI NOVAG VLA (C
RANDY JO HOBBS	B	(D	RICK SCHLOSSER D (E EDGAR WINTER K (E	TED TEMPLEMAN PROD(A

M188 MONTY PYTHON'S FLYING CIRCUS M188

Personnel	Inst	Albums	Title	Release
JOHN CLEESE		(	(A) MONTY PYTHON'S FLYING CIRCUS	1970 BBC REB 73M
ERIC IDLE		(	(b) ANOTHER MONTY PYTHON RECORD	1971 CHARISMA UK CAS 1049
MICHAEL PALIN		(	(C) PREVIOUS RECORD	1972 CHARISMA UK CAS 1063
TERRY WILLIAMS		(	(D) MATCHING TIE & HANKERCHIEF	1973 CHARISMA UKCAS1080 US ARISTA 4039
GRAHAM CHAPMAN		(	(E) LIVE AT DURY LANE	1974 CHARISMA UK CLASS 4
TERRY GILLIAM		(	(F) MONTY PYTHON & THE HOLY GRAIL	1975 CHARISMA UKCAS1102 US ARISTA 4050
DOUGLAS ADAMS		(	(G) LIVE AT THE CITY CENTRE	1976 ARISTA US 4073
JOHN YOUNG		(	(H) INSTANT RECORD COLLECTION	1977 CHARISMA UK CAS1134
BEE DUFFELL		(	(I) WORST OF MONTY PYTHON	19 BUDDAH US 5656/2
CONNIE BOOTH		(	(J) LIFE OF BRIAN	1979 WB UK K56757
CAROL CLEVELAND		(	CONTRACTUAL OBLIGATION ALBUM	1980 CHARISMA UK CAS 1152

M188A MONUMENT M188A

Personnel	Inst	Albums	Title	Release
STEVEN LOWE	V K	(A	(A) MONUMENT	1971 BEACON BEAS15
WES TRUVOR	G	(A		
JAKE BREWSTER	D	(A	MARVE FLETCHLEY B (A	

M189 MOODY BLUES M189

Personnel	Inst	Albums	Title	Release
DENNY LAINE	G V	(AB	(A) GO NOW , THE MOODY BLUES	1965 LONDON US LP 428
CLINT WARWICK	B	(AB	(B) MAGNIFICENT MOODIES	1966 DECCA UK LK 4711
MIKE PINDER	K V	(ABCDEFGHJKLMN	(C) DAYS OF FUTURE PAST	1967 DERAM UK SML 707 US LONDON 18012
GRAEME EDGE	D	(ABCDEFGHJKLMN1R	(D) IN SEARCH OF THE LOST CHORD	1968 DERAM UK SML 717 US LONDON 18017
RAY THOMAS	FLT V	(ABCDEFGHJKLMN1R	(E) ON THE THRESHOLD OF A DREAM	1969 DERAM UK SML 1035 US LONDON 18025
JUSTIN HAYWARD	G V	(CDEFGHJKLMN1R	(F) TO OUR CHILDRENS CHILDREN	1969 THRESHOLD UK/US THS 1
JOHN LODGE	B V	(CDEFGHJKLMN1R	(G) QUESTION OF BALANCE	1970 THRESHOLD UK/US THS 3
PATRICK MORAZ	K	(1R	(H) EVERY GOOD BOY DESERVES FAVOUR	1971 THRESHOLD UK/US THS 5
			(J) SEVENTH SOJOURN	1972 THRESHOLD UK/US THS7 NL 9299139
(1) 1978 TOUR			(K) THIS IS THE MOODY BLUES	1974 THRESHOLD US 2 12/13 UK MB1/2
			(K) THIS IS THE MOODY BLUES	1974 DECCA NL 6645 302
			(K) THIS IS THE MOODY BLUES	19 TELDEC GERM DX6 28316
			(L) IN THE BEGINNING	1975 DERAM US 18051 TELDEC GERM 769
			(L) IN THE BEGGINING	197 DECCA NL 6454 307
			(M) CAUGHT LIVE PLUS FIVE	1977 LONDON US 690/1 UK DECCA MB3/4
			(M) CAUGHT LIVE PLUS FIVE	1977 TELDEC GERM DP& 24812
			(N) DREAM	1977 TELDEC GERM DP6 28362
			(O) OCTAVE	1978 LONDON US PS 708 UK DECCA TXS 129
			(P) OUT OF THIS WORLD (COMP)	1979 K TEL NE1051
			(Q) MOODY BLUES (PROFILE)	19 TELDEC GERM 624004
			(R) LONG DISTACE VOYAGER	1981 THRESHOLD UK 139 US 2901
			(S) THE GREAT	19 DERAM BEL 159/60
			(T) BOULEVARD DELA MADELEINE	19 DECCA NL 6454 041
			(EP) MOODY BLUES(EP)	1965 DECCA UK DFE8622

M189A **EVE MOON** M189A

EVE MOON G V (A (A) EVE MOON 1981 CAPITOL ST 12132
JIMMY RIPP G (A
TOM WOLK B (A BOB RILEY D (A ELAINE CASWELL PERC (A

M190 **MOON(UK)** M190

NOEL McCALLA V (AB (A) TOO CLOSE FOR COMFORT 1976 EPIC UK 81456
LOZ NETTO G V (AB (B) TURNING THE TIDE 1977 EPIC UK 82084
GRAHAM COLLYER G (AB
DOUG BAINBRIDGE WIND (AB NICKY PAYN WIND (AB JOHN SHEARER (B RON LAWRENCE B (AB
LUIGI SALVONI D (A GARY MOBERLEY K (A BOB JACKSON K (A DAVE DENNIS V (A

M190A **MOON(US)** M190A

MATTHEW MOORE V PNO(A (A) MOON WITHOUT EARTH 196 IMPERIAL US LP12381 LIBERTY GER 83146
DAVID MARKS G ((B) MOON 196 IMPERIAL US LP12444
DAVE JACKSON B (
LARRY BROWN D (

M191 **KEITH MOON** M191

KEITH MOON D V PERC(A (A) TWO SIDES OF THE MOON 1975 POLYDOR UK 2442 134 MCA US 2136
CURLY SMITH D (A
CAM DAVIES D (A MIGUEL FERRER D (A MICKEY McGEE D (A RON GRINEL D (A
JIM KELTNER D (A RINGO STARR D V (A JIMMIE RANDALL B (A PAUL STALLWORTH B (A
JEAN MILLINGTON B (A DAVID BIRKETT B (A KLAUS VOORMANN B (A SPENCER DAVIS G (A
AL STAEHELY G (A MIKE CONDELLO G (A DANNY KOOTCH B (A JOHN STAEHELY G (A
JESSE ED DAVIS G (A PATTI QUATRO G (A JOE WALSH G SYN(A BEAU GUSS G (A
JOHN SEBASTIAN G (A STEVE ADAMICK G (A JAMES ED HAYMER D (A DICK DALE G (A
PAUL LENART G (A JAY FERGUSON K (A NICKEY BARCLAY K (A BLAIR AARONSON K (A
DAVID FOSTER K (A NORMAN KURBAN K (A HARRY NILSSON V (A SHIRLEY MATTHEWS V (A
LORNA WILLARD V (A JULIA TILLMAN V (A JAMES GILSTRAP V (A CLYDIE KING V (A
MARK VOLMAN V (A HOWARD KAYLAN V (A DENNIS LARDEN V (A JAY WHITE V (A
RON HICKLIN V (A AUGUST JOHNSON V (A GREG MATTA V (A IRMA ROUTEN V (A
ANDREA WILLIS V (A IRA HAWKINS V (A GERALD GARRETT V (A CAROLYN WILLIS V (A
SKIP EDWARDS STEEL(A OLLIE MITCHELL HRNS (A STEVE DOUGLAS HRNS (A BOBBY KEYS SAX(A
ROBERT GREENIDGE PERC (A RICK NELSON V (A

M191A **MOONDOGS** M191A

GERRY McCANDLESS G V (A (A) THAT'S WHAT FRIENDS ARE FOR 1981 SIRE GER 204 061
AUSTIN BARRETT D (A
JACKIE HAMILTON B V (A

M192 **MOONDOG** M192

LOUIS HARDIN V PERC HCA(ALL (A) MOONDOG 19 CBS US 7335 UK63906
FRITZ STORFINGER K (D (B) MOONDOG 2 1971 CBS US 30897
(C) MOONDOG IN EUROPE 19 KOPF RRF 33014
(D) H'ART SONGS 19 KOPF GER RRF 33016

M192A **JOHN MOONEY** M192A

JOHN MOONEY G V (A (A) COMIN' YOUR WAY 19 BLIND PIG US BP 779
BRIAN WILLIAMS B (A
BOB COOPER PNO (A NICK LANGAN HCA K(A TOM McDERMOTT D (A STEVE NARDELLA HCA(A
GREG PICCOLO SAX (A DOUG JAMES SAX (A RICH LATAILLE SAX (A DAVID SWAIN SECTION (A

M192B **MOONQUAKE** M192B

HOVANESS HAGOPIAN G V (B (A) MOONQUAKE 197 FANTASY US 9450
JACK AUGUST B V (B (B) STARSTRUCK 197 FANTASY US 9486
DEREK KENDRICK D V (B

M192C **MOONGLOWS** M192C

BOBBY LESTER ((A) MOONGLOWS 1972 CHESS US 701
HARVEY FUQUA (A (B) RETURN OF THE MOONGLOWS 1972 RCA US 4722

M192D **MOONRAKERS** M192D

DENNIS FLANNIGAN K V (A (A) TOGETHER WITH HIM 1968 SHAMLEY 704
VAN DORN G V (A
JOEL BRANDES B (A RANDY WALRATH G V (A BOB SAVNAR D (A BOB WEBBET G (A
JERRY CORBETTA D (A

M193 **MOONRIDER** M193

KEITH WEST G V (A (A) MOONRIDER 1975 ANCHOR US ANCL2010
CHICO GREENWOOD D (A
JOHN WEIDER G V (A BRUCE THOMAS B (A

M194 **MICHAEL MOORCOCK & DEEP FIX** M194

MICHAEL MOORCOCK G V MAND(A (A) THE NEW WORLDS FAIR 1975 UA UK UAG 29732
STEVE GILMORE G (A
DEBI ROSS V (A ALAN POWELL D (A KUMA HARADA B (A GRAHAM CHARNOCK G (A
SIMON HOUSE VLN K(A DAVE BROCK G (A PETE PAVLI CELLO(A SHIRLEY RODEN V (A
SIMON KING D (A SNOWY WHITE G (A HERBERT NORTH G (A

M194A **BOBBY MOORE & THE RHYTHM ACES** M194A

BOBBY MOORE (A (A) SEARCHING FOR MY LOVE 19 CHECKER US 3000

M195 **G T MOORE & THE REGGAE GUITARS** M195

G T MOORE G V (AB (A) G T MOORE & THE REGGAE GUITARS 1974 CHARISMA UK CAS1095 MERCURY US 1065
TOM WHYTE B (AB (B) REGGAE BLUE 1975 CHARISMA UK CAS1105
MARTIN HAYWARD G (AB (C) MOVE IT ON UP 1980 CHARISMA NL 9124 057
TIM JONES K (AB
CHRIS MERCER SAX (B TOM ROBINSON V PERC (A RABBIT BUNDRICK K (A PETER VAN DER PUIJE SAX (A
TONY HANNAFORD V PERC(A EDDIE QUANSAH TPT (A TONY REDUNZO D V (B MALCOLM MORTIMER D (A
GEORGE LARNYOH SAX (A

M196 **GARY MOORE** M196

GARY MOORE G V (ABC (A) GRINDING STONE 1973 CBS UK 65527 US PETERS 9004
PHIL LYNOTT B V (B (B) BACK ON THE STREETS 1978 MCA UK MCF2853 US CBS 35991
BRIAN DOWNEY D (B (B) BACK ON THE STREETS 1978 MCA GER 62/122
MO FOSTER B (C (C) CORRIDORS OF POWER 1982 VIRGIN UK 2245
DON AIREY K (B
SIMON PHILLIPS D (B JOHN MOLE B (B PEARCE KELLY D (A JOHN CURTIS B (A
JAN SCHELLHAAS K (A FRANK BOYLAN B (A PHILLIP DONNELLY G (A JACK BRUCE B (C
IAN PAICE D (C NEIL MURRAY B (C TOMMY EYRE K (C BOBBY CHOUINARD D (C

M196A **PAMELA MOORE** M196A

PAMELA MOORE V (A — (A) TAKE A LOOK 1981 FIRST AMERICAN US FA7754

M197 **MERRILL MOORE** M197

MERRILL MOORE PNO (ALL
(A) TREE TOP TALL 1969 B &C CAS 1001
(B) BELLYFULOF BLUE THUNDER 1972 EMBER EMB 3392
(C) ROUGH HOUSE 88 1972 EMBER EMB 3394
(D) MERRILL MOORE 19 CAPITOL US 1 608

M197A **SCOTTY MOORE** M197A

SCOTTY MOORE G (A
BOOTS RANDOLPH SAX (A
BILL PURSELL PNO (A
JERRY KENNEDY G (A   BOB MOORE B (A   D J FONTANA G (A   BUDDY HARMAN D (A
JORDANAIRES V (A
(A) GUITAR THAT CHANGED THE WORLD 1973 EPIC US 26103
(B) BIG ELVIS HITS 1976 CBS NL 53343

M197B **STEVIE MOORE** M197B

R STEVIE MOORE G V K (AB
(A) STANCE 1978 HP MUSIC US EP 30733
(B) PHONOGRAPHY 1978 HP MUSIC US 30734

M198 **TIM MOORE** M198

TIM MOORE G B K V (ALL
RUSS KUNKEL (B
ROY MANKOWITZ D (B
BERNARD PURDIE D (B
BILL McCORD D (B
BILL PAYNE K (D
MARK VOLMAN V (D   JEFF PORCARO D (D   ELLIOT RANDALL G (D   HOWARD KAYLAN V (D
FRED TACKETT G (D   MIKE UTLEY K (D   LEE SKLAR B (D   MICHAEL McDONALD V (D
JOEL BISHOP OBRIEN D (C   FRANK SIMS V (C   GEORGE SIMMS V (C   DAVE KONDZIELA V (C
PAUL GLANZ V (C   ANDY ROBINSON V (C   ALLAN SCHWARZBERG D (C   JOHN WILCOX D (C
BENNETT CARLISLE D (C   DON PAYNE B (C   WILL LEE B (C   BOB LIZIK B (C
JOHN TROPEA G (C
(A) A FOOL LIKE YOU 1974 MOONCREST UK CREST 16
(B) TIM MOORE 1975 POLYDOR 2310 363 UK US ASYLUM 7E 1019
(C) BEHIND THE EYES 1975 POLYDOR 2310 412 UK US ASYLUM 7E 1042
(D) WHITE SHADOWS 1977 POLYDOR 2310 512 UK US ASYLUM 7E 1088
(E) HIGH CONTRAST 1979 US ASYLUM 179

M199 **JOHNNY MOPED** M199

JOHNNY MOPED(PAUL HALFORD)V(A
SLIMEY TOAD G (A
FRED BERK K B (A   PHIL BURNS B (A   DAVE BERK D (A   RAY BURNS G (
(A) CYCLEDELIC 1978 CHISWICK UK WIK8 NL550 108 GER 67 060

M200 **PATRICK MORAZ** M200

PATRICK MORAZ K (A
VIVIENNE McAULIFFE V (A
JOHN McBURNIE V (AB
RAY GOMEZ G (AB
JEFF BERLIN B (A
ALPHONSE MOUZON D (A
ANDY NEWMARK D (AB
JEAN RISTORI B (A
VERONIQUE MUELLER V (A   FRANCOIS ZMIROU V (B   RICHIE MORALES D (E   JEAN LUC BOURGEOIS PERC (A
AUGUSTE DE ANTHONY G (A   PHILIPPE STAEHLI PERC (A   RENE MORAZ PERC (A   WORNELL JONES B (B
SYRINX (E   JOHN WOOLOFF G (E   JOY YATES V (C   DJALMA CORRIEA PERC(CE
(A) "I" 1976 CHARISMA CDS 4002
(A) "I" 1976 ATLANTIC US 18175
(B) OUT OF THE SUN 1977 CHARISMA CDS 4007
(B) OUT OF THE SUN 1977 VISA US 1015
(C) PATRICK MORAZ 1978 CHARISMA US 2201 UK CDS4015
(D) FUTURE MEMORIES LIVE ON TV 1979 CARRERE FR 67435
(E) CO EXISTENCE 1980 CARRERE CAL 117

M200A **A.MORE** M200A

A MORE
(A) FLYING DOESN'T HELP 1979 QUANGO UK HMG 98 FR 200139

M200B **MORE** M200B

(A) WARHEAD 1981 ATLANTIC UK K50775

M201 **MORGAN** M201

MORGAN FISHER K (ABC
MAURICE BACON D (ABC
TIM STAFFELL G V (ABC
BOB SAPSTEAD B (BC
(A) THE SLEEPER WAKES 1979 CHERRY RED UK A RED1
(B) NOVA SOLIS 19 RCA
(C) BROWN OUT 1976 IMPORT US 1006

M201A **GIORGIO MORODER** M201A

GORGIO MORODER (AB
(A) MIDNIGHT EXPRESS 1978 CASABLANCA CAL 2030
(B) E=MC² 19 OASIS 507

M202 **RON PAUL MORIN** M202

RON PAUL MORIN G V (A
LUKE P WILSON G V BAN (A
GRAHAM TODD K (A   JOHNNY VAN DERRICK FDL (A   JOHN PEARSE G V (A   RICK KEMP B (A
CAMILLA DE CRESPIGNY V (A   CHRIS LAURENCE B (A   PETE WILLSHER STEEL(A   SUSAN JAMES V (A
(A) PEACEFUL COMPANY 1972 SOVEREIGN SVNA 7252

M202A **ROGER MORRIS** M202A

ROGER MORRIS G V (A
LISLE HARPER B (A
BRUCE ROWLAND D (A   TERRY STANNARD D (A   ROD COOMBES D (A   TOMMY EYRE PNO (A
JOHN WEIDER G (A   KEITH WEST G (A   GLEN CAMPBELL STEEL(A   JOHNNY ALMOND SAX (A
CHRIS MERCER SAX (A   KEN BURGESS V (A
(A) FIRST ALBUM 1972 REGAL ZONOPHONE UK SRZA 8509

M202B **MORRIS & THE MINORS** M202B

(A) STATE THE OBVIOUS(EP) 19 ROUND UK MOR 1

M202C **TOMMY MORRISON** M202C

TOMMY MORRISON V (A
PAUL RODGERS V (A
JOHN WATCHMAN (A   ROD DEATH D (A   DAVE RAMSEY (A   BOB MARSHALL (A   JAMES HONEYMANSCOTT(A
KUMA HARADA B (A   STEWART McDONALD (A   GARY WINDO (A   LOU MARTIN K(A   PETE FARNDON (A
(A) PLACE YOUR BETS 1979 REAL RAL 2

M203 VAN MORRISON M203

VAN MORRISON V SAX G K(ALL (A) BLOWIN' YOUR MIND 1967 BANG US BLB21 LONDON UK 8346
RICHARD DAVIS B (B (B) ASTRAL WEEKS 1968 WB US WS 1768 UK K46024 RI 26004
CONNIE KAY D (BFG (C) BEST OF 1970 BANG US BLP222
WARREN SMITH PERC (B (C) BEST OF 1970 PRESIDENT UK 1045
JOHN PAYNE FLT (B (D) MOONDANCE 1970 WB US WS 1835 UK K46040
JOHN PLATANIA G (DEHJ (E) HIS BAND & STREET CHOIR 1970 WB US WS 1884 UK K46066
JOHN KLINGBERG B (DE (F) TUPELO HONEY 1971 WB US WS 1950 UK K46114
GARY MALLABER D PERC (DFGHS (G) ST DOMINICS PREVIEW 1972 WB US BS 2633 UK k46172
JACK SCHROER SAX PNO (DEFGHJL (H) HARD NOSE THE HIGHWAY 1973 WB US BS 2712 UK K46242
COLLIN TILTON WIND (D (J) ITS TOO LATE TO STOP NOW 1974 WB US BS 2760 UK K86007
JEFF LABES K (DHJL (K) TB SHEETS 1974 BANG US BLP400 LONDON UK HSM5008
CHRIS MICHIE G (S (K) TB SHEETS 1974 BELLAPHON GER 15103
EMILY HOUSTON V (D (L) VEEDON FLEECE 1974 WB US BS 2805 UK K56068
JUDY CLAY V (D (EF) HIS BAND/TUPELO HONEY 1975 WB UK K86009
JACKIE VERDELL V (D (M) THIS IS WHERE I CAME IN(COMP) 1977 BANG UK 6467 625
DAVID SHAW PERC CLAR (DEJL (N) PERIOD OF TRANSITION 1977 WB US BS 2987 UK K56322
BILL CHURCH B (FG (O) WAVELENGTH 1978 WB US BSK3212 UK K56526
KEITH JOHNSON TPT K(E (P) INTO THE MUSIC 197 MERCURY US 3390 UK 9102 852 JAP7630
ALAN HAND PNO SAX (E (Q) CHAIRFELLOWS(BOOTLEG) 1978 IMPOSSIBLE IMP118
ELLEN SCHROER V (EFG (R) COMMON ONE 1980 MERCURY UK 6302 021
CHRIS HAYES G (S (S) BEAUTIFUL VISION 1982 MERCURY UK 6302 122
JAY BERLINER G (B (1) 1979 TOUR
MARTHA VELEZ V (E
LARRY GOLDSMITH V (E ANDY ROBINSON V (E JANET PLANET V (EFG JIM ROTHERMEL WIND(L
MARK JORDAN PNO (FGP LUIS GASCA TPT (F RONNIE MONTROSE G V (FG TED TEMPLEMAN ORG (F
JOHN McFEE STEEL(FG BRUCE ROYSTON FLT (F BOOTS STUART HOUSTON V FLT(F JULES BROUSSARD SAX(GH
TOM SALISBURY K (G DOUG MESSENGER G (G MARK SPRINGER V (G PAT O'HARA HRNS(G
MARK NAFTALIN PNO (G RICK SCHLOSSER D (FGH ROLF HOUSTON (G BERNIE KRAUSE SYN (G
RON ELLIOTT G (G MARTY DAVID B (H DAVID HAYES B (HJLPRS BILL ATWOOD HCA (H
JOSEPH ELLIS HRNS (H JACKIE DE SHANNON V (H RALPH WASH G (L JAMES TRUMBO K (L
JOE MACHO B (L NATHAN RUBIN STRINGS (HJL ZAVEN MALIKIAN VLN (H NANCY ELLIS VLA (HJ
JOHN TENNEY VLN (H MICHAEL GIRLING VLN (H TIM KOVATCH VLN (J TOM HAPLIN VLN (J
ALLEN SCHWARZBERG D (L JOHN TROPEA G (L DR JOHN K (N REGGIE McBRIDE B (N
OLLIE BROWN D (N MARLO HENDERSEN G (N JERRY JUMONVILLE SAX (N ROBBIE MONTGOMERY V (N
JOE POWELL V (N GARY GARRETT V (N CARLENA WILLIAMS V (N GREGORY WRIGHT V (N
TONY McVEY V (N CANDY NASH V (N PAULETTE PARKER V (N ROGER KENERLY SAINT V(N
JOEL PESKIN SAX (N MARK UNDERWOOD TPT (N BOB TENCH G (1QOQ JOHN ALTMAN SAX (1
KATIE KISSOON V (1PQ TONI MARCUS VLN (P PEE WEE ELLIS SAX (PRS MARK ISHAM SYN TPT (PRS
PETER VAN HOOKE D (OPQR ROBIN WILLIAMSON WHISTLE(P KURT WORTMAN D (P MICK COX G (R
ZAKIR HUSSAIN PERC (P RY COODER G (P JOHN ALLAIR K (RS PETE BREWIS V (R
GARTH HUDSON K SYN(O MITCH DALTON G (O GINGER BLAKE V (O LAURA CREAMER V (O
LINDA DILLARD V (O MICKEY FEAT B (OQ ANNA PEACOCK V (Q LEE CHARLTON D (R
HERBIE ARMSTRONG G V(OPQRS BIANCA THOPNTON V (S TOM DOLLMEYER D (S ROB WASSERLAN B (S
SEAN FULSOM PIPES(S PAULINE LOSANA V (S MARK KNOPFLER G (S ERIC GALE G (K
AL GORGONI G (K BOB BUSHNELL B (K HUGH McCRACKEN G (K DONALD THOMAS G (K
RUSSEL SAVKAS B (K HERBIE LOVELLE D (K GEORGE DEVINS PERC (K PAUL GRIFFIN K (K
SELDON POWELL WIND (K CISSY HOUSTON V (K MYRNA SMITH V (K BROOKS ARTHUR V (K
GARY CHESTER D (K ARTIE BUTLER K (K ARTIE KAPLAN WIND (K JEFF BARRY PERC V(K
DEE DEE WARWICK V (K BERT BERNS V (K

M204 MORNING M204

JAY LEWIS G V (A (A) MORNING 1970 LIBERTY UK LBS83463 US VAULT 138
JIM HOBSON K V (A (B) STRUCK LIKE SILVER 1974 UA UAS29337 US FANTASY 9402
BARRY BROWN G D (A
BRUCE WALLACE B (A AL PERKINS STEEL(A JIM KEHN D V (A TERRY JOHNSON G B (A
JAY DONNELLAN G (

M205 MORNING GLORY(EURO) M205

JOHN SURMAN SAX (A (A) MORNING GLORY 1973 ISLAND UK ILPS 9237
JOHN MARSHALL D (A
TERJE RYPDAL G (A MALCOLM GRIFFITHS TROM (A CHRIS LAURENCE B (A JOHN TAYLOR K (A

M205A MORNING STAR M205A

RICK BACUS G K V(AB (A) MORNING STAR 1978 CBS US 35316
JERRY CHAMBERS G V (AB (B) VENUS 1979 CBS US 35713
MICHAEL EDMUNDS G V (AB
GREG HARRIS D PERC (AB GREG LEECH B (AB

M205B MORNING GLORY (US) M205B

ALLEN WEHR D (A (A) A TWO SUNS WORTH 1968 FONTANA 67573
DANNY NU DELMAN G V (A
LARRY GERUGHTY K V (A GINI GRAYBEAL PERC V(A BOB BOHANNA B G V (A

M206 DICK MORRISSEY & JIM MULLEN M206

DICK MORRISSEY SAX (AB (A) UP 1977 EMBRYO US SD 536
JIM MULLEN G (AB (B) CAPE WRATH 1979 FUSION UK SHSP 4098
ROBERT AHWAI G (B (C) BADNESS 1981 BEGGARS BANQUET UK BEGA 27
MALCOLM DUNCAN SAX (A
HAMISH STUART G (A ONNIE McINTYRE G (A PAT REBILLOT K (A ROGER BALL K (A
ALAN GORRIE B (A STEVE FERRONE D (A SAMMY FIGUEROA PERC (A RAFAEL CRUZ PERC (A
RICHARD BAILEY D (B TONY CARR PERC (B MAX MIDDLETON K (B KUMA HARADA B (B

M206A MORTIMER M206A

T SMITH (A (A) MORTIMER 19 PHILIPS US 600 267
G MASSON (A
T VAN BENSCHOTEN (A

M206B MORTY M206B

(A) LOVE BLIND 1980 BELLAPHON BPLP 001

M207 PABLO MOSE M207

PABLO MOSES (ALL (A) REVOLUTIONARY DREAM 1976 SOUNDTRACS + DIFF 1978 GETL 104
(B) I LOVE I BRING 1978 UA LA 798
( ) A SONG 19 ISLAND UK 9541

M208 MOSE JONES M208

RANDY LEWIS B V (AC — (A) MOSE KNOWS — 1974 MCA — MCA 394
JIMMY O'NEILL G V (A — (B) GET RIGHT — 1974 MCA US 329 — MCF 2673
BRYAN GLENNCOLE D V (A — (C) BLACKBIRD — 1978 RCA — 12793
STEVE McRAY K V (AC
CHRIS SEYMOUR D V (C — MARTIN TAYLOR G V (C

M209 BOB MOSLEY M209

BOB MOSLEY G V (A — (A) BOB MOSLEY — 1972 WB US MS 2068
ED BLACK STEEL(A
WOODIE BERRY V (A — FRANK SMITH V (A — WAYNE JACKSON HRNS (A — ALLEN WEHR V (A
ANDREW LOVE HRNS (A

M210 ELTON MOTELLO M210

ELTON MOTELLO V (AB — (A) POP ART — 1980 EDGE UK HOG1 PASSPORT US 9846
MIKE BUTCHER G V (A — (B) VICTIMS OF TIME — 1978 PINBALL GER 6 23650
WALTER METER D V (A
PAUL KIDSLEY V (A — ANDREW GOLDBERG K V (A — J P MARTINS G B (A — NOBBY GAFF G (B
PETER GOFF G (B — WILLIE CHANGE B (B — JET STAXX G (B — TONY BOAST G (B
TWINK D (B — DANNY CELLO(B — PIETRO SAX (B — ROBBIE K (B
JEAN K (B — MITZI V (B — TIME V (B — FRISOI V (B
YVONNE V (A — HILDE V (A — COOKY K (A

M210A MOTELS M210A

JEFF JOURARD G (A — (A) MOTELS — 1979 CAPITOL 11996 NL 85999
MARTHA DAVIS V G (AB — (B) CAREFUL — 1980 CAPITOL EST 12070
MARTIN JOURARD K SAX(AB
TIM McGOVERN G (B — MICHAEL GOODROE B (AB — BRIAN GLASCOCK D (AB

M211 MOTHER EARTH M211

TRACY NELSON K V (ALL — (A) REVOLUTION(+ STEVE MILLER ETC) — 1968 UA US 5185
MARTIN FIERRO SAX (AB1 — (B) LIVING WITH THE ANIMALS — 1968 MERCURY US SR 61194
MARK NAFTALIN K (AB — (C) MAKE A JOYFUL NOISE — 1969 MERCURY UK SMCL20143 US SR61226
BOB ARTHUR B V (ACDB — (D) TRACY NELSON COUNTRY — 1969 MERCURY UK SMCL20179 US 61230
JOHN ANDREWS G (ABDEFG — (E) SATISFIED — 1970 MERCURY UK 6338 023 SR61270
GEORGE RAINS D SAX(AB — (F) BRING ME HOME — 1971 REPRISE UK K44133 US 6431
TIM DRUMMOND B (F — (G) POOR MANS PARADISE — 1973 CBS US 31759
KARL HIMMEL D (EF — (1) EARLY LINE UP
IRV KANE TROM (G
JOHN GIMBLE FDL (CDF — SAMMY DODGE FDL (F — BEN KEITH G (CF — TERRY BURNSIDE SAX (G
BILLY PUETT SAX (G — REV STALLINGS V (C — JOSEPH ARNOLD SAX (C — PETE DRAKE STEEL(CD
PIG ROBBINS K (C — R P ST JOHN HCA V(CBA1 — CLAYBORNE BROTHER COTTON(C — SHORTY LAVENDER FDL (CD
ANDREW MACMAHON K (EFG — BOB CARDWELL G (EF — JAMES DAY STEEL(E — DAVE ZETTNER B (E
IRMA JEAN ROUTEN V (CF — SADIE CANTRELL V (CF — LADY CORDER V (CF — LONNIE CASTILLE D (1
SCOTTY MOORE G (D — JORDANAIRES V (D — JACK DRAKE B (D — DENNIS GOODE TROM (G
JACK LEE G V (G — STEVE MANDELL B (G — BEAU DOLLAR D (G — JERRY CARRIGAN D (G
MAC GAYDEN G (G — RANDY SCRUGGS G (G — TOMMY SMITH TPT (G — LOUIS GASCA TPT (B
LINK DAVIS SAX (B — FRANK MORIN SAX (B — RON TAORMINA SAX (B — BOB SALISBURY SAX (B
LOSELLA FUNQUE V (B — SYLVIA CALDWELL V (B — SHALIMAR SAMUELSON V (B — MAKAL BLUMFELD G (B
DANY GOLDBERG ORG (B — SPENCER PERSKIN VLN (B — JOSE EMILIO RODRIQUEZ D(B

M211A MOTHER GONG M211A

GILLI SMYTH V (A — (A) FAIRY TALES — 19 CHARLY UK CRL 5018
HARRY WILLIAMSON G (A
DIDIER MALHERBE WIND (A — RONNIE WATHEN PIPES (A — NIC TURNER WIND (A — TREVOR DARKS B (A
MO VICARAGE K (A — EDUARDO NIEBLA G (A — MARIANNE OBERASHER HARP (A — CORRINA V (A
ERMANO GHISIO ERBA D (A

M211B MOTHER GOOSE(AUST) M211B

STEVE YOUNG K (— (A) MOTHER GOOSE — 1978 ?
CRAIG JOHNSTON V (— (B) DONT BELIEVE IN FAIRY TALES — 1979 ?
KEVIN COLLINGS G (
MARCEL RODEKE D (— DENIS GIBBINS B (— JUSTIN McCARTHY G (

M211C MOTHER HEN M211C

CLARENCE WHITE G (A — (A) MOTHER HEN — 196 RCA US LSP 4641
JERRY McGEE G (A
DANNY KOOTCH G (A — SNEAKY PETE KLEINOW STEEL(A — JERRY SCHEFF B (A — LEE SKLAR B (A
JAMIE FAUNT B V (A — RUSS KUNKEL D (A — RON TUTT D (A — DAVID CAMPBELL VLN (A
EMIL RICHARDS PERC (A

M212 MOTHERS FINEST M212

B B BORDEN D (BCDEF — (A) MOTHERS FINEST — 1972 RCA US 4790
JOYCE BABY] V PERC(BCDEF — (B) MOTHERS FINEST — 1976 EPIC US 34179 UK 81595
JEAN KENNEDY] — (C) ANOTHER MOTHER FURTHER — 1977 EPIC US 34699 UK 82037
GLENN MURDOCK V (BCDF — (D) MOTHER FACTOR — 1978 EPIC US 35546 UK 83011
JAMES CUNNINGHAM PERC (D — (E) LIVE — 1980 CBS US 35976
SKIP SCARBOROUGH PNO (D — (F) IRON AGE — 1981 EPIC UK 84424
MOSES MO G V (BCDEF
WIZZARD B V (BCDEF — MIKE K (BCD

M212A MOTHERS RUIN M212A

SYLVIA V (A — (A) WANT MORE — 1981 OFF COURSE GER 3303
RETO G (A
MARKUS G V (A — BAYER D (A — GULY B (A

M212B MOTHERLODE M212B

(A) TUFFED OUT — 1973 BUDDAH US 5108

M212C MOTION M212C

(A) MOTION — 1981 DOUBLE D UK DDLP4

M213 MOTORHEAD M213

LEMMY B V (ALL — (A) MOTORHEAD — 1977 CHISWICK UK WIK2 + CWK 3008
LARRY WALLIS G (AE — (B) OVERKILL — 1979 BRONZE UK BRON 515
LUCAS FOX D (AE — (C) BOMBER — 1979 BRONZE UK BRON 523
PHIL TAYLOR D (ABCDEFG — (D) ACE OF SPADES — 1980 BRONZE UK BRON 531
GIRLSCHOOL (X — (D) ACE OF SPADES — 1980 MERCURY US 4011
EDDIE CLARKE G (ABCDEFG — (E) ON PAROLE (ROCKFILE) — 1980 LIBERTY LBR 1004
(F) NO SLEEP TILL HAMMERSMITH — 1981 BRONZE UK BRON535 GER 203 801
(G) IRON FIST — 1982 BRONZE GER 204 636
(X) ST VALENTINES DAY MASSACRE — 1981 BRONZE (EP) UK BROX116

M214 MOTT THE HOOPLE M214

PETE OVEREND WATTS B (ABCDEFGHJKLMN (A) MOTT THE HOOPLE 1969 ISLAND UK ILPS9108 US ATLANTIC 8258
DALE GRIFFIN D (ABCDJKH (B) MAD SHADOWS 1970 ISLAND UK ILPS9119 US ATLANTIC 8272
MICK RALPHS G (ABCD (C) WILD LIFE 1971 ISLAND UK ILPS9144 US ATLANTIC 8284
VERDEN ALLEN K (ABCD (D) BRAIN CAPERS 1971 ISLAND UK ILPS9178 US ATLANTIC 8304
STAN TIPPENS V (CJ (E) ROCK'N' ROLL QUEEN 1972 ISLAND UK ILPS9215 US ATLANTIC 7297
IAN HUNTER V K G(ABCDEFGHJLN (F) ALL THE YOUNG DUDES 1972 CBS UK 65184 US 31750 EMBASSY UK 31205
ARIEL BENDER G (JH (G) MOTT 1973 CBS UK 69038 US 32425
BLUE WEAVER K (J (H) THE HOOPLE 1974 CBS UK 69062 US 32871
MORGAN FISHER K (JKH (J) MOTT THE HOOPLE LIVE 1974 CBS UK 69093 US 33282
MICK RONSON G V ((K) DRIVE ON 1975 CBS UK 69154 US 33705
RAY MAJOR G (K (L) POP CHRONIK 1975 ISLAND IMP VOL 11
NIGEL BENJAMIN V (KM (M) SHOUTING & POINTING 1976 CBS UK 81289 US 34236
STEVE HYMANS V ((N) GREATEST HITS 1976 CBS UK 81225 US 34368
MICK BOLTON ORG (J ( ) SHADES OF 1979 CBS UK 88476
GUY STEVENS PNO (BAD ( ) 2 MILES FROM HEAVEN 198 ISLAND IRSP 8 ARIOLA EURO 202429
JAMES ARCHER VLN (C
HOWIE CASEY SAX (H JOCK McPHERSON SAX (H GERRY HOGAN STEEL (C JESS RODEN V (C
JIM PRICE TPT (D PAUL BUCKMASTER CELLO(G GRAHAM PRESKETT VLN (GH THUNDERTHIGHS V (G
ANDY MACKAY SAX (G BARRY ST JOHN V (H SONNY LESLIE V (H SUE GLOVER V (H

M215 MOTORS M215

ANDY McMASTER V B K(ABC (A) MOTORS 1 1977 VIRGIN UK V2089 US 34924 GER 25457
NICK GARVEY G V (ABC (B) APPROVED BY THE MOTORS 1978 VIRGIN UK V2101 US 35348
BRAM TCHAIKOVSKY G V (AB (C) TENEMENT STEPS 1979 VIRGIN UK V2151 US 13139 GER 202 022
RICHARD SLAUGHTER WERNHAM D(AB (C) TENEMENT STEPS 1979 VIRGIN EURO 2473 755
MARTIN ACE B (C
TERRY WILLIAMS D (C MICHAEL DESMARAIS D (C

M216 MOUNTAIN M216

LESLIE WEST G V (ALL (A) MOUNTAIN 1970 WINDFALL US 4500
FELIX PAPPALARDI PROD B(ALL (B) MOUNTAIN CLIMBING 1970 WINDFALL US 4501 UK BELL SBLL133
STEVE KNIGHT K PERC(ABCDH (C) NANTUCKET SLEIGHRIDE 1971 WINDFALL US 5500 UK ISLAND 9148
CORKY LAING D (BCDEFHJ (D) FLOWERS OF EVIL 1971 WINDFALL US 5501 UK ISLAND 9179
(D) FLOWERS OF EVIL 1971 ISLAND GER 85549
NORMAN SMART D ((E) MOUNTAIN LIVE 1972 WINDFALL US 5502 UK ISLAND 9199
(E) MOUNTAIN LIVE 1972 ISLAND FR 6427 014
DAVID PERRY G (J (F) ROAD GOES ON FOREVER 1972 WINDFALL US 5503
BOB MANN G K (K (G) POP HISTORY (AB) 1972 POLYDOR 2625 022
ALLEN SCHWARTBERG D (K (H) BEST OF 1973 CBS US 32079 UK ISLAND 9236
(J) AVALANCHE 1974 EPIC US 33088 UK 80492
(K) TWIN PEAKS (DBL) 1974 CBS US 32818 UK 88095

M216A MOUNTAIN BUS M216A

BILL KEES G (A (A) SUNDANCE 1974 GOOD US G101
LEE SIMS D (A
CRAIG TAKEHARA B BAN(A TOM JURKENS V (A STEVE KRATER D (A ED MOONEY G (A

M216B MOUNTAIN ASH M216B

HANS GERD FUCHS B V (A (A) MOMENTS 1980 NO FUN GER 80001
THOMAS MANZEL D (A
UWE BODEKER PERC V(A ECKHARD WAHMANN K V (A

M216C MOUNT RUSHMORE M216C

BULL G (A (A) HIGH ON MOUNT RUSHMORE 1968 DOT US DLP 25898
KIMBALL B (A (B) MOUNT RUSHMORE 1969 DOT US 25934
TRAVIS D (A
SMITTY V (A

M217 MOUSE M217

(A) LADY KILLER 1974 SOVEREIGN SVNA 7262

M218 ALPHONSE MOUZON M218

ALPHONSE MOUZON D K (ALL (A) THE ESSENCE OF MYSTERY 1975 BLUENOTE BNLA 059
TOMMY BOLIN G (C (B) FUNKY SNAKEFOOT 1975 BLUENOTE BNLA 222
JAY GRAYDON G K (C (C) MIND TRANSPLANT 1975 BLUENOTE BNLA 398
LEE RITENOUR G (CD (D) THE MAN INCOGNITO 1976 BLUENOTE US 584 UA UK UAG 20005
JERRY PETERS K (C (E) BACK TOGETHER AGAIN 1977 ATLANTIC UK K 50382
HENRY DAVIS B (C (F) ALPHONSE MOUZON 19 SONOPRESSE FR 036 99400
LARRY CORYELL G (E (G) IN SEARCH OF A DREAM 1978 MPS
PHILIP CATHERINE G (E (H) VIRTUE 197 MPS 15498
JOHN LEE B (E (J) THE DRUM 19 IMPULSE 9272
CHERYL P ALEXANDER V (E (K) BY ALL MEANS 1980 MPS 0068 266
TAWATHA AGEE V (E
JERRY HEY HRNS (K FREDDIE HUBBARD HRNS (K KIM HUTCHCROFT WIND (K LARRY WILLIAMS WIND (K
LARRY TIM OBOE (K HERBIE HANCOCK K (K PAUL JACKSON G (K SCOTT EDWARDS B (K
DAWILLI GONGA K SYN(D TIM DEHUFF G (D CHARLES MEEKS B (D DAVE GRUSIN K (D
DAVE BENOIT K (D IAN UNDERWOOD SYN (D VICTOR FELDMAN PERC (D EMIL RICHARDS PERC(D
TOM SCOTT HRNS (D RAY PIZZI HRNS (D GEORGE BOHANON TROM (D GARY GRANT TPT (D
MARTY McCALL V (D JACKIE WARD V (D CAROLINE WILLIS V (D DAVID T WALKER G (D
JOHN MALLER K (D RANDY BRECKER RPR (B ANDY GADSDEN SAX (B LEON PENDARVIS K (B
RICHIE RESNICOFF G (B GARY KING B (B STEVE BERRIOS PERC (B BARRY ROGERS TROM(B
HARRY WHITAKER K (B MIKE MANDEL K (B MARK HAROWITZ STEEL(B RAY ARMANDO PERC(B
ANGEL ALLENDE (B

M219 THE MOVE M219

ROY WOOD WIND G V (ALL (A) THE MOVE 1966 REGAL ZONOPHONE UK SLRZ1002
BEV BEVAN D V(ALL (A) THE MOVE 1974 M F P UK 50158
ACE KEFFORD B G V(ACF (A) THE BEST OF MOVE (REPACKAGE) 19 A&M UK SP3625
TREVOR BURTON G B V(ACF (B) SHAZAM 1970 REGAL ZONOPHONE UK SLRZ1012
CARL WAYNE V B (ABCF (B) SHAZAM 197 A&M US SP4259
RICK PRICE B G V (BCD (B) SHAZAM 197 POLYDOR 2310 012
JEFF LYNNE G V K B(DEH (C) BEST OF 1970 FLY UK TON 3 KARUSSELL 2345020
DENNY CORDELL PROD (E (D) LOOKING ON 1971 FLY UK FLY1 CAPITOL US ST658
RICHARD TANDY K (CF (E) MESSAGE FROM THE COUNTRY 1971 HARVEST UK SHSP 4013
(E) MESSAGE FROM THE COUNTRY 197 CAPITOL US ST811
(E) SHINES ON 1979 HARVEST UK SHSM 2029
(F) FIRE BRIGADE 1971 M F P UK 5276
(G) SPLIT ENDS (COMP) 1972 UA US UAS 5666

(CONTINUED)

M219 (CONTINUED)

THE MOVE M219

(AB) MOVE /SHAZAM 1972 CUBE UK TOOFA5/6 GER 2635 003
(H) CALIFORNIA MAN 1974 HARVEST UK SHSP 4035
(I) MASTERS OF ROCK 1974 HARVEST EURO 054 05696
(EP) SOMETHING ELSE 1968 REGAL ZONOPHONE UK TR2 2001
(J) GREATEST HITS VOL 1 1978 HALLMARK UK SHM 952

M220
MOVIES (UK) M220

JON COLE G V (ABCD — (A) THE MOVIES 1975 FIREFLY UK AMLH33002
GREG KNOWLES G V (ABCD — (B) DOUBLE A 1977 GTO UK GTLP 026
DAG SMALL K V (A — (C) BULLETS THROUGH THE BARRIER 1978 GTO UK GTLP 031
JULIAN DIGGLE PERC V(ABCD — (D) INDIA 1980 GEM UK LP105 US RCA 3552
JAMIE LANE D V (ABCD — (E) MOTOR MOTOR 1981 RCA UK 5054 UK 3854
DURBAN LAVERE B V (A
STAN SULZMANN SAX (B MICK PARKER K CLAR(BC DAVE QUINN B V (BC COLIN GIBSON B V (D
RAY WARLEIGH SAX (B

M221
MOVIES(US) M221

TED MEDBURY (A — (A) MOVIES 1976 ARISTA US AL 4085
PETER BARNES (A
MICHAEL MORGAN (A

M221A
MOVING FINGER M211A

KEN ELLIOT V K (A — (A) REALITY 1969 POLYDOR 583045
NICK SOUTH B (A
KIERAN O'CONNOR D (A BOB GIBBONS G (A

M221B
MOVING GELATINE PLATES M221B

GERARD BERTRAM G V (AB — (A) MOVING GELATINE PLATES 19 CBS 64399
MAURICE HELMINGER K FLT(AB — (B) THE WORLD OF GENIUS HANS 1971 CBS 64146
DIDIER THIBAUT B V (AB
GERARD PONS D (AB MICHEL CAMICAS TROM (B JEAN PIERRE LAROQUE BASSOON (B GUY BOYER VIBES (B
CLAUDE DELCLOO V (B

M221C
MOVING SIDEWALKS M211C

BILLY GIBBONS G V (A — (A) FLASH 19 TANTARA US TS 6919
DON SUMMERS B (A
DAN MITCHELL D (A TOM MOORE K (A

M221D
JUDY MOWATT M221D

JUDY MOWATT V (A — (A) BLACK WOMAN 1980 GROVE MUSIC ILPS 9649
FREDDIE McGREGOR D K V(A
DALTON BROWNE G (A LEROY WALLACE D (A HOWARD SPREAD BADESSIE B(A TONY CHIN G (A
EWAN LEWIS B (A EARL SMITH G (A MASKEL I B (A CAT COORE G (A
MIKEY HEWLETTE K (A GEOFFREY CHUNG K (A TYRONE DOWNIE K (A WIRE K (A
STELLEY K (A ARNOLD BRACKENRIDGE TPT(A HEADLEY BENNETT SAX (A DONALD GREAVES TPT (A
HERBERT CHANG FLT (A ENROY GRANT SAX (A SCULLY PERC (A EVERTON CARRINGTON PERC (A
ORVILLE WOOD PERC (A RAS INEFIRE TROI PERC (A ANICEA BANKS V (A HAROLD BUTLER MELODICA (A
JOY TULLOCH V (A SHARON TUCKER V (A PAM HALL V (A

M221E
MOVING HEARTS M221E

DONAL LUNNY K V (A — (A) DOUBLE SINGLE 1981 WAE LANDFORD IR 1 8826
DECLAN SINNOTT G V (A
MICK HANLY (A EOGHAN O(NEILL B V (A KEITH DONALD SAX V(A BRIAN CALNAN D (A
DANY SPILLANE PIPES(A CHRISTIE MOORE G V (A

M222
MOXY M222

BUDDY CAINE G (BCD — (A) MOXY 1 1976 MERCURY US SRM11087 UK POLYDOR 2480 460
BILL WADE D (BC — (B) MOXY 2 1976 MERCURY US SRM11115 UK POLYDOR 2480 372
BUZZ SHERMAN V (BC — (C) RIDIN HIGH 1977 MERCURY US SRM11161 UK POWER EXCHANGE022
TERRY JURIC B (DBC — (D) UNDER THE LIGHTS 1978 MERCURY US SRM13723 UK POLYDOR 2480 400
EARL JOHNSON G (DBC
MICHAEL RYNOSKI V (D DANNY BELAN D (D JACK RICHARDSON PROD (D TRACY RICHARDSON V (D
COLINA PHILLIPS V (D SHARONLEE WILLIAMS V (D SCOT CUSHINE PNO (D

M222A
MTUME M222A

MTUME V K PERC(A — (A) IN SEARCH OF THE RAINBOW SEEKERS 1980 EPIC US 36017 UK 84629
TAWATHA AGEE V PERC(A
REGGIE LUCAS G V (A HOWARD KING D V (A SINCLAIR ACEY HRNS (A DANNY COLEMAN HRNS (A
GWEN GUTHRIE V (A BRENDA WHITE V (A BASIL FEARRINGTON B V (A ED TREE MOORE G (A
HUBERT EAVES K V (A ED WALSH SYN (A PETE CANNAROZZI SYN (A LUTHER VAN DROSS V (A

M222B
MU M222B

MERREL FRANKHAUSER G V (A — (A) MU 19 RTV US 300 + UK UA UAG29709
JEFF COTTON SAX G V (A
RANDY WIMER PERC (A LARRY WILLEY B V (A

M222C
MUCKRAM WAKES M222C

CHRIS COE DULC (B — (A) MAP OF DERBYSHIRE 1973 TRAILER UK LER 2085
JOHN ADAMS FDL BAN TROM(BC — (B) MUCKRAM WAKES 1976 TRAILER UK LER2093
SUZIE ADAMS D (BC — (C) WARBLES,JANGLES & REEDS 1980 HIGHWAY UK SHY7009
PETER COE DULC (B
HELEN WATSON K (BC ROGER WATSON CONC (BC BILL LEADER PERC (B SONIA JACKSON CELLO (B

M222D
MUD ACRES M222D

MARIA MULDAUR G FDL V(A — (A) MUD ACRES 1972 ROUNDER US 3001
HAPPY TRAUM BAN G B V(A
ARTIE TRAUM G B BAN V(A JIM ROONEY G V (A ERIC KAZ G HCAV(A JOHN HERALD G V (A
BILL KEITH BAN G B(A TONY BROWN B (A LEE BERG V (A

M223
MUD M223

LES GRAY V (ALL — (A) MUD ROCK 1974 RAK UK SRAK 508
ROB DAVIS G (ALL — (B) USE YOUR IMAGINATION 1975 PRIVATE STOCK UK PVLP 1003
ROY STILES B (ALL — (C) GREATEST HITS 1975 RAK UK SRAK 6755
DAVE MOUNT D (ALL — (D) MUD ROCK VOL 2 1975 RAK UK SRAK 513
(E) ITS BETTER THAN WORKING 1976 PRIVATE STOCK UK PVLP 1011
(F) ROCK ON 1978 RCA PL25170
(G) MUD PACK 1977 PRIVATE STOCK UK PVLP 1022
( ) AS YOU LIKE IT 1980 RCA UK 25256

M223A **MUFFINS** M223A

(A) MANNA/MIRAGE 19 RANDOM RADAR RRR003
(B) AIR/LIVE 19

M224 **MUGWUMPS** M224

CASS ELLIOT V (| (A) MUGWUMPS 1967 WB US W 1697
DENNY DOHERTY V (| (B) HISTORICAL RECORDINGS 197 VALIANT UK VS 134
ZAL YANOVSKY (
JAMES HENDRICKS (

M225 **IDRIS MUHAMMAD** M225

IDRIS MUHAMMAD D V (ALL | (A) BLACK RHYTHM REVOLUTION 1972 PRESTIGE US 10005
JERRY HEY HRNS (J | (B) YOU TALK THAT TALK 19 PRESTIGE US 10019
LARRY HALL HRNS (J | (C) PEACE & RHYTHM 1973 PRESTIGE US 10036
BILL REICHENBACH HRNS (J | (D) POWER OF SOUL 1974 KUDU KU 17
CARLBERG JONES HRNS (J | (E) IDRIS MUHAMMAD 1976 KUDU KU 27
HERB JIMMERSON K (J | (F) TURN THIS MUTHA OUT 1977 KUDU KU 34
ROLAND BAUTISTA G (J | (G) BOOGIE TO THE TOP 1978 KUDU KU 38
TIP WIRRICK G (J | (H) YOU AIN'T NO FRIEND OF MINE 1978 FANTASY FT 552
NATHANIEL PHILLIPS B (J | (I) FOX HUNTIN' 1979 FANTASY US 9581 UK F 562
CLAY TOVEN V (J | (J) MAKE IT COUNT 1980 FANTASY US F 9598
MAXINE WATERS V (J
JULIA TILLMAN V (J | CLYDENE JACKSON V (J | PAUL SMITH K V (J | DAVID FRAZIER PERC (J
PAT HENDERSON V (J | KEITH HATCHER B (J | DAVID STONE FLT (J | WILL LEE B (G
CLIFF CARTER K (G | DAVID FRIEDMAN VIBES(G | RONNIE CUBER SAX (G | HIRAM BULLOCK G (G
DANIEL CAHN TPT (G | JEREMY STEIG FLT (G | FRANK FLOYD V (G | SAM FIGUEROA PERC(G
JOHN GATCHELL HRNS (G | HUGH McCRACKEN HCA (G | ZACHARY SANDERS V (G | NICKY MARRERO PERC(G
RAY DAVIS SAX (G | GLORIA AGOSTINI HARP (G | RAY SIMPSON V (G | KEN WILLIAMS V (G

M227 **GEOFF MULDAUR** M227

GEOFF MULDAUR V G K(ALL | (A) GEOFF MULDAUR 1964 PRESTIGE US 14004
JAMES JAMESON B (D | (B) SLEEPY MAN BLUES 1965 PRESTIGE US 7727
KLAUS VOORMANN B (D | (C) IS HAVING A WONDERFUL TIME 1975 REPRISE US 2220 UK K54046
AMOS GARRETT G (CEF | (D) MOTION 1976 REPRISE US MS 2255
DOC CHEATHAM TPT (C | (E) GEOFF MULDAUR & AMOS GARRETT 197 FLYING FISH US 061
JIMMY NOTTINGHAM TPT (C | (F) BLUES BOY 1979 FLYING FISH US FF 201
TOM PRINEIPATO G V (G | (G) I AINT DRUNK 1981 ISLAND 203 546
TAFT JORDON TPT (C
RON CARTER B (C | STEPHEN BRUTON G V (CF | ED DANIELS FLT (C | JAMES BOOKER K (C
DENSIL LANG V PERC(C | BENNY MORTON TROM (C | QUENTON JACKSON TROM (C | BILL BUTLER G (C
PETER GORDON HRNS (C | KENNETH BERGER CLAR (C | JOHN CALE VLN (C | BOB WILBUR WIND(C
RUSSELL PROCOPE SAX (C | BOB SIGGINS BANJ (C | FRANK WESS SAX (C | ROMEO PENQUE CLAR(C
JOHN CLARK HRN (C | GEORGE DORSEY SAX (C | HOWARD JOHNSON SAX (C | DAVID SIMON HCA V(C
HERSCHEL HOLDER TPT (C | DON BUTTERFIELD TUBA (C | JENNY MULDAUR V (CF | JERRY JEMMOTT B (C
MICHAEL AVERY D (G | RICK HAMMET TPT (G | KENNY CRANE HRNS (G | JOE CALO SAX (G
KAZ KAZANOFF SAX V(G | RICO ROYAL SAX (G | GEORGE LEH V (G | DAVE BURGIN HCA V (E
BARBARA MENDELSOHN DULC(E | NICHOLAS TEN BROEK TROM(E | TEM NITMAR SAX (E | SCOTT MATHAOS D SAX(E
MICHAEL MELFORD MAND V(E | DWIGHT BRAINERD V (E | SAMMY CREASON D (F | MIKE UTLEY K (F
DENNIS WHITTED D (F | GEORGE LEN V (F | PIERRE BEAUREGARD HCA (F | SARAH BROWN V (FG
STEVE BURDETT V (F | CRIS CIOE SAX (F | RICH DISHMAN D (F | PETER ECKLUND HRNS(F
WHIT GRISWOLD V (F | EARL MACINTYRE TROM (A | MARIA MULDAUR FDL V(C | RICHARD THOMPSON G (C
BERNARD PURDIE D (C | HAROLD VICK SAX (C | LLOYD SMITH SAX (C | MERLE SAUNDERS K (C
CHARLES WILLIAMS SAX (C | CORNELL DUPREE G (C | JIMMY SHIRLEY BANJO(C | LIONEL KINGHAM SAX (C
FRITZ RICHMOND JUG V(CE | BILLY RICH B (CDEF | GRAHAM LYONS BASSOON (C | SELDON POWELL SAX (C
EDDIE LOCKE D (C | PAUL HUMPHREY D (C | CHRIS PARKER D (C | BILL KEITH STEEL (C
GREG PRESTOPINO V (CD | PATTI BONE K (C | LEWIS SOLOFF HRNS (C | JOE FARRELL OBOE(C
ED GREENE D (D | MIKE BAIRD D (D | STEVE MADAIO HRNS (D | BOBBY KEYS HRNS(D
TREVOR LAWRENCE HRNS (D | LYNDA LAURENCE V (D | JIM KELTNER D (D | ABIGAIL HANESS V (D
DAVID KEMPER D (D | CINDY BULLENS V (D | DR JOHN K (D | DEIDRA ASKEY V (D
TOM COSTER K (D | SUSAN MOORE V (D | JAMES GETZ K (D | MARTIN MULL V (D
DENNIS COFFEY G (D | DONNIE RAITT V (D | JAY GRAYDON G (D | SID SHARP STRINGS (D
JESSE ED DAVIS G (D | DEAN PARKS G (D | MIKE ANTHONY G (D | JOHN MORELL G (D
DAVID WOLFERT G (D | MICHAEL BODDICKER SYN (D | BOBBYE HALL PERC (D | JIM PRICE HRNS(D
GUS BIVONA CLAR (A

M228 **GEOFF & MARIA MULDAUR** M228

GEOFF MULDAUR V G K(AB | (A) POTTERY PIE 1970 REPRISE US RS 6350
MARIA MULDAUR V (AB | (B) SWEET POTATOES 1972 WB US MS 2073
BILL KEITH STEEL(AB
AMOS GARRETT G (AB | BILLY WOLF B (AB | RICK MARCUS D (A | BILLY MUNDI D (AB
BETSY SIGGINS V (A | HAL GROSSMAN HRNS (A | PETER ECKLUND TPT (AB | JOHN KAHN B (B
STU BROTMAN TROM (B | JUNIOR TURLOCK B (B | JEFF GUTCHEON K (B | PAUL BUTTERFIELD HCA (B
MUNE BLACKBURN WIND (B | GENE DINWIDDIE SAX (B | BOBBY NOTKOFF VLN (B | TREVOR LAWRENCE SAX (B

M229 **MARIA MULDAUR** M229

MARIA MULDAUR V (ALL | (A) MARIA MULDAUR 1974 REPRISE UKK44255 US 2148
DAVID LINDLEY G (AB | (B) WAITRESS IN A DONUTSHOP 1974 REPRISE UK K54925 US 2194
JIM KELTNER D (A | (C) SWEET HARMONY 1976 REPRISE UK K54059 US 2235
JIM DICKINSON K (A | (D) SOUTHERN WINDS 1978 WB UK K56463 US 2162
MARK JORDAN K (AB | (E) OPEN YOUR EYES 1979 WB UK K56634 US 3305
KLAUS VOORMANN B (A | (F) GOSPEL NIGHTS 1980 TAKOma US 7084
RY COODER G (A
RAY BROWN B (AB | AMOS GARRETT G B V (ABCDE | GLORIA JONES V (A | DAVID NICHTERN G (ABCE
CHRIS ETHRIDGE B (A | SPOONER OLDHAM K (AB | BILL KEITH BANJ STEEL(A | LARRY PACKER VLN (AB
DAVE HOLLAND B (A | KAREN ALEXANDER V (A | ANDREW GOLD G (A | ED SHAUGHNESSY D (A
JAMES CALHOUN B (A | BETTY LAVETTE V (A | GREG PRESTOPINO V K (ABD | CHRIS PARKER D (A
CLARENCE WHITE G (A | DAVID GRISMAN MAND (AB | RICHARD GREENE VLN (AE | ELLEN KEARNEY V (ABC
MAC REBENNACK K (AB | JIM GORDON SAX CLAR K(ACE | FREEBO B (ABE | JOHN BOUDREAUX D (A
JESSIE M SMITH V (A | PAUL BUTTERFIELD HCA (B | JEFF GUTCHEON K (B | BOBBYE HALL PERC(BE
JIM GORDON D (B | BOBBY KING V (B | PAUL HUMPHREY D (B | DENNIS BUDIMIR G (B
JOHN KAHN B (B | ROSENDO CERVANTES TPT (B | RED CALLENDER B (B | DOC WATSON G (B
JAMES BOOKER K (BC | BUD SHANK SAX (B | TERRY LEE EVANS V (B | HARRY SWEETS EDISON TPT(B
SNOOKY YOUNG TPT (B | GEORGE BOHANON TROM (B | KATE McGARRIGLE V (B | LOWELL GEORGE G (B
MILT HOLLAND PERC (B | JOSE ORDAZ DURANTE TPT (B | EARL PALMER D (BC | MERLE WATSON G (B
JOHN COLLINS G (B | ABE MOSS SAX (B | PLAS JOHNSON SAX (BC | SHAHIB SHIHAH SAX (BC
ROGER KELLAWAY K (B | LINDA RONSTADT V (BC | TOM TEDESCO REQUINTO (B | EMIL RICHARDS PERC(B
PAUL HARRIS K (B | ANNA McGARRIGLE V (B | ALVIN BISHOP ROBINSON G (B | FRED STAEHLE D (B

(CONTINUED)

M229 (CONTINUED) **MARIA MULDAUR** M229

VI REDD SAX (C WADDY WACHTEL G (C BILL PAYNE K (CE WILLIE WEEKS B (CE
FRED JACKSON SAX (C HOWARD JOHNSON SAX (C AL AARONS TPT (C BENNY POWELL TROM(C
JOHN GIRTON G (C MICHAEL FINNIGAN K V (CD MICHAEL MOORE B (C VICTOR FELDMAN PERC(CE
DAVID WILCOX G (C BILL DICKINSON B (C MARY ANN PRICE V (C TREVOR LAWRENCE SAX (C
JOHNNY ROTELLA WIND (C STEVE MADAIO TPT (C LEW McCREARY TROM (CD MARSHAL ROYAL SAX (CE
GENE COE TPT (C OSCAR BRASHEAR TPT (C WENDY WALDMAN V (CD ARTHUR ADAMS V (C
WILLIAM SMITH K (C J J CALE G (C LARRY GALES B (C JOE HARNELL PNO (C
KENNY BURRELL G (C BRITT WOODMAN TROM (C CHRISTOPHER BOND G SYN(D THOM ROTELLA G (D
JOHN HUG G (DEG ED GREENE D (D SCOTT EDWARDS B (D LES DUDEK G (D
GARY COLEMAN PERC (D DAVE BURGIN HCA (D PHIL AABERG K (D PEPPER WATKINS V (D
ROSEMARY BUTLER V (D JIM ANDERSON V (D ERNIE WATTS HRNS (D DON MENZA HRNS(D
JIM HORN HRNS (D CHUCK FINDLEY HRNS (D ROBERT BRYANT HRNS (D GARY MALLABER D (C
STEVIE WONDER HCA (E JUNIOR WALKER SAX (E PAT HENDERSON (E TOMMY McCLURE B (AB
DOUG LIVINGSTON STEEL(E DAVID WODFORD SAX (E RICK VITO G (E MARTY PAICH STR (E
JIM PETTAWAY G (E ROBBEN FORD G (E DEAN PARKS G (E RON TUTT D (E
PETER BUNETTA D (E JAI WINDING PNO (E BRIAN CUMMINGS SAX (E CURT STEVENS TPT (E
RICK SCHLOSSER V (E

M229A **MULESKINNER** M229A

PETER ROWAN G V (A (A) MULESKINNER 1973 WB US 2787
DAVID GRISMAN MAND V(A
BILL KEITH BAN (A RICHARD GREENE VLN (A CLARENCE WHITE G V (A JOHN KAHN B (A
JOHN GUERIN D (A

M229B **MARTIN MULL** M229B

MARTIN MULL G V K(A (A) MARTIN MULL 1973 CAPRICORN UK K47506
RICHARD ADELMAN D (A
DEAN ADRIAN CONGA(A LEVON HELM D (A BILLY ELGART D (A JACK BONE B (A
BILL ELLIOTT V K HRNS (A STUART SHULMAN STR (A PHIL WILSON TROM (A

M230 **MUNGO JERRY** M230

RAY DORSET G V PERC (ALL (A) MUNGO JERRY 1970 DAWN UK DNLS3008 JANUS US 7000
COLIN EARL PNO V(ABCJ (B) ELECTRONICALLY TESTED 1971 DAWN UK DNLS 3020
PAUL KING BAN G V (ABC (C) YOU DONT HAVE TO BE IN THE ARMY 1971 DAWN UK DNLS 3028
( ) MEMOIRS OF A STOCKBROKER 1971 JANUS US 3027
MIKE COLE B (A (D) BOOT POWER 1972 DAWN UK DNLS 3041
JOHN GODFREY V G K(BCD (E) GREATEST HITS 1973 DAWN UK DNLS 3045
JOE RUSH PERC (C (F) LONG LEGGED WOMAN 1974 DAWN UK DNLS 3051
TIM REEVES D (D (G) GOLDEN HOUR 1974 PYE UK GH 586
JON POPE K (D (H) IMPALA SAGA 1976 POLYDOR UK 2383 364
CHRIS WARNES B (J (I) FILE 1977 PYE UK FILD 003
PETE SULLIVAN D (J (J) LOVE IN THE ALLEY 1977 POLYDOR UK 2383 435
(K) IN THE SUMMERTIME 197 PYE H121/6
(L) RAY DORSET & MUNGO JERRY 1978 POLYDOR UK 2383 485

M232 **MICHAEL MURPHEY** M232

MICHAEL MURPHEY G V HCA PNO(ALL (A) GERONIMO'S CADILLAC 1972 A&M US SP4358 UK REGAL ZONO8512
LEONARD ARNOW G STEEL (A (B) COSMIC COWBOY SOUVENIR 1973 A&M US SP4388 UK EMI EMA 754
GARY NUNN G B K V (AB (C) MICHAEL MURPHEY 1974 EPIC US 32835 UK EMI EMC2037
ROBERT LIVINGSTON B V G (AB (D) BLUE SKY NIGHT THUNDER 1975 EPIC US 33290 UK EPIC 80741
BOOMER CASTLEMAN G (A (E) SWANS AGAINST THE SUN 1975 EPIC US 33851 UK EPIC 69224
KENNY BUTTREY D PERC(AC (F) FLOWING FREE FOREVER 1976 EPIC US 34220 UK EPIC 81713
KARL HIMMEL D (A (G) LONE WOLF 1978 EPIC US 35013
CHARLES JOHN QUARTO V (A (H) PEAKS, VALLEYS,HONKY-TONKS & ALLEYS 79 EPIC US 35742
MICHAEL McGEARY D (B
HERB STEINER STEEL (BC CRAIG HILLIS G (BC W ALAN RAMSEY V (B TOMMY COGBILL B (C
JOHN HILL D (C BILL FARMER PNO (C BUDDY SPICHER FDL (C BOB HOLMES ORG(C
CLYDIE KING V (C MERRY CLAYTON V (C PATTIE HENDERSON V (C PAT POWDRILL V (C
ANDY JOHNSTON V (C CHARLIE DANIELS FDL G V(E RICHARD DEAN G (E JOHN DENVER G V(E
JAMES GUERCIO B (E JEFF HANNA V (E JOHN McEUEN BAN FDL G (EF MICHAEL McKINNEY B V(EF
JERRY MILLS MAND (E JAE MURPHY K SYN(EF TRACY NELSON V (E WILLIE NELSON V (E
EARL PALMER D (E MICKEY RAPHAEL HCA (E STEVE WEISBERG G (E SAM BROUSSARD G V (FGH
JAI WINDING K (GH HARRY WILKINSON PERC D(EF BOB GLAUB B (GH JOHN MACY STEEL(F
RAY BONNERVILLE HCA (F DAVID LUELL SAX (F DEBORAH McCOLL V (F STEVE FROMHOLZ V (F
MIKE BOTTS D (GH DENNIS CHRISTIANSON HRNS(G DICK HYDE HRNS (G JERRY JUMONVILLE HRNS(G
STEVE MADAIO HRNS (G BILL PAYNE K SYN HRNS(G LON PRICE HRNS (G VICTOR FELDMAN PERC(FG
ROBERT GREENIDGE PERC(G JOEY DE LAURO V (G JOHN BOYLAN V (G WENDY WEBB V (G
ROD PHILLIPS K (H DON BROOKS HCA (H BYRON BERLINE FDL (H DAN DUGMORE STEEL(H
DOUG DILLARD BANJO(H GARY COLEMAN PERC (H KATY MOFFATT V (H TOM KELLY V (H
BOBBY KIMBALL V (H TIM SCHMIT V (H

M232A **J F MURPHY & SALT** M232A

J F MURPHY V K G(ALL (A) J F MURPHY & SALT 19 MGM?
RON ALLARD V HRNS(ALL (B) LIVE 1972 ELEKTRA US 75024
JOE PARRINO V G HRNS(ALL (C) LAST ILLUSION 1973 CBS US 32539
GEORGE CHRIST V HCA PERC(ALL (D) URBAN RENEWAL(MURPHY'S LAW) 1975 DUNHILL US 50194
RUSSELL WARMOLTS B V (ALL (E) ALMOST HOME 19 MGM US 4708
JOHN REILLY D (CD
BOB PAVIA D (B DENNIS COOLEY V (B GLORIA GOLDMAN V (B DELORES HALL V (B
VICTORIA MEDLIN V (B ALLAN NICHOLLS V (B AL PERKINS STEEL(B BOBBY KURTZ D (E

M233 **ELLIOTT MURPHY** M233

ELLIOTT MURPHY V G K HCA(ALL (A) AQUASHOW 1974 POLYDOR US 5061 2391 100
MATTHEW MURPHY B V (A (B) LOST GENERATION 1975 RCA US APLI0916
GENE PARSONS D V (A (C) NIGHT LIGHTS 1976 RCA US APLI1318
PAT REBILLOT K (A (D) JUST A STORY FROM AMERICA 1977 CBS US 34653 UK 81881
LINDA NOVEMBER V (A
DENNIS FERRANTE V (A JIM MASON V (A EDDIE MOTTAU V (A MAERETHA STEWART V (A
TEDDY IRWIN G (A FRANK OWENS K (A DICK WAGNER V (A TASHA THOMAS V (A
MICK TAYLOR G (D GORDON EDWARDS B (B JACKIE CLARK G (B SONNY LANDRETH G (B
JIM GORDON D PERC(B WAYNE DEVILLIER K (B RICHARD TEE K (B JON SMITH SAX (B
BOBBY KIMBALL V (B TERRY HARRISON K (C ANDY PALEY D (C ERNIE BROOKS B (C
BILLY JOEL PNO (C MIKE BRAUN D (C RALPH SCHUCKETT ORG (C DOUG YULE G (C
RICHARD DAVIS B (C STEVE KATZ V (C MARK HOROWITZ STEEL(C LEW SOLOFF HRNS (C
LOU MARINI HRNS (C TOM MALONE HRNS (C MICHAEL BRECKER HRNS (C HOWARD JOHNSON HRNS(C
HARRY LOOKOFSY VLN (C PHIL COLLINS D (D DAVE MARKEE B (D PETER OXENDALE K (D
CHRIS MERCER SAX (D STEVE GREGORY SAX (D MORRIS PERT PERC (D BARRY DE SOUZA D (D
MIKE MORAN K (D NICKY HARRISON RECORDER(D NICK CARAWAY V (D STRINGS (D

M233A **PAULINE MURRAY** M233A

PAULINE MURRAY V (A — (A) & THE INVISIBLE GIRLS 1980 ILLUSIVE 2394 277
MARTIN HANNETT (A
STEVE HOPKINS (A

M234 **JUNIOR MURVIN** M234

JUNIOR MURVIN G (A — (A) POLICE & THIEVES 1977 MANGO/ISLAND ILPS 9499
(B) TEDIOUS 1978 MANGO 2009

M235 **MUSCLE SHOALS** M235

SPOONER OLDHAM G (— (A) DOIN' IT TO THE BONE 1971 ARIOLA ST 50021
BARRY BECKETT K (ABC — (B) CREAM OF MUSCLE SHOALS 197 ATLANTIC UK K 50283
JIMMY JOHNSON G (BC — (C) BORN TO GET DOWN 1976 BANG BLP 403 + SHOT 001
DAVE HOOD B (AB
CHARLES ROSE HRNS (ABC ROGER HAWKINS D (ABC HARRISON CALLOWAY HRNS (ABC HARVEY THOMPSON HRNS(ABC
RONNIE EADES HRNS (ABC CLAYTON IVEY K (B PETE CARR G (B TRAVIS WAMMACK G (B
ROGER CLARK D (A BOB WRAY B (AC TIM HENSON K (A KEN BELL G (AC
LARRY BYROM G (A TOM ROADY PERC (AC ANTHONY PARSONS FLT (A RANDY McCORMICK K (C
KATHERINE HILL V (C

M236 **MUSCLES** M236

(A) MUSCLES 197 BIG BEAR BEAR 24
( ) MUSCLES 1978 BIG BEAR BBR 1001

M236A **MUSIC EXPLOSION** M236A

JAMES LYONS V (A — (A) LITTLE BIT O' SOUL 1967 LAURIE US SLLP 2040
DON ATKINS G (A
RICK NESTA G (A BUTCH STAHL B ORG(A BOB AVERY D HCA(A

M236B **MUSICAL JANEENS** M236B

ORPHEUS ROVERS D (A — (A) SELL OUT 1980 PLUREX 1500

M237 **MUSIC MACHINE** M237

SEAN BONNIWELL G (AB — (A) TURN ON THE MUSIC 1966 ORIGINAL SOUND US OSRLPS8875
KEITH OLSEN B (A — (B) BONNIWELL MUSIC MACHINE 1968 WB US 1732
RON EDGAR D (A
DOUG RHODES ORG (A MARK LANDON G (A

M237A **HARRY MUSKEE BAND** M237A

HARRY MUSKEE V HCA(A — (A) HARRY MUSKEE BAND 1977 NEGRAM NN3
MARTIN VAN DIJK K (A
BERNARD REINKE G (A LOURENS LEEUW B (A JAN GROENINK D (A PETER SCHON SYN (A
PIET VAN BLAUW PERC (A CARL KALFF HRNS (A FRANS MIJTS HRNS (A FRED LEEFLANG HRNS(A
BART VAN LIER HRNS (A JAN SCHUURMAN BELLS(A MONICA V (A FLOUR V (A
JOSEE VAN IERSEL V (A

M237B **HARRY MUSKEE & EELCO GELLING** M237B

HARRY MUSKEE (A — (A) BALLADS 1973 ? RI 80 PHILIPS NL 6423 339
EELCO GELLING (A

M238 **CHARLIE MUSSELWHITE** M238

CHARLIE MUSSELWHITE V G HCA(ALL — (A) STAND BACK HERE COMES C M S'SIDE 1966 VANGUARD US VSD 79232
TIM KAIHATSU G (BFK — (B) STONE BLUES 1968 VANGUARD UK SVRL19012
CLAY COTTON K V (B — (C) CHARLIE MUSSELWHITE 1968 VANGUARD US VSD 79287
CARL SEVEREID B (BFK — (D) LOUISIANA FOG 1968 CHERRY RED US CR 5102
EDDIE HOH D (B — (E) BLUES FROM CHICAGO 1968 CHERRY RED US CR 5104
ROBBEN FORD G V (G — (F) TENNESSEE WOMAN 1969 VANGUARD US VSD 6528
JACK MYERS B (H — (G) TAKIN' MY TIME 1971 ARHOOLIE US 1056
LANCE DICKERSON D (GF — (H) MEMPHIS TENNESSEE 197 PARAMOUNT PAR 5012
GERALD PEDERSEN B (G — (J) GOIN' BACK DOWN SOUTH 1974 ARHOOLIE US 1074
BOB HALL PNO (L — (K) LEAVE THE BLUES TO US 1975 CAPITOL US 11450
SAM MITCHELL G (L — (L) HARMONICA ACCORDING TO CHARLIE 1978 KICKING MULE US 305 UK SNKF
EUGENE BLACKNELL G (M — (M) TIMES GETTIN TOUGHER THAN TOUGH 1978 CRYSTAL CLEAR(DIRECT) US CCS 005
PEE WEE ELLIS SAX (M
BIG JOHN EVANS D (M BOBBY FORTE SAX (M JOHNNY HEARTSMAN G (M STEVEN B JONES D (M
JOHN TURK TPT (M DARRELL BROADNAX B (M PAT FORD D (DG STU FELDMAN B (D
WORIN BELLAS ORG (D MIKE OSBORN G (D STAN POPLIN G (D VICTOR VIGEANT B (D
MICHAEL KONCALSKI D (D DARYL DRAGON PNO (D ED CARTER G (D SKIP ROSE PNO (FKM
FRED ROULETTE STEEL(F? LARRY MARTIN D (K RAY ARBIZU HRNS (K MIKE BLOOMFIELD G (K
LYNN CAREY'MAMA LION' V(K STEVE YORK B (L LONNIE CASTILLE D (H JEFF RICH D (L
STEFAN GROSSMAN G PROD(L ROD PIAZZA HCA (F FRED BELOW D (A BOB ANDERSON B (A
HARVEY MANDEL G (A BARRY GOLDBERG K PROD(ABK LARRY WELKER G (BF

M238A **MYLES & LENNY** M238A

MYLES COHEN G V (AB — (A) MYLES & LENNY 1974 CBS US 33366
LENNY SOLOMON VLN (AB — (B) IT ISNT THE SAME 1975 CBS US 33938
BOB MANN G (
MICKY ERBE B (RHONDA SILVER V (A SHARON LEE WILLIAMS V (DICK SMITH CONGAS (
DOUG RILEY K (BRIAN LEONARD D (LAUREL WARD V (HAGOOD HARDY VIB(
PATRICK McNEILLY S/D (MARIBETH SOLOMON K (BRIAN RUSSELL G (BILL MACKAY D (
LAURIE HOOD V (DICK BERG HRNS (DAVID BROMBERG G DOB(PAUL BLANEY B (
CHARLIE McCOY HCA (JUDY TATE V (

M238B **LOUIS MYERS** M238B

LOUIS MYERS V G HCA(A — (A) I'M A SOUTHERN MAN 1978 ADVENT US 2809
FREDDY ROBINSON G (A
NATHANIEL DOVE PNO (A DENNIS WALKER B (A BUSTER JONES D (A

M238C **SAM MYERS** M238C

SAM MYERS HCA V (A — (A) DOWN HOME IN MISSISSIPPI 19 TJ US 1030
TOMMY LEE THOMPSON G (A

M239 **RICHARD MYHILL** M239

RICHARD MYHILL V (AB — (A) RICHARD MYHILL ALBUM 1974 EMI UK EMC3024
PAUL KEOGH G (A — (B) 21 DAYS IN SOHO 1974 EMI UK EMC3051
GRAHAM PRESKETT B MAND(A
BRIAN COLE STEEL(A MIKE MORGAN G (A FRANK RICOTTI PERC (A TONY CARR PERC(A
HENRY SPINETTI D (A

M240 **MYOFIST** M240

RON CHENIER G V (A
ED EAGAN K (A
JOHN CHENIER D V (A
JEFF NYSTROM B V (A

(A) HOT SPIKES 1980 A&M UK AMLH64823

M240A **GARY MYRICK & THE FIGURES** M240A

GARY MYRICK G V (AB
DAVID DENNARD B (A
ED BEYER K (A
JACK WHITE D (A

(A) GARY MYRICK & THE FIGURES 1980 EPIC US 36524 UK 84450
(B) LIVING IN A MOVIE 1981 EPIC

M241 **MYSTERY GIRLS** M241

(A) FAMOUS MEN (EP) 19 STRANGE UK HAM 001

M242 **MYSTERYS** M242

(A) MYSTERYS (EP) 1979 DEAD GOOD UK DEAD 4

M242A **MYSTIC NUMBER NATIONAL BANK** M242A

GLENN WALTERS D V (A
BOB SEBBO G (A
RUSS BOOTH B (A
DAVE LORENZ G (A

(A) A MYSTIC NUMBER NATIONAL BANK 1969 PROBE CPLPS 4501

M243 **MYTHOS** M243

STEPHAN KASKE V K SYN D G(A

(A) QUASAR 1980 SKY SKY 046

M244 **CEDRIC MYTON & THE CONGOS** M244

CEDRIC MYTON (A

(A) FACE THE MUSIC 1981 GO FEET UK BEAT 4

N1 **N C C U** N1

(A) SUPER TRICK 1977 UA UK UAS30122

N2 **N R B Q** N2

TERRY ADAMS K WIND V (ALL
TOM ARDOLINI D (D
STEVE FERGUSON G V (ABC
AL ANDERSON G V (CDE
FRANK GADLER V (BC
[JODY ST NICOLAS B V (ABCD
JOE SAMPINAIO]
G T STALEY D (ABCD
DON ADAMS TROM (CDA

(A) N R B Q 1969 CBS UK 63653
(B) BOPPIN THE BLUES 1970
(C) SCAPS 1971 POLYDOR UK 2329018 US KAMA S 2045
(D) WORKSHOP 1972 US KAMA S 2065
(E) AT YANKEE STADIUM 1978 MERCURY US 3712
(F) ALL HOPPED UP 1978 RED ROOSTER 101 +ROUNDER 3029
(G) KICK ME HARD 1979 ROUNDER US 3030

N2A **N Y C C** N2A

ARTHUR FREEMAN (A
BENNY DIGGS (A
JOSEPH JOUBERT (A
LEON PENDARVIS K (A
CLIFF MORRIS G (A
ERROL BENNETT PERC (A
GREG COLE PNO (A
WILL LEE B (A
JEFF MIRANOV G (A
RICHARD TEE K (A
JOHN TROPEA G (A
STEVE GADD D (A
PAUL SCHAEFFER PNO (A
WILLIAM SEADMAN G(A
GEORGE DEVENS PERC(A

(A) MAKE EVERY DAY COUNT 1978 RCA PL12782

N2B **NA FILI (The POETS)** N2B

THOMAS O CANAINN V PIPES(A
TOM BARRY WIND(A
MATT CRANITCH FDL (A

(A) CHANTERS TUNE 1977 TRANSATLANTIC UK TRA353

N2C **STEVE NARDELLA** N2C

STEVE NARDELLA (A

(A) ITS ALL ROCK'N'ROLL 1980 BLIND PIG US 879

N2D **NANTUCKET** N2D

(A) NANTUCKET 1978 EPIC US 35253
(B) YOUR FACE OR MINE 1979 EPIC US 36023
(C) LONG WAY TO THE TOP 1980 EPIC US 36523

N3 **NAPOLEON XIV** N3

JERRY SAMUELS V (A

(A) THEY'RE COMING TO TAKE ME AWAY 1966 WB US W1661

N4 **GRAHAM NASH** N4

GRAHAM NASH K HCA G V (AB
JOHN BARBATA D (AB
CALVIN SAMUELS B (A
JOEL BERNSTEIN K V (ABC
DAVID MASON G (AB
DALLAS TAYLOR D (A
PHIL LESH B (A
CHRIS ETHRIDGE B (A
CLYDIE KING V (A
TIM DRUMMOND B (BC
JOE VITALE D K FLT(C
CECE BULFORD V (C
STEVE LUKATHER G (C
BRENDA EAGER V (C
STEPHEN STILLS G (C
RITA COOLIDGE V (A
JERRY GARCIA G (A
BOBBY KEYS SAX (A
DOROTHY MORRISON V (A
BEN KEITH STEEL (B
JOE WALSH G (C
JOHN BRENNAN G (C
ARMANDO HURLEY V (C
GLORIA COLEMAN V (C
LEAH KUNKEL V (C
JOE YANKEE PNO (AB
DAVID CROSBY G V (ABC
VANETTA FIELDS V (A
DORIAN RUDNYTSKY CELLO (A
HARRY HALEX PNO (B
RUSS KUNKEL PERC (C
DANNY KORTCHMAR G (C
NICOLETTE LARSON V (C
JOE LALA PERC (C
PAT P ARNOLD V (A
DAVID LINDLEY FDL G V(ABC
SHIRLEY MATTHEWS V (A
LARRY COX (A
JONI MITCHELL V (B
CRAIG DOERGE K (C
JACKSON BROWNE V (C
CLEO KENNEDY V (C
GEORGE PERRY B (C

(A) SONGS FOR BEGINNERS 1971 ATLANTIC UK 2401 011 US SD 7204
(A) SONGS FOR BEGINNERS 1971 ATLANTIC UK IR K40237
(B) WILD TALES 1973 ATLANTIC UK K50025 US SD 7288
(C) EARTH & SKY 1980 EMI US UK 12014

N4A **NASH THE SLASH** N4A

(A) CHILDREN OF THE NIGHT 1980 ARIOLA 203 406 SINDISC UK DID9

N4B **JOHNNY NASH** N4B

JOHNNY NASH V (ALL

(A) SOUL FOLK 196 JAD US 1006
(B) HOLD ME TIGHT 196 JAD US 1207
(C) JOHNNY NASH 19 ABC US 244
(D) QUIET HOUR 19 ABC US 276
(E) I GOT RHYTHM 19 ABC US 299
(F) LETS GET LOST 19 ABC US 334
(G) TEARDROPS IN THE RAIN 19 CADET US 50034
(H) STARRING JOHNNY NASH STUDIO TIME 19 ABC US 383
(I) I CAN SEE CLEARLY NOW 1972 CBS US 31607 UK 64840
(J) MY MERRY GO ROUND 1973 CBS US 32158 UK 65449
(K) CELEBRATE LIFE 1974 CBS US 32828 UK 80039
(L) GREATEST HITS 1974 CBS UK 69096
(M) TEARS ON MY PILLOW 197 CBS UK 69148
(N) WAHT A WONDERFUL WORLD 1977 EPIC UK 81783
(O) THE JOHNNY NASH COLLECTION 1977 EPIC UK 10008
(P) LETS GO DANCING 1979 EPIC UK 83043
(Q) THE JOHNNY NASH ALBUM 1980 CBS UK 31779
(R) STIR IT UP 1981 HALLMARK UK 3063

N5 NASHVILLE TEENS N5

ARTHUR SHARP V ((A) TOBACCO ROAD 19 LONDON US 3407
RAY PHILLIPS V B ((B) NASHVILLE TEENS 19 NEW WORLD AW 6002
JOHN ALLEN G ((C) REMEMBERING 19 DECCA
PATER SHANNON B G ((D) NASHVILLE TEENS (EP) 1964 DECCA UK DFE8600
BARRY JENKINS D (
JOHN HAWKEN K (ROGER GROOM D (NEIL KORNER B (

N5A NASHVILLE WEST N5A

CLARENCE WHITE G V (A (A) NASHVILLE WEST 178 SIERRA US 8701
GENE PARSONS D V (A
GIB GUILBEAU G V (A WAYNE MOORE B V (A

N5B NASMAK N5B

JOOP VAN BRAKEL G V (A (A) NASMAK & INSTUMENTS 1980 PLUREX NL 1800
TOON BRESSERS D (A
HENK JANSSEN G (A THEO VNA EENBERGEN B (A TRUUS DE GROOT V SYN G(A

N6 NASTY POP N6

TONY WILMSHURST G V (AB (A) NASTY POP 1975 ISLAND UK ILPS 9340
KEITH WILKINSON B V (AB (B) MISTAKEN IDENTITY 1977 POLYDOR UK 2302 056
STEVE GRACE G HCA(AB
JON FITZPATRICK V (AB STEVE CORDUNER D (B CHRIS MERCER SAX (B MARTYN FORD HRNS (B
JOHN HEATH D (A

N6A NANETTE NATAL N6A

NANETTE NATAL G V (A (A) THE BEGINNING 19 EVOLUTION US 3009
JERRY FRIEDMAN G (A
KEN ASCHER K (A ANDY MUSON B (A ALLAN SCHWARZBERG D (A

N7 NATCHEZ TRACE N7

(A) TO NASHVILLE 197 PINE RIDGE 6414 104
(B) BEST OF 1975 SWEETFOLK SFA 048

N8 NATIONAL HEAD BAND N8

LEE KERSLAKE D K V(A (A) ALBERT ONE 1971 WB UK K46094
JAN SCHELHAAS K (A
DAVE PAUL B G K V(A NEIL FORD G V (A

N9 NATIONAL HEALTH N9

AMANDA PARSONS V (12A (A) NATIONAL HEALTH 1978 AFFINITY UK AFF 6
DAVE STEWART K (1345AB (B) OF QUEUES & CURES 1978 CHARLY UK CRL5010
RICK BIDDULPH B K (B (1) 1977 (2) 1977 (3) 1978 (4) 1978 (5) 1978
BILL BRUFORD D (1
ALAN GOWAN K (12A PHIL MILLER G (ALL NEIL MURRAY B (123A PIP PYLE D (AB2345
JOHN GREAVES B (45B GEORGE BORN CELLO B V (45B LINDSAY COOPER WIND (5 JOHN MITCHELL PERC(A
JIMMY HASTINGS WIND (AB PAUL NIEMAN TROM (B PHIL MINTON TPT (B SELWYN BAPTISTE (B
KEITH THOMPSON OBOE (B PETER BLEGVAD V (B

N10 NATIONAL LAMPOON N10

JOHN BELUSHI (* (A) RADIO DINNER 1972 ISLAND UK HELP 8 BLUE THUMB US 38
CHRISTOPHER CERF (* (D) LEMMINGS 1973 BLUE THUMB US BTS6006
CHEVY CHASE (* (C) MISSING WHITE HOUSE TAPES 1974 BLUETHUMB US BTS6008
RHONDA COULLET (* (D) GOLD TURKEY 1975 EPIC US 33410
BRIAN DOYLE-MURRAY (* (E) GOODBYE POP 1976 EPIC US 33956
TONY HENDRA (* (F) THATS NOT FUNNY THATS SICK 1978 RADAR UK RAD 4
MARK HOROWITZ (* (G) ANIMAL HOUSE 1979 MCA UK MCF 2868 US 3046
DAVID HURDON (* (*) GREATEST HITS 1978 VISA IMP
HAROLD RAMIS (* (J) WHITE ALBUM 1980 LABEL 21 US 2002
PHIL JACOBS (*
BILL MURRAY (* ALICE PLAYTEN (* NORMAN ROSE (* MELISSA MANCHESTER (*
JOSEPH O'FLAHERTY (* GILDA RADNER (* PAUL SHAFFER (* CHRISTOPHER GUEST (*

N11 NATURAL ACCUSTIC BAND N11

KRYSIA KOCJAN V ((A) LEARNING TO LIVE 1972 RCA UK SF 8272
TOM HOY G V ((B) BRANCHING IN 1974 RCA UK SF 8314
ROBIN THYNE G V (
JEAN CARLIN V (AYMIN MUHAMMED B (GRAHAM MORGAN D (

N11A NATIVE N11A

WAYNE JOBSON G V (A (A) 1ST ALBUM 1979 ARISTA UK NEW 2
BRIAN JOBSON G (A
WARREN MENDES B (A PETER COUCH K (A PERRY TOLE G (A CHRIS LOPEZ PERC (A
RICHARD SINCLAIR D (A

N11B NAUGHTY SWEETIES N11B

LAN JACK G V (A (A) LIVE (EP) 1981 RHINO US RNDP 906
VOLLA SMITH G V (A
SIMEON PILLICH B V (A ANDY DOERSCHUK D (A

N12 NATURAL GAS N12

JERRY SHIRLEY D (A (A) NATURAL GAS 1976 PRIVATE STOCK US 2011 UK PVLP1007
PETER WOOD K (A
MARK CLARKE B V (A JOEY MOLLAND G V (A FELIX PAPPALARDI V (A

N12A NAVARRO N12A

ROBERT McENTEE G V (B (A)LISTEN 1977 CAPITOL US SW 11670
MARK HALLMAN G V K(B (B) STRAIGHT TO THE HEART 1978 CAPITOL US SW 11784
RICHARD HARDY WIND (B
MICHAEL WOOTEN D (B STEVE SIROTKIN K (B ROB GALLOWAY B (B MIGUEL RIVERA PERC (B
JOEY CONWAY PNO (B

N13 NAVASOTA N13

JEFF BAXTER G (A (A) ROOTIN' 1972 ABC US ABCX 757
RAY PAWLIK G (A
STEVE LONG G (A PAUL MINTER B (A LINDSEY MINTER D (A DICKY SONY PNO (A
CLYDIE KING V (A SHIRLEY MATTHEWS V (A JACKIE WARD V (A DONALD FAGEN K (A
BYRON BERLINE FDL (A MARK VOLMAN V (A HOWARD KAYLAN V (A

N14 NAZARETH N14

Musician	Inst	On	Album	Release
DAN McCAFFERTY	V	(ALL	(A) NAZARETH	1971 PEGASUS UK PEG 10 MOONCREST CREST 10
PETE AGNEW	G B	(ALL	(A) NAZARETH	197 MOUNTAIN TOPC5001 US WB BS 2615
MANNY CHARLTON	G	(ALL	(B) EXERCISES	1972 MOONCREST CREST14
DARRELL SWEET	D	(ALL	(B) EXERCISES	19 MOUNTAIN TOPS103 US WB BS 2639
PETE WINGFIELD	K	(A	(C) RAZAMANAZ	1973 MOONCREST CREST 1
PETE YORK	PERC	(A	(C) RAZAMANAZ	197 MOUNTAIN TOPS104 US A&M SP 4396
B J COLE	STEEL	(A	(D) LOUD & PROUD	1974 MOONCREST CREST 4
DAVE STEWART	K	(A	(D) LOUD & PRO'D	1974 MOUNTAIN TOPS105 US A&M SP 3609
ZAL CLEMINSON	SYN G	(MNO	(E) HAIR OF THE DOG	1975 MOONCREST CREST27
MAX MIDDLETON	K	(E	(E) HAIR OF THE DOG	197 MOUNTAIN TOPS107 US A&M SP 4511
VICKI BROWN	V	(E	(F) RAMPANT	1975 MOONCREST CREST15
SIMON PHILLIPS	PERC	(E	(F) RAMPANT	197 MOUNTAIN TOPS106 US A&M SP 3641
LISA STRIKE	V	(E	(G) GREATEST HITS	1975 MOUNTAIN TOPS108 US A&M 9020
BARRY ST JOHN	V	(E	(H) CLOSE ENOUGH FOR ROCK'N'ROLL	1976 MOUNTAIN TOPS109 US A&M SP 4562
VICKY SILVA	V	(E	(J) PLAY 'N' THE GAME	1977 MOUNTAIN TOPS113 US A&M SP 4610
JEFF BAXTER	SYN	(O	(K) EXPECT NO MERCY	1977 MOUNTAIN TOPS115 US A&M SP 4666
JOHN LOCKE	K	(OP	(L) HOT TRACKS (EP)	1977 MOUNTAIN NAZ 001 US A&M 4643
BILLY RANKIN	G	(P	(M) NO MEAN CITY	1978 MOUNTAIN TOPS123 US A&M SP 4741
PAULINHO DA COSTA	PERC	(N	(N) MALICE IN WONDERLAND	1980 MOUNTAIN TOPS126 US A&M SP 4799
VANETTA FIELDS	V	(N	(O) FOOL CIRCLE	1981 NEMS UK NEL 6019
SHIRLEY MATTHEWS	V	(N	(P) SNAZ	1981 NEMS UK NAL 102 US A&M SP 6703
PAULETTE BROWN	V	(N		
ALAN ESTES	VIBES	(N		

N15 NAZTY N15

Album	Release
(A) I GOT TO MOVE	197 CONTEMPO CLP 542

N16 NAZZ N16

Musician	Inst	On	Album	Release
TODD RUNDGREN	G	(AB	(A) NAZZ	1968 SCREEN GEMS US SD 5001
THOM MOONEY	D	(AB	(B) NAZZ NAZZ	1969 SCREEN GEMS US SD 5002
ROBERT ANTONI	K V	(AB	(C) NAZZ 3	1969 SCREEN GEMS US SD 5004
CARSON VAN OSTEN	B V	(AB		

N16A TED NEELEY N16A

Musician	Inst	On	Album	Release
TED NEELEY	V	(A	(A) 1974 AD	1973 RCA US APLI 0317
MICHAEL OMARTIAN	K	(A		

Musician	Inst	On	Musician	Inst	On	Musician	Inst	On	Musician	Inst	On
LEW McCREARY	TROM	(A	JIM GORDON	D	(A	MARK TULIN	B	(A	DEAN PARKS	G	(A
BEN BENAY	G	(A	KING ERRISSON	CONG	(A	BARRY FASMAN	K	(A	PAUL HUBINON	TPT	(A
JACKIE KELSO	SAX	(A	DAVID DUKE	HRNS	(A	BARBARA CARLSON	HRNS	(A	CHUCK FINDLEY	TPT	(A
FRED SELDON	SAX	(A	SID SHARP	STR	(A						

N16B NEGATIVLAND N16B

Musician	Inst	On	Album	Release
DAVID WILLS	SYN V	(A	(A) NEGATIVLLAND	1980 SEELAND US 001
MARK HODLER	K CLAR	(A	(B) POINTS	1981 SEELAND US 002
RICHARD LYONS	K CLAR	(A		
PETER DAYTON	G B VLA	(A		
W KENNEDY	G	(A		
BOB JACKSON	CLAR	(B		
JAN ALLEN		(B		

N17 FRED NEIL N17

Musician	Inst	On	Album	Release
FRED NEIL	G V	(ALL	(A) HOOTENANNY LIVE AT THE BITTER END	1964 FM RECORDS US FM 309
PETE CHILDS	G	(D	(B) WORLD OF FOLK MUSIC	1964 FM RECORDS US FM 319
DOUGLAS HATFIELD	B	(D	(C) TEAR DOWN THE WALLS	1964 ELEKTRA US EKS 7248
FELIX PAPPALARDI	B	(D	(D) BLEECKER & MACDOUGAL	196 ELEKTRA US EKS 7293
JOHN SEBASTIAN	HCA	(D	(D) LITTLE BIT OF RAIN	1970 ELEKTRA US EKS 74073
			(E) FRED NEIL	1966 CAPITOL US ST 2665
			(E) EVERYBODY'S TALKIN'	1969 CAPITOL US ST 2665
			(F) SESSIONS	1971 CAPITOl US ST 2862
			(G) OTHER SIDE OF THIS LIFE	1971 CAPITOL US ST 657

N18 NEKTAR N18

Musician	Inst	On	Album	Release
MICK BROCKETT		(ALL	(A) JOURNEY TO THE CENTRE OF THE EYE	1972 BELLAPHON/BACILLUS BLPS19064
ALLAN FREEMAN	K	(ALL	(B) TAB IN THE OCEAN	1972 BELLAPHON/BACILLUS BLPS19118
ROY ALBRIGHTON	G V	(ABCDEFGHK	(B) " " " "	1974 UA UAS 29499
RON HOWDEN	D	(ALL	(B) " " " "	1976 PASSPORT US 98017
DEREK MOORE	B V	(ALL	(C) REMEMBER THE FUTURE	1973 BELLAPHON/BACILLUS BLPS19164
DAVE NELSON	G V	(JKLMN	(C) " " " "	1974 UA UAS 29545
CHRIS MERCER	SAX	(E	(C) " " " "	1974 PASSPORT US 98002
LARRY FAST		(J	(D) SOUNDS LIKE THIS	1973 BELLAPHON/BACILLUS BDA7506
STEVE GREGORY	SAX	(E	(D) " " " "	1973 UA UAD60041/2
ROBERT CALVERT	V	(E	(E) (E) DOWN TO EARTH	1974 BELLAPHON/BACILLUS BLPS19190
P P ARNOLD	V	(E	(E) " " "	1973 UA UAG29680
KEN COLE	V	(E	(E) " " "	197 PASSPORT 98005
PHIL BROWN	B	(E	(F) LIVE AT THE ROUNDHOUSE	1974 BELLAPHON BLPS19182
STEPHEN WICK	TUBA	(E	(F) " " " "	197 BACILLUS BAC 2028
BUTCH HUDSON	TPT	(E	(G) RECYCLED	1976 BELLAPHON BLPS19219
RON CARTHY	TPT	(E	(G) " "	1976 DECCA UK SKLR5250 PASSPORT US 98011
CHRIS PYNE	TROM	(E	(H) NEKTAR	1976 BELLAPHON BLPS19224
WALT NEKTROID	G	(J	(J) MAGIC IS A CHILD	1977 BELLAPHON BAC 2050
STRING SECTION		(J	(J) " " "	1977 POLYDOR US PD 6115
			(K) LIVE IN NEW YORK	1977 BELLAPHON BAC 2004
			(L) MORE LIVE IN NEW YORK	1978 BELLAPHON BAC 2058
			(M) THRU THE EARS	1978 VISA IMP 9001
			(N) MAN IN THE MOON	19

N19 BILL NELSON N19

Musician	Inst	On	Album	Release
BILL NELSON	G V	(A	(A) NORTHERN DREAM	1971 SMILE LAF 2182
			(A) NORTHERN DREAM	1980 BUTT RI BUTT002

N20 BILL NELSONS RED NOISE N20

Musician	Inst	On	Album	Release
BILL NELSON	G V		(A) SOUND ON SOUND	1979 HARVEST UK SHSP 4095 US ST 11931
ANDREW CLARK	K	(ABC	(B) QUIT DREAMING AND GET ON THE BEAM	1981 MERCURY UK 6359 055
IAN NELSON	SAX	(ABC	(C) SOUNDING OF THE RITUAL ECHO	1981 FREE WITH B
RICK FORD	B	(ABC		

Musician	Inst	On	Musician	Inst	On	Musician	Inst	On	Musician	Inst	On
STEVE PEER	D	(ABC	DAVE MATTACKS	D	(ABC	RICHARD BROWN	K D	(A	GARETH EILLEDGE	B	(A
LEOM ARTHURS	B	(A	TOM KELLICHEN	D	(BC						

N20A JIMMY NELSON N20A

Musician		
JIMMY NELSON		(A

Album	Year	Release
(A) JIMMY'Mr T99' NELSON	1981	ACE UK 10CH 35

N21 RICKY NELSON N21

Musician	Instrument	Albums
RICK NELSON	G V	(ALL
JAMES BURTON	G	(
JOE OSBORN	B	(
JAMES KIRKLAND	B	(
RICHIE FROST	D	(
RAY JOHNSON	PNO	(
JOE MAPHIS	G	(
BARNEY KESSEL	G	(
GENE GARTH	PNO	(
JIM CETERA	B V	(J
TOM BRUMLEY	STEEL	(JKLMN
ALLEN KEMP	G V	(JKL
PATRICK SHANAHAN	D	(JKL
RANDY MEISNER	B V	(K
ANDY BELLING	K	(K
STEPHEN A LOVE	B V	(L
DON NELSON	FLT	(L
DENNIS LARDEN	G	(MN
JAT DE WITT WHITE	B V	(MN
TY GRIMES	D	(M
RICHIE HAYWARD	D	(
SNEAKY PETE KLEINOW	STEEL	(
BUDDY EMMONS	STEEL	(
STEVE DUNCAN	D PERC V	(N
JAI WINDING	K	(N
ROGER BUSH	B	(N

Album	Year	Release	Other release
RICKY	1957	US IMPERIAL 9048	UK LONDON HAP 2080
RICKY (RI 2 TRACKS LESS)	1979	US IMPERIAL M1004	
RICKY NELSON	1958	US IMPERIAL 9050	UK LONDON HAP 2119
RICKY SINGS AGAIN	1959	US IMPERIAL 9061	UK LONDON HAP 2159
SONGS BY RICKY	1959	US IMPERIAL 9082	UK LONSDON HAP 2206
SONGS BY RICKY	1959	US IMPERIAL 12030	
MORE SONGS BY RICKY	1960	US IMPERIAL 9122	UK LONDON HAP 2290
MORE SONGS BY RICKY	1960	US IMPERIAL 12059	
RICK IS 21	1961	US IMPERIAL 9152	UK LONDON HAP 2379
RICK IS 21	1961	US IMPERIAL 12071	
ALBUM SEVEN	1962	US IMPERIAL 9167	UK LONDON HAP 2445
ALBUM SEVEN	1962	US IMPERIAL 12082	
BEST SELLERS BY RICK NELSON	1963	US IMPERIAL 9218	US IMPERIAL 12218
ITS UP TO YOU	1963	US IMPERIAL 9223	US IMPERIAL 12223
ITS UP TO YOU (DIFF TRACKS)	1963		UK LONDON HAP 8066
MILLION SELLERS	1963	US IMPERIAL 9232	US IMPERIAL (S) 12232
MILLION SELLERS(DIFF TRACKS)	1964	UK	BRUNSWICK LBY 3027
HELLO MARY LOU (SAME AS ABOVE)	197	NL SUNSET	DA 5026
ROCK 'N' ROLL CLASSICS(AS ABOVE)	197	NL U A	52 92968
STORY OF R'N'R (RI OF IMP 9232)	19	GERM U A	UA 30050
A LONG VACATION	1963	US IMPERIAL 9244	US (S) 12244
SINGS FOR YOU	1964	US IMPERIAL 9251	US (S) 12251
FOR YOUR SWEET LOVE	1963	US DECCA DL 74419	UK BRUNSWICK LAT 8545
SINGS FOR YOU	1964	US DECCA DL 74479	UK BRUNSWICK LAT 8562
THE VERY THOUGHT OF YOU	1964	US DECCA DL 74559	UK BRUNSWICK LAT 8581
SPOTLIGHT ON RICK	1964	US DECCA DL 74608	UK BRUNSWICK LAT 8596
BEST ALWAYS	1965	US DECCA DL 74660	UK BRUNSWICK LAT 8615
LOVE & KISSES	1965	US DECCA DL 74678	UK BRUNSWICK LAT 8630
BRIGHT LIGHTS & COUNTRY MUSIC	1966	US DECCA DL 74779	UK BRUNSWICK LAT 8657
ON THE FLIP SIDE (4 TRACK BY RICK)	66	US DECCA DL 74836	
COUNTRY FEVER	1967	US DECCA DL 74837	UK BRUNSWICK LAT 8680
COUNTRY FEVER	197	US MCA RI MCA2	
ANOTHER SIDE OF RICK	1968	US DECCA DL 74944	UK MCA MUPS 302
PERSPECTIVE	1969	US DECCA DL 75014	
RICK NELSON IN CONCERT	1970	US DECCA DL 75162	UK MCA MUPS 409
RICK NELSON IN CONCERT	197	US MCA RI MCA 3	
GOLDEN GREATS	19	US LIBERTY 8674	
(J)RICK SINGS NELSON	1970	US DECCA DL 75236	UK MCA MUPS 442
(J)RICK SINGS NELSON	197	US MCA RO MCA20	UK MCA RI MCF 2644
(K)RUDY THE FIFTH	1971	US DECCA DL 75297	UK MCA MUPS 440
(K)RUDY THE FIFTH	197	US MCA RI MCA37	UK MCA RI MCF 2535
(L)GARDEN PARTY	1972	US DECCA DL 75391	UK MCA MDKS8009
(L)GARDEN PARTY	1974	US MCA RI MCA62	UK MCA RI NCG 3515
(M)WINDFALL	1974	US MCA 383	UK MCA MCG 3516
(N)INTAKES	1977	US EPIC 34420	UK EPIC 81802
VERY BEST OF	1970	SUNSET	UK SLS 50164
VERY BEST OF (DIFF TRACKS)	197	UA	US UALA 330E
LEGENDARY MASTERS	1971	UA US 9960	UK UA UAD 60029/30
POP CHRONICLE (RI OF ABOVE)	197	UA	GERM UA 29962
RICK NELSON COUNTRY	1973	MCA	US MCA 24004
RICK NELSON	197	SUNSET	US SUS 5118
I NEED YOU	197	SUNSET	US SUS 5205
RICKY NELSON STORY (TRIPLE)	197	ARI	US ARI 1003
RICKY NELSON SINGLES	1977	MCA US CDL 8053	UK RI MFP MFP 50411
RICKY NELSON ALBUMS	1979	UK UA	UAK 30246
STARS OF THE 60s	19	NL UA	50 94953
RICK NELSON STORY	19	JAP JET	JET 7070
BIG HITS	19	JAP UA	UA GXH18
RICKY	1980	UA US 1004	
PLAYING TO WIN	1981	CAPITOL	12109

N22 SANDY NELSON N22

Musician	Instrument	Albums
SANDY NELSON	D	(ALL

Album	Year	Release
TEENBEAT	1960	IMPERIAL US (M)9105(S)12044
HES A DRUMMER BOY	1961	IMPERIAL US (M)9136(S)12159
LET THERE BE DRUMS	1961	IMPERIAL US (M)9159(S)12080
LET THERE BE DRUMS	1961	LONDON UK HAP 2425
DRUMS ARE MY BEAT	1962	IMPERIAL US (M)9168(S)12083
COMPELLING PERCUSSION	1962	LONDON UK HAP 8029
DRUMMING UP A STORM	196	IMPERIAL US (M)9189(S)12189
DRUMMING UP A STORM	196	LONDON UK HAP 8009
GOLDEN HITS	196	IMPERIAL US (M)9202(S)12202
ON THE WILD SIDE	196	IMPERIAL US (M)9203(S)12203
AND THEN THERE WERE DRUMS	196	IMPERIAL US (M)9204(S)12204
AND THEN THERE WERE DRUMS	1968	SUNSET US 5224
TEENAGE HOUSE PARTY	1963	IMPERIAL US (M)9215(S)12215
TEENAGE HOUSE PARTY	1963	LONDON UK HAP 8051
BEST OF THE BEATS	196	IMPERIAL US (M)9224(S)12224
BEAT THAT DRUM	196	IMPERIAL US (S)12237
SANDY NELSON PLAYS	196	IMPERIAL US (M)9249(S)12249
SANDY NELSON PLAYS	1964	LIBERTY UK BY 3007
BE TRUE TO YOUR SCHOOL	196	IMPERIAL US (M)9258(S)12258
LIVE IN LAS VEGAS	196	IMPERIAL US (S)12272
LIVE IN LAS VEGAS	196	LIBERTY UK LBY 3035
TEENBEAT 65	196	IMPERIAL US (M)9278(S)12278
DISCOTHEQUE DRUMS	196	IMPERIAL US (M)9283(S)12283
DRUMS A GOGO	196	LIBERTY UK LBY 3061
BOSS BEAT	196	IMPERIAL US (M)9298(S)12298

SUPERDRUMS	196	IMPERIAL	US	(M)9314(S)12914
SUPERDRUMS	196	LIBERTY	UK	LBY 3080
IN BEAT	196	IMPERIAL	US	(M)9305(S)12305
BEAT THAT *?!! DRUM	196	IMPERIAL	US	(M)9329(S)12329
SOUL DRUMS	196	IMPERIAL	US	(M)9362(S)12362
BOOGALOO BEAT	196	IMPERIAL	US	(M)9367(S)12367
ROCK'N'ROLL REVIVAL	196	IMPERIAL	US	(M)9400(S)12400
MANHATTAN SPIRITUAL	1969	IMPERIAL	US	(M)9439(S)12439
HEAVY DRUMS	1969	SUNSET	US	5261
GROOVY	196	IMPERIAL	US	(M)9451(S)12451
WALKING BEAT	19	SUNSET	US	5114
TEENDRUMS	19	SUNSET	UK	SLS50061
DRUMS DRUMS DRUMS	19	SUNSET	UK	SLS50060
FATS DOMINO HITS	19	SUNSET	US	5291
GOLDEN GREATS VOL 1	19	LIBERTY	US	8679
THE BEST OF	1974	LIBERTY	UK	LBS83387
HOCUS POCUS	1976	EMI	IMP	UAS29509
VERY BEST OF	1974	UA	US	LA 440
VERY BEST OF	1978	SUNSET	UK	SLS50411

N23 TRACY NELSON N23

TRACY NELSON	G K	(ALL									
REGGIE YOUNG	G	(BC									
MAC GAYDEN	G	(AB									
BOBBY EMMONS	K	(B									
BOBBY WOODS	K	(B									
JIM GORDON	D	(D									
RON CORNELIUS	G	(BC									
ED GREENE	D	(D									
JIM HUGHART	B	(D	DAVID FOSTER	K	(D	CLARENCE McDONALD	K	(D	LARRY MUHOBERAC	K	(D
LARRY CARLTON	G	(D	DEAN PARKS	G	(D	JESSE ED DAVIS	G	(D	DANNY KORTCHMAR	G	(D
JIM HORN	SAX	(D	LAURA CREAMER	V	(D	GERALD GARRETT	V	(CE	MAXINE WILLARD	V	(D
JULIA TILLMAN	V	(D	MARK CREAMER	V	(D	IRMA ROUTEN	V	(D	SUSAN STEWARD	V	(D
OMA DRAKE SINGERS	V	(D	DARLENE GRONCKI	V	(D	LEON PENDARVIS	K	(BC	JACK LEE	G V K	(B
TOMMY COGBILL	B	(B	KENNY MALONE	D	(B	STEVE HOWARD	TPT	(B	MARSHALL CYR	TPT	(B
LON PRICE	SAX	(B	MICHAEL PIERCE	SAX	(B	CLARENCE FORD	HRNS	(B	CLYDIE KING	V	(B
BEAU CECCHINO	V	(B	MERRY CLAYTON	V	(B	JIM GILSTRAP	V	(B	JOE GREEN	V	(B
PAT POWDRILL	V	(B	WILLIE NELSON	V	(B	LINDA RONSTADT	V	(B	ANDY MACMAHON	K V	(F
BILLY PUETT	SAX³	(F	BOB BABITT	B	(C	WILLIE HALL	D	(C	MYRNA SMITH	V	(C
DANNY SANDERS	SAX	(E	SYLVIA SHEMWELL	V	(C	JOHNNY GIMBLE	FDL	(C	RICHARD TEE	K	(C
ESTELLE BROWN	V	(C	PETE DRAKE	STEEL	(C	HARVEY THOMPSON	HRNS	(C	CHARLES ROSE	HRNS	(C
RON EADES	HRNS	(C	HARRISON CALLOWAY	HRNS	(C	LANNY BOLES	PERC	(EF	LARRY CHANEY	G	(F
BARRY CHANCE	G	(F	CHRIS LEUZINGER	G	(F	LISA SILVER REYNOLDS	V	(F	SHERRY KRAMER	V	(F
DONNA McELROY	V	(F	JAMIE BRANTLEY	V	(F	JACK GROCHMAL	V	(F	TED REYNOLDS	B	(EF
WAYNE JACKSON	HRNS	(F	ANDREW LOVE	HRNS	(F	PEBBLE DANIEL	V	(F	MARCIA ROUTH	V	(F
SHERRY GROOMS	V	(F	YVONNE HODGES	V	(F	STEVE BRANTLEY	V	(F	BRUCE DEES	V	(F
WAYNE JACKSON	HRNS	(E	CARLENE CARTER	V	(E	STEVE HOSTACK	G V	(E	SWEET INSPIRATION	V	(C
JOHN SALEM	K V	(E	CHARLIE MUSSELWHITE	HCA	(A						

(A) DEEP ARE THE ROOTS	1966	PRESTIGE	US 7393
(B) TRACY NELSON	1974	ATLANTIC US SDD7310	UK K50091
(C) SWEET SOUL MUSIC	1975	MCA	US MCA 494
(D) TIME IS ON MY SIDE	1976	MCA	US 2203 UK MCF2765
(E) HOMEMADE SONGS	197	FLYING FISH	US FF 052
(F) COME SEE ME ABOUT ME	1980	FLYING FISH	US FF 209
(G) DOIN' IT MY WAY	1980	AUDIO DYN US 101 ADELPHI	4119

N23A WILLIE NELSON N23A

WILLIE NELSON	G V	(ALL
PAUL ENGLISH	D	(RSZX
JODY PAYNE	G V	(SRXZ
BUCKY MEADOWS	G	(RXZ
MICKEY RAPHAEL	HCA	(RSXZ
DAVID ALLEN COE	V	(S
TOM MORRELL	STEEL	(S
BOBBIE NELSON	PNO	(RSX
BILLY ENGLISH	D	(R
BILL SPEARS	B	(RSXZ
GUZENSLAW BROTHERS	V	(S
STEVE FROMHOTZ	V	(S
CHRIS ETHRIDGE	B	(XZ
MOSES CALDERON	K	(Z
JOHNNY GIMBLE	FD	(Z
BOOKER T JONES	K	(X
RAY PRICE	V	(Z
GRADY MARTIN	G	(Z
BUDDY EMMONS	STEEL	(Z
CRYSTAL GAYLE	V	(Z

...AND THAN I WROTE	1962	LIBERTY	US	LST7239
HERE'S WILLIE NELSON	1963	LIBERTY	US	LST7308
COUNTRY WILLIE	1965	RCA	US	LSP3418
HELLO WALLS	1966	SUNSET	US	SUS5138
HELLO WALLS	197	PICKWICK	US	SPC3584
COUNTRY FAVOURITES	1966	RCA	US	LSP3528
COUNTRY MUSIC CONCERT	1966	RCA	US	LSP3659
MAKE WAY FOR	1967	RCA	US	LSP3748
THE PARTYS OVER	1967	RCA	US	LSP3858
TEXAS IN MY SOUL	1968	RCA US LSP3937	UK	RD 7997
GOOD TIMES	1968	RCA	US	LSP4057
MY OWN PECULIAR WAY	1969	RCA	US	LSP4111
BOTH SIDES NOW	1970	RCA	US	LSP4294
LAYING MY BURDENS DOWN	1970	RCA	US	LSP4404
COLUMBUS STOCKADE	1970	CAMDEN	US	CAS2444
COLUMBUS STOCKADE	197	CAMDEN	US	ACL7018
WILLIE NELSON & FAMILY	1971	RCA	US	LSP4489
YESTERDAYS WINE	1971	RCA	US	LSP4568
YESTERDAYS WINE	197	CAMDEN	US	ANL1102
YESTERDAYS WINE	1980	INTERNATIONAL		INT5014
THE WORDS DONT FIT	1972	RCA	US	LSP4653
THE WILLIE WAY	1972	RCA	US	LSP4760
COUNTRY WINNERS	1973	CAMDEN	US	ACLI0326
THE BEST OF(RI LST7239)	1973	UA	US	UALA086
SPOTLIGHT ON	1974	CAMDEN	US	ACLI0705
COUNTRY WILLILE	1973	UA		UALA420
SHOTGUN WILLIE	1973	ATLANTIC	US	SD 7262
PHASES & STAGES	1974	ATLANTIC	US	SD 7291
WHAT CAN YOU DO TO ME	1975	RCA	US	APLI1234
(R)RED HEADED STRANGER	1975	CBS UK 69200	US	33482
FAMOUS COUNTRY (DBL)	1975	RCA	UK	DPS2062
(S)SOUND IN YOUR MIND	1976	CBS UK 81252	US	34092
(S)SOUND IN YOUR MIND	1980	EMBASSY	UK	31828
TROUBLEMAKER	1976	CBS UK 81565	US	34112
WANTED THE OUTLAWS	1976	RCA	US	APLI1321
WANTED THE OUTLAWS	1976	RCA	UK	RS 1048
WILLIE NELSON LIVE	1976	RCA UK APLI1487 US		LSA3277
& FRIENDS	1976	PLANTATION U	US	PLP214
& FRIENDS	1976	CHARLY	UK	CR30120
WILLIE NELSON 1961	1977	DOUBLE BARREL		LT1961
BEFORE HIS TIME	1977	RCA	US	APLI2210
TEXAS COUNTRY (DBL)	1976	U A	US	LA574H2
TO LEFTY FROM WILLIE	1977	CBS	US	34695
WAYLON & WILLIE	1978	RCA	UK/ US	APL12686
(X)STARDUST	1978	CBS US35305		UK 82710

(CONTINUED)

N23A WILLIE NELSON (CONTINUED) N23A

FACE OF A FIGHTER 1978 LONE STAR US L4602
THERE'LL BE NO TEARS 1978 UA US LA930 UK UAS 30215
WILLIE & FAMILY LIVE 1978 CBS US 35642 UK 88333
PRETTY PAPER 1979 CBS US 36189 UK 83877
SWEET MEMORIES 1979 RCA US AHL13243
CLASSIC WILLIE NELSON 1979 SUNSET SLS50430
ONE FOR THE ROAD 1979 CBS US 36064 UK 88641
ELECTRIC HORSEMAN 1979 CBS US 36327 UK 70177
(Z)SAN ANTONIO ROSE 1980 CBS US 36476 UK 84358
HONEYSUCKLE ROSE 1980 CBS US 36752 UK 22080
FAMILY BIBLE 1980 SONGBIRD US MCA 3258
MINSTREL MAN 1980 RCA US 4045
SOMEWHERE OVER THE RAINBOW 19 CBS US 36883
ALWAYS ON MY MIND 1982 CBS UK 85688
GREATEST HITS 1982 CBS UK 88567

N24 NEON N24

PETER BRANNIGAN G V (A — (A) NEON 19 PARAMOUNT US PAS 5024
FRANCIS CRABTREE K V (A
FUNG PORTER V B (A RUSSELL LESLIE V PERC (A

N24A NEON HEARTS N24A

PAUL RAVEN B (A — (A) POPULAR MUSIC 1979 SATRIL UK SATL4012
KEITH ALLEN D (A
STEVE HEART SAX (A MARTIN RATCLIFFE G (A

N24B NEON BABIES N24B

NIKOLAUS POLAK G (AB — (A) NEON BABIES 1981 GOOD NOISE GER 2005
CONNY COOL B (AB — (B) HARMLOS 1982 ARIOLA GER 204 530
REINHARD MEERMAN SAX (AB
TONI NISSL D (AB INGA'DILEMMA'HUMP K V(AB MIKO V (A

N24C NEON ROSE N24C

ROGER HOLEGUARD G V (AB — (A) NEON ROSE 1973 VERTIGO 6316 250
BENNO MENGARELLI B V (AB — (B) RELOAD 1974 VERTIGO
STANLEY LARSSON D (AB
PIERO MENGARELLI G (AB

N24D NERVES N24D

(A) NOTRE DEMO 1981 GOOD VIBRATIONS UK

N24E NERVOUS EATERS N24E

STEVE CATALDO G V (A — (A) NERVOUS EATERS 1980 ELEKTRA 6E282
JEFF WILKINSON D (A
JONATHAN PALEY G V (A ROBB SKEEN B V (A NICKY HOPKINS K (A ANDY PALEY K (A
HARRY MASLIN PERC (A STEVE CROPPER G (A

N24F NERVOUS REX N24F

SHAUN BRIGHTON V G (A — (A) NERVOUS REX 1980 DREAMLAND US 5002 UK 2394 270
LAUREN AGNELLI K V (A
DIANNE ATHEY B (A JONATHAN LEE GILDERSLEEVE D (A

N25 MICHAEL NESMITH N25

MICHAEL NESMITH G V (ALL — (A) WICHITA TRAIN WHISTLE SINGS 1968 DOT US 25861 SLPD 516
RED RHODES STEEL(ABCDEFGH — (A) WICHITA TRAIN WHISTLE SINGS 1978 PACIFIC ARTS US RI PACB 7113
JAMES BURTON G (AD — (B) MAGNETIC SOUTH 1970 RCA US LSP4371 UK SF8136
SHORTY ROGERS D (A — (C) LOOSE SALUTE 1970 RCA US LSP4415
HAL BLAINE D (A — (D) NEVADA FIGHTER 1971 RCA US LSP4497 UK SF8209
JOHN AUDINO TPT (A — (E) TANTAMOUNT TO TREASON 1972 RCA US LPS4563 UK SF8276
CHUCK BERGHOFFER B (A — (F) AND THE HITS JUST KEEP ON COMING 1972 RCA US LSP4695
MILT BERNHART TROM (A — (F) AND THE HITS JUST KEEP ON COMING 1977 ISLAND UK ILPS 9439
BUD BRISBOIS TPT (A — (F) AND THE HITS JUST KEEP ON COMING 1979 PACIFIC ARTS UK RI PAC 116
FRANK CAPP PERC (A — (G) PRETTY MUCH YOUR STANDARD STASH 1973 RCA US APLI 0164
BUDDY CHILDERS TPT (A — (G) PRETTY MUCH YOUR STANDARD STASH 1977 ISLAND UK ILPS 9440
GENE CIPRIANO WIND (A — (G) PRETTY MUCH YOUR STANDARD STASH 1979 PACIFIC ARTS US RI PAC 117
TOM SAVIANO SAX (MN — (H) THE PRISON 1975 ISLAND UK ILPS9428
GARY COLEMAN PERC (A — (H) THE PRISON 1979 PACIFIC ARTS US RI PAC 101
BUDDY COLLETTE WIND (A — (J) FROM A RADIO ENGINE TO PHOTON WING 1977 ISLAND UK ILPS 9486
JIM DECKER HRNS (A — (J) FROM A RADIO ENGINE TO PHOTON WING 1979 PACIFIC ARTS US PAC 107
DOUG DILLARD BANJO(A — (K) BEST OF 1976 RCA US RS 1064
VICTOR FELDMAN PERC (A — (L) LIVE AT THE PALAIS 1978 PACIFIC US PAC 7118
JOHN HOBBS K V (MN — (M) COMPILATION 1977 ISLAND UK ILPS 9425
JUSTIN GORDON WIND (A — (M) COMPILATION 197 PACIFIC ARTS US PAC106 +PAC 7106
BILL HINSHAW HRNS (A — (N) INFINITE RIDER ON THE BIG DOGMA 1979 PACIFIC ARTS US PAC 7130
LENNY CASTRO PERC (MN — (EP) & FIRST NATIONAL BAND 1976 ISLAND UK IEP4
JOE HOWARD TROM (A
DICK HYDE TROM (A JULES JACOB TROM (A JOHN KITZMILLER TUBA (A MANNY KLAIN TPT (A
LARRY KNECHTEL PNO (A JOHN LOWE WIND (A LEW McCREARY TROM (A JACK NIMITZ WIND(A
BARRETT O'HARA TROM (A EARL PALMER D (A LONNIE MACK G (J DICK PERISSI HRNS(A
DON RANDI PNO (A SAM RICE TUBA (A KENNY SHROYER TROM (A TOMMY TEDESCO G (A
TONY TERRAN TPT (A JIMMY ZITO TPT (A LOUISE BLACKBURN TROM (A JULES CHAIKEN TPT (A
JIM HORN WIND (A OLLIE MITCHELL TPT (A JOHN WARE D (BCDL JOHN LONDON B (BCD
EARL P HALL K (B AL CASEY G (D JACK PANELLI D (E JOHNNY MEEKS B (E
DAVID MACKAY B (JLMN LARRIE LONDIN D (J JERRY CARRIGAN D (J GLEN D HARDIN K (CD
JOSE FELICIANO CONGAS (E DAVID BRIGGS K (J JOE OSBORN B (D JAY LACY G (G
JOHN SHANE KEISTER K (J MAX BENNETT B (D DAVID BARRY K (G JOE CHEMAY V (MN
MICHAEL COHEN K (DEH BILL GRAHAM B FDL(G LISA SILVER VLN (J GREG TAYLOR HCA (J
DANNY LANE D (G WELDON MYRICK STEEL(J LINDA HARGROVE V (J MARCIA ROUTH V (J
PEBBLE DANIEL V (J JACK RANELLI (J AL PERKINS STEEL(LMN JAMES TRUMBO K (L
RON TUTT D (D PAUL LEIM D (MN

N25A NETWORK N25A

MICHAEL RICCIARDELLA D V(A — (A) NETWORK 1977 EPIC 34979
MIKE COXTON K (A — (B) NIGHTWORK
JEAN PAUL GASPAR PERC V(A
GEORGE BITZER K V (A JOHN VINCI V (A RICHIE G (A

N26 NEU N26

KLAUS DINGER G V D K ALL (A) NEU 1972 UA UK UAS 29396 BRAIN 000 1004
HANS LAMPE D (C (A) NEU 197 BILLINGATE US 1001
MICHAEL ROTHER G B K(ALL (B) NEU 2 1973 UA UK UAS 29500 BRAIN 000 1028
THOMAS DINGER D (C (C) NEU 75 1977 UA UK UAS 29782 BRAIN 000 1062
CONREAD PLANK PROD (AC (D) HALLOGALLO 197 BRAIN 0040 145
(AB) 2 ORIGINALS 197 BRAIN 008 0114

N26A RICK NEUFELD N26A

RICK NEUFELD G V (A (A) PRAIRIE DOG 1974 RCA UA APLI 0074 UK SF 8413
DON ZUEFF FDL MAND V G (A
HUMPHREY DUMPTRUCK BAN V(A BURTON CUMMINGS K FLT V(A BILL WALLACE B HRNS V(A GARY PETERSON D PERC(A
AL BRISCOE STEEL(A TERRY BUSH G V (A TOM JACKSON V (A LORNA HIBBERT V (A
LUCILLE LEPING V (A GRAEME GARD V (A

N26B NEUSCHWANSTEIN N26B

(A) BATTLEMENT 19 RACKET RAK 15002

N27 NEUTRONS N27

WILL YOUATT G B (AB (A) BLACK HOLE STAR 1974 UA US 1010 UK UAG 29652
MARTIN WALLACE G V (AB (B) TALES FROM THE BLUE COCOONS 1975 UA UK UAG 29726
PHIL RYAN K (AB
STUART HALLIDAY D (B CAROMAY DIXON V (AB JOHN WEATHERS D (A RAY TAFF WILLIAMS G (AB
STUART GORDON VLN (A DAVID CHARLES D (AB PICK WITHERS PERC (A

N27A NEVILLE BROTHERS N27A

(A) THE NEVILLE BROTHERS 1979 CAPITOL UK US 11865
(B) FI YO ON BAYOU 1980 A&M US 4866

N27B NEW ADVENTURE N27B

PETER BOOTSMAN G V (A (A) NEW ADVENTURE 1980 POLYDOR US 6278 UK 2925 098
HARRY DE WINTER K B V(A
HENK TORPEDO D PERC(A

N27C NEW BARBARIANS N27C

RON WOOD G V (A (A) LIVE 1979 NO RECORDS
PHIL CHEN B (A
KEITH RICHARDS G (A BOBBY KEYS SAX (A SUGAR BLUE HCA(A IAN MACLAGAN K (A

N27D NEW AGE STEPPERS N27D

BRUCE SMITH D SYN (A (A) NEW AGE STEPPERS 1980 ONU UK LP1
'STYLE' SCOTT D (A (B) ACTION BATTLEFIELD 1981 STATIK UK STAT2
CECIL D (A
NOBBY TURNER PERC (A GEORGE OBAN B (A STEVE BERESFORD K B (A JOHN WADDINGTON G (A
VIV ALBERTINE G V (A 'CRUCIAL' TONY G (A SEAN K (A ARI V (A
MARK V (A 'SHOES' D (A DAN D (A VIKKI VLN (A

N28 NEW BIRTH N28

MELVIN WILSON (C (A) NEW BIRTH 197 RCA US LSP 4450
ROBIN RUSSELL D (E (B)AINT NO BIG THING 1971 RCA US LSP 4526
LESLIE WILSON V PERC(E (C) COMIN TOGETHER 1972 RCA US LSP 4697
LONDIE WIGGINS V PERC(E (D) BIRTHDAY 1973 RCA UK SF 8368 US LSP 4797
CARL McDANIEL G V (C (D) BIRTHDAY 197 RCA APLI2145
JAMES BAKER K HRNS(C (D) ITS BEEN A LONG TIME 1974 RCA ALPI0285
TONY CHURCHILL SAX V(CE (E) BLIND BABY 1975 BUDDAH UK 4034 US 5636
LEROY TAYLOR B G (E (F) LOVE POTION 1976 WB US BS2953
VERNON BULLOCK (C (G) COMIN' FROM ALL ENDS 19 RCA US APLI0494
ALAN FREY V PERC(E (H) BEST OF 197 RCA US AHLI1021
ROBERT JACKSON TPT V(CE (J) REINCARNATION 1977 RCA US APLI1801
AUSTIN LANDER SAX V(E (K) DISCO 1977 RCA US 1535
CHARLIE HEARNDON G (E (L) BEHOLD(THE MIGHTY ARMY) 1978 WB US BS3071
JOSEPH PORTER III V (E (M) PLATINUM CITY 1979 CAPITOL US 50062

N29 NEW CACTUS BAND N29

DUANE HITCHINGS K V FLT(A (A) SON OF CACTUS 1973 ATLANTIC US SD7917 UK K40488
ROLAND ROBINSON B V (A
MANNY BERTEMATTI D V (A MIKE PINERA G V (A JERRY NORRIS D V (A

N29A NEW ENGLAND N29A

JOHN FANNON G V (ABC (A) NEW ENGLAND 1979 INFINITY US 9007 UK INS 2005
JIMMY WALDO K V (ABC (B) EXPLORER SUITE 1980 ELEKTRA US 6E307
HIRSH GARDNER D V (ABC (C) WALKING WILD 1981 ELEKTRA US 6E346
GARY SHEA B (ABC
TODD RUNDGREN G (C

N29B NEW COLONY SIX N29B

BILLY HERMAN D V (D (A) BREAKTHROUGH 1966 SENTAR US 101
CHUCK LOBES K (CD (B) COLONIZATION 1967 SENTAR US 3001
LES KUMMEL B (BCD (C) REVELATIONS 1969 MERCURY US 61165
JERRY KOLLENBERG G V (ABCD (D) ATTACKING A STRAWMAN 1970 MERCURY US 61228
PAT McBRIDE V (ABCD
RAY GRAFFIA V TAMB(ABCD WALLY KEMP B (AB CRAIG KEMP ORG (A CHICK JAMES D (ABC
RONNIE RICE V G K B(BCD

N29C NEW GRASS REVIVAL N29C

SAM BUSH MAND FDL G V(ALL (A) FLY THROUGH THE COUNTRY 197 FLYING FISH US 016
COURTNEY JOHNSON BAN V(ALL (B) THE NEW GRASS REVIVAL 197 STARDAY US 482
CURTIS BURCH G V (ALL
JOHN COWAN B V (A CHUCK COCHRAN PNO (A EBO WALKER B V (B

N29D NEW HEAVENLY BLUE N29D

(A) NEW HEAVENLY BLUE 1972 ATLANTIC US 7247

N29E NEW MIX N29E

(A) THE NEW MIX 1968 UA UAS 6678

N30A NEW MUSIK N30A

TONY MANSFIELD V G K(B (A) FROM A TO B(STRAIGHT LINES) 1980 GTO UK GTLP041 EPIC US 36450
TONY HIBBERT B (B (B) ANYWHERE 1981 GTO UK GTLP044
CLIVE GATES K (B (C) SANCTUARY 1981 GTO UK
PHIL TOWNER D (B (D) WARP 1982 EPIC UK 85567

N31 NEW ORDER N31

RON ASHETON G (A (A) NEW ORDER 1978 RCA/FUN ISL 6443
DENNIS THOMPSON D (A (B) BRADFORD RED LIGHT DISTRICT 1981 COME UK CARA 12
RAY GUNN G (A
JIMMY RECCA B (A SCOTT THURSTON K (A JEFF SPREY V (A DAVE GILBERT V (A

N31A NEW ORDER N31A

(A) MOVEMENT 1981 FACTORY UK FAC 50

N32 NEW RIDERS OF THE PURPLE SAGE N32

JOHN DAWSON G V (ALL (A) NEW RIDERS OF THE PURPLE SAGE 1971 CBS US 30888 UK 64843
DAVID NELSON G V MAND (ALL (B) POWERGLIDE 1972 CBS US 31284 UK 64843
DAVE TORBERT B G V(ABCDE (C) GYPSY COWBOY 1973 CBS US 31930 UK 65008
SPENCER DRYDEN D V (ALL (D) ADVENTURES OF PANAMA RED 1973 CBS US 32450 UK 65687
MICKEY HART D ((E) HOME HOME ON THE ROAD 1974 CBS US 32870 UK 80060
JERRY GARCIA G (ABEG (F) BRUJO 1975 CBS US 33145 UK 80405
PHIL LESH B ((G) OH WHAT A MIGHTY TIME 1975 CBS US 33688 UK 69182
COMMANDER CODY PNO ((H) NEW RIDERS 1976 MCA US 2196 UK MCF2758
BUDDY CAGE STEEL(BCDEFGHK (J) BEST OF 1976 CBS US 34367 UK 81742
BILLY KREUTZMAN PERC (B (K) WHO ARE THESE GUYS 1977 MCA US 2248 UK MCF2793
NICKY HOPKINS K (B (L) MARIN COUNTY LINE 1978 MCA US 2307 UK MCF2830
SKIP BATTIN B V (FGH
NORBERT PUTNAM B (SLY STONE K V (G JOHN HUG G (K BILL STEWART D (K
JEFF NARELL PERC (G PEPPER WATKINS V (G BOOTCHE ANDERSON V (G MARILYN SCOTT V (G
RAY PARK FDL (G DONNA GODCHAUX V (CD BUFFY ST MARIE V (D MEMPHIS HORNS HRNS (D
STEPHEN LOVE B (K PENE BLANCA V (G JACK SCHROER HRNS (C LUCHA CARDENAS V (G
RICHARD GREENE VLN (C PATTIE SANTOS V (G ANDREA AHLGREN V (G DARLENE DIDOMENICO V (C
MARK NAFTALIN PNO (C ANDT STEIN SAX (E

N32A NEW TWEEDY BROS N32A

(A) NEW TWEEDY BROS 1966 RIDON US 234

N33 NEW VICTORY BAND N33

JOHN ADAMS TROM FDL (A (A) ONE MORE DANCE & THEN 1978 TOPIC 12 TS 382
SUZIE ADAMS BANJO(A
CHRIS COE DULCIMER(A PETER COE MELODEON(A HELEN WATSON K (A IAN WORDSWORTH PERC (A
ROGER WATSON TUBA (A LINDA WORDSWORTH (A

N33A NEW YORK CITY N33A

(A) I'M DOIN' FINE 19 CHELSEA US 0198
(B) SOULFUL ROAD 19 CHELSEA US 500

N34 NEW YORK DOLLS N34

DAVID JOHANSEN V (12345ABC (A) NEW YORK DOLLS 1973 MERCURY UK 6338 270 US SRM1 675
JOHNNY THUNDERS G (1234ABC (B) TOO MUCH TOO SOON 1974 MERCURY UK 6338 498 US SRMI 1001
RICK RIVETS G (1 (AB)N Y DOLLS/TOO MUCH 1977 MERCURY UK 6641 631
TODD RUNDGREN K PROD(A (C) LIPSTICK KILLERS 1981 ROUR A104 CASS
ARTHUR KANE B (123AC (1) 1972 (2) 1972 (3) 1972/73 (4) 1974 1975 (5) 1975/77
BILLY MURCIA d (12C
TONY MACHINE (5 CHRIS ROBINSON K (5 SYLVAIN SYLVAIN G K(2345GC JERRY NOLAN D (34AB
PETER JORDAN B (45B BOBBY BLAIN K (5 MARTY THALL PROD (C SHADOW MORTON PROD (B
BUDDY BOWSER SAX (A

N34A NEW YORK GONG N34A

DAEVID ALLEN G V (A (A) ABOUT TIME 1980 CHARLY CRL 5021
BILL LASTWELL B (A
BILL BACON D (A FRED MAHER D (A CLIFF CLIFTON G (A GARY WINDO SAX (A
MICHAEL BEINHORN SYN (A DON DAVIS SAX (A MARK KRAMER ORG (A

N35 NEW YORK MARY N35

BRUCE JOHNSTONE WIND (B (A) NEW YORK MARY 197 FREEDOM US 1019
RICK PETRONE B (B (B) A PIECE OF THE APPLE 1977 FREEDOM UK 41035 US 1035
JOE CORSELLO D (B
ROBERT FRIEDMAN HRNS (B GENE BERTONCINI G (B DON ELLIOTT SINGERS V(B PETE LEVIN SYN (B

N36 NEW YORK ROCK & ROLL ENSEMBLE N36

DORIAN RUDNYTSKY K H HRNS(BDE (A) NEW YORK ROCK AND ROLL EMSEMBLE 1968 ATCO US 33240
MARTIN FULTERMAN D OBOE (BDE (B) FAITHFUL FRIENDS 1969 ATCO UK 228 932 US 33294
BRIAN CORRIGAN G V (B (C) REFLECTIONS 1970 ATCO US 33312
CLIFFORD NIVISON G (BDE (D) ROLL OVER 1971 CBS UK 64126 US 30033
MICHAEL KAMEN K G V WIND(BDE (E) FREEDOMBURGER 1972 CBS UK 64324 US 31317
LARRY PACKER FDL (
DAVID SANBORN SAX (HANK DE VITO STEEL(D DENNIS WHITTED D (

N37 MICKEY NEWBURY N37

MICKEY NEWBURY G V (ALL (A) HARLEQUINN MELODIES 1968 RCA US LSP 4043
JERRY KENNEDY S SITAR (B (B) LOOKS LIKE RAIN 1969 MERCURY US SR 61236
CHARLIE McCOY HCA G(BEGC (C) FRISCO MABEL JOY 1971 ELEKTRA UK K42105 US EKS74107
WAYNE MOSS G (BEJC (D) SINGS HIS OWN 1972 RCA UK SF 8268 US LPS 4675
FARRELL MORRIS PERC (BEIJGC (E) HEAVEN HELP THE CHILD 1973 ELEKTRA UK K42137 US EKS75055
DENNIS LINDE G V (EC (F) LIVE AT MONTEZUMA 1973 ELEKTRA US 7E 2007
KENNY BUTTREY D (B (BF)LOOKS LIKE RAIN/LIVE AT MONTEZUMA 197 ELEKTRA US 72001
KENNY MALONE D (EG (G) I CAME TO HEAR THE MUSIC 1974 ELEKTRA UK K42162 US 7E 1007
WELDON MYRICK STEEL(Ec (H) LOVERS 1975 ELEKTRA UK K52017 US 7E 1030
CHET ATKINS G (E (I) RUSTY TRACKS 1977 HICKORY US AH44002
NORBERT PUTNAM B (EI (I) RUSTY TRACKS 1977 ABC UK ABCL5215
BOB SEYMOUR (E (J) HIS EYE ON THE SPARROW 1978 HICKORY US HA44011
BUDDY SPICHER FDL (EGC (K) THE SAILOR 1979 HICKORY US HB44017
VASSAR CLEMENTS FDL (E (L) FUNNY FAMILIAR FORGOTTEN FEELINGS 19 RCA UK
JAMES CAPPS (C (M) AFTER ALL THESE YEARS 1981 MERCURY US SRMI4024
EMORY GORDY B (E
RICHARD BENNETT G (E DENNIS ST JOHN D (E DON RANDI PNO (E MARLINE GREENE G (E
JOE OSBORN B (E BOBBY WOOD K (EIK BOBBY THOMPSON G BAN (EIJKC TOMMY COGBILL B (EG
BOB BECKHAM (EC DAVID BRIGGS K (EG JIMMY HASKELL ACC/STRINGS(E JIMMY GETZOFF VLN(E
TOM BAYLOR V (E BILLY SANFORD G (EIK STAN FARBER V (E JOE ALLEN B (I
CHARLES NAVARRO (C DON GANT V (CG DR JOHN HARRIS (C JOHN MOSS (C
BILLY PUETT HRNS (G BEEGIE CRUISER (C WALKER SILL (C JAMES ISBELL (CI
HENRY STRZELECKI B (GI HAYWARD BISHOP D PERC(IJ LARRIE LONDON D PERC(I BOBBY EMMONS K (IG
ALAN MOORE K (IJK RON OATES K (I PHIL BAUGH G (I JOHNNY CHRISTOPHER G(I
DAVE KIRBY G (I REGGIE YOUNG G (GI BUDDY EMMONS STEEL(I LLOYD GREEN STEEL (IG

(CONTINUED)

N37 (CONTINUED) MICKEY NEWBURY N37

TERRY McMILLAN HCA (IJK EVERHARD RAMM HRNS (I CINDY REYNOLDS HARP(I ROBERT S GALBRAITH K (J
THOMAS C GAIN K (J DONALD L POTTER G (J STEVE COLLOM G (J JESSE BOYCE B (J
JOHN C WILLIAMS B (J DAN ECKLEY MAND (J RAFE VAN HOY G (K DON ROTH G (K
RAY EDENTON G (GK BARRY BURTON G (K JOSEPH PELLECUIA SAX (K BOB L MOORE B (K
JERRY CARRIGAN D (GK MARK B MORRIS PERC (K MIKE LEECH B (G SHANE KEISTER SYN (G
PETE WADE G (G JERRY SHOOK G (G GORDON STOKER V (G LAVERNA MOORE V (G
WENDY SUITS V (G GEORGE TIDWELL HRNS (G BUDDY HARMON D (G HOYT HAWKINS V (G
DOTTIE DELEONIBUS V (G BERGEN WHITE V (G DENNIS GOODE HRNS (G HAROLD BRADLEY B (G
RAY WALKER V (G NEAL MATTHEWS V (G DIANE TIDWELL V (G CHIP YOUNG G (G
DON SHEFFIELD HRNS(G

N38 ANDY NEWMAN N38

ANDY NEWMAN K (A (A) RAINBOW 1971 track UK 2406 103

N38A COLIN NEWMAN N38A

COLIN NEWMAN G V K(ABC (A) A-Z 1980 BEGGARS BANQUET UK BEGA20
DESMOND SIMMONS G B V(AC (B) PROVISIONALLY ENTITLED 1981 4AD UK CAD108
ROBERT GOTOBED D (ABC (C) NOT TO 1981 4AD UK CAD201 B BANQUET GER 58425
MIKE THORN K (A
BILLY BRAGG CLAR (A SIMON GILLHAM B V (C BRUCE GILBERT G (A

N39 DAVID 'FATHEAD' NEWMAN N39

DAVID FATHEAD NEWMAN SAX(ALL (A) BEST OF 1971 ATLANTIC US SD 1590
IDRIS MUHAMMAD D (H (B) LONELY AVE 197 ATLANTIC US SD 1600
CLAUDE JOHNSON PNO G(G (C) THE WEAPON 19 ATLANTIC US SD 1638
ROGER BOYKIN G B (G (D) CAPTAIN BUCKLES 19 ATLANTIC US SD 18002
GEORGE CABLES K (H (E) STRAIGHT AHEAD 19 ATLANTIC US SD 1366
HILTON RUIZ K (H (F) MR FATHEAD 1976 W B US 1304 UK K56201
GEORGE DAVIS G (H (G) FRONT MONEY 1977 W B US BS 2984
LEE RITENOUR G (H (H) KEEP THE DREAM ALIVE 1978 PRESTIGE US P10106
BILL SUMMERS PERC (HJ (J) SCRATCH MY BACK 1979 PRESTIGE US P10108
JEFF DAVIS TPT (H
LARRY MOSES TPT (H JANICE ROBINSON TROM (H EARL McINTYRE TROM (HJ KENNETH HARRIS FLT (HJ
ED XIQUES SAX (H RENE MANNING V (H YVONNE FLETCHER V (H RANDY BRECKER TPT (J
JERRY DODGION FLT (J JAMES BUFFINGTON HRNS (J BEN CARTER V (J KEVIN TONEY K (J
RICHARD TEE K (J ERIC GALE G (J CORNELL DUPREE G (J RON CARTER B (J
WILBUR BASCOMB B (J HARVEY MASON D (J TANYETTE V (J BESSIE RUTH SCOTT V (J
JON FADDIS TPT (J GEORGE MARGE FLT (J FLAME BRAITHWAITE V (J DEBORAH McGRIFF V (J

N39A JIMMY C NEWMAN N39A

JIMMY C NEWMAN (ALL (A) PROGRESSIVE CC 1977 PLANT US 544 CHARLY UK CRL 5005
(B) HAPPY CAJUN 1979 CHARLY UK CR 30177
(C) CAJUN COWBOY 1980 PLANT US 530

N39B JOE NEWMAN N39B

JOE NEWMAN (A (A) I LOVE MY BABY 1981 BLACK & BLUE UK 33155

N40 RANDY NEWMAN N40

RANDY NEWMAN PNO V(ALL (A) RANDY NEWMAN 1968 REPRISE US 6286
RY COODER G (DEFB (B) 12 SONGS 1970 REPRISE US 6373 UK K44084
RUSS TITELMAN G B (DE (C) LIVE 1971 REPRISE US 6459 UK K44151
JIM KELTNER D (DEF (D) SAIL AWAY 1972 REPRISE US 2064 UK K44185
GENE PARSONS D (DB (E) GOOD OLD BOYS 1974 WB US 2193 UK K54022
EARL PALMER D (D (F) LITTLE CRIMINALS 1977 WB US 3079 UK K56404
CHRIS ETHRIDGE B (D (G) BORN AGAIN 1979 WB US 3346 UK K56663
WILTON FELDER B (D
JIMMY BOND B (D MILT HOLLAND PERC (DEF ABE MOST SAX (D RED CALLENDER B (E
DON HENLEY V (EF J D SOUTHER V (F KLAUS VOORMANN B (F TIM SCHMIT V (F
DAVID SHIELDS B (G VICTOR FELDMAN K PERC (G CHUCK FINDLEY TPT (G STEPHEN BISHOP V (G
VALERIE CARTER V (G ARNO LUCAS V (G ANDY NEWMARK D (EFG BOBBYE HALL PERC(E
RON ELLIOTT G (DB JOHN PLATANIA G (E DENNIS BUDIMIR G (E AL PERKINS STEEL(E
WILLIE WEEKS B (EFG GLENN FREY G V (EF RICK MAROTTA D (F WADDY WACHTEL G (FG
JOE WALSH G (F RALPH GRIERSON PNO (F MICHAEL BODDICKER SYN (FG LENNY CASTRO PERC(G
TOM SCOTT HRNS (G BUZZY FEITEN G (G MILT HOLLAND PERC (B AL McKIBBON B (B
CLARENCE WHITE G (B LYLE RITZ B (B JIM GORDON D (B ROY HARTE PERC (B

N41 TOM NEWMAN N41

TOM NEWMAN G V K(ALL (A) FINE OLD TOM 1975 VIRGIN UK V2022 US ANTILLES 7042
MIKE OLDFIELD G (A (B) LIVE AT THE ARGONAUT(NOT RELEASED)197 VIRGIN UK V2042
FRED FRITH G B (A (C) FAERIE SYMPHONY 1977 DECCA UK TXS 123
CHRIS BUTLER D (A
JOHN VARNOM G (A HUGH FLINT D (A MIKE STOREY K (A DAVID DUHIG G (A
NED CALLAN B (A JON FIELD D WIND PERC V(AC PETER COOK HCA (A LOL COXHILL SAX(A
SUZI SHUTE V (A JOHN OBYTON V (A TED MACDOWELL G (A NEIL INNES K G(A
MICK TAYLOR G (A TOM NORDEN G (C PETE GIBSON TROM D(C DEBBIE HALL VLN(C
TERRY EDWARDS V (C JOE O'DONNELL VLN (C TINA JONES V (C GEOFF WESTLEY PNO(C
WARD KELLY CONOVER D (C JON COLLINS VLN (C JANE GIBSON D (C

N42 OLIVIA NEWTON-JOHN N42

OLIVIA NEWTON JOHN V (ALL (A)(A) FIRST IMPRESSIONS 1974 EMI UK EMC 3056
JAHN FARRAR PROD G B V SYN(GHJL (B) LONG LIVE LOVE 1974 EMI UK EMC 3028
LEE SKLAR B (H (C) HAVE YOU EVER BEEN LONELY 1975 EMI UK EMC 3069
MYRNA MATTHEWS V (H (D) CLEARLY LOVE 1976 EMI UK EMA 774
JULIA RINKER V (H (E) COME ON OVER 1976 EMI UK EMC 3124
SNEAKY PETE KLEINOW STEEL(H (F) DONT STOP BELIEVING 1976 EMI UK EMC 3162
JEFF PORCARO D (H (G) GREATEST HITS 1976 EMI UK EMA 785
GREG MATHIESON PNO (H (H) MAKING A GOOD THING BETTER 1877 EMI UK EMA 789 MFSL US MFSL 01
JOE PORCARO PERC (H (J) TOTALLY HOT 1977 EMI UK EMA 789 MFSL US 1 01
LAURA CREAMER V (H (K) MUSIC MAKES MY DAY 1979 PYE UK 28185
JAMES NEWTON HOWARD STR(H (L) PHYSICAL 1981 EMI UK EMC 3381
BYRON BERLINE VLN (H
TOMMY MORGAN HCA (H PETER MYERS STR (H MARTI McCALL V (H PATTIE BROOKS V (HJ
GEORGE MARGE WIND (H DAVID CAMPBELL STR (H DOUG LIVINGSTON STEEL(H RANDY EDELMAN K (H
MIKE BOTTS D (JK DAVID HUNGATE B (JK STEVE LUKATHER G (J PHYLLIS ST JAMES V (J
CARLOS VEGA D PERC(L MICHAEL BODDICKER SYN (L BILL CUOMO SYN (L GARY HERBIG HRNS(L
VICTOR FELDMAN PERC (L TOM SNOW SYN (L LENNY CASTRO PERC (L JOHN HOBBS K SYN(L

N43 JUICE NEWTON N43

JUICE NEWTON G V (ALL (A) & SILVER SPUR 1975 RCA APLI1004
TOM KEALEY G B V(AC (B) AFTER DUST SETTLED 1977 RCA APLI1722
OTHA YOUNG G V (ACE (C) COME TO ME 1977 CAPITOL 11682
JEFF PORCARO D (A (D) WELL KEPT SECRET 1978 CAPITOL 11811
HAL BLAINE D PERC(A (E) TAKE A HEART 1979 CAPITOL 12000
DENNY SEIWELL D (C (F) JUICE 1981 CAPITOL 12136
TEDDY IRWIN G (C
MIKE MELVOIN PNO (A RUSTY YOUNG STEEL(A R GILLMAN K V (C BUZZY BUCHANAN D (C
SMIGGY G (C MICHAEL O'NEILL G (C TONY SAUNDERS B (C BOB HOGINS K (C
MATTHEW KELLY HCA (C MIKE PORCARO B (E BILLY WALKER G (E JOHN HATTON B (E
MIKE BAIRD D (E DOUG LIVINGSTON K (E ALAN ESTES PERC (E RICK SCHLOSSER D (E
FRED TACKETT G (E STEVE FOREMAN PERC (E WILLIE ORNALES D (E THOM ROTELLA G (E
ALBERT LEE G (E JOHN HUNT G (E JOHN HOBBS K (E STANLEY BERENS HCA (E
JOHN HUG G (E JOHN HERRON K (E

N43A NIAGARA N43A

KLAUS WEISS D (AB (A) NIAGARA 1971 UA GER UAS 29232
KEITH FORSEY D (A (B) S.U.B. 1972 UA GER UAS 29343
COTCH BLACKMON PERC (A (C) AFIRE 1973
JUAN ROMERO PERC (A
UDO LINDENBERG D (A DANNY FICHELSCHER PERC (AB GEORGE GREEN D (A JOE HARRIS PERC (B
GARY UNWIN B (B PAUL VINCENT G (B CHRISTIAN SCHULZE K (B ACK VAN ROOYEN HRNS(B
FERDINAND)B MILAN PILAR B (B

N44 NICE N44

KEITH EMERSON V K (ALL (A) THOUGHTS OF EMERLIST DAVJACK 1967 IMMEDIATE IMSP016 US 52004
BRIAN DAVISON D (ALL (A) " " " " " 1973 CBS IMP 11633
LEE JACKSON B G V(ALL (A) " " " " " 1978 CHARLY UK CR300021
DAVY O'LIST G (AF (B) ARS LONGA VITA BREVIS 1968 IMMEDIATE IMSP020 US 52020
SINFONIA OF LONDON (D (B) " " " " 1973 CBS IMP 11634
GORDON LONGSTAFF G (1 (B) " " " " 1978 CHARLY UK CR300019
ALAN SKIDMORE HRNS (D (C) NICE 1969 IMMEDIATE IMSP026 US 52022
KENNY WHEELER HRNS (D (C) EVERYTHING AS NICE AS MOTHER 1973 CBS us 11635
JOHN WARREN HRNS (D (C) NICE 1978 CHARLY UK CR300014
PETE KING HRNS (D (D) FIVE BRIDGES SUITE 1970 CHARISMA UK CAS1014
JOE HARRIOT HRNS (D (D) " " " 1970 MERCURY US SR61295
CHRIS PINE HRNS (D (E) ELEGY 1971 CHARISMA UK CAS1030
(E) ELEGY 1971 MERCURY US SR61324
(1) 1968 (F) AUTUMN 67,SPRING 68 1972 CHARISMA UK CS1
( ) BEST OF NICE 197 ELECTROLA IMP 04890674
( ) IN MEMORIAM 197 PATHE FR 05491951
( ) IMMEDIATE STORY 1 1975 SIRE US 3710
( ) HANG ON TO A DREAM 197 EMI IMP 04850722
( ) AMOENI REDIVIVI 1976 IMMEDIATE IML1003
( ) NICE WITH KEITH EMERSON 1976 PHONOGRAM 6641 119
( ) KEITH EMRSON & THE NICE 197 MERCURY US SRM26500
( ) AMERICA 1976 PICKWICK US SHM 917
( ) POP GROUPS OF THE 60s(WITH H PIE) 197 MFP GERM 14694319/20
( ) GREATEST HITS 1977 IMMEDIATE IML 2003

N45 NICO N45

NICO V HARMONIUM (ALL (A) CHELSEA GIRL 1968 MGM UK 2353 025
PHIL MANZANERA G (D (B) MARBLE INDEX 1968 ELEKTRA US EKS74029 UK K 42065
BRIAN ENO SYN (E (C) DESERT SHORE 1971 REPRISE US 6424 UK K 44102
JOHN CALE K B G(BCD (D) THE END 1974 ISLAND ILPS9311
ADAM MILLER V (C (E) JUNE 1st 1974 1974 ISLAND ILPS9291
VICKI WOOD V (C (F) DRAMA OF EXILE 1981 AURA AUZ 715
ANNAGH WOOD V (C
FRAZIER MOHAWK PROD (B JOE BOYD PROD (C

N45A LEA NICHOLSON N45A

LEA NICHOLSON CONC V(ALL (A) HORSE MUSIC 1971 TRAILER UK LER 3010
STAN ELLISON G V (AB (B) GOD BLESS THE UNEMPLOYED 1972 TRANSATLANTIC UK TRA 254
CHRIS NICHOLSON PERC (A (C) THE CONCERTINA RECORD 1980 KICKING MULE SNKF165
RICK KEMP B (B
IAN WHITEMAN K (B ROD ARGENT K (C MIKE OLDFIELD G PERC (C RUSS BALLARD G (C
ROBIN DRANSFIELD G (C

N45B STEVIE NICKS N45B

STEVIE NICKS V (A (A) BELLA DONNA 1981 WEA UK K99169 US MODERN 38139
SHARON CELANI V (A
LORI PERRY V (A RUSS KUNKEL D (A WADDY WACHTEL G (A DAVEY JOHNSTONE G (A
BOB GLAUB B (A BILL ELLIOTT PNO (A BOBBYE HALL PERC (A BENMONT TENCH K (A
DAVID ADELSTEIN SYN (A ROY BITTAN PNO (A TOM PETTY G V (A MICHAEL CAMPBELL G (A
DUCK DUNN B (A STAN LYNCH D (A PHIL JONES PERC (A BILLY PAYNE PNO(A
DAN DUGMORE STEEL(A DON HENLEY D V (A TOM MONCRIEFF B (A DON FELDER G (A
RICHARD BOWDEN B (A

N45C NICOL & MARSH N45C

KEN NICOL G V (AB (A) NICOL & MARSH 1974 EPIC UK 80468 CAPRICORN US 174
PETER MARSH G V (AB (B) NICOL & MARSH 1978 POLYDOR POLD5012
RANDY BISHOP K (B
DAVID KEMPER D (B JEFF EYRICH B (B BILL PAYNE K SYN(B TONY BERG G (B
VICTOR FELDMAN VIBES(B DAVID LUELL SAX (B MARTY GWINN V (B KRYSIA KRISIANNE V (B
LEE SKLAR B (B TOM HENSLEY K (B CHRIS DOERGE PNO (B BARRY DE SOUZA D (A
PETE ZORN B SAX(A B J COLE STEEL(B FRANK COLLINS V (A RAY DUFFY D (A
GRAHAM SMITH HCA (A DYAN BIRCH V (A DOUG WRIGHT D (A PADDIE McHUGH V (A
BILL ZORN BANJO(A

N46 NIELSEN /PEARSON BAND N46

MARK PEARSON (AB (A) NIELSEN PEARSON BAND 1978 EPIC
REED NIELSEN (AB (B) NIELSEN PEARSON 1980 CAPITOL US 12101

N46A **NIGHT** N46A

CHRIS THOMPSON G V (AB — (A)NIGHT — 1979 PLANET US P3 UK K52200 GER 52144
STEVIE LANGE V (AB — (B)LONG DISTANCE — 1980 PLANET US P10 UK K52251 GER 52251
NICKY HOPKINS PNO (A
ROBBIE McINTOSH G (AB BILLY KRISTIAN B (AB RICK MAROTTA D (A BOBBY GUIDOTTI D (B
BOBBY WRIGHT K (B STEVE PORCARO SYN (A BILL PAYNE K SYN(A MICHAEL McDONALD PNO (A
BOBBY LAKIND PERC (A DEREK AUSTIN K SYN(A JAMES ALBERT JOHNSON D (A VINCE MELAMED K (A
VICKY BROWN V (B KEN SAVIGAR K (B MORRIS PERT PERC (B GRAHAM TODD PNO (B

N46B **NIGHTCAPS** N46B

(A) WINE WINE WINE — 197 CHARLY UK CR30183

N46C **ROBERT NIGHTHAWK** N46C

ROBERT NIGHTHAWK G V (ALL — (A) BRICKS ON MY PILLOW — 19 PEARL US P11
JOHNNY YOUNG G (C — (B) MASTERS OF MODERN BLUES — 19 TESTAMENT US T 2215
ROBERT WHITEHEAD D (C — (C) LIVE ON MAXWELL STREET 1964 — 1979 ROUNDER US 2022
CAREY BELL HCA (C
HOUSTON STACKHOUSE (C

N46D **NIGHTHAWKS** N46D

JIM THACLERY G V (ACE — (A) OPEN ALL NIGHT — 1976 ADELPHI US 4105
PETE RAGUSA D (ACE — (B) LIVE AT THE PSYCHEDELLY — 1977 ADELPHI US 4110
DAVE MAXWELL PNO (CE — (C) SIDE POCKET SHOT — 1978 ADELPHI US 4115
GUITAR JUNIOR G V (E — (D) JACKS & KINGS — 1978 ADELPHI US 4120
MARK WENNER HCA V(ACE — (E) JACKS & KINGS FULL HOUSE — 1979 ADELPHI US 4125
JAN ZUKOWSKI B (ACE — (F) TEN YEARS LIVE — 1982 CHESAPEAKE US 101
PINETOP PERKINS PNO V(E — (G) ROCK'N'ROLL — 1982 ALADDIN US 101
BOB MARGOLIN G (E — ( ) HOT TRACKS — 19 VANGUARD VSD79424

N46E **NIGHTHAWKS(EURO)** N46E

PETER LA BONTE V PERC(A — (A) SHANK IT UP — 1980 ROCKTOPUS NL 201 428 320
OLIVER STEPHEN G V (A
HANS GLINKA K V (A SVEN VAN STRAUCH B V (A JORGEN NITSCH D (A MATZI ENSINGER (A
FRANZ DIEZ G (A PIT TROJER PERC (A DIDI ZILL PROD (A

N47 **MAXINE NIGHTINGALE** N47

MAXINE NIGHTINGALE V (ALL — (A) RIGHT BACK WHERE WE STARTED — 1976 UA US LA 626 UK UAG29953
(B) LOVE HIT ME — 1977 UA UK UAS30076
(C) NIGHT LIFE — 1977 UA UA LA 731 UK UAS30105
(D) LOVE LINES — 1978 UA UK UAG30179
(E) LEAD ME ON — 1979 WINDSONG US 3404
(F) BITTERSWEET — 1981 LIBERTY UK LBG30323
(F) BITTERSWEET — 1981 RCA US 3528

N47A **NIGHTWING** N47A

ALEC JOHNSON G (B — (A) SOMETHING IN THE AIR — 1980 OVATION UK 1757
(B) BLACK SUMMER — 1982 GULL UK GULP 1036

N47B **NIKKI & THE CORVETTES** N47B

LORI V (A — (A) NIKKI & THE CORVETTES — 1980 BOMP US 4012 LINE GER LLP5087
KRYSTI V (A
NIKKI V (A

N48 **NIGHTRIDERS** N48

MIKE SHERIDAN V (— (PRE IDLE RACE CIRCA 1963)
ALAN JOHNSON G (
BRIAN COPE B (DAVE PRITCHARD G (JEFF LYNNE G V (ROGER SPENCER D (
GREG MASTERS (ROY WOOD G (

N48A **WILLIE NILE** N48A

WILLIE NILE G PNO V (AB — (A) WILLIE NILE — 1980 ARISTA US AB4260 UK SPART1126
FRED SMITH B (A — (A) WILLIE NILE — 1980 ARISTA GER 201 734
CLAY BARNES G V (AB — (B) GOLDEN DAWN — 1981 ARISTA US AB4284 GER 203 416
PETER HOFFMAN G (AB
TOM ETHRIDGE B (A JAY DEE DAUGHERTY D (AB MARK JOHNSON V (AB PAUL SCHAEFFER K (B
GERG HUSTED K (B PAUL PRESTOPINO DULC G(B LOWRY HAMMER V (B TERRE ROCHE V (B
ARNO HECHT SAX (B

N48B **NINE BELOW ZERO** N48B

DENNIS GREAVES G V (ABC — (A) PACKED FAIR & SQUARE(EP) — 1979 M&L UK ML1
PETER CLARK B V (ABC — (B) LIVE AT THE MARQUEE — 1980 A&M UK AMLE68515
MARK FELTHAM V HCA (ABC — (C) DON'T POINT YOUR FINGER — 1981 A&M US 4859 UK AMLH68521
STIX BURKEY D (BC
KENNY BRADLEY D (A MICKEY MODEM PROD (B GLYN JOHN PROD (C

N48C **NINE DAYS WONDER** N48C

WALTER SEYFFER V D (ABC — (A) NINE DAYS WONDER — 1971 BACILLUS GER 19073
JOHN EARLE V SAX G(A — (B) WE NEVER LOST CONTROL — 1973 BACILLUS GER 19163
ROLF HENNING G K (A — (C) ONLY THE DANCERS — 1975 BACILLUS GER 19200
FREDDIE MUNSTER SAX SYN K(B
KARL MUTSCHLECHNER B(A MARTIN ROSCOE D (A MICHAEL BUNDT B (BC HANS FRAUENSCHAH G (B
HYAZ INTUS D (B SIDHATTA GAUTAMA D 'C DAVE JACKSON WIND (C STEVE ROBINSON K (C

N49 **NINE NINE NINE(999)** N49

NICK CASH G V (ABCD — (A) 9 9 9 — 1978 UA UK UAG 30199
PABLO LABRITAIN D (ABCD — (B) SEPARATES — 1978 UA UK UAG 30209
JOHN WATSON B (ABCD — (C) BIGGEST PRIZE IN SPORT — 1980 POLYDOR UK POLS1013 US 6256
ED CASE D V (C — (C) BIGGEST PRIZE IN SPORT — 1980 ALBION GERM201 331
GUY DAYS G (ABD — (D) CONCRETE — 1981 ALBION UK ITS 999 GER 203 320
(D) CONCRETE — 1981 POLYDOR US 6323
(E) SINGLES ALBUM — 1980 ALBION UK SOS 999
(F) HIGH ENERGY PLAN — 1981 PVC US 7999

N50 **NINE SENSE** N50

ELTON DEAN SAX (AB — (A) OH! FOR THE EDGE — 1976 OGUN OG 900
ALAN SKIDMORE SAX (AB — (B) HAPPY DAZE — 1977 OGUN OG 910
HARRY BECKETT HRNS (AB
NICK EVANS TROM (AB MARK CHARIG HRNS (AB KEITH TIPPETT PNO (AB HARRY MILLER B (AB
LOUIS MOHOLO D (AB RADU MALFATI TROM (B

N50A 1994 N50A

KAREN LAWRENCE V (AB — (A) 1994 — 1978 A&M US 4709 UK AMLH64709
JOHN DESAUTELS D (AB — (B) PLEASE STAND BY — 1979 A&M US 4769
STEVE SCHIFF G (AB
BILL RHODES B G V(AB — BRAD WHITFORD G (A — ERIC TROYER V (A — RICK ARMOND G K (B
TERRY LINVILL B (B — JIM ALCIVER SYN (B — LANCER GREIG SYN (B — JIM HORNS SAX (B

N50B 90 DEGREES INCLUSIVE N50B

HUGH FRANCIS G V (AB — (A) 90' INCLUSIVE — 1976 VERTIGO UK 6360 139
HENRY BARNES G V (AB — (B) FIRE OVER YONDER — 1978 ICE ICEL 1005
WEBSTER DYER K (AB
WINSTON HENRY B (AB — DELFORD DAVIS D (AB — EDDIE GRANT SYN HCA(A — LLOYD TYRELL V (B

N50C NINETEEN TEN FRUITGUM COMPANY N50C

PAT SORIANO K V (E — (A) SIMON SAYS — 19 BUDDAH US BDS 5010
RALPH COHEN TPT (E — (B) A RED LIGHT — 19 BUDDAH US BDS 5022
JERRY ROTH SAX (E — (C) GOODY GOODY GUM DROPS — 19 BUDDAH US BDS 5027
DON CHRISTOPHER G V (E — (D) INDIAN GIVER — 19 BUDDAH US BDS 5036
RICHIE GOMEZ G V (E — (E) HARD RODE — 19 BUDDAH US BDS 5043
JIMMY CASAZZA D (E — (F) JUCIEST FRUITGUM — 19 BUDDAH US BDS 5057

N50D NINTH CREATION N50D

BILL ERIKSEN K WIND(A — (A) FALLING IN LOVE — 1979 RITE TRACK US 01 PYE US 12138
J D BURRISE PERC V(A
STEVEN RUBIO SAX V(A — LAURENCE HOLMAN HRNS(A — A D BURRISE B V (A — DON ROY ALLEN D V (A
MIKE MICENHEIMER HRNS(A — W THAD BOURLAND TPT V(A — HENRY ANADON HENS(A — ROBERT E CLARK G (A

N50E NIPS(NIPPLE ERECTORS) N50E

(A) ONLY THE END OF THE BEGINNING — 19 SOHO HOHO1

N51 NIRVANA N51

PATRICK CAMPBELL-LYONS (ABC — (A) SIMON SIMOPATH — 1967 ISLAND UK ILPS9059
ALEX SPRYOPOULOS PNO (ABC — (B) ALL OF US — 1968 ISLAND UK ILPS9087
BRIAN HENDERSON B (A — (C) DEDICATED TO MARKOS III — 1970 PYE 28132
RAY SINGER G V (A — (D) LOCAL ANAESTHETIC — 1971 VERTIGO 6360 031
SYLVIA SCHUSTER CELLO(A — (E) SONGS OF LOVE & PRAISE — 1972 PHILIPS 6308 089
PETER KESTER D (A — ( ) NIRVANA — 19 METROMEDIA US 1018
BILLY BREMNER G (C
LESLEY DUNCAN V (C — SPOOKY TOOTH (C

N52 NITE CITY N52

RAY MANZAREK K (AB — (A) NITE CITY — 1977 20TH CENTURY T 528
NOAH JAMES V (A — (B) GOLDEN DAYS DIAMOND NIGHTS — 1978 20TH CENTURY 6370 263
PAUL WARREN G V (AB
NIGEL HARRISON B (AB — JIMMY HUNTER D V (AB

N52A NITS N52A

HENK HOFSTEDE K V (A — (A) TENT — 1979 CBS NL 84051
ROB KLOET D V (A
ALEX ROELOFS B V (A — MICHAEL PETERS G V (A

N53 NITTY GRITTY DIRT BAND (DIRT BAND) N53

JEFF HANNA G V (ALL — (A) NITTY GRITTY DIRT BAND — 1967 LIBERTY US LST 7501
JIMMIE FADDEN G HCA(ALL
BRUCE KUNKEL (ACE — (C) RICOCHET — 1967 LIBERTY US LST 7516
GLEN CROSLOSE (— (D) RARE JUNK — 1967 LIBERTY US LST 7611
STEVE PRYKA (— (E) PURE DIRT — 1968 LIBERTY UK 83122
MICHAEL WHITTAKER (— (F) ALIVE — 1969 LIBERTY US LST 7615
RALPH BARR G V (ACDEFG — (G) DEAD & ALIVE(COMP) — 1969 LIBERTY UK LBS83286
WILLIAM McEUEN (— (H) UNCLE CHARLIE & HIS DOG — 1970 LIBERTY US LST7642 UK LBG83345
LES THOMPSON B G V(ACDEFGHJK — (J) ALL THE GOOD TIMES — 1972 UA US UAS5553 UK UAS29284
JACKSON BROWNE V (— (K) WILL THE CIRCLE BE UNBROKEN — 1973 UA US UAT9801
JOHN McEUEN STEEL G V (DEFHJKLMNOPQR — (L) STARS & STRIPES FOREVER — 1974 UA US LA 184 UK UAS29570
DUANE ALLMAN G (— (M) DREAM — 1975 UA US LA469 UK UAS29850
GREGG ALLMAN K V (— (N) DIRT SILVER & GOLD(TRIPLE) — 1976 UA US 9802 + LA 670
STEVE GILLETTE (— (O) DIRT BAND (DIRT BAND) — 1978 UA US LA 854 UK UAK30174
STEVE MARTIN (— (P) AMERICAN DREAM(DIRT BAND) — 1979 UA US LA 974 UK UAG30271
JIM IBBOTSON G V K D (HJKLMN — (Q) GOLD FROM DIRT — 1980 UA UK UAG30275
CHRIS DARROW G V VLN (DFG — (R) MAKE A LITTLE MAGIC — 1980 UA US LT1042 UK UAG30300
JOHN LONDON (H — (S) JEALOUSY — 1981 LIBERTY US LW1106
MIKE RUBINI (H
BYRON BERLINE FDL (H
RUSS KUNKEL (H — JOHN CABLE G V (HJKLMN — JACKIE CLARK B (AJLMN — BILL CUNNINGHAM (H
MAURICE MANSEAU II (H — AL GARTH VLN V SAX(OPR — MEREL BREGANTE D V (OP — RICHARD HATHAWAY B (OPRQR
MICHAEL McDONALD V (O — JAN GARRETT V (O — HADEN GREGG V (O — ROSEMARY BUTLER V (OR
BOB CARPENDER V K(OPQR — MICKEY THOMAS V (O — LEON MEDICA B (OP — BRYAN SAVAGE HRNS(OR
DENNY CHRISTENSEN HRNS (O — AL KOOPER SYN (O — BOBBY MASON G (O — GREG TAYLOR HARP (O
JEFF POLLARD G (P — TONY HASELDON G (P — JIM GORDON HRNS K (H — DAVID PETERS D(P
ROD RODDY K (P — LINDA RONSTADT V (P — LEAH KUNKEL V (P — FUNKY LESTER HRNS(P
MARTY GUINN V (P — BOBBY LAKIND PERC (P — STEVE SHLOSSER D (R — STEVE LUKATHER G (R
KAREN SILVER V (R — M L BENOIT PERC (R — JOHN MACY STEEL(R — KENNY LOGGINS V (R
DAVID HOLSTER V (R — LISA SILVER V (R

N53A NITZINGER N53A

JOHN NITZINGER G V (ABC — (A) NITZINGER — 1972 CAPITOL SMAS 11091
LINDA WARING V D (AB — (B) ONE FOOT IN HISTORY — 1973 CAPITOL SMAS 11122
CURLY BENTON B V (AB — (C) LIVE BETTER ELECTRICALLY — 1976 20TH CENTURY US 518 UK 6370 251
BUGS HENDERSON G (B
PAUL LEIM D (C — JERRY HARRIS B (C — KENNETH WHITFIELD K (C — LAYTON DE PENNING V (C
THE AUSTIN SINGERS (C — DARRELL NORRIS D (C — LARRY WHITE STEEL(C — RANDY REEDE D (C
MARIANNE LINDSEY V (C — PHYLLIS LINDSEY V (C — WHITNEY THOMAS K (C

N54 JACK NITZSCHE N54

JACK NITZSCHE K (ALL — (A) THE LONELY SURFER — 1963 REPRISE US 6101
DAVID MEASHAM (E — (B) HITS OF THE BEATLES — 1964 REPRISE US 6115
LONDON SYPHONY ORCHESTRA(E — (C) CHOPIN' 66 — 1966 REPRISE US 6200
(D) PERFORMANCE — 1970 WB WS 2554
(E) ST GILES CRIPPLEGATE — 1972 REPRISE US 2092
(E) ST GILES CRIPPLEGATE — 197 HARVEST RI UK 2031 INITIAL 006
(F) ONE FLEW OVER THE CUCKOO'S NEST — 1976 FANTASY UK FTA 3004

N55 DON NIX N55

DON NIX (ALL — (A) IN GOD WE TRUST 1971 SHELTER SHE 8902
BARRY BECKETT K (ABC — (B) LIVING BY THE DAYS 1971 ELEKTRA UK K 42096 US EKS74101
CHRIS STAINTON K (B — (C) HOBOS HEROES & STREET CORNER CLOWNS 74 ENTERPRISE ENS 1032
WAYNE PERKINS G V (BC — (D) GONE TOO LONG 1976 CREAM US 1001
JIMMY JOHNSON G (B — (E) SKYRIDER 1979 CREAM US 1011
LARRY RASPBERRY G (AC
ROGER HAWKINS D (BCA DAVID HOOD B (ABC DONALD DUCK DUNN B (B LON PRICE (C
TIPPY ARMSTRONG G (B GIMMER NICHOLSON G (B CLAUDIA LENNEAR V (B JOEY COOPER V (B
MARLINE GREENE V (B KATHI McDONALD V (B DON PRESTON V (B JEANNIE GREENE V (B
FURRY LEWIS V (ABC PETE CARR (C EDDIE HINTON G (CA KLAUS VOORMANN B (C
STEVE SMITH K G (C TIM SMITH (C BOBBY MANUEL (C J A SPELL FDL (A
DARRELL NORRIS D (E ROB KENDRICK G (E ERNIE CHAPMAN B (E LEN GROOME K (E
ROY HALLE G (E JOHN FRY ACC (E WILLIAM C BROWN V (E ORCHESTRA (C

N56 NO DICE N56

ROGER FERRIS V (AB1 — (A) NO DICE 1977 EMI UK EMC 3198 US CAPITOL11733
DAVE MOORE G (AB1 — (B) TWO FACED 1979 EMI UK EMC 3282 US CAPITOL11925
DAVE MARTIN G (AB1 — (1) 1979 SEPT
GARY STRANGE B (AB1
CHRIS WYLES D PERC(AB TONY FERNANDEZ D PERC(1 STEVE SMITH HCA PROD(AB JIMMY JEWEL SAX(AB

N56A NO ENTRY BAND N56A

KENNETH TURLEWICZ V (A — (A) COLD & LONELY LIVES(EP) 1978 KUBE ARTS KA1
ILONA TURLEWICZ G V (A
KENNETH LITTLE G V (A DOUGIE BURNS D (A ROBERT KIRK B (A

N56B EDDIE NOACK N56B

EDDIE NOACK (A — (A) EDDIE NOACK 1980 CHISWICK UK CH21

N57 RAB NOAKES N57

RAB NOAKES G V (ALL — (A) DO YOU SEE THE LIGHT 1970 DECCA UK SKL 5061
GERRY RAFFERTY V (BCD — (B) RAB NOAKES 1972 A&M UK AMLS68119
JOE EGAN V (BCD — (C) RED PUMP SPECIAL 1974 WB US 2777 UK K46284
SID CAIRNS B (B — (D) NEVER TOO LATE 1975 WB UK K56114
DAVIE CRAIG FDL V(B — (E) RESTLESS 1978 RING O RECORDS UK 2339 201
ROBIN McKIDD G HCA(AB — (F) RAB NOAKES 1981 MCA US 3082 UK MCA 3251
ALAN NOAKES G (B
RAY JACKSON HCA (C REGGIE YOUNG G (C WAYNE JACKSON TPT (C JACK HALE TROM (C
TOMMY JACKSON HCA (C ANDREW LOVE HRNS (C SHEL TALMY TAMB (C JOHN CHRISTOPHER G (C
TEDDY IRWIN G (CD WELDON MYRICK G (C JOHN HARRIS K (CD TOMMY COGBILL B (C
KENNY BUTTREY D (C ED LOGAN SAX (C JAMES MITCHELL SAX (C DANNY SEIWELL D (D
CHRISSY STEWART B (D BEN KEITH V G K D (D RALPH MOLINA V (D ARTIE TRAUM G (D
BOB BERTLES SAX (D MIKE DEACON K (D JACK EMBLOW ACC (D RICKY FATAAR D PERC (E
JOHN PERRY B (E RICHARD BRUNTON G (EF JEFF ALLEN D PERC(E PETE ZORN B (E
MARTIN JENNER G (E ALY BAIN FDL (E TERRY MELCHER K V (E MEL COLLINS HRNS (E
TOMMY McCARTHY PIPES(E SUZANNE LYNCH V (E BARBARA DICKSON V (E CHARLIE DORE V (E
BARRY ST JOHN V (E ROGER BROWN V (E TOMMY EYRE K (F ROD CLEMENTS B (F
LIAM GENOCKEY D (F KARL HIMMEL D (B BILL KEMP D (A ALLAN TRAJAN K (A
RONNIE RAE B (A

N57A NOAH N57A

(A) PEACEMAN'S FARM 1972 DUNHILL US 50117

N57B NOBODY'S BUSINESS N57B

BOBBIE HARRISON V PERC(A — (A) NOBODY'S BUSINESS 1978 CBS JAP 7210
JOE JAMMER G (A
TONY STEVENS B (A JERRY FRANK D (A

N57C NOEL & THE RED WEDGE N57C

NOEL V (A — (A) PEER PRESSURE 1982 CBS US 37944
JOHN OTTEN G V (A
THOM MOONEY D (A VEYLER HILDEBRAND B (A KURT KEARNES G (A RICKY PHILLIPS B V (A
FRANKIE BANALI D (A MITCHELL FROOM K (A

N57D NOIR N57D

BARRY FORD D V (A — (A) WE HAD TO LET YOU HAVE IT 1971 DAWN UK DNLS3029
GORDON HUNTE G V (A
TONY COLE K (A ROY WILLIAMS B (A

N58 STEVE NOONAN N58

STEVE NOONAN (A — (A) STEVE NOONAN 196 ELEKTRA US EKS 74017

N58A IAN NORTH N58A

IAN NORTH G V SYN (AB — (A) NEO 1979 AURA AUL 706
(B) MY GIRLFRIENDS DEAD 1981 CACHALOT US CA 900

N58B LARRY NORMAN N58B

LARRY NORMAN K V (ALL — UPON THIS ROCK 1969 KINGSWAY UK DOVE 6
JOHN WETTON B (C — (B) SO LONG AGO THE GARDEN 1973 PHYDEAUX 7776 MGM 4942
KEITH SMART D (C — (C) ONLY VISITING THIS COUNTRY 1974 VERVE US 5092
MICKY KEEN G (C — (D) ROLL AWAY THE STONE 1980 PHYDEAUX US 999/2
ROD EDWARDS K V (C — (E) SOMETHING NEW UNDER THE SUN 1981 PHYDEAUX US
ROGER HAND V (C — (F) ROUGH MIX 2 19 PHYDEAUX US
GORDON GILTRAP G (C
BOB BRADY K (C MIKE GILES D (B MICKEY KEENE G (B MALCOLM DUNCAN SAX(B
ROGER BALL SAX (B GRAHAM PRESKETT VLN (B MARK HEARD G (D JON LINN G (D
TOM HOWARD PNO (D ALEX MACDOUGAL D (D DAVID COY B (D RANDY STONEHILL G V (D
BILLY BATSONE B (D

N58C NEIL NORMAN N58C

NEIL NORMAN G V (A — (A) NOT OF THIS EARTH 1978 GNP US 2111
KIRK BUCHANAN D (A
JOHN GUERIN D (A LARRY KLEIN D (A GARY BRASWELL B (A SAM TAGLIAVORE B (A
LES BAXTER K (A MAX BENNETT B (A KEN HOFFMAN B (A HALL DANIELS K (A
BOB KENT K (A GREG VITO FLT (A LARRY DUNN SYN (A

N59 NORTHWIND N59

HUGH BARR G (A — (A) SISTER BROTHER LOVER — 1971 REGAL ZONOPHONE UK SLRZ 1020
COLIN SOMERVILLE K (A
DAVE SCOTT D (A TOM BRANNAN B V (A BRIAN YOUNG G V (A

N59A NOTATIONS N59A

(A) NOTATIONS — 1976 GEMIGO US 5501 UK WB K56212

N59B NOTE FROM THE UNDERGROUND N59B

(A) NOTES FROM THE UNDERGROUND — 19 VANGUARD US 6502
(B) PSYCHEDELIC VISIONS — 1967 MERCURY 16337 US

N59C NOVA COMBO N59C

STEPHEN DEES B V (A — (A) NOVA COMBO — 1981 POLYDOR UK 2391 523
MICHAEL SHRIEVE D (A
JACK GRIFFITH (A PETE HEWLETT (

N60 NOVA N60

CORRADO RUSTICI G MARIMBA V(ABCD — (A) BLINK — 1976 ARISTA UK ARTY 118
ELIO D'ANNA WIND (ABCD — (B) VIMANA — 1976 ARISTA US 4110 UK ARTY 138
RENATO ROSSET K V (ABCD — (C) WINGS OF LOVE — 1977 ARISTA US 4150 UK SPARTY 102
PERCY JONES B (B — (D) SUN CITY — 1978 ARISTA US 4203
NARADA MICHAEL WALDEN G K(BC
PHIL COLLINS PERC (B ZAKIR HUSSAIN CONGA(B RICK PARNELL D (ACD BARRY JOHNSON B V (AC
LUCIANO MILANESE B V (A FRANCO LOPREVITE D (A DANIELO RUSTICI G (A BARRY SUNJON V B (D
STATIA QAMAR PERC (D
NECLAR SMILE CHOIR V(C

N60A NOVAKS KAPELLE N60A

ERWIN NOVAK D (A — (A) NAKED — 1978 ARIOLA GERM 25 784
HARRY STOJKA G V (A
WALLA MAURITZ V SAX HCA(A PAETER TRAVNICEK B V (A PAUL BRAUNSTEINER G V (A GITTA WALTHER V (A
RENATE MAUERER V (A MARIA NEUHAUSE V (A

N60B NOVA LOCAL N60B

RANDY WINBURN G (A — (A) NOVA 1 — 196
JOE MENDYK G (A
CAM SCHINHAN K (A JIM OPTON B (A BILL LEVASSEUR D (A PHIL LAMBETH G (A

N61 NOVALIS N61

DETLEF JOB G V (BFG — (A) BANISHED BRIDGE — 1973 BRAIN 0001029
FRED MUHLBOCK G V (F — (B) NOVALIS — 1975 BRAIN 0001070
LUTZ RAHN K SYN(ABFG — (C) SOMMERABEND — 1976 BRAIN 0001087
HARTWIG BIEREICHEL D (ABFG — (D) KONZERTE — 1977 BRAIN 0060065
HEINO SCHUNZEL B V (ABF — (E) BRANDUNG — 1977 BRAIN 0060094
CARLO KARGES K G (B — (F) VIELLEICHT BIST DU EIN CLOWN — 1978 BRAIN 0060164
JURGEN WENZEL G V (A — (G) NEUMOND — 1982 VERTIGO UK 6435150
( ) FLOSSENENGER — 1979 AHORN 6 23980

N61A NOYES BROTHERS N61A

STEVE SOLAMAR V G K SYN B D(A — (A) SHEEP FROM GOATS (DBL) — 1980 OBJECT MUSIC OBJ009/0010
STUART PICKERING G (A
STEVE MIRO V G K(A JAE BOYER V (A

N61B NOW N61B

BOBBY ORE (A — (A) THE NOE — 1979 MIDSONG INT MSI014
ROBIN DEE (A
JEFF LENNON (A MANNIE FRANCIS (A

N61C RALF NOWY GROUP N61C

RALF NOWY WIND (AB — (A) LUCIFERS DREAM — 1973 INTERCORD GER 26 015 8
PAUL VINCENT G (AB — (B) ESCALATION — 1974 ATLANTIC GER 40556
LOTHAR MEID B (A
DON ANDERSON K (A BERNIE PROCK PERC (A LIZ VAN NEYENHOFF SITAR(A THOR BALDURSON K (B
VIKTOR DEHRENS TPT V(B MARTIN HARRISON D V(B GARY UNWIN B (AB KEITH FORSEY D (AB
SYLVESTER LEVAY K (AB ANDY MARX G (A AL GROMER SITAR(A SANKAR CHATTEERJEL TAB(A

N62 NUCLEUS N62

IAN CARR TPT (ALL — (A) ELASTIC ROCK — 1970 VERTIGO UK 6360 065 RI 6360 008
KARL JENKINS SAX K(ABCK — (B) WE'LL TALK ABOUT IT LATER — 1970 VERTIGO UK 6360 027
JOHN MARSHALL D (ABCK — (C) SOLAR PLEXUS — 1971 VERTIGO UK 6360 039
CHRIS SPEDDING G (ABCK — (D) BELLADONNA — 1972 VERTIGO UK 6360 076
BOB BERTLES SAX (GHJK — (E) LABYRINTH — 1973 VERTIGO UK 6360 091
KEN SHAW G (GHJK — (F) ROOTS — 1973 VERTIGO UK 6360 100
GEOFF CASTLE K (GHJLMN — (G) UNDER THE SUN — 1974 VERTIGO UK 6350 110
ROGER SUTTON B (GHJFK — (H) SNAKE HIPS ETCETERA — 1975 VERTIGO UK 6360 119 SIRE US 7508
ROGER SELLERS D (HJLM — (J) ALLEY CAT — 1975 VERTIGO UK 6360 124
KENNY WHEELER TPT (CEK — (K) DIRECT HITS (COMP) — 1976 VERTIGO UK 9286 019
BRIAN SMITH WIND (ABCDEFKLM — (L) IN FLAGRANTE DELICTO — 1977 CAPITOL UK 11771 CONTEMP GER 1
TONY ROBERTS WIND (CK — (M) OUT OF THE LONG DARK — 1979 CAPITOL UK 11916 GER 85788
CHRIS KARAN PERC (CK — (N) AWAKENING — 1980 MOOD 24000
TONY LEVIN D (EK
KEITH WINTER K (C JEFF CLYNE B (ABCK DAVE MacRAE K (DEFK ALLAN HOLDSWORTH G (DK
RON MATHESON B (CK ROY BABBINGTON B (DEK CLIVE THACKER D (DEFK GORDON BECK K (DEGK
TREVOR TOMKINS PERC(DEJK JOCELYN PITCHEN G (GFK BRYAN SPRING D (GK KIERAN WHITE V (G
HARRY BECKETT TPT (C CHUCHO B (N NIC FRANCE D (N TONY COE WIND (EK
NORMA WINSTONE V (EK PADDY KINGSLAND SYN (E AUREO DE SOUZA PERC (FK JOY YATES V (F
BILL KRISTIAN B (LM NEIL ARDLEY SYN (M RICHARD BURGESS PERC (M CHRIS FLETCHER PERC (M

N62A NUCLEUS (US) N62A

BOB HORNE K (A — (A) NUCLEUS — 196 MAINSTREAM US 6120
GREG FITZPATRICK B K V(A
JOHN RICHARDSON G (A HUGHIE LEGGAT B V (A DANNY TAYLOR D (A

N63 TED NUGENT & AMBOY DUKES N63

TED NUGENT G B V(ALL (A) THE AMBOY DUKES 1968 MAINSTREAM US 6104
DAVE PALMER D (ABCD (B) JOURNEY TO THE CENTRE OF THE MIND 1968 LONDON UK 8378
STEVE FARMER G (AB (B) " " " " 1968 MAINSTREAM US 6112 GER VOGUE7715
RICK LOBER K (A (C) MIGRATION 1969 LONDON UK 8392
BILL WHITE B (A (C) " " 1969 MAINSTREAM US 6118
JOHN DRAKE V (AB (D) MARRIAGE ON THE ROCKS/ROCK BOTTOM 1970 POLYDOR US 6073 24 4012
ANDY JEZOWSKI V (FG (ABC) JOURNEYS & MIGRATIONS (COMP) 1975 MAINSTREAM US 2/ 801
GREG ARAMA B (BCD (E) SURVIVAL OF THE FITTEST 1974 POLYDOR US 4035 UK 2675 141
ANDY SOLOMON K (BCE (DE) MARRIAGE/SURVIVAL 1977 POLYDOR UK 2664 344
WALT MONAGHAN B (N ( ) BEST OF AMBOY DUKES 19 MAINSTREAM US 6125
ROB RRUZGA B (E (F) CALL OF THE WILD 1974 DISCREET US 2181 UK K59203
K J KNIGHT D (E (G) TOOTH FANG & CLAW 1975 DISCREET US 2203 UK K59205
JOHN ANGELOS V ((FG) CALL/TOOTH(2 ORIGINALS) 1977 WB UK K69202
ROB GRANGE B (EFHJKLG (H) DR SLINGSHOT (COMP) 1975 MAINSTREAM US 414
JOE VITALE D ((I) TED NUGENT 1975 EPIC US 33692 UK 81196
CLIFF DAVIES D V(IJKLMNOP (J) FREE FOR ALL 1976 EPIC US 34121 UK 81397
DEREK ST HOLMES V G (IJKLR (K) CAT SCRATCH FEVER 1977 EPIC US 34700 UK 82010
VIC MASTRIANNI D (FG (L) DOUBLE LIVE GONZO 1978 EPIC US 35069 UK 88282
BRIAN STAFFELD PERC (I (M) WEEKEND WARRIOR 1978 EPIC US 35551 UK 83036
CHARLIE HUHN G V (MNOP (N) STATE OF SHOCK 1979 EPIC US 36000 UK 86092
JOHN SAUTER B (M (O) SCREAM DREAM 1980 EPIC US 36404 UK 86111
GABE MAGNO K FLT(F (P) INTENSITIES IN TEN CITIES 1981 EPIC US 37084 UK 84917
MEATLOAF V (J (Q) GREAT GONZO THE BEST OF 1981 EPIC US 37667 UK 85408
STEVE McRAY K (IJ (R) NUGENT 1982 ATLANTIC UK K50898
BOZ BURRELL V (K
RORY DODD V (K ALAN SPENNER V(K MONTEGO JOE PERC (K TOM WERMAN PERC (IJK
CARMINE APPICE D (R DAVE KISWENEY B V (OPR DAVID HULL B (M RUSTY DAY V PERC(C
LEAH KILBURN V (N REV ATROCIOUS THEODOSIUS G V(G

N63A GARY NUMAN N63A

GARY NUMAN K V G(ALL (A) PLEASURE PRINCIPLE 1979 BEGGARS BANQUET UK BEGA10 GER 146522
JAMES FRIEND (E (A) PLEASURE PRINCIPLE 1979 ATCO US 38120
PAUL GARDINER B (ABCD (B) TELEKON 1980 BEGGARS BANQUET UK BEGA19 GER 146603
JOHN WEBB SYN (EF (B) TELEKON 1980 ATCO US 32103
CHRISTOPHER PAYNE K VLA(ABCD (C) LIVING ORNAMENTS '79 1981 BEGGARS BANQUET UK BEGA24
GARRY ROBSON V (A (D) LIVING ORNAMENTS '80 1981 BEGGARS BANQUET UK BEGA25
CEDRIC SHARPLEY D (ABCD (CD)BOX SET +SINGLE 1981 BEGGARS BANQUET UK BRX 1
BILL CURRIE VLN (A (E) DANCE 1981 BEGGARS BANQUET UK BEGA 28
ROGER TAYLOR D (E (F) I ASSASSIN 1982 BEGGARS BANQUET UK BEGA 40
MICK PRAGUE B (E
MIKE KARN B (E ROB DEAN (E CONNIE FILLIPLOT V (E RUSSELL BELL G V (BCDE
ROGER MASON SYN (CDF DENNIS HAINES K V (EB JESS LIDYARD D(E PINO PALLADINO B (F
CHRIS SLADE D (F JAMES FREUD (B

N63B CRAIG NUTTYCOMBE N63B

CRAIG NUTTYCOMBE G V (A (A) ITS JUST A LIFETIME 1978 A&M US SP 4683
HENRY SPINETTI D (A
DAVE PEGG B (A ANDY FAIRWEATHER LOW V G(A TIM RENWICK G (A DICK MORRISSEY SAX (A
DAVE MARKEE B (A GLYN JONES G (A PETER HOPE EVANS HCA (A DAVE MATTACKS D (A
PAT DONALDSON B (A GEORGIE FAME K (A TONY CARR PERC (A STEVE GREGORY SAX (A
BUD BEADLE SAX (A MALCOLM GRIFFITHS TROM (A BERNIE LEADON G (A

N63C NUMBERS N63C

COLEMAN YORK D V (A (A) ADD UP 1979 BASE CAN 6000
ED BLOCKI B V (A
PETER EVANS V G K(A JIM KENNEDY G V (A

N63D STEVE NUNNERY N63D

STEVE NUNNERY K G V (A (A) STEVE NUNNERY 1973 CREST CREST 6
RICK MAROTTA D (A
PAUL GRIFFIN K SYN(A BUZZY FEITEN G B (A AL GORGONI G (A HUGH McCRACKEN G (A
ELLIOTT RANDALL G (A DAVID SPINOZZA G (A JOHN TROPEA G (A STU WOODS B (A
KIRK HAMILTON B (A ANDY MUSON B (A ALAN SCHWARZBERG D (A

N63E NUNS N63E

(A) THE NUNS 1981 BUTT UK ALSO 001

N63F NURSE WITH WOUND N63F

(A) CHANCE MEETING 1979 UNITED DAIRIES UK 001

N64 NUTZ N64

MICK DEVONPORT G V (ABCD (A) NUTZ 1974 A&M US 3648 UK AMLS68256
DAVID LLOYD G V (ABCD (B) NUTZ TOO 1975 A&M UK AMLS68306
KEITH MULHOLLAND B (ABCD (C) HARD NUTZ 1977 A&M US 4623 UK AMLH64623
JOHN MYLETT D (ABCD (D) NUTZ LIVE CUTZ 1977 A&M UK AMLH68453
RABBIT K (A
CHRIS HUGHES HRNS (A PAUL CARRACK K (B NEIL KERNON K (B KENNY NEWTON K (D

N64A NYL N64A

STEPHANE ROSSINI D (A (A) NYL 1976 URUS FR 000 013
MICHAEL PETEAU G (A
OLIVER PAMELA B V (A BERNARD LAVALLE G (A ELIZABETH WIENER V (A ARIEL KALMA SAX (A
PATRICK QUENTIN SAX (A LOY K (A JANIK TOP B (A

N65 LAURA NYRO N65

LAURA NYRO G V K(ALL (A) MORE THAN A NEW DISCOVERY 1966 VERVE US FTS3020
JOHN TROPEA G (GHJ (B) ELI & 13TH CONFESSION 1968 CBS US 9626 UK 63346
MICHAEL MAINIERI VIBES(H (C) NEW YORK TENDABERRY 1969 CBS US 9737 UK 63510
ANDY NEWMARK D (HJ (D) XMAS & THE BEADS OF SWEAT 1970 CBS US 30259 UK 64157
RICHARD DAVIS B (DGH (E) GONNA TAKE A MIRACLE 1971 CBS US 30987 UK 64770
NYDIA MATA PERC (EGHJ (F) THE FIRST SONGS 1973 CBS US 31410 UK 64991
ELLEN SEELING TPT (H (G) SMILE 1976 CBS US 33912 UK 81171
JEFF KING SAX (H (H) SEASON OF LIGHT 1977 CBS US 34786 UK 82183
JEANIE FINEBERG WIND (H (J) NESTED 1978 CBS US 35449 UK 82917
CARTER COLLINS PERC (GH (K) IMPRESSIONS (COMP) 1980 EMBASSY UK 31864
LABELLE V (E
JIM HELMER D (E LARRY WASHINGTON PERC (E RONNIE BAKER B (E ROLAND CHAMBERS G (E
NORMAN HARRIS G (E LENNY PAKULA ORG (E VINCE MONTANA PERC (E ROGER HAWKINS D (D
EDDIE HINTON G (D BARRY BECKETT VIBES(D DAVID HOOD B (D FELIX CAVALIERE K (DJ

(CONTINUED)

N65 **LAURA NYRO** (CONTINUED) N65

STU SHARF G (D DINO DANELLI D (D CHUCK RAINEY B (D CORNELL DUPREE G (D
RALPH McDONALD PERC (D ASHAD GARABEDIAN OUD (D MICHAEL SZITTAI CIM (D ALICE COLTRANE HARP(D
JOE FARRELL WIND (DG DUANE ALLMAN G (D WILL LEE B (GJ CHRIS PARKER D (G
PAUL MESSING PERC (G HUGH McCRACKEN G (G BOB BABITT B (G ALLEN SCHWARZBERG D (G
JEFF MIRANOV G (G JERRY FRIEDMAN G (G DAVID FRIEDMAN VIBES (G JIMMY MAELEN PERC(G
MICHAEL BRECKER WIND (G RANDY BRECKER TPT (G JOE BECK G (G GEORGE YOUNG FLT(G
RUBENS BASSINI PERC (G GREG BENNETT G (G RICK MAROTTA D (G REIKA KAMOTA KOTO(G
VINNIE CUSANO G (J JOHN SEBASTIAN HCA (J CYRIL CIANFLONE B (J TONY LEVIN B (J
JACK JENNINGS PERC (D NISAKO KOSHIDA KOTO (G

N66 **NYTRO** N66

RONALD A SMITH K (B (A) NYTRO 1977 WHITFIELD US 3019
MARK ENGEL HCA (B (B) RETURN TO NYTROPOLIS 1979 WHITFIELD US WHK3275 UK K56614
CHRIS POWELL SAX (B
ROBERT JUSTICE V (B THEODORE WILLINGHAM B (B JOHN JACKSON D (B EARNEST REDD G (B
KENNETH SCOTT TPT (B LAMORRIS PAYNE TPT (B JAMES GADSON D (B TREY STONE G (B
TERRY SANTIEL PERC (B

O1 **'O' BAND** O1

PIX G V (ABCD (A) A BAND CALLED O 1974 EPIC UK 80120
PETER FILLEUL K (AB (B) OASIS 1975 EPIC UK 80596
MARK ANDERS B (ABCD (C) WITHIN REACH 1976 UA UK UAG29942
DEREK BALLARD D (ABCD (D) THE KNIFE 1977 UA UK UAG30077
CRAIG ANDERS G (ABCD
JEFF BANNISTER K V (CD

O1A **O LEVEL** O1A

(A) WE LOVE MALCOLM McLAREN(EP) 19 KINGS ROAD 002

O2 **OAK** O2

SCOTT WEATHERSPOON G V (A (A) OAK 1979 MERCURY US 3802
RICK PINETTE G V K(A (B) SET THE NIGHT ON FIRE 1980 MERCURY US 4009
GEORGE BORDEN B V (A
DAVID STONE K (A DANNY CARON D (A

O2A **OAKLAHOMA** O2A

STEVE CROSSLEY G V (A (A) OAKLAHOMA 1977 CAPITOL US 11646
SAM FLORES D (A
BEN BLAKEMORE B V (A DON JUNTUNEN G (A

O2B **JOHN O'BANNION** O2B

JOHN O'BANNION V (A (A) JOHN O'BANNION 1981 ELEKTRA US 6E342 UK K52284
JOEY CARBONE K V PERC(A
CARLOS VEGA D (A JAMES NEWTON HOWARD STR(A JIMMY HAAS V (A STAN FARBER V (A
RICHIE ZITO G K (A DENNIS BELLFIELD B (A LENNY CASTRO PERC (A JON JOYCE V (A
BOBBY KIMBALL V (A

O2C **DEKE O'BRIEN** O2C

DEKE O'BRIEN G V (A (A) NIGHTBUS 1976 MILLIGAN LUN 3
MICK MOLLOY G (A
RUAN O'LOCHLAIRN CLAR (A BRENDAN BONASS G (A BOBBY KELLY G (A FIACHRE FRENCH K (A
ROBBIE BRENNAN D (A BRIAN MASTERSON B (A DONAL LUNNY BOUZ(A

O3 **OAKLEY** O3

RITCHIE OAKLEY G (A (A) OAKLEY 1980 NOVA WRCI 957
WAYNE NICHOLSON V (A
BRUCE DIXON B (A BILL McCAULEY K (A DOUG MACKAY D (A

O4 **OBSERVER ALL STARS** O4

(A) DUBBING WITH THE OBSERVER 1978 ATTACK ATLP1017

O5 **OCCASIONAL WORD ENSEMBLE** O5

(A) THE YEAR OF THE GREAT LEAP SIDEWAYS 1970 DANDELION UK 63753

O6 **PHIL OCHS** O6

PHIL OCHS G V (ALL (A) ALL THE NEWS THATS FIT TO SING 1964 ELEKTRA US 7269
VAN DYKE PARKS (E (A) " " " " 19 CHARTERLINE ITALY 22016
JACK ELLIOT (E (B) I AINT MARCHIN' ANYMORE 1965 ELEKTRA US 7287
LINCOLN MAYORGA PNO (EH (C) IN CONCERT 1966 ELEKTRA US 7310
BOB RAFKIN G (H (D) PLEASURE OF THE HARBOUR 1967 A&M US 4133 UK AML 913
KENNY KAUFMAN B (H (E) TAPE FROM CALIFORNIA 1968 A&M US 4148 UK AMLS 919
KEVIN KELLEY D (H (F) REHEARSALS FOR RETIREMENT 1969 A&M US 4181 UK AMLS 934
(G) GREATEST HITS 1970 A&M US 4253 UK AMLS 973
(H) GUNFIGHT AT CARNEGIE HALL 1971 A&M US 9010
(J) CHORDS OF FAME 1974 A&M US 4599 UK AMLM64599
(K) PHIL OCHS SINGS 19 FOLKWAYS US 5320
(L) INTERVIEWS 19 FOLKWAYS US 5321
(M) BROADSIDE TAPES 19 FOLKWAYS US 5362

O6A **HAZEL O'CONNOR** O6A

HAZEL O'CONNOR K V (ABC (A) BREAKING GLASS 1980 A&M US 4820 UK AMLH64820
BOB CARTER G K V(AB (B) SONS & LOVERS 1980 ALBION NL 203215 UK ALB 104
WESLEY McGOOGAN SAX (ABC (C) COVER PLUS 1981 ALBION GER 204047 UK ALB 108
MARY HOPKIN V (C
RICK FORD B (AB ANDY QUNTA K (C NEIL O'CONNOR G (BC ANDY DUNCAN D (AB
TONY VISCONTI PROD K V (AB ED CASE D (C WILD OSCAR B (C GARY TIBBS B (C
JESSICA VISCONTI V (C STEVE KMCH B V (C DELANEY VISCONTI V (C LIZZIE DONOVAN V (C
NICHOLCHAS DONOVAN V (C

O6B **OCTOBER CHERRIES** O6B

PHIL TOWNER D (A (A) BAKING HOT 1980 BAAL BAL89014
STEVE COOPER D (A ( ) WORLD HITS '76 1976 BAAL BE 603
JOHN EDMED STEEL(A
CHRIS GOULSTONE G (A PETER DIAZ G V (A JAY SHOTAM V B (A JEREMIAH STAR K VIBES (A

O6C **OCTOPUS** O6C

TOM MILLER SAX V(A (A) OCTOPUS 1969 ESP DISK US 2000
LANNY BROOKS B V (A
TREVOR KOEHLER SAX (A DION GRODY G K V(A CRAIG JUSTIN D (A

O7 **OCTOPUS** O7

WERNER LITTAU K (ABC (A) THE BOAT OF THOUGHTS 1976 SKY SKY009
SEPP NIEMEYER D PERC (B (B) AN OCEAN OF ROCKS 1978 SKY SKY016
JENNIFER HENSEL V (ABC (C) RUBBER ANGEL 1979 SKY SKY035
CLAUS D KNIEMEYER B (ABC (D) DE 14 BESTE VAN OCTOPUS 1980 GNOME NL 12563
PIT HENSE+ G (ABC
FRANK EULE D (A

O7A **MARTIN O'CUTHBERT** O7A

MARTIN O'CUTHBERT (A (A) NAVIGATOR THROUGH NOWHERE 19 ESOTERIC EEE3

O7B **ODDSOCKS** O7B

ROBIN BROOKS G V (A (A) MEN OF THE MOMENT 1975 SWEET FOLK SFA 030
GERALD CLARIDGE G V BAN(A
NICK PERROT D PERC(A NICK SALOMAN B K(A

O8 **ANN ODELL** O8

ANN ODELL K V (A (A) A LITTLE TASTE 1973 DJM DJLPS 434
MADELINE BELL V (A
LIZA STRIKE V (A DORIS TROY V (A BRUCE ROWLAND D (A BARRY DE SOUZA V (A
RAY COOPER PERC (A RAY FENWICK G (A GARY BOYLE G (A CALEB QUAYE G (A
JOHN GUSTAFSON B (A CHRISTOPHER NEAL HARP (A RICHARD TAYLOR REC (A PETER ROBINSON K (A
ANDREW CAUTHENY WIND (A

O8A **ANDREW ODOM** O8A

ANDREW ODOM V (AB (A) GOING TO CALIFORNIA 197 MCM FR 900 297
EARL HOOKER G (B (B) FARTHER ON THE ROAD 1973 BLUESWAY US 6055
JOHNNY WALKER K (B
JIMMY BOND B (B DAVID FRANCIS D (B

O8B **ODIN** O8B

STUART FORDHAM D PERC (A (A) ODIN 1972 VERTIGO 6360 608
JEFF BEER K PERC V(A
RAY BROWN B V (A ROB TERSTALL G V (A

O9 **JOE O'DONNELL BAND** O9

JOE O'DONNELL VLN (A (A) GAODHAL'S VISION 1978 POLYDOR 2383 465
THEODORE THUNDER D (A
STEVE BOLTON G (A DAVE LENNOX K (A BILL SMITH B (A

O9A **BUDDY ODOR** O9A

(A) BUDDY ODOR IS A GAS 198 ARIOLA UK 5045 NL 200 931

O10 **ODYSSEY** O10

GENE PELLO D (A (A) ODYSSEY 1972 MOWEST US MW 115
BILLY PIERCE V (A
KATHLEEN WARREN K V (A WARNER SCHWEBKE B (A DON DACUS G (A DON PEAK G (A
ROYCE JONES V (A CHRIS DARROW FDL BANJ (A BUDDY EMMONS STEEL(A DAVID T WALKER G (A
CARTER C C COLLINS CONGA(A ROBERT JAMES FLT (A

O10A **OFF BROADWAY** O10A

CLIFF JOHNSON V (AB (A) QUICK TIMES 1980 ATLANTIC US SD 19286
JOHN IVAN G (AB (B) ON 1980 ATLANTIC NL 50695 US 19263
ROB HARDING G (AB
KEN HARCK D (AB MIKE GORMAN B (AB

O10B **OFFENBACH** O10B

GERALD BOULEL V K G(A (A) NEVER TOO TENDER 1976 A&M US 4630 UK AMLH69025
JEAN GRAVEL G V (A
ROGER BELVAL D V (A MICHEL LAMOTHE B V (A

O11 **OHIO EXPRESS** O11

DALE POWERS G ((A) OHIO EXPRESS 1968 BUDDAH US BDS 5018
DEAN KASTRAN B ((A) OHIO EXPRESS 1968 PYE UK NSPL28117
JIM PFAYLER K ((B) SALT WATER TAFFY 1968 BUDDAH US BDS 5021
TIM CORWIN D ((C) CHEWY CHEWY 1968 BUDDAH UK203015 US BDS 5026
DOUGALAS GRASSEL G ((D) MERCY 1969 BUDDAH US BDS 5037
(E) VERY BEST OF THE OHIO EXPRESS 196 BUDDAH US BDS 5058
(F) BEG, BORROW & STEAL 1968 CAMEO US 20000

O12 **OHIO KNOX** O12

PAUL HARRIS K (A (A) OHIO KNOX 1971 REPRISE US 6435
PETER GALLWAY V G (A
RAY NEOPOLITAN B (A DALLAS TAYLOR D (A RUSS KUNKEL CONGAS (A LYNN BLESSING VIBES (A
JOHN SEBASTIAN G V HCA (A DANNY WEIS G (A

O13 **OHIO PLAYERS** O13

CLARENCE 'PEE WEE'SATCHWELL SAX V(MRT FIRST IMPRESSIONS 1968 TRIP US 8029
LEROY 'SUGAR'BONNER G V (MRT OHIO PLAYERS 19 TRIP US 3506
JAMES WILLIAMS D V (MRT OBSERVATIONS IN TIME 1969 CAPITOL US 192
MERVIN PIERCE HRNS (MRT OHIO PLAYERS 19 CAPITOL 11291
MARSHALL JONES B (MRT PAIN 1972 WESTBOUND US 2015
RALPH MIDDLEBROOKS TPT (MR PLEASURE 1973 WESTBOUND US 2017
WILLIE BECK K V (MR ECSTACY 197 WESTBOUND US 2021
RUBENS BASSINI PERC (R PAIN+PLEASURE=ECSTACY 1974 WESTBOUND UK 6309 103
CLARENCE WILLIS G V (R BEST OF 19 WESTBOUND US 304
AZZEDIN WESTON PERC (R SKIN TIGHT 1974 MERCURY UK SRM1 705 UK 6338 497
L DAVID JOHNSON K (T CLIMAX 1974 WESTBOUND US 1003
JIMMY SAMPSON D V (T FIRE 1974 MERCURY US SRM1 1013 UK 9100 009
VINCENT THOMAS PERC V(T FIRE 1974 MERCURY EURO 6338 527
RENNEE ARMAND V (T HONEY 1975 MERCURY US SRM1 1038 UK 9100 014
DANIELLE FOREMAN V (T CONTRADICTION 1976 MERCURY US SRM1 1088 UK 9100 024
ELLEN GOLDMAN V (T RATTLESNAKE 1976 WESTBOUND US 211
SUSAN GRINDELL V (T (M) GOLD 1976 MERCURY US SRM1 1122 UK 9100 030
IRENE REVETS V (T ANGEL 1977 MERCURY US SRM1 3701 UK 9100 037
ABBIE RUBIN V (T MR MEAN 197 MERCURY US SRM1 3717
SALLY STEVENS V (T JASS AY LAY DEE 1978 MERCURY US SRM1 3730
ANN WHITE V (T (R) EVERYBODY UP 1979 ARISTA US AB 4226
VINCE ANDREWS HRNS (T YOUNG & READY 1980 ACCORD US 7120
BRYAN CUMMINGS HRNS (T SKIN TIGHT 1981 MERCURY US 8009
GARY PLATT HRNS (T (T) TENDERNESS 1981 BOARDWALK US 37090 UK EPIC 85041
MARK THOMAS D (T OUCH 1981 BOARDWALK US 33247 UK EPIC 85562
CHUCK RICH STEEL(T
MIKE McDONOUGH G (T CINCINNATI SYM ORCH (T

O13A OINGO BOINGO O13A

STEVE BARTEK G (B — (A) OINGO BOINGO (10" EP) — 1980 IRS US 70400
DANNY ELFMAN G V (B — (B) ONLY A LAD — 1981 A&M NL 64863
RICHARD GIBBS K TROM(B
KERRY HATCH B (B — JOHNN HERNANDEZ D (B — DALE TURNER SAX (B — SAM PHIPPS SAX (B
KON SCHNEIDERMAN SAX (B

O14 O JAYS O14

Musician	Inst		Title	Year / Label		No.
EDDIE LAVERT	V	(ALL	COMIN' THROUGH	1965 IMPERIAL	US	9290
WALTER WILLIAMS	V	(ALL	SOUL SOUNDS	1967 MINIT	US	40008
WILLIAMS POWELL	V	(ALL	(C) BACKSTABBER	1972 EPIC	UK	65257
BOBBY MASSEY	V	(LEFT 72	(C) BACKSTABBER	1973 PHILADELPHIA US 31712	UK	65932
BILL ISLES	V	(LEFT 66	BACK ON TOP	197 BELL US 6014		
			IN PHILADELPHIA	1973 EPIC	UK	65469
WITH			IN PHILADELPHIA	1973 PHILADELPHIA US 32120	UK	65933
LEON CHANCLER	PERC	(MN	LIVE IN LONDON	1974 PHILADELPHIA US 32953	UK	80169
KENNY GAMBLE	PROD	(CFL	LIVE	1974 MFP	UK	50124
THOM BELL	PROD STR	(CL	(F)SHIP AHOY	1974 PHILADELPHIA US 32408	UK	65860
EARL YOUNG	D	(C	SURVIVAL	1975 PHILADELPHIA US 33150	UK	80765
MTUME	PERC	(MN	PEACE	1975 POWER EXCHANGE		PXL2001
LEON HUFF	K	(NCFL	FAMILY REUNION	1976 PHILADELPHIA US 33807	UK	69196
VICTOR CARSTARPHEN	K	(N	MESSAGE IN THE MUSIC	1976 PHILADELPHIA US 34245	UK	81460
DENNIS WILLIAMS	K	(NL	O'JAYS	1976 DJM	UK	22009
MIKE JACKSON	K	(N	(L)SO FULL OF SOUL	1978 PHILADELPHIA US 35355	UK	86066
ROLAND CHAMBERS	G	(CLN	GREATEST HITS	1978 PHILADELPHIA	UK	86058
RAYMOND EVIL	B	(N	(M) IDENTIFY YOURSELF	1979 PHILADELPHIA US 36027	UK	83666
CHARLES COLLINS	D	(NL	(N) YEAR 2000	1980 PHILADELPHIA US 36416	UK	84221
SHORTY MILLER	D	(NL	MY FAVOURITE PERSON	1982 PHILLY	UK	85712
DAVID CRUSE	PERC	(NL				
WALTER SIGLER	PNO	(N				
JAMES SIGLER	K	(NL				

LENNY PAKULA	K	(NC	DENNIS RICHARDSON	K	(NL	DENNIS HARRIS	G	(NC	KIM MILLER	G	(N
WILLIE ROSS	G	(N	MICHAEL FOREMAN	B	(NL	JAMES WILLIAMS	B	(NL	QUINTON JOSEPH	D	(NL
LARRY WASHINGTON	PERC	(CLN	CHARLES WILLIAMS	CONGA	(NL	BUNNY SIGLER	K PROD	(CL	RONNIE BAKER	B	(C
NORMAN HARRIS	G	(C	BOBBY ELI	G	(CL	VINCE MONTANA	PERC	(C	DON RENALDO	STR HRNS	(CL
CECILLE DUVALLE	PNO	(L	JAMES CARTER	D	(L	ALFRED POLLITT	PNO	(L	DAVID WILLIAMS	D	(L
BOB BABBIT	B	(L	JAMES WALKER	B	(L	KIM SIGLER	G	(L	RICKY HICKS	PERC	(L
RAYMOND EARL	B	(L	MORMAN SMITH	B	(L	ROBERT LE GRAND	G	(L	BARBARA INGRAM	V	(L
EVETTE BENTON	V	(L	CARLA BENSON	V	(L						

O15 DANNY O'KEEFE O15

Musician	Inst		Title	Year / Label		No.
DANNY O'KEEFE	G V	(ALL	(A) DANNY O'KEEFE	1971 ATLANTIC	UK	2466001
DOUG HASTINGS	G	(A	(A) DANNY O'KEEFE	1971 COTILLION	US	9036
BILL McPHERSON	WIND	(A	(B) O'KEEFE	1972 SIGNPOST	US	8404
BOB NIXON	K	(A	(B) O'KEEFE	1972 SIGNPOST	UK	4252
CHRIS ETHRIDGE	B	(A	(B) O'KEEFE	1979 CRIMINAL RI	UK	TAKE 1
RICH CROOKS	D	(A	(C) BREEZY STORIES	1973 ATLANTIC	US	SD 7264
EDDIE HINTON	G	(A	(D) SO LONG HARRY TRUMAN	1975 ATLANTIC	US	SD18125
JIMMY JOHNSON	G	(A	(E) AMERICAN ROULETTE	1977 WB	US	BS 3050
ROGER HAWKINS	D	(A	(F) SEATTLE TAPES	1977 FIRST AMERICAN	US	7700
BARRY BECKETT	K	'A	(G) GLOBAL BLUES	1978 WB	US	BS 3314
JOEL TEPP	G	(G	(H) INTRODUCING	1966 PANORAMA	US	105
MIKE BODDIKER	SYN	(G	(I) SEATTLE TAPES VOL 2	1978 FIRST AMERICAN	US	7721
DAVID HOOD	B	(A				

REGGIE YOUNG	G	(B	JOHN CHRISTOPHER	G	(B	BOBBY WOOD	K	(B	SHANE KEISTER	K	(B
BOBBY EMMONS	K	(B	MIKE LEECH	B	(B	GENE CHRISMAN	D	(B	HAYWARD BISHOP	D	(B
HOWARD McNATT	VLN	(B	LEO LEBLANC	STEEL	(B	MARKIE MARKOWITZ	TPT	(B	PHIL OLIVELLA	CLAR	(B
EDDIE BRIGATI	V	(B	DAVID BRIGATI	V	(B	HUGH McCRACKEN	G	(C	DONNY HATHAWAY	K	(C
GORDON EDWARDS	B	(C	BERNARD PURDIE	D	(C	NORMAN PRIDE	PERC	(C	AIRTO MOREIRA	PERC	(C
DOMINIC CORTESE	ACC	(C	MONTEGO JOE	CONGA	(C	ARIF MARDIN	VIBES	(C	DAVID BRUMBERG	G	(C
RICHARD DAVIS	B	(C	CISSY HOUSTON	V	(C	MYRNA SMITH	V	(C	SYLVIA SHEMWELL	V	(C
ANDY STATMAN	MAND	(C	KEN KOSEK	FDL	(C	DR JOHN	K	(C	HUGH McDONALD	B	(C
STEVE MOSLEY	D	(C	GENE ORLOFF	VLN	(C	EMANUEL GREEN	VLN	(C	RICHARD DICKLER	VLA	(C
NORMAN FORREST	VLA	(C	CHARLES McCRACKEN	CELLO	(C	PETR ECKLUND	TPT	(C	JOHN PAYNE	SAX	(C
TOM SCOTT	WIND	(DE	DAVID GRISMAN	MAND	(D	LARRY VANOVER	JUG	(D	RANDY MEISNER	B	(D
LARRY KNECHTEL	K B	(D	DON HENLEY	D V	(D	BERNIE LEADON	V	(D	LINDA RONSTADT	V	(D
ANDREW GOLD	K	(D	JIM FIELDER	B	(D	GARY MALLABER	D	(DE	SNEAKY PETE	STEEL	(D
JOHN BOYLAN	K	(D	ROGER KELLAWAY	K	(DEG	CHUCK DOMANICO	B	(D	JOHN GUERIN	D	(D
JOYCE EVERSON	V	(D	RICHARD GREENE	VLN	(D	JIMMY BOND	B	(D	GLENN FREY	G	(D
DAVID LINDLEY	STEEL	(DE	VEYLER HILDEBRAND	B	(G	MIKE MELVOIN	PNO	(E	REGGIE McBRIDE	B	(E
ALVIN TAYLOR	D	(E	OLIVER BROWN	CONGA	(E	SCOTT STRONG	G	(E	KING ERRISSON	CONGA	(E
CHARLES IRWIN	K	(EG	VINCE MELAMED	K	(EG	DAVE PARLATO	B	(E	ROGER BETHELMY	D	(E
LAUDIR DE OLIVEIRA	PERC	(E	BOBBYE HALL	PERC	(E	STEVE SCHAEFFER	D	(E	PETER WOODFORD	G	(E
JOHN HOBBS	K	(E	THOM MOONEY	D	(G	TONY WILLIAMS	D	(G	BILL CUOMO	PNO	(G
JIM GORDON	D	(G	STEVE FORMAN	PERC	(G	VENETTE GLOUD	V	(G	JIM KELTNER	D	(G
SHARON ROBINSON	V	(G	LARRY MUHOBERAC	PNO	(G	CARMEN TWILLIE	V	(G	BOBBY KING	V	(G
FRANK MAROCCO	ACC	(G	'BIGGY' McFADDEN	V	(G	KAZU MATSUI	SHAKAHACHI	(G	RONNIE BARRON	V	(G
JAY LEWIS	G	(G	JOHN EWING	TROM	(G	BILL BRAUN	PERC	(G	RICHARD NASH	TROM	(G
RUSTY BUCHANAN	V	(G	MIKE BAIRD	CLAR	(G	SUE RICHMAN	V	(G	JOHN ROTELLA	CLAR	(G
LYNDA LAWLEY	V	(G	JOHN COAN	CORNET	(G	PAUL WOLTZ	TUBA	(G			

O16 OKLAHOMA MAFIA O16

LEON RUSSELL K V (
LEVON HELM MAND V(
BOBBY KEYS SAX (— CARL RADLE B (— JESSE ED DAVIS G (— JIMMY MARKHAM (

O17 OLD & IN THE WAY O17

JERRY GARCIA BANJ G V (A — (A) OLD & IN THE WAY — 1975 ROUND RX 103
DAVID GRISMAN MAND V(A
PETER ROWAN G V (A — JOHN KAHN B (A — VASSAR CLEMENTS VLN (A

O18 MIKE OLDFIELD O18

MIKE OLDFIELD G B K+++(ALL — (A) TUBULAR BELLS 1973 VIRGIN US 13135 UK V 2001
STEVE BROUGHTON D (A — (B) HERGEST RIDGE 1974 VIRGIN US 13109 UK V 2013
MUNDY ELLIS V (A — (C) OMMADAWN 1975 VIRGIN US 33913 UK V 2043
JON FIELD FLT (A — (X) BOXED (4LP SET) 1976 VIRGIN UK VBOX1
VIV STANSHALL V (A — (D) INCANTATIONS 1978 VIRGIN UK VDT 101
JABULA PERC (D — (E) EXPOSED (LIVE DBL) 1979 VIRGIN UK VD 2511
SALLY OLDFIELD V (ABDC — (F) PLATINUM 1979 VIRGIN UK V 2141
TERRY OLDFIELD FLT (BCD — (G) Q E 2 1980 VIRGIN UK V 2181
LINDSAY COOPER B OBOE (AB — (H) AIRBORNE 1980 VIRGIN US 13135
CHRIS CUTLER PERC (X — (I) MUSIC WONDERLAND 1981 VIRGIN
WILLIAM MURRAY D (XC — (J) FIVE MILES OUT 1982 VIRGIN EURO 204500
PHIL COLLINS D (G
JUNE WHITING OBOE (B — TED HOBART TPT (B — CHILI CHARLES D (B — CLODAGH SIMMONDS V (BC
PIERRE MOERLEN D (CDF — MIKE FRYE PERC K (EGJ — BENOIT MOERLEN PERC (E — DAVID BEDFORD PERC (EXG
RINGO McDONOUGH BOD (E — NICO RAMSDEN G (EF — PHIL BEER G V (E — PEKKA POHJOLA B (E
PETE LEMER K (EF — TIM CROSS K (EG — MADDY PRIOR V (DE — RAY GAY TPT (E
RALPH IZEN TPT (E — SIMO SALMINEN TPT (E — COLIN MOORE TPT (E — SEBASTIAN BELL FLT (DE
CHRIS NICHOLLS FLT (E — DEBRA BRONSTEIN V (E — EMMA ACHESON V (E — DIANA COULSON V (E
MARY ELLIOTT V (E — MARY CREED V (E — CECILY HAZELL V (E — WENDY LAMPITT V (E
CLARA HARRIS V (E — EMMA SMITH V (E — CATHERINE LOEWE V (E — MIKE LAIRD TPT (D
DAVID HENTSCHEL SYN (G — TIM COOK B (G — MAGGIE RILEY V (G — MORRIS PERT PERC (JC
TOM CROSS K (J — RICK FENN G (G — PADDY MALONEY WIND (BJC — CARL PALMER PERC (J
GRAHAM BROAD D (J — DAVID STRANGE CELLO(C — EDDIE TATANE D (C — PENRHOS KIDS V (C
BRIDGET ST JOHN V (C — ERNEST MOTHLE V (C — JULIAN BAHULA V (C — DON BLAKESON TPT (C
LESLIE PENNING REC (CX — HERBIE PIPES(C — HEREFORD CITY BAND (C — TOM NEWMAN G (A
STRING SECTION (E — ROYAL PHIL (X — LUCKY RANKU D (C — ALLAN SCHWARTZBERG D (F
NEIL JASON B (F — HANSFORD ROWE B (F — FRANCISCO CENTENO B (F — WENDY ROBERTS V (F
SALLY COOPER BELLS(F — DEMELZA C CONGA(F — GUY BARKER TPT (G — RAUL D'OLIVEIRA TPT (G
PAUL NEIMAN TROM (G — PHILIP TODD SAX (G

O18A SALLY OLDFIELD O18A

SALLY OLDFIELD V G K WIND(ABC — (A) WATER BEARER 1978 BRONZE UK BRON 511
DAVE LAWSON SYN (A — (A) WATER BEARER 1978 CHRYSALIS US 1211
FRANK RICOTTI PERC (A — (B) EASY 1979 BRONZE UK BRON 522
BRIAN BURROWS SAX (A — (C) CELEBRATION 1980 BRONZE UK BRON 528
JEAN PRICE HARP (A
TIM WHEATER PERC (A — TREVOR SPENCER PERC (A

O18B KAI OLSSON O18B

KAI OLSSON G V (A — (A) CRAZY LOVE 1979 CHRYSALIS UK CHR 1226
TERRY BRITTEN G (A
MICK GRABHAM G (A — TAFF WILLIAMS G (A — DAVE WINTOUR B (A — HERBIE FLOWERS B (A
COLIN PATTENDEN B (A — ALAN COULTER D (A — STUART ELLIOTTD (A — CHRIS SLADE D (A
BARRIE GUARD G K (A — CLIFF HALL K (A — DAVID MACKAY K (A — RON ASPERY SAX (A
STUART BROOKS TPT (A — TERRY JOHN HRNS (A — STEPHEN NYE OBOE (A — ANDREW JACKMAN MAND(A
STEVE SIMPSON VLN (A — TONY HARRIS VLA (A — DIGBY RICHARDS V (A — LINDA TAYLOR V (A
WAYNE OLSSON V (A

O19 NIGEL OLSSON O19

NIGEL OLSSON D V PERC(ABC — (A) DRUM ORCHESTRA 1972 DJM UK DJLPS417 US UNI 73113
(B) NIGEL OLSSON 1975 ROCKET UK ROLL 2 US PIGL 2158
(C) DRUMMERS CAN SING TOO 1978 ROCKET US PIG 1932
(D) CHANGING TIDES 19 BANG 3649 NL EPIC 84360
(E) NIGEL 1979 CBS US 35792

O19A OLYMPIC O19A

PETR JANDA G V (A — (A) HOLIDAY ON EARTH 1979 SUPRAPHON CZECH 1113 2714
MILAN BROUM B (A
MIROSLAV BERKA K (A — PETR HEJDUK D V (A

O20 OLYMPIC RUNNERS O20

PETE WINGFIELD K V (BDEFG — (A) PUT YOUR MONEY WHERE YOUR MOUTH IS1974 LONDON US PS653
GLEN LEFLEUR D (BDEG — (B) OUT IN FRONT 1975 LONDON US PS658 UK SHU 8483
JO JAMMER G (BDEFG — (C) DONT LET UP 1975 LONDON US PS668
GEORGE CHANDLER V (BDEFG — (D) HOT TO TROT 1977 LONDON US PS678
DELISLE HARPER B (BDEFG — (D) HOT TO TROT 1977 CHIPPING NORTON UK NOR 1
MIKE VERNON PERC (BDEFG — (E) KEEPING IT UP 1978 RCA PL 25124
PEARLY GATES V (B — (F) PUTTIN' IT ON YOU 1978 POLYDOR POLD5015
JIMMY HAYNES V (B — (G) OUT OF THE GROUND 1979 RCA PL 25195
GLEN PENNISTON D (F — (H) ITS A BITCH 1979 POLYDOR 2383 549
STEVE GREGORY WIND (F — (I) DANCEALOT 1979 POLYDOR US 16196
JOY YATES V (D
SIMON PHILLIPS D (F — JACQUIE SULLIVAN V (D — GEORGE CHISHOLM HRNS (F

O21 OLYMPICS O21

WALTER WARD V (ALL — HULLY GULLY 19 ARVEE US 423
EDDIE LEWIS V (ALL — DANCE BY THE LIGHT OF THE MOON 19 ARVEE US 424
CHARLES FIZER V (ALL — PARTY TIME 19 ARVEE US 429
MELVIN KING V (ALL — OLYMPICS 19 JAYBOY SSX 2008
DO THE BOUNCE 19 TRIDISC US 1001
SOMETHING OLD SOMETHING NEW 19 MIRWOOD US 7003
OLYMPICS SING 19 POST US 8000

O22 OMAHA SHERRIFF O22

PAUL MUGGLETON G V (A — (A) COME HELL OR HIGH WATER 1977 GOODEARTH UK GDS803 US RCA 2022
BOB NOBLE K (A
CHRIS BIRKETT G V PERC(A — TONY VISCONTI B (A — MICHAEL SPENCER ARSCOTT D HCA V(A

O23 MICHAEL OMARTIAN O23

MICHAEL OMARTIAN K (ALL — (A) ONWARD 197 ABC ABC 903
STORMIE OMARTIAN (D — (B) WHITE HORSE 197 MYRRH MYRA1048 US DUNHILL 50185
(C) ADAM AGAIN 1979 MYRRH MYR 1058
(D) SEASONS OF THE SOUL 1979 MYRRH MYR 1073

O24 OMEGA O24

JANOS KABOR V (ALL — (A) RED STAR — 1963 QUALITON HUN
GYORGY MOLNAR G (ALL — (B) FREDDIE THE BUGLER & TERRIBLE — 1969 QUALITON HUN
LASLO BENKO K SYN (ALL — (C) ON THE HIGHWAY AT NIGHT — 19 QUALITON HUN SLPX17426
TAMAS MIHALY B (ALL — (C) OMEGA — 1973 BELLAPHON BLP19147 BAC2017
FERENC DEBRECENI D PERC(ALL — (C) OMEGA — 1975 PASSPORT US 98007
(D) 10000 LEPES — 19 QUALITON HUN LPX17400
(E) ELO — 19 PEPITA HUN 17443
(E) ON TOUR — 197 BELLAPHON GER 2527
(F) OMEGA 5 — 19 PEPITA HUN 17457
(F) 2000 YEARS — 19 BELLAPHON GER 19175
(G) NEM TUDOM A NEVED — 19 PEPITA HUN 17483
(H) HALL OF FLOATERS IN THE SKY — 1976 DECCA UK 5219 BELLAPHON GER 19218
(I) III — 19 BELLAPHON GER 19191 BAC 2030
(J) IDORABLO — 19 PEPITA HUN 17523
(J) TIME ROBERS — 1976 DECCA UK 5243
(K) SKYROVER — 19 PEPITA HUN 17570 FANTASY US 9560
(K) SKYROVER — 1978 BELLAPHON GER BAC2052
(L) ELO KISSTADITION — 19 PEPITA HUN 17619/20
(M) GANNAPOLIS — 1978 BELLAPHON GER 2061
(N) WORKING — 1981 WEA 58329

O24A ONE (UK) O24A

ALAN MARSHALL G V HCA (A — (A) ONE — 1969 FONTANA UK STL 5539
BOBBY SASS G K (A
NORMAN LEPPARD WIND (A — KEVIN FOGARTY G (A — BRENT FORBES B (A — CONRAD ISADORE D (A

O24B ONE (US) O24B

MARK BAKER D (A — (A) ONE — 1972 GRUNT US FTR 1008
REALITY D BLIPCROTCH V PERC(A
ROGER CRISSINGER K (A — FRANK TREVOR FEE B (A — DONALD ENSSLIN G BAN(A — THEODORE TEIPEL FLT HCA K(A
MARV GRANAT G SITAR DULC(A — SARAH OPPENHEIM AUTOHARP(A — LAURIE PAUL V (A

O24C 100% PROOF O24C

STEVE WRIGHT G V (A — (A) 100% PROOF — 1981 MYRRH MYR 1007
CHARLIE WILSON G V (A
STEVE HANSON B (A — PHIL WRIGHT D (A

O25 ONE O ONERS (101ERS) O25

CLIVE TIMPERLEY G (A — (A) ELGIN AVE BREAKDOWN — 1981 ANDALUCIA UK AND101
RICHARD DUDANSKI D V (A
DAN KELLEHER B K V(A — JOE STRUMMER G V (A — MOLE B (A

O26 ONLY ONES O26

MIKE KELLIE D (ABC — (A) THE ONLY ONES — 1978 CBS UK 82830
ALAN MAIR B (ABC — (B) EVEN SERPENTS SHINE — 1979 CBS UK 83451
JOHN PERRY G K (ABC — (C) BABY'S GOT A GUN — 1980 CBS US 36504 UK 84089
PETER PERRETT G V (ABC — (D) SPECIAL VIEW — 1979 EPIC US 36199
KOULLA KAKOULLI V (AB
ADAM MAITLAND K SAX(B — RABBIT BUNDRICK K (B — ROBERT ASH PROD (A — MICK GALLAGHER K(A
GORDON EDWARDS K (A — RAPHAEL & FRIENDS HRNS(A

O27 YOKO ONO O27

YOKO ONO V (AB — (A) FLY (DBL) — 1971 APPLEUS 3380 UK SPTU 101/2
JOHN LENNON G V (A — (B) FEELING THE SPACE — 1973 APPLE US 3412 UK SAPCOR26
ERIC CLAPTON G (A — (C) SEASONS OF GLASS — 1981 GEFFEN US 2004 UK K99164
HUGH McCRACKEN G (C
RINGO STARR D (A — KLAUSS VOORMANN B (A — JIM KELTNER D (AB — JIM GORDON D (A
BOBBY KEYS SAX (A — CHRIS OSBORNE (A — JOE JONES (A — DAVID SPINOZZA G (A
KEN ASCHER K (B — BOB BABITT B (B — ANDREW SMITH D (B — JEREMY STEIG FLT(B
GORDON EDWARDS B (B — ARTHUR JENKINS PERC (BC — DAVID FRIEDMAN VIBES(BC — RICK MAROTTA D (B
DON BROOKS HCA (B — SNEAKY PETE STEEL (B — MICHAEL BRECKER SAX (BC — JOHN OCEAN G (B
EARL SLICK G (C — GEORGE SMALL K (C — ANTHONY DAVILIO G (C — TONY LEVIN B (C
JOHN SIEGLER B (C — ANDREW NEWMARK D (C — GEORGE'YOUNG'OPALISKY SAX(C — RONNIE CUBER SAX(C
HOWARD JOHNSON TUBA (C

O27A OPA O27A

HUGO FATTORUSO K V (AB — (A) GOLDEN WINGS — 1976 MILESTONE M9069
GEORGE FATTORUSO D V (AB — (B) MAGIC TIME — 1977 MILESTONE M9078
RINGO THIELMANN B V (AB
HERMETO PASCOAL FLT (AB — DAVID AMRO G (AB

O27B THE OPEN MIND O27B

(A) THE OPEN MIND — 19 PHILIPS UK SBL 7893

O28 OPEN ROAD O28

JOHN CARR D (A — (A) WINDY DAZE — 1971 GREENWICH GSLP 1001
MIKE THOMSON B (A
SIMON LANZON K (A — BARRY HUSBAND G V (A

O28A OPERATION BASEBALL O28A

(A) ON THE CASE — 19 CHESS US 1549

O28B ORAN UTAN O28B

(A) ORAN UTAN — 1974 BELL US 6054

O28C ORANGE JUICE O28C

EDWYN COLLINS G V (A — (A) YOU CANT HIDE YOUR LOVE FOREVER — 1982 POLYDOR POLS 1057
JAMES KIRK G V (A
DAVID McCLYMONT B (A — STEVEN DALY D (A — MIKE McEVOY K (A — JACKIE CHALLENOR V(A
ESTHER BYRD V (A — LORENZA JOHNSON V (A — ADAM KIDRON PROD (A

O28D ORANGE PEEL O28D

PETER BISCHOF V PERC(A — (A) ORANGE PEEL — 19 BELLAPHON GER 19036
CURT CRESS D (A
LESLIE LINK G (A — HEINE MOHN B (A — RALPH WILRHEISS ORG (A

Musician	Instruments	Title	Year	Label	Country	Number
ROY ORBISON	G V (ALL	LONELY & BLUE	1963	LONDON		SHU2342
		LONELY & BLUE	196	MONUMENT		14002
		GREATEST HITS	196	MONUMENT	US	18000
		CRYING	1963	LONDON		SHU6229
		CRYING	19	MONUMENT	US	14007
		CRYING	19	MONUMENT	US	6620
		IN DREAMS	1963	LONDON	UK	SHU8108
		IN DREAMS	196	MONUMENT	US	18003
		IN DREAMS	196	MONUMENT	US	6620
		EXCITING SOUNDS	1964	EMBER		
		OH PRETTY WOMAN	1964	LONDON	UK	8207
		THERE IS ONLY ONE	1965	LONDON	UK	8252
		THERE IS ONLY ONE	1965	MGM	US	4683
		THE ORBISON WAY	1966	LONDON	UK	8279
		THE ORBISON WAY	1966	MGM	US	4322
		THE CLASSIC	1966	LONDON	UK	8297
		THE CLASSIC	1966	MGM	US	4379
		SINGS DON GIBSON	1967	LONDON	UK	8318
		SINGS DON GIBSON	1967	MGM	US	4424
		CRY SOFTLY LONELY ONE	1968	LONDON	UK	8357
		CRY SOFTLY LONELY ONE	1968	MGM	US	4514
		FASTEST GUITAR ALIVE	1968	LONDON	UK	8358
		ORBISONGS	196	MONUMENT		5004
		ORBISONGS	196	MONUMENT		18035
		EARLY ORBISON	196	MONUMENT		5013
		EARLY ORBISON	196	MONUMENT		18023
		GREATEST HITS	19	MONUMENT		5007
		GREATEST HITS	19	MONUMENT		64663
		GREATEST HITS	19	MONUMENT	US	6619
		GREATEST HITS	19	MONUMENT		14009
		MORE GREATEST HITS	19	MONUMENT		5014
		MORE GREATEST HITS	19	MONUMENT		6621
		MORE GREATEST HITS	19	MONUMENT		18024
		VERY BEST OF	19	MONUMENT		18045
		VERY BEST OF	19	MONUMENT		6622
		AT THE ROCKHOUSE	196	SUN	US	1260
		AT THE ROCKHOUSE	1980	CHARLY	UK	CRM2007
		MANY MOODS OF	1969	MGM	US	4636
		GREAT SONGS	1969	MGM	US	4659
		HANK WILLIAMS SONGS	1969	MGM	US	4683
		THE BIG O	1970	LONDON		8496
		THE ORIGINAL SOUND	1970	SUN	US	113
		THE ORIGINAL SOUND	197	SUN	UK	6467 005
		ROY ORBISON SINGS	1972	LONDON	UK	8435
		ROY ORBISON SINGS	197	MGM	US	4835
		MEMPHIS	1973	LONDON	UK	8445
		MEMPHIS	1973	MGM	US	4867
		THE BEST OF	1973	BOVEMA	EURO	05491411
		THE BEST OF	19	TRIP	US	
		ALL TIME GREATEST HITS	1973	MONUMENT		67290
		ALL TIME GRESTEST HITS	197	MONUMENT		8600
		ALL TIME GREATEST HITS	1973	MONUMENT	US	31484
		THE EXCITING	1974	HALLMARK	UK	SHM 824
		MILESTONES	1974	MGM	US	4934
		IM STILL IN LOVE WITH YOU	1976	MERCURY	US	SRMI1045
		ORBITING	19	DESIGN	US	DLP 164
		STARS OF THE 60s	1974	EMI	EURO	05092542
		THE BIG O	1975	CHARLY	UK	CRR300008
		THE BEST OF	1975	ARCADE	UK	ADEP19
		MONUMENTAL HITS	1975	MONUMENT	UK	69147
		MONUMENTAL HITS VOL2	1975	MONUMENT	UK	69188
		FOCOS ON	1976	DECCA		FOS/U15/6
		REGENERATION	1977	MONUMENT	UK	81809
		REGENERATION	1977	MONUMENT	US	7600
		LAMINAR FLOW	1979	ASYLUM	UK	K53092
		LAMINAR FLOW	1979	ELEKTRA	US	6E 198
		AT THE ROCK HOUSE	1980	CHARLY	UK	CRM2007

O29A ORCHESTRAL MANOEUVRES IN THE DARK O29A

Musician	Instruments	Title	Release
PAUL HUMPHREYS	V K PERC(ABC	(A) ORCHESTRAL MANOEUVRES IN THE DARK	1980 DINDISC UK DID2 GER 20297
ANDY McCLUSKEY	V G K(ABC	(B) ORGANISATION	1980 DINDISC UK DID6 GER 202971
DAVE FAIRBAIRN	G (A	(C) ARCHITECTURE & MORALITY	1981 DINDISC UKDID12 GER 204016
MALCOLM HOLMES	PERC D(ABC	(C) ARCHITECTURE & MORALITY	1981 CBS US 37721
MARTIN COOPER	SAX (AC		
MIKE HOWLETT	PROD (BC		
RICHARD MAINWARING	(C		

MICHAEL DOUGLAS K (C DAVID HUGHES TAPES (C CHESTER VALENTINE PROD(A

O29B ORCHIDS O29B

Musician	Instruments	Title	Release
LAURIE BELL	D V (A	(A) ORCHIDS	1980 MCA UK MCF3067 US 3235 GER 202177
JAN KING	V G K(A		
LAURIE McALLISTER	B V (A		

SUNBIE SINN G PNO V(A CHE ZURO G K V(A KIM FOWLEY PROD (A

O29C ORIENTAL WIND O29C

Title	Year	Label	Country	Number
(A) BAZAAR	1981	SONET	UK	SNTF 864

O30 OREGON O30

Musician	Instruments	Title	Year	Label	Country	Number
PAUL McCANDLESS	(FG	(A) MUSIC OF ANOTHER PRESENT ERA	1974	VANGUARD		VSD79326
GLEN MOORE	(FG	(B) DISTANT HILLS	1974	VANGUARD		VSD79341
RALPH TOWNER	(FG	(C) WINTER LIGHT	1975	VANGUARD		VSD79350
COLLIN WALCOTT	(FG	(D) IN CONCERT	1975	VANGUARD		VSD79358
ELVIN JONES	(FG	(E) FRIENDS	1975	VANGUARD		VSD 79370
ZBIGNIEW	VLN (G	(F) TOGETHER	1977	VANGUARD		VSD79377
		(G) VIOLIN	197	VANGUARD		VSD79397
		(H) OUT OF THE WOODS	1978	ELEKTRA		K52101
		(I) IN PERFORMANCE	1980	eELEKTRA	US	304

O30A ORGANISATION O30A

RALF HUTTER ORG (A (A) TONE FLOAT 1970 RCA SF8111
BASIL HAMMOUDI PERC V (A
FLORIAN SCHNEIDER-ESLEBEN FLT(A BUTCH HAUF B PERC (A FRED MONICKS D PERC(A

O30B ORGINAL MIRRORS O30B

PETE KIRCHER D (AB (A) ORIGINAL MIRRORS 1980 MERCURY UK 9102 039 6310 050
STEVE ALLEN V (AB (B) ORIGINAL MIRRORS 1980 ARISTA US 4269
IAN BROUDIE G (AB (B) HEART TWANGO & RAW BEAT 1981 VERTIGO UK 6359 046
JONATHAN PERKINS K (AB
PHIL SPALDING B (B JIMMY HUGHES B (AB MIKE HOWLETT PROD(B

O31 ORIGINALS O31

WALTER GAINES ((A) GREEN GROW THE LILACS 1969 SOUL US 716
C P SPENCER (A (B) PORTRAIT 1970 SOUL US 724
HENRY DIXON ((C) NATURALLY TOGETHER 1971 SOUL US 729
FREDERICK GORMAN ((D) DEFINITIONS 1972 SOUL US 734
JOE STUBBS ((E) GAME CALLED LOVE 1974 SOUL US 740
TY HUNTER ((F) CALIFORNIA SUNSET 1975 MOTOWN US 826 UK 11287
(G) COMMUNIQUE 1976 SOUL US 746 UK TAMLA12034
(H) DOWN TO LOVE TOWN 1977 SOUL US 749 UK TAMLA12054
(J) ANOTHER TIME ANOTHER PLACE 1978 FANTASY US 9546 UK FT542
(K) COME AWAY WITH ME 1978 FANTASY US 9577
(L) YESTERDAY & TODAY 19 POLYDOR US 37075

O31A ORION O31A

(A) SOMETIMES WORDS JUST GET IN THE WAY 75 LONDON US 44230
REBORN 197 CHARLY CRL 5020
SUNRISE 1980 SUN US 1017
ROCKABILLY 1981 SUN US 1021
COUNTRY 1981 SUN US 1019

O32 ORLEANS O32

LARRY HOPPEN G V (ABCDEFG (A) ORLEANS 1975 ABC US 795 UK 5107 NL 27141
LANCE HOPPEN B V (ABCDEFG (B) LET THERE BE MUSIC 1975 ASYLUM US 7E 1029 UK SYL 9023
JOHN HALL G V (ABCDF (B) LET THERE BE MUSIC 1975 ASYLUM UK K53011
WELLS KELLY D V K(ABCDEF (C) WAKING & DREAMING 1976 ASYLUM US 7E 1070 UK K53044
JERRY MAROTTA D (CFG (D) BEFORE THE DANCE 1977 ABC US 1058 UK ABCL6224
MICHAEL BRECKER SAX (C (E) FOREVER 1979 INFINITY US 9006 UK 2004
RICK MAROTTA D (F (F) ORLEANS 1980 MCA US 5110
GERALDO VALEZ PERC(F (G) ONE OF A KIND 1982 RADIO US 90012/1
BLUE MITCHELL TPT (C
LINDA RONSTADT V (C BOB LEINBACH K V (EF R A MARTIN HRNS K V(AEF JIMMY MAELEN PERC(EG
RUBENS BASSINI PERC (E BASIL TYLER HRNS (F PHIL COLLINS V (F MORRIS PERT PERC(F
LANE HOPPEN V K (FG JAY BECKINSTEIN SAX (F BILL BROWN HRNS (F MIKE MUGRAGE G V (G
BEN WISCH PROD (G DENNIS AMERO G (G DON SILVER PROD (G STRING SECTION (E

O32A ROBERT ELLIS ORRALL O32A

ROBERT ELLIS ORRALL K V (A (A) FIXATION 1981 WHY UK WH02
KOOK LAWRY G V (A
DAVID STEFANELLI D V (A DON WALDEN B V (A JOHN PAYNE SAX (A ED GRENGA (A
DOUG MILLETT G V (A JIMMY MAELEN PERC (A RANDY ROOS G (A JOSIAH SPAULDING PROD(A
MICHAEL PILLOT PROD (A

O33 ORLONS O33

STEVE CALDWELL V (12 ALL THE HITS 19 CAMEO US 1033
MARLENA DAVIS V (12 SOUTH STREET 19 CAMEO US 1041
ROSETTA HIGHTOWER V (12 NOT ME 19 CAMEO US 1054
AUDREY BRICKLEY V (1 BIGGEST HITS 19 CAMEO US 1061
SHIRLEY BRICKLEY V (1 GOLDEN HITS 196 CAMEO US 1067
DOWN MEMORY LANE 19 CAMEO US 1073
THE BEST OF 1977 LONDON UK HAU 8594
(1) PRE 1959 (2) POST 1959

O33A ORPHAN O33A

ERIC LILLEQUIST V G (C (A) EVERYONE LOVES TO SING 1972 LONDON US PS 614 UK SHU 8438
STUART SCHULMAN B K V((B) ROCK & REFLECTION 1973 LONDON US PS 630 UK SHU 8452
RICHARD ADELMAN D ((C) MORE ORPHAN THAN NOT 1974 LONDON US PS 645 UK SHU 8475
BILL KEITH STEEL(
DAVE CONRAD B (C BILL ELLIOTT K (BOB CHOUINARD D (C DEAN ADREN G V (C
BRUCE McPHERSON K V (C DAVID WOODFORD SAX (C KERRY BLOUNT SAX (C JAY DEWALD TPT (C
BILL SEISM TPT (C LLOYD BASKIN ORG (C DAN FRYE K (C SANDRA BASKIN V (C
SUZANNE SWAN V (C SHARON BROWN V (C

O33B ORPHAN EGG O33B

JIM BATE V (A (A) ORPHAN EGG 1968 CAROLE GER 9621 US CARS8004
GEORGE LORIX D (A
PAT GALLAGHER G V (A LARRY SMITH B (A DAVE MONLEY G K (A

O33C ORPHEUS O33C

ERIC GULLIKSEN B V (ABC (A) ORPHEUS 1967 MGM US 4524
K P BURKE HCA (D (B) ASCENDING 1968 MGM US SE4569
JACK McKENES G V (ABC (C) JOYFUL 1968 MGM US 4599
BRUCE ARNOLD G V (ABCD (D) ORPHEUS 1969 BELL US 6061
HARRY SANDLER D V (ABC
STEVE MARTIN V (D BERNARD PURDIE D (D HOWARD HARSH B (D ELLIOTT SHERMAN K (D

O33D OSANNA O33D

ELIO D'ANNA SAX (ABCDE (A) L'UOMO 197 FONIT LPX 10 +1976 MF 103
DANIEL RUSTICI G (ABCDE (B) MILANO CALIBRO 9 1974 FONIT LPX 14 +PETER PILPS9001
MASSIMO GUARINO D (ABCD (C) PALEPOLI 197 FONIT LPX 19
LELLO BRANDI B (ABCD (D) LANDSCAPE OF LIFE 197 FONIT LPX 32 +PETER PILPS9007
LINO VAIRETTI K SYN V(ABCD (E) UNO 1974 FONIT LPX 26 +MOTORS MT 44027
ENZO VALICELLI D (E

O33E OZZY OSBOURNE(BLIZZARD OF OZ) O33E

OZZY OSBOURNE V (ALL (A) BLIZZARD OF OZ 1980 JET US 36812 UK JETLP234
BOB DAISLEY B V (ABC (B) DIARY OF A MADMAN 1981 JET UK 237
RANDY RHODES G (ABC (C) MR CROWLEY (EP) 1981
LEE KERSLAKE D (A (D) TALK OF THE DEVIL 1982 JET UK 401
BRAD GILLIS G (D
RUDI SARZO B (DB (TOMMY ALDRIDGE D (AB DON AVERY K (A BERNIE TORME G (

O33F OSCAR O33F

BRIAN McGLADDERY G V (A — (A) OSCAR — 1975 BUK UK 2001 US 22301
GARY McDOUGAL B (A — (B) TWILIGHT ASYLUM — 1976 DJM UK DJF 20494
TONY BANFORD K (A — (C) COBBLESTONE HEROES — 1977 DJM UK DJF 20516
KEVIN PARROT G (A
ROGER TWEEDALE PERC (A

O33G OSAMU O33G

OSAMU KITAJIMA G KOTO V(A — (A) OSAMU — 1977 ISLAND ILPS9426 US ANTILLES7016
JOHN HUG G MAND (A
GEOFFREY HALES D PERC(A DENNIS BELFIELD B (A BRIAN WHITCOMB G K SYN(A TATSUYA SANO (A
GEORGE MARINELLI G (A MINNIE RIPERTON V (A

O33H WAVIS O'SHAVE O33H

WAVIS O'SHAVE V (— (A) DENNIS SMOKES TABS(EP) — 19 COMPANY CR 003
(B) ANNA FORD'S BUM — 19 ANTI POP AP 2

O33J JEFF OSBORNE O33J

JEFF OSBORNE (A — (A) AYMUK — 1982 A&M UK AMLH 64896

O33K JOHNNY OSBOURNE O33K

JOHNNY OSBOURNE ~~V~~ (AB — (A) FALLY OVER — 1981 GREENSLEEVES UK GREL12
~~(B) IN NAH DISCO STYLE~~ — 1981 CHA CHA UK 0010

O34 OSIBISA O34

TEDDY OSEI FLT PERC (ALL — (A) OSIBISA — 1971 MCA UK MDKS8001 +74 MCG 3508
LOUGHTY AMAO SAX (ABCD — (A) OSIBISA — 197 DECCA US 75285 +MCA MCA32
ROBERT BAILEY K (ABCDGK — (B) WOYAYA — 1971 MCA UK MDKS8005 +74 MCD 3506
SPARTACUS R B (ABCD — (B) WOYAYA — 197 DECCA US 75327 +MCA MCA43
WENDEL RICHARDSON G (ABCDHK — (C) HEADS — 1972 MCA UK MDKS8007 +74 MCG 3514
MAC TONTOH TPT (ALL — (C) HEADS — 197 DECCA US 75368 MCA GER MAPS6283
SOL AMARFIO D (ALL — (D) BEST OF — 1974 MCA UK MCF 2575
KIKI GYAN K (FH — (E) HAPPY CHILDREN — 1973 WB US BS 2732 UK K56022
KOFI AYIVOR PERC (EFGH — (F) OSIBIROCK — 1974 WB US BS 2802 UK K56048
PAUL GOLLY G (FH — (G) SUPER FLY TNT — 1974 BUDDAH US 5136 UK 2318 087
GORDON HUNTE G V (G — (G) SUPER FLY TNT — 197 BUDDAH UK BDLP4020
JEAN ROUSSEL K (E — (H) WELCOME HOME — 1975 BRONZE UK ILPS9355 RI BRNA355
MIKE ODUMUSU B (HK — (H) WELCOME HOME — 1977 ANTILLES US 7051
JEAN MANDENGUE B (EFGHL — (J) OJAH AWAKE — 1976 BRONZE UK ILPS9411 RI BRNA 411
DAKU 'POTATO' K (KL — (J) OJAH AWAKE — 197 ANTILLES US 7058
SONIA LEKHELA V (K — (K) BLACK MAGIC NIGHT — 1977 BRONZE UK BRSP 3
NTOBI MDUDU V (K — (L) MYSTIC ENERGY — 1980 CALIBRE UK CAB1002
TINY CONCO V (K
LINDA CONCO V (K KARI BANNERMAN G (L EMA YAWKOBA RENTZOS K V(L KATHY T V (L
ROBERT ABIA G B (L ALTON EDWARDS V (L REBOP KWAKU BAAH PERC (L PAM DOUGLAS V (L
MIQUEL BROWN V (L CANDY McKENZIE V (L

O35 LEE OSKAR O35

LEE OSKAR HCA V (AB — (A) LEE OSKAR — 1976 UA US UALA 594
(OSKAR LEVETIN HANSEN) — (B) BEFORE THE RAIN — 1978 MCA UK MCF2870 US ELEKTRA 6E150
B B DICKERSON B (A — (C) LEE OSKAR — 1980 MCA UK MCF3060 US 37114
GREG ERRICO K D (A
ROBERT VEGA B (A STEVE BUSFELD G (A CHEPITO AREAS CONGA(A WENDY HAAS V (A
HERMAN EBERITZSCH PNO (A MOSES WHEELOCK CONGA(A HAROLD BROWN D (A MONTY STARK PERC (A
JULIA TILLMAN V (A MAXINE WILLARD V (A LANI GROVES V (A EDNA WRIGHT V (A
CHARLES MILLER SAX (A JERRY FISHER V (A CONNIE FISHER V (A NITO MEDINA G (A
LONNIE JORDAN PERC K (A PAPA DEE ALLEN PERC (A HOWARD SCOTT G V (A

O36 OSMOSIS O36

CHARLIE MARIANT WIND (A — (A) OSMOSIS — 1970 RCA US LSA3010 LSP 4369
BOBBY KNOW V (A
DANNY COMFORT B (A LOU PETERSON D (A BOBBY CLARK PERC (A CHARLIE BECHLER K (A
ANDY STENBORN G (A

O36A OS MUNDI O36A

ANDREAS VILLAIN B (A — (A) LATIN MASS — 1980 METRONOME GER 15381
CHRISTOPH BURSE G D V(A — (B) 43 MINUTEN — 1972 BRAIN GER 1015
CONNY PLANK G (B
DIETRICH MARKGRAF WIND (A HARTMUT SEIDEL B (A UDO ARNDT G K (A DAVID KALCKREUTH K (A
BUDDY MANDLER D (A MIKRO RILLING STR V(A ERIK SPIEKERMAN G (B

O37 OTGER DICE O37

ANTON VERHAGEN V (A — (A) GARDEN OF PLEASURE — 19 TRIANGLE 150 330020
OTGER COOYMANS K V (A
FRED BERGER G (A DAVID KEMPER D (A PAUL HAPPENER B (A EEF ALBERS G (A
JAN PIJNENBERG D (A DEAN PARKS G (A VICTOR FELDMAN PERC (A

O37A OTHER HALF O37A

RANDY HOLDEN G (— (A) THE OTHER HALF — 19 ATCO 38004
MIKE PORT (

O38 JOHNNY OTIS O38

JOHNNY OTIS D V PNO(ALL — (A) COLD SHOT — 1969 SONET UK SNTF613 US KENT 534
SHUGGIE OTIS G B (A — (B) CUTTIN' UP — 1970 EPIC US 26524
MIGHTY MOUTH EVANS V (A — (C) LIVE AT MONTEREY — 1971 EPIC UK 66295 US 30473
AL RIVERA B (A — (D) GREAT R & B — 19 BLUES SPECTRUM US BS 103
HOOTIE GALVAN D (A — (E) ROCK'N'ROLL HIT PARADE — 197 DIG US 104
DON SUGARCANE HARRIS VLN(A — (F) FORMIDABLE — 19 EMBER UK SPE 6604
BROADWAY THOMAS B (A — (G) THE JOHNNY OTIS SHOW — 19 BOVEMA EURO 052 80676
BUDDY REDD D (A — (H) THE JOHNNY OTIS SHOW — 19 SAVOY US 2221
ESTHER PHILLIPS V (— (I) THE JOHNNY OTIS SHOW — 19 CAPITOL US 940
MEL WALKER (— (J) PIONEERS OF ROCK — 1973 STARLINE UK SRS 5129
CLIFFORD SOLOMON (— (K) JOHNNY OTIS — 1975 BULLDOG BDL1002
MIGHTY FLEA TROM (— (L) ROCK'N'ROLL HISTORY — 1979 CAPITOL FR 038 85085
LADY DEE WILLIAMS (— (M) ROCK'N'ROLL — 1979 FLYRIGHT UK 550
PETE LEWIS (
ROBINS V (BIG JIM WYNN (OTISETTES V (MARGIE EVANS V (
BIG DADDY RUCKER (EDDIE VINSON G V (BIG JOE TURNER V (

O39 SHUGGIE OTIS O39

SHUGGIE OTIS G B V(ALL (A) AL KOOPER INTRODUCES 1969 CBS US 9951 UK 63797
JOHNNY OTIS D PNO(BC (B) HERE COMES SHUGGIE OTIS 1970 CBS US 26511 UK 63996
AL KOOPER K V (A (C) FREEDOM FLIGHT 1971 EPIC US 30752
RAY JOHNSON K (B (D) INSPIATION INFORMATION 1975 EPIC US 33059
LEON HAYWOOD K (B (E) OMAHA BAR B Q 19 KENT US 540
WILTON FELDER B (BC (1) 1969 LIVE
AL McKIBBON B (B
STIX HOOPER D (B PAUL LAGOS D (B ABE MILLS D (B PRESTON LOVE WIND (B1
PLAS JOHNSON SAX (B TANK JERNIGAN WINS (AB JIM HORN SAX (B JACK KELSO SAX (BD1
MELVIN MOORE TPT (B BOB MITCHELL TPT (B GENE'MIGHTY FLEA'CONNERS(B WILLIE RUFF HRNS (B
WELLS KELLY D (A STU WOODS B (A MARK KLINGMAN PNO (A CLIFFORD SOLOMON SAX (1
ED PLEASANCE SAX (1 WALLACE BRODIE SAX (1 JOE EPPS SAX (1 BILL CATER SAX (1
RON SELICO D (1 MIKE KOWALSKI D (C GEORGE DUKE K (C AYNSLEY DUNBAR D (C
JIM BRADSHAW HCA V(C RICHARD APLANALP FLT (C CLYDIE KING V (C VANETTA FIELDS V (C
SHIRLEY MATTHEWS V (C CURT SLETTEN TPT (D RON ROBBINS TPT (D DOUG WINTZ TROM (D
JIM PRINGLE TROM (D JEFF MARTNEY HRNS (D STRINGS SECTION (AD RICHARD MACKAY HRNS (B

O40 JOHN OTWAY O40

JOHN OTWAY G V (ALL (A) JOHN OTWAY & WILD WILLY BARRETT 1977 EXTRACKED ELP1+POLYDOR 2383 453
WILD WILLY BARRETT G V (A F (B) DEEP & MEANINGLESS 1978 POLYDOR 2383 501
PETE TOWNSHEND G PROD(A (C) WHERE DID I GO RIGHT 1979 POLYDOR 2383 532
PAUL WARD (ABD (D) WAY & BAR 1980 POLYDOR 2383 581
NIGEL PEGRUM D (ABD (E) DEEP THOUGHT 198 STIFF US USE5
BARON ANTHONY PROD (A (F) GONE WITH THE BIN 1981 POLYDOR POLS1039
ROGER CAREY (D
PHIL CUTLER (A STUART EATON (A LYN FLETCHER (A FIONA BUTT (B
MARTIN LOVEDAY (A MILTON REAME JAMES (A LISA STRIKE V (A MORGAN FISHER K (C
OLLIE HALSALL G (C PAUL MARTINEZ B (C CHARLIE MORGAN D (C MAGGIE RYDER V (CD
JULIAN SMEDLEY FDL (C MARK FREEMAN (BD MAURICE BACON (D LOL COXHILL (D
DAVE HULMES (B YVONNE GRECH (D SIMON HANSON (B

O40A OUTCASTS O40A

COLIN COWAN D (A (A) SELF CONSCIOUS OVER YOU 1979 GOOD VIBRATIONS BIG 1
MARTIN COWAN G V (A
GREG COWAN B V (A GETTY G (A SIMON LLOYD SAX (A D SMYTH G (A
IZZY TURNER K (A

O40B OUT OF FOCUS O40B

REMIGIUS DRECHSLER G (AB (A) WAKE UP 1971 KUCKUCK GER 2375 006
MORAN NEUMULLER SAX (AB (B) OUT OF FOCUS 1972 KUCKUCK GER 2375 010
HENNES HERING K (AB (C) FOUR LETTER MONDAY AFTERNOON(DBL) 1972
STEFAN WISHEU B (AB
KLAUS SPORI D (AB

O40C OUTDOOR PLUMBING CO O40C

(A) MOONSHINE MOUNTAIN 1980 REBEL US 1578

O41 OUTLAW BLUES BAND O41

LEON RUBENHOLD (AB (A) OUTLAW BLUES BAND 1968 BLUESWAY US BLS 6021
JOE WHITEMAN (AB (B) BREAKING IN 1969 STATESIDE UK SSL10290
PHILLIP JOHN (AB (B) BREAKING IN 1969 BLUESWAY US BLS 6030
VICTOR ALEMAN (AB
LAWRENCE DICKENS (AB

O42 THE OUTLAWS (UK) O42

MIKE BERRY V ((A) DREAM OF THE WEST 1961 HMV UK CLP 1489
CHAS HODGES B (A
REG HAWKINS G (BILLY KUY G (A BOBBY GRAHAM D (A DON GROOM D (
KEN WINDGREN G (A ROGER MINGAY G (LORNE GREENE G (RITCHIE BLACKMORE G (
MICK UNDERWOOD D (HARVEY HINSLEY G (

O43 OUTLAWS(US) O43

BILLY JONES G V (ABCDEFG (A) THE OUTLAWS 1975 ARISTA US AL 4042 UK ARTY 115
FRANK O'KEEFE B (AB (B) LADY IN WAITING 1976 ARISTA US 4070 UK ARTY 126
HENRY PAUL G V (ABC (C) HURRY SUNDOWN 1977 ARISTA US AL 4135 UK SPART1010
HUGHIE THOMASSON G V (ABCDEFGH (D) BRING IT BACK ALIVE 1978 ARISTA US AL 8300 UK DARTY 5
MONTE YOHO D (ABCDEF (E) PLAYING TO WIN 1978 ARISTA US 4205 UK ARTY 156
JOE LALA PERC (B (F) IN THE EYE OF THE STORM 1979 ARISTA US AL 9507
HARVEY ARNOLD B V (CDEF (G) GHOST RIDERS IN THE SKY 1981 ARISTA US 9542 UK SPART1160
JOE VITALE SYN STRING(C (H) LOS HOMBERS MALO 1982 ARISTA US 9584 UK 204558
MANUAL LABOUR PERC (C
DAVID DIX D PERC(DEFGH FREDDIE SALEM G V(DEFGH RICK CUA B V (GH J D SOUTHER V (A
CAROL BRISTOW V (H LU MOSS V (H GARY LYONS K V (H DAVE LANE FDL (H

O44 OUTSIDERS O44

ADRIAN BORLAND G V (AB1 (A) CALLING ON YOUTH 1977 RAW EDGE RER 001
ADRIAN JANES D V (AB1 (B) CLOSE UP 1978 RAW EDGE RER 003
BOB LAWRENCE B (AB (1) 1979
GRAHAM GREEN B (1

O44A OUTSIDERS (US) O44A

TOM KING G (A) TIME WONT LET ME IN 19 CAPITOL US 2501
BILL BRUNO (B) ALBUM 2 19 CAPITOL US 2568
MERDIN MADSEN B G HCA (C) IN 19 CAPITOL US 2636
SONNY GERACI V (D) HAPPENING LIVE 19 CAPITOL US 2745
RICKY BAKER D

O45 OVARY LODGE O45

KEITH TIPPETT K (AB (A) OVARY LODGE 1973 RCA UK SF8372
JULIE TIPPETT V (B (B) OVARY LODGE 1976 OGUN OG 600
HARRY MILLER B (B
FRANK PERRY V PERC(AB ROY BABBINGTON B (A

O46 OZARK MOUNTAIN DAREDEVILS O46

JOHN DILLON G V K(ABCDEFG (A) OZARK MOUNTAIN DAREDEVILS 1973 A&M US 4411 UK AMLH64411
RANDLE CHOWNING G V HCA(ABCD (B) IT'LL SHINE WHEN IT SHINES 1974 A&M US 3654 UK AMLH63654
STEVE CASH HCA V(ABCDEFG (C) CAR OVER THE LAKE ALBUM 1975 A&M US 4549 UK AMLH64549
BUDDY BRAYFIELD K (ABCD (D) MEN FROM EARTH 1976 A&M US 4601 UK AMLH64601
LARRY LEE D G K(ABCDF (E) DONT LOOK DOWN 1978 A&M US 4662 UK AMLH64662
MICHAEL GRANDA B V (ABCDFG (F) ITS ALIVE 1978 A&M US 6006 UK AMLM66006
NICK DE CARO ACC (B (G) OZARK MOUNTAIN DAREDEVILS 1980 CBS US 36375 UK 84193
WELDON MYRICK STEEL(C
FARRELL MORRIS PERC (C JODY TROUTMAN V (B NANCY BLAKE CELLO (C BILL JONES WIND K V(CD
GLYN JOHNS G (B STEVE CANADY G D V (D JERRY MILLS MAND (DF RUNE WALLE G (DFG
RUSSELL CHAPPELL K V (F CONNIE CANADAY V (D BOBBYE HALL PERC (D STEVE KENNEDY G (F
MIKE BOTTS D (G JOHN GOIN G (G CLINTON THOMPSON G (G JAI WINDING K (G
JOHN BOYLAN G (G PAUL GRUUP PERC (G GARY COLEMAN PERC (G BUDDY EMMONS STEEL(G
VANETTA FIELDS V (G ROSEMARY BUTLER V (G PAULETTE BROWN V (G TOM KELLY V (G

O47 OZO O47

JOHN MIZEROLLO G (AB (A) LISTEN TO THE BUDDAH 1976 DJM US DJM 4 UK 20488
BETH KUSTRA V (A (B) MUSEUM OF THE WORLD 1978 DJM UK 20517
VAL MACDONALD D PERC (A
VERNON CUMMINGS PERC V(A EDDIE DAVIES K V (A MARTIN ABRAHAMS G (A FRANZ KOCK WIND(A
TREVOR STEPHENS B (A HELEN DENISTON V (A KIM WENDELS V (A DEREK MANDL G (A
HUGH ASHTON G (A MICK WAYNE G (A KATHY TONTO V (B

O48 OZZ O48

ALEXIS T ANGEL V (A (A) NO PRISONERS 1980 CBS 36198
GREGG PARKER G V (A
DONNELL HAGAN D (A CRAIG GRUBER B (A WILLIE BASS B (A MICHAEL CAVANAUGH K SYN(A

O49 OZONE O49

(A) WALK ON 1980 MOTOWN US 938
(B) JUMP ON IT 1981 MOTOWN US 950
(C) NO PRISONERS 1980 EPIC US 36198

P1 P F M P1

FLAVIO PREMOLI K V (ALL (A) STORIA DI UN MINOTO 1972 NUMERO UNO IT ZSLN55055
FRANZ DI CIOCCIO D V (CDFGH (B) PER UN AMICO 1972 NUMERO UNO IT ZSLN55155
FRANCO MUSSIDA G V (CFGHD (C) PHOTO'S OF GHOSTS 1973 MANTICORE 2003 US 66668 UK KK43502
MAURO PAGANI FLT V VLN(CFHD (D) WORLD BECAME THE WORLD 1974 MANTICORE US 66673 UK K53502
PATRIC DJIVAS B (FHD (E) COOK 1975 MANTICORE US 6502 UK K53506
BERNARDO LANZETTI G V (FH (F) CHOCOLATE KINGS 1976 MANTICORE UK K53508
GIORGIO PIAZZA B (CG (F) CHOCOLATE KINGS 1976 NUMERO UNO IT 55684
GREGORY BLOCH VLN (G (F) CHOCOLATE KINGS 1976 ASYLUM US 7E1071
PETE SINFIELD PROD (C (G) MARCONI BAKERY 1976 PETERS INT 9014
CLAUDIO FABI PROD (CE (H) JET LAG 1977 MANTICORE UK K53511
(H) JET LAG 1977 ASYLUM US 7E1101
(J) PASS PARTU 197 ZOO 34032
(K) SUONARESUONARE 197 ZOO 34092
(L) LIVE USA 197 NUMERO UNO 55676

P1A P H D P1A

(A) P H D 1981 WEA UK K99150

P1B P G R S P1B

GEOFFREY STOCKER K D (A (A) PHOTOGRAPHS OF SOUND 1979 RISKYDISC FUNC 1
PAUL RAMSAY G D (A
ROBIN WATTS G K PERC(A SHANE JARVIS K (A

P1C P.M. P1C

CARL PALMER D (A (A) ONE P M 1980 ARIOLA UK 5048 GER 201 659
TODD COCHRAN K V (A
BARRY FINNERTY G V (A JOHN NITZINGER G V (A ERIK SCOTT B V (A

P2 AUGUSTOS PABLO P2

AUGUSTOS PABLO V K (ABC (A) ITAL DUB 1975 TROJAN TRLS 115
BAGGA B (B (B) EAST OF THE RIVER NILE 1978 MESSAGE
ROBERT SHAKESPEARE B (B (C) ORIGINAL ROCKERS 1979 GREENSLEEVES GREL 8
CARLTON BARRETT D (B (D) THRILLER 1981 ECHO UK STLP1002
EARL 'CHINNA'SMITH G (B
NOEL BENBOW D (B C DOWNIE B (B MAX EDWARDS D (B EVERTON DA SILVA PERC (B
ASTON BARRETT B (B

P3 PABLO CRUISE P3

DAVE JENKINS G B V(ABCDEF (A) PABLO CRUISE 1975 A&M US 4528 UK AMLH64528
CORY LERIOS PNO (ABCDEF (B) LIFE LINE 1976 A&M US 4575 UK AMLH64575
STEPHEN PRICE D PERC(ABCDEF (C) A PLACE IN THE SUN 1977 A&M US 4625 UK AMLH64625
BRUCE DAY B V (E (D) WORLDS AWAY 1978 A&M US 4597 UK AMLH64697
BUD COCKRELL B V (ABC (E) PART OF THE GAME 1980 A&M US 3712 UK AMLK63712
GENE MEROS SAX (E (F) REFLECTOR 1981 A&M US 3726 UK AMLK63726
BOBBYE HALL PERC (A
MIKE PORCARO B (E VICTOR FELDMAN PERC (E DAVID FOSTER SYN (E MICHAEL BODDICKER SYN(E
STEVE PORCARO SYN (E ANGELO ROSSI G V (F JOHN PIERCE B V (F CAROLYN BRAND V (A
MIKE UTLEY K (A DAVID PAICH STR (A

P3A TOM PACHECO P3A

TOM PACHECO ((A) PACHECO & ALEXANDER 1971
(B) SWALLOWED UP IN AMERICAN HEARTLAND 1976 RCA APLI 1254
(C) THE OUTSIDER 1977 RCA APLI 1887

P4 PACIFIC DRIFT P4

LAWRENCE ARENDS D PERC V(A (A) FEELIN' FREE 1970 NOVA UK SND13 US DECCA 18040
BARRY REYNOLDS G V (A
BRIAN SHAPMAN K V (A GRAHAM HARROP B G (A JACK LANCASTER FLT (A DAVE DAVANI HRNS(A
SUE GLOVER V (A SUNNY LESLIE V (A

P5 PACIFIC EARDRUM P5

DAVE MACRAE K (AB (A) PACIFIC EARDRUM 1977 CHARISMA CAS1133
ISAAC GUILLORY G (AB (B) BEYOND PANIC 1978 CHARISMA CAS1136
GEOFF SEOPARDIE D (AB
JOY YATES V (AB BILLY KRISTIAN B (AB BRIAN SMITH WIND PERC(B JIM CUOMO SAX (A
MORRIS PERT PERC (A SIMON MORTON PERC (B

P6 PACIFIC GAS & THE ELECTRIC P6

CHARLI ALLEN V (ALL — (A) PACIFIC GAS & THE ELECTRIC 1969 CBS US 9900 UK 63822
BRENT BLACK B (AC — (B) GET IT ON 1969 KENT US 547 UK B&C CAS1003
FRANK COOK D (AC — (B) GET IT ON 19 ORANGE US 701 METRONOME15379
TOM MARSHALL G (AC — (C) ARE YOU READY 1970 CBS US 1017 UK 64026
GLENN SCHWARTZ G (AB — (D) P G & E (HARD BURN) 1971 CBS US 30362 UK 64295
FREDDY HILL TPT (AC — (E) P G & E WITH CHARLIE ALLEN 1973 DUNHILL US 157
BUD BRISBOIS TPT (A — (F) BEST 1973 CBS US 32019
WAYNE HENDERSON TROM (A — (G) LIVE & KICKING AT LEXINGTON 187 CBS UK 66264
ALLEN SCHWARZBERG D (E
WILTON FELDER SAX (E — GORDON EDWARDS B (E — JOHN HILL K (E — BOB MANN G (E
CHARLIE BROWN G (E — JON STROLL PNO (E — GEORGE YOUNG SAX (E — ARTIE KAPLAN SAX(E
JOE GRIMM SAX (E — SELDON POWELL SAX (E — MICHAEL BRECKER SAX (E — PHIL BODNER SAX(E
CORNELL DUPREE G (E — ERNIE HAYES K (E — LOU SOLOFF HRNS (E — AL DE RISI HRNS (E
BURT COLLINS HRNS (E — MICKEY GRAVINE HRNS (E — RAY ROLLARD V (E — J R BAILEY V (E
JIM MADEN TAMB V (E — TASHA THOMAS V (E — BARBARA MASSEY V (E — CARL HALL V (E
KENNY WILLIAMS V (E — LOU COURTNEY V (E — JERRY FRIEDMAN G (E — SAMMY TURNER V (E
SHERMAN LEWIS V (E — TROY KEYES V (E — BILL FOSTER V (E — JON LUCAS V (E
RON MARSHALL V (E — LANI GROVES V (E — GLORIA BARLEY V (E — SHIRLEY BREWER V (E
MANNY SEYMOUR V (E — MELVIN KENT V (E — JOHN BROWN V (E — CHARLOTTE GILBERT V (E
JAMES RYAN V (E — DELORES HARVIN V (E — ALBERTINE ROBERTSON V (E — JOSHIE ARMSTEAD V (E
VANETTA FIELDS V (C — DELORES HALL V (C — GINGER SCHACKNE V (C — RUSTY YOUNG G (C
SHERRILL ATWOOD V (C — CLYDIE KING V (C — LORNA WILLARD V (C — MERRY CLAYTON V (C
SHIRLEY MATTHEWS V (C — ALFRED GALLEROS SAX (D — KEN UTTERBACK G (D — RON WOODS SAX(D
JERRY AIELLO K (D — JOE LALA PERC (D — STANLEY ABERNATHY TPT (D — FRANK PETRICCA B (D
BLACKBERRIES V (D

P6A CLEO PAGE P6A

(A) LEAVING MISSISSIPPI 1979 JSP UK 1003

P6B THE PACK P6B

JORG EVERS G V (A — (A) THE PACK 1978 VINYL GER 6 23450
DASHIEL DYNAMITE D (A
GERARD CARBONEL B V (A

P6C PACKARDS P6C

PAUL JOHNSON G (A — (A) PRAY FOR SURF 19 SURFSIDE 001
CHRIS DARROW B G (A
JOHN RUSSELL D (A

P7 GENE PAGE P7

GENE PAGE — BLACULA 197 RCA US LSP 4806
HOT CITY 1975 ATLANTIC US 18111 UK K50105
LOVELOCK 1976 ATLANTIC US 18161 UK K50221
CLOSE ENCOUNTERS 1978 ARISTA US 4174 SPART1052
LOVE STARS AFTER DARK 1980 ARISTA US 4262

P8 JIMMY PAGE P8

JIMMY PAGE G (A — (A) DONT SEND ME NO FLOWERS 1969 MARMALADE UK 608004
SONNY BOY WILLIAMSON V (A — (A) SONNY BOY WILLIAMSON 1975 SPRINGBOARD 4038
BRIAN AUGER K (A — (A) JAM SESSION 1975 CHARLY UK CR 30011
JOE HARRIOT SAX (A — (B) FACES & PLACES VOL 8 19 BYG FR 529 908
ALAN SKIDMORE SAX (A
MICK WALLER D (A

P8A PAGES P8A

RICHARD PAGE V PNO(ABC — (A) PAGES 1978 EPIC US
JOHN LANG LYRICS(C — (B) FUTURE STREET 1979 EPIC US 36209
NEIL STUBENHAUS B (C — (C) PAGES 1981 CAPITOL US 12123
PAULINHO DACOSTA PERC(C
RALPH HUMPHREY D (C — PAUL JACKSON G (C — JAY GRAYDON G (C — ABRAHAM LABORIEL B (C
STEV GEORGE V K SYN (C — STEVE KAHN G (C — JEFF PORCARO D (C — CHARLES JOHNSON G (C
VINCE CALAIUTA D (C — TOM SCOTT SAX (C — MIKE BAIRD D (C — AL JARREAU V (C

P8B PAGLIARO P8B

(A) PAGLIARO 1972 PYE UK NSPL 18380

P9 PAICE ASHTON & LORD(PAL) P9

IAN PAICE D (A — (A) MALICE IN WONDERLAND 1977 WB JAPAN P10360 US BS3088
JON LORD K (A — (A) MALICE IN WONDERLAND 1977 OYSTER UK 2391269 RI 80 2482485
TONY ASHTON K V (A
PAUL MARTINEZ B (A — BERNIE MARSDEN G (A — HOWIE CASEY SAX (A — REG BROOKS TROM (A
SHEILA McKINLEY V (A — DAVE CASWELL HRNS (A — GILBERT DALL'ENESE SAX (A — JEANETTE McKINLEY V (A

P9A PAINTER P9A

(A) PAINTER 1974 ELEKTRA US 75071

P10 RONNIE PAISLEY BAND P10

RONNIE PAISLEY V (A — (A) SMOKING MIRROR 1979 PYE UK NSPL18582
ANDY BROWN (A
STEVE GREGORY HRNS (A — JOHN MARK (A — TONY HILL (A — KIM HAKINSSON (A
PETE KELLY (A — DAVID PAISLEY (A — ALAN PARK (A — PETE PAVLI (A
FRANK RICOTTI PERC (A — JIM TOOMEY (A — PAUL TURNER (A — DIGGER DAVIES (A
LADYBIRDS V (A

P10A PAKALAMEREDITH P10A

(A) PAKALAMEREDITH 1978 ELEKTRA US 1106

P10B PALACE FLOPHOUSE P10B

CASPAR FALKE G MAN(A — (A) BONTEBURG 1980 UNIVERSE NL DLS30
WILLY EBBES D V (A
ANDRE PASMAN WIND (A — HENNY HEGMAN PERC (A — HANS HEGMAN G V (A — WOLF OVERKAMP VLN G(A
ELINE HARBES V (A — GERARD HEGMAN B V(A — ERNST JAN WITKAP FLT (A

P11 PALADIN P11

KEITH WEBB D (AB1 — (A) PALADIN 1971 BRONZE UK ILPS9150 US EPIC 31137
PETE SOLLEY K V VLN (AB1 — (B) CHARGE 1972 BRONZE ILPS 9190
PETE BECKETT B V (AB1 — (1) 1972
LOU STONEBRIDGE K V (AB
DEREK FOLEY G V (AB — JOE JAMMER G (1

P13 PALEY BROTHERS P13

ANDY PALEY V G HCA(A (A) PALEY BROTHERS 1978 SIRE US SRK6052 GER 200 161*
JONATHAN PALEY G V (A * DIFF TRACKS
JEFF LASS K (A
ERIC ROSENFELD G (A JAN UVENA D (A LEIGH FOXX B (A JIM HASLIP B (A
RAMONES G B D(PHIL JUSTICE B (JEFF WILKINSON D (

P14 BRUCE PALMER P14

BRUCE PALMER G B (A (A) THE CYCLE IS COMPLETE 1971 VERVE FORCAST US vrf 3086
ED ROTH K (A
RICK MATTHEWS PERC V(A BIG BLACK CONGA(A PAUL LAGOS D (A JEFF KAPLAN K (A
TEMPLETON PARCELY VLN (A RICHARD APLAN WIND (A

P15 ROBERT PALMER P15

ROBERT PALMER G B V K D (ALL (A) SNEAKIN' SALLY THROUGH THE ALLEY 1974 ISLAND UK ILPS 9294
SPIDER WEBB D (C (B) PRESSURE DROP 1975 ISLAND UK ILPS 9372
JEFF PORCARO D (C (C) SOME PEOPLE CAN DO WHAT THEY LIKE 1976 ISLAND UK ILPS 9420
ALLEN SCHWARZBERG D (D (D) DOUBLE FUN 1978 ISLAND UK ILPS 9476
KEITH BENSON D (E (E) SECRETS 1979 ISLAND UK ILPS 9544
CHRIS PARKER D (D (F) CLUES 1980 ISLAND UK ILPS 9595
MICHAEL DAWE D (G (G) MAYBE IT'S ALIVE 1982 ISLAND UK ILPS 9665
RITCHIE HAYWARD D (BCD
ED GREENE D (B FREDDIE HARRIS G (CD CHUCK RAINEY B (C BILL PAYNE K V (BCD
SAM CLAYTON PERC (BC PAUL BARRERE G V (BCD PIERRE BROCK B (CDE JAMES ALAN SMITH K (CD
CHILI CHARLES PERC (C CAROL KAYE G (C JAMES JAMESON B (B JEAN ROUSSEL K (B
JODY LINSCOTT CONGA(C FREDDIE WALL G (C KEN GRADNEY B (B LOUIS JOHN DAVIS K (D
ROBERT GREENRIDGE PERC (CD LOWELL GEORGE G (B BOB BABITT B (D STEVE ROBBINS K (DE
LENNY CASTRO PERC (D JAMES MAHONEY G (D JIMMY WILLIAMS B (D RON KERSEY K (D
DAVID SNELL HARP (B DONOVAN McKITTY G (D ANDY FRASER B (F EDWARD PUTMON K (D
DONY WYNN D (EFG NEIL HUBBARD G (D PAUL GARDINER B (F GARY NUMAN K (F
GREG CARROLL HCA (C T J TINDALL G (D RANDY BRECKER HRNS (D WILLIAM SMITH K (C
CHRIS FRANTZ PER (F ALAN MANSFIELD G (FG MICHAEL BRECKER HRNS (D JACK WALDMAN K (EF
STEVE YORK HCA (B KENNY MAZUR G (EFG MEL COLLINS SAX (B ART SMITH OCARINA (C
BRIAN RUSSELL V (D BRENDA RUSSELL V (D MARTIN FRY TUBA (B RAY ALLEN HRNS(B
FRAN TATE V (B VICKI BROWN V (B MONGEZI FEZA HRNS (B MUSCLE SHOALS HRNS(B
GORDON DEWITTE K (B JOE BROWN BANJO(B CHRIS BISHOP B (G JACK WALDMAN K (G
GARY NUMAN K (G ADRIAN BELEW G (G DANNY WILDE G B(G

P16 PAN P16

RON ELLIOTT (A (A) PAN 1973 CBS US 32062
KEITH BARBOUR V (A
JIM HASKELL K SYN(A ARTHUR RICHARDS STEEL G V(A DON FRANCISCO D PERC V(A GABRIEL MEKLER K(A
SHERMAN HAYES B V (A VAL GARAY G V (A SANDRA KROUCH TAMB (A BOBBYE HALL PERC(A

P16A PANAMA P16A

PANAMA 1978 PETERS US 9023

P17 PANAMA FRANCIS BLUES BAND P17

(A) TOUGH TALK 196 STATESIDE SL 10070

P18 PANAMA LIMITED JUG BAND P18

DENNIS PARKER (A (A) PANAMA LIMITED JUG BAND 1969 HARVEST UK SHVL 753
LIZ HANNS (A (B) INDIAN SUMMER 1970 HARVEST UK SHVL 779
BRIAN STRACHAN (A
GARY COMPTON (A RON NEEDS (A

P18A PANDEMONIUM P18A

JEAN BAPTISTE BARRIERE SYN(AB (A) VILLE OUVERTE 1979 ATEM 7003
JEAN MARIE BARRIERE SYN(AB (B) NON JAMAIS L'ESPERANCE 1979 ATEM 7004

P18B PANTHER P18B

KLAUS SCULZ G V (A (A) WIR WOLLEN ALLES 1974 PANTHER GER 2667
GERT LANGE G V (A
OLAF LIETZEN D (A KLAUS AHRENS G B V(A GREGOR AHRENS D (A

P18C PANIC P18C

REINHARD ROFFEL D (A (A) 13 1978 ARIOLA NL 26388
PETER PENTHOUSE V (A
MIKE DECOURT G V (A PETE PASSION B V (A

P18D PANIC SQUAD P18D

NORMAN NORMAL G V (A (A) PANIC SQUAD EP 1980 WHIRLED US NOno
ANDY GRAY G V (A
LONIE LONIE D (A MICHAEL MAXWELL B (A BILLY GOOD G K (A JIMMIE O'BRIEN G (A

P19 JOHN PANTRY P19

JOHN PANTRY K V(ABC (A) EMPTY HANDED 19 KINGSWAY UK DOVE 56
TONY COE WIND (C (B) NOTHING IS IMPOSSIBLE 19 KINGSWAY UK KMR 303
BARRY DE SOUZA D (C (C) HOT COALS 19 MARSHALLS MRT 1003
BILL ELDRIDGE TPT (C
RONNIE GOODMAN PERC (C GEORGE HALL SYN (C TIM HARRIES B (C 'FRESH AIR' V (C
DAVE MARTIN G (C ROB McKAY SAX (C BRUCE NOCKLES TPT (C CHRIS NORTON K (C
RAY WEHRSTEIN SAX (C

P19A PAPA NEBO P19A

MICHAEL PACKER G V (A (A) PAPA NEBO 197 ATLANTIC US SD 8280
BRENDAN HARKIN G V (A
SANDY ALLEN B V (A SAL COSTANZO K (A ALL LEATHERS VLN(A BOB MINTZER WIND (A
KEN ADAMS D (A

P20 FELIX PAPPALARDI P20

FELIX PAPPALARDI B V K(A (A) FELIX PAPPALARDI & CREATION 1976 A&M US 4586 UK AMLH64586
ERIC GALE G (B (B) DONT WORRY MUM? 1979 A&M US 4729 UK AMLH64729
PAUL BUTTERFIELD HCA (A
RALPH MOSS PERC (A SHIGERU MATSUMOTO B (A KAZUO TAKEDA G (A YOSHIAKI IIJIMA G (A
MASAYUKI HIGUCHI D (A RICHARD TEE K (B CHUCK RAINEY B (B BERNARD PURDIE D (B

P20A JOHANNES 'ALTO' PAPPERT P20A

JOHANNES PAPPERT SAX G(AB (A) ALTO 1978 SPIEGELEI GER 160609 JOJO NL19002
ALLEN MEIER V (AB
WOLFGANG GRASEKAMP K (A HELMUT HATTLER B (A GEORG KOCKBECK K V(B MICKI STICKDORN G V (AB
PETER WOLFBRANDT G BAN(A ANDY GOLDNER G V (A LOU MARIGNAN B(A HEINZ GENBUS B (B
JAN FRIDE D PERC(A BERND KIEFER B (A ZABBA LINDNER D(A

P21 **PARADISE EXPRESS** P21

VI ANN V (A — (A) PARADISE EXPRESS — 1979 FANTASY US 9574 UK FT557
HERB JIMMERSON K (A — (B) LETS FLY — 1980 FANTASY US 9589
SHARON HYMES V (A
KENNETH ELLIOTT D (A DAVID PRUITT G (A DAVID FRAZIER PERC (A ROMEO WILLIAMS B (A
BRIAN CABANAS D (A FRED BERRY HRNS (A AL BENT HRNS (A CHARLES McCARTHY HRNS(A
MARTHA WASH V (A IZORA RHODES V (A

P22 **PARAFFIN JACK FLASH LTD** P22

(A) MOVERS & GROOVERS — 1968 PYE NSPL18252

P22A **PARAGONS** P22A

SLY DUNBAR (A — (A) SLY & ROBBIE MEETS THE PARAGONS — 1981 ISLAND UK ILPS 9632
ROBBIE SHAKESPEARE (A

P23 **PARAMOUNTS** P23

GARY BROOKER V K (A12 — (A) PARAMOUNTS (EP) — 196 PARLOPHONE GEP8908
B J WILSON D (A12 — (A) 1962 (2) 1963/66
ROBIN TROWER G (A12
CHRIS COPPING B (1 DIZ DERRICK B (A2

P23A **PARASITES OF THE WESTERN WORLD** P23A

PATRICK BURKE V B G K SYN(A — (A) SUBSTRATA — 1980 MATCHBOX US MB 1004
TERRY CENSKY K V G B D HRN(A
MIKE AUDRY D (A MIKEY CASCADDEN G V (A

P24 **PARIS** P24

HUNT SALES D V(B — (A) PARIS — 1976 CAPITOL UK/US 11464
ROBERT WELCH G V (AB — (B) BIG TOWNE 2061 — 1976 CAPITOL UK/US 11560 GER 85010
GLEN CORNICK K B (AB
BERNIE MARSDEN G (THOM MOONEY D (A

P24A **PARISH HALL** P24A

GARY WAGNER G PNO V (A — (A) PARISH HALL — 1970 LIBERTY UK LBS83374
STEVE ADAMS D (A — (A) PARISH HALL — 1970 FANTASY US 8398
JOHN HADEN B (A

P24B **DENNIS PARKER** P24B

DENNIS PARKER V (A — (A) LIKE AN EAGLE — 1979 MERCURY UK 9109 622
RUSSELL DABNEY D (A
ALFONSO CAREY B V (A JIMMI LEE G (A RODGER LEE G (A BARRY FINNERTY G (A
TOM POLITE K (A NATHANIEL WILKIE K (A RICHARD TRIFAN SYN (A PHIL HURTT V (A
MILT GREGSON V (A FRANK FLOYD V (A ARTHUR WILLIAMS V (A TONY WELLS V (A
LENNY ROBERTS V (A MARTY NELSON V (A

P25 **GRAHAM PARKER & THE RUMOUR** P25

GRAHAM PARKER V G (ALL — (A) HOWLIN' WIND — 1976 MERCURY US SRM1 1095
STEVE GOULDING PERC (ABCDEFGH — (A) " " — 1976 VERTIGO UK 6360 129
BRINSLEY SCHWARZ G (ABCDEFGH — (B) HEAT TREATMENT — 1976 MERCURY US SRM1 1117
ANDREW BODNAR D B (ABCDEFGH — (B) " " — 1976 VERTIGO UK 6360 137
MARTIN BELMONT G (ABCDEFGH — (C) AT MARBLE ARCH — 1976 VERTIGO UK GP1
BOB ANDREWS K (ABCDEFG — (D) STICK TO ME — 1977 MERCURY US SRM1 3706
STEWART LYNAS SAX (A — (D) STICK TO ME — 1977 VERTIGO UK 9102 017
HERSCHEL HOLDER TPT (A — (E) PARKERILLA DBL — 1978 MERCURY US SRM 2100
DAVE CONNERS SAX (A — (E) PARKERILLA DBL — 1978 VERTIGO UK 6641 797
DANNY ELLIS TROM (AB — (F) SQUEEZING OUT SPARKS — 1979 VERTIGO UK 9102030 GER 6360 168
JOHN EARLE SAX (ABE — (G) BEST OF — 1980 VERTIGO UK 9102 042
ALBE DONNELLY SAX (B — (H) THE UP ESCALATOR — 1980 STIFF UK SEEZ23 GER 6 24355
ROBERT JOHN LANGE PROD (B — (H) UP THE ESCALATOR — 1980 ARISTA US 9517
DAVE EDMUNDS G (A — (J) ANOTHER GREY AREA — 1982 RCA LP6027
NICK LOWE PROD (ABD — (EP) PINK PARKER — 1977 VERTIGO UK PARK 001
NOEL BROWN G (A — (EP) PINK PARKER — 1977 MERCURY US 6831 040
DICK HANSON TPT (BED
ED DEAN G (A CHRIS GOWER TROM (ED RAY BEAVIS SAX (E NICKY HOPKINS K (HJ
DANNY FEDERICI K (H PETER WOOD SYN (H JIMMY MAELEM PERC (H BRUCE SPRINGSTEEN V(H
JOHN EARLE SAX (D JOHN ALTMAN SAX (D DARRYL LEEQUE PERC (D HUGH McCRACKEN G (J
DAVID BROWN G (J DOUG STEGMEYER B (J MICHAEL BROWN D (J KURT McGETTRICK WIND(J
GEORGE SMALL K (J JIM CLOUSE SAX (J PAUL PRESTOPINO BAN (J JACK DOUGLAS PERC(J
KRYSTAL DAVIS V (J KAREN LAWRENCE V (J ERIC TROYER V (J FRED HOSTETLER V (J

P26 **JUNIOR PARKER** P26

JUNIOR PARKER HCA V(ALL — DRIVING — 19 DUKE US DLP 76
MATT MURPHY G (— BLUES CONSOLIDATED — 19 DUKE US
PAT HARE G (— BEST OF — 19 DUKE US DLP 83
JOHN BOWERS D (— JUNIOR PARKER — 1974 BLUESWAY US 6066
KENNETH BANKS B (— OUTSIDE MAN — 19 CAPITOL US ST 564
JAMES WHEELER SAX (— LIKE IT IS — 19 MERCURY UK SMCL20097
BILL JOHNSON PNO (— BLUE SHADOWS FALLING — 1972 GROOVE MERCHANT GM 502
RAYMOND HILL SAX (— (X) GOOD THINGS DONT HAPPEN EVERYDAY — 1972 GROOVE MERCHANT GM2205
HOUSTON STOKES D (— YOU DONT HAVE TO BE BLACK — 1973 PEOPLE PLEO 4
IKE TURNER PNO (— LOVE AIN' NOTHIN' BUT BUSINESS — 1974 PEOPLE PLEO18
JIMMY McGRIFF ORG (X — BLUES FOR MR CRUMP (APPEARED ON) — 1974 POLYDOR UK 2383 257
AL SMITH B (— BLUESMAN — 19 MINIT US 24024
OTIS JACKSON B (— BAREFOOT — 1975 DU US
L C DRANES D (— (EP) JUNIOR PARKER(LOVE MY BABY) — 1976 CHARLY UK CEP 104
FLOYD MURPHY G (— LEGENDARY SUN PERFORMERS(1 SIDE) — 1978 CHARLY UK CR 30135
JIM STEWART TPT (— DUDES DOIN — 19 CAPITOL US 569
JOE FRITZ SAX (— I TELL STORIES — 1972 UA US 6823
JIMMY JOHNSON SAX (— 100% PROOF — 19 UA US 6814
RAY FIELDS SAX (— BABY PLEASE — 19 WING 16401
JOE SCOTT TPT (— HONEYDRIPPER — 19 BLUE ROCK US 64004
DALE McJOWN PNO (
HAMP SIMMONS B (BILL HARVEY SAX (PLUMA DAVIS TROM(SONNY FREEMAN D (

P26A RAY PARKER JR P26A

RAY PARKER JR V G B K PROD(A (A) THE OTHER WOMAN 1982 ARISTA GER 204 673
CHARLES GREEN WIND (A
MICHAEL BODDICKER SYN (A ANITA SHERMAN V (A J D NICHOLAS V (A LYNN SMITH V (A
OLLIE BROWN PERC (A LARRY TOLBERT D (A AMELL CARMICHAEL V (A JERRY KNIGHT V (A

P27 ROBERT PARKER P27

ROBERT PARKER V (ALL (A) BAREFOOTIN' 1966 ISLAND UK ILP942
(B) BAREFOOTIN' 196 NOLA US LP1001
(EP) BAREFOOTIN' 1980 CHARLY UK CTD123

P28 VAN DYKE PARKS P28

VAN DYKE PARKS V (ALL (A) SONG CYCLE 1968 WB US WS 1727
HUGH BORDE (C (B) DISCOVER AMERICA 1972 WB NL26043 GER 46166 US 2589
MALCOLM CECIL (C (C) CLANG OF YANKEE REAPER 1975 WB UK K56161 US BS 2878
CHILLI CHARLES D (C
JESSE ED DAVIS G (C HOLLIS DURITY (C ROBERT GREENIDGE (C FRED TACKETT G (C
JIM KELTNER D (C KLAUS VOORMANN B (C BOBBY KEYS SAX (C NOBLE WILLIAMS (C
GARVIN ADAMS (B MURRAY ADLER (B LAURINDO ALMEIDA (B JOHN AUDINO (B
ISRAEL BAKER (B JOHN BERGAMO (B CHARLES BERGHOFER (B ROGER BOBO (B
NORM BOTNICK (B GARY COLEMAN (B BONNIE DOUGLAS (B JESSE EHRLICH (B
KAREN ERVIN (B ROY ESTRADA (B GEORGE FIELDS (B LOWELL GEORGE G (B
ANNE GOODMAN (B JIM GORDON D (B RICHIE HAYWARD (B KENRICK HEADLEY (B
MILT HOLLAND PERC (B KIRBY JOHNSON (B JERRY KESSLER (B MYRA KESTENBAUM (B
GAYLE LEVANT (B LEW McCREARY HRN (B AL McKIBBON (B MALCOLM McNAB (B
GORDON MARRON (B JAY MIGLIORI (B BUELL NEIDLINGER (B DAN NEUFELD (B
JEFFREY REYNOLDS (B TOM SCOTT WIND (B FREDERICK SCYKORA (B PAUL SHURE (B
DENNIS SMITH (B TONY TERRAN (B ESSO TRINIDAD STEELBAND (B

P29 PARLIAMENT P29

GEORGE CLINTON V (ALL (A) OSMUIM 1970 INVICTUS US 7302
CALVIN SIMON V (BCE (B) UP FOR THE DOWN STROKE 1974 CASABLANCA UK CAL2011 US 7002
FUZZY HASKINS V (BCE (C) CHOCOLATE CITY 1975 CASABLANCA UK CAL2012 US 7014
RAYMOND DAVIS V (BCE (D) MOTHERSHIP CONNECTION 1976 CASABLANCA UK CAL2013 US 7022
GRADY THOMAS V (BCE (E) CLONES OF DR FUNKENSTEIN 1976 CASABLANCA UK CAL2001 US 7034
GARRY SHIDER V (BCE (F) GET DOWN & BOOGIE 197 CASABLANCA US 7042
EDDIE HAZAL G V (BCE (G) LIVE (DBL) 1977 CASABLANCA UK CALD5002 US 7053
MICHAEL HAMPTON G V (E (H) FUNKENSTEIN VsTHE PLACEBO SYNDROME1977 CASABLANCA UK CALN2021 US 7084
GLEN COLLINS G V (E (J) MOTOR BOOTY AFFAIR 1978 CASABLANCA UK CALH2044 US 7125
WILLIAM NELSON G (B (K) GLORY HALLASTOOPID 1980 CASABLANCA UK/US 7195
BERNIE WORRELL K (E (L) TROMBIPULATION 1981 CASABLANCA UK/US 7294
JEROME BRAILEY D (E
BOOTSY COLLINS B D G(BCE GARY COOPER D (E PRAKASH JOHN B (C RON BYKOWSKI G (B
GARY BRONSON D (B TIKI FULWOOD D (BC FRED WESLEY HRNS (E MACEO PARKER HRNS(E
RICK GARDNER HRNS (E MICHAEL BRECKER HRNS (E RANDY BRECKER HRNS (E CORDELL MOSSON B(BC
PETER CHASE WHISTLE(B

P29A PARLOUR BAND P29A

PETER FILLEUL K V (A (A) IS A FRIEND 1972 DERAM UK SDL10
PIX G (A
CRAIG ANDERS G (A MARK ASHLEY G (A JERRY ROBBINS D PERC(A

P29B PARRISH & GURVITZ P29B

BRIAN PARRISH G V (A (A) PARRISH & GURVITZ 1971 REGAL ZONOPHONE SRZA8506
PAUL GURVITZ G V (A
MIKE KELLIE D (A

P30 BRIAN PARRISH P30

BRIAN PARRISH G V (A (A) LOVE ON MY MIND 1976 BARN UK 2314 101
BRIAN CHATTON K (A
PETER VAN HOOKE D (A JEROME RIMSON B (A PETE WHITFIELD K (A

P31 ALAN PARSONS PROJECT P31

ALAN PARSONS K V (ALL (A) TALES OF MYSTERY & IMAGINATION 1976 CHARISMA CDS 4003 US 20CENT 339
B J COLE STEEL(ABD (B) I ROBOT 1977 ARISTA US 7002 UK SPARTY1012
STUART TOSH D (ABD (C) PYRAMID 1978 ARISTA US 4180 UK SPART 1054
IAN BAIRNSON G (ABCDEF (D) EVE 1979 ARISTA US 9504 UK SPART1100
DAVID PATON V B G(ABCDEF (E) TURN OF A FRIENDLY CARD 1980 ARISTA US 9518 UK DLART 1
STEVE HARLEY V (BD (F) EYE OF THE SKY 1982 ARISTA US 9599 UK 3484
JOHN PERRY V (B
ALLAN CLARKE V (BD ERIC WOOLFSON K(BCDE COLIN BLUNSTONE V (CF JACK HARRIS V (BCD
DUNCAN MACKAY K (BCD LENNY ZAKATEK V(BCDEF DEAN FORD V (C STUART ELLIOTT D (BCDEF
JOE PUERTA B (A DARRYL RUNSWICK B (A BURLEIGH DRUMMOND D (A DAVID PACK G (A
ARTHUR BROWN V (A CHRIS RAINBOW V (EDF ELMER GANTRY V (EF MUNICH CHAM OPERA ORCH(E
JOHN LEACH (B LESLIE DUNCAN V (D CLARE TORRY V (D DAVE TOWNSEND V (BD
PETER STRAKER V (BD JAKI WHITREN V (BD HILLARY WESTON V (B TONY RIVERS V (B
SMOKEY PARSON V (B STUART CALVER V (B ORCH & CHORUS (B MEL COLLINS SAX (F

P32 GENE PARSONS P32

GENE PARSONS V G B D(A (A) KINDLING 1974 WB US 2687 UK K46257
RED CALLENDER TUBA (A (B) MELODIES 1979 SIERRA US 8703
CLARENCE WHITE G MAND(A
VASSAR CLEMENTS FDL (A GIB GUILBEAU FDL (A ROGER BUSH B (A
RALPH STANLEY SAX (A BILL PYNE SYN (A NICK DECARO ACC (A ANDY NEWMARK D (A

P33 GRAM PARSONS P33

GRAM PARSONS G V (ALL (A) G P 1973 REPRISE US MS 2123 UK K44228
GEORGE WRIGLEY BAN G(D (B) GRIEVOUS ANGEL 1974 REPRISE US MS 2171 UK K54018
PAUL SURRATT G BAND (C) SLEEPLESS NIGHTS(BURRITO BROS) 1976 A&M US 4578 UK AMLH64578
JOE KELLY V B (D (D) EARLY YEARS 1979 SIERRA US 8702 ARIOLA200750
LEWIS MORFORD V (A (E) & THE FALLEN ANGELS 1982 SIERRA US 1973
MITCH WRIGLEY V (A (*) GRAM PARSONS 197 SHILOH US 4088
TOM BAHLER V (A ( ) GRAM PARSONS 1982 WB UK K57008
RON HICKLIN V (A ( ) LIVE 1973 1982 REPERTOIRE UK 6 25106
KYLE TULLIS B (E (*) RI OF INTERNATIONAL SUBMARINE BANDS SAFE OF HOME'
JOCK BARTLEY B (E
GLEN D HARDIN K (ABC NEIL FLANZ STEEL(E RICK GRECH B (ABC N D SMART D (BE
HERB PEDERSEN G (BC BERNIE LEADON G V (BC JAMES BURTON G (ABC AL PERKINS STEEL (ABC

(CONTINUED)

P33 GRAM PARSONS (CONTINUED) P33

BYRON BERLINE FDL (ABC STEVE SNYDER VIBES(B LINDA RONSTADT V (B CHRIS HILLMAN B (C
SNEAKY PETE STEEL(C MICHAEL CLARKE D (C EMORY GORDY B (BC RONNIE TUTT D (ABC
EMMYLOU HARRIS V (ABCE JOHN CONRAD B (A JOHN GUERIN D (A SAM GOLDSTEIN D (A
BARRY TASHIAN G V (A BUDDY EMMONS STEEL(A ALAN MUNDE BANJO(A HAL BATTISTE SAX (A

P33A PASSAGE P33A

JOEY McKECHNIE (B (A) PINDROP 1980 OBJECT UK OBJ011
ANDREW WILSON (B (B) FOR ALL & NONE 1981 VIRGIN UK 3200
DICK WITTS (B (EP) NEW LOVE SONGS 19 OBJECT OM 02
TERESA SHAW (B (EP) ABOUT TIME 19 OBJECT OM 08

P33B PASSIONS P33B

BARBARA GOGAN G V (12AB (A) MICHAEL & MIRANDA 1980 FICTION FIX003 2383573 NL 2442184
DAVID AGAR B (2B (B) 30000 FEET OVER CHINA 1981 POLYDOR 2383 616 POLS1041
CLIVE TIMPERLEY G K V VLN(12AB (1) 1978 (2) 1981
RICHARD WILLIAMS D (12A
CLAIRE BIDWELL B (1A PETE WILSON PROD (B NIGEL GRAY PROD (B

P33C ANDY PARTRIDGE P33C

ANDY PARTRIDGE (A (A) THE LURE OF SALVAGE 1980 VIRAN UK 2145

P33E PARZIVAL P33E

LOTHAR SIEMS G V (AB (A) LEGEND 1971 TELDEC GER 14635
WALTER QUINTUS B K VLN(AB (B) BA-ROCK 19 TELDEC GER 14685
THOMAS OLIVER D (AB
MATTHIAS MULLER-MENCKENS K(A JOACHIM REICHOLD CELLO(A HANS JASPER VLA (A WALTER V SEYDLITZ CELLO(B
MAT McMILLER K (B HARALD KONIETZKO B V (B

P33F NIK PASCAL P33F

NIK PASCAL D SYN(ABC (A) BEYOND THE END......ETERNITY 1971 NARCO NR 102
GYPSY FLEMING ORG ((B) SIXTH EAR 1972 NARCO NR 666
(C) MAGNETIC WEB 1973 NARCO NR 321

P34 PASSPORT P34

KLAUS DOLDINGER SAX K(ALL (A) PASSPORT 1971 ATLANTIC 40299
OLAF KUBLER WIND (A (B) SECOND 1972 ATLANTIC 40417
LOTHAR MEID B (A (C) HAND MADE 1973 ATLANTIC 40483
JIMMY JACKSON ORG (A (D) LOOKING THRU 1973 ATLANTIC US 7042 UK K50024
UDO LINDENBERG D (A (E) DOLDINGER JUBILEE(TRIPLE) 1973 ATLANTIC 60073
JOHN MEALING K (B (F) DOLDINGER 1973 ATLANTIC UK K44243
BRYAN SPRING D (B (G) DOLDINGER JUBILEE CONCERT 1974 ATLANTIC 50070
FRANK ROBERTS K (C (H) CROSS COLLATERAL 1975 ATLANTIC US 36107 50111
VOLKER KRIEGER G (G (J) DOLDINGER JUBILEE 75 1975 ATLANTIC US 18162 50186
ALEXIS KORNER G (G (K) INFINITY MACHINE 1976 ATLANTIC US 36132 UK K50354
BRIAN AUGER K (G (L) IGUACU 1977 ATLANTIC US 36149
WOLFGANG SCHMID B G (BCDEGHK (M) SKY BLUE 1978 ATLANTI US 19177
CURT CRESS D (CDGHKL (N) ATARAXIA 1978 ATLANTIC UK K50456
KRISTIAN SCHULTZE K (DGHK (O) GARDEN OF EDEN 1979 ATLANTIC US 19233 UK K50586
WILLY KETZER D (MONO (P) OCEANLINER 1980 ATLANTIC US 19265 50688
HENDRIK SCHAPER K (MOPN (Q) LIFELIKE 1980 ATLANTIC NL 60150
PEDRO SANTOS PERC (L
ELMER LOUIS PERC (MNL DIETER PETEREIT B (MNOP ROY LOUIS G (LMN GUILLERNO MARCHENA V PERC(MN
KEVIN MULLIGAN G V (OP HORST RAMTHOR HCA (O KATHY BARTNEY V (O DAVID CRIGGER D (P
MATS BJORKLIND G (L JOHNNY GRIFFIN SAX (G PETE YORK (G

P35 JACO PASTORIUS P35

JACO PASTORIUS B (AB (A) JACO PASTORIUS 1976 EPIC US 33949 UK 81453
DON ALIAS CONGA(A (B) JACO 1978 IMPRO ARTS IAI373846
DAVE PRATER V (A (C) WORD OF MOUTH 1981 WB UK K 56897 US 3535
RANDY BRECKER HRNS (A
RON TOOLEY TPT (A PETER GRAVES TROM (A DAVID SANBORN SAX (A MICHAEL BRECKER HRNS (A
HOWARD JOHNSON SAX (A HERBIE HANCOCK K (A NARADA MICHAEL WALDEN D (A SAM MOORE V (A
ALEX DAROU K (A LENNY WHITE D (A BOBBY ECONOMOU D (A STRING SECTION (A
WAYNE SHORTER SAX (A OTHELLO MOLINEAUX PERC (A LEROY WILLIAMS PERC (A PETER GORDON HRNS (A
HUBERT LAWS WIND (A PAUL BLEY (B

P35A PATAPHONE P35A

ANDRE VIAUD G (AB (A) PATAPHONE 19 POLE 003
GILLES ROUSSEAU D (AB LE MATIN BLANC 1978 FEERI 178
PIERRE DEMOURON B K (A

P36 BRIAN PATTEN P36

BRIAN PATTEN V (ABC (A) BRIAN PATTEN 1970 CAEDMON TC 1300
ROGER McGOUGH V (C (B) VANISHING TRICK 1971 TANGENT TGS 116
LINDA THOMPSON V (B (C) PATTEN & McGOUGH 1976 ARGO ZLP 1190
CLEO LAINE V (D (D) THE SLY CORMORANT 1977 ARGO UK ZSW607
DAVE RICHARDS, B (B
GERRY CONWAY D (B JOHN TAYLOR K (B NEIL INNES K (B JONNO DELMAR G (B
RICHARD THOMPSON G (B NORMA WINSTONE V (B ANDY ROBERTS G (B ALAN DALZIEL CELLO(B
PHIL LEE G (B STAN SULZMANN FLT (B BRIAN GASCOIGNE K (D CATHY WEISS VLN(D
SUKI TOWB CELLO(D DAVID LAWRENCE CLAR (D JOHN WILLIAMS G (D DAVID VORHAUS SYN (D

P36A BOBBY PATTERSON P36A

BOBBY PATTERSON V (AB (A) ITS JUST A MATTER OF TIME 1972 PAULA US LPS 2215
(B) SHE DONT HAVE TO SEE YOU(EP) 1980 CHARLY CTD 112

P37 PATTO P37

MIKE PATTO V (ABC (A) PATTO 1970 VERTIGO VEL 1001 + 6360 016
OLLIE HALSALL G K V(ABC (B) HOLD YOUR FIRE 1971 VERTIGO VEL 1008 6360 032
CLIVE GRIFFITHS B (ABC (C) ROLL EM SMOKE EM 1972 ISLAND UK ILPS9210 US 9322
JOHN HALSEY D (ABC

P37A HENRY PAUL BAND P37A

HENRY PAUL G V (ABC (A) GREY GHOST 1979 ATLANTIC US 19232
BILLY CRAIN G (ABC (B) FEEL THE HEAT 1980 ATLANTIC US 19273
DAVID FIESTER G V (ABC (C) ANYTIME 1981 ATLANTIC US 19325
WALLY DENTZ B (ABC
BILL HOFFMAN D (ABC BARRY RAPP K V (ABC JAI WINDING K (C MONTE YOHO D (AB
JOE LALA PERC (B JOE VITLAE SYN (B JON MATHIES SYN (B JIM FISH V (B
VALERIE WILSON V (B

P37B **BILLY PAUL** P37B

BILLY PAUL V (ALL — (A) WAR OF THE GODS — 1973 PHILADELPHIA US 32409
NORMAN FARRINGTON D(A — (B) 360 DEGREES OF — 1973 PHILADELPHIA UK 65930
ANTHONY JACKSON B (A — (C) WHEN LOVE IS NEW — 1976 PHILADELPHIA UK 69202
EDDIE GREEN K (A — (D) ONLY THE STRONG SURVIVE — 1977 PHILADELPHIA UK 82236
(E) FIRST CLASS — 1979 PHILADELPHIA UK 83481
(F) GREATEST HITS — 1980 PHILADELPHIA UK 84169

P38 **LES PAUL** P38

LES PAUL G (ALL — NEW SOUND 10 INCH — 195 CAPITOL 226
MARY FORD V (— NEW SOUND VOL2 10 INCH — 195 CAPITOL 286
CHET ATKINS G (* — BYE BYE BLUES 10 INCH — 195 CAPITOL 356
HIT MAKERS — 19 CAPITOL 416
LES & MARY — 19 CAPITOL 577
TIME TO DREAM — 19 CAPITOL 802
LOVER — 19 CAPITOL 1276
HITS OF LES & MARY — 19 CAPITOL 1476
LES PAUL & MARY FORD — 1965 HARMONY US 11133
LES PAUL NOW — 1968 DECCA UK LK 4924 + PFS 4138
LES PAUL NOW — 1968 LONDON US SP44101
VERY BEST OF — 1974 CAPITOL 23321
LES & MARY — 19 PICKWICK 3122
TIGER RAG — 19 PICKWICK 3145
STORY VOL 1 — 1974 CAPITOL EURO 052 81050
STORY VOL 2 — 1974 CAPITOL EURI 052 81359
WORLD IS WAITING FOR THE SUNRISE — 1974 CAPITOL US 11308
LES & MARY — 1975 CAPITOL 11308
GUIAR TAPESTRY — 19 PROJECT 3 US6-19/20
(*) GUITAR MONSTERS — 1978 RCA PL 12786
(*) CHESTER & LESTER — 1977 RCA LSA 3290
MULTI TRACKIN — 1979 LONDON US 50016

P39 **PAUPER** P39

SKIP PROKOP D V G(AB — (A) MAGIC PEOPLE — 1967 VERVE US 3026
ADAM MITCHELL G K V D(AB — (B) ELLIS ISLAND — 1968 VERVE US 3051
CHUCK BEAL G MAND (AB
DENNY GERRARD B (A — BRAD CAMPBELL G B D V(B — AL KOOPER K (B

P40 **PAVLOVS DOG** P40

DAVID SURKAMP G V (AB — (A) PAMPERED MENIAL — 1975 CBS US 33552 UK 80872
DOUG RAYBURN FLT B K (AB — (B) THE SOUND OF THE BELL — 1976 CBS US 33694 UK 81163
STEVE SCORFINA G (AB
DAVID HAMILTON K (AB — RICHARD STOCKTON B (AB — TOM NICKESON G V (B — MIKE SAFRON D (A
SIEGFRIED CARVER VLN (A — BILL BRUFORD D (B — MIKE ABEBE ORG (A — MICHAEL BRECKER SAX(B
GEORGE GENCH ORG (B — ANDY MACKAY SAX (B — LES NICOL G (B — PAUL PRESTOPINO MAND(B
ELLIOTT RANDALL G B (B — GAVIN WRIGHT VLN (B — MURRAY KRUGMAN PROD (A — SANDY PEARLMAN PROD(A

P41 **TOM PAXTON** P41

TOM PAXTON G V (ALL — (A) RAMBLIN BOY — 1964 ELEKTRA US EKS 7277 UK K42003
JACK BONUS WIND (E — (B) AIN'T THAT NEWS — 1965 ELEKTRA US EKS 7289 UK K42005
ALBERT BOUCHARD D (E — (C) OUTWARD BOUND — 1966 ELEKTRA US EKS 7317 UK K42007
DAVID BROMBERG G (EF — (D) MORNING AGAIN — 1968 ELEKTRA US EKS74019 UK K42019
HERB BUSHLER B (EFO — (E) THINGS I NOTICE NOW — 1969 ELEKTRA US EKS74043 UK K42028
JOHNNY COLES HRNS (E — (F) NUMBER 6 — 1970 ELEKTRA US EKS74066 UK K42047
RICHARD GRAND WIND (E — (G) THE COMPLEAT TOM PAXTON — 1971 ELEKTRA US 7E 2003 UK K62004
DAVID HOROWITZ K (EFH — (H) HOW COME THE SUN — 1971 REPRISE US RS 6443 UK K44129
HUBERT LAWS FLT (E — (J) PEACE WILL COME — 1972 REPRISE US RS 2096 UK K44182
JIMMY MADISON D (E — (K) NEW SONGS OLD FRIENDS — 1973 REPRISE US RS 2144 UK K44237
MAX POLLIKOFF VLN (E — (L) CHILDRENS SONG BOOK — 1974 BRADLEYS UK BRADN601
ROBERT SYLVESTER CELLO(E — (M) SOMETHING IN MY LIFE — 1975 MAM UK MAM 1002
STEVE GOODMAN G V (O — (M) SOMETHING IN MY LIFE — 1975 PRIVATE STOCK US 2002
ANGEL ALLENDE V (O — (N) SATURDAY NIGHT — 1976 MAM UK MAMS1003
IAN HUNT G (M — (O) NEW SONGS FROM THE BRIAR PATCH — 1977 MAM UK MAMS1005
DAVE WILLIS B (KMH — (O) NEW SONGS FROM THE BRIAR PATCH — 1977 VANGUARD US VSD79395
PETER WOOD K (M — (P) HEROES — 1978 VANGUARD VSD79411
BARRY DE SOUZA D (M — (Q) UP & UP — 1980 MOUNTAIN RAILWAY US 52792
BARRY KORNFIELD BAN G(A — (Q) UP & UP — 1980 EVOLUTION UK E2
FELIX PAPPALARDI G (A
CHRIS KARAN PERC (KM — NANCY LEE BAXTER V (P — KENNETH KOSEK VLN (P — ERIC WEISSBERG G MAND (P
GARY CHESTER D (P — PETER SARSTEDT V (K — RALPH McTELL G V HCA (K — GARY MURE D (P
TONY VISCONTI G (K — MARY VISCONTI V (K — RAYMOND MANTILLA PERC (P — JENNIFER PAXTON V (K
DANNY THOMPSON B (K — PAUL PRESTOPINO G (F — TEDDY SOMMER D (F — MARK HOROWITZ G BAN (H
MIKE MORGAN G (H — JULIAN CUMMINGS VLN (H — BRIAN ODGERS B (H — SUE EVANS D (H
CHRIS SLADE D (H — DIANA CUMMINGS VLN (H — HARRY PITCH HCA (H — LUCIANO JORIO VLN (H
DOUGLAS CUMMINGS CELLO(H — KATY PAXTON V (K — MIKE BRITTAIN B (H — CHRIS LAURENCE B (H
JEFF CLYNE B (H

P41A **PAYOLAS** P41A

PAUL HYDE G V K(— (A) IN A PLACE LIKE THIS — 1981 A&M UK 70017
BOB ROOK G V K(
GARY MIDDLECLASS B K (— TAYLOR NELSON LITTLE D V K(

P42 **JOHN PAYNE** P42

JOHN PAYNE (AB — (A) BEDTIME STORIES — 19 ARISTA AL 1025
(B) RAZOR'S EDGE — 1977 ARISTA AL 1036

P42A **PAZ** P42A

BRIAN SMITH FLT (A — (A) KANDEEN LOVE SONG — 1977 SPOTLIGHT SPJ 507
GEOFF CASTLE K (A
PHIL LEE G (A — RON MATTHEWSON B (A — DICK CROUCH PERC (A — DAVE SHEEN D (A
SIMON MORTON PERC (A — RAY WARLEIGH FLT (A — CHRIS FLETCHER CONGA(A

P42B DAVE PEABODY P42B

DAVE PEABODY G HCA(AB (A) PEABODY HOTEL 1973 VILLAGE THING VTS 22
HUGH McNULTY B (B (B) KEEP IT CLEAN 1974 MATCHBOX SDM 261
BILL SHORTT WASHB(B
DAVE GRIFFITHS MAND (B DIZ WATSON K (B IAN A ANDERSON G (B ANDY LEGGETT JUG(B

P43A DAVE PEACE P43A

DAVE PEACE K V (A (A) GOOD MORNING 1969 saga FID 2155
MICK WALSH D (A
DAVE 'LILLY' LLOYD G (A DAVE PEGG B (A

P44 PEACHES & HERB P44

FRANCINE'PEACHES'HURD V(ALL (A) LETS FALL IN LOVE 1967 CBS UK 62966 US DATE 4004
HERB FAME V (ALL (B) FOR YOUR LOVE 1967 CBS UK 63119 US DATE 4005
PETE ROBINSON K SYN(FG (C) GOLDEN DUETS 19 DATE US TES 4007
FREDDIE PERREN PNO VIBES(FG ( ) GREATEST HITS 1968 DATE US 4017
JOHN BARNES K SYN(E (D) PEACHES & HERB 1977 MCA UK MCF2802 US 2261
EDDIE WATKINS B (FG (E) 2 HOT 1979 POLYDOR US 1 6172 UK 2391 378
JAMES GADSON D (FGE (F) TWICE THE FIRE 1979 POLYDOR US 1 6239 UK 2391 433
BOB BOWLES G (EFG (G) WORTH THE WAIT 1980 POLYDOR UK 2391 484
DAVID T WALKER G (E (H) LOVE IS STRANGE 1979 CBS US 36089
WAH WAH WATSON G (FEG
PAULINHO DA COSTA PERC (EFG BOB ZIMITTI PERC (FEG CLARENCE McDONALD K (G JOSE FELICIANO G (G
EDDIE BROWN CONGA(G KATIE KIRKPATRICK HARP (G GARY HERBIG SAX (G MAXINE WILLARD V (G
JULIA TILLMAN V (G LUTHER WATERS V (G OREN WATERS V (G LARRY FARROW K (E
BOB RABATAILLE SYN (E

P45 ANNETTE PEACOCK P45

ANNETTE PEACOCK V K SYN(ALL (A) BLEY/PEACOCK SYNTHESIZER SHOW 1971 POLYDOR 2425 043
MICK RONSON G (E (B) I'M THE ONE 1972 RCA US LSP 4578 UK SF 8255
BILL BRUFORD D (E (C) IMPROVISE 1973 AMERICA FR 6121
GEORGE KHAN SAX (E (D) DUAL UNITY 1973 FREEDOM UK 40109 GERM 2383 105
DAVE CHAMBERS HRNS (E (E) X DREAMS 1978 AURA UK AUL702 US TOMATO 7025
TOM COSGROVE G (ABE (F) PERFECT DREAMS PERFECT RELEASE 1979 AURA UK AUL707 US TOMATO 7044
STEVE HAAS D (A (G) SKY SKATING 1982 IRONIC UK IRON2
JEFF CLYNE B (E (1) 1974 TOUR (NO ALBUM)
CHRIS SPEDDING G (E
SAM PHIPPS SAX (1 ROBBIE SCHWIMMER K (1 PETE LA ROCCA D (1 PAUL BLEY K (ABCD
STU WOODS B (ABE RICK MAROTTA D (ABE MICHAEL GARSON K (AB GLEN MOORE B (AB
LAURENCE COOK D (ABD MICHAEL MOSS SAX (B BARRY ALTSCHUL D PERC (AB AIRTO MOREIRA PERC(B
ORESTES VILATO PERC (B DOMIUN ROMAO PERC (B APACHE BLEY PNO (B RICHARD YOUNGSTEIN B(A
BOB MASSON K (A PERRY ROBINSON CLAR (A MARK WHITECAGE SAX (A HAN BENNINK PERC(CD
MARIO PAVONE B (D JIM MULLEN G (E BRIAN GODDING G (E PHIL LEE G (E
KUMA HARADA B (E PETER PAVLI B (E STEVE COOK B (E JOHN HALSEY D (E
DAVE SHEEN D (E DARRYL LE QUE PERC (EF BROTHER JAMES PERC (E RAY WARLIEGH SAX (E
PETER LEMER K (E MAX MIDDLETON K (F ROBERT AHWAI G (F RICHARD BAILEY D (F
JOHN MacKENZIE B (F LENNOX LANGTON PERC (F A R FOX V (G

P46 PEANUT BUTTER CONSPIRACY P46

JIM VOIGHT D (AB (A) IS SPREADING 1968 CBS US 9454
AL BRACKETT B (AB (B) GREAT CONSPIRACY 1968 CBS US 9590
LANCE FENT G (AB (C) FOR CHILDREN OF ALL AGES 196 CHALLENGE US 2000
JOHN MERRILL G (AB
SANDI ROBINSON V (AB BILL WOLF G HCA (AB

P47 BOB PEARCE BLUES BAND P47

BOB PEARCE G V HCA(ALL (1) BLUES CRUSADE (EP) 1968 AVENUE BEV 1054
BOB GORMAN G V (1 (2) LET'S GET DRUNK AGAIN(SOLO) 1974 WESTWOOD WRS 040
ROGER CHANTLER D (1 (3) COLOUR BLIND 1979 FOREST TRACKS FT 3015
PETE HARRIS G V K(4Za (4)I'M A BLUEMAN (EP) 1981 WHITE ELEPHANT UK RIOCH 2
PAUL BRYER G V(NOPQRSTUVWXY3 (5) NEW ALBUM 1983 ?
KEVIN FRANCIS B V (1
DANNY KELLY D (C (A) 68/FEB 69 (B) FEB 69/JUL 70 (C) JUL 70/OCT 70 (D) OCT 70/NOV 70
GLENN'JUDGE'LEE D(ACDEFGHJKLMVWX (E) NOV 70/NOV 71 (F) NOV 71/FEB 72 (G) FEB 72/OCT 74 (H) OCT 74/NOV 74
TONY BURNETT D (NO (J) NOV 74/DEC 74 (K) DEC 74/FEB 75 (L) FEB 75/NOV 75 (M) NOV 75/APR 76
JOHN PICKEN D (PQ (N) APR 76/JUL 76 (O) JUL 76/AUG 76 (P) AUG 76/OCT 76 (Q) OCT 76/NOV 76
CHRIS NEWMAN D (R (R) NOV 76/JUL 77 (S) JUL 77/AUG 77 (T) AUG 77/SEP 77 (U) SEP 77/JAN 78
BARRY FREEMAN D (ST (V) JAN 78/JUL 78 (W) JUL 78/DEC 78 (X) DEC 78/FEB 79 (Y) FEB 79/MAY 80
HENRY WRIGHT D (UY34Zab (Z) MAY 80/MAY 81 (a) MAY 81/MAY 82 (b) MAY 82/SEPT 82 (c) SEPT82/JAN 83
BIG JOHN McATEE B (CD
BOB WILLIAMS B (H PETE 'BALDY' WARD B(MNOPQR ERNEST FAGG B (ST KEN WHEELER B (UVW
JOSS JONES B (XY34Z CHRIS GODDEN G (F MICK WILLIAMS G (H DEREK GARDENER G (J
DOUG WALKER G (K VERNON CHUTER G (MNOP JOHN MARSHALL SAX (O LEE GOODALL SAX (N
PAPA JOHN LIVERMORE GK(3BY DAVE 'DOMINO'WARD HCA(TUV JOHN CARTWRIGHT B (* PETE HUNT D (*
CARL'SONNY'LEYLAND PNO(4Zabc PETE PLASCOTT B (abc
MIKE STEEL G (bc DANNY KELLY D (c (*) INVALUABLE ASSISTANCE THROUGH THE YEARS

P48 PEARL P48

DEBBIE PEARL V (A (A) PEARL 1977 LONDON US 692 UK SHU 8508
LESLIE PEARL V (A
DEAN PARKS G (A RUSS KUNKEL D (A MARK LEVINE B (A

P48A PEARL HARBOUR P48A

PEARL E GATES V PERC (AB (A) AND THE EXPLOSIONS 1980 WB US BSK 3404 UK K56769
PETER BILT G V (A (B) DON'T FOLLOW ME, I'M LOST TOO 1980 WB US BSK 3515 UK K56885
HILARY STENCH B V (A
JOHN STENCH D (A

P49 PEARLS BEFORE SWINE P49

TOM RAPP G V (ALL (A) ONE NATION UNDERGROUND 1967 ESP US 1054 NL 858115
WAYNE HARLEY BAN V(ABC (B) BALAKLAVA 1968 ESP US 1075
LANE LEDERER B G HRNS V(AB (C) THESE THINGS TOO 1969 REPRISE RSLP 6364
ROGER CRISSINGER K (A (D) THE USE OF ASHES 1970 REPRISE RSLP 6405
WARREN SMITH D (A (E) CITY OF GOLD 1971 REPRISE RSLP 6442
JIM BOHANNON K (B (F) BEAUTIFUL LIES YOU COULD LIVE 1971 REPRISE RSLP 6467
RICHARD ALDERSON PROD(A (AB) BEST OF(DBL)? 1980 ADELPHI US 4111
JOE FARRELL WIND (B
LU CRABTREE K FLT(B BILL SALTER B (BC AL SHACKMAN G (B DAVID NOYES V (E
ELIZABETH V (CDEF RICHARD GREENE VLN (C MORRIE E BROWN B (F GRADY TATE D (C

(CONTINUED)

P49 (CONTINUED)

PEARLS BEFORE SWINE P49

GORDON HAYES B (F MICHAEL KRAWITZ PNO (F BILLY MUNDI D (F BOB DOROUGH PNO(F
STU SCHARF G (F AMOS GARRETT G (F HERB LOVELL D (F JOHN DUKE WIND(D
JERRY JEMMOTT B (F CHARLIE McCOY V G B HCA(D BUDDY SPICHER VLN (F HUTCH DAVIE WIND(D
NORBERT PUTNAM B (D BILL PIPPIN WIND (D KEN BUTTREY D (D MAC GAYDEN G (D
DAVID BRIGGS K (D JOHN TOOKER G (F JIM FAIRS G V K(C STEVE GRABLE K (F

P49A

KEITH PEARSON P49A

KEITH PEARSON G V BAN(A (A) RIGHT HAND BAND 1976 ERON 014
PAUL CRASWELL B V (A
DAVE CRASWELL G V PERC(A DAVE ARBUS VLN SAX V (A

P49B

PEDDLER P49B

KENNY WEIR G V PERC((A) STREETCORNER STUFF 1976 UA US LA665G
RUSSELLL TAYLOR D V (A
BO GOOLIAK B G K V(A JOHN CASCELLA K SAX(A RANDY STIERER K SYN(A

P50

HERB PEDERSEN P50

HERB PEDERSEN V (AB (A) SOUTHWEST 1976 EPIC US 34225
CHRIS SMITH G (A (B) SANDMAN 1977 EPIC US 34933
ED CARTER (A
JIM GORDON D (A JOHN GUERIN D (A LARRY CARLTON G (A JOSH GRAVES DOBRO (A
AL PERKINS G (A MIKE BAIRD D (A ROY DEAN WEBB MAND (A DAVID LINDLEY (A
GARY COLEMAN PERC (A EMMYLOU HARRIS V (A LEE SKLAR B (AB LINDA RONSTADT V (AB
DOLLY PARTON V (B LOWELL GEORGE G (B JOEY SCARBURY (B JOHNNY RIVERS (AB

P50A

PEE WEE & SPECIALS P50A

PEE WEE & SPECIALS 1980 ROCKHOUSE NL 8004

P51

ANN PEEBLES P51

ANN PEEBLES V (ALL (A) THIS IS 1969 HI US 32053
HOWARD GRIMES D (DF (B) PART TIME LOVE 1971 HI US 32059
LEROY HODGES B (DF (C) STRAIGHT FROM THE HEART 1972 HI US 32065 UK LONDON SHU8434
CHARLES HODGES K (DF (D) CANT STAND THE RAIN 1974 HI US 32079 UK LONDON SHU8468
ED LOGAN SAX (DF (E) TELLIN' IT 1976 HI US 32091 UK LONDON SHU8490
WAYNE JACKSON TPT (DF (F) STAR PORTRAIT 1977 CREAM US 58100 GER 6002
JAMES DROY D (F (G) IF THIS IS HEAVEN 1978 HI US 6002
JAMES MITCHELL SAX (B (H) HANDWRITING IS ON THE WALL 197 HI US 6007
TEENIE HODGES G (DF (J) STRAIGHT 1970 HI US 8009
ANDREW LOVE SAX (DF
JACK HALE TROM (DF ARCHIE TURNER K (DF BEN CAULEY TPT (F EDGAR MATTOUS TPT(F
BILL EASLEY SAX (F DONNA RHODES V (F SANDRA RHODES/CHALMERS V(F

P52

KEVIN PEEK P52

KEVIN PEEK G (A (A) AWAKENING 1982 ARIOLA UK 5065
(B) LIFE & OTHER GAMES 1982 ARIOLA UK 5067

P53

DAVID PEEL & LOWER EAST SIDE P53

DAVID PEEL V G (ALL (A) HAVE A MARIJUANA 1968 ELEKTRA US EKS74032
HAROLD C BLACK V TAMB(ABHI (B) AMERICAN REVOLUTION 1970 ELEKTRA UK 2410 001 US EKS74069
LARRY ADAM G (A (C) THE POPE SMOKES DOPE 1972 APPLE US SW 3391
TONY BARTOLI D (B (D) SANTA CLAUS ROOFTOP JUNKIE 1974 RLF 001 RI 79 ORANGE 711
BILLY JOE WHITE G (AB (E) AN EVENING WITH 1976 ORANGE US ORA 713
GEORGE CORI B (A (F) BRING BACK THE BEATLES 1977 ORANGE US 004
CHRIS OSBORNE (C (G) KING OF PUNK 1978 ORANGE US 700
EDDIE MOTTAU (C (H) JOHN LENNON FOR PRESIDENT 1980 ORANGE US 005
EDDIE RYAN (C (I) DEATH TO DISCO 1980 ORANGE US 666
HERB BUSHLER B (B
DAVID HOROWITZ ORG (B RICHARD GRANDO SAX (B LES FRADKIN G K B V(DFI PAUL THORTON G V PERC(DF
MICHAEL ANGELO G V (DF ANDY FRIEDMAN D PERC(D GRIMES TPT(D RON SKOLER V (D
MARK SHATASKY V (D A J WEBERMAN V (D JEFF GILLMAN G (F ANDY PIERCE G (FI
TOM DOYLE B V G (FGHI MIKE MURRAY B (F FRED KRAMER D (F SCOTT BAILEY D V (F
SAL SPICOLLA SAX (F DEREK LIPMAN PERC (F DANNY LIPMAN PERC(F TOMMY ACOSTA V (G
RON BLOTTER V (GH CHRIS BOVASSO G V (G EDDIE CRISS G (GHI BOB DELIA G (G
AL DONNELLY V (G STEVE GIORDANO B (G BARRY GUBER G (G SHANE HARRIS V (G
RICHARD HOFFMAN V (G GREG LANNER G (G PHYLISS LEE PERC V (GHI MARUGA D V (GI
JOHN MICHAELS PERC (G PETE MONTANO PERC (G PAT RAMPEY G V (G DAVID A SCHURE G V (G
HANK SHUSTER G V (G NICK TRIP V (G PEPE VALENTINE PERC G V(GH PAUL S WEISS PERC V(G
DAVID YIFRACH G (G MITCH BLOTTER PERC V K (HI MARGOT DAY FLT (H GARY DORFMAN V (HI
BILL DOWNING V PERC(HI CURTIS FIELDS PERC SAX(HI MARK TRUTHE TAMB V (H B B GUN PERC(H
JOHN HAGEL G (H ANDY LLOYD CONGA(HI YOKO ONO PERC V(H ED PERPER V (H
GABRIEL REXACH V B (HI STEVE ROSENTHAL V K (HI NAGED ABELL V G (H FLOYD AVERY FLEMING PERC(H
JOE BOZZA PERC (H ADELE EVANS G V (H BOB GURTLRT V (H ISHMAEL G V (H
YES LEVY G V (H HANK NUESSLEIN V TAMB(H DONNA SCHALL V K (H JOHN STASIC V PERC(HI
WAYNE KRAMER G (I TERRY MANN B (ISACHA NELSON FLT (I CLANCEY MORALES PERC(I
DAVID GALE B (I TOM DE GENNO G (I ADELE KRAUS V (I SHEENA MITCHELL V (I
STEVE BENJAMIN G (I HANK WYATT G V (I SCOTT SEVERIN V (I EDDIE RHODES V (I
GARY SCHWARTZ PERC (I MICHAEL SUBRIZI PERC (I RIK CHEN YOUNG V (I JOEY BELL G (I
MIKE GIRAO G (I ROB BASSO G (I STEVE VICTIM B (I PHIL LOONEY K (I
RODIE KAISER TPT (I FRANKY CADILLAC B (I G G ALLIN G (I ALAN CHAPPLE G (I

P54

BOB PEGG P54

BOB PEGG G V WIND(ABC (A) BOB PEGG & NICK STRUTT 1973 TRANSATLANTIC TRA 265
NICK STRUTT G MAND(AB (B) SHIPBUILDER 1974 TRANSATLANTIC TRA 280
STEVE SIMPSON G VLN(B (C) ANCIENT MAPS 1975 TRANSATLANTIC TRA 299
RICHIE BULL B (B
DAVE HAMMEL D (B CHRIS TAYLOR RECORDER(C RICHARD McNICOL RECORDER (C ADRIAN BRETT RECORDER(C
ROGER BRENNER SACKBUT (C MALCOLM FISHER SACKBUT (C JOHN EDNEY SACKBUT(C DAVID PURSER SACKBUT (C
TONY COE CLAR (C DAVID CROPPER HRNS (C MIKE LAIRD CORNETTO (C IAN WILSON CORNETTO(C
BILL STOKES CORNETTO (C RAY WARLEIGH FLT (C PAUL HARVEY CLAR (C NORMAN WEBB HARP(C
BRENT FORBES B (C GRAHAM FIELD K (C HAROLD FISHER D (C RICK RUSSELL G (C
B J COLE STEEL(A MICK YARROW (B

P55

BOB & CAROLANNE PEGG P55

BOB PEGG G V WIND(A (A) HE CAME FROM THE MOUNTAIN 1971 TRAILER UK LER 3016
CAROLANNE PEGG V (A

P56 CAROLANNE PEGG P56

CAROLANNE PEGG V (A (A) CAROLANNE PEGG 1973 TRANSATLANTIC UK TRA 266
ALBERT LEE G K (A
KEITH NELSON BANJO(A MICHAEL LAVELLE CELLO(A ALUN EDEN D (A PAUL ROWAN HCA(A
DAVE PEACOCK B G (A

P56A JIM PEMBROKE P56A

JIM PEMBROKE (ABC (A) WICKED IVORY 19
RONNIE OSTERBERG D (C (B) PIGWORM 1974 LOVE SWED
REKKU RECHARDT G (C (C) CORPORAL CAULIFLOWERS MENTAL FUNCTION 1977
CASTE APRETREA G (C
PAAVO MAIJANEN B V (C EERO KOIVISTOINEN HRNS(C HESSU HIETANEN ACC (C

P56B TEDDY PENDERGASS P56B

TEDDY PRENDERGRASS V (ALL (A) TEDDY PRENDERGRASS 1977 P I R UK 81756
VICTOR CARSTARPHON K (A (B) LIFE IS A SONG WORTH SINGING 1978 P I R UK 82555
DEXTER WANSEL K (AD (C) TEDDY 1979 P I R UK 83656
ROLAND CHAMBERS G (AD (D) T P 1980 P I R UK 84542
DENNIS HARRIS G (AD (E) READY FOR TEDDY 1981 P I R UK 84903
MICHAEL FOREMAN B (A (F) ITS TIME FOR LOVE 1981 P I R UK 85220
JAMES WILLIAMS B (ADF (G) THIS ONES FOR YOU 1982 P I R UK 85937
KEITH BENSEN D (AD
KARL CHAMBERS D (A LARRY WASHINGTON CONGA(A M F S B HRNS STR (AF VALERIE SIMPSON K V (D
ERIC GALE G (D BARBARA INGRAM V (D FRANCISCO CENTENO B (D CHRIS PARKER D (D
RALPH MACDONALD PERC(D NICKOLAS ASHFORD V (D STEPHANIE MILLS V (D CECIL WOMACK G (D
THE FUTURES V (D SAM REED SAX (F LENNY PAKULA ORG (F JAMES CARTER D (F
LEON HUFF K (F KENNETH GAMBLE V (F

P57 ALVARO PENA ROJAS P57

ALVARO PENA ROJAS K V B FLT(A (A) DRINKING MY OWN SPERM 197 SQUEAKY SHOE SSRDR 1
ANTONIO NARVAEZ D V (A
CATHY WILLIAMS V (A

P58 PENETRATION P58

PAULINE MURRAY V (ABC (A) MOVING TARGETS 1978 VIRGIN UK V 2109 GER 200170
FRED PURSER G K (ABC (B) DANGER SIGNS (EP) 1979 VIRGIN UK V25712
GARY SMALLMAN D (ABC (C) COMING UP FOR AIR 1979 VIRGIN UK V 2131 GER 200 964
NEALE FLOYD G (ABC (D) RACE AGAINST TIME(OFFICIAL BOOT) 1980 CLIFDAYN
ROBERT BLAMIRE B (ABC
STEVE JACOBS D (

P59 PENGUINS P59

CLEVELAND DUNCAN V ((A) COOL COOL PENGUINS 19 DOOTONE US DTE 242
DEXTER TISBY V (
CURTIS WILLIAMS V (BRUCE TATE V (RANDY JONES V (TEDDY HARPER V (

P59A PEOPLE P59A

ROBB LEVIN B (ABC (A) I LOVE YOU 1968 CAPITOL US 2924
DENNY FRIDKIN D (ABC (B) BOTH SIDE OF PEOPLE 1968 CAPITOL US 151
ALBERT RIBISI ORG (ABC (C) THERE ARE PEOPLE 19 PARAMOUNT US 5013
JOHN TRISTAO V (ABC
TOM TUCKER G V (C GENE MASON V (AB LAWRENCE V (AB JEFF LEVIN G (AB

P59B PEOPLE BAND P59B

CHARLIE WATTS D (A (A) PEOPLE BAND 1970 TRANSATLANTIC UK TRA 214
MEL DAVIS (A
TERRY DAY (A LYN DOBSON (A EDDIE EDEM (A GEORGE KHAN (A
TONY EDWARDS (A MICK FIGGIS (A FRANK FLOWERS (A TERRY HALMAN (A
RUSS HERNEY (A

P59C PEOPLES CHOICE P59C

FRANKIE BRUSON K V (AB (A) BOOGIE DOWN U S A 1975 PIR UK 69175
DAVID THOMDSON PERC (AB (B) WE GOT THE RHYTHM 1976 PIR UK 81370
ROGER ANDREWS B (AB
GUY FISKE G (AB BOBBY ELI G (A NORMAN HARRIS G (A VICTOR CARSTARPHEN ORG(AB
ZACK ZACHERY SAX (A M F S B HRNS (A DONALD FORD K (B DARNELL JORDON G (B
LEON HUFF V SYN(B JOHN WHITEHEAD V (B GENE McFADDEN V (B SAM PEAKE SAX (B

P60 PENTANGLE P60

BERT JANSCH G V (ALL (A) THE PENTANGLE 1960 TRANSATLANTIC UK TRA162 US REPRISE 6315
JACQUI McSHEE V (ALL (B) SWEET CHILD (DBL) 1968 TRANSATLANTIC UK TRA178 US REPRISE 6334
TERRY COX D PERC(ALL (C) BASKET OF LIGHT 1969 TRANSATLANTIC UK TRA205 US REPRISE 6372
JOHN RENBOURNE G V SITAR(ALL (C) BASKET OF LIGHT 1969 METRONOME GER 201 051
DANNY THOMPSON B (ALL (D) CRUEL SISTER 1970 TRANSATLANTIC UK TRA228 GER 44005
(D) RUEL SISTER 197 XTRA UK 1172 REPRISE US 6430
(E) REFLECTIONS 1971 TRANSATLANTIC UK TRA240 US REPRISE 6463
(F) SOLOMONS SEAL 1972 REPRISE UK K44197 US 2100
(G) HISTORY BOOK (COMP) 1972 TRANSATLANTIC UK TRASAM23
(H) PENTANGLING 1973 TRANSATLANTIC UK TRASAM29 RI 81 TRS 106
(J) PENTANGLE COLLECTION(COMP 1975 TRANSATLANTIC UK 89503/4
(K) ANTHOLOGY (COMP) 1978 TRANSATLANTIC UK MTRA 2013

P60A JIM PEPPER P60A

JIM PEPPER V SAX D(A (A) PEPPERS POW WOW 1971 ATLANTIC UK 2400 149
RAVIE PEPPER FLT V(A
LARRY CORYELL G (A TOM GRANT PNO V(A CHUCK RAINEY B (A BILLY COBHAM D (A
JERRY JEMMOTT B (A SPIDER RICE D (A GIB PEPPER V D (A

P60B VICTOR PERAINO'S KINGDOM COME P60B

VICTOR PERAINO K V (A (A) NO MANS LAND 1975 MKC 5121 N10
DAVID WILD D (A
EDWARD HOWLEHAN D (A PAUL ROGERSON B V (A JON LAFLOTTE FLT G V (A DAVID CHRISTIAN G (A
HERMAN DALDIN B (A

P61 PERE UBU P61

DAVID THOMAS V (1234ABCDEFG (A) MODERN DANCE 1978 BLANK US 001 UK MERCURY 9100052
ALLEN RAVENSTINE K (134ABCEG (A) MODERN DANCE RI 198 ROUGH TRADE UK ROUGH 22
THOMAS LAUGHNER G (1234CBEG (B) DUB HOUSING 1978 CHRYSALIS UK CHR1207 GER 6307646
TOM HERMAN G (2134ACBEG (C) DATAPANIK IN THE YEAR ZERO(EP) 1978 RADAR UK RDR1
TIM WRIGHT B (123CG (D) DATAPANIK IN THE YEAR ZERO(LP) 1979 ATLANTIC UK K50587
SCOTT KRAUSS D (1234ABDEG (E) NEW PICNIC TIME 1979 CHRYSALIS UK CHR1248 NL 511248
TONY MAIMONE B (ABCEG (F) ART OF WALKING 1980 ROUGH TRADE UK ROUGH 14
ALAN GREENBLATT G (4C (G) 390' SIMULATED STEREO 198 ROUGH TRADE UK ROUGH "£
DAVID TAYLOR K (2CG (1) 1975 (2) 1976 (3) 1976 (4) 1977

P62 CHRISTINE PERFECT P62

CHRISTINE(McVIE) PERFECT K V(ALL (A) CHRISTINE PERFECT 1970 BLUE HORIZON UK 7 63860
TOP TOPHAM G (AC (B) ALBATROSS (1 SIDE) 1977 EMBASSY UK 31569
RICK HAYWARD G (AC (C) THE LENGENDARY CP ALBUM 1978 SIRE SASD 7522
MARTIN DUNSFORD B (A
DANNY KIRWAN G (AC JOHN McVIE B (AC ANDY SYLVESTER B (B STAN WEBB G (B
DAVE BIDWELL D (B CHRIS HARDING D (A

P63 CARL PERKINS P63

CARL PERKINS G V (ALL (A) DANCE ALBUM "TEENBEAT" 1959 LONDON UK HA 2202 US SUN 1225
WES HOLLAND D (1 (B) WHOLE LOTTA SHAKIN' 1959 CBS US 1234
JAY PERKINS G (1 (C) COUNTRY BOY DREAMS 1968 LONDON UK SHP8366 US DOLLIE4001
CLAYTON PERKINS B (1 (D) ON TOP 1969 CBS US 9931
STAN PERKINS D (2 (E) BLUE SUEDE SHOES 1969 LONDON UK HAS2202 US SUN 112
GREG PERKINS B (2 (E) BLUE SUDE SHOES 1974 SUN UK 6467 009
DAVID SEA SAX (2 (F) ORIGINAL GOLDEN HITS 1970 SUN UK 6467 004 US 111
LEE McALPIN PNO (2 (G) KING OF ROCK 19 CBS UK 63309
HAROLD BRADLEY G (P (H) BOPPIN THE BLUES(N R B Q) 1970 CBS UK 63826 US 9981
RAY EDENTON G (P (I) CARL PERKINS 19 HARMONY US 11385
JERRY KENNEDY G (P (J) BROWN EYED HANDSOME MAN 1972 HARMONY US 31179
JERRY SHOOK G (PV (K) GREATEST HITS 1973 HARMONY US 31792
PETE WADE G (P (K) GREATEST HITS 19 CBS US 9833 UK 63676
CHIP YOUNG G (P (L) MATCHBOX 19 PICKWICK US JS6103 HILLTOP 6103
BUDDY HARMON D (P (M) MAN BEHIND JOHNNY CASH 1972 CBS 64892
BOB MOORE B (P (N) BEST OF 19 TRIP US TLX8503
HENRY STRZELECKI B (P (O) GREATEST HITS 197 EMBASSY UK 31527
PIG ROBBINS K (P (P) MY KIND OF COUNTRY 1974 MERCURY US SRM1691 UK 6338 475
MICHAEL LEECH B (V (Q) ROCKIN GUITAR MAN 1975 CHARLY UK CR30003
GAYLE WHITFIELD SAX (V (R) ORIGINAL CARL PERKINS 1976 CHARLY UK CR30110
HOYT HAWKINS V (V (S) CARL PERKINS SHOW 1976 SUEDE US NR 6778
GINGER HOLLADAY V (V (T) LONG TALL SALLY 1977 EMBASSY UK 31554
STEVE FERGUSON G V HCA(H (U) FROM JACKSON TENNESSEE 1977 LAKE COUNTY US LC 505
PETE DRAKE STEEL(P (V) OL' BLUE SUEDES BACK 1978 JET US JTLA 856 UK 30146
CHARLIE McCOY HCA (P (W) OL' BLUE SUEDES BACK 1978 JET US 35604
HAYWARD BISHOP D (V (X) SUN SOUNDS SPECIAL 1978 CHARLY UK CR30152
DAVID BRIGGS PNO (V (Y) SUN STORY VOL 3 1979 SUN US 9330 903
WELDON MYRICK STEEL(V (Z) TENNESSEE 19 DESIGN US DLP 611
HUGH STOKER V (V ( ) ROCKIN' GUITAR MAN 1982 CHARLY UK 1015
NEAL MATTHEWS V (V
RAYMOND L WALKER V (V LEA JANE BERINATI V (V LISA SILVER V (V JODY STNICHOLAS B V (H
TOM STALEY D (H FRANK GADLEY V PERC(H DONN ADAMS TROM(H
(1) EARLY BANDS (2) 1978 TOUR

P63A JOE PERRY(PROJECT) P63A

JOE PERRY G V (AB (A) LET THE MUSIC DO THE TALKING 1980 CBS US 36888 UK 84213
RALPH MORMAN V (A (B) IVE GOT THE ROCK'N'ROLLS AGAIN 1981 CBS US 37374 NL 85145
DAVID HULL V B (AB
RONNIE STEWART D (AB CHARLIE FARREN G V (B

P64 JOHN PERRY P64

JOHN PERRY B V K(A (A) SUNSET WADING 1976 DECCA UK SKL 5233
RUPERT HINE K SYN V(A
MIKE GILES D (A GEOFF RICHARDSON VLA FLT(A BERYL STREETER V (A MORRIS PERT PERC(A
ELIO D'ANNA WIND (A CARRADO RUSTICCI G (A ROGER GLOVER SYN (A SIMON JEFFES KOTO(A
STRING SECTION (A

P65 LEE PERRY P65

LEE PERRY (ALL AFRICA BLOOD 19 TROJAN TBL 166
REVOLUTION DUB 1979 CACTUS CTLP 112
BEST OF LEE PERRY & UPSETTERS 19 JET STAR PTLP1023

P65A MARK PERRY P65A

MARK PERRY G V WIND(A (A) SNAPPY TURNS 1980 UK DEPTFORD FUN CITY DLP06
DENNIS BURNS V SAX B(A
ANNE VLN (A GRANT SHOWBIZ B (A HAG SYN V(A TYRONE THOMAS G (A

P65B PAUL PERSONNE P65B

PAUL PERSONNE G V HCA(A (A) PAUL PERSONNE 1982 EPIC UK 85445
DANIEL ANTOINE K (A
PHILIPPE FLORIS D (A GINO B (A PHIL MARLO G (A BOBBY BRUNO PROD(A

P66 PERSUADERS P66

PERSUADERS 1974 ATLANTIC UK K40476 US 7021
BEST THING THATS HAPPENED TO ME 1976 ATLANTIC US 7046
THIN LINE BETWEEN LOVE & HATE 1974 ATLANTIC UK K40370 US 33387
ITS ALL ABOUT LOVE 1976 CALLA US 34802

P67 PERSUASIONS P67

JERRY LAWSON V (BDG (A) WE CAME TO PLAY 19 CAPITOL US 791
JIMMY HAYES V (BDG (B) STREET CORNER SYMPHONY 1972 CAPITOL US 872
JOSEPH RUSSELL V (BDG (B) STREET CORNER SYMPHONY 1972 ISLAND UK ILPS 9201
WILLIE C DANIELS V (D (C) SPREAD THE WORD 197 CAPITOL US 11101
HERBERT RHOAD V (BD (D) MORE THAN BEFORE 1974 A&M UK AMLS 63835 US SP3635
BENORCE BLACKMON G (D (E) I JUST WANNA SING 1976 A&M US SP3656
HENRY DAVIS B (D (F) ACAPELLA 19 STRAIGHT STS1062 REPRISE US 6394
JAY OTIS WASHINGTON V (B (G) CHIRPIN' 1977 ELEKTRA US 7E1099
JEFF BARRY PERC (D (H) WE STILL AIN'T GO NO BAND 197 MCA US 326
RICK BEILKE G (D
OLLIE BROWN D (D RANDY KOONTZ B (D JOE AGLIO D (D CLARENCE McDONALD K (D

P67A PERTH COUNTY CONSPIRACY P67A

(A) ALIVE 19 COLUMBIA IMP GES 90037

P68 PESKY GEE P68

(A) EXCLAMATION MARK 1969 PYE UK NSPL18293

P68A JIM PETERIK P68A

JIM PETERIK (A (A) DON'T FIGHT THAT FEELING 1976 EPIC US 34196

P68B COLLEEN PETERSON P68B

COLLEEN PETERSON V (ALL — (A) BEGINNING TO FEEL LIKE HOME 1976 CAPITOL
(B) COLLEEN 1977 CAPITOL US ST 11714
(C) TAKIN' MY BOOTS OFF 1978 CAPITOL UK/US 11835

P68C PETARDS P68C

KLAUS EBERT G V (ABC — (A) A DEEPER BLUE 1968 EUROPA GER E313
HORST EBERT G V (ABC — (B) HITSHOCK 1969 LIBERTY GER LBS 83325
ARNO DITTRICH D (ABC — (C) PETARDS 1970 LIBERTY GER LBS 83481 (CASS)
ROGER B (ABC

P68D PETER & GORDON P68D

PETER ASHER V (ALL — PETER & GORDON 1964 COLUMBIA UK SCX3518
GORDON WALLER V (ALL — IN TOUCH 1964 COLUMBIA UK SCX3532
PETER & GORDON 1966 COLUMBIA UK SCX6045
HURTIN 'N' LOVIN' 1965 COLUMBIA UK SCX3565
SOMEWHERE 1966 COLUMBIA UK SCX6097
A WORLD WITHOUT LOVE 196 CAPITOL US 2115
I DONT WANT TO SEE YOU AGIAN 196 CAPITOL US 2220
I GO TO PIECES 196 CAPITOL US 2324
TRUE LOVE WAYS 196 CAPITOL US 2368
SING & PLAY THE HITS OF NASHVILLE 196 CAPITOL US 2430
WOMAN 196 CAPITOL US 2477
BEST OF 196 CAPITOL US 2549
LADY GODIVA 196 CAPITOL US 2664
KNIGHT IN RUSTY ARMOUR 196 CAPITOL US 2729
IN LONDON FOR TEA 196 CAPITOL US 2747
HOT COLD & CUSTARD 196 CAPITOL US 2882
THE BEST OF 1977 EMI UK NUT8
GORDON (SOLO) 1972 VERTIGO UK 6360 069

P68E PETER PAUL & MARY P68E

PETER YARROW G V (ALL — (A) PETER PAUL & MARY 196 WB US 1449
PAUL STOOKEY V (ALL — (B) MOVING 196 WB US 1473
MARY TRAVERS V (ALL — (C) IN THE WIND 196 WB US 1507
(D) IN CONCERT 196 WB US 1555
(E) A SONG WILL RISE 196 WB US 1589
(F) SEE WHAT TOMORROW BRINGS 196 WB US 1615
(G) PETER PAUL & MARY ALBUM 196 WB US 1648
(H) ALBUM 1700 196 WB US 1700
(J) LATE AGAIN 196 WB US 1751
(K) PETER PAUL & MOMMY 196 WB US 1785
(L) 10 YEARS TOGETHER THE BEST OF 196 WB US 2552 UK K46051
(M) REUNION 1978 WB US 3231

P69 PETS P69

GREG SUTTON B V (A — (A) WET BEHIND THE EARS 1978 ARISTA UK SPART 1061 US AB4154
GREG LEROY G WIND(A
VINCE MELAMED K V (A — DEANE HAGEN D (A — IRA INGBER G V (A — ALAN ESTES PERC (A
STEVE FORMAN PERC (A — EDDIE TUDURI D (A — MIKE BAIRD D (A — SCOTT STRONG G (A
JOANNE HARRIS V (A

P70 TOM PETTY & THE HEARTBREAKERS P70

TOM PETTY G V (ALL — (A) TOM PETTY & THE HEARTBREAKERS 1977 ISLAND UK ISA5014 US SHELTER 52006
BENMONT TENCH K V (ABCDEF — (B) YOURE GONNA GET IT 1978 ISLAND UK ISA5017 US SHELTER 52029
RON BLAIR B (ABCDEF — (C) OFFICIAL LIVE BOOTLEG 197 US SHELTER 12677
STAN LYNCH D K (ABCDEF — (D) DAMN THE TORPEDOES 1979 BACKSTREET US 5105 UK MCF 3044
MIKE CAMPBELL G K HCA(ABCDEF — (E) HARD PROMISES 1981 BACKSTREET US 5160 UK MCA MCF 3098
HOWIE EPSTEIN B (F — (F) LONG AFTER DARK 1982 UK MCA MCF 3155
JIMMY LOVINE PROD (E
DUCK DUNN B (E — PHIL JONES PERC (E — STEVIE NICKS V (E — SHARON CEYLANI V (E
A BUGS WEIDEL PNO (F — PHIL SEYMOUR V (D — NOAH SHARK PERC (B

P71 PEZBAND P71

MIMI BETINIS G K V(ABCDE — (A) PEZBAND 1977 PASSPORT US 98021
MIKE GORMAN B V (ABCDE — (B) LAUGHING IN THE DARK 1978 PASSPORT US 9826 UK RADAR RAD 6
TOMMY GAWENDA G (ABCDE — (C) COVER TO COVER 1981 PASSPORT US 9837
MICK RATN D V (ABCDE
MEL COLLINS SAX(ABCDE — TOMMY EYRE PNO (ABCDE — CLARENCE CLEMMONS SAX (A — JOHN PAYNE SAX (A
RANDY BRECKER TPT (A — ALAN RUBIN TPT (A — LARRY FAST SYN (A

P71A PHANTOM BAND P71A

JAKI LIEBEZEIT D (AB — (A) PHANTOM BAND 1980 SKY SKY 048
ELEK GELBA PERC (AB — (B) FREEDOM OF SPEECH 1981 SKY GER SKY 065
HELMUT ZERLETT K (AB
DOMINIK VON SENGER G (AB — ROSKO GEE V B (A

P71B PHEW P71B

(A) PHEW 1981 PASS 3F28002

P71C GREG PHILLINGANES P71C

(A) SIGNIFICANT GAINS 1981 PLANET UK K52299

P72 ANTHONY PHILLIPS P72

ANTHONY PHILLIPS G V (ABCD — (A) THE GEESE & THE GHOST 1977 HIT & RUN UK 001 US PASSPORT 98020
MICHAEL RUTHERFORD G B K D(A — (B) WISE AFTER THE EVENT 1978 ARISTA UK SPARTY1063 US PASSPORT9828
PHIL COLLINS V (A — (C) PRIVATE PARTS AND PIECES 1978 APL UK AFLP 1 PASSPORT US 7905
ROB PHILLIPS OBOE (AB — (D) SIDES 1978 ARISTA UK SPART1085 US PASSPORT9834
LAZA MOMULOVICH OBOE (A — (D) SIDES 1978 VERTIGO GER 9124 362
JOHN HACKETT FLT (A — (E) PRIVATE PARTS 2 1980 PVC 7913
WIL SLEATH FLT (A — (F) 1984 1981 RCA UK 5036 US PASSPORT6006
JACK LANCASTER FLT (A
CHARLIE MARTIN CELLO(A
KIRK TREVOR CELLO(A — NICK HAYLEY VLN (A — MARTIN WESTLAKE PERC (A — VIV McAULIFFE V (A
THE VICAR G V K(BD — MIKE GILES D (BD — JOHN G PERRY B (BD — FRANK RICOTTI PERC (D
RALPH BERNASCONE V (DA — VIC STENCH B (BD — JEREMY GILBERT K (B — RUPERT HINE V PERC (B
DALE NEWMAN V (D — DAN OWEN V (D — RAY COOPER PERC (D — MORRIS PERT PERC (D
HUMBERT RUSE PERC HRNS(ABD — MEL COLLINS SAX (BD — PERKIN ALANBECK SYN (B — TOM NEWMAN (A

P72A ESTHER PHILLIPS P72A

ESTHER PHILLIPS V (ALL (A) AND I LOVE HIM 19 ATLANTIC US 8102
DON GROLNICK K (N (B) SINGS 1966 ATLANTIC UK 587010
JEFF BERLIN B (N (C) ESTHER 19 ATLANTIC US 8122
RANDY BRECKER TPT (N (D) COUNTRY SIDE 19 ATLANTIC US 8130
MICHAEL BRECKER SAX (N (E) BURNIN 1970 ATLANTIC US 1565
SAN BURTIS TROM (N (F) FROM A WHISPER TO A SCREAM 19 KUDU US 05 UK 2
ANTHONY JACKSON B (N (G) ALONE AGAIN NATURALLY 1973 KUDU US 09 UK 6
STEVE KHAN G (N (H) BLACK EYED BLUES 1974 KUDU US UK 11
BARRY ROGERS TROM (N (J) PERFORMANCE 1975 KUDU US 18 UK 18
JOHN BLAIR VLN (N (K) WITH JOE BECK 1975 KUDU UK 23
BOBBY LYLE K (N (L) CONFESSIN' THE BLUES 1976 ATLANTIC US 1680 UK K50222
ALLAN HOLDSWORTH G (N (M) FOR ALL WE KNOW 1976 KUDU UK 28
HUGH McCRACKEN G (N (N) CAPRICORN PRINCESS 1977 KUDU UK 31
BARRY MILES SYN (N (O) YOU'VE COME A LONG WAY BABY 1977 MERCURY US SRM1187
ANDY NEWMARK D (N (P) ESTHER PHILLIPS 1978 KUDU UK SCU001
JOHN TROPEA G (N (Q) ALL ABOUT ESTHER 1978 PHILIPS UK 6338885
JON FADDIS TPT (N (R) HERE'S ESTHER ARE YOU READY 1979 MERCURY US 9111030 UK 9100065
RONNIE CUBER SAX (N (S) GOOD BLACK IS HARD TO CRACK 1981 MERCURY US SRM14005
MIKE ABENE K (N
STEVE GADD D (N JOHN GATCHELL TPT (N SUE EVANS V (N JOE FARRELL WIND (N
CREED TAYLOR PROD (N GORDON EDWARDS B (FGJ RON CARTER B (G BOZ BURRELL B (H
WILL LEE B (M AIRTO MOREIRA PERC (F RALPH MACDONALD PERC(GJMNK ARTHUR JENKINS PERC(H
CORNELL DUPREE G (FG ERIC GALE G (EFN JOE BECK G (KMO GEORGE BENSON G (G
CHARLIE BROWN G (HJ RICHARD TEE K (FGJ RICHARD WYNARDS K (G TIM HINKLEY K (H
DON GROLNICK K (KM JOSHIE ARMSTEAD V (FH HILD HARRIS V (FM BILL VATON V (N
BARBARA MASSEY V (F TASHA THOMAS V(FGHJM LANI GROVES V (GHJ DENISE WILLIAMS V (J
LOUIS ST LOUIS V (F CAL CALDWELL V (GHJ PATTI AUSTIN V (JM ROBIN CLARK V (M
BABI FLOYD V (N ZACHARY SARDEN V (N MAERETHA STEWART V (M

P73 GLENN PHILLIPS P73

GLENN PHILLIPS G V (AB (A) LOST AT SEA 1975 CAROLINE UK C1519 US SNOWSTAR SSR1
JOHN CARR HARRIMAN CELLO(A (B) SWIM IN THE WIND 1977 VIRGIN UK V2087
MIKE HOLBROOK B (A
JIM PRESMANES D (A BILL REA G (AB SANT RAM SINGH KHALSA K (AB JERRY FIELDS D (AB
DAVID LANDSBERG D (B JANIE GEISER REA V (B BILLY McPHERSON WIND (B CHUCK MOON V (B
JOHN CURRIE (B DANA HOWARD NELSON K V (B BILLY McKINLEY BANJO (B PHOEBE PNO (B
DAVID BYRD STEEL(B JIM MARETT PNO (B BILL SHEFFIELD HCA V (B

P74 JOHN PHILLIPS P74

JOHN PHILLIPS G V HCA (A (A) WOLFKING OF L A 1970 STATESIDE UK 5027 US DUNHILL 50077
LARRY KNECHTEL K (A
DAVID COHEN G (A DARLENE LOVE V (A FANITA JAMES V (A BUDDY EMMONS STEEL (A
GORDON TERRY FDL (A HAL BLAINE D (A JOE OSBORNE B (A DR HORD G (A
JEAN KING V (A JAMES BURTON G (A RED RHODES STEEL(A

P75 MICHELLE PHILLIPS P75

MICHELLE PHILLIPS V (A (A) VICTIM OF ROMANCE 1977 A&M US 4651 UK AMLH64651
JACK NITZSCHE K PERC(A
SCOTT FREE D G ACC V (A DAVID C ALLEN G (A GREGORY LEE B (A TIM DRUMMOND B (A
DON RANDI PNO (A JOHN MOON MARTIN G V (A STEVE DOUGLAS WIND PERC(A RON NAGLE PERC (A
GENE ESTES PERC (A BEN BENAY G MAND (A JERRY DONAHUE G (A MIKE BODDIKER SYN(A
SID SHARP STRINGS (A JERRY JUMONVILLE WIND (A JAY MIGLIORI WIND (A DENNIS DREITH WIND(A
JACK NIMITZ WIND (A BOB FINDLEY TPT (A BILL PETERSON TPT (A MARK UNDERWOOD TPT(A
TRICIA JOHNS V (A LAURA CREAMER V (A CHERIE ENGLISH V (A MYRNA MATTHEWS V (A
MAXINE WILLARD V (A KATHY WARD V (A BILLY GUY V (A GRADY CHAPMAN V (A
JEROME EVANS V (A

P76 SHAWN PHILLIPS P76

SHAWN PHILLIPS V G SITAR(ALL (A) I'M A LONER 1965 COLUMBIA UK 33SX 1748
ADRIAN GAYE G (C (B) SHAWN 1966 COLUMBIA UK SCX 6006
MICK WEAVER K (C (C) CONTRIBUTION 1970 A&M US 4241 UK AMLS 978
SNEAKY PETE STEEL(HL (D) SECOND CONTRIBUTION 1971 A&M US 4282 UK AMLS 2006
JIM PRICE HRNS (H (E) COLLABORATION 1972 A&M US 4323 UK AMLS64324
JIM HORN SAX (HL (F) FACES 1973 A&M US 4363 UK AMLS64363
CRAIG DOERGE (H (G) FURTHERMORE 1974 A&M US 3662 UK AMLH68278
BOBBY KEYS SAX (H (H) BRIGHT WHITE 1974 A&M US 4402 UK AMLH64402
LEE SKLAR B (LF (J) DO YOU WONDER 1975 A&M US 4539 UK AMLH64539
RUSS KUNKEL D (L (K) RUMPLESTILTSKIN'S RESOLVE 1976 A&M US 4582 UK AMLH64582
JOE SAMPLE K (L (L) SPACED 1977 A&M US 4650 UK AMLH64650
PETER ROBINSON K (DKCG (M) TRANSCENDENCE 1978 RCA US APLI13028
MICHAEL BAIRD D (L
CHUCK RAINEY B (L MIKE MILLER G B (KL AL WING SAX (KL STEVE NEILEN D (L
ANTHONY NEDZA K (L JOSEPH GAETA G B (L DANIEL TIMMS G (L BRUCE ROWLAND D (L
BRIAN ODGERS B (DFL CHRIS MERCER SAX (CFL JOHNNY ALMOND SAX (L MIKE CLARKE D (KL
PAUL JACKSON B (KL BOBBY LICHTIG B (K STEVE HAMMOND G (K JOHN GUSTAFSON B (KG
BARRY DE SOUZA D (KG CALEB QUAYE G (KFG PAUL BUCKMASTER K (FKCG JOHN PULLEN OBOE(K
BILL SUMMERS PERC (K STEVE WINWOOD K (CF CHRIS WOOD WIND (C MOX HCA (C
JIM CAPALDI D (C CANDY JOHN CARR D (C REMI KABAKA PERC (CF JIMMY COFF PERC(C
HARVEY BURNS G (D JIM CREGAN G (D MARTYN FORD HRNS (F GLEN CAMPBELL STEEL(F
JACK CONRAD B (F ED GREEN D (F JOHN PIGNEGUY HRNS (F SKAILA KANGA HARP(F
SNEAKY PEYE KLEINOW STEEL(F ED MORIN D (F JOE SAMPLE PNO (F DAVID KATZ ORCH (F
ANN O'DELL K (G RAUL MAYORA PERC (G

P76A PHILLIPS MACLEOD P76A

ROBERT PHILLIPS G V (AB (A) LE PARTIE DU COCKTAIL 1979 POLYDOR US PD1 6198
SEAN MacLEOD G V (AB (B) PHILLIPS & MACLEOD 1980 POLYDOR US PD1 6255
JIM DIVISEK (A
ANDREW STEELE (A BRIAN WHITCOMB (A BOB CONTI (A DAVID KEMPER (A
ANDY NEWMARK D (B ART WOOD D (B

P76B PHLUPH P76B

BENSON BLAKE (A (A) PHLUPH 196 US VERVE US 5054
JOHN PELL (A
JOEL MAISANO (A

P76C **PHONEY & HARDCORE** P76C

ERIK STRACK G V (A — (A) PHONEY HITS 1979 ARIOLA NL 200 894
KEES ALKEMA V D (A — (B) PHONEY HITS 1980 ARIOLA NL 202 878
TOMMY VANDERSCHOOT B (A
BURNY REINKE G (A BIEM VISSER K (A NEIL MERRYWEATHER V(A

P76D **PHOTOGLO** P76D

(A) PHOTOGLO 1980 20 TH CENT UK 604

P77 **PHOENIX** P77

JOHN VERITY V D G(AB — (A) PHOENIX 1976 CBS US 34476 UK 81621
ROBERT HENRIT D (AB — (B) IN FULL VIEW 1980 CHARISMA UK CAS1150
ROD ARGENT K (B
JIM RODFORD D (A MICHAEL DES BARRES V (A RAY MINHINNIT G V (B RUSS BALLARD V (B
BRUCE TURGON V (B RONNIE LEE CUNNINGHAM K V(B

P77A **PHOTOS** P77A

WENDY WU V (AB — (A) PHOTOS 1980 EPIC US 36515 UK PHOTO 5
STEVE EAGLES G V (AB — (B) BLACKMAIL TAPES[FREE WITH (A)]
DAVE SPARROW B V (AB
OILY HARRISON D (AB

P77B **PICCADILLY LINE** P77B

ROD EDWARDS V G K(A — (A) HUGE WORLD OF EMILY SMALL 1967 CBS 63129
ROGER HAND G V (A
NORRIE McLEAN B (A KEITH HODGE D (A

P77C **PIBLIKO** P77C

JIM MULLEN G (AB — (A) ART SCHOOL DANCE GOES ON FOREVER 1970 HARVEST UK SHVL768
ROGER BRUNN B (A — (B) THOUSANDS ON A RAFT 1970 HARVEST UK SHVL782
DAVE THOMPSON D (AB
ROB TAIT D (AB PETE BROWN (AB STEVE GLOVER PERC(B

P77D **PIC & BILL** P77D

CHARLES PICKINS V (A — (A) 30 MINUTES OF SOUL 1978 12 O'CLOCK US LD 303
BILL SMITH

P78 **BOBBY'BORIS' PICKETT** P78

BOBBY 'BORIS' PICKETT V(A — (A) MONSTER MASH 1973 LONDON UK ZGU 133
( ) MONSTER MASH 1962 GARPAX US SGP 67001
( ) ORIGINAL MONSTER MASH 1973 PARROT UK 71063

P79 **COURTLAND PICKETT** P79

COURTLAND PICKETT V B (A — (A) FANCY DANCER 1973 ELEKTRA UK K42147 US EKS 75060
DAVID HOOD B (A
ROGER HAWKINS D (A BARRY BECKETT K (A PETE CARR G (A JIMMY JOHNSON G (A
CHARLES STRATFORD TROM (A BOBBY BRUCE VLN (A SONNY ROYAL CLAR (A WAYNE HILL TPT(A
HARVEY THOMPSON SAX (A RONNIE EADES SAX (A CHARLES ROSE TROM (A JO ANN CARR V (A
LAURA STRUZICK V (A SUZY STORM V (A

P80 **WILSON PICKETT** P80

WILSON PICKETT V (ALL — (A) IN THE MIDNIGHT HOUR 196 ATLANTIC UK 587 032 US 8114
JEAN ROUSSEL K (Z — EXCITING WILSON PICKETT 196 ATLANTIC US 8129
MARTY SIMON D (Z — WICKED PICKETT 196 ATLANTIC UK 588 057 US 8138
JERRY KNIGHT B V (Z — THE SOUND OF 196 ATLANTIC UK 588 050 US 8145
WALTER ROSSI G (Z — THE BEST OF 196 ATLANTIC UK 588 092 US 8151
GARY BROWN SAX (Z — I'M IN LOVE 196 ATLANTIC US 8175
CLYDE KERR TPT (Z — MIDNIGHT MOVER 196 ATLANTIC US 8183
JIMMY TANAKA PERC (Z — GREAT HITS 196 WAND US 672
GARY WILSON V (Z — (I) HEY JUDE 196 ATLANTIC UK 588 170 US 8215
BILLY NELSON V (Z — RIGHT ON 196 ATLANTIC UK 2465 002 US 8250
PETSYE POWELL V (Z — (K) IN PHILADELPHIA 1970 ATLANTIC US 8270
ROGER HAWKINS D (I — BEST OF VOL 2 1971 ATLANTIC US 8290
DAVID HOOD B (IX — IF YOU NEED ME 19 JOY JOYS101
ALBERT LOWE G (I — BEST OF 197 ATLANTIC UK K40015 US 2 501
BARRY BECKETT K (I — GREATEST HITS 1973 ATLANTIC UK K60038 US 2501
JERRY JEMMOT B (I — MR MAGIC MAN 1973 RCA US 4858
JAMES JOHNSON G (I — DONT KNOCK MY LOVE 1974 ATLANTIC UK K40319 US 8300
DUANE ALLMAN G (I — TONIGHT I'M MY BIGGEST AUDIENCE 1974 RCA UK SF 8344 US 4858
MARVEI THOMAS ORG (I — MIZ LENA3 BOY 1974 RCA UK SF 8390 US 0312
GENE MILLER TPT (I — LIVE IN JAPAN 1974 RCA APL 20669
JACK PECK TPT (I — PICKETT IN POCKET 1974 RCA APL1 0495
AARON VARNELL SAX (I — JOIN ME & LETS BE FREE 1975 RCA UK SF8439 USAPL1 0856
JOE ARNOLD SAX (I — PEACE BREAKER 1975 DJM UK DJSL064 US 26064
SWEET INSPIRATIONS V (I — ITS TOO LATE 19 DOUBLE L US 2300
UGENE DOZIER PNO (K — KEEP THE DREAM ALIVE 19 RCA VSPX 6097
LENNY PAKULA PNO (X — STAR COLLECTION 1978 WEA UK MID26001 FR 20017
THOM BELL ORG (X — (X) FUNKY SITUATION 1978 BIG TREE 76011
NORMAN HARRIS G (X — (Z) I WANT YOU 1979 EMI UK 3007 US 17019
ROLAND CHAMBERS G (X — RIGHT TRACK 1981 EMI UK 3016 US 17043
BOBBY ELI G (X — BEST OF 1981 ATLANTIC UK K20017
RONNIE BAKER B (X — BESTS OF 2 1981 ATLANTIC UK K20078
EARL YOUNG D (X
VINCE MONTANA PERC (X RANDY McCORMICK K (X LARRY BYROM G (X KEN BELL G (X
BOB WRAY B (X ROGER CLARK D (X MICKEY BUCKINS PERC (X SANDRA RHODES V (X
DONNA RHODES V (X CHARLES CHALMERS V (X AVA ALDRIDGE V (X CINDY RICHARDSON V(X
CINDY STORM V (X DON DAILY PERF (X PETE CARR G (X

P80A **PIERCE ARROW** P80A

DOUG LUBAHN B V (AB — (A) PIERCE ARROW 1977 CBS US 34805
JEFF KENT K G V(AB — (B) PITY THE RICH 1978 CBS US 35307
DAVID BUSKIN G V (AB
ROBIN BATTEAU G V (AB WERNER FRITZSCHING G V (AB BOBBY CHOUINARD D (AB

P80B **PIECES** P80B

GEOFFREY LEIB K SYNV(A — (A) PIECES 1979 UA US UALA 966 UK UAG 30252
MIKE LINGLE D V (A
KENNY LEE LEWIS B V (A LARRY LINGLE G V (A

P80C MARIE PIERRE P80C

MARIE PIERRE V (A (A) LOVE AFFAIR 1979 TROJAN TRLS 177
JAH BUNNY D (A
DENNIS BOVELL K B (A WEBSTER JOHNSON PNO (A JOHN KPIAYE G (A PATRICK TENYUE TPT (A
HENRY TENYUE TROM (A

P80D PIDGEON P80B

BILL STRONG SMITH D V(A (A) PIDGEON 196 DECCA US 75103
CHERI GAGE V (A
JOBRIATH SALISBURY K G V(A RICHARD T MARSHALL (A

P80E PIG IRON P80E

BILL PETERS G V (A (A) PIG IRON 1970 CBS NL 64044
GARY VAN SCYOC B TPT(A
MARTY FOGEL SAX (A ADAM IPPOLITO K TPT V(A PAUL SQUIRE HRNS (A

P81 PIGSTY HILL LIGHT ORCHESTRA P81

ANDY LEGGETT V G SAX (A (A) PIGGERY JOKERY 1971 VILLAGE THING VTS 8
DAVID CREECH V TPT(AC (B) CUSHION FOOT STOMP 197 VILLAGE THING VTS 1
BARRY BLACK G V (A (C) PIGSTY HILL LIGHT ORCHESTRA 1976 PHLO 001
BILL COLE B (A
JON HAYS PERC V(C ROBERT GREENFIELD G V (C CHRIS NEWMAN G B (C

P81A PIIRPAUKE P81A

SAKARI KUKKO SAX PNO(ALL (A) I 19 LOVE LRLP 148
HASSE WALLI G PERC(ALL (B) II 19 LOVE LRLP 192
ANTTI HYTTI B V (AB (C) LIVE 19 LOVE LRLP 251
JUKKA WASAMA D (ALL
ILLI-PECKA WASAMA B PERC(C

P81B PILOT P81B

DAVID PATON B V (ALL (A) FROM THE ALBUM OF THE SAME NAME 1974 EMI US 11368 EMC 3045
BILLY LYALL K V FLT(AB (B) SECOND FLIGHT 1975 EMI GER 05879 UK EMC 3075
ALAN PARSONS PROD (A (C) MORIN HEIGHTS 1976 EMI EMA 779
STUART TOSH D V (ABC (D) TWOS A CROWD 1977 ARISTA SPARTY 1014
IAN BAIRNSON G (ABCD (E) BEST OF 1980 EMI NUT 29
DAVID MASON TPT (A
PETER OXENDALE K (C TREVOR SPENCER D (D HENRY SPINETTI D (D STEVE SWINDELLS K V (D

P81C PILOT (2) P81C

BRUCE STEPHENS G V K(AB (A) PILOT 1972 RCA US LSP 4730
LEIGH STEPHENS G (AB (B) POINT OF VIEW 197 RCA US LSP 4825
MICK WALLER D (AB
MARTIN QUITTENTON G (AB NEVILLEWHITEHEAD BAN (AB

P82 PILTDOWN MEN P82

ED COBB (EP) PILTDOWN RIDES AGAIN 19 CAPITOL EAP 1 20155
LINCOLN MAYORGA

P83 MICHAEL PINDER P83

MICHAEL PINDER G K V(A (A) THE PROMISE 1976 THRESHOLD UK THS 18
BILL BERG D (A
FLYN J JOHNSON B (A MAXINE WILLARD V (A JEANIE KING V (A JULIA TILLMAN V (A
JIM DILLAN G V (A FRED BECKMEIER B (A WILLIAM'SMITTY'SMITH ORG(A SUSAN McDONALD HARP(A
JOEL DIBARTELLO B (A TOM PETERSON WIND (A MICHAEL AZEVEDO CONGA(A DEAN OLCH WIND(A
STEVE MADAIO TPT (A BOBBY KEYS SAX (A

P83A MIKE PINERA P83A

MIKE PINERA G V (A (A) ISLA 1978 CAPRICORN US 0202
DUANE HITCHINGS K (A (B) FOREVER 1979 SPECTOR US 0001
TERRY WEISS K V (A
DONNY VOSBURGH D (A FLACO CONGOS(A

P83B RICHARD PINHAS P83B

RICHARD PINHAS SYN G (ALL (A) RHIZOSPERE 1979 COBRA FR COB37005
FRANCOIS AUGER D (AB (B) CHRONOLYSE 1979 COBRA FR COB37015
JEAN PHILIPPE GOUDE SYN(C (C) ICE LAND 1980 PULSE 001
DIDIER BATARD B (B (D) EAST WEST 1980 PULSE 003

P84 PINK FAIRIES P84

DUNCAN SANDERSON B (ABCD (A) NEVER NEVER LAND 1971 POLYDOR UK 2383 045
RUSSEL HUNTER D (ABCD (B) WHAT A BUNCH OF SWEETIES 1972 POLYDOR UK 2383 132
MARTIN STONE G ((C) KINGS OF OBLIVION 1975 POLYDOR US5537 UK 2383 212
LARRY WILLIS G V (CD (D) PINK FAIRIES (COMP) 1975 POLYDOR UK 2384 071
PAUL RUDOLPH G (ABD (1) 1969 70
TWINK D (A1D
MICK FARREN (1 STEVE TOOK (1 NEIL SLAVEN PROD (AD JON ALDER PROD (A
PETER KNIGHT PROD (D TREVOR BURTON G (B DAVID HITCHCOCK PROD (D

P85 PINK FLOYD P85

ROGER WATERS B V G(ALL (A) PIPER AT THE GATES OF DAWN 1967 TOWER US 5093 UK COLUMBIA SCX 6157
VANETTA FIELDS V (K (A) PIPER AT THE GATES OF DAWN 1967 COLUMBIA GER 04292
RICHARD WRIGHT K V (ALL (B) SAUCERFUL OF SECRETS 1968 TOWER US 5131 UK COLUMBIA SCX 6258
CARLENA WILLIAMS V (K (B) SAUCERFUL OF SECRETS 1968 COLUMBIA GER 04190
NICK MASON D (ALL (C) MORE 1969 HARVEST US 11198 UK COLUMBIA SCX 6346
DICK PARRY SAX (K (C) MORE 1969 COLUMBIA GER 04096
SYD BARRETT G V (ABGZX (D) UMMAGUMMA 1969 HARVEST US 388 UK HARVEST SHDW 1/2
NORMAN SMITH PROD (ABG (D) UMMAGUMMA 1969 HARVEST GER 04222/23
DAVE GILMOUR G V (BCDEFGHJKLMXZ(E) ATOM HEART MOTHER 1970 HARVEST US 382 UK HARVEST SHVL 781
JOE BOYD PROD (G (E) ATOM HEART MOTHER 1970 HARVEST GER 297
ROY HARPER V (K (F) MEDDLE 1971 HARVEST US 832 UK HARVEST SHVL 795
JIM HAAS V (M (F) MEDDLE 1971 HARVEST GER 04917
SNOWY WHITE G (M (G) RELICS (COMP) 1971 HARVEST US 759 UK STARLINE SRS 5071
PETER WOOD K ((G) RELICS (COMP) 1971 HARVEST EURO 50740 1978 UK MFP 50397
JOHN'WILLIE'WILSON D ((H) OBSCURED BY CLOUDS 1972 HARVEST US 11078 UK HARVEST SHSP4020
JOE CHEMAY V (M (H) OBSCURED BY CLOUDS 1972 HARVEST GER 05054
ANDY BOWN B ((J) DARK SIDE OF THE MOON 1973 HARVEST US 11163 UK HARVEST SHVL 804
STAN FARBER V (M (J) DARK SIDE OF THE MOON 19 HARVEST GER 05249 US MOBILE 17
TONI TENNILLE V (M (K) WISH YOU WERE HERE 1976 CBS US 33453 UK HARVEST SHVL 814
JON JOYCE V (M (K) WISH YOU WERE HERE 1976 HARVEST GER 06918
LESLEY DUNCAN V (J (L) ANIMALS 1977 CBS US 34474 UK HARVEST SHVL 815
BRUCE JOHNSTON V (M (L) ANIMALS 1977 HARVEST EURO 98434

(CONTINUED)

P85 PINK FLOYD (CONTINUED) P85

CLAIRE TORRY V (J — (M) THE WALL — 1979 CBS US 36183 UK HARVEST SHDW 411
BARRY ST JOHN V (J — (M) THE WALL — 1979 HARVEST EURO 63410/11
LIZA STRIKE V (J — (N) COLLECTION OF GREAT DANCE — 1981 CBS US 37680 UK HARVEST SHVL 822
DORIS TROY V (J — (O) THE FINAL CUT — 1983 HARVEST UK
ISLINGTON GREEN SCHOOL V(M — (AB) A NICE PAIR — 1973 HARVEST US 11257 UK HARVEST SHDW 403
(AB) A NICE PAIR — 1973 HARVEST GER 50203/04
(X) MASTERS OF ROCK — 1970 EMI IMP EURO 054 04299 1976 062 04299
(Y) ZABRISKIE POINT (SOUNDTRACK)*1970 MGM 2315 002 — 2354 040
(Z) TONIGHT LETS ALL MAKE LOVE *1968 INSTANT ANALYSIS INLP 002
(*) BOTH SOUNDTRACK LPS WITH OTHER ARTISTS

P85A PINK MILITARY P85A

JAYNE V (A — (A) DO ANIMALS BELIEVE IN GOD — 1980 VIRGIN UK ERICS004 GER 202 512
NICKY G SYN(A
CHARLIE K (A MARTIN B G (A NEIL PERC (A CHRIS JOYCE D (A

P86 PINPOINT P86

ARTURO BASSICK G (— (A) THIRD STATE (WITH FREE EP) — 1980 ALBION UK ALB 103 GER 203383
A P BILLINGSLEY G V (A
DAVE ALLEN B (A HUGH GRIFFITHS D (A M R RUSHENT SYN (A I P HARTNELL K (A
MOSLEY K (A

P87 PIONEERS P87

GEORGE DEKKER(AGARD) V (— LONGSHOT — 1970 TROJAN TBL 103
SYDNEY CROOKS V (— BATTLE OF THE GIANTS — 197 TROJAN TBL 139
LAUREN 'JACKIE'ROBINSON V(— YEAH — 1971 TROJAN TRL 24
I BELIEVE IN LOVE — 1972 TROJAN TRLS 48
FREEDOM FELING — 1973 TROJAN TRLS 64
I'M GONNA KNOCK ON YOUR DOOR — 1974 TROJAN TRLS 98
FEEL THE RHYTHM — 1976 MERCURY 9286 172
ROLL ON MUDDY RIVER — 1877 TROJAN TRLS 144
PUSHER MAN — 1979 TROJAN TRLS 156
GREATEST HITS — 1979 TROJAN TRLS 172

P87A PIPER P87A

BILLY SQUIER V G PERC(AB — (A) PIPER — 1976 A&M US SP 4615 RI 3194
ALAN LAINE NOLAN G PERC(AB — (B)CANT WAIT — 19 A&M US SP 4654
TOMMY GUNN G (AB — (B) BILLY SQUIER — 19 A&M US RI 3195
DANNY McGARY B (AB
RICHIE FONTANA D (AB

P88 PIPS P88

(A) AT LAST THE PIPS — 1978 CASABLANCA US 7081 UK CAL 2022
(B) CALLIN' — 1978 CASABLANCA US 7113 UK CAL 2031

P88A PIRANA P88A

JIM YONGE D (AB — (A) PIRANA — 19 HARVEST SHVL 603
GRAEME THOMPSON B (AB — (B) PIRANA II — 1972 HARVEST SHVL 609
TONY HAMILTON G B V PERC(AB
STAN WHITE K V (A COL LAUGHNAN FLT (A KEITH GRIEG K PERC(B

P88B PIRANHAS P88B

DICK SLEXIA D (A — (A) PIRANHAS — 1980 SIRE SRK 6098
BOB GROVER (A
JOHNNY HELMER G (A ZOOT SAX (A RICHARD MYHILL K (A MIKE COOK VLN (A
REG (A GRAHAM PRESKETT VLN (A

P89 PIRATES P89

MICK GREEN G (ABC — (A) OUT OF THEIR SKULLS — 1977 WB US 3155 UK K56411
JOHN SPENCER B V (ABC — (B) SKULL WARS — 1978 WB US 3224 UK K56468
FRANK FARLEY D (ABC — (C) HAPPY BIRTHDAY ROCK'N'ROLL — 1979 CUBE UK HIFLY33
(C) HARD RIDE — 1979 PACIFIC ARTS US 7140

P89A PLAIN SAILING P89A

PAUL STEWART V HCA(A — (A) DANGEROUS TIMES — 1980 CHARISMA UK CHR 1282
ROBERT FREEMAN G V (A
ALAN STEWART G V (A COLIN STEWART K V (A DAVE WINTOUR B (A ALAN COULTER D (A

P89B PLAIN JANE P89B

BARRY RAY G V (A — (A) PLAIN JANE — 19 HOBBITT US 5000
DON GLEICHER G V (A
DAVID SCHOENFELD D (A JERRY SCHOENFELD B K V(A

P90 PLAINSONG P90

IAN MATTHEWS G V (AB — (A) IN SEARCH OF AMELIA EARHART — 1972 ELEKTRA NL ELK 22013 UK K42120
ANDY ROBERTS G V (AB — (B) PLAINSONG III RELEASED AS A WHITE LABEL PROMO ONLY
DAVE RICHARDS G V (AB
BOB RONGA B V (AB TIMI DONALD D (A DAVE MATTACKS D (A MARTIN JENKINS MAND(A

P91 PLANET EARTH P91

COLIN GREEN G (A — (A) PLANET EARTH — 1978 PYE UK NSPL18556
KEVIN PEEK G (A
BILLY CHRISTIAN B (A TREVOR BARTON K (A RONNIE ASPERY SAX (A BARRY MORGAN D (A
MIKE RATLEDGE K (A TRISTRAN FRY PERC (A KARL JENKINS K (A

P92 PLANET GONG P92

DAEVID ALLEN G V (A — (A) FLOATING ARNACHY LIVE 77 — 1978 CHARLY UK CRM 2000 FR LTM1002
GILLI SMYTH V (A
PEPI MILAN G V (A JUANE BIBLIONI G V (A SAM GOPAL PERC SYN(A

P92A PLANETS P92A

(A) GOONHILLY DOWN — 1979 RIALTO TENOR102 US MOTOWN 934
(B) SPOT — 1980 RIALTO TENOR10?

P92B PLANT P92B

GERRIT VEEN B V (A — (A) LIFETIME GUARANTEE — 1978 POLYDOR NL 2925 071
RUDY LENTZE G V (A
RUUD BANUS ORG V(A HEDDY VANDER LAAN G V (A EDDY KORMA D (A EELCO GELLING G (A
BEA WILLEMSTEIN V (A MARISKA VERES V (A MARTHA HOLLESTELLE V (A OKKIE HUYSDENS V (A

P92C ROBERT PLANT P92C

ROBERT PLANT V (A (A) PICTURES AT ELEVEN 1982 SWANSONG UK SSK 59418
ROBBIE BLUNT G (A
PAUL MATINEZ B (A JEZZ WOODROFFE K (A PHIL COLLINS D (A COZY POWELL D (A
RAPHAEL RAVENSCROFT SAX(A

P92D PLANNING BY NUMBERS P92D

STEPHEN MILFORD G V SYN(A (A) '1' 198 BEGGARS BANQUET UK BEGA 32
TREVOR STEEL G (A
IAN CURNOW SYN K(A JOHN HOLIDAY B V (A MILAN ZELAVICA D (A

P93 PLANXTY P93

CHRISTY MOORE G V (EF (A) PLANXTY 1973 POLYDOR UK 2383 186
MATT MOLLOY FLT (EF (B) WELL BELOW THE VALLEY 1973 POLYDOR UK 2383 232
DONAL LUNNY G SYN(EF (C) COLD BLOW & THE RAINY NIGHT 1974 POLYDOR UK 2383 301
PAUL BRADY ((D) PLANXTY COLLECTION 1976 POLYDOR UK 2389 397
ANDY IRVINE (ALL (E) AFTER THE BREAK 1979 TARA 3001
LIAM O'FLYNN WIND (ALL (F) WOMAN I LOVED SO WELL 1980 TARA 3005
JOHNNY MOYNIHAN (
NOEL HILL CONC (F TONY LINNANE FDL (F BILL WHELAN K (F

P93A PLASMATICS P93A

WENDY'O' WILLIAMS V (AB (A) NEW HOPE FOR THE WRETCHED 1980 STIFF UK 24 US USE9 GER 624496
STU DEUTSCH D (A (B) METAL PRIESTESS 1981 STIFF US WOW666
RICHIE STOTTS G (AB
WES BEACH G (AB JEAN BEAUVIOR B (AB JIMMIY MILLER PERC(A CHRIS ROMANELLI B (B
JOEY REESE D (B TONY PETRI D (A

P93B PLASTER CASTER BLUES BAND P93B

ART ADAMS G (A (A) PLASTER CASTERS 1969 BLUES TIME BTS 9001
CLIFFORD SOLOMON SAX (A
GEORGE SMITH HCA(A GILDO MAHONES K (A BOGGY BRYANT TPT(A JULES CHAIKIN V (A
ELLEN SANDER V (A MAX HARDY D (A

P94 PLASTIC BERTRAND P94

PLASTIC BERTRAND V (A (A) AN 1 1978 SIRE 9103 258

P94A PLASTIC PEOPLE OF THE UNIVERSE P94A

VRATISSLAV WIND (A (A) EGON BONDY'S HAPPY HEART CLUB BANNED 19 INVISIBLE SCOPA 10001
MILAN HLAVSA B (A
JOSEF JANICEK G K (A JIRA KABES VLA G(A JAROSLAV VOZNIAK D (A IVAN JIROUS (A

P95 PLASTIC PENNY P95

PAUL RAYMOND ORG ((A) 2 SIDES OF PENNY 1968 PAGE ONE UK 005
NIGEL OLSSON D ((B) CURRENCY 1969 PAGE ONE UK 014
TONY MURRAY B ((C) HEAD I WIN,TAILS YOU LOOSE 1970 PAGE ONE UK 611
BRIAN KEITH V (
MICK GRABHAM G (

P95A PLASTICS P95A

HAJIME TACHIBANA (A (A) WELCOME BACK 1981 ISLAND GER 203 435
TOSHI NAKANICHI (A
CHICA SATO (A TEKEMI SHIMA (A MA-CHAN SAKUMA (A

P96 PLATINUM HOOK P96

STEPHEN DANIELS D V (A (A) PLATINUM HOOK 1978 MOTOWN US 899 UK STML12086
TINA RENNE STANFORD PERC V(A (B) IT'S TIME 1979 MOTOWN US 918 UK STML12140
ROBERT DOUGLAS K V (A
ELISHA INGRAMS B V (A VICTOR JONES G V (A ROBIN D CARLEY WIND V(A GLENN WALLACE TROM V(A
JEROME JUMONVILLE HRNS (A STEVE MADAIO HRNS (A DENNIS CHRISTIANSON HRNS (A RONNIE VANN G (A
TYRELL DEADRICK PERC (A MICHAEL BODDICKER SYN (A

P97 PLATTERS P97

DAVID LYNCH V (ABCDE
HERB REED V (ABCDE
TONY WILLIAMS V (ABC
ALEX HODGE V (AB
PAUL ROBBI V (BCD
ZOLA TAYLOR V (CD
SONNY TURNER V (DE
SANDRA DAWN V (E
NATE NELSON V (E

(A) 1953
(B) 1954
(C) 1955
(D) 1961
(E) 1963

ALL TIME MOVIE HITS 19 MERCURY US SR 60782
BEST OF VOL 1 1973 PHILIPS UK 6336 218
BEST OF VOL 2 1973 PHILIPS UK 6336 219
CHRISTMAS WITH THE PLATTERS 19 MERCURY US SR 60841
COLLECTION 1976 HALLMARK UK PDA 003
DOUBLE GOLD PLATTERS 19 MUSICOR US 4601
ENCORE OF BROADWAY GOLDEN HITS 19 MERCURY US SR 60613
ENCORE OF GOLDEN HITS 19 MERCURY US SR 60243
ENCORE OF GOLDEN HITS OF THE GROUPS 19 MERCURY US SR 60893
ENCORES 19 WING US SRW 16112
THE FLYING PLATTERS 19 MERCURY US MG 20298
FLYING PLATTERS AROUND THE WORLD 19 MERCURY US SR 60043
GOING BACK TO DETROIT 19 MUSICOR US MS 3125
GOING BACK TO DETRIT 1967 STATESIDE UK SSL 10208
GOLDEN HOUR 19 PYE UK GH 808
GREAT PRETENDER 1974 HALLMARK UK SHM 843
HAVE THE MAGIC TOUCH 19 MUSICOR US 3111
I GET THE SWEETEST FEELING 1968 MUSICOR US MS 3171
I LOVE YOU A THOUSAND TIMES 1966 MUSICOR US MS 3091
IN THE STILL OF THE NIGHT 19 PICKWICK US 3120
JUKE BOX GIANTS 1981 AUDIO FIDELITY UK 007
LIVE 1974 CONTOUR UK 6870 627
LIFE IS JUST A BOWL OF CHERRIES 19 MERCURY US MG 20589
MOONLIGHT MEMORIES 19 MERCURY US SR 60759
MORE ENCORE OF GOLDEN HITS 19 MERCURY US SR 60252
MUSIC FROM ACROSS THE WAY 1975 PHILIPS UK 6382 117
MY PRAYER 1975 HALLMARK UK SHM 876
NOW 1975 CONTOUR UK 6870 640
NEW GOLDEN HITS OF THE PLATTERS 19 MUSICOR US MS 3141
NEW GOLDEN HITS OF THE PLATTERS 1968 STATESIDE UK SSL 10227
NEW SOUL OF THE PLATTERS 19 MERCURY US SR 60983
ONLY YOU 19 GUEST STAR US NG 1419
ONLY YOU 19 MUSICOR US 1002
OUR WAY 19 PYE UK NSPL28149
PLATTERS 19 SPRINGBOARD 4059
THE ORIGINAL 1978 FESTIVAL UK ALB 281
THE ORIGINAL 1978 PHILIPS UK 9100 049

(CONTINUED)

P97 **PLATTERS** (CONTINUED) P97

PLATTERS 19 KING US LP549
THE PLATTERS 19 STARDAY US K5002
THE PLATTERS 19 MERCURY US MG 20146
THE PLATTERS 19 IMPACT UK 6886 401
THE PLATTERS 19 MERCURY US SR 60245
PLATTERS HITS 1976 SONIC SON 002
PLATTERS HAVE THE MAGIC TOUCH 19 MUSICOR US MS 3111
REFLECTIONS 19 MERCURY US SR 60160
REFLECTIONS 19 WING RI US SRW 16672
REFLECTIONS 1968 WING UK WL1174
REMEMBER WHEN 19 MERCURY US SR 60087
SING LATINO 19 MERCURY US SR 60808
SING LATINO 1968 FONTANA UK SFL13040
SIXTEEN GREATEST HITS 19 TRIP US TOP 1611
SONG FOR THE LONELY 19 MERCURY US SR 60669
SPOTLIGHT ON 1974 PHILIPS UK 6641 202
SUPER HITS 19 PICKWICK US 3236
SWEET SWEET LOVIN' 19 MUSICOR US MS 3156
SWEET SWEET LOVIN' 1968 STATESIDE UK SSL 10245
TWO DECADES OF HITS 19 PYE UK PKL 4411
TWENTY CLASSIC HITS 1976 MERCURY UK 9100 048
TEHTH ANNIVERSARY ALBUM 1968 WING UK WL 1174
WONDER OF YOU 1976 HALLMARK UK SHM 896

P98 **PLAYER** P98

J C CROWLEY K G V(AB
PETER BECKETT G V (ABC
JOHN FRIESEN D (ABC
RON MOSS B (ABC
WAYNE COOK K (AB
JAY LEWIS G STEEL(A JIM HORN SAX (A MICHAEL OMARTIAN SYN (A REED KAILING G (A
GARY COLEMAN PERC (A JACK WHITE D (A

(A) PLAYER 1978 RSO US 1 3036 UK 2394 193
(B) DANGER ZONE 1978 RSO US 1 3026 UK 2394 208
(B) DANGER ZONE 1978 RSO UK RSS 3
(C) ROOM WITH A VIEW 19 CASABLANCA UK NBLP7217

P99 **PLAYERS ASSOCIATION** P99

CHRIS HILLS G V K B D (BD
WENDELL MORRISSON V (D
MICHAEL BRECKER SAX (B
DAVE SANBORN SAX (B
MARIAN ROLLE V (D
JON FADDIS TPT (B
STEVE KHAN G (B VICTOR PAZ TPT (D JOHN DEARTH TPT (D TOM HARREL HRNS (D
WILBUR BASCCOMB B (B MTUME CONG (B LORRAINE MOORE V (B WAYNE ANDRE TROM(B
MIKE MANDEL SYN (B LEON PENDARVIS K (B FREDDIE HARRIS G (B DANNY TRIFAN B (B
NICKY MARRERO CONG (B DAVID EARLE JOHNSON PERC(B ED'EASY' ZANT V (B JIM McELWAINE K (D
CALEB MARTIN G (D LUCIO HOPPER B (D RAY MANTILLA PERC (D BOB BERG SAX(D
ONNIE CUBER SAX (D

(A) PLAYERS ASSOCIATION 1978 VANGUARD VSD 79384
(B) BORN TO DANCE 1978 VANGUARD VSD 79398
(C) TURN THE MUSIC UP 1979 VANGUARD VSD 79421
(D) WE GOT THE GROOVE 1980 VANGUARD VSD 79431
(E) LET YOUR BODY GO 1980 VANGUARD VSD 79434

P100 **COUSIN JOE PLEASANT** P100

COUSIN JOE PLEASANT V PNO(A
ROGER HILL G (A
GRAHAM GALLERY B (A PETE YORK D (A DYAN BIRCH V (A FRANK COLLINS V (A
PADDY McHUGH V (A GEORGE CHISHOLM TROM (A COLIN SMITH TPT (A JOHNNY BARNES CLAR(A

(A) BLUESMAN FROM NEW ORLEANS 1974 BIG BEAR BEAR3

P102 **PLEASURE** P102

(A) DUST YOURSELF OFF 1975 FANTASY 9473
(B) ACCEPT NO SUBSTITUTES 1976 FANTASY 9506
(C) JOYOUS 19 FANTASY 9526
(D) GET TO THE FEELING 1978 FANTASY FT 543 9550
(E) FUTURE NOW 1979 FANTASY 9578
(F) SPECIAL THINGS 19 FANTASY 9600

P102A **PLUGS** P102A

(A) PLUGROCK (EP) 19 CATHEDRAL CATH1

P102B **PLIMSOULS** P102B

LOU RAMIREZ D (A
DAVE PAHOA B V (A
EDDIE MUNOZ G (A PETER CASE G V (A JACKIS KELSO SAX (A DOUG RICHARDSON SAX (A
HERMAN RILEY SAX (A

(A) THE PLIMSOULS 1981 PLANET US P13

P102C **PLUGZ** P102C

TITO LARRIVA G V (A
BARRY McBRIDE B V (A
CHARLIE QUINTANA D (A CLIFF ROMAN SAX (A

(A) ELECTRIFY ME 1979 PLUG 001

P102D **PLUM NELLY** P102D

RIC PRINCE K V (A
JOHN E WALKER G (A
STEVE RESS G V (A PETER HARRIS B V (A CHRISTOPHER LLOYD D PERC(A

(A) DECEPTIVE LINES 19 CAPITOL UK 692

P103 **PLUMMET AIRLINES** P103

DARRYL HUNT B V (1A
RICHARD BOOTH G V (1A
DUNCAN KERR G V (1A
KEITH GOTHERIDGE D (1A HARRY STEPHENSON G V (1A GASPAR LAWAL PERC (A

(1) 1977
(A) ON STONEY GROUND (DBL) 1981 HEDONICS UK HEDON1/2

P103A **PLUTO(1)** P103A

PAUL GARDNER G V (A
ALLAN WARNER G V (A
MICHAEL WORTH B (A DEREK JERVIS D (A

(A) PLUTO 197 DAWN UK DNLS 3030

P104 **PLUTO (2)** P104

WENCHE KJAERSTAD V (A
GUNNAR BERG-NIELSEN D(A

(A) VOYAGE INTO A DREAMERS MIND 1980 STRWBERRY SRLP 103

P104A **POACHER** P104A

TIM FLAHERTY G (A
PETE ALLEN STEEL(A
PETE LONGBOTTOM BANJ (A ADRIAN HART G (A ALLAN CROOKES B (A STAN BENNETT D (A

(A) POACHER 1978 RK RKLP 5002

P105 **POCKETS** P105

(A) COME GO WITH US 1977 CBS US 34897 UK 82288
(B) TAKE IT ON UP 1978 CBS US 35384
(C) SO DELICOUS 1979 CBS US 36001

P106 POCO P106

RUSTY YOUNG V STEEL G(ALL — (A) PICKING UP THE PIECES — 1969 EPIC US 26460 UK 65327
GEORGE GRANTHAM D(ABCDEFGHIJKLM — (B) POCO — 1970 EPIC US 26522 UK 64082
RICHIE FURAY G V(ABCDEH — (C) DELIVERIN' — 1971 EPIC US 30209 UK 64204
RANDY MEISNER B V G(A — (D) FROM THE INSIDE — 1971 EPIC US 30753 UK 64543
JIM MESSINA G V (ABC — (E) GOOD FEELIN' TO KNOW — 1973 EPIC US 31601 UK 65126
TIM SCHMIT B V(BCDEFGHIJKLM — (F) CRAZY EYES — 1973 EPIC US 32354 UK 65631
PAUL COTTON G V(DEFGHIJKLMNRST — (G) SEVEN — 1974 EPIC US 32895 UK 80082
CHARLIE HARRISON B V (ST — (H) CANTAMOS — 1975 EPIC US 33192 UK 80596
STEVE CHAPMAN D (STN — (I) THE VERY BEST OF POCO — 1975 EPIC US 33537 UK 88135
MILT HOLLAND PERC (JL — (J) HEAD OVER HEELS — 1975 ABC US 890 UK ABCL 5137
STEVE FORMAN PERC (JMOT — (K) LIVE — 1975 EPIC US 33336 UK 80705
DONALD FAGEN SYN (M — (L) ROSE OF CIMARRON — 1976 ABC US 946 UK ABCL 5166
KIM BULLARD K V (OST — (L) ROSE OF CIMARRON — 1982 MCA MCL 1638
MARK HENRY HARMAN K PROD(JL — (M) INDIAN SUMMER — 1977 ABC US 989 UK ABCL 5220
AL GARTH VLN (JLG — (N) LEGEND — 1978 ABC US 1099 UK ABCL 5264
VICTOR FELDMAN PERC (J — (O) UNDER THE GUN — 1980 MCA US 5132 UK MCF 3076
MICHAEL VON VERDICK V (J — (P) SONGS OF RICHIE FURAY — 1980 EPIC US 36211
CHRIS HILLMAN MAND (F — (Q) SONGS OF PAUL COTTON — 1980 EPIC US 36210
PAUL HARRIS PNO (F — (R) BLUE & GRAY — 1981 MCA US 5227
JOE LALA PERC (F — (S) COWBOYS & ENGLISHMEN — 1982 MCA US 5288
BILL GRAHAM FDL (F — (T) GHOST TOWN — 1982 ATLANTIC UK K50902
BOBBYE HALL PERC (G
SID SHARP STRINGS (LM — JOHN LOGAN BANJO(L — STEVE FERGUSON PNO (L — GARTH HUDSON K (J
JIM HASKELL STRING(JM — BARRY FAST PNO (E — JAI WINDING K (N — TOM STEPHENSON K (N
PHIL KENZIE SAX (NOT — MICHAEL BODDICKER SYN (N — BURTON CUMMINGS K (G — DENISE SUBOTNIL G V (T
ARMAND KAPROFF CELLO(T — BUELL NEIDLINGER (T

P106A POE P106A

(A) UP THROUGH THE SPIRAL — 1972 UNI US 73099

P107 POET & THE ONE MAN BAND P107

TONY COLTON V PERC(A — (A) POET & THE ONE MAN BAND — 1969 VERVE FORECAST UK SVLP6012
RAY SMITH G V (A — (A) POET & THE ONE MAN BAND — 1969 PARAMOUNT US 5010
BARRY MORGAN D (A
PAT DONALDSON B V (A — ALBERT LEE G V (A — NICKY HOPKINS PNO (A — ROGER COULAM ORG (A
WILLIAM DAVIES ORG (A — SPEEDY ACQUAYE CONGA(A — JERRY DONAHUE V (A — JOHN BELL CLAR (A
MIKE O'NEIL K (— PETE GAVIN V D (

P108 POET & THE ROOTS P108

LINTON KWESI JOHNSON V(A — (A) DREAD BEAT AN' BLOOD — 1978 FRONT LINE UK FL1017
VIVIAN WEATHERS B G V(A
DENNIS BOVELL G K (A — WINSTON CURNIFFE D (A — JAH BUNNY D (A — DESMOND CRAIG K (A
EVERALD FORREST PERC (A — LILA WEATHERS V (A — JOHN VARNOM G (A

P109 PEKKA POHJOLA P109

PEKKA POHJOLA B SYN K (ALL — (A) PIHKASILMA KAARNAKORVA — 1972 LOVE LRLP 71
EERO KOIVISTOINEN SAX (B — (B) HARAKKA BIALOIPOKKU — 1975 LOVE LRLP 118
PEKKA POYRY SAX (B — (B) B THE MAGPIE — 1975 VIRGIN UK V 2036
PAVONI PAAKUNAINEN WIND(B — (C) SKUGGORNAS TJUVSTART — 1977 LOVE LRLP 219
BERTIL LOFGREN TPT (B — (C) MATHEMATICIANS AIR DISPLAY — 1977 VIRGIN UK V 2084
COSTE APETREA G (B — (D) VISITATION — 1980 DIG IT DIGLP 4
TOMI PARKKONEN D (B
GEORGE WADENIUS G PERC(C — WLODEK GULGOWSKI SYN K(C — PIERRE MOERLEN D PERC(C — VESA AALTONEN D (C
MIKE OLDFIELD G PERC(C — SALLY OLDFIELD V (C

P109A POINT BLANK P109A

RUSTY BURNS G V (ABCDEF — (A) POINT BLANK — 1976 ARISTA US AL 4087 UK ARTY 135
KIM DAVIS G V (ABCDEF — (B) SECOND SEASON — 1977 ARISTA US AL 4137 UK SPARTY1019
PETER GRUEN D (ABCDEF — (C) AIRPLAY — 1979 MCA US 3160 UK MCF 3049
JOHN O'DANIEL V (ABCD — (D) THE HARD WAY — 1980 MCA US 5114 GER 202 431
PHILIP PETTY B (AB — (E) AMERICAN EXCESS — 1981 MCA US 5189 GER 203 692
BILL RANDOLPH B V (CDEF — (F) ON A ROLL — 1982 MCA US 5288 UK MCF3141
STEVE HARDIN K V HCA (CD
KARL BERKE K V (D — MIKE HAMILTON K (EF — BUBBA KEITH V (EF

P109B POINT OF VIEW P109B

(A) POINT OF VIEW — 1973 RCA 4825

P110 POLECAT P110

GRAHAM BROAD D PERC V (A — (A) MONEY TALKIN' — 1976 DJM UK DJH 40475
BERNIE LEE G V (A
GEOFF KNOWLES G V (A — DAVE GOODMAN B (A — STEPHEN COTTON K V (A — ROGER DELL PERC V(A
ROBIN LAWRENCE SAX (A — MARTIN HAYES TPT V (A

P110A POLECATS P110A

TIM WORMAN (A — (A) CULT HEROES 1981 — NERVOUS NERD 001
BOZ BOORER (A
PHIL BLOOMBERG (A — NEIL ROONEY (A

P111 POLICE P111

GORDON 'STING'SUMNER V B(ALL — (A) OUTLANDOS D'AMOUR — 1978 A&M US 4753 UK AMLH68502
ANDY SUMMERS G V (ALL — (B) REGATTA DE BLANC — 1979 A&M US 4792 UK AMLH64792
STEWART COPELAND D V (ALL — (C) ZENYATTA MONDATTA — 1980 A&M US 4831 UK AMLH64831
HENRY PALOVANI G (— (D) GHOST IN THE MACHINE — 1981 A&M US 3730 UK AMLK63730
JEAN ROUSSEL K (D
HUGH PADHAM PROD (D

P112 PAMELA POLLAND P112

PAMELA POLLAND K V (A — (A) PAMELA POLLAND — 1972 CBS US 31116 UK 64934
TAJ MAHAL G (A
MARC McCLURE V (A — DENNIS LOCORRIERE V (A — RAY SAWYER V (A — GEORGE CUMMINGS V (A
ROWAN BROS. V (A — GEORGE DALY V (A — JIMMY SPHEERIS V (A — MARC McCALLEN V (A
MEMPHIS HRNS (A — ART ROSCH PERC (A — PAUL FALLERSO K (A — ROSCOE HIRSCHBERG PERC(A
NICKY HOPKINS K (A — DAVID BRIGGS K (A — JOHN SHINE G (A — EDDIE HINTON G (A
RICHARD SCHLOSSER D (A — KENNY BUTTREY D (A — BING NATHAN B (A — NORBERT PUTNAM B (A
TOMMY COGBILL B (A — BOBBY WOOD K (A

P113 BONNIE POINTER P113

BONNIE POINTER V (A — (A) BONNIE POINTER — 1978 MOTOWN US M7 911 UK STML12101
TRUMAN THOMAS K (A — (B) BONNIE POINTER 2 — 1980 MOTOWN US 929 UK STML12129
NIGEL OLSSON D (A
OLLIE BROWN D (A — EDDIE HAZEL G (A — JACK ASHFORD PERC (A — JAMES JAMESON B (A
DONALD BALDWIN G B (A

P114 POINTER SISTERS P114

ANITA POINTER V (ALL — (A) THE POINTER SISTERS — 1973 BLUE THUMB US BT 48 UK ILPS 9243
RUTH POINTER V (ALL — (B) THATS A PLENTY — 1974 BLUE THUMB US 6009 UK ILPS 9276
JUNE POINTER V (ALL — (C) LIVE AT THE OPERA HOUSE — 1974 ABC US 8002 UK ABCD 608
BONNIE POINTER V (ABCDF — (D) STEPPIN' — 1975 BLUE THUMB US 6021 UK ANCHOR 5133
GAYLORD BIRCH D (ACDF — (E) BEST OF — 1976 BLUE THUMB US 6026 UK ABC ABCD 611
TOM SALISBURY K (ACDF — (F) HAVING A PARTY — 1978 BLUE THUMB US 6023 UK ABC ABCL 5163
RON McCLURE B (A — (G) ENERGY — 1978 PLANET US P1 UK K52107
WILLIE FULTON G (A — (H) PRIORITY — 1979 PLANET US 9003 UK K52161
JOHN REWIND G (A — (J) SPECIAL THINGS — 1980 PLANET US P9 UK K52242
SKIP MESQUITE SAX (A — (K) BLACK & WHITE — 1981 PLANET UK K52300
JOHN NEWMAN B (C — (L) SO EXCITED — 1982 PLANET UK RPLP6001
CHRIS MICHIE G (CDF
SONNY BURKE K (F — STEVIE WONDER K (DF — OLLIE BROWN D (J — NATHAN WATTS B (JKL
JAMES GADSON D (FJ — ED GREENE D (F — LOUIS JOHNSON B (F — CHUCK DOMANICO B (F
JAMES JAMESON B (F — WILLIE WEEKS B (F — GENE SANTINI B (FD — WAH WAH WATSON G (DF
RAY PARKER G (F — DAVID T WALKER G (F — ROBERT BOWLES G (F — ERNIE WATTS SAX(F
ANDY NARELL STEEL(F — ED MARSHAL D (A — ROD ELLICOTT B (A — NORMAN LANDSBERG K (A
JOE CRANE K (A — DEXTER C PLATES B (A — JEROME KIMSEY D (A — KENNETH NASH PERC(F
GERALD JOHNSON B (G — MICHAEL BAIRD D (G — ABRAHAM LABORIEL B (G — RANDY BACHMAN G (G
EDDIE WATKINS JNR (G — BRYAN CUMMING SAX (G — JEFF PORCARO D (G — DAVID HUNGATE B (G
WADDY WACHTEL G (GH — DANNY KORTCHMAR G (G — DAVID PAICH K (G — LENNY CASTRO PERC(G
JIMMY PHILLIPS K (G — MIKE PORCARO B (G — STEVE PORCARO K (G — JAMES NEWTON HOWARD K(G
DAVEY JOHNSTONE G (G — JAI WINDING K (G — RICHARD PERRY PERC (G — RICK JAEGER D (G
FRED TACKETT G (G — HERBIE HANCOCK K (D — PAUL JOHNSON B (D — BILL SUMMERS PERC(D
JIM ROTHERMEL CLAR (D — DAVID SPINOZZA G (H — RICK MAROTTA D (H — DAN DUGMORE G (H
BILL PAYNE PNO (H — WILLIAM'SMITTY'SMITH K(MKL — SCOTT CHAMBERS B (H — BOBBY GUIDOTTI PERC(H
NICKY HOPKINS PNO (H — GREG PHILLINGANES K (JKL — PAUL JACKSON G (JKL — PAULINHO DACOSTA PERC(JKL
STEVE MADAIO TPT (J — JAY HUTSON FLT (J — HENRY SIGISMONTE HRNS (J — TIM MAY G (JK
LANCE ONG SYN (J — BURT BACHARACH K STR(J — MARLO HENDERSON G (J — GARY GRANT TPT (JL
JOHN PIERCE B (J — CLARENCE McDONALD K (J — RICKY LAWSON D (J — DAVID WILLIAMS G (J
JOHN ROBINSON D (KL — DAVID FOSTER SYN (K — ED WALSH SYN (KL — LEE RITENOUR G (L
NATHAN EAST B (L — ROBBIE BUCHANAN K SYN(K — JIM HORN SAX (L — RANDY WALDMAN K (L
JOHN PARKER K SYN(L — CHUCK FINDLEY TPT (JL — DON MYRICK WIND (J — BILL REOCHENBACH TROM(J
TREVOR LAWRENCE HRNS (JK — TOM SNOW K SYN(J — MICHAEL BODDICKER SYN (JL — WARREN LOONEY HRN(J
RAYMOND POUNDS D (J — BEN BRIDGES G (J — LARRY GITTENS TPT (J — JOHN BARNES K (JKL
MARK GOLDENBURG G (J — JAMES JAMERSON B (J — RICHARD PERRY PROD (JLK — JAMES NEWTON HOWARD K(K
MIKE PORCARO B (K — MIKE COTTON SYN (K — DANNY FARAGHER G (L — GEORGE DOERING G (L
WADDY WACHTEL G (L — GARY HERBIG SAX (L — DICK HYDE TROM(L — IRA NEWBORN G (L

P114A POISON GIRLS P114A

VI SUBVERSA G V (C — (A) FATAL MICROBES MEET THE POISON GIRLS(EP — 1979 SMALL WONDER UK WEENY3
RICHARD FAMOUS G V (C — (B) HEX (EP) — 1979 SMALL WONDER UK WEENY4
BERNHARDT REBOURS V B K(C — (C) CHAPPAQUIDDICK BRIDGE — 1980 CRASS UK 421984/2
LANCE D'BOYLE D V (C
NIL VLN (C — GEM STONE V (C

P114B MICHEL POLNAREFF P114B

MICHEL POLNAREFF — (A) MICHEL POLNAREFF — 1976 ATLANTIC US SD 18153 UK K50195
LEE RITENOUR G (A — (B) LIPSTICK — 1976 ATLANTIC UK K50281
CLIFF GIVENS V (A
ANDREW GOLD G V (A — STEVE CROPPER G (A — GARY STOVALL G (A — FRED TACKETT G (A
DONNIE DACUS G (A — DAVID HENSCHEL K (A — LEE SKLAR B (A — DAVID HUNGATE B (A
REINY PRESS B (A — WILLIE WEEKS B (A — NIGEL OLSSON D (A — JIM GORDON D (A
JIM KELTNER D (A — DAVID KEMPER D (A — RUSS KUNKEL PERC (A — STAR RICHARDS SAX(A
ELLEN KEARNEY V (A — LEAH KUNKEL V (A — JENNIFER WARNES V (A — VALERIE CARTER V 'A
BROOKS HUNNICUTT V (A — EUGENE GARFIN V (A — LEWIS FUREY V (A — BOBBY KING V (A
TERRY EVANS V (A

P114C POLLUTION P114C

JOHN LAMBERT B V (A — (A) POLLUTION — 19 ATCO US 6051
RICHARD LEWIS TPT K V(A
CHRISTIAN MOSERT WIND K V(A — DENNIS KENMORE PERC V(A — JAMES QUILL SMITH G V (A — DOBIE GRAY V PERC(A
TATA V (A — JOE LALA CONGA (A — PAUL LEWINTHAL SYN (A

P114D POLYROCK P114D

(A) POLYROCK — 1980 RCA 3714

P115 JEAN LUC PONTY P115

JEAN LUC PONTY VLN (ALL — (A) SUNDAY WALK — 1967 MPS 0068 226 15045
WOLFGANG DAUNER PNO (AR — (A) SUNDAY WALK — 1975 BASF BAP 5070 20645
NIELS HENNING PEDERSEN B(AE — (B) ELECTRIC CONNECTION — 1968 PACIFIC JAZZ 20156 UK LIBERTY 83262
DANIEL HUMAIR D (A — (C) EXPERIENCE — 1969 PACIFIC JAZZ 20168 UK RI SUNSET 50232
GEORGE DUKE PNO (BCD — (C) EXPERIENCE — 1980 PAUSA RI US 7065
WILBERT LONGMIRE G (B — (D) KING KONG — 1970 PACIFIC JAZZ 20172 UK LIBERTY 83375
BUD SHANK SAX (B — (E) ASTRORAMA — 1970 FAR EAST 65016
TONY ORTEGA FLT (B — (F) OPEN STRINGS — 1972 MPS 68088 BASF 75 21288
RICHARD ALPAN SAX (B — (G) LIVE IN MONTREUX — 1972 INNER CITY IC1003
TONY RISCH TPT (B — (H) PONTY/GRAPPELLI — 1973 AMERICA 6139
LARRY McGUIRE TPT (B — (J) UPON THE WINGS OF MUSIC — 1975 ATLANTIC US 18138 UK K50149
WILLIAM PETERSON TPT (B — (K) IMAGINARY VOYAGE — 1976 ATLANTIC US 18195 UK K50317
PAUL HUBINON TPT (B — (L) CANTELOUPE ISLAND(1969) — 1976 BLUENOTE US BNLA 632 UK BND 4018
THURMAN GREEN TROM (B — (M) AURORA — 1977 ATLANTIC US 18163 UK K50228
FRANK STRONG TROM (B — (N) ENIGMATIC OCEAN — 1977 ATLANTIC US 19110 UK K50409
FRANK WIMBERLEY TROM (B — (O) COSMIC MESSENGER — 1979 ATLANTIC US 29289 UK K50505
BOB WEST B (B — (P) CIVILIZED EVIL — 1980 ATLANTIC US 16020 UK K50744
PAUL HUMPHREY D (B — (Q) A TASTE FOR PASSION — 1979 ATLANTIC US 19253
SUGARCANE HARRIS VLN (R — (R) NEW VIOLIN SUMMIT — 1972 MPS GER 33 21285/8
MICHAEL URBANIAK VLN (R — (S) MYSTICAL ADVENTURES — 1982 ATLANTIC UK K50872

(CONTINUED)

P115 (CONTINUED) **JEAN LUC PONTY** P115

JOHN HEARD B (CL DICK BERK D (CL GENE ESTES VIBES PERC (DL BUELL NEIDLINGER B (DL
ARTHUR TRIPP D (DL IAN UNDERWOOD SAX (DL WILTON FELDER B (DL JOHN GUERIN D (DL
ERNIE WATTS SAX (DL FRANK ZAPPA G (DL DONALD CHRISTLIEB WIND(DL GENE CIPRIANO WIND(DL
VINCENT DE ROSA HRNS (DL ARTHUR MAEBE HRNS (DL JONATHAN MEYER FLT(DL HAROLD BEMKO CELLO(DL
MILTON THOMAS VLA (DL MASAHIKO SATO PNO (E YOSHIAKI MASUO G (E MOTOHIKO HINO D (E
JOACHIM KUHN PNO (FG PHILIP CATHERINE G (FH OLIVER JOHNSON D (FG PETER WARREN B (F
J F JENNY CLARKE B (G NANA PERC (G STEPHANE GRAPPELLY VLN(H MAURICE VANDER PNO(H
NIPSO BRANTHER VLN (R TERJE RYPDAL G (R NEVILLE WHITEHEAD B (R ROBERT WYATT D (R
TONY BONFILS B (H ANDRE CECCARELLI D (H DARRYL STUERMER G(KMNP PATRICE RUSHEN K (MJ
TOM FOWLER B (KM NORMAN FEARRINGTON D (M ALLAN HOLDSWORTH G (N RALPHE ARMSTRONG B (NO
ALLAN ZAVOD K (KNPQ STEVE SMITH D (K MARK CRANEY D (OP CASEY SCHEUERELL D (OQ
PETER MAUNU G (O JOAQUIN LIEVANO G (OPQ CHRIS RHYNE K (P RANDY JACKSON B (P

P115A **PONY EXPRESS** P115A

(A) PONY EXPRESS 1972 REBEL US 1513

P116 **THE POP** P116

DAVID SWANSON G V (B (A) THE POP 1977 ARISTA ARTY 170
ROGER PRESCOTT G V (B (B) THE POP 1978 AUTOMATIC SA 101
JOEL MARTINEZ D ((C) GO! 1979 ARISTA US 4243 UK SPART 1107
TIM HENDERSON B V (B
IVAN KRAL (TIM McGOVERN G (B DAVID ROBINSON (STEPHEN T (
DAVID HOSKOT D (TIM HENDERSON V (

P117 **THE POP GROUP** P117

MARK STEWART V (A (A) THE POP GROUP 'Y' 1979 RADAR UK RAD 20
PAUL STEWART D ((B) FOR HOW MUCH LONGER DO WE TOLERATE1980 ROUGH TRADE UK ROUGH9
BRUCE SMITH D (A (C) WE ARE TIME 1980 ROUGH TRADE UK ROUGH 12
GARETH SAGER G (A
SIMON UNDERWOOD B (A JOHN WADDINGTON G (A

P117A **POPOL ACE** P117A

ARNE SCHULZE G ((A) POPOL ACE 1973 POLYDOR 2480 270
THOR ANDREASSEN D ((B) STOLEN FROM TIME 1975 POLYDOR 2480 332
TERJE METHI B ((C) CURLY SOUNDS 1978 POLYDOR 2483 498
PETE KNUDSEN G K SYN (
JAHN TEIGEN V (

P117B **POP RIVETS** P117B

WILD BILLY CHILDISH V(AB (A) GREATEST HITS 1979 HIPOCRITE HIP 007
WILL POWER G V (AB (B) EMPTY SOUNDS FROM ANARCHY RANCH 1979 HIPOCRITE HIP 0
RUSSELL SQUARE B V (AB
VALENTINE LAX D V (A LI'L RUSS D (B

P117C **POPOL VUH (NORWAY)** P117C

JOHN TEIGEN V (AB (A) POPOL VUH 19 POLYDOR
TERJE METHI B (AB (B) QUICHE MAYA 19 POLYDOR
PETE KNUDSEN K G (AB
ARNE SCHULTZE G (AB PJOUKEN EIDE TROM (AB THOR ANDREASSEN D (AB

P118 **POPOL VUH (GERM)** P118

FLORIAN FRICKE PNO (ALL (A) AFFENSTUNDE 1971 LIBERTY GER LBS 83460
DANIEL FISCHELSCHER G (DEFGHJKLMN (A) AFFENSTUNDE 1980 INNOVATIVE COMMINICATION 58159
TED DE JONG PERC (HKL (B) IN DEN GARTEN PHARAOS 1972 PILZ GER 212769
BOB ELISCU OBOE (CDL (C) HOSIANNA MANTRA 1973 PILZ GER 291431
MATTIAS V TIPPELSKIRCH FLT(J (C) HOSIANNA MANTRA 1981 CELESTRIAL HARMONIES US CEL 004
HOLGER TRULKSCH PERC (AB (D) SELIGPREISUNG 1974 KOSMISCHE GER 58 009
ALOIS GROMER SITAR(FHJKLM (E) EINSJAGER UND SIEBENJAGER 1975 KOSMISCHE GER 58 017
FRANK FIELDER SYN (AB (F) DAS HOELIED 1975 UA GER UAS 29781
CONNY VEIT G (CD (G) AGUIRRE 1975 PDA IT 6040
DJONG YUN SAX (CEFGHM (G) AGUIRRE 1975 BARCLAY FR 840103
KLAUS WIESE PERC (C (H) LETZTE TAGE LETZTE NACHTE 1976 UA GER UAS 29916
FRITZ SONNLEITNER VLN (C (I) YOGA 1976 PDU IT 6060
SHANA KUMA TABLAS(F ( ) PERLENKLANGEO THE BEST OF 1977 PDU IT 6073
SUSAN GOETTING OBOE (M (J) HERZ AUS GLAS (HEART OF GLASS) 1977 BRAIN GER 0060 079
RENATE KNAUP V (MN (J) COEUR DE VERRE (" " ") 1977 EGG FR 900536
CHRIS KARRER SAX (N (K) ON THE WAY TO A LITTLE WAY/NOSFERATU78 EGG FR 900573
(L) BRUDER DES SCHATTENS- 1978 BRAIN GER 0060 167
(M) DIE NACHT DER SEELE 1979 BRAIN GER 0060 242
(N) SEI STILL, WISSE ICH BIN 1981 INNOVATIVE COMMUNICATION 80007
(CE) DISCOVER COSMIC 1973 OHR DBL GER 94011920

P118A **POTTER ST CLOUD** P118A

DAVE POTTER (A (A) POTTER ST CLOUD 1971 MEDIARTS 41 7
ENDLE ST CLOUD (A
JAMES HARRELL (A DANNY BAKER K V (A BUZZ CLIFFORD V (A GENE TREEK G V (A
SNEAKY PETE STEEL(A BILLY CALDWELL ORG (A LEE KIEFER (A MATT MOORE V (A
GARY MONTGOMERY V (A EDDIE FISHER G (A

P118B **POPPEES** P118B

(A) IF SHE CRIES 1978 LINE GER EP 3001

P118C **PORK DUKES** P118C

VILOS STYLES G V (A (A) PORK DUKES 19 WOOD PORK 001
HARRENDUS STYLES G (A
MARK E VALLEY K (A GERMUM LE PIG D (A

P118D **PORTLAND** P118D

GARY OGAN G V (A (A) PORTLAND 1972 ELEKTRA US 75048
BILL LAMB G V (A
DAVID BRIGGS PNO (A RUSSELL DASHIEL G (A BOB WRAY B (A FRED PROUDY D (A
EMORY GORDY B (A DENNIS ST JOHN D (A BOBBY BRUCE FDL (A JOHN BERGMAN PNO (A
RICHARD BENELF STEEL(A

P118E **POSITIVE NOISE** P118E

ROSS MIDDLETON V K B(A (A) HEART OF DARKNESS 1981 STATIC UK STAT LP1
GRAHAM MIDDLETON K V (A
FRASER MIDDLETON B V (A RUSSELL BLACKSTONE G V (A LES GAFF D V (A

P118F **POT LIQUOR** P118F

GEORGE RATZLAFF K G V(A — (A) FIRST TASTE 1972
JERRY AMOROSO D V (A — (B) LEVEE BLUES 19 JANUS US 3033
GUT SCHAEFFER B V (A — (C) LOUISIANA ROCK'N'ROLL 19 JANUS US 3036
LES WALLACE G V (A

P118G **NIC POTTER & GUY EVANS** P118G

NIC POTTER (A — (A) LONG HELLO VOL 2 1981 BUTT UK NOTT004
GUY EVANS (A

P118H **POUSSEZ** P118H

(A) LEAVE THAT BOY ALONE 1980 VANGUARD VSD 79433

P119 **POUSSETTE DART BAND** P119

JOHN POUSSETTE DART G (ABCD — (A) POUSSETTE DART 1976 CAPITOL EST 11507
JOHN CURTIS G (ABCD — (B) AMNESIA 1977 CAPITOL EST 11608
JOHN TROY B (CBD — (C) 3 1978 CAPITOL SW 11781
MICHAEL DAWE D (CD — (D) NEVER ENOUGH 1979 CAPITOL 11935
NORMAN PRIDE PERC (CD
DAVE APPELL STRINGS (CD HANK MEDRESS PERC (C DAVID LASLEY V (CD STAN SCHWARTZ K (CD
ARNOLD McCULLER V (CD

P119A **POWDER BLUES BAND** P119A

TOM LAVIN G V (AB — (A) UNCUT 1980 RCA PL 10365
JACK LAVIN B V (AB — (B) THIRSTY EARS 1981
WILL MAC CALDER K V (AB
DURIS MAXWELL D (AB DAVE WOODWARD SAX V(AB WAYNE KOZAK SAX (A GORD BERTRAM SAX (AB
MARK HASSELBACH TPT (AB

P119B **COZY POWELL** P119B

COZY POWELL D (AB — (A) OVER THE TOP 1979 ARIOLA NL201178 UK ARL5038
JACK BRUCE B (AB — (A) OVER THE TOP 1979 POLYDOR US 6312
DON AIREY K (AB — (B) TILT 1981 POLYDOR UK5047 US 1 6342
GARY MOORE G (AB
CLEM CLEMPSON G (AB MAX MIDDLETON K (A BERNIE MARSDEN G (AB JEFF BECK G (B
DAVID SANCIOUS K (B CHRIS GLENN B (B ELMER GANTRY V (B MEL COLLINS SAX(B
KIRBY G (B NEIL MURRAY B (B FRANK AIELLO B V (B JOHN COOK K (B

P119C **ROGER POWELL** P119C

ROGER POWELL K (A — (A) AIR POCKET 1980 BEARSVILLE US 6994 UK ILPS9607

P120 **DUFFY POWER** P120

DUFFY POWER V (ALL — (A) INNOVATIONS 1971 TRANSATLANTIC TRA229
JOHN McLAUGHLIN G (A — (B) DUFFY POWER 1973 SPARK SRLM 2005
COLIN PINCOTT G (A — (C) DUFFY POWER 1973 GSF GS 502
JACK BRUCE B (A — (D) POWERHOUSE 1976 BUK BULP2010
DANNY THOMPSON B (A
TERRY COX D (A PHIL SEAMAN D (A RED REECE D (A MARTIN KERSHAW G (D
GRAHAM JONES G (D MARY ZINOVIEFF PNO (D MIKE THOMPSON B (D RAY COOPER PERC (D
ALLAN JAMES B (D PETER KIRKE B (D MIKE GILES D (D PERE AHERN D (D
BRYSON GRAHAM D (D CHRIS BAILEY D (D DANA GILLESPIE V (D ALEXIS KORNER V (D
BOZ BURRELL V (D PAM McKENNA V (D JOY YATES V (D MISTY BROWING V (D

P122 **POWERHOUSE FOUR** P122

ERIC CLAPTON G (A — (A) WHAT'S SHAKIN' (3 TRACKS) 1966 ELEKTRA 4002 UK RI UK EUK 260
STEVE WINWOOD K V (A
PAUL JONES V HCA(A JACK BRUCE B V (A BEN PALMER PNO (A PETE YORK D (A

P122A **PRAGVEC** P122A

NICHOLAS CASH D (B — (A) NO COWBOYS 1980 SREC UK
JOHN STUDHOLME G V (B — (B) PRAGVEC (EP) 198 CELLULOID FR 1040
DAVID BOYD V B (B
SUSAN GOGAN V SYN(B

P123 **ANDY PRATT** P123

ANDY PRATT V PNO(ALL — (A) RECORDS ARE LIKE LIFE 1969 POLYDOR UK 2489 003
ANDY MENDELSON K (D — (B) ANDY PRATT 1973 EPIC US 31722 UK 65646
GARY LINK B V (D — (C) RESOLUTION 1976 NEMPEROR US NE438 UK K50279
RICK SCHLOSSER D (D — (D) SHIVER IN THE NIGHT 1977 NEMPEROR US NE443 UK K50386
MARK DOYLE K G V (BCD — (E) MOTIVES 1979 NEMPEROR US 35701
LUTHER VANDROSS V (D
STEVE GADD D (C G DIANE SUMLER V (D DAVID LASLEY V (D MICHAEL BRECKER SAX (D
LOUIS MARINI SAX (D LEWIS DEL GATTO SAX (D RANDY BRECKER TPT (D RUBENS BASSINI PERC(DC
ANDY NEWMARK D (DC HUGH McDONALD B (CD GENE ORLOFF STRINGS (D ARIF MARDIN PERC(C
DIANE SUMLER V (C ANDY MENDELSON SYN (C CARLOS MARTIN PERC (C TONY LEVIN B (C
KEN BICHEL SYN (C RICHARD MENDELSON D (C LUTHER VANDROSS V (C DAVID LASLEY V (C
THE ROWANS V (C

P123A **PRAYING MANTIS** P123A

TINO TROY G V (A — (A) TIME TELLS NO LIES 1981 ARISTA UK SPART1153 GER 203 449
CHRIS TROY B V (A
STEVE CARROLL G V (A DAVE POTTS D (A TIM FRIESE GREENE PNO(A

P124 **PRELUDE** P124

BRIAN HUME G V (ABCDE — (A) HOW LONG IS FOREVER 1973 DAWN UK DNLS 3052
IAN VARDY G V (ABCDE — (B) AFTER THE GOLDRUSH 1974 ISLAND ILPS 9282
IRENE HUME V PERC(ABCDE — (C) DUTCH COURAGE 1974 DAWN UK DNLS 3061
TONY HYMAS K (E — (D) OWLCREEK INCIDENT 1975 DAWN DNLH 3 PYE 12120
HUGH BURNS G (E — (E) BACK INTO THE LIGHT 1976 PYE NSPL19448
DAVE MATTACKS D (E
DAVE PEACOCK B (A ISAAC GUILLORY B K G(D MIKE DRISCOLL D (D ALAN CARNEY B (E
JIM HORNSBY BANJO(D PATRICE LEMOINE K (D ROGER RETTIG G STEEL (D LINDA CURTIS PERC (D
STEVE GREGORY SAX (D ROD CLEMENTS B (D PICK WITHERS D (D

ELVIS PRESLEY G V (ALL

BILL BLACK	B	SCOTTY MOORE	G	D J FONTANA	D	FLOYD CRAMER	PNO
JAMES BURTON	G	HANK GARLAND	G	CHET ATKINS	G	KENNY BURRELL	G
HAL BLAINE	D	JORDANAIRES	V	BUDDY HARMON	D	RONNIE TUTT	D
JOHN WILKINSON	G	JERRY SCHEFF	B	GLEN D HARDIN	K	SONNY BROWN	PNO
DAVID BRIGGS CLAR	K	CHARLIE HODGES	G V	BOOTS RANDOLPH	SAX	MARVIN HUGHES	PNO
SHORTY LONG	PNO	NEAL MATTHEWS	SAX	HUGH JARRETT	V	HOYT HAWKINS	V
DUDLEY BROOKS	PNO	MIKE STOLLER	PNO	MILLIE KIRKHAM	V	KITTY WHITE	V
H J TUIMBRELL	G	BOB MOORE	B	HAROLD BRADLEY	G	CHIP YOUNG	G
PETE DRAKE	G	TOM TEDESCO	G	DON RANDI	K	LARRY KNECHTEL	B
MIKE DEASY	G	TOMMY COGBILL	B G	BOBBY EMMONS	PNO	GLEN SPREEN	ORG
MIKE LEECH	B	HENRY SLAUGHTER	ORG	CHARLIE McCOY	HCA	GRADY MARTIN	G
PETE HALLIN	K	JERRY REED	G	DARLENE LOVE	V	FANITA JAMES	V
JEAN KING	V	JEANNIE GREENE	V	LARRY MUHOBERAC	PNO	NORBERT PUTNAM	B
JERRY CARRIGAN	D	TEMPLE RISER	V	KEN BUTTREY	D	EMORY GORDY	B
JOHN CHRISTOPHER	G	KATH WESTMORELAND	V	J D SUMNER	V	STAMPS	V
RONNIE MILSAP	V	ED LOGAN	HRNS	MARY HOLLADAY	V	GINGER HOLLADAY	V
BOB TAYLOR	HRNS	WAYNE JACKSON	HRNS	GENE CHRISMAN	V	JUBILEE FOUR	V
CAROLE LOMBARD QUARTET		BOB WOOD	PNO	REGGIE YOUNG	G	SANDY POSEY	V

			MONO UK	STER UK	MONO US	STER US	
ELVIS (ROCK'N'ROLL No1)	HMV	1956	CLP 1093				
" " " "	RCA				LPM 1254	LSP 1254	
ELVIS (ROCK'N'ROLL No2)	HMV	1956	CLP 1105				
" " " "	RCA	1956	RD 7528	SF 7526	LPM 1382	LSP 1382	RI INT 5142 1981
THE BEST OF ELVIS	HMV	1956	DLP 1159				
LOVING YOU	RCA	1957	RC 24001		LPM 1515	LSP 1515	
LOVING YOU RI 12"	RCA	1977		PLG 2358			
ELVIS CHRISTMAS ALBUM	RCA	1957	RD 27052		LOC 1035		
" " "	RCA	195			LPM 1951	LSP 1951	
" " " "	CAMDEN	19	INT 1126		CAS 2428		RI 1980 INT 5060
KING CREOLE	RCA	1958	RD 27088	SF 8231	LPM 1884	LSP 1884	
GOLDEN RECORDS VOL 1	RCA	1958	RD 16069	SF 8129	LPM 1707	LSP 1707	RI 1980 INT 5143
ELVIS FOR LP FANS ONLY	RCA	1959	RD 27120	SF 8378	LPM 1990	LSP 1990	
A DATE WITH ELVIS	RCA	1959	RD 27128		LPM 2011	LSP 2011	
ELVIS GOLDEN RECORDS VOL 2	RCA	1959	RD 27159	SF 8151	LPM 2075	LSP 2075	RI 1981 INT 5144
ELVIS IS BACK	RCA	1960	RD 27171	SF 5060	LPM 2231	LSP 2231	RI 1981 INT 5141
G I BLUES	RCA	1960	RD 27192	SF 5078	LPM 2256	LSP 2256	
HIS HAND IN MINE	RCA	1960	RD 27211	SF 5094	LPM 2328	LSP 2328	
" " "	RCA RI	19		SF 8207			
SOMETHING FOR EVERYBODY	RCA	1961	RD 27244	SF 5106	LPM 2370	LSP 2370	RI 1981 INT 5135
BLUE HAWAII	RCA	1961	RD 27238	SF 5115	LPM 2426	LSP 2426	RI 1981 INT 5136
" "	RCA RI	19		SF 8145			
POT LUCK	RCA	1962	RD 27265	SF 5135	LPM 2523	LSP 2523	
GIRLS GIRLS GIRLS	RCA	1963	RD 7534	SF 7534	LPM 2621	LSP 2621	
IT HAPPENED AT THE WORLD FAIR	RCA	1963	RD 7565	SF 7565	LPM 2697	LSP 2697	
" " " "	RCA RI	19		1025		APLI2568	
FUN IN ACAPULCO	RCA	1963	RD 7609	SF 7609	LPM 2756	LSP 2756	
GOLDEN RECORDS VOL 3	RCA	1964	RD 7630	sf 7630	LPM 2765	LSP 2765	RI 1981 INT 5145
KISSIN COUSINS	RCA	1964	RD 7645	SF 7645	LPM 2894	LSP 2894	
ROUSTABOUT	RCA	1965	RD 7678	SF 7678		LSP 2999	
GIRL HAPPY	RCA	1965	RD 7714	SF 7714	LPM 3338	LSP 3338	
FLAMING STAR	RCA	1965	RD 7723		PRS 279		
" " "	RCA	19		INT 1017			
" "	CAMDEN	19				CAS 2304	
ELVIS FOR EVERYONE	RCA	1965	RD 7751	SF 7751	LPM 2450	LSP 3450	
" " "	RCA	19		SF 8232			RI 1981 INT 5073
HARUM SCARUM	RCA	1965			LPM 3468	LSP 3468	
HAREM HOLIDAY	RCA	1965	RD 7767	SF 7767			
HAREM HOLIDAY	RCA	19		46 1022			
FRANKIE & JOHNNY	RCA	1966	RD 7793	SF 7793	LPM 3553	LSP 3553	
" " "	RCA	19		46 1024		ACL 7007	
" " "	RCA	19				APLI2559	
PARADISE HAWAIIAN STYLE	RCA	1966	RD 7810	SF 7810	LPM 3643	LSP 3643	
CALIFORNIA HOLIDAY	RCA	1966	RD 7820	SF 7820			
" " "	RCA	19		46 1020			
SPIN OUT	RCA	1966			LPM 3702	LSP 3702	
" "	RCA	197				APLI2560	
HOW GREAT THOU ART	RCA	1967	RD 7867	SF 7867	LPM 3758	LSP 3758	
" " "	RCA	19		SF 8206			RI 1981 INT 5147
DOUBLE TROUBLE	RCA	1967	RD 7892	SF 7892	LPM 3787	LSP 3787	
" " "	RCA	196				AFLI2564	
CLAMBAKE	RCA	1967	RD 7917	SF 7917	LPM 3893	LSP 3893	
" "	RCA	19		46 1021		APLI2565	
GOLDEN RECORDS VOL 4	RCA	1968	RD 7924	SF 7924	LPM 3921	LSP 3921	RI 1981 INT 5146
SPEEDWAY	RCA	1968	RD 7957	SF 7957	LPM 3989	LSP 3989	
NBC TV SPECIAL	RCA	1968	RD 8011			LSP 4088	
FROM ELVIS IN MEMPHIS	RCA	1969	RD 8029	SF 8029		LSP 4155	
FROM MEMPHIS TO VEGAS	RCA	1970		SF 8080		LSP 6020	
ON STAGE FEB 1970	RCA	1970		SF 8128		LSP 4362	
WORLDWIDE 50 GOLD HITS VOL 1	RCA	1970	LPM 6401		LPM 6401		
IN PERSON AT THE INTERNATIONAL	RCA	1970				LSP 4428	
BACK IN MEMPHIS	RCA	1970				LSP 4429	
LETS BE FRIENDS	RCA INT	1970		INT 1103			
" " "	CAMDEN	1970				CAS 2408	
ALMOST IN LOVE	RCA INT	1970		INT 1023			
" " "	CAMDEN	1970				CAS 2440	
THATS THE WAY IT IS	RCA	1971		SF 8162		LSP 4445	RI 1981 INT 5137
ELVIS COUNTRY I'M 10,000 YEARS OLD	RCA	1971		SF 8172		LSP 4460	
LOVE LETTERS FROM ELVIS	RCA	1971		SF 8202		LSP 4530	
50 GOLD AWARD (THE OTHER SIDES)	RCA	1971	LPM 6402		LPM 6402		

(CONTINUED)

C'MON EVERYBODY	RCA INT	1971	INT 1280		
" " "	CAMDEN	1971		CAS 2518	
I GOT LUCKY	RCA INT	1971	INT 1322	CAS 2533	
" "	CAMDEN	1971	CDS 1154	CAS 2611	
YOU'LL NEVER WALK ALONE	CAMDEN	1971	CMD 1088	CAS 2472	
WONDERFUL WORLD OF CHRISTMAS	RCA	1971	SF 8221	LSP 4579	
" " " "	RCA	197		ANI 1936	
ELVIS NOW	RCA	1972	SF 8266	LSP 4671	
LIVE AT MADISON SQUARE GARDENS	RCA	1972	SF 8296	LSP 4776	
HE TOUCHED ME	RCA	1972	SF 8275	LSP 4690	
HITS FROM THE MOVIES	CAMDEN	1972	CDS 1110	CAS 2567	
HITS FROM THE MOVIES VOL2	CAMDEN	1972		CAS 4776	
ALOHA FROM HAWAII	RCA	1973	DPS 2040	VPSX6089	
ELVIS	RCA	1973	PL 10283	APL10283	
BURNING LOVE	RCA INT	1973	INT 1414		
" "	CAMDEN	1973		CAS 2595	
RAISED ON ROCK	RCA	1973	PL 10388	APL10388	
SEPARATE WAYS	CAMDEN	1973	CDS 1118	CAS 2611	
LEGENDARY PERFORMER 1	RCA	1974	LP 10341	CPL10341	
GOOD TIMES	RCA	1974	PL 10475	APL10475	
LIVE ON STAGE IN MEMPHIS	RCA	1974	PL 10606	APL10606	
HAVING FUN ON STAGE	RCA	1974	PM 10828	AFM10818	
40 GREATEST HITS	ARCADE	1975	ADEP 12		
HITS OF THE 70s	RCA	1974	FL 17527		
PROMISED LAND	RCA	1974	PL 10873	APL10873	
PURE GOLD	RCA	1975		ANL10971	
TODAY	RCA	1975	PL 11039	APL11039	
LEGENDARY PERFORMER VOL 2	RCA	1975		CLP11349	
US MALE	CAMDEN	1974	CDS 1150		
PICTURES OF ELVIS	RCA	1975	HY 1023		
DOUBLE DYNAMITE	PICKWICK	1975		DL 25001	
THE SUN COLLECTION	RCA	1975	HY 1001		
THE SUN SESSIONS	RCA	1976	PM 11675	APL11675	
FROM ELVIS PRESLEY BOULEVARD	RCA	1976	PL 11506	APL11506	
WELCOME TO MY WORLD	RCA	1976	PL 12274	APL12274	RI 1981 LP 3020
MOODY BLUE	RCA	1977	PL 12428	APL12428	RI 1981 LP 3021
THE SUN YEARS	CHARLY	1977	SUN 1001		
IN DEMAND	RCA	1977	PL 42003		
THE '56 SESSIONS	RCA	1978	PL 42101		
40 GREATEST HITS	RCA	1978	PL 42691		
ELVIS TAPES	CHISWICK /ACE	197	RED 1		
ELVIS PRESLEY COLLECTION	PICKWICK	1978	PDA 042		
HE WALKS BESIDE ME	RCA	1978	PL 12772	APL12772	
TV SPECIAL	RCA	1978	PL 42370		RI 19 5093
LEGENDARY PERFORMER VOL 3	RCA	1978	PL 13082		
RETURN TO SENDER	PICKWICK	19	CDS 1200		
ELVIS	PICKWICK	19	CDS 1201		
WONDERFUL WORLD	PICKWICK	19	PDA 073		
THE '56 SESSIONS VOL 2	RCA	1979	PL 42102		RI 1981 INT 3025
OUR MEMORIES OF YOU	RCA	1979	PL 13448		
ELVIS AARON PRESLEY (8 RECORD SET)	RCA	1980	CPL83699	3699	
INSPIRATION	K TEL	1980	NE 1101		
GUITAR MAN	RCA	1980	RCALP5010	3917	
THE '56 SESSIONS VOL 2	RCA	1981	3030		
HEARTBREAK HOTEL	CAMDEN	1981	CDS 1204		
ITS NOW OR NEVER	CAMDEN	1981	CDS 1202		
ARE YOU LONSOME TONIGHT	CAMDEN	1982	CDS 1207		
GREATEST HITS	RCA	1982	INT 5116		
ROCK & ROLL REBEL	K TEL	1982	NE 1170		
SUSPICIOUS MINDS	CAMDEN	1982	CDS 1206		
THE SOUND OF YOUR CRY	RCA	1982	ALP 3060		
OTHER RELEASES					
PORTRAIT IN MUSIC	RCA	1975	SRS 558		
LID ROCKS	RCA	1975	RJS27120		
GOLD THIRTY	RCA	1975	6176 77		
TODAY TOMORROW & FOREVER	RCA	1971	LSP 10220 GER		
ELVIS THE ROCKIN DAYS	RCA	1972	LSP 10204 GER		
ELVIS FOREVER	RCA	1974	PJL 8024		
SONGS FOR CHILDREN	RCA	1978	PL 12901 GER		
CANADIAN TRIBUTE	RCA	1978	KKL 1 7065 GER		
RARE ELVIS	RCA	1980	PL 42935 GER		
JAILHOUE ROCK/TICKLE ME	RCA	1979	PL 42792 GER		
EASY COME/KID GALLAHAD	RCA	1979	PL 42791 GER		
BURBANK SESSIONS	AUDIFON	19	AFNS 62768 GER		
THIS IS ELVIS	RCA	1981	PL 4031 GER		
GOOD ROCKIN' TONIGHT 10"	RCA	19	130 252		
ELVIS GOLDEN RECORDS 10"	RCA	19	HP 50X		
PANEL DELUXE	RCA	19	9201		
ON STAGE FEB 1970	RCA	19	R4P 5009		
GREAT HITS	RCA	19	SR1 9062		
CHRISTMAS ALBUM	RCA	19	5028		
GIRL HAPPY	RCA	19	5436		
GOLDEN BOY	HORZU	19	SHZT521		
GOLDEN BOY	RCA	1981	GER 43559		
ROCKIN' ON VOL 1	RCA	19	135		
ROCKIN' ON VOL 2	RCA	19	141		
MAGICAL ROCKIN' SOUND	JUBILEE	19	MLP1956		
BLUE CHRISTMAS	RCA	19	KNLI7047		
ELVIS PRESLEY 10"	RCA	19	CML 3009		
ELVIS PRESLEY	IMPACT	1978	6886807		
GREATEST HITS (7 RECORD SET)	RCA	19	GELV 6A		

(CONTINUED)

EPS

Title	Year	Label	US	UK
ELVIS PRESLEY	1956	RCA	US 1254	
ELVIS PRESLEY	1956	RCA	US 747	
ELVIS PRESLEY	1956	RCA	US 830	
LOVE ME TENDER	1956	RCA	US 4006	
THE REAL ELVIS	1956	RCA	US 940	
ELVIS VOL 1	1956	RCA	US 992	
ELVIS VOL 2	1956	RCA	US 993	
ANYWAY YOU WANT ME	1956	RCA	US 965	
JUST FOR YOU	1956	RCA	US 4041	
LOVING YOU VOL 1	1956	RCA	US 1515	
PEACE IN THE VALLEY	1957	RCA	US 4354	UK RCX 101
ELVIS PRESLEY	1957	RCA		UK RCX 104
JAILHOUSE ROCK	1957	RCA	US 4114	UK RCX 106
KING CREOLE VOL 1	1958	RCA	US 4319	UK RCX 117
KING CREOLE VOL 2	1958	RCA	US 4321	UK RCX 118
CHRISTMAS SONGS	1958	RCA	US 4108	UK RCX 121
CHRISTMAS WITH ELVIS	1958	RCA	US 4340	
ELVIS SAILS	1958	RCA	US 4325	UK RCX 131
IN A TENDER MOOD	1959	RCA		UK RCX 135
TOUCH OF GOLD	1959	RCA	US 5088	UK RCX 1045
STRICTLY ELVIS	1959	RCA		UK RCX 175
" "	1957	RCA	US 994	
TOUCH OF GOLD VOL 2	1959	RCA	US 5101	UK RCX 1048
TOUCH OF GOLD VOL 3	1959	RCA	US 5141	
SUCH A NIGHT	1960	RCA		UK RCX 190
FLAMING STAR	1961	RCA	US 128	
FOLLOW THAT DREAM	1962	RCA	US 4368	UK RCX 211
KID GALLAHAD	1963	RCA	US 4371	UK RCX 7106
VIVA LAS VEGAS	1964	RCA	US 4382	UK RCX 7141
ELVIS FOR YOU 1	1964	RCA		UK RCX 7142
ELVIS FOR YOU 2	1964	RCA		UK RCX 7143
TICKLE ME 1	1965	RCA	US 4383	UK RCX 7173
" " 2	1965	RCA		UK RCX 7174
EASY COME EASY GO	1967	RCA	US 4387	UK RCX 7187

P125A PRESSURE P125A

Musician	Inst		Album	Year	Label	UK
MELVIN ROBINSON	G	(A	(A) PRESSURE	1979	MCA US 3195	UK MCF3055
BARNABY FINCH	K	(A				

BOBBY VEGAS		(A	PAT KELLY	G V	(A	ART RODRIGUEZ	D	(A	RONNIE LAWS	SAX V	(A
JOHNNY LAWS	V	(A	SAMUEL MOORE	V	(A	REGGIE ALEXANDER	V	(A	SANDRA	V	(A

P126 BILLY PRESTON P126

Musician	Inst		Album	Year	Label / Catalogue
BILLY PRESTON	K V	(ALL	(A) THE WILDEST ORGAN IN TOWN	1966	CAPITOL (RI 76) ST 2532
OLLIE BROWN	D	(PMN	(B) MOST EXCITING ORGAN EVER	1967	SUE UK ILP 935 US V JAY1123
KEN BURKE	B	(PMN	(B) MOST EXCITING ORGAN EVER	196	JOY UK JOYS 112
JULIA WATERS	V	(M	( ) CLUB MEETING	19	CAPITOL 2607
TRUMAN THOMAS	K	(P	(C) GOSPEL IN MY SOUL	19	JOY UK JOYS 174
MANUEL KELLOUGH	D	(HKLP	(D) THE APPLE OF THEIR EYE	1969	PRESIDENT PTLS1034
BOBBY WATSON	B	(K	(E) THAT'S THE WAY GOD PLANNED IT	1969	APPLE UK SAPCOR 9 US ST 3359
TONY MAIDEN	G	(MNKP	(F) ENCOURAGING WORDS	1969	APPLE UK SAPCOR14 US ST 3370
JOE WALSH	G	(K	(G) I WROTE A SIMPLE SONG	1971	A&M UK AMLH63507 US 3507
ALBERT PERKINS	BANJ	(K	(H) MUSIC IS MY LIFE	1972	A&M UK AMLS63516 US 3516
KENNETH LUPPER	K	(KL	(J) EVERYBODY LIKES SOME KIND OF MUSIC	1973	A&M UK AMLH63526 US 3526
HUBERT HEARD	K	(HKL	(K) THE KIDS & ME	1974	A&M UK AMLH63645 US 3645
ALVIN TAYLOR	D	(PN	(L) LIVE EUROPEAN TOUR	1974	A&M UK AMLH68265 US 3657
WELTON GITE	B	(P	(M) ITS MY PLEASURE	1975	A&M UK AMLH64532 US 4532
WYNELL MONTGOMERY	SAX	(P	(N) BILLY PRESTON	1976	A&M UK AMLH64587 US 4587
EUGENE HENDERSON	G	(P	(O) BILLY'S BAG	1976	DJM UK DJB 26082
MICHAEL McGLOIRY	G	(P	(P) WHOLE NEW THING	1977	A&M UK AMLH64656 US 4656
CHARLES GARNETT	TPT	(GP	( ) THE GENIUS OF	1975	SPRINGBOARD US 4034
KENNETH L MOORE	K	(P	( ) SIXTEEN YEAR OLD SOUL	19	DERBY US 701
BOBBYE HALL	PERC	(P	( ) SOUL'D OUT	1974	GNP US 2 2071
ANGELO RICHARDS	TPT	(P	( ) GREAZEE SOUL	1969	SOUL CITY SCM 002
GLORIA JONES	V	(P	( ) ORGAN TRANSPLANT	19	PICKWICK SPC 3315
GWEN GUTHRIE	V	(H	(Q) BEHOLD	1979	MYRRH MYR 1070
SYREETA WRIGHT	V	(RM	(R) & SYREETA(FASTBREAK)	1979	MOTOWN US 915 UK STML12107
JESSE KIRKLAND	V	(G	(S) LATE AT NIGHT	1979	MOTOWN US 925 UK STML12116
LUTHER WATERS	V	(M	( ) BILLY PRESTON	19	BUDDAH US 7502
STEVIE WONDER	HCA	(M	(U) BILLY & SYREETA	19	MOTOWN UK STML12155
OREN WATERS	V	(M	(V) THE WAY I AM	19	MOTOWN US 941
SHUGGIE OTIS	G	(M	(W) UNIVERSAL LOVE	1980	MYRRH 1080
ROCKY DZIDZORNU	PERC	(M	( ) EARLY HITS	19	EXODUS US 304
ANDRE CROUCH	V	(P			
ROBERT MARGOULEFF	SYN	(M			

FRANKIE SPRING	V	(P	CLYDIE KING	V	(GHP	JOE GREEN	V	(P	VANETTA FIELDS	V	(GH
OMA DRAKE	V	(H	TOM SCOTT	HRNS	(H	JIM HORN	HRNS	(H	GEORGE BOHANON	HRN	(H
BUCK MONARI	HRNS	(H	PAUL HUBINON	HRNS	(H	LOUIS JOHNSON	B	(H	GEORGE JOHNSON	G B	(HN
DAVID T WALKER	G	(G	GEORGE HARRISON	G	(GM	MERRY CLAYTON	V	(G	PATRICE HOLLOWAY	V	(G
MYRNA MATTHEWS	V	(G	KING ERRISSON	CONGA	(G	ROCKY PEOPLES	SAX	(G	SHERRILL ATWOOD	V	(G
EUGENE BRYANT	V	(G	DOUG GIBBS	V	(G	DUANE ROGERS	V	(G	STEVE BECKMEIER	G	(N
STEPHANIE SPRUILL	V	(N	OLIVIA FOSTER	V	(N	REGGIE McBRIDE	B	(M	MALCOLM CECIL	SYN	(M
TOWER OF POWER	HRNS	(N	MERRY CLAYTON	V	(N	JEFF BECK	G	(N			

P126A DON PRESTON P126A

Musician	Inst		Album	Year	Label	
DON PRESTON	G V	(A	(A) SACRE BLUES	1981	RAG BABY	US RAG1005
BARRY FROST	B	(A				

DAVE JOHNSON	B	(A	JERRY ZARIMBA	G	(A	BUD DEAL	SAX	(A	JOHN HOBBS	K	(A

P127 **PRETENDERS** P127

CHRIS HYNDE G V (AB (A) PRETENDERS 1979 REAL UK RAL 3 US SIRE6083
PETE FARNDON B V (AB (B) 2 1981 SIRE UK K56924 US 3572
MARTIN CHAMBERS D V (AB
JAMES HONEYMAN-SCOTT G K V(AB CHRIS THOMAS PROD K(A NICK LOWE PROD (A CHRIS MERCER SAX (B
HENRY LOWTHER TPT (B JIM WILSON TPT (B GEOFF BRYANT HRNS (B

P128 **PRETTY THINGS** P128

PHIL MAY B G V(ALL (A) THE PRETTY THINGS 1965 FONTANA US 67544 UK TL5239
DICK TAYLOR BG V(ABCDEFJKLMNOX (A) THE PRETTY THINGS 1967 WING RI UK WL1167
VICTOR UNITT G (FL (B) THE PRETTY THINGS 1965 FONTANA US 67544
BRIAN PENDLETON G (ABCJKNX (C) GET THE PICTURE 1965 FONTANA UK TL5280
JOHN STAX B (ABCJKNX (C) WE WANT YOUR LOVE 1967 FONTANA 858039
PETE TOLSON G B (GHILM (D) EMOTIONS 1967 FONTANA UK 13140 UK TL5425
GORDON EDWARD V G B K (HI (E) S F SORROW 1968 COLUMBIA UK SCX 6306
WALLY ALLEN WALLER B V(DEFJKLMO (E) S F SORROW 1969 RARE EARTH US 506
JOHN ADLER (TWINK) D (EL (E) S F SORROW 1978 COLUMBIA EURO 062 04004
STUART BROOKS B (G (F) PARACHUTE 1970 HARVEST UK SHVL 774
VIV PRINCE D (ABCJKNX (F) PARACHUTE 1970 RARE EARTH US 515
(F) PARACHUTE 1982 GI UK WAX 6
JOHN POVEY PERC V(DEFGHIJKLMO (EF(SF SORROW/ PARACHUTE 1975 HARVEST UK SHDW 406
NICKY HOPKINS K (JK (EF) REAL PRETTY 19 RARE EARTH US R7 549
JIMMY PAGE G (C (EF) MILESTONES 19 COLUMBIA NL
SKIP ALLAN D V(BCDFGHIJKLMNO (G) FREEWAY MADNESS 1972 W B US 2680 UK K46190
GORDON HUNTLEY STEEL(G (H) SILK TORPEDO 1974 SWANSONG US 8411 UK SSK 59400
JOHN'WILLY' WILSON D (M (I) SAVAGE EYE 1975 SWANSONG US 8414 UK SSL 59401
STRING SECTION (G (J) GREATEST HITS DBL (COMP) 1975 PHILIPS 6625 015
(K) VINTAGE YEARS 1976 SIRE US SASH37132
(L) THE SINGLES A's & B's 1977 HARVEST UK SHSM 2022
(M) CROSS TALK 1980 WB US 3466 UK K56842
(N) ATTENTION 1971 FONTANA GER 6438059 RI 6438 202
(O) LIVE 1978 JADE EURO 6812 728
(X) DONT BRING ME DOWN 1967 FONTANA NL
(EPs)
PRETTY THINGS 1964 FONTANA UK TE 17434
RAINING IN MY HEART 1965 FONTANA UK TE 17442
ON FILM 1966 FONTANA UK TE 17472
PRETTY THINGS 1965 WING UK WL 1167

P129 **DORY PREVIN** P129

DORY PREVIN G V (ALL (A) MYTHICAL KINGS & IGUANAS 1972 UA US 4110 UK UAG 29186
PETER JAMESON G (ACF (B) REFLECTIONS IN A MUD PUDDLE 1972 UA US 5536 UK UAG 29346
DAVID COHEN G (ACDF (C) MARY C BROWN 1972 UA US 5657 UK UAG 29435
LAURINDO ALMEIDA G (C (D) ON MY WAY TO WHERE 1973 UA UK UAG 29176
BUDDY COLLETTE WIND (DF (D) ON MY WAY TO WHERE 1976 SUNSET RI UKSLS 50385
BRYAN GAROFALO B (C (E) LIVE AT CARNEGIE HALL(DBL) 1973 UA US 108 1/2 UK UAD 60045
JOE OSBORN B (ACF (F) DORY PREVIN 1974 WB US 5336 UK K56066
REINHOLD PRESS B (C (G) WERE CHILDREN OF COINCIDENCE 1976 WB US 2908 UK K56213
PEGGY SANDVIG K (C (H) ONE AM PHONE CALLS 1977 UA UK UAS 30070
TOM KEENE K (ACF
MICHAEL LANG K (CD EARL PALMER D (C RON TUTT D (ACD BRIAN DAVIES G (AF
JOHN P GUERIN D (C CLARK MAFFITT G (A LAWRENCE W KNECHTEL K (AD LOUIE SHELTON G (A
HAMILTON WESLEY WATT G (A DENNY BROOKS V (A MICHAEL McGINNIS V (A PETER MORSE V (A
B G DAVIES V (A FLOYD C MAFFITT V (A JUDY MAYHAN V (A WEST VENET V (A
D VERONICA LANGDEN V (A JIMMY BOND (D JOHN WILKIN G (D BERNIE LEADON G (D
CAROL KAYE B (D JOE SAMPLE K (D FRANK CAPP PERC (D DENNIS BUDIMIR G (D
HERB ELLIS (D DON RANDI K (D JOHN MORELL G (D TOM TEDESCO G (D
ROBERT WACHTEL G (F RON TUTT D (F LYLE RITZ B (F DAN DUGMORE STEEL (F
MARTI McCALL V (F CAROLYN MATTHEWS V (F LISA ROBERTS V (F RAY BROWN B (F
LINCOLN MAYORGA PNO (F BOBBY BRUCE FDL (F PERRY BOTKIN STR (F MYRNA MATTHEWS V (F
PATRICIA HENDERSON V (F SHIRLEY MATTHEWS V (F

P130 **JIM PRICE** P130

JIM PRICE V K HRNS (AB (A) KIDS NOWADAYS AINT GOT NO SHAME 1971 A&M UK AMLS64321
JOHN URIBE G V (AB (B) SUNDEGOS TRAVELLING ORCHESTRA 1974 DUNHILL US 50126
DAVE FARRELL B (B (B) SUNDEGOS TRAVELLING ORCHESTRA 1974 CBS UK 65245
KLAUS VOORMANN B (A
JIM KELTNER D (A BOBBY KEYS SAX (AB NICKY HOPKINS K (A DON PONCHER D (B

P130A **JIM PRICE** P130A

JIM PRICE V K HRNS (AB (A) KIDS NOWADAYS AINT GOT NO SHAME 1971 A&M UK AMLS64321
JOHN URIBE G V (AB (B) SUNDEGOS TRAVELLING ORCHESTRA 1974 DUNHILL US 50126
DAVE FARRELL B (B (B) SUNDEGOS TRAVELLING ORCHESTRA 1974 CBS UK 65245
KLAUS VOORMANN B (A
JIM KELTNER D (A BOBBY KEYS SAX (AB NICKY HOPKINS K (A DON PONCHER D (B

P131 **ALAN PRICE** P131

ALAN PRICE K V (ALL (A) THE PRICE TO PLAY 1966 DECCA UK LK4839
CLIVE BURROWS D B WIND ((B) A PRICE ON HIS HEAD 1967 DECCA UK LK4907
STEVE GREGORY WIND (JO (C) THE AMAZING (EP) 1967 DECCA UK 8670
JOHN WALTERS HRNS ((D) PRICE IS RIGHT 1968 PARROT US PAS 71018
ROD 'BOOTS'SLADE B (1 (E) THE WORLD OF ALAN PRICE 1970 DECCA UK SPA 77
LITTLE ROY WIND ((F) FAME & PRICE 1971 CBS UK 64392
RICK MORCOMBE G V (L (G) O LUCKY MAN 1973 WB US 2710 UK K46227
THEODORE THUNDER D V (L (H) BETWEEN YESTERDAY & TODAY 1974 WB US 2783 UK K56032
JOHN GORDON B V (LO (J) METROPOLITAN MAN 1975 POLYDOR UK 2442 133
COLIN GREEN G B (HJG (K) PERFORMING PRICE 1975 POLYDOR UK 2683 062
DAVE MARKEE B (HGJ (L) SHOUTS ACROSS THE STREET 1976 POLYDOR UK 2383 410
GRAHAM SMITH HCA (J (M) RAINBOWS END 1977 JET UK UAG 30133
LYN DOBSON WIND (1 (N) ENGLAND MY ENGLAND 1978 JET JET DL 300
HARRY BECKETT TPT (1 (O) ALAN PRICE 1978 JET US LA809G UK JETLP 207
BERNIE GEORGE WIND (J (P) FOCUS ON 1979 DECCA UK FOS 65/6
DAVID ROSE K SYN(O (Q) LUCKY DAY 1979 JET US 35710
BOB HENDRY G V (O (R) RISING SUN 1980 JET US 36510 UK 227
BILLY SMITH B (O (S) IN A WORD 1980 JET UK 13/162
GEORGE CHISHOLM TROM (O ( ) PROFILE 19 TELDEC GER 624 284
HUGHIE FLINT D (1 (1) FLOATING BAND

(CONTINUED)

P131 (CONTINUED) — ALAN PRICE — P131

DEREK WADSWORTH	HRNS (1							TONY CARR	D PERC(J
JOHN MUMFORD	HRNS (1	WILLY PAINE		(1	DENIS ANDRE		(1	DON WELLER	SAX (0
BARRY MORGAN	D (J	ALAN PARKER	G	(J	PAUL KEOGH	G	(J	ALAN DOWNEY	TPT(J
CLIVE THACKER	D (JGH	KENNY BAKER	TPT	(J	KENNY WHEELER	TPT	(J	PETER CIVIL	HRNS(J
CHRIS PYNE	TROM (J	CLIFF HARDY	TROM	(J	BILL GELDARD	TROM	(J	TONY BURROWS	V(0
FRED CROSSMAN	HRNS (J	VIC ASH	WIND	(J	JACQUIE SULLIVAN	V	(0	GEOFF DRISCOLL	SAX(0
CHAS MILLS	V (0	THEODORE THUNDER	D V	(0	MARTIN DROVER	TPT	(0		
KAY GARNER	V (0	JOY YATES	V	(0	NEIL LANCASTER	V	(0		

P132 LLOYD PRICE P132

LLOYD PRICE V (ALL

Title	Year	Label	Country	Number
A B C COLLECTION	1976	ABC	US	AC 30006
BEST OF	1970	STARLINE	UK	SRS 5025
BEST OF	19	TEEM	US	5007
COME TO ME	19	GUEST STAR	US	1910
COOKIN'	19	ABC	US	382
EXCITING LLOYD PRICE	19	ABC	US	277
FANTASTIC	19	ABC	US	346
FUNKY	19	UPFRONT	US	128
JUKE BOX GIANTS	1981	AUDIO FIDELITY	UK	1009
LLOYD PRICE	19	SPECIALTY US 2105	UK	SNTF5007
LLOYD AT ANY PRICE	19	JOY	UK	JOYS 179
LLOYD SWINGS FOR SAMMY	1965	MONUMENT	US	8032
LLOYD PRICE ORCHESTRA	19	DOUBLE	US	8301
MR PERSONALITY	1959	ABC	US	297
MR PERSONALITY SINGS THE BLUES	19	ABC	US	315
MR PERSONALITYS BIG 15	196	ABC	US	324
MISTY	19	DOUBLE	US	8308
MISTY	1976	DJM	UK	DJB26074
MISTY	19	UPFRONT	US	UPF 126
MR RHYTHM & BLUES	19	GRAND PRIX	US	422
NOW	19	TURNTABLE	US	5001
NOW	19	JAD	US	1002
PERSONALITY	1972	INTERCORD	GER	128613
ROCK'N'ROLL CLASSICS	1973	PATHE	FR 052	91361
SINGS THE MILLIONS SELLERS	19	ABC	US	366
SIXTEEN GREATEST HITS	19	ABC	US	AC 30006
SIXTEEN GREATEST HITS	19	STRIP	US	TOP16/5
STAGGER LEE	19	JOY	UK	JOY 202
THIS IS MY BAND	19	DOUBLE	US	2301

P132A RICK PRICE P132A

RICK PRICE G B V(A

(A) TALKING TO THE FLOWERS — 1971 GEMINI UK GME 1017

P132B PRIMA VERA P132B

JOHN TEIGEN V (
TOM MATHISEN V (
HERODES FALSK V (

(A) PRIMA VERA	1977	RCA	NOR	40020
(B) BRAKARA	1978	RCA	NOR	40029
(C) SALMER OG SANGER VI GERNE HIVER	1979	RCA	NOR	40163
(D) DEN STE	1981	RCA	NOR	40233

P132C ROLAND PRINCE P132C

(A) COLOR VISIONS — 1976 VANGUARD VSD 79371

ROLNAD PRINCE	G (A						
RANDY BRECKER	TPT (A						
JOE FARRELL	FLT (A	KENNY BARON	K (A	FRANK FOSTER	SAX (A	BOB CRANSHAW	B (A
AL CHALK	PERC (A	AL FOSTER	D (A	JOHN HICKS	K (A	ART JARDINE	D (A
VIRGIL JONES	TPT (A	EDDIE MOORE	D (A	THOMAS NICHOLAS	PER (A	BUSTER WILLIAMS	B (A

P133 PRINCE BUSTER P133

PRINCE BUSTER V (ALL

FABULOUS GREATEST HITS	19	MELODISC		M 51
SISTERS BIG STUFF	19	MELODISC		M12156
BIG 5	19	MELODISC		M12157
WRECK A PUM PUM	19	BLUE BEAT		BBLP 821
TEN COMMANDMENTS	19	RCA	US	LSP 3792
SHE WAS A ROUGH RIDER	1978	BLUE BEAT		BBLP 820

P134 PRINCE FAR I P134

Musician		Album	Year	Label	Country	Number
PRINCE FAR I	PERC V(ALL	(A) MESSAGE FROM THE KING	1978	FRONT LINE	UK	FL1013
CHINNAAS MELCHEZ INICK	G(BE	(B) LONG LIFE	1978	FRONT LINE	UK	FL1021
BINGY BUNNY	G (BDF	(C) CRY TUFF DUB ENCOUNTER	1978	FRONT LINE	UK	
BOBBY KALPHAT	K (BDF	(D) FREE FROM SIN	1979	TROJAN	UK	TRLS 125
TARZAN	K (B	(E) DUB TO AFRICA	1979	HIT & RUN		APLP 9006
SNAPPY	K (BD	(F) SHOWCASE	1979	PRE		PREFIX 3
ROBBIE SHAKESPEARE	B (B	(G) CRY TUFF DUB ENCOUNTER II	1979	FRONT LINE	UK	FL4002
GEORGE FULLWOOD	B (B	(H) CRY TOUGH DUB ENCO UNTER III	1980	DADDY COOL	UK	DKLP 15
SLY DUNBAR	D (B	(J) JAMAICAN HEROES	1980	TROJAN	UK	190
ROY JOHNSON KONGO	PERC(F					

SANTA	D (B	BONGO HERMAN	PERC (BD	DIRTY HARRY	HRNS (B	DON DRUMMOND	HRNS (B
STYLE SCOTT	D (DEF	ERROL HOLT	B (DEF	SOWELL	G VLN(DEF	EARL CHINNA SMITH	G (D
DEADLY HEADLEY	HRNS (D	RAS MILLINER	PERC (D	SCULLY	PERC (F	GLADSTONE ANDERSON	K (F

P135 PRINCE HAMMER P135

(A) BIBLE — 1978 FRONT LINE UK FL1004

PRINCE HAMMER	(A						
ERROL NELSON	K (A						
FRANKLIN WAUL	K (A	ERIC LAMONT	K (A	BO PEE	G (A	SLY DUNBAR	D (A
LLOYD PARKS	B (A	ROBBIE SHAKESPEARE	B (A	STICKY	PERC (A	TOMMY McCOOK	HRNS(A
VIN GORDON	HRNS (A	HERMAN MARQUIS	HRNS (A				

P135A PRINCE JAMMY P135A

(A) KAMIKAZI DUB — 1979 TROJAN TRLS 174

P135B PRINCE MOHAMMED P135B

(A) PEOPLE ARE YOU READY — 1978 BALLISTIC UK UAS 30192

P136 PRINCIPAL EDWARDS MAGIC THEATRE P136

BELINDA BOURQUIN K VLN V(ABC (A) SOUNDTRACK 1969 DANDELION US D9103 UK S63752
DAVID JONES PERC (ABC (B) THE ASMOTO RUNNING BAND 1971 DANDELION UK DAN8002
JEREMY ENSOR B (AB (C) ROUND ONE 1974 DERAM UK SML1108
MARTIN STELLMAN V (AB
ROGER SWALLOW D (B JOHN HILL DANCE (A CHRIS RUNCIMAN LIGHTS(A ROOTS CARTWRIGHT G (ABC
LESLIE ADEY LIGHTS(A MONICA NETTLES V (A VIVIENNE McAULIFFE V (AB DAVID WEEKS (
GILLIAN HADLEY (EVA DARLOW DANCE (A HARRY HOSMAN STAGE(A LYN EDWARDS PERC (A
RICHARD JONES B V (C NICK PALLETT G V (C GEOFF NICHOLS D (C NICK MASON PROD(B

P137 JOHN PRINE P137

JOHN PRINE G V (ALL (A) JOHN PRINE 1972 ATLANTIC US SD 8296 UK K40357
REGGIE YOUNG G (ACE (B) DIAMONDS IN THE ROUGH 1973 ATLANTIC US SD 7240 UK K40427
STEVE GOODMAN G (BCDEF (C) SWEET REVENGE 1974 ATLANTIC US SD 7274 UK K40524
DAVID BRIGGS K (CE (D) COMMON SENSE 1975 ATLANTIC US SD18127 UK K50137
MIKE LEECH B (ACE (E) PRIME PRINE 1976 ATLANTIC US SD18202 UK
KENNY MALONE D (CE (F) BRUISED ORANGE 1978 ASYLUM US 6E 139 UK K53084
JOHN CHRISTOPHER G (ACE (G) PINK CADILLAC 1979 ASYLUM US 6E 222 UK K52164
DAVE PRINE G (CDE (H) STORM WINDOWS 1980 ASYLUM US 280 NL 52248
GRADY MARTIN G (C
JERRY SHOOK HCA (C STEVE BURGH G (C KENNY ASCHER K (C HUGH McDONALD B (C
STEVE MOSLEY D (C RALPH McDONALD PERC (C JOHN BURNS G V (FG DOYLE GRISHAM STEEL(C
BOBBY WOOD K (ACE BILL SLATER B (C RAUN McKINNON V (CE JUDY CLAY STEEL (C
DEIRDRE TUCK V (CE CISSY HOUSTON V (CE SID SIMS B V (F TOM RADTKE D PERC (F
JIM ROTHERMEL WIND V(DE RICK VITO G (DE LEN DRESSLAR V (F DON SHELTON V (F
BOB BOWKER V (F LEO LEBLANC STEEL G(ACDEFG CORKY SIEGEL HCA (F BONNIE HERMAN V (F
JACKSON BROWNE V (DF MIKE UTLEY K (F VICKI HUBLEY V (F KITTY HAYWOOD V (F
DIANE HOLMES V (F BONNIE KOLOC V (F HOWARD LEVY K SAX(FG BOB HOBAN K V (F
HARRY WALLER V (F MIKE JORDAN V (F STEVE RODBY B (F SAM BUSH G V (F
JETHRO BURNS MAND V(F DAN CRONIN V (DF RAMBLIN JACK ELLIOT V (F JOHN COWAN V (F
FRED HOLSTEIN V (F BRYAN BOWERS V (F TOM HANSON V (F HANK NEUBERGER V (F
EARL PIONKE V (F JAMES TALLEY V (F ED HOLSTEIN V (F ALDO BOTTALLA V (F
MIKE URSCHEL V (F JAMES McNAMARA V (F AL BUNETTA V (F TYLER WILSON V (F
TIM MESSER V (F PETER BUNETTA D V (DE TOMMY CATHEY B (DE JAMES BROWN K (DE
PAUL CANNON G (DE WAYNE JACKSON HRNS (DE ANDREW LOVE HRNS (DE JACK HALE HRNS(DE
JAMES MITCHELL HRNS (DE LEWIS COLLINS HRNS (DE LARRY MUHOBERAC PNO (DE JOHN DAVID SOUTHER V(D
GLENN FREY V (D BONNIE RAITT V (DE HERB PEDERSEN V (D DUCK DUNN B (DE
ALAN HAND V K (DE MAILTO CORREA PERC (DE BROOKS HUNNICUTT V (DE PAT COULTER V (DE
GWENN EDWARDS V (DE JIM HORN HRNS (D CHUCK FINDLEY HRNS (D JACKIE KELSO HRNS(D
GREG JACKSON V (D CARL MARSH STR (D STEVE SPEAR B (D BOBBY EMMONS K (A
TOM PIEKARSK B (G ANGIE VARIAS D (G JERRY PHILLIPS G (G BILLY LEE RILEY G V (G
PHYLLIS DUNCAN V (G HELEN BERNARD V (G BEVERLEY WHITE V (G

P138 MADDY PRIOR P138

MADDY PRIOR V (AB (A) WOMAN IN THE WINGS 1978 CHRYSALIS GER 6307627 UK CHR1185
CHRIS STAINTON K (B1 (A) WOMAN IN THE WINGS 1978 TAKOMA US 7078
BARBARA DICKSON V (B (B) CHANGING WINDS 1978 CHRYSALIS UK CHR 1203
PHILIP TODD WIND (B (B) CHANGING WINDS 1978 TAKOMA US 7079
PAT DONALDSON B (1 (1) 1978 TOUR
JOHN LINGWOOD D (1B
KEVIN SAVIGAR SYN (1B ANDY ROBERTS G (A BARRIEMORE BARLOW D (A JOHN GLASCOCK B (A
DAVID PALMER K (A DAVID OLNEY B (A MARTIN BARRE G (A IAN ANDERSON FLT(A
JOHN HALSEY D (A BARRY BOOTH PNO (A SHONA ANDERSON V (A CHERRY GILLESPIE V (A
BOB GILL G (A RAY FLACKE G (1 RICHIE CLOSE K (B SARAH DECO V PNO (B
DOUG MORTER G V (B JOHN O'CONNOR G V (B RICK KEMP B V (B B J COLE STEEL (B
DAVID HASSALL PERC (B GLYN THOMAS PERC (B MALCOLM PEET G (B

P139 PRISM P139

RON TABAK B (ABCDEF (A) PRISM 1978 EMI UK INS 3014 ARIOLA US 50020
LINDSAY MITCHELL G V (ABCDEF (B) SEE FOREVER EYES 1978 ARIOLA ARL 5014 US 50034
JOHN HALL K V (ABCD (C) ARMAGEDDON 1979 CAPITOL UK 12051 ARIOLA US 50063
ALLEN HARLOW B G (BCDEF (D) YOUNG & RESTLESS 1980 CAPITOL 12072
ROCKET NORTON D (BCDEF (E) GREATEST HITS 1980 CAPITOL
A B BRYANT B (A (F) SMALL CHANGE 1982 CAPITOL UK 12184
RODNEY HIGGS K D (A
TOM KEENLYSIDE HRNS (A BRUCE FAIRBAIRN HRNS(A HENRY SMALL G B (F

P139A PRISONAIRES P139A

JOHNNY BRAGG V (A (A) FIVE BEATS BEHIND BARS 1979 CHARLY UK CR 30176
ED THURMAN V (A

P139B PRIVATE EYE P139B

HUGHIE LEGGAT G V (A (A) PRIVATE EYE 1979 CAPITOL EST 11980
HOWARD WARDEN B (A
GORDY LEGGAT G (A PAUL 'BOOMER' STAMP D V (A

P139C PRIVATE SECTOR P139C

(A) I WANNA STAY FREE (EP) 19 TJM UK TJM 8

P139D PROCESSION P139D

CRAIG COLLINGE D (A (A) PROCESSION 1969 MERCURY UK SMCL 20132
TREVOR GRIFFIN K V (A
MICK ROGERS V G B(A BRIAN PEACOCK B G K(A

P139E PRIVATE LINES P139E

RYCHE CHLANDA G V (A (A) TROUBLE IN SCHOOL 1980 PASSPORT US 9848
BILL PANKOW K (A
SPIKE BIGLIN B (A JOHNNY McLAUGHLIN D V (A

P139F PRIVATE LIGHTNING P139F

PATTY VAN NESS V (A (A) PRIVATE LIGHTNING 1980 A&M US 4791 UK AMLK 64791
PAUL VAN NESS G (A
STEVE KEITH B (A ERIC KAUFMAN K (A SCOTT WOODMAN D (A

P139G P J PROBY P139G

Name	Instr.	Albums
P J PROBY	V	(ALL
JOHN PAUL JONES	B K	(F
CLEM CATTINI	D	(F
JIMMY PAGE	G	(F
ALAN HAWKSHAW	K	(F
ALAN PARKER	G	(F
ROBERT PLANT	HCA	(F
DENNIS LOPEZ	PERC	(F
STAN BARRETT	PERC	(F
JOHN BONHAM	D	(F
AMORY KANE	G	(F

- (A) SOMEWHERE — 1965 LIBERTY US 7406
- (B) P J PROBY — 1965 LIBERTY US 7421
- (C) ENIGMA — 1967 LIBERTY US 7497
- (D) PHENOMENON — 1967 LIBERTY US 7515
- (E) WHAT'S WRONG WITH MY WORLD — 1968 LIBERTY US 7561
- (F) THREE WEEK HERO — 1969 LIBERTY UK LBS83219
- (G) LETS DANCE — 19 SUNSET GER 501072
- (H) SOMEWHERE — 1977 SUNSET UK 50404

P139H SAMUEL PRODY P139H

Name	Instr.	Albums
TONY SAVVA	G V	(A
JOHN BOSWELL	D V	(A
STEPHEN DAY	B	(A
DEREK SMALLCOMBE	GV	(A

- (A) SAMUEL PRODY — 19 GLOBAL 6306 906

P140 PROCOL HARUM P140

Name	Instr.	Albums
GARY BROOKER	K V	(ALL
KEITH REID	LYRICS	(ABCDEFG1
B J WILSON	D	(ABCDEFGHJK
CHRIS COPPING	K B	(DEFGHJK
DAVE KNIGHTS	B	(ABC1
B J COLE	STEEL	(H
RAY ROYER	G	(1
BOBBY HARRISON	D	(1
BILL EYDEN	D	(1
MATTHEW FISHER	K	(ABC1
ALAN CARTWRIGHT	B	(FGHJ
MICK GRABHAM	G	(GHJK
ROBIN TROWER	G	(ED
DAVE BALL	G	(F
PETE SOLLEY	K	(K
CHRISTIANNE LEGRAND	V	(G
DA CAMERA SINGERS	V	(F
EDMONTON SYN ORCH		(F

(1) 1967

- (A) PROCOL HARUM — 1967 REGAL ZONOPHONE UK LRZ 1001
- (A) PROCOL HARUM — 1967 DERAM US 18008
- (B) SHINE ON BRIGHTLY — 1969 REGAL ZONOPHONE UK SLRZ 1004
- (B) SHINE ON BRIGHTLY — 1969 A&M US SP 4151
- (C) A SALTY DOG — 1969 REGAL ZONOPHONE UK SLRZ 1009
- (C) A SALTY DOG — 1969 A&M US SP 4179
- (C) A SALTY DOG(RI DIFF TRACKS) — 1972 M F P UK MFP 5277
- (D) HOME — 1970 REGAL ZONOPHONE UK SLRZ 1014
- (D) HOME — 1970 A&M US SP 4261
- (E) BROKEN BARRICADES — 1971 CHRYSALIS UK ILPS 9158 US A&M SP 4294
- (E) BROKEN BARRICADES — 1971 CHRYSALIS NL 94566
- (E) BROKEN BARRICADES — 1974 CHRYSALIS UK RI CHR1056 GER 6499 659
- (F) LIVE IN CONCERT — 1972 CHRYLALIS UK CHR 1004 US A&M SP 4335
- (F) LIVE IN CONCERT — 1972 CHRYSALIS GER 6307 503
- (G) GRAND HOTEL — 1973 CHRYSALIS UK/US CHR 1037 GER 6307 511
- (H) EXOTIC BIRDS & FRUIT — 1974 CHRYSALIS UK/US CHR 1058
- (J) PROCOL NINTH — 1975 CHRYSALIS UK/US CHR 1080 GER 6307 555
- (K) SOMETHING MAGIC — 1977 CHRYSALIS UK/US CHR 1130 GER 6307 593
- ( ) BEST — 1975 A&M US 4401
- (AC) WHITER SHADE/SALTY DOG — 1972 CUBE UK TOOFA 7 GER 2635 004
- (BD) SHINE ON/HOME — 1972 CUBE UK TOOFA 10 GER 2635 009
- ( ) WHITER SHADE OF PALE — 19 INTERCORD GER 126 300
- ( ) WHITER SHADE OF PALE — 19 A&M US SP4373
- ( ) ROCK ROOTS — 1976 DECCA UK ROOTS 4
- ( ) BEST OF — 1971 FLY UK TON 4
- ( ) PORTRAIT — 1975 POLYDOR 2434 059
- ( ) HITS (DBL) — 1976 POLYDOR GER 2647 102
- ( ) GREATEST HITS — 1977 IMPACT FR 6886 555
- ( ) GREATEST HITS — 1978 HALLMARK UK SHM 956

P140A PRODUCT P140A

- (A) STYLE WARS(45 RPM LP) — 1981 CLAY RECORDS UK PLATE 1

P140B PROLES P140B

- (A) CONDEMNED (EP) — 19 ROCK AGAINST RACISM

P140C MICHAEL PROPHET P140C

Name	Instr.	Albums
MICHAEL PROPHET	V	(A
SANTA	D	(A
CLINTON FERRON	B	(A
ANSEL COLLINS	K	(A
BOBBY ELLIS	HRNS	(A
ALBERT GRIFFITHS	G	(A
PATRICK ANDY	V	(A
TONY TUFF	V	(A
CHINNA SMITH	G	(A
SCULLY	PERC	(A
YABBY U(VIV JACKSON)	V	(A
BERNARD HARVEY	K	(A
TOMMY McCOOK	HRN	(A

- (A) SERIOUS REASONING — 1980 GROVE MUSIC UK ILPS9606

P140D PROFFESIONALS P140D

Name	Instr.	Albums
STEVE JONES	G V	(A
PAUL COOK	D V	(A
PAUL MEYRS	B	(A
RAY McVEIGH	G V	(A

- (A) PROFFESIONALS — 1980 VIRGIN UK V2167
- (B) I DIDN'T SEE — 1981 VIRGIN GER 204 234

P140E. PROOF P140E

- (A) ITS SAFE — 1981 NEMPORER US 36546

P141 BRIAN PROTHEROE P141

Name	Instr.	Albums
BRIAN PROTHEROE	V K G	(ALL
BRIAN ODGERS	B	(B
BARRY MORGAN	D	(B

- (A) PINBALL — 1974 CHRYSALIS UK/US CHR 1065
- (B) PICK UP — 1975 CHRYSALIS UK/US CHR 1090
- (C) I.YOU — 1976 CHRYSALIS CHR 1108
- (D) LEAVE HIM TO HEAVEN — 1976 CHRYSALIS CHR 1118

P141A PROVIDENCE P141A

Name	Instr.	Albums
JIM COCKNEY	VLN V	(A
BARTHOLOMEW BISHOP	K V	(A
TIM TOMPKINS	CELLO V PERC	(A
BOB BARRIATUA	B V	(A
TOM TOMPKINS	VLN V	(A
ANDY GUZIE	G V	(A

- (A) EVER SENSE THE DAWN — 1972 THRESHOLD UK THS 9

P141B PRUDENCE P141B

Name	Instr.	Albums
AGE ALEXANDERSEN	G V	(A
TERJE TYSLAND	G K	(A
JOHAN TANGEN	MAND	(A
PER ERIK WALLUM	FLT V	(A
KARE SKEVIK	D	(A
JAN DEVIK	B	(A

- (A) 11.12.75 LIVE DBL — 1975 ARTIC NORWAY 7602

P142 JAMES 'SNOOKY' PRYOR P142

Name	Instr.	Albums
JAMES 'SNOOKY'PRYOR	HCA V	(ALL
HOMESICK JAMES	G V	(C
BOB HALL	PNO	(C
JOHN HUNT	D	(B
BOB BRUNNING	B	(C
MOODY JONES	G	(E
EARL PHILLIPS	D	(
LEE COOPER	G	(
SUNNYLAND SLIM	PNO	(E
ALFRED ELKINS	B	(E
ALFRED WALLACE	D	(E
LEROY FOSTER	G	(
EDDIE TAYLOR	G	(

- (A) SNOOKY — 19 MAGPIE US 1813
- (B) SNOOKY PRYOR — 19 FLYRIGHT UK LP 100
- (C) HOMESICK JAMES & SNOOKY PRYOR — 1973 CAROLINE UK C 1502
- (C) HOMESICK JAMES & SNOOKY PRYOR — 1979 BIG BEAR UK BEAR21
- (D) DO IT IF YOU WANT — 19 BLUEWAY US 6076
- (E) SNOOKY & MOODY — 1980 FLYRIGHT UK FLY565
- ( ) SHAKE YOUR BOOGIE — 1976 BIG BEAR UK BEAR14
- ( ) CHAKE YOUR BOOGIE — 1979 INTERCORD GER 146406

P142A ARTHUR PRYSOCK P142A

ARTHUR PRYSOCK (ALL — ART & SOUL 1967 VERVE US 65009
ARTHUR PRYSOCK'74 1973 OLDTOWN US 12001
LOVE MAKES IT RIGHT 1974 OLDTOWN US 12002
ALL MY LIFE 1974 OLDTOWN US 12004
ALL MY LIFE 1977 POLYDOR UK 2383 441
BEST OF ARTHUR PRYSOCK 19 VERVE 6 5011
THIS IS MY BELOVED 19 VERVE 6 5070
SILK & SATIN 19 POLYDOR US 2 8901
DOES IT AGAIN 1978 POLYDOR UK 2383 481
UNFORGETABLE 1978 KING US 1134

P142B PSEUDO EXISTERS P142B

NICK ARMSTRONG G (123A — (A) STAMP OUT NORMALITY(EP) 1979 DEAD GOOD UK DEAD 2
GES HALL B (12 — (1) JULY 1978 (2) AUTUMN 1978 (3) DECEMBER 1978
PAUL STEEL G V (123A
JOHN CARTWRIGHT V (1 MARK SIDDY D (123A JOHN LOONAM G B (23A

P142C PSYCHEDELIC FURS P142C

BUTLER REP V (AB — (A) PSYCHEDELIC FURS 1980 CBS US 36791 UK 84084
JOHN ASHTON G (AB — (B) TALK TALK TALK 1981 CBS US 37339 UK 84892
DUNCAN KILBURN SAX (AB
ROGER MORRIS G (AB VINCE ELY D (AB TIM BUTLER B (AB

P142D PSYCHOTIC PINEAPPLE P142D

(A) WHERE'S THE PARTY 19 US

P142E PSYCHEDELIC PSOUL P142E

(A) THE FREAK SCENE 1968 CBS CS US 9456

P143 PUBLIC FOOT THE ROMAN P143

DAG SMALL K V (A — (A) PUBLIC FOOT THE ROMAN 1973 SOVEREIGN UK SVNA 7259
SEAN BYRNE G V (A
JAMIE LANE D V (A GREG KNOWLES G (A WARD B (A

P144 PUBLIC IMAGE LTD P144

JOHN LYDON V (ALL — (A) PUBLIC IMAGE LTD 1978 VIRGIN UK V2114 GER 200301 US WB 3288
KEITH LEVINE G (AB — (B) SECOND EDITON 1979 VIRGIN UK VD2512 GER300863
JIM WALKER D (A — (B) METAL BOX(3X 12" EPS) 1979 VIRGIN UK METAL1
JAH WOBBLE B (AB — (C) PARIS AU PRINTEMPS 1980 VIRGIN UK V2183 GER 203095
JEANNETTE LEE (B — (D) FLOWERS OF ROMANCE 1981 VIRGIN GER 203410 US WB 3536
DAVE CROWE (B

P145 GARY PUCKETT & THE UNION GAP P145

GARY PUCKETT V (ALL — WOMAN WOMAN 1968 CBS US 9612
DWIGHT BEMENT SAX (ALL — YOUNG GIRL 1968 CBS US 9664 UK 63342
KERRY CHATER B (ALL — INCREDIBLE 1968 CBS US 9715 UK 63429
PAUL WHEATBREAD D (ALL — NEW ALBUM 1970 CBS US 30862 9935 UK 63794
GARY WITHEM PNO (ALL — GREATEST HITS 1970 CBS UK 64115
LADY WILLPOWER 1972 CBS US 31184

P145A PUDDLETOWN EXPRESS P145A

ARTHUR BROWN V (AB — (A) APRIL 1969 (B) JULY 1969
DRACHEN THEAKER SYN D(AB
DENNIS TAYLOR B (AB GEORGE KHAN SAX (B JOHN MARSHALL D (A JONAH MITCHELL ORG (B
McCULLOCH ORG (A ANDROID FUNNEL G (A

P146 DUDU PUKWANA P146

DUDU PUKWANA SAX V K PERC(ABC — (A) IN THE TOWNSHIPS 1974 CAROLINE UK C 1504
MONGEZI FEZA TPT PERC V(ABC — (B) FLUTE MUSIC 1975 CAROLINE UK CA2005
LOUIS MOHOLO D (AC — (C) DIAMOND EXPRESS 1978 FREEDOM FLP 41044
BIZO MNGQIKANA SAX PERC V(A
HARRY MILLER B (A ELTON DEAN SAX (C NICK EVANS TROM (C KEITH TIPPETT PNO (C
LUCKY RANKU G (C VICTOR NTONI B (C FRANK ROBERTS K (C ERNEST MOTHLE B (C
JAMES MENE D (C VICTOR WILLIAMS K (B PETE COWLING B (B JOHN STEVENS D (B
BOB STIGNEC PERC (B AUDREY MOTAUNA V (B

P147 PULSAR P147

JACQUES ROMAN K B (ABC — (A) POLLEN 1976 DECCA UK SKLR5228 CBS FR 82769
VICTOR BOSCH D PERC(ABC — (B) THE STRANDS OF THE FUTURE 1976 DECCA UK TXS 119 CBS FR 82703
GILBERT GANDIL G V (ABC — (C) HALLOWEEN 1977 CBS FR 82477
PHILIPPE ROMAN B V (A
ROLAND RICHARD FLT (ABc MICHEL MASSON B (BC

P147A PUNCHIN' JUDY P147A

BARBARA O'MEARA V (A — (A) PUNCHIN' JUDY 1973 TRANSATLANTIC UK TRA 272
JOHN PHILLIPS G V (A
KEITH EVANS B V (A ALAN BROOKS D V (A ROBIN LANGRIDGE K (A

P148 PUNISHMENT OF LUXURY P148

NEVILLE LUXURY G (— (A) LAUGHING ACADEMY 1979 UA UK UAG30258 GER 82735
BRIAN BOND V (
RED HELMIT G (JIMMY GIRO B (LES DENHAM D (

P148A PUPILS P148A

(A) A TRIBUTE TO THE ROLLING STONES 1966 WING UK WL 1150

P149 BERNARD PURDIE P149

BURNARD PURDIE D V (ALL — (A) SOUL FINDERS 1968 CAMDEN CAS 2170
RALPH McDONALD CONGA(E — (B) SOUL DRUMS 1968 DIRECTION 8 63290
HORACE OTT K (E — (C) STAND BY ME 1971 MEGA 51 5001
CORNELL DUPREE G (E — (D) PURDIE GOOD 1971 PRESTIGE US 10013
LLOYD DAVIS G (E — (E) SOUL IS ... PRETTY PURDIE 1972 PHILIPS 6369 421 FLY US 10154
GARNETT BROWN TROM (E — (F) SHAFT 1974 PRESTIGE US 10038
BILLY NICHOLS G (E — (G) DELIGHTS OF THE GARDEN 19 CASABLANCA US 7051
ARTHUR CLARKE SAX (E
NORMAN PRIDE PERC (E MAERETHA STEWART V (E RICHARD TEE K (E JAY BERLINER G (E
PAUL MARTINEZ B (E DANNY MOORE TPT (E SELDON POWELL SAX (E JAMES POWELL SAX(E
HILDA HARRIS V (E CHARLIE BROWN SAX (E GORDON POWELL PERC (E JERRY JEMMOTT B (E
EILEEN GILBERT V (E PAUL GRIFFIN K (E ERNIE ROYAL TPT (E HAROLD VICK SAX (E
CARL HALL V (E BARBARA MASSEY V (E

P150 **PURE FOOD & DRUG ACT** P150

HARVEY MANDEL G (A — (A) CHOICE CUTS — 1972 EPIC US 31401 NL 65197
DON 'SUGARCANE 'HARRIS VLN(A
PAUL LAGOS D (A VICTOR CONTE B (A COLEMAN HEAD G V (A RANDY RESNICK G V (A

P151 **PURE PRAIRIE LEAGUE** P151

CRAIG FULLER G V (AB — (A) PURE PRAIRIE LEAGUE — 1972 RCA UK SF 8320 RI 73 SF8453
GEORGE POWELL G V (ABCDEFG — (A) PURE PRAIRIE LEAGUE — 1972 RCA US LSP4650
JOHN CALL STEEL(ACDE — (B) BUSTIN' OUT — 1972 RCA UK SF 8417 US LSP 4769
JIM LANHAM B V (A — (C) TWO LANE HIGHWAY — 1975 RCA UK SF 8445 US APLI 0933
BILLY HINDS D (BCDEGJK — (D) IF THE SHOE FITS — 1976 RCA UK RS 1040 US AFLI 1247
MICK RONSON G V (B — (E) DANCE — 1976 RCA UK PL 11924 US APLI 1924
MICHAEL O'CONNOR K (CDEGJK — (F) LIVE TAKIN' THE STAGE — 1977 RCA US CPLL 2404
JAMES ROLLESTON B (B — (G) JUST FLY — 1978 RCA UK PL 12590 US AFLI 2590
LARRY GOSHORN G (CDEG — (H) HOLD BACK — 1979 RCA UK PL 13335 US APLI 3335
MICHAEL REILLY B (CDEGJ — (J) FIRIN' UP — 1980 CASABLANCA NBLP 7212
AL BRISCOE STEEL(B — (K) SOMETHING IN THE NIGHT — 1981 CASABLANCA US 7255
ANDY STEIN FDL (E
CHET ATKINS G (C TIM GOSHORN G V (G DAVID SANBORN SAX (JK GARY MIELKE SYN (JK
JANIS GILL V (JK KRISTINE ARNOLD V (JK VINCE GILL G V FDL BAN (JK JEFF WILSON G V (JK
JIM CAUGHLAN D (A DIANNE BROOKS V (B LITTLE BOBBY RING PERC (B BOB RING PROD (A
ASHAN ABRAHAMS PROD (E CHARLIE VEAL VLN (E DON FELDER MAND (C JOHNNY GIMBLE FDL (C
EMMYLOU HARRIS V (C JOHN ROTELLA K (C VINCE DEROSA HRNS (C JOHN BOYLAN PROD (CE

P152 **PURIFY BROTHERS** P152

JAMES PURIFY V (AB — (A) JAMES & BOBBY PURIFY — 1977 MERCURY UK 9110 028 US SRM11134
BOBBY PURIFY V (ALL — (B) YOU & MEE TOGETHER FOREVER — 1978 CASABLANCA US 7011 UK CAL2025
( ) PURE SOUND OF — 19 BELL US 6010

P153 **PURPLE GANG** P153

PETE'LUCIFER' WALKER V KAZOO(A — (A) PURPLE GANG STRIKES — 1968 TRANSATLANTIC UK SIRE US 97006
DEL ROBINSON HCA MAND(A
ANK LANGLEY BAN (A GEOFF BOURJER PNO (A JAMES BEARD G (A TONY MOSS B (A

P154 **PURPLE HEARTS** P154

ROBERT MANTON V (A — (A) BEAT THAT — 1980 FICTION UK FIX2 GER 60 280
GARY SPARKS D (A
JEFF SHADBOLT B V (A SIMON STEBBING G V (A CHRIS TSANGARIDES K (A

P155 **JIMMY PURSEY** P155

JIMMY PURSEY (AB — (A) IMAGINATION CAMOUFLAGE — 1980 POLYDOR UK 2442180 GER 2383 600
(B) ALIEN ORPHAN — 1982 EPIC UK 85235

P156 **PUSSYCAT** P156

(A) SOUVENIRS — 19 EMI NL 064 25565
(B) FIRST OF ALL — 1976 SONET SNTF 725

P156A **PUZZLE** P156A

JOHN LIVIGNI D V (AB — (A) PUZZLE — 1973 MOTOWN US 768
ANTHONY SICILIANO B (AB — (B) 2ND ALBUM — 1974 MOTOWN US 807
JOSEPH SPINAZOLA K (AB
BOBBY VILLALOBOS G (B RALF RICHERT G TPT (B BOB WILLIAMS TPT (B LARRY KLIMAS WIND(BA
BOB CULLEN PROD (B

P156B **PUZZLES** P156B

REUS PLASCHEK G (A — (A) LETS HAVE A PUZZLEPARTY — 1980 METRONOME GER 60350
JOHNNY LITTLEGIRL SAX (A
MARIO LUCCI B (A MARCEL MELLEMA D (A ARNO ARTS ORG (A

P157 **PYLON** P157

(A) GYRATE — 1980 ARMAGEDDON UK ARM5

P158 **PYRYMYD** P158

(A) PYRYMYD — 1980 CAPITOL US 12027

P159 **PYTHON LEE JACKOSN** P159

DAVE BENTLEY K V (A — (A) IN A BROKEN DREAM — 1974 YOUNGBLOOD 3001 US GNP 2066
DAVE MONTGOMERY D (A
MICK LIBER G (A TONY CAHILL B (A ROD STEWART V (A GARY BOYLE G (A

Q1 **EDDIE QUANSAH** Q1

EDDIE QUANSAH HRNS PERC V(A — (A) CHE CHE KULE — 1977 ISLAND UK ILPS 9446
ROSETTA HIGHTOWER V (A — (B) AWO AWO — 1981 ISLAND UK ILPS 9546
DICK CUTHELL TPT (A
MAC TONTOH TPT (A GEORGE LARNYOH SAX (A RAY ALLEN SAX (A PETE VANDER PUIJE SAX(A
CHRIS MERCER SAX (A GRAHAM MORGAN D (A KOFI AYIVOR D PERC(A TERRY WILSON B (A
COLIN BASS B (A WILLY CHEETHAM CONGA(A JIMMY CHAMBERS V (A PATRICE EBIGWE V (A
JOANNA WHYTE V (A ESTHER BYRD V (A WINSTON DELANDRO G V (A JUNIOR KERR G (A
JANOS BAJTALA K (A KIKI GYAN K (A EMMANUEL RENTZOS K V (A JOE SCOTT K (A
PETE WINGFIELD K (A TONY BRAUNAGEL D (A REMI KABAKA D (A SPARTACUS R B (A
JEROME RIMSON B (A REEBOP KWAKU BAAH PERC (A IAN GREEN SYN (A CLIFFORD MATAYA V (A
PAMELA DOUGLAS V (A

Q1A **'Q'** Q1A

VAN CROZIER (— (A) DANCIN' MAN — 1977 EPIC US 34691
DON GARVIN (
JOHN HOGUE (ED JONNET (ROBERT PECKMAN (CHRIS PATARINO (
BILL THOMAS (BILL VOGEL (

Q1B **Q65** Q1B

FRANK NUYENS G (A — (A) REVOLUTION — 1966 DECCA NL 6440675
PETER VINK B (A — (B) GREATEST HITS — 196 DECCA NL 6454409
WILLIAM BIELER HCA V(A
JOOP ROELOFS G (A JAY BAAR D (A

Q1C **'Q TIPS'** Q1C

PAUL YOUNG V (A — (A) Q TIPS — 1980 CHRYSALIS UK CHR 1255
BARRY WATTS D (A
MICK PEARL B (A GARTH WATT ROY G V (A IAN KEW K (A TONY HUGHES TPT (A
STEVE FARR SAX V(A STEWART BLANDMER SAX V(A

Q2 QUANTUM JUMP Q2

MARK WARNER G V (AC (A) QUANTUM JUMP 1976 ELECTRIC UK TRIX1
TREVOR MORAIS D (ABC (B) BARRACUDA 1977 ELECTRIC UK TRIX3
JOHN PERRY B (ABC (C) MIXING 1979 ELECTRIC UK TRIX11
ROY ALBRIGHTON G (
RUPERT HINE K V (ABC GEOFFREY RICHARDSON G VLN(B MORRIS PERT PERC (A RAY COOPER PERC (AB
PAUL KEOGH G (B ELKIE BROOKS V (B GEOFF DALY HRNS (B HENRY LOWTHER HRNS(B
PENGUIN CAFE STRINGS (B GAVIN WRIGHT STRINGS (B HELEN LIEBMANN STR (B

Q2A QUARTZ(FRANCE) Q2A

LAURENT TAIEB SYN (A (A) CAMEL IN THE CITY 1979 POLYDOR PD 1 6203
PATRICK LANGLADE B (A
DIDIER PLUS D (A

Q3 QUARTZ Q3

DEREK ARNOLD B (ABCDE (A) QUARTZ 1977 JET UK UAG 30081
MALCOLM COPE D (ABCDE (B) QUARTZ 1978 PYE UK NSPL28261
MICK HOPKINS G (ABCDE (C) DELETED 1979 JET UK JETLP 223
MIKE 'TAFFY' TAYLOR V (ABCDE (D) LIVE COUNT DRACULA 1980 REDDINGTON UK 001 LOGO 4007
GEOFF NICHOLS G K (A (E) STAND UP & FIGHT 1980 MCA UK MCF 3080

Q3A BILL QUATEMAN Q3A

BILL QUATEMAN G V (ALL (A) BILL QUATEMAN 1972 CBS US 31761
TOM RADTKE PERC (C (B) NIGHT AFTER NIGHT 1977 RCA UK PL12027 US AFLI 2027
CALEB QUAYE G V (BC (C) SHOT IN THE DARK 197 RCA US AFLI 2434
DENNY SEIWELL D (BC (D) JUST LIKE YOU 1979 RCA US 2879
JOHN MARSH B (BC
IRA KART PNO (B DAVE SHIELDS B (C TERRY REID V (B RICHARD SUPA V (B
LENNY CASTRO CONGA(BCD IAN UNDERWOOD K (B BRUCE JOHNSTON V (B CINDY BULLENS V (B
JIMMY HAAS V (B ERNIE WATTS HRNS (B NOLAN SMITH HRNS (B SHIRLEY MATTHEWS V (BD
GEORGE BOHANON HRNS (B OSCAR BRASHEAR HRNS (B VANETTA FIELDS V (BD MAXAYN LEWIS V (B
JACKIE KELSO HRNS (B JON JOYCE V (B STRING SECTION (B BILL PAYNE SYN (C
NEIL LARSEN K (D RICK SCLOSSER D (D JAMES NEWTON HOWARD SYN(D GARY HERBIG SAX(D
BUZZY FEITEN G (D DAVID HUNGATE B (D MICHAEL McDONALD V (D STEVE PORCARO SYN (D
JULIA TILLMAN V (D JOHN JARVIS K (D JEFF BAXTER G (D
CHUCK RAINEY B (C DAVID SANBORN SAX (C

Q3B QUARTER FLASH Q3B

RINDY ROSS V SAX (A (A) QUARTER FLASH 1982 GEFFEN UK 85438 US 2003
JACK CHARLES G V (A
MARV ROSS G (A RICH GOOCH B (A BRIAN WILLIS D (A RICK DIGIALLONARDO K(A
BRUCE SWEETMAN VLN (A TIM SCHMIT V (A JOHN BOYLAN V (A MARCY LEVY V(A
PAULINHO DACOSTA PERC (A

Q4 QUATERMASS Q4

JOHN GUSTAFSON B V (A (A) QUATERMASS 1970 HARVEST UK SHVL 775 US 314
PETE ROBINSON K (A (A) QUATERMASS 1975 HARVEST RI UK SHSM 2002
MICK UNDERWOOD D (

Q4A QUATRAIN Q4A

BUFF LINDSAY B V (A (A)QUATRAIN 1968 TETRAGRAMMATON US 5002
DON SENNEVILLE G V (A
ERIC PEASE G V (A
JIM LEKAS D V (A

Q5 MICHAEL QUATRO Q5

MICHAEL QUATRO K V (ALL (A) PAINTINGS 1972 EVOLUTION 3011
TED NUGENT G (AB (B) LOOK DEEP IN THE MIRROR 1973 EVOLUTION 3021
PATTI QUATRO (AB (C) IN COLLABORATION WITH THE GODS 1975 UA US LA 420 UK UAS 29785
TEDDY HALE G (CH (D) DANCERS ROMANCERS & DREAMERS 1976 PRODIGAL UK PDL 2001
RICK DERRINGER G (C (E) GETTING READY 197 PRODIGAL US P7 10016
DAVE KISWINEY B V (C (F) GOLDEN HITS 1976 RAK UK SKRA 6756
KIRK TRACHSEL D (BC (G) LIVE & KICKIN 1977 RAK JAP 5U009/10
HOWARD KAYLAN V (C (H) MICHAEL QUATRO BAND 1980 LOTUS SWED 4099
MARK VOLMAN V (C
TERRY MULLEN PERC (A
NANCY QUATRO V (A JOHN FINBY V (A STUART LOVE PROD (D TOM CLUPAK G (H
JOHN THORPE (H GREG KOBE (H GARY JACKSON (H ARTSKT (H
LYN ROUSKO (H JOHN BAUER (H DAVID GURKAMP (H JOHN MACINTYRE (H
BILL REYNA D (H BELINDA MCCLURE V (H TRACY RICHARDSON (H STEVE ARGY (H

Q6 SUZI QUATRO Q6

SUZI QUATRO B V (ALL (A) SUZI QUATRO 1973 RAK UK SRAK505 US BELL 1302
KEITH HODGE D ((B) QUATRO 1974 RAK UK SRAK509 US BELL 1313
LENNIE TUCKEY G (ALL (C) YOUR MAMA WON'T LIKE ME 1975 RAK UK SRAK514 US ARISTA 4035
MIKE DEACON K (DE (D) AGGRO PHOBIA 1977 RAK UK SRAK525
BILL HURD K ((E) IF YOU KNEW SUZI 1978 RAK UK SRAK532 US RSO 3044
ALASTAIR McKENZIE K (ABC (F) GREATEST HITS 1980 RAK UK EMTV24
DAVE NEAL D (ABCDE (G) ROCK HARD 1980 DREAMLAND US 15006 UK 2479 275
MICK EVE SAX (C
STEVE GREGORY SAX (C BUD BEADLE SAX (C RON CARTHY TPT(C

Q7 QUAZAR Q7

(A) QUAZAR 1978 ARISTA US 4187 UK ARTY 157

Q8 QUEEN Q8

FREDDIE MERCURY V PNO(ALL
BRIAN MAY G K V BANJO (ALL
JOHN DEACON G B (ALL
ROGER TAYLOR D V (ALL
DAVID BOWIE V (M

		UK	UK	US	US	JAP	JAP
(A) QUEEN	1973	EMI	EMC 3006	ELEKTRA	75064	ELEKTRA	P10118E
(B) QUEEN II	1974	EMI	EMC 767	ELEKTRA	75082	ELEKTRA	P10119E
(C) SHEER HEART ATTACK	1974	EMI	EMC 3061	ELEKTRA	7E1026	ELEKTRA	P10137E
(D) A NIGHT AT THE OPERA	1875	EMI	EMTC 103	ELEKTRA	7E1053	ELEKTRA	P10075E
(E) A DAY AT THE RACES	1976	EMI	EMTC 104	ELEKTRA	6E 101	ELEKTRA	P10300E
(F) NEWS OF THE WORLD	1977	EMI	EMA 784	ELEKTRA	7E 112	ELEKTRA	P10430E
(G) JAZZ	1978	EMI	EMA 788	ELEKTRA	6E 166	ELEKTRA	P10601E
(H) LIVE KILLERS	1979	EMI	EMSP 330	ELEKTRA	702		
(J) THE GAME	1980	EMI	EMA 795	ELEKTRA	513		
(K) FLASH GORDON (S TRCK)	1980	EMI	EMC 3351	ELEKTRA	518		
(L) GREATEST HITS	1981	EMI	TV 30	ELEKTRA	5E 564		
(M) HOT SPACE	1982	EMI	EMC 797	ELEKTRA	60128		
(EP) GOOD OLD FASHIONED	1977	EMI	EMI 2623				

Q9 QUESTION MARK & THE MYSTERIANS Q9

RUDY MARTINEZ V ((A) 96TEARS 1966 CAMEO US C2004
ROBERT MARTINEZ ((B) ACTION 1966 CAMEO US C2006
BOBBY BALDERAMMA G (
EDDIE SERRATI D (FRANK LUGO B (FRANK RODRIGUEZ ORG (LARRY BORJAS (

Q10 QUICK Q10

DANNY WILDE V (A (A) MONDO DECO 1977 MERCURY US SRM1 1114
DANNY BENAIR D (A
BILLY BIZEAU K V (A IAN AINSWORTH B (A STEVE HUFSTETER G (A

Q11 QUICKSAND Q11

JIMMY DAVIES (A (A) HOME IS WHERE I BELONG 1974 DAWN UK DNLS 3056
PHIL DAVIES (A
ROBERT COLLINS (A ANTHONY STONE (A

Q12 QUICKSILVER MESSENGER SERVICE Q12

GREG ELMORE D (ALL (A) QUICKSILVER MESSENGER SERVICE 1968 CAPITOL UK/US 2904
GARY DUNCAN V G B(ABDEFGHJ1 (B) HAPPY TRAILS 1969 CAPITOL UK/US 120 EURO 80543
BUD BRISBOIS TPT (G (B) HAPPY TRAILS 1981 GREENLIGHT UK 2012
JOHN CIPOLLINA G (ABCDEJ1 (C) SHADY GROVE 1969 CAPITOL UK/US 391
DAVID FREIBERG B V G(ABCDEJ1 (D) JUST FOR LOVE 1970 CAPITOL UK/US 498
JIM MURRAY V HCA(1 (D) JUST FOR LOVE 197 EMI GERM 038 80543
NICKY HOPKINS K (CDEJ (E) WHAT ABOUT ME 1971 CAPITOL UK/US 630
DINO VALENTI FLT G V (DEFGJ (E) WHAT ABOUT ME 19 CAPITOL US/RI 16092 GER 80722
JOSE REYES PERC (E (F) QUICKSILVER 1972 CAPITOL UK/US 819
MARK RYAN B (FG (G) COMIN' THRU' 1972 CAPITOL UK/US 11002 GER 81121
CHUCK STEAKS K (FG (H) ANTHOLOGY (COMP)(DBL) 1978 CAPITOL UK ESTSP 13 US 11165
PETE SEARS PNO (J (J) SOLID SILVER 1975 CAPITOL UK/US 11462
MICHAEL LEWIS K (J (K) BEST OF 197 CAPITOL EURO 054 80691
SKIP OLSON B (J (L) HIT ROAD 1976 EMI EURO 048 51874
MARIO CIPOLLINA B (J (1) 1965/67
KEN BALZALL TPT (EG
KATHI McDONALD V (J MARK NAFTALIN PNO (E MARTIN FIERRO WIND (E RON TAORMINA SAX (E
FRANK MORIN SAX (E PAT O'HARA TROM (EG DALTON SMITH TPT (G SONNY LEWIS SAX (G
CHARLES CALOPER TROM (G DON MENZE SAX (G

Q13 QUIET SUN Q13

PHIL MAZANERA G K (A (A) MAINSTREAM 1975 ISLAND UK HELP19
DAVE JARRETT K (A (A) MAINSTREAM 1977 POLYDOR RI UK 2343 093
BRIAN ENO K (A (A) MAINSTREAM 1975 ANTILLES US 7008
IAN MACCORMICK V (A
BILL MACCORMICK B V (A CHARLES HAYWARD D K V(A

Q14 QUIET WORLD Q14

(A) THE ROAD 1970 DAWN UK DNLS 3007

Q15 QUILL Q15

JU UNK KHOL (A (A) QUILL 1970 COTILLION US SD 9017
DA ANK KHOL (A
R WILLY NORTH (A PHIL STAN D'THERE (A RED ROCKET ROGERS (A

Q15A QUINAIMES BAND Q15A

DAVID PALMER V (A (A) QUINAIMES BAND 1971 ELEKTRA US EKS 74096
KENNY PINE G V (A
MIKE ROSA D (A JERRY BURNHAM B V (A DANNY MANSOLINO K V (A DANIEL BEN ZEBULON CONGA(A
DANNY KOOTCH G (A ALLAN JACOBS G (A RICHARD GREENE FDL (A BILL KEITH STEEL (A
RICHARD GRANDO SAX (A

Q16 QUINTESSENCE Q16

RAJA RAM FLT V PNO (ALL (A) IN BLISSFUL COMPANY 1969 ISLAND UK ILPS 9110
SHIVA SHANKAR JONES V K(ABCD (B) QUINTESSENCE 1970 ISLAND UK ILPS 9128
SAMBHU BABAJI B (ALL (C) DIVE DEEP 1970 ISLAND UK ILPS 9143
JAKE MILTON D (ALL (D) SELF 1971 RCA UK SF8273
MAHA DEV(DAVE CODLING)G(ABCD (E) INDWELLER 1972 RCA UK SF8317
ALAN MOSTERT G (ALL (F) BAND REFORMED

Q17 QUIVER Q17

TIM RENWICK G (AB (A) QUIVER 1971 WB US 1939 UK K46089
WILLIE WILSON D (AB (B) GONE IN THE MORNING 1972 WB US 2630 UK K46153
CAL BATCHELOR V G K(AB
BRUCE THOMAS B (AB DICK PARRY SAX (A

R1 R.A.F. R1

DAVID VALENTINE V K (AB (A) R.A.F. 1980 A&M US 4816 UK AMLH64816
DOUGLAS A BOGIE G (AB (B) THE HEAT'S ON 1981 A&M US 4865 UK AMLH68525
BILLY McGHEE B (AB
TOM ANNAN PERC (AB BOBBY HEATLIE SAX (A ANDY GROSSART B (A WENDY BOGIE V (A
PETER VETTESE KV (B STEVE DONELLY G (B

R1A REO SPEEDWAGON R1A

TERRY LUTTRELL V (ABD (A) R E O SPEEDWAGON 1971 EPIC US31089 UK 64813 RI 32096
KEVIN CRONIN G V (DEFHJLMN (B) R E O 2 1972 EPIC US 31745
ALAN GRATZER D (EHJLABDEFGMN (D) RIDING THE STORM 1973 EPIC US 32378
GARY RICHRATH G V (EHJLMN (E) LOST IN A DREAM 1974 EPIC US 34143 32948
NEAL DOUGHTY K (EHJLABDFGMN (F) THIS TIME WE MEAN IT 1975 EPIC US 33338
MIKE MURPHY V (E (G) R E O 1976 EPIC US 34143
SLY STONE G B K(E (H) YOU GET WHAT YOU PLAY FOR 1977 EPIC US 34494 UK 88265
LON PRICE SAX (J (J) YOU CAN TUNE A PIANO ..... 1978 EPIC US 35082 UK 82554
BRUCE HALL B (JLMN (K) NINE LIVES 1979 EPIC US 35988 UK 83647
TOM KELLY V (MN (L) DECADE OF ROCK'N'ROLL (DBL COMP) 1980 EPIC US 36444 UK 88488
STEVE FORMAN PERC (MN (M) HI INFIDELITY 1980 EPIC US 36844 UK 84700
RICHARD PAGE V (MN (N) GOOD TROUBLE 1982 CBS US 38100
N YOLLETTA V (MN

R2 R M O R2

(A) BEYOND THE LIMIT 19 BRAIN 0060 115
(B) GET THE BALL 19 BRAIN 0001 083
(C) GARUDA 19 BRAIN 0001 072

R3 RABBIT R3

JOHN'RABBIT' BUNDRICK V K G B(AB (A) BROKEN ARROWS 1973 ISLAND UK ISPS 9238
TETSU YAMAUCHI B (AB (B) DARK SALOON 1974 ISLAND UK ILPS 9289
SNUFFY WALDEN G (AB
RE BOP PERC (A RANDY D (A GEORGE LARNYOH HRNS (AB EDDY QUANSAH HRNS (AB
PETER VANDER PUIJE (AB CHRIS LAURENCE B (A GERRY MASTERS B (A JIM CAPALDI D (A
PETE CARR G (A RICHARD REEVES G (A DUNDEE HORNS (A ALAN GERRI G B (AB
SIMON KIRKE D (A JUNIOR KERR G (A CONRAD ISADORE D (A TERRY WILSON B (B
TONY BRAUNAGEL D (B DAVID KEELEY G (B JANNE SCHAFFER G (B OLA BRUNKERT D (B
MIKE B (B BRYSON GRAHAM D (B

R3A RABBITT R3A

TREVOR RABIN G V K SYN (AB (A) BOYS WILL BE BOYS 1976 CAPRICORN US 0175
RONNIE ROBOT B (AB (A) BOYS WILL BE BOYS 1976 JET UK JETLP 17
NEIL CLOUD D PERC (AB (B) CROAK & GRUNT IN THE NIGHT 1977 CAPRICORN US 0190
DUNCAN FAURE K V (

R4 EDDIE RABBITT R4

EDDIE RABBITT G V (ALL (A) EDDIE RABBITT 1975 ELEKTRA US CM3
MIKE LEECH B (A (B) ROCKY MOUNTAIN MUSIC 1976 ELEKTRA UK K52037 US 7E1065
JACK WILLIAMS B (BC (C) RABBITT 1977 ELEKTRA UK K52054 US 7E1105
JOE OSBORN B (B (D) VARIATIONS 1978 ELEKTRA US 6E 127
LARRY LONDIN D (BC (E) LOVELINES 1979 ELEKTRA UK K52135 US 6E 181
HARGUS ROBBINS PNO (BC (F) BEST OF 1979 ELEKTRA NL 52184 US 6E 235
NORBERT PUTNAM B (EG (G) HORIZONS 1981 ELEKTRA UK K52225 US 276
SHANE KEISTER PNO (B (H) STEP BY STEP 1981 MERCURY UK 6302 152
JAMES STROUD D PERC(G
DAVID BRIGGS PNO (B MICHAEL SPRIGGS G (B PETE WADE G (B JOHN CHRISTOPHER G (B
BOBBY THOMPSON G (BC STEVE GIBSON G (BC REGGIE YOUNG G (BC SONNY GARRISH STEEL(BC
HAL RUGG STEEL(B BUDDY SPICHER FDL (B FARRELL MORRIS PERC (BCG LEA JANE SINGERS (B
NASHVILLE EDITION (B KENNY MALONE D (C MIKE SUTTLE V (C DAVID HOOD B (E
DENNIS BELFIELD B (E ROGER HAWKINS D (E RANDY McCORMICK K (EG STEVE FORMAN PERC (E
MICHELE GRUSKA V (E DAVID HUNGATE B (EG BARRY BECKETT K (E LARRY BYROM G (EG
JIMMY JOHNSON G (E TIM MAY G (E ERNIE WATTS FLT (E SARAH TAYLOR V (E
SHERRY GROOMS V (EG DAVID MALLOY V (G DON BARRETT B (G ALAN FEINGOLD K (G
PAUL OVERSTREET V (G

R4A RABBLE R4A

(A) LEPS & OTHER NEW WORDS 19 M80 US 801

R5 TREVOR RABIN R5

TREVOR RABIN G B K V (ABC1 (A) TREVOR RABIN 1978 CHRYSALIS UK CHR 1196
KEVIN KRUGER D (AB (B) FACE TO FACE 1979 CHRYSALIS UK CHR 1221
SIMON PHILLIPS D (C (C) WOLF 1981 CHRYSALIS UK CHR 1295
JACK BRUCE B (C (1) 1979 TOUR
MO FOSTER B (C
SIMON FOX D (1 MANFRED MANN V (C CHRIS THOMPSON V (C STEVIE LANGE V (C
RABBIT K (C NOEL McCALLA V (C JOHN GALLEY K (1 LES GOODE B (1
DAVE MATTACKS D (B RENE ARNELL V (B

R6 RACING CARS R6

RAY ENNIS G V (ABC (A) DOWNTOWN TONIGHT 1976 CHRYSALIS UK CHR 1099
GRAHAM WILLIAMS G V (ABC (B) WEEKEND RENDEZVOUS 1977 CHRYSALIS UK CHR 1149
GARETH MORTIMER G V (ABC (C) BRING ON THE NIGHT 1978 CHRYSALIS UK CHR 1178
DAVE LAND B V (ABC
ROBERT WILDING D V (ABC ROY EDWARDS K (A ROGER HAND K (A BOWLES BROTHERS BAND V(A
TONY CARR PERC (A GERAINT WATKINS K (AB TIN HINKLEY K (C VEC FELDMAN PERC(C
JERRY JUMONVILLE SAX (C JIM MASON G (C SKIP EDWARDS K (C

R6A MAXIM RAD R6A

MAXIM RAD G V (A (A) TIMES AINT THAT BAD 1980 DISQUES MOTORS 77016
CLAUDE ANGEL G (A
DOMINIQUE PERRIER K (A SAUVEUR MALLIA B (A JEAN PAUL PRATT D V (A RICHARD PRATT SAX (A
YVONE JONES V (A

R7 RADIATOR R7

ALAN HULL G V (A (A) ISN'T IT STRANGE 1977 ROCKET UK ROLL 14
RAY LAIDLAW D (A
KENNY CRADDOCK K (A PETE KIRTLEY G (A COLIN GIBSON B (A TERRY POPPLE D (A

R7A RADIATOR(AUST) R7A

GEOFF TURNER B (A (A) FEEL THE HEAT 1980 WEA 60059
BRIAN NICHOL V (A
CHRIS TAG D (A FESS PARKER G (A BRENDAN CALLINAN K (A

R8 RADIATORS FROM SPACE R8

PETER HOLIDAI G V (AB (A) T V TUBE HEART 1977 CHISWICK UK WIK 4 GER 67051
PHILIP CHEVRON G V SYN(AB (B) GHOSTOWN 1979 CHISWICK UK CWK3003 GER 67064
MARK MEGARAY B V K(AB
JAMES CRASH D V (AB STEVE RAPID V (A TONY VISCONTI PROD SYN V(B RUAN O'LOCHLAINN SAX (B

R9 RADIO BIRDMAN R9

ROB YOUNGER V (A (A) RADIOS APPEAR 1978 SIRE UK 9103 332 US 6050
WARWICK GILBERT B (A
CHRIS MASNAK G (A DENIZ TEK G (A JOHNNY KANNIS V (A RON KEELEY D (A
PIP HOYLE K (A JOHN SAGEN PROD (A CHARLES FOWLER PROD (A

R10 RADIO STARS R10

ANDY ELLISON V SYN(AB (A) SONG FOR SWINGING LOVERS 1977 CHISWICK UK WIK 5 RI CWK 3005
PAUL JONES HCA (B (A) SONG FOR SWINGING LOVERS 1977 CHISWICK GER 67061
MARTIN GORDON B V K(AB (B) HOLIDAY ALBUM 1978 CHISWICK UK CWK3001 NL 550011
THE STARLETS V (B (C) TWO MINUTES MR SMITH 1982 MOONLIGHT UK 001
STEVE PERRY D (A (EP) STOP IT 19 CHISWICK SW 17
IAN MACLEOD G (AB
STEVE PRATTLE D (B DANNY GOODWIN V (B GRAHAM CHAPMAN V (B CHRIS GENT SAX (B
JANNIE CROMPTON D (B QUASIMODO BROS V (B RED ARMY BOY CHOIR V (B

R11 GERRY RAFFERTY R11

GERRY RAFFERTY V G K(ALL (A) CAN I HAVE MY MONEY BACK 1971 TRANSATLANTIC UK TRA 241
ROGER BROWN G V (AD1 (A) CAN I HAVE MY MONEY BACK 197 BLUE THUMB US BTS 58 +RI 78 6031
TOM PARKER K (A (A) ?THE ORIGINAL 1980 TRANSATLANTIC NL 44010
MORRIS PERT PERC (G (B) GERRY RAFFERTY REVISITED 1974 TRANSATLANTIC UK TRA 270
GARY TAYLOR B V (ADE1 (C) GERRY RAFFERTY 1978 LOGO UK MOGO4002 US VISA 7006
HENRY SPINETTI D (AD (D) CITY TO CITY 1978 UA US 840 UK UAS 30104
JOE EGAN V (A (E) NIGHT OWL 1979 UA US LA958 UK UAS 30238
ROD KING STEEL(A (F) SNAKES & LADDERS 1980 UA US 1039 UK UAS 32098
ALAN PARKER G (A (G) SLEEPWALKING 1982 LIBERTY UK LBS 30352
CHRISTOPHER NEIL D SYN(G (1) 1978 TOUR BAND
VIV McAULIFFE V (D
GLEN LEFLEUR PERC (D BARBARA DICKSON V (DE RAB NOAKES G V (AD HUGH MURPHY V (AD
JOHN VANDERRICK FDL (A ANDREW STEELE D (A ANDY FAIRWEATHER LOW G (D HUGH BURNS G (DEG
GRAHAM PRESKETT K FDL V(DE TOMMY EYRE K (DE1 RAPHAEL RAVENSCROFT SAX(DEF1 LIAM GENOCKEY D (EF1G
BRIAN COLE STEEL(D MICK MOODY G (D NIGEL JENKINS G (D WILLY RAY ACC (D
JERRY DONAHUE G (DF PAUL JONES HCA (D JOHN McBURNIE V (D RICHARD BRUNTON G(EF
RICHARD THOMPSON G MAND(E PETE WINGFIELD ORG (EF MO FOSTER B (EFG FRANK RICOTTI PERC(EFG
JOHN KIRKPATRICK ACC (E RICHARD HARVEY WIND SYN(EF BETSY COOKE V (EF LINDA THOMPSON V(E
IAN LYNN K (FG BRYN HAWORTH G (F BILLY LIVSEY K (F PETE ZORN B (F
MEL COLLINS SAX (FG ALAN CLARK K (G KEN CRADDOCK K (G

R12 JIM RAFFERTY R12

JIM RAFFERTY G V (AB (A) DONT TALK BACK 1978 DECCA UK SKL8291 US LONDON 722
HENRY SPINETTI D (A (B) SOLID LOGIC 1979 DECCA UK SKLR5314
PICK WITHERS D (A
DAVE MATTACKS D (A PETER VAN HOOKE D (A LYNTON NAIFF PNO (A BRIAN ODGERS B (A
GRAHAM PRESKETT FDL K(AB ROD CLEMENTS B (A HUGH BURNS G (AB LAWRENCE JUBER G (A
FRANK BOGIE G (AB B J COLE STEEL(A GARY TAYLOR B (A FRANCIS MONKMAN K (A
BARRY MORGAN D (A MIKE DAY D PERC (A TIM RENWICK G (A GERRY RAFFERTY G V SYN(AB
HERBIE FLOWERS B (A JOHN JAMES G (A MADELINE BELL V (A KAY GARNER V (A
PETE SWETTENHAM (A CHRIS MERCER SAX (A JOHN NIVEN CONC (A GEORGE McCRAE PIPES(A
FRANK SHERPAS V (A MIKE SHERPAS V (A BILL McGEACHY V (A FIONA McGEACHY V (A
RAB NOAKES V (AB PRESTON HEYMAN D (B BEN BARSON K (B DON AIREY K (A
JOHN GIBLIN B (B MEL COLLINS SAX (B MORRIS PERT PERC (B MARTIN LEVAN PERC(B
PEPI LEMER V (B RICKY HITCHCOCK G (B TERRY JONES HRNS (B

R12A RAGE R12A

KEITH MULHOLLAND G (A (A) NICE 'N' DIRTY 1982 CARRERE US CAL 138
JOHN MYLETT D (A
DAVE LLOYD V (A TONY STEERS G V (A MICK DEVONPORT B (A

R13 RAH BAND R13

PETER KING SAX (A (A) THE CRUNCH & BEYOND 1978 EBONY EBY1001
BARRY DE SOUZA D (A (B) THE RAH BAND 1981 DJM UK DJF 20573
TONY CARR PERC (A
RICHARD HEWSON K SYN B(A

R13A RAICES R13A

JUAN MELENDEZ WIND V(A (A) RAICES 1975 NEMPEROR US NE 434
CARLOS MELENOEZ G V (A
GONCHI SIFRE D HCA(A SAMMY FIGUEROA PERC V(A AMAURY LOPEZ K G SYN(A ROBERT PURAS B (A
RAFAEL CRUZ D FLT(A

R14 (RITCHIE BLACKMORES)RAINBOW R14

RITCHIE BLACKMORE G (ALL (A) RITCHIE BLACKMORE'S RAINBOW 1975 OYSTER OYA 2001
COZY POWELL D (BCDEHJ (A) RITCHIE BLACKMORE'S RAINBOW 1978 POLYDOR US 6049 UK RI 2490 141
GARY DRISCOLL D (AHJ (B) RAINBOW RISING 1976 OYSTER US 1601 UK 2490 137
CRAIG GRUBER B (AHJ (C) ON STAGE 1977 OYSTER OYA21801
MICKY LEE SOULE K (AHJ (C) ON STAGE 1977 POLYDOR 2490 016
TONY CAREY K (BCHJ (D) LONG LIVE ROCK'N'ROLL 1978 POLYDOR US 6143 UK 2490 142
JIM BAIN B (BCHJ (E) DOWN TO EARTH 1979 POLYDOR UK POLD5023
RONNIE DIO V (BCDHJ (F) DIFFICULT TO CURE 1981 POLYDOR UK 6316 UK POLD5036
MARK CLARKE B (HJ (G) JEALOUS LOVER (EP) 1981 POLYDOR US 1/502
GRAHAM BONNET V (EHJK (H) BEST OF 1981 POLYDOR UK PODV 2
DAVID STONE K (DHJ (J) BEST OF 1981 POLYDOR JAP 139/40
BOB DAISLEY B (DH (K) STRAIGHT BETWEEN THE EYES 1982 POLYDOR UK POLD5056
ROGER GLOVER B(EFGHJK (K) STRAIGHT BETWEEN THE EYES 1982 MERCURY US 4041
DON AIREY K(EFGHJK (AB) RISING/RAINBOW 1980 POLYDOR UK 2683 078
BOB RONDINELLI D(FGHK
JOE LYNN TURNER V (FGHJK

R15 CHRIS RAINBOW R15

CHRIS RAINBOW V (ABC (A) HOME OF THE BRAVE 1975 POLYDOR UK 2383 467
SIMON PHILLIPS D (BC (B) LOOKING OVER MY SHOULDER 1978 POLYDOR UK 2383 338
PETE ZORN B (BC (C) WHITE TRAILS 1979 EMI UK EMC 3305
MO FOSTER B (BC
DAVE LAWSON SYN (CB IAN BAIRNSON G (C LINDA TAYLOR V (C SHUG BARR G (C
MART JENNER G (BC MAX MIDDLETON K (C DEREK QUINN PERC (C DICK MORRISSEY SAX(C
MARLYN BAIRNSON V (C CHRISTY THOMPSON V (C MALCOLM CECIL HRN (A ROBERT MARGOULEFF PROD(A
MAXINE WILLARD V (A OREN WATERS V (A JULIA TILLMAN V (A OLLIE BROWN D (A
DON GRUSIN K (A SEYMOUR DUNCAN B (AB HENRY SPINETTI D (B DAVE MARKEE B (B
JOHN HAMILTON SYN (B PAT DONALDSON B (B CLIVE CHAMAN B (B PETE BARON D (B
DAVE WINTOUR B (B JAN COCHRANE D (B ANDY STEELE D (B CHRIS KARAN D (B
JOHN BARHAM STR(B

R15A RAINBOW CANYON R15A

(A) ROLLIN' 1975 CAPITOL US 11272

R15B RAINBOW PRESS R15B

DAVE TROUP B (A (A) SUNDAY FUNNIES 1969 MR G US 9004
MARC ELLIS G (A
LARRY MILTON K G(A CHARLIE OSBORNE K (A JOE GROFF PERC(A BILLY YERGIN PERC(A

R16 RAINBOW FFOLLY R16

(A) SALLIES FORTH 1967 PARLOPHONE PCS 7050

R16A RAINBOW RED OXIDISER R16A

ED CASSIDY D (? (A) RECORDED LIES 1980 LINE GER 5084
MARS BONFIRE G (A
LEON RUBINHOLD G (A GARY MARKER B (A NIKKI & THE CORVETTES V (A JANA LEE DARC (A
CHERYL JONES (A JIM EPPOLITO (A TIPPI CANOE (A SPECIAL OCCASIONS (A

R16B A RAINCOAT R16B

ANDY ARTHUR G V (A (A) DIGALONGAMACS 1975 EMI UK EMC 3090
ROD SYERS B (A
PHILLIPE CHAMBON G (A DAVE HUDSON K (A JOHN PUNTER D (A ROSS PEARLSTONE D (A
STEVE WILSON D (A

R17 RAINCOATS R17

JEREMIE FRANK G V (123 (A) RAINCOATS 1979 ROUGH TRADE UK ROUGH 3
RICHARD DUDANSKI D (3B (1) 1978 (2) 1978 (3) 1978 JULY (4) 1979
NICK TURNER D (12 (EP) FAIRYTALE IN THE SUPERMARKET 1979 ROUGH TRADE UK
KATE KORUS G (1 (B) ODYSHAPE 1981 ROUGH TRADE UK ROUGH13
ANA DA SILVA G V(1234AB
KADIR DURVESH SHEHNAI (B GINA BIRCH B V (1234AB PALMOLIVE D (4A VICKI ASPINALL VLN G B(4AB
LORA LOGIC SAX (A SHIRLEY O'LOCHLIN (B ROBERT WYATT D (B CHARLEY HAYWARD D (B
INGRID WEISS PERC(B DICK O'DELL (B GEORGIE BORN CELLO(B

R18 MARVIN RAINWATER R18

MARVIN RAINWATER V (ALL (A) GONNA FIND ME A BLUEBIRD 196 MGM US 4046
(B) SONGS 196 MGM US 3534
(C) WITH A HEART 19 MGM US 3721
(D) MARVIN RAINWATER 19 CROWN US 5307
(E) GETS COUNTRY FEVER 1972 PHILIPS UK 6414 110
(F) NEW COUNTRY SOUND 1974 GEM GES 1108
(G) ESPECIALLY FOR YOU 1976 WESTWOOD WRS 101
(H) ROCKIN' ROLLIN' RAINWATER 1982 BEAR FAMILY UK 15079

R18A RAINY DAZE R18A

BOB HECKENDORF ORG (A (A) THAT ACAPULCO GOLD 1967 UNI 73002
KIP GILBERT D (A
MAC FERRIS G (A SAM FULLER B (A TIM GILBERT G V (A

R19 RAM JAM R19

PETER CHARLES D (A (A) RAM JAM 1977 EPIC US 34885 UK 82215
BILL BARTLETT G V (A (B) PORTRAIT OF THE ARTIST 19 EPIC US 35287
HOWIE BLAUVELT B V (A
MYKE SCAVONE V PERC(A

R20 RAMASES R20

RAMASES (AB (A) SPACE HYMNS 1971 VERTIGO UK 6360 046
SEL (AB (A) SPACE HYMNS 1980 VERTIGO NL 9199 134
ERIC STEWART G SYN(A (B) GLASS TOP COFFIN 1975 VERTIGO UK 6360 115
LOL CREME G SYN(A
KEVIN GODLEY D FLT(A GRAHAM GOULDMAN G B (A MARTIN RAPHAEL SITAR(A PETE KINGSMAN B (B
ROGER HARRISON D (B BARRY KIRSCH K (B JO ROMERO G (B SUE GLOVER V (B
BOB BERTLES SAX (B COLIN THURSTON B (B SUNNY LESLIE V (B KAY GARNER V (B
EDDIE LESTER CHORALE V (B

R20A RAMSES R20A

WINFRIED LANGHORST K V ((A) LA LEYLA 1975 SKY 002 ANNUIT US 003
HANS KLINKHAMMER B ((B) ETERNITY RISE 1978 SKY 020
NORBERT LANGHORST G (
HERBERT NATHO V (REINHARD SCHROTER D (A

R21 RAMATAM R21

APRIL LAWTON G B V HCA (AB (A) RAMATAM 1972 ATLANTIC UK K40415 US SD7236
TOMMY SULLIVAN K G V WIND(AB (B) IN APRIL CAME THE DAWNING 1973 ATLANTIC US SD7261
MITCH MITCHELL D (A
MIKE PINERA G V (A RUSS SMITH B V (A JIMMY WALKER V PERC(B BRUCE MORGENHEIM VLN (B
SELDON POWELL HRNS (B GARNETT BROWN HRNS (B ARTHUR KAPLAN HRNS (B JOE NEWMAN HRNS(B
MARVIN STAMM HRNS (B RAYMOND BECKENSTEIN HRN(B JOE SHEPLEY HRNS (B DOMINICK GRAVINE HRNS(B
STRING SECTION (B

R22 BONIE RAITT R22

BONNIE RAITT G V (ALL (A) BONNIE RAITT 1971 WB US WS 1953 UK K56255
JUNIOR WELLS HCA (A (B) GIVE IT UP 1972 WB US BS 2643 UK K46189
A C REED SAX (A (C) TAKIN' MY TIME 1973 WB US BS 2729 UK K46261
WILLY MURPHY V K (A (C) TAKIN' MY TIME 1975 WB RI UK K56254
FREEBO B V (ABCDEFG (D) STREET LIGHTS 1974 WB US BS 2818 UK K56075
PETER BELL G (A (E) HOME PLATE 1975 WB US BS 2864 UK K56160
DOUGLAS SPURGEON TROM (A (F) SWEET FORGIVNESS 1977 WB US BS 2990 UK K56323
PETER ASHER V (G (G) THE GLOW 1979 WB US 3369 UK K56706
JOHNNY LEE SCHELL G V K(H (H) GREEN LIGHT 1982 WB UK K56980
RUSSELL HAGEN G (A
STEPHEN BRADLEY D (A VOYLE HARRIS TPT (A MAURICE JACOX WIND (A EUGENE HOFFMAN SAX (A
PAUL BARRERE G (C JOHN HALL G (BCDE BILL PAYNE K V (CEFG JIM KELTNER D (C
MILT HOLLAND PERC (C EARL PALMER D (C TAJ MAHAL B V HCA (C GEORGE BOHANON TROM(CE
OSCAR BRASHEAR HRNS (C ERNIE WATTS SAX (C SAM CLAYTON CONGA(CF VAN DYKE PARKS K V (C
ANTHONY TERRAN HRNS (C GLEN FERRIS HRNS (C JOEL PESKIN HRNS (C MARTIN KRYSTALL HRNS(C
ROBERT HARDAWAY HRNS (C BUD BRISBOIS HRNS (C LOWELL GEORGE G (C DON GROLNICK K (DG
STEPHEN GADD D (D DAVID SPINOZZA G (D ARTHUR JENKINS PERC (D LEON PENDARVIS K (D
BOB KREINAR B (D CHARLES BROWN G (D JEFF MIRANOV G (D DAVID LASLEY V (D
LOU COURTNEY V (D JERRY FRIEDMAN G (D CARL HALL V (D SHARON REDD V (D
TASHA THOMAS V (D JOHN TROPEA G (D RALPH McDONALD PERC (D PAUL GRIFFIN K (D
JOHN MAYER K (D RICHARD DAVIS B (D ROBERT MANN G (D TERRY REID V (E
EMMYLOU HARRIS V (E GREG PRESTOPINO V (E WILLOW VANDER HOEK V (E JEFF LABES K (F
MICHAEL McDONALD V (F CARLENA WILLIAMS V (F NATALIE VENABLE V (D GARY MALLABER D (E
WILL McFARLANE G. (EF FRED TACKETT K G (EF JAY WINDING K (E DENNIS WHITTED D (BEF
WILLIAM'SMITTY'SMITH K (EH JOE PORCARO PERC (E JEFF PORCARO PERC (E JOHN SEBASTIAN A'HARP(E
JERRY JUMONVILLE SAX (E JIM GORDON SAX (E DICK HYDE HRNS (E VANETTA FIELDS V (E
ROBBIE MONTGOMERY V (E MAXAYN LEWIS V (EFG JACKSON BROWNE V (EH ROSEMARY BUTLER V (EFG
JOHN D SOUTHER V (EFG DEBBIE GREENE V (E JOHN HERALD V (E TOM WAITS V (E
DAVID GRISMAN MAND (F LESTER CHAMBERS V (F TERRY EATON SAX (B TIM MOORE V (B
PAUL BUTTERFIELD HCA (BG GENE STASHUK CELLO (B MARTY GREBB SAX (B MERL SAUNDERS PNO (B

(CONTINUED)

R22 (CONTINUED)

BONIE RAITT R22

KAL DAVID G (B   AMOS GARRETT G (B   ERIC KAZ VIBES(B   WELLS KELLY CONGA(B
T J TINDALL G (B   MARK JORDAN K (B   JACKIE LOMAX V (B   JACK VIERTEL G (B
DAVE HOLLAND B (B   LOU TERRICIANO PNO (B   CHRIS PARKER D (B   JOHN PAYNE WIND(B
PETER ECKLUND CORNET (B   WADDY WACHTEL G V (G   DANNY KORTHCHMAR G V (G   BOB GLAUB B (G
RICK MAROTTA D (G   KEN EDWARDS V (G   TREVOR LAWRENCE SAX (G   LARRY WILLIAMS SAX (G
DAVID SANBORN SAX (G   STEVE MADAIO TPT (G   CRAIG FULLER V (G   JOHN GUERIN D (G
BOB MAGNUSSON B (G   RAY CHARA B (H   DAVID WOODFORD SAX (H   STEVE RAITT V (H
BOB FRABONI PROD (H   RICKY FATAAR V D (H   MELANIE ROSALES V (H   RICK VITO G (H
RICHARD MANUEL V (H   VINCE GILL V (H   IAN McLAGAN G K (H

R22A

RAMBLERS R22A

FRANK BECKING G (C
RUDIGER BRAUNE D V (C
RUDIGER ELZE G (C
JURGEN MEIER B V (C
CHRISTIAN SCHNEIDER V(C   NICK GENNIE SMITH K (C

(A) THE KIDS ARE BACK TO ROCK'N'ROLL 1978 CRYSTAL GER CRY 45103
(B) STREETHEAT 1979 ANTAGON GER ALP3231
(C) STRANGE LIFE 1980 CBS NL 8456=

R23

PHIL RAMBOW R23

PHILIP RAMBOW G V (ALL
MICK RONSON G (1
MAGGIE RONSON V (1
DAVE DRILL B (1
LAURIE JELLYMAN D (1   HUGH BURNS G (A   DAVE COCHRAN B (AB   JOHN MACKENZIE (A
BLAIR CUNNINGHAM D (AB   PETE WINGFIELD K V (A   JOE BREEN (A   JOHN KIRKPATRICK (A
TONY BEARD (A   DAVE DONEN D PERC(PETER GORIN B (TOM SPAHN K (
JANN NEILSON V (B   MATT BATT V (B   JO SUC V (B   MATT IRVING B (B
STEVE BOLTON G (B   JOHN WETTON B (B   BERNIE CLARKE K (B   MARK PINDER D (B
STEVE HOLLY D (B   LAWRENCE JUBER G (B   DAVID BENDETH G (B   DAVEY PAYNE SAX(B
JAMIE WEST G (B

(A) SHOOTING GALLERY 1979 EMI UK EMC3304 US CAPITOL 12074
(1) 1977 TOUR
(B) JUNGLE LAW 1981 PARLOPHONE UK PCS7216

R24

RAMONES R24

JOHNNY RAMONE G (ABCDEF
JOEY RAMONE V (ABCDEF
DEE DEE RAMONE B (ABCDEF
TOMMY RAMONE D (ABCE
MARC BELL RAMONE D (DF
BARRY GOLDBERG K (F
STEVE DOUGLAS SAX (F

(A) RAMONES 1976 SIRE UK 9103 253
(A) RAMONES 1976 SIRE US 7520 RI 1977 6020
(B) RAMONES LEAVE HOME 1976 SIRE UK 9103 254
(B) RAMONES LEAVE HOME 1976 SIRE US 7528 RI 1977 6031
(C) ROCKET TO RUSSIA 1977 SIRE US 6042 UK 9103 255
(D) ROAD TO RUIN 1978 SIRE UK/US 6063 philips 6370810
(E) ITS ALIVE (DBLE) 1979 SIRE SRK26074 GER 300 504
(F) END OF THE CENTURY 1980 SIRE SRK 6077
(G) PLEASANT DREAMS 1981 SIRE UK 357 GER 203 891

R24A

RAMP R24A

(A) COME INTO KNOWLEDGE 1977 BLUE THUMB US 6028

R24B

WILLIS ALAN RAMSEY R24B

WILLIS ALAN RAMSEY V B G (A
NICK DECARO ACC (A
ERNEST WATTS SAX (A   LEON RUSSELL K VIBES(A   TYLLER COLLIE D (A   LARRY STEDMAN PNO (A
ROBERT ABERG G (A   RED RHODES STEEL (A   CARL RADLE B (A   JIM KELTNER D (A
KENNY BULBEY D (A   RUSS KUNKEL D (A   TIM SELF FDL (A   CATHY PRUITT CELLO(A
LEE SKLAR B (A   DUSTY RHODES FDL (A

(A) WILLIS ALAN RAMSEY 1972 A&M UK AMLS 68158

R25

ELLIOTT RANDALL R25

ELLIOTT RANDALL G V (ABC
BOB PIAZZA B V (A
ALLEN HERMAN D PERC(AB
PAUL FLEISHER WIND (AB
GEORGE ANDREWS PNO (A   ANDY ALISON B (A   TERRY ADAMS K (A   RICHARD BOCK CELLO(A
POT PNO (AB   BOB BABITT B (C   RUBENS BASSINI PERC (C   GENE BIANCO HARP (C
KEN BISCHEL K (C   SUZANNE CIANI K (C   JERRY FRIEDMAN G (C   STEVE GADD D (C
PAUL GRIFFIN K (C   WILL LEE B (C   TONY LEVIN B (C   JESSE LEVY CELLO(C
RALPH MACDONALD PERC (C   JIMMY MAELEN PERC (C   MITCH MARGO V G K(C   LESLIE MILLER V (C
JEFF MIRANOV G (C   JEFF PORCARO D (C   ALLEN SCHWARZBERG D (C   JAY SIEGEL V (C
THE TOKENS V (C   GARY KING B (B

(A) RANDALLS ISLAND 1970 POLYDOR US 24/4044 UK 2489 004
(B) ROCK'N'ROLL CITY 1973 POLYDOR US 5026
(C) RANDALLS NEW YORK 1977 KIRSHNER US 34351

R26

BOOTS RANDOLPH R26

BOOTS RANDOLPH SAX (ALL
WITH
MAYBELLE CARTER (*
CHET ATKINS G (*
JOSH GRAVES G (*

YAKETY SAX (EP) 1960 RCA GER 9752
YAKETY SAX 1964 MONUMENT US 18002 US RI MC6600
HIP BOOTS 19 MONUMENT UK 5002 US RI MC6601
HIP BOOTS 1964 MONUMENT US 18015
MORE YAKETY SAX 1965 MONUMENT US 18037 RI MC6602
THE YANKIN' SAX MAN 1964 CAMDEN CAS825
SWEET TALK 1965 CAMDEN CAS865
THE FANTASTIC BOOTS RANDOLPH 1966 MONUMENT UK 5012 US RI MC6603
BOOTS WITH STRINGS 1967 MONUMENT US 18066 US RI MC6604
BOOTS WITH STRINGS 1967 MONUMENT UK 5003
SAX-SATIONAL 1967 MONUMENT US 18079 US RI MC6605
SAX SATIONAL 1967 MONUMENT UK 5022
VOICES & STRINGS 19 MONUMENT US 18082 US RI MC6606
SUNDAY SAX 1968 MONUMENT US 18092 US RI MC6607
THE SOUND OF BOOTS 1968 MONUMENT US 18099 US RI MC6608
WITH LOVE 1969 MONUMENT US 18111 US RI MC6609
BOOTS & STOCKING 19 MONUMENT US RI MC6610
YAKETY REVISTED 19 MONUMENT US 18128 US RI MC6611
YAKETY REVISITED 19 MONUMENT UK 5040
BOOTS WITH BRASS 1970 MONUMENT US 18147 US RI MC6613
HIT'S 1970 MONUMENT US 18144
HOMER LOUIS RANDOLPH 1971 MONUMENT US 30678 US RI MC6614
YAKETY SAX 1971 CANDEN US 9003
GREAT HITS OF TODAY 1972 MONUMENT US 31908 US RI MC6615
THE WORLD OF 1972 MONUMENT US 30963 UK 68203
SENTIMENTAL JOURNEY 1973 MONUMENT US 32292 US RI MC6616
(*)COUNTRY BOOTS 1974 MONUMENT US 32912 US RI MC6617
COOL BOOTS 1976 MONUMENT US 33803 US RI MC6618
GREATEST HITS 1976 MONUMENT UK 80548 US RI MG7602
PARTY BOOTS (DBL) 1976 MONUMENT US 34082 US RI MP8604
COOL BOOTS 1976 MONUMENT US 33803
SAX APPEAL 1978 MERCURY US MG7611

R26A ERIC RANDOM R26A

ERIC RANDOM V K B G SYN(A — (A) THAT'S WHAT I LIKE ABOUT ME — 1980 NEW HORMONE UK ORG 6
LYN WALTON K (A

R27 RANDOM ELEMENT R27

(A) RAMDOM ELEMENT — 1978 ROCKING HORSE US 5521

R28 RANDY PIE R28

DICKY TARRACH D (ABCDe — (A) SIGHTSEEING TOUR — 1974 POLYDOR 2371 491
FRANK DIEZ G (E — (A) RANDY PIE — 1974 ZEBRA GER 2949 015
MANFRED THIERS B V (ABCE — (B) HIGHWAY DRIVER — 1974 POLYDOR US 6515 2371 555
WERNER BECKER K V (ABC — (C) KITSCH — 1975 POLYDOR US 6518 2371 666
PETER FRENCH (DE — (D) ENGLAND ENGLAND — 1976 POLYDOR 2664 160
BERND SCHULZ (D — (E) FAST FORWARD — 1977 POLYDOR US 6113 2371 807
BERND WIPPICH G V (ABC
RAINER BAUMANN G (A — JEAN JACQUES KRAVETZ K (BC — JOCHEN PETERSEN V G SAX(BC — GEORGE MEYER (D
HERBERT HILDEBRAND G V (D — CARL GRAVES V (E — LARRY BROWN PERC(C

R28A RANK STRANGERS R28A

CHRIS DARROW G V MAND (A — (A) RANK STRANGERS — 1977 PACIFIC ARTS US PAC7 112
JOHN SELK V B (A
ROBB STRANDLUND G V (A — CINDY EDWARDS V (A — TEMPLETON PARCELY VLN (A =FENRUS EPP
POPE TERMAN B (A — MAX BUDA HCA (A

R28B KENNY RANKIN R28B

KENNY RANKIN V G K(A — (A) SILVER MORNING — 1974 LITTLE DAVID UK K59651
RICHARD BENNETT (A — (B) INSIDE — 1975 LITTLE DAVID UK K 59653
JOHN GUERIN D (AB
JOHN SEBASTIAN HCA (A — KING ERRISIN PERC (A — BOBBYE HALL PERC (AB — WILLIAM SMITH K (AB
JIM GORDON D (A — PETER MARSHALL B (AB — RON TUTT D (A — RICHARD GREEN (A
JIM NICHOLS (A — JIM GILSTRAP V (A — LANI GROVES V (A — ANGIE JOHNSON V (A
YVONNE RANKIN V (A — STEPHANIE SPRUELL V (A — DENIECE WILLIAMS V (AB — WILLIE WEEKS B (B
WADDY WACHTEL G (B — YVONNE RANKIN V (B — AL CASEY STEEL(B — GARY DURTON VIBES(B
WILTON FELDER D (D — JULIA TILLMAN V (B — ORAN WATERS V (B — MICHAEL STEWART G (B
ROY McCURDY D (B — BILL CHAMPLIN K (B — MICHAEL O'MARTIAN K (B — PAUL STALLWORTH B (B
MAYUTO PERC (B — MAX BENNETT B (B — JAMES GADSON D (B — MAXINE WILLARD V (B
LUTHER WATERS V (B — STEVE CROPPER G (B — JIM HORN SAX (B — SID SHARP STR (B

R28C RANKING DREAD R28C

(A) LOTS OF LOVING — 1980 STAND FIRM 01

R29 RANKING JOE R29

RANKING JOE V (ABC — (A) WEAKHEART FADE AWAY — 1978 GREENSLEEVES GREL2
SLY DUNBAR D (C — (B) DUB IT IN A DANCE — 1980 TROJAN TRLS 194
SANTA D (C — (C) SATURDAY NIGHT JAMDOWN STYLE — 1980 GREENSLEEVES GREL16
STYLE D (C — (D) ROUND THE WORLD — 1980 STUDENT UK 009
JIMMY BECKER HCA (C
FLABBA B (C — STEELIE K (C — ANSEL COLLINS K (C — GLADSTONE ANDERSON K (C
SOREL G (C — BINGY BUNNY G (C — BONGO HERMAN PERC (C — SKY JUICE PERC (C
STICKY PERC (C — HEADLEY BENNETT SAX (C — VAL BENNETT TROM (C — BOBBY ELLIS TPT (C

R30 RANKING TREVOR R30

RANKING TREVOR V (ABC — (A) IN FINE STYLE — 1978 FRONT LINE UK FL1015
SLY DUNBAR D (A — (B) 3 PIECE CHICKEN — 1978 CHA CHA CHALP 001
RANCHIE McLEAN G B (A
ROBBIE SHAKESPEARE B (A — ANSEL COLLINS K (A — TOUTER HARVEY K (A — DUGGIE G (A
STICKY PERC (A — BARNABAS PERC (A

R30A RAPED R30A

(A) PRETTY PAEDOPHILES(EP) — 19 PAROLE UK KNIT 1

R31 TOM RAPP R31

TOM RAPP G V (ABC — (A) TOM RAPP (FAMILIAR SONGS) — 1972 REPRISE US MS 2069
ART ELLIS FLT CONC V (BC — (B) STARDANCER — 1972 BLUE THUMB US BTS 44
BILL ROLLINS CELLO(BC — (C) SUNFOREST — 1973 BLUE THUMB US BTS 56
STEVE McCORD G (BC
JIM COLVARD G DOBR(BC — CHARLIE McCOY HCA V G K(BC — BUZZ CASON B (C — DIANE HARRIS V (C
CHUCK COCHRAN PNO (C — BUDDY SPICHER VLN (BC — DAVID BRIGGS PNO (BC — MIKE LEECH B (BC
FARRELL MORRIS PERC (C — BOBBY WOOD PERC (BC — REGGIE YOUNG PNO (BC — KARL HIMMEL D (C
BOBBY THOMPSON G BANJ(C — CHIP YOUNG G (C — BOB MOORE B (C — KENNY BUTTREY D (C
BOB DOROUGH PNO (C — BILL SALTER B (C — WARREN SMITH PERC (C — JIM ISBELL D PERC(B
WELDON MYRICK STEEL(B — FLORENCE WARNER V (B — HARRY ORLOVE G V MAND (B — STRING SECTION (B

R32 RARE EARTH R32

JERRY LA CROIX V (H — (I) DREAM ANSWERS — 1968 VERVE US 5056
GIL BRIDGES FLT V SAX (ABCDEFGHJI — (A) GET READY — 1970 TAMLA UK STML11156 RARE EARTH US 507
PETE RIVERA D V (ABCDEFI]SAME? — (B) ECOLOGY — 1971 TAMLA UK STML11180 RARE EARTH US 514
PETE HOORELBEKE D V (EFJ — (C) ONE WORLD — 1971 RARE EARTH UK 4001 US 520
ROD RICHARDS G V (ABI — (D) IN CONCERT — 1972 RARE EARTH UK 301 US 534
KENNY JAMES K (ABI — (E) WILLIE REMEMBERS — 1973 RARE EARTH UK 3008 US 543
RAY MONETTE G V (CDEFGH — (F) MA — 1973 RARE EARTH UK 3010 US 546
FRANK WESTBROOK K (H — (G) BACK TO EARTH — 1975 RARE EARTH US 6 548
MIKE URSO B V (EFJ — (H) MIDNIGHT LADY — 1976 RARE EARTH UK 3013 NL 97575 US 550
ED GUZMAN PERC (CEDGHJ — (J) RARE EARTH — 1977 PRODIGAL UK 2007 US 10019
MARK OLSON K V (CEFD — (K) BAND TOGETHER — 1978 PRODIGAL UK 2008 US 10025
REGGIE McBRIDE B (GH — (L) GRAND SLAM — 1978 PRODIGAL UK 2009
PAUL WARREN G V (GH — ( ) DISQUE DO'R — 1976 PATHE FR 064 95295
GABRIEL KATONA K V (G — ( ) MASTERS OF ROCK — 19 RARE EARTH GER 95926
BARRY FROST PERC (G
MAXINE WATERS V (H — RON FRANSEN K (J — JULIA TILLMAN V (H — JESSICA SMITH V (H
DANIEL FERGUSON G (J

R32A HERMAN RAREBELL R32A

HERMAN REREBELL D (A — (A) NIP IN THE BUD — 1981 HARVEST SHSP 4118
D H COOPER G (A
GEORGE PHILLIPS B V (A

R33 RAREBIRD R33

Member	Instr.	(Albums	Album	Release
STEVE GOULD	V SAX B G	(ALL	(A) RAREBIRD	1969 CHARISMA UK CAS1005 PHILIPS GER 6369900
FRED KELLY	D V	(CDEF	(B) AS YOUR MIND FLIES BY	1970 CHARISMA UK CAS1011 US ABC 716
JOHN WETTON	B	(D	(B) AS YOUR MIND FLIES BY	1970 PHILIPS GER 6369904
DAVE KAFFINETTI	K SYN	(ALL	(C) EPIC FOREST	1972 POLYDOR UK 2442 101 US5530
ANDY RAE	B	(E	(D) SOMEBODYS WATCHING	1973 POLYDOR UK 2383 211 US 6502
KEVIN LAMB	ORG V	(BEG	(E) BORN AGAIN	1974 POLYDOR UK 2383 274 US 6506
GRAHAM FIELD	ORG	(ABG	(F) RAREBIRD	1975 POLYGRAM UK 9299 008 US 4514
MARK ASHTON	D V	(ABG	(G) SYMPATHY	1976 CHARISMA UK CS 4
ANDY CURTIS	G	(CDH	(H) RARE BIRD(POLYDOR SPECIAL)	1977 POLYDOR UK 2384 078
AL MATTHEWS	PERC	(D		
NIC POTTER	B	(DH	SAMMY ABU PERC (D	PAUL HOLLAND PERC (DC PAUL KORDA V (D
PAUL KARAS	B	(CH	NICKY JAMES V (D	

R33A RAS MICHAEL & THE SONS OF NEGUS R33A

Member	Instr.	(Albums	Album	Release
RAS MICHAEL	V	(ALL	(A) NYAHBINGHI	1975 TROJAN TRS 113
ALVIN JACK HEWITT	V	(C	(B) TRIBUTE	1976 TROJAN TRS A£"
THOMAS MARTIN	V	((C	(C) MOVEMENTS	1978
ISON FUNDE		(C	(D) FREEDOM SUITE	1979 DYNAMIC 3004
SYDNEY WOLFE	D	(C		
DENNIS FERRON	ORG	(C	EARL'CHINNA' SMITH G (C	MICHAEL MASKIL G B (C RICA BACA V (C
S CHUNG CLANNER	V	(C	PUMA JONES V (C	

R34 THE YOUNG RASCALS R34

Member	Instr.	(Albums	Album	Release
FELIX CAVALIERE	K V	(ALL	(A) THE YOUNG RASCALS	1966 ATLANTIC UK 587974 US SD8123
DINO DANELLI	D	(ALL	(B) COLLECTIONS	1966 ATLANTIC US SD8134
GENE CORNISH	G	(ABCDEFGH	(C) GROOVIN'	1967 ATLANTIC US SD8148
EDDIE BRIGATI	G V	(ABCDEFH	(D) ONCE UPON A DREAM	1968 ATLANTIC UK 588 098 US SD8169
ROBERT POPWELL	B	(JK	(E) GREATEST HITS (TIMEPEACE)	1968 ATLANTIC UK 588 120 US SD8190
ANN SUTTON	V	(JK	(F) FREEDOM SUITE	1969 ATLANTIC UK 588 183 US SD8901
BUZZY FEITEN	G	(JK	(G) SEARCH & NEARNESS	1971 ATLANTIC UK 2400113 US SD8246
HAROLD COWART	B	(G	(H) SEE	1969 ATLANTIC UK 588 183 US SD8246
CHUCK RAINEY	B	(GHF	(J) PEACEFUL WORLD	1971 CBS UK 66292 US 30462
JOE NEWMAN	TPT	(GJ	(K) ISLAND OF REAL	1972 CBS UK 64756 US 31103
JOE FARRELL	SAX	(GJ	(L) STAR COLLECTION	1973 MIDI UK 30049 GERM 20022
SELDON POWELL	SAX	(G		
MOLLY HOLT	V	(J	HUBERT LAWS FLT (HJ	RON CARTER B (HJ DANNY LABBATE SAX (H
JOE BUSHKIN	PNO	(H	KING CURTIS SAX (F	DAVID SHEWMAN SAX (F RICHARD DAVIS B (F
GERALD GEMOTTA	B	(FJ	LINK CHAMBERLAIN G (J	RALPH MACDONALD PERC (J CYNTHIA WEBB V (J
GARNETT BROWN	HRNS	(J	ERNIE ROYAL TPT (J	ERNIE WILKING SAX (J WILLIAM SALTER B (J
BRUCE BUONO	V	(J	BUDDY BUONO V (J	PEPPER ADAMS SAX (J JOM SMITH SAX(J
ALICE COLTRANE	HARP	(J		

R35 RASPBERRIES R35

Member	Instr.	(Albums	Album	Release
WALLY BRYSON	G	(AB	(A) RASPBERRIES	1972 CAPITOL UK/US 11036
ERIC CARMEN	G V K	(ABED	(B) FRESH	1973 CAPITOL UK/US 11123
DAVE SMALLEY	G B	(AB	(C) SIDE THREE	1974 CAPITOL UK/US 11220
JIM BONFANTI	D	(AB	(D) STARTING OVER	1974 CAPITOL UK/US 11329
SCOTT McCARL	B	(D	(E) BEST OF	1975 CAPITOL UK/US 11524
MIKE McBRIDE	D	(D	(E) BEST OF	1976 CAPITOL CAPS 1026
JEFF HUTTON	K	(D		
JIMMY LENNER	PROD	(ABD		

R35A RASPUTIN'S STASH R35A

Album	Release
(A) RASPUTIN'S STASH	19 COTILLION US 9046
(B) DEVIL MADE ME DO IT	19 GEMIGO US 5500

R35B (ROYAL) RASSES (ROYALS) R35B

Member	Instr.	(Albums	Album	Release
LINCOLN THOMPSON	G V	(BC	(A) HUMANITY	1979 BALLISTIC UAG 30227
KEITH PETERKIN	V	(B	(B) EXPERIENCE	1979 BALLISTIC UAG 30259
CLINTON HALL	V	(B	(C) NATURAL WILD	1980 BALLISTIC UAG 30309
LEROY WALLACE	D	(BD	(D) HARDER NA RASS	1980 BALLISTIC LBR 1031
MIKEYBOOTH	D	(BCD		
BOBBY ELLIS	TPT	(BD	STICKY PERC (BD	VAL DOUGLAS B (BD WIRE LINDO K (BD
PABLO BLACK	K	(BD	GEOFFREY CHUNG K (BD	CECIL LLOYD K (BD BUBBLER HRNS(BD
BROTHER JOMO	PERC	(BD	JOE JACKSON K (C	GEORGE MILLER G (BD DIGGLES G (BD
ERNEST RANGLIN	G	(BD	TOMMY McCOOK HRNS (BD	HEADLEY BENNETT SAX (BD BAGGA B (BD
GRAHAM MABY	B	(C	RANCHIE McLEAN B (C	GARY SANFORD G (C WILLIE LINDO G (BC
DOUGIE	G	(C	DAVE HOUGHTON D (C	ANSEL COLLINS K (C TONY GAD SYN (C
GEORGE OBAN	PERC	(C	CRIS ALNE DUB SOUNDS(C	MO PERC(C

R36 RASTUS R36

Member	Instr.	(Albums	Album	Release
DANIEL MAGALEN	V SAX	(A	(A) LIVE RASTUS	1971 GRT US 30004
MARC ROMAN	V TROM	(A	(B) STEAMIN'	1972 NEIGHBORHOOD NH3002
DAVE SMELKO	D V	(A		
TONY CORRAO	G	(A	ARTHUR APPLETON TROM (A	MIKE GERACI SAX V (A VIC WALKUSKI SAX(A
DON NAGY	B TPT	(A	GEORGE SOPUCH G (A	

R36A RATIONALS R36A

Member	Instr.	(Albums	Album	Release
SCOTT MORGAN	V	(A	(A) RATIONALS	1969 CREWE US 1334
STEVE CORREL	G	(A		
TERRY TRABANDT	B	(A	BILL FIGG D (A	

R36B RATCHELL R36B

Member	Instr.	(Albums	Album	Release
LARRY BYROM		(A	(A) RATCHELL	197 MCA US 5330
CHRIS COUCHOIS		(A		
PAT COUCHOIS		(A	HOWARD MESSER (A	

R37 RATS R37

Album	Release
(A) RATS FIRST	1974 GOODEAR EARLH5003

R38 RATTLES R38

ACHIM REICHEL G V (1 — (A) TWIST AT THE STAR CLUB — 1964 PHILIPS BL 7614
HERBERT HILDEBRAND K B(1 — (B) THE RATTLES — 1965 FONTANA
DICKY TARRACH D (1 — (C) HURRA! DIE RATTLE KOMMEN — 1966 FONTANA
RUGY RUGINSTEIN G (1 — (D) ATTENTION — 19 FONTANA 6434 162
AL BROCK D (3H — ( ) REMEMBER FINALE LIGURE — 1967 STARCLUB GER 158 031
DIETER SADLOWSKI D (— (E) GREATEST HITS — 1969 FONTANA 701707 US MERCURY 61127
HAJO KREUTZFELD G (— (F) THE RATTLES — 1971 DECCA UK SKL 5008
ZAPPO LUNGREN B (23GH — (G) TONIGHT STARRING EDNA — 1972 PHILIPS 6305 176
FRANK MILLER G (23GH — (H) GIN MILL — 1974 RCA PPLI 4016
LUDE LAFAYETTE K (3GH — (J) THE WITCH — 19 PHILIPS GER 6305 072
HERBERT BORNHOLD D (2G — ( ) THE BEST OF — 19 LUXOR GOLD GER 41034
GEORGE MAYER G V (3 — (EP) TEENBEAT — 19 ARIOLA S41174
EDNA BEJARANO V (2G — (EP) TEENBEAT 2 — 19 DECCA DFE 8568
LINDA FIELDS V (3H — (EP) RATTLES — 19 PHILIPS 423 560
(EP) RATTLES — 19 FONTANA 466 030
(1) 1961 (2) 1970 (3) 1975

R38A RATTLESNAKE R38A

(A) RATTLE SNAKE — 1873 KAMA SUTRA US 2047

R39 GENYA RAVAN R39

GENYA RAVAN V HCA PERC(ALL — (A) GENYA RAVAN WITH BABY — 1972 CBS UK 64872 US 31001
BOBBY KEYS SAX (C — (B) THEY LOVE ME /THEY LOVE ME NOT — 1973 DUNHILL US 50143
KENNETH RICE D (C — (C) GOLDIE ZELKOWITZ — 1974 JANUS US 3060
FRED BECKMAIER B (C — (D) URBAN DESIRE — 1978 20th CENTURY BTH8007 T 562
KEN MARCO G (C — (E) AND I MEAN IT — 1979 20th CENTURY T 595
DANNY KORTCHMAR G (C
STEVE BECKMAIER G (C — LARRY NASH K (C — GABRIEL MAKLER K (C — TREVOR LAWRENCE K HRNS(C
WILLIAM SMITH K (C — MAILTO CORREA PERC (C — STEVE MADAIO HRNS (C — ABIGALE HANESS V (C
GWENDOLYN EDWARDS V (C — C C WILLIAMSON V (C — CHARLIE GIORDANO K (DE — CONRAD TAYLOR G (DE
RITCHIE FLIEGLER G MAND(D — DON NOSSOV B (D — BOBBY CHEN D (DE — STUART DAYE G (D
JOEY RIBAUDO V (D — PAUL OPALACH B (D — JOHN PAUL FETTA B (D — DAVID LASLEY V (D
IVAN KRAL V (D — LOU REED V (D — MITCH STYLES G (A — NICK OLIVA K (A
JOHN PLATANIA G (A — PETER HODGSON B (A — BRIAN KEENAN D (A — BERNARD WILLIAMS CONGA(A
MIKE LOMBARDI B (E — IAN HUNTER V (E — MICK RONSON G (E

R40 RAVEN R40

JOHN CIPOLLINA G (AB — (A) 1976
ANDY KIRBY D V (A — (B) JOHN CIPOLLINAS RAVEN — 198 LINE GER 5041
DAVID WEBER D (A
SKIP OLSEN B (A — NICKY HOPKINS K (A — GREG DOUGLAS G (A — HUTCH HUTCHINSON K (A
DAVE WALKER (

R40A RAVEN R40A

JOHN WEITZ G (AB — (A) LIVE AT THE INFERNO — 19 DISCOVERY US 36133
TONY GALLA V HCA(AB — (B) RAVEN — 196 CBS US 9903
JAMES CALIRE K V (AB
GARY MALLABER D (AB — THOMAS CALANDRA B (AB

R40B RAPHAEL RAVENSCROFT R40B

RAPHAEL RAVENSCROFT SAX FLT(A — (A) HER FATHER DIDN'T LIKE ME ANYWAY — 1979 PORTRAIT US 35683
GARY TAYLOR B (A
KUMA HARADA B (A — PETE ZORN B FLT(A — STEVE YORK B (A — LIAM GENOCKEY D (A
PRESTON HEYMAN D (A — STRETCH D (A — GEOFF BRITTON D (A — TOMMY EYRE K (A
JEFF BANNISTER K (A — BETSY COOKE K V (A — PETE SOLLEY K (A — NIGEL JENKINS G (A
JULIAN LITTMAN G (A — RICHARD BRUNTON G (A — STEVE WALLER G (A — BRIAN HOLLOWAY G (A
FRANK RICOTTI PERC (A — DAVID ULM PERC (A — CHARLES BOROMEO V (A — PAUL DA VINCI V (A
MAGGIE RYDER V (A — VIVIAN V (A — DENNIS O'BRIEN V (A — ALBERT WING WIND (A
BIL SKEAT WIND (A — VIC ASH SAX (A — MANNY WINTER SAX (A — KEITH BIRD SAX(A
JOHN WILBRAHAM TPT (A — DEREK WATKINS TPT (A — EDDIE BLAIR TPT (A — KENNY BAKER TPT(A
DEREK HEALEY TPT (A — JOHN HUCKRIDGE TPT (A — DON LUSHER TROM (A — WALLY SMITH TROM(A
BOBBY LAMB TROM (A — KEN GOLDIE TROM (A — JIM BROWN HRNS (A — JOHN PIGNEGNY HRNS(A

R40C RAVENNA & THE MAGNETICS R40C

(A) ROCKABILLY FOOL — 1981 RONDELET UK ABOUT1001

R41 RAVERS R41

(A) PUNK ROCK CHRISTMAS (EP) — 1978 RHINO RNEP 503

R41A RAW HOLLY R41A

IAN CAMPBELL V (A — (A) RAW HOLLY — 1971 CORAL 757515 MCA GER MAPS4067
ZED JENKINS G SIT(A

R42 RAW MATERIAL R42

DAVE GREEN (A — (A) TIME IS — 1971 NEON NE 8
COLIN CATT (A — (B) RAW MATERIAL ALBUM — 1970 EVOLUTION UK 21006
PAUL YOUNG (A
PHIL GUNN CLIFFORD (A — MIKE FLETCHER (A

R42A DAVE'SNAKER' RAY R42A

DAVE RAY (A — (A) KID MAN — 1977 MONUMENT US 52780

R43 JAMES RAY R43

JAMES RAY V (A — (A) JAMES RAY — 1961 CAPRICE US 1002

R44 RAY OWEN'S MOON R44

RAY OWEN G V PNO(A — (A) RAY OWEN'S MOON — 1971 POLYDOR UK 2425 061
SID GARDNER G B K(A
DICK STUBBS G (A — LES NICOL G (A — IAN McLEAN D (A

R44A RAYBEATS R44A

(A) GUITAR BEAT — 1981 D F O T M X7

R45 RAYDIO R45

RAY PARKER G (ABC (A) RAYDIO 1978 ARISTA US 4163 UK SPART 1041
VINCENT BONHAM (A (B) ROCK ON 1979 ARISTA US 4212 UK SPART 1087
JERRY KNIGHT B (A (C) TWO PLACES AT THE SAME TIME 1980 ARISTA US 9515 UK SPART 1121
NORMA JEAN BELL SAX (B (D) JUST LOVE 1981 ARISTA US 9543 UK SPART 1152
ARNELL CARMICHAEL (ABC
CHARLES FEARING G (ABC LARRY TOLBERT (BC DARREN CARMICHAEL (BC OLLIE BROWN D V (BC
SYLVESTER RIVERS PNO (BC JACK ASHFORD PERC (BC KEN PETERSON V TPT(BC HORATIO GORDON SAX (BC
VALORIE JONES V (B FRANCIS PEARMAN V (B CHERYL BROWN V (B HERBIE HANCOCK K (C
GARY COLEMAN VIBES(C DEBORAH THOMAS V (C

R46 CHRIS REA R46

CHRIS REA V G K SYN (ALL (A) WHATEVER HAPPENED TO BENNY SANTINI 1978 MAGNET UK MAG5021 US UALA 879
ROD ARGENT K (A (B) DELTICS 1979 MAGNET UK MAGL5028 US UA 959
PETE WINGFIELD K (ACD (C) TENNIS 1980 MAGNET UK MAGL5032 US CBS 36435
DAVE MATTACKS D (AD (D) CHRIS REA 1982 US CBS 37664
PAT DONALDSON B (A
PAUL KEOGH G (A STEVE GREGORY SAX (A GUS DUDGEON PROD PERC(A DAVE MARKEE B (A
FRANK RICOTTI PERC (A PHIL CURTIS (A NORMAN NOSEBAIT D (AC EDDIE GUY G (A
GEORGE WOODHEAD PERC (A STUART EPPS V (C WATSONI V (C STUART ELLIOTT D (D
DAVE BURTON G (C MICK HUTCHINSON B (C GRAHAN WATSON K (C MARK REA PERC(C
GEOFF DRISCOLL SAX (C RAPHAEL RAVENSCROFT SAX(C LEE THORNBERG TPT (C RAOUL GONZALES TROM(C
IRENE CHANTER V (A DOREEN CHANTER V (A GEORGE CHANDLER V (C JIMMY CHAMBERS V (C
BRUCE LYNCH B (C JIM MULLEN G (D SIMON NICOL G (D CAROL KENYON V (D
LINDA TAYLOR V (D KATY KISSOON V (D DAVID PACK V (D JOE PUERTA V (D
BURLEIGH DRUMMOND V (D STEVE LAWRENCE B (D RON ASPERY SAX (D DAVE PATON B (D
ANDREW POWELL B (D ALLAN MURPHY G (D RAY COOPER PERC (D MAX MIDDLETON K (D
MIKE MORAN K (D DAVE SKINNER PNO (D SKALA KANGA HARP (D DAVID SNELL HARP(D

R47 DAVID REA R47

DAVID REA G V BANJO (AB (A) MAVERICK CHILD 19
(B) BY THE GRACE OF GOD 19
(C) SLEWFOOT 1975 CBS US 32485

R48 JOHN DAWSON READ R48

JOHN DAWSON READ G V (AB (A) A FRIEND OF MINE 1975 CHRYSALIS UK CHR 1075
ALAN HODGE G (A (B) READ ON 1976 CHRYSALIS UK CHR 1102
B J COLE STEEL(A
LES HURDLE B (A TERRY COX D (A ALBERT HALL HRNS (A RAY SWINFIELD FLT (A
DEAN FORD V (A GUY FLETCHER V (A

R50 REAL KIDS R50

JOHN FELICE G V (A (A) THE REAL KIDS 1977 BRONZE BRON 509 RED STAR RS2
ALAN PAULINO B V (A (A) THE REAL KIDS 1977 RED STAR GER 26206
HOWARD FERGUSON D (A
BILL BORGEOLLI G (A MONO MANN PNO (A

R50A ROGER C REALE & RUE MORGE R50A

ROGER C REALE B V (AB (A) RADIO ACTIVE 1978 BIG SOUND US 028
MICHAEL CAVADINI PNO (B (B) ROGER C REALE & RUE MORGUE 1979 LONDON/BIG SOUND SHY 8528
BILLY MICHAELS D V (B
G E SMITH G (B

R51 REBEL R51

TONY RIVERS V STUART ELLIOTT D GEORGE FORD B DUNCAN MACKAY K

R51A RECORD PLAYERS R51A

(A) GIVE AN INCH (EP) 1979 WRECKORD UK AERO1004

R51B RECKLESS R51B

STEVE MADDEN G V (A (A) RECKLESS 1981 EMI UK AMC 3362
JAN MELANSON V (A
GENE STOUT B V (A GIL ROBERTS D (A

R51C EUGENE RECORD R51C

EUGENE RECORD (ALL (A) THE EUGENE RECORD 1977 WB US 3018
(B) TRYING TO GET YOU 1978 WB US 3097
(C) WELCOME 1979 WB UK K56639 US 3284

R51D RECREATION R51D

FRANCIS LONNEUX D (AB (A) MUSIC OR NOT MUSIC 19 BARCLAY FR 920 356
J PAUL VANDER BOSSCHE B(AB (B) RECREATION 19 BELLAPHON GER 19006
JEAN JACQUES ORG (AB

R52 RECORDS R52

JOHN WICKS G V (ABC (A) SHADES IN BED 1979 VIRGIN US 13130 UK V2122
HUW GOWER G V (A (B) CRASHES 1980 VIRGIN US 13140 UK V2155
JUDE COLE G B (B (C) MUSIC ON BOTH SIDES 1982 VIRGIN GER 204464 UK V2206
PHIL BROWN B V (ABC (EP) HIGH HEELS(FREE WITH A) 1979 VIRGIN
WILL BIRCH D (ABC
IAN GIBBONS K (AB ROBERT J LANGE PROD (A BARRY MARTIN G (B CLEM CLEMPSON G (B
DAVE WHELAN G (C CHRIS STEIN (B CHRIS GENT V SAX(B

R52A RED CLAY RAMBLERS R52A

BILL HICKS FDL V(CD (A) THE RED CLAY RAMBLERS 1975 FOLKWAYS US 31039
TOMMY THOMPSON G V (CD (B) STOLEN LOVE 1976 FLYING FISH US 009
MIKE CRAVER D K G(CD (C) TWISTED LAUREL 1977 FLYING FISH US 030 SONET UK 731
JIM WATSON MAND G V B(CD (D) MERCHANTS LUNCH 1978 FLYING FISH US SONET UK 745
JACK HERRICK B V HCA TPT(CD (E) CHUCKIN' THE FRIZZ 1979 FLYING FISH US 089
AL McCANLESS FDL (C

R53 RED CRAYOLA R53

MAYO THOMPSON (ABC (A) PARABLE OF ARABLE LAND 1967 INTERNATIONAL ARTISTS US IALP 2
STEVE CUNNINGHAM (AB (A) PARABLE OF ARABLE LAND 1978 RADAR UK RAD12
TOMMY SMITH D (AB (B) GOD BLESS THE RED CRAYOLA 1968 INTERNATIONAL ARTISTS US IALP 7
RICK BARTHELME (A (B) GOD BLESS THE RED CRAYOLA 1978 RADAR UK RAD16
HOLLY PRITCHARD V (B (C) SOLDIER TALK 1979 RADAR UK RAD18
JESSE CHAMBERLAIN (C (D) KANGAROO 1981 ROUGH TRADE UK ROUGH 19
DICK CUTHELL (C
SCOTT KRAUSS (C CHRISTINE THOMPSON (C TOM HERMAN (C LORA LOGIC SAX (C
DAVID THOMAS (C TONY MAIMONE (C ALLEN RAVENSTINE (C LELAN ROGERS PROD(A

R53A
RED EYE
R53A

DAVE HODGKINS G V (AB — (A) REDEYE — 1971 PENTAGRAM US PE 10003
DOUGLAS 'RED' MARK G V (AB — (B) ONE MANS POISON — 19 PENTAGRAM US PE 10006
BOB BEREMAN D (AB
BILL KIRKHAM B V (AB

R53B
RED HELICOPTER
R53B

(EP) BRACKNELL — 19 PAY FOR

R53C
RED NOISE
R53C

PATRICK VIAN G V (A — (A) SARCELLES LOCHERES — 1970 FUTURA FR RED01
JEAN CLAUDE CENCU WIND V(A
DANIEL GEOFFROY B V (A PHILIP BARRY D G (A JOHN LIVENGOOD ORG (A AUSTIN BLUE PERC (A

R53D
RED RIDER
R53D

TOM COCHRANE G V (AB — (A) DONT FIGHT IT — 1980 CAPITOL 12028
PETER BOYNTON K (AB — (B) AS FAR AS SIAN — 1981 CAPITOL 12145
KIM GREEN G K (AB
ROB BAKER D (AB KEN GREER STEEL K G V(AB

R53E
RED WILDER BLUE
R53E

MIKE BALLEW G (A — (A) RED WILDER BLUE — 1972 PENTAGRAM US PE 10007
DANNY WILDER B K (A
LUCKY FLOYD D (A MACK TUBB G (A

R54
REDBONE
R54

TONY BELLAMY G V (ABCDEF — (A) REDBONE — 1970 CBS US 501 UK 64069
PAT VEGAS B (ABCDEF — (B) POTLATCH — 1971 EPIC US 30109 UK 64198
LOLLY VEGAS G V (ABCDEF — (C) WITCH QUEEN OF NEW ORLEANS — 1971 EPIC UK 64709
PETER DEPOE D (ABCD — (C) MESSAGE FROM A DRUM — 1971 EPIC US 30815
DON BRANKER (C — (D) ALREADY HERE — 1973 EPIC US 31598 UK 65072
WARREN WINSTON (C — (E) WOVOKA — 1973 EPIC US 32462 UK 65500
EDDIE CAICEDO (C — (F) BEADED DREAMS — 1974 EPIC US 33053 UK 80429
JOHN D'ANDREA (C — (G) COME & GET YOUR REDBONE — 1975 EPIC US 33456 UK 22003
RASMUSSEN TOWER (C — (H) CYCLES — 1978 RCA AFLI 2352
CLARENCE McDONALD (C — (J) BEST OF — 19 EPIC UK 65678
BUTCH PILLERA D V (EF
RED RHODES STEEL(D TERRY FURLONG G (D GORDON DE WITTE PNO (D ELIJAH HORN SECTION (D
CHIPPER LAVERONE PERC (D RONNIE BARRON PERC (D DAVID OLIVER V (D MICHAEL FREDA V (D
BONNIE BRAMLETT V (F MERRY CLAYTON V (F CLYDIE KING V (F ED GREENE (C

R55
NOEL REDDING
R55

NOEL REDDING G V B(AB — (A) CLONAKILTY COWBOYS — 1975 RCA UK RS 1030 APLI 1237
ERIC BELL G V (AB — (B) BLOWIN' — 1976 RCA UK RS 1084 APLI 1863
LES SAMSON D (AB
DAVE CLARKE K V (AB DON MICHAEL YOUNG K (B STANLEY SCHNIER B (B ANDY KEELY V (B

R56
OTIS REDDING
R56

OTIS REDDING V (ALL — (A) THE PAIN IN MY HEART — 1965 ATLANTIC US 33161 UK 587042
(1941/1967) — (B) OTIS BLUE — 1966 ATLANTIC US 33284 UK 587036
STEVE CROPPER G (B — (B) OTIS BLUE — 19 ATLANTIC RIUK K40003 US VOLT412
JOE CURTIS V (QS — (C) DICTIONARY OF SOUL — 1966 ATLANTIC US 33284 UK 587 050
JIMMY KING (— (C) DICTIONARY OF SOUL — 19 US VOLT416
RON CALDWELL (— (D) LIVE IN EUROPE — 1966 ATLANTIC US 33286 UK 228 017
PHALIN JONES (— (D) LIVE IN EUROPE — 19 ATLANTIC UK 589 011 US VOLT416
CARL CUNNINGHAM (— (E) DOCK OF THE BAY — 1968 ATLANTIC US 33288 UK 228 022
BEN CAULEY (— (E) DOCK OF THE BAY — 19 ATLANTIC UKRI K40076 US VOLT419
CARLA THOMAS V (P — (F) IMMORTAL OTIS REDDING — 1968 ATLANTIC US 33252 UK 588 113
SAMMIE COLEMAN TPT (GZ — (F) IMMORTAL OTIS REDDING — 1966 ATLANTIC UKRIK40019
(G) IN PERSON AT THE WHISKEY — 1968 ATLANTIC UK 588 148 US 33265
JOHN FARRIS TPT (GZ — (H) LOVE MAN — 1969 ATLANTIC US 33289 UK 228 025
CLARENCE JOHNSON TROM (GZ — (H) LOVE MAN — 19 ATLANTIC UKRI K40078
BOB HOLLOWAY SAX (GZ — (I) HISTORY OF OTIS REDDING — 1969 ATLANTIC US 33261 UK 228 001
BOBBY PITTMAN SAX (GZ — (I) HISTORY OF OTIS REDDING — 197 ATLANTIC UKRI K40066 US VOLT418
DONALD HENRY SAX (GZ — (J) TELL THE TRUTH — 1970 ATLANTIC UK 2400 018 US 33333
JAMES RANDOLF YOUNG G((GZ — (K) THE BEST OF — 1972 ATLANTIC UK K 60016 US 31801
ELBERT WOODSON D (GZ — (L) SINGS SOUL BALLADS — 1966 ATLANTIC UK 587035 US VOLT411
RALPH STEWART B (Z — (M) SOUL ALBUM — 19 ATLANTIC UK 500 011 US 33285
(N) REMEMBERING — 19 ATLANTIC UK 2464 003
(P) KING & QUEEN — 19 ATLANTIC UK 589007 STAX US 716
(Q) HERE COMES SOME SOUL — 19 MARBLE ARCH UK MAL 772
(R) MONTEREY POP (1 SIDE) — 19 REPRISE US 2029
(S) SOUL AS SUNG BY — 19 ALLSHIRE US 5082
(T) OTIS REDDING STORY (DBL) — 19 ATCO FR 60013
(U) OTIS REDDING STORY VOL 2 — 19 ATCO FR 60016
(V) OTIS REDDING VOL 1 — 1981 ATLANTIC UK K20043
(Z) RECORDED LIVE — 1982 ATLANTIC 450881

R56A
THE REDS
R56A

RICK SCHAFFER G V (— (A) THE REDS — 1979 A&M US 4772 UK AMLH64772
TOM GEDDES D (— (B) STRONGER SILENCE — 1981 KINGDOM 9005
BRUCE COHEN K (
JIM PETER B (

R56B
REDUCERS
R56B

(A) MAN WITH GUN(EP) — 19 VIBES UK VR 003

R57
REDWING
R57

RON FLOEGEL G V (ABC — (A) REDWING — 1971 FANTASY US 8409
ANDREW SAMUELS G V B(ABC — (A) REDWING — 1971 UA UK UAS29188
GEORGE HULLIN D V (ABC — (B) WHAT THIS COUNTRY NEEDS — 1972 FANTASY US 9405
TOM PHILLIPS G K STEEL (ABC — (C) TAKE ME HOME — 1973 FANTASY UK FT518 US 9439
JOHN MYERS B (BC — (D) DEAD OR ALIVE — 1974 FANTASY US 9459
ED BOGAS FDL MAND(C — (E) BEYOND THE SUN & STARS — 1975 FANTASY US 9488
TIM MOORE FDL (C
DAVE FRASER PNO (CDE KENNETH NASH PERC (DE BUDDY HARPHAN B V (E DEBBIE MOORE V (D

R58 HERB REED R58

HERB REED		(A	(A) SWEET RIVER	197	PVK UK PVK002

R59 JIMMY REED R59

JIMMY REED	G V	(ALL	(A)I'M JIMMY REED	19	US VEEJAY1004
PHIL UPCHURCH	B	(KLCEDMR	(B)ROCKIN WITH JIMMY REED	19	US VEEJAY1008
LEFTY BATES	G	(BCEFJKLMDRQ	(C) FOUND LOVE	19	US VEEJAY1022
AL DUNCAN	D	(KMR	(D)NOW APPEARING	19	US VEEJAY1025
JIMMY REED JR	B	(KMR	(E)AT CARNEGIE HALL	1962	STATESIDE UK SL10012 US VEEJAY1035
EDDIE TAYLOR	G	(KLQABEFJMCDNP	(E)AT CARNEGIE HALL	19	BLUESWAY BLX60732 JOY JOYS 120
WAYNE BENNETT	G	(L	(E) AT CARNEGIE HALL	19	EXODUS US 307
JIMMY TILLMAN	D	(L	(O) PREACHIN THE BLUES(4 TRACKS)	1963	STATESIDE UK SL10046
JOHN LEE HOOKER		(O	(F)THE BEST OF	196	US VEEJAY1039
MEMPHIS SLIM		(O	(R)JUST JIMMY REED	1964	STATESIDE UK SL10055 US VEEJAY1050
MORRIS WILKERSON	D	(QABEFJP	(R)JUST JIMMY REED	196	RI JOY JOYS146
W C DALTON	G	(QACEFM	(G)T'AINT NO BIG THING	196	US VEEJAY1067
HENRY GRAY	PNO	(ACEFMQ	(H)SINGS THE BEST OF THE BLUES	196	STATESIDE UK SL10069 US VEEJAY1072
MILTON RECTOR	B	(QAEFMC	(J)PLAYS 12 STRING GUITAR BLUES	1964	STATESIDE UK SL10086 US VEEJAY1073
EARL PHILLIPS	D	(ACEDFBJMQ	(J)PLAYS 12 STRING GUITAR BLUES	1968	JOY JOYS132
VERNELL FOURNIER	D	(Q	(M)BOSS MAN OF THE BLUES	1964	STATESIDE UK SL10091 US VEEJAY1080
REMO BIONDI	G	(QABEFM	(N)AT SOUL CITY	196	JOY JOYS 127 US VEEJAY1095
LEE BAKER	G	(QCEFM	(P)THE LEGEND,THE MAN	196	JOY JOYS 111 US VEEJAY8501
WILLIE DIXON	B	(QCEFM	(P) THE LEGEND,THE MAN	19	EXODUS US 324
MARY LEE REED	V	(QEJM	(K) SOULIN'	1968	STATESIDE UK SL10221
MARCUS JOHNSON	B	(CEFJM	(K) SOULIN'	19	BLUESWAY US BLS 6009
CURTIS MAYFIELD	B	(E	JIMMY REED	19	ARC FOLK US 234
JOHNNY JONES	PNO	(N	VERY BEST	19	BUDDAH US 4003
HUBERT SUMLIN	G	(N	ROOTS OF THE BLUES	19	KENT US 5037
SCREAMING JAY HAWKINS	V	(Z	SOMETHING ELSE	19	SUNSET 5218
			SOUL GREATS	19	UPFRONT US 101
			SOULFUL SOUND	19	UPFRONT US 108
			THE BEST	19	UPFRONT US 125
			NEW JIMMY REED	19	HMV UK CLP 3611 BLUESWAY 6004
			WAILIN' THE BLUES	19	MUSIDISC FR 6088 TRADITION US2069
			(L) BIG BOSS MAN	1973	BLUESWAY US BLS 6015
			DOWN IN VIRGINIA	197	BLUESWAY US BLS 6024
			I AIN'T FROM CHICAGO	1973	BLUESWAY US BLS 6054
			THE ULTIMATE	1973	BLUESWAY US BLS 6067
			THE BEST OF JIMMY REED	1974	G N P CRESENDO US GNP 10006
			JIMMY REED IS BACK	1976	JOY JOYS 264
			(Q)MEMORIAL ALBUM VOL 1	1976	DJM 28033
			LET THE BOSSMAN SPEAK	19	BLUE ON BLUES US 10001
			AS JIMMY IS	197	ROKER US 6067
			COLD CHILLS	1976	ANTILLES US 7007
			HISTORY OF	1972	TRIP US 8012
			JIMMY REED	19	EVEREST US 234
			UPSIDE YOUR HEAD	1980	CHARLY UK CRB 1003
			(Z) FUNKY FNKY SOUL	1981	MANHATTAN 5041
			HIGH & LONESOME	1981	CHARLY UK CRB 1013
			GOT ME DIZZY	1982	CHARLY UK CRB 1028
			SHAME SHAME SHAME (EP)	1980	CHARLY UK CTD 105

R60 LOU REED R60

LOU REED	G V	k8ALL	(A) LOU REED	1972	RCA US LSP 4701 UK SF8281
JO'ANNA KAMERON	V	(L	(A) LOU REED	1981	RCA RI UK 43214
CLEM CATTINI	PERC	(A	(B) TRANSFORMER	1972	RCA US LSP4807 UK RI INTS5061
CALEB QUAYE	G PNO	(A	(C) BERLIN	1973	RCA US 10207 UK RS1002
RICK WAKEMAN	K	(A	(C) BERLIN	1981	RCA UK RI INT5150
STEVE HOWE	G	(A	(D) ROCK'N'ROLL ANIMAL	1974	RCA US APLI0472 UK PL 10472
CHRISTINE WILTSHIRE	V	(L	(D) ROCK'N'ROLL ANIMAL	1981	RCA US 3664 UK INTS 5086
AUL KEOGH	G	(A	(E) SALLY CANT DANCE	1974	RCA US APLI0611 UK PL 10611
LES HURDLE	B	(A	(F) LOU REED LIVE	1975	RCA US APLI0959 UK RS1007
BRIAN ODGERS	B	(A	(G) METAL MACHINE MUSIC	1975	RCA CPL2 1101
DAVID BOWIE	V	(B	(H) CONEY ISLAND BABY	1976	RCA US APLI0915 UK RS1035
MICK RONSON	G	(B	(H) CONEY ISLAND BABY	197	RCA US ANLI2480 GER 21665
THUNDERTHIGHS	V	(B	(J) ROCK'N'ROLL HEART	1976	ARISTA US 4100 UK 142 GER 98284
KLAUS VOORMANN	B	(B	(K) WALK ON THE WILD SIDE (BEST OF)	1977	RCA US APLI2001 UK PL 12001
HERBIE FLOWERS	B	(B	(L) STREET HASSLE	1978	ARISTA US 4169 UK 1045 GER 60445
JOHN HALSEY	D	(B	(M) LIVE TAKE NO PRISONERS(DBL)	1978	ARISTA US 8502 UK 03066
BARRY DE SOUZA	D	(B	(N) VICIOUS	1979	RCA NL 42731
RONNIE ROSS	SAX	(B	(O) THE BELLS	1979	ARISTA US 4229 UK 1093 GER 62630
STEVE HUNTER	G	(CDF	(P) GROWING UP IN PUBLIC	1980	ARISTA US 9522 UK 1131 GER 202120
ALLAN MacMILLAN	K	(C	(Q) ROCK'N'ROLL DIARY(67/80)	1980	ARISTA US 8603 UK DART8
MICHAEL BRECKER	SAX	(C	(R) THE BLUE MASK	1982	RCA UK RCALP6028

RANDY BRECKER	TPT	(C	JACK BRUCE	B	(C	AYNSLEY DUNBAR	D	(C	BOB EZRIN	K V	(C
TONY LEVIN	B	(C	GENE MARTYNEC	G K V	(C	JON PIERSON	TROM	(C	DICK WAGNER	G V	(CDF
BLUE WEAVER	K	(C	B J WILSON	D	(C	STEVE WINWOOD	K	(C	DENNIS FERRANTE	V	(C
STEVE HYDEN	V	(C	ELIZABETH MARSH	V	(C	RAY COLCORD	K	(DF	PENTTI GLAN	D	(DEF
PRAKASH JOHN	B V	(DEF	MICHAEL WENDROFF	V	(EH	DANNY WEIS	G V	(E	MICHAEL FONFARA	K	(EJMPLO
RITCHIE DHARMA	D	(BE	PAUL FLEISHER	SAX	(E	JOANNE VENT	B V	(E	STEVE KATZ	HCA	(E
GODFREY DIAMOND	V	(H	BOB KULICK	G	(H	MICHAEL SUCHORSKY	D	(HJLMOP	BRUCE YAW	B	(HJ
GARLAND JEFFREYS	V	(J	KAY GARNER	V	(A	HELENE FRANCOIS	V	(A	STUART HEINRICH	G V	(PML
CHUCK HAMMER	SYN G	(P	ELLARD BOWLES	V SYN G B	(PMO	MARTY FOGEL	SAX	(MLO	ANGELA HOWELL	V	(ML
CHRISSY FAITH	V	(M	KAY GARNER	V	(A	HELENE FRANCOIS	V	(A	GENYA RAVAN	V	(L
DON CHERRY	TPT	(O									

R60A REELS R60A

DAVID MASON	V	(A	(A) THE REELS	1979	POLYDOR US PD1 6275
COLIN NEWMAN	K	(A			

PAUL ABRAHAMS	B	(A	JOHN BLISS	D	(A	CRAIG HOOPER	G	(A

R60C MARTHA REEVES R60C

MARTHA REEVES V (ALL (A) MARTHA REEVES 1974 MCA US 414 UK MCF2565
RICHARD PERRY PERC(A (B) THE REST OF MY LIFE 1977 ARISTA US 4105 UK SPART1030
JAMES JAMERSON B (A (C) WE MEET AGAIN 1978 MILESTONE US 9549 FANTASY UK544
LON VAN EATON G (A
DANNY FARAGHER K (A STEVE MADAIO HRNS (A JAMES GADSON D (AC RUSS TURNER V K (A
LEON PATILLO V K (A &LENNY LEE GOLDSMITH K (A NICKY HOPKINS K (A ARTHUR ADAMS G (A
MALCOLM CECIL SYN (A TREVOR LAWRENCE HRNS (A BOBBY KEYS HRNS (A MELVIN RAGIN G (A
HENRY DAVIS B (A JIMMIE CALHOUN B (A TRAVIS FULLERTON D (A CAROL KAFI V (A
KING ERRISSON PERC (A DENNIS COFFEY G (A DEAN PARKS G (A WILLIAM SMITH K (A
LARRY NASH K (A BILLY PRESTON K (A CLARENCE MACDONALD K (A JIM KELTNER D (A
KLAUS VOORMANN B (A JOE SAMPLE K (A CLYDIE KING V (A JAMES TAYLOR HRNS(A
D LLOYD GREGORY G (A VINI PONCIA G V (A DEREK VAN EATON G (A MILT HOLLAND VIBES(A
BASIL GREEN B (A KENNY ASHER K (A JESSE BUTLER K (A HOYT AXTON G (A
JIM GILSTRAP V (A TOM HENSLEY K (A AVALON COMM CHOIR V (A RALPH MACDONALD PERC(A
SYLVESTER RIVERS K (C DALE WARREN K (C GEORGE SPENCER K (C GREG LEVIAS K (C
CHARLES FEARING G (C CORNELIUS GRANT G (C DAVID PRUITT G (C GREG CROCKETT G (A
ROMEO WILLIAMS B (C GARNETT BROWN TROM (C MAURICE SPEARS TROM (C BUBBA CHAMBERS PERC(C
PHILLIP RANELIN TROM (C ROBERT BRYANT TPT (C GROVER MITCHELL TROM (C ANANIAS CHAMBERS CONGA(A
ALBERT AARONS TPT (C BENJAMIN POWELL TROM(C ROBERT ZIMITTI PERC (C BANJAMIN KIRK TPT (C
WILLIAM PETERSON TPT (C DONALD CHRISTLIEB WIND (C JOHN ROBERTS TPT (C WILLIAM GREEN WIND(C
ERNIE FIELDS FLT (C STRING SECTION (C FRED JACKSON FLT (C

R61 REFUGEE R61

LEE JACKSON B (A (A) REFUGEE 1974 CHARISMA UK CAS 1087
BRIAN DAVISON D (A
PATRICK MORAZ K (A JOHN BURNS PROD (A

R61A REGULARS R61A

ALLAN'KINGPIN'KING V (A (A) VICTIM 1978 CBS UK 83541
ANTHONY ROOKWOOD V (A
NORMAN EBANKS G (A PATRICK DONEGAN G (A GEORGE CLARKE K (A TREVOR SALMON B (A
ERROLL FRANCIS D (A ERROLL FORREST PERC (A GEORGE CHISHOLM TPT (A DEREK WADSWORTH TROM(A
STEVE GREGORY SAX (A

R61B JOHN REID R61B

(A) FACADE 19 CBS US PC 34298

R61C ROY REID R61C

ROY REID V (A (A) WHAP'N BAP'N 1980 VIRGIN UK V2164
ANGUS GAYE D (A
JAH BUNNY D (A
WEBSTER JOHNSON PNO (A JOHN KPIAYE G (A EUTON JONES PERC (A GLAISTER VENN PERC (A
ZENON (A DELROY CLARKE FLT (A BAGGA FAGAN PERC B V (A TONY ROBINSON B (A
DENNIS BOVELL K B G(A PATRICK TENYUE HRNS (A HENRY TENYUE HRNS (A PHIL TOWNER D (A
NICK BAILEY K (A JANET KAY V (A

R62 TERRY REID R62

TERRY REID G V (ALL (A) BANG BANG, YOU'RE TERRY REID 1968 EPIC US 26427
ERIC LEESE K (A (B) MOVE OVER FOR TERRY REID 1969 EPIC US 26477 UK EMI SCX 6370
KEITH WEBB D (AB (B)THE MOST OF TERRY REID 1971 MFP UK 5220
CONRAD ISADORE D (C (C) RIVER 1973 ATLANTIC US 7259 UK WB K40340
WILLIE BOBO PERC (C (D) SEED OF MEMORY 1976 ABC US 935 UK ABCL 5162
AL VIOLA SAX (D (E) ROGUE WAVES 1979 CAPITOL UK 11857
PETE SOLLEY K (B
LEE MILES B (CDE DAVID LINDLEY G VLN(CD SOKO RICHARDSON D (D BEN KEITH STEEL(D
JOEL BERNSTEIN G (D JESSE ERLICH CELLO (D BLUE MITCHELL HRNS (FRED WESLEY HRNS(
PLAS JOHNSON SAX (GRAHAM NASH V (D TIM WEISBERG FLT (D CLIFFORD SOLOMON HRNS(
JAMES GADSON D (D AL PERKINS STEEL(D DOUG RODRIGUES G (E JOHN SIOMOS D (E
STERLING SMITH (E JAMES JOHNSON (E CHRIS STEWART B (

R63 RELEASE MUSIC ORCHESTRA R63

NORBERT JACOBSON PNO WIND V(AB (A) LIFE 1974 BRAIN GER 1056
WOLFGANG'ZABBA'INDNER D V (ABC (B) GARUDA 1975 BRAIN GER 1072
JOCHEN PETERSON SAX (B (C) GET THE BALL 1977 BRAIN 1083
BERND KIEFER B V (A (D) BEYOND THE LIMIT 1978 BRAIN GER 60 115
MANNE RURUP K SYN V(ABCDE (E) NEWS 1979 BRAIN GER 60 194
FRANK FISCHER D (CDE
HOLGER DUNKEL B (B MARGIT MAYA HABERLAND PERC V G(BC WOLFGANG THIERFELDT D (DE
JOHANNES'ALTO'PAPPERT SAX(B JOCHEN PETERSON SAX (B ERHARD SCHAFER TPT (C CPT SNATTY STORTEBECKER(B
MIKE GONG G (C CARLOS KARGES G (C TOMMY GOLDSCHMIDT PERC(DE HANS BEHRENDT PERC(D
NURI EFFENDI V (E

R63A RELUCTANT STEREOTYPES R63A

PAUL KING V ((A) THE LABEL 1980 WEA UK K58201
TONY WALL B (
COLIN HEANES D (STEVE EDGSON CLAR (PAUL SAMPSON G (

R63B REMA REMA R63B

MARK COX K SYN (A (A) WHEEL IN THE ROSES(EP) 1980 4AD UK BAD5
GARY ASQUITH G V (A
MICHAEL ALLEN B V (A MARCO G (A MAX D (A

R64 REMAINS R64

BARRY TASHIAN G V (A (A) REMAINS 1967 SPOONFED US 3305
CHIP DAMIANI D (A (A) REMAINS(ADDITIONAL TRACKS) 1978 EPIC US 24214
VERN MILLER B G HRNS(A
WILLIAM BRIGGS K (A

R64A REMIPEDS R64A

(A) THE TAHITI SYNDROME 1981 BANANA UK EAT 1

R64B REMO 4 R64B

COLIN MANLEY G V (AB (A) SMILE 1967 STARCLUB GER 158 034
TONY ASHTON V K (AB (B) ATTENTION 1973 PHONOGRAM GER 6434 158
ROY DYKE D (AB
PHIL ROGERS B (AB

R65 RENAISSANCE R65

KEITH RELF V G HCA (AB (A) RENAISSANCE 1969 ISLAND UK ILPS 9114 US ELEKTRA 74068
JIM McCARTY D (AB (B) ILLUSION 19 ISLAND UK HELP 27 EURO 80895
JANE RELF V (AB (C) PROLOGUE 1972 SOVEREIGN UK 7253 US CAPITOL 11116
NEIL KORNER B (B (C) PROLOGUE 1972 SOVEREIGN GER 94663
JOHN HAWKEN K (AB (D) ASHES ARE BURNING 1973 SOVEREIGN UK 7261 US CAPITOL 11216
LOUIS CENNAMO B (AB (E) TURN OF THE CARDS 1975 BTM UK 1000 US SIRE 6015
TERRY SLADE D (B (E) TURN OF THE CARDS 1975 RCA GER 21490 US RI SIRE 7502
ANNIE HASLAM V PERC(CDEFGHJLM (F) SCHEHERAZADE & OTHER STORIES 1975 BTM UK 1006 US SIRE 6017 + 7510
MIKE DUNFORD G V (BDEFGHJLM (G) LIVE AT CARNEGIE HALL(DBL) 1976 BTM UK 2001 US SIRE 6029 + 3902
JON CAMP V B G(CDEFGHJLM (H) NOVELLA 1977 WB UK K56422 US SIRE 6024 + 7526
JOHN TOUT K V (CDEFGHJL (J) A SONG FOR ALL SEASONS 1978 WB UK K56460 US SIRE 6049
TERENCE SULLIVAN D V (CDEFGHJL (K) IN THE BEGINNING 19 CAPITOL US 11871
ROB HENDRY G V MAND(C (L) AZURE D'OR 1979 WB UK K56633 US SIRE 6068
ANDY POWELL G (D (M) CAMERA CAMERA 1981 ILLEGAL UK ILP008 US IRS 70019
FRANCIS MONKMAN SYN (C (EF) ROCK GALAXY (DBL) 1980 RCA NL 25282
TERRY CROWE V (B
DON SHINN K (B PETER GOSLING K (M PETER BARRON D (M BINKY CULLUM V (
RICHARD HEWSON STR (D

R65A RENALDO & THE LOAF R65A

RENALDO M G MAND D V(A (A) SONGS FOR SWINGING LARVAE 1981 RALPH US 8108 UK DOIT RIDE 6
THE LOAF G WIND B(A

R65B RENEGADES R65B

DENYS GIBSON G (A (A) THE RENEGADE STORY 1978 MIDI GER 26070
KIM BROWN G V (A
IAN MALLETT B (A GRAHAM JOHNSON D (A

R66 JOHN RENBOURN R66

JOHNRENBOURN G V (ALL (A) JOHN RENBOURN 1965 TRANSATLANTIC UK TRA135 US REPRISE 6482
BERT JANSCH G (AB (B) BERT & JOHN 1966 TRANSATLANTIC UK TRA144
JACQUI McSHEE V (CLN (C) ANOTHER MONDAY 1967 TRANSATLANTIC UK TRA149
JENNIFER DE MONTFORTE JONES OBOE(C (D) SIR JOHN ALOT OF M ENGLAND1968 TRANSATLANTIC UK TRA167 US REPRISE 6344
TERRY COX PERC (DGE (E) LADY & THE UNICORN 1970 TRANSATLANTIC UK TRA224 US REPRISE 6407
RAY WARLEIGH FLT (DE (F) JOHN RENBOURN SAMPLER 1971 TRANSATLANTIC UK TRASAM20
DOMINIQUE TREPEAU G (K (G) FARO ANNIE 1971 TRANSATLANTIC UK TRA247 US REPRISE 2082
JOHN JAMES G (K (H) SO CLEAR 1973 TRANSATLANTIC UK TRASAM28
TONY ROBERTS V WIND(LNOE (J) HEADS & TAILS 1974 TRANSATLANTIC UK TRASAM18
SUE DRAHEIM V FDL(GL (K) THE HERMIT 1976 TRANSATLANTIC UK TRA 336
KESH SATHIE PERC (LO (L) MAID IN BEDLAM 1977 TRANSATLANTIC UK TRA 348
DON HARPER VLA (E (L) MAID IN BEDLAM 1977 SHANACHIE 79004 US
GLEN TOMMY D (O (M) JOHN RENBOURN & S GROSSMAN1978 KICKING MULE UK SNKF139 GER SONET 69081
JOHN MOLINAUX V DULC MAND(O (N) BLACK BALLOON 1979 TRANSATLANTIC UK TRA 355
LEE NICHOLSON CONC (E (N) BLACK BALLOON 1979 KICKING MULE US 163
STEFAN GROSSMAN G (M (O) ENCHANTED GARDEN 1980 TRANSATLANTIC UK TRA 356
STUART GORDON TABLA(N (P) UNDER THE VOLCANO 1980 SONET UK SNTF 161
PETE DYER HCA (G
DORRIS HENDERSON V (G DANNY THOMPSON B (G DAVE SWARBRICK VLN (E

R66A RENIA R66A

PETER SUTHERLAND K V (A (A) FIRST OFFENDERS 1973 TRANSATLANTIC UK TRA261
KENNY STEWART V (A
JOHN ROBINSON G V (A MALCOLM SUTHERLAND B K V(A DAVE MATTHEWS D (A

R66B ROBERT RENTAL & THE NORMAL R66B

A) LIVE AT WEST RUNTON PAVILLION 1980 ROUGH TRADE UK ROUGH 17

R66C REPAIRS R66C

PETER McCANN V G K(A (A) REPAIRS 1972 MOWEST US MW1211
SUKIE HONEYCUTT V K PERC(A (B) ALREADY A HOUSEHOLD WORD 1973 RARE EARTH US 532
LARRY TREADWELL V K G HCA(A
MICHAEL KAMEN HRNS (A MIKE FOLEY V B G TROM(A JIM HONEYCUTT B G (A ACE HOLLERAN D PERC(A
DAVID McCANN FDL (A BOB BONEFANT HRNS (A BARRY MARSHALL HRNS (A

R66D KLAUS RENFT COMBO R66D

KLAUS RENFT B (ALL (A) KLAUS RENFT COMBO 19 AMIGA GER 855326
THOMAS SCHOPPE G V (A (B) RENFT 19 AMIGA GER 855396
PETER KSCHENTZ WIND (A (C) ROCK AUS LEIPZIG(LIVE) 19 TELDEC GER 6622093
JOCHEN HOHL D (A
CHRISTIAN KUNERT K TROM G V(A PETER GLASER G V (A

R66E TIM RENWICK R66E

TIM RENWICK G V (A (A) TIM RENWICK 1980 CBS UK 84082

R67 THE RESIDENTS R67

THE RESIDENTS V G K B D VLN HRNS (A) MEET THE RESIDENTS 1974 RALPH US RR0274
WITH (A) MEET THE RESIDENTS 1977 RALPH US RR0677
PAMELA ZEIBAK V (CD (B) NOT AVAILABLE 1978 RALPH US RR1174
SNAKEFINGER LITHMAN G V VLN(CGJ (C) 3RD REICH & ROLL 1976 RALPH US RR1075
DON JACKOVICH PERC (DJ (D) FINGER PRINCE 1977 RALPH US RR1276
A DEKBAR VLN (D (E) DUCK STAB /BUSTER & GLEN 1978 RALPH US RR0278
T LOGAN PERC (D (F) NIBBLES (COMP) 1979 VIRGIN UK VR3 NL 200 598
RUBY V (E (G) COMMERCIAL ALBUM 1980 RALPH UK PREX2 US 6559
PEGGY HONEYDEW V (C (H) MARK OF THE MOLE 1981 RALPH US 8152
DON PRESTON SYN (G (J) THE TUNES OF TWO CITIES 1982 RALPH UK RZ 8202
CHRIS CUTLER D (GJ
FRED FRITH (J SANDY SANDWICH (J MUD'S SIS (J

R68 RESISTERS R68

DAVE OWYNNE-JONES G (A (A) THE RESISTERS 1979 TRIKONT GERM 0052
SUSY BARRY D (A
ILSE ZANBOUINI B (A GEOFF HOLLAND V (A PETE HULLINEAUX G (A KIM PARKER K (A

R69 RETAINERS R69

PAUL CARRACK K (1 (A) MAY 1978
TONY O'MALLEY K (1
ALAN SPENNER B (1 NEIL HUBBARD G (1 MEL COLLINS SAX (1

R69A MARTIN REV R69A

MARTIN REV V (A (A) MARTIN REV 1980 INFIDELITY US 228

R69B REVELATION R69B

BENNY DIGGS V (A (A) REVELATION 1975 RSO US 4810 UK 2394 161
(B) GET IN TOUCH 1979 RCA US 3287

R70 PAUL REVERE & THE RAIDERS R70

PAUL REVERE ORG (ALL (A) PAUL REVERE & THE RAIDERS 19 SANDE US 1001
MARK LINDSAY K SAX V(K (A) IN THE BEGINNING 1966 JERDEN US 7004
DRAKE LEVIN G ((B) HERE THEY COME 1965 CBS US 9107
MICHAEL SMITH D ((C) JUST LIKE US 1966 CBS UK 62406 US 9251
JOE CORRERO D V (K (D) MIDNIGHT RIDE 1966 CBS UK 62397 US 9308
PHILIP VOLK B ((E) SPIRIT OF 67 1967 CBS US 9395
CHARLIE COE B ((F) GREATEST HITS 1967 CBS US 9462
JIM VALLEY G ((G) REVOLUTION 1967 CBS UK 63095 US 9521
FREDDY WELLER G V (K (H) CHRISTMAS PAST & PRESENT 1968 CBS US 9555
KEITH ALLISON G V K(K (I) GOIN' TO MEMPHIS 1968 CBS UK 63265 US 9605
(J) SOMETHINGS HAPPENING 1968 CBS US 9665
(K) HARD & HEAVY 1969 CBS UK 63649 US 9753
(L) SPIRIT OF 69 1969 CBS US GP12
(M) ALIAS PINK PUZZ 1967 CBS US 9905
(N) COLLAGE (RAIDERS) 1970 CBS UK 63973 US 9964
(O) PAUL REVERE & THE RAIDERS 19 HARMONY US 30089
(P) GREATEST HITS VOL 2 1967 CBS US 30386
(Q) INDIAN RESERVATION 1971 CBS UK 64461 US 30768
(E+) GOOD THING (E) + 1 TRACK) 1969 CBS UK 62963 HARMONY 30975
(S) MOVIN' ON 1972 HARMONY US 31183
(T) COUNTRY WINE 19 CBS US 31196
( ) PAUL REVERE & THE RAIDERS 1970 CBS NL 52 830
( ) PAUL REVERE & THE RAIDERS 19 PICKWICK US 3176
( )GREATEST HITS 1979 CBS 35593
( ) LIKE LONG HAIR 196 GARDENA US 1000
( ) THE FALCONAIRES WITH MARK LINDSAY 19 USAF US 70 3
(U) ALL TIME GREATEST HITS 1972 CBS US 31464

R70A REVILLOS R70A

FAY FIFE V (A (A) REV UP 1980 DINDISC UK DID 3
EUGENE REYNOLDS K V (A
HI FI HARRIS G (A D K SMYTHE B (ROCKY RHYTHM D (A KID KRUPA G (A
BABS & CHERRY HANDJIVE (A WILLIAM MYSTERIOUS B (A

R71 REVOLUTIONAIRES R71

SLY DUNBAR D (A (A) REACTION IN DUB 1978 CHACHA CHALP 002
ERROLL NELSON PNO (A (B) GOLDMINE DUB 1979 GREENSLEEVES GREL 4
SCULLY SIMMS PERC (A (C) REVOLUTIONAIRES SOUNDS VOL2 1978 BALLISTIC UAG 30237
BOBBY ELLIS TPT (A (D) NEGREA LOVE DUB 1979 TROJAN TRLS 153
ROBBIE SHAKESPEARE G B(A (E) OUTLAW DUB 1979 TROJAN TRLS 169
HERMAN MARQUIS SAX (A ( ) LEGGO DUB 19 CASH & CARRY
RED BRYAN G (A ( ) GREEN BAY DUB 19 BURNING VIBRATIONS 1004
TOMMY McCOOK SAX (A ( ) BLACK ASH 1980 TROJAN 186
( ) JONKANOO DUB 19

R72 REVOLUTIONARY BLUES BAND R72

TOM SCOTT SAX (A (A) REVOLUTIONARY BLUES BAND 1970 MCA UK MUPS402 CORAL US 757506
DAVID COHEN G (A
ARTHUR ADAMS G (A LIGHTNIN' ROD V (A

R73 REX(SMITH) R73

REX SMITH V (AB (A) REX 1977 CBS US 34399 UK 63439
MIKE RATTI D (AB (B) WHERE DO WE GO FROM HERE 1978 CBS US 34865 UK 82186
ORVILLE DAVIS B (Ab
LARS HANSON G (AB LOU VANDORA G (AB

R73A REXY R73A

(A) RUNNING OUT OF TIME 1981 ALIEN UK BEALIEN2

R74 REZILLOS R74

FAY FIFE V (AB (A) CANT STAND THE REZILLOS 1978 SIRE 9103 257 K56530 US 6057
EUGENE REYNOLDS V (AB (B) MISSION ACCOMPLISHED 1979 SIRE SRK6069 GER 200 654
ANGEL PATERSON D (AB
LUKE WARM G (B SIMON TEMPLAR B (B JO CALLIS G (A GAIL WARNING V (B
WILLIAM MYSTERIOUS SAX B(AB D K SMYTHE B (HI FI HARRIS G (

R75 RHINOCEROS R75

BILL MUNDI D (AB (A) RHINOCEROS 1969 ELEKTRA US 74030 71RI UK K42042
MIKE FONFARA K (ABC (B) SATIN CHICKEN 1969 ELEKTRA US 74056 71RI UK K42036
DANNY WEIS K G (ABC (C) BETTER TIMES ARE COMING 1970 ELEKTRA US 74075 UK 2469 006
DOUG HASTINGS G (AB (C) BETTER TIMES ARE COMING 1971 ELEKTRA UK RI K42049
JERRY PENROD B (A
JOHN FINLEY V (ABC ALAN GERBER K V (AB DUKE EDWARDS D (C PETER HODGSON B (BC
LARRY LEISHMAN G (C

R76 EMITT RHODES R76

EMITT RHODES ALL INST (ALL (A) AMERICAN DREAM 1971 A&M US SP4254 UK AMLS64254
CHUCK BERGHOFFER B (A (B) EMITT RHODES 1971 DUNHILL US 50089 UK PROBE SPBA6256
HAL BLAINE D (A (C) MIRROR 1971 DUNHILL US 50111 UK PROBE SPBA6262
DAVID COHEN G (A (D) FAREWELL TO PARADISE 1972 DUNHILL US 50122 UK PROBE SPBA6266
JIM GORDON D (A (D) FAREWELL TO PARADISE 1974 ABC RI UK ABCL 5041
JOHN GUERIN D (A
PETE JOLLY (A LARRY KNECHTEL K (A GARY KATO (A MICHAEL RICE (A
JOEL LARSON D (A JAMES LEITCH (A DRAKE LEVIN (A DON PEAK (A
JOE PORCARO PERC (A EMIL RADOCCHIA (A DON RANDI K (A TOM REYNOLDS (A
BILL RHEINHART (A LYLE RITZ B (A

R77 RED RHODES R77

ORVILLE J 'RED'RHODES STEEL(ALL (A) ONCE A DAY 19 CROWN US CST 520
JAY LACY G (F (B) BLUE BLUE DAY 19 CROWN US CST 528
ROBERT K WARFORD G (F (C) STEEL GUITAR RAG 19 CROWN US CST 535
COLIN CAMERON B (F (D) GUITARS GO COUNTRY 19 CROWN US
DANNY LANE D (F (E) LIVE AT THE PALOMINO 19 HAPPY TIGER US HT10035
DAVID BARNY PNO (F (F) VELVET HAMMER IN A COWBOY BAND 1973 COUNTRYSIDE US CS 102
JIM STALLINGS B (F

R77A RHYTHM CATS R77A

(A) ROCK WITH THE RHYTHM(EP) 19 TYGER TYG 3

R77B RHYTHM DEVILS R77B

MICKEY HART D (A (A) PLAY RIVER MUSIC 1980 PASSPORT US PB 9844
BILLY KREUTZMANN D (A
AIRTO MOREIRA PERC (A MIKE HINTON (A JIM LOVELESS PERC (A GREGG ERRICO (A
JORDAN AMARANTHA PERC (A PHIL LESH (A

R77C RHYTHM HAWKS R77C

(A) WALK OUT ON YOU(EP) 19 REDBALL RR 011

R78 RHYTHM HERITAGE R78

MICHAEL OMARTIAN K V (ABC (A) DISCO FIED 1976 ABC UK ABCL 5174 US ABCD 934
STEVE MADAIO TPT (C (B) LAST NIGHT ON EARTH 1977 ABC US 987
ED GREENE D (ABC (C) SKY'S THE LIMIT 1978 ABC US 1037
DEAN PARKS G (A
SCOTT EDWARDS B (ABC TONY TERRAN TPT (A TOM SCOTT WIND (A ERNIE WATTS SAX (AC
FRED SELDON WIND (AC LEW McCREARY TROM (A SID SHARP STRINGS(ABC LEE RITENOUR G (A
DAVID DUKE (A GALE ROBINSON (A ORRIN WATERS V (AC LUTHER WATERS V (AC
MICHAEL PRICE V (A MARVIN DEANE PERC (A PAT McCOY PERC (A RAY PARKER G (A
BEN BENAY G (A VICTOR FELDMAN PERC (AC PAUL HUBINON TPT (A JAY GRAYDON G (C
CHUCK FINDLEY B (C

R78A CATHERINE RIBEIRO & LES ALPES R78A

CATHERINE RIBEIRO V (AB (A) LE RAT DEBILE ET L'HOMME DES CHAMPS 1974 PHILIPS FR 9101 003
DANIEL MOTRON K (A (B) PAIX 19 PHILIPS 6325 019
GERALD RENARD B (A
PATRICE MOULLET G (AB DENIS COHEN PERC (A JEAN JACQUES LEURION K (A JEAN SEBASTIAN LEMORNE B(B
PATRICE LEMORNE K (A MICHAEL SANTANGELLI D(A

R78B BOYD RICE R78B

BOYD RICE (A (A) BOYD RICE 1981 MUTE UK STUMM 4

R78C TONY RICE R78C

TONY RICE G B (A (A) GUITAR 197 REBEL US SLP 1582
J D CROWE BAN (A
LARRY RICE MAND (A BOBBY SLOAN FDL B(A

R79 RICH KIDS R79

GLEN MATLOCK B V (A (A) GHOSTS OF PRINCES IN TOWERS 1978 EMI UK EMC 3263
RUSTY EGAN D (A
MIDGE URE G V (A STEVE NEW G (A IAN McLAGAN PNO (A MICK RONSON PROD (A

R79A RICH MOUNTAIN TOWER R79A

DAVID CARR G (A (A) RICH MOUNTAIN TOWER 1970
SANDY GARRETT B V (A
DANA PAUL G K V(A BOB TUCCILLO D (A RANDY HASPEL G V (A LAMONTE OUSLEY CONGA(A
CHARLIE McCOY HCA (A WELDON MYRICK STEEL(A

R80 CLIFF RICHARD R80

CLIFF RICHARD(HARRY WEBB) V(ALL CLIFF 1959 COLUMBIA UK 33SX1147
HANK MARVIN G (CLIFF SINGS 1959 COLUMBIA UK 33SX1192
BRIAN BENNETT D (T CLIFF SINGS 19 ABC US ABC 321
BRUCE WELCH G V (ST ME & MY SHADOWS 1960 COLUMBIA UK SCX3330 33SX1261
TONY MEEHAN D (LISTEN TO CLIFF 1961 COLUMBIA UK SCX3375 33SX1320
IAN SAMWELL (LISTEN TO CLIFF 19 ABC US ABC 391
JET HARRIS B (THE YOUNG ONES 1961 COLUMBIA UK SCX3397 33SX1384
TERRY SMART (21 TODAY 1961 COLUMBIA UK SCX3409 33SX1368
JOHN ROSTILL B (32 MINUTES 17 SECONDS 1962 COLUMBIA UK SCX3436 33SX1431
ALAN TARNEY B PROD(TW CLIFFS HITS ALBUM 1962 COLUMBIA UK SCX1512
JOHN FARRAR G B (WHEN IN SPAIN 1963 COLUMBIA UK SCX3488 33SX1541
TERRY BRITTEN G (T IN SPAIN WITH THE SHADOWS 196 EPIC US 24115
GRAHAM TODD K (TZ SUMMER HOLIDAY 1963 COLUMBIA UK SCX3462 33SX1472
FRANK RICOTTI PERC (T SUMMER HOLIDAY 1963 EPIC US 24063
JOHN PERRY V (T WONDERFUL LIFE 1963 COLUMBIA UK SCX3515 33SX1628
RICHAR HURSON STR (T HIT ALBUM 1963 COLUMBIA UK 33SX1512
ROGER POPE D (T IT'S ALL IN THE GAME 19 EPIC US 26089
ALAN JONES B (T SWINGERS PARADISE 19 EPIC US 26145
MO WITHAM G (T ALADDIN & HIS WONDERFUL LAMP 1965 COLUMBIA UK SCX3522 33SX1676
ALAN HAWKSHAW K (T WONDERFUL TO BE YOUNG 19 DOT US 3474
TONY RIVERS V (T CLIFF RICHARD 1965 COLUMBIA UK SCX3546 33SX1709
CRAIG PRUESS K SYN(Z WHEN IN ROME 1965 COLUMBIA UK SX1762
NIGEL PERRIN V (Z MORE HITS 1965 COLUMBIA UK SCX3555 SX1737
MART JENNER G (Z LOVE IS FOREVER 1965 COLUMBIA UK SCX3569 SX1769
DAVE COOKE SYN (Z KINDA LATIN 1966 COLUMBIA UK SCX6039 SX6039
MEL COLLINS SAX (Z FINDERS KEEPERS 1966 COLUMBIA UK SCX6079 SX6079
JOHN CLARK G (Z CINDERELLA 1967 COLUMBIA UK SCX6103 SX6103
MO FOSTER B (Z DON'T STOP ME NOW 1967 COLUMBIA UK SCX6133
GRAHAM JARVIS D (Z GOOD NEWS 1967 COLUMBIA UK SCX6167
BILL ROBERTS G (Z CLIFF IN JAPAN 1968 COLUMBIA UK SCX6244 GER 05553
DAVE MATTACKS D (Z TWO A PENNY 1968 COLUMBIA UK SCX6262
MARK GRIFFITHS B (Z ESTABLISHED 1958 1968 COLUMBIA UK SCX6282
PAUL WESTWOOD B (Z BEST OF 1969 COLUMBIA UK SCX6343
ANDY PASK B (Z SINCERELY 1969 COLUMBIA UK SCX6357
IT'LL BE ME 1969 STARLINE UK 5011
ABOUT THAT MAN 1970 COLUMBIA UK SCX6408
ALL MY LOVE 1970 MFP UK 1420 GER RECORD CLUB68/9
LIVE AT THE TALK OF THE TOWN 1970 STARLINE UK 5031
TRACKS & GROOVES 1970 COLUMBIA UK SCX6435

(CONTINUED)

R80 CLIFF RICHARD (CONTINUED) R80

HIS LAND 1970 COLUMBIA UK SCX6443
BEST OF VOL 2 1972 COLUMBIA UK SCX6519
CLIFF & THE SHADOWS 197 ELECTROLA EURO 048 04318
HISTORY OF 1973 EMI IMP EURO 052 05019
TAKE ME HIGH 1973 EMI UK EMC3016
POWER TO ALL MY FRIENDS 1973 EMI IMP EURO 062 05355
EDITION 2000 19 CONTEMPORARY C2027/8
HELP IT ALONG 1974 EMI EMA 768
31ST OF FEBRUARY 1974 EMI EMC 3048
JAPAN TOUR 1974 1975 IRL IMP EMS67037
WHEN IN FRANCE 19 EMI BELG 06234
CLIFF RICHARD & THE SHADOWS 19 DIE VOLKSPLATTE GER 6084
HIER IST CLIFF 19 HOR ZU GER 261
FAMOUS POP GROUPS OF THE 60'S 19 MFP GER 05285/6
ICH TRAUME DEINE TRAUME 19 RECORD CLUB GER 27301/1
LIVE 1976 MFP UK MFP50307
(S)I'M NEARLY FAMOUS 1976 EMI UK EMC 3122
(S)I'M NEARLY FAMOUS 1976 ROCKET US 2210 RI 3004
(T)EVERY FACE TELLS A STORY 1977 EMI UK EMC 3172
(T)EVERY FACE TELLS A STORY 1977 ROCKET US 2268
MY KIND OF LIFE 1977 EMI UK EMI12584
40 GOLDEN GREATS 1977 EMI UK EMTVS 6
SMALL CORNERS 1978 EMI UK EMC 3219
GREEN LIGHT 1978 EMI UK EMC 3231
ROCK'N'ROLL JUVENILLE 1979 EMI UK EMC 3307
STARS OF R'N'R 1978 EMI EURO 052 04740
THANK YOU VERY MUCH 1979 EMI UK EMTV 151
20 ROCK'N'ROLL HITS 1979 EMI GER 07145
I'M NO HERO 1980 EMI UK EMA796 US 17039 NL 07342
WE DONT TALK ANYMORE 1980 EMI US 17018
WIRED FOR SOUND 1981 EMI UK EMC3377 GER 07541
LOVE SONGS 1981 EMI UK EMTV27
(Z) NOW YOU SEE ME ...NOW YOU DON'T 1982 EMI UK EMC3415

R80A DIGBY RICHARDS R80A

DIGBY RICHARDS G V (AB
RICHARD BENNETT G (A
TAFF WILLIAMS G (B
PETE KING STEEL(B ROGER BARA K (B KEVIN DUNN B (B MICKEY GIBBONS D PERC(B
ALAN LINDGREN K SYN(A JOE OSBORN B (A JIM GORDON D (A JIM KELTNER D (A
DENNIS CONWAY D (A

(A) DIGBY RICHARDS 1974 RCA US UPLI 0001
(B) WHISKEY SUNDOWN 1978 RCA UK PL 25154

R81 TURLEY RICHARDS R81

TURLEY RICHARDS V (ALL
LEE SKLAR B (B
DANNY KORTCHMAR G (B
BRYAN GAROFALO B (B
RUSS KUNKEL D (b
JIM HORN FLT (b MICK FLEETWOOD D (D KENNY MALONE D (D FARRELL MORRIS PERC(D
JACK WILLIAMS B (D BOB WELCH B (D DAVID BRIGGS K (D TOM SNOW K (D
JAY GRUSKA K (D SHANE KIESTER K SYN(D JOHN GOIN G (D REGIE YOUNG G (D
STEVE GIBSON G (D DANNY FERGUSON G (D PAUL WORLEY G (D TODD SHARP G (D
BILL JONES SAX (D ROGER WILLIAMS SAX (D MARIE TOMLINSON V (D CINDY RICHARDSON V (D
AVA ALDRIDGE V (D

(A) TURLEY RICHARDS 197 WB US 1870
(B) EXPRESSIONS 1971 WB US 1918 UK K46086
(C) WEST VIRGINIA SUPERSTAR 19 EPIC US 34306
(D) THERFU 1980 ATLANTIC US 19260

R82 DEL RICHARDSON R82

DEL RICHARDSON G B V(A
CHILI CHARLES D (A
REMI KABAKA PERC (A ROSETTA HIGHTOWER V (A JEAN ROUSSEL K (A ROGER BALL HRNS (A
DONNY PERKINS V (A ALAN SPENNER B (A MALCOLM DUNCAN HRNS (A

(A) A PIECES OF A JIGSAW 1973 MCA UK MUPS 491 +RI MCF 2513

R83 JONATHAN RICHMOND & THE MODERN LOVERS R83

JONATHAN RICHMAN G V (ALL
ERNIE BROOKS B (A
SKIP DUELKS V (E
JERRY HARRISON K V (A
DON GLADSTONE B (E
DAVID ROBINSON D V (AB
LEROY RADCLIFFE G V (BCDE
GREG KERANEN B V (BC
ASA BREBNER B (DE
D SHARPE D V (CDE
JOHN FELICE G (RALPH ANDERSON B (KENNY LAGUNA K (E ANDY PALEY G (E
STEVE TRACEY V (E

(A) MODERN LOVERS 1977 BESERKLEY US 0048 UK BSERK 1
(B) MODERN LOVERS 1977 BESERKLEY US 0050 UK BSERK 2
(B) MODERN LOVERS 19 BESERKLEY US 34755
(C) ROCK'N' ROLL WITH THE MODERN LOVER1977 BESERKLEY US 0053 UK BSERK 9
(C) ROCK'N' ROLL WITH THE MODERN LOVER1977 BESERKLEY US 34800
(D) MODERN LOVERS LIVE 1977 BESERKLEY US 055 UK BSERK12
(E) BACK IN YOUR LIFE 1979 BESERKLEY US 060 UK BSERK17
(F) BEST OF 1980 BESERKLEY UK BSERK 19
( ) THE ORIGINAL MODERN LOVERS 1981 BOMP BOM 1

R84 RICO R84

RICO RODRIGUES TROM (A
RAY ALLEN SAX (A
HERMAN MARQUIS SAX (A
SLY DUNBAR D (A
BUNNY McKENZIE B (A ROBBIE SHAKESPEARE B (A JACKO D (A DUGGIE RAD BRYAN G(A
KARL PITTERSON G K PERC(A JUNIOR HANSON MARVIN G (A LLOYD PARKS G (A PHIL CHEN G (A
TOUTER HARVEY K (A ANSEL COLLINS K (A TARZAN NELSON K (A TONY WASHINGTON K (A
SKULLY PERC (A TONY UTER PERC (A SATCH DIXON PERC (A FLICK PERC(A
CANDY McKENZIE V (A DICK CUTHELL HRNS (A VIV TALENT HALL TPT (A BOBBY ELLIS TPT(A
EDDIE THORNTON TPT (A DIRTY HARRY SAX (A GEORGE LEE SAX (A KEITH GEMMELL SAX(A

(A) MAN FROM WAREIKA 1977 ISLAND UK ILPS9485
(B) MIDNIGHT IN ETHIOPIA 1978 ISLAND UK ILPS9516
(C) THAT MAN IS FORWARD 1981 2 TONE UK TT 5005

R84A FRANK RICOTTI R84A

FRANK RICOTTI PERC SAX(A
CHRIS LAWRENCE B (A
CHRIS SPEDDING G (A BRYAN SPRING D (A

(A) OUR POINT OF VIEW 1969 CBS UK 52668

R85 RICOTTI & ALBUQUERQUE R85

FRANK RICOTTI (A
MICHAEL D'ALBUQUERQUE (A
JOHN TAYLOR K (A CHRIS LAWRENCE B (A TREVOR TOMKINS D (A MICHAEL KEEN TPT(A
HENRY LOWTHER TPT (A

(A) FIRST WIND 1971 PEGASUS UK PEG 2

R85A **BOB RIEDY BLUES BAND** R85A

BOB RIEDY PNO (A — (A) JUST OFF HALSTED — 1976 FLYING FISH US 006
JOHN REDA G (A — (B) LAKE MICHIGAN — 1977 ROUNDER US 2005
MIKE COGAN SAX (A
DAN DRAHER G (A MARK GASTON TPT (A BOB FALVEY B (A RICHARD ROBINSON D (A
CAREY BELL HARRINGTON HCA(A EDDY CLEARWATER V (A MIKE WILLENS SAX (A

R85B **RIDERS IN THE SKY** R85B

(A) THREE ON THE TRAIL — 1980 ROUNDER US 0102

R85C **WOLFGANG RIECHMANN** R85C

WOLFGANG RIECHMANN G K B(A — (A) WONDERBAR — 1978 SKY GER 017
HANS SCHWEISS D (A

R86 **RIFF RAFF** R86

AUREO DE SOUZA D (AB — (A) RIFF RAFF — 1973 RCA UK SF 8351
TOMMY EYRE K V (AB — (B) ORIGINAL MAN — 1974 RCA LPLI5023
PETE KIRTLEY G V (AB
ROGER SUTTON B V (AB BUD BEADLE SAX (AB JOE O'DONNELL VIOLA(B STEVE GREGORY WIND (B
JO NEWMAN V (B

R86A **RIFF RAFF (2)** R86A

MARK KAUFFMAN D (A — (A) VINYL FUTURE — 1981 ATLANTIC UK K50819 ATCO US 32108
WERNER FRITZSCHING G V(A — () COSMONAUT (EP) — 19 CHISWICK UK SW 34
DOUG LUBAHN B V (A
NED LIBER G V (A

R86B **RIGGS** R86B

JERRY RIGGS G V (A — (A) RIGGS — 1982 FULLMOON UK FMM3655
STEPHEN ROY CARLISLE D(A
DAVID RIDARICK B (A JEREMY GRAF K (A

R87 **RIGHTEOUS BROTHERS** R87

BOBBY HATFIELD V (ALL — RIGHT NOW — 1964 MOONGLOW US 1001 UK PYE NPL 28059
BILL MEDLEY V(ALL EXCEPT *? — SOME BLUE EYED SOUL — 1965 MOONGLOW US 1002 UK PYE NPL 28056
JIMMY WALKER V (* — THIS IS NEW — 1965 MOONGLOW US 1003
WITH — BEST OF THE RIGHTEOUS BROTHERS — 1966 MOONGLOW US 1004
DAVID PAICH K (S — YOU'VE LOST THAT LOVIN FEELIN' — 1965 PHILLES US 4007 UK LONDON HA 8226
TOM SELLERS K (S — JUST ONCE IN MY LIFE — 1965 PHILLES US 4008 UK LONDON HA 8245
DENNIS LAMBERT K PERC(S — (G)BACK TO BACK — 1966 PHILLES US 4009 UK LONDON HA 8278
DAVID HUNGATE B (S — (H)SOUL & INSPIRATION — 1966 VERVE US 65001 UK VERVE SVLP9131
DEAN PARKS G (S — GO AHEAD & CRY — 1966 VERVE US 65004 UK VERVE SVLP9140
ED GREENE D (S — IN ACTION — 1966 GNP US 2029 UK SUE ILP 937
GARY COLEMAN PERC (S — SAYIN' SOMETHIN' — 1967 VERVE US 65010 UK VERVE SVLP9168
BRIAN POTTER PERC (S — GREATEST HITS — 1967 VERVE US 5020 UK VERVE SVLP9183
CHUCK FINDLEY HRNS (S — GREATEST HITS — 197 VERVE UK RI 2352 018
PAUL HUBINON HRNS (S — GREATEST HITS VOL 2 — 1967 VERVE US 65071 UK SVLP9240
ERNIE WATTS SAX (S — GREATEST HITS VOL 2 — 1969 VERVE UK RI 2352 019
TOM SCOTT SAX (S — SOULED OUT — 1967 VERVE US 5031 UK SVLP9190
DON MENZA HRNS (S — STANDARDS — 1967 VERVE US 65051 UK SVLP9204
DICK HYDE TROM (S — ONE FOR THE ROAD — 1968 VERVE US 65058 UK SVLP9228
GINGER BLAKE V (S — (*)REBIRTH — 1970 VERVE US &5076 UK VERVE SVLP9249
JULIA TILLMAN V (S — RIGHTEOUS BROTHERS — 1970 MGM US 102
MAXINE WILLARD V (S — 2 BY 2 — 1973 POLYDOR UK 2683 033
CARLENA WILLIAMS V (S — GIVE IT TO THE PEOPLE — 1974 HAVEN US 9201 UK CAPITOL 9201
STRING SECTION (S — (S)SONS OF MRS RIGHTEOUS — 1975 HAVEN US 9203 UK CAPITOL 9203
MICHAEL PATTERSON K (H — PORTRAIT — 1975 POLYDOR UK 2348 119
BILL BAKER SAX (H — UNCHAINED MELODY — 1975 METRONOME 200 115
DREW JOHNSON D (H — HISTORY — 1977 MCM US 4885
ART MUSON G (H
JIM BOND B (H
DICK SHEARER TROM (H BILL KING TPT (H SANDFORD SKINNER TPT (H BOB FAUST TPT (H
BARNEY KESSEL G (G CAROL KAYE G (G DON PEAKE G (G DON RANDI K (G
LARRY KNECHTEL K (G HAROLD BATTISTE K (G MIKE RUBINI K (G LYLE RITZ B(G
JIMMY BOND B (G PAT SMITH B (G EARL PALMER D (G RITCHIE FROST D (G
FRANK CAPP PERC (G JULIUS WECHTER PERC (G GENE ESTES PERC (G JAY MIGLIORI HRNS(G
JIM HORN HRNS (G LOU BLACKBURN HRNS (G ROY CATON HRNS (G MIKE PATTERSON BAND (G
PHIL SPECTOR PROD (G

R88 **RIKKI & THE LAST DAYS OF EARTH** R88

RIKI SYLVAN (A — (A) FOUR MINUTE WARNING — 1978 DJM UK DJF 20526

R89 **BILLY LEE RILEY** R89

BILLY LEE RILEY (ALL — FUNK HARMONICA — 19 CRESCENDO US 2020
IN ACTION — 19 CRESCENDO US 2028
HARMONICA & THE BLUES — 19 CROWN US 5277
HARMONICA BEATLEMANIA — 19 MERCURY US SR60974
BIG HARMONICA SPECIAL — 19 MERCURY US SR60965
WHISKEY A GO GO PRESENTS — 19 MERCURY US SR60985
SOUTHERN SOUL — 19 MOJO US 1933
LEGENDARY SUN PERFORMER — 1978 CHARLY UK CR30131
SUN SOUNDS SPECIAL — 1978 CHARLY UK CR30151
(EP) BILLY LEE RILEY — 1977 CHARLY UK CEP 112

R89A **JIMMY RILEY** R89A

(A) TELL THE YOUTHS THE TRUTH — 19 TROJAN TRLS 167
(B) JIMMY RILEY EXPLOSIVE SHOW — 1978 BURNING SOUNDS BS 1011

R90 **TERRY RILEY** R90

TERRY RILEY K (ALL — (A) REED STREAMS — 1967 MASS,ART,INC US M131
JOHN CALE (D — (B) KEYBOARD STUDIES — 1969 BYG
DAVID BEHMAN PROD(E — (C) IN 'C' — 1970 CBS US 7178 UK 64565
(D) CHURCH OF ANTHRAX — 1971 CBS US 30131 UK 64259
(E) RAINBOW IN CURVED AIR — 1971 CBS US 7315 UK 64564
(F) PERSIAN SURGERY DERVISHES — 1972 SHANDAR 83501/2
( ) HAPPY ENDING — 1972 WB FR 46125
(G) LE SECRET DE LA VIE — 1975 PHILIPIS 9120 037
(H) SHRI CAMEL — 1980 CBS US 35164 73929

R91 LAURIN RINDER & W MICHAEL LEWIS R91

LAURIN RINDER D SAX(AB (A) SEVEN DEADLY SINS 1978 PYE UK NSPL28252
W MICHAEL LEWIS K SAX(AB (B) WARRIORS 1979 AVI US 6073
ADAM STRANGE G (B
DAVID TURNER G (B VENETTE GLOUD V (B AZAR LAWRENCE SAX (B JIMBO ROSS VLA (B
CARMEN TWILLIE V (B

R92 RING OF TRUTH R92

VICTOR BROX K V (A (A) 1970
ANNETTE BROX V (A
JIM KING SAX (A ANNIE MATTHEWS PNO (A GERRY FIELDS VLN (A FLOYD LAWSON B (A
RAY DRAPER V (A JOHN PEARSON D (A

R92A RINGS (US) R92A

BOB GIFFIRD B V (A (A) THE RINGS 1980 MCA US 5165
MARK SUTTON G (A (B) RHYTHM METHOD 1981 MCA
MIKE BAKER G (A
MATT THURBER D (A

R93 RINGS R93

TWINK D V (PAUL RUDOLPH G (SANDY ROBERTSON B (RUSSELL HUNTER D (

R93A RINKY DINK & THE CRYSTAL SETS R93A

ALLAN BLACK G (A (A) CAMEO ROLES 1975 HARVEST US 11438 UK SHSP4047
NIGEL WARD K V (A
JANE HUTCHINSON V (A BILL WARD D (A KEN COOK B (A GRAHAM BLYTH K (A
RON ASPERY SAX (A

R93B RIO GRANDE R93B

DAVID STANLEY G B V(A (A) RIO GRANDE 1971 RCA LSP 4454
RONNY'MOUSE'WEISS G V (A
TOM RUSSELL G B V(A BOBBY TUTTLE STEEL G V(A KEN MURRAY D (A DALE HAWKINS PROD(A

R94 RIOT R94

GUY SPERANZA V PERC(ABC (A) RIOT CITY 1978 ARIOLA ARL 5007
MARK REALE G V (ABC (B) NARITA 1979 CAPITOL US12081 +ATTIC 1067
PETER BITELLI D (AB (C) FIRE DOWN UNDER 1981 ELEKTRA UK K 52315
JIMMY IOMMI B (AB (D) RESTLESS BREED 1982 ELEKTRA UK K 52398
RICK VENTURA G (BC L A KOUVARIS G (A KIP LEMING B (C SANDY SLAVIN D (C

R95 RIOT ROCKERS R95

(A) RIOT ROCKERS 1978 CHARLY UK CR 30158

R96 RIOT SQUAD R96

MITCH MITCHELL ((A) 1965/67
JON LORD (
TERRY CLIFFORD (GRAHAM BONNET (DELL ROLL (ROGER CRISP (
BUTCH DAVIS (BOB EVANS (NERO (

R96A RIP CHORDS R96A

PHIL STEWART (B (A) HEY LITTLE COBRA 1964 CBS UK 8951
ARNIE MARKUS (B (B) THREE WINDOW COUPE 1965 CBS UK 9016
RICH ROTKIN (B
BERNIE BRINGAS (A BRUCE JOHNSON (B TERRY MELCHER (A

R96B RIP RIG & PANIC R96B

(A) GOD 1981 VIRGIN UK V2213

R97 MINNIE RIPPERTON R97

MINNIE RIPPERTON V ((A) COME TO MY GARDEN 19 JANUS US 7011 GRT US 30001
JOSE FELICIANO (E (B) PERFECT ANGEL 1974 EPIC US 32561 UK 80426
HUBERT LAWS FLT (EF (C) ADVENTURES IN PARADISE 1975 EPIC US 33454 UK 69142
TOM SCOTT SAX (EF (D) STAY IN LOVE 1977 EPIC US 34191 UK 81457
DAVID HUNGATE (E (E) MINNIE 1979 CAPITOL 11936
CHUCK RAINEY B (E (F) LOVE LIVES FOREVER 1980 CAPITOL 12097
PHIL UPCHURCH B (F
HARVEY MASON D (EF GERRY VINCI VLN (EF OSCAR NEVES (E CLAUDIO SLOAN (E
STEVE FORMAN (E ART PHILLIPS (E LARRY WILLIAMS HRNS (E KIM HUTCHCROFT HRNS(E
VICTOR FELDMAN PERC (E JERRY HEY HRNS (E ABE LABORIEL B (EF BILL REICHENBACH (E
MARLO HENDERSON (E LEON CHANCLER (E RANDY WALDMAN (E BUDDY COLLETTE (E
JEREMY LUBBOCK (E BILL GREEN (E PAULINHO DA COSTA PERC (EF SHERIDAN STOKES (E
HENRY GIBSON (E VINCE DE ROSA (E RICHARD PERISSI (E DAVID DUKE (E
LENNY CASTRO PERC (F GREG PHILLINGANES K (F PAUL JACKSON G (F LEE RITENOUR G (F
TENNYSON STEPHENS PNO (F GAYLE LEVANT HARP (F MAXINE WILLARD V (F ROBERTA FLACK V (F
JULIA TILLMAN V (F PEABO BRYSON V (F STEPHANIE SPRUILL V (F MICHAEL JACKSON V (F
MICHAEL BODDICKER SYN (F STEVIE WONDER HCA (F GEORGE BENSON V (F PATRICE RUSHEN V K(F

R97A RISERS (US) R97A

(A) SHE'S A BAD MOTORCYCLE 196 IMPERIAL US 12269

R98 RISING SONS R98

ED CASSIDY D (TAJ MAHAL V (RY COODER G (JESSIE ED DAVIS G (
JESSE LEE KINCADE PNO (KEVIN KELLEY D (GARY MARKER B (

R99 LEE RITENOUR R99

LEE RITENOUR G V SYN(ALL (A) FIRST CHOICE 1976 EPIC US 33847
PATRICE RUSHEN K (ABC (B) CAPTAIN FINGERS 1977 EPIC US 34426
DAVID GRUSIN SYN (ABCFGJ (C) CAPTAINS JOURNEY 1978 ELEKTRA UK K52094 US 136
STEVE GADD D (CF (D) GENTLE THOUGHTS 1978 JVC JAP VIDC1
DAVID NADIEN STRINGS (C (E) SUGAR LOAF EXPRESS 1978 JVC JAP VIDC2
ALEX ACUNA PERC (BCFG HJ (F) FEEL THE NIGHT 1979 ELEKTRA UK K52141 US 6E192
CARMEN TWILLIE V (C (G) FRIENDSHIP 1979 JVC JAP VIDC3
JOHNNY MANDEL STR (H ( ) THE BEST 1980 EPIC US 36527
DAVID FOSTER C (BCFH (H) RIT 1981 ELEKTRA UK K52273 US 6E331
LARRY WILLIAMS HRNS (F (J) RIO 1982 ELEKTRA UK K52350
SUE EVANS PERC (C
LOUIS JOHNSON B (AH PAULINHO DA COSTA PERC (CH RAY BECKENSTEIN FLT (C IAN UNDERWOOD SYN (ABFC
JAY GRAYDON G (BC BILL REICHENBACH HRNS (FH VENETTE GLOUD V (C STEVE THORNTON PERC(C
PATTI AUSTIN V (CF DAVE VALENTIN FLT (B ABRAHAM LABORIEL B(CFGHJ ANTHONY JACKSON B (BC
BILL CHAMPLIN V (BCH MITCH HOLDER G (BC ERNIE WATTS SAX(ABCFGJ TOM BAYLOR V (C
EDDY DANIELS FLT (C STEVE FORMAN PERC(BCFHJ JERRY STEINHOLTZ PERC (A JERRY PETERS K (A
LARRY NASH K (A MIKE OMARTIAN K (A CHUCK RAINEY B (A GREG PHILLINGANES K(H

(CONTINUED)

R99 (CONTINUED) **LEE RITENOUR** R99

ED GREENE D (A | TOM SCOTT SAX (A | JEROME RICHARDSON SAX (A | CHUCK FINDLEY TPT (AFH
FRANK ROSELINO TROM (A | DAWILLI GONGA K (B | DENNIS BUDIMIR G (B | RAY PARKER G (B
ALPHONSO JOHNSON B (B | BILL DICKINSON B (AB | CHARLES MEEKS B (B | MIKE PORCARO B (B
HARVEY MASON D (ABH | JEFF PORCARO D (BH | MIKE BODDICKER SYN (FH | VICTOR FELDMAN PERC(F
CHARLES LOPER HRNS (H | STEVE LUKATHER G (F | JOE SAMPLE PNO (F | TOM BAHLER V (F
JERRY HEY HRNS (FH | GARY GRANT HRNS (FH | LEW McCREARY HRNS (FH | GREG MATHIESON K (H
ERIC TAGG V (H | JOHN PIERCE B (H | RICHARD TEE K (H | DAVID HUNGATE B (H
RICK SHLOSSER D (H | MARCUS MILLER B (J | JEFF MIRANOV G (J | PAULINHO BRAGO D (J
OSCAR NEVES G (J | JOSE DA SILVA PERC (J | ARMANDO MARCAL PERC (J | BUDDY WILLIAMS D (J
RUBINS BASSINI PERC (J | LUIZAO MAIA B (J | CHICO BATERA PERC (J | ROBERTO PINHEIRO PERC(J
DON GRUSIN K (HJ

R100 **SCARLET RIVERA** R100

SCARLET RIVERA VLN (AB — (A) SCARLET RIVERA 1977 WB US 3060
KRISTIN PIMPINELLA V (A — (B) SCARLET FEVER 1978 WB US BSK3174
DOMINIC CARDINALE K (A

BERNARD PURDIE D (A | MIKE MAINIERI VIBES(A | GARY BURKE D (A | FRANCISCO SANTANA B (A
URBIE GREEN TROM (A | ED MIKENAS B (A | PAUL GRIFFIN K (A | PAUL PRESTOPINO MAND (A
LANI GROVES V (A | ULLANDA McCULLOUGH V (A | MICHELLE LEWIS V (A | JAMIE LEE V (A
REGGIE YOUNG G (A | VINNIE BELL G (A | ELLIOTT RANDALL G (A | CLARENCE CLEMONS SAX V(A
SREDNI VOLLNER HCA (A | DAVE SANBORN SAX (A | MICHAEL BRECKER SAX (A | RANDY BRECKER SAX (A
BURT COLLINS TPT (A | ARTIE KAPLAN WIND (A | VIVIAN CHERRY V (A | DEDE WASHBURN V (A
HELENE MILES V (A

R101 **JOHNNY RIVERS** R101

Musician			Album	Year	UK label	UK no.	US label	US no.
JOHNNY RIVERS	V	(ALL	AT THE WHISKY A GO GO	1964	LIBERTY	UK LBY3031	US IMPERIAL	12264
			AT THE WHISKY A GO GO	1970	SUNSET	UK 50157	US	5157
WITH			HERE WE GOGO AGAIN	1964	LIBERTY	UK LBY3036	US IMPERIAL	12274
JIM GORDON	D	(ABLMOP	IN ACTION	1965			US IMPERIAL	12280
JOE OSBORNE	B	(ABHMGP	BACK AT THE WHISKY	1965			US IMPERIAL	12284
LARRY KNECHTEL	PNO	(ABHGNSP	ROCKS THE FOLK	1965	LIBERTY	UK LBY3064	US IMPERIAL	12293
MICHAEL OMARTIAN	K V	(ABMOP	AND I KNOW YOU WANNA DANCE	1966			US IMPERIAL	12307
JIM WEBB	K STR	(AR	(C)CHANGES	1967	LIBERTY	UK LBY3087	US IMPERIAL	12334
JERRY ALLISON	D	(A	GOLDEN HITS	196			US IMPERIAL	12324
MICHAEL GEORGIADES	V	(ABMOPR	(G)REWIND	1967			US IMPERIAL	12341
HERB PEDERSEN	V	(ABLMOPR	REALIZATION	1969			US IMPERIAL	12372
KEITH ALLISON	B	(A	A TOUCH OF GOLD	1969	LIBERTY	UK 83141	US IMPERIAL	12427
DEAN PARKS	G	(ABLMOP	JOHN LEE HOOKER	1970	SUNSET	UK 50025		
LARRY CARLTON	G	(ABMP	(S) SLO SLIM SLIDER	19			US IMPERIAL	16001
BOBBYE HALL	PERC	(A	WILD NIGHT	1976	LIBERTY	UK 83383	US UA	LA486
GARY COLEMAN	PERC	(ABMOP	JOHNNY RIVERS	19			US UA	LA593
JIM HORN	SAX	(ABHLMSP	(A) LA REGGAE	1973	UA	UK 29298	US	LA5650
CHUCK FINDLEY	HRNS	(ABLMOP	(H) HOME GROWN	1973			US UA	LA5532
JACKIE KELSO	SAX	(ABMP	HISTORY OF	197	LIBERTY	UK 83461		
JACK CONRAD	B	(L	GO JOHNNY GO	19			UA UA	LA3386
MICHAEL MELVOIN	K	(LP	(B) BLUE SUEDE SHOES	1973	UA	UK 29473	US	LA 075
MICKEY JONES	D	(L	(L) LAST BOOGIE IN PARIS	1974	ATLANTIC	UK K50033		
JAMES HENDRICKS	V	(B	(R)ROAD	1974	ATLANTIC	UK K50063	US	7301
RON TUTT	D	(HS	(M) HELP ME RHONDA	1975	EPIC	UK 80987		
GLEN TOWNSEND	G	(H	(P)NEW LOVES AND OLD FRIENDS	1975	CBS	UK 80946	US	33681
RITA COOLIDGE	V	(H	(O) OUTSIDE HELP	1978	POLYDOR	UK 2310603	US SOULCITY	76004
CLYDIE KING	V	(H	MR TEENAGE	19			US SEARS	417
RON MICO DUQUETTE	G V	(H	SENSATIONAL	19			US CAPITOL	2161
CHARLES D HARRIS	V	(H	JOHNNY RIVERS	19			US PICKWICK	3191
MIKE DEASY	G V	(GH	VERY BEST OF	1975	UA		US	444
FRANK KINSEL	V	(H	SUPER PAK	1973	UA		UK UX593	
CHRIS ETHRIDGE	B	(H	SWINGING SHINDIG	19			US CORNET	246
VANETTA FIELDS	V	(H	20 GREATEST HITS	19			CAN TEEVEE	1062
KATHY DEASY	V	(H	BORROWED TIME	1980	RSO		US	13082
JIM KELTNER	D	(HO						
MICHAEL AMILIUS	V	(H						

JAMES BURTON G (HS | JERRY SCHEFF B (HS | WAYNE MINCY V HCA(H | TOMMY COE G V (H
MIKE SHANKLIN G V (H | GURU RAMDAS SINGERS (H | SCOTT EDWARDS B (MOP | GINGER BLAKE V (MOP
JULIA TILLMAN V (MOP | MAXINE WILLARD V (MOP | JOHN RAINES D (MP | JIM HUGHART B (MP
TAY UHLER G (MOP | BEN BENAY G (MP | TOM SCOTT SAX (MPO | BRIAN WILSON V (MP
MARK BOOKIN V (MRP | BARRY BOOKIN V (MP | TOM LEADON V (MP | ED GREENE D (MOP
BOB ALCIVER HRNS (S | MARTY PAICH HRNS (S | GARY ILLINGSWORTH PNO (S | JOE SAMPLE PNO(O
WAYNE BERRY G V (O | RICHARD CUOMO K (O | M L BENOIT PERC (O | LUTHER WATERS V (O
ORRIN WATERS V (O | JERRY JUMONVILLE HRNS (O | JOHN PHILLIPS HRNS (O | JOEL PESKIN HRNS(O
FRED TACKETT G (O | HAL BLAINE D (OGS | DAVID HUNGATE B (O | JON DOUGLAS HAYWOOD V(O
JAMES E HAAS V (O | DAVID KEMPER D (MP | NED DOHENY G (MP | DAVID T WALKER G (MP
JIM HELMER D (MP | SKIP EDWARDS K (MP | DUITCH HELMER V (MP | MARTY GWINN V (MP
PLAS JOHNSON SAX (MP | GARY HERBIG HRNS (O | GARY GRANT HRNS (O | MILT HOLLAND PERC(OR
MARC F LEVINE B (O | HARLAN ROGERS K (O | ROGER HAWKINS D (R | DAVID HOOD B (R
BARRY BECKETT G (R | PETE CARR G (R | JIMMY JOHNSON G (R | ERNIE FREEMAN SAX (R
JORDONAIRES V (R | MIKE LEECH B (R | JERRY CARRIGAN D (R | BOBE SEYMOUR STEEL(R
REGGIE YOUNG G (R | RON OATES K (R | JOHN REID G (R

R101A **RIVITS** R101A

JESS RODEN D V (A — (A) MULTIPLAY 1980 ISLAND UK ILPS9617 US ANTILLES7072
PETER WOOD K V (A
STEVE DWIRE B (A | DOANE PERRY D (A | LEE GOODALL SAX (A

R101B **RIVIERAS** R101B

BILL DOBSHAW V (A — (A) LET'S HAVE A PARTY 1964 ? US LP102
PAUL DENNERT D (A
OTTO NUSS ORG (A | DOUG GEAN B (A | JIM BOAL G (A | WILLIE GAUT G (A

R102 ROAD R102

JERRY HUDSON G V (AB — (A) ROAD — 1972 KAMA SUTRA US 2012 RAREEARTH3006
NOEL REDDING B V (A — (A) ROAD — 1972 NATURAL RESOURCES US 105
PHIL HUDSON V (AB — (B) COGNITION — 1973 KAMA SUTRA US 2032
JOE HESSE B (AB
NICK DISTEFANO D V (AB JIM HESSE K (AB RALPH PARKER G (A DON JAKE JAKUBOWSKI K(B
HUGH McCRACKEN G (B KEN KAUFMAN K (B RON BURRANO K (B DAN TURBEVILLE K (B
ROD RICHARDS G V (A LES SAMPSON D V (A

R102A ROADMASTER R102A

BOBBY JOHNS D (BAC — (A) SWEET WORLD — 1979 MERCURY US SRMI3760
RICK BENICK G (ABC — (B) FORTRESS — 1979 MERCURY US SRMI3814
STEPHEN McNALLY V (BCA — (C) HEY WORLD — 1979 MERCURY US SRMI3774
TOBY MYERS B (BCA
MICHAEL READ K (BCA

R102B ROAD HOME R102B

GREG SHANNON G (A — (A) PEACEFUL CHILDREN — 196 DUNHILL US 50104
WILLY SPROUSE K PERC V(A
DEE ARCHER V (A JIMMY SIMS D (A PETER WICKERSHAM V (A JIMMY HASKELL HRNS STR(A

R103 HARGUS ROBBINS R103

HARGUS 'PIG' ROBBINS PNO(ALL — (A) HARGUS ROBBINS — 1969 CHART US 1011
(B) COUNTRY INSTRUMENTALIST — 1977 ELEKTRA US 7E1110
(C) A PIG IN A POKE — 1978 ELEKTRA UK K52071 US 6E 129
(D) UNBREAKABLE HEARTS — 1979 ELEKTRA US 6E 185

R103A ROBBS R103A

JOE ROBB (A — (A) THE ROBBS — 1966 MERCURY 21130
BRUCE ROBB (A
CRAIG ROBB (A DEE ROBB (A

R104 TEX ROBERG BAND R104

TEX ROBERG V (A1 — (A) FIRST PRESSING — 1979 ARNIES SHACK UK AS 029
BRUCE ROBERTS G V (A1 — (1) 1979 SPRING
VERNON CHUTER G (A
DAVE NASH STEEL(A MICK WILLIAMS G (A BOB PHILLIPS B (A CHRIS BROWN G V (1
CHRIS PNO (A DAVE WARD HCA (1 BOB WILLIAMS B (1 PETE HUNT D (A1

R105 AL ROBERTS JR R105

AL ROBERTS JR (AB — (A) ROCKABILLY GUITAR MAN — 1978 FROG 001
(B) FROGABILLY — 1979 FROG 002

R106 ANDY ROBERTS R106

ANDY ROBERTS G V PERC FLT(ALL — (A) HOME GROWN — 1971 B&C CAS 1034 RCA UK SF 8086
IAN WHITEMAN K V (AB — (B) HOME GROWN(SOMR DIFF TRACKS) — 1971 AMPEX US 10120
JOHN PEARSON D (BCD — (C) ANDY ROBERTS WITH EVERYONE — 1971 B&C UK CAS1028 AMPEX US 10117
RAY WARLEIGH SAX (BD — (D) NINA & THE DREAM TREE — 1971 PEGASUS UK PEG5 PHILIPS 6303039
MIKE EVANS K V (AB — (E) URBAN COWBOY — 1973 ELEKTRA UK K42139
DAVE RICHARDS B V (ABCDE — (F) & THE GREAT STAMPEDE — 1973 ELEKTRA UK K42151
ROGER POWELL D V (ABD — (G) ANDY ROBERTS — 1973 CHARISMA UK CS6
GORDON HUNTLEY STEEL(AB
MAC KISSOON V (ABD MIKE LONDON V (ADD KATHY KISSOON V (ABD ZOOT MONEY K V (DEF
IAN MATTHEWS V (DE TIMI DONALD D (E BOB RONGA B V (E B J COLE STEEL (EF
DICK PARRY SAX (E RICHARD THOMPSON G (E NEIL INNES G (E JOHN MEGGINSON K (E
MIKE KELLIE D (E MARTIN CARTHY BANJO(E GILLIAN NOEL V (E PAUL KENT V (E
KARENE WALLACE V (E GERRY CONWAY D(ABDEF MICK KAMINSKI VLN (F PAT DONALDSON B (F
OLLIE HALSALL G (F SONNY FRANCIS K (F RAY WEHRSTEIN SAX (F BOB SARGEANT V G K HCA(C
JOHN PORTER G (C PAUL KRIWACZEK ORG (B CHARLENE COLLINS V (BD CAROL GRIMES V (BD

R107 BRUCE ROBERTS R107

BRUCE ROBERTS K V (A — (A) BRUCE ROBERTS — 1978 ELEKTRA US 7E119 UK K52061
DAVID FOSTER K (A — (B) COOL FOOL — 1980 ELEKTRA US 262
GRADY TATE D (A
JIM CREGAN G (A BOBBYE HALL PERC (A RON CARTER B (A JOHN JARVIS K (A
STEVE CROPPER G (A IAN UNDERWOOD K (A BROOKS HUNNICUTT V (A DONALD DUCK DUNN B(A
JEFF PORCARO D (A FRED TACKETT G (A TOMMY VIG PERC (A MIKE PORCARO B(A
BOB GLAUB B (A

R108 HOWARD ROBERTS R108

HOWARD ROBERTS G (ABCD — (A) THE REAL HOWARD ROBERTS — 19 CONCORD US 53
DAVE GRUSIN ORG (B — (B) ANTELOPE FREEWAY — 19 IMPULSE AS9207
MIKE WOFFORD PNO (D — (C) SOUNDS — 1974 CAPITOL 11247
JERRY SCHEFF B (D — (D) EQUINOX EXPRESS ELEVATOR — 1975 IMPULSE US 9299 IMPL 8004
JOHN GUERIN D (D
MAILTO CORREA PERC (D DIANA LEE V (D ED MICHAL SYN (D

R108A LAVADA JUNE ROBERTS R108A

LAVADA JUNE ROBERTS V PNO(A — (A) LAVADA — 1976 PYE 12126
RICHARD CROOKS D (A
WELDON MYRICK STEEL(A FRANK OWENS ORG (A DON PAYNE B (A PAUL PRESTOPINO G (A
BOB SYLVESTER CELLO(A

R109 RICK ROBERTS R109

RICK ROBERTS G V (ABC — (A) WINDMILLS — 1972 A&M UK AMLH64372 US SP 4372
DON HENLEY D V (A — (B) SHE IS A SONG — 1973 A&M US SP 4404
BERNIE LEADON G V (A — (C) BEST OF — 19 A&M US SP 4744
RANDY MEISNER B (A
JACKSON BROWNE V (A AL PERKINS STEEL(AB JOE LALA PERC (AB CHRIS HILLMAN B (A
DALLAS TAYLOR D (A DAVID CROSBY V (A JANE GETZ PNO V(A BYRON BERLINE FDL(A
LEE SKLAR B (A MIKE UTLEY ORG (A MARC BENNO G (A PAUL HARRIS K (B
GEORGE GRANTHAM D V (B KENNY PASSARELLI B (B JOE WALSH G (B JOE VITALE D (B
RUSTY YOUNG G (B STEVE FROMHOLZ B V (B

R110 B A ROBERTSON R110

BRIAN ALEXANDER ROBERTSON V(ABC — (A) WRINGING APPLAUSE — 1973 ARDENT US ADS 2804
GRAHAM JARVIS D (B — (B) INITIAL SUCCESS — 1980 ASYLUM UK K52216
ALAN JONES B (B — (C) BULLY FOR YOU — 1981 ASYLUM UK K52275
BILLY LIVSEY K (B — (D) R & BA — 1982 ASYLUM UK K52383
TERRY BRITTEN G (B

R111 ROBINS R111

BOBBY NUNN V ((A) ROCK'ROLL WITH ROBINS 1976 WHIPPETT US 703
TY TERRELL V ((B) THE BEST OF 1976 GNP CRESCENDO US 9034
ROY RICHARDS V (
BILLY RICHARDS V (GRADY CHAPMAN V (CARL GARDNER V (RICHARD BERRY V (
PETE LEWIS G (MARIO DELAGARDE B (JOHNNY OTIS D (DEVONIA WILLIAMS PNO(
LEARD BELL D (DON JOHNSON TPT (LEE GRAVES TPT (LORENCE HOLDEN SAX(
JAMES VON STREETER SAX (WALTER HENRY B (GEORGE WASHINGTON TROM (GIL BERNAL SAX(
MIKE STOLLER G (BARNEY KESSEL G (CHARLIE NORRIS G (RALPH HAMILTON B (
JESSE SAILES D (

R111A ROBEY, FALK & BOD R111A

BILL ROBEY G V (A (A) KENTUCKY GAMBLER 19 EPIC US 31796
DON FALK B G V(A
BOD NOUBARIAN G V (A KENNETH BUTTREY D (A WELDON MYRICK STEEL(A RICK POWELL SYN(A
BUD SPICHER FDL (A

R111B ANDY ROBINSON R111B

ANDY ROBINSON G V (A (A) PATTERNS OF REALITY 1968 PHILIPS 600289
ARTIE BUTLER K (A
LINCOLN MAYORGA K (A JIM GORDON D (A EARL PALMER D (A CAROL KAYE B (A
DAVID COHEN G (A DENNIS BUDIMIR G (A AL CASEY G (A KEN WATSON PERC (A
GENE ESTES PERC (A VICTOR FELDMAN PERC(A GARY COLEMAN PERC (A SID SHARP VLN (A
BILL NUTTYCOMBE VLN (A SAM BOGHOSSIAN VLA (A JESS EHRLICH CELLO(A

R111C ΩΩΩ ROBINSON CRUISER R111C

JAN HOLLESTELLE (A (A) CATCH A THRILL 1980 CBS UK 84600
HANS HOLLESTELLE (A
ROBIN LENT V (A TOMMY BACHMAN D (A

R112 FENTON ROBINSON R112

FENTON ROBINSON G V (ALL (A) SOMEBODY LOAN ME A DIME 197 SONET SNTF686 ALLIGATOR 4705 TRIO6218
STEVE DITZELL G (B (B) I HEAR SOME BLUES DOWNSTAIRS 1978 SONET SNTF712 ALLIGATOR 4710 TRIO6219
BILL HEID K (AB (C) & LARRY DAVIS 19 PYTHON FR PLP 24
LARRY EXUM B (B (D) MONDAY MORNING BOOGIE & BLUES1972 77 US 7200 UK 2001
EARL CROSSLEY SAX (B (E) GETAWAY 19 77 US 77 109
D BALDWIN SAX (A
ASHWARD GATES D (B BILL MACFARLAND TROM (AB BILL BRIMFIELD TPT (B LARRY DAVIS (C
MIGHTY JOE YOUNG G (A CORNELIUS BOYSON B (A TONY GOODEN D (A NORVAL D HODGES TPT(A
ELMER BROWN JR TPT (A

R113 FREDDY ROBINSON R113

FREDDY ROBINSON G V (AB (A) AT THE DRIVE IN 19 POLYDOR UK 2325 085 US ENTERPRISE1025
AL VESOVO G (A (B) BLACK FOX 19 PACIFIC JAZZ 20162
HARVEY MASON D (A (C) HOT FUN SUMMERTIME 197 PACIFIC JAZZ 20176
PAUL HUMPHREY D (A
JOE SAMPLE K (A WILTON FELDER B (A MONK HIGGINS ORG (A BOBBYE HALL PERC(A
CLYDIE KING V (B

R114 L C ROBINSON R114

L C ROBINSON G V VLN STEEL(AB (A) UPS & DOWNS 1972 ARHOOLIE US 1062
JAMES MADISON G (A (B) HOUSE CLEANING BLUES 1974 BLUESWAY US BLS 6082
SAMUEL LAWHORN G (A
CALVIN JONES B (A WILLIE SMITH D (A JOE'PINETOP'PERKINS PNO(A CHARLIE MUSSELWHITE HCA(A
DAVID ALEXANDER PNO (A WILLIAM HYATT B (A TEDDY WINSTON D (A KEN SWANK D (B
ROBERT HOOKER PNO (B LEX BOYD SILVA B (B LUTHER TUCKER G (B

R115 SMOKEY ROBINSON & THE MIRACLES R115

SMOKEY ROBINSON V(ALL EXCEPT ** HI WE'RE THE MIRACLES 1961 TAMLA US 220
WILLIAM GRIFFIN V (** COOKIN' WITH THE MIRACLES 196 TAMLA US 223
WAH WAH WATSON G (ZS SHOP AROUND 1962 TAMLA US 224
RICHARD LITTLEFIELD G (Z I'LL TRY SOMETHING NEW 196 TAMLA US 230
MARLO HENDERSEN G (SZ CHRISTMAS WITH THE MIRACLES 196 TAMLA US 236
DAVID T WALKER G (SZ FABULOUS MIRACLES 1964 TAMLA UK STML11003 US 238
PHIL UPCHURCH G (S MIRACLES ON STAGE 1964 TAMLA UK STML10055 US 241
MARV TARPIN D (STZ DOIN' MICKEY'S MONKEY 1963 TAMLA US 245
JAMES GADSON D (SZ TEARS OF A CLOWN 196 TAMLA US 246
ED GREENE D (Z I LIKE IT LIKE THAT 196 TAMLA UK TML11003
SCOTTIE HARRIS D (ZS GREATEST HITS 196 TAMLA UK STML11072 US 254
JOSEPH A BROWN D (T THE FABULOUS MIRACLES 1964 STATESIDE UK SL 10099
CHUCK RAINEY B (Z GOING TO A GO GO 1964 TAMLA UK STML11024 US 267
KENNETH BURKE B (S MIRACLES FROM THE BEGINNING 1965 TAMLA UK TML11031
JAMES JAMESON B (Z AWAY WE GO GO 1965 TAMLA UK STML11044 US 271
WAYNE TWEED B (STZ MAKE IT HAPPEN 1968 TAMLA UK STML11067 US 276
DAVID SHIELDS B (Z GREATEST HITS VOL 2 196 TAMLA UK STML11233 US 280
SCOTT EDWARDS B (STZ LIVE 1969 TAMLA UK STML11107 US 289
SONNY BURKE K (ZST SPECIAL OCCASION 1969 TAMLA UK STML11089 US 290
SYLVESTER RIVERS K (Z TIME OUT 1970 TAMLA UK STML11129 US 295
MICHAEL B SUTTON K (Z FOUR IN BLUE 1970 TAMLA UK STML11151 US 297
JOHN BARNES K (Z WHAT LOVE HAS JOINED TOGETHER 1970 TAMLA US 301
RODERICK RANCIFER K (S POCKETFUL OF MIRACLES 197 TAMLA US 306
RONNIE McNEIR K (Z ONE DOZEN ROSES 197 TAMLA US 312
BOB SMITTY VIBES(Z FLYING HIGH TOGETHER 197 TAMLA US 318
FRED SMITH WIND (STZ SMOKEY & THE MIRACLES 1971 TAMLA UK STML11172
PATRICIA HENLEY V (ZT 1957/1972 1973 TAMLA UK STMA 8008 US 320
CLAUDETTE ROBINSON V (ZS (**) RENAISSANCE 1973 TAMLA UK STMA 8010
JESSIE RICHARDSON V (Z SMOKEY 1973 TAMLA UK STMG 8012 US 328
JAMES BRADFORD PNO (Z ANTHOLOGY 1974 TAMLA 793
JAMES SLEDGE CONGA(ZST PURE SMOKEY 1974 TAMLA UK STML11265 US 331
PAULINHO DA COSTA PERC (Z (**) DO IT BABY 1974 TAMLA UK STML11276 US 334
IVORY DAVIS V (ZST QUIET STORM 1974 TAMLA UK STML11288 US 337
CAROLYN DENNIS V (Z (**) CITY OF ANGELS 1974 TAMLA UK STML12010 US 339
MELBA JOYCE V (T LOVE MACHINE 1975 TAMLA UK STML12020
MELBA BRADFORD V (Z (T)SMOKEYS FAMILY ROBINSON 1975 TAMLA UK STML12021 US 341
FREDRICK ROCHE K (Z (**) POWER OF THE MUSIC 1975 TAMLA UK STML12038
MICHAEL JACOBSEN CELLO(ZT DEEP IN MY SOUL 1977 TAMLA UK STML12055 US 350
ROBERT ZIMMITTI PERC (Z BIG TIME(SOUNDTRACK) 1977 TAMLA UK STML12068 US 355
CHERYL COOPER V (ZS (**) LOVE CRAZY 1977 CBS UK 81696 US 34450
(CONTINUED

R115 SMOKEY ROBINSON & THE MIRACLES R115

PAT TALBERT V (S — (**) MIRACLES — 1977 CBS US 34910
STEVIE WONDER PROD (S — SMOKEY'S WORLD — 1978 TAMLA UK STML12076
BRENDA SUTTON V (Z — (Z) LOVE BREEZE — 1978 TAMLA UK STML12081 US 359
RONNIE WHITE V (— SMOKIN' (LIVE) — 1978 TAMLA US 363
BOBBY ROGERS V (— WHERE THERES SMOKEY — 1979 TAMLA UK STML12115 US 366
PETE MOORE V (— TEARS OF A CLOWN — 19 PICKWICK US 3389
MARV TAMPLIN G (— FROM THE BEGINNING — 19 BELL US 1063
TEARS OF A CLOWN — 1979 MFP UK 50422
(S) WARM THOUGHTS — 1980 TAMLA UK STML12134 US 367
BEING WITH YOU — 1981 MOTOWN UK STML12151 US 375
YES ITS YOU LADY — 1981 TAMLA US6001
SHOP AROUND — 19 LONDON US 1295
PURE SMOKEY — 1982 TAMLA UK STMS 5043 RI
QUIET STORM — 1982 TAMLA UK STMS 504$ RI

R116 TOM ROBINSON BAND R116

TOM ROBINSON B V (ALL — (A) POWER IN THE DARKNESS — 1978 EMI EMC 3226 CAPITOL US 11778
DEREK QUINTON PERC (C — (A) POWER IN THE DARKNESS — 1978 EMI EURO 06687
DANNY KUSTOW G V (AB1 — (B) TRB2 — 1979 EMI EMC 3296 HARVEST US 11930
STEVE B G (C — (B) TRB2 — 1979 EMI EURO 06977
DOLPHIN TAYLOR D V (A1 — (C) SECTOR 27 — 1980 FONTANA 6359 039
JO BURT B (C — (C) SECTOR 27 — 1980 MERCURY 6359 039
MARK AMBLER K (A — (1) MAY 1978
NICK PLYTAS K (1 — ( ) TOM ROBINSON BAND — 1982 FAME UK FA 3028
IAN 'QUINCE' PARKER K V(B — PRESTON HEYMAN D V (B — KASIM SULTON V (B — CAROL GRIMES V (B
BARRY ST JOHN V (B — NIAMH CHAMBERS V (B

R117 VICKI SUE ROBINSON R117

VICKI SUE ROBINSON V (ABC — (A) NEVER GONNA LET YOU GO — 1976 RCA UK RS 1051 US APLI 1256
(B) VICKI SUE ROBINSON — 1976 RCA UK RS 1095 US APLI 1829
(C) HALF & HALF — 1978 RCA UK PL12294 US APLI 2294

R117A MAGGIE & TERRE ROCHE R117A

MAGGIE ROCHE V G (A — (A) SEDUCTIVE REASONING — 1975 CBS US 33232
TERRE ROCHE G V (A
BARRY BECKETT K (A — PETE CARR G (A — JOHNNY GIMBLE FDL (A — JOHN HALL G (A
ROGER HAWKINS D (A — DAVID HOOD B (A — JIMMY JOHNSON G (A — GEORGE MARGE CLAR(A
JERRY MASTERS B (A — OAK RIDGE BOYS V (A — PAUL SIMON G (A

R118 THE ROCHES R118

SUZZY ROCHE G V (AB — (A) THE ROCHES — 1979 WB GER 56683 US 3298
MAGGIE ROCHE SYN G V (AB — (B) NURDS — 1980 WB UK K56855 US 3475
TERRE ROCHE G V (AB
ROBERT FRIPP G (A — TONY LEVIN B (A — JIM MAELEN PERC (A — LARRY FAST SYN (A
JAY DEE DAUGHERTY D (B — FRED SMITH B (B — LINCOLN GOINES B (B — JON MATHIAS B (B
GABRIEL KATONA SYN (B — BOB CONTI PERC (B — BOBBY GORDON (B

R118A ROCCO R118A

RUSSELL DUNLOP D (A — (A) ROCCO — 1976 20TH CENTURY US T505
TIM PARTRIDGE B (A
LEO DE CASTRO V (A — HARRIS CAMPBELL G V (A — SUNIL DE SILVA PERC (A — TONY ANSELL K (A
SPOONS BUCHANAN SAX (A — MICK KENNY SYN (A — MARK PUNCH G (A — RALPH WHITE HRNS(A
TUI RICHARDS G (A

R119 ROCK'N'ROLL ALL STARS R119

(A) RED CHINA ROCKS — 1972 B+C BCM 104

R120 ROCK FOLLIES(TV SHOW) R120

JULIE COVINGTON V (AB — (A) ROCK FOLLIES — 1976 ISLAND ILPS 9362 POLYDOR 2302054
CHARLOTTE CORNWELL V (AB — (B) ROCK FOLLIES 77 — 1977 POLYDOR 2302072 GER 2344 067
RULA LENSKA V (AB
SUE JONES DAVIS V (B — RAY RUSSELL G (AD — ANDY MACKAY SAX (AB — TONY STEVENS B (AB
CHRIS PARREN K (B — PETER VAN HOOKE D (AB — BRIAN CHATTON K (A — ROBIN WILLIAMS VLN(A
SADIE MACKENZIE V (A

R121 ROCK HOUSE R121

MARTIN STONE G (— (A) ROCK HOUSE (EP) — 1979 LIMP KOOL1
PETE SHELLEY D (
KEITH TILLMAN B (— DAVID COXHILL SAX (— MICK O'NEAL SAX (

R121A ROCK ROSE R121A

CHRIS BARR K V (A — (A) ROCK ROSE — 1979 CBS US 35819
JACK D'AMORE D (A
FRANK DEMME B V (A — CARL JOHNSON G (A

R122 ROCK WORKSHOP R122

HARRY BECKETT HRNS (AB — (A) ROCK WORKSHOP — 1970 CBS UK 64075
BUD PARKES HRNS (AB — (B) THE VERY LAST TIME — 1971 CBS UK 64394
TONY ROBERTS WIND (AB
BOB DOWNES WIND (AB — DEREK WADSWORTH TROM (AB — ROBIN JONES D (A — BRIAN MILLER K (AB
PHIL WAINMAN PERC (B — ALAN RUSHTON D (AB — DARYL RUNSWICK B (AB — RAY RUSSELL G (AB
ALAN GREED K V (AB — GINGER HARPER V (B — ALEX HARVEY V (A — TONY UTER PERC(B

R122A ROCKET 88 R122A

ALEXIS KORNER G V (A — (A) ROCKET 88 — 1981² ATLANTIC US SD19293 UK K50776
JACK BRUCE B (A
CHARLIE WATTS D (A — IAN STEWART PNO (A — BOB HALL PNO (A — DON WELLER SAX (A
GEORGE GREEN PNO (A — COLIN SMITH TPT (A — JOHN RICARD TROM (A

R123 ROCKETS (US) R123

DAVID GILBERT V (ABCDE — (A) LOVE TRANSFUSION — 1977 RCA US/UK PL 12572
JIM McCARTY G V (ABCDE — (B) ROCKETS — 1979 RSO US 3047 UK 2394 224
JOHN BADANJEK D V (ABCDE — (C) NO BALLADS — 1980 RSO US 3071 UK 2394 250
DENNIS ROBBINS G V (ABCD — (D) BACK TALK — 1981 ELEKTRA US 6E351 UK K52309
JOHN FRAGA B (AB — (E) ROCKET ROLL — 1982 ELEKTRA US 60143
DONNIE DACUS PNO V(BCDE
DAVID HOOD B (B — CHUCK LEAVELL K (BANITA POINTER V (C — RUTH POINTER V(C
LEE MICHAELS ORG (C — DAN KRYLA B (C — BOBBY HARALSON B (DE — JACK DOUGLAS PERC(D
JIMMY Z HCA (D

R123A ROCKETS(60s) R123A

DANNY WHITTEN G V (A (A) ROCKETS 1968 WHITEWHALE US WWS7116
LEON WHITSELL G V (A
GEORGE WHITSELL G (A RALPH MOLINA D (A BILLY TALBOT B (A BOBBY NOTKOFF VLN (A

R123B ROCKETS (FRANCE) R123B

CHRISTIAN LEBARTZ V (B (A) ROCKETS 19 DORBY DBR 20005
ALAIN GROETZINGER D (B (B) ON THE ROAD AGAIN 1978 DORBY 20014 IPG FR 170/008
GERARD L'HER B V (B (C) PLASTEROID 19 ROCKLAND RKL 20137
ALAIN MARATRAT G K V(B (D) LIVE 19 ROCKLAND RKL 20197
FABRICE QUAGLIOTTI K (B (E) GALAXY 1980 ROCKLAND RKL 20208
ZEUS B HELD V (B

R124 ROCKIN' BERRIES R124

ROY AUSTIN (IN TOWN 1964 PICCADILLY NPL 38013
TERRY BOND (* LIFE IS JUST A BOWL OF BERRIES 1965 PICCADILLY NPL 38022
CHUCK BOTFIELD (* EP I DIDN'T MEAN TO HURT YOU 1964 PICCADILLY NEP 34639
CLIVE LEA (EP NEW FROM THE ROCKIN' BERRIES 1965 PICCADILLY NEP 34043
GEOFF TURTON ((*) BLACK GOLD 1976 SATRIL SATL 4002
KEN RODWAY (
BOBBY THOMPSON (* TERRY WEBSTER G V (* HENRY HADAWAY PROD (*

R124A ROCKIN' DOPSIE & THE CAJUN TWISTERS R124A

ROCKIN' DOPSIE RUBIN V ACC(ALL (A) DOIN' THE ZYDECO 1976 SONET UK SNTF 718
CHESTER ZENO PERC (ABCD (B) ZY DE BLUE 1977 SONET UK SNTF 761
MAJOR HANDY HARRIS G (ABCD (C) HOLD ON! 1979 SONET UK SNTF 800
AUGUST CHARLES SAX (AB (D) BIG BAD ZYDECO 1980 SONET UK SNTF 851
JOSEPH EDWARDS D (ABC
MORRIS FRANCES B V (ABCD JOHN PARKER HART SAX (CD ALTON RUBIN D (D

R124C ROCKIN' LOUIE & THE MAMMA JAMMERS R124C

(A) IT WILL STAND 19 CHARLY CR 30185

R124D ROCKIN' FOO R124D

WAYNE ERWIN G (A (A) A ROCKIN' FOO 1971 HOBBIT 5001
LESTER BROWN D (A
MICHAEL RACOON PNO (A

R124E ROCKIN' JIMMY & THE BROTHERS OF THE NIGHT R124E

'ROCKIN' JIM BYFIELD G V (A (A) BY THE LIGHT OF THE MOON 1981 SONET UK SNTF 857
STEVE HICKERSON G (A
CHUCK DEWALT D (A GARY GILMORE B (A WALT RICHMOND K (A DEBBIE CAMPBELL V (A
JIM SWENEY V (A

R124F ROCKSPUR R124F

RICH TANNUM B V (A (A) ROCKSPUR 1978 DJM 15
MICHAEL FESTA G STEEL K(AB (B) GETTING OFF 1979 DJM GER 64223
MICK MORAN G V K(AB
PETER BRILLON D (AB GREG HOLLISTER B V (B

R125 JESS RODEN R125

JESS RODEN V (ALL (A) JESS RODEN 1974 ISLAND UK ILPS 9286
ALLEN TOUSSAINT PNO (A (B) YOU CAN KEEP YOUR HAT ON 1976 ISLAND UK ILPS 9349
ART NEVILLE ORG (A (C) PLAY IT DIRTY PLAY IT CLASS 1977 ISLAND UK ILPS 9442
JOESEPH MODELISTE D (A (D) BLOWIN' 1977 ISLAND UK ILPS 9496
GEORGE PORTER B (A (E) PLAYER NOT THE GAME 1977 ISLAND UK ILPS 9506
LEO NOCENTELLI G (A (F) STONECHASER 1980 ISLAND UK ILPS 9531
NEW ORLEANS HRNS (A (EP) LIVE 1976 ISLAND UK IEP 3
SIMON KIRKE D (A
JOHN BUNDRICK K (A RICHARD BAILEY D (A MICK FEAT B (A ROY DAVIES K (A
GEORGE LEE SAX (A ALLAN SHARP CONGA (A STEVE GREGORY FLT (A RICHARD DIGA SMITH K(A
REBOP KWAKU BAAH PERC (A MICK WEAVER K (A PAT DONALDSON B (A STEVE WEBB G V(ABCD
BRUCE ROBERTS G V (BCD CHRIS GOWER TROM (BCD RONNIE TAYLOR SAX (BCD JOHN CARTWRIGHT B G (BCDF
PETE HUNT D (BCD BILLY LIVSEY K (BCD LEON PENDARVIS K (EF ROB MOUNSEY K (EF
SHIRLEY SCOTT K (E ANTHONY JACKSON B (EF FRANCISCO CENTENO B (E MILT HINTON B (E
CLIFFORD MORRIS G (EF JOHN TROPEA G (E LANCE QUINN G (E JEFF MIRONOV G (EF
FRANKLIN MICARE G (E GARY MURE D (E BUDDY WILLIAMS D (E ERROL BENNETT PERC(EF
RUBENS BASSINI PERC (E DAVID CAREY VIBES(EF SCOTT HAMILTON SAX (E BARRY ROGERS HRNS(F
MICHAEL LEE GRAY V (E DOLORES HALL V (E BENNY DIGGS V (E ARNOLD McCULLER V (E
LOU MARINI WIND (E RAYMOND BECKENSTEIN WIND(EF GEORGE MARGE HRNS (E ALAN RUBIN HRNS(E
JON FADDIS HRNS (E VIRGIL JONES HRNS (EF BURT COLLINS HRNS (E MICHAEL LAWRENCE HRNS(E
VICTOR PAZ HRNS (E ALAN RAPH TROM (EF TOM MALONE TROM (E WAYNE ANDRE TROM(EF
HOWARD JOHNSON WIND (EF STRING SECTION (EF PAT REBILLOT K (F GEORGE T CLINTON K (F
JEFF LAYTON G (F DAVE TAYLOR HRNS (F DAVID LANDALL G (F JAKI WHITREN V (F
JANICE PENDARVIS V (F LUTHER VANDROSS V (F JOSHIE ARMSTEAD V (F PAT RYAN SAX (F
DAVE TOFANI WIND (F HAROLD VICK WIND (FE ALEX FOSTER WIND (F BILLY SLAPIN WIND(F
ROMEO PENQUE WIND (F CHRIS PARKER D (F RICHARD CROOKS D (F PETER BUNETTA D (F
NEIL BUNETTA D (F RICK CHUDAKOFF B (F ARNO LUCAS PERC(F CHANDRA ARMSTEAD V (F
ZACHARY SANDERS V (F BARBARA MASSEY V (F LEE GOODALL CLAR(F LEW SOLOFF HRNS (F
ALLAN TOUSSAINT PROD (A CHRIS BLACKWELL PROD (A

R125A THE RODS R125A

DAVID FEINSREIN G V (AB (A) THE RODS 1981 ARISTA UK SPART1182 US 9558
GARRY BORDONARO B V (AB (B) WILD DOGS 1982 ARISTA UK SPART1196
CARL CANEDY D (AB

R126 TOMMY ROE R126

Musician	Instr	Albums	Title	Year	Label	Country	No.
TOMMY ROE	G V	(ALL	SHEILA	1963	ABC	US	ABC432
JACK SARGENT	D	(*	SOMETHING FOR EVERYBODY	1963	ABC	US	ABC467
HAL BLAINE	D	(*	SWEET PEA	1966	ABC	US	ABC575
JOE OSBORN	B	(*	ITS NOW A WINTERS DAY	196	ABC	US	ABC594
KEITH ALLISON	B	(*	PHANTASY	1967	ABC	US	ABC610
RICHARD LAWS	G	(*	DIZZY	196	ABC	US	ABC683
MAXINE WILLARD	V	(*	12 IN A ROE	1970	ABC	US	ABC700
BEN BENAY	G	(*	WE CAN MAKE MUSIC	1970	ABC	US	ABC714
LARRY KNECHTEL	K	(*	GREATEST HITS	1970	STATESIDE	UK	SSL10296
DON RANDI	PNO	(*	(*) BEGINNINGS	1971	ABC	US	ABC732
DAVE BOONE	FDL	(*	16 GREATEST HITS	1971	ABC UK ABCL5157	US	ABC762
PLAS JOHNSON	SAX	(*	ENERGY	1976	MONUMENT US 34182		MG 7604
GINGER BLAKE	V	(*	FULL BLOOM	1978	MONUMENT	US	MG 7614
JULIA TILLMAN	V	(*					

R127 JOACHIM ROEDELIUS R127

Musician	Instr	Albums	Title	Year	Label	Country	No.
HANS JOACHIM ROEDELIUS	K SYN V	(ALL	(A) DURCH DIE WUSTE	1978	SKY		SKY014
SCHAGZERIG GREENE	CELLO	(B	(B) JARDIN AU FOU	1979	BARCLAY		90291
CONRAD PLANK	PERC G	(CA	(C) SELBSTPORTRAIT	1979	SKY	GER	028
JASO CHRISTO	G B	(CA	(D) SELBSTPORTRAIT II	1980	SKY	GER	SKY040
DIETER MOEBIUS	SYN	(CA	(E) SELBSTPORTRAIT III	1980	SKY	GER	SKY044
WOLFGANG DIUMSHEDE	FLT	(B	(F) LUSTWANDEL	1981	SKY		SKY058
ULRIKE LAI	CELLO	(B	(G) WENN DER SUDWIND WEHT	1981	SKY	GER	SKY064
HANS BRANDEIS	G	(B	(H) OFFENE TUREN	1982	SKY	GER	SKY072

R127A KENNY ROGERS(& THE FIRST EDITION) R127A

Musician	Instr	Albums	Title	Year	Label	Country	No.
KENNY ROGERS	V	(ALL	(A) ROLLIN	196	JOLLY ROGER	US	5003
TERRY WILLIAMS	G	(	(B) MONUMENTAL	196	JOLLY ROGER	US	5004
MIKE SETTLE	G	(	(C) THE FIRST EDITION	1968	REPRISE	US	6276
THELMA CAMACHO	V	(	(D) THE SECOND EDITION	1969	REPRISE	US	6328
MARY ARNOLD	V	(	(E) RUBY DONT TAKE YOUR LOVE TO TOWN	196	REPRISE	US	6352 UK K44075
KIM VASSY	G B K	(	(F) SOMETHINGS BURNIN'	1979	REPRISE	US	6385
MICKEY JONES	D	(	(G) TELL IT ALL BROTHER	1972	REPRISE	US	6414
BOB MOORE	B	MQ	(H) BALLAD OF CALICO	1972	REPRISE	US	6426
DENNIS WILSON	B V	(MR	(I) TRANSITION	1972	REPRISE	US	2039
TOMMY ALLSUP	B	(M	(J) DAY TIME FRIENDS	1977	UA	UK	UAG 30256
BILLY SANFORD	G	(MQR	(K) EVERYTIME 2 FOOLS COLLIDE	1978	UA	UK	UAS 30170
RAY EDENTON	G	(MQ	(L) LOVE OR SOMETHING LIKE IT	1978	UA	UK	UAG 30194
JIMMY CAPPS	G	(MQ	(M) THE GAMBLER	1978	UA US 934	UK	UAG 30220
RANDY DORMAN	G V	(MQR	(N) SINGLES ALBUM	1979	UA	UK	UAK 30263
JERRY SHOOK	G	(MQ	(O) CLASSICS	1979	UA	UK	UAG 30235
RICK HARPER	G	(MQ	(P) SHINE ON	1980	RADAR	UK	K24037
TONY JOE WHITE	G	(M	(Q) KENNY	1980	UA US 979	UK	UAG 30273
REGGIE YOUNG	G	(MQ	(R) GIDEON	1980	UA US 1035	UK	UAK 30303
HARGUS ROBBINS	K	(MQ	(S) LOVE LIFTED ME	1980	LIBERTY	UK	LBR 1015
GENE GOLDEN	K V	(MQR	(T) RUBY	1981	MFP	UK	50514
STEVE GLASSMEYER	K SAX V	(MQR	(U) SHARE YOUR LOVE	1981	LIBERTY	UK	30339
THOMAS CAIN	K	(M	(V) LADY	1981	LIBERTY	UK	LBC 30334
JERRY CARRIGAN	D	(MQR					

Musician	Instr	Albums	Musician	Instr	Albums	Musician	Instr	Albums	Musician	Instr	Albums
BOBBY DANIELS	D V	(MQR	BYRON METCALF	D	(M	EDDY ANDERSON	D	(M	PETE DRAKE	STEEL	(M
EDGAR STRUBLE	SYN V	(M	JORDONAIRES	V	(M	MICKEY NEWBURY	V	(M	BILL MEDLEY	V	(M
CHUCK JACOBS	B	(QR	JOE OSBORNE	B	(Q	DAVID BRIGGS	K	(Q	LARRY KEITH	K	(Q
CHUCK COCHRAN	K	(Q	SHANE KEISTER	K	(Q	BOBBY WOOD	K	(Q	DAVE KIRBY	G	(Q
JOHNNY CHRISTOPHER	G	(Q	BOBBY THOMPSON	BAN	(Q	FARRELL MORRIS	PERC	(Q	LEA JANE BERINATI	V	(QR
DONNA McELROY	V	(Q	YVONNE HODGES	V	(Q	BUZZ CASON	V	(QR	TOM BRANNON	V	(Q
BERGEN WHITE	V	(Q	DON GANT	V	(Q	KIM CARNES	V	(RV	WILLIAM CUOMO	K	(R
LARRY BUTLER	K	(R	PATRICK HARPER	G	(R	DAVID ELLINGTON	V	(R	WENDY SUITS	V	(R
DOTTIE WEST	V	(KOV									

R128 JIMMY ROGERS R128

Musician	Instr	Albums	Title	Year	Label	Country	No.
JIMMY ROGERS	G V	(ABCD	(A) THATS ALL RIGHT	1974	BLACK & BLUE		33504
FRED BELOW	D	(BCE	(B) CHICAGO BOUND	19	CHESS		407
WILLIE MABRON	PNO	(A	(C) BLUESMASTERS	1976	CHESS		2ACMB207
DAVE MYERS	B	(AE	(D) & LEFT HAND FRANK	1979	JSP		1008
LOUIS MYERS	G	(AE	(E) GOLD TAILED BIRD	19			
FREDDIE KING	G	(E					

Musician	Instr	Albums	Musician	Instr	Albums	Musician	Instr	Albums	Musician	Instr	Albums
LEFT HAND FRANK	G V	(D	BIG CRAWFORD	B	(D	BOB BRUNNING	B	(D	RAY WESTON	D	(D
ERNEST COTTON	SAX	(BC	EDDIE WARE	PNO	(BC	WALTER HORTON	HCA	(B	LITTLE WALTER	HCA	(BC
ELGIN EVANS	D	(BC	MUDDY WATERS	G	(BC	BOB WOODFORK	G	(C	JOHNNY JONES	PNO	(C
WILLIE DIXON	B	(BC	A J GLADNEY	D	(C	J T BROWN	SAX	(BC	HENRY GRAY	PNO	(BC
OTIS SPANN	PNO	(BC	JOE YOUNG	G	(C	WAYNE BENNETT	G	(C	S P LEARY	D	(C
LUTHER TUCKER	G	(C	FRED ROBINSON	G	(C	GEORGE HUNTER	D	(C	BOB REED	PNO	(E

R129 ROGUE R129

Musician	Instr	Albums	Title	Year	Label	Country	No.
TREVOR SPENCER	D	(B	(A) FALLEN ANGEL	1975	EPIC	UK	69235
BARRY MORGAN	D	(ABC	(B) LET IT GO	1977	EPIC	UK	81987
ALAN TARNEY	B	(B	(C) WOULD YOU LET YOUR DAUGHTER	1979	ARIOLA		ARL 5028
LES HURDLE	B	(ABC					

Musician	Instr	Albums	Musician	Instr	Albums	Musician	Instr	Albums	Musician	Instr	Albums
J W HODGKINSON	V	(ABC	GUY FLETCHER	K V	(ABC	TERRY BRITTEN	G	(B	RITCHIE BULL	BANJO	(B
AL HODGE	G	(AC	FRANK RICOTTI	PERC	(A	JIMMY JEWELL	SAX	(C	B J COLE	STEEL	(AC

R129A CHRIS ROHMANN R129A

Musician	Instr	Albums	Title	Year	Label	Country	No.
CHRIS ROHMANN		(	(A) THE MAN I AM TODAY	1974	RCA	UK	SF 8364

R129B ROKES R129B

Musician	Instr	Albums	Title	Year	Label	Country	No.
SHEL SHAPIRO		(A	(A) THESE WERE THE ROKES	1977	RCA	IT	33037
MIKE ROGERS		(					
BOBBY POWELL		(	JOHNNY CHARLTON (				

R130 ROKOTTO R130

Musician	Instr	Albums	Title	Year	Label	Country	No.
CLEVELAND WALKER	V	(A	(A) ROKOTTO	1977	STATE		ETAT15
SISTER B	V	(A					
STEWART GARDEN	K	(A					
HOWARD McLEOD	D	(A					

Musician	Instr	Albums	Musician	Instr	Albums	Musician	Instr	Albums
HOWARD LLOYD WISDON	B	(A	DEREK HENDERSON	G	(A	HUGH PAUL	V	(A

R131 ROLL UPS R131

Name	Inst	On	Album	Release
LEA HART JR	G V	(A	(A) LOVE DIVE FOR HIGH BALLS	197 BRIDGEHOUSE BHLP 004
PAUL AIRE	K V	(A		
JEFF PETERS	B V	(A	RICKY ANDREO D (A	

R132 ROLLERCOASTER R132

Name	Inst	On	Album	Release
RAY WARLEIGH	SAX	(A	(A) WONDERIN'	1981 CALIBRE UK CABLP1006
DICK MORRISSEY	SAX	(A		
DEREK WATKINS	TPT	(A	CHRIS PYNE TROM (A ALAN PARKER G (A MIKE PYNE PNO (A	
RON MATTHEWSON	B	(A	BARRY MORGAN D (A KARL JENKINS K (A MIKE RATLEDGE K (A	

R133 ROLLING STONES R133

Name	Inst	On	Album	Release
MICK JAGGER	G K V	(ALL	(A) THE ROLLING STONES	1964 DECCA UK LK4605 US LONDON PS375
KEITH RICHARD	G V K	(ALL	(A) THE ROLLING STONES	196 DECCA GER 16300 RI 17005 RI70 621695
			(B) THE ROLLING STONES 2	1965 DECCA UK SLK4661 NOVA GER 621393
BRIAN JONES	G V	(ABCDEFGHJKLMRN	(C) 12X5	1965 US LONDON PS402
IAN STEWART	PNO	(ABGEPQUZ,JJ,LL	(D) THE ROLLING STONES NOW	1965 US LONDON PS420
MICK AVORY	D	(	(E) OUT OF OUR HEADS	1965 DECCA UK SKL4733 US LONDON PS429
DICK TAYLOR	G B	(	(F) DECEMBERS CHILDREN	1965 US LONDON PS451
CHARLIE WATTS	D	(ALL	(G) AFTERMATH	1966 DECCA UK SKL4786 US LONDON PS476
BILL WYMAN	V B SYN	(ALL	(H) HIGHTIDE & GREEN GRASS	1966 DECCA UK TXA 101 US LONDON NPS 1
RON WOOD	G B V	(LL,MM,NN,OO,	(I) GOT LIVE IF YOU WANT IT	1967 LONDON US SL226/7 DECCA UK SLK 4838
MICK TAYLOR	G V	(QUZYN	(J) BETWEEN THE BUTTONS	1967 DECCA UK SKL4852 US LONDON PS499
TONY CHAPMAN	D	(	(K) FLOWERS	1967 DECCA SKL16487 US LONDONPS509
AL KOOPER	K	(N	(K) FLOWERS	19 NOVA RI 621407
JIM PRICE	HRNS	(QU	(L) SATANIC MAJESTIES REQUEST	1967 DECCA UK TKS 103 US LONDON NPS 2
BOBBY KEYS	HRNS	(QUN,LL,	(M) BEGGARS BANQUET	1968 DECCA UK SKL4955 US LONDON PS539
NICKY HOPKINS	K	(LMMQUZ,HH,LL	(N) LET IT BLEED	1969 DECCA UK SKL5025 US LONDON NPS 4
LEON RUSSELL	PNO	(N	(N) LET IT BLEED	1970 NONA GER 621412
ILLY PRESTON	K	(QUZ,HH,JJ	(O) THROUGH THE PAST DARKLY	1969 DECCA UK SKL5019 US LONDON NPS 3
RY COODER	G MAND	(QN	(P) GET YER YA YAS OUT	1970 DECCA UK SKL5065 US LONDON NPS 5
OLLIE BROWN	PERC	(HH,JJ,	(Q) STICKY FINGERS	1971 ROLLING STONE COC 59100
WAYNE PERKINS	G	(HH,	(R) STONE AGE	1971 DECCA UK SKL5084
HARVEY MANDEL	G	(HH,	(S) GIMME SHELTER	1971 DECCA UK SKL5101
PAUL BUCKMASTER		(Q	(T) MILESTONES	1971 DECCA UK SKL5098
JACK NITZSCHE	K	(EGQB	(U) EXILE ON MAIN STREET	1972 ROLLING STONE UK 69100 US 2900
J W ALEXANDER	PERC	(E	(V) ROCK'N'ROLLIN' STONES	1972 DECCA UK SKL5149
JIM DICKINSON	PNO	(Q	(W) HOT ROCKS 1964/71	1972 US LONDON 606/7
JIMMY MILLER	PERC	(QUN	(X) MORE HOT ROCKS	1972 US LONDON 626/7
ROCKY DZIDZORNU	PERC	(QN	(Y) GOATS HEAD SOUP	1973 ROLLING STONE 59101 US 39106
CLYDIE KING	V	(U	(Z) ITS ONLY ROCK'N'ROLL	1974 ROLLING STONE UK 59103 US RS 79101
VANETTA FIELDS	V	(U	(AA) NO STONE UNTURNED	1973 DECCA UK SKL5173
JESSE KIRKLAND	V	(U	(BB) ROLLED GOLD	1975 DECCA UK ROST 1/2 GER NOVA 628356
TAMMY LYNN	V	(U	(CC) METAMORPHOSIS	1975 DECCA UK SKL5212 US ABCKO ANA 1
SHIRLEY GOODMAN	V	(U	(CC) METAMORPHOSIS	1975 CAN LONDON PS 573
DR JOHN	V	(U	(DD) MADE IN THE SHADE	1975 ROLLING STONE UK 59104 US 79102
JOE GREEN	V	(U	(EE) STONE AGE/GOT LIVE	1975 TELDEC EURO SD3024 GER 6645 400
KATHI McDONALD	V	(U	(FF) AROUND & AROUND	197 DECCA UK SLK6315 GER 16315 RI70 621392
BILL PLUMMER	B	(U	( ) LIVE	197 LONDON JAPAN SL226/7
AL PERKINS	STEEL	(U	(HH) BLACK & BLUE	1976 ROLLING STONE UK 59106 US 79104
RAY COOPER	PERC	(Z	(JJ) LOVE YOU LIVE	1977 ROLLING STONE UK 89101 US 2 9001
BLUE MAGIC	V	(Z	(KK) SOME GIRLS	1978 ROLLING STONE UK/US CUN 39108
MERRY CLAYTON	V	(N	(LL) EMOTIONAL RESCUE	1979 ROLLING STONE UK CUN 39111
NANNETTE NEWMAN	V	(N	(MM) TATTOO YOU	1981 ROLLING STONE UK CUN39114 US 16052
MADELINE BELL	V	(N	(MM) TATTOO YOU	1981 ROLLING STONE GER 64553
DORIS TROY	V	(N	(NN) STILL LIFE	1982 ROLLING STONE UK CUN 39115
CHARLIE JOLLY	TABLA	(Z	( ) ROLLING STONES SOLID ROCK	19 DECCA UK TAB1
MAX ROMEO	V	(LL	( ) SLOW ROLLERS	1981 DECCA UK TAB 30
ED LEACH	PERC	(Z	( ) ROLLING STONES (PROFILE)	19 TELDEC GERM 624001
KENNY JONES	D	(Z	( ) DECEMBERS CHILDREN	1981 DECCA 24314
SUGAR BLUE	HCA	(KK,	( ) SUCKING IN THE SEVENTIES	1981 ROLLING STONES UK 39112 US 16028
MICHAEL SHRIEVE	PERC	(LL	( ) 30 GREAT HITS (DBL)	1970 ABKCO IT 3042
GENE PITNEY	V	(A	( ) GET STONED	1977 ARCADE UK ADE 32
PHIL SPECTOR	PERC	(A	( ) IN CONCERT	1982 POLYGRAM IMP 6640 037
WILLY WEEKS	B	(Z	(EP) ROLLING STONES	1964 DECCA UK DFE 8560
IAN MACLAGAN	K	(KK,	(EP) 5X5	1964 DECCA UK DFE 8590
MEL COLLINS	SAX	(KK,	(EP) GOT LIVE IF YOU WANT	1965 DECCA UK DFE 8620

R133A ROMANTICS R133A

Name	Inst	On	Album	Release
MIKE SKILL	G V	(AB	(A) ROMANTICS	1980 EPIC US 36273 UK 84095
WALLY PALMAR	G V	(ABC	(B) NATIONAL BREAKOUT	1980 EPIC US 36881 UK 84176
RICH COLE	B V	(ABC	(C) STRCTLY PERSONAL	1981 EPIC UK 85721
JIMMY MARINOS	D V	(ABC		
PETE SOLLEY	PROD	(AB	MIKE STONE PROD (C COZ CANTHER G (C	

R134 MAX ROMEO R134

Name	Inst	On	Album	Release
MAX ROMEO	V	(ALL	(A) REVELATION TIME	1975 SOUNDTRAC TSL 1000
BARRY LLEWELLYN	V	(B	(B) WAR IN A BABYLON	1976 ISLAND UK ILPS 9392
EARL MORGAN	V	(B	(C) RONDOS	19 KING KONG KANT1
MARCIA GRIFFITHS	V	(B	(D) OPEN THE IRON GATES	1978 UA US LA 803
CYNTHIA SCOLAS	V	(B	(E) RECONSTRUCTION	1978 MANGO UK MLPS 9503
BORIS GARDNER	B	(E		
MICKY RICHARDS	D	(E	KEITH STERLING PNO (E EARL LINDO K CLAR(E DAVID MADDEN TPT (E	
BOBBY ELLIS	HRNS	(E	GLEN DA COSTA SAX (E VIN GORDON TROM (E EARL SMITH G (E	
ERNIE RANGLIN	G	(E	SHEENA V (E JIMMY RILEY V (E RICKY STORME V (E	

R134A ROMEO VOID R134A

Name	Inst	On	Album	Release
DEBORA JYALL	V	(A	(A) ITSACONDITION	1981 415 US 0004
PETER WOODS	G	(A		
JOHN STENCH	D	(A	BEN BOSSI SAX (A FRANK ZINCAVAGE B (A	

R134B ROMEO'S R134B

Name	Inst	On	Album	Release
			ROCK'N'ROLL & LOVE & DEATH	1980 CBS US 36544

R135 RONETTES R135

VERONICA BENNETT(SPECTOR) V(ALL (A) TODAYS HITS 1963 PHILLES US 4004
ESTELLE BENNETT V ((B) CHRISTMAS GIFT 1963 PHILLES US 4005 UK LONDON HAU8141
NEDRA TALLEY V ((C) FABULOUS RONETTES 1964 PHILLES US 4006 UK LONDON HAU8212
CAROL KAYE B ((D) THE RONETTES 1965 COLPIX US 486
HAL BLAINE D ((E) CHA CHA CHA 1967 ROPER US 1009
DENISE EDWARDS V ((F) SING THEIR GREATEST HITS 1975 PHIL SPECTOR UK 2307 003
LEON RUSSELL K (
CHIP FIELDS V (

R135A RONIN R135A

WADDY WACHTEL G (A (A) RONIN 1980 MERCURY US 1 3832
RICK MAROTTA D (A
DAN DUGMORE G (A STANLEY SHELDON B V (A DON GROLNICK K (A

R136 MICK RONSON R136

MICK RONSON G V K(AB (A) SLAUGHTER ON THE TENTH AVENUE 1974 RCA APL10353
IAN HUNTER G V ((B) PLAY DONT WORRY 1975 RCA APL10681
TREVOR BOLDER B HRN(AB
DAVID HENTSCHEL K (A AYNSLEY DUNBAR D (AB MIKE GARSON K (AB MARGARET RONSON V (A
BEVERLY BAXTER V (B RITCHIE DHARMA D (B VICKY BROWN V (B TONY NEWMAN D (B
PAUL FRANCIS D (B

R137 LINDA RONSTADT R137

LINDA RONSTADT V (ALL (A) HAND SOWN HOME GROWN 1969 CAPITOL(RI 1975) ST208
DAN DUGMORE G (GJKOPHQ (B) SILK PURSE 1970 CAPITOL ST407
WADDY WACHTEL G V (JKOPHQ (C) LINDA RONSTADT 1972 CAPITOL ST635 RI GREENLIGHT 2013
KENNY EDWARDS B V (FGJKIOP HQ (D) DONT CRY NOW 1974 ASYLUM UK SYL9012 US SD5064
RICK MAROTTA D (JOPQ (D) DONT CRY NOW 1974 ASYLUM UK K43002 RI
DON GROLNICK K (JKOP (E) DIFFERENT DRUM 1974 CAPITOL US 11269
BRIAN AHERN PROD (Q (E) DIFFERENT DRUM 1975 CAPITOLUK VMP1010 RI CAPS 1004
PETER ASHER G V PERC (FGJKOPHQ (F) HEART LIKE A WHEEL 1974 CAPITOL 11358
CHARLES VEAL VLN (JH (G) PRISONER IN DISGUISE 1975 ASYLUM UK SYL8761 US 7E1045
DAVID CAMPBELL VLA (FJH (G) PRISONER IN DISGUISE 1975 ASYLUM UK K53015 RI
DENNIS KARMAZYN CELLO(FJHQ (H) HASTEN DOWN THE WIND 1976 ASYLUM UK K53045 US 7E1072
RICHARD FEVES B (FJH (I) GREATEST HITS 1976 ASYLUM UK K53055 US 6E 106
MIKE AULDRIDGE G (JP (J) SIMPLE DREAM 1977 ASYLUM UK K53065 US 6E 104
DOLLY PARTON V (JQ (K) LIVING IN THE USA 1978 ASYLUM UK K53085 US 6E 155
STEVE FORMAN PERC (JOP (L) RETROSPECTIVE 1977 CAPITOL UK CAPSP102 US 11629
DON HENLEY V D (CFJOH (M) THE SOUTHERN BELLE 1978 EMI IMP 05085068
LARRY HAGLER V (JO (N) STONE PONEYS FEATURING L.RONSTADT 1975 CAPITOL 11383
JOHN DAVID SOUTHER V (CFGIJQ (O) GREATEST HITS VOL 2 1980 ASYLUM UK K52255 US 5E 516
HERB PEDERSEN V (FCGJIH (P) MAD LOVE 1980 ASYLUM UK K52210 US 510
EDIE LEHMANN V (Q (Q) GET CLOSER 1982 ASYLUM 960185
DAVID SANBORN SAX (KO
ANDREW GOLD K G V(FGHIKOPQ RUSS KUNKEL D(FGHKOPQ DAVID LINDLEY FDL (FG JIM CONNOR HCA (G
LOWELL GEORGE G (G NIGEL OLSSON D (G DANNY KORTCHMAR G (GOPQ DAVID KEMPER D (GI
DAN FRANCISCO V (G EMMYLOU HARRIS V (FGQ GLEN D HARDIN PNO (G DAVID GRISMAN MAND(GQ
JAMES TAYLOR G (GQ MARIA MULDAUR V (FG EDDIE BLACK G (FG PAT HENDERSON V (GHKO
JULIA TILLMAN V (G MAXINE WILLARD V (C MIKE MAINIERI VIBES(K SHIRLEY MATTHEWS V(FIKUH
JIM GILSTRAP V (KOH JOHN LEHMAN V (KO DAVID LASLEY V (K ARNOLD McCULLER V (K
CLYDIE KING V (FIH SNEAKY PETE STEEL(FIC JIMMY FADDEN HRNS (CFI WENDY WALDMAN V (FIOH
CHRIS ETHRIDGE B (FI BOB WARFORD G (F DENNIS ST JOHN D (F EMORY GORDY B (F
CISSY HOUSTON V (F JOYCE NESBITT V (F LLOYD MYERS D (F PAUL CRAFT G (F
JOHN STARLING G (F TOM GUIDERA B (F DANNY PENDLETON STEEL(F JOHN BOYLAN G (CFI
GLENN FREY G (CF TIM SCHMIT B (F JIM GORDON D (I JIMMY GORDON HRNS(I
BERNIE LEADON G (IC AL CAIOLA B (I MARK GOLDENBERG G (OP BOB GLAUB B (OPQ
BILL PAYNE K (OPQ ROSEMARY BUTLER V (OPQ NICOLETTE LARSON V (OP KARLA BONOFF V (HO
PETER BERNSTEIN G (P MICHAEL BODDICKER SYN (P MIKE BOWDEN B (CI RICHARD BOWDEN G (CI
GIB GUILBEAU FDL V(CI TIPPY ARMSTRONG G (C WELDON MYRICK STEEL(C BARRY BECKETT K (C
DAVID HOOD B (C DEAN WEBB MAND (C JOHN MARTIN G V (C RANDY MEISNER B V(C
ROGER HAWKINS D (C MERRY CLAYTON V (C DIANNE DAVIDSON V (C MISS ONA V (C
JIM HORN SAX (Q WESLEY PRITCHETT B (C BUDDY EMMONS STEEL(C LYLE RITZ B (C
ANDY JOHNSON G (I PETE WADE G (I SPOONER OLDHAM PNO(I NORBERT PUTNAM B (IB
MICKY McGEE D (I MARTI McCALL V (I MICHAEL BOTTS D (IH GAIL MARTIN TROM(I
DON RANDI K (I NINO TEMPO SAX (I MACK JOHNSON TPT (I DARRELL LEONARD TPT(I
BUDDY SPICHER BAN FDL (I GINGER HOLLADAY V (I MARY HOLLADAY V (I JERRY PETERSON SAX (Q
DEBBIE PEARL V (Q PATTI AUSTIN V (Q LINDSEY BUCKINGHAM ACC (Q RICK SHLOSSER D (Q
KEN YERKE VLA (H RON HICKLAND V (H CLARENCE McDONALD K (H BECCI LOUIS V (H
BILL THEDFORD V (H GERRY GARRETT V (H PAUL POLENICK VLA (H BEECHWOOD RANGERS (B
ELLIOTT MAZER (B ADAM MITCHELL (B KEN BUTTREY D (B

R138 ROOGALATOR R138

DANNY ADLER G (A1 (A) PLAY IT BY EAR 1977 DO IT UK RIDE 1
NICK PLYTAS K (A (1) 1978
JUSTIN HILDRETH D (A1
JULIAN SCOTT B (A1

R138A ROOMFUL OF BLUES R138A

GERG PICCOLO SAX ((A) ROOMFUL OF BLUES 1979 ISLAND 9474
DOUG JAMES SAX ((B) LETS HAVE A PARTY 1980 ANTILLES US 7071
RICH LATAILLE SAX ((C) HOT LITTLE MAMA 1981 ACE UK CH39

R139 ROOT BOY SLIM & THE SEX CHANGE BAND R139

ROOT BOY SLIM (FOSTER MACKENZIE III) V(AB (A) ROOT BOY SLIM & THE SEX CHANGE BAND 1978 WB US 3160 ILLEGAL 79 003
(B) ZOOM 1979 ILLEGAL UK 004
RATTLESNAKE RATTLES (BOB GREENLEE) B(AB
COSMO GREEK(WALT ANDREWS G(A ERNIE E LOCKEROOM G(A RON HOLLOWAY SAX (A TOMMY RUGER D (A
MICKI LEE JONNIE V (A CHERIE GRASSO V (A FLACO FALCON PERC (A KATHE'SPECIAL K'RUSSELL V(A
WINSTON 'SPOTS'KELLY K(A

R139A BIFF ROSE R139A

BIFF ROSE V K (A (A) CHILDREN OF LIGHT 1968 TETRAGRAMMATON US T116
VAN DYKE PARKS SYN (A
NICK WOODS SYN (A BENNY BARTH D (A

R139B ROSE R139B

DAVID ROSE V VLN (A (A) ROSE 1979 RCA US XL17749
SERJE PERATHONER K SYN(A
STEVE SHEHAN PERC (A CLAUDE SALMIERI D (A

R139C ROSE R139C

GARY PALONNE B V (AB (A) TASTE OF NEPTUNE 1977 POLYDOR 2424 135
RON GLATLEY K V (AB (B) JUDGEMENT DAY 1977 POLYDOR 2424 168
JAMES FOX D V (AB
BRIAN ALLEN G V (AB

R140 TIM ROSE R140

TIM ROSE V (ALL (A) TIM ROSE 1967 CBS UK 63168 US 9577
BERNARD PURDIE D (A (B) THROUGH ROSE COLOURED SPECS 1969 CBS UK 63636 US 9772
FELIX PAPPALARDI B (A (C) LOVE A KIND OF HATE STORY 1970 CAPITOL US 673
JAY BERLINER G (A (D) TIM ROSE 1972 PLAYBOY US 101
HUGH McCRACKEN G (A (E) TIM ROSE 1974 DAWN UK DNLS3062
GARY WRIGHT K (E (F) THE MUSICIAN 1975 ATLANTIC UK K50183
BRYSON GRAHAM D (E (G) RETROSPECTIVE 1977 CAPITOL
ARCHIE LEGGETT B (E
MICK JONES G (RICHARD HUSSAN B (A ART BUTLER K (A JIM FISCHOFF PERC(A
CHARLES SMALLS PNO (A PATTI BROWN K (A CHUCK RAINEY B (A ERNEST HAYES K (A
RICHARD KILLGROVE D (A ERIC WEISSBERG B (A DAVE CHARLES D (E TOMMY EYRE K (E
B J COLE STEEL(E BOBBY JONES PERC (A JONATHAN ROWLANDS TAMB(E PAUL COBBOLD B (E
RAY MARTINEZ G (E KEN FREEMAN SYN (E ROGER SUTTON B (E RICHARD BURGESS D(E
JOHN VERITY G (E ANDY SUMMERS G (E LEE JACKSON K (E

R140A ROSE GARDEN R140A

DIANA DI ROSE G (A (A) ROSE GARDEN 1968 ATCO SD 33225
JOHN NORDEN G (A
JAMES GROSHONG G (A WILLIAM FLEMING B (A BRUCE BOUDIN D (A

R141 ROSE ROYCE R141

ROSE NORWALT V (C (A) CAR WASH 1976 MCA UK MCSP 278
GWEN 'ROSE' DICKEY V (D (B) BEST OF CARWASH 1977 MCA UK MCF 2799 UK RI 1609
TERRY SANTIEL CONGA(CDH (C) IN FULL BLOOM 1977 WHITFIELD US 3074 UK K56394
HENRY GARNER D V (CDH (D) STRIKES AGAIN 1978 WHITFIELD US 3227 UK K56527
LEQUEINT JOBE B V (CDH (E) RAINBOW CONNECTION IV 1979 WHITFIELD US 3387 UK K56714
MICHAEL MOORE SAX (CDH (F) GOLDEN TOUCH 1980 WHITFIELD US 3512 UK K56881
KENNY COPELAND TPT V(CDH (G) GREATEST HITS 1980 WHITFIELD RRTV1
KENJI BROWN G V (CD (H) JUMP STREET 1981 WHITFIELD UK K56958
RICHIE BENSON V (H
MICHAEL NASH K (CDH FREDDIE DUNN TPT (CDH MARK DAVIS K (CD WAH WAH WATSON G (CDEH
JAMES GADSON D (C JACK ASHFORD D (CDE VICTOR NYX K (D CORNELIUS GRANT G (D
JIMMY VALDEZ D (D WALTER DOWNING K (DE MARK KENOLY B (D LAFAYETTE TREY STONE G(E
ISY MARTIN G (E WALTER McKINSEY G (H

R141A ROSE TATTOO R141A

'ANGRY ANDERSON TROAT V(AB (A) ROSE TATTOO 1980 WEA UK 58144 US MIRAGE 19280
PETER WELLS G V (AB (B) ASSAULT & BATTERY 1981 CARRERE UK CAL127 US MIRAGE19342
DALLAS ROXAL D (AB (B) ASSAULT & BATTERY 1981 WEA FR 58359
GEORDIE LEECH B (AB
MICHAEL COCKS G (AB

R142 ALAN ROSS R142

ALAN ROSS G V (ABCD (A) ROSS 1974 RSO US 878 UK 2394 127
STEVE EMERY V B (AB (B) PIT & THE PENDULUM 1975 RSO US 4802 UK 2394 144
BOB JACKSON K V (AB (C) ARE YOU FREE ON SATURDAY 1977 EBONY EBY 1000
TONY FERNANDEZ D (AB (D) RESTLESS NIGHTS 1978 EBONY UK EBY 1003
REUBEN WHITE PERC (AB
FRANK WILSON K V (C JOHN COOKE K V (CD ED SPEVOCK D (CD PETE DENNIS B V (CD
TOM COMPTON D (C CHRIS FLETCHER PERC V(C CRAIG ANDERS D V (D STRINGS (C

R142A DIANA ROSS R142A

DIANA ROSS V (ALL (A) DIANA ROSS 1970 MOTOWN UK STML11159 US 711
NICKOLAS ASHFORD PROD (ACER (B) EVERYTHING IS EVERYTHING 1971 MOTOWN UK STML11178 US 724
VALERIE SIMPSON PROD (ACER (C) I'M STILL WAITING 1971 MOTOWN UK STML11193
DEBE RICHARDS PROD (CE (D) DIANA 1971 MOTOWN UK STMA 8001
ALBERT AARONS TPT (G (E) GREATEST HITS 1972 MOTOWN UK STMA 8006
BOBBY BRYANT TPT (G (F) TOUCH ME IN THE MORNING 1973 MOTOWN UK STML11239 US 772
GOERGIE AULD SAX (G (G) LADY SINGS THE BLUES 1973 MOTOWN UK TMSP 1131 US 758
PLAS JOHNSON SAX (G (H) DIANA & MARVIN 1974 MOTOWN UK STMA 8015
MARVIN GAYE V (H (I) LIVE AT CAESARS PALACE 1974 MOTOWN UK STML11248 US 801
MARSHALL ROYAL SAX (G (J) LAST TIME I SAW HIM 1974 MOTOWN UK STML11255 US 812
GEORGE BOHANON TROM (G (K) MAHOGANY 1975 MOTOWN UK STML12004 US 858
HENRY COKER TROM (G (L) DIANA ROSS 1976 MOTOWN UK STML12022 US 861
MAURICE SPEARS TROM (G (M) GREATEST HITS 1976 MOTOWN UK STML12036 US 869
GEORGE'RED' CALLENDER B(G (N) AN EVENING WITH DIANA ROSS 1977 MOTOWN UK TMSP 6005 US 877
EARL PALMER D (G (O) BABY ITS ME 1977 MOTOWN UK STMA 8031 US 890
WILLIAM ANDERSON TPT (G (P) ROSS 1978 MOTOWN UK STML12093 US 907
HARRY EDISON TPT (G (Q) THREE ORIGINALS 1979 EMI FR 53013
WILLIAM COLLETTE SAX (G (R) THE BOSS 1979 MOTOWN UK STML12118
JACK NIMITY SAX (G (S) 20 GOLDEN GREATS 1979 MOTOWN UK EMTV 21
ERNIE WATTS SAX (G (T) DIANA 1980 MOTOWN UK STMA 8033
JIMMY CLEVELAND TROM (G (U) TO LOVE AGAIN 1981 MOTOWN UK STML12152
GROVER MITCHELL TROM (G (V) WHY DO FOOLS FALL IN LOVE 1981 CAPITOL UK 26733
MAX BENNETT B (G (W) DIANA'S DUETS 1982 MOTOWN UK STML12163
JOHN COLLINS G BAN(G (X) SICK ELECTRIC 1982 CAPITOL UK 27313
DON ABNEY PNO (G
GERALD WIGGINS PNO (G CHESTER LANE PNO (G TEDDY BUCKNER TPT (G ARTHUR EDWARDS B (G
JESSE SAILES D (G JOHN EWING TROM (G 'LAUGHEY' ROBERTS SAX (G MICHEL LEGRAND STR (G
GIL ASHEY STR (G OLIVER NELSON STR (G RICHARD PERRY PROD (O JEFF PORCARO D (O
DAVID HUNGATE B (O STEVE LUKATHER G (O TOM SNOW PNO (O TOM SCOTT SAX (O
JACK ASHFORD PERC (O GENE PAGE STR (O RAY PARKER G B (O LEE RITENOUR G (O
MICHAEL OMARTIAN K (O LENNY CASTRO PERC(O BECKY LEWIS V (O PETSYE POWELL V (O
PATTI BROOKS V (O DONALD DUCK DUNN B (O DAVID FOSTER HRNS (O JAMES NEWTON HOWARD K(O
DEL NEWMAN STR (O KEN PETERSON K SYN(O JIM HORN HRNS (O CHUCK FINDLEY HRNS(O

(CONTINUED)

R142A DIANA ROSS (CONTINUED) R142A

DAVID PAICH V ORG K(O BOBBY KIMBALL V (O CLYDIE KING V (O SHIRLEY MATTHEWS V(O
ED GREENE D (O RICH ZITO G (O IRA NEWBORN G HCA(O BOBBYE HALL PERC(O
BUD SHANK FLT (O RICHARD HEWSON STR (O RICHARD SHLOSSER D (OU BRYAN GAROFALO B (O
STANLEY SCHWARTS PNO (O OLLIE BROWN D (O SCOTT EDWARDS B (O BEN BENAY G (O
LENNY CASTRO PERC (O RAY CHEW K (RVX ERIC GALE G (RVX ANTHONY JACKSON B(R
FRANCISCO CENTENO B (RV JOHN SUSSEWELL D (R SAMMY FIGUEROA PERC (R ERROL BENNETT PERC(RX
MICHAEL BRECKER SAX (RV ULLANDO McCULLOUGH V(R RAYMOND SIMPSON V (R PAUL RISER STR HRNS(RVX
ROBERT MOUNSEY STR HRNS(RVX JOHN DAVIS STR HRN(R BERNARD EDWARDS B PROD(T NILE RODGERS G PROD(T
RAYMOND JONES K (T ANDY SCHWARTZ K (T TONY THOMPSON D (T EDDIE DANIELS SAX (T
MECO MONARDO TROM (T BOB MILLIKEN TPT (T ALFA ANDERSON V (T LUCI MARTIN V (T
FONZI THORNTON V (T MICHELLE COBBS V (T MICHAEL MESSER PROD K(U LARRY KNECHTEL PNO (U
BILLY PAYNE K (U LEE SKLAR B (U TIM MAY G (U BECKY LOPEZ V (U
MAXINE WILLARD WATERS V(UX JULIA TILLMAN WATERS V (UX NEIL JASON B (VX JEFF MIRANOV G (VX
YOGI HORTON D (VX BURT DE COTEAUX STR HRNS(V GEORGE MACDONALD PERC (V DON BROOKS HCA (V
RANDY BRECKER HRNS (V PATRICK REBILLOT PNO (V ED WALSH SYN (VX LEON PENDARVIS K (V
RON FRANGIPANE K (V MARGARET DORN V (V LEOTA GALLOWAY V (V MILLIE WHITESIDE V (V
STEVE GOLDSTEIN SYN (X RICK MAROTTA D (X PAUL SHAFFER K (X LUCIO HOPPER B (X
JOE BARGER PNO (X NATHAN WATTS B (X JONATHAN MOFFETT D (X DAVID WILLIAMS G (X
DENZIL MILLER K (X LUTHER VANDROSS V (X CISSY HOUSTON V (X PAULETTE McWILLIAMS V(X
TAWATHA AGEE V (X PATTI AUSTIN V (X MICHAEL BODDICKER SYN (X BILL WOLFER SYN (X
GREGORY SMITH SYN (X

R143 DOCTOR ROSS R143

DOCTOR ROSS V HCA G PERC(ALL (A) HIS FIRST RECORDINGS 19 ARHOOLIE F1065
BOB HALL PNO (C (B) LIVE AT MONTREUX 19 ATLANTIC 2460 169 BIG BEAR 18
LAFAYETTE LEAKE PNO (B (C) THE HARMONICA BOSS 1974 BIG BEAR BEAR 2
LOUIS MYERS G (B (D) JIVIN' THE BLUES 197 BIG BEAR BEAR15
DAVID MYERS B (B (E) CALL THE DOCTOR 19 TESTAMENT 2206

R143A ROSSINGTON COLLINS BAND R143A

GARY ROSSINGTON G (AB (A) ANY TIME ANYWHERE 1980 MCA UK MCG 4011 US 5130
ALLEN COLLINS G (AB (B) THIS IS THE WAY 1981 MCA UK MCG 4018
BILLY POWELL K (AB
LEON WILKESON B (AB DALE KRANTZ V (AB BARRY HARWOOD G V (AB DEREK HESS D (AB

R144 ROTARY CONNECTION R144

MINNIE RIPPERTON V ((A) ROTARY CONNECTION 1968 CHESS CRL 4538 CADET LPS 312
SIDNEY BARNES V ((B) ALADDIN 196 CADET LPS 317
BOBBY SIMS V ((C) PEACE AT LAST 1969 CADET LPS 318
JUDY HAUF V ((D) SONGS 196 CADET LPS 322
MITCH ALIOTTA V ((E) DINNER MUSIC 19 CADET LPS 328
KENNY VENEGAS V ((F) TRIP ONE 1973 CHECKER 6467 300
(G) HEY LOVE 19 CADET US 50006

R144A ARLEN ROTH R144A

ARLEN ROTH G V (AB (A) HOT PICKUPS 1980 SONET UK SNTF845 ROUNDER 3044
MICHAEL BRAUN D (A (B) GUITARIST 1978 ROUNDER US 3022
VAN ELIAS B (A
DEAN KRAUS K (A STEPHANIE DAVY V (A THE PERSUASIONS V (A KEVIN KELLY V (A
TONY BROWN B (B TIM CAPPELLO SAX (A RICHARD CROOKS D (B AUBRAY SCHRAM V (B
RALPH SCHUCKETT K (B

R145 MICHAEL ROTHER R145

MICHAEL ROTHER G B SYN (ALL (A) FLAMMENDE HERZEN 1976 SKY SKY 007
JAKI LEIBEZEIT D (ABCD (A) FLAMMENDE HERZEN 197 RADAR (UNRELEASED) RAD 8
(B) STERNTALER 1978 SKY SKY 013
(C) KATZENMUSIK 1979 SKY SKY 033
(D) FERNWARME 1982 POLYDOR GER 2372 111

R146 ROUGH DIAMOND R146

DAVID BYRON V (A (A) ROUGH DIAMOND 1977 ISLAND ILPS 9490
DAVE CLEMPSON G (A
GEOFF BRITTON D (A DAMON BUTCHER K (A WILLIE BATH B (A

R146A ROUGH TRADE R146A

MICHAEL FONFARA K (A (A) LIVE 1976 UMBRELLA CAN DD1
PETER HOGSON B (A
CAROLE POPE V (A JOANNE BROOKS V PERC(A KEVAN STAPLES G K (A RICK GRATTON D (A

R147 ROUNDABOUT R147

CHRIS CURTIS V (A (A) 1967
DAVE CURTIS V (A
BOBBY CLARK D (A JON LORD K (A RITCHIE BLACKMORE G (A

R148 ROWAN BROTHERS R148

PETER ROWAN V G MAND(ALL (A) THE ROWAN BROTHERS 1972 CBS US 31297
LORIN ROWAN G V (ALL (B) ROWANS 1975 ASYLUM SYL9026 US 7E1038
CHRIS ROWAN G V (ALL (B) ROWANS 197 ASYLUM RI K53023
JACK BONUS WIND (B (C) SIBLING RIVALRY 1976 ASYLUM US 7E1073
BILL ELLIOTT PNO (C (D) JUBILATION 19 ASYLUM US 7E1114
JOE CARROLL B (C
RICHARD GREENE VLN (C PETER WALSH B (C WALLY DROGAS D (C JORDAN AMARANTHA CONGA(C
K DUDLEY GLANZ D (C JIMMY HODDER D (C MARK STEIN D (C DAVID HAYES B (B
RUSS KUNKEL D (B

R148A ROXY R148A

BOB SEGARINI G B V PERC(A (A) ROXY 1970 ELEKTRA US EKS74063
RANDY BISHOP G B K V (A
JIM DE COCQ K G (A JOHN McDONALD D PERC(A JAMES MORRIS K (A JOHN HAENY PROD (A

R149 ROXY MUSIC R149

BRYAN FERRY V K (ALL — (A) ROXY MUSIC — 1972 UK ISLAND ILPS9200 RI POLYDOR 2302 048
PAUL THOMPSON D (ALL — (A) ROXY MUSIC — 197 US REPRISE RS2114 RI ATCO 36133
PETE SINFIELD PROD (A — (A) ROXY MUSIC — 1972 ISLAND EURO 88179
ROGER BUNN G (1 — (B) FOR YOUR PLEASURE — 1973 ISLAND UK ILPS9232
DAVY OLIST G (— (B) FOR YOUR PLEASURE — 197 US WB 2629 ATCO 36134
RHETT DAVIES PROD (H — (B) FOR YOUR PLEASURE — 1978 UK POLYDOR RI 2302 049
ANDY MACKAY SAX (ALL — (C)STRANDED — 1973 UK ISLAND ILPS9252 RI POLYDOR 2302 050
BRIAN ENO SYN K(AB12I — (C)STRANDED — 1974 US ATCO 7045 ISLAND EURO 63313
PHIL MANZANERA G (ALL — (D) COUNTRY LIFE — 1974 UK ISLAND ILPS9303 RI POLYDOR 2302 051
GRAHAM SIMPSON B (A12 — (D) COUNTRY LIFE — 197 US ATCO 36106 EURO POLYDOR 2459 344
RIK KENTON B (I — (E) SIREN — 1975 UK ISLAND ILPS9344 RI POLYDOR 2302 052
JOHN GUSTAFSON B (BCEFI — (E) SIREN — 1975 US ATCO 36127 EURO POLYDOR 2344 090
JOHN PORTER B (CI — (F) VIVA — 1976 UK ISLAND ILPS9400 RI POLYDOR 2302 053
JOHN WETTON B (F — (F) VIVA — 1976 US ATCO 36139 EURO ISLAND 27553
EDDIE JOBSON K VLN(CDEFI — (G) MANIFESTO — 1979 UK POLYDOR POLH001 EURO 2310 651
CHRIS LAURENCE B (C — (H) FLESH & BLOOD — 1980 UK POLYDOR 2302 099 POLH 002
CHRIS THOMAS PROD (C — (H) FLESH & BLOOD — 1980 US ATCO 32102
SAL MAIDA B (F — (I) GREATEST HITS — 1977 UK POLYDOR 2302 073 US ATCO 38103
RICK WILLS B (F — (1) 1970/71 (2) 1971/72
NEIL HUBBARD G (H
SIRENS V (F — GARY TIBBS B (GH — PAUL CARRACK K (GH — ALLEN SCHWARZBERG D (H
ANDY NEWMARK D (H — SIMON PHILLIPS D (H — ALAN SPENNER B (H — NEIL JASON B (H
DEXTER LLOYD D (1

R149A ROYAL GUARDSMEN R149A

(A) SNOOPY Vs THE RED BARON — 1966 LAURIE 2038
(B) RETURN OF THE RED BARON — 19 LAURIE 2039
(C) SNOOPY & HIS FRIENDS — 19 LAURIE 2042
(D) SNOOPY FOR PRESIDENT — 19 LAURIE 2046

R150 THR ROYALS R150

ROY COUSINS (ALL — (A) PICK UP THE PIECES — 1977 MAGNUM DEAD1004 RI UA LBR1010
LEROY WALLACE D (B — (B) ISRAEL BE WISE — 1978 BALLISTIC UAG 30206
MIKEY D (B — (C) TEN YEARS AFTER — 1978 UA UAS 30189
WINSTON WRIGHT K (B
ANSEL COLLINS K (B — VIN GORDON HRNS (B — HEADLEY BENNETT HRNS (B — LLOYD PARKS B (B
BAGGA B (B — ROBBY SHAKESPEARE B (B — RANCHIE McLEAN G (B — PABLO BLACK G (B
BUBBLER G (B — ROBERT LYN G (B — WINSTON G (B — SKULLY PERC (B
STICKY PERC (B

R151 RUBBER CITY REBELS R151

ROD 'FIRESTONE'BENT V G(AB — (A) FROM AKRON(1 SIDE) — 1977 CLONE US 001
BUZZ CLICK G V (AB — (B) RUBBER CITY REBELS — 1980 CAPITOL US 12100
DONNIE DAMAGE B (
MICHAEL VON HAMMER D (— PETE SAKE K V (A — STIX PELTEN D (A — BRANDON MATHESON D V (B
JOHNNY BETHESDA B V (B

R151A RUBBER DOLLS R151A

CHRIS MARCH B (A — (A) MEAT THE RUBBER DOLLS — 1981 HAFENKLANG GER 6 24638
MARTIN NEAL D (A
J HILBIG EFFECTS(A — PWC HOBSON V (A — GOFFO G V (A

R152 RUBEN & THE JETS R152

RUBEN LADRON DE GuEVARA V TAM(AB — (A) FOR REAL — 1973 MERCURY SRM 1 659
TONY DURAN G V K(AB — (B) CON SAFOS — 1973 MERCURY SRM 1694
ROBERT CAMARENA G V (AB
JOHNNY MARTINEZ B V ORG(AB — ROBERT ROBERTS SAX (AB — BILL WILD B V (AB — BOB ZAMORA D (AB
JIM SHERWOOD SAX (A

R153 RUBETTES R153

ALAN WILLIAMS G FLT K (— (A) WE CAN DO IT — 1975 STATE ETAT 001
TONY THORPE G K D(— (B) RUBETTES — 1975 STATE US 2193 ETAT 004
MICK CLARKE B (— (C) SIGN OF THE TIMES — 1976 STATE ETAT 006
BILL HURD K (— (D) BEST OF — 1976 STATE ETAT 008
JOHN RICHARDSON D (— (E) WHERE ITS AT — 1976 POLYDOR 2383 306
PETER ARNESEN K (— (F) BABY I KNOW — 1977 STATE ETAT 012
(G) SOMETIME IN OLDCHURCH — 1978 POLYDOR 2383 480
(H) STILL UNWINDING — 1978 POLYDOR 2383 520

R154 RUBICON R154

DENNIS MARCELLINO WIND (AB — (A) RUBICON — 1978 20TH CENTURY BT 552
BRADLEY GILLIS G (AB — (B) AMERICAN DREAMS — 1980 20TH CENTURY BT 557
GREG ECKLER D (AB
JERRY MARTINI SAX (AB — MAX HASKETT TPT (AB — JIM PUGH K (AB — JACK BLADES B (AB

R155 RUBINOOS R155

JOHN RUBIN G V (A — (A) THE RUBINOOS — 1977 BESERKLEY US 0051 UK BSERK10
TOMMY DUNBAR G (A — (B) BACK TO THE DRAWING BOARD — 1979 BESERKLEY US 0080 UK BSERK18
ROYSE ADER B (A
DONN SPINDT D (A

R156 RUBY (UK) R156

MIKE LENTON G (A — (A) RED CRYSTAL FANTASIES — 1974 CHRYSALIS CHR 1061
JOHN ABBOTT G V (A
DAVID KNIGHTS V G B(A — RAB MUNRO V PERC (A — GERRY SHURY STRINGS(A — GEOFF SWETTENHAM D (A
COLIN FAIRLEY D (A

R157 RUBY (US) R157

TOM FOGERTY G V (AB — (A) RUBY — 1977 PBR INT US 7001 UK PBRL5001
RANDY ODA G K V(AB — (B) ROCK'N'ROLL MADNESS — 1978 PBR INT US 7004 UK PBRL5003
BOBBY COCHRAN D V (AB
ANTHONY DAVIS B V (AB — ED BOGAS B (A

R157A RUBY & THE ROMANTICS R157A

(A) GREATEST HITS — 19 MCA US 541

R158 RUEFREX R158

JACKIE FORGE G (A — (A) ONE BY ONE(EP) — 1979 GOOD VIBRATION GOT 8
ALAN CLARKE V (A
TOM COULTER B (A PAUL BURGESS D (A

R159 DAVID RUFFIN R159

DAVID RUFFIN V (ALL — MY WHOLE WORLD ENDED — 1969 TAMLA US 685
VAN McCOY V PROD K(H — FEELIN' GOOD — 1969 TAMLA US 695
GORDON EDWARDS B (H — DOIN HIS THING — 196 TAMLA US 696
ERIC GALE G (H — DAVID RUFFINS — 1973 TAMLA UK STML11228 US 762
PAUL GRIFFIN K (H — ME & ROCK'N'ROLL IS HERE TO STAY — 1975 TAMLA UK STML11283 US 7818
CRUSHER BENNETT PERC (H — WHO AM I — 1975 TAMLA UK STML12012 US 7849
HUGH McCRACKEN G (H — EVERYTHING'S COMING UP LOVE — 1976 TAMLA UK STML12030 US 7866
VICTOR PAZ TPT (H — (H) IN MY STRIDE — 1977 TAMLA UK STML12064 US 7885
MICKEY GRAVINE TROM (H — AT HIS BEST — 1978 TAMLA UK STML12079 US 7895
WAYNE ANDRE TROM (H — SO SOON WE CHANGE — 1979 WB US 3306
PAUL FAULISE TROM (H — G ENTLEMAN RUFFIN — 1981 WB US 3416
CHARLES KIPPS PROD (H
CORNELL DUPREE G (H STEVE GADD D (H DON GROLNICK K (H JON FADDIS TPT (H
MARVIN STAMM TPT (H BOB ALEXANDER TROM (H JANIS ROBBINSON TROM (H ALBERT DAILEY V (H

R160 JIMMY RUFFIN R160

JIMMY RUFFIN V (ALL — JIMMY RUFFIN — 1967 POLYDOR UK 2383 240
SINGS TOP TEN — 1967 SOUL US 704
JIMMY RUFFIN WAY — 1967 TAMLA UK STML11048
RUFF & READY — 1969 TAMLA UK STML11106
RUFF & READY — 1969 SOUL US 708
FOREVER — 1970 TAMLA UK STML11161
GROOVE GOVERNOR — 1970 SOUL US 727
I AM MY BROTHERS KEEPER — 1970 SOUL US 728
JIMMY & DAVID RUFFIN — 1971 TAMLA UK STML11176
GREATEST HITS — 1974 TAMLA UK STML11259
LOVE IS ALL WE NEED — 1975 POLYDOR UK 2383 337
20 GOLDEN CLASSIC — 1980 TAMLA UK 9012
SUNRISE — 1980 RSO US 30784 UK 2394 258

R161 RUFUS R161

CHAKA KHAN V (ABCDEFH — (A) RUFUS — 1973 ABC UK ABCL5114 US 783
RON STOCKERT K V (AB — (B) RAGS TO RUFUS — 1974 ABC UK ABCL5952 US 809
KEVIN MURPHY K V (ABCDEFGH — (C) RUFUSIZED — 1974 ABC UK ABCL5063 US 837
ANDRE FISCHER D V (ABCDE — (D) RUFUS FEATURING CHAKA KHAN — 1975 ABC UK ABCL5151 US 909
AL CINER G V (AB — (E) ASK RUFUS — 1977 ABC UK ABCL5203 US 975
DENNIS BELFIELD B V (AB — (F) STREET PLAYER — 1978 ABC UK ABCL5239 US 1049
ERIC FISCHER V (A — (G) NUMBERS — 1979 ABC UK ABCL5263 US 1098
TONY MAIDEN G V (CDEFGH — (H) MASTERJAM — 1979 MCA MCG 4007
BOBBY WATSON B V (CDEFGH — (J) PARTY TILL YOU'RE BROKE — 1981 MCA UK MCF3108 US 5151
DAVE GROVER HRNS (G
TOWER OF POWER HRNS (D RON WOOD G (E MILT HOLLAND PERC (E JERRY HEY TPT (FH
KIM HUTCHCROFT HRNS (FH BILL REICHENBACH TROM (FH LARRY WILLIAMS WIND (FH HELEN LOWE V (F
EVERETT BRYSON PERC (FG JOHN ROBINSON D (GH DAVID WOLINSKI K V(EFGH RICHARD CALHOUN D PERC(F
LEW McCREARY TROM (H GARY GRANT HRNS (H LARRY HALL HRNS (H LOUIS JOHNSON PERC (H
GEORGE JOHNSON PERC (H RICHARD HEATH PERC (H FREDDIE HUBBARD TPT (G HARVEY MASON D (G
TRUMAN THOMAS K (G CHUCK BROOKE WIND (G JOHN ERVIN TROM (G RICHARD MIKULS G (G
BOB GREVE WIND (G MAXAYN LEWIS V (G LALOMIE WASHBURN V (G BILL LAMB HRNS(G

R161A RUGBYS R161A

STEVE McNICOL G (A — (A) HOT CARGO — 1969 AMAZON US 1000
MIKE MORNER B (A
ED VERNON K (A GLENN HOWERTON D (A

R162 RUMOUR R162

BRINSLEY SCHWARZ G (ABC — (A) MAX — 1977 VERTIGO UK 6360149
BOB ANDREWS K (AD — (A) MAX — 1977 MERCURY US SRM1 1174
STEVE GOULDING PERC (ABC — (B) FROGS SPROUTS CLOGS & KRAUTS — 1979 STIFF UK SEEZ13 GER 6 23756
ANDREW BODNAR D (ABC — (B) FROGS SPROUTS CLOGS & KRAUTS — 1979 ARISTA US 4235
ROGER BECHIRAN PROD (B — C) PURITY OF ESSENCE — 1980 STIFF UK SEEZ 27
DAN ELLIS TROM (A
MARTIN BELMONT G (ABC ALBIE DONNELLY SAX (A BOB ROBERTSON SAX (A DICK HANSON TPT (AB

R162A INGA RUMPF R162A

INGA RUMPF G V (AB — (A) MY LIFE IS A BOOGIE — 1977 RCA PL28321
ALAN SPENNER B (A — (B) I KNOW WHO I AM — 1980 RCA PL13499
GERRY CONWAY D (A
PAUL CARRACK K (A NEIL HUBBARD G (A ROBERT AWHAI G (A VINCE WEBER PNO (A

R162B RUMPLESTILTSKIN R162B

PETER CHARLES GREENE V (A — (A) RUMPLESTILTSKIN — 1969 BELL US 6047
JEREMY EAGLES K (A
ANDREW BALMAIN G (A RUPERT BAER D (A JACKSON PRIMROSE B (A HUGH MURPHY (A

R163 RUNAWAYS R163

LITA FORD G V (ABCDEF — (A) THE RUNAWAYS — 1976 MERCURY US SRMI1090
SANDY WEST D V (ABCDEF — (B) QUEENS OF NOISE — 1977 MERCURY UK 9100 032 US SRMI1126
VICKI BLUE G V (DE — (B) " " " — 1977 MERCURY GER 6338 780
JOAN JETT G V (ABCDEF — (C) LIVE IN JAPAN — 1977 MERCURY UK 9100 046
CHERIE CURRIE K V (ABF — (C) " " " — 1977 MERCURY GER 6338 833
JACKie FOX B V (ABF — (D) WAITIN' FOR THE NIGHT — 1977 MERCURY UK 9100 047 US SRMI3705
LAURIE McALLISTER B (— (D) " " " " — 1977 MERCURY GER 6338 844
DUANE HITCHINGS K (E — (E) AND NOW THE RUNAWAYS — 1979 MERCURY 6304 505
(E) AND NOW THE RUNAWAYS — 1979 CHERRY RED ARED 3
(F) FLAMIN' SCHOOLGIRLS — 1980 CHERRY RED ARED 9
(F) " " " — 1980 MERCURY GER 6337 944

R164 TODD RUNDGREN (& UTOPIA) R164

Name	Instr	Albums
TODD RUNDGREN	G V	(ALL
DAVID LASLEY	V	(H
KEVIN ELLIMAN	PERC	(EFG
DAVID SANBORN		(DG
MOOGY KLINGMAN	K	(CDEFGH
FROG LABAT	SYN	(DF
RALPH SHUCKETT	B	(DEFGH
JOHN SIEGLER	CELLO B	(CFJDGHE
ROGER POWELL	K TPT	(FJKOPLGH
KASIM SULTON	B	(KOPL
JOHN WILCOX	D	(JKOPLGH
HUNT SALES	D	(CB
TONY SALES	B	(CB
N D SMART	D	(B
JOHN SIOMOS	D	(CD
STU WOODS	B	(C
RANDY BRECKER	HRNS	(CDE
MICHAEL BRECKER	HRNS	(CDE
BARRY ROGERS	TROM	(CDE
RICK DERRINGER	G	(CDG
EDWARD OLMOS	C	(C

Name	Instr	Albums	Name	Instr	Albums	Name	Instr	Albums	Name	Instr	Albums
AMOS GARRETT	G	(C	BEN KEITH	STEEL	(C	ROBBIE KAGALE	G	(C	BUGSY MAUGH	B	(C
RALPH WASH	G	(C	BILLY MUNDI	D	(C	GENE DINWIDDIE	SAX	(C	SERGE KAKEN	CONGA	(C
JIM COLGROVE	B	(C	RICK VITO	G	(C	CHARLIE SCHONING	PNO	(C	JIM HORN	SAX	(C
JOHN KELSO	SAX	(C	HOPE RUFF	V	(C	RICHARD COREY	V	(C	VICKI ROBINSON	V	(C
DENNIS COOLEY	V	(C	CECILIA NORFLEET	V	(C	BROOKS BAXES	V	(C	ANTHONY CARRABBA	V	(C
HENRY FANTON	V	(C	ARNOLD McCULLER	V	(H	PHILLIP BALLOU	V	(H	WELLS KELLY	D	(E
BILL GELBER	B	(E	PETER POROZEL	SAX	(E	TOM COSGROVE		(D	JERRY SCHEFF	B	(B
JOHN GUERIN	D	(B	ROY MARKOWITZ	D	(G	BARBARA BURTON	PERC	(G	LEE PASTORA	PERC	(G
JOHN MILLER	B	(GE	RICK MAROTTA	D	(G	BERNARD PURDIE	D	(G	CHRIS PARKER	D	(E
BARRY LAZAROWITZ	D	(G	DAN HARTMAN	B	(G	EDGAR WINTER	SAX	(G			

Album	Release
(A) RUNT	1970 BEARSVILLE UK K45505 US 2046
(A) RUNT	1970 US AMPEX 10105
(B) BALLAD OF TODD RUNDGREN	1971 BEARSVILLE UK K45506 US 2046
(B) " " " "	1971 AMPEX US 10116
(C) SOMETHING ANYTHING	1972 BEARSVILLE UK K65501 US 2BX2066
(D) A WIZARD A TRUE STAR	1973 BEARSVILLE UK K45513 US 2133
(D) A WIZARD A TRUE STAR	1980 BEARSVILLE RI IRSP10
(E) TODD	1974 BEARSVILLE UK K85501 US 6952
(F) TODD RUNDGRENS UTOPIA	1974 BEARSVILLE UK K55501 US 6954
(G) INITIATION	1975 BEARSVILLE UK K55504 US 6957
(H) ANOTHER LIVE	1976 BEARSVILLE UK K55508 US 6961
(J) FAITHFUL	1976 BEARSVILLE UK K55510 US 6963
(K) R A	1977 BEARSVILLE UK K55514 US 6965
(L) OOPS WRONG PLANET	1977 BEARSVILLE UK K55517 US 6970
(M) HERMIT OF MINK HOLLOW	1978 BEARSVILLE UK K55521 US 6981
(M) HERMIT OF MINK HOLLOW	1980 BEARSVILLE RI IRSP11
(N) BACK TO THE BARS	1978 BEARSVILLE UK K65511 US 6986
(O) ADVENTURES IN UTOPIA	1980 BEARSVILLE UK ILPS9602 US 6991
(P) DEFACE THE MUSIC	1980 BEARSVILLE UK ILPS9614 US 3487
(Q) HEALING	1981 BEARSVILLE UK ILPS9657 US WB 3522

R164A RUNNER R164A

Name	Instr	Albums	Name	Instr	Albums	Name	Instr	Albums	Name	Instr	Albums
STEVE GOULD	G V	(A									
MICKIE FEAT	B V	(A									
DAVE DOWLE	D	(A	ALLAN MEWRILL	G K V	(A	RAY COOPER	PERC	(A	JON COLE	G	(A
IAN LYNN	K	(A	WILLIAM C LYALL	SYN	(A						

Album	Release
(A) RUNNER	1979 ACROBAT ACRO 1 US ISLAND 9536

R165 RUNNING MAN R165

Name	Instr	Albums	Name	Instr	Albums	Name	Instr	Albums	Name	Instr	Albums
RAY RUSSELL	G B K V	(A									
ALAN GREED	V K B	(A									
ALAN RUSHTON	D	(A	HARRY BECKETT	HRNS	(A	GARY WINDO	SAX	(A	ROY CAMERON	V	(A

Album	Release
(A) RUNNING MAN	1972 NEON NE 11

R166 RUPHUS R166

Name	Instr	Albums
SYLVI LILLEGARD	V	(CD
JAN SIMONSEN	K	(CD
KJELL LARSON	G	(CD
THOR BENEDIKSEN	D	(CD
ASLE NILSEN	B	(CD
TROND VILLA	VLN	(C

Album	Release
(A) LET YOUR LIGHT SHINE IN	19 BRAIN 0060 031
(B) INNER VOICE	1977 BRAIN 0060 060
(C) FLYING COLOURS	197 BRAIN 0060 108
(D) HOT RHYTHMS AND HIGH NOTES	1978 ELECTRIC TRIX 8

R167 RUSH R167

Name	Instr	Albums
JOHN RUTSEY	D	(A
ALEX LIFESON	G	(ABCDEFHJKLMN
GEDDY LEE	G K B V	(ABCDEFHJKLMN
NEIL PEART	D	(BCDEFHJKLMN
ERWIG CHUAPCHUADUA	STEEL D	(J
HUGH SYME	K	(CJ

Album	Release
(A) RUSH	1974 MERCURY US SRMI1011 UK 9100 011
(B) FLY BY NIGHT	1975 MERCURY US SRMI1023 UK 9100 013
(C) 2112	1976 MERCURY US SRMI1079 UK 9100 039
(D) CARESS OF STEEL	1977 MERCURY US SRMI1046 UK 9100 018
(AB) RUSH/FLY BY NIGHT	19 MERCURY GER 9111 065
(E) ALL THE WORLD'S A STAGE	1976 MERCURY US SRM27508 6672 015
(F) FAREWELL TO KINGS	1977 MERCURY US SRM11184 UK 9100 042
(G) ARCHIVES (TRIPLE)(ABD)	1978 MERCURY US SRM39200 6641 799
(H) HEMISPHERES	1978 MERCURY US SRM13743 UK 9100 059
(I) CLOSER TO THE HEART (12" EP)	1978 MERCURY UK RUSH12
(J) PERMANENT WAVES	1980 MERCURY US 4001 9100 071
(K) MOVING PICTURES	1981 MERCURY US 4013 UK 6337 160
(L) EXIT STAGE LEFT	1981 MERCURY UK 6619 053
(M) RUSH THROUGH TIME	1981 MERCURY UK 6331 171
(N) SIGNALS	1982 MERCURY UK 6337 243

R167A BOBBY RUSH R167A

Name	Instr	Albums
BOBBY RUSH		(A

Album	Release
(A) RUSH HOUR	1979 PHILADELPHIA US 35509

R168 OTIS RUSH R168

Name	Instr	Albums
OTIS RUSH	G V	(ALL
WALTER HORTON	HCA	(AKL
HAROLD ASHBY	SAX	(AKL
LITTLE BRO MONTGOMERY	PNO	(AKL
JESSE GREEN	D	(F
LOUIS MILES	G	(AKL
WILLIE DIXON	B	(AKL
ODIE PAYNE	D	(AKL
RONALD EADES	SAX	(B
JIMMY JOHNSON	G	(BD
AARON VARNELL	SAX	(B
BARRY BECKETT	K	(B
BOB LEVIS	G	(F
GENE MILLER	TOT	(B

Name	Instr	Albums	Name	Instr	Albums	Name	Instr	Albums	Name	Instr	Albums
DUANE ALLMAN	G	(B	MARK NAFTALIN	K	(B	JOE ARNOLD	SAX	(B	ROGER HAWKINS	D	(B
JERRY JEMMOTT	B	(B	RED HOLLOWAY	SAX	(KL	LAYFAYETTE LEAKE	K	(KL	WAYNE BENNETT	G	(KL
AL DUNCAN	D	(KL	LUCIUS WASHINGTON	SAX	(KL	JODY WILLIAMS	G	(KL	REGGIE BOYD	G	(KL
FRED BELOW	D	(KL	JACKIE BRENSTON	SAX	(KL	IKE TURNER	G	(KL	JIMMY DAWKINS	G	(C
JEROME VAN JONES	K	(C	SUNNYLAND SLIM	PNO	(C	WILLIE MABON	PNO	(C	JAMES GREEN	B	(C
BOB PLUNKETT	D	(C	SYLVESTER BOINES	B	(D	TYRONE CENTURY	D	(D	DOUG KILMER	B	(E
JOHN KAHN	B	(E	BOB JONES	D	(E	FRED BURTON	G	(E	IRA KAMIN	ORG	(E
JOHN WILMETH	TPT	(E	RON STALLINGS	SAX	(E	HART McNEE	SAX	(E	AB LOCKE	SAX	(F
CHUCK SMITH	SAX	(F	BIG MOOSE WALKER	K	(F	MIGHTY JOE YOUNG	G	(F	BOB STROGER	B	(F

Album	Release
(A) THIS ONE'S A GOOD UN	1968 BLUE HORIZON UK 763222
(B) MOURNING IN THE MORNING	1969 COTILLION US 9006 UK ATCOK40495
(C) SCREAMING & CRYING	1974 BLACK & BLUE FR 33516
(D) BLUES LIVE	1975 TRIO JAP PA3086
(D) SO MANY ROADS (1 DIFF TRACK)	1978 DELMARK US DS 643
(E) RIGHT PLACE WRONG TIME	1976 BULLFROG US 301
(F) COLD DAY IN HELL	1976 DELMARK DS 638
(G) DOOR TO DOOR (1 SIDE)	1976 CHESS US 1538
(H) CHICAGO BLUES TODAY VOL 2	1966 VANGUARD VSD 79217
(J) TROUBLES TROUBLES	1978 SONET UK SNTF 756
(K) GROANING THE BLUES	1980 FLYRIGHT UK LP 560
(L) OTHER TAKES 1956/58 (1 SIDE)	1980 FLYRIGHT UK LP 562
(M) OTIS RUSH	1972 BLUE HORIZON US 4602

TOM RUSH

TOM RUSH V (ALL (A) MIND RAMBLIN' 1963 PRESTIGE US 14003
HERBIE LOVELLE D (I (B) BLUES SONGS & BALLADS 1965 PRESTIGE US 7374
TREVOR VEITCH G (I (B) BLUES & FOLK 1965 TRANSATLANTIC UK XTRA5024
WARREN BERNHARDT K (I (C) TOM RUSH 1965 ELEKTRA EKS 7288
DUKE BARDWELL B (I (D) TAKE A LITTLE WALK WITH ME 1966 ELEKTRA EKS 7308
DAVID BROMBERG G (I (E) I GOT A MIND TO RAMBLE 1968 TRANSATLANTIC UK XTRA5053
JOHN SEBASTIAN HCA (CD (E) I GOT A MIND TO RAMBLE 1968 PRESTIGE US 7536
PAUL GRIFFIN K (I (F) TOM RUSH 19 FANTASY 24709
RED RHODES STEEL(I (G) THE CIRCLE GAME 1968 ELEKTRA EKS74018UK RI K42018
ED FREEMAN G (I (H) CLASSIC RUSH 196 ELEKTRA EKS74062 UK RI K42073
RON CARTER B (I (I) TOM RUSH 1970 CBS US 9972 UK 63940
FELIX PAPPALARDI G (CD (J) WRONG END OF A RAINBOW 1970 CBS US 30402 UK 64268
DADDY BONES G (CD (K) MERRIMACK COUNTY 1972 CBS US 31306 UK 64887
HARVEY BROOKS B (D (L) LADIES LOVE OUTLAWS 1976 CBS US 33054 UK 80282
AL KOOPER K (D (M) BEST OF 19 CBS US 33907
BILL LEE B (C
FRITZ RICHMOND JUG (C JACK ELLIOT G V (C

JIMMY RUSHING

JIMMY RUSHING (ALL BLUES I LOVE TO SING 1977 ACE OF HEARTS UK AH 119
RAY CHARLES (* LISTEN TO THE BLUES 1767 VANGUARD SRV73007
IVORY JOE HUNTER (* GOIN' TO CHICAGO 19 VANGUARD VRS 8518
THE YOU & ME THAT USED TO BE 19 RCA UK SF 8234
EVERY DAY I HAVE THE BLUES 1967 BLUESWAY BLS 6005
SENT FOR YESTERDAY 1968 BLUESWAY BLS 6057
IF THIS AIN'T THE BLUES 1974 VANGUARD UK VRS 8513
ESSENTIAL JIMMY RUSHING 1976 VANGUARD VJD 65/66
(*) THREE OF A KIND 19 DESIGN US DLP 909
GEE BABY 19 MASTER US 8104
LIVING THE BLUES 19 BLUESWAY US 6017
WHO WAS IT 19 MASTER US 8120

RICK RUSKIN

RICK RUSKIN G V (ABC (A) RICHARD RUSKIN 1974 TAKOMA US 1039
DAVID JACKSON PNO (B (B) MICROPHONE FEVER 1975 TAKOMA US 1044
MIKE BOTTS D (B (C) SIX STRING CONSPIRACY 1976 TAKOMA US 1057
COLIN CAMERON B (B
DICK ROSMINI K V B(B MARC CHOVER B (B CASSANDRA THOMAS V (B PAULA THOMAS V (B
CLAUDIA CRUTZINGER V (B

JOHNNY RUSSELL

JOHNNY RUSSELL (ALL (A) MR & MRS UNTRUE 1972 RCA US LSP4588
(B) CATFISH JOHN 1973 RCA US LSP4851
(C) RED NECKS WHITE SOCKS 1974 RCA UK AFLI0345
(D) SHE'S IN LOVE WITH A RODEO MAN 1974 RCA AFLI0542
(E) HERE COMES JOHNNY RUSSELL 1975 RCA APLI1211

LEON RUSSELL

LEON RUSSELL V K G B PERC(ALL (A) LOOKING INSIDE (ASYLUM CHOIR)1968 SMASH 67107 UK MERCURY 20141
CHRIS STAINTON K (BD (B) LEON RUSSELL 1970 A&M AMLS 982 RI ISLAND ISA 5005
GEORGE HARRISON G (B (B) LEON RUSSELL 1970 SHELTER US 8901 RI 52008
RINGO STARR D (B (C) ASYLUM CHOIR II 1971 SHELTER US 8910 RI 52010
CHARLIE WATTS D (B (C) ASYLUM CHOIR II 1971 SHELTER UK AMLS 68089
BILL WYMAN B (B (D) AND THE SHELTER PEOPLE 1971 SHELTER US 8903 RI 52008 RI US 2119
KLAUS VOORMANN B (B (D) AND THE SHELTER PEOPLE 1971 A&M AMLS65003 RI ISLAND ISA 5006
B J WILSON D (B (E) CARNEY 1972 SHELTER US 8911 RI 52011
ALAN SPENNER B (B (E) CARNEY 1972 A&M AMLH68911 RI ISLAND ISA 5007
JIM GORDON D (BD (F) HANK WILSON'S BACK 1973 A&M AMLS68923 US SHELTER 8923
BUDDY HARMON D (B (G) LEON LIVE 1973 SHELTER US 8917
GREG DEMPSEY (B (H) STOP ALL THAT JAZZ 1974 A&M AMLS68262 RI ISLAND ISA 5009
STEVE WINWOOD K (B (H) STOP ALL THAT JAZZ 1974 SHELTER US 2108 RI 52016
JIM HORN SAX (BIJ (I) WILL O THE WISP 1975 A&M AMLS68309 RI ISLAND ISA 5008
DELANEY BRAMLETT G (B (I) WILL O THE WISP 1975 SHELTER US 2138 RI 52020
BONNIE BRAMLETT V (B (J) LIVE IN JAPAN 1975 SHELTER RS 5117
BOBBY WHIPLASH (B (K) WEDDING ALBUM 1976 PARADISE US 2943 UK K56244
CLYDIE KING (B (L) BEST OF LEON RUSSELL 1976 SHELTER US 52004 ISLAND ISA 5013
BOB MOORE B (F (M) MAKE LOVE TO THE MUSIC 1977 PARADISE US 3066
MERRY CLAYTON V (B (N) AMERICANA 1978 PARADISE US 3172 UK K56534
JOE COCKER V (B (O) WILLIE & LEON 1979 CBS UK 88461
J J CALE G (FI (P) LIFE & LOVE 1979 PARADISE US 3341 UK K56891
BILLY SANFORD G (F (Q) & NEW GRASS REVIVAL LIVE 1981 WB UK K56891
DIANNE DAVIDSON G (F ( ) LOOKING BACK 1974 OLYMPIC US 7112
BEN KEITH DOB (M
ERIC CLAPTON G (B CHUCK BLACKWELL D (EHDG CARL RADLE B EFHIDG JIM KELTNER B (EHID
DON PRESTON G V (EHIDG HAROLD BRADLEY B (F JOEY COOPER G V(EHDG JOHN GALLIE K (DEHGO
JOE ZINKAN B (F RAY EDENTON G (F PETE DRAKE STEEL(FH DAVID BRIGGS K (F
PETE WADE G (F CHARLIE McCOY HCA (F JOHNNY GIMBLE FDL (F BOBBY THOMPSON BAN(F
CURLY CHALKER STEEL(F JIM BUCHANAN FDL (F BUTCH ROBINS G (F TUT TAYLOR G (F
JERRY CARRIGAN D (F PIG ROBBINS K (F WELDON MYRICK STEEL(F JESSE ED DAVIS G (D
BILLY BYRD G (F CHIP YOUNG G (F GRADY MARTIN G (F HAL RUGG STEEL (F
KARL HIMMEL D (HM HENRY BEST B (H WILLIAM KENNER MAND (H LINDA HARGROVE G (H
EDWIN SCRUGGS G (H JOHN CALE G (H WILLIE NELSON G (HO ODELL STOKES G (H
JAMIE OLDAKER D (H ROBERT WILSON B (HK CHARLES WILSON K V (H RONNIE WILSON HRNS(H
TOMMY LOKEY HRNS (H CHRIS CLAYTON HRNS (H MARCY LEVY V (H ANN BELL V (H
PAM THOMPSON V (H LENA STEPHENS V (H TEDDY JACK EDDY D (IKM MARY RUSSELL K V(IKM
MOON CALHOUN D (I MASAKO HIRAYAMA BIWA (I AL JACKSON D (I STEVE CROPPER G (I
BOBBY MANUEL G (I DONALD DUCK DUNN B (I TOMMY ALLSUP G (I PATRICK HENDERSON K PERC(IG
AMBROSE CAMPBELL PERCD(IKOGO STEVE DOUGLAS FLT (K DENNIS MANSFIELD D (K RICHARD TORRANCE G (K
ROGER LINN G (KP DAVID MINER B (IM TRUMAN THOMAS K (K JULIUS WECHTER K (K
MARTY GREBB SAX (KNOPM GREG THOMAS D (KM WILLIE WEEKS B (K NIGEL OLSSON D (K
GARY ROWLES G (K BOBBY WOMACK G (K MARC BENNO (AC BRENT NELSON D (N
JOE CHEMAY B (NP JOHN WOODHEAD G (N MIKE MEROS K (N LEE LOUGHNANE TPT(N
JAMES PANKOW TROM (N WALTER PARAZEIDER SAX (N WORNELL JONES V (NP PAUL ENGLISH D (O
JIM BOATMAN V (O REX LUDWICK D (O JODY PAYNE G V (O CHRIS ETHRIDGE B (O
BEE SPEARS B (O MICKEY RAPHAEL HCA(OMP MARIA MULDAUR V (O BONNIE RAITT G (O
BERNETTA RAND V (P LENA LUCKEY V (P CLAUDIA LENNEAR V (D KATHI McDONALD V (D
BARRY BECKETT K (D JIMMY JOHNSON G (D DAVID HOOD B (D ROGER HAWKINS D (D
JIM PRICE K (D

R174 RAY RUSSELL R174

RAY RUSSELL G (ALL — (A) TURN CIRCLE — 1968 CBS 52586
TONY ROBERTS SAX (CDF — (B) DRAGON HILL — 1969 CBS 52663
DARYL RUNSWICK B (CDE — (C) RITES & RITUALS — 1971 CBS 64271
ALAN RUSHTON D (CABD — (D) JUNE 11TH 1971 — 1971 RCA UK SF8214
HARRY BECKETT TPT (CBDE — (E) SECRET ASYLUM — 1973 BLACK LION BLP12100 2460 207
NICK EVANS TROM (CB — (F) READY OR NOT — 1977 DJM DJH20506
SIMON PHILLIPS D (F
PETER VAN HOOKE D (F — MO FOSTER B (F — TONY HYMAS K (F — CHRIS PARREN K (F
JOHN PUNTER PERC (F — KAPLAN KAYE PERC (F — MARTIN DROVER TPT (F — MALCOLM GRIFFITHS TROM(F
AL GREED V (F — ANNIE KAVANAGH V (F — MOON WILLIAMS V (F — ANDY MACKAY SAX (F
TIM WHITEHEAD SAX (F — DENNY McCAFFREY V (F — HELEN WRIGHT CELLO(F — LIZ EDWARDS VLN (F
LEVINE ANDRADE VLA (F — GAVIN WRIGHT VLN (F — MIKE RUTHERFORD (— GARY WINDO SAX (E
ROY FRY PNO (AB — RON MATTEWSON B (AB — BUD PARKES TPT (B — LYN DOBSON SAX (B
DONALD BEICHTOL TROM (B

R174A RUSSIA R174A

(A) RUSSIA — 1980 WB US BSK 3414

R174B MIKE RUTHERFORD R174B

MIKE RUTHERFORD G B (AB — (A) SMALLCREEPS DAY — 1980 CHARISMA UK CAS 1149
ANTHONY PHILLIPS K (A — (B) ACTING VERY STRANGE — 1982 WEA UK K99249
NOEL McCALLA V (A
SIMON PHILLIPS D (A — MORRIS PERT PERC (A — DARYL STUERMER G (B — JOHN ALEXANDER G (B
STEWART COPELAND D (B — PETE PHIPPS D (B — PETE ROBINSON K (B — PAUL FISHMAN K (B
GARY BARNACLE SAX (B — LUKE TUNNEY TPT (B — STEVE GOULD V (B — NOEL McCALLA V (B
DALE NEWMAN V (B

R175 RUTLES R175

OLLIE HALSALL G K (A — (A) THE RUTLES — 1978 WB UK K56459 US 3151
NEIL INNES G K V(A
RICKI FATAAR G B V(A — JOHN HALSEY D V (A — ANDY BROWN B (A

R175A THE RUTS R175A

MALCOLM OWEN V (AB — (A) THE CRACK — 1979 VIRGIN UK V2132 GER 200 988
PAUL FOX G (ABC — (B) GRIN & BEAR IT — 1980 VIRGIN UK V2188 GER 203 056
DAVE RUFFY D (ABC — (C) ANIMAL NOW — 1981 VIRGIN UK V2193 GER 203 705
VINCE SEGS B (ABC
BILL BARNACLE TPT (BC — GARY BANACLE SAX K V(ABC — LUKE TUNNEY TPT (A — MANNAH V (A
MICK GLOSSOP SYN (A

R175B PAUL RYAN R175B

PAUL RYAN K V (A — (A) SCORPIO RISING — 1976 CHARISMA UK CAS 1121
RAY ROBERTS K (A
DAVE CAKEBREAD B (A — KEVIN STEPHENSON G (A — TONY BEARD D (A

R175C PAUL & BARRY RYAN R175C

PAUL RYAN V (A — (A) TWO OF A KIND — 1967 DECCA UK LK 4878
BARRY RYAN V (A

R176 MAGGIE RYDER R176

MAGGIE RYDER V (A — (A) MAGGIE RYDER — 1978 POLYDOR UK 2383 496
STEVE JAMES PROD(A

R177 MITCH RYDER R177

MITCH RYDER V (ALL — (A) TAKE A RIDE — 1966 NEW VOICE US 2000
JIM McCARTY G (ABCEFI — (A) TAKE A RIDE — 1966 STATESIDE UK 10178
JOE CUBERT G (ABCEFI — (B) BREAKOUT — 1967 NEWVOICE US 2002
TONY SUEHY B (J — (B) BREAKOUT — 1967 STATESIDE UK 10189
EARL ELIOT B (AEFI — (C) SOCK IT TO ME — 1967 NEW VOICE US 2003
JOHN'BEE' BADANJEK D (ABCEFHI — (D) WHAT NOW MY LOVE — 1967 DYNAVOICE US 31901
DAVE OPATIK G (J — (D) WHAT NOW MY LOVE — 1967 STATESIDE UK 10229
JIM McCALLISTER B (CDEFI — (E) MITCH RYDER SINGS THE HITS — 1968 NEW VOICE US 2005
BOOKER T JONES K (G — (F) ALL MITCH RYDERS HITS — 196 CREWE US 1335
DUCK DUNN B (G — (G) THE DETROIT MEMPHIS EXPERIMENT — 1969 DOT US 25963
AL JACKSON D (G — (H) DETROIT — 1971 PARAMOUNT SPFL277 + 6010
STEVE CROPPER G PROD(G — (I) GREATEST HITS — 1972 BELLAPHON 15163
STEVE HUNTER G (H — (J) HOW I SPENT MY VACATION — 1979 LINE GERM 5002
JOHN VASS G (J — (J) HOW I SPENT MY VACATION — 197 SEEDS & STEMS US 7801
W R COOKE B (H — (K) ROCK'N'ROLL LIVE(EP) — 1979 LINE GERM 3004
BRETT TUGGLE G (H — (L) NAKED BUT NOT DEAD — 1980 LINE GERM 5046
WAYNE GABRIEL G (J — (L) NAKED BUT NOT DEAD — 198 SEEDS & STEM US 7804
DIRTY ED PERC (H — (M) WE'RE GONNA WIN (EP) — 1980 LINE GERM 3013
HARRY PHILLIPS K (H — (N) GOT CHANGE FOR A MILLION — 1981 LINE GERM 5100
BOOT HILL K HCA(H — (O) LIVE TALKIES (DBL) — 1982 LINE GER 8001
BILLY CSERNITS K (JKLMN — (P) SMART ASS — 1982 LINE GER 5200
MARK GOUGEON B (JKLMN
JOHN SAUTER B (H — MARK MANKO G (H — RICHARD SCHEIN G (JKLMN — JOE GUTE G (KLMN
WILSON OWENS D (JKLMN — BILLY LAVERE(ITCH RYDER) V

R177A RYE WHISKEY ROAD BAND R177A

MIKE WHITE G V (A — (A) RUNNING KIND 1979 — FOLK HERITAGE FHR 1017
PETE HANDLEY V B (A
KEN BYNG V G STEEL (A — MICK WILLIAMS G (A — MAI JONES V (A — BERYL WATKINS V (A
KIP GLADWELL D (A

R178 TERJE RYPDAL R178

TERJE RYPDAL G V FLT(ALL — (A) TERJE RYPDAL — 1971 ECM ECM 1016
BOBO STENSSON K (AX — (B) WHAT COMES AFTER — 1974 ECM ECM 1031
TOM HALVERSEN K (A — (C) WHENEVER I SEEM TO BE FAR AWAY — 1974 ECM ECM 1045
ARILD ANDERSEN B (A — (D) ODYSSEY (DBL) — 1975 ECM ECM1067/8
BJØRNAR ANDERSEN B (A — (E) AFTER THE RAIN — 1976 ECM ECM 1083
JON CHRISTENSEN B (ABCFH — (F) WAVES — 1978 ECM ECM 1110
BARRE PHILLIPS B (B — (G) RYDAL,VITOUS,DeJOHNETTE — 1979 ECM ECM 1125
ERIK NIORD LARSEN HRNS (B — (H) DESCENDRE — 1980 ECM ECM 1144
INGER LISE RYPDAL V (AE — (X) SART — 1971 ECM ECM1915
JACK DeJOHNETTE D (G — (Y) BLEAK HOUSE — 1968 KARUSSEL GER 2915 053
MIROSLAV VITOUS B PNO(G — ( ) DREAM — 19 KARUSSEL GER 2915 068
PALLE MIKKELBORG HRNS (FH

(CONTINUED)

R178 TERJE RYPDAL (CONTINUED) R178

SVEIN CHRISTIANSEN D (D C M NEUMANN WIND (Y HANS KNUDSEN B (Y KNUR RIISNAES SAX (Y
FRODE THINGNAES HRNS (Y ØRVIND WESTBY SAX (Y TORE NILSEN SAX (Y KJELL HANJEN SAX (Y
DITLEF ECHHAFF TPT (Y KARE FUFUHOLMEN TPT (Y JARL JOHANSEN TPT (Y FROYDRS REE HAUFE HRNS(Y
ODD ULLEBERG HRNS (Y CHRISTAIN REIM K (Y TERJE VENAAS B (Y JOHN CHRISTENSEN D (Y
TOM KARLSEN D (Y ECKEHARD FINTL WIND (A JAN GARBAREK WIND (AXY SVEINUNG HOVENSJØ B(BCDF
PETE KNUTSEN K (C ODD ULLEBERG HRN (C SUDFUNK SYMPHONY ORCH (C TORBJØRN SUNDE TROM(D
BRYNJOLF BLIX K (D

S1 S F F (SCHICKE, FURHS & FROHLING) S1

EDWARD SCHICKE D (AB (A) SYMPHONIC PICTURES 1976 BRAIN 0060 010
GERHARD FUHRS K SYN(ABCDE (B) SUNBURST 1977 BRAIN 0060 068
HEINZ FROHLING G (ABCDE (C) AMMERLAND 1978 BRAIN GER 0060 105
EDWARD BRUMUND RUTHER B(ABC (D) TICKET TO EVERYWHERE 1979 BRAIN 0060 173
(E) STRINGS 1979 BRAIN GER 0060 223

S1A S A F T S1A

(A) THE BEST OF 1974 PHILIPS NOR 6478 019

S1B S B B S1B

JOSEF SZRZEK K V (A (A) FOLLOW MY DREAM 1978 SPIEGELEI GER 913272
JERZY PIOTROWSKI D (A
APOSTOLIS ANTYMOS G (A

S2 S R C S2

SCOTT RICHARDSON V (ABC (A) SRC 1968 CAPITOL US 2991
GLENN QUACKENBUSH K V (ABC (B) MILESTONES 1969 CAPITOL US 134
STEVE LYMAN G V (AB (C) TRAVELLER'S TALE 1970 CAPITOL US 273
E G CLAWSON D V (BC
ROBIN DALE B V (A AL WILMOT B V (CB RAY GOODMAN G (C GARY QUACKENBUSH G (AB

S3 S V T S3

JACK CASADY B (A (A) EXTENDED PLAY (EP) 19 415A US 0002
BILL GIBSON D (
NICK BUCK K (A BRIAN MARNELL G V (PAUL ZAHL D V (A

S3A SUE SAAD & THE NEXT S3A

SUE SAAD V (A (A) SUE SAAD & THE NEXT 1980 PLANET P4
JAMES LANCE D V (A
BILLY ANSTATT G (A TONY RIPARETTI G (A BOBBY MANZER B (A

S3B SABATAGE S3B

(A) SUBTERFUGE(EP) 19 OPTIMISTIC OPT004

S3C SABREJETS S3C

(A) RADIOLAND (EP) 1979 BLUEPORT BLU5

S3D SABU S3D

PAUL SABU G V (A (A) SABU 1979 MCA
DAN HOLMES D (A (B) SABU 1980 MCA 202209
RICK BOZZO B (A
STEFFEN PRESLEY K (A

S4 SAD CAFE S4

PAUL YOUNG V (BCDEFH (A) SAD CAFE (MATERIAL USED ON (B) 1976 CHRYSALIS (NOT RELEASED) 1114
ASHLEY MULFORD G (BCDEFH (B) FANX TARA 1977 RCA PL25101 RI INTS 5132
TONY CRESSWELL D (BCD (C) HUNGRY EYES 1977 RCA PB 5062
JOHN STIMPSON B V (BCDEFH (D) MISPLACED IDEALS 1978 RCA PL25133 RI INTS 5133
LENNI ZAKSEN SAX (FH (D) MISPLACED IDEALS 1978 A&M US 4737
VIC EMERSON G V (BCDEF (E) FACADES 1979 RCA PL25249 RI 80 3033
IAN WILSON G V (BDEFH (E) FACADES 1979 A&M US 4779
LENNY SACHS SAX (D (F) SAD CAFE 1980 RCA SAD LP4 + PL 25319
DALE IRVING D (EF (F) SAD CAFE 1980 POLYDOR US 5045
JOHN PUNTER PERC (D (G) LIVE 1981 RCA UK SAD LP5
DOREEN CHANTER V (D (H) SAD CAFE 1981 SWANSONG
IRENE CHANTER V (D

S5 SADISTIC MIKA BAND S5

MIKA KATOH V (ABC (A) SADISTIC MIKA BAND 1974 HARVEST US 11375 UK SHSP 4029
KAZUHIKO KATOH G V (ABC (B) BLACK SHIP 1975 HARVEST UK SHSP 4043
REI OHARA B V (AB (C) HOT MENU 1976 HARVEST UK SHSP 4049
YUKIHORO TAKAHASHI D (ABC
MASAYOSHI TAKANAKA G (ABC HIROSHI IMAI K SAX(BC TSUGUTSHI GOTO B (C

S5A SAGA S5A

MICHAEL SADLER K V (ABCDE (A) SAGA 1978 MAZE US 8001 POLYDOR 6209
PAUL RECHON K (A (B) IMAGES AT TWILIGHT 1980 MAZE US 8002 POLYDOR 2391 437
STEVE NEGUS D (ABCDE (C) SILENT KNIGHT 1980 POLYDOR 2374 166
IAN CRICHTON G (ABCD (D) WORLDS APART 1981 MAZE US 8004 PORTRAIT 25054
JIM CRIGHTON SYB B(ABCDE (E) IN TRANSIT 1982 MAZE US 8006
JIM GILMOUR K V (BCDE
GREG CHADD K V (B

S6 SAGITTARIUS S6

CURT BOETCHER (AB (A) PRESENT TENSE 1968 CBS US 9644
MIKE FENNELLY (A (B) THE BLUE MARBLE 1969 TOGETHER US 1002
LEE MALLORY (A
DOUG RHODES (A SANDY SALISBURY (A JOE STEC (A RON EDGAR (A
KEITH OLSEN (AB GLEN CAMPBELL (A BRUCE JOHNSTON (A STEVE CLARK (A
GARY USHER (AB

S6A SAHARA S6A

PAUL VINCENT G (A (A) SUBJECT 1972 EPIC GER 64998
MICHAEL HOFMANN WIND SYN(ABC (B) SAHARA 1973 DAWN UK DNLS 3068
ALEX PITTWOHN HCA SAX V(ABC (C) SUNRISE 1974 PAN GER 87306 US PETERS 9006
HARRY ROSENKIND D PERC(ABC
STEFAN WISSNET B V (ABC NICHOLAS WOODLAND G(BC PETER STADLER K (A

DOUG SAHM & THE SIR DOUGLAS QUINTET

DOUG SAHM G V FDL(ALL (A) BEST OF SIR DOUGLAS QUINTET 1965 TRIBE US 37001 UK LONDONHAU8311
MARTIN FIERRO SAX (G (A) BEST OF SIR DOUGLAS QUINTET 1976 CRAZY CAJUN RI 1003
WAYNE TALBERT PNO ((B) HONKY BLUES(SIR DOUGLAS) 1968 SMASH US 67108
TERRY HENRY HRNS ((C) MENDOCINO 1969 SMASH US 67115
WHITNEY FREEMAN B ((C) MENDOCINO 1975 OVAL 5001 MERCURY 9279 125
FRANK MORIN V HRNS (CKMDI (D) 1+1+1=4 1970 PHILIPS 600 344
MEL MARTIN SAX (G (E) TOGETHER AFTER FIVE 1970 SMASH US 67130
BILL ATWOOD SAX ((F) RETURN OF DOUG SALDANA 1971 PHILIPS 600 353
JOHN PEREZ D (CDFIMR (G) DOUG SAHM & THE BAND 1973 ATLANTIC US 7254 UK K40466
AUGIE MEYER K (CDGIKMR (H) TEXAS TORNADO 1974 ATLANTIC US 7287
KEN KOSEK FDL (G (I) ROUGH EDGES 1973 MERCURY US SRMi 655
HARVEY KAGAN B (CKMDI (J) GROOVERS PARADISE 1974 WB US 2810 K56067
JIM STALLINGS B (MFI (K) TEXAS ROCK FOR COUNTRY ROLLERS 1976 DOT US 2057 ABC UK 5186
GEORGE RAINS D (GK (L) LIVE LOVE 1977 TEXAS US 1007
JACK BARBER B V (GOF (N) SIR DOUG WAY BACK 1979 HARLEM US 1005
BOB DYLAN V G K HCA (G (O) HELL OF A SPELL 1980 TAKOMA US 7075
DR JOHN K (G (O) HELL OF A SPELL 1980 CHRYSALIS UK CHR1249
DAVID BROMBERG G (G (P) WAY BACK WHEN HE WAS JUST D SAHM 1980 ROCKHOUSE NL 8001
DAVID NEWMAN SAX (G (Q) BEST OF SIR DOUGLAS QUINTET 1980 TAKOMA US 7086
WAYNE JACKSON TPT (G (R) BORDER WAVE 1981 TAKOMA US 7088 CHRYSALIS 203258
WILLIE BRIDGES SAX (G
JACK WALRATH TPT (G
CHARLIE OWENS STEEL(G ANDY STATMAN MAND (G ARIF MARDIN PNO (G FLACO JIMINEZ ACC (G
ATWOOD ALLEN G V (GF DOUG CLIFFORD D (J STU COOK D (J LINK DAVIS K FDL V(J
GARY POTTERTON STEEL(J RON STALLINGS SAX (J JOE RAE MARIMBA (J ROCKY MORALES SAX (O
LEON BAEBY (JOHN OXENDINE D (O KELLY DUNN K (O LOUIE BUSTOS SAX (O
CHARLES McBURNEY TPT (O ALVIN CROW G V (R SPEEDY SPARKS B (R

S7A SAILCAT S7A

COURT PICKETT (A (A) MOTORCYCLE MAMMA 1972 ELEKTRA US 75029
JOHN WYKER (A
CHUCK LEAVEL K (A

S8 SAILOR S8

GRANT SERPELL D V (ABCDG (A) SAILOR 1974 EPIC US 33248 UK 80337
GEORG KAJANUS G V K(ABCDG (B) TROUBLE 1975 EPIC US 34039 UK 69192
HENRY MARSH K V (ABCDFG (C) THIRD STOP 1976 EPIC NL 81701 UK 81637
PHIL PICKETT G K V(ABCFG (D) CHECK POINT 1977 EPIC UK 82256
VIRGINIA TAYLOR (F (E) GREATEST HITS 1978 EPIC UK 82754
GAVIN TAYLOR (F (F) DRESSED TO DROWN 1981 CARIBOU US 36746 UK 84534
PENGUIN CAFE ORCH (G (G) HIDEAWAY 1978 EPIC NL 83249

S8A ENDLE ST CLOUD S8A

ENDLE ST CLOUD (A (A) THANK YOU ALL VERY MUCH 19 INT ARTISTS IALP 12
D F POTTER (A
PETE BLACK (A JAMES HARRELL (A

S8B JOHN ST FIELD S8B

JOHN ST FIELD(JACKIE LEVEN) V G K(A (A) CONTROL 19 MCA
JOE KUCCER WIND (A
JOHN HAYNES D (A PHIL RYAN K (A

S9 BRIDGET ST JOHN S9

BRIDGET ST JOHN G V K(ALL (A) ASK ME NO QUESTIONS 1969 DANDELION US 101 UK 62750
RON GEESIN G K (B (B) SONGS FOR A GENTLE MAN 1971 DANDELION UK DAN8007
RICK SANDERS G (BC (B) SONGS FOR A GENTLE MAN 1971 ELEKTRA US 74104
JOHN MARTYN G (C (C) THANK YOU FOR 1972 DANDELION UK 2310 193
RICK KEMP B (C (D) JUMBLE QUEEN 1974 CHRYSALIS UK CHR 1062
PIP PYLE D (C
GORDON HUNTLEY STEEL(C IAN WHITEMAN K (C ANDY ROBERTS G (C DAVE MATTACKS D (C
TIM RENWICK G (C WILLIE WILSON D (C BRUCE THOMAS B (C

S9A ROY ST JOHN S9A

ROY ST JOHN (A (A) ROY ST JOHN(EP) 1977 VIRGIN UK VEP 1002

S9B ST PARADISE S9B

ROB GRANGE B V (A (A) ST PARADISE 1979 WB US BSK 3281 UK K56689
DENNY CARMASSI D V (A
DEREK ST HOLMES G V (A JOHN CORY K V (A MARTY CONN K (A

S9C ST JOHN GREEN S9C

ED BISSOT B V (A (A) ST JOHN GREEN 19 FLICK US 45001
SHEL SCOTT D (A
VIC SABINO HCA V(A BILL KIRKLAND (A MIKE BAXTER K V (A

S10 BUFFY SAINTE MARIE S10

BUFFY ST MARIE V G (ALL (A) IT'S MY WAY 1964 VANGUARD VSD79142
CHARLIE McCOY HCA (JH (A) IT'S MY WAY 196 FONTANA UK TFL 6040
BILLY SANFORD G (JH (B) MANY A MILE 1965 VANGUARD VSD79171
DAVID BRIGGS K (JH (B) MANY A MILE 196 FONTANA UK TFL 6047
NORBERT PUTNAM B (JH (C) LITTLE WHEEL SPIN 1966 VANGUARD VSD79211
KENNY BUTTREY D (JH (C) LITTLE WHEEL SPIN 196 FONTANA UK TFL 6071
SID SHARP STRINGS(J (D) FIRE ,FLEET & CANDLE LIGHT 1967 VANGUARD VSD79250
MEMPHIS HORNS (JH (E) I'M GONNA BE A COUNTRY GIRL AGAIN 1968 VANGUARD VSD79280
JACK NITZSCHE PNO (G (F) ILLUMINATIONS 1970 VANGUARD VSD79300
MERRY CLAYTON V (G (G) SHE USED TO WANNA BE A BALLERINA 1971 VANGUARD VSD79311
RY COODER G (G (H) MOON SHOT 1972 VANGUARD VSD79312
RUSS TITELMAN (G (J) QUIET PLACES 1973 VANGUARD VSD79330
GAYLE LEVANT HARP (G (K) BEST OF (DBL) 1973 VANGUARD VSD 3/4
JESSE ED DAVIS G (G (L) NATIVE NORTH AMERICAN CHILD 1974 VANGUARD VSD79340
BOBBY WEST (G (M) BEST OF VOL 2 (DBL) 1974 VANGUARD VSD33/44
DANNY WHITTEN (G (N) BUFFY 1974 MCA US 405 MCG 3517
RALPH MOLINA (G (O) CHANGING WOMAN 1975 MCA US 451 UK MCF 2594
BILLY TALBOT (G (P) GOLDEN HOUR 1976 PYE UK GH 825
NEIL YOUNG (G (Q) SWEET AMERICA 1976 ABC US 929 UK ABCL5168
CARLOS PARDEIRO (G

(CONTINUED)

S10 BUFFY SAINTE MARIE (CONTINUED) S10

ARIEL GONZALES (G BOB BOZINA G (F BRUCE LANGHORN G (DC MONTE DUNN MAND (D
BOB SIGGINS BAN (D RUSS SAVAKUS B (BD AL RODGERS D (D ERIC WEISSBERG G (C
GRADY MARTIN G (E RAY EDENTON G (E VELMA SMITH G (E HARALD RUGG STEEL(E
LLOYD GREEN STEEL (E WAYNE MOSS B (E JERRY SHOOK B (E JUNIOR HUSKY B (E
FLOYD CRAMER PNO (E GROVER LAVENDER VLN (E SONNY OSBORNE BJO (E BUDDY HARMAN D (E
BILL ACKERMAN D (E JORDONAIRES V (E BOB BOZINA G (F JOHN CRAVIOTTO D (F
RICK OXENDINE B (F GLORIA JONES V (H RHETTA HUGHES V (H OMA DRAKE V (H
PATRICE HOLLOWAY V (H

S11 SAINTS S11

CHRIS BAILY V (ABCD (A) I'M STRANDED 1977 HARVEST UK SHSP 4065
ED KUEPPER G (ABC (A) I'M STRANDED 1977 SIRE US 6039
IVOR HAY D (ABCD (B) ETERNALLY YOURS 1978 HARVEST UK SHSP 4078
KIM BRADSHAW B (A (C) PREHISTORIC SOUNDS 1978 HARVEST UK SHSP 4094
ALASTAIR WARD B (BC (D) MONKEY PUZZLE 1981 NEW ROSE ROSE 1
MARTIN BRUCE TPT (C
MARTIN DROVER TPT (C PAUL NIEMAN TROM (C ROGER CAWKWELL SAX PNO (C BARRINGTON G (D
JANINE HALL B (D ROD COE PROD (A MARK BIRMINGHAM D (D PATRICE MATHE HCA (D

S11A RIUIDHI SAKAMATO S11A

RIUICHI SAKAMATO (A (A) B 2 UNIT 1981 ISLAND UK ILPS9656

S11B FREDDIE SALEM & THE WILDCATS S11B

MYRON GROMBACKER (A (A) CAT DANCE 1982 EPIC US 38018

S12 SALLYANGIE S12

MIKE OLDFIELD G V (A (A) CHILDREN OF THE SUN 1968 TRANSATLANTIC UK TRA176
SALLY OLDFIELD V (A
TERRY COX D (A REY WARLEIGH FLT (A

S12A SALUKI S12A

KJELL RONNINGEN K (A (A) SALUKI 1976 COMPENDIUM FIN FIDARO 6
PETER BERG NILSEN V SAX(A
SVERRE BEYER B (A BJORN JENSEN D PERC (A FREDDY DAHL G V (A

S12B SALVATION (ARMY BANNED) S12B

AL LINDE V (A (A) SALVATION 1968 ABC US ABCS 623 UA UK UAS 29062
ARTIE McLEAN B (A
JOE TATE G (A TEDDY STEWART D (A TOM SCOTT WIND (A BILL PLUMMER SIT (A
ART RESNICK K (A

S13 SAM & DAVE S13

SAM DAVID MOORE V (ALL (A) SAM & DAVE 1966 ROULETTE US 25323
DAVE PRATER V (ALL (B) HOLD ON I'M COMIN' 1966 ATLANTIC US 8708
(C) DOUBLE DYNAMITE 1966 ATLANTIC US 8712 UK588181
(D) SOUL MEN 1967 ATLANTIC US 8725 UK580185
(E) I THANK YOU 1968 ATLANTIC US 8205 UK588154
(F) BEST OF 1969 ATLANTIC US 8218 UK588155
(F) BEST OF 1972 ATLANTIC RI UK K40027
(F) BEST OF 1982 ATLANTIC RI UK K50748
(G) STAR COLLECTION 1974 WB GERM 20073
(H) BACK ATCHA 1975 UA US LA 524

S14 SAM APPLE PIE S14

SAM SAMPSON (AB (A) SAM APPLE PIE 1969 DECCA UK SKLR5005 US SIRE 97020
ANDY'SNAKEHIP'JOHNSON (AB (B) EAST 17 1973 DJM UK DJLPS429
MARTIN BELL D (
MARK DeMAJO B (DAVE CHARLES D (A ANDY JOHNSON G (BOB RENNIE B (AB
MIKE'TINKERBELL'SMITH G(A DENNY BARNES G (B LEE BAXTER HAYES D (B MALCOLM MORLEY K(A
REX MORRIS SAX (A HARRY KLEIN SAX (A STEVE JOLLY G (A ANDY CLARK K(A

S14A SAM THE SHAM & THE PHARAOHS S14A

DOMINGO 'SAM' SAMUDIO V K(ALL (A) WOOLY BULLY 1965 MGM US 4297
DAVID MARTIN B (ABCDE (B) THEIR SECOND ALBUM 1965 MGM US 4314
RAY STINNET G (ABCDE (C) ON TOUR 1966 MGM US 4347
JERRY PATTERSON D (ABCDE (D) 'LIL RED RIDING HOOD 1966 MGM US 4407
BUTCH GIBSON SAX (ABCDE (E) BEST OF 1967 MGM US 4422
(F) NEFERTITI(REVUE) 1967 MGM US 4479
(G) TEN OF PENTACLES 196 MGM US 4526
(H) SAM,HARD & HEAVY 1970 ATLANTIC US SD 8271

S14B SAMLA MAMMAS MANNA(SWED) S14B

HANS BRUNIUSSON D (ALL (A) SAMLA MAMMAS MANNA 1971 SILENCE SRS 4604
LARS HOLLMER K (ALL (B) MALTID 1973 SILENCE SRS 4621
LARS KRANTZ B (ALL (C) KLOSSA KNAPITATET 1974 SILENCE SRS 4627
BEBBEN OBERG CONGA(A1 (D) SNORUNGARNAS SYMFONI 1976 MUSIKNATET WAXHOLM MNW 70P
COSTE APETREA G (BC3D (E) FOR ALDRE NYBEGYNNARE 1978 SILENCE SRS 4640
KALLE ERIKSSON TPT ((1) 1970 (2) 1972
ULF ARTAN WALLANDER SAX(D (3) 1972 (4) 1976
EINO HAAPALA G (E5 (5) 1977
GREGORY FITZPATRICK (D

S14C JOE SAMPLE S14C

JOE SAMPLE K (ALL (A) RAINBOW SEEKER 1978 ABC US AA1050 UK ABCL5245
JOHN COLLINS G (D (A) RAINBOW SEEKER 1982 MCA RI UK 1624
STIX HOOPER D (AC (B) FANCY DANCE 1979 SONET UK SNTF 788
ROBERT POPWELL B (A (C) CARMEL 1979 ABC US AA1126 UK ABCL 5366
JERRY HEY HRNS (D (C) CARMEL 1982 CRUSADERS UK RI 16001
PAULINHO DA COSTA PERC (ACD (D) VOICES IN THE RAIN 1981 MCA UK MCG 4016
L SUBRAMANIAM VLN (D (E) SING STREET CAFE 1982 CRUSADERS UK 16004
GARNETT BROWN TROM (A
ERNIE WATTS WIND (A FRED JACKSON SAX (A WILLIAM GREEN WIND (A ROBERT O BRYANT TPT(A
JAY DAVERSA TPT (A STEVE MADAIO TPT (A RAY PARKER G (A RAY BROWN B (D
DEAN PARKS G (ACD BARRY FINNERTY G (A BILLY ROGERS B (A DAVID T WALKER G (AE
FLORA PURIM V (D JOSIE JAMES V (D PAULINE WILSON V (D ABRAHAM LABORIEL B (CD
NIKA REJTO FLT (D

S14D SAMSON S14D

PAUL SAMSON G V (ABCD (A) SURVIVORS 1979 LASER LAP 1
CHRIS AYLMER B (AB (B) HEAD ON 1980 GEM UK GEMLP108
BRUCE BRUCE V (AB (C) SAMSON 1981 GEM UK GEMLP113
THUNDERSTICKS D (AB (D) SHOCK TACTICS 1981 RCA UK LP 5031

S15 FUZZY SAMUELS S15

CALVIN'FUZZY' SAMUELS G B V(A (A) FUZZY SAMUELS 1974 CAROLINE UK CA2002

S16 SAMURAI S16

DAVE LAWSON K V (A (A) SAMURAI 1971 GREENWICH UK GSLP 1003
TONY EDWARDS G V (A
JOHN EATON B (A LENNIE WRIGHT D PERC (A KENNY BEVERIDGE D (A TONY ROBERTS WIND(A
DON FAY SAX (A

S17 DAVID SANBORN S17

DAVID SANBORN SAX K (ALL (A) TAKING OFF 1975 WB US 2873 UK K56148
HERB BUSHLER B (B (B) SANBORN 1976 WB US 2957
HIRAM BULLOCK G V (BCE (C) DAVID SANBORN BAND 1977 WB US 3051
ROSALINDA DELEON K (BC (D) HEART TO HEART 1978 WB US 3189
PAUL SIMON V (B (E) HIDEAWAY 1980 WB US 3379 NL 56766
JAMES TAYLOR V (E (F) VOYEUR 1981 WB UK K 56900
DANNY KORTCHMAR G (E (G) AS WE SPEAK 1982 WB US 3650
WADDY WACHTEL G (E
VICTOR LEWIS D V (B PATTI AUSTIN V (B PHOEBE SNOW V (B JUMMA SANTOS PERC(BC
LANI GROVES V (BC MICHAEL BRECKER SAX (A RANDY BRECKER TPT (A HOWARD JOHNSON HRNS(A
TOM MALONE TROM (A STEVE KHAN G (A BUZZY FEITEN G (A JOE BECK G (A
DON GROLNICK K (AE WILL LEE B (A CHRIS PARKER D (A RICK MAROTTA D (AE
RALPH MACDONALD PERC (AE PETER GORDON HRNS (A JOHN CLARK HRNS (A JOSE MADERA PERC(A
WARREN SMITH PERC (A STEVE GADD D (AE MARK EGAN B (C DALE OEHLER K (C
KAT McCORD V (C CHRISTINE FAITH V (HAMISH STUART V (C STRINGS (AE
DAVID SPINOZZA G (E

S18 DAVID SANCIOUS S18

DAVID SANCIOUS K G V PERC(ALL (A) FOREST OF FEELING 1975 EPIC US 33441
GERALD CARBOY B (ABC (B) TRANSFORMATION (& TONE) 1976 EPIC US 33939
ERNEST CARTER D V (ABC (C) TRUE STORIES (& TONE) 1978 ARISTA US 4201 UK SPART1082
GAIL BOGGS (C (D) DAVID SANCIOUS 1977 CHELSEA US 548
ALEX LIGERTWOOD (C (E) JUST AS I THOUGHT 1980 ARISTA US 4247
GAYLE MORAN V (B (F) DANCE OF THE AGE OF ENLIGHTENMENT 197 ARISTA US 4130
BRENDA MADISON (C (G) BRIDGE 1981 ARISTA UK SPART1162

S18A SAND S18A

JACK MEUSSDORFFER G V (A (A) SAND 1973 BARNABY US BR 15006
DAN ROSS G V STEEL (A
DAN WILSON V (A RICH GOOCH B V (A STEVE (A

S18B SANDALS S18B

(A) ENDLESS SUMMER (SOUNDTRACK) 19 WORLD PACIFIC US ST1832

S18C ED SANDERS S18C

ED SANDERS (AB (A) SANDERS TRUCKSTOP 19 REPRISE US 6374
(B) BEER CANS ON THE MOON 19 REPRISE US 2105

S18D SANDII & THE SUNSETZ S18D

SANDII V (A (A) HEAT SCALE 1981 ALFA ALF 85642
MAKOTO KUBOTA G V K (A
KENI INOVE G V (A KING CHAMP B V (A HIDEO D (A CHARLES K (A

S19 SANTANA S19

CARLOS SANTANA G V (ALL (A) SANTANA 1968 CBS US 9781 UK 63815 RI 32003
WITH (B) ABRAXAS 1970 CBS US 30130 UK 64087 RI 32032
GREGG ROLIE K V (ABDE1234T (C) WITH BUDDY MILES 1971 CBS US 30308 UK 65142
DAVID BROWN B (ABDL235G (D) SANTANA III 1972 CBS US 30595 UK 69015
MIKE SHRIEVE D (ABDEJK34G (E) CARAVANSERAI 1972 CBS US 31610 UK 65299
MIKE CARABELLO PERC (ABCD3 (F) LOVE DEVOTION SURRENDER 1973 CBS US 32034 UK 69037
NEAL SCHON G (CDE34 (G) WELCOME 1974 CBS US 32445 UK 69040
JOSE CHEPITOS AREAS PER(ABDEKGJMN345 (H) ILLUMINATIONS 1974 CBS US 32900 UK 69063
RICO REYES PERC (DE34B (I) GREATEST HITS 1974 CBS US 33050 UK 69081
TOM COSTER K V(EJKLH5678GMNO (J) BORBOLETTA 1974 CBS US 33135 UK 69084
ARMANDO PERAZA G V(EFJKLR56GHOPQRS(K) LOTUS (TRIPLE) 1975 CBS UK 66325
LEON PATILLO V PERC (57JS (L) AMIGOS 1976 CBS US 33576 UK 86005
TOM FRAZER G (1 (M) FESTIVAL 1977 CBS US 34423 UK 86020
ROD HARPER D (1 (N) MOONFLOWER 1977 CBS US 34914 UK 88272
GUS RODRIGUES B (1 (O) ONENESS 1979 CBS US 35686 UK 86037
MARCUS MALONE PERC (2 (P) INNER SECRETS 1979 CBS US 35600 UK 86075
BOB LIVINGSTONE D (2 (Q) MARATHON 1979 CBS US 36154 UK 86098
TOM RUTLEY B (34E (R) SWING OF DELIGHT (DBL) 1980 CBS US 36590 UK 22075
COKE ESCOVEDO PERC (3C4D (S) ZEBOP 1981 CBS US 37158 UK 84946
VICTOR PANTOJA PERC (3C (T) SHANGO 1982 CBS US 38122 UK 85914
WILLIE BOBO PERC (3 (1) 1966/67 (2) 1967/69 (3) 1971 (4) 1971
PHIL FORD TABLAS (H (5) 1974/74 (6) 1976 (7) 1976 (8) 1976
PETE ESCOVEDO PERC(NOP LEON THOMAS V (KG RICHARD KERMODE K (KG MINGO LEWIS PNO (CEF
BYRON MILLER B (6 GREG WALKER V(56JLM LEON CHANCLER D (56JLM JULES BROUSSARD (HGJ5
FRANCISCO AQUABELLA PERC(R6 TOM CROUCHER V (7 RAUL REKOW PERC (78RQPS PABLO TELLEZ B V (78MN
JOHN SANTOS PERC (7 DAVID PRATER D (7 GAYLORD BIRCH D (7M LUTHER RABBS V (8
GRAHAM LEAR D (8NOPQRST JOEL (8 DOUGLAS RAUCH B G(EFJGK TOWER OF POWER HRNS(D
LUIS GASCA TPT (DC LINDA TILLERY V (D MARIO OCHOA K (D GREG ERRICO PERC(DC
HADLEY CALIMAN SAX (EC WENDY HAAS K (DGE DAVID RODRIGUES G (E LENNY WHITE PERC(E
JAMES BOND B (PHIL BROWNE PERC (FH DAVID HOLLAND B (H JACK DeJOHNETTE PERC(H
ALICE COLTRANE K HARP (H JULIA TILLMAN WATERS V (LM IVORY STONE B (L MAXINE WILLARD WATERS V(LM
JOHN McLAUGHLIN G (FG BILLY COBHAM D (F JAN HAMMER K (F LARRY YOUNG ORG (F
DON ALIAS D (F STANLEY CLARKE B (J AIRTO MOREIRA D (J FLORA PURIM V (JG
HERBIE HANCOCK K (R WAYNE SHORTER SAX (R RON CARTER B (R TONY WILLIAMS D (R
ORESTES VILATO PERC (R HARVEY MASON D (R RUSSELL TUBBS WIND (R DAVID MARGEN B(RNOPQRST
ALEX LIGERTWOOD V (QRST STRINGS (H ALBERTO GIANQUINTO PNO (B BUDDY MILES D V (C
RON JOHNSON B (C ROBERT HIGGINS ORG (C PAUL JACKSON B (M FRANCISCO ZAVALA V (M
JULES BROUSSARD SAX (G GREG ADAMS STR (G MICHAEL CARPENTER G (J ORIN WATERS V (M
FRANCISCO ZAINLA V (M CHRIS RHYME K (OP RICHARD BAKER K (ST ORESTES VILATO V PERC(ST
ALAN PASQUA K V (QS CHRIS SOLBERG G K V(PQSO BOB LEVY SYN (O URMILA SANTANA V (O
SAUNDERS KING G V (O CLARE FISHER PNO (O NARADA MICHAEL WALDEN K (O TONY SMITH D (G
BOB YANCE FLT (G DOUG RODRIGUEZ G (G

S20 SANFORD & TOWNSEND S20

JOHN TOWNSEND V (ABCD (A) SMOKE FROM A DISTANT FIRE 1976 WB US BS 2966
ED SANFORD K V (ABCD (B) DUOGLIDE 1977 WB US BS 3081 UK K56476
STEVE CROPPER G (B (C) NAIL ME TO THE WALL 1979 WB US BS 3343
OTIS HALE G SAX(ABC
ROGER JOHNSON G (AC FRED TACKETT G (B PAUL BARRERE G (B DAVID PAICH K (B
HERB PEDERSEN V (B JERRY McGEE G (B MIKE UTLEY PNO (B JEFF PORCARO D (C
DAVID HUNGATE B (B MILT HOLLAND PERC (B BILL PAYNE K (B RICHARD TORRANCE V (B
JERRY RIGHTMER B (AC CHRIS MEYER D (C TOM ROADY PERC (AC DICK HALLIGAN STRINGS(B
JIM VARLEY D (A BARRY BECKETT K (A KENNY LOGGINS V (A GEORGE HAWKINS V(A
BILLY TOWNSEND V (A JOHN CLARKE WIND (A TEX WEX V (A

S21 VERONIQUE SANSON S21

VERONIQUE SANSON (AB (A) AMOUREUSE 1972 ELEKTRA K42106
(B) HOLLYWOOD 1978 ELEKTRA K52063

S22 SANTA BARBARA MACHINEHEAD S22

JON LORD K (AB (A) TRACKS ON(BLUES ANTHOLOGY VOL3) 1968 IMMEDIATE UK IMLP019
RON WOOD G (AB (B) TRACKS ON(BEST OF BRITISH BLUES) 19 IMMEDIATE GERM 048 90677
KIM GARDNER B (AB (C) TRACKS ON(ANTHOLOGY OF BRITISH) 19 IMMEDIATE UK IMA 06
TWINK D (AB THE ONLY THREE TRACKS THEY RECORDED ARE ON THE ABOVE COMPILATION ALBUMS

S23 BOB SARGEANT S23

BOB SARGEANT G V K(A (A) FIRST STARRING ROLE 1975 RCA LPLI 5076
COZY POWELL D (A
JOHN WOODS (A JACK LANCASTER WIND (A JERRY SMITH (A CLIVE CHAMAN B (A
ROBIN LUMLEY (A RITCHIE DHARMA D (A MIKE GARSON (A WALT MONAGHAN B (A
HERBIE FLOWERS B (A

S23A SARACEN S23A

RICHARD LOWE K (A (A) HEROES SAINTS & FOOLS 1982 NUCLEUS 492

S24 SAROFEEN & SMOKE S24

(A) DO IT 1971 PYE UK NSPL28153
(B) SAROFEEN & SMOKE 197 GWP US 2029

S26 SASSAFRAS S26

DAI SHELL G (ABC1 (A) EXPECTING COMPANY 1973 POLYDOR 2383 245
TERRY BENNETT V (ABC (B) WHEELIN' & DEALIN' 1975 CHRYSALIS CHR 1076
RALPH EVANS G V (ABC1 (C) RIDING HIGH 1976 CHRYSALIS CHR 1100
DICK OWEN D (B (D) SASSAFRAS 1978 H&L US 69027
RICKY JOHN HOLT B V (ABC1 (1) MAY 1978
ROBERT JONES D V (AC
STEVE FINN B (B EDDIE WILLIAMS G V (1 CHRIS SHARLEY D (B JEFF JONES D (1
ROB REYNOLDS D (A

S26A SATIN WHALE S26A

THOMAS BRUCK B V (A (A) DESERT PLACES 197 BRAIN GERM 0040 120
HORST SCHATTGEN D V (A
DIETER ROESBERG G WIND(A GERALD DELLMAN K (A

S27 SATISFACTION S27

MIKE COTTON HRNS (A (A) SATISFACTION 1971 DECCA UK SKL5075
LEM LUBIN B (A
JOHN BEECHAM TROM (A DEREK GRIFFITHS G V (A NICK NEWELL SAX (A BERNIE HIGGINSON DV(A

S27A SATISFACTION UNLIMITED S27A

(A) THINK OF THE CHILDREN 19 HOT WAX US 716

S27B MERL SAUNDERS S27B

MERL SAUNDERS K V (ALL (A) HEAVY TURBULENCE 1971
JERRY GARCIA G V (ABC (B) FIRE UP 1973
TOM FOGERTY G (AB (C) LIVE AT KEYSTONE 1973 FANTASY US 79002
JOHN KAHN B (ABC (D) YOU CAN KEEP YOUR HAT ON 1976 FANTASY US 9503
BILL VITT D (ABC
EDDIE MOORE D SAX(A SKIP MESQUITE SAX (A MIC GILLETTE HRNS (A PAT O'HARA TROM(A
DAVID GRISMAN MAND (C MARTIN FIERRO WIND (C ARTHUR ADAMS G (D BILLY FENDER G (D
CHRIS HAYES G (D TONY SAUNDERS B (D PAUL HUMPHREY D (D LARRY VANN D (D
SHEILA ESCOVEDO PERC (D JACKIE KING G (D

S28 SATURNALIA S28

ALETTA V (A (A) MAGICAL LOVE MATRIX 1973 TRIX 1
TOM CROMPTON D (A
ROD ROACH G (A ADRIAN HAWKINS V (A RICHARD HOUGHTON B (A

S28A SAVAGE GRACE S28A

JOHN SEANOR K (AB (A) SAVAGE GRACE 1970 REPRISE US RS6399
LARRY ZACK D (AB (B) SAVAGE GRACE 2 1972 REPRISE US RS6434
AL JACQUEZ B V (AB
RON KOSS G V (AB

S29 SAVAGE RESURRECTION S29

BILL HARPER (A (A) SAVAGE RESURRECTION 1968 MERCURY US SR61156 UK SMCL20123
RANDY HAMMON (A
JEFF MYER (A STEVE LANGE (A JOHN PALMER (A

S30 SAVAGE ROSE S30

ANNISETTE V (ALL (A) SAVAGE ROSE 1968 POLYDOR 543 031 184 144
ANDERS KOPPEL K (ALL (B) IN THE PLAIN 1968 POLYDOR 543051 46292 US 246001
THOMAS KOPPEL K V (ALL (C) TRAVELLIN' 1969 POLYDOR 184 316
ILSE MARIA KOPPEL K (ABCEK (D) YOUR DAILY GIFT 1971 POLYDOR 2380 004
NILS TUXEN G (BCDF (D) YOUR DAILY GIFT 1971 RCA UK SF8169 US GREGAR 103
ALEX RIEL D (BCDEF (E) REFUGEE 1972 POLYDOR 2380 014
FLEMMING OSTERMANN G (A (E) REFUGEE 1972 RCA UK SF8250 US GREGAR 104
JOHN URIBE G (E (F) POP HISTORY 1972 POLYDOR 2675 018
KEN GUDMAND D (J (G) DODENS TRIUMF 1972 POLYDOR 2380 016
RUDOLF HANSEN B (J (H) BABYLON 1973 POLYDOR 2380 019
BEN WEBSTER SAX (H (J) WILD CHILD 1973 POLYDOR 2380 021
JENS RUGSTED V B (ABCDF (K) I'M SATISFIED 197 KARUSSEL 2499 010
PEER FROST G (J (L) SOLE VAROGSA DIN 1980 SONET SLP 1556

S31 SAVOY BROWN S31

KIM SIMMONDS G HCA(ALL (A) SHAKE DOWN 1967 DECCA UK SKL4883
BRYCE PORTIUS V (A (B) GETTING TO THE POINT 1968 DECCA UK SKL4925 US PARROT 71024
MARTIN STONE G (A (C) BLUE MATTER 1968 DECCA UK SKL4994 US PARROT 71027
RAY CHAPPELL B (A (D) A STEP FURTHER 1969 DECCA UK SKL5013 US PARROT 71029
LEO MANNING D (A (E) RAW SIENNA 1970 DECCA UK SKL5030 US PARROT 71036
BOB HALL PNO (ABCD (F) LOOKING IN 1970 DECCA UK SKL5066 US PARROT 71042
CHRIS YOULDEN V (BCDE (G) STREET CORNER TALKING 1971 DECCA UK TXS 104 US PARROT 71047
LONESOME DAVE PEVERETT G(BCDEF (H) HELLBOUND TRAIN 1972 DECCA UK TXS 107 US PARROT 71024
RIVERS JOBE B (BC (J) LIONS SHARE 1973 DECCA UK SKL5152 US PARROT 71057
ROGER EARL D (BCDEF (K) JACK THE TOAD 1973 DECCA UK TXS 112 US PARROT 71059
TONY STEVENS PERC B(CDEF (L) BOOGIE BROTHERS 1974 DECCA UK SKL5186 US LONDON PS638
OWEN FINNEGAN PERC (F (M) WIRE FIRE 1975 US LONDON PS659
DAVE WALKER V (GHJ (N) SKIN'N'BONE 1976 NOVA GER 622547 US LONDON PS670
ANDY SYLVESTER B (GH (O) BEST OF 1977 US LONDON 50000
RALPH MOMAN V (R (P) SAVAGE RETURN 1978 US LONDON PS718
DAVE BIDWELL D (GHJK (Q) BLUES ROOTS 1978 DECCA UK ROOTS 7
KEITH BOYCE D (R (R) ROCK'N'ROLL WARRIOR 1981 US CAPITOL 7002
BARRY PAUL G (R (S) JUST LIVE 1981 LINE GER 5122
JOHN HUMPHREY B V (R ( ) GREATEST HITS LIVE 1981 US ACCORD
PAUL RAYMOND V K G(GHJKNM
JACKIE LYNTON V (K STAN WEBB G V (L MILLER ANDERSON G V (L RON BERG D PERC(K
ERIC DILLON D (L JIMMY LEVERTON B (L IAN ELLIS B V (NOP TOM FARNELL D (MNPO
MIKE VERNON PERC (CD PHIL REID VLN (D DEREK WADSWORTH TROM (C BRIAN PERRIN TROM (C
TERRY FLANNERY TROM (C KEITH MARTIN TROM (C ALAN MOORE TROM (C BUTCH HUDSON TPT (D
KENNY WHEELER TPT (D EDDIE BLAIR TPT (D RAY DAVIS HRNS (D BOBBY HAUGHEY HRNS (D
DON LUSHER TROM (D JOHN EDWARDS TROM (D BOB EFFORD SAX (D REX MORRIS SAX (D
DON HONEYWILL SAX (D STAN SULZMAN SAX (K SUE GLOVER V (K SUNNY LESLIE V (K
FRANK RICOTTI PERC (K ANDY PYLE B (JK BARRY MURRAY PERC (K ANDY RAE B (M
JOHN SINCLAIR K (R LINDA LAWLEY V (R ANDREA ROBINSON V (R SUE RICHMAN V (R
RIBA GLEICH V (A

S31A SAWBUCK S31A

STARR DONALDSON G V (A (A) SAWBUCK 1972
CHUCK RUFF G D V(A
NINE YEAR B (A STEPHAN HATLEY K G V(A MOJO G V (A

S32 RAY SAWYER S32

RAY SAWYER G V (A (A) RAY SAWYER 1977 CAPITOL 11591
STEVE GIBSON G (A
DOYLE GRISHAM STEEL(A SHANE KEISTER K (A BOBBY OGDIN PNO (A LARRY LONDIN D (A
KENNY MALONE D (A TED REYNOLDS B (A LISA SILVER FDL V(A BUDDY SPICHER FDL(A
SHERI KRAMER V (A DIANE TIDWELL V (A STRING SECTION (A

S32A SAXON S32A

PETER'BIFF' BYFORD V (ABCD (A) SAXON 1979 CARRERE CAL110
PAUL QUINN G (ABCD (B) WHEELS OF STEEL 1980 CARRERE US 38 126 UK CAL115
STEVE DAWSON B (ABCD (B) WHEELS OF STEEL 1980 CARRERE GER 2934 124
GRAHAM OLIVER G (ABCD (C) STRONG ARM OF THE LAW 1980 CARRERE GER 2934 129 CAL120
PETE GILL D (ABCD (D) DENIM & LEATHER 1981 CARRERE GER 2934 138 UK CAL 128

S33 SKY SAXON BLUES BAND(SEEDS) S33

SKY SAXON (A (A) FULL SPOON OF SEEDY BLUES 1967 GNP US 2040 RI GER LINE 5033
DARYL HOOPER K (A
JAN SAVAGE G (A RICK ANDRIDGE D (A

S34 LEO SAYER S34

LEO SAYER V HCA G(ALL (A) SILVERBIRD 1973 CHRYSALIS UK CHR1050 WB US 2738
MIKE GILES D (ABC (B) JUST A BOY 1974 CHRYSALIS UK CHR1068 WB US 2836
HENRY SPINETTI D (A (C) ANOTHER YEAR 1975 CHRYSALIS UK CHR1087 WB US 2885
BOB HENRIT D (A (D) ENDLESS FLIGHT 1976 CHRYSALIS UK CHR1125 WB US 3101
RUSS BALLARD K G (AC (E) THUNDER IN MY HEART 1977 CHRYSALIS UK CHR1154 WB US 3089
DAVE WINTOUR B (A (F) LEO SAYER 1978 CHRYSALIS UK CHR1198 WB US 3200
DAVE COURTNEY PNO (ABH (G) THE VERY BEST OF 1979 CHRYSALIS UK CHR1222
MAX CHETWYN G (A (H) HERE 1979 CHRYSALIS UK CDL1240 WB US 3374
CLIFF HALL PNO (B (I) SHOW MUST GO ON 1979 PICKWICK UK SHM3035
PAUL KEOGH G (BC (J) LIVING IN A FANTASY 1980 CHRYSALIS UK CDL1297 WB US 3483
DAVE MARKEE B (BC ( ) LEO SAYER 1980 PICKWICK UK 8030
BOBBYE HALL PERC (EFH (K) WORLD RADIO 1982 CHRYSALIS UK CHR 1345
DAVE ROSE PNO (B JAMES LITHERLAND G (B BILL SMITH B (B JOHN MEALING ORG (B
LIZA STRIKE V (B THEODORE THUNDER D (B BARRY ST JOHN V (B KEITH NELSON BANJ(B
FRANK FARRELL K (C TERRY STARR TPT (C NICK NEWELL FLT (C JOHNNY VAN DERRICK VLN(C
DAVID KATZ ORCHESTRA (C JEFF PORCARO D (EF ABE LABORIEL B (E LEE RITENOUR G (E
FRED TACKETT G (EFH TOM SNOW PNO (EFH LENNY CASTRO CONGA(EF MICHAEL OMARTIAN K (E
LARRY CARLTON G (E JAY GRAYDON G (EF CLYDIE KING V (E BEN ADKINS B (E
DAVID HUNGATE B (E IRA NEWBORN G (E TOM SCOTT SAX (E SHIRLEY MATTHEWS V (E
RAY PARKER G (E JACK ASHFORD PERC (E JAMES NEWTON HOWARD K (EF BECKY LEWIS V (E
DEAN PARKS G (F STEVE LUKATHER G (F DAVID LINDLEY STEEL FDL(F SCOTTY EDWARDS B (F
DAVID PAICH K (F RUSS KUNKEL D (F LELAND SKLAR B (F WADDY WACHTEL G (F
GREG PHILLINGANES K (F STEVE PORCARO SYN (F JIM GILSTRAP V (F BOBBY KIMBALL V (F
BILL CHAMPLIN V (F LINDSAY BUCKINGHAM G (F BEN BENAY G (F CHUCK RAINEY B (FH
OLLIE E BROWN PERC (F TOM SAVIANO HRNS (F MIKE CARNAHAN HRNS (F RICHARD FELTS HRNS(F
DAVEY JOHNSTONE G (F RICK SHLOSSER D (H PAULINHO DACOSTA PERC (H MITCH HOLDER G (H
BILLY LIVSEY K (H VICTOR FELDMAN PERC (H MICHAEL BODDICKER SYN (H ED GREENE D (H
DUCK DUNN B (H STEVE CROPPER G (H DAVE LUELL SAX (H STEVE MADAIO HRNS(H
JEFF BAXTER G (H AL KOOPER K (H CHRIS DESMOND (H JOHN BARNES K(H
JERRY JUMONVILLE SAX(H ARNELL CARMICHAEL V (H MARK DOYLE G (H BILL PAYNE SYN K(H
BOB GLAUB B (H ALAN TARNEY V G K B(J TREVOR TARNEY D (J NICK GLENNIE SMITH K(J

S34A SCABS S34A

(A) LEAVE ME ALONE (EP) 1980 CLUBLAND

S35 SCAFFOLD S35

MIKE McGEAR V (ABCDE — (A) McGOUGH & McGEAR(NOT SCAFFOLD) 1967 PARLOPHONE UK PCS 7047
ROGER McGOUGH V (ABCDE — (B) AN EVENING WITH SCAFFOLD 1968 PARLOPHONE UK PCS 7051
JOHN GORMAN V (BCDE — (C) LILY THE PINK 1969 PARLOPHONE UK PCS 7077
JOHN MEGGINSON K (DE — (D) FRESH LIVER 1973 ISLAND UK ILPS 9234
GERRY CONWAY D (DE — (E) SOLD OUT 1975 WB UK K56097
LOL CREME GYSMO(E — (B) THANK YOU VERY MUCH 1968 BELL US 6018
HELEN COX V (E
ZOOT MONEY K (DE · ANDY ROBERTS G V (DE · OLLIE HALSALL G (DE · BRIAN JONES SAX (E
FRANK RICOTTI PERC (E · NEIL INNES K G (D · RAY WARLEIGH FLT (D · ANTHONY WHITE G (D
NORMAN YARDLEY HCA (D · TIM RICE V (D · ROGER BALL SAX (D · MALCOLM DUNCAN SAX (D
MIKE ROSEN TPT (D · HARRY BECKETT TPT (D · DORIS TROY V (D · PAUL KORDA V (D
JIMMY HELMS V (D · ALAN GORRIE V (D · DAVE RICHARDS B V (E · ROB TOWNSEND D (E
JIMI HENDRIX G (A · DAVE MASON G (B · MIKE VICKERS (B

S36 BOZ SCAGGS S36

BOZ SCAGGS G V (ALL — (A) BOZ 1965 POLYDOR LPHM 46253
GEORGE RAINS D (CDE — (B) BOZ SCAGGS 1969 ATLANTIC UK 588 205 US 8239
BOB ARTHUR B (— (B) BOZ SCAGGS RI 1971 ATLANTIC UK K40419 US 19166
JOHN ANDREWS G (— (C) MOMENTS 1971 CBS UK 64248 US 30454
DAVID BROWN B (CDE — (D) BOZ SCAGGS & HIS BAND 1971 CBS UK 64431 US 30796
JOACHIM YOUNG K (CDE — (D) BOZ SCAGGS & HIS BAND 1981 CBS RI US 31848
MEL MARTIN HRNS (CD — (E) MY TIME 1972 CBS UK 64975 US 31384
DOUG SIMRIL G PNO(D — (F) SLOW DANCER 1974 CBS UK 65953 US 33760
RAY PARKER G (HK — (F) SLOW DANCER 1981 CBS UK RI 32072
TOM POOLE HRNS (D — (G) SILK DEGREES 1976 CBS UK 81193 US 33920
CAROLYN WILLIS V (GH — (G) SILK DEGREES 1981 CBS UK RI 32036
ART O'HARA (— (H) DOWN TWO THEN LEFT 1977 CBS UK 86028 US 34729
PAT O'HARA HRNS (CD — (J) HITS 1980 CBS UK 84706 US 36846
PAUL BECKER HRNS (— (K) MIDDLEMAN 1980 CBS UK 86094 US 36106
ROGER HAWKINS D (BE
EDDIE HINTON G (BE · JIM JOHNSON G (BE · PETER CARR G (E · DAVE HOOD B (BE
CLAYTON IVEY K (E · SID SHARP STRINGS(· JOE PORCARO (· JEFF PORCARO (GHK
FRED TACKETT G (G · LES DUDEK G (G · DUANE ALLMAN G DOB(B · JOHN MADRID HRNS (
ADRIA TAPIA SAX (K · LENNY CASTRO PERC (K · SCOTT EDWARDS B (H · STEVE LUKATHER G (HK
JAI WINDING K (H · JOHN McFEE STEEL (C · CURLEY COOKE G (C · COKE ESCOVEDO PERC(C
PETE ESCOVEDO PERC (C · BILL ATWOOD HRNS (C · RITA COOLIDGE V (CD · BEN SIDRAN VIBES (C
CHEPITO AREAS PERC (D · DOROTHY MORRISON V (DE · MIKE CARABELLO PERC (D · LEE CHARLTON (D
BARRY BECKETT K (BE · CHARLES CHALMERS SAX (BE · FLOYD NEWMAN SAX (B · BEN CAULEY TPT (B
GENE MILLER TPT (B · JOE ARNOLD SAX (B · JAMES MITCHELL SAX (B · JEANNIE GREENE V (B
MARY HOLLADAY V (B · DONNA THATCHER V (B · TRACY NELSON V (B · IRMA ROUTEN V (B
JOYCE DUNN V (B · AL LESTER FDL (B · DAVID PAICH K SYN(GK · LOUIS SHELTON G (G
PLAS JOHNSON SAX (G · JIM HORN HRNS (G · CHUCK FINDLEY HRNS (G · BUD SHANKS SAX (G
MARTY McCALL V (G · AUGIE JOHNSON V (G · MAXINE GREEN V (G · PEPPER SWENSON V (G
JOHN PIERCE B (K · RICK MAROTTA D (K · DON GROLNICK K (K · CARLOS SANTANA G (K
JOE VITALE D (K · JAMES NEWTON HOWARD K (K · PAULETTE BROWN V (K · DAVID LASLEY V (K
SHARON REDD V (K · CHARLOTTE CROSSLEY V (K · BILI THEDFORD V (K · OREN WATERS V (K
BILL CHAMPLIN V (K · CHARLES IRWIN V (K · DAVID HUNGATE B (GHK · ZEDRIC TURNBOUGH V (H
VICTOR FELDMAN K (H · PHYLLIS ST JAMES V (H · ELDRIGE KING V (H · CHUCK FINDLEY HRN (GH
JULIA TILLMAN V (HK · STAN FARBER V (H · ERNIE WATTS SAX (H · DON MENZA HRNS(H
MICHAEL OMARTIAN K (H · JAY GRAYDON B (H · BOBBYE HALL PERC (H · JIM GILTRAP V (H
JOHN LEHMAN V (H · VENETTA FIELDS V (H · ROY GALLOWAY V (H · BOBBY KING V (H
TERRY EVANS V (H · ALAN ESTES CONGA(H · MYRNA MATTHEWS V (H · JAMES HAAS V (H
STEVE MADAIO HRNS (H · FRED SELDON HRNS (H · DAVID DUKE HRNS (H · BARBARA KORN HRNS(H

S36A SCARECROW S36A

JOHN STEWART G V (A — (A) SCARECROW LIVE 1978 SPILT MILK SMFM1127(
DAVE RUMSEY D (A
BILL PUPLETT G (A · DICK WILLIAMSON B (A

S37 SCARS S37

PAUL RESEARCH G (A — (A) 1979
CALUNN MACKAY D (A — ( ) AUTHOR! AUTHOR! 1981 PRE UK PREX 5
BOBBY KING V (A
JOHN MACKIE D (A

S37A SCENE STEALER S37A

(A) FIRST OFFENCE 1978 EMI 066 60275

S38 SCHADEL BROS! S38

EKKI SCHADEL V (AB — (A) QUITE LIKE THIS 1978 PHOX GER 2013
HEINER SCHADEL K V (AB — (B) CAN YOU MATCH A SUPRISE 1980 VERTIGO GER 6360 644
KLAUS PETER REINICKE (AB
HEINER LURIG G (A · RENE GILLY G (A · ARNULF'BRETT'SCHULDT G (H · DIETER AHLERS G (A
MATZ STEINKE B (AB · DIRK ERDMANN B (A · ERWIN GIEBELHAUSEN B (AB · HAJO HOFFMANN VLN(A
WOLFGANG STURWOHLD K (A · BRIGITTE THIELEPAPPE HRNS(A · JIM McGILLIVRAY D (A · LOTHAR HITZEK V (A
GERD WENNEMUTH D (AB · WENER LOHR D (B · MICKY STICKDORN D (B · LOTHAR KRIST SAX (B
KLAUS LENZ TPT (B · JENS FISCHER G (B · HASSO ANHOECK D (A · ACHIM GIESELER K (B
ARNDT SCHULZ G (B · MICK RAUSCH G (B · MICHAEL THIELEPAPPE SAX (A · HORST MICHAEL DURING PERC(A
KARSTEN SEIDENBERG PERC(A · RAINER HOLST PERC (A · WERNER KUCKUCK PERC (A · MICHAEL MELLENTHIN PERC(A
SEPPL KREUTZFELD PERC (A · MICHAEL NULLENTHIN PERC (A · BILLY KABUS B (B · NORBERT DOMLING B(B

S39 JANNE SCHAFFER S39

JANNE SCHAFFER G V (ALL — (A) JANNE SCHAFFER 1973 4LEAF SWED EFG 7232
BJORN LINDH K FLT(ABD — (A) THE CHINESE 1974 VERTIGO UK 6360 107
STEFAN BROLUND B (ABD — (B) ANDRA LP 1974 EUROPA FILM SWED EFG 501 2106
OLA BRUNKERT D (AB — (B) SECOND ALBUM 1975 VERTIGO UK 6360 118
JAN TOLF PERC (A — (C) KARTHARSIS 1977 CBS US 34499 UK 81733
JAN BANDEL PERC VIBES(AB — (D) EARMEAL 1979 CBS US 35508 UK 83002
MALANDO GASSAMA PERC (ABD
SLIM NOTINI V PNO(A · HALAN NYQVIST TPT (A · SVEN LARSSON TROM (A · BENGT KARLSSON G (A
LUCAS LINDHOLM B (B · PETER OSTLUND D (B · PER SAHLBERG G (B · PETER ROBINSON K (BD
JOHN GUSTAFSON B (B · MADS WINDING B (B · JEFF PORCARO D (D · STEVE PORCARO K (D
MIKE PORCARO B (D · JOE PORCARO PERC (D

S40 ARMAND SCHAUBROECK S40

ARMAND SCHAUBROECK (ALL (A) A LOT OF PEOPLE WOULD LIKE TO SEE US DEAD 19 MIRROR
BRIAN ORMOND K (DE (B) SHAKIN' SHAKIN' 1978 MIRROR MIRROR 5
JACK BEARCE G V (DE (C) I CAME TO VISIT 19 MIRROR
BOBBY HUBER V PERC(DE (D) RATF*CKER 1978 MIRROR 7
JAY PORTER D (DE (E) LIVE AT THE HOLIDAY INN DBL 1978 MIRROR 4
GENE D'AGOSTINO V (D
BERNARD HEVERON B (DE ETHAN PORTER G (DE RILEY NEILSON V (D FRANK M DICESARE WIND(D
JERRY PORTER HCA (E

S41 MICHAEL SCHENKER GROUP S41

MICHAEL SCHENKER G (ALL (A) MICHAEL SCHENKER GROUP 1980 CHRYSALIS UK CHR 1302
GARY BARDEN V (AB (B) M S G 1981 CHRYSALIS UK CHR 1336
SIMON PHILLIPS D (A (C) ASSULT ATTACK 1982 CHRYSALIS UK CHR 1393
MO FOSTER B (A (D) ONE NIGHT AT BUDOKAN 1982 CHRYSALIS UK CHR 1375
DON AIREY K (A
CHRIS GLEN B (ABC COZY POWELL D (A TED McKENNA D (C GRAHAM BONNET V (C
PAUL RAYMOND K G (B

S41A GUNTER SCHICKERT S41A

GUNTER SCHICKERT (AB (A) UBERFALLIG 1979 SKY SKY 032
CHARLES M HEUZ (A (B) SAMTVOGEL 1975 BRAIN GER 0040 176

S41B TON SCHERPENZEEL S41B

TON SCHERPENZEEL K B (A (A) LE CARNIVALDES ANIMALS 1978 ARIOLA NL 26327
HANS HOLLESTELLE G (A
THEO DE JONG B (A FRANS PETERS HCA (A IRENE LINDERS V (A ADDY DE WILDE HCA (A
CLOUS VAN MECHELEN SAX (A MAX WERNER D PERC (A ELLEN NEEFJES V (A

S42 CONRAD SCHNITZLER S42

CONRAD SCHNITZLER ELECTRONICS(ALL (A) SCHWARZ 1971 BLOCK KS 1001
(B) ROT 1971 BLOCK KS 1002
(C) BLAU 1972 BLOCK KS 1003
(D) CON 1977 BARCLAY EGG 90184
(E) WORK IN PROGRESS 1978 BLOCK

S42A EBERHARD SCHOENER S42A

EBERHARD SCHOENER K (ALL (A) DESTRUCTION OF HARMONY 1971
TONY ASHTON K V (E (B) DIE SCHACHTEL 1971
STING B V (N (C) DAYS LULLABY 1971
ANDY SUMMERS G (N (D) MEDITATION 1974 ARIOLA GER 87131
STEWART COPELAND D (N (E) WINDOWS 1974 ELECTROLA EURO 95634
EVERT FRATERMAN D (N (F) BALI AGUNG 1976 HORZU GER 29647
OLAF KUBLER SAX (N (G) BASTIEN UND BASTIENNE 1977 EMI EURO 30231
HANSI STROER G B (N (H) DER SCHAUSPIELDIREKTOR 1977 EMI EURO 30230
NEPPI NOYA PERC(N (J) TRANCE FORMATION 1977 HARVEST EURO 32526
ORCHESTRA (N (K) THE BOOK 1978 ARIOLA EURO 28706
DAVID COVERDALE V (B (L) FLASH BACK 1978 HARVEST EURO 32839
RAY FENWICK G (B (M) VIDEO MAGIC 1978 HARVEST EURO 45234
GLENN HUGHES G V B(B (N) VIDEO FLASHBACK 1979 HARVEST UK SHSM2030
JON LORD K (B (O) EVENTS 1980 HARVEST EURO 45879

S42B SCHOENHERZ S42B

RICHARD SCHOENHERZ K V (A (A) WHAT A NIGHT 1878 WB UK K56504
CHRISTIAN KOLONOVITS K (A
GEORG LISZT B (A RAINER MARZ G (A JOHAN DAANSEN G (A JURGEN ZOLLER D (A
HARTMUT PFANMULLER D (A CARO V (A

S42C NEAL SCHON & JAN HAMMER S42C

NEAL SCHON G SYN V(A (A) UNTOLD PASSION 1981 CBS UK 85355 US 37600
JAM HAMMER D K SYN(A
COLIN HODGKINSON B (A

S42D JOHN SCHROEDER S42D

JOHN SCHROEDER (A (A) PARTY DANCE VIBRATION 19 POLYDOR 2460 145

S42E ERNST SCHULTZ S42E

ERNST SCHULTZ G V (A (A) PARAMOIA PICKNICK 1972 KUCKUCK GER 2375 014
JACK GRUMSKY G HCA (A
THEO BINO G (A TOMMI ROEDER K (A SONNY HENNIG K (A WALTI SCHNEIDER B (A
GUNTHER STORCH D (A WOLF STUMM G (A ALO SCHNURRER VLN (A

S42F ROBERT SCHROEDER S42F

ROBERT SCHROEDER (A (A) HARMONIC ASCENDANT 1980 WEA 58087

S43 KLAUS SCHULZE S43

KLAUS SCHULZE K SYN(ALL (A) IRRLICHT 1972 OHR GER 556022
HAROLD GRASSKOPF D (FJG (A) IRRLICHT 1978 ISADORA FR 9004
ARTHUR BROWN V LM (A) IRRLICHT 1975 BRAIN GER 1077
WOLFGANG TIEPOLD CELLO (LMO (B) CYBORG DBL 1973 KOSMISCHE GER 2 58 005
ERNST WALTER SIEMON V (C (B) CYBORG 1978 ISADORA 9005/6
MICHAEL SHRIEVE D (O (C) BLACKDANCE 1974 BRAIN GER 1051
(C) BLACKDANCE 1975 CAROLINE UK 2003
(C) BLACKDANCE 1981 BRAIN GER RI 0060 406
(D) PICTURE MUSIC 1974 BRAIN GER 1067
(D) PICTURE MUSIC 1976 CLEMENTINE FR 33007
(D) PICTURE MUSIC 1977 ISADORA FR 9007
(D) PICTURE MUSIC 1980 BRAIN GER RI 0040 146
(E) TIMEWIND 1975 BRAIN GER 1975
(E) TIMEWIND 1975 CAROLINE UK 2005
(F) MOONDAWN 1976 BRAIN GER 1008
(F) MOONDAWN 1976 VIRGIN NOT ISSUED ? 2064
(F) MOONDAWN 1977 ISADORA FR 9001
(G) BODY LOVE 1977 METRONOME GER 0060 047
(H) MIRAGE 1977 ISLAND UK ILPS9461
(H) MIRAGE 1977 BRAIN GER 0060 040
(I) BODY LOVE II 1977 BRAIN GER 0060 097
(I) BODY LOVE II 1977 ISLAND UK ILPS9510
(J) "X" 1978 BRAIN GER 0080 023
(K) BLANCHE 1979 LOGO NOT RELEASED UK 1011

(CONTINUED)

S43 **KLAUS SCHULZE** (CONTINUED) S43
(L) DUNE 1979 BRAIN GER 0060 225
(M) ...LIVE DBL 1980 BRAIN GER 0080 048
(N) DIG IT 1980 BRAIN GER 0060 353
(O) TRANCEFER 1981 INNOVATIVE COMM GER 80 014
( ) ROCK ON DBL 1981 BRAIN GER 0080 046

S44 **SCHUNGE** S44
SCHUNGE G V (A — (A) BALLAD OF A SIMPLE LOVE 1972 REGAL ZONOPHONE SLRZ 1033
BOB RICARDO V (A
CHRIS SPEDDING G (A JEFF CLYNE B (A HAIM ROMANO G (A BARRY DE SOUZA D (A
ROY BABBINGTON B (A DAVE MACRAE K (A

S45 **SCIENTIST** S45
PRINCE JAMMY (A — (A) BIG SHOWDOWN 1980 GREENSLEEVES UK GREL10
SOWELL G (C — (B) HEAVYWEIGHT DUB CHAMPION 1980 GREENSLEEVES UK GREL11
BINGY BUNNY G (C — (C) SCIENTIST MEETS THE SPACE INVADERS 1981 GREENSLEEVES UK GREL 19
FLABBA HOLT B (C — (D) SCIENTIST IN THE KINGDOM 1981 KINGDOM UK 9004
STLE D (C
SANTA D (C SKY JUICE PERC (C GLADDIE K (C SKULLY PERC (C
STEELY K (C WINSTON WRIGHT K (C

S45A **SCISSORS FITS** S45A
(A) SOON AFTER DARK 19 TORCH TOR 005

S45B **SCOPE** S45B
RIK SYN K B(AB — (A) SCOPE 1975 ATLANTIC GER 40553
HENK ZOMER D (AB — (B) SCOPE II 1975 ATLANTIC GER 50078
ROB FRANKEN K SYN(AB
RENS NIEUWLAND G (AB

S45C **SCOOTERS(US)** S45C
LARRY LEE B V G(A — (A) YOUNG GIRLS 1978 EMI UK AML3011 US 17026
BOBBY DEAN WICKLAND D (A
LUKE ZAMPERINI G V (A ROBERT FERRERO G V (A HELLEN TURNER PNO (A

S46 **ERROL SCORCHER** S46
ERROL SCORCHER (A — (A) RASTA FIRE 19 BALLISTIC UAS 30198

S47 **SCORPIONS** S47
HERMAN RAREBELL D (HEFG — (A) LONESOME CROW 1972 BRAIN 0040 023+METRONOME200191
RUDOLF SCHENKER G (ALL — (A) GOLD ROCK 197 BRAIN 00040016
KLAUS MEINE V (ALL — (A) ACTION 197 BRAIN 0040 0150
ULRICH ROTH G (BCDEFH — (A) I'M GOING MAD 1974 BILLINGSGATE 1004
MICHAEL SCHENKER G (AG — (B) FLY TO THE RAINBOW 1974 RCA US 1023 APL1 4025
RUDY LENNERS D PERC(CDH — (C) IN TRANCE 1976 RCA APL1 4128
FRANCIS BUCHOLZ B (BCDEFGH — (D) VIRGIN KILLER 1977 RCA 3659 APL1 4225
WOLFGANG DZIONY D (A — (E) TAKEN BY FORCE 1978 RCA RI3024 PL28309 APL1 2628
LOTHAR HEIMBERG B (A — (F) TOKYO TAPES 1979 RCA PL28331 APL2 3039
JURGEN ROSENTHAL D (A — (G) LOVE DRIVE 1979 HARVEST SHSP4097 MERCURY US 3795
MATTHIAS JABS G (J — (H) THE BEST 1979 RCA 3035 +3516 US 28356
ACHIM KIRSCHNING K SYN(D — (J) ANIMAL MAGNETISM 1980 HARVEST SHSP4113 MERCURY US 3825
GEORGE SIMPSON HRNS (J — ( ) ROCK GALAXY 1980 RCA 28390
BRAD WARNAAR HRNS (J — (L) BLACKOUT 1982 HARVESTUK SHVL823

S47A **CALVIN SCOT** S47A
CALVIN SCOT (A — (A) I'M NOT BLIND I JUST CANT SEE 19 STAX 2046

S48 **COLIN SCOT** S48
COLIN SCOT G V (ALL — (A) COLIN SCOT WITH FRIENDS 1971 UA EURO 038 60520 UK UAG29154
RAY GLYNN MAND G (C — (B) JUST ANOTHER CLOWN 1973 WB K46236
DAVE ETHRIDGE B (C — (C) OUT OF THE BLUE 1974 WB K46281
KIRK DUNCAN K (C — (A) COLIN SCOT 197 VISA IMP 1010
BARRY DE SOUZA D (C
JUANITA FRANKLIN V (C SPARKIE V (C TARAGON V (C MOX FLT HCA (C
BRIAN ODGERS B (C PHILLIP GOODHAND TAIT K(C TONY LUKYN SYN (C ERIC HASTINGS VLN(C
JULIA TURNER VLN (C KEITH SMITH VLN (C GERRY RICH VLA (C KEITH THATCHER CELLO(C
RUTH LOCK CELLO(C PETER GABRIEL (A PHIL COLLINS D (A PETER HAMMILL (A
ROBERT FRIPP G (A JON ANDERSON V (A RICK WAKEMAN K (A

S48A **ESTER MAE SCOTT** S48A
ESTER MAE SCOTT V (A — (A) MAM AINT NOBODYS FOOL 1976 BOMP 1

S48B **ISAAC SCOT BLUES BAND** S48B
ISAAC SCOT (A — (A) ISAAC SCOT BLUES BAND 1979 RED LIGHTNIN' UK 0023

S49 **JACK SCOTT** S49
JACK SCOTT V (ALL — (A) WHAT IN THE WORLD 1960 TOP RANK UK 12/024 US 626
(B) I REMEMBER HANK WILLIAMS 1960 TOP RANK UK 12/034 US 619
(C) THE SPIRIT MOVES ME 1961 TOP RANK UK 35/109 US 648
(D) JACK SCOTT 19 CARLTON US 12107
(E) WHAT AM I LIVING FOR 19 CARLTON US 12122
(F) BURNING BRIDGES 19 CAPITOL US ST2035
(G) JACK SCOTT GREATEST HITS 197 PONIE US 563
(H) SECOND ALBUM 1977 PONIE US 7055

S50 **TOM SCOTT** S50
TOM SCOTT SYN WIND (ALL — (A) HONEYSUCKLE BREEZE 1968 IMPULSE US AS 9163
ERIC GALE G (FKG — (B) RURAL STILL LIFE 1970 IMPULSE US AS 9171
HUGH McCRACKEN G HCA(FG — (C) GREAT SCOTT 19 A&M US AM 4330
BOB JAMES K (F — (D) TOM SCOTT & L A EXPRESS 1974 ODE 87969 US 77021
RALPH MACDONALD PERC (FKG — (E) TOM CAT 1975 ODE US 77029
GARY KING B (FKG — (F) NEW YORK CONNECTION 1975 ODE US 77033
GEORGE HARRISON G (F — (G) BLOW IT OUT 1977 EPIC UK 82285 US 34966
RICHARD TEE K (FKG — (H) TOM SCOTT IN L A 1977 RCA UK SF8429
CHUCK FINDLEY TPT (FKG — (H) TOM SCOTT IN L A 1977 FLYING DUTCHMAN BXLI 0833
JACO PASTORIUS B (H — (I) INTIMATE STRANGERS 1979 CBS UK 83309 US 35705
STEVE GADD D (FKG — (J) STREET BEAT 1979 CBS US 36437
DICK HYDE HRNS (FKG — (K) BEST OF 1980 CBS UK 84347 US 36352
MAX BENNETT B (DEK

(CONTINUED)

S50 (CONTINUED) **TOM SCOTT** S50

JOHN GUERIN D (KBDE LARRY CARLTON G (KD LARRY NASH K (KE RICK MAROTTA D (KG
ROBBEN FORD G (KE JINI MITCHELL V (E CHUCK DOMANICO B (B JOE SAMPLE K (D
CHUCK RAINEY B (G JOHN TROPEA G (D KENNY ASCHER K (G DENNIS BUDIMIR G (G
RAY PARKER G (G WILL LEE B (G CHRIS PARKER D (G

S50A **TONY SCOTT** S50A

TONY SCOTT (A (A) MUSIC FOR MEDITATION & OTHER JOYS 1968 VERVE 2304 471

S51 **GIL SCOTT HERON** S51

GILL SCOTT HERON G PNO(ALL (A) SMALL TALK AT 125TH & LENNOX 1972 FLYING DUTCHMAN
BRIAN JACKSON FLT K (GJK (B) FREE WILL 1972 FLYING DUTCHMAN 10153
BARNETT WILLIAMS PERC (KJ (C) PIECES OF A MAN 1973 FLYING DUTCHMAN BXLI0833 10143
LEON WILLIAMS SAX (K (D) WINTER IN AMERICA 1975 STRATA EAST 19742
HARVEY MASON D (K (E) REVOLUTION WILL NOT BE TELEVISED 1975 RCA UK SF8428
GREG PHILLINGANES K (K (E) REVOLUTION WILL NOT BE TELEVISED 1975 FLYING DUTCHMAN BXLI0613
ALVIN TAYLOR D (K (F) FIRST MINUTE OF A NEW DAY 1975 ARISTA UK ARTY 106 US 4030
RALPH PENLAND D (K (G) FROM S AFRICA TO S CAROLINA 1976 ARISTA UK ARTY 121 US 4044
MAXINE WILLARD V (K (H) IT'S YOUR WORLD 1976 ARISTA UK DARTY 1 US 5001
JULIA TILLMAN V (K (J) BRIDGES 1977 ARISTA UK SPARTY1031 US 4147
MARTI McCALL V (K (K) SECRETS 1978 ARISTA UK SPARTY1073 US 4189
MARLO HENDERSON G (J ( ) REAL EYES 1980 ARISTA US 9540
DANNY BOWENS B (J ( ) REFLECTIONS 1981 ARISTA UK SPARTY 1180
JO BLOCKER D (J ( ) THE BOTTLE 19 AUDIO FIDELITY 1017
BILAL SUNNI ALI SAX (J
DELBERT TAILOR TPT (J REGGIE BRUBANE D (J TONY DUNCANSON PERC (J FRED PAYNE G (J

S52 **SCOTTSVILLE SQUIRREL** S52

CHRIS HILLMAN MAND B V (12 (A) BLUEGRASS FAVOURITES 196 CROWN US CST 346
ED DOUGLAS B (12 (1) 1958 (2) 1962
GARY CARR G (12
LARRY MURRAY G (12 KENNY WERTZ BANJO(1 BERNIE LEADON BANJO(2

S53 **SCRATCH & UPSETTERS** S53

(A) CLOAK & DAGGER 1973 RHINO SRNO 8002
(B) SUPER APE 1976 ISLAND ILPS 9417

S53A **THE SCRATCH BAND** S53A

ROBERT ORSI V HCA G(A (A) THE SCRATCH BAND 1977 BIG SOUND US 1009 LONDON UKSHY8529
CHRISTINE OHLMAN V (A (A) THE SCRATCH BAND 1977 KUCKUCK GER 2375 043
G E SMITH G (A
PAUL J OSSOLA B (A MICKEY CURRY D V (A THOMAS CAVALIER PROD (A TOMMY GREGORY SAX(A

S53B **SCREEN IDOLS** S53B

CHED CHEESMAN G (A (A) PREMIERE 1979 COBRA CBR 1001
TONY SMITH G (A
MICHELLE NIEDDU V (A GEOFF APPLEBY B (A WOODY WOODMANSEY D (A

S53C **SCRITTI POLITTI** S53C

(A) HEGEMONY(4 A SIDES)(EP) 1979 ROUGH TRADE RT 027
(B) PEEL SESSIONS (EP) 1979 ROUGH TRADE RT 034

S53D **SCREAMS** S53D

(A) SCREAMS 1979 INFINITY US 9009

S54 **SCROUNGER** S54

PAUL LEWIS V (A (A) SNAP 1976 ANCHOR ANCL 2021
IAN CURNOW K V (A
PAUL KEOGH G (A RAY RUSSELL G (A MO FOSTER B (A FRANK McDONALD B(A
MIKE NICHOLLS D (A PETER VAN HOOKE D (A JOHN CAMERON STRINGS (A

S55 **THE SCRUFFS** S55

DAVE BRANYAN G V (A (A) WANNA MEET THE SCRUFFS 1977 POWERPLAY US 5050
STEPHEN BURNS G V PNO (A
RICK BRANYAN B PNO V (A ZEPH PAULSON D V (A

S55A **EARL SCRUGGS** S55A

EARL SCRUGGS BAN G (ALL (A) NASHVILLE ROCK 19 CBS US 1007
GARY SCRUGGS (HJ (B) HIS FAMILY & FRIENDS 1972 CBS US 30584 uk 64777
STEVE SCRUGGS (J (C) I SAW THE LIGHT 1972 CBS US 31354 UK 65023
RANDY SCRUGGS (J (D) LIVE AT KANSAS STATE 1972 CBS US 31758
JODY MAPHIS (HJ (E) DUELING BANJOS 1973 CBS US 32268
JOAN BAEZ (J (F) EARL SCRUGGS REVUE 197 CBS US 32426
BONNIE BRAMLETT V (HJ (G) WHERE LILLIES BLOOM 19 CBS US 32806
DAVID BRIGGS (J (H) ROCKING ACROSS THE COUNTRY 1973 CBS US 32943
KENNY BUTTREY D (J (J) ANNIVERSARY SPECIAL 197 CBS US 33416 UK 80821
JOHNNY CASH V (J (K) EARL SCRUGGS REVUE 2 1976 CBS US 34090
LEONARD COHEN V (J (L) FAMILY PORTRAIT 1976 CBS UK 34346
RON CORNELIUS (J (M) LIVE FROM AUSTIN CITY LIMITS 1977 CBS UK 34464
CHARLIE DANIELS (J (N) STRIKE ANYWHERE 1977 CBS UK 34878
RAMBLIN' JACK ELLIOTT (J (O) BOLD & NEW 1978 CBS 35319
DAN FOGELBERG (J (P) TODAY & FOREVER 1979 CBS US 36084
LARRY GATLIN (J
WILLIE HALL (J BILLY JOEL (J BOB JOHNSON (J JIM KELTNER D (J
DOUG KERSHAW FDL (J ALVIN LEE G V (J KENNY LOGGINS (J ROGER McGUINN (J
MIRABAI (J JIM MESSINA (J MICHAEL MURPHY (J TRACY NELSON V (J
DON NIX (J LEON PENDARVIS (J POINTER SISTERS V (J BUFFY ST MARIE V (J
REGGIE YOUNG (J LOUDEN WAINWRIGHT III V(J TIM WIPPERMAN (J RUSTY YOUNG (J
SHANE KEISTER K (H JOSH GRAVES DOB (H TEDDY IRWIN G (H LINDA RONSTADT V (H
DAVID ALLAN COE V (H

S55B **EDDIE SCWARTZ** S55B

EDDIE SCWARTZ V (A (A) NO REFUGE 1981 ATCO US 38141
GARY CRAIG D (A
BOB WILSON B (A DAVE TYSON K B (A PETER FOLLET G (A JIM McGRATH TPT (A

S55C **SEA CRUISE** S55C

JAY (A (A) SEA CRUISE 1978 LOLLIPOP GER 623783
GERMAIN (A
NANETTE SAAB V (A

S55D SEA DOG S55D

PAUL WESTON G V (A — (A)SEA DOG — 196 BUDDAH US BDS 5104
JOHN REDMOND K V (A
BRIAN KIRKWOOD B V (A — JIM NORRIS D V (A — DOUG VARTY K V (A

S56 SEA LEVEL S56

CHUCK LEAVELL V PERC K (ABCDE — (A) SEA LEVEL — 1977 CAPRICORN US 0178 UK 2429 150
LAMAR WILLIAMS B (ABCDE — (B) CATS ON THE COAST — 1978 CAPRICORN US 0198 UK 2429 158
JAI JOHANSON D (AB — (C) ON THE EDGE — 1978 CAPRICORN US 0212
ED DOWLING TPT (D — (D) LONG WALK ON A SHORT PIER — 1979 CAPRICORN US 0227
JIMMY NALLS G (ABCDE — (E) BALLROOM — 1980 ARISTA US 9531 UK SPARTY 1145
RANDALL BRAMBLETT SAX V(BCDE
GEORGE WEAVER D (B — DAVIS CAUSEY G (BCDE — DON McCLURE HRNS (A — LEO LABRANCHE HRNS (A
EARL FORD HRNS (A — CHARLES FAIRLEY HRNS (A — RUDOLPH CARTER HRNS (A — JOE ENGLISH D V (CDE
MATT GREELEY PERC V(DE — TOMMY TALTON V (D — DAVID EARLE JOHNSON PERC(D — CHARLIE BRENT SAX (D
TONY DAGRADI SAX (D — RODNEY LAFON TPT (C — JON ROBERT SMITH SAX (D — JOE WOOLIE TPT (D
HAROLD WILLIAMS SAX (D — RONNIE EADES HRNS (B — DENNIS GOODE HRNS (B — HARVEY THOMPSON SAX(B
HARRISON CALLOWAY TPT (B

S57 SON SEALS S57

SON SEALS G V (ALL — (A) THE SON SEALS BLUES BAND — 1974 SONET UK SNTF 679 US ALLIGATOR 4703
JOHNNY WALKER ORG (A — (B) MIDNIGHT SON — 1977 SONET UK SNTF 728 US ALLIGATOR 4708
JOHN RILEY B (A — (C) LIVE & BURNING — 1978 SONET UK SNTF 782 US ALLIGATOR 4712
CHARLES CALDWELL D (A — (D) CHICAGO FIRE — 1980 SONET UK SNTF 838 US ALLIGATOR 4720
A C REED SAX (C
LACY GIBSON G (C — SNAPPER MITCHUM B (BCD — TONY GOODEN D (C — ALBERTO GIANQUINTO PNO(BC
BERT ROBINSON D (B — REG ALLMON SAX (B — KEN COOPER TPT (BD — BILL McFARLAND TROM (BD
MARK WEAVER G (D — PAUL HOWARD TPT (D — DAVID D ANDERSON D (D — KING SOLOMON K (D

S57A TROY SEALS S57A

TROY SEALS V (AB — (A) PRESENTING TROY SEALS — 1973 ATLANTIC US SD7281
(B) TROY SEALS — 1977 CBS US 34271

S58 SEALS & CROFTS S58

JIM SEALS G V SAX FDL (ALL — (A) SEALS & CROFT — 1970 TA US 5001
DASH CROFTS D MAND V K G(ALL — (B) DOWN HOME — 1970 BELL UK SBLL 139 TA US 5004
LOUIE SHELTON G V (DEFGIJL — (C) YEAR OF SUNDAY — 1972 WB UK K46133 US 2568
BOBBY LICHTIG WIND B(DEJ — (D) SUMMER BREEZE — 1972 WB UK K46173 US 2629
WILTON FELDER B (DEGIJ — (CD) YEAR/SUMMER — 1974 WB UK K66033 US 2809
DAVID PAICH K (EFGI — (E) DIAMOND GIRL — 1973 WB UK K46218 US 2699
JOHN GUERIN D (DE — (F) UNBORN CHILD — 1974 WB UK K56028 US 2761
JIM GORDON D (DE — (G) I'LL PLAY FOR YOU — 1975 WB UK K56116 US 2848
JEFF PORCARO D (EFGI — (H) GREATEST HITS — 1975 WB UK K56176 US 2886
HARVEY MASON D (E — (I) GET CLOSER — 1976 WB UK K56209 US 2907
BOBBYE HALL PERC (EF — (J) SUDAN VILLAGE — 1976 WB UK K56307 US 2976
JOHN FORD COLEY V (DE — (K) ONE ON ONE — 1977 WB UK K56402
BUDDY EMMONS STEEL(F — (L) TAKIN' IT EASY — 1978 WB UK K56484 US 3163
ENGLAND DAN SEALS V (CE — (M) LONGEST ROAD — 1980 WB UK K56719 US 3365
DAVID HUNGATE B (FI
JACK LENZ FLT K(G — ED GREENE D (GIJ — JIM VARLEY D (G — ANTOINE DEARBORN PERC (G
LARRY FORD TPT (G — RON KING TPT (G — PAUL HUBINUN TPT (G — BOBBY SHEW TPT (G
BOBBY CROSBY WIND (G — JIM HORN WIND (DGI — STEVE LEEDS WIND (G — GENE CIPRIANO WIND (G
HENRY SIGISMONTI WIND (G — DICK HYDE TROM (G — JOHN LEYS TROM (G — LEW McCREARY TROM (G
MIKE PORCARO B (G — OVID STEVENS G (G — BILL CUOMO K (J — RALPH HUMPHREY D (JL
MARTY WALSH G (JL — JOE PORCARO PERC (J — DONNA GIPSON V (J — SHIRLEY MATTHEWS V (IJL
MARTY McCALL V (J — BECKY LOUIS V (J — CAROLYN WILLIS V (IJ — DEAN PARKS G (J
LEE RITENOUR G (IJ — JOE SAMPLE K (IJ — RON KRASINSKI D (L — JIM KELTNER D (DL
JAMES DIVISEK D (L — TONY PELUSO V SYN G (L — LARRY ROLANDO G (L — DENNIS BELFIELD B (L
DAVID PARLATO B (L — DOMINIC GENOVA B (L — TOM HENSLEY K (L — DAVID FOSTER K (L
STEVEN OLITZKY K (L — DAN FERGUSON DOBRO(L — BRIAN WHITCOMB K (L — DANNY DEARDORFF HCA (L
DON MENZA SAX (L — ALAN ESTES VIBES(L — MANOUCHEHR SADEGHI V (L — SEAN MACLEOD V (L
BOB PHILLIPS V (L — GARY SIMS V (L — DOUG STRAWN V (L — TANYA TUCKER V (L
JAMES GILSTRAP V (L — VANETTA FIELDS V (L — LARRY LICHTIG PNO (D — CLARENCE MACDONALD PNO(D
MIKE LANG PNO (D — MICHAEL OMARTIAN PNO (D — RUSS KUNKEL D (D — HARVEY BROOKS B (D
JOE OSBORN B (D — MILT HOLLAND PERC (DI — KING ERRISSON CONGA(D — RED RHODES STEEL(D
JOHN HARTFORD BANJO(D — DEL HIGGINS V (D — DONNIE SHELTON V (DI — LARRY CARLTON G (I
RAY PARKER G (I — CAROL CARMICHAEL V (I — MYRNA MATTHEWS V (I

S59 PHIL SEAMAN S59

PHIL SEAMAN (ABC1 — (A) PHIL SEAMAN NOW...LIVE — 1968 VERVE UK SVLP 9220
WITH — (B) THE PHIL SEAMAN STORY — 1974 DECIBEL BSM 103
ERIC CLAPTON G (1 — (C) PHIL ON DRUMS — 1975 77 77SEV 12/53
GINGER BAKER D (1 — (1) AT BLUES FESTIVAL 1968

S59A SEANOR & KOSS S59A

JOHN SEANOR K (A — (A) SEANOR & KOSS — 1972 REPRISE US 2091
RON KOSS G V (A
KENNY ALTMAN B (A — KING ERRISSON PERC (A — JOHN SEBASTIAN HCA (A — JOHN SEITER D (A

S60 SEARCHERS S60

JOHN McNALLY G V (ALL — (A) MEET THE SEARCHERS — 1963 PYE UK NPL18086
MIKE PENDER G V (ALL — (A) MEET THE SEARCHERS — 1963 KAPP US 3363
CHRIS CURTIS D V (ABCDEFGHKLM — (A) MEET THE SEARCHERS — 1966 GOLDEN GUINEA UK RI GGL 0349
TONY JACKSON B V (ABCDE — (B) SUGAR & SPICE — 1963 PYE UK NPL18089
FRANK ALLEN B (FGHIJKLMNOPQRSTU — (B) SUGAR & SPICE — 1967 MARBLE ARCH UK RI MAL 704
BILLY ADAMSON D PERC(TU — (C) THIS IS — 196 KAPP US 3409
BOB JACKSON K (T — (D) NEW SEARCHERS LP — 196 KAPP US 3412
MICK WEAVER K (U — (E) IT'S THE SEARCHERS — 1964 PYE UK NPL 18092
ED STASIUM K (U — (E) IT'S THE SEARCHERS — 1968 MARBLE ARCH US MAL 798
MARTIN HUGHES PERC (U — (F) SOUNDS LIKE THE SEARCHERS — 1964 PYE UK NPL 18111
DAVE CHARLES PERC (U — (G) SEARCHERS No4 — 196 KAPP US 3449
(H) TAKE ME FOR WHAT I'M WORTH — 1965 PYE UK NPL 18120
(H) TAKE ME FOR WHAT I'M WORTH — 196 KAPP US 3477
(I) SMASH HITS — 1967 MARBLE ARCH UK MALS 640
(J) SMASH HITS VOL 2 — 1967 MARBLE ARCH UK MALS 673
(K) NEEDLES & PINS — 1971 HALLMARK UK HMA 203
(L) GOLDEN HOUR — 1972 PYE UK GH 541
(M) SECOND TAKE — 1972 RCA UK SF 8298

(CONTINUED)

S60 (CONTINUED)

SEARCHERS S60

(N) GOLDEN HOUR VOL 2 1973 PYE UK GH 564
(O) NEEDLES & PINS 1974 RCA INT UK INTS 1480
(P) ROCK MUSIC FROM BRITAIN 197 MODE FR 9029
(Q) ATTENTION 197 PHONOGRAM EURO 6434 127
(R) HEAR HEAR 19 MERCURY US SR 60916
( ) HISTORY OF BRITISH POP 1976 PYE US 501
( ) HISTORY OF BRITISH POP 2 1976 PYE US 508
(S) THE SEARCHER FILE 1977 PYE UK FILD002
(T) THE SEARCHERS 1980 SIRE UK SRK 6086
(T) THE SEARCHERS(DIFFERENT TRACKS) 1980 SIRE GER 200986 UK SRK 6082
( ) ROCK MUSIC FROM 60'S 1980 VOGUE NL 9039
( ) WHEN YOU WALK IN THE ROOM 1980 PYE 18617
(U) PLAY FOR TODAY 1981 SIRE UK SRK 3523
(V) LOVE MELODYS 1981 SIRE UK SRK 3523
(W) 100 MINUTES 1982 PRT CASS UK 103

S61

SEASTONES S61

NED LAGIN K (A (A) SEASTONES 1975 ROUND US RX 106
PHIL LESH B (A
JERRY GARCIA G (A DAVID FREIBERG V (A DAVID CROSBY V (A MICKEY HART PERC(A
GRACE SLICK V (A SPENCER DRYDEN PERC (A

S62

B B SEATON S62

B B SEATON (ABC (A) THIN LINE BETWEEN LOVE & HATE 1973 TROJAN TRLS 59
(B) DANCING SHOES 1974 CAROLINE CA 2002
(C) COLOUR IS NOT THE ANSWER 1976 JAMA JALP 002

S63

SEATRAIN S63

RICHARD GREENE VLN (ABC (A) SEATRAIN 1969 A&M US4171 UK AMLS941 GER 212061
ANDY KULBERG FLT B(ABCD (B) SEATRAIN 1971 CAPITOL US SMAS659 UK EAST 659
JILL SHIRES FLT (D (B) SEATRAIN 1971 CAPITOL GER 80726
DON KRETMAR SAX (A (C) MARBLEHEAD MESSENGER 1972 CAPITOL US SMAS829 UK EAST 829
JOHN GREGORY G V (A (D) WATCH 1973 WB US BS 2692 UK K 46222
ROY BLUMENFELD D (A
PETER ROWAN G (BC LARRY ATAMANUIK D (BC LLOYD BASKIN K V (BCD JULIO CORONADO D (D
WILLIAM ELLIOTT K (D PETER WALSH G V (D JIM ROBERTS (ABC ANDY MUSAR B (
SANDRA LEE V (D PAUL PRESTOPINO G (D BOB STUART TUBA (D BILL KEITH BAN(D
SHA NA NA V (D PAUL SHURE VLN (D BONNIE DOUGLAS VLN (D MYRA KESTENBAUM VLA(D
DOUG DAVIES CELLO(D ALLAN VOGEL OBOE (D BUELL NEIDLINGER B (D WAYNE DALEY V (D

S64

SEAWIND S64

PAULINE WILSON V (ABC (A) SEAWIND 1976 CTI 5002
BOB WILSON D (ABC (B) WINDOW OF A CHILD 1977 CTI 5007
BUD NUANEZ G V (AB (B) WINDOW OF A CHILD 1978 PYE NSPL18561
BUD JUANEZ HRNS (C (C) LIGHT THE LIGHTS 1979 HORIZON US 734
KEN WILD B V (ABC (D) SEAWIND 1980 A&M US SP4824 UK AMLH 64824
BILL REICHENBACH TROM (BC
JERRY HEY HRNS (ABC KIM HUTCHCROFT SAX V(ABC LARRY WILLIAMS K WIND V(ABC PAULINHO DA COSTA PERC(AC
RALPH MACDONALD PERC (A IAN UNDERWOOD SYN (AB HARVEY MASON PERC V(AB BILL SUMMERS PERC(B
CHARLES VEAL STRINGS (B GARY GRANT HRNS (C BERNARD IGNER V (C

S65

JOHN SEBASTIAN S65

JOHN SEBASTIAN G V PERC HCA(ALL (A) JOHN B SEBASTIAN 1970 REPRISE US 6379 UK K44086
MILT HOLLAND D (D (A) JOHN B SEBASTIAN (WITHDRAWN) 1970 MGM US 4654
RUSSELL DASHIELL G (D (B) CHEAPO CHEAPO PRODUCTION PRESENTS 1971 REPRISE US 2036 UK K44127
AMOS GARRETT G (D (B) CHEAPO CHEAPO (WITHDRWAN) 1971 MGM US 4720
KENNY ALTMAN B (CDE (C) FOUR OF US 1971 REPRISE US 2041 UK K44149
POINTER SISTERS V (D (D) TARZANA KID 1974 REPRISE US 2187 UK K54028
RITCHIE OLSON CLAR (D (E) WELCOME BACK 1976 REPRISE US 2249 UK K54074
GREG REEVES B (C
KELLY SHANAHAN D (D DAVID LINDLEY FDL (D RON KOSS G (D JIM GORDON D (D
JERRY McKUEN G (D LOWELL GEORGE G V (D BOBBYE HALL PERC (D BUDDY EMMONS STEEL (D
EMMYLOU HARRIS V (D DAVID GRISMAN MAND (D PHIL EVERLY V (D PAUL HARRIS K (ABC
RY COODER MAND G(D RICHARD BELL K (E DAVID HUNGATE B (E JEFF PORCARO D (E
MICHAEL OMARTIAN K (E JEFF BAXTER STEEL(E REGGIE KNIGHTON G (E JON LIND V (E
MURRAY WEINSTOCK PNO (E DALLAS TAYLOR D (C JOHN BARBATA D (C FELIX PAPPALARDI B (C
MAC REBENNACK PNO (C ESSO STEEL BAND (C PAUL A ROTHCHILD PROD (D HARVEY BROOKS B (A
RAY NEOPOLITAN B (A DALLAS TAYLOR D (A LUCIAN BARNES G (B SAN ARMSTRONG G (B

S65A

SECOND LAYER S65A

(A) FLESH AS A PROPERTY(EP) 197 TORCH TOR 001
(B) STATE OF EMERGENCY (EP) 197 TORCH TOR 006
(C) WORLD OF RUBBER 1981 CHERRY RED UK BRED 14

S66

SECOND VISION S66

RIC SANDERS VLN (A (A) FIRST STEPS 1980 CHRYSALIS CHR 1289
DAVE BRISTOW K (A
JONATHAN DAVIE B (A JOHN ETHERIDGE G (A MICKEY BARKER D PERC(A

S66A

SECOND MOVEMENT S66A

HARALD KESSELHACK V (A (A) BLIND MAN'S MIRROR 1976 CASTLE GER 1003
MANNI GREINER B (A
SIGGI ZEIDLER K (A THOMAS MOECKL G (A MATTHIAS HELK D (A MANNI BIERBACH WIND(A

S67

SECONDHAND S67

KEN ELLIOT K V (AB (A) REALITY 1968 POLYDOR
ROB ELLIOT V (AB (B) DEATH MAY BE YOUR SANTA CLAUS 1971 MUSHROOM MRE 200 6
KIERAN O'CONNOR PERC (B
GEORGE HART V VLN(B MOGGY MEAD G (B NICK SOOTH B (A BOB GIBBONS G (A
TONY McGILL G (B CHRIS WILLIAMS WIND (A PAUL GREEDUS V (B

S67A

THE SECRET S67A

(A) THE SECRET 1979 OVAL AMLH68504

S68 SECRET AFFAIR S68

IAN PAGE V TPT K (AB (A) GLORY BOYS 1979 ISPY UK ISPY1 GER 201 179
MAGGIE RYDER V (A (A) GLORY BOYS 1979 SIRE US 6089
DAVID CAIRNS G V (AB (B) BEHIND CLOSED DOORS 1980 ISPY UK ISPY2 GER ARISTA 202862
DENNIS SMITH B V (Ab (C) BUSINESS AS USUAL 1982 ARISTA UK ISPY3
SEB SHELTON D (AB
DAVE WINTHROP SAX (AB

S69 SECRET OYSTER S69

BO THRIGE ANDERSEN D(A (A) FURTIVE PEARL 1976 PETERS INT US 9003
JESS STAEHR B (BE (A) SECRET OYSTER 1973 CBS EURO 65769
CLAUS BØHLING G (ABE (B) SEA SON 1974 CBS UK 80489 EURO 19009
MADS VINDING B (A (B) SEA SON 1974 PETERS INT US 9009
KENNETH KNUDSEN K (ABE (C) VIDUNDERLIGE 1975 CBS EURO 81044
FINN ZIEGLER VLN (B (D) ORLAVER 1976 CHRISTIANA P1
ERLIN CHRISTENSEN CELLO(B (E) STRAIGHT TO THE KRANKENHAUS 1976 CBS UK 80489
PALLE MIKKELBORG TPT (E
KASPER WINDING PERC (BE KARSTEN VOGEL SAX K (ABE HANS NIELSEN VLN (B BJARNE BOIE RASMUSSEN VLA(B
OLE STREENBERG D (BE

S69A SECRET SERVICE S69A

(A) OH SUSIE 1980 SONET UK SNTF 823

S70 SECTION S70

DANNY KORTCHMAR G (ABC (A) THE SECTION 1972 WB US 2661 UK K46191
LELAND SKLAR B (AB (B) FORWARD MOTION 1973 WB UK K46251
CRAIG DOERGE K (AB (C) FORK IT OVER 1977 CAPITOL 11656
RUSS KUNKEL D (AB
LEE PASTORA PERC (B SERGIO PERC (B DAVID CROSBY V (C JAMES TAYLOR V (C

S70A SECTION 25 S70A

(A) ALWAYS NOW 1981 FACTORY UK FACT 45

S70B SECTOR 27 S70B

TOM ROBINSON G V (A (A) SECTOR 27 1980 FONTANA UK 6359 039 US IRS 70013
JOE BUTT B V (A
STEVE B G V (A GARY D (A

S71 THE SEEDS S71

SKY SAXON K V HCA (ABCDE (A) THE SEEDS 1966 GNP 2023 LINE RI 5021
DARYL HOOPER K V (BCAE (B) WEB OF SOUND 1966 VOCALION 8062 +GNP 2033 LINE RI 5022
RICK ANDRIDGE D (BCAE (C) FUTURE 1967 VOCALION 8070 +GNP 2038 LINE RI 5030
JAN SAVAGE G V (ABCE (D) MERLINS MUSIC BOX(RAW & ALIVE)1967 GNP 2043 LINE RI 5036
HARVEY SHARPE B (BC (E) FALLIN' OFF THE EDGE 1977 GNP 2107 LINE RI 5042
COOKER G (B (F) SEEDS 1978 SONET UK SNTF 746
(G) FULL SPOON OF SEEDY BLUES 1967 GNP US 2040 RI GER LINE GER 5033

S71A SEEMON & MARIJKE S71A

SEEMON V K(A (A) SON OF AMERICA 197 A&M US SP4309
MARIJKE V K (A
COLLEEN FORTUNE V (A RICHARD FURTUNE G (A JOHN BARBATA D (A KING CHARLES STEEL DR(A
RITA COOLIDGE V (A NICK DE CARO ACC (A CHRIS ETHRIDGE B K (A MARIO JAMES STEEL DR(A
BOOKER T JONES K (A FRANK MAYES SAX (A JONI MITCHELL V (A GEROLD LAWRENCE STEEL DR(A
GRAHAM NASH G C (A SNEAKY PETE STEEL(A MORREEN THORNTON V (A MAC NILES STEEL DR(A
KAZEM RAZZAZAN VLN (A GEORGE ST JOHN SAX (A

S72 BOB SEGARINI S72

BOB SEGARINI G V K(AB (A) GOTTA HAVE POP 1978 BOMB 7027 UK EPIC EPC 83806
PET KASHUR G (B (A) GOTTA HAVE POP 198 LINE GER 5096
MIKE ST DENIS G V (AB (B) GOODBYE L A 1979 BOMP 90576 UK EPIC EPC 84086
WAYNE MILLS HRNS (B (B) GOODBYE L A 198 LINE GER 5051
PHIL ANGERS B (AB (C) THE RADIO 1980 BOMP 7030 LINE GER 5085
MARK BRONSON D (AB
GARWOOD WALLACE G V (B DAVID HENMAN G (A DAVID CLAYTON THOMAS V (A GORD PATON PERC (A
GABOR HEGEDUS G (A KIER BROWNSTONE B (A PAUL IRVINE SAX (A DREW WINTERS V K (AB
DAVID NORRIS ELYE HRNS (B

S73 BOB SEGER S73

BOB SEGER V (ALL (A) RAMBLIN' GAMBLIN' MAN 1969 CAPITOL US 172 UKRI77 CAPS 1013
SAM CLAYTON V (M (A) RAMBLIN' GAMBLIN' MAN 1981 GREENLIGHT RI 2010
DREW ABBOTT G (KLGJMNH (B) NOAH 1969 CAPITOL US 236
ALTO REED HRNS (GKLJMN (C) MONGREL 1970 CAPITOL US 499 UKRI77 CAPS 1010
LINDA DILLARD V (M (C) MONGREL 1981 GREENLIGHT RI 2022
CHARLIE ALLEN MARTIN D (GJKLM (D) BRAND NEW MORNING 1971 CAPITOL US 731
ROBYN ROBBINS K (GJKLM (E) SMOKIN' OPs 1972 REPRISE US 2109 UK K44214
GLEN FREY G (LM (E) SMOKIN' OPs 1977 CAPITOL RI 11746 GER 85348
CHRIS CAMPBELL B (GKLJMNH (F) BACK IN 72 1973 REPRISE US 2126 UK K44227
PAUL HARRIS K (M (F) BACK IN 72 197 CAPITOL 11747
DAVID TEEGARDEN D (LMN (G) SEVEN 1974 REPRISE US 2184 UK K44262
DON FELDER G (L (G) SEVEN 1977 CAPITOL RI 11748 GREENLIGHT 2006
BARRY BECKETT K (KLM (H) BEUTIFUL LOSER 1975 CAPITOL 11378
PETE CARR G (KLMH (J) LIVE BULLET 1976 CAPITOL US 11523 UK ESTSP 16
JIMMY JOHNSON H (KLM (K) NIGHT MOVES 1977 CAPITOL US/UK11557 GER 85027
DAVE HOOD B (KLM (L) STRANGER IN TOWN 1978 CAPITOL US/UK11698 GER 85333
ROGER HAWKINS D (KLM (M) AGAINST THE WIND 1980 CAPITOL US/UK12041 GER 86097
CRAIG FROST K (N (N) NINE TONIGHT 1981 CAPITOL US UK 12182
BILL PAYNE K (L (EP) GET OUT OF DENVER 1977 REPRISE K12476
DOUG RILEY K (KL
BOB SCHULTZ K SAX V(B VANETTA FIELDS V (L JAMES LAVELL V (L CLYDIE KING V (L
EASLEY STANLEY CARTER V(L SHIRLEY MATTHEWS V (L GEORGE JACKSON V (L LUTHER WATERS V (L
ORRIN WATERS V (L JULIA TILLMAN V (L MAXINE WILLARD WATERS V (L BRANDY V (L
DAN HONAKER B V G(ABC PEP PERRINE D (BC DAN WATSON K V (C JERRY LUCK ACC(K
JOE MIQUELON G (K SHARON DEE WILLIAMS V (K LAUREL WARD V (K RICK MANSKA K (GJ
DAVID BRIGGS PNO (G TOMMY COGBILL B (G KENNY BUTTREY D (G DAVE DORAN G (G
TOM CARTMELL SAX (G BILL MUELLER G (G RANDY MEYERS D (G CHARLIE McCOY G (G
JIM McCARTY G (G JOHN HARRIS ORG (G TOM NEME V G K(B SHAUN MURPHY V (N
KATHY LAMB V (N COLLEN BEATON V (N JUNE TILTON V (N PAM MOORE V (N
DON HENLEY V (M TIM SCHMIT V (M DR JOHN K (M LAURA CREAMER V (M

(CONTINUED)

S73 (CONTINUED) **BOB SEGER** S73

RANDY McCORMICK K (M MIKE ERELWINE HARP (A PEP PERRINE V (A BON SCHULTZ (A
SKIP KNAPE K B (E PAM TODD V (E CRYSTAL JENKINS V (E JACK ASHFORD PERC(E
EDDIE BONGO PERC (E JIM BUZZESE PERC (E HARVEY THOMPSON SAX (H HARRISON CALLOWAY TPT(H
CHARLES ROSE TROM (H CHARLIE MARTIN (H RON EADES SAX (H STONEY & ROCKY V (H
KENNY BELL G (H ROBIN ROBBINS K (H PAUL KINGERY G (H TOM CARTMELL SAX (H

S73B SELDOM SCENE S73B

MIKE AULDRIDGE G DOB V(ALL (A) ACT ONE 1972 REBEL US SLP1511
BEN ELDRIDGE BAN G V(ALL (B) ACT TWO 1973 REBEL US SLP1520
JOHN DUFFY G V MAND(ALL (C) ACT THREE 1973 REBEL US SLP1536
JOHN STARLING V G (ABCDEFG (D) OLD TRAIN 1974 REBEL US SLP1538
LINDA RONSTADT V (FD (E) RECORDED LIVE 1975 REBEL US SLP1547/48
TOM GRAY B V (ALL (F) THE NEW SELDOM SCENE ALBUM 1976 REBEL US SLP1561
RICKY SCAGGS FDL (CDG (G) BAPTIZING 1978 REBEL US 1573
CLAYTON HAMBRICK G (C (H) ACT FOUR 1979 SUGAR HILL 3709
PAUL CRAFT G (D (I) AFTER MIDNIGHT 1981 SUGAR HILL 3721
BOB WILLIAMS HCA (D
MARK CUFF D (F PHIL ROSENTHAL G V (GHI CARL NELSON VLN (I

S73C ZBIGNIEW SEIFERT S73C

ZBIGNIEW SEIFERT VLN (ALL (A) MAN OF THE LIGHT 19 MPS 15489
JACK DEJONETTE D (A (B) SOLO VIOLIN 19 MRC 066 45 088
JOHN SCOFIELD G (A (C) PASSION 19 CAPITOL 11923
EDDIE GOMEZ B (A (D) ZBIGNIEW SEIFERT 19 CAPITOL 11618
RICHIE BEIROICH PNO (AE (E) WE'LL REMEMBER ZBIGGY(74 78 19 MOOD 24500
NANA VASCONCELES PERC (A
JOACHIM KUHN K (BE CECIL McBEE B (B HUBERT EAVES K (D PHILIP CATHERINE G (DE
BILLY HART D (B DWIGHT BREWSTER K (D JOHN TURNER B (D JASPER VAN'THOF K (B
MIKE MANDEL SYN (D JOHN LEE B (D JAMES BATRON K (D REGGIE LUCAS G (D
HAKIN THOMPSON PERC(D GERRY BROWN D (D ROB FRANKEN SYN (D STEFAN DIEZ G (D
MTUME PERC V(D JOE CARO G (D DARYL BROWN PERC (D JOHN FADDIS TPT (D
MICHAEL BRECKER SAX (D CHRIS HINZE FLT (D MICHAEL LAWRENCE TPT (D DAVID TAYLOR TROM(D
CHERYL ALEXANDER V (D WOLFGANG DAUNER K (E GLEN MOORE B (E TAWATHA AGEE V (D
CHARLIE MARIANO SAX (E DAVID DARLING STR (E JOE HAIDER K (E ADELHARD ROIDINGER B(E
JAM HAMMER D (E ISLA ECKINGER B (E JOCNUSZ STEFANSKI D (E URSZULA DUDZIAK V (E
JOHN NAY D (E ALBERT MONGELSOLORFF TROM(E LESZEK ZADLO SAX (E HANS KOLLER SAX (E

S74 SELECTOR S74

NOEL DAVIES G (AB (A) TOO MUCH PRESSURE 1980 TWO TONE UK 5002 GER 6703 693
NORMAN WATT-ROY B (B (A) TOO MUCH PRESSURE 1980 CHRYSALIS US 1274
DESMOND BROWN K (A (B) CELEBRATE THE BULLET 1981 CHRYSALIS UK CHR 1306
PAULINE BLACK V (AB
CHARLEY ANDERSON B (A RICO RODRIGUES TROM (A DICK CUTHELL TPT (A JOE REYNOLDS SAX (A
CHARLEY H BEMBRIDGE D (AB COMPTON AMANOR D V (AB ARTHUR HENDRICKSON V (AB HILLFIELD BOYS CHOIR (A
ROGER COMAS B (B BARRY JONES TPT (B ADAM WILLIAMS B V (B JAMES MACKIE SAX K V(B

S74A SENSATION FIX S74A

FRANCO FALSINI SYN G V (ALL (A) PORTABLE MADNESS 1974 POLYDOR 2448 034
RICHARD URSILLO B (ALL (B) FRAGMENT OF LIGHT 1974 POLYDOR IT 2448 023
STEVE HEAD K D (CDE (C) FINEST FINGER 1976 POLYDOR IT 2448 048
MARCO MARCOVECCHIO D (F (D) BOXES PARADISE 1977 POLYDOR IT 2448 068
MATT NOBLE B (E (E) FLYING TAPES 1978 POLYDOR IT 2448 074
KEITH EDWARDS D (A (F) VISION'S FUGITIVES 197 ALL EARS US SF 11478

S74B SEMUTA S74B

(A)SEMUTA 1979 LEE LAMBERT LAM 101

S74C SERPENT POWER S74C

DAVID MELTZER G VHCA(A (A) SERPENT POWER 1967 VANGUARD US VSD 79252
DENNY ELLIS G (A
JOHN PAYNE K (A J P PICKENS BAN (A TINA MELTZER V (A DAVID STENSON B (A
CLARK COOLIDGE D (A

S75 JOHN SERRY S75

JOHN SERRY K V D (A (A) EXHIBITION 1979 CHRYSALIS UK CHR 1230
BOB SHEPPARD SAX (A (B) JAZZIZ 1981 CHRYSALIS UK CHR 1279
BARRY FINNERTY G (A
GORDON JOHNSON B (A FLIM JOHNSON B (A NANCY SHANX V (A CARLOS VEGA D(A
GORDON GOTTLIEB PERC (A

S75A SEVEN O SEVEN(707) S75A

PHIL BRYANT B V (ABC (A) '707' 1980 CASABLANCA US 7213
JIM McCLARTY D (ABC (B) THE SECOND ALBUM 1981 CASABLANCA US 7248
KEVIN RUSSELL G V (ABC (C) MEGAFORCE 1982 BOARDWALK US 33523
DUKE McFADDEN K G V(A
DAVID CARR K (A TOD HOWARTH K G V (C KEVIN CHALFANT V (C SANDY WELCH V (C
ZOE FOX V (C

S76 SEVENTH WAVE S76

KEN ELLIOT K V (AB (A) THINGS TO COME 1974 GULL UK GULP1001 JANUS US 7009
KIERAN O'CONNOR PERC (AB (B) PSI FI 1975 GULL UK GULP1010 US JANUS 7021
TONY UTER PERC (B
BRIAN GOULD K (B PEPI LEMER V (B CHRIS ANSON SYN (B PETER LEMER K (B
STEVE COOK B (B HUGH BANTON K (B TONY ELLIOT PERC (B

S77 SEX PISTOLS S77

JOHN ROTTEN LYDON V (ABCDE12 (A) NEVER MIND THE BOLLOCKS 1977 VIRGIN UK V2086 US WB 3142
STEVE NEW G (1 (A) " " " " 1977 VIRGIN GER 25593
STEVE JONES G (ABCDE12 (B) GREAT ROCK'N'ROLL SWINDLE(DBL) 1978 VIRGIN UK VD2510 GER 300 279
PAUL COOK D (ABCDE12 (C) SOME PRODUCT 1979 VIRGIN UK VR2
SID VICIOUS B V (ABCD (D) FLOGGING A DEAD HORSE 1979 VIRGIN UK V2142 GER 201 165
GLEN MATLOCK B (12 (E) GREAT ROCK'N'ROLL SWINDLE 1980 VIRGIN UK V 2168
MALCOLM McLAREN V (B ( ) BEST OF ...WE DONT CARE 1980 FLYOVER JAP IMP 7247
NICK KENT G V (1 (1) 1975 (2) 1976/77
RONNIE BIGGS V (B
M

S77A PHIL SEYMOUR S77A

Member	Instr.	Albums	Title	Release
PHIL SEYMOUR	G D V	(A	(A) PHIL SEYMOUR	1980 BOARDWALK US 36996 UK EPIC 85000
BILL PITCOCK	G	(A		
EMORY GORDY	B	(A		
ROGER LINN	G	(A		
WAYNE COOK	K	(A		

DUANE HITCHINGS K (A   DAVID CROCKETT D (A   LARRY BYROM G (A
STEVE ALLEN G (A   RON FLYNT B (A   CARLA OLSON G (A

S78 SHA NA NA S78

Member	Instr.	Albums	Title	Year	Label	Country	Number
JOCKO MARCELLINO	D	(BC	(A) IS HERE TO STAY	1969	KAMA SUTRA	US	2010 RI 2077
LONNIE BAKER	SAX	(BC	(A) IS HERE TO STAY	1971	KAMA SUTRA	UK	2319 025
SCOTT POWELL		(B	(A) IS HERE TO STAY	197	MODE	FR	9023
JOHNNY CONTARDO	K D	(CB	(A) IS HERE TO STAY	1974	KAMA SUTRA RI	UK	KSLP7003
DENNIS GREENE		(CB	(B) SHA NA NA	1971	KAMA SUTRA	UK	2319 007
DON YORK		(CB	(B) SHA NA NA	1971	KAMA SUTRA	US	2034
RITCH JOFFE	D	(CB	(B) SHA NA NA	1974	KAMA SUTRA RI	UK	KSLP7002
ELLIOT CAHN	G	(B	(C) THE NIGHT IS STILL YOUNG	1972	KAMA SUTRA	US	2050
CHRIS DONALD	G	(B	(C) THE NIGHT IS STILL YOUNG	1972	KAMA SUTRA	UK	2319 019
BRUCE CLARKE	B	(CB	(C) THE NIGHT IS STILL YOUNG	1974	KAMA SUTRA RI	UK	KSLP8001
SCOTT SIMON	K B	(CB	(D) GOLDEN AGE OF ROCK'N'ROLL	1973	KAMA SUTRA	UK	2623 102
DAVID BROMBERG	G	(B	(D) GOLDEN AGE OF ROCK'N'ROLL	1973	KAMA SUTRA	US	2073
ELLIOTT RANDALL	G	(	(D) GOLDEN AGE OF ROCK'N'ROLL	197	K TEL		NE 495
TONY SARTINI		(	(E) FROM THE STREETS OF NEW YORK	1974	KAMA SUTRA	UK	2319 038
VINNIE TAYLOR	G	(C	(E) FROM THE STREETS OF NEW YORK	1974	KAMA SUTRA	US	2075
GINO	G	(C	(E) FROM THE STREETS OF NEW YORK	1974	KAMA SUTRA	UK	KSLP7004
JOHN BOWZER BAUMAN	K	(CB	(F) HOT SOX	1974	KAMA SUTRA	US	2605
HENRY GROSS	G	(	(F) HOT SOX	1974	KAMA SUTRA	UK	KSLP7001
CHICO RYAN		(	(G) SHA NA NA NOW	1975	KAMA SUTRA	US	2603
ERIC WEISSBERG	STEEL	(B	(H) BEST OF	1976	KAMA SUTRA	US	KSLP2609
RICHARD DAVIS	B	(B	(J) ROCK'N'ROLL REVIVAL	1977	PYE	UK	GH 867
			( ) REMEMBER THEN	1981	ACCORD	US	7115

S78A SHADES OF JOY S78A

Member	Instr.	Albums	Title	Release
MARTIN FIERRO	WIND V	(A	(A) SHADES OF JOY	1969 FONTANA UK STL 5498
JACKIE KING	G SITAR	(A	(A) SHADES OF JOY	196 DOUGLAS UA 30920
EDWARD ADAMS	B	(A		
LEE CHARLTON	VLN	(A		

JYMM YOUNG K HRN(A   JOSE RODRIGUEZ D (A   MILLIE FOSTER V (A

S78B SHABBY TIGER S78B

Member	Instr.	Albums	Title	Release
HENDERSON GIBSON	V	(A	(A) SHABBY TIGER	1977 RCA PL 25046
TONY BAKER	K V	(A		
DAVE ALMOND	G FLT V	(A		

MIKE RYAN B (A   GRAHAM FIELDEN D PERC(A

S78C BOBBY SHAD S78C

BOBBY SHAD (A — (A) ... AND THE BADMEN — 196 MAINSTREAM US 306

S78D SHADES S78D

(A) ACE OF SHADES — 1981 MAGNUN FORCE UK MFLP 005

S78E SHADOW S78E

(A) LOVE LIFE — 1980 ELEKTRA US 233
(B) SHADOW — 1981 ELEKTRA US 293

S79 SHADOWFAX S79

Member	Instr.	Albums	Title	Release
CHICK GREENBERG	WIND	(A	(A) WATERCOURSE WAY	1976 PASSPORT PPSD98013
PHIL MAGGINI	B	(A		
DOUG MALUCHNIK	K	(A		

STUART NEVITT D PERC(A   GREG STINSON G V (A

S80 THE SHADOWS S80

Member	Instr.	Albums	Title	Release
HANK MARVIN	G V	(ALL	THE SHADOWS	1962 COLUMBIA UK (M)33SX1374 (S)SCX3414
BRUCE WELCH	G V	(ALL	OUT OF THE SHADOWS	1962 COLUMBIA UK (M)33SX1458 (S)SCX3449
IAN SAMWELL	B	(A	GREATEST HITS	1963 COLUMBIA UK (M)33SX1522 (S)SCX1522
TERRY SMART	D	(A	DANCE WITH THE SHADOWS	1964 COLUMBIA UK (M)33SX1619 (S)SCX3511
JET HARRIS	B	(BC	THE SOUND OF THE SHADOWS	1965 COLUMBIA UK (M)33SX1736 (S)SCX3554
TONY MEEHAN	D	(B	MORE HITS	1965 COLUMBIA UK (M)33SX1791 (S)SCX3578
BRIAN BENNETT	D	(CDEGIJ	SHADOW MUSIC	1966 COLUMBIA UK (M)33SX6041 (S)SCX6041
BRIAN LOCKING	B	(D	JIGSAW	1967 COLUMBIA UK SCX6148
JOHN ROSTILL	B	(E	HANK,BRUCE,BRIAN & JOHN	1967 COLUMBIA UK SCX6199
JOHN FARRAR	G V B	(FGH	ESTABLISHED 1958	1968 COLUMBIA UK SCX6282
ALAN JONES	B	(HIJ	IT'LL BE ME	1969 STARLINE UK SRS 5011
FRANCIS MONKMAN	K	(H	SOMETHING ELSE	1969 STARLINE UK SRS 5012
CLIFF HALL	K	(IJ	SHADES OF ROCK	1970 COLUMBIA UK SCX6420
DAVE LAWSON	SYN	(J	MUSTANG	1972 MFP UK MFP 5266
NORRIE PARAMOUR	STR	(	THE BEST OF	1973 EMI IMP EURO 14804859
ALAN TARNEY	B	(	I MAESTRI	1974 COLUMBIA 04532
DAVE RICHMOND			OUT OF THE SHADOWS 2	19 COLUMBIA GER 04502
GRAHAM TODD	K	(A	THE SHADOWS	19 CRYSTAL 04203
(A)1958			THE BEST OF	197 EMI IMP EURO 05404300
(B) 1959			SHADOOGIE (TRIPLE)	19 EMI IMP EURO 154 061 129
(C) 1961			ROCKIN' WITH CURLY LEADS	1973 EMI EMA 762
(D) 1962			SPECS APPEAL	1975 EMI EMC 3066
(E) 1962			LIVE AT PARIS OLYMPIA	1975 EMI EMC 3095
(F) 1970			RARITIES	1976 EMI NUT 2
(G) 1973			THE SHADOWS	1975 EMBER SE 8031
(H) 1977			TASTY	1977 EMI EMC 3195
(I) 1979			20 GOLDEN GREATS	1977 EMI EMTV 3
(J) 1980			BEST OF THE SHADOWS	1977 EMI EMTV 33
			AT THE MOVIES	1978 MFP 50347
			CHANGE OF ADDRESS	1980 POLYDOR UK 2442 179
			STRING OF HITS	1979 EMI EMC 3310
			ANOTHER STRING OF HITS	1980 UK 3339
			HITS RIGHT UP YOUR STREET	1981 POLYDOR UK 5046

S81 SHADOWS OF KNIGHT S81

Member	Instr.	Albums	Title	Year	Label	Country	Number
JIM SOHNS	V	(ABC	(A) GLORIA	1966	DUNWICH	US	666
WARREN ROGERS	G	(ABC	(A) GLORIA (RI)	1979	RADAR	UK	RAD 11
JERRY McGEORGE	G	(ABC	(B) BACK DOOR MEN	1967	DUNWICH	US	667
TOM SCHIFFOUR	D	(ABC	(C) SHADOWS OF KNIGHT	1968	SUPER K	US	6002
JOE KELLEY	B	(ABC					
THE HAWK	K	(B					

S81A SHAFTESBURY S81A
ROGER GRIGG D K V(A (A) THE LULL BEFORE THE STORM 1980 O K RECORDS OKA001
DAVE MARTIN B V (A
PETER ROFFEY G (A

S81B SHAGGS S81B
BETTY WIIGINS D (A (A) PHILOSOPHY OF THE WORLD 1972 THIRD WORLD 3001 RED ROOSTER US 103
HELEN WIGGIN G (A (A) " " " " 1980 ROUNDER US 3032
DOROTHY WIGGIN G (A

S82 SHAGRAT THE VAGRANT S82
MICK FARREN V (
STEVE TOOK V PERC(
PAUL BUCKMASTER CELLO(RUSS HUNTER B (TWINK D (SID BISHOP G (
CORD REES PNO (

S82A SHAKATAK S82A
GEORGE ANDERSON B (B (A) DRIVING HARD 1981 POLYDOR UK POLS 1030
NIGEL WRIGHT K SYN(AB (B) NIGHTBIRDS 1982 POLYDOR UK POLS 1059
ROGER ODELL D (B
JACKIE RAWE V (B SIMON MORTON V PERC(B DICK MORRISSEY SAX (B BILL SHARPE K SYN(B
KEITH WINTER G (B JILL SAWARD V (B LORNA BANNON V (B STUART BROOKS TPT (B

S83 SHAKE S83
JOHN CALLIS G (A (A) CULTURE SHOCK (EP) 1979 SIRE UK SIR 4016
SIMON TEMPLAR B (A
ANGEL PATERSON D (A TROY TATE G (A

S83A SHAKERS S83A
JANET SMALL K V (A (A) YANKEE REGGAE 1976 ASYLUM US7E1057 UK K53036
CHRIS SOLBERG G V (A
BILL WALLACE G V (A DON FULTON B (A RON RHODES D (A

S84 SHAKIN STREET S84
FABIENNE SHINE V (Ab (A) VAMPIRE ROCK 1978 CBS UK 82610
DYAN BIRCH V (A (B) SHAKIN' STREET 1980 CBS UK 84115
ERIC LEWY G (AB (C) SKIN EM 1981 VIRGIN UK 2199
ROSS THE BOSS G (B
MIKE WINTER B (AB JEAN LOU KALONOWSKI D(AB FRANK COLLINS V (A ARMIK TIGRANE G (A
IAN STEWART PNO (A BONNIE V (A PATRICE FABIEN PROD (A

S84A SHAKEY LEGS S84A
NICK LAURITZEN K V (A (A) SHAKEY LEGS 197 PARAMOUNT US 6022
TED DEMOS G (A
JACK BRUNO D (A TOM ENRIGHT B (A JOHN MASTORY B (A

S84B SHAKEY VICK S84B
GRAHAM VICKERY HCA V (A (A) LITTLE WOMAN YOURE SO SWEET 1969 PYE UK NSPL18276
NED BALIN D (A
BRUCE LANGSMAN G (A NIGEL TICKLER B (A

S84C SHAKIN' PYRAMIDS S84C
DAVIE DUNCAN V HCA PERC(A (A) SKIN EM UP 1981 VIRGIN UK 2199 GER 802 088
JAMES G CREIGHTON G V (A (B) CELTS & COBRAS 1982 VIRGIN UK 2216
RAILROAD KEN G V (A
NICK CLARK B (A

S85 SHAKTI S85
JOHN McLAUGHLIN G (ABC (A) SHAKTI 1976 CBS US 34162 UK 81388
L SHANKAR VLN V(ABC (B) HANDFUL OF BEAUTY 1977 CBS US 34372 UK 81664
ZAKIR HUSSAIN PERC (ABC (C) NATURAL ELEMENTS 1978 CBS US 34980 UK 82329
T H VINYAKRAM PERC V(ABC

S85A SHALAMAR S85A
JODY WATNEY V (CD (A) UPTOWN FESTIVAL 1977 SOUL TRAIN UK 12289
JEFF DANIEL V (CD (B) DISCO GARDENS 1978 RCA UK 12895
HOWARD HEWITT V (CD (C) BIG FUN 1979 SOLAR UK 13479
LEON SYLVERS B (C (D) THREE FOR LOVE 1980 SOLAR US 13577
ERNEST REED G (C (E) FRIENDS 1982 SOLAR UK 52345
FRED LEWIS PERC (C (F) GREATEST HITS 1982 SOLAR UK 3001
STEVE SHOCKLEY G (C
GREG DAWKINS CONGA(C FRED RHEIMERT G (C JAMES DAVIS B (C WARDELL POTTS D (C
ERNEST BILES B (C GERALD THOMPSON D (C FREEMAN BROWN D (C JOEY GALLO K (C
JOHN BARNES K (C RON ARTISTS K (C WILLIAM SHELBY K (C GIP NOBELS K (C
KEVIN SPENCER K (C GENE DOZIER K (C KOSSI GARDNER K (C STRING SECTION (C

S86 SHAM 69 S86
JIMMY PURSEY V ((A) TELL US THE TRUTH 1978 POLYDOR UK 2383 491 SIRE US 6060
DAVE TREGANNA B ((B) THATS LIFE 1978 POLYDOR UK POLD5010+2442 158
MARK CAIN D ((C) HERSHAM BOYS 1979 POLYDOR UK POLD5025+2442 165
DAVE PARROS G ((D) THE GAME 1979 POLYDOR UK POLD5033+2442 173
ALBIE SLIDER B ((E) FIRST, THE BEST & THE LAST 1980 POLYDOR UK 2383 596

S86A SHAMROCKS S86A
(A) THE SHAMROCKS 1965 ARIOLA 72151
( ) THE SHAMROCKS IN PARIS 19 POLYDOR FR 658032
(EP) CADILLAC 19 POLYDOR FR 60122
(EP) CANT SAY 19 POLYDOR FR 60124

S86B SHANDI S86B
SHANDI V (A (A) SHANDI 1980 DREAMLAND 2394 257
PAUL HERTZOG K (A
JAMES ROLLENSTON B (A STEVE SYKES G (A TIM PIERCE G (A PAT MASTELLOTTO D (A

S86C SHANGHAI (80's) S86C
ANTON FIG D V (A (A) SHANGHAI 1982 CHRYSALIS UK CHR 1389
BOB HANLON SAX (A
KEITH LENTIN G V (A GARY VALENTE TROM (A JIMMY LOWELL B V (A BEAU HILL K G V (A
NEIL BALM TPT (A

S87 SHANGHAI (70's) S87

CLIFF BENNETT V (B — (A) SHANGHAI 1974 WB UK K56093
BRIAN ALTERMAN G (B — (B) FALLEN HEROES 1976 THUNDERBIRD THR 2000
MICK GREEN G (AB
SPEEDY KING B (AB PETE KIRCHER D (AB CHUCK BEDFORD V HCA(A MIKE DEMIAN K B (A
BARBARA BEDFORD V (A

S87A SHANGO S87A

RICHIE HERNANDEZ G (A — (A) TRAMPIN' 1970 DUNHILL US D5 50082
JOE BARILE D (A
MALCOLM EVAN B (A TOMMY REYNOLDS PERC K(A

S88 SHANGRILAS S88

MARY WEISS V (— LEADER OF THE PACK 1964 RED BIRD US RB 20101
MARYANN GANSER V (— SHANGRILAS '65 1965 RED BIRD US RB 20104
MARGIE GANSER V (— I CAN NEVER GO HOME 1966 RED BIRD US RI RB 20104
BETTY WEISS V (— GOLDEN HITS 1966 MERCURY US 61099 UK 20096
SHADOW MORTON PROD (— GOLDEN HITS 1973 PHILIPS 6336 215 NL 6430 154
TEEN ANGUISH VOL 2 197 CHARLY UK CRM 2005
(EP) REMEMBER (WALKING IN THE SAND) 1976 CHARLY UK CEP 109

S89 DEL SHANNON S89

DEL SHANNON G V (ALL — HATS OFF TO LARRY 1963 LONDON UK 8071
MIKE CAMPBELL B G (* — RUNAWAY 1963 LONDON UK 2402 US BIG TOP 1303
BENMONT TENCH K (* — LITTLE TOWN FLIRT 1963 LONDON UK 8091 US BIG TOP 1308
STAN LYNCH D (* — ANDY MAN 1965 STATESIDE UK 10115 AMY US 8003
RON BLAIR B (* — SINGS HANK WILLIAMS 1965 STATESIDE UK 10130 AMY US 8004
DAVID WHITE B (* — 1,661 SECONDS OF 1965 STATESIDE UK 10140 AMY US 8006
HOWIE EPSTEIN B (* — THIS IS MY BAG 196 LIBERTY UK SLBY1320 US LST 7452
PHIL JONES V (* — TOTAL COMMITMENT 1966 LIBERTY UK SLBY1335 US LST 7479
PHIL SEYMOUR V (* — FURTHER ADVENTURES OF C WESTOVER 196 LIBERTY US LST 7539
MARTY TOUVARD SAX (* — BEST OF 1967 DOT US 25824
KYM WESTOVER V (* — VINTAGE YEARS 19 SIRE US 3708/2
JUDE COLE V (* — DEL SHANNON SINGS 19 POST US 9000
TOM PETTY HCA V PROS(* — 10TH ANNIVERSARY 1971 SUNSET UK 50211
LIVE IN ENGLAND 1973 UA UK UAS29474 US LA 151
LIVE IN ENGLAND 1982 FAME RI UK 3020
BEST OF 1973 POLYDOR EURO 2870 323
VERY BEST OF 1975 CONTEMPO CRMD 1001
HIT PARADE 1980 LONDON UK HAR 8545
(*) DROP DOWN AND GET ME 1981 ELEKTRA US 5E568
AND THE MUSIC PLAYS ON 1978 SUNSET UK SLS50412
(EP) DELS OWN FAVOURITES 196 LONDON UK REX 1383
(EP) No2 196 LONDON UK REX 1346

S91 SHANTI S91

ASHISH KHAN SAROD(A — (A) SHANTI 1971 ATLANTIC US SD 8302
ZAKIR HUSSAIN TABLA(A
NEIL SEIDEL G (A STEVE HAEHL G V (A STEVE LEACH V D (A FRANK LUPICA D (A
PRANESH KHAN TABLA(A

S92 SHARKS S92

CHRIS SPEDDING G (AB — (A) FIRST WATER 1973 ISLAND UK ILPS9233 US MCA351
ANDY FRASER B (A — (B) JAB IT IN YOUR EYE 1974 ISLAND UK ILPS9271 US MCA415
SNIPS V (AB
MARTY SIMON D (AB NICK JUDD K (B BUSTA CHERRY JONES B (B

S92A DEE DEE SHARP S92A

DEE DEE SHARP V (ALL — (A) ITS MASHED POTATO TIME 196 CAMEO US C 1018
(B) SONGS OF FAITH 196 CAMEO US C 1022
(C) ALL THE HITS 196 CAMEO US C 1032
(D) DO THE BIRD 196 CAMEO US C 1050
(E) BIGGEST HITS 196 CAMEO US C 1062
(F) DOWN MEMORY LANE 196 CAMEO US C 1074
(G) 18 GOLDEN HITS 196 CAMEO US C 2002
(H) THE CAMEO PARKWAY SESSIONS 1979 LONDON UK HAU 8514
( ) HAPPY 'BOUT 1976 PHILADELPHIA US 33839
( ) WHAT COLOUR IS LOVE 1978 PHILADELPHIA US 34437
( ) DEE DEE 1980 PHILADELPHIA US 36370

S92B BILLY JOE SHAVER S92B

BILLY JOE SHAVER V (— (A) OLD FIVE & DIMERS LIKE ME 1974 MONUMENT KZ32293 MG 7621
(B) WHEN I GET MY WINGS 1976 CAPRICORN US CPN 0171
(C) GYPSY BOY 197 CAPRICORN US CPN 0192

S92C ROCKY SHARPE S92C

ROCKY SHARPE V (ABC
(A) RAMA LAMA (REPLAYS) 1979 CHISWICK UK CWK 3010
(B) ROCK IT TO MARS 1980 CHISWICK UK CWK3013 GER 67072
(C) DRIP DROP (EP) (RAZORS) 19 ACE UK SW6

S93 GARY SHEARSTON S93

GARY SHEARSTON G V HCA (AB — (A) DINGO 1974 CHARISMA UK CAS1091
TOMMY EYRE K SYN (A — (A) THE GREATEST STONE ON EARTH & ... 1975 CHARISMA UK CAS1106
DAVE OLNEY B (A
ANDREW STEELE D (A GRAHAME SMITH VLN (A JOHN TURNBALL G (A JON FIELDS CONGA(A
ROD KING STEEL(A PHIL CHAPMAN K (A CARL LEVY K (A JIM PARKER K (A
GARY TAYLOR G (A FRANKLYN DUNN B (B LOCKSLEY GICHIE G (B ROYSTON MITCHELL K (B
MAURICE ELLIS D (B FRANK McDONALD B (B CHRIS RAE G (B B J COLE STEEL(B
BARRY DE SOUZA D (B JOHNNY VAN DERRICK VLN (B HENRY LOWTHER VLN (B KEITH NELSON BAN (B
ROBERT KIRBY V K (B DAVID KATZ VLN (B IAN HAMMER HRNS (B EDDIE MORDUE SAX (B
DAVE HORLER HRNS (B DOREEN CHANTER V (B MARTHA SMITH V (B JON ASTLEY V SYN(B
DEBORAH WOOD V (B CAMILLA WIGAN V (B LATIFA BALSTON V (B LYNN GIBSON V (B
CHRISTIANE KONCZEWSKI V(B MICHAEL THOMAS V (BJOHN JAMES V (B STABLE STEVENS V (B

S93A SHEENA & THE ROCKETS S93A

SHEENA V (A — (A) SHEENA & THE ROSKETS 1980 A&M US SP4875
MAKOTO AYUKAWA G V (A
TAKESHI ASADA B V (A KAZU KAWASHIMA D (A

S93B SHERBET(SHERBS) S93B

DARYL BRAITHWAITE V (— (A) HOWZAT 1976 MCA US 2226
TONY MITCHELL B (— (B) MAGAZINE 1977 MCA US 2304
GARTH PORTER K (— (C) COLLECTION 1977
ALAN SANDOW D (— (D) PHOTOPLAY 1978 MCA US UK EPIC 82251
HARVEY JANES G (— (E) THE SKILL 1981 ATCO 38137 UK K50783

S93C SHERIDAN/PRICE S93C

DAVE SHERIDAN V (A — (A) THIS IS TO CERTIFY THAT 1970 GEMINI UK GME 1002
RICK PRICE V B G(A

S94 PETE SHELLEY S94

PETE SHELLEY V (AB — (A) SKY YEN 1980 GROOVY STP2
(B) HOMOSAPIENS 1981 GENETICS GER 204 163

S94A SHEPPARDS S94A

(A) SHEPPARDS 1980 SOLID SMOKE US CS4

S95 SHILOH S95

JIM ED NORMANS K G (A — (A) SHILOH 1970 AMOS/BELL AAS7015
DON HENLEY D (A
MIKE BOWDEN B (A RICHARD BOWDEN G (A AL PERKINS STEEL G (A

S95A PLUTO SHERVING S95A

(A) PLUTO 1976 OPAL PL1002

S95B DON SHINN S95B

DON SHINN K (AB — (A) TEMPLES WITH PROPHET 1969 COLUMBIA UK SCX 6319
STAN TRACY K PERC(B — (B) DEPARTURES 1969 COLUMBIA UK SCX 6355
BARRY MORGAN PERC (B
TREVOR TOMKINS D (B

S96 JOHNNY SHINES S96

JOHNNY SHINES G V (ALL — (A) LAST NIGHTS DREAM 1969 BLUE HORIZON UK 763212
WALTER HORTON HCA (AC — (B) MASTERS OF MODERN BLUES 1969 TESTAMENT US 2212
WILLIE DIXON B (A — (C) JOHNNY SHINES & BIG WALTER HORTON 1969 TESTAMENT US 2217
CLIFTON JAMES D (A — (D) STANDING AT THE CROSSROADS 1969 TESTAMENT US 2221
OTIS SPANN PNO (AC — (E) CHICAGO BLUES FESTIVAL 1972 BLACK & BLUE 33502
LEE JACKSON B (C — (F) JOHNNY SHINES & CO 1972 BIOGRAPH US 12048
PRINCE CANDY B (C — (G) SITTING ON TOP 1972 BIOGRAPH US 12044
RICHARD BAKER G (H — (H) COUNTRY BLUES 1974 XTRA UK XTRA1142
ROBERT LOCKWOOD (L — (J) JOHNNY SHINES 1974 ADVENT 2803
PHILIP WALKER G (J — (K) HEY BA BA RE BOP 1978 ROUNDER 2020
DAVID II SAX (J — (L) DUST MY BROOM 1980 FLYRIGHT UK FLY 563
NATHANIEL DOVE PNO (J — ( ) JOHNNY SHINES 19 BLUE HORIZON US 4607
CHARLES JONES B (J
DAVID BROMBERG G (F DOWNY MURL D (J FRED BELOW D (C BILL BROWN B (C
LUTHER ALLISON G (C DON AUDET HCA (H BOB DERKACH B (H

S96A THE SHIP S96A

SHIP MELSHENKER G (A — (A) THE SHIP 1972 ELEKTRA UK K42122
MARE NAMBY K V FLT(A — (A) A CON FOLK MUSIC JOURNEY 1972 ELEKTRA USEKS 75036
STEVE COWAN G V (A
TODD BROADSHAW B (A TIM SCOTT CELLO (A STEVE REINWAND G V (A

S97 ELLEN SHIPLEY S97

ELLEN SHIPLEY V (AB — (A) ELLEN SHIPLEY 1979 RCA US BXL1 3428 UK FL13428
RALPH SCHUCKETT K V (B — (B) BREAKING THROUGH THE ICE AGE 1980 RCA US 3626 UK PL13626
RICHIE CERNIGLIA G V (B
NICHOLAS LYNN G V (B STEVE VITALE B V (B DENNY McDERMOTT D V (B ALFA ANDERSON V (B
ONY KAYE V (B JEAN PAUL GASPAR V (B ROBIN LUMLEY SYN (B

S98 SHIRELLES S98

ADDIE HARRIS V (— (A) TONIGHTS THE NIGHT 1961 SCEPTER US 501
SHIRLEY ALSTON V (— (A) TONIGHTS THE NIGHT 1961 WAND UK 1001
DORIS KENNER V (— (B) SHIRELLES SING 1961 SCEPTER US 502
BEVERLY LEE V (— (B) SHIRELES SING 1961 TOP RANK UK 35 115
(C) BABY IT'S YOU 1962 SCEPTER US 504
(C) BABY IT'S YOU 1962 STATESIDE UK 10006
(D) & KING CURTIS TWIST PARTY 196 SCEPTER US 505
(E) GREATEST HITS 196 SCEPTER US 507
(E) GREATEST HITS 1963 STATESIDE UK 10041
(F) FOOLISH LITTLE GIRL 196 SCEPTER US 511
( ) ITS A MAD MAD MAD WORLD 196 SCEPTER US 514
(G) SING THE GOLDEN OLDIES 196 SCEPTER US 516
(H) GREATEST HITS VOL2 196 SCEPTER US 560
(J) SPONTANEOUS COMBUSTION 196 SCEPTER US 562
(K) REMEMBER WHEN 196 SCEPTER US 2 599
(L) REMEMBER WHEN VOL 1 19 WAND 1009
(M) REMEMBER WHEN VOL 2 19 WAND 1010
(N) ETERNALLY SOUL 1970 WAND UK WNS 4 US SCEPTER 569
(O) HAPPY IN LOVE 197 RCA US LSP4581 UK SF8237
(P)SHIRELLES 1972 RCA US 4698 UK SF8279
(Q) SWINGS THE MOST 19 PRICEWISE US 4001
(R) SING THEIR BEST 1972 SPRINGBOARD US 4006
(S) VERY BEST OF 19 UA US LA 340
(T) GOLDEN HOUR 1973 PYE UK GH 824
( ) HERE & NOW 19 PRICEWISE US 4002
( ) JUKE BOX GIANTS 1981 AUDIO FIDELITY 1008
( ) LETS GIVE EACH OTHER 1976 RCA APLI0102
(EP) WILL YOU LOVE ME TOMORROW 19&" TOP RANK UK 3012

S98A **SHIRLEY & CO** S98A

(A) SHAME SHAME SHAME 1975 PHILIPS UK 6310604 VIBRATION US 218

S99 **SHIRLEY & LEE** S99

SHIRLEY GOODMAN V (ALL
LEONARD LEE V (ALL

(A) LET THE GOOD TIMES ROLL 19 JAYBOY JSX 2005
" " " " 19 ALADDIN 807
" " " " 19 SCORE US 4023
" " " " 1960 WARWICK US 2028
" " " " 19 IMPERIAL 9179
" " " " 1975 UA US UALA 069
LEGENDARY MASTERS 19 UA US UALA 026
RESPECTFULLY YOURS 1980 MANHATTAN UK 5040
HAPPY DAYS 1980 MANHATTAN UK 5025

S100 **SHIRTS** S100

ANNIE GOLDEN V (ABC — (A) THE SHIRTS 1978 HARVEST UK SHSP4089 GER 06717
ART LAMONICA G V K(ABC — (A) THE SHIRTS 1978 CAPITOL US SW 11791
RONNIE ARDITO G V K(ABC — (B) STREET LIGHT SHINE 1979 HARVEST UK SHSP4104 GER 07111
JOHN PICCOLO G V K(ABC — (B) STREET LIGHT SHINE 1979 CAPITOL US 11986
JOHN CRISCIONE D V (ABC — (C) INNER SLEEVE 1980 CAPITOL UK/US 12085 GER 86184
ROBERT RACIOPPO G (ABC
LYLE DEDRICK WIND (B URBIE GREEN WIND (B DIANA HALPRIN VLN (B PAUL EISLER WIND(B
HARVEY ESTRIN FLT (B DAVID TOFANI WIND (B

S101 **SHIVA'S HEAD BAND** S101

SPENCER PERSKIN V VLN G(ABC — (A) TAKE ME TO THE MOUNTAINS 19 CAPITOL US 538
SUZY PERSKIN V ORG (ABC — (B) COMING TO A HEAD 19 ARMADILLO US NO No
BRIAN'RED' MOORE B (C — (C) YESTERDAYS 1978 APE . US 1001
JERRY BRAZIL D (C
ROBERT FLYNN JR G (C SHAWN SIEGEL K V (A KENNY PARKER B G V(A ROBERT GLADWIN G B(C
RICHARD FUNNELL D (A

S101A **SHOCKING BLUE** S101A

CORNELIUS VAN DER BEEK D(A — (A) SHOCKING BLUE 1969 PENNY FARTHING UK PELS500 METRONOME 15373
MARISKA VERES V (A — (B) SCORPIOS DANCE 1969 PENNY FARTHING UK PELS510
KASSJE VAN DER WAL B (A — ( ) SHOCKING BLUE 19 COLOSSUS CS 1000 NL GNR 447 009
ROBBY VAN LEEUWEN G (A — ( ) GREATEST HITS 19 GNR NL 657 574
( ) POP POWER 1970 POLYDOR

S102 **SHOES** S102

GARY KLEBE G V (ABC — (A) BLACK VINYL SHOES 1978 PVC 7904 + BLACK VINYL 51477
JEFF MURPHY G V (ABC — (A) BLACK VINYL SHOES 1979 SIRE UK SRK 6075
JOHN MURPHY V B (ABC — (B) PRESENT TENSE 1979 ELEKTRA US 6E244 UK K52187
SKIP MEYER D (ABC — (C) TONGUE TWISTER 1980 ELEKTRA US 6E303 UK K52261

S102A **SHOES FOR INDUSTRY** S102A

BASSETT DAVIES V SAX(A — (A) TALK LIKE A WHELK 1980 FRIED EGG FRY 1
JOHN SCHOFIELD D (A
ANDY BOOT G (A TIM NORFOLK G (A STEVE LONNEN B (A LAZLO K V(A

S102B **SHOOT** S102B

CRAIG COLLINGE D (A — (A) ON THE FRONTIER 1973 EMI US 11229 UK EMA 753
DAVE GREENE G V (A
JIM McCARTY K V (A BILL RUSSELL B (A

S103 **SHOOTER** S103

DAVE MATTHEW G V (A — (A) SHOOTER 1978 EMI UK INS3026
STEVE ST CLAIR G V (A
JOHN TOWE D PERC(A SPENCER SHIRES K G V(A SIMON JAMES DUNN B V(A

S103A **SHOOTING STAR** S103A

STEVE THOMAS D (ABC — (A) SHOOTING STAR 1979 VIRGIN UK V 2130
RON VERLIN B (ABC — (B) HANG ON FOR YOUR LIFE 1981 VIRGIN US 37407
CHARLIS WALTZ V VLN K (ABC — (C) III WISHES 1982 VIRGIN UK V 2235
VAN McCLAIN G (ABC
GARY WEST V K G D(ABC BILL GUFFEY K (AB

S103B **BRIAN SHORT** S103B

BRIAN SHORT V (A — (A) ANYTHING FOR A LAUGH 1971 TRANSATLANTIC UK TRA 245
ALAN WHITE D (A
MAX MIDDLETON K (A KEN CRADDOCK G K V (A RAY COOPER PERC (A ED SPEVOCK PERC(A
PETE KIRTLEY G MAND V (A COLIN GIBSON B (A LYN DOBSON WIND (A COLERIDGE GOODE B (A

S103C **SHORTWAVEBAND** S103C

STUART GORDON G K V(A — (A) SHORTWAVEBAND 1975 RCA UK SF 8400
PHIL HARRISON K G FLT(A
PICK WITHERS D (A PAUL COBBOLD B (A

S104 **WAYNE SHORTER** S104

WAYNE SHORTER SAX (ALL — (A) FREEFORM 196 BLUENOTE US BST 84118
(B) SEARCH FOR NEW LAND 196 BLUENOTE US BST 84169
(C) NIGHT DREAMER 1964 BLUENOTE US BST 84173
MICHELIN PRELL D (L — (D) SOME OTHER DTUFF 196 BLUENOTE US BST 84177
(E) JU JU 1964 BLUENOTE US BST 84182
MIROSLAV VITOUS G (KO — (F) SPEAK NO EVIL 1965 BLUENOTE US BST 84194
CHICK COREA K (KO — (G) ALL SEEING EYE 1966 BLUENOTE US BST 84219
RON CARTER B (O — (H) ADAMS APPLE 1966 BLUNOTE US BST 84232
DAVE HOLLAND B G (O — (I) SCHIZOPHRENIA 1968 BLUNOTE UK BNS40026 US BST84297
JOHN McLAUGHLIN G (KO — (J) ODYSSEY OF ISKA 1970 BLUENOTE US BST84363
AIRTO MORIERA PERC (K — (K) SUPER NOVA 1970 BLUENOTE UK BNS40028 USBST84332
MILTON NASCIMENTO (P — (L) SHORTER MOMENTS 19 TRIP US 5009
SONNY SHARROCK G (K — (M) SECOND GENESIS 19 VEE JAY US
JACK DE JOHNETTE D (K — (N) WAYNE SHORTER 1974 GNP US GNPS22075
MARIA BOOKER V (K — (O) MOTO GROSSO FEIO 1975 BLUENOTE US BNLA 014
WALTER BOOKER G (K — (P) NATIVE DANCER 1975 EPIC UK 80721 US 33418
(Q) ETCETERA 1981 BLUENOTE UKLBR 1037 US 1056
(R) SOOTHSAYER 1980 UA UK LBR 1021

S104A SHOT GUN S104A

(A) SHOTGUN 1977 ABC US ABCD 979
(B) GOOD THE BAD & FUNKY 197 ABC US 1060
(C) SHOTGUN 197 ABC US 1118

S104B SHOT IN THE DARK S104B

KRYSIA KRYSTIANNE K V (A
ADAM YURMAN G V (A
BRYAN SAVAGE WIND (A ROBIN LAMBLE G V B VLN (A PETER WHITE G K B V(A HARRY STINSON D V (A

(A) SHOT IN THE DARK 1981 POLYDOR UK 2394 297

S104C JAY SHOTAM S104C

JAY SHOTAM B V (A
PETER DIAZ G (A
JULIAN LINDSAY K (A PHIL TOWNER D (A

(A) MANHATTAN SKYLINE 1979 BAAL BAL89011

S105 SHOTGUN EXPRESS S105

PETER BARDENS K (
DAVE AMBROSSE B (
PETER GREEN G (MICK FLEETWOOD D (ROD STEWART V (PHIL SAWYER G (
JOHN MOORSHEAD G (BERYL MARSDEN V (

(A) SHOTGUN EXPRESS (EP) 196 COLUMBIA FR ESRF1864

S106 SHOW OF HANDS S106

RICK CUTLER D (A
JACK JACOBSEN K (A
JERRY McCANN FLT G V (A

(A) FORMERLY ANTHRAX 1970 ELEKTRA EKS74084

S107 SHOWADDYWADDY S107

DAVE BARTRAM V (ALL
ROMEO CHALLENGER D (ALL
AL JAMES B (ALL
BJ COLE STEEL(E
JEFF DALY SAX (E
JOHN ACOCK PNO (AE
MARTYN FORD ORCHESTRA (E
RUSS FIELD G (ALL
ROD DEES B (ALL
TREVOR OAKLEY G (ALL
BUDDY CIASK V (ALL MALCOLM ALLURED D (ALL

(A) SHOWADDYWADDY 1974 BELL UK BELLS 248
(B) STEP TWO 1975 BELL UK BELLS 256
(C) TROCADERO 1976 BELL UK SYBKL 8003
(D) SHOWADDYWADDY 1977 MFP UK 50353
(E) RED STAR 1977 ARISTA UK SPARTY 1023
(F) GREATEST HITS 1978 ARISTA UK ARTY 145
(G) CREPES & DRAPES 1979 ARISTA UK ARTV 3
(H) BRIGHT LIGHTS 1980 ARISTA UK SPART 1142
( ) SHOWADDYWADDY 1981 HALLMARK UK SHM 3085

S108 SHUSHA S108

SHUSHA V (ALL
G T MOORE G K (CDEF
MARTIN HAYWARD G (CDE
CHRIS LAURENCE B (DE
TOM WHYTE B (CE
TERRY WILSON B (E
RICHIE BULL BANJO(E
B J COLE STEEL(E
TONY BRAUNAGEL PERC (E BRIAN GASCOIGNE K ACC(E RABBIT BUNDRICK K (E GERRY CONWAY D(E
DUSTER BENNETT HCA (E THUNDERTHIGHS V (E TIM JONES PERC K (E JACK EMBLOW ACC (E
GEORGE LARNYOH HRNS (E EDDIE QUANSAH HRNS (E PETER VANDER PUIJE HRNS (E BILL POVEY OCCARINA (E
ROY CARTER WIND (E FRANK CLARKE B (B MARTIN KERSHAW G (B DUNCAN LAMONT FLT (AB
DAVID SNELL HARP (B JOHNNY DEANE D (B STANLEY MYERS PNO (B GRAHAM MATTHEWS D(C
PAUL ROBINSON D (F KUMU HARADA B (F JAMES LASCELLES K (F BROTHER JAMES PERC(F
BAGER AMINI (F BRIAN SMITH FLT (F CHAKO YAMASHTA VLN (F PAUL BUCKMASTER SYN(F
MOX HCA (D BEHBOUDI ZARB (A PAT DONALDSON B (D FRANK RICOTTI PERC(D
JOHN KIRKPATRICK ACC (DG RICHARD BAILEY D (G DARRYL LE QUE PERC (G PATRICK TISON G (G
LESLEY DUNCAN V (G JOHN McKENZIE B (G J A GARDET K (G DAVID WINTHROP SAX (G
GAYLE CUNNINGHAM V (G

(A) PERSIAN LOVE SONGS & MYSTIC CHANTS1973 LYRICORD LLST7235 +TANGENT 108
(B) SONG OF LONG TIME LOVERS 1972 TANGENT TGS114
(C) SHUSHA 1974 UA UK UAS29575
(D) THIS IS THE DAY 1974 UA UK UAS29684
(E) BEFORE THE DELUGE 1975 UA UK UAS29879
(F) FROM EAST TO WEST 1978 TANGENT TGS 138
(G) HERE I LOVE YOU 1980 RHAPSODY RHAP 2

S108A MORT SHUMAN S108A

MORT SHUMAN V (ALL

(A) MY DEATH 1969 REPRISE US 6358
(B) MORT SHUMAN 1973 PHILIPS US 700 005
(C) VOILA COMMENT 1973 PHILIPS FR 6499 630
(D) DES CHANSONS SENTIMENTALES 1974 PHILIPS US 6325 172
(E) IMAGINE 1976 PHILIPS FR 9101 029
(F) MY NAME IS MORTIMER 1977 PHILIPS FR 9101 107

S108B SUHRS / SHROLING S108B

(A) DIARY 1981 BRAIN GER/UK 0060 333

S108C SHU BI DUA S108C

BOSSE HALL CHRISTENSEN D V(ABCDE
JENS TAGE NIELSEN K V (ABCDE
MICHAEL HARDINGER GV (ABCDE
MICHAEL BUNDESEN V (ABCDE
PAUL MEYENDORF G V (A
NIELS GRONBECH B V (ABCD
SVEND ASMUSSEN VLN (ABCD
TOMMY SEEBACH SYN (AB
MORTEN LANGEBFEK K (A
PER STAN PERC (AB KASPER WINDING (A CLAUS ASMUSSEN G B(BCDE JESPER THILO SAX (B
ALLAN BOTSCHINSKY HRNS (B FINN MADSEN HRNS (B VINCENT NIELSSON HRNS (B MICHAEL ELO V (C
JENS HYLLESTAD CELLO(C KIM DAUGAARD B V (E NIELS ERIK CLAUSEN CELLO(E

(A) SHU BI DUA 1974 POLYDOR DK 2380 024
(B) "2" 1975 POLYDOR DK 2380 040
(C) "3" 1976 POLYDOR DK 2380 046
(D)"4" 1977 POLYDOR DK 2380 053
(E) 78 EREN 1978 POLYDOR DK 2380 061
(F) LEIF I PARKEN 1979 POLYDOR DK 2444 070
(G) "7" 1980 POLYDOR DK
(H) "8" 1981 POLYDOR DK

S109 SIDE EFFECT S109

(A) SIDE EFFECT 197 FANTASY US 9491
(B) GOIN' BANANAS 1978 FANTASY FTA 3008 US 9537
(C) WHAT YOU NEED 197 FANTASY US 9513
(D) RAINBOW VISIONS 1979 FANTASY US 9569
(E) AFTER THE RAIN 1980 ELEKTRA US 261
(F) PORTRAITS 1981 ELEKTRA UK K52295
(G) ALL ABOARD 1982 ELEKTRA UK 160049

S110 SIDE WINDER S110

STUART SMITH G (
FRED SCARRET G (
NEIL HARVEY V (STEVE McLAUGHLIN B (YATTA YATES D (

(A) ALL WOUND UP 1979 TANK UK 332

S110A SIDEWINDERS S110A

ANDY PALEY V HCA (A
LEIGH LISOWSKI B V (A
MIKE READ G (A ERIC ROSENFELD G V (A HENRY STERN D PERC V(A

(A) SIDEWINDERS 1972 RCA US LSP 4696

S111 BEN SIDRAN S111

BEN SIDRAN V PNO (ALL — (A) FEEL YOUR GROOVE — 1971 CAPITOL US ST 825
CLYDE STUBBLEFIELD D (BCD — (B) I LEAD A LIFE — 1972 BLUE THUMB US BTS 40
GEORGE BROWN D (BC — (C) DONT LET GO — 1972 BLUE THUMB US BTS 6012
PHIL UPCHURCH D G B(BCDEF — (D) PUTTIN' IN TIME ON PLANET EARTH — 1973 BLUE THUMB US BTS 55
CURLEY JAMES COOKE G (ABCDE — (E) FREE IN AMERICA — 1976 ARISTA US AL 4081
JERRY ALEXANDER HCA (C — (F) DOCTOr IS IN — 1977 ARISTA SPARTY1022 US AL 4131
BUNKY GREEN SAX (C — (G) A LITTLE KISS IN THE NIGHT — 1978 ARISTA SPART 1064 US AB 4178
SONNY SEALS SAX (CE
KIP MERKLEIN B (C — RANDY FULLERTON B (F — JIM PETERMAN ORG (CD — TOM PIAZZA D (C
RICHARD DAVIS B (F — CHUCK DOMANICO B (F — JOHN GUERIN D (F — TONY WILLIAMS D (DF
BLUE MITCHELL TPT(ABFG — LARRY CARLTON G (F — RAY ARMONDO PERC (F — DAVID WOODFORD (G
PHIL WOODS SAX (G — GARY MALLABER D PERC(AF — GAVIN CHRISTOPHER V (BE — CHEEBA SWITZER V (B
JOHNNY ALMOND FLT (B — BRUCE BOTNICK V (B — CURT ROADS SYN (B — DENNIS OLIVER B (B
TIM DAVIS CONGA(BD — CHARLES DAVIS SAX (B — BOB FOLKEDAHL HRNS (B — BOB CORBET HRN(B
JIM GORDON SAX (B — JIM KELTNER D (A — SANDY KONIKOFF PERC (A — JUDY SIDRAN V (A
BOZ SCAGGS G (A — PETER FRAMPTON G (A — GREG RIDLEY B (A — CHRIS DRISCOE SAX(A
DAVID BROWN B (A — GEORGE RAINS D (A — MIMI FARINA MELVIN V (A — CHARLIE WATTS D (A
BILL PERKINS SAX (D — LAUDIR DE OLIVEIRA PERC(D — JOSE SOARES PERC (D — STEVE MILLER G (D
JESSE ED DAVIS G (AG — ABE LABORIEL B (G — ARTHUR ADAMS G (G — GERALD JOHNSON G (G
ROSE BUTLER V (G — MAX GRONENTHAL V (G — MIKE FINNIGAN K V (G — JAY GRAYDON G (G
GARY COLEMAN PERC (G — BOB GLAUB B (G — GARY ZAPPA B (E — BILL MEEKER D (E
HENRY GIBSON PERC (E — MARY ANN STEWART V (E — RICHARD TEE K (E — WOODY SHAW TPT(E
RANDY BRECKER HRNS (E — MICHAEL BRECKER HRNS (E — KITTY HAYWOOD V (E — VIVIAN HAYWOOD V (E

S112 PAUL SIEBEL S112

PAUL SIEBEL G V (ALL — (A) WOODSMOKE AND ORANGES — 1970 ELEKTRA EKS 74064 RI UK K42040
DAVID BROMBERG G (C — (B) JACK KNIFE GYPSY — 1971 ELEKTRA EKS 74081 RI UK K42076
GARY WHITE (C — (C) LIVE — 1981 RAG BABY UK 1006

S112A DAN SIEGEL S112A

DAN SIEGEL K V (A — (A) THE HOT SHOT — 1980 INNER CITY US 1C1111
GARRY HAGBERG G (A
ROB THOMAS B VLN(A — GARY HOBBS D (A — JEFF HOMAN SAX (A — MARC SIEGEL V (A
EDWARD McMANUS HRNS (A — CINDY McMANUS HRNS (A — SUE DAVIS HARP (A

S112B CORKY SIEGEL S112B

CORKY SIEGAL V K HCA(A — (A) CORKY SIEGAL — 1974 DHARMA US 806
SHELLY PLOTKIN D (A
VASSAR CLEMENTS STR (A

S113 SIEGEL SCHWALL BAND S113

CORKY SIEGEL V K HCA(ALL — (A) SIEGEL SCHWALL BAND — 1966 VANGUARD VSD 79235
JIM SCHWALL G V (ALL — (B) SAY SIEGEL SCHWALL — 1967 VANGUARD VSD 79249
JOS DAVIDSON B (ABCDEFGHIJ — (C) SHAKE — 1968 VANGUARD UK SVRL19044+VSD 79289
RUSS CHADWICK D (ABCDJ — (D) SIEGEL SCHWALL 70 — 1970 VANGUARD VSD 6562
JACK DAWSON B (BCDJ — (E) THE SIEGEL SCHWALL BAND — 1971 WOODEN NICKEL US WNS 1002
SHELDON IRA PLOTKIN D (EFGHIK — (E) THE SIEGEL SCHWALL BAND — 1971 RCA UK SF 8246
(E) THE SIEGEL SCHWALL BAND — 198 LINE GER 5034
ROLLOW RADFORD B (EFGHIK — (F) SLEEPY HOLLOW — 1972 WOODEN NICKEL US WNS 1010
SAN FRANCISCO SYM ORCH (K — (F) SLEEPY HOLLOW — 1972 RCA LSP10394 GER RI 5043
(G) 953 WEST — 1973 TELDEC 10121 GER RI LINE 5049
(H) LIVE LAST SUMMER — 1974 TELDEC 6 24215 GER RI LINE 5032
(H) LIVE LAST SUMMER — 1974 WOODEN NICKEL US WNS 1 288
(I) R.I.P. SIEGEL SCHWALL — 1974 TELDEC 6 24217
(I) R.I.P. SIEGEL SCHWALL — 1974 WOODEN NICKEL US WNS 1 554
(I) R.I.P. SIEGEL SCHWALL — 1980 LINE GER 5054
(J) BEST OF — 1974 VANGUARD VSD 79336
(K) THREE PIECES FOR BLUES BAND & ORCH — 1974 POLYDOR 2530 309
(K) S S B & SYM ORCH — 1980 POLYDOR 2344 157 2261 031

S114 SIERRA S114

SNEAKY PETE STEEL(A — (A) SIERRA — 1977 MERCURY US SRM1 1179
GIB GUILBEAU FDL (A
MICKY McGEE D V (A — FELIX PAPPALARDI PROD (A — THAD MAXWELL B V (A — BOBBY COCHRAN G V (A

S114A DAVITT SIGERSON S114A

DAVITT SIGERSON V (A — (A) DAVITT SIGERSON — 1980 ISLAND/ZE ILPS 7011
KENWOOD DENNARD D (A
RICHARD CROOKS D (A — JIMMY RIPPETOE G B (A — GORDON JOHNSON B (A — NED ALBRIGHT PNO (A
MICHAEL DELUGG PROD (A

S115 BUNNY SIGLER S115

BUNNY SIGLER K (A — (A) LET THE GOOD TIMES ROLL — 19 PARKWAY US PS 50000
RAYMOND EARL B (F — (B) THAT'S HOW LONG I'LL BE LOVING — 1974 PHILADELPHIA UK 80253 US 32589
IM MILLER G (F — (C) KEEP SMILIN' — 197 PHILADELPHIA US 33249
SCOTTY MILLER D (F — (D) MY MUSIC — 19 PHILADELPHIA UK 81755 US 34267
DENNIS RICHARDSON K (F — (E) LET ME PARTY WITH YOU — 1978 SALSOUL UK 1502 GOLD US 9500
LARRY DAVIS PERC V(F — (F) I'VE ALWAYS WANTED TO SING — 1979 SALSOUL UK 1512 GOLD US 9503
JIMMY SIGLER K V (F — (G) LET IT SNOW — 1980 SALSOUL UK 8531
CHARLES COLLINS PERC (F
CARLA BENSON V (F — EVETTE BENTON V (F — BARBARA INGRAM V (F

S115A SILENT TYPES S115A

(A) WAR ECONOMY(EP) — 1980 DOUBLE DOSE SHOT 13

S115B SILICON TEENS S115B

DARRYL V (A — (A) MUSIC FOR PARTIES — 1980 MUTE UK STUMM2 US SIRE 6092
JACKI SYN (A
PAUL PERC (A — DIANE SYN (A

S115C SILENCERS S115C

(A) ROCK'N'ROLL ENFORCEMENT — 19 PRECISION US 36529
(B) ROMANIAC — 1981 PRECISION US 37083

S115D THE SILKIE S115D

KEV SILKIE B (A — (A) YOU'VE GOT TO HIDE YOUR LOVE AWAY 1965 FONTANA US 67548
MIKE SILKIE G V (A
SILVIE SILKIE V (A IVOR SILKIE D (A JOHN LENNON G (A PAUL McCARTNEY G (A
GEORGE HARRISON G (A

S116 JUDEE SILL S116

JUDEE SILL G V (ABC — (A) JUDEE SILL 1971 ASYLUM UK SYLA 8751
CLYDIE KING V (A — (B) HEART FOOD 1973 ASYLUM UK SYL9006 US 5063
VANETTA FIELDS V (A — (C) TULIPS FROM AMSTERDAM 1979
RITA COOLIDGE V (A
DAVID BEARDEN (B LYNN BLESSING (B GENE CIPRIANO (B VINCE DE ROSA (B
DOUG DILLARD (B OMA DRAKE (B ASSA DRORI (B BUDDY EMMONS (B
JESSE EHRLICH (B CHRIS ETHRIDGE (B RON FULSOM (B HARRIS GOLDMAN (B
JIM GORDON (B BOBBYE HALL PERC (B GLORIA JONES V (B RAY KELLY (B
WILLIAM KURASCH (B LEONARD MALARSKY (B SPOONER OLDHAM (B RICHARD PERISSI (B
BILL PLUMMER (B EMIL RICHARDS (B RALPH SCHAEFFER (B LOUIE SHELTON (B
DAVID SCHWARTZ (B CAROLYN WILLIS (B TIBOR ZELIG (B

S116A SILLY WIZARD S116A

JOHNNY CUNNINGHAM FDL MAND(ABC — (A) SILLY WIZARD 1976 XTRA UK XTRA 1158
PHIL CUNNINGHAM K (ABC — (B) CALEDONIA'S SONS 1978 HIGHWAY SHY 7004
ANDY STEWART V BAN(ABC — (C) SO MANY PARTINGS 1979 HIGHWAY UK SHY 7007
GORDON JONES G MAND(ABC
BOB THOMAS G (ABC MARTIN HODDEN B (ABC

S117 SILVER S117

JOHN BATDORF G V (A — (A) SILVER 1976 ARISTA US 4076 UK ARTY 144
BRENT MYDLAND V K (A
RICK GILES (GREG COLLIER G V (A HARRY STINSON V D(A TOM LEADON B V (A

S117A SILVER APPLES S117A

SIMEON BAN V(A — (A) SILVER APPLES 1968 KAPP US 3562
DAN TAYLOR PERC V(A — (B) CONTRACT 1969 KAPP US 3584

S117B SILVER CONDOR S117B

CLAUDE PEPPER D (A — (A) SILVER CONDOR 1981 CBS US
JOE CERISCNO V (A
EARL SLICK G (A JOHN CAREY G K V(A JAY DAVIS B (A

S118 SILVERADO S118

EARL GOODWIN G V (AB — (A) SILVERADO 1976 RCA US APLI 1792
CARL SHILLO G V (AB — (B) TAKING IT ALL IN STRIDE 1977 RCA US APLI 2421
JAY D MANESS G (A — (C) READY FOR LOVE 1981 RCA
J F KEITHLINO B (B
RON TUTT D (A VICTOR FELDMAN PERC VIBES(A AL CASEY G MAND(A ALAN ESTES PERC(A
JAMES B GORDON D (A EMORY GORDY B (A TOM HENSLEY K (A MIKE HAYDEN D (B
DON ORIOTO K (B

S118A SILVERBIRD S118A

(A) GETTING TOGETHER 1972 CBS US 31570

S119 SILVERHEAD S119

MICHAEL DES BARRES V (ABC — (A) SILVERHEAD 1972 PURPLE UK TPSA 7506 US MCA 306
NIGEL HARRISON B (ABC — (B) SIXTEEN & SAVAGED 1973 PURPLE UK TPSA 7511 US MCA 391
ROD DAVIES PERC V G (ABC — (C) LIVE AT RAINBOW 1976 PUPLE JAP 80351
PETE THOMPSON D K (ABC
ROBBIE BLUNT G (B MARTIN BIRCH PROD (A STEVE FOREST G V (A JOHN MUMFORD TROM(A
LYLE JENKINS SAX (A

S119A SILVERMETRE S119A

LEIGH STEVENS G (A — (A) SILVERMETRE 1969 NATIONAL GENERAL 2000
MICK WALLER D (A
JACK REYNOLDS V (A PETE SEARS B K (A

S120 SHEL SILVERSTEIN S120

SHEL SILVERSTEIN (ALL — (A) HAIRY JAZZ 1961 ELEKTRA US 176
PIG ROBBINS K (J — (B) INSIDE SHEL SILVERSTEIN 196 ATLANTIC US 8257
RAY SAWYER V (G — ( ) INSIDE FOLK MUSIC 1962 ATLANTIC US SD 8072
DENNIS LOCORRIERE V (G — (C) IM SO GOOD , I DONT HAVE TO BRAG 196 CADET US 4052
JAY DAVID (G — (D) DRAIN MY BRAIN 196 CADET US 4054
GEORGE CUMMINGS (G — (E) CROUCHING ON THE OUTSIDE 197 JANUS 2JLS 3052
BILLY FRANCIS (G — (F) A BOY NAMED SUE 1968 RCA US LSP 4192
RIK ELSWIT (G — (G) FREAKIN' AT THE FREAKERS BALL 1973 CBS UK 65452 US 31119
AMOS GARRETT G (J — (G) FREAKIN' AT THE FREAKERS BALL 1979 CBS RI UK 31766
JANCE GARFAT (G — (H) SONGS & STORIES 1978 PARACHUTE US RRLP9007
MIKE FINNIGAN (G — (J) GREAT CONCH TRAIN ROBBERY 1980 FLYING FISH US
ART TWAIN (G
JELLY ROLL TURNER (G TURK MURPHY (G CHARLES H PETERSON (G CHARLES DAY (G
DELL DUCKWORTH (G CLYDE GRAVES (G PHILLIP HOWE (G JAMES MAIHACH (G
LEON OAKLEY (G RICHARD SHUBB (G FRED MERGY (G SAM BUSH (J
JOHN HARTFORD (J D J FONTANA D (J

S120A DENNIS SIMMONDS S120A

DENNIS SIMMONDS (A — (A) ALONE ON PENGUIN ISLAND 1981 DOME UK DOM331

S120B DAVID SIMMONS S120B

DAVID SIMMONS V (AB — (A) HEAR ME OUT 1978 FANTASY US F9561
WILLIAM INGRAM G (AB — (B) THE WORLD BELONGS TO ME 1979 FANTASY US F9588
JAMES RAMSEY G (A
JAMES INGRAM G K (AB JOHN INGRAM D (AB TIMMI INGRAMS CONGOS(AB BARBARA INGRAM V (AB
JAMES MINGRAM SAX (A MARK PRATER K (B BUTCH INGRAM TPT V (B

S121 GENE SIMMONS S121

GENE SIMMONS G V (A — (A) GENE SIMMONS — CASABLANCA UK NBLP 7120

ALLEN SCHWARZBERG D (A

NEIL JASON B (A — ELLIOTT RANDALL G (A — SEAN DELANEY PERC V(A — BOB SEGER V (A

JOE PERRY (A — HELEN REDDY V (A — MITCH WEISSMAN (A — RICHIE RANNO (A

GORDON GRODY V (A — RICK NIELSEN G (A — MICHAEL DES BARRES V (A — DIVA GRAY V (A

KATE SAPAL V (A — FRAN EISENBERG V (A — CAROLYN RAY V (A — ERIC TROYER PNO(A

JANIS IAN (A — STEVE LACEY G (A — JOHN SHANE HOWELL G (A — RICHARD GERSTEIN PERC(A

JEFF BAXTER G (A — DONNA SUMMER V (A — JOE PECORINO (A — CHER (A

S122 JEFF SIMMONS S122

JEFF SIMMONS B V K(AB — (A) NAKED ANGELS SOUNDTRACK — 1969 STRAIGHT STS 1056

FRANK ZAPPA G (B — (B) LUCILLE HAS MESSED UP MY MIND — 1969 STRAIGHT STS1057 REPRISE 6391

CRAIG TARWATER G (B

IAN UNDERWOOD SAX (B — RON WOODS D PERC(B — JOHN KEHLIOR D (B

S122A SIMMS BROTHERS BAND S122A

GEORGE SIMMS V PERC(A — (A) SIMMS BROTHERS BAND — 1979 ELEKTRA US 6E220

FRANK SIMMS G V (A — (B) ATTITUDE — 1980 ELEKTRA US 289

BUDD TUNICK D (A

DAVID SPINNER V CONG(A — ROBERT SABINO K (A — SHIMMY MAKI B (A — MICKEY LEONARD G (A

S123 SIMON & GARFUNKEL S123

PAUL SIMON G V (ALL — (A) WEDNESDAY MORNING 3 AM — 1966 CBS UK 63370 US 9049

ART GARFUNKEL V (ALL — (B) THE SOUND OF SILENCE — 1966 CBS UK 62690 US 9269

FRED CARTER G (F — (C) PARSLEY SAGE ROSEMARY & THYME — 1966 CBS UK 62860 US 9363

HAL BLAINE D (F — (D) BOOKENDS — 1968 CBS UK 63101 US 9529

JOE OSBORN B (F — (E) THE GRADUATE(SOUNDTRACK) — 1968 CBS UK 70042 US 3180

LARRY KNECHTEL K (F — (F) BRIDGE OVER TROUBLED WATERS — 1970 CBS UK 63699 US 9914

JIMMY HASKELL STRINGS(F — (G) GREATEST HITS — 1972 CBS UK 69003 US 31350

ERNIE FREEMAN STRINGS(F — ( ) SIMON & GARFUKEL — 1967 ALLEGRO ALL 836

STEVE GADD D (K — ( ) SIMON & GARFUkel — 19 PICKWICK US 3059

GRADY TATE D (K — ( ) SIMON & GARFUNKEL — 19 FONTANA 6430 006

DAVID BROWN G (K — (K) CONCERT IN CENTRAL PARK — 1981 GEFFEN UK 96008

JOHN GATCHELL TPT (K — (EP) WEDNESDAY MORNING 3 AM — 1965 CBS

PETE CARR G (K — (EP) I AM A ROCK — 1966 CBS 6034

ANTHONY JACKSON B (K — (EP) MRS ROBINSON — 1968 CBS 6400

RICHARD TEE K (K — (EP) FEELING GROOVY — 1967 CBS 6360

ROB MOUNSEY SYN (K

DAVE TOFANI SAX (K — GERRY NIEWOOD SAX (K — JOHN ECKERT TPT (K

S124 CARLY SIMON S124

CARLY SIMON V G PNO (ALL — (A) CARLY SIMON — 1971 ELEKTRA US 74082 UK K42077

JAMES TAYLOR G V (DEFGHJK — (B) ANTICIPATION — 1971 ELEKTRA US 75016 UK K42101

JIM RYAN G B (BCDF — (AB) CARLY SIMON /ANTICIPATION — 1975 ELEKTRA UK K62015

JOHN RYAN B (BF — (C) NO SECRETS — 1972 ELEKTRA US 75049 UK K42127

PAUL KEOGH G (C — (D) HOTCAKES — 1974 ELEKTRA US 7E1002 UK K52005

KLAUS VOORMANN B (CDEFG — (E) PLAYING POSSUM — 1975 ELEKTRA US 7E1033 UK K52020

LOWELL GEORGE G (CG — (F) THE BEST OF CARLY SIMON — 1976 ELEKTRA US 7E1048 UK K52025

ANDREW GOLD G D (EFG — (G) ANOTHER PASSAGE — 1976 ELEKTRA US 7E1064 UK K52036

WILLIE WEEKS B (EF — (H) BOYS IN THE TREES — 1978 ELEKTRA US 6E 128 UK K52066

LEE SKLAR B (E — (J) SPY — 1979 ELEKTRA US 5E 506 UK K52147

JOE MONDRAGON B (E — (K) COME UPSTAIRS — 1980 WB US BSK3443 UK K56828

JEFF BAXTER G (EG — (L) TORCH — 1981 WB US 3592 UK K56935

ANTHONY JACKSON B (L

PAUL GLANZ	PNO	(BF	ANDY NEWMARK	D PERC	(BCDEFG	ALVIN ROBINSON	G	(E	PETER ROBINSON	PNO	(C
JIM GORDON	D	(CDEF	TONY LEVIN	B	(FJK	NICKY HOPKINS	PNO	(CF	JIM KELTNER	D	(BDFG
ROBBIE ROBERTSON	G	(FD	JAMES NEWTON HOWARD	K	(E	RAY COOPER	PERC	(CF	PAUL BARRERE	G	(G
PAUL GRIFFIN	PNO	(F	RINGO STARR	D	(E	GLENN FREY	G	(G	KIRBY JOHNSON	K	(F
RUSS KUNKEL	D	(DC	PATRICK SIMMONS	G	(G	BILL PAYNE	ORG	(G	IVY COTTLER	D	(E
LAURINDO ALAMEIDA	G	(G	NICK DE CARO	ACC	(G	FREDDIE STAEHLE	PERC	(E	STEVE BRUTON	G	(G
RICHARD TEE	K	(HJ	ALAN ESTES	PERC	(E	KENNY GRADNEY	G	(G	KEN BISCHEL	K	(HJ
JIMMY JOHNSON	D	(F	BOB GLAUB	B	(G	DON GROLNICK	K	(HJK	EDDIE BONGO	CONGA	(F
TIRAN PORTER	B	(G	BILLY MERNIT	PNO	(EJK	RALPH MACDONALD	PERC	(FD	ERIC GALE	G	(H
DR JOHN	K C	(DEFG	RICHARD PERRY	PERC	(F	CORNELL DUPREE	G	(H	DAVE SANBORN	SAX	(HJL
RITCHIE HAYWARD	D V	(G	GORDON EDWARDS	B	(H	HARVEY ESTRIN	RECORDER	(H	RICK JAEGER	D V	(G
JOHN HALL	G	(HJ	GEORGE MARGE	RECORDER	(H	ROBERT GREENIDGE	D	(G	JEFF MIRANOV	G	(H
BOBBY KEYS	SAX	(DCF	JOHN HARTMAN	D	(G	HUGH McCRACKEN	G	(HL	TREVOR LAWRENCE	SAX	(E
KEITH KNUDSEN	D	(G	WILL LEE	B	(HJ	DERREK VAN EATON	FLT	(E	MILT HOLLAND	PERC	(G
FRED TACKETT	MANDOCELLO	(G	MICHAEL BRECKER	SAX	(DFJL	VICTOR FELDMAN	PERC	(G	ANDREW LOVE	SAX	(G
STEVE GADD	D	(HJK	CRUSHER BENNETT	PERC	(HJ	RUBENS BASSINI	PERC	(H	TOMMY MORGAN	HCA	(E
JOE CARO	G	(J	DAVID SPINOZZA	G	(JD	IAN McLAUGHLIN	K	(J	WARREN BERNHARDT	K	(KL
RANDY BRECKER	TPT	(JL	RICK MAROTTA	D	(JKLD	KEN LANDRUM		(K	MIKE MAINIERI	K V	(JKL
HUBERT LAWS	FLT	(J	FRANK CARILLO	G	(G	CLIFF CARTER	SYN	(J	RAPHAEL CRUZ	PERC	(J
PETER BALLIN	SAX	(J	TOM MALONE	TROM	(J	LEW DELGATTO	SAX	(J	PETE HEWLETT	G V	(K
SID McGINNIS	G V	(K	ED WALSH	OBERHEIM	(K	JERRY GROSSMAN	CELLO	(K	NOVI NOVAG	VLA	(G
DAVID CAMPBELL	VLA	(G	BUD SHANK	FLT	(G	PHIL BODNER	OBOE	(H	MARGARET ROSS	HARP	(K
GLORIA AGOSTINI	HARP	(H	RITA COOLIDGE	V	(E	RODNEY RICHMOND	V	(E	LIZA STRIKE	V	(E
VICKI BROWN	V	(CF	BONNIE BRAMLETT	V	(CF	DORIS TROY	V	(CF	PAUL McCARTNEY	V	(CF
LINDA McCARTNEY	V	(CF	CLYDIE KING	V	(E	CAROLYN WILLIS	V	(E	CAROLE KING	V	(EF
VINI PONCIA	V	(E	MAXINE WILLARD	V	(E	JULIA TILLMAN	V	(E	ABIGALE HANESS	V	(EF
KENNY MOORE	V	(EF	CARL HALL	V	(FD	TASHA THOMAS	V	(FD	LANI GROVES	V	(FD
MIKE McDONALD	V	(G	LUCY SIMON	V	(GJ	ALEX TAYLOR	V	(GK	ELLEN KEARNEY	V	(G
LINDA RONSTADT	V	(G	DOOBIE BROTHERS	V	(G	JACKSON BROWNE	V	(G	LIBBY TITUS	V	(G
LEAH KUNKEL	V	(G	TIM CURRY	V	(J	ULLANDA McCULLOUGH	V	(J	LORAINE NEWMAN	V	(K
MARIA AGUIAR	V	(K	CHRISTINE MARTIN	V	(K	GAIL BOGGS	V	(J	HUGH TAYLOR	V	(K
SARAH MARIA TAYLOR	V	(K	LEE RITENOUR	G	(EL	LON VAN EATON	SIT SYN	(E	ANTHONY JACKSON	B	(L
MARTY PAICH	STR	(L	EDDIE GOMEZ	B	(L	JIMMY WISNER	STR	(L	JAY BERLINER	G	(L
DON SEBESKY	STR	(L	ROBERT M FREEDMAN	STR	(L	PHIL WOODS	SAX	(L	GRADY TATE	D	(L
JERRY MAROTTA	D	(L	DAVID NADIEN	VLN	(L	MICK JAGGER	C	(C	KEN ASHER	K	(D
RICHARD DAVIS	B	(D	GEORGE DEVONS	PERC	(D	TODD GRAFF	V	(D	LARRY BREAN	B	(D
HOWARD JOHNSON	SAX	(D	BARRY ROGERS	TROM	(D	BILLY COBHAM	D	(D	BENNIE DIGGS	V	(D
REVELATIONS	V	(D	CARL HALL	V	(D	BUCKY PIZZARELLI	G	(D	PAUL BUCKMASTER	STR	(D
STEVE MADAIO	TPT	(D									

S124A JOE SIMON S214A

JOE SIMON V (ALL
ROLAND CHAMBERS G (G
T J TINDALL G (G
EARL YOUNG PERC (G
VINCE MONTANA VIBES (G
LEON HUFF PNO (G
NORMAN HARRIS G (G
RONALD BAKER B (G
LARRY WASHINGTON PERC (G
LEONARD PAKULA ORG (G
THOM BELL STR (G

(A) JOE SIMON 19 JOY UK JOYS 176
(B) SOUNDS OF SIMON 19 POLYDOR UK 2918 001
(C) POWER OF SIMON 19 POLYDOR UK 2391 090
(D) GREATEST HITS 1973 MONUMENT UK 65419 US 231916
(E) MOOD HEART & SOUL 1974 POLYDOR UK 2391 132
(F) GET DOWN 1975 POLYDOR UK 2391 181
(G) DROWNING IN THE SEA OF LOVE 1976 POLYDOR UK 2482 278
(H) CHOKIN' WIND 1976 MONUMENT UK 22008
(I) TODAY 1976 SPRING UK 2391 216
(J) EASY TO LOVE 1977 SPRING UK 2391 260
(K) BEST OF 1977 POLYDOR UK 2391 311
(L) BAD CASE OF LOVE 1978 SPRING UK 2391 307
(M) LOVE VIBRATIONS 1979 SPRING UK 2391 375

S125 PAUL SIMON S125

PAUL SIMON G V (ALL
HUX BROWN G (BF
DAVID SPINOZZA G (BCF
WALLACE WILSON G (B
JERRY HAHN G (B
STEFAN GROSSMAN G (B
NEVILLE HINDS ORG (BF
JACKIE JACKSON B (BF

(A) THE PAUL SIMON SONGBOOK 1965 CBS UK 62579
(B) PAUL SIMON(MOTHER & CHILD REUNION)1972 CBS US 30750 UK 69007
(C) THERE GOES RHYMIN' SIMON 1973 CBS US 32280 UK 69035
(D) LIVE RHYMIN' 1974 CBS US 32855 UK 69059
(E) STILL CRAZY AFTER ALL THESE YEARS 1975 CBS US 33540 UK 86001
(F) GREATEST HITS ETC 197 CBS US 35032 UK 86047
(G) ONE TRICK PONY 1980 WEA US 3472 UK K56846

RON CARTER B (B | RUSSELL GEORGE B (BF | JOE OSBORN B (B | WINSTON GRENNAN D (BF
HAL BLAINE D (B | VICTOR MONTANEZ D (B | DENSIL LANG PERC (BF | LOS INCAS PERC FLT (BF
AIRTO MOREIRA PERC (BCF | LARRY KNECHTEL K HCA(BF | MIKE MAINIERI VIBES(B | FRED LIPSIUS HRNS(B
JOHN SCHROER HRNS (B | STEVEN TURRE HRNS (B | CHARLIE McCOY HCA (B | CISSY HOUSTON B (BF
RONELLE STAFFORD V (BF | DEIRDRE TUCK V (BF | VON EVA SIMS V (BF | STEPHANE GRAPPELLY VLN(B
PETE CARR G (CEF | CORNELL DUPREE G (C | ALEXANDER GAFA G (CF | JERRY PUCKETT G (C
DAVID HOOD B (CEF | GORDON EDWARDS B (CEF | BOB CRANSHAW B (CF | RICHARD DAVIS B (CF
VERNIE ROBBINS B (C | ROGER HAWKINS D (CEF | RICK MAROTTA D (C | GRADY TATE D (CEF
JAMES STRAUD D (C | BARRY BECKETT K (CEF | BOB JAMES K (CEF | PAUL GRIFFIN PNO(C
BOBBY SCOTT PNO (CF | ONWARD BRASS BAND (CF | DON ELLIOTT VIBES(C | CARSON WHITSETT ORG(C
DIXIE HUMMINGBIRDS V (CF | MAGGIE ROCHE V (C | TERRE ROCHE V (C | JIMMY JOHNSON G (CF
JESSY DIXON SINGERS (DEF | URUBAMBA (D | RICHARD TEE K V (GEF | HIRAM BULLOCK G (G
RALPH MACDONALD PERC (GEF | ERIC GALE G (G | JEFF MIRONOV G (G | JOHN TROPEA G (GEF
JOE BECK G (GEF | STEVE GADD D (GEF | TONY LEVIN B (G | HUGH McCRACKEN G (GEF
DON GROLNICK SYN (G | JON FADDIS HRNS (G | PATTI AUSTIN V (GEF | MIKE BRECKER HRNS(EF
ART GARFUNKEL V (E | SIVUKA V ACC(EF | TONY LEVIN B (EF | PHOEBE SNOW V (EF
DAVE MATTHEWS HRNS (EF | JERRY FRIEDMAN G (EF | KEN ASHER K (EF | VALERIE SIMPSON V (EF
TOOTS THIELMANS HCA (E | DAVE SANBORN SAX (EF | PHIL WOODS SAX (EF | EDDIE DANIELS SAX (E
LEON PENDARVIS K (E | ANTHONY JACKSON B (F | CHICAGO COMM CHOIR V (E | RANDY BRECKER TPT (F
THE OAK RIDGE BOYS V (F | MARVIN STAMM TPT (F | IRVIN MARKOWITZ TPT (F | LOU DELGATTO SAX (F
QUINCY JONES STR (F | WALLACE WILSON G (F | RONELLE STAFFORD V (F | VON EVA SIMS V (F
REV CLAUDE JITER V (F

S126 SIMPLE MINDS S126

JIM KERR V (ABCDE
CHARLIE BURCHILL G V (ABCDE
MICHAEL McNEIL K V (ABCDE
BRIAN McGEE D V (ABCD
DEREK FORBES B V (ABCDE
KEN LOCKIE V (D
JACQUIE V (D | MIKE OGLETREE D PERC(E | MEL GAYNOR D (E | KENNY HYSLOP D (A
SHARON CAMPBELL V (E | HERBIE HANCOCK K (

(A) LIFE IN A DAY 1979 ZOOM ZULP 001
(B) REAL TO REAL CACOPHONY 1979 ZOOM SPART1109
(C) EMPIRES AND DANCE 1980 ARISTA SPART1140
(D) SONS AND FASCINATION 1981 VIRGIN V 2207
(E) NEW GOLD DREAM 1982 VIRGIN V 2230

S127 MARTIN SIMPSON S127

MARTIN SIMPSON G V BAN(A
AL SCHMIDT HCA (A
PETER THOMPSON B (A

(A) GOLDEN VANITY 1976 TRAILER LER 2099

S128 VALERIE SIMPSON S128

VALERIE SIMPSON V K (AB
JAMES JAMESON B (A
ANDREW SMITH D (A
ROBERT WHITE G (A
JOE MESSINA G (A | DENNIS COFFEY G (A | URIEL JONES D (A | JOHNNY GRIFFITH PNO (A
LEONARD CASTON PNO (A | EDDIE BROWN PERC (A | JACK ASHFORD PERC (A | JACK BROKENSHAW PERC(A
JOSHIE ASMSTEAD V (AB | PAUL RISER STR (AB | NAT ADDERLEY PNO (B | RAY LUCAS D (B
BUDDY WILLIAMS D (B | CHARLES COLLINS D (B | FRANCISCO CENTENO B (B | KEITH ILLIDGE G (B
RALPH MACDONALD PERC (B

(A) VALERIE SIMPSON EXPOSED 1971 TAMLA US 311 UK STML11194
(B) VALERIE SIMPSON 1972 TAMLA US 317 UK STML11219
(C) KEEP 1977 TAMLA US 351

S129 FRANKIE LEE SIMS S129

FRANKIE LEE SIMS (A
HUBERT WASHINGTON D (A

(A) LUCY MAE BLUES 19 SPECIALTY UK SNTF 5004

S130 SINCEROS S130

DON SNOW K V (AB
BOBBI IRWIN D (AB
MARK KJELDSEN G V (AB
RON FRANCIS B (AB | GUS DUDGION PROD (B

(A) SOUND OF SUNBATHING 1979 EPIC US 36134 UK CBS 83632
(B) PET ROCK 1981 EPIC UK 85003

S131 PETE SINFIELD S131

PETE SINFIELD G SYN V (A
RICHARD BRUNTON G (A
B J COLE STEEL(A | GREG LAKE G V (A | SNUFFY WALDEN G (A | MEL COLLINS WIND(A
DON HONEYWELL SAX (A | CHRIS PYNE TROM (A | GREG BOWEN TPT (A | STAN RODERICK TPT (A
ROBIN MILLER WIND (A | TIM HINKLEY PNO (A | PHIL JUMP K (A | KEITH TIPPETT PNO (A
BOZ BURRELL B (A | STEVE DOLAN B (A | JOHN WETTON B (A | MIN D PERC (A
IAN WALLACE D (A

(A) STILL 1973 MANTICORE 2001 UKK43501 US 66667

S131A SINS OF SATAN S131A

(A) SINS OF SATAN 1977 BUDDAH US 5673

S132 SIOUXSIE & THE BANSHEES S132

SIOUXSIE V (ALL (A) THE SCREAM 1978 POLYDOR UK POLD5009 US 6207 GER 2383523
SID VICIOUS D (1 (B) JOIN HANDS 1979 POLYDOR UK 2442 264 GER 2383551
STEVE SEVERIN B G K SYN(ABC123DE (C) KALEIDOSCOPE 1980 POLYDOR UK 2442 177 GER 2383568
MARCO PIRRONI G (1 (D) JU JU 1981 POLYDOR UK POLS1034
P FENTON G (2 (E) ONCE UPON A TIME 1981 POLYDOR UK POLS1056
STEVE JONES G (C (1) SEPT 1976 (2) NOV 1976 (3) 1977
KENNY MORRIS D (23A
JOHN McKAY G(3A JOHN McGEOCH SAX (BC THE SIRENS V (C BUDGIE D B V(C

S132A SIR LORD BALTAMORE S132A

JOHN GARNER V D (AB (A) SIR LORD BALTIMORE 19 MERCURY US 1613
GARY JUSTIN B G V(AB (B) KINGDOM COME 19 MERCURY US 61328
LOUIS DAMBRA G K (AB
JOEY DAMBRA G K V(A

S133 SIREN S133

KEVIN COYNE G V (AB (A) SIREN 1969 DANDELION US D9 104 63755
DAVE CLAGUE G B (AB (B) STRANGE LOCOMOTION 1971 ELEKTRA US74087 DANDELION GER 2310152
NICK CUDWORTH K V G(AB (B) STRANGE LOCOMOTION 1971 DANDELION UKDAN8001
TAT MEAGER D (AB
JOHN CHICHESTER G (A COLIN WOOD K FLT(A MICK GRATTON G (B

S134 SIRKEL & CO S134

ERIC SIRKEL G V (A (A) SIRKEL & CO 1976 CHARLY CRL5003
MICK TAYLOR G (A (A) SIRKEL & CO 1977 AFFINITY AFF 1
MARC FRENTZEL D (A
GORDON RAITT B (A CHRIS MERCER SAX (A JOY YATES V (A RONNIE LEAHY K (A
MICK EVE SAX (A LIZA STRIKE V (A COLIN ALLEN D (A ROBIN MILLAR K (A
RON CARTHY TPT (A JACKIE SULLIVAN V (A

S135 SISTER SLEDGE S135

KATHIE SLEDGE V (BCD (A) CIRCLE OF LOVE 1975 ATLANTIC UK K50097 US 36105
NARADA MICHAEL WALDEN PROD(D ( ) TOGETHER 1977 COTILLION US 9919
DEBBIE SLEDGE V (BCD (B) WE ARE FAMILY 1979 COTILLION UK K50587 US 5209
KIM SLEDGE V (BCD (C) LOVE SOMEBODY TODAY 1980 COTILLION UK K50693 US 16012
JONI SLEDGE V (BCD (D) ALL AMERICAN GIRLS 1981 COTILLION UK K50774 US 16072
NILE RODGERS G (B ( ) SISTER SLEDGE 1981 COTILLION UK K50853 US 5231
ELLEN SEELING TPT (B ( ) THE SISTERS 1982 COTILLION UK K50853
BARRY ROGERS TROM (B
BERNARD EDWARDS B (B TONY THOMPSON D (B ROBERT SABINO K (B KAREN MILNE STRINGS(B
CHERYL HONG STRINGS (B MARIANNE CARROLLSTRINGS(B ANDY SCHWARTZ PNO (B RAYMOND JONES K (B
SAMMY FIGUEROA PERC (B ALEX FOSTER WIND (B JEAN FINEBERG SAX (B JON FADDIS TPT(B

S135A EARL SIXTEEN S135A

EARL SIXTEEN (A (A) REGGAE SOUND 1981 DREAD AT THE CONTROLS UK 003

S135B 6680 LEXINGTON S135B

DAVE GARLAND K V (A (A) 6680 LEXINGTON 196 MGM US 4783
ART MUNSON G V (A
JOE LAMANNO B (A MIKE PATTERSON K V (A ERNIE EARNSHAW D (A VIRGIL BECKHAM G (A
BONNIE BOWDEN V (A DARLENE LOVE V (A GEORGE POOLE VLN (A TONY McCASHEN HCA (A

S136 64 SPOONS S136

TAM NEAL K D V((A) LADIES DONT HAVE WILLIES(EP) 19 BUSHBABY
LYNDON CANNACH D V K(
ANDY CRAWFORD FLT B G (TED EMMET TPT K(JACKO FLT G V(

S137 SIXTY NINE(69) S137

ARMIN STOUWE K G V(A (A) CIRCLE OF THE CRAYFISH 19 PHILIPS 6305 164
ROLAND SCHUPP PERC (A (B) 69 LIVE 1974 PHILIPS 6623 046

S137A SKAFISH S137A

KEN BRONOWSKI G V (A (A) SKAFISH 1979 ILLEGAL UK ILP007 US A&M 008
JIM SKAFISH K V (A
JAVIER CRUZ K V (A BARBIE GOODNICK G V (A LARRY MAZALAN B V (A LARRY MYSLIWIEC D (A
GAYLE CROWDER V (A

S138 SKATELITES S138

(A) AFRICAN ROOTS 19 UA US LA 799

S139 SKID ROW S139

GARY MOORE G V (A (A) SKID 1970 CBS UK 63965
ADRIAN FISHER ((B) 34 HOURS 1971 CBS US 30913 UK 64411
ED DEAN ((C) ALIVE & KICKING 1976 RELEASE RRL 8001
KEVIN McALEA (
NOEL BRIDGEMAN D V (A BRENDAN'BRUSH' SHIELS B V(A

S140 SKIDS S140

STUART ADAMSON G K V(ABC (A) SCARED TO DANCE 1979 VIRGIN UK V2116
RICHARD JOBSON V (ABCD (B) DAYS IN EUROPA 1979 VIRGIN UK V2138 GER 201 049
WILLIE SIMPSON B (AB (C) ABSOLUTE GAME 1980 VIRGIN UK V2174 GER 202 859
RUSSELL WEBB B (C (D) JOY 1981 VIRGIN GER 204 167
MIKE BAILLIE D (C (E) FANFARE 1982 VIRGIN UK VM 2
NICK GRIFFITHS V (D
TOM FELLICHAN D (MICK GLOSSOP PROD (C RUSTY EGAN D (B BILLNELSON K (B
JUDE NETTLETON V (C FRANCES LYNCH V (D NICKY HOLLAND V (D MIKE OLDFIELD (D
DAVE DUNCAN BOD (D SALLY NETTLETON V (C JULIUS NEWELL V (C ANDREW SIGSWORTH V (C
TIM CROSS K (D ALAN RANKIN V (D ALISON PIPKIN V (C JOHN SIGSWORTH V (C
DAVID PIPKIN V (C BILLY MACKENZIE V (D HANNAH YEADON V (C ESTER MARSHALL V (C
CHLOE DYMOTT V (C KEN LOCKIE CELLO (D MARLIS DUNKLAN V (C GRACIE BENSON V (C
HARRIET BAKEWELL V (C VIRGINIA ASHLEY FLT (D MARY VOLKE V (C PAUL WISHART WIND K (D
J J JOHNSON D (D ALAN DARBY G (D DEBBIE MITCHELL V (D

S141 SKIN ALLEY S141

KRZYSZTOF HENRYK JUSKIEWICZ K(ABCD (A) SKIN ALLEY 1969 CBS UK 63847
BOB JAMES G SAX(ABCD (B) TO PAGHAM & BEYOND 1970 CBS UK 64140
THOMAS CRIMBLE B K V(AB (C) TWO QUID DEAL 1972 TRANSATLANTIC UK TRA 260
FRITZ FREYER PROD (C (C) TWO QUID DEAL 1972 STAX US 3013
ALVIN POPE D (AB (D) SKINTIGHT 1973 TRANSATLANTIC UK TRA 273
NICK GRAHAM V K B FLT (BCD (D) SKINTIGHT 197 STAX US STS3022
TONY KNIGHT D V (DC
MARTIN DROVER HRNS (D GEOFF DRISCOLL SAX (D PHIL KENZIE SAX (D DAVE COXHILL SAX (D
BUD PARKES HRNS (D

S142 SKIP BIFFERTY S142

MICK GALLAGHER K (A — (A) SKIP BIFFERTY — 1967 RCA US LSP9761 UK SF7941
GRAHAM BELL V (A
JOHN TURNBULL G (A COLIN GIBSON B (A TOM JACKMAN (A

S143 SKREWDRIVER S143

IAN STEWART V (A — (A) ALL SKREWED UP (45 RPM LP) — 1977 CHISWICK UK WIK3+CH3 GER 550200
RON HARTLEY G (A — (A) ALL SKREWED UP (33 LP) — 1977 CHISWICK GER 67057
KEVIN McKAY B (A — (EP) SKREWDRIVER — 197 TJM TJM4
GRINNY D (A

S144 SKY S144

JOHN WILLIAMS G (ABC — (A) SKY — 1979 ARIOLA UK ARLH 5022
HERBIE FLOWERS B (ABC — (B) SKY2 — 1980 ARIOLA UK AD SKY 2
KEVIN PEEK G (ABC — (C) SKY 3 — 1981 ARIOLA UK ASKY 3
TRISTAN FRY D (ABC — (D) FORTHCOMING — 1982 ARIOLA UK A SKY 4
FRANCIS MONKMAN K (AB STEVE GRAY K (C

S145 PATRICK SKY S145

PATRICK SKY (A — (A) PATRICK SKY — 1965 VANGUARD VSD 79179
(B) HARVEST OF A GENTLE CLANG — 1966 VANGUARD SVRL19054 VSD 79207
(C) REALITY IS BAD ENOUGH — 1968 VERVE US FTS 3052
(D) PHOTOGRAPHS — 1969 VERVE US FTS 3079
(E) SONGS THAT MADE AMERICA FAMOUS — 1973 ADELPHI US AR 4101
(F) TWO STEPS FORWARD ONE STEP BACK — 1975 LEVIATHAN US 2006

S146 SKY BAND S146

(A) SKYBAND — 1975 RCA US APLI0839 UK SF 8409

S147 SKYHOOKS S147

GRAEME STRACHEN V (ABC — (A) EGO IS NOT A DIRTY WORD — 1975 MERCURY UK 6306 900 US SRM11066
ROBERT STARKIE G (AB — (B) LIVING IN THE SEVENTIES — 19 MERCURY US SRM11124
REDMOND SYMONS G V (A — (C) GUILTY UNTIL PROVEN INSANE — 1979 UA UK UAG30241
GREG MACINTOSH B (AB
FREDDIE KABOODLESCHNITZER D(A PETER JONES K (A COL LOUGHNAN SAX (A IMANTS STRAUKS D V (B
ROBERT SPENCER G V (B WILBUR WILDE SAX (B TONY ANSELL K (B EDDIE LEONETH K (B

S147A SKYKING S147A

CHRIS BRUBECK B K HRNS V(A — (A) SECRET SAUCE — 1975 CBS US 33367
DAVID ROSS MASON G B V (A
RICK JACOBS G V B(A RICHIE MORALES D V (A CHRIS COAN V (A PETER RUTH HCA V(A
LEE PASTORA PERC (A JERRY BERGONZI SAX PERC(A PERRY ROBINSON CLAR (A LENNY PICKETT WIND (A
EMILIO CASTILLO SAX (A STEPHEN KUPKA SAX (A GREG ADAMS HRNS (A JOSHIE ARMSTEAD V (A
MAERETHA STEWART V (A CISSY HOUSTON V (A

S148 SKYLARK S148

DOUG EDWARDS G (A — (A) SKYLARK — 1972 CAPITOL 11048
STEVE PUGSLEY B (A — (B) 2 — 1974 CAPITOL 11256
ROBBIE KING K (A
BOBBY TORRES CONGA(A PAUL BEAVER SYN (A PATRICE HOLLOWAY V (A KITTY DITTO V (A
DOMENIC TROIANO G (

S149 SKYROCKETS S149

STEVE BONNETT G V (A — (A) 1974
ANDREW BODNAR B (A
STEVE GOULDING D (A WILL STALLIBRASS HCA (A NOEL BROWN G (A

S149A SKYWHALE S149A

STEVE ROBSHAW G K (A — (A) THE WORLD AT MINDS END — 1977 FIREBRAND DM0013
STAN THEWLIS HRNS (A
PAUL TODD HRNS (A DOUGALL AIRMOLE B (A MICK AVORY D (A GWYO ZEPIX K (A
JOHN SCHOFIELD D (A

S149B SKYY S149B

(A) SKYY — 1981 EPIC UK 85494 US SALSOUL 8548

S150 SLACK ALICE S150

ALICE SPRINGS V (A — (A) SLACK ALICE — 1974 PHILIPS UK 6308 214
PETE FINBERG G V (A
JOHN COOK K V (A EDDIE LEACH D (A MICK HOWARD B V (A

S151 SLADE S151

NODDY HOLDER G V (ALL — (A) BEGINNINGS(AMBROSE SLADE) — 1969 FONTANA UK STL 5494 US 67592
( ) BALLZY — 1969 FONTANA US 67598
JIM LEA B V K VLN (ALL — (B) PLAY IT LOUD — 1970 POLYDOR UK 2383 026 US COTILLION9035
DAVE HILL G V (ALL — (C) SLADE ALIVE — 1972 POLYDOR UK 2383 101 US POLYDOR 5508
DON POWELL D (ALL — (D) SLAYED — 1972 POLYDOR UK 2383 163 US POLYDOR 5524
(E) SLADEST — 1973 POLYDOR UK 2442 119 US REPRISE 2173
(F) OLD NEW BORROWED BLUE — 1974 POLYDOR UK 2383 261
( ) STOMP YOU HANDS — 1974 WB US 2770
(G) IN FLAME (SOUNDTRACK) — 1975 POLYDOR UK 2442 126 US WB 2865
(H) THE BEST OF SLADE — 1975 POLYDOR UK 2664 124
(J) NOBODY'S FOOLS — 1976 POLYDOR UK 2383 377 US WB 2936
(K) WHATEVER HAPPENED TO SLADE — 1977 POLYDOR UK 2314 103
(L) ALIVE VOL 2 — 1978 BARN UK 2314 106
(M) RETURN TO BASE — 1979 BARN UK BARN 10 + NARB 003
(M) RETURN TO BASE — 1979 WEA NL 58192
(N) SLADE SMASHES — 1980 POLYDOR UK POLTV 13
(O) WE'LL BRING THE HOUSE DOWN — 1981 CHEAPSKATE UK SKATE 1
(EP) 6 OF THE BEST — 19 S O T B UK SUPER 45

S152 SLAPP HAPPY S152

ANTHONY MOORE K V (ALL — (A) SORT OF SLAPP HAPPY — 1972 POLYDOR UK 2310 204 RI RECOMMENDED
PETER BLEGVAD G V CLAR(ALL — (B) SLAPP HAPPY — 1974 VIRGIN UK V2014
DAGMAR KRAUSE PNO V(ALL — (C) DESPERATE STRAIGHTS(H COW) — 1974 VIRGIN UK V2024
MARC SINGER D (B — (D) IN PRAISE OF LEARNING — 1975 VIRGIN UK V2027
DAVE WINTOUR B (B — (E) CASABLANCA MOON — 19 RECOMMENDED UK
GRAHAM PRESKETT VLN MAND(B
JEREMY BAINES BASSOON(B ROGER WOOTON V (B EDDIE SPARROW D (B CLAIRE DENIZ CELLO(B
JEAN HERVE-PERON B (B NICK WORTERS B (B ANDY LEGGETT JUGS (B CLEM CATTINI D (B
HENRY LOWTHER TPT (B KESHAVE SATHE PERC (B GEOFF LEIGH WIND (BC JOHN GREAVES B PNO(C
CHRIS CUTLER D (C TIM HODGKINSON CLAR PNO(C FRED FRITH G VLN (C PIERRE MOERLEN PERC(C
MONGEZI FEZA TPT (C MUCHSIN CAMPBELL HRNS (C LINDSAY COOPER WIND (C NICK EVENAS TROM(C

S152A NELSON SLATER S152A

NELSON SLATER (A) WILD ANGEL 19 RCA US APL1 1306

S153 SLAUGHTER & THE DOGS S153

WAYNE BARRETT V (AB (A) DO IT DOG STYLE 1978 DECCA UK SKL 5292
BRIAN CRANFORD D ((B) LIVE 1978 RABID UK HAT 23
HOWARD BATES B (ABC (C) BITE BACK 1980 DJM DJM 20566
MIKE ROSSI G (ABC (EP) BUILD UP NOT DOWN 19 TJM UK TJM 3
MAD MUFFET D (A
EDDIE GARRITY V (C PHIL ROWLAND D (C MORGAN FISHER K (C CHRIS GENT SAX (C
MICK RONSON (A

S154 SLAVE S154

MARK ADAMS B (ADE (A) SLAVE 1977 COTILLION UK K50358 US 5200
FLOYD MILLER V HRNS(ADE (A) SLAVE 198 COTILLION US RI 9914
STEVE ARRINGTON D V (DE (B) HARDNESS OF THE WORLD 1978 COTILLION UK K50435 US 5201
CHARLES CARTER SAX (DE (C) CONCEPT 1978 COTILLION UK K50512 US 5206
JIMMY DOUGLAS V (E (D) JUST A TOUCH OF LOVE 1979 COTILLION UK K50684 US 5217
MARK HICKS G (ADE (E) STONE JAM 1980 COTILLION UK K50761 US 5224
CURT JONES G V (DE
T LOCKETT SAX V(ADE O WILHOITE SAX (A RAYE TURNER K (DE S WASHINGTON V TPT(DEA
DANNY WEBSTER G V (DEA STARLEANA YOUNG V (DE TINY DOZIER D V (A C BRADLEY K (A

S155 PERCY SLEDGE S155

PERCY SLEDGE V (ALL WHEN A MAN LOVES A WOMAN 1966 ATLANTIC UK 2464 002 US 8125
WARM & TENDER SOUL 1966 ATLANTIC UK 588 048 US 8132
THE PERCY SLEDGE WAY 1967 ATLANTIC UK 587 081 US 8146
TAKE TIME TO KNOW HER 1968 ATLANTIC
THE BEST OF 1969 ATLANTIC UK 588 153 US 8210
THE BEST OF 1972 ATLANTIC UK RI K40026
GOLDEN VOICE OF SOUL 1974 ATLANTIC UK K50169
I'LL BE YOUR EVERYTHING 197 CAPRICORN US 0147
STAR COLLECTION VOL 1 197 MIDI 20019
STAR COLLECTION VOL 2 197 MIDI 20065
WHEN A MAN LOVES A WOMAN 19 K TEL NL TN1451

S155A SLEEPLESS NIGHTS S155A

COR ZWANN V (A (A) SLEEPLESS NIGHTS 1980 SLEEPLESS NIGHTS NL SNLP01
JAN VANDER PIAS G V (A
GIJSBERT B V (A JAN VAN EGMOND D (A

S156 EARL SLICK BAND S156

EARL SLICK G (AB (A) EARL SLICK BAND 1976 CAPITOL UK/US 11493 EURO 82194
JIMMIE MACK G V (AB (B) RAZOR SHARP 1976 CAPITOL UK/US 11570
GENE LEPPIK B V (AB
BRYAN MADEY D (AB JAY FERGUSON K (A MICHAEL KAMEN PNO (A CLAUDE PEPPER PERC (A

S157 GRACE SLICK S157

GRACE SLICK V G K(ALL (A) MANHOLE 1974 GRUNT BFLI 0347
PETER KAUKONEN G B (A (B) THE BEST OF(GREAT SOCIETY 1975 CBS 80172
DAVID FREIBERG G V (AC (C) DREAMS 1980 RCA PL 13544
DAVID CROSBY V (A (D) WELCOME TO THE WRECKING BALL 1981 RCA 5007 PL 13851
RON CARTER B (A
JACK CASADY B (A CRAIG CHAQUICO G (A JOHN BARBATA D (A DAVID SNELL HARP(A
JACK ELLORY FLT (A TIMOTHY WALKER G (A PAUL KANTNER G V (A GARY DUNCAN G (A
SEEDER PEARS B (A CHRIS TAYLOR FLT (A ANDREW McGAVIN HRN (A DOUGLAS MOORE HRNS(A
MICHAEL LAIRD TPT (A GEORGE WHITING TPT (A RAYMOND PREMRU TPT (A HAROLD NASH TPT (A
PETER HARVEY TROM (A TERENCE MACDONAGH OBOE (A PHILIP HILL OBOE (A FRANK REIDY CLAR(A
ALAN HAKIN PERC (A TERENCE EMERY PERC (A ERIC ALLEN PERC (A STAN BARRETT PERC(A
FRANK OWEN K (C SCOTT ZITO G HCA V(AC NEIL JASON B (C ALLAN SCHWARZBERG D(C
GEOFF FARR SYN (C GEORGE WADENIUS G (C JIM MAELIN PERC (C ED WALSH SYN (C
RON FRANGOPANE SYN (C JOE SHEPLEY TPT (C JOE D'ELIA PNO (C PHIL BODNER SAX (C
RONNIE CUBER SAX (C ARTIE KAPLAN SAX (C STEVE PRICE D (C GEORGE DEVENS PERC(C
DANNY GULINO G (D PHIL STONE B (D JOE LALA PERC (D PAUL HARRIS K (D
BOBBY T D (D

S158 SLIK S158

MIDGE URE G V (A (A) SLIK 1976 BELL UK SYBEL8004 ARISTA US 4115
BILLY McISAAC D (A
JIM McGINLAY (A KENNY HYSLOP (A

S158A SLIME S158A

DIRK JORN V (ALL (A) SLIME 19 RAUBBAU GER 6622277
MICHAEL MAYER G (ALL (B) YANKEES RAUS 19 ARP 006
CHRISTIAN MEWS G (ALL
SVEN RAETHER B (ALL PETER WODOK D (A STEPHEN MAHLER D (B

S159 SLITS S159

PALMOLIVE D (12 (A) CUT 1979 ISLAND UK ILPS9573 US ANTILLES7072
BRUCE SMITH D (C (A) CUT 1979 ISLAND GER 200874
TESSA POLLITT B (12C (B) RETROSPECTIVE 1980 ROUGH TRADE UK Y 3
VIV ALBERTINE (2C (C) RETURN OF THE GIANT SLITS 1981 CBS UK 85269
ARI UP V (12C (1) 1976 (2) 1977
KATE KORUS G (12
STEVE BERESFORD K (C

S160 P F SLOAN S160

P F SLOAN G V HCA (ALL (A) SONGS OF OUR TIME 1965 DUNHILL US 50004
JOE OSBORN D (D (B) 12 MORE TIMES 1966 DUNHILL US 50007
HAL BLAINE D (D (C) MEASURE OF PLEASURE 1968 ATCO US 33268
MIKE OMARTIAN K (D (D) RAISED ON RECORDS 1972 EPIC UK 65179 MUMS US 31260
WAYNE PERKINS K G (D
CHRIS ETHRIDGE B (B JOHN BARBATA D (D ALAN ESTES CONGA(D BEN BENAY BANJO G (D
LARRY KNECHTEL PNO (D BARRY BECKETT ORG (D MIKE MELVOIN B (D JAMES BURTON DOBRO(D
RICHARD BENNETT STEEL(D BOBBYE HALL PERC (D TONY TERRAN TPT (D DUANE EDDY G (D
SID SHARP STRINGS (D ROBERT KRANTZ VLN (D LOREN FARBER V (D RON HICKLIN V (D
JOHN BAYLOR V (D TATA VEGA V (D PHYLLIS BROWN V (D JACKIE KELSO WIND (D
JIM HORN SAX (D OLLIE MITCHELL TPT (D CONTE CANDOLI TPT (D DICK HYDE TROM (D
MITCH GORDON V (D SALLY STEVENS V (D IDA McCUNE V (D EVANGELINE CARMICHAEL V(D

S160A SLOW CHILDREN S160A

(A) SLOW CHILDREN 1981 ENSIGN UK ENVY 501

S161 SLY(& THE FAMILY)STONE S161

SLY STONE V G K(ALL
FREDDIE STONE G (DH
CYNTHIA ROBINSON TPT (DH
LARRY GRAHAM B (D
GREG ERRICO D (D
ROSE STONE V PNO(DH
JERRY MARTINI SAX (DH
RUSTY ALLEN B (H
ANDY NEWMARK D (H
PAT RIZZO SAX (H
LITTLE SISTER VOCAL GROUP (H

(A)DANCE TO THE MUSIC 1968 EPIC US 26371 US RI 30334
(A) DANCE TO THE MUSIC 1968 DIRECTION UK 8 63412
(B) LIFE 1968 EPIC US 26397 US RI 30333
(C) M'LADY 1968 DIRECTION UK 8 63461
(D) STAND 1969 EPIC US 26456 UK 63655
(E) WHOLE NEW THING 1970 EPIC US 26456 US RI 30335
(F) THERE'S A RIOT GOING ON 1971 EPIC US 30986 UK 64613
(G) GREATEST HITS 1971 EPIC US 30325 UK 69002
(H) FRESH 1973 EPIC US 32134 UK 69039
(I) SMALL TALK 1974 EPIC US 32930 UK 69070
(J) HIGH ENERGY 1975 EPIC US 22004 US RI 33462
(K) HIGH ON YOU 1975 EPIC US 33835 UK 69165
(L) HEARD YOU MISSED ME .... 1976 EPIC US 34348 UK 81641
(M) 10 YEARS TOO SOON (E REMIXED) 1979 EPIC UK 83640
(N) BACK ON RIGHT TRACK 1979 WB US 3303 UK K56640
( ) RECORDED 1964 67 19 SCULPTURE US SCP 2001
( ) LIFE 1979 EPIC US 30333

S161A DRINK SMALL S161A

DRINK SMALL G V (A

(A) I KNOW MY BLUES ARE DIFFERENT 19 SOUTHLAND US SLP 1

S162 SMALL FACES S162

STEVE MARRIOTT G V (ALL
RONNIE LANR B V (ALL
KENNY JONES D (ALL
IAM McLAGAN G ORG V(CDEFLPST
JIMMY WINSTON ORG (A
RICK WILLS B (
STAN UNWIN V (C
JOE BROWN G V (S
VICKI BROWN V (ST
P P ARNOLD V (JOPRVRS
DAVE HYNES V (S
GREG RIDLEY V (S
TONY WILLIAMS V (S
MEL COLLINS HRNS (S
SAUL SHECKNER (S
HWLWN CHAPPPELLE V (T
LAVINA ROBERTS V (T
MADELINE BELL V (T
LIZA STRIKE V (T
SAM BROWN (T
JIMMY McCULLOCH (T

(A) SMALL FACES 1966 DECCA LK4790
(B) FROM THE BEGINNING 1967 DECCA LK 4879
(C) ODGENS NUT GONE FLAKE 1967 IMMEDIATE IMSP012 IML 1001
(C) ODGENS NUT GONE FLAKE 1968 IMMEDIATE US Z1252 008
(C) OGDENS NUT GONE FLAKE 1978 CHARLY UK CR 300015
(C) OGDENS NUT GONE FLAKE 19 OXFORD 3158
(C) ODGENS NUT GONE FLAKE 1980 VIRGIN UK RI V2159
(D) AUTUMN STONE (DBL) 1969 IMMEDIATE UK IMA101/2
(D) AUTUMN STONE (DBL) 19 IMMEDIATE GER SMIM2107/8
(E) IN MEMORIAM 1970 IMMEDIATE IMM 022
(E) IN MEMORIAM 1975 EMI IMP GERM 048 90201
(F) WHAM BAM 1970 EMI IMP GERM 048 50719
(G) ROCK ROOTS 1976 DECCA UK ROOTS 5
(H) AMEN CORNER & SMALL FACES 1975 NEW WORLD NW 6001
(J) VINTAGE YEARS 1975 SIRE 3709
(K) HISTORY OF SMALL FACES 197 IMMEDIATE 052 05108
(K) HISTORY OF SMALL FACES 197 PRIDE US PRD0014
(L) SMALL FACES 19 NEW WORLD NW6000
(M) FIRST STEPS 19 WB UK 1851
(N) ARCHETYPES 1974 MGM US 4955
(O) FAMOUS POP GROUPS (WITH A CORNER) 19 EMI 148 51812/3
(P) THERE ARE BUT FOUR SMALL FACES 19 IMMEDIATE US Z1252 002
(Q) SMALL FACES PROFILE 19 TELDEC GERM 624002
(R) GREATEST HITS 1977 IMMEDIATE IML 2008
(S) PLAYMATES 1977 ATLANTIC US SD19113 UK K50375
(T) 78 IN THE SHADE 1978 ATLANTIC US SD19171 UK K50468
(U) LIVE UK 1969 1978 CHARLY UK CR 300025
(V) BIG HITS 1980 VIRGIN UK V2166
(W) FOR YOUR DELIGHT 1980 VIRGIN UK V2178
(X) SMALL FACES(DBL)(C+) 19 CHARLY 3001
(Y) IMMEDIATE STORY VOL 2(DBL) 1975 SIRE US 3709/2
(Z) SHA LA LA LEE 1981 DECCA UK TAB 16
( ) MAGIC MOMENTS 1976 IMMEDIATE UK AML1008
( ) BIG HITS 1980 VIRGIN UK V2166

S162A SMALL WONDER S162A

JERRY MORIN G V (AB
JIMMY PHILLIPS K V (AB
HENRY SMALL V VLN(AB

(A) SMALL WONDER 1976 CBS US 34100
(B) GROWIN 19 CBS US 34425

S163 LEROY SMART S163

LEROY SMART (ALL

(A) SUPERSTAR 1977 THIRD WORLD TWS 601
(B) DREAD HOT IN AFRICA 1978 BURNING SOUNDS BSLP 1004
(C) IMPRESSIONS 1978 BURNING SOUNDS BSLP 1005
(D) JAH LOVES EVERYONE 1978 BURNING SOUND BSLP 1008

S164 SMIRKS S164

SIMON MILNER G V (A
NEIL FITZPATRICK G (A
IAN MORRIS B (A MIKE DOHERTY V (A

(A) AMERICAN PATRIOTS(EP) 1979 SMIRKSOUND DHSS 01

S164A A GROUP CALLED'SMITH' S164A

GAYLE McCORMICK V (AB
LARRY MOSS K (AB
JERRY CARTER B (AB
ROBERT EVANS D (A RICK CLIBURN G (A ALAN PARKER G (A JADE HASS (B

(A) A GROUP CALLED SMITH 1969 DUNHILL US 50056
(B) MINUS PLUS 196 DUNHILL US 50081

S164B BOB SMITH S164B

BOB SMITH G V (A
JOHN LATINI B (A
DON PRESTON SYN (A STAN KEISER FLT (A SKIP SCHNEIDER D (A MIKE DEGREVE G (A
JAMES CURTIS D (A LARRY CHAPMAN VLN (A

(A) THE VISIT FROM BOB SMITH 1971

S165 GEORGE'HARMONICA' SMITH S165

GEORGE SMITH HCA (ALL
J D NICHOLSON PNO (A
BUDDY REED G (A
GREGG SCHAEFER G (A
MARSHALL HOOKS G (A
PEE WEE CRAYTON G (A JERRY SMITH B (A DICK INNES D (A

(A) NO TIME TO JIVE 1970 BLUE HORIZON UK 763856
(B) ARKANSAS TRAP 1971 DERAM SML 1082 US 18059
(C) GEORGE SMITH OF THE BLUES 1973 BLUESWAY US BLS 6029
(D) TRIBUTE TO LITTLE WALTER 197 WORLD PACIFIC US 21887

S166 GORDON SMITH S166

GORDON SMITH	V HCA G	(ALL	(A) LONG OVERDUE	1968	BLUE HORIZON UK	763211
PETER GREEN	HCA	(A	(B) TAKIN' TIME	1979	APPALOOSA ITALY	AP002
DEREK HALL	PNO	(A	(C) DOWN ON THE STREETS	1980	APPALOOSA ITALY	AP005
JOHN McVIE	B	(A				
MICK FLEETWOOD	D	(A				
PAT GROVER	HCA D	(BC				
BERNIE PALLO	ACC G	(BC				
CRAIG MACKIE	PNO	(C				

S167 HUEY 'PIANO' SMITH S167

HUEY SMITH	PNO	(ALL	(A) HAVING FUN	19	ACE US	(EP) 104
			(B) HAVING A GOOD TIME	19	ACE US	1004
			(C) FOR DANCING	19	ACE US	1015
DR JOHN	K	(D	(D) NIGHT BEFORE CHRISTMAS	19	ACE US	1027
			(E) ROCK'N' ROLL REVIVAL	19	ACE US	2021
			(F) ROCKIN' PNEUMONIA	1978	ACE US	
			(F) ROCKIN' PNEUMONIA	1978	CHISWICK UK	CH9

S168 JIMMY SMITH S168

JIMMY SMITH	ORG	(ALL	(A) THE INCREDIBLE	1962	HMV	CLP 1595
WITH			(B) HOBO FLATS	1963	VERVE	SVLP 9039
RICHARD DAVIS	B	(F	(C) ANY NUMBER CAN WIN	1963	VERVE	SVLP 9057
MILT HINTON	B	(C	(D) WHO'S AFRAID OF VIRGINIA WOLF	1964	VERVE	VLP 9068
BOB BUSHNELL	B	(C	(E) THE CAT	1964	VERVE VLP 9079 RI	2317 010
WES MONTGOMERY	G	(Z	(E) THE CAT	19	'ERVE US 68587	
ART DAVIS	B	(C	(F) MONSTER	1959	VERVE US 68618 UK	SVLP 9093
GEORGE DUVIVIER	B	(AE	(G) ORGAN GRINDER SWING	1965	VERVE US 68628 UK	SVLP 9108
VINCE GAMBELLA	G	(A	THE BEST OF	196	VERVE	2304 004
BARCY GALBRAITH	G	(A	(J) I GOT MY MOJO WORKING	1966	VERVE US 68641 UK	SVLP 9123
JIMMY WARREN	G	(A	PETER & THE WOLF	1967	VERVE	SVLP 9159
KENNY BURRELL	G	(CEFGJ	RESPECT	1967	VERVE US 68705 UK	SVLP 9182
BILLY MURE	G	(C	STAY LOOSE	1968	VERVE	SVLP 9182
GRADY TATE	D	(EFGJ	CHRISTMAS COOKING	1968	VERVE	SVLP 9218
PHIL KRAUS	PERC	(E	FURTHER ADVENTURE	1969	VERVE US 68766	1969 9241
ED SHAUGHNESSY	D	(A	THE BOSS	1969	VERVE	SVLP 9247
DON BAILEY	D	(A	JAZZ SPECTRUM	19	VERVE	2355 005
HERB LOVELL	D	(C	I'M GONNA GIT MYSELF TOGETHER	19	VERVE	2304 020
GEORGE DEVENS	PERC	(C	THE OTHER SIDE OF JIMMY SMITH	19	VERVE	2304 021
BOBBY DONALDSON	D	(C	THE INCREDIBLE JIMMY SMITH	1967	MFP	MFP 1292
DOUG ALLAN	PERC	(C	THE INCREDIBLE JIMMY SMITH	196	BLUENOTE US 81525	1525
ART MAROTTI	PERC	(C	FURTHER	19	VERVE	V 68766
MEL LEWIS	D	(C	WALK ON THE WILD SIDE	19	VERVE	2682 025
WARREN T SMITH	PERC	(F	PORTUGUESE SOUL	1974	VERVE US 8832	2304 167
JOE NEWMAN	TPT	(AC	JIMMY SMITH	1975	VERVE	2356 080
DON SEVERINSEN	TPT	(A	BLACK SMITH	1975	DJM	DJLPS 451
JOE WILDER	TPT	(A	A NEW STAR SOUND	19	BLUENOTE	BST 81512
ERNIE ROYAL	TPT	(AE	A NEW STAR SOUND VOL 2	19	BLUENOTE	BST 81514
CHARLIE SHAVERS	TPT	(C	AT THE LOWRY ORGAN	1973	DECCA	SKL 5146
JIMMY MAXWELL	TPT	(CE	AT THE ORGAN	19	BLUENOTE	BST 81525
SNOOKY YOUNG	TPT	(CE	AT THE BABY GRAND(DBL)	19	BLUENOTE	BST 81528/9
BERNIE GLOW	TPT	(E	A DATE WITH (DBL)	19	BLUENOTE	BST 81547/8
THAD JONES	TPT	(E	AT THE ORGAN VOL 2	1958	BLUENOTE	BST 81551
TOMMY MITCHELL	TROM	(A	SOUND OF JIMMY SMITH	1959	BLUENOTE	BST 81556
JIMMY CLEVELAND	TROM	(ACE	PLAYS PRETTY FOR YOU	1959	BLUENOTE	BST 81563
URBIE GREEN	TROM	(AE	GROOVIN' AT SMALLS PARADISE	1958	BLUENOTE	BST 81585/6
KAI WINDING	TROM	(C	GREATEST HITS VOL 2	19	BLUENOTE	BST 83367
MELBA LISTON	TROM	(C	SERMON	1960	BLUENOTE	BST 84011
PAUL FAULISE	TROM	(C	HOME COOKING	1961	BLUENOTE	BST 84050
BILLY BYERS	TROM	(E	CRAZY BABY	1960	BLUENOTE	BST 84030
TONy STUDD	TROM	(E	MIDNIGHT SPECIAL	1961	BLUENOTE	BST 84078
DADE CLARKE	SAX	(A	PLAYS FATS WALLER	19	BLUNOTE	BST 84100
ROBERT ASHTON	SAX	(AF	BACK AT THE CHICKEN SHACK	19	BLUENOTE	BST 84117
GERRY DODGION	SAX	(AG	ROCKIN THE BOAT	1963	BLUENOTE	BST 84141
PHIL WOODS	SAX	(ACF	PRAYER MEETING	1964	BLUENOTE	BST 84164
GEORGE BARROW	SAX	(A	BUCKET	1966	BLUENOTE	BST 84235
OLIVER NELSON	HRNS	(Z	(Z) THE DYNAMIC DUO	1967	VERVE UK	SVLP 9160
MARVIN HOLLADAY	SAX	(C	I'M MOVIN' ON	19	BLUENOTE	BST 84255
BUDD JOHNSON	SAX	(CF	OPEN HOUSE	1968	BLUENOTE	BST 84269
SELDON POWELL	SAX	(C	PLAIN TALK	19	BLUENOTE	BST 84296
JEROME RICHARDSON	SAX	(CF	GREATEST HITS	1968	BLUENOTE	BST 89901
DANNY BANKS	WIND	(F	JIMMY SMITH	19	BLUENOTE	BNLA 400
RAY BECKENSTEIN	WIND	(F	TOMORROWS SOUND TODAY	1978	GROSVENOR	GRS 1065
GEORGE DORSEY	WIND	(F				
HARVEY ESTRIN	WIND	(F				
BILL CORREA	HRNS	(E				
MARKY MARKOWITZ	TPT	(E				
RAY ALONGE	HRNE	(E				
DON BUTTERFIELD	HRNS	(E				
BRITT WOODMAN	TROM	(A				
JIMMY BUFFINGTON	HRNS	(E				
CREED TAYLOR	PROD	(Z				
EARL CHAPIN	HRNS	(				
JAMES SEDLAR	TPT	(C				

S169 LONNIE LISTON SMITH S169

LONNIE LISTON SMITH	G V	(ALL	ASTRAL TRAVELLING	1974	FLYING DUTCHMAN	BNLI 0163
MARCUS MILLER	B	(ELS	EXPANSIONS	1975	RCA UK SF 8434	BXLI 0934
DONALD SMITH	V FLT	(BEL	AFRO DESIA	1975	GROOVEMASTER	GM 3308
RONALD D MILLER	G	(ESL	REFLECTIONS	1976	RCA UK RS 1053	US 1460
LINO REYES	D	(ES	VISIONS OF A NEW WORLD	1976	RCA UK SF 8461	BXLI 1196
STEVE THORNTON	PERC	(ES	COSMIC FUNK	1974	FLYING DUTCHMAN	BXLI 0591
DAVE HUBBARD	FLT	(BESL	THINK	19	BLUENOTE	BST 84290
AURELL RAY	G	(ES	TURNING POINT	19	BLUENOTE	BST 84313
BUTCH CAMPBELL	G	(ES	MOVE YOUR HAND	19	BLUENOTE	BST 84326
JIMMY OWENS	TPT	(E	DRIVES	19	BLUENOTE	BST 84351
ROBERT FORTUNATO	TPT	(E	RENAISSANCE	1977	RCA	APLI11822
VIRGIL JONES	TROM	(E	(L) LOVELAND	1978	CBS	82837
TOM MALONE	TROM	(E	GOTCHA	1978	TK	TKR 83356
SAM BURTIS	TROM	(E	(S)SONG FOR THE CHILDREN	1979	CBS	83609
STRING SECTION		(E	(E) EXOTIC MYSTERIES	1979	CBS	83331
GWEN GUTHRIE	V	(E	(F) LOVE IS THE ANSWER	1980	CBS US 36373 UK	84365
BRENDA WHITE	V	(E	(B) BEST OF	1980	RCA US 36366 UK PL	12897
ULLANDA McCULLOUGH	V	(ES	BEST OF	1980	CBS	84348

(CONTINUED)

```
S169     (CONTINUED)                    LONNIE LISTON SMITH                                              S169
   RAY SIMPSON         V    (E
   ZACHARY SANDERS     V    (E   JAMES ROBINSON    V    (S   PETER BROWN        B    (S   KEVIN J PERRY    G  (S
   YVONNE LEWIS        V    (S   JANET WRIGHT      V    (S   CECIL McBEE        B    (B   LAWRENCE KILLIAN PERC(B
   MICHAEL CARVIN      PERC (B   ART GORE          D    (B   LEOPOLDO FLEMING   PERC (B   GREG MAKER       B  (B
   WILBY FLETCHER      D    (B   RAY ARMANDO       PERC (B   ANGEL ALLENDE      PERC (B   AL ANDERSON      B  (BL
   KEN BISCHEL         SYN  (B   LEON PENDARVIS    K    (B   GENE BERTONCINI    G    (B   GUILHERME FRANCO PERC(B
S169A                                   MACK ALLEN SMITH                                                 S169A
   MACK ALLEN SMITH         (A           (A) GOTTA ROCK TONIGHT          1981 CHARLY      UK   CR 30201
S169B                                   ROBERT CURTIS SMITH                                              S169B
   ROBERT CURTIS SMITH   (A              (A) ROBERT CURTIS SMITH         19   BLUESVILLE   US 1064
S169C                                   TIGER B SMITH                                                    S169C
   HOLGER SCHMIDT      G V(B             (A) TIGER ROCK                  1973
   CLAUS MEINHARD      B    (B           (B) WERE THE TIGER BUNCH        1974 BACILLUS    GER  19176
   KARL HEINZ TRAUT    D    (B
   LINDA FIELD         V    (B   RAINER MARZ  G V      (B   PETER TRUNK   B     (B   CURT CRESS   D  (B
   VEIT MARROS         K SYN(B   HANUS BERKA       WIND (B
S169D                                   T V SMITH'S EXPLORERS                                            S169D
   TV SMITH                 (A           (A) THE WORDS OF THE GREAT EXPLORER   1981 KALEIDOSCOPE 85087
   COLIN STONER        B V  (A
   MEL WESSON          K    (A   ERIK RUSSELL G    (A   DAVID SINCLAIR    D     (A
S170                                    PATTI SMITH                                                      S170
   PATTI SMITH         V G  (ALL         (A) HORSES                   1975 ARISTA US 4066 UK ARTY122 EURO 97237
   RICHARD SOHL        PNO  (1236ABCD    (B) RADIO ETHIOPIA           1976 ARISTA US 4097 UK SPARTY1001 EURO98283
   LENNY KAYE          G B V(A1234567BCD (C) EASTER                   1978 ARISTA US 4171 UK SPARTY1043 EURO60561
   IVAN KRAL           B G K(A234567CD   (D) WAVE                     1979 ARISTA US 4221 UK SPARTY1086 EURO62516
   J D DAUGHERTY       D    (A34567BCD   (EP) SET FREE                1978 ARISTA         UK ARIST 12197
   TOM VERLAINE        G    (A           (1) 1974      (4) OCT 1976 TOUR  (7) SEPT 1977
   ANDY PALEY          PNO  (4           (2) EARLY 1975(5) LATE  76
   LEIGH FOXX          B    (5           (3) 1975/76   (6) 1977
   BRUCE BRODY         K    (C7
   ALLEN LANIER        G K  (AC  ANDI OSTROWE PERC (CD     JIM MAXWELL   PIPES(C   JOHN PAUL FETTA B    (C
   TODD RUNDGREN       B    (C
S170A                                   WARREN SMITH                                                     S170A
   WARREN SMITH        V G  (ABC         (A) FIRST COUNTRY COLLECTION  1961 LIBERTY         US  LRP 3198
                                         (B) LEGENDARY SUN PERFORMERS  1977 CHARLY UK CR31132 US LAKE   506
                                         (EP) WARREN SMITH             1977 CHARLY UK CEP 113
                                         (C) MEMORIAL ALBUM            1982 MAGNUM FORCE UK 001
S171                                    WHISPERING SMITH                                                 S171
   MOSES SMITH         V HCA(A           (A) OVER EASY                 19 EXCELLO EX8020+ CONTEMPO  CRM 116
   BOBBY POWELL        K V  (A           (A) OVER EASY                 19   BLUE HORIZON   UK    2431 015
   MELVIN HILL         G    (A
   HARVEY LEXING       G    (A   ALFRED LUCAS      B    (A   GREG 'DOC' JOHNSON PERC (A   NOLAN SMITH      PERC(A
   LEROY PERO          HRNS (A   WILLIE SINGLETON  HRNS (A   JOHNNIE CAGE  HRNS (A   NAPOLEON MARTIN HRNS(A
   REGGIE MORRISON     HRNS (A   TROMBONE OBRY     TROM (A
S172                                    SMITH PERKINS SMITH                                              S172
   STEVE SMITH         K G V(A           (A) SMITH PERKINS SMITH       1972 ISLAND US 9317        ILPS 9198
   WAYNE PERKINS       G V  (A
   TIM SMITH           K G V(A   BARRY BECKETT     K    (A   JAMIE GRANT    V    (A   DAVID HOOD       B    (A
   EDDIE HINTON        G    (A   ROGER HAWKINS     D    (A   LARRY NICHOLSON    G    (A
S173                                    CHRIS SMITHERS                                                   S173
   CHRIS SMITHERS      G V  (A           (A) DON'T IT DRAG ON          1972 POPPY       US         PYS  5704
   ERIC KAZ            PNO  (A
   BEN KEITH  DOBRO STEEL   (A   ROD HICKS         B    (A   ROY MARKOWITZ      D    (A   MARIA MULDAUR    V  (A
   BONNIE RAITT        V    (A   KATHY ROSE        V    (A   STU SCHULMAN       VLN  (A   HAPPY TRAUM      BAN(A
S173A                                   SMOKE (UK)                                                       S173A
   MICK ROWLEY         V    (A           (A) THE SMOKE                 1966 GULL        25114
   GEOFF GILL          D    (A
   MAL LUBEN           G    (A   ZEKE LUND    B    (A
S173B                                   SMOKE (US)                                                       S173B
                                         (A) SMOKE                     19   UNI         US   73052
                                         (B) AT GEORGES COFFE SHOP     19   UNI         US   73065
                                         (C) THE SMOKE                 1968 SIDEWALK US 5912
S173C                                   SMOKESTACK LIGHTNING                                             S173C
   RIC EISERLING       G    (A           (A) OFF THE WALL              1969 BELL US 6026    UK SBLL116
   RONNIE DARLING      V    (A
   ART GUY             D    (A   KELLY GREEN       B    (A   THE BLOSSOMS       V    (A   MIKE DEASEY      G  (A
   LARRY KNECHTEL      K    (A   SANDY ZEVON  K G       (A   HAL BLAINE         D    (A   WILD BILL HOLMAN HRNS(A
S174                                    SMOKIE                                                           S174
   PETER SPENCER   V D SAX(ALL           (A) PASS IT AROUND            1975 RAK          UK          SRAK  510
   TERRY UTTLEY        V B  (ALL         (B) CHANGING ALL THE TIME     1975 RAK          UK          SRAK  517
   ALAN SILSON         G V  (ALL         (C) MIDNIGHT CAFE             1976 RAK UK SRAK 520 RSO US     13005
   CHRIS NORMAN        V G K(ALL         (D) GREATEST HITS             1977 RAK          UK          SRAK  526
                                         (E) BRIGHT LIGHTS & BACK ALLEYS  1977 RAK UK SRAK 530  RSO US  13029
                                         (F) MONTREUX ALBUM            1978 RAK          UK          SRKA 6757
                                         (G) THE OTHER SIDE OF THE ROAD   1979 RAK       UK          SRAK  539
                                         (H) VERY BEST OF              1980 RAK          UK          SRAK  540
S174A                                   OTIS 'SMOKEY' SMOTHERS                                           S174A
   OTIS SMOKEY SMOTHERS   (A             (A) DRIVIN BLUES              19   KING        US    779
                                         (B) SMOKEY SMOTHERS 1960/62   19   KRAZY KAT   UK    7406
```

S175 GILLI SMYTH S175

GILLI SMYTH V (A — (A) MOTHER — 1978 CHARLY UK CRL 5007
ORLANDO ALLEN V (A — (B) FAIRY TALES — 1979 CHARLY UK CRL 5018
VERA BLUM VLN (A
PIP PYLE D (A — TONY PASCHAL K (A — DIDIER MALHERBE SAX (A — DAEVID ALLEN B G V(A
CHRISTIAN TRITSCH B (A — RAFEL AGUILO D (A — TALIESEN ALLEN V (A — PETER LEWIS V (A
SAM GOPAL TABLAS(A — ANNIE TRUXELL V (A — MARTIN TALLENTS WHISTLE(A — TOM LIPPS V (A
MARTI KLARWEIN V (A — PEPE MILAN G (A — JOAN BIBILON G (A — PATRICK MEADOWS V (A
FRANK FEHLING V (A — PHIL SHEPHERD V (A — STEPHANIE SHEPHERD V (A — ANDREW PAGE V (A
OONA LIND V (A

S176 SNAFU S176

BOBBY HARRISON V PERC(ABC — (A) SNAFU — 1974 W W A UK 003 US CAPITOL 11292
MICK MOODY HCA G V (ABC — (B) SITUATION NORMAL — 1974 W W A UK 013 US CAPITOL 11343
PETE SOLLEY K VLN V(AB — (C) ALL FUNKED UP — 1975 CAPITOL 11473
COLIN GIBSON B (ABC
TERRY POPPLE D B (ABC — MEL COLLINS SAX (BC — STEVE GREGORY SAX (B — BUD BEADLE SAX (B
TIM HINKLEY K (C — BRIAN CHATTON K (C — VIOLA WILLS V (C — LIZA STRIKE V (C

S176A SNATCH S176A

(A) SHOPPING FOR CLOTHES(EP) — 1980 FETISH FET 004

S177 SNAIL S177

BOB O'NEILL G V (AB — (A) SNAIL — 1978 CREAM US 1009
KEN KRAFT G V (AB — (B) FLOW — 1979 CREAM US 1012
BRETT BLOOMFIELD B V (AB
DON BALDWIN D V (AB

S177A SNAKEFINGER S177A

PHIL'SNAKEFINGER' LITHMAN — (A) GREENER PASTURES — 1980 RALPH US 8053
THE RESIDENTS (B — (B) CHEWING THE SOUND — 1979 RALPH US 7909 VIRGIN UK 2149
DON JACKOVICH PERC (B
PHIL CULP B (B — STEVEN BROWN SAX (B

S177B SNEAKER S177B

MICHAEL CAREY SCHNEIDER K V (A — (A) SNEAKER — 1981 HANDSHAKE
MITCH OARE G V (A
MICHAEL COTTAGE B (A — MICHAEL HUGHES D (A — TIM TORRANCE G (A — JIM KING K (A

S177C SNEAKERS S177C

CHRIS STANLEY V G K(A — (A) IN THE RED — 1978 CAR 0398
MITCH EASTER V B G D(A
WILL RIGBY V (A — ROBERT KEELY B (A — JAMES SIMS K (A — PHIL THOMAS B (A
FAYE HUNTER FLT (A

S177D ADRIAN SNELL S177D

ADRIAN SNELL K G V(ALL — (A) FIREFLAKE — 1975 KINGSWAY UK 34
GARRY PAGE B (BC — (B) GOODBYE OCTOBER — 1976 KINGSWAY UK 41
JOE KING K G (B — (C) LISTEN TO THE PEACE — 1978 KINGSWAY UK 51
KEN PAGE WIND (B — (D) SOMETHING NEW UNDER THE SUN — 1979 KINGSWAY UK 63
BERNARD SHAW D (BC — (E) THE PASSION — 1980 KINGSWAY UK 308
GORDON CARR HRNS (B — (F) CUT — 1981 KINGSWAY UK 324
ELIZABETH KAUFMANN V ((B
BILL THORP STR (C — BRYN HAWORTH G (D — B J COLE STEEL(D — TONY CARR PERC (D
TONY CARR PERC (D — ROGER HAND PERC V(DE — MARK WILLIAMSON V (E — MICHAEL HARDING TROM(C
GEOFF TURTON V (E — TONY HEPWORTH TPT (C — SHIRLIE RODEN V (EF — ROB McKAY WIND(C
RICHARD BARNES V (E — MO WITHAM G (C — DEBI DOSS V (EF — FRANCES KELLY HARP(C
SIMON PHILLIPS D (E — JULIAN SULLIVAN CONGA(C — GORDON GILTRAP G (E — JOHN PERRY B (DEF
ROD EDWARDS K STR(D — DAVID MARTIN G (EF — KEVIN PEEK G (DE — EDDY SPENCE K (F
FRANK RICOTTI VIBES (F — NICK PENTELOW SAX (F — IAN MOSLEY D (F — MO McCAFFERTY V (E
ANNIE McCRAIG V (E — LONDON WELSH MALE CHOIR V(E — ENGLISH CHAMBER SINGER V(E — ROYAL PHIL ORCH (E

S178 SNIFF N THE TEARS S178

PAUL ROBERTS G V (ALL — (A) FICKLE HEART — 1978 CHISWICK WIK9 UK +UK RI CWD3002
NINK SOUTH B (BCD — (A) FICKLE HEART — 1978 ATLANTIC US 19242
LOZ NETTO G (ABC — (A) FICKLE HEART — 1982 CHISWICK UK RI SNIP 1
LEW LEWIS HCA (D — (B) THE GAMES UP — 1980 CHISWICK UK CWK3014
MICK DYCHE G (A — (B) THE GAMES UP — 1980 ATLANTIC US 19272
DEREK WADSWORTH TROM (D — (B) THE GAMES UP — 1982 CHISWICK UK SNIP 2
CHRIS BIRKIN B (A — (C) LOVE ACTION — 1981 CHISWICK UK 2018 RI UK SNIP 3
RON LAWRENCE B (A — (D) RIDE BLUE DIVIDE — 1982 CHISWICK UK 3020 RI UK TOSS 3
KEITH MILLER SYN (A
LUIGI SALVONI D (A — NOEL McCALLA V (A — ALAN FELDMAN K (A — JIM NELLIS V (A
MIKE TAYLOR K (BCD — PAUL ROBINSON D (B — RICHARD BAILEY D (B — RICHARD MARCANGELO D(B
JAMIE LANE D (CD — LES DAVIDSON G V (CD — RICK FENN G V (C — MO McCAFFERTY V (C
ANNIE McCRAIG V (C — MARK WILLIAMSON V (C — PAT CRUNLEY SAX (C — STEVIE LANGE V (D
MARTIN JAY V (D — JULIAN DIGGLE CONGA(D — DICK MORRISEY SAX (D — MARTIN DROVER TPT (D

S179 SNIPS S179

SNIPS V (AB — (A) VIDEO KING — 1976 JET UK LP 212
MICK DYCHE G (A — (B) LA ROCCA — 1981 EMI UK EMC 3359
GRAHAM DEACON D (A
JOHN BENTLEY G (A — JACKIE BADGER B (AB — CHRIS SPEDDING G (B — BILL NELSON SYN (B
DAVE MATTACKS D (B — CLEM CATTINI D (B

S179A SNOPEK S179A

(A) THINKING OUT LOUD — 1979 MOUNTAIN RAILROAD US 52789
(B) FIRST BAND ON THE MOON — 1981 MOUNTAIN RAILROAD US

S180 PHOEBE SNOW S180

PHOEBE SNOW G V (ALL — (A) PHOEBE SNOW — 1974 A&M UK AMLS68283
SONNY BURKE K (C — (A) PHOEBE SNOW — 1974 SHELTER US2109 UK ISA 5010
DAVID POMERANZ K (C — (C) IT LOOKS LIKE SNOW — 1976 CBS US 34387 UK 81794
JAMES GADSON D (C — (D) SECOND CHILDHOOD — 1976 CBS US 33952 UK 81162
REGGIE McBRIDE B (C — (E) AGAINST THE GRAIN — 1978 CBS US 34456 UK 82195
STEVE BURGH G (BCF — (F) NEVER LETTING GO — 1978 CBS US 34875 UK 82224
ED GREENE D (C — ( ) ROCK AWAY — 1981 ATLANTIC UK K50780
STEVE KHAN G (F — (H) SNOWBIRD — 1974 CAMDEN US 0124
JEROME RICHARDSON FLT(D

(CONTINUED)

S180 CONTINUED) PHOEBE SNOW S180

CHUCK DOMANICO B (CB RAY PARKER JR G (C HARVEY MASON D (C DAVID BROMBERG G (BC
GREG POREE G (C ANDY NARELL PERC (C KURT McGETTRICK HRNS (C MEL MARTIN HRNS(C
HADLEY CALIMAN HRNS (C BOB YANCE HRNS (C GOLDEN AGE JAZZ BAND (C PHIL KEARNS V (CD
MAXINE WILLARD V (C JULIA TILLMAN V (C ORRIN WATERS V (C HUGH McDONALD B (B
STEVE MOSLEY D (B PERSUASIONS V (B TEDDY WILSON PNO (B RALPH McDONALD PERC(BDF
JOHN ZOOT SIMS SAX (B MARGARET ROSS HARP (B DAVE MASON G (B CHUCK ISRAELS B (B
BOB JAMES K (BF TONY LEVIN B (DF STEVE GADD D (B KEN ASCHER K (DF
HUGH McCRACKEN G (DF JOHN TROPEA G (D KEN BISCHEL SYN (D RICHARD TEE K (DF
DAVID SANBORN SAX (D STUART SCHARF G (D RON CARTER B (D JESSE DIXON SINGERS (D
JIMMY YOUNG D (D DON GROLNICK K (D GORDON EDWARDS B (D GRADY TATE D (DF
PHIL RAMONE V (D WILL LEE B (DF

S180A SOCIAL SECURITY S180A

(A) I DONT WANT MY HEART TO RULE MY HEAD(EP) 19 HEARTBEAT UK PULSE1

S180B SOCRATES S180B

(A) ON THE WINGS 1976 PETERS INT PILPS9002
(B) PHOS 19 PETERS INT PILPS9013

S180C SODS S180C

PETER PETER V (A (A) MINUTES TO GO 1979 STEP FORWARD UK SFLP 3
KNUD SORENSEN B (A
THOMAS ORTVED D (A STEEN JORGENSON G (A

S180D ERROL SOBER S180D

ERROL SOBER K (A (A) DAY DREAMER 1976 CAPITOL ST11485
MICHAEL OMARTIAN K (A
BEN BENAY G (A LEE RITENOUR G (A DEAN PARKS G (A ED GREENE D (A
MAX BENNETT B (A LEE SKLAR B (A VICTOR FELDMAN PERC(A STEVE BARRI PERC(A
JIMMY HASKELL K (A ERNIE WATTS WIND (A JOHNNY ROTELLA WIND (A GINGER BLAKE V (A
JULIA TILLMAN V (A MAXINE WILLARD V (A DON WALSH V (A MICHAEL PRICE V (A
SID SHARP STR (A

S181 SOFT BOYS S181

ANDY METCALFE B (1A (A) CAN OF BEES 1979 TWO CRABS CLAW 101
TIM MELTON D HCA(A (A) CAN OF BEES 1979 AURAL AUL709 GER 60301
ROBYN HITCHCOCK G V B(1ABC (B) UNDERWATER MOONLIGHT 1980 ARMAGEDDON UK ARM002
ROB APPLETON HCA (C (C) 2 HALFS FOR THE PRICE OF ONE 1981 ARMAGEDDON UK BYE 1
KIMBERLEY REW G (AB1C (EP) NEAR THE SOFT BOYS 1980 ARMAGEDDON UK ARM001
MORRIS WINDSOR D (B1AC (1) APRIL 1978
MATTHEW SELIGMAN B (B
ANDY KING SITAR(B GERRY HALE VLN (B MATTHEW SELIGMANN B (C

S181A SOFT HEAP S181A

HUGH HOPPER B (A (A) SOFT HEAP 1979 CHARLY UK CRL 5014
ELTON DEAN SAX (A
ALAN GOWAN K (A PIP PYLE D (A RADU MALFATTI TROM (A MARC CHARIG CORN(A

S182 SOFT MACHINE S182

LARRY NOLAN G (1 (A) THE SOFT MACHINE 1968 PROBE US 4500
MIKE RATLEDGE K(12345ABCDEJFGHMN (B) VOLUME 2 1969 PROBE US 4505 UK SPB 1002
KEVIN AYERS B V (A1BMN (B) VOLUME 2 1974 ABC RI UK ABCL 5004
DAEVID ALLEN G (1MN (AB) 1&2 1973 PROBE US 204 RI UK ABC 602
ROBERT WYATT D (123ABCDMN (C) THIRD 1970 CBS US 30339 UK 66246
HUGH HOPPER B (ABCDE2345FN (D) FOURTH 1971 CBS US 30754 UK 64280
ANDY SUMMERS G (1 (E) FIFTH 1972 CBS US 31604 UK 64806
ELTON DEAN SAX (2345CDEN (E) FIFTH 1979 EMBASSY RI UK 31748
PHIL HOWARD D (4EN (F) SIXTH 1973 CBS US 32260 UK 68214
JOHN MARSHALL D (5EJKLGFHN (G) SEVENTH 1973 CBS US 32716 UK 65799
ROY BABBINGTON B (DEGHJN (H) BUNDLES 1975 HARVEST UK SHSP4044 GER 96356
KARL JENKINS (5FGHJNO (J) SOFTS 1976 HARVEST UK SHSP4056
ALLAN HOLDSWORTH G (HLN (K) ALIVE & WELL IN PARIS 1978 HARVEST UK SHSP4083
ALAN WAKEMAN SAX (J (L) LAND OF COCKAYNE 1981 EMI UK EMC3348 GER 07439
JOHN ETHERIDGE G (JKN (M) AT THE BEGINNING 1977 CHARLY GER 3011 UK CR300014
RICK SANDERS VLN (K (N) TRIPLE ECHO (TRIP)(COMP) 1977 HARVEST UK SHTW 800
STEVE COOK B (K FACES & PLACES VOL 7 1971 BYG FR 529907
NICK EVANS TROM (C2DN ROCK GENERATION 7 (1 SIDE) 197 BYG FR 529707
MARK CHARIG HRNS (2DN ROCK GENERATION 8 (1 SIDE) 197 BYG FR 529708
LYN DOBSON HRNS (23CDN RUBBER RIFF 1976 DEWOLFE UK 3331
AB SPALL VLN (CN (1) 1967/68 (2) 1969 (3) 1970 (4) 1971/72 (5) 1972
JIMMY HASTINGS WIND (CDN
JACK BRUCE B (L DICK MORRISEY SAX (L ALAN PARKER G (L GIORGIO GOMELSKY PROD (
TOM WILSON PROD (A ALAN SKIDMORE SAX (DN PERCY JONES B (JIMI HENDRIX G(N
BRIAN HOPPER SAX (ABN RAY WARLEIGH FLT (HL JOHN TAYLOR K (L TONY RIVERS V (L
STU CALVER V (L JOHN PERRY V (L WILLIAM BURROUGH V (N

S184 SOFTIES S184

KEITH LANE D (A (A) NICE & NASTY 1979 CHARLY UK CRL 5012
MIKE SMITH G V (A
JACK BOOTHE B G K V (A

S185 MIKE SOFTLEY S185

MICK SOFTLEY V G K(ABC (A) SUNRISE 1970 CBS UK 64098
JERRY DONAHUE G (ABC (B) STREET SINGER 1971 CBS UK 64395
PAT DONALDSON B (ABC (C) ANY MOTHER DOESN'T GRUMBLE 1972 CBS UK 64841
TONY COX K (ABC
GERRY CONWAY D (ABC SUE GLOVER V (A SUNNY LESLIE V (A LYN DOBSON WIND SITAR(AC
LESLEY DUNCAN V (A NED BALEN TABLAS (A BARRY CLARKE G (A MIKE VICKERS K (A
GRINGO V (A TONY CARR PERC (B STEVE HAYTON G HCA(B DAVID HOROWITZ K (B
KARL JENKINS SAX (B DUDU PUKWANA SAX (B FRANK RICOTTI PERC (B RICHARD THOMPSON G (B
LIZA STRIKE V (B DORIS TROY V (B JIMMY THOMAS V (B BARRY DE SOUZA PERC(C

S186 SOLAR PLEXUS S186

TOMMY KORBERG V ((A) CONCERTO GROSSO(SWEDISH) 1972 ODEON SWED 154 34 573/4
MONICA GROSSO ORG (A) CONCERTO GROSSO(ENGLISH) 1972 ODEON SWED 154 34 684/5
CARL AXEL DOMINIQUE PNO((B) SOLAR PLEXUS 2 1973 ODEON SWED 062 34 797
BOSSE HAGGSTROM B ((C) SOLAR PLEXUS 1973 POLYDOR UK 2383 222
TOMMY BORGUDD D ((D) DET ER INTE BATEN 1974 HARVEST 062 34 975
GEORG WADENIUS G (A (E) HELLRRE GYCKLARE AN HYCKLARE 1975 HARVEST 062 35 166

S186A SOLID GOLD CADILLAC S186A

BRIAN GODDING G (B (A) SOLID GOLD CADILLAC 1972 RCA UK SF 8311
ROY BABBINGTON B (A (B) BRAIN DAMAGE 1973 RCA UK SF 8365
MALCOLM GRIFFITHS TROM (AB
ALAN JACKSON D PERC (AB PHIL MINTON V TPT (AB GEORGE AHMAD KHAN WIND K(AB BUTCH POTTER G B K BAN(B
MIKE WESTBROOK PNO (AB CHRIS SPEDDING G (A DICK MORECOMBE G (A FIACHA TRENCH K (A

S187 SOLUTION S187

TOM BARLAGE K WIND(ABCD (A) SOLUTION 1972 DECCA UK SKLR 5124
WILLEM ENNES K (ABCD (B) DIVERGENCE 1973 EMI UK EMC 3002
GUUS WILLEMSE B V (BCD (C) CORDON BLEU 1975 ROCKET US 2189 UK ROLL 1
HANS WATERMAN D (ABCD (D) FULLY INTERLOCKING 1977 ROCKET UK ROLL 8
RAY COOPER PERC (D (E) ITS ONLY JUST BEGIN 1980 CBS NL 84119
STUART EPPS V (D
PETER VAN DER SANDE B (A FRANKIE FISH V (C MICHIEL POS G SAX(C

S187A ERWIN SOMER GROUP S187A

ERWIN SOMER VIBES PERC(A (A) ERWIN SOMER GROUP 1973 UNIVERSE UP 110
RUDY VAN DIJK SAX (A
HELMIG VAN DER VEGT K(A HANS LAFAILLE D (A JAAP VAN EUCKY B (A

S187B SONICS S187B

GEORGE FENCIL WALLACE G V K(A (A) SINDERELLA 1980 LINE GERM LLP5052AP
TOM KATTICA PNO (A (A) SINDERELLA 1980 BOMP US 4011
BILL SHAW D V (A (1) HERE ARE THE SONICS 196 ETIQUETTE US 024
MICHAEL GONE G (A (2) SONICS BOOM 196 ETIQUETTE US 027
GEORGE CROWE B (A ( ) INTRODUCING THE SONICS 196 JERDEN US 7007
GERRY ROSLIE K V (A12 ( ) EXPLOSIVES 196 BUCKSHOT US 001
JAMES N BUTSCH D (A ( ) SONICS 1977 SRT 77079
ANDY PARYPA B V (12 ( ) ORIGINAL NORTHWEST PUNK 1979 FIRST US 7715
LARRY PARYPA G V (12 ( ) UNRELEASED 1980 FIRST US 7719
ROB LIND V SAX(12
LES CLIN KINGBEARD SAX (A BOB BENNETT D (12

S187C JOEL SONNIER S187C

JOEL SONNIER G V D HCA(A (A) CAJUN LIFE 1980 SONET UK SNTF 839 US ROUNDER
MICHEL DOUCET G (A (A) CAJUN VALENTINE 19 GOLDBAND US 7742
MERLIN FONTENOT FDL (A ( ) HURRICANE AVORY 19 GOLDBAND US 7747
JAY STUTES DOB (A ( ) SCENE TODAY IN CAJUN MUSIC 19 GOLDBAND US 7753
ROY HUSKY B (A
BUDDY HARMON D (A
EARL BALL PNO (A HENRY STRZELECKI B (A KENNY KENNERSON PNO (A GENE O'NEAL STEEL(A
PETE DRAKE STEEL(A BOB MILSAP G (A JOE ALLEN B (A WILLIE ACKERMAN D (A
BOB WHITE FDL (A PHIL BALL G (A VIC JORDAN G (A BILLY REYNOLDS D (A
TOMMY WILLIAMS FDL (A

S187D SONOMA S187D

(A) SONOMA 1974 DUNHILL US 50156

S188 SONNY & CHER S188

SONNY BONO V (ALL LOOK AT US 1964 ATLANTIC US UK 5036 US 33177
CHER BONO V (ALL WONDROUS WORLD OF 1966 ATLANTIC US 33183
IN CASE YOUR IN LOVE 1967 ATLANTIC US 33203
GOOD TIMES 1967 ATLANTIC US 33214
BEST OF 196 ATLANTIC UK 588083 US 33219
BEST OF 1972 ATLANTIC RI UK K40012
LIVE 196 KAPP US 3654
LIVE 1972 MCA RI UKMUPS435 US 2009
BEST OF 1972 CHARTERLINE ITALY 20024
BABY DON'T GO 19 REPRISE US 6177
LIVE IN LAS VEGAS 1974 MCA UK MCSP 257 US 2/8004
MAMA WAS A ROCK'N' ROLL SINGER 1974 MCA UK MCF 3672
ALL I EVER NEED IS YOU 1971 KAPP US 3660
ALL I EVER NEED IS YOU 1974 MCA UK MCF 2517 US ri 2021
GREATEST HITS 1975 MCA UK MCF2586 US2117 GER 7527
THE BEAT GOES ON 1975 ATCO US 11000
GREATEST HITS 1981 ATLANTIC UK K20026

S189 SONS OF CHAMPLIN S189

BILL CHAMPLIN V G K SAX(ALL (A) LOOSEN UP NATURALLY 1969 CAPITOL US SWBB 200
TERRY HAGGERTY G V (ABCDEFGH (B) THE SONS 1969 CAPITOL US SKAO 322
GEOFFREY PALMER K B V SAX(ABCDEFGH (C) MINUS SEEDS & STEMS (LIMITED) 1970
JAMES PRESTON D (EFGH (D) FOLLOW YOUR HEART 1971 CAPITOL US ST 675
DAVID SCHALLOCK B V (EFG (E) WELCOME TO THE DANCE 1973 CBS US 32341 UK 65663
ROB MOITOZA B HCA V (H (F) THE SONS OF CHAMPLIN 1975 ARIOLA US 50002 UK AAS 1501
STEVE FREDIANI WIND (GH (G) CIRCLE FILLED WITH LOVE 1976 ARIOLA US 50007 GER 27690
JIM HORN SAX (H (H) LOVING IS WHY 1977 ARIOLA US 50017 UK AAS 1505
CHRIS BOND SYN (H
DAVID FAREY HRNS (H CHUCK FINDLEY TPT (H GARY COLEMAN PERC (H DON MENZA SAX (H
PAUL HUBINON TPT (H AL STRONG B (ABCD TIM CAINE SAX (ABC PHIL WOODS HRNS(E
BILL BOWEN D (ABCD MARK USHAM HRNS(EF MIKE ANDREAS HRNS (EF ERNIE WATTS SAX (H

S190 SONS OF JAH S190

BUNNY McKENZIE G (A (A) REGGAE HIT SHOWCASE 1980 PLASTIC FANTASTIC PFULP 350
WIRE LINDO K (A (B) BURNING BLACK 1979 NATTY CONGO UK 3502
NEGUS DAWTAS V (A
SANTA DAVIS (A T BOW G (A BROTHER NAT K (A RICO BRASS (A
RANKING REUBEN (A SPEEGO G (A ASTON BARRETT B (A TUNGA OF SABANDIS G (A
TONY ROBINSON K (A TAN TAN HRNS (A CARLTON BARRETT D (A CHINNA SMITH G (A
TENDA I OF ZABANDIS K (A

S191

SOPWITH CAMEL S191

PETER KRAEMER V WIND K (AB — (A) SOPWITH CAMEL 1967 KAMA SUTRA US KLPS 8060
TERRY MACNEIL K G (AB — (A) HELLO HELLO 1973 KAMA SUTRA US RI KSBS 2063
MARTIN BEARD B (AB — (B)MIRACULOUS HUMP RETURNS FROM THE MOON 1973 REPRISE US MS 2108 UK K44251
NORMAN MAYELL D HCA SITAR(AB
WILLIAM SIEVERS G (A

S192

SORE THROAT S192

MATT FLOWERS K (A — (A) SOONER THAN YOU THINK 1979 HURRICANE UK FLAK 101
DAN FLOWERS B (A
JUSTIN WARD V (A REID SAVAGE G (A ROBIN KNAPP D (GREGORY MASON SAX (A

S192A

SORROWS S192A

DON FARDON V (A — (A) TAKE A HEART 1965 PYE UK NPL38023
WEZ PRICE G (A — (A) TAKE A HEART 1982 RAVEN AUSTR 1004
PHILIP WITCHER G (A
PHILIP PACKHAM B (A BRUCE FINLEY D (A

S192B

SORROWS(US) S192B

ARTHUR ALEXANDER G V (AB — (A) TEENAGE HEARTBREAK 1980 PAVILLION 36369
SHEL TALMY PROD (B — (B) LOVE TOO LATE 1981 PAVILLION 37015
JOEY COLA G (AB
RICKY STREET B V (AB JETT HARRIS D (AB ELLIE GREENWHICH V (A ELLEN FOLEY V (A
KARLA DEVITO V (A SUSAN HALL V (A MIKEY HARRIS V (A

S193

SORRY S193

J P CECCARELLI D (A — (A) OH KATHY 1978 KISWELL FR 29 33109
CLIVE EDWARDS D (A
DOUDON WEISS D (A BUNNY BRUNEL B (A STEVE CARMEN B (A RONNIE DEVILLE B (A
MAX MESUMECCI K (A PAUL IVES K V (A DOMINIQUE RUIZ G (A MICKY V (A
JOYCE V (A FLO V (A JACKY V (A RAY HENDRIKSEN V (A
STRING SECTION (A

S193A

MARK SOSKIN S193A

MARK SOSKIN K (A — (A) RHYTHM VISION 1980 PRESTIGE P10109
BENNIE MAUPIN WIND (A
OSCAR BRASHEAR HRNS (A SNOOKY YOUNG HRNS (A GEORGE BOHANON TROM (A MEL MARTIN WIND (A
RAY OBIEDO G (A PAUL SOCOLOW B (A HARVEY MASON D (A SAMMY FIGUEROA CONGA(A

S193B

SOUND S193B

GRAHAM GREEN B (CDE — (A) PHYSICAL WORLD (EP) 19 TORCH UK TOR003
ADRIAN BORLAND G V (CDE — (B) THE SOUND 19 TORCH UK TOR008
BENITA MARSHALL K (C — (C) JEOPARDY 1980 KOROVA UK KODE 2
MICHAEL DUDLEY D (CDE — (D) FROM THE LIONS MOUTH 1981 KOROVA UK KODE 5
MAX MAYERS K (E — (E) ALL FALL DOWN 1982 WEA 240019/1

S193C

SOUND CEREMONY S193C

RON WARREN GANDERTON G (AB — (A) GUITAR STAR 1979 CELESTIAL SOUND RWG1
(B) SOUND CEREMONY 1980 CELESTIAL SOUND RWG2
(C) PRECIOUS AS ENGLAND 1981 CELESTIAL SOUND RWG123

S194

SOUNDS INCORPORATED S194

ALAN HOLMES SAX (— (A) SOUNDS LIKE 196 COLUMBIA UK SCX 2531
BARRY CAMERON SAX (— (B) SOUNDS INCORPORATED 1964 COLUMBIA 33SX1659 SCX 3531
TONY NEWMAN D (— (C) TWIST AT THE STAR CLUB HAMBURG 1964 PHILIPS P48 036L
JOHN ST JOHN GILLARD G (— (D) TOP GEAR (EP) 1964 COLUMBIA UK SEG 8360
TERRY FOGG D (— (E) SOUNDS INCORPORATED 1966 STUDIO TWO UK TWO 1449
GRIFF WEST WIND (— (F) RINKY DINK 1973 REGAL UK SREG1071
WES HUNTER B (

S194A

SOUP S194A

(A) SOUP 19 BIG TREE US 2007

S194B

SOUNDS NICE S194B

TIM MYCROFT K (A — (A) LOVE AT FIRST SIGHT 1969 PARLOPHONE UK PCS7089
PAUL BUCKMASTER STR (A
HERBIE FLOWERS B (A CHRIS SPEDDING G (A BRIAN ODGES B (A CLEM CATTINI D (A

S195

SOUR GRAPES S195

RICHARD THOMPSON G V (A — (A) 1974 NO LPS
LINDA THOMPSON V (A
SIMON NICOL G V (A WILLIE MURRAY D (A STEVE BORRILL B (A

S195A

TIM SOUSTER S195A

TIM SOUSTER K (AB — (A) SWIT DRIMZ 1977 TRANSATLANTIC UK TRA 343
(B) THE FUTURE IS NOW(EP) 1977 TRANSATLANTIC UK TBG1

S195B

JOE SOUTH S195B

JOE SOUTH G V (ALL — (A) INTROSPECTIVE 196 CAPITOL US 108
( ) DONT IT MAKE YOU WANT TO GO HOME 19 CAPITOL US 392
( ) GREATEST HITS 196 CAPITOL US 450
( ) SO THE SEEDS ARE GROWING 19 CAPITOL US 637
( ) JOE SOUTH 19 CAPITOL US 845
( ) YOU'RE THE REASON 19 NASHVILLE US 2092
( ) THE JOE SOUTH STORY 19 MINE US 1100

S196

J D SOUTHER S196

JOHN DAVID SOUTHER G V (ABC — (A) JOHN DAVID SOUTHER 1972 ASYLUM US SD 5055 UK SYL 9003
NED DOHENY G (AB — (A) JOHN DAVID SOUTHER 1975 ASYLUM UK K53026
BRYAN GAROFALO B (A — (B) BLACK ROSE 1976 ASYLUM US 7E1059 UK K53037
GARY MALLABER D K (A — (C) YOU'RE ONLY LONELY 1979 CBS US 36093 UK 83753
GIB GUILBEAU FDL (A
DAVID JACKSON K B (A MIKE BOWDEN B (A MICKY McGEE D (A JOEL TEPP B (A
JOHN BARBATA D (A WAYNE PERKINS G (A DANNY KOOTCH G (BC WADDY WACHTEL G (BC
PAUL STALLWORTH B (B JIM KELTNER D (B DAVID CROSBY V (B ART GARFUNKEL V (B
ANDREW GOLD V G K(B GLENN FREY G (BC KENNY EDWARDS B (BC RUSS KUNKEL D (B
LINDA RONSTADT V (B PETER ASHER V (B STANLEY CLARKE B (B DAVID DUKE HRNS (B
VINCENT DEROSA HRNS (B MIKE BOTTS D (BC ROY POPER HRNS (B DONALD BYRD HRNS (B
LOWELL GEORGE G (B CHUCK DOMANICO B (B JOHN GUERIN D (B JAMES BOND B (B
DON MENZA FLT (B EARL DUMLER WIND (B JOE WALSH G (B DON HENLEY V (BC
DON GROLNICK PNO (C RICK MAROTTA D (C DAVID SANBORN SAX (C DAN DUGMORE G (C
TOM SCOTT SAX (C JACKSON BROWNE V (C JORGE CALDERON V (C PHIL EVERLY V (C
JAI WINDING ORG (C DON FELDER G (C FRED TACKETT G (C JOHN SEBASTIAN HCA(C

S197 SOUTHER HILLMAN FURAY BAND S197

JOHN DAVID SOUTHER G V (AB (A) SOUTHER HILLMAN FURAY BAND 1974 ASYLUM US 7E1006 UK SYLA 8758
CHRIS HILLMAN B V (AB (B) TROUBLE IN PARADISE 1975 ASYLUM US 7E1036 UK SYLA 8760
RICHIE FURAY G V (AB
PAUL HARRIS K (AB AL PERKINS G STEEL (AB JIM GORDON D (A JAMES GUERCIO G (B
RON GRINEL D (B GLENN FREY V (B JOE LALA PERC (AB DON HENLEY V (B

S198 SOUTHERN COMFORT S198

GORDON HUNTLEY STEEL V(ABC (A) FROG CITY 1971 HARVEST UK SHSP4012 CAPITOL US800
CARL BARNWELL G V K(ABC (B) SOUTHERN COMFORT 1971 HARVEST UK SHSP 799
MARK GRIFFITHS G V K(ABC (B) SOUTHERN COMFORT 1971 CBS NL 64125 US 1011
ANDY LEIGH B V (ABC (C) STIR DON'T SHAKE 1972 HARVEST UK SHSP 4021
RAY DUFFY D (ABC (D) DISTILLED (COMP) 1976 HARVEST UK SHSM 2009
DON HARPER VLN (C
KEITH CUMMINGS VLA (C PETER MORRIS K (C BOB JONES D V (B JOHN WILMETH TPT (B
STEVE FUNK K (B ART STAVRO B (B REV RON STALLINGS SAX V(B FRED OLSON G (B

S198A SOUTHROAD CONNECTION S198A

DELWIN GILLMAN B TROM K V(A (A) POSITIVE ENERGY 1980 UA US LT1047 UK UAG 30316
STEVEN FIELDS D (A
LINDA WATSON V PERC K (A ELLSWORTH FORRESTER K (A HAROLD HUTTON SAX (V LOU BARBARIN TROM(A
MAERETHA STEWART V (A KRYSTAL DAVIS V (A YVONNE LEWIS V (A JEFF MEDINA G V (A
MICHAEL JONES V (A ALBERT JONES TPT (A RAY BLUE SAX (A

S198B SOUTHERN FRIED S198B

MAURICE ROGERS K V PERC(A (A) SOUTHERN FRIED 1971 MERCURY 6338 058
PAT ST CLAIR VPERC(A
HARRY HOLT B V (A BOB FERGUSON G V (A TODD ROBERTS D (A GENE PELLO D (A
KENT SPRAGUE D (A LARRY TAYLOR B (A LARRY KNECHTAL B (A DAVID T WALKER G (A
GERRY McGEE G (A LOUIE SHELTON G (A DENNY WALLY G (A MIKE O'MARTIAN K (A
ALLAN BEUTLER HRNS (A CHUCK FINDLEY HRNS (A JACK REDMAN HRNS (A

S199 SOUTHSIDE JOHNNY & THE ASBURY DUKES S199

JOHNNY LYON G V (ALL (A) LIVE AT THE BOTTOM LINE 1976 EPIC AS 275
TONY PALLIGROSI TPT V(BC (B) I DON'T WANT TO GO HOME 1976 EPIC US 34180 UK 81515
RICKY GAZDA TPT V(BCDFE (B) HAVING A PARTY (RI + 1 TRACK) 1979 EMBASSY RI UK 31772
CARLO NOVI SAX V(BC (C) THIS TIME IT'S FOR REAL 1977 EPIC US 34668 UK 81909
RICHIE'LA BAMBA'ROSENBERG TROM(BCDFE (D) HEARTS OF STONE 1978 EPIC US 35488 UK 82994
KENNY PENTIFALLO D V (BC (E) THE JUKES 1979 MERCURY US 3793 UK 9100 067
KEVIN KAVANAUGH K V (BCDE (F) LOVE IS A SACRIFICE 1980 MERCURY US 3836 UK 9111 081
EDDIE MANION SAX V(BCDEF (G) LIVE REACH UP & TOUCH THE SKY 1981 MERCURY US 8602 UK 6619 052
AL BERGER B V (BCDEF
BILLY RUSH G V (EF STEVE VAN ZANT G (D STEVE BUSLOWE B (F MAX WEINBERG D (D
STEVE BECKER D (FE STAN HARRISON SAX (DE BOB MUCKLIN TPT (DE JOE GRAMILINI G (EF

S199A SOUTHWEST S199A

JOHN FORD COLEY V (A (A) SMELL OF INCENSE 1968 HIP US HIS 7001
ENGLAND DAN SEALS V (A

S199B SOUTHWIND S199B

JOHN MOON MARTIN G V (Bc (A) SOUTHWIND 19 VENTURE US VTS 4002
JIM PULTE B (BC (B) READY TO RIDE 19 BLUE THUMB US BTS 13
ERIK DALTON D (BC (C) WHAT A PLACE TO LAND 1973 BLUE THUMB US BTS 26
FONTAINE BROWN K V G(BC

S200 BOB B SOXX & THE BLUE JEANS S200

DARLENE LOVE V (A (A) ZIP A DEE DOO DAH 1963 PHILLES PHLP4002 LONDON 8121
BOBBY SHEEN V (A (B) WALL OF SOUND VOL 2 1976 PHIL SPECTOR 2307 004
FANITA JAMES V (A
GLEN CAMPBELL G (A BILLY STRANGE G (A AL DELORY (A LEON RUSSELL PNO (A
NINO TEMPO SAX (A

S201 SPACE ART S201

(A) SPACE ART 1977 ARIOLA AHAL 8001

S202 SPACE OPERA S202

BRETT WILSON D PERC(A (A) SPACE OPERA 1973 EPIC US 32117 UK 65557
PHILIP WHITE B G K V (A
SCOTT FRASER G K V(A DAVID BULLOCK G FLT HCA V(A

S203 SPANKY & OUR GANG S203

ELAINE'SPANKY'McFARLANE V PERC(ALL (A) SPANKY & OUR GANG 1967 MERCURY UK SMCL20114 US SR61124
NIGEL PICKERING G D (ABCDEF (B) LIKE TO GET TO KNOW YOU 1968 MERCURY UK SMCL20121 US SR61161
JOHN SEITER D (ABCDE (C) WITHOUT RHYME OR REASON 1968 MERCURY US SR61183
MALCOLM HALE D (ABCDE (D) SPANKY'S GREATEST HITS 1970 MERCURY US SR61227
KENNY HODGES B ((E) LIVE 1970 MERCURY US SR61326
LEFTY BAKER G V (ABCDE (F) CHANGE 1975 EPIC US33580
GEOFFREY MYERS B (
CARLOS BERNAL B (F GENE GARLIN D (F GAIL LAUGHTON HARP (F JOHN LOGAN HCA (F
MARC McCLURE B V G(F JIM MOON D (F RAY NEAPOLITAN B (F HERB PEDERSEN BAN (F
RICK VITO G (F BILL PLUMMER B V (F JOHN RHYTHM HCA (F RICHARD THOMPSON PNO(F
BOBBY WOOD PNO (F JERRY YESTER V (F TOWER OF POWER HRNS (F

S203A SPANDAU BALLET S203A

JOHN KEEBLE D V (AB (A) JOURNEY TO GLORY 1981 CHRYSALIS UK CHR1331 GER 203428
MARTIN KEMP B V (AB (B) DIAMOND 1982 CHRYSALIS UK CHR1353 GER 204514
GARY KEMP G SYN(AB
STEVE NORMAN G V (AB
TONY HADLEY V SYN(AB CANUTE WEELINGTON TPT (B DAVID BAPTISTE SAX (B NATHANIEL AUGUSTIN TROM(B

S204 OTIS SPANN S204

OTIS SPANN PNO V(ALL (A) OTIS SPANN IS THE BLUES 1960 CANDID 8001 + BARNABY US 30246
BARRY MELTON G (O (B) BLUES ARE WHERE ITS AT 1963 HMV UK CSD3609 BLUESWAY BLS6003
LUTHER JOHNSON G (OBH (C) PORTRAIT IN BLUES 1963 STORYVILLE SLP157
LONNIE JOHNSON G (C (D) PIANO BLUES 196 STORYVILLE SLP168
JOS DAVIDSON B (O (E) BLUES OF OTIS SPANN 1964 DECCA UK LK 4615
LONNIE TAYLOR D (O (F) BLUES NEVER DIE 1965 PRESTIGE US 7319
LUCILLE SPANN V (OH (F) BLUES NEVER DIE 1966 STATESIDE UK SL 10169
MUDDY WATERS G V (LBHQT (G) NOBODY KNOWS MY TROUBLES 1967 POLYDOR 545 030 +BOUNTY BY 6037
SAMMY LAWHORN G (BH (H) BOTTOM OF THE BLUES 1968 BLUESWAY US BLS 6013
MAC ARNOLD B (B (H) BOTTOM OF THE BLUES 1968 STATESIDE UK SL 10255
FRANCIS CLAY D (B (J) FATHERS & SONS 1969 CHESS CRLS 4556
GEORGE SMITH HCA (B (K) BIGGEST THING SINCE COLOSSUS 1969 BLUE HORIZON US4802 UK 763217

(CONTINUED)

S204 (CONTINUED) **OTIS SPANN** S204

```
LITTLE WILLIE SMITH D  (BC     (L) CRACKED SPANNER HEAD            1969 DERAM            UK   SML  1036
RANSOM KNOWLING   B    (LQ     (M) HEART HEAVY WITH TROUBLE        19   BLUESWAY             BLS  6063
SPIT JAMES        G    (L      (N) WALKING BLUES                   1972 EPIC       US 31290  UK  64888
STEVE GREGORY     SAX  (L      (O) CRYING TIME                     1978 VANGUARD                VSD 6514
BUD BEADLE        SAX  (L      (P) OTIS SPANN                      19   EVEREST             US     216
DANNY KIRWAN      G    (K      (Q) HALF AIN'T BEEN TOLD            19   BLACK CAT           NL     001
ROD M LEE         TPT  (L      (R) CHICAGO BLUES                   19   TESTAMENT           US    2211
S P LEARY         D    (K      (S) THE EVERLASTING BLUES           19   SPIVEY              US    1013
PETER GREEN       G    (K      (T) WITH MUDDY WATERS BAND          19   MUSE                US    5008
JOHN McVIE        B    (K      (U) SWEET GIANT OF THE BLUES        19   BLUESTIME  US 9006
JOHNNY YOUNG      G    (G      (V) CRY BEFORE I GO                 1974 BLUESWAY . US 6070
JAMES COTTON      HCA V(FG
JIMMY LEE MORRIS  B    (G
ROBERT WHITEHEAD  D    (G   GEORGE BUFORD    HCA  (H   LAWRENCE WIMBERLEY B   (H   MEMPHIS SLIM      K(Q
PAUL HUMPHREY     D    (U   MAX BENNETT  B        (U   LOUIS SHELTON      G   (U   TOM SCOTT  WIND   (U
```

S204A **SPARGO** S204A

```
                               (A) GOOD TIME SPIRIT                1980 SCREAM     NL   2604
```

S205 **SPARKS** S205

```
RON MAEL          K V  (ALL    (A) SPARKS                          1971 BEARSVILLE US 2048   UK K45511
RUSSELL MAEL      V    (ALL    (B) WOOFER IN TWEETERS CLOTHING     1972 BEARSVILLE US 2110   UK K45510
ADRIAN FISHER     G    (C      (AB) SPARKS/WOOFER                  1975 BEARSVILLE          UK   K85505
HARLEY FEINSTEIN  D    (B      (C) KIMONO MY HOUSE                 1974 ISLAND              UK ILPS 9272
EARL MANKEY       G    (B      (D) PROPAGANDA                      1974 ISLAND              UK ILPS 9312
JIM MANKEY        G B  (B      (E) INDISCREET                      1975 ISLAND              UK ILPS 9345
TREVOR WHITE      G    (       (F) BIG BEAT                        1976 CBS US 34359 ISLANDUK ILPS 9445
IAN HAMPTON       B    (       (G) INTRODUCING SPARKS              1977 EPIC     34901      UK     82284
DINKY DIAMOND     D    (C      (H) No 1 IN HEAVEN                  1979 VIRGIN              UK     V2115
PETER OXENDALE         (       (J) BEST OF                         1979 ISLAND              UK ILPS 9493
MARTIN GORDON     B    (C      (K) TERMINAL JIVE                   1980 VIRGIN              UK     V2137
JEFF SAILIN       G V  (F      (L) WHOMP THAT SUCKER               1981 RCA US 4091
TODD RUNDGREN     PROD (A
HILLY MICHAELS    D    (F   SAL MAIDA          B    (F   THAD JAMES LOWE PROD   (F   MUFF WINWOOD    PROD(C
```

S205A **SPARROW** S205A

```
                               (A) HATCHING OUT                    1974 SPARK       US    05
```

S206 **ROGER RUSKIN SPEAR** S206

```
ROGER RUSKIN SPEAR V K B SAX(AB  (A) ELECTRIC SHOCKS               1972 UA US 097          UK UAS 29508
CHRIS WELCH       D    (A        (B) UNUSUAL                       1973 UA                 UK UAG 29381
PETER BANKS       G    (A
ROY HOLLINGWORTH  G    (A   TONY NEWMAN      SAX  (A   DAVE GLASSON     PNO  (A   JERRY GARDINER     G  (A
GRAHAM PRESKETT   VLN  (A   SAM SPOONS            (A   CYRIL JORDAN     G    (A   ROGER C MITCHELL   V  (A
JAMES FERRELL     G    (A   DANNY MIHM       D    (A   CHRIS WILSON     V    (A   STEVE WALLER       G  (A
DAVE CLAGUE       B    (A   B J COLE         STEEL(A   ANDY NEWMAN      K V  (B   DAVE CHARLES       D  (B
RICHARD PERSELL   G    (B   JOE RYAN         G    (B   RICHARD TREECE   G    (B   MAGGIE STREDDER SINGERS(B
ARRAN ROE         D    (AB  KEN WHALEY       B    (B   JOHN SAWYER      B    (B
```

S207 **SPECIALS** S207

```
TERRY HALL        V    (AB     (A) THE SPECIALS                    1979 TWO TONE UK 5001
PAUL HESATT       SAX  (B      (A) THE SPECIALS                    1979 CHRYSALIS US 1256 GER 202 685
LYNVAL GOLDING    G V  (AB     (B) MORE SPECIALS                   1980 TWO TONE UK CHRTT5003
JERRY DAMMERS     K    (AB     (B) MORE SPECIALS                   1980 CHRYSALIS US 1303 GER 202 848
RODDY RADIATION   G    (AB
HORACE GENTLEMAN  B    (AB  NEVILLE STAPLES   V PERC(AB JOHN BRADBURY   D    (A   RHODA DAKER V       (B
KIX THOMPSON      SAX  (B   RICO RODRIGUES    HRNS  (AB DICK CUTHELL    HRNS(AB   THE GO GO'S       V (B
```

S207A **SPECKLED RED** S207A

```
RUFUS PERRYMAN    V PNO(ALL    (A) DIRTY DOZENS                    19   DELMARK                 DL  601
                               ( ) IN LONDON 1960                  19   VJM                     LC   11
                               ( ) PIANO BLUES                     19   STORYVILLE              SLP  188
                               ( ) BLUES IN EUROPE                 19   STORYVILLE              SLP  187
                               ( ) BARRELHOUSE BLUES               19   FOLKWAYS        3555
```

S208 **RONNIE SPECTOR** S208

```
RONNIE SPECTOR    V    (A      (A) SIREN                           1981 REDSHADOW UK 002 POLISH US  808
```

S209 **CHRIS SPEDDING** S209

```
CHRIS SPEDDING    G V  (ALL    (A) BACKWOODS PROGRESSION           1970 HARVEST        UK   SHSP 4004
PAUL ABRAHAMS     K    (A      (B) SONGS WITHOUT WORDS             1970 HARVEST EURO SHVL776
STEVE CURRY       B    (F      (C) ONLY LICK I KNOW                1972 HARVEST        UK   SHSP 4017
MICK OLIVER       G    (F      (D) CHRIS SPEDDING                  1976 RAK            UK   SRAK  519
DAVE LUTTON       D    (F      (E) HURT                            1977 RAK            UK   SRAK  529
HERBIE FLOWERS    B    (E      (F) GUITAR GRAFFITI                 2979 RAK            UK   SRAK  534
CLEM CATTINI      D    (E      (G) I'M NOT LIKE EVERYBODY ELSE     1980 RAK            UK   SRAK  542
RAY COOPER        PERC (EF     (H) FRIDAY THE 13TH                 1981 PASSPORT US 6007
JACK EMBLOW  MUSETTE   (E
CHAS MILLS        V    (DE  CHRISSIE HYNDE   V    (E   JOHN CARTER      V    (E   ROYSTON MITCHELL K HCA(A
NEIL LANCASTER    V    (DE  TONY NEWMAN      D    (F   LINDA LEWIS      V    (C   LAURIE ALLEN     D  (C
HAROLD FISHER     D    (E   ALAN HAWKSHAW    PNO  (C   PAUL FRANCIS     D    (C   PHIL DENNYS      K  (C
LES HURDLE        B    (D   BRIAN BENNETT    D    (D   DAVE COCHRAN     B    (D   TONY CARR        D  (D
TONY BURROWS      V    (D   BARRY MORGAN     D    (D   SUE GLOVER       V    (D   SUNNY LESLIE     V  (D
DAVE MATTACKS     D    (G   RICHARD GOWER    V    (G   PHIL LANZON      PNO  (G   PAUL WESTWOOD    B  (G
PHIL FURSDON      V    (G   CHRIS GREEN  CELLO    (G   CHRIS MERCER     SAX  (G   PETE MILLER      V  (G
PETE WILLIAMSON   CELLO(G   TONI CAMPO       B    (C   ROY BABBINGTON   B    (A   LAWRIE ALLEN     D  (A
FRANK RICOTTI     PERC (A   PAUL RUTHERFORD  TROM (B   JOHN MITCHELL    K    (B   ROGER POTTER     B  (B
JOHN MITCHELL     D    (B   BUSTA JONES      B V  (H   TONY MACHINE     D V  (H
```

S210 **SPEED LIMIT** S210

```
ACKER APPLEBY     V    (A      (A) FIRST OFFENCE                   1978 SATRIL                  SATL 4011
TONY BAYLIS       D    (A
DOUGIE DENNIS     B    (A   BRIAN SMITH      G    (A   DAVID MORRIS     G    (A
```

S210A **SPEEDOMETERS** S210A

```
ROBBIE WATSON     B V  (A      (A) DAY IN THE LIGHTS               1979 ACROBAT        UK        ACRO5
IAN TAYLOR        G V  (A
LEE DALLON        K    (A   TOMMY EYRE       K    (A   MARTIN FINLEY    G V  (A   STEVE PARRY D     (A
CHRIS GENT        SAX V(A   PAUL SPENCER     D    (A
```

S210B SPEEDWAY BLVD S210B

GREGG HOFFMAN G V (A — (A) SPEEDWAY BLVD — 1980 EPIC US 36533
DENNIS FELDMAN B V (A
ROY HERRING JR V K PERC(A — GLENN DOVE D (A — JORDAN RUDES K (A

S210C SKIP SPENCE S210C

ALEXANDER 'SKIP' SPENCE(A — (A) OAR — 1968 CBS US CS 9831

S211 JEREMY SPENCER S211

JEREMY SPENCER G V (ABC — (A) JEREMY SPENCER — 1970 REPRISE US RSLP 9002 UK K44105
MICK FLEETWOOD D (A — (B) & THE CHILDREN — 1973 CBS US 31990 UK 65387
JOHN McVIE B (A — (C) FLEE — 1979 ATLANTIC US 19236 UK K50624
DANNY KIRWAN G V (A
PETER GREEN BAN (A — STEVE GREGORY SAX (A — PHIL HAM G FLT(B — BOAZ B V (B
MICHAEL HCA G V (B — GINNETHON D PERC (B — MICHAEL FOGARTY K V (C — JEFF SCHOEN K (C
NEAL JASON B (C — AL IZZO D (C — BUZ BUCHANAN D (C — VICTOR SALAZAR PERC(C
RAY GOMEZ G (C — STEVE THOMPSON B (C — SIMON PHILLIPS D (C

S212 JOHN SPENCER'S LOUTS S212

JOHN SPENCER G V K(A — (A) THE LAST LP — 1978 BEGGARS BANQUET BEGA3
JOHNNY G G D V HCA (A
DAVE THORNE B BAN(A — CHAS AMBLER K D (A — ANDY McDONALD WIND (A — SIAN DANIELS V (A
ADAM SKEAPING CELLO(A

S213 JIMMY SPHEERIS S213

JIMMY SPHEERIS V G K(ALL — (A) ISLE OF VIEW — 19 CBS US 30988 UK 64919
GEOFF LEVIN G (ABCD — (B) ORIGINAL TAP DANCING KID — 1973 CBS US 32157
DAVID CAMPBELL VLN (ACD — (C) DRAGON IS DANCING — 1975 EPIC US 33565
LEE CALVIN NICOLI G FLT B V(A — (D) PORTS OF THE HEART — 1976 CBS US 34276
DAVID HAROWITZ K (A
EMIL LATIMER CONGO(A — BUDDY SALZMAN D (A — FELIX CAVALIERE K V(B — RUSS KUNKEL D (B
LELAND SKLAR B (B — DOREEN DAVIS V (B — VINNIE JOHNSON D (B — BOBBYE HALL PERC(B
SNEAKY PETE STEEL(B — JANE GETZ K V (BC — JOHN SUMMERS B (B — HARVEY MASON D (B
NOVAR TROTTER (B — CHARLIE LARKY B (B — BART HALL D (CD — JOHNNY PIERCE B V (CD
HENRY LEWY PERC (C — MORGAN AMES V (C — MIKE KALLEN G (C — PAUL LEWINSON K (C
DOROTHY REMSEN HARP (C — CHICK COREA K (DC — STANLEY CLARKE B (D — JIM COWGER WINDB(CD
JIM CALIGER FLT (B — JOHN GUERIN D (D — EMILE PANDALF K (D — JAY ELLINGTON HARP(D
RICHARD FEVES B (D — JACKSON BROWNE V (D — ROBIN WILLIAMSON (D — DAN ORBACH MAND(D

S214 SPHERICAL OBJECTS S214

STEVE SOLAMAR V G HCA(AB — (A) PAST & PARCEL — 1978 OBJECT UK OBJ001
DUNCAN PRESTBURY K V (AB — (B) ELIPTICAL OPTIMISM — 1979 OBJECT UK OBJ004
ROGER HILTON D (ABCD — (C) FURTHER ELLIPSES — 1980 OBJECT UK OBJ012
FREDERICK BURROWS B G (AB — (D) NO MANS LAND — 1981 OBJECT UK OBJ016
JOHN BISSET-SMITH G V (AB
MIKE RABBIT G (D — MIKE ZEE B (D — ROGER BLACKBURNS G (D

S214A SPIDER S214A

AMANDA BLUE V (AB — (A) SPIDER — 1980 RSO 2394260
KEITH LENTIN G V (AB — (B) BETWEEN THE LINES — 18 DREAMLAND
JIMMY LOWELL B (AB
ANTON FIG D (AB — HOLLY KNIGHT K (AB

S214B SPIDERZ S214B

GUUS BOERS V (A — (A) PRESSURE — 1980 HURRICANE FLAK103
BART BROUWER K V (A
KOOS CORNELISSEN G (A — JOHN SNEP B (A — HENRI HOEYMANS D (A — APPIR BAARS SAX (A

S214C SPIDERS FROM MARS S214C

PETE McDONALD V (A — (A) SPIDERS FROM MARS — 1976 PYE US 12125 UK NSPL18479
WOODY WOODMANSEY D (A
DAVE BLACK G (A — TREVOR BOLDER B (A — MIKE GARSON K (A

S214D SPIN S214D

REIN VAN DER BROEK HRNS (A — (A) SPIN — 1976 ARIOLA US ST 50013
JAN VANNIK WIND (A
HANS HOLLESTELLE G (A — JAN HULLESTELLE B SYN(A — HANS JANSEN K (A — CEES KRANENBURG (A

S214E SPIDERS S214E

SNIFFA G (A — (A) ROCK'N' ROLL GYPSIES — 1982 RCA UK RC3101
COL HARKNESS G V (A
ROB BURROWS D (A — BRIAN BURROWS V B (A

S215 DAVID SPINOZZA S215

DAVID SPINOZZA G V (A — (A) SPINOZZA — 1978 A&M US SP4677
JOE CARO G (A
ANTHONY JACKSON B (A — RICK MAROTTA D (A — MIKE MAINIERI SYN (A — LEON PENDARVIS PNO (A
LUTHER VANDROSS V (A — DAVID LASLEY V (A — DIVA GRAY V (A — STEVE JORDAN D (A
ROB MOUNSEY PNO (A — ALAN RUBIN TPT (A — RANDY BRECKER TPT (A — JOHN FADDIS TPT (A
WAYNE ANDRE TROM (A — BARRY ROGERS TROM (A — DAVID TAYLOR TROM (A — TONY PRICE TUBA(A
JOHN TREVOR CLARK HRNS (A — SHARON MOE HRNS (A — GEORGE MARGE WIND (A — GEORGE YOUNG WIND(A
DAVID TOFANI WIND (A — KIM CARLSON V (A — GORDON GRODY V (A — WARREN BERNHARDT K (A
GARY MURE PERC (A — DAVID CAREY PERC (A — RUBENS BASSINI PERC (A — DON GROLNICK PNO (A
MICHAEL BRECKER SAX (A — LEW SOLOFF TPT (A — DAVID SANBORN SAX (A — RONALD CUBER SAX (A
STRING SECTION (A

S216 SPIRIT S216

RANDY CALIFORNIA G V B(ABCDFGHJKLMNOP (A) SPIRIT 1968 CBS UK 63278 US 31457
ED CASSIDY D (ABCDEFGHJKLMNOP (A) SPIRIT 1968 ODE US Z1244004
JAY FERGUSON K V(ABCDF (A) BEST OF(REPACKAGED) 1979 EMBASSY UK 31693
MARK ANDES B (ABCDFJ (AC) SPIRIT/CLEAR (DBL) 1973 EPIC US 31457
MIKE FONDALIER D ((B) THE FAMILY THAT PLAYS TOGETHER 1968 CBS UK 63523 US 31461
ROB ARKIN B ((B) THE FAMILY THAT PLAYS TOGETHER 1968 ODE US Z1244014
JOHN LOCKE K (ABCDEFJO (BE)FAMILY/FEEDBACK(DBL) 1975 EPIC US 33761
MATT ANDES G (J (C) CLEAR SPIRIT 1969 CBS UK 63729 ODE Z1244016
JOHN ARLISS B ((D) 12 DREAMS OF Dr SARDONICUS 1970 EPIC UK 64191 US 30267
AL STAEHELY B V (E (E) FEEDBACK 1971 EPIC UK 64507 US 31175
CHRIS STAEHELY G V (E (F) BEST OF SPIRIT 1973 EPIC UK 65585 US 32271
LARRY KNIGHT B (LMN (G) SPIRIT OF 76 (DBL) 1975 MERCURY UK 6672 012 US SRM2 804
MIKE THORNBURGH HRNS (O (G) SPIRIT OF 76 (DBL) 1975 MERCURY GER 6641 323
COZY POWELL D ((H) SON OF SPIRIT 1975 MERCURY UK 9100 019 US SRM11053
STU PERRY D ((J) FARTHER ALONG 1976 MERCURY US SRM11094
BARRY KEENE B (GH (K) FUTURE GAMES 1977 MERCURY UK 9100 036 US SRM11133
JOHN TERLEP B ((L) LIVE 1977 ILLEGAL UK ILP 001
ERNIE WATTS SAX (J (M) LIVE (MADE IN GERMANY) 1978 POTATO 172200
MICHAEL D TEMPLE MAND (J (N) LIVE 1978 POTATO US PR 2001
IAN UNDERWOOD (J (O) POTATOLAND 1981 LINE GER 6 24641
DAVID BLUMBERG HRNS (J (O) POTATOLAND 1981 BEGGARS BANQUET UK BEGA 23
NICK DE CARO HRNS (J (O) POTATOLAND 1981 RHINO US
LAWRENCE WEISBERG B (J (P) INTERVIEW RECORD 1981 RHINO US 1984
TERRY ANDERSON V (K
GEORGE VALUNE K (O MIKE BUNNELL K (O KARI NILE K (O BENJI K (O
JEFF JARVIS HRNS (O CHUCK SNYDER HRNS (O JOE GREEN STR (O BERYL K (G
AL SCHNUTT PROD (J LOU ADLER PROD(J PAUL WALKINS PROD (L DAVID BRIGGS PROD (D
STEVE LARRENCE PERC (J MICHAEL LEE PROD(O ROBERT LEE PROD (O

****NOTE (L.M.N. ARE DIFFERENT RECORDS BUT OF THE SAME TOUR ,TRACKS & MIX ARE DIFFERENT.)

S217 SPIRIT OF JOHN MORGAN S217

JOHN MORGAN K V (ABC (A) SPIRIT OF JOHN MORGAN 1969 CARNABY UK CNLS 6002
MICK WALKER D V (ABC (B) AGE MACHINE 1970 CARNABY UK CNLS 6007
DON WHITAKER G V (A (C) KALEIDOSCOPE(AS JOHN MORGAN) 1972 CARNABY UK 6302 010
PHIL SHUTT B (ABC
TREVOR THOMS G (BC

S218 SPIROGYRA S218

MARTIN COCKERHAM G V (B (A) ST RADIGUNDS 1971 B&C CAS 1042
STEVE BORRILL B (B (B) OLD BOOT WINE 1972 PEGASUS PEG 13
MARK FRANCIS G V K(B (C) BELLS BOOTS & SHAMBLES 1973 POLYDOR 2310 246
BARBARA GASKIN V (B
DAVE MATTACKS D (B JULIAN CUSACK VLN K (B ALAN LAING CELLO (B RICK BIDDULPH MAND(A

S219 SPITBALLS S219

(A) SPITBALLS 1978 BESERKLEY NL 530057 UK BSERK15

S219A SPIZZ(SPIZZELS) S219A

MARK COALFIELD K (A (A) DO A RUNNER 1980 A&M UK AMLE68514
DAVE SCOTT G (A (B) SPIKEY DREAM FLOWERS 1981 A&M US 4861 UK AMLE68523
C P SNARE D (AB
JIM SOLAR B (AB SPIZZ V (B LU G (B

S219B SPLIFF S219B

(A) SPLIFF RADIO SHOW 1981 CBS UK 84555
(B) 85555 1982 CBS UK 85739

S220 SPLINTER S220

BILL ELLIOTT V (ABC (A) THE PLACE I LOVE 1974 DARK HORSE AMLH22001
BOBBY PURVIS V (ABC (B) HARDER TO LIVE 1975 DARK HORSE AMLH22006
BILLY PRESTON K (AB (C) TWO MAN BAND 1977 DARK HORSE US 3073 UK K56403
KLAUS VOORMAN B (A ( ) SLPINTER 1980 BELLAPHON UK 002
EARL PALMER D (B
BILL DICKINSON B (B GEORGE HARRISON G (BA CHRIS SPEDDING G (B JOHN TAYLOR K (B
JIM KELTNER D (AB TOM SCOTT HRNS (B RALPH MACDONALD PERC (B WADDY WACHTEL G (B
BILL NUTTYCOMBE (B GARY WRIGHT K (A WILLIE WEEKS B (A MIKE KELLY D (A
GRAHAM MAITLAND ACC (A

S221 SPLIT ENZ S221

TIM FINN V K (ALL (A) MENTAL NOTES 1975 MUSHROOM AUST 35588
IAN SHARP CELLO((B) MENTAL NOTES 1976 CHRYSALIS UK CHR 1131
NEIL FINN G V (FGH (C) SECOND THOUGHTS 1976 MUSHROOM AUST 35981
MILES GOLDING VLN ((D) DIZRHYTHMIA 1977 CHRYSALIS UK CHR 1145
WALLY WILKINSON G (A (D) DIZRHYTHMIA 1977 MUSHROOM AUST 36347
NOEL CROMBIE (ALL (E) FRENZY 1978 MUSHROOM AUST 36921
EDDIE RAYNER K (ALL (F) TRUE COLOURS 1980 A&M UK 64822
JON CHUNN B (AB (G) WAIATA 1981 A&M UK 64848
PHIL JUDD G V (ABC (H) TIME & TIDE 1982
EMLYN CROWTHER PERC (AB (I) BEGINNING OF THE ENZ 1980 CHRYSALIS UK 64822
ROBERT COLES HRNS ((J) BEGINNING OF THE ENZ(DIFF TRACKS) 1980 MUSHROOM AUST
MAL GREEN PERC (G
NIGEL GRIGGS B (FG ROBERT GILLIES SAX (B PHIL MANZANERA PROD (B DAVID MUSSEL PROD(A
MILES GOLDING VLN (

S221A SPLODGENESSABOUNDS S221A

MAX SPLODGE V (A (A) SPLODGENESSABOUNDS 1981 DERAM UK SML 1121

S222 MARK SPOELSTRA S222

MARK SPOELSTRA (ALL (A) 5 & 20 QUESTIONS 1965 ELEKTRA EKS 7283
(B) STATE OF MIND 1966 ELEKTRA EKS 7307
(C) MARK SPOELSTRA 1969 CBS 9793
(D) MARK SPOELSTRA 197 FOLKWAYS 3572
( ) SONGS 197 FOLKWAYS 2449
( ) THIS HOUSE 197 FANTASY US 8412

S223 SPONTANEOUS COMBUSTION S223

GARY MARGETTS G V (A — (A) SPONTANEOUS COMBUSTION — 1972 HARVEST UK SHVL801 US CAPITOL 11021
TRIS MARGETTS B V (A — (B) TRIAD — 1972 HARVEST UK SHVL805 US CAPITOL 11095
TONY BROCK D (A

S224 SPOOKY TOOTH S224

MIKE HARRISON K V(ABCDEFG — (A) ITS ALL ABOUT SPOOKY TOOTH — 1968 ISLAND UK ILPS9080 GER 85682
GARY WRIGHT K V(ABCEFG — (B) SPOOKY TWO — 1969 ISLAND UK ILPS9098 US A&M 4194
PIERRE HENRY ELEC (C — (B) SPOOKY TWO — 1969 ISLAND 6339 004 RI 85785
LUTHER GROSVENOR G (ABCD — (C) CEREMONY — 1969 ISLAND UK ILPS9107 A&M 4225
VAL BURKE B V (G — (C) CEREMONY — 1969 PHILIPS FR 849 512
BRYSON GRAHAM D (EFG — (C) CEREMONY — 1969 FONTAN GER 6444 540
GREG RIDLEY G B (AB — (D) THE LAST PUFF — 1970 ISLAND UK ILPS9117 US A&M 4266
MICK JONES G (EFG — (D) THE LAST PUFF — 1970 ISLAND GER 85685
MIKE KELLIE D (ABCDG — (E) YOU BROKE MY HEART..... — 1973 ISLAND UK ILPS9227 US A&M 4385
CHRIS STEWART B (EF — (E) YOU BROKE MY HEART..... — 1973 ISLAND GER 86687
ANDY LEIGH B (C — (F) WITNESS — 1973 ISLAND UK ILPS9255 US 9255
MIKE PATTO V D K(G — (F) WITNESS — 1973 ISLAND GER 87332
CHRIS STAINTON K (D — (G) THE MIRROR — 1974 ISLAND US 9292
HENRY McCULLOUGH G (D — (G) THE MIRROR — 1974 GOODEAR UK EARL2001
ALAN SPENNER (D — (G) THE MIRROR — 1979 CHARLY UK CR 30167
(H) POP CHRONIK (DBL COMP) — 1975 ISLAND EURO VOL 10 GER 88133
(I) THE BEST OF — 1976 ISLAND UK ILPS9368

S224A SPORTS S224A

ROBERT GLOVER B (B — (A) RECKLESS — 1978 MUSHROOM AUST 36571
STEPHEN CUMMINGS V (AB — (B) DONT THROW STONES — 1978 MUSHROOM AUST 36844
ANDREW PENDLEBURY G V (AB — (B+) DONT THROW STONES(DIFF TRACKS) — 1979 SIRE UK 6001 US ARISTA 4249
ED BATES G V (B — (B+) DONT THROW STONES — 1979 ARIOLA GER 201 020
JIM NIVEN K V (B — (C) SPORTS — 1979 STIFF SEEZ 15
PAUL HITCHINGS D (AB — (D) SPORTS (EP) — 1979 STIFF LAST 5
MARTIN ARMIGER G V (B — (E) SUDDENLY — 1980 ARISTA US 4266
W WILDE SAX (B
M BURNS SYN (B — PETE SOLLEY K (B — G HYDE PERC (B — HERBIE FLOWERS B (B
CHANTER SISTERS V (D

S225 SPOTNICKS S225

BO LANDER G (— (A) SPOTNICKS IN LONDON — 1961 KARUSSELL GER 1012 UK ORIOLE
BO WINBERG G (ALL — (B) SPOTNICKS IN PARIS — 1963 KARUSSELL GER 1014 UK ORIOLE
BJORN THELIN B (— (C) SPOTNICKS IN SPAIN — 1963 SWEDISC SWELP 1
OVE JOHANNSON D (— (D) OUTTA SPACE — 1963 ORIOLE UK SPS 40037
PETER WIBERG (P — (E) IN JAPAN — 1966 SWEDISC SWELP 38
LENNART HERMENSSON (P — (F) IN WINTERLAND — 1966 SWEDISC SWELP 48
BO MANIEETE (P — (G) THE SPOTNICKS — 1975 POLYDOR 2482 051
JOHAN DIELEMANS (P — (H) BEST OF — 19 POLYDOR 184 151
MATZ NILSSON (P — (I) POP GIANTS No8 — 19 BRUNSWICK 2911 519
JAN SVENSSON BAN (P — (J) VERY BEST OF — 1977 AIR CHM 1171
(K) LE TOUR DE MONDE DES SPOTNICKS — 19 PRESIDENT FR 279 (4LP SET)
(L) BEST — 19 KARUSSELL 2499 017 GER
(M) SPOTNICKS — 19 POLYDOR 27501 6 GER
(N) ON TOUR — 19 KARUSSELL 2499 050 GER
(O) NEVER TRUST ROBOTS — 1978 POLYDOR 2344 116 GER
(P) TODAY — 1973 POLYDOR 2480 164 GER
(Q) SOMETHING IN THE COUNTRY — 19 POLYDOR 2480 112 GER
(R) SATURDAY NIGHT MUSIC — 19 M RECORDS MILP1304
(S) GREAT SNOWMAN — 19 M RECORDS MILP1300
(EP)ON THE AIR — 196 ORIOLE UK 7075
(EP) IN PARIS — 196 ORIOLE UK 7078
(EP) AT THE OLYMPIA — 196 ORIOLE UK 7079

S226 SPREADEAGLE S226

ANDY BLACKFIELD G V (A — (A) A PIECE OF PAPER — 1972 CHARISMA UK CAS 1055
SAM LLEWELLYN B V PERC(A
JIM COPLEY D (A — JOHN FIELD PERC (A — TIM PHILLIPS V G K(A — NICK PERC (A
SHELL PERC (A

S227 SPRIGUNS S227

MANDY MORTON G V (ABC — (A) REVEL WEIRD & WILD — 1976 DECCA SKL 5262
TOM LING VLN V(AB — (B) TIME WILL PASS — 1977 DECCA SKL 5286
DICK POWELL G V K(AB — (C) MAGIC LADY — 1979 BANSHEE BAN 1101
MIKE MORTON B V (AB
CHRIS WOODCOCK D (A — WAYNE MORRISON G MAND V(B — TIM HART (C — B J COLE STEEL(A
LEA NICHOLSON CONCERTINA(B — DENNIS DUNSTAN PERC D(B — GRAEME TAYLOR (C — GORDON FOLKARD CONC (C
SARAH FOLKARD V (C — BYRON GILES D (C — ALEX COOPER D (C

S227A SPRING S227A

MARILYN WILSON-POWELL V(A — (A) SPRING — 1974 UA UK UAS 29363 US UAS 5577
DIANE POWELL V (A
KEITH ALLISON B (A — RAY POHMAN B (A — DAVID COHEN G (A — LARRY CARLTON G (A
CARL WILSON G (A — JOHN GUERIN D (A — LINCOLN MAYORGA PNO (A — DAVID SANDLER PNO (A
ALAN BEUTLER HRNS (A — IGOR HOROSHEFSKY CELLO(A — BRIAN WILSON (A

S228 DUSTY SPRINGFIELD S228

DUSTY SPRINGFIELD V (A — (A) A GIRL CALLED DUSTY — 1964 PHILIPS UK BL 7594
RONALD CHAMBERS G (P — (B) EVERYTHING IS COMING UP DUSTY — 1965 PHILIPS UK SBL 1002
DICK HYDE TROM (b — (B) SHEER MAGIC RI — 197 AUDIO CLUB 6856 020
NORMAN HARRIS G (P — (C) STAY AWHILE — 196 PHILIPS US 600 133
VINCE MONTANA VIBES(P — (D) DUSTY — 196 PHILIPS US 600 156
UGENE DOZIER PNO (P — (E) OOOOOOOWEEEEE1111 — 196 PHILIPS US 600 174
RONALD BAKER B (P — (F) YOU DONT HAVE TO SAY YOU LOVE ME — 196 PHILIPS US 600 210
EARL YOUNG D (P — (G) GOLDEN HITS — 1966 PHILIPS UK SBL 7737 US 600 220
DON RENALDO STR (P — (H) THE PEKING MEDALION(SOUNDTRACK) — 1967 PHILIPS UK SBL 7782
SAM REED HRNS (P — (I) WHERE AM I GOING — 1967 PHILIPS UK SBL 7820
RICHARD TEE K (a — (J) STAY AWHILE — 1968 FONTANA UK 131189 UK RI WING1211
JOE SAMPLE K (a — (K) DUSTY DEFINITELY — 1968 PHILIPS UK SBL 7864
BILL PAYNE K (a — (L) THE LOOK OF LOVE — 196 PHILIPS US 600 256

(CONTINUED)

S228 (CONTINUED)

DUSTY SPRINGFIELD S228

DAVID PAICH K (a — (M) DUSTY SPRINGFIELD(LTD EDITION) 196 WORLD RECORD CLUB ST 848
JAI WINDING K (a — (N) DUSTY IN MEMPHIS 1969 PHILIPS UK SBL 7889
WILLIAM SMITH K (a — (N) DUSTY IN MEMPHIS 1969 ATLANTIC US 8214
JOHN BARNES K (a — (O) BEST OF BACHARACH 1970 FONTANA UK SFL 13193
JAY GRAYDON G (a — (P) FROM DUSTY WITH LOVE 1970 PHILIPS UK SBL 7927
DAVID T WALKER G (a — (P) A BRAND NEW ME 1970 ATLANTIC US 8249
CHARLES FEARING G (a — (Q) A GIRL CALLED DUSTY 1970 FONTANA UK 6438024 RI 6870 555
THOM ROTILLA G (a — (R) THIS IS DUSTY SPRINGFIELD 1971 PHILIPS UK 6382 016
JEFF BAXTER G (a — (S) STAR DUSTY 197 AUDIO CLUB OF GB 6850 002
BOB GLAUB B (a — (U) SEE ALL HER FACES 197 PHILIPS UK 6308 117
KENNETH BURKE B (a — (V) MAGIC GARDEN(THIS IS VOL 2) 1973 PHILIPS UK 6382 063
COLIN CAMERON B (a — (W) CAMEO 1973 PHILIPS UK 6308 152
CHUCK RAINEY B (a — (W) CAMEO 1973 DUNHILL US 50128
ED GREENE D (a — (X) LONGINGS (NOT ISSUED) 197 DUNHILL US 50186
RICHARD SCHLOSSER D (a — (Y) SINGS BACHARACH & KING 1975 PHILIPS UK 6382 105
OSCAR NEVES PERC (a — (Z) YOU DONT HAVE TO SAY YOU LOVE ME 1976 CONTOUR UK 2016
MR M PERRC(a — (a) IT BEGINS AGAIN 1978 MERCURY UK 9109 607
TIMMY VIG VIBES(a — (b) LIVING WITHOUT YOUR LOVE 1979 MERCURY UK 9109 629
JERRY JUMONVILLE SAX (a — (c) GRESTEST HITS 1979 PHILIPS UK 9109 629
PATTI BROOKS V (ab — (d) DUSTY IN MEMPHIS PLUS 1981 MERCURY UK 6381 023
DIANE BROOKS V (ab — (e) THE VERY BEST OF 1981 UK KTEL UK NE 1139
BRENDA RUSSEL V (ab — (EP) I ONLY WANT TO BE WITH YOU 1964 PHILIPS UK 12560
MICHELLE ALLER V (a — (EP) DUSTY 1964 PHILIPS UK 12564
SCOT EDWARDS B (b — (EP) MADEMOISELLE DUSTY 1964 PHILIPS UK 12579
WILL LEE B (b — (EP) DUSTY IN NEW YORK 1965 PHILIPS UK 12572
NEIL LARSEN K (b — (EP) IF YOU GO AWAY 1967 PHILIPS UK 12605
LINCOLN MAYORGA K (b
DENNIS BUDMIR G (b — DAVID WOLFERT G (b — IAN UNDERWOOD SYN (b — LENNY CASTRO PERC(b
GARY COLEMAN PERC (b — STEVE MADAIO HRNS (b — TOM SAVIANO SAX (b — MIKE CANAHAN SAX (b
DAVID LUELL SAX (b — ARIF MARDIN PROD (d — TOM DOWD PROD (d — JERRY WEXLER PROD (d

S228A

RICK SPRINGFIELD S228A

RICK SPRINGFIELD V G K B(ABC — (A) WAIT FOR THE NIGHT 1976 CHELSEA US 2306 UK CHL 515
NIGEL OLSSON D V (A — (B) WORKING CLASS DOG 1981 RCA US
DEE MURRAY B V (A — (C) SUCCESS HASN'T SPOILED ME YET 1982 RCA UK 6033
JOE LAMANO B (A
JIM HAAS V (A — LES EMERSON V (A — BILL CUOMO K (A — GABRIEL KATONA K (A
JIMMIE HASKELL STR (A

S229

BRUCE SPRINGSTEEN S229

BRUCE SPRINGSTEEN G V HCA B(ALL — (A) GREETINGS FROM ASBURY PARK N J 1973 CBS US 31903 UK 65480
CLARENCE CLEMONS SAX V(ABCDEX — (B) WILD, INNOCENT & THE EAST STREET 1973 CBS US 32432 UK 65780
GARRY TALLENT B HRN(ABCDEX — (C) BORN TO RUN 1975 CBS US 33795 UK 69170
MAX WEINBERG D (CDEX — (D) DARKNESS ON THE EDGE OF TOWN 1978 CBS US 35318 UK 86061
ROY BITTAN K (CDEX — (E) THE RIVER 1980 CBS UK 88510
VINI LOPEZ D V HRNS (AB — (ABC)BRUCE SPRINGSTEEN(TRIPLE) 1979 CBS UK 66353
DANNY FEDERICI K V (BCDEX — (X) REQUESTED AROUND THE WORLD(PROMO) 1981 CBS US AS978
HOWARD KAYLAN V (E — (F) NEBRASKA 1982 CBS UK 85669
MARK VOLMAN V (E
DAVID SANCIOUS K SAX(ABC — RICHARD BLACKWELL PERC (B — ALBANY TELLONE SAX (B — STEVE VAN ZANDT G (CEDX
MIKE APPEL V (C — ERNEST CARTER D (C — RANDY BRECKER HRNS (C — MICHAEL BRECKER HRNS(C
DAVID SANBORN SAX (C — WAYNE ANDRE TROM (C — RICHARD DAVIS B (AC — HAROLD WHEELER PNO (A

S230

SPUD S230

DON KNOX V FDL(AB — (A) A SILK PURSE 1975 PHILIPS 9108 002
MICHAEL SMITH V B (AB — (B) THE HAPPY HANDFUL 1975 PHILIPS 9108 003
AUSTIN KENNY G V (AB — (C) SMOKING ON THE BOG 1977 SONET SNTF 742
DERMOT O'CONNOR G SYN(A
MALCOLM WRAY V (A — DON HARRIS D (B — DANNY SMITH PERC (B — JIMMY FAULKNER G (B
RICK EPPING CONGA(B — STEVE MOORE PERC (B — DONAL LUNNY G SYN(A

S230A

SPY S230A

DANNY SEIDENBERG VLN (A — (A) SPY 1980 KIRSHNER US 36378
DAVID NELSON G V (A
BOB GOLDMAN D (A — MICHAEL VISCEGLIA B (A — DAVE LEBOLT K (A — JOHN VISLOCKY V (A

S231

SPYRO GYRA S231

JAY BECKENSTEIN PERC SAX(ALL — (A) MORNING DANCE 1978 INFINITY US 9004 UK INS 2003
TOM SCHUAMAN K (ABCD — (B) SPYRO GYRA 1977 INFINITY US 9011 UK INS 2008
STEVE KROON PERC (D — (B) SPYRO GYRA 1982 MCA UK MCL 1628
DAVID SAMUELS PERC VIBES(BD — (C) CATCHING THE SUN 1980 MCA US 5108 UK 4009
RICK STRAUSS G (ABCD — (D) CARNIVAL 1980 MCA US 5149 UK 3087
JEREMY WALL K PERC(ALL — (E) FREE TIME 1981 MCA US 5238 UK 3119
STEVE JORDAN D (D — (BC) MORNING DANCE/CATCHING (CASS) 1982 MCA UK 2/100
JIM KURZDORFER B (ABCD
DAVID WOFFERN B (E — TOM WALSH D (B — EMILE LATIMER PERC (B — RICK BELL TROM(B
FRED MARSHALL TROM (B — RUBENS BASSINI CONGA(B — FREDDY RAPILLO G (B — GREG MILLAR G (B
TONY GARUSSO TPT (B — CHET CATALLO G (ALL — WILL LEE B (D — ELI KONIKOFF D (ALL
CRUSHER BENNETT PERC (D — ROB MOUNSEY SYN (D — MICHAEL BRECKER FLT (D — HIRAM BULLOCK G (D
GERARDO VELEZ PERC (D — RANDY BRECKER TPT (D — DAVID DARLING CELLO(D — JOHN TROPEA G (DE

S231A

SPYS S231A

ED GAGLIARDI B (A — (A) SPYS 1982 EMI US ST 17073
AL GREEN WOOD K (A
JOHN BLANCO V (A — BILLY MIKE D (A

S232

SQUEEZE S232

CHRIS DIFFORD G V (ABCDEFG — (A) SQUEEZE 1978 A&M US 4687 UK AMLH68465
GLENN TILBROOK G V (ABCDEFG — (B) COOL FOR CATS 1979 A&M SU 4759 UK AMLH68003
JULIAN HOLLAND K (ABCD — (C) SQUEEZE (10") 1979 A&M US SP3413
GILSON LAVIS D (ABCDEFG — (D) ARGY BARGY 1980 A&M US 4802 UK AMLH64802
JOHN BENTLEY B (CDEFG — (E) EAST SIDE STORY 1981 A&M UK AMLH64854
ROGER BECHIRIAN PROD (E — (F) SWEETS FORM A STRANGER 1982 A&M UK AMLH64899
DAVE EDMUNDS PROD (E — (G) SINGLES 45's & UNDER 1982 A&M UK AMLH68552
PHIL McDONALD PROD (F — (EP) PACKET OF THREE 197 DEPTFORD FUN CITY DFC 01
HARRY KAKOULLI B (ABC
DEL NEWMAN STR (E — ELVIS COSTELLO VPROD(F — DON SNOW K V (F — PAUL YOUNG B (F

S232A **BILLY SQUIER** S232A

BILLY SQUIER G V (ALL (A) A TALE OF THE TAPE 1980 CAPITOL UK/US 12062 NL 86138
BRUCE KULICK G (A (B) DONT SAY NO 1981 CAPITOL 12146
BUCKY BALLARD B (A (C) EMOTIONS IN MOTION 1982 CAPITOL 12217
BOBBY CHOUINARD D (ABC
DAVID SANCIOUS K (A RICHARD T BEAR K (A ERNEST CARTER PERC (A MARK CLARKE B V (B
ALAN ST JOHN K (BC GARY SHARAF G (B DOUG LUBAHN B (C JEFF GOLUB G (C
KENNY AARONSON B (

S233 **CHRIS SQUIRE** S233

CHRIS SQUIRE B G V(A (A) FISH OUT OF WATER 1975 ATLANTIC US 18159 UK K50203
BILL BRUFORD D (A
MEL COLLINS SAX (A JIM HASTINGS FLT (A PATRICK MORAZ K SYN(A BARRY ROSE K (A
ANDREW BRYCE JACKMAN K (A ORCHESTRA (A

S235 **STACKRIDGE** S235

ANDREW CRESWELL-DAVIS V G K D(ALL (A) STACKRIDGE 1971 MCA UK MDKS8002 UK 74RI MCG3505
BOB LAMB TROM (DF (A) STACKRIDGE 1971 DECCA US 75317
JAMES WARREN V B G(ABCF (B) FRIENDLINESS 1972 MCA UK MKPS2025 UK 74RI MCF2504
MARTIN FRY TUBA (F (B) FRIENDLINESS 1972 MCA US 308
MICHAEL SLATER V FLT K(ABCDEF (C) MAN IN A BOWLER HAT 1973 MCA UK MCG3501
MICHAEL EVANS V VLN(ABCF (D) EXTRAVAGANZA 1974 ROCKET ROLLA1 + PIGL 11
BILLY BRENT D (A (D) EXTRAVAGANZA 1974 SIRE US 7509
JIM CRUN WALTER G B (BCEF (E) MR MICK 1976 ROCKET UK ROLL 3
BILLY SPARKLE D (BCF (F) PINAFORE DAYS 1974 SIRE US 7503
REG LEOPOLD VLN (CF (G) DO THE STANLEY(COMP) 1976 MCA UK MCF2747
WILLIAM REID VLN (CF
GRAEME SCOTT VLN (CF VIVIAN JOSEPH CELLO(CF JACK EMBLOW ACC (CF RAY DAVIS TPT (CF
DEREK TAYLOR HRNS (CF R CHAMBERLAIN HRNS (CF ROD BOWKETT K (DF KEITH GEMMELL WIND(DEF
PAUL KARAS B V (DF ROY MORGAN D (DF PETER VAN HOOKE D (E JOANNA CARLIN V (E
DAVE LAWSON K (E RAY RUSSELL G (

S236 **STACKWADDY** S236

JOHN KNAIL V HCA(1 (A) STACKWADDY 1971 DANDELION DAN 8003 + 2310 154
MICK SCOTT G (1 (B) BUGGER OFF 1972 DANDELION 2310 231
STUART BARNHAM B (12 (1) 1966/71 (2) 1973 /76
STEVE REVELL D (1
MIKE SWEENEY V (2 WAYNE JACKSON B (2 ROBIN GOODWIN D (2

S237 **STADIUM DOGS** S237

PETE COUSINS B V (A (A) WHAT'S NEXT 1978 MAGNET MAG 5025
PAUL GRIFFITHS G V (A
STAN PEARCE D (A JONATHAN PERKINS K V (A KIRK THORN G V (A KEVIN WILKINSON D (A

S237A **STAINED GLASS** S237A

(A) CRAZY HORSE ROADS 19 CAPITOL ST 154
(B) AURORA 19 CAPITOL ST 242

S238 **STAINLESS STEEL** S238

(A) CAN CAN 1978 EMI UK EMC 3259 WB US 3274

S238A **STALLION** S238A

WALLY DAMRICK V K SYN(A (A) STALLION 1977 CASABLANCA UK CAL2014 US 7040
JORG GONZALEZ B V (A (B) HEY EVERYBODY 19 CASABLANCA US 7083
LARRY THOMPSON D (A
STEVE STEPHENSON SAX (A DON BUZZARD STEEL (A PAUL VASTOLA SYN (A BRUCE FOWLER TROM(A
STAN ROGERS TROM (A JIM OATTS TPT (A AL WING SAX (A CHUCK SNEIDENER SAX (A
DIK DARNELL V (A DANNY O'NEIL G V (A BUDDY STEPHENS V PERC(A JOHN MACY STEEL(A
PATTY GREER HARP (A DAVE KAHN TROM (A WALT FOWLER TPT (A TOM HOWARD TPT (A
STEVE FOWLER SAX (A

S238B **STAIRSTEP** S238B

(A) 2ND RESURRECTION 1976 DARK HORSE US 22004

S238C **TERRY STAMP** S238C

TERRY STAMP V (A (A) EASTSTICKS 1975 A&M UK AMLH 63329
OLLIE HALSALL K G (A
TONY NEWMAN D (A HERBIE FLOWERS B (A MIKE MORAN K (A ALAN SPENNER B (A
JIM AVORY B (A

S239 **STAMPEDERS** S239

RONNIE KING (ALL (A) STAMPEDERS 1972 REGAL ZONOPHONE UK SLPZ 1032
BOB ADDUONO HRNS (E (B) SWEET CITY WOMAN 1973 BELL US 6068
RICH DODSON (ALL (C) FROM THE FIRE 1974 REGAL ZONOPHONE UK SLRZ 1039
KIM BERLY (ALL (D) NEWDAY 1975 EMI UK INS 3003
GIBBY LACASSA PERC (E (E) HIT THE ROAD 1976 QUALITY US QLP 1001
GUY MARCHI HRNS (E
RANDY MARCHI HRNS (E

S240 **STANDELLS** S240

LARRY TAMBLYN K V (C (A) DIRTY WATER 196 TOWER US ST5027
TONY VALENTINO G (C (B) WHY PICK ON ME 196 TOWER US ST5044
GARY LANE ((C) HOT ONES 196 TOWER US ST5049
DICK DODD D (C (D) TRY IT 196 TOWER US ST5098
DAVE BURKE G B (C (E) LIVE & OUT OF SIGHT 196 SUNSET US 5136
(F) IN PERSON AT P Js 196 LIBERTY US LST 7384

S241 **MICHAEL STANLEY** S241

MICHAEL STANLEY G V (ALL (A) ROSEWOOD BITTERS 1973 TUMBLEWEED TW 3505
RICK BELL SAX (J (B) MICHAEL STANLEY 1974 TUMBLEWEED TW 106
JONAH KOSLEN G V (DEFG (C) FRIENDS & LEGENDS 1975 MCA MCA 372
DANNY PECCHIO B V (DEFG (D) YOU BREAK IT YOU BOUGHT IT 1975 EPIC US 33492
TOMMY DOBECK D (DEFGHJ (E) LADIES CHOICE 1976 EPIC US 33917
BOB PELANDER K (FGHJ (F) STAGE PASS 1977 EPIC US 34661
GARY MARKASKI G (GHJ (G) CABIN FEVER 1978 ARISTA US 4182 UK SPART 1066
KEVIN RALEIGH K V (HJ (H) HEARTLAND 1980 EMI UK AML 3015 US 17040
MICHAEL GISMONDI B (HJ (I) GREATEST HITS 1979 ARISTA US 4236
MUTT LANGE B V (G (J) NORTH COAST 1981 CAPITOL US 17056
DARRYL TOOKES V (J
CURTIS KING V (J YVONNE LEWIS V (J ED KRAMER V (J

S242 PAUL STANLEY S242

PAUL STANLEY V G B(A (A) PAUL STANLEY 1978 CASABLANCA NBLP7123
BOB KULICK G (A
RICHIE FONTANA D (A CRAIG KRAMPF D (A CARMINE APPICE D (A MARIA VIDAL V (A
DIANA GRASSELLI V (A MIRIAM NAOMI VALLE V (A STEVE BUSLOWE B (A ERIC NELSON B (A
DOUG KATSAROS PNO (A STEVE LACEY G (A PEPPI CASTRO V (A

S243 VIV STANSHALL S243

VIV STANSHALL V WIND(AB1 (A) MEN OPENING UMBRELLAS AHEAD 1974 WB UK K56052
BUBS WHITE G (A1 (B) SIR HENRY AT RAWLINSON END 1978 CHARISMA UK CAS 1139
STEVE WINWOOD B ORG(AB (C) TEDDY BOYS DONT KNIT 1981 CHARISMA UK CAS 1153
JIM CUOMO WIND (B (1) BIG GRUNT 1969
GASPAR LAWAL PERC V(A
NEIL INNES K G (A JIM CAPALDI D (A DEREK QUINN PERC (A RIC GRECH VLN (A
REBOP K BAAH PERC (A DORIS TROY V (A MADELINE BELL V (A BARRY ST JOHN V (A
AYUS APE V (A GANI V (A IAN WALLACE D (1 DENNIS COWAN B (1
ROGER RUSKIN SPEAR SAX (1 FRED MUNT (1 ZOOT MONEY PNO (JULIAN SMEDLEY B MAND(B
JIM FRENCH V HRNS(B PETE MOSS ACC FDL (B

S243A HOLLY STANTON S243A

HOLLY STANTON V (A (A) TEMPTATION 1981 SOLIS SMOKE US WB 9004
JOHN REWIND K G (A
BILLY CARMASSI D (A MICKEY RAZOR D (A J D SHARP K (A GREG SMITH G (A
ALEX BENDAHAN G (A

S244 STAR PARK S244

COLIN MOULDING B ((NO RECORDS)
ANDY PARTRIDGE G (
TERRY CHAMBERS D (DAVE CARTNER G (STEVE HUTCHINS V (JOHNNY PERKINS K (

S245 STARBUCK S245

BRUCE BLACKMAN K V (BC (A) MOONLIGHT FEELS RIGHT 1976 PRIVATE STOCK US 2013 1008
JIMMY COBB B V (BC (B) ROCK'N'ROLL ROCKET 1977 PRIVATE STOCK US 2027 UK 1023
KEN CRYSLER D (BC (C) SEARCHING FOR A THRILL 1978 UA US LA918 UK UAS 30221
SLOAN HAYES K V (B
DARRYL KUTZ G V (B DAVID SHAVER G V (CB BO WAGNER PNO (B JOHN WALKER G V (C
JOHN FRISTOE G V (C

S246 STARCASTLE S246

STEPHEN HAGLER G V (ABCD (A) STARCASTLE 1976 EPIC US 33914 UK 81347
GARY STRATER B V (ABCD (B) FOUNTAINS OF LIGHT 1977 EPIC US 34375 UK 81665
HERB SCHILDT K (ABC (C) CITADEL 1977 EPIC US 34935 UK 82232
STEPHEN TASSTER D V (ABC (D) REAL TO REEL 1978 EPIC US 35441 UK 82916
MATTHEW STEWART G V (B
TERRY LUTTRELL V (B

S247 STARDRIVE S247

ROBERT MASON SYN (AB (A) INTERGALATIC TROT 1973 ELEKTRA US EKS75058 UK K42140
JAIME AUSTRIA B (AB (B) STARDRIVE 1974 CBS US 33047
BRUCE DITMAS PERC (A
HARVEY SARCH G (AB MICHAEL BRECKER SAX (A STEPHEN GADD D (A HOWARD REGO D (B

S248 STARDUST S248

(A) STARDUST 1977 SATRIL SATL 4008

S249 ALVIN STARDUST S249

ALVIN STARDUST V (ALL (A) UNTOUCHABLE 1974 MAGNET UK MAG 5001
(B) ALVIN STARDUST 1974 MAGNET UK MAG 5004
(C) ROCK WITH ALVIN 1975 MAGNET UK MAG 5007
(D) GREATEST HITS 1977 MAGNET UK MAG 4002
(E) ROCK ON WITH ALVIN 1980 MFP UK 50464

S249A STARFIGHTERS S249A

STEVE BURTON V (A (A) STARFIGHTERS 1981 JIVE HOP 200
STEVE YOUNG G (A
PAT HAMBLY G (A DOUG DENNIS B (A STEVE BAILEY D (A

S249B STARF*CKERS S249B

OLE FRO (A (A) VOGT DEM FOR EFTERLIGNINGER 1978 CBS DK 83511
THOMAS GRUE (A
JESS STAEHR (A KIM LARGEN (A STIG MOLLER (A KEN GUDMAND (A

S249C STARFYRE S249C

JOHN W EDWARDS K V TPT(ABCD (A) STARFYRE 1977 AI US 0016
EUGENE J HOLDT K V (ABC (B) HERE WE GO AGAIN 1978 AI US 0016
EDWARD ABRIL SAX (ABC (C) MUSIC AFTER MIDNIGHT 1979 AI US 0021
ROSI HOFFNER V (A (D) LAY IT ON THE LINE 1981 AI US 0028
HOWARD TAYLOR SAX G V(A
SANTOS HERNANDEZ G V (A JOEY ROSELES B G V(A TERRY ROSALES D (A ALAN FOSTER K V (BC
NEIL McQUEEN K V (D BILL HUDSPETH SAX (D KAREN BURGHARD V VLN(BC KELLY LOVEGROVE V VLN(D
STEVE CHRISTIANSEN G CLAR(AB JAMES GIUSTI G B (BC RUSS McCALLEY G V (D BOB CRAVEN G V (ABC
CAREY CLELAND G (D JIM CURRENT G V FLT (CD TUCKER BURLING B G (CD TROY MARHN B G V(D
BOB SPRAGUE D (BC CURT TANTILLO D V (D RICHARD TUCKER PERC (CD

S250 STARGARD S250

ROCHELLE RUNNELS V K (ABC (A) STARGARD 1978 MCA UK MCF2834 US 2321
DEBRA ANDERSON V (ABC (B) WHAT YOU WAITING FOR 1978 MCA UK MCF2859 US 3046
JANICE C WILLIAMS V (ABC (C) CHANGING OF THE GARD 1979 WB US BSK3386 UK K56746
KENI BURKE B (C (D) BACK TO BACK 1980 WB US 3456 UK K56854
VERDINE WHITE B (C
BEVERLEY ASHBY HARP (C BUTCH AZEVEDO D (C LARRY TOLBERT D (C JOSEPH BAKER G (C
CHARLES FEARING G (C ROBERT PALMER G (C MARK DAVIS K (C DEAN GANT K (C
ROBERT WRIGHT K (C EDDIE BROWN PERC (C PAULINHO DA COSTA PERC (C DON MYRICK HRNS (C
LOUIS SATTERFIELD HRNS (C RAHEEM LEE MICHAEL DAVIS(C FRED JACKSON HRNS (C OSCAR BRASHAR HRNS (C
JEROME RICHARDSON HRNS (C GARNETT BROWN HRNS (C

S250A STARJETS S250A

PAUL BOWEN (A (A) GOD BLESS THE STARJETS 1979 EPIC US 36245 UK 83534
TERRY SHARPE (A
SEAN MARTIN (A LIAM L'ESTRANGE (A

S250B STARK NAKED S250B

PAUL VENIER V K PERC(A (A) STARK NAKED 1971 RCA US LSP 4592
LYNE BUNN V PERC(A
JIM MONAHAN G V (A JOHN FRAGOS D PERC(A TOM RUBINS B (A RICHARD BELSKIN G (A

S251 EDWIN STARR S251

EDWIN STARR V (ALL (A) SOUL MASTER 1969 TAMLA UK STML11094 US GORDY 931
L MIDDLETON G (L (B) 25 MILES 197 US GORDY 940
J ROBERTS B (L (C) WAR & PEACE 197 US GORDY 948
SPIKE K (L (D) INVOLVED 1972 TAMLA UK STML11199 US GORDY 956
R REED D (L (E) HITS OF EDWIN STARR 1974 TAMLA UK STML11209
M SINGER D (L (F) HELL UP IN HARLEM 1974 TAMLA UK STML11210 US TAMLA 802
E FLETCHER PERC (L (G) FREE TO BE MYSELF 1976 GRANITE US 1005
K PEACHY HRNS (L (H) AFTERNOON SUNSHINE 1977 GTO UK GTLP 019
E HILL HRNS (L (J) EDWIN STARR 1977 20THCENTURY UK 538 GTO US 518
A HAMILTON HRNS (L (K) CLEAN 1979 20TH CENTURY UK BT 559
CURT SLETTEN HRNS (L (L) HAPPY RADIO 1979 20TH CENTURY UK BT 591
JOEL PESKIN FLT (L (M) STRONGER THAN YOU THINK I AM 1980 20TH CENTURY UK BT 615
HARRY KIM FLT (L ( ) JUST WE TWOO 19 GORDY US 945
MAURICE YOUNG V (M
H PRESTON FLT (L D STOUT FLT (L DAVID SHIELDS B (M JAMES GADSON D (M
MELVIN D WEBB D (M DAVID T WALKER G (M HOWARD FEITEN G (M RALPH E HAMMER G (M
GLENNIS JONES G (M CLARK E SPANGLER SYN (M JIMMY McAFEE B (M JOHN J BARNES K (M
LARRY FARROW K (M RONALD COLEMAN K (M EARL VAN DYKE K (M RICK McAFEE K (M
EDDIE BROWN PERC (M LUKE METOYER PERC (M LUTHER WATERS V (LM CLIFTON CURTIS V M
ORRIN WATERS V (LM MAXINE WILLARD V (LM JULIA TILLMAN V (LM JERRY PETERSON SAX(M
WILLIAM CLARK V (M MONROE WRIGHT V (M

S252 RINGO STARR S252

RINGO STARR V PERC D (ALL (A) SENTIMENTAL JOURNEY 1970 APPLE UK PCS 7101 US 3365
JOHN LENNON V PNO(CFD (B) BEACOUPS OF BLUES 1970 APPLE UK PAS 10002 US 3368
GEORGE HARRISON G (C (C) RINGO 1973 APPLE UK PCTC 252 US 3413
PAUL McCARTNEY K V SAX (CF (D) GOODNIGHT VIENNA 1974 APPLE UK PLS 7168 US 3417
KLAUS VOORMANN B (CFD (E) BLAST FROM YOUR PAST 1975 APPLE UK PCS 7170 US 3422
BILLY PRESTON K (CD (F) ROTOGRAVURE 1976 POLYDOR UK 2302 040 US ATCO 18193
JIM KELTNER D (CDF (G) RINGO THE FOURTH 1977 POLYDOR UK 2310 556 US ATCO 19108
MILT HOLLAND PERC (C (H) BAD BOY 1978 POLYDOR UK 2310 599 US PORTRAIT35378
LON VAN EATON PERC (CGD (I) RINGO STARR 1980 MFP 50508
DERREK VAN EATON PERC (CD (J) STOP & SMELL THE ROSES 1981
LEVON HELM MAND (CF (NB) RE ISSUES OF APPLE RECORD ARE ON PARLOPHONE/CAPITOL SAME NUMBERS
HARRY NILSSON V (CFD DIFFERENT PREFIX
CHARLIE DANIELS G (B
MARTHA REEVES V (C LINDA McCARTNEY V (CF RICHARD PERRY V (C MELISSA MANCHESTER V(FG
JESSE ED DAVIS G (DF VAN DYKE PARKS V K (F JOE ESPOSITO V (FG SNEAKY PETE STEEL(F
MARC BOLAN G (C TOM SCOTT HRNS (C VINI PONCIA G V (CFG JAMES BOOKER PNO (C
NICKY HOPKINS PNO (CD JIMMY CALVERT G (C BOBBY KEYS SAX (CD ROBBIE ROBERTSON G (CD
RICK DANKO FDL (C GARTH HUDSON ACC (C MERRY CLAYTON V (C STEVE CROPPER G (CD
TOM HENSLEY PNO (C CHUCK FINDLEY HRNS (CD ROBERT GREENIDGE PERC (F JOHN JARVIS K (F
COOKER LOPRESTI B (F DUITCH HELMER V (FG ERIC CLAPTON G V (F PAUL STALLWORTH B (F
DANNY KORTCHMAR G V (FG DR JOHN K V (FD PETER FRAMPTON (F DAVID SPINOZZA G (G
JEFF MIRANOV G (G JOHN TROPEA G (G DON GROLNICK K (G TONY LEVIN B (G
HUGH McDONALD B (G STEVE GADD D (G CORNELL DUPREE G (G RICHARD TEE K (G
NICK MARRERO PERC (G JEFF GUTCHEON K (G MARIETTA WATERS V (G MAXINE ANDERSON V (G
DAVID LASLEY V (G ROBIN CLARK V (G DEBRA GRAY V (G LUTHER VANDROSS V (G
JIM GILSTRAP V (GD DICK FEGY G (G DAVID BROMBERG FDL G (CG CHUCK RAINEY B (G
BRIE HOWARD V (G LYNN PITNEY V (G ARNOLD McCULLER V (G REBECCA LOUIS V (G
BETTE MIDLER V (G RANDY BRECKER HRNS(G MICHAEL BRECKER HRNS (G KEN BISCHEL SYN (G
DON BROOKS HCA (G CHUCK HOWARD G (B SORRELLS PICKARD G (B JERRY REED G (B
PETE DRAKE STEEL(B CHARLIE McCOY HCA (B ROY HUSKY B (B BUDDY HARMAN (B
DAVE KIRBY (B JERRY KENNEDY (B JERRY SHOOK (B GEORGE RICHEY (B
GROVER LAVENDER (B JIM BAUCHANAN (B D J FONTANA D (B BEN KEITH (B
JEANNIE KENDAL (B ALVIN ROBINSON G (D TREVOR LAWRENCE SAX (D LOU McCREARY SAX (D
STEVE MADAIO TPT (D VINI PONCIA V (D CLYDIE KING V (D LINDA LAWRENCE V (D
JOE GREENE (D RICHARD PERRY (D CYNTHIA WEBB V (D IRA HAWKINS V (D
DAVID FOSTER K (D CARL FORTIA ACC (D THE BLACKBERRIES V (D TOM HENSLEY K (D
LINCOLN MAYORGA K (D DENNIS COFFEY G (D ELTON JOHN K (D JAMES NEWTON HOWARD SYN(D

S253 STARRY EYED & LAUGHING S253

TONY POOLE G V K(AB (A) STARRY EYED & LAUGHING 1974 CBS UK 80450
IAIN WHITMORE B V (AB (B) THOUGHT TALK 1975 CBS US 33837 UK 80907
MIKE WACKFORD D (AB
ROY CARR BONGO(A ROSS McGEENEY G V (AB PAUL TURNER D (DAVID POMEROY B V (
ARTHUR MAY G V (B J COLE STEEL(A RAY JACKSON MAND (A PETER WOODS K (A
RUSS BALLARD PNO (A DAN LOGGINS HCA (B JEFF BANNISTER K (B MICHAEL GORE CELLO(B
COLIN WALKER CELLO(B FRANK RICOTTI VIBES(B PETE ZORN SAX (B

S253A STARS & STIPS S253A

CESAR ZUIDERWIJK D (A (A) NEVERGREEN 1976 POLYDOR UK 2925 041
BERTUS BORGERS SAX V(A
RINUS GERRITSEN B (A ROBERT JAN STIPS K PERC(A

S254 STARZ S254

BRENDAN HARKIN G (ALL (A) STARZ 1976 CAPITOL 11539
RICHIE RANNO G (ALL (B) VIOLATION 1977 CAPITOL 11617
MIKE LEE SMITH V (ALL (C) ATTENTION SHOPPERS 1978 CAPITOL 11730
PETE SWEVAL B (ALL (D) COLISEUM ROCK 1979 CAPITOL 11861
JOE X DUBE D (ALL (E) STARZ LIVE (PROMO) 1978 US SPRO8857
BOBBY MESSANNO G (D

S254A STATES S254A

JIMMY McDONNELL G (A — (A) STATES — 1979 CHRYSALIS CHR 1229
DOMINIC GERMANO B (A — (B) PICTURE ME WITH YOU — 19 BOARDWALK US 37180
STEPHEN CHANDLER G V (A
BARRY SCOTT G V (A — ROBERT SCHINDLER K (A — JIMMY WILKINS D (A — GARY COLEMAN PERC(A
JOHN JANSEN PROD(A — C B SYN G V (A

S254B CANDI STATON S254B

CANDI STATON V (ALL — (A) CANDI STATON — 19 FAME US 1800
CORNELL DIUPREE G (F — (B) STAND BY YOUR MAN — 19 FAME US 4202
RON MILLER G (F — (C) YOUNG HEARTS RUN FREE — 11976 WB UK K56360
CAROL COLMAN B (F — (D) MUSIC SPEAKS LOUDER THAN WORDS — 1977 WB UK K56259
CRUSHER BENNETT PERC(F — (E) HOSE OF LOVE — 1978 WB UK K56510
RAY CHEW K (F — (F) CHANCE — 1979 WB UK K56641
CHRISTOPHER PARKER D (F — (G) CANDI — 1980 WB UK K56803
STAN LUCAS G (F
JAMES SMITH K (F — OLLIE BROWN D (E — SCOTT EDWARDS B (E — TIMMA I G (E
DERYLL INMAN G (E — DAVE CRAWFORD K V (E — RAY PARKER G (E — SONNY BURKE K (E
JIM GILSTRAP V (E — CAROLYN DENNIS V (E

S255 STATUS QUO S255

FRANCIS ROSSI G V (ALL — (A) PICTURESQUE MATCHSTICKABLE — 1968 PYE NSPL18220
RICK PARFITT K G V(ALL — (B) SPARE PARTS — 1968 PYE NSPL18301
JOHN COUGHLAN D (ALL — (C) MESSAGES FROM THE STATUS QUO — 1968 CADET LSP 315
ALAN LANCASTER V B G (ALL — (D)STATUS QUOTATION — 1969 MARBLE ARCH MAL 1193
(E) MA KELLYS GREASY SPOON — 1970 PYE UK NSPL18344 US JANUS 3018
(F) DOG OF TWO HEAD — 1971 PYE UK NSPL18371 US JANUS 3301
(G) BEST OF STATUS QUO — 1972 PYE NSPL18402
ROY LYNES K (PQSTXWY — (I) GOLDEN HOUR — 1973 PYE GH 556
ROB YOUNG HCA (FIKORZc — (I) PILE DRIVER — 1973 VERTIGO 6360 082 US A&M 4381
JIMMY HOROWITZ PNO (I — (J) HELLO — 1974 VERTIGO 6360 098 US A&M 3615
BRUCE FOSTER K (F — (K) QUO — 1974 VERTIGO 9102 001 US A&M 3649
STEWART BLANDMER SAX (J — (L) ON THE LEVEL — 1975 VERTIGO 9102 002 US CAPITOL11381
JOHN MEALING PNO (J — (M) GOLDEN HOUR — 1975 PYE GH 604
DAVID KATZ HRNS (V — (N) STATUS QUO — 1975 VERTIGO QUO 13 US CAPITOL11509
STEVE FARR SAX (J — (O) POP CHRONIK VOL 5 — 1975 PYE 87099
BUD REVO V (V — (P) THE REST OF STATUS QUO — 1976 PYE PKL 5546
FRANK RICOTTI PERC (UV — (Q) BLUE FOR YOU — 1976 VERTIGO 9102 006
ANDY BOWN K (JORUVZc — (R) LIVE — 1977 VERTIGO 6641 580 US CAPITOL11623
BERNIE FROST V (c — (S) STATUS QUO FILE — 1977 PYE FLD 005
JOY YATES V (V — (T) PICTURES OF MATCHSTICK MEN — 1977 HALLMARK HMA 257
GRASS V (F — (U) ROCKIN ALL OVER THE WORLD — 1977 VERTIGO 9102 014 US CAPITOL11749
TOM PARKER K (K — (V) IF YOU CANT STAND THE HEAT — 1978 VERTIGO 9102 027
JAQUIE SULLIVAN V (V — (W) COLLECTION — 1978 PICKWICK PDA 046
(X) STATUS QUO — 1978 HALLMARK HMA 260
(Y) IN MY CHAIR — 1979 MODE FR 9018
(Z) WHATEVER YOU WANT — 1979 VERTIGO 9102 037
(a) MEAN GIRL — 1979 MODE FR 9053
(b) JUST FOR THE RECORD — 1979 PYE NSPL18607
(c) JUST SUPPOSIN' — 1980 VERTIGO 6302 057
(d) GOLD BARS — 1980 VERTIGO QUOTV1
(e) NEVER TOO LATE — 1981 VERTIGO 6302 104
( ) STATUS QUO — 198= PICKWICK UK 8035
( ) SPOTLIGHT — 1981 PRT UK 1010
( ) NOW HEAR THIS — 1981 RIVA US 7402
( ) FRESH QUOTE — 1981 PRT DOW 2
( ) VOL 1 (1972/74) — 1981 VERTIGO 7215 038

S257 STEALERS WHEEL S257

GERRY RAFFERTY G V (ABC — (A) STEALERS WHEEL — 1973 A&M US 4377 UK AMLH68121
JOE EGAN K V (ABC — (B) FERGUSLIE PARK — 1974 A&M US 4419 UK AMLH68209
RAB NOAKES (— (C) RIGHT OR WRONG — 1975 A&M US 4517 UK AMLH68293
ROGER BROWN (— (D) STUCK IN THE MIDDLE WITH YOU (COMP197 A&M US 4708 UK AMLH64708
IAN CAMPBELL B (— (E) BEST OF — 1981 MFP UK 50501
STEVE GREGORY SAX (B
PAUL PILNICK G (A — ROD COOMBES D (A — TONY WILLIAMS B (A — DELISLE HARPER B (
LUTHER GROSVENOR G (— ANDY STEELE D PERC(BC — DAVE WINTOUR B (C — CHRIS MERCER SAX(BC
CHRIS NEILL HCA (BC — BERNIE HOLLAND G (BC — HUGH BURNS G (C — DAVID BRIGGS K (C
GERALDINE JOSEPHINE K G(C — PETER ROBINSON K (B — GARY TAYLOR B SYN(B — JOE JAMMER G (B
MIKE STOLLER K (B — CORKY HALE HARP (B

S258 STEAMHAMMER S258

KIERAN WHITE HCA G V(ABC — (A) STEAMHAMMER — 1968 CBS US 26490 UK 63611
MARTIN PUGH G V (ABCD — (A) STEAMHAMMER — 1970 REFLECTION REFL1
PETE SEARS PNO (A — (A) STEAMHAMMER — 1970 BELLAPHON GER RI 15134
STEVE DAVY B V (ABC — (B) STEAMHAMMER MARK 2 — 197 CBS UK 63694
HAROLD McNAIR FLT (A — (B) STEAMHAMMER MARK 2 — 1970 BELLAPHON GER RI 14012
MICK BRADLEY D (CD — (C) MOUNTAINS — 1970 METRONOME 15 376
LOUIS CENNAMO B (CD — (C) MOUNTAINS — 1971 BRAIN 201 006
KEITH NELSON BAN (C — (D) SPEECH — 1972 BRAIN 1009 0040 054
MIKE RUSHTON (A — (E) THIS IS (CD) (DBL) — 1972 BRAIN 201 042 0021 043
MICKY WALLER (
MARTIN QUITTENTON G (A — STEVE JOLLIFFE WIND V(B

S259 STEAMPACKET S259

BRIAN AUGER K V (A — (A) FIRST OF THE SUPERGROUPS — 1977 CHARLY UK CR 30020
JULIE DRISCOLL V (A — (B) THE STEAMPACKET — 197 BYT FR 529 706
VIC BRIGGS G (A — (C) PLACES & FACES — 197 BYG FR 529 906
RICKY BROWN B (A
MICK WALLER D (A — LONG JOHN BALDRY V (A — ROD STEWART V (A — PETER GREEN G (
MICK FLEETWOOD D (

S259A WALTER STEDING S259A

WALTER STEDING (A — (A) WALTER STEDDING — 1980 RED STAR 101
ROBERT FRIPP G (A
CHRIS STEIN (A RICHARD LLOYD G (A JOEY PINTER B G (A RICHARD LLOYD G (A
JAN MAREK PAKULSKI B (A JERRY RYAN D (A

S260 STEEL MILL S260

TERRY WILLIAMS G (A — (A) GREEN EYED GOD — 1975 PENNYFARTHING UK PELS 549
JEFF WATTS B (A
CHRIS MARTIN D (A DAVE MORRIS K V (A JOHN CHALLENGER WIND (A

S261 STEEL PULSE S261

DAVID HINDS G V (ABC — (A) HANDSWORTH REVOLUTION — 1978 ISLAND UK ILPS 9502
BASIL GABBIDON G V (ABC — (B) TRIBUTE TO THE MARTYRS — 1979 ISLAND UK ILPS 9568
RONNIE McQUEEN B (ABC — (C) CAUGHT YOU/REGGAE FEVER — 1980 ISLAND UK ILPS 9613
SELWYN BROWN K V (ABC
FONSO MARTIN V PERC(ABC STEVE NESBITT D (ABC MICHAEL RILEY V PERC(A RICO RODRIGUES TROM(B
GODFREY MADURA SAX (ABC DICKAGE HRNS (B

S261A STEEL RIVER S261A

RAY ANGROVE D (AB — (A) A BETER ROAD — 19 EVOLUTION 3006
TONY DUMMING G (AB — (B) WHEIGHING HEAVY — 19 EVOLUTION 2018
LAFE BUCKNER PERC V(A
ROB COCKELL B (AB JOHN DUDGEON G V (AB ROBERT FORRESTER K (AB HEDGEHOGS PERC V(A

S261B JAN STEELE/JOHN CAGE S261B

JAN STEELE K (A — (A) VOICES & INSTRUMENTS — 1976 OBSCURE UK OBS5
JANET SHERBOURNE V K (A
FRED FRITH G (A STUART JONES G (A KEVIN EDWARDS VIBES(A ROBERT WYATT V (A
STEVE BERESFORD B (A PHIL BUCKLE PERC (A UTAKO IKEDA FLT (A DOMINIC MULDOWNEY VLA(A
MARTIN MAYES K (A CARLA BLEY V (A ARTHUR RUTHERFORD PERC (A RICHARD BERNAS K PERC(A

S262 STEELY DAN S262

WALTER BECKER B V G(ALL — (A) YOU GOTTA WALK IT(SOUNDTRACK) — 1971 VISA US 7005 UK SPARK 78 124
DONALD FAGEN K V (ALL — (B) CANT BUY A THRILL — 1972 ABC US 758 UK PROBE SPB1062
DENNY DIAS G (ABCDEFG — (B) CANT BUY A THRILL — 1974 ABC UK ABCL 5024
VALERIE SIMPSON V (J — (B) CANT BUY A THRILL — 1982 MCA US 37040
JOE DISCEPOLO D (A — (C) COUNTDOWN TO ECSTASY — 1973 ABC US 779 UK PROBE SPB1079
JIM HODDER D (BCD — (C) COUNTDOWN TO ECSTASY — 1974 ABC UK ABCL 5034
DAVID PALMER V K (BC — (C) COUNTDOWN TO ECSTACY — 1982 MCA RI UK 1664 US 37041
MICHAEL BRECKER SAX (J — (D) PRETZEL LOGIC — 1974 ABC US 808 UK PROBE SPBA6282
JEFF BAXTER G (BCD — (D) PRETZEL LOGIC — 1974 ABC UK ABCL 5045
RALPH MACDONALD PERC (J — (D) PRETZEL LOGIC — 198 MCA RI US 37042
JEFF PORCARO D (DEJ — (E) KATY LIED — 1975 ABC US 846 UK ABCL 5094
RON MOUNSEY PNO (J — (E) KATY LIED — 198 MCA US RI 37043
MIKE McDONALD V (EFGJ — (F) THE ROYAL SCAM — 1976 ABC US 931 UK ABCL 5161
ANTHONY JACKSON B (J — (F) THE ROYAL SCAM — 198 MCA US RI 37044
RICK DERRINGER G (CEJ — (G) AJA — 1977 ABC US 1006 UK ABCL 5225
ZACK SANDERS V (J — (G) AJA — 1981 MOBILE 033
ELLIOTT RANDALL G (BEF — (H) GREATEST HITS (DBL) — 1978 ABC US 1107 UK ABCD 616
FRANK FLOYD V (J — (H) GREATEST HITS — 1982 MCA UK MCLD 608
DEAN PARKS G (DEFG — (I) PLUS FOUR (EP) • — 1977 ABC UK ABE 12003
HUGH McCRACKEN G (EJ — (J) GAUCHO — 1980 MCA US 6102 UK MCF 3090
LARRY CARLTON G (EFGJ — (BG) CANT BUY A THRILL/AJA (CASS ONLY) — 1982 MCA UK 101
BEN BENAY G (CD — ( ) GOLD — 1982 MCA UK MCF 3145
GORDON GRODY V (J
DIVA GRAY V (J LEE RITENOUR G (G STEVE KHAN G (GJ JAY GRAYDON G (G
MICHAEL OMARTIAN K (DEG DAVID PAICH K (BDE VICTOR FELDMAN PERC K(BCDEFGJ ROYCE JONES V (C
CHUCK RAINEY B (EFGJ WILTON FELDER B (DE HAL BLAINE D (E TIM SCHMIT B V (DFG
PLAS JOHNSON SAX (DFG OLLIE MITCHELL TPT (D JEROME RICHARDSON SAX (BD LEW McCREARY HRNS (DG
ERNIE WATTS SAX (CD RAY BROWN B (C TOM SCOTT SAX (GJ WAYNE SHORTER SAX (G
PAUL HUMPHREY D (G CLYDIE KING V (BFG VANETTA FIELDS V (BFG SHIRLEY MATTHEWS V (BCEFG
REBECCA LOUIS V (G JOE SAMPLE K (GJ BERNARD PURDIE D (FGJ PETE CHRISTLIEB SAX (G
JIM HORN SAX (FG BILL PERKINS HRNS (EG JACKIE KELSO HRNS (G CHUCK FINDLEY HRNS(FG
SLYDE HYDE TROM (FG RICK MAROTTA D (FGJ PAUL GRIFFIN K V (FG DON GROLNICK K (FGJ
GARY COLEMAN PERC (FG ED GREENE D (G JIM KELTNER D (G SNOOKY YOUNG HRNS(B
MYRNA MATTHEWS V (CE PATRICIA HALL V (C JAMES ROLLESTON V (C MICHAEL FENELLY V (C
LANNY MORGAN SAX (C JOHN ROTELLA SAX (C BOB FINDLEY HRNS (F TUBBY BRUCE (D
STEVE GADD D (GJ JOHN KLEMMER HRNS (F JIM GORDON D (D CAROLYN WILLIS V (E
JIMMIE HASKELL HRNS (E PHIL WOODS HRNS (E ERROL BENNETT PERC (J MARK KNOPFLER G (J
DAVE TOFANI SAX (J DAVID SANBORN SAX (J RON CUBER SAX (J RANDY BRECKER HRNS (J
PAT REBILLOT K (J GEORGE MARGE CLAR (J HIRAM BULLOCK G (J WALTER KANE CLAR (J
LESLIE MILLER V (J NICHOLAS MARRERO PERC(J PATTI AUSTIN V (J WAYNE ANDRE TROM (J
TONI WINE V (J LANI GROVES V (J

S263 STEELEYE SPAN S263

ASHLEY HUTCHINGS B (ABCE — (A) HARK THE VILLAGE WAIT — 1970 RCA UK SF8113
TIM HART V G DULCIMER (ALL — (A) HARK THE VILLAGE WAIT — 1971 UA UK UAG 29160
MADDY PRIOR V (ALL — (A) HARK THE VILLAGE WAIT — 1974 MOONCREST UK CREST 22
GAY WOODS V CONC(A — (A) HARK THE VILLAGE WAIT — 1976 CHRYSALIS US 1120
TERRY WOODS G V MAND(A — (B) PLEASE TO SEE THE KING — 1971 B&C UK CAS 1029
MARTIN CARTHY G V (BCLO — (B) PLEASE TO SEE THE KING — 1974 MOONCREST UK CREST 8
PETER KNIGHT K V VLN (BCDEFGHJKP — (B) PLEASE TO SEE THE KING — 1976 CHRYSALIS US 1119
GERRY CONWAY D (A — (B) PLEASE TO SEE THE KING — 1976 BIG TREE US 2004
RICK KEMP B V (DEFGHJKLOP — (C) TEN MAN MOP — 1971 PEGASUS UK PEG 9
BOB JOHNSON G V (DEFGHJKP — (C) TEN MAN MOP — 1974 MOONCREST UK CREST 9
NIGEL PEGRUM D FLT(GHJKLP — (C) TEN MAN MOP — 1976 CHRYSALIS US 1121
JOHN KIRKPATRICK V ACC(LO — (D) BELOW THE SALT — 1972 CHRYSALIS CHR1008 GER 6307 508
DAVID BOWIE SAX (G — (E) INDIVIDUALLY & COLLECTIVELY(COMP) — 1972 CHARISMA UK CS5
PETER SELLERS V UKE(H — (F) PARCEL OF ROGUES — 1973 CHRYSALIS CHR 1046
DAVE MATTACKS D (A — (G) NOW WE ARE SIX — 1974 CHRYSALIS CHR1053 GER 6307 529
(H) COMMONERS CROWN — 1975 CHRYSALIS CHR1071 GER 6307 543
(I) ALMANACK (COMP) — 1973 CHARISMA UK CS12
(J) ALL AROUND MY HAT — 1975 CHRYSALIS CHR 1091
(K) ROCKET COTTAGE — 1976 CHRYSALIS CHR1123 GER 6307 584
(L) STORM FORCE 10 — 1977 CHRYSALIS CHR1151 GER 6307 615
(M) ORIGINAL MASTERS(COMP DBL) — 1977 CHRYSALIS US 2 1136 UK CJT 3
(M) ORIGINAL MASTERS — 1977 CHRYSALIS GER 6441 636
(N) TIME SPAN — 1977 MOONCREST UK CRD 1
(O) LIVE AT LAST — 1978 CHRYSALIS CHR 1199
(P) SAILS OF SILVER — 1980 CHRYSALIS CHR1304 GER 203 003
( ) STEELEYE SPAN — 1980 HALLMARK UK 3040

S263A **STEPASIDE** S263A

(A) SIT DOWN & RELAPSE — 1980 STEPASIDE STEP 001

PAUL ASHFORD B V (A
BRENNY BONASS G V (A
ROBBIE BRENNAN D V (A
DAVE KODAK K V (A

S263B **JIM STEINMAN** S263B

(A) BAD FOR GOOD — 1981 CBS UK 84361 US 36531

JIM STEINMAN V K(A
ROY BITTAN K (A
JOE STEFKO D (A
DAVEY JOHNSTONE G (A
MAX WEINBERG D (A
ROGER POWELL SYN (A
STEVE BUSLOWE B (A
LARRY FAST (A
KASIM SULTAN B V (A
JIMMY MAELEN PERC(A
KARLA DEVITO V (A
ALAN SCHWARTZBERG D (A
RORY DODD V (A
NEIL JASON (A
ELLEN FOLLEY V (A
TODD RUNDGREN G V (A
ERIC TROYER V (A

S264 **LEIGH STEPHENS** S264

(A) RED WEATHER — 1969 PHILIPS UK SBL7897
(B) CAST OF THOUSANDS — 1971 CHARISMA UK CAS 1040

LEIGH STEPHENS G V K(AB
PETE SEARS B (B
KEVIN WESTLAKE D (AB
MICK WALLER D (AB
DICK MORRISSEY SAX (B
TONY ASHTON PNO (B
ALIKI ASHMAN V (B
DAVE JACKSON SAX (B
ELIZABETH LEGWORTHY V (B
NICKY HOPKINS K (A
DAVE CASWELL TPT (B
ROY DYKE D (B
GLENN CORNICK B (B
PETER ROSS V (B
IAN STEWART (A
CHARLENE COLLINS V (B
DAVE QUINCY SAX (B
JEFF PEACH SAX (B
PAUL MAINTENANCE V G (B
BOB ANDREWS PNO (B
KIM GARDNER B (B
NOEL NORRIS TPT (B
LYLE JENKINS SAX (B
TREVOR OP V G (B

S265 **STEPPENWOLF** S265

(A) STEPPENWOLF — 1968 DUNHILL US 50029 UK STATESIDE 5020
(A) STEPPENWOLF — 19 MCA GER 201 578
(A) STEPPENWOLF — 1968 RCA UK RD 7974
(B) THE SECOND — 1968 DUNHILL US 50037 UK STATESIDE 5003
(C) AT YOUR BIRTHDAY PARTY — 1969 DUNHILL US 50053 UK STATESIDE 5011
(D) EARLY STEPPENWOLF — 1969 DUNHILL US 50060 UK STATESIDE 5015
(E) MONSTER — 1970 DUNHILL US 50066 UK STATESIDE 5021
(F) STEPPENWOLF LIVE — 1970 DUNHILL US 50075 UK STATESIDE 5029
(F) STEPPENWOLF LIVE — 197 ABC RI UK ABCL5007
(G) STEPPENWOLF 7 — 1970 DUNHILL US 50090 UK PROBE SPBA6254
(H) FOR LADIES ONLY — 1970 DUNHILL US 50110 UK PROBE SPBA6260
(J) STEPPENWOLF GOLD — 1971 DUNHILL US 50099 UK PROBE SPB 1033
(J) STEPPENWOLF GOLD — 197 ABC UK ABCL8613
(K) REST IN PEACE — 1972 DUNHILL US 50124 UK PROBE SPB 1059
(L) 16 GREATEST HITS — 1974 DUNHILL US 50135 UK PROBE SPB 1071
(L) 16 GREATEST HITS — 197 ABC UK RI ABCL5028
(M) SLOW FLUX — 1974 EPIC US 33093 UK 80358
(N) HOUR OF THE WOLF — 1975 EPIC US 33583 UK 69151
(O) SKULLDUGGERY — 1976 EPIC US 34120 UK 81328
(P) MASTERS OF ROCK — 1975 ABC EURO 054 95147
(Q) THE ABC COLLECTION — 197 ABC US 30008
(R) REBORN TO BE WILD — 1977 EPIC US 34382
(S) 16 GREAT PERFORMANCES — 197 ABC US 4001
(T) BEST — 1979 PICKWICK US 3603
(U) GOLD — 1980 MCA UK 1502

JOHN KAY G V (123456HDMNO
TOM SCOTT HRNS (N
GEORGE BIONDO B V (456HMNO
JERRY EDMONTON D (123456HMNOD
BOBBY COCHRAN G (56MNO
WAYNE COOK K (60
GOLDY McJOHN K (12345HD
JOHN MORGAN B (2
RUSHTON MOREVE B (1
NICK ST NICHOLAS B (3D
LARRY BYROM G (34
MICHAEL MONARCH G (12
(1) 1967
(2) 1967
(3) 1969
(4) 1970
(5) 1974
(6) 1974
GABRIEL MEKLER PROD (A
KENT HENRY (H
ANDY CHAPIN K (N
MARS BONFIRE G (D

S265A **STEPSON** S265A

(A) STEPSON — 197 ABC 826

JEFF HAWKS V (A
BRUCE HAUSER B V (A
JOEY NEWMAN G V (A
DON GALLUCI HCA (A
LEN FAGAN D (A
JIMMY GREENSPOON K (A
JEFF SIMMONS HCA (A

S265B **STERLING** S265B

(A) CITY KIDS — 1980 A&M 4807 US UK AMLH64807

S266 **CAT STEVENS** S266

(A) MATTHEW & SON — 1967 DERAM UK SML1004 US 18005
(B) NEW MASTERS — 1968 DERAM UK SML1018 US 18010
(AB) MATTHEW /NEW MASTERS — 197 DERAM US 18005
(C) WORLD OF CAT STEVENS — 1970 DECCA UK SPA 93
(D) MONA BONE JAKON — 1970 ISLAND UK ISLP 9118 US A&M 4260
(E) TEA FOR THE TILLERMAN — 1971 ISLAND UK ILPS 9135 US A&M 4280
(F) TEASER & THE FIRECAT — 1971 ISLAND UK ILPS 9154 US A&M 4313
(G) CATCH BULL AT FOUR — 1972 ISLAND UK ILPS 9206 US A&M 4365
(H) FOREIGNER — 1973 ISLAND UK ILPS 9240 US A&M 4391
(I) THE BEST OF — 1973 TELDEC EURO 17009
(J) BUDDAH & THE CHOCOLATE BOX — 1974 ISLAND UK ILPS 9274 US A&M 3623
(K) VIEW FROM THE TOP(A+B) — 1974 DERAM UK DPA3019/20
(L) NUMBERS — 1975 ISLAND UK ILPS 9370 US A&M 4555
(M) GREATEST HITS — 1975 ISLAND UK ILPS 9310 US A&M 4519
(N) IZITSO — 1977 ISLAND UK ILPS 9451 US A&M 4702
(O) BACK TO EARTH — 1978 ISLAND UK ILPS 9565 US A&M 4735
( ) CATS CRADLE — 1978 LONDON US 50010
( ) VERY YOUNG & EARLY SONGS — 19 DERAM US 18061
( ) FIRST CUT IS THE DEEPEST — 1981 ROCK ECHOES TAB 25

CAT STEVENS V G K(ALL
ALUN DAVIES G V (DEFGJL
GERRY CONWAY D V (FGHLJ
JEAN ROUSSEL K (GHJLN
BRUCE LYNCH B (JLN
JIM RYAN G (J
MARK WARNER G (J
ROLAND HARKER BANJ (J
JOHN RYAN B (DE
HARVEY BURNS D (DEF
PETER GABRIEL FLT (D
JACK ROSTEIN VLN (E
LARRY STEELE B PERC (F
ANDREAS TOUMAZIS (FG
ANGELOS HATZIPAVLI (F
ALAN JAMES B (G
LINDA LEWIS V (G
BERNARD PURDIE D (H
DAVID SANBORN SAX (L
PHIL UPCHURCH (H
PAUL MARTINEZ (H
TASHA THOMAS V (H
CHICK COREA K (N
BARRY BECKETT (N
SUZANNE LYNCH (N
BRODERICK SMITH (N
BARBARA INGRAM (N
GORDIE FLEMING ACC (L
HERBIE FLOWERS B (H
JIM JOHNSON (N
ELKIE BROOKS V (N
PETE CARR (N
WELDON MYRICK (N
MARJORIE LAGERWALL (N
RAY GOMEZ G (N
PATTI AUSTIN V (H
ANDY NEWMARK (N
ROGER HAWKINS D (N
TIM HENSON (N
REGGIE YOUNG (N
CARLA BENSON (N
SIMON NICOL G (L
BARBARA MASSEY V (H
BILL BERG (N
DAVID HOOD B (N
DAVID CAMPBELL (N
BARRY MORGAN (N
EVETTE BENTON (N
CHRIS BATERA PERC(L

S267 **JOHN STEVENS** S267

JOHN STEVENS D (ALL — (A) CHALLENGE — 1966 EYEMARK EMPL 1002
ALLAN HOLDSWORTH G (P — (B) KARYOBIN — 1968 ISLAND UK ILPS 9097
JEFF YOUNG K (PO — (C) SPONTANEOUS MUSIC ENSEMBLE(OLIV) — 1969 MARMALADE 608 008 + 2384 009
RON MATTHEWSON B (PD — (D) SOURCE FROM & TOWARDS — 1971 TANGENT UK TNGS 107
NICK STEPHENS B (MLO — (E) BIRDS OF A FEATHER — 1972 BYG FR 529 023
RON HERMAN B (EHLMO — (F) SO WHAT DO YOU THINK — 1973 TANGENT UK TGS 118
ROBERT CALVERT SAX (MLO — (G) FOR YOU TO SHARE — 1974 'A' 001
DAVID COLE G (MLO — (H) BOBBY BRADFORD PLUS SME — 1974 FREEDOM 24865
EVAN PARKER SAX (STB — (J) SMO — 1975 'A' 003
NIGEL COOMBES VLN (R — (K) JOHN STEVENS AWAY — 1976 VERTIGO 6360 131
ROGER SMITH G (R — (L) SOMEWHERE INBETWEEN — 1976 VERTIGO 6360 135
COLIN WOOD CELLO(R — (M) 'MAZIN' ENNIT — 1977 VERTIGO 6360 141
TREVOR WATTS SAX (QUACDEFGHKNV — (N) CHEMISTRY — 1977 VINYL VS 1978
BARRY GUY (QUV — (O) 'AH — 1978 VINYL VS 111
HOWARD RILEY PNO (U — (P) TOUCHING ON — 1978 VINYL VS 105
BOBBY BRADFORD TPT (H — (Q) NO FEAR — 1978 SPOTLITE SPJ 556
KENNY WHEELER HRNS (ABCDFN — (R) BIO SYSTEMS — 1978 INCUS 24
PAUL RUTHERFORD TROM (A — (S) LONGEST NIGHT VOL 1 — 1978 OGUN OG 120
BRUCE COLE B (A — (T) LONGEST NIGHT VOL 2 — 1978 OGUN OG 420
JEFF CLYNE B (AN — (U) END GAME — 1979 JAPO 600 28
DAVE HOLLAND B (BF — (V) APPLICATION — 197 SPOTLITE SPJ 513
DEREK BAILEY G (BCF — (W) & SME VOL 1 — 1981 NESSA N17
PETE LEMER K V (C
JOHNNY DYANNI B (C — MAGGIE NICHOLLS (C — ROLAND NICHOLLS (C — RAY WARLEIGH WIND(DN
BRIAN SMITH WIND (D — BOB NORDERN TROM (DH — CHRIS PYNE TROM (D — MIKE PYNE PNO (D
MARCO MATTOS B (D — JULIE TIPPETTS G V (EH — WORKSHOP GROUP (G — STEVE HAYTON G (K
PETE COWLING D (K — NIGEL MOYSE G (O — BRENT D'FORDO PERC (L

S268 **SHAKIN' STEVENS** S268

SHAKIN'MIKE BARRATT'STEVENS V(ALL — (A) THE LEGEND — 1970 PARLOPHONE UK PCS 7112
STEVE PRIOR (— (A) LEGEND — 1979 EMI UK RI NUT 25
DICK BLAND B (M — (B) I'M NO D J — 1971 CBS UK 52901
BRIAN WILLIAMS (— (C) ROCKIN'N' SHAKIN' — 1972 CONTOUR UK 2870152
CARL PETERSON G (A — (D) SHAKIN' STEVENS & THE SUNSETS — 1973 EMERALD GES1121
TREVOR HAWKINS PNO (A — (E) SHAKIN' STEVENS & THE SUNSETS — 1974 PHILIPS UK 6478010
STEVE PERCY B (A — (F) SHAKIN STEVENS — 1978 TRACK UK 2406011
ROBERT LOU LLEWELLYN D (AE — (H) MARIE MARIE (ONE TRACK DIFF) — 198 EPIC UK 84547
PAUL DALLAS SAX (A — (H) THIS OLD HOUSE — 1981 EPIC UK 84985
IAN LAWRENCE G (E — (I) AT THE ROCKHOUSE — 1981 MAGNUM FORCE UKMFLP004
TONY BRITNALL SAX (E — ( ) TAKE ONE — 1980 EPIC UK 83978
MIKE SKUDDER PNO (E — ( ) SHAKEY — 1981 EPIC UK 10027
GEORGE CHICK B (E — ( ) MANHATTAN — 1981 MINT 29
LLOYD JONES G (— ( ) SHAKIN STEVENS — 19 HALLMARK SHM3065
MATCHBOX (H — (M) GIVE ME YOUR HEART — 1982 EPIC UK 10035
PETE WINGFIELD K (M — ( ) HOT DOG — 1982 EPIC UK 32126
ALBERT LEE G (H
STU COLEMAN B (HM — GERAINT WATKINS K (HM — BILLY BREMNER G (M — ROGER McKEW G (A
GAVIN POVEY K ACC(M — CHRIS WYLES D (M — RAY BEAVIS SAX (M — JOHN EARLE SAX (M
CHRIS GOWER TROM (M — DICK HANSON TPT (M — B J COLE STEEL(M — MICKEY GEE G (M
HOWARD TIBBLE D (M

S269 **B W STEVENSON** S269

B W STEVENSON G V (ALL — (A) B W STEVENSON — 1972 RCA US LSP 4685
SID SIMS B (A — (B) LEAD FREE — 1972 RCA US LSP 4794
DON SIMMONS D (A — (C) MY MARIA — 1973 RCA US APLI 0088
PAT FERRARI G (A — (D) CALABASAS — 1974 RCA US APLI 0410
RONALD STEELE G (A — (E) WE BE SAILIN' — 1975 WB US 2901
MICKEY RAPHAEL HCA (AB — (F) LOST FEELING — 1977 WB US 3012
ED SHOOK PERC V(A — (G) BEST OF — 1977 RCA US APLI 2394
RICHARD SILEN PERC (A — (H) LIFELINE — 1980 MCA US MCA 3215
KITTY APPLING V (A
RAY TATE STEEL(A — SHANE APPLING B (A — BRIAN CHRISTIAN TAMB (A — JIM GORDON D (BCD
DENNIS ST JOHN D (B — LARRY CARLTON G (BCD — DEAN PARKS G (B — EMORY GORDY B (B
RED RHODES STEEL(BD — LARRY MUHOBERAC K (BCD — GIB GUILBEAU FDL (B — LARRY MURRAY V (B
THAD MAXWELL V (B — LINDA DILLARD V (B — JOE OSBORN D (CDE — HERB STEINER STEEL MAND(C
LAYTON DE PENNING G (C — RODNEY GARRISON B (C — DONNIE DOLAN D (C — BOBBY RAMBO G (D
JAY PRUITT K (D — BOBBYE HALL PERC (D — JIMMY HASKELL SYN (D — LINDA RONSTADT V (D
DANIEL MOORE V (DE — ANDREW GOLD V (D — KEN EDWARDS V (D — KIM CARNES V (D
DAVE ELLINGTON V (D — JULIA TILLMAN V (D — DARLA GRISER V (D — CASSELL WEBB V (E
FRED KRC D (E — RILEY OSBORNE PNO G(E — STUART SCHULMAN STEEL G (E — WALLER COLLIE B (E
TREVOR LAWRENCE SAX (E — LARRY BUNKER PERC (E — JIM HORN SAX (E — NICK DE CARO STRINGS(E
REGGIE YOUNG G (F — STEVE GIBSON G (FGH — CASEY KELLY G (F — DENNIS LINDE G (F
LARRY LONDIN D (F — SHANE KEISTER PNO (FGH — BOBBY WOOD PNO (F — RON OATES PNO(F
FARRELL MORRIS PERC (F — BUZZ CASON V (F — BERGEN WHITE V STRINGS(FH — CAROL MONTGOMERY V (F
SANDY POSEY V (F — DOTTIE DELEONIBUS V (F — ROGER CLARK D (H — TERRY McMILLAN PERC HCA(H
STEVE SCHAFFER B (H — CHRIS CHRISTIAN G (H — JON GION G (H — BOBBY OGDIN K (H
DIANE TIDWELL V (H — SHERI CRAMER V (H — LISA SILVER V (H

S270 **AL STEWART** S270

AL STEWART G V K(ALL — (A) BEDSITTER IMAGES — 1967 CBS UK 63087 RI 64023
MARVIN PRESTWICK G (B — (B) LOVE CHRONICLES — 1969 CBS UK 63460
JIMMY PAGE G (B — (C) ZERO SHE FLIES — 1970 CBS UK 63848
SIMON BRECKENRIDGE G (B — (D) ORANGE — 1972 CBS UK 64730
ASHLEY HUTCHINGS B (B — (E) PAST, PRESENT & FUTURE — 1974 CBS UK 65726 US JANUS 3063
BRIAN ODGERS B (BDE — (F) MODERN TIMES — 1975 CBS UK 80477 US JANUS 7012
BRIAN BROCKLEHURST B (B — (G) YEAR OF THE CAT — 1976 RCA UK RS1082 US JANUS 7072
MARK VOLMAN V (L — (G) YEAR OF THE CAT — 1981 ARISTA 9503 3015
MARTYN FRANCIS D (B — (H) THE EARLY YEARS — 1978 RCA UK PL25131
HOWARD KAYLAN V (L — (H) THE EARLY YEARS (DBL) — 1978 US JANUS 2 7026
HARVEY BURNS D (B — (J) TIME PASSAGES — 1978 RCA UK PL25173 US ARISTA 4190
ROBIN LAMBLE B V (JKLM — (J) TIME PASSAGE — 1981 RCA UK RI 3026
HIL PHILLIPS K (B — (K) 24 CARROTS — 1980 RCA UK PL25306 US ARISTA 9520
STEPHEN GRAY G (C — (K) 24 CARROTS — 1981 RCA UK RI 3042
GEORG HULTGREEN (C — (L) INDIAN SUMMER — 1981 RCA UK LP 9001 ARISTA US

(CONTINUED)

S270 (CONTINUED) S270

AL STEWART

GERRY CONWAY D (CF — (M) THE LIVE RADIO CONCERT ALBUM 1979 ARISTA SP40
ART TRIPP PERC (J — (N) LIVE INDIAN SUMMER 1981 RCA UK PL 25391
MIKE WOODS (C
LARRY STEELE (C | ADAN YURMAN G V (KLMN | BRYAN SAVAGE WIND (LKN | HARRY STINSON D V (LKMN
TIM HINKLEY K (CE | DUFFY POWER (C | LOUIS CENNAMO B (C | PETER GAVIN D (C
TIM RENWICK G (DEFGJ | CAL BATCHELOR B (D | TIM WALKER G (D | BRINSLEY SCHWARZ G (D
RICK WAKEMAN K (DE | BOB ANDREWS K (DE | BRUCE THOMAS B (DE | JOHN WILSON D (DE
ROGER POPE D (D | GRAHAM HUNT D (D | JOHN DONELLY V (DE | MICK WELTON V (DE
KEVIN POWERS V (DE | PETE BERRYMAN G (E | ISAAC GUILLORY G (EF | B J COLE STEEL (E
PETER WOOD K (EFGJ | BOB SARGEANT K (E | ALISTAIR ANDERSON CONC (E | DAVE SWARBRICK MAND(E
HAIM ROMANO MAND (E | LUCIANO BRAVO PERC (E | LENNOX JAMES PERC (E | MICHAEL OLIVER PERC(E
FRANK RICOTTI PERC (E | ROGER MEDDOWSTAYLOR PERC(E | FRANCIS MONKMAN SYN (E | KRYSIA KOCJAN (E
DAVE ELLIS G (F | SIMON NICOL G (F | STUART COWELL G (F | PETE WINGFIELD K (F
GEORGE FORD B (FG | PETER MOSS B (F | BARRY DE SOUZA D (F | TONY CARR PERC(F
GRAHAM SMITH HCA (FG | CHAS MILLS V (F | BRIAN BENNETT V (F | NEIL LANCASTER V (F
PETER WHITE G K(GJKLM N | DON LOBSTER K (G | STUART ELLIOTT D (GJ | BOBBY BRUCE VLN (G
PHIL KENZIE SAX (GJ | MARION DRISCOLL PERC (G | DAVID PACK V (GJ | TONY RIVERS V (G
JOHN PERRY V (G | PETER ROBINSON K (J | JEFF PORCARO D (J | TREVOR LUCAS G (C
STEVE CHAPMAN PERC (LK | JERRY McMILLAN VLN (LK | KEN NICOL V (K | ROBERT MARLETTE K (K
RUSS KUNKEL D (K | MARK SANDERS D (K | JEFF PORCARO D (K | BEAU SEGAL D (K
LENNY CASTRO PERC (K | ROBIN WILLIAMSON MAND (K | SYLVIA WOODS HARP (K | PHIL KENZIE SAX (M
ROBERT ALPERT K (M | MARK GOLDENBURG G (J | PETE SOLLEY K (J | AL PERKINS STEEL(J
KRYSIA KRISTIANNE V(HJKLMN | JOE PUERTA V (J | JAMES ROBERT WEST V (J | BRIAN HUDDY V (J
JEFF BORGESON V (J

S270A

BILLY STEWART

S270A
BILLY STEWART (A — (A) CROSS MY HEART 1976 CHESS US 50059

S271

GARY STEWART

S271
GARY STEWART G V (ALL — (A) YOU'RE NOT THE WOMAN 1975 MCA US 488
HAROLD BRADLEY G B (F — (B) OUT OF HAND 1975 RCA LSA 3215 APLI 0900
TERRY McMILLAN HCA (F — (C) STEPPIN' OUT 1976 RCA LSA 3266 APLI 1225
HAL RUGG STEEL(F — (D) YOUR PLACE OR MINE 1977 RCA PL12199 APLI 2199
WELDON MYRICK STEEL(F — (E) LITTLE JUNIOR 1978 RCA APLI 2779
REGGIE YOUNG G (F — (F) GARY 1979 RCA PL 13288 APLI 3288
BOBBY WOOD PNO (F — (G) CACTUS & ROSE 1981 RCA PL 3637
PIG ROBBINS K (F — (H) GREATEST HITS 1981 RCA 3981
HENRY STRZELECKI B (F
MIKE LEECH B (F | JERRY SHOOK G (F | BUDDY HARMON D (F | JERRY CARRIGAN D (F
HAYWARD BISHOP D (F | DALE SELLERS G (F | BOB EMMONS K (F

S272

JOHN STEWART

S272
JOHN STEWART G V (ALL — (A) SIGNALS THROUGH THE GLASS 1968 CAPITOL US ST 2975 RI 1975 SM2975
WENDY WALDMAN V (K — (A) SIGNALS THROUGH THE GLASS 1979 CAPITOL 11988
BUFFY FORD V (ACDEGIJL — (B) CALIFORNIA BLOODLINES 1969 CAPITOL US ST 203 UK EST203
BLAISE TOSTI V (K — (B) CALIFORNIA BLOODLINES 1979 CAPITOL 11987
FRED CARTER G B (BCD — (C) WILLARD 1970 CAPITOL US ST 540 UK EST540
LINDA RONSTADT V (K — (C) WILLARD 1979 CAPITOL 11989
CHARLIE McCOY HCA (BCF — (D) LONESOME PICKER RIDES AGAIN 1971 WB US WS1948 UK K46135
KENNY BUTTREY D (BCI — (E) SUNSTORM 1972 WB US BS2611
LLOYD GREEN STEEL(B — (F) CANNONS IN THE RAIN 1973 RCA US LSP 4827 UK SF 8359
NORBERT PUTNAM B (BC — (G) CANNONS IN THE RAIN 197 RCA US AYLI 3731
BUDDY HARMON D (BF — (G) PHOENIX CONCERTS LIVE 1974 RCA US CPLZ 0265 UK PL20265
HARGUS ROBBINS PNO (BF — (H) WINGLESS ANGELS 1975 RCA US APLI 0816 UK SF 8437
JERRY SMITH K (B — (I) FIRE IN THE WIND 1977 RSO US RS 13027 UK 2394 194
BEEGIE CRUZER K (B — (J) BOMBS AWAY DREAM BABIES 1979 RSO US RS 13051 UK 2394 228
BERGEN WHITE V (BF — (K) DREAM BABIES GO HOLLYWOOD 1980 RSO US RS 13074 UK RSD 5007
JOHN'BUCK' WILKIN G (BF — (L) IN CONCERT 1980 RCA US AFLI 3513
MARI JOHN WILKIN V (B — (M) FORGOTTEN SONGS... 1980 RCA UK PL43155
JAMES TAYLOR G V (C
JOEL BISHOP O'BRIEN D (C | RUSS KUNKEL D (CDEHJK | BILL MUNDI PERC (CE | PETER ASHER V PERC(CD
BRYAN GAROFALO B V(CDEIJ | CAROLE KING PNO (C | MICHAEL STEWART G V(CDEGL | DOUG KERSHAW FDL V (C
BOBBY THOMPSON BANJ (C | RALPH SCHUCKETT K (C | ABIGALE HANESS V (C | DANNY KOOTCH G (C
CHRIS DARROW FDL DOBRO(CDF | PETER FULLERTON V (D | HENRY DILTZ V HCA (DEK | RICK CUNHA V (D
JENNIFER V (D | KATE TAYLOR V (D | JIMMY HASKELL ACC STRING(DE | LOREN NEWKIRK PNO (DEGL
KING ERRISON PERC (DE | BUDDY EMMONS STEEL(DE | GLEN D HARDIN PNO (DE | LEE SKLAR B (D
ARNIE MOORE B V(DEFGHL | RON TUTT D (EH | DAVID KEMPER D (E | JERRY SCHEFF B (E
LARRY KNECHTEL PNO (E | JAMES BURTON G DOB(E | BILL CUNNINGHAM FDL (E | MIKE DEASY G (E
LARRY CARLTON G (E | GARY DAVID PERC (E | JIM HORN HRNS (E | CHARLES FINDLEY HRNS (E
PAUL HUBINON HRNS (E | JACK CARONE V (E | LAURA CREAMER V (E | JONATHAN DOUGLASK PERC(GHL
JIM GORDON D (GL | DAN DUGMORE STEEL(GHL | MIKE SETTLE V (GHL | DENNY BROOKS V (GHIL
JOE OSBORN B (H | PETER JAMESON G (H | ROBERT WACHTEL G (H | TOM KEENE PNO (H
STEPHANIE FORD V (H | DANIEL MOORE V (H | MARTI McCALL V (H | JACKIE WARD V (H
LISA FREEMAN ROBERTS V (H | JON WOODHEAD G (I | TROY SEALS G (I | REGGIE YOUNG G (I
JOEY HARRIS G V (IJ | DAVE KIRBY G (I | SHANE KEISTER K (I | DAVID BRIGGS K (I
BILL CUOMO K (I | MICKEY RAPHAEL HCA (I | GARY WEISBERG D PERC(IJ | CHRIS WHALEN V (IJK
JOHN WILLIAMS B (I | HERB PEDERSEN V (I | LINDSEY BUCKINGHAM G V (J | JOEY CARBONE K (JK
MIKE BOTTS D (J | STEVE NICKS V (J | MARY TORREY V (J | RICHARD SCHLOSSER D(J
CHRISTINE DE LISLE V (J | MARY KAY PLACE B (J | DAVID JACKSON B (J | CROXLEY GUARD V (J
DEBORAH TOMPKINS V (J | CATHERINE GUARD V (J | WAYNE HUNT K (J | DAVID PLATSHON D (K
STEVE ROSS PERC (K | PHIL EVERLY V (K | SYDNEY FOX V (K | NICOLETTE LARSON V (K

S273

ROD STEWART

S273
ROD STEWART V (ALL — (A) AN OLD RAINCOAT ... 1970 VERTIGO UK VO4 US MERCURY SR61237
CARMINE APPICE D V (JMQ — (B) GASOLINE ALLEY 1970 VERTIGO UK 6360 500 US MERCURY SR61264
PHIL CHEN B V (JM — (C) EVERY PICTURE TELLS A STORY 1971 MERCURY UK 6338 063 US SRM1 609
RICK GRETCH VLN (F — (C) EVERY PICTURE TELLS A STORY 1977 MERCURY CAN 6336 548
JOHN JARVIS K (JH — (D) NEVER A DULL MOMENT 1972 MERCURY UK 6499 153 US SRMI 646
BILLY PEEK G (JMH — (E) SING IT AGAIN ROD 1973 MERCURY UK 6499 484 US SRMI 680
JIM CREGAN G (JMOPQ — (F) SMILER 1974 MERCURY UK 9104 001 US SRM11017
GARY GRAINGER G (JM — (G) ATLANTIC CROSSING 1975 WB UK K56151 US WB 2875
PETE CARR G (G — (H) A NIGHT ON THE TOWN 1976 RIVA UK RVLP 1 US WB 3116
STEVE CROPPER G (GH — (I) SHOT OF RHYTHM & BLUES 1976 CRYSTAL 98198 +PRIVATE STOCK PS 2021
KEITH EMERSON K (A — (AB) VINTAGE YEARS 1969/70 1976 MERCURY UK 6672 013 GER 6641 414
JESSE ED DAVIS G (G — (J) FOOTLOOSE & FANCY FREE 1977 RIVA UK RVLP5 WB US 3092 GER 56423

(CONTINUED)

S273 ROD STEWART (CONTINUED) S273

JIMMY JOHNSON G (G (K) THE BEST OF 1977 MERCURY UK 6643 030 US SRM27507
FRED TACKETT G (GMH (L) BEST OF VOL 2 1977 MERCURY US SRM27509
DAVID LINDLEY VLN MAND (GH (M) BLONDES HAVE MORE FUN 1978 RIVA UK RVLP8 WB US 3261 PIC DISC 3276
DONALD DUNN B (GH (N) GREATEST HITS 1979 RIVA UK RODTV1 US WB 3373
BOB CLAN B (G (O) HOT RODS 1980 MERCURY UK 6463 061
DAVID HOOD B (G (P) FOOLISH BEHAVIOUR 1980 RIVA UK RVLP 11 US WB 3485
MEMPHIS HORNS (GH (Q) TONIGHT I'M YOURS 1981 RIVA UK RVLP14 WB US 3602
ELTON JOHN K V (F ( ) MAGGIE MAY 1981 CONTOUR UK 2043
ANDY NEWMARK D (FH ( ) VOL 1 1981 MERCURY UK 7145 069
WILLIE WEEKS B (FH
MICK WALLER D (ABCDF PETE SEARS PNO(BCDF RON WOOD B G(ABCF MARTIN QUITTENTON G (ABCDF
IAN McLAGAN ORG(ABCDF DANNY THOMPSON B (C ANDY PYLE B (C DICK POWELL VLN(BCDF
MADELINE BELL V (C KENNY JONES D (BDF MARTIN PUGH G (A TOM VIG PERC(MHQ
LINDA LEWIS V (MQ MIKE FINNIGAN V (M MAX GRONENTHAL V (M SPIKE HEATLEY B (DF
GORDON HUNTLEY STEEL(D RONNIE LANE B (BD DUANE HITCHINGS K (MQ ROGER BETHELMY D (M
PAULINHO DA COSTA PERC (MQ NICKY HOPKINS K (M GARY HERBIG FLT (M PHIL KENZIE HRNS(M
STEVE MADAIO TPT (M TOM SCOTT WIND(M SAM MITCHELL G (BC DENNIS O'FLYNN VLN(B
MIKE D'ABO PNO (A RAY JACKSON MAND(F DUCK DUNN B (H RON GLAUB B (H
LEE SKLAR B (H JOE WALSH G (H DAVID FOSTER K (H J SMITH K (H
RICK SCLOSSER D (H ROGER HAWKINS D (H AL JACKSON D (H JOE LALA PERC(H
JIMMY HOROWITZ STR (H MEL LEWIS STR (H A MARDIN STR (H TOWER OF POWER HRNS(H
JERRY JUMONVILLE SAX (H PLAS JOHNSON SAX (H TONY BROCK D V (Q JAY DAVIS B (Q
JEFF BAXTER G (Q KEVIN SAVIGAR K (Q DANNY JOHNSON G (Q ROBIN LEMESURIER G (Q
BYRON BERLINE FDL (Q PENTECOSTAL COMM CHOIR V(Q TROPIC ISLE STEEL BAND (F CHRIS BARBERS JAZZ BAND (F
PENNY JONES V (Q

S274 STICKY FINGERS S274

BARRY KEANE D (A (A) STICKY FINGERS 1978 EPIC UK 83612
ERROL THOMAS B (A
MICHAEL TOLES G (A BRIAN RUSSELL G (A CARL MARSH K (A DICK SMITH PERC (A
GUIDO BASSO HRNS (A AL STANWICK HRNS (A RUSS LITTLE HRNS (A GARY MORGAN HRNS (A
ROB McCONNELL HRNS (A EUGENE AMARO HRNS (A PHYLLIS DUNCAN V (A HELEN DUNCAN V (A

S274A ARBEE STIDHAM S274A

ARBEE STIDHAM (AB (A) ARBEES BLUES 19 FOLKWAYS US 3824
(B) TIRED OF WONDERING 19 BLUESVILLE US 1021

S275 STIFF LITTLE FINGERS S275

BRIAN FALOON D (AB (A) INFLAMMABLE MATERIAL 1979 ROUGH TRADE UK ROUGH 1
HENRY CLUNEY G (ABCD (B) NOBODYS HERO 1980 CHRYSALIS UK CHR 1270 NL 511270
JAKE BURNS G V (ABCD (C) HANX 1980 CHRYSALIS UK CHR1300 GER 202916
JIM REILLY D (BCD (D) GO FOR IT 1981 CHRYSALIS UK CHR1339 GER 203645
ALI McMORDIE B (ABCD

S275A STILL LIFE S275A

(A) STILL LIFE 1971 VERTIGO UK 6360 026

S275B STILL ROCK S275B

DON PRESTON (A (A) STILL ROCK 19 ENTERPRISE US 731016

S276 STEPHEN STILLS S276

STEPHEN STILLS G V (ALL (A) STEPHEN STILLS 1970 ATLANTIC UK 2401 004 US 7202
PAUL HARRIS K (BG (A) STEPHEN STILLS 1972 ATLANTIC UK K40341 RI
DALLAS TAYLOR D (ABC (B) STEPHEN STILLS TWO 1971 ATLANTIC UK 2401 013 US 7206
CALVIN SAMUELS B V (ABC (B) STEPHEN STILLS TWO 1972 ATLANTIC UK K40249 RI
JERRY AIELLO K (CDE (C) STILLS 1975 CBS UK 69146 US 33575
JOE LALA PERC (CDEG (D) STILLS LIVE 1975 ATLANTIC UK K50214 US 18156
DONNIE DACUS G V (CDE (E) ILLEGAL STILLS 1976 CBS UK 81330 US 34148
RUSS KUNKEL D (CD (F) THE BEST OF(STILL STILLS) 1976 ATLANTIC UK K50327 US 18201
KENNY PASSARELLI B (CD (G) THOROUGHFARE GAP 1978 CBS UK 82859 US 35380
RICK ROBERTS G V (C (AB) TWO ORIGINALS 1975 ATLANTIC GER 60063
MIKE FINNIGAN B (G (X) SUPER SESSIONS(SEE AL KOOPER)
DAVE MASON V (G
NEIL YOUNG G V (F GERRY TOLMAN G (G MIKE FINNIGAN B (G VERNA RICHARDSON V(G
GEORGE TERRY G (CG JOE VITALE D (EG DAVID CROSBY V (ACD GRAHAM NASH V (AC
BETTY WHITE V (C LEE SKLAR B (C TUBBY ZIEGLER D (CE GEORGE PERRY B (EG
HOWARD KAYLAN V (E MARK VOLMAN V (E JEFF WHITTAKER CONGA(A RITA COOLIDGE V (A
PRISCILLA JONES V (A JOHN SEBASTIAN V (A SHIRLEY MATTHEWS V (A CONRAD ISADORE D (AB
JUDITH POWELL V (A LIZA STRIKE V (A LARRY STEELE V (A TONY WILSON V (A
JIMI HENDRIX G (A ERIC CLAPTON G (A JOHN BARBATA D (A CLAUDIA LENNEAR V (A
CASS ELLIOT V (A RICHIE HAYWARD D (A BOOKER T JONES K (A SYDNEY GEORGE WIND (AB
GASPAR LAWAL PERC (B DR JOHN K (B NILS LOFGREN G K V(B JAMES MITCHELL SAX (B
FLOYD NEWMAN SAX (B ED LOGAN SAX (B JACK HALE TROM (B ANDREW LOVE SAX (B
ROGER HOPPS HRNS (B WAYNE JOHNSON HRNS (B ROCKY DZIDZORNU PERC (B HENRY DILTZ V (B
FEARLESS FREDDY V (B DANNY KORTCHMAR G V (G ANDY GIBB V (G PAUL LEE D (G
AL GOULD FDL (G KENNY KIRKLAND PNO (G RICHARD O'CONNELL D (G GERALD JOHNSON B (G
ALBY GALUTEN K (G KITTY PRITIKEN V (G BROOKS HUNNICUTT V (G LISA ROBERTS V (G
JOEY MERCIA V (G JOHN SAMBATERO V (G WHIT SIDENER FLT (G

S276A STILLS/ YOUNG BAND S276A

STEPHEN STILLS G V (A (A) LONG MAY YOU RUN 1976 REPRISE UK K54081 US 2253
NEIL YOUNG G V (A
JOE LALA PERC (A JERRY AIELLO K (A JOE VITALE FLT D(A GEORGE PERRY B (A

S277 STILLWATER S277

MIKE CAUSEY G (AB (A) STILLWATER 1977 CAPRICORN US 0186 UK 2429 155
JIMMY HALL V PERC(AB (B) I RESERVE THE RIGHT 1979 CAPRICORN US 0210 UK 2429 176
BOBBY GOLDEN G (AB
SEBIE LACEY D V (AB ALLISON SCARBOROUGH B V(AB ROB WALKER G V (AB BOB SPEARMAN K (AB

S278 STINGRAY S278

DENNIS EAST V (A (A) STINGRAY 1979 CARRERE US 38127 CAL 113
ALLAN GOLDSWAIN K (A
MIKE PILOT G V (A EDDIE BOYLE B (A SHAUN WRIGHT D (A DANNY ANTHILL ORG (A

S279 STINKY TOYS S279

ELLI MEDEIROS V (A (A) STINKY TOYS 1977 POLYDOR UK 2393 174
BRUNO CARONE G (A
JACNO G (A ALBIN DERIAT B (A HERVE ZENOUDA D (A

S280 ALAN STIVELL S280

ALAN STIVELL V FLT PIPES(ALL (A) RENAISSANCE OF CELTIC HARP 1972 PHILIPS FR 6414406
YANN JAKEZ HASSOLD V (EG (B) A L'OLYMPIA 1972 FONTANA FR 6325321 6399 005
DAN AR BRAS G (ABCEFGK (C) ALAN STIVELL REFLECTIONS 1973 FONTANA 6399 008
RENE WERNEER FDL (BCEFK (D) FROM CELTIC ROOTS 1974 FONTANA 6325 304
ALAN KLOATR FLT BOD(AEF (E) A LANGONNED 1975 FONTANA 9101 500 6325 332
LIAM WELDON BOD (E (F) IN DUBLIN 1975 FONTANA 9299 547
YANN-FANCH AR MERDY D(AE (G) BEFORE LANDING 1977 FONTANA 9286 999
LOEIZ ROUJON D (E (H) SUZI MACGUIRE 1978 IMPACT 6886 122
JANNLUG FAUCHON D (E (J) SYMPHONIE CELTIQUE (DBL) 1980 CBS 88487
JEAN LUC HALLERAU B V (K (K) CELTIC ROCK 19 VERTIGO GER 6325 251
BERNARD LEVASSELLY B (C (L) 3RD INTERNATIONAL TOUR 1979 METRONOME GER 60 200
YOVENN SICARD BOMBA(E
GABRIEL YACOUB G DULC (BCK PASCAL STIVE K(BCFK GERARD LEVASSEUR B (AB HENRI DELAGARDE CELLOFLT(ABC
MICHEL SANTANGELI D(BCFK SERJ PARAYRE PERC (BC MIKAEL KLEC'H FLT (BC DANIELE BAROLLETTI V (A
MICHEL DELAPORTE PERC (AK GUY CASCALES D (A GERARD SALKOWSKY B (A GILLES TINAYJRE K (A
MIK AR BIZ BOMBA(AF JEAN MARC DOLLEZ B (A ANNE GERMAIN V (A CLAUDE GERMAIN V (A
JEAN CLAUDE BRION V (A FRANCOISE WALL V (A JACQUES HENDRIX V (A PADRIG KERRE FDL DULC(A
ANDREW HERVE K (G MIKAEL HERVE B (G JEAN LUC DANNA D (G DAVE SWARBRICK FDL(G
MARIA POPKIEWICZ V (G CLEMENT BAILLY D (G DOMINIQUE LURO K (G PATRICK KIFFER B (G
ALAIN HATOT SAX (G ADAM SKEAPING CELLO(G LYN DOBSON FLT SITAR PERC(G RICHARD HARVEY WIND(G
BAGAD BLEIMOR WIND D (GK CHRIS HAYWARD FLT PERC(JL ROBBY FINKEL K (J MICHEL PREZMAN K (J
DOMINIQUE WIDIEZ K (J MARC PERRU G (JL MIKAEL VALY B (J ROGER SECCO D (J
PADRIG KERRE FDL MAND(JL ORCHESTRA & CHOIR (J MARIE YACOUB PERC V(K ELYANE WERNEER V (K
MIREILLE WERNEER V (K JACKY THOMAS B (K PADRIG SICARD BOMB (F DOMINIQUE MOLLARD D(F
PADRIG MOLLARD PIPES(F PIERRE MAYEL PIPES(F MIKAEL AR VALY B (L CHRISTIAN PIGET K (L
UJAN HERVE D (L

S280A ORVILLE STOEBER S280A

ORVILLE STOEBER G V (A (A) ORVILLE STOEBER 1971 UNI UNLS 120
HARRY PALMER G (A
RAY BARRETT K (A GEORGE DUVIVIER B (A

S281 SIMON STOKES S281

SIMON STOKES V (ALL (A) SIMON STOKES & THE NIGHTHAWKS 1971 MGM US MGM S4677
BUTCH SENNEVILLE G (AB (B) & THE BLACK WHIP THRILL BAND 1973 SPINDIZZY US 32075
RANDALL KEITH G (A (C) BUZZARD OF LOVE 197 U A
ROBERT LEDGER B (A
JOE YUELE D (A JOHN LOCKE K (B HARRY GARFIELD K (B CHRISTIAN PENNICK G (B
MARTY TRYON B (A BILLY GOODNICK D (B DAVID LUELL SAX (C CLARK GASSMAN SYN (C
MAX MENNITT B (C JAT GRAYDON G (C JIM SHULMAN PERC (C FRANK CAPP PERC(C
HAL BLAINE D (C PETER MAUFFU G (C STANLEY SCHWARTZ K (C MAXINE WATERS V (C
JULIA WATERS V (C ORIN WATERS V (C

S281A STONE CITY BAND S281A

(A) IN'N'OUT 1980 GORDY US 991
(A) BOYS ARE BACK 1981 GORDY US 1001 UK MOTOWN 12150

S282 STONE PONEYS S282

LINDA RONSTADT V (ABCDE (A) STONE PONEYS 1967 CAPITOL US ST 2666
BOB KIMMEL G (ABCDE (B) EVERGREEN VOL 2 1967 CAPITOL US ST 2763
KEN EDWARDS G (ABCDE (C) STONE PONEYS & FRIENDS VOL 3 1968 CAPITOL US ST 2863
BILLY MUNDI D (A (D) STONE PONEYS FEATURING L RONSTADT 1976 CAPITOL US ST 11383
JOHN T FORSHA G (A (E) STONEY END 1972 PICKWICK SPC 3298
JAMES E BOND JR B (A
CYRUS FARYAR G (A PETE CHILDS G (A

S283 STONE THE CROWS S283

LES HARVEY G (ALL (A) STONE THE CROWS 1970 POLYDOR US 244019 UK 2425 017
MAGGIE BELL V (ALL (B) ODE TO JOHN LAW 1970 POLYDOR UK 2425 042
JOHN McGINNIS K (ABE (C) TEENAGE LICKS 1971 POLYDOR US PD5020 UK 2425 071
COLIN ALLEN D (ALL (D) 'ONTINUOUS PERFORMANCE 1972 POLYDOR US 5037 UK 2391 043
JIM DEWAR B (ABE (E) STONE THE CROWS(COMP) 1976 POLYDOR/FLASHBACK UK 2482 279
RONNIE LEAHY K (CDE
STEVE THOMPSON D (CDE JIMMY McCULLOCH G (DE ROGER BALL HRNS (D MALCOLM DUNCAN HRNS(D
WEE MARIE (C DUNDEE HORNS (C

S283A STONEBOLT S283A

BRIAN LOUSLEY D V (A (A) STONEBOLT 1978 PARACHUTE US 9006 UK RRL 2006
JOHN WEBSTER K (A (B) KEEP IT ALIVE 1980 RCA PL 10357
DAVID WILLS V (A (C) A NEW SET OF CHANGES 1980 RCA US 1 3825
DANNY AITCHISON B (A
RAY ROPER G V (A

S283B STONEBRIDGE McGUINNESS S283B

LOU STONEBRIDGE HCA G K V(A (A) CORPORATE MADNESS 1980 RCA UK PL 25275
TOM McGUINNESS G (A
ROY MORGAN D (A PAUL KARAS B (A MO FOSTER B (A MIKE MORAN PROD K (A
NICKY PAYNE SAX (A DICK HANSON TPT (A CHRIS GOWER TROM (A JOHN 'IRISH' EARLE SAX(A
RAY BEAVIS SAX (A FRANK RICOTTI PERC (A CHARLIE FAWN V (A MORRIS PERT PERC(A

S284 STONEGROUND S284

SAL VALENTINO G V (ABC (A) STONEGROUND 1971 WB US WS 1895 UK K46087
TIM BARNES G V (ABCDE (B) FAMILY ALBUM 1971 WB US WS 1956 UK K53999
JOHN BLAKELEY G B (ABC (C) STONEGROUND THREE 1972 WB US BS 2645
PETE SEARS K B (A (D) FLAT OUT 1976 FLAT OUT US FOR 001
MICHAEL MAU D (A (E) HEARTS OF STONE 1978 WB US BSK3187 GER 56543
LUTHER BILDT G V (A (F) PLAY IT LOUD 1980 CRYSTAL US 5009
AMANDO PERAZA CONGA(D
LYNNE HUGHES V (ABC DEIRDRE LAPORTE V (ABC ANNIE SAMPSON V (ABCD LYDIA PHILLIPS V (A
RON NAGLE K (A BRIAN CRODULA V (B LYDIA MORERO V (BC STEPHEN PRICE (B
CORY LERIOS V (BC JO BAKER V (ED TERRY DAVIS B V (ED LENNY LEE GOLDSMITH V(E
SAMMY PIAZZA D (D FRED WEBB K (ED BOB GAUDIO K (E JERRY PETERSON SAX(D
STEVE FONTANA PERC (E TERRY CLEMENTS HRNS (C DAVID McCULLOUGH B (C DANNY ARMSTRONG TROM(D
JULES BROUSSARD SAX (D CAL LEWISTON TPT (D JACK SCHROER SAX (D

S284A STONEHOUSE S284A

PETER SEARING G V (A (A) STONEHOUSE CREEK 1971 RCA UK SF 8197
JAMES SMITH V (A
IAN SNOW D (A TERRY PARKER B (A

S284B ROB STONER S284B

ROB STONER (A (A) PATRIOTIC DUTY 1980 MCA US 5118

S284C **PAUL STOOKEY** S284C

PAUL STOOKEY (A — (A) PAUL AND.... — 197 WB US 1912 RI UK MYRRH 1074
MAKEL LEWIS G STEEL (A — (B) ONE NIGHT STAND — 197 WB US 2674
DANNY TURBEVILLE V (A — (C) BAND & BODY WORKS — 1980 MYRRH UK 1087
JIMMY NAILS G V (A
MICHAEL EPSTEIN D V (A BARRY FLAST K (A EDDIE MOTTAU V G PERC(A JIM MASON B V (A
PAUL PRESTOPINO G (A CAMERON KOTLER CELLO(A

S284D **RONNIE STOOTS** S284D

RONNIE STOOTS V (A — (A) ASHES TO ASHES — 1972 TMI US 1002
STEVE CROPPER G (A
PAUL CANNON G (A TIM GOODWIN G (A DAVID MAYO G V (A JIM JOHNSON B (A
J A SPELL K (A RICHIE SIMPSON D (A JOEL WILLIAMS D (A PAT TAYLOR V (A
JOSE FELICIANO G (A BOB LEHNERT V (A DAVID BREWER V (A NASHVILLE EDITION V(A

S285 **MIKE STOREY** S285

MIKE STOREY K V HCA PERC(AB — (A) STOREY — 1974 MAM MAMAS1011
NEIL HUBBARD G (A — (B) WHO ARE YOU PLAYING TO — 1975 MAM AS 1013
WINSTON DELANDRO G (AB
MICK WEAVER K (A MIKE WOODS G (A STEVE CHAPMAN D (AB RICHARD BAILEY D(A
CHARLIE HARRISON B V (A SMILEY DEJONNES PERC (A RAY SINGER PERC V(A CHRIS MERCER HRNS(A
RON CARTHY HRNS (A STEVE GREGORY HRNS (A MICK EVE HRNS (A BUD BEADLE HRNS(A
FRANK COLLINS V (A DYAN BIRCH V (A PADDIE McHUGH V (A CLIVE SARSTEDT V (A
STUART BROOKS B (B

S286 **STORIES** S286

IAN LLOYD B V (ABC — (A) STORIES — 1972 KAMA SUTRA US KSBS 2051
MICHAEL BROWN K SYN(ABC — (B) ABOUT US — 1973 KAMA SUTRA US KSBS 2068
STEVE LOVE G V B(ABC — (C) TRAVELLING UNDERGROUND — 1973 KAMA SUTRA US KSBS 2078
BRYAN MADEY D PERC(ABC
KENNETH BISCHEL K SYN(C KENNY AARONSON B (C RICH RANNO G (PETER HOFFMAN G (B
PETER BUONCONSIGILIO VLN(B HARRY LOOKAFSLAV VLN (B

S286A **STORMY SIX** S286A

FRANCO FABBRI G (1 — (A) L'UNITA — 1970
UMBERTO FIORI (1 — (B) UN BIGLIETTO DEL TRAM — 197 L'ORCHESTRA OLP 10001
TOMMASO LEDDI (1 — (C) CLICKE — 197 L'ORCHESTRA OLP 10010
CARLO DE MARTINI (1 — (D) L'APPRENDISTA — 197 L'ORCHESTRA OLP 10012
(1) 1973

S286B **STORM** S286B

JANNETTE CHASE V (A — (A) STORM — 1979 MCA US 3179
LEAR STEVENS G (A
RONNI HANSON B (A DAVID DEVON D (A

S286C **BILLY STORM** S286C

BILLY STORM (A — (A) BILLY STORM & THE VALIANTS — 19 FAMOUS US 504
(B) BILLY STORM — 19 VISTA US 3315

S286D **JOHNNY STORM** S286D

JOHNNY STORM (A — (A) FLAME ON — 1981 MAGNUM FORCE MFLP003

S287 **STORYTELLER** S287

CAROLINE ATTARD V (AB — (A) STORYTELLER — 1970 TRANSATLANTIC UK TRA220
RODNEY CLARK V D (A — (B) MORE PAGES — 1971 TRANSATLANTIC UK TRA232
ROGER MOON G V (AB
MIKE ROGERS V (AB CHRIS BELSHAW B V (B TERRY DURHAM V (AB HARRY BECKETT HRNS(B
HENRY SPINETTI D (B

S288 **DAVIS STOUGHTON** S288

DAVIS STOUGHTON (A — (A) TRANSFORMER — 19 ELEKTRA US 74034

S288A **STRAIGHT EIGHT** S288A

RICK CASSMAN G K V(AB — (A) NO NOISE FROM HERE — 1979 EEL PIE UK EPRP 001
BOOT KINGSMAN G V SAX(AB — (B) SHUFFLE & CUT — 1980 LOGO UK FLUSH 1UK GER 64026
STEVE CHERRY B V (AB
PAUL SCHOFIELD B (A TIM BEETON VLN (A RUAN O'LOCHLAINN SAX (A GARY HOLTON V (A
PAUL TURNER K D (B ROD BERRIEDALE JOHNSON D(A RABBIT K (A ANDY HAAS SAX(B

S289 **STRAIGHT SHOOTER** S289

GEORG BUSCHMANN V (AB — (A) MY TIME HOUR TIME — 1974 SKY SKY 034
FRIEDHELM MISLEJUK D (A — (B) GET STRAIGHT — 1978 SKY SKY 018
GUNTHER STRIEPLING G (AB — (C) FLYING STRAIGHT — 1981 SKY SKY 054
HANS PLANKERT K (AB
ROLAND HAASE B (AB PETER KEGLER D PERC (B

S289A **NICK STRAKER BAND** S289A

NICK STRAKER K V (A — (A) A WALK IN THE PARK — 1980 CBS UK 84608
ANDY MANSFIELD G (A
DAVE McSHERA G (A TONY HIBBERT B (A PETER HAMMOND B (A PHIL TOWNER D (A
FERNANDO BUSTAMENTE D (A

S289B **STRAND** S289B

RICK CALHOUN V (A — (A) THE STRAND — 1980 ISLAND UK ILPS 9594
SCOTT SHELLY G V (A
PETER REILICH K V (A DEAN COTEZ B V (A KELLY SHANAHAN D (A

S290 **RICHARD STRANGE** S290

RICHARD STRANGE (A — (A) PHENOMENAL RISE OF RICHARD STRANGE 1981 VIRGIN UK 2203 GER 203 763
ANGUC McLEAN G (A — (A) " " " " " 1981 PVC 7917
MARTIN GRIFFIN D (A
PETE O'SULLIVAN B (A DAVE WINTHROP SAX (A STEVE BOLTON G (A JIM TELFORD SYN (A
J L HELLAWELL K SYN(A REBOP KWAKU BAAH PERC (A RADIO JONES V (A RENE EYRE V (A
SUE SHARP V (A ROSS MIDDLETON V (A

S291 **STRANGE DAYS** S291

GRAHAM WARD G V (A — (A) NINE PARTS TO THE WIND — 1975 RETREAT UK RTL6005
PHIL WALMAN B V (A
EDDIE McNEIL D PERC(A EDDIE SPENCE K (A

S291A **STRANGER** S291A

(A) STRANGER — 1982 EPIC US 37940

S292 STRANGLERS S292

HUGH CORNWELL	G V	(ABCDEF	(A) RATTUS NORVEGICUS	1977 A&M US 4648 UA UK UAG30045
JET BLACK	D	(ABCDEF	(B) NO MORE HEROES	1978 A&M US 4659 UA UK UAG30200
DAVE GREENFIELD	K V	(ABCDEF	(C) BLACK & WHITE	1978 A&M US 4706 US UK UAK30222
JEAN JACQUES BURNEL	B V	(ABCDEF	(D) LIVE(X CERT)IV	1979 IRS US 70011 UA UK UAG30224
LORA LOGIC	SAX	(C	(D) LIVE(X CERT)	1979 UA GER 62412
ERIC CLARK	SAX	(A	(E) THE RAVEN	1979 UA UK UAG30262
ALAN WINSTANLEY		(F	(F) THE MEN IN BLACK	1981 LIBERTY NL 83084 UK LBG30313
ALDO BOCCA		(F	(G) THE COLLECTION	1982 LIBERTY UK LBG 30353
LAURENCE DIANA		(F		
MARTIN RUSHENT	PROD	(A		

S292A STRANGELOVES S292A

RICHARD GOTTEHRER		(A	(A) I WANT CANDY	1965 BANG US 211 RI GER LOLLIPOP 624341
BOB FELDMAN		(A		
JERRY GOLDSTEIN		(A		

S293 STRAPPS S293

ROSS STAGG	G V	(AB	(A) STRAPPS	1976 HARVEST UK SHSP 4055
JOE READ	B V	(AB	(B) SECRET DAMAGE	1977 HARVEST US 11621 UK SHSP 4064
NOEL SCOTT	K V	(AB	(C) SHARP CONVERSATION	1978 HARVEST UK SHSP 4088
MICK UNDERWOOD	D	(AB		

S294 STRAWBERRY ALARM CLOCK S294

MARK WEITZ	K	(ABCD	(A) INCENSE & PEPPERMINTS	1968 PYE UK 28106 US UNI 73014
LEE FREEMAN	V D WIND B	(ABCD	(B) WAKE UP ,ITS TOMORROW	1968 UNI US 73025
ED KING	G V	(ABCD	(C) WORLD IN A SEA SHELL	1968 UNI US 73035
GARY LOVETRO	B V	(A	(D) GOOD MORNING STARSHINE	19 UNI US 73054
GEORGE BUNNELL	B	(ABC	(E) BEST OF	19 UNI US 73074
RANDY SEOL	D V	(ABC	(F) PSYCH OUT(3 TRACKS) (SOUNDTRACK)	1968 SIDEWALK US ST 5913
JIMMY PITMAN	G V	(D	(G) CHANGES	19 VOCALION 73915
GENE GUNNELS	D	(D		

S295 STRAWBS S295

DAVE COUSINS	G V	(ABCDEFGHIJKLMNO	(A) ALL OUR OWN WORK (1968 RECORDING)	1973 HALLMARK SHM 813
RICHARD HUDSON	PERC	(BCDEFG	(B) STRAWBS	1969 A&M UK AMLS 936
JOHN FORD	B V	(BCDEFG	(C) DRAGONFLY	1970 A&M UK AMLS 970
RICK WAKEMAN	K	(BCDEK	(D) JUST A COLLECTION OF ANTIQUES	1970 A&M US 4288 UK AMLS 994
TONY HOOPER	G V	(ABCDE	(E) FROM THE WITCHWOOD	1971 A&M US 4304 UK AMLS64304
DAVE LAMBERT	G V	(FGHJKMNLX	(F) GRAVE NEW WORLD	1972 A&M US 4344 UK AMLS68078
ROD COOMBES	D	(HJKML	(G) BURSTING AT THE SEAMS	1973 A&M US 4383 UK AMLH68144
CHAS CRONK	B	(HJKMNLX	(H) HERO & HEROINE	1974 A&M US 3607 UK AMLH63607
NICKY HOPKINS	K	(B	(I) STRAWBS BY CHOICE	1974 A&M UK AMLH68259
BLUE WEAVER	K	(FG	(J) GHOSTS	1975 A&M US 4506 UK AMLH68277
JOHN HAWKEN	K	(HJ	(K) NOMADNESS	1976 A&M US 4544 UK AMLH68331
CLAIRE DENIZ	CELLO	(CJ	(L) DEEP CUTS	1976 OYSTER US 1 1603 UK 2391 234
RON CHESTERMAN	B	(AC	(M) BURNING FOR YOU	1977 OYSTER US 1 1604 UK 2391 287
SANDY DENNY	V	(A	(N) DEAD LINES	1978 ARISTA US 4172 UK SPART 1036
KEN GUDMAND	D	(A	(O) BEST OF	1978 A&M US 6005 UK AMLM66005
RUPERT HOLMES	K	(L	(BC) EARLY STRAWBS	1974 A&M CAN 9014
ROY HILL	G V	(X	(X) 1980 BAND	
ALAN PARKER	G	(B		
ANDY WEIGHELL	B	(B	ANNE COLLINS V (F	RON VERRALL D (B TREVOR LUCAS V(F
JOHN MEALING	K	(MNKL	ROBERT KIRBY K (MN	TONY FERNANDEZ D (NX TONY VISCONTI PROD(F
JOHN KNIGHTSBRIDGE	G	(X	ANDY RICHARDS K (X	JACK EMBLOW ACC (K TOMMY EYRE K (K
TONY CARR	PERC	(K	JOHN LUMLEY-SAVILE K (K	MADDY PRIOR V (X

S295A STRAWHEAD S295A

GREGG BUTLER	V WIND	(A	(A) SONGS FROM THE BOOK OF ENGLAND(DBL)	1980 TRADITION UK TRS 0356
CHRIS POLLINGTON	G K V SYN	(A		
MALCOLM GIBBONS	G V	(A	PETE ASHWORTH VLN (A	STUART GRILLS TPT (A LAWRENCE YATES HRNS(A
IAN DUCKWORTH	TUBA	(A	EDWARD HOYLE TROM (A	MICHAEL LORMOR HRNS (A

S296 STRAY S296

DEL BROMHAM	G V K	(ABCDEFGH	(A) STRAY	1970 TRANSATLANTIC UK TRA216
STEVE GADD	HCA G V	(ABCDE	(B) SUICIDE	1971 TRANSATLANTIC UK TRA233
RITCHIE COLE	D	(ABCDEFGH	(C) SATURDAY MORNING PICTURES	1972 TRANSATLANTIC UK TRA248 RI TRS110
GARY G GILES	B	(ABCDEFGH	(C) SATURDAY MORNING PICTURES	1972 MERCURY US SRM1 624
JIMMY HELMS	TPT	(E	(D) MUDANZAS	1973 TRANSATLANTIC UK TRA268
PETE DYER	G V	(GH	(E) MOVE IT	1974 TRANSATLANTIC UK TRA281
MIKE EVANS	VLN	(C	(F) TRACKS	1975 TRANSATLANTIC UK TRASAM3066
KEITH BLEASBY	CONGAS	(C	(G) STAND UP & BE COUNTED	1975 DAWN UK DNLS 3066 US PYE 12017
ANDY BEARNE	HCA	(C	(H) HOUDINI	1976 PYE UK NSPL18482 US 12129
P P ARNOLD	V	(C	(J) HEARTS OF FIRE	1976 PYE UK NSPL18512
LISA STRIKE	V	(C		
BARRY ST JOHN	V	(C	KAY GARDNER V (C	

S296A STRAY CATS S296A

BRIAN SETZER	G V	(ABC	(A) STRAY CATS	1981 ARISTA UK STRAY 1
SLIM JIM PHANTOM	D	(ABC	(B) GONNA BALL	1981 ARISTA GER 204 019
LEE ROCKER	B V	(ABC	(C) BUILT FOR SPEED	1982 CAPITOL US 17070
IAN STEWART	K	(B		
JOHN LOCKE	K	(B	STEVE PONCAR SAX (B	BRIAN McDONALD HCA (A LEE ALLEN SAX (B
GARY BARNACLE	SAX	(A		

S297 STRAY DOG S297

SNUFFY WALDEN	G V	(AB	(A) STRAY DOG	1974 MANTICORE US 66671 UK K43506
TIM DULAINE	G V	(B	(B) WHILE YOU'RE DOWN THERE	1974 MANTICORE US 501s1 UK K53504
ALAN ROBERTS	B V	(AB		
LES SAMPSON	D	(AB	LUIS CABAZA K V(B	

S298 STRAY GATOR S298

NEIL YOUNG	G V	(		
BEN KEITH	STEEL	(	JACK NITZSCHE (	JOHN BARBATA D (KENNY BUTTREY D (
TIM DRUMMOND	B	(		

S298A STREET CORNER SYMPHONY S298A

JAMES GADSON D ((A) HARMONY GRITS 1975 BANG US 406
JAMES JAMESON B ((B) LITTLE FUNK MACHINE 1977 ABC US ABC 974

S298B STREET S298B

ANYA COHEN V PERC(A (A) STREET 19 VERVE US FTS 3057
MICHAEL LYNNE G B V(A
JOHN WILLIAMSON G B V(A AL CAMARDO PERC (A TOM CHAPSON D (A WILL BETZ G (A

S299 STREETBAND S299

PAUL YOUNG HCA K V (AB (A) LONDON 1979 LOGO UK 1012
ROGER KELLY G V (AB (B) DILEMMA 1979 LOGO UK 1017
JOHN GIFFORD G V (AB
MICK PEARL B V (AB VINCE CHAULK D (AB CHAZ JANKEL V K G(A JOOLS HOLLAND K (B
TREVOR RABIN K (B

S299A STREETHEART S299A

DARYL GUTHEIL K V (AB (A) MEANWHILE BACK IN PARIS 1978 ATLANTIC KCA 92002
MATTHEW FRENETTE D V (AB (B) UNDER HEAVEN OVER HELL 1979 ATLANTIC KSD 19228
KENNY SHIELDS V (ABC (C) STREETHEART 1982 CAPITOL CAN ST 6491
SPIDER SINNAEVE B V (AB
JOHN HANNAH G V (B PAUL DEAN G V (A

S299B STREETMARK S299B

DOROTHEA RAUKES K ((A) NORDLAND 1975 SKY SKY003
THOMAS SCHREIBER G ((B) EILEEN 1978 SKY SKY011
GEORG BUSCHMANN V ((C) DRY 1979 SKY SKY023
WOLFGANG WESTPHAL B ((D) SKY RACER 1981 SKY SKY050
HANS SCHWEISS D (

S299C STREETNOISE S299C

TINA NEWKIRK V (A (A) STREETNOISE 19 EVOLUTION US 2010
TOM TRICKS D (A
PAUL PATOS G V (A TOM GRAVES K (A WALLACE B (A

S300 STREETWALKERS S300

ROGER CHAPMAN HCA V(ALL (A) STREETWALKERS 1974 REPRISE UK K54017
CHARLIE WHITNEY G (ALL (A) STREETWALKERS 1975 MERCURY US SRMI 1060
BOB TENCH G V (BCDE (B) DOWNTOWN FLIER 1975 VERTIGO UK 6360 123
TIM HINKLEY K V (A (C) RED CARD 1976 VERTIGO UK 9102 010
MAX MIDDLETON K (A (C) RED CARD 1976 MERCURY US SRMI 1083
JOHN WETTON B V (A (D) VICIOUS BUT FAIR 1977 VERTIGO UK 9102 012 NL 6360 140
RIC GRECH B (A (D) VICIOUS BUT FAIR 197 MERCURY US SRMI 1135
NEIL HUBBARD G (A (E) STREETWALKERS LIVE(DBL) 1977 VERTIGO UK 6641 703
IAN WALLACE D (A
MIKE GILES D (A GODFREY McLEAN PERC (A POLI PALMER VIBES(ABD LINDA LEWIS V (A
PETE WINGFIELD K (B BOZ BURRELL V (A JIM CREGAN V (A NICKO D (BC
JON PLOTEL B (BC MICKEY FEAT B (DE BRIAN JOHNSTON K (DE DAVID DOWLE D (DE
MEL COLLINS HRNS (D

S301 STRETCH S301

KIRBY G (ABCD (A) ELASTIQUE 1975 ANCHOR UK ANCL 2014
ELMER GANTRY G V (ABC (B) CANT BEAT YOUR BRAIN FOR ENTERTAINMENT 1976 ANCHOR UK ANCL 2016
STEVE EMERY B (ABCD (C) LIFE BLOOD 1977 ANCHOR UK ANCL2023 GER 25698
JEFF RICH D (BC (D) FORGET THE PAST 1978 HOT WAX UK HW1
ROSHI G (A
PAUL MARTINEZ B (A JIM RUSSELL D (A JOHN COOK K (AD CHRIS MERCER HRNS(AD
MICK EVE HRNS (A RON CARTHY HRNS (A MIKE BAILEY HRNS (A NICKO McBAIN D (D
CHRIS FLETCHER PERC (D FRAN BYRNE D (D NIGEL WATSON G V (A

S302 WILLIAM R STRICKLAND S302

WILLIAM R STRICKLAND (A (A) WILLIAM R STRICKLAND IS ONLT THE NAME 1969 DERAM UK SML 1041

S302A PETE STRIDE & JOHN PLAIN S302A

PETE STRIDE G V (A (A) NEW GUITAR IN TOWN 1980 BEGGARS BANQUET UK BEGA 17
JOHN PLAIN G V (A
TONY BATEMAN V B (A JACK BLACK D (A PETE EDWARDS HCA V(A MICK TALBOT K (A

S303 STRIDER S303

JIM HAWKINS B (A (A) EXPOSED 1973 G M GML 1002
IAN KEWLEY K V (A (B) MISUNDERSTANDING 1974 G M UK GML 1012
BOB MURRAY G (
GARY GRAINGER G (BA ROB ELLIOT V (B LEE STRELLEZYK B (BA COSMO G (
JAY WILLIAMS G (MALCOLM MORTIMER D (LES OLBINSON PERC (TONY MILLS (
MARK PINDER D (TONY BROCK D V (B JENNY HAAN V (B

S304 STRIFE S304

JOHN REID HCA G V (AB (A) RUSH 1975 CHRYSALIS CHR 1063
GORDON ROWLEY B V (AB (B) BACK TO THUNDER 1978 GULL UK GULL 1029
PAUL H ELLSON D (A
DAVID WILLIAMS D V (B DON AIREY K (B

S305 STRIKER S305

SCOTT ROSBURG V B G((A) STRIKER 1978 ARISTA US 4165 SPART1059
RICK TAYLOR D V (
RICK RANDLE V K G(RICK RAMIREZ G (

S306 STRING DRIVEN THING S306

CHRIS ADAMS G V (ABE (A) STRING DRIVEN THING 1972 CHARISMA UK CAS 1062
PAULINE ADAMS V (ABE (B) MACHINE THAT CRIED 1973 CHARISMA US 6063 UK CAS 1070
GRAHAME SMITH VLN (ABCDE (C) PLEASE MIND YOUR HEAD 1974 CHARISMA UK CAS1097 US 20TH 470
COLIN WILSON G B (AB (D) KEEP YER'AND ON IT 1975 CHARISMA UK CAS1112 US 20TH 503
BILLY FAIRLEY D (B (E) STRING DRIVEN THING 19 CONCORD UK CON 1001
CLARE SEALEY CELLO(B
BILL HATJE B (B JAMES EXELL B V (CD KENNY ROWE V (C GRAHAME WHITE V (C
COLIN FAIRLEY D V (CD ALUN ROBERTS G V (CD KIMBERLEY BEACON V (CD HENRY McDONALD K (C
ALAN SKIDMORE SAX (C PETER WOOD PNO (D CUDDLY JUDDLY HCA (D

S306A STRINGBAND S306A

SUSIE EVERETT G V PERC(A (A) STREET SINGERS HEAVEN 1974 INTERCORD GER 26467
JOHN EVERETT VLN BAN G (A
JOHN BERQUIST B BAN V (A BOB DOUGLAS G B V (A

S308 **BARRETT STRONG** S308

BARRETT STRONG V (A — (A) STRONGHOLD 1975 CAPITOL EST 11376
(B) LIVE & LOVE 1976 CAPITOL 11490

S308A **STRONGBOW** S308A

BILL BENDER V K HRNS(A — (A) STRONGBOW 1975 SOUTHWIND UK SWS 6401
JOHN STELZER K WIND V(A
DAVID SMITH D V (A MICHAEL SHORTLAND G V (A JOHN DURZO B V (A

S308B **BABE STOVALL** S308B

BABE STOVALL (A — (A) BABE STOVALL 19 VERVE US

S309 **STUD** S309

JIM CREGAN G V (A — (A) STUD 1971 DERAM AML1084 POLYDOR 2310 097
RICHARD McCRACKEN G B (A — (B) SEPTEMBER 1972 BASF GERM 20 29054
JOHN WILSON D (A — (C) GOODBYE -LIVE AT COMMAND 1973 BASF GERM 20 29117
JOHN WEIDER VLN G K V(BC

S310 **STUFF** S310

CORNELL DUPREE G (— (A) STUFF 1977 WB UK K56305 US BS2968
STEVE GADD D (— (B) MORE STUFF 1977 WB US BS3061
ERIC GALE G (— (C) STUFF IT 197 WB US BS3262
RICHARD TEE K (— (D) LIVE IN JAPAN 1979 WEA JAP 10629
GORDON EDWARDS B (— (E) LIVE STUFF 1978 WB GER 56720
CHRIS PARKER D (— (F) LIVE IN NY 1980 WB EURO 56833 US 3417

S310A **STUMBLEBUNNY** S310A

DAVID WHITE G V (A — (A) WHILE YOU WERE OUT 1979 MERCURY GER 9198 135
PETER JORDON B (A
CHRIS ROBINSON G K V(A SAMMY BROWN D V (A STAN BRONSTEIN SAX (A

S311 **JEFF STURGES & UNIVERSE** S311

DEAN PARKS G (A — (A) JEFF STURGES & UNIVERSE 197 MAM US MAM1 UK MAMAS1002
DENNIS KELLY B (A
DON BALDWIN B (A HAL STESCH K (A ROGER RAMPTON PERC (A MIKE LEWIS PERC(A
JIMMY MANONE D (A BOBBY SHAW TPT (A TOM PORRELLO TPT (A JON MURAKAMI TPT (A
RICH COOPER TPT (A DEREK WATKINS TPT (A JIM TRIMBLE TROM (A BILL BOOTH TROM(A
STAN NISHAMURA TROM (A ARCHIE WHEELER SAX (A BURT ESTERMAN SAX (A DON MENZA SAX (A
JOHN PHILLIPS SAX (A GARY FREYMAN SAX (A ART MAEBE HRNS (A DICK PERISSI HRNS(A
AUBREY BOUCK HRNS (A RALPH POLLACK HRNS (A JEFF STURGES (A

S311A **STYLISTICS** S311A

RUSSELL THOMPKINS JR V (E — (A) THE STYLISTICS 1971 H&L US 33023 UK AVCO 6466 008
JAMES SMITH V (E — (B) 2 1972 H&L US 11006 UK AVCO 6466 010
JAMES DUNN V (E — (C) ROCK'N'ROLL BABY 1973 H&L US 11010 UK AVCO 6466 012
AIRRION LOVE V (E — (D) LETS PUT IT ALL TOGETHER 1974 H&L US 69001 UK AVCO 6466 013
HERB MURRELL V (E — (E) HEAVY 197 H&L US 69004
(F) FROM THE MOUNTAIN 197 UK AVCO 9109 002
(G) THE BEST OF 1975 H&L US 69005 UK AVCO 9109 003
(H) THANK YOU BABY 1975 H&L US 69008 UK AVCO 9109 005
(I) YOU ARE BEAUTIFUL 1975 H&L US 69010 UK AVCO 9109 006
(J) FABULOUS 1976 H&L US 69013 UK 9109 008
(K) BEST OF VOL 2 1976 H&L UK 9109 010
(L) ONCE UPON A JUKE BOX 197 H&L US 69015
(M) SUN & SOUL 1977 H&L US 69019 UK 9109 014
(N) SPOTLIGHT ON 1977 H&L UK 6641 622
(O) WONDER WOMAN 1978 H&L US 69032 UK 9109 016
(P) LIVE IN JAPAN 1979 FLYOVER JAP 594
(Q) BLACK SATIN 1979 H&L UK 9198 230
(R) IN FASHION 19 MERCURY US 3727

S312 **STYLUS** S312

PETER JONES STRINGS HRNS(A — (A) STYLUS 1978 PRODIGAL PDL 2011
GRAHAM LYALL HRNS (A
MIKE CLARKE HRNS (A SAM McNALLY K (A PETER CUPPLES V K G(A ASHLEY HENDERSON B V (A
RON PEERS G V (A TREVOR COURTNEY D (A

S312A **POLY STYRENE** S312A

POLY STYRENE V (A — (A) TRANSLUCENCE 1980 UA UAG 30320
RICHARD MOORE G (A
KUMA HARADA B (A TED BUNTING WIND (A DARYL LEE QUE PERC (A KEVIN McALEA K (A
RICHARD BAILEY D (A G T MOORE G (A

S313 **LAURIE STYVERS** S313

LAURIE STYVERS K V (AB — (A) SPILT MILK 1972 CHRYSALIS UK CHR1007 US WB1946
TOM PARKER K (AB — (B) COLORADO KID 1973 CHRYSALIS UK CHR1038
ANDREW STEELE D (AB
HENRY SPINETTI D (AB GARY TAYLOR B (AB BRIAN DALY G (A ROD KING STEEL(A
MIKE RICHARDS D (A ADRIAN LEGG G (A JIM LAWLESS PERC (A CLAIRE TORRY V (A
SUE LYNN V (A NOELEEN BATLEY V (A ALAN PARKER G (A JERRY DONAHUE G (B
DYAN BIRCH V (B FRANK COLLINS V (B PADDY McHUGH V (B RODNEY WYATT G (B
TOMMY EYRE K (B TRISTRAM FRY PERC (B BILLY BEHNKE G (B PETE WILLSHER STEEL(B
CHRISSIE STEWART B (B MICK COX G (B MAL LUKER SITAR(B JERRY HOVELL V (B
GEORGE LEE SAX (B JON FIELD CONGA(B

S314 **STYX** S314

JAMES YOUNG G (ALL — (A) STYX 1972 WOODEN NICKEL US BXLI 1008
DAN BARBER HRNS(L — (A) STYX 1980 RCA RI UK 3593
DENNIS DE YOUNG K (ALL — (B) STYX II (LADY) 1973 WOODEN NICKEL US BXLI 1012
MIKE HALPIN HRNS (L — (B) STYX II (LADY) 1980 RCA RI UK 3694
CHUCK PANOZZO B (ALL — (C) SERPENT IS RISING 1973 WOODEN NICKEL US BXLI 0287
MARK OHLSEN HRNS (L — (C) SERPENT IS RISING 1980 RCA RI UK 3595
JOHN PANOZZO D (ALL — (D) MAN OF MIRACLES 1974 WOODEN NICKEL US BWLI 0638
BILL SIMPSON HRNS (L — (D) MAN OF MIRACLES 1980 RCA RI UK 3596
JOHN CURULEWSKI G (ABCDE — (E) EQUINOX 1975 A&M US 4559 UK AMLH64559
TOM NARDIN G (— (F) CRYSTAL BALL 1976 A&M US 4604 UK AMLH64604
TOMMY SHAW G (FGHJL — (G) GRAND ILLUSION 1977 A&M US 4637 UK AMLH64637
JOHN HAYNOR HRNS (L — (G) GRAND ILLUSION 197 MOBILE US 026
BILL THAUT SAX (B — (H) PIECES OF EIGHT 1978 A&M US 4724 UK AMLH64724
STEVE EISEN SAX (JL — (J) CORNERSTONE 1979 A&M US 3711 UK AMLK63711
(K) BEST OF 1977 WOODEN NICKEL US BXLI 2250
(K) BEST OF 1979 RCA US 3597 UK PL 13116
(L) PARADISE THEATRE 1980 A&M US 3719 UK AMLK63719

S315 SUBURBAN STUDS S315

(A) SLAM 1978 POGO UK POW 001

S315A SUBURBS S315A

HUGO KLAERS D (A — (A) IN COMBO 1980 TWINTONE US 8014
BLAINE JOHN BEEJTAR V (A
BRUCE B C ALLEN G V (A CHAN POLING K V (A MICHAEL HALLIDAY B (A

S316 SUBWAY SECT S316

VIC GODDARD V (123A — (A) WHAT'S THE MATTER BOY 1980 MCA UK 3070
MARK LAFF D (2 — (1) 1977 (2) 1977 (3) 1978
PAUL MYERS B (123
ROBERT MILLER G (123 PAUL SMITH D (1 ROB WARD D (3

S317 SUE & SUNNY S317

SUE GLOVER V (A — (A) SUE & SUNNY 1970 CBS UK 63740
SUNNY LESLIE V (A

S318 SUGARLOAF S318

JERRY CORBETTA K V (ABCD — (A) SUGARLOAF 1970 LIBERTY US LST7640 UK LBS83415
BOB WEBBER G B (ABCD — (B) I GOT A SONG 1973 BRUT US 6006
BOB RAYMOND SAX G B (ABCD — (C) SPACE SHIP EARTH 1974 UA UK UAS29165 US LIBERTY 11010
BOB MACVITTIE D (AC — (D) DON'T CALL US, WE'LL CALL YOU 1975 POLYDOR UK 2310 394
ROBERT YEAZEL G V (C — (D) DON'T CALL US, WE'LL CALL YOU 1975 CLARIDGE US 1000
BOB PICKETT G B (
MYRON POLLOCK D (D LARRY FERRIS D (B

S319 SUICIDE S319

ALAN VEGA V (ALL — (A) SUICIDE 1977 BRONZE BRON 508+RED STAR IMP
MARTY REV INST (ALL — (B) LIVE(LIMITED EDITION) 1979 FRANKI 1
RIC OCASEK PROD (C — (C) SUICIDE 1980 ZE US 7080 UK ILPS 7007
CRAIG LEON PROD (A — (D) HALF ALIVE 1981 ROIR A103
MARTY THAU PROD (A

S320 SUICIDE COMMANDOS S320

(A) MAKE A RECORD 1978 BLANK US 002 NL MERCURY 6336673

S320A SUICIDE ROMEO S320A

PIERRE GODDARD G V (A — (A) PICTURES 1980 ZE UK ILPS 7010
MICHEL BELLOCQ G SYN(A
JEAN LOUIS WINBERG B(A DANIEL BRUNETTI SAX (A FREDERICK D (A

S321 BIG JIM SULLIVAN S321

BIG JIM SULLIVAN G (ABCD — (A) SITAR BEAT 1968 MERCURY US SR61137 UK SML30001
BUDDY CHILDERS HRNS (B — (B) JIM SULLIVAN 1972 PLAYBOY US 103
CHAS HODGES K FDL G V (C — (C) BIG JIMS BACK 1974 RETREAT RTA 4001
IAN WALLACE D V (C — (D) SULLIVAN PLAYS OSULLIVAN 1977 MAM RAM 3003
DAVE PEACOCK B BAN V (C
CHUCK FINDLEY HRNS (B DICK HYDE TROM (B VINCE DE ROSA HRNS (B KEN SHROYER HRNS(B
GEORGE ROBERTS HRNS (B JIM HORN SAX (B TOM SCOTT WIND (B JIM HUGHART B (B
COLIN BAILEY PERC (B MIKE MELVOIN PNO (B DAVID COHEN G BAN(B ALLEN REUSS BAZ (B
GENE ESTES PERC (B

S321A JOHN L SULLIVAN S321A

JOHN L SULLIVAN V (A — (A) WOMAN LEAVE ME ALONE 1972 NUGGET US 101

S322 ROCKY SULLIVAN S322

JOHN CIPOLLINA G (A — (A) ILLEGAL ENTRY 1981 RAG BABY 1010 JUPITER US 2006
ROCKY SULLIVAN V (A
JOEY COVINGTON D (MARIO CIPOLLINA G B (JARRETT WASHINGTON K (MIKE VARNEY G (A
STEVE LIND B (A GREG ANTON D (A SCOTT METHEWS D (A MAC CRIDLIN B (A
MARK CUMMINGS SYN (A CAROLE STEELE PERC (A MARK SHAIMAN K (A JEFF COHEN G (A
GREGG DOUGLASS (A NICKY HOPKINS K (A JANET MORRISON V (A JEANETTE SARTAIN V (A
PAM MOORE V (A

S323 HUBERT SUMLIN S323

HUBERT SUMLIN G V (ALL — (A) HUBERT'S AMERICAN BLUES 19 SCOUT SC4
LONNIE BROOKS G (B — (B) GROOVE 1976 BLACK & BLUE 33511
FRED BELOW D (BC — (C) KINGS OF CHICAGO BLUES VOL 2 19 VOGUE LDM 30175
SUNNYLAND SLIM V PNO(AD — (D) BLUES ANYTIME (1964) 1980 L+R GERM 42004
WILLIE MABON PNO (B — (E) GAMBLIN' WOMAN 1980 L+R GERM 42008
CLIFTON JAMES D (AD
CAREY BELL V HCA(B JIMMY DAWKINS G (C JAMES GREEN B (C BILLY BOY ARNOLD V HCA(C
EDDIE SHAW SAX (C JOE CARTER G V (C DAVE MYERS B (B WILLIE DIXON B (D

S323A DONNA SUMMER S323A

DONNA SUMMER V (A — (A) STAR COLLECTION 1977 ATLANTIC UK 20109
PAUL JABARA (G — (B) LOVE TO LOVE YOU BABY 1977 GTO UK 008 US OASIS 5001
(C) LOVE TRILOGY 1977 US OASIS 5004
(D) FOUR SEASONS OF LOVE 1977 GTO UK 018 US CASABLANCA 7038
(E) I REMEMBER YESTERDAY 1977 GTO UK 025 US CASABLANCA 7056
(F) THE DEEP 1977 CASABLANCA UK 2018
(G) SHUT OUT 1977 CASABLANCA UK 2019
(H) ONCE UPON A TIME 1977 CASABLANCA UK 5003 US 5003
(I) GREATEST HITS 1977 GTO UK 028
(J) LIVE AND MORE 1978 CASABLANCA UK 5006 RI 81 6680030
(K) I REMEMBER YESTERDAY 1979 EMBASSY UK 31718
(L) BAD GIRLS 1979 CASABLANCA UK 5007 RI 81 6635035
(M) ON THE RADIO(GREATEST HITS) 1979 CASABLANCA UK 5008 RI 81 6685049
(N) WANDERER 1980 GEFFEN UK K99124
(O) WALK AWAY 1981 CASABLANCA UK 6302 070
(P) DONNA SUMMER 1982 WB UK 99163

S324 SAFFRON SUMMERFIELD S324

SAFFRON SUMMERFIELD V G K(AB — (A) SALISBURY PLAIN 1974 MOTHER EARTH MUM 1001
GEORGE NORRIS G V (A — (B) FANCY MEETING YOU HERE 1976 MOTHER EARTH MUM 1202
LAURIE RHODES B (A
ALISON BAILEY CELLO(A

S325 BILL SUMMERS S325

BILL SUMMERS V PERC FLT(AB (A) STRAIGHT TO THE BANK 1978 PRESTIGE PR 10105
LEO MILLER V (A (B) ON SUNSHINE 1979 PRESTIGE PR 10107
VIRGINIA AYERS V (A
RAY OBIEDO G (AB FRED WASHINGTON B (A GEORGE BOHANON TROM (A BENNY POWELL TROM(A
DARRYL JACKSON D (A OSCAR BRASHEAR HRNS (A JOHN BARNES K (A RAY BROWN HRNS(A
LEON CHANCLER D (A JERRY HEY HRNS (AB DICK HYDE TROM (A BILL GREEN SAX (A
PATTIE BROOKS V (A ERNIE WATTS SAX (A MAXINE ANDERSON V (A LORI HAM V (B
JOSIE JAMES V (A CALVIN TILLERY V (B PETSYE POWELL V (A TOM POOLE TPT (B
LARRY BATISTE TROM V PNO(B BO FREEMAN B (B CLAYTOVEN SAX PNO V (B PAUL VAN WAGENINGEN D(B
PAUL SMITH K (B SCOTT ROBERTS PERC V(B TIM GORMAN SYN (B MARLON McCLAIN G (B
GARY GALVIN B (B GREG PHILLINGANES PNO (B LLOYD ADAMS D (B GAYLORD BIRCH D (B
DWAYNE SWEET K (B TONY LEWIS D (B PHILLIP RICHARDSON V (B WAYNE WALLACE TROM(B
MARK SOSKIN PNO (B COLIN PAYNE ORG (B LARRY WILLIAMS SAX (B MAXINE WILLARD V (B
MYYA LARK V (B CARLBERG JONES HRNS (B JULIA TILLMAN V (B PAT HENDERSON V (B
STRINGS (B

S326 SUN S326

BARON BYRD WIND K V(C (A) LIVE ON DREAM ON 1976 CAPITOL 11461
KEITH CHEATHAM G TROM V(C (B) SUN POWER 1977 CAPITOL 11609
KYM YANCEY D V(C (C) SUNBURN 1978 CAPITOL 11723
CURTIS HOOKS B SAX(V(C (D) DESTINATION SUN 1979 CAPITOL 11941
SONNY TALBERT K G V SYN(C (E) SUN OVER THE UNIVERSE 1980 CAPITOL 12088
NIGEL BOULTON HRNS V(C (F) FORCE OF NATURE 1981 CAPITOL 12142
ERNIE KRISLEY HRNS (C
GARY KING TROM V(C ROBERT ARNOLD TPT V(C

S326A SUN ALSO RISES S326A

GRAHAM HEMINGWAY G V (A (A) SUN ALSO RISES 1970 VILLAGE THING UK VTS 2
ANNE HEMINGWAY V DULC(A
JOHN TURNER B (A ANDY LEGGETT WIND (A

S326B SUN RAYS S326B

RICKY HENN D V (A (A) ANDREA 1967 TOWER US 5017
EDDIE MEDORA G V (A
VINCE HOZIER B V (A MARTY DI GIOVANNI K (A BYRON CASE G D V(A MURRY WILSON PROD(A

S327 SUNDANCE S327

BOB BOWMAN G V BAN(A (A) RAIN STEAM SPEED 1973 DECCA UK TXS111 US KAPP 3659
JOHN LYNAM G V MAND(A (B) CHUFFER 1974 DECCA UK SKL5183
PHIL SAVAGE B V HCA((A (C) SUNDANCE 1975 20TH CENTURY US 477
STEPHEN GRIFFIN K V (A
ALAN MOORE D V (A

S327A SUNDAY FUNNIES S327A

RICHARD KOSINSKI K V (A (A) SUNDAY FUNNIES 1971 RARE EARTH US RS 526
RICHARD MITCHELL D (A
RICHARD FIDGE V (A RONALD AITKEN G V (A

S327B ROY SUNDHOLM S327B

ROY SUNDHOLM G V (AB (A) CHINESE METHOD 1979 ENSIGN ENVY 10
ALAN PLATT D PERC(A (B) EAST TO WEST 1981 ENSIGN ENVY 503
BRUCE DOUGLAS G B (A
GUY HUMPHRIES G (A BRIAN ROBERTSON G (A CARMEN DEMICHI G (A PATRICK BROWNE K (A
BOB ANDREWS K (A RAY BEAVIS HRNS (A JOHN EARLE HRNS (A DICK HANSON HRNS (A
CHRIS GOWER TROM(A SHARON CAMBELL V (A LINDA TAYLOR V (A

S328 SUNFOREST S328

(A) SOUND OF SUNFOREST 19 NOVA UK SDN17

S238A SUNNY JIM BAND S238A

MARTIN ALLEN G V (A (A) JAY 1981 VERTIGO GER 6435 100
JOHN BARRY B (A
DIDIER LAGET G PERC(A J J VRENEGOOR D (A DOREEN CHANTER V (A JILL MACKINTOSH V (A
STEVE NYE K (A

S329 SUNNYLAND SLIM S329

SUNNYLAND SLIM V PNO(ALL (A) SLIM'S GOT THIS THING GOIN' ON 1968 WORLD PACIFIC US WPS 21890
ERNEST DONABLE D (A (A) SLIM'S GOT THIS THING GOIN' ON 1969 LIBERTY UK LBS 83237
MICKEY BAKER G (K (B) MIDNIGHT JUMP 1969 BLUE HORIZON UK 763213
LAYFAYETTE HUDSON B (K (C) PEARL HARBOUR BLUES(1 SIDE) 1970 RCA INT UK INT 1176
GEORGE SMITH HCA (A (D) SAD & LONESOME 1972 JEWEL US LPS 5010
LUTHER ALLISON G (A (E) PLAYS RAGTIME BLUES 1973 BLUESWAY BLS 6068
MICK TAYLOR G (A (F) & LITTLE BROTHER MONTGOMERY 19 77 77LA 1221
CURTIS TILLMAN B (A (G) SUNNYLAND SLIM 19 STORYVILLE SLP 169
RANDY FULLERTON G (A (H) LEGACY OF THE BLUES 1975 SONET UK SNTF 671
BIG MAMA THORNTON D (A (I) BLUES MASTERS VOL 8 19 BLUE HORIZON US 4608
ROBERT ELEM B (A (J) DECORATION DAY 1980 L+R GERM 42015
FRANCIS CLAY D (A (K) DEPRESSION BLUES 19 FESTIVAL FLD 648
HENRY VESTINE G (A ( ) PATIENCE LIKE JOB 1979 AIRWAY US LP 4746
ODIE PAYNE D (J ( ) SHE GOT THAT JIVE 19 AIRWAY US 3220
BOB STROGER B (J ( ) CHICAGO BLUES 19 SPIVEY US 1003
CAREY BELL HCA (J
AL WILSON G (A LARRY TAYLOR B (A PAUL LAGOS D (A GUS WRIGHT D (A
SHAKEY JAKE HCA (A FRED BELOW D (E DAVE MYERS B (E LOUIS MYERS D (E
JOHNNY SHINES G (B WILLIE DIXON B (B WALTER HORTON HCA (B CLIFTON JAMES D (B
BLIND JOHN DAVIS PNO (C BIG BILL BROONZY G (C RANSOM KNOWLING B (C JUDGE RILEY D (C
HUBERT SUMLIN G (J JEFF SWAN G (J

S329A SUNSHINE S329A

JACK GREEN B G V(A (A) SUNSHINE 1972 WB UK K46169
GORDON EDWARDS G K V(A
PETER OLIVER G V (A TERRY SLADE PERC D(A JOANNE WHITE PERC V(A ETHEL COLEY PERC V(A

S329B **SUNSHINE** S329B

JACK GREEN B G V(A (A) SUNSHINE 1972 WB UK K46169
GORDON EDWARDS G K V(A
PETER OLIVER G V (A TERRY SLADE PERC D(A JOANNE WHITE PERC V(A ETHEL COLEY PERC V(A

S329C **SUNSET BOMBERS** S329C

NICK ARMAND V (A (A) SUNSET BOMBERS 1978 ARIOLA US 50025
RICK ARMAND G (A
BRENDON MATHESON D (A DOUGLAS FIEGER B (A

S330 **SUNSHINE COMPANY** S330

MARY NANCE V PERC(ABC (A) HAPPY IS THE SUNSHINE COMPANY 1967 IMPERIAL US 12359
MAURICE MANSEAU V K G(ABC (B) SUNSHINE COMPANY 1968 IMPERIAL US 12368
LARRY SIMS G V (ABC (C) SUNSHINE & SHADOWS 1968 LIBERTY UK LBS 83159
MEREL BREGANTE D V (ABC (C) SUNSHINE & SHADOWS 1968 IMPERIAL US 12399
DOUGLAS MARK G VLN V (ABC
DAVE HODGKINS G (C

S331 **SUNTREADER** S331

MORRIS PERT D (AB (A) ZIN ZIN 1973 ISLAND UK HELP13
PETER ROBINSON K (AB (B) MUSIC OF MORRIS PERT 1976 CHANTRY UK ABM 21
ALYN ROSS B (A
ROBIN THOMPSON SAX (A NEVILLE WHITEHEAD B PERC(B PAUL BUCKMASTER CELLO (B MARTYN FORD HRN (B
VERONICA HAYWARD V (B GEORGIA DOBREE HRN (B

S331A **RICHARD SUPA** S331A

RICHARD SUPA G V (A (A) SUPAS JAMBOREE 19 PARAMOUNT PAS 6009
LIBERTY DEVITTO D (A
IVAN ELIAS B (A JOHNATHAN HIPPS K (A DEAN DOUGHTRY K (A HOWIE EMERSON G (A
J R COBB G (A BARRY BAILEY G (A ROBERT NIX D (A PAUL GODDARD D (A

S332 **SUPERCHARGE** S332

ALBIE DONNELLY WIND V(AB (A) LOCAL LADS MAKE GOOD 1976 VIRGIN UK V 2053
DALE IRVING D V (A (B) HORIZONTAL REFRESHMENT 1977 VIRGIN UK V 2067
IAIN BRADSHAW K (A (C) BODY RHYTHM 1979 VIRGIN UK V 2118
LES KARSKI G V (A (D) NOW JUMP 19 CRIMINAL UK STEAL 10
OZZIE YUE G V (A (EP) 4 BY 6 1976 VIRGIN UK VEP 1001
TONY DUNMORE B V (A
BOB ROBERTSON SAX V(A DICK HANSON TPT (A

S332A **SUPERFINE DANDELION** S332A

MIKE McFADDEN V G HCA (A (A) SUPERFINE DANDELION 196 MAINSTREAM US S6102
MIKE COLLINS D V (A
ED BLACK G K V(A RICK ANDERSON B G (A

S332B **SUPERMAX** S332B

KURT HAVENSTEIN V B K(A (A) WORLD OF TODAY 1977 ATLANTIC K50423
CYNTHIA ARRICH V (A (B) DONT STOP THE MUSIC 1977 ATLANTIC GER 50325
TEBLES REYNOLDS V (A (C) FLY WITH ME 1979 ELEKTRA US 193
RICHARD SCHOENHERZ SYN K(A (D) TYPES OF SKIN 1980 ELEKTRA NL 52253
RAINER MARZ G (A
JUANITA SCHULZ V(A JUANITA FORD PERC (A HARTMUT PFANNMULLER D(A

S332C **SUPERSEPFFT** S332C

DIETER KOLB SYN (A (A) ROBOTER WERK 1979 CBS 83712
ROBOTERWERKE D (A

S332D **SUPERSISTER** S332D

ROBERT JAN STIPS K (ALL (A) PRESENT FROM NANCY(SUPERSISTER) 1970 POLYDOR 2419061 US DWARF 2001
RON VAN ECK B (ALL (B) TO THE HIGHEST BIDDER 1971 DANDELION 2310 146 POLY2925002
MARCO VROLIJK D (ABC (C) PUDDING AND GISTEREN 1972 POLYDOR 2925 007 + 2419 058
SACHA VAN GEEST WIND (ABCD (D) ISKANDER 1973 POLYDOR 2485 134 2925 021
CHARLIE MARIANO WIND (D (E) SUPER STRASHINE 3 197 POLYDOR 2419 030
HERMAN VAN BOEYEN D (D (F) SWEET OKAY 1974 POLYDOR NL 2441 048
PIERRE MOERLEN PERC (D

S333 **SUPERTRAMP** S333

ROGER HODGSON V G (ABCDEFGJ (A) SUPERTRAMP 1970 A&M US 4665 UK AMLS 981
RICHARD DAVIES K V (ABCDEFGJ (B) INDELIBLY STAMPED 1971 A&M US 4311 UK AMLS64306
RICHARD PALMER G (A (C) CRIME OF THE CENTURY 1974 A&M US 3647 UK AMLS68258
DAVE WINTHROP SAX (B (D) CRISIS? WHAT CRISIS? 1975 A&M US 4560 UK AMLH60347
BOB MILLER D (A (E) EVEN IN THE QUIETEST MOMENTS 1977 A&M US 4634 UK AMLK64634
KEVIN CURRIE D (B (F) BREAKFAST IN AMERICA 1979 A&M US 3708 UK AMLK63708
FRANK FARRELL B (B (G) PARIS 1980 A&M US 6702 UK AMLM66702
BOB BENBERG D (CDEFGJ ( ) EXTREMES(SOUNDTRACK) 1973 DERAM UK AML 1095
JOHN HELLIWELL SAX (CDEFGJ (DE) CRISIS?/EVEN IN THE (CASS) 1981 A&M UK CAMCR7
DOUGIE THOMPSON B (CDEFG (J) FAMOUS LAST WORDS 1982 A&M UK AMLK63732
DICK HYDE TROM (F
KEN SCOTT PROD(C ANN WILSON V (J NANCY WILSON V (J CLAIRE DIAMENT V (J

S333A **SUPREMES** S333A

DIANA ROSS V (MEET THE SUPREMES 1964 TAMLA US 606 UK STATESIDE10109
MARY WILSON V (LIVE AT THE APOLLO 1964 TAMLA US 609
FLORENCE BALLARD V (A BIT OF LIVERPOOL 1965 TAMLA US 621
BARBARA MARTIN V (WHERE DID OUR LOVE GO 1965 TAMLA US 623
CINDY BIRDSONG V (COUNTRY WESTERN & POP 1965 TAMLA US 625 UK TML11018
JEAN TERRELL V (HITS (EP) 1965 TAMLA UK TME 2008
LYNDA LAURENCE V (MORE HITS 1965 TAMLA US 627 UK TML 11020
SHARI PAYNE V (WE REMEMBER SAM COOKE 1965 TAMLA US 629 UK TML 11012
SUSAYE GREEN V (WITH LOVE 1965 TAMLA UK TML 11002
KAREN JACKSON V (AT THE COPA 196 TAMLA US 636 UK STML11026
MERRY CHRISTMAS 1965 TAMLA US 638
WITH I HEAR A SYMPHONY 1966 TAMLA US 643 UK STML11028
JAMES GADSON D (" . " " " 1981 TAMLA UK RI STMS 5012
JULIUS WECHTER B (AGO GO 1966 TAMLA US 649 UK STML11039
RAY PARKER G ("." 1981 TAMLA UK RI STMS 5013
EDDIE BONGO BROWN CONGA(SING MOTOWN 1967 TAMLA UK STML11047
JOE SAMPLE K (" " 1981 TAMLA UK RI STMS 5014
GARY COLEMAN PERC (SING HOLLAND DOZIER HOLLAND 1967 TAMLA US 650

(CONTINUED)

S333A (CONTINUED) **SUPREMES** S333A

SCOTT EDWARDS B (SING RODGERS & HART 1967 TAMLA US 659 UK STML11054
OLIVER BROWN CONGA(GREATEST HITS 1968 TAMLA US 663 UK STML11063
JAY GRAYDON G (FUNNY GIRL 1968 TAMLA US 672 UK STML11288
DAN WYMAN SYN (LIVE AT THE TALK OF THE TOWN 1968 TAMLA US 676 UK STML11070
HENRY DAVIS B (" " " " 1979 MFP UK 50449
WAH WAH WATSON G (REFLECTIONS 1968 TAMLA US 665 UK STML11073
BEN BENAY G (LOVE CHILD 1969 TAMLA UK STML11095
JOHN BARNES G (JOIN THE TEMPTATIONS 1969 TAMLA US 679 UK STML11096
CLARENCE McDONALD K (" " " " 1981 TAMLA UK RI STMS 5015
ROBERT ZIMMITTI PERC (T C B 1969 TAMLA US 682 UK STML11110
CHUCK RAINEY B (LET THE SUN SHINE IN 1969 TAMLA US 689 UK STML11114
GREG POREE G (TOGETHER(TEMPTATIONS) 1969 TAMLA US 692 UK STML11122
SONNY BURKE K (CREAM OF THE CROP 1970 TAMLA US 694 UK STML11137
ON BROADWAY(TEMPTATIONS) 1970 TAMLA US 699
GREATEST HITS VOL 2 1970 TAMLA US 702 UK STML11146
FAREWELL 1970 TAMLA US 708 UK STML11154
RIGHT ON 1970 TAMLA US 705 UK STML11157
NEW WAYS BUT LOVE STAYS 1971 TAMLA US 720 UK STML11175
MAGNIFICENT SEVEN 1971 TAMLA US 717 UK STML11179
SURRENDER 197 TAMLA US 723
TOUCH 1971 TAMLA US 737 UK STML11189
RETURN OF THE MAGNIFICENT SEVEN 1971 TAMLA US 736 UK STML11192
DYNAMITE 1972 TAMLA US 745 UK STML11203
FLOY JOY 1972 TAMLA US 751 UK STML11210
BABY LOVE 1973 MFP UK SPR 90001
GREATEST HITS 1974 TAMLA UK STML11256
SUPREMES PRODUCED BY JIM WEBB 1973 TAMLA US 756 UK STML11222
ANTHOLOGY 1974 TAMLA UK A3/1
ANTHOLOGY 1975 TAMLA US 794 UK TMSP 6001
SUPREMES 1975 TAMLA US 879 UK STML11293
HIGH ENERGY 1976 TAMLA US 863 UK STML12027
MARY,SHARI & SUSAYE 1976 TAMLA US 873 UK STML12047
STOP IN THE NAME OF LOVE 1976 MFP UK MFP 50291
AT THEIR BEST 197 TAMLA US 904 UK STML12091
DIANA ROSS & THE SUPREMES 1977 TAMLA UK STMX 6001
SUPREMES & TEMPTATIONS 1977 TAMLA UK STMX 6003
20 GOLDEN GREATS 1977 TAMLA UK EMTV 5
IT'S HAPPENING 19 MCA 734727
EARLY DAYS 1980 TAMLA UK STMR 9008

S333B **THE SURF PUNKS** S333B

DENNIS DRAGON D V (A (A) MY BEACH 1980 EPIC UK EPC 84346
DREW STEELE G V K(A
JOHN HUNT B (A JOHNNY MALIBU G V (A RAY BAN B (A THE HULK HCA (A
SPINO URCHIN G (A

S333C **SURFERS** S333C

(A) ALIVE & WELL 1971 DAYBREAK US 2001

S333D **SUPPLY & DEMAND** S333D

GREG BOLAND G (A (A) SUPPLY DEMAND 1976 MULLIGAN UK LUN009
PAUL McATEER D (A
JOLYON JACKSON K V (A BRIAN MASTERSON B V (A

S333E **SURPLUS STOCK** S333E

ROBERT GIDDENS SYN (A (A) HOLLAND IN NOT 1980 OUTATUNE GER 8004
GARY GIDDENS (A
JOSEF SCHENK D (A PHIL RENSHAW G (A ROB RISIKO (A IAN DERBYSHIRE (A
PHIL FALSETTO (A

S334 **SURPRISE SISTERS** S334

PATRICIA V (A (A) SURPRISE SISTERS 1976 GOOD EARTH GDS801 US RCA 1404
LINDA V (A
SUSAN V (A ELLEN V (A RAY RUSSELL G (A BRUCE LYNCH G (A
JEAN ROUSSEL K (A BRENT FORBES B (A RAY WARLEIGH SAX (A FRANK RICOTTI VIBES(A
BLUE WEAVER K (A GERRY CONWAY D (A PHIL KENZIE SAX (A

S335 **SURFARIS** S335

PAT CONNOLLY B V ((A) WIPE OUT 1963 DOT US 25535 UK LONDON HAD8110
JIM FULLER G ((B) SURFARIS PLAY 1963 DECCA US 4470 UK BRUNSWICK 8561
BOB BERRYHILL G ((C) HIT CITY '64 1964 DECCA US 4487 UK BRUNSWICK 8567
RON WILSON D ((D) FUN CITY 1964 DECCA US 4560 UK BRUNSWICK 8582
JIM PASH G WIND ((E) HIT CITY '65 1965 DECCA US 4614 UK BRUNSWICK 8605
(F) WHEELS 19 DIPLOMAT US 2309
(G) YESTERDAYS POP SCENE 1973 CORAL COPS 6354
(H) WIPE OUT 1973 POLYDOR 2870 335
(J) SURFERS RULE 1976 MCA US MCF 2761
(K) GONE WITH THE WAVE 1977 CORAL CDL 8050

S335A **SURRENDER** S335A

PETER CURRY K (A (A) SURRENDER 1979 CAPITOL CAN 11935
PAUL DELANEY D (A
ALFIE ZAPPACOSTA G V (A GEOFF WADDINGTON B (A STEVE JENSON G (A

S336 **SURVIVOR** S336

FRANKIE SULLIVAN G V (ABC (A) SURVIVOR 1979 SCOTTI US 7107 UK K50698
DAVE BICKLER V K (ABC (B) PREMONITION 1981 SCOTTI US 37549 UK K85289
JIM PETERIK G (ABC (C) EYE OF THE TIGER 1982 SCOTTI US 38062 UK K85845
GARY SMITH D (A
DENNIS KEITH JOHNSON B(A MARC DROUBAY D (BC STEPHAN ELLIS B (BC DARYL DRAGON K (B
FERGIE V (B

S337 **SUSAN** S337

TOM DICKIE G V (A (A) FALLING IN LOVE 1979 CHAMP US 3372
CHARLES LELAND B V (
JOHN KALISHES G (MICHAEL LELAND D (

S337A SUSTAIN S337A

FRANK V HELVOIRT SAX PERC(A (A) SUSTAIN 19 XILOVOX NL 0105
HANS GRANDIA D (A
GIEZEL VOORSLUIJS B V (A WALLIE LATUMETEN G V (A COERT COEHOORN V PERC(A

S338 SCREAMING LORD SUTCH S338

LORD SUTCH V (ABC (A) LORD SUTCH & HEAVY FRIENDS 1970 ATLANTIC UK 2400 008 US COTILLION 9015
JIMMY PAGE G (A (B) HANDS OF JACK THE RIPPER 1972 ATLANTIC UK K40313 US COTILLION 9049
NICKY HOPKINS K (A (C) ALIVE & WELL 1980 BABYLON GERM B 80010
JOHN BONHAM D (A
NOEL REDDING B (A JEFF BECK G (A DANIEL EDWARDS G B (A CARLO LITTLE D (A
KENT HENREY G (A MARTIN KOHL B (A RICK BROWN B (A BOB METKE D (A
SID PHILLIPS SAX (B MATTHEW FISHER K (B NICK SIMPER B (B ANNETTE BROX V (B
BRIAN KEITH V TROM(B RITCHIE BLACKMORE G (B KEITH MOON D (B VICTOR BROX V (B
PAT TRAVERS G (C JIM GREEN G (C RICK NIELSEN G (C RICHARD PRUT SAX (C
COLIN SOLMAN D (C DETLEV RESHOFT K (C MARS COWLING B (C KLAUS VOORMANN B (C
REINHARD STROEMER B (C

S339 SUTHERLAND BROTHERS (& QUIVER) S339

GAVIN SUTHERLAND B G V(ALL (A) THE SUTHERLAND BROTHERS BAND 1972 ISLAND UK ILPS9181 US 9315
IAIN SUTHERLAND V G K(ALL (A) THE SUTHERLAND BROTHERS BAND 1976 CBS UK RI 82297
BRIAN BENNETT PERC (H (B) LIFEBOAT 1972 ISLAND UK ILPS9212 US 9326
RICK WILLS B (H (B) LIFEBOAT 1977 CBS UK RI 82298
TIM RENWICK G (CDEFGH (C) DREAM KID 1973 ISLAND UK ILPS9259 US 8341
ANDY PYLE B (H (C) DREAM KID 1977 CBS UK RI 82299
WILLIE WILSON D (2CDEFGH (D) BEAT OF THE STREET 1974 ISLAND UK ILPS9288 RT CBS 82300
BRUCE THOMAS K (C (E) REACH FOR THE SKY 1975 CBS UK 69191 US 33982
KIM LUDMAN B (A (F) SAILING (COMP) 1976ISLAND UK ILPS9358 US CBS 33982
NEIL HOPWOOD D (A (G) SLIPSTREAM 1976 CBS UK 81593 US 34376
PETE WOOD K (CD (H) DOWN TO EARTH 1977 CBS UK 82255 US 35293
MICK GRABHAM G (H (J) WHEN THE NIGHT COMES DOWN 1979 CBS UK 83427 US 35703
TEX COMER B (D (1) MARCH 1978 (2) OCT 1977
ALAN ROSS G (2
MICK WEAVER K (2 GLEN SPREEN K (J JIM HORN HRNS (J STEVE PORCARO SYN (J
STEVE FORMAN PERC (J JOHN SHEARER PERC (2H BILL SMITH (J1 BOB GLAUB (J1
MIKE BAIRD (J1 RITCHIE ZETO (J1 ALBHY GALUTEN K (G FLACO PADRON PERC(G
JOHN HAWKEN K (B BOB RONGA B (B STEVE WINWOOD K (B DAVE MATTACKS D (B
PAT DONALDSON B (B RABBIT BUNDRICK K (B

S339A SWALLOW S339A

GEORGE LEH V (A (A) OUT OF THE NEST 1972 WB US 2606 UK K56174
PARKER WHEELER V HCA(A
VERN MILLER V G B(A DAVID WOODFORD WIND K(A PHIL GREEN G (A MICK ARANDA D(A
BOB CAMACHO K (A JAY DEWALD TPT (A ANDY HARP TPT (A KERRY BLOUT SAX (A
GEORGE KENNEDY TROM (A JEFF BAXTER STEEL(A

S340 SWAMP DOGG S340

JERRY WILLIAMS V PNO(ALL (A) TOTAL DESTRUCTION OF YOUR MIND 1970 CANYON US LP 7706
STACY GOSS HRNS (BG (B) SWAMP DOGG(RAT ON) 1971 ELEKTRA UK EKS 74089
SONNY ROYAL WIND (B (C) CUFFED COLLARED & TAGGED 1972 CREAM US 9009
MIKE STOUGH HRNS (B (D) FINALLY CAUGHT UP WITH MYSELF 197 MCA 2504
ROBERT POPS POPWELL B (B (E) SWAMP DOGG 19 WIZARD US 1122
JESSE CARR G V (B (F) GAG A MAGGOT 1975 PRESIDENT PTLS 1059
JASPER GUARINO D (B (F) GAG A MAGGOT 1973 STONEDOGG 3001
JIMMY EVANS D (G (G) HAVE YOU HEARD THIS STORY 1975 ISLAND UK ILPS 9299
HARRISON CALLOWAY TPT (G (H) NEVER TOO OLD TO BOOGIE 1976 DJM UK DJF 20476
CHARLES ROSE TROM (G ( ) UNCUT & CLASSIFIED 19 CHARLY UK CRB 1026
TRAVIS WAMMACK G HCA(G
AUDIE WATKINS PERC (G RANDY McCORMICK K (G LENNY LEBLANC B (G DAVE'BABY'JOHNSON WIND(G
HARVEY THOMPSON WIND (G RON EADES SAX (G

S340A SWAMP GAS S340A

JACK DAVIS B (A (A) SWAMP GAS 19 BUDDAH US BDS 5102
BAIRD HERSEY G (A
KIM ORNITZ V (A RICKY SALTER D (A

S340B SWAMP RATS S340B

BOB HOCKO V (A (A) DISCO SUCKS 1980 KEYSTONE US K111541

S341 SWAMPWATER S341

THAD MAXWELL B V (A (A) SWAMPWATER 1971 RCA US LSP 4572+ KING US 1122
STAN PRATT D V (A
GIB GUILBEAU FDL G V (A HERB PEDERSEN G V (A JOHN BELAND G V (A GLEN D HARDIN G (A

S342 BILLY SWAN S342

BILLY SWAN V (ALL (A) I CAN HELP 1975 MONUMENT UK 80615 US CBS 33279
KRIS KRISTOFFERSON V (E (B) ROCK'N'ROLL MOON 1975 MONUMENT UK 69192 US CBS 33805
RITA COOLIDGE V (E (C) BILLY SWAN 1976 MONUMENT UK 81387 US CBS 34183
LEO SAYER HCA (E (D) FOUR 1977 MONUMENT UK 81867 US CBS 34473
JORDANAIRES V (E (E) YOUR OK I'M OK 1978 A&M UK AMLH64886 US 4686
SCOTTY MOORE G (E (F) BILLY SWAN 1978 EMBASSY UK 31674
DONALD DUNN B (E (G) AT HIS BEST 1978 MONUMENT US MG7629
ROGER HAWKINS (D (H) I'M IN TO YOU 1981 EPIC US 37079
DAVID HOOD (D
PETE CARR D (BARRY BECKETT (D JIMMY JOHNSON (D TIM HENSON K (D
MIKE UTLEY K (E STEVE BRUTON G (E SAMMY CREASON D (E JERRY McGEE G (E
BOOKER T JONES K (E OTIS BLACKWELL PNO (E DON ROBERTSON PNO (E CLYDIE KING V (E
VANETTA FIELDS V (E PAULETTE BROWN V (E NEAL MATTHEWS V (E LOUIS NUNLEY V (E
GORDON STOKER V (E

S343 SWAN ARCADE S343

DAVE BRADY V (A (A) SWAN ARCADE 1973 TRAILER UK LER2032
HEATHER BRADY V (A (B) MATCHLESS 197 SHANACHIE MU 7428
FRANK TOWARD V (A
JIM BOYES G V (A DAVE FARRER V (A RAB NOAKES G (A DAVE BURLAND G V (A
JIMMY HUTCHISON V (A DIXIE KIDD B (A ALASDAIR CAMERON V (A

S344 **DAVE SWARBRICK** S344

DAVE SWARBRICK FDL MAND VLA(ABCD (A) RAGS,REELS & AIRS 1967 POLYDOR 236 514
BERYL MARRIOTT K (BCD (B) SWARBRICK 1976 TRANSATLANTIC UK TRA 337
MARTIN CARTHY G (ABC (C) SWARBRICK 2 1977 TRANSATLANTIC UK TRA 341
SIMON NICOL G (BCD (D) LIFT THE LID & LISTEN 1978 SONET UK SNTF 763
DAVE PEGG B (BCD (E) THE CEILIDH ALBUM 1978 SONET UK SNTF 764
BRUCE ROWLAND PERC (BCD (F) SMIDDY BURN 1981 LOGO UK 1029
DIZ DIZLEY G (A
SAVOURNA STEVENSON CLAR (BCD KATE GRAHAM FDL (BC ROGER MARRIOTT MELODIAN(BCD ALAN ROBERTSON ACC(BCD

S344A **SWEAT** S344A

NO MORE RUNNING 1980 DOUBLE D UK DDLP 2

S345 **SWEATHOG** S345

LENNY LEE GOLDSMITH K V(B (A) SWEATHOG 1971 CBS US 30601
BOB JONES G V (B (B) HALLELUJAH 1972 CBS US31144 UK 64784
DAVID LEONARD JOHNSON B V(B
BARTHOLOMEW SMITH-FROST D(B

S346 **SWEENEYS MEN** S346

ANDY IRVINE (AB12 RATTLIN' & ROARIN' WILLY 1968 TRANSATLANTIC UK TRA 170
JOW DOLAN (1 (B) TRACKS OF SWEENEY 1969 TRANSATLANTIC UK TRA 200
TERRY WOODS (AB234 (B) TRACKS OF SWEENEY 1977 TRANSATLANTIC UK TRANAM 40
AL O'DONNELL (4 (C) SWEENEYS MEN 1976 TRANSATLANTIC UK TRASAM 37
HENRY McCULLOUGH G (3
JOE MOYNIHAN (AB1234

S347 **THE SWEET** S347

BRIAN CONNOLLY V (*ABCDEFGHIK (*) GIMME DAT DING (ONE SIDE) 1970 MFP UK 5248
STEVE PRIEST HCA V B (ALL (A) FUNNY HOW SWEET COCO CAN BE 1971 RCA UK SF8288
MIKE TUCKER D V (ALL (B) SWEETS BIGGEST HITS 1972 RCA UK SF8316
FRANK TORPY G ((C) SWEET 1973 BELL US 1124
MICK STEWART G ((D) SWEET FANNY ADAMS 1974 RCA LPLI5039
ANDY SCOTT G SYN V (ALL (E) DESOLATION BOULEVARD 1975 RCA UK LPLI5080 US CAPITOL11395
GARY MOBERLEY K (M (F) STRUNG UP 1975 RCA SPC 0001
(G) GIVE US A WINK 1976 RCA UK RS 1036 US CAPITOL11496
(H) OFF THE RECORD 1977 RCA UK PL25172 US CAPITOL11636
(I) GOLDEN GREATS 1977 RCA UK PL25111
(J) LEVEL HEADED 1978 POLYDOR POLD 5001 2302 077
(J) LEVEL HEADED 1978 CAPITOL US 11744
(K) THE SWEET 1978 CAMDEN UK CDS 1168
(L) CUT ABOVE THE REST 1979 POLYDOR POLS 5022 US CAPITOL11929
(M) WATERS EDGE 1980 POLYDOR POLS 1021 US CAPITOL12106
(O) IDENTITY CRISIS 1982 POLYDOR UK 2311 179

S348 **RACHEL SWEET** S348

RACHEL SWEET V (AB (A) FOOL AROUND 1978 STIFF US 36101 UK SEEZ 12
CHARLIE CHARLES D (A (B) PROTECT THE INNOCENT 1980 STIFF US 36337 UK SEEZ 18
NORMAN WATT ROY B (A (B) PROTECT THE INNOCENT 1980 STIFF GER 624251
BRINSLEY SCHWARZ G (A (C) AND THEN HE KISSED ME 1981 CBS UK 85006
MICKEY GALLAGHER K (A
PIETRO NARDINI B G K(A LENE LOVICH V (A MARK SURGEON D (A PAUL GILLIERON SAX (A
JOHN EARLE SAX (A DICK HANSON TPT (A CHRIS GOWER TROM (A SIMON CLIMIE PERC(A
RAY BEAVIS SAX (A LEAH SWEET PERC (A STIFF CHORUS V (A

S348A **SWEET 'D BUSTER** S348A

BERTUS BORGERS V WIND(ABCD (A) SWEET'D BUSTER 1977 ARIOLA 25177 XOT
PAUL SMEENK G (ABCD (B) FRICTION 1978 ARIOLA 25861 XOT
HERMAN DEINUM B (ABCD (C) GIGS 1979 ARIOLA 200 337
HANS LAFAILLE D (ABC (D) SHOT INTO THE BLUE 1979 ARIOLA 200 651
ROBERT JAN STIPS K (ABC
ARNOLD BOGAARL PERC (A
FRANS MIJTS TPT (A JONS PISTOOR K (D PIERRE VAN DER LINDEN D(D

S348B **SWEET F.A.** S348B

CAROL GRIMES V (A (A) SWEET F.A. 1980 MNW SWED 103P
PETE KIRTLEY G V (A
GARY TWIGG B (A TONY HICKS D (A OLLIE MALLARD K V (A

S349 **SWEET PAIN (US)** S349

DAVID ROIRDAN (A (A) SWEET PAIN 1970 UA UK UAS 29161 US 6793
BOB SPALDING ((B) SWEET PAIN II 1974 20TH CENTURY US 410
CARL JOHNSON (
MARTY FOLTZ (FRANK DEMME (J C PHILLIPS (

S349A **SWEET PAIN (UK)** S349A

JOHN O'LEARY HCA (A (A) SWEET PAIN 1969 MERCURY UK SMCL20146
KEITH TILLMAN B (A (A) ENGLANDS HEAVY BLUES SUPER SESS 19 MERCURY US SR 61231
STUART COWELL G (A
DICK HECKSTALL SMITH SAX(A ANNETTE BROX V (A SAM CROZIER PNO V(A JUNIOR DUNN D(A
ALAN GREED V (A

S349B **SWEET SLAG** S349B

MICK KARANSKY G V (A (A) TRACKING WITH CLOSE UPS 1971 TRANSATLANTIC UK XTRA 1112
PAUL JOLLY WIND (A
NOTH O'NEIL B TROM(A AL CHAMBERS D (A

S350 **SWEET SMOKE** S350

MARVIN KAMINOWITZ G V (C (A) JUST A POKE 197 HARVEST IMP IC062 28886
MARTIN ROSENBERG PERC (C (A) JUST A POKE 197 HARVEST 5C054 24311
ANDREW DERSHIN B (C (B) DARKNESS TO LIGHT 197 HARVEST IMP IC062 29471
JAY DORFMAN D (C (C) LIVE 1974 HARVEST IMP IC062 29513
RICK GREENBERG G (C
JOHN CLASSI PERC (C

S351 **SWEET THUNDER** S351

(A) SWEET THUNDER 1978 FANTASY FT 545
(B) HORIZONS 1979 FANTASY US 576

S352 SWEET THURSDAY S352

NICKY HOPKINS K (A
JON MARK G V (A
ALUN DAVIES G V (A
HARVEY BURNS D (A
BRIAN ODGERS B WIND (A

(A) SWEET THURSDAY 1969 TETRAGRAMMATON US T 12
(A) SWEET THURSDAY 1969 POLYDOR UK 2310 051
(A) SWEET THURSDAY 1973 CBS UK 65573
(A) SWEET THURSDAY 198 LINE GER LLP 5044

S353 SWEET WATER S353

FRED HERRERA B V (BC
ALEX DELZOPPO K V HCA (BC
ALBERT B MOORE FLT B(CB
ELPIDIO COBIAN PERC (BC
NANSI NEVINS G V (CB ALAN MALAROWITZ D (CB AUGUST BURNS CELLO(CB RICKY FATAAR D(C

(A) SWEET WATER 19 REPRISE US RS6313
(B) JUST FOR YOU 1970 REPRISE US RS6417
(C) MELON 1971 REPRISE US RS6473

S354 SWEETBOTTOM S354

WARREN 'VITO' WIEGRATZ K WIND V(AB
MARK TORROLL D (AB
DUANE STUERMER B V (AB
MARTIN J APPEL G (AB

(A) ANGELS OF THE DEEP 1978 ELEKTRA UK K52110 US 6E 156
(B) TURN ME LOOSE 1979 ELEKTRA US 6E 210

S354A SWELL MAPS S354A

BIGGLES BOOKS G K V B'ABC
BARRY K (B
NIKKI MATTRESS K G V(ABC
JOWE HEAD B HCA G V(ABC
EPIC SOUNDTRACK K D SYN(ABC PHONES B SPORTSMAN B VLN G(ABC GORDON B V (BC GOLDEN COCKRILL B G V(A
LORA LOGIC SAX (C

(A) TRIP TO MARINEVILLE 1979 ROUGH TRADE ROUGH 2
(B) IN 'JANE FROM OCCUPIED EUROPE' 1980 ROUGH TRADE ROUGH 15
(C) WHATEVER HAPPENS NEXT 1981 ROUGH TRADE ROUGH 21

S355 JONATHAN SWIFT S355

JONATHAN SWIFT G V (AB
PETER MORGAN B (B
HAROLD FISHER D (B
ALAN SPARKES G (B PAT KELLY K (A JACK BRAND B (A COLIN DAVY D (A
STEVE HAMMOND G (A LAURIE ALLEN D (B LES HARVEY G (B ANN ODELL K (B

(A) INTROVERT 1971 CBS UK 64412
(B) SONGS 1972 CBS UK 64751

S355A STEVE SWINDELLS S355A

STEVE SWINDELLS K V (A
JOHN GUSTAFSON B (A
BARRY DE SOUZA D (A
CALEB QUAYE G (A DAVE WINTOUR B (A MIKE GILES D (A BRUCE KNAPP G (A
MARK WARNER G (A DORIS TROY V (A ROSETTA HIGHTOWER V (A BARRY ST JOHN V (A
CHRIS MERCER SAX (A MORRIS PERT PERC (A DANNY THOMPSON B (A MOUNTAIN FJORD ORCH(A
HUW LLOYD-LANGTON G (B NIC POTTER B (A SIMON KING D (A

(A) MESSAGES 1974 RCA UK 5057
(B) FRESH BLOOD 1980 ATCO UK K50738 US 38128

S355B SWIMMING POOL Q's S355B

(A) THE DEEP END 1981 ARMAGEDDON UK ARM 12

S356 SWINGING BLUE JEANS S356

RAY ENNIS G (ALL
RALPH ENNIS G (
LES BRAID B (
NORMAN KUHLKE D (

(A) TUTTI FRUTTI 1964 REGAL UK SREG 1073
(B) BLUE JEANS A SWINGING 1964 HMV UK CLP(M)1802 +CSD(S) 1570
(C) HIPPY HIPPY SHAKE 1964 IMPERIAL US LPS 12261
(D) SHAKING TIME 1964 EMI EURO 83716 SWE 94823
(E) HEY HEY HEY HEY (LIVE) 1965 ELECTROLA EURO 83927
(F) THE SWINGING BLUES JEANS 1966 LIVERPOOL SOUND UK PSQ030
(G) THE SWINGING BLUE JEANS 1967 MFP UK MFP1163
(H) HIPPY HIPPY SHAKE 1973 BELLAPHON EURO 15100
(J) BRAND NEW & FADED 1974 DART BULL1001
(K) SWINGING BLUE JEANS 1978 EMI UK NUT 15
(EP) SHAKE WITH 196 HMV UK 7EG 8850
(EP) YOUR NO GOOD 196 HMV UK 7EG 8868

S356A SWINGING MEDA LLIONS S356A

JOHN McELRATH V K (A
CARROLL BLEDSOE TPT (A
CHARLIE WEDDER TPT (A JIM PERKINS SAX D(A STEVE CALDWELL SAX D K(A JIMBO DOARES G (A
JOE MORRIS D (A BRENT FORTSON K WIND(A

(A) DOUBLE SHOT 1966 SMASH UK 67083

S357 SWITCH S357

(A) SWITCH 1978 MOTOWN UK STML12096 US GORDY 980
(B) SWITH II 1979 MOTOWN UK STML12112 US GORDY 988
(C) THIS IS MY DREAM 1980 US GORDY 999
(D) REACHING FOR TOMORROW 1980 MOTOWN UK STML12135

S358 ROOSEVELT SYKES S358

ROOSEVELT SYKES PNO V(ALL
JUSTIN ADAMS G (I
CLARENCE FORD SAX (I
GEORGE FRENCH B (I
ALONZO STEWART D (I
DON LAWSON D (F
LITTLE BROTHER MONTGOMERY(R
J T BROWN SAX (B
WILLIE JAMES LACEY G(B
ARMAND JACKSON D (B
JOHNNY WALKER K (B
JOHN FRAZIER B (B
CHARLES SAUNDERS D (B
JOHNNY MORTON TPT (B
OETT MALLARD SAX (B
LEON WASHINGTON SAX (B
LEONARD GASTON G (B
ALFRED ELKINS B (B
BILL CASIMIR SAX (B
ERNEST CRAWFORD B (B
W B NELSON D (B
ROBERT PETE WILLIAMS G(A
HOMESICK JAMES G B (K

(A) BLUES FROM BAR ROOMS 1967 77 UK 77LEU1250
(B) BLUE BIRD No10 19 RCA FR PM 42028
(C) BLUE & RIBALD 1977 SOUTHLAND US RI 2
(D) BLUES 19 FOLKWAYS 3827
(E) BARRELHOUSE BLUES & STOMPS 19 EUPHONIC US 1205
(F) BIG MAN OF BLUES 1961 EMI UK ENC 183
(G) CHICAGO BLUES FESTIVAL 19 BLACK & BLUE FR 33513
(H) COUNTRY BLUES PIANO ACE 1974 YAZOO L 1033
(I) DIRTY DOUBLE MOTHER 1973 BLUESWAY US BL 6077
(J) FEEL LIKE BLOWING MY HORN 19 DELMARK DS 632
(K) HARD DRIVING BLUES 19 DELMARK DL 607
(L) HONEYDRIPPER'S DUKE'S MIXTURE 1971 BARCLAY IMP 920 294 + 80604
(M) HONEYDRIPPER 19 FANTASY US 24717
(N) IN EUROPE 19 DELMARK DS 616
(O) MUSIC IS MY BUSINESS 19 BLUE LABOR US BL111
(P) ORIGINAL HONEYDRIPPER 19 BLIND PIG US 005
(Q) ROOSEVELT SYKES 19 STORYVILLE SLP 189
(R) URBAN BLUES 19 FANTASY US 24717
( ) SINGS THE BLUES 19 CROWN US 5287
( ) SINGS THE BLUES 19 UNITED US 7792
( ) RETURN OF ROSSEVELT SYKES 19 BLUESVILLE 1006
( ) HONEYDRIPPER 19 BLUESVILLE 1014

S358A TERRY SYLVESTER S358A

TERRY SYLVESTER G V (AB

(A) TERRY SYLVESTER 1974 EPIC US 33076
(B) I BELIEVE 1976 POLYDOR UK 2383 394

S358B SYLVAIN SYLVAIN S358B

SYLVAIN SYLVAIN G V (A (A) SYLVAIN SYLVAIN 1979 RCA US/UK 13475
BOBBY BLAIN K (A (B) AND THE TEARDROPS 1981 RCA 3913
JON GERBER SAX (A
BUZ VERNO B (A JOHNNY RAO G (A LEE CRYSTAL D (A

S358C RIKKI SYLVAN S358C

RIKKI SYLVAN V SYN(A (A) THE SILENT HOURS 1981 KALEIDOSCOPE UK 85198
ANDY PRICE B (A
STEVE WILKIN G (A CHARLIE CHARLES D (A EUGENE MOULE K V (A

S358D SYLVERS S358D

OLYMPIA SYLVERS ((A) SYLVERS 19 PRIDE US 007
JAMES SYLVERS ((B) SYLVERS II 19 PRIDE US 026
RICKY SYLVERS ((C) SYLVERS III 1974 MGM US 4940
CHERMAINE SYLVERS ((D) SHOWCASE 197 CAPITOL US 11465
EDMUND SYLVERS (( ) SOMETHING SPECIAL 197 CAPITOL US 11580
LEON SYLVERS (( ) NEW HORIZONS 197 CAPITOL US 11705
( ) BEST OF 197 CAPITOL US 11868
( ) FOREVER YOURS 197 CASABLANCA US 7103

S358E SYLVESTER S358E

SYLVESTER K V (ALL (A) SCRATCH MY FLOWER 1973 US BTS 45
JAMES Q SMITH G V HCA(AB (B) BAZAAR 1973 US BTS 60
KERRY HATCH B V K(AB ( ) STARS 1979 FANTASY UK 556 US 9579
TRAVIS FULLERTON D V (AB ( ) MIGHTY REAL 19 FANTASY UK 3009
CHRIS MOSTERT WIND (AB ( ) STEP TWO 19 FANTASY US 9556
BOBBY BLOOD TPT (AB ( ) SYLVESTER 19 FANTASY US 9531
PETER MINTUN K (A ( ) LIVING PROOF 19 FANTASY UK 573
( ) SELL MY SOUL 1980 FANTASY US 9601

S358F SYN S358F

CHRIS SQUIRE B ((A) THE SYN 1967 DERAM
ANDREW JACKSON K (
STEVE NARDELLI V (PETER BROCKLAND(BANKS) G(A GUNNAR HAKARNARSON D (A RAY STEELE D (
CHRIS ALLEN D (A

S358G SYNATHESIA S358G

DENNIS HOLMES G VIBES(A (A) SYNATHESIA 1969 RCA UK SF 8058
JIMMY FRASER WIND (A
LESLIE COOK V VLN MAND(A

S359 SYMPHONIC SLAM S359

TIMO LAINE SYN G V(A (A) SYMPHONIC SLAM 1976 A&M UK AMLH69023
JOHN LOWRY D V (A.
DAVID STONE K V (A

S360 SYNDICATE OF SOUND S360

BOB GONZALES B (A (A) LITTLE GIRL 19 BELL US 6001 STATESIDE UK SSL10185
JOHN SHARKEY G K (A
DON BASKIN SAX V(A JOHN DUCKWORTH D V (A JIM'BO' SAWYERS G V (A

S361 SYNERGY S361

LARRY FAST ((A) SEQUENCER 1976 SIRE UK 9103326 US PASSPORT 98014
RON HOWDEN ((A) SEQUENCER 1979 RI US PASSPORT 6002
MORTY SCOTT ((B) ELECTRONIC REALIZATIONS 1976 SIRE UK 9299752 US PASSPORT 98009
(B) ELECTRONIC REALIZATIONS 1979 RI US PASSPORT 6001
(C) CHORDS 1979 US PASSPORT 6000
(D) GAMES 1979 US PASSPORT 6003
(E) AUDION 1982 LOGO UK 1033

S362 SYREETA S362

SYREETA WRIGHT V (ALL (A) SYREETA 1972 MOWEST US 7001
BUZZY FEITON G (A (B) STEVIE WONDER PRESENTS 1974 TAMLA UK STML11268
STEVIE WONDER (AB (C) SYREETA 1975 TAMLA US 808 M6 84451
KEITH COPELAND D (A (D) ONE TO ONE 1977 TAMLA US 349 UK STML12053
G C CAMERON (E (E) RICH LOVE POOR LOVE 1978 TAMLA US 891 UK STML12073
LANI GROVES V (AB (F) SYREETA 1980 MOTOWN US 382 UK STML12137
JIM GILSTRAP V (A (G) BEST OF 1981 MOTOWN UK STMR 9014
TREVOR LAWRENCE PERC (A (H) SET MY LOVE IN MOTION 1982 MOTOWN UK ST 12162
SCOTT EDWARDS B (A
LINDA TUCKER V (A GLORIA BARLEY V (A JULIAN GAILLARD ORCH(A OLLIE BROWN D (B
MARLO HENDERSON G (B STEVE MADAIO TPT (B DENIECE WILLIAMS V(B ANITA SHERMAN V (B
PAUL RISER STR (B REGGIE McBRIDE B (B MIKE SEMBELLO G(B DENNIS MOROUSE SAX (B
SHIRLEY BREWER V (B MINNIE RIPPERTON V (B DENNIS MORRISON V(B

T1 STEVEN T T1

STEVEN T G V K (A (A) WEST COAST CONFIDENTIAL 1978 DREAM US DA 3500 GER 6 23359
WILTON FELDER B (A
DON MENZA SAX (A MIKE BAIRD D (A DAN FERGUSON G (A BECKY HOBBS PNO (A
BEN BENAY HCA (A DAVE CARR K (A LEE SKLAR B (A HAL BLAINE D (A
CHRIS DARROW ACC V(A RICK HENN SYN (A MIKE MELVOINE K (A EMIL RICHARDS PERC(A
MIKE POCARO B (A LEE RITENOUR G (A MARY HYLAN V (A STEVE LUKATHER G (A
WILLIE ORNELAS D (A JAI WINDING K (A DAVID FOSTER PNO (A

T2 T FORD & THE BONE SHAKERS T2

(A) ROCK RATTLE & ROLL 1978 SPLASH CPLP1004
(B) JUST KEEP IT UP 1979 SPLASH CPLP 2001

T3 T.I.M.E. (TRUST IN MEN EVERYWHERE) T3

LARRY BYROM G (B (A) T.I.M.E. 1968 LIBERTY US LST7558
BILL RICHARDSON G (B (B) SMOOTH BALL 1969 LIBERTY US LST7605 UK LBS83232
STEVE RUMPH D (
NICK ST NICHOLAS B (PAT COUCHOIS D (B RICHARD TEPP B (B

T4 T.K.O. (TECHNICAL KNOCK OUT) T4

BRAD SINSEL V (A (A) LET IT ROLL 1979 INFINITY INS 2002
RICK PIERCE G (A
MARK SEIDENVERG B (A DARRYL SIGUENZA D (A TONY BORTKO K G (A

T4A **T T REUTER** T4A

PETER STRAUSS D (A (A) KONTROLL KLUBB KASHBAN 1980 SKAN HEART WORK 01
PETER IVARSS B V (A
PETER PUDERS G V (A HENRIK VANANT G V (A

T5 **T 2** T5

KEITH CROSS G K V(A (A) IT'LL ALL WORK OUT IN BOOMLAND 1970 DECCA UK SKL 5050
PETER DUNTON D V (A
BERNARD JINKS B V (A

T5A **T V KIDS** T5A

(A) TV KIDS 197 BRAIN BOOSTER TA 001

T5B **T V 21** T5B

IAN BROUDIE V PERC PROD(A (A) A THIN RED LINE 1981 DERAM UK SML 1123
ALAN WINSTANLEY PROD (A
NEIL BALDWIN B (A DAVE HAMPTON TPT V(A ALLY PALMERR G V(A ALI PATERSON D (A
NORMAN RODGER G V (A STEVE BROWN PERC(A

T6 **JUNE TABOR** T6

JUNE TABOR V (ALL (A) SILLY SISTERS 1976 CHRYSALIS UK CHR 1101
MADDY PRIOR V (A (B) AIRS & GRACES 1976 TOPIC UK 12TS 298
TONY HALL MEL (AC (C) ASHES & DIAMONDS 1977 TOPIC UK 12TS 360
BOB DAVENPORT (D (D) BEES ON HORSEBACK 1977 FREE REED UK FRR 016
MARTIN CARTHY G PERC(A (1) 1977 TOUR
NIC JONES FDL G(A
ANDY IRVINE MAND (A DANNY THOMPSON B (A GABRIEL McKEON PIPES(A JON GILLASPIE K WIND(ABC1
JOHNNY MOYNIHAN WIND (A BRIAN GOLBEY FDL (A LUIS JARDIM PERC (A RICK KEMP B (C
NIGEL PEGRUM D (C DOUG MORTER G (C MARTIN SIMPSON G (1

T6A **TAGGETT** T6A

COLIN HORTON JENNINGS G (A (A) TAGGETT 1974 EMI UK EMC3015 US UA UALA407
TIM WHEATLEY B V (A
TERRY FOGG D (A PETE ARNESON K (A

T6B **TALBOT BROTHERS** T6B

TERRY TALBOT HCA G V (A (A) TALBOT BROTHERS 1974 WB US BS2767 UK K56039
JOHN TALBOT BAN G V(A
RUSS KUNKEL D (A LEE SKLAR B (A RANDY SCRUGGS G (A JOSH GRAVES G DOBRO (A
SNEAKY PETE KLEINOW STEEL(A CREEPER KURNOW HCA (A DON DACUS G (A JOHN JARVIS PNO(A
DAVID LINDLEY G (A

T6C **WAYNE TALBERT** T6C

WAYNE TALBERT (AB (A) HOUSTON NICKEL KICKS 196 MERCURY US 61259
(B) DUES TO PAY 196 MERCURY US 10603

T7 **TALISKER** T7

MARK MEGGIDO B (A (A) DREAMING OF GLENISLA 1975 CAROLINE CA 1513
LINDSAY COOPER WIND (A (B) LAND OF STONE 1977 ECM JAP060018
DAVE WEBSTER SAX (ABC (C) THE LAST BATTLE 1978 VINYL VS 107
JOHN RANGECROFT SAX (ABC
KEN HYDER D (ABC JOHN LAWRENCE B

T8 **TALKING HEADS** T8

DAVID BYRNE G V (ALL (A) TALKING HEADS '77 1977 SIRE US SR6306 UK 9103 328
TINA WEYMOUTH B (ALL (B) MORE SONGS OF BUILDING & FOOD 1978 SIRE US SR6058 UK K56531
BRIAN ENO SYN K G V (BCD (B) MORE SONGS OF BUILDING & FOOD 1979 SIRE GER 200 880
CHRIS FRANTZ D (ALL (C) FEAR OF MUSIC 1979 SIRE US SRK 6076 UK/GER K56707
JERRY HARRISON G V K(ALL (D) REMAIN IN LIGHT 1980 SIRE US/UK SRK 6095
GENE WILDER PERC (C (E) THE NAME OF THIS BAND IS T HEADS 1982 SIRE 23590 GER K66112
ARI PERC (C (EP) HOUSE IN MOTION 1981 SIRE UK 4050
ROBERT FRIPP G (C
JULIE LAST V (C ADRIAN BELEW G (DE JON HASSELL HRNS (DE NONA HENDRYX V (D
ROBERT PALMER PERC (D JOSE ROSSY PERC (DE DOLETTE McDONALD V PERC(E BERNIE WORRELL K V (E
BUSTA JONES G B (E STEVE SCALES PERC (E SWEETBREATHES V (C TOMMY BONGIOUR PROD(A
LANCE QUINN PROD (A

T9 **JAMES TALLEY** T9

JAMES TALLEY G V (ALL (A) GOT NO BREAD,NO MILK NO MONEY 1975 CAPITOL 11416
BYRON BACH CELLO(C (B) TRYIN' LIKE THE DEVIL 1976 CAPITOL 11494
RICK DURRETT PNO (C (C) BLACKJACK CHOIR 1977 CAPITOL 11605
DAVE GILLON G (C (D) AIN'T IT SOMETHIN' 1978 CAPITOL 11695
JOHNNY GIMBLE G (C
JOSH GRAVES FDL (C DOYLE GRISHAM STEEL(C STEVE HOSTAK G (C IRV KANE TROM(C
B B KING G (C PEBBLE DANIEL V (C MARCIA ROUTH V (C MIKE LEECH B (C
ANDY McMAHON K (C CLARK PIERSON D V (C BILLY PUETT WIND (C JOHN SAYLES FDL (C
DON SHEFFIELD TPT (C JERRY SHOOK G B HCA (C TOMMY SMITH TPT (C KYLE TULLIS B (C
REGGIE YOUNG G (C MARY JO TALLEY V (C

T9A **TALTON,STEWART,SANDLIN** T9A

TOMMY TALTON G V (A (A) HAPPY TO BE ALIVE 1976 CAPRICORN US 0167
BILL STEWART D G PERC(A
JOHN SANDLIN G B (A SCOTT BOYER (A BONNIE BRAMLETT (A JOE ENGLISH (A
CHUCK LEAVELL (A DRU LOMBAR (A STEVE MILLER (A JOE WALK (A

T9B **TAMPA RED** T9B

HUDSON'RED'WHITTAKER G V(ALL (A) TAMPA RED 19 BLUESVILLE US BVLP1030
GEORGIA TOM DORSEY PNO (C (B) HOW LONG 19 BLUESVILLE US BVLP1043
BLACK BOB PNO (DE (C) BOTTLENECK GUITAR 1928 1937 1974 YAZOO US 1039
BIG MACEO PNO (DE (D) THE GUITAR WIZARD 19 RCA AMX2 5501
WILLIE WILLIAMSON HCA (DE (E) THE GUITAR WIZARD 1935 1953 1974 BLUES CLASSICS US 25
WALTER HORTON HCA (DE
JOHNNY JONES PNO (
WILLIE LACEY G (ODIE PAYNE D (SUGARMAN PENIGAR SAX (BILL CASIMIR SAX (
JUDGE RILEY D (ARMAND JACKSON SAX (ERNEST CRAWFORD B (OETT MALLARD WIND(
TYRELL DIXON D (RANSOM KNOWLING B (BLIND JOHN DAVIS PNO (

T10 NORMA TANEGA T10

NORMA TANEGA G V AUTOHARP(AB	(A) WALKING MY CAT NAMED DOG	1966 NEW VOICE 2001 UK STATESIDE10182
MIKE MORAN K B V(B	(B) I DONT THINK IT WILL HURT	1977 RCA UK SF8217
DON PAUL V (B		

T11 TANGERINE DREAM T11

EDGAR FROESE SYN K G B (ALL	(A) ELECTRONIC MEDITATION	1970 OHR GER OMM556004
CHRIS FRANKE SYN K(BCDEFHJKLMNRS	(B) ALPHA CENTAURI	1971 OHR GER OMM556012
PETER BAUMANN SYN K(CDEFHJKL	(B) ALPHA CENTAURI	1975 POLYDOR 2383 314
CONRAD SCHNITZLER FLT (A	(C) ZEIT	1972 OHR GER OMM256021
KLAUS SCHULZE K (A	(C) ZEIT	1976 VIRGIN UK VD 2503
UDO DENNEBOURG FLT (B	(D) ATEM	1972 OHR GER OMM566031
ROLAND PAULCYK SYN (B	(D) ATEM	1974 POLYDOR 2383 297
STEVE SCHROYDER ORG (BC	(BD) ATEM /ALPHA	1976 VIRGIN UK VD2504 GER 87761
MICHAEL HOENIG K (	(E) PHAEDRA	1974 VIRGIN UK V 2010 GER 81761
FLORIAN FRICKE SYN (C	(E) PHAEDRA	1974 VIRGIN US 13108
STEVE JOLLIFFE HRNS FLT(M	(F) RUBYCON	1975 VIRGIN UK V 2025 US 13166
KLAUS KRIEGER D (MN	(F) RUBYCON	1975 VIRGIN FR 2933 716
JOHANNES SCHMOELLING K (PRS	(H) RICOCHET	1976 VIRGIN UK V 2044 GER 89679
VOLKER HOMBACH FLT VLN(	(J) STRATOSFEAR	1976 VIRGIN US 34427 UK V 2068
JOHANNES LUCKE CELLO(C	(J) STRATOSFEAR	1976 VIRGIN GER 28146
LANSE HAPSHASH D (	(K) SORCERER	1977 MCA UK MCF2806 GER 62085
KIRT HERKENBERG B (	(L) ENCORE (DBL)	1977 VIRGIN US 35014 UK VD 2506
JOCHEN VON GRUMBCOW CELLO(A	(L) ENCORE (DBL)	1977 VIRGIN GER 25495
SVEN JOHANNSON D (	(M) CYCLONE	1978 VIRGIN UK V 2097 GER 25843
HANS JOCHEN BRUNE CELLO(C	(N) FORCE MAJEURE	1978 VIRGIN UK V 2111 GER 200347
EDUARD MEYER CELLO(N	(O) 70/80 (4 LP SET)	1980 VIRGIN UK V BOX2
HANS ULRICH WEIGEL PROD(A	(P) TANGRAM	1980 VIRGIN UK V 2147 GER 202169
KLAUS FREUDIGMANN PROD(A	(Q) THIEF	1981 VIRGIN UK V 2189
	(R) EXIT	1981 VIRGIN UK V 2212 GER 203998
	(S) WHITE EAGLE	1982 VIRGIN UK V 2226

T11A TANGERINE PEEL T11A

	(A) SOFT THOUGHTS	1970 RCA US LSA 3002

T11B TANGERINE ZOO T11B

DONALD SMITH D (A	(A) TANGERINE ZOO	19 MAINSTREAM US 6107
TONY TAVARES B (A	(B) OUTSIDE LOOKING ON	19 MAINSTREAM US 6116
ROBERT BENEVIDES G (A		
WAYNE GAGNOH G (A	RONALD MEDEIROS K HCA(A	

T11C TANK T11C

	(A) FILTH HOUNDS OF HADES	1981 KAMAFLAGE KAM LP1

T12 MARC TANNER T12

MARC TANNER (	(A) NO ESCAPE	1979 ELEKTRA US 168
MIKE BAIRD D (A	(B) TEMPTATION	1980 ELEKTRA US 240 NL 52192
BOB GLAUB B (A		

RITCHIE ZITO G (AB	GLEN SPREEN K (A	WILLIAM SMITH K (A	JIM HORN FLT (A
VANETTA FIELDS V (A	GARY MALLABER D (A	JAY GRAYDEN G (A	BEN BENAY G (A
MAX GRONENTHAL V (A	TOMMY VIG PERC (A	JEFF PORCARO D (A	STEVE LUKATHER G (A
MIKE FINNIGAN V (A	ROSE BUTTER V (A	DAVID PAICH K (A	JOE TURANO V (A
DAVID PIET B (A	MICHAEL STEVENS G (B	RON EDWARDS B (B	JOE ROMERSA D (B
STEVE MANN WIND (B	LINDA STEVENS V (B	ED TREE G (B	IRVIN KRAMER G (B
MARC GREEN SYN (B	JOHN JARVIS K (B	BILL PAYNE K (B	RICHARD PAGE V (B
GARY GRANT HRNS (B	BILLY LAMB HRNS (B	CHUCK BROOKE HRNS (B	

T12A TAPES T12A

ROLF HERMSEN G V (AB	(A) YOU JUST CANT SLEEP	1978 VERTIGO GER 9198 108
MICK BRANDES G V (AB	(B) PARTY	1980 PASSPORT US 9842 NL 58129
DICK VANDERVAART D (A		
IGOR ROOVERS B (AB	PETER MEURIS D (B	

T12B TANTRUM T12B

BARB ERBER V (AB	(A) TANTRUM	1978 OVATION US 1735 GER 146 206
BILL SYNIAR B (AB	(B) RATHER BE ROCKIN'	1979 OVATION US 1747
SANDY CAULFIELD V (AB		
VERN WENNERSTROM D (AB	PAM BRADLEY V (AB PHIL BALSANO K (AB	RAY SAPKO G (AB

T13 TAOS T13

ALBIE CIAPPA D V (A	(A) TAOS	196 MERCURY US 61257
BURT LEVINE G BAN(A		
STEVE OPPENHEIM G K V(A	JEFF BAKER G K V(A KIT BEDFORD	B K V(A

T13A TARGET T13A

JIM JAMISON V (AB	(A) TARGET	1976 A&M US 4607
DAVID SPAIN D (AB	(B) CAPTURED	1977 A&M US 4652
TOM CATHEY B (AB		
PAUL CANNON G (AB	BUD DAVIS K (AB	

T13B TARHEEL SLIM T13B

ALLEN 'SLIM' BUNN V G (A	(A)NUMBER 9 TRAIN(EP)	1980 CHARLY UK CTD 125
JIMMY SPRUIL G (A		

T14 TARNEY SPENCER T14

ALAN TARNEY G V K(ABC	(A) TARNEY SPENCER	1976 BRADLEYS UK BRADL1011
TREVOR SPENCER D (ABC	(B) THREE'S A CROWD	1978 A&M US 4692 UK AMLH68466
LYNTON NAIFF K (B	(C) RUN FOR YOUR LIFE	1979 A&M US 4757 UK AMLH64757
COLIN COOPER (B		
JOE POLLARD (B	PETER HAYCOCK (B TONY RIVERS	(B JOHN PERRY (B
STU CALVER (B	JOHN CUFFLEY (B PETER FILLEUL	(B DEREK HOLT (B

T15 TASAVALLAN PRESIDENTTI T15

JUKKA TOLONEN G PNO(ABC	(A) TASAVALLAN PRESIDENTTI	1969 EMI 062 34264 LOVE SWEDLRLP 7
PEKKA POYRY WIND (BC	(B) LAMBERTLAND	1972 SONET SWED SLP2533
VESA AALTONEN D (ABC	(B) LAMBERTLAND	1973 SONET SNTF636 LOVE SWED LRLP 60
FRANK ROBSON K V (A	(B) LAMBERTLAND	1974 BRAIN GER 1063
MANS GROUNDSTROEM B K (AB	(C) MILKY WAY MOSES	1974 SONET SNTF658 LOVE SWED LRLP102
JUHANN AALTONEN WIND (A	(C) MILKY WAY MOSES	1974 BRAIN GER 1058 US JANUS 3065
HEIKKI VIRTANEN B (C		
EERO RAITTINEN V PERC(BC		

T16 TASTE T16

RORY GALLAGHER G V HCA(ALL (A) TASTE 1969 POLYDOR UK 583042 US ATCO 33296
RICHARD McCRACKEN B (ALL (B) ON THE BOARDS 1970 POLYDOR UK 583083 US ATCO 33322
(B) ON THE BOARDS 1970 POLYDOR EURO 184 366
JOHN WILSON D (ALL (C) LIVE TASTE 1971 POLYDOR UK 2310 082
(D) FIRST TASTE(1967) 1971 BASF GERM20 29084 0
(E) LIVE AT I O W 1972 POLYDOR UK 2383 120
(F) POP HISTORY 197 POLYDOR 2668 003
(G) POP GIANTS No 5 197 BRUNSWICK EURO 2911 516
(H) MOVIN' ON 197 KARUSSEL EURO
(J) TASTE 1977 POLYDOR 2384 076
(K) TASTE 19 VIOLENT SYSTEM PN100001
(L) GREATEST ROCK SENSATION 1977 POLYDOR GER 2499 115
(M) IN CONCERT AT THE MARQUEE '68 1977 ARIOLA EURO 25001

T16A TASTE OF HONEY T16A

JANCE M JOHNSON B V (A (A) A TASTE OF HONEY 1978 CAPITOL UK 11754
PERRY L KIBBLE K V (A
HAZEL P PAYNE G V (A WARE MARCUS STR (A LARRY MIZELL PROD (A DONALD JOHNSON D V (A
FONCE MIZELL PROD (A

T17 TATTO T17

THOM MOONEY D (A (A) TATTO 1976 PRODIGAL US 10014 PDL2003
JEFF HUTTON K V (A
WALLY BRYSON G V (A DAN KIAWON B (A DAVIS THOMAS G V (A

T18 BERNIE TAUPIN T18

BERNIE TAUPIN (ALL (A) BERNIE TAUPIN 19 ELEKTRA US EKS 75020
CALEB QUAYE G (A (B) TAUPIN 1971 DJM UK DJLPS 415
DAVEY JOHNSTONE G MAND(A (C) HE WHO RIDES THE TIGER 1980 ASYLUM US 6E263 UK K52220
SHAWN PHILLIPS G SIT V(A
RICHARD COFF VLN (A DIANA LEWIS K (A

T18A TAXI GIRL T18A

MAR WAIS G (A (A) SEPPUKU 1981 VIRGIN 1981 GER 201 899
DANIEL DARC V (A
LAURENT SINCLAIR K (A
J J BURNEL V PROD(A VIVIENNE VOG V (A JET LE NOIR D (A PHILIPPE B (A

T19 TAX LOSS T19

PAUL PHILLIPS G K V(A (A) HEY MISTER RECORD MAN 1979 LOGO UK LOGO 1015
PETE ZORN B G WIND V (A
MATT FINISH G (A ALLEN KEYS K SYN (A RICHARD BURGESS D (A NAPOLEON GLOSS D PERC(A
JETT SEOPARDIE CONGA(A BILL ZORN V (A KEN NICOL V (A

T19A TAXXI T19A

DAVID CUMMING G V (A (A) DAY FOR NIGHT 1980 FANTASY US 9603
COLIN PAYNE K (A
JEFF NEAD D (A TIM GORMAN K (A MAC GARDIN B (A

T20 ALEX TAYLOR T20

ALEX TAYLOR V (AB (A) WITH FRIENDS & NEIGHBOURS 1971 ATCO 2400 177 US CAPRICORN 860
JOHNNY SANDLIN B (AB (B) DINNERTIME 1972 CAPRICORN US 0101
PAUL HORNSBY K (AB (C) THIRD FOR MUSIC 1974 DUNHILLUS 50151
TOMMY TALTON G (A
STEVE SMITH V (B BILL STEWART D (AB SCOTT BOYER G V (AB JAMES TAYLOR G (A
KING CURTIS SAX (A FRANK WESS SAX (A WILLIE BRIDGES SAX (A RONNIE CUBER SAX(A
DANNY MOORE TPT (A P KOWALKE G (A JOE RUDD G (A LOU MULLENIX PERC(B
CHARLES HAYWARD B (B ROGER HAWKINS PERC (B CHUCK LEAVELL K (B WAYNE PERKINS G B(B
JOHN HUGHEY STEEL(B JAI JOHANNY JOHANSON PERC(B EARL SIMS PERC (B CHARLES CHALMERS V (B
SANDY RHODES V (B DONNA RHODES V (B GINGER HOLLADAY V (B MARY HOLLADAY V (B
TEMPLE RISER V (B

T21 ALLAN TAYLOR T21

ALLAN TAYLOR G V (ALL (A) SOMETIMES 1971 LIBERTY US 5529 LBG 83483
DAVE MATTACKS D (A (B) THE LADY 1972 UA UAS 29275
DAVE PEGG B (A (C) AMERICAN ALBUM 1973 UA UAG 29408
DAVE SWARBRICK VLN (A (C) AMERICAN ALBUM 1977 MOONCREST UK CREST 28
D KELSO HERSTON (C (C) AMERICAN ALBUM 1978 ROCKBURGH UK ROC 101
SPANKY McFARLANE V (C (D) TRAVELLER 1978 RUBBER UK RUB 026
BILLY SANFORD G (C (E) ROCK ON THE DAY 1979 RUBBER UK RUB 040
MARY CASLIN (C
MIKE LEECH (C BILLY RILEY (C PETE WADE G (B JOHN BUCK WILKIN G (C
DAVID BRIGGS PNO (C JERRY CARRIGAN (C BUDDY SPICHER FDL (C JOHNNY GIMBLE FDL (C
TOMMY COGBILL B (C LARRY BUTLER K (C REGGIE YOUNG G (C STEVE MILLER K (C
JAMES COLVARD G (C KARL HIMMEL D (C DON GRANT (C JAMES CASON B (C
D BERGEN WHITE (C PETER JAMESON G (C MIKE OMARTIAN K (C JOHN GUERIN D (C
WADDY WACHTEL G (C BRYAN GAROFALO B (C NICK VAN MAARTH (C JAMES E BOND JR (C
MAX HOCH (C

T22 CHIP TAYLOR T22

CHIP TAYLOR V G FDL (ALL (A) GASOLINE 1972 POLYDOR 2318074 US BUDDAH 5118
GEORGE KIRIAKIS G V (BCDF (B) LAST CHANCE 1974 WB UK K56036 US WB 2718
JOHN PLATANIA G (BCDF (C) SOME OF US 1974 WB UK K56077 US WB 2824
JOE RENDA K (BCDF (D) THIS SIDE OF THE BIG RIVER 1975 WB UK K56152 US WB 2882
TOM REILLY STEEL(C (E) ANGEL OF THE MORNING (CASSETTE) 1975 BUDDAH UK CBDS 4026
JOHN REGAN B (C (F) SOMEBODY SHOOT OUT THE JUKEBOX 1976 CBS US 34345
CHUCK FIORE B (C (G) SAINT SEBASTIAN 1979 CAPITOL US 11909
ERIK'RICK' NELSON D (BC
CHARLIE POWERS D (CD LEE HARRISON V (C JOHN NAGY PERC (BC MARGARET McGUINN V (C
ANN McGUINN V (C ANN HEIMBUCH V (C DAVE KAPELL B (BDF PETE DRAKE STEEL(BD
BUDDY SPICHER FDL (D DAVID MANSFIELD FDL (DF KEN GARRETSON WIND (D SANDY BULL WIND(D
VIC SERMAN HRNS (DF JOE STELLITTI HRNS (DF RON CARRAN HRNS (DF DAVE GRISMAN MAND (B
THE JORDANAIRES V (B BEAU SEGAL D (F 'THUMBS' TAYLOR PNO (F

T22A DAVE TAYLOR T22A

DAVE TAYLOR (A) ROCKIN' IN THE SAME OLD WAY 1979 CHARLY UK CRL 5016

T22B

DREW TAYLOR

T22B

Personnel			
DREW TAYLOR (A			

Record	Year	Label	Issue
(A) WINDOW	1981	ROXON	UK ROX 004

T23

EDDIE TAYLOR

T23

Personnel			
EDDIE TAYLOR G V (ALL			
BIG WALTER HORTON HCA (A			
OTIS SPANN PNO (A			
FRED BELOW D (A			
BOB HALL PNO (B			
STEVE BEAL G (F			
ROGER HILL G (B			
BOB BRUNNING B (B	GRAHAM GALLERY B (B	PETE YORK D (B	PHILIP WALKER G(C
GEORGE SMITH HCA (C	JIMMY JONES PNO (C	CHUCK JONES B (C	JOHNNY TUCKER D(C
LITTLE H WILLIAMS TAMB (C	GEORGE KITTA B (F	ODIE PAYNE D (F	CAREY BELL HCA (F
SUNNYLAND SLIM PNO (F	FLOYD JONES (A		

Record	Year	Label	Issue
(A) MASTER OF THE MODERN BLUES	1966	TESTAMENT	US 2214
(B) READY FOR EDDIE	1975	BIG BEAR	BEAR 6
(C) FEEL SO BAD	1976	DJM	UK DJM 22065
(D) BAD BOY A LONG WAY FROM CHICAGO	1978	P/VINE	JAP PLP 3501
(E) BIG TOWN PLAYBOY	1980	CHARLY	UK CRB 1015
(F) MY HEART IS BLEEDING	1980	L&R	GER 42009

T24

HOUND DOG TAYLOR

T24

Personnel			
HOUND DOG TAYLOR G V (ALL			
BREWER PHILLIPS G (ABC*			
TED HARVEY D (ABC*			

Record	Year	Label	Issue
(A) & THE HOUSE ROCKERS	1974	SONET	UK SNTF676 ALLIGATOR US 4701
(B) NATURAL BOOGIE	197	SONET	UK SNTF678 ALLIGATOR US 4704
(C) BEWARE OF THE DOG	197	SONET	UK SNTF701 ALLIGATOR US 4707
(D) LIVE AT FLORENCES(1969)	1980	JSP	1020
(*) 1972 ANN ARBOR FESTIVAL			

T25

JAMES TAYLOR

T25

Personnel			
JAMES TAYLOR G V (ALL			
DANNY KORTCHMAR G (BDEJKLN			
RUSS KUNKEL D (DEKLHJN			
PETER ASHER V (ADEJLN			
ALEX TAYLOR V (EJ			
KATE TAYLOR V (ED			
HUGH TAYLOR V (E			
CAROLE KING PNO V(BEKD			
ABIGALE HANESS V (ED			
CARLY SIMON V (EFHJKLN			
LELAND SKLAR B (DEHJKLN			
BOBBYE HALL PERC (EJ			
GEORGE BOHANON TROM (EHJ			
CHRIS DARROW FDL (B			
MICHAEL BRECKER SAX (EFJK			
LINDA RONSTADT V (EL			
JOHN McLAUGHLIN G (E			
BARRY ROGERS TROM (EF	ART BARON TROM (E	LOUIS CENAMO G V (A	DON SCHINN K (A
RANDY BRECKER TPT (EF	DAN DUGMORE G STEEL(KL	DAVID SPINOZZA G (KFN	DASH CROFTS MAND(E
JOHN LONDON B (BK	RANDY MEISNER B (BK	JOHN HARTFORD FDL (ED	ANDY MUSON B (KF
CLARENCE MACDONALD PNO(KHJL	RED RHODES STEEL(BEK	RALPH MACDONALD PERC (KF	MILT HOLLAND PERC (KHJ
BYRON BERLINE FDL (K	KENNY ASCHER K (KF	ANDREW GOLD V HCA(K	RICK MAROTTA D (KF
JIM KELTNER D (KHJ	BOBBY WEST B (BK	GAYLE LEVANT HARP (KHJ	DAVID SANBORN SAX (KLHLN
NICK DE CARO ORG (KHJ	VICTOR FELDMAN PERC (KHJ	HERB PEDERSEN V (K	JONI MITCHELL V (KD
GRAHAM NASH V (KHJL	DAVID CROSBY V (KHJ	CRAIG DOERGE K (EKJ	KEVIN KELLY K (D
BISHOP O'BRIEN D (A	SKAILA KANGA HARP (A	PAUL McCARTNEY B (AF	GENE ORLOFF STR (F
HUGH McCRACKEN G (F	RALPH SHUCKETT K (FN	KENNY BERGER SAX (F	RICHARD HEWSON STR (A
MICK WAYNE G (A	FREDDIE REDD K (A	LINDA McCARTNEY V (F	DON GROLNICK K (FN
HOWARD JOHNSON TUBA (F	GEORGE YOUNG SAX (F	ALAN RUBIN TPT (F	GEORGE MARGE OBOE(F
PETER GORDON HRNS (F	ANDY NEWMARK D (H	AL PERKINS STEEL(H	WILLIE WEEKS B (HJ
DAVID GRISMAN MAND (HJ	JULES JACOB CLAR (H	ARTHUR ADAMS G (H	CHUCK FINDLEY HRNS(H
RANDY NEWMAN K (H	LOWELL GEORGE V (H	VALERIE CARTER V (HJ	ART GARFUNKEL V (J
KENNY WATSON PERC (J	RED CALLENDER B TUBA (JL	OSCAR BRASHEAR HRNS (J	ERNIE WATTS SAX (J
WADDY WACHTEL G (JN	STEVIE WONDER HCA (J	RUSS TITELMAN PERC (J	DAVID LINDLEY G (J
HERB PEDERSEN BANJ (J	BONNIE RAITT V (J	STEVE MADAIO HRNS (J	DAVID CAMPBELL STR (L
LEAH KUNKEL V (L	STEVE FORMAN PERC (N	DAVID LASLEY V (N	ARNOLD McCULLER V (N
LOUISE SCHULMANN VLA (N	JESSE LEVY CELLO (N	ARIF MARDIN STR (N	RICHARD GREEN FDL (D

Record	Year	Label	Issue
(A) JAMES TAYLOR	1968	APPLE	UK SAPCOR 3 US 3352
(B) SWEET BABY JAMES	1970	WB	UK K46043 US 1843
(C) & THE ORIGINAL FLYING MACHINE	1971	EUPHORIA	EUPH 2
(C) & THE ORIGINAL FLYING MACHINE	197	SPRINGBOARD	US 4023
(D) MUD SLIDE SLIM	1971	WB	UK K46085 US 2561
(E) ONE MAN DOG	1972	WB	UK K46185 US 2660
(F) WALKING MAN	1974	WB	UK K56042 US 2794
(G) RAINY DAY MAN	1975	DJM	UK DJSLM2007 TRIP US 9513
(H) GORILLA	1975	WB	UK K56137 US 2866
(J) IN THE POCKET	1976	WB	UK K56197 US 2912
(K) THE BEST OF	1976	WB	UK K56309 US 2979
(L) J.T.	1977	CBS	UK 86029 US 34811
(M) GREATEST HITS	1977	WB	US 3113 US 2979
(N) FLAG	1979	CBS	UK 86091 US 36058
(O) DAD LOVES HIS WORK	1980	CBS	US 37009
(BD) TWO ORIGINALS	1975	WB	UK K66029

T26

JOHNNIE TAYLOR

T26

Personnel			
JOHNNIE TAYLOR V (ALL			
EDDIE WILLIS G (S			
GEORGE ROUNDTREE K (S			
GREG COLES B (S			
LEE NATHAN D (S			
JERRY JONES D (S			
CARL SMITH PERC (S			
BRANDYE V (S			

Record	Year	Label	Issue
WANTED ONE SOUL SINGER	19	ATLANTIC	US 7715
WHP'S MAKIN' LOVE	1968	STAX	US 2005
RAW BLUES	196	STAX	US 2008
RARE STAMPS	196	STAX	US 2012
J T PHILOSOPHY CONTINUES	1969	STAX	UK 1024 US 2023
ONE STEP BEYOND	19	STAX	US 2030
GREATEST HITS	197	STAX	US 2032
TAYLORED IN SILK	1973	STAX	UK STX1012 US 3014
SUPER TAYLOR	1974	STAX	UK STX5022 US 5509
BEST OF	1976	STAX	UK STX1049 US 5522
EARGASM	1976	CBS	UK 81201 US 33951
RATED EXTRAORDINAIRE	1977	CBS	US 34401
EVER READY	197	CBS	US 35340
REFLECTIONS	19	RCA	US APLI 2527
CHRONICLE VOL 1	1978	STAX	UK 7001 US 88001
CHRONICLE VOL 2	1978	STAX	UK 7002 US 88009
DISCO 9000	197	CBS	38004
SHE'S KILLING ME	1979	CBS	US 36061
(S) A NEW DAY	1980	CBS	US 36548
BEST OF	1981	CBS	US 37127

T27

KATE TAYLOR

T27

Personnel			
KATE TAYLOR V (AB			
DANNY KORTCHMAR G PERC(A			
J D SOUTHER V (A			
CHARLES LARKEY B (A			
JOEL O'BRIEN D (A	SANDRA CROUCH PERC (A	DONNA PRATER V (A	LEE SKLAR B (A
JOHN HARTFORD BAN (A	LINDA RONSTADT V (A	JAMES TAYLOR G (A	CAROLE KING V (A
MERRY CLAYTON V (A	RUSS KUNKEL D (A	ANDREW LOVE HRNS (A	JOHN BIELAND G (A
ABIGAIL HANESS V (A	WAYNE JACKSON HRNS (A	RALPH SCHUCKETT K (A	OMA DRAKE V (A
PETER ASHER V (A	MEMPHIS HORNS (A		

Record	Year	Label	Issue
(A) SISTER KATE	1971	COTILLION	US SD9045
(B) KATE TAYLOR	1978	CBS	US 35089
(C) ITS IN THERE	1979	CBS	US 36034

T27A KING SIZE TAYLOR T27A

KING SIZE TAYLOR V (AB (A) LIVE IM STAR CLUB HAMBURG 19 ARIOLA GER 200 868 241
(B) LIVE IM STAR CLUB VOL 2 19 ARIOLA GER 200 869 241

T28 KOKO TAYLOR T28

KOKO TAYLOR V (ABC (A) I GOT WHAT IT TAKES 1975 SONET UK SNTF687 US ALLIGATOR 4706
MIGHTY JOE YOUNG G (A (B) SOUTHSIDE BABY 1975 BLACK & BLUE 33505
SAMMY LAWHORN G (AC (C) EARTHSHAKER 1978 SONET UK SNTF775 US ALLIGATOR 4711
ABE LOCKE SAX (AC ( ) KOKO TAYLOR 19 CHESS US 1532
VINCE CHAPPELLE D (AC ( ) BASIC SOUL 19 CHESS US 50018
BILL HEID K (A ( ) HEART OF A WOMAN 1982 SONET UK SNTF 868
CORNELIUS BOYSON B (AC
JOHNNY B MOORE G (C PINETOP PERKINS K (C MERVYN HINDS HCA(C

T29 LITTLE JOHNNY TAYLOR T29

LITTLE JOHNNY TAYLOR (ALL (A) EVERYBODY KNOWS ABOUT MY GOODTHING 197 POLYDOR UK 2916 015 US RONN 7530
(B) OPEN HOUSE 1973 CONTEMPO 1003 US RONN 7532
(C) SUPER TAYLORS 1974 CONTEMPO CLP 502
(D) PART TIME LOVE 1980 CHARLY UK CRB 1012
(D) PART TIME LOVE 197 GALAXY US 0207
(E) I SHOULDA BEEN A PREACHER 1981 RED LIGHTNING UK RL 0030
( ) GREATEST HITS 19 GALAXY US 8207
( ) LITTLE JOHNNY TAYLOR 1979 RONN US 7535
(EP AS LONG AS I DONT SEE YOU 1980 CHARLY UK CTD 118

T30 LIVINGSTON TAYLOR T30

LIVINGSTON TAYLOR G K V(ABCDE (A) LIVINGSTON TAYLOR 1970 WB US WS 3006 + ATCO 33334
PAUL HORNSBY K (AB (B) LIV 1971 WB UK K46131 US CAPRICORN 863
ROBERT POPWELL B (AB (C) OVER THE RAINBOW 1973 CAPRICORN US CP 0114
DAVE WOODFORD WIND (B (D) THREE WAY MIRROR 1979 EPIC US 35540
BILL STEWART D (BC (E) ECHOES 1979 CAPRICORN US 0220
TOMMY TALTON G (BC (F) MANS BEST FRIEND 1980 EPIC US 36155
WALTER ROBINSON B (BC
JOHNNY SANDLIN B (AB GREG PRESTOPINO V (B PETE CARR G (A BUZZ FEITON G (C
NEIL LARSEN K (C JIN NAILS G (C RICK MAROTTA D (C TONY LEVIN B (C
VICTOR BRADY STEEL(C MIKE MAINIERI PERC (C GEORGE MARGE CLAR (C GLORIA AGOSTINI HARP(C
ED FREEMAN STR (C JAMES TAYLOR V (C CARLY SIMON V (C MERETHA STEWART V (C

T31 MICK TAYLOR T31

MICK TAYLOR G V (A1 (A) MICK TAYLOR 1979 CBS 35076 UK 82600
LOWELL GEORGE G (A (1) 1977 LIVE BAND
PIERRE MOERLEN D (A
JEAN ROUSSEL PNO (A NORMAN MITCHELL TAMB (A MIKE DRISCOLL D (A KUMA HARADA B (A
RICHARD BAILEY D (A ALAN SPENNER B (A RONNIE LEAHY K (1 STEVE THOMPSON B (1
COLIN ALLEN D (1

T32 R DEAN TAYLOR T32

R DEAN TAYLOR V (ALL (A) I THINK THEREFORE I AM 1970 RARE EARTH RS 522
SCOTT ROGERS V (C (A) INDIANA WANTS ME 197 TAMLA US STML11185 90007
(B) L A SUNSET 1975 POLYDOR UK 2383 399

T32A TED TAYLOR T32A

TED TAYLOR V (ALL (A) & LITTLE JOHNNY 1974 RONN US 0011
DINO ZIMMERMAN G (C (B) SHADES OF BLUE 19 RONN US 7528
DON BARRETT B (C (C) TED TAYLOR 1976 CONTEMPO UK 538
JAMES STROUD D (C (D) KEEPING MY HEAD ABOVE WATER 1978 MCA US 3059
WARDELL QUEZERQUE K (C (E) KEEP ON WALKING 1980 CHARLY CRB 1011
MUSCLE SHOALS HRNS (C (F) IT'S TOO LATE(EP) 1980 CHARLY CTD 111
DOROTHY MOORE V (C
JEWEL BASS V (C DENNIS BELFIELD B (D BOBBY RUFFINO D (D JOEY BRASLER D (D
RAY BRAVERMAN K (D MICHAEL GIRARD PERC (D PAT ZICARI SAX (D TONY COLEMAN TROM(D

T32B ROD TAYLOR T32B

ROD TAYLOR G V (A (A) ROD TAYLOR 1973 ASYLUM SYLA 8755
BONNIE BRAMLETT V (A
DON CAVERHILL K (A RY COODER G (A JESSE ED DAVIS G (A KENNY EDWARDS B (A
STEVE FERGUSON PNO (A CRAIG SAFAN PNO (A STEVE VAN GELDER G FDL(A ERNIE WATTS SAX (A
CHUCK FINDLEY TPT (A ANDREW GOLD G ACC(A JIM HORN SAX (A JIM KELTNER D (A
LARRY KNECHTEL PNO (A DAVID LA FLAMME FDL (A LEE SKLAR B (A GARY MALLABER D (A
LEW McCREARY HRN (A JONI MITCHELL V (A BUELL NEIDLINGER B (A BILL PAYNE K (A
CHUCK PLOTKIN K (A RED RHODES STEEL (A JOEL TEPP HCA CLAR(A

T32C RODERICK TAYLOR T32C

RODERICK TAYLOR V (A (A) STRAIGHT 1980 METRONOME GER 60379
EARL SLICK G (A
JEAN MILLINGTON B V (A CURLEY SMITH D V (A DUANE HITCHING K (A PETER IVERS HCA (A
JIMMY GREENSPOON K (A MARK OLSON K (A JEFFY RICH B (A

T32D ROGER TAYLOR T32D

ROGER TAYLOR (A (A) FUN IN SPACE 1981 ELEKTRA US 522 UK EMC 3369

T32E TUT TAYLOR T32E

TUT TAYLOR G (ALL (A) DORBROLIC PLECTORAL SOCIETY 19 TAKOMA US 1050
CLARENCE TAYLOR G (D (B) FRIAR TUT 19 ROUNDER US 0011
ROLAND WHITE (D (C) THE OLD POST OFFICE 19 FLYING FISH US 008
CHRIS HILLMAN (D (D) DOBRO COUNTRY 19 UA UK 29711
BILLY RAY LATHAM (D
BILL KEITH (D

T33 VINCE TAYLOR T33

VINCE TAYLOR V (ALL (A) VINCE TAYLOR 19 BARCLAY 280 149
(B) 100% ROCK 1977 BARCLAY 80984/5 RI 81088/9
(C) VINCE TAYLOR (EP) 1979 SPADE PFE 1

T33A TAZMANIAN DEVILS T33A

BARRY LOWENTHAL M D (A (A) TAZMANIAN DEVILS 1980 WB US 3400 EURO 56812
DUANE VAN DEMAN B (A
DENNIS HEGAN G V (A PAT CRAIG K (A DAVID CARLSON G (A

T34 BRAM TCHAIKOVSKY T34

BRAM TCHAIKOVSKY G V (ABCD123 (A) STRANGE MAN CHANGED MAN 1979 RADAR UK 17 POLYDOR US 6211
KEITH BOYCE D (A123 (B) RUSSIANS ARE COMING 1980 RADAR UK 26
MICKY BROADBENT V B G K(AB123 (C) PRESSURE 1980 POLYDOR US 6273
DENIS FORBES G(BCD123 (D) FUNLAND 1981 ARISTA UK 1164 GER 203 654
KEITH LINE D (BC3 (1) SARAH SMILES 1978 CRIMINAL UK BRAM1
ALBIE DONNELLY SAX (C (2) LULLABY OF BROADWAY 1979 CRIMINAL UK BRAM5
ANDY PARKER SAX (C (3) PRESSURE(EP) 1980 RADAR UK RDR 3
MIKE KEARNS SAX (C
BOB ANDREWS K (C NICK GARVEY B V (ACD23 RICHARD ITCHINGTON B (D BERNIE CLARKE K (D
ANDY McMASTER V (D LEW SOLOFF TPT (D JIMMY MAELEN PERC (D MIKE OLDFIELD PERC(A

T35 TEA T35

MARK STORACE V (AB (A) TEA 1975 PHILIPS 6305 238
TURO PASCHAYAN B V (AB (B) THE SHIP 1975 PHILIPS 9118 001
ARMAND VOLKER G V (AB
PHILIPPE KIENHOLZ K V (AB ROLI EGGLI D (A DIETER DIERKS D (B

T35A TEA COMPANY T35A

(A) COME & HAVE SOME TEA WITH TEA COMPANY 196 SMASH US 67105

T36 TEA & SYMPHONY T36

JEFF DAW FLT G V (A (A) AN ASYLUM FOR THE MUSICALLY INSANE 1969 HARVEST UK SHVL 761
JAMES LANGSTON G V WIND(A (B) JO SAGA 1970 HARVEST UK SHVL 785
NIGEL PHILLIPS K V PERC(A
BOB LAMB D (A RON CHESTERMAN B (A MICK HINCKS B (A GUS DUDGEON PERC (A
CLEM CLEMPSON G (A

T36A TEA SET T36A

NICK HAEFFNER G ((A) CUPS & SAUCERS (EP) 1979 WALDOS RECORDS BS 003
RON WEST B (
DUNCAN STRINGER G (CALLY D (NICK EGAN V (

T37 TEAR GAS T37

ZAL CLEMINSON G (AB (A) PIGGY GO GETTER PARAMOUNT US 5029 UK FAMOUS SFMA5751
CHRIS GLEN B V (AB (B) TEAR GAS REGAL ZONOPHONE UK SLRZ1021
HUGH McKENNA K (B
TED McKENNA D (B DAVEY BATCHELOR V (A EDDIE CAMPBELL K V (A WILLIE MONRO D V (A

T37A TEARDROP EXPLODES T37A

JULIAN COPE B V (AB (A) KILIMANJARO 1980 MERCURY US 4016 UK 6359 035
DAVID BALFE K SYN(AB (B) WILDER 1981 MERCURY UK 6359 056
GARY DWYER D (AB
ALAN GILL G (A MICHAEL FINKLER G (A RAY MARTINEZ TPT (A HURRICANE SMITH TPT (A
CLIVE LANGER PROD(AB JAMES ELLER (B TROY TATE (B LUKE TUNNEY (B
TED EMMETT (B JEFF HAMMER (B ALFIE AGIUS (B

T37B TEARDROPS T37B

BOK BOK (A (A) FINAL VINYL 1980 ILLUMINATED JAMS 2
TONY FRIEL (A
STEVE GARVEY (A TREV WAYNE (A HELEN BARBROOK (A

T37C TEAZE T37C

BRIAN DANTER B V (A (A) ON THE LOOSE 1978 AQUARIUS AQR 516
MIKE KOZAK D (A (B) LIVE 1978 AQUARIUS 520
CHUCK PRICE G (A (C) ONE NIGHT STANDS 1979 CAPITOL US 11919
MARK BIADAC G (A (D) BODY SHOTS 1980 AQUARIUS AQR 528

T37D TEDDY BEARS T37D

PHIL SPECTOR V (A (A) TEDDY BEARS SING 19 IMPERIAL US LP 12010
ANNETTE KLEINBARD V (A
MARSHALL LIEB V (A

T37E RICHARD TEE T37E

RICHARD TEE K (AB (A) STROKIN' 1979 CBS US 35695 UK 83339
STEVE GADD D (B (B) NATURAL INGREDIENTS 1980 CBS US 36380 UK 84194
ERIC GALE G (B
MATTHEW BRAGG B (B RALPH MACDONALD PERC (B HUGH McCRACKEN HCA (B TOM SCOTT SAX (B
JON FADDIS HRNS (B RANDY BRECKER HRNS (B BARRY ROGERS HRNS (B SELDON POWELL HRNS(B
VALERIE SIMPSON V (B ULLANDA McCULLOUGH V (B LANI GROVES V (B STRING SECTION (B

T37F WILLIE TEE T37F

WILLIE TEE (A) ANTICIPATION 19 UA US UALA 655

T37G TEE SET T37G

FRANKLIN MADJA B (A (A) MY BELLE AMI 19 QUALITY BM 597
DILL BENWICK G (A
JOOP BLOM D (A HANS VAN EIJCK K (A

T37H TED T37H

TED GARDESTAD V (A (A) BLUE VIRGIN ISLE 1978 EPIC UK 83653 POLS 300 IMP
JEFF PORCARO D (A
JIM KELTNER D (A DAVID HUNGATE B (A RAY BROWN B (A BOB GLAUB B (A
JAI WINDING B K SYN V(A JAY GRAYDON G (A LEE RITENOUR G (A STEVE LUKATHER G(A
FRED TACKETT G (A JOHN COLLINS G (A LARRY MUHOBERAC K (A MIKE MELVOIN K (A
JAMES NEWTON HOWARD K (A DR JOHN K (A VICTOR FELDMAN PERC (A JERRY WILLIAMS PERC(A
HAL BLAINE PERC (A GARY COLEMAN PERC (A AL HENDRICKSON BAN (A STEVE PORCARO SYN (A
EMIL RICHARDS PERC (A JOHN MAYALL HCA V (A STEVE MADAIO TPT (A BOB FOWLER TPT (A
GENE COE TPT (A JERRY HEY TPT (A CAPPY LEWIS TPT (A DICK HYDE TROM(A
TOM SHEPARD TROM (A ABE MOST WIND (A JOHN LOWE WIND (A JIM HORN WIND(A
BUDDY COLETTE HRNS (A DAVID LUELL WIND (A TED NASH WIND (A WILLIE SCHWARTZ WIND(A
GARY HERBIG WIND (A STEPHEN NILSSON (A JANNE SCHAFFER G (A MIKE WATSON (A
ROGER PALM (A DAVIS CASSIDY V (A VANETTA FIELDS V (A SHIRLEY MATTHEWS V (A
STRINGS (A

T37i TEEGARDEN & VANWINKLE T37i

SKIP'VANWINKLE'KNAPE V K B(ABC (A) AN EVENING AT HOME 19 ATCO US 33272
DAVE TEEGARDEN D V (ABC (B) BUT, ANYHOW 19 WESTBOUND US 2003
MIKE BRUCE G V (C (C) ON OUR WAY 19 WESTBOUND US 2010
BOB SEGER V G (C
ERNIE FILEDS HRNS (C BRENDA KNIGHT V (C MARLENE DRISCOLL V (C JO ANN HILL V (A
JERRY SMITH PNO (C TRACY NELSON V (C

T37J TEENAGE HEAD T37J

NICK STIPANITZ D V (AB — (A) TEENAGE HEAD — 1979 EPIC CAN 90534
STEVE MAHON B (AB — (B) FRANTIC CITY — 1980 ATTIC GER 6 24407
GORDON LEWIS G (AB
FRANKIE KERR/VENOM V (AB DAVE RAVE G (A GRANT SLATER PNO (A KELLY JAY K (A
RICK MORRISON SAX (B THE SHAKERS V (B WALTER ZWOL SYN (B

T37K TELEPHONE T37K

JEAN LOUIS AUBERT G V (BC — (A) TELEPHONE — 1977 MARCONI FR 14506
LOUIS BRTIGNAC G V (BC — (B) CACHE TON VENIM — 1979 EMI FR 14737
RICHARD KOLINKA D (BC — (C) AU COEUR DE LA NUIT — 1980 EMI FR 72279 VIRGIN UK 2195
CORINE MARIENNEAU B V (BC
COWBOY SAX (C

T37L JAHN TEIGEN T37L

JAHN TEIGEN K V (A — (A) THIS YEARS LOSER — 1978 RCA NOR 40028
B HADAWAY B (A
S COOLING G (A H BORNHOLT TIMB (A L NIELSEN VLN (A PETE KNUDSEN STR (A
T METALL D (A JONAS FIELD G (A A STAV SAX (A TORE SYVERTSEN V PERC(A
WALTER QUINTUS VLN (A BAARD SVENDSEN K (A

T38 TELEVISION T38

TOM VERLAINE G V (AB1 — (A) MARQUEE MOON — 1977 ELEKTRA US 7E1098 UK K52046
RICHARD LLOYD G V (AB1 — (B) ADVENTURE — 1978 ELEKTRA US 6E 133 UK K52072
BILLY FICCA D (AB1 — (1) 1974/5
FRED SMITH B (AB
RICHARD HELL B (1 JOHN JANSEN PROD (B

T38A TELEVISION PERSONALITIES T38A

(A) WHERE'S BILL GRUNDY — 19 KINGS ROAD 001
(B) AND DONT THE KIDS JUST LOVE IT — 198 ROUGH TRADE UK ROUGH24

T38B TELEX T38B

DAN LACKSMAN (AB — (A) LOOKING FOR ST TROPEZ — 1979 SIRE UK SRK 6072
MICHAEL MOERS (AB — (B) NEUROVISION — 1980 SIRE NL50142 UK SRK 6090
MARC MOULIN (AB

T39 JACK TEMPCHIN T39

JACK TEMCHIN (A — (A) JACK TEMPCHIN — 1978 ARISTA US 4193 UK SPART 1078
PETE CARR G (A
ROGER CLARK D (A BOB WRAY B (A BARRY BECKETT K (A ANTHONY PARSONS FLT (A
GLENN FREY G V (A HARVEY THOMPSON SAX (A RANDY McCORMICK K (A GAY BAKER B (A
EDDIE STRUZICK V (A THOM FLORA V (A JENNIFER WARNES V (A JACKSON BROWNE V (A

T40 TEMPEST T40

JON HISEMAN D (AB — (A) TEMPEST — 1973 BRONZE GER 86626 ILPS 9220
MARK CLARKE B K V(AB — (B) LIVING IN FEAR — 1974 BRONZE ILPS 9267
PAUL WILLIAMS V G K(A
ALLAN HOLDSWORTH G V VLN(A OLLIE HALSALL G K V(B

T41 TEMPLE CITY KAZOO BAND T41

DR JIM ZANE KAZOO(A — (A) SOME KAZOOS (EP) — 1978 RHINO RNEP 501
RICHIE BALANCE KAZOO(A — (B) PLATE FULL OF KAZOOS(KAZOO BROS) — 1979 RHINO EP RNEP 504
ZAZOOT SIMS KAZOO(A
TOM'CAT'KNAPP KAZOO(A DAVID ANDREWS KAZOO(A DON BUCHANAN KAZOO(A GLEN COBAR KAZOO(A
PAUL SANOIAN KAZOO(A JEFF GINSBERG KAZOO(A GREG GORDON KAZOO(A TED KAZOOSKI KAZOO(A
ELIJAH GOLDSTEIN KAZOO(A THE KAZOO BROTHERS BAND(B ELVIN KAZOOS KAZOO(B JACKSON KAZOOS KAZOO(B

T42 TEMPTATIONS T42

OTIS MILES V (1234567 — MEET THE TEMPTATIONS — 1964 TAMLA UK STML11009 US GORDY 911
MELVIN FRANKLIN V (1234567 — SING SMOKEY — 1965 TAMLA UK TML11016 US GORDY 912
EDDIE KENDRICKS V (1234 — TEMPTIN' TEMPTATIONS — 1966 TAMLA UK STML11023 US GORDY 914
ELDRIDGE BRYANT V (2 — GETTIN' READY — 1966 TAMLA UK STML11035 US GORDY 918
RICHARD STREET V (Z — GREATEST HITS — 1967 TAMLA UK STML11042 US GORDY 919
DAVID RUFFIN V (3 — LIVE — 1967 TAMLA UK STML11053 US GORDY 921
DENNIS EDWARDS V (4567Z — WITH A LOT OF SOUL — 1967 TAMLA UK STML11057 US GORDY 922
RICKY OWENS V (5 — IN A MELLOW MOOD — 1967 TAMLA UK STML11068 US GORDY 924
DAMON HARRIS V (67 — WISH IT WOULD RAIN — 1968 TAMLA UK STML11079 US GORDY 927
PAUL WILLIAMS V (123456 — T V SHOW — 1967 TAMLA US GORDY 933
WITH THE SUPREMES — 1969 TAMLA UK STML11096
(1) 1959(DISTANTS) — LIVE AT THE COPA — 1969 US GORDY 938
(2) 1960 — CLOUD NINE — 1969 TAMLA UK STML11109 US GORDY 939
(3) 1962 — TCB (SUPREMES) — 1969 TAMLA UK STML11110 US TAMLA 682
(4) 1968 — TOGETHER(SUPREMES) — 1970 TAMLA UK STML11122
(5) 1971 — PSYCHEDELIC SHACK — 1970 TAMLA UK STML11147 US GORDY 947
(6) 1971 — PUZZLE PEOPLE — 1970 TAMLA UK STML11133 US GORDY 949
(7) 1971 — LIVE AT THE TALK OF THE TOWN — 1970 TAMLA UK STML11141 US GORDY 953
ROBERT WARD G (ML — LIVE AT THE TALK OF THE TOWN RI — 1979 MFP US 50419
JOE MESSINA G (LM — CHRISTMAS CARD — 1970 US GORDY 951
ROBERT WHITE G (LM — GREATEST HITS VOL 2 — 1970 TAMLA UK STML11170 US GORDY 954
AARON SMITH D (LM — THE SKY'S THE LIMIT — 1971 TAMLA UK STML11184 US GORDY 957
URIEL JONES D (LM — SOLID ROCK — 1972 TAMLA UK STML11202 US GORDY 961
EARL VAN DYKE K (LM — (L) ALLDIRECTIONS — 1972 TAMLA UK STML11218 US GORDY 962
BOB BABBITT B (MLZ — (M)MASTERPIECE — 1973 TAMLA UK STML11229 US GORDY 965
WAH WAH RAGIN G (LMQ — GET READY — 1973 SOUNDS SUPERB UK 90004
PAUL WARREN G (ML — 1990 — 1974 TAMLA UK STMA 8016
LEDDIE WILLIS G (ML — ANTHOLOGY 1964/73 — 1974 TAMLA UK TMSP 6003 US GORDY 974
RICHARD ALLEN D (ML — 10TH ANNIVERSARY — 1974 TAMLA M782
ANDREW SMITH D (LM — HOUSE PARTY — 1975 TAMLA UK STML12006 US GORDY 973
LEROY TAYLOR B (LM — (Q)A SONG FOR YOU — 1975 TAMLA UK STMA 8021 US GORDY 969
EDDIE WATKINS B (ML — WINGS OF LOVE — 1976 TAMLA UK STMA 8025 US GORDY 971
EDDIE BROWN PERC (LM — DO THE TEMPTATIONS — 1976 TAMLA UK STML12040 US GORDY 975
MAURICE DAVIS TPT (ML — GREATEST HITS VOL 3 — 1977 TAMLA UK STML12061 US
JACK BROCKENSHA PERC (LM — TEMPTATIONS — 1977 TAMLA UK STMX 6002
LJACK ASHFORD PERC (ML — HEAR TO TEMPT YOU — 1978 ATLANTIC UK K50413 US 19143
TED LUCAS HCA (ML — BARE BACK — 1978 ATLANTIC UK K50504 US 19188
DON BALDWIN K WIND SYN(Q — SING SMOKEY — 1979 MOTOWN UK STMR 9005
OLLIE BROWN D (Q — 20 GOLDEN GREATS — 1980 MOTOWN UK STML12140
ZACHARY FRAZIER D (Q — POWER — 1980 MOTOWN UK STML12136 US 994
JAMES GADSON D (Q — TEMPTATIONS — 1981 MOTOWN UK STML12159

(CONTINUED)

T42 (CONTINUED)

TEMPTATIONS T42

EDDIE HAZEL G (Q
WILLY NELSON B (Q OTIS WILLIAMS V (Z GLENN LEONARD V (Z DAVID ENGLISH V (Z
DON RENALDO SRT (Z BILL NEALE STR G(Z LARRY WASHINGTON PERC (Z JOHNNY GRIFFIN ORG (LM
PAUL RISER STR (LM NORMAN WHITFIELD PROD (LM BILLY COOPER G (L THOM BELL PROD K(Z
BOBBY ELI G (Z CHARLES COLLINS D (Z ED W SHEA PERC (Z

T43 TEN C C T43

ERIC STEWART G V (ALL (A) TEN CC 1973 UK UK UKAL 1005 US 53105
GRAHAM GOULDMAN G V (ALL (B) SHEET MUSIC 1974 UK UK UKAL 1007 US 53107
KEVIN GODLEY D V (ABCDE (C) 100CC 1975 UK UK UKAL 1012 US 53110
LOL CREME G V (ABCDE (D) ORIGINAL SOUNDTRACK 1975 MERCURY UK 9102 500 US SRM1 1029
TERRY BOZZIO D (F (D) ORIGINAL SOUNDTRACK ½ SPEED 1981 MERCURY UK 9102 500
PAUL BURGESS D (FGHK (E) HOW DARE YOU 1976 MERCURY UK 9102 501 US SRMI 1061
RICK FENN G (GHK (F) DECEPTIVE BENDS 1977 MERCURY UK 9102 502 US SRMI 3702
STUART TOSH D (GHK (G) LIVE & LET LIVE 1977 MERCURY UK 6641 698 US SRM2 8600
TONY O'MALLEY K (G (H) BLOODY TOURISTS 1978 MERCURY UK 9102 503 US SRMI 6160
TONY SPATH PNO (FH (I) GREATEST HITS 1979 MERCURY UK 9102 504 US POLYDOR6244
JEAN ROUSSEL K (F (J) THINGS WE DO FOR LOVE 1979 POLYDOR US 6186
DUNCAN MACKAY K (HK (K) LOOK HEAR 1980 MERCURY UK 9102 505 US WB 3442
DEL NEWMAN SRT (F ( ) THE BEST OF 1980 MERCURY NL 9279 567
(L) 10 OUT OF 10 1981 MERCURY UK 6359 048

T44 TEN WHEEL DRIVE T44

GENYA RAVAN V HCA(ABC (A) CONSTRUCTION No1 1969 POLYDOR US 4008 UK 583 577
ARAM SCHEFRIN G V (ABCD (B) BRIEF REPLIES 1970 POLYDOR US 4024 UK 2425 022
MIKE ZAGER K CLAR (ABCD (C) PECULIAR FRIENDS 1971 POLYDOR US 4062 UK 2425 065
BILL TAXAS B (A (D) TEN WHEEL DRIVE 1974 CAPITOL US ST 11199
LEON RIX D CELLO(A
LOUIS HOFF WIND (A DENNIS PARISI TROM (AB JAY SILVA WIND (A RICHARD MEISTERMAN TPT(A
PETER HYDE HRNS (A BOB PIAZZA B (B STEVE SATTEN HRNS (A JOHN GATCHELL HRNS(BD
DAVE LIEBMAN WIND (B JOHN ECKERT HRNS (B ALLEN HERMAN D (B BLAKE HINES B (C
DAVID WILLIAMS D (C ALAN GAUVIN WIND (C DEAN PRATT TPT (CD TOM MALONE TROM (C
DANNY STILES TPT (C FRANK FRINT TPT (C ANN SUTTON V (D GERRY CHAMBERLAIN TROM(D
ED XIQUES WIND (D DON GROLNICK K (D HARRY MAX VLN (D BARRY LARAROWITZ D (D

T45 TEN YEARS AFTER T45

ALVIN LEE V (ALL (A) TEN YEARS AFTER 1967 DERAM US 18009 UK SML1015
LEO LYONS B (ALL (B) UNDEAD 1968 DERAM US 18016 UK SML1023
(B) UNDEAD 19 NOVA GER 6 21585
CHICK CHURCHILL D (ALL (C) STONEDHENGE 1969 DERAM US 18021 UK SML1029
(AC) T Y A/STONEDHENGE (DBL) 19 DERAM GER 3026/1 RI NOVA 628110
RIC LEE D(ABCDEFGHIJKLMN (D) SSSSSSSH 1969 DERAM US 18029 UK SML1052
DAVID POTTS D (1 (D) SSSSSSSH 1975 CHRYSALIS RI UK CHR 1083
GUS DUDGEON PERC (A (E) CRICKLEWOOD GREEN 1970 DERAM US 18038 UK SML1065
MIKE VERNON V (C (E) CRICKLEWOOD GREEN 1975 CHRYSALIS RI UK CHR 1084
(E) CRICKLEWOOD GREEN 19 DERAM GER 6 21589
SIMON STABLE PERC (C (F) WATT 1970 DERAM US 18050 UK SML1078
HAROLD BURGON V (K (F) WATT 1975 CHRYSALIS RI UK CHR 1085
(G) ALVIN LEE & CO 1972 DERAM US 18064 UK SML1096
(1) 1967 (G) ALVIN LEE & CO 1979 LONDON US RI 50013
(H) A SPACE IN TIME 1972 CHRYSALIS UK 1001 US CBS 30801
(I) ROCK'N'ROLL TO THE WORLD 1972 CHRYSALIS UK 1009 US CBS 31779
(J) RECORDED LIVE 1973 CHRYSALIS UK 1049 US CBS 32288
(K) POSITIVE VIBRATIONS 1974 CHRYSALIS UK 1060 US CBS 32851
(L) GOIN' HOME 1975 CHRYSALIS UK 1077 US DERAM18072
(M) ANTHOLOGY 1976 CHRYSALIS UK 1107
(N) CLASSIC PERFORMANCES 1977 CHRYSALIS UK 1134 US CBS 34366
(O) PROFILE 19 TELDEC GERM 624011
(P) LONDON COLLECTION 19 LONDON US LC 50013
(Q) HEAR ME CALLING 1981 DECCA UKTAB24
( ) TEN YEARS AFTER 1980 PICKWICK UK SHM3038

T46 TEN YEARS LATER T46

ALVIN LEE G V (AB (A) ROCKET FUEL 1978 POLYDOR 2310 605 + 2344 103
TOM COMPTON D (AB (B) RIDE ON 1979 POLYDOR 2310 678
MICK HAWKSWORTH B (AB
BERNIE CLARKE K (A MICK WEAVER K (A

T47 TENNENT MORRISON T47

DAVID MORRISON (AB (A) TENNENT MORRISON 1972 POLYDOR UK 2383 152
JOHN TENNENT G V (AB (B) KEEP IT CLEAN(AS JOE SOAP) 1973 POLYDOR UK 2383 233
RONNIE LEAHY K (A
HERBIE FLOWERS B (A JIMMY McCULLOCH (AB BRIAN ODGERS (A CLEM CATTINI (A
ROGER McKEW (A STEVE THOMPSON (A COLIN ALLEN (A DENNIS LOPEZ (A
MIK KAMINSKI VLN (B GERRY CONWAY D (B JEFF PEARCE B (B

T47A TENNESSEE FARM BAND T47A

LINDA HERSHFIELD V (A (A) COMMUNION 1977 FARM 1013
DAVID CHALMERS D (A
THOMAS DOTZLER V K SAX(A MICHAEL SULLENS B (A WALTER RABIDEAU G V (A

T47B TENNIS SHOES T47B

(A) MEDIUM WAVE (EP) 19 BONAPARTE UK BONE 3

T47C TERENCE T47C

(A) AN EYE FOR AN EAR 19 DECCA IMP DL75137

T47D TENT T47D

(A) 6 EMPTY PLACES 1981 CHERRY RED BRED 17

T47E TERESA T47E

(A) CLASS REUNION 1980 DREAM US 3502

T47F TERPSICHORE T47F

(A) TERPSICHORE (SILLY NOT TO) 1981 EMI UK EMS 1004

T48 TERRA COTTA T48

TOM ATKINSON G (1 (A) HARD TO KNOW (EP) 197 TERRA COTTA TC 001
STEVE LUDLAM G (1 (1) 1978
CHRIS WOODCOCK D (1
TERRY COTTAM V (1 KELLY CANTLON B (1

T51 TAMMI TERRELL T51

Musician	Instr	Albums	Title	Year	Label	Country	Cat. No.
TAMMI TERRELL	V	(ALL	(A) UNITED	1968	TAMLA	UK	STML11062
MARVIN GAYE	V	(A	(B) YOU'RE ALL I NEED	1968	TAMLA	UK	STML11084
			(C) IRRESISTIBLE	1969	TAMLA	US	652
			(D) EARLY SHOW	1969	MARBLE ARCH	UK	MAL 1110

T52 DEWEY TERRY T52

Musician	Instr	Albums	Title	Year	Label	Country	Cat. No.
DEWEY TERRY	V	(A	(A) CHIEF	1973	TUMBLEWEED		TW 3502
HARVEY MANDEL	G	(A					

T53 KARL TERRY & THE CRUISER T53

Musician	Instr	Albums	Title	Year	Label	Country	Cat. No.
KARL TERRY		(A	(A) CRUISIN'	1978	RAW		RWLP 105

T53A SONNY TERRY & BROWNIE MCGHEE T53A

Musician	Instr	Albums	Title	Year	Label	Country	Cat. No.
SONNY TERRY	V HCA	(	AT SUGARHILL	19	AMERICA		AM 6071
BROWNIE McGHEE	G V	(	AT THE BUNKHOUSE	19	SMASH	US	27067
DAVE LEE	PNO	(	BACK COUNTRY BLUES	1978	MUSIDISC	FR	CV 956
SVEND ERIK NORREGARD		(	BLUES IS MY COMPANION	19	VERVE	US	3008
PEPPERMINT HARRIS		(	BROWNIE & SONNY	19	ARC FOLK	US	242
			BLUES & SHOUTS	19	FANTASY	US	3317
			BROWNIE & SONNY	19	FANTASY	US	3340
			BROWNIE & SONNY	19	FANTASY	US	8091
			BROWNIE McGHEE BLUES	19	FOLKWAYS	US	2030
			BROWNIE McGHEE & SONNY TERRY	19	FOLKWAY	US	2327
			BROWNIE McGHEE SINGS THE BLUES	19	FOLKWAYS	US	3557
			BEST OF	19	PRESTIGE	US	7715
			BLUES FROM EVERYWHERE	19	TRANSATLANTIC		XTRA 1099
			BEST OF	19	STORYVILLE		SLP 217
			BROWNIE McGHEE SONNY TERRY	1971	STORYVILLE	FR	21020
			BROWNIE & SONNY'S BLUES	1960	ROULETTE	US	
			BROWNIE & SONNY'S BLUES	197	VOGUE	FR	12505
			BLUES & FOLK	19	BLUESVILLE	US	1005
			BLUES ALL ROUND	19	BLUEVILLE	US	1020
			BLUES IN MY SOUL	19	BLUESVILLE	US	1033
			BROWNIES BLUES	19	BLUESVILLE	US	1042
			COULDN'T BELIEVE MY EYES	197	BLUESWAY		BLS 6059
			DOWN HOME BLUES	19	SHARP	US	2003
			DOWN HOME BLUES	19	BLUESVILLE	US	1002
			GOING DOWN SLOW	1974	MAINSTREAM		L35784
			GOING DOWN SLOW	197	MAINSTREAM	US	MRL 407
			GUITAR HIGHWAY	19	VERVE	US	9019
			GET ON BOARD	19	FOLKWAYS	US	2028
			GET TOGETHER	19	VERVE	US	9010
			HOMETOWN BLUES	1974	MAINSTREAM	US	MRL 1019
			HOMETOWN BLUES	197	MAINSTREAM		56049
			HOMETOWN BLUES	19	MAINSTREAM		308
			HOMETOWN BLUES	1969	ACE OF HEARTS		ZAHT 182
			HOOTIN' & HOLLERIN'	1975	VOGUE	FR	LDE 894
			HOOTIN' & HOLLERIN'	19	CHOICE	US	503
			IN LONDON	1969	MARBLE ARCH	UK	MAL 843
			KEY TO THE HIGHWAY	1957	TRANSATLANTIC		XTRA 1004
			LONG WAY FROM HOME	1969	BLUESWAY		BLS 6028
			LIVE AT THE 2ND FRET	19	PRESTIGE	US	7803
			LIVIN' WITH THE BLUES	1960	FONTANA		688006
			LIGHTNIN' SONNY & BROWNIE	1965	SOCIETY		SOC 1009
			MIDNIGHT SPECIAL	1978	FANTASY	US	FAN 5973
			ON THE ROAD	19	TRANSATLANTIC		XTRA 1110
			PREACHIN' THE BLUES	1960	FOLKWAY	US	31024
			PREACHIN' THE BLUES	19	FOLKWAY	US	9019
			PENETENTIARY BLUES	1960	FONTANA		688 007
			SONNY TERRY & WOODY GUTHRIE	19	EMBER		CW 136
			SONNY TERRY	19	ARC FOLK		206
			SING & PLAY	19	SOCIETY	UK	1015
			SONNY TERRYS WASHBOARD BAND	19	FOLKWAYS		2006
			SONNY TERRY GUITAR & HARMONICA	19	FOLKWAYS		2035
			SONNY TERRY'S NEW SOUND	19	FOLKWAYS		3821
			SONNY IS KING	19	PRESTIGE		7802
			SONNY'S STORY	19	BLUESVILLE		1025
			SONNY'S STORY	1967	XTRA	UK	5025
			SONNY TERRY & LIGHTNIN' HOPKINS	19	BLUESVILLE		1059
			SONNY TERRY & HIS MOUTH HARP	19	STINSON		55
			SONNY TERRY	19	TRANSATLANTIC		XTRA 1064
			SHOUTS & BLUES	19	AMERICA		AM 6075
			SONNY & BROWNIE	1973	A&M	UK	AMLH64379
			TRADITIONAL BLUES	1977	CHANT DUMONDE	FR	FL 52421
			TERRY & McGHEE	19	FANTASY	US	3254
			THE SOUND OF AMERICA	19	CHOICE		509
			TERRY McGHEE	19	FANTASY	US	3254
			WALK ON	1977	BULLDOG	UK	BDL 1018
			WHERE THE BLUES BEGAN	19	fontana		67599
			WORK SONGS PLAY SONGS	19	CHOICE		500
			YOU HEAR ME TALKING	1979	MUSE	FR	MR 5131

T54 TERRY & THE PIRATES T54

Musician	Instr	Albums	Title	Year	Label	Country	Cat. No.
TERRY DOLAN	G V	(AB12	(A) THE DOUBTFUL HANDSHAKE	1980	LINE	GERM	LLP 5062
DAVID HAYES	B v	(A23B	(B) TOO CLOSE FOR COMFORT	1979	WILD BUNCH	ITALY	WB 5001
DAVE CARTER	B V	(B	(1) 1974 (2) 1975 (3) 1977				
ANDY KIRBY	D	(23					

Musician	Instr	Albums	Musician	Instr	Albums	Musician	Instr	Albums	Musician	Instr	Albums
JEFF MYER	D	(A3	MICHAEL WHITE	B	(3	STEVE DERR	G	(B	LONNIE TURNER	B	(B3
JOHN CIPOLLINA	G	(A123	GREG DOUGLASS	G	(A123	DAVID WEBER	D	(1	HUTCH HUTCHINSON	B	(12
SID PAGE	VLN	(2	NICKY HOPKINS	K	(B2	JIM McPHERSON	K	(2	BONES JONES	D	(B2
BILL BARON	D	(B									

T55 JOE TEX T55

Personnel	Inst	LPs	Title	Year	Label / Catalogue
JOE TEX	V	(ALL	THE BEST OF	19	KING US 935
HAYWARD BISHOP	D	(S	THE BEST OF	1965	PARROT US S71002
KARL HIMMEL	D	(S	HOLD ON TO WHAT YOU'VE GOT	1965	ATLANTIC US SD8106
BUDDY KILLEN		(R	HOLD ON	1965	CHECKER 2993
BOBBY WOOD	K	(SR	NEW BOSS	1965	ATLANTIC US SD8115
LOUIS JOHNSON		(R	GREATEST HITS	1967	ATLANTIC UK 588089
BOBBY EMMONS	K	(RS	LOVE YOU SAVE	1966	ATLANTIC US SD8124
JOHN CHRISTOPHER	G	(S	I'VE GOT TO DO A LITTLE BETTER	19	ATLANTIC US SD8133
REGGIE YOUNG	G	(SR	BEST OF	196	ATLANTIC US SD8144
TOMMY COGBILL	B	(S	LIVE & LOVELY	1968	ATLANTIC UK 588104 US SD8156
LARRIE LONDIN		(R	SOUL COUNTRY	1968	ATLANTIC UK 588118 US SD8187
CHARLES ROSE	HRNS	(R	HAPPY SOUL	1969	ATLANTIC US SD8211
JOSEPH THOMAS		(R	YOU BETTER GET IT	1969	ATLANTIC UK 588130
MIKE LEECH	B	(S	BUYING A BOOK	1969	ATLANTIC UK 588193 US SD8231
DALE QUILLEN	HRNS	(S	SINGS WITH STRINGS	19	ATLANTIC UK 2465001 US SD8254
LEROY HADLEY		(R	FROM THE ROOTS CAME THE RAPPER	196	ATLANTIC US SD8292
BEN CAULEY	HRNS	(S	SHOW ME	19	ATLANTIC UK 2464004
HARRISON CALLOWAY	HRNS	(SR	I GOTCHA	1972	DIAL US 6002
HARVEY THOMPSON	HRNS	(SR	I GOTCHA	1972	MERCURY UK 6338 093
RON EADES	HRNS	(SR	(S) SPILL THE BEANS	197	DIAL US 6004
JAMES BOOKER	PNO	(R	HE WHO IS WITHOUT FUNK	197	DIAL US 6100
FARRELL MORRIS	PERC	(R	LONDON COLLECTOR SUPER SOUL	19	LONDON US 50017
PAULA BEBEFIELD		(R	ANOTHER MANS WOMAN	1977	POWERPAK US 305
BETH HAVIS	V	(R	HISTORY OF	19	PRIDE US 0020
WAYNE BUTLER	HRNS	(R	BUMPS & BRUISES	1977	EPIC UK 81931 US 34666
CHARLES CHALMERS	V	(R	(R) RUB DOWN	1978	EPIC UK 82581 US 35079
SANDRA RHODES	V	(R	TURN BACK THE HANDS	19	PICKWICK
DONNA RHODES	V	(R	SUPER SOUL	1979	LONDON US 50017
WAYNE JACKSON	HRNS	(R			
STRING SECTION		(R			

T56 THE WAY WE LIVE T56

Personnel	Inst	LPs	Title	Year	Label / Catalogue
JIM MILNE	G K V	(A	(A) A CANDLE FOR JUDITH	1971	DANDELION UK DAN 8004
STEPHEN CLAYTON	D PERC	(A			
JOHN BRIERLEY	PROD	(A			

T56A THEATRE OF HATE T56A

Personnel	Inst	LPs	Title	Year	Label / Catalogue
			(A) WHO DARES WINS	1981	SSSSS UK SS1

T56B THEE IMAGE T56B

Personnel	Inst	LPs	Title	Year	Label / Catalogue
MIKE PINERA	G V	(AB	(A) THEE IMAGE	1975	MANTICORE US MA6 504
DUANE HITCHINGS	K V SYN	(AB	(B) INSIDE THE TRIANGLE	1975	MANTICORE US MA6 506
DANNY VOLBERG	D	(AB			

T56C THEIVES T56C

Personnel	Inst	LPs	Title	Year	Label / Catalogue
			(C) YUCATAN	1980	ARISTA US 4232

T57 THEM T57

Personnel	Inst	LPs	Title	Year	Label / Catalogue
VAN MORRISON	HVA V	(	ANGRY YOUNG THEM	1965	DECCA UK LK4700 GER 17029
BILLY HARRISON	G	(1	THEM	1965	PARROT US PAS71005
ALAN HENDERSON	B	(1JK	THEM AGAIN	1966	DECCA LK 4751 US PARROT 71008
RONNIE MILLINGS	D	(1	NOW & THEM	1968	TOWER US ST 5104
ERIC WIKSEN	PNO	(	TIME OUT,TIME IN FOR THEM	1968	TOWER US ST 5116
JACKIE McAULEY	ORG	(1	WORLD OF THEM (COMP)	1970	DECCA UK SPA 86
PAT McAULEY	D	(	(J)THEM	1970	HAPPY TIGER US HT 1004
PETER BARDENS	ORG	(	(K)THEM IN REALITY	197	HAPPY TIGER US HT 1012
JIMMY PAGE	G	(	BACKTRACKIN'	1974	LONDON US PS 639
RAY ELLIOT	K	(	THE BEGINNING	1972	DECCA GERM ND 772
DAVID HARVEY	D	(	BAD OR GOOD (COMP) (DBL)	1972	DECCA GERM 3008 1/2
JIM ARMSTRONG	G	(	STORY OF THEM (COMP)	1977	LONDON US 50001
KEN McDOWELL	V	(	THEM (COMP) (DBL)	1973	PARROT US 71053
JOHN WILSON	D	(	THEM	1973	DERAM UK DPA 3001
KEN McLEOD		(	PROFILE (COMP)	197	DECCA GER 624 005
MARK SCOTT		(	ITS ALL OVER NOW	1975	DECCA GER 628 339
JERRY COLE	V	(J	HERE COMES GLORIA (COMP) (DBL)	1976	DECCA GER 628 361
RAY RUFF		(J	ROCK ROOTS (COMP)	1976	DECCA UK ROOTS3
JOHN STARK	D	(K	BELFAST GYPSIES	1977	SONET UK SNTF 738
JIM PARKER	G	(K	BELFAST GYPSIES	19	GRAND PRIX SWED GP 9923

(1) 1963

T58 THERAPY T58

Personnel	Inst	LPs	Title	Year	Label / Catalogue
			(A) BRINGING THE HOUSE DOWN	19	
			(B) ONE NIGHT STAND	19	
			(C) ALMANAC	1976	CBS 69017 +DJM DJF 20492

T59 THIN LIZZY T59

Personnel	Inst	LPs	Title	Year	Label / Catalogue
PHIL LYNOTT	B V	(ALL	(A) THIN LIZZY	1971	DECCA UK SKL 5082 US LONDON 594
BRIAN DOWNEY	D	(ALL	(B) SHADES OF A BLUE ORPHANAGE	1972	DECCA UK TXS 108
ERIC BELL	G	(ABC	(C) VAGABONDS OF WESTERN WORLD	1973	DECCA UK SKL 5170 US LONDON 636
GARY MOORE	G	(DK	(D) NIGHT LIFE	1974	VERTIGO UK 6360 116 US MERCURY SRM11107
JOHN HELLIWELL	SAX	(H	(D) NIGHT LIFE	1975	VERTIGO US 2002
SCOTT GORHAM	G	(DEFGHJKLMNO	(E) FIGHTING	1975	VERTIGO UK 6360 121 US MERCURY SRM11108
SNOWY WHITE	G	(NL	(E) FIGHTING	1975	VERTIGO US 2005
BRIAN ROBERTSON	G	(DEFGHJN	(F) JAILBREAK	1976	VERTIGO UK 9102 008 US MERCURY SRM11081
PHIL COLLINS	PERC	(G	(G) JOHNNY THE FOX	1976	VERTIGO UK 9102 012 US MERCURY SRM11119
KIMBERLEY BEACON	V	(G	(H) BAD REPUTATION	1977	VERTIGO UK 9102 016 US MERCURY SRM11186
ROGER CHAPMAN	V	(E	(I) REMEMBERING	1976	DECCA UK SKL 5249
IAN MACLAGAN	PNO	(E	(J) LIVE & DANGEROUS	1978	VERTIGO UK 6641 807 US WB 2 3213
DARREN WHARTON	K	(NLO	(K) BLACK ROSE	1979	VERTIGO UK 9102 032 US WB 3338
JEAN ROUSSEL	K	(D	(L) CHINA TOWN	1980	VERTIGO UK 6359 030 US UK 3496
FRANKIE MILLER	V	(D	( ) THE ROCKER	1977	LONDON US 50004
MARY VISCONTI	V	(H	( ) PROFILE	19	TELDEC GERM 624013
MIDGE URE	V	(LO	(M) ADVENTURES OF (COMP)	1981	VERTIGO LIZ TV 1
TIM HINKLEY	K	(LO	(N) KILLERS LIVE (EP)	1981	VERTIGO LIZZY 812
JON BOJIC	V	(H	(O) RENEGADE	1981	VERTIGO UK 6359 083
KEN MORRIS	V	(H			
TONY VISCONTI	REC	(H			
JOHN EARLE	SAX	(J			

T60 THIRD EAR BAND T60

COLIN SWEENEY PERC (ABC — (A) ALCHEMY — 1969 HARVEST UK SHVL 756
PAUL MINNS OBOE (ABC — (B) THIRD EAR BAND — 1970 HARVEST UK SHSP 773
RICHARD COFF VLN (AB — (C) MACBETH — 1972 HARVEST UK SHSP 4019
MEL DAVIS CELLO(A — (D) EXPERIENCES (COMP) — 1976 HARVEST HERITAGE UK SHSM 2007
JOHN PEEL JEWS HARP (A
DAVE TOMLIN VLN (A URSULA SMITH (B SIMON HOUSE VLN (C DENIM BRIDGES G (C
PAUL BUCKMASTER CELLO(C

T60A THIRD POWER T60A

DREW ABBOTT G V (A — (A) BELIEVE — 1970 VANGUARD US VSD 6554
JEM TARGAL B V (A
JIM CRAIG D V (A

T61 THIRD RAIL T61

ART RESNICK K (A — (A) IN MUSIC — 1967 EPIC US 26327
K RESNICK (A
JOEY LEVINE (A

T62 THIRD WORLD T62

PRILLY V (A
CAT COORE G B (ABCDE — (A) THIRD WORLD — 1976 ISLAND UK ILPS 9369
RICHIE B G (ABCDE — (B) 96 DEGREES IN THE SHADE — 1977 ISLAND uk ILPS 9443
IBO K V (ABCDE — (C) JOURNEY TO ADDIS — 1978 ISLAND UK ILPS 9554
CORNEL D (A — (D) STORY'S BEEN TOLD — 1979 ISLAND GER 200663 UK ILPS 9569
CARROT PERC (ABCDE — (E) PRISONER IN THE STREET — 1980 ISLAND UK ILPS 9616
RUGS G V (BCDE — (F) RISE IN HARMONY — 1980 ISLAND US 9574
WILLIE D (BCDE — (G) ROCKS THE WORLD — 1981 CBS UK 85027
CHRIS WOOD SAX (D
REBOP PERC (B

T62A THIRD WORLD T62A

STEVE WINWOOD K G V(A — (A) AIYE KETA — 1973 ISLAND UK HELP 14
REMI KABAKA V G D B(A
ABDUL LOUGHTY AMAO V WIND(A

T63 THIRD WORLD WAR T63

TERRY STAMP G V (AB — (A) THIRD WORLD WAR — 1971 FLY UK HIFLY4 GER POLYDOR 2310123
JIM AVERY B (AB — (B) THIRD WORLD WAR II — 1972 TRACK UK 2406 108 GERM 2310 123
MICK LIEBER G (A — (B) THIRD WORLD WAR II — 1972 POLYDOR GER 2310 200
JOHN KNIGHTSBRIDGE G (B
RAY FLACKE G (B JOHN HAWKEN PNO (B CRAIG COLLINGE D (B JIM PRICE HRNS (AB
WINGY HCA (A SPEEDY PERC (A FRED SMITH D (A BOBBY KEYS SAX (A
TONY ASHTON K (A PETE MARTIN G (A JOHN FENTON PROD (AB

T63A THIRSTY MOON T63A

NORBERT DROGIES D (ABCD — (A) THIRSTY MOON — 1973 BRAIN GER1021
MICHAEL KOBS K (AB — (B) YOU'LL NEVER COME BACK — 1973 BRAIN GER 1041
WILLI PAPE WIND (AB — (C) YELLOW SUNSHINE — 197 BRAIN GERM 0040 124
JUNIOR WEERASINGHE D(D — (D) STARCHASER — 1981 SKY GER 053
HARALD KONIETZKO G B V(AB
ERWIN NOACK PERC (AB JURGEN DROGIES G PERC(ABD HANS WENER RANWIG K V (AD SIEGFRIED PISALLA G V(A

T64 THIRTEENTH FLOOR ELEVATORS T64

ROCKY ERICSON V (ABC — (A) PSYCHEDELIC SOUNDS OF — 1966 INTERNATIONAL ARTIST US LP1
DAN GALINDO B (B — (A) PSYCHEDELIC SOUNDS OF — 1978 RADAR RI UK RAD13
JOHN IKE WALTON D (A — (B) EASTER EVERYWHERE — 1968INTERNATIONAL ARTIST US IA5
DANNY THOMAS D (B — (B) EASTER EVERYWHERE — 1979 RADAR RI UK RAD15
STACY SUTHERLAND G PROD(AB — (C) 13TH FLOOR ELEVATORS LIVE — 1968 INTERNATIONAL ARTIST US IA8
BENNY THURMAN B VLN(A — (D) BULL OF THE WOODS — 1969 INTERNATIONAL ARTIST US IA9
TOMMY HALL JUG (ABC — (E) AVALON 66 — 1977 FP 1001
RONNIE LEATHERMAN D (A — (F) YOU REALLY GOT ME (EP) — 1978 AUSTIN UK RE1
LELAN ROGERS PROD (AB
GORDON BYNUM PROD (A

T64A THIRTY DAYS OUT T64A

PHIL LOWE D V (A — (A) THIRTY DAYS OUT — 1971 REPRISE US 6450
JACK MALKEN G V (A
MONTE MELNICK B V K(A JOHN MILCALLEF G V (A JIM DICKENSON K (A LARRY KNECHTEL K (A

T65 THIRTY EIGHT SPECIAL T65

DONNIE VAN ZANT V (ALL — (A) THIRTY EIGHT SPECIAL — 1977 A&M US 4638 UK AMLH64638
STEVE BROOKINS D (ALL — (B) SPECIAL DELIVERY — 1978 A&M US 4684 UK AMLH64684
JACK GRONDIN D (ALL — (C) ROCKIN' THE NIGHT — 1980 A&M US 4782
KEN LYONS B (A — (D) WILD EYED SOUTHERN BOYS — 1981 A&M US 4835 UK AMLH64835
DON BARNES G V (ALL — (E) SPECIAL FORCES — 1982 A&M US 4888
JEFF CARLISI G STEEL(ALL — (EP) HOLD ON LOOSELY — 1981 A&M UK AMS 9160
TERRY EMERY PNO (ABDE
LARRY JUNSTROM B (ALL DAN HARTMAN V (A LANI GROVES V (A JOSLYN BROWN V (A
CARL HALL V (A BILLY POWELL K (C DALE KRANTZ V (C STEVE McRAY HCA (E
JIM BARNES HCA (E CAROL BRISTOW V (E LU MOSS V (E

T66 THIS HEAT T66

GARETH WILLIAMS K G B V(AB — (A) THIS HEAT — 1979 PIANO UK THIS 1
CHARLES HAYWARD PERC K V (AB — (B) DECEIT — 1981 ROUGH TRADE UK ROUGH26
CHARLES BULLEN G VLA V CLAR(AB

T67 JACQUES THOLLOT T67

JACQUES THOLLOT D K (ABCD — (A) QUAND LE SON DEVIENT TROP AIGU — 1971 FUTURA GER 24
FRANCOIS JEANNEAU SAX (BCD — (B) WATCH DEVIL GO — 19 PALM 17
SIEGFRIED KESSLER PNO (C — (C) RESURGENCE — 1977 MUSICA MUS 3021
BOB GUERIN B (C — (D) CINQ HOPS — 1978 FREE BIRD FLY 03
NANA VASCONCELOS PERC (C
FREDERIQUE GEGENBACH V (C ELISE ROSS V (D FRANCOIS COUTURIER PNO (D JEAN PAUL CELEA B (D
CHRIS HOWARD FLT (D MICHEL GRAILLIER CLAR (D JEAN FRANCOIS CLARK B (B CHARLINE SCOTT V (B

T67A B J THOMAS T67 A

B J THOMAS V (ALL
PAUL WILLIAMS V (IM
MENTOR WILLIAMS V (I
MARK JAMES V (IM
JON STROLL K V (IL
AL GORGONI G V (IKL
DOMINIC CORTESE ACC (I
TEDDY IRWIN G (I
KIRK HAMILTON B (IK
ALLAN SCHWARTZBERG D (ILK
JIMMY MAELEN PERC (ILK
GLEN SPREEN STR (IK
BARRY MANN K V (IK
DUANE EDDY G (I
GEORGE DEVENS VIBES(I
DAVE CARY VIBES(I
DARLENE LOVE V (I
FANITA JAMES B (I
JEAN KING V (I
DAVE SOMERVILLE V (I
RON HICKLIN V (I
TOM BAHLER V (I
GENE MORFORD V (I
CHARLIE LARKEY B (I
STEVE TYRELL PERC V(IKL
JOHN SEBASTIAN G (I
GENE CHRISMAN D (M
REGGIE YOUNG G (M
BOB MANN G (LK
LINDA LAWLEY V (K
LOU MARINI SAX (KL
SHARON WALKER V (K
ERIC THORNGREN V (K
MIKE BRECKER SAX (L
ELLIOTT RANDALL G (L
PROF BRADFORD SINGERS V(L
STEVIE WONDER HCA (I
RON TUTT D (I
WAYNE CARSON G (I
PETE DRAKE STEEL (IM
MIKE LEECH B (M
SHANE KEISTER SYN (M
ERIC WEISSBERG BAN (K
MARGRET DORN V (K
DAVE BARGERON TROM (KL
GENE CORNISH V (K
JOHN TURI V (K
RANDY BRECKER TPT (L
RICHIE SUPA G (L
JIMMY WEBB K (I
HUGH McCRACKEN G (IKL
CHIP TAYLOR V (I
BOBBY EMMONS K (M
CHIPS MOMAN G (M
STEVE GIBSON G (M
PAUL GRIFFIN K (KL
TOM MALONE TPT (K
GINI EASTWOOD V (K
DINO DANELLI V (K
GERRY GOFFIN V (K
RANDALL BRAMBLETT K V (L
RICK MAROTTA D (L
CAROLE KING K (I
DAVE BOONE FDL (I
RODNEY JUSTO V (ILK
BOBBY WOODS (M
JOHNNY CHRISTOPHER G(M
GEORG WADENIUS G (KL
ANDY MUSON B (KL
LOU SOLOFF TPT (KL
DON GROLNICK K (KL
BILLY HOCHER V (K
BARRY GOLDBERG V (K
PETER GORDON HRNS(L
BELL TREE G (L

(A) I'M SO LONELY I COULD CRY 19 SCEPTER US 535
(B) ON MY WAY 19 SCEPTER US 570
(C)YOUNG & IN LOVE 19 SCEPTER US 576
(D) GREATEST HITS 19 SCEPTER US 518
(E) RAINDROPS KEEP FALLING 19 SCEPTER US 580
(F) EVERYBODY'S OUT OF TOWN 19 SCEPTER US 582
(G) MOST OF ALL 1971 SCEPTER US 586
(H) GREATETS HITS VOL 2 197 SCEPTER US 597
(I) ROCK'N'ROLL LULLABY 1972 SCEPTER US 5101
(J) B J THOMAS COUNTRY 1972 SCEPTER US 5108
(K) SONGS 1973 PARAMOUNT US 6052
(L) LONGHORN & LONDON BRIDGES 1974 PARAMOUNT US 1020
(M) REUNION 197 ABC US 858
(N) HELP ME MAKE IT 197 ABC US 912
(O) BEST OF 19 STARDAY US 992
(P) ABC COLLECTION 19 ABC US 30028
(Q) 16 GREATEST HITS 197 TRIP US 16/18
(R)HOME WHERE I BELONG 1977 MYRRH UK 1060
(S) B J THOMAS 1977 MCA US 2286
(T) EVERYBODY LOVES 1978 MCA US 3035
(U) HAPPY MAN 1979 MYRRH US 1072

T68 CARLA THOMAS T68

CARLA THOMAS V (ALL

(A) GEE WHIZ 1961 ATLANTIC US SD8057
(B) COMFORT ME 1966 STAX/ATLANTIC US 7706
(C) CARLA 1966 STAX/ATLANTIC US 7709
(D) KING & QUEEN 1967 STAX/ATLANTIC US 7716
(E) QUEEN ALONE 1967 STAX/ATLANTIC US 7 718
(F) LOVE MEANS 1971 STAX US 2044 UK PLORDOR 2362023
(G) MEMPHIS QUEEN 1975 STAX Us 2019 UK STAX STX 1038
(H) BEST OF 19 ATLANTIC US SD8232
(J) CHRONICLE 1979 STAX STX 4124

T68A DAVID THOMAS T68A

DAVID THOMAS (A

(A) SOUND OF SOUND 1981 ROUGH TRADE ROUGH 30

T69 IAN THOMAS T69

IAN THOMAS (AB

(A) GOODNIGHT MRS CALABASH 1976 CHRYSALIS UK CHR 1126
(B) IAN THOMAS 1976 DJM UK DJM 20440

T69A IAN THOMAS BAND T69A

DAVE COOPER G (AB
MICK OBERLE D V (AB
DAVE SAWYER B V (AB
HUGH SYME K V (AB
IAN THOMAS G K V(AB

(A) STILL HERE 1978 ATLANTIC US 19167
(B) SLIDER 1979 ATLANTIC

T70 IRMA THOMAS T70

IRMA THOMAS V (ALL
JERRY WILLIAMS PNO (A
JESSE CARR G (A
POPS POPWELL B (A
SQUIRM D (A
PAUL HORNSBY K (A
SWAMP DOGG BAND (A
MIKE THOMAS D (E
STAN KEMPER D (E
PETE VERDOIS SAX (E
RANDY JACKSON B (EF
HAROLD COWART B (E
HAROLD COWART STR (E
CARSON WHITSITT K (F
FREDDY WALL G (E
CORA JEFFERSON V (E
JAMES STROUD D (F
ROD ANTOON K (E
ALICE JACKSON V (E
ROGER HAWKINS D (F

(A) IN BTWEEN TEARS 1973 FUNGUS US 25150 UK RI CHARLY1020
(B) WISH SOMEONE WOULD CARE 19 IMPERIAL US
(C) TAKE A LOOK 196 MINIT UK 40004
(D) LIVE 1976 ISLAND UK HELP 29
(E) SOUL QUEEN OF NEW ORLEANS 1978 MAISON SOUL US 1005
(F) SAFE WITH ME 1979 RCS US 1004
(G) HIP SHAKIN' MAMA 1981 CHARLY UK 2019

T71 JOE THOMAS T71

JOE THOMAS FLT (AB
MARVIN STAMM HRNS (B
GEORGE YOUNG SAX (B
HIRAM BULLOCK G (B
RICHARD TRIFAN SYN (B

(A) JOY OF COOKIN' 1974 PEOPLE PLEO 15
(B) MAKE YOUR MOVE 1979 LRC 9327 + TK TKR 83374

T71A MICKEY THOMAS T71A

MICKEY THOMAS PERC V(A
JOE VITALE D SYN V(A
DON FELDER G (A
DON BALDWIN SYN V(A
JULIA TILLMAN V (A
CORY LERIOS K (A
KEN FAULK TPT (A
GEORGE PERRY B V (A
MIAMI STRINGS (A
OREN WATERS V (A
DON BONSANTI SAX (A
PAUL HARRIS PNO (A
MARTY GREBB SAX (A
CRAIG CHAQUICO G (A
NEAL BONSANTI SAX (A
STEVE PORCARO SYN (A
MAXINE WILLARD V (A
NORTON BUFFALO HCA (A
ROGER HOMEFIELD TROM (A

(A) ALIVE ALONE 1981 ELEKTRA US 5E530

T72 NICKY THOMAS T72

NICKY THOMAS (ALL

(A) TELL IT LIKE IT IS 1971 TROJAN TRLS 25
(B) IMAGES OF YOU 19 HORSE HRLP 701
(C) LOVE OF THE COMMON PEOPLE 1976 TROJAN TBL 143

T73 **RAY THOMAS** T73

RAY THOMAS V FLT(AB (A) FROM MIGHTY OAKS 1975 THRESHOLD UK THS 16
NICKY JAMES V PERC(AB (B) HOPES WISHES & DREAMS 1976 THRESHOLD UK THS 17
JOHN JONES G V (AB
MIKE MORAN K (AB B J COLE STEEL(A DAVE POTTS D (A MIKE SILVER G V (A
TREVOR JONES B V (B GRAHAM DEACON D (B BARRY ST JOHN V (B LIZA STRIKE V (B
HELEN CHAPPELLE V (B

T74 **RUFUS THOMAS** T74

RUFUS THOMAS V (ALL WALKING THE DOG 1964 STAX US 704
BILLY RED LOVE PNO ((E) MAY I HAVE YOUR TICKET PLEASE 19 STAX US 2022
JOE HILL LOUIS G (E FUNKY CHICKEN 1970 STAX US 2028
HOUSTON STOKES D (E LIVE AT PJs DOIN' THE PUSH & PULL 1970 STAX US 2039
DID YOU HEAR ME 197 STAX US 3004 UK POLYDOR 2362028
CROWN PRINCE OF DANCE 1974 STAX US 3008 UK STAX STX1002
(E)RUFUS THOMAS(EP) 1977 CHARLY UK CEP 101
I AINT GETTIN' OLDER 19 AVID US 6046
IF THERE WERE NO MUSIC 1977 PYE UK NSPL28241 US AVI 6015
CHRONICLE(1 SIDE RUFUS /1 SIDE CARLA) 1979 STAX US STX 4124

T75 **TIMMY THOMAS** T75

TIMMY THOMAS ((A) TOUCH TO TOUCH 1978 TK TKR 82510
( ) WHY CANT WE LIVE TOGETHER 19 GLADES US 6501 POLYDOR 2956 002
( ) YOU'RE THE SONG 1975 POLYDOR 2310 377
( ) MAGICIAN 1977 TK UK XL 14044

T75A **MALCOLM THOMLINSON** T75A

MALCOLM THOMLINSON V (A (A) ROCK'N'ROLL HERMIT 1980 CASABLANCA US 7199

T75B **THOMPSON TWINS** T75B

(A) A PRODUCT OF 1981 T UK TELP1
(B) SET 1982 T UK TELP2

T76 **BARBARA THOMPSON** T76

BARBARA THOMPSON SAX PERC(ALL (A) PARAPHERNALIA 1978 MCA UK MCF 2852
JON HISEMAN D (DC (B) JUBIABA 1978 MCA UK MCF 2867
DILL KATZ B (DC (C) WILDE TALES 1979 MCA UK MCF 3047
COLIN DUDMAN K SYN(DAC (D) LIVE IN CONCERT 1980 MCA MCSP 309
ROY BABBINGTON B (AB
HAROLD FISHER D (A DEREK WADSWORTH HRN (B HENRY LOWTHER TPT (B IAN HAMMER TPT (B
GLYN THOMAS PERC (B PETER LEMER K (B TREVOR TOMKINS D (B BILL LESAGE PERC (B

T77 **ALI THOMPSON** T77

ALI THOMPSON (A (A) TAKE A LITTLE RHYTHM 1980 A&M UK AMLH68512
DURBAN LAVERDE B (AB (B) DECEPTION IS AN ART 1981 A&M UK AMLH64846
PHILIP WRIGHT G V (AB
JAMES LACELLES PNO (A WILLIAM C LYALL SYN (AB TED McKENNA D (A DAVE ROACH SAX (AB
JULIAM DIGGLE PERC (A DEBI DOSS V (AB PETE FILLEUL PNO (A STUART ELLIOT D (B
JEFF PHILLIPS D (A ALAN MURPHY G (A CHARLIE SPITERI PERC (A CAROL KENYON V (AB
RICHARD BAILEY D (A SONJA JONES V (A JON KELLY PROD (AB RAY COOPER PERC(B
JOHN HELLIWELL SAX (B ED GOODMAN HRNS (B SYLVIA MASON V (B ELLIE WARREN V (B

T78 **MAYO THOMPSON** T78

MAYO THOMPSON V (A (A) CORKY'S DEBT TO HIS FATHER 19 TEXAS REVOLUTION US CFS 2270

T79 **RICHARD & LINDA THOMPSON** T79

RICHARD THOMPSON G V (ALL (A) HENRY THE HUMAN FLY 1972 ISLAND UK ILPS9197 US REPRISE2112
LINDA THOMPSON(PETERS)V(ALL (B) I WANT TO SEE THE BRIGHT LIGHTS 1974 ISLAND UK ILPS 9266
TIMI DONALD D (ABCDEG (C) HOKEY POKEY 1974 ISLAND GER 00598 UK ILPS 9305
PAT DONALDSON B (ABCDEG (D) POUR DOWN LIKE SILVER 1975 ISLAND UK ILPS 9348
SANDY DENNY K V (AE (E) GUITAR & VOCAL 1976 ISLAND UK ICD8
DAVID SNELL HARP (A (E) R T LIVE!(MORE OR LESS)(DBL) 1977 ISLAND US ISLA 9421
JEFF COLE TROM (A (F) FIRST LIGHT 1978 CHRYSALIS GER 6307640 UK CHR1177
JOHN DEFERERI SAX (A (G) SUNNY VISTA 1979 CHRYSALIS NL 511247 UK CHR1247
CLAY TOYANI TPT (A (H) STRICT TEMPO 1981 ELIXIR UK LP1
ABDU RAHIM V (G
SUE DRAHEIM FDL (A BARRY DRANSFIELD FDL (A JOHN KIRKPATRICK ACC (ALL ASHLEY HUTCHINGS V B(ADE
SIMON NICOL G K V (BCEFG BRIAN GULLAND KRUMM(B RICHARD HARVEY KRUMM(B ROYSTON WOOD V (B
TREVOR LUCAS V (BF C W S SILVER BAND (BC IAN WHITEMAN K FLT(CDE ALY BAIN FDL(CD
SIDONIE GOOSSENS HARP (C DAVE MATTACKS D (DEFGH NIC JONES FDL (D HENRY LOWTHER TPT(D
JUDY DYBLE V (E IAN MATTHEWS V (EF MARTIN LAMBLE D (E PETE ROSS HCA(E
DAVE SWARBRICK FDL (E DAVID PEGG (EG ANDY NEWMARK D (F WILLIE WEEKS B (F
NEIL LARSEN K (F CHRIS KARAN PERC (F DOLORES KEANE WHISTLE (F DAVE BRADY V (F
HEATHER BRADY V (F BILL CADDICK V (F PHILIPPA CLARE V (F JULIE COVINGTON V (F
ANDY FAIRWEATHER LOW V (F MADDY PRIOR V (F PETA WEBB V (F ANDY ROBERTS DULC(A
DAVE BURLAND V (F MICHAEL SPENCER ARSCOTT D(G SUE HARRIS WIND (G PETE WINGFIELD K (G
RABBIT BUNDRICK K (G LUIS JARDIM PERC (G KATE McGARRIGLE V (G ANNA McGARRIGLE V (G
GLEN TILBROOK V (G JULIAN LITTMAN V (G MARC ELLINGTON V (G OLIVE SIMPSON V (G
NICOLE TIBBELS V (G LINDSAY BENTON V (G DAVID BEAVAN V (G BRUCE LYNCH B (G
GERRY RAFFERTY V (G HAFSA ABDUL JABBAS V (G

T79A **ROBBIN THOMPSON** T79A

ROBBIN THOMPSON G V (AB (A) ROBBIN THOMPSON 1976 NEMPEROR US 440
VELPO ROBERTSON G V (A (B) TWO B'S PLEASE 1980 NEMPEROR US
ERIC HIEBERG K V (
BOB ANTONELLI D V (MIKE LANNING B V (

T79B **BIG MAMA THORNTON** T79B

BIG MAMA THORNTON V (ALL (A) STRONGER THAN DIRT 1969 MERCURY UK SMCL 20176 US 61225
CORNELL DUPREE G (H (B) SHES BACK 1968 BACKBEAT US 68
RONNIE MILLER G (H (C) IN EUROPE 1966 ARHOOLIE US F 1028
PAUL GRIFFIN K (H (D) CHICAGO BLUES 1967 ARHOOLIE US F 1032
WILBUR BASCOMB B (H (E) BALL & CHAIN 1968 ARHOOLIE US F 1039
JIMMY JOHNSON D (H (F) JAIL 1975 VANGUARD 79351
BUDDY LUCAS SAX (H (G) SASSY MAMA 1975 VANGUARD 79354
GEORGE SMITH HCA (H (H) MAMA'S PRIDE 1978 VANGUARD VPC4000<
STEVE WACHSMAN G (H (I) SAVED 1973 PENTAGRAM US 10005
WALTER HORTON HCA (C ( ) THATS THE WAY IT IS 19 MERCURY 61249
BEE HOUSTON G (H
FRANCIS CLAY D (D J D NICHOLSON K (H BRUCE SIEVERSON B (H TODD NELSON D (H
BILL POTTER SAX (H EDDIE BOYD K (C BUDDY GUY G (C JIMMY LEE ROBINSON B(C
FRED BELOW D (C FRED McDOWELL G (C JAMES COTTON HCA (D OTIS SPANN PNO (D
MUDDY WATERS G (D

T79C THOR T79C

THOR V (A — (A) KEEP THE DOGS AWAY 1978 MIDSONG US 2337
JOHN SHAN G (A
TERRY McKEO

T79D PETER THORUP T79D

PETER THORUP G B V(A — (A) THIN SLICES 1978 METRONOME EURO 15635
KEN GUDMAN D (A
SANNE SALOMONSEN V (A KENNETH KNUDSEN K (A HANS FJELDSTED K (A

T80 GEORGE THOROGOOD & THE DESTROYERS T80

GEORGE THOROGOOD G V (ALL — (A) GEORGE THOROGOOD & THE DESTROYERS 1977 ROUNDER 3013 US UK SONET SNTF760
MICHAEL LEVINE B (C — (A) GEORGE THOROGOOD & THE DESTROYERS 1978 SONET GER 69082
JEFF SIMON D (ALL — (B) MOVE IT ON OVER 1978 ROUNDER 3024 US UK SONET SNTF781
BILLY BLOUGH B (ABE — (C) BETTER THAN THE REST (1974) 1979 MCA US 3091 GER 62136 UKMCL1623
RON SMITH G (BA — (D) MORE GEORGE THOROGOOD 1980 ROUNDER US 3045 UK SONET SNTF850
UNCLE MEAT PENNINGTON PERC(B — (E) BAD TO THE BONE 1982 EMI US 17076
HANK CARTER SAX (DE

T80A BILLY THORPE T80A

BILLY THORPE G V (AB — (A) CHILDREN OF THE SUN 1979 POLYDOR UK 2391424
GIL MATTHEWS D (B — (A) CHILDREN OF THE SUN 1979 CAPRICORN US 0221
LEE SKLAR B (AB — (B) 21ST CENTURY MAN 1980 ELEKTRA US 6E 294
ALVIN TAYLOR D (A — (C) STIMULATION 1981 PASHA US 37499

T80B THOSE NAUGHTY LUMPS T80B

(A) ICE CREAM 19 OPEN EYE UK OE 1002

T80C THREE D T80C

RICK ZWIC V (A — (A) 3D 1980 POLYDOR US 6254 UK 2391 445
KEW GINSBERG G V (A
TED WENDER K V (A NICK STEVENS B V (A MIKE FINK D (A

T81 THREE DOG NIGHT T81

DANNY HUTTON V (12K — (A) THREE DOG NIGHT 1969 UK STATESIDE 5006 US DUNHILL 50048
CHUCK NEGRON V (12K — (B) SUITABLE FOR FRAMING 1969 UK STATESIDE 5013 US DUNHILL 50058
CORY WELLS V (12K — (C) LIVE AT THE FORUM 1970 UK STATESIDE 5023 US DUNHILL 50068
MIKE ALLSUP G (12K — (D) IT AINT EASY 1970 UK PROBE SPBA6251 US DUNHILL 50078
JIM GREENSPOON K (12K — (E) NATURALLY 1971 UK PROBE SPBA6257 US DUNHILL 50088
JOE SCHERMIE B (1K — (F) GOLDEN BISCUITS 1971 UK PROBE SPB 1035 US DUNHILL 50098
FLOYD SNEED D (12K — (F) GOLDEN BISCUITS 1974 UK ABC ABCL5014
JACK RYLAND B (2K — (G) HARMONY 1971 UK PROBE SPB 1047 US DUNHILL 50108
SKIP KONTE K (2K — (H) SEVEN SEPARATE FOOLS 1972 UK PROBE SPTC 1 US DUNHILL 50118
(1) 1968/73 (2) 1973/ — (I) AROUND THE WORLD 1973 UK PROBE PBSP 113 US DUNHILL 50138
(J) CYAN 1974 UK ABC ABCL5039 US DUNHILL 50158
(K) HARD LABOUR 1974 UK ABC ABCL5049 US DUNHILL 50168
(L) GREATEST HITS 1974 UK ABC ABCL5064 US DUNHILL 50178
(M) DOG STYLE 1974 US DUNHILL 50198
(N) COMING DOWN YOUR WAY 1975 UK ABC ABCL5120 US ABC 888
(O) AMERICAN PASTIME 1976 UK ABC ABCL5159 US ABC 928

T82 THREE MAN ARMY T82

PAUL GURVITZ(CURTIS[illegible] (ALL — (A) A THIRD OF A LIFETIME 1971 PEGASUS UK PEG3
ADRIAN GURVITZ(CURTIS G(ALL — (A) A THIRD OF A LIFETIME (DIFF TRACKS) KAMA SUTRA 2044
PETE ROBINSON PNO (BC — (B) THREE MAN ARMY 1973 REPRISE UK K44254 US 2150
MIKE KELLIE D (A — (C) THREE MAN ARMY 2 1974 REPRISE UK K54015
BUDDY MILES D (A — (D) MAHESHA 1974 POLYDOR 2310 241
TONY NEWMAN D (BC
BRIAN PARRISH G (A RUBY JAMES V (C MADELINE BELL V (C DORIS TROY V (C

T82A PERCY THRILLINGTON T82A

PERCY THRILLINGTON (A — (A) THRILLINGTON 1978 CAPITOL US 11642
(PAUL McCARTNEY)

T82B THRILLS T82B

TONY MONACO K V (AB — (A) FIRST THRILLS 1980 CBS
DAVE FULLERTON G V (AB — (B) FRONY PAGE NEWS 1981 CBS
BILL GILBERT B V (A
ROB OWENS D V (AB

T83 THROBBING GRISTLE T83

GENESIS P ORRIDGE B C (ABCDE — (A) 1ST ANNUAL REPORT 197 INDUSTRIAL UK IR0001
COSEY FANNI TUTTI G V(ABCDE — (B) 2ND ANNUAL REPORT 1977 INDUSTRIAL UK IR0002
CHRIS CARTER K (ABCDE — (B) 2ND ANNUAL REPORT(RECUT RI) 1979 FETISH UK FR2001
PETER CHRISTOPHERSON EFFECTS(ABCDE — (C) D O A 1978 INDUSTRIAL UK IR0004
(D) 20 JAZZ FUNK GREATS 1979 INDUSTRIAL UK IR0008
(E) HEATHEN EARTH 1980 INDUSTRIAL UK IR0009
(F) GREATEST HITS 1981 ROUGH TRADE UK 23

T83A THUMBS T83A

STEVE WILSON V (A — (A) THUMBS 1979 RAMONA US RR1
MARTY OLSON K (A
KEVIN SMITH G V (A KARL HOFFMANN G B (A MARK MOOSE BRENNAN G B(A

T83B THUNDER T83B

JOHN PORTER McMEARS G V(A — (A) THUNDER 1980 ATCO US 38129 EURO 50746
MO WERT G V (A — (B) HEADPHONES FOR COWS 1981 ATCO
DANNY HERSON K V (A
CHOPPER ANDERSON B V (A TRIS IMBODEN D (A

T84 THUNDERCLAP NEWMAN T84

ANDY NEWMAN K (A — (A) HOLLYWOOD DREAM 1970 TRACK UK 2406 003
JIMMY McCULLOCH G (A
SPEEDY KEEN V G D(A PETE TOWNSHEND (BIJOU DRAINS)B(A JIM AVERY B (JACK McCULLOCH D (
CHRIS MORPHET HCA (A

T84A THUNDERHEAD T84A

MIKE DAGGER V (A — (A) THUNDERHEAD 1975 ABC US 919
PAT RUSH G (A
RONNIE DOBBS G (A

T85 **THUNDERMUG** T85

BILL DURST G (A — (A) THUNDERMUG STRIKES — 1972 AXE UK AXS502 US EPIC 32464

JOE DE ANGELIS V (A — (B) TA DAA — 1975 MERCURY US SRM1 1039

JIM CORBETT B (A

ED PRANSKUS D (A

T86 **JOHNNY THUNDERS** T86

JOHNNY THUNDERS G V (A — (A) SO ALONE — 1978 REAL UK RAL1 GER WB 56571

STEVE MARRIOTT K (A

PETER PERRETT G V (A STEVE JONES G (A BILLY RATH B (A PAUL GRAY D(A

PHIL LYNOTT B (A MIKE KELLIE D (A WALTER LURE G (A PAT PALLADIN V (A

PAUL COOK D (A JOHN IRISH EARLE SAX (A STEVE NICOL D (A HENRI PAUL G (A

STEVE LILLYWHITE PROD K(A CHRISSIE HYNDES V (A KOULLA KAKOULLI V (A

T87 **THUNDERTHIGHS (VOCAL BACKING)** T87

CASEY SYNGE V (KAREN FRIEDMAN V (DARI LALOU V (JUANITA FRANKLIN V (

T88 **THUNDERTRAIN** T88

GENE PROVIST G (1 — (A) TEENAGE SUICIDE — 1977 JELLY JPLP1

RICK PROVOST B (1 — (1) 1976

MACH BELL V (1 STEVEN SILVA G (1 BOB EDWARDS D (1

T88A **TICKETS** T88A

STEVE RAPPO D (A — (A) 0001 — 1980 CBS 84423

KEVIN CARLSEN FLYNN G V(A

DOM TORCHE K V (A HUBERT HERITIER B V (A

T88B **TIERRA** T88B

(A) TIERRA — 1974 20TH CENTURY US 412

T88C **ASMUS TIETCHENS** T88C

HANS TIM CESSTEU SYN (A — (A) BIOTOP — 1981 SKY GER 057

TUSSI SCHEMANTE SYN (A

STY SEEMI (A SAM SENS SYN (A ACHIM STUTESSEN SYN (A MISCHA SUTTENSE SYN (A

T89 **TIGER** T89

BIG JIM SULLIVAN G (AB — (A) TIGER — 1976 RETREAT RTL6006 US WB 2940

ALAN PARK K (B — (B) GOING DOWN LAUGHING — 1976 EMI UK EMC 3153 US 11660

DAVID McCRAE K (A

NICKY MOORE HCA V G (AB ANDY BROWN B V (B PHIL CURTIS B (A LES WALKER G V (AB

BILL McGILLIVRAY G K V(B RAY FLACKE G (A BILLY RANKIN D (A

T89A **TIGERS** T89A

TONY JACKS G V (A — (A) SAVAGE MUSIC — 1980 A&M US AP4817 EURO WEA 58163

NICK COLA K V (A

ROSS McGEENEY G V (A NIC POTTER B (A PETE DOBSON D (A

T90 **TIGHT LIKE THAT** T90

DAVID H PEABODY G V HCA(A — (A)HOKUM — 1972 VILLAGE THING VTS 12

DAVID GRIFFITHS VLN G V(A

BILL SHORTT PERC (A HUGH McNULTY B V (A ANDY LEGGETT JUG (A

T90A **TILLER BOYS** T90A

(A) BIG NOISE FROM THE JUNGLE(EP) — 198 NEW HORMONE ORG 3

T91 **ROGER TILLISON** T91

ROGER TILLISON (A — (A) ROGER TILLISON'S ALBUM — 19 ATCO US SD 33355

JESSE ED DAVIS G (A

JIM KELTNER D (A LARRY KNECHTEL K (A

T92 **STEVE TILSTON** T92

STEVE TILSTON G V (A — (A) ACOUSTIC CONFUSION — 1971 VILLAGE THING UK VTS 5

( ) COLLECTION — 1972 TRANSATLANTIC UK TRA252

( ) SONGS FOR THE DRESS REHERSAL — 1977 CORNUCOPIA UK

T92A **TILT** T92A

JOHN PONDER D V (A — (A) MUSIC — 1978 PARACHUTE US 9008

FRANK EWING B (A

MIKE HARNER G V (A DOUG KAHN K (A

T93 **TIMBER** T93

JUDY ELLIOTT V (AB — (A) PART OF WHAT YOU HEAR — 19 KAPP US KS3633

WAYNE BERRY B G V(AB — (B) BRING AMERICA HOME — 19 ELEKTRA US 74095 UK K42093

GEORGE CLINTON K V HRNS(AB

ROGER JOHNSON G V TPT (AB WARNER DAVIS D (AB

T93A **TIMBERLINE** T93A

(A) GREAT RUSH — 1977 EPIC US 34681

T93B **TIME** T93B

GARY MARGETZ G V (A — (A) TIME — 1975 BUK UK BULP 2005

TORRIS MARGETZ B (A

ALEX JOHNSON G V (A JOE DOLLY D V (A

T94 **TIME BOX** T94

MIKE PATTO V (— (A) ORIGINAL MOOSE ON THE LOOSE — 1977 COSMOS COLLECTOR US CCLPS9016

JOHN HALSEY D (

OLLIE HALSALL G (CHRIS HOLMES K (CLIVE GRIFFITHS B (

T94A **TIN HUEY** T94A

HARVEY GOLD SYN K(A — (A) CONTENTS DISLODGED DURING SHIPMENT 1979 WB US BSK 3297

RALPH CARNEY K WIND V(A

MICHAEL AYLWARD G V (A CHRIS BUTLER G V (A JIM HAAS V (A MARK PRICE B V (A

STUART AUSTIN D V (A STAN FARBER V (A

T94B **TIN TIN** T94B

(A) TIN TIN — 1970 ATCO US

(B) ASTRAL TAXI — 1971 ATCO US 33370

T94C **TINY TIM** T94C

TINY TIM V UKE(ALL — (A) GOD BLESS TINY TIM — 1968 REPRISE US 6292

(B) 2ND ALBUM — 1968 REPRISE US 6323

(C) FOR ALL MY LITTLE FRIENDS — 1969 REPRISE US 6351

(D) WITH LOVE & KISSES — 19 BOUQUET 771

T95 KEITH TIPPETT T95

KEITH TIPPETT PNO (ALL — (A) YOU ARE HERE I AM THERE — 1970 POLYDOR GER 2383 050 UK 2384004
ELTON DEAN SAX (ABG — (B) DEDICATED TO YOU — 1971 VERTIGO 6360 024
MARK CHARIG HRNS (ABG — (C) BLUE PRINT — 1972 RCA UK SF 8290
NICK EVANS TROM (ABG — (D) T'N'T — 1976 EMANEM US 3307
JEFF CLYNE B (A — (E) T'N'T — 1978 STEAM SJ104
ALAN JACKSON D (A — (F) WARM SPIRITS COOL SPIRITS — 1977 VINYL VS 101
GIORGIO GOMELSKY BELLS(A — (G) FRAMES (ARK) — 1978 OGUN OGD 003/4
ROBERT WYATT D (B — (H) BOTH SIDES NOW — 19 POLYDOR 2359 007
BRYAN SPRING D (B
PHIL HOWARD D (B — TONY UTER CONGA(B — ROY BABBINGTON B (BC — NEVILLE WHITEHEAD B (B
GARY BOYLE G (B — KEITH BAILEY PERC (C — FRANK PERRY PERC (C — JULIE TIPPETTS G V (CFG
TREVOR WATTS SAX (FG — COLIN McKENZIE B (F — STAN TRACEY PNO (DEG — BRIAN SMITH WIND (G
LARRY STABBINS WIND (G — HENRY LOWTHER TPT (G — PETER KOWALKE HRNS (G — HARRY MILLER B (G
LOUIS MOHOLO D (G — DAVE AMIS TROM (G — MAGGIE NICHOLLS V (G

T96 TIR NA NOG T96

SONNY CONDELL G V PERC(ABC — (A) TIR NA NOG — 1971 CHRYSALIS UK ILPS 9153
LEO O'KELLY G V VLN (ABC — (B) A TEAR & A SMILE — 1972 CHRYSALIS UK CHR 1006
BRIAN ODGERS B (C — (C) STRONG IN THE SUN — 1973 CHRYSALIS UK CHR 1047
DAVE MARKEE B (C
JIM RYAN B (C — BARRY DE SOUZA D (BC — ACE FOLLINGTON D (C — JEFF JONES D (C
MATTHEW FISHER K (C — LARRY STEELE B (B

T97 TITANIC T97

KJELL'CHAPPY'ASPERUD D (ACD — (A) TITANIC — 1971 CBS 64104
JANNY LOSETH G (ACD — (B) SEA WOLF — 1972 CBS 64791
JOHN LORCK D (AC — (C) EAGLE ROCK — 1973 CBS 65661
ARICA SIGGS B (— (D) BALLAD OF A ROCK'N'ROLL LOSER — 1975 CBS 80786
HELGE GROSLIE K (C — (E) RETURN OF DRAKKAR — 1978 EGG 900542
ROY ROBINSON V (ACD — (F) EYE OF THE HURRICANE — 1980 SOUPLET NL 201 856
JOHN WILLIAMS B G V(D
KENNY AAS ORG (A — ANDREW RAILSTON D (D

T97A TITANS T97A

RON RHOADES K V (A — (A) THE FABULOUS TITANS (EP) — 1980 EPIPHANY US 003
LLOYD ADAMS D (A
DON FULTON B V (A — SCOTT HILL G V (A — CARROLL KNAPP SAX (A

T98 LIBBY TITUS T98

LIBBY TITUS V (A — (A) LIBBY TITUS — 1977 CBS US PC 34152
GRADY TATE D (A
TONY LEVIN B (A — DON GROLNICK K (A — HUGH McCRACKEN G (A — ALAN RUBIN HRNS(A
DAVID NADIEN VLN (A — KATHY KIENKE VLN (A — ALFRED BROWN VLA (A — JANET HAMILTON CELLO(A
PAUL SIMON V (A — RONNY ZITO D (A — CHUCK ISRAELS B (A — GEORGE YOUNG SAX (A
JOE BECK G (A — CHRIS PARKER D (A — RUSSELL GEORGE D (A — JOHN GUERIN D (A
MAX BENNETT B (A — HIRTH MARTINEZ G V (A — MICHAEL MELVOIN K (A — GARTH HUDSON K (A
RICK MAROTTA D (A — JOHN TROPEA G (A — PATTI AUSTIN V (A — LANI GROVES V (A
WILL LEE B (A — GWEN GUTHRIE V (A — ROBBIE ROBERTSON G (A — LARRY MUHOBERAC PNO (A
MARVIN STAMM TPT (A — DAVE TOFANI FLT (A — PHIL BODNER FLT (A — DON BROOKS HCA (A
CRAIG DOERGE K (A — CARLY SIMON V (A — JAMES TAYLOR V (A

T99 TITUS GROAN T99

JIM YOOMEY D (A — (A) TITUS GROAN — 1970 JANUS US 3024 UK DAWN DNLS3012
STUART COWELL K G (A
TONY PRIESTLAND WIND (A — JOHN LEE B (A

T100 TO BE T100

LEMMIE LEMBRECHT B V (A — (A) TO BE — 1977 BRAIN GER 0060 053
PETER FRANKEN D (A
PETER WICHE G (A — ROLF KOHLER B (A — CLAUS ROBERT KRUSE K (A

T101 TOAD T101

(A) TOAD — 1972 RCA UK SF8241

T102 TOAD HALL T102

GARY RAZZANTE B (A — (A) TOAD HALL — 1968 LIBERTY US 7580
JOHN RICHARDSON V PERC(A
CHRIS SIGWALD D (A — THOMAS O MARCUS G V (A — CLAPTON GUGLIAMO G (A

T102A TOBY BEAU T102A

BALDE SILVA G V HCA (AB — (A) TOBY BEAU — 1978 RCA UK PL 12771
STEVE ZIPPER B V (AB — (B) MORE THAN A LOVE SONG — 1979 RCA UK PL 13119
RON ROSE G V BAN(AB — (C) IF YOU BELIEVE — 1980 RCA 3575
DANNY McKENNA G V (AB
ROB YOUNG D PERC(AB

T103 TOEFAT T103

CLIFF BENNETT V (AB — (A) TOEFAT — 1970 PARLOPHONE UK 7097
KEN HENSLEY G V (AB — (A) TOEFAT — 1970 RARE EARTH US RS 511
LEE KERSLAKE D V (A — (B) TOEFAT II — 1971 REGAL ZONOPHONE UK SLRZ 1015
JOHN GLASCOCK B (— (B) TOEFAT II — 1971 RARE EARTH US RS 525
JOE KONAS B (A
MOX HCA FLT (A

T103A TOLLHOUSE T103A

IAN CUSSICK V (A — (A) TOLLHOUSE — 1978 NOVA GER 623430
DIRK STEFFENS G (A
PETER WEIHE G (A — ROLF KOHLER B V (A — PETER FRANKEN D PERC(A — JEAN JACQUES KRAVETZ K(A
HERB GELLER SAX (A — BOB LANESE TPT (A — HANS UWE REIMERS SAX (A — RALE V (A
JIM HOPKINS V (A — HEIKO EFFERTZ V (A

T103B TOKYO T103B

KEN TAYLOR B V (A — (A) TOKYO — 19 ARIOLA GER 203 430
FRITZ MATZKA D (A
PETER WICHE G (A — ROLF KOHLER B (A — KLAUS LULEY G V (A

T104 JUKKA TOLONEN T104

JUKKA TOLONEN G (ALL | (A) TOLONEN | 1974 SONET UK SNTF652 SW LOVE LP 47
BILL OHRSTROM PERC V(K | (A) TOLONEN | 1974 BRAIN GER 1059 US JANUS 3066
PEKKA POHJOLA B (A | (B) THE SUMMER GAMES | 197 SW LOVE LP91
PEKKA POYRY SAX (AD | (C) THE HOOK | 197 SW LOVE LP113
REINO LAING D (A | (D) CROSSECTION | 1976 SONET UK SNTF699 US JANUS 7017
HEIKKI VIRTANEN B (AD | (E) HYSTERICA | 197 SW LOVE LP149
RONNE OSTERBERG D (A | (F) A PASSENGER TO PARAMARIBO | 1978 SONET UK SNTF768 SW LOVE LP231
NORMAN FEARINGTON D SYN(K | (F) A PASSANGER TO PARAMARIBO | 1978 SONET NL 3028
JUKKA GUSTAVSON K (A | (G) MONTREUX BOOGIE | 1979 SONET UK SNTF789 SW LOVE LP278
PARONI PAAKKUNAINEN SAX(D | (H) MOUNTAIN STREAM | 1980 SONET UK SNTF818
ESA KOTILAINEN K SYN(DF | (J) J T B | 1979 PICK UP PULP79302
ESKO ROSNELL D (D | (K) DUMS HAVE MORE FUN | 1981 POLYDOR UK 2380 087
SAKARI KUKKO WIND (D | (L) TOUCH WOOD | 1981 SONET SNTF865
JOSSI AALTO TROM (D
HARRY MERILAHTI B (JK | COSTE APETREA G V(FJKL | CHRIS EKLUND SAX (JF | BILL CARSON D (FJ
JOACHIM KUHN K (J | MANS GRUNDSTROEM B (F | ILKA HANSKI B (F

T104A TOM TOM CLUB T104A

BEN ARMBRISTER (A | (A) TOM TOM CLUB | 1981 ISLAND UK ILPS9686 GER 204 102
LORIC WEYMOUTH (A
LAURA WEYMOUTH (A | LANI WEYMOUTH (A | TINA WEYMOUTH (A | JAMES RIZZI (A
ADRIAN BELEW (A | STEVE STANLEY (A | STICKY (A | CHRIS FRANTZ (A
MONTE BROWNE (A | TYRONE DOWNIE (A | KENDALL STUBBS (A

T105 TOMITA T105

ISAO TOMITA K SYN(ALL | (A) SNOWFLAKES ARE DANCING | 1975 RCA ARL1 0488 RI 81 LP3008
(B) PICTURES AT AN EXHIBITION | 1975 RCA ARLI 0838 RI 81 LP 3010
(C) FIREBIRD SUITE | 1976 RCA ARL1 1312
(D) THE PLANETS(WITHDRAWN) | 1977 RCA RL 11919
(E) BERMUDA TRIANGLE | 1979 RCA RL 12885
(F) KOSMOS | 1979 RCA RL 42652
( ) DAPHRIS ET CHLOE | 19 RCA FR PL13412
( ) GREATEST HITS | 1981 RCA LP 3037

T106 TOMORROW T106

KEITH WEST V (A | (A) TOMORROW | 1968 PARLOPHONE PCS 7042
JOHN WOOD B (A | (A) TOMORROW | 1976 HARVEST UK SHSP 2010
STEVE HOWE G (A | (A) TOMORROW | 1968 SIRE US 1003 97012
TWINK D (A | (A) TOMORROW | 1978 VISA 1002
KEN LAWRENCE D (A
JOHN BURGESS (| MARK P WIRTZ PROD K (A

T106A TOMORROW'S GIFT T106A

ELLEN MEYER V (A | (A) TOMORROWS GIFT (DBL) | 19 PLUS GER 1+2
WOLFGANG TRESCHER FLT (A | (B)GOODBYE FUTURE | 1973 AAMOK GER 28515
CARLOS KARGES G PERC(A
BERND KIEFER B (AB | GERD PAETZKE D (A | MANFRED RURUP K (AB | JOCHEN PETERSEN SAX (A

T107 TONI & TERRY BROWN GARTHWAITE T107

TONI BROWN V G K(ABDG | (A) CROSS COUNTRY (TONI & TERRY) | 1973 CAPITOL 11137
TERRY GARTHWAITE V G (ABCDEF | (B) GOOD FOR YOU TOO (TONI) | 1974 MCA MCF 2558
BILL AIKENS K (A | (C) TERRY | 1975 ARISTA US 4055 UK ARTY 124
DENNIS LINDE V B (A | (D) THE JOY (TONI & TERRY) | 1977 FANTASY FT 537
KENNY MALONE D (A | (E) HAND IN GLOVE (TERRY) | 1978 FANTASYUS 9564 UK FT 554
RUSS HICKS G V (A | (F) SAN FRANCISCO LTD(TERRY) | 1976 CRYSTAL CLEAR US 5004
JIM COLVARD G (A | (G) ANGEL OF LOVE (TONI) | 1980 FANTASY US 9585
VASSAR CLEMENTS VLN (A
CHARLIE McCOY HCA V(A | BOBBY THOMPSON G BAN(A | ROBERT EARL SCOTT D (F | DAVID AUSTIN K (D
DAVE DORAN G (A | JIM METHENY V (A | BILLY PUETT HRNS (B | LLOYD GREEN STEEL(B
CHUCK COCHRAN ACC (B | MARY HOEPFINGER HARP (B | KURT McGETTRICK SAX (BC | TOMMY COGBILL D (D
JERRY CARRIGAN D (B | BOBBY WOOD K (B | BILLY SANFORD G (B | REGGIE YOUNG G (B
JOHN CHRISTOPHER G (B | CHIP YOUNG G (B | FARRELL MORRIS PERC (B | GEORGE TIDWELL HRNS (B
DENNIS GOODE HRNS (B | BOBBY EMMONS K (B | BUDDY SPICHER FDL (B | WILLOW WRAY V (CDE
SONNY BURKE K (C | WILLIAM SMITH K (CD | PATRICE RUSHEN K (C | ROGER KELLAWAY K (C
PEGGY STERN K (CE | JAMES GADSON D (CD | HARVEY MASON D (C | JOHN GUERIN D (CE
VALENTINOS V (C | BOBBY WOMACK V (C | SCOTT MATTHEWS D (C | BILL SUMMERS PERC (C
WILLIE WEEKS B (C | RON CARTER B (C | CHUCK DOMANICO B (C | DAVID GARTHWAITE B (C
WAH WAH WATSON G (C | HOWARD ROBERTS G (C | JOE CRANE G (C | BOB FLURIE G (C
REGGIE McBRIDE B (D | STEVE MITCHELL D (D | JOHN BLAKELY G (D | ELVIN BISHOP G (D
BOBBYE HALL PERC (D | TAJ MAHAL G HCA(D | J D MANESS STEEL(D | JIM HORN HRNS (D
STEVE MADAIO HRNS (D | JIMMY ROBERTS WIND (D | BILL NAPIER CLAR (D | JOHNNY ROTELLA CLAR (D
MICHELLE HARRIS DULC MAN(D | MARJIE ORTEN DULC MAND(D | KENNETH NASH PERC (E | JAY GRAYDON G (E
VICTOR FELDMAN K (E | CLARK GASSMAN K (E | MAC CRIDLIN B (E | GEORGE MRAZ B (E
SHEILAH GLOVER V (E | VICKI RANDLE V (E | DEE DEE DICKERSON V (E | DON SHEFFIELD HRNS (B
KENT MIDDLETON PERC HCA(F | JOHN STAFFORD HRNS (F | BRIAN ATKINSON TPT VIBES(F | CHUCK METCALF B (F
BILL SCHWARTZ G (F | PHILIP G SMITH SAX (C

T108 TONTON MACOUTE T108

CHRIS GAVIN G B (A | (A) TONTON MACOUTE | 1971 NEON UK NE 4
PAUL FRENCH K V (A
NIGEL REVELER D (A | DAVE KNOWLES WIND V(A

T109 TONTOS EXPANDING HEADBAND T109

ROBERT MARGOULEFF SYN K(AB | (A) ZERO TIME | 1971 UK ATLANTIC K40251 US EMBRY0732
MALCOLM CECIL SYN K(AB | (A) ZERO TIME | 1975 ATLANTIC US RI 18123
STEVE GADD D (B | (B) ITS ABOUT TIME | 1974 POLYDOR 2383 308
REG McBRIDE B (B
MARLO HENDERSON G (B | ARMAND HABDURIAN PERC (B | MICHAEL CEMBALO G (B

T109A DAVID TOOP T109A

DAVID TOOP INSTR(A (A) NEW & REDISCOVERED MUSICAL 1975 OBSCURE UK OBS 48
BRIAN ENO PROD (A

T110 TOOTS & THE MAYTALS T110

TOOTS HIBBERT V (ALL (A) FROM THE ROOTS 1973 TROJAN TRLS 63
HUX BROWN G (DFJ (B) FUNKY KINGSTON 1973 DRAGON DRLS5002 ISLAND ILPS9186
HAROLD BUTLER K (HJ (B) FUNKY KINGSTON 1973 ISLAND US 9330
JACKIE JACKSON B (DHJ (C) IN THE DARK 1974 DRAGON DRLS5004 ISLAND ILPS9231
PAUL DOUGLAS B (DFHJ (D) REGGAE GOT SOUL 1976 ISLAND ILPS9374
RAD BRYAN G (DF (E) THE MAYTALS 1978 STATE ETAT 16
RALEIGH GORDON V (DFGHJ (F) PASS THE PIPE 1979 ISLAND NL 200471 UK ILPS9534
JERRY MATHIAS V (DFGHJ (G) BEST OF 1979 TROJAN TRLS 171
WINSTON WRIGHT K (DFHJ (H) JUST LIKE THAT 1980 ISLAND UK ILPS9590
RANCHY McLEAN B (F (J) LIVE 1980 ISLAND ILPS9647
JUNIOR KERR G (D (K) BEST OF TROJAN 1980 TROJAN UK 171
CHINNA LINDO G (D
CARL HARVEY G (J GLADSTONE ANDERSON K (D SONNY BINNS K (D STEVE WINWOOD K (D
EMMANUEL RENTZOS K (D CHICAGO STEVE HCA (D BOBBY ELLIS TPT (D EDDIE QUANSAH TPT(D
JEROME FRANCISQUE TROM (D RICO RODRIGUES TROM (D RAY ALLEN SAX (D DUDU PUKWANA SAX(D
TOMMY McCOOK SAX (D GEORGE LEE SAX (D DENSIL LANG PERC (D BROTHER JAMES PERC(D
TONY UTER PERC (D BRUCE ROWLAND PERC (D PABLO BLACK K (D WILLIE LINDO G (H
MIKEY CHUNG G (H

T110A TOPAZ T110A

ROB STONER (A (A) TOPAZ 19 CBS US 34934

T111 TOP TOPHAM T111

TOP TOPHAM G (A (A) ASCENSION HEIGHTS 1970 BLUE HORIZON UK 763857
RICK HAYWARD G (A
JOHN MARSHALL D (A COLIN ALLEN D (A HERBIE FLOWERS B (A EDDIE TRIPP B (A
BRIAN ODGERS B (A STRING SECTION (A PETE WINGFIELD K (A STEVE GREY K (A
DUSTER BENNETT HCA (A MIKE VERNON PERC (A TERRY NOONAN TPT (A BUTCH HUDSON TPT(A
GREG BOWEN TPT (A NIGEL CARTER TPT (A CHRIS PYNE TROM (A DANNY ELWOOD TROM(A
JACK THIRLWELL TROM (A ALAN SKIDMORE SAX (A DANNY MOSS SAX (A TONY COE SAX (A
STEVE GREGORY SAX (A DON HONEYWELL SAX (A

T111A TORNADER T111A

SANDY TORANO G (A (A) HIT IT AGAIN 1977 POLYDOR US PL 1 6098
LARRY ALEXANDER V (A
JOHNNY WINTER G (A JOE BECK G (A STEVE FERRONE D (A RANDY BRECKER HRNS(S
MICHAEL BRECKER HRNS (A

T111B BERNIE TORME T111B

BERNIE TORME G V HCA FLT(A (A) TURN OUT THE LIGHTS 1972 KAMAFLAGE UK KAMLP2
PHIL SPALDING B V (A
NIGEL GLOCKLER D (A MARK HARRISON D (A COLIN TOWNS K FLT(A

T112 TORNADOS T112

HEINZ BURT V B G((A) SOUND OF (EP) 1962 DECCA UK DFE 8510
ROGER JACKSON K ((B) TELSTAR (EP) 1963 DECCA UK DFE 8511
GEORGE BELLAMY G ((C) MORE SOUNDS FROM (EP) 1963 DECCA UK DFE 8521
ALAN CADDY VLN G((D) TORNADO ROCK 1963 DECCA UK DFE 8533
CLEM CATTINI D ((E) TELSTAR 196 LONDON US 3279
(F) AWAY FROM IT ALL 1963 DECCA UK LK 4552
(G) WORLD OF 1972 DECCA UK SPA 253
(H) REMEMBERING 1976 DECCA UK ROOTS 4

T112A TORONTO T112A

NICKI COSTELLO B (AB (A) LOOKING FOR TROUBLE 1980 SOLIDGOLD US 1000 A&M UK 64821
JIMMY FOX D (AB (B) HEAD ON 1981 A&M UK 64872
SHERON ALTON G V (A (C) GET IT ON CREDIT 1982 SOLIDGOLD US 1011
HOLLY WOODS V (A
SCOTT KREYER K (A BRIAN ALLEN G V (A

T113 RICHARD TORRANCE T113

RICHARD TORRANCE V B G K(ALL (A) EUREKA 1974 A&M UKAMLH68266 US SHELTER 2112
GARY ROWLES G V PERC STEEL(ABC (B) BELLE OF THE BALL 1975 A&M UKAMLH68312 US SHELTER 2134
MONTY STARK B SYN(A (B) BELLE OF THE BALL 1979 SHELTER RI 52019
KEN WEISSMAN (A (C) EUREKA III 1977 PHILIPS NL 6363133 US SHELTER?
DENNIS MANSFIELD V D VIBES(ABCE (D) BAREBACK 1977 CAPITOL SW 11610
JON LAMB G B V PERC(BC (E) DOUBLE TAKE 1978 CAPITOL SW 11699
RICHARD CANTU PERC (BC (F) ANYTHINGS POSSIBLE 1979 CAPITOL
DUANE SCOTT V K PERC (AB
TERRY LEE LICK G V (E DAVID WHITE B V (E MELODY JEAN HORNEY K V (E BILLY PAYNE K (ED
VANDER LOCKETT PERC (E STEPHANIE BLACK V (A BILL LINCOLN G B (A JOE McSWAYNE B (A
BILL CUOMO K (A EDDIE TUDUR D (A JAY SPELL K V (C JIM RICHARDSON HRNS(C
FRED TACKETT G (D DAVID HUNGATE B (D JEFF PORCARO D (D SAM CLAYTON PERC(D
VANETTA FIELDS V (D MAXINE WILLARD V (D JULIA TILLMAN V (D THOMAS SNOW V (D
ERNIE WATTS HRNS (D HARVEY MASON D (D WILTON FELDER B (D PETER CHRISTLIEB HRNS(D
BUDDY COLLETTE HRNS (D JOHN HAENY PROD (D BOB FINDLEY HRNS (D

T114 PETER TOSH T114

PETER TOSH G V K(ALL (A) LEGALIZE IT 1976 VIRGIN UK V2061 US CBS 34253
CARLTON BARRETT D (A (B) EQUAL RIGHTS 1978 VIRGIN UK V2081 US CBS 34670
ASTON BARRETT B (A (C) BUSH DOCTOR 1978 ROLLING STONES CUN 39109
ROBBIE SHAKESPEARE B (ABCD (D) MYSTIC MAN 1979 ROLLING STONES CUN 39111
TYRONE DOWNEY K (A (E) WANTED DREAD OR ALIVE 1981 ROLLING STONES CUN 39113
LARRY McDONALD PERC (C
RITA MARLEY V (A JUDY MOWATT V (A BUNNY WAILER V (AB AL ANDERSON G (AB
DONALD KINSEY G (AC ROBBIE LEE HCA (A RAS LEE HCA (A EARL LINDO (B
MIKEY CHUNG K G (CD SLY DUNBAR D (BCD ROBBIE LYN K (DC YVONNE LEWIS V (D
KEITH STERLING PNO (DC STICKY PERC (DC ED ELIZALDE G (D SAMMY FIGUEROA CONGA(D
SKULLY D (D ED WALSH SYN (D GEORGE YOUNG WIND (D LOU MARINI WIND (D
HOWARD JOHNSON SAX (D BARRY ROGERS TROM (D MIKE LAWRENCE TPT (D TAMLINS V (D
GWEN GUTHRIE V (D BRENDA WHITE V (D LUTHOR FRANCOIS SAX (C KEITH RICHARDS G (C
MICK JAGGER V (C

T114A **TOTALLY HOT** T114A

(A) TOTALLY HOT 1981 MOBILE US 040

T115 **TOTO** T115

DAVID PAICH K V (ABCD (A) TOTO 1978 CBS US 35317 UK 83148
DAVID HUNGATE B G (ABCD (B) HYDRA 1979 CBS US 36229 UK 83900
JEFF PORCARO D (ABcD (C) TURN BACK 1980 CBS US 36813 UK 84609
JOE PORCARO PERC (ABCD (D) IV 1982 CBS UK 85529
BOBBY KIMBALL V (ABCD
GARY GRANT TPT (D STEVE PORCARO K (ABCD STEVE LUKATHER G V(ABCD LENNY CASTRO PERC(ABD
JIM HORN SAX (AD CHERYL LYNN (A MICHAEL BODDICKER K (AB RALPH DYCK SYN(CD
CHUCK FINDLEY HRNS (A ROGER LINN (ABC MARTY PAICH STR (ABD SID SHARP STR (A
REGGIE FISHER (B MIKE PORCARO CELLO (D JAMES NEWTON HOWARD STR(D TOM SCOTT SAX (D
JERRY KEY TPT (D JIM PANKOW TROM (D JON SMITH SAX (D TOM KELLY V (D
TIMOTHY SCHMIDT V (D

T116 **TOUCH** T116

DON TULLUCCI K V (A (A) TOUCH 1969 DERAM UK SML 1033
JOHN BORDONARO PERC V(A
JOEY NEWMAN G V (A BRUCE HAUSER B V (A JEFF HAWKES V (A

T116A **TOUCH** T116A

CRAIG BROOKS G V (AB (A) ENERGIZER 1977 BRUNSWICK US 754214
GLENN KITHCART D (B (B) TOUCH 1980 ATCO US SD 38123
MARK MANGOLD K V (B (B) TOUCH 1980 ARIOLA UK 5036
DOUG HOWARD B V (B

T116B **TOUCHSTONE** T116B

TOM CONSTANTEN K (A (A) TAROT 1972 UA US 5563
PAUL DRESHER G FLT(A
GARY HIRSH PERC (A WES STEELE B CELLO(A ART FAYER VLN (A JIM BYERS G (A
RUBBER DUCK TAMB (A

T117 **TOURISTS** T117

ANNIE LENNOX V K FLT(ABC (A) TOURISTS 1979 LOGO UK 1018 GER 64019
PETE COOMBES G V (ABC (B) REALITY EFFECT 1979 LOGO UK 1019 GER 64021
DAVE STEWART G (ABC (B) REALITY EFFECT 1979 EPIC US 36386
JIM TOOMEY D (ABC (C) LUMINOUS BASEMENT 1980 RCA RCALP5001 + PL 25323
EDDY CHIN B (ABC (A) THE TOURIST 1981 RCA INT UK INTS5096

T118 **ALLEN TOUSSAINT** T118

ALLEN TOUSSAINT K G HCA(ALL (A) WILD SOUNDS OF NEW ORLEANS 1958 RCA VICTOR US 1767
VINCENT TOUSSAINT G (C (B) TOUSSAINT 1971 TIFFANY US014 WAND WNS 14
LEO NOCENTELLI G (C (B) TOUSSAINT 1977 DJM UK DJF 22070
GEORGE PORTER B (C (C) LIFE LOVE & FAITH 1972 REPRISE US 2062 UK K44202
GEORGE PLUMMER G (C (D) SOUTHERN NIGHTS 1975 REPRISE US 2186 UK K54021
WALTER PAYTON B (C (E) MOTION 1978 WB US 3142 UK K56473
JOSEPH MODELISTE D (C (F) BOMP CITY 1973 WB US 2616
VANETTA FIELDS V (B
JOE LAMBERT D (C ALFRED ROBERTS CONGA(C SQUIRREL CONGA(C GARY BROWN SAX (C
ALVIN THOMAS SAX (C RED TYLER SAX (C CLYDE KERR TPT (BC FRANCIS ROUSSELLE TPT(C
JEFF PORCARO D (E POPS POPWELL B (E CHUCK RAINEY D (E LARRY CARLTON G (E
VICTOR FELDMAN PERC (E RICHARD TEE K (E PAULINHO DA COSTA PERC (E ETTA JAMES V (E
BONNIE RAITT V (E DR JOHN G K (B TERRY KELLMAN G (B FRED STAEHLE D (B
EDDIE HOHNER B (B ED GREENE D (B EARL TURBINTON SAX (B FRED KEMP SAX(B
MERRY CLAYTON V (B

T118A **MEIKE TOUW** T118A

MEIKE TOUW V (A (A) TUTTI FRUTTI 1980 ARIOLA NL 202 160
HENK TORPEDO (A
HARRY DEWINTER (A DICK SCHULTE NORDHOLT B V(A ROBERT JAN STIPS K (A MARC BOON (A
PETE CALICKER (A MAX MOLLINGER (A JAN CEES TANS (A JOHN KRIEK (A
ERNST GLERUM (A HENK WIJTMAN D (A

T119 **TOWER OF POWER** T119

HUBERT TUBBS V (EG (A) EAST BAY GREASE 1970 SAN FRANCISO US SD204
LENNY PICKETT SAX (QBCDEGHJ (B) BUMP CITY 1972 WB UK K46167 US 2616
GREG ADAMS HRNS (ABCDEGHJ (C) TOWER OF POWER 1974 WB UK K46223 US 2681
MIC GILLETTE HRNS (ABCDEGHJ (D) BACK IN OAKLAND 1974 WB UK K46282 US 2749
STEVE KUPKA SAX (ACEGHJ (E) IN THE SLOT 1975 WB UK K56155 US 2880
BRUCE CONTE G V (CEGHJ (F) URBAN RENEWAL 1975 WB UK K56093 US 2834
CHESTER THOMPSON K (CEGHJ (G) LIVE & LIVING COLOUR 1976 WB UK K56221 US 2924
FRANCIS PRESTIA B (ABCCFGH (H) AINT NOTHIN' STOPPIN' US NOW 1976 CBS UK 81572 US 34302
DAVID GARIBALDI D (CFGABD (J) WE CAME TO PLAY 1978 CBS UK 82239 US 34906
LENNY WILLIAMS (C (K) BACK ON THE STREETS 1979 CBS US 35784
EMILIO CASTILLO SAX V(AC
BRENT BYARS (CA RICK STEVENS V (A WILLIE FULTON G V (A JAY SPELL PNO (C
BRUCE STEINBERG HCA (C BOOTCHE ANDERSON V (E MARILYN SCOTT V (E PEPPER WATKINS V (E
DAVID BARTLETT V (E RON BECK V D (EHJ FRANK BINER V (E ROGER RIFKIND V (D
EDWARD McGEE V (H MICHAEL JEFFRIES V (J VICTOR CONTE B (J SKIP MESQUITE V WIND(A

T119A **RALPH TOWNER** T119A

RALPH TOWNER G K (ALL (A) TIROS:SOLOS 1975 ECM UK 1025
JACK DEJONETTE D (G (B) DIARY 1975 ECM UK 1032
EDDIE GOMEZ B (G (C) MATCHBOX 1975 ECM UK 1056
GARY BURTON VIBES(C (D) SOLTICE 1975 ECM UK 1060
JOHN ABERCROMBIE (E (E) SARGASSO SEA 1976 ECM UK 1080
(F) SOUND OF SHADOWS 1977 ECM UK 1095
(G) BATIK 1978 ECM UK 1127

T119B **COLIN TOWNLEY** T119B

COLIN TOWNLEY V (AB (A) TOWNLEY 1980 HARVEST US 12007
(B) MORE THAN A DREAM 1981 EMI UK 3371

T120 **COLIN TOWNS** T120

COLIN TOWNS (A (A) FULL CIRCLE 1978 VIRGIN UK V 2093

T121 PETE TOWNSHEND T121

PETE TOWNSHEND G V K(AB (A) WHO CAME FIRST 1972 TRACK UK 2408 201 US MCA 2026
TONY BUTLER B (B (A) WHO CAME FIRST 197 DECCA US 79189
RONNIE LANE G V (A (B) EMPTY GLASS 1980 ATCO UK K 50699 US 32100
BILLIE NICHOLLS G V (A
CALEB QUAYE G (A RABBIT BUNDRICK K (B KENNY JONES D (B MARK BRZEZICKI D (B
RAPHAEL BUDD HRNS (B SIMON PHILLIPS D (B JAMES ASHER D (B PETE HOPE-EVANS HCA (B
CHRIS THOMAS PROD (B

T122 TONWSHEND/LANE T122

PETE TOWNSHEND G (A (A) ROUGH MIX 1977 POLYDOR UK 2442 147 US MCA 2295
RONNIE LANE B G V(A (A) ROUGH MIX 1080 POLYDOR RI 2482 488
CHRIS LAURENCE B (A
ERIC CLAPTON G (A CHARLIE WATTS D (A RABBIT BUNDRICK K (A HENRY SPINETTI D (A
PETER HOPE EVANS HCA (A GRAHAM LYLE G (A BENNY GALLAGHER ACC (A CHARLIE HART VLN (A
DAVE MARKEE B (A MEL COLLINS SAX (A IAN STEWART PNO (A JULIAN DIGGLE PERC (A
TONY GILBERT (A CHARLES VORZANGER VLN (A STEVE SHINGLES VLA (A CHRIS GREEN CELLO(A
BOZ BURRELL B (A JOHN ENTWISTLE HRNS V(A BILLY NICHOLLS V (A

T122A TOY T122A

ALBERT HARRY WOODS K G V(AB (A) BAD NIGHT 1970 PAYOLA NL 939/1 LOGO UK 4010
THEO VAN HEMELRYK G V (AB (B) SPIT 1981 PAYOLA NL 64389
RENATO MARCIANO B (A
PAUL ILLE D (A MARK BOURNE G PERC(B PAOLO DAMANTS K (B RENAAT BOEYKENS B (B

T122B TOYAH T122B

TOYAH WILCOX V (ABCDE (A) SHEEP FARMING IN BARNET 1979 SAFARI UK SAP1 GER 63442
PETE BUSH K (AC (B) TOYAH TOYAH TOYAH 1980 SAFARI UK LIVE2 GER 63866
MARK HENRY B (A (C) BLUE MEANING 1980 SAFARI UK IEYA666
JOEL BOGEB G (AC (D) FOUR FROM TOYAH(EP) 1981 SAFARI UK TOY1
STEVE BRAY D (AC (E) ANTHEM 1981 SAFARI UK VOOR1
CHARLES FRANCIS B (C

T122C TOYAN T122C

(A) HOW THE WEST WAS WON 1981 GREENSLEEVES UK GREL20

T123 TRACE T123

RICK VAN DER LINDEN K (ABC (A) TRACE 1974 VERTIGO UK 6360852 US SIRE 7504
COR DEKKER B (C (A) TRACE 1974 PHILIPS GER 6423 075
JAAP VAN EIK G (AB (B) BIRDS 1975 VERTIGO UK 6413080 SIRE US 7514
PIERRE VANDER LINDEN D (A (C) THE WHITE LADIES 1976 RCA GER 21815
IAN MOSLEY D (B
DARRYL WAY VLN (B PETER DE LEEUWE G D (C DICK REMELINCK WIND (C HANS JACOBSE K (C
HETTI SMIT V (C HARRY SCHAFER V (C

T123A TRACKS T123A

ANDREW ASHTON G V (A (A) EVEN A BROKEN CLOCK IS RIGHT TWICE A DAY 1972 CAPITOL 1118
SCOTT KENNETH B V (A
ROY BITTAN K B G V(A STEV MEROLA D HCA(A EARL SLICK G (A

T124 TRACTOR T124

JIM MILNE G V B(A (A) TRACTOR 1972 DANDELION UK 2310 217
STEVE CLAYTON B K D FLT(A
DAVE ADDISON B (

T124A JEANIE TRACY T124A

JEANIE TRACY V (A (A) ME AND YOU 1982 FANTASY US 6414

T125 TRADER HORNE T125

JUDY DYBLE K V (A (A) MORNING WAY 1970 DAWN UK DNLS3004 JANUS US 3012
JACKIE McAULEY K G V(A1 (1) 1970 SUMMER
RAY ELLIOT WIND (A
SAFFRON SUMMERFIELD G V(1 ANDY WHITE D (A JOHN GODFREY B (A

T126 TRADITION T126

(A) SHOWCASE 1980 VENTURE UK CUT 10
(B) CAPTAIN GANGA & THE SPACE AGE 1981 VENTURE UK CUT 9

T127 TRAFFIC T127

STEVE WINWOOD G K V(ALL (A) Mr FANTASY 1967 ISLAND UK ILPS 9061 US UA 6651
JIMMY JOHNSON G (G (A) MR FANTASY 1967 ISLAND GER 85784
JIM CAPALDI D V K(ALL (B) TRAFFIC 1968 ISLANDUK ILPS 9081 US UA 6676
CHRIS WOOD WIND (ALL (C) LAST EXIT 1969 ISLAND UK ILPS 9097 US UA 6702
DAVE MASON G V (ABCE (D) JOHN BARLEYCORN MUST DIE 1970 ISLAND UK ILPS 9116 US UA 5504
BARRY BECKETT K (GH (D) JOHN BARLEYCORN MUST DIE 1970 ISLAND GER 6339 016
RICK GRECH B (EF (E) WELCOME TO THE CANTEEN 1971 ISLAND UK ILPS 9166 US UA 5550
REBOP BAAH CONGA(EGHF (F) LOW SPARK OF HIGH HEELED BOY 1971 ISLAND UK ILPS 9180 US 9306
ROSKO GEE B (J (F) LOW SPARK OF HIGH HEELED BOY 1971 ISLAND GER 85867
JIM GORDON D (EF (G) SHOOT OUT AT THE FANTASY FACTORY 1973 ISLAND UK ILPS 9224 US 9323
DAVE HOOD B (GH (H) ON THE ROAD (LIVE DBL) 1973 ISLAND UK ILSD 2 US 9336
ROGER HAWKINS D (GH (J) WHEN THE EAGLE FLIES 1974 ISLAND UK ILPS 9273 GER 88334
(J) WHEN THE EAGLE FLIES 1974 ASYLUM US 7E1020
( ) COLOURED RAIN 1967 ISLAND SWED ILP800
( ) LIVE (NOT RELEASED) 1970 ISLAND UK ILPS 9142
( ) BEST OF 1969 ISLAND UK ILPS 9112 US UA 5500
( ) BEST OF 19 ISLAND GER 88066
( ) HEAVY TRAFFIC 1975 US UA 4211
( ) MORE HEAVY TRAFFIC 1975 US UA LA526
(EP) HOLE IN MY SHOE 1978 ISLAND UK I EP 7

T128 TRAMLINE T128

JOHN McCOY V HCA(A (A) SOMEWHERE DOWN THE LINE 1968 ISLAND UK ILPS9088
TERRY SIDGWICK B V (A (B) MOVES OF VEGETABLE CENTURIES 1969 ISLAND UK ILPS9095
TERRY POPPLE D (A
MICK MOODY G (A CHRIS BLACKWELL PROD (

T129 **BOBBY LEE TRAMMELL** T129

BOBBY LEE TRAMMELL (AB (A) ARKANSAS TWIST 19 ATLANTA US 1503
(B) I DARE AMERICA TO BE GREAT 19 SUNCOT US 1102

T130 **TRAMP** T130

MICK FLEETWOOD D (BA (A) TRAMP 1969 MUSIC MAN 603 RI SPARK UK SRLM2001
DANNY KIRWAN G (BA (B) PUT A RECORD ON 1974 SPARK UK SRLP 112
DAVE BROOKS SAX (B
DAVE KELLY V (BA JO ANN KELLY V (BA BOB BRUNNING B(BA BOB HALL K (BA
IAN MORTON PERC (B

T131 **TRANQUILITY** T131

TONY LUKYN K V (A (A) TRANQUILITY 1972 EPIC UK 64729 US 31084
KEVIN McCARTHY G (A (B) SILVER 197 EPIC US 31989
TERRY SHADDICK G V (A
BERNARD HAGLEY G (A BERKELEY WRIGHT G V (A PAUL FRANCIS D (A

T131A **TRANSISTOR** T131A

ROBERT JAN STIPS K (A (A) ZIG ZAG 1980 ARIOLA NL 201 163
HENK WIJTMAN D V (A
HUBA DE GRAFF K V (A DICK SCHULTE NORDHOLT B V (A

T132 **TRANSMITTERS** T132

CHRIS GEORGE LYRIC(A (A) 24 HOURS 1978 EBONY UK EB1002
MIKEL LEE G (A (B) AND WE CALL THAT LEISURE TIME 1981 HEARTBEAT UK HB4
SAM DODSON B G K(AB
JIM CHASE D (AB VINCE CUTLIFFE G (A JOHN QUINN V (A DAVE BABY SAX (B
SID WEELS B (B JULIAN TREASURE D (B ROB CHAPMAN V K(B

T133 **TRAPEZE** T133

GLENN HUGHES B (ABCF (A) TRAPEZE 1970 THRESHOLD UK THS 2
MEL GALLEY G (ABCEFGH (B) MEDUSA 1970 THRESHOLD UK THS 4
DAVE HOLLAND D (BCEFGA (C) YOU ARE THE MUSIC 1972 THRESHOLD UK THS 8
PETE WRIGHT B (EFGH (D) FINAL SWING 1974 THRESHOLD UK THS11
ROB KENDRICK G (EF (E) HOT WIRE 1974 WB US 2828 UK K56064
PETE GALBY G V (GH (F) TRAPEZE 1975 WB US 2887 UK K56165
B J COLE STEEL(C (G) HOLD ON/RUNNING 1978 AURA AUL 708
STEVE BRAY D (H (H) LIVE IN TEXAS/DEAD ARMADILLOS 1980 AURA UK AUL 717
ROD ARGENT K (C
TERRY ROWLEY G K FLT (EGA JOHN JONES V TPT (A KIRK DUNCAN K (C JOHN OGDEN PERC (CE
FRANK RICOTTI PERC (C JIMMY HASTINGS SAX (C KENNY COLE V (E MISTY BROWNING V(E
CHRIS MERCER SAX (E

T133A **TRASHMEN** T133A

BOB REEDS B (A (A) SURFIN' BIRD 1964 SOMA US 200
DAL WINSLOW (A

T134 **HAPPY & ARTIE TRAUM** T134

HAPPY TRAUM G (ABCDEF (A) HAPPY & ARTIE TRAUM 1969 CAPITOL ST 586
ARTIE TRAUM G (ABCFDG (B) DOUBLEBACK 1971 CAPITOL ST 799
PATRICK ALGER MAND (EF (C) MUD ACRES 1972 ROUNDER US 3001 UK MATCHBOX 239
RICK DANKO B ((D) HARD TIMES IN THE COUNTRY 1975 ROUNDER US 3007
ERIC KAZ ((E) RELAX YOUR MIND(HAPPY) 1976 KICKING MULE US 110 UK SNKF 111
TRACY NELSON ((F) AMERICAN STRANGER 1978 KICKING MULE US 301 UK SNKF 142
AMOS GARRETT G ((G) LIFE ON EARTH 1974 ROUNDER US 3014
MARIA MULDAUR V ((H) BRIGHT MORNING STARS 1980 GREENHAYS US 703
BILL KEITH STEEL(
DOUG JAMES PERC (F BETTY McDONALD V FDL(F ANDY ROBINSON VPERC(F ROLY SALLEY B (F
JOHN SEBASTIAN V HCA(F HOWARD VOGEL REC (F JODI VOGEL CELLO(F ERIC WEISSBERG FDL(F

T134A **TRAVEL AGENCY** T134A

(A) TRAVEL AGENCY 1968 VIVA US 36017

T135 **PAT TRAVERS** T135

PAT TRAVERS G V K(ALL (A) PAT TRAVERS 1976 POLYDOR US 1 6079 UK 2383 395
PETER MARS COWLING B(ABCDEFGH (B) MAKIN' MAGIC 1977 POLYDOR US 1 [illegible] UK 2383 436
NICKO McBAIN D (CB (C) PUTTIN' IT STRAIGHT 1977 POLYDOR US 1 6121 UK 2383 471
TONY CAREY K (C (D) HEAT IN THE STREET 1979 POLYDOR US 1 6170 UK POLD5005
SUZIE McKINLEY V (C (E) GO FOR WHAT YOU KNOW(LIVE) 1979 POLYDOR US 6202 UK POLS1011
BERT HERMISTON SAX (C (F) CRASH & BURN 1980 POLYDOR US 6262 UK POLS1017
SCOTT GORHAM G (C (G) RADIO ACTIVE 1981 POLYDOR US 6313 UK 2391 499
ROY DYKE D (A (H) BLACK PEARL 1982 POLYDOR UK 2391 553
TOMMY ALDRIDGE D (DEFG
PAT THRALL G SYN(DEFG CLIVE EDWARDS D (B GLENN HUGHES V (B MICHAEL SCHRIEVE PERC(FG
DAWN SHAHAN V (F SANDY GENNARO D (GH DON HARRISS K SYN(H

T135A **PAUL TRAVIS** T135A

PAUL TRAVIS G K V(A (A) RETURN OF THE NATIVE 1975 A&M UK AMLS 68290
TONY BRAUNAGEL D (A
TERRY WILSON B (A RABBIT BUNDRICK K (A MARK WARNER G (A SANDY DAVIS V (A
HELEN CHAPPELLE V (A BARRY LORD V (A CHRIS MERCER SAX (A EDDIE QUANSAH SAX (A
PETER VANDERPIUSE SAX (A JACK EMBLOW ACC (A CHRIS LAURENCE B (A

T135B **TRAX** T135B

(A) HOME (EP) 19 LONELY UK LONSOME 1

T136 **JACK TRAYLOR & STEELWIND** T136

JACK TRAYLOR G V (A (A) CHILD OF NATURE 1973 GRUNT FTR 0194
CRAIG CHAQUICO G (A
DANNY VIRDIER B V (A SKIP MORAIRTY G V (A DIANA HARRIS K V (A KENT MIDDLETON HCA PERC(A
BILL LAUDNER V (A RICK QUINTANAL V (A DAVID FREIBERG K (A

T137 **TREES** T137

CELIA HUMPHRIS K V (AB1 (A) THE GARDEN OF JANE DELAWNEY 1970 CBS 63837
BIAS BOSHELL G V B(AB (B) ON THE SHORE 1970 CBS 64168
BARRY CLARKE G (AB1 (1) 1972
DAVID COSTA G (AB1
UNWIN BROWN D V (AB TONY COX B (B MICHAEL JEFFERIES HARP (B BARRY LYONS B (1
ALUN EDEN D (1 CHUCK FLEMING VLN (1

T137A TREMBLERS T137A

PETER NOONE V G K B (A — (A) TWICE NIGHTLY — 1980 EPIC UK 84448 US JOHNSTON 36532
GREGG INHOFER K G V(A
ROBERT WILLIAMS D V (A GEO CONNER G V (A MARK BROWNE B (A MIKE CAMPBELL (A
STAN LYNCH (A RON BLAIR (A JOHN FARRAR (A STEPHEN HAGUE (A
STEVE ALLEN (A NIGEL OLSSON (A BILL PITCOCK (A DARYL DRAGON (A

T138 (BRIAN POOLE &) THE TREMELOES T138

BRIAN POOLE V (ABCHP — (A) BIG HITS OF 1962 — 1963 ACE OF CLUBS UK ACL 1146
RICK WESTWOOD G V (— (B) TWIST & SHOUT — 1963 DECCA UK LK 4550
ALAN BLAKELY G V (— (C) IT'S ABOUT TIME — 1965 DECCA UK LK 4685
DAVE MUNDEN D V (— (D) HERE COME THE TREMELOES — 1967 CBS UK 63017
LEN'CHIP'HAWKES B V (— (E) HERE COMES MY BABY — 1967 CBS US 26310
AARON WOOLLEY (— (F) EVEN THE BAD TIMES ARE GOOD — 1967 CBS US 26326
BOB BENHAM (— (G) SUDDENLY YOU LOVE ME — 1967 CBS US 26363 UK 63138
(G) SILENCE IS GOLDEN — 1975 EMBASSY UK 31206
(H) 58/68 WORLD EXPLOSION — 1968 CBS US 26388
(J) LIVE IN CABARET — 1969 CBS UK 63547
(K) MASTER — 1970 CBS UK 64242
(L) GREATEST HITS — 1970 CBS UK 64206
(M) REACH OUT FOR THE TREMELOES — 1973 EMBASSY UK 31031
(N) SHINER — 1974 DJM UK DJLP 5441 + DJF 20441
(O) DON'T LET THE MUSIC DIE — 1976 DJM UK DJF 20447
(P) REMEMBERING — 1977 DECCA UK REM 5

T138A TRETTIOARIGA KRIGET T138A

STEFAN FREDIN (B — (A) KRIGSSANG — 1975 CBS UK 80900
DAG LUNDQUIST (B — (B) HEJ PA ER! — 1978 MISTLUR SWED MRL 4
ROBERT ZIMA (b — ( ) TRETTIOARIGA KRIGET — 19 CBS UK 80220
CHRISTER AKERBERG (B — ( ) MO ALLA ODDS — 19 MISTLUR SWED MLR 9
MATS LINDBERG SAX K(B

T138B TRICKSTER T138B

PHIL BATES G V (AB — (A) FIND THE LADY — 1977 JET UAS 30132 RI JETLP 206
JOHN FINCHAM B V (B — (A) FIND THE LADY — 1977 JET US 35478
COLIN HEWINSON K SYN(AB — (B) BACK TO ZERO — 1979 JET UK JETLP221 US 35968
MIKE SHEPPARD G B V(A
PAUL ELLIOTT D PERC(AB MICHAEL GROTH G V (B

T138C TRIANA T138C

JESUS DE LA ROSA V (ALL — (A) TRIANA — 1975 MOVIE PLAY 17 0678/7
EDUARDO RODRIGUEZ G V (ALL — (B) HYOS DEL AGOBIO — 1977 GONG 170907/9
JUAN JOSE PALACIOS D V(ALL — (C) SOMBRA Y LUZ — 1979 MOVIE PLAY 17 1439/4
(D) UN ENCUENTRO — 1980 MOVIE PLAY 53 0678/5
(E) TRIANA CASSETTE — 1981 MOVIE PLAY 53 2770/8

T138D TRIBE T138D

(A) ETHNIC STEW — 1974 ABC US 807
(B) TRIBAL BUMPIN' — 1975 ABC US 859

T139 TRIGGER T139

JIMMY DUGGAN (A — (A) TRIGGER — 1978 CASABLANCA UK NBLP 7092
RITCHIE HOUSE (A
TOM NIGRA (A DEREK REMINGTON (A

T139A TRILLION T139A

RON ANAMAN B V (AB — (A) TRILLION — 1978 EPIC US 35460
PAT LEONARD K (BA — (B) CLEAR APPROACH — 1980 CBS US 36206
FRANK BARBALACE G V (BA
THOM GRIFFIN G V (B BILL WILKINS D PERC(BA DENNIS FREDRICKSON V (A

T139B TRINITY T139B

(A) UPTOWN GIRL — 1977 MAGNUM DEAD 1003
(B) ROCK IN THE GHETTO — 1979 TROJAN TRLS 170

T140 TRINITY RIVER BOYS T140

MICHAEL MURPHEY G (A — (A) TRINITY RIVER BOYS — 1964 PROSPECTOR NOT RELEASED
MICHAEL NESMITH G V (A
JOHN RAINES D (A JOHN LONDON B (A

T141 TRIO T141

JOHN SURMAN SAX (ABC — (A) THE TRIO — 1970 DAWN UK DNLS 3006
BARRE PHILLIPS B (ABC — (B) CONFLAGRATION — 1971 DAWN UK DNLS 3022
STU MARTIN D (ABC — (C) LIVE AT WOODSTOCK TOWN HALL — 1976 DAWN UK DNLS 3072
HARRY BECKETT TPT (B
MARC CHARIG CORN(B CHICK COREA K (B NICK EVANS TROM (B MALCOLM GRIFFITHS TROM(B
DAVE HOLLAND B (B JOHN TAYLOR PNO (B JOHN MARSHALL D (B MIKE OSBORNE CLAR(B
ALAN SKIDMORE WIND (B STAN SULOMAN WIND (B KENNY WHEELER HRNS(B

T141A TRITONUS T141A

PETER K SEILER K (A — (A) TRITONUS — 1975 BASF GERM 17 223841
RONALD J D BRAND B V G(A
CHARLIE JOST D PERC(A

T142 TRIUMPH T142

RIK EMMET G (ABCDE — (A) TRIUPH — 1976 ATTIC LAT 1012
G L MOORE D (ABCDE — (B) ROCK'N'ROLL MACHINE — 1977 ATTIC LAT 1036
MIKE LEVINE B (ABCDE — (C) ROCK'N'ROLL MACHINE(COMP OF A B) — 1979 RCA 12982
LAURIE DELGRANDE K (A — (D) JUST A GAME — 1979 RCA 13224 RI INT5154
BEAR DAVID V (B — (E) PROGRESSIONS OF POWER — 1980 RCA 13524 RI INT LP3039
GORD WASZEK V (B — (F) ALLIED FORCES — 1981 RCA LP 6002

T143 TRIUMVIRAT T143

Member	Inst	Albums	Album	Release
HELMUT KOELLEN	B G V	(B	(A) MEDITERRANEAN TALES	1972 HARVEST EURO IC 062 29441
CURT CRESS	D	(E	(B) ILLUSION ON A DOUBLE DIMPLE	1974 HARVEST US 11311 UK SHSP 4030
BARRY PALMER	V	(DE	(B) ILLUSION ON A DOUBLE DIMPLE	1977 EMI EURO IC 062 29441
DIETER PETEREIT	B	(E	(C) SPARTACUS	1975 HARVEST US 11392 UK SHSP 4048
HANS JUERGEN FRITZ	K V	(ABCDEFG	(D) OLD LOVES DIE HARD	1976 CAPITOL US 11551 EURO 29622
HANS PAPE	B V	(AB	(E) POMPEII	1977 CAPITOL US 11697 EURO LC1305
HANS BATHELT	D	(ABCD	(F) A LA CARTE	1978 CAPITOL US 11862
DICK FRANGENBERG	B	(D	(G) RUSSIAN ROULETTE	1980 HARVEST 45834
ULLA WIESNER	V	(B		

Member	Inst	Albums	Member	Inst	Albums	Member	Inst	Albums	Member	Inst	Albums
HANNA DOHTISCH	V	(B	PETER CADERA	V	(B	BRIGITTE THOMAS	V	(B	ARNO STEFFEN	V	(G
JEFF PORCARO	D	(G	STEVE LUKATHER	G B	(G	TIM MAY	G	(G	ROBERT GREENRIDGE	D	(G
NEAL STUBENHAUS	B	(G	ALAN ESTES	PERC	(G	PETER CHRISTLIEB	SAX	(G	MIKE GONG	G V	(G
DAVID HUNGATE	B	(G	JIM HITE		(G	VANETTA FIELD	V	(G	MAXINE WILLARD	V	(G
JULIA TILLMAN	V	(G	BRIGITTE WITT	V	(G	HINNA DOLITZSCH	V	(G	CATRIN PROPPER	V	(G

T144 TROGGS T144

Member	Inst	Albums	Album	Release
REG PRESLEY	V	(1	FROM NOWHERE	1966 FONTANA UK ST 5355
CHRIS BRITTON	G	(1	TROGGLODYNAMITE	1966 PAGE ONE UK POL 001
PETE STAPLES	B	(1	WILD THING	1966 ATCO US SD 33193
RONNIE BOND	D	(1	WILD THING	1966 FONTANA 27556
TONY MURRAY	B	(	GIVE IT TO ME	1966 FONTANA 85001
COLIN FLETCHER	G	(	CELLOPHANE	1967 PAGE ONE POL 003
CALEB QUAYE	G	(	BEST OF VOL 1	1967 PAGE ONE FPR 001
IAN AMEY	G	(	BEST OF VOL 2	1967 PAGE ONE FOR 002
RICHARD MOORE	G	(	LOVE IS ALL AROUND	1968 FONTANA SRF 67576
PETER GREEN	G	(	MIXED BAG	1968 PAGE ONE POLS 012
			HIP HIP HOORAY	1968 HANSA GERM 78595
			THE TOP OF THE TROGGS	1968 HANSA GERM 77817
			TROGGLOMANIA	1969 PAGE ONE POS 602
			CONTRAST	1970 SILVERLINE DJSL 009
			THE TROGGS	1975 PENNYFARTHING UK PEN 543
			THE TROGGS	1975 PYE US 12112
			THE TROGG TAPES	1976 PENNYFARTHING UK PELS 551
			A GIRL LIKE YOU	1975 DJM DJML26047
			THE ORIGINAL TROGG TAPES	1976 DJM DJM 44314
			THE ORIGINAL TROGG TAPES	1976 PRIVATE STOCK US 2008
			POP CHRONIK	19 HANSA GERM 87574
			VINTAGE YEARS	1976 SIRE 3714 2
			WILD THING	1979 CHEVRON CHV 155
			LIVE AT MAX'S KANSAS CITY	1980 BASEMENT 6006
			LIVE AT MAX'S KANSAS CITY	1981 MKC US 214 UK 100
			BLACK BOTTON	1981 NEW ROSE FR 4

T145 DOMENIC TROIANO T145

Member	Inst	Albums	Album	Release
DOMENIC TROIANO	G V	(ALL	(A) DOMENIC TROIANO	1972 MERCURY US SRM1 639 UK 6338105
PENTI GLEN	D	(A	(B) TRICKY	1973 MERCURY US SRM1 670
HUGH SULLIVAN	K	(A	(C) BURNING AT THE STAKE	1977 CAPITOL 11665
PRAKASH JOHN	B	(A	(D) JOKES ON ME	197 CAPITOL 11772
WILLIAM SMITH	K V	(AB	(E) FRET FEVER	1979 CAPITOL GERM 064 85893 US 11932
ROY KENNER	PERC V	(ABE		

Member	Inst	Albums	Member	Inst	Albums	Member	Inst	Albums	Member	Inst	Albums
TESSE CALDERONE	V	(AB	SHAUN JACKSON	V	(AB	BUNK GARDNER	SAX	(A	BUZZ GARDNER	TPT	(A
TJAY CANTRELLI	SAX	(A	LONNIE SHETTER	CLAR	(A	PAUL DELONG	D	(E	DAVE TYSON	K V	(E
BOB WILSON	B V	(E	KEN RICE	D	(B	WILLIE WEEKS	B	(B	MONT STARK	SYN	(B
GAYLE LEVANT	HARP	(B	PAT HOLLOWAY	V	(B	JOHN WEIDER	VLN	(B	ERNIE WATTS	SAX	(B
MARION CHILDERS	TPT	(B	DOUG RICHARDSON	SAX	(B	TOM SCOTT	TPT	(B	WILLIAM GREEN	WIND	(B
JOHN KELSO	SAX	(B	RED RHODES	STEEL	(A						

T145A TRONICS T145A

Member	Inst	Albums	Album	Release
GABY DE VIVUENNE		(A	(A) LOVE BACKED BY FORCE	1981 ALIEN BEALIEN UK 3

T146 TROOPER T146

Member	Inst	Albums	Album	Release
RAY McGUIRE	V HCA	(ALL	(A) TROOPER	1976 EPIC UK 81618 US MCA 2149
BRIAN SMITH	G V	(ALL	(B) TWO FOR THE SHOW	1977 US MCA 2214
HARRY KALENSKY	B V	(A	(C) KNOCK 'EM DEAD KID	1977 EPIC UK 82296 US MCA 2275
TOMMY STEWART	D V	(ALL	(D) FLYING COLOURS	1979 MCA UK MCF3039 US MCA 3173
RANDY BACHMAN	G	(ABC	(E) THICK AS THIEVES	1978 MCA US 2377
FRANK LUDWIG	K V	(BCDE	(F) TROOPER	1980 MCA US 5151
DONI UNDERHILL	B V	(BCDEF	(G) HOT SHOT	1980 MCA US 3222
ROBERT DEANS	K	(F		

T147 JOHN TROPEA T147

Member	Inst	Albums	Album	Release
JOHN TROPEA	G V SYN	(ALL	(A) JOHN TROPEA	1976 JAYBOY JSL7 MARLIN 2200
WILL LEE	B V	(ABC	(B) SHORT TRIP TO SPACE	1977 TK 14061
RICK MAROTTA	D	(ABC	(C) TO TOUCH YOU AGAIN	1979 MARLIN US 2222 +TK UK 83355
EARL CHAPIN	HRNS	(B		

Member	Inst	Albums	Member	Inst	Albums	Member	Inst	Albums	Member	Inst	Albums
DON GROLNICK	K	(ABC	LEON PENDARVIS	ORG	(BC	RUBENS BASSINI	PERC	(ABC	DAVE TAYLOR	TROM	(ABC
RALPH MACDONALD	PERC	(B	JEFF KING	SAX	(B	RON CARTALEMI	V	(B	RANDY BRECKER		(ABC
JEFF KAWALEK	V	(B	MICHAEL BRECKER	WIND	(ABC	CHARLES BLACKWELL	V	(B	DAVID SPINOZZA	G	(B
DUNCAN CLEARY	V	(B	MARGARET ROSS	HARP	(B	BRIAN DRAKE	V	(B	RICHARD DAVIS	B	(B
BRUCE GOLDBERG	V	(B	MIKE MAINIERI	VIBES	(B	BILL GUERRA	V	(B	ROMEO PENQUE	WIND	(B
STEVE GADD	D	(AB	RON JANNELLI	WIND	(B	LANI GROVES	V	(B	GEORGE YOUNG	HRNS	(ABC
JIM BUFFINGTON	HRNS	(B	LEW DEL GATTO	WIND	(ABC	LOU MARINI	WIND	(BC	EUMIR DEODATO	K	(A
ELLEN SEELING	TPT	(B	TONY PRICE	HRNS	(BC	JOHN GATCHELL	HRNS	(A	ALAN RUBIN	HRNS	(AC
ALLEN SCHWARZBERG	D	(A	DON PAYNE	B	(A	KENNY ASCHER	K	(A	RON TROPEA	PERC	(AC
NICK REMO	PERC	(A	C CONRAD		(A	DAVE SANBORN	SAX	(AC	BOB MINTZER	FLT	(A
GEORGE OPALISKY	WIND	(A	KEN BERGER	WIND	(A	JEANNIE FINEBERG	SAX	(B	SAM BURTIS	TROM	(ABC
STEVE JORDAN	D	(C	PAUL SCHAEFFER	K	(C	RICHARD TEE	K	(C	JON FADDIS	WIND	(C
LUTHER VANDROSS	V	(C	DIVA GRAY	V	(C	JOCELYN SHAW	V	(C	JIM MAELEN	PERC	(C
BARRY ROGERS	HRNS	(C	STRING SECTION		(ABC						

T148 ROBIN TROWER T148

ROBIN TROWER G (ALL (A) TWICE REMOVED FROM YESTERDAY 1973 CHRYSALIS CHR1039 GER 6307 513
JIMMY DEWAR B V (ABCDEFGH (B) BRIDGE OF SIGHS 1974 CHRYSALIS CHR 1057
REG ISADORE D (AB (C) FOR EARTH BELOW 1975 CHRYSALIS CHR1073
BILL LORDAN D (CDEFGHJ (D) LIVE 1975 CHRYSALIS CHR1089
RUSTY ALLEN B (FG (E) LONG MISTY DAYS 1976 CHRYSALIS CHR1107
PAULINHO DA COSTA PERC (G (F) CITY DREAMS 1977 CHRYSALIS CHR1148 GER 6307 610
JACK BRUCE B (J (G) CARAVAN TO MIDNIGHT 1978 CHRYSALIS CHR1189 GER 6307 630
(H) VICTIM OF FURY 1980 CHRYSALIS CHR1215
(J) BRUCE, LORDAN, TROWER B L T 1981 CHRYSALIS CHR1324 GER 203 384

T149 DORIS TROY T149

DORIS TROY V (ALL (A) DORIS TROY 1970 APPLE US ST3371 UK SAPCOR 13
WINSTON DELANDRO G (B (B) STRETCHING OUT 1974 POLYDOR PLEO 12
KEN ELLIOT SYN (B (C) RAINBOW TESTAMENT 19 POLYDOR 2956 001
HUX BROWN G (B (D) JUST ONE LOOK 19 ATLANTIC UK 2464 001 US 8088
JACKIE JACKSON B (B
ROSETTA HIGHTOWER V (B PHIL CHEN B (B ROY DAVIES SYN (B RAD BRYAN G (B
WINSTON WRIGHT K (B JOANNE WILLIAMS V (B GLADSTONE ANDERSON V (B WINSTON GRENNAN V (B
DORIS PAYNE V (B

T149A ROGER TROY T149A

ROGER TROY (A (A) ROGER TROY 1976 RCA US APLI 1910

T149B TROYKA T149B

MIKE RICHARDS V D (A (A) TROYKA 1970 COTILLION US SD9020
ROBERT EDWARDS G MAND V(A
RUMOR LUKAWIETSKY B PERC V(A

T149C TRUCK STOP T149C

LUCIUS REICHLING V (ABC (A) TRUCK STOP 1973 TELEFUNKEN GER 14742
RAINER BACH G K V(ABC (B) CANT STOP TRUCK STOP 1974 TELEFUNKEN GER 14783
ERICH DOLL G BAN(ABC (C) KEEP ON TRUCKING 1975 TELEFUNKEN GER 622142
CISCO BERND B V (ABC
ECKART (ABC HOFFMAN WIND (ABC TEDDY IBING D (ABC MICHAEL REINECKE K G V(C

T150 WILLIAM TRUCKAWAY T150

WILLIAM TRUCKAWAY V G K(A (A) BREAKAWAY 1976 REPRISE US 6469 UK K44165
ED BOGAS VLN MAND VIBES(A
BOBBY CASTRO PERC (A RUSSELL DASHIELL G (A TERRY DOLAN G (A BILL DOUGLAS B (A
JOHN NONZIATO CONG V(A BUDDY EMMONS STEEL(A RICHARD GREENE VLN (A LARRY HANKS JEWSHARP(A
DAVID HAYES B (A DOUG KILMER B (A WALT KOKEN BANJO FDL (A FRANK MESTROPASQUA V (A
DOC STORCH V (A JOHN WATSON V (A CHARLES LLOYD FLT (A NORM MAYELL D V (A
DALLAS WILLIAMS V PERC(A STOVALL SISTERS V (A ARCELLO GARCIA V (A VICTOR QUINONES V (A
JOHN RODRIGUEZ V (A

T150A ANDREA TRUE CONNECTION T150A

ANDREA TRUE V (A (A) WHITE WITCH 1977 BUDDAH 5702
CHRISTOPHER CARROLL D (A
KEN WALLACE K (A RALPH AGRESTA G V (A TOM CAREY B V (A JOE BARBOSA G V (A

T150B TRUE CONFESSIONS T150B

JULIA BOURQUE G V (A (A) TRUE CONFESSIONS 1980 BOMB US 7033 LINE GER LLP5089
GLEN BINMORE G V (A
BLANCHE BEUBE K V (A TERRY McCUBBEN D (A MARK FOURNIER B (A JOHN HAMILTON D (A

T151 TRUK T151

MOBY ANDERSON B (A (A) TRUK TRACKS 1971 CBS US 30005 UK 64367
BILL DAFFERN D (A
MIKE GRAHAM V (A PAT GRAHAM K (A GLENN TOWNSEND G (A

T151A TRUST T151A

BERNARD BONVOISIN V (AB (A) REPRESSION 1981 CBS UK 84958
NONO G (B (B) SAVAGE 1982 EPIC UK 85546
VIVI B (B
MOHO G (B NICKO D (B

T151B TRUTH T151B

(A) TRUTH 1975 ROULETTE US 3014

T152 TUBES T152

FEE WAYBILL V (ALL (A) THE TUBES 1975 A&M US SP 4534 UK AMLH64534
BILL SPOONER G (ALL (B) YOUNG & RICH 1976 A&M US SP 4580 UK AMLH64580
VINCE WELNICK K (ABCDEFG (C) NOW 1977 A&M US SP 4632 UK AMLH64632
RICK ANDERSON B (ABCDEFG (D) WHAT DO YOU WANT FROM LIVE 1978 A&M US SP 6003 UK AMLM68460
MICHAEL COTTEN SYN (ABCDEFG (E) REMOTE CONTROL 1979 A&M US SP 4751 UK AMLH64751
ROGER STEEN G (ABCDEFG (F) COMPLETION BACKWARDS PRINCIPLE 1981 CAPITOL US 12151 UK 26285
PRAIRIE PRINCE D (ABCDEFG (G) BEST OF 1981 A&M
RE STYLES V DANCE(ACDE (EP) WHITE PUNKS ON DOPE 1978 A&M AMS 7323
MINGO LEWIS PERC (CDEF

T153 TUBEWAY ARMY T153

GARY NUMAN V K G(ABC (A) TUBEWAY ARMY 1978 BEGGARS BANQUET UK BEGA 4
PAUL GARDINER B (AB (A) TUBEWAY ARMY 1978 BEGGARS BANQUET GER 146510
JESS LIDYARD D (AB (A) TUBEWAY ARMY 1978 BEGGARS BANQUET NL 660048
(B) REPLICAS 1979 BEGGARS BANQUET UK BEGA7
(B) REPLICAS 1979 ATCO US 38117
(B) REPLICAS 1979 BEGGARS BANQUET GER 146519
(C) THAT'S TOO BAD(EP) 1979 BEGGARS BANQUET UK BACK2

T153A TANIA TUCKER T153A

TANIA TUCKER V (ALL (A) DELTA DAWN 1972 CBS US 31742
PIG ROBBINS K (F (B) WHATS YOUR MAMA'S NAME 1973 CBS US 32272
JERRY CARRIGAN D (F (C) WOULD YOU LAY WITH ME 1974 CBS US 32744
JACK WILLIAMS B (F (D) GREATEST HITS 1975 CBS US 33355
BILLY SANFORD G (F (E) GREATEST HITS 1975 EMBASSY 31180
GLENN KEENER G (F (F) LOVIN' & LEARNIN' 1976 MCA US 2167 UK MCF2741
STEVE GIBSON G (F (G) TANYA TUCKER 1976 MCA US 2141 UK MCF 2713
PETE DRAKE STEEL(F (H) HERES SOME LOVE 197 MCA US 2213 UK MCF 2722
CHARLIE McCOY HCA (F (J) RIDIN RAINBOWS 1976 MCA US 2253
BERGEN WHITE V (F (K) YOU ARE SO BEAUTIFUL 1977 EMBASSY UK 31568
CHARLIE DANIELS FDL (F (L) WOULD YOU LAY WITH ME 1978 EMBASSY UK 31690

(CONTINUED)

T153A **TANIA TUCKER** (CONTINUED) T153A

JANIE FRICKE V (F (M) GREATEST HITS 1978 MCA US 3032
LARRY GATLIN V (F (N) TEAR ME APART 1979 MCA UK MCF 3048
JERRY CRUTCHFIELD V (F (O) DREAM LOVERS 1981 MCA UK MCF 3109
JERRY SWALLOW G MAND(N
BILL ANDERSON G V (N BEAU SEGAL D (N STEVE GOLDSTEIN K V (N JEFF EYRICH B (N
LUTHER WATERS V (N MAXINE WILLARD V(N JULIA TILLMAN V (N RUSTY BUCHANAN V (N
LYNDA LEE LAWLEY V (N SUE RICHMAN V (N SNDREA ROBINSON V (N JERRY PETERSON SAX (N
OREN WATERS V (N

T154 **TOMMY TUCKER** T154

TOMMY TUCKER V K D(A (A) MOTHER TUCKER 1977 RED LIGHTNING UK RL 022
LARRY HOLLOWAY D (A ( ) HIGH HEELED SNEAKERS 19 CHECKER US 2990
WELDON DEAN YOUNG G (A
BRENDA JONES B (A JOHNNY WILLIAMS D (A EDDIE WILLIAMS TPT (A MICKEY BAKER G (A
SCOTT ALLEN B (A GENE ROBERTS PNO (A DONNY HATHAWAY K (A PAUL WILLIAMS SAX (A
BUDDY LEWIS SAX (A DONNIE FITZ V (A ROBERT BANKS K (A GENE JOHNSON K (A
GREG FITZ K (A PAZANT BROTHERS HRNS (A LEO GATEWOOD D (A

T155 **TUCKY BUZZARD** T155

TERRY TAYLOR G (ABCD (A) WARM SLASH 1969 CAPITOL US 787
DAVE BROWN B (ABCD (B) COMING ON AGAIN 1971 CAPITOL US 864
TIM HENDERSON V (ABCD (C) ALRIGHT ON THE NIGHT 1973 PURPLE UK TPSA 7510 BASF 291367
NICK GRAHAM K (AB (C) ALRIGHT ON THE NIGHT 1973 PASSPORT US 97001
DON WELLER HRNS (C (D) BUZZARD 1973 PURPLE UK TPSA 7512
JOHN LEE TROM (D (D) BUZZARD 1973 PASSPORT US 98001
PAUL FRANCIS D (AB
CHRIS JOHNSON D (CAD RON TAYLOR G (C PHIL TALBOT G (D PAUL KENDRICK G V (CD
TONY ASHTON K (D RICKY DODD SAX (D JEFF WORKMAN PNO (C BILL WYMAN PNO (D
NOEL NORRIS TPT (D PHIL CORDELL PNO (C

T155A **TONY TUFF** T155A

SANTA D (A (A) TONY TUFF 1980 GROVE MUSIC UK ILPS9619
CLINTON FERRON B (A
ALRICK FORBES G V (A ALBERT GRIFFITHS G (A ANSEL COLLINS K (A SKULLY PERC(A
MICHAEL PROPHET V (A YABBY U V (A

T155B **TENPOLE TUDOR** T155B

TENPOLE TUDOR (AB (A) EDDIE, OLD BOB, DICK & GARY 1980 STIFF UK SEEZ 31
(B) LET THE FOUR WINDS BLOW 1981 STIFF UK SEEZ 42

T156 **TUFF DARTS** T156

JEFF SALEN G (A (A) TUFF DARTS 1978 SIRE UK 6048
JOHN DI SALVO B (A
BOB BUTANI G (A JAMES MORRISON D (ROBERT GORDON V (KEVIN COLNEY V (
TOMMY FRENZY V (A JOHN MORELLI D (A JOHN CRISCIONE V (A RONALD ARDITO V (
ART LAMONICA V (A GEORGE YOUNG SAX (A LEW DELGATTO SAX (A RALPH SCHUCKETT PNO (A
LANCE QUINN G (A ERIC WEISSBERG STEEL(A IAN HUNTER K (A BOB CLEARMOUNTAIN B(A

T157 **TUNDRA** T157

CHRIS STAINTON K (A (A) TUNDRA 1976 DECCA UK SKLR5259
GLEN TURNER B (A
HENRY SPINETTI D (A CHARLIE HARRISON B V (A

T157A **GORDON TURNER** T157A

GORDON TURNER (A (A) MEDITATION 1969 CHARISMA UK CAS 1009

T157B **TUNES** T157B

(A) TRUTH JUSTICE & MANCUNIAN WAY(EP) 19 RHESUS GO APE1

T157C **TURN UPS** T157C

JOE GEAR D (A (A) TURN UP 1980 CRACKED US CRLP2
STEVINYL G V (A
R FINGERS DELLER B (A

T157D **TURKEY** T157D

(A) TURKEY 197 CHRYSALIS UK/US 1010

T158 **IKE & TINA TURNER** T158

IKE TURNER G V ACID QUEEN (TINA) 1975 UA US LA495 UK UNS29875
TINA TURNER V AIRWAVES 1979 UA US LA917
P P ARNOLD V AND THE RAELETTES 19 TANGERINE US 15611
VANETTA FIELDS V (R BAD DREAMS 1973 US UK UAS29549
MERRY CLAYTON V BEST OF 19 BLUE THUMB US 49
BONNIE BRAMLETT V BLACK ANGEL 1976 MUSIDISC CV1342
EDWARD BURKS TROM (NP BLUES ROOTS (IKE) 1972 UA US 5576 UK UAG29326
McKINLEY JOHNSON TPT (NP BLACK MANS SOUL 19 POMPEII US 6003
MARY REED SAX (N COME TOGETHER 1970 LIBERTY US 7637 UK LBS83350
JACKIE CLARK G (NP CONFINED TO SOUL (IKE) 19 UA US 061
SOKO RICHARDSON D (NP THE COUNTRY OF TINA TURNER 19 UA US 200
WARREN DAWSON B (NP CUSSIN' CRYIN' AND CARRYING ON 19 POMPEII US 6004
J D REED SAX (N DELILAHS POWER 1977 UA US 707 UK UAS30040
DAVID GARLAND (P DANCE WITH 19 SUE US 2003
CLAUDE WILLIAMS (P DYNAMITE 19 SUE US 2004
JIMMIE SMITH (P DONT PLAY ME CHEAP 19 SUE US 2005
ANDRE CECCARELLI D (M FANTASTIC 1969 SUNSET US 5265 UK SLS50205
BERNIE ARCADIO K (M FEEL GOOD 1972 UA US 5598 UK UAS29377
JAYCEE CHANAVAT G (M FUNKY MULE 1975 DJM DJSLM2010
TONY BONFILS B (M FESTIVAL OF LIVE PERFORMANCES 19 KENT US 538
MANU ROCHE PERC (M FESTIVAL OF LIVE PERFORMANCES 19 UNITED US 7755
GEORGES RODI SYN (M GREATEST HITS 19 WB US 1810 UK K36001
GEORGE MARGE OBOE (M GREATEST HITS 197 UA US LA592
TOM MALONE TROM (M GREATEST HITS 197 SUNSET US 5285
WAYNE ANDRE TROM (M GREATEST HITS 196 SUE US 1038
BARRY ROGERS TROM (M GREATEST HITS 19 HALLMARK 563
DAVE TAYLOR TROM (M GREATEST HITS 196 LONDON UK HAC8248
MICHAEL BRECKER SAX (M GREAT ALBUM 1974 ALBUM ALB 148
LAWRENCE FELDMAN SAX (M GOSPEL ACCORDING TO 19 UA
GEORGE YOUNG SAX (M GET IT GET IT 19 CENCO US 104
LEW DELGATTO SAX (M HER MAN HIS WOMAN 1970 CAPITOL US ST 571 VMP 1013
RANDY BRECKER TPT (M HUNTER 1970 BLUE THUMB US BTS11

(CONTINUED)

T158 (CONTINUED) IKE & TINA TURNER T158

JON FADDIS TPT (M
ALAN RUBIN TPT (M
PETER BUNETTA D (R
BILL HAYNES B (R
RONNY STOCKERT K (R
MICHAEL BODDICKER SYN (R
AIRTO MOREIRA PERC (R
MAXAYN LEWIS V (R
STEPHANIE SPRUILL V (R
DEBORAH LINDSEY V (R
JULIA TILLMAN V (R
DENISE ECHOLS V (R
AL CINER G (R
KEN MOORE PNO V(R
W D SMITH ORG (R
TONY WALTHERS V (R
MICHAEL STEPHENSON V (R
ED GREENE D (R
DENNIS BELFIELD B (R
MARY RUSSELL V (R
RICK KELLIS SAX (R
BILL OZ HCA (R

Title	Year	Label	Catalogue
HUNTER	1970	HARVEST	UK SHSP4001
IKE & TINA	1975	DJM	DJMD 8006
IKE & TINA SHOW II	19	TOMATO	US
IKE & TINA SHOW II	19	WB	US 1568
IKE & TINA SHOW	19	LOMA	5112
IKE & TINA SHOW	1966	WB	1579
IKE TURNER ROCKS THE BLUES(IKE)	19	CROWN	US 367
IKE TURNER & THE KINGS OF RHYTHM	1980	ACE	UK CH22
IKE TURNER & THE KINGS OF RHYTHM	19	SUE	US 2004
ITS GONNA WORK OUT FINE	19	SUE	2007
IKE & TINA TURNER	19	CENCO	US 5031
IN PERSON	1969	MINIT	US 24018 UK 40014
I'M TORE UP	1978	RED LIGHTNIN'	UK RL0016
LIVE IN PARIS	19	LIBERTY	LBS83468/9
(L) LET ME TOUCH YOUR MIND(TINA)	1973	UA	US 5660 UK UAS29423
(M) LOVE EXPLOSION	1978	UA	UK UAG30267
(N) NUFF SAID	1971	UA	US 5530 UK UAG29256
NUTBUSH CITY LIMITS	1973	UA	US 180 UK UAS29557
OOH POO PAH DOO	19	HARMONY	US 30400
OUTTA SEASON	19	SUNSET	UK SLS50314
OUTTA SEASON	19	BLUE THUMB	US BT5
ON STAGE	19	VALIANT	UK VS 118
PEACHES	19	POLYDOR	UK 2916 020
PLEASE PLEASE PLEASE	19	KENT	US 550
QUEEN	1975	SPRINGBOARD	US 4033
(R) ROUGH (TINA)	1979	UA	UK UAG30211
REVUE	1975	NEW WORLD	MW 6006
RIVER DEEP & MOUNTAIN HIGH	1975	A&M	US 4178 UK AMLP8013
RIVER DEEP & MOUNTAIN HIGH	197	PHILLES	118 4011
RIVER DEEP & MOUNTAIN HIGH	1966	LONDON	UK SHU 8298
RIVER DEEP & MOUNTAIN HIGH	1970	MAYFAIR	UK AMLB1021
RIVER DEEP & MOUNTAIN HIGH	197	MFP	UK 50443
SO FAR	19	MUSIDISC	CV 1262
SOUL OF	19	KENT	US 519
SOUL OF	19	SUE	2001
SOUL SELLERS(COMP)	1980	LIBERTY	UK LBR 1002
SOMETHINGS GOT A HOLD OF ME	19	HARMONY	US 30567
STRANGE FRUIT	1974	UA	UK UAG29316
SWEET RHODE ISLAND RED	1974	UA	UK UAS29681
SIXTEEN GREAT PERFORMANCES	1975	ABC	US 4014 UK ABCL5123
SOULED FROM THE VAULTS	1975	DJM	DJLMD8006
SUPER ORIGINAL SESSIONS	1975	MUSIDISC	ALB 169
SO FINE	196	LONDON	UK SHU 8370
SO FINE	196	POMPEII	US 6000
TOO HOT TO HOLD	19	SPRINGBOARD	4011
TOO HOT TO HOLD	19	PICKWICK	US 3284
VERY BEST OF	1976	UA	UK UAS29948
WORLD OF	1973	UA	US 064 UK UAD60043
WORKING TOGETHER	1971	LIBERTY	US 7650 UK LBS83455
WHAT YOU HEAR	1971	UA	US 995 UAD60005/6

T159 NIK TURNER T159

NIK TURNER V WIND(AB
STEVE HILLAGE G (A
TIM BLAKE SYN (A
ALAN POWELL PERC (A MIQUETTE GIRAUDY SYN (A MORRIS PERT PERC (A MIKE HOWLETT B(A

Title	Year	Label	Catalogue
(A) XITINTODY	1978	CHARISMA	UK CDS 4011
(B) PASS OUT (INNER CITY)	19		

T160 TURNING POINT T160

JEFF CLYNE B (AB
BRIAN MILLER K (AB
DAVID T D BALL SAX (AB
PEPE LEMER V (AB PAUL ROBINSON D (AB

Title	Year	Label	Catalogue
(A) CREATURES OF THE NIGHT	1977	GULL	UK GULP 1022
(B) SILENT PROMISES	1978	GULL	UK GULP 1027

T161 TURTLES T161

HOWARD KAYLAN K V (ALL
MARK VOLMAN G V (ALL
JOHN SEITER K V D(EGF
AL NICHOL K V B G(ALL
DON MURRAY D (1
JIM PONS G B V(3F
CHUCK PORTZ B (12
JIM TUCKER G (123
JOHN BARBATA D (3E
(1) 1965
(2) 1965
(3) 1966

Title	Year	Label	Catalogue
(A) IT AINT ME BABY	1965	WHITE WHALE	US WWS 7111
(B) YOU BABY	1966	WHITE WHALE	US WWS 7112
(C) HAPPY TOGETHER	1966	WHITE WHALE	US WWS 7114
(C) HAPPY TOGETHER	1967	LONDON	UK HAU 8330
(D) GOLDEN HITS	1967	WHITE WHALE	US WWS 7115
(E) BATTLE OF THE BANDS	1968	WHITE WHALE	UK 8904 US WWS7118
(E) BATTLE OF THE BANDS	1968	LONDON	UK SHU 8376
(F) TURTLE SOUP	1969	WHITE WHALE	US WWS 7124
(G) MORE GOLDEN HITS	1970	WHITE WHALE	US WWS 7127
(H) WOODEN HEAD	1970	WHITE WHALE	US WWS 7133
(J) HAPPY TOGETHER AGAIN	1975	PHILIPS	9299 425
(K) HAPPY TOGETHER AGAIN(DBL)	1975	SIRE	US 3703
(EP) 1968	1978	RHINO	US RNPD 901

T161A TUXEDOMOON T161A

STEVE BROWN K V SAX (AB
BLAINE REININGER VLN V K G B(AB
PETER PRINCIPLE B G SYN(AB
WINSTON TONG V (B VICKY ASPINALL VLN (B AL ROBINSON CELLO(B

Title	Year	Label	Catalogue
(A) HALF MUTE	1980	RALPH	US TX 8004
(B) DESIRE	1981	RALPH	US UK PRE PREX4

T161B TUSH T161B

DANNY LADEMACHER (A

Title	Year	Label	Catalogue
(A) WE'RE JUST THE BOYS	1980	EMI	EURO 29679

T161C TOMMY TUTONE T161C

TOMMY HEATH G V (AB
JIM KELLER G (A
MICKEY SHINE D (AB
TERRY NAILS B (AB

Title	Year	Label	Catalogue
(A) TOMMY TUTONE	1980	CBS	US 36372
(B) 2	1981	CBS	

T161D TWEEDS T161D

JEFF MEZZROW G V B(A — (A) PERFECT FIT — 1980 AUTOBAHN TDS 1230
GEORGE GODDING V PERC(A
MARK McHUGH G V (A — GORDON WALLACE D V (A — KENNY G PNO (A

T162 TWENTIETH CENTURY STEEL BAND T162

MARTIN JAMES PERC V(B — (A) WARM HEART, COLD STEEL — 1975 UA UK UAK 29878
MIKEY BRUMONT PERC V(B — (B) YELLOW BIRD IS DEAD — 1976 UA UK UAS 29980
WINSTON FINDLEY PERC V(B
MICHAEL OLIVER PERC(B — GODFRUN MOORE PERC (B — GIDEON ROGERS PERC (B — LUCIANO BRAVO PERC(B
TREVOR WILLIAMS PERC V(B — COLLINS MOORE D V (B — MIKE D'ALBERQUERQUE B (B — TERRY TAYLOR G (B

T162A TWENTY SIXTY SIX T162A

VEIT MARVOS K V (A — (A) AND THEN — 1972 UA UK UAS 29314
STEVE ROBINSON SYN K(A
GEFF HARRISON V (A — GAGEY MROZECK G V (A — DIETER BAUER B (A — KONSTANTIN BOMMARIUS D(A

T162B 20/20 T162B

STEVE ALLEN G V (A — (A) 20/20 — 1980 PORTRAIT US 36205 UK PRT 83898
RON FLYNT B V (A — (B) LOOK OUT — 1981 PORTRAIT US 37050
MIKE GALLO D (A
CHRIS SILAGYI G V SYN(A — PHIL SEYMOUR V (A

T163 TWICE AS MUCH T163

DAVE SKINNER (AB — (A) OWN UP — 1966 IMMEDIATE UK IMSP 007
ANDREW ROSE (AB — (B) THAT'S ALL — 1968 IMMEDIATE UK IMSP 013
NICKY HOPKINS K (
JOHN McLAUGHLIN G (A — ANDY WHITE D (A — JIMMY PAGE G (A — JIM SULLIVAN G (A
ALAN WEIGHALL G (A — JOE MORETTI G (A — ERIC FORD (A

T164 DWIGHT TWILLEY T164

DWIGHT TWILLEY G K V PERC(ALL — (A) SINCERELY — 1976 SHELTER UK ISA5012 US 52001
PHIL SEYMOUR D B V(ABC — (B) TWILLEY DONT MIND — 1977 SHELTER UK ISA5015 US ARISTA4140
BILL PITCOCK IV B G (ABCDE — (C) TWILLEY — 1979 ARISTA US 4214
JOHNNY JOHNSON B (AB — (D) BLUE PRINT — 1980 ARISTA US 4251
LEON RUSSELL PNO B(A — (E) SCUBA DIVER — 1982 EMI US 17064
ROGER LINN G (A
JERRY NAIFEH D (ACD — JIM LEWIS B D (CD — JIMMY HASKELL STR (A — NOAH SHARK PERC(CE
GREG BLOCH VLN (C — BENMONT TENCH K (E — BRIAN QUALIS B (E

T165 TWINK T165

TWINK D V (AB — (A) THINK PINK — 1970 POLYDOR GER 2310057 UK 2343 032
KID ROGERS G V (B — (B) DO IT (EP) WITH THE FAIRIES) — 1978 CHISWICK UK SW 26
CHRIS CHESNEY G (B
LITTLE JOHN G (B — DANGER SUN B (B — FINGERS FALCONER K (B

T165A TWINKEYZ T165A

DONNIE JUPITER G B V(A — (A) ALPHA JERK — 1979 PLUREX 1000
HONEY V G B(A
KEITH McKEE D V (A — TOM DARLING G V B (A — DAVID L HOUSTON B SYN(A

T166 THE TWINKLE BROTHERS T166

RALSTON GRANT G V (CD — (A) DO YOUR OWN THING — 1977 CARIB' GEMS
ERIC BERNARD B V PNO (CD — (B) LOVE (10") — 1978 FRONT LINE UK FCL 5001
NORMAN GRANT D V (CD — (C) PRAISE JAH — 1979 FRONT LINE UK FL 1041
BONGO ASHER PERC (CD — (D) COUNTRYMEN — 1980 VIRGIN UK V 2169
KARL HYATT V PERC(CD — (E) ME NO YOU — 1981 TWINKLE NG 632
DERRICK BROWN B (C
TERRY BARHAM G (D — ASHTON GRANT G (C — P HURLOCK G (C — MICHAEL DAN PNO (C
ARNOLD BRECKENRIDGE SYN(C — TOMMY McCOOK HRNS (C — VIN GORDON HRNS (C — RANCHIE B (C
DAVIDSON DUBOIS G B (D — MICHAEL SMITH D (D

T166A TWIST T166A

STEVE CORDUNER D (A — (A) THIS IS YOUR LIFE — 1979 POLYDOR UK 2383 552
WIMS G V (A
PETE MARSH G V (A — ANDY PASK B (A — STEVE NAIVE K (A — ELVIS COSTELLO V (A
JIMMY EDWARDS V (A

T166B TWISTED SISTER T166B

DEE SNYDER V (A — (A) UNDER THE BLADE — 1982 SECRET UK SEC x9
EDDIE OJEDA G (A
JAY JAY FRENCH G (A — MARK MENDOZA B (A — A J PERO D (A — EDDIE CLARKE G (A

T167 CONWAY TWITTY T167

CONWAY TWITTY G V (ALL
LORETTA LYNN V (GKPRT
BOBBY WOOD K (C
MIKE LEECH B (C
HENRY STRZELECKI B (C
JERRY CARRIGAN D (C
REGGIE YOUNG G (C
JOHNNY CHRISTOPHER G (C
TROY SEALS G (C
JOHN HUGHEY STEEL(C
JACK HICKS BAN (C
DON SANDERS SAX (C
TOM BRANNON SAX V(C
LISA SILVER FDL (C
FARRELL MORRIS (C
SHELLEY KURLAND STR (C
LEA JANE BERINATI V (C
GINGER HOLLADAY V (C
JANIE FRICKE V (C
DWAYNE WEST V (C

SATURDAY NIGHT WITH CONWAY — 1959 MGM US C801 3786
HITS — 1960 MGM US 4799
GREATEST HITS — 19 MGM US 3849
TOUCH — 1961 MGM US 3943
HIT THE ROAD — 1964 MGM US 4217
CONWAY TWITTY — 1965 MGM METRO US 110
ROCK'N'ROLL STORY — 19 CONTOUR UK 2870 151
CONWAY TWITTY SINGS — 19 DECCA US 74724
LOOK INTO MY TEARDROPS — 19 DECCA US 74828
COUNTRY — 19 DECCA US 74913
HERE'S CONWAY TWITTY — 19 DECCA US 74990 UK MCA MUPS342
HERE'S CONWAY TWITTY — 1974 MCA UK MCF 2622
NEVER ENDING SONG OF LOVE — 1974 CORAL UK CDL 8006
I'M SO USED TO LOVING YOU — 197 CORAL US 20000
SHAKE IT UP — 19 PICKWICK US 3360
STAR SPANGLED SONGS — 19 M F P UK SPR90064
NEXT IN LINE — 1968 DECCA US 75062 MCA UK MUPS363
YOU KNOW I WOULDN'T LIE — 1969 DECCA US 75105 MCA UK MUPS386
YOU CANT TAKE COUNTRY OUT OF CONWAY — 1969 MGM US 4650
HELLO DARLIN' — 1970 DECCA US 75209 US MCA 19
I LOVE YOU MORE TODAY — 1970 MCA UK MUPS404
TO SEE MY ANGEL CRY — 1970 MCA UK MUPS412 UK RI MCF2639
TO SEE MY ANGEL CRY — 1970 DECCA US 75172
(G)WE ONLY MAKE BELIEVE — 1971 DECCA US 75251 MCA UK MUPS423
CONWAY TWITTY — 1971 MGM UK 2351 006
15 YEARS AGO — 1971 MCA UK MUPS426 MCA RI MCF2647

(CONTINUED)

T167 (CONTINUED) **CONWAY TWITTY** T167

15 YEARS AGO 1971 DECCA US 75248
I WONDER WHAT SHE'LL THINK 1972 MCA UK MUPS443 MCA RI MCF2653
HOW MUCH MORE CAN SHE STAND 1971 DECCA US 75276
I CAN'T SEE ME WITHOUT YOU 1972 DECCA US 75335
(P) LEAD ME ON 1972 DECCA US 75326
GREATEST HITS VOL 1 1972 DECCA US 75352
I CANT STOP LOVING YOU 1972 DECCA US 75361
SINGS THE BLUES 1972 MGM US 4837
TWENTY GREAT HITS 1972 MGM US 4884
SHE NEEDS SOMEONE TO HOLD HER 1973 MCA US 303
(K) LOUISIANA WOMAN/MISSISSIPPI MAN 1974 MCA US 335 UK MCF2539
YOU'VE NEVER BEEN THIS FAR BEFORE 1974 MCA US 359 UK MCF2557
CLINGING TO A SAVING HAND 1973 MCA US 376
HONKY TONK ANGEL 1974 MCA US 406
COUNTRY PARTNERS 1974 MCA US 427
I'M NOT THROUGH LOVING YOU YET 1974 MCA US 441
LINDA ON MY MIND 1975 MCA US 469 UK MCF2706
(R) FEELIN'S 1975 MCA UK MCF2717
HIGH PRIEST OF COUNTRY MUSIC 197 MCA US 2144
TWITTY 197 MCA US 2176
BEST OF 1976 MCA UK MCF2737
NOW & THEN 1976 MCA US 2206 UK MCF2760
(T) UNITED TALENT 1976 MCA UK MCF2764
GREATEST HITS 1976 MCA US 2235
BEST OF VOL 2 1977 MCA UK MCF2788
PLAY GUITAR PLAY 1977 MCA US 2262 UK MCF2798
DYNAMIC DUO 1977 MCA US 2278
I'VE ALREADY LOVED YOU IN MY MIND 1977 MCA US 2293
GEORGIA KEEPS PULLING MY RING 1978 MCA US 2328 UK MCF 2845
GREATEST HITS 1977 MCA US 2345
HONKY TONK HEROES 1978 MCA US 2372
VERY BEST OF 1978 MCA US 3043
ROCK'N'ROLL (DBL) 1978 POLYDOR FR 2624 031
SINGS THE GREAT COUNTRY HITS 1978 TEE VEE US 1010
CONWAY 1978 MCA US 3063 UK MCF 2878
(C)CROSSWINDS 1979 MCA US 3086 UK MCF 3038
VERY BEST OF LOETTA & CONWAY 1979 MCA US 3162
COUNTRY ROCK 1979 MCA FR 414039
TWO'S A PARTY 1980 MCA US 3190
HEART & SOUL 1981 MCA US 3210
REST YOUR LOVE 1980 MCA US 5138

T168A **TWO GUNS** T168A

KENNY BARKER G V (A — (A) BALL OUT 1979 CAPRICORN US 0224
BOBBY WILLIAMS G V (A
MIKE SCONCE B V (A PAT SPENCE D (A

T169 **TYCOON** T169

MARK KREIDER B V K(AB — (A) TYCOON 1979 ARISTA US 4215 UK ARTY 167
NORMAN MERSHON V (Ab — (B) TURN OUT THE LIGHTS 1981 ARISTA US 9555
MICHAEL FONFARA K SYN (A
MARK RIVERA SAX V(AB JON GORDON G SYN(AB RICHARD STEINBERG D(A BOB MESSANO G V (B
MIKE BROUN D (B KEITH TAYLOR K (B

T169A **TYGERS OF PAN TANG** T169A

ROBB WEIR G V (ABCD — (A) WILD CAT 1980 MCA US 3270 UK MCF3075 GER 202966
JESS COX V (A — (B) SPELLBOUND 1981 MCA UK MCF3104 GER 203621
BRIAN'BIG' DICK D (ABCD — (C) CRAZY NIGHTS 1981 MCA UK MCL3123 GER 204671
ROCKY B (ABCD — (D) THE CAGE 1982 MCA UK 3150
JOHN SYKES G (BC — (EP) CRAZY NIGHT 1981 MCA GER MCAT723
CHRIS GARIDES K (B
FRED PURSER K G (D JON DEVERILL V (BCD

T170 **SEAN TYLA & THE TYLA GANG** T170

SEAN TYLA G V (ABCD — (A) YACHTLESS 1977 BESERKLEY UK BSERK 11 US 0057
GERALD MOFFETT G (D — (A) YACHTLESS 1977 BESERKLEY GER 623 370
BRIAN TURRINGTON B (AB — (B) MOONPROOF 1978 BESERKLEY UK BSERK 16 US 0059
PAUL SIMMONS D (D — (B) MOONPROOF 1978 BESERKLEY GER 623 637
KEN WHALEY B (BC — (C) JUST POPPED OUT 1980 LINE GER 5068 POLYDOR 2391 463
REEBOP KWAKU BAAH PERC (D — (C) JUST POPPED OUT 1980 POLYDOR US 6281
BRUCE IRVINE G (ABC — (D) REDNECK IN BABYLON 1981 ZILCH GER 2324 184 UK RIEN 1
STEVE JONES V (C
PETER O'SULLIVAN B (A MIKE DESMARAIS D (ABC DEKE LEONARD G V K(A BAM KING G (C
MARTYN WATSON G V (C BUZZ CHANTER G (C MALCOLM MORLEY G (C TEX COMER B (C
NICK GARVEY B V (C MICK GROOM B V (CD BOB DAISLEY B (C ANDY BENNIE B (C
KEVIN KINSON K (C KENNY LAGUNA K V (C FRAN BYRNE D (C TIM ROPER D (C
PETE THOMAS D (C MIKE KELLIE D (C JOHN EARLE SAX (CD CARLENE CARTER V (CD
JOAN JETT V (C MARK DODSON V (C

T170A **ALVIN 'RED' TYLER** T170A

ALVIN'RED' TYLER (AB — (A) ROCKIN & ROLL 19 ACE US 1006
(B) TWISTIN' WITH MR SAX 19 ACE US 1021

T171 **BONNIE TYLER** T171

BONNIE TYLER V (ABC — (A) THE WORLD STARTS TONIGHT 1977 CHRYSALIS US 1140 RCA UK PL25063
KEVIN DUNN B (B — (B) NATURAL FORCE 1978 RCA UK PL25152
MICKY GIBBONS D (B — (B) ITS A HEARTACHE 1978 RCA US AFLI12821
ROGER BARM K (B — (C) DIAMOND CUT 1979 RCA US AFLI3072 UK PL25194
TAFF WILLIAMS G V (B
STEVE WOLFE G V (B PETER KING V (B

T172 **TYNDALL** T172

RUDOLF LANGER K (A — (A) SONNENLICHT 1980 SKY GERM SKY036
JURGEN KREHAN K (A — (B)
(C) REFLEXIONEN 1982 SKY GER SKY074

T173 JUDIE TZUKE T173

JUDIE TZUKE V (ALL — (A) WELCOME TO THE CRUISE — 1979 ROCKET UK TRAIN7
MO FOSTER B (A — (B) SPORTSCAR — 1980 ROCKET US 3249 UK TRAIN9
PETER VAN HOOKE D (A — (C) I AM PHOENIX — !)(! ROCKET UK TRAIN15
RAY RUSSELL G (A — (D) STAY WITH ME TILL DAWN — 1981 ROCKET US 27001
CHRIS PARREN K (A — (E) ROAD NOISE — 1982 CHRYSALIS UK CTY1405
JOHN PUNTER PERC (A — (F) SHOOT THE MOON — 1982 CHRYSALIS UK CDL 1382
ROY BABBINGTON B (A
MIKE PAXMAN PERC G(ABCDEF — SIMON PHILLIPS D (A — PAUL HART K SYN (A — PAUL MUGGLETON V (BCDE
JOHN EDWARDS B (BCEF — BOB NOBLE K (BCEF — CHARLIE MORGAN D (BCF — JEFF RICH D (BCEF
ANDY CLARK SYN CF — MARTIN DITCHAM PERC (C — EUGENE ORGAN G (C — MIKE ROGERS G (C
DON SNOW K (F — THE DRIBBLE BROS V (F

U1 UB40 U1

ALISTAIR CAMPBELL G V (ABC — (A) SIGNING OFF — 1980 GRADUATE GRADLP 2
ROBIN CAMPBELL G (ABC — (B) PRESENT ARMS — 1981 DEP DEP 1
BRIAN TRAVERS SAX (ABC — (C) PRESENT ARMS IN DUB — 1981 DEP DEP 2
MICHAEL VIRTUE K (ABC — (D) THE SINGLES ALBUM — 1982 DEP DEP 5
EARL FALCONER B (ABC
JIM BROWN D (ABC — NORMAN HASSAN PERC (ABC

U1A U BROWN U1A

U BROWN V (ALL — (A) SATTA DREAD — 1977 KLIK KLP 9018
SANTA D (E — (B) LONDON ROCK — 1977 THIRD WORLD TWS 909
ROBERT SHAKESPEARE B (E — (C) REVELATION TIME — 1977 LIVE & LOVE LALP 002
WINSTON WRIGHT K (E — (D) STARSKY & HUTCH — 1978 CANCER CANSLP 001
WIRE LINDO K (E — (E) MI BROWN SOMETHING — 1978 FRONT LINE UK FL1003
BO PEE G (E — (F) CAN'T KEEP A GOOD MAN DOWN — 1979 FRONT LINE FL1030
CHINNA G (E
SCULLY PERC (E

U2 U.F.O. U2

PETER WAY B (ALL — (A) U F O — 1971 BEACON UK BEAS12 US RARE EARTH 524
ANDY PARKER D (ALL — (B) FLYING — 1972 BEACON UK BES19 GERM NOVA21438
PHIL MOGG V (ALL — (AB) U F O /FLYING — 1973 DECCA UK SD30311/2
BERNIE MARSDEN G (— (C) LIVE — 1972 NOVA GER 6 21454
MICK BOLTON G (ABC — (D) PHENOMENON — 1974 CHRYSALIS CHR 1059
MICHAEL SCHENKER G (DEFHJK — (E) FORCE IT — 1975 CHRYSALIS UK CHR 1074
DANNY PEYRONEL K (F — (F) NO HEAVY PETTING — 1976 CHRYSALIS UK CHR 1103
PAUL RAYMOND K (HJKL — (G) SPACE METAL — 1976 NOVA GERM 6 28363
PAUL CHAPMAN G (MLO — (H) LIGHTS OUT — 1977 CHRYSALIS UK CHR 1127
NEIL CARTER G K V(OK — (J) STRANGERS IN THE NIGHT — 1978 CHRYSALIS CJT5 CHR 1209
LARRY WALLIS G (— (K) OBSESSIONS — 1978 CHRYSALIS CDL 1182
(L) NO PLACE TO RUN — 1979 CHRYSALIS CDL 1239
(M) THE WILD, THE WILLING & INNOCENT — 1981 CHRYSALIS CHR 1307
(O) MECHANIX — 1982 CHRYSALIS CHR 1360
( ) PROFILE — 19 TELDEC GERM 624007
( ) C'MON EVERYBODY(1971) — 1981 TELEFUNKEN GER 624836

U3 U.K. U3

JOHN WETTON B G V(ADC — (A) U K — 1978 POLYDOR UK 2302 080 US 1 6146
TERRY BOZZIO D (BC — (A) U K — 1978 POLYDOR GER 2344 104
EDDIE JOBSON VLN K(ABC — (B) DANGER MONEY — 1979 POLYDOR UK 2302 089 US 1 6194
BILL BRUFORD D (A — (C) NIGHT AFTER NIGHT — 1979 POLYDOR UK 2302 096 US 1 6234
ALLAN HOLDSWORTH G (A

U4 UK SUBS U4

CHARLIE HARPER V HCA(ABCDE — (A) ANOTHER KIND OF BLUES — 1979 GEM UK GEMLP 100
NICK GARRATT G (ABCD — (B) BRAND NEW AGE — 1980 GEM UK GEMLP 106
PAUL SLACK B (ABC — (C) CRASH COURSE(WITH LTD EDITION EP) — 1980 GEM UK GEMLP 111 GER 43423
PETE DAVIES D (ABC — (D) DIMINISHED RESPONSIBILITY — 1981 GEM UK GEMLP 112
STEVE ROBERTS D (D — (F) LIVE KICKS — 1980 UNIVERSE NL 23
ALVIN GIBBS B (D
MEL WESSON SYN (D — CAPTAIN SENSIBLE K (D

U4A U ROY U4A

U ROY(EWART BECKFORD) (ALL — (A) DREAD IN A BABYLON — 1976 VIRGIN US 34234 UK V 2048
ROBBIE SHAKESPEARE B (C — (B) NATTY REBEL — 1976 VIRGIN UK V 2059
SLY DUNBAR D (C — (C) RASTA AMBASSADOR — 1977 VIRGIN UK V 2092
CLINTON FEARON B (C — (D) DREADLOCKS IN JAMAICA — 1977 LIVE & LOVE LALP 05
ALBERT GRIFFITHS G V (C — (E) BEST OF — 1977 LIVE & LOVE LALP 08
RANCHIE V G (C — (F) VERSION GALORE — 1978 FRONT LINE UK FL1018
DUGGIE G (C — (G) JAH SON OF AFRICA — 1977 LIVE & LOVE LALP 08
ANSEL COLLINS K (C
EARL 'WIRE' LINDO SYN(C — STICKY PERC (C — WAYNE JARRETT V (C — NAGGO MORRIS V (C

U5 US SKY U5

BOB GREENFIELD D (A — (A) DON'T HOLD BACK — 1971 RCA UK SF 8168
DOUG FIEGER B (A
JOHN COURY K G (A — ROB STAWINSKI D (A — PAT ARNOLD V (A — BOBBY KEYS SAX (A
GARY WRIGHT K (A — JIMMY MILLER PERC (A — JIM PRICE SAX (A — DORIS TROY V (A
ALAN WHITE D (A — CHRIS WOOD FLT (A — FLO BENDER (A

U5A U2 U5A

LARRY MULLIN D (AB — (A) BOY — 1980 ISLAND UK ILPS9646 GER 202 913
ADAM CLAYTON B (AB — (B) OCTOBER — 1981 ISLAND UK ILPS9680 GER 204 185
THE EDGE G (AB
BONO HEWSON V (AB

U5B UBIQUITY U5B

(A) STARBOOTY — 19 ELEKTRA UK K52068

U5C UGLY DUCKLINGS U5C

DAVE BINGHAM V HCA(AB — (A) SOMEWHERE OUTSIDE — 1966 YORKTOWN
JOHN READ B (AB — (B) OFF THE WALL — 1980 RAZOR CAN 003
GLYN BELL G V (AB
ROGER MAYNE G (AB — ROBIN BOERS D (AB — SCOTT CUSHINE K (B — ANDY GRAUTITUS (B
BERT HERMISTON SAX (B — SIMON WALLIS SAX (B

U6 JAMES'BLOOD'ULMER U6

JAMES BLOOD ULMER G (ABC (A) NO WAVE 1980 MOERS MUSIC MM01072
AMIN ALI B (C (B) MUSIC REVELATION ENSEMBLE 1980 GERM
SHANNON JACKSON D (C (C) ARE YOU GLAD TO BE IN AMERICA 1980 ROUGH TRADE UK ROUGH 16
DAVID MURRAY SAX (C
G CALVIN WESTON D (C OLIVER LAKE SAX (C OLU DARA TPT (C WILLIAM PATTERSON G(C

U7 ULTIMATE SPINACH U7

BARBARA HUDSON G V (ABC (A) ULTIMATE SPINACH 1968 MGM UK 8071 US SE4518
IAN BRUCE DOUGLAS V K G HCA(AB (B) BEHOLD & SEE 1968 MGM UK 8094 US SE4570
KEITH LAHTEINEN D V (AB (C) ULTIMATE SPINACH 1969 MGM US SE4600
GEOFFREY WINTHROP G V SIT(AB
RICHARD NESE B (AB JEFF BAXTER G V (C MIKE LEVINE B (C RUSS LEVINE D (C
TED MYERS G V (A TONY SCHEUREN K (C ALAN LORBER PROD (A

U7A ULTRA VIOLET U7A

(A) ULTRA VIOLET 1974 CAPITOL 11244

U8 ULTRAVOX U8

JOHN FOXX V (ABCD (A) ULTRAVOX 1977 ISLAND UK ILPS9449 GER 28193
STEVE SHEARS K V (ABD (B) HA HA HA 1977 ISLAND UK ILPS9505 GER 25499
BILLY CURRIE K VLN(ABCDE123 (C) SYSTEMS OF ROMANCE 1978 ANTILLES US 7069 UK ISLAND 9555
ROBIN SINE G (D (C) SYSTEMS OF ROMANCE 1978 ISLAND GER 26453
WARREN CANN D (ABCDE123 (D) THREE INTO ONE (COMP) 1980 ISLAND UK ILPS 9614
MIDGE URE G V (E23 (D) THREE INTO ONE (COMP) 1980 ANTILLES US 7079
CHRIS CROSS B (ABCDE123 (E) VIENNA 1981 CHRYSALIS UK CHR1296 GER 202701
(F) RAGE IN EDEN 1981 CHRYSALIS UK CHR1338 GER 203959
(G) QUARTER 1982 CHRYSALIS UK CHR1338
(1) MAN WHO DIES (EP) 1978 ISLAND UK IEP8
(2) VIENNA (EP) 1981 CHRYSALIS GER 600352
(3) ALL STOOD STILL(EP) 1981 CHRYSALIS GER 12 2522

U8A UMPS & DUMPS U8A

ALAN HARRIS B V (A (A) THE MOON IS FIT 1980 TOPIC UK 12TS 416
SUE HARRIS DULC (A
TUFTY SWIFT FDL HCA(A JOHN KIRKPATRICK CONC V(A DEREK PEARCE BANJO PERC V(A

U9 UNCLE DOG U9

CAROLE GRIMES V (A (A) OLD HAT 1972 SIGNPOST UK SG 4253
DAVID SKINNER K V (A
PHILLIP CROOKS G (A TERRY STANNARD D (A JOHN PORTER G B (A SAMMY MITCHELL G (A
JOHN PEARSON D (A RABBIT BUNDRICK K (A

U9A UNCLE JIM'S MUSIC U9A

GARY TOLBERT NICHOLSON G V (A (A) THERE'S A SONG IN THIS 19 / / US
THOMAS DUNSTAN STEEL BAN V(A
WESLEY PRITCHARD B V (A JIM NORMAN K G V (A MICHAEL MINDEL VLN (A ST PERRY D (A
MARK HOFSTEIN SAX (A

U10 UNDERTAKERS U10

JACKIE LOMAX G V (A (A) UNDERTAKERS 1964 PYE NOT RELEASED
BUGS PEMBERTON D (A
CHRIS HUSTON G (A GEORGE NUGENT G (A BRIAN JONES SAX(A

U11 UNDERTONES U11

FEARGAL SHARKEY V (ABC (A) THE UNDERTONES 1979 SIRE UK SRK6071 GER 200 681
MICKEY BRADLEY B (ABC (A) THE UNDERTONES (1 EXTRA TRACK) 1979 SIRE UK/US SRK 6081
JOHN O'NEILL G (ABC (B) HYPNOTISED 1980 SIRE UK SRK6088 GER 202 203
BILLY DOHERTY D (ABC (EP) TEENAGE KICKS 197 GOOD VIBRATION GOT 4
DAMIAN O'NEILL G (ABC (C) POSITIVE TOUCH 1981 ARDECK UK 103 EMI GER 64367
NEILL KING TPT (C
DICK BLEWETT SAX (C PAUL CARRACK K (C

U12 UNDISPUTED TRUTH U12

(A) UNDISPUTED TRUTH 1971 TAMLA UK STML11197 US GORDY 955
(B) FACE TO FACE 1972 TAMLA UK STMG 8004 US GORDY 959
(C) LAW OF THE LAND 1973 TAMLA UK STML11240 US GORDY 963
(D) HIGHER THAN HIGH 1975 TAMLA UK STML12009 US GORDY 972
(E) DOWN TO EARTH 1975 TAMLA UK STML11277 US GORDY 968
(F) COSMIC TRUTH 1975 TAMLA UK STMA 8023 US GORDY 970
(G) BEST OF 1977 TAMLA UK STMA 8029
(H) METHOD TO THE MADNESS 197 WB UK K56289 US 2967
(I) SMOKIN' 1979 WB UK K56497 US 3202

U13 UNICORN U13

PETER PERRIER D V (ABCD (A) UPHILL ALL THE WAY 1971 TRANSATLANTIC UK TRA238
TREVOR MEE G V FLT (A (B) BLUE PINE TREES 1974 CHARISMA UK 1092 US CAPITOL 11334
KEN BAKER V K G(ABCD (C) TOO MANY CROOKS 1976 HARVEST UK SHSP4054
PAT MARTIN B V (ABCD (C) UNICORN II 1976 CAPITOL US ST 11453
KEVIN SMITH G (BCD (D) ONE MORE TOMORROW 1977 HARVEST UK SHSP 4067
DAVID GILMOUR STEEL(BC (D) ONE MORE TOMORROW 1977 CAPITOL US ST 11692
CHRIS PIDGEON K (CD
HOWIE CASEY SAX (D BILLY LIVSEY K (D

U13A UNIQUES U13A

(A) YOU DONT MISS YOUR WATER 1980 CHARLY UK CTD 121

U13B UNION U13B

RANDY BACHMAN G V (A (A) ON STRIKE 1981 POTRAIT UK 85121 US 37368
FRED TURNER B V (A
FRANK LUDWIG K V (A CHRIS LEIGHTON D PERC(A

U14 UNIT 4+ 2 U14

BRIAN PARKER LYRICS ((A) FIRST ALBUM 1965 DECCA UK LK 4697
DAVE MEIKLE G V (1 (B) UNIT 4+2 FEATURING CONCRETE & CLAY196 LONDON US PS 427
TOMMY MOELLER K V (1 (C) REMEMBERING 1977 DECCA UK REM 6
PETE MOULES V (1 (1) 1962
HOWARD LUBIN G V (1
BOB GARWOOD B (HUGH LEM HALLIDAY D (RUSS BALLARD G V (ROBERT HENRIT D (

U15A UNITED SONS OF AMERICA U15A

GERRY BLAKE K V (A — (A) GREETINGS FROM THE U S OF A 19 MERCURY SR 61312 + 6338 036
STEVE WOODS V PERC(A
RICHARD FREEMAN G (A JERRY RITCHLEY B (A MIKE HUESTIS D PERC (

U15B UNITED JAZZ & ROCK ENSEMBLE U15B

(A) LIVE IM SCHUTZENHAUS 19 MOOD GER 22666
(B) TEAMWORK 19 MOOD GER 22999
(C) THE BREAK EVEN POINT 1979 MOOD GER 23600

U16 UNITED STATES OF AMERICA U16

JOSEPH BYRD K SYN(A — (A) UNITED STATES OF AMERICA 1968 CBS US 9619 UK 63340
DOROTHY MOSKOWITZ V (A
GORDON MARRON VLN SYN V(A RAND FORBES B V (A CRAIG WOODSON D PERC (A ED BOGAS K (A

U16A UNITS U16A

SCOTT RYSER SYN V (A — (A) DIGITAL STIMULATION 1980 '415' US 003
RACHEL WEBBER SYN V (A
BRAD SAUNDERS D (A JIM REYNOLDS VIBES (A

U17 UNIVERS ZERO U17

DANIEL DENIS PERC (AB — (A) UNIVERS ZERO 1978 ATEM 7001
MICHEL BERCKMANS WIND (AB — (B) HERESIE 1979 ATEM 7005 UK RECOMMENDED RR4
MARCEL DUFRANE VLN (A
CHRISTIAN GENET B (A PATRICK HANAPPIER VLN (AB EMMANUEL NICAISE HCA (A ROGER TRIGAUX G K(AB
GUY SEGERS B V (B

U17A UNIVERSAL ENERGY U17A

(A) UNIVERSAL ENERGY 1977 HARVEST UK SHSP 4075

U17B UNIVERSE U17B

GARY PAUL VAN K V (A — (A) UNIVERSE 1977 PBR INTERNATIONAL PBR 7002
DENNIS LEE ASKEW G V (A
WALFREDO REYES PERC (A

U17C UP WITH THE PEOPLE U17C

(A) LIVE IT LIVE 1970 BUDDAH US ?

U18 PHIL UPCHURCH U18

PHIL UPCHURCH G B V(ALL — (A) YOU CANT SIT DOWN 1961 BOYD US 398
TENNYSON STEVENS (J — (B) YOU CANT SIT DOWN II 196 UA US 6162
ERIC GALE G (J — (C) TWIST THE BIG HIT DANCES 196 UA US 6175
ARTHUR ADAMS G (H — (D) UPCHURCH 196 CADET US 826
HARVEY MASON D (H — (E) THE WAY I FEEL 1969 CADET US 840
BOBBYE HALL PERC (H — (F) FEELING BLUE 1968 MILESTONE US 9010
DOUG BASCOMB B (J — (G) PHIL UPCHURCH 19 MARLIN US 2209
BOB JAMES K (J — (H) DARKNESS DARKNESS 1972 BLUE THUMB US 6005 UK ILPS9219
STEVE GADD D (J — (J) UPCHURCH TENNYSON 1975 KUDU KU 22
ANDREW SMITH D (J — (K) PHIL UPCHURCH 1978 TK TKR82542
DAVID SANBORN SAX (J
CHUCK RAINEY B (H JOE SAMPLE K (H ELSA HARRIS V (E CASH McCALL V (E
KITTY HAYWOOD V (E DON SIMMONS D (H BEN SIDREN K (H DONNY HATHAWAY K (H

U19 UPP U19

ANDY CLARK K V (AB — (A) UPP 1975 EPIC US 33439 UK 80625
STEVEN AMAZING B (AB — (B) THIS WAY UPP 1976 EPIC US 34177 UK 81322
JAMES COPLEY D (AB
DAVID BUNCE G (B JEFF BECK G (AB TOM SCOTT SAX (B JEANIE ARNOLD V (B
CHRISTY THOMPSON V (B GARY COLEMAN PERC (B JIMMY GETZOFF (B

U20 UPSETTERS U20

LEE PERRY (— (A) RETURN OF DJANGO 1970 TROJAN TRL 19
JOHNNY MOORE (— (B) THE GOOD THE BAD & THE UPSETTERS 1970 TROJAN TBL 119
VAL BENNETT (— (C) EASTWOOD RIDES AGAIN 1970 TROJAN TBL 125
WINSTON WRIGHT (— (D) PRISONER 1970 TROJAN TBL 127
JIM JACKSON (— (E) SUPER APE 1977 ISLAND UK ILPS9417
HUX BROWN (— (F) AFRICA'S BLOOD 1980 TROJAN TBL 166
EASY BECKFORD (— (G) THE UPSETTERS COLLECTION 1981 TROJAN UK TRLS195
BOB AITKENS (
GLEN ADAMS (ALVA LAVIS (CARLTON BARRETT (ASTON BARRETT (

U20A URBAN VERBS U20A

ROBIN ROSE (AB — (A) URBAN VERBS 1 1980 WB US BSK3418 UK K56810
RODDY FRANTZ (AB — (B) EARLY DAMAGE 1981 WB US BSK3533 UK K56896
LINDA FRANCE (AB
ROBERT GOLDSTEIN (AB DANNY FRANKEL D (AB

U20B URBAN HEROES U20B

EVERT NIEUWSTEDE V (A — (A) WHO SAID... 1980 FLEET NL 202026 HANDSHAKE US 36962
MARTIN ZONDEROP B (A
JAAP DE JONCKHEERE G (A JEROEN ERNST K (A AD VAN DER REE D (A

U20C URBAN RENEWAL U20C

(A) MURPHYS LAW 1975 DUNHILL US 50194

U20D URBAN SAX U20D

GILBERT ARTMAN (AB — (A) UBRAN SAX 1978 COBRA FR 37004
SAX ORCHESTRA(16 SAX) (— (B) URBAN SAX 2 1979 COBRA FR 37017

U21 MICHAEL URBANIAK U21

MICHAEL URBANIAK VLN SAX(ALL — (A) FUSION 1974 CBS US 32852 UK 65744
URSZULA DUDZIAK PERC V(BCDF — (B) ATMA 1974 CBS US 33184
CZESLAW BARTKOWSKI D (BD — (C) FUSION III 1975 CBS US 33542
WOJCIECH KAROLAK K (B — (D) INACTIN' 1975 SPIEGELEI GERM 287847U
RAY MANTILLA PERC (B — (E) PARATYPHUS B 1975 SPIEGELEI GERM 28771
JOHN ABERCROMBIE G (C — (F) BODY ENGLISH 1976 ARISTA US AL 4086
ROMAN DYLAG B (D — (G) TRIBUTE TO KOMEDA 1976 BASF US 21657
WLODEK GULGOWSKI K (C — (H) ECSTASY 1978 MARLIN 2221
ANTHONY JACKSON B (C — (I) SERENADE FOR THE CITY 1980 MOTOWN US M 7944
BRANISLAV KOVACEK D (D — (J) HERITAGE 1980 PAUSA US 7047
GERRY BROWN D (C
STEVE GADD D (C LARRY CORYELL G (C JOE CARO G (CF BERNARD KAFKA V (CF
HAROLD IVORY WILLIAMS K(F BASIL FEARRINGTON B (F STEVE JORDAN D (F ERROL CRUSHER BENNETT PERC(F
ADAM MAKOWICZ PNO (D

U22 — URIAH HEEP — U22

MICK BOX G(ABCDEFGHJKLMNOPS (A) VERY'UMBLE VERY 'EAVY 1970 VERTIGO UK 6360 006 MERCURY US SR61294
KEN HENSLEY K V(ABCDEFGHJKLMNOP(A) VERY'UMBLE VERY 'EAVY 1971 BRONZE RI ILPS9142 BRONZE 77RI BRNA142
DAVID BYRON V (ABCDEFGHJKL (B) SALISBURY 1971 VERTIGO UK 6360 028 MERCURY US SR61319
PAUL NEWTON B (ABCK (B) SALISBURY 1971 BRONZE RI ILPS9152 BRONZE 77RI BRNA152
KEITH BAKER D (BK (C) LOOK AT YOURSELF 1971 BRONZE UK ILPS9169 MERCURY US SRM1614
AL NAPIER D (AK (C) LOOK AT YOURSELF 1977 BRONZE RI BRNA169
NIGEL OLSSON D (A (D) DEMONS & WIZARDS 1972 BRONZE UK ILPS9193 MERCURY US SRM1630
IAN CLARKE D (CK (D) DEMONS & WIZARDS 1977 BRONZE RI BRNA193
GARY THAIN B (DEFGH (E) MAGICIANS BIRTHDAY 1971 BRONZE UK ILPS9213 MERCURY US SRM1652
LEE KERSLAKE D (DEFGHJKLMNOS (E) MAGICIANS BIRTHDAY 1977 BRONZE RI BRNA213
JOHN WETTON B (JL (F) LIVE 1973 BRONZE UK ILSD1 MERCURY US SRM7503
TREVOR BOLDER B V (MNOP (F) LIVE 1977 BRONZE RI BRSP 1
COLIN WOOD K (A (G) SWEET FREEDOM 1973 BRONZE UK BRNA245 WB US 2724
JOHN LAWTON V (MNO (G) SWEET FREEDOM 1977 BRONZE RI BRNA245
MEL COLLINS SAX (J (H) WONDERWORLD 1974 BRONZE UK ILPS9280 WB US 2800
B J COLE STEEL (J (H) WONDERWORLD 1975 BRONZE RI BRNA280
CHRIS MERCER SAX (O (J) RETURN TO FANTASY 1975 BRONZE UK ILPS9335 WB US 2869
JOHN SLOMAN V (P (J) RETURN TO FANTASY 1977 BRONZE RI BRNA335
MARK CLARKE V (1 (K) THE BEST OF 1975 BRONZE UK ILPS9375 MERCURY US SRM11070
CHRIS SLADE D (P (K) THE BEST OF 1977 BRONZE RI BRNA375
JOHN SINCLAIR K (S (L) HIGH & MIGHTY 1976 BRONZE UK ILPS9384 WB US 2949
PETE GOALBY V (S (L) HIGH & MIGHTY 1977 BRONZE RI BRNA384
BOB DAISLEY B (S (M) FIRE FLY 1977 BRONZE UK ILPS9483 WB US 3013
(M) FIRE FLY 1977 BRONZE RI BRNA383
(N) INNOCENT VICTIM 1977 BRONZE UK BRON504 WB US 3145
(O) FALLEN ANGEL 1978 BRONZE UK BRNA 512 CHRYSALIS US S 1204
(P) CONQUEST 1980 BRONZE UK BRNA 524
(Q) URIAH HEEP 1980 MERCURY US 8004
(R) WONDERFUL 1980 CHRYSALIS US 1227
(S) ABOMINOG 1982 BRONZE UK BRAN 538 GER 204 532
(T) ABOMINOG JUNIOR (EP) 1982

U22A — URSA MAJOR — U22A

DICK WAGNER G V (A (A) URSA MAJOR 1972 RCA US LSP 4777
GREG ARAMA B (A
RICKY MANGONE D V (A

U23 — UTOPIA — U23

DENNY FISCHELSCHER D (A (A) UTOPIA 1973 UA UK UAG 29438
JIMMY JACKSON K (A
LOTHAR MEID B (A ANDY MARX G (A JOE NAY D (A CHRIS KARRER VLV (A
ROLF ZACHER V (A JOHN WEINZIERL G (A GEO GREEN D (A JOE QUICK G (A
GEORGE BROWN D (A KRISTIAN SCHULZE K (A RENATE KNAUP V (A FALK ROGNER K (A
OLAF KUBLER SYN PROD(A SIEGFRID SCHWAB G (A PETER KRAMPER SYN (A EDGAR HOFFMAN SAX (A
KEITH FORSEY D (A RALF BASTEN V (A

V1 — V.H.F — V1

RITCHIE TEETER D (A (A) 1979
BRUCE BRODY K (A RITCHIE FLIEGLER G (A DONNIE NOSSOV B(A

V1A — VACANTS — V1A

(A) PUNK ROCK 19 FESTIVAL FR 680

V2 — VAGRANTS — V2

JAY STORCH K
PETER SABATINO V LARRY WEST B LESLIE WEST G ROGER MANSOUR D

V3 — VALDY — V3

VALDY V (AB (A) VALDY 1975 A&M US 4538 UK AMLH64538
JIM KELTNER D (A (B) VALDY & THE HOMETOWN BAND 197 A&M US 4592
JERRY SCHEFF B (A
FRED TACKETT G (G DAVID PAICH K (A RICHARD GREENE VLN (A DALLAS TAYLOR D(A
JERRY McGEE G (A ELEANOR SEATKIN CELLO(A JOHN SEBASTIAN HCA (A JIM GORDON D (A
JIM HORN FLT (A ALAN MUNDE BANJO(A JESSE ED DAVIS G (A JAY DEE MANESS G (A
WILLIAM SMITH K (A KLAUS VOORMANN B (A

V4 — RITCHIE VALENS — V4

RITCHIE VALENS V (A RITCHIE VALENS 19 DELFI US 1201
RITCHIE 19 DELFI US 1206
RITCHIE 19 LONDON US HA 2390
IN CONCERT 19 DELFI US 1214
GREATEST HITS 19 DELFI US 1225
GREATEST HITS II 19 DELFI US 1247
GREATEST HITS 19 LONDON UK HA 8196
ORIGINAL 19 GUEST STAR US 1484
ORIGINAL LA BAMBA 19 GUEST STAR US 1469
RITCHIE VALENS 19 APEX US 1201
HIS GREATEST HITS 19 PRESIDENT PTL 1001
ROCK LI'L DARLIN' 19 JOY JOYS 254
RITCHIE VALENS 1979 LONDON UK HAR 8535

V5 — DINO VALENTI — V5

DINO VALENTI (CHESTER POWERS) V (A (A) DINO VALENTI 1968 CBS UK 63443 US EPIC 26335

V6 — DAVE VALENTIN — V6

DAVE VALENTIN FLT (ABC (A) THE HAWK 1979 ARISTA US 5006
DAVE GRUSIN K SYN(ABC (B) LAND OF THE THIRD EYE 1980 ARISTA US 5009
MICHAEL VINAS G (ABC (C) PIED PIPER 1981 ARISTA US 5505
MARCUS MILLER B (ABC
BUDDY WILLIAMS D (ABC CRUSHER BENNETT PERC (AC OSCAR HERNANDEZ K (ABC LINCOLN GOINES B (ABC
TITO MARRERO D (ABC ROGER SQUITERO PERC (ABC RAFAEL DE JESUS PERC (ABC LARRY ROSEN PERC(A
ANGELA BOFILL V (A DENNIS BELL K (B JEFF MIRONOV G (B PATTI AUSTIN V (B
LUTHER VANDROSS V (B BOBBY BROOM G (C VIVIAN CHERRY V (C YVONNE LEWIS V (C
KACEY CYSIK V (C BILL O'CONNELL K (C

V7 VAMPIRES V7

GARY GAREIS V (A — (A) WE'RE ON THE ROAD AGAIN — 1978 NITTRIBITT GER 1006
UDO WALDER G (A
DIETER KLIER K V (A NORBERT ROSCH B (A JURGEN FECHTER D (A

V8 JOEL VANCE V8

JOEL VANCE G V (A — (A) WHAT I DID ON MY VACATION — 19 CADET US 325

V9 MARTHA & THE VANDELLAS V9

MARTHA REEVES V (ALL — (A) COME & GET YOU MEMORIES — 1963 US GORDY 902
ROSALIND ASHFORD V (123 — (B) HEAT WAVE — 1963 TAMLA UK STML11005 US GORDY 907
LOIS REEVES V (34 — (C) DANCE PARTY — 1965 TAMLA UK STML11013 US GORDY 915
BETTY KELLY V (2 — (D) WATCH OUT — 1966 TAMLA UK STML11051 US GORDY 920
ANNETTE BEARD V (1 — (E) GREATEST HITS — 1966 TAMLA UK STML11040 US GORDY 917
SANDRA TILLEY V (4 — (F) LIVE — 1968 US GORDY 925
(G) RIDIN HIGH — 1968 US GORDY 926
(H) SUGAR & SPICE — 196 US GORDY 944
(J) NATURAL RESOURSES — 196 US GORDY 952
(K) BLACK MAGIC — 1974 TAMLA UK STML11204 US GORDY 958
(L) GREATEST HITS VOL 2 — 1974 TAMLA UK STML11223
(M) ANTHOLOGY — 1974 TAMLA UK STML12060 US TAMLA 778
(N) GREATEST HITS — 1981 TAMLA UK STMS5042

V9A GINO VANELLI V9A

GINO VANELLI V PROD (ALL — (A) CRAZY LIFE — 1973 A&M US 4395
JOE VANELLI K PROD SYNBFGH — (B) POWERFUL PEOPLE — 1974 A&M US 3661 UK AMLS 63630
ROSS VANELLI V PROD (FGH — (C) STORM AT SUNUP — 1975 A&M US 4533
JIMMY HASLIP B (F — (D) THE GIST OF THE GEMINI — 1976 A&M UK AMLH64596
MANUEL BADRENA PERC (F — (E) A PAUPER IN PARADISE — 1977 A&M UK AMLH 64664
STEPHANIE SPRUILL V (F — (F) BROTHER TO BROTHER — 1978 A&M US 4722 UK AMLH 64722
JULIA TILLMAN V (F — (G) NIGHTWALKER — 1980 ARISTA UK START 1148
MARK CRANEY D (F — (H) THE BEST OF GINO VANELLI — 1980 A&M UK AMLE 69043
CARLOS RIOS G (F
LEON GAER B (F ERNIE WATTS SAX (F VICTOR FELDMAN VIBES (F MAXINE WILLARD V (F
RICHARD BAKER STR HRNS K(B JOHN J MANDEL PERC (B LANI HALL V (B GRAHAM LEAR D (B
TONY GOLIA PERC (B

V9B VANDENBERG V9B

ADJE VANDENBERG G (A — (A) VANDENBERG — 1982 ATCO UK 50904
JOS ZOOMER D (A
DICK KEMPER B (A BERT HEERINK V (A

V10 CHRISTIAN VANDER V10

CHRISTIAN VANDER K (A — (A) TRISTAN ET ISEULT — 1978 EGG FR 90171
JANIK TOP B (A
STELLA VANDER V (A KLAUS BLASQUIZ V PERC (A LAURENT THIBAULT PROD (A

V11 VAN DER GRAAF GENERATOR V11

PETER HAMMILL K V G(ALL — (A) AEROSOL GREY MACHINE — 1968 FONTANA UK 6430 083
NIC POTTER B (BCJKMH — (A) AEROSOL GREY MACHINE — 1968 MERCURY US SR 61238
DAVE JACKSON WIND K(BCDEFGJKMH — (A) AEROSOL GREY MACHINE — 1968 VERTIGO ITALY 6360 510
GUY EVANS D (ABCDEFGLKMHJ — (B) THE LEAST WE CAN DO IS WAVE — 1969 CHARISMA CAS1007 GER PHILIPS 6369901
HUGH BANTON K G B(ABCDEFGKM — (C) H TO HE WHO AM THE ONLY ONE — 1970 CHARISMA CAS1027 GER PHILIPS 6369915
JOHN ANTHONY PROD (ABC — (C) H TO HE WHO AM THE ONLY ONE — 1970 DUNHILL US 50097
KEITH ELLIS B (AK — (D) PAWN HEARTS — 1971 CHARISMA CAS 1051
GRAHAM SMITH K V VLN (HJ — (E) GODBLUFF — 1975 CHARISMA CAS1109 US MERCURY 1069
CHARLES DICKIE K CELLO(J — (F) STILL LIFE — 1976 CHARISMA CAS1116 US MERCURY 1096
CED CURTIS G B (M — (G) WORLD RECORD — 1976 CHARISMA CAS1120 US MERCURY 1116
PIERO MESSINA K G (M — (H) THE QUIET ZONE — 1977 CHARISMA CAS1132
JERRY SALISBURY HRNS (B — (J) VITAL LIVE (DBL) — 1978 CHARISMA CVLD101 US PVC 9901
MIKE HURWITZ CELLO(B — (K) 1968//1971 — 1973 CHARISMA CS 2
JEFF? FLT (A — (M) LONG HELLO — 1973 NO LABEL
ROBERT FRIPP G (CD — (N) REPEAT PERFORMANCE — 1980 CHARISMABG8
(O) REFLECTION — 19 FONTANA GER 9286 002

V12 LON & DERREK VAN EATON V12

LON VAN EATON G V K D SAX(AB — (A) BROTHER — 1973 APPLE UK SAPCOR 25
DERREK VAN EATON V B G D (AB — (B) WHO DO YOU OUT DO — 1975 A&M US SP 4507
RINGO STARR D (A
JIM GORDON D (AB KLAUS VOORMANN B (AB ANDY NEWMARK D (A PAUL GLANZ ORG (A
T J TINDALL G (A MIKE HUGG D (A ALEX GUEVARA CONGA(A RICHARD DAVIS B (A
JIM KELTNER D (B RICHARD PERRY PERC (B TOM HENSLEY K (B VANETTA FIELDS V (B
BOBBY HARTNAGLE G (B CYNTHIA WEBB V (B FRITZ POASKETT V (B RUSS TURNER ORG (B
DAVID BEEBE D (B TOM SEUFERT G (B CHUCK FINDLEY HRNS (B LANI GROVES V (B
MARTHA REEVES V (B TREVOR LAWRENCE SAX (B LYNDA LAURENCE V (B JAMES GADSON D (B
CLYDIE KING V (B GARY WRIGHT K (B

V13 VANGELIS V13

VANGELIS K (ALL — (A) DRAGON — 1971 CHARLY UK CRL 5013
MICHEL RIPOCHE B (AHK — (B) L'APOCALYPSE DES ANIMAUX — 1973 POLYDOR 2489 113
BRIAN ODGERS B (AH — (C) EARTH — 1974 VERTIGO US 1019 UK 6499 693
TONY OXLEY D (AH — (D) HEAVEN & HELL — 1975 RCA UK RS1025 RI 3012 US 5110
MICK WALLER D (A — (E) ALBEDO .39 — 1976 RCA UK RS1080 RI 3017 US 5136
ARCHIRIS G (A — (F) SPIRAL — 1977 RCA UK PL25116 RI3022 US 2627
YEUNK HAK FUN V (K — (G) BEAUBOURG — 1978 RCA UK PL25155 US 3020
KOON FOOK MAN V (K — (H) HYPOTHESIS — 1978 AFFINITY AFF 11
JON ANDERSON V (DL — (J) BEST OF — 1978 RCA UK PL25174 RI 3028
VANA VEROUTIS V (D — (K) CHINA — 1979 POLYDOR UK POLD5018 US 1 6199
ENGLISH CHAMBER CHOIR (D — (L) SEE YOU LATER — 1980 POLYDOR UK 2302 101
PETER MARSH V (L — (M) CHARIOTS OF FIRE — 1981 POLYDOR UK POLS1026
CHERRY VANILLA V (L — (N) TO THE UNKNOWN MAN — 1981 RCA US 4397
CORI JOSIAS V (L

V14 **VAN HALEN** V14

EDWARD VAN HALEN G (ABCDE (A) VAN HALEN 1978 WB US BSK3075 UK K56470
ALEX VAN HALEN D (ABCDE (B) VAN HALEN II 1979 WB US HS 3312 UK K56616
MIKE ANTHONY B (ABCDE (C) WOMEN & CHILDREN FIRST 1980 WB US 3415 UK K56793
DAVE ROTH V (ABCDE (EP) VAN HALEN 12" 197 WB PRO 705
JAN VAN HALEN CLAR (E (D) FAIR WARNING 1981 WB US 3540 UK K56899
(E) DIVER DOWN 1982 WB UK K57003

V15 **VANILLA FUDGE** V15

MARK STEIN K (ABCDEFG (A) VANILLA FUDGE 1967 ATLANTIC UK 587 086 US 33224
VINCE MARTELL G (ABCDEFG (B) THE BEAT GOES ON 1968 ATLANTIC UK 587 100 US 33237
TIM BOGERT B (ABCDEFG (C) RENAISSANCE 1968 ATLANTIC UK 587 110 US 33244
CARMINE APPICE D (ABCDEF (C) RENAISSANCE 1973 MIDI GER 20045
(D) NEAR THE BEGINNING 1969 ATLANTIC UK 228 020 US 33278
(D) NEAR THE BEGINNING 1981 ATLANTIC RI UK K40075
(E) ROCK'N'ROLL 1970 ATLANTIC UK 288 029 US 33303
(F) STAR COLLECTION 1974 MIDI MID 0033
(AS THE PIGEONS)>>>(G) WHILE THE WORLD WAS EATING 1970 WAND US 687 METRONOME GER 200108
(BE) TWO ORIGINALS 1976 ATLANTIC GERM 60116

V16 **CHERRY VANILLA** V16

CHERRY VANILLA V (AB (A) BAD GIRL 1978 RCA UK PL 25122
LOUIS LE PERE G K V(AB (B) VENUS DE VINYL 1979 RCA UK PL 25217
ZECCA ESQUIBEL K (A
HOWIE FINKEL B (A IAN STUART V (B STUART ELLIOTT D (AB ALUN EDEN D (B
DAVE QUINN B (B GEORGE FORD B (B ROY BABBINGTON B (B MORRIS PERT PERC(B
MICHAEL MANUSCE D (

V17 **THIJS VAN LEER** V17

THIJS VAN LEER FLT K SYN(ALL (A) INTROSPECTION 1972 CBS US 32346 UK 65589
LETTY DE JONG V (A (B) INTROSPECTION II 1975 CBS 65913
PAUL BUCKMASTER K (C (C) O MY LOVE 1975 PHILIPS 6303 143
VICTOR FELDMAN PERC (C (D) MUSICA PER LA NOTTE DI NATALE 1976 CBS 69239
WILTON FELDER B (C (E) INTROSPECTION III 1978 CBS 86034
JAMES GADSON D (C (F) NICE TO HAVE MET YOU 1978 CBS US 35345 UK 86059
EUGENE CIPRIANO OBOE (C
DAVID KEMPER D (C ROSELIE VAN LEER V (C NORMAN BENNO OBOE(C LOUIE SHELTON G (C
KING ERRISON CONGA(C RALPH MACDONALD PERC (F RICHARD TEE K (F ERIC GALE G (F
ANTHONY JACKSON B (F HARVEY MASON D (F EEF ALBERS G (F STEVE KHAN G (F
JON FADDIS HRNS (F RANDY BRECKER TPT (F BARRY ROGERS TROM (F DAVE TAYLOR TROM(F
JAMES BUFFINGTON HRNS (F JOHN CLARK HRNS (F FRED GRIFFIN HRNS (F ALEX FOSTER SAX(F
MICHAEL BRECKER SAX (F RONNIE CUBER SAX (F TOM SCOTT SAX (F BROOKS TILLOTSON HRNS(F
DON CORRADO HRNS (F LOU MARINI SAX (F VIVIAN CHERRY V (F BRENDA WHITE V (F
KEN WILLIAMS V (F GWEN GUTHRIE V (F RAYMOND SIMPSON V (F ZACH SANDERS V (F
BILL EATON V (F LOUIS VAN DIJK K (D ROGIER VAN OTTERLOO (D STRINGS (DF

V18 **TOWNES VAN ZANDT** V18

TOWNES VAN ZANDT G V (ALL (A) FOR THE SAKE OF A SONG 1968 POPPY PYS40001
PHILLIP DONNELLY G V (H (B) OUR MOTHER THE MOUNTAIN 1969 POPPY PYS40004 TOMATO TOM 7015
BILLY EARL McLELLAND G V(H (C) TOWNES VAN ZANDT 1970 POPPY PYS40007 TOMATO TOM 7014
CHIPS MOMAN G V (H (D) DELTA MOMMA BLUES 1971 POPPY PYS40012 TOMATO TOM 7013
RANDY SCRUGGS G MAND (H (E) HIGH,LOW & IN BETWEEN 1971 POPPY PYS5700 TOMATO TOM 7012
TOMMY COGBILL B (H (F) LATE GREAT 1973 POPPY LA 004 UA UK UAS29442
BOBBY EMMONS K (H (F) LATE GREAT 197 TOMATO TOM 7011
EDDY ANDERSON D (H (G) LIVE AT THE OLD QUARTER 1977 TOMATO TOM27001
TONI WINE V (H (H) FLYING SHOES 1978 TOMATO TOM 7017
JIMMY DAY STEEL(H
GARY SCRUGGS HCA (H SPOONER OLDHAM PNO (H BILLY BURNETTE V (H

V18A **JOHNNY VAN ZANT** V18A

JOHNNY VAN ZANT G V (AB (A) NO MORE DIRTY DEALS 1980 POLYDOR US 6289 NL 2391 472
ROBBIE GAY G (A (B) ROUND TWO 1981 POLYDOR US 6322
ERIK LUNDGREN G (A
DANNY CLAUSMAN B (A ROBBIE MORRIS D (A PAUL BARRERE G (A AL KOOPER K (A
ERNIE WATTS WIND (A JULIA TILLMAN V (A RON HICKLIN V (A JOHN BALHLER V (A
JERRY WHITMAN V (A GENE MORFORD V (A MARTI McCALL V (A MYRNA MATTHEWS V (A
LORNA WILLARD V (A

V18B **VAPOUR TRAILS(VTs)** V18B

JOHN McBURNIE G V (AB (A) VAPOUR TRAILS 1979 WB US BSK3363 UK K56722
ANDY DALBY G (AB (B) V T s 1980 CRIMINAL UK STEAL1
PHIL CURTIS B (AB
JOHN FERRARO D (AB STEVE HOLLY D V (AB BRIAN MANN K (AB WILLIAM D SMITH K (AB
MICHAEL OMARTIAN K (AB DAVE ROSE K (AB BRIAN CHATTON K (AB DAVID BENOIT K (AB
BETSY COOKE K V (AB PAULINHO DA COSTA PERC (AB TOM SCOTT SAX (AB MEL COLLINS SAX(AB
VIVIENNE McAULIFFE V (AB BILL CHAMPLIN V (AB

V18C **VARDIS** V18C

STEVE ZODIAC G V (ABC (A) 100MPH 1980 LOGO UK MOGO 4012
ALAN SELWAY B V (ABC (B) WORLD'S INSANE 1981 LOGO GER 64029 UK LOGO 1026
GARY PEARSON D (ABC (C) QUO VARDIS 1981 LOGO UK LOGO 1034
JUDD LANDER HCA (B
ANDY BOWN K (B

V18D **VAPORS** V18D

DAVID FENTON G V (A (A) NEW CLEAR DAYS 1980 UA US 1049 UK UAG 3030
HOWARD SMITH D (A (B) MAGNETS 1981 LIBERTY US 1090 UK LBG 30324
EDWARD BAZALGETTE G (A
STEVE SMITH B V (A

V19 BOBBY VEE V19

Musician	Inst	Albums	Title	Year	Label / Catalogue
BOBBY VEE	V	(ALL	DEVIL OR ANGEL	196	LIBERTY US LST7165
SONNY CURTIS	G V	(C	BOBBY VEE	196	LIBERTY US LST7181
BOB BOGLE	G	(D	WITH STRINGS & THINGS	196	LIBERTY US LST7186
NOKIE EDWARDS	B	(D	HITS OF THE 50s	19	LIBERTY US LST7205
JERRY ALLISON		(C	TAKE GOOD CARE OF MY BABY	196	LIBERTY US LST7211 UK LBY 1004
JOE MAULDIN		(C	(C) MEETS THE CRICKETS	1962	LIBERTY US 7228 UK LBY 1086
DON WILSON	G	(D	(C) MEETS THE CRICKETS	1974	SUNSET UK SLS50357
MEL TAYLOR	D	(D	RECORDING SESSION	196	LIBERTY US LST7232 UK LBY 1084
			GOLDEN GREATS	1962	LIBERTY US LST7245
			MERRY CHRISTMAS	196	LIBERTY US LST7267
			NIGHT HAS A THOUSAND EYES	196	LIBERTY US LST7285 UK LBY 1139
			(D) MEETS THE VENTURES	1963	LIBERTY US LST7289 UK LBY 1147
			I REMEMBER BUDDY HOLLY	196	LIBERTY US LST7336 UK SBY 1188
			SING NEW SOUND FROM ENGLAND	196	LIBERTY US LST7352
			HITS OF THE SIXTIES	196	LIBETRY US LST7385
			LIVE ON TOUR	196	LIBERTY US LST7393
			GOLDEN GREATS VOLII	196	LIBERTY US LST7464
			LOOK AT ME GIRL	196	LIBERTY US LST7482 UK SBY 1341
			COME BACK WHEN YOU GROW UP	1967	LIBERTY US LST7534
			JUST TODAY	196	LIBERTY US LST7554 UK 83112
			DO WHAT YOU GOTTA DO	196	LIBERTY US LST7592 UK 83130
			GRITS GRILLS & RAILINGS	19	LIBERTY US LST7612
			FOREVER KIND OF LOVE	1967	SUNSET UK 5162
			BOBBY VEE	1966	SUNSET 5111
			FAVOURITES	19	SUNSET 1019
			VERY BEST OF	1971	SUNSET UK SLS50271
			NOTHING LIKE A SUNNY DAY	19	UA UK 29457
			LEGENDARY MASTERS	1974	UA US LA 025 UK UAD60055
			VERY BEST OF	1975	UA US LA 332
			TRIBUTE TO BUDDY HOLLY	1978	SUNSET UK SLS50417

V20 TATA VEGA V20

Musician	Inst	Albums	Title	Year	Label / Catalogue
TATA VEGA	V	(AB	(A) FULL SPEED AHEAD	1976	TAMLA US 347 UK STML12039
			(B) TOTALLY TATA	1977	TAMLA US 353 UK STML12058
			(C) TRY MY LOVE	19	TAMLA US 360

V21 MARTHA VELEZ V21

Musician	Inst	Albums	Title	Year	Label / Catalogue
MARTHA VELEZ	V	(ALL	(A) FIENDS & ANGELS	1969	LONDON UK SHK8395 SIRE US 97008
ERIC CLAPTON	G	(A	(A) FIENDS & ANGELS	1969	BLUE HORIZON UK 763867
JACK BRUCE	B	(A	(B) HYPNOTIZED	1972	POLYDOR US PD5034
MITCH MITCHELL	D	(A	(C) MATINEE WEEPERS	1973	SIRE US 7409 UK 0598
RICK HAYWARD	G	(A	(D) ESCAPE FROM BABYLON	1976	SIRE US 7515 UK 9103 252
DUSTER BENNETT	HCA	(A	(E) AMERICAN HEARTBEAT	1977	SIRE US 6040 UK 9103 256
DAVE BIDWELL	D	(A			

Musician	Inst	Albums	Musician	Inst	Albums	Musician	Inst	Albums	Musician	Inst	Albums
ANDY SYLVESTER	B	(A	STAN WEBB	G	(A	JEFF CONDON	HRNS	(A	CHRIS WOOD	SAX	(A
CHRISTINE PERFECT	K	(A	MICK WEAVER	K	(A	BRIAN AUGER	ORG	(A	PETER SHELLEY		(A
KEEF HARTLEY	D	(A	TERRY NOONAN	HRNS	(A	PAUL KOSSOFF	G	(A	GARY THAIN	B	(A
SPIT JAMES	G	(A	JIM CAPALDI	D	(A	BUD PARKES	HRNS	(A	DEREK WADSWORTH	HRNS	(A
CHRIS MERCER	SAX	(A	KEITH JOHNSON	HRNS	(B	DAHAUD SHAAR	D	(B	JOHNNY ALMOND	SAX	(A
JOHN PLATANIA	G	(B	NANCY WADE	K	(B	DON MOORE	B	(B	MIKE WINFIELD	B	(B
ALAN HAND	K	(B	JOHN KLINGBERG	B	(B	GERARDO VELEZ	CONGA	(B	BILLY CURTIS	CONGA	(B
COLLIN TILTON	WIND	(B	GEORGE DEVENS	PERC	(B	SPIDER BARBOUR	G	(B	CISSY HOUSTON	V	(B
JOSHIE ARMSTEAD	V	(B	JACKIE VERDELL	V	(B	RONNELLE STAFFORD	V	(B	ASTON BARRETT	B	(D
CARLTON BARRETT	D	(D	AL ANDERSON	G	(D	EARL SMITH	G	(D	TYRONE DOWNIE	K	(D
WINSTON WRIGHT	K	(D	GLADSTONE ANDERSON	K	(D	BERNARD HARVEY	K	(D	LEE PERRY	PERC	(D
BOB MARLEY	PERC	(D	RITA MARLEY	V	(D	JUDY MOWATT	V	(D	MARCIA GRIFFITH	V	(D
DAVID SCANCE	V G K	(E	BRIAN CUOMO	K	(E	JOHN SIEGLER	B	(E	PAUL MARCHETTI	D	(E
JOEL KRANTZ	V	(E	JOHN DI ROBERTIS	V	(F	KEN NEMIROFF	V	(E	FRANK D'AGOSTINO	V	(E
PAT ELLINGTON	V	(E	JOAN ELLINGTON	V	(E	JUDY ELLINGTON	V	(E	RON CARTALEMI	V	(E
JOHN ZANGRANDO	SAX	(E	JOHN PAYNE	WIND	(E	STEVE SAVAGE	PERC	(E	BOB GERLAND	WIND	(E
GEORGE CONSTANINOU	STEEL	(E	LARRY FAST	SYN	(E	ERNEST ROYAL	HRNS	(E	JOHN CLARK	HRNS	(E
JAMES BUFFINGTON	HRNS	(E	WAYNE ANDRE	HRNS	(E	JOHN GATCHELL	HRNS	(E	JANICE ROBINSON	HRNS	(E
DUD MARTIN	SAX	(E	MICHAEL CULLEN	SAX	(E	PETER SOBEL	ZITHER	(E			

V21A VELVET FOGG V21A

Title	Year	Label / Catalogue
(A) VELVET FOGG	1967	PYE UK NSPL18272

V22 VELVET OPERA V22

Musician	Inst	Albums	Title	Year	Label / Catalogue
COLIN FOSTER	G	(A	(A) RIDE A HUSTLERS DREAM	1969	CBS UK 63692
JOHN FORD	B	(A			
RICHARD HUDSON	D	(A			
JOHN JOYCE	V	(A			

V23 VELVET UNDERGROUND V23

Musician	Inst	Albums	Title	Year	Label / Catalogue
LOU REED	V G K	(ABCDEFHJ	(A) VELVET UNDERGROUND WITH NICO	1967	VERVE UK SVLP 9184 US 5008
JOHN CALE	B K	(ABE	(A) VELVET UNDERGROUND WITH NICO	196	VERVE 665114
STERLING MORRISON	G	(ABCDEFJ	(A) VELVET UNDERGROUND WITH NICO	1971	MGM UK 2315056 GER RI 2428 506
ANDY WARHOL	PROD	(AE	(B) WHITE LIGHT WHITE HEAT	1967	VERVE UK SVLP9201 US 5046
BILLY YULE	D	(DF	(B) WHITE LIGHT WHITE HEAT	1971	MGM UK 2353 024 GER 710 015
MO TUCKER	B	(ABCDEJ	(C) VELVET UNDERGROUND	1969	MGM UK CS 8108 US4617
DOUG YULE	G B D V K	(CDFGJ	(C) VELVET UNDERGROUND	1971	MGM UK 2353 022 GER 665 114
NICO	V	(AE	(D) LOADED	1970	ATLANTIC 2400 111 COTILLION US 9034
TOM WILSON	PROD	(B	(D) LOADED	1972	ATLANTIC UK K40113 MIDI GER 20049
			(E) ANDY WARHOL'S V UNDERGROUND	1971	MGM UK 2683 006
			(F) LIVE AT MAX'S KANSAS CITY	1972	ATLANTIC UK K30022 COTILLION 9500
			(G) SQUEEZE	1972	POLYDOR UK 2383 180
			(H) VELVET UNDERGROUND ,LOU REED	1973	VERVE UK 2315 258 PRIDE US 0022
			(J) VELVET UNDERGROUND LIVE	1974	MERCURY UK 6643 900 US SRM27504
			(J) LIVE	1976	MERCURY GER 6643 017
			( ) POP HISTORY No12	19	KAMA SUTRA UK 2612 021
			( ) POP HISTORY No19	19	KAMA SUTRA UK 2625 019
			( ) VELVET UNDERGROUND	1970	MGM IMP GAS131
			( ) VELVET UNDERGROUND	1976	MGM UK 2354 033
			( ) ARCHETYPES	1974	MGM US 4950
			( ) EVIL MOTHERS	19	SKYDOG US LP 003

V24 VENTURES V24

BOB BOGLE G (12345R
DON WILSON G (12345R
MEL TAYLOR D (2345R
NOKIE EDWARDS B (12
HOWIE JOHNSON D (1
JERRY McGEE G (345R
JOHNNY DURRILL PNO (45R
JOE BARILE PERC (SR
RED RHODES STEEL(S
LARRY LINSTROT PROD (R
MIKE GUTIERREZ PERC (R
(1) 1960 (2) 1963 (3) 1967
(4) 1967 (5) 1968

Title	Year	Label	UK	US
WALK DONT RUN	196	LIBERTY	UK LBY1002	US DOLTON 8003
THE VENTURES	196			US DOLTON 8004
ANOTHER SMASH	196			US DOLTON 8006
COLORFUL VENTURES	196			US DOLTON 8008
TWIST PARTY	1962	LIBERTY	UK LBY1072	
TWIST WITH THE VENTURES	196			US DOLTON 8010
TWIST PARTY VOL 2	196			US DOLTON 8014
MASHED POTATOES & GRAVY	196			US DOLTON 8016
DANCE PARTY	196			US DOLTON 8017
PLAY TELSTAR & LONELY BULL	1963			US DOLTON 8019
SURFING	1963	LIBERTY	UK LBY1150	US DOLTON 8022
COUNTRY CLASSICS	196			US DOLTON 8023
LETS GO	1963	LIBERTY	UK LBY1169	US DOLTON 8024
IN SPACE	1964	LIBERTY	UK LBY1189	US DOLTON 8027
FABULOUS	196			US DOLTON 8029
WALK DONT RUN VOL 2	196	LIBERTY	UK SLBY1228	US DOLTON 8031
KNOCK ME OUT	1965	LIBERTY	UK SLBY1252	US DOLTON 8033
ON STAGE	1965	LIBERTY	UK SLBY1270	US DOLTON 8035
A GO GO	196	LIBERTY	UK SLBY1274	US DOLTON 8037
CHRISTMAS ALBUM	196	LIBERTY	UK SLBY1285	US DOLTON 8038
WHERE THE ACTION IS	196	LIBERTY	UK SLBY1297	US DOLTON 8040
BATMAN THEME	19			US DOLTON 8042
GO WITH	196	LIBERTY	UK SLBY1323	US DOLTON 8045
WILD THING	196			US DOLTON 8047
GUITAR FREAKOUT	196	LIBERTY	UK SLBY1345	US DOLTON 8050
SUPER PSYCHEDELICS	196	LIBERTY	UK SLBY1372	US DOLTON 8052
BEST OF	196	LIBERTY	UK SLBY1375	
GOLDEN GREATS	1965	LIBERTY	UK 83046	US 8053
MILLION DOLLAR WEEKEND	1965	LIBERTY		US 8054
FLIGHTS OF FANCY	196	LIBERTY		US 8055
I LIKE IT LIKE THAT	1965	LIBERTY	UK 83116	
THE HORSE	196	LIBERTY		US 8057
GENIUS	1967	SUNSET		US 5160
UNDERGROUND FIRE	1969	LIBERTY	UK 83193	US 8059
MORE GOLDEN GREATS	19	LIBERTY	UK 83175	US 8060
HAWAII FIVE O	1969	LIBERTY	UK	US 8061
SWAMP ROCK	1969	LIBERTY	U K 83289	US 8062
DECADE	196	SUNSET		5137
10TH ANNIVERSARY ALBUM	1970	LIBERTY		US 35000
VENTURES	197	UA		US UAX 80
JIM CROCE SONGBOOK	197	UA		US 217
(R) NEW TESTAMENT	1971	UA		US 6769
(S) SHAFT	197	UA	UK UAS29280	US 5547
SECRET AGENT MAN	19	LIBERTY		
8 MILES HIGH	19	LIBERTY		US 8811
GUITAR POWER	19	SUNSET 1012		
THE VENTURES DBL COMP	19	SUNSET NL 60022/3		
SUPER GROUP	19	SUNSET 5271		
LEGENDARY MASTERS	1974	UA	UK UAD 60051	
JOY	1974	UA	UK UAS29340	US 5575
BEST OF THE POPS	1974	UA	UK UAS29249	
VERY BEST OF	1975	US	EURO 050 96470	US UALA331
VERY BEST OF	1976	SUNSET	UK SLS50386	
RUNNING STRONG	197	SUNSET		US 5116
ROCKY ROAD	197	UA		US LA586
ROCK'N'ROLL FOREVER	1973	UA		US 5649
IN SPACE	1978	PICKWICK		US 3604

V25 VENUS & THE RAZOR BLADES V25

(A) SONGS FROM SUNSHINE JUNGLE 1978 SPARK srlp125 NL ARIOLA 26121

V25A VIC VERGAT V25A

VIC VERGAT

(A) DOWN TO THE BONE 1981 HARVEST UK SHSP4117

V25B TOM VERLAINE V25B

TOM VERLAINE G V (AB
FRED SMITH B PERC V(AC
JIMMY RIPP G (C
TOMMY PRICE D (C
JOE VASTA B (C
DEERFRANCE V (A
RICKY WILSON G (A
JAY DEE DAUGHERTY D (AC
TOM THOMPSON D (A
ALLAN SCHWARTZBERG D (AC
MARK ABEL G (A
LENE LOVICH SAX V(C
BRUCE BODY K (A

(A) TOM VERLAINE 1979 ELEKTRA US 216 UK 52156
(B) DREAMTIME 1981 WB UK K56919
(C) WORDS FROM THE FRONT 1982 VIRGIN UK 2227

V26 JOHN VERITY BAND V26

JOHN VERITY G V (A
GEOFF LYTH K G (A
GERRY SMITH B (A
RON KELLY D (A
THUNDERTHIGHS V (A

(A) JOHN VERITY BAND 1974 PROBE UK SPB1087 US DUNHILL 50170

V26A MIKE VERNON V26A

MIKE VERNON V HCA PERC(AB
COLIN ALLEN D (B
LAWRENCE GARMAN HCA (B
LEO LYONS B (B
RICK HAYWARD G (A
JOE JAMMER G (B
NICK SOUTH B (B
BILLY GRAHAM TROM (B
LAURIE GARMON HCA (A
FUZZY SAMUELS B (B
PETE WINGFIELD K (AB
MITCH MITCHELL D (B
BRUCE ROWLAND D (B
HOWIE CASEY SAX (B
PAUL KOSSOFF G (A
ANDY SYLVESTER B (B
KENNY LAMB D (A
PAUL BUTLER G (B
CECIL MOSS TPT(B
RORY GALLAGHER G (A
RIC LEE D (B
DICK PARRY SAX (A
DEREK GRIFFITHS G (B
JOHN DONNELLY TPT (B
PAUL BUTLER G (A

(A) BRING IT BACK HOME 1971 BLUE HORIZON UK 2931 003
(B) MOMENT OF MADNESS 1973 SIRE US SAS 7410

V26B

VERTO

V26B

JEAN PIERRE GRASSET G SYN(AB (A) KRIG / VOLUBILIS 1976 TAPIOCA FR 10007 POLE 0009
GILLES GOUBIN B (A (B) REEL 19/36 1978 FLEAU FL 7004
CHARLES GOUBIN G (A
CYRIL LEFEBVRE G (B OCTAVE AGOBERT (B BENOIT WIDEMANN SYN (B DOMINIQUE GRASSET G(B
PHILIPPE PERRONET D (B JEAN PIERRE FOUQUET B K(B FRANCOIS ARTIGE G (B PH GOUBIN D (A
XAVIER VIDAL VLN (A MICHAEL DEPALLE D (A SERGE SOULIE D (A DOMINIQUE DUBUISSON B(A
OKAMOTO V (A ALAIN THOMAS B (A F ARTIGE G (A MICHEL GOUBIN

V26C

EDWARD VESALA

V26C

EDWARD VESALA V D (ALL (A) NANA 1970 BLUE MASTER BLULP 125
JUHANN AALTONEN WIND (ABDEF (B) HOT LOTTA 1973 BLUE MASTER SPEL 306
ARILD ANDERSON B (A (C) I'M HERE 1973 BLUE MASTER SPEL 311
PETER KOWALD B (B (D) NAN MADOL 1974 JAPO 60007 + ECM 1077
PETER BROTZMANN SAX (B (E) SATU 1976 ECM 1088
KAJ BACKLUND TPT (D (F) RODINA 1976 LOVE LRLP 189
SAKARI KUKKO FLT (D
JOHANN POUTANEN V (D TEPPO HAUTOANO B (D ELISABETH LEISTOLA HARP (D MIRCEA STANKO HRNS (DF
SEPPO PAAKKUNAINEN WIND(D PENTTI LANTI WIND (DF CHARLIE MANANO SAX (D TOMASZ STANKO TPT (EF
PALLE MIKKELBERG HRNS (E TOMASZ SZUKALSKI SAX (EF KNUT RIISNAES FLT (E ROLF HALM WIND(E
TORBJØRN SUNDE HRNS (E TERJE RYPDAL G (E PALLE DAUIELGSON B (E PEKKA POYRY SAX (F
ESA HELALSVUO PNO (F PEKKA RECHARDIT (F PEKKA SARMANTO (F IRINA MILAN V (F

V27

PATRICK VIAN

V27

PATRICK VIAN (A (A) BRUITS ET TEMPS ANALOGUES 1978 EGG EURO 900 541

V28

VIBRATORS

V28

IAN CARNOCHAN G V (1 (A) PURE MANIA 1977 EPIC US 35038 CAN 90433 UK 82097
KNOX G V K(ABC1 (B) V 2 1978 EPIC UK 82495
JOHN ELLIS G V SYN(ABC (C) BATTERIES INCLUDED (COMP) 1980 CBS UK 31840
PAT COLLIER G (A (1) 1978
JOHN EDWARDS D (ABC1
GARY TIBBS B (BC1 DON SNOW K SAX(1 DAVE BIRCH G (1 CHRIS SPEDDING G (
GREG VANCOOK G (C BEN BRIERLEY B (C SISTERS OF MERCY V (B

V28A

SID VICIOUS

V28A

SID VICIOUS V (A (A) SID VICIOUS 1979 VIRGIN UK V2144

V29

MIKE VICKERS

V29

MIKE VICKERS (AB (A) I WISH I WERE A GROUP AGAIN 1968 COLUMBIA UK SCX 6180
HUGH BURNS G (B (B) A DAY AT THE RACES 1976 DJM UK DJSLM2034
PAUL KEOGH G (B
MIKE MORAN K (B ALAN TARNEY B (B TREVOR SPENCER D (B CHRIS KARAN PERC (B

V29A

VICTIMS

V29A

RICHARD V HCA(A (A) THE REAL WILD CHILD 1979 GOLDEN DISC US 1001
BARRY RYAN G V (A
CHRIS DEY B V (A M T HEART D (A STEVE BERMAN B (A JAMES ALEXANDER D (A

V30

VIGRASS & OSBORNE

V30

PAUL VIGRASS V (AB (A) QUEUES 1972 UNI US 73129 UK UDLS 501
GARY OSBORNE G V (AB (A) QUEUES 1974 MCA UK RI MCG 3521
BARRY CLARKE G MAND(B (B) STEPPIN' OUT 1974 CBS US 33077 UK 80119
MARK GRIFFITHS G (B
PETER MORGAN B (B TETSU YAMAUCHI B (B PETER WATKINS B (B HERBIE FLOWERS B (B
BARRY DE SOUZA D (B KENNEY JONES D (B RAY COOPER PERC (B PETER WOOD K (B
ALAN HAWKSHAW K (B JEFF WAYNE K (B DOREEN CHANTER V (B IRENE CHANTER V (B
JUANITA FRANKLIN V (B JUDITH POWELL V (B TIM RENWICK G (B

V31

VICTORIAN PARENTS

V31

CLINTON BEALE G V (A (A) SILENCE FOLLOWS 1981 POLYDOR UK POLS 1049
DAVID PHIZACKLEA B V (A
RAY THOMAS D (A STEVE JOHNSON G V (A

V32

GENE VINCENT

V32

GENE VINCENT V (ALL BLUEJEAN BOP 195 CAPITOL T764
CLIFF GALLUP G (1 & THE BLUECAPS 196 CAPITOL T811
JACK NEAL B (1 VINCENT ROCKS,BLUECAPS ROLL 196 CAPITOL T970
WILLIE WILLIAMS G (1 RECORD DATE 196 CAPITOL T 1059
DICKIE HARRELL D (12 SOUNDS LIKE 196 CAPITOL T 1207
PAUL PEEK (2 CRAZY TIMES 1960 CAPITOL T 1342
TOMMY FACENDA (2 CRAZY BEAT 196 CAPITOL T20452
BOBBY LEE JONES (2 SHAKIN UP A STORM 196 CAPITOL 33SX 1646
JOHN MEEKS G (* GENE VINCENT 1967 LONDON UK HAU 8333
JIM GRANT K (* BEST OF GENE VINCENT 1967 CAPITOL T20957
RED RHODES STEEL(* BEST OF VOL 2 1969 CAPITOL ST21144
(*) I'M BACK & I'M PROUD 1969 DANDELION US 102 UK 63754
JIM GORDON D (* GENE VINCENT 1970 KAMA SUTRA UK 2019
MARS BONFIRE G (* THE DAY THE WORLD TURNED BLUE 1971 KAMA SUTRA 2027
SKIP BATTIN B (* PIONEERS OF ROCK 1972 STARLINE UK SRS 5117
STORY VOL 1 1956/57 1973 PATHE FR 064 81081
STORY VOL 2 1958 1973 PATHE FR 064 81082
(1) 1956 STORY VOL 3 1959 1973 PATHE FR 064 81083
(2) 1957 STORY VOL 4 1960 1973 PATHE FR 064 81084
MEMORIAL ALBUM 19 PATHE FR 154 81001
KING OF FOOLS 1974 STARLINE UK SRS 5177
GREATEST 19 CAPITOL IMP 052 80230
SINGLE ALBUM 1981 CAPITOL 26233
THE BOP THEY COULDN'T STOP 1982 MAGNUM FORCE UK 007
BOP THAT WONT STOP 1974 CAPITOL ST 11287
GENE VINCENT STORY 1975 CAPITOL IMP 178 81798
GREATEST 1977 CAPITOL UK CAPS 1001
ROCK'N'ROLL LEGEND(4LP BOXED SET) 1977 EMI IMP 85071/4
GREATEST 1979 CAPITOL UK CAPS 1028
BIRD DOGGIN 1982 LINE GER BULLDOG UK 3001

V32A JAMES VINCENT V32A

JAMES VINCENT G (A (A) SPACE TRAVELLER 1977 CARIBOU US 34237
RONALD STOCKHERT K (A
VERDINE WHITE B (A HARVEY MASON D (A PATRICK M MURPHY PERC (A

V32B MADS VINDING V32B

MADS VINDING B (A (A) DANISH DESIGN 1974 SONET SLP 2560
JAN SCHAFFER G (A
KJELL OHMAN K SYN(A OLA BRUNKERT D (A SABU MARTINEZ CONGA (A

V33 VINEGAR JOE V33

ELKIE BROOKS V K (ABC (A) VINEGAR JOE 1972 ISLAND UK ILPS9183 ATCO US 7007
ROBERT PALMER G V (ABC (B) ROCK'N'ROLL GYPSIES 1972 ISLAND UK ILPS9214 ATCO US 7016
PETE GAGE K G V(ABC (C) SIX STAR GENERAL 1973 ISLAND UK ILPS9262
STEVE YORK HCA B(ABC
TIM HINKLEY K (A ROB TAIT D (A DAVE THOMPSON K SAX(A DAVE BROOKS SAX (A
CONRAD ISADORE D (A KEEF HARTLEY D (AB GASPAR LAWAL PERC (A ROGER BALL HRNS(A
MALCOLM DUNCAN HRNS (A JIM MULLEN G (B MIKE DEACON K V (BC JOHN WOODS (BC
PETE GAVIN D (C

V34 EDDIE 'CLEANHEAD' VINSON V34

EDDIE VINSON V SAX(ALL EDDIE CLEANHEAD VINSON 19 TRIP US 5590
LARRY CORYELL G (H THE ORIGINAL CLEANHEAD 1972 PHILIPS UK 6369 406
NEAL CREQUE K (H CHERRY RED BLUES 19 KING STARDAY US 1087
CORNELL DUPREE G (H JAMMING THE BLUES 1975 BLACK LION BLP 30168
CHUCK RAINEY B (H EDDIE VINSON 19 B&B 33021
BERNARD PURDIE D (H CLEANHEADS BACK IN TOWN 19 BETHLEHEM US BCP 5005
MIKE BLOOMFIELD G (G CLEAN MACHINE 1979 MUSE FR MR 5116
PATTI BROWN K (G (G)CHERRY RED 1967 BLUESWAY 6007
BUDDY LUCAS SAX HCA(G (H) YOU CANT MAKE LOVE ALONE 19 MEGA US 1012
( ) I WANT A LITTLE GIRL 1982 PABLO UK 2310 866

V35 VIOLINSKI V35

MIK KAMINSKI VLN (AB (A) NO CAUSE FOR ALARM 1979 JET US 36133 UK JETLP 219
JOHN MARCANGELO K (AB (B) STOP CLONING ABOUT 1980 JET UK JETLP 232
JOHN HODSON D (AB
MIKE DE ALBUQUERQUE G V(AB BAZ DUNNERY G V (A PAUL MANN V B (A ANDY BROWN B V(A
IAIN WHITMORE B V (B

V35A VISAGE V35A

STEVE STRANGE (A (A) VISAGE 1980 POLYDOR US 16304 UK 2490 157
MIDGE URE G (A (A) VISAGE 1980 POLYDOR NL 2391 494
BILLY CURRIE VLN (A (B) THE ANVIL 1982 POLYDOR UK 5060
JOHN McGEOCH G (A (AB) VISAGE / THE ANVIL 1982 POLYDOR CASS UK DBMC1
RUSTY EGAN D (A
DAVE FORMULA K (A BARRY ADAMSON B (A

V35B FRANKIE VIRTUE & THE VIRTUES V35B

(A) GUITAR BOOGIE SHUFFLE 1980 PRESIDENT UK PRX 16

V36 VISITOR 2035 V36

CRAIG PRUESS KTPT VIBES((A) VISITOR 2035 1978 ARIOLA AHAL 8003
RAY DEEFHOLTS G ((B) CAIN (D) 19
PETER STROUD B (
NIGEL ROBINSON D PERC(

V37 VITAL DUB V37

(A) WELL CHARGED 1977 VIRGIN UK V 2055

V38 JOE VITALE V38

JOE VITALE D V (AB (A) ROLLERCOASTER WEEKEND 1975 ATLANTIC US SD18114 UK K50121
JOE WALSH G (AB (B) PLANTATION HABOR 1980 ASY US 529
RICK DERRINGER G (A
NELSON'FLACO' PADRON PERC(A PHIL KEAGY G (A GEORGE PERRY B V (B RICKY WASHINGTON V (B
WILLIE HALE G (B MARILYN MARTIN V (B JOEAN PERRY V (B PAUL HARRIS K (B
MICKEY THOMAS V (B JOE LALA PERC (B TIM SCHMIT V (B DON FELDER G (B
GREG DROMAN V (B BILL SZYMCZYK PROD (B BOBBY MAYO K (B JIMMY PANKOW TROM(B
LEE LOUGHNANE TPT (B WALT PARAZAIDER SAX (B MARTY GREBB SAX (B GRAHAM NASH V (B

V38A VITESSE V38A

PETER VAN STRATEN B V (E (A) VITESSE 1975 REPRISE RI NL 54058
HERMAN BROOD K V (A (B) VITESSE 1977 NEGRAM NL 25754
PAUL BAGMEIER B (A (C) OUT IN THE COUNTRY 1978 EMI GER 26013
HERMAN VAN BOEYEN D V (ABCDEF (D) ROCK INVADER 1979 NEGRAM NL 26378
RON TEN BOKUM G B V(A (E) LIVE 1980 RCA UK 44024
"BIG" JOHN HCA (A (F) GOOD NEWS 1981 RCA UK 30086
ROB VAN DON SELAAR K (A (CD) VITESSE 1979 UA UK 30250
FERRY WIENECKE K (B
MARGRIET V (A HILDE V (A RUDY DE QUELJOE G (BCD MARK BOON G V (F
ANDRE VERSLUYS B V (BF JAN VANDER MEY G V(BCDE HANRY VAN DIJK G V (B NAPPA NOYA PERC(C
PIM KOOPMAN K VIBE(C WILCO TORROE LEERDAM B V(CD JERNEY & JODY V (C SANDER JANSSEN K (F
FRED LEEFLANG SAX (D TONY DE BRUIN V (D PETER LANGERAK G V (F JOCHEN FLUITSMA G V (F

V39 MIROSLAV VITOUS V39

MIROSLAV VITOUS B SYN G(ALL (A) INFINITE SEARCH 1969 EMBRYO US SD 524
JOE ZAWINUL PNO (B (B) PURPLE 1970 CBS SONY US 37181
JOE HENDERSON SAX (AC (C) MOUNTAIN IN THE CLOUDS 1972 ATLANTIC UK K50406 US SD1622
BILLY COBHAM D (B (D) BASS =(C) 1972 ATLANTIC 30024
JOHN McLAUGHLIN G (ABC (E) MAGICAL SHEPHERD 1976 WB UK K56219 US BS2925
HERBIE HANCOCK K (ACE (F) MIROSLAV 1978 FREEDOM UK 41040 US 1040
JACK DE JOHNETTE D (ACE (G) FIRST MEETING 1980 ECM 1145
JON CHRISTENSEN D (GH (H) M V GROUP 1981 ECM 1185
JOE CHAMBERS D (AC
JAMES GADSON D (E AIRTO MOREIRA PERC (E CHERYL GRAINGER V (E ONIKE V (E
JOHN SURMAN WIND (GH KENNY KIRKLAND PNO (GH

V39A **VIVA** V39A

BANARA SCHENKER K (A — (A) WHAT THE HELL IS GOING ON — 1982 CBS GER 85372
ANDY FACK G (A
RALPH MURPHY G (A

V39B **VIVABEAT** V39B

(A) PARTY IN THE WAR ZONE — 1981 CHARISMA US 3102

V39C **VOG** V39C

ONY KAYE V (A — (A) VOG — 1981 RCA PL 28466
RENNIE XOSA B V (A
JIMI JOHALLIS D (A ROBERT LEPICOLO SYN K(A BOBBY DIMONTE G V (A

V40 **VOICES OF EAST HARLEM** V40

BERNICE COLE V (— (A) RIGHT TO BE FREE — 1970 ELEKTRA US 74080 UK 2469 007
GERRI GRIFFIN V (— (B) BROTHERS & SISTERS — 197 ELEKTRA UK K42119
CYNTHIA SESSIONS V (— (C) VOICES OF EAST HARLEM — 1973 JUST US JUST 7
JAMES MISSOURI V (— (D) CAN YOU FEEL IT — 1974 JUST US JUST3504

V40A **VOLKSMUSIC** V40A

ALBRECHT METZGER G V (B — (A) SONGSAUS DER SCHAN — 19
WOLFGANG KALLERT B V (B — (B) MORGENS UM 7 ABENDS UM 8 — 1979 PLANE GER
STEFAN POPOVIC D V (B
PETER SCHICK K G V(B HANS DIETER SUMPF G V (B

V41 **ADELBERT VON DEYEN** V41

ADELBERT VON DEYEN ALL INST(AB — (A) STEMGAT — 1978 SKY SKY 019
(B) MORDBORG — 1979 SKY SKY 029
(C) ATMOSPHERE — 1980 SKY 041

V41A **ROGER VOUDOURIS** V41A

ROGER VOUDOURIS (ABC — (A) RADIO DREAM — 1979 WB
(B) A GUY LIKE ME — 1980 WB
(C) ON THE HEELS OF LOVE — 1981 BOARDWALK US

V42 **VOYAGER** V42

PAUL FRENCH K V (AB — (A) HALFWAY HOTEL — 1979 MOUNTAIN UK TOPS124 US ELEKTRA 208
PAUL HIRSH K G V(AB — (B) ACT OF LOVE — 1980 MOUNTAIN UK TOPS127 US RCA 3662
CHRIS HOOK B V (AB — (C) THE WEB — 1981 RCA UK 5020
JOHN MARTER D (AB

W1 **THE WACKERS** W1

BOB SEGARINI G V (ABCD — (A) WACKERING HEIGHTS — 1971 ELEKTRA US EKS 74098
ANDY BISHOP V G B K (ABCD — (B) HOT WACKS — 1972 ELEKTRA US EKS 75025
MICHAEL STULL G V PNO(AB — (C) SHREDDER — 1972 ELEKTRA US EKS 75046
BILL KOOTCH TROCHIM V B G(ABCD — (D) WACK'N' ROLL (NOT RELEASED)
SPENCER T EARNSHAW D (ABC
BILL HENDERSON D (A JACK SCHAEFFER SAX (AC KATHIE KODAMA KOTO (B J P LAUZON B G PNO(C
DAN YEN MANTOR CONGAS(C FRANKIE HART V PERC (C JERRY MERCER D (C RAY BLAKE V (C
JANET ABRAMSON V (C MARK ABRAMSON PROD (C

W2 **WAGES OF SIN** W2

TIM RENWICK G (A — (A) 1968
COLIN FREEMAN (A PETER DINES K (A VIC FARRAR (A JERRY SHIRLEY D(A

W3 **ADRIAN WAGNER** W3

ADRIAN WAGNER K (ABC — (A) DISTANCES BETWEEN US — 1974 ATLANTIC UK K50082
JOHN CORNWALL B (C — (B) INSTINCTS — 1977 CHARISMA UK CAS 1124
MEL COLLINS SAX (B — (C) THE LAST INCA — 1978 CHARISMA UK CAS 1135
IVO HATFIELD G (C
MORRIS PERT D (BC BOB WESTON G (B THUNDERTHIGHS V (B

W3A **WAH** W3A

(A) NAH POO THE ART OF BLUFF — 1981 ETERNAL CLASSIC1

W3B **THE WAILERS** W3B

KENT MORRILL K (— TALL COOL ONE — 1964 IMPERIAL US 12262 UK LONDON
MARK MARUSH SAX (— FABULOUS WAILERS AT THE CASTLE — 19 ETIQUETTE US ALB1
RICK DANGEL G (— WAILERS WAILERS EVERYWHERE — 19 ETIQUETTE US ALB23
BUCK ORMSBY B (— WAILERS & COMPANY — 19 ETIQUETTE US ALB22
MIKE BURK D (— OUT OF OUR TREE — 19 ETIQUETTE US ALB26
GAIL HARRIS V (— OUTBURST — 19 UA US 6557
ROBIN ROBERTS V (— WAILERS — 19 GOLDEN CREST US 3075
WALK THRU' THE PEOPLE — 1967 BELL US 6016

W4 **BUNNY WAILER** W4

BUNNY WAILER V (ABC — (A) BLACK HEART MAN — 1976 ISLAND uk ILPS 9415
CARLTON BARRETT D (A — (B) PROTEST — 1977 ISLAND UK ILPS 9512
ASTON BARRETT G (A — (C) SINGS THE WAILERS — 1981 ISLAND UK ILPS 9629
HEADLEY BENNETT HRNS (C — (D) ROCK'N' GROOVE — 1981 SOLOMONIC IMP
ROBBY SHAKESPEARE B (ABC
TYRONE DOWNIE K (A TOMMY McCOOK FLT (AB PETER TOSH G (AB WINSTON WRIGHT K (AC
DIRTY HARRY HRNS (AB BOBBY ELLIS HRNS (AB HERMAN MARQUIS HRNS (AB WILLY PEP PERC(A
HAROLD BUTLER K (A EARL CHINNA SMITH G (AC FRATTER G (A HORSE MOUTH D (B
MIKE RICHARDS D (B EARL LINDO K (B TOUTER K (B KEITH STERLING K (BC
SOLOMONIC ENCHANTERS V (B STICKY PERC (C DEAN FRASER HRNS (C NAMBO HRNS(C
SLY DUNBAR D (C

W4A **WAILING SOULS** W4A

WINSTON'PIPE'MATTHEWS V(AB — (A) WILD SUSPENSE — 1979 ISLAND UK ILPS 9523
LLOYD McDONALD V (AB — (B) FIREHOUSE ROCK — 1981 GREENSLEEVES UK GREL 21
HEADLEY BENNETT SAX (A
RAD BRYAN G (A ANSELL COLLINS K (A GEORGE HAYE V (AB TARZAN NELSON PNO (A
RUDOLPH DENNIS V (AB NOEL SLY DUNBAR D (A RANCHIE McLEAN B (A VIN GORDON TROM(A
STICKY THOMPSON PERC (A RICO TROM (A CEDRIC BROOKS SAX (A NOEL SIMMS PERC(A
ROBBIE SHAKESPEARE G (A BOPEE BOWEN G (A DICKAGE HRNS (A

W5 LOUDON WAINWRIGHT III W5

LOUDON WAINWRIGHT II G V(ALL (A) ALBUM 1 1971 ATLANTIC US SD8260 UK 2400 103
RICHARD CROOKS D (CEFG (A) ALBUM 1 1971 ATLANTIC UK K40107
JOHN CROWDER B (FG (B) ALBUM 2 1972 ATLANTIC US SD8291 UK K40272
STEPHEN TUBIN K (FG (C) ALBUM 3 1972 CBS US 31462 UK 65238
RON GETMAN STEEL G (FG (D) ATTEMPTED MOUSTACHE 1974 CBS US 32710 UK 65837
JIMMY MAELEN CONGA(F (E) UNREQUITED 1975 CBS US 33369 UK 80696
ELLIOTT RANDALL G (F (F) T SHIRT 1976 ARISTA US 4063 UK ARTY 127
JOANNE VENT V (F (G) FINAL EXAM 1978 ARISTA US 4173 UK SPART1042
GWYNNE MICHAELS V (F (H) LIVE ONE 1979 ROUNDER US 3050 RADAR UK RAD 24
ERIN ARNOLD DICKINS (F
JEAN ARNOLD V (F CHRISTIE THOMPSON V (F JON COBERT V (F GEORGE MARGE REC (F
MARVIN STAMM HRNS (F HANK JONES K (F MARKIE MARKOWITZ HRNS (F RICHARD DAVIS B (F
JOE COCUZZO D (F PETER LA BARBERA VIBES(F MAGGIE ROCHE V (F TERRE ROCHE V (F
ERIC WEISSBERG BANJO(FG CHARLES BROWN III G (CF KENNETH KOSEK FDL (CFG GLEN MITCHELL K V (FG
DAVID SANBORN SAX (CF PAUL PRESTOPINO (F DAVE TAYLOR TROM (F JOHN LISSAUER CLAR(FG
DON HAMMOND REF (F HARVEY ESTRIN REC (F JOHN HALL G (EG ARLEN ROTH G (G
HUGH McCRACKEN G (G LARRY PACKER FDL (G ERROL BENNETT PERC (G TEDDY WENDER PNO (C
GREG THOMAS D (E RON COLBERTSON (E HARVEY BROOKS B (E KLAUS VOORMANN B (E
LYLE RITZ B (E RICHARD GREENE VLN (E MARTIN FIERRO SAX (E ANNA McGARRIGLE V (E
THOMAS JEFFERSON KAYE G(C DON PAYNE B (E CALVIN HARDY (FRANK KLEIGER (E
RANDY WALLACE (E MARTY GREBB K (E CHRIS GUEST (E GEORGE GERDES (E
JIM KELTNER D (E JAY MIGLIORI WIND (E AUSTIN DELONE (E KATE McGARRIGLE V (E

W5A JOHN WAITE W5A

JOHN WAITE V (A (A) IGNITION 1982 CHRYSALIS UK CHR 1376
IVAN KRAL G K (A
DONNIE NOSSOV B V (A TIM PIERCE G (A FRANKIE LA ROCKA D (A CRISPIN CIOE HRNS(A
ARNO HECHT HRNS (A PAUL LITTERAL HRNS (A PATTY SMYTH V (A RAHNI KUGEL V (A
ILANA MORRILLO V (A BRUCE BRODY K (A

W5B THE WAITRESSES W5B

PATTY DONAHUE V (A (A) WASN'T TOMORROW WONDERFUL 1982 polydor us 6346
ARIEL WARNER V (A
MARS WILLIAMS WIND (A DAVID HOFSTRA B (A BILLY FICCA D (A DAN KLAYMAN K (A
CHRIS BUTLER G (A TRACY WORMWORTH B (A DON CHRISTENSEN D (A RALPH CARNEY SAX HCA(A
STUART AUSTIN D (A RICK DAILEY K (A

W6 TOM WAITS W6

TOM WAITS G V (ALL (A) CLOSING TIME 1973 ELEKTRA US SD5061 UK SYL 9007
MIKE MELVOIN K (C (A) CLOSING TIME 1976 ELEKTRA UK K53030
PETE CHRISTLIEB SAX (C (B) HEART OF A SATURDAY NIGHT 1974 ASYLUM US 7E1015 UK K53035
JIM HUGHART B (CFGD (C) NIGHTHAWKS AT THE DINER 1975 ASYLUM US 7E2008 UK SYSP 903
SHELLEY MANNE D (CD (C) NIGHTHAWKS AT THE DINER 1976 ASYLUM UK K63002
LEW TABACKIN SAX (CD (D) SMALL CHANGE 1976 ASYLUM US 7E1078 UK K53050
DA WILLIE GONGA K (F (E) FOREIGN AFFAIRS 1977 ELEKTRA US 7E1117 UK K53068
RICK LAWSON D (F (F) BLUE VALENTINE 1978 ASYLUM US 6E 162 UK K53088
ROLAND BAUTISTA G (FG (G) HEART ATTACK & VINE 1980 ASYLUM US 6E 295 UK K52252
BYRON MILLER B (F (1) TV SHOW ENGLAND 1979
FRANK VICARI SAX (F
RAY CRAWFORD G (F CHARLES KYNARD B (F CHIP WHITE D (F BOBBYE HALL PERC (F
HAROLD BATTISTE PNO (F SHINE ROBINSON G (F SCOTT EDWARDS B (F EARL PALMER D (F
BIG JOHN THOMASSIE D (G PLAS JOHNSON SAX (G GREG COHEN B (G RONNIE BARRON K (G
VICTOR FELDMAN PERC (G MICHAEL LANG PNO (G MEL COLLINS SAX (1 TIM HINKLEY K (1
CLEM CLEMPSON G (G HERBERT HARDESTY SAX (F BILL GOODWIN D (C BONES HOWE PROD (BD
DELBERT BENNETT TPT (A SHEP COOKE G V (A ARNI EGILSSON B (A JESSE EHRLICH CELLO(AD

W6A JOHNNY WAKELIN W6A

JOHNNY WAKELIN V (ALL (A) REGGAE SOUL & ROCK'N'ROLL 1976 PYE US 12131 UK NSPL 18521
(B) AFRICAN MAN 1977 PYE UK NSPL 18487
(C) DOUBLE TROUBLE 1978 PYE UK NSPL 18561
(D) GOLDEN HOUR 1979 PYE UK GH 680

W7 RICK WAKEMAN W7

RICK WAKEMAN K PROD(ALL (1) PIANO VIBRATIONS 1971 POLYDOR UK 2460 135
TIM RICE V (K (A) 6 WIVES OF HENRY VIII 1973 A&M US 4361 UK AMLH64361
DAVE WINTOUR B (A (B) JOURNEY TO THE CENTRE OF EARTH 1974 A&M US 3621 UK AMLH63621
CHRIS SQUIRE B (AG (C) KING ARTHUR 1975 A&M US 4515 UK AMLH64515
CHAS CRONK B (A (D) LISZTOMANIA 1975 A&M US 4546 UK AMLK64546
LES HURDLE B (A (E) NO EARTHLY CONNECTION 1976 A&M US 4583 UK AMLK64583
MIKE EGAN G (AGB (F) WHITE ROCK 1976 A&M US 4614 UK AMLH64614
DAVE LAMBERT G (A (G) CRIMINAL RECORD 1977 A&M US 4660 UK AMLK64660
STEVE HOWE G (A (H) BEST KNOWN WORKS 1978 A&M UK AMLH68447
ALAN WHITE D (AG (J) RHAPSODIES 1979 A&M US 6501 UK AMLX68508
BILL BRUFORD D (A (K) 1984 1981 CHARISMA UK CDS 4022
TONY VISCONTI G (J (L) THE BURNING 19
BARRY DE SOUZA D (A
RAY COOPER PERC (A DAVID HEMMINGS V (B FRANK RICOTTI PERC (AGK DAVE COUSINS BANJO (A
LISA STRIKE V (A LAURA LEE V (A BARRY ST JOHN V (A SYLVIA McNEILL V (A
JUDY POWELL V (A ASHLEY HOLT V (BCE GARY PICKFORD HOPKINS V (BC JEFF CRAMPTON G (C
ROGER NEWELL B (BCE BARNEY JAMES D (BC JOHN HODGSON PERC (C JOHN DUNSTERVILLE G V(E
TONY FERNANDEZ D (EFK MARTY SHIELD HRNS V (E REG BROOKS HRNS V(E BILL ODDIE V (B
ARS LAETA CHOIR V (B ROGER DALTREY V (D PAUL NICHOLAS V (D LINDA LEWIS V (D
DAVID WILDE PNO (D GEORGE MICHIE (D JOHN FORSYTHE (D ENG ROCK ENSEMBLE (D
NAT PHILHARMONIC ORCH (D BRUCE LYNCH B (J FRANK GIBSON D (J NICO RAMSDEN G (J
STEVE BARNACLE B (K TIM STONE G (K VICKIE BROWN V (K STEVIE LANGE V (K
KEVIN KELLY B (L MIKE GAREAU G (L RONNIE LAWSON K (L BRIAN MATHEWS V (L
CHAKA KHAN V (K STEVE HARLEY V (K JON ANDERSON V (K KENNY LYNCH V (K
SONIA JONES V (K GARRY BARNACLE SAX (K ALAN BRAWER G (L MIKE BRAUN D (L
ARLEN ROTH G (L LIBERTY DEVITTO D (L LONDON SYMP ORCHESTRA (B ENGLISH CHAMBER CHOIR(B

W8 NARADA MICHAEL WALDEN W8

NARADA MICHAEL WALDEN D V(ALL (A) GARDEN OF LOVE LIGHT 1977 ATLANTIC US 18199 UK K50329
JEFF BECK G (A (B) I CRY, I SMILE 1978 ATLANTIC UK K50417
RAY GOMEZ G (AB (C) AWAKENING 1979 ATLANTIC US SD19222 UK K50570
T M STEVENS B (D (D) THE DANCE OF LIFE 1979 ATLANTIC UK K50678
CARLOS SANTANA G (AC (E) VICTORY 1980 ATLANTIC US SD19279 UK K50473
HIRAM BULLOCK G (BC
NEIL JASON B (B CLIFF CARTER K (BC HERBIE MANN SAX (B NORMA JEAN BELL SAX (AB
SAMMY FIGUEROA PERC (AB RAFAEL CRUZ PERC (B CHRISTINE FAITH V (B ELLEN DELESTON V (B
CHERYL ALEXANDER V (BC WILL LEE B (A DAVID SANCIOUS K (A CISSY HOUSTON B V (A
PATTY SCALFA V (AC BOB KNAPP HRNS (A ICARUS JOHNSON G (A DON MERO SYN (A
LOIS COLIN HARP (A JAY GRAYDON G (C PAT THRALL G (C KENNY MAZUR G (C
KENI BURKE B (C NATE PHILLIPS B (C NORBERT SCOLEY B (C GREG PHILLINGANES K (C
BOBBY LYLE K (C MICHAEL BRECKER HRNS (C RANDY BRECKER HRNS (C AIRTO MOREIRA PERC (C
POINTER SISTERS V (C JIM GILSTRAP V (CD CARLA VAUGHN V (CD ALEX BROWN V (C
ANGELA WINBUSH V (C BILL LAMB TPT (E TAWATHA AGEE V (C CORRADO RUSTICI G V (DE
RANDY JACKSON B (E FRANK MARTIN K (DE MARC RUSSO SAX (DE DAVID GROVER TPT (DE
WAYNE WALLACE TROM (E DANNY NOE TROM (D VICKI RANDLE V (D NUHAD SABA MARTIN V (D

W9 WENDY WALDMAN W9

WENDY WALDMAN V PNO G DULC(ALL (A) LOVE HAS GOT ME 1973 WB US BS 2735
DAVID KEMPER D (D (B) GYPSY SYMPHONY 1974 WB US BS 2792
KENNY EDWARDS B G V(ABCD (C) WENDY WALDMAN 1975 WB US BS 2859
ANDREW GOLD G V PNO (ABCD (D) THE MAIN REFRAIN 1976 WB US BS 2974
WADDY WACHTEL G (D (E) STRANGE COMPANY 1978 WB US BS 3178
EMIL RICHARDS PERC (C (F) WHICH WAY TO MAIN STREET 1982 EPIC US
LINDA RONSTADT V (D
MICHAEL BOTTS D (D KARLA BONOFF V (ABCD NICK DE CARO ACC (D PETER BERNSTEIN B (DE
DAVID FOSTER K (CD STEVE CROPPER G (D KING ERRISSON PERC (D TAJ MAHAL V (D
JIM HORN WIND (ABD MILT HOLLAND CONGA(D VICTOR FELDMAN PERC (AD STEVE FERGUSON K G V(ACD
JAI WINDING ORG (D CHUCK FINDLEY HRNS (ABD DON MENZA HRNS (ABD JAY MIGLIORI HRNS(D
STEVE BEERS D (E MARK GOLDENBERG G PNO G V(E CRAIG HULL G V (E DEBBIE DOBKIN V PERC(E
KAT HENDRIKSE D (E PETER ROBINSON PNO (E PETER WHITE K (E JENNIFER WARREN V (C
RON TUTT D (C RUSS KUNKEL D (A JOHN JOSEPH KELSON HRNS (A JOE PORCARO PERC(A
BOBBYE HALL PERC (A MARIA MULDAUR V (AB KAREN ALEXANDER V (A PETER IVERS HCA (A
BARRY BECKETT K SYN(B ROGER HAWKINS D (B JIMMY JOHNSON G (B THOMAS ROADY PERC(B
JOEL TEPP HCA (B GENE GARFIN D (A LARRY BUNKER VIBES(A LEE SKLAR B (A
STEPEN PAIETLA ACC (A FRED STREINER STR (A CARMI SIMON MAND G (AB GREG PRESTOPINO V (AB
DAVID CAMPBELL STR (A PETE CARR G (B DAVID HOOD B (B JERRY MASTERS B (B
PAUL HUBINON HRNS (B

W9A WALDORF & TRAVERS W9A

M WALDORF V (A (A) NIGHT BLINDNESS 19 UA UK UAG30234
G TRAVERS V (A
HENRY SPINETTI B (A DAVE MARKEE B (A LAWRENCE JUBER G (A PHIL PALMER G (A
BILLY LIVSEY K (A SIMON MORTON PERC (A PETER HOPE EVANS HCA (A STAN SULZMANN HRNS(A
KENNY WHELLER HRNS (A RAY WARLIEGH HRNS (A

W10 WALES /O'REGAN W10

ERIC WALES V G MAND K(A (A) READY TO RUN 1977 MOUNTAIN UK TOPC5010
JERRY O'REGAN G V (A
JEFF ALLEN D (A BARRY DE SOUZA D (A ALLAN MAIR D (A PETE ZORN B (A
ROGER SUTTON B (A DAVE MARKEE B (A RICHARD BRUNTON G (A DAVE ROSE K (A
GEOFF WESTLEY K (A B J COLE STEEL(A TONY COLE WIND (A STAN SULZMANN HRNS(A
RON ASPERY HRNS (A JACK EMBLOW ACC (A VICKY BROWN V (A LIZA STRIKE V (A
BARRY ST JOHN V (A IRENE CHANTER V (A ANNE CULLEN V (A

W10A DAVID T WALKER W10A

DAVID T WALKER G (AB (A) DAVID T WALKER 1973 ODE US SP 77011
JOE SAMPLE K (A (B) PRESS ON 1974 ODE US SP 77020
JOHN LEHMAN V (A (C) SIDEWALK 19 REVUE US RS 7297
JERRY PETERS K (A (D) PLUMM HAPPY 19 ZEA 1000
BILLY PRESTON K (A (E) ON LOVE 1976 ODE US SP 77035
CLARENCE McDONALD K (A
PAUL HUMPHREY D (A WILTON FELDER B (A JIM GILSTRAP V (A STEPHANIE SPRUILL V (A
BOBBYE HALL PERC (A CURTIS AMY SAX (A MERRY CLAYTON V (A PATRICE HOLLOWAY V (A
ANN ESTHER DAVIS V (A

W11 JERRY JEFF WALKER W11

JERRY JEFF WALKER G V (ALL (A) MR BOJANGLES 1968 ATCO US 33259
DAVID BROMBERG G (ABE (B) DRIFTIN' WAY OF LIFE 1969 VANGUARD US VSD 6521
GARY ILLINGSWORTH K (A (C) FIVE YEARS GONE 1969 ATCO US 33297
DONNY BROOKS HARP (A (D) BEIN' FREE 1970 ATCO US 33336
DANNY MILTON DOBRO(A (E) JERRY JEFF WALKER 1972 MCA US 510 RI 1976 2358
JODY STECHER FDL MAND(A (E) JERRY JEFF WLAKER 1973 MCA UK MUPS 488 RI 1974 MCF 2518
BOBBY CRANSHAW B (A (E) JERRY JEFF WALKER 1973 DECCA US 75384
JERRY JEMMOTT V (A (F) VIVA TERLINGUA 1973 MCA US 382 RI 76 2350
RON CARTER B (A (F) VIVA TERLINGUA 1973 MCA UK MAPS7164
BILL LAVORGNA D (A (G) WALKERS COLLECTIBLES 1974 MCA US 450 RI 76 2355
KENNETH BUTTREY D (BIJ (G) WALKERS COLLECTIBLES 1974 MCA UK MCF 2592
NORBERT PUTNAM B (BIJ (H) RIDIN' HIGH 1975 MCA US 2156
PETE WADE DOBRO(B (I) ITS A GOOD NIGHT FOR SINGING 1976 MCA US 2202 UK MCG 3522
HAROLD RUGG STEEL(B (J) A MAN MUST CARRY ON (DBL) 1977 MCA US 2 8013 UK MCSP 281
WAYNE MOSS G (B (K) CONTRARY TO ORDINARY 1978 MCA US 3041 UK MCF 2851
DAVID BRIGGS K (BIJ (L) JERRY JEFF 1978 ELEKTRA US 6E163 UK K52106
PATTERSON BARRETT STEEL(EJ (M) TOO OLD TO CHANGE 1979 ELEKTRA US 6E239
BEN CARUSO B (E (N) BEST OF 1980 MCA US 5128
RAY WYLIE HUBBARD V (J (O) REUNION 1981 MCA US 5199
WILLIE NELSON G V (J
DAVID COOK STEEL(E JEFF DUFINE PNO (E MARY EGAN VLN (EF CRAIG HILLIS G (EF
ELLEN KEARNEY V (E BOB LIVINGSTON K B V(EFHIJL RAUN MACKINNON PNO (E MICHAEL McGARRY D (E
MICHAEL MURPHEY G (E ANDY NEWMARK D (E GARY P NUNN K V (EFHIJ LARRY PACKER G VLN(E
MICKEY RAPHAEL HARP (EF JIM RICHMOND D (E JONATHAN SIMMONS MAND (E HERB STEINER STEEL(EFJ
JOANNE VENT V (EF KELLY DUNN ORG (FHIJ JOHN INMON G V (HIJ TOMAS RAMIREZ WIND(HJLM
DONNY DOLAN D (HIJ WELDON MYRICK STEEL(IJ JOHNNY GIMBLE FDL (IM CHIP YOUNG G V (I

(CONTINUED)

W11 (CONTINUED)

JERRY JEFF WALKER
W11

BOBBY THOMPSON BAN (I SHANE KEISTER K (I DEBORAH ALLEN V (I REESE WYNANS K (I
BOBBY RAMBO G B V(JLM RON COBB SAX (JLM LEO LEBLANC STEEL(JLM FRED KRC D PERC V(JLM
DAVE PERKINS G (JLM KEITH SYKES G (L PENNY NEY V (L STEVE ZIRKEL HRNS(L
MICHAEL MORDECAI HRNS (LM CAROLE KING V (M RICHARD PRICE B (M MARK HALLMAN D (M
DAVID AMRAM HRNS (M FINGERS TAYLOR HCA (M GEORGE M JONES PERC (M STEVE KEITH FDL (J
KAREN BROOKS V (J SHARI NEUWELL V (J VASSAR CLEMENTS FDL (J BEE SPEARS B (J
DON McCLURE K (J SUSAN WALKER V (J HONDO CROUCH V (J CHARLES JOHN QUATRO V(J
BILL JOOR (J JIMMY BAKER TROM (J

W11A
JOHNNY' BIG MOOSE' WALKER
W11A

JOHNNY WALKER K (A (A) RAMBLIN WOMAN 1969 ABC BLUESWAY US 6036

W12
JUNIOR WALKER & THE ALL STARS
W12

JUNIOR WALKER	SAX V(	SHOTGUN	1965	TAMLA UK STML11017 US SOUL	701
WILLIE WOODS	G (	SOUL SESSION	1966	TAMLA UK STML11029 US SOUL	702
VIC THOMAS	K (	ROADRUNNER	1966	TAMLA UK STML11038 US SOUL	703
		LIVE	196	TAMLA UK STML11152 US SOUL	705
JAMES GRAVES	D (	HOME COOKIN'	196	TAMLA UK STML11097 US SOUL	710
		GREATEST HITS	196	TAMLA UK STML11120 US SOUL	718
		WHAT DOES IT TAKE TO WIN YOUR LOVE	196	US SOUL	721
		A GASSSS	1970	TAMLA UK STML11167 US SOUL	726
		LIVE	1970	US SOUL	725
		RAINBOW FUNK	1971	TAMLA UK STML11198 US SOUL	732
		MOODY JUNIOR	1972	TAMLA UK STML11211 US SOUL	733
		PEACE & UNDERSTANDING	1973	TAMLA UK STML11234 US SOUL	738
		GREATEST HITS VOL 2	1973	TAMLA UK STML11224	
		ANTHOLOGY	1974	TAMLA UK TMSP 1129 US M2	786
		JR WALKER & THE ALL STARS	1974	TAMLA UK STML11274	
		HOT SHOT	1976	TAMLA UK STML12018 US SOUL	745
		SAX APPEAL	1976	TAMLA UK STML12033 US SOUL	747
		WHOPPER BOPPER SHOW STOPPER	1976	TAMLA UK STML12048 US SOUL	748
		MOTOWN SPECIAL	1977	TAMLA UK STMX 6005	
		20 SUPER HITS	1978	EMI EURO 062 60061	
		SMOOTH SOUL	1978	TAMLA UK STML12089 US SOUL	750
		BACK STREET BOOGIE	1979	WHITFIELD US 3331	

W12A
PHILLIP WALKER
W12A

PHILLIP WALKER	G V (AB	(A) SOMEDAY YOU'LL HAVE THESE BLUES	1980	SONET UK SNTF831 US ALIGATOR 4715
AL BRUNO	G (A	(B) BLUES SHOW LIVE AT PIT INN	1980	YUPITERU JAP YR 23 4002
BILL MURRAY	K (A	( ) THE BOTTOM OF THE TOP	1975	PLAYBOY US 118
JUNSHI YAMAGISHI	G (B			

DENNIS WALKER B (AB FREDDIE LEWIS D (A AL DEVILLE TPT (A ARCHIE FRANCIS D (A
VICTOR HILL D (A DAVID II HRNS (A JOHNNY BANKS ORG (A AARON TUCKER D (A
MILTON THOMAS PERC (A GEORGE SMITH HCA (B JOHNNY TUCKER D (B MITSUYOSHI AZUMA G (B

W13
T BONE WALKER
W13

T BONE WALKER	G V (ALL	T B WALKER	196	CAPITOL	T 1958
MIKE OMARTIAN	K (V	THE TRUTH	1968	BRUNSWICK US	754126
CHARLES BROWN	K (V	THE TRUTH	1968	MCA UK MUPS331	RIMCF2617
JAMES BOOKER	K (V	STORMY MONDAY BLUES	1968	STATESIDE UK	SSL 10223
MAX BENNETT	B (V	STORMY MONDAY	1973	BLUESWAY	BLS 6008
PAUL HUMPHREY	D (V	STORMY MONDAY	197	WET SOUL US	1002
BEN BENAY	G HCA(V	STORMY MONDAY BLUES	1978	CHARLY UK	CR 30144
RICHARD BENNETT	G (V	FUNKY TOWN	1969	STATESIDE UK	SSL 10265
JERRY LACROIX	HCA (V	FUNKY TOWN	1973	BLUESWAY	BLS 6014
DAVID FATHEAD NEWMAN	SAX(V	WELL DONE	19	HOME COOKING US	HCS103
MIKE STOLLER	K (V	DIRTY MISTREATER	1973	BLUESWAY	BLS 6058
JOE OSBORN	B (V	(I) I WANT A LITTLE GIRL	1973	DELMARK US	DS 633
DEAN PARKS	G (V	FEELIN' THE BLUES	197	B & B	33019
SWEET INSPIRATIONS	V (V	(V) VERY RARE	1974	WB UK	K94001
DIZZY GILLESPIE	TPT (V	(T) T BONE BLUES	1975	ATLANTIC UK K40131	US SD8256
JON FADDIS	TPT (V	SINGING THE BLUES	197		
TONY STUDD	TROM (V	CLASSICS OF MODERN BLUES	1976	BLUENOTE	BLAD 533
ZOOT SIMS	SAX (V	JUMPS AGAIN	1980	CHARLY UK	CRB 1019
HERBIE MANN	FLT (V	FLY WALKER AIRWAYS	1974	POLYDOR US 5521	
WARREN BERNHARDT	K (V	EVERYDAY I HAVE THE BLUES	19	BLUESTIME US 9004	
LOUIE SHELTON	G (V	GOOD FELLING	19	POLYDOR 24 4502	
KING ERRISSON	CONGA(V				

JOHN TROPEA SITAR(V WILTON FELDER B (V LARRY CARLTON G (V AL COHN SAX(V
DAVID T WALKER G (V GERRY MULLIGAN SAX (V JERRY DODGION WIND (V JOE FARRELL WIND (V
FRANK VICARI WIND (V GARNETT BROWN TROM (V PAUL FAULISE TROM (V SELDON POWELL WIND(V
MARVIN STAMM TPT (V DANNY STILES TPT (V MIKE GIBSON TROM (V R S RANKIN G (T
BARNEY KESSEL G (T PLAS JOHNSON SAX (T JOE COMFORT B (T LLOYD GLENN PNO (T
OSCAR BRADLEY D (T GEORGES ARVANITAS PNO (I S P LEARY D (I RAY JOHNSON PNO (T
EARL PALMER D (T BILLY HADNOTT B (T HAL SINGER SAX (I JACKIE SAMSON B (I
JIM GORDON D (V

W13A
WALKER BROTHERS
W13A

JOHN MAUS WALKER	G VV (ALL	(A) THE WALKER BROTHERS	1965	STAR CLUB	158 026 STY
SCOTT ENGEL	V G K(ALL	(B) PORTRAIT	1966	STAR CLUB	158 028 STY
GARY LEEDS	V D (ALL	(B) PORTRAIT	1966	PHILIPS	BL 7732
STEVE GREY	K G (FJ	(C) IMAGES	1967	STAR CLUB GER 158 032	
CHRIS MERCER	SAX (K	(C) IMAGES	1967	PHILIPS UK SBL7770	
DAVE McRAE	K (FJK	(D) STORY (COMP)	1967	PHILIPS 843476/7	6640 001
BARRY MORGAN	D (FJ	(E) MAKE IT EASY ON YOURSELF	1972	PHILIPS UK	6336 214
RONNIE ROSS	SAX (K	(E) MAKE IT EASY ON YOURSELF	19	CONTOUR RI	CN 2017
DOUG WRIGHT	D (F	(F) NO REGRETS	1975	GTO	GTLP 007
CHRIS KARAN	PERC (F	(G) GREATEST HITS	1975	PHILIPS	6640 009
ALAN PARKER	G (FJ	(H) IMMORTAL	1970	PHILIPS	6870 564
RITCHIE HITCHCOCK	G (F	(J) LINES	1976	GTO	6321 114
JUDD PROCTOR	G (F	(K) NITE FLIGHTS	1978	GTO	GTLP 033
LEN WALKER	G (F	( ) TAKE IT EASY ON YOURSELF	1965	PHILIPS UK	SBL 7691
B J COLE	STEEL(F	( ) SPOTLIGHT ON	1979	PHILIPS UK	6640 013
BRIAN ODGERS	B (F	( ) SUN AINT GONNA SHINE	1966	SMASH US	27082
BRIAN BENNETT	D (J				

(CONTINUED)

W13A WALKER BROTHERS (CONTINUED) W13A

MORRIS PERT PERC (K
SIMON PHILLIPS D (J ALAN JONES B (J JOHN MEALING G (J PAUL KEOGH G (J
ALAN SKIDMORE WIND (JK JEFF DALY WIND (J DAVE WILUS WIND (J TRISTAN FRY PERC (J
LES DAVIDSON G (K JIM SULLIVAN G (K PETER VAN HOOKE D (K MO FOSTER B (K
FRANK GIBSON D (K DILL KATZ B (K ROGER CHURCHYARD VLN (J

W13B WALL W13B

KELLY V (A (A) BEACHEAD 19 FRESH UK FLP 2
NICK WARD G (A (B) PERSONAL TROUBLES & PUBLIC ISSUES 1980 FRESH LP 2
ANDY GRIFFITHS B (A (EP) GHETTO 1980 FRESH FRESH 17
RAB RAE BEITH D (A
PETE WILSON K G (A

W13C ALWYN WALL BAND W13C

ALWYN WALL G V (A (A) THE PRIZE 1977 MYRRH MYR 1057
NORMAN BARRETT G V (A
PHIL HOLMES K V (A TONY HUDSON B (A NICK BROTHERWOOD D (A

W13D WALLENSTEIN W13D

BILL BARONE G V (ABCD (A) BLITZKRIEG 1971 BASF 20 290646
HARALD GROSSKOPF D (ABC (B) MOTHER UNIVERSE 1972 BASF 20 291138
JURGEN DOLLASE K V (ALL (C) COSMIC CENTURY 19 OHR KM 58 006
JERRY BERKERS B V (AB (D) STORIES SONGS & SYMPHONIES 19 OHR KM 58 014
JURGEN PLUTA B PERC(DE (E) NO MORE LOVE 1977 RCA PL 30010
JOACHIM REISER VLN (CD (F) CHARLINE 1978 RCA PL 30045
NICKY GEBHARD D (E (G) BLUE EYED BOYS 1979 RCA PL 30061
GERD KLOCKER G V (E (H) FRAULEINS 1980 RCA EURO 064 45932
DIETER MEIER B (C
ROLF DOLLASE FLT (C KIM MERZ V (FGH PETE BROUGH G (FGH MICHAEL DOMMERS G(FGH
CHARLY TERSTAPPEN D (FGH TERRY PARK B (FGH

W13E WALKIE TALKIES W13E

TONY BEARD D (A (A) SURVEILLANCE 1980 RIALTO UK 101 US 44059
ROB SPENSLEY B V (A
DAVE FULLER G V (A ALAN MURPHY G (A DAVE STEWART K (A KEITH GEMMELL WIND (A
TONY MARONIE BONGO(A KIM BEACON V (A

W13F WALLACE COLLECTION W13F

RAYMOND VINCENT VLN (AB (A) FIRST COLLECTION 19 PARLOPHONE UK 7076
CHRISTIAN JANSEN B (B (B) WALLACE COLLECTION 1070 PARLOPHONE UK 7099 US CAPITOL 350
JACQUES NAMOTTE CELLO(B
MARC HEROVETT K (B SYLVAIN VAN HOLMAN G (B FREDDY NIEULAND D V (B

W14 WALLY W14

PETE COSKER G B V(AB (A) WALLY 1974 ATLANTIC US 18115 UK K50051
PAUL GERRETT K V (A (B) WALLY GARDENS 1975 ATLANTIC UK K50180
PAUL MIDDLETON STEEL B (AB
ROGER NARRAWAY D (AB NICK GLENNIE SMITH K V(B JAN GLENNIE SMITH V (B MADELINE BELL V (B
PETE SAGE VLN MAND B (AB ROY WEBBER G V (AB RAY WEHRSTEIN SAX(B

W15 WALRUS W15

DON RICHARDS TPT (A (A) WALRUS 1971 DERAM UK SML1072 US JANUS 3051
ROY VOCE SAX (A
BILL HOAD WIND(A STEVE HAWTHORN B (A JOHN SCATES G (A NICK GABB D (A
BARRY PARFITT K (A NOEL GREENAWAY V (A

W15A SHEILA WALSH W15A

SHEILA WALSH V (A (A) FUTURE EYES 1981 CHAPEL LANE UK CLS 8006
COLIN VALLANCE B (A
CHRIS ROBINSON K (A RAY GOUDIE D (A RALPH BOLLARD B (A ROB MARSHALL G (A
NORMAN BARRETT G (A DAVE MORRIS K (A PETE BROOKS G (A DAVE BOLLARD B (A
DAVE KASAK G (A

W15B STEVE WALSH W15B

STEVE WALSH V K D(A (A) SCHEMER DREAMER 1980 KIRSHNER US 36320
PHIL EHART D (A
TIM GEHRT D (A STEVE MORSE G (A ALAN SLOAN VLN (A JEFF LUX G VIBES FLT(A
KERRY LIVGREN G (A TURNER GAUGH B (A CECIL WELCH TPT (A SKIP LANE SAX (A
RICH WILLIAMS G (A DAVID BRYSON G (A DUANE BUCKLER B (A MERLE McLAIN B (A

W16 JOE WALSH W16

JOE WALSH G V SYN B(ALL (A) BARNSTORM 1973 DUNHILL US 50130 PROBE UK 6268
KENNY PASSARELLI B V(ABC (A) BARNSTORM 1974 ANCHOR RI UK ABCL 5022
JOE VITALE FLT D K(ABCDF (B) THE SMOKER YOU DRINK 1973 DUNHILL US 50140 PROBE UK 6275
AL PERKINS STEEL(A (B) THE SMOKER YOU DRINK 1974 ANCHOR RI UK ABCL 5033
PAUL HARRIS K (A (C) SO WHAT 1974 DUNHILL US 50171
ROCKE GRACE K V (B (C) SO WHAT 1974 ANCHOR UK ABCL 5055
TOM STEPHENSON K (C (D) YOU CANT ARGUE WITH A SICK MIND 1975 ABC US ABCD 932 ANCHOR UK 5156
RANDY MEISNER V (C (D) YOU CANT ARGUE WITH A SICK MIND 1981 MCA UK RI 1613
CLYDIE KING V (B (E) SO FAR SO GOOD 1978 ANCHOR UK ABCL 5240
VANETTA FIELDS V (B (F) BUT SERIOUSLY FOLKS 1978 ASYLUM US 6E 141 UK K53081
JOE LALA PERC (B (G) BEST OF 1979 ABC US 1083
RICKY FATAAR D ((EP) PLUS FOUR 1977 ANCHOR UK ABE 1202
JOHN STRONACH V (C (H) THERE GOES THE NEIGHBORHOOD 1981 ELEKTRA US 5E523 UK K52285
BRYAN GAROFALO B V (C
J D SOUTHER G V (C DAN FOGELBERG G V (C DAVID MASON K (D WILLIE WEEKS B (DF
JAY FERGUSON K V (DF DON FELDER G V (D GLENN FREY V (CDF DON HENLEY V (CDF
ROCKY DZIDZORNU PERC (D ANDY NEWMARK D (D JOEY MURCIA G (F TIM SCHMIT V (F
CHUCK RAINEY (A RON GRINEL D (C GUILLE GARCIA PERC (C JODY BOYER V (C

W16A TRAVIS WAMMACK W16A

TRAVIS WAMMACK G V HCA (AB (A) TRAVIS WAMMACK 1973 FAME US 1801
RICK HALL V (B (B) NOT FOR SALE 1975 CAPRICORN US 162 UK 2493 133
LEON SHERRILL G (B
PETE CARR G (B DON CARTEE D (B RANDY McCORMICK K (B BARRY BECKETT K (B
JOE HAMILTON B (B LENNY LE BLANC B (B JIMMY EVANS D (B RONNIE OLDHAM K (B
STACY GOSS HRNS (B ROGER CLARK D (B

W16B THE WANDERERS W16B

STIV BATORS V (A — (A) ONLY LOVERS LEFT ALIVE 1981 POLYDOR POLS 1028
DAVID FREGANNA B V (A
DAVE PARSONS G V (A RICK ROCK D (A

W17 WAR W17

ERIC BURDON V (ABK — (A) BLACKMANS BURDON 1970 LIBERTY LDS 8400 314
DEACON JONES V (— (B) ERIC BURDON DECLARES WAR 1970 POLYDOR UK 2310 041
HAROLD BROWN D (ABCDEFGHJKLMNO — (C) WAR 1971 UA US LA5508 UK LBG83478
HOWARD SCOTT G PERC(ABCDEFGHJKLMNO — (C) WAR RI 1979 MCA UK MCG4003 ISLAND 76 ILPS 9164
B B DICKERSON B PERC(ABCDEFGHJKLMNO — (D) ALL DAY MUSIC 1972 UA US LA5546 UK UAS29269
CHARLES MILLER WIND(ABCDEFGHJKLMNO — (D) ALL DAY MUSIC RI 1979 MCA UK MCF3020 ISLAND 76 ILPS 9177
(D) ALL DAY MUSIC RI 1981 LAX US 37111
LONNIE JORDAN K (ABCDEFGHJKLMNO — (E) THE WORLD IS A GHETTO 1973 UA US LA5652 UK UAS29400
PAPA DEE ALLEN PERC(BCDEFGHJKLKNO — (E) THE WORLD IS A GHETTO RI 1979 MCA UK MCF3021 ISLAND 76 ILPS 9171
(E) THE WORLD IS A GHETTO RI 1981 LAX US 37112
LEE OSKAR HCA (ABCDEFGHJKLMNO — (F) DELIVER THE WORD 1973 UA US LA 128 UK UAG29521
(F) DELIVER THE WORD RI 1979 MCA· UK MCF3022 ISLAND 76 ILPS 9194
(G) LIVE 1974 UA US LA 193 UK UAD60067/8
(G) LIVE RI 1979 MCA UK MCF3040 ISLAND 76 ILSD 8
(H) WHY CANT WE BE FRIENDS 1975 UA US LA 441 UK UAG29843
(H) WHY CANT WE BE FRIENDS RI 1981 LAX US 37113
(H) WHY CANT WE BE FRIENDS RI 1979 MCA UK MCF3023 ISLAND 76 ILPS 9378
(I) GREATEST HITS 1976 UA US LA 648 ISLAND ILPS 9413
(J) PLATINUM 1977 UA US 690 ISLAND UK ILPS 9507
(K) LOVE IS ALL AROUND 1976 ABC US ABCD 988 UK ABCL 5207
(K) LOVE IS ALL AROUND 1979 MCA UK MCF3025
(L) YOUNGBLOOD(SOUNDTRACK) 1978 UA US LA904 MCA UK MCF 2864
(M) GALAXY 1978 MCA US MCA 3030 UK MCF 2822
(N) MUSIC BAND 1979 MCA 3085 UK RI 79 MCF 4001
(O) MUSIC BAND 2 1979 MCA UK 3050 US 3193
(P) PLATINUM JAZZ (DBL) 1979 MCA 305

W18 CLIFFORD T WARD W18

CLIFFORD T WARD V K(ALL — (A) SINGER SONGWRITER 1972 DANDELION UK 2310 216
DEREK THOMAS GABCDF — (B) HOME THOUGHTS FROM ABROAD 1973 CHARISMA US 6061 UK CAS 1066
KEN WRIGHT D (ABCD — (C) MANTLEPIECES 1973 CHARISMA US 6065 UK CAS 1077
BEV PEGG B (A — (D) NO MORE ROCK'N'ROLL 1975 PHILIPS 8109 500
DAVID SKINNER K (A — (E) ESCALATOR 1975 CHARISMA UK CAS 1098
JOHN SAWYER VIBES(A — (F) WAVES 1976 PHILIPS 9109 216
WILL ROPER FLT (A — (G) NEW ENGLAND DAYS 1977 PHILIPS 9109 605
JOHN MEALING K (F
PAUL KEOGH G (F PETE KING SAX (F TERRY EDWARDS B(BCDF CHRIS SPEDDING G (D
ALAN PARKER G (D MIKE MORAN K (D BRIAN ODGERS B (D ANDREW STEELE D (D
CHRIS KARAN PERC (D B J COLE STEEL(D PETE WINGFIELD PNO(D MARTIE ECHITO K D(G
GENE HOLMES G V (G MARC LEVINE B (G MARC SINGER D (G SID SHARP STRINGS (G
KEITH SMART D (F MICHAEL EASLEY G (G

W18A HAYES WARE W18A

HAYES WARE V (A — (A) GHETTO WOMAN 1979 BASH US 426
BILLY BRANCH HCA (A
SHORT GARY D (A CRAIG 'SLOE GIN' WALTON B(A

W18B LEON WARE W18B

LEON WARE V (A — (A) ROCKIN YOU ETERNALLY 1981 ELEKTRA UK K52282

W19 WARHORSE W19

NICK SIMPER (AB — (A) WARHORSE 1970 VERTIGO UK 6360 015
MAC POOLE D (AB — (B) RED SEA 1972 VERTIGO UK 6360 066
ASHLEY HOLT V (AB
FRANK WILSON K PNO(AB PETER PARKER G (B GED PECK G (A

W19A WARLOCK W19A

(A) WARLOCK 1972 BUDDAH US 102

W20 WARM DUST W20

PAUL CARRACK K (ABC — (A) AND IT CAME TO PASS 1970 TREND UK TNLS 700
DAVE PEPPER D (AC — (A) AND IT CAME TO PASS 1970 UNI US 73109
TEX COMER B (ABC — (B) PEACE FOR OUR TIME 1971 TREND UK 6480 001
LES WALKER V (ABC — (C) THIRD ALBUM 1972 BASF
ALAN SOLOMON SAX K V (ABC
JOHN SURGUY SAX G V (ABC KEITH BAILEY D (B

W20A JOHNNY WARMAN W20A

JOHNNY WARMAN (A — (A) WALKING INTO MIRRORS 1981 ROCKET UK TRAIN 17
JERRY MAROTTA D (A
JOHN GIBLIN B (A TONY LEVIN B (A DAVE LAWSON K (A LARRY FAST SYN(A

W20B DAVE WARNERS W20B

DAVE WARNERS V (A — (A) MUG'S GAME 1978 MUSHROOM AUST 36759
JOHN DENNISON K V (A
JOHN RYAN G (A PAUL NOONAN B V (A ALI JOHNSTONE PERC (A TONY DURANT STEEL V(A
TREVOR LUCAS V (A PETER SCHULTZ BAN (A BOB SPENCER G (A GAIL V (A
DANNY V (A DR PEPPER V (A MARK MOFFAT V (A

W21 JENNIFER WARNES W21

JENNIFER WARNES K V (ALL — ( ) I CAN REMEMBER 1968 PARROT US 71020
KENNY EDWARDS V G (B — ( ) SEE ME 1968 PARROT US 71034
MIKE FINNIGAN V (B — ( ) JENNIFER 1972 REPRISE US 2065
BRIAN RUSSELL V (B — (A) JENNIFER WARNES 1977 ARISTA US 4062 UK SPARTY 1006
NICKY HOPKINS K (A — (B) SHOT THROUGH THE HEART 1979 ARISTA US 4217 UK SPART 1097
PEGGY SANDVIG K (A
JAY GRAYDON G (A JIM HORN WIND (A DAVE McDANIELS B (A RUSS KUNKEL D (A
JOE CORRERO D (A JIM PRICE K V TROM (A DANIEL MOORE V (A MATTHEW MOORE V (A
DAN SAWYER G (A STEVE MADAIO TPT (A SKIP MESQUITE SAX (A MAX HASKETT TPT(A
LAUDIR DE OLIVEIRA PERC(A JIM MOORE V (A ALAN LINDGREN PNO (A JOHN HUG G (A
DOUG ROAHNE G (A REINIE PRESS B (A DENNIS ST JOHN D (A BETH FICHET V (A
HERB PEDERSEN V (A DOUG G LIVINGSTON PNO (AB BRIAN WHITCOMB PNO (A GAYLE LEVANT HARP (A
MICHAEL BOWDEN B (A MATT BETTON D (A DOUG HAYWOOD V (A BEN BENAY G (A

(CONTINUED)

W21 JENNIFER WARNES (CONTINUED) W21

DANNY KOOTCH G (A ANDREW GOLD D B K G (B BLONDIE CHAPLIN G V (B JIM GORDON D (B
BOB GLAUB D (B BROCK WALSH K V (B DENNY SEIWELL D (B BUZZY FEITEN G (B
ABRAHAM LABORIEL B (B MARK OLSON K (B MARTY GREBB K (B BILL ELLIOTT PNO (B
WALT RICHMOND K (B RICKY FATAAR D (B CHICO GOLDSMITH PERC(B ROB FRABONI V (B
PENNY NICHOLS V (B

W21A WARSAW PAKT W21A

ANDY CALQUHOUN B (A (A) WARSAW PAKT 1977 ISLAND ILPS 9515
LUCAS FOX D (A
JOHN WALKER (A CHRIS UNDERHILL (A JIMMY COULL (A

W21B DIONNE WARWICK W21B

DIONNE WARWICK V (ALL PRESENTING 1964 PYE UK NPL28037 SCEPTER US 508
ISAAC HAYES V (M ANYONE WHO HAD A HEART 1964 SCEPTER US 517
KARL RICHARDSON PROD (Z MAKE WAY FOR 1964 PYE UK NPL28046 SCEPTER US 523
BARRY GIBB V PROD G SRT(Z THE SENSITIVE SOUND OF 1965 PYE UK NPL28055 SCEPTER US 528
STEVE GADD D (Z THE BEST OF 1966 PYE UK NPL28064
GEORGE BITZER K SYN(Z HERE I AM 1966 PYE UK NPL29071 SCEPTER US 531
GEORGE TERRY G (Z IN PARIS 1966 PYE UK NPL28076 SCEPTER US 534
JOE LALA PERC (Z HERE WHERE THERE IS LOVE 1967 PYE UK NPL28096 SCEPTER US 555
DANIEL BEN ZEBULON PERC(Z ON STAGE AND IN THE MOVIES 1967 PYE UK NPL28101 SCEPTER US 559
GARY BORION SAX (Z WINDOWS OF THE WORLD 1967 PYE UK NPL28105 SCEPTER US 563
WHIT SIDENER HRNS (Z MAGIC OF BELIEVING 1967 SCEPTER US 567
BRETT MURPHEY HRNS (Z VALLEY OF THE DOLLS 1968 PYE UK NPL28114 SCEPTER US 568
DAN BONSANTI HRNS (Z FREEWHEELIN' 1969 PYE UK NPL28120
KEN FAULK HRNS (Z SOULFUL 1969 PYE UK NPL28122 SCEPTER US 573
NEAL BONSANTI HRNS (Z SOULFUL 1971 WAND UK WNS12
ALBHY GALUTEN PROD SYN K(Z GREATEST MOTION PICTURE HITS 1969 PYE UK NPL28126 SCEPTER US 575
RICHARD TEE PNO (Z GOLDEN HITS VOL 1 1969 WAND UK WNS 1 SCEPTER US 565
TIM RENWICK G (Z GOLDEN HITS VOL 2 1970 WAND UK WNS 2 SCEPTER US 577
I'LL NEVER FALL IN LOVE AGAIN 1970 SCEPTER US 581
GEORGE PERRY B (Z VERY DIONNE 1971 WAND UK WNS 10 SCEPTER US 587
DENNIS BRYON PERC (Z PROMISES PROMISES 1971 WAND UK WNS 11 SCEPTER US 571
ANITA LOPEZ PERC (Z FROM WITHIN VOL 1 1972 WAND UK 1007 SCEPTER US 598
PETER GRAVES HRNS (Z FROM WITHIN VOL2 1972 WAND UK 1008
GREATEST HITS VOL 1 1973 HALLMARK UK 789
GREATEST HITS VOL 2 1973 HALLMARK UK 803
DIONNE 1973 WB UK K46140 US 2585
THE DIONNE WARWICK STORY 1 1973 GOLDEN HOUR UK826
THE DIONNE WARWICK STORY 2 1973 GOLDEN HOUR UK 827
JUST BEING MYSELF 1973 WB UK K46186 US 2658
GREATEST HITS 3 1974 HALLMARK UK 829
THEN CAME YOU 1975 WB UK K56109 US 2846
GREATEST HITS 4 1975 HALLMARK UK 883
TRACK OF THE CAT 1975 WB UK K56178 US 2893
DIONNE WARWICK COLLECTION 1976 PICKWICK UK 001
FOREVER OLD 19 SCEPTER US 5110
VERY BEST OF 19 UA US UALA 388
(M) A MAN & A WOMAN 1976 ABC UK ABCD613
LOVE AT FIRST SIGHT 1977 WB UK K56429 US 3119
DIONNE 1978 ARISTA UK SPART1096
NO NIGHT SO LONG 1980 ARISTA UK SPART1132
HOT LIVE & OTHERWISE 1981 ARISTA UK DARTY 10
GOLDEN COLLECTION 1981 K TEL UK NE1137
20 GREATEST HITS 1981 ORCHID UK 003 CASSETTE
FRIENDS IN LOVE 1982 ARISTA UK SPART1192
20 GOLDEN PIECES 1982 BULLDOG UK
HEARTBREAKER 1982 ARISTA UK 204974

W21C WAS(NOT WAS) W21C

DAVID WAS SAX K V(A (A) WAS(NOT WAS) 1981 ISLAND UK ILPS 7015
JACK TANN PROD (A
DAN WAS B SYN V(A

W22 WASA EXPRESS W22

BO HALLGREN K (ABC (A) WASA EXPRESS 1977 LOVE SWED 239
MALLA RONNANDER HCA (C (B) ON WITH THE ACTION 1978 LOVE SWED 279 SONET UK SNTF771
CARY SHARRAF EL DIN G (ABC (C) WASA EXPRESS 1979 SONET SNTF 810
BO HAGGSTROM B (ABC
AKE ERIKSSON D (ABC

W22A WASHBOARD DOC,LUCKY & FLASH W22A

JOSEPH'WASHBOARD'DOCTOR (A (A) EARLY MORNING BLUES 1980 L&R 42010
CAB LUCKY G V (A
JOHN'FLASH'WHITNER B V (A LOUISIANA RED G V (A

W22B BABY WASHINGTON W22B

BABY WASHINGTON (ALL THATS HOW HEARTACHES ARE MADE 1965 SUE US 1014 LONDON UK HAC8260
ONLY THOSE IN LOVE 1966 SUE US 1042 LONDON UK HAC8292
THE ONE & ONLY 196 TRIP US 8009
SOUL OF BABBY WASHINGTON 196 UA US 21020
WITH YOU IN MIND 19 DEEP US 16528 UK UA 1217

W23 DELROY WASHINGTON W23

DELROY WASHINGTON B V G PERC(AB (A) I SUS 1976 VIRGIN UK V2060
CANDY McKENZIE V (B (B) RASTA 1977 VIRGIN UK V2088
BUNNY McKENZIE B G (AB
JUNIOR MARVIN G (B KARL PITTERSON PERC (B ANGUS GAYE D (AB AL ANDERSON G (AB
TREVOR STARR G (B DICK CUTHELL PERC HRNS (B COURTNEY HEMMINGS K (AB GEORGE OBAN PERC(AB
TONY ROBINSON K (AB RICO TROM (AB EDDIE THORNTON HRNS (AB KEITH GEMMELL WIND(AB
JUNIOR KERR G (A LADBROKE GROVE ST CHOIR(A DONALD GITS G (A PAT THRALL G (A

W24 GENO WASHINGTON(& THE RAM JAM BAND) W24

GENO WASHINGTON V (ALL — (A) HAND CLAPPIN' FOOT STOMPIN' 1966 PICCADILLY UK NPL38026
HERB PRESTIDGE (— (A) HAND CLAPPIN' FOOT STOMPIN' 1980 PYE UK NSPL18618
STEVE GREGORY WIND (— (B) SHAKE A TAIL FEATHER 1968 PICCADILLY UK NSPL38029
BUD BEADLE SAX (— (C) HIPSTERS FLIPSTERS 1968 PICCADILLY UK NSPL38032
JEFF WRIGHT (— (D) RUNNING WILD 1968 PYE UK NSPL18219
JOHN ROBERTS (— (E) SIFTERS,SHIFTERS,FINGER CLICK MAMA1969 MARBLE ARCH UK MAL 816
CARL PALMER D (— (F) UP TIGHT 1969 MARBLE ARCH UK MAL 1162
PETE GAGE G (— (G) GOLDEN HOUR 1975 PYE UK GH 594
ROD BABY (— (H) GENO'S BACK 1976 DJM UK DJF 20486
BILLY DAVEY (— (J) LIVE 1976 DJM UK DJF 20457
LIONEL KINGHAM SAX (— (L) THAT'S WHY HOLLYWOOD LOVES ME 1979 DJM UK DJF 20561
BARRIE MARTIN PERC (J — ( ) PUT OUT THE CAT 197 TELDEC GER 24665
DONNA FEIN V (L
PETE LAMONT TROM (J — ROGER CHANTLER D (J — DAVID BALLENTINE G V (J — CHRIS STAINES B V(J
MIKE MEROS K (L — JOE CHEMAY B V (L — MIKE BAIRD D (L — BRENT NELSON D (L
PAULINHO DA COSTA PERC (L — GEORGE DOERING G (L — JOEL PESKIN SAX (L — CURT BOETCHER V (L
MUFFY HENDRIX V (L

W25 GROVER WASHINGTON W25

GROVER WASHINGTON SAX (ALL — (A) SOUL BOX (DBL) 1973 KUDU US 1213 KULD 501
BOB JAMES K (DE — (B) INNER CITY BLUES 197 KUDU KULD 11 KUL 3
LOUIS JOHNSON B (E — (C) ALL THE KINGS MEN 197 KUDU KUL 7
GARY KING B (DE — (D) MISTER MAGIC 1975 KUDU KUL 20
STEVE GADD D (E — (E) FEEL SO GOOD 1975 KUDU KU 24
RALPH MACDONALD PERC(DEFN — (F) SECRET PLACE 1976 KUDU KU 32
RANDY BRECKER TPT (E — (G) SOUL BOX 1 1976 KUDU KU 12
JON FADDIS TPT (DEN — (H) SOUL BOX 2 1976 KUDU KU 13
JOHN FROSK TPT (E — (J) LIVE AT THE BIJOU 1978 KUDU SOUL D02
BOB MILLIKAN TPT (E — (K) REED SEED 1978 TAMLA STML12099
ALAN RAPH TROM (E — (L) PARADISE 1979 ELEKTRA US6E182 UK K52130
BARRY ROGERS TROM (E — (M) WINELIGHT 1980 ELEKTRA US 6E305 UK K52262
DAVE TAYLOR TROM (E — (N) SKYLARKIN' 1980 MOTOWN UK STML12131
PHIL UPCHURCH B (D — (O) BADDEST 1981 MOTOWN UK TMSP 604
HARVEY MASON D (DF — (P) COME MORNING 1981 ELEKTRA US 562 UK K52337
ERIC GALE G (DFN
DAVID GRUSIN PNO (F — TONY JACKSON B (F — GEORGE MRAZ B (F — STEVE KHAN G (F
GERRY NIEWOOD SAX (F — JOHN BLAKE VLN V K (K — TYRONE BROWN B (K — LEONARD GIBBS V PERC(K
JAMES SIMMONS K (K — RICHARD L STEACKER G V (K — MILLARD VINSON D (K — ED WALSH K (N
JORGE DALTO PNO (N — ALEXANDER OTEY TPT (N — MARCUS MILLER B (N — RICHARD TEE K (N
IDRIS MUHAMMAD D (N — PAUL GRIFFIN K (N — MARVIN STAMM TPT (D — KENNETH RICE D (E
JIMMY MADISON D (E

W26 WASTED YOUTH W26

KEN SCOTT (A — (A) WILD & WANDERING 1981 BRIDGEHOUSE UK BHLP 006

W26A WASTELAND W26A

(A) WANT NOT (EP) 1979 DISASTER

W27 SADAO WATANABE W27

SADAO WATANABE SAX FLT(ABCD — (A) ROUND TRIP 1970 CBS SONY 50320
CHICK COREA K (A — (B) AUTUMN BLOW 1977 INNERCITY US IC 6064
LEE RITENOUR G (BC — (C) CALIFORNIA SHOWER 1979 MIRACLE MLP3005
ERNIE WATTS SAX (BC — (D) HOW'S EVERTHING (DBL LIVE) 1980 CBS 22081
PATRICE RUSHEN K (B — ( ) ORANGE EXPRESS 19 ?
JACK DEJOHNETTE D (A
ANTHONY JACKSON B (BD — JON FADDIS TPT (D — TOKYO PHILHARMONIC ORCH(D — HARVEY MASON D (BC
STEVE FORMAN PERC (B — DAVE GRUSIN K (CD — CHUCK RAINEY B (C — PAULINHO DA COSTA PERC(C
OSCAR BRASHEAR TPT (C — GEORGE BOHANON TROM (C — RICHARD TEE K (D — ERIC GALE G (D
JEFF MIRANOV G (D — STEVE GADD D (D — RALPH MACDONALD PERC (D — MIROSLAV VITOUS B (A

W27A WATER W27A

(A) DAMBURST 19 VERTIGO UK 9286 575

W27B WATER & POWER W27B

RACHEL SANDERS V (A — (A) WATER & POWER 1975 FANTASY F9494
WARREN SAMS V (A
CHRISTINE ADAMS V (A — JAMES GADSON D (A — JAMES JAMERSON B (A — SONNY BURKE K (A
RAY PARKER JR G (A — BUD BRISBOIS HRNS (A — GEORGE BOHANON TROM (A — GARY COLEMAN PERC(A

W27C WATERFALL W27C

(A) BENEATH THE STARS 1981 GUNDOG UK LP003

W28 MUDDY WATERS W28

MUDDY WATERS (McKINLEY MORGANFIELD) G V(ALL — (A) AT NEWPORT 1960 CHESS 1449 + CRL 4513
(A) AT NEWPORT 1967 MARBLE ARCH UK MAL 661
JIMMIE ROGERS G (RSYa — (A) AT NEWPORT 1973 CHECKER UK 6467 306
WILLIE DIXON B (RSY — (B) MUDDY WATERS 1964 PYE INT UK NPL28040 US CHESS203
PAUL BUTTERFIELD HCA (X — (B) MUDDY WATERS 1967 MARBLE ARCH UK MAL 723
FRED BELOW D (RSY — (C) FOLK SINGER 1964 PYE INT NPL28048 US CHESS 1483
LEROY FOSTER G (S — (D) SINGS BIG BILL BROONZY 1964 US CHESS 1444
BIG CRAWFORD B (RSY — (E) MUDDY BRASS & THE BLUES 1967 CHESS US 1507
ANDREW STEPHENS B (ARSY — (F) REAL FOLK BLUES 1966 CHESS UK CRL4515 US 1501
PAT HARE G (AS — (G) MORE REAL FOLK BLUES 196 CHESS US 1511
FRANCIS CLAY D (ARSVY — (H) SUPER BLUES 1966 CHESS UK CRL4529
WILLIE SMITH D (SZabcde — (I) SUPER SUPER BLUES BAND 1968 CHECKER LPS 3010 CHESS CRL 4537
ELGIN EVANS D (SL — (J) ELECTRIC MUD 1968 CADET LPS 314
LITTLE WALTER HCA (RSY — (K) SAIL ON 19 CHESS 1539
JERRY PORTNOY HCA (ade — (L) DOWN ON STOVALLS PLANTATION 19 TESTAMENT US T2210
SAM LAWHORN G (STVXd — (M) AFTER THE RAIN 1969 CADET LPS 320 CHESS 50017
OTIS SPANN PNO (PRSVYQ — (N) THEY CALL ME MUDDY WATERS 19 CHESS 1553
LEVON HELM D B (X — (O) THE BEST OF MUDDY WATERS 19 CHESS FR 9124 224
JAMES MADISON G (Sd — (M) AFTER THE RAIN 1969 CHESS CRL 4553
PAUL OSCHER HCA (PSc — (Q) FATHERS & SONS 1969 CHESS 2 127 CRL 4556
SONNY WIMBERLEY B (S — (Q) FATHERS & SONS 1969 CHESS 50033
BO DIDDLEY G V (I — (R) McKINLEY MORGANFIELD AKA M WATERS 1972 CHESS 60006

(CONTINUED)

W28 **MUDDY WATERS** (CONTINUED) W28

JOE NEWMAN TPT (T — (S) VINTAGE MUD — 1970 SUNNYLAND KS 100
MARCUS JOHNSON SAX (S — (T) LONDON SESSIONS — 1972 CHESS 6310 121 60013
CHARLES CALMESE B (Zd — (U) CANT GET NO GRINDING — 1973 CHESS 6310 129 50023
RORY GALLAGHER G (TW — (V) MUD IN YOUR EAR — 1973 MUSE 5008
CAREY BELL HARRINGTON HCA(TW — (W) LONDON REVISTED — 1974 CHESS 60026
RICK GRECH B (TW — (X) WOODSTOCK ALBUM — 1975 CHESS 60035
STEVE WINWOOD K (TW — (Y) CHESS BLUES MASTERS — 1977 CHESS NL 6641 639 2ACBM 203
GEORGE FORTUNE K (TW — (Z) HARD AGAIN — 1977 BLUE SKY US 34449 UK 81853
MITCH MITCHELL D (TW — (a) I'M READY — 1977 BLUE SKY US 34928 UK 82235
JOHNNY WINTER G (UZade — (b) 'UNK IN FUNK — 1974 CHESS 60031
BOB MARGOLIN G (XZabde — (c)LIVE — 1972 CHESS 50012
HERBIE LOVELL D (T — (d) LIVE — 1977 BLUE SKY US 35712 UK 83422
CHARLES'CHUCK' BERRY G(L — (e) KING BEE — 1980 BLUE SKY US 37064 UK 84918
GEORGE BUFORD HCA (V — ( ) CHICAGO 5 GOLDEN YEARS — 1980 CHESS FR 427005
LEONARD CHESS PERC(RY — ( ) BACK IN THE GOOD OLD DAYS — 19 SYNDICATE CHAPTER 001
LUTHER TUCKER G (RY — ( ) GOOD NEWS — 19 SYNDICATE CHAPTER 002
CHARLES STEPNEY ORG (P
SELDON POWELL SAX (T — GARTH HUDSON ACC K SAX(X — HOWLIN WOLF V HCA(I — PHIL UPCHURCH G (PQ
ROSETTA HIGHTOWER V (T — WALTER HORTON HCA (RYa — FRED CARTER B G (U — ERNIE ROYAL TPT(T
PINETOP PERKINS PNO(XZabcde — HOWARD JOHNSON SAX (X — JOE DENIM HCA (c — PETE COSEY G (P
GARNETT BROWN TROM (T — LUTHER JOHNSON G (Vbde — MORRIS JENNINGS D (P — JAMES COTTON HCA(ARSYZd
CALVIN JONES B(bcde — LOUIS SATTERFIELD B (P — LITTLE WILLIE SMITH HCA (— TAT HARRIS G (ARY
PERCY THOMAS G V (L — LOUIS FORD V MAND(L — HENRY SIMS G VLN(L — MIKE BLOOMFIELD G (Q
DONALD DUNN B (Q — SAM LAY D (Q — BUDDY MILES D (Q — JEFFREY CARP HCA(Q
PAUL ASBELL G (Q

W29 **ROGER WATERS** W29

ROGER WATERS (A — (A) THE BODY (SOUNDTRACK) — 1970 HARVEST UK SHSP 4008
RON GEESIN (A

W29A **GERAINT WATKINS** W29A

GERAINT WATKINS K V (A — (A) GERAINT WATKINS & THE DOMINATORS — 1979 VERTIGO 9102 033
ANDY FAIRWEATHER LOW G V(A
MICKY GEE G PERC V B(A — JOHN DAVID B V PERC(A — DAVE CHARLES D V (A — HENRY SPINETTI D V(A
STEVE GREGORY SAX V(A — BUD BEADLE SAX V (A

W29B **JOHN L WATSON** W29B

JOHN L WATSON V (A — (A) WHITE HOT BLUE BLACK — 1970 DERAM UK SMLR 1061

W30 **JOHNNY GUITAR WATSON** W30

JOHNNY GUITAR WATSON G V(ALL — (A) JOHNNY GUITAR WATSON — 196 KING US 857
EMRY THOMAS D (MNOPHQ — (B) BLUES SOUL — 196 CHESS US 1490
TOMMY ROBERTSON TROM (MNO — (C) LARRY WILLIAMS SHOW WITH J G W — 1965 DECCA UK LK 4691
KNUD JENSEN SAX (N — (D) BAD — 1966 OKEH OKS 14118
WALT FOWLER TPT (NOQ — (E) TWO FOR THE PRICE OF ONE — 1967 OKEH OKS 14122
MAXWELL DAVIS SAX (J — (F) I CRIED FOR YOU — 1967 CADET LPS 4056
JIM WYNN SAX (J — (G) IN THE FATS BAG — 1968 OKEH OKS 14124
RENE HALL G (J — (H) LISTEN — 1973 FANTASY EURO 03861279 US 9437
TED BRUNSON G (J — (I) GANSTER OF LOVE — 19 POWERPAK 306
BARNEY KESSEL G (J — (J) THE GANGSTER IS BACK — 1975 RED LIGHTNING UK RL 0013
RUDY COPELAND K V (H — (K) I DONT WANT TO BE A LONE RANGER — 1976 FANTASY US 9484
ANDRE LEWIS K B (H — (L) CAPTURED LIVE — 1976 DJM
J D REED SAX (H — (M) AIN'T THAT A BITCH — 1976 DJM US DJM 3 UK DJF 20485
HENRY REED G SAX(H — (N) A REAL MOTHER FOR YA — 1977 DJM US DJLPA7 UK DJF 50505
DARCUS V (P — (O) FUNK BEYOND THE CALL OF DUTY — 1977 DJM US 714 UK DJF 20525
BILL HALEY SAX (OQ — (P) GIANT — 1978 DJM US 19 UK DJF 20551
MAXAYN LEWIS V (H — (Q) WHAT THE HELL IS THIS — 1979 DJM US 24 UK DJF 20557
PAUL DUNMALL SAX (M — (R) LOVE JONES — 1980 DJM UK DJF 20568
GREGORY DUVAS TPT (Q — (S) GETTIN DOWN — 1978 CADET US 4056
ALBERT WING SAX (Q — (T) VERY BEST OF — 1981 DJM UK DJF 20576
TONY COLEMAN TRUM (Q — (U) JOHNNY & THE FAMILY CLONE — 1981 DJM UK DJF 20574
BOBBY HOWARD B (Q — (V) HOT LITTLE MAMA — 19 BIG TOWN BT1002
MARCY THOMAS V (P
PETER MARTIN TPT (M — WILMA WILSON V (Q — DEON ESTUS B (Q

W30A **ROBERT WATSON** W30A

ROBERT WATSON SAX K(A — (A) ESTIMATED TIME OF ARRIVAL — 1978 PYE UK NSPL28250
WILBY FLETCHER D (A — (B) ALL BECAUSE OF YOU — 1979 PYE UK NSPL28276
PAT PATRICK SAX (A
CHARLES DAVIS SAX (A — SINCLAIR ACEY TPT (A — FRANK WILLIAMS TPT (A — DICK GRIFFIN TROM(A
MICHAEL TRENI TROM (A — ARTHUR WHITE SAX (A — VALERI PONOMAREN TPT (A — RICHARD CARUSO TROM(A
BILL SAXTON SAX (A — CURTIS LUNDY B (A — TERUMASA HINO TPT (A — DENNIS IRWIN B (A
JOE CARO G (A — ROLAND PRINCE G (A — MONTI ELLISON PERC (A — JABALI BILLY HART D(A
WALTER DAVIS K (A — BILLY HIGGINS D (A — PAMELA WATSON K V (A

W31 **WAH WAH WATSON** W31

WAH WAH WATSON G V (A — (A) ELEMENTARY — 1976 CBS UK 81582 US 34328
JULIA TILLMAN V (A
MAXINE WILLARD V (A — ORRIN WATERS V (A — LUTHER WATERS V (A — RAY PARKER JR G (A
OLLIE BROWN D (A — LOUIS JOHNSON B (A — SONNY BURKE K (A — JOHN BARNES K (A
JOE SAMPLE PNO (A — CLARENCE McDONALD PNO (A — MARK DAVIS PNO (A — WILLIE WEEKS B (A
HERBIE HANCOCK K (A — BENNIE MAUPIN SAX (A — ERNIE WATTS SAX (A — AARON SMITH D (A
WILTON FELDER B (A — HENRY DAVIS B (A — JAMES JAMESON B (A — DAVID T WALKER G (A
DAVID GRUSIN K (A

W32 **WATSONIAN INSTITUTE** W32

JOHNNY GUITAR WATSON G V(A — (A) MASTER FUNK — 1978 DJM US 13 UK DJF 20529
BOBBY HOWARD B V (A — (B) EDP — 1981 DJM US 27
GIP NOBLE K (A
EMRY THOMAS D V (A — TOMMY ROBERTSON TROM B V(A

W32A **ERNIE WATTS** W32A

ERNIE WATTS SAX FLT PERC V(AB | (A) LOOK IN YOUR HEART | 1980 ELEKTRA | US | 6E 285
PETE ROBINSON K (A | (B) CHARIOTS OF FIRE | 1982 QWEST | US | 3637
DAN DEAN B (A
ALEX ACUNA D (A | RON COOK G (A | PAULINHO DA COSTA PERC(AB | RICHARD TEE K (B
CARLOS RIOS G (B | JOHN ROBINSON D ((B | IAN UNDERWOOD SYN (B | LARRY HALL TPT (B
JAMES INGRAM V K (B | HOWARD HEWITT V (B | STEVE LUKATHER G (B | DON GRUSIN K SYN(B
QUINCY JONES PROD (B | MICHAEL OMARTIAN K STR(B | NEIL STUBENHAUS B (B | JERRY HEY HRNS (B
BILL REICHENBACH TPT (B | PHILLIP INGRAM V (B | DAVID WILLIAMS G (B | GREG PHILLINGANES SYN(B

W33 **WATTS 103RD STREET BAND** W33

CHARLES WRIGHT V (| (A) CORNBREAD & GRITS | 1967 WB | US | 1741
MELVIN DUNLOP B (| (B) IN THE JUNGLE BABE | 1969 WB | US | 1801
AL McKAY G (| (C) EXPRESS YOURSELF | 1970 WB | US | 1864
BERNARD BLACKMAN G (| (D) YOU'RE SO BEAUTIFUL | 19 WB | US | 1904
RAY JACKSON TROM (
JOHN RAYFORD SAX (| GABRIEL FLEMMING TPT (| BILL CANNON SAX (| JAMES GADSON D (

W34 **WAVEMAKER** W34

JOHN LEWIS K (AB | (A) WHERE ARE WE CAPTIAN | 1975 POLYDOR | UK | 2383 331
BRIAN HODGSON K (AB | (B) NEW ATLANTIS | 1977 POLYDOR | UK | 2383 434
TONY McVEY PERC (AB
JON KEHLIOR PERC (A

W34A **WAX** W34A

(A) WAX ATTACK | 1981 RCA | US | 3608

W35 **DARRYL WAY** W35

DARRYL WAY VLN K(ALL | (A) SATURATION POINT | 1973 DERAM UK SML1104 | LONDON JAP LAX1037
DEK MESSECAR B V (ABCE | (B) CANIS LUPUS | 1973 DERAM UK SDL 14 | LONDON JAP LAX1036
JOHN ETHERIDGE G (ABCE | (AB) SATURATION/CANIS | 19 LONDON IMP 23113 | NOVA GER 8005/1-2
IAN MOSLEY D (ABCDE | (C) NIGHT MUSIC | 1974 DERAM UK SML1116 | LONDON JAP LAX1116
JOHN HODKINSON V (C | (D) CONCERTO FOR ELEC VLN & SYN | 1978 ISLAND | UK | ILPS 9550
FRANCIS MONKMAN SYN (D | (E) DARRYL WAY'S WOLF | 1974 LONDON | US | PS 644
( ) ANTHOLOGY | 1976 KING JAP 1008

W35A **JEFF WAYNE** W35A

JEFF WAYNE (A | (A) WAR OF THE WORLDS | 1978 CBS 96000

W35B **WAZMO NARIZ** W35B

JEFF BOYNTON K (A | (A) THINGS AREN'T RIGHT | 1979 ILLEGAL | UK | ILP 003
JEFF HILL G V (A
BRUCE ZELESNIK D (A | JAMES E McGEEVY III B (A

W35C **WEAPON OF PEACE** W35C

(A) WEAPON OF PEACE | 1981 SAFARI | UK SWOP 1

W36 **WEATHER REPORT** W36

WAYNE SHORTER SAX (ALL | (A) WEATHER REPORT | 1971 CBS UK 64521 | US 30661 | JAP 25AP 941
JOE ZAWINUL K (ALL | (B) I SING THE BODY ELECTRIC | 1972 CBS UK 64943 | US 31356 | JAP 25AP 944
ALEJANDRO ACUNA PERC (FH | (C) SWEETNIGHTER | 1973 CBS UK 65532 | US 32210 | JAP 25AP 945
CHESTER THOMPSON D (F | (D) MYSTERIOUS TRAVELLER | 1974 CBS UK 80027 | US 32494 | JAP 25AP 946
JACO PASTORIUS B (FHJ | (E) TAIL SPINNIN' | 1975 CBS UK 80734 | US 33417 | JAP 25AP 947
NARADA MICHAEL WALDEN D(F | (F) BLACK MARKET | 1976 CBS UK 81325 | US 34099 | JAP 25AP 57
MIROSLAV VITOUS B (ABCDG | (G) LIVE IN TOKYO | 1977 CBS SONY | SOPJ 12/13XR
DON ALIAS PERC (F | (H) HEAVY WEATHER | 1977 CBS UK 81775 | US 34418 | JAP 25AP 357
MANOLO BADRENA PERC (HJ | (J) Mr GONE | 1978 CBS UK 82775
ALPHONSO JOHNSON B (DEF | (K) 8.30 | 1979 CBS UK 83670
DOM UM ROMAO PERC (BCDG | (L) NIGHT PASSAGE | 1980 CBS UK 84597
ISHMAEL WILBURN D (D
AIRTO MOREIRA D (A | ALPHONZE MOUZON D (A | ERIC GRAVATT D (BCG | ANDREW WHITE HRNS B(BC
HUBERT LAWS FLT (B | WILMER WISE HRNS (B | YOLANDE BAVAN V (B | JOSHIE ARMSTEAD V (B
ROBERT CHAPMAN V (B | RALPH TOWNER G (B | HERSCHEL DWELLINGHAM D (E | ALYRIO LIMA PERC (E
NGUDU CHANCLER D (E | TONTO K (E | MURUGA PERC (C | STEVE GADD D (J
TONY WILLIAMS D (J | PETER ERSKINE D (J | DENIECE WILLIAMS V (J | MAURICE WHITE V (J
JON LUCIEN V (J

W36A **JIM WEATHERLY** W36A

JIM WEATHERLY G V (AB | (A) THE SONGS OF JIM WEATHERLY | 1974 BUDDAH | US | 5608
(B) MAGNOLIAS & MISFITS | 1975 BUDDAH | US | 5637

W37 **VIVIAN WEATHERS** W37

VIVIAN WEATHERS V PERC(A | (A) BAD WEATHER | 1978 FRONT LINE | FL1025
WINSTON BENNETT G (A
KOJO OSEI D (A | WINSTON CURNIFFE D (D | TONY OSEI K (A | EVER DEE B (A
FLOYD LAWSON B PERC(A | JOHN VARNOM PERC G(A | JANOS BAJTALA K (A

W38 **THE WEB** W38

JOHN L WATSON V (AB | (A) FULLY INTERLOCKING | 1968 DERAM US 18018 | UK | SML 1025
TOM HARRIS WIND (ABC | (B) THERAPHOSA BLONDI | 1970 DERAM | UK | SML 1058
JOHN EATON G (ABC | (C) I SPIDER | 1970 POLYDOR | UK | 2383 024
TONY EDWARDS G (ABC
DICK LEE SMITH B (AB | LENNIE WRIGHT D PERC (ABC | KENNY BEVERIDGE PERC D(ABC | STRING SECTION (AB
DAVE LAWSON K V (C

W39 **JIMMY WEBB** W39

JIMMY WEBB V K (ALL | (A) JIM WEBB SINGS JIM WEBB | 1968 EPIC | US | 26401
DAVID PAICH K SYN(F | (B) WORDS & MUSIC | 1970 REPRISE UK K44101 | US | 6421
GEORGE MARTIN K SYN(F | (C) & SO ON | 1971 REPRISE | US | 6448
FRED TACKETT G (BDEF | (D) LETTERS | 1972 REPRISE UK K44173 | US | 2055
DEAN PARKS G (FE | (E) LANDS END | 1974 ASYLUM UK SYL9014 | US | 5070
B J COLE STEEL(E | (E) LANDS END | 1974 ASYLUM GER 43006
DEE MURRAY B (FE | (F) EL MIRAGE | 1977 ATLANTIC UK K50370 | US | 18218
HARVEY MASON PERC (F
DAVID HUNGATE B (F | LARRY KNECHTEL B (F | NIGEL OLSSON D (FE | JIM GORDON D (F
LOWELL GEORGE G (F | BARRY DE SOUZA D (E | PHILIP GOODHAND TAIT K (E | DAVID HENTSCHEL SYN (E
BRIAN HODGES B (E | DAVEY JOHNSTONE MAND(E | PAUL KEO G (E | JONI MITCHELL V (DE
JIM RYAN G (E | TOM SCOTT SAX (BE | RINGO STARR D (E | SUSAN WEBB V (DE
RAY RICH D (D | SKIP MOSHER B SAX (D

W39A EBERHARD WEBER W39A

EBERHARD WEBER B CELLO(ALL (A) COLOURS OF CHLOE 1974 ECM 1042
RAINER BRUNINGHAUS K(ABCD (B) YELLOW FIELDS 1976 ECM 1066
PETER GIGER D (A (C) THE FOLLOWING MORNING 197 ECM 1084
RALF HUBNER D (A (D) SILENT FEET 197 ECM 1107
ACK VAN ROOYEN HRNS (A (E) FLUID RUSTLE 197 ECM 1137
GARY BURTON VIBES(E
CHARLIE MARIANO SAX (BCD JOHN CHRISTENSEN D (B JOHN MARSHALL D (D BILL FRISELL G (E
BONNIE HERMAN V (E NORMA WINSTON V (E

W39B VINCE WEBER W39B

VINCE WEBER PNO (A (A) BLUES 'N' BOOGIE 1977 RUSSEL GER 32295
INGA RUMPF V (A

W39C THE WEDGE W39C

TOM BROWN D (A (A) THE BIG BAD BOSS BEAT OF(EP) 1980 RHINO RNEP 509
FRED GRABERT G (A
LOU MAXFIELD G (A ACE THE BASS B (A HAROLD BRONSON PROD (A

W39D WEEKEND MILLIONAIRE W39D

NICOLAS GORODETSKY V G K WIND(A (A) WEEKEND MILLIONAIRE 1978 WB UK K56449
JEAN MARESKA PROD (A
JEAN MICHEL NAVARRE V G (A ALAIN THOMAS B K V(A NICOLAS DEGAULEJAC D (A FRANCOIS SRTIGE G(A
PHILIPPE BENZEL PERC (A JEAN PHILIPPE DELRIEU K(A CLAUDE ALVAREZ PEREYNE G K(A ROGER LOUBET SYN (A

W40 RANDY WEBSTER W40

RANDY WEBSTER (A (A) BLUES TO AFRICA 19 FREEDOM FLP 41014

W40A RITCHIE WEEMS W40A

RITCHIE WEEMS (A (A) NATURAL BORN MAN 1965 DUNHILL 202

W41 JOHN WEIDER W41

JOHN WEIDER G V (A (A) JOHN WEIDER 1976 ANCHOR UK ANCL 2018
CHARLIE McCRACKEN B (A
PIERCE KELLY D (A

W41A WEIDORJE W41A

MICHEL ETTORI G (A (A) WEIDORJE 1978 COBRA COB 37014
JEAN PHILIPPE GOUDE K (A
PATRICK GAUTHIER K (A KIRT RUST D (A ALAIN GAILLARD SAX (A YVON GAILLARD TPT V(A
BERNARD PAGANOTTI B V (A

W42 BOB WEIR W42

BOB WEIR G V (AB (A) ACE 1972 WB US BS2627 UK K 46165
DAVID PAICH K (B (B) HEAVEN HELP THE FOOL 1978 ARISTA US 4155 UK SPART1044
DAVID FOSTER K (B (B) HEAVEN HELP THE FOOL 1978 ARISTA GER 60467
CARMEN TWILLIE V (B (C) BOBBT & THE NIDNITES 1981 ARISTA
DAVE TORBERT B (A
MIKE BAIRD D (B MIKE PORCARO B (B TOM SCOTT WIND (B BILL CHAMPLIN K V (B
TOM KELLY V (B NIGEL OLSSON D (B DEE MURRAY B (B WADDY WACHTEL G (B
PEGGY SANDVIG K (B LYNETTE GLOUD V (B BILL KREUTZMANN D (A PHIL LESH B V (A
JERRY GARCIA G STEEL (A KEITH GODCHAUX PNO (A DONNA GODCHAUX V (A ED BOGAS STRINGS(A

W43 RUSTY WEIR W43

RUSTY WEIR G V (ALL (A)STONED SLOW RUGGED 1975 ABC US AB 820
LEONARD ARNOLD G STEEL V(C (B) DONT IT MAKE YOU WANNA DANCE 1975 20TH CENTURY US T 469
RUSTY YOUNG (A (C) RUSTY WEIR 1976 20TH CENTURY US T 495
CHRIS HILLMAN B V (A (D) BLACK HAT SALOON 1976 CBS US 34319
RICHIE FURAY (A (E) STACKED DECK 1977 CBS US 34775
HERB PEDERSEN (A
GIB GUILBEAU (A JIM MARRIOTT V D (C BOBBT SMITH B V (C TODD POTTER G V (C
KIM SNIDER K V (C BILL SMITH K (C GLENN SPREEN PNO (C MIKE BALLEW G (C
DON FRANCISCO V (C SHANE KEISTER K SYN(C

W43A WEIRDO'S W43A

JOHN DENNY V (AB (A) WHO? WHAT? WHEN? WHERE? WHY? 1979 BOMP EP US W3 LINE GER LSLP4001
DIX DENNEU G SYN(AB (B) ACTION DESIGN 1980 RHINO EP US RNEP 508
WILLY WILLIAMS B (B
CLIFF ROMAN G SAX SYN (AB DANNY BENAIR D (A ART FOX D (B BILLY PERSONS B (A
KELLY QUINN K (A

W44 TIM WEISBERG W44

TIM WEISBERG FLT V(ALL (A) TIM WEISBERG 1971 A&M US 3039
TODD ROBINSON G (DEGH (B) DREAMSPEAKER 1972 A&M US 3045
DOUG ANDERSON B (DEGBH (C) HURTWOOD EDGE 1973 A&M US 4352
TY GRIMES D (EG (D) TIM WEISBERG 4 1974 A&M US 3658 UK AMLH63658
TOM DOUGHERTY PERC (G (E) LISTEN TO THE CITY 1975 A&M US 4545 UK AMLH64545
BILL STEWART D (H (F) LIVE AT LAST 197 A&M US 4600
RICK JAEGER D (BGH (G) TIM WEISBERG BAND 1977 UA US LA773 UK UAG 30113
JOHN HUG G (GKH (H) ROTATIONS 1978 US UA LA857 UK UAG 30175
TOWER OF POWER HRNS (G (I) TWIN SONS OF DIFFERENT MOTHERS 1978 EPIC US 35339
CHUCK LEAVELL K (GH (J) NIGHT RIDER 1979 MCA US 3084
JIM KRUEGER G (B (K) PARTY OF ONE 1980 MCA US 5125
MILT HOLLAND PERC (B (L) SMILE (BEST OF) 1979 A&M US 4749
DAN FOGELBERG G V (I
MIKE MELVOIN PNO (B BOBBYE HALL PERC (H RONNIE EADES SAX (H NEIL LARSEN K (GHK
MICKEY RAPHAEL HCA (H HARRISON CALLOWAY TPT (H HARVEY THOMPSON SAX (B BEN CAULEY TPT (H
FRED SELDON SAX (H ERNIE CARLSON TROM (H LYNN BLESSING K SYN(BDEK MARTY FOLTZ D (D
JUDEE SILL G V K(D TOM PELTIER V (D ART JOHNSON V (D LARRY KNECHTEL B (B
ED GREENE D (K NEIL STUBENHAUS B (K ABRAHAM LABORIEL B (K GREG PHILLINGANES PNO(K
JOHN JARVIS PNO (K RUSSEL FERRANTE PNO (K BUZZ FEITEN G (K MIKE SEMBELLO G (K
MICHAEL BODDICKER SYN (K STEVE FORMAN PERC (K BILL CHAMPLIN V (K CARMEN GRILLO V (K
LAURA CREAMER V (K WILLIAM SMITH K (K

W44A
LARRY WEISS
W44A

LARRY WEISS V (A (A) BLACK & BLUE SUITE 1974 20TH CENTURY T428
TOM HENSLEY PNO (A
LEE SKLAR B (A RICK MAROTTA D (A HUGH McCRACKEN G K(A JIMMIE HASKELL K (A
JAMES HENDRIX G (A JIM KELTNER D (A DEAN PARKS G (A DAVID PARLATO B (A
STRING SECTION (A

W45
ERIC WEISSBERG
W45

ERIC WEISSBERG G V FDL (ALL (A) FOLK BANJO STYLES 1966 POLYDOR UK
STEVE MANDELL G V BANJ(CD (B) NEW DIMENSIONS IN BANJO BLUEGRASS 19 ELEKTRA US EKS 7238
CHARLIE BROWN G V HCA (D (C) DUELLING BANJO'S 1973 WB US BS2683 UK K46214
MARSHALL BRICKMAN (AB (D) RURAL FREE DELIVERY(DELIVERANCE) 1973 WB US 2720 UK K46260
TONY BROOKS B V (D
RICHARD BROOKS D (D

W46
BOB WELCH
W46

BOB WELCH G V (ALL (1) BOB WELCH WITH HEAD EAST 1970 VOGUE LDA 20344
ROBERT HUNT K V (1 (A) FRENCH KISS 1977 CAPITOL UK/US EST11663 GER 85266
CHRISTINE McVIE K (AB (B) THREE HEARTS 1979 CAPITOL UK/US EST11907 GER 85807
MICK FLEETWOOD D (AB (C) I'M THE ONE 1979 CAPITOL UK/US EST12017 GER 86050
STEVE NICKS V (B (D) MAN OVERBOARD 1980 CAPITOL UK/US EST12107 GER 86231
ALVIN TAYLOR D (ABDE (E) BOB WELCH 1981 RCA UK 6019 US 4107
LINDSAY BUCKINGHAM G V(A
TODD SHARP G (BCD DAVID ADELSTEIN SYN K(BCDE STEVE FOREMAN PERC (B DONNY FRANCESCO D V (CD
BRAD PALMER B (DE ALAN BRAN B (D RANDY MEISNER V (D WENDY WALDMAN V (D
MARTY JOWARD SAX K(D VENETTA FIELDS V (D PAULETTE BROWN V (D BUNNY HILL V (D
NORTON BUFFALO HCA (D DAVE RODRIGUEZ B (E JOEY BRASLER G (E AL BRAN B (D
TOM KELLY V (E ROBBIE PATTON PERRC(E ROGER VOUDOURIS G (C HENRY MOORE D V (1

W46A
BRANDI WELLS
W46A

BRANDI WELLS V (A (A) WATCH OUT 1981 WMOT UK 2224 US 37668

W46B
CORY WELLS
W46B

CORY WELLS (A (A) TOUCH ME 197 A&M US 4673

W47
JUNIOR WELLS
W47

JUNIOR WELLS V HCA(ALL (A) ON TAP 1966 DELMARK US DS 635
BUDDY GUY G (BCDKF (B) IT'S MY LIFE BABY 1966 VANGUARD UKSRVL19028 US VSD79231
FRED BELOW D (BEJ (B) IT'S MY LIFE BABY 1966 FONTANA TFL6084
LEROY STEWART B (B (C) SOUTH SIDE JAM 196 DELMARK US DS 612
WALTER BEASLEY G (B (D) HOODOO MAN BLUES 196 DELMARK US DS 628
LITTLE AL D (B (E) BLUES HIT BIG TOWN 196 DELMARK US DS 640
WALTER WILLIAMS G (F (F) COMING AT YOU 1968 VANGUARD UKSVRL19011 US VSD79262
DOUGLAS FAGAN SAX (F (G) YOU'RE TUFF ENOUGH 1968 MERCURY UK SMCL20130
TOM CRAWFORD B (F (G) YOU'RE TUFF ENOUGH 1968 BLUE ROCK US 64002
LEVI WARREN D (F (H) SINGS AT THE GOLDEN BEAR 1968 BLUE ROCK US 64003
CLARK TERRY TPT (F (J) IN MY YOUNGER DAYS 1971 RED LIGHTNING UK RL 007
WALLACE DAVENPORT TPT (F (K) PLAY THE BLUES 1972 ATLANTIC US 33364 UK K40240
JIMMY OWEN TPT (F (L) PLEADING THE BLUES 19 ISABEL FR 900501
TOM McINTOSH TROM (F (EP) BLUES WITH A BEAT 197 DELMARK DJB 1
HENRY GRAY K (J
LOUIS MYERS G EJ DAVID MYERS B (EJ SYL JOHNSON G (J WILLIE DIXON B (EJ
EUGENE LOUNGE D (J EARL HOOKER G (J LAFAYETTE LEAKE K (J DONALD HAWKINS SAX(J
JARRETT GIBSON SAX (J JOHN WALKER K (JA JACK MEYERS B (DJ MUDDY WATERS G (E
ELMORE JAMES G (E ODIE PAYNE D (E OTIS SPANN G (E JOHNNIE JONES PNO(E
A C REED SAX (A ROOSEVELT SHAW D (A CHARLES MILES SAX (A PHILIP GUY G (A
HERMAN APPLEWHITE B (A SAM LAWHORN G (A (**) SEE BUDDY GUY ENTRY FOR K LINE UP

W48
MARY WELLS
W48

MARY WELLS V (ALL BYE BYE BABY 1961 TAMLA US 600 ORIOLE 63 UK 40051
MARVIN GAYE V (* ONE WHO REALLY LOVES YOU 1962 TAMLA US 605
TWO LOVERS 1962 TAMLA US 607 ORIOLE 63 UK 40045
ON STAGE 1962 TAMLA US 611
GREATEST HITS 1963 TAMLA US 616 UK TML 11032
TOGETHER * 1964 STATESIDE UK 10097
TOGETHER * 1964 TAMLA US 613
MY GUY 1964 STATESIDE UK 10095
MY GUY 1964 TAMLA US 617
MY GUY 197 PICKWICK CAN 3395
MARY WELLS 1965 STATESIDE UK 10133
MARY WELLS 196 20TH CENTURY US 4171
MY BABY JUST CARES FOR ME 1966 TAMLA UK STML11006
LOVE SONGS OF THE BEATLES 196 STATESIDE UK 10171
LOVE SONGS OF THE BEATLES 196 20TH CENTURY US 4178
GREATEST HITS 196 TAMLA US 616
OOH! 1966 MOVIETONE US 71010
VINTAGE STOCK 1967 TAMLA US 653
TWO SIDES OF 196 ATCO US 33199
SERVIN' UP SOME SOUL 1968 JUBILEE US 8018
SERVIN' UP SOME SOUL 1968 STATESIDE UK 10266
MY GUY 1970 MOTOWN UK SRS5040
(EP) MARY WELLS 1966 TAMLA TME 2007

W48A
PHILLIP J WELLS
W48A

PHILLIP J WELLS ALL INST(A (A) THE LAST SURVIVORS 1978 SOLID GOLD SGRLP 101

W48B
MICHAEL WENDROFF
W48B

MICHAEL WENDROFF G HCA V(A (A) SOUTHPAW 1974 BUDDAH BDS 5609
BOB KULICK G (A (B) LIVE 1977 BUDDAH US 5687
STEVE MORGAN V (A
MIKE MONTGOMERY K (A JIM GREGORY B (A GREGG DIAMOND PERC D V (A JIMMY MAELEN PERC V(A
P J ROSS V (A RALPH MOSS V (A JOANNE VENT V (A STRING SECTION (A

W48C
WEREWOLVES
W48C

BRIAN PAPGEORGE V (A (A) THE WEREWOLVES 1978 RCA AFLI2746 uk PL 12746
BUCKNER BALLARD V G B(A (B) SHIP OF FOOLS 197 RCA AFLI3079
KIRK BREWSTER G V (A
SEAB MEADOR G (A BOBBY BARANOWSKI D (A MICHAEL KINDRED K (A JOEY STANN HRNS (A
PETER WOOD ACC (A

W48D DAVID WERNER W48D

DAVID WERNER G V K(ABC (A) WIZZ KID 1975 RCA US 0350
MAX KENDRICK G (A (B) IMAGINATION 1976 RCA UK 0922
GARY LINK B (A (C) DAVID WERNER 1979 EPIC US 36126 UK 83862
MARK DOYLE G K B V (C
MOONEY D (C ALBRITTON McLAIN B (C KEN BISCHEL SYN (C RICHARD HUNTER HCA (C
TIM CAPELLO SAX (C IAN HUNTER V (C MAXINE DIXON V (C TOM GLAISTER D (A
JOE FARRELL SAX (A LINDA NOVEMBER V (A MAERETHA STEWART V (A TASHA THOMAS V (A

W48E WENCHIN' W48E

(A) WENCHIN' 1975 BUDDAH US 5642

W48F WEREWOLVES OF LONDON W48F

PAUL ROLAND G V (A (A) MIDNIGHT RAGS 1980 ARMAGEDDON UK ARM9
JOHN DANIELS G (A
BRIAN GOULD K (A PAUL NESBIT SAX (A SIMON BALESTRINI B (A ROGER DIAMOND D PERC(A
MARTIN MEADS D (A MAURICE MEMMOTT VLN (A

W49 HOWARD WERTH & THE MOONBEAMS W49

HOWARD WERTH G V (A (A) KING BRILLIANT 1975 CHARISMA UK CAS11-04 US ROCKET2180
MIKE MORAN K (A
FRED GANDY B (A BOB WESTON G (A ROGER POPE D (A PHIL DUNNE (A
GUS DUDGEON PERC (A

W50 FRANK WESS W50

FRANK WESS (AB (A) FLUTE OF THE LOOM 1973 ENTERPRISE ENS5006
(B) COMMODORE YEARS 1973 ATLANTIC SD 2 306
(C) WESS TO MEMPHIS 197 ENTERPRISE ENS5001

W51 LESLIE WEST W51

LESLIE WEST G V (ALL (A) MOUNTAIN 1969 WINDFALL/BELL 4500
N D SMART D (A (B) LESLIE WEST BAND 1975 PHANTOM PHS 701 1976 1258
FELIX PAPPALARDI K B PROD(A (C) THE GREAT FATSBY 1875 RCA US RS1009 PHANTOM US 0954
NORMAN LANDSBERG K (A
CORKY LAING D (BC MICK JONES G (B DON KRETMAR B (BC SREDNI VOLLNER HCA (BC
KEN ASCHER K (B BILL GELBER B (B HILDA HARRIS V (B TASHA THOMAS V (B
SHARON REDD V (B CARL HALL V (B MICK JAGGER G (C JOEL TEPP G (C
HOWIE WYETH PNO (C GARY WRIGHT PNO (C MARTY SIMON PNO (C NICK FERRANTELLA D (C
KEN HINKLE B (C FRANK VICARI HRNS (BC DANA VALERY V (C JAY TRAYNOR V (C

W51A TOMMY WEST W51A

TOMMY WEST G V (A (A) HOMETOWN FROLICS 1976 LIFESONG US 6003 2794
ROB STEVNS K (A
CHARLIE BROWN G (A WARREN NICHOLS B (A DAVID SANBORN SAX (A GEORGE DEVENS PERC(A
PAUL PRESTOPINO DOBRO(A SUSAN MANCHESTER V (A ERIC WEISSBERG STEEL(A TOM ROSSETLER D (A
MARTY NELSON V (A DAVID SPINOZZA G (A DAVID MANSFIELD STEEL(A TASHA THOMAS V (A
RICK RICARDO V (A GENI JACKSON V (A MICHAEL KAMEN HRNS (A TERRY CASHMAN V (A
KENNY KOSEK FDL (A RICHARDS CROOKS D (A JOHN CROWDER B (A MICHAEL RAGOGNE V (A

W52 WEST BRUCE & LAING W52

LESLIE WEST G V (ABC (A) WHY DONTCHA 1972 CBS UK 65314 WINDFALL US 31929
JACK BRUCE B V K SYN HCA(ABC (B) WHAT EVER TURNS YOU ON 1973 RSO UK 2394 107 WINDFALL US 32216
CORKY LAING D (ABC (C) LIVE & KICKIN' 1974 RSO UK 2394 128 WINDFALL US 32899

W53 WEST COAST POP ART EXPERIMENTAL BAND W53

BOB MARKLEY PROD (ABCD (A) PART ONE 1967 REPRISE US 6247 RI MIDI K24024
DAN HARRIS G V (ALL (B) VOL2 1967 REPRISE US 6270
SHAUN HARRIS G B V(ALL (C) A CHILD'S GUIDE TO GOOD & EVIL 1968 REPRISE 5106 6298
JIMMY BOWEN PROD ((D) WHERE'S MY DADDY? 19 AMOS US AAS 7004
MICHAEL LLOYD G K V(E (E) LEGENDARY UNRELEASED ALBUM 1980 RASPBERRY SAWFLY SAW 8001

W53A WEST ROAD BLUES BAND W53A

TAKASHI NAGAI V (A (A) WEST ROAD 1975 BOURBON JAP BUC3001
SHINJI SHIOTSUGU G (A
JUNGHI YAMAGIGHI G (A TADASHI KOBORI B (A TERUO MATSUMOTO D (A RYUICHIRO SENOH HCA(A
HIROSHI SATO K (A RYUICHI IDE K (A MARI KANEKO V (A

W53B KEVIN WESTLAKE W53B

KEVIN WESTLAKE (A (A) STARS FADE 1976 UTOPIA US 1388
JIMMY JEWELL SAX (A

W54 WET WILLIE W54

JIMMY HALL SAX V HCA(ALL (A) WET WILLIE 1971 CAPRICORN UK K40281 US SD 861
JACK HALL B V (ALL (A) WET WILLIE 1971 CAPRICORN RI US 0138
RICKY HIRSCH G V (ABCDEFGH (B) WET WILLIE II 1972 CAPRICORN US 0109
JOHN ANTHONY K V (ABCDEFGH (C) DRIPPIN' WET 1973 CAPRICORN UK K47512 US 0113
LEWIS ROSS D (ABCDEFGH (D) KEEP ON SMILIN' 1974 CAPRICORN UK 2429 115 US 0128
WICK LARSEN G (B (E) DIXIE ROCK 1975 CAPRICORN UK 2429 124 US 0149
ELLA AVERY V (BDE (F) WETTER THE BETTER 1976 CAPRICORN UK 2429 137 US 0166
SUZI STORM V (B (G) LEFT COAST LIVE 1977 CAPRICORN UK 2429 151 US 0182
SCOTT BOYER STEEL(B (H) GREATEST HITS 1977 CAPRICORN US 0200
JAI JOHANNY JOHANSON (BC (J) MANORISMS 1978 EPIC UK 82330 US 34983
DONNA HALL V (DEF (K) WHICH ONE'S WILLIE 1979 EPIC US 35794
JOYCE KNIGHT V (DE
EARL FORD TROM (DE MIKE DUKE K V(EFGJK TOM DOWD PERC (E MAMA HALL K V (E
SUSAN HALL V (E PAUL HORNSBY K (F LEO LABRANCHE TPT (F SKIP LANE SAX (F
DEZSO LAKATOS SAX (F JEROME JOSEPH CONGA(F LESLIE PHILUS LIVELY D V(J LESLIE HAWKINS V (F
LARRY BERWALD G (JK MARSHALL SMITH G V (JK THEOPHILUS LIVELY D V (JK PAULETTE BROWN B (K
VANETTA FIELDS V (K ANGELLE TROSCLAIR V (K MIGHTY CLOUDS OF JOY V (K STEVE MADAIO TPT (K
LENNY CASTRO PERC (K VICTOR FELDMAN PERC (K CHUCK FINDLEY HRNS (K GARY HERBIG SAX (K
DAVID LUELL SAX (K BOB PAYNE TROM (K

W54A JOHN WETTON W54A

JOHN WETTON G V K B (A (A) CAUGHT IN THE CROSSFIRE 1980 POLYDOR EG UK EGLP 107
SIMON KIRKE D PERC(A
MALCOLM DUNCAN SAX (A MARTIN BARRE G (A PHIL MANZANERA G (A

W54B (BIG) WHA KOO W54B

DAVID PALMER V (ABC (A) BIG WHA KOO 1977 ABC UK ABCL5208 US 971
RICK VAN MAARTH G V (AC (B) FRAGILE LINE 1977 EPIC US 36173
DANNY DOUMA G V (AC (C) BERKSHIRE 1978 ABC UK ABCL5238
DON FRANCISCO PERC V(ABC
CLAUDE PEPPER D VIBES(AC PETER FREIBERGER (C RICHARD KOSINSKI K V (ABC ANDREW SYLVESTER G B (A
REINIE PRESS B SAX (AC LEE RITENOUR G (A EDDIE TUDURI D (B ERIC GOTTHELF B (B
CHUCK COCHRAN G V (B WILLIAM D SMITH SAX (B DAVID WOODFORD K (B STEVE FORMAN TROM(C
BRADFORD THOELKE TROM (C DAN LEMELLE SAX (C BUDDY McDANIEL SAX (C CLIFF ERVIN TPT (C

W55 WHALEFEATHER W55

MICHAL JONES G V (A (A) WHALEFEATHER 1971 BLUE HORIZON UK2431 009 NASCO 9005
M E BLACKMON K V (A
LEONARD LE BLANC B V (A STEPHEN BACON PERC (A

W55A MIKE WHELLANS W55A

MIK. WHELLANS G (A (A) DIRT WATER FOX 1976 DARA MPA016
COLIN BAINE G V (A
BILLY JACKSON B (A CILLA FISHER V (A

W55B WHIPPING POST W55B

ASTRID COTTI K V (A (A) AFTER & REALLY LIVE 1978 MUSK PROJEKT 7777/2-3
GEORGE KLEE WIND V PERC(A
FABI TONON B (A PUMI BRUNNER D PERC V(A C B BUSSER G V (A PIMI BENDEL G (A

W56 WHIRLWIND W56

NIGEL DIXON V (AB (A) BLOWING UP A STORM 12" 1978 CHISWICK WIK 7 CWK 3007
MICHAEL LEWIS G (AB (A) BLOWING UP A STORM 10" 1978 CHISWICK CH4 GER 67058
CHRIS EMO B (AB (B) MIDNIGHT BLUE 1980 CHISWICK CWK 3012 GER 67069
PHIL HARDY D (A
GARY HASSETT (B

W57 WHIRLY WORLD W57

IAN OLSON V K SYN(A (A) WIN OR LOSE (EP) 1980 MISSING LINK MLEP 4
JOHN MURPHY D PERC(A
GREG SUN B PERC(A ARNIE HANNA G (A

W58 ALAN WHITE W58

ALAN WHITE D V (A (A) RAMSHACKLED 1976 ATLANTIC US SD18167 UK K50217
PETER KIRTLEY G V (A
COLIN GIBSON B PERC(A KEN CRADDOCK K V (A ALAN MARSHALL V (A BUD BEADLE WIND(A
ANDY PHILLIPS PERC (A STEVE GREGORY WIND (A HENRY LOWTHER TPT (A
JON ANDERSON V (A STEVE HOWE G (A

W59 BUKKA WHITE W59

BUKKA WHITE G V (ALL (A) BUKKA WHITE(37/40 1964 CBS 52629
WASHBOARD SAM PERC (A (B) SIC 'EM DOGS 196 HERWIN US 201
HARMONICA BOY HCA (C (C) MEMPHIS HOT SHOTS 1968 BLUE HORIZON UK 7 63229
BILL BARTH G (C (D) BLUES MASTERS VOL 4 196 BLUE HORIZON US 4604
TREVOR KEOHLER PNO (C (E) MISSISSIPPI BLUES 1969 TAKOMA US 1001 GNP US 10011
ANCHOR B (C (F) LEGACY OF THE BLUES 19 SONET UK SNTF 609
JIM CROSTHWAIT PERC (C (G) SKY SONGS VOL 1 63 1975 ARHOOLIE F1019
BIG WILLIE PERC (GH (H) SKY SONGS VOL 2 1975 ARHOOLIE F1020
JOE GRAY D (C (J) PARCHMENT FARM 19 CBS US 30036
LIGHTNIN' SLIM (L (K) BIG DADDY 1974 BIO US 12049
WHISPERIN' SMITH (L (L) BATON ROUGE, MOSBY ST 1972 CAR 1932119

W60 CHRIS WHITE W60

CHRIS WHITE V PERC(A (A) MOUTH MUSIC 1976 CHARISMA CAS 1118
TOM PARKER K (A
CLEM CATTINI D (A Z JENKINS G (A DAVE OLNEY B (A SHEL TALMY PERC (A

W61 KIERAN WHITE W61

KIERAN WHITE V G B HCA (A (A) OPEN DOOR 1975 GULL UK GULP1011 GER 622307
DAVE SHEEN B D (A
CHAS JANKEL K G V(A ROGER BUNN B (A DONAL LUNNEY SYN G V(A GEOFF DRISCOLL WIND(A
TIM STAFFEL V (A

W62 LENNY WHITE W62

LENNY WHITE D K B(ALL (A) VENUSIAN SUMMER 1975 NEMPEROR US 435 UK K50213
DOUG RAUCH B (A (B) BIG CITY 1977 NEMPEROR US 441 UK K50345
DOUG RODRIGUEZ G (A (C) ADVENTURES OF ASTRAL PIRATES 1978 ELEKTRA US 6E121 UK K52065
RAY GOMEZ G (AB (D) STREAMLINE 1978 ELEKTRA UK K52108
JIMMY SMITH ORG (A (E) BEST OF FRIENDS 1979 ELEKTRA US 223
DON BLACKMAN K SYN(A (F) 29 1980 ELEKTRA UK K52257
DAVID SANCIOUS K (A
JEFF SIGMAN G (C WELDON IRVINE K (A ONAJE ALLAN GUMBS K (AB PATRICK GLEASON K (AB
PETER ROBINSON K (A HUBERT LAWS FLT (A DENNIS MACKAY PERC (A LARRY YOUNG ORG (A
TOM HARREL (A LARRY CORYELL G (A AL DIMEOLA G (A BRIAN AUGER K (B
HERBIE HANCOCK K (B VERDINE WHITE B (B TOWER OF POWER HRNS (B JAN HAMMER K (B
JERRY GOODMAN VLN (B NEAL SCHON G (B LINDA TILLERY V (B ALEX LIGERTWOOD G (B
JACK MILLS G (B CLIVE CHAMAN B (B BENNIE MAUPIN SAX (B LENNOX LAINGTON CONGA(B
PAUL JACKSON B (B MARCUS MILLER B (B ALEX BLAKE B (BC MIROSLAV VITOUS B (B
MIKE GIBBS PNO (B LOIS COLIN HARP (B GARY KING D (B DAVID JOHNSON CONGA(B
NICK MOROCH G (C

W63 MICHAEL WHITE W63

MICHAEL WHITE (ALL (A) THE SUN & MOON HAVE COME TOGETHER 1969 CAPITOL US SKOA 423
BABATUNDE (J (B) WEREWOLF 1970 CAPITOL US
JOSEPH BARBOZA (J (C) 4TH WAY 1971 CAPITOL US
NAPOLEON BROCK (J (D) SPIRIT DANCE 1972 IMPULSE US AS9215
DAVID DANIEL (J (E) PNEUMA 1973 IMPULSE US AS9221
BRUCE FOWLER (J (F) THE LAND OF SPIRIT & LIGHT 1974 IMPULSE US AS9241
WALT FOWLER (J (G) FATHER MUSIC MOTHER DANCE 1974 IMPULSE US AS9268
DEWILLI GONGA (J (H) GO WITH THE FLOW 1975 IMPULSE US AS9281
MUFFY JAMES (J (J) THE X FACTOR 1978 ELEKTRA US 138 UK K52095
HUBERT LAWS (J (K) WHITE NIGHT 1979 ELEKTRA US 183
KING ERRISON PERC (J
BYRON MILLER (J AIRTO MOREIRA (J EDWARD MYERS (J GREGORY PHILLINGANES (J
PETSYE POWELL (J DUANE ROBERSON (J PATRICE RUSHEN (J MIKE SEMBELLO (J
ALBERT WING (J ROLAND BAUTISTA (J MARVIN BOXLEY (J PATTY BROOKS (J
LEON CHANCLER (J RAUL DE SOUZA (J

W64 TONY JOE WHITE W64

TONY JOE WHITE G V HCA(ALL (A) BLACK & WHITE 1968 MONUMENT US 18114 UK SMO 5027

TOMMY McCLURE B (BFE (B) CONTINUED 1969 MONUMENT US 18133 UK SMO 5035

SAMMY CREASON D (BFE (C) TONY JOE 1970 MONUMENT US 18142 UK SMO 5043

JAMES MILHART D (BF (D) TONY JOE WHITE 1971 WB US 1900 UK K46068

MIKEE UTLEY ORG (BFE (E) THE TRAIN I'M ON 1972 WB US 2580 UK K46147

DAVID BRIGGS K (AFE (F) BEST OF 1973 WB EURO 054 92274 UK K56149

JERRY CARRIGAN D (AFE (G) HOME MADE ICE CREAM 1973 WB US 2708 UK K46229

NORBERT PUTNAM B (AFE (H) EYES 197 20TH CENTURY BT523

CHIP YOUNG G (A (J) TONY JOE WHITE 1977 20th CENTURY PS2030

JIMMY ISBELL D (A (K) REAL THANG 1980 CASABLANCA US 7233

TIPPY ARMSTRONG G (C (DE) TWO ORIGINALS 1973 WEA GER 66028

JOHN HUGHEY STEEL(C

ROGER HAWKINS D (C DAVID HOOD B (C BARRY BECKETT K (C RONNIE BARON K (C

CHARLES CHALMERS SAX (C TOM DOWD V (C

W65 WHITE HORSE W65

JON LIND G V (A (A) WHITE HORSE 1977 CAPITOL US ST 11687

BILLY NICHOLLS PNO G V(A

KENNY ALTMAN G B (A JEFF PORCARO D (A PAUL BARRERE G (A BILL PAYNE SYN K(A

JOE PORCARO PERC (A GARY MALLABER D (A BOB GLAUB B (A CALEB QUAYE G (A

RUSS KUNKEL D (A FRED TACKETT G (A CHUCK DOMANICO B (A REGGIE KNIGHTON G(A

DAVY LIVINGSTONE STEEL(A DAVID PAICH PNO (A

W65A WHITE CLOUD W65A

THOMAS JEFFERSON KAYE G V (A (A) WHITE CLOUD 1972 ?

JOANNE VENT V (A

RICHARD CROOKS PERC (A TEDDY WENDER K V (A KENNETH KOSEK FDL V(A DONALD PAYNE B (A

CHARLIE BROWN G (A ERIC WEISSBERG BAN STEEL (A

W65B WHITE HEAT W65B

BOB SMEATON V (A (A) IN THE ZERO HOUR 1981 VALIUM UK VALP 101

ALAN FISH G (A

BRYAN YOUNGER G (A COLIN ROBERTS B (A JOHN ROBERTS D (A SIMON BOSWELL K (A

JOHN EARLE SAX (A GEORGE WATERS D (

W66 WHITE LIGHTNING W66

BUSTA CHERRY JONES B V (A (A) WHITE LIGHTNIN' 1975 ISLAND US ILPS9325

DONALD KINSEY G V (A

WOODY KINSEY D V (A

W67 WHITE MANSIONS (CONCEPT) W67

JESSI COLTER V (A (A) WHITE MANSIONS 1978 A&M US 6004 UK AMLX64691

WAYLON JENNINGS G V (A

JOHN DILLON V G K FDL (A STEVE CASH HCA V(A ERIC CLAPTON G (A BERNIE LEADON G V (A

HENRY SPINETTI D (A DAVE MARKEE B (A TIM HINKLEY K (A PAUL KENNERLEY V (A

W68 WHITE NOISE W68

DAVID VORHAUS (ABC (A) AN ELECTRIC STORM 1969 ISLAND US 9303 UK ILPS 9099

JOHN WHITMAN V (A (A) AN ELECTRIC STORM 1976 ANTILLES US 7011

DELIA DERBYSHIRE (A (B) WHITE NOISE 1975 VIRGIN v2032

BRIAN HODGSON (A (C) RE ENTRY 1980

PAUL LYTTON PERC (A

ANNIE BIRD V (A VAL SHAW V (A

W68A WHITE WATER W68A

JOHN VASTANO G (A (A) OUT OF THE DARKNESS 1973 RCA US APLI 0091

RICHARD DOMANE K TPT(A

PAUL PHILLIPS HRNS (A JOHN EMMA SAX (A BOB FIOCCO B (A CONRAD CATALANO D(A

W68B WHITE RUSSIA W68B

TREVOR WATKINS V (A (A) EAST SIDE STORY 1981 ALADIN 85055

GERRIT MEYER G (A

UWE HOFFMAN D (A T PIERS HEADLEY B (A

W69 WHITE WITCH W69

RON GOEDART V (AB (A) WHITE WITCH 1972 CAPRICORN UK K47505

BUDDY PENDERGRASS K (AB (A) WHITE WITCH 1972 CAPRICORN US 0107

BUDDY RICHARDSON G (AB (B) A SPIRITUAL GREETING 1974 CAPRICORN US 0129

BOBBY SHEA PERC (AB

BILL PETERSON PERC (B CHARLIE SOUZA B (B BEAU FISHER D V (A

W69A WHITEFACE W69A

STEVE HARDWICK G V (A (A) WHITEFACE 1979 MERCURY US SRM13765

KYLE HENDERSON B V (A (B) CHANGE OF FACE 1981 MERCURY US SRM14017

DOUG BARE K V (A

BENNY RAPPA D V (A

W69B WHITESPIRIT W69B

MALCOLM PEARSON K (A (A) WHITESPIRIT 1980 MCA UK MCF 3079

PHIL BRADY B (A

BRUCE RUFF V (A JANICK GERS G (A GRAEME VRALLEN D (A

W69C WHITEHEAT W69C

WHITEHEAT 1975 RCA US 0853

W69D WHITEHOUSE W69D

(A) ERECTOR 1980 COME UK 881007

W69E GEOFF WHITEHORN W69E

GEOFF WHITEHORN G V (A (A) WHITEHORN 1974 STATESIDE JAP ISS 80164

GERRY MORRIS B (A

JOHN RICHARDSON D (A PETE ARNESON K (A CLIFF DAVIS D (A DICK MORRISSEY SAX (A

TONY ATKINS V (A

W69F WHITFORD- ST HOLMES W69F

BRAD WHITFORD G (A (A) WHITFORD- ST HOLMES 1981 CBS US

DEREK ST HOLMES V (A

DAVE HEWITT B (A STEVE PACE D (A

W70 BOBBY WHITLOCK W70

Musician	Instrument	Albums
BOBBY WHITLOCK	G V	(ABCD
RICK VITO	G	(B
DON PONCHER	D	(B
KEITH ELLIS	B	(B
T J TINDALL	G BAN	(C
DICKIE BETTS	G	(C
CHUCK LEAVELL	PNO	(C
KENNY TIBBETTS	B	(C
RICK ECKSTEIN	D	(C

Album	Year	Label	Number
(A) BOBBY WHITLOCK	1972	DUNHILL US 50121 UK CBS	65109
(B) RAW VELVET	1972	DUNHILL US 50131 UK CBS	65301
(C) ONE OF A KIND	1975	CAPRICORN US 0160	
(D) ROCK YOUR SOX OFF	1976	CAPRICORN US 0168 UK	2429 139

W71 JAKI WHITREN W71

Musician	Instrument	Albums
JAKI WHITREN	G V BANJO	(A
PAT DONALDSON	B	(A
GERRY CONWAY	D	(A
ROB YOUNG	FLT	(A
FRANK RICOTTI	PERC	(A
BRIAN BROCKLEHURST	B	(A
LINDSAY COOPER	BASSOON	(A
HENRY VIII	JUG	(A
IVAN CHANDLER	K	(A
STUART COWELL	G	(A
ALBERT LEE	G	(A
JOHN VAN DERRICK	VLN	(A
HARRY BECKETT	HRNS	(A
MIKE LESLIE	G V	(A
MARIE GOOSENS	HARP	(A
GORDON HUNTLEY	STEEL	(A
STAN SULZMANN	SAX	(A

Album	Year	Label	Country	Number
(A) RAW BUT TENDER	1973	EPIC	UK	65465

W72 THE WHO W72

Musician	Instrument	Albums
PETE TOWNSHEND	G K V	(ALL
ROGER DALTREY	V HCA	(ALL
JOHN ENTWISTLE	B K V	(ALL
KEITH MOON	D V	(ALL TO 1978
KENNY JONES	D	(F
NICKY HOPKINS	PNO	(KR
DAVE ARBUS	VLN	(RK
ROD ARGENT	K	(T
ANDY FAIRWEATHER LOW	V	(T
CHRIS STAINTON	K	(NL
ELTON JOHN	PNO V	(G
ERIC CLAPTON	G	(G
RON WOOD	G	(G
FUZZY SAMUELS	B	(G
CALEB QUAYE	G	(G
MICK RALPHS	G	(G
GRAHAM DEACON	D	(G
PHIL CHEN	B	(G
ALAN ROSS	G	(G
RICHARD BAILEY	D	(G
DAVE WINTOUR	B	(G
TONY MURRAY	B	(G
NIGEL OLSSON	D	(G
RAY COOPER	PERC	(G
DAVEY JOHNSTONE	G	(G
GERALD SHAW	ORG	(G
TONY STEVENS	B	(G
ANN MARGARET	V	(G
OLIVER REED	V	(G
JACK NICHOLSON	V	(G
ROBERT POWELL	V	(G
PAUL NICHOLAS	V	(G
TINA TURNER	V	(G
BARRY WINCH	V	(G
ARTHUR BROWN	V	(G
VICTORIA RUSSELL	V	(G
BEN ARIS	V	(G
MARY HOLLAND		(G
JENNIFER BAKER		(G
SUSAN BAKER		(G
IMOGEN CLAIRE		(G
JULIET KING		(G
GILLIAN KING		(G
SIMON TOWNSHEND		(G
LIZA STRIKE	V	(G
MYLON LEFEVRE	V	(G
BILLY NICHOLLS		(G
JESS RODEN	V	(G
MARGO NEWMAN		(G
SARAH McINTOSH		(G
VICKI BROWN	V	(G
KIP TREVOR		(G
HELEN CHAPPELLE		(G
PAUL GURVITZ		(G
ALISON DOWLING		(G

Album	Year	Label	Country	Number
(A) MY GENERATION	1965	BRUNSWICK	UK	LAT 8616
(A) " " "	1966	DECCA	US	74664
(A) " " "	1972	MCA	US	2044
(A) " " "	1980	VIRGIN	UK	V2179
THE WHO	1966	POLYDOR	FR	2383 137
A QUICK ONE	1966	REACTION	UK	593002
" " "	1970	BACKTRACK	UK	2407 008
WHO SELL OUT	1967	TRACK 612002	UK	613 002
" " "	1970	BACKTRACK	UK	2407 009
" " "	1967	DECCA	UK	74950
" " "	1974	POLYDOR	GERM	2675 089
A QUICK ONE/SELL OUT	19	TRACK		2683 038
" " " "	19	TRACK	GER	2644 002
" " " "	197	MCA	US	2046
HAPPY JACK	1967	DECCA	US	74892
" " "	197	MCA	US	2045
MAGIC BUS	1968	DECCA	US	75064
" " "	1972	MCA	US	2047
MAGIC BUS/MY GENERATION	1975	MCA	US	2 4068
DIRECT HITS	1969	TRACK	UK	613 006
TOMMY DBL	1969	TRACK	UK	613 013/4
" " DBL	1972	TRACK		2657 002
" "	19	POLYDOR	GER	2612 006
" "	196	DECCA	US	7205
" "	197	MCA	US	2-1005
TOMMY PART ONE	1972	TRACK	UK	2406 007
TOMMY PART TWO	1972	TRACK	UK	2406 008
(G) TOMMY SOUNDTRACK	1975	POLYDOR		PD 29502
THE BEST OF TOMMY	197	POLYDOR	NL	2383 130
LIVE AT LEEDS	1970	TRACK	UK	24-6 001
" " "	1970	DECCA	US	79175
" " "	1972	MCA	US	2022
" " "	197	MCA	US	3023
" " "	19	POLYDOR	NL	65 124
MEATY BEATY BIG & BOUNCY	1971	TRACK	UK	2406 006
" " " " "	1971	DECCA	US	79184
" " " " "	1972	MCA	US	2025
" " " " "	19	MCA	US	3025
POP HISTORY VOL 4 (DBL)	1971	POLYDOR	GERM	2675 012
(K)WHO'S NEXT	1971	TRACK	UK	2408 102
(K) " "	1971	DECCA	US	79182
" " "	1972	MCA	US	2023
(L)QUADROPHENIA (DBL)	1973	TRACK	UK	2657 013
" " "	1973	MCA	US	10004
" " "	1973	POLYDOR	GER	2644 001
(N) " " " SOUNDTRACK	1979	POLYDOR	UK	2625 037
INSTANT PARTY	19	BRUNSWICK	NL	173 269
POP HEROES	19	POLYDOR	GERM	2459 410
THE WHO & JIMI HENDRIX(DBL)	19	KARUSSELL	GERM	2674 001
WHO DID IT (WITHDRAWN)	19	TRACK	UK	2856 001
GREATEST ROCK SENSATION	19	KARUSSELL	GERM	2345 104
VERY BEST OF	19	POLYDOR	JAP	MFP 1163
THE STORY OF THE WHO	19	POLYDOR	JAP	MPZ81012
PERFECT COLLECTION	19	POLYDOR	JAP	MP 94478
I'M A BOY	19	POLYDOR	JAP	SLPM1354
EXCITING	19	POLYDOR	JAP	MP 1385
GOLDEN DOUBLE ALBUM	19	POLYDOR	JAP	MP93556
ODDS & SODS	1974	TRACK	UK	2406 116
" " "	1974	MCA	US	2126
BEST OF 1964 74	1975	POLYDOR	UK	2674 017
BEST OF	1975	POLYDOR		2482 172
BEST OF	19	POLYDOR	GERM	185 152
BEST OF LAST TEN YEARS (DBL)	197	KARUSSEL GER 26740017		2662 323
PORTRAIT OF	1975	POLYDOR		2482 100
WHO (COMP)	197	IMPACT		6886 551
WHO (COMP)	197	POLYDOR	FR	6371 450
(R) WHO BY NUMBERS	1975	POLYDOR	UK	2490 129
(R) " " "	1975	MCA	US	2161
(R) " " "	19	MCA	US	3026
(R) " " "	1975	POLYDOR	GER	2480 309
STORY OF THE WHO	1976	POLYDOR	UK	2683 069
" " " "	19	POLYDOR	GERM	2668 015
(T) WHO ARE YOU	1978	POLYDOR	UK	WHOD5004
(T) " " "	1978	MCA	US	3050
(T) " " "	1978	POLYDOR	EURO	2417 325
WHO ARE YOU/LIVE AT LEEDS (DBL)	1980	POLYDOR CASS		3574 089
KIDS ARE ALRIGHT	1979	POLYDOR	UK	2675 179
(F) FACE DANCES	1981	POLYDOR	UK	WHOD 5037
(F) FACE DANCES	1981	POLYDOR	EURO	2302 106
HOOLIGANS	1981	MCA	US	
PHASES (BOXED SET)	1981	POLYDOR	UK	2675 216
ITS HARD	1982	POLYDOR	UK	WHODC5066

W73 WICHITA FALL W73

LARRY WATSON B (A (A) LIFE IS BUT A DREAM 1969 LIBERTY UK83208 IMPERIAL US12417
DANNY ROUSH G V (A
LEN FEIGIN D (A PHILIP BLACK G V (A

W73A BENOIT WIDEMANN W73A

BENOIT WIDEMANN K (A (A) STRESS 1980 BALLON NOW BAL 13002
CLEMENT BAILLY D (A

W74 WIDOWMAKER W74

ARIEL BENDER G (AB (A) WIDOWMAKER 1976 JET UK 2310 432 UK RI JETLP 15
STEVE ELLIS V (A (A) WIDOWMAKER 1976 UA US LA 642
PAUL NICHOLS D (AB (B) TOO LATE TO CRY 1977 UA UK UAG30038 US LA 723
LLOYD LANGTON G (A
BOB DAISLEY B (AB JOHN BUTLER V (B ZOOT MONEY K (A

W74A WIGGY BITS W74A

(A) WIGGY BITS 1976 POLYDOR US 1 6081

W75 WIGWAM W75

JIM PEMBROKE K V (BCDHJKLM (A) HARD & HORNEY 1969 LOVE SWED LRLP 9
RONNIE OSTERBERG D (CHJKLMBD (B) TOMBSTONE VALENTINE 1970 LOVE SWED LRLP19
JUKKA GUSTAVSON K (BCDHL (C) FAIRYPORT 1971 LOVE SWED LRLP44/55
PEKKA POHJOLA B VLN(BCDH (D) WIGWAM 1972 LOVE SWED LRLP 511
PEKKA RECHARDT G (HJKLM (E) WICKED IVORY 1972 LOVE SWED LRLP52
MANS GROUNDSTROEM B (JKLM (F) BEING 1974 LOVE SWED LRLP 92
ESA KOTILAINEN K (JM (G) PIGWORM 1974 LOVE SWED LRLP 103
PAAVO MAIJANEN B V (JKLM (H) LIVE FROM TWILIGHT ZONE 1975 LOVE SWED LXLP517/8
ILMARI VARILA OBOE (C (J) DEAD AT THE NUCLEAR NIGHTCLUB 1975 LOVE SWEDLRLP129 UK VIRGIN 2035
TAPIO LOUHENSALO (C (K) LUCKY GOLDEN STRIPES 1976 VIRGIN UK 2051
HANNU SAXELIN WIND (C (L) DARK ALBUM 1978 LOVE IMP LRLP 227
RISTO RENSOLA WIND (C (M) RUMOURS ON THE REBOUND (DBL COMP) 1979 VIRGIN UK VGD 3503
UNTO HAAPA AHO WIND (C
EERO KOIVISTOINEN SAX (CM PEKKA POYRY SAX (C HESSU HIETANEN K (KLM TIMO KOJO V (L
COSTA APETREA G (M MATS HULDEN B (D JUKKA TOLONEN G (D NIKKE NIKAMO G (D

W76 DANNY WILD W76

DANNY WILD (A (A) WILD IN THE COUNTRY 1978 RAW RWLP 102

W77 WILD ANGELS W77

JOHN HAWKINS G (C (A) OUT AT LAST 1972 DECCA UK SKL 5134
ROD COTTER B (C (B) LETS GET BACK TO ROCK 1975 PYE UK GH 614
ROB O'CONNOR D (c (C) LIVE AT THE REVOLUTION 1970 B+C BCM 101
BILL KINGSTON V (C (D) RED HOT'N'ROCKIN' 1970 B+C BCM 102
MAL GRAY (C (E) TOO LATE TO CRY 19 JET UK UAG 30038
MITCH MITCHELL G (
GEOFF BRITTON D (

W77A WILD BUTTER W77A

RICK GAREN G V (A (A) WILD BUTTER 196
JOHN SENNE G V (A
STEVE PRICE B V (A JERRY BUCKNER K V (A

W77B WILD BLUE YONDER W77B

(A) ENTHUSIASM 1980 TOTALLYOUTOFCONTROLL US 1

W77C WILD CHERRY W77C

TAMPA LANN V (A (A) I LOVE MY MUSIC 1978 EPIC US 35011
BECK GOLDSTEIN V (A
RANDY BRECKER HRNS (A MICHAEL BRECKER HRNS (A

W78 WILD HORSES W78

BRIAN ROBERTSON G (AB (A) THE FIRST ALBUM 1980 EMI UK EMC 3326
JIM BAIN B (AB1 (B) STAND YOUR GROUND 1981 EMI UK EMC 3368
NEIL CARTER G (A
CLIVE EDWARDS D (AB JOHN LOCKTON G (B REUBEN ARCHER V (1 LAURENCE ARCHER G (1
FRANK NOON D (1

W78A WILD MAGNOLIAS W78A

BO DOLLIE V TAMB(A (A) WILD MAGNOLIAS 19 BARCLAY 80529
MONK BOUDREAUX V CONGA(A
'GATOR JUNE' JOHNSON V TAMB(A
'CRIP' ADAMS V PERC(A QUARTER MOON TOBIAS V PERC(A GALE JOHNSON PERC V(A BUBBA SCOTT PERC V(A
JAMES SMOTHERS PERC V(A GITCHIE D(A EARL TURBINTON WIND(A JULIUS FARMER B (A
SNOOKS EAGLIN G (A LARRY PANNA D (A ALFRED ROBERTS CONGA(A

W78B WILD TCHOUPITOULAS W78B

(A) WILD TCHOUPITOULAS 1976 ISLAND US 9360

W79 WILD TURKEY W79

GLEN CORNICK B G K(AB (A) BATTLE HYMN 1971 CHRYSALIS UK CHR 1002
TWEKE LEWIS G (AB (B) TURKEY 1972 CHYSALIS UK CHR 1010
MICK DYCHE G V (B
JEFF JONES D (AB STEVE GURL K (B GARY PICKFORD HOPKINS G V(AB JON BLACKMORE G V(A

W80 WILD WALLY W80

WILD WALLY ((A) I GO APE 1971 CONSTELLATION CCS 5001

W81 MARTY WILDE W81

MARTY WILDE V (ALL DR DOOLITTLE 1968 MARBLE ARCH UK MAL 738
BIG JIM SULLIVAN G (AB ROCK'N'ROLL 1970 PHILIPS 6308 010
BRIAN BENNETT D (AB GOOD ROCKIN' THEN & NOW 1974 PHILIPS 6382 102
LICORICE LOCKING B (AB BAD BOY 19 EPIC US EPC 3686
TONY BELCHER G (AB (A)WILDE ABOUT MARTY (RI) 1969 EPIC US 3711 PHILIPS UK 13147
WILDCAT 198 PHILIPS SWED
(B) SHOWCASE 1960 PHILIPS UK

W82 WILDERNESS ROAD W82

NATE HERMAN G K V(ABC (A) WILDERNESS ROAD 19 CBS US 31118
WARREN LEMING G V BANJ (ABC (B) THREE GENUINE TRANSPLANT 19 REPRISE US PRO 556
ANDY HABAN B V (ABC (C) SOLD FOR PREVENTION OF DISEASE 1973 REPRISE US 2125
RAY WARD (A
TOM HABAN D V OBOE(ABC J A RICHARDSON B (A RICK MANN STEEL (C JIM HORN SAX (C
DON MENZA SAX (C VENETTA FIELDS V (C CLYDIE KING V (C SHIRLEY MATTHEWS V (C

W82A

WILDING BONUS

W82A

DANNY WILDING FLT (A — (A) PLEASURE SIGNALS — 1978 DJM UK DJF 20553 US VISA 7003
PETE BONUS G (A
PHIL COLLINS D (A — PHIL CHEN B (A — KIKI GYAN K (A — REBOP KWAKU BAAH PERC(A
ASHTON TOOTLE HRNS (A — PHIL TODD HRNS (A — JOHN GOODSALL G (A — BAYETE K (A
GREGG SHEEHAN D (A — JOHN GIBLIN B G (A — PRESTON HEYMAN D (A — ROBIN LUMLEY K (A
ANDY CLARK K (A — KATE ST JOHN OBOE (A — MIKE SHRIEVE D (A — CHRIS PARREN K (A

W82B

WILDLIFE

W82B

STEVE OVERLAND G V (A — (A) BURNING — 1980 CHRYSALIS UK CHR 1288
MARK BOOTY K (A
CHRIS OVERLAND G (A — ROB SKEAT K B (A — PETE JUPP D (A — RUPERT HINE K PERC V(A
TREVOR MORAIS D (A — JOHN GIBLIN B (A — GEOFFREY RICHARDSON (A

W83

MIKE WILHELM

W83

MIKE WILHELM (A — (A) WILHELM — 1976 ZIG ZAG UK UA ZZ1
RICHARD OLSEN WIND PROD B K (A
GINO RYMER D (A — KENNY STREIGHT B (A — DENNIS WILSON V (A — PETER MINTUM K (A
J BETHARDS TPT PERC B (A — CHRIS WILSON G V (A — RICK KUNSTER G V (A — SID PAGE VLN (A
DENNIS CORSO V (A — RICK PADEN V (A — CAPRICE REYNOLDS V (A — JOHN ILLY V (A

W84

BIG JOE WILLIAMS

W84

BIG JOE WILLIAMS G V (ALL
MARY WILLIAMS V (U
SAM FOWLER V HCA(M
WILLIE EALEY V PNO(M
LEE WILLIAMS V (M
CHARLIE MUSSELWHITE HCA(T
ROGER ALLEN CLARK D (I
JERRY BRIDGES B (I
RANSOM KNOWLING B (PB
J D SHORT G V HCA(S

Title	Year	Label	Country	No.
BIG JOE WILLIAMS	1975	STORYVILLE		SLP224
BIG JOE WILLIAMS(LEGACY No6)	197	SONET UK SNTF635 US GNP		10016
BIG JOE WILLIAMS	19	EVEREST	US	218
BIG JOE WILLIAMS	19	WORLD PACIFIC	US	21897
BLUES FROM MISSISSIPPI DELTA	19	BLUES ON BLUE	US	10003
BIG JOE & ROBERT PETE WILLIAMS	1975	STORYVILLE		SLP225
(B) BLUE ON HIGHWAY 49	196	DELMARK	US	DL 604
BACK TO THE COUNTRY	19	TESTAMENT	US	2205
(F)CLASSIC DELTA BLUES	1964	CBS	UK	63813
COUNTRY BLUES	19	SPECIALTY	UK	SNTF5014
DONT LEAVE ME	19	POLYDOR		616 011
(I)DONT YOUR PLUMS LOOK MELLOW	19	BLUESWAY	UK	BLS 6080
EARLY RECORDINGS	197	MAMLISH	US	3810
HAND ME DOWN MY OLD WALKING STICK	1968	LIBERTY		LBS83207
HELL BOUND & HEAVEN SENT	1964	FOLKWAYS	US	FTS31004
(M)MALVINA MY SWEET WOMAN	1974	OLDIE BLUES	NL	OL 2814
MISSIPPIPPI JOE WILLIAMS	19	FOLKWAYS	US	3820
BLUES FOR NINE STRING	19	BLUESVILLE	US	1056
LIVE AT FOLK CITY	1968	BLUESVILLE US 1067 XTRA UK		5059
MISSIPPIPPI DELTA BLUES	19	SPIVEY	US	1005
STUDIO BLUES	196	BLUESVILLE	US	1083
BIG CRAWLIN' SNAKE	1970	RCA	US	INT 1087
(P)NINE STRING GUITAR BLUES	196	DELMARK	US	627
(P) " " " "	196	FOLKWAYS	US	3820
PINEY WOOD BLUES	196	DELMARK	US	602
RAMBLIN' WANDERIN' BLUES	19	STORYVILLE		SLP 163
(S) STAVIN' CHAIN BLUES	196	DELMARK	US	609
(S) SUPER BLACK BLUES	196	GOODY	FR	10006
(T)THINKING OF WHAT THEY DID	1969	ARHOOLIE	US	1053
(U)TOUGH TIMES	1960	ARHOOLIE	US	1002

W84A

CLAUDE WILLIAMS

W84A

CLAUDE WILLIAMS (A — (A) KANSAS CITY GREATS — 197 BIG BEAR UK BEAR 25

W84B

JERRY WILLIAMS & ROADWORK

W84B

JERRY WILLIAMS V (A — (A) TOO FAST TO LIVE — 1977 SONET SWED SLP 2604 UK SNTF791
PEDER SUNSAHL D (A
INGEMAR RAGEFEDT G (A — CAJ HOGBERG B G PNO V (A — DOUGIE LAWTON G (A — LARS AKE JOHANSSON PERC G(A

W84C

DENIECE WILLIAMS

W84C

DENIECE WILLIAMS V (ALL — (A) THIS IS NIECY — 1977 CBS UK 81869
AL McKAY G (AB — (B) SONGBIRD — 1977 CBS UK 86946
FREDDIE WHITE D (AB — (C) THATS WHAT FRIENDS ARE FOR — 1978 CBS UK 86068
JOHNNY MATHIS V (C — (D) WHEN LOVE COMES CALLING — 1979 CBS UK 83202
SYDNEY BARNES V (ABC — (E) MY MELODY — 1981 CBS UK 84874
STEVE MADAIO TPT (AB
RANDALL ALDCROFT TROM (A — GALE ROBINSON HRNS (A — RAY PIZZI SAX (A — ERNIE WATTS SAX (A
CHARLES FEARING G (BC — JOHN ROWIN G (A — PAULINHO DACOSTA PERC (A — VICTOR FELDMAN VIBES(B
MICHAEL HARRIS TPT (B — LOUIS SATTERDFIELD TROM(B — DON MYRICK SAX (BC — ANDREW WOOLFOLK SAX (B
MARILYN ROBINSON HRNS (B — JEFF PORCARO D (C — MAURICE WHITE D V PROD (AB — JERRY PETERS K (AB
VERDINE WHITE B (AB — OSCAR BRASHEAR TPT (AB — GEORGE BOHANON TROM (AB — SIDNEY MULDROW HRNS(A
PLAS JOHNSON SAX (A — TERRY HARRINGTON SAX (A — NATHAN WATTS B (B — MARLO HENDERSON SAX(B
DAVID GARIBALDI D (B — LARRY DUNN SYN (B — CHUCK FINDLEY TPT (B — CHARLES LOPER TROM (B
AZAR LAWRENCE SAX (B — GEORGE PATTERSON SAX (B — ALAN ROBINSON HRNS (B — RAY PARKER G PROD(B
DAVID SHIELDS B (B — GREG PHILLINGANES K (C — GARY COLEMAN VIBES(C — MAXINE WILLARD V (C
STEVE LUKATHER G (C — MIKE PORCARO B (C — GARY HERBIG SAX (C — JULIA TILLMAN V(C
JERRY HEY HRNS (C — WAH WAH WATSON G (C — EDDIE BROWN PERC (C — LARRY JACOBS V (C
LARRY FARROW K (C — OLLIE BROWN PERC (C — DYANNE CHANDLER V (C — GENE PAGE STR HRN(C
ED GREENE D (C — DAVID FOSTER K PROD(C — BILL CHAMPLIN V (C — DAVID HUNGATE B (C
RICHARD FELDMAN G (C — SCOTT EDWARDS B (C — JACK ASHFORD PERC (C — SYLVESTER RIVERS K (C

W84D

DUKE WILLIAMS & THE EXTREMES

W84D

DUKE WILLIAMS K V(ALL — (A) FANTASTIC FEDORA — 1974 CAPRICORN US
T J TINDALL G V B(AB — (B) A MONKEY IN A SILK SUIT — 1974 CAPRICORN US 0119
BOBBY HARTNAGLE G (AB
COTTON KENT K (AB — TOMMY HOUGH B V (A — EARL SCOOTER PERC V(A — DIMITRI CHIMES G (A
EARL YOUNG D (B — SKIP DRINKWATER PERC (B — RON BAKER B (B — RALPH SCHUCKETT K (B
LARRY WASHINGTON PERC (B — BRUCE STEINBERG HCA (B — CHRIS BOND SYN (B

W85

JODY WILLIAMS

W85

JODY WILLIAMS G V (A — (A) LEADING BRAND(6 TRACKS) — 1977 RED LIGHTNIN RL0018
BERNARD BARKSON SAX (A
HAROLD ASHBY SAX (A — LAFAYETTE LEAKE PNO (A — RED HOLLOWAY SAX (A — WILLIE DIXON B (A
BOB GUTHRIE D (A

W86 JOHN WILLIAMS W86

JOHN WILLIAMS G (ALL (A) CHANGES 1971 FLY UK HIFLY 5 US CBS 31091
HERBIE FLOWERS G B (ABH (B) HEIGHT BELOW 1973 FLY UK HIFLY 16
FRANCIS MONKMAN K (H (C) GREATEST HITS 1974 CBS 30051
BARRY MORGAN D (AH (D) RHAPSODY 1974 CBS 73350
ADRIAN BRETT WIND (H (E) & FRIENDS 1976 CBS 73487
RICHARD HARVEY REC (H (F) SPANISH GUITAR 1976 WESTMINSTER UK WG1001
VIC FLICK G (H (G) BEST FRIENDS 1976 RCA UK RS1094
LAWRENCE JUBER G (H (AB) CHANGES /HEIGHT BELOW 1977 CUBE RI UK TOOFA12
LES THATCHER G (H (H) TRAVELLING 1978 CUBE UK HIFLY27
HAROLD FISHER D (H (J) BRIDGES 1979 LOTUS UK WH 5015
STUART ELLIOTT D (H
PATRICK GOWERS K (H DANNY THOMPSON B (A JIM LAWLESS PERC (A CHRIS LAURENCE B (A
JOE MUDELE B (A RAY COOPER PERC (A BARRY GUARD PERC (A ALAN PARKER G (A
CHRIS SPEDDING G (A RICK WAKEMAN K (A DAVID SNELL HARP (A CHRIS TAYLOR WIND (AB
ROY WILCOX WIND (A TONY COE WIND (A RONNIE CHAMBERLAIN WIND (A KENNY WHEELER TPT (A
STANLEY RODERICK TPT (A RALPH IZEN TPT (A DEREK WATKINS TROM (A NAT PECK TROM (A
DON LUSHER TROM (A PAT HARLEY TROM (A RAY PREMRU TROM (A RONNIE VERRALL PERC (A
TERRY COX PERC (A TRISTAN FRY PERC (AB BRIAN GASCOIGNE PERC (B CHARLOTTE NASSIM KOTO (B
VIRAM JASANI TABLA(B ROY BABBINGTON B (B JOHN MARSHALL D (B WILLIAM DE MONT CELLO (B
MORRIS LUBAN VLA (B BRIAN MOLLINSON B (B CHRIS BOWERS-BROADBENT K(B DARRYL RUNSWICK B (B
PETE MORGAN B (B BARRY DE SOUZA D (B KENNY CLAIRE D (B TREVOR TOMKINS D (B
ALAN BRANSCOMBE VIBES(B DAVID CORKHILL FLT (B JACK ELLORY FLT (B GEORGE CROZIER FLT (B
DUDLEY MOORE ORG (B ROLAND HARKER G (B DICK ABEL G (B

W87 LARRY WILLIAMS W87

LARRY WILLIAMS V (ALL (A) LIVE 1965 SUE UK ILP 922
JOHNNY GUITAR WATSON G (ABD (B) THE LARRY WILLIAMS SHOW 1965 DECCA UK LK 4691
PLAS JOHNSON SAX (C (C) HERE'S LARRY WILLIAMS 196 SPECIALITY US 2109 UK SNTF5008
ALVIN'RED'TAYLOR SAX (C (D) TWO FOR THE PRICE OF ONE 19 OKEH OKS 14122
ERNIE FREEMAN PNO (C (E) MISSING & UNISSUED SIDES 19 SPECIALITY FR 2225
RENEE HALL G (C (F) GREATEST HITS 19 OKEH OKS 12123
BARNEY KESSEL G (C
TED BRINSON B (C RAY BROWN B (C EARL PALMER D (C GERALD WILSON TPT (C
DAVE SHERIDAN SAX (AB TONY HURLEY SAX (AB PHILIP GOODHAND TAIT K (AB IVOR SHAKLETON G (AB
KIRK RIDDLE B (AB DICK FORCEY D (AB

W88 MASON WILLIAMS W88

MASON WILLIAMS G V (ALL (A) PHONOGRAM RECORD 1969 WB US WS1729
BILL CUNNINGHAM G (H (B) MASON WILLIAMS EAR SHOW 1969 WB US WS1766
RICK CUNHA G (H (C) MUSIC 1969 WB US WS1788
AL CASEY G (H (D) HAND MADE 19 WB US WS1838
LARRY KNECHTEL B (H (E) THEM POEMS & THINGS 196 JOY JOY 118
HAL BLAINE D (H (F) SHAREPICKERS 10 WB US WS1941
TOMMY MORGAN HCA (H (G) FEUDIN BANJOS 19 OLYMPIC US 7105
STEVE LA FEVER B (H (H) IMPROVED 1971 WB UK K46120
MILT HOLLAND PERC (H (I) FRESH FISH 197 FLYING FISH US FF059
PATTER SMITH B (H (J) LISTENING MATTER 19 EVEREST US 3265
DAVE DAWSON V (H
SUZETTE GRANT G V (H NANCY AMES V (H ARTIE AZENZOR PNO (H JAN HYDE D (H
GARY CARLSON G (H RONNIE TUTT D (H

W89 PAUL WILLIAMS W89

PAUL WILLIAMS V (ALL (A) DELTA BLUES SINGER 1973 SONET UK SNTF 654
ROGER SUTTON B (2 (A) IN MEMORY OF ROBERT JOHNSON 1973 INTERCORD GER 28754
GLENN CAMPBELL G (A (1) PAUL WILLIAMS SET 1967
BOB HALL K (A (2) PAUL WILLIAMS SET 1968
KEITH ELLIS B (A
EDDIE YARLETT (A PAT DONALDSON B (A ALUN DAVIES G (A SPENCER DAVIS G (A
JON MARK G (A ROY MILLS (1 ROD SLADE B (1 TEDDY CHILDS (1
JOHN ALMOND WIND (12 JIMMY CRAWFORD (12 JEFF CONDON HRNS (12 ALAN WHITE D (2
JOHN WIGGINS (2

W90 TONY WILLIAMS W90

TONY WILLIAMS D (A (A) JOY OF FLYING 1979 CBS US 35705 UK 83338
RONNIE MONTROSE G (A
HERBIE HANCOCK K (A BRIAN AUGER K (A JAN HAMMER K (A STANLEY CLARKE B (A
GEORGE BENSON G (A

W91 HOMESICK JAMES WILLIAMSON W91

JAMES WILLIAMSON (ALL (A) CHICAGO 19 B&B FR 33034
DAVE MYERS B (B (B) AIN'T SICK NO MORE 1973 BLUESWAY BLS 6071
EDDIE TAYLOR B (B (C) & SNOOKY PRYOR 197 CAROLINE UK C1502 BIGBEAR 21
SNOOKY PRYOR HCA (BCD (D) HOME SWEET HOMESICK JAMES 1976 BIG BEAR BEAR10
WILLIE SMITH D (B
BOB HALL PNO (CD BOB BRUNNING B (CD JOHN HUNT D (CD PETE YORK D (D
JIMMIE LEE ROBINSON B (D

W92 ROBIN WILLIAMSON W92

ROBIN WILLIAMSON (ALL (A) MYRRH 1972 ISLAND HELP 2
SYLVIA WOODS K HCA V B (C (B) JOURNEY EDGE 1977 FLYING FISH US 033
CHRISTOPHER CASWELL WIND V(C (C) AMERICAN STONEHENGE 1978 FLYING FISH US 062
JERRY McMILLAN VLN V(C (C) AMERICAN STONEHENGE 1978 CRIMINAL UK STEAL 4
PETE GRANT BAN G(C (D) GLINT AT THE KINDLING 1979 CRIMINAL UK STEAL 6
LOUIS KILLEN CONC (C (D) GLINT AT THE KINDLING 1979 FLYING FISH US 096
DIRK DALTON B (C (E) SONGS OF LOVE & PARTING 1981 FLYING FISH US 257
STU BROTMAN B (C
CAROL SHRIVE VLN (F MIKE GARSON K (E DAVID CAMPBELL VLA (E JESSE ERLICH CELLO(E
JUDY GAMERAL DULC(E

W93 SONNY BOY WILLIAMSON (1) W93

SONNY BOY WILLIAMSON V HCA(A (A) SONNY BOY WILLIAMSON 19 RCA FXM1 7215
(JOHN LEE WILLIAMSON) (B) BLUEBIRD BLUES 1970 RCA INT INT 1088
JOE WILLIAMS G (B (C) SONNY BOY VOL 1 1975 BLUES CLASSICS BC3
YANK RACHELL MAND (B (D) SONNY BOY VOL 2 1975 BLUES CLASSICS BC20
SPECKLED RED PNO (B (E) SONNY BOY VOL 3 1975 BLUES CLASSICS BC24
WILLIE HATCHER MAND (B
ROBERT LEE McCOY G (B WALTER DAVIS PNO (B JOSH ALTHEIMER PNO (C FRED WILLIAMS D (C
WASHBOARD SAM PERC (C ARMAND JACKSON D (C BLIND JOHN DAVIS PNO (C ALFRED WLKINS B (C
BILL BROONZY G (C MATT MURPHY G (D TED SUMMIT G (C RANSOM KNOWLING B (C
CHARLIE McCOY G (C WALTER DAVIS PNO (C

W94 SONNY BOY WILLIAMSON (II) W94

SONNY BOY WILLIAMSON V (ALL (A) SONNY BOY & MEMPHIS SLIM 1963 VOGUE LD 63930
(RICE MILLER) (B) DOWN & OUT BLUES 1964 CHESS US 1437 UK PYE NPL 28036
BRIAN AUGER K (M (B) DOWN & OUT BLUES 1967 MARBLE ARCH UK RI MAL 662
JOE HARRIOT SAX (M (C) HELP ME 1964 CHESS CRE 6001
ALAN SKIDMORE SAX (M (D) & THE YARDBIRDS 1964 FONTANA UK TL5277
JIMMY PAGE G (M (D) & THE YARDBIRDS 1964 MERCURY US 21071
RICKY BROWN B (M (D) & THE YARDBIRDS 196 FONTANA 858 025
MICK WALLER D (M (D) & THE YARDBIRDS 1968 FONTANA SFJL 960
ERIC CLAPTON G (D (D) & THE YARDBIRDS 1975 PHILIPS 6435 011
DUKE HUDDLESTON SAX(P (D) & THE YARDBIRDS 1980 MERCURY US 8003
KEITH RELF HCA (D (E) ONE WAY OUT 196 CHESS US 1417 RI CHV 417
JIM McCARTY D (D (F) IN MEMORIUM 1965 CHESS CRL 4510
CHRIS DREJA G B (D (G) REAL FOLK BLUES 196 CHESS US 1503
PAUL SAMWELL SMITH B (D (H) MORE FOLK BLUES 196 CHESS US 1509
ERIC BURDON (Q (I) SONNY BOY WILLIAMSON 19 STORYVILLE SLP 158
JOHN STEEL D (Q (J) BLUES OF 19 STORYVILLE 671 170
HILTON VALENTINE G (Q (K) PORTRAIT IN BLUES 19 STORYVILLE US 4016 UK 671 158
MATT MURPHY G (QJKPVW (L) DONT SEND ME NO FLOWERS 1968 MARMALADE 608 004
CHAS CHANDLER B (Q (M) THE ORIGINAL 19 BLUES CLASSICS BC 9
ALAN PRICE K (Q (N) BUMMER ROAD 19 CHESS US 1536
MEMPHIS SLIM PNO (AJKX (O) THIS IS MY STORY 19 CHESS 50027
BILLY STEPNEY D (JKW (P) DONT MAKE A MISTAKE 19 BLUES BALL US 2004
MUDDY WATERS G (EV (M) JAM SESSION 1975 CHARLY UK CR 30011
WILLIE DIXON B (EPVW (Q) & THE ANIMALS 1975 CHARLY UK CR 30018
BUDDY GUY G (PVW (U) KING BISCUIT TIME 1976 ARHOOLIE R 2020
LAFAYETTE LEAKE PNO (PVW (V) BLUES MASTERS 19 CHESS 2ACBM 206
OTIS SPAN PNO (EPVW (V) CHICAGO GOLDEN YEARS 1976 VOGUE FR 427 804
WALTER DAVIS PNO (R (W) BYE BYE BIRD 1979 BLUES NIGHT 073 1668
BIG JOE WILLIAMS G (Y (X) CHEST MASTERS 1981 CHESS UK CXMD 4001
OLIVER HARRIS B (P (Y) & BIG JOE WILLIAMS (1 SIDE) 1980 P VINE JAP PLP 9014
CLIFF BIVENS V B (PU
S P LEARY D (P JOE WILLIE WILKINS G (PU FRED BELOW D (EPV ODIE PAYNE D (V
MILTON RECTOR B (V JARRETT GIBSON SAX (PV CLIFTON JAMES D (PV DAVE CAMPBELL PNO (PU
FROCK D (U CLARENCE LONNIE PNO (U JIMMY ROGERS G (EV ROBERT LOCKWOOD G (EPNV
LUTHER TUCKER G (ENV AL DUNCAN D (V JACK MYERS B (PV

W95 WILLIE & THE RED RUBBER BAND W95

WILLIE REDDEN G V (AB (A) WILLIE & THE RED RUBBER BAND 1968 RCA US LSP 4074
GLEN BALLARD G B (AB (B) WE'RE COMING UP 1969 RCA US LSP 4193
CHARLES ADDINGTON K (AB
CONLAY BRADFORD D (AB LARRY FIELD G (AB JOHN BUCK WILKEN G (B BEGIE CRUZER K (B

W96 PETE WILLSHER W96

PETE WILLSHER STEEL G(AB (A) GUITAR MAGIC 19 JOY JOYS 158
STUART COWELL G (B (B) STEEL SEASONS 1977 PYE NSPL18539
ROB HENDRY G (B
TONY KELLY G V (B LUCE LANGRIDGE D (B BOB LOVEDAY FDL (B GRAHAM WAYNE B (B
TRISTRAM FRY PERC (B RAPH RAVENSCROFT WIND (B KEITH MILLER K (B KEITH NELSON BANJ(B
MANDI WILSON V (B

W96A CHUCK WILLIS W96A

CHUCK WILLIS V (AB (A) STOOP DOWN BABY.. LET YOUR DADDY SEE 1972 LAVAL US LVB 1327
(B) THE KING OF THE STROLL 19 PIONEER JAP P4587A

W96B WILLOW W96B

(A) WILLOW 1974 20TH CENTURY US 420
(B) BRANCHING OUT 1974 20TH CENTURY US 450

W96C VIOLA WILLS W96C

VIOLA WILLS V (A (A) WITHOUT YOU 1979 LINE GER LLP 5023

W97 DENNIS WILSON W97

DENNIS WILSON V K D STR(A (A) PACIFIC OCEAN BLUE 1977 CARIBOU US 34354 UK 81672
JAMIE JAMERSON B (A (B) ONE OF THOSE PEOPLE 1980 ELEKTRA US 230
ED TULIJA G V (A
JOHN KANTON G (A BOBBY FIGUEROA D (A BILL LAMB HRNS (A LANCE BULLER HRNS(A
CHARLIE McCARTHY HRNS (A ED CARTER G B (A CHUCK DOMANICO B (A EARLE MARKEY G (A
HAL BLAINE D (A RICKY FATAAR D (A MICHAEL ANDREAS HRNS (A JANICE HUBBARD HRNS(A
KAREN LAMM-WILSON V (

W97A CARL WILSON W97A

CARL WILSON V G K (A (A) CARL WILSON 1981 CARIBOU UK 84840 US 37010
MYRNA SMITH V (A
GERALD JOHNSON B (A
JAMES STROUD D (A JOEL PESKIN SAX (A JAMES GUERCIO G B PERC (A
JOHN DALY STEEL(A ALAN KRIGGER D (A RANDY McCORMICK CLAR K(A

W98 JACKIE WILSON W98

JACKIE WILSON V (ALL

HES SO FINE 195 BRUNSWICK US 54042
LONELY TEARDROPS 1958 BRUNSWICK US 54045
DOGGIN' AROUND 1959 BRUNSWICK
NIGHT 1960
SO MUCH 1960 BRUNSWICK US 754050
SINGS THE BLUES 1960 BRUNSWICK US 754055
MY GOLDEN FAVOURITES 1960 BRUNSWICK US 754058
MY GOLDEN FAVOURITES 196 CORAL UK LVA9135
A WOMAN A LOVER A FRIEND 1960 BRUNSWICK US 754059
TRY A LITTLE TENDERNESS 1961
YOU AIN'T HEARD NOTHING YET 1961 BRUNSWICK US 754100
BY SPECIAL REQUEST 1961 BRUNSWICK US 754101
BY SPECIAL REQUEST 1961 CORAL UK LVA9151
BY SPECIAL REQUEST 1961 CORAL UK SVL3018
BODY & SOUL 1962 BRUNSWICK US 754105
BODY & SOUL 1962 CORAL UK LVA9202
WORLDS GREATEST MELODIES 196 BRUNSWICK US 754106
WORLDS GREATEST MELODIES 196 CORAL UK LVA9214
AT THE COPA 196 BRUNSWICK US 754108
AT THE COPA 196 CORAL UK LVA9209
BABY WORK OUT 1962 BRUNSWICK US 754110
MERRY CHRISTMAS 196 BRUNSWICK US 754112
SHAKE A HAND 1962 BRUNSWICK US 754113
GOLDEN FAVOURITES 196 BRUNWICK US 754115
SOMETHIN' ELSE 1964 BRUNSWICK US 754117
SOUL TIME 196 BRUNSWICK US 754118
SPOTLIGHT ON 1965 BRUNSWICK US 754119
SOUL GALORE 1966 BRUNSWICK US 754120
SOUL GALORE 196 CORAL UK LVA9232
WHISPERS 1966 BRUNSWICK US 754122
HIGHER & HIGHER 1967 BRUNSWICK US 754130
HIGHER & HIGHER 1967 MCA UK MUPS304
MANUFACTURES OF SOUL 196 BRUNSWICK US 754134
TOO MUCH 196 MCA UK MUPS333
I GET THE SWEETEST FEELING 1968 BRUNSWICK US 754138
I GET THE SWEETEST FEELING 1968 MCA UK MUPS361
GREATEST HITS 19 BRUNSWICK US 754140
DO YOUR THING 19 BRUNSWICK US 754154
DO YOUR THING 19 MCA UKMUPS 405
ITS ALL A PART OF LOVE 1971 BRUNSWICK US 754158
YOU GOT ME WALKING 1973 BRUNSWICK US 754172
YOU GOT ME WALKING 1973 BRUNSWICK BRLS3001
GREATEST HITS 197 BRUNSWICK US 754185
GREATEST HITS 1973 BRUNSWICK BRLS3004
VERY BEST OF 1975 BRUNSWICK BRLS3016
THIS LOVE IS REAL 1973 BRUNSWICK US 754167
BEAUTIFUL DAY 197 BRUNSWICK US 754189
NOWSTALGIA 19 BRUNSWICK US 754199
NOBODY BUT YOU 1977 BRUNSWICK US 754212
NOBODY BUT YOU 1977 BRUNSWICK BRLA5002

W98A LARRY JON WILSON W98A

LARRY JON WILSON (ALL

(A) NEW BEGINNINGS 1975 MONUMENT US 33382 RI MC 6635
(B) LET ME SING MY SONGS 1976 MONUMENT US 34041 RI MC 6636
(C) LOOSE CHANGE 1977 MONUMENT US MG 7615
(D) THE SOJOURNER 1979 MONUMENT US MG 7631

W99 LEROY WILSON W99

LEROY WILSON (A

(A) BEST OF 1978 UA US LA 807

W99A WILSON /GALE W99A

FRANK WILSON K V (A
MELVYN GALE K V (A
ALAN ROSS G V (A STEVE STROUD B (A ADRIAN SHEPARD D (A

(A) GIFT WRAPPED SET 1980 JET UK JETLP223

W99B WIND CHASE W99B

MARIO MILLO K V (A
TOWO PILT K V (A
DOUG BLIGH D (A DUNCAN MCGUIRE B (A

(A) SYMPHINITY 1976 FESTIVAL 36216

W100 WIND IN THE WILLOWS W100

DEBORAH HARRY V PERC(A
GIL FIELDS D (A
WAYNE KIRBY B V K(A
IDA ANDREWS WIND (A PETER BRITTAIN G V (A PAUL KLEIN G V (A ANTON CARYSFORTH D(A
STEVE DE PHILLIPS B V (A PETER C LEEDS PERC (A ARTIE KORNFELD PROD PERC(A HARRIS WIENER K V (A

(A) WIND IN THE WILLOWS 1968 CAPITOL 2956
(A) WIND IN THE WILLOWS 1979 CAPITOL RI CAPS 1030

W101 JESSE WINCHESTER W101

JESSE WINCHESTER G V K(ALL
AMOS GARRETT G (BC
MARTY HARRIS B V (DE
CHRIS CASTLE D (D
BOB COHEN G (DE
CHRISTIAN STROCH D (D
MAURICE BEAUCHAMP K (D
DONALD BROWN K (G
RON DAWN STEEL(DE
CARLISLE MILLER SAX (D BRUCE MURCHISON VLN (D KEN PEARSON K (AD DON HABIB B (D
BOB LUCIER STEEL(D DAVE LEWIS D (AE LORRI ZIMMERMANN V (D SHARON RYAN V (D
MICKEY RAPHAEL HCA (E PAUL BUTTERFIELD HCA (D RICKY SKAGGS FDL (E TOM SZCZESNIAK ACC(E
JON CLARKE SAX (E JAMES BURTON G (E EMMYLOU HARRIS V (E HERB PEDERSEN V (E
ANNE MURRAY V (E DIANNE BROOKS V (E NICOLETTE LARSON V (E ROBBIE ROBERTSON G (A
LEVON HELM D (A BOB BOUCHER B (AB DAVID REA G V (A GUY BLACK D (A
AL CHERNEY VLN (A ANDRE BENICHOU G (B DOUG SCHMOLZE G (B CHARLES VIBER VLN(B
GORD FLEMING PNO (B JIMMY OLIVER B (B GENE COTTON B (B NORMAN SMART D (B

(A) JESSE WINCHESTER 1971 AMPEX US A10104
(B) 3RD DOWN 110 TO GO 1972 BEARSVILLE US 2102 UK K45512
(AB) JESSE WINCHESTER/3RD DOWN 1976 BEARSVILLE UK K85507
(C) LEARN TO LOVE IT 1974 BEARSVILLE US 6953 UK K55506
(D) LET THE ROUGH SIDE DRAG 1976 BEARSVILLE US 6964 UK K55512
(E) NOTHIN' BUT A BREEZE 1977 BEARSVILLE US 6968 UK K81853
(F) A TOUCH ON THE RAINY SIDE 1978 BEARSVILLE US 6984
(G) TALK MEMPHIS 1981 BEARSVILLE US 6989

W101 (CONTINUED) **JESSE WINCHESTER** W101

RON FRANKEL D (B SAM KELLY CONGA(B DON ABRAMS PERC (B CARL MARSH SYN (G
EDDIE FISHER D (G BLAIR CUNNINGHAM D (G STEVE COBB B (G WILLIE MITCHELL K (G
WALTER PERSON PERC (G MICHALE TOLES G (G ERMA SHAW V (G CINDY FARR V (G
ELIZABETH SMITH V (G GARY BURKE D (G BRAD STAHL B (G

W102 **WINDS OF CHANGE** W102

BRIAN ADDISON WIND (A (A) ILLUSIONS 1979 EMI UK EMA 791
STAN SULZMANN WIND (A
ANTON WEINBERG WIND (A DAVID WHITE WIND (A TONY HYMAS K SYN (A JIM LAWLESS PERC(A
STEVE GREY K (A BARRY DE SOUZA D (A RICHARD HARVEY SYN (A RICKY HITCHCOCK G (A
PAUL WESTWOOD B (A SIMON PHILLIPS D (A HERBIE FLOWERS B (A FRANK RICOTTI PERC(A
LITTLECHAP STRINGS (A

W103 **PETE WINGFIELD** W103

PETE WINGFIELD K V (AB (A) BREAKFAST SPECIAL 1975 ISLAND UK ILPS9333
DELISLE HARPER B (A (B) LOVE BUMPS & DIZZY SPELLS 1976 ISLAND NOT RELEASED
NEIL HUBBARD G (A
JOSEPH EDWARD WRIGHT G (A GLEN LE FLEUR D (A CHRIS MERCER SAX (A

W103A **WINGS (US)** W103A

(A) WINGS 19 DUNHILL US DS50046

W104 **THE WINKIES** W104

MICHAEL DESMARAIS D (A (A) THE WINKIES 1975 CHRYSALIS US CHR 1066
PHILIP RAMBOW G V (A
GUY HUMPHREYS G V (A BRIAN TURRINGTON B V K(A

W104A **COLIN WINSKI** W104A

COLIN WINSKI (A (A) ROCK THERAPY 1980 CHRYSALIS 1318

W105 **WINTER** W105

(A) WINTER 197 EMI UK EMC 3266

W106 **EDGAR WINTER** W106

EDGAR WINTER V SAX K (ALL (A) ENTRANCE 1970 EPIC US 26503 UK 64083
JIMMY GILLEN D (A (B) WHITE TRASH 1971 EPIC US 30512 UK 64298
RANDAL DOLANON G (A (AB) ENTRANCE WHITE TRASH 1976 EPIC US 33770 UK 81191
GENE KURTZ B (A (C) ROAD WORK 1972 EPIC US 31249 UK 67244
JOHNNY WINTER G HCA V (ABCF (D) THEY ONLY COME OUT AT NIGHT 1973 EPIC US 31584 UK 65074
RAY ALONGE HRNS (A (E) SHOCK TREATMENT 1974 EPIC US 32461 UK 65640
EARL W CHAPIN HRNS (A (F) JASMINE NIGHTDREAMS 1975 BLUE SKY US 33483 UK 80772
BROOKS TILLOTSON HRNS (A (G) WITH RICK DERRINGER 1975 BLUE SKY US 33798 UK 69181
JERRY LA CROIX V SAX HCA(BCH (H) RECYCLED 1977 BLUE SKY US 34858 UK 82228
JON SMITH V SAX(BCH (J) EDGAR WINTER ALBUM 1979 BLUE SKY US 35989 UK 83648
MIKE McCLELLAN V TPT(BC (K) STANDING ON ROCK 1981 BLUE SKY US 36494
KEITH BENSON D (J
BOBBY RAMIREZ D (BC GEORGE SHECK B (B FLOYD RADFORD G (BH RICK DERRINGER G V(BCDEFG
TASHA THOMAS V (B JANICE BELL V (B CARL HULL V (B MAERETHA STEWART V (B
ALBERTINE ROBINSON V (B EILEEN GILBERT V (B RAY BARRETTO CONGA(B RANDY HOBBS B (CD
MARSHALL CYR TPT (CH TILLY LAWRENCE TPT (C DAN HARTMAN B V G PERC(EDFGH CHUCK RUFF D V (EDFG
PAUL PRESTOPINO G BAN(G JOHN SIEGLER B (G ROBERT ARNOLD B (H BOZ SCAGGS G (
JERRY WEEMS G (RONNIE MONTROSE G (D GEORGE RECILE D (H DAN MINATRE G (H
JOHNNY BADANAJEK D (D RICK MAROTTA D (F JAMES WILLIAMS B (J CRAIG SNYDER G (J
LARRY WASHINGTON PERC(J AL FERRANTE G MAND (K RONNIE LAWSON K V (K SCOTT SPRAY B (K
GREG CARTER D PERC(K MONIQUW WINTER V (K

W107 **JOHNNY WINTER** W107

JOHNNY WINTER G V HCA(ALL (A) JOHNNY WINTER 1969 CBS US 9826 UK 63619
EDGAR WINTER SAX K V (ADMQSN (B) PROGRESSIVE BLUES EXPERIMENT 1969 LIBERTY US LBR1001 UK 83240
JOHN TURNER D (ABDS (B) PROGRESSIVE BLUES EXPERIMENT 1969 IMPERIAL US 12431
TOMMY SHANNON B (ABDS (B) PROGRESSIVE BLUES EXPERIMENT 1973 SUNSET UK 50264
DENNIS COLLINS B (D (C) FIRST WINTER 1970 CBS US 7513 BUDDAH UK 2359 011
MUDDY WATERS V G (PS (D) SECOND WINTER (3 SIDES) 1970 CBS US 9947 UK 66231
RICK DERRINGER G (FGLMSN (E) STORY 1971 GRT US 101 MARBLE ARCH UK 34
KENNY ASCHER K (N (E) STORY 19 SONET SWED 9972
RANDY JO HOBBS B (FLMOSGn (F) JOHNNY WINTER AND... 1971 CBS US 30221 UK 64117
RICHARD HUGHES D (LOMSN (G) JOHNNY WINTER AND..LIVE 1971 CBS US 30475 RI 33651 UK 64289
JAMES COTTON HCA (PS (H) ABOUT BLUES 1971 JANUS US 3008
PINETOP PERKINS PNO (PS (I) EARLY TIMES 1971 JANUS US 3023
BOB MARGOLIN G (PS (J) BEFORE THE STORM 197 JANUS US 3056
CHARLES CALMESE B (PS (K) AUSTIN TEXAS 1976 UA US LA139
WILLIE SMITH D (PS (L) STILL ALIVE & WELL 1973 CBS US 32188 UK 65484
DAN HARTMAN B (MSR (M) SAINTS & SINNERS 1974 CBS US 32715 UK 65842
BOBBY CALDWELL D (GMS (N) JOHN DAWSON WINTER III 1974 BLUE SKY US 33292 UK 80568
TASHA THOMAS V (M (O) CAPTURED LIVE 1976 BLUE SKY US 33944 UK 69230
CARL HALL V (M (P) NOTHIN' BUT THE BLUES 1977 BLUE SKY US 34813 UK 82141
LANI GROVES V (M (Q) WHITE HOT & BLUE 1978 BLUE SKY US 35475 UK 82963
KANSAS PERC (M (R) RAISIN' CAIN 1980 BLUE SKY US 36343 UK 84103
BARBARA MASSEY V (M (S) THE JOHNNY WINTER STORY(DBL) 1980 BLUE SKY UK 22112
RANDY BRECKER TPT (MN
ALAN RUBIN TPT (M LEW DELGATTO SAX (MN JO JO GUNNE PERC (M JON SMITH SAX (M
I P SWEAT B (QS BOBBY TORELLO D (QRS PAT RAMSEY HCA (QS PAT RUSH G (QS
RANDY ZEHRINGER D (FS JEREMY STEIG FLT (L TODD RUNDGREN K (L MARK KLINGMAN PNO (LS
FLOYD RADFORD G (OS CHUCK RUFF D (S A WYNN BUTLER SAX (AS KARL GARIN TPT (AS
JERRY PORTNOY HRNS (S PAUL PRESTOPINO PERC (SN JACKDAW V (S DENNIS FERRANTE V (S
WILLIE DIXON B (AS WALTER HORTON HCA (AS NORMAN RAY SAX (A CARRIE HOSSELL V (A
PEGGY BOWERS V (A ELSIE SENTER V (A JON PARIS B V HCA G (R SUSAN WARFORD V (R
KRISTY GRIGGS V (R ALLAN MARTIN V (R BERNADETTE MAZUR V (R TOM STROHMAN SAX (R
DAVE STILL PERC (R CINDY MURRAY V (R MIKE BRECKER SAX (N DAVE TAYLOR TROM(N

W108 JOHNNY & EDGAR WINTER W108

JOHNNY WINTER G V (A — (A) TOGETHER ,LIVE — 1976 BLUE SKY US 34033 UK 81338
EDGAR WINTER SAX V(A
RICK DERRINGER G (A — FLOYD RADFORD G (A — RANDY JO HOBBS B (A — DAN HARTMAN K (A
RICHARD HUGHES D (A — CHUCK RUFF D (A

W109 RUBY WINTERS W109

RUBY WINTERS V (AB
(A) RUBY WINTERS — 1978 CREOLE CRLP 512
(B) SONGBIRD — 1979 K TEL NE 1045
(C) I WILL — 1980 MILLENIUM US 8006

W110 WINTERS BROTHERS BAND W110

DONNIE WINTERS G V (AB — (A) COAST TO COAST — 197 ATLANTIC US 38106
DENNIS WINTERS G V (AB — (B) WINTER BROTHERS BAND — 1977 ATLANTIC UK K50343 US 36145
GENE WATSON B (B
KENT HARRIS D (B — DAVID DAVIS K (B — CHARLIE DANIELS FDL (B — DON MURRAY CONGAS(B
DON WINTERS SNR V (B — TAZ DIGREGORIO PNO (B

W110A WINTERGARDEN W110A

(A) WINTERGARDEN — 1979 HARVEST EURO 45265

W111 STEVE WINWOOD W111

STEVE WINWOOD K G V(ALL — (A) WINWOOD — 197 UA 9964
NICOLE WINWOOD V (CE — (B) WINWOOD & FRIENDS — 197 SPRINGBOARD US SPB4040
BROTHER JAMES PERC (A — (C) STEVE WINWOOD — 1977 ISLAND UK ILPS 9494
ALAN SPENNER B (C — (D) ARC OF A DIVER — 1980 ISLAND UK ILPS 9576
WILLIE WEEKS B (C — (E) TALKING BACK TO THE NIGHT — 1982 ISLAND UK ILPS 9777
ANDY NEWMARK D (C
JOHN SUSSWELL D (C — JUNIOR MARVIN G (D — JIM CAPALDI D V (CA — REBOP PERC(C
ERIC CLAPTON G (BA — YARDBIRDS (B — JEFF BECK G (B — GINGER BAKER D (BA
LONG JOHN BALDRY V (B — JACK BRUCE B (B — SONNY BOY WILLIAMSON (B — MUFF WINWOOD (A
SPENCER DAVIS (A — PETER YORK (A — DAVE MASON G (A — CHRIS WOOD FLT(A
RICK GRETCH B (A — NB (A&B) ARE COMPILATION ALBUMS OF STEVE'S PREVIOUS BANDS AND OTHER OUT TAKES

W112 WIRE W112

ROBERT GOTOBED D (ABCD — (A) PINK FLAG — 1977 HARVEST US 11757 UK SHSP 4076
GRAHAM LEWIS B V (ABCD — (B) CHAIRS MISSING — 1978 HARVEST UK SHSP 4093
BRUCE CLIFFORD GILBERT G(AD — (C) 154 — 1979 HARVEST UK SHSP 4105
COLIN NEWMAN G V (ABCD — (C) 154 — 1979 WB US 3398
MIKE THORNE PROD K (BC — (D) DOCUMENT & EYEWITNESS — 1981 ROUGH TRADE UK ROUGH 29
KATE LUCAS FLT (BC
TIM SOUSTER VLA (C — HILLY KRISTAL V (C — JOAN WHITING WIND (C

W113 WIRELESS W113

MIKE CRAWFORD G (AB — (A) POSITIVELY HUMAN ,RELATIVELY SANE — 1979 MERCURY US 3750
STEVE McMURRAY G (AB — (B) NO STATIC — 1980 ANTHEM ANR 11025
ALAN MARSHALL B V (AB
MARTY MORIN D (AB

W114 WISHBONE ASH W114

STEVE UPTON D (ALL
MARTIN TURNER B(A TO O
GLEN TURNER G (
ANDY POWELL G (ALL
TED TURNER G (ABCDE
LAURIE WISEFIELD G(FJKMNOPR
JOHN TOUT K (C
GEORGE NASH K (D
GRAHAM MAITLAND PNO (D
PHIL KENZIE HRNS (D
DAVE COXHILL HRNS (D
BUD PARKES HRNS(D
FLACO PADRON CONGAS(F
ALBHY GALUTEN SYN (F
JOHN WETTON B (P
CLAIRE HAMMILL V (P
TREVOR BOLDER B (R
GASPAR LAWAL PERC (P
IAN KEW K (P
CISSY HOUSTON V (J
EUNICE PETERSON V (J
SYLVIA SHEMWELL V (J
PETE WOOD K (J

(A) WISHBONE ASH — 1970 MCA UK MKPS2014 RI MCG3507
(A) " " — 1970 DECCA US 75249 RI MCA 2343
(A) " " — 197 BARCLAY FR 510002
(B) PILGRIMAGE — 1971 MCA UK MDKS8004 RI MCG3504
(B) " " — 197 DECCA US 75295 RI MCA 36
(B) " " — 197 BARCLAY FR 510007
(C) ARGUS — 1972 MCA UK MDKS8006 RI MCG3510
(C) " — 197 DECCA US 75437 RI 2344
(C) " — 197 BARCLAY FR 410003
(D) WISHBONE FOUR — 1973 MCA UK MDKS8011 RI MCG3503
(D) " " — 197 MCA US 327 RI 2348
(D) " — 197 MCA MAPS6673
(D) " " — 197 BARCLAY FR410008
(E)LIVE DATES — 197 MCA UK MCSP254 US 2 8006
(E)" " — 197 BARCLAY FR 41012/13
(F) THERES THE RUB — 1974 MCA UK MCF2575 US 464
(F) " " — 197 BARCLAY FR 410029
(G) MILESTONES — 1974 EMI EURO 184 50373
(H) MASTERS OF ROCK — 1975 EMI EURO 054 98289
(J) LOCKED IN — 1976 MCA UK MCF2750
(J) " — 19 BARCLAY FR 410055
(K) NEW ENGLAND — 1976 MCA UK MCG 3523
(K) " — 1976 ATLANTIC US 18200
(K) " " — 197 BARCLAY FR 414006
(L) CLASSIC ASH — 1977 MCA UK MCF2795
(L) " " — 197 BARCLAY FR 414015
(M) FRONT PAGE NEWS — 1977 MCA UK MCG3524 US 2311
(M) " " — 197 BARCLAY FR 511001
(N) NO SMOKE WITHOUT FIRE — 1978 MCA UK MCG3528 US 3060
(O) JUST TESTING — 1979 MCA UK MCF3052
(P) NUMBER THE BRAVE — 1981 MCA UK MCF3103
(Q) LIVE DATES II — 1981 MCA UK MCG4012 NL 203050
(R) TWIN BARRELS BURNING — 1982 AVM UK ASH 1
( ) THE ORIGINAL WISHBONE ASH — 1977 MCA US 42006

W115 WISHFUL THINKING W115

KEVIN SCOTT V (B — (A) LIVE — 1967 DECCA UK SKL 4900
BRIAN ALLEN D V (AB — (B) HIROSHIMA — 1971 B&C CAS 1038
TONY COLLIER B V (BC — (C) WISHFUL THINKING — 19 ?
JOHN FRANKLIN G V (ABC
TERRY NEW G V (— RAY DANIEL V (A — ROGER CHARLES B V (A

W116 WITCHFYNDE W116

STEVE BRIDGES V (AB — (A) GIVE 'EM HELL — 1980 RONDOLET UK ABOUT 1
PETE SURGEY B (AB — (B) STAGEFRIGHT — 1980 RONDELET UK ABOUT 2
GRA SCORESBY D (AB
MONTALO G (AB

W116 BILL WITHERS W116

BILL WITHERS V (ALL — (A) JUST AS I AM — 1971 SUSSEX LPSX3 7006
BRYAN GAROFALO G (J — (B) STILL BILL — 1972 SUSSEX LPSX1 7014
JERRY KNIGHT B (GHJ — (C) LIVE AT CARNEGIE HALL — 1973 SUSSEX LPDX101 7025/2
KEN BURKE B (HJ — (D) 'JUSTMENTS — 1974 SUSSEX LPSX2 8032
RUSS KUNKEL D (HJ — (E) BEST OF — 1975 SUSSEX LPSX 10 US 8037
RALPH MACDONALD PERC (HJ — (F) MAKING MUSIC — 1975 CBS US 33704 UK 69183
PAUL SMITH K (J — (G) NAKED & WARM — 1976 CBS US 34327 UK 81580
MIKE JONES SYN (H — (H) MENAGERIE — 1978 CBS US 34903 UK 82265
RAY PARKER G (H — (J) 'BOUT LOVE — 1978 CBS US 35596 UK 83176
DEAN GANT K (H — (K) 20 BEST OF — 1978 METRONOME GERM 69 030
CLIFF COULTER K (GH — (L) BEST OF — 1980 CBS UK 84710
GROVER WASHINTON JR SAX (K — (M) GREATEST HITS — 1981 CBS UK 85049
ALVIN TAYLOR D (H

GEOFFREY LEIB (G — DON FREEMAN (G — LARRY NASH K (G — LARRY TOLBERT PERC(G
CLARENCE McDONALD K (H — MELVIN DUNLOP B (GB — DOROTHY ASHBY (G — ERROL BENNETT PERC(G
YOUSEFF RAHMAN (G — BENORCE BLACKMON G (GB — ROCKY DZIDZORNU PERC (G — STEPHEN STILLS V (A
AL JACKSON D (A — DONALD DUNN B (A — BOOKER T JONES K G PROD (A — JIM KELTNER D (A
BOBBYE HALL PERC (A — CHRIS ETHRIDGE B (A — JAMES GADSON D (B — RAY JACKSON K WIND (A

W116A JIMMY WITHERSPOON W116A

JIMMY WITHERSPOON V G (ALL — GROOVIN' & SPOONIN' — 19 ORIGINAL SOUND 7107
GROOVE HOLMES ORG (B — (B) SINGS THE BLUES — 1964 SOCIETY UK SOC968
TEDDY EDWARDS SAX (B — EVENING BLUES — 1964 STATESIDE 10088 US PRESTIGE7300
FRANK BUTLER D (B — BLUES AROUND THE CLOCK — 1965 STATESIDE 10105 US PRESTIGE7314
JIMMY BOND B (B — SOME OF MY BEST FRIENDS ARE THE BLUES — 1965 STATESIDE 10114 US PRESTIGE7356
DANNY KALB G (J — BLUE SPOON — 1965 STATESIDE 10139 US PRESTIGE7327
HARVEY MANDEL G (J — IN PERSON — 1966 VOGUE VRL3005 RI MODE 546
BARRY GOLDBERG K (J — LIVE — 1968 STATESIDE 10232
CHARLIE MUSSELWHITE HCA(J — (J) BLUES SINGER — 1969 STATESIDE 10289 US BLUESWAY6026
SPOON IN LONDON — 1966 US PRESTIGE7418
BLUES FOR EASY LIVERS — 1967 US PRESTIGE7475
ROBBEN FORD G (L — BEST OF — 19 US PRESTIGE7713
MEAN OLD FRISCO — 19 US PRESTIGE7855
(*) LINE UP SEE ERIC BURDON ENTRY — GOING TO KANSAS CITY — 19 RCA US LPM 1639 RI ANL11048
(*) GUILTY — 1971 UA UK UAG29251 MGM US 4791
SPOONFUL — 19 BLUENOTE US LA534
HEY MRS JONES — 19 REPRISE US 6012
SPOON CONCERTS — 19 FANTASY 24701
AT MONTEREY FESTIVAL — 19 HI FI JAZZ US 421
& BEN WEBSTER — 19 VERVE US V68835
BEST OF — 1973 BLUESWAY BLS 6051
LOVE IS A 5 LETTER WORD — 1975 CAPITOL 11360 US LAX RI 37115
AINT NOBODYS BUSINESS — 197 POLYDOR UK 2460 206
LIVE — 1979 MCA UK MCF 3027
BABY BABY BABY — 19 PRESTIGE US 7290
HANDBAGS & GLADRAGS — 19 ABC US 717
HUHH — 1973 BLUESWAY US 6040
TAKE THIS HAMMER — 19 CONSTELLATION US 1422
JIMMY WITHERSPOON — 19 CROWN US 5156
SINGS THE BLUES — 19 CROWN US 5192
FEELIN THE SPIRIT — 19 HIFI US 422
AT THE RENAISSANCE — 19 HIFI US 426

W116B WIZARDS FROM KANSAS W116B

ROBERT MENADIER B V (A — (A) THE WIZARDS FROM KANSAS — 196 MERCURY US 61309
MARC CAPLAN PERC (A
JOHN COFFIN G (A — ROBERT CRAIN G (A — HAROLD PIERCE D (A — MARK NAFTALIN K (A

W117 WIZARDS CONVENTION W117

RAY FENWICK G B V(A — (A) WIZARDS CONVENTION — 197 RCA UK RS 1085
MO FOSTER B (A
RICK VAN DER LINDEN K (A — EDDIE HARDIN SYN V(A — RIC LEE D (A — MARK NAUSEEF D (A
JOHN CROCKER SAX (A — JON LORD PNO (A — JOHN SLAUGHTER G (A — TONY ASHTON V K(A
PETE YORK D (A — LESLIE BINKS D (A — GLEN HUGHES V (A — HENRY SPINETTI D (A
ROGER GLOVER B (A — DAVID COVERDALE V (A — MIKE D'ABO V (A — MIKE SMITH (A
JIMMY HELMS (A — CHRIS BARBER BAND (A

W117A JAH WOBBLE W117A

JAH WOBBLE (AB — (A) LEGEND LIVES ON — 1980 VIRGIN UK V2159 GER 203 050
MARTIN ATKINS D (A — (B) V.I.E.P. (EP) — 1980 VIRGIN UK V36112
SNOW WHITE V (A

W117B WOOLY WOLSTENHOLME W117B

WOOLY WOLSTENHOLME V K B G(A — (A) MAESTOSO — 1980 POLYDOR UK 2374 165
STEVE BROOMHEAD V MAND G(A
KIM TURNER D V (A — BILL NIXON PERC (A — BRIAN DAY B (A

W118 BOBBY WOMACK W118

BOBBY WOMACK G V (ALL — (A) LIVE — 19 LIBERTY LST 7645
BARRY BECKETT K (BCDELMN — (B) COMMUNICATION — 1972 UA US 5539 UK UAS 29306
CLAYTON IVEY K (BCDELMN — (C) UNDERSTANDING — 1972 UA US 5577 UK UAS 29365
ROGER HAWKINS D (BCDELMN — (D) FACTS OF LIFE — 1973 UA US LA043 UK UAS 29456
JIMMY JOHNSON G (BCDELMN — (E) LOOKING FOR A LOVE AGAIN — 1974 UA US LA199 UK UAS 29574
DAVID HOOD B (DEC — (F) ICAN UNDERSTAND IT — 1975 UA UK UAS 29715
DAVE TURNER G (D — (G) GREATEST HITS — 1975 UA US LA346
TRUMAN THOMAS K (BCDE — (H) I DONT KNOW WHAT THE WORLDS COMING TO — 1975 UA US LA353 UK UAS 29762
TIPPY ARMSTRONG G (EC — (J) SAFETY ZONE — 1976 UA US LA544 UK UAS 29907
LARRY RHEINHARDT G (E — (K) B W GOES C W — 1976 UA US LA638 UK UAS 29979
GERRY MASTERS B (D — (L)HOME IS WHERE THE HEART IS — 1976 CBS US 34384 UK 81693
HARVEY THOMPSON SAX (BCLN — (M) PIECES — 1978 CBS US 35083
DALE QUILLEN TROM (BC — (N) ROADS OF LIFE — 1979 ARISTA US 4222 UK ARTY 165
HARRISON CALLOWAY TPT (BCLN — (O) THE POET — 1982 BG US 10000
PAM GRIER V (BC
PATRICE HOLLOWAY V (BC — JANICE SINGLETON V (BC — PETE CARR G (DE — BRANDYE V (M
KERRY CAMPBELL SAX (M — WAH WAH WATSON G (J — SONNY BURKE K SYN(JL — JAMES GADSON D (JO
BILL SUMMER PERC (F — WILLIE WEEKS B (F — LOUIS JOHNSON B (F — HERBIE HANCOCK K (F

(CONTINUED)

W118 BOBBY WOMACK (CONTINUED) W118

Name	Inst	Code	Name	Inst	Code	Name	Inst	Code	Name	Inst	Code
POINTER SISTERS	V	(F	VALENTINOS	V	(FL	DETROIT HORNS		(M	DETROIT SYMPHONY STRINGS		(M
LAWRENCE FRATENGELO	PERC	(M	GLEN GOINS	G	(M	MICHAEL HENDERSON	B	(M	BARBARA HUDY	HRNS	(M
DWAYNE LOMAX	D	(M	RUDY ROBINSON	K	(M	DAVID RUFFIN	V	(M	CANDI STATON	V	(M
AARON WILLIS	G	(MN	ANTHONY WILLIS	G	(MN	EDDIE WILLIS	G	(MN	CHARLES FULLILVE	G	(L
EDDIE HINTON	G	(L	TOM ROADY	PERC	(L	MUSCLE SHOALS		(L	BEN CULLEY	TPT	(L
BROTHERHOOD	HRNS	(L	ALAN DEVILLE	TPT	(L	LESTER SMITH	TPT	(L	DASHIELL HUMAY	SAX	(L
ZAIMUS ROWAN	TROM	(L	FRIENDLY WOMACK JR	V	(LO	CECIL WOMACK	V	(JLNO	CURTIS WOMACK	V	(LO
REGGIE YOUNG	G	(CJ	RANDY McCORMICK	K	(N	JACK ASHFORD	D	(N	WAYNE JACKSON	HRNS	(N
HODGES/JAMES?SMITH	V	(N	ROBERT ROBERTIE	D	(H	CATHERINE GOTTHOFFER	HARP	(H	BOBBY BABIES	V	(H
PEACE	HRNS	(H	BILL WITHERS	V	(H	SOKO RICHARDSON	D	(H	DAVID SHIELDS	B	(O
DAVID T WALKER	G	(O	PATRICK MOTEN	K	(O	DALE RAMSEY	K	(O	DOROTHY ASHBY	HARP	(O
PAULINHO DACOSTA	PERC	(O	THE WATERS	V	(O	SALLY WOMACK		(O	VINCENT WOMACK		(O
REGINA WOMACK		(O	BOBBY EMMONS	K	(C	MIKE LEECH	B	(C	BOBBY WOOD	K	(C

W119 STEVIE WONDER W119

Album	Year	US		UK	
(A)TRIBUTE TO UNCLE RAY	1963	TAMLA	232	ORIOLE	40049
(B)LITTLE STEVIE WONDER	196	TAMLA			54191
(C)JAZZ SOUL OF LITTLE STEVE	1963	TAMLA	233	STATESIDE	10078
(D)12 YEAR OLD GENIUS	1963	TAMLA	240	ORIOLE	40053
(D)12 YEAR OLD GENIUS	1980	TAMLA			STMR 9003
(E)WITH A SONG IN MY HEART	196	TAMLA	250		
(F)AT THE BEACH(HEY MR HARMONICA MAN)	1965	TAMLA	255	STATESIDE	10108
(G)UPTIGHT	1966	TAMLA	268		STML11036
(H)DOWN TO EARTH	1966	TAMLA	272		STML11045
(J)I WAS MADE TO LOVE HER	1967	TAMLA	279		STML11059
(K)GREATEST HITS	1968	TAMLA	282		STML11075
(L)SOMEDAY AT CHRISTMAS	1969	TAMLA			STML11085
(M)FOR ONCE IN MY LIFE	1969	TAMLA	291		STML11098
(N)EIVETS REDNOW	1969	GORDY	932		
(O)MY CHERIE AMOUR	1970	TAMLA	296		STML11128
(P)LIVE	1970	TAMLA	298		STML11150
(Q)TALK OF THE TOWN	1970	TAMLA			STML11164
(R)SIGNED SEALED DELIVERED	1970	TAMLA	304		STML11169
(S)WHERE I'M COMING FROM	1971	TAMLA	308		STML11183
(T)GREATEST HITS	1972	TAMLA	313		STML11196
(U)MUSIC OF MY MIND	1972	TAMLA	314		STMA 8002
(V)TALKING BOOK	1972	TAMLA	319		STMA 8007
(W)INNERVISIONS	1973	TAMLA	326		STMA 8011
(X)FULFILLINGNESS FIRST FINALE	1974	TAMLA	332		STMA 8019
(X)FULFILLINGNESS FIRST FINALE	197	TAMLA	T633 251		
(Y)SONGS IN THE KEY OF LIFE	1976	TAMLA	340		TMSP 6002
(a)PORTRAIT	1976	EMI	EURO		064 92636
(b)ANTHOLOGY	1977	TAMLA	804		M 9 804
(c)WONDERLAND	197	EMI	EURO 064 95182		
(d)THE SECRET LIFE OF PLANTS	1979	TAMLA			TMSP 6009
(e)LIGHT MY FIRE	1979	M F P			50420
(f)HOTTER THAN JULY	1980	TAMLA			STMA 8035
(g)ORIGINAL MUSIQUARIUM (DBL)	1982	TAMLA			TMSD 6012
( )GREATEST HITS 2	19	TAMLA	EURO 91056		
(EP)A CALL IT PRETTY MUSIC	1964	STATESIDE			
(EP) STEVIE WONDER	1965	TAMLA			TME 2006
(EP) FREE WITH SONGS IN THE KEY OF LIFE	76	TAMLA			TME 2020

Name	Inst	Code
STEVIE WONDER	V HCA K	(ALL
SCOTT EDWARDS	B	(WV
DANIEL BEN ZEBULON	PERC	(V
GLORIA BARLEY	V	(V
LANI GROVES	V	(VWX
JIM GILSTRAP	V	(VWX
RAY PARKER	G	(V
SHIRLEY BREWER	V	(VXYfg
DENIECE WILLIAMS	V	(VXY
TREVOR LAWRENCE	SAX	(VYf
DAVID SANBORN	SAX	(V
STEVE MADAIO	TPT	(VY
JEFF BECK	G	(V
BUZZY FEITEN	G	(VY
DEBRA WILSON	V	(V
LORIS HARVIN	V	(V
BEN BRIDGES	SITAR G	(Ydfg
MICHAEL SEMBELLO	G	(dXY
LARRY GITTENS	TPT	(dgf
JOSIE JAMES	V	(dgY
RON KERSEY	K	(d
JACQUELINE F ENGLISH	V	(Y
PHILLIP KIMBLE	V	(Y
EARL DEROUEN	V	(dfg
NATHAN WATTS	B	(Ydfg
HANK REDD	SAX	(Ydf
RICK ZUNIGAR	G	(dfg
ABDOULAYE SOUMARE	V	(d
JOE JOHNSON	V	(d
ALEXANDRA BROWN	V	(dfg
LAMINE KONTE	PERC V	(d
IDRAHIM CAMARA	PERC	(d
KATHY COLLIER	V	(d
SUSAYE GREENE BROWN	V	(dYf
DENNY DAVIS	D	(d
ANGELA ISAIAH WINBUSH	V	(df
MARVA HOLCOLM	V	(df
HANK DEVITO	STEEL	(f

Name	Inst	Code	Name	Inst	Code	Name	Inst	Code	Name	Inst	Code
CHARLES K WILSON	V	(f	MELODY McCULLY	V	(fg	JANICE ROBINSON	HRNS	(g	VIRGIL JONES	HRNS	(g
VICTOR PAZ	HRNS	(g	EARL McINTYRE	HRNS	(g	ROBERT RATLEDGE	HRNS	(g	J D PARRAN	HRN	(g
ALFRED WILSON	HRNS	(g	ROBERT ELDRIDGE	HRNS	(g	LORENZO WYCHE	HRNS	(g	FRANK WESS	HRN	(g
CLIFTON ANDERSON	HRNS	(g	ANTHONY TOOLEY	HRNS	(g	BRITT WOODMAN	HRNS	(g	EUGENE GHEE	HRNS	(g
DELORES BARNES	V	(fg	RONNIE WILSON	V	(f	DEAN PARKS	G	(WY	CLARENCE BELL	ORG	(W
LARRY LATIMER	V PERC	(WXY	YUSUF ROAHMAN	PERC	(W	WILLIE WEEKS	B	(W	REGGIE McBRIDE	B	(X
SYREETA WRIGHT	V	(XYf	JAMES JAMERSON	B	(X	ROCKY	PERC	(X	JACKSON 5	V	(X
ART BARON	TROM	(U	TASHA THOMAS	V	(W	DAVID T WALKER	G	(W	MALCOLM CECIL	B	(W
RALPH HAMMER	G	(W	SHEILA WILKERSON	PERC	(W	BOBBYE HALL	PERC	(XY	PAUL ANKA	V	(X
SNEAKY PETE	STEEL	(X	MINNIE RIPPERTON	V	(XY	EDDIE BROWN	PERC	(Yf	SURDRAY TUCKER	V	(Y
GREG PHILLINGANES	K	(Y	MICHAEL GRAY	V	(Y	ARTICE MAY	V	(Y	RAYMOND MALDONADO	TPT	(Y
RONNIE FOSTER	ORG	(Y	MARY LEE WHITNEY	V	(Yf	LINDA LAWRENCE	V	(Y	TERRY HENDRICKS	V	(Y
CHARITY McCRARY	V	(Y	LINDA McCRARY	V	(Y	MADELAINE JONES	V	(Y	GEORGE BOHANON	TROM	(Y
GLEN FERRIS	TROM	(Y	DOROTHY ASHBY	HARP	(Y	HERBIE HANCOCK	K	(Y	GREG BROWN	D	(Y
BOBI HUMPHREY	FLT	(Y	GEORGE BENSON	G V	(Y	NATHAN ALFRED	PERC	(Y	CARMELLO GARCIA	PERC	(Y
JIM HORN	SAX	(Y	SNUFFY WALDEN	G	(Y	DENNIS DAVIS	D	(fg	ISAIAH SANDERS	K	(fg
EDDIE LEVERT	V	(f	MICHAEL JACKSON	V	(f	BETTY WRIGHT	V	(f	ROBERT MALACK	SAX	(f
NOLAN SMITH	TPT	(f	WALTER WILLIAMS	V	(f	JAMIL RAHEEM	V	(f	PAUL RISER	STR	(fg
CHARLIE COLLINS	V	(f	RAY POUNDS	D	(Y	STEPHANIE ANDREWS		(f	BILL WOLFER		(f
DENNIS MORRISON		(f	KIMBERLEY JACKSON		(f	RENEE HARDAWAY	V PERC	(Y	ADDIE COX	V	(Y
LONNIE MORGAN	V	(Y	ROSONA STARKS	V	(Y	MICHAEL WYCOFF	V	(Y	DURYODHANA GURU DASA	V	(Y
JAYASACINANDANA DASA	V	(Y	VEDAVYASA DASA	V	(Y	YOGAMAYA DASI	V	(Y	BHAKTA GREGORY	V	(Y
RUKMINI	V	(Y	ETHEL ENOEX	V	(Y	CAROLYN JOHNSON	V	(Y	JAMES LAMBERT	V	(Y
DENNIS SWINDELL	V	(Y	SHERYL WALKER	V	(Y	BARADRAS	V	(Y	AGNIDEVA DASA	V	(Y
JITAMRTYI DASA	V	(Y	CINMAYI DASA	V	(Y	BHAKTA EDDIE	V	(Y	BHAKTA KEVIN	V	(Y
BRENDA BARRETT	V	(Y	COLLEEN CARLETON		(Y	CAROLE COLE		(Y	NELSON HAYES	PERC	(Y
DAVE HENSON		(Y	EDNA ORSO		(Y	JOSETTE VALENTINO		(Y	GLEN FERRIS	TROM	(Y
SUDANA BOBATOON	V	(Y	BERRY BRIGES	V	(Y	CECILIA BROWN	V	(Y	GARY BYRD	V	(Y
AL FANN	V	(Y	BARBARA FANN	V	(Y	SHELLEY FANN	V	(Y	MILDRED GIVENS	V	(Y
MIMI GREEN	V	(Y	ADRIAN JAMES	V	(Y	PAT JOHNSON	V	(Y	WILLIE MOORE	V	(Y
LARRI NUCKENS	V	(Y	GARY VENEY	V	(Y	TAN ADAMS	V	(Y	HENRY AMERICA	V	(Y
LINDA AMERICA	V	(Y	STARSHEMAH BOBATOON	V	(Y	KHALIF BOBATOON	V	(Y	JEAN BROWN	V	(Y
RODNEY BROWN	V	(Y	DOE RANI EDWARDS	V	(Y	AL JOCKO FANN	V	(Y	MELANI FANN	V	(Y
TRACY FANN	V	(Y	SUSIE FUZZELL	V	(Y	AUDREY GIVENS	V	(Y	ANTONIO GIVENS	V	(Y
ANTHONY GIVENS	V	(Y	DERRICK GIVENS	V	(Y	JEANIA HARRIS	V	(Y	TROY HARRIS	V	(Y
CALVIN JOHNSON	V	(Y	IRMA LESLIE	V	(Y	CARL LOCKHART	V	(Y	GAIL LOCKHART	V	(Y
KIM LEWIS	V	(Y	CAROLYN MASSENBURG	V	(Y	KIM NIXON	V	(Y	LISA NIXON	V	(Y
GWEN PERRY	V	(Y	GREGORY RUDD	V	(Y	KEITH SLAUGHTER	V	(Y	CHARLES BREWER	PERC	(Y
MARIETTA WATERS	PERC	(Y	JOHN FISHBACH	PERC	(Y	AMALE MATHEWS	PERC	(Y	YOLANDA SIMMONS		(Y

W119A

BRENTON WOOD

W119A

BRENTON WOOD V (AB (A) OOGUM BOOGUM 19 DOUBLE SHOT US 1002
(B) BABY YOU GOT IT 19 DOUBLE SHOT US 1003

W119B

LAUREN WOOD

W119B

LAUREN WOOD K V (ALL (A) LAUREN WOOD 1979 WB US BSK 3278
JIM KELTNER D (A (B) CAT TRICK 1981 WB US BSK 3517
MICHAEL BAIRD D (A
JEFF PORCARO D (A ALVIN TAYLOR D (A RICK SCHLOSSER D (A ERNIE EREMUTA B PERC(A
ABRAHAM LABORIEL B (A DAVID HUNGATE B (A BILL PAYNE K SYN(A JAI WINDING K (A
JAY GRAYDON G (A STEVE LUKATHER G (A RONNIE MONTROSE G (A SUMNER MERING G (AB
FRED TACKETT G (A NOVI NOVOG VLA SYN (AB JOHN KLEMMER SAX (A ANDREW LOVE SAX (A
PAUL LANI PERC V(A STEVE FORMAN PERC (A BOBBY LAKIND PERC V (A MICHAEL JACKSON PERC(A
SINCLAIR ROGERS LOTT PERC(A MICHAEL McDONALD V (A JOHN TOWNSEND V (A BILL CHAMPLIN V (A
ROSEMARY BUTLER V (A PAT SIMMONS V (A ARNO LUCAS V (A BOBBY KIMBALL V (A
RICARDO LECAMPOS V (A KIKI KOURY V (AB DUNCAN MACKAY SYN (A BEN CAULEY HRNS (A
BILL ELLIOTT K SYN STR(B BRIAN RAY G (A RICK CHUDACOFF B K (B PETER BUNETTA D (B
ALAN ESTES PERC (B ARNOLD McCULLER V (B LESLIE SMITH V (B TOMMY FUNDERBURK V (B
CARRIE BARTON B (B JOE KELLY G (B LARRY TRENDWELL G (B GEORGE SOPUCH G (B
AIRTO MOREIRA PERC (B JOHN BERGAMO PERC (B MICHAEL BODDICKER SYN (B MARK PELSONE K (B
JERRY HEY TPT (B GARY GRANT TPT (B BILL REICHENBACH TROM (B GARY HERBIG SAX (B
PHIL AYLING SAX (B DAVID WOODFORD SAX (B ROBBIE DUPREE V (B TATA VEGA V (B

W119C

ROBERT WOOD

W119C

ROBERT WOOD VIBES(ALL (A) TAROT 19 EDICI FR ED 6102
STEVE POTTS WIND (A (B) SONABULAR 19 EDICI FR ED 6103
KENT CARTNER B (A (C) VIBRAROCK 19 POLYDOR 2393 137
RON PITTNER D (A (D) TOMBAC VIBE 19 POLYDOR 2393 150
GILBERT ARTMAN D (B
OLIVER ZDRZALIK G B (C MARCEL BEL D (C PATRICK FONTAINE B (C OLIVER DIDIER (C
PIERRE MOERLIN D (C DIDDIER MALHERBE WIND (C MIKE HOWLET B (C PERRY YELDHAM B (D
PATRICE CRAMER D (D

W120

RON WOOD

W120

RON WOOD G V (ABC (A) I'VE GOT MY OWN ALBUM TO DO 1974 WB US 2819 UK K56065
WILLIE WEEKS B (AB (B) NOW LOOK 1975 WB US 2872 UK K56145
IAN MacLAGAN K (ABCD (C) GIMME SOME NECK 1979 CBS US 35702 UK 83337
KEITH RICHARD G (ABC (D) 1234 1981 CBS US 37473 UK 85227
MICK JAGGER G V (AC
ALVIN TAYLOR D (D MICK TAYLOR G B (ABC JEAN ROUSSEL K (AB MICK WALLER D (A
PETE SEARS B (A MARTIN QUITTENTON G (A ROD STEWART V (A IRENE CHANTER V (A
DOREEN CHANTER V (A ANDY NEWMARK D (AB BOBBY WOMACK G (BD KENNY JONES D (B
BOBBY KEYS SAX (CD JIM KELTNER D (CD DAVE MASON G (C CHARLIE WATTS D (CD
MICK FLEETWOOD D (C ROBERT POPWELL B (C JIM HORN HRNS (D IAN WALLACE D (D
CLYDIE KING V (D SHIRLEY MATTHEWS V (D NICKY HOPKINS K (D ANITA POINTER V (D
ALAN MYERS D (D CARMINE APPICE D (D JAY DAVIS B (D ROBIN LEMESURIER G (D
JIMMY HASLIP B (D WADDY WACHTEL G (D

W121

RON WOOD & RONNIE LANE

W121

RON WOOD G V (A (A) MAHONEYS LAST STAND 1976 ATLANTIC US SD36126 UK K50308
RONNIE LANE B BAN G V (A
KENNEY JONES D (A PETE TOWNSHEND G PERC (A IAN McLAGAN K (A
BOBBY KEYS HRNS (A JIM PRICE HRNS (A BRUCE ROWLAND D V (A BENNY GALLAGHER B (A
MICK WALLER PERC (A RICK GRECH B D VLN (A IAN STEWART K (A GLYN JOHNS V (A
BILLY NICHOLLS V (A

W122

ROY WOOD

W122

ROY WOOD G V B K HRNS WIND(ALL (A) BOULDERS 1973 HARVEST SHVL803 RI SHSM 2021
MOVE (F (A) BOULDERS 1974 UA US UALA168
PAUL ROBINS K G (GH (B) WIZZARD BREW (WIZARD) 1973 HARVEST SHSP4025 US UA LA042
PETER MACKIE B V (H (C) SEE MY BABY JIVE (WIZARD) 1974 HARVEST SHSP4034
BILLY PAUL SAX (GH (D) EDDIE & THE FALCONS (WIZARD) 1974 WB UK K56029 US UA LA219
JOHN KURLANDER K (A (E) MUSTARD 1975 JET UK JETLP12 US UA LA575
ANDY FAIRWEATHER LOW V (H (F) THE ROY WOOD STORY 1976 HARVEST SHDW408
JOHN BONHAM D (H (G) SUPER ACTIVE WIZZO (WIZZO) 1977 WB UK K56388 US 3065
CARL WAYNE V (H (H) ON THE ROAD AGAIN 1979 WB US BSK3247
ANNIE HASLAM V (HE
DAVE DONOVAN D (HE DICK PLANT V (HE RICK PRICE B V PERC(BCDEFG BILL HUNT K HRNS V (BCDF
HUGH McDOWELL CELLO SYN(BCF NICK PENTELOW WIND V (BCDF MIKE BURNEY WIND (BCDF KEITH SMART D (BCDF
CHARLIE GRIMA D(BCDFH CARBAG CHOIR V (B BOB BRADY K V (D PHIL EVERLY V (E
ELECTRIC LIGHT ORCH (F BEACH BOYS (F NIGHTRIDERS (F GRAHAM GALLERY B (G
BOB WILSON TROM (G

W123

ROYSTON & HEATHER WOOD

W123

ROYSTON WOOD V CONC(A (A) NO RELATION 1977 TRANSATLANTIC UK TRA 342
HEATHER WOOD V (A
PETER BELLAMY V (A SIMON NICOL G (A PENNIE HARRIS V DULC(A PETE KIRTLEY G MAND(A
TONY HALL MELODEON (A ASHLEY HUTCHINGS B (A

W124

WOODY WOODMANSEYS U BOAT

W124

WOODY WOODMANSEY D (A (A) U BOAT 1977 BRONZE BRON 501
PHIL PLANT B (A
MARTIN SMITH G (A FRANK MARSHALL K SYN(A PHIL MURRAY V (A

W124A

JEZZ WOODROFFE

W124A

JEZZ WOODROFFE K (A (A) OPPOSITE DIRECTIONS 1980 GRADUATE UK GRADLP1
ERIC CAIRNS D (A
IRWEN SYLVESTER D (A GIBSON JOHN B (A

W124B

STEVIE WOODS

W124B

STEVIE WOODS V (A (A) TAKE ME TO YOUR HEAVEN 1982 COTILLION US 5229

W125 TERRY & GAY WOODS W125

TERRY WOODS V G B MANS(ALL — (A) WOODS BAND — 1971 GREENWICH UK GSLP 1004
GAY WOODS V CONC DULC(ALL — (A) WOODS BAND — 1977 ROCKBURGH UK ROC 102
ED DEANE B G K(AB — (A) WOODS BAND — 197 MOONCREST UK CREST 29
PAT NASH D V (A — (B) BACKWOODS — 197 POLYDOR UK 2383 322
AUSTIN CORCORAN B G (A — (C) THE TIME IS RIGHT — 1976 POLYDOR UK 2383 375
JOHN RYAN K (A — (D) RENOWNED — 1976 POLYDOR UK 2383 406
TONY REEVES B (A — (E) TENDERHOOKS — 1978 rockburgh UK ROC 104
MIKE GILES D (B
DAVE WINTOUR B (B — TONY CARR CONGA (B — DAVE MATTACKS D (C — GEOFF WHITEHORN G (B
PETER ARNESEN K (B — JOE O'DONNELL VLN (B — DAVE PEGG B (C — PAT DONALDSON B (CE
TIMI DONALD D (C — B J COLE STEEL(C — BRIAN GOLBEY FDL (C — JON GILLASPIE K (C
DAVID MORRISON G (C — TRISTIAN FRY VIBES (C — PHIL PALMER G (E — JIM RUSSELL D (E
KATE McGARRIGLE V PNO(E — KEITH DONALD SAX (E — MARTIN O'CONNOR ACC (E — NEIL TONER MAND (E
FRAN BREEN PERC (E — JOLYON JACKSON ORG (E

W125A WOOL W125A

ED WOOL G V (A — (A) WOOL — 19 ABC US ABCS &'&
TOM HASKELL G V (A
PETER LULIS D (A — CLAUDIA WOOL V (A — ED BARRELLA B (A

W126 HENRY WOOLF W126

HENRY WOOLF (A — (A) TIBETAN BELLS — 1972 ISLAND UK HELP3
NANCY HEMMING (A
DREW GLADSTONE (A

W126A BRUCE WOOLLEY W126A

BRUCE WOOLLEY V (AB — (A) ENGLISH GARDEN — 1979 EPIC UK 83893
DAVID BIRCH G (A — (B) BRUCE WOOLLEY & THE CAMERA CLUB — 1981 CBS US 36301
ROD JOHNSON D (A
MATTHEW SELIGMAN D (A — TOM DOLBY B (A

W127 WORLD OF OZ W127

CHRISTOPHER ROBIN (A — (A) WORLD OF OZ — 1969 DERAM UK SML1034
DAVID KUBINEC (A
TONY CLARKSON (A — DAVID REA (A

W127A WORLD SERVICE W127A

ROLY KERRIDGE D (A — (A) DEFINITE UNCERTAINTIES — 1979 COOPER WARP001
KEVIN DUNFORD B (A
STEVEN LODDER K VLN(A — GERRY HUNT G SAX (A — ALAN HAYMAN PERC FLT(A

W128 SONNY WORTHING W128

SONNY WORTHING K V (A — (A) TEENAGE DREAM — 1977 TRANSATLANTIC UK TRA 344
JIM CUOMO WIND (A
ELLIOTT RANDALL G (A — PETE WINGFIELD K V (A — PETER VAN HOOKE D (A — PETE WILSHER STEEL(A
ISAAC GUILLORY G (A — MO FOSTER B (A — RITCHIE G (A — KEITH NELSON BANJO(A
BARBARA SEXTON V (A — MARTIN DROVER TPT (A — GEORGE CHISHOLM TPT (A — TONY ROBERTS SAX (A
JEFF DALY SAX (A — DAVID SNELL HARP (A

W128A WRABIT W128A

LOU NADEAU V (A — (A) WRABIT — 1982 MCA UK MCF3126
DAVID APLIN G (A
SCOTT JEFFERSON SLECK D(A — JOHN ALBANI G V (A — CHRIS BROCKWAY B V (A — LES PAULHUS K V (A
DAVID KIRBY K (A — RON SMITH B (A — ROB LOUDEN V (A

W128B BILL WRAY W128B

BILL WRAY V (A — (A) FIRE & ICE — 1981 LIBERTY LT1098
JAMES BENTLEY WRAY G V B(A
GEORGE ENETE K (A — GREG WORLEY D (A — JERRY HEY HRNS (A — GARY GRANT TPT (A
BILL REICHENBACH TROM (A — LARRY WILLIAMS SAX (A — JIM HORN SAX (A — JERRY PATERSON SAX (A
PAULINHO DACOSTA PERC (A — WENDY WALDMAN V (A — DEBRA DABKIN V (A — LISA DALBELLO V (A
RANDY BISHOP V (A

W129 LINK WRAY W129

LINK WRAY G V (ALL — (A) LINK WRAY & THE WRAY MEN — 1960 EPIC US LN3661
BILLY HODGES K V (CF — (B) JACK THE RIPPER — 1963 SWAN US SLP 510
MORDICAI JONES K MAND (F]SAME ? — (C) LINK WRAY — 1971 POLYDOR US 24 4064 UK 2489 029
BOBBY HOWARD K MAND (C — (D) THERES GOOD ROCKIN TONIGHT — 1973 UNION PACIFIC UP 002
DOUG WRAY D V G(CFQ — (E) BE WHAT YOU WANT — 1973 POLYDOR US 5047 UK 2391 063
STEVE VERROCA D V (CF — (F) BEANS & FATBACK — 1973 VIRGIN UK V 2006
COMMANDER CODY (E — (G) ROCKIN' & HANDCLAPPIN' — 1973 EPIC UK 63267
JERRY GARCIA G (E — (H) RUMBLE — 1974 POLYDOR US 6025 UK 2391 128
DAVID BROMBERG G (E — (J) INTERSTATE 10 — 1975 CAROLINE UK C 1511
BOBBY BLACK STEEL(E — (K) STUCK IN GEAR — 1976 VIRGIN UK V 2050
RUAN OLOCHLAINN K SAX(K — (L) ROCK'N'ROLL RUMBLE — 19 CHARLY UK CR 30171
GORDON SMITH B (K — (M) EARLY RECORDINGS(B)? — 1978 CHISWICK /ACE CH 6
ARCHIE LEGGET B (K — (N) GREAT GUITAR HITS — 19 VERMILLION US 1924
FREDDIE SMITH D (K — (O) SINGS & PLAYS — 19 VERMILLION US 1925
DAVE GREAVES (J — (P) YESTERDAY & TODAY — 19 RECORD FACTORY US 1929
CHARLEY CHARLES D (J — (Q) BULLSHOT — 1979 CHARISMA UK CAS1143 US VISA 7009
JOHN DZERIGAN G (H — (R) LIVE AT THE PASADISO — 1980 LINE GER LLP5019 US VISA 7010
BOZ SCAGGS G V (H — (R) LIVE AT THE PARADISO — 1980 MAGNUMFORCE UK 008 RCA NL 44012
ROBIN WRAY V (Q
RHONDA WRAY V (Q — MARK JORDAN K V (H — RICK SCHLOSSER D (H — TOM RUTLEY B (H
JOE CRANE B V K(H — ANDY NARELL PERC K (H — BERNIE KRAUSE K (H — PETE ESCOVEDO CONGA(H
BRUCE STEINBERG HCA (H — LENNY PICKETT SAX (H — EMILIO CASTILLO SAX (H — STEVE KUPKA SAX(H
MIC GILLETTE TPT (H — GREG ADAMS TPT (H — GLENN WALTERS V (H — SKIP DRINKWATER V (H
DOROTHY MORRISON V (H — ZELLER HURD V (H — BILL COMBS V (H — JOE SCOTT V (H
BILLY CROSS G (Q — ANTON FIG D PERC(Q — RICHARD GOTTEHRER K PERC(Q — CHRIS ROBINSON K (Q
ROB STONER B (Q — HOWIE WYETH D (Q — JOANNA MASSEY V (Q

W130 WRECKLESS ERIC W130

Personnel	Inst	Albums	Album	Year / Label / Catalogue
WRECKLESS ERIC	G V	(ABC	(A) WRECKLESS ERIC	1978 STIFF UK SEEZ 6
DAVEY PAYNE	SAX	(AC	(B) WONDERFUL WORLD OF W ERIC	1978 STIFF UK SEEZ 9
DAVID WITTON	D	(AC	(C) BIG SMASH (DBL)(COMP)	1980 STIFF UK SEEZ21 GER 6 28499
CHARLIE HART	K	(AC	(C) BIG SMASH (DBL)(COMP)	1980 STIFF US 36463
MARTIN ACE	V	(C		

BARRY PAYNE B (AC STEVE CURRIE B (AC JOHN GLYN SAX (AC STEVE GOULDING D (AC
NICK LOWE G B (AC GEIR WAADE D (B JOHN BROWN B (BC EUNON BRADY G (B
PETE SOLLEY K (B MALCOLM MORLEY G (BC JOHN EARLE HRNS (BC DICK HANSON HRNS (BC
JOE PARTRIDGE G (B GARY TAYLOR V (B PETE GOSLING G (C WALTER HACON G (C
DAVE OTWAY D (AC ROGER RETTIG STEEL(C

W131 BIG JOHN WRENCHER W131

Personnel	Inst	Albums	Album	Year / Label / Catalogue
BIG JOHN WRENCHER	V HCA	(AB	(A) BIG JOHNS BOOGIE	1975 BIG BEAR BEAR 5
EDDIE TAYLOR	G	(A	(B) MAXWELL STREET ALLEY BLUES	1978 BARRELHOUSE BH 2
BOB HALL	PNO	(A	(C) MEMPHIS TO MAXWELL	19 JAWES 9999
BOB BRUNNING	B	(A		
PETE YORK	D	(A		

W132 BETTY WRIGHT W132

Personnel	Inst	Albums	Album	Year / Label / Catalogue
BETTY WRIGHT	V	(ALL	(A) MY FIRST TIME AROUND	1968 ATCO US 33260
GREGORY WILKERSON	D	(G	(B) I LOVE THE WAY YOU LOVE ME	1971 ALSTON US 33388 ATLANTIC UK K40364
MICHAEL WILKERSON	B	(G	(C) HARD TO STOP	1973 ALSTON US 7026 ATLANTIC UK K40514
WILL BRIDGEFORTH	G	(G	(D) DANGER HIGH VOLTAGE	1975 ALSTON US 4400 RCA UK SF8408
ROBERT WEBB	V PERC	(G	(E) EXPLOSION	1976 ALSTON US 4402 RCA UK RS1063
GARRY GREENE	SAX	(G	(F) THIS TIME FOR REAL	1977 ALSTON US 4406 TK UK XL14053
MICHAEL SCOTT	TPT	(G	(G) LIVE	1978 ALSTON US 4408 TK UK TKR82541
KEVIN KENDRICKS	K	(G	(H) TRAVELING IN THE CIRCLE	1979 ALSTON US 4410 TK UK TKR83352
			(J) BETTY WRIGHT	1981 EPIC US 36879 UK 84882

W133 GARY WRIGHT W133

Personnel	Inst	Albums	Album	Year / Label / Catalogue
GARY WRIGHT	K V	(ALL	(A) EXTRACTION	1970 A&M US 4277 UK AMLS2004
JIM KELTNER	D	(DEC	(B) RING OF CHANGES (WONDERWHEEL)	1972 A&M UKAMLH64362
ANDY NEWMARK	D	(DG	(C) FOOT PRINT	1971 A&M US 4296 UK AMLS64296
DAVID FOSTER	K	(DE	(D) DREAM WEAVER	1976 WB US 2868 UK K56141
BOBBY LYLE	K	(DFG	(E) LIGHT OF SMILES	1976 WB US 2951 UK K56278
LORNA WRIGHT	V	(DEGJ	(F) TOUCH & GONE	1977 WB US 3137 UK K56435
BETTY SWEET	V	(DE	(G) HEADIN' HOME	1979 WB US 3244 UK K56585
DAVID POMERANZ	V	(DE	(H) THAT WAS ONLY YESTERDAY	1976 A&M US 3528
SPOOKY TOOTH		(H	(J) THE RIGHT PLACE	1981 WB US 3511 UK K56877
JIM GORDON	D	(C		

HUGH McCRACKEN G (ACG ALAN WHITE D (ACG TREVOR BURTON B (A KLAUS VOORMAN B (AC
MIKE KELLIE D (A MICK ABRAHAMS G (A RONNIE MONTROSE G (D DORIS TROY V (AC
MADELINE BELL V (A NANETTE NEWMAN V (AC BRYSON GRAHAM D (C MIKE JONES G (C
TOM DUFFY B (C ART WOOD D (EF PETER REILICH K (E STEVE PORCARO B (E
JUSTIN WRIGHT V (E COLLIN ALLAN D (C JERRY DONAHUE G (C GEORGE P'HARA G (C
JIM PRICE HRNS (C BOBBY KEYS SAX (C KING CURTIS SAX (C LIZA STRIKE V (C
BARRY ST JOHN V (C PAT P ARNOLD V (C JIMMY THOMAS V (C RICHARD BAKER K (F
CLYDIE KING V (F VANETTA FIELDS V (FG SHIRLEY MATTHEWS V (FG PETER REILICH SYN (F
HIROSHI UPSHUR SYN (F GARY MIELKE SYN (F STEVE LUKATHER G (G LENNY CASTRO PERC(GJ
AUDIE WATKINS PERC (G MICHAEL BODDICKER SYN (G JAI WINDING SYN (G MICHAEL McDONALD V (G
PAULINHO DACOSTA PERC (G FRED TACKETT G (G JIM HORN SAX (G EMIL RICHARDS PERC(G
RALPH HUMPHREY PERC (G BUZZY FEITON G (G NEIL LARSEN SYN (G DAVID CROSBY V (G
GRAHAM NASH V (G JEFF PORCARO D (G ROLAND BAUTISTA G (G DEAN PARKS G SAX B PROD(J
MARTY WALSH G (J TRIS IMBODEN D (J BOB C BENBERG D (J DAVID KEMPER D (J
GEORGE HAWKINS B (J ROD PIAZZA HARP (J DAVID PACK V (J TIM SCHMIT V (J

W133A LORNA WRIGHT W133A

Personnel	Inst	Albums	Album	Year / Label / Catalogue
LORNA WRIGHT	V	(A	(A) CIRCLE OF LOVE	19 ROCKET 2902
LARRY CARLTON	G	(A		

BILL CUOMO K (A JIM KELTNER D (A ANDRE FISHER D (A STEVE FORMAN PERC(A
MIKE PORCARO B (A ERNIE WATTS SAX (A JAY LEWIS G B (A KIM CARNES V (A
JAY GRAYDON G (A FRED TACKETT G (A RALPH HUMPHREY D (A CHET McCRACKEN D (A
DAVID FOSTER SYN (A KLAUS VOORMANN B (A

W134 RICHARD WRIGHT W134

Personnel	Inst	Albums	Album	Year / Label / Catalogue
RICHARD WRIGHT	K V	(A	(A) WET DREAM	1978 HARVEST UK SHVL818 US CBS 35559
MEL COLLINS	SAX	(A		

LARRY STEELE B (A REG ISADORE D (A SNOWY WHITE G (A

W134A WRITING ON THE WALL W134A

Personnel	Inst	Albums	Album	Year / Label / Catalogue
WILLY FINLAYSON	G V	(A	(A) POWER OF THE PICTS	1969 MIDDLE EARTH MDLS 303
BILL SCOTT	K	(A		

JAKE SCOTT V B (A LINNIE PATERSON V (JIMMY HUSH D (A ALBY GREENHALGH WIND(A
SMIGGY G (

W134B STEVE WRIGHT W134B

Personnel	Inst	Albums	Album	Year / Label / Catalogue
STEVE WRIGHT			(A) HARD ROAD	1975 POLYDOR UK 2480 249

W134C WRITZ W134C

Personnel	Inst	Albums	Album	Year / Label / Catalogue
STEVE ROWLES	G V	(A	(A) WRITZ	1979 ELECTRIC UK TRIX 12 GER 146352
STEVE FAIRNIE	V	(A		

JULES HARDWICK G SYN(A BEV SAGE V (A NICK BATTLE B (A ARRY AXELL D (A

W135 ROBERT WYATT W135

Personnel	Inst	Albums	Album	Year / Label / Catalogue
ROBERT WYATT	V K D	(ALL	(A) THE END OF AN EAR	1970 CBS UK 64189 RI 80 EMBASSY 31846
NEVILLE WHITEHEAD	B	(A	(B) ROCK BOTTOM	1974 VIRGIN US 13112 UK V2017
MARK CHARIG	CORNET	(A	(C) RUTH IS STRANGER THAN RICHARD	1975 VIRGIN UK V2034
BRIAN ENO	K G	(C	(BC) ROCK BOTTOM/RUTH IS STRANGER	1981 VIRGIN UK VGD 3505
ELTON DEAN	SAX	(A		

DAVE SINCLAIR ORG (A CYRIL AYERS PERC (A RICHARD SINCLAIR B (B LAURIE ALLEN D (BC
HUGH HOPPER B (B IVOR CUTLER K V (B MONGESI FEZA TPT (B GARY WINDO WIND(BC
ALFREDA BENGE V (B FRED FRITH VLA PNO (BC MIKE OLDFIELD G (B BILL McCORMICK B (C
NISAR AHMAD KHAN SAX (C JOHN GREAVES B (C

W136 BILL WYMAN W136

BILL WYMAN V B G K (AB (A) MONKEY GRIP 1974 ROLLINGSTONE US COC79100 UK COC59102
DANNY KOOTCH G (AB (B) STONE ALONE 1976 ROLLINGSTONE US COC79103 UK COC59105
JOE LALA PERC (A (C) GREEN ICE(SOUNDTRACK) 1981 POLYDOR UK POLS1031
DAVE MATTACKS D (D (D) BILL WYMAN 1981 A&M UK AMLH 68540
CHRIS REA G (D
MAC REBENNACK PNO (AB DALLAS TAYLOR D (AB JOEY MURCIA G (A DUANE SMITH PNO (A
GEORGE TERRY G (A BYRON BERLINE FDL (A JACKIE GRAVES TROM (A JOHN McEUEN BANJ(A
ABIGALE HANESS V (A LEON RUSSELL PNO (A WILLIAM SMITH PNO (A HUBIE HEARD K (AB
BETTY WRIGHT V (A GEORGE McCRAE V (A GWEN McCRAE V (A MARK COLBY HRNS(AB
KEN FAULK HRNS (A NEAL BONSANTI HRNS (A DAVE LAWSON SYN (DGUILLE GARCIA PERC (B
MARK NAFTALIN K (B BONNIE POINTER V (B CLYDIE KING V (B ALBHY GALUTEN SYN (B
PAUL HARRIS K (B JOE VITALE K D (B NICKY HOPKINS K (B AL KOOPER K (B
GREGG ERRICO D (B BOB WELCH G (B VAN MORRISON SAX HCA G (B RUTH POINTER V (B
WANETTA FIELDS V (B TERRY TAYLOR G (BD JACKIE CLARK G (B ROBERT GREENRIDGE D(B
JOE WALSH G (B JIM KELTNER D (B RON WOOD G (B ROCKY DZIZDORNU PERC(B
JOHN McFEE FDL (B FLOYD COOLEY TUBA (B

W137 MICHAEL WYCOFF W137

MICHAEL WYCOFF K V (A (A) COME TO MY WORLD 1981 RCA UK PL13823

W138 MICHAEL WYNN W138

MICHAEL WYNN G V (A (A) READY TO FLY 1978 ARIOLA GER 26484
ROBERT MUSENBICHLER G V (A (B) QUEEN OF THE NIGHT 1979 ARIOLA 50027
NORBERT SCHMITT B V (A
TOMMY SCHMITT K V (A FRITZ MATZKA D (A JOHAN DAANSEN G (A DAVE SPRUNG V (A
ACHIM FARR SAX (A

X1 "X" X1

JOHN DOE B (AB (A) LOS ANGELES 1980 SLASH US 104
BILLY ZOOM G (AB (B) WILD GIFT 1981 SLASH US 107
CHRISTINE CERVENKA V(A
EXENE V (AB DON BONEBRAKE D (AB RAY MANZAREK K PROD (A

X2 X RAY SPECS X2

POLY STYRENE V (A (A) GERM FREE ADOLESCENTS 1978 EMI INS 3023
LARA LOGIC SAX (
JACK AIRPORT STAFFORD G(A PAUL DEAN B (A CHRIS CHRYSLER D (RUDI THOMPSON SAX (A
GLYN JOHNS SAX (B P HARDING D (A RICHARD BP TEES D (

X3 "XTC" X3

COLIN MOULDING B V (ABCDE (A) WHITE MUSIC 1978 VIRGIN UK V2095
ANDY PARTRIDGE G V (ABCDE (B) GO TWO 1978 VIRGIN UK V2108
TERRY CHAMBERS D (ABCDE (C) DRUMS & WIRES 1979 VIRGIN US 13134 UK V2129
BARRY ANDREWS K (AB (D) BLACK SEA 1980 VIRGIN US 13147 UK V2173
DAVID GREGORY K G (CDE (E) ENGLISH SETTLEMENT (DBL) 1982 VIRGIN UK V2223
JOHN LECKIE PROD (A (EP) GO PLUS 1978 VIRGIN UK VS23312
STEVE LILLYWHITE PROD (A
HUGH PADGHAM PROD V(E

X4 XIT X4

MICHAEL MARTIN G V (A (A) PLIGHT OF REDMAN 1972 RARE EARTH US R5361 UK SREA4002
JUMAC SUAZO B (A (A) PLIGHT OF REDMAN 1972 RARE EARTH NL 058 93622
R C GARISS G PNO(A ( ) XIT 19
LEEJA HERRERA D PERC(A ( ) SILENT WARRIOR 19

X4A XDREAMISTS X4A

ROE BUTCHER B (A (A) XDREAMISTS 1980 POLYDOR NL 2442 181
JOHN DOC DOCHERTY G (A
BRIAN MOFFAT D (A UEL WALLS G V (A

Y1 YACHTS Y1

J J CAMPBELL V ((A) YACHTS 1979 RADAR UK RAD19
GLYNN HAVARD B V (B (A) S O S 1970 POLYDOR US 6220
MARTIN DEMPSEY B (A (B) WITHOUT RADAR 1980 RADAR UK RAD27 US POLYDOR16270
MARTIN J WATSON G V (AB
BOB BELLIS D (AB HENRY PRIESTMAN K (AB MICK SKINNER B (GLYN HAVARD B V (B

Y2 STOMU YAMASHTA Y2

STOMU YAMASHTA K PERC(ALL (A) CONTEMPORARY 1972 L'OISEAU DGL01
STEVE WINWOOD K V (HI (B) RED BUDDHA 1972 BARCLAY 920376 GER 16063
MICHAEL SHRIEVE D (HJI (B) RED BUDDHA 1974 VANGUARD US 79343
ANDY POWELL B (C (C) COME TO THE EDGE 1973 ISLAND HELP 12
PAT THRALL G (HI (D) THE MAN FROM THE EAST 1973 ISLAND ILPS9228
PHIL MANZANERA G ((E) FREEDOM IS FRIGHTENING 1973 ISLAND GER 87703 UK ILPS9242
AL DIMEOLA G (HJI (F) ONE BY ONE 1974 ISLAND ILPS9269
ROSCO GEE B (H (G) RAINDOG 1975 ISLAND ILPS9319
KLAUS SCHULZE K (HJI (H) GO 1976 ISLAND GER 27448 UK ILPS9387
HUGH HOPPER B (EF (I) GO LIVE FROM PARIS 1976 ISLAND UK ISLD 10
GARY BOYLE G (EFG (J) GO TOO 1977 ARISTA US4138 UK SPARTY1011
DAVE WHITE SAX (C (J) GO TOO 1977 ARISTA GER 99228
BRIAN GASGOIGNE (EFG
HISAKO YAMASHTA VLN(DEFGH DONI HARVEY (J PAUL JACKSON (J BROTHER JAMES PERC(HIJ
JEROME RIMSON B (I LINDA LEWIS V (J KAREN FRIEDMAN V (K PETER ROBINSON (CDJ
JESS RODEN V (J R HARRIS TPT (C MORRIS PERT PERC (CD PHIL PLANT B (CD
HIDEO FUNAMOTO PERC (D ALYN ROSS B (D GARY BOYLE G (DE ROBIN THOMPSON SAX (CD
JOJI HIROTA C (D GORO KUII V (D MIKAKO TAKESHITA V (D SHIRO MURATA FLT (D
YOSHIO TAIRA K (D MAGGIE NEWLANDS K (D SAMMI ABU V (EF NIGEL MORRIS D (EF
FRANK TANKOWSKI G (F BERNIE HOLLAND G (FH DAITO FUJITA B (G HOZUMI TANAKA D (G
TSUNEO MATSUMOTO G (G MURRAY HEAD V (G MAXINE NIGHTINGALE V (G JULIAN MARVIN G (H
LENNOX LAINGTON PER (H KAREN FRIEDMAN V (H CASEY SYNGE V (H DARI LALOU V (H
THUNDERTHIGHS V (H HANS WERNER HENZE (A PETER MAXWELL DAVIES (A TORU TAKEMITSU (A
DOREEN CHANTER V (J RUBY JAMES V (J LIZA STRIKE V (J J GIFFE TROM (C

Y2A YAMBU Y2A

RAMON RODRIGUEZ B (A — (A) YAMBU — 1975 MONTUNO MLP 506
MILTON HAMILTON K (A
REINALDO ALCANTARA TIMB(A — MANNY RIVERA BONGO(A — JOSE GONZALES CONGA(A — JAY SIVA TPT (A
JOSE MORRISON TPT (A — SAM BURTIS TROM (A — FRANKIE MALABE CONGA(A — EDDIE RODRIGUEZ CONGA(A
FREDDY HARRIS G (A — RODNEY JONES G (A — MIGUEL SEVILLA D (A — LESETTE WILSON V (A
CATY SEVITTA V (A — IZZY DAVILA CORO (A — NESTOR SANCHEZ CORO(A — WILLIE TORRES CORO(A

Y3 JIMMY YANCEY Y3

JIMMY YANCEY V PNO(ALL — (A) PURE BLUES — 196 ATLANTIC US SD1283
MAMA YANCEY V (AB — (B) CHICAGO PIANO VOL 1 — 1972 ATLANTIC US SD7229 UK K40406
MICHAEL CROSBY B (B — (C) JIMMY YANCEY VOL 1 — 19 OLDIE BLUES US 2802
(D) JIMMY YANCEY VOL 2 — 19 OLDIE BLUES US 2813

Y3A YANKEES Y3A

JON TIVEN V SAX(A — (A) HIGH 'N' INSIDE — 1978 LONDON UK SHY8531 US BIGSOUND 037
SALLY YOUNG G V (A
PAUL OSSOLA K B (A — MICKEY CURRY D (A — ROGER C REALE B V (A — IVAN JULIAN B V (A
HILLY MICHAELS D (A — JIMMY McALLISTER B (A — ROBERT ORSI HCA V(A — VAN DUREN V (A
CHRISTINE OHLMAN V (A — DOC CAVALIER V (A — ALEX CHILTON V (A — TOMMY HOEHN V (A
JOHNNY PARADISE V (A — EDYTH V (A — NELSON ADELARD V (A — FREDERICK BOV V (A

Y4 ZAL YANOVSKY Y4

ZAL YANOVSKY (A — (A) ALIVE & WELL IN ARGENTINA — 1971 KAMA SUTRA UK 2316 003

Y4A YAQUI Y4A

RUDY REGALDO D (A — (A) YAQUI — 1974 ?
RONNIE REYES G V (A
LARRY CRONIN K SYN V(A — GEORGE OCHOA HCA V K G(A — ART SANCHEZ B G V(A — EDDIE SERRANO V CONGA(A
ROY RODRIGUEZ D PERC(A

Y4B PETER YARROW Y4B

PETER YARROW V (A — (A) THAT'S ENOUGH FOR ME — 1973 WB UK K46263
GLADY ANDERSON PNO (A
CHRIS DEDRICK V K G(A — JACKIE JACKSON B (A — BARRY BECKETT K (A — JESSE DIXON SINGERS V(A
JIMMY JOHNSON G (A — DAVID BROMBERG MAND (A — FONTZ B (A — DENZIL LANG PERC(A
HUKS BROWN G (A — WINSTON GRENNAN D (A — COLIN LOUGHAN SAX (A — BRAD BRYAN G (A
ROGER HAWKINS D (A — ROY MARKOWITZ D (A — TONY BUCHANAN SAX (A — TOOTS HIBBERT V (A
DAVID SPINOZZA G (A — PAUL BUTTERFIELD HCA (A — JOHN HUCKRIDGE TPT (A — WINSTON WRIGHT K (A
PETE CARR G (A — DAVID HOOD B (A

Y4C YATHA SIDHRA Y4C

ROLF FICHTER K SYN G V (A — (A) MEDITATION MASS — 1974 BRAIN GER 1045
KLAUS FICHTER D PERC(A
MATTHIAS NICOLAR G B (A — PETER ELBRACHT FLT (A

Y5 YARDBIRDS Y5

TONY TOP TOPHAM G (1
KEITH RELF V HCA(12345
JIM McCARTY D (12345
CHRIS DREJA G (12345
PAUL SAMWELL-SMITH B (123
ERIC CLAPTON G (2
JEFF BECK G (34
JIMMY PAGE G (45

(1) 1963 (2) 1964 (3) 1965
(4) 1966 (5) 1967

Album	Release
WITH SONNY BOY WILLIAMSON	1964 FONTANA TL5277 RI SFJL 960
" " " "	1967 FONTANA UK 858 025
" " " "	1966 MERCURY US SR 61071
" " " "	1975 PHILIPS 756435 011
FIVE LIVE YARDBIRDS	1964 COLUMBIA UK 33SX 1677
FIVE LIVE YARDBIRDS RI	1979 CHARLY GER 3066 UK CR 30173
FOR YOUR LOVE	1965 EPIC US 26167
HAVING A RAVE UP	1965 EPIC US 26177 CBS GER GCXC 28
THE YARDBIRDS	1966 COLUMBIA UK SCX 6063
OVER UNDER SIDEWAYS DOWN	1966 EPIC US 26210 CAPITOL CAN 6202
GREAT HITS	1967 EPIC US 26246 US RI 34491
LITTLE GAMES	1967 EPIC US 26313
PERFORMANCES BY CLAPTON BECK PAGE	1970 EPIC US 30135
ROCK GENERATION	19 BYG FR 529701/2
LIVE YARDBIRDS WITH J PAGE	1971 EPIC US 30615
REMEMBER	1971 STARLINE UK SRS 5069
HITS OF THE YARDBIRDS	197 CAPITOL US DT 6229
MORE GOLDEN EGGS	19 BERKELEY US 1003
ERIC CLAPTON & YARDBIRDS	19 SPRINGBOARD US 4036
FAVOURITES	1977 EPIC US 34490
WITH ERIC CLAPTON	1975 CHARLY GER 3008 UK CR 30012
WITH JEFF BECK	1975 CHARLY UK CR 30013
WITH JEFF BECK	1975 BYG FR 200 139
YARDBIRDS (DBL)	1975 CHARLY GER 3088
SHAPES OF THINGS	19 BOMB US 1045
SHAPES OF THINGS	19 SPRINGBOARD US 4039
SHAPES OF THINGS	1977 CHARLY UK CDX 1
ATTENTION	19 FONTANA GER 9294 902
YARDBIRDS (EP)	1977 CHARLY UK CEP 116
REFLECTIONS/EARLY YARDBIRDS	19 FONTANA GER 9294 904

Y5A YELLO Y5A

BORIS BLANK ELECT V(AB — (A) SOLID PLEASURE — 1980 RALPH US YL 80L
DIETER MEIER V (AB — (B) CLARO QUE SI — 1981 RALPH US YL8159 UK DOIT 008
CARLOS PERON TAPES (AB — (B) CLARO QUE SI — 1981 VERTIGO GER 6435 123
CHICO HABLAS G (AB
BEAT ASH D (B — ZINE EL ABADINE V (B — WALT KAISER D (A — FELIX HAUG D (A

Y5B ATLEE YEAGER Y5B

ATLEE YEAGER B V (AB — (A) PLANT ME NOW AND DIG ME LATER — 1973 CHELSEA US 0366
MICHAEL STEVENS G (AB — (B) FLYING AHEAD — 197 DUNHILL US 50084
FRED STAEHLE D (A
MARK PAUL D (A — ROBERT WACHTEL D G(A — ROCKY HILTON G (A — BILL COWSILL G (A
RICH CLYBURN G (A — KEITH JOHNSON G (A — SAM McCUE G (A — JIM GORDON K SAX (A
BUD DEAL SAX (A — BRUCE SHAFFER K V (A — DON FRANCISCO D V (A

Y6 YELLOW DOG Y6

HERBIE ARMSTRONG G V (AB — (A) YELLOW DOG — 1977 VIRGIN UK V2083 GER 28936
KENNY YOUNG G V (AB — (B) BEWARE OF THE DOG — 1978 VIRGIN UK V2103 GER 26189
PETE SOLLEY (B — ( )STRANGERS IN PARADISE — 1981 ESCAPE ES001
ROD DEMICK B (B
GARY TAYLOR B (A — GERRY CONWAY D (A — ANDY ROBERTS G (A — PHIL PALMER G (B
JIM GANNON G (A — MICK FEAT B (B — PETER VAN HOOKE D (B — PETER BARDENS K (B
PAUL ATKINSON D (B — MO FOSTER B (B — JACK HALL B (B — NEVILLE ROBERTS (B
SIMON PHILLIPS D (B — JIMMY HALL SAX (B — THEOPHILUS K LIVELY D (B — JACK SPENCE PERC(B

Y6A YELLOW MAGIC ORCHESTRA Y6A

RYUICHI SAKAMOTO K PERC(A — (A) YELLOW MAGIC ORCHESTRA — 1979 A&M UK AMLH68506 HORIZON US 736
KENJI OHUMURA G (B — (B) XOO MULTIPLES — 1980 A&M UK AMLH68516 US 4813
YUKIHIRO TAKAHASHI D V (A — (C) B G M — 1981 A&M UK AMLH64853 US 4853
HARUOMI HOSONO K B (B — (D) SOLID STATE SURVIVOR — 1982 ALFA UK 85664
HIDEKI MATSUTAKE (A
BSHUNICHI HASHIMOTO V (A — MASAYOSHI TAKANAKA G(A — SANDI V (B

Y6B YELLOW JACKETS Y6B

RUSSELL FERRANTE K (A — (A) YELLOWJACKETS — 1981 WB US 3573 UK K56920
JIMMY HASLIP B (A
RICKY LAWSON D (A — ROBBEN FORD G (A — LENNY CASTRO PERC (A — PAULINHO DACOSTA PERC(A
BOBBY LYLE K (A — LARRY WILLIAMS WIND (A — JERRY HEY TPT (A — ERNIE WATTS SAX (A
BILL REICHENBACH TROM (A — GARY HERBIG WIND (A — KIM HUTCHCROFT SAX (A

Y6C YELLOW PAYGES Y6C

BILL HAM G (A — (A) VOLUME 1 — 1969 UNI US 73045
BOB BARNES B (A
DAN HORTTER V HCA(A — DAN GORMAN D (A

Y7 YES Y7

CHRIS SQUIRE B V (ALL — (A) YES — 1969 ATLANTIC US 8243 UK 588 190
JON ANDERSON V (A>M — (A) YES — 1971 ATLANTIC RI UK K40034
BILL BRUFORD D (ABCDEF — (B) TIME & A WORD — 1970 ATLANTIC US 8273 UK 2400 006
TONY KAYE K (ABC — (B) TIME & A WORD — 1971 ATLANTIC RI UK K40085
PETER BANKS G (AB — (C) THE YES ALBUM — 1971 ATLANTIC US 8283 UK 2400 101
STEVE HOWE G (C>N — (C) THE YES ALBUM — 1971 ATLANTIC RI UK K40106
RICK WAKEMAN K (DEFGJKLM — (C) THE YES ALBUM — 1980 ATLANTIC US 19131
ALAN WHITE D (FGHJKLM — (D) FRAGILE — 1971 ATLANTIC US 7211 UK 2401 019
PATRICK MORAZ K (HM — (D) FRAGILE — 1971 ATLANTIC RI UK K50009
TREVOR HORN V B (N — (D) FRAGILE — 1980 ATLANTIC US 19132
GEOFF DOWNES K (N — (E) CLOSE TO THE EDGE — 1972 ATLANTIC US 7244 UK K50012
COLIN GOLDRING REC (C — (E) CLOSE TO THE EDGE — 1980 ATLANTIC US 19133
(F) YESSONGS (TPL) — 1973 ATLANTIC US 3 100 UK K60045
(G) TOPOGRAPHIC OCEANS (DBL) — 1973 ATLANTIC US 2908 UK K80001
(H) RELAYER — 1974 ATLANTIC US 18122 UK K50096
(H) RELAYER — 1980 ATLANTIC US 19135
(J) YESTERDAYS — 1975 ATLANTIC US 18103 UK K50048
(J) YESTERDAYS — 1980 ATLANTIC US 19134
(K) GOING FOR THE ONE — 1977 ATLANTIC US 19106 UK K50379
(L) TORMATO — 1978 ATLANTIC US 19202 UK K50518
(M) YESSHOWS (DBL) — 1980 ATLANTIC US 2/510 UK K60142
(N) DRAMA — 1980 ATLANTIC US 16019 UK K50736
(O) CLASSIC YES — 1981 ATLANTIC US 19320

Y8 YESTERDAY & TODAY(Y&T) Y8

DAVE MENIKETTI G V(ABCD — (A) YESTERDAY & TODAY — 1976 LONDON US PS 677
JOEY ALVES G V(ABCD — (B) STRUCK DOWN — 1978 LONDON US PS 711
PHIL KENNEMORE B V(ABCD — (C) EARTHSHAKER — 1981 A&M UK AMLH64872
LEONARD HAZE D V(ABCD — (D) BLACK TIGER — 1982 A&M UK AMLH64910

Y8A YOBS Y8A

NODDY OLDFIELD (A — (A) CHRISTMAS ALBUM — 1980 SAFARI UK RUDE 1
EBENEZER POLAK (A
KID VICIOUS (A — H J BEDWETTER (A

Y8B YIPES Y8B

PETE STRAND B (AB — (A) YIPES — 1979 MILLENIUM
PAT McCURDY V K (AB — (B) A BIT IRRATIONAL — 1980 MILLENNIUM 7750
ANDY BARTEL G V (AB
TEDDY FREESE D (AB — MICHAEL HOFFMAN G (AB

Y9 PETE YORK Y9

PETE YORK D (A — (A) PETE YORK PERCUSSION BAND — 19 DECCA UK TXS 109

Y9A RUSTY YORK Y9A

RUSTY YORK (A — (A) ROCK'N' MEMORIES — 1981 JEWEL US 917

Y10 STEVE YORK'S CAMELO PARDALIS Y10

STEVE YORK B (A — (A) MANOR LIVE — 1973 VIRGIN UK V 2003
ELKIE BROOKS V (A
OLLIE HALSALL G V (A — GRAHAM BOND K SAX (A — TIM HINKLEY K (A — IAN WALLACE D (A
MARC CHARIG HRNS (A — JOHN LEE TROM (A — BOZ BURRELL V (A — DAVE THOMPSON K (A
DAVE BROOKS SAX (A — MIKE PATTO V (A — ROB TAIT D (A — DIANE STEWART CONGA V(A
MICK MOODY G (A — PETE GAVIN D (A — LOL COXHILL SAX (A — BARRY DUGGAN SAX (A
JIM MULLEN G (A — PETE GAGE (A

Y11 CHRIS YOULDEN Y11

CHRIS YOULDEN V (AB — (A) NOWHERE CITY — 1973 DERAM UK SML 1099 US LONDON 633
DEREK GRIFFITHS G (B — (B) CITY CHILD — 1974 DERAM UK SML 1112 US LONDON 642
PETE WINGFIELD K (AB — (C) LEGEND — 1979 US LONDON 50016
CHRIS SPEDDING G (A
ROSCO GEE B (B — JACK MILLS G (B — TERRY STANNARD D (B — NICK NEWELL SAX (B
MIKE COTTON TPT (B — DAVE CASWELL TPT (B — JOHN BEECHAM TROM (B — JOY YATES V (B
ANNA PEACOCK V (B — SUZANNA LYNCH V (B — DANNY KIRWAN G (A — RAY FENWICK G (A
FOGGY LYTTLE G (A — ROY BABBINGTON B (A — ANDY SYLVESTER B (A — BRUCE ROWLAND D (A
MIKE McNAUGHT K (A

Y12 | JESSE COLIN YOUNG | Y12

JESSE COLIN YOUNG G V (ALL (A) SOUL OF A CITY BOY 1964 CAPITOL US 2070 RI 74 11267
JEFF MYER D (CDEFGHJ (A) SOUL OF A CITY BOY 1975 VINE US 1009
SCOTT LAWRENCE K (CDEFGHJ (B) YOUNGBLOOD 1965 MERCURY US SR 61005
JIM ROTHERMEL WIND (EFGHJ (C) TOGETHER 1972 WB US 2588
KELLY BRYAN B (EF (D) SONG FOR JULI 1973 WB US 2734 UK K46262
OZZIE AHLERS PNO (E (E) LIGHT SHINE 1974 WB US 2790 UK K56037
MARTY DAVID B (E (F) SONGBIRD 1975 WB US 2845 UK K56110
JERRY CORBITT V (CEF (G) ON THE ROAD 1976 WB US 2913 UK K56223
SUZI YOUNG V (CEFGHJ (H) LOVE ON A WING 1977 WB US 3033 UK K56358
RON STALLINGS SAX (CF (J) AMERICAN DREAMS 1978 ELEKTRA US 6E157 UK K52105
PETER WELKER TPT (FH
REX ALLEN TROM (G CHUCK PETERSON SAX (H HANK DE VITO STEEL(FH FELIX PAPPALARDI V (H
JEFF NEIGHBOR B (H ZANE WOODWORTH TPT (JH CHUCK BENNETT TROM (H NICOLETTE LARSON V (H
JOHN BLAKELEY G (H EVERETT FAREY HRNS (H GORDON MESSICK TROM (H DAVID HAYES B V(GHJD
RICHARD ANDERSON HCA (DC PETER CHILDS G (BC EDDY OFFENSTEIN G (DC JOHN WILMETH HRNS(C
JEFF LABES K (J MICHAEL O'NEILL G (J ALVIN TAYLOR D (J DAVID LINDLEY VLN (J
ANNA RIZZO V (J PAMELA MOORE V (J PAULETTE McWILLIAMS V (J GREG WRIGHT V (J
STEPHANIE SPRUILL V (J ROGER KENERLY SAINT V (J JIM GILSTRAP V (J GWEN EVANS V (J
JOHN LEHMAN V (J FRITZ HEIBRON TROM (J RAYMOND LOECKLIE SAX (J BENNETT FRIEDMAN SAX (J
OSIE JOHNSON D (B JOHN SEBASTIAN HCA (B GEORGE DUVIVIER B (B

Y13 | JOHNNY YOUNG | Y13

JOHNNY YOUNG G V HCA (ALL (A) CHICAGO BLUES BAND 1966 ARHOOLIE US 1029
LOUIS MYERS G (E (B) CHICAGO BLUES 1968 ARHOOLIE US 1037
PAUL OSCHER HCA (D (C) BLUES MASTER No9 197 BLUE HORIZON US 4609
SAMMY LAWHORN G (D (D) FAT MANDOLIN 1970 BLUE HORIZON UK 763852
S P LEARY D (AD (E) I CANT KEEP MY FOOT FROM JUMPING 1973 BLUESWAY BLS 6075
RICHARD EVANS B (E (F) & HIS FRIENDS 197 TESTAMENT US 2226
OTIS SPANN PNO (AD
BILL WARREN D (E
WALTER HORTON HCA (B LAFAYETTE LEAKE PNO (B JAMES COTTON HCA (A JIMMY DAWKINS G (B
ERNEST GATEWOOD B (B JIMMY LEE MORRIS B (A LESTER DORSIE D (B

Y14 | KENNY YOUNG | Y14

KENNY YOUNG (AB (A) CLEVER DOG CHASE THE SUN 1972 WB US 2579
BOB FALLOON G (A (B) LAST STAGE FOR SILVERWOOD 19 WB US 2676
BRUCE EPSTIEN G (A
MARK WARNER G (AB CHRIS SPEDDING G (A DAVE EDMUNDS G (A GERRY HOGAN STEEL(A
FIACHRA TRENCH K (A DAVE WINTOUR B (A BARRY DESOUZA PERC (A DEAN PARKS G (B
LELAND SKLAR B (B RUSS KUNKEL D (B TOM CANNING K (B JIM HORN SAX (B
RABBIT BUNDRICK K (B CHRIS GUNNING STR (B BOBBYE HALL PERC (B LOUIS SHELTON G (B
WILTON FELDER B (B GARY COLEMAN PERC (B DAVE COHEN G (B WAYNE PERKINS G (B
TRACY HARRILL B (B MIKE KELLIE D (B SUSAN TRAYNOR V (B JOE SAMPLE K (B

Y14A | LARRY YOUNG | Y14A

LARRY YOUNG K (ALL GROOVE STREET 196 PRESTIGE US 7237
OF LOVE & PEACE 19 BLUENOTE BST 84242
CONTRASTS 19 BLUENOTE US BST 84266
HEAVEN ON EARTH 19 BLUENOTE US BST 84304
LAWRENCE OF NEWARK 1973 PERCEPHON US 34
FUEL 1976 ARISTA US AL 4051
SPACEBALL 197 ARISTA US AL 4072

Y15 | MIGHTY JOE YOUNG | Y15

MIGHTY JOE YOUNG G V (ALL (A) CHICKEN HEADS 1974 OVATION US 1437
BOB REIDY PNO (E (B) LOVE GONE 19 OVATION US 1443
SYLVESTER BOINES B (E (C) MIGHTY JOE YOUNG 19 OVATION US 1706
ALVINO BENNETT D (E (D) BLUES WITH A TOUCH OF SOUL 19 DELMARK US DS 629
CHARLES BEECHAM TPT (E (E) LEGACY OF THE BLUES (VOL 4) 1972 SONET UK SNTF633 US GNP 10014
KEN SAJDAK K (F (F) BLUESY JOSEPHINE 1976 BLACK & BLUE 33521
WILLIE MABON PNO (F
CORNELIUS BOYSON B (F WILLIE HAYES D (F WALTER HAMBRICK SAX (E

Y16 | NEIL YOUNG | Y16

NEIL YOUNG G V HCA(ALL (A) NEIL YOUNG 1969 REPRISE US RS6317 UK K44059
JOHN BARBATA D (F (B) EVERYBODY KNOWS THIS IS NOWHERE 1969 REPRISE US RS6349 UK K44073
PATRICE HOLLOWAY V (A (B) EVERYBODY KNOWS THIS IS NOWHERE 19 REPRISE US RI 2282
TIM DRUMMOND B (DFHLJNOG (C) AFTER THE GOLDRUSH 1970 REPRISE US RS6383 UK K44088
SHIRLEY MATTHEWS V (A (C) AFTER THE GOLDRUSH 19 REPRISE US RI 2283
JACK NITZSCHE K G (ADFH (D) HARVEST 1972 REPRISE US RS2032 UK K54005
BOBBY NOTKOFF VLN (B (D) HARVEST !) REPRISE US RI 2277
BEN KEITH STEEL G V (DFHLNGO (E) JOURNEY THROUGH THE PAST(COMP) 1972 REPRISE US RS2480 UK K54015
DAVID CROSBY G V (DFJG (F) TIME FADES AWAY 1973 REPRISE US RS2151 UK K54010
JOE YANKEE B (FG (G) ON THE BEACH 1974 REPRISE US RS2180 UK K54014
NICOLETTE LARSON V (LNP (H) TONIGHTS THE NIGHT 1975 REPRISE US RS2221 UK K54040
KENNY BUTTREY D (DH (J) ZUMA 1975 REPRISE US MS2242 UK K54057
BILLY TALBOT B (BCHJLNOGQR (K) LONG MAY YOU RUN 1976 REPRISE US 2253 UK K54081
GREG REEVES B (C (L) AMERICAN STARS & BARS 1977 REPRISE US 2261 UK K54088
NILS LOFGREN PNO V(CH (M) DECADE (TRIPLE) 1978 REPRISE US 3 2257 UK K64037
RALPH MOLINA D V (BCHJLNOGQR (N) COMES A TIME 1978 REPRISE US 2266 UK K54099
DANNY WHITTEN G V (BCH (O) HAWKS & DOVES 1979 REPRISE US 2297 UK K54109
STEPHEN STILLS V (CDJK (P) RUST NEVER SLEEPS 1979 REPRISE US 2295 UK K54105
JAMES TAYLOR V (D (Q) LIVE RUST 1980 REPRISE US 2 2296 UK K64041
GRAHAM NASH V (DFJG (R) REACTOR 1981 REPRISE US 2304 UK K54116
RICK DANKO B (G
JIM MESSINA B (A LINDA RONSTADT V (DL JOHN HARRIS PNO (D EMMYLOU HARRIS V (L
KARL HIMMEL D (LNP FRANK SAMPEDRO G STR(JLNOPQR CAROLE MAYEDO VLN (L SPOONER OLDHAM PNO (N
STRINGS (N RUFUS THIBODEAUX FDL (NO JOE OSBORN B (NP LARRIE LONDIN D (N
J J CALE G (N FARRELL MORRIS PERC (N GRANT BOATRIGHT G (N BUCKY BARRETT G (N
JOHN CHRISTOPHER G (N JERRY SHOOK G (N STEVE GIBSON G (N RUSS KUNKEL CONGA(N
DALE SELLERS G (N RAY EDENTON G (N RITA FEY AUTOHARP (N TIM MULLIGAN SAX(N
LONDON SYM ORCH (D RUSTY KERSHAW G FDL(G GLORIA R JONES V (A GRACIA NITZSCHE V (A
ROBIN LANE V (A LEVON HELM D (GO GEORGE WHITSELL G (G TOM SCRIBNER SAW (O
DENNIS BELFIELD B (O ANN HILARY O'BRIEN V(O GONE WITH THE WIND ORCH (N

Y17 ROY YOUNG Y17

ROY YOUNG K V (AB (A) THE ROY YOUNG BAND 1971 RCA UK SF8161
JON LEE TROM (AB (B) MR FUNKY 1972 MCA UK MKPS2022 RI MCF2690
ALAN DAVIES D (AB
DAVE WENDELLS G (AB HOWIE CASEY SAX (A PAUL SIMMONS B (EDDIE THORNTON TPT (B
RICKY DODD SAX (B RONNIE MACDONALD SAX (B ONNIE McINTYRE G (B NICK SOUTH B (B
ROD COOMBES D (B ROBIN JONES PERC (B DORIS TROY V (A BARRY ST JOHN V (A
SUE GLOVER V (A SUNNY LESLIE V (A LIZA STRIKE V (A KATHY KISSOON V (A
ALAN TOWNSEND HRNS (AB

Y18 STEVE YOUNG Y18

STEVE YOUNG G V (ALL (A) ROCK,SALT & NAILS 1969 A&M US 4177
JOE ALLEN B (E (B) SEVEN BRIDGES ROAD 1972 REPRISE US 2081
KENNY MALONE D (E (B) SEVEN BRIDGES ROAD 1975 BLUE CANYON US 505
CHUCK COCHRAN K (E (B) SEVEN BRIDGES ROAD 1976 SONET UK SNTF 705
JIM COLVARD G (E (C) HONKY TONK MAN 1976 MOUNTAIN RAILROAD US 52776
DAVE KIRBY G (E (D) RENEGADE PICKER 1976 RCA US APL11759 UK PL11759
LLOYD GREEN STEEL(E (E) NO PLACE TO FALL 1978 RCA US AHL12510 UK PL12510
KRISTIN WILKINSON VLA (E (F) TO SATISFY YOU 1981 ROUNDER US 3057
KARL HIMMEL D (BDE
BOBBY WOOD K (D MIKE LEECH B (DE JERRY SHOOK G HCA(DE DALE SELLERS G (BDE
MAC GAYDEN G (DE BUDDY EMMONS STEEL(DE TRACY NELSON V (ED KIM YOUNG V (DE
CHARLIE McCOY HCA (BE BUDDY SPICHER VLN (BE LARRY BYROM G (E TERRY McMILLAN HCA(D
JOHNNY GIMBLE FDL MAND (D WELDON MYRICK STEEL(B JOSH GRAVES DOBRO(B PETER WADE G (B
BOBBY THOMPSON G (B HENRY STRZELECKI B (B JERRY SMITH K (B PETE DRAKE STEEL(B
FRED CARTER B (B DAVID BRIGGS K (B RAY EDENTON G (B JERRY CARRIGAN D (B
D J FONTANA D (B WILLIE ACKERMAN D (B BOB MOORE G (B J B BROWN (B
GEORGE BOURQUE (B SPOOK JAMES (B CHARLIE JOBES (B STEVE KEITH (B
NASHVILLE EDITION V (B PAUL TANNEN V (B MARY HOLLADAY V (B GINGER HOLLADAY V (B
ANITA BALL V (D KIM MORRISON V (D

Y19 YOUNG & MOODY Y19

BOB YOUNG V HCA(A (A) YOUNG & MOODY 1977 MAGNET UK MAG5015 UA UA LA759
MICK MOODY G V (A
GRAHAM PRESKETT VLN B K(A KAY GARNER V (A TERRY STANNARD D (A JEAN HAWKER V (A
CLAIRE TORRY V (A

Y19A YOUNG & RENSHAW Y19A

PAUL YOUNG (A (A) THIS IS YOUNG AND RENSHAW 1972 BELL UK 201
FRANK RENSHAW (A

Y19B YOUNG CANADIANS Y19B

BARRY TAYLOR D (A (A) THIS IS YOUR LIFE 1980 QUINTESSENCE EP CAN 1205
ART BERGMANN G V (A
JIM BESCOTT B V (A HOWARD OGILVIE VLA (A

Y19C YOUNG LIONS Y19C

TIM BENJAMIN B G (A (A) NO NEWS 1980 PLUREX EP NL 0013
RONALD HEILOO K V (A
HAROLD SCHELLINK G B (A PETER MERTENS G B (A RON SCHOLTE D V (A

Y20 YOUNG MARBLE GIANTS Y20

ALISON STRATTON V (AB (A) COLOSSAL YOUTH 1980 ROUGH TRADE UK ROUGH 8
PHILIP MOXHAM B (AB (B) FINAL DAY(EP) 1980 ROUGH TRADE UK
STUART MOXHAM G K (AB

Y21 YOUNG TRADITION Y21

HEATHER WOOD V (A (A) GALLERIES 1968 VANGUARD VSD 79295
DAVE SWARBRICK FDL MAND(A (A) GALLERIES 1968 TRANSATLANTIC UK TRA 172
ROYSTON WOOD V TAMB(A (B) THE YOUNG TRADITION 19 TRANSATLANTIC UK TRA 142
DOLLY COLLINS V (A (C) SO CHEERFULLY ROUND 19 TRANSATLANTIC UK TRA 155
CHRIS HOGWOOD PERC (A (D) YOUNG TRADITION SAMPLER 1977 TRANSATLANTIC TRANSAM13
PETE BELLAMY V G CONC (A (E) GALLERIES REVISITED 1979 TRANSATLANTIC TRANSAM30
DAVID MUNROW SHAWN (A
ROD SKEAPING VLN (A ADAM SKEAPING VLN (A

Y22 YOUNGBLOODS Y22

JESSE COLIN YOUNG G V B(ALL (A) YOUNGBLOODS 1967 RCA US LSP3724
JERRY CORBITT G B (A (B) EARTH MUSIC 1967 RCA US LSP3865
JOE BAUER D (DHJKL (C) ELEPHANT MOUNTAIN 1969 RCA US LSP4150
LOWELL LEVINGER K G (DHKL (D) ROCK FESTIVAL 1970 WB US WS 1878
MICHAEL KANE B (LK (E) CRABTUNES NOGGINS 197 WB US WS 1944
RICHARD'EARTHQUAKE'ANDERSON HCA(DKL (F) THE BEST OF 1970 RCA US LSP4399
(F) THE BEST OF 19 RCA RI AYL13680
(G) TWO TRIPS 1970 MERCURY US SR 61273
(H) RIDE THE WIND 1971 WB UK K46100 US WS 2563
(J) SUNLIGHT 1971 RCA UK SF8218 US LSP4561
(K) GOOD & DUSTY 1971 WB US BS 2566
(L) HIGH ON A RIDGETOP 1972 WB US BS 2653
(M) GET TOGETHER 19 RCA INT INTS1170
(N) THIS IS (DBL) 1972 RCA US 6051

Y23 'YS' Y23

RENE WERNEER VLN V(A (A) MADAME LA FRONTIERE 1976 PHILIPS FR 9101 056
PASCAL STIVE K V (A
JACKY THOMAS B V (A JACQUES HIGELIN ACC (A MICHEL SANTANGELI D V (A GABRIEL YACOUB G (A
PIERRE CHEREEZ G (A JACQUES WIEDERKER CELLO(A

Y24 COLE YOUNGER Y24

COLE YOUNGER G K V(A (A) COLE YOUNGER 1975 ANCHOR UK ANCL 2008
LINTON NAIFF K (A
ROD ALEXANDER G (A JIM RYAN G (A STEVE WALLER G V (A DELISLE HARPER B (A
TOM CROMPTON D (A LITTLE STEVIE SMITH HCA (A KEN FREEMAN SYN (A DORIS TROY V (A
ROSETTA HIGHTOWER V (A JIM EVANS V (A BILL KIMBLE V (A

Y25 YOUR GANG Y25

BEN BENAY G (A (A) THE DAILY TRIP 1964 MERCURY US 21094
MIKE DEASY B (A
JERRY SCHEFF B (A BUTCH PARKER K (A JIM BELL OBOE V(A JIM TROXELL D (A
CURT BOETTCHER PERC (A TOXIE FRENCH VIBES(A MIKE HENDERSON ORG (A

TIMI YURO V (A

HURT 1961 LIBERTY US LST7208
HURT 19 LIBERTY RI SLS 50201
SOUL 1962 LIBERTY LRP 3212 LBY 1042
WHATS A MATTER BABY 1962 LIBERTY LRP 3263 LBY1154
WHATS A MATTER BABY 19 LIBERTY RI 50399
LET ME CALL YOU SWEETHEART 19 LIBERTY LST7234 LRP 3234 LBY1275
MAKE THE WORLD GO AWAY 19 LIBERTY LST 7319
THE AMAZING TIMI YURO 19 MERCURY US 60963
SOMETHINGS BAD IN MY MIND 1968 LIBERTY LST 7594 LBL 83198
THE TIMI YURO ALBUM 1976 EMI NL 97969
IN THE BEGINNING 1968 LIBERTY UK LBS 83128
timi yuro 19 LIBERTY 5107 RI 50032
BEST OF 19 LIBERTY LRP 3289 LBY 1290
GREAT PERFORMANCES 19 LIBERTY UK 83115

Z1

Z Z TOP

Z1

BILLY GIBBONS G V (ALL
DUSTY HILL B V (ALL
FRANK BEARD D (ALL

(A) FIRST ALBUM 1970 LONDON US PS 584
(A) FIRST ALBUM RI 1980 WB RI EURO 56601 US 3268
(B) RIO GRANDE MUD 1972 LONDON UK SHU8433 US PS 612
(B) RIO GRANDE MUD 1980 WB RI EURO 56602 US 3269
(C) TRES HOMBRES 1973 LONDON UK SHU8459 US PS 631
(C) TRES HOMBRES 1980 WB RI EURO 56602 US 3270
(D) FANDANGO 1975 LONDON UK SHU8482 UK PS 656
(D) FANDANGO 1980 WB RI EURO 56603 US 3271
(E) TEJAS 1976 LONDON UK LDU 1 US PS 680
(E) TEJAS 1980 WB RI EURO 56604 US 3272
(F) BEST OF 197 LONDON US PS 706
(F) BEST OF 197 TELEFUNKEN/NOVA GER 623361
(F) BEST OF 1980 WB RI US 3273
(G) DEGUELLO 1979 WB UK K56701 US 3361
(H) EL LOCO 1981 WB UK K56929 US 3593

Z2

Z.N.R

Z2

JOSEPH RACAILLE K SYN V(AB
HECTOR ZAZOU K SYN B(AB
ANDRE JAUME SAX (A
HARVEY NENEUX G (A PATRICK PORTELLA CLAR (A DAVID RUEFF WIND (AB GILLY BELL SYN (A
FERNAND D'ARLES D (A MANFRED LE LALO SAX (B CATHERINE ARMAND SAX (B LOLA TALOT SAX (B
HUMPHREY NENEUX V (B REMI DEMILLAC VLN (B

(A) BARRICADE 3 1976 RECOMMENDE RR7 ISADORA FR 9002
(B) TRAITE DE MECANIQUE POPULAIRE 1970 SCOPA 1002

Z3

Z.O.U.(ZON ORCHESTRA UNLIMITED)

Z3

ANDRE HERVE K G V(A
MICHEL HERVE B V (A
JOEL HERVE G V (A STEPHAN HERVE D (A MARIA POPKIEWICZ V (A

(A) Z.O.U. 1975 POLYDOR FR 2393 103

Z3A

ZAGER & EVANS

Z3A

DENNY ZAGER G V(ALL
RICK EVANS G V (ALL
MARK DALTON B (A
NORM CHRISTIAN D (A

(A) 2525 1969 RCA US 4214
(B) IN THE YEAR 2525 19 RCA US ANL1 1077
( ) FOOD FOR THE MIND 19 VANGUARD US 6568
( ) ZAGER & EVANS 1970 RCA US 4302

Z3B

MICHAEL ZAGER BAND

Z3B

MICHAEL ZAGER K (ABC
ROB MOUNSEY SYN K (A
FRANCISCO CENTANO B (A
CLIFF MORRIS G (A
RAY CRISARA TPT (A ALAN SCHWARTZBERG D (A JEFF MIRANOV G (A RUBENS BASSINI PERC(A
GEORGE MARGE WIND (A DAVE GAREY PERC (A GLORIA AGOSTINI HARP (A PHIL BODNER WIND(A
JOHN GATCHELL HRNS (A ALAN RUBIN HRNS (A ROBERT MILLIKAN HRNS (A TOM MALONE TROM (A
GERALD CHAMBERLAIN TRROM(A DAVE TAYLOR TROM (A WALTER KANE WIND (A RONALD CUBER WIND(A
JAMES BUFFINGTON HRNS (A BROOKS TILLOTSON HRNS (A ALVIN FIELDS V (A YOLANDA McCULLOGH V(A
DOLLETTE McDONALD V (A LONI CLARK V (A MAERETHA STEWART V (A FRANK FLOYD V (A
BILLY BAKER V (A

(A) LETS ALL CHANT 1978 PRIVATE STOCK UK 1042
(B) LIFE'S A PARTY 1979 PRIVATE STOCK UK 1045
(C) ZAGER 1980 EMI UL EMC 3328

Z4

LENNY ZAKATEK

Z4

LENNY ZAKATEK V (A
JOHN GIBLIN B V (A
STUART ELLIOTT D PERC(A MAX MIDDLETON K (A ROBERT AHWAI G (A IAN BAIRNSON G V (A
MARILYN BAIRNSON V (A STEVE GREGORY SAX (A GEORGE CHISHOLM HRNS (A STRINGS (A

(A) LENNY ZAKATEK 1979 A&M US 4777 UK AMLH64777

Z5

ZAL BAND

Z5

ZAL CLEMINSON G (A
LEROI JONES G (A CHRIS GLEN B (A BILLY RANKIN (A TED McKENNA D (A

Z5A

ZAO

Z5A

MAUNCIA PLATON V (A
FRANCOIS CAHEN K (A
JEFF SEFFER SAX (A JOEL DUGREN B (A JEAN YVES PIZAUD VLN (A JEAN MYTRUONG D (A

(A) Z=7L 1973 VERTIGO UK 6499 738

Z6

ZAP POW

Z6

(A) ZAP POW WOW 1976 VULCAN VULP 004
(B) REVOLUTION 1976 TROJAN TRLS 130
(C) ZAP POW 1978 ISLAND UK ILPS 9547
(D) REGGAE RULES 1981 RHINO US 015

FRANK ZAPPA PROD G V (ALL
DON SUGARCANE HARRIS VLN(HJKLS
DON PRESTON K B (BCDEFGHLMOPQT
IAN UNDERWOOD G K WIND(CEFHJKL
(MOQSRYNG
RUTH UNDERWOOD K PERC (NRSTYZcGU
DAVID ANDERLE (A
RONNIE AMBLER WIND (
MIKE ALTSCHUL WIND (PQ
HAROLD AYRES (
JIMMY CARL BLACK D(ABCEFGHLNfDj
TERRY BOZZIO D (XYZbK
BIANCO K (
MAX BENNETT B (JK
TERRY BOLIN D (
NAPOLEON MURPHY BROCK SAX(STUYbcX
JACK BRUCE B (S
RANDY BRECKER HRNS (Z
MICHAEL BRECKER HRNS (Z
CAPTAIN BEEFHEART V (KYX
BILL BYERS TROM (PQ
DALE BOZZIO (ef
EDWIN BEACH (A
BEN BARRETT (A
JOHN BERGAMO PERC (Z
BLOODSHOT ROLLIN'RED HCA(U
ADRIAN BELEW G (Abl
ARTHUR BARROW (efhjkm
GARY BARONE TPT (
JIMMY BUND B (D
DENNIS BUDIMIR G (D
JOHN BALKIN B (D
CHUCK BERGHOFFER B (D
DICK BARBER V (DC
RAY COLLINS (ABEGHS
DAVE CORONADO SAX (
ROBERT CAMARENA V (ST
RONNIE CUBER REEDS(Z
LEE CLEMENT PERC (P
HERB COHEN (B
LISA COHEN (B
VINCE COLAIUTA (efhk
GENE CIPRIANO WIND (D
ERIC CLAPTON G (CD
DON CHRISTLIEB WIND (D
MARGINAL CHAGRIN SAX (e
FRANKIE CAPP D (D
CHUNCKY (P
WARREN CUCURULLO (efhk
AYNSLEY DUNBAR D (GMNOPQJS
TONY DURAN G (PQ
VINCENT DE ROSA HRNS (D
EARL DUMLER WIND (P
GEORGE DUKE K V (JNPQRSTUXac
EUGENE DINOVI (A
ALEX DMOCHOWSKI(ERRONEOUS B(PRSQ
DEBBIE (ST
ROY ESTRADA B V(ABCDEFGHLYkm
VIRGIL EVANS (A
ALAN ESTES PERC (PD
GENE ESTES (AD
DON ELLIS (B
JIM FIELDER B (
KIM FOWLEY (A
GABBY FURGGY V (L
LARRY FANOGA (D
VICTOR FELDMAN PERC (D
TOM FOWLER B (RSTUXY
JANET FERGUSON V (PQ
BRUCE FOWLER TROM (RSTXY
CARL FRANZONI (A
WALT FOWLER TPT (TY
LOWELL GEORGE G (HKL
ROY GATON (A
BUZZ GARDNER HRNS (HL
BUNK GARDNER WIND (BCEFGHL
RUBEN DE GUEVARA B V (STY
JIM GORDON D (S
SUSIE GLOVER V (S
JOHN GUERIN (DJKS
JIM HAYNES G (D
RALPH HUMPHREY D (RST
PAUL HUMPHREYS D (K
BOB HARRIS K V (M
GEORDIE HORMEL (f
ELLIOT INGBER G (A
JOHN JOHNSON (A
DR JOHN K (
PETE JOLLY K (D
JULES JACOB WIND (D
FRED JACKSON WIND (P
PLAS JOHNSON (A
EDDIE JOBSON K VLN V (ZK
SNEAKY PETE KLEINOW STEEL(Q
HOWARD KAYLAN V (JMNO
RAY KELLOFF (A
RUTH KOMANOFF (

(A) FREAK OUT 1966 VERVE UK SVLP9154
(A) " " (DBL) 1966 VERVE US 5005
(A) " " (DBL) 197 VERVE UK 2683 004
(A) " 196 VERVE GERM 710007
(B) ABSOLUTELY FREE 1967 VERVE UK SVLP9174 RI 2317 035
(B) " " " 1967 VERVE US 5013
(B) " " " 1967 VERVE GERM 710006
(C) WE'RE ONLY IN IT FOR THE MONEY 1967 VERVE UK SVLP9199 RI 2317 034
(C) " " " " 1967 VERVE US 5045
(C) " " " " 1967 VERVE GERM 710012
(D) LUMPY GRAVY 1967 VERVE UK SVLP9223 RI 2317 046
(D) " " 1967 VERVE US 8741
(E) CRUISIN WITH RUBEN & THE JETS 1968 VERVE UK SVLP9237 RI 2317 069
(E) " " " 1969 VERVE US 5055
(E) " " " " 1969 VERVE GERM 710020
(F) MOTHER MANIA 1969 VERVE UK SVLP9239 RI 2317 047
(F) " " " 19 VERVE 2351 017
(F) " " " 1969 VERVE US 5068
(F) " " " 1969 VERVE GERM 710021
(G) UNCLE MEAT 1969 BIZARRE UK 52024 US 2024
(G) " " " 1969 REPRISE GERM 64005
(G) " " " 196 TRANSATLANTIC UK TRA197
(H) WEASELS RIPPED MY FLESH 1970 REPRISE UK K44019
(H) " " " " 1970 BIZARRE US 2028
(J) CHUNGAS REVENGE 1970 REPRISE UK K44020
(J) " " " " 1970 BIZARRE US 2030
(K) HOT RATS 1970 REPRISE UK K44078 RI K59021
(K) " " " 1970 BIZARRE US 6356
(L) BURNT WEENY SANDWICH 1970 REPRISE UK K44083
(L) " " " " 1970 BIZARRE US 6370
(HL) WEASELS/BURNT WEENY(2 ORIGINALS) 19 REPRISE UK K64024
(M) LIVE AT FILLMORE EAST 1971 REPRISE UK K44150
(M) " " " " " 1971 BIZARRE US US 2042
(N) 200 MOTELS 1971 UA UK 50003 US LA9956
(N) " " 1971 UA GERM 29218/9
(O) JUST ANOTHER BAND FROM LA 1972 REPRISE UK K44179
(O) " " " " 1972 BIZARRE US 2075
(P) THE GRAND WAZOO 1972 REPRISE UK K44209
(P) " " " 1972 BIZARRE US 2093
(Q) WAKA JAWAKA 1972 REPRISE UK K44203
(Q) " " 1972 BIZARRE US 2094
(R) OVERNIGHT SENSATION 1973 DICREET UK K41000 US 2149
(S) APOSTROPHE 1974 DISCREETUK K59201 US 2175
(T) ROXY & ELSEWHERE 1974 DISCREET UK K69201 US 2202
(U) ONE SIZE FITS ALL 1974 DISCREET UK K59207 US 2216
(V) MOTHERS DAY 197 VERVE 2626 002
(W) ROCK FLASHBACKS 1975 VERVE 2352 057
(X) BONGO FURY 1975 DISCREET UK K59209 US 2234
(Y) ZOOT ALLURES 1976 WB UK K56298 US 2970
(Z) IN NEW YORK 1978 DISCREET UK K69204 US 2/2290
(a) STUDIO TAN 1978 DISCREET UK K59210 US 2291
(b) SHEIK YERBOUTI 1979 CBS UK 88339
(b) " " 1979 ZAPPA US 2/1501
(c) SLEEP DIRT 1979 DISCREET UK K59211 US 2292
(d) ORCHESTRAL FAVOURITES 1979 DISCREET UK K59212 US 2294
(e) JOE'S GARAGE ACT 1 1980 CBS UK 86101
(e) " " " " 1980 ZAPPA US 1/1603
(f) JOE'S GARAGE ACTS 2&3 1980 CBS UK 88475
(f) " " " " 1980 ZAPPA US 2/1502
(g) ZAPPA & THE MOTHERS 19 VERVE 2352 057
(h) TINSELTOWN REBELLION 1981 CBS UK 88516 US 37336
(J) YOU ARE WAHAT YOU IG 1981 CBS UK 88560
(k) SHUT UP 'N PLAY YER GUITAR 1981 CBS UK 66368
(m) SHIP ARRIVING TOO LATE 1982 CBS UK 85804

CAROL KAYE (A
MICHAEL LICKERT (,
LYNN (ST
MIKE LANG K (D
DAVID LOGERMAN (hj
ANDRE LEWIS K (bY
RICKY LANCELOTTI (R
BILL MUNDI (BCG
DAVID MOIRE V (Yb
SAL MARQUEZ TPT (PQRS
LOU MARINI REED (Z
KERRY McNABB V (S
ARTHUR MAEBE HRNS (D
ED MANN PERC(Zbelfkjm
TOM MALONE HRNS (Z
MALCOLM McNABB HRNS (P
LINCOLN MAYORGA K (D
SHELLEY MANNE D (D
BOB MARTON SAX V K (m
JOANNE CALDWELL McNABB (P
TOM MARIANO K (1
AL MANN (efhm
AL MALKIN (e
TOMMY MARS K V (behjkm
LOU ANNE NEIL HARP (ZY
TED NASH WIND (D
SHUGGIE OTIS G (K
TONY ORTEGA WIND (P
PAT O'HEARN B WIND(DZkm
DAVID OCKER CLAR (bj
JIM PONS V (OMN

MARK PINSKE (j
JOEL PESKIN SAX (PQ
LISA POPEIL V (m
VAN DYKE PARKS (
DAVE PARLATO B (Y
GEORGE PRICE (A
RICHARD PERISSI HRNS (D
SPARKY PARKER B V (Y
JEAN LUC PONTY K (KRSk
DON PARDO V (Z
CHRIS PETERSON V (Q
JOHN ROTELLA PERC (ABDP
KURT RETAR (AB
EMIL RICHARDS PERC (D
TONY RIZZI G (D
ALICE STUART (
STUMUK SAX (e
CRAIG STEWART (ej
KEN SHROYER TROM (DPQ
PAUL SMITH K (D
JEFF SIMMONS B G V(JOTQ
JIM SHERWOOD WIND (BCEFGHLj
EMMET SARGEANT (A
JOE SAXON (A
DAVID SAMUELS PERC (Z
RON SELICO D (K
ARTIE TRIPP (EFGHL
TOMMY TEDESCO G (D
RANDY THORNTON V (b
SCOTT THUNES B (m
CHESTER THOMPSON D (TUXc

ERNIE TACK HRNS (P
VITO (A
AL VIOLA G (D
STEVE VAI G(hjkm
KEN VASSEY (R
NEIL VANG (A
HENRY VESTINE (
MARK VOLMAN V (JMNO
RAY WHITE G(Zhjkm
CHAD WACKERMANN V (jm
DAVID WELLS (A
TOM WILSON PROD (A
KEN WATSON (A
ERNIE WATTS SAX (P
BOB WEST B (D
PETER WOLF K(efhk
RON WILLIAMS (D
JOHNNY GUITAR WATSON
G V(U
DENNIS WALLEY G(Xefhjk
NELLY WALKER (G
IKE WILLIS (efhjk
JAMES YOUMAN (Uc
BOB ZIMMITTI PERC (P
PAMELA ZARUBICA (BC
GAIL ZAPPA V (Y
AHMET ZAPPA (j
MOON ZAPPA (jm
JIMMY ZITO TPT (D

Z9 ## JOE ZAWINUL Z9

JOE ZAWINUL K (ALL (A) ZAWINUL 1971 ATCO US 1579 UK 2400 151

GEORGE DAVIS FLT (A (A) ZAWINUL 1971 ATLANTIC UK RI K40349

EARL TURBINTON SAX (A (B) RISE & FALL 19 VORTEX US 2002

WOODIE SHAW TPT (A (C) MONEY IN THE POCKET 19 ATCO US 3003

MIROSLAV VITOUS B (A (D) CONCERTO RETITLED(COMP) 1976 ATLANTIC US 1694

JIMMY OWENS TPT (A

HUBERT LAWS FLT (A HERBIE HANCOCK K (A WALTER BOOKER B (A JOE CHAMBERS PERC(A

BILLY HART PERC (A DAVID LEE PERC (A WAYNE SHORTER SAX (A JACK DE JOHNETTE WIND(A

Z9A ## ZAZU Z9A

JOHN MELNICK K V (A (A) ZAZU 1975 WOODEN NICKEL US 0791

RANDY CURLEE B V (A

PAUL RIPUPERO G V (A MICKEY LEHOCKY PERC (A

Z9B ## ZED Z9B

NIGEL JENKINS G B (A (A) ZED 1981 ATLANTIC US 19299 DOUBLE 003

GRAHAM JARVIS D (A

PAUL WESTWOOD B (A DAVE LAWSON SYN (A MIKE MORAN K (A

Z9C ## ZEN Z9C

(A) RUSSIAN ROULETTE 1981 LASER UK LPIP2

Z10 ## ZEPHYR Z10

TOMMY BOLIN G V (AB (A) ZEPHYR 1970 PROBE UK SPB 1006 US CP4510

CANDY GIVENS K V (ABC (B) GOING BACK TO COLORADO 1971 WB US WS1897

JOHN FARIS K SAX(AB (C) SUNSET RIDE 1972 WB US WS2603

ROBBIE CHAMBERLAIN D(A

BOBBY BERGE D (B DAVID GIVENS B V (ABC PAUL CONLEY SYN (B BUZZY LINHART V (B

P M WOOTEN D (C JOHN ALFONSE CONGA(C DAN SMYTH K (C JOCK BARTLEY G V (C

BOBBY NOTKOFF VLN (C

Z11 ## WARREN ZEVON Z11

WARREN ZEVON G V K B HCA(ALL (A) WANTED DEAD OR ALIVE 1969 IMPERIAL US LP 12456

DAVID LINDLEY FDL (BD (B) WARReN ZEVON 1976 ASYLUM US 7E1060 UK K53039

WADDY WACHTEL PROD G V (BCDF (C) EXCITABLE BOY 1978 ASYLUM US 6E 118 UK K53973

BOB GLAUB B (BC (D) BAD LUCK STREAK IN DANCING SCHOOL 1980 ASYLUM US 5E 509 UK K52191

LARRY ZACK D (B (E) STAND IN THE FIRE 1980 ASYLUM US 5E 519 UK K52265

PHIL EVERLY V (B (F) THE ENVOY 198 ASYLUM UK K52354

GREG LADANY PROD(DEF

J D SOUTHER V (BDCF JACKSON BROWNE G V (BDC LINDSEY BUCKINGHAM G V (B MARTY DAVID B (B

GARY MALLABER D (A SID SHARP STRINGS (B BOBBY KEYS SAX (B JAI WINDING K V(B

GLENN FREY G V (BD DON HENLEY V (BDF ROY MARINELL B (BF JORGE CALDERON V (BCDF

NED DOHENY G (B BONNIE RAITT V (B ROSEMARY BUTLER V (B CARL WILSON V (B

JEFF PORCARO D (CF GREG LADANYI PERC (C KENNY EDWARDS B (CF RICK MAROTTA D (CDF

ARTHUR GERST HARP (C LUIS DAMIAN JARANA (C DANNY KORTCHMAR G (CF MANUEL VASQUEZ (C

RUSS KUNKEL D (CF LEE SKLAR B (CDF JIM HORN SAX (CF LINDA RONSTADT V (CD

LINDA WARNES V (C JOHN McVIE B (C MICK FLEETWOOD D (C KARLA BONOFF V (C

SKIP BATTIN B (A DRACHEN THEAKER D (A ED CARAEFF PERC (A SWEET TRIFLES V (A

BRENT SEAWELL B (A TOXEY FRENCH D (A JON CORNEAL D (A GENTLEMEN BOYS V (BC

DON FELDER G (D JOE WALSH G (D STEVIE NICKS V (B JORDON ZEVON V (F

DAVID LANDAU G (EF ZEKE ZIRNGIRBEL G V (E BOB HARRIS K V (E ROBERTO PIRON B V (E

MARTY STINGER D (E STEVE LUKATHER G (F MIKE POTTS D (F STEVE FORMAN PERC(F

BOB GLAUB B (F GRAHAM NASH V (F

Z11A ## ZIGGYBYFIELD & THE BLACKHEART BAND Z11A

(A) RUNNING 1980 PVK UK PVK 1

Z12 ## ZIOR Z12

KEITH BONSOR V K B FLT(A (A) ZIOR 1971 NEPENTHA 6437 005

JOHN TRUBA G V (A

PETER BREWER D PNO HCA(A BARRY SKEELS B V (A

Z15 ## ZOMBIES Z15

COLIN BLUNSTONE V (B (A) BEGINS HERE 1965 DECCA UK LK 4679

ROD ARGENT K (B (B) ODESSEY & ORACLE 1968 CBS UK 63280 US DATE TES 4013

HUGH GRUNDY D (B (C) WORLD OF THE ZOMBIES 1970 DECCA UK SPA 85

PAUL ATKINSON G (B (D) TIME OF THE ZOMBIES 1973 EPIC UK 65728 RI 68262

CHRIS WHITE B (B (D) TIME OF THE ZOMBIES 1973 EPIC US 32861

PAUL ARNOLD B ((E) ROCK ROOTS (COMP) 1976 DECCA UK ROOTS2

(F) EARTHDAYS 19 LONDON US PS 557

(G) ZOMBIES (COMP) 19 PARROT US PAS71001

(H) SHES NOT THERE (DBL)(COMP) 1976 NOVA GERM 6/28378

Z16 ## ZON Z16

DENTON YOUNG V ((A) ASTRAL PROJECTOR 1978 EPIC PEC 90442

HOWARD HELM K ((B) BACK DOWN TO EARTH 1979 EPIC 80026

KIM HUNT D ((C) I'M WORRIED ABOUT THE BOYS 1980 FALCON 80003

JIM SAMSON B (

BRIAN MILLER G (

Z17 ## ZONES Z17

WILLY GARDNER G V (A (A) UNDER INFLUENCE(4 DIFF COVERS) 1979 ARISTA UK SPART 1095

BILLY McISAAC K V (A

RUSSELL WEBB B V (A KENNY HYSLOP D (A

Z18 ## ZOO Z18

PIERRE FANEN G (A (A) ZOO 19 BARCLAY 521172 RIVIERA521118

JOEL DAYDE V (A (A) ZOO 19 MAJOR MINOR UK SMLP 74

DANIEL CARLET VLN SAX (AB (B) I SHALL BE FREE 1971 RIVIERA 521147

MICHEL RIPOCHE VLN SAX (AB

TONY CANAL TPT (A ANDRE HERVE K (AB MICHEL BONNECARRERE G(AB MICHEL HERVE B (AB

CHRISTIAN DEVAUX D (AB IAN BELLAMY V (B

Z19 ## ZOO Z19

TROND NYRUD WIND (B (A) CAPTURED BY ZOO 1979

KETIL STOKKAN G V (B (B) NOREGS HEITASTE 1980 SNOWFLAKE CLP 3017

SVERRI DAHL K V (B (C) Z PA MAKEN 1981 SNOWFLAKE 3022

RUDI HOYNES TROM (b (D) GAYA 1981 SNOWFLAKE 3029

ROYER LARSEN B (B

Z20 ZORRO Z20

(A) 'ARRODS DON'T SELL 'EM (EP) 19 BRIDGE HOUSE BHEP 1

Z20A ZOUNDS Z20A

(A) CURSE OF THE ZOUNDS 1981 ROUGH TRADE UK

Z21 TAPPER ZUKIE Z21

TAPPER ZUKIE (ALL

MAN AH WARRIOR 1977 MER MER 101
IN DUB 19 STARS RI FRONT LINE FL1029
M P L A 19 KLICK RI FRONT LINE FL1006
MAN FROM BOSRAH 19 STARS
PEACE IN THE GHETTO 1978 FRONT LINE FL1009
TAPPER ROOTS 1978 FRONT LINE FL1032

Z22 ZWOL Z22

WALTER ZWOL K V (A
WOODY WEST G (A
RALPH MURPHY V (A
DENNIS PINHAM B V (A
GHIA CONGA(A
RACHEL SIMPSON V (A
CHARLES CHALMERS V SAX(A
DANNY SMITH D (A
DONNA RHODES V (A
KATHY JOHNSON V (A
SANDRA RHODES V (A
MARL GENDLE G (A
ROGER COOK V (A
STACEY HAYDEN G (A
JIM ISBELL D (A
PHILIP DONNELLY G (A
TONY NEWMAN B (A

(A) ZWOL 1978 EMI AMS 2003
(B) EFFECTIVE IMMEDIATELY 1981 EMI US 17014

Z22A ZYANKALI Z22A

PETER JAKOBI K V (A
DIETER BECK B G V(A
SOL DE SULLY PERC (A
WILLY MICHL V G PERC(A
BERNHARD TREUTWEIN EFFECTS(
KLAUS WEISS D (A
WALTER BRANDT G B (A

(A) I COULD CRY A LOTTA BLUES 1972 PLANE GER 1001

Z23 ZYGOAT Z23

(A) ZYGOAT 1975 POLYDOR 2383 270

Z24 ZZEBRA Z24

TERRY SMITH G (A
GUS YEADON PNO G V (A
LIAM GENOCKEY D V (AB
JOHN McCOY B (AB
LOUGHTY AMAO PERC SAX V(AB
KIM MOORE V (B
STEVE BYRD G (B
DAVE QUINCY SAX (AB
ALAN MARSHALL V (B
JO NEWMAN V (B
TOMMY EYRE K (B
LESLEY DUNCAN V (B

(A) ZZEBRA 1974 POLYDOR 2383 296
(B) PANIC 1975 POLYDOR 2383 326

Index

The index lists the main headings of each entry and all the musicians included. The references are to entry codes not page numbers. Main entries are indicated by a line under the code, e.g. ACE A7.

Various cross references have been provided between maiden, former, stage, real names etc.; all elements of composite group names have been indexed.

BALLARD Russ A50 A77 B25 B160 B174B C201A D9 F7B F36 N45A P77 S34 S253 U14
BALLBY Dave I20
BALLENTINE David W24
BALLERINI Freddie H19B
BALLEW Mike R53E W43
BALLEW Tom F90C
BALLIN Dixie C59
BALLIN Peter S124
BALLIN' JACK B25A
BALLINGER Dave B45
BALLINGER Dennis F22
BALLISTER Ann E18B
BALLOU Philip A102 H8 R164
BALLS B26
BALLUFF Thomas E77B
BALM Neil S86C
BALMAIN Andrew see PARKER Alan
BALSANO Phil T12B
BALSTON Latifa S93
BALTIK B26A
BALTIMORE Sir Lord S132A
BALZALL Ken B177 G9 Q12
BALZER Andre A114
BAMA B26B
BAMBOO B27
BAMBOO ZOO B27A
BAMI Eric K19
BAN Ray S333B
BANALI Frankie N57C
Banana see LEVINGER Lowell (K G)
Banana (STEEL) M46
BANCHEE B27B
BANCO B28
BAND B29
BAND CALLED 'O' O1
BAND OF GYPSYS H99
BAND OF JOY B30
BAND OF THIEVES B30A
BANDEL Jan L79 S39
BANDERA B31B
BANDIT (UK) B31
BANDIT (US) B31A
BANDOGGS B32
BANFORD Tony O33F
BANG B32A
BANHAM PETE B250
BANGOR FLYING CIRCUS B33
BANISTER John G15
BANJO Banjo D12
BANKES Carl J22
BANKS Anicea M221D
BANKS Brenton D139 M11
BANKS Brian J10E
BANKS Danny D27 S168
BANKS Darrell B33A
BANKS Don B37
BANKS Gordon G17
BANKS Homer B238
BANKS John M136
BANKS Johnny W12A
BANKS Kenneth E52B P26
BANKS Martin K51
BANKS Patryce D24 G80 L71B
BANKS Peter (G) B34 B136 D100 F63 S206 S358F Y7
BANKS Peter (K) A19
BANKS Robert L126 T154
BANKS Ron L143
BANKS Rose B34A
BANKS Stanley B85 M102
BANKS Tony B34B B178 G21
BANNERMAN Kari O34
BANNISTER Jeff B188 B222 R40B S253
BANNON Lorna S82A
BANUS Ruud P92B
BANSHEES S132
BANTON Hugh H13 S76 V11
BANZAI B35
Baps F4B
BAPTISTE David L71B S203A
BAPTISTE Selwyn N9
BAR-KAYS B36 E55
BARA Roger R80A
BARADOS Miguel H70
Baradras W119
BARAJAS George D127B
BARAKAN Mick B288 H185
BARANOWSKI Bobby W48C
BARARD David G4 L65 M149
BARBALACE Frank T139A
BARBARELLA B36A
BARBARIANS B36B
BARBARIN Lou S198A
BARBATA John B47A B149 C233 C234 E69 E75 J46 K10 M101 M144 N4 S65 S71A S157 S160 S196 S276 S298 T161 Y16
BARBATO Eddie F102
BARBE Dave A10
BARBEDA John C179
BARBER Bill D27 K88
BARBER Chris A101 G27 J97 S273 W117
BARBER Dan S314
BARBER Dick Z8
BARBER Don F139
BARBER Jack S7
BARBER John D27
BARBER Perry L80C
BARBER Trevor M145
BARBIER Dennis C113A
BARBIERI Gato B131
BARBIERI Richard J40
BARBOUR J. Spider C111 V21
BARBOUR Keith P16
BARBOZA Joseph T150A W63
BARBROOK Helen T37B
BARCLAY Bill B36C
BARCLAY Cynthia C155
BARCLAY Hamilton L16E
BARCLAY Nicole'Nickey' B38 C155 D26 F18 M191
BARCLAY JAMES HARVEST B37
BARCLAY JAMES HARVEST SYMPHONY ORCHESTRA B37
BARCUS Allen K77
BARDEN Gary S41
BARDEN Mike S45
BARDEN Phil S45
BARDENS Peter B39 C19 C97 G94 G110 M95 S105 T57 Y6
BARDOT B40 B174B
BARDUCCI Alfredo C24B
BARDWELL Duke H35 M95D R169
BARDWELL Gary B233
BARE Doug M111 W69A
BAREFOOT JERRY B41
BARENBERG Russ C199C
BARETH Harald A67K
BARFIELD Eluriel F60
BARFIELD Tinker H39A
BARGE Gene D66 H170
BARGER Joe R142A
BARGERON Dave B141 F4C J20 T67A
BARGERON Lee H162A
BARHAM John K4 L51 L111 R15
BARHAM Terry T166
BARIACHER Tom B197A
BARILE Joe S87A V24
BARISH Jesse B41B
BARKDULL Wiley K32
BARKER Baz H163
BAKER Buzz C250C
BARKER Criston A22C
BARKER David H110 I16 M50
BARKER Duke B233
BARKER George J8 K52
BARKER Guy C39A J16A O18
BARKER John (D) G32
BARKER John (K) F97A
BARKER Kenny J107 T168A
BARKER Mickey S66
BARKER Mike M15A
BARKER Ronnie J107
BARKER Ted F70B G29A
BARKHAM Terry G1
BARKOU Kaare B36A
BARKS Cliff H145
BARKSDALE Chuck D44
BARKSDALE Everett C146 F27A F128 M26
BARKSON Bernard W85
BARLAGE Tom A27 S187
BARLEY Gloria P6 S362 W119
BARLOW Barriemore D68 J58 L95C P138
BARLOW Bruce C173 M27
BARM Roger T171
Barnabas D130 J17C J17D R30
BARNABY Dick A68A
BARNACLE Bill R175A
BARNACLE Gary C210 H124B M1A R174B R175A S296A W7
BARNACLE Peter B220A G31 G36A
BARNARD Anne F74C
BARNARD Dave D51
BARNCARD Stephen C232
BARNES Billy M53
BARNES Bob Y6B
BARNES Clay F83A N48A
BARNES David F7C
BARNES Delores W119
BARNES Denny S14
BARNES Don T65
BARNES George C146 D139
BARNES Henry N50B
BARNES James (PERC) C153
BARNES Jim (V) C158A
BARNES Jim (HARP) T65
BARNES John (K) B226 C30 E30 F128 M75 M78 P44 P114 R115 S34 S85A S228 S251 S325 S333A W31
BARNES Johnny (Sax) A50A M5 P100
BARNES Max.D. B41C
BARNES Lucian S65
BARNES Mike L48A
BARNES Patrick B41A D77D
BARNES Peter M221
BARNES Phil A67C
BARNES Richard H66A H67 S177D
BARNES Sid C17 L126 R144 W84C
BARNES Sylvia B51
BARNES Tim C208A S284
BARNETT Bob K94B M51
BARNETT Brian H58A
BARNETT Marcus K45
BARNETT Mike F71
BARNETTE Frances F48
BARNEY Tom C164
BARNHAM Stuart S236
BARNHELDT Terge B36A
BARNHILL KEVIN B31A
BARNSTORM W16
BARNUM Billy H179
BARNUM H.B. B281
BARNWELL Bill I25B
BARNWELL Carl H43 M108 S198
BARNY David R77
BAROLLETTI Danielle S280
BARON Art T25 W119
BARON Bill F74B T54
BARON Greg J84
BARON Kenny C44 R132C
BARON Mike F26
BARON Pete R15
BARON Ronnie W64
Baron Samedi E78
BARONE Bill W13D
BARONE Gary K94A M86 M101 Z8
BARONE Mike A65C M68
BAROOGA BANDIT B42
BAROOSHIAN Eleanor C11
BAROQUES B42A
BARR Chris R121A
BARR George A121B
BARR Hugh N59
BARR John C113
BARR Ralph N53
BARR Shug R15
BARR Walt B42B
BARRABAS B43
BARRACLOUGH Elizabeth B43C
BARRACLOUGH Nick T37H
BARRACUDAS B43D
BARRADA Antonio C26 H150
BARRADAS Miguel A99A B48
BARRANCO John B57A
BARRATT BAND B43E
BARRATT Mike see STEVENS SHAKIN S268
BARRATT Norman B43E
BARRAZA Steve A130
BARRE Bruno G123
BARRE Martin C112 J58 P138 W54A
BARRELHOUSE B43A
BARRELHOUSE BUCK B43B
BARRELLA Ed W125A
BARRERE Paul C45 D8 H10 J85A K17 L19 L89 P15 R22 S20 S124 V18A W65A
BARRETT Aston 'Family Man' B276 D71A M53 M88 P2 S190 T114 U20 V21 W4
BARRETT Austin 'Doughnut' M191A
BARRETT Ben A131D Z8
BARRETT Bucky Y16
BARRETT Carlton M88 P2 S190 T114 U20 V21 W4
BARRETT Clive F53
BARRETT Don G92B R4 T32A
BARRETT Malcolm B211
BARRETT Marcia B174
BARRETT Mike A74
BARRETT Norman G85 M67 W13C W15A
BARRETT Patterson W11
BARRETT Ray S280A
BARRETT Stan P139G S157
BARRETT Syd B44 P85
BARRETT Wayne S153
BARRETT Wild Willy (G) H172 O40
BARRETT Willy (FDL) F76
BARRETTO Ray A131 B71 C147 C234 C255 D50 F17 M78 W106
BARRI Steve B127 C51 D74 E40 F18B F92 M30 S108D
BARRIATUNA Bob P141A
BARRIERE Jean Baptiste P18A
BARRIERE Jean Marie P18A
Barrington S11
BARRINO BROTHERS B44B
BARRIO Rick E71A
BARRON Kenny C44
BARRON Peter A28B R65
BARRON Ronnie B44A B268 B282 C38A C123 C179 D86 K45 M111 O15 R54 W6
BARRON KNIGHTS B45
BARROW Arthur Z8
BARROW Dave H108
BARROW George M41 M79 S168
BARROWMAN Mike C15B
BARRY Alan F44 H54
BARRY Auburn M36
BARRY David J41 M108 N25
BARRY Gary F128
BARRY Jeff L51 M203 P67
BARRY John S328A
BARRY Len D106D
BARRY Lloyd A45
BARRY Philip C175 R53C
BARRY Sandra also ALICE SPRING S150
BARRY Susi R68
BARRY Tom N2B
BARRY & THE REMAINS R64
BARSON Ben L16C L135 R12
BARSON Mike M46A
BARTA Tamas L103
BARTEK Steve O13A
BARTEL Andy Y8B
BARTEL Beate L66C
BARTEL Jon B45B
BARTELMES Karl B174
BARTES Ellis B233
BARTH Bill I21 W59
BARTH Bobby A131C B7B
BARTH Peter H18B
BARTH Steve I22
BARTHELME Rick R53
BARTHOL Bruce F85C M18
Bartholomew A67H
BARTHOLOMEW Dave D96
BARTI Kim L100A
BARTKOWSKI Czeslaw U21
BARTLE John D1D
BARTLETT Bill L49 R19
BARTLETT David T119
BARTLETT Larry C6
BARTLETT Michael see Henry VIII
BARTLETT Richie B228A F81D
BARTLETT Roger B261
BARTLETT Ted A94
BARTLEY Jock F50 H120 P33 Z10
BARTLEY John C174A
BARTNEY Kathy P34
BARTOLI Tony P53
BARTOLIN Bill 'Cupid' B149A
BARTON Carrie W119B
BARTON Cliff B23 D99 F14
BARTON Dee G15
BARTON Gordon A63A E60
BARTON Kristi C35C
BARTON MICHAEL & THE GROOVERS B45C
BARTON Robert B66 L63
BARTON Trevor P91
BARTOS Karl K92
BARTZ Gary B45D D27 G122 J75A L41
BARUTZKY Chris A3A
BARWELL Buzz L62
BARWISE Alan C132
BARWISE Mic C132
BASBERRY Larry N55
BASCOMB Doug U18
BASCOMB Wilbur B64 B85 B87 B169A D66 D97A H137 J92 J93D M69 N39 P99 T79B
BASCOMBE Dud C146
BASEMENT 5 B45F
BASEORE Stu A95 B17A
BASHAN Neil B45A
BASHFORD Chris C95
BASHO Robbie B45E
BASKERVILLE Priscilla M12
BASKIN Don S360
BASKIN Lloyd O33A S63
BASKIN Sandra O33A
BASORE Stu K30
BASS Carvel M18
BASS Colin C19 C119 H119 Q1
BASS Fontella A89 L90
BASS James G92
BASS Jewel T32A
BASS Keith B238
BASS Michael B46 L119A
BASS Stella I27
BASS Willie O48
BASSICK Arturo L142 P86
BASSIL Richard B23A
BASSINI Rubens A131 C103C D50 G113A H156 H164C I2 J48 K38 M26 M41 M111 N65 O13 O32 P123 R25 R99 R125 S124 S215 S231 T147
BASSINSON Kevin D87B
BASSO Guido S274
BASSO Rob P53
BASTARD B47
BASTARDOS Carlos B47
BASTEN Ralf U23
BASTOW Geoff J10A
BATAAN Joe L21
BATARD Didier H89A P83B
BATCHELL Forrest B141
BATCHELOR Cal A133 C148 K38 M108 Q17 S270
BATCHELOR David H52 T37
BATCHELOR Keith A133
BATCHELOR Leroy M129
BATDORF John A59 B47A M101 S117
BATDORF & RODNEY B47A
BATE Jim O33B
BATEMAN Rick J86
BATEMAN Tony S302A
BATERA Chico R99
BATERA Chris D103 S266
BATES David (Perc) M41A
BATES David (V) D6B
BATES Ed S224A
BATES Frank G17
BATES Howard S153
BATES Kenneth F133
BATES Lefty G122 R59
BATES Martyn E78A
BATES Phil F14 H11 L57 T138B
BATEY Peter H40 J109
BATH Brian B280
BATH Willie C70 R146
BATHELT Hans T143
BATISE Javier C26
BATISTE Larry S325
BATISTE Paul L63
BATLES Peter A6D
BATLEY Noeleen S313
BATORS Stiv B47D D32 W16B
BATRON James S73C
BATSON Billy H139A H19B
BATSON Ernest H19B
BATSTONE Billy F139
BATT Matt R23

COLLIER Greg S117
COLLIER Jack F70B
COLLIER Kathryn A116 C107 E40 G101B H156 W119
COLLIER Pat V28
COLLIER Tom C179
COLLIER Tony W115
COLLINGE Craig M80 P139D S102B T63
COLLINGS Kevin M211B
COLLINS Albert C162
COLLINS Allen L146 R143A
COLLINS Anne S295
COLLINS Ansel B95A B117 B234 C163 C245 D63 D130 G39 J17B J17C J17D L58A P140C R29 R30 R35B R84 R150 T155A U4A W4A
COLLINS Bernard A6
COLLINS Bill (D) M173
COLLINS Bill (V) M18
COLLINS Bobby L100B
COLLINS Burt B85 B168 D50 I2 J48 L58B M75 M107 P6 R100 R125
COLLINS Carter C.C. B256 H59 M68 N65 O10
COLLINS Charlene B247 R106 S264
COLLINS Charles (D) A96 A123 C203 C249 L69 O14 S115 S128 T42
COLLINS Charlie(SAX) C140C
COLLINS Charlie (V) W119
COLLINS Clarence L85
COLLINS Dave C163
COLLINS Dennis W107
COLLINS Denver C164
COLLINS Dolly C165 D17 E41 M108 Y21
COLLINS Edmund L86
COLLINS Edwyn O28C
COLLINS Elmira B238 G17
COLLINS Frank A85 B21 B189 C7 D9 D54 F8 F42 G32 H56 H65 K76 K84 L37 M5 M41A N45C P100 S84 S285 S313
COLLINS Glen P29
COLLINS Glyn G67A
COLLINS Harlan K99A
COLLINS Howard D139 F27A H59
COLLINS Jack M47C
COLLINS John (G) M229 R142A S14C T37H

LOFGREN Nils C216 L107 M16 S276 Y16
LOFGREN Tom L107
LOGAN Bud E54
LOGAN Ed B202 C62 D86 G92 G101A M130 N57 P51 P125 S276
LOGAN John P106 S203
LOGAN Mal G26A
LOGAN T. R67
LOGAN Todd A37 H195
LOGEMAN David Z8
LOGGINS Dan S253
LOGGINS Dave B261 H7D L108
LOGGINS Ken C70A G15 G106A L109 L110 M16A N53 S20 S55A
LOGGINS AND MESSINA L110
LOGIC Lora E66A R17 R53 S292 S354A X2
LOGIC SYSTEM L110A
LOHMANN Michael J4B
LOHR Tommy H125B
LOHR Werner H26B S38
LOHSE Wertehr L70A
LOILE Jim F139
LOIZZO Gary A51
LOJEWSKI Rainer E56B
LOKEY Tommy R173
LOLLIPOP SHOPPE L110B
LOMAS Roger D90
LOMAX Dwayne K46 W118
LOMAX Jackie B17 B149 B26 D26 H84 L111 L112 R22 U10
LOMAX ALLIANCE L112
LOMBAR Dru C207 G104 T9A
LOMBARD Carole P125
LOMBARDI Mike R39
LOMBARDO Sam E71A
LONDIN Larry A95 B57F C124 C194 C237 E57 E75 H35 H49 H117 J53 K30 K77 L108 M157 N25 N37 R4 S32 S269 T55 Y16
LONDON L113
LONDON Dobbie J93D
LONDON John C188 F109 M113 N25 N53 T25 T140
LONDON Lew G72
LONDON Mark B77
LONDON Mike K28B M19 R106
LONDON Richard (Svor Naan) C213B
LONDON CHAMBER CHOIR M15A
LONDON PHILHARMONIC ORCHESTRA E34
LONDON SYMPHONY ORCHESTRA G27 L120 N54 W7 Y16
LONDON WELSH CHOIR S177D
Lone Groover L113A
LONE STAR L114
Lonesome Sundown (GREEN Cornelius) L115
LONEY Roy A. F61 L115A
LONG Danny K77
LONG Dino L81 M158B
LONG Gary C173A
LONG Joey F91
LONG Julie B42B
LONG Mike C156
LONG Shorty P125
LONG Steve N13
LONG HELLO L117A
LONG TALL ERNIE L115B
LONGBOTTOM Pete P104A
LONGBRANCH PENNYWHISTLE L116
LONGDANCER E41 L117
LONGHAIR Professor L118
LONGMIRE Wilbert L119 P115
LONGO John L4 M46B M149 M157
LONGORIA Carlos B242B
LONGSTAFF Gordon N44
LONIE Clive J94
LONIE Lonie P18D
LONNEN Steve S102A
LONNEUX Francis R51D
LONNIE Clarence W94
LONSDALE Shep C85
LOOK Richard C86A
LOOKING GLASS L119B
LOOKOFSKY Harry L45 M233 M233
LOONAM John P142B
LOONEY Phil P53
LOONEY Warren P114
LOOP Bill E19B
LOOS Charles C190 J105B L26A
LOOSIGIAN Billy A32
LOPAC Gary L16B
LOPER Charles C70A C156 C213E E7 F92 H8A H156 K48 Q12 R99 W84C
LOPEZ Amaury R13A
LOPEZ Anita W21B
LOPEZ Barbara B246A
LOPEZ Becky B9 C246 J10B R142A
LOPEZ Chris N11A
LOPEZ Dennis A98 J72 M15A P139G T47
LOPEZ Vini 'Mad Dog' S229
LOPRESTI John 'Cooker' B157 C107 C182 M65A S252
LOPREVITE Franco N60
LORANGE Kirk D121 H40 L101
LORBER Alan U7
LORBER Jeff L119C
LORCK John T97
LORD Barry T135A
LORD David K83
LORD Jon A92 A100 B174B B208B C204 D40 H91 L120 M90A P9 R96 R147 S22 W117
LORD Tracy L85
LORDAN Bill A53A T148
LORDAN Erin J110
LORDAN Petrina J110
LORDS L121
LORENZ Dave M242A
LORENZ Ding B145A
LORENZ Gene G117C
LORENZ Wolfgang B92
LORENZINI Mimi E18B
LORENZO Randy C179
LORIX George O33B
LORMANN Klaus E34A
LORMOR Michael S295A
LOS BRAVOS L121B
LOSEKAMP Michael C255
LOSEKES BLUES GANG L121C
LOSETH Janny T97
LOSIER Gilles M21
LOS INCAS S125
LOST AND FOUND L121A
LOST GONZO BAND L122
LO TEMPIO Rick B17A
LOTHAR AND THE HAND PEOPLE L122A
LOTT Carl B233
LOTT Sinclair Rogers W119B
LOUBET Roger W39D
Loud Lance M226
LOUDEN Rob W128A
LOUDERMILK John D. L123
LOUDSPEAKERS L124
LOUENS Paul G47
LOUGHAN Colin S147 Y4B
LOUGHNANE Lee A65 B71 C100 R173 V38
LOUHENSALO Tapio W75
LOUIE Doug J15A
LOUIS Becky (or Becci) R137 S34 S58
LOUIS Daniel B43
LOUIS Elmer D43A H57A P34
LOUIS Huey see LEWIS Huey
LOUIS Joe Hill L125 T74
LOUIS Rebecca D124 S252 S262
LOUIS Roger Hayward D96
LOUIS Roy P34
Louisiana Red (MINTER Iverson) L126 W22A
LOUNDER MAN Gus B280A
LOUNGE Eugene W47
LOUNGE LIZARDS L126A
LOU'S L127
LOUSLEY Brian S283A
LOUSTAU Henri A64
LOUTS S212
LOVE L128
LOVE Airrion S31A
LOVE Andrew B43C B202 C133 C231 D86 D101 F50 G92 G101A H65 J85A K45 L19 M85 M130 M209 N23 N57 P51 P137 S124 S276 T27 W119B
LOVE Arthur L128
LOVE Billy 'Red' L125 T74
LOVE Brad A131A
LOVE Candy H19
LOVE Charles B143
LOVE Clayton L128A
LOVE Darlene B224A B226 C38A J73A P74 P125 S135B S200 T67A
LOVE Jerry M32
LOVE Mike B56 C62B K58 L97 L129
LOVE Preston O39
LOVE Stephen H9 H164C I2 J65A L98 M27 N21 N32 S286
LOVE Steve JM46B
LOVE Stuart Q5
LOVE AFFAIR L129A
LOVE COMMITTEE L130
LOVE SCULPTURE L130C
LOVE TOGETHERNESS DEVOTION L2
LOVECRAFT L130A
LOVEDAY Billy E31F
LOVEDAY Bob W96
LOVEDAY Martin O40
LOVEGROVE Kelly S249C
LOVELACE David C160 K68C M27
LOVELACE Jimmy B85 D67 R77B
LOVELACE Ken L64
LOVELADY Billy M114A
LOVELADY Dave F93
LOVELESS Jim D67 R77B
LOVELL Herbie A59 A68 B149 B157 B160B B194 B262 D139 K45 M94 M203 P49 R169 S168 W28
LOVELL Mike J2
LOVERBOY L130B
LOVERING John F30C
LOVETRO Gary S294
LOVGREN Bertil L79
LOVICH Lene D78E L131 S348 V25B
LOVIN' SPOONFUL L133
LOVINE Jimmy P70
LOVING Jim M141
LOVING Keith H58
LOVING AWARENESS L132
LOW Andy Fairweather see FAIRWEATHER LOW Andy
LOW Pit M136B
LOW NUMBERS L134
LOWARCH Dave B247
LOWE Albert J22
LOWE Colin M52
LOWE Dan F90B
LOWE Helen R161
LOWE Jeff A82A
LOWE Jim E35
LOWE John N25 T37H
lowe Mundell C213E
LOWE Nick (Bazza) B218 C42 C105 C193 C234E D10 D123 E19 F3B G79 J110 K62 L135 M10C M157 P25 W130
LOWE Phil T64A
LOWE Richard S23A
LOWE Sammy H63
LOWE Steven M188A
LOWE Thadeus James S205
LOWELL Jimmy S86C S214A
LOWENTHAL Barry T33A
LOWER EAST SIDE P53
LOWERY Jim H7
LOWERY Robert A51B
LOWNER Peter F8D
LOWREY Gene C50
LOWRY John S359
LOWTHER Clare D111 F6
LOWTHER Henry A60A A74 B98 B237 B248 C2 C34 C109 C145A C159 C204 C251 D7 D108 E24 E38 F6 F14 F42 F86 F125 G11 G32 G71A G102 H50 H64 H70 H116C H176 I20 K84 L104 L136 M6 M80 M83 M111 P76 P127 Q2 R85 S93 S152 T76 T79 T95 W58
Loy N64A
LOYA Bobby E30
LOYALE Dale H146A
LOYDE Lobby A137
LOZAGA Bon G66
LOZANO Pauline M203
Lu see EDMUNDS Robert
LUANDREW Albert see Sunnyland Slim
LUBAHN Douglas C138 D103 D115 E75 P80A R86A S232A
LUBAN Morris W86
LUBBOCK Jeremy L56C R97
LUBIN Howard Lem H185 M180 S27 U14
LUCAFO Phil H78
LUCAS Alfred C146 S171
LUCAS Arno C213 D133A J93C N40 R125 W119B
LUCAS Buddy B85 C146 D97A H99 R169 T79B V34
LUCAS David B154
LUCAS Douglas J3
LUCAS Harold C144A
LUCAS Jon P6
LUCAS Kate W112
LUCAS Keith see CASH Nick
LUCAS Paulina K54
LUCAS Pete D20
LUCAS Ray A27 C146 F60 H58 K17 K55 S128
LUCAS Reggie D27 F60 L41 M222A
LUCAS Rob B45C
LUCAS Roy B45C
LUCAS Sharalee L136A
LUCAS Soo I23C
LUCAS Stan s254B
LUCAS Ted T42
LUCAS Trevor B222 B266 C206 D49 E12 F6 F89 G110 G111 L137 S270 S295 T79 W20B
LUCCA Papo F17
LUCCI Mario P156B
LUCE John A104
LUCERO Geno G112A
LUCHESSI Joe B13A
LUCIA Peter H126A J30
LUCIANO Bravo T162
LUCIEN Jon J75A W36
LUCIER Bob W101
Lucifer see WALKER Pete
LUCIFER L138
LUCIFER'S FRIEND L139
LUCK Jerry S73
LUCKE Johannes T11
LUCKEY Lena R173
LUCKLEY Margi H87
LUCKLEY Stu H87
LUCKY Cab W22A
LUDDECKE Larry F19A
LUDEWIG Peter E31D
LUDLUM Steve T48
LUDMAN Kim S339
LUDUS L139A
LUDWICK Rex F128 R173
LUDWIG Frank A69 I25A T146 U13B
LUDWIG Rex N23A
LUELL David A37 B225 C39 C158 F103C F128 K72 L1 M65A M93 M232 N45C S34 S281 T37H W54
LUENING Warren B53 D86 L50
LUER Karl Hermann L139
LUFT Lorna B139
LUGO Frank Q9
LUHRING Les G7e
LUHRMANN Joachim f8D
LUKATHER Steve A35C A50 A123 B53 B85 B194 C6B C45 C63D C70A C213E C227 D104 E7 E57 F100 H9 J10B J72 J93C K17 K99A L9A L56C M10B M16A M75 M102 M111 M170 N4 N42 N53 R99 R142A S34 S36 T1 T12 T37H T115 T143 W32A W84C W119B W133 Z11
LUKAWIETSKY Rumor T149B
LUKENS Malcolm B253 S173B
LUKER Mal S313
LUKISKI Terry B81
LUKYN Tony H73 S48 T131
LULEY Klaus T103B
LULIS Peter W125A
Lulu (LAWRIE Marie L27 L140
LUMAN Robert Glynn 'Bob' L141
LUMIA Guy S215
LUMLEY Robin B195 B203 C251 E77A H169 L15 S23 S97 W82A
LUMLEY-SAULE John S295
LUMSDEN Allan C165 D17 H194
LUNCH Lydia C177D L141A
LUND Zeke S173B
LUNDGREN Erik V18A
LUNDGREN Ken B89
LUNDQUIST Dag T138A
LUNDY Curtis W30A
LUNETTA Rick D77
LUNGREN Zappo R38
LUNNY Andy M41A
LUNNY Donal B185 C120 K24 M221E O2C P93 S230 W61
LUNT Tony C41A
LUPICA Frank S91
LUPPER Kenneth P126
LURE Walter H76 T86
LURIE Elliot L119B
LURIG Heiner S38
LURKERS L142
LURO Dominique S280
LUSHER Don C2 K84 R40B S31 W86
LUSSENDEN Bill B158
LUSTGARTEN Edgar B17 F19
LUSTGARTEN Robert A59
LUSTREA Robert M115
Luther D139
LUTHER Donald D122C
LUTHJENS Gustav A19A
LUTTICK Johannes F133A
LUTTON Davey B168 E26 E46 H84 S209
LUTTRELL Terry R1A S246
LUTZ Michael B246
LUVVERS L140
LUX Casimierz B197A
Lux Interior C212B
LUX Jeff W15A
LUX Kaz A27
LUXURY Neville P148
LYALL Graham L92 S312
LYALL William L142A P81B R164A
LYCETT Kevin M124
LYDON John see ROTTEN Johnny
LYEFOOT Byron B160 K24
LYLE Bobby B52A B85 C11B C147 H96 L28 L65 L71B L128 L143 M68 P72A W8 W133 Y6B
LYLE Graham A82 C121 D49 E22 F6 F7 G6 G10 L16A M29 T122
LYLE Joy G76C
LYLES Chipper I25B
LYMAN Mel K101
LYMAN Steve S2
LYMON Frankie L144
LYN Robert 'Robbie' B117 D63 D130 F86 I12 R150 T114
LYNAM John S327
LYNAS Stewart P25
LYNCH Bruce B224B B280 C201A H70 I20 J110 R46 S266 S334 T79 W7
LYNCH Carl A59B C146 D66 F133 J93D
LYNCH David P97
LYNCH Eddie C30B C97
LYNCH Frances S140
LYNCH George D93H
LYNCH Kenny W7
LYNCH Larry K40
LYNCH Sean N73A
LYNCH Stan N45B P70 S89 T137A
LYNCH Suzanne H70 I24A M80 N57 S266 Y11
LYNCH Tim F61
LYNDON Dewey see OLDHAM Spooner
LYNDON Frank B80A
LYNES Roy S255
LYNG Karsten D31
LYNGSTAD-FREDRIKSSON Frida A4
LYNN Barbara L144A

LYNN Bill F127
LYNN Bonnie see BRAMLETT Bonnie
LYNN Brenda E8
LYNN Cheryl M111 T115
LYNN Ian B174B B237 D54 E8 L80A R11 R164A
LYNN Loretta T167
LYNN Nicholas S97
LYNN Roger T!&$
LYNN Sue F13 S313
LYNN Tammy D86 R133
LYNN-DEAN Jesse W26
LYNNE Jeff E34 I7 M219 N48
LYNNE Michael S298B
LYNON George G85
LYNOTT Phil L144B M196 T59 T86
LYNTON Jackie H74 L145 S31
LYNYRD SKYNYRD L146
LYON Anthony Del Monte B224A
LYON Jimmy M179
LYON Johnny S199
LYONS Barry F59 M166 T137
LYONS Gary O43
LYONS Gerry C182
LYONS Graham M227
LYONS James (V) M236A
LYONS Jamie C30A
LYONS Jill C63
LYONS Jimmy (Sax) B56 M79
LYONS Ken H193 T65
LYONS Leo B166A C112 I45 V26A
LYONS Richard N14B
LYONS Sean M140
LYONS Tim D38
LYONS Trigger C6
LYONS Willie James E35C L145A
LYRICKS Mattie C52B
LYSHOLMORTENSEN Borge D83A
LYTH Geoff V26
LYTTON Paul W68

'M' M1A
M.C.5 M1
M.F.S.B. K80 M2 P56B P59C
M.G's B180 M3
M.P.G. M3A
M.X.80 SOUND M4
MAAHN Wolf F81B
MAAOCH William F. F51
MAAS Kees K32C
MAASS Antonia B186
MAASS Jurgen L47C
MAASS M.M. C219B
MAAT Ferry A27
MABEL M4A
MABON Willie B21 M5 R128 R168 S323 Y15
MABOUL Aqeak A71A
MABRY Bill A102
MABRY Lynn F137
MABY Graham J10 R35B
MAC Bill (or Willie) A104A B205A
MAC Tony F94
McAFEE Jimmy S251
McAFEE Rick S251
McALEA Kevin B37 B73 S139 S312A
McALLISTER Don D53C
McALLISTER Jimmy Y3A
McALLISTER Laurie O29B R163
McALLISTER Mayo James B68
McALPIN Lee P63
MACALUSO Lenny B224A L53
McANDREW Snake L81
MACARA Nigel A79
McARDLE George L92
MACARTHUR Neil see BLUNSTONE Colin
McARTHUR Neil F16A
McATEE Big John P47
McATEER Paul S333D
McAULEY Jackie C30 M6 T57 T125
McAULEY Matthew H117
McAULEY Robin G81A
McAULEY Pat T57
McAULIFFE Kim G37
McAULIFFE Pat K33
McAULIFFE Vivienne C78 M200 P72 P136 R11 V18B
McAVOY Gerry G5
MACAVOY Grant B135
McBAIN Neil D54 E62 H11
McBAIN Nicko S300 S301 T135
McBEE Cecil S73C S169
MACBETH Peter F90A
McBOOKER Lonnie P26
McBRAIN Nicko T151A
McBRIDE Barry F102C
McBRIDE Bob H31 L74 L75 L115
McBRIDE Curtis A35D
McBRIDE Danny (G) B57F K53
McBRIDE Danny (D) G112A
McBRIDE Mike (D) C38 R35
McBRIDE Mike (B/G) B41
McBRIDE Pat N29B
McBRIDE Reggie B149 C6B C179 F8B H119 J72 K94A L79A M203 O15 P126 R15 R32 S180 s362 T107 T109 W119
McBRIDE Richie H12A
McBRIDE Robin M151
McBURNEY Charles D13 S7
McBURNIE John B231 C78 D39 J14 J112A M200 R11 V18B
McCABE Bruce L14
McCAFFERTY Dan E77A M7 N14
McCAFFERTY Mo S177D S178
McCAFFREY Denny C108 R174
McCAFFREY Mary M125
McCAFFREY Pat B123 B246
McCAIN Alva C146
McCAIN Tiemeyer G26A L10A
McCALL Cash U18
McCALL Debbie B261
McCALL Marti B8 C76 C217 C234D E40 E71 F103C G121 H150 I32 M18 M179 M218 N42 P129 R137 S36 S51 S58 S272 V18A
McCALLA Everton L71B
McCALLA Noel C39A D54 M7A M190 R5 R174B S178
McCALLEN Marcus P112
McCALLEY Russ S249C
McCALLISTER Don G61
McCALLISTER Jim R177
McCANDLESS Gerry M191A
McCANDLESS Paul O30
McCANN David R66C
McCANN Jerry S106
McCANN Peter R66C
McCARL Scott R35
McCARTHY Charles M53 P21 W97
McCARTHY David G124
McCARTHY Dennis F62A
McCARTHY Eldridge F134
McCARTHY Jeff J8
McCARTHY Jim G58 M8
McCARTHY John D99
McCARTHY Justin M211B
McCARTHY Kevin C223 T131
McCARTHY Mike see PATTO Mike
McCARTHY Michael C174A
McCARTHY Patrick Daniel C185H
McCARTHY Tommy L117 N57
McCARTNEY Linda L7 M9 M23 S124 S252 T25
McCARTNEY Mike see McGEAR Mike
McCARTNEY Paul B59 B89A C222 L7 L111 M9 M100E M159 S115D S124 S252 T25
McCARTNEY Sheila F30C
McCARTY Jim (D/G-U.K.) C59 C121 H188 I13 M151 R65 W94 Y5
McCARTY Jim (G-U.S.) C5 H99 K46 M151 R123 R177 S73
McCARTY Jim (K) S102B
McCARTY Mike C200 H9
MACCARTY Ray C198 H150
McCASHEN Tony S135B
McCASLIN Mary T21
McCAULEY Bill O3
McCAULEY Matthew E15 K99A M10B
McCAULEY Mavis I25A
McCAULEY Mike I34
McCLAIN James D72B
McCLAIN Marlon S325
McCLAIN Van S103A
McCLARTY Jim S75A
McCLARY Tommy C174
McCLAVAN Doug B47E
McCLELLAN David M113
McCLELLAN Mike W106
McCLELLAND Billy Earl M9A V18
McCLEOD Ernest 'Sterling' C139
McCLEOD Race J14
McCLINTON Delbert M10
McCLMORE Mary Beth M10
McCLOONE Annie E23 G101B
McCLOUD Andrew M26
McCLURE Belinda 'Bomb' Q5
McCLURE Donald (Hrns) S56
McCLURE Don (K) W11
McCLURE John C13 C15 F70
McCLURE Les H64
McCLURE Marc E45 M10A P112 S203
McCLURE Patrick C52A
McCLURE Ron B131 D141 F115 M79 P114
McCLURE Tommy B97 B202 C179 C180 M229 W64
McCLUSKEY Andy O29A
McCLUSKY David M10B
McCLYMONT David O28C
McCOLL Deborah M232
MACCOLL Kirsty A23 M10C
McCOLL Lachlan H69
McCONNELL Rob S274
McCONVILLE Tom M50
McCOOK Tommy A6 B234 C139 C245 D71A D130 G39 M149 P135 P140C R35B T110 T166 W4
McCORD Bill M198
McCORD Kat F3A S17
McCORD Steve A28C R31
McCORKLE George D12 M93
MACCORMICK Bill E24C E59 H129B M81 M106 Q13 W135
McCORMICK Charles B143
McCORMICK Gayle S164A
McCORMICK Herman L128
MACCORMICK Ian M81 Q13
McCORMICK Kevin M111
McCORMICK Maureen M179
McCORMICK Randy A123 B126 B213 C39D C155 C213E G85A H7D H92 J11 J14A L34A L35 L146 M10 M65A M235 P80 R4 S73 S340 T39 W16A W97A W118
McCOY Billy B127
McCOY Bob M75
McCOY Charlie (Hca) A59 A75 B17A B41 B43C B210 C14 C50 C194 D21 D104 D139 F7 F35A G72 G85A H62 J13 J30 J31 J53 K30 K81 K95 K96 L72 L108 M11 M75 M159 M238A N37 P49 P63 P125 R31 R79A R173 S10 S73 S125 S252 S272 T107 T153A Y18
McCOY Charlie (G) W93
McCOY Gregory K47
McCOY John (V/Harm) T128
McCOY John (B) G31 Z24
McCOY Larry C50
McCOY Pat R78
McCOY Robert Lee W93
McCOY Van F103 M12 R159
McCOYS M13
McCRACKEN Charles (Cello) C164 G72 O15 S215
McCRACKEN Charlie (B) A131E A133 D28 F12 F94 M121 W41
McCRACKEN Chester A50 E72
McCRACKEN Chet D101 F99A G29 W133A
McCRACKEN Gary M112
McCRACKEN Hugh A59 A96 A123 B53 B77 B110 B125E B141 B199B C40 C44 C51 C134 C164 C185F C213D C213E C234A C236 D86 D97A E40 F4C F60 F84 F103D F108A G10 G27 G72 G102 G109 H9 H136A I2 I21 J20 J48 J69 K45 K51 K84A L4A L109 M9 M12 M21 M41 M125 M143 M203 M225 N63D N65 O15 O27 P25 P72A R102 R140 R159 R169 S50 S124 S125 S180 S262 T25 T37E T67A T98 W5 W44A W133
McCRACKEN Jodi C185F
McCRACKEN Richard G5 S309 T16
McCRACKEN Scot C185F
McCRACKLIN Jimmy B233 M13A
McCRAE Dave A74 B195 C161C T89
McCRAE George R12
McCRAE George (V) L24 W136
McCRAE Gwen L24 W136
McCRAE Shel F87
McCRAIG Annie S177D S178
McCRARY Charity M65A W119
McCRARY Everett H150
McCRARY Linda M65A W119
McCRAY Steve A111
McCREARY Lew A131 A131D B127 C162 C164 C180 C213E C234D D36A D99 E7 F92 F134 H8A L50 M65A M68 M229 N16A N25 P28 R78 R99 R161 S58 S252 S262 T32B
McCREARY Macey L7
McCREARY Mary see RUSSELL Mary
McCRORIE Shand Andrew D122
McCRORY Martha D139 G72 J53 M11
McCUBBEN Terry T150B
McCUBBON Bill B268
McCUE Sammy A1 E74 Y5B
McCUEN John A132
McCULLER Andrew M65A
McCULLER Arnold B110 B242A C249 H8 H164C J48 K86 M177 P119 R125 R137 R164 S252 T25 W119B
McCULLEY Melody B123 W119
McCulloch B231 P145A
McCULLOCH Andrew F44 G97 K54 M35 M80
McCULLOCH Danny A67 K52
McCULLOCH Jack A63A T84
McCULLOCH Ian E11B
McCULLOCH Jimmy D9 D127C E60 G29 H29 K20 L27 M9 M23 M111 S283 T47 T84
McCULLOUGH David S284
McCULLOUGH Henry B268 C35D C78 C155 D84 E26 F7 F104 G86 H29 H116C H123 L7 L101 M9 M15 M157 S224 S346
McCULLOUGH Ullanda A96 A123 B141 B155 D63 F60 G64C H164C M93 M111 R100 R142A S124 S169 T37E Z3B
MACCULLUM Paul M178
McCULLUM Robert see NIGHTHAWK Robert
McCUNE Ida S160
McCUNE Susie L72
McCURDY Pat Y8B
McCURDY Ron M111
McCURDY Roy B141 R28B
McCURN George C179
McCUSKER Phil E78B
McCUSKER Terry C165A
McCUSKER Vince F131
McCUTCHEON Donnie K59A
McDADE Butch A45
McDADE Steve S55B
McDANIEL Carl N28
McDANIEL Elias see DIDDLEY Bo
McDANIEL Lenny L21B M111
McDANIEL Wally L21B
McDANIEL Willard J21
McDANIELS Buddy M111 W54B
McDANIELS David A35C A120 F23A H166 W21
McDANIELS Ernie H8A J41
McDANIELS Eugene F60
McDANIELS Pete B106
McDERMOTT Denny S97
McDERMOTT Tom M192A
McDONAGH Johnny D38
McDONAGH Terence S157
McDONALD Al M93
McDONALD Andy S212
McDONALD Barry D139
MACDONALD Bertie L71A
MACDONALD Betty T134
McDONALD Billy John G112B
McDONALD Brian S296A
McDONALD Bonnie G112C
McDONALD Carol I27
McDONALD Clarence C153 C220 E55 E57 G60 H8A H9 H112 J93C K56A L26B L38 M75 M130 M151 N23 P44 P67 P114 R54 R60C R137 S58 S333A T25 W10A W31 W116
McDONALD Country Joe M18
McDONALD Dollette H39A T8 Z3B
MACDONALD Donald H23 H59 H136A I21 J54 K84A M55A M125
McDONALD Frank B47B E74 K44A S54 S93
MACDONALD Henry K94 S306
McDONALD Howie W118
McDONALD Hugh B221 C42 F83A G72 O15 P123 P137 S180 S252
McDONALD Ian (D) B168 F84
MACDONALD Ian (K/Wind) B168 C63 C109 F48F F131 K54 L63 L98 M20 M78 M81
MACDONALD Ian (V) see MATTHEWS Ian
McDONALD John R148A
McDONALD Kathi B23 B94 D24 K25 K51 L107 M16 M101 N55 Q12 R133 R173
McDONALD Larry B283 D53C M53 T114
McDONALD Laverne C184B
McDONALD Lennie M15A
McDONALD Lloyd W4A
McDONALD Maureen B134A C180 D101 L19 M16A
McDONALD Mike B53 B110 B134A C180 C234D D101 G106A J72 J85A J93C L19 L89 L109 M16A M198 N46A N53 Q3A R22 S124 S262 W119B W133
McDONALD Paul I1
McDONALD Pete S214C
McDONALD Phil S232
MACDONALD Ralph A35A A96 A123 A131 B71 B77 B85 B186 B208 B208E C9A C44 C164 C213D C213E C241 D86 D132B E40 G4 G10 G61 H9 H58 J20 J43 J48 J69 J93D K48 K69 L4A L18 L109 L119B M17 M41 M75 M78 M86 M102 N65 P56B P72 P137 P149 R22 R25 R34 R60C R142A S17 S50 S64 S124 S125 S128 S180 S220 S262 T25 T37E T147 V17 W25 W27 W116
McDONALD Robin D6 K93 M18
MACDONALD Ronnie Y17
McDONALD Shelagh C109 M19
McDONALD Stewart K43 M202C
McDONALD Susan P83
McDONALD Tesfa C139
MACDONALD Val O47
MACDONALD AND GILES M20
McDONNELL Jimmy S254A
McDONNELL M.J. D58
McDONNELL Pat A126
McDONOUGH Mike O13
McDONOUGH Ringo O18
McDOUGAL Don G115
McDOUGAL Gary O33F
McDOUGALL Al F139
McDOUGALL Alex N58C
McDOUGALL Allan G115
McDOUGALL Brad M106C
McDOUGALL Dave A63A K20
MACDOWELL Al C177D
McDOWELL Annie Mae M22
McDOWELL Fred L61 M22 T79B
McDOWELL Gary M175D
McDOWELL Hugh D39 E34 W122
McDOWELL Ken T57
MACDOWELL Ted N41
McDUFF Brother Jack B85

RUTHERFORD Paul A74 G47 M29 S209 S267
RUTLEDGE Jim B142
RUTLEDGE Robert W119
RUTLES R175
RUTLEY Tom A136 C63C S19 W129
RUTS R175A
RUTSEY John R167
RUVIE Joe B224C
RUZGA Rob N63
RYAN Barry R175C V29A
RYAN Chico S78
RYAN Craig C86
RYAN Eddie P53
RYAN James F115 P6
RYAN Jerry S259A
RYAN Jim C228 C229 D39 E60 F56 G32 G117C J16B M156 S124 S266 T96 W39 Y24
RYAN Joe S206
RYAN John (B) H48 M19 S124 S266 W20B W125
RYAN John (K) G81B
RYAN John (Prod) A38
RYAN Mark B165 K13 M18 Q12
RYAN Mike S78B
RYAN Nicky C120
RYAN Pat A102 R125
RYAN Paul R175B R175C
RYAN Paul (Sex) F47
RYAN Phil A58 B96 B237 E80 G6 J71 L80C M63 N27 S88
RYAN Roz H98
RYAN Sharon W101
RYAN Terry B268
RYAN PAUL & BARRY R175C
RYAN-CARTER Tosh B247
RYANS R175C
RYDELL Bobby C93
RYDER Maggie L60 O40 R40B R176 S68
RYDER Mitch (LA VERE Billy) R177
RYE Steve B250 E41 G112 K22A
RYE WHISKEY ROAD BAND R177A
RYECROFT Frank J84
RYERSON Art C146
RYGA Andy Patty Pei K22A
RYKIEL Jean Philippe H119
RYLAND Jack T81
RYMER Gino W38
RYNAT Eulalie see CHANET Chris
RYNOSKI Michael M222
RYPDAL Inger Lise R178
RYPDAL Terje H34 M79 M205 P115 R178 V26C
RYSER Scott U16A

S.Michael C86
S.A.F.T. S1A
S.A.H.B. H52
S.B.B. S1B
S.F.F. S1
S.R.C. S2
S.V.T. S3
SAAB Nanette S55C
SAAD Sue S3A
SAARLOUIS Berry L47C
SAATCHI Philip A5A
SABATINI Bill G96
SABATINO Peter V2
SABEL Peter I22
Saber M75
SABER Andy M139A
Sabicas B65
SABIN John C111
SABINO Robert A96 C99 H42A S122A S135
SABINO Vic S9C
SABOTAGE S3B
SABREJETS S3C
SABU Paul S3D
SABU S3D
SABY Paul H122A
SACHER Martin B199
SACHS Jon E37
SACHS Lenny S4
SACK Nick D93D
SAD CAFE S4
SADEGHI Manouchehr S58
Sadie The Cat F47
SADISTIC MIKA BAND S5
SADLER John L57C
SADLER Larry H51
SADLER Michael S5A
SADLER Tim B23
SADLER Tony H169
SADLOWSKI Dieter R38
SAFAN Craig H35 T32B
SAFAN Mark G60
Safanya M160A
SAFKA Melanie see Melanie
SAFRON Mike P40
SAGA S5A
SAGAL Katy M178A
SAGE Bev W134C
SAGE Pete G62B W14
SAGER Gareth F74C P117
SAGITTARIUS S6
SAHARA S6A
SAHL Michael C164
SAHLBERG Per A4 S39
SAHM Doug D13 G84 M141 S7
SAHM Shawn S7
SAIBI Lahmi 'Puce' F4B
SAIDI Mohamed Ben Hamou B4
SAILCAT S7A
SAILES Jessie C96 C146 J21 R111 R142A
SAILIN Jeff S205
SAILOR S8
SAIN Oliver E52B L90
ST.CLAIR Gary B253
ST.CLAIR Micki K16A
ST.CLAIR Pat S198B
ST.CLAIR Steve S103
ST.CLAIR-SHEETS Scott B80B
ST.CLAIRE Alex (Snouffer) B72 K49A
ST.CLOUD Endle S8A
ST.CLOUD POTTER P118A
ST.DENIS Mike S72
ST.FIELD John (LEVIN Jackie) D95 S8B
ST.HOLMES Derek see HOLMES Derek St.
ST.JAMES Phyllis C213E C246 F103C H62 N42 S36
ST.JAMES Sylvia D127 H96
ST.JAMES Tony F103C
ST.JOHN Barry A35 A133 B20 B23 B83 C13 C204 C210 D39 D54 E8 E18 E38 F7 F42 G50 G98 H26A H52 H74 H175 J72 K11 K81 L63 M7 M214 N14 N57 P85 R116 S34 S243 S257 S296 S355A T73 W7 W10 W133 Y17
ST.JOHN Bridget A133 C78 O18 S9
ST.JOHN Dennis A59 B29 B53 B80 C38A H52A N37 P118D R137 S269 W21
ST.JOHN Dick D63A
ST.JOHN George S71A
ST.JOHN John G77C
ST.JOHN Kate W82A
ST.JOHN Phillip A82
ST.JOHN R.Powell Jnr M211
ST.JOHN Roy S9A
ST.JOHN Wayne C140
ST.JOHN-GILLARD John S194
ST.JOHN GREEN S9C
ST.JON Alan S232A
ST.JULIEN Robert M48
ST.KENERLY Roger C156 M102
ST.LOUIS Louis P72A
ST.MARYS CHOIR G10
ST.NICHOLAS Jody also SPAMPINATO Joseph N2 P63
ST.NICHOLAS Nick S265 T3
ST.PARADISE S9B
ST.Perry U9A
ST.PIERRE Bill M36A
ST.ROCH Christian W101
SAINT GERMAIN Ronnie G64C
SAINT ROCK Chris H196
SAINTE MARIE Buffy D99 N32 S10 S55A
SAINTS S11
SAINTY Ian M121
SAISSE Phillipe D72
SAJDAK Ken Y15
SAKAMOTO Meguni G55
SAKAMOTO Ryuichi S11A Y6A
SAKS Toby C11A
SAKUMA Ma-Chan P95A
SAKURAI Tetsuo C51C
SALARGIE Jim M86
SALAMONE Ross L13
SALAS Jerry E30
SALAS Rudy E30
SALAS Steve E30
SALAZAR Marcello P34
SALAZAR Victor S211
SALBER Gunter L120
SALEEM Kashif B3
SALEH Jens E56B
SALEM Freddie O43
SALEM FREDDIE & THE WILDCATS S11B
SALEM John N23
SALEN Jeff T156
SALERNE Pasquale B203A
SALES Hunt I10 M82 P24 R164
SALES Tony I10 M82 R164
SALESTROM Jim L108
SALGADO Curtis C214B
SALINAS Tony L23C
SALISBURY Bob M211
SALISBURY Dave L14
SALISBURY Jerry B22 B171 V11
SALISBURY Jobraith P80D
SALISBURY Sandy S6
SALISBURY Tom A59 K16A L10B M203 P114
SALKOWSKY Gerard S280
SALLEY Roley B135 T134
SALLYANGIE S12
SALM Ulrich L47C
SALMIERI Claude R139B
SALMINEN Simo O18
SALMON Andy C234D
SALMON Godfrey E66
SALMON Kenny D28
SALMON Trevor 'Seal' R61A
SALOMAN Nick O7B
SALOMONE Ross L13
SALOMONSEN Sanne T79D
SALT Morton K. M65A
SALT Pete F7B
SALTER Ricky S340A
SALTER William B77 M17 P49 R31 R34
SALTSBERG Mike B269A
SALTZMAN Larry C103C
SALTZMAN Stan D2
SALUKI S12A
SALVATION S12B
SALVONI Luigi S178 M190
SALZMAN Buddy C76 C108D C146 C255 H23 I2 I21 M125 S213
SALZMAN Danny B223
Sam see SAMUELS Carlton
SAM Robert G80
SAM AND DAVE S13
SAM APPLE PIE S14
SAM GOPAL G73
SAM THE SHAM AND THE PHARAHUS S14A
SAMARTINO Leonard F54
SAMARTINO Sandra F54
SAMBARATO John M28 M101 S276
SAMLA MAMMAS MANNA S14B
SAMPEDRO Frank C216 Y16
SAMPINAIO Joe N2
SAMPLE Joe A11 A52 A131D A132 B174 B281 C36 C96 C153 C213E C241 E71 F33 F103D G17 H8 H156 H193B J43 J91A K45 K46 K72 L28 M170 P76 P129 R60C R99 R101 R113 S50 S14C S58 S228 S262 S333A U18 W10A W31 Y14
SAMPLE William D97A
SAMPSON Annie B109 D24 S284
SAMPSON Charles C20
SAMPSON Jimmy A35D O13
SAMPSON Paul R63A
SAMPSON Leslie S297
SAMPSON Sam F26A S14
SAMS David H110 W102
SAMS Warren W27B
SAMSON S14D
SAMSON Jackie W13
SAMSON Jim Z16
SAMSON Les C35D R55
SAMSON Paul S14D
SAMUDIO Domingo 'Sam' S14A
SAMUEL Bill B233
SAMUELS Andrew R57
SAMUELS Bruce B278
SAMUELS Calvin 'Fuzzy' A133 C83 C180 C234 D86 F8 H120 M64 M78 N4 S15 S276 V26A W72
SAMUELS Carlton 'Sam' B276
SAMUELS David B105 S231 Z8
SAMUELS Jerry see Napoleon XIV
SAMUELS Keith 'Doc' B213
SAMUELSON John D81A
SAMUELSON Lars T37H
SAMUELSON Shalimar M211
SAMURAI S16
SAMWELL Ian R80 S80
SAMWELL-SMITH Paul C121 I13 W94 Y5
SAN FRANCISCO SYMPHONY ORCHESTRA S113
San Frisco Jeff B233 M13A
SANAELL Robert D77
SANBORN David A31 B65 B169 B169A B175 B183B B186 B208 B282 C44 C51B C62 C94 C189 C195 C213 C213E C249 D39 E2 F3A F83A F103D G109 H8 H58 H185 J20 J48 J72 J93C K36 K37 K45 L4A L41 L107 L119 M17 M40 M41 M69 M75 M107 M125 M143 N36 P35 P99 P151 Q3A R22 R100 R137 R164 S17 S124 S125 S180 S196 S215 S229 S262 S266 T25 T147 U18 W5 W51A W119
SANCHEZ Art Y4A
SANCHEZ Freddie E30
SANCHEZ Mario C241B
SANCHEZ Nestor Y2A
SANCIOUS David L. B248 C129 D124 G64C P119B S18 S229 S232A W8 W62
SAND S18A
SANDALS S18B
SANDELL Bruce G26A
SANDRE Ellen P93B
SANDERS Billy M10
SANDERS Charlie B95B
SANDERS Don I13A N23 T167
SANDERS Doug L12A
SANDERS Ed F133 S18C
SANDERS Issiah W119
SANDERS Kevin M62
SANDERS Mark S270
SANDERS Marty J44
SANDERS Neil C2 K84
SANDERS Pharaoh M79
SANDERS Rachel W27B
SANDERS Ric A30 C230 G35 S9 S66 S182
SANDERS Rick (G) H46
SANDERS Steve L44
SANDERS Stu C153
SANDERS Zachary B139 B141 F4C F60 G4 J20 J69 L119 M17 M225 P72A R125 S169 S262 V17
SANDERSON Duncan D58 P84
SANDERSON John K29A
SANDFORD Butch K20
Sandi Y6A
Sandii E34 S18D
SANDII & THE SUNSETS S18D
SANDKE Jordan H170
SANDLER David S227A
SANDLER Harry O33C
SANDLER Myron A131D
SANDLES Verlin M53
SANDLIN Johnny A37 A38 B91 B109 B200 C207 D126B H164 H195 J52 K30 K60 T9A T20 T30
SANDON Alan H116 S93B
SANDOVAL Everado C156
SANDOVAL Pablo C156
SANDS Kenny K45
SANDVIG Peggy B221 B255 C155 G24 L12B P129 W21 W42
SANDWICH Sandy R67
SANDY McCLELLAND AND THE BACKLINE M41A
Sanford B42B
SANFORD Billy B43C C77A C194 F126 G72 H7D H65 J13 J53 K77 L42 L108 M11 M41 N37 R127A R173 S10 T21 T107 T153A
SANFORD Ed L110 M16A S20
SANFORD Gary A82 J10 R55B
SANFORD Laurie K33
SANFORD Richard G86B
SANFORD Rick D61 L47A
SANFORD AND TOWNSEND S20
SAN FRISCO Jeff M13A
SANG Samantha C38
SANO Tatsuya O33G
SANOIAN Paul T41
SANSON Marilyn J41
SANSON Veronique S21
Santa see DAVIS Carlton
SANTA BARBARA MACHINEHEAD S22
SANTAMARIA Mongo F17 J20
SANTANA S19
SANTANA Carlos B144 C217 D139 G26D H19 K81 M40 S19 S36 W8
SANTANA Francisco R100
SANTANA Jorge F17 M59
SANTANA Jose M59
SANTANA Urmila S19
SANTANDEREA Giorgio A41B
SANTANGELI Michel A72A R78A S280 Y23
SANTANGELO Joe B228A
SANTARELLA Tony J88
SANTHIER Michelle M49
SANTI Erminia L120
SANTI Richard B144
SANTIAGO Adalberto F17
SANTIAGO Herman L144
SANTIAGO Neftali M72
SANTIEL Robert L2
SANTIEL Terry N66 R141
SANTINI Gene A27 P114
SANTKIN Marc L48B
SANTOS John S19
SANTOS Jumma E49 L67B M53 S17
SANTOS Patti C151B I31 N32
SANTOS Pedro P34
SAPADIN Janet C185F
SAPAL Kate S121
SAPAN Mark G60
SAPKO Ray T12B
SAPPHIN Craig J31
SAPSTEAD Bob M201
SARACEN S23A
Sarah F71
SARAKUS Russ B17A
SARANDON Chris F27A
SARANDON Sue F27A
SARCH Harvey S247
SARGEANT Bob A5 B58B C23 C251 E76 J107 M181C R106 S23 S270
SARGEANT Emmet Z8
SARGEANT Will E11B
SARGENT Jack R126
SARKIN Frank G81E
SARKISSIAN Louis M49
SARLIN Don F115
SARMANTO Pekka V26C
SARNEY Joy J110
SAROFEEN AND SMOKE S24
SAROYAN Kathleen M101
SARSTEDT Clive J70A S285
SARSTEDT Peter P41
SARTAIN Jeanette S322
SARTI Mauro C24B
SARTINI Tony S78
SARUMI Shamsi A82 D37 E31
SARZE Robert B286
SARZO Rudi O33E
SASAKI Michael C158
SASHATUNES M170
SASPARELLA Simeon see HILLAGE Steve
SASS Bobby O24A
SASSAFRAS S26
SASSER Larry D104 L42
SATCHELL Clarence O13
SATCHFIELD Keith F56A
SATHIE Kesh C191 F35 G78 J36A L80C L117 M94 R66 S152
SATIN Arnie D106D
SATIN WHALE S26A
SATISFACTION S27
SATISFACTION UNLIMITED S27A
SATO Chica P95A
SATO Hiroshi G10B W53A
SATO Masahiko P115
SATTEN Steve L67B T44
SATTERFIELD Louis C45 C164B E7 E55 H170 L65 S250 W28 W84C

STERN Peggy T107

THRONE Bob J51
THUMBS T83A
THUNDER Margo A27
THUNDER Theodore B31 E8 L47 O9 P131 S34
THUNDER T83B
THUNDERBIRDS F21
THUNDERBOLTS M44 M99
THUNDERBYRD M27
THUNDERCLAP NEWMAN T84
Thundercloud J104D
THUNDERHEAD T84A
THUNDERMUG T85
THUNDERS Johnny H76 N34 T86
Thundersticks S14D
THUNDERTHIGHS A42 B231 E37 F65 K24 M214 R60 S108 T87 V26 W3 Y2
THUNDERTRAIN T88
THUNES Scott Z8
THURBER Matt R92A
THURMAN Benny T64
THURMAN Ed P139A
THUROW Mathies D19A
THURSTON Colin H178A R20
THURSTON Scott H129A I10 N31
THYNE Robin M50 N11

Z

An interesting spin off from the production of the index has been to see how often musicians have appeared in different entries

We have prepared a list of these musicians in the form of a small chart. If you would like a copy send a stamped addressed envelope or outside U.K. send an international reply coupon (from post offices)

Write to :

'Chart'
13,Stanton Road
Regents Park,
Southampton
England,
SO1 ?HF.

'Thats all folks'